W9-BRS-900

ProQuest Statistical Abstract of the United States 2018

ProQuest Statistical Abstract of the United States 2018

Issued December 2017

Published by Rowman & Littlefield
A wholly owned subsidiary of The Rowman & Littlefield Publishing Group, Inc.
4501 Forbes Boulevard, Suite 200, Lanham, Maryland 20706
www.rowman.com
800-462-6420
Unit A, Whitacre Mews, 26-34 Stannary Street, London SE11 4AB, United Kingdom

ISBN 13: 978-1-59888-945-1

Suggested Citation:
ProQuest LLC. ProQuest Statistical Abstract of the United States, 2018. (6th ed.) Bethesda, MD, 2017

Preface

The *Statistical Abstract of the United States,* published since 1878, is the best-known statistical reference publication in the country. As a comprehensive collection of statistics on the social, political, and economic conditions of the United States, it is a snapshot of America and its people. In the spring of 2011, the Census Bureau announced that the edition published that year would be the last one produced at government expense. Beginning in 2012, ProQuest took on responsibility for updating and releasing this publication, the most used statistical reference tool in U.S. libraries.

The editors at ProQuest have endeavored to continue the tradition established by the Census Bureau Statistical Compendia Branch. Like its predecessors, the *ProQuest Statistical Abstract of the United States* is designed to serve as a convenient volume for statistical reference and as a guide to other statistical publications and sources. The latter function is served by the introductory text to each section; source citations appearing below each table; and Appendix I, which is comprised of the *Guide to Sources of Statistics,* including a list of international statistical abstracts, and the *Guide to State Statistical Abstracts.*

This volume includes a selection of data from many statistical sources, both government and private. Publications cited as sources usually contain additional statistical detail and more comprehensive discussions of definitions and concepts. Data not available in publications issued by the contributing agency, but obtained from the internet or unpublished records are identified in the source notes. More information on the subjects covered in the tables may generally be obtained from the source.

Except as indicated, figures are for the United States as presently constituted. Although emphasis in the *ProQuest Statistical Abstract* is primarily given to national data, many tables present data for regions and individual states and a smaller number for metropolitan areas and cities. "Appendix II, Metropolitan and Micropolitan Statistical Areas: Concepts, Components, and Population," presents explanatory text, a complete current listing, and population data for metropolitan and micropolitan areas defined as of July 2015. Statistics for the Commonwealth of Puerto Rico and for Island Areas of the United States are included in many state tables and are supplemented by information in Section 29.

Statistics in this edition are generally for the most recent year or period available, as of early September 2017. Each year over 1,400 tables are reviewed and evaluated, new tables of current interest are added,

continuing series are updated, and less timely data are condensed or eliminated. Text notes and appendices are revised as appropriate.

Changes in this edition—This year ProQuest introduces 38 new tables, presenting data on topics including health insurance enrollment and coverage, use and misuse of prescription drugs, presidential pardons, foodborne disease outbreaks, household electronics, characteristics of employer firms, living arrangements of young adults, Federal Highway Trust Fund, high school English as a second language (ESL) programs, organic farms, cost of attendance for undergraduate education, and Freedom of Information Act (FOIA) requests. For a complete list of new tables, see "New Tables," p. xi.

Additionally, within the Elections section, tables presenting data on election results have been arranged into two separate subsections - voter registration and vote results and elected officials.

Online edition—*ProQuest Statistical Abstract* is also available in an online edition. This dynamic edition features table-specific capabilities for narrowing results by source, data date, subject, and type of data breakdown. Importantly, the online edition is updated with new statistical content on a monthly basis, enabling users to regularly access new and revised data. The online product functions as a repository for additional back year's data that cannot fit into the print publication. Users will find spreadsheets that correspond to each table in the book. In many cases, these spreadsheets present expanded coverage of the data shown in print. It is available as a stand-alone product or a fully integrated component of *ProQuest Statistical Insight.*

Limitations of the data—The contents of this volume were taken from many sources. All data from censuses, surveys, and administrative records are subject to error arising from a number of factors including the following: sampling variability (for statistics based on samples), reporting errors in the data for individual units, incomplete coverage, nonresponse, and imputation and processing errors (see also Appendix III). ProQuest cannot accept responsibility for the accuracy or limitations of the data presented here. However, selection of the material and its proper presentation is the responsibility of ProQuest.

For additional information on data presented—Please consult the source publications available in local libraries and on the internet, or contact the agency or organization indicated in the source notes.

Contents

[Numbers following subject are page numbers]

Sec. 9. Federal Government Finances and Employment 327

Sec. 10. National Security and Veterans Affairs 345

Sec. 11. Social Insurance and Human Services 365

Sec. 12. Labor Force, Employment, and Earnings 393

Sec. 13. Income, Expenditures, Poverty, and Wealth 451

Sec. 14. Prices 491

Sec. 15. Business Enterprise 507

Sec. 16. Science and Technology 541

Sec. 17. Agriculture 555

New and Deleted Tables for the 2018 Edition

New Tables for 2018

Tables Deleted Since the 2017 Edition of the Statistical Abstract

[Tables are deleted for several reasons, including: source data has been discontinued, source data was monographic and new data is not expected to be available, data are no longer reliable, and data was previously unpublished and cannot be replicated. Some tables have been replaced with tables illustrating similar content. Where applicable, please see reference to new table number]

2017 Table	Section and Table Title	Replaced by...
	Section 1: Population	
Table 46........	Estimated Unauthorized Immigrants by Selected Country of Birth and State: 2000 to 2012	
Table 76........	Householders' Children Under 18 Years Old by Whether Adopted, Biological, and Stepchildren and Selected Child Characteristics: 2009 to 2011	Table 75
Table 77........	Householders' Children Under 18 Years Old by Whether Adopted, Biological, and Stepchildren and Selected Characteristics of Householder: 2009 to 2011	Table 75
	Section 2: Births, Deaths, Marriages, and Divorces	
Table 98........	Women's Relationship Status at First Birth by Selected Characteristics: 2012	Table 97
Table 105......	Contraceptive Use of Women by Method and Selected Characteristics: 2011 to 2013	Table 104
Table 110.......	Women's Use of Infertility Services by Type of Service and Selected Characteristics: 2006 to 2010	
	Section 3: Health and Nutrition	
Table 173......	Physicians and Nurses by State: 2013 and 2014	Table 176
Table 186......	Procedures for Inpatients Discharged From Short-Stay Hospitals: 1990 to 2010	
Table 191......	Hospital Utilization Rates by Sex: 1990 to 2010	
Table 192......	Hospital Utilization Measures for HIV Patients: 1990 to 2010	
Table 193......	Hospital Discharges and Days of Care: 2009 and 2010	
Table 194......	Hospital Discharges and Days of Care by Selected Diagnosis by Patient Sex and Age: 2010	
Table 218......	Prescription Drug Use in Past 30 Days by Selected Characteristics: 2005 to 2012	Table 217
Table 227......	Autism, Intellectual Disability, Learning Disability, and Other Developmental Delays Among Children by Selected Characteristics: 2011	
Table 238......	Prevalence of Allergies Among Children by Allergy Type and Age, Race/Ethnicity, and Poverty Status: 2003 to 2014	Table 226
	Section 4: Education	
Table 321......	Mean Student Loan Debt of Households: 1989 to 2010	
Table 323......	Private for Profit Colleges—Summary: 2000 to 2012	
	Section 7: Elections	
Table 455......	Political Action Committees—Number by Committee Type: 1980 to 2015	
Table 457......	Presidential Campaign Finances—Federal Funds for General Election: 2000 to 2012	
Table 458......	Presidential Campaign Finances—Primary Campaign Receipts and Disbursements: 2003 to 2012	
	Section 9: Federal Government Employment and Finances	
Table 502......	Tax Expenditure Estimates Relating to Individual and Corporate Income Taxes by Selected Function: 2015 to 2018	
	Section 10: National Security and Veterans Affairs	
Table 545......	Federal Funding Obligations for Selected Homeless Veterans Programs: 1988 to 2015	
Table 552......	U.S. Border Patrol Apprehensions by Border, Gender, Age, and Country of Nationality: 2007 to 2010	
	Section 11: Social Insurance and Human Services	
Table 578......	Defined Contribution 401(k) Plans—Participants, Assets, Contributions, and Benefits by Type of Plan: 2013	Table 577
	Section 12: Labor Force, Employment, and Earnings	
Table 676......	Median Earnings of College Graduates by Degree and Occupation: 2012	
	Section 14: Prices	
Table 754......	Cost of Living Index for Selected Urban Areas, Annual Average: 2015	
	Section 15: Business Enterprise	
Table 807......	Information and Communications Technology (ICT) Equipment and Computer Software Expenditures: 2010 and 2013	
	Section 19: Energy and Utilities	
Table 985......	Public Drinking Water Systems by Size of Community Served and Source of Water: 2014	
Table 986......	Public Drinking Water Systems—Number and Population Served by State: 2013	
	Section 24: Information and Communication	
Table 1149.....	Book Publishers' Net Shipments: 2010 to 2013	
Table 1170.....	Household Computer and Internet Use by Selected Characteristics: 2013	Table 1175
	Section 30: International Statistics	
Table 1399.....	Foreign Stock Market Activity—MSCI Indexes: 2010 to 2014	

Guide to Tabular Presentation

Example of Table Structure

Table 1287. Top 20 U.S. Gateway Airports for Nonstop International Air Travel Passengers: 2016

[215,266 represents 215,266,000. International passengers are residents of any country traveling nonstop to and from the United States on U.S. and foreign carriers. The data cover all passengers arriving and departing from U.S. airports on nonstop commercial international flights with 60 seats or more]

Gateway airport	Airport code	Passengers, (1,000)	Gateway airport	Airport code	Passengers, (1,000)
Total, all airports................	**(X)**	**215,266**	Dallas-Ft. Worth, TX................	DFW	7,854
Total, top 20 airports..............	**(X)**	**191,596**	Washington (Dulles), DC..............	IAD	7,203
Top 20, percentage of total...........	**(X)**	**89.0**	Boston, MA............................	BOS	6,233
			Fort Lauderdale, FL...................	FLL	5,879
New York (JFK), NY.....................	JFK	31,595	Orlando, FL..........................	MCO	5,476
Los Angeles, CA.......................	LAX	22,544	Honolulu, HI.........................	HNL	5,131
Miami, FL.............................	MIA	20,533	Seattle-Tacoma, WA...................	SEA	4,663
San Francisco, CA.....................	SFO	12,197	Philadelphia, PA.....................	PHL	3,692
Chicago (O'Hare), IL..................	ORD	12,118	Las Vegas, NV........................	LAS	3,509
Newark, NJ............................	EWR	11,867	Detroit, MI..........................	DTW	3,331
Atlanta, GA...........................	ATL	11,209	Guam Island, GU......................	GUM	2,986
Houston (G. Bush), TX.................	IAH	10,598	Charlotte, NC........................	CLT	2,980

X Not applicable.

Source: U.S. Department of Transportation, Research and Innovative Technology Administration, Bureau of Transportation Statistics, Office of Airline Information, "T-100 International Segment data," <http://www.transtats.bts.gov/Fields.asp?Table_ID=261>, accessed July 2017.

Headnotes immediately below table titles provide information important for correct interpretation or evaluation of the table as a whole or for a major segment of it.

Footnotes below the bottom rule of tables give information relating to specific items or figures within the table.

Unit indicators show the *specified quantities* in which data items are presented. They are used for two primary reasons. Sometimes data are not available in absolute form and are estimates (as in the case of many surveys). In other cases we round the numbers in order to save space to show more data, as in the case above.

When a table presents data with more than one unit indicator, they are found in the headnotes and column headings (Tables 4 and 28), spanner (Table 36), stub (Table 27), or unit column (Table 240). When the data in a table are shown in the same unit indicator, it is shown as the first part of the headnote (Table 2). If no unit indicator is shown, data presented are in absolute form (Table 1).

Vertical rules are used to separate independent sections of a table (Table 1), or in tables where the stub is continued into one or more additional columns (Table 2).

Averages—An average is a single number or value that is often used to represent the "typical value" of a group of numbers. It is regarded as a measure of "location" or "central tendency" of a group of numbers.

The *arithmetic mean* is the type of average used most frequently. It is derived by summing the individual item values of a particular group and dividing the total by the number of items. The arithmetic mean is often referred to as simply the "mean" or "average."

The *median* of a group of numbers is the middle number or value when each item in the group is arranged according to size (lowest to highest or vice versa); it generally has the same number of items above it as well as below it. If there is an even number

of items in the group, the median is taken to be the average of the two middle numbers.

Per capita (or per person) quantities—a per capita figure represents an average computed for every person in a specified group (or population). It is derived by taking the total for an item (such as income, taxes, or retail sales) and dividing it by the number of persons in the specified population.

Index numbers—An index number is the measure of difference or change, usually expressed as a percent, relating one quantity (the variable) of a specified kind to another quantity of the same kind. Index numbers are widely used to express changes in prices over periods of time, but may also be used to express differences between related subjects for a single point in time.

To compute a price index, a base year or period is selected. The base year price (of the commodity or service) is then designated as the base or reference price to which the prices for other years or periods are related. Many price indexes use the year 1982 as the base year; in tables this is shown as "1982 = 100." A method expressing the price relationship is: The price of a set of one or more items for a related year (e.g. 1990) **divided by** the price of the same set of items for the base year (e.g. 1982). The result multiplied by 100 provides the index number. When 100 is subtracted from the index number, the result equals the percent change in price from the base year.

Average annual percent change—Unless otherwise stated in the *Abstract* (as in Section 1, Population), average annual percent change is computed by use of a *compound interest formula*. This formula assumes that the rate of change is constant throughout a specified compounding period (1 year for average annual rates of change). The formula is similar to that used to compute the balance of a savings account that receives compound interest. According to this formula, at the end of a compounding period the amount of accrued change (e.g., school enrollment or bank interest) is added to the amount that existed at the beginning of the period. As a result, over time (e.g., with each year or quarter), the same rate of change is applied to a larger and larger figure.

The *exponential formula,* which is based on continuous compounding, is often used to measure population change. It is preferred by population experts, because they view population and population-related subjects as changing without interruption, ever ongoing. Both exponential and compound interest formulas assume a constant rate of change. The former, however, applies the amount of change continuously to the base rather than at the end of each compounding period. When the average annual rates are small (e.g., less than 5 percent) both formulas give virtually the same results. For an explanation of these two formulas as they relate to population, see U.S. Census Bureau, *The Methods and Materials of Demography,* Vol. 2, 3d printing (rev.), 1975.

Current and constant dollars—Statistics in some tables in a number of sections are expressed in both current and constant dollars (see, e.g., Table 690 in Section 13, Income, Expenditures, Poverty, and Wealth). Current dollar figures reflect actual prices or costs prevailing during the specified year(s). Constant dollar figures are estimates representing an effort to remove the effects of price changes from statistical series reported in dollar terms. In general, constant dollar series are derived by dividing current dollar estimates by the appropriate price index for the appropriate period (e.g., the Consumer Price Index). The result is a series as it would presumably exist if prices were the same throughout, as in the base year—in other words, as if the dollar had constant purchasing power. Any changes in this constant dollar series would reflect only changes in real volume of output, income, expenditures, or other measure.

Explanation of Symbols

The following symbols, used in the tables throughout this book, are explained in condensed form in footnotes to the tables where they appear:

— Represents zero or rounds to less than half the unit of measurement shown.

B Base figure too small to meet statistical standards for reliability of a derived figure.

D Figure withheld to avoid disclosure pertaining to a specific organization or individual.

NA Data not enumerated, tabulated, or otherwise available separately.

P Data are preliminary or projected.

S Figure does not meet publication standards for reasons other than that covered by symbol B, above.

X Figure not applicable because column heading and stub line make entry impossible, absurd, or meaningless.

Z Entry would amount to less than half the unit of measurement shown.

In many tables, details will not add to the totals shown because of rounding.

Section 1
Population

This section presents statistics on the growth, distribution, and characteristics of the U.S. population. The principal source of these data is the U.S. Census Bureau, which conducts a decennial census of population, a monthly population survey, a program of population estimates and projections, and a number of other periodic surveys.

Decennial censuses—The U.S. Constitution provides for a census of the population every 10 years, primarily to establish a basis for apportionment of members of the House of Representatives among the states. For over a century after the first census in 1790, the census organization was a temporary one, created only for each decennial census. In 1902, the Census Bureau was established as a permanent federal agency, responsible for enumerating the population and also for compiling statistics on other population and housing characteristics.

Historically, the enumeration of the population has been a complete (100 percent) count. That is, an attempt is made to account for every person, for each person's residence, and for other characteristics (sex, age, family relationships, etc.). In the twentieth century, the questions were divided between a "short" and "long" form. Only a subset of the population was required to answer the long-form questions. The most recent census consisted only of a short form, which included basic questions about age, sex, race, Hispanic origin, household relationship, and owner/renter status. After the 2000 Census, the long form became the American Community Survey (ACS) and continues to collect long-form-type information. The ACS includes not only the basic short-form questions, but also detailed questions about population and housing characteristics. It is a nationwide, continuous sample survey designed to provide communities with reliable and timely demographic, housing, social, and economic data every year. Since its start, the ACS has been providing a continuous stream of updated information for states and local areas. Sample data may be used with confidence where large numbers are involved and assumed to indicate trends and relationships where small numbers are involved.

Current Population Survey (CPS)—The CPS sample is a probability sample designed primarily to produce national and state estimates of labor force characteristics of the civilian non-institutional population 16 years of age and older. The sample consists of independent samples in each state and the District of Columbia, and each state sample is specifically tailored to the demographic and labor market conditions that prevail in that particular state. About 60,000 housing units are required in order to meet the national and State reliability criteria, drawn from 824 sample areas.

The CPS also serves as a vehicle for inquiries on other subjects. Using CPS data, the Census Bureau issues a series of publications under the general title of *Current Population Reports*.

Estimates of population characteristics based on the CPS will not agree with the counts from the census because the CPS and the census use different procedures for collecting and processing the data for racial groups, the Hispanic population, and other topics. Caution should also be used when comparing estimates for various years because of the periodic introduction of changes into the CPS. Beginning in January 1994, a number of changes were introduced into the CPS that affect all data comparisons with prior years. These changes included the results of a major redesign of the survey questionnaire and collection methodology and the introduction of 1990 census population controls, adjusted for the estimated undercount. Beginning with the 2001 CPS Annual Demographic Supplement, the independent estimates used as control totals for the CPS are based on civilian population benchmarks consistent with Census 2000. In 2003 the name of the March supplement was changed to Annual Social and Economic Supplement (ASEC). Beginning with the 2012 March CPS supplement, the estimates are based on Census 2010 population controls. These changes in population controls had relatively little impact on derived measures such as means, medians, and percent distribution, but did have a significant impact on levels.

In 2002, the ASEC incorporated a significant sample expansion. The sample was expanded primarily to improve state estimates of children's health insurance coverage (CHIP). This sample increase of 19,000 households added to the regular sample of 72,500 households and the Hispanic sample of 6,500 gives a total sample size of about 98,000 households. The 2014 CPS ASEC included redesigned questions for income and health insurance coverage. All of the approximately 98,000 addresses were selected to receive the improved set of health insurance coverage items. The improved income questions were implemented using a split panel design. Approximately 68,000 addresses were selected to receive a set of income questions similar to those used in the 2013 CPS ASEC. The remaining 30,000 addresses were selected to receive the redesigned income questions.

Population estimates and projections—Each year, the United States Census Bureau produces and publishes estimates of the population for the nation, states, counties, state/county equivalents, and Puerto Rico. With each annual release of population estimates, the Population Estimates Program revises and updates the entire time series of estimates from April 1, 2010 to July 1 of the current year, which is referred to as the vintage year. "Vintage" denotes an entire time series created with a consistent population starting point and methodology. The release of a new vintage of estimates supersedes any previous series and incorporates the most up-to-date input data and methodological improvements.

Estimates of the United States population are derived by updating the resident population enumerated in Census 2010 with information on the components of population change: births, deaths, and net international migration. The population estimates base reflects changes to the decennial census population due to the Count Question Resolution program, geographic program revisions, and modifications to the 2010 Census race categories for consistency with the race categories in input data.

Registered births and deaths are estimated from data supplied by the National Center for Health Statistics and the Federal-State Cooperative for Population Estimates (FSCPE). The net international migration component consists of four parts: (1) the net international migration of the foreign born, (2) the net migration of natives to and from the United States, (3) the net migration between the United States and Puerto Rico, and (4) the net overseas movement of the Armed Forces population. Data from the ACS are used to estimate the annual net migration of the foreign-born population. The estimated net migration of the native-born population is produced using the foreign-census method which utilized data from over 80 countries. This work compared estimates of the United States born or United States citizen population living overseas measured by population registers and censuses in other countries at two consecutive time periods. The residual was used to develop estimates of net native migration. Estimates for net migration between Puerto Rico and the U.S. are derived from the ACS and the Puerto Rico Community Survey. Estimates of the net overseas movement of the Armed Forces are derived from data collected by the Defense Manpower Data Center.

Estimates for state and county areas are based on the same components of change data and sources as the national estimates with the addition of net internal migration. Estimates of net internal migration are derived from federal income tax returns from the Internal Revenue Service; group quarters data from the branches of the military, the Department of Veterans Affairs, and the FSCPE; and Medicare data from the Centers for Medicare and Medicaid Services.

Population estimates and projections are available on the Census Bureau website, see <http://www.census. gov>. These estimates and projections are consistent with official decennial census figures with no adjustment for estimated net census coverage. For details on methodology, see "Methodology for the United States Population Estimates: Vintage 2016," <https://www.census.gov/programs-surveys/popest/ technical-documentation/methodology.html>.

Immigration—Immigration (migration to a country) is one component of international migration; the other component is emigration (migration *from* a country). In its simplest form, international migration is defined as any movement across a national border. In the United States, federal statistics on international migration are produced primarily by the U.S. Census Bureau and the Office of Immigration Statistics of the U.S. Department of Homeland Security (DHS).

The Census Bureau collects data used to estimate international migration through its decennial censuses and numerous surveys of the U.S. population.

The Office of Immigration Statistics publishes immigration data in annual flow reports and the *Yearbook of Immigration Statistics.* Data for these publications are collected from several administrative data sources including the DS-230 *Application for Immigrant Visa and Alien Registration,* the DS-260 *Electronic Application for Immigrant Visa and Alien Registration* of the U.S. Department of State (used by applicants living abroad), and the I-485 *Application to Register Permanent Residence or Adjust Status* of U.S. Citizenship and Immigration Services (USCIS) for applicants living in the United States.

An immigrant, or lawful permanent resident (LPR), is a foreign national who has been granted lawful permanent residence in the United States. New arrivals are foreign nationals living abroad who apply for an immigrant visa at a consular office of the Department of State, while individuals adjusting status are already living in the United States and file an application for adjustment of status to lawful permanent residence with USCIS. Individuals adjusting status include refugees, asylees, and various classes of nonimmigrants. A refugee is an alien outside the United States who is unable or unwilling to return to his or her country of nationality because of persecution or a well-founded fear of persecution. Asylees must meet the same criteria as refugees, but are located in the United States or at a port of entry. Refugees are required to apply for adjustment to legal permanent resident status after one year of residence in the United States. Asylees are eligible to apply one year after they are granted asylum.

Nonimmigrants are foreign nationals granted temporary entry into the United States. The major activities for which nonimmigrant admission is authorized include temporary visits for business or pleasure, academic or vocational study, temporary employment, and to act as a representative of a foreign government or international organization. DHS collects information on the characteristics of a proportion of nonimmigrant admissions, those recorded on the I-94 Arrival/Departure Record.

U.S. immigration law gives preferential immigration status to persons with a close family relationship with a U.S. citizen or legal permanent resident, persons with needed job skills, persons who qualify as refugees or asylees, and persons who are from countries with relatively low levels of immigration to the United States (diversity immigrants). Immigration to the United States can be divided into two general categories: (1) classes of admission subject to the annual worldwide limitation and (2) classes of admission exempt from worldwide limitations. Numerical limits are imposed on visas issued and not on admissions. In 2015, the annual limit for family-sponsored preferences was 226,000 and the limit for employment-based preferences was 144,796.

The Diversity Visa Program is available to nationals of countries with fewer than 50,000 persons granted LPR status during the preceding five years in the employment-based and family-sponsored preferences and immediate relative classes of admission. The annual diversity visa limit has been 50,000 since 1999.

The number of persons who may be admitted to the United States as refugees each year is established by the President in consultation with Congress. The ceiling was 70,000 for 2015. There is no numerical limit on the number of persons who can be granted asylum status in a year.

Classes of admission exempt from the worldwide limitation include immediate relatives of U.S. citizens, refugees and asylees adjusting to permanent residence, and other various classes of special immigrants.

Metropolitan and micropolitan areas—Metropolitan and micropolitan statistical areas (metro and micro areas) are geographic entities delineated by the U.S. Office of Management and Budget (OMB) for use by Federal statistical agencies in collecting, tabulating, and publishing Federal statistics. These areas are the result of the application of published standards to Census Bureau data. Generally, the areas are delineated using the most recent set of standards following each decennial census. Between censuses, the delineations are updated annually to reflect the most recent Census Bureau population estimates. Areas based on the 2010 standards and Census Bureau data were delineated in July of 2015.

The term "Core Based Statistical Area" (CBSA) is a collective term for both metro and micro areas. A metro area contains a core urban area of 50,000 or more population, and a micro area contains an urban core of at least 10,000 (but less than 50,000) population. Each metro or micro area consists of one or more counties and includes the counties containing the core urban area, as well as any adjacent counties that have a high degree of social and economic integration (as measured by commuting to work) with the urban core.

Urban and rural—The Census Bureau's urban-rural classification is fundamentally a delineation of geographical areas, identifying both individual urban areas and the rural areas of the nation. The Census Bureau's urban areas represent densely developed territory, and encompass residential, commercial, and other non-residential urban land uses.

For the 2010 Census, an urban area comprises a densely settled core of census tracts and/or census blocks that meet minimum population density requirements, along with adjacent territory containing non-residential urban land uses as well as territory with low population density included to link outlying densely settled territory with the densely settled core. To qualify as an urban area, the territory identified according to criteria must encompass at least 2,500 people, at least 1,500 of which reside outside institutional group quarters. The Census Bureau identifies two types of urban areas: Urbanized Areas of 50,000 or more people; and Urban Clusters of at least 2,500 and less than 50,000 people. "Rural" encompasses all population, housing, and territory not included within an urban area. For Census 2010, many more geographic entities, including metropolitan areas, counties, and places, contain both urban and rural territory, population, and housing units.

Residence—In determining residence, the Census Bureau counts each person as an inhabitant of a usual place of residence (i.e., the place where one lives and sleeps most of the time). While this place is not necessarily a person's legal residence or voting residence, the use of these different bases of classification would produce the same results in the vast majority of cases.

Race—Census 2000 and 2010 adhere to the federal standards for collecting and presenting data on race and ethnicity as established by the OMB in October 1997. Starting with Census 2000, the OMB requires federal agencies to use a minimum of five race categories: White, Black or African American, American Indian or Alaska Native, Asian, and Native Hawaiian or Other Pacific Islander. Additionally, to collect data on individuals of mixed race parentage, respondents were allowed to select one or more races. For respondents who did not identify with any of these five race categories, the OMB approved and included a sixth category—"Some other race" on the Census 2000 and 2010 questionnaire. The Census 2000 and 2010 question on race included 15 separate response categories and three areas where respondents could write in a more specific race group. The response categories and write-in answers can be combined to create the five minimum OMB race categories plus "Some other race." People who responded to the question on race by indicating only one race are referred to as the *race alone* population, or the group that reported only one race category. Six categories make up this population: White alone, Black or African American alone, American Indian and Alaska Native alone, Asian alone, Native Hawaiian and Other Pacific Islander alone, and Some other race alone. Individuals who chose more than one of the six race categories are referred to as the *Two or More Races* population, or as the group that reported more than one race. Additionally, respondents who reported one race together with those who reported the same race plus one or more other races are combined to create the race alone or in *combination* categories. For example, the *White alone or in combination group* consists of those respondents who reported only White or who reported White combined with one or more other race groups, such as "White and Black or African American," or "White and Asian and American Indian and Alaska Native." Another way to think of the group who reported White alone or in combination is as the total number of people who identified entirely or partially as White. This group is also described as people who reported White, whether or not they reported any other race.

The *alone or in combination* categories are tallies of *responses* rather than *respondents*. That is, the alone or in combination categories are not mutually exclusive. Individuals who reported two races were counted in two separate and distinct alone or in combination race categories, while those who reported three races were counted in three categories, and so on. Consequently, the sum of all alone or in combination categories equals the number of races reported, which exceeds the total population.

The racial categories included in the census questionnaire generally reflect a social definition of race recognized in this country and not an attempt to define race biologically, anthropologically, or genetically. It is also recognized that the categories of the race item include racial and national origin or sociocultural groups. For example, data are available for the American Indian and Alaska Native tribes. A detailed explanation of race can be found at <https://www.census.gov/prod/cen2010/doc/sf1.pdf>.

Data for the population by race for April 1, 2000 and 2010, (shown in Tables 7 and 9) are modified counts and are not comparable to Census 2000 and 2010 race categories. These numbers were computed using Census 2000 and 2010 data by race and had been modified to be consistent with the 1997 OMB's "Revisions to the Standards for the Classification of Federal Data on Race and Ethnicity," (Federal Register Notice, Vol. 62, No 210, October 1997). A detailed explanation of the race modification procedure appears at <https://www.census.gov/programs-surveys/popest/technical-documentation/research/modified-race-data.html>.

In the CPS and other household sample surveys conducted through personal interview, respondents are asked to classify their race as: (1) White; (2) Black, African American, or Negro; (3) American Indian or Alaska Native; (4) Asian; or (5) Native Hawaiian or Other Pacific Islander. Beginning January 2003, respondents were allowed to report more than one race to indicate their mixed racial heritage.

Hispanic population—People who identify with the terms "Hispanic" or "Latino" are those who classify themselves in one of the specific Hispanic or Latino categories listed on the decennial census questionnaire and various Census Bureau survey questionnaires – "Mexican, Mexican American, Chicano" or "Puerto Rican" or "Cuban" – as well as those who indicate that they are "another Hispanic, Latino, or Spanish origin." Origin can be viewed as the heritage, nationality group, lineage, or country of birth of the person or the person's ancestors before their arrival in the United States.

Traditional and current data collection and classification treat race and Hispanic origin as two separate and distinct concepts in accordance with guidelines from the OMB. Race and Hispanic origin are two separate concepts in the federal statistical system. People who are Hispanic may be of any race and people in each race group may be either Hispanic or Not Hispanic. Also, each person has two attributes, their race (or races) and whether or not they are Hispanic. The overlap of race and Hispanic origin is the main comparability issue. For example, Black Hispanics (Hispanic Blacks) are included in both the number of Blacks and in the number of Hispanics. For further information, see <http://www.census.gov/population/www/socdemo/compraceho.html>.

Foreign-born and native populations—The Census Bureau separates the U.S. resident population into two groups based on whether or not a person was a U.S. citizen or U.S. national at the time of birth. Anyone born in the United States, Puerto Rico, or a U.S. Island Area (such as Guam), or born abroad to a U.S. citizen parent is a U.S. citizen at the time of birth and consequently included in the *native population*. The term *foreign-born population* refers to anyone who is not a U.S. citizen or a U.S. national at birth. This includes naturalized U.S. citizens, legal permanent resident aliens (immigrants), temporary migrants (such as foreign students), humanitarian migrants (such as refugees), and people illegally present in the United States. The Census Bureau provides a variety of demographic, social, economic, geographic, and housing information on the foreign-born population in the United States at <https://www.census.gov/topics/population/foreign-born.html>.

Mobility status—The U.S. population is classified according to mobility status on the basis of a comparison between the place of residence of each individual at the time of the survey or census and the place of residence at a specified earlier date. Nonmovers are all persons who were living in the same house or apartment at the end of the period as at the beginning of the period. Movers are all persons who were living in a different house or apartment at the end of the period than at the beginning of the period. Movers are further classified as to whether they were living in the same or different county, state, or region, or were movers from abroad. Movers from abroad include all persons whose place of residence was outside the United States (including Puerto Rico, other U.S. Island Area, or a foreign country) at the beginning of the period.

Living arrangements—Living arrangements refer to residency in households or in group quarters. A "household" comprises all persons who occupy a "housing unit," that is, a house, an apartment or other group of rooms, or a single room that constitutes "separate living quarters." A household includes the related family members and all the unrelated persons, if any, such as lodgers, foster children, or employees who share the housing unit. A person living alone or a group of unrelated persons sharing the same housing unit is also counted as a household. See text, Section 20, Construction and Housing, for definition of housing unit.

All persons not living in housing units are classified as living in group quarters. These individuals may be institutionalized, e.g., under care or custody in juvenile facilities, jails, correctional centers, hospitals, or nursing homes; or they may be residents in noninstitutional group quarters such as college dormitories, group homes, or military barracks.

Householder—The householder is the person, or one of the people, in whose name the home is owned, being bought, or rented. If a home is owned or rented jointly by a married couple, either spouse may be listed first. Two types of householders are distinguished: a family householder and a nonfamily householder. A family householder is a householder living with one or more people related to him or her by birth, marriage, or adoption. The householder and all people in the household related to him or her are family members. A family household may contain people not related to the householder, but those people are not included as part of the householder's family in census tabulations. Thus, the number of family households is equal to the number of families, but family households may include more members than do families.

Nonfamily—A nonfamily householder is a householder living alone or with nonrelatives only.

Subfamily— A subfamily is a married couple with or without children, or a single parent with one or more own never-married children under 18 years old, who does not maintain their own household, but lives in the home of someone else (the householder). Subfamilies are divided into "related" and "unrelated" subfamilies. A related subfamily is related to, but does not include, the householder or the spouse of the householder. Members of a related subfamily are also members of the family with whom they live. The number of related subfamilies, therefore, is not included in the count of families. An unrelated subfamily may include persons such as guests, lodgers, or resident employees and their spouses and/or children; none of whom is related to the householder. The number of unrelated subfamily members is included in the total number of household members, but is not included in the count of family members.

Married couple—A married couple is defined as a husband and wife living together in the same household, with or without children and other relatives.

Statistical reliability—For a discussion of statistical collection and estimation, sampling procedures, and measures of statistical reliability applicable to Census Bureau data, see Appendix III.

Figure 1.1
Percent Change in Population for States: April 1, 2000 to April 1, 2010

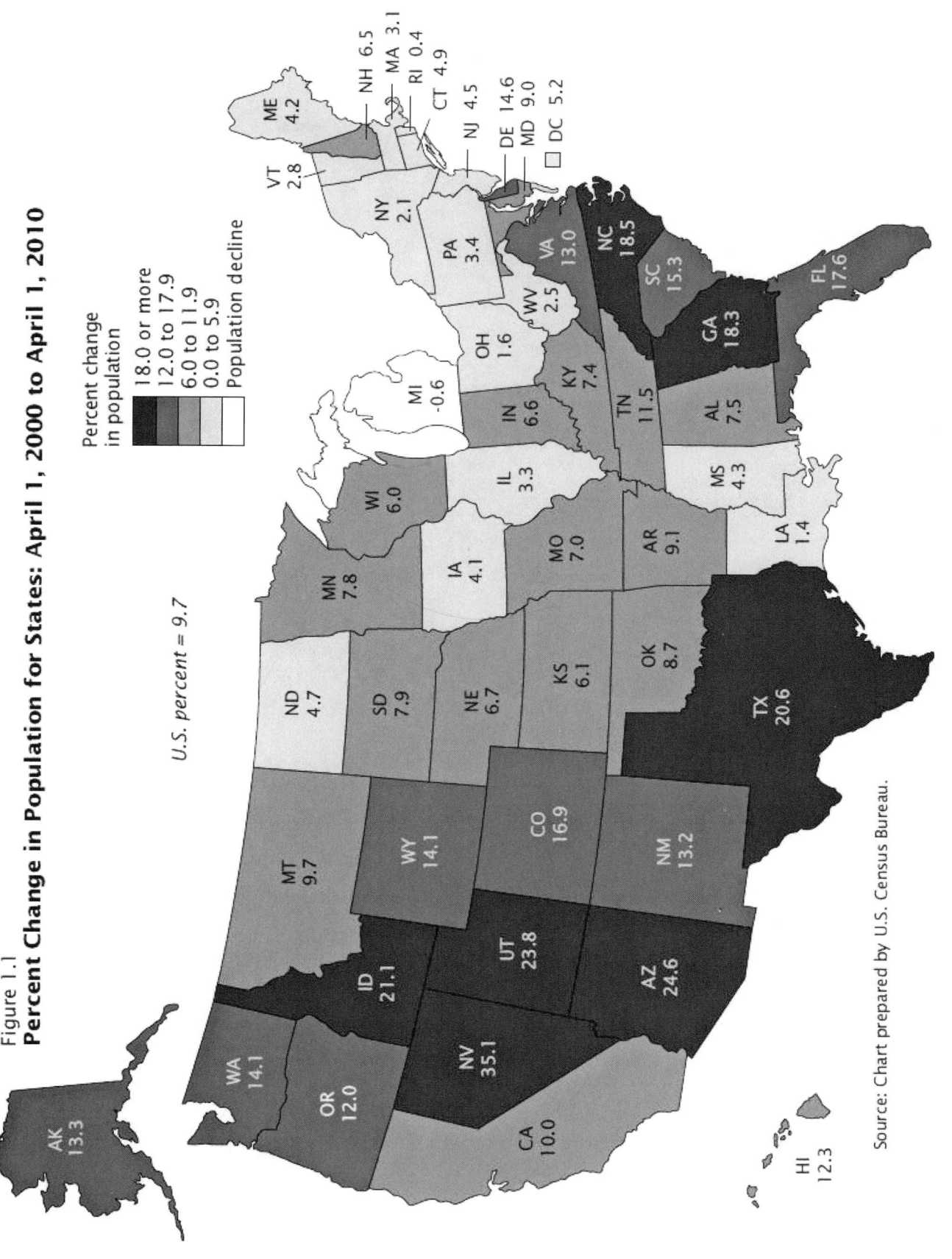

Percent change
in population

- 18.0 or more
- 12.0 to 17.9
- 6.0 to 11.9
- 0.0 to 5.9
- Population decline

U.S. percent = 9.7

Source: Chart prepared by U.S. Census Bureau.

Mean Center of Population for the United States: 1790 to 2010

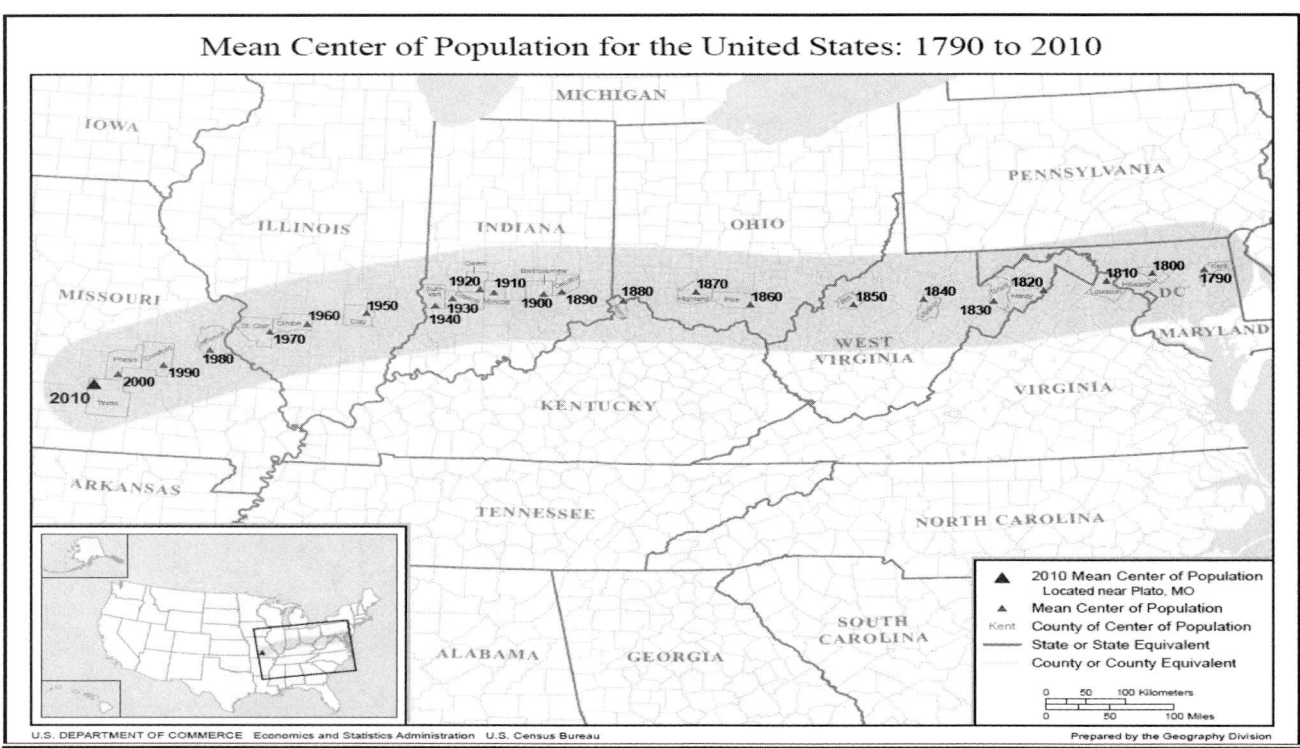

Legend:
- ▲ 2010 Mean Center of Population Located near Plato, MO
- ▴ Mean Center of Population
- Kent County of Center of Population
- State or State Equivalent
- County or County Equivalent

0   50   100 Kilometers
0   50   100 Miles

U.S. DEPARTMENT OF COMMERCE   Economics and Statistics Administration   U.S. Census Bureau

Prepared by the Geography Division

Median Center of Population for the United States: 1880 to 2010

Legend:
- ● 2010 Median Center of Population Located near Petersburg, IN
- • Median Center of Population
- State
- County

0   20   40 Kilometers
0   20   40 Miles

U.S. DEPARTMENT OF COMMERCE   Economics and Statistics Administration   U.S. Census Bureau

Prepared by the Geography Division

Table 1. Population and Area: 1790 to 2010

[Area figures represent area on indicated date including in some cases considerable areas not then organized or settled, and not covered by the census. Area data include Alaska beginning in 1870 and Hawaii beginning in 1900. Total area figures for 1790 to 1970 have been recalculated on the basis of the remeasurement of states and counties for the 1980 census, but not on the basis of subsequent censuses. The land and water area figures for past censuses have not been adjusted and are not strictly comparable with the total area data for comparable dates because the land areas were derived from different base data, and these values are known to have changed with the construction of reservoirs, draining of lakes, etc. Density figures are based on land area measurements as reported in earlier censuses]

| Census date | Resident population | | | | Area (square miles) | | |
| | Number | Per square mile of land area | Increase over preceding census | | Total | Land | Water [1] |
			Number	Percent			
1790 (Aug. 2).......	3,929,214	4.5	(X)	(X)	891,364	864,746	24,065
1800 (Aug. 4).......	5,308,483	6.1	1,379,269	35.1	891,364	864,746	24,065
1810 (Aug. 6).......	7,239,881	4.3	1,931,398	36.4	1,722,685	1,681,828	34,175
1820 (Aug. 7).......	9,638,453	5.5	2,398,572	33.1	1,792,552	1,749,462	38,544
1830 (June 1)......	12,866,020	7.4	3,227,567	33.5	1,792,552	1,749,462	38,544
1840 (June 1)......	17,069,453	9.8	4,203,433	32.7	1,792,552	1,749,462	38,544
1850 (June 1)......	23,191,876	7.9	6,122,423	35.9	2,991,655	2,940,042	52,705
1860 (June 1)......	31,443,321	10.6	8,251,445	35.6	3,021,295	2,969,640	52,747
1870 (June 1)......	[2] 39,818,449	[2] 11.2	8,375,128	26.6	3,612,299	3,540,705	68,082
1880 (June 1)......	50,189,209	14.2	10,370,760	26.0	3,612,299	3,540,705	68,082
1890 (June 1)......	62,979,766	17.8	12,790,557	25.5	3,612,299	3,540,705	68,082
1900 (June 1)......	76,212,168	21.5	13,232,402	21.0	3,618,770	3,547,314	67,901
1910 (Apr. 15).....	92,228,496	26.0	16,016,328	21.0	3,618,770	3,547,045	68,170
1920 (Jan. 1)......	106,021,537	29.9	13,793,041	15.0	3,618,770	3,546,931	68,284
1930 (Apr. 1).......	123,202,624	34.7	17,181,087	16.2	3,618,770	3,554,608	60,607
1940 (Apr. 1)........	132,164,569	37.2	8,961,945	7.3	3,618,770	3,554,608	60,607
1950 (Apr. 1).......	151,325,798	42.6	19,161,229	14.5	3,618,770	3,552,206	63,005
1960 (Apr. 1).......	179,323,175	50.6	27,997,377	18.5	3,618,770	3,540,911	74,212
1970 (Apr. 1).......	203,302,031	57.5	23,978,856	13.4	3,618,770	3,536,855	78,444
1980 (Apr. 1).......	[3] 226,542,199	64.0	23,240,168	11.4	3,618,770	3,539,289	79,481
1990 (Apr. 1).......	[4] 248,718,302	70.3	22,176,103	9.8	[5] 3,717,796	3,536,278	[5] 181,518
2000 (Apr. 1).......	[6] 281,424,603	79.6	32,706,301	13.1	3,794,083	3,537,438	256,645
2010 (Apr. 1)........	[7] 308,746,065	87.4	27,321,462	9.7	3,796,742	3,531,905	264,837

X Not applicable. [1] Data for 1790 to 1980 cover inland water only. Data for 1990 comprise Great Lakes, inland, and coastal water. Data for 2000 and 2010 comprise Great Lakes, inland, territorial, and coastal water. [2] Revised to include adjustments for underenumeration in southern states; unrevised number is 38,558,371 (10.9 per square mile). [3] Total population count has been revised since the 1980 census publications. Numbers by age, race, Hispanic origin, and sex have not been corrected. [4] The April 1, 1990, census count includes count question resolution corrections processed through December 1997, and does not include adjustments for census coverage errors. [5] Data reflect corrections made after publication of the results. [6] Reflects modifications to the Census 2000 population as documented in the Count Question Resolution program. [7] Reflects modifications to the Census 2010 population as documented in the Count Question Resolution program (updated February 11, 2014).

Source: U.S. Census Bureau, *Notes and Errata, 2010 Census of Population and Housing*, SF/10-1, 2014; 2000 Census of Population and Housing, *Population and Housing Unit Counts, United States Summary*, Series PHC-3-1, and *Notes and Errata*, (2000), SF/01-ER; *Areas of the United States: 1940*; Area data for 1990: unpublished data from TIGER ®; and Davis, Warren, personal correspondence, U.S. Census Bureau, 23 June 2006.

Table 2. Population: 1970 to 2016

[In thousands (205,052 represents 205,052,000). Estimates as of July 1. Civilian population excludes Armed Forces. For basis of estimates, see text, this section]

Year	Resident population, including Armed Forces overseas	Resident population	Civilian population	Year	Resident population, including Armed Forces overseas	Resident population	Civilian population
1970........	205,052	203,984	201,895	1994........	263,436	263,126	261,714
1972........	209,896	209,284	207,511	1995........	266,557	266,278	264,927
1973........	211,909	211,357	209,600	1996........	269,667	269,394	268,108
1974........	213,854	213,342	211,636	1997........	272,912	272,647	271,394
1975........	215,973	215,465	213,789	1998........	276,115	275,854	274,633
1976........	218,035	217,563	215,894	1999........	279,295	279,040	277,841
1977........	220,239	219,760	218,106	2000........	(NA)	282,162	(NA)
1978........	222,585	222,095	220,467	2001........	(NA)	284,969	(NA)
1979........	225,055	224,567	222,969	2002........	(NA)	287,625	(NA)
1980........	227,726	227,225	225,621	2003........	(NA)	290,108	(NA)
1981........	229,966	229,466	227,818	2004........	(NA)	292,805	(NA)
1982........	232,188	231,664	229,995	2005........	(NA)	295,517	(NA)
1983........	234,307	233,792	232,097	2006........	(NA)	298,380	(NA)
1984........	236,348	235,825	234,110	2007........	(NA)	301,231	(NA)
1985........	238,466	237,924	236,219	2008........	(NA)	304,094	(NA)
1986........	240,651	240,133	238,412	2009........	(NA)	306,772	(NA)
1987........	242,804	242,289	240,550	2010........	309,768	309,348	308,113
1988........	245,021	244,499	242,817	2011........	312,080	311,663	310,446
1989........	247,342	246,819	245,131	2012........	314,335	313,998	312,758
1990........	250,132	249,623	247,983	2013........	316,506	316,205	314,962
1991........	253,493	252,981	251,370	2014........	318,839	318,563	317,338
1992........	256,894	256,514	254,929	2015........	321,132	320,897	319,700
1993........	260,255	259,919	258,446	2016........	323,349	323,128	321,925

NA Not available.

Source: U.S. Census Bureau, Population Division, data prior to 2010, <http://www.census.gov/programs-surveys/popest.html>; and 2010 to 2016, "Monthly Population Estimates for the United States: April 1, 2010 to December 1, 2017," <http://www.census.gov/data/tables/2016/demo/popest/nation-total.html>, accessed January 2017.

Table 3. Resident Population Projections and Components of Change: 2015 to 2060

[In thousands, except as indicated (321,369 represents 321,369,000). As of July 1. The 2014 National Projections are based on the July 1, 2013 population estimates, which are based on the 2010 Census. The projections were produced using a cohort-component method and are based on assumptions about future births, deaths, and net international migration. More information on methodology and assumptions is available at <http://www.census.gov/population/projections/files/methodology/methodstatement14.pdf>]

Year	Population			Components of Change			
	Total	Numeric change	Percent change [1]	Natural increase	Births	Deaths	Net international migration [2]
2015.................	321,369	2,621	0.8	1,380	3,999	2,619	1,241
2016.................	323,996	2,627	0.8	1,377	4,027	2,650	1,250
2017.................	326,626	2,630	0.8	1,374	4,055	2,681	1,256
2018.................	329,256	2,631	0.8	1,369	4,080	2,712	1,262
2019.................	331,884	2,628	0.8	1,361	4,104	2,743	1,267
2020.................	334,503	2,619	0.8	1,349	4,125	2,777	1,271
2021.................	337,109	2,606	0.8	1,331	4,142	2,811	1,275
2022.................	339,698	2,589	0.8	1,307	4,155	2,848	1,282
2023.................	342,267	2,569	0.8	1,279	4,165	2,887	1,291
2024.................	344,814	2,547	0.7	1,246	4,174	2,927	1,301
2025.................	347,335	2,521	0.7	1,210	4,181	2,971	1,310
2026.................	349,826	2,491	0.7	1,171	4,187	3,016	1,320
2027.................	352,281	2,456	0.7	1,127	4,191	3,064	1,329
2028.................	354,698	2,417	0.7	1,079	4,194	3,115	1,338
2029.................	357,073	2,374	0.7	1,028	4,196	3,168	1,347
2030.................	359,402	2,329	0.7	974	4,198	3,224	1,355
2031.................	361,685	2,283	0.6	919	4,200	3,281	1,363
2032.................	363,920	2,235	0.6	864	4,203	3,339	1,371
2033.................	366,106	2,187	0.6	808	4,207	3,399	1,379
2034.................	368,246	2,139	0.6	753	4,212	3,459	1,386
2035.................	370,338	2,093	0.6	699	4,219	3,520	1,394
2036.................	372,390	2,052	0.6	651	4,227	3,576	1,401
2037.................	374,401	2,012	0.5	604	4,235	3,631	1,407
2038.................	376,375	1,974	0.5	560	4,245	3,685	1,414
2039.................	378,313	1,938	0.5	518	4,255	3,737	1,420
2040.................	380,219	1,906	0.5	479	4,266	3,787	1,426
2041.................	382,096	1,877	0.5	445	4,278	3,833	1,432
2042.................	383,949	1,852	0.5	414	4,290	3,876	1,438
2043.................	385,779	1,831	0.5	388	4,303	3,916	1,443
2044.................	387,593	1,814	0.5	365	4,317	3,952	1,448
2045.................	389,394	1,801	0.5	348	4,332	3,984	1,453
2046.................	391,187	1,792	0.5	335	4,347	4,012	1,458
2047.................	392,973	1,786	0.5	324	4,362	4,038	1,462
2048.................	394,756	1,783	0.5	317	4,377	4,060	1,466
2049.................	396,540	1,784	0.5	314	4,391	4,077	1,470
2050.................	398,328	1,788	0.5	315	4,406	4,091	1,473
2055.................	407,412	1,840	0.5	352	4,470	4,117	1,488
2060.................	416,795	1,898	0.5	403	4,519	4,116	1,495

[1] Percent change from immediate preceding year. 2015, change from 2014. [2] Net international migration includes the international migration of both native and foreign-born populations. Specifically, it includes: (a) the net international migration of the foreign born, (b) the net international migration of the native born, and (c) the net migration between the United States and Puerto Rico.

Source: U.S. Census Bureau, Population Division, "Table 1. Projections of the Population and Components of Change for the United States: 2015 to 2060 (NP2014-T1)," December 2014, <https://www.census.gov/programs-surveys/popproj/data/tables.html>, accessed March 2015.

Table 4. Components of Population Change: 2010 to 2016

[In thousands, except as indicated (308,758 represents 308,758,000). Resident population]

Period	Population as of beginning of period	Net increase		Births	Deaths	Net international migration [2]	Population as of end of period
		Total	Percent [1]				
April 1, 2010 to July 1, 2010 [3].....................	308,758	590	0.2	988	599	201	309,348
July 1, 2010 to July 1, 2011.................	309,348	2,315	0.7	3,973	2,512	854	311,663
July 1, 2011 to July 1, 2012.................	311,663	2,335	0.7	3,937	2,502	900	313,998
July 1, 2012 to July 1, 2013.................	313,998	2,207	0.7	3,941	2,608	874	316,205
July 1, 2013 to July 1, 2014.................	316,205	2,359	0.7	3,963	2,582	978	318,563
July 1, 2014 to July 1, 2015.................	318,563	2,333	0.7	3,983	2,687	1,037	320,897
July 1, 2015 to July 1, 2016.................	320,897	2,231	0.7	3,978	2,746	999	323,128

[1] Percent of population at beginning of period. [2] Net international migration includes the international migration of both native and foreign-born populations. Specifically, it includes: (a) the net international migration of the foreign born, (b) the net migration between the United States and Puerto Rico, (c) the net migration of natives to and from the United States, and (d) the net movement of the Armed Forces population between the United States and overseas. [3] The April 1, 2010 population estimates base reflects changes from the Count Question Resolution program and geographic program revisions.

Source: U.S. Census Bureau, Population Division, "Population estimates, population change, and components of population change: April 1, 2010 to July 1, 2016 (NST-EST2016-alldata)," <http://www.census.gov/data/tables/2016/demo/popest/nation-total.html>, accessed January 2017.

Table 5. Components of Population Change by Race and Hispanic Origin: 2010 to 2016

[In thousands (14,369 represents 14,369,000). Resident population. Covers period April 1, 2010 to July 1, 2016. The April 1, 2010 population estimates base reflects changes to the Census 2010 population from the Count Question Resolution program and geographic program revisions. Responses of "Some Other Race" from the 2010 Census are modified. This results in differences between the population for specific race categories shown for the 2010 Census population in this table versus those in the original 2010 Census data. Minus sign (-) indicates decrease]

Race and Hispanic origin	April 1, 2010 to July 1, 2016				
	Net increase	Natural increase	Births	Deaths	Net international migration [1]
Total	**14,369**	**8,527**	**24,763**	**16,236**	**5,842**
One race	12,874	7,182	23,281	16,099	5,692
White	6,557	4,109	17,839	13,730	2,448
Black or African American	2,746	1,895	3,785	1,890	851
American Indian and Alaska Native	315	285	402	117	30
Asian	3,159	829	1,180	351	2,330
Native Hawaiian and Other Pacific Islander	97	64	75	10	33
Two or more races	1,495	1,345	1,482	137	150
Race alone or in combination: [2]					
White	7,937	5,362	19,203	13,841	2,576
Black or African American	3,562	2,651	4,587	1,936	911
American Indian and Alaska Native	568	516	702	186	51
Asian	3,742	1,326	1,721	396	2,417
Native Hawaiian and Other Pacific Islander	199	155	181	26	45
Hispanic [3]	6,992	5,369	6,389	1,020	1,623
White alone, not Hispanic	643	-399	12,401	12,800	1,042

[1] Net international migration includes the international migration of both native and foreign-born populations. Specifically, it includes: (a) the net international migration of the foreign born, (b) the net migration between the United States and Puerto Rico, (c) the net migration of natives to and from the United States, and (d) the net movement of the Armed Forces population between the United States and overseas. [2] In combination with one or more other races. The sum of the five race groups adds to more than the total population because individuals may report more than one race. [3] Hispanic origin is considered an ethnicity, not a race. Persons of Hispanic origin may be of any race.

Source: U.S. Census Bureau, Population Division, "Estimates of the Components of Resident Population Change by Race and Hispanic Origin for the United States: April 1, 2010 to July 1, 2016," <http://factfinder.census.gov>, accessed June 2017.

Table 6. Resident Population by Sex and Age: 2000 to 2016

[In thousands, except as indicated (281,425 represents 281,425,000). As of April 1, except 2015 and 2016 as of July 1. Excludes Armed Forces overseas]

Age	2000 [1]			2010 [1]			2015			2016		
	Total	Male	Female	Total	Male	Female	Total	Male	Female	Total	Male	Female
Total	**281,425**	**138,056**	**143,368**	**308,758**	**151,789**	**156,969**	**320,897**	**157,960**	**162,937**	**323,128**	**159,079**	**164,049**
Under 5 years	19,176	9,811	9,365	20,201	10,319	9,882	19,912	10,181	9,732	19,927	10,187	9,740
5 to 9 years	20,550	10,523	10,026	20,349	10,390	9,959	20,481	10,455	10,026	20,430	10,430	10,000
10 to 14 years	20,528	10,520	10,008	20,677	10,580	10,097	20,606	10,511	10,094	20,618	10,519	10,100
15 to 19 years	20,219	10,391	9,828	22,042	11,305	10,737	21,085	10,785	10,299	21,130	10,802	10,328
20 to 24 years	18,963	9,688	9,275	21,588	11,015	10,572	22,693	11,645	11,048	22,381	11,491	10,890
25 to 29 years	19,382	9,799	9,583	21,103	10,637	10,467	22,401	11,379	11,022	22,891	11,631	11,259
30 to 34 years	20,511	10,322	10,189	19,963	9,997	9,966	21,618	10,861	10,757	21,786	10,968	10,818
35 to 39 years	22,707	11,319	11,388	20,180	10,043	10,138	20,313	10,142	10,170	20,774	10,376	10,397
40 to 44 years	22,442	11,130	11,313	20,892	10,395	10,497	20,157	10,002	10,155	19,696	9,776	9,920
45 to 49 years	20,093	9,890	10,203	22,709	11,210	11,500	20,801	10,309	10,493	20,948	10,376	10,572
50 to 54 years	17,586	8,608	8,978	22,299	10,934	11,365	22,290	10,941	11,348	21,839	10,730	11,109
55 to 59 years	13,469	6,509	6,961	19,665	9,524	10,141	21,768	10,577	11,191	21,980	10,683	11,297
60 to 64 years	10,806	5,137	5,669	16,818	8,078	8,741	19,039	9,100	9,938	19,483	9,316	10,167
65 to 74 years	18,391	8,303	10,088	21,714	10,097	11,617	27,527	12,878	14,649	28,630	13,391	15,239
75 to 84 years	12,361	4,879	7,482	13,062	5,477	7,585	13,919	6,020	7,899	14,234	6,177	8,057
85 years and over	4,240	1,227	3,013	5,495	1,790	3,705	6,289	2,173	4,116	6,380	2,225	4,155
5 to 13 years	37,026	18,964	18,062	36,860	18,834	18,026	36,905	18,832	18,073	36,954	18,861	18,093
14 to 17 years	16,093	8,285	7,808	17,121	8,792	8,329	16,799	8,586	8,213	16,761	8,561	8,200
18 to 24 years	27,141	13,873	13,268	30,674	15,663	15,011	31,160	15,979	15,182	30,844	15,819	15,025
18 years and over	209,130	100,996	108,133	234,576	113,843	120,733	247,280	120,361	126,919	249,485	121,470	128,016
55 years and over	59,267	26,055	33,212	76,755	34,966	41,789	88,541	40,748	47,792	90,707	41,792	48,915
65 years and over	34,992	14,410	20,582	40,271	17,364	22,907	47,734	21,071	26,664	49,244	21,793	27,451
75 years and over	16,601	6,106	10,495	18,557	7,267	11,290	20,207	8,193	12,014	20,614	8,402	12,212

[1] The April 1, 2000 and April 1, 2010 population estimates bases reflect changes to the Census 2000 and Census 2010 population from the Count Question Resolution program and geographic program revisions.

Source: U.S. Census Bureau, "Intercensal Estimates of the United States Population by Age and Sex, 1990-2000: All Months," September 2002, <https://www.census.gov/data/tables/time-series/demo/popest/intercensal-national.html>; and "Annual estimates of the resident population by single year of age and sex for the United States: April 1, 2010 to July 1, 2016 (NC-EST2016-AGESEX-RES)," <https://www.census.gov/data/tables/2016/demo/popest/nation-detail.html>, accessed May 2017.

Table 7. Resident Population by Sex, Race, and Hispanic Origin: 2000 to 2016

[281,425 represents 281,425,000. Data shown are modified race counts; see text, this section]

Characteristic	Number (1,000)					Percent change	
	2000 [1] (April)	2010 [1] (April)	2014 (July)	2015 (July)	2016 (July)	2000 to 2010	2010 to 2016
BOTH SEXES							
Total....................	**281,425**	**308,758**	**318,563**	**320,897**	**323,128**	**9.7**	**4.7**
One race...................	277,527	301,774	310,576	312,663	314,648	8.7	4.3
White...................	228,106	241,945	246,512	247,543	248,503	6.1	2.7
Black or African American....................	35,705	40,254	42,131	42,574	43,001	12.7	6.8
American Indian and Alaska Native.....................	2,664	3,740	3,955	4,006	4,055	40.4	8.4
Asian...................	10,589	15,160	17,238	17,785	18,319	43.2	20.8
Native Hawaiian and Other Pacific Islander...............	463	675	740	756	771	45.9	14.4
Two or more races...................	3,898	6,984	7,988	8,233	8,480	79.2	21.4
Race alone or in combination: [2]							
White...................	(NA)	248,076	253,569	254,826	256,013	(NA)	3.2
Black or African American....................	(NA)	43,217	45,640	46,217	46,779	(NA)	8.2
American Indian and Alaska Native.....................	(NA)	6,139	6,525	6,617	6,706	(NA)	9.2
Asian...................	(NA)	17,677	20,146	20,789	21,419	(NA)	21.2
Native Hawaiian and Other Pacific Islander...............	(NA)	1,333	1,467	1,500	1,532	(NA)	15.0
Not Hispanic...................	246,118	258,279	263,373	264,558	265,657	4.9	2.9
One race...................	242,712	252,675	256,992	257,987	258,895	4.1	2.5
White...................	195,577	197,326	197,902	197,964	197,970	0.9	0.3
Black or African American....................	34,314	37,926	39,508	39,877	40,229	10.5	6.1
American Indian and Alaska Native.....................	2,097	2,263	2,351	2,370	2,387	7.9	5.5
Asian...................	10,357	14,662	16,687	17,221	17,741	41.6	21.0
Native Hawaiian and Other Pacific Islander...............	367	497	544	556	567	35.4	14.1
Two or more races...................	3,406	5,605	6,381	6,571	6,762	64.5	20.7
Race alone or in combination: [2]							
White...................	(NA)	202,237	203,533	203,770	203,953	(NA)	0.8
Black or African American....................	(NA)	40,287	42,290	42,761	43,219	(NA)	7.3
American Indian and Alaska Native.....................	(NA)	4,042	4,225	4,266	4,306	(NA)	6.5
Asian...................	(NA)	16,795	19,150	19,765	20,367	(NA)	21.3
Native Hawaiian and Other Pacific Islander...............	(NA)	1,020	1,118	1,142	1,166	(NA)	14.3
Hispanic [3]...................	35,306	50,479	55,190	56,339	57,470	43.0	13.9
One race...................	34,815	49,099	53,583	54,676	55,753	41.0	13.6
White...................	32,530	44,619	48,610	49,579	50,533	37.2	13.3
Black or African American....................	1,391	2,328	2,623	2,698	2,771	67.4	19.0
American Indian and Alaska Native.....................	566	1,476	1,604	1,636	1,667	160.6	12.9
Asian...................	232	498	551	564	577	114.2	15.9
Native Hawaiian and Other Pacific Islander...............	95	177	195	200	204	85.9	15.1
Two or more races...................	491	1,380	1,607	1,662	1,717	180.8	24.5
Race alone or in combination: [2]							
White...................	(NA)	45,839	50,036	51,055	52,060	(NA)	13.6
Black or African American....................	(NA)	2,930	3,350	3,456	3,560	(NA)	21.5
American Indian and Alaska Native.....................	(NA)	2,097	2,300	2,351	2,400	(NA)	14.4
Asian...................	(NA)	881	996	1,025	1,052	(NA)	19.4
Native Hawaiian and Other Pacific Islander...............	(NA)	312	349	358	366	(NA)	17.3
MALE							
Total....................	**138,056**	**151,789**	**156,780**	**157,960**	**159,079**	**9.9**	**4.8**
One race...................	136,146	148,362	152,843	153,897	154,890	9.0	4.4
White...................	112,478	119,703	122,105	122,643	123,134	6.4	2.9
Black or African American....................	16,972	19,208	20,156	20,378	20,592	13.2	7.2
American Indian and Alaska Native.....................	1,333	1,890	1,996	2,021	2,045	41.8	8.2
Asian...................	5,128	7,219	8,210	8,472	8,728	40.8	20.9
Native Hawaiian and Other Pacific Islander...............	235	343	376	384	392	45.8	14.2
Two or more races...................	1,910	3,426	3,937	4,063	4,189	79.4	22.3
Race alone or in combination: [2]							
White...................	(NA)	122,721	125,594	126,247	126,855	(NA)	3.4
Black or African American....................	(NA)	20,635	21,861	22,152	22,435	(NA)	8.7
American Indian and Alaska Native.....................	(NA)	3,055	3,247	3,293	3,338	(NA)	9.3
Asian...................	(NA)	8,468	9,661	9,972	10,276	(NA)	21.3
Native Hawaiian and Other Pacific Islander...............	(NA)	668	736	753	769	(NA)	15.2
Not Hispanic...................	119,894	126,169	128,882	129,500	130,063	5.2	3.1
Hispanic [3]...................	18,162	25,620	27,898	28,460	29,016	41.1	13.3
FEMALE							
Total....................	**143,368**	**156,969**	**161,783**	**162,937**	**164,049**	**9.5**	**4.5**
One race...................	141,381	153,411	157,733	158,766	159,758	8.5	4.1
White...................	115,628	122,242	124,407	124,900	125,368	5.7	2.6
Black or African American....................	18,733	21,047	21,976	22,197	22,409	12.4	6.5
American Indian and Alaska Native.....................	1,331	1,850	1,959	1,985	2,010	39.0	8.7
Asian...................	5,461	7,941	9,027	9,312	9,591	45.4	20.8
Native Hawaiian and Other Pacific Islander...............	227	332	364	372	380	45.9	14.5
Two or more races...................	1,987	3,558	4,050	4,170	4,291	79.0	20.6
Race alone or in combination: [2]							
White...................	(NA)	125,355	127,975	128,579	129,158	(NA)	3.0
Black or African American....................	(NA)	22,582	23,779	24,066	24,344	(NA)	7.8
American Indian and Alaska Native.....................	(NA)	3,084	3,278	3,324	3,368	(NA)	9.2
Asian...................	(NA)	9,209	10,486	10,817	11,143	(NA)	21.0
Native Hawaiian and Other Pacific Islander...............	(NA)	665	731	747	763	(NA)	14.8
Not Hispanic...................	126,224	132,110	134,491	135,058	135,594	4.7	2.6
Hispanic [3]...................	17,144	24,859	27,292	27,878	28,455	45.0	14.5

NA Not available. [1] The April 1, 2000 and 2010 population estimates base reflects changes to the Census 2000 and 2010 population from the Count Question Resolution program and geographic program revisions. [2] In combination with one or more other races. The sum of the five race groups adds to more than the total population because individuals may report more than one race. [3] Persons of Hispanic origin may be of any race.

Source: U.S. Census Bureau, Population Division, "Table 2. (US-EST00INT-02)," September 2011, <https://www.census.gov/data/tables/time-series/demo/popest/intercensal-2000-2010-national.html>; and "Monthly Postcensal Resident Population, by single year of age, sex, race, and Hispanic origin," <https://www.census.gov/data/tables/2016/demo/popest/nation-total.html>; accessed June 2017.

Table 8. Resident Population Projections by Sex and Age: 2020 to 2060

[In thousands, except as indicated (334,503 represents 334,503,000). As of July 1. The 2014 National Projections are based on the July 1, 2013 population estimates, which are based on the 2010 Census. The projections were produced using a cohort-component method and are based on assumptions about future births, deaths, and net international migration. More information on methodology and assumptions is available at <https://www.census.gov/programs-surveys/popproj/technical-documentation/methodology.html>]

Age	2020 Total	2020 Male	2020 Female	2025	2030	2035	2040	2045	2050	2060	Percent distribution 2020	2030	2040	2050	2060
Total	334,503	165,036	169,467	347,335	359,402	370,338	380,219	389,394	398,328	416,795	100.0	100.0	100.0	100.0	100.0
FIVE-YEAR AGE GROUPS															
Under 5 years	20,568	10,520	10,047	21,010	21,178	21,268	21,471	21,775	22,147	22,778	6.1	5.9	5.6	5.6	5.5
5 to 9 years	20,274	10,360	9,914	20,889	21,347	21,529	21,632	21,845	22,158	22,894	6.1	5.9	5.7	5.6	5.5
10 to 14 years	20,735	10,584	10,150	20,555	21,182	21,650	21,842	21,952	22,171	22,871	6.2	5.9	5.7	5.6	5.5
15 to 19 years	21,048	10,749	10,299	21,219	21,060	21,706	22,190	23,383	22,516	23,067	6.3	5.9	5.8	5.7	5.5
20 to 24 years	22,059	11,300	10,759	22,077	22,299	22,183	22,866	24,098	23,615	23,999	6.6	6.2	6.0	5.9	5.8
25 to 29 years	23,722	12,161	11,561	23,103	23,179	23,450	23,377	24,259	24,646	25,065	7.1	6.4	6.1	6.2	6.0
30 to 34 years	23,168	11,781	11,387	24,450	23,878	23,995	24,302	24,813	25,004	25,845	6.9	6.6	6.4	6.3	6.2
35 to 39 years	22,060	11,099	10,961	23,586	24,360	24,360	24,507	24,838	24,813	26,151	6.6	6.9	6.4	6.2	6.3
40 to 44 years	20,568	10,272	10,296	22,291	23,840	25,176	24,668	24,840	25,190	25,949	6.1	6.6	6.5	6.3	6.2
45 to 49 years	20,204	10,010	10,195	20,613	22,351	23,919	25,274	24,798	24,995	25,368	6.0	6.2	6.6	6.3	6.1
50 to 54 years	20,638	10,182	10,456	20,063	20,506	22,257	23,844	25,219	24,781	25,395	6.2	5.7	6.3	6.2	6.1
55 to 59 years	21,879	10,651	11,228	20,294	19,777	20,260	22,023	23,629	25,023	24,893	6.5	5.5	5.8	6.3	6.0
60 to 64 years	21,141	10,147	10,993	21,265	19,799	19,351	19,880	21,653	23,275	24,357	6.3	5.5	5.2	5.8	5.8
65 to 69 years	18,194	8,567	9,626	20,202	20,397	19,071	18,704	19,283	21,054	24,112	5.4	5.7	4.9	5.3	5.8
70 to 74 years	14,882	6,900	7,982	16,891	18,830	19,091	17,940	17,664	18,294	21,662	4.4	5.2	4.7	4.6	5.2
75 to 79 years	10,112	4,538	5,574	13,154	15,013	16,819	17,143	16,212	16,042	18,393	3.0	4.2	4.5	4.0	4.4
80 to 84 years	6,527	2,783	3,744	8,191	10,737	12,343	13,924	14,294	13,634	14,274	2.0	3.0	3.7	3.4	3.4
85 to 89 years	3,964	1,545	2,420	4,521	5,747	7,622	8,867	10,114	10,492	10,184	1.2	1.6	2.3	2.6	2.4
90 to 94 years	2,024	686	1,337	2,114	2,464	3,192	4,320	5,127	5,951	6,184	0.6	0.7	1.1	1.5	1.5
95 to 99 years	649	181	468	728	782	940	1,254	1,751	2,141	2,752	0.2	0.2	0.3	0.5	0.7
100 years and over	89	20	69	119	138	154	193	267	387	604	(Z)	(Z)	0.1	0.1	0.1
SPECIAL AGE CATEGORIES															
5 to 13 years	36,824	18,806	18,018	37,316	38,322	38,848	39,087	39,389	39,887	41,193	11.0	10.7	10.3	10.0	9.9
14 to 17 years	16,737	8,547	8,190	16,689	16,773	17,330	17,627	17,746	17,854	18,338	5.0	4.7	4.6	4.5	4.4
18 to 24 years	30,555	15,641	14,915	30,736	30,794	30,890	31,815	32,440	32,717	33,300	9.1	8.6	8.4	8.2	8.0
16 years and over	268,750	131,438	137,312	280,749	291,500	301,559	310,879	319,400	327,402	343,677	80.3	81.1	81.8	82.2	82.5
18 years and over	260,375	127,163	133,212	272,319	283,129	292,892	302,034	310,484	318,440	334,486	77.8	78.8	79.4	79.9	80.3
15 to 44 years	132,625	67,362	65,262	136,726	139,154	140,869	141,910	143,813	145,784	150,076	39.6	38.7	37.3	36.6	36.0
16 to 64 years	212,309	106,218	106,091	214,829	217,393	222,326	228,535	234,688	239,406	245,513	63.5	60.5	60.1	60.1	58.9
55 years and over	99,461	46,018	53,441	107,479	113,684	118,843	124,248	129,994	136,293	147,415	29.7	31.6	32.7	34.2	35.4
65 years and over	56,441	25,220	31,221	65,920	74,107	79,233	82,344	84,712	87,996	98,164	16.9	20.6	21.7	22.1	23.6
75 years and over	23,365	9,753	13,612	28,827	34,881	41,070	45,701	47,765	48,647	52,391	7.0	9.7	12.0	12.2	12.6
85 years and over	6,727	2,432	4,295	7,482	9,132	11,909	14,634	17,259	18,972	19,724	2.0	2.5	3.8	4.8	4.7
Median age (years)[1]	38.5	37.3	39.8	39.3	40.1	41.0	41.6	42.0	42.4	43.0	(X)	(X)	(X)	(X)	(X)

X Not applicable. Z Less than 0.05 percent. [1] For definition of median, see Guide to Tabular Presentation.

Source: U.S. Census Bureau, "Table 3. Projections of the Population by Sex and Selected Age Groups for the United States: 2015 to 2060 (NP2014-T3)," and "Table 9. Projections of the Population by Sex and Age for the United States: 2015 to 2060 (NP2014-T9)," December 2014, <https://www.census.gov/programs-surveys/popproj/data/tables.html>; accessed June 2016.

Table 9. Resident Population by Race, Hispanic Origin, and Age: 2010 and 2016

[In thousands, except as indicated (308,758 represents 308,758,000). 2010 data as of April 1. 2016 data as of July 1]

Age	Total 2010[1]	Total 2016	White alone 2010[1]	White alone 2016	Black or African American alone 2010[1]	Black or African American alone 2016	American Indian, Alaska Native alone 2010[1]	American Indian, Alaska Native alone 2016	Asian alone 2010[1]	Asian alone 2016	Native Hawaiian, Other Pacific Islander alone 2010[1]	Native Hawaiian, Other Pacific Islander alone 2016	Two or more races 2010[1]	Two or more races 2016	Hispanic origin[2] 2010[1]	Hispanic origin[2] 2016	Not Hispanic White alone 2010[1]	Not Hispanic White alone 2016
Total	**308,758**	**323,128**	**241,945**	**248,503**	**40,254**	**43,001**	**3,740**	**4,055**	**15,160**	**18,319**	**675**	**771**	**6,984**	**8,480**	**50,479**	**57,470**	**197,326**	**197,970**
FIVE-YEAR AGE GROUPS																		
Under 5 years	20,201	19,927	14,691	14,256	3,055	3,038	330	322	948	1,055	59	62	1,119	1,194	5,114	5,145	10,307	9,885
5 to 9 years	20,349	20,430	15,044	14,727	3,013	3,100	321	327	972	1,060	56	61	944	1,154	4,791	5,271	10,885	10,208
10 to 14 years	20,677	20,618	15,399	15,112	3,155	3,050	318	326	922	1,080	54	59	829	991	4,525	5,022	11,449	10,762
15 to 19 years	22,042	21,130	16,347	15,557	3,573	3,223	340	322	999	1,097	60	57	723	873	4,532	4,791	12,387	11,381
20 to 24 years	21,588	22,381	16,247	16,362	3,240	3,538	319	336	1,149	1,311	66	62	566	772	4,322	4,803	12,468	12,158
25 to 29 years	21,103	22,891	16,061	16,796	2,912	3,498	300	332	1,279	1,569	64	71	488	625	4,311	4,611	12,269	12,769
30 to 34 years	19,963	21,786	15,185	16,306	2,746	3,020	275	304	1,284	1,577	56	69	420	511	4,125	4,454	11,534	12,393
35 to 39 years	20,180	20,774	15,473	15,632	2,707	2,872	261	282	1,334	1,478	49	61	357	449	3,856	4,293	12,018	11,846
40 to 44 years	20,892	19,696	16,342	14,912	2,752	2,659	251	258	1,188	1,450	45	51	314	366	3,442	3,956	13,250	11,381
45 to 49 years	22,709	20,948	18,103	16,258	2,902	2,741	255	251	1,105	1,320	43	48	302	330	3,022	3,572	15,387	13,056
50 to 54 years	22,299	21,839	18,009	17,253	2,753	2,813	228	248	1,004	1,180	37	45	268	301	2,442	3,113	15,813	14,460
55 to 59 years	19,665	21,980	16,144	17,681	2,246	2,694	177	227	863	1,065	28	39	207	274	1,841	2,537	14,476	15,402
60 to 64 years	16,818	19,483	14,089	15,914	1,715	2,209	134	179	703	936	21	30	156	216	1,372	1,932	12,839	14,169
65 to 69 years	12,436	16,820	10,564	14,017	1,181	1,710	89	135	483	772	14	23	105	162	949	1,434	9,694	12,715
70 to 74 years	9,278	11,810	7,911	9,992	865	1,094	60	85	361	519	9	15	72	105	700	968	7,266	9,108
75 to 79 years	7,318	8,368	6,341	7,111	625	755	39	56	255	368	6	9	51	69	511	670	5,867	6,495
80 to 84 years	5,744	5,866	5,079	5,039	430	501	25	34	171	242	4	6	35	44	351	452	4,752	4,621
85 to 89 years	3,621	3,885	3,244	3,400	248	292	13	19	94	146	2	3	20	26	185	279	3,072	3,140
90 to 94 years	1,449	1,883	1,300	1,652	101	140	5	8	35	69	1	1	7	12	65	126	1,240	1,535
95 to 99 years	371	530	328	459	31	44	1	2	9	21	(Z)	(Z)	2	3	18	35	312	427
100 years and over	53	82	45	67	7	10	(Z)	(Z)	1	4	(Z)	(Z)	(Z)	1	3	7	42	61
SPECIAL AGE CATEGORIES																		
5 to 13 years	36,860	36,954	27,331	26,826	5,530	5,537	576	590	1,707	1,930	99	109	1,617	1,963	8,426	9,323	20,002	18,800
14 to 17 years	17,121	16,761	12,724	12,338	2,732	2,545	263	258	756	853	45	46	601	721	3,591	3,877	9,582	8,963
18 to 24 years	30,674	30,844	22,982	22,594	4,719	4,829	459	464	1,579	1,765	92	84	844	1,108	6,154	6,686	17,606	16,745
16 years and over	243,288	257,955	193,656	201,322	30,361	33,176	2,706	3,015	12,130	14,907	495	578	3,939	4,957	35,154	41,055	162,310	164,880
18 years and over	234,576	249,485	187,200	195,082	28,937	31,881	2,571	2,886	11,749	14,480	471	555	3,647	4,602	33,348	39,125	157,436	160,321
16 to 64 years	203,016	208,711	158,843	159,585	26,874	28,632	2,474	2,675	10,720	12,765	459	521	3,646	4,534	32,373	37,086	130,066	126,778
55 years and over	76,755	90,707	65,045	75,337	7,449	9,448	543	747	2,976	4,142	85	127	656	913	5,996	8,438	59,559	67,672
65 years and over	40,271	49,244	34,812	41,737	3,488	4,545	232	341	1,410	2,141	36	58	293	423	2,782	3,969	32,244	38,101
75 years and over	18,557	20,614	16,338	17,727	1,442	1,741	83	120	566	850	13	20	116	156	1,133	1,568	15,285	16,279
85 years and over	5,495	6,380	4,918	5,578	386	485	19	30	140	240	3	5	30	42	271	446	4,666	5,163
Median age (years)[3]	37.2	37.9	39.0	39.8	32.0	33.4	29.0	31.0	35.1	36.3	28.3	31.0	19.1	20.2	27.3	29.0	42.0	43.4

Z Less than 500. [1] The April 1, 2010 population estimates base reflects changes to the Census 2010 population from the Count Question Resolution program and geographic program revisions. [2] Hispanic origin is considered an ethnicity, not a race. Persons of Hispanic origin may be of any race. [3] For definition of median, see Guide to Tabular Presentation.

Source: U.S. Census Bureau, National Population by Characteristics: 2010-2016, "Median Age and Age by Sex, Race, and Hispanic Origin," <https://www.census.gov/data/tables/2016/demo/popest/nation-detail.html>, and "Annual Estimates of the Resident Population by Sex, Race, and Hispanic Origin for the United States: April 1, 2010 to July 1, 2016," <http://factfinder.census.gov>; accessed June 2017.

Table 10. Resident Population by Race, Hispanic Origin, and Single Years of Age: 2016

[In thousands, except as indicated (323,128 represents 323,128,000). As of July 1. For derivation of estimates, see text, this section]

Age	Total	Race						Hispanic origin [1]	Non-Hispanic White alone
		White alone	Black or African American alone	American Indian, Alaska Native alone	Asian alone	Native Hawaiian and Other Pacific Islander alone	Two or more races		
Total..........................	323,128	248,503	43,001	4,055	18,319	771	8,480	57,470	197,970
Under 5 years old............	19,927	14,256	3,038	322	1,055	62	1,194	5,145	9,885
Under 1 year old............	3,970	2,841	604	64	205	12	243	1,025	1,972
1 year old..................	3,995	2,853	611	64	214	13	241	1,037	1,973
2 years old.................	3,992	2,854	610	65	211	12	240	1,028	1,982
3 years old.................	3,982	2,846	607	64	216	12	237	1,024	1,975
4 years old.................	3,988	2,862	607	65	209	12	233	1,031	1,983
5 to 9 years old............	20,430	14,727	3,100	327	1,060	61	1,154	5,271	10,208
5 years old.................	4,033	2,909	610	63	205	12	233	1,059	1,999
6 years old.................	4,030	2,897	608	65	211	12	236	1,047	2,001
7 years old.................	4,030	2,899	614	65	210	12	230	1,032	2,016
8 years old.................	4,159	2,996	634	67	218	12	231	1,066	2,082
9 years old.................	4,179	3,026	633	68	215	12	224	1,067	2,109
10 to 14 years old..............	20,618	15,112	3,050	326	1,080	59	991	5,022	10,762
10 years old.................	4,144	3,018	619	67	214	12	214	1,045	2,117
11 years old.................	4,131	3,019	610	66	218	12	206	1,023	2,135
12 years old.................	4,140	3,039	606	65	219	12	199	1,001	2,171
13 years old.................	4,110	3,023	603	64	218	12	190	983	2,170
14 years old.................	4,094	3,013	613	64	210	11	183	970	2,170
15 to 19 years old.............	21,130	15,557	3,223	322	1,097	57	873	4,791	11,381
15 years old.................	4,197	3,086	636	64	217	11	183	977	2,235
16 years old.................	4,265	3,137	655	66	216	12	180	979	2,284
17 years old.................	4,205	3,103	641	64	211	11	175	951	2,274
18 years old.................	4,219	3,107	646	64	221	11	170	943	2,284
19 years old.................	4,243	3,125	646	64	232	11	165	941	2,304
20 to 24 years old.............	22,381	16,362	3,538	336	1,311	62	772	4,803	12,158
20 years old.................	4,286	3,159	649	64	241	12	162	941	2,335
21 years old.................	4,387	3,219	683	65	249	12	159	954	2,384
22 years old.................	4,481	3,270	716	67	261	12	155	963	2,426
23 years old.................	4,553	3,313	737	69	272	13	149	965	2,467
24 years old.................	4,674	3,401	753	71	288	13	147	979	2,545
25 to 29 years old.............	22,891	16,796	3,498	332	1,569	71	625	4,611	12,769
25 years old.................	4,758	3,462	762	71	308	14	142	968	2,618
26 years old.................	4,747	3,464	749	69	318	15	133	954	2,632
27 years old.................	4,559	3,335	701	66	320	14	123	905	2,546
28 years old.................	4,452	3,286	657	64	314	14	116	898	2,501
29 years old.................	4,375	3,248	630	62	309	14	111	886	2,472
30 to 34 years old.............	21,786	16,306	3,020	304	1,577	69	511	4,454	12,393
30 years old.................	4,392	3,277	620	62	313	14	107	893	2,493
31 years old.................	4,424	3,308	618	61	318	14	105	900	2,518
32 years old.................	4,283	3,204	590	60	315	13	100	875	2,435
33 years old.................	4,346	3,258	597	61	316	14	101	892	2,475
34 years old.................	4,342	3,259	596	60	316	14	98	894	2,472
35 to 39 years old.............	20,774	15,632	2,872	282	1,478	61	449	4,293	11,846
35 years old.................	4,293	3,231	590	59	304	13	96	883	2,454
36 years old.................	4,376	3,283	614	60	309	13	96	909	2,483
37 years old.................	4,103	3,082	572	55	294	12	89	839	2,342
38 years old.................	4,022	3,034	551	54	286	11	85	835	2,296
39 years old.................	3,980	3,002	544	54	285	11	83	827	2,270
40 to 44 years old.............	19,696	14,912	2,659	258	1,450	51	366	3,956	11,381
40 years old.................	3,862	2,912	523	52	286	11	78	813	2,191
41 years old.................	3,980	3,010	536	53	295	11	75	819	2,279
42 years old.................	3,855	2,916	517	51	289	10	72	785	2,214
43 years old.................	3,912	2,958	532	51	290	10	71	774	2,266
44 years old.................	4,088	3,116	550	51	289	10	71	766	2,430
45 to 49 years old.............	20,948	16,258	2,741	251	1,320	48	330	3,572	13,056
45 years old.................	4,320	3,329	573	53	282	10	72	761	2,648
46 years old.................	4,372	3,382	573	53	283	10	71	757	2,704
47 years old.................	4,143	3,221	531	50	266	9	65	706	2,588
48 years old.................	4,055	3,149	534	48	254	9	62	688	2,532
49 years old.................	4,058	3,176	531	48	234	9	60	661	2,583
50 to 54 years old.............	21,839	17,253	2,813	248	1,180	45	301	3,113	14,460
50 years old.................	4,131	3,228	550	49	237	9	59	653	2,642
51 years old.................	4,376	3,438	576	51	240	9	61	657	2,849
52 years old.................	4,453	3,519	571	50	242	9	61	629	2,955
53 years old.................	4,446	3,525	562	49	241	9	60	599	2,987
54 years old.................	4,434	3,543	554	49	220	9	59	575	3,026
55 to 59 years old.............	21,980	17,681	2,694	227	1,065	39	274	2,537	15,402
55 years old.................	4,485	3,600	555	48	216	8	58	551	3,105
56 years old.................	4,519	3,612	567	48	226	8	58	551	3,117
57 years old.................	4,363	3,507	539	45	210	8	54	502	3,056
58 years old.................	4,333	3,499	521	43	210	7	53	475	3,072
59 years old.................	4,281	3,464	514	42	203	7	51	458	3,053

See footnotes at end of table.

Table 10. Resident Population by Race, Hispanic Origin, and Single Years of Age: 2016-Continued.

See headnote on page 13.

| Age | Total | Race | | | | | | Hispanic origin [1] | Non-Hispanic White alone |
		White alone	Black or African American alone	American Indian, Alaska Native alone	Asian alone	Native Hawaiian and Other Pacific Islander alone	Two or more races		
60 to 64 years old............	19,483	15,914	2,209	179	936	30	216	1,932	14,169
60 years old................	4,124	3,337	490	40	201	7	49	436	2,945
61 years old................	4,084	3,317	475	39	200	6	47	421	2,937
62 years old................	3,911	3,197	443	36	187	6	43	385	2,849
63 years old................	3,757	3,087	412	33	179	6	40	358	2,763
64 years old................	3,606	2,976	388	31	169	5	37	332	2,675
65 to 69 years old............	16,820	14,017	1,710	135	772	23	162	1,434	12,715
65 years old................	3,491	2,877	382	30	162	5	35	319	2,587
66 years old................	3,404	2,798	369	29	169	5	34	307	2,519
67 years old................	3,295	2,737	340	27	156	5	32	282	2,480
68 years old................	3,252	2,725	320	25	147	4	30	270	2,480
69 years old................	3,378	2,881	301	25	137	4	30	256	2,648
70 to 74 years old............	11,810	9,992	1,094	85	519	15	105	968	9,108
70 years old................	2,487	2,084	240	19	117	4	23	222	1,882
71 years old................	2,446	2,053	236	18	112	3	23	210	1,862
72 years old................	2,371	2,008	218	17	103	3	21	192	1,833
73 years old................	2,414	2,067	212	16	95	3	20	182	1,901
74 years old................	2,092	1,779	188	14	91	2	18	163	1,630
75 to 79 years old............	8,368	7,111	755	56	368	9	69	670	6,495
75 years old................	1,900	1,611	174	13	84	2	16	152	1,471
76 years old................	1,784	1,507	166	12	81	2	15	145	1,374
77 years old................	1,665	1,417	148	11	73	2	14	134	1,295
78 years old................	1,579	1,347	139	10	68	2	13	125	1,232
79 years old................	1,440	1,228	127	9	63	2	11	114	1,123
80 to 84 years old............	5,866	5,039	501	34	242	6	44	452	4,621
80 years old................	1,358	1,160	120	8	58	1	11	107	1,061
81 years old................	1,284	1,101	111	8	53	1	10	101	1,007
82 years old................	1,135	974	98	6	47	1	9	88	892
83 years old................	1,079	929	91	6	45	1	8	80	855
84 years old................	1,009	876	80	5	40	1	7	75	806
85 to 89 years old............	3,885	3,400	292	19	146	3	26	279	3,140
85 years old................	938	819	71	5	36	1	6	69	755
86 years old................	876	764	67	4	34	1	6	65	703
87 years old................	766	671	57	4	29	1	5	55	620
88 years old................	694	609	51	3	25	1	5	48	564
89 years old................	610	536	45	3	22	(Z)	4	41	498
90 to 94 years old............	1,883	1,652	140	8	69	1	12	126	1,535
90 years old................	521	457	39	2	19	(Z)	3	36	424
91 years old................	450	395	33	2	16	(Z)	3	30	367
92 years old................	373	328	27	2	14	(Z)	2	24	305
93 years old................	300	263	23	1	11	(Z)	2	20	244
94 years old................	239	210	18	1	9	(Z)	2	16	195
95 to 99 years old............	530	459	44	2	21	(Z)	3	35	427
95 years old................	186	163	14	1	7	(Z)	1	12	152
96 years old................	136	117	11	1	5	(Z)	1	9	109
97 years old................	94	81	8	(Z)	4	(Z)	1	6	76
98 years old................	69	59	6	(Z)	3	(Z)	(Z)	5	55
99 years old................	45	38	4	(Z)	2	(Z)	(Z)	3	35
100 years old and over.......	82	67	10	(Z)	4	(Z)	1	7	61
Median age (years) [2].........	37.9	39.8	33.4	31.0	36.3	31.0	20.2	29.0	43.4

Z Less than 500. [1] Persons of Hispanic origin may be of any race. [2] For definition of median, see Guide to Tabular Presentation.

Source: U.S. Census Bureau, Population Division, "Annual Estimates of the Resident Population by Sex, Single Year of Age, Race, and Hispanic Origin for the United States: April 1, 2010 to July 1, 2016," <http://factfinder.census.gov>, accessed June 2017.

Table 11. Resident Population Projections by Race, Hispanic Origin, and Age: 2020

[In thousands (334,503 represents 334,503,000). As of July 1. The 2014 National Projections are based on the July 1, 2013 population estimates, which are based on the 2010 Census. The projections were produced using a cohort-component method and are based on assumptions about future births, deaths, and net international migration. More information on methodology and assumptions is available at <https://www.census.gov/programs-surveys/popproj/technical-documentation/methodology.html>]

Age group	Total	White alone	Black or African American alone	American Indian/ Alaska Native alone	Asian alone	Native Hawaiian/ Other Pacific Islander alone	Two or more races	Hispanic origin [1]	Not Hispanic White alone
Total	334,503	255,357	44,590	4,242	19,869	806	9,639	63,551	199,400
Under 5 years	20,568	14,586	3,063	304	1,153	54	1,407	5,304	10,047
5 to 9 years	20,274	14,515	3,030	315	1,123	58	1,233	5,257	10,021
10 to 14 years	20,735	14,976	3,117	334	1,113	61	1,134	5,374	10,355
15 to 19 years	21,048	15,450	3,090	327	1,159	59	963	5,157	10,957
20 to 24 years	22,059	16,193	3,294	329	1,325	59	859	5,182	11,638
25 to 29 years	23,722	17,244	3,714	351	1,589	66	758	5,303	12,569
30 to 34 years	23,168	17,052	3,397	329	1,720	73	597	4,925	12,718
35 to 39 years	22,060	16,543	2,996	304	1,645	67	505	4,706	12,386
40 to 44 years	20,568	15,491	2,798	277	1,510	59	433	4,398	11,589
45 to 49 years	20,204	15,377	2,687	258	1,472	50	361	4,003	11,788
50 to 54 years	20,638	16,068	2,677	244	1,289	46	314	3,509	12,917
55 to 59 years	21,879	17,392	2,740	241	1,167	43	295	3,022	14,675
60 to 64 years	21,141	17,055	2,528	211	1,053	36	258	2,413	14,884
65 to 69 years	18,194	14,931	1,992	159	888	27	195	1,793	13,309
70 to 74 years	14,882	12,461	1,446	115	698	20	141	1,291	11,286
75 to 79 years	10,112	8,595	903	70	445	12	88	838	7,828
80 to 84 years	6,527	5,575	571	41	280	7	52	544	5,074
85 to 89 years	3,964	3,432	327	22	152	4	29	319	3,136
90 to 94 years	2,024	1,775	158	10	67	2	13	155	1,631
95 to 99 years	649	568	55	3	19	(Z)	4	48	523
100 years and over	89	76	10	(Z)	3	(Z)	1	7	70
5 to 13 years	36,824	26,442	5,526	581	2,013	107	2,154	9,561	18,252
14 to 17 years	16,737	12,256	2,449	264	912	48	808	4,173	8,634
18 to 24 years	30,555	22,437	4,556	458	1,795	82	1,227	7,237	16,085
16 years and over	268,750	208,227	34,768	3,223	16,252	620	5,660	46,567	166,834
18 years and over	260,375	202,073	33,552	3,093	15,790	597	5,270	44,513	162,467
16 to 64 years	212,309	160,812	29,309	2,803	13,701	547	5,136	41,570	123,978
55 years and over	99,460	81,862	10,727	872	4,771	152	1,076	10,432	72,415
65 years and over	56,441	47,415	5,460	420	2,551	73	523	4,997	42,855
75 years and over	23,366	20,022	2,022	145	965	25	187	1,913	18,261
85 years and over	6,727	5,852	549	35	240	6	46	530	5,359

Z Less than 500. [1] Hispanic origin is considered an ethnicity, not a race. Persons of Hispanic origin may be of any race.

Source: U.S. Census Bureau, "Table 1. Projected Population by Single Year of Age, Sex, Race, and Hispanic Origin for the United States: 2014 to 2060," December 2014, <https://www.census.gov/programs-surveys/popproj/data/tables.html>, accessed June 2016.

Table 12. Resident Population Projections for Native and Foreign-Born Populations by Age Group: 2020 to 2060

[In thousands (334,503 represents 334,503,000), except as indicated. As of July 1. Data shown are modified race counts; see text, this section. Based on 2014 National Projections, see headnote Table 11.]

Nativity and age group	2020	2025	2030	2035	2040	2045	2050	2060
Total population	334,503	347,335	359,402	370,338	380,219	389,394	398,328	416,795
Under 18 years	74,128	75,015	76,273	77,446	78,185	78,910	79,888	82,309
Under 5 years	20,568	21,010	21,178	21,268	21,471	21,775	22,147	22,778
5 to 13 years	36,824	37,316	38,322	38,848	39,087	39,389	39,887	41,193
14 to 17 years	16,737	16,689	16,773	17,330	17,627	17,746	17,854	18,338
18 to 64 years	203,934	206,400	209,022	213,659	219,690	225,772	230,444	236,322
18 to 24 years	30,555	30,736	30,794	30,890	31,815	32,440	32,717	33,300
25 to 44 years	89,518	93,429	95,795	96,981	96,854	98,034	99,653	103,010
45 to 64 years	83,861	82,235	82,434	85,788	91,021	95,298	98,074	100,013
65 years and over	56,441	65,920	74,107	79,233	82,344	84,712	87,996	98,164
Native population	286,611	294,909	302,545	309,235	315,103	320,534	326,030	338,564
Under 18 years	71,683	72,394	73,486	74,549	75,189	75,828	76,735	79,055
Under 5 years	20,260	20,687	20,842	20,920	21,113	21,408	21,773	22,396
5 to 13 years	35,558	35,928	36,868	37,336	37,525	37,782	38,244	39,497
14 to 17 years	15,866	15,779	15,776	16,292	16,551	16,637	16,718	17,161
18 to 64 years	166,565	166,749	167,447	170,403	175,039	179,786	183,194	186,633
18 to 24 years	27,353	27,678	27,650	27,546	28,345	28,862	29,049	29,499
25 to 44 years	72,016	75,434	77,496	78,350	77,708	78,399	79,385	81,642
45 to 64 years	67,196	63,637	62,302	64,507	68,986	72,525	74,761	75,493
65 years and over	48,362	55,766	61,612	64,283	64,876	64,920	66,101	72,876
Foreign-born population	47,892	52,426	56,857	61,103	65,116	68,860	72,299	78,230
Under 18 years	2,445	2,622	2,787	2,897	2,996	3,082	3,153	3,254
Under 5 years	308	323	336	348	358	367	374	382
5 to 13 years	1,266	1,388	1,454	1,512	1,563	1,607	1,644	1,695
14 to 17 years	871	911	997	1,038	1,075	1,108	1,136	1,177
18 to 64 years	37,369	39,651	41,575	43,256	44,651	45,986	47,250	49,689
18 to 24 years	3,202	3,057	3,144	3,344	3,471	3,578	3,669	3,801
25 to 44 years	17,502	17,996	18,299	18,631	19,146	19,635	20,268	21,368
45 to 64 years	16,665	18,598	20,132	21,281	22,035	22,773	23,313	24,520
65 years and over	8,079	10,154	12,495	14,950	17,469	19,792	21,895	25,288

Source: U.S. Census Bureau, "2014 National Population Projections: Summary Tables," <https://www.census.gov/programs-surveys/popproj/data/tables.html>, accessed June 2015.

Table 13. Resident Population Projections by Race/Ethnicity and Hispanic Origin: 2020 to 2060

[In thousands, except as indicated (334,503 represents 334,503,000). As of July 1. Data shown are modified race counts; see text, this section. The 2014 National Projections are based on the July 1, 2013 population estimates, which are based on the 2010 Census. The projections were produced using a cohort-component method and are based on assumptions about future births, deaths, and net international migration. More information on methodology and assumptions is available at <https://www.census.gov/programs-surveys/popproj/technical-documentation/methodology.html>]

Characteristic	2020	2025	2030	2035	2040	2045	2050	2060
Total	**334,503**	**347,335**	**359,402**	**370,338**	**380,219**	**389,394**	**398,328**	**416,795**
One race	324,865	336,170	346,571	355,706	363,637	370,701	377,357	390,772
White	255,357	261,825	267,459	271,981	275,447	278,153	280,503	285,314
Black or African American	44,590	46,725	48,768	50,678	52,485	54,244	56,007	59,693
American Indian and Alaska Native	4,242	4,475	4,694	4,895	5,074	5,232	5,370	5,607
Asian	19,869	22,278	24,726	27,175	29,603	31,997	34,359	38,965
Native Hawaiian/Other Pacific Islander	806	866	923	977	1,028	1,075	1,118	1,194
Two or more races	9,639	11,165	12,831	14,632	16,582	18,693	20,971	26,022
Race alone or in combination: [1]								
White	263,969	271,873	279,081	285,312	290,635	295,360	299,896	309,567
Black or African American	49,052	52,081	55,121	58,132	61,158	64,260	67,499	74,530
American Indian and Alaska Native	7,071	7,526	7,968	8,386	8,777	9,146	9,497	10,169
Asian	23,380	26,358	29,426	32,550	35,709	38,891	42,099	48,575
Native Hawaiian/Other Pacific Islander	1,631	1,784	1,940	2,098	2,257	2,420	2,586	2,929
Not Hispanic	**270,952**	**276,895**	**281,939**	**285,795**	**288,593**	**290,750**	**292,778**	**297,750**
One race	263,275	268,019	271,761	274,217	275,504	276,027	276,293	277,374
White	199,400	199,867	199,403	197,810	195,197	191,919	188,419	181,930
Black or African American	41,594	43,404	45,118	46,694	48,162	49,580	51,006	54,028
American Indian and Alaska Native	2,432	2,499	2,555	2,597	2,623	2,637	2,641	2,637
Asian	19,255	21,608	23,999	26,389	28,756	31,090	33,391	37,879
Native Hawaiian/Other Pacific Islander	595	641	685	726	765	802	836	900
Two or more races	7,678	8,876	10,178	11,578	13,089	14,723	16,485	20,376
Race alone or in combination: [1]								
White	206,256	207,854	208,626	208,368	207,201	205,493	203,691	200,963
Black or African American	45,140	47,665	50,174	52,623	55,054	57,533	60,124	65,773
American Indian and Alaska Native	4,449	4,637	4,810	4,960	5,087	5,199	5,303	5,507
Asian	22,224	25,053	27,960	30,906	33,872	36,847	39,835	45,822
Native Hawaiian/Other Pacific Islander	1,239	1,352	1,466	1,578	1,691	1,805	1,920	2,155
Hispanic [2]	**63,551**	**70,440**	**77,463**	**84,543**	**91,626**	**98,644**	**105,550**	**119,044**
One race	61,590	68,150	74,810	81,490	88,133	94,674	101,064	113,398
White	55,957	61,959	68,056	74,171	80,250	86,233	92,084	103,384
Black or African American	2,997	3,321	3,650	3,984	4,323	4,664	5,002	5,665
American Indian and Alaska Native	1,810	1,975	2,139	2,298	2,451	2,595	2,729	2,970
Asian	614	670	727	786	847	908	968	1,086
Native Hawaiian/Other Pacific Islander	211	225	238	251	262	273	282	293
Two or more races	1,961	2,289	2,653	3,054	3,493	3,970	4,486	5,646
Race alone or in combination: [1]								
White	57,713	64,019	70,455	76,943	83,434	89,867	96,205	108,605
Black or African American	3,912	4,416	4,947	5,509	6,103	6,727	7,375	8,756
American Indian and Alaska Native	2,623	2,889	3,158	3,426	3,690	3,947	4,194	4,662
Asian	1,157	1,305	1,467	1,644	1,837	2,044	2,264	2,753
Native Hawaiian/Other Pacific Islander	392	432	475	519	567	616	666	774
PERCENT DISTRIBUTION								
Total	**100.0**	**100.0**	**100.0**	**100.0**	**100.0**	**100.0**	**100.0**	**100.0**
One race	97.1	96.8	96.4	96.0	95.6	95.2	94.7	93.8
White	76.3	75.4	74.4	73.4	72.4	71.4	70.4	68.5
Black or African American	13.3	13.5	13.6	13.7	13.8	13.9	14.1	14.3
American Indian and Alaska Native	1.3	1.3	1.3	1.3	1.3	1.3	1.3	1.3
Asian	5.9	6.4	6.9	7.3	7.8	8.2	8.6	9.3
Native Hawaiian/Other Pacific Islander	0.2	0.2	0.3	0.3	0.3	0.3	0.3	0.3
Two or more races	2.9	3.2	3.6	4.0	4.4	4.8	5.3	6.2
Not Hispanic	**81.0**	**79.7**	**78.4**	**77.2**	**75.9**	**74.7**	**73.5**	**71.4**
One race	78.7	77.2	75.6	74.0	72.5	70.9	69.4	66.5
White	59.6	57.5	55.5	53.4	51.3	49.3	47.3	43.6
Black or African American	12.4	12.5	12.6	12.6	12.7	12.7	12.8	13.0
American Indian and Alaska Native	0.7	0.7	0.7	0.7	0.7	0.7	0.7	0.6
Asian	5.8	6.2	6.7	7.1	7.6	8.0	8.4	9.1
Native Hawaiian/Other Pacific Islander	0.2	0.2	0.2	0.2	0.2	0.2	0.2	0.2
Two or more races	2.3	2.6	2.8	3.1	3.4	3.8	4.1	4.9
Hispanic [2]	**19.0**	**20.3**	**21.6**	**22.8**	**24.1**	**25.3**	**26.5**	**28.6**
One race	18.4	19.6	20.8	22.0	23.2	24.3	25.4	27.2
White	16.7	17.8	18.9	20.0	21.1	22.1	23.1	24.8
Black or African American	0.9	1.0	1.0	1.1	1.1	1.2	1.3	1.4
American Indian and Alaska Native	0.5	0.6	0.6	0.6	0.6	0.7	0.7	0.7
Asian	0.2	0.2	0.2	0.2	0.2	0.2	0.2	0.3
Native Hawaiian/Other Pacific Islander	0.1	0.1	0.1	0.1	0.1	0.1	0.1	0.1
Two or more races	0.6	0.7	0.7	0.8	0.9	1.0	1.1	1.4

[1] In combination with one or more other races. The sum of the five race groups adds to more than the total population because individuals may report more than one race. The original race data from Census 2010 are modified to eliminate the "some other race" category. [2] Persons of Hispanic origin may be of any race.

Source: U.S. Census Bureau, "Table 10. Projections of the Population by Sex, Hispanic Origin, and Race for the United States: 2015 to 2060 (NP2014-T10)," December 2014, <https://www.census.gov/programs-surveys/popproj/data/tables.html>, accessed June 2016.

Table 14. Resident Population by Region and State: 1990 to 2016

[In thousands (248,791 represents 248,791,000). 1990, 2000, and 2010 data as of April 1, data for other years as of July 1. Insofar as possible, population shown for all years is that of present area of state. See Appendix III]

State and region	1990, estimates base [1]	2000, estimates base [2]	2010, estimates base [3]	2011	2012	2013	2014	2015	2016
United States.........	248,791	281,425	308,758	311,663	313,998	316,205	318,563	320,897	323,128
Northeast................	50,828	53,595	55,318	55,633	55,829	55,989	56,117	56,185	56,210
Midwest.................	59,669	64,397	66,930	67,153	67,332	67,544	67,726	67,838	67,941
South....................	85,456	100,235	114,563	116,062	117,299	118,424	119,696	121,039	122,320
West.....................	52,837	63,199	71,947	72,815	73,538	74,248	75,024	75,834	76,657
Alabama.................	4,040	4,447	4,780	4,800	4,816	4,829	4,843	4,854	4,863
Alaska...................	550	627	710	723	731	737	737	738	742
Arizona..................	3,665	5,130	6,392	6,467	6,550	6,625	6,720	6,818	6,931
Arkansas................	2,351	2,673	2,916	2,939	2,951	2,959	2,967	2,978	2,988
California...............	29,811	33,872	37,255	37,677	38,011	38,335	38,681	38,994	39,250
Colorado................	3,294	4,302	5,029	5,118	5,190	5,268	5,350	5,449	5,541
Connecticut.............	3,287	3,406	3,574	3,590	3,594	3,596	3,592	3,585	3,576
Delaware................	666	784	898	908	917	925	935	944	952
District of Columbia......	607	572	602	620	635	649	659	670	681
Florida..................	12,938	15,983	18,805	19,097	19,344	19,582	19,889	20,245	20,612
Georgia.................	6,478	8,187	9,689	9,812	9,915	9,985	10,087	10,199	10,310
Hawaii..................	1,108	1,211	1,360	1,378	1,392	1,406	1,416	1,425	1,429
Idaho...................	1,007	1,294	1,568	1,584	1,596	1,612	1,634	1,653	1,683
Illinois..................	11,431	12,420	12,832	12,860	12,871	12,880	12,868	12,839	12,802
Indiana..................	5,544	6,081	6,484	6,516	6,538	6,569	6,595	6,613	6,633
Iowa....................	2,777	2,927	3,047	3,065	3,076	3,092	3,108	3,122	3,135
Kansas..................	2,478	2,689	2,853	2,870	2,885	2,893	2,899	2,907	2,907
Kentucky................	3,687	4,042	4,339	4,369	4,385	4,400	4,413	4,425	4,437
Louisiana...............	4,222	4,469	4,533	4,575	4,603	4,626	4,648	4,669	4,682
Maine...................	1,228	1,275	1,328	1,328	1,329	1,329	1,331	1,329	1,331
Maryland................	4,781	5,297	5,774	5,844	5,890	5,931	5,967	5,995	6,016
Massachusetts...........	6,016	6,349	6,548	6,612	6,658	6,707	6,750	6,784	6,812
Michigan................	9,295	9,939	9,884	9,876	9,887	9,899	9,916	9,918	9,928
Minnesota...............	4,376	4,920	5,304	5,349	5,380	5,419	5,453	5,482	5,520
Mississippi..............	2,575	2,845	2,968	2,978	2,985	2,990	2,992	2,989	2,989
Missouri.................	5,117	5,597	5,989	6,011	6,025	6,043	6,061	6,076	6,093
Montana.................	799	902	989	998	1,005	1,014	1,023	1,032	1,043
Nebraska................	1,578	1,711	1,826	1,842	1,856	1,869	1,881	1,894	1,907
Nevada..................	1,202	1,998	2,701	2,718	2,753	2,786	2,833	2,884	2,940
New Hampshire..........	1,109	1,236	1,316	1,318	1,321	1,323	1,329	1,330	1,335
New Jersey..............	7,748	8,415	8,792	8,841	8,873	8,899	8,925	8,935	8,944
New Mexico.............	1,515	1,819	2,059	2,078	2,084	2,085	2,083	2,080	2,081
New York................	17,991	18,977	19,378	19,520	19,603	19,674	19,719	19,747	19,745
North Carolina...........	6,632	8,046	9,536	9,651	9,746	9,842	9,934	10,035	10,147
North Dakota.............	639	642	673	685	702	724	740	757	758
Ohio....................	10,847	11,353	11,537	11,545	11,551	11,570	11,594	11,605	11,614
Oklahoma...............	3,146	3,450	3,752	3,786	3,817	3,852	3,877	3,907	3,924
Oregon.................	2,842	3,422	3,831	3,868	3,899	3,926	3,968	4,025	4,093
Pennsylvania............	11,883	12,281	12,703	12,744	12,772	12,781	12,791	12,792	12,784
Rhode Island............	1,003	1,048	1,053	1,052	1,053	1,053	1,054	1,056	1,056
South Carolina..........	3,486	4,012	4,625	4,673	4,721	4,768	4,828	4,895	4,961
South Dakota............	696	755	814	824	834	845	853	858	865
Tennessee..............	4,877	5,689	6,346	6,398	6,454	6,495	6,545	6,595	6,651
Texas...................	16,986	20,851	25,146	25,646	26,072	26,474	26,945	27,430	27,863
Utah....................	1,723	2,233	2,764	2,816	2,856	2,903	2,942	2,991	3,051
Vermont.................	563	609	626	627	626	627	627	626	625
Virginia.................	6,189	7,079	8,001	8,110	8,192	8,263	8,317	8,368	8,412
Washington..............	4,867	5,894	6,725	6,823	6,895	6,968	7,054	7,160	7,288
West Virginia............	1,793	1,808	1,853	1,855	1,857	1,853	1,849	1,841	1,831
Wisconsin...............	4,892	5,364	5,687	5,710	5,726	5,743	5,758	5,768	5,779
Wyoming................	454	494	564	568	577	583	584	587	586

[1] The April 1, 1990 census counts include corrections processed through August 1997, results of special censuses and test censuses, and do not include adjustments for census coverage errors. [2] The April 1, 2000 population estimates base reflects changes to the Census 2000 population from the Count Question Resolution program, legal boundary updates, and other geographic program revisions. [3] The April 1, 2010 population estimates base reflects changes to the Census 2010 population from the Count Question Resolution program and geographic program revisions.

Source: U.S. Census Bureau, "Table CO-EST2001-12-00 - Time Series of Intercensal State Population Estimates: April 1, 1990 to April 1, 2000," April 2002, <http://www2.census.gov/programs-surveys/popest/tables/1990-2000/intercensal/st-co/co-est2001-12-00.pdf>; "Table 1. Intercensal Estimates of the Resident Population for the United States, Regions, States, and Puerto Rico: April 1, 2000 to July 1, 2010 (ST-EST00INT-01)," September 2011, <http://www.census.gov/data/tables/time-series/demo/popest/intercensal-2000-2010-state.html>; and "Table 1. Annual Estimates of the Population for the United States, Regions, States, and Puerto Rico: April 1, 2010 to July 1, 2016 (NST-EST2016-01)," December 2016, <http://www.census.gov/data/tables/2016/demo/popest/state-total.html>.

Table 15. State Population—Rank, Percent Change, and Population Density: 1990 to 2016

[As of April 1, except 2016 as of July 1. Insofar as possible, population shown for all years is that of present area of state. For land area by State, see Table 394. Minus sign (-) indicates decrease. See Appendix III]

State	Rank				Percent change			Population per square mile of land area [1]		
	1990	2000	2010	2016	1990–2000	2000–2010	2010–2016 [2]	2000	2010	2016
United States.........	(X)	(X)	(X)	(X)	**13.1**	**9.7**	**4.7**	**79.7**	**87.4**	**91.5**
Alabama................	22	23	23	24	10.1	7.5	1.7	87.8	94.4	96.0
Alaska..................	49	48	47	48	14.0	13.3	4.5	1.1	1.2	1.3
Arizona.................	24	20	16	14	40.0	24.6	8.4	45.2	56.3	61.0
Arkansas...............	33	33	32	33	13.7	9.1	2.5	51.4	56.0	57.4
California..............	1	1	1	1	13.8	10.0	5.4	217.4	239.1	252.0
Colorado...............	26	24	22	21	30.6	16.9	10.2	41.5	48.5	53.5
Connecticut............	27	29	29	29	3.6	4.9	0.1	703.3	738.1	738.6
Delaware...............	46	45	45	45	17.6	14.6	6.0	402.1	460.8	488.6
District of Columbia....	(X)	(X)	(X)	(X)	-5.7	5.2	13.2	9,370.6	9,856.9	11,157.6
Florida..................	4	4	4	3	23.5	17.7	9.6	298.0	350.7	384.4
Georgia................	11	10	9	8	26.4	18.4	6.4	142.3	168.5	179.3
Hawaii..................	41	42	40	40	9.3	12.3	5.0	188.6	211.8	222.4
Idaho...................	42	39	39	39	28.5	21.2	7.4	15.7	19.0	20.4
Illinois..................	6	5	5	5	8.6	3.3	-0.2	223.7	231.1	230.6
Indiana.................	14	14	15	17	9.7	6.6	2.3	169.7	181.0	185.1
Iowa....................	30	30	30	30	5.4	4.1	2.9	52.4	54.5	56.1
Kansas.................	32	32	33	35	8.5	6.1	1.9	32.9	34.9	35.6
Kentucky...............	23	25	26	26	9.6	7.4	2.2	102.4	109.9	112.4
Louisiana..............	21	22	25	25	5.9	1.4	3.3	103.4	104.9	108.4
Maine...................	38	40	41	42	3.8	4.2	0.2	41.3	43.1	43.2
Maryland...............	19	19	19	19	10.8	9.0	4.2	545.6	594.8	619.8
Massachusetts..........	13	13	14	15	5.5	3.1	4.0	814.0	839.5	873.3
Michigan...............	8	8	8	10	6.9	-0.5	0.4	175.8	174.8	175.6
Minnesota..............	20	21	21	22	12.4	7.8	4.1	61.8	66.6	69.3
Mississippi.............	31	31	31	32	10.5	4.3	0.7	60.6	63.3	63.7
Missouri................	15	17	18	18	9.3	7.0	1.7	81.4	87.1	88.6
Montana................	44	44	44	44	12.9	9.7	5.4	6.2	6.8	7.2
Nebraska...............	36	38	38	37	8.4	6.7	4.4	22.3	23.8	24.8
Nevada.................	39	35	35	34	66.3	35.2	8.9	18.2	24.6	26.8
New Hampshire........	40	41	42	41	11.4	6.5	1.4	138.0	147.0	149.1
New Jersey.............	9	9	11	11	8.9	4.5	1.7	1,144.2	1,195.5	1,216.2
New Mexico............	37	36	36	36	20.1	13.2	1.1	15.0	17.0	17.2
New York...............	2	3	3	4	5.5	2.1	1.9	402.7	411.2	419.0
North Carolina.........	10	11	10	9	21.4	18.5	6.4	165.6	196.1	208.7
North Dakota...........	47	47	48	47	0.5	4.7	12.7	9.3	9.7	11.0
Ohio....................	7	7	7	7	4.7	1.6	0.7	277.8	282.3	284.2
Oklahoma..............	28	27	28	28	9.7	8.7	4.6	50.3	54.7	57.2
Oregon.................	29	28	27	27	20.4	12.0	6.8	35.6	39.9	42.6
Pennsylvania...........	5	6	6	6	3.4	3.4	0.6	274.5	283.9	285.7
Rhode Island...........	43	43	43	43	4.5	0.4	0.3	1,014.0	1,018.5	1,021.9
South Carolina.........	25	26	24	23	15.1	15.3	7.3	133.5	153.9	165.0
South Dakota...........	45	46	46	46	8.5	7.9	6.3	10.0	10.7	11.4
Tennessee..............	17	16	17	16	16.7	11.5	4.8	138.0	153.9	161.3
Texas...................	3	2	2	2	22.8	20.6	10.8	79.8	96.3	106.7
Utah....................	35	34	34	31	29.6	23.8	10.4	27.2	33.6	37.1
Vermont................	48	49	49	49	8.2	2.8	-0.2	66.1	67.9	67.8
Virginia.................	12	12	12	12	14.4	13.0	5.1	179.2	202.6	213.0
Washington.............	18	15	13	13	21.1	14.1	8.4	88.7	101.2	109.7
West Virginia...........	34	37	37	38	0.8	2.5	-1.2	75.2	77.1	76.2
Wisconsin..............	16	18	20	20	9.6	6.0	1.6	99.0	105.0	106.7
Wyoming...............	50	50	50	50	8.9	14.2	3.9	5.1	5.8	6.0

X Not applicable. [1] Persons per square mile were calculated on the basis of land area data from the 2010 Census. [2] Based on 2010 population estimates base that reflects changes to the Census 2010 population from the Count Question Resolution program and geographic program revisions.

Source: U.S. Census Bureau, *2000 Census of Population and Housing, PHC-3-1, United States Summary*, 2004, <http://www.census.gov/prod/cen2000/phc3-us-pt1.pdf>; *2010 Census Briefs, Population Distribution and Change: 2000 to 2010*, March 2011, <http://www.census.gov/prod/cen2010/briefs/c2010br-01.pdf>; and "Table 1. Annual Estimates of the Population for the United States, Regions, States, and Puerto Rico: April 1, 2010 to July 1, 2016 (NST-EST2016-01)," December 2016, <http://www.census.gov/data/tables/2016/demo/popest/state-total.html>.

Table 16. State and Region Resident Population—Components of Change: 2010 to 2016

[Covers period April 1, 2010 to July 1, 2016. Minus sign (-) indicates net decrease or net outflow]

State	Numeric population change [1]	Births	Deaths	Natural increase (births minus deaths)	Net migration Total	Net migration Inter-national [2]	Net migration Domestic
United States...........	14,369,408	24,762,895	16,235,690	8,527,205	5,842,203	5,842,203	(X)
Northeast.................	891,157	3,976,268	2,975,566	1,000,702	-35,901	1,581,612	-1,617,513
Midwest..................	1,011,604	5,206,369	3,736,233	1,470,136	-417,977	773,061	-1,191,038
South....................	7,756,569	9,495,205	6,294,582	3,200,623	4,459,788	2,165,692	2,294,096
West.....................	4,710,078	6,085,053	3,229,309	2,855,744	1,836,293	1,321,838	514,455
Alabama..................	83,169	367,421	312,625	54,796	27,555	29,630	-2,075
Alaska...................	31,645	71,088	25,713	45,375	-13,454	13,791	-27,245
Arizona..................	538,770	539,307	320,404	218,903	305,233	81,853	223,380
Arkansas.................	72,223	238,842	187,626	51,216	21,775	19,238	2,537
California...............	1,995,495	3,135,219	1,563,968	1,571,251	443,210	826,554	-383,344
Colorado.................	511,221	411,768	213,620	198,148	306,202	62,531	243,671
Connecticut..............	2,338	228,277	185,383	42,894	-34,774	100,910	-135,684
Delaware.................	54,129	68,977	51,096	17,881	35,621	15,135	20,486
District of Columbia......	79,404	58,893	30,473	28,420	50,470	23,794	26,676
Florida..................	1,807,847	1,353,262	1,150,096	203,166	1,562,390	695,906	866,484
Georgia..................	621,691	817,366	468,825	348,541	263,358	144,659	118,699
Hawaii...................	68,256	117,502	68,045	49,457	20,050	48,549	-28,499
Idaho....................	115,490	142,224	76,045	66,179	47,053	9,986	37,067
Illinois.................	-30,035	992,140	649,058	343,082	-361,646	178,520	-540,166
Indiana..................	148,917	521,319	372,748	148,571	4,511	63,671	-59,160
Iowa.....................	87,824	243,461	178,416	65,045	24,643	35,326	-10,683
Kansas...................	54,160	246,116	157,380	88,736	-34,632	35,867	-70,499
Kentucky.................	97,630	346,968	273,427	73,541	26,135	40,051	-13,916
Louisiana................	148,187	393,453	267,075	126,378	21,958	44,308	-22,350
Maine....................	3,115	79,584	83,138	-3,554	7,753	9,715	-1,962
Maryland.................	242,661	457,026	286,739	170,287	77,875	161,392	-83,517
Massachusetts............	263,966	452,120	341,961	110,159	163,483	236,088	-72,605
Michigan.................	44,171	710,867	573,859	137,008	-87,519	128,353	-215,872
Minnesota................	216,028	431,430	254,314	177,116	42,028	80,206	-38,178
Mississippi..............	20,623	241,975	187,223	54,752	-35,013	14,296	-49,309
Missouri.................	104,072	470,801	356,501	114,300	-6,804	51,332	-58,136
Montana..................	53,106	76,644	58,129	18,515	33,673	3,945	29,728
Nebraska.................	80,782	163,686	96,895	66,791	14,572	24,303	-9,731
Nevada...................	239,367	222,508	134,927	87,581	146,626	42,594	104,032
New Hampshire............	18,334	78,003	68,798	9,205	9,804	12,587	-2,783
New Jersey...............	152,516	649,061	447,845	201,216	-39,135	297,224	-336,359
New Mexico...............	21,817	165,723	106,138	59,585	-37,780	15,183	-52,963
New York.................	367,179	1,495,760	949,141	546,619	-147,221	699,448	-846,669
North Carolina...........	611,100	751,818	523,384	228,434	370,369	128,086	242,283
North Dakota.............	85,361	66,088	38,052	28,036	56,271	9,475	46,796
Ohio.....................	77,646	865,493	706,188	159,305	-70,390	112,592	-182,982
Oklahoma.................	171,946	331,103	238,568	92,535	78,417	38,804	39,613
Oregon...................	262,393	284,655	210,571	74,084	184,204	38,917	145,287
Pennsylvania.............	81,370	887,430	804,358	83,072	11,424	195,038	-183,614
Rhode Island.............	3,486	68,094	60,437	7,657	-3,159	25,406	-28,565
South Carolina...........	335,709	358,823	277,145	81,678	243,861	36,963	206,898
South Dakota.............	51,259	75,478	45,707	29,771	21,072	9,563	11,509
Tennessee................	304,896	502,451	392,451	110,000	191,384	55,613	135,771
Texas....................	2,716,496	2,437,794	1,117,880	1,319,914	1,375,776	508,843	866,933
Utah.....................	287,329	321,460	99,031	222,429	65,017	32,159	32,858
Vermont..................	-1,147	37,939	34,505	3,434	-4,076	5,196	-9,272
Virginia.................	410,767	641,455	392,605	248,850	157,996	202,410	-44,414
Washington...............	563,455	549,553	323,987	225,566	333,395	142,595	190,800
West Virginia............	-21,909	127,578	137,344	-9,766	-10,139	6,564	-16,703
Wisconsin................	91,419	419,490	307,115	112,375	-20,083	43,853	-63,936
Wyoming..................	21,734	47,402	28,731	18,671	2,864	3,181	-317

X Not applicable. [1] Total population change includes a residual. This residual represents the change in population that cannot be attributed to any specific demographic component. [2] Net international migration includes the international migration of both native and foreign-born populations. Specifically, it includes: (a) the net international migration of the foreign born, (b) the net migration between the United States and Puerto Rico, (c) the net migration of natives to and from the United States, and (d) the net movement of the Armed Forces population between the United States and overseas.

Source: U.S. Census Bureau, Population Division, "Cumulative Estimates of the Components of Resident Population Change for the United States, Regions, States, and Puerto Rico: April 1, 2010 to July 1, 2016 (NST-EST2016-04)," December 2016, <http://www.census.gov/data/tables/2016/demo/popest/nation-total.html>.

Table 17. Resident Population by Age and State: 2016

[In thousands (323,128 represents 323,128,000), unless otherwise noted. As of July 1]

State	Total	Under 5 years	5 to 14 years	15 to 24 years	25 to 34 years	35 to 44 years	45 to 54 years	55 to 64 years	65 to 74 years	75 to 84 years	85 years and over	Median age (years)	Percent 65 years old and over
United States	323,128	19,927	41,048	43,511	44,677	40,470	42,787	41,463	28,630	14,234	6,380	37.9	15.2
Alabama	4,863	293	610	654	637	596	644	645	465	233	87	38.9	16.1
Alaska	742	54	103	105	120	92	94	95	52	18	6	33.9	10.4
Arizona	6,931	439	913	951	933	845	847	831	683	351	137	37.6	16.9
Arkansas	2,988	190	394	402	393	365	379	378	284	146	57	38.0	16.3
California	39,250	2,487	5,062	5,392	5,918	5,160	5,195	4,689	3,089	1,535	722	36.4	13.6
Colorado	5,541	337	713	745	842	742	718	699	458	200	86	36.6	13.4
Connecticut	3,576	185	425	495	442	423	524	505	324	164	90	40.7	16.1
Delaware	952	55	114	121	128	109	128	131	100	48	19	40.2	17.5
District of Columbia	681	44	62	96	155	99	78	70	46	22	11	33.9	11.6
Florida	20,612	1,126	2,297	2,463	2,683	2,464	2,756	2,727	2,278	1,261	556	42.1	19.9
Georgia	10,310	661	1,415	1,441	1,422	1,363	1,417	1,237	839	377	138	36.5	13.1
Hawaii	1,429	92	169	176	208	177	178	184	139	66	39	38.6	17.1
Idaho	1,683	115	248	231	222	206	199	208	154	73	28	36.2	15.1
Illinois	12,802	773	1,640	1,728	1,774	1,647	1,713	1,656	1,073	539	259	37.8	14.6
Indiana	6,633	422	878	936	860	815	866	864	576	287	128	37.6	14.9
Iowa	3,135	199	408	446	394	368	390	416	281	154	79	38.0	16.4
Kansas	2,907	194	401	417	385	347	354	372	245	127	65	36.5	15.0
Kentucky	4,437	276	561	594	575	553	597	590	412	201	78	38.7	15.6
Louisiana	4,682	311	616	630	682	574	592	603	402	195	77	36.6	14.4
Maine	1,331	65	142	157	157	151	191	210	152	73	32	44.6	19.4
Maryland	6,016	367	750	778	834	761	855	794	516	245	115	38.5	14.6
Massachusetts	6,812	361	766	955	952	825	961	917	613	303	159	39.4	15.8
Michigan	9,928	574	1,217	1,375	1,252	1,157	1,348	1,393	941	458	213	39.7	16.2
Minnesota	5,520	353	720	723	748	677	727	739	472	241	119	37.9	15.1
Mississippi	2,989	189	407	421	394	366	380	381	266	134	51	37.1	15.1
Missouri	6,093	374	774	818	813	731	790	816	560	290	128	38.4	16.1
Montana	1,043	63	127	137	133	119	126	152	110	52	23	39.8	17.7
Nebraska	1,907	133	264	269	253	231	230	241	160	84	43	36.3	15.0
Nevada	2,940	184	380	364	428	388	393	363	276	124	42	37.8	15.0
New Hampshire	1,335	64	147	177	161	152	201	206	136	62	29	43.0	17.0
New Jersey	8,944	521	1,110	1,140	1,162	1,146	1,296	1,196	777	397	199	39.7	15.3
New Mexico	2,081	129	278	284	280	243	252	273	203	100	40	37.6	16.5
New York	19,745	1,160	2,296	2,629	2,891	2,463	2,706	2,568	1,713	881	438	38.5	15.4
North Carolina	10,147	606	1,293	1,366	1,335	1,290	1,386	1,301	942	450	178	38.7	15.5
North Dakota	758	55	95	117	114	86	86	95	59	33	18	34.8	14.5
Ohio	11,614	698	1,450	1,539	1,507	1,380	1,548	1,605	1,081	551	254	39.3	16.2
Oklahoma	3,924	267	536	541	545	479	477	488	342	178	71	36.4	15.0
Oregon	4,093	236	484	514	575	532	516	548	416	188	85	39.3	16.8
Pennsylvania	12,784	712	1,486	1,665	1,678	1,481	1,735	1,804	1,237	652	334	40.7	17.4
Rhode Island	1,056	55	116	152	143	123	147	147	97	49	28	40.0	16.5
South Carolina	4,961	293	616	657	655	599	652	658	513	233	84	39.2	16.7
South Dakota	865	61	118	118	112	99	102	116	77	40	22	37.0	16.0
Tennessee	6,651	408	835	877	892	831	894	867	628	303	116	38.7	15.7
Texas	27,863	2,019	4,067	3,976	4,086	3,726	3,519	3,116	2,008	957	388	34.5	12.0
Utah	3,051	253	520	491	449	411	314	291	191	94	36	30.8	10.5
Vermont	625	31	66	90	73	70	86	97	68	31	14	42.7	18.1
Virginia	8,412	511	1,041	1,131	1,172	1,086	1,162	1,080	735	349	145	38.1	14.6
Washington	7,288	455	904	932	1,081	941	948	946	657	292	132	37.7	14.8
West Virginia	1,831	101	209	227	219	223	243	266	203	101	39	42.2	18.8
Wisconsin	5,779	337	725	788	728	687	780	806	531	268	129	39.3	16.1
Wyoming	586	38	79	77	82	71	69	81	53	24	11	37.1	15.0

Source: U.S. Census Bureau, "Annual Estimates of the Resident Population for Selected Age Groups by Sex for the United States, States, Counties, and Puerto Rico Commonwealth and Municipios: April 1, 2010 to July 1, 2016," <http://factfinder.census.gov>, accessed June 2017.

Table 18. Age Dependency Ratios by State: 2000 to 2016

[As of April, except 2016 as of July]

State	Age dependency ratio [1]			Child dependency ratio [2]			Old-age dependency ratio [3]		
	2000	2010	2016	2000	2010	2016	2000	2010	2016
United States	**61.6**	**58.9**	**61.4**	**41.5**	**38.2**	**36.8**	**20.1**	**20.7**	**24.6**
Alabama	62.1	59.9	63.1	40.9	37.9	36.8	21.1	22.0	26.3
Alaska	56.5	51.8	55.4	47.6	40.0	39.2	8.9	11.7	16.2
Arizona	65.7	64.7	67.9	44.2	42.0	39.5	21.6	22.7	28.4
Arkansas	65.1	63.4	66.3	42.0	39.9	39.2	23.1	23.5	27.1
California	61.1	57.1	58.2	44.0	39.2	36.6	17.1	17.9	21.5
Colorado	54.5	54.6	56.7	39.5	37.7	35.7	14.9	16.9	21.0
Connecticut	62.7	58.8	59.3	40.2	36.3	33.5	22.5	22.5	25.7
Delaware	60.8	59.5	63.9	39.9	36.6	35.2	20.9	23.0	28.7
District of Columbia	47.8	39.3	41.4	29.7	23.3	25.1	18.1	15.9	16.3
Florida	67.7	62.9	66.6	38.3	34.7	33.5	29.5	28.2	33.1
Georgia	56.5	57.2	60.0	41.5	40.4	39.0	15.0	16.7	21.0
Hawaii	60.4	57.9	63.0	39.2	35.3	35.1	21.3	22.7	27.8
Idaho	66.1	66.1	69.8	47.4	45.5	44.1	18.7	20.6	25.7
Illinois	61.8	58.6	59.9	42.3	38.7	36.6	19.5	19.9	23.4
Indiana	62.0	60.7	63.1	41.9	39.9	38.7	20.1	20.9	24.4
Iowa	66.6	63.3	65.9	41.8	39.0	38.7	24.8	24.3	27.2
Kansas	66.0	63.0	65.6	44.0	41.5	40.7	22.0	21.5	24.9
Kentucky	59.0	58.5	62.2	39.1	37.4	36.9	19.9	21.1	25.2
Louisiana	63.6	58.6	61.8	44.6	39.1	38.5	18.9	19.5	23.3
Maine	61.3	57.6	62.6	38.1	32.6	31.1	23.2	25.0	31.5
Maryland	58.5	55.5	58.7	40.6	36.4	35.6	17.9	19.1	23.1
Massachusetts	59.2	54.9	56.2	37.6	33.6	31.6	21.6	21.4	24.6
Michigan	62.3	60.0	62.1	42.4	37.9	35.8	19.9	22.0	26.3
Minnesota	61.9	59.0	62.4	42.4	38.5	37.9	19.6	20.5	24.5
Mississippi	64.8	62.0	64.5	44.9	41.2	39.7	19.9	20.8	24.8
Missouri	64.0	60.8	63.4	41.8	38.3	37.2	22.1	22.5	26.2
Montana	63.7	59.8	65.5	41.7	36.1	36.1	21.9	23.7	29.4
Nebraska	66.3	63.0	66.3	43.8	41.0	41.3	22.6	22.0	25.0
Nevada	57.6	57.8	61.4	40.4	38.9	37.2	17.3	19.0	24.2
New Hampshire	58.8	54.7	57.5	39.8	33.8	30.8	19.0	20.9	26.8
New Jersey	61.4	58.7	60.1	40.0	37.3	35.5	21.4	21.4	24.6
New Mexico	65.6	62.4	66.8	46.3	40.9	39.3	19.3	21.5	27.4
New York	60.3	55.8	57.6	39.6	34.8	33.4	20.7	21.1	24.2
North Carolina	57.3	58.4	61.6	38.4	37.9	36.6	19.0	20.5	25.0
North Dakota	66.0	58.2	60.7	41.6	35.2	37.4	24.4	22.9	23.3
Ohio	63.2	60.6	63.2	41.5	38.0	36.7	21.7	22.6	26.5
Oklahoma	64.1	62.1	65.4	42.4	40.2	40.5	21.7	21.9	24.9
Oregon	60.1	57.6	61.4	39.6	35.6	34.3	20.5	21.9	27.2
Pennsylvania	65.1	59.8	62.1	39.3	35.1	33.9	25.8	24.6	28.2
Rhode Island	61.8	55.5	56.7	38.2	33.1	30.9	23.5	22.5	25.8
South Carolina	59.4	58.8	63.6	40.1	37.1	36.2	19.3	21.7	27.4
South Dakota	70.0	64.5	68.6	45.6	41.0	41.5	24.4	23.6	27.0
Tennessee	58.6	58.8	62.1	39.0	37.4	36.6	19.6	21.4	25.5
Texas	61.7	60.4	61.9	45.7	43.8	42.4	16.1	16.6	19.5
Utah	68.6	68.2	68.7	54.3	53.0	51.0	14.4	15.2	17.8
Vermont	58.6	54.3	58.9	38.4	31.9	30.1	20.2	22.5	28.7
Virginia	55.6	54.7	58.3	38.2	35.9	35.2	17.4	18.9	23.1
Washington	58.5	55.8	59.2	40.7	36.6	35.6	17.8	19.2	23.6
West Virginia	60.2	58.6	64.6	35.6	33.2	33.7	24.5	25.5	30.9
Wisconsin	62.9	59.3	62.2	41.6	37.5	36.1	21.3	21.8	26.1
Wyoming	60.7	57.4	63.2	41.9	37.8	38.7	18.8	19.6	24.5

[1] The age dependency ratio is derived by dividing the sum of populations age under 18 and age 65/over by the population age 18-64, and multiplying by 100. [2] The child dependency ratio is derived by dividing the population under age 18 by the population age 18-64, and multiplying by 100. [3] The old-age dependency ratio is derived by dividing the population age 65/over by the population age 18-64, and multiplying by 100.

Source: U.S. Census Bureau, Census 2010 Briefs, "Age and Sex Composition: 2010," May 2011; and "Annual Estimates of the Resident Population for Selected Age Groups by Sex for the United States, States, Counties, and Puerto Rico Commonwealth and Municipios: April 1, 2010 to July 1, 2016," <http://factfinder.census.gov>, accessed June 2017.

Table 19. Resident Population by Hispanic Origin and State: 2016

[In thousands, except as indicated (323,128 represents 323,128,000). As of July 1. Hispanic origin is considered an ethnicity, not a race. Persons of Hispanic origin may be of any race]

State	Number (1,000)				Percent		
	Total population	Hispanic or Latino	Total Non-Hispanic	Non-Hispanic White alone	Hispanic or Latino	Total Non-Hispanic	Non-Hispanic White alone
United States.........	**323,128**	**57,470**	**265,657**	**197,970**	**17.8**	**82.2**	**61.3**
Alabama................	4,863	204	4,659	3,202	4.2	95.8	65.8
Alaska.................	742	52	690	454	7.0	93.0	61.2
Arizona................	6,931	2,145	4,786	3,845	30.9	69.1	55.5
Arkansas...............	2,988	219	2,770	2,178	7.3	92.7	72.9
California.............	39,250	15,281	23,969	14,803	38.9	61.1	37.7
Colorado...............	5,541	1,181	4,359	3,802	21.3	78.7	68.6
Connecticut............	3,576	562	3,014	2,420	15.7	84.3	67.7
Delaware...............	952	87	865	598	9.2	90.8	62.9
District of Columbia....	681	74	607	248	10.9	89.1	36.4
Florida................	20,612	5,127	15,485	11,315	24.9	75.1	54.9
Georgia................	10,310	973	9,338	5,504	9.4	90.6	53.4
Hawaii.................	1,429	148	1,280	316	10.4	89.6	22.1
Idaho..................	1,683	208	1,475	1,386	12.3	87.7	82.4
Illinois...............	12,802	2,181	10,620	7,896	17.0	83.0	61.7
Indiana................	6,633	450	6,183	5,283	6.8	93.2	79.6
Iowa...................	3,135	183	2,952	2,703	5.8	94.2	86.2
Kansas.................	2,907	338	2,569	2,218	11.6	88.4	76.3
Kentucky...............	4,437	156	4,281	3,770	3.5	96.5	85.0
Louisiana..............	4,682	236	4,446	2,761	5.0	95.0	59.0
Maine..................	1,331	21	1,310	1,245	1.6	98.4	93.5
Maryland...............	6,016	587	5,430	3,099	9.8	90.2	51.5
Massachusetts..........	6,812	781	6,031	4,972	11.5	88.5	73.0
Michigan...............	9,928	492	9,436	7,487	5.0	95.0	75.4
Minnesota..............	5,520	289	5,231	4,448	5.2	94.8	80.6
Mississippi............	2,989	91	2,897	1,700	3.1	96.9	56.9
Missouri...............	6,093	250	5,843	4,858	4.1	95.9	79.7
Montana................	1,043	38	1,005	901	3.6	96.4	86.5
Nebraska...............	1,907	203	1,704	1,518	10.7	89.3	79.6
Nevada.................	2,940	837	2,103	1,468	28.5	71.5	49.9
New Hampshire..........	1,335	47	1,288	1,213	3.5	96.5	90.8
New Jersey.............	8,944	1,787	7,158	4,991	20.0	80.0	55.8
New Mexico.............	2,081	1,010	1,071	792	48.5	51.5	38.1
New York...............	19,745	3,747	15,998	11,009	19.0	81.0	55.8
North Carolina.........	10,147	932	9,215	6,447	9.2	90.8	63.5
North Dakota...........	758	28	730	644	3.6	96.4	85.0
Ohio...................	11,614	425	11,190	9,230	3.7	96.3	79.5
Oklahoma...............	3,924	404	3,520	2,597	10.3	89.7	66.2
Oregon.................	4,093	523	3,571	3,126	12.8	87.2	76.4
Pennsylvania...........	12,784	901	11,883	9,849	7.0	93.0	77.0
Rhode Island...........	1,056	157	899	775	14.9	85.1	73.3
South Carolina.........	4,961	275	4,687	3,170	5.5	94.5	63.9
South Dakota...........	865	32	833	714	3.7	96.3	82.5
Tennessee..............	6,651	349	6,302	4,937	5.2	94.8	74.2
Texas..................	27,863	10,881	16,981	11,873	39.1	60.9	42.6
Utah...................	3,051	420	2,631	2,405	13.8	86.2	78.8
Vermont................	625	12	613	581	1.9	98.1	93.1
Virginia...............	8,412	766	7,646	5,253	9.1	90.9	62.4
Washington.............	7,288	907	6,381	5,063	12.4	87.6	69.5
West Virginia..........	1,831	28	1,803	1,690	1.5	98.5	92.3
Wisconsin..............	5,779	388	5,391	4,720	6.7	93.3	81.7
Wyoming................	586	58	527	492	10.0	90.0	84.1

Source: U.S. Census Bureau, "Annual Estimates of the Resident Population by Sex, Race, and Hispanic Origin for the United States, States, and Counties: April 1, 2010 to July 1, 2016," <http://factfinder.census.gov>, accessed June 2017.

Table 20. Resident Population by Race and State: 2016

[In thousands, except as indicated (323,128 represents 323,128,000). As of July 1]

State	Number (1,000)							Percent distribution					
	Total population	White[1]	Black[1]	American Indian[1,2]	Asian[1]	Native Hawaiian[1,3]	Two or more races	White[1]	Black[1]	American Indian[1,2]	Asian[1]	Native Hawaiian[1,3]	Two or more races
U.S.	323,128	248,503	43,001	4,055	18,319	771	8,480	76.9	13.3	1.3	5.7	0.2	2.6
AL	4,863	3,373	1,304	34	69	5	79	69.3	26.8	0.7	1.4	0.1	1.6
AK	742	490	28	112	47	10	54	66.1	3.8	15.2	6.3	1.3	7.3
AZ	6,931	5,773	339	372	237	18	192	83.3	4.9	5.4	3.4	0.3	2.8
AR	2,988	2,374	469	29	47	9	61	79.4	15.7	1.0	1.6	0.3	2.0
CA	39,250	28,539	2,547	648	5,818	197	1,501	72.7	6.5	1.7	14.8	0.5	3.8
CO	5,541	4,846	249	88	181	11	166	87.5	4.5	1.6	3.3	0.2	3.0
CT	3,576	2,882	421	19	168	4	83	80.6	11.8	0.5	4.7	0.1	2.3
DE	952	668	215	6	38	1	24	70.1	22.6	0.6	4.0	0.1	2.6
DC	681	304	325	4	28	1	19	44.6	47.7	0.6	4.1	0.2	2.7
FL	20,612	15,996	3,472	102	588	23	431	77.6	16.8	0.5	2.9	0.1	2.1
GA	10,310	6,311	3,302	52	420	12	213	61.2	32.0	0.5	4.1	0.1	2.1
HI	1,429	369	31	6	539	145	338	25.8	2.2	0.4	37.7	10.2	23.7
ID	1,683	1,571	14	29	25	4	40	93.3	0.8	1.8	1.5	0.2	2.4
IL	12,802	9,885	1,878	76	709	8	246	77.2	14.7	0.6	5.5	0.1	1.9
IN	6,633	5,679	641	27	149	4	133	85.6	9.7	0.4	2.2	0.1	2.0
IA	3,135	2,865	115	16	79	4	57	91.4	3.7	0.5	2.5	0.1	1.8
KS	2,907	2,519	180	35	86	3	85	86.6	6.2	1.2	3.0	0.1	2.9
KY	4,437	3,903	368	13	66	4	83	88.0	8.3	0.3	1.5	0.1	1.9
LA	4,682	2,957	1,525	36	85	3	76	63.2	32.6	0.8	1.8	0.1	1.6
ME	1,331	1,262	20	9	17	1	23	94.8	1.5	0.7	1.2	(Z)	1.7
MD	6,016	3,567	1,846	34	396	6	167	59.3	30.7	0.6	6.6	0.1	2.8
MA	6,812	5,571	587	33	454	7	159	81.8	8.6	0.5	6.7	0.1	2.3
MI	9,928	7,903	1,406	72	306	4	237	79.6	14.2	0.7	3.1	(Z)	2.4
MN	5,520	4,691	344	74	272	4	134	85.0	6.2	1.3	4.9	0.1	2.4
MS	2,989	1,773	1,127	18	32	2	37	59.3	37.7	0.6	1.1	0.1	1.2
MO	6,093	5,072	721	34	122	9	136	83.2	11.8	0.6	2.0	0.1	2.2
MT	1,043	930	6	69	8	1	28	89.2	0.6	6.6	0.8	0.1	2.7
NE	1,907	1,695	95	27	47	2	40	88.9	5.0	1.4	2.5	0.1	2.1
NV	2,940	2,209	281	48	254	23	124	75.1	9.6	1.6	8.7	0.8	4.2
NH	1,335	1,252	20	4	36	1	22	93.8	1.5	0.3	2.7	0.1	1.7
NJ	8,944	6,474	1,338	54	877	9	193	72.4	15.0	0.6	9.8	0.1	2.2
NM	2,081	1,718	52	220	35	3	52	82.6	2.5	10.6	1.7	0.2	2.5
NY	19,745	13,798	3,488	191	1,751	26	491	69.9	17.7	1.0	8.9	0.1	2.5
NC	10,147	7,206	2,252	158	297	13	221	71.0	22.2	1.6	2.9	0.1	2.2
ND	758	666	22	42	12	1	16	87.9	2.9	5.5	1.5	0.1	2.1
OH	11,614	9,576	1,487	32	255	7	257	82.5	12.8	0.3	2.2	0.1	2.2
OK	3,924	2,926	304	360	88	7	238	74.6	7.8	9.2	2.2	0.2	6.1
OR	4,093	3,578	87	73	183	18	154	87.4	2.1	1.8	4.5	0.4	3.8
PA	12,784	10,531	1,505	47	443	9	249	82.4	11.8	0.4	3.5	0.1	1.9
RI	1,056	892	85	11	38	2	29	84.4	8.1	1.0	3.6	0.2	2.7
SC	4,961	3,397	1,363	27	80	5	90	68.5	27.5	0.5	1.6	0.1	1.8
SD	865	737	17	78	13	1	20	85.2	2.0	9.0	1.5	0.1	2.3
TN	6,651	5,234	1,137	30	120	6	124	78.7	17.1	0.4	1.8	0.1	1.9
TX	27,863	22,136	3,515	283	1,350	39	539	79.4	12.6	1.0	4.8	0.1	1.9
UT	3,051	2,778	41	48	77	32	76	91.1	1.4	1.6	2.5	1.0	2.5
VT	625	591	8	2	11	(Z)	12	94.6	1.3	0.4	1.8	(Z)	1.9
VA	8,412	5,892	1,665	46	556	9	245	70.0	19.8	0.5	6.6	0.1	2.9
WA	7,288	5,830	302	138	625	55	338	80.0	4.1	1.9	8.6	0.8	4.6
WV	1,831	1,714	66	5	15	1	31	93.6	3.6	0.2	0.8	(Z)	1.7
WI	5,779	5,057	382	66	164	3	108	87.5	6.6	1.1	2.8	0.1	1.9
WY	586	543	8	16	6	1	12	92.8	1.3	2.7	1.0	0.1	2.1

Z Less than 500 or 0.05 percent. [1] Data shown for each race alone. [2] Includes Alaska Natives. [3] Includes other Pacific Islanders.

Source: U.S. Census Bureau, "Annual Estimates of the Resident Population by Sex, Race, and Hispanic Origin for the United States, States, and Counties: April 1, 2010 to July 1, 2016," <http://factfinder.census.gov>, accessed June 2017.

Table 21. Large Metropolitan Statistical Areas—Population: 2000 to 2016

[In thousands, except as indicated (695 represents 695,000). As of April 1, except 2016 as of July 1. Covers metropolitan statistical areas with population of 250,000 and over in 2016, as delineated by the U.S. Office of Management and Budget as of July 2015. All geographic boundaries for 2010 to 2016 population estimates are defined as of January 1, 2016. For definitions and components of all metropolitan and micropolitan areas, see Appendix II. Minus sign (-) indicates decrease]

Metropolitan statistical area	2000	2010, esti- mates base [1]	2016	Change 2000–2010 [2] Number	Change 2000–2010 [2] Percent	Change 2010–2016 Number	Change 2010–2016 Percent	Rank, 2016
Akron, OH	695	703	702	8	1.2	-1	-0.1	80
Albany-Schenectady-Troy, NY	826	871	882	45	5.4	11	1.3	63
Albuquerque, NM	730	887	910	157	21.6	23	2.6	60
Allentown-Bethlehem-Easton, PA-NJ	740	821	836	81	10.9	14	1.8	69
Amarillo, TX	229	252	263	23	10.2	11	4.5	184
Anchorage, AK	320	381	403	61	19.2	22	5.7	133
Ann Arbor, MI	323	345	365	22	6.9	20	5.7	146
Asheville, NC	369	425	452	56	15.1	27	6.5	116
Atlanta-Sandy Springs-Roswell, GA	4,263	5,287	5,790	1,023	24.0	503	9.5	9
Atlantic City-Hammonton, NJ	253	275	271	22	8.7	-4	-1.3	176
Augusta-Richmond County, GA-SC	508	565	595	57	11.2	(Z)	5.3	93
Austin-Round Rock, TX	1,250	1,716	2,056	467	37.3	340	19.8	31
Bakersfield, CA	662	840	885	178	26.9	45	5.4	62
Baltimore-Columbia-Towson, MD	2,553	2,711	2,799	158	6.2	88	3.3	21
Baton Rouge, LA	706	803	835	97	13.7	33	4.1	70
Beaumont-Port Arthur, TX	400	403	410	3	0.8	7	1.7	130
Birmingham-Hoover, AL	1,052	1,128	1,147	76	7.2	19	1.7	49
Boise City, ID	465	617	691	152	32.6	75	12.1	81
Boston-Cambridge-Newton, MA-NH	4,391	4,553	4,794	161	3.7	242	5.3	10
Boulder, CO [3]	270	295	322	25	9.2	28	9.4	155
Bremerton-Silverdale, WA	232	251	265	19	8.3	14	5.4	182
Bridgeport-Stamford-Norwalk, CT	883	917	944	34	3.9	27	3.0	57
Brownsville-Harlingen, TX	335	406	422	71	21.2	16	3.9	126
Buffalo-Cheektowaga-Niagara Falls, NY	1,170	1,136	1,133	-34	-2.9	-3	-0.2	50
Canton-Massillon, OH	407	404	401	-3	-0.6	-(Z)	-(Z)	134
Cape Coral-Fort Myers, FL	441	619	722	178	40.3	104	16.7	78
Cedar Rapids, IA	237	258	268	21	8.7	10	3.8	179
Charleston-North Charleston, SC	549	665	761	116	21.1	97	14.5	74
Charlotte-Concord-Gastonia, NC-SC	1,717	2,217	2,474	500	29.1	257	11.6	22
Chattanooga, TN-GA	477	528	552	52	10.8	23	4.4	100
Chicago-Naperville-Elgin, IL-IN-WI	9,098	9,462	9,513	363	4.0	51	0.5	3
Cincinnati, OH-KY-IN	1,995	2,115	2,165	120	6.0	50	2.4	28
Clarksville, TN-KY	220	261	282	41	18.7	22	8.3	168
Cleveland-Elyria, OH	2,148	2,077	2,056	-71	-3.3	-22	-1.0	32
College Station-Bryan, TX	185	229	255	44	23.7	26	11.5	187
Colorado Springs, CO	537	646	712	108	20.1	67	10.3	79
Columbia, SC	647	767	817	120	18.6	50	6.5	71
Columbus, GA-AL	282	296	309	14	4.9	13	4.5	161
Columbus, OH	1,675	1,902	2,042	227	13.6	140	7.3	33
Corpus Christi, TX	403	428	455	25	6.2	27	6.2	115
Crestview-Fort Walton Beach-Destin, FL	211	236	267	25	11.7	31	13.2	180
Dallas-Fort Worth-Arlington, TX	5,204	6,426	7,233	1,222	23.5	807	12.6	4
Davenport-Moline-Rock Island, IA-IL	376	380	382	4	1.0	3	0.7	138
Dayton, OH	806	799	801	-7	-0.8	1	0.2	72
Deltona-Daytona Beach-Ormond Beach, FL	493	590	638	97	19.7	47	8.0	88
Denver-Aurora-Lakewood, CO [3]	2,179	2,544	2,853	364	16.7	309	12.2	19
Des Moines-West Des Moines, IA	481	570	635	88	18.3	65	11.4	89
Detroit-Warren-Dearborn, MI	4,453	4,296	4,298	-156	-3.5	1	0.0	14
Duluth, MN-WI	275	280	279	4	1.6	-(Z)	-(Z)	171
Durham-Chapel Hill, NC	426	507	560	80	18.8	53	10.4	97
El Paso, TX	683	804	842	121	17.7	38	4.7	68
Erie, PA	281	281	276	-(Z)	-0.1	-4	-1.6	172
Eugene, OR	323	352	370	29	8.9	18	5.1	144
Evansville, IN-KY	296	312	316	15	5.2	4	1.4	158
Fayetteville, NC	337	366	380	30	8.8	14	3.8	139
Fayetteville-Springdale-Rogers, AR-MO	347	463	525	116	33.5	62	13.3	105
Flint, MI	436	426	409	-10	-2.4	-17	-4.0	131
Fort Collins, CO	251	300	340	48	19.1	40	13.5	150
Fort Smith, AR-OK	255	281	281	25	9.8	(Z)	0.2	169
Fort Wayne, IN	390	416	432	26	6.7	16	3.7	125
Fresno, CA	799	930	980	131	16.4	49	5.3	56
Gainesville, FL	232	264	281	32	13.7	16	6.2	170
Grand Rapids-Wyoming, MI	931	989	1,047	58	6.3	58	5.9	52
Greeley, CO [3]	181	253	295	72	39.7	42	16.7	163
Green Bay, WI	283	306	318	24	8.4	12	3.9	157
Greensboro-High Point, NC	643	724	756	80	12.5	32	4.5	75
Greenville-Anderson-Mauldin, SC	726	824	885	98	13.6	61	7.4	61
Gulfport-Biloxi-Pascagoula, MS	364	371	391	7	1.9	20	5.5	136
Hagerstown-Martinsburg, MD-WV	208	252	264	44	21.1	12	4.9	183
Harrisburg-Carlisle, PA	509	549	568	40	7.9	19	3.4	96
Hartford-West Hartford-East Hartford, CT	1,149	1,212	1,207	64	5.6	-6	-0.5	47
Hickory-Lenoir-Morganton, NC	342	366	364	24	7.0	-2	-0.4	147
Houston-The Woodlands-Sugar Land, TX	4,693	5,920	6,772	1,227	26.2	852	14.4	5
Huntington-Ashland, WV-KY-OH	362	365	360	3	0.7	-5	-1.5	148
Huntsville, AL	342	418	450	75	22.0	32	7.7	117

See footnotes at end of table.

Table 21. Large Metropolitan Statistical Areas—Population: 2000 to 2016-Continued.

See headnote on page 24.

Metropolitan statistical area	2000	2010, esti-mates base [1]	2016	Change 2000–2010 [2] Number	Change 2000–2010 [2] Percent	Change 2010–2016 Number	Change 2010–2016 Percent	Rank, 2016
Indianapolis-Carmel-Anderson, IN	1,658	1,888	2,004	230	13.8	116	6.2	34
Jackson, MS	525	568	579	42	8.1	12	2.0	94
Jacksonville, FL	1,123	1,346	1,478	223	19.8	133	9.9	40
Kalamazoo-Portage, MI	315	327	337	12	3.7	10	3.1	152
Kansas City, MO-KS	1,811	2,009	2,105	198	10.9	95	4.7	30
Kennewick-Richland, WA	192	253	284	62	32.1	31	12.0	165
Killeen-Temple, TX	331	405	436	75	22.6	31	7.5	123
Kingsport-Bristol-Bristol, TN-VA	298	310	306	11	3.7	-3	-1.0	162
Knoxville, TN	748	838	869	89	11.9	31	3.7	64
Lafayette, LA	425	467	492	42	9.8	25	5.3	108
Lakeland-Winter Haven, FL	484	602	666	118	24.4	64	10.6	82
Lancaster, PA	471	519	539	49	10.4	19	3.7	103
Lansing-East Lansing, MI	448	464	475	16	3.6	11	2.4	110
Laredo, TX	193	250	271	57	29.6	21	8.3	175
Las Vegas-Henderson-Paradise, NV	1,376	1,951	2,156	576	41.8	204	10.5	29
Lexington-Fayette, KY	408	472	507	64	15.6	35	7.3	106
Lincoln, NE	267	302	327	35	13.3	25	8.2	154
Little Rock-North Little Rock-Conway, AR	611	700	735	89	14.6	35	5.0	76
Los Angeles-Long Beach-Anaheim, CA	12,366	12,829	13,310	463	3.7	481	3.8	2
Louisville/Jefferson County, KY-IN	1,121	1,236	1,283	115	10.2	48	3.9	44
Lubbock, TX	256	291	315	35	13.5	24	8.2	159
Lynchburg, VA	229	253	260	24	10.5	8	3.0	185
Madison, WI	535	605	649	70	13.1	43	7.2	86
Manchester-Nashua, NH	381	401	408	20	5.2	7	1.8	132
McAllen-Edinburg-Mission, TX	569	775	850	205	36.1	75	9.7	66
Memphis, TN-MS-AR	1,213	1,325	1,343	112	9.2	18	1.4	42
Merced, CA	211	256	269	45	21.5	13	5.0	178
Miami-Fort Lauderdale-West Palm Beach, FL	5,008	5,566	6,066	559	11.2	500	9.0	8
Milwaukee-Waukesha-West Allis, WI	1,501	1,556	1,572	55	3.7	17	1.1	39
Minneapolis-St. Paul-Bloomington, MN-WI	3,032	3,349	3,551	317	10.5	202	6.0	16
Mobile, AL	400	413	415	13	3.3	2	0.4	128
Modesto, CA	447	514	542	67	15.1	27	5.3	102
Montgomery, AL	347	375	374	28	8.1	-1	-0.2	142
Myrtle Beach-Conway-North Myrtle Beach, SC-NC	270	377	449	107	39.6	73	19.3	118
Naples-Immokalee-Marco Island, FL	251	322	365	70	27.9	44	13.6	145
Nashville-Davidson-Murfreesboro-Franklin, TN	1,381	1,671	1,865	290	21.0	194	11.6	36
New Haven-Milford, CT	824	862	857	38	4.7	-6	-0.6	65
New Orleans-Metairie, LA	1,338	1,190	1,269	-148	-11.1	79	6.6	46
New York-Newark-Jersey City, NY-NJ-PA	18,945	19,566	20,154	622	3.3	587	3.0	1
North Port-Sarasota-Bradenton, FL	590	702	788	112	19.0	86	12.3	73
Norwich-New London, CT	259	274	270	15	5.8	-4	-1.6	177
Ocala, FL	259	331	349	72	28.0	18	5.3	149
Ogden-Clearfield, UT	485	597	654	112	23.0	57	9.6	85
Oklahoma City, OK	1,095	1,253	1,373	158	14.4	120	9.6	41
Olympia-Tumwater, WA	207	252	275	45	21.7	23	9.1	173
Omaha-Council Bluffs, NE-IA	767	865	924	98	12.8	59	6.8	59
Orlando-Kissimmee-Sanford, FL	1,645	2,134	2,441	490	29.8	307	14.4	23
Oxnard-Thousand Oaks-Ventura, CA	753	823	850	70	9.3	26	3.2	67
Palm Bay-Melbourne-Titusville, FL	476	543	579	67	14.1	36	6.6	95
Pensacola-Ferry Pass-Brent, FL	412	449	486	37	8.9	37	8.2	109
Peoria, IL	367	379	376	12	3.3	-3	-0.8	141
Philadelphia-Camden-Wilmington, PA-NJ-DE-MD	5,687	5,966	6,071	279	4.9	105	1.8	7
Phoenix-Mesa-Scottsdale, AZ	3,252	4,193	4,662	941	28.9	468	11.2	12
Pittsburgh, PA	2,431	2,356	2,342	-75	-3.1	-14	-0.6	26
Port St. Lucie, FL	319	424	465	105	32.8	41	9.7	111
Portland-South Portland, ME	488	514	530	27	5.4	16	3.0	104
Portland-Vancouver-Hillsboro, OR-WA	1,928	2,226	2,425	298	15.5	199	8.9	25
Providence-Warwick, RI-MA	1,583	1,601	1,615	18	1.1	14	0.8	38
Provo-Orem, UT	377	527	603	150	39.8	76	14.5	92
Raleigh, NC	797	1,130	1,303	333	41.8	172	15.3	43
Reading, PA	374	412	415	38	10.2	3	0.8	129
Reno, NV	343	425	458	83	24.1	32	7.6	114
Richmond, VA	1,056	1,208	1,282	152	14.4	74	6.1	45
Riverside-San Bernardino-Ontario, CA	3,255	4,225	4,528	970	29.8	303	7.2	13
Roanoke, VA	288	309	314	20	7.1	5	1.6	160
Rochester, NY	1,062	1,080	1,079	17	1.6	-1	-0.1	51
Rockford, IL	320	349	339	29	9.1	-10	-2.9	151
Sacramento-Roseville-Arden-Arcade, CA	1,797	2,149	2,296	352	19.6	147	6.9	27
Salem, OR	347	391	418	44	12.5	27	7.0	127
Salinas, CA	402	415	435	13	3.3	20	4.9	124
Salisbury, MD-DE	313	374	400	61	19.6	26	7.1	135
Salt Lake City, UT	939	1,088	1,186	149	15.8	98	9.0	48
San Antonio-New Braunfels, TX	1,712	2,143	2,430	431	25.2	287	13.4	24
San Diego-Carlsbad, CA	2,814	3,095	3,318	282	10.0	222	7.2	17
San Francisco-Oakland-Hayward, CA	4,124	4,336	4,679	212	5.1	344	7.9	11
San Jose-Sunnyvale-Santa Clara, CA	1,736	1,837	1,979	101	5.8	142	7.7	35
San Luis Obispo-Paso Robles-Arroyo Grande, CA	247	270	283	23	9.3	13	4.9	166
Santa Cruz-Watsonville, CA	256	262	275	7	2.6	12	4.7	174

See footnotes at end of table.

Table 21. Large Metropolitan Statistical Areas—Population: 2000 to 2016-Continued.

See headnote on page 24.

Metropolitan statistical area	2000	2010, esti-mates base [1]	2016	Change				Rank, 2016
				2000–2010 [2]		2010–2016		
				Number	Percent	Number	Percent	
Santa Maria-Santa Barbara, CA	399	424	446	25	6.2	22	5.2	119
Santa Rosa, CA	459	484	503	25	5.5	19	4.0	107
Savannah, GA	293	348	384	55	18.6	36	10.5	137
Scranton-Wilkes-Barre-Hazleton, PA	561	564	555	3	0.5	-8	-1.5	99
Seattle-Tacoma-Bellevue, WA	3,044	3,440	3,799	396	13.0	359	10.4	15
Shreveport-Bossier City, LA	418	440	442	22	5.3	2	0.4	121
Sioux Falls, SD	187	228	256	41	22.0	27	12.0	186
South Bend-Mishawaka, IN-MI	317	319	321	3	0.8	2	0.5	156
Spartanburg, SC	284	313	329	30	10.4	16	5.1	153
Spokane-Spokane Valley, WA	470	528	557	58	12.4	29	5.5	98
Springfield, MA	608	622	630	13	2.2	9	1.4	90
Springfield, MO	368	437	459	68	18.6	22	5.1	113
St. Louis, MO-IL [4]	2,675	2,788	2,807	112	4.2	19	0.7	20
Stockton-Lodi, CA	564	685	734	122	21.6	48	7.1	77
Syracuse, NY	650	663	657	12	1.9	-6	-0.9	84
Tallahassee, FL	320	369	380	48	15.1	11	2.9	140
Tampa-St. Petersburg-Clearwater, FL	2,396	2,784	3,032	388	16.2	249	8.9	18
Toledo, OH	618	610	605	-8	-1.3	-5	-0.8	91
Trenton, NJ	351	368	371	17	4.8	4	1.0	143
Tucson, AZ	844	980	1,016	137	16.2	36	3.7	53
Tulsa, OK	860	938	987	78	9.1	50	5.3	55
Urban Honolulu, HI	876	953	993	77	8.8	39	4.1	54
Utica-Rome, NY	300	299	294	-(Z)	-0.2	-6	-1.9	164
Vallejo-Fairfield, CA	395	413	440	19	4.8	27	6.5	122
Virginia Beach-Norfolk-Newport News, VA-NC	1,580	1,677	1,727	97	6.1	50	3.0	37
Visalia-Porterville, CA	368	442	460	74	20.2	18	4.1	112
Waco, TX	232	253	265	21	8.9	12	4.9	181
Washington-Arlington-Alexandria, DC-VA-MD-WV	4,837	5,636	6,132	799	16.5	496	8.8	6
Wichita, KS	580	631	645	51	8.8	14	2.2	87
Wilmington, NC	201	255	283	53	26.6	28	10.9	167
Winston-Salem, NC	569	641	662	71	12.5	21	3.4	83
Worcester, MA-CT	860	917	936	57	6.6	19	2.1	58
York-Hanover, PA	382	435	444	53	13.9	9	2.0	120
Youngstown-Warren-Boardman, OH-PA	603	566	545	-37	-6.2	-21	-3.7	101

Z Less than 500 or .05 percent. [1] The April 1, 2010 population estimates base reflects changes to the Census 2010 population from the Count Question Resolution program and geographic program revisions. [2] Based on census data. [3] Broomfield County, CO, was formed from parts of Adams, Boulder, Jefferson, and Weld Counties, CO, on November 15, 2001, and is coextensive with Broomfield city. For purposes of defining and presenting data for metropolitan statistical areas, Broomfield city is treated as if it were a county at the time of the 2000 census. [4] The portion of Sullivan city in Crawford County, Missouri, is legally part of the St. Louis, MO-IL MSA. Data shown here do not include this area.

Source: U.S. Census Bureau, "CPH-T-5. Population Change for Metropolitan and Micropolitan Statistical Areas in the United States and Puerto Rico (February 2013 Delineations): 2000 to 2010," March 2013, <http://www.census.gov/population/www/cen2010/cph-t/cph-t-5.html>; and Metropolitan and Micropolitan Statistical Areas, Tables, "Annual Estimates of the Resident Population: April 1, 2010 to July 1, 2016" and "Cumulative Estimates of Resident Population Change and Rankings: April 1, 2010 to July 1, 2016," March 2017, <https://www.census.gov/programs-surveys/popest/data/tables.html>; accessed March 2017.

Table 22. The 50 Largest Metropolitan Statistical Areas in 2016—Components of Population Change: 2010 to 2016

[503 represents 503,000. Covers period April 1, 2010 to July 1, 2016. Covers metropolitan statistical areas as delineated by the U.S. Office of Management and Budget as of July 2015. For definitions and components of all metropolitan and micropolitan areas, see Appendix II. Minus sign (-) indicates decrease or outmigration]

| Metropolitan statistical area | Number (1,000) | | | | | | | |
| | Total change [1] | Natural increase | | | Net migration | | | Percent change |
		Total	Births	Deaths	Total	International	Domestic migration	
Atlanta-Sandy Springs-Roswell, GA	503	241	455	214	258	104	153	9.5
Austin-Round Rock, TX	340	105	162	57	230	38	192	19.8
Baltimore-Columbia-Towson, MD	88	63	211	148	28	55	-26	3.3
Birmingham-Hoover, AL	19	19	91	72	1	6	-5	1.7
Boston-Cambridge-Newton, MA-NH	242	103	324	221	146	182	-36	5.3
Buffalo-Cheektowaga-Niagara Falls, NY	-3	1	76	75	-1	21	-22	-0.2
Charlotte-Concord-Gastonia, NC-SC	257	78	186	108	176	33	143	11.6
Chicago-Naperville-Elgin, IL-IN-WI	51	322	753	431	-261	149	-409	0.5
Cincinnati, OH-KY-IN	50	53	169	116	-1	23	-23	2.4
Cleveland-Elyria, OH	-22	14	146	132	-34	25	-58	-1.0
Columbus, OH	140	76	169	93	65	36	29	7.3
Dallas-Fort Worth-Arlington, TX	807	358	612	254	445	140	304	12.6
Denver-Aurora-Lakewood, CO	309	115	218	103	192	37	155	12.2
Detroit-Warren-Dearborn, MI	1	63	314	252	-59	72	-131	(Z)
Hartford-West Hartford-East Hartford, CT	-6	11	75	65	-14	33	-47	-0.5
Houston-The Woodlands-Sugar Land, TX	852	373	600	227	477	194	283	14.4
Indianapolis-Carmel-Anderson, IN	116	69	166	97	47	26	21	6.2
Jacksonville, FL	133	37	111	74	93	25	68	9.9
Kansas City, MO-KS	95	70	173	103	26	20	6	4.7
Las Vegas-Henderson-Paradise, NV	204	75	167	92	126	38	88	10.5
Los Angeles-Long Beach-Anaheim, CA	481	554	1,049	494	-57	316	-373	3.8
Louisville/Jefferson County, KY-IN	48	25	99	74	24	16	8	3.9
Memphis, TN-MS-AR	18	47	118	71	-28	9	-37	1.4
Miami-Fort Lauderdale-West Palm Beach, FL	500	121	419	298	375	381	-7	9.0
Milwaukee-Waukesha-West Allis, WI	17	43	125	82	-25	18	-43	1.1
Minneapolis-St. Paul-Bloomington, MN-WI	202	148	285	138	57	65	-8	6.0
Nashville-Davidson-Murfreesboro-Franklin, TN	194	62	146	85	130	26	104	11.6
New Orleans-Metairie, LA	79	31	99	68	47	19	27	6.6
New York-Newark-Jersey City, NY-NJ-PA	587	672	1,564	893	-54	849	-903	3.0
Oklahoma City, OK	120	48	119	70	71	19	52	9.6
Orlando-Kissimmee-Sanford, FL	307	71	171	100	231	100	132	14.4
Philadelphia-Camden-Wilmington, PA-NJ-DE-MD	105	115	451	336	-5	123	-128	1.8
Phoenix-Mesa-Scottsdale, AZ	468	182	371	189	277	62	215	11.2
Pittsburgh, PA	-14	-21	150	170	11	23	-12	-0.6
Portland-Vancouver-Hillsboro, OR-WA	199	71	174	103	125	30	94	8.9
Providence-Warwick, RI-MA	14	12	104	92	3.8	33	-29	0.8
Raleigh, NC	172	55	97	42	114	24	91	15.3
Richmond, VA	74	30	93	63	43	22	21	6.1
Riverside-San Bernardino-Ontario, CA	303	206	383	177	93	34	59	7.2
Sacramento-Roseville-Arden-Arcade, CA	147	69	172	103	76	37	39	6.9
Salt Lake City, UT	98	79	118	39	21	19	2	9.0
San Antonio-New Braunfels, TX	287	102	202	100	180	34	147	13.4
San Diego-Carlsbad, CA	222	148	277	129	74	90	-15	7.2
San Francisco-Oakland-Hayward, CA	344	142	327	185	207	165	43	7.9
San Jose-Sunnyvale-Santa Clara, CA	142	90	153	63	55	102	-47	7.7
Seattle-Tacoma-Bellevue, WA	359	138	286	148	220	114	106	10.4
St. Louis, MO-IL [2]	19	53	213	159	-33	25	-58	0.7
Tampa-St. Petersburg-Clearwater, FL	249	11	197	186	231	67	163	8.9
Virginia Beach-Norfolk-Newport News, VA-NC	50	58	142	84	-8	34	-42	3.0
Washington-Arlington-Alexandria, DC-VA-MD-WV	496	297	504	207	199	246	-46	8.8

Z Less than 500 or .05 percent. [1] Total population change includes residual. This residual represents the change in population that cannot be attributed to any specific demographic component of change. [2] The portion of Sullivan city in Crawford County, Missouri, is legally part of the St. Louis, MO-IL MSA. Data shown here do not include this area.

Source: U.S. Census Bureau, Metropolitan and Micropolitan Statistical Areas, Tables, "Estimates of the Components of Resident Population Change: April 1, 2010 to July 1, 2016," <https://www.census.gov/data/tables/2016/demo/popest/total-metro-and-micro-statistical-areas.html>, accessed March 2017.

Table 23. Population by Core Based Statistical Area (CBSA) Status and State: 2016

[323,128 represents 323,128,000. As of July 1. Covers core based statistical areas (metropolitan and micropolitan statistical areas) as delineated by the U.S. Office of Management and Budget as of July 2015. For definitions and components of all metropolitan and micropolitan statistical areas, see Appendix II. Minus sign (-) indicates decrease]

State	Total population, 2016 (1,000)	Inside Core-Based Statistical Area (metropolitan or micropolitan statistical area), 2016 — Total Number (1,000)	Total Percent	Metropolitan (1,000)	Micropolitan (1,000)	Outside CBSA, 2016 Number (1,000)	Percent	Percent change, 2010–2016 Metropolitan	Micropolitan	Outside CBSAs
United States..........	323,128	304,786	94.3	277,080	27,706	18,342	5.7	5.5	0.3	-1.5
Alabama................	4,863	4,420	90.9	3,717	703	443	9.1	3.0	-1.0	-3.9
Alaska..................	742	549	74.1	503	46	193	25.9	5.2	3.2	2.9
Arizona.................	6,931	6,828	98.5	6,581	247	103	1.5	8.8	0.6	2.6
Arkansas...............	2,988	2,452	82.1	1,852	600	536	17.9	5.7	-1.3	-3.4
California...............	39,250	38,980	99.3	38,417	563	270	0.7	5.5	-0.9	-2.7
Colorado................	5,541	5,231	94.4	4,838	393	309	5.6	11.4	3.2	1.1
Connecticut............	3,576	3,576	100.0	3,394	183	–	–	0.3	-3.9	(X)
Delaware...............	952	952	100.0	952	–	–	–	6.0	(X)	(X)
District of Columbia....	681	681	100.0	681	–	–	–	13.2	(X)	(X)
Florida..................	20,612	20,266	98.3	19,903	363	346	1.7	10.0	1.9	-1.1
Georgia.................	10,310	9,526	92.4	8,532	994	784	7.6	7.8	0.9	-0.7
Hawaii..................	1,429	1,429	100.0	1,158	270	–	–	4.5	7.3	(X)
Idaho...................	1,683	1,544	91.7	1,126	418	139	8.3	10.1	3.2	-0.5
Illinois..................	12,802	12,198	95.3	11,324	874	603	4.7	0.2	-3.4	-3.4
Indiana.................	6,633	6,175	93.1	5,170	1,005	458	6.9	3.3	-0.7	-1.8
Iowa....................	3,135	2,406	76.7	1,859	547	729	23.3	6.4	-1.0	-2.5
Kansas.................	2,907	2,518	86.6	1,973	545	389	13.4	4.0	-1.3	-3.6
Kentucky...............	4,437	3,486	78.6	2,604	882	951	21.4	4.2	1.8	-2.3
Louisiana..............	4,682	4,355	93.0	3,921	434	326	7.0	4.3	-1.3	-2.7
Maine..................	1,331	909	68.3	789	121	422	31.7	1.7	-1.3	-1.9
Maryland...............	6,016	5,934	98.6	5,865	70	82	1.4	4.4	-1.2	-1.6
Massachusetts.........	6,812	6,801	99.8	6,713	88	11	0.2	4.1	-0.3	8.2
Michigan...............	9,928	9,267	93.3	8,132	1,135	662	6.7	0.8	-(Z)	-2.8
Minnesota..............	5,520	5,009	90.7	4,282	727	511	9.3	5.4	0.7	-1.9
Mississippi.............	2,989	2,348	78.6	1,378	970	641	21.4	3.7	-1.2	-2.6
Missouri................	6,093	5,264	86.4	4,548	716	829	13.6	2.7	0.1	-1.9
Montana................	1,043	684	65.6	368	316	359	34.4	5.2	9.3	2.3
Nebraska...............	1,907	1,568	82.2	1,240	328	339	17.8	7.5	0.5	-2.1
Nevada.................	2,940	2,908	98.9	2,668	240	32	1.1	9.7	1.9	-3.6
New Hampshire........	1,335	1,288	96.5	838	449	47	3.5	2.4	-0.1	-1.1
New Jersey.............	8,944	8,944	100.0	8,944	–	–	–	1.7	(X)	(X)
New Mexico............	2,081	2,009	96.5	1,388	621	72	3.5	1.3	1.7	-7.6
New York...............	19,745	19,353	98.0	18,364	989	392	2.0	2.3	-2.6	-3.5
North Carolina..........	10,147	9,514	93.8	7,940	1,574	633	6.2	8.2	1.3	-1.9
North Dakota...........	758	560	73.8	378	182	198	26.2	14.0	18.4	5.7
Ohio....................	11,614	11,164	96.1	9,255	1,910	450	3.9	1.2	-1.4	-1.6
Oklahoma..............	3,924	3,383	86.2	2,642	740	541	13.8	6.8	1.5	-1.3
Oregon.................	4,093	3,994	97.6	3,430	564	99	2.4	7.9	1.6	1.5
Pennsylvania...........	12,784	12,409	97.1	11,314	1,095	376	2.9	1.1	-2.5	-3.2
Rhode Island...........	1,056	1,056	100.0	1,056	–	–	–	0.3	(X)	(X)
South Carolina.........	4,961	4,657	93.9	4,214	442	305	6.1	9.1	-0.4	-4.7
South Dakota..........	865	647	74.8	416	231	218	25.2	10.4	4.0	1.6
Tennessee.............	6,651	6,021	90.5	5,149	872	630	9.5	6.0	2.0	-0.4
Texas..................	27,863	26,477	95.0	24,807	1,670	1,385	5.0	12.0	2.0	1.3
Utah....................	3,051	2,904	95.2	2,727	178	147	4.8	10.7	11.0	3.9
Vermont................	625	462	74.0	217	245	163	26.0	2.9	-2.2	-1.0
Virginia.................	8,412	7,633	90.7	7,365	269	779	9.3	6.3	-4.4	-1.6
Washington.............	7,288	7,132	97.9	6,557	575	156	2.1	8.9	4.0	2.3
West Virginia...........	1,831	1,431	78.2	1,131	300	400	21.8	-0.1	-2.0	-3.4
Wisconsin..............	5,779	5,057	87.5	4,279	778	721	12.5	2.4	-0.1	-1.0
Wyoming...............	586	425	72.6	179	246	161	27.4	7.1	3.3	1.4

– Represents zero. Z less than .05. X Not applicable.

Source: U.S. Census Bureau, Metropolitan and Micropolitan Statistical Area Population Totals Tables: 2010-2016, "Datasets, CBSA-EST2016-alldata," <https://www.census.gov/data/tables/2016/demo/popest/total-metro-and-micro-statistical-areas.html>, accessed March 2017.

Table 24. Population of Incorporated Places With 170,000 or More Inhabitants in 2016: 1990 to 2016

[In thousands, except as indicated (223 represents 223,000). Census years as of April 1; all other years, as of July 1. Data for the 2010 estimates base and July estimates are based on the 2010 Census and reflect changes to the April 1, 2010 population due to the Count Question Resolution program and geographic program revisions. All geographic boundaries for the 2016 population estimates series are defined as of January 1, 2016. For 1990 and 2000, the counts relate to places as defined on January 1, 2010. Minus sign (-) indicates decrease. See Appendix III]

City	Number (1,000)					Percent change			Rank, 2016
	1990	2000	2010, estimates base	2015	2016	1990 to 2000 [1]	2000 to 2010 [1]	2010 to 2016	
Akron, Ohio	223	217	199	198	198	-2.7	-8.3	-0.7	118
Albuquerque, New Mexico	385	449	546	557	559	16.6	21.7	2.4	32
Amarillo, Texas	158	174	191	198	200	10.2	9.8	4.7	116
Anaheim, California	267	328	336	349	351	23.0	2.5	4.3	56
Anchorage, Alaska	226	260	292	298	298	15.0	12.1	2.2	66
Arlington, Texas	262	333	365	389	393	27.2	9.8	7.5	48
Atlanta, Georgia	394	416	420	463	473	5.7	0.8	12.4	38
Augusta-Richmond County, Georgia [2]	186	200	196	197	197	7.3	-2.0	0.6	120
Aurora, Colorado	222	276	325	358	362	24.6	17.6	11.4	54
Aurora, Illinois	100	143	198	201	201	43.6	38.4	1.6	111
Austin, Texas	466	657	811	930	948	41.0	20.4	16.9	11
Bakersfield, California	175	247	348	372	376	41.2	40.6	8.3	53
Baltimore, Maryland	736	651	621	621	615	-11.5	-4.6	-1.0	30
Baton Rouge, Louisiana	223	228	230	228	228	2.2	0.7	-0.8	97
Birmingham, Alabama	265	243	212	213	212	-8.5	-12.6	0.0	104
Boise City, Idaho	126	186	208	220	223	48.0	10.7	7.1	99
Boston, Massachusetts	575	589	618	666	673	2.5	4.8	9.0	22
Brownsville, Texas	114	140	175	183	184	22.6	25.3	5.0	132
Buffalo, New York	328	293	261	258	257	-10.8	-10.7	-1.7	81
Cape Coral, Florida	75	102	154	175	180	36.1	50.9	16.5	136
Chandler, Arizona	90	177	236	244	247	96.5	33.7	4.8	84
Charlotte, North Carolina	428	541	736	826	842	26.4	35.2	14.5	17
Chattanooga, Tennessee	153	156	170	176	178	1.5	7.8	4.3	139
Chesapeake, Virginia	152	199	222	235	238	31.1	11.6	7.0	92
Chicago, Illinois	2,783	2,896	2,696	2,714	2,705	4.1	-6.9	0.3	3
Chula Vista, California	135	174	244	265	267	28.4	40.5	9.5	74
Cincinnati, Ohio	364	331	297	299	299	-9.0	-10.4	0.6	65
Cleveland, Ohio	506	478	397	388	386	-5.5	-17.1	-2.7	51
Colorado Springs, Colorado	280	361	417	456	465	28.7	15.4	11.4	40
Columbus, Georgia	179	186	191	200	197	3.9	2.2	3.6	119
Columbus, Ohio	633	711	789	850	860	12.4	10.6	9.0	14
Corpus Christi, Texas	258	277	305	325	326	7.4	10.0	6.7	58
Dallas, Texas	1,008	1,189	1,198	1,297	1,318	18.0	0.8	10.0	9
Denver, Colorado	468	555	600	680	693	18.6	8.2	15.5	19
Des Moines, Iowa	193	199	204	215	215	2.8	2.4	5.5	102
Detroit, Michigan	1,028	951	714	676	673	-7.5	-25.0	-5.8	23
Durham, North Carolina	137	187	228	258	263	36.9	22.1	15.1	78
El Paso, Texas	515	564	648	679	683	9.4	15.2	5.4	20
Fayetteville, North Carolina	76	121	201	204	205	59.5	65.7	2.1	110
Fontana, California	88	129	196	207	210	47.3	52.1	6.7	106
Fort Lauderdale, Florida	149	152	166	178	179	2.1	8.6	8.0	138
Fort Wayne, Indiana	173	206	254	263	264	18.9	23.3	4.3	76
Fort Worth, Texas	448	535	745	834	854	19.5	38.6	14.7	16
Fremont, California	173	203	214	231	233	17.3	5.2	8.9	96
Fresno, California	354	428	496	519	522	20.8	15.7	5.2	34
Garden Grove, California	143	165	171	175	175	15.5	3.4	2.3	143
Garland, Texas	181	216	227	236	235	19.4	5.1	3.6	95
Gilbert, Arizona	29	110	208	232	237	276.7	90.0	13.8	93
Glendale, Arizona	148	219	226	243	246	48.0	3.6	8.6	86
Glendale, California	180	195	192	200	201	8.3	-1.7	4.8	112
Grand Prairie, Texas	100	127	175	187	191	27.9	37.6	8.7	127
Grand Rapids, Michigan	189	198	188	195	196	4.6	-4.9	4.4	121
Greensboro, North Carolina	184	224	269	285	287	21.8	20.4	6.7	68
Henderson, Nevada	65	175	257	285	293	170.0	47.0	13.9	67
Hialeah, Florida	188	226	225	237	236	20.4	-0.8	5.2	94
Houston, Texas	1,631	1,954	2,100	2,285	2,303	19.8	7.5	9.7	4
Huntington Beach, California	182	190	191	201	201	4.4	0.2	5.0	114
Huntsville, Alabama	160	158	180	191	193	-1.0	13.8	7.0	124
Indianapolis, Indiana [2]	731	792	820	852	855	8.3	3.6	4.2	15
Irvine, California	110	143	212	256	266	29.7	48.4	25.6	75
Irving, Texas	155	192	216	236	238	23.6	12.9	10.2	91
Jacksonville, Florida	635	736	822	867	881	15.8	11.7	7.2	12
Jersey City, New Jersey	229	240	248	264	264	5.0	3.1	6.7	77
Kansas City, Missouri	435	442	460	475	481	1.5	4.1	4.7	37
Knoxville, Tennessee	165	174	178	185	186	5.4	2.9	4.4	129
Laredo, Texas	123	177	236	255	257	43.7	33.7	8.9	80
Las Vegas, Nevada	258	478	585	622	633	85.3	22.0	8.3	28
Lexington-Fayette, Kentucky	225	261	296	315	318	15.6	13.5	7.7	60
Lincoln, Nebraska	192	226	258	277	280	17.5	14.5	8.5	71
Little Rock, Arkansas	176	183	193	198	199	4.2	5.7	2.6	117
Long Beach, California	429	462	462	471	470	7.5	0.2	1.7	39
Los Angeles, California	3,486	3,695	3,793	3,949	3,976	6.0	2.6	4.8	2
Louisville/Jefferson County, Kentucky [2]	[3] 270	[3] 256	596	615	616	[3] -4.9	(X)	3.3	29
Lubbock, Texas	186	200	229	249	253	7.2	15.0	10.0	83
Madison, Wisconsin	191	208	233	249	253	9.1	12.1	8.4	82
McKinney, Texas	21	54	131	163	172	155.5	141.2	31.5	147

See footnotes at end of table.

Table 24. Population of Incorporated Places With 170,000 or More Inhabitants in 2016: 1990 to 2016-Continued.

See headnote on page 29.

City	Number (1,000)					Percent change			Rank, 2016
	1990	2000	2010, estimates base	2015	2016	1990 to 2000 [1]	2000 to 2010 [1]	2010 to 2016	
Memphis, Tennessee..................	610	650	652	654	653	6.5	-0.5	0.1	25
Mesa, Arizona...........................	288	396	440	478	485	37.6	10.8	10.1	36
Miami, Florida...........................	359	362	400	441	454	1.1	10.2	13.5	42
Milwaukee, Wisconsin................	628	597	595	599	595	-5.0	-0.4	0.0	31
Minneapolis, Minnesota..............	368	383	383	410	414	3.9	0.0	8.1	46
Mobile, Alabama.......................	196	199	195	193	193	1.4	-1.9	-0.9	125
Modesto, California....................	165	189	203	210	212	14.6	6.5	4.5	103
Montgomery, Alabama................	188	202	206	201	200	7.5	2.1	-2.7	115
Moreno Valley, California............	119	142	193	203	205	19.9	35.8	6.3	109
Nashville-Davidson, Tennessee [2]....	488	570	603	654	660	16.7	5.5	9.4	24
New Orleans, Louisiana..............	497	485	344	390	391	-2.5	-29.1	13.9	49
New York, New York...................	7,323	8,008	8,175	8,517	8,538	9.4	2.1	4.4	1
Newark, New Jersey..................	275	274	277	281	282	-0.6	1.3	1.7	70
Newport News, Virginia..............	171	180	181	182	182	5.1	0.3	0.4	135
Norfolk, Virginia........................	261	234	243	246	245	-10.3	3.6	0.9	88
North Las Vegas, Nevada...........	48	115	217	234	239	141.4	87.9	10.2	90
Oakland, California....................	372	399	391	418	420	7.3	-2.2	7.4	45
Oceanside, California.................	128	161	167	175	175	25.7	3.8	5.1	141
Oklahoma City, Oklahoma..........	445	506	580	631	638	13.8	14.6	10.1	27
Omaha, Nebraska.....................	336	390	432	445	447	16.2	4.9	3.5	44
Ontario, California.....................	133	158	164	171	173	18.6	3.7	5.7	146
Orlando, Florida........................	165	186	239	270	277	12.9	28.2	15.9	73
Overland Park, Kansas..............	112	149	173	186	189	33.4	16.3	9.0	128
Oxnard, California.....................	143	170	198	207	208	19.5	16.2	5.0	108
Philadelphia, Pennsylvania.........	1,586	1,518	1,526	1,565	1,568	-4.3	0.6	2.7	6
Phoenix, Arizona.......................	983	1,321	1,448	1,583	1,615	34.3	9.4	11.6	5
Pittsburgh, Pennsylvania............	370	335	306	304	304	-9.5	-8.6	-0.7	63
Plano, Texas............................	128	222	260	283	286	73.6	17.0	10.1	69
Port St. Lucie, Florida................	56	89	165	179	185	59.2	85.4	12.4	130
Portland, Oregon......................	439	529	584	631	640	20.6	10.3	9.6	26
Providence, Rhode Island...........	161	174	178	179	179	8.0	2.5	0.7	137
Raleigh, North Carolina..............	212	276	404	450	459	30.2	46.3	13.6	41
Rancho Cucamonga, California......	101	128	165	175	177	26.0	29.4	6.8	140
Reno, Nevada..........................	134	180	226	241	245	34.8	24.8	8.5	87
Richmond, Virginia....................	203	198	204	220	223	-2.5	3.2	9.3	98
Riverside, California..................	227	255	304	321	325	12.6	19.1	6.8	59
Rochester, New York..................	230	220	211	210	209	-4.6	-4.2	-0.9	107
Sacramento, California...............	369	407	466	489	495	10.2	14.6	6.2	35
Salt Lake City, Utah...................	160	182	186	191	194	13.6	2.6	3.9	123
San Antonio, Texas...................	935	1,145	1,328	1,468	1,493	22.4	16.0	12.4	7
San Bernardino, California..........	165	185	210	216	216	12.6	13.2	3.0	100
San Diego, California.................	1,111	1,223	1,302	1,391	1,407	10.2	6.9	8.1	8
San Francisco, California...........	724	777	805	862	871	7.3	3.7	8.2	13
San Jose, California..................	782	895	953	1,023	1,025	14.4	5.7	7.6	10
Santa Ana, California.................	294	338	325	334	334	15.0	-4.0	2.9	57
Santa Clarita, California.............	111	151	176	181	182	36.5	16.7	3.2	134
Santa Rosa, California...............	113	148	168	175	175	30.3	13.7	4.4	142
Scottsdale, Arizona...................	130	203	217	240	247	55.8	7.2	13.4	85
Seattle, Washington..................	516	563	609	684	704	9.1	8.0	15.7	18
Shreveport, Louisiana................	199	200	200	197	195	0.8	-0.4	-2.7	122
Sioux Falls, South Dakota..........	101	124	154	172	174	22.9	24.1	13.3	145
Spokane, Washington................	177	196	209	213	216	10.4	6.8	3.1	101
St. Louis, Missouri....................	397	348	319	315	311	-12.2	-8.3	-2.5	61
St. Paul, Minnesota...................	272	287	285	300	302	5.5	-0.7	6.1	64
St. Petersburg, Florida...............	240	248	245	257	261	3.3	-1.4	6.4	79
Stockton, California...................	211	244	292	305	307	15.6	19.7	5.3	62
Tacoma, Washington.................	177	194	198	208	211	9.6	2.5	6.5	105
Tallahassee, Florida..................	125	151	181	190	191	20.7	20.4	5.2	126
Tampa, Florida.........................	280	303	336	368	377	8.4	10.6	12.3	52
Tempe, Arizona........................	142	159	162	178	182	11.7	2.0	12.8	133
Toledo, Ohio............................	333	314	287	280	279	-5.8	-8.4	-3.0	72
Tucson, Arizona.......................	405	487	521	528	531	20.1	6.9	1.9	33
Tulsa, Oklahoma......................	367	393	392	403	403	7.0	-0.3	2.8	47
Urban Honolulu CDP, Hawaii [4]........	(NA)	(NA)	338	352	352	(NA)	(NA)	4.2	55
Vancouver, Washington..............	46	144	162	172	175	209.5	12.7	7.6	144
Virginia Beach, Virginia.............	393	425	438	452	453	8.2	3.0	3.4	43
Washington, District of Columbia.....	607	572	602	670	681	-5.7	5.2	13.2	21
Wichita, Kansas.......................	304	344	382	389	390	13.2	11.1	2.0	50
Winston-Salem, North Carolina.......	143	186	230	241	242	29.5	23.6	5.5	89
Worcester, Massachusetts...........	170	173	181	184	185	1.7	4.9	1.9	131
Yonkers, New York....................	188	196	196	200	201	4.3	-0.1	2.5	113

NA Not available. X Not applicable. [1] Based on census data. [2] Represents the portion of a consolidated city that is not within one or more separately incorporated places. [3] Data are for the incorporated place of Louisville city before consolidation of the city and county governments. [4] CDP=Census Designated Place.

Source: U.S. Census Bureau, 1990, 2000 and 2010 census data: *Census of Population and Housing, 2010, CPH-2. Population and Housing Unit Counts*; and beginning 2010: City and Town Population Totals Tables: 2010-2016, "Annual Estimates of the Resident Population for Incorporated Places Over 50,000, Ranked by July 1, 2016 Population: April 1, 2010 to July 1, 2016," May 2017, <https://www.census.gov/programs-surveys/popest/data/tables.2016.html>.

Table 25. Incorporated Places by Population Size: 1990 to 2016

[153.1 represents 153,100,000. See Appendix III]

Population size	Number of incorporated places				Population (mil.)				Percent of total			
	1990	2000	2010	2016	1990	2000	2010	2016	1990	2000	2010	2016
Total..................	19,262	19,452	19,540	19,510	153.1	173.5	192.0	203.3	100.0	100.0	100.0	100.0
1,000,000 or more.........	8	9	9	10	20.0	22.9	23.6	25.9	13.1	13.2	12.3	12.8
500,000 to 999,999.......	15	20	24	24	10.1	12.9	16.1	16.9	6.6	7.4	8.4	8.3
250,000 to 499,999.......	41	37	40	49	14.2	13.3	14.0	17.0	9.3	7.7	7.3	8.4
100,000 to 249,999.......	131	172	200	220	19.1	25.5	30.2	32.8	12.5	14.7	15.7	16.1
50,000 to 99,999.........	309	363	432	454	21.2	24.9	30.1	31.8	13.8	14.4	15.7	15.6
25,000 to 49,999..........	567	644	723	736	20.0	22.6	25.2	25.7	13.1	13.0	13.1	12.6
10,000 to 24,999..........	1,290	1,435	1,542	1,555	20.3	22.6	24.2	24.6	13.3	13.0	12.6	12.1
Under 10,000..............	16,901	16,772	16,570	16,462	28.2	28.7	28.7	28.6	18.4	16.5	14.9	14.1

Source: U.S. Census Bureau, *1990 Census of Population and Housing, Population and Housing Unit Counts (CPH-2-1)*; *Census 2000 PHC-3, Population and Housing Unit Counts*; 2010 Census Redistricting Data (Public Law 94-171) Summary File; and City and Town Population Totals Datasets: 2010-2016, Incorporated Places and Minor Civil Divisions Datasets, "SUB-EST2016: Subcounty Resident Population Estimates: April 1, 2010 to July 1, 2016," May 2017, <https://www2.census.gov/programs-surveys/popest/datasets/2010-2016/cities/totals/>.

Table 26. Urban and Rural Population by State: 2000 and 2010

[222,361 represents 222,361,000. As of April 1. Resident population. Based on current urban definitions, see text, this section]

State	2000 Urban (1,000)	2000 Rural (1,000)	2010 Urban Number (1,000)	2010 Urban Percent	2010 Rural (1,000)	State	2000 Urban (1,000)	2000 Rural (1,000)	2010 Urban Number (1,000)	2010 Urban Percent	2010 Rural (1,000)
U.S......	222,361	59,061	249,253	80.7	59,492	MO.........	3,883	1,712	4,218	70.4	1,771
AL.........	2,466	1,981	2,822	59.0	1,958	MT.........	488	414	553	55.9	436
AK.........	411	216	469	66.0	241	NE.........	1,194	518	1,336	73.1	491
AZ.........	4,524	607	5,741	89.8	651	NV.........	1,829	170	2,544	94.2	157
AR.........	1,404	1,269	1,638	56.2	1,278	NH.........	732	503	794	60.3	523
CA.........	31,990	1,882	35,374	95.0	1,880	NJ.........	7,939	475	8,324	94.7	468
CO.........	3,633	668	4,333	86.2	696	NM.........	1,364	456	1,594	77.4	465
CT.........	2,988	418	3,145	88.0	429	NY.........	16,603	2,374	17,028	87.9	2,350
DE.........	628	156	748	83.3	150	NC.........	4,849	3,200	6,302	66.1	3,234
DC.........	572	0	602	100.0	0	ND.........	359	283	403	59.9	270
FL.........	14,270	1,712	17,140	91.2	1,661	OH.........	8,782	2,571	8,990	77.9	2,547
GA.........	5,864	2,322	7,272	75.1	2,416	OK.........	2,255	1,196	2,485	66.2	1,266
HI.........	1,108	103	1,250	91.9	110	OR.........	2,694	727	3,104	81.0	727
ID.........	859	434	1,106	70.6	461	PA.........	9,464	2,817	9,991	78.7	2,711
IL.........	10,910	1,510	11,354	88.5	1,477	RI.........	953	95	955	90.7	98
IN.........	4,304	1,776	4,697	72.4	1,787	SC.........	2,427	1,585	3,068	66.3	1,558
IA.........	1,787	1,139	1,950	64.0	1,096	SD.........	391	363	461	56.7	353
KS.........	1,921	768	2,117	74.2	736	TN.........	3,620	2,069	4,213	66.4	2,133
KY.........	2,254	1,788	2,533	58.4	1,806	TX.........	17,204	3,648	21,298	84.7	3,848
LA.........	3,246	1,223	3,318	73.2	1,216	UT.........	1,970	263	2,504	90.6	260
ME.........	513	762	514	38.7	815	VT.........	232	376	243	38.9	382
MD.........	4,559	738	5,034	87.2	739	VA.........	5,170	1,909	6,037	75.5	1,964
MA.........	5,801	548	6,022	92.0	526	WA.........	4,831	1,063	5,652	84.1	1,073
MI.........	7,419	2,519	7,370	74.6	2,514	WV.........	833	976	903	48.7	950
MN.........	3,490	1,429	3,886	73.3	1,418	WI.........	3,664	1,700	3,990	70.2	1,697
MS.........	1,387	1,457	1,464	49.4	1,503	WY.........	321	172	365	64.8	199

Source: U.S. Census Bureau, 2000 Census of Population and Housing, *Population and Housing Unit Counts PHC-3*; 2010 Census of Population and Housing, *Population and Housing Unit Counts, CPH-2-1, United States Summary*; and "Percent Urban and Rural in 2010 by State," <https://www.census.gov/geo/reference/ua/urban-rural-2010.html>, accessed March 2013.

Table 27. Population in Coastal Counties: 1990 to 2016

[3,537 represents 3,537,000. Data for 1990 to 2010 as of April 1; beginning 2013, data as of July 1. Data for 1990 and 2000 are based on 675 counties in areas as defined by U.S. National Oceanic and Atmospheric Administration, 1992. Beginning 2010, data cover 678 counties and equivalent areas in a coastal watershed; see headnote, Table 28. See Appendix III]

Year	Total	Counties in coastal regions					Balance of United States
		Total	Atlantic	Gulf of Mexico	Great Lakes	Pacific	
Land area, 2010 (1,000 sq. mi.)......	3,537	888	147	116	115	510	2,649
POPULATION							
1990 (millions).........................	248.7	133.4	59.0	15.2	25.9	33.2	115.3
2000 (millions).........................	281.4	148.3	65.2	18.0	27.3	37.8	133.1
2010 (millions).........................	308.7	159.7	70.2	20.9	27.2	41.4	149.0
2013 (millions).........................	316.2	163.7	72.0	21.7	27.3	42.7	152.5
2014 (millions).........................	318.6	164.9	72.5	22.0	27.3	43.2	153.6
2015 (millions).........................	320.9	166.1	72.9	22.4	27.2	43.6	154.8
2016 (millions).........................	323.1	167.1	73.3	22.7	27.2	43.9	156.0
1990 (percent).........................	100.0	53.6	23.7	6.1	10.4	13.3	46.4
2000 (percent).........................	100.0	53.0	23.0	6.0	10.0	13.0	47.0
2010 (percent).........................	100.0	51.7	22.7	6.8	8.8	13.4	48.3
2013 (percent).........................	100.0	51.8	22.8	6.9	8.6	13.5	48.2
2014 (percent).........................	100.0	51.8	22.7	6.9	8.6	13.5	48.2
2015 (percent).........................	100.0	51.8	22.7	7.0	8.5	13.6	48.2
2016 (percent).........................	100.0	51.7	22.7	7.0	8.4	13.6	48.3

Source: U.S. Census Bureau, *1990 Census of Population and Housing (CPH1)*; "Annual Estimates of the Resident Population for Counties: April 1, 2000 to July 1, 2009," March 2011, <http://www.census.gov/popest/data/counties/totals/2009/CO-EST2009-01.html>; and "PEPANNRES: Annual Estimates of the Resident Population: April 1, 2010 to July 1, 2016," <http://factfinder.census.gov>, accessed September 2017.

Table 28. States With Coastal Counties—Population and Housing Units, Establishments, and Employees by Coastal Region and State: 2010 to 2016

[308,758 represents 308,758,000. Data for 2010 as of April 1 and reflect population estimates base. Data for 2016 as of July 1. Beginning in 2010, data cover 678 counties and equivalent areas in a coastal watershed. A county is considered a coastal watershed county if one of the following criteria is met: (1) at a minimum, 15 percent of the county's total land area is located within a coastal watershed or (2) a portion of, or an entire county accounts for at least 15 percent of a coastal watershed. The 15- percent rule was selected as an appropriate level for capturing counties with a significant impact on coastal and ocean resources. See Appendix III. Minus sign (-) indicates decrease]

Coastal region and state	Number of counties	Population 2010 (1,000)	Population 2016 Number (1,000)	Population 2016 Percent of state total	Population 2016 Percent change, 2010–2016	Population 2016 Per square mile 2016[1]	Housing units Number 2010 (1,000)	Housing units Number 2016 (1,000)	Housing units Percent change, 2010–2016	Housing units Per square mile 2016[1]	Private nonfarm Establishments, 2015 (1,000)	Private nonfarm Employees, 2015 (1,000)
United States, total	3,142	308,758	323,128	(X)	4.7	91	131,705	135,698	3.0	38	7,664	124,086
Interior U.S.	2,464	149,009	155,998	(X)	4.7	59	64,631	66,835	3.4	25	3,569	(NA)
Coastal counties, total	678	159,749	167,129	(X)	4.6	188	67,074	68,863	2.7	78	4,095	(NA)
Atlantic	286	70,242	73,291	(X)	4.3	497	29,916	30,639	2.4	208	1,898	28,645
Maine	14	1,239	1,247	93.6	0.6	62	667	676	1.4	33	38	472
New Hampshire	6	1,073	1,095	82.0	2.0	260	485	494	1.9	118	31	450
Massachusetts	12	6,318	6,580	96.6	4.1	1,001	2,712	2,761	1.8	420	169	3,040
Rhode Island	5	1,053	1,056	100.0	0.3	1,022	463	463	-0.2	447	28	421
Connecticut	8	3,574	3,576	100.0	0.1	739	1,488	1,499	0.8	310	89	1,476
New York	18	13,952	14,377	72.8	3.0	1,861	5,601	5,701	1.8	738	418	5,869
New Jersey	20	8,683	8,838	98.8	1.8	1,263	3,509	3,559	1.4	509	228	3,411
Pennsylvania	12	6,108	6,241	48.8	2.2	909	2,512	2,537	1.0	370	145	2,636
Delaware	3	898	952	100.0	6.0	489	406	426	5.0	219	25	392
Maryland	20	5,288	5,517	91.7	4.3	734	2,176	2,237	2.8	298	125	2,018
District of Columbia	1	602	681	100.0	13.2	11,158	297	314	5.7	5,139	23	513
Virginia	61	5,426	5,743	68.3	5.8	414	2,216	2,304	4.0	166	136	2,239
North Carolina	38	2,254	2,311	22.8	2.5	117	1,078	1,123	4.2	57	46	625
South Carolina	22	1,932	2,110	42.5	9.2	139	953	1,003	5.2	66	47	642
Georgia	25	945	997	9.7	5.4	84	414	427	3.1	36	20	286
Florida	21	10,896	11,971	58.1	9.9	643	4,940	5,115	3.6	275	331	4,156
Gulf of Mexico	144	20,888	22,710	(X)	8.7	197	9,294	9,794	5.4	85	486	7,543
Florida	41	7,535	8,252	40.0	9.5	256	3,887	4,022	3.5	125	193	2,460
Georgia	3	98	97	0.9	-0.7	61	43	43	0.2	27	2	26
Alabama	8	765	788	16.2	3.0	90	363	373	2.9	43	17	250
Mississippi	12	629	650	21.8	3.5	96	280	292	4.4	43	12	182
Louisiana	39	3,574	3,726	79.6	4.3	143	1,543	1,601	3.8	61	84	1,372
Texas	41	8,288	9,198	33.0	11.0	230	3,178	3,463	9.0	86	178	3,253
Great Lakes	158	27,191	27,200	(X)	0.0	236	12,128	12,199	0.6	106	635	11,062
New York	21	3,635	3,606	18.3	-0.8	169	1,647	1,663	1.0	78	83	1,376
Pennsylvania	1	281	276	2.2	-1.6	346	119	120	0.8	150	6	114
Ohio	24	4,326	4,277	36.8	-1.1	406	1,967	1,970	0.1	187	100	1,801
Michigan	74	8,797	8,853	89.2	0.6	174	4,050	4,077	0.7	80	198	3,283
Indiana	9	1,433	1,437	21.7	0.3	353	607	615	1.3	151	31	580
Illinois	2	5,898	5,907	46.1	0.1	4,252	2,441	2,444	0.1	1,760	152	2,684
Wisconsin	23	2,569	2,594	44.9	1.0	169	1,165	1,178	1.1	77	59	1,124
Minnesota	4	252	252	4.6	(Z)	24	132	134	1.0	13	7	101
Pacific	90	41,429	43,927	(X)	6.0	86	15,737	16,230	3.1	32	1,076	(NA)
Washington	19	5,229	5,704	78.3	9.1	232	2,264	2,379	5.1	97	147	2,112
Oregon	12	1,982	2,111	51.6	6.5	101	895	925	3.3	44	61	821
California	29	32,259	34,057	86.8	5.6	438	11,803	12,130	2.8	156	819	12,663
Alaska	25	598	627	84.5	4.8	2	255	259	1.5	1	18	235
Hawaii	5	1,360	1,429	100.0	5.0	222	520	537	3.4	84	32	(NA)

NA Not available. X Not applicable. Z Less than .05 percent. [1] Calculated on the basis of land area data from the 2010 census. [2] Covers establishments with payroll. Excludes most government employees, railroad employees, and self-employed persons. Employees are for the week including March 12.

Source: U.S. Census Bureau, "PEPANNRES: Annual Estimates of the Resident Population: April 1, 2010 to July 1, 2016"; "PEPANNHU: Annual Estimates of Housing Units for the United States, Regions, Divisions, States, and Counties: April 1, 2010 to July 1, 2016"; and "2015 County Business Patterns", <http://factfinder.census.gov>, accessed September 2017.

Table 29. Geographic Mobility Status of the Population by Selected Characteristics: 1981 to 2016

[221,641 represents 221,641,000. As of March. For persons 1 year old and over, unless otherwise noted. Based on comparison of place of residence in year shown vs. previous year. Excludes members of the Armed Forces except those living off post or with their families on post. 2011 data based on population controls from Census 2000. 2016 data based on population controls from Census 2010. Based on Current Population Survey, Annual Social and Economic Supplement. See text, this section and Appendix III. For composition of regions, see map, inside front cover]

Mobility period and characteristic	Total persons (1,000)	Non–movers	Movers (different house in United States)					Movers from abroad
			Total	Same county	Different county			
					Total	Same state	Different state	
1981..................................	221,641	82.8	16.6	10.4	6.2	3.4	4.3	0.6
1991..................................	244,884	83.0	16.4	10.3	6.1	3.2	4.3	0.6
2001..................................	275,611	85.8	13.5	8.0	5.6	2.7	2.8	0.6
2011..................................	302,005	88.4	11.3	7.7	3.5	2.0	1.6	0.4
2016, total............................	**314,992**	**88.8**	**10.7**	**6.9**	**3.9**	**2.4**	**1.5**	**0.4**
By age:								
1 to 4 years old.............................	16,046	82.2	17.2	11.6	5.6	3.4	2.2	0.6
5 to 9 years old..............................	20,469	87.0	12.6	8.4	4.2	2.5	1.7	0.4
10 to 14 years old..........................	20,573	89.8	9.9	6.7	3.2	1.9	1.3	0.3
15 to 19 years old..........................	20,915	89.6	10.0	6.6	3.4	2.1	1.3	0.4
20 to 24 years old..........................	21,973	77.0	22.2	14.3	7.9	5.1	2.7	0.8
25 to 29 years old..........................	22,434	76.0	23.0	14.4	8.6	5.1	3.4	1.1
30 to 44 years old..........................	61,334	87.2	12.2	7.7	4.5	2.7	1.9	0.6
45 to 64 years old..........................	83,701	93.4	6.4	3.8	2.6	1.6	1.0	0.2
65 to 74 years old..........................	27,942	96.8	3.2	2.0	1.2	0.7	0.5	0.1
75 to 84 years old..........................	14,058	97.2	2.8	1.8	1.0	0.6	0.4	0.1
85 years old and over.......................	5,547	96.4	3.7	2.3	1.4	1.0	0.4	–
By region:								
Northeast...................................	55,282	91.1	8.4	5.3	3.1	2.1	1.1	0.5
Midwest....................................	66,281	88.7	11.0	7.3	3.7	2.5	1.2	0.2
South......................................	118,611	88.5	11.1	6.6	4.5	2.8	1.7	0.4
West.......................................	74,817	87.9	11.6	8.0	3.6	1.9	1.8	0.5
Persons 16 years old and over............	**253,680**	**89.3**	**10.3**	**6.4**	**3.8**	**2.4**	**1.5**	**0.4**
Civilian labor force..........................	158,875	87.8	11.8	7.5	4.3	2.7	1.6	0.4
Employed...................................	150,562	88.1	11.5	7.3	4.2	2.6	1.6	0.3
Unemployed................................	8,313	81.7	17.2	10.3	6.9	3.8	3.1	1.1
Armed Forces...............................	914	71.1	26.5	12.9	13.6	3.6	10.0	2.4
Not in labor force...........................	93,891	92.0	7.5	4.6	2.9	1.8	1.1	0.4
By occupation:								
Employed civilians, 16 years old and over...	150,562	88.1	11.5	7.3	4.2	2.6	1.6	0.3
Management, business, and financial.......	25,003	89.7	10.0	6.0	4.0	2.3	1.6	0.3
Professional...............................	34,968	88.1	11.3	6.7	4.6	2.6	2.1	0.5
Service....................................	26,216	85.7	13.9	9.6	4.3	2.8	1.5	0.4
Sales.....................................	15,662	88.7	11.0	7.2	3.8	2.5	1.2	0.4
Office and administrative support...........	17,588	88.4	11.3	7.3	4.0	2.6	1.4	0.2
Farming, fishing, and forestry..............	1,082	89.4	9.7	7.0	2.7	1.3	1.4	0.8
Construction and extraction.................	7,429	88.3	11.5	7.2	4.4	2.7	1.7	0.2
Installation, maintenance, and repair........	4,802	90.3	9.5	5.5	4.0	3.1	0.9	0.2
Production.................................	8,522	88.2	11.5	7.7	3.9	2.8	1.0	0.3
Transportation and material moving.........	9,292	87.8	11.9	7.7	4.2	3.0	1.2	0.2
By housing tenure:								
Owner occupied units.........................	206,767	95.0	4.9	3.0	1.9	1.3	0.6	0.1
Renter occupied units........................	108,224	77.1	21.9	14.1	7.8	4.5	3.3	1.0

– Represents or rounds to zero.

Source: U.S. Census Bureau, "Geographical Mobility: 2015 to 2016," November 2016, and earlier releases, <https://www.census.gov/topics/population/migration.html>.

Table 30. Movers by Type of Move and Reason for Moving: 2016

[35,138 represents 35,138,000. As of March. For persons 1 year old and over. Based on comparison of place of residence in 2016 vs. 2015. Excludes members of the Armed Forces except those living off post or with their families on post. Based on Current Population Survey, Annual Social and Economic Supplement. See text, this section and Appendix III]

Reason for move	All movers	Intra-county	Inter-county	From abroad	Reason for move	All movers	Intra-county	Inter-county	From abroad
Total (1,000).....................	**35,138**	**21,588**	**12,269**	**1,281**	**Housing–related reasons**......	**42.2**	**53.3**	**26.1**	**8.4**
PERCENT DISTRIBUTION					Wanted to own home/not rent.....	5.9	6.9	4.6	1.7
Total...........................	100.0	100.0	100.0	100.0	New/better house/apartment.....	17.4	23.3	8.7	3.0
Family–related reasons........	**27.4**	**28.0**	**26.6**	**25.8**	Better neighborhood/less crime...	3.1	3.6	2.4	1.8
Change in marital status...........	4.8	5.3	3.6	7.1	Cheaper housing....................	8.2	10.1	5.6	1.4
To establish own household.......	12.2	15.0	8.1	3.4	Foreclosure/eviction................	0.9	1.1	0.5	–
Other family reasons [1]..........	10.5	7.7	14.9	15.3	Other housing [1]...................	6.7	8.4	4.3	0.5
Work–related reasons..........	**20.2**	**10.8**	**34.3**	**42.6**	**Other reasons**...................	**10.2**	**7.8**	**13.0**	**23.1**
New job/job transfer...............	10.8	3.2	22.2	30.8	Attend/leave college...............	3.2	2.0	4.4	12.3
To look for work/lost job...........	1.5	0.6	3.2	1.6	Change of climate..............	0.8	0.3	1.6	0.1
Closer to work/easier commute...	6.0	5.8	6.5	2.7	Health reasons....................	1.8	1.7	2.1	1.1
Retired............................	0.6	0.6	0.9	0.2	Natural disaster....................	–	0.1	–	–
Other job–related reason [1]........	1.2	0.7	1.5	7.3	Other reason [1]....................	4.4	3.8	4.9	9.7

– Represents or rounds to zero. [1] Beginning in 2016, respondents who selected "other family," "other job-related," "other housing," and "other reason" were asked to provide their specific reason for move. These responses could potentially be coded to more specific reasons. Prior to 2016, only respondents who selected "other reason" were asked to specify a reason.

Source: U.S. Census Bureau, "Geographical Mobility: 2015 to 2016," November 2016, <https://www.census.gov/topics/population/migration.html>.

Table 31. Geographic Mobility Status of Resident Population by State: 2015

[In percent, except as indicated (317,636 represents 317,636,000). Based on comparison of place of residence in 2015 vs. 2014. The American Community Survey universe includes the household population and the population living in institutions, college dormitories, and other group quarters. Based on a sample and subject to sampling variability. See text, this section and Appendix III]

| State | Population 1 year old and over (1,000) | Same house in 2014 | Different house in United States in 2014 | | | | | Abroad in 2014 |
| | | | Total | Same county | Different county | | | |
					Total	Same state	Different state	
United States	**317,636**	**85.3**	**14.1**	**8.5**	**5.6**	**3.2**	**2.4**	**0.7**
Alabama	4,802	85.7	14.1	8.5	5.5	3.1	2.4	0.2
Alaska	728	80.1	19.3	11.9	7.4	2.7	4.8	0.6
Arizona	6,748	82.0	17.3	11.8	5.4	1.7	3.8	0.7
Arkansas	2,938	83.1	16.6	9.9	6.7	3.9	2.8	0.3
California	38,675	86.5	12.6	8.6	4.1	2.8	1.3	0.9
Colorado	5,393	81.7	17.7	8.6	9.1	4.9	4.2	0.6
Connecticut	3,555	87.5	11.7	7.4	4.4	2.2	2.2	0.8
Delaware	936	85.6	13.9	7.9	6.1	1.3	4.8	0.5
District of Columbia	663	79.2	19.2	10.1	9.0	0.0	9.0	1.6
Florida	20,068	83.9	15.1	9.0	6.1	3.1	2.9	1.1
Georgia	10,089	84.2	15.3	7.8	7.5	4.7	2.8	0.6
Hawaii	1,414	85.3	13.5	9.1	4.4	0.6	3.8	1.3
Idaho	1,635	81.6	17.9	10.3	7.6	3.1	4.5	0.6
Illinois	12,706	86.8	12.7	8.4	4.2	2.6	1.7	0.5
Indiana	6,541	84.5	15.1	9.2	5.9	3.6	2.3	0.3
Iowa	3,081	84.3	15.3	8.7	6.7	3.9	2.8	0.3
Kansas	2,876	83.7	15.7	9.1	6.6	3.4	3.2	0.6
Kentucky	4,373	84.8	14.9	8.3	6.5	4.1	2.4	0.4
Louisiana	4,612	86.9	12.8	7.7	5.1	3.1	2.0	0.3
Maine	1,317	85.6	14.1	8.7	5.4	3.2	2.3	0.3
Maryland	5,934	85.6	13.6	7.8	5.8	3.0	2.8	0.8
Massachusetts	6,726	87.6	11.4	6.6	4.8	2.8	2.0	1.0
Michigan	9,811	85.6	14.0	9.0	5.0	3.6	1.5	0.5
Minnesota	5,420	85.2	14.2	7.6	6.6	4.6	2.0	0.6
Mississippi	2,959	86.3	13.4	7.6	5.8	3.5	2.3	0.3
Missouri	6,016	84.1	15.6	8.6	7.0	4.3	2.6	0.4
Montana	1,020	83.9	15.8	8.3	7.5	3.3	4.2	0.3
Nebraska	1,869	84.0	15.5	9.0	6.4	3.6	2.8	0.5
Nevada	2,859	80.1	19.2	13.6	5.6	0.9	4.8	0.6
New Hampshire	1,318	86.1	13.3	7.3	6.0	2.0	4.1	0.6
New Jersey	8,854	90.2	9.0	5.2	3.8	2.2	1.6	0.7
New Mexico	2,060	85.8	13.8	8.8	5.0	2.3	2.7	0.4
New York	19,570	89.5	9.8	6.0	3.8	2.5	1.3	0.8
North Carolina	9,928	84.4	15.2	8.4	6.7	3.6	3.1	0.5
North Dakota	745	81.6	17.9	8.9	9.0	3.3	5.7	0.5
Ohio	11,482	84.7	14.9	9.7	5.3	3.5	1.8	0.4
Oklahoma	3,865	82.9	16.7	9.4	7.3	4.4	2.9	0.5
Oregon	3,986	82.2	17.2	10.1	7.1	3.6	3.5	0.6
Pennsylvania	12,662	87.7	11.8	7.3	4.5	2.6	1.8	0.5
Rhode Island	1,045	86.2	13.0	7.8	5.3	1.6	3.7	0.7
South Carolina	4,840	84.8	14.7	8.1	6.7	3.1	3.5	0.4
South Dakota	848	82.8	16.9	8.7	8.2	5.1	3.2	0.3
Tennessee	6,522	84.9	14.8	8.6	6.2	3.2	3.0	0.4
Texas	27,093	83.9	15.3	9.3	6.0	4.0	2.0	0.8
Utah	2,947	82.6	16.6	10.2	6.3	3.0	3.3	0.8
Vermont	620	85.9	13.4	7.6	5.8	2.4	3.4	0.7
Virginia	8,284	83.9	15.2	6.8	8.4	5.1	3.4	0.8
Washington	7,089	81.5	17.6	10.9	6.7	3.4	3.3	0.9
West Virginia	1,824	88.3	11.5	6.3	5.2	2.9	2.3	0.2
Wisconsin	5,708	85.7	14.0	8.6	5.3	3.5	1.9	0.3
Wyoming	579	82.0	17.5	8.4	9.1	2.9	6.2	0.5

Source: U.S. Census Bureau, 2015 American Community Survey, B07003, "Geographical Mobility in the Past Year by Sex for Current Residence in the United States," <http://factfinder.census.gov/>, accessed December 2016.

Table 32. Persons 65 Years Old and Over—Characteristics by Sex: 2000 to 2016

[In percent except as noted (32.6 represents 32,600,000). As of March, except as noted. Covers civilian noninstitutional population. Excludes members of Armed Forces except those living off post or with their families on post. Data for 2000 data based on 1990 Census population controls; data for 2010 based on 2000 Census population controls; and data for 2015 and 2016 based on 2010 Census population controls. Beginning 2005, data based on an expanded sample of households. Based on Current Population Survey. See text, this section]

Characteristic	Total				Male				Female			
	2000	2010	2015	2016	2000	2010	2015	2016	2000	2010	2015	2016
Total (million)	**32.6**	**38.6**	**46.0**	**47.5**	**13.9**	**16.8**	**20.4**	**21.2**	**18.7**	**21.8**	**25.5**	**26.3**
PERCENT DISTRIBUTION												
Marital status:												
Never married	3.9	4.3	4.8	5.2	4.2	4.1	4.9	5.0	3.6	4.5	4.8	5.3
Married	57.2	57.6	58.6	58.8	75.2	74.5	72.4	73.0	43.8	44.5	47.6	47.4
Spouse present	54.6	55.2	56.2	56.5	72.6	71.7	70.0	70.4	41.3	42.4	45.2	45.2
Spouse absent [1]	2.6	2.4	2.4	2.3	2.6	2.8	2.4	2.6	2.5	2.1	2.4	2.1
Widowed	32.1	28.1	24.4	24.0	14.4	12.7	11.9	12.1	45.3	39.9	34.3	33.6
Divorced	6.7	10.0	12.2	12.0	6.1	8.7	10.8	9.9	7.2	11.1	13.3	13.7
Educational attainment:												
Less than 9th grade	16.7	10.2	7.5	7.1	17.8	10.2	7.5	7.3	15.9	10.1	7.4	6.9
Completed 9th to 12th grade, but no high school diploma	13.8	10.3	8.2	7.5	12.7	9.7	7.0	7.2	14.7	10.8	9.2	7.8
High school graduate	35.9	36.4	34.6	33.2	30.4	32.0	30.8	29.2	39.9	39.8	37.6	36.5
Some college or associate's degree	18.0	20.6	23.1	24.0	17.8	19.7	22.8	23.1	18.2	21.2	23.3	24.8
Bachelor's or advanced degree	15.6	22.5	26.7	28.1	21.4	28.4	31.8	33.2	11.4	18.0	22.5	24.0
Labor force status: [2]												
Employed	12.4	16.2	18.2	18.6	16.9	20.5	22.5	23.1	9.1	12.9	14.7	14.9
Unemployed	0.4	1.2	0.7	0.7	0.6	1.6	0.9	0.9	0.3	0.9	0.6	0.6
Not in labor force	87.2	82.6	81.1	80.7	82.5	77.9	76.6	76.0	90.6	86.2	84.7	84.5
Percent below poverty level [3]	9.7	8.9	10.0	8.8	6.9	6.6	7.4	7.0	11.8	10.7	12.1	10.3

[1] Includes separated. [2] Annual averages of monthly figures. Source: U.S. Bureau of Labor Statistics, "Labor Force Characteristics," <http://www.bls.gov/cps/lfcharacteristics.htm#laborforce>. [3] Poverty status based on income in preceding year.

Source: Except as noted, U.S. Census Bureau, Current Population Reports, P20-546, and earlier reports; series P-23, No. 59; series P-60, No. 226; "The Older Population in the United States: March 2002 Detailed Tables (PPL-167)," May 2003; and "Educational Attainment," <https://www.census.gov/topics/education/educational-attainment.html>, "Families and Living Arrangements," <https://www.census.gov/topics/families/families-and-households.html>, and "Poverty," <https://www.census.gov/data/tables/time-series/demo/income-poverty/cps-pov.html>, accessed April 2017.

Table 33. Persons 65 Years Old and Over by Living Arrangement: 2010 to 2015

[In thousands (40,434 represents 40,434,000), except as indicated. Based on the American Community Survey (ACS). Based on a sample and subject to sampling variability; see text, this section and Appendix III]

Relationship by household type	2010		2013		2014		2015	
	Number	Percent distribution	Number	Percent distribution	Number	Percent distribution	Number	Percent distribution
Total	**40,434**	**100.0**	**44,664**	**100.0**	**46,215**	**100.0**	**47,732**	**100.0**
In households	38,869	96.1	43,157	96.6	44,728	96.8	46,232	96.9
In family households	26,809	66.3	30,044	67.3	31,118	67.3	32,232	67.5
Householder	13,379	33.1	14,783	33.1	15,279	33.1	15,801	33.1
Spouse	9,563	23.7	10,882	24.4	11,279	24.4	11,707	24.5
Parent	2,208	5.5	2,426	5.4	2,544	5.5	2,637	5.5
Parent-in-law	661	1.6	721	1.6	727	1.6	766	1.6
Other relatives	807	2.0	982	2.2	1,034	2.2	1,030	2.2
Nonrelatives	191	0.5	250	0.6	255	0.6	291	0.6
In nonfamily households	12,060	29.8	13,113	29.4	13,610	29.5	14,000	29.3
Householder	11,495	28.4	12,418	27.8	12,867	27.8	13,199	27.7
Male	3,417	8.5	3,885	8.7	4,096	8.9	4,244	8.9
Living alone	3,124	7.7	3,531	7.9	3,721	8.1	3,851	8.1
Female	8,078	20.0	8,534	19.1	8,771	19.0	8,955	18.8
Living alone	7,784	19.3	8,195	18.3	8,401	18.2	8,563	17.9
Nonrelatives	565	1.4	695	1.6	744	1.6	801	1.7
In group quarters	1,565	3.9	1,507	3.4	1,487	3.2	1,500	3.1

Source: U.S. Census Bureau, American Community Survey, B09020, "Relationship by Household Type (Including Living Alone) for the Population 65 Years and Over," <http://factfinder.census.gov>, accessed January 2017.

Table 34. Persons 65 Years Old and Over with a Disability by Type and Sex: 2015

[In thousands (16,461 represents 16,461,000). Based on data from the American Community Survey (ACS). Disability data limited to civilian noninstitutionalized population. Based on a sample and subject to sampling variability; see text in this section, and Appendix III]

Type of disability	Number					Percent				
	Total age 65 and over	Males		Females		Total age 65 and over	Males		Females	
		Age 65 to 74	Age 75 and over	Age 65 to 74	Age 75 and over		Age 65 to 74	Age 75 and over	Age 65 to 74	Age 75 and over
Persons with any disability	**16,461**	**3,422**	**3,781**	**3,496**	**5,763**	**35.4**	**26.9**	**48.0**	**24.0**	**51.1**
With a hearing difficulty	6,862	1,708	2,172	824	2,158	14.8	13.4	27.6	5.7	19.1
With a vision difficulty	3,005	544	692	606	1,164	6.5	4.3	8.8	4.2	10.3
With a cognitive difficulty	4,165	714	973	734	1,744	9.0	5.6	12.4	5.0	15.5
With an ambulatory difficulty	10,491	1,772	2,152	2,464	4,104	22.6	13.9	27.3	16.9	36.4
With a self-care difficulty	3,818	534	854	673	1,757	8.2	4.2	10.8	4.6	15.6
With an independent living difficulty	6,910	832	1,489	1,254	3,335	14.9	6.5	18.9	8.6	29.6

Source: U.S. Census Bureau, American Community Survey, Tables B18101, B18102, B18103, B18104, B18105, B18106, and B18107, <http://factfinder.census.gov>, accessed January 2017.

Table 35. Selected Characteristics of Racial Groups and Hispanic or Latino Population: 2015

[In thousands (216,447 represents 216,447,000), except as indicated. The American Community Survey universe includes the household population and the population living in institutions, college dormitories, and other group quarters. Based on a sample and subject to sampling variability; see text, this section and Appendix III]

Characteristic	Total population	White alone	Black or African American alone	American Indian, Alaska Native alone	Asian alone	Native Hawaiian and Other Pacific Islander alone	Some other race alone	Two or more races	Hispanic or Latino origin[1]	White alone, not Hispanic or Latino
EDUCATIONAL ATTAINMENT										
Persons 25 years old and over, total	**216,447**	**163,863**	**25,578**	**1,584**	**12,076**	**335**	**8,911**	**4,099**	**31,653**	**142,711**
Less than 9th grade	11,988	7,376	1,109	129	991	17	2,148	218	6,382	3,354
9th to 12th grade, no diploma	15,838	10,523	2,796	202	636	25	1,354	302	4,382	7,690
High school graduate (includes equivalency)	59,663	45,637	8,062	503	1,869	117	2,545	928	8,738	39,858
Some college, no degree	44,910	34,167	6,335	389	1,467	94	1,424	1,034	5,576	30,395
Associate's degree	17,807	13,907	2,102	137	795	30	455	381	1,899	12,590
Bachelor's degree	41,152	32,574	3,267	147	3,622	38	718	788	3,223	30,241
Graduate degree	25,089	19,679	1,908	77	2,695	15	267	449	1,455	18,583
OCCUPATION										
Employed civilian population, 16 years old and over, total	**150,535**	**112,857**	**17,199**	**1,002**	**8,634**	**253**	**7,179**	**3,410**	**24,846**	**96,494**
Management, business, science, and arts occupations	55,873	43,876	4,928	264	4,403	59	1,172	1,171	5,093	40,267
Management, business, and financial occupations	22,658	18,300	1,815	106	1,481	27	494	436	2,119	16,790
Computer, engineering, and science occupations	8,277	6,044	539	32	1,321	9	139	194	606	5,613
Education, legal, community service, arts, and media occupations	16,183	12,928	1,617	89	788	16	377	368	1,664	11,756
Healthcare practitioners and technical occupations	8,756	6,605	957	38	813	8	161	173	704	6,107
Service occupations	27,048	18,231	4,299	239	1,445	58	2,037	740	6,372	14,222
Sales and office occupations	35,511	26,822	4,341	234	1,707	74	1,468	865	5,439	23,188
Natural resources, construction, and maintenance occupations	13,543	10,819	882	122	254	20	1,197	249	3,883	8,263
Farming, fishing, and forestry occupations	1,102	852	44	14	16	1	156	19	572	454
Construction and extraction occupations	7,663	6,076	470	72	102	12	795	136	2,458	4,488
Installation, maintenance, and repair occupations	4,777	3,890	368	36	136	8	245	95	853	3,322
Production, transportation, and material moving occupations	18,559	13,109	2,749	142	825	42	1,306	385	4,059	10,555
Production occupations	8,970	6,469	1,106	67	513	15	635	165	1,965	5,232
Transportation occupations	5,570	3,961	936	40	189	14	309	120	996	3,324
Material moving occupations	4,019	2,680	707	35	123	13	362	100	1,098	1,999
FAMILY INCOME IN THE PAST 12 MONTHS										
Total families	**77,531**	**59,442**	**8,851**	**553**	**3,974**	**111**	**3,174**	**1,426**	**11,499**	**51,674**
Less than $10,000	3,340	1,976	871	52	125	7	217	91	755	1,485
$10,000 to $19,999	4,940	3,089	1,072	63	217	9	370	119	1,250	2,271
$20,000 to $29,999	6,279	4,306	1,071	66	244	10	449	132	1,511	3,311
$30,000 to $39,999	6,734	4,892	980	64	265	10	400	123	1,381	3,978
$40,000 to $49,999	6,496	4,912	815	50	246	10	346	117	1,196	4,112
$50,000 to $59,999	6,087	4,704	697	47	237	11	279	113	982	4,047
$60,000 to $74,999	8,366	6,608	851	55	352	11	337	152	1,196	5,802
$75,000 to $99,999	10,975	8,858	992	62	519	17	341	186	1,297	7,964
$100,000 to $124,999	7,979	6,551	604	37	455	17	189	132	779	5,999
$125,000 to $149,999	5,009	4,133	339	25	318	11	100	88	428	3,828
$150,000 to $199,999	5,474	4,502	334	20	432	6	92	88	415	4,203
$200,000 or more	5,853	4,912	224	13	562	4	53	84	309	4,674
Median family income in the past 12 months (in dollars)[2]	68,260	72,730	45,014	46,006	88,858	58,991	43,698	61,231	46,690	77,072
POVERTY STATUS IN THE PAST 12 MONTHS[3]										
Persons below poverty level	46,153	28,027	9,906	666	2,037	102	3,633	1,782	12,506	19,985
Families below poverty level	8,233	4,929	1,909	119	345	18	700	214	2,317	3,428
HOUSING TENURE										
Total householders	**118,208**	**91,024**	**14,505**	**824**	**5,369**	**148**	**4,076**	**2,263**	**15,062**	**80,847**
Owner-occupied	74,507	62,329	5,934	437	3,100	59	1,558	1,090	6,808	57,390
Renter-occupied	43,702	28,695	8,571	387	2,269	89	2,517	1,174	8,254	23,457

[1] Persons of Hispanic origin may be of any race. [2] For definition of median, see Guide to Tabular Presentation. [3] For explanation of poverty level, see text, Section 13.
Source: U.S. Census Bureau, 2015 American Community Survey, Tables B15002, B17001, B17010, B19101, B19113, B24010, and B25003, <http://factfinder.census.gov/>, accessed January 2017.

Table 36. Social and Economic Characteristics of the Hispanic Population: 2014

[54,268 represents 54,268,000. As of March, except labor force status is annual average. Excludes members of the Armed Forces except those living off post or with their families on post. Based on Current Population Survey, Annual Social and Economic Supplement; see text, this section and Appendix III]

Characteristic	Number (1,000)						Percent distribution					
	His-panic, total[1]	Mexi-can	Puerto Rican	Cuban	Central Ameri-can[2]	South Ameri-can[2]	His-panic, total[1]	Mexi-can	Puerto Rican	Cuban	Central Ameri-can[2]	South Ameri-can[2]
Total persons	**54,268**	**34,764**	**5,025**	**2,025**	**4,875**	**2,863**	**100.0**	**100.0**	**100.0**	**100.0**	**100.0**	**100.0**
Under 5 years old	5,126	3,621	447	90	403	203	9.4	10.4	8.9	4.4	8.3	7.1
5 to 14 years old	9,962	6,822	857	248	762	463	18.3	19.6	17.1	12.2	15.6	16.2
15 to 44 years old	25,710	16,534	2,359	846	2,605	1,312	47.5	47.6	47.0	41.8	53.3	46.0
45 to 64 years old	10,065	5,892	997	532	943	648	18.5	16.9	19.8	26.3	19.4	22.6
65 years old and over	3,405	1,895	364	310	162	236	6.2	5.5	7.2	15.3	3.3	8.2
EDUCATIONAL ATTAINMENT												
Persons 25 years old and over	**29,932**	**18,221**	**2,768**	**1,422**	**2,943**	**1,821**	**100.0**	**100.0**	**100.0**	**100.0**	**100.0**	**100.0**
Less than ninth grade	5,527	4,012	198	102	847	128	18.5	22.0	7.2	7.2	28.8	7.0
Ninth to twelfth grade (no diploma)	4,485	3,190	347	94	444	101	15.0	17.5	12.5	6.6	15.1	5.5
High school graduate	8,929	5,415	991	453	801	470	29.8	29.7	35.8	31.9	27.2	25.8
Some college or associate degree	6,372	3,618	694	303	498	471	21.3	19.9	25.1	21.3	16.9	25.9
Bachelors degree	3,219	1,455	352	345	237	422	10.8	8.0	12.7	24.3	8.1	23.2
Advanced degree	1,400	532	186	124	116	229	4.7	2.9	6.7	8.7	3.9	12.6
Less than high school graduate	10,013	7,202	545	196	1,290	229	33.5	39.5	19.7	13.8	43.9	12.6
High school graduate or more	19,920	11,020	2,223	1,226	1,652	1,592	66.5	60.5	80.3	86.2	56.1	87.4
Bachelor's degree or more	4,619	1,987	539	470	353	651	15.4	10.9	19.5	33.0	12.0	35.7
NATIVITY AND CITIZENSHIP STATUS												
Total	**54,268**	**34,764**	**5,025**	**2,025**	**4,875**	**2,863**	**100.0**	**100.0**	**100.0**	**100.0**	**100.0**	**100.0**
Native	35,775	23,665	4,985	842	1,925	1,152	65.9	68.1	99.2	41.6	39.5	40.2
Foreign born	18,493	11,099	40	1,183	2,951	1,712	34.1	31.9	0.8	58.4	60.5	59.8
Naturalized citizen	6,212	2,990	16	697	855	876	11.4	8.6	0.3	34.4	17.5	30.6
Not a citizen	12,281	8,108	24	486	2,096	835	22.6	23.3	0.5	24.0	43.0	29.2
LABOR FORCE STATUS[3]												
Civilians 16 years old and over	**38,400**	**23,829**	**3,515**	**1,659**	**(NA)**	**(NA)**	**100.0**	**100.0**	**100.0**	**100.0**	**(NA)**	**(NA)**
Civilian labor force	25,370	15,768	2,114	1,009	(NA)	(NA)	66.1	66.2	60.1	60.8	(NA)	(NA)
Employed	23,492	14,629	1,891	950	(NA)	(NA)	61.2	61.4	53.8	57.3	(NA)	(NA)
Unemployed	1,878	1,139	224	59	(NA)	(NA)	4.9	4.8	6.4	3.6	(NA)	(NA)
Unemployment rate[4]	7.4	7.2	10.6	5.8	(NA)	(NA)	(X)	(X)	(X)	(X)	(X)	(X)
Male	6.8	6.4	11.0	4.9	(NA)	(NA)	(X)	(X)	(X)	(X)	(X)	(X)
Female	8.2	8.4	10.1	6.9	(NA)	(NA)	(X)	(X)	(X)	(X)	(X)	(X)
Not in labor force	13,030	8,061	1,401	650	(NA)	(NA)	33.9	33.8	39.9	39.2	(NA)	(NA)
HOUSEHOLDS[5]												
Total	**15,874**	**9,500**	**1,713**	**763**	**1,376**	**913**	**100.0**	**100.0**	**100.0**	**100.0**	**100.0**	**100.0**
Family households	12,167	7,542	1,128	543	1,132	684	76.7	79.4	65.9	71.2	82.2	74.9
Married-couple families	7,495	4,767	601	372	680	461	47.2	50.2	35.1	48.8	49.4	50.4
Male householder, no spouse present	1,380	851	126	52	163	64	8.7	9.0	7.3	6.8	11.9	7.0
Female householder, no spouse present	3,292	1,925	401	119	288	160	20.7	20.3	23.4	15.6	21.0	17.6
Nonfamily households[6]	3,706	1,957	584	220	244	229	23.3	20.6	34.1	28.8	17.8	25.1
Male householder	1,970	1,134	282	113	142	106	12.4	11.9	16.5	14.9	10.3	11.6
Female householder	1,736	824	302	107	102	123	10.9	8.7	17.6	14.0	7.4	13.4

NA Not available. X Not applicable. [1] Includes other Hispanic groups not shown separately. [2] Refers to people whose origin is from Spanish-speaking Central or South American countries. Central American totals exclude Mexican and Cuban. [3] Source: U.S. Bureau of Labor Statistics, "Employment and Earnings Online, Household data from the Current Population Survey," <http://stats.bls.gov/opub/ee/home.htm>, accessed August 2017. [4] Total unemployment as percent of civilian labor force. [5] Household type is shown by the Hispanic origin of the householder. [6] A nonfamily household consists of a householder living alone (a one-person household) or where the householder shares the home exclusively with people to whom he/she is not related.

Source: Except as noted, U.S. Census Bureau, Hispanic Origin Data Tables, "The Hispanic Population in the United States: 2014," <https://www.census.gov/topics/population/hispanic-origin/data/tables.html>, accessed August 2017.

Table 37. Native and Foreign-Born Population by State: 2015

[278,128 represents 278,128,000. The term foreign-born refers to anyone who is not a U.S. citizen at birth. This includes naturalized U.S. citizens, legal permanent residents (immigrants), temporary migrants (such as foreign students), humanitarian migrants (such as refugees), and persons illegally present in the United States. The American Community Survey universe includes the household population and the population living in institutions, college dormitories, and other group quarters. Based on a sample and subject to sampling variability; see text, this section and Appendix III]

State	Native population (1,000)	Foreign-born population Number (1,000)	Foreign-born population Percent of total population	Foreign-born population Percent entered 2010 or later	State	Native population (1,000)	Foreign-born population Number (1,000)	Foreign-born population Percent of total population	Foreign-born population Percent entered 2010 or later
U.S.	278,128	43,290	13.5	15.6	MO	5,841	243	4.0	23.5
AL	4,689	170	3.5	20.7	MT	1,012	21	2.1	(NA)
AK	680	59	7.9	17.8	NE	1,768	128	6.8	23.9
AZ	5,914	914	13.4	14.6	NV	2,333	558	19.3	11.7
AR	2,835	143	4.8	16.3	NH	1,251	80	6.0	17.6
CA	28,456	10,688	27.3	11.2	NJ	6,981	1,977	22.1	14.8
CO	4,920	537	9.8	15.2	NM	1,888	197	9.4	13.7
CT	3,071	520	14.5	17.0	NY	15,266	4,530	22.9	14.9
DE	858	88	9.3	19.1	NC	9,248	795	7.9	17.0
DC	577	95	14.1	26.3	ND	728	29	3.8	(NA)
FL	16,185	4,086	20.2	16.9	OH	11,110	504	4.3	25.8
GA	9,191	1,024	10.0	16.4	OK	3,676	235	6.0	19.7
HI	1,178	253	17.7	15.3	OR	3,632	397	9.9	15.2
ID	1,561	94	5.7	18.7	PA	11,965	837	6.5	21.8
IL	11,034	1,826	14.2	13.0	RI	914	142	13.5	16.9
IN	6,298	321	4.9	21.6	SC	4,663	233	4.8	18.1
IA	2,975	149	4.8	25.4	SD	831	28	3.2	(NA)
KS	2,706	206	7.1	21.0	TN	6,269	332	5.0	22.7
KY	4,268	157	3.6	28.3	TX	22,798	4,671	17.0	16.3
LA	4,484	186	4.0	21.9	UT	2,751	244	8.2	14.7
ME	1,285	45	3.4	19.3	VT	598	28	4.5	(NA)
MD	5,095	912	15.2	17.5	VA	7,364	1,019	12.2	18.2
MA	5,698	1,096	16.1	19.7	WA	6,190	980	13.7	17.5
MI	9,270	652	6.6	20.8	WV	1,815	30	1.6	27.0
MN	5,032	457	8.3	23.5	WI	5,492	279	4.8	17.4
MS	2,920	72	2.4	21.8	WY	564	22	3.8	(NA)

NA Not available.

Source: U.S. Census Bureau, 2015 American Community Survey, B05002, "Place of Birth by Nativity and Citizenship Status"; and B05007, "Place of Birth by Year of Entry by Citizenship Status for the Foreign-Born Population"; <http://factfinder.census.gov>, accessed January 2017.

Table 38. Nativity and Place of Birth of Resident Population—25 Largest Cities: 2015

[Largest cities are based on 2016 population; see Table 24. The American Community Survey universe includes the household population and the population living in institutions, college dormitories, and other group quarters. Based on a sample and subject to sampling variability; see text, this section and Appendix III. See headnote, Table 37]

City	Total population	Native population Total	Native population Born in United States	Native population Born outside United States	Foreign born Total Number	Foreign born Total Percent of total population	Foreign born Entered 2010 or later Number	Foreign born Entered 2010 or later Percent of foreign-born population
Austin, TX	931,840	750,154	734,059	16,095	181,686	19.5	39,298	21.6
Boston, MA	669,469	479,346	457,567	21,779	190,123	28.4	46,348	24.4
Charlotte, NC	827,121	698,224	686,700	11,524	128,897	15.6	29,572	22.9
Chicago, IL	2,720,556	2,147,093	2,095,816	51,277	573,463	21.1	79,582	13.9
Columbus, OH	849,067	747,938	739,093	8,845	101,129	11.9	32,379	32.0
Dallas, TX	1,300,082	973,257	959,812	13,445	326,825	25.1	55,383	16.9
Denver, CO	682,545	569,323	558,132	11,191	113,222	16.6	16,382	14.5
Detroit, MI	677,124	637,263	630,860	6,403	39,861	5.9	7,678	19.3
El Paso, TX	681,136	521,427	504,716	16,711	159,709	23.4	17,675	11.1
Fort Worth, TX	836,969	693,565	681,244	12,321	143,404	17.1	18,496	12.9
Houston, TX	2,298,628	1,602,418	1,576,463	25,955	696,210	30.3	157,936	22.7
Indianapolis, IN [1]	848,423	775,967	768,962	7,005	72,456	8.5	14,984	20.7
Jacksonville, FL	868,031	782,381	763,012	19,369	85,650	9.9	12,806	15.0
Los Angeles, CA	3,971,896	2,486,471	2,437,638	48,833	1,485,425	37.4	156,492	10.5
Memphis, TN	655,760	612,442	607,948	4,494	43,318	6.6	9,960	23.0
Nashville–Davidson, TN [1]	654,596	566,403	558,555	7,848	88,193	13.5	25,060	28.4
New York, NY	8,550,405	5,337,905	5,016,221	321,684	3,212,500	37.6	482,497	15.0
Philadelphia, PA	1,567,442	1,362,103	1,308,588	53,515	205,339	13.1	47,478	23.1
Phoenix, AZ	1,563,001	1,262,299	1,237,750	24,549	300,702	19.2	36,532	12.1
San Antonio, TX	1,469,824	1,261,778	1,231,728	30,050	208,046	14.2	31,776	15.3
San Diego, CA	1,394,907	1,021,065	992,680	28,385	373,842	26.8	61,524	16.5
San Francisco, CA	864,816	567,617	549,302	18,315	297,199	34.4	42,306	14.2
San Jose, CA	1,026,919	625,426	607,732	17,694	401,493	39.1	60,610	15.1
Seattle, WA	684,443	564,603	550,608	13,995	119,840	17.5	27,680	23.1
Washington, DC	672,228	577,111	564,275	12,836	95,117	14.1	24,999	26.3

[1] Represents the portion of a consolidated city that is not within one or more separately incorporated places.

Source: U.S. Census Bureau, 2015 American Community Survey, C05002, "Place of Birth by Nativity"; and C05005, "Period of Entry by Nativity and Citizenship Status in the United States"; <http://factfinder.census.gov>, accessed January 2017.

Table 39. Native and Foreign-Born Populations by Selected Characteristics: 2014

[In thousands (313,401 represents 313,401,000). As of March. The foreign-born population includes anyone who is not a U.S. citizen at birth. This includes legal permanent residents (immigrants), temporary migrants (such as students), humanitarian migrants (such as refugees), and persons illegally present in the United States. Based on Current Population Survey, Annual Social and Economic Supplement, which includes the civilian noninstitutional population plus Armed Forces living in housing units on or off post with at least one other civilian adult; see text, this section, and Appendix III]

Characteristic	Total population	Native population	Foreign-born population			
			Total	Natural-ized citizen	Not a U.S. citizen	Year of entry: 2000 or later
Total...................................	**313,401**	**272,658**	**40,743**	**19,134**	**21,609**	**17,287**
Under 5 years old............................	19,865	19,596	269	80	189	269
5 to 9 years old..............................	20,522	19,914	607	189	418	607
10 to 14 years old............................	20,642	19,789	853	262	591	848
15 to 19 years old............................	20,807	19,337	1,470	415	1,055	1,116
20 to 24 years old............................	22,278	19,981	2,297	584	1,713	1,656
25 to 29 years old............................	21,474	18,102	3,372	874	2,497	2,462
30 to 34 years old............................	20,974	16,791	4,184	1,277	2,907	2,725
35 to 39 years old............................	19,407	14,947	4,460	1,526	2,935	2,165
40 to 44 years old............................	20,382	15,831	4,551	2,018	2,533	1,654
45 to 49 years old............................	20,668	16,538	4,130	2,219	1,911	1,162
50 to 54 years old............................	22,355	18,663	3,693	2,111	1,581	872
55 to 59 years old............................	21,109	18,055	3,055	1,966	1,088	607
60 to 64 years old............................	18,440	16,007	2,432	1,653	779	424
65 to 69 years old............................	14,986	13,195	1,790	1,252	538	288
70 to 74 years old............................	10,805	9,473	1,332	967	365	194
75 to 79 years old............................	7,804	6,767	1,037	787	250	116
80 to 84 years old............................	5,627	4,987	640	499	141	65
85 years and over............................	5,255	4,684	571	454	117	56
Median age (years) [1]	38	36	43	50	37	33
Male................................	153,595	133,983	19,612	8,650	10,962	8,364
Female............................	159,806	138,676	21,131	10,484	10,647	8,924
MARITAL STATUS						
Persons 15 years old and over.....................	**252,372**	**213,359**	**39,013**	**18,603**	**20,411**	**15,562**
Married......................................	127,240	103,026	24,214	12,169	12,044	9,031
Widowed....................................	14,283	12,493	1,790	1,270	520	323
Divorced....................................	25,356	22,604	2,752	1,672	1,080	619
Separated................................	5,400	4,232	1,168	471	697	451
Never married............................	80,092	71,002	9,090	3,020	6,070	5,138
EDUCATIONAL ATTAINMENT						
Persons 25 years old and over..................	**209,287**	**174,041**	**35,246**	**17,603**	**17,643**	**12,790**
Less than 9th grade.........................	9,893	3,816	6,077	1,838	4,240	2,152
9th to 12th grade (no diploma)...............	14,486	10,624	3,862	1,243	2,619	1,440
High school graduate.......................	62,113	53,308	8,805	4,525	4,280	2,958
Some college or associate's degree.........	55,854	50,139	5,715	3,538	2,177	1,848
Bachelor's degree.........................	42,420	35,914	6,506	3,969	2,537	2,622
Master's degree...........................	17,800	14,884	2,916	1,650	1,266	1,301
Professional degree.......................	3,072	2,605	467	319	148	140
Doctorate degree..........................	3,648	2,751	897	522	376	330
Less than high school diploma...............	24,380	14,440	9,940	3,081	6,859	3,592
High school graduate or more...............	184,908	159,601	25,307	14,523	10,784	9,198
EMPLOYMENT STATUS						
Persons 16 years old and over......................	**155,620**	**130,144**	**25,476**	**11,903**	**13,573**	**10,221**
Employed...................................	144,920	121,087	23,833	11,255	12,578	9,484
Full-time [2].................................	116,351	96,410	19,942	9,543	10,399	7,852
Part-time [2].................................	28,568	24,677	3,891	1,712	2,179	1,633
Unemployed................................	10,701	9,057	1,643	648	996	736
HOUSEHOLD TYPE [3]						
Total households............................	**123,229**	**105,518**	**17,712**	**9,476**	**8,236**	**5,976**
Family households...........................	81,353	67,716	13,637	7,237	6,400	4,620
Married couple............................	59,629	49,722	9,908	5,491	4,417	3,233
Male family householder.................	6,304	5,196	1,107	443	664	478
Female family householder...............	15,420	12,798	2,622	1,303	1,319	909
Nonfamily households.....................	41,877	37,802	4,075	2,239	1,836	1,357
Male householder.......................	19,658	17,661	1,997	863	1,134	807
Female householder.....................	22,219	20,140	2,078	1,376	702	550
HOUSEHOLD SIZE [3]						
Total households............................	**123,229**	**105,518**	**17,712**	**9,476**	**8,236**	**5,976**
One person.................................	34,185	30,880	3,305	1,977	1,328	953
Two people.................................	41,589	37,218	4,371	2,560	1,811	1,381
Three people...............................	19,369	15,999	3,369	1,735	1,634	1,370
Four people................................	16,244	12,865	3,380	1,669	1,711	1,221
Five or more people........................	11,842	8,555	3,287	1,534	1,753	1,051
HOUSEHOLD TENURE [3]						
Total households............................	**123,230**	**105,518**	**17,712**	**9,476**	**8,236**	**5,977**
Owner occupied unit.......................	79,603	70,684	8,919	6,065	2,854	1,863
Renter occupied unit [4].....................	43,626	34,833	8,792	3,410	5,382	4,112

[1] For definition of median, see Guide to Tabular Presentation. [2] Those who report working 35 hours a week or more are employed full-time; those who report working less than 35 hours a week are employed part-time. [3] Based on citizenship of householder. [4] Includes occupiers who paid no cash rent.

Source: U.S. Census Bureau, Foreign Born Data Tables, "Foreign-Born: 2014 Current Population Survey Detailed Tables," <https://www.census.gov/topics/population/foreign-born/data/tables.html>, accessed August 2017.

Table 40. Foreign-Born Population—Selected Characteristics by Region of Origin: 2014

[In thousands (40,743 represents 40,743,000). As of March. The term foreign-born refers to anyone who is not a U.S. citizen at birth. This includes naturalized U.S. citizens, legal permanent residents (immigrants), temporary migrants (such as foreign students), humanitarian migrants (such as refugees), and persons illegally present in the United States. Based on Current Population Survey, Annual Social and Economic Supplement; see text, this section and Appendix III]

Characteristic	Total foreign-born	Europe	Asia	Latin America Total	Mexico	Other Latin America	Other areas [1]
Total.	**40,743**	**4,373**	**12,176**	**21,066**	**11,268**	**9,797**	**3,128**
0 to 4 years old.	269	27	119	91	46	45	32
5 to 9 years old.	607	54	240	235	99	136	78
10 to 14 years old.	853	78	281	401	211	190	93
15 to 19 years old.	1,470	122	418	785	466	319	144
20 to 24 years old.	2,297	172	632	1,326	726	600	167
25 to 29 years old.	3,372	221	938	1,937	1,148	789	275
30 to 34 years old.	4,184	284	1,204	2,364	1,378	986	331
35 to 39 years old.	4,460	319	1,208	2,578	1,495	1,082	355
40 to 44 years old.	4,551	367	1,261	2,545	1,495	1,050	378
45 to 49 years old.	4,130	346	1,182	2,278	1,224	1,053	324
50 to 54 years old.	3,693	344	1,140	1,966	955	1,012	242
55 to 59 years old.	3,055	387	939	1,490	676	814	240
60 to 64 years old.	2,432	367	871	1,044	481	563	150
65 to 69 years old.	1,790	346	624	714	322	391	106
70 to 74 years old.	1,332	297	456	504	220	284	76
75 to 79 years old.	1,037	274	302	383	165	218	77
80 to 84 years old.	640	169	214	217	71	146	39
85 years old and over.	571	196	146	207	88	119	21
Median age [2].	43	53	44	42	40	44	41
EDUCATIONAL ATTAINMENT							
Persons 25 years old and over.	**35,246**	**3,919**	**10,486**	**18,227**	**9,719**	**8,507**	**2,615**
Less than ninth grade.	6,077	220	763	4,942	3,508	1,434	152
Ninth to twelfth grade (no diploma).	3,862	147	543	3,064	2,142	921	108
High school graduate.	8,805	996	2,127	5,105	2,495	2,611	576
Some college or associate's degree.	5,715	809	1,603	2,726	983	1,744	578
Bachelor's degree.	6,506	970	3,145	1,685	451	1,234	705
Master's degree.	2,916	532	1,562	507	98	410	315
Professional degree.	467	64	243	86	17	69	73
Doctorate degree.	897	180	499	111	26	85	107
Less than high school diploma.	9,940	368	1,306	8,005	5,650	2,355	261
High school graduate or more.	25,307	3,551	9,179	10,221	4,069	6,152	2,354
Less than bachelor's degree.	24,460	2,173	5,036	15,837	9,127	6,710	1,414
Bachelor's degree or more.	10,786	1,746	5,450	2,390	592	1,797	1,201

[1] Africa, Oceania, Northern America, and born at sea. [2] For definition of median, see Guide to Tabular Presentation.

Source: U.S. Census Bureau, Foreign Born Data Tables, "Foreign-Born: 2014 Current Population Survey Detailed Tables," <https://www.census.gov/topics/population/foreign-born/data/tables.html>, accessed August 2017.

Table 41. Foreign-Born Population by Citizenship Status and Place of Birth: 2015

[The term foreign-born refers to anyone who is not a U.S. citizen at birth. This includes naturalized U.S. citizens, legal permanent residents (immigrants), temporary migrants (such as foreign students), humanitarian migrants (such as refugees), and persons illegally present in the United States. The American Community Survey universe includes the household population and the population living in institutions, college dormitories, and other group quarters. Based on a sample and subject to sampling variability; see text, this section and Appendix III]

Region and country	Foreign-born population, total	Naturalized citizens	Not a U.S. citizen Number	Percent of foreign-born
Total [1].	**43,290,372**	**20,697,103**	**22,593,269**	**52.2**
Latin America.	22,111,409	8,265,629	13,845,780	62.6
Caribbean.	4,165,453	2,433,683	1,731,770	41.6
Cuba.	1,210,674	(NA)	(NA)	(NA)
Central America.	15,027,927	4,318,416	10,709,511	71.3
Mexico.	11,643,298	3,207,284	8,436,014	72.5
Other Central America.	3,384,629	1,111,132	2,273,497	67.2
El Salvador.	1,352,357	(NA)	(NA)	(NA)
South America.	2,918,029	1,513,530	1,404,499	48.1
Asia.	13,249,179	7,734,379	5,514,800	41.6
China, excluding Hong Kong and Taiwan.	2,065,431	(NA)	(NA)	(NA)
India.	2,389,639	(NA)	(NA)	(NA)
Korea.	1,060,019	(NA)	(NA)	(NA)
Philippines.	1,982,369	(NA)	(NA)	(NA)
Vietnam.	1,300,515	(NA)	(NA)	(NA)
Europe.	4,789,662	3,091,439	1,698,223	35.5
Africa.	2,062,257	1,119,184	943,073	45.7
North America.	838,476	389,986	448,490	53.5
Oceania.	238,663	96,195	142,468	59.7

NA Not available. [1] Includes persons born at sea.

Source: U.S. Census Bureau, 2015 American Community Survey, B05002, "Place of Birth by Nativity and Citizenship Status"; B05006, "Place of Birth for the Foreign-Born Population in the United States"; and B05007, "Place of Birth by Year of Entry by Citizenship Status for the Foreign-Born Population"; <http://factfinder.census.gov/>, accessed January 2017.

Table 42. American Indian Reservations and Alaska Native Village Statistical Areas With Largest American Indian and Alaska Native Populations: 2010

[As of April. Rankings of the American Indian reservations and Alaska Native village statistical areas are based on the American Indian and Alaska Native alone-or-in-combination population]

Area	Total population	American Indian and Alaska Native			Not American Indian and Alaska Native alone or in combination [1]
		Alone or in combination [1]	Alone	In combination [1]	
AMERICAN INDIAN RESERVATION					
Navajo Nation Reservation and Off-Reservation Trust Land, AZ–NM–UT..........	173,667	169,321	166,824	2,497	4,346
Pine Ridge Reservation, SD–NE..........	18,834	16,906	16,580	326	1,928
Fort Apache Reservation, AZ..........	13,409	13,014	12,870	144	395
Gila River Indian Reservation, AZ..........	11,712	11,251	10,845	406	461
Osage Reservation, OK..........	47,472	9,920	6,858	3,062	37,552
San Carlos Reservation, AZ..........	10,068	9,901	9,835	66	167
Rosebud Indian Reservation and Off-Reservation Trust Land, SD..........	10,869	9,809	9,617	192	1,060
Tohono O'odham Nation Reservation and Off-Reservation Trust Land, AZ..........	10,201	9,278	9,139	139	923
Blackfeet Indian Reservation and Off-Reservation Trust Land, MT..........	10,405	9,149	8,944	205	1,256
Flathead Reservation, MT..........	28,359	9,138	7,042	2,096	19,221
ALASKA NATIVE VILLAGE STATISTICAL AREA					
Knik Alaska Native village statistical area..........	65,768	6,582	3,529	3,053	59,186
Bethel Alaska Native village statistical area..........	6,080	4,334	3,953	381	1,746
Kenaitze Alaska Native village statistical area..........	32,902	3,417	2,001	1,416	29,485
Barrow Alaska Native village statistical area..........	4,212	2,889	2,577	312	1,323
Ketchikan Alaska Native village statistical area..........	12,742	2,605	1,692	913	10,137
Kotzebue Alaska Native village statistical area..........	3,201	2,585	2,355	230	616
Nome Alaska Native village statistical area..........	3,681	2,396	1,994	402	1,285
Chickaloon Alaska Native village statistical area..........	23,087	2,373	1,369	1,004	20,714
Dillingham Alaska Native village statistical area..........	2,378	1,583	1,333	250	795
Sitka Alaska Native village statistical area..........	4,480	1,240	855	385	3,240

[1] In combination with one or more other race groups.

Source: U.S. Census Bureau, 2010 Census Briefs, *The American Indian and Alaska Native Population: 2010*, January 2012. See also <http://www.census.gov/2010census/data/>.

Table 43. American Indian and Alaska Native Population by Selected Tribal Groupings: 2010

[As of April. Data shown for American Indian and Alaska Native tribes alone or in combination of tribes or races]

Tribal grouping	American Indian and Alaska Native tribal grouping alone or in any combination [1]	Tribal grouping	American Indian and Alaska Native tribal grouping alone or in any combination [1]
Total [2]..........	**5,220,579**	Navajo..........	332,129
AMERICAN INDIAN TRIBES		Osage..........	18,576
Apache..........	111,810	Ottawa..........	13,033
Arapaho..........	10,861	Paiute..........	13,767
Blackfeet..........	105,304	Pima..........	26,655
Canadian and French American Indian.....	14,822	Potawatomi..........	33,771
Central American Indian..........	27,844	Pueblo..........	62,540
Cherokee..........	819,105	Puget Sound Salish..........	20,260
Cheyenne..........	19,051	Seminole..........	31,971
Chickasaw..........	52,278	Shoshone..........	13,002
Chippewa..........	170,742	Sioux..........	170,110
Choctaw..........	195,764	South American Indian..........	47,233
Colville..........	10,549	Spanish American Indian..........	19,951
Comanche..........	23,330	Tohono O'odham..........	23,478
Cree..........	7,983	Ute..........	11,491
Creek..........	88,332	Yakama..........	11,527
Crow..........	15,203	Yaqui..........	32,595
Delaware..........	18,264	Yuman..........	10,089
Hopi..........	18,327	**ALASKA NATIVE TRIBES**	
Houma..........	10,768	Alaskan Athabascan..........	22,484
Iroquois..........	81,002	Aleut..........	19,282
Kiowa..........	13,787	Inupiat..........	33,360
Lumbee..........	73,691	Tlingit-Haida..........	26,080
Menominee..........	11,133	Tsimshian..........	3,755
Mexican American Indian..........	175,494	Yup'ik..........	33,889

[1] The numbers by American Indian and Alaska Native tribal grouping do not add to the total American Indian and Alaska Native population. This is because the American Indian and Alaska Native tribal groupings are tallies of the number of American Indian and Alaska Native responses rather than the number of American Indian or Alaska Native respondents. Respondents reporting several American Indian or Alaska Native groups are counted several times. [2] Includes other tribal groupings not shown separately.

Source: U.S. Census Bureau, 2010 Census Briefs, *The American Indian and Alaska Native Population: 2010*, January 2012. See also <http://www.census.gov/2010census/data/>.

Table 44. Persons Obtaining Legal Permanent Resident Status: 1901 to 2015

[8,795 represents 8,795,000. For fiscal years ending in year shown; see text, Section 8. Rates based on Census Bureau estimates as of July 1 for resident population through 1929 and for total population thereafter (excluding Alaska and Hawaii prior to 1959)]

Period/year	Number (1,000)	Rate [1]	Period/year	Number (1,000)	Rate [1]
1901 to 1910	8,795	10.4	1990	1,536	6.1
1911 to 1920	5,736	5.7	2000	841	3.0
1921 to 1930	4,107	3.5	2005	1,122	3.8
1931 to 1940	528	0.4	2007	1,052	3.5
1941 to 1950	1,035	0.7	2008	1,107	3.6
1951 to 1960	2,515	1.5	2009	1,131	3.7
1961 to 1970	3,322	1.7	2010	1,043	3.4
1971 to 1980	4,399	2.0	2011	1,062	3.4
1981 to 1990	7,256	3.0	2012	1,032	3.3
1991 to 2000	9,081	3.4	2013	991	3.1
2001 to 2010	10,501	3.5	2014	1,017	3.2
2011 to 2015	5,152	3.3	2015	1,051	3.3

[1] Annual rate per 1,000 U.S. population. Rate computed by dividing sum of annual immigration totals by sum of annual U.S. population totals for same number of years.

Source: U.S. Department of Homeland Security, Office of Immigration Statistics, "2015 Yearbook of Immigration Statistics," <https://www.dhs.gov/immigration-statistics/yearbook>, accessed January 2017.

Table 45. Refugee Arrivals and Individuals Granted Asylum by Country of Nationality: 2007 to 2015

For year ending September 30. Data shown provide information on the number of persons admitted to the U.S. as refugees or granted asylum in the United States in the year shown. In cases with no country of nationality, the applicant's last country of residence is assigned. For definitions of refugee and asylee, see text, this section. The refugee data were derived from data on refugee admissions that are maintained in the Worldwide Refugee Admissions Processing System (WRAPS) of the Bureau of Population, Refugees, and Migration (PRM) of the U.S. Department of State. The asylee data were derived from data on applications for asylum maintained in the Refugee, Asylum, and Parole System (RAPS) of the U.S. Citizenship and Immigration Services (USCIS) of the U.S. Department of Homeland Security and obtained from the Executive Office for Immigration Review (EOIR) of the U.S. Department of Justice]

Country of nationality	2007	2008	2009	2010	2011	2012	2013	2014	2015
REFUGEE ARRIVALS									
Total	**48,218**	**60,107**	**74,602**	**73,293**	**56,384**	**58,179**	**69,909**	**69,975**	**69,920**
Burma	13,896	18,139	18,202	16,693	16,972	14,160	16,299	14,598	18,386
Iraq	1,608	13,822	18,838	18,016	9,388	12,163	19,487	19,769	12,676
Somalia	6,969	2,523	4,189	4,884	3,161	4,911	7,608	9,000	8,858
Congo, Democratic Republic	848	727	1,135	3,174	977	1,863	2,563	4,540	7,876
Bhutan	0	5,320	13,452	12,363	14,999	15,070	9,134	8,434	5,775
Iran	5,482	5,270	5,381	3,543	2,032	1,758	2,579	2,846	3,109
Syria	17	24	25	25	29	31	36	105	1,682
Eritrea	963	251	1,571	2,570	2,032	1,346	1,824	1,488	1,596
Sudan	705	375	683	558	334	1,077	2,160	1,315	1,578
Cuba	2,922	4,177	4,800	4,818	2,920	1,948	4,205	4,062	1,527
Ukraine	1,605	1,022	601	449	428	372	227	490	1,451
Afghanistan	441	576	349	515	428	481	661	753	910
Ethiopia	1,028	299	321	668	560	620	765	728	626
Russia	1,773	426	495	326	165	197	125	139	281
Vietnam	1,500	1,112	1,486	873	79	41	69	67	22
Liberia	1,606	992	385	244	121	69	94	31	12
All other countries [1]	6,855	5,052	2,689	3,574	1,759	2,072	2,073	1,610	3,555
ASYLEES									
Total	**25,307**	**23,021**	**22,280**	**19,746**	**23,557**	**28,146**	**25,151**	**23,374**	**26,124**
China, People's Republic	6,384	5,498	6,166	6,318	8,188	9,767	8,585	7,884	6,192
El Salvador	556	487	323	280	234	293	252	369	2,173
Guatemala	675	547	506	421	433	505	384	486	2,082
Egypt	427	419	482	511	1,003	2,854	3,376	2,842	1,666
Honduras	105	95	86	106	117	216	199	242	1,416
Syria	31	34	26	23	52	356	798	914	974
Ethiopia	867	905	1,112	1,043	1,010	1,077	890	833	879
Mexico	152	250	255	170	264	416	357	592	870
Iraq	668	996	909	391	361	410	466	617	766
Iran	279	400	349	460	454	695	675	631	674
Nepal	413	500	665	624	727	950	853	554	617
Venezuela	1,151	1,057	586	610	1,057	1,073	680	410	504
India	434	374	411	308	309	346	416	485	493
Haiti	1,651	1,260	1,006	768	863	671	497	521	417
Russia	493	573	494	525	634	692	532	334	400
Eritrea	272	302	435	354	619	450	326	314	385
Colombia	2,175	1,663	1,006	546	500	433	249	310	305
All other countries [1]	8,574	7,661	7,463	6,288	6,732	6,942	5,616	5,036	5,311

[1] Includes unknown.

Source: U.S. Department of Homeland Security, Office of Immigration Statistics, *Annual Flow Report, Refugees and Asylees: 2015*, November 2016; and "2015 Yearbook of Immigration Statistics," <https://www.dhs.gov/immigration-statistics/yearbook>, accessed March 2017.

Table 46. Immigrant Orphans Adopted by U.S. Citizens by Sex, Age, Region, and Country of Birth: 2015

[For year ending September 30]

Region and country of birth	Total	Sex		Age		
		Male	Female	Under 1 year old	1 to 4 years old	5 years old and over
Total [1]	5,462	2,756	2,706	148	3,091	2,223
REGION						
Africa	1,018	453	565	45	501	472
Asia	3,171	1,637	1,534	64	2,264	843
Europe	714	377	337	(D)	(D)	529
North America	333	170	163	(D)	(D)	236
Oceania	32	12	20	20	9	3
South America	194	107	87	10	44	140
COUNTRY						
Armenia	18	10	8	4	9	5
Bulgaria	184	101	83	–	75	109
Cameroon	12	7	5	–	–	12
China, People's Republic	2,343	1,268	1,075	28	1,705	610
Colombia	144	80	64	10	34	100
Congo, Democratic Republic	129	72	57	(D)	76	(D)
Costa Rica	15	12	3	–	(D)	(D)
Ethiopia	322	109	213	18	188	116
Ghana	78	39	39	(D)	(D)	62
Guatemala	13	8	5	–	–	13
Guyana	27	15	12	–	6	21
Haiti	137	71	66	–	52	85
Honduras	24	9	15	–	9	15
Hong Kong	17	4	13	–	10	7
Hungary	18	7	11	–	10	8
India	136	101	35	–	91	45
Jamaica	43	19	24	–	3	40
Japan	17	8	9	10	7	–
Korea, South	320	84	236	–	320	–
Kyrgyzstan	25	12	13	–	9	16
Latvia	156	93	63	–	15	141
Marshall Islands	21	8	13	(D)	(D)	(D)
Mexico	25	11	14	–	–	25
Morocco	20	8	12	10	6	4
Nicaragua	26	16	10	–	10	16
Nigeria	151	82	69	9	69	73
Pakistan	25	15	10	13	5	7
Philippines	141	79	62	–	31	110
Poland	58	36	22	–	29	29
Sierra Leone	24	13	11	–	12	12
South Africa	32	10	22	–	14	18
Taiwan	55	25	30	(D)	(D)	26
Thailand	45	21	24	–	34	11
Uganda	190	84	106	3	100	87
Ukraine	265	123	142	8	35	222

– Represents zero. D Data withheld to limit disclosure. [1] Includes countries not shown separately.

Source: U.S. Department of Homeland Security, Office of Immigration Statistics, "2015 Yearbook of Immigration Statistics," <https://www.dhs.gov/immigration-statistics/yearbook>, accessed January 2017.

Table 47. Petitions for Naturalization Filed, Persons Naturalized, and Petitions Denied: 1990 to 2015

[For years ending September 30. Naturalizations refer to persons 18 and over who become citizens of the United States]

Year	Petitions filed	Persons naturalized				Petitions denied
		Total	Civilian	Military	Not reported	
1990	233,843	267,586	245,410	1,618	20,558	6,516
1995	959,963	485,720	472,518	3,855	9,347	46,067
2000	460,916	886,026	812,579	836	72,611	399,670
2001	501,643	606,259	575,030	758	30,471	218,326
2002	700,649	572,646	550,835	1,053	20,758	139,779
2003	523,370	462,435	449,123	3,865	9,447	91,599
2004	662,796	537,151	520,771	4,668	11,712	103,339
2005	602,972	604,280	589,269	4,614	10,397	108,247
2006	730,642	702,589	684,484	6,259	11,846	120,722
2007	1,382,993	660,477	648,005	3,808	8,664	89,683
2008	525,786	1,046,539	1,032,281	4,342	9,916	121,283
2009	570,442	743,715	726,043	7,100	10,572	109,832
2010	710,544	619,913	604,410	9,122	6,381	56,994
2011	756,008	694,193	677,385	8,373	8,435	57,065
2012	899,162	757,434	745,932	7,257	4,245	65,874
2013	772,623	779,929	769,073	6,652	4,204	83,112
2014	773,824	653,416	642,431	7,468	3,517	66,767
2015	783,062	730,259	720,645	7,234	2,380	75,810

Source: U.S. Department of Homeland Security, Office of Immigration Statistics, "2015 Yearbook of Immigration Statistics," <https://www.dhs.gov/immigration-statistics/yearbook>, accessed January 2017.

Table 48. Persons Obtaining Legal Permanent Resident Status by Class of Admission: 2000 to 2015

[For years ending September 30. For definition of immigrants, see text, this section]

Class of admission	2000	2005	2010	2013	2014	2015
Total.............	841,002	1,122,257	1,042,625	990,553	1,016,518	1,051,031
New arrivals.................	407,279	383,955	476,049	459,751	481,392	508,716
Adjustments.................	433,723	738,302	566,576	530,802	535,126	542,315
Family-sponsored preferences.................	235,092	212,970	214,589	210,303	229,104	213,910
Unmarried sons/daughters of U.S. citizens and their children......	27,635	24,729	26,998	24,358	25,686	24,533
Spouses, children, and unmarried sons/daughters of alien residents........	124,540	100,139	92,088	99,115	105,641	104,892
Married sons/daughters of U.S. citizens [1]..........	22,804	22,953	32,817	21,294	25,830	24,271
Brothers or sisters of U.S. citizens age 21 and older [1]............	60,113	65,149	62,686	65,536	71,947	60,214
Immediate relatives of U.S. citizens................	346,350	436,115	476,414	439,460	416,456	465,068
Spouses................	196,405	259,144	271,909	248,332	238,852	265,367
Children [2]................	82,638	94,858	88,297	71,382	61,217	66,740
Parents................	67,307	82,113	116,208	119,746	116,387	132,961
Employment-based preferences................	106,642	246,865	148,343	161,110	151,596	144,047
Priority workers [1]................	27,566	64,731	41,055	38,978	40,554	41,688
Professionals with advanced degrees or aliens of exceptional ability [1]................	20,255	42,597	53,946	63,026	48,801	44,344
Skilled workers, professionals, unskilled workers [1]...............	49,589	129,070	39,762	43,632	43,156	37,243
Special immigrants [1]................	9,014	10,121	11,100	6,931	8,362	10,584
Employment creation (investors) [1]................	218	346	2,480	8,543	10,723	10,188
Diversity (lottery) [3]................	50,920	46,234	49,763	45,618	53,490	47,934
Refugees................	56,091	112,676	92,741	77,395	96,066	118,431
Asylees................	6,837	30,286	43,550	42,235	38,176	33,564
Parolees................	3,162	7,715	1,592	556	95	23
Children born abroad to alien residents................	(NA)	571	716	643	594	403
Nicaraguan Adjustment and Central American Relief Act (NACARA)................	20,364	1,155	248	138	70	49
Cancellation of removal................	12,154	20,785	8,180	5,763	5,248	4,713
Haitian Refugee Immigration Fairness Act (HRIFA)................	435	2,820	386	62	22	9
Other................	2,955	4,065	6,103	7,270	25,601	22,880

NA Not available. [1] Includes spouses and children. [2] Includes orphans. [3] The Diversity Visa Program is a lottery available to nationals of countries with fewer than 50,000 persons granted legal permanent residency status during the preceding 5 years in the employment-based and family-sponsored preferences and immediate relative classes of admission. Includes categories of immigrants admitted under three laws intended to diversify immigration: P.L. 99-603, P.L. 100-658, and P.L. 101-649.

Source: U.S. Department of Homeland Security, Office of Immigration Statistics, "2015 Yearbook of Immigration Statistics," <https://www.dhs.gov/immigration-statistics/yearbook>, accessed January 2017.

Table 49. Persons Obtaining Legal Permanent Resident Status by Selected Country of Birth and Selected Characteristics: 2015

[For year ending September 30]

Age, marital status, occupation, class of admission	All countries [1]	Mexico	China	India	Philippines	Cuba	Dominican Republic	Vietnam	Iraq
Total................	1,051,031	158,619	74,558	64,116	56,478	54,396	50,610	30,832	21,107
AGE									
Under 18 years old................	195,345	24,777	11,879	7,936	11,055	7,863	15,542	5,368	5,608
18 to 24 years old................	127,362	21,866	6,007	5,075	6,399	5,497	7,551	4,981	2,750
25 to 34 years old................	258,528	37,542	18,112	15,316	10,306	11,057	9,110	5,875	4,730
35 to 44 years old................	201,674	35,669	15,126	17,418	10,063	10,431	7,366	4,260	3,317
45 to 54 years old................	127,551	23,098	10,218	7,147	7,322	9,795	5,667	5,092	2,012
55 to 64 years old................	81,870	9,500	6,961	5,851	6,930	4,809	3,326	3,935	1,488
65 years old and over................	58,696	6,166	6,254	5,373	4,403	4,944	2,048	1,320	1,202
Unknown................	5	1	1	–	–	–	–	1	–
MARITAL STATUS									
Married................	615,259	103,217	50,161	47,559	32,148	23,561	20,763	18,582	9,337
Single................	363,590	45,428	19,849	13,004	20,224	22,737	25,966	10,063	10,586
Other................	68,824	9,318	4,429	3,422	4,026	7,888	3,800	2,142	1,036
Unknown................	3,358	656	119	131	80	210	81	45	148
OCCUPATION [2]									
Management, professional, and related...	151,755	10,418	17,356	17,461	7,868	2,064	6,826	4,476	1,137
Service................	25,130	3,831	2,319	344	874	2,292	1,105	279	728
Sales and office................	18,666	2,567	1,668	754	780	949	639	951	286
Farming, fishing, and forestry................	4,157	(D)	(D)	437	284	(D)	(D)	373	(D)
Construction, extraction, maintenance and repair................	24,112	13,023	1,352	126	203	912	1,663	594	137
Production, transportation, and material moving................	22,445	6,406	975	304	239	3,592	517	258	1,127
MAJOR CLASS OF ADMISSION									
Family-sponsored preferences............	213,910	41,529	14,384	14,591	15,695	2,211	26,432	16,065	209
Employment-based preferences..........	144,047	6,479	22,531	27,514	10,545	9	369	872	68
Immediate relatives of U.S. citizens.......	465,068	97,816	27,659	20,558	29,955	3,882	23,554	13,690	866
Diversity programs................	47,934	9	24	53	9	428	(D)	(D)	37
Refugees and asylees................	151,995	726	9,727	978	19	47,803	(D)	(D)	18,973
Other................	28,077	12,060	233	422	255	63	147	55	954

– Represents zero. D Data withheld to avoid disclosure. [1] Includes other countries not shown separately. [2] Those in the military and without an occupation and unknown occupation are not shown.

Source: U.S. Department of Homeland Security, Office of Immigration Statistics, "Profiles on Lawful Permanent Residents: 2015," <https://www.dhs.gov/profiles-lawful-permanent-residents-2015-country>, accessed April 2017.

Table 50. Persons Obtaining Legal Permanent Resident Status by Country of Birth: 1991 to 2015

[In thousands (9,080.5 represents 9,080,500). For years ending Sept. 30. Persons by country prior to 1996 are unrevised]

Region and country of birth	1991–2000	2001-2010	2011-2014	2015
All countries [1]	9,080.5	10,501.1	4,100.7	1,051.0
Europe [1]	1,226.0	1,263.9	335.3	85.8
Albania	26.2	50.5	14.0	4.7
Bulgaria	23.1	39.2	10.9	2.7
France	27.4	39.6	16.2	4.7
Germany	67.6	77.7	23.6	5.4
Italy	22.5	26.5	11.4	3.5
Poland	169.5	116.8	25.3	5.3
Romania	57.5	53.6	14.6	3.4
Russia	[2] 127.8	139.7	36.7	8.8
Spain	13.7	15.8	9.1	3.3
Ukraine	[2] 141.0	149.3	31.9	8.0
United Kingdom	135.6	153.5	48.8	12.6
Asia [1]	2,973.2	3,784.6	1,712.2	419.3
Afghanistan	17.4	24.3	16.0	8.3
Armenia	[2] 26.6	29.9	11.3	3.0
Bangladesh	66.0	106.7	58.2	13.6
Bhutan	–	7.0	36.6	6.3
Burma	11.0	45.0	57.6	12.8
China	424.4	662.7	316.7	74.6
India	383.0	662.5	281.8	64.1
Iran	112.5	125.9	52.2	13.1
Iraq	40.7	65.0	70.2	21.1
Israel	31.9	46.6	15.8	4.0
Japan	61.4	76.1	23.7	5.4
Jordan [3]	39.7	38.7	17.4	4.7
Korea, South [4]	171.1	221.5	87.3	17.1
Lebanon	43.4	39.5	12.2	2.8
Nepal	3.6	33.1	46.9	12.9
Pakistan	124.5	157.0	62.1	18.1
Philippines	505.3	587.2	218.8	56.5
Syria	26.1	25.9	12.7	3.8
Taiwan	106.3	87.9	21.6	4.9
Thailand	48.4	68.3	33.2	7.5
Turkey	26.3	41.1	16.5	4.2
Uzbekistan	[2] 22.9	36.0	19.4	4.0
Vietnam	420.8	306.1	119.8	30.8
Yemen	16.3	24.6	13.0	3.2
Africa [1]	382.5	860.4	404.3	101.4
Cameroon	5.8	23.2	16.4	4.4
Congo, Dem. Rep. of the	2.5	7.9	13.3	5.3
Egypt	46.7	73.1	38.5	12.1
Ethiopia	49.3	109.7	53.7	11.4
Ghana	35.6	65.3	36.8	6.2
Kenya	14.0	59.7	26.8	5.6
Liberia	16.0	45.2	15.5	3.8
Morocco	20.0	44.4	15.0	3.7
Nigeria	67.2	111.2	52.1	11.5
Somalia	20.1	64.2	18.6	6.8
Oceania	47.9	58.1	20.1	5.4
North America [1]	3,910.1	3,605.1	1,301.7	366.1
Canada	137.2	168.2	50.5	12.7
Cuba	178.7	318.4	148.2	54.4
Dominican Republic	340.8	329.1	173.6	50.6
El Salvador	217.3	252.8	72.5	19.5
Guatemala	103.0	160.7	41.9	11.8
Haiti	181.7	213.8	80.6	17.0
Honduras	66.7	65.4	30.1	9.3
Jamaica	173.4	180.7	78.8	17.6
Mexico	2,250.5	1,693.2	558.9	158.6
Nicaragua	94.6	60.9	12.4	3.3
Trinidad and Tobago	63.2	61.8	18.9	3.2
South America [1]	539.3	906.0	320.2	72.3
Argentina	24.3	50.5	17.1	3.7
Brazil	52.2	123.8	44.7	11.4
Colombia	130.8	251.3	82.9	17.3
Ecuador	76.3	112.5	42.0	10.2
Guyana	73.8	76.2	24.4	5.5
Peru	105.6	145.7	49.8	10.1
Venezuela	29.9	84.4	36.6	9.1

– Represents or rounds to zero. [1] Includes other countries not shown separately. [2] Covers years 1992–2000. [3] Prior to 2003, includes Palestine; beginning in 2003, Palestine included in Unknown. [4] Prior to 2009, includes a small number of cases from North Korea.

Source: U.S. Department of Homeland Security, Office of Immigration Statistics, "2015 Yearbook of Immigration Statistics," <https://www.dhs.gov/immigration-statistics/yearbook>, accessed January 2017.

Table 51. Refugees and Asylees Obtaining Legal Permanent Resident Status by Country of Birth: 2001 to 2015

[For years ending September 30]

Country of birth	2001–2010	2011–2014	2015
Total [1]	1,325,365	572,946	151,995
Europe [1]	296,794	16,892	3,317
Albania	10,905	1,071	152
Belarus	9,310	1,296	199
Moldova	10,813	2,025	241
Russia	32,819	3,299	532
Soviet Union [2]	6,794	1,666	272
Ukraine	57,186	2,784	471
Asia [1]	389,469	301,428	67,603
Afghanistan	13,533	2,052	691
Armenia	12,408	1,967	225
Bhutan	6,762	36,455	6,290
Burma	32,904	51,630	11,443
China	111,632	71,924	9,727
India	24,010	3,743	978
Indonesia	7,618	1,423	187
Iran	45,515	13,818	3,756
Iraq	40,789	55,911	18,973
Jordan	1,013	1,427	581
Malaysia	1,125	3,783	1,296
Nepal	6,000	22,939	5,261
Pakistan	8,339	2,624	803
Sri Lanka	1,852	1,442	238
Syria	2,223	1,674	1,137
Thailand	22,405	15,460	3,439
Uzbekistan	14,047	1,685	306
Vietnam	36,990	2,692	148
Africa [1]	242,839	92,125	27,104
Burundi	3,387	1,355	234
Cameroon	7,564	4,844	825
Congo, Dem. Rep. of the	5,643	6,571	2,043
Congo, Rep. of the	5,243	1,721	313
Cote d' Ivoire	4,404	1,631	305
Egypt	7,987	7,463	4,194
Eritrea	4,534	5,623	1,352
Ethiopia	31,900	15,899	3,808
Guinea	4,467	2,827	481
Kenya	15,351	6,358	1,173
Liberia	28,808	4,306	414
Mauritania	3,420	1,003	154
Rwanda	2,939	1,440	444
Somalia	59,069	13,818	5,630
Sudan	23,580	4,488	1,975
Tanzania	3,503	1,929	211
Uganda	2,482	1,256	531
Zimbabwe	1,563	1,080	189
Oceania	1,453	193	37
North America [1]	326,846	145,632	51,535
Cuba	276,331	127,968	47,803
El Salvador	4,061	1,684	366
Guatemala	7,399	2,921	667
Haiti	29,824	8,077	1,240
Mexico	2,780	2,328	726
South America [1]	65,912	16,143	2,346
Brazil	1,680	1,010	116
Colombia	40,321	5,379	785
Peru	7,258	1,389	157
Venezuela	10,726	5,737	806

[1] Includes other countries and unknown not shown separately. [2] Data are for unknown republic only.

Source: U.S. Department of Homeland Security, Office of Immigration Statistics, "2015 Yearbook of Immigration Statistics," <https://www.dhs.gov/immigration-statistics/yearbook>, accessed January 2017.

Table 52. Population by Selected Ancestry Group and Region: 2015

[In thousands (321,419 represents 321,419,000), except percent. Covers single and multiple ancestries. Ancestry refers to a person's ethnic origin or descent, "roots," or heritage; or the place of birth of the person, the person's parents, or ancestors before their arrival in the United States. The American Community Survey universe includes the household population and the population living in institutions, college dormitories, and other group quarters. Based on a sample and subject to sampling variability; see text, this section, and Appendix III. For composition of regions of the United States, see map, inside front cover]

Ancestry group	Total, (1,000)	North-east	Mid-west	South	West	Ancestry group	Total, (1,000)	North-east	Mid-west	South	West
Total population [1]	**321,419**	**18**	**21**	**38**	**24**	Irish	32,713	25	24	32	18
Afghan	96	14	6	30	50	Israeli	138	40	8	23	29
Albanian	198	53	26	15	6	Italian	17,070	43	17	23	17
American	21,845	13	19	54	14	Latvian	85	29	26	20	25
Arab [1]	1,963	24	24	28	23	Lithuanian	630	36	27	20	16
Egyptian	252	37	11	29	22	Northern European	297	13	18	23	46
Iraqi	145	10	35	24	31	Norwegian	4,433	6	48	13	33
Jordanian	89	22	21	33	24	Pennsylvania German	307	53	28	12	6
Lebanese	508	24	26	29	21	Polish	9,231	32	37	19	12
Moroccan	114	36	11	37	16	Portuguese	1,373	44	4	15	37
Palestinian	119	13	34	31	22	Romanian	469	23	26	23	28
Syrian	171	35	20	24	21	Russian	2,723	35	16	22	27
Arab	303	17	31	27	25	Scandinavian	631	7	31	20	42
Armenian	461	22	8	9	61	Scotch-Irish	2,982	12	16	53	19
Assyrian/ Chaldean/Syriac	108	3	55	3	40	Scottish	5,511	16	20	38	26
Australian	100	16	14	30	39	Serbian	191	20	40	18	22
Austrian	678	30	24	23	23	Slavic	117	28	24	23	25
Belgian	350	10	54	19	17	Slovak	705	43	33	17	8
Brazilian	387	43	7	35	15	Slovene	165	14	56	13	17
British	1,398	14	17	40	29	Sub-Saharan African [1]	3,482	20	18	47	15
Bulgarian	97	20	31	24	25	Cape Verdean	116	89	1	7	4
Cajun	106	2	4	89	6	Ethiopian	280	6	17	44	32
Canadian	673	25	16	30	29	Ghanian	123	39	14	37	10
Croatian	410	22	39	16	23	Nigerian	390	23	13	51	13
Czech	1,391	11	44	28	17	Somali	145	7	57	15	21
Czechoslovakian	311	20	33	26	21	African	1,925	16	16	54	14
Danish	1,315	8	30	16	45	Swedish	3,829	13	37	17	32
Dutch	4,141	15	36	26	23	Swiss	915	16	33	21	31
Eastern European	507	42	14	22	22	Turkish	204	37	11	29	23
English	23,959	16	21	38	25	Ukrainian	987	38	19	18	24
European	3,931	12	19	35	34	Welsh	1,777	19	22	31	28
Finnish	642	12	46	14	28	West Indian [1,2]	2,950	44	4	48	5
French (except Basque)	7,970	24	22	34	20	British West Indian	105	60	3	35	3
French Canadian	2,072	42	19	25	14	Haitian	1,063	37	3	58	2
German	45,526	16	39	26	19	Jamaican	1,097	47	5	44	5
Greek	1,281	33	22	24	20	Trinidadian and Tobagonian	218	57	2	38	4
Guyanese	251	74	3	21	2	West Indian	264	57	4	34	5
Hungarian	1,411	32	30	21	17	Yugoslavian	271	20	32	21	27
Iranian	487	12	7	27	54						

[1] Includes other groups, not shown separately. [2] Excludes Hispanic-origin groups.

Source: U.S. Census Bureau, 2015 American Community Survey, B04006, "People Reporting Ancestry," <http://factfinder.census.gov/>, accessed December 2016.

Table 53. Language Spoken at Home and English Speaking Ability: 2015

[See headnote, Table 52]

Language	Number of speakers of language at home	Percent who speak English less than "very well"	Language	Number of speakers of language at home	Percent who speak English less than "very well"
Total population 5 years old and over	**301,625,014**	**(X)**	Urdu	481,391	29.4
			Other Indic languages	992,222	40.9
Speak only English	236,908,935	(X)	Other Indo-European languages	463,883	34.2
Spanish or Spanish Creole	40,045,795	41.0	Chinese	3,333,588	55.7
French (including Patois, Cajun)	1,266,366	20.1	Japanese	446,084	41.7
French Creole	863,449	41.2	Korean	1,108,798	53.2
Italian	605,651	27.7	Mon-Khmer, Cambodian	219,817	51.4
Portuguese or Portuguese Creole	717,643	35.1	Hmong	228,721	40.9
German	933,441	14.9	Thai	159,208	51.8
Yiddish	169,814	35.7	Laotian	152,139	49.5
Other West Germanic languages	336,626	25.6	Vietnamese	1,468,251	58.9
Scandinavian languages	116,735	9.1	Other Asian languages	1,201,392	31.0
Greek	289,291	26.8	Tagalog	1,737,186	32.4
Russian	905,149	44.0	Other Pacific Island languages	445,947	37.5
Polish	541,914	39.2	Navajo	159,995	20.7
Serbo-Croatian	253,604	35.3	Other Native North American	182,710	16.5
Other Slavic languages	317,407	37.7	Hungarian	78,877	25.0
Armenian	235,526	44.0	Arabic	1,156,908	37.2
Persian	429,510	38.3	Hebrew	200,632	14.6
Gujarathi	404,831	34.5	African languages	1,104,617	31.8
Hindi	812,818	21.2	Other and unspecified languages	148,143	40.6

X Not applicable.

Source: U.S. Census Bureau, 2015 American Community Survey, B16001, "Language Spoken at Home by Ability to Speak English for the Population 5 Years and Over," <http://factfinder.census.gov/>, accessed December 2016.

Table 54. Language Spoken at Home by State: 2015

[In thousands (301,625 represents 301,625,000), except percent. The American Community Survey universe includes the household population and the population living in institutions, college dormitories, and other group quarters. Based on a sample and subject to sampling variability; see text, this section, and Appendix III]

State	Population 5 years old and over (1,000)	English only (1,000)	Language other than English		State	Population 5 years old and over (1,000)	English only (1,000)	Language other than English	
			Number (1,000)	Percent of population 5 years and over				Number (1,000)	Percent of population 5 years and over
U.S.	301,625	236,909	64,716	21.5	MO	5,709	5,367	342	6.0
AL	4,574	4,341	233	5.1	MT	973	931	41	4.2
AK	684	573	110	16.2	NE	1,766	1,570	196	11.1
AZ	6,398	4,665	1,733	27.1	NV	2,714	1,894	820	30.2
AR	2,790	2,587	202	7.3	NH	1,267	1,168	99	7.8
CA	36,637	20,311	16,326	44.6	NJ	8,429	5,833	2,596	30.8
CO	5,123	4,242	881	17.2	NM	1,951	1,281	669	34.3
CT	3,404	2,642	762	22.4	NY	18,611	12,864	5,747	30.9
DE	890	773	117	13.1	NC	9,444	8,361	1,083	11.5
DC	629	519	110	17.4	ND	705	663	42	5.9
FL	19,173	13,620	5,553	29.0	OH	10,924	10,165	759	6.9
GA	9,566	8,228	1,338	14.0	OK	3,648	3,280	369	10.1
HI	1,340	990	349	26.1	OR	3,800	3,227	573	15.1
ID	1,543	1,385	158	10.2	PA	12,088	10,774	1,314	10.9
IL	12,080	9,300	2,780	23.0	RI	1,002	780	222	22.2
IN	6,200	5,679	522	8.4	SC	4,609	4,297	311	6.8
IA	2,929	2,704	225	7.7	SD	799	746	53	6.6
KS	2,715	2,395	319	11.8	TN	6,201	5,773	428	6.9
KY	4,152	3,932	220	5.3	TX	25,502	16,475	9,027	35.4
LA	4,366	4,010	356	8.2	UT	2,746	2,338	408	14.8
ME	1,265	1,188	77	6.1	VT	596	560	36	6.1
MD	5,640	4,595	1,045	18.5	VA	7,872	6,620	1,252	15.9
MA	6,429	4,953	1,476	23.0	WA	6,726	5,430	1,296	19.3
MI	9,352	8,466	886	9.5	WV	1,742	1,697	45	2.6
MN	5,139	4,550	588	11.5	WI	5,434	4,963	471	8.7
MS	2,803	2,694	109	3.9	WY	548	507	41	7.5

Source: U.S. Census Bureau, 2015 American Community Survey, C16005, "Nativity by Language Spoken at Home by Ability to Speak English for the Population 5 Years and Over," <http://factfinder.census.gov/>, accessed December 2016.

Table 55. Language Spoken at Home—25 Largest Cities: 2015

[In thousands (870 represents 870,000), except percent. Data shown for population aged 5 and over. Largest cities are based on 2016 population; see Table 24. The American Community Survey universe includes the household population and the population living in institutions, college dormitories, and other group quarters. Based on a sample and subject to sampling variability; see text, this section, and Appendix III]

City	Population 5 years old and over (1,000)	English only (1,000)	Language other than English, total [1]		Speak English less than "very well" (1,000)	Spanish (1,000)	Other Indo-European languages (1,000)	Asian and Pacific Island languages (1,000)
			Number (1,000)	Percent				
Austin, TX	870	579	291	33.4	113	215	28	39
Boston, MA	632	394	238	37.7	109	105	73	47
Charlotte, NC	771	616	156	20.2	76	93	26	29
Chicago, IL	2,545	1,620	925	36.4	385	630	152	103
Columbus, OH	787	673	113	14.4	44	31	31	23
Dallas, TX	1,195	671	524	43.9	280	465	22	22
Denver, CO	637	460	177	27.8	73	135	16	16
Detroit, MI	628	557	71	11.4	29	45	11	2
El Paso, TX	628	193	435	69.3	175	420	6	7
Fort Worth, TX	770	511	260	33.7	111	213	20	18
Houston, TX	2,122	1,075	1,047	49.3	517	825	83	96
Indianapolis, IN [2]	785	687	98	12.5	45	63	12	14
Jacksonville, FL	808	701	107	13.3	40	51	23	27
Los Angeles, CA	3,716	1,490	2,226	59.9	965	1,592	261	322
Memphis, TN	603	543	60	9.9	25	35	8	9
Nashville–Davidson, TN [2]	609	501	108	17.7	60	55	18	12
New York, NY	7,981	4,034	3,946	49.4	1,831	1,964	1,055	712
Philadelphia, PA	1,458	1,132	326	22.3	150	144	82	79
Phoenix, AZ	1,450	905	545	37.6	190	456	35	31
San Antonio, TX	1,366	765	601	44.0	183	548	19	26
San Diego, CA	1,305	764	540	41.4	202	312	60	149
San Francisco, CA	825	463	362	43.9	173	91	51	210
San Jose, CA	958	410	548	57.2	243	221	63	252
Seattle, WA	651	518	133	20.5	50	27	27	65
Washington, DC	629	519	110	17.4	34	56	30	11

[1] Includes other language groups, not shown separately. [2] Represents the portion of a consolidated city that is not within one or more separately incorporated places.

Source: U.S. Census Bureau, 2015 American Community Survey, C16005, "Nativity by Language Spoken at Home by Ability to Speak English for the Population 5 Years and Over," <http://factfinder.census.gov/>, accessed January 2017.

Table 56. Marital Status of the Population by Sex, Race, and Hispanic Origin: 2000 to 2016

[In millions, except percent (213.8 represents 213,800,000). As of March. Data shown are for persons aged 15 years and over. Excludes members of Armed Forces except those living off post or with their families on post. Beginning 2005 based on an expanded sample of households. Data for 2010 based on population controls from Census 2000. 2015 and 2016 data based on population controls from Census 2010. Based on Current Population Survey, see text, this section and Appendix III]

Marital status, race and Hispanic origin	Total				Male				Female			
	2000	2010	2015	2016	2000	2010	2015	2016	2000	2010	2015	2016
Total [1]	**213.8**	**242.0**	**255.0**	**257.6**	**103.1**	**117.7**	**123.6**	**125.0**	**110.7**	**124.4**	**131.4**	**132.7**
Never married	60.0	74.2	81.0	83.1	32.3	40.2	43.1	44.1	27.8	34.0	38.0	39.0
Married [2]	120.2	129.7	133.6	134.1	59.7	64.5	66.3	66.7	60.5	65.2	67.2	67.5
Widowed	13.7	14.3	14.6	14.9	2.6	3.0	3.3	3.5	11.1	11.4	11.3	11.4
Divorced	19.9	23.7	25.8	25.5	8.6	10.0	11.0	10.7	11.3	13.8	14.9	14.8
Percent of total	100.0	100.0	100.0	100.0	100.0	100.0	100.0	100.0	100.0	100.0	100.0	100.0
Never married	28.1	30.7	31.8	32.2	31.3	34.2	34.8	35.3	25.1	27.4	28.9	29.4
Married [2]	56.2	53.6	52.4	52.1	57.9	54.8	53.7	53.4	54.7	52.4	51.2	50.8
Widowed	6.4	5.9	5.7	5.8	2.5	2.5	2.6	2.8	10.0	9.1	8.6	8.6
Divorced	9.3	9.8	10.1	9.9	8.3	8.5	8.9	8.6	10.2	11.1	11.3	11.2
White, total [3]	**177.6**	**195.5**	**200.1**	**201.5**	**86.4**	**96.2**	**98.1**	**98.9**	**91.1**	**99.3**	**102.1**	**102.6**
Never married	45.3	54.7	57.3	58.5	25.1	30.6	31.4	32.0	20.2	24.1	25.9	26.5
Married [2]	104.2	109.6	110.1	110.3	51.9	54.7	55.0	55.2	52.3	54.8	55.1	55.1
Widowed	11.5	11.8	11.9	12.2	2.2	2.5	2.7	2.9	9.3	9.3	9.3	9.3
Divorced	16.5	19.4	20.8	20.5	7.2	8.3	9.0	8.8	9.3	11.1	11.8	11.7
Percent of total	100.0	100.0	100.0	100.0	100.0	100.0	100.0	100.0	100.0	100.0	100.0	100.0
Never married	25.5	28.0	28.6	29.1	29.1	31.8	32.0	32.4	22.1	24.3	25.4	25.9
Married [2]	58.7	56.1	55.0	54.7	60.0	56.9	56.1	55.9	57.4	55.2	54.0	53.7
Widowed	6.5	6.0	6.0	6.0	2.5	2.6	2.7	2.9	10.2	9.3	9.1	9.0
Divorced	9.3	9.9	10.4	10.2	8.4	8.7	9.2	8.9	10.2	11.2	11.6	11.4
Black, total [3]	**25.9**	**29.4**	**32.0**	**32.5**	**11.7**	**13.3**	**14.6**	**14.9**	**14.2**	**16.0**	**17.4**	**17.6**
Never married	11.3	13.7	15.5	15.9	5.2	6.5	7.3	7.5	6.0	7.2	8.2	8.4
Married [2]	10.1	10.6	11.1	11.2	5.0	5.2	5.5	5.6	5.1	5.4	5.6	5.6
Widowed	1.7	1.8	1.8	1.8	0.3	0.4	0.4	0.4	1.4	1.5	1.4	1.4
Divorced	2.8	3.2	3.6	3.6	1.1	1.2	1.4	1.4	1.7	2.0	2.2	2.2
Percent of total	100.0	100.0	100.0	100.0	100.0	100.0	100.0	100.0	100.0	100.0	100.0	100.0
Never married	43.5	46.8	48.5	49.0	44.9	48.8	49.9	50.4	42.4	45.2	47.4	47.8
Married [2]	39.2	36.1	34.7	34.4	42.8	39.4	37.8	37.5	36.2	33.4	32.0	31.7
Widowed	6.6	6.2	5.7	5.6	2.8	2.7	2.9	2.8	9.6	9.1	8.0	7.9
Divorced	10.7	10.9	11.2	11.1	9.5	9.1	9.4	9.3	11.8	12.4	12.6	12.6
Asian, total [3]	**8.4**	**11.2**	**14.6**	**15.1**	**4.0**	**5.3**	**6.9**	**7.1**	**4.4**	**5.9**	**7.7**	**8.0**
Never married	2.8	3.2	4.5	4.6	1.5	1.7	2.4	2.5	1.3	1.4	2.1	2.1
Married [2]	4.9	7.0	9.0	9.4	2.3	3.3	4.2	4.4	2.6	3.7	4.8	5.0
Widowed	0.3	0.5	0.6	0.6	0.0	0.1	0.1	0.1	0.3	0.5	0.5	0.5
Divorced	0.4	0.5	0.7	0.5	0.1	0.2	0.2	0.2	0.2	0.3	0.4	0.4
Percent of total	100.0	100.0	100.0	100.0	100.0	100.0	100.0	100.0	100.0	100.0	100.0	100.0
Never married	33.1	28.3	30.4	30.3	37.7	32.8	34.8	34.7	28.8	24.2	26.6	26.4
Married [2]	58.6	62.8	61.2	62.2	57.8	62.6	60.7	61.6	59.4	62.9	61.6	62.8
Widowed	4.0	4.7	3.9	3.9	1.2	1.3	1.5	1.4	6.6	7.7	6.1	6.2
Divorced	4.3	4.3	4.5	3.6	3.2	3.3	3.0	2.3	5.3	5.2	5.7	4.7
Hispanic, total [4]	**22.8**	**34.3**	**40.4**	**41.5**	**11.3**	**17.7**	**20.2**	**20.7**	**11.5**	**16.6**	**20.2**	**20.8**
Never married	7.5	13.3	16.1	16.7	4.2	7.7	8.8	9.1	3.3	5.6	7.3	7.5
Married [2]	12.7	17.2	19.8	20.3	6.2	8.6	9.7	9.9	6.5	8.6	10.1	10.4
Widowed	0.9	1.2	1.3	1.3	0.2	0.3	0.3	0.3	0.7	0.9	1.0	1.0
Divorced	1.6	2.6	3.1	3.2	0.7	1.1	1.3	1.3	1.0	1.5	1.8	1.8
Percent of total	100.0	100.0	100.0	100.0	100.0	100.0	100.0	100.0	100.0	100.0	100.0	100.0
Never married	33.1	38.7	39.9	40.2	37.5	43.4	43.7	44.0	28.9	33.7	36.1	36.3
Married [2]	55.9	50.1	49.1	48.9	55.1	48.7	48.1	48.0	56.6	51.7	50.1	49.9
Widowed	3.9	3.5	3.2	3.2	1.5	1.7	1.5	1.5	6.2	5.4	5.0	4.9
Divorced	7.1	7.7	7.8	7.7	5.9	6.2	6.6	6.5	8.3	9.2	8.9	8.9

[1] Includes persons of other races not shown separately. [2] Includes persons who are married with spouse present, married with spouse absent, and separated. [3] Beginning 2003, data represent persons who selected this race group only and exclude persons reporting more than one race. Prior to 2003, the CPS only allowed respondents to report one race group. See also comments on race in the text for this section. [4] Hispanic persons may be of any race.

Source: U.S. Census Bureau, America's Families and Living Arrangements, Historical Time Series, "Table MS-1. Marital Status of the Population 15 Years Old and Over, by Sex, Race and Hispanic Origin: 1950 to Present," <http://www.census.gov/hhes/families/data/historical.html>, accessed January 2017.

Table 57. Marital Status of the Population by Sex and Age: 2016

[124,953 represents 124,953,000. As of March. Data shown for population aged 15 and older. Excludes members of Armed Forces except those living off post or with their families on post. Population controls based on Census 2010. Based on Current Population Survey, see text, this section, and Appendix III]

Sex and age	Number of persons (1,000)					Percent distribution				
	Total	Never married	Married [1]	Widowed	Divorced	Total	Never married	Married [1]	Widowed	Divorced
MALE										
Total	**124,953**	**44,079**	**66,695**	**3,469**	**10,708**	**100.0**	**35.3**	**53.4**	**2.8**	**8.6**
15 to 17 years old	6,603	6,487	93	7	16	100.0	98.2	1.4	0.1	0.2
18 years old and over	118,349	37,592	66,602	3,462	10,692	100.0	31.8	56.2	2.9	9.0
18 to 19 years old	3,968	3,875	84	–	9	100.0	97.7	2.1	–	0.2
20 to 24 years old	11,055	10,056	897	13	89	100.0	91.0	8.1	0.1	0.8
25 to 29 years old	11,283	7,711	3,304	19	249	100.0	68.3	29.2	0.2	2.2
30 to 34 years old	10,556	4,616	5,361	23	555	100.0	43.7	50.8	0.2	5.3
35 to 39 years old	10,054	2,716	6,478	31	829	100.0	27.0	64.5	0.3	8.2
40 to 44 years old	9,640	1,807	6,796	50	987	100.0	18.7	70.5	0.5	10.2
45 to 49 years old	10,125	1,799	6,782	124	1,420	100.0	17.8	66.9	1.2	14.0
50 to 54 years old	10,708	1,613	7,372	178	1,546	100.0	15.1	68.8	1.7	14.4
55 to 64 years old	19,768	2,342	14,048	464	2,914	100.0	11.8	71.0	2.3	14.7
65 to 74 years old	12,952	784	9,736	916	1,516	100.0	6.1	75.2	7.1	11.7
75 to 84 years old	6,254	209	4,555	974	517	100.0	3.3	72.8	15.6	8.3
85 years old and over	1,988	63	1,190	673	61	100.0	3.2	59.9	33.8	3.1
FEMALE										
Total	**132,662**	**38,995**	**67,450**	**11,387**	**14,831**	**100.0**	**29.4**	**50.8**	**8.6**	**11.2**
15 to 17 years old	6,468	6,368	77	10	12	100.0	98.5	1.2	0.2	0.2
18 years old and over	126,194	32,626	67,374	11,376	14,819	100.0	25.9	53.4	9.0	11.7
18 to 19 years old	3,782	3,658	107	–	15	100.0	96.7	2.8	–	0.4
20 to 24 years old	10,864	9,240	1,501	14	109	100.0	85.1	13.8	0.1	1.0
25 to 29 years old	11,146	6,244	4,496	29	378	100.0	56.0	40.3	0.3	3.4
30 to 34 years old	10,766	3,624	6,352	62	727	100.0	33.7	59.0	0.6	6.8
35 to 39 years old	10,329	2,187	6,996	119	1,027	100.0	21.2	67.7	1.2	9.9
40 to 44 years old	9,973	1,615	6,757	154	1,446	100.0	16.2	67.7	1.5	14.5
45 to 49 years old	10,552	1,304	7,350	233	1,665	100.0	12.4	69.7	2.2	15.8
50 to 54 years old	11,167	1,239	7,538	410	1,980	100.0	11.1	67.4	3.7	17.7
55 to 64 years old	21,347	2,117	13,830	1,528	3,872	100.0	9.9	64.8	7.2	18.1
65 to 74 years old	14,964	875	8,587	2,956	2,545	100.0	5.8	57.5	19.8	17.0
75 to 84 years old	7,796	381	3,188	3,365	861	100.0	4.9	40.9	43.2	11.0
85 years old and over	3,509	141	667	2,506	194	100.0	4.0	19.0	71.4	5.5

– Represents or rounds to zero. [1] Includes persons who are married with spouse present, married with spouse absent, and separated.

Source: U.S. Census Bureau, America's Families and Living Arrangements, Detailed Tables, Adults (A table series), "Table A1. Marital Status of People 15 Years and Over, by Age, Sex, and Personal Earnings: 2016," <http://www.census.gov/hhes/families/data/cps.html>, accessed January 2017.

Table 58. Living Arrangements of Persons 18 Years Old and Over by Age and Sex: 2016

[In thousands (244,544 represents 244,544,000), except percent. As of March. Excludes members of Armed Forces except those living off post or with their families on post. Population controls based on Census 2010 and an expanded sample of households. Based on Current Population Survey (CPS); see text, this section, and Appendix III]

Living arrangement	Total	18 to 24 years old	25 to 34 years old	35 to 64 years old	65 to 74 years old	75 years old and over
NUMBER (1,000)						
Total	**244,544**	**29,669**	**43,750**	**123,663**	**27,916**	**19,547**
Male	118,350	15,023	21,838	60,295	12,952	8,242
Female	126,195	14,646	21,912	63,368	14,964	11,305
PERCENT DISTRIBUTION						
Male, total	**100.0**	**100.0**	**100.0**	**100.0**	**100.0**	**100.0**
Alone	(NA)	5.3	11.5	13.6	18.0	23.8
With spouse [1]	(NA)	5.1	36.3	64.7	72.8	66.8
Child of householder [2]	(NA)	58.3	18.5	4.8	–	–
Living with partner	(NA)	7.2	15.0	6.8	2.9	1.7
Other relatives	(NA)	13.9	9.4	7.5	4.6	6.4
Nonrelatives	(NA)	10.3	9.3	2.6	1.3	1.3
Female, total	**100.0**	**100.0**	**100.0**	**100.0**	**100.0**	**100.0**
Alone	(NA)	5.1	8.4	12.2	27.5	45.6
With spouse [1]	(NA)	9.1	44.9	62.4	54.9	32.5
Child of householder [2]	(NA)	51.4	11.6	2.4	–	–
Living with partner	(NA)	10.8	14.7	5.9	2.4	1.1
Other relatives	(NA)	14.5	15.6	15.7	13.4	19.5
Nonrelatives	(NA)	9.0	4.7	1.4	1.5	1.3

– Represents or rounds to zero. NA Not available. [1] Includes only adults who are married, spouse present in the household. This living arrangement supersedes the others shown in the table. For example people living with their parents and a spouse are counted as living with a spouse, not as a child of the householder. [2] Children of the householder are not living with a spouse or unmarried partner, and are residing in the household of a parent. In CPS, unmarried college students living in dormitories are counted as living in the parental home.

Source: U.S. Census Bureau, America's Families and Living Arrangements, Historical Time Series, "Table AD-3. Living Arrangements of Adults 18 and Over, 1967 to Present," <http://www.census.gov/hhes/families/data/cps.html>, accessed January 2017.

Table 59. Households, Families, Subfamilies, and Married Couples: 1990 to 2016

[In thousands (93,347 represents 93,347,000), except as indicated. As of March. Excludes members of the Armed Services except those living off post or with their families on post. Beginning 2001, based on an expanded sample of households. Population controls for 2010 based on Census 2000; beginning 2014, population controls based on Census 2010. Based on Current Population Survey (CPS), see text, this section and Appendix III. Minus sign (-) indicates decrease]

Type of unit	1990	2000	2010	2014	2015	2016	Percent change 1990 to 2000	Percent change 2000 to 2010	Percent change 2010 to 2016
Households...................	93,347	104,705	117,538	123,229	124,587	125,819	12.2	12.3	7.0
Persons per household..................	2.63	2.62	2.59	2.54	2.54	2.53	(X)	(X)	(X)
White [1].................................	80,163	87,671	95,489	98,052	98,679	99,313	9.4	8.9	4.0
Black [1].................................	10,486	12,849	14,730	16,064	16,437	16,539	22.5	14.6	12.3
Asian [1].................................	(NA)	(NA)	4,687	5,749	6,040	6,328	(NA)	(NA)	35.0
Hispanic [2].............................	5,933	9,319	13,298	15,874	16,239	16,667	57.1	42.7	25.3
Family households.......................	66,090	72,025	78,833	81,353	81,716	82,184	9.0	9.5	4.3
Married couple.......................	52,317	55,311	58,410	59,629	60,010	60,251	5.7	5.6	3.2
Male householder [3].................	2,884	4,028	5,580	6,304	6,162	6,310	39.7	38.5	13.1
Female householder [3]..............	10,890	12,687	14,843	15,420	15,544	15,622	16.5	17.0	5.2
Nonfamily households..................	27,257	32,680	38,705	41,877	42,871	43,635	19.9	18.4	12.7
Male householder....................	11,606	14,641	18,263	19,658	20,143	20,542	26.2	24.7	12.5
Female householder..................	15,651	18,039	20,442	22,219	22,728	23,093	15.3	13.3	13.0
One person...........................	22,999	26,724	31,399	34,185	34,866	35,388	16.2	17.5	12.7
Families.............................	66,090	72,025	78,833	81,353	81,716	82,184	9.0	9.5	4.3
Persons per family...................	3.17	3.17	3.16	3.13	3.14	3.14	(X)	(X)	(X)
With own children under age 18.........	32,289	34,605	35,218	34,955	34,979	34,769	7.2	1.8	-1.3
Without own children under age 18......	33,801	37,420	43,615	46,398	46,737	47,415	10.7	16.6	8.7
Married couple.......................	52,317	55,311	58,410	59,629	60,010	60,251	5.7	5.6	3.2
With own children under age 18......	24,537	25,248	24,575	23,933	24,040	23,772	2.9	-2.7	-3.3
Without own children under age 18...	27,780	30,062	33,835	35,697	35,970	36,480	8.2	12.6	7.8
Male householder [3].................	2,884	4,028	5,580	6,304	6,162	6,310	39.7	38.5	13.1
With own children under age 18......	1,153	1,786	2,224	2,472	2,388	2,472	54.9	24.5	11.2
Without own children under age 18...	1,731	2,242	3,356	3,832	3,774	3,838	29.5	49.7	14.4
Female householder [3]..............	10,890	12,687	14,843	15,420	15,544	15,622	16.5	17.0	5.2
With own children under age 18......	6,599	7,571	8,419	8,550	8,551	8,525	14.7	11.2	1.3
Without own children under age 18...	4,290	5,116	6,424	6,870	6,993	7,097	19.3	25.6	10.5
Unrelated subfamilies [4]..................	534	571	484	511	566	485	6.9	-15.2	0.2
Married couple.......................	68	37	93	107	76	80	(B)	(B)	-14.0
Male reference persons [3]..........	45	57	44	52	63	56	(B)	(B)	(B)
Female reference persons [3]........	421	477	347	352	428	348	13.3	-27.3	0.3
Related subfamilies [4]....................	2,403	2,984	4,300	4,502	4,508	4,540	24.2	44.1	5.6
Married couple.......................	871	1,149	1,881	2,114	2,144	2,297	31.9	63.7	22.1
Father-child [3].....................	153	201	313	337	308	374	31.4	55.7	19.5
Mother-child [3].....................	1,378	1,634	2,106	2,051	2,056	1,870	18.6	28.9	-11.2
Married couples........................	53,256	56,497	60,384	61,850	62,230	62,628	6.1	6.9	3.7
With own household....................	52,317	55,311	58,410	59,629	60,010	60,251	5.7	5.6	3.2
Without own household.................	939	1,186	1,974	2,221	2,220	2,377	26.3	66.4	20.4
Percent without....................	1.8	2.1	3.2	3.6	3.6	3.8	(X)	(X)	(X)

B Base less than 75,000. NA Not available. X Not applicable. [1] Beginning with the 2003 CPS, respondents could choose more than one race. Beginning in 2003, data represent persons who selected this race group only and exclude persons reporting more than one race. The CPS in prior years only allowed respondents to report one race group. See also comments on race in text for this section. [2] Persons of Hispanic origin may be of any race. [3] No spouse present. [4] A subfamily is a married couple or parent/child group that does not maintain its own household. A subfamily may be related to the householder, or unrelated to the householder.

Source: U.S. Census Bureau, America's Families and Living Arrangements, Historical Time Series, Households Table HH-6; and Detailed Tables F1, FG1, FG7, and H1; <http://www.census.gov/hhes/families/data/cps.html>, accessed January 2017, and earlier releases.

Table 60. Interracially Married Couples by Race and Hispanic Origin of Spouses: 1980 to 2016

[In thousands (49,714 represents 49,714,000). As of March. Persons 15 years old and over. Persons of Hispanic origin may be of any race. Population controls for 2010 based on Census 2000; beginning 2013, based on Census 2010. Based on Current Population Survey; see headnote, Table 59 and Appendix III]

Race and origin of spouses	1980	1990	2000	2010	2013	2014	2015	2016
Married couples, total [1].............................	49,714	53,256	56,497	60,384	61,295	61,850	62,230	62,628
Interracial married couples, total [1].................	651	964	1,464	2,413	2,731	2,910	2,920	2,998
White [2] and Black [2].................................	167	211	363	558	571	602	562	594
Black husband and White wife...........................	122	150	268	390	402	400	383	417
White husband and Black wife...........................	45	61	95	168	169	202	179	177
White [2] and other race [3]...........................	450	720	1,051	1,723	1,994	2,108	2,171	2,218
Black [2] and other race [3]...........................	34	33	50	132	166	200	187	186
HISPANIC ORIGIN								
Hispanic and Hispanic....................................	1,906	3,085	4,739	6,166	6,789	6,898	7,176	7,481
Hispanic and other origin (not Hispanic)................	891	1,193	1,743	2,289	2,714	2,711	2,830	2,849
All other couples (not of Hispanic origin).............	46,917	48,979	50,015	51,928	51,792	52,242	52,224	52,297

[1] Includes other married couples not shown separately. [2] See footnote 1, Table 59. [3] "Other race," is any race other than White or Black, such as Asian; and, beginning 2003, includes other single race alone or any combination of races.

Source: U.S. Census Bureau, America's Families and Living Arrangements, Historical Time Series, "Table MS-3. Interracial Married Couples: 1980 to 2002"; and Detailed Tables, Family groups (FG table series), "Table FG3. Married Couple Family Groups, By Presence Of Own Children Under 18, And Age, Earnings, Education, And Race And Hispanic Origin Of Both Spouses," <http://www.census.gov/hhes/families/data/cps.html>; accessed January 2017, and earlier releases.

Table 61. Households and Persons Per Household by Type of Household: 2000 to 2016

[104,705 represents 104,705,000. As of March. See headnote, Table 59]

Type of household	Households						Persons per household		
	Number (1,000)			Percent distribution					
	2000	2010	2016	2000	2010	2016	2000	2010	2016
Total households.............	**104,705**	**117,538**	**125,819**	**100.0**	**100.0**	**100.0**	**2.62**	**2.59**	**2.53**
Family households................	72,025	78,833	82,184	68.8	67.1	65.3	3.24	3.24	3.21
Married couple family.............	55,311	58,410	60,251	52.8	49.7	47.9	3.26	3.24	3.19
Male householder, no spouse present........	4,028	5,580	6,310	3.8	4.7	5.0	3.16	3.24	3.23
Female householder, no spouse present.....	12,687	14,843	15,622	12.1	12.6	12.4	3.17	3.23	3.27
Nonfamily households...........	32,680	38,705	43,635	31.2	32.9	34.7	1.25	1.26	1.25
Living alone..................	26,724	31,399	35,388	25.5	26.7	28.1	1.00	1.00	1.00
Male householder..............	14,641	18,263	20,542	14.0	15.5	16.3	1.34	1.35	1.32
Living alone..................	11,181	13,971	15,804	10.7	11.9	12.6	1.00	1.00	1.00
Female householder..............	18,039	20,442	23,093	17.2	17.4	18.4	1.17	1.18	1.19
Living alone..................	15,543	17,428	19,585	14.8	14.8	15.6	1.00	1.00	1.00

Source: U.S. Census Bureau, Current Population Reports, P20-537, 2001, and earlier reports; and America's Families and Living Arrangements, Detailed Tables, "Table AVG1" and "Table H1," <http://www.census.gov/hhes/families/data/cps.html>, accessed January 2017, and earlier releases.

Table 62. Households by Age of Householder and Size of Household: 1990 to 2016

[In millions (93.3 represents 93,300,000). As of March. Based on Current Population Survey; see headnote, Table 59]

Age of householder and size of household	1990	2000	2005	2010	2011	2012	2013	2014	2015	2016
Total.....................	**93.3**	**104.7**	**113.3**	**117.5**	**118.7**	**121.1**	**122.5**	**123.2**	**124.6**	**125.8**
15 to 24 years old.........	5.1	5.9	6.7	6.2	6.1	6.2	6.3	6.4	6.4	6.4
25 to 29 years old.........	9.4	8.5	9.2	9.4	9.3	9.2	9.3	9.3	9.4	9.5
30 to 34 years old.........	11.0	10.1	10.1	9.8	10.2	10.6	10.8	10.7	10.7	10.6
35 to 44 years old.........	20.6	24.0	23.2	21.5	21.3	21.2	21.3	21.1	21.1	21.2
45 to 54 years old.........	14.5	20.9	23.4	24.9	24.5	24.2	24.1	23.7	23.6	23.3
55 to 64 years old.........	12.5	13.6	17.5	20.4	21.8	22.8	22.8	23.2	23.5	23.9
65 to 74 years old.........	11.7	11.3	11.5	13.2	13.3	14.5	15.3	16.0	16.9	17.6
75 years old and over.....	8.4	10.4	11.6	12.1	12.0	12.3	12.6	12.8	13.1	13.4
One person...............	23.0	26.7	30.1	31.4	32.7	33.2	33.6	34.2	34.9	35.4
Male..................	9.0	11.2	12.8	14.0	14.5	14.8	15.0	15.2	15.5	15.8
Female..................	14.0	15.5	17.3	17.4	18.2	18.4	18.6	19.0	19.4	19.6
Two persons...............	30.1	34.7	37.4	39.5	39.7	41.0	41.5	41.6	41.9	42.8
Three persons............	16.1	17.2	18.3	18.6	18.5	19.2	19.3	19.4	19.3	19.4
Four persons.............	14.5	15.3	16.4	16.1	15.9	16.0	16.4	16.2	16.5	16.3
Five persons.............	6.2	7.0	7.2	7.4	7.3	7.3	7.4	7.5	7.5	7.5
Six persons.............	2.1	2.4	2.5	2.8	2.8	2.7	2.7	2.8	2.8	2.8
Seven persons or more...	1.3	1.4	1.4	1.7	1.7	1.6	1.6	1.6	1.7	1.6

Source: U.S. Census Bureau, Current Population Reports, P20-537, and earlier reports; and America's Families and Living Arrangements, Detailed Tables, Households (H table series), <http://www.census.gov/hhes/families/data/cps.html>, accessed January 2017.

Table 63. Family Households With Own Children Under 18 Years of Age by Type of Family, 2000 to 2016, and by Age of Householder, 2016

[34,605 represents 34,605,000. As of March. See headnote, Table 64]

Age of householder	Family households with children		Married couple households with children		Male householder with children [1]		Female householder with children [1]	
	Number (1,000)	Percent of all family households	Number (1,000)	Percent of all married couple households	Number (1,000)	Percent of all male householder families [1]	Number (1,000)	Percent of all female householder families [1]
2000, total................	34,605	48	25,248	46	1,786	44	7,571	60
2010, total................	35,218	45	24,575	42	2,224	40	8,419	57
2015, total................	34,979	43	24,040	40	2,388	39	8,551	55
2016, total..............	**34,769**	**42**	**23,772**	**39**	**2,472**	**39**	**8,525**	**55**
15 to 24 years old.......	1,403	44	465	52	152	16	785	58
25 to 34 years old......	9,393	73	5,733	70	779	55	2,880	87
35 to 44 years old......	13,593	80	9,704	81	813	66	3,075	84
45 to 54 years old......	8,299	49	6,310	49	535	43	1,454	49
55 to 64 years old......	1,686	11	1,276	10	168	20	241	12
65 years old and over...	395	2	283	2	23	4	89	4

[1] No spouse present.

Source: U.S. Census Bureau, Current Population Reports, P20-537, 2001; and America's Families and Living Arrangements, Detailed Tables, Family households (F table series), "Table F1. Family Households, by Type, Age of Own Children, Age of Family Members, and Age of Householder," <http://www.census.gov/hhes/families/data/cps.html>, accessed January 2017, and earlier releases.

Table 64. Family Groups With Children Under 18 Years of Age by Race and Hispanic Origin: 2000 to 2016

[In thousands (37,496 represents 37,496,000). As of March. Family groups are family households, related subfamilies, and unrelated subfamilies; each married couple or parent/child group is counted separately, even if they reside in the same household. Excludes members of Armed Forces except those living off post or with their families on post. Beginning 2005, based on an expanded sample of households. Data for 2005 and 2010 based on Census 2000 population controls. Data for 2015 and 2016 based on Census 2010 population controls. Based on Current Population Survey, Annual Social and Economic Supplement, see text, this section and Appendix III]

Race and Hispanic origin of householder or reference person	Number (1,000)				Percent distribution			
	2000	2010	2015	2016	2000	2010	2015	2016
All races, total [1]........	**37,496**	**39,947**	**39,934**	**39,490**	**100**	**100**	**100**	**100**
Two-parent family groups [2]........	25,771	27,082	26,862	26,462	69	68	67	67
One-parent family groups........	11,725	11,686	11,780	11,814	31	29	29	30
Maintained by mother........	9,681	9,924	9,891	9,781	26	25	25	25
Maintained by father........	2,044	1,762	1,889	2,033	5	4	5	5
Grandparent householder with grandchild(ren) under 18...	(NA)	1,179	1,292	1,214	(NA)	3	3	3
White, total [3]........	**30,079**	**30,933**	**30,131**	**29,673**	**100**	**100**	**100**	**100**
Two-parent family groups [2]........	22,241	22,457	21,664	21,272	74	73	72	72
One-parent family groups........	7,838	7,729	7,639	7,607	26	25	25	26
Maintained by mother........	6,216	6,396	6,177	6,019	21	21	21	20
Maintained by father........	1,622	1,333	1,462	1,588	5	4	5	5
Grandparent householder with grandchild(ren) under 18...	(NA)	747	828	794	(NA)	2	3	3
Black, total [3]........	**5,530**	**5,903**	**5,837**	**5,782**	**100**	**100**	**100**	**100**
Two-parent family groups [2]........	2,135	2,275	2,209	2,159	39	39	38	37
One-parent family groups........	3,396	3,280	3,262	3,308	61	56	56	57
Maintained by mother........	3,060	2,977	2,971	3,007	55	50	51	52
Maintained by father........	335	303	291	301	6	5	5	5
Grandparent householder with grandchild(ren) under 18...	(NA)	348	366	315	(NA)	6	6	5
Asian, total [3]........	**1,469**	**2,025**	**2,443**	**2,467**	**100**	**100**	**100**	**100**
Two-parent family groups [2]........	1,184	1,694	2,071	2,159	81	84	85	88
One-parent family groups........	285	292	340	273	19	14	14	11
Maintained by mother........	236	235	291	217	16	12	12	9
Maintained by father........	49	57	49	56	3	3	2	2
Grandparent householder with grandchild(ren) under 18...	(NA)	39	32	35	(NA)	2	1	1
Hispanic, total [4]........	**5,503**	**7,572**	**8,345**	**8,593**	**100**	**100**	**100**	**100**
Two-parent family groups [2]........	3,625	4,856	5,407	5,575	66	64	65	65
One-parent family groups........	1,877	2,499	2,688	2,744	34	33	32	32
Maintained by mother........	1,565	2,186	2,338	2,321	28	29	28	27
Maintained by father........	313	313	350	423	6	4	4	5
Grandparent householder with grandchild(ren) under 18...	(NA)	217	250	274	(NA)	3	3	3
Non-Hispanic White, total [3]........	**24,847**	**23,911**	**22,657**	**22,067**	**100**	**100**	**100**	**100**
Two-parent family groups [2]........	18,750	17,911	16,738	16,222	75	75	74	74
One-parent family groups........	6,096	5,457	5,317	5,293	25	23	23	24
Maintained by mother........	4,766	4,404	4,171	4,090	19	18	18	19
Maintained by father........	1,331	1,053	1,146	1,203	5	4	5	5
Grandparent householder with grandchild(ren) under 18...	(NA)	543	602	552	(NA)	2	3	3

NA Not available. [1] Includes other race/ethnicities, not shown separately. [2] Beginning 2007, includes children living both with married and unmarried parents. [3] Beginning with the 2003 Current Population Survey (CPS), respondents could choose more than one race. Beginning 2003, data represent persons who selected this race group only and exclude persons reporting more than one race. The CPS prior to 2003 allowed respondents to report only one race group. See also comments on race in the text for this section. [4] Hispanic persons may be of any race.

Source: U.S. Census Bureau, Families and Living Arrangements, Current Population Reports, P20-537, 2001; and America's Families and Living Arrangements, Family groups (FG table series), "Table FG10. Family Groups: 2016," <http://www.census.gov/hhes/families/data/cps.html>, accessed January 2017, and earlier releases.

Table 65. Parents and Children in Stay-At-Home Parent Family Groups: 1995 to 2016

[In thousands (22,973 represents 22,973,000), except percent. Family groups with children include those families that maintain their own household (family households with own children); those that live in the home of a relative (related subfamilies); and those that live in the home of a nonrelative (unrelated subfamilies). Stay-at-home family groups are married-couple family groups with children under age 15 where one parent is in the labor force all of the previous year and the other parent is out of the labor force for the entire year with the reason 'taking care of home and family.' Only married couples with children under age 15 are included. Based on Current Population Survey; see Appendix III]

Year	Married-couple family groups with children under 15 years old					Children under 15 years old in married-couple family groups				
	Total	With stay-at-home mothers	With stay-at-home fathers	With stay-at-home mothers	With stay-at-home fathers	Total	With stay-at-home mothers	With stay-at-home fathers	With stay-at-home mothers	With stay-at-home fathers
	Number			Percent		Number			Percent	
1995........	22,973	4,440	64	19.3	0.3	41,008	9,106	125	22.2	0.3
2000........	22,953	4,785	93	20.8	0.4	41,860	10,087	180	24.1	0.4
2005........	23,305	5,584	142	24.0	0.6	41,111	11,224	247	27.3	0.6
2010........	22,138	5,020	154	22.7	0.7	41,026	10,833	287	26.4	0.7
2012........	21,334	5,091	189	23.9	0.9	39,222	10,675	369	27.2	0.9
2013........	21,547	5,215	214	24.2	1.0	39,448	10,818	434	27.4	1.1
2014........	21,549	5,203	211	24.1	1.0	39,424	10,791	420	27.4	1.1
2015........	21,586	5,210	199	24.1	0.9	39,621	10,758	368	27.2	0.9
2016........	21,531	5,031	209	23.4	1.0	39,693	10,360	392	26.1	1.0

Source: U.S. Census Bureau, America's Families and Living Arrangements, Historical Time Series, "Table SHP-1. Parents and Children in Stay-At-Home Parent Family Groups: 1994 to Present," <http://www.census.gov/hhes/families/data/historical.html>, accessed December 2016.

Table 66. Children Under 18 Years of Age by Presence of Parents: 2000 to 2016

[72,012 represents 72,012,000. As of March. Excludes persons under 18 years old who maintained households or family groups and their spouses. Based on Current Population Survey; see headnote, Table 64]

Race, Hispanic origin, and year	Number (1,000)	Both parents [1]	Percent living with—						
			Mother only					Father only	Neither parent
			Total	Divorced	Married, spouse absent [2]	Never married	Widowed		
ALL RACES [3]									
2000	72,012	69.1	22.4	7.9	4.5	9.2	1.0	4.2	4.2
2005	73,494	67.3	23.4	7.9	4.6	10.1	0.8	4.8	4.5
2010	74,718	69.4	23.1	7.1	5.1	10.1	0.8	3.4	4.1
2015	73,623	69.2	23.1	6.6	4.4	11.3	0.8	3.7	3.9
2016	73,745	68.7	23.4	7.0	4.4	11.1	0.8	4.1	3.8
WHITE [4]									
2000	56,455	75.3	17.3	(NA)	(NA)	(NA)	(NA)	4.3	3.1
2005	56,234	73.5	18.4	7.9	4.0	5.8	0.7	4.7	3.4
2010	56,416	74.9	18.3	6.9	4.5	6.1	0.8	3.5	3.4
2015	53,621	74.9	18.2	6.6	4.0	6.7	0.8	3.7	3.2
2016	53,628	74.3	18.1	7.0	3.8	6.5	0.8	4.2	3.3
BLACK [4]									
2000	11,412	37.6	49.0	(NA)	(NA)	(NA)	(NA)	4.2	9.2
2005	11,293	35.0	50.2	8.7	8.1	32.0	1.3	5.0	9.8
2010	11,272	39.2	49.7	8.6	8.4	31.5	1.2	3.6	7.5
2015	11,091	38.7	49.4	7.6	6.7	33.9	1.1	4.2	7.7
2016	11,101	38.7	51.5	8.2	8.2	34.2	1.0	4.0	5.8
ASIAN [4]									
2005	2,843	83.6	10.2	4.0	2.3	2.7	1.3	3.6	2.5
2010	3,300	85.5	10.1	3.8	3.7	2.1	0.6	2.2	2.1
2015	3,736	85.7	10.6	2.8	3.4	3.9	0.5	2.0	1.7
2016	3,758	88.6	7.4	2.2	2.4	1.9	0.9	1.8	2.2
HISPANIC [5]									
2000	11,613	65.1	25.1	(NA)	(NA)	(NA)	(NA)	4.4	5.4
2005	14,241	64.7	25.4	6.1	7.1	11.4	0.8	4.8	5.2
2010	16,941	67.0	26.3	5.8	8.1	11.7	0.7	2.7	4.0
2015	17,981	67.0	25.9	5.3	7.1	13.0	0.6	3.0	4.1
2016	18,231	67.2	25.3	5.4	6.7	12.4	0.6	3.8	3.7
NON-HISPANIC WHITE [4]									
2005	43,106	75.9	16.4	8.5	3.1	4.2	0.7	4.8	2.9
2010	41,089	77.5	15.5	7.5	3.1	4.2	0.8	3.8	3.1
2015	38,084	77.5	15.5	7.2	2.7	4.7	0.8	4.1	2.9
2016	37,951	76.5	15.9	7.8	2.6	4.7	0.9	4.4	3.2

NA Not available. [1] Beginning in 2007, includes children living both with married and unmarried parents. [2] Includes separated. [3] Includes other races and non-Hispanic groups, not shown separately. [4] Beginning with the 2003 Current Population Survey (CPS), respondents could choose more than one race. Data represents persons who selected this race group only and exclude persons reporting more than one race. Prior to 2003, the CPS allowed respondents to report only one race group. See also comments on race in the text for this section. [5] Hispanic persons may be of any race.

Source: U.S. Census Bureau, America's Families and Living Arrangements, Detailed Tables, Children (C table series), "Table C3. Living Arrangements of Children Under 18 Years and Marital Status of Parents, by Age, Sex, Race, and Hispanic Origin and Selected Characteristics of the Child for All Children: 2016," <http://www.census.gov/hhes/families/>, accessed December 2016, and earlier releases.

Table 67. Grandparents Living With Grandchildren by Race, Hispanic Origin, and Sex: 2015

[In thousands (7,292 represents 7,292,000), except percent. Covers both grandparents living in own home with grandchildren present and grandparents living in grandchildren's home. The American Community Survey universe includes the household population and the population living in institutions, college dormitories, and other group quarters. Based on a sample and subject to sampling variability; see text, this section, and Appendix III]

Race, Hispanic origin, and sex	Grandparents living with own grandchildren, total	Grandparents responsible for grandchildren		
		Total	30 to 59 years old	60 years old and over
Grandparents living with own grandchildren under 18 years old (1,000)	**7,292**	**2,572**	**1,549**	**1,023**
PERCENT DISTRIBUTION				
Total	100.0	100.0	100.0	100.0
White alone	62.6	66.1	65.6	66.8
Black or African American alone	17.2	20.7	21.5	19.5
American Indian and Alaska Native alone	1.4	2.0	2.1	1.8
Asian alone	8.9	3.3	2.1	5.2
Native Hawaiian and Other Pacific Islander alone	0.3	0.3	0.3	0.3
Some other race alone	7.7	5.6	6.3	4.5
Two or more races	1.8	2.0	2.1	1.9
Hispanic origin [1]	25.9	20.0	22.5	16.2
White alone, not Hispanic	45.5	52.7	50.6	56.1
Male	35.8	37.1	33.9	42.0
Female	64.2	62.9	66.1	58.0

[1] Persons of Hispanic origin may be of any race.

Source: U.S. Census Bureau, 2015 American Community Survey, S1002, "Grandparents," <http://factfinder.census.gov/>, accessed December 2016.

Table 68. Group Quarters Population by Type of Group Quarter and Selected Characteristics: 2015

[In percent, except as indicated. The American Community Survey universe includes the household population and the population living in institutions, college dormitories, and other group quarters. Based on a sample and subject to sampling variability]

Characteristic	Total group quarters population [1]	Institutionalized group quarters population			Noninstitutionalized group quarters population	
		Total [1]	Adult correctional facilities	Nursing facilities/ skilled nursing facilities	Total [1]	College/ university housing
Total population........................	**8,070,896**	**3,938,749**	**2,218,725**	**1,497,148**	**4,132,147**	**2,660,344**
PERCENT DISTRIBUTION						
Male........................	61.3	69.1	91.1	36.0	53.7	45.9
Female........................	38.7	30.9	8.9	64.0	46.3	54.1
Under 15 years old........................	0.9	1.1	(X)	(X)	0.7	(X)
15 to 17 years old........................	1.7	2.3	0.2	(X)	1.1	1.0
18 to 24 years old........................	41.3	9.2	14.6	0.2	71.8	96.5
25 to 34 years old........................	12.8	19.1	32.9	0.6	6.8	2.1
35 to 44 years old........................	9.5	14.9	25.1	1.4	4.3	0.2
45 to 54 years old........................	8.6	11.8	17.7	4.2	5.5	0.1
55 to 64 years old........................	6.7	8.5	7.4	10.6	4.9	0.1
65 to 74 years old........................	4.8	7.6	1.7	17.0	2.2	–
75 to 84 years old........................	5.7	10.2	0.2	26.4	1.3	(X)
85 years old and over........................	8.1	15.1	–	39.6	1.4	(X)
Median age (years)........................	29.4	47.6	35.7	81.7	20.5	19.7
One race........................	100.0	100.0	100.0	100.0	100.0	100.0
White........................	67.6	63.7	52.0	81.3	71.4	74.0
Black........................	23.2	29.2	39.0	14.4	17.4	13.6
American Indian and Alaska Native.........	1.1	1.5	2.2	0.5	0.7	0.4
Asian........................	4.4	1.3	0.9	1.9	7.3	9.5
Native Hawaiian/Pacific Islander............	0.2	0.2	0.2	0.1	0.3	0.2
Some other race........................	3.5	4.1	5.6	1.7	2.9	2.3
Hispanic origin [2]........................	13.0	14.7	20.3	5.8	11.4	9.7
Not Hispanic........................	87.0	85.3	79.7	94.2	88.6	90.3
White alone, not Hispanic........................	57.0	52.6	37.2	76.7	61.2	64.4

– Represents or rounds to zero. X Not applicable. [1] Includes other types of group quarters, not shown separately. [2] Persons of Hispanic origin may be of any race.

Source: U.S. Census Bureau, 2015 American Community Survey, S2601A, "Characteristics of the Group Quarters Population"; and S2601B, "Characteristics of the Group Quarters Population by Group Quarters Type"; <http://factfinder.census.gov/>, accessed December 2016.

Table 69. Population in Group Quarters by State: 2000 to 2016

[In thousands (7,780 represents 7,780,000). 2000 and 2010, as of April. 2015 and 2016, as of July. For definition of group quarters, see text, this section]

State	2000 [1]	2010 [2]	2015	2016	State	2000 [1]	2010 [2]	2015	2016
United States........	**7,780**	**7,999**	**8,097**	**8,080**	Missouri.............	164	174	175	175
Alabama................	115	116	120	120	Montana.............	25	29	29	29
Alaska.................	19	26	28	28	Nebraska.............	51	51	52	52
Arizona.................	110	140	157	157	Nevada.............	34	36	37	38
Arkansas................	74	79	85	85	New Hampshire....	36	40	42	42
California..............	820	820	820	814	New Jersey.........	195	187	187	186
Colorado...............	103	116	118	118	New Mexico.........	36	43	43	43
Connecticut............	108	118	116	115	New York............	581	586	576	576
Delaware...............	25	24	25	25	North Carolina......	254	257	256	256
District of Columbia....	36	40	39	40	North Dakota.......	24	25	26	26
Florida.................	389	425	435	434	Ohio.................	299	306	312	313
Georgia................	234	254	261	257	Oklahoma...........	112	112	110	110
Hawaii.................	36	43	44	44	Oregon..............	77	87	89	89
Idaho..................	31	29	30	30	Pennsylvania.......	433	427	427	427
Illinois..................	322	302	301	301	Rhode Island.......	39	43	43	43
Indiana................	178	187	189	187	South Carolina.....	135	139	137	137
Iowa...................	104	99	100	101	South Dakota......	28	34	34	34
Kansas................	82	79	79	79	Tennessee.........	148	154	154	153
Kentucky..............	115	126	132	131	Texas..............	561	582	608	608
Louisiana..............	136	128	129	129	Utah...............	40	46	45	46
Maine.................	35	36	36	36	Vermont............	21	25	25	25
Maryland..............	134	139	141	141	Virginia.............	231	240	243	242
Massachusetts.........	221	239	252	253	Washington.........	136	139	141	143
Michigan..............	250	230	230	230	West Virginia.......	43	49	48	48
Minnesota.............	136	135	134	133	Wisconsin..........	156	151	148	146
Mississippi............	95	93	93	93	Wyoming...........	14	14	14	14

[1] The April 1, 2000, population estimates base reflects changes to the Census 2000 population from the Count Question Resolution program and geographic program revisions. [2] The April 1, 2010 population estimates base reflects changes to the Census 2010 population from the Count Question Resolution program and geographic program revisions.

Source: U.S. Census Bureau, "Annual Resident Population Estimates, Estimated Components of Resident Population Change, and Rates of the Components of Resident Population Change for States and Counties: April 1, 2000 to July 1, 2009," <https://www.census.gov/data/datasets.2009.html>, and "Population, population change and estimated components of population change: April 1, 2010 to July 1, 2016 (CO-EST2016-alldata)," <https://www.census.gov/data/datasets/2016/demo/popest/counties-total.html>; accessed May 2017.

Table 70. Opposite-Sex and Same-Sex Couple Households by Selected Characteristics: 2015

[In percent, except as indicated (56,290 represents 56,290,000). The American Community Survey universe includes the household population and the population living in institutions, college dormitories, and other group quarters. Based on a sample and subject to sampling variability. See text, this section and Appendix III]

Characteristics	Married opposite-sex couples	Unmarried opposite-sex couples	Married and unmarried same-sex couples			Married same-sex couples
			Total	Male-male couples	Female-female couples	
Total households (1,000)........................	**56,290**	**6,914**	**859**	**412**	**447**	**425**
Age of householder:						
15 to 24 years old.............................	1.2	11.7	4.0	3.0	4.9	1.9
25 to 34 years old.............................	13.1	35.2	17.8	15.5	19.9	12.6
35 to 44 years old.............................	19.9	21.3	19.3	18.6	19.9	18.9
45 to 54 years old.............................	22.0	15.8	25.3	27.0	23.7	24.9
55 to 64 years old.............................	21.2	10.1	19.0	20.4	17.7	21.3
65 years old and over.........................	22.5	5.9	14.6	15.4	13.9	20.4
Average age of householder (years)...........	52.0	39.2	48.2	49.4	47.2	51.7
Average age of spouse/partner (years)........	51.3	38.4	46.3	46.8	45.9	50.5
Race of householder:						
White...	81.8	76.2	83.0	84.7	81.4	84.3
Black or African American......................	6.9	11.4	7.8	5.8	9.7	6.6
American Indian or Alaska Native..............	0.5	1.1	0.7	0.4	0.9	0.5
Asian...	5.7	2.4	3.1	3.6	2.5	3.8
Native Hawaiian or Pacific Islander............	0.1	0.2	0.3	0.3	0.3	0.2
Some other race...............................	3.3	5.8	2.6	2.6	2.6	2.3
Two or more races.............................	1.6	2.9	2.6	2.6	2.6	2.2
Percent of couples interracial...................	7.0	13.5	15.1	17.8	12.6	12.9
Hispanic origin of householder:						
Hispanic [1]...................................	12.7	19.1	11.4	11.6	11.2	10.9
White alone, not Hispanic......................	72.9	64.0	75.0	76.5	73.7	76.4
Children in the household:						
Children in the household [2]..................	39.4	40.2	17.2	9.7	24.1	20.1
Own children in the household.................	39.3	37.1	16.0	9.2	22.2	19.9
Household income:						
Less than $35,000.............................	14.3	25.5	14.1	10.7	17.2	13.0
$35,000 to $49,999............................	11.2	15.7	10.4	8.6	12.0	8.8
$50,000 to $74,999............................	19.1	22.1	17.3	16.8	17.9	16.5
$75,000 to $99,999............................	16.1	14.6	15.4	14.6	16.1	14.8
$100,000 or more..............................	39.3	22.0	42.8	49.3	36.8	46.9
Median household income (dollars) [3].........	82,293	58,879	87,300	98,486	79,494	93,940
Housing tenure:						
Owner occupied................................	79.0	41.8	66.2	68.1	64.4	75.0
Renter occupied...............................	21.0	58.2	33.8	31.9	35.6	25.0

[1] Persons of Hispanic origin may be of any race. [2] Includes own children and nonrelatives of the householder under 18 years old. [3] Prior to 2015, this table displayed estimates of mean (average) household income.

Source: U.S. Census Bureau, 2015 American Community Survey, "Characteristics of Same-Sex Couple Households: 2015," <http://www.census.gov/hhes/samesex/data/acs.html>, accessed March 2017.

Table 71. Opposite Sex Unmarried Couples by Presence of Biological Children: 2016

[In thousands (8,075 represents 8,075,000), except percent. As of March. Excludes members of Armed Forces except those living off post or with their families on post. All opposite-sex unmarried couples are included, regardless of householder status. Unmarried couples of the opposite sex with children under 18 years old are included in the estimates if either partner had at least one never-married biological child living with them. Population controls based on Census 2010. Based on Current Population Survey; see text, this section and Appendix III]

Sex and age of partner	Unmarried couples, total	Without children under 18 years old	With children under 18 years old	
			Number	Percent of total
Total...	**8,075**	**5,044**	**3,031**	**37.5**
Age of male partner:				
15 to 24 years old..............................	1,050	704	347	33.0
25 to 29 years old..............................	1,702	1,107	594	34.9
30 to 34 years old..............................	1,340	694	647	48.3
35 to 39 years old..............................	858	317	541	63.1
40 to 44 years old..............................	696	309	387	55.6
45 to 49 years old..............................	659	395	264	40.1
50 to 54 years old..............................	570	433	137	24.0
55 to 64 years old..............................	759	657	102	13.4
65 years old and over..........................	440	429	11	2.5
Age of female partner:				
15 to 24 years old..............................	1,569	1,023	546	34.8
25 to 29 years old..............................	1,805	1,121	684	37.9
30 to 34 years old..............................	1,222	583	639	52.3
35 to 39 years old..............................	781	278	503	64.4
40 to 44 years old..............................	695	312	383	55.1
45 to 49 years old..............................	564	392	172	30.5
50 to 54 years old..............................	481	404	77	16.0
55 to 64 years old..............................	594	569	25	4.2
65 years old and over..........................	363	361	2	0.6

Source: U.S. Census Bureau, America's Families and Living Arrangements, Detailed Tables, Unmarried couples (UC table series), "Table UC3. Opposite Sex Unmarried Couples by Presence of Biological Children under 18, and Age, Earnings, Education, and Race and Hispanic Origin of Both Partners," <http://www.census.gov/hhes/families/data/cps.html>, accessed January 2017.

Table 72. Opposite and Same-Sex Unmarried-Partner Households by Region: 2015

[The American Community Survey universe includes the household population and the population living in institutions, college dormitories, and other group quarters. For composition of regions, see map inside front cover. Based on a sample and subject to sampling variability; see text, this section and Appendix III]

Item	Total	Northeast	Midwest	South	West
Total households	**118,208,250**	**21,006,538**	**26,371,735**	**44,441,974**	**26,388,003**
Unmarried-partner households	7,347,757	1,316,989	1,676,391	2,536,256	1,818,121
Male householder and male partner	210,222	40,154	37,175	75,763	57,130
Male householder and female partner	3,505,774	617,995	811,214	1,211,021	865,544
Female householder and female partner	223,317	39,798	44,683	83,792	55,044
Female householder and male partner	3,408,444	619,042	783,319	1,165,680	840,403
All other households	110,860,493	19,689,549	24,695,344	41,905,718	24,569,882

Source: U.S. Census Bureau, 2015 American Community Survey, B11009, "Unmarried-Partner Households by Sex of Partner," <http://factfinder.census.gov/>, accessed December 2016.

Table 73. Young Adults Living in Parental Home by Sex and Age: 1990 to 2016

[In thousands (12,450 represents 12,450,000), except percent. As of March. Excludes members of Armed Forces except those living off post or with their families on post. Unmarried college students living in dormitories are counted as living in their parent(s) home. Beginning 2005, based on an expanded sample of households. Population controls for 2005 to 2010 based on Census 2000; beginning 2011, population controls based on Census 2010. Based on Current Population Survey; see text, this section and Appendix III]

Year	Male young adults Total	Child of householder living at home Number	Percent of total	Female young adults Total	Child of householder living at home Number	Percent of total
18 TO 24 YEARS OLD						
1990	12,450	7,232	58.1	12,860	6,135	47.7
1995	12,545	7,328	58.4	12,613	5,896	46.7
2000	13,291	7,593	57.1	13,242	6,232	47.1
2005	14,060	7,448	53.0	13,933	6,413	46.0
2007	14,409	7,880	54.7	13,976	6,648	47.6
2008	14,378	8,066	56.1	13,983	6,736	48.2
2009	14,498	8,219	56.7	14,161	6,923	48.9
2010	14,824	8,501	57.3	14,469	7,123	49.2
2011	14,979	8,772	58.6	14,820	7,448	50.3
2012	15,154	9,161	60.5	14,971	7,765	51.9
2013	15,137	8,864	58.6	14,867	7,732	52.0
2014	15,280	8,892	58.2	14,852	7,645	51.5
2015	15,123	8,808	58.2	14,893	7,714	51.8
2016	15,023	8,875	59.1	14,646	7,664	52.3
25 TO 34 YEARS OLD						
1990	21,462	3,213	15.0	21,779	1,774	8.1
1995	20,589	3,166	15.4	20,800	1,759	8.5
2000	18,563	2,387	12.9	19,222	1,602	8.3
2005	19,656	2,660	13.5	19,632	1,597	8.1
2007	20,002	2,849	14.2	19,828	1,850	9.3
2008	20,182	3,044	15.1	19,922	2,053	10.3
2009	20,419	3,178	15.6	20,069	1,988	9.9
2010	20,685	3,387	16.4	20,383	2,133	10.5
2011	20,223	3,462	17.1	20,526	1,996	9.7
2012	20,458	3,459	16.9	20,743	2,155	10.4
2013	20,803	3,490	16.8	20,967	2,324	11.1
2014	21,186	3,755	17.7	21,219	2,478	11.7
2015	21,417	3,896	18.2	21,574	2,613	12.1
2016	21,839	4,284	19.6	21,912	2,736	12.5

Source: U.S. Census Bureau, America's Families and Living Arrangements, Living Arrangements of Adults, Historical Time Series, "Table AD-1. Young Adults, 18-34 Years Old, Living At Home: 1960 to Present," <http://www.census.gov/hhes/families/data/adults.html>, accessed January 2017.

Table 74. Children of Householders by Age and Whether Biological, Adopted, and Stepchildren: 2010

[88,820 represents 88,820,000. As of April. Includes children of the householder regardless of marital status and excludes persons under age 18 who are not children of the householder. Includes Puerto Rico. Based on 2010 Census of Population; see Appendix III]

Type of relationship	Total	Under 18 years old Total	Under 6 years old	6 to 11 years old	12 to 14 years old	15 to 17 years old	18 years old and over Total	18 to 24 years old	25 years old and over
NUMBER (1,000)									
Total children of householders	**88,820**	**64,778**	**20,277**	**21,903**	**11,188**	**11,410**	**24,042**	**13,649**	**10,393**
Adopted children	2,072	1,527	351	569	304	303	545	325	220
Stepchildren	4,166	2,785	284	978	718	806	1,381	889	492
Biological children	82,582	60,467	19,643	20,356	10,166	10,301	22,115	12,435	9,681
PERCENT DISTRIBUTION									
Total children of householders	100.0	100.0	100.0	100.0	100.0	100.0	100.0	100.0	100.0
Adopted children	2.3	2.4	1.7	2.6	2.7	2.7	2.3	2.4	2.1
Stepchildren	4.7	4.3	1.4	4.5	6.4	7.1	5.7	6.5	4.7
Biological children	93.0	93.3	96.9	92.9	90.9	90.3	92.0	91.1	93.1

Source: U.S. Census Bureau, *Adopted Children and Stepchildren: 2010*, Current Population Reports, P20-572, April 2014. See also <https://www.census.gov/library/publications.html>.

Table 75. Children in Households by Relationship to Householder: 2010 to 2015

[Data shown for population under age 18 in households, excluding householders, spouses, and unmarried partners. Based on a sample and subject to sampling variability; see text this section and Appendix III]

Type of relationship	2010	2011	2012	2013	2014	2015
NUMBER						
Total children in households	**73,904,493**	**73,650,025**	**73,461,927**	**73,336,382**	**73,324,581**	**73,386,395**
Own child	65,472,116	65,214,152	64,952,641	64,594,807	64,426,004	64,445,292
Biological child	61,539,878	61,392,262	61,139,414	60,766,301	60,628,258	60,631,741
Adopted child	1,581,562	1,546,309	1,519,987	1,496,123	1,447,057	1,422,968
Stepchild	2,350,676	2,275,581	2,293,240	2,332,383	2,350,689	2,390,583
Grandchild	5,396,969	5,499,443	5,602,780	5,712,157	5,829,891	5,886,720
Other relatives	1,826,283	1,768,058	1,731,717	1,737,898	1,792,059	1,793,069
Foster child or other unrelated child	1,209,125	1,168,372	1,174,789	1,291,520	1,276,627	1,261,314
PERCENT DISTRIBUTION						
Total children in households	100.0	100.0	100.0	100.0	100.0	100.0
Own child	88.6	88.5	88.4	88.1	87.9	87.8
Biological child	83.3	83.4	83.2	82.9	82.7	82.6
Adopted child	2.1	2.1	2.1	2.0	2.0	1.9
Stepchild	3.2	3.1	3.1	3.2	3.2	3.3
Grandchild	7.3	7.5	7.6	7.8	8.0	8.0
Other relatives	2.5	2.4	2.4	2.4	2.4	2.4
Foster child or other unrelated child	1.6	1.6	1.6	1.8	1.7	1.7

Source: U.S. Census Bureau, American Community Survey, B09018, "Relationship to Householder for Children Under 18 in Households," <https://factfinder.census.gov>, accessed August 2017.

Table 76. Living Arrangements of Young Adults by Selected Characteristics: 2015

[In thousands (15,795 represents 15,795,000), except as noted. Based on the American Community Survey; see Appendix III]

Characteristics	Young adults aged 18 to 24				Young adults aged 25 to 34			
	Living in parents' home [1]		Living independ- ently [2]	Living with room- mates [3]	Living in parents' home [1]		Living independ- ently [2]	Living with room- mates [3]
	Number	Percent			Number	Percent		
Total	**15,795**	**100.0**	**4,458**	**7,757**	**8,382**	**100.0**	**24,362**	**10,118**
By sex:								
Female	7,317	46.3	2,587	3,851	3,679	43.9	12,662	5,252
Male	8,479	53.7	1,871	3,907	4,702	56.1	11,700	4,866
By race/ethnicity:								
White alone, non-Hispanic	8,148	51.6	2,852	4,054	4,192	50.0	15,525	4,702
Black alone, non-Hispanic	2,350	14.9	463	1,203	1,428	17.0	2,168	1,837
Asian alone, non-Hispanic	769	4.9	137	534	571	6.8	1,554	750
Other race, non-Hispanic	665	4.2	179	338	326	3.9	746	365
Hispanic [4]	3,864	24.5	828	1,628	1,864	22.2	4,369	2,464
Has a disability [5]	1,044	6.6	224	413	904	10.8	1,019	630
Work status:								
Employed	9,033	57.2	3,399	4,981	5,778	68.9	19,869	7,863
Worked full-time, year-round	2,813	17.8	2,109	2,174	3,651	43.6	15,557	5,617
Mean hours worked per week	29.9	(X)	38.3	33.3	37.1	(X)	41.6	39.5
Unemployed	1,594	10.1	247	643	851	10.2	830	682
Not in labor force	5,168	32.7	812	2,133	1,752	20.9	3,662	1,573
Educational attainment:								
High school diploma or less	7,850	49.7	1,681	3,209	3,474	41.4	6,834	4,044
Associate's degree or some college	6,632	42.0	1,930	3,544	2,840	33.9	7,563	3,211
Bachelor's degree or higher	1,312	8.3	848	1,004	2,068	24.7	9,965	2,864
Enrolled in school	8,463	53.6	1,198	3,586	1,276	15.2	2,564	1,425
Personal income: [6]								
$0 to $29,999	14,973	94.8	3,416	6,917	6,247	74.6	10,998	6,402
$30,000 to $59,999	736	4.7	885	715	1,730	20.7	8,292	2,706
$60,000 to $99,999	71	0.4	135	101	336	4.0	3,653	806
$100,000 or more	13	0.1	22	23	65	0.8	1,408	201
Housing type:								
Single-family home	12,512	79.2	1,628	3,975	6,687	79.8	14,531	5,478
Apartment or multifamily building	2,421	15.3	2,507	3,391	1,233	14.7	8,610	4,136
Other housing type	863	5.5	324	391	462	5.5	1,222	504
Lived at same address a year ago	14,127	89.4	2,158	4,506	7,341	87.6	18,005	7,178
Tenure:								
Own home	10,831	68.6	802	2,459	6,230	74.3	10,918	3,439
Rent home	4,965	31.4	3,656	5,298	2,152	25.7	13,444	6,679

X Not applicable. [1] Child of the householder, regardless of the young adult's marital status. [2] The young adult lives alone, or is the householder living with a spouse or unmarried partner, or is the spouse or unmarried partner of the householder. [3] Living with other relatives or nonrelatives. [4] Persons of Hispanic origin may be of any race. [5] "Has a disability" means the young adult reported having at least one of the following six types of disabilities: hearing, vision, cognitive, ambulatory, self-care, or independent living difficulty. [6] Excludes young adults with incomes less than $0.

Source: U.S. Census Bureau, *The Changing Economics and Demographics of Young Adulthood: 1975-2016*, Current Population Reports, P20-579, April 2017. See also <https://www.census.gov/topics/families.html>.

Table 77. Self-Described Religious Identification of Adult Population: 1990, 2001, and 2008

[In thousands (175,440 represents 175,440,000). The methodology of the American Religious Identification Survey (ARIS) 2008 replicated that used in previous surveys. The three surveys are based on random-digit-dialing telephone surveys of residential households in the continental U.S. (48 states): 54,461 interviews in 2008, 50,281 in 2001, and 113,723 in 1990. Respondents were asked to describe themselves in terms of religion with an open-ended question. Interviewers did not prompt or offer a suggested list of potential answers. Moreover, the self-description of respondents was not based on whether established religious bodies, institutions, churches, mosques or synagogues considered them to be members. Instead, the surveys sought to determine whether the respondents regarded themselves as adherents of a religious community. Subjective rather than objective standards of religious identification were tapped by the surveys]

Religious group	1990	2001	2008
Adult population, total [1]	**175,440**	**207,983**	**228,182**
Christian, total [2]	**151,225**	**159,514**	**173,402**
Catholic	46,004	50,873	57,199
Baptist	33,964	33,820	36,148
Methodist	14,174	14,039	11,366
Lutheran	9,110	9,580	8,674
Presbyterian	4,985	5,596	4,723
Episcopalian/Anglican	3,043	3,451	2,405
Orthodox (Eastern)	502	645	824
United Church of Christ	438	1,378	736
Disciples of Christ	144	492	263
Reformed/Dutch Reform	161	289	206
Quaker	67	217	130
Christian unspecified	8,073	14,190	16,834
Nondenominational Christian [3]	194	2,489	8,032
Protestant unspecified [3]	17,214	4,647	5,187
Evangelical/Born Again [3]	546	1,088	2,154
Independent Christian Church	25	71	86
Pentecostal unspecified	3,116	4,407	5,416
Assemblies of God	617	1,105	810
Church of God	590	943	663
Holiness/Holy	610	569	352
Church of the Nazarene	549	544	358
Foursquare Gospel	28	70	116
Churches of Christ	1,769	2,593	1,921
Jehovah's Witness	1,381	1,331	1,914
Apostolic/New Apostolic	117	254	970
Seventh-day Adventist	668	724	938
Mennonite	235	346	438
Christian Reform	40	79	381
Christian Science	214	194	339
Church of the Brethren	206	358	231
Mormon/Latter-day Saints	2,487	2,697	3,158
Other Christian [4]	105	254	206
Other religions, total [2]	**5,853**	**7,740**	**8,796**
Jewish	3,137	2,837	2,680
Buddhist	404	1,082	1,189
Hindu	227	766	582
Sikh	13	57	78
Muslim	527	1,104	1,349
Unitarian/Universalist	502	629	586
Spiritualist	(NA)	116	426
Wiccan	8	134	342
Pagan	(NA)	140	340
Native American	47	103	186
Other unclassified [4]	991	774	1,030
No religion specified, total [2]	**14,331**	**29,481**	**34,169**
Agnostic	[5]1,186	991	1,985
Atheist	(5)	902	1,621
Humanist	29	49	90
No Religion [4]	13,116	27,486	30,427
Other No Religion [4]	(NA)	57	45
Refused to reply to question	4,031	11,246	11,815

NA Not available. [1] Refers to the total number of adults in all fifty states. All other figures are based on projections from surveys conducted in the continental United States (48 states). [2] Includes other groups, not shown separately. [3] Because of the subjective nature of replies to open-ended questions, these categories are the most unstable as they do not refer to clearly identifiable denominations as much as underlying feelings about religion. Thus they may be the most subject to fluctuation over time. [4] Estimates for subpopulations smaller than 75,000 adults are aggregated to minimize sampling errors. [5] Atheist included in Agnostic.

Source: 1990 data, Barry A. Kosmin and Seymour P. Lachman, "One Nation Under God: Religion in Contemporary American Society, 1993"; 2001 data, Barry A. Kosmin and Ariela Keysar, *Religion in A Free Market: Religious and Non-Religious Americans, Who, What, Why, Where, 2006*; and 2008 data, Barry A. Kosmin & Ariela Keysar, *American Religious Identification Survey (ARIS 2008) Summary Report, 2009*, Institute for the Study of Secularism in Society and Culture, Trinity College, Hartford, CT <http://www.trincoll.edu/Academics/centers/ISSSC/Pages/ARIS-Data-Archive.aspx> and <www.AmericanReligionSurvey-ARIS.org> ©.

Table 78. Religious Adherents and Jewish Population—States: 2010 to 2011

[137,450 represents 137,450,000. Adherents were defined as "all members, including full members, their children and others who regularly attend services." The Jewish population includes Jews who define themselves as Jewish by religion as well as those who define themselves as Jewish in cultural or ethnic terms. Data on Jewish population are based on both scientific studies and informant estimates provided by local Jewish communities]

State	Number (1,000)			Percent of population [3]		
	Christian adherents, [1] 2010	Other religious adherents, [2] 2010	Jewish population, 2011	Christian adherents, [1] 2010	Other religious adherents, [2] 2010	Jewish population, 2011
United States	**137,450**	**10,890**	**6,588**	**44.5**	**3.5**	**2.1**
Alabama	2,948	52	9	61.7	1.1	0.2
Alaska	200	40	6	28.1	5.7	0.9
Arizona	1,894	466	106	29.6	7.3	1.7
Arkansas	1,573	40	2	53.9	1.4	0.1
California	15,021	1,530	1,220	40.3	4.1	3.3
Colorado	1,684	199	91	33.5	4.0	1.8
Connecticut	1,735	48	116	48.6	1.3	3.2
Delaware	349	22	15	38.9	2.5	1.7
District of Columbia	298	16	28	49.6	2.7	4.7
Florida	6,829	400	639	36.3	2.1	3.4
Georgia	4,702	186	128	48.5	1.9	1.3
Hawaii	421	140	7	31.0	10.3	0.5
Idaho	384	417	2	24.5	26.6	0.1
Illinois	6,529	486	298	50.9	3.8	2.3
Indiana	2,793	69	17	43.1	1.1	0.3
Iowa	1,592	46	6	52.3	1.5	0.2
Kansas	1,375	61	18	48.2	2.1	0.6
Kentucky	2,182	49	11	50.3	1.1	0.3
Louisiana	2,688	50	11	59.3	1.1	0.2
Maine	345	19	14	26.0	1.4	1.0
Maryland	2,214	118	238	38.3	2.0	4.1
Massachusetts	3,546	122	278	54.2	1.9	4.2
Michigan	3,910	211	82	39.6	2.1	0.8
Minnesota	2,894	69	46	54.6	1.3	0.9
Mississippi	1,709	33	2	57.6	1.1	0.1
Missouri	2,806	123	59	46.9	2.0	1.0
Montana	326	50	1	33.0	5.0	0.1
Nebraska	974	38	6	53.3	2.1	0.3
Nevada	725	196	74	26.8	7.3	2.8
New Hampshire	444	14	10	33.7	1.1	0.8
New Jersey	4,321	272	504	49.1	3.1	5.7
New Mexico	940	87	12	45.6	4.2	0.6
New York	8,529	611	1,635	44.0	3.2	8.4
North Carolina	4,372	140	31	45.9	1.5	0.3
North Dakota	443	8	(Z)	65.9	1.2	0.1
Ohio	4,861	146	148	42.1	1.3	1.3
Oklahoma	2,148	75	5	57.3	2.0	0.1
Oregon	998	187	41	26.1	4.9	1.1
Pennsylvania	6,530	206	295	51.4	1.6	2.3
Rhode Island	558	10	19	53.1	0.9	1.8
South Carolina	2,337	70	13	50.5	1.5	0.3
South Dakota	464	13	(Z)	57.0	1.6	(Z)
Tennessee	3,425	82	20	54.0	1.3	0.3
Texas	13,062	872	140	51.9	3.5	0.6
Utah	256	1,929	6	9.3	69.8	0.2
Vermont	199	9	5	31.8	1.4	0.9
Virginia	3,206	351	97	40.1	4.4	1.2
Washington	1,945	364	46	28.9	5.4	0.7
West Virginia	635	22	2	34.3	1.2	0.1
Wisconsin	2,973	62	28	52.3	1.1	0.5
Wyoming	158	65	1	28.0	11.5	0.2

Z Fewer than 500 or less than 0.05 percent. [1] Comprises evangelical Protestants, Black Protestants, mainline Protestants, Orthodox and Catholic groups. [2] Includes counts of Jain, Shinto, Sikh, Tao, National Spiritualist Association, Church of Jesus Christ of Latter Day Saints, Unitarian Universalist, Jehovah's Witnesses, Church of Christ Scientist, Bahá'í, three Buddhist groupings, four Hindu groupings, Muslims, and Zoroastrians. Excludes four Judaism groups. [3] Based on U.S. Census Bureau data for resident population enumerated as of April 1, 2010 and estimated as of July 2012.

Source: Religious adherents: Clifford Grammich, Kirk Hadaway, Richard Houseal, Dale E. Jones, Alexei Krindatch, Richie Stanley, and Richard H. Taylor, *2010 U.S. Religion Census: Religious Congregations & Membership Study* ©, 2012, Association of Statisticians of American Religious Bodies. See also <http://www.asarb.org>. Jewish population: Ira M. Sheskin and Arnold Dashefsky, University of Miami and University of Connecticut, *Jewish Population of the United States, 2011*, published by the Mandell L. Berman North American Jewish Data Bank in cooperation with the Association for the Social Scientific Study of Jewry and the Jewish Federations of North America, see also <http://www.jewishdatabank.org>

Table 79. Religious Adherents by Metropolitan Area Status and Religious Groups: 2010

[Groups shown have 500,000 adherents or more. Adherents were defined as all members, including full members, their children and the estimated number of other participants who are not considered members. Based on a study of 236 religious bodies sponsored by the Association of Statisticians of American Religious Bodies. Participants included 217 Christian denominations, associations, or communions (including Latter-day Saints, Messianic Jews, and Unitarian/Universalist groups); counts of Jain, Shinto, Sikh, Tao, and National Spiritualist Association congregations, and counts of congregations and individuals for Bahá'í, three Buddhist groupings, four Hindu groupings, four Jewish groupings, Muslims, and Zoroastrians. For definition of metropolitan and micropolitan areas, see Appendix II]

Religious group	Total adherents (1,000)	Percent		
		In metropolitan area	In micropolitan area	Outside metro/micro area
U.S. population, total............................	308,746	83.7	10.0	6.3
Total adherents.................................	**150,686**	**83.5**	**10.0**	**6.5**
Catholic..	58,929	90.5	6.2	3.3
Southern Baptist Convention.................	19,897	69.3	17.2	13.5
Non-denominational Christian Churches........	12,241	88.7	7.8	3.5
United Methodist Church........................	9,948	73.6	15.3	11.1
Church of Jesus Christ of Latter-day Saints.....	6,145	82.8	11.6	5.6
Evangelical Lutheran Church in America........	4,181	70.4	16.0	13.6
Assemblies of God................................	2,945	82.7	11.0	6.3
Muslim, estimate..................................	2,600	97.4	2.0	0.6
Presbyterian Church (U.S.A.).................	2,452	82.5	11.4	6.1
Lutheran Church—Missouri Synod..............	2,271	72.7	13.7	13.6
Episcopal..	1,952	88.2	8.1	3.7
National Baptist Convention, USA, Inc...........	1,881	90.3	7.0	2.7
Churches of Christ................................	1,584	69.8	17.1	13.1
American Baptist Churches in the USA.........	1,561	83.8	9.8	6.4
Christian Churches and Churches of Christ.....	1,453	72.6	15.9	11.5
United Church of Christ.........................	1,284	79.3	13.5	7.2
Seventh-day Adventist Church..................	1,195	87.7	8.2	4.1
Church of God (Cleveland, Tennessee)..........	1,110	72.2	17.5	10.3
African Methodist Episcopal Church.............	1,010	77.7	12.3	10.0
Orthodox Judaism................................	947	99.6	0.0	0.4
Church of the Nazarene.........................	894	76.2	15.6	8.2
Christian Church (Disciples of Christ)...........	786	70.3	17.7	12.0
Reform Judaism...................................	766	98.3	1.3	0.4
Mahayana Buddhism.............................	733	92.8	6.8	0.4
Church of God in Christ.........................	624	87.8	7.3	4.9
Conservative Judaism............................	502	99.5	0.4	0.1

Source: Clifford Grammich, Kirk Hadaway, Richard Houseal, Dale E. Jones, Alexei Krindatch, Richie Stanley, and Richard H. Taylor. *2010 U.S. Religion Census: Religious Congregations & Membership Study*, 2012 ©. Association of Statisticians of American Religious Bodies.

Table 80. Religious Bodies—Selected Data: 1988 to 2010

[Includes the self-reported membership of religious bodies with 750,000 or more as reported to the Yearbook of American and Canadian Churches. Groups may be excluded if they do not supply information. The data are not standardized so comparisons between groups are difficult. The definition of "church member" is determined by the religious body]

Religious body	Year reported	Churches reported	Membership
African Methodist Episcopal Church............................	2009	4,100	2,500,000
African Methodist Episcopal Zion Church.....................	2010	(NA)	1,400,000
American Baptist Churches in the USA........................	2010	5,366	1,308,054
Assemblies of God...	2010	12,457	3,030,944
Catholic Church..	2010	18,199	68,202,492
Christian Churches and Churches of Christ..................	1988	5,579	1,071,616
Christian Methodist Episcopal Church.........................	2006	3,500	850,000
Church of God in Christ..	1991	15,300	5,499,875
Church of God (Cleveland, Tennessee)........................	2010	6,481	1,074,047
Church of Jesus Christ of Latter-day Saints..................	2010	13,601	6,157,238
Churches of Christ...	2006	13,000	1,639,495
Episcopal Church..	2010	6,794	1,951,907
Evangelical Lutheran Church in America.......................	2010	9,995	4,274,855
Greek Orthodox Archdiocese of America......................	2006	560	1,500,000
Jehovah's Witnesses..	2010	13,021	1,184,249
Lutheran Church—Missouri Synod.............................	2010	6,158	2,278,586
National Baptist Convention of America Inc..................	2000	(NA)	3,500,000
National Baptist Convention, U.S.A., Inc.....................	2010	10,358	5,197,512
National Missionary Baptist Convention of America........	1992	(NA)	2,500,000
Pentecostal Assemblies of the World, Inc....................	2010	2,550	1,800,000
Presbyterian Church (U.S.A.)...................................	2010	10,560	2,675,873
Progressive National Baptist Convention, Inc................	2009	1,500	1,010,000
Seventh-day Adventist Church..................................	2010	4,916	1,060,386
Southern Baptist Convention....................................	2010	45,727	16,136,044
United Church of Christ..	2010	5,227	1,058,423
United Methodist Church...	2009	33,583	7,679,850

NA Not available.

Source: National Council of Churches of Christ in the USA, *2012 Yearbook of American and Canadian Churches* ©. See also <http://nationalcouncilofchurches.us/>.

Births, Deaths, Marriages, and Divorces

This section presents vital statistics data on natality, mortality, marriages, and divorces, as well as factors that help explain fertility, such as use of contraception, sexual activity, and prevalence of abortions and fetal deaths. Vital statistics are collected and disseminated for the nation through the National Vital Statistics System by the National Center for Health Statistics (NCHS) and published annually in *Vital Statistics of the United States, National Vital Statistics Reports (NVSR),* and other selected publications. Reports are also issued by various state bureaus participating in the National Vital Statistics System. Factors influencing fertility are collected in NCHS's National Survey of Family Growth and the U.S. Census Bureau's American Community Survey and Current Population Reports (published in *Fertility of American Women*).

Additionally, data on births, deaths, and other public health topics can be accessed via the Center for Disease Control's WONDER Online Databases at <https://wonder.cdc.gov/>. Data on abortions are published by the Guttmacher Institute in selected issues of *Perspectives on Sexual and Reproductive Health.*

Registration of vital events—The registration of births, deaths, fetal deaths, and other vital events in the United States is primarily a state and local function. There are 57 vital registration jurisdictions in the United States: the 50 states, five territories (Puerto Rico, etc.), District of Columbia, and New York City. Each of the 57 jurisdictions has a direct statistical reporting relationship with NCHS. Vital events occurring to U.S. residents outside the United States are not included in the data.

Births and deaths—The live-birth, death, and fetal-death statistics prepared by NCHS are based on vital records filed in the registration offices of all states, New York City, and the District of Columbia. The annual collection of death statistics on a national basis began in 1900 with a national death-registration area of ten states and the District of Columbia; a similar annual collection of birth statistics for a national birth-registration area began in 1915, also with ten reporting states and the District of Columbia. Since 1933, the birth- and death-registration areas have comprised the entire United States, including Alaska (beginning 1959) and Hawaii (beginning 1960). National statistics on fetal deaths were first compiled for 1918 and annually since 1922. Prior to 1951, birth statistics came from a complete count of records received in the Public Health Service (now received in NCHS). From 1951 through 1971, they were based on a 50-percent sample of all registered births (except for a complete count in 1955 and a 20- to 50-percent sample in 1967). Since 1972, they have been based on a complete count for states participating in the Vital Statistics Cooperative Program (VSCP) (for details, see the technical appendix in *U.S. Vital Statistics System: Major Activities and Developments, 1950-95*) and on a 50-percent sample of all other areas. Beginning in 1986, all reporting areas participated in the VSCP. Mortality data have been based on a complete count of records for each area (except for a 50-percent sample in 1972). Beginning in 1970, births to and deaths of nonresident aliens of the United States and

U.S. citizens outside the United States have been excluded from the data. Fetal deaths and deaths among Armed Forces abroad are excluded. Data based on samples are subject to sampling error; for details, see annual issues of *National Vital Statistics Reports.*

Mortality statistics by cause of death are compiled in accordance with World Health Organization regulations according to the *International Classification of Diseases* (ICD). The ICD is revised approximately every 10 years. The tenth revision of the ICD was employed beginning in 1999. Deaths for prior years were classified according to the revision of the ICD in use at the time. Each revision of the ICD introduces a number of discontinuities in mortality statistics; for a discussion of those between the ninth and tenth revisions of the ICD, see *National Vital Statistics Reports*, Vol. 65, No. 4. Information on tests of statistical significance, differences between death rates, and standard errors can also be found in the aforementioned report.

Some of the tables present age-adjusted death rates in addition to crude death rates. Age-adjusted death rates shown in this section were prepared using the direct method, in which age-specific death rates for a population of interest are applied to a standard population distributed by age. Age adjustment eliminates the differences in observed rates between points in time or among compared population groups that result from age differences in population composition.

Fertility and life expectancy—The total fertility rate, defined as the number of births that 1,000 women would have in their lifetime if at each year of age they experienced the birth rates occurring in the specified year, is compiled and published by NCHS. See *Births: Final Data for 2015, National Vital Statistics Reports*, Vol. 66, No. 1. Data on life expectancy, the average remaining lifetime in years for persons who attain a given age, are also computed and published by NCHS. See *Deaths: Final Data for 2014, National Vital Statistics Reports*, Vol. 65, No. 4 and <https://www.cdc.gov/nchs/nvss/deaths.htm> for details.

Marriage and divorce—In 1957 and 1958 respectively, the National Office of Vital Statistics established marriage- and divorce-registration areas. Originally the marriage-registration area comprised 30 states, plus Alaska, Hawaii, Puerto Rico, and the Virgin Islands; it currently includes 42 states and the District of Columbia. The divorce-registration area, originally 14 states, Alaska, Hawaii, and the Virgin Islands, currently includes a total of 31 states and the Virgin Islands. Procedures for estimating the number of marriages and divorces in the registration states are discussed in *Vital Statistics of the United States, Vol. III—Marriage and Divorce.* Total counts of events for registration and nonregistration states are gathered by collecting already summarized data on marriages and divorces reported by state offices of vital statistics and by county offices of registration. The collection and publication of detailed marriage and divorce statistics was suspended beginning in January 1996. For additional information, contact the National Center for

Health Statistics online at <https://www.cdc.gov/nchs/nvss/marriage-divorce.htm>.

With the suspension of detailed data collection by the NCHS, data on marriage and divorce can be found in the Census Bureau's American Community Survey data tables. See <https://www.census.gov/programs-surveys/acs/> for information and data access.

Vital statistics rates—Except as noted, vital statistics rates computed by NCHS are based on decennial census population figures as of April 1 for 1960, 1970, 1980, 1990, 2000, and 2010; and on midyear population figures for other years, as estimated by the Census Bureau (see text, Section 1).

Race—Data by race for births, deaths, marriages, and divorces from NCHS are based on information contained in the certificates of registration. The Census Bureau's Current Population Survey obtains information on race by asking respondents to classify their race as (1) White, (2) Black, (3) American Indian or Alaska Native, (4) Native Hawaiian or Other Pacific Islander, or (5) Asian. Beginning with the 1989 data year, NCHS has tabulated birth data primarily by race of the mother. In 1988 and prior years, births were tabulated by race of the child, which was determined from the race of the parents as entered on the birth certificate. Trend data by race shown in this section are by race of mother beginning with the 1980 data. Hispanic origin of the mother is reported and tabulated independently of race. Thus, persons of Hispanic origin may be of any race. The majority of women of Hispanic origin are reported as White.

Statistical reliability—For a discussion of statistical collection, estimation, and sampling procedures and measures of reliability applicable to data from NCHS and the Census Bureau, see Appendix III.

Table 81. Live Births, Deaths, Marriages, and Divorces: 1960 to 2015

[4,258 represents 4,258,000. Beginning 1970, excludes births to, and deaths of nonresidents of the United States. See Appendix III]

Year	Number (1,000)					Rate per 1,000 population				
	Births	Deaths Total	Infant [1]	Marriages [2]	Divorces [3]	Births	Deaths Total	Infant [1]	Marriages [2]	Divorces [3]
1960	4,258	1,712	111	1,523	393	23.7	9.5	26.0	8.5	2.2
1970	3,731	1,921	75	2,159	708	18.4	9.5	20.0	10.6	3.5
1975	3,144	1,893	51	2,153	1,036	14.6	8.8	16.1	10.0	4.8
1980	3,612	1,990	46	2,390	1,189	15.9	8.8	12.6	10.6	5.2
1981	3,629	1,978	43	2,422	1,213	15.8	8.6	11.9	10.6	5.3
1982	3,681	1,975	42	2,456	1,170	15.9	8.5	11.5	10.6	5.1
1983	3,639	2,019	41	2,446	1,158	15.6	8.6	11.2	10.5	5.0
1984	3,669	2,039	40	2,477	1,169	15.6	8.6	10.8	10.5	5.0
1985	3,761	2,086	40	2,413	1,190	15.8	8.8	10.6	10.1	5.0
1986	3,757	2,105	39	2,407	1,178	15.6	8.8	10.4	10.0	4.9
1987	3,809	2,123	38	2,403	1,166	15.7	8.8	10.1	9.9	4.8
1988	3,910	2,168	39	2,396	1,167	16.0	8.9	10.0	9.8	4.8
1989	4,041	2,150	40	2,403	1,157	16.4	8.7	9.8	9.7	4.7
1990	4,158	2,148	38	2,443	1,182	16.7	8.6	9.2	9.8	4.7
1991	4,111	2,170	37	2,371	1,187	16.2	8.6	8.9	9.4	4.7
1992	4,065	2,176	35	2,362	1,215	15.8	8.5	8.5	9.3	4.8
1993	4,000	2,269	33	2,334	1,187	15.4	8.7	8.4	9.0	4.6
1994	3,953	2,279	31	2,362	1,191	15.0	8.7	8.0	9.1	4.6
1995	3,900	2,312	30	2,336	1,169	14.6	8.7	7.6	8.9	4.4
1996	3,891	2,315	28	2,344	1,150	14.4	8.6	7.3	8.8	4.3
1997	3,881	2,314	28	2,384	1,163	14.2	8.5	7.2	8.9	4.3
1998	3,942	2,337	28	2,244	[4] 1,135	14.3	8.5	7.2	8.4	[4] 4.2
1999	3,959	2,391	28	2,358	(NA)	14.2	8.6	7.1	8.6	[4] 4.1
2000	4,059	2,403	28	2,315	[5] 944	14.4	8.5	6.9	8.2	[5] 4.0
2001	4,026	2,416	28	2,326	[5] 940	14.1	8.5	6.9	8.2	[5] 4.0
2002	4,022	2,443	28	2,290	[6] 955	14.0	8.5	7.0	8.0	[6] 3.9
2003	4,090	2,448	28	2,245	[7] 927	14.1	8.4	6.9	7.7	[7] 3.8
2004	4,112	2,398	28	2,279	[8] 879	14.0	8.2	6.8	7.8	[8] 3.7
2005	4,138	2,448	28	2,249	[9] 847	14.0	8.3	6.9	7.6	[9] 3.6
2006	4,266	2,426	29	2,193	[9] 872	14.3	8.1	6.7	[10] 7.5	[9] 3.7
2007	4,316	2,424	29	2,197	[9] 856	14.3	8.0	6.8	7.3	[9] 3.6
2008	4,248	2,472	28	2,157	[9] 844	14.0	8.1	6.6	7.1	[9] 3.5
2009	4,131	2,437	26	2,080	[9] 840	13.5	7.9	6.4	6.8	[9] 3.5
2010	3,999	2,468	25	2,096	[9] 872	13.0	8.0	6.2	6.8	[9] 3.6
2011	3,954	2,515	24	2,118	[9] 877	12.7	8.1	6.1	6.8	[9] 3.6
2012	3,953	2,543	24	2,131	[9] 851	12.6	8.1	6.0	6.8	[9] 3.4
2013	3,932	2,597	23	2,081	[11] 832	12.4	8.2	6.0	6.8	[11] 3.3
2014	3,988	2,626	23	2,140	[11] 814	12.5	8.2	5.8	6.9	[11] 3.2
2015	3,978	2,713	23	2,222	[11] 801	12.4	8.4	5.9	6.9	[11] 3.1

NA Not available. [1] Infant mortality rate; infants under 1 year, excluding fetal deaths. [2] Marriages and marriage rates are by place of occurrence. Beginning 1991, data are provisional. Includes estimates for some States through 1965 and for 1976-1977, and marriage licenses for some states for all years except 1973 and 1975. Beginning 1978, includes nonlicensed marriages in California. [3] Divorces and divorce rates are by place of occurrence. Includes reported annulments and some estimated state figures for all years. Beginning 1991, data are provisional. [4] Excludes data for California, Colorado, Indiana, and Louisiana. [5] Excludes data for California, Indiana, Louisiana, and Oklahoma. [6] Excludes data for California, Indiana, and Oklahoma. [7] Excludes data for California, Hawaii, Indiana, and Oklahoma. [8] Excludes data for California, Georgia, Hawaii, Indiana, and Louisiana. [9] Excludes data for California, Georgia, Hawaii, Indiana, Louisiana, and Minnesota. [10] Excludes Louisiana. [11] Excludes data for California, Georgia, Hawaii, Indiana, and Minnesota.

Source: U.S. National Center for Health Statistics, *Births: Final Data for 2015*, Vol. 66, No. 1, January 2017; *Deaths: Final Data for 2014*, Vol. 65, No. 4, June 2016; *Health, United States, 2016*, May 2017; and "National Marriage and Divorce Rate Trends," <https://www.cdc.gov/nchs/nvss/marriage-divorce.htm>, accessed August 2017.

Table 82. Live Births, Birth Rates, and Fertility Rates by Hispanic Origin: 2010 to 2015

[Births in thousands (3,999 represents 3,999,000). Represents registered births. Excludes births to nonresidents of the United States. Data are based on Hispanic origin and race of mother. Persons of Hispanic origin may be of any race. See Appendix III]

Hispanic-origin status and race of mother	Number of births (1,000)				Birth rate per 1,000 population				Fertility rate [1]			
	2010	2013	2014	2015	2010	2013	2014	2015	2010	2013	2014	2015
Total [2]	3,999	3,932	3,988	3,978	13.0	12.4	12.5	12.4	64.1	62.5	62.9	62.5
Hispanic	945	901	914	924	18.7	16.7	16.5	16.3	80.2	72.9	72.1	71.7
Mexican	598	545	546	546	18.2	15.8	15.5	(NA)	78.2	68.4	67.0	(NA)
Puerto Rican	66	68	70	71	14.1	13.3	13.3	(NA)	59.7	57.8	57.5	(NA)
Cuban	17	19	20	21	9.0	9.4	9.9	(NA)	46.4	48.0	52.1	(NA)
Central and South American [3]	143	131	137	142	23.4	21.9	22.0	(NA)	97.1	94.4	94.9	(NA)
Other and unknown Hispanic [4]	121	137	141	144	([3])	([3])	([3])	([3])	([3])	([3])	([3])	([3])
Non-Hispanic [4]	3,027	3,004	3,044	3,022	11.8	11.6	11.7	11.5	60.4	59.9	60.7	60.2
White	2,162	2,129	2,149	2,130	10.9	10.7	10.8	10.7	58.7	58.7	59.5	59.3
Black	590	584	589	589	15.1	14.4	14.4	14.2	66.6	64.6	64.5	64.1

NA Not available. [1] Live births per 1,000 women aged 15 to 44 years in specified group. [2] Includes all races and Hispanic origin status not stated. [3] Rates for the Central and South American population include other and unknown Hispanic. [4] Includes other races not shown separately.

Source: U.S. National Center for Health Statistics, National Vital Statistics Reports, *Births: Final Data for 2015*, Vol. 66, No. 1, January 2017. See also <https://www.cdc.gov/nchs/nvss/births.htm>.

Table 83. Births, Birth Rates, and Fertility Rates by Sex and Mother's Race and Age: 1980 to 2015

[Births in thousands (3,612 represents 3,612,000). Excludes births to nonresidents of the United States. For population bases used to derive these data; see text, this section and Appendix III]

Item	1980	1990	2000	2005	2009	2010	2011	2012	2013	2014	2015
Live births [1]	**3,612**	**4,158**	**4,059**	**4,138**	**4,131**	**3,999**	**3,954**	**3,953**	**3,932**	**3,988**	**3,978**
Male	1,853	2,129	2,077	2,119	2,114	2,047	2,024	2,021	2,013	2,041	2,036
Female	1,760	2,029	1,982	2,019	2,017	1,952	1,930	1,931	1,919	1,947	1,942
Males per 100 females (sex ratio)	105	105	105	105	105	105	105	105	105	105	105
Race and age of mother:											
White	2,936	3,290	3,194	3,229	3,173	3,069	3,020	3,000	2,986	3,020	3,013
Black	568	684	623	633	658	636	633	634	635	641	640
American Indian or Alaska Native	29	39	42	45	49	47	46	46	46	45	44
Asian or Pacific Islander	74	142	201	231	251	247	254	273	266	283	281
Under 20 years	562	533	478	421	415	372	334	309	276	252	232
20 to 24 years	1,226	1,094	1,018	1,040	1,006	952	925	917	897	883	851
25 to 29 years	1,108	1,277	1,088	1,132	1,167	1,134	1,128	1,124	1,121	1,145	1,152
30 to 34 years	550	886	929	951	955	962	987	1,013	1,037	1,081	1,095
35 to 39 years	141	318	452	483	474	465	464	472	484	509	528
40 to 44 years	(NA)	(NA)	90	105	106	107	109	110	109	110	112
45 to 54 years	(NA)	(NA)	4	6	8	8	8	8	8	8	9
Mean age of mother at first birth (years)	22.7	24.2	24.9	25.2	25.2	25.4	25.6	25.8	26.0	26.3	26.4
Birth rate per 1,000 population	**15.9**	**16.7**	**14.4**	**14.0**	**13.5**	**13.0**	**12.7**	**12.6**	**12.4**	**12.5**	**12.4**
Race and age of mother:											
White	15.1	15.8	13.9	13.6	13.0	12.5	12.2	12.1	12.0	12.0	12.0
Black	21.3	22.4	17.0	16.1	15.8	15.1	14.8	14.7	14.5	14.5	14.3
American Indian or Alaska Native	20.7	18.9	14.0	12.6	11.8	11.0	10.7	10.5	10.3	9.9	9.7
Asian or Pacific Islander	19.9	19.0	17.1	15.9	15.1	14.5	14.5	15.1	14.3	14.6	14.0
10 to 14 years	1.1	1.4	0.9	0.6	0.5	0.4	0.4	0.4	0.3	0.3	0.2
15 to 19 years	53.0	59.9	47.7	39.7	37.9	34.2	31.3	29.4	26.5	24.2	22.3
20 to 24 years	115.1	116.5	109.7	101.8	96.2	90.0	85.3	83.1	80.7	79.0	76.8
25 to 29 years	112.9	120.2	113.5	116.5	111.5	108.3	107.2	106.5	105.5	105.8	104.3
30 to 34 years	61.9	80.8	91.2	96.7	97.5	96.5	96.5	97.3	98.0	100.8	101.5
35 to 39 years	19.8	31.7	39.7	46.4	46.1	45.9	47.2	48.3	49.3	51.0	51.8
40 to 44 years	3.9	5.5	8.0	9.1	10.0	10.2	10.3	10.4	10.4	10.6	11.0
45 to 54 years [2]	0.2	0.2	0.5	0.6	0.7	0.7	0.7	0.7	0.8	0.8	0.8
Fertility rate per 1,000 women [3]	**68.4**	**70.9**	**65.9**	**66.7**	**66.2**	**64.1**	**63.2**	**63.0**	**62.5**	**62.9**	**62.5**
White [3]	65.6	68.3	65.3	66.8	66.4	64.4	63.4	63.0	62.7	63.2	63.1
Black [3]	84.7	86.8	70.0	68.5	68.8	66.3	65.5	65.1	64.7	64.6	64.0
American Indian or Alaska Native [3]	82.7	76.2	58.7	53.6	51.6	48.6	47.7	47.0	46.4	44.8	43.9
Asian or Pacific Islander [3]	73.2	69.6	65.8	63.0	61.3	59.2	59.9	62.2	59.2	60.7	58.5

NA Not available. [1] Includes other races not shown separately. [2] The number of births shown is the total for women aged 45–54 years. The rate is computed by relating the births to women aged 45–54 years to women aged 45–49 years. [3] Number of live births per 1,000 women, 15 to 44 years old in specified group.

Source: U.S. National Center for Health Statistics, National Vital Statistics Reports, *Births: Final Data for 2015*, Vol. 66, No. 1, January 2017, and earlier reports; and CDC WONDER Online Database, "Natality for 2007-2015," <http://wonder.cdc.gov/natality.html>, accessed February 2017.

Table 84. Births and Multiple Births by Race and Hispanic Origin of Mother: 1990 to 2015

[Represents registered births. Excludes births to nonresidents of the United States. Data are based on Hispanic origin and race of mother. Persons of Hispanic origin may be of any race. See Appendix III]

Birth order	1990 [1]	2000	2010	2013	2014	2015
All births, total number [2]	**4,158,212**	**4,058,814**	**3,999,386**	**3,932,181**	**3,988,076**	**3,978,497**
Twin births	93,865	118,916	132,562	132,324	135,336	133,155
Triplet and higher order multiple births	3,028	7,325	5,503	4,700	4,526	4,123
Multiple birth rate [3]	23.3	31.1	34.5	34.8	35.1	34.5
Twin birth rate [4]	22.6	29.3	33.1	33.7	33.9	33.5
Triplet and higher order multiple birth rate [5]	72.8	180.5	137.6	119.5	113.5	103.6
Non-Hispanic White births, total number	**2,626,500**	**2,362,968**	**2,162,406**	**2,129,196**	**2,149,302**	**2,130,279**
Twin births	60,210	76,018	79,728	78,072	78,788	76,848
Triplet and higher order multiple births	2,358	5,821	3,842	3,134	3,028	2,617
Multiple birth rate [3]	23.8	34.6	38.6	38.1	38.1	37.3
Twin birth rate [4]	22.9	32.2	36.9	36.7	36.7	36.1
Non-Hispanic Black births, total number	**661,701**	**604,346**	**589,808**	**583,834**	**588,891**	**589,047**
Twin births	17,646	20,173	21,804	22,346	23,546	23,204
Triplet and higher order multiple births	306	506	574	623	528	615
Multiple birth rate [3]	27.1	34.2	37.9	39.3	40.9	40.4
Twin birth rate [4]	26.7	33.4	37.0	38.3	40.0	39.4
Hispanic births, total number	**595,073**	**815,868**	**945,180**	**901,033**	**914,065**	**924,048**
Twin births	10,713	16,470	21,359	21,511	22,051	22,593
Triplet and higher order multiple births	235	659	721	643	588	611
Multiple birth rate [3]	18.4	21.0	23.4	24.6	24.8	25.1
Twin birth rate [4]	18.0	20.2	22.6	23.9	24.1	24.5

[1] Data by Hispanic-origin status exclude data for New Hampshire and Oklahoma, which did not report Hispanic origin. [2] Includes other races not shown separately. [3] Number of live births in all multiple deliveries per 1,000 live births. [4] Number of live births in twin deliveries per 1,000 live births. [5] Births in greater than twin deliveries per 100,000 live births.

Source: U.S. National Center for Health Statistics, National Vital Statistics Reports, *Births: Final Data for 2015*, Vol. 66, No. 1, January 2017. See also <https://www.cdc.gov/nchs/nvss/births.htm>.

Table 85. Births—Number and Rate by State and Island Area: 2015

[Number of births, except rates. Registered births by place of residence. Excludes births to nonresidents of the United States. Based on race and Hispanic origin of mother. See Appendix III]

State and Island Area	All races [1]	Non-Hispanic White	Non-Hispanic Black	American Indian or Alaska Native	Asian or Pacific Islander	Hispanic [2]	Birth rate [3]	Fertility rate [4]
United States [5]...............	3,978,497	2,130,279	589,047	44,299	281,264	924,048	12.4	62.5
Alabama...............	59,657	35,826	18,261	190	1,193	4,295	12.3	62.2
Alaska..................	11,282	6,543	423	2,415	1,114	810	15.3	77.0
Arizona................	85,351	36,976	4,582	5,316	3,518	35,247	12.5	64.7
Arkansas...............	38,886	25,714	7,589	353	1,234	4,008	13.1	67.5
California..............	491,748	141,592	27,035	3,510	80,269	234,237	12.6	60.8
Colorado..............	66,581	40,878	3,453	803	2,973	18,139	12.2	60.2
Connecticut...........	35,746	20,395	4,439	97	2,497	8,275	10.0	52.5
Delaware..............	11,166	5,959	2,986	16	675	1,532	11.8	61.8
District of Columbia....	9,578	2,976	4,802	16	499	1,327	14.2	52.8
Florida................	224,269	102,549	49,609	373	7,603	64,078	11.1	60.0
Georgia...............	131,404	60,328	45,461	298	6,468	17,836	12.9	62.0
Hawaii.................	18,420	4,803	579	35	11,443	2,775	12.9	68.7
Idaho..................	22,827	18,087	240	406	516	3,645	13.8	71.8
Illinois................	158,116	85,424	27,160	205	10,222	33,902	12.3	61.3
Indiana................	84,040	63,472	10,343	120	2,523	7,634	12.7	64.8
Iowa...................	39,482	32,028	2,503	242	1,364	3,418	12.6	67.1
Kansas................	39,154	28,236	2,912	330	1,483	6,300	13.4	69.9
Kentucky..............	55,971	46,344	5,269	88	1,315	3,000	12.6	65.7
Louisiana.............	64,692	34,047	24,064	392	1,498	4,826	13.9	68.5
Maine.................	12,607	11,563	463	143	186	251	9.5	54.3
Maryland..............	73,616	32,412	23,626	279	5,849	11,750	12.3	61.3
Massachusetts.........	71,492	43,651	7,019	141	6,713	13,015	10.5	52.0
Michigan..............	113,312	78,960	21,822	786	4,294	7,431	11.4	60.3
Minnesota.............	69,834	49,673	8,030	1,415	5,659	4,852	12.7	66.3
Mississippi............	38,394	19,635	16,419	259	559	1,613	12.8	64.0
Missouri...............	75,061	57,092	11,304	359	2,129	4,042	12.3	63.8
Montana...............	12,583	10,270	89	1,560	152	573	12.2	67.3
Nebraska..............	26,679	19,201	1,872	557	987	4,249	14.1	72.8
Nevada................	36,298	14,937	4,455	510	3,337	13,225	12.6	63.3
New Hampshire........	12,433	10,928	237	26	527	638	9.3	51.3
New Jersey............	103,127	47,425	14,880	172	12,192	27,919	11.5	60.0
New Mexico............	25,816	7,157	472	3,452	517	14,431	12.4	65.3
New York..............	237,274	114,643	36,392	738	26,556	55,796	12.0	58.8
North Carolina.........	120,843	67,122	28,866	1,964	5,861	18,091	12.0	60.7
North Dakota..........	11,314	8,796	573	985	344	580	14.9	76.4
Ohio..................	139,264	103,586	23,739	253	4,367	6,974	12.0	63.1
Oklahoma.............	53,122	33,293	4,995	5,924	1,762	7,406	13.6	69.1
Oregon...............	45,655	32,147	1,335	813	2,895	8,518	11.3	58.1
Pennsylvania..........	141,047	97,845	20,160	391	6,961	14,950	11.0	58.7
Rhode Island..........	10,993	6,702	952	138	639	2,622	10.4	52.5
South Carolina........	58,139	33,927	17,801	217	1,289	4,942	11.9	61.1
South Dakota..........	12,336	9,063	328	2,166	322	559	14.4	78.2
Tennessee.............	81,685	55,420	16,792	211	2,153	7,264	12.4	62.8
Texas.................	403,618	140,553	49,662	1,270	21,775	191,157	14.7	70.2
Utah..................	50,778	38,473	644	699	1,875	7,876	16.9	78.0
Vermont...............	5,903	5,370	131	25	175	139	9.4	51.1
Virginia...............	103,303	59,244	21,777	254	8,535	13,930	12.3	61.3
Washington............	88,990	55,352	4,619	2,036	10,611	16,073	12.4	62.8
West Virginia..........	19,805	18,442	698	28	225	331	10.7	59.4
Wisconsin.............	67,041	49,024	7,098	1,029	3,276	6,604	11.6	61.8
Wyoming..............	7,765	6,196	87	294	135	963	13.2	70.2
Puerto Rico...........	31,157	1,454	134	40	52	29,464	9.0	44.8
Virgin Islands.........	1,325	104	946	1	15	237	12.8	69.6
Guam.................	3,366	197	34	13	3,098	31	20.8	98.0
American Samoa.......	1,078	–	–	–	1,075	(NA)	19.8	86.3
Northern Marianas.....	427	3	–	–	424	–	8.2	33.0

– Represents zero. NA Not available. [1] Includes persons of other groups, not shown separately. [2] Persons of Hispanic origin may be of any race. [3] Per 1,000 estimated population. [4] Number of births per 1,000 women aged 15 to 44 years. [5] Does not include data for the Island Areas.

Source: U.S. National Center for Health Statistics, National Vital Statistics Reports, *Births: Final Data for 2015*, Vol. 66, No. 1, January 2017. See also <https://www.cdc.gov/nchs/nvss/births.htm>.

Table 86. Total Fertility Rate by Race and Hispanic Origin: 1980 to 2015

[Based on race of mother. Excludes births to nonresidents of United States. The *total fertility rate* is the number of births that 1,000 women would have in their lifetime if, at each year of age, they experienced the birth rates occurring in the specified year. A total fertility rate of 2,100 represents "replacement level" fertility for the total population under current mortality conditions (assuming no net immigration). See Appendix III]

Race and Hispanic origin	1980	1990	2000	2010	2011	2012	2013	2014	2015
Total [1]	**1,840**	**2,081**	**2,056**	**1,931**	**1,895**	**1,881**	**1,858**	**1,863**	**1,844**
White	1,773	2,003	2,051	1,948	1,905	1,886	1,868	1,876	1,864
Black	2,177	2,480	2,129	1,957	1,920	1,900	1,883	1,872	1,853
American Indian or Alaska Native	2,165	2,185	1,773	1,404	1,374	1,350	1,335	1,289	1,263
Asian or Pacific Islander	1,954	2,003	1,892	1,689	1,707	1,770	1,681	1,716	1,646
Hispanic [2]	(NA)	2,960	2,730	2,350	2,240	2,190	2,149	2,131	2,124

NA Not available. [1] For 1980 and 1990, includes births to races not shown separately. Beginning 1992, unknown race of mother is imputed. [2] Persons of Hispanic origin may be of any race.

Source: U.S. National Center for Health Statistics, National Vital Statistics Report, *Births: Final Data for 2015*, Vol. 66, No. 1, January 2017. See also <https://www.cdc.gov/nchs/nvss/births.htm>.

Table 87. Teenagers—Births and Birth Rates by Age, Race, and Hispanic Origin: 1990 to 2015

[Birth rates per 1,000 women in specified group. Based on race and Hispanic origin of mother. See text this section]

Item	Number of births					Birth rate				
	1990	2000	2010	2014	2015	1990	2000	2010	2014	2015
All races, 15 to 19 years	[1] 521,826	468,990	367,678	249,078	229,715	59.9	47.7	34.2	24.2	22.3
15 to 17 years	183,327	157,209	109,173	66,791	61,184	37.5	26.9	17.3	10.9	9.9
18 to 19 years	338,499	311,781	258,505	182,287	168,531	88.6	78.1	58.2	43.8	40.7
White	354,482	333,013	259,058	179,489	165,934	50.8	43.2	31.9	23.0	21.3
Black	151,613	118,954	94,950	59,951	54,746	112.8	77.4	51.1	35.1	32.0
American Indian or Alaska Native	(NA)	8,055	7,408	5,001	4,738	81.1	58.3	38.7	27.3	25.7
Asian or Pacific Islander	(NA)	8,968	6,262	4,637	4,297	26.4	20.5	10.9	7.7	6.9
Hispanic [2]	(NA)	129,469	121,798	85,970	80,364	100.3	87.3	55.7	38.0	34.9
Non-Hispanic	(NA)	335,567	243,634	161,756	148,103	54.8	40.7	28.8	20.3	18.6
Non-Hispanic White	(NA)	204,056	144,102	99,220	90,833	42.5	32.6	23.5	17.3	16.0
Non-Hispanic Black	(NA)	116,019	88,329	54,819	50,039	116.2	79.2	51.5	34.9	31.8

NA Not available. [1] Includes races other than White and Black, not shown separately. [2] Persons of Hispanic origin may be of any race.

Source: U.S. National Center for Health Statistics, National Vital Statistics Reports, *Births: Final Data for 2015*, Vol. 66, No. 1, January 2017, and earlier reports. See also <https://www.cdc.gov/nchs/nvss/births.htm>.

Table 88. Births to Unmarried Women by Race, Hispanic Origin, and Age of Mother: 1990 to 2015

[1,165 represents 1,165,000. Excludes births to nonresidents of the United States. Persons of Hispanic origin may be of any race. Marital status is inferred from a comparison of the child's and parents' surnames on the birth certificate for those states that do not report on marital status. No estimates included for misstatements on birth records or failure to register births. See also Appendix III]

Race/ethnicity and age of mother	Number (1,000)				Percent distribution				Birth rate [1]			
	1990	2000	2010	2015	1990	2000	2010	2015	1990	2000	2010	2015
Total live births [2]	**1,165**	**1,347**	**1,633**	**1,602**	**100.0**	**100.0**	**100.0**	**100.0**	**43.8**	**44.1**	**47.5**	**43.4**
White	670	866	1,102	1,078	57.5	64.3	67.5	67.3	32.9	38.2	44.5	40.4
Black	455	427	459	449	39.1	31.7	28.1	28.0	90.5	70.5	65.3	59.6
American Indian or Alaska Native	(NA)	(NA)	31	29	(NA)	(NA)	1.9	1.8	(NA)	(NA)	(NA)	(NA)
Asian or Pacific Islander	(NA)	(NA)	42	46	(NA)	(NA)	2.6	2.9	(NA)	20.9	22.3	20.4
Hispanic	[3] 219	348	504	489	[3] 18.8	25.8	30.9	30.6	[3] 89.6	87.2	80.6	67.4
Non-Hispanic White	[3] 443	522	628	621	[3] 38.0	38.7	38.4	38.8	[3] 24.4	28.0	32.9	31.6
Non-Hispanic Black	(NA)	415	428	416	(NA)	30.8	26.2	25.9	(NA)	(NA)	(NA)	(NA)
Under 15 years	11	8	4	2	0.9	0.6	0.3	0.2	(NA)	(NA)	(NA)	(NA)
15 to 19 years	350	369	324	204	30.0	27.4	19.8	12.7	42.5	39.0	31.1	20.2
20 to 24 years	404	504	601	561	34.7	37.4	36.8	35.0	65.1	72.2	70.0	59.7
25 to 29 years	230	255	385	435	19.7	18.9	23.6	27.2	56.0	58.5	69.2	66.9
30 to 34 years	118	130	203	252	10.1	9.7	12.5	15.8	37.6	39.3	56.3	60.3
35 to 39 years	44	65	91	117	3.8	4.8	5.6	7.3	17.3	19.7	29.6	34.1
40 years and over [4]	9	16	25	30	0.7	1.2	1.5	1.9	3.6	5.0	8.0	9.0

NA Not available. [1] Rate per 1,000 unmarried women (never-married, widowed, and divorced) estimated as of April 1 for census years and as of July 1 for all other years. Total rate and rates by race/ethnicity cover women 15 to 44 years old. [2] Includes other race/ethnicities, not shown separately. [3] Excludes data for New Hampshire and Oklahoma, which did not report Hispanic origin. [4] Beginning in 1997, birth rates computed by relating births to unmarried mothers aged 40 years and over to unmarried women aged 40–44 years.

Source: U.S. National Center for Health Statistics, National Vital Statistics Reports, *Births: Final Data for 2015*, Vol. 66, No. 1, January 2017, and earlier reports. See also <https://www.cdc.gov/nchs/nvss/births.htm>.

Table 89. Percent of Births to Teenagers, Unmarried Mothers, and Births With Low Birth Weight by Race and Hispanic Origin of Mother: 1990 to 2015

[Represents registered births. Excludes births to nonresidents of the United States. See Appendix III]

Characteristics of mother	1990	2000	2010	2011	2012	2013	2014	2015
Percent of births to teenage mothers [1]	**12.8**	**11.8**	**9.3**	**8.4**	**7.8**	**7.0**	**6.3**	**5.8**
White	10.9	10.6	8.5	7.8	7.3	6.6	6.0	5.6
Black	23.1	19.7	15.2	13.7	12.4	10.8	9.5	8.7
American Indian or Alaska Native	19.5	19.7	16.1	14.9	14.2	12.6	11.3	10.8
Asian or Pacific Islander	5.7	4.5	2.6	2.3	2.0	1.9	1.7	1.5
Hispanic origin [2]	16.8	16.2	13.1	12.1	11.5	10.5	9.5	8.8
Mexican	17.7	17.0	13.8	12.8	12.2	11.1	10.1	9.3
Puerto Rican	21.7	20.0	15.3	14.0	13.3	11.8	10.4	9.8
Cuban	7.7	7.5	6.2	5.6	5.3	4.6	4.2	3.7
Central and South American	9.0	9.9	7.2	6.5	6.1	5.8	5.9	5.9
Other and unknown Hispanic	(NA)	18.8	16.3	14.7	13.7	12.4	11.0	10.0
Non-Hispanic	(NA)	10.7	8.1	7.3	6.7	6.0	5.4	5.0
White	(NA)	8.7	6.7	6.1	5.7	5.1	4.6	4.3
Black	(NA)	19.8	15.2	13.7	12.4	10.8	9.5	8.6
Percent of births to unmarried mothers	**26.6**	**33.2**	**40.8**	**40.7**	**40.7**	**40.6**	**40.2**	**40.3**
White	16.9	27.1	35.9	35.7	35.9	35.8	35.7	35.8
Black	66.7	68.5	72.1	71.8	71.6	71.0	70.4	70.1
American Indian or Alaska Native	53.6	58.4	65.6	66.2	66.9	66.4	65.7	65.8
Asian or Pacific Islander	13.2	14.8	17.0	17.2	17.0	17.0	16.4	16.4
Hispanic origin [2]	36.7	42.7	53.4	53.3	53.5	53.2	52.9	53.0
Mexican	33.3	40.7	52.0	52.0	52.1	51.9	51.6	51.5
Puerto Rican	55.9	59.6	65.2	65.0	65.1	64.6	63.9	64.2
Cuban	18.2	27.3	47.0	48.2	48.8	50.1	49.8	50.7
Central and South American	41.2	44.7	51.8	51.2	50.8	50.1	50.4	51.0
Other and unknown Hispanic	(NA)	46.2	56.3	55.9	56.4	56.1	55.5	55.1
Non-Hispanic	(NA)	30.8	36.9	36.8	36.9	36.8	36.5	36.4
White	(NA)	22.1	29.0	29.0	29.3	29.3	29.2	29.2
Black	(NA)	68.7	72.5	72.3	72.1	71.5	70.9	70.5
Percent of births with low birth weight [3]	**7.0**	**7.6**	**8.1**	**8.1**	**8.0**	**8.0**	**8.0**	**8.1**
White	5.7	6.5	7.1	7.1	7.0	7.0	7.0	7.0
Black	13.3	13.0	13.2	13.0	12.8	12.8	12.8	13.0
American Indian or Alaska Native	6.1	6.8	7.6	7.5	7.6	7.5	7.6	7.5
Asian or Pacific Islander	(NA)	7.3	8.5	8.4	8.2	8.3	8.1	8.4
Hispanic origin [2]	6.1	6.4	7.0	7.0	7.0	7.1	7.1	7.2
Mexican	5.5	6.0	6.5	6.5	6.5	6.6	6.6	6.8
Puerto Rican	9.0	9.3	9.6	9.7	9.4	9.4	9.5	9.4
Cuban	5.7	6.5	7.3	7.1	7.4	7.3	7.5	7.2
Central and South American	5.8	6.3	6.5	6.7	6.6	6.8	6.7	6.7
Other and unknown Hispanic	(NA)	7.8	8.4	8.0	8.0	8.0	7.9	8.1
Non-Hispanic	(NA)	7.9	8.5	8.4	8.3	8.3	8.3	8.3
White	(NA)	6.6	7.1	7.1	7.0	7.0	7.0	6.9
Black	(NA)	13.1	13.5	13.3	13.2	13.1	13.2	13.3

NA Not available. [1] Mothers under 20 years old. [2] Hispanic persons may be of any race. [3] Births less than 2,500 grams (5 pounds, 8 ounces).

Source: U.S. National Center for Health Statistics, National Vital Statistics Reports, *Births: Final Data for 2015*, Vol. 66, No. 1, January 2017, and earlier reports. See also <https://www.cdc.gov/nchs/nvss/births.htm>.

Table 90. Births by Race, Hispanic Origin, and Method of Delivery: 1990 to 2015

[In thousands (4,111 represents 4,111,000), except rate. Persons of Hispanic origin may be of any race. See Appendix III]

Method of delivery	1990 [1]	2000	2010	2013	2014	2015 Total [2]	2015 Hispanic	2015 Non-Hispanic White	2015 Non-Hispanic Black
Births, total	**4,111**	**4,059**	**3,999**	**3,932**	**3,988**	**3,978**	**924**	**2,130**	**589**
Vaginal	3,111	3,108	2,681	2,643	2,700	2,704	631	1,466	380
Cesarean	914	924	1,309	1,284	1,285	1,273	293	663	209
Not stated	85	27	9	5	4	2	(Z)	1	(Z)
Cesarean delivery rate [3]	22.7	22.9	32.8	32.7	32.2	32.0	31.7	31.1	35.5

Z represents less than 500. [1] 1990 excludes data for New Hampshire and Oklahoma, which did not report data by Hispanic origin. Oklahoma also did not report method of delivery on the birth certificate. [2] Includes other races, not shown separately. [3] Percent of all live births by cesarean delivery.

Source: U.S. National Center for Health Statistics, National Vital Statistics Reports, *Births: Final Data for 2015*, Vol. 66, No. 1, January 2017, and earlier reports. See also <https://www.cdc.gov/nchs/nvss/births.htm>.

Table 91. Percent of Births to Teenage Mothers, Unmarried Women, and Births with Low Birth Weight by State: 2014 and 2015

[In percent. By place of residence. Excludes nonresidents of the United States. Data for teenage mothers are not comparable to data in previous editions of this table, as the definition of teenage mothers has changed from women under age 20 to women aged 15-19]

State	Births to teenage mothers [1] 2014	2015	Births to unmarried women 2014	2015	Births with low birth weight [2] 2014	2015	State	Births to teenage mothers [1] 2014	2015	Births to unmarried women 2014	2015	Births with low birth weight [2] 2014	2015
U.S...........	6.2	5.8	40.2	40.3	8.0	8.1	MO.............	6.9	6.4	40.2	40.4	8.2	8.3
AL.............	8.4	7.9	43.3	43.9	10.1	10.4	MT.............	6.5	6.1	36.9	36.3	7.4	7.1
AK.............	5.7	5.9	35.6	36.1	5.9	5.8	NE.............	5.2	5.2	33.0	32.9	6.6	7.1
AZ.............	7.6	6.9	45.1	45.5	7.0	7.2	NV.............	6.8	6.5	45.8	46.7	8.3	8.5
AR.............	9.8	9.5	43.9	45.0	8.9	9.2	NH.............	3.9	3.8	33.7	34.0	6.9	6.9
CA.............	5.4	4.9	38.8	38.8	6.7	6.8	NJ.............	3.6	3.3	35.5	35.1	8.1	8.1
CO.............	5.1	4.9	22.4	22.7	8.8	9.0	NM.............	9.8	9.0	51.3	52.1	8.8	8.7
CT.............	3.9	3.5	37.1	37.5	7.6	7.9	NY.............	4.2	3.8	39.6	39.5	7.9	7.8
DE.............	5.6	4.8	46.6	46.3	8.3	9.3	NC.............	6.8	6.3	41.0	41.0	8.9	9.1
DC.............	5.9	5.2	50.2	49.3	9.8	10.0	ND.............	5.0	4.7	32.4	31.6	6.2	6.2
FL.............	5.8	5.3	47.9	47.8	8.7	8.6	OH.............	6.8	6.3	43.5	43.3	8.5	8.5
GA.............	7.4	6.7	45.4	45.2	9.5	9.5	OK.............	9.0	8.3	42.2	41.8	8.0	7.9
HI.............	4.8	4.3	37.1	37.1	7.9	8.3	OR.............	5.2	5.0	36.1	36.0	6.2	6.4
ID.............	5.7	5.6	27.8	27.7	6.4	6.6	PA.............	5.5	5.1	41.0	41.2	8.3	8.2
IL.............	6.0	5.5	40.1	40.4	8.2	8.3	RI.............	5.5	4.8	45.4	45.1	7.1	7.6
IN.............	7.4	6.9	43.3	43.3	8.0	8.0	SC.............	7.5	6.9	47.3	46.5	9.4	9.5
IA.............	5.2	4.9	35.1	35.3	6.7	6.7	SD.............	6.0	5.8	37.7	37.2	6.5	6.1
KS.............	6.8	6.3	36.5	36.0	7.0	6.8	TN.............	8.3	7.7	44.0	43.9	9.0	9.2
KY.............	8.7	8.0	41.9	41.6	8.8	8.7	TX.............	8.8	8.1	41.7	41.5	8.2	8.2
LA.............	8.2	7.8	52.7	52.9	10.5	10.6	UT.............	4.2	4.0	18.6	18.8	7.0	7.0
ME.............	5.2	4.8	41.2	40.5	7.6	6.9	VT.............	5.0	4.2	39.5	40.2	7.1	6.6
MD.............	4.6	4.4	39.7	40.1	8.6	8.6	VA.............	4.7	4.4	33.9	34.4	7.9	7.9
MA.............	3.3	3.0	33.2	33.4	7.5	7.5	WA.............	4.6	4.2	32.1	32.1	6.4	6.4
MI.............	6.1	5.6	41.8	41.9	8.4	8.5	WV.............	9.7	8.7	44.9	43.8	9.1	9.6
MN.............	3.9	3.4	32.3	32.2	6.6	6.4	WI.............	5.0	4.5	37.8	37.5	7.3	7.3
MS.............	9.9	9.2	54.0	53.5	11.3	11.4	WY.............	7.1	6.6	33.2	33.9	9.2	8.6

[1] Defined as teenage mothers aged 15-19. [2] Less than 2,500 grams (5 pounds, 8 ounces).

Source: U.S. National Center for Health Statistics, National Vital Statistics Reports, *Births: Final Data for 2015, Supplemental Tables*, Vol. 66, No. 1, January 2017, and earlier reports; and CDC WONDER Online Database, "Natality for 2007-2015," <https://wonder.cdc.gov/natality.html>, accessed February 2017.

Table 92. Rate of Pregnancy Risk Factors, Obstetric Procedures and Labor or Delivery Characteristics, and Birth Defects by Age of Mother: 2015

[Rates are number of live births with specified risk factor, procedure, or characteristic per 1,000 live births in specified group; birth defects are per 100,000 live births. In 2015, total number of births to residents of areas reporting risk factors, procedure, or defects was 3,978,497]

Factor/characteristic	Births with factor reported (number)	Rates by age All ages	Under 20 years	20-24 years	25-29 years	30-34 years	35-39 years	40-54 years
RISK FACTORS IN CURRENT PREGNANCY								
Diabetes........................	259,282	65.2	23.3	36.4	56.0	77.5	107.0	142.6
Hypertension, pregnancy-associated........	222,710	56.0	60.7	54.5	53.8	54.0	60.3	79.2
Hypertension, chronic.................	65,223	16.4	5.9	9.6	13.5	18.5	28.0	42.8
OBSTETRIC PROCEDURES AND LABOR OR DELIVERY CHARACTERISTICS								
Induction of labor...................	948,418	238.5	274.2	258.2	242.1	223.8	215.4	230.3
Breech or malpresentation................	209,764	53.6	40.6	44.0	49.8	57.6	67.2	85.7
BIRTH DEFECTS (CONGENITAL ANOMALIES)								
Anencephaly.......................	410	10.3	14.7	12.4	9.9	9.5	8.5	(B)
Meningomyelocele or spina bifida............	500	12.6	13.4	11.5	14.4	12.3	11.0	(B)
Omphalocele or gastroschisis................	1,470	37.0	107.8	66.4	30.6	18.1	15.0	22.4
Cleft lip or palate...................	2,943	74.1	75.9	83.5	74.0	68.2	65.1	98.7
Down syndrome.....................	2,057	51.8	27.2	27.3	27.8	41.0	107.5	354.2

B Base figure too small to meet statistical standards for reliability of a derived figure.

Source: U.S. National Center for Health Statistics, National Vital Statistics Reports, *Births Final Data for 2015: Supplemental Tables*, Vol. 66, No. 1, January 2017. See also <https://www.cdc.gov/nchs/nvss/births.htm>.

Table 93. Induction of Labor by Gestational Age: 1990 to 2014

[In percent. Data are for singleton births]

Gestational age	1990 [1]	1995	2000	2005	2008	2009	2010	2011	2012	2013	2014
All gestations...........	9.2	15.9	19.7	22.2	22.9	23.1	23.3	23.2	22.8	23.0	23.2
Under 20 weeks............	8.2	11.3	13.9	12.0	10.0	10.2	12.5	11.8	10.9	12.9	11.9
20-27 weeks................	4.1	5.7	6.5	5.5	5.6	5.7	5.7	5.3	5.6	5.6	5.6
28-31 weeks................	4.6	7.8	9.0	8.7	8.8	8.8	9.0	8.8	9.0	9.0	9.6
32-35 weeks................	6.4	11.1	13.8	13.9	13.8	13.8	14.0	13.8	13.7	14.1	14.7
36 weeks....................	7.5	12.8	16.3	17.3	17.0	16.6	16.7	16.2	16.1	16.3	17.0
37-39 weeks................	7.6	14.2	18.7	21.6	22.0	21.8	21.9	21.7	21.2	21.2	21.4
40 weeks....................	8.6	16.1	20.6	24.9	26.1	27.1	27.3	27.2	26.7	26.9	26.7
41 weeks....................	13.0	22.4	26.9	30.7	32.2	32.9	33.6	33.7	33.4	34.4	35.1
42 weeks and over..........	14.4	21.1	24.1	26.0	27.2	27.8	28.2	28.0	27.5	27.8	28.4

[1] Oklahoma did not report induction of labor.

Source: U.S. National Center for Health Statistics, "VitalStats," <http://www.cdc.gov/nchs/vitalstats.htm>, accessed April 2016.

Table 94. Premature Births by Whether Early or Late Preterm and by Age, Race, and Hispanic Origin of Mother: 2015

[Based on race and Hispanic origin of mother. Preterm/premature births are those with less than 37 completed weeks of gestation. Based on obstetric estimates; see Technical Notes in source for details]

Characteristic	Number			Percent		
	Total [1]	Early [2]	Late [3]	Total	Early [2]	Late [3]
Total [4]...........................	**382,786**	**109,660**	**273,126**	**9.6**	**2.8**	**6.9**
Age of mother:						
Under 15 years...........................	343	143	200	13.8	5.8	8.0
15 to 19 years...........................	22,735	6,989	15,746	9.9	3.1	6.9
15 years...........................	801	251	550	10.6	3.3	7.3
16 years...........................	1,938	635	1,303	10.5	3.5	7.1
17 years...........................	3,493	1,074	2,419	9.9	3.1	6.9
18 years...........................	6,310	1,982	4,328	10.0	3.1	6.8
19 years...........................	10,193	3,047	7,146	9.7	2.9	6.8
20 to 24 years...........................	78,833	22,812	56,021	9.3	2.7	6.6
25 to 29 years...........................	102,751	28,932	73,819	8.9	2.5	6.4
30 to 34 years...........................	102,345	28,785	73,560	9.4	2.6	6.7
35 to 39 years...........................	58,419	16,801	41,618	11.1	3.2	7.9
40 to 44 years...........................	15,288	4,530	10,758	13.7	4.1	9.6
45 years and older...........................	2,072	668	1,404	23.2	7.5	15.7
Race and Hispanic origin of mother:						
Non-Hispanic White...........................	189,146	49,817	139,329	8.9	2.3	6.5
Non-Hispanic Black...........................	78,911	28,438	50,473	13.4	4.8	8.6
Hispanic [5]...........................	84,418	23,266	61,152	9.1	2.5	6.6

[1] Total includes those unknown, not shown separately. [2] Less than 34 completed weeks of gestation. [3] 34-36 completed weeks of gestation. [4] Includes races other than White and Black, not shown separately. [5] Persons of Hispanic origin may be of any race.

Source: U.S. National Center for Health Statistics, *Births, Final Data for 2015*, Vol. 66, No. 1, January 2017. See also <https://www.cdc.gov/nchs/nvss/births.htm>.

Table 95. Women Who Had a Birth in the Past 12 Months by Selected Characteristics: 2015

[For women aged 15 to 50 years old. Based on the 2015 American Community Survey (ACS). The ACS sample includes the household population and the population living in institutions, dormitories, and other group quarters. Based on a sample and subject to sampling variability. See Appendix III for details]

Characteristic	Total women (number)	Women who had a child in the past 12 months			
		Number	Percent distribution	Rate per 1,000 women	Percent unmarried
Total, aged 15 to 50 years...........................	**76,551,119**	**3,931,053**	**(X)**	**51**	**35.7**
Age:					
15 to 19 years...........................	10,460,193	166,984	4.2	16	84.2
20 to 34 years...........................	32,738,955	2,925,125	74.4	89	37.3
35 to 50 years...........................	33,351,971	838,944	21.3	25	20.1
Race/ethnicity:					
One race...........................	74,218,234	3,812,768	97.0	51	35.4
White...........................	53,356,902	2,698,271	68.6	51	29.6
Black or African American...........................	10,817,292	569,659	14.5	53	66.6
American Indian and Alaska Native...........................	667,604	39,553	1.0	59	55.3
Asian...........................	4,967,052	247,130	6.3	50	12.2
Native Hawaiian and Other Pacific Islander...........................	158,980	11,005	0.3	69	49.5
Some other race...........................	4,250,404	247,150	6.3	58	45.6
Two or more races...........................	2,332,885	118,285	3.0	51	45.2
Hispanic origin:					
Hispanic or Latino origin (of any race)...........................	14,966,229	879,122	22.4	59	44.0
White alone, not Hispanic or Latino...........................	43,528,688	2,114,920	53.8	49	26.0
Nativity:					
Native...........................	63,571,102	3,150,052	80.1	50	38.4
Foreign born [1]...........................	12,980,017	781,001	19.9	60	24.6
Education:					
Less than high school graduate...........................	13,233,416	520,398	13.2	39	56.8
High school graduate (includes equivalency)...........................	16,274,932	908,204	23.1	56	51.9
Some college or associate's degree...........................	24,962,758	1,253,050	31.9	50	40.4
Bachelor's degree...........................	14,664,312	780,653	19.9	53	12.5
Graduate or professional degree...........................	7,415,701	468,748	11.9	63	6.6
Poverty status in past 12 months:					
Women 15 to 50 years old with poverty status determined......	74,826,771	3,919,986	(X)	52	35.5
Below 100 percent of poverty level...........................	13,150,145	1,000,721	25.5	76	67.3
100 to 199 percent of poverty level...........................	13,787,845	834,653	21.3	61	39.9
200 percent or more above poverty level...........................	47,888,781	2,084,612	53.2	44	18.5
Labor force status:					
In labor force [2]...........................	53,431,276	2,446,961	62.4	46	36.5
Public assistance income in past 12 months:					
Received public assistance income...........................	1,720,373	199,637	5.1	116	70.9
Did not receive public assistance income...........................	74,830,746	3,731,416	94.9	50	33.8

X Not applicable. [1] Excludes persons born outside of the United States to a parent who is a U.S. citizen. [2] Data are shown for women aged 16-50 years old.

Source: U.S. Census Bureau, 2015 American Community Survey, S1301, "Fertility," <http://factfinder.census.gov>, accessed December 2016.

Table 96. Women by Number of Children Ever Born by Age, Marital Status, and Race/Ethnicity: 2016

[75,919 represents 75,919,000. As of June. Data shown are for women aged 15 to 50. Based on the Current Population Survey; for more information, see <http://www.census.gov/cps/methodology>]

Age and marital status	Total women (1,000)	Percent distribution by number of children ever born						
		None	One	Two	Three	Four	Five and six	Seven or more
Total women: [1]............................	**75,919**	**43.4**	**17.1**	**21.5**	**11.1**	**4.4**	**2.1**	**0.4**
By age:								
15 to 19 years old............................	10,292	96.2	2.9	0.5	0.3	0.2	–	–
20 to 24 years old............................	10,833	75.8	16.2	6.1	1.6	0.2	0.1	–
25 to 29 years old............................	11,190	53.8	20.9	16.0	6.7	2.2	0.4	–
30 to 34 years old............................	10,779	30.8	21.8	26.8	12.8	5.1	2.6	0.2
35 to 39 years old............................	10,364	18.5	18.9	31.7	18.1	7.7	4.2	1.0
40 to 44 years old............................	9,924	14.4	18.3	34.9	19.6	7.9	3.9	1.0
45 to 50 years old............................	12,537	17.1	19.7	33.6	18.2	7.7	3.4	0.5
By marital status:								
Women ever married.........................	41,441	17.2	21.2	33.6	17.3	6.9	3.2	0.6
Women never married........................	34,478	74.9	12.1	6.9	3.7	1.5	0.7	0.2
By race and Hispanic origin:								
White alone....................................	56,263	43.4	16.2	22.4	11.5	4.3	2.0	0.4
White alone, non-Hispanic................	43,002	44.9	16.4	23.0	10.4	3.6	1.5	0.3
Black alone....................................	11,188	40.6	21.0	17.7	10.9	5.8	3.3	0.6
Asian alone...................................	5,190	47.6	18.8	22.6	7.5	2.8	0.5	0.1
Hispanic alone [2]...........................	15,091	38.8	15.8	20.2	14.7	6.6	3.5	0.5

– Represents or rounds to zero. [1] Includes women of other races, not shown separately. [2] Persons of Hispanic origin may be of any race.

Source: U.S. Census Bureau, "Fertility of Women in the United States: 2016," <https://www.census.gov/topics/health/fertility/data/tables.html>, accessed May 2017.

Table 97. Women's Relationship Status and Age at First Birth by Current Age and Race/Ethnicity: 2016

[In percent, except as noted (42,984 represents 42,984,000). As of June. Data are from the Current Population Survey; for more information, see <https://www.census.gov/programs-surveys/cps.html>.]

Current age and race/ethnicity	Total mothers, 1,000	Married at first birth			Not married at first birth					
					Living with unmarried partner			Neither married nor living with unmarried partner		
		Under age 20 at first birth	Age 20 to 25 at first birth	Over age 25 at first birth	Under age 20 at first birth	Age 20 to 25 at first birth	Over age 25 at first birth	Under age 20 at first birth	Age 20 to 25 at first birth	Over age 25 at first birth
TOTAL										
15 to 50 years old....	**42,984**	**6.4**	**22.4**	**33.7**	**6.3**	**10.0**	**4.2**	**7.4**	**7.5**	**2.2**
15 to 19 years old.......	391	16.9	(X)	(X)	23.3	(X)	(X)	59.8	(X)	(X)
20 to 24 years old.......	2,619	7.6	15.4	(X)	17.7	22.4	(X)	19.4	17.5	(X)
25 to 29 years old.......	5,174	6.9	23.7	11.2	10.9	17.8	4.4	11.2	12.7	1.3
30 to 34 years old.......	7,463	8.4	20.1	30.6	7.4	11.6	5.0	6.9	7.6	2.4
35 to 39 years old.......	8,447	6.7	23.6	37.1	5.6	7.8	5.0	6.4	5.6	2.2
40 to 44 years old.......	8,491	6.3	23.1	42.2	4.4	7.0	3.9	5.4	4.9	2.8
45 to 50 years old.......	10,399	3.8	24.7	46.9	2.0	6.4	4.2	3.2	6.2	2.7
WHITE ALONE										
15 to 50 years old.....	31,861	7.1	24.6	36.3	6.1	9.8	4.0	5.3	5.4	1.6
15 to 19 years old.......	265	17.1	(X)	(X)	29.7	(X)	(X)	53.3	(X)	(X)
20 to 24 years old.......	1,851	10.0	17.7	(X)	18.3	24.7	(X)	15.7	13.6	(X)
25 to 29 years old.......	3,706	7.8	27.4	13.7	10.9	18.0	4.3	7.5	9.5	0.8
30 to 34 years old.......	5,483	9.9	22.1	32.7	6.6	11.3	5.2	5.2	5.4	1.7
35 to 39 years old.......	6,251	7.0	26.0	39.0	5.5	7.7	4.9	4.5	3.8	1.6
40 to 44 years old.......	6,339	6.7	24.6	45.2	4.2	6.7	3.2	4.0	3.8	1.6
45 to 50 years old.......	7,966	4.2	26.3	49.7	2.0	5.9	3.8	1.9	4.2	2.0
BLACK ALONE										
15 to 50 years old.....	6,650	3.8	13.1	15.3	7.3	12.7	5.1	17.9	19.4	5.6
15 to 19 years old.......	75	15.7	(X)	(X)	3.5	(X)	(X)	80.8	(X)	(X)
20 to 24 years old.......	524	2.0	8.6	(X)	13.0	12.8	(X)	30.6	33.0	(X)
25 to 29 years old.......	994	3.6	7.1	3.4	11.9	17.4	3.0	23.8	26.8	2.9
30 to 34 years old.......	1,145	3.2	12.0	11.5	9.5	15.4	5.9	16.7	20.2	5.7
35 to 39 years old.......	1,232	5.9	14.0	18.2	6.9	11.2	5.6	17.5	15.3	5.4
40 to 44 years old.......	1,215	3.5	16.4	19.1	6.1	12.1	7.4	14.5	12.3	8.7
45 to 50 years old.......	1,464	2.7	16.7	26.8	1.8	9.7	5.6	10.3	19.1	7.3
HISPANIC [1]										
15 to 50 years old.....	9,240	11.0	25.2	20.5	9.4	11.8	4.4	7.9	7.6	2.0
15 to 19 years old.......	120	7.8	(X)	(X)	44.2	(X)	(X)	48.0	(X)	(X)
20 to 24 years old.......	772	14.5	15.4	(X)	16.5	19.7	(X)	19.7	14.2	(X)
25 to 29 years old.......	1,269	12.9	22.8	4.5	13.6	17.7	3.2	12.4	12.2	0.7
30 to 34 years old.......	1,630	14.8	19.5	18.8	11.1	14.2	3.6	7.6	8.1	2.4
35 to 39 years old.......	1,822	11.5	27.6	20.6	9.7	10.8	6.8	6.6	4.6	1.8
40 to 44 years old.......	1,768	9.1	30.1	27.9	6.1	7.8	5.2	4.9	5.7	3.3
45 to 50 years old.......	1,859	6.7	30.7	35.5	2.8	7.9	5.1	2.0	6.6	2.7

– Represents or rounds to zero. X Not applicable. [1] Persons of Hispanic origin may be of any race.

Source: U.S. Census Bureau, "Fertility of Women in the United States: 2016," <https://www.census.gov/topics/health/fertility/data/tables.html>, accessed August 2017.

Table 98. Women Who Had a Birth in the Past Year Who Are in the Labor Force by Educational Attainment: 2010 to 2015

[In thousands (2,562 represents 2,562,000), except percent. For women aged 16 to 50 years old. Based on the American Community Survey (ACS). The ACS universe includes the household population and population living in institutions, college dormitories, and other group quarters. Based on a sample and subject to sampling variability, see Appendix III]

Year	Number of women who had a birth in the past year who are in the labor force					Percent of women who had a birth in the past year who are in the labor force				
	Total	Less than high school diploma	High school diploma or GED	Some college	Bachelor's degree or higher	Total	Less than high school diploma	High school diploma or GED	Some college	Bachelor's degree or higher
2010........	2,562	278	589	859	836	61.6	39.7	57.9	66.4	72.7
2011........	2,547	275	541	849	882	62.1	41.4	57.5	65.5	73.4
2012........	2,554	256	536	869	893	62.1	41.0	56.4	65.7	73.4
2013........	2,418	221	513	805	879	61.7	38.8	56.4	64.4	73.8
2014........	2,436	203	508	815	909	61.8	38.2	55.4	64.9	73.7
2015........	2,447	196	508	816	927	62.4	38.2	56.0	65.1	74.2

Source: U.S. Census Bureau, "Fertility: Historical Time Series Tables," <https://www.census.gov/topics/health/fertility/data/tables.html>, accessed May 2017.

Table 99. Women With Births in the Past 12 Months by Citizenship Status, Educational Attainment, and Poverty Status by State: 2015

[In percent, except for total. For women 15 to 50 years old. Based on 2015 American Community Survey (ACS). See headnote, Table 95]

State	Total (number)	Citizenship status		Educational attainment					Below poverty [3]
		Native born	Foreign born [1]	Less than high school graduate	High school graduate [2]	Some college or associate's degree	Bachelor's degree	Graduate or professional degree	
United States......	**3,931,053**	**80.1**	**19.9**	**13.2**	**23.1**	**31.9**	**19.9**	**11.9**	**25.5**
Alabama..............	59,374	92.9	7.1	14.2	22.6	38.4	17.1	7.7	32.0
Alaska...............	11,144	90.5	9.5	9.5	32.5	29.9	18.9	9.3	18.3
Arizona..............	85,798	81.5	18.5	17.6	22.0	35.8	17.8	6.8	30.6
Arkansas.............	41,817	91.6	8.4	16.5	27.0	35.8	13.1	7.6	38.5
California............	478,813	64.6	35.4	15.9	22.0	31.0	19.3	11.8	24.0
Colorado.............	65,555	82.9	17.1	12.3	21.5	27.8	24.9	13.5	19.7
Connecticut..........	34,705	76.2	23.8	8.6	20.6	28.4	22.0	20.5	18.8
Delaware.............	9,736	77.4	22.6	10.2	20.7	26.1	24.8	18.1	18.3
District of Columbia...	8,575	86.1	13.9	10.1	19.2	17.7	14.5	38.5	16.1
Florida...............	208,713	72.9	27.1	14.2	28.2	30.9	17.4	9.3	28.8
Georgia..............	137,866	84.3	15.7	15.7	23.8	32.9	18.5	9.1	28.0
Hawaii...............	18,465	80.3	19.7	10.7	21.9	40.3	18.0	9.1	21.6
Idaho................	22,597	89.5	10.5	9.0	25.2	39.2	21.7	5.0	25.5
Illinois...............	159,167	79.1	20.9	10.7	20.7	31.4	21.8	15.4	23.7
Indiana..............	80,320	90.1	9.9	13.5	23.6	33.8	19.5	9.6	25.1
Iowa.................	43,263	91.2	8.8	10.7	18.1	38.2	25.1	7.9	22.7
Kansas...............	38,186	87.5	12.5	14.3	20.3	31.1	22.3	12.0	26.3
Kentucky.............	53,925	92.5	7.5	13.2	25.2	36.9	14.6	10.1	33.0
Louisiana............	62,415	93.7	6.3	13.8	25.3	36.8	16.5	7.6	30.2
Maine................	11,600	95.2	4.8	12.2	22.1	33.1	22.9	9.6	24.6
Maryland.............	76,129	78.2	21.8	11.4	19.3	27.4	22.9	19.0	19.0
Massachusetts........	72,160	72.8	27.2	10.0	19.0	23.2	24.5	23.4	19.9
Michigan.............	114,616	89.1	10.9	13.0	23.7	35.1	17.7	10.5	29.7
Minnesota............	74,614	82.7	17.3	8.8	17.0	36.1	26.3	11.8	19.0
Mississippi...........	34,417	95.8	4.2	14.6	24.6	37.9	12.5	10.3	35.4
Missouri.............	72,010	93.8	6.2	11.4	21.8	33.2	19.9	13.7	25.6
Montana.............	12,432	97.7	2.3	8.5	27.4	27.9	25.5	10.7	28.3
Nebraska.............	29,431	86.6	13.4	9.9	21.7	34.1	23.8	10.5	26.5
Nevada..............	33,774	71.7	28.3	19.7	27.6	34.1	15.0	3.7	27.8
New Hampshire.......	15,223	84.7	15.3	10.7	23.1	25.4	24.8	16.0	15.3
New Jersey...........	101,634	66.5	33.5	9.1	20.2	26.6	26.8	17.3	20.8
New Mexico..........	24,412	89.6	10.4	20.1	25.1	37.0	8.7	9.1	34.7
New York............	219,972	69.1	30.9	12.7	21.1	26.4	20.3	19.5	24.3
North Carolina........	119,725	83.9	16.1	13.2	19.8	34.4	19.7	12.8	27.5
North Dakota.........	12,118	97.1	2.9	6.5	19.0	38.6	28.3	7.5	16.4
Ohio.................	141,168	90.7	9.3	14.0	24.5	31.4	17.7	12.4	27.8
Oklahoma............	47,490	88.9	11.1	15.5	26.6	31.7	19.4	6.8	29.3
Oregon..............	46,087	83.2	16.8	10.9	25.9	32.3	18.5	12.3	26.8
Pennsylvania.........	149,372	89.0	11.0	11.5	26.5	25.8	21.6	14.6	25.0
Rhode Island.........	13,820	77.5	22.5	8.7	23.8	33.3	23.0	11.3	22.8
South Carolina........	61,316	91.8	8.2	11.4	28.1	34.5	15.0	11.0	27.7
South Dakota.........	10,875	95.2	4.8	10.2	24.5	33.8	25.4	6.2	29.5
Tennessee............	80,773	88.8	11.2	12.6	26.6	31.2	19.2	10.5	29.4
Texas................	395,878	75.0	25.0	17.0	24.9	31.9	18.2	8.0	27.5
Utah................	51,060	88.6	11.4	7.0	19.0	42.0	27.4	4.6	17.9
Vermont.............	5,651	92.7	7.3	7.2	25.3	33.9	20.9	12.7	14.2
Virginia..............	102,870	78.5	21.5	10.1	19.9	31.2	22.4	16.3	19.0
Washington...........	86,668	76.0	24.0	10.3	22.2	34.8	21.0	11.7	20.4
West Virginia.........	19,670	97.5	2.5	12.4	32.9	29.4	14.2	11.1	33.3
Wisconsin............	65,927	92.6	7.4	8.2	21.9	35.4	23.2	11.3	20.1
Wyoming.............	7,727	94.1	5.9	5.9	28.5	43.8	15.1	6.8	29.3

[1] Foreign born excludes people born outside the U.S. to a parent who is a U.S. citizen. [2] Includes equivalency. [3] The population universe used when determining poverty status excludes people institutionalized, in military group quarters, and in college dormitories, and unrelated individuals under 15 years old.

Source: U.S. Census Bureau, 2015 American Community Survey, Tables B13008, B13010, and B13014, <http://factfinder.census.gov>, accessed December 2016.

Table 100. Women Who Had a Birth in the Past 12 Months by Household Income and Marital Status: 2015

[In thousands (3,827.1 represents 3,827,100), except percent. Data shown for women aged 15 to 50 years old; does not include women living in group quarters. Based on the American Community Survey (ACS). Based on a sample and subject to sampling variability]

Annual household income	Total women	Women with a birth in the past 12 months			Percent of total women	Percent of women with a birth in the past 12 months		
		Total	Married [1]	Unmarried [2]		Total	Married [1]	Unmarried [2]
Under $10,000.................	3,827.1	247.8	56.5	191.3	5.1	6.3	2.3	13.1
$10,000-$14,999..............	2,330.4	141.4	44.7	96.7	3.1	3.6	1.8	6.6
$15,000-$24,999..............	5,618.4	347.5	139.7	207.8	7.5	8.9	5.7	14.2
$25,000-$34,999..............	6,148.0	365.9	188.7	177.3	8.2	9.4	7.7	12.1
$35,000-$49,999..............	9,069.5	499.2	284.8	214.4	12.2	12.8	11.6	14.7
$50,000-$74,999..............	13,705.6	712.7	473.5	239.3	18.4	18.2	19.4	16.4
$75,000-$99,999..............	10,670.9	532.5	397.1	135.4	14.3	13.6	16.2	9.3
$100,000-$149,999..........	12,780.0	600.2	472.1	128.1	17.1	15.4	19.3	8.8
$150,000-$199,999..........	5,317.0	237.1	196.4	40.7	7.1	6.1	8.0	2.8
$200,000 or more............	5,151.2	222.4	192.7	29.7	6.9	5.7	7.9	2.0

[1] Includes women who are married, spouse present. [2] Includes women who are widowed, divorced, separated, and never married.

Source: U.S. Census Bureau, "Fertility of Women in the United States: 2016," <https://www.census.gov/topics/health/fertility/data/tables.html>, accessed May 2017.

Table 101. Sexually Active High School Students and Birth Control Use by Sex, Race/Ethnicity, and Grade: 2015

[In percent. For public and private school students in grades 9 to 12. Current sexual activity defined as having had sexual intercourse with at least one person during the 3 months before the survey. Based on the Youth Risk Behavior Survey; see source for details]

Item	Total	Race/ethnicity			Grade level			
		White [1]	Black [1]	Hispanic	9th	10th	11th	12th
TOTAL								
Ever had sexual intercourse......................	41.2	39.9	48.5	42.5	24.1	35.7	49.6	58.1
Currently sexually active..........................	30.1	30.3	33.1	30.3	15.7	25.5	35.5	46.0
Condom use [2].....................................	56.9	56.8	63.4	55.6	60.5	59.9	57.7	52.9
Birth control use [3]..................................	26.8	33.3	15.9	17.8	16.4	24.4	30.9	29.6
No pregnancy prevention method [2]..............	13.8	10.4	15.9	20.0	16.5	12.3	11.1	15.5
MALE								
Ever had sexual intercourse......................	43.2	39.5	58.8	45.1	27.3	37.9	51.2	59.0
Currently sexually active..........................	30.3	29.1	40.0	30.5	17.3	26.4	34.5	45.4
Condom use [2].....................................	61.5	58.1	73.6	62.5	63.3	65.6	62.5	57.4
Birth control use [3]..................................	20.2	27.0	13.1	12.3	13.1	15.5	25.5	22.7
No pregnancy prevention method [2]..............	12.2	10.3	9.9	17.2	12.1	11.7	9.9	14.2
FEMALE								
Ever had sexual intercourse......................	39.2	40.3	37.4	39.8	20.7	33.5	48.2	57.2
Currently sexually active..........................	29.8	31.4	25.7	30.1	14.0	24.7	36.7	46.5
Condom use [2].....................................	52.0	55.9	46.7	48.3	56.7	54.0	52.9	48.8
Birth control use [3]..................................	33.7	39.2	20.5	23.2	20.8	33.6	36.2	36.2
No pregnancy prevention method [2]..............	15.2	10.2	25.6	22.7	22.0	12.9	12.3	16.2

[1] Non-Hispanic. [2] During last sexual intercourse. [3] Includes use of birth control pills, an IUD or implant, or a shot, patch, or birth control ring.

Source: U.S. Centers for Disease Control and Prevention, *Morbidity and Mortality Weekly Report, Surveillance Summaries*, 65:6, June 10, 2016, "Youth Risk Behavior Surveillance—United States, 2015." See also <http://www.cdc.gov/healthyyouth/data/yrbs/index.htm>.

Table 102. Adults Reporting Sexual Contact with Opposite- and Same-Sex Partners by Sex, Age, and Race/Ethnicity: 2011 to 2013

[In percent, except as indicated (55,271 represents 55,271,000). Data shown for persons aged 18 to 44 years old who have ever had specified types of sexual contact. Based on the 2011-2013 National Survey of Family Growth. See Appendix III]

Sex and selected characteristics	Number (1,000)	Percent reporting type of sexual contact [1]				
		Opposite-sex sexual contact [2]	Vaginal intercourse with opposite-sex partner	Oral sex with opposite-sex partner	Anal sex with opposite-sex partner	Same-sex sexual contact [3]
Women [1].................................	**55,271**	**95.3**	**94.2**	**86.2**	**35.9**	**17.4**
By age:						
18 to 24 years old...........................	14,269	85.6	81.7	77.3	28.4	19.4
25 to 44 years old...........................	41,002	98.7	98.5	89.3	38.5	16.7
By race/ethnicity:						
White alone, non-Hispanic..................	31,880	95.4	93.9	91.9	40.5	19.6
Black alone, non-Hispanic..................	7,581	96.3	95.6	82.7	27.5	19.4
Hispanic.......................................	10,811	95.8	95.5	77.7	32.3	11.2
Men [1]..................................	**54,685**	**93.5**	**92.0**	**87.4**	**42.3**	**6.2**
By age:						
18 to 24 years old...........................	14,718	83.5	79.9	77.6	29.3	6.6
25 to 44 years old...........................	39,967	97.2	96.5	91.0	47.0	6.0
By race/ethnicity:						
White alone, non-Hispanic..................	31,423	93.7	92.0	91.0	44.1	6.9
Black alone, non-Hispanic..................	6,304	96.3	95.4	90.4	35.4	5.3
Hispanic.......................................	11,292	93.3	92.4	78.6	40.4	6.2

[1] Includes other race/ethnicities not shown separately. [2] Includes vaginal, oral, or anal sex. [3] For women, any sexual contact with same-sex (female) partners includes oral sex or any sexual experience. For men, includes oral or anal sex with male partners.

Source: U.S. National Center for Health Statistics, National Health Statistics Reports, *Sexual Behavior, Sexual Attraction, and Sexual Orientation Among Adults Aged 18-44 in the United States: Data From the 2011-2013 National Survey of Family Growth*, No. 88, January 2016. See also <http://www.cdc.gov/nchs/nsfg/>.

Table 103. Sexual Attraction and Orientation by Sex, Age, and Race/Ethnicity: 2011 to 2013

[In percent, except as indicated (55,271 represents 55,271,000). Data shown for persons aged 18 to 44 years old. Based on the 2011-2013 National Survey of Family Growth. See Appendix III]

Sex and sexual attraction and orientation	Total [1]	Age				Race/ethnicity		
		18 to 24 years old	25 to 44 years old			White, Non-Hispanic	Black, Non-Hispanic	His-panic
			Total	25 to 34 years old	35 to 44 years old			
Women (1,000)	**55,271**	**14,269**	**41,002**	**20,790**	**20,212**	**31,880**	**7,581**	**10,811**
Percent distribution								
Sexual attraction:								
Total	100.0	100.0	100.0	100.0	100.0	100.0	100.0	100.0
Only opposite sex	81.0	75.9	82.8	79.1	86.6	79.6	84.2	84.7
Mostly opposite sex	12.9	14.4	12.4	15.4	9.2	15.2	9.1	9.3
Equally to both	3.2	5.3	2.5	3.3	1.7	2.9	3.7	3.5
Mostly same sex	0.8	1.7	0.5	0.3	0.7	0.8	0.6	1.1
Only same sex	0.8	1.0	0.8	0.9	0.6	0.9	0.8	0.8
Not sure	1.2	1.6	1.1	0.9	1.3	0.7	1.7	0.5
Sexual orientation:								
Total	100.0	100.0	100.0	100.0	100.0	100.0	100.0	100.0
Heterosexual or straight	92.3	89.5	93.3	92.5	94.2	93.1	93.1	92.6
Homosexual, gay, or lesbian	1.3	1.8	1.1	1.2	0.9	1.3	1.1	1.2
Bisexual	5.5	7.8	4.7	5.4	4.0	5.4	4.9	4.2
Not reported [2]	0.9	0.9	0.9	1.0	0.9	0.2	0.9	1.9
Men (1,000)	**54,685**	**14,718**	**39,967**	**20,453**	**19,514**	**31,423**	**6,304**	**11,292**
Percent distribution								
Sexual attraction:								
Total	100.0	100.0	100.0	100.0	100.0	100.0	100.0	100.0
Only opposite sex	92.1	88.6	93.4	92.7	94.1	92.5	93.5	91.5
Mostly opposite sex	4.1	5.9	3.4	3.4	3.5	3.9	2.8	3.9
Equally to both	0.9	1.0	0.7	0.9	0.6	0.9	0.4	1.1
Mostly same sex	0.8	0.7	0.8	1.2	0.3	0.6	1.1	0.8
Only same sex	1.5	2.5	1.2	1.0	1.4	1.7	0.9	1.8
Not sure	0.7	1.3	0.5	0.8	(S)	0.3	1.3	0.8
Sexual orientation:								
Total	100.0	100.0	100.0	100.0	100.0	100.0	100.0	100.0
Heterosexual or straight	95.1	94.0	95.4	95.4	95.5	95.4	96.5	93.2
Homosexual, gay, or lesbian	1.9	2.6	1.7	1.6	1.7	2.0	1.5	2.1
Bisexual	2.0	2.5	1.8	2.2	1.3	2.2	1.6	2.0
Not reported [2]	1.0	0.9	1.1	0.8	1.4	0.4	0.4	2.7

S Figure does not meet publication standards. [1] Includes other race/ethnicities not shown separately. [2] Includes "don't know" and "refused" survey responses.

Source: U.S. National Center for Health Statistics, National Health Statistics Reports, *Sexual Behavior, Sexual Attraction, and Sexual Orientation Among Adults Aged 18-44 in the United States: Data From the 2011-2013 National Survey of Family Growth*, No. 88, January 2016. See also <http://www.cdc.gov/nchs/nsfg/>.

Table 104. Contraceptive Use Among Women by Race/Ethnicity, Age, and Method: 1995 to 2015

[In percent. Covers women who are sexually active. Based on National Survey of Family Growth interviews of women of childbearing age. Survey collects up to four methods of contraception used in the month of interview; percents may not add to total because more than one method could have been used in month of interview]

Year and race/ethnicity	By age [1,2]					By method					
	15 to 44 years, total	15 to 19 years	20 to 24 years	25 to 34 years	35 to 44 years	Female steril-ization	Inject-able	Pill [3]	Intra-uterine device	Con-dom	With-drawal
Total women: [4]											
1995	92.5	80.2	91.7	94.0	93.9	27.8	3.0	27.0	0.8	23.4	6.1
2002	89.3	82.0	87.9	90.2	90.7	27.0	5.5	31.0	2.1	23.8	8.8
2006 to 2010	89.0	82.0	87.0	89.8	90.6	26.6	3.9	28.4	5.6	23.1	10.1
2011 to 2015	89.7	84.9	89.1	89.9	90.9	23.2	4.2	26.6	11.5	22.2	14.0
White alone, non-Hispanic:											
1995	93.0	81.7	93.0	93.9	94.2	24.5	2.4	28.7	0.7	22.5	6.4
2002	90.9	84.4	90.9	91.5	91.7	23.9	4.3	34.9	1.7	21.7	9.5
2006 to 2010	90.5	85.7	89.1	91.6	91.2	23.6	2.5	33.1	5.6	20.8	10.3
2011 to 2015	91.2	89.4	90.0	91.3	92.2	20.7	2.8	30.9	11.4	20.9	13.8
Black alone, non-Hispanic:											
1995	90.0	80.0	91.3	91.6	90.9	39.9	5.4	23.7	(S)	24.9	3.3
2002	84.7	82.2	74.8	88.9	86.0	39.2	9.4	23.1	(S)	29.6	4.8
2006 to 2010	82.8	77.3	79.4	82.1	86.3	37.3	8.9	18.7	5.0	29.9	7.1
2011 to 2015	86.5	78.5	85.4	89.0	86.6	30.9	10.0	19.5	8.8	25.6	12.4
Hispanic or Latina: [5]											
1995	91.4	75.5	82.5	95.4	95.2	36.6	4.7	23.0	(S)	21.2	5.7
2002	88.4	76.4	87.5	87.4	92.3	33.8	7.8	22.0	5.3	24.1	6.3
2006 to 2010	89.6	75.5	87.0	89.7	93.4	31.7	6.0	20.2	6.8	22.2	10.4
2011 to 2015	87.1	72.0	87.5	87.1	90.4	28.2	5.0	18.3	14.3	21.3	13.9

S Figure does not meet standards of reliability or precision. [1] Includes women using contraception in the month of interview, or not using contraception in the month of interview but who had sexual intercourse in the 3 months prior to interview. [2] Any contraceptive use. Includes other methods not shown separately. [3] For 2011-2015, includes the oral contraceptive pill only. Prior to 2011, also includes the emergency contraception/morning-after pill. [4] Includes women of other or multiple races, not shown separately. [5] Persons of Hispanic origin may be of any race.

Source: U.S. National Center for Health Statistics, *Health, United States, 2016*, May 2017. See also <https://www.cdc.gov/nchs/hus/.htm>.

Table 105. Abortions—Number and Rate by Race: 1990 to 2010

[In thousands (58,700 represents 58,700,000), except rate. Data for 2000-09 have been revised based on Census Bureau intercensal population estimates, as of October 2012]

Year	All races Women aged 15 to 44	All races Abortions Number (1,000)	All races Abortions Rate per 1,000 women [1]	White Women aged 15 to 44	White Abortions Number (1,000)	White Abortions Rate per 1,000 women [1]	Black Women aged 15 to 44	Black Abortions Number (1,000)	Black Abortions Rate per 1,000 women [1]	Other Women aged 15 to 44	Other Abortions Number (1,000)	Other Abortions Rate per 1,000 women [1]
1990 [2]	58,700	1,609	27.4	48,224	1,039	21.5	7,905	505	63.9	2,571	65	25.1
1991	59,305	1,557	26.2	48,560	982	20.2	8,053	507	62.9	2,692	68	26.2
1992	59,417	1,529	25.7	48,435	943	19.5	8,170	517	63.3	2,812	69	24.4
1993 [2]	59,712	1,495	25.0	48,497	908	18.7	8,282	517	62.4	2,933	70	23.9
1994 [2]	60,020	1,423	23.7	48,592	856	17.6	8,390	492	58.6	3,039	76	23.7
1995	60,368	1,359	22.5	48,719	817	16.8	8,496	462	54.4	3,153	80	25.3
1996	60,704	1,360	22.4	48,837	797	16.3	8,592	483	56.2	3,275	81	24.6
1997 [2]	61,041	1,335	21.9	48,942	777	15.9	8,694	479	55.1	3,405	79	23.1
1998 [2]	61,326	1,319	21.5	49,012	762	15.5	8,785	476	54.2	3,528	81	23.1
1999	61,475	1,315	21.4	48,974	743	15.2	8,851	485	54.8	3,650	87	24.0
2000	61,642	1,313	21.3	48,939	733	15.0	8,911	488	54.8	3,792	92	24.3
2001 [2]	61,795	1,291	20.9	48,877	717	14.7	8,977	476	53.0	3,941	99	25.1
2002 [2]	61,856	1,269	20.5	48,735	706	14.5	9,034	468	51.8	4,088	96	23.4
2003 [2]	61,888	1,250	20.2	48,570	695	14.3	9,092	458	50.4	4,227	97	23.0
2004	61,969	1,222	19.7	48,438	674	13.9	9,168	453	49.4	4,364	95	21.8
2005	62,071	1,206	19.4	48,321	662	13.7	9,246	452	48.9	4,504	92	20.5
2006 [2]	62,190	1,242	20.0	48,205	681	14.1	9,335	464	49.7	4,649	97	20.8
2007	62,292	1,210	19.4	48,082	668	13.9	9,421	448	47.6	4,789	93	19.5
2008	62,360	1,212	19.4	47,943	664	13.8	9,499	458	48.2	4,918	90	18.4
2009 [2]	62,373	1,152	18.5	47,771	621	13.0	9,562	445	46.6	5,040	86	17.0
2010	62,414	1,103	17.7	47,644	591	12.4	9,613	427	44.4	5,157	85	16.6

[1] Aged 15–44. [2] Total numbers of abortions in 1990, 1993, 1994, 1997, 1998, 2001-2003, 2006, and 2009 have been estimated by interpolation.

Source: R.K. Jones and K. Kooistra, "Abortion Incidence and Access to Services in the United States, 2008," *Perspectives on Sexual and Reproductive Health*, 43.1 (2011) ©; R.K. Jones and J. Jerman, "Abortion Incidence and Service Availability in the United States, 2011," *Perspectives on Sexual and Reproductive Health*, 46.1 (2014) ©; and unpublished data from the Guttmacher Institute ©. See also <http://www.guttmacher.org/>.

Table 106. Abortions by Selected Characteristics: 1990 to 2010

[1,609 represents 1,609,000. Number of abortions from surveys conducted by source; characteristics from the U.S. Centers for Disease Control's (CDC) annual abortion surveillance summaries, with adjustments for changes in states reporting data to the Centers for Disease Control each year. Data for 2000 have been revised based on Census Bureau intercensal population estimates, as of October 2012]

Characteristic	Number (1,000) 1990	Number (1,000) 2000	Number (1,000) 2010	Percent distribution 1990	Percent distribution 2000	Percent distribution 2010	Abortion rate per 1,000 women 1990	Abortion rate per 1,000 women 2000	Abortion rate per 1,000 women 2010
Total abortions	**1,609**	**1,313**	**1,103**	**100.0**	**100.0**	**100.0**	**27.4**	**21.3**	**17.7**
Age of woman:									
Less than 15 years [1]	13	9	5	0.8	0.7	0.5	7.9	4.3	2.5
15 to 19 years	351	235	157	21.8	17.9	14.3	40.6	23.9	14.7
20 to 24 years	532	430	362	33.1	32.7	32.9	56.7	45.9	34.1
25 to 29 years	360	303	272	22.4	23.0	24.7	34.0	31.7	26.0
30 to 34 years	216	190	172	13.4	14.5	15.6	19.7	18.6	17.1
35 to 39 years	108	110	97	6.7	8.4	8.8	10.7	9.7	9.6
40 years and over [2]	29	37	37	1.8	2.8	3.3	3.2	3.2	3.3
Race/ethnicity of woman:									
White	1,039	733	591	64.6	55.8	53.6	21.5	15.0	12.4
Black	505	488	427	31.4	37.2	38.7	63.9	54.8	44.4
Other	65	92	85	4.0	7.0	7.7	25.1	24.3	16.6
Hispanic	195	261	239	12.1	19.8	21.7	35.1	30.3	20.2
Non-Hispanic White	852	479	366	52.9	36.5	33.2	19.7	11.7	9.5
Marital status of woman: [3]									
Married	341	246	164	21.0	19.0	14.8	10.6	7.9	5.8
Unmarried	1,268	1,067	939	79.0	81.0	85.2	47.7	35.0	27.4
Number of prior live births:									
None	780	533	448	49.0	41.0	40.6	32.0	20.2	15.2
One	396	361	296	25.0	28.0	26.8	36.9	32.5	28.0
Two	280	260	208	17.0	20.0	18.9	20.5	18.9	16.3
Three	102	104	95	6.0	8.0	8.6	15.6	14.9	14.5
Four or more	50	56	56	3.0	4.0	5.1	14.7	16.4	17.4
Number of prior induced abortions:									
None	891	699	585	55.0	53.0	53.0	(NA)	(NA)	(NA)
One	443	355	288	28.0	27.0	26.2	(NA)	(NA)	(NA)
Two or more	275	259	229	17.0	20.0	20.8	(NA)	(NA)	(NA)
Weeks of gestation:									
Less than 9 weeks	825	749	696	51.3	57.1	63.1	(NA)	(NA)	(NA)
9 to 10 weeks	416	269	182	25.8	20.5	16.5	(NA)	(NA)	(NA)
11 to 12 weeks	195	138	102	12.1	10.5	9.2	(NA)	(NA)	(NA)
13 weeks or more	173	156	129	10.8	11.9	11.2	(NA)	(NA)	(NA)

NA Not available. [1] Denominator of rate is women aged 14. [2] Denominator of rate is women aged 40–44. [3] Separated women are included with married.

Source: R.K. Jones and K. Kooistra, "Abortion Incidence and Access to Services in the United States, 2008," *Perspectives on Sexual and Reproductive Health*, 43.1 (2011) ©; R.K. Jones and J. Jerman, "Abortion Incidence and Service Availability in the United States, 2011," *Perspectives on Sexual and Reproductive Health*, 46.1 (2014) ©; and unpublished data from the Guttmacher Institute ©. See also <http://www.guttmacher.org/>.

Table 107. Abortions—Number and Rate by State of Occurrence: 2000 to 2010

[Number of abortions by state of occurrence from surveys of hospitals, clinics, and physicians identified as providers of abortion services conducted by the Guttmacher Institute. The Guttmacher Institute reallocates abortions to the woman's state of residence for survey years. Abortion rates are computed per 1,000 women 15 to 44 years of age on July 1 of specified year. Estimates for 2000-08 have been revised based on Census Bureau intercensal population estimates, as of October 2012]

| State | State of occurrence | | | | | | State | State of occurrence | | | | | |
| | Number | | | Rate [1] | | | | Number | | | Rate [1] | | |
	2000	2005	2010	2000	2005	2010		2000	2005	2010	2000	2005	2010
U.S.....	1,312,990	1,206,200	1,102,670	21.3	19.4	17.7	MO......	7,920	8,400	6,160	6.6	7.0	5.2
AL.......	13,830	11,340	10,280	14.3	11.9	10.7	MT.......	2,510	2,150	2,220	13.5	11.9	12.4
AK.......	1,660	1,880	1,930	11.8	13.3	13.4	NE.......	4,250	3,220	2,490	11.6	9.0	7.0
AZ.......	17,940	19,480	15,180	16.5	16.3	12.0	NV......	13,740	13,530	11,850	32.1	26.8	21.6
AR.......	5,540	4,710	4,680	9.8	8.3	8.2	NH......	3,010	3,170	3,040	11.2	11.9	12.2
CA......	236,060	208,430	191,550	31.1	26.8	24.3	NJ......	65,780	61,150	48,840	36.2	34.2	28.1
CO......	15,530	16,120	15,060	15.9	16.3	14.7	NM......	5,760	6,220	5,630	14.7	15.7	14.1
CT.......	15,240	16,780	15,430	21.1	23.6	22.3	NY......	164,630	155,960	142,790	39.1	37.9	35.3
DE......	5,440	5,150	6,570	31.3	28.9	36.6	NC......	37,610	34,500	32,700	21.1	18.7	16.8
DC......	9,800	7,230	4,660	68.2	50.2	28.6	ND......	1,340	1,230	1,290	9.9	9.5	10.0
FL.......	103,050	92,300	86,180	31.9	26.2	24.2	OH......	40,230	35,060	30,220	16.5	15.0	13.5
GA......	32,140	33,180	35,590	16.9	16.7	17.1	OK......	7,390	6,950	6,290	10.1	9.6	8.5
HI.......	5,630	5,350	5,520	22.2	20.7	21.0	OR......	17,010	13,200	11,010	23.5	18.1	14.6
ID.......	1,950	1,810	1,740	7.0	6.2	5.7	PA......	36,570	34,150	38,650	14.3	13.7	15.8
IL.......	63,690	50,970	44,400	23.2	19.1	16.9	RI.......	5,600	5,290	4,290	24.1	23.2	20.0
IN.......	12,490	11,150	10,400	9.4	8.6	8.1	SC......	8,210	7,080	6,730	9.3	7.9	7.2
IA.......	5,970	6,370	6,000	9.8	10.8	10.4	SD......	870	790	740	5.5	5.1	4.8
KS......	12,270	10,410	7,240	21.4	18.6	13.0	TN......	19,010	18,140	17,850	15.2	14.5	14.0
KY.......	4,700	3,870	4,040	5.3	4.5	4.7	TX......	89,160	85,760	79,390	18.7	17.2	14.9
LA.......	13,100	11,400	12,710	13.0	11.6	13.7	UT......	3,510	3,630	3,540	6.6	6.5	5.9
ME......	2,650	2,770	2,490	9.9	10.7	10.3	VT......	1,660	1,490	1,370	12.7	11.9	11.6
MD.....	34,560	37,590	34,310	29.0	31.1	28.7	VA......	28,780	26,520	27,660	18.1	16.2	16.7
MA......	30,410	27,270	24,360	21.4	19.8	18.0	WA......	26,200	23,260	22,240	20.2	17.7	16.4
MI......	46,470	40,600	30,770	21.6	19.7	16.1	WV......	2,540	2,360	2,540	6.8	6.7	7.4
MN.....	14,610	13,910	11,570	13.5	13.0	11.1	WI......	11,130	9,800	8,080	9.6	8.6	7.4
MS......	3,780	3,090	2,300	6.0	5.0	3.8	WY......	100	70	90	1.0	0.7	0.8

[1] Rate per 1,000 women, 15 to 44 years old on July 1 of specified year.

Source: R.K. Jones et al., "Abortion in the United States: Incidence and Access to Services, 2005," *Perspectives on Sexual and Reproductive Health*, 40.1 (2008) ©; R.K. Jones and K. Kooistra, "Abortion Incidence and Access to Services in the United States, 2008," *Perspectives on Sexual and Reproductive Health*, 43.1 (2011) ©; R.K. Jones and J. Jerman, "Abortion Incidence and Service Availability in the United States, 2011," *Perspectives on Sexual and Reproductive Health*, 46.1 (2014) ©; and unpublished data from the Guttmacher Institute ©. See also <http://www.guttmacher.org/>.

Table 108. Percent of Babies Breastfed by Selected Characteristics of Mother: 1986 to 2013

[In percent. Annual averages for 3-year period shown. Based on the National Survey of Family Growth. Data are from household interviews with a sample of women aged 15-44 years old]

Mother's characteristics	1986-1988	1989-1991	1992-1994	1995-1998	1999-2001	2002-2004	2005-2007	2008-2010	2011-2013
PERCENT OF BABIES EVER BREASTFED 3 MONTHS OR MORE									
Total..................................	34.6	31.8	33.6	45.8	48.4	50.6	46.6	50.2	56.6
Age at baby's birth:									
Under 20 years......................	18.5	(S)	(S)	30.0	30.0	37.6	26.6	35.5	38.4
20-24 years.........................	26.1	24.1	25.1	36.6	41.8	38.0	38.6	37.6	43.8
25-29 years.........................	36.9	32.3	35.6	46.3	43.7	50.2	49.0	54.8	58.3
30-44 years.........................	50.1	46.8	46.7	57.5	62.4	63.9	56.3	59.6	65.6
Race and Hispanic origin: [1]									
Not Hispanic or Latina									
White alone........................	37.7	35.2	36.6	47.8	49.7	54.5	49.5	48.4	57.8
Black or African American alone...........	11.6	11.5	13.3	29.6	33.7	29.2	26.3	35.7	37.0
Hispanic or Latina............................	38.2	33.9	35.0	49.7	54.3	55.9	49.4	55.6	58.8
Education: [2]									
No high school diploma or GED.............	21.8	17.6	25.2	33.9	37.0	39.9	41.3	42.8	50.8
High school diploma or GED.................	28.2	28.0	27.4	36.9	43.1	41.9	36.8	44.4	45.1
Some college, no bachelor's degree........	38.7	33.1	38.7	49.6	52.8	43.2	48.7	46.7	52.3
Bachelor's degree or higher..................	55.0	56.1	59.3	64.5	64.1	75.9	65.8	63.7	73.9
Region:									
Northeast..	29.9	37.2	36.4	48.2	48.8	59.9	51.5	46.9	57.7
Midwest...	30.3	31.5	30.1	42.0	42.8	46.8	41.6	42.1	50.8
South...	27.7	20.1	26.2	38.9	44.4	42.7	40.5	45.6	51.8
West...	52.4	42.9	45.3	58.2	59.2	62.6	57.8	66.0	68.5

S Figure does not meet publication standards. [1] Starting with 1995 data, race-specific estimates are tabulated according to 1997 Revisions to the Standards for the Classification of Federal Data on Race and Ethnicity and are not strictly comparable with estimates for earlier years. Starting with 1995 data, race-specific estimates are for persons who reported only one racial group. Prior to data year 1995, data were tabulated according to the 1977 Standards. Estimates for single-race categories prior to 1995 included persons who reported one race or, if they reported more than one race, identified one race as best representing their race. [2] Educational attainment is presented only for women age 22 to 44 years old, as of day of interview.

Source: U.S. National Center for Health Statistics, *Health, United States, 2016*, May 2017. See also <http://www.cdc.gov/nchs/hus.htm>.

Table 109. Assisted Reproductive Technology (ART) Procedures and Outcomes: 2000 to 2015

[Covers ART procedures with the intent to transfer at least one embryo; excludes freezing/banking cycles. In 1996, Centers for Disease Control (CDC) initiated data collection regarding Assisted Reproductive Technology (ART) procedures performed in the United States, as mandated by the Fertility Clinic Success Rate and Certification Act. ARTs include those infertility treatments in which both eggs and sperm are handled in the laboratory for the purpose of establishing a pregnancy (i.e., in vitro fertilization and related procedures)]

Year	Procedures started [1]	Number of pregnancies [2]	Live birth deliveries [3]	Live born infants
2000	99,629	30,557	25,228	35,025
2005	134,260	47,651	38,910	52,041
2010	147,260	57,773	47,090	61,564
2011	151,923	59,132	47,818	61,610
2012	157,662	62,977	51,267	65,160
2013	163,209	65,580	54,323	67,996
2014	173,198	68,988	57,323	70,354
2015	186,157	(NA)	60,778	72,913

NA Not available. [1] Excludes procedures for which new treatments were being evaluated. [2] Beginning in 2012, excludes pregnancies from procedures performed in U.S. territories other than Puerto Rico; and, beginning in 2013, excludes pregnancies resulting from oocyte thaw procedures. [3] A live birth delivery is defined as the delivery of one or more live born infants.

Source: U.S. Centers for Disease Control and Prevention, *2014 Assisted Reproductive Technology, National Summary Report*, October 2016, and earlier reports; *Assisted Reproductive Technology Surveillance - United States, 2014*, MMWR Surveillance Summaries Vol. 66, No. 6, February 2017 and earlier reports; and "ART Success Rates," <http://www.cdc.gov/art/artdata/index.html>, accessed July 2017.

Table 110. Life Expectancy at Birth, 1940 to 2015, and Projected, 2020 to 2060

[In years. Beginning in 1970, excludes deaths of nonresidents of the United States. See Appendix III]

Year	Total			White			Black		
	Total	Male	Female	Total	Male	Female	Total	Male	Female
1940	62.9	60.8	65.2	64.2	62.1	66.6	(NA)	(NA)	(NA)
1950	68.2	65.6	71.1	69.1	66.5	72.2	60.8	59.1	62.9
1960	69.7	66.6	73.1	70.6	67.4	74.1	63.6	61.1	66.3
1970	70.8	67.1	74.7	71.7	68.0	75.6	64.1	60.0	68.3
1980	73.7	70.0	77.4	74.4	70.7	78.1	68.1	63.8	72.5
1990	75.4	71.8	78.8	76.1	72.7	79.4	69.1	64.5	73.6
2000	76.8	74.1	79.3	77.3	74.7	79.9	71.8	68.2	75.1
2010 [1, 2]	78.7	76.2	81.0	78.9	76.5	81.3	75.1	71.8	78.0
2013 [1, 2, 3]	78.8	76.4	81.2	79.1	76.7	81.4	75.5	72.3	78.4
2014 [1, 2, 3]	78.9	76.5	81.3	79.1	76.7	81.4	75.6	72.5	78.5
2015 [1, 2, 3]	78.8	76.3	81.2	79.0	76.6	81.3	75.5	72.2	78.5
Projections: [4]									
2020	80.2	78.0	82.4	80.7	78.6	82.9	77.0	74.0	79.8
2030	81.7	79.6	83.7	82.2	80.2	84.1	78.8	76.1	81.3
2040	83.0	81.2	84.8	83.5	81.7	85.2	80.5	78.0	82.8
2050	84.4	82.7	86.0	84.8	83.2	86.4	82.0	79.8	84.1
2060	85.6	84.0	87.1	86.0	84.5	87.4	83.4	81.4	85.3

NA Not available. [1] Beginning 2001, life expectancies calculated using revised methodology and may differ from those previously published. [2] Multiple-race data were bridged to the single-race categories of the 1977 OMB standards for comparability with other reporting areas. [3] Life expectancy estimates for 2013 based on final Medicare data; estimates for 2014-15 are based on preliminary Medicare data. [4] Based on mortality assumptions, see source: U.S. Census Bureau, 2014 National Population Projections, "Table 17: Projected Life Expectancy at Birth by Sex, Race, and Hispanic Origin for the United States: 2015 to 2060 (NP2014-T17)," December 2014, <https://www.census.gov/programs-surveys/popproj.html>.

Source: Except as noted. U.S. National Center for Health Statistics, National Vital Statistics Reports (NVSR), *Deaths: Final Data for 2014*, Vol. 65, No. 4, June 2016; and *Health, United States, 2016*, May 2017. See also <http://www.cdc.gov/nchs/deaths.htm>.

Table 111. Life Expectancy by Sex, Age, and Race: 2014

[Average number of years of life remaining. Excludes deaths of nonresidents of the United States]

Age	Total [1]			White			Black		
	Total	Male	Female	Total	Male	Female	Total	Male	Female
0	78.9	76.5	81.3	79.1	76.7	81.4	75.6	72.5	78.5
1	78.3	76.0	80.7	78.5	76.1	80.8	75.5	72.4	78.3
5	74.4	72.0	76.8	74.5	72.2	76.8	71.6	68.5	74.4
10	69.5	67.1	71.8	69.6	67.3	71.9	66.7	63.6	69.4
15	64.5	62.1	66.8	64.6	62.3	66.9	61.7	58.6	64.5
20	59.7	57.3	61.9	59.8	57.5	62.0	56.9	53.9	59.6
25	54.9	52.7	57.0	55.0	52.8	57.1	52.2	49.3	54.7
30	50.2	48.0	52.2	50.2	48.1	52.3	47.5	44.8	49.9
35	45.4	43.4	47.4	45.5	43.5	47.5	42.9	40.3	45.2
40	40.7	38.8	42.6	40.8	38.9	42.7	38.3	35.8	40.5
45	36.1	34.2	38.0	36.2	34.3	38.0	33.9	31.4	36.0
50	31.7	29.8	33.4	31.7	29.9	33.4	29.5	27.2	31.5
55	27.4	25.6	29.0	27.4	25.7	29.0	25.5	23.2	27.4
60	23.3	21.7	24.7	23.3	21.8	24.7	21.7	19.6	23.4
65	19.4	18.0	20.6	19.4	18.0	20.6	18.2	16.4	19.7
70	15.7	14.5	16.7	15.7	14.5	16.6	14.9	13.3	16.1
75	12.3	11.2	13.1	12.2	11.2	13.0	11.9	10.6	12.8
80	9.2	8.4	9.8	9.2	8.3	9.7	9.2	8.2	9.8
85	6.7	6.0	7.1	6.6	5.9	7.0	6.9	6.1	7.3
90	4.6	4.1	4.9	4.6	4.1	4.8	5.1	4.5	5.4
95	3.2	2.9	3.4	3.2	2.8	3.3	3.8	3.3	3.9
100	2.3	2.1	2.3	2.2	2.0	2.3	2.8	2.5	2.9

[1] Includes races other than White and Black.

Source: U.S. National Center for Health Statistics, National Vital Statistics Reports (NVSR), *United States Life Tables, 2014*, Vol. 66, No. 4, August 2017. See also <https://www.cdc.gov/nchs/products/life_tables.htm>.

Table 112. Selected Life Table Values—Life Expectancy and Percent Surviving by Age: 1959 to 2013

[Decennial life tables are based on population data from a decennial census and reported deaths of the 3-year period surrounding the census year; the census year is the middle year. The annual tables are based on deaths in a single year, and except for census years, on postcensal population estimates. Beginning in 1970, data exclude deaths of nonresidents of the United States. See Technical Notes, source]

Age and sex	All races 1959-1961	1969-1971	1979-1981	1989-1991	1999-2001	2013	White 1959-1961	1969-1971	1979-1981	1989-1991	1999-2001	2013	Black[1] 1959-1961	1969-1971	1979-1981	1989-1991	1999-2001	2013
LIFE EXPECTANCY IN YEARS																		
Male by age:																		
At birth	66.8	67.0	70.1	71.8	74.1	76.4	67.6	67.9	70.8	72.7	74.8	76.7	61.5	60.0	64.1	64.5	68.2	72.3
Age 20	49.8	49.5	51.9	53.3	55.2	57.3	50.3	50.2	52.5	54.0	55.7	57.5	45.8	43.5	46.5	46.7	49.9	53.7
Age 30	40.6	40.5	42.8	44.1	45.9	48.0	41.0	41.1	43.3	44.7	46.3	48.1	37.1	35.4	37.8	38.1	41.0	44.6
Age 40	31.4	31.5	33.6	35.1	36.6	38.7	31.7	31.9	34.0	35.6	37.0	38.8	28.7	27.6	29.5	30.1	32.2	35.6
Age 50	23.0	23.1	25.0	26.4	27.8	29.7	23.2	23.3	25.3	26.7	28.1	29.9	21.3	20.7	22.0	22.5	24.1	27.0
Age 60	15.9	16.0	17.5	18.5	19.7	21.7	16.0	16.1	17.6	18.7	19.9	21.7	15.3	14.9	15.9	16.0	17.2	19.5
Age 65	13.0	13.0	14.2	15.1	16.1	17.9	13.0	13.0	14.3	15.2	16.2	18.0	12.8	12.5	13.3	13.3	14.1	16.2
Age 70	10.3	10.4	11.4	12.1	12.8	14.4	10.3	10.4	11.4	12.1	12.9	14.4	10.8	10.4	10.9	10.9	11.4	13.2
Age 80	6.0	6.3	6.8	7.1	7.4	8.3	5.9	6.2	6.8	7.1	7.4	8.3	6.9	7.4	7.0	7.0	7.1	8.0
Age 90	3.2	3.6	3.9	3.9	4.0	4.1	3.2	3.5	3.8	3.9	3.9	4.0	3.4	4.7	4.5	4.2	4.2	4.4
Female by age:																		
At birth	73.2	74.6	77.6	78.8	79.5	81.2	74.2	75.5	78.2	79.5	80.0	81.4	66.5	68.3	72.9	73.7	75.2	78.4
Age 20	55.6	56.6	59.0	59.9	60.3	61.9	56.3	57.2	59.4	60.4	60.7	62.0	50.1	51.2	54.9	55.5	56.5	59.5
Age 30	46.0	47.0	49.3	50.2	50.6	52.1	46.6	47.6	49.8	50.7	51.0	52.2	40.8	42.0	45.4	46.0	47.0	49.9
Age 40	36.6	37.6	39.8	40.7	41.0	42.6	37.1	38.1	40.2	41.0	41.3	42.7	32.2	33.3	36.3	37.0	37.7	40.5
Age 50	27.7	28.8	30.7	31.4	31.8	33.3	28.1	29.1	31.0	31.7	32.0	33.4	24.3	25.5	27.8	28.4	29.1	31.5
Age 60	19.5	20.6	22.3	22.9	23.1	24.6	19.7	20.8	22.5	23.1	23.3	24.6	17.8	18.7	20.4	20.7	21.2	23.3
Age 65	15.8	16.8	18.4	19.0	19.1	20.5	15.9	16.9	18.6	19.1	19.5	20.5	15.1	15.7	17.1	17.4	17.7	19.5
Age 70	12.4	13.4	14.8	15.4	15.4	16.6	12.4	13.4	14.9	15.5	15.5	16.5	12.5	13.0	14.1	14.3	14.4	16.0
Age 80	6.7	7.7	8.7	9.1	9.1	9.7	6.7	7.6	8.7	9.1	9.0	9.7	7.7	8.9	9.0	9.1	9.0	9.7
Age 90	3.3	4.1	4.7	4.7	4.7	4.8	3.2	4.1	4.6	4.7	4.7	4.7	3.5	5.4	5.5	5.2	5.2	5.3
PERCENT SURVIVING OUT OF 100,000 BORN ALIVE																		
Male by age:																		
At birth	100.0	100.0	100.0	100.0	100.0	100.0	100.0	100.0	100.0	100.0	100.0	100.0	100.0	100.0	100.0	100.0	100.0	100.0
Age 20	95.5	96.1	97.3	97.9	98.4	98.8	95.9	96.5	97.5	98.1	98.6	98.9	93.1	94.1	96.1	96.1	97.3	98.0
Age 30	93.8	94.1	95.4	96.2	97.1	97.5	94.4	94.7	95.8	96.7	97.4	97.7	90.3	89.6	93.1	93.1	94.9	96.1
Age 40	91.6	91.5	93.3	93.8	95.4	95.9	92.4	92.6	94.0	94.6	95.9	96.1	85.7	83.4	88.5	87.9	91.9	93.7
Age 50	86.2	86.1	89.0	89.9	91.8	92.9	87.4	87.7	90.1	91.1	92.6	93.2	77.2	73.3	80.1	80.0	85.7	89.7
Age 60	73.9	74.0	79.0	81.4	84.6	86.1	75.5	76.0	80.6	83.2	85.8	86.6	61.7	57.5	65.0	66.3	73.6	80.4
Age 65	64.2	64.3	70.6	74.0	78.2	80.7	65.8	66.3	72.4	76.0	79.7	81.3	51.4	47.5	55.1	56.8	65.0	72.7
Age 70	52.2	52.3	59.7	64.1	69.5	73.7	53.8	54.1	61.4	66.2	71.0	74.4	39.9	36.9	44.2	45.7	54.3	63.7
Age 80	25.3	24.9	31.8	36.7	42.8	51.3	26.0	25.9	32.8	38.2	44.1	51.9	20.0	16.6	22.0	22.5	28.5	39.6
Age 90	4.6	5.1	7.7	9.9	12.5	18.2	4.6	5.1	7.9	10.2	12.8	18.4	5.2	4.7	5.7	6.0	7.6	13.1
Female by age:																		
At birth	100.0	100.0	100.0	100.0	100.0	100.0	100.0	100.0	100.0	100.0	100.0	100.0	100.0	100.0	100.0	100.0	100.0	100.0
Age 20	96.8	97.3	98.2	98.6	98.9	99.1	97.1	97.6	98.4	98.8	99.0	99.2	94.7	95.7	97.2	97.6	98.1	98.5
Age 30	96.0	96.5	97.5	98.0	98.4	98.7	96.5	96.9	97.8	98.3	98.6	98.7	93.1	94.1	96.2	96.5	97.3	97.9
Age 40	94.6	95.1	96.5	97.0	97.5	97.7	95.3	95.8	96.9	97.5	98.0	97.9	89.7	90.8	94.1	94.4	95.6	96.7
Age 50	91.3	91.9	94.1	94.9	95.4	95.8	92.5	92.9	94.7	95.6	96.0	96.0	83.0	84.2	89.6	90.3	91.7	93.9
Age 60	84.4	85.1	88.4	89.7	91.8	91.5	86.3	86.7	89.5	90.8	91.6	91.9	69.9	72.8	80.3	81.9	84.0	87.7
Age 65	78.5	79.7	83.5	85.1	86.4	88.0	80.7	81.6	84.8	86.3	87.4	88.5	60.8	64.7	73.3	75.0	77.9	82.8
Age 70	70.1	72.0	76.7	78.5	80.2	83.0	72.5	74.1	78.1	80.0	81.4	83.5	51.3	54.9	64.7	66.3	69.8	76.4
Age 80	43.1	46.4	54.4	57.0	58.5	64.4	44.7	48.2	55.8	58.5	59.7	64.9	30.3	31.8	41.7	43.6	46.5	56.3
Age 90	10.1	14.2	20.6	23.7	23.9	29.7	10.2	14.4	21.0	24.3	24.5	29.8	9.7	12.2	16.3	17.5	18.3	25.2

[1] Prior to 1970, data for the black population are not available. Data shown for 1959–1970 are for the non-white population.

Source: U.S. National Center for Health Statistics, National Vital Statistics Reports (NVSR), *United States Life Tables, 2013*, Vol. 66, No. 3, April 2017. See also <http://www.cdc.gov/nchs/products/life_tables.htm>.

Births, Deaths, Marriages, and Divorces   77

Table 113. Life Expectancy at Birth by Sex, Race, and State: 1989 to 2001

[Average number of years of life remaining. Excludes deaths of nonresidents of the United States. Decennial life tables are based on population data from a decennial census and reported deaths of the 3-year period surrounding the census year; the census year is the middle year. The annual tables are based on deaths in a single year, and except for census years, on postcensal population estimates]

State	Total, 1989–1991	1999-2001						
		Total	Male			Female		
			Total	White	Black	Total	White	Black
United States	**75.37**	**76.83**	**74.10**	**74.74**	**68.08**	**79.45**	**79.97**	**75.12**
Alabama	73.64	74.80	71.32	72.85	66.42	78.34	79.14	74.94
Alaska	74.83	76.63	74.18	75.45	(B)	79.41	80.10	(B)
Arizona	76.10	78.15	75.25	75.51	70.95	81.16	81.64	77.70
Arkansas	74.33	75.43	72.05	73.17	67.30	78.99	79.59	73.58
California	75.86	78.80	76.02	76.11	69.97	81.63	81.36	76.67
Colorado	76.96	78.72	76.29	76.23	71.71	81.16	81.31	76.59
Connecticut	76.91	78.90	76.13	76.73	71.73	81.63	81.92	77.71
Delaware	74.76	77.04	74.24	75.05	70.27	79.78	80.55	75.21
District of Columbia	67.99	73.09	68.57	78.94	64.59	77.59	84.31	74.46
Florida	75.84	78.10	74.97	75.64	68.98	81.40	82.14	75.53
Georgia	73.61	75.27	72.28	73.88	68.29	78.22	79.53	76.16
Hawaii	78.21	80.23	77.17	78.40	(B)	83.65	83.31	(B)
Idaho	76.88	78.29	76.18	76.46	(B)	80.50	80.53	(B)
Illinois	74.90	77.06	73.91	75.33	66.81	80.26	80.78	74.20
Indiana	75.39	76.47	73.55	74.24	67.47	79.45	79.69	76.55
Iowa	77.29	78.76	76.11	76.19	70.81	81.39	81.35	75.16
Kansas	76.76	77.78	74.84	75.46	68.47	80.88	81.00	75.02
Kentucky	74.37	75.20	72.25	72.73	69.01	78.20	78.42	74.46
Louisiana	73.05	74.28	71.12	73.47	66.45	77.44	79.41	75.30
Maine	76.35	77.46	75.23	75.59	(B)	79.63	80.88	(B)
Maryland	74.79	76.36	73.55	75.58	68.41	79.08	80.66	75.78
Massachusetts	76.72	78.76	75.79	76.35	73.14	81.68	81.63	79.33
Michigan	75.04	76.90	73.98	75.26	67.38	79.83	80.59	75.95
Minnesota	77.76	79.26	76.74	77.03	71.59	81.80	82.61	76.60
Mississippi	73.03	73.88	70.30	72.25	66.72	77.62	79.13	73.68
Missouri	75.25	76.52	73.59	74.29	67.22	79.46	79.93	74.50
Montana	76.23	77.74	75.18	75.07	(B)	80.56	81.24	(B)
Nebraska	76.92	78.37	76.00	76.17	69.15	80.78	81.14	74.67
Nevada	74.18	76.05	73.34	73.49	70.56	79.24	78.97	74.75
New Hampshire	76.72	78.79	76.24	76.46	(B)	81.40	81.30	(B)
New Jersey	75.42	77.58	74.77	75.82	68.85	80.32	81.32	75.54
New Mexico	75.74	77.26	74.52	75.19	71.63	80.06	80.69	74.37
New York	74.68	78.20	75.13	75.78	70.13	81.16	81.49	77.84
North Carolina	74.48	76.27	73.05	74.27	66.33	79.56	80.34	76.68
North Dakota	77.62	79.06	75.96	76.65	(B)	82.61	82.67	(B)
Ohio	75.32	76.49	73.94	74.58	68.60	78.95	80.01	74.91
Oklahoma	75.10	75.61	72.75	73.00	68.97	78.59	78.75	74.34
Oregon	76.44	78.09	75.82	75.72	70.67	80.37	80.20	78.24
Pennsylvania	75.38	77.02	74.09	75.03	67.26	79.90	80.65	75.34
Rhode Island	76.54	78.65	75.83	76.06	72.18	81.42	81.60	77.39
South Carolina	73.51	75.04	71.68	73.76	67.34	78.49	79.77	75.41
South Dakota	76.91	78.34	75.19	76.35	(B)	81.79	82.61	(B)
Tennessee	74.32	75.29	71.98	73.31	66.86	78.66	79.28	74.16
Texas	75.14	77.04	74.12	74.74	69.18	80.05	80.35	74.76
Utah	77.70	78.89	76.84	76.95	(B)	80.95	80.93	(B)
Vermont	76.54	78.24	76.18	76.30	(B)	80.29	80.90	(B)
Virginia	75.22	76.95	74.48	75.62	69.37	79.34	80.69	76.20
Washington	76.82	78.64	76.18	76.10	71.90	81.14	80.98	77.11
West Virginia	74.26	75.28	72.75	72.75	69.87	77.84	78.36	72.65
Wisconsin	76.87	78.56	75.61	76.12	68.41	81.64	81.87	74.34
Wyoming	76.21	76.64	74.83	75.33	(B)	78.55	80.41	(B)

B Base figure too small to meet statistical standards for reliability.

Source: U.S. National Center for Health Statistics, National Vital Statistics Reports (NVSR), *U.S. Decennial Life Tables for 1999-2001: State Life Tables*, Vol. 60, No. 9, September 2012, and earlier reports. See also <http://www.cdc.gov/nchs/products/life_tables.htm>.

Table 114. Deaths and Death Rates by Sex, Race, and Hispanic Origin: 1970 to 2015

[Deaths in thousands (1,921 represents 1,921,000). Rates are per 1,000 population for specified groups. Excludes deaths of nonresidents of the United States and fetal deaths. Rates are based on population enumerated as of April 1 for census years and estimated as of July 1 for all other years. Data for Hispanic origin and specified races other than White and Black should be interpreted with caution because of inconsistent reporting of race and Hispanic Origin on death certificates and censuses and surveys]

Sex and race	1970	1980	1990	2000	2005	2010	2011	2012	2013	2014	2015
Deaths [1]	**1,921**	**1,990**	**2,148**	**2,403**	**2,448**	**2,468**	**2,515**	**2,543**	**2,597**	**2,626**	**2,713**
Male [1]	1,078	1,075	1,113	1,178	1,208	1,232	1,255	1,274	1,306	1,328	1,373
Female [1]	843	915	1,035	1,226	1,240	1,236	1,260	1,270	1,291	1,298	1,339
White	1,682	1,739	1,853	2,071	2,098	2,115	2,156	2,175	2,217	2,238	2,307
Male	942	934	951	1,007	1,028	1,052	1,072	1,085	1,111	1,129	1,164
Female	740	805	902	1,064	1,070	1,063	1,084	1,090	1,106	1,109	1,143
Black	226	233	265	286	293	287	290	295	303	309	320
Male	128	130	145	145	149	146	147	151	155	158	165
Female	98	103	120	141	144	141	143	145	148	151	155
American Indian or Alaska Native	6	7	8	11	14	16	16	17	17	18	19
Male	3	4	5	6	8	9	9	9	9	10	10
Female	2	3	3	5	6	7	7	7	8	8	9
Asian or Pacific Islander	(NA)	11	21	35	43	51	53	56	60	62	67
Male	(NA)	7	12	19	23	27	27	29	31	32	34
Female	(NA)	4	9	16	20	25	26	28	29	30	33
Hispanic origin [2]	(NA)	(NA)	(NA)	107	131	144	150	156	163	169	179
Male	(NA)	(NA)	(NA)	60	74	80	82	85	89	92	98
Female	(NA)	(NA)	(NA)	47	57	65	68	71	74	77	81
Non-Hispanic, White	(NA)	(NA)	(NA)	1,960	1,967	1,970	2,006	2,017	2,053	2,067	2,124
Male	(NA)	(NA)	(NA)	945	954	972	990	999	1,021	1,035	1,064
Female	(NA)	(NA)	(NA)	1,015	1,013	998	1,016	1,018	1,032	1,032	1,060
Death rates [1]	**9.5**	**8.8**	**8.6**	**8.5**	**8.3**	**8.0**	**8.1**	**8.1**	**8.2**	**8.2**	**8.4**
Male [1]	10.9	9.8	9.2	8.5	8.3	8.1	8.2	8.2	8.4	8.5	8.7
Female [1]	8.1	7.9	8.1	8.6	8.3	7.9	8.0	8.0	8.0	8.0	8.2
White	9.5	8.9	8.9	9.0	8.8	8.6	8.7	8.8	8.9	8.9	9.2
Male	10.9	9.8	9.3	8.9	8.7	8.7	8.8	8.8	9.0	9.1	9.3
Female	8.1	8.1	8.5	9.1	8.9	8.6	8.7	8.7	8.8	8.8	9.0
Black	10.0	8.8	8.7	7.8	7.5	6.8	6.8	6.8	6.9	7.0	7.1
Male	11.9	10.3	10.1	8.3	8.0	7.3	7.2	7.3	7.4	7.4	7.7
Female	8.3	7.3	7.5	7.3	7.0	6.4	6.4	6.4	6.5	6.6	6.7
American Indian or Alaska Native	(NA)	4.9	4.0	3.8	3.9	3.7	3.7	3.8	3.8	4.0	4.2
Male	(NA)	6.0	4.8	4.2	4.3	4.0	4.0	4.1	4.2	4.3	4.5
Female	(NA)	3.8	3.3	3.5	3.5	3.3	3.4	3.4	3.5	3.6	3.8
Asian or Pacific Islander	(NA)	3.0	2.8	3.0	3.0	3.0	3.1	3.1	3.2	3.2	3.3
Male	(NA)	3.8	3.3	3.3	3.3	3.3	3.3	3.3	3.5	3.4	3.5
Female	(NA)	2.2	2.3	2.6	2.7	2.8	2.8	2.9	3.0	3.0	3.1
Hispanic origin [2]	(NA)	(NA)	(NA)	3.0	3.0	2.9	2.9	3.0	3.0	3.1	3.2
Male	(NA)	(NA)	(NA)	3.3	3.4	3.1	3.1	3.2	3.2	3.3	3.4
Female	(NA)	(NA)	(NA)	2.7	2.7	2.6	2.6	2.7	2.8	2.8	2.9
Non-Hispanic, White	(NA)	(NA)	(NA)	9.9	9.9	9.8	10.0	10.0	10.2	10.3	10.6
Male	(NA)	(NA)	(NA)	9.8	9.8	9.9	10.0	10.1	10.3	10.5	10.7
Female	(NA)	(NA)	(NA)	10.1	10.0	9.8	10.0	10.0	10.1	10.1	10.4
Age-adjusted death rates [1,3]	**12.2**	**10.4**	**9.4**	**8.7**	**8.2**	**7.5**	**7.4**	**7.3**	**7.3**	**7.2**	**7.3**
Male [1]	15.4	13.5	12.0	10.5	9.7	8.9	8.8	8.7	8.6	8.6	8.7
Female [1]	9.7	8.2	7.5	7.3	6.9	6.3	6.3	6.2	6.2	6.2	6.2
White	11.9	10.1	9.1	8.5	8.0	7.4	7.4	7.3	7.3	7.3	7.4
Male	15.1	13.2	11.7	10.3	9.5	8.8	8.7	8.6	8.6	8.5	8.6
Female	9.4	8.0	7.3	7.2	6.8	6.3	6.3	6.2	6.2	6.2	6.3
Black	15.2	13.1	12.5	11.2	10.4	9.0	8.8	8.6	8.6	8.5	8.5
Male	18.7	17.0	16.4	14.0	12.8	11.0	10.7	10.6	10.5	10.3	10.4
Female	12.3	10.3	9.8	9.3	8.6	7.5	7.4	7.2	7.2	7.1	7.1
American Indian or Alaska Native	(NA)	8.7	7.2	7.1	7.0	6.3	6.0	6.0	5.9	5.9	6.0
Male	(NA)	11.1	9.2	8.4	8.2	7.3	6.9	6.9	6.9	6.9	6.9
Female	(NA)	6.6	5.6	6.0	6.0	5.4	5.2	5.1	5.1	5.1	5.1
Asian or Pacific Islander	(NA)	5.9	5.8	5.1	4.6	4.2	4.1	4.1	4.1	3.9	3.9
Male	(NA)	7.9	7.2	6.2	5.6	5.1	4.9	4.8	4.9	4.6	4.7
Female	(NA)	4.3	4.7	4.2	3.9	3.6	3.5	3.5	3.4	3.3	3.4
Hispanic origin [2]	(NA)	(NA)	(NA)	6.7	6.3	5.6	5.4	5.4	5.4	5.2	5.3
Male	(NA)	(NA)	(NA)	8.2	7.7	6.8	6.5	6.4	6.4	6.3	6.3
Female	(NA)	(NA)	(NA)	5.5	5.1	4.6	4.5	4.5	4.5	4.4	4.4
Non-Hispanic, White	(NA)	(NA)	(NA)	8.6	8.1	7.6	7.5	7.5	7.5	7.4	7.5
Male	(NA)	(NA)	(NA)	10.4	9.6	8.9	8.9	8.8	8.8	8.7	8.8
Female	(NA)	(NA)	(NA)	7.2	6.9	6.4	6.4	6.4	6.4	6.3	6.4

NA Not available. [1] Includes other races not shown separately. [2] Persons of Hispanic origin may be of any race. [3] Age-adjusted death rates are better indicators than crude death rates for showing changes in the risk of death over time when the age distribution of the population is changing, and for comparing the mortality of population subgroups that have different age compositions. All age-adjusted death rates are standardized to the year 2010 population.

Source: U.S. National Center for Health Statistics, National Vital Statistics Reports (NVSR), *Deaths: Final Data for 2014*, Vol. 65, No. 4, June 2016; and CDC Wonder Online Database, "Multiple Cause of Death, 1999-2015," <https://wonder.cdc.gov/>, accessed August 2017. See also <http://www.cdc.gov/nchs/nvss/deaths.htm>.

Table 115. Death Rates by Age, Sex, and Race: 1960 to 2015

[Rates per 100,000 population]

Characteristic	All ages [1]	Under 1 year	1 to 4 years	5 to 14 years	15 to 24 years	25 to 34 years	35 to 44 years	45 to 54 years	55 to 64 years	65 to 74 years	75 to 84 years	85 years and over
MALE												
Total:												
1960	1,105	3,059	120	56	152	188	373	992	2,310	4,914	10,178	21,186
1970	1,090	2,410	93	51	189	215	403	959	2,283	4,874	10,010	17,822
1980	977	1,429	73	37	172	196	299	767	1,815	4,105	8,817	18,801
1990	918	1,083	52	29	147	204	310	610	1,553	3,492	7,889	18,057
2000	853	807	36	21	115	139	255	543	1,231	2,980	6,973	17,501
2010	812	680	30	15	98	142	213	506	1,076	2,275	5,694	15,414
2015	868	639	28	15	100	161	226	496	1,104	2,190	5,376	14,796
White:												
1990	931	896	46	26	131	176	268	549	1,467	3,398	7,845	18,268
2000	888	668	33	20	106	124	234	497	1,163	2,906	6,933	17,716
2010	866	584	27	14	92	136	207	492	1,033	2,232	5,704	15,640
2013	899	566	26	14	87	140	208	492	1,051	2,152	5,507	15,220
2014	909	551	24	14	88	145	213	489	1,064	2,143	5,419	15,000
2015	933	542	25	14	92	157	221	487	1,071	2,160	5,427	15,203
Black:												
1990	1,008	2,112	86	41	252	431	700	1,261	2,618	4,946	9,130	16,955
2000	834	1,568	55	28	181	261	453	1,018	2,080	4,254	8,486	16,791
2010	725	1,207	43	20	143	217	308	716	1,662	3,206	6,722	14,715
2013	739	1,120	41	20	136	219	312	679	1,628	3,064	6,362	13,657
2014	743	1,125	42	21	135	212	309	672	1,612	3,047	6,173	13,292
2015	765	1,150	46	21	151	229	326	678	1,613	3,042	6,205	13,066
Asian or Pacific Islander: [2]												
1990	334	605	45	21	76	80	131	287	789	2,041	5,009	12,446
2000	333	529	23	13	55	55	105	250	642	1,661	4,328	12,125
2010	327	434	19	8	43	53	84	214	519	1,226	3,439	10,825
2013	347	409	19	11	42	54	89	220	518	1,126	3,240	10,143
2014	341	384	14	10	45	54	83	212	520	1,107	3,048	9,263
2015	355	438	15	10	49	56	85	205	508	1,131	3,092	9,406
American Indian or Alaska Native: [2]												
1990	476	1,057	77	33	220	256	365	620	1,211	2,462	5,389	11,244
2000	416	700	45	20	136	179	295	520	1,090	2,478	5,351	10,726
2010	398	543	34	18	116	156	258	496	951	1,971	4,452	10,268
2013	417	493	42	12	98	173	244	506	938	1,846	4,225	9,034
2014	433	510	41	12	104	179	264	509	985	1,830	4,098	8,610
2015	455	486	35	15	101	191	281	544	994	1,841	4,171	8,277
FEMALE												
Total:												
1960	809	2,321	98	37	61	107	229	527	1,196	2,872	7,633	19,008
1970	808	1,864	75	32	68	102	231	517	1,099	2,580	6,678	15,518
1980	785	1,142	55	24	58	76	159	413	934	2,145	5,440	14,747
1990	812	856	41	19	49	74	138	343	879	1,991	4,883	14,274
2000	855	663	29	15	43	64	143	313	772	1,921	4,815	14,719
2010	787	564	23	11	36	64	129	311	644	1,528	4,138	13,219
2015	821	538	22	11	38	72	135	315	662	1,451	3,971	13,081
White:												
1990	847	690	36	18	46	62	117	309	823	1,924	4,839	14,401
2000	912	551	26	14	41	55	126	281	731	1,868	4,785	14,891
2010	857	488	22	11	36	61	123	295	618	1,505	4,165	13,419
2013	879	457	20	11	36	65	127	303	623	1,453	4,072	13,316
2014	877	458	20	10	36	67	131	306	635	1,433	4,001	13,079
2015	899	455	20	11	38	72	132	307	640	1,444	4,028	13,443
Black:												
1990	748	1,736	68	28	69	160	299	639	1,453	2,866	5,688	13,310
2000	733	1,280	45	20	58	122	272	588	1,227	2,690	5,697	13,941
2010	643	994	33	15	43	93	199	481	972	2,021	4,581	12,590
2013	651	981	33	15	41	91	188	454	962	1,909	4,418	11,929
2014	656	956	32	14	43	89	194	456	975	1,880	4,357	11,657
2015	666	970	32	15	46	93	192	447	970	1,864	4,310	11,741
Asian or Pacific Islander: [2]												
1990	234	518	32	13	29	38	70	183	483	1,089	3,128	10,254
2000	262	434	20	12	22	28	66	156	391	996	2,882	9,052
2010	277	342	16	8	17	27	49	128	299	789	2,446	8,590
2013	297	329	18	9	18	26	52	128	287	704	2,347	8,240
2014	296	339	13	7	18	25	49	122	283	701	2,238	7,945
2015	311	358	15	7	19	26	51	128	288	705	2,264	8,142
American Indian or Alaska Native: [2]												
1990	330	689	38	26	69	102	156	381	806	1,679	3,073	8,201
2000	346	492	40	18	59	85	172	285	772	1,900	3,850	9,118
2010	332	366	24	11	44	86	147	326	624	1,482	3,392	9,278
2013	348	306	26	11	43	94	172	335	617	1,315	3,222	8,008
2014	364	413	20	11	47	88	179	354	606	1,369	3,227	7,894
2015	376	431	27	14	47	105	171	354	622	1,360	3,193	7,637

[1] Figures for age not stated are included in "All ages" but not distributed among age groups. [2] The death rates for specified races other than White and Black should be interpreted with caution because of inconsistencies between reporting race on death certificates and censuses and surveys.

Source: U.S. National Center for Health Statistics, *Health, United States, 2016*, May 2017. See also <http://www.cdc.gov/nchs/hus.htm>.

Table 116. Age-Adjusted Death Rates by Sex, Race, and Hispanic Origin: 1980 to 2015

[Age-adjusted rates per 100,000 population. Age-adjusted death rates are better indicators than crude death rates for showing changes in the risk of death over time when the age distribution of the population is changing, and for comparing the mortality of population subgroups that have different age compositions. Populations enumerated as of April 1 for census years and estimated as of July 1 for all other years. Excludes fetal deaths and deaths of nonresidents of the United States. Data for Hispanic-origin and specified races other than White and Black should be interpreted with caution because of inconsistent reporting of race on death certificates and on censuses and surveys. See text this section and Appendix III]

Sex, race, and Hispanic origin	1980	1990	2000	2005	2010	2011	2012	2013	2014	2015
ALL RACES [1]										
Total	1,039	939	869	815	747	741	733	732	725	733
Male	1,348	1,203	1,054	972	887	875	865	864	855	863
Female	818	751	731	692	635	632	625	624	617	624
WHITE										
Total	1,013	910	850	801	742	739	731	731	725	735
Male	1,318	1,166	1,029	953	879	870	860	859	853	862
Female	796	729	715	681	631	630	624	624	618	627
BLACK										
Total	1,315	1,250	1,121	1,035	898	877	865	861	849	852
Male	1,698	1,645	1,404	1,281	1,104	1,067	1,059	1,053	1,034	1,040
Female	1,033	975	928	863	753	740	724	721	713	711
AMERICAN INDIAN OR ALASKA NATIVE										
Total	867	716	709	701	628	601	595	592	594	597
Male	1,112	916	842	825	730	692	691	689	685	694
Female	662	562	605	602	542	523	512	508	514	511
ASIAN OR PACIFIC ISLANDER										
Total	590	582	506	460	424	410	407	405	388	338
Male	787	716	624	561	512	491	484	488	462	468
Female	426	469	417	385	359	350	349	343	331	395
HISPANIC ORIGIN [2]										
Total	(NA)	(NA)	666	628	559	541	539	535	523	525
Male	(NA)	(NA)	818	771	678	647	644	640	627	629
Female	(NA)	(NA)	546	514	463	453	453	449	438	438
NON-HISPANIC, WHITE										
Total	(NA)	(NA)	856	810	755	754	746	747	743	753
Male	(NA)	(NA)	1,035	962	893	887	876	877	872	881
Female	(NA)	(NA)	722	691	643	645	638	638	634	644
NON-HISPANIC, BLACK										
Total	(NA)	(NA)	1,137	1,055	920	902	887	885	871	876
Male	(NA)	(NA)	1,422	1,306	1,132	1,098	1,086	1,083	1,060	1,070
Female	(NA)	(NA)	941	879	771	760	742	741	731	731

NA Not available. [1] For 1980 and 1990, includes deaths among races not shown separately. [2] Persons of Hispanic origin may be of any race.

Source: U.S. National Center for Health Statistics, National Vital Statistics Reports (NVSR), *Deaths: Final Data for 2014*, Vol. 65. No. 4, June 2016; and CDC WONDER Online Database, "Multiple Cause of Death, 1999-2015," <https://wonder.cdc.gov/> accessed August 2017. See also <http://www.cdc.gov/nchs/nvss/deaths.htm>.

Table 117. Death Rates by Hispanic-Origin Status, Sex, and Age: 2010 to 2015

[Rates per 100,000 U.S. standard population. Rates are based on populations enumerated as of April 1 for census years and estimated as of July 1 for all other years. Excludes deaths of nonresidents of the United States. Data for Hispanic-origin should be interpreted with caution because of inconsistent reporting of Hispanic origin and race on death certificates and censuses and surveys]

Age	Hispanic male			Hispanic female			Non-Hispanic White male			Non-Hispanic White female		
	2010	2014	2015	2010	2014	2015	2010	2014	2015	2010	2014	2015
Age adjusted [1]	**678**	**627**	**629**	**463**	**438**	**438**	**893**	**872**	**881**	**643**	**634**	**644**
Crude [2]	**311**	**330**	**343**	**261**	**281**	**290**	**988**	**1,045**	**1,073**	**981**	**1,011**	**1,039**
Under 1 year	557	508	500	463	432	437	576	550	541	480	451	446
1 to 4 years	25	20	22	20	17	18	28	25	26	22	20	20
5 to 14 years	11	13	12	9	10	9	14	14	15	11	10	11
15 to 24 years	79	75	82	26	27	29	93	91	93	38	38	40
25 to 34 years	101	104	112	39	41	45	144	156	168	67	73	79
35 to 44 years	146	149	153	75	79	78	219	227	238	133	144	146
45 to 54 years	352	341	340	194	185	184	508	511	510	308	326	328
55 to 64 years	815	788	788	450	443	435	1,046	1,085	1,093	632	654	661
65 to 74 years	1,775	1,655	1,674	1,086	1,037	1,049	2,257	2,170	2,184	1,536	1,463	1,473
75 to 84 years	4,462	4,103	4,127	3,067	2,931	2,937	5,770	5,499	5,501	4,233	4,079	4,103
85 years and over	11,780	10,318	10,146	10,237	9,250	9,266	15,817	15,286	15,526	13,544	13,290	13,683

[1] Age-adjusted death rates are better indicators than crude death rates for showing changes in the risk of death over time when the age distribution of the population is changing, and for comparing the mortality of population subgroups that have different age compositions. [2] The total number of deaths in a given time period divided by the total resident population.

Source: U.S. National Center for Health Statistics, *Health, United States, 2016*, May 2017. See also <http://www.cdc.gov/nchs/hus.htm>.

Table 118. Deaths and Death Rates by State: 1990 to 2015

[2,148 represents 2,148,000. By state of residence. Excludes deaths of nonresidents of the United States. Caution should be used in comparing death rates by state; rates are affected by the population composition of the area. See also Appendix III]

State	Number of deaths (1,000)						Death rate per 1,000 population [1]						Age-adjusted rate, 2015 [1,2]
	1990	2000	2010	2013	2014	2015	1990	2000	2010	2013	2014	2015	
United States........	2,148	2,403	2,468	2,597	2,626	2,713	8.6	8.5	8.0	8.2	8.2	8.4	7.3
Alabama................	39	45	48	50	50	52	9.7	10.1	10.1	10.4	10.4	10.7	9.3
Alaska..................	2	3	4	4	4	4	4.0	4.6	5.2	5.4	5.6	5.8	7.5
Arizona.................	29	41	47	51	52	54	7.9	7.9	7.3	7.6	7.7	8.0	6.7
Arkansas...............	25	28	29	30	30	32	10.5	10.6	9.9	10.3	10.3	10.6	9.0
California..............	214	230	234	248	246	259	7.2	6.8	6.3	6.5	6.3	6.6	6.2
Colorado..............	22	27	31	34	35	36	6.6	6.3	6.3	6.4	6.6	6.7	6.6
Connecticut...........	28	30	29	30	30	31	8.4	8.8	8.0	8.2	8.3	8.5	6.6
Delaware..............	6	7	8	8	8	9	8.7	8.8	8.6	8.6	8.8	9.1	7.4
District of Columbia....	7	6	5	5	5	5	12.0	10.5	7.8	7.3	7.2	7.2	7.5
Florida.................	134	164	174	181	186	192	10.4	10.3	9.2	9.3	9.3	9.5	6.6
Georgia................	52	64	71	75	77	80	8.0	7.8	7.4	7.5	7.6	7.8	8.1
Hawaii.................	7	8	10	11	11	11	6.1	6.8	7.1	7.5	7.6	7.7	5.9
Idaho..................	7	10	11	12	13	13	7.4	7.4	7.3	7.7	7.7	7.9	7.3
Illinois.................	103	107	100	103	105	107	9.0	8.6	7.8	8.0	8.2	8.3	7.3
Indiana.................	50	55	57	61	61	63	8.9	9.1	8.8	9.2	9.2	9.5	8.3
Iowa...................	27	28	28	29	29	30	9.7	9.6	9.1	9.4	9.4	9.5	7.3
Kansas................	22	25	25	25	26	27	9.0	9.2	8.6	8.8	8.9	9.2	7.8
Kentucky..............	35	40	42	44	45	47	9.5	9.8	9.7	10.0	10.2	10.5	9.2
Louisiana..............	38	41	41	43	44	44	8.9	9.2	9.0	9.4	9.4	9.4	8.8
Maine..................	11	12	13	14	14	14	9.0	9.7	9.6	10.2	10.2	10.9	7.8
Maryland..............	38	44	43	46	46	47	8.0	8.3	7.5	7.7	7.7	7.9	7.1
Massachusetts.........	53	57	53	55	55	58	8.8	8.9	8.0	8.2	8.2	8.5	6.8
Michigan...............	79	87	88	92	94	95	8.5	8.7	8.9	9.3	9.5	9.6	7.9
Minnesota.............	35	38	39	41	41	43	7.9	7.7	7.3	7.6	7.6	7.8	6.5
Mississippi.............	25	29	29	31	31	32	9.8	10.1	9.8	10.3	10.2	10.6	9.6
Missouri...............	50	55	55	57	58	60	9.8	9.8	9.2	9.5	9.6	9.8	8.2
Montana...............	7	8	9	10	9	10	8.6	9.0	8.9	9.4	9.2	9.6	7.6
Nebraska..............	15	15	15	16	16	17	9.4	8.8	8.3	8.4	8.5	8.8	7.4
Nevada................	9	15	20	21	22	23	7.8	7.6	7.3	7.7	7.7	7.9	7.6
New Hampshire........	8	10	10	11	12	12	7.7	7.8	7.7	8.2	8.7	9.0	7.2
New Jersey............	70	75	69	71	71	72	9.1	8.9	7.9	8.0	8.0	8.1	6.7
New Mexico............	11	13	16	17	18	18	7.0	7.4	7.7	8.1	8.4	8.5	7.4
New York..............	169	158	146	151	150	154	9.4	8.3	7.6	7.7	7.6	7.8	6.4
North Carolina.........	57	72	79	83	85	89	8.6	8.9	8.3	8.5	8.6	8.9	7.9
North Dakota...........	6	6	6	6	6	6	8.9	9.1	8.8	8.6	8.4	8.2	7.0
Ohio...................	99	108	109	113	115	118	9.1	9.5	9.4	9.8	9.9	10.2	8.3
Oklahoma..............	30	35	37	38	38	39	9.7	10.2	9.7	10.0	9.9	10.1	9.0
Oregon................	25	30	32	34	34	36	8.8	8.6	8.3	8.6	8.6	8.9	7.2
Pennsylvania..........	122	131	125	129	128	133	10.3	10.7	9.8	10.1	10.0	10.4	7.7
Rhode Island...........	10	10	10	10	10	10	9.5	9.6	9.1	9.3	9.3	9.6	7.2
South Carolina.........	30	37	42	45	45	47	8.5	9.2	9.0	9.3	9.4	9.6	8.4
South Dakota..........	6	7	7	7	8	8	9.1	9.3	8.7	8.4	8.8	9.0	7.1
Tennessee.............	46	55	60	63	65	67	9.5	9.7	9.4	9.8	9.9	10.1	8.9
Texas..................	125	150	167	179	184	190	7.4	7.2	6.6	6.8	6.8	6.9	7.5
Utah...................	9	12	15	16	17	17	5.3	5.5	5.3	5.6	5.7	5.8	7.1
Vermont...............	5	5	5	6	6	6	8.2	8.4	8.6	9.0	9.0	9.5	7.2
Virginia................	48	56	59	63	64	66	7.8	8.0	7.4	7.6	7.6	7.8	7.2
Washington............	37	44	48	51	52	55	7.6	7.5	7.2	7.4	7.4	7.6	6.9
West Virginia...........	19	21	21	22	22	23	10.8	11.7	11.5	11.8	12.0	12.3	9.4
Wisconsin..............	43	46	47	50	50	51	8.7	8.7	8.3	8.7	8.7	8.9	7.2
Wyoming..............	3	4	4	5	5	5	7.1	7.9	7.9	7.8	8.0	8.2	7.5

[1] Rates based on enumerated resident population as of April 1 for 1990, 2000, and 2010; estimated resident population as of July 1 for all other years. [2] Age-adjusted death rates are better indicators than crude death rates for showing changes in the risk of death over time when the age distribution of the population is changing, and for comparing the mortality of population subgroups that have different age compositions. See text this section.

Source: U.S. National Center for Health Statistics, CDC WONDER Online Database, "Multiple Cause of Death, 1999-2015," <http://wonder.cdc.gov/>; and National Vital Statistics Reports (NVSR), *Deaths: Final Data for 2014*, Vol. 65, No. 4, June 2016 and earlier reports. See also <http://www.cdc.gov/nchs/nvss/deaths.htm>.

Table 119. Fetal and Infant Deaths: 1990 to 2013

[The term "fetal death," defined on an all inclusive basis to end confusion arising from the use of such terms as stillbirth, spontaneous abortion, and miscarriage, has been adopted by the National Center for Health Statistics (NCHS) as the nationally recommended standard. Fetal deaths do not include induced terminations of pregnancy. See also Appendix III]

Year	Fetal deaths[1]			Infant deaths		Fetal mortality rate[2]			Perinatal mortality rate	
	Total[1]	20 to 27 weeks[3]	28 weeks or more[3]	Less than 7 days	Less than 28 days	Total[1]	20 to 27 weeks[3]	28 weeks or more[3]	Definition I[4]	Definition II[5]
1990.....	31,386	13,427	17,959	19,439	23,591	7.49	3.22	4.30	8.95	13.12
1995.....	27,294	13,043	14,251	15,483	19,186	6.95	3.33	3.64	7.60	11.84
2000.....	27,003	13,497	13,506	14,893	18,733	6.61	3.31	3.32	6.97	11.19
2001.....	26,373	13,122	13,251	14,622	18,275	6.51	3.25	3.28	6.90	11.02
2002.....	25,943	13,072	12,871	15,020	18,791	6.41	3.24	3.19	6.91	11.05
2003.....	26,004	13,348	12,656	15,152	18,935	6.32	3.25	3.08	6.78	10.92
2004.....	26,001	13,068	12,933	14,836	18,602	6.28	3.17	3.14	6.73	10.78
2005.....	25,894	13,326	12,568	15,013	18,782	6.22	3.21	3.03	6.64	10.73
2006.....	25,972	13,269	12,703	15,148	19,041	6.05	3.10	2.97	6.51	10.49
2007.....	26,593	13,822	12,771	15,139	19,094	6.12	3.19	2.95	6.45	10.52
2008.....	26,335	13,347	12,988	14,648	18,238	6.16	3.13	3.05	6.49	10.43
2009.....	24,872	12,813	12,059	13,768	17,261	5.99	3.09	2.91	6.23	10.14
2010.....	24,258	12,388	11,870	12,900	16,193	6.03	3.09	2.96	6.18	10.05
2011.....	24,289	12,432	11,857	12,960	16,065	6.11	3.13	2.99	6.26	10.14
2012.....	24,073	12,334	11,739	12,911	15,887	6.05	3.11	2.96	6.22	10.05
2013.....	23,595	11,874	11,721	12,900	15,893	5.96	3.01	2.97	6.24	9.98

[1] Fetal deaths with stated or presumed gestation of 20 weeks or more. [2] Rate per 1,000 live births and fetal deaths in specified age group. [3] Not stated gestational age proportionally distributed. [4] Infant deaths of less than 7 days and fetal deaths with stated or presumed period of gestation of 28 weeks or more, per 1,000 live births and fetal deaths. [5] Infant deaths of less than 28 days and fetal deaths with stated or presumed period of gestation of 20 weeks or more per 1,000 live births and fetal deaths.

Source: U.S. National Center for Health Statistics, National Vital Statistics Reports (NVSR), *Fetal and Perinatal Mortality, United States, 2013*, Vol. 64. No. 8, July 2015. See also <http://www.cdc.gov/nchs/fetal_death.htm>.

Table 120. Fetal, Infant, Neonatal, and Maternal Mortality Rates by Race: 1980 to 2015

[Deaths per 1,000 live births, except as noted. Data based on death certificates, fetal death records, and birth certificates. Excludes deaths of nonresidents of the United States. See also Appendix III]

Race and year	Infant[1]	Neonatal[1]		Post-neonatal[1]	Fetal mortality rate[2]	Late fetal mortality rate[3]	Perinatal mortality rate[4]	Maternal mortality rate[5]
		Under 28 days	Under 7 days					
ALL RACES								
1980.........................	12.6	8.5	7.1	4.1	9.1	6.2	13.2	9.2
1990.........................	9.2	5.8	4.8	3.4	7.5	4.3	9.0	8.2
1995.........................	7.6	4.9	4.0	2.7	7.0	3.6	7.6	7.1
2000.........................	6.9	4.6	3.7	2.3	6.6	3.3	7.0	9.8
2005.........................	6.9	4.5	3.6	2.3	6.2	3.0	6.6	[6] 15.1
2010.........................	6.1	4.0	3.2	2.1	6.0	3.0	6.2	(NA)
2013.........................	6.0	4.0	3.3	1.9	6.0	3.0	6.2	(NA)
2014.........................	5.8	3.9	3.2	1.9	6.0	2.8	6.0	(NA)
2015.........................	5.9	3.9	3.2	2.0	(NA)	(NA)	(NA)	(NA)
WHITE[7]								
1980.........................	10.9	7.4	6.1	3.5	8.1	5.7	11.8	6.7
1990.........................	7.6	4.8	3.9	2.8	6.4	3.8	7.7	5.4
1995.........................	6.3	4.1	3.3	2.2	5.9	3.3	6.5	4.2
2000.........................	5.7	3.8	3.0	1.9	5.6	2.9	5.9	7.5
2005.........................	5.7	3.8	3.0	1.9	5.3	2.7	5.7	[6] 11.1
2010.........................	5.2	3.5	2.7	1.7	(NA)	(NA)	(NA)	(NA)
2013.........................	5.1	3.5	2.8	1.6	(NA)	(NA)	(NA)	(NA)
2014.........................	4.9	3.4	2.7	1.6	(NA)	(NA)	(NA)	(NA)
2015.........................	4.9	3.3	2.7	1.6	(NA)	(NA)	(NA)	(NA)
BLACK[7]								
1980.........................	22.2	14.6	12.3	7.6	14.7	9.1	21.3	22.4
1990.........................	18.0	11.6	9.7	6.4	13.3	6.7	16.4	22.4
1995.........................	15.1	9.8	8.2	5.3	12.7	5.7	13.8	22.1
2000.........................	14.1	9.4	7.6	4.7	12.4	5.4	13.0	22.0
2005.........................	13.7	9.1	7.3	4.7	11.4	4.9	12.1	[6] 36.5
2010.........................	11.6	7.5	6.0	4.1	(NA)	(NA)	(NA)	(NA)
2013.........................	11.2	7.4	6.1	3.8	(NA)	(NA)	(NA)	(NA)
2014.........................	11.0	7.3	6.0	3.7	(NA)	(NA)	(NA)	(NA)
2015.........................	11.4	7.4	6.0	4.0	(NA)	(NA)	(NA)	(NA)

NA Not available. [1] Infant (under 1 year of age), neonatal (under 28 days), early neonatal (under 7 days), and postneonatal (28 days–11 months). [2] Number of fetal deaths of 20 weeks or more gestation per 1,000 live births plus fetal deaths. [3] Number of fetal deaths of 28 weeks or more gestation (late fetal deaths) per 1,000 live births plus late fetal deaths. [4] Number of late fetal deaths plus infant deaths within 7 days of birth per 1,000 live births plus late fetal deaths. [5] Per 100,000 live births from deliveries and complications of pregnancy, childbirth, and the puerperium. Beginning 2000, deaths are classified according to the tenth revision of the International Classification of Diseases; earlier years classified according to the revision in use at the time; see text, this section. [6] Increase partially reflects the use of a separate item on the death certificate on pregnancy status by an increasing number of states. [7] Infant deaths are tabulated by race of decedent; fetal deaths and live births are tabulated by race of mother.

Source: U.S. National Center for Health Statistics, *Fetal and Perinatal Mortality, United States, 2013*, Vol. 64, No. 8, July 2015; and *Health, United States, 2016*, May 2017. See also <http://www.cdc.gov/nchs/hus.htm>.

Table 121. Infant Mortality Rates by Race, State, and Island Area: 1990 to 2014

[Deaths per 1,000 live births, by place of residence. Represents deaths of infants under 1 year old, exclusive of fetal deaths. Excludes deaths of nonresidents of the United States]

State and Island Area	Total [1]				White				Black			
	1990	2000	2010	2014	1990	2000	2010	2014	1990	2000	2010	2014
United States	**9.2**	**6.9**	**6.2**	**5.8**	**7.6**	**5.7**	**5.2**	**4.9**	**18.0**	**14.1**	**11.6**	**11.1**
Alabama	10.8	9.4	8.7	8.7	8.1	6.6	6.6	6.1	16.0	15.4	13.7	14.6
Alaska	10.5	6.8	3.8	6.6	7.6	5.8	3.3	4.3	(B)	(B)	(B)	(B)
Arizona	8.8	6.7	6.0	6.2	7.8	6.2	5.5	5.6	20.6	17.6	12.1	12.7
Arkansas	9.2	8.4	7.3	7.5	8.4	7.0	6.7	6.6	13.9	13.7	10.3	11.9
California	7.9	5.4	4.7	4.3	7.0	5.1	4.6	4.1	16.8	12.9	9.8	10.6
Colorado	8.8	6.2	5.9	4.8	7.8	5.6	5.6	4.4	19.4	19.5	13.1	11.2
Connecticut	7.9	6.6	5.3	4.9	6.3	5.6	4.5	4.2	17.6	14.4	11.6	9.9
Delaware	10.1	9.2	7.7	6.7	9.7	7.9	6.4	5.1	20.1	14.8	11.9	10.7
District of Columbia	20.7	12.0	7.9	7.3	(B)	(B)	(B)	(B)	24.6	16.1	10.5	9.8
Florida	9.6	7.0	6.5	6.1	6.7	5.4	5.0	4.6	16.8	12.6	11.3	10.8
Georgia	12.4	8.5	6.4	7.5	7.4	5.9	5.1	4.9	18.3	13.9	9.1	12.0
Hawaii	6.7	8.1	6.2	4.5	6.1	6.5	3.9	3.3	(B)	(B)	(B)	(B)
Idaho	8.7	7.5	4.8	5.5	8.6	7.5	4.8	5.6	(B)	(B)	(B)	(B)
Illinois	10.7	8.5	6.8	6.6	7.9	6.6	5.4	5.4	22.4	17.1	13.6	12.5
Indiana	9.6	7.8	7.6	7.1	7.9	6.9	6.7	6.1	17.4	15.8	15.0	14.3
Iowa	8.1	6.5	4.9	4.8	7.9	6.0	4.6	4.6	21.9	21.1	11.2	8.5
Kansas	8.4	6.8	6.2	6.3	8.0	6.4	5.7	5.5	17.7	12.2	12.4	13.2
Kentucky	8.5	7.2	6.8	7.1	8.2	6.7	6.4	6.6	14.3	12.7	11.1	12.6
Louisiana	11.1	9.0	7.6	7.5	8.1	5.9	4.9	5.6	16.7	13.3	11.8	10.6
Maine	6.2	4.9	5.4	6.7	6.7	4.8	5.4	6.6	(B)	(B)	(B)	(B)
Maryland	9.5	7.6	6.8	6.5	6.8	4.8	4.4	4.5	17.1	13.2	11.6	10.3
Massachusetts	7.0	4.6	4.4	4.4	6.1	4.0	4.0	4.2	11.9	9.9	7.2	6.6
Michigan	10.7	8.2	7.1	6.5	7.4	6.0	5.5	5.1	21.6	18.2	14.1	12.3
Minnesota	7.3	5.6	4.5	5.0	6.7	4.8	4.2	4.1	23.7	14.6	6.4	10.5
Mississippi	12.1	10.7	9.7	8.2	7.4	6.8	6.6	6.1	16.2	15.3	13.8	10.9
Missouri	9.4	7.2	6.6	6.1	7.9	5.9	5.8	5.2	18.2	14.7	11.8	11.2
Montana	9.0	6.1	5.9	5.5	6.0	5.5	5.9	4.5	(B)	(B)	(B)	(B)
Nebraska	8.3	7.3	5.3	5.1	6.9	6.4	4.7	5.2	18.9	20.3	13.4	(B)
Nevada	8.4	6.5	5.6	5.5	8.2	6.0	4.8	5.2	14.2	12.7	13.8	8.9
New Hampshire	7.1	5.7	4.0	4.3	6.0	5.5	3.9	4.4	(B)	(B)	(B)	(B)
New Jersey	9.0	6.3	4.8	4.4	6.4	5.0	3.6	4.0	18.4	13.6	10.4	7.5
New Mexico	9.0	6.6	5.6	5.4	7.6	6.3	5.5	5.3	(B)	(B)	(B)	(B)
New York	9.6	6.4	5.1	4.7	7.4	5.4	4.2	4.2	18.1	10.9	9.2	7.8
North Carolina	10.6	8.6	7.0	7.1	8.0	6.3	5.4	5.4	16.5	15.7	12.3	12.1
North Dakota	8.0	8.1	6.8	5.0	7.2	7.5	5.4	4.5	(B)	(B)	(B)	(B)
Ohio	9.8	7.6	7.7	6.9	7.8	6.3	6.3	5.4	19.5	15.4	14.8	14.0
Oklahoma	9.2	8.5	7.6	8.1	9.1	7.9	6.3	7.0	14.3	16.9	12.4	13.2
Oregon	8.3	5.6	4.9	5.1	7.0	5.5	4.7	5.0	(B)	(B)	(B)	(B)
Pennsylvania	9.6	7.1	7.3	5.9	7.4	5.8	6.3	4.8	20.5	15.7	12.6	11.5
Rhode Island	8.1	6.3	7.1	4.4	7.0	5.9	6.7	3.9	(B)	(B)	(B)	(B)
South Carolina	11.7	8.7	7.4	6.5	8.1	5.4	5.3	4.7	17.3	14.8	11.3	10.1
South Dakota	10.1	5.5	6.9	5.9	8.0	4.3	6.0	4.6	(B)	(B)	(B)	(B)
Tennessee	10.3	9.1	7.9	6.9	7.3	6.8	6.6	5.5	17.9	18.0	13.3	12.3
Texas	8.1	5.7	6.1	5.9	6.7	5.1	5.6	5.2	14.7	11.4	11.2	10.9
Utah	7.5	5.2	4.9	4.9	6.0	5.1	4.5	4.9	(B)	(B)	(B)	(B)
Vermont	6.4	6.0	4.2	4.6	5.9	6.1	4.4	4.8	(B)	(B)	(B)	(B)
Virginia	10.2	6.9	6.8	5.8	7.4	5.4	4.8	4.6	19.5	12.4	14.3	10.8
Washington	7.8	5.2	4.5	4.5	7.3	4.9	4.0	4.2	20.6	9.4	8.2	10.9
West Virginia	9.9	7.6	7.3	7.0	8.1	7.4	7.1	6.8	(B)	(B)	(B)	(B)
Wisconsin	8.2	6.6	5.8	5.7	7.7	5.5	4.9	4.9	19.0	17.2	14.6	12.7
Wyoming	8.6	6.7	6.8	6.4	7.5	6.5	6.4	6.3	(B)	(B)	(B)	(B)
Puerto Rico	(NA)	9.7	8.1	7.0	(NA)	10.2	8.8	7.6	(NA)	(B)	(B)	(B)
Virgin Islands	(NA)	13.4	(B)	(NA)	(NA)	(B)	(B)	(NA)	(B)	(B)	(B)	(NA)
Guam	(NA)	5.8	14.1	8.3	(NA)	(B)	(B)	(B)	(B)	(B)	(B)	(B)

B Base figure too small to meet statistical standards for reliability. NA Not available. [1] Includes other races, not shown separately.

Source: U.S. National Center for Health Statistics, National Vital Statistics Reports (NVSR), *Deaths: Final Data for 2014*, Vol. 65, No. 4, June 2016 and earlier reports. See also <http://www.cdc.gov/nchs/nvss/deaths.htm>.

Table 122. Age-Adjusted Death Rates by Major Cause: 1960 to 2015

[Age-adjusted rates per 100,000 population. Age-adjusted death rates were prepared using the direct method, in which age specific death rates for a population of interest are applied to a standard population distributed by age. Age adjustment eliminates the differences in observed rates between points in time or among compared population groups that result from age differences in population composition. Beginning 1999, deaths classified according to tenth revision of International Classification of Diseases; for earlier years, causes of death were classified according to the revisions then in use. Changes in classification of causes of death due to these revisions may result in discontinuities in cause-of-death trends. See Appendix III]

Year	Diseases of the heart	Malignant neoplasms (cancer)	Accidents[1]	Chronic lower respiratory diseases	Cerebrovascular diseases	Alzheimer's disease	Diabetes mellitus	Influenza and pneumonia	Nephritis, nephrotic syndrome and nephrosis	Intentional self-harm (suicide)
1960	559.0	193.9	63.1	12.5	177.9	(NA)	22.5	53.7	10.6	12.5
1961	545.3	193.4	60.6	12.6	173.1	(NA)	22.1	43.4	10.0	12.2
1962	556.9	193.3	62.9	14.2	174.0	(NA)	22.6	47.1	9.6	12.8
1963	563.4	194.7	64.0	16.5	173.9	(NA)	23.1	55.6	9.2	13.0
1964	543.3	193.6	64.1	16.3	167.0	(NA)	22.5	45.4	8.9	12.7
1965	542.5	195.6	65.8	18.3	166.4	(NA)	22.9	46.8	8.3	13.0
1966	541.2	196.5	67.6	19.2	165.8	(NA)	23.6	47.9	7.9	12.7
1967	524.7	197.3	66.2	19.2	159.3	(NA)	23.4	42.2	7.3	12.5
1968	531.0	198.8	65.5	20.7	162.5	(NA)	25.3	52.8	6.1	12.4
1969	516.8	198.5	64.9	20.9	155.4	(NA)	25.1	47.9	6.0	12.7
1970	492.7	198.6	62.2	21.3	147.7	(NA)	24.3	41.7	5.5	13.1
1971	492.9	199.3	60.3	21.8	147.6	(NA)	23.9	38.4	5.2	13.1
1972	490.2	200.3	60.2	22.8	147.3	(NA)	23.7	41.3	5.2	13.3
1973	482.0	200.0	59.3	23.6	145.2	(NA)	23.0	41.2	5.0	13.1
1974	458.8	201.5	52.7	23.2	136.8	(NA)	22.1	35.5	4.7	13.2
1975	431.2	200.1	50.8	23.7	123.5	(NA)	20.3	34.9	4.7	13.6
1976	426.9	202.5	48.7	24.9	117.4	(NA)	19.5	38.8	4.9	13.2
1977	413.7	203.5	48.8	24.7	110.4	(NA)	18.2	31.0	4.8	13.7
1978	409.9	204.9	48.9	26.3	103.7	(NA)	18.3	34.5	4.8	12.9
1979	401.6	204.0	46.5	25.5	97.1	(NA)	17.5	26.1	8.6	12.6
1980	412.1	207.9	46.4	28.3	96.4	(NA)	18.1	31.4	9.1	12.2
1981	397.0	206.4	43.4	29.0	89.5	0.9	17.6	30.0	9.1	12.3
1982	389.0	208.3	40.1	29.1	84.2	1.3	17.2	26.5	9.4	12.5
1983	388.9	209.1	39.1	31.6	81.2	2.2	17.6	29.8	9.6	12.4
1984	378.8	210.8	38.8	32.4	78.7	3.1	17.2	30.6	10.0	12.6
1985	375.0	211.3	38.5	34.5	76.6	4.1	17.4	34.5	10.4	12.5
1986	365.1	211.5	38.6	34.8	73.1	4.6	17.2	34.8	10.4	13.0
1987	355.9	211.7	38.2	35.0	71.6	5.5	17.4	33.8	10.4	12.8
1988	352.5	212.5	38.9	36.5	70.6	5.8	18.0	37.3	10.4	12.5
1989	332.0	214.2	37.7	36.6	66.9	6.1	20.5	35.9	9.6	12.3
1990	321.8	216.0	36.3	37.2	65.3	6.3	20.7	36.8	9.3	12.5
1991	312.5	215.2	34.7	37.9	62.9	6.3	20.7	34.7	9.3	12.3
1992	304.0	213.5	33.2	37.7	61.5	6.3	20.7	32.8	9.4	12.0
1993	308.1	213.5	34.2	40.7	62.7	7.1	21.9	35.0	9.7	12.1
1994	297.5	211.7	34.2	40.3	62.6	7.7	22.6	33.6	9.4	11.9
1995	293.4	209.9	34.4	40.1	63.1	8.4	23.2	33.4	9.5	11.8
1996	285.7	206.7	34.5	40.6	62.5	8.5	23.8	32.9	9.6	11.5
1997	277.7	203.4	34.2	41.1	61.1	8.7	23.7	33.3	9.8	11.2
1998	267.4	202.1	35.6	43.8	62.8	8.6	24.2	24.2	9.8	11.1
1999	266.5	200.8	35.3	45.4	61.6	16.5	25.0	23.5	13.0	10.5
2000	257.6	199.6	34.9	44.2	60.9	18.1	25.0	23.7	13.5	10.4
2001	249.5	196.5	35.7	43.9	58.4	19.3	25.4	22.2	14.1	10.7
2002	244.6	194.3	37.1	43.9	57.2	20.8	25.6	23.2	14.4	10.9
2003	236.3	190.9	37.6	43.7	54.6	22.1	25.5	22.6	14.7	10.8
2004	221.6	186.8	38.1	41.6	51.2	22.6	24.7	20.4	14.5	11.0
2005	216.8	185.1	39.5	43.9	48.0	24.0	24.9	21.0	14.7	10.9
2006	205.5	181.8	40.2	41.0	44.8	23.7	23.6	18.4	14.8	11.0
2007	196.1	179.3	40.4	41.4	43.5	23.8	22.8	16.8	14.9	11.3
2008	192.1	176.4	39.2	44.7	42.1	25.8	22.0	17.6	15.1	11.6
2009	182.8	173.5	37.5	42.7	39.6	24.2	21.0	16.5	15.1	11.8
2010	179.1	172.8	38.0	42.2	39.1	25.1	20.8	15.1	15.3	12.1
2011	173.7	169.0	39.1	42.5	37.9	24.7	21.6	15.7	13.4	12.3
2012	170.5	166.5	39.1	41.5	36.9	23.8	21.2	14.4	13.1	12.6
2013	169.8	163.2	39.4	42.1	36.2	23.5	21.2	15.9	13.2	12.6
2014	167.0	161.2	40.5	40.5	36.5	25.4	20.9	15.1	13.2	13.0
2015	168.5	158.5	43.2	41.6	37.6	29.4	21.3	15.2	13.4	13.3

NA Not available. [1] Unintentional injuries.

Source: U.S. National Center for Health Statistics, National Vital Statistics Reports (NVSR), *Deaths: Final Data for 2014*, Vol. 65, No. 4, June 2016 and earlier reports; and CDC WONDER Online Database, "Multiple Cause of Death, 1999-2015," <https://wonder.cdc.gov/>, accessed August 2017. See also <http://www.cdc.gov/nchs/nvss/deaths.htm>.

Table 123. Deaths by Leading Cause and Race: 2015

[Cause of death based on International Classification of Diseases, Tenth Revision (ICD-10)]

Cause of death	White			Black			American Indian/ Alaska Native			Asian/ Pacific Islander		
	Rank [1]	Deaths	Per-cent	Rank [1]	Deaths	Per-cent	Rank [1]	Deaths	Per-cent	Rank [1]	Deaths	Per-cent
All causes.................	(X)	2,306,861	100.0	(X)	320,072	100.0	(X)	19,016	100.0	(X)	66,681	100.0
Diseases of heart............	1	540,857	23.4	1	75,249	23.5	1	3,463	18.2	2	14,273	21.4
Malignant neoplasms........	2	505,613	21.9	2	69,389	21.7	2	3,358	17.7	1	17,570	26.3
Chronic lower respiratory diseases....................	3	141,766	6.1	6	10,475	3.3	6	883	4.6	8	1,917	2.9
Accidents (unintentional injuries)......................	4	125,773	5.5	4	15,745	4.9	3	2,078	10.9	4	2,975	4.5
Cerebrovascular diseases...	5	116,788	5.1	3	17,988	5.6	7	676	3.6	3	4,871	7.3
Alzheimer's disease.........	6	99,866	4.3	9	8,156	2.5	11	327	1.7	6	2,212	3.3
Diabetes mellitus............	7	61,938	2.7	5	13,869	4.3	4	1,087	5.7	5	2,641	4.0
Influenza and pneumonia. . .	8	48,877	2.1	12	5,641	1.8	10	342	1.8	7	2,202	3.3
Intentional self harm (suicide)....................	9	39,796	1.7	16	2,504	0.8	8	577	3.0	10	1,316	2.0
Nephritis, nephrotic syndrome and nephrosis......	10	39,078	1.7	8	9,170	2.9	9	352	1.9	9	1,359	2.0
Chronic liver disease and cirrhosis...................	11	35,386	1.5	15	3,254	1.0	5	1,061	5.6	14	625	0.9
Septicemia..................	12	32,998	1.4	10	6,647	2.1	12	308	1.6	12	820	1.2
Assault (homicide)..........	18	8,007	0.3	7	9,173	2.9	13	286	1.5	19	327	0.5

X Not applicable. [1] Rank based on number of deaths.

Source: U.S. National Center for Health Statistics, National Vital Statistics Reports (NVSR), *Deaths: Leading Causes for 2014*, Vol. 65, No. 5, June 2016; and CDC WONDER Online Database, "Multiple Cause of Death, 1999-2015," <https://wonder.cdc.gov/>, accessed August 2017. See also <http://www.cdc.gov/nchs/nvss/deaths.htm>.

Table 124. Deaths by Leading Cause and Hispanic Origin: 2015

[Race and Hispanic origin are reported separately on death certificates. Persons of Hispanic origin may be of any race. Cause of death based on International Classification of Diseases, Tenth Revision (ICD-10). See Appendix III]

Cause of death	Hispanic			Non-Hispanic White			Non-Hispanic Black		
	Rank [1]	Deaths	Per-cent	Rank [1]	Deaths	Per-cent	Rank [1]	Deaths	Per-cent
All causes....................................	(X)	179,457	100.0	(X)	2,123,631	100.0	(X)	315,254	100.0
Malignant neoplasms...........................	1	37,804	21.1	2	467,208	22.0	2	68,523	21.7
Diseases of heart..............................	2	36,401	20.3	1	503,172	23.7	1	74,093	23.5
Accidents (unintentional injuries)..............	3	13,806	7.7	4	111,827	5.3	4	15,366	4.9
Cerebrovascular diseases......................	4	9,795	5.5	5	106,830	5.0	3	17,760	5.6
Diabetes mellitus..............................	5	8,278	4.6	7	53,590	2.5	5	13,693	4.3
Alzheimer's disease............................	6	6,444	3.6	6	93,325	4.4	9	8,072	2.6
Chronic liver disease and cirrhosis............	7	6,018	3.4	12	29,343	1.4	15	3,185	1.0
Chronic lower respiratory diseases............	8	5,159	2.9	3	136,228	6.4	6	10,327	3.3
Nephritis, nephrotic syndrome and nephrosis.	9	3,581	2.0	10	35,481	1.7	7	9,083	2.9
Influenza and pneumonia......................	10	3,497	1.9	8	45,242	2.1	12	5,554	1.8
Intentional self harm (suicide).................	11	3,303	1.8	9	36,465	1.7	16	2,415	0.8
Septicemia....................................	13	2,692	1.5	11	30,240	1.4	10	6,576	2.1
Assault (homicide).............................	12	2,886	1.6	20	5,222	0.2	8	9,038	2.9

X Not applicable. [1] Rank based on number of deaths.

Source: U.S. National Center for Health Statistics, National Vital Statistics Reports (NVSR), *Deaths: Leading Causes for 2014*, Vol. 65, No. 5, June 2016; CDC WONDER Online Database, "Multiple Cause of Death, 1999-2015," <https://wonder.cdc.gov/>, accessed August 2017. See also <http://www.cdc.gov/nchs/nvss/deaths.htm>.

Table 125. Deaths and Death Rates by Selected Causes: 2014 and 2015

[Rates per 100,000 population. Figures are weighted data rounded to the nearest individual, so categories may not add to total or subtotal. Excludes deaths of nonresidents of the United States. Deaths classified according to the International Classification of Diseases, Tenth Revision (ICD-10). See also Appendix III]

Cause of death	2014			2015		
	Number	Rate	Age-adjusted rate [1]	Number	Rate	Age-adjusted rate [1]
All causes [2]............	**2,626,418**	**823.7**	**724.6**	**2,712,630**	**844.0**	**733.1**
Major cardiovascular diseases [2]........................	803,227	251.9	218.6	832,024	258.9	221.5
Diseases of heart........................	614,348	192.7	167.0	633,842	197.2	168.5
Acute rheumatic fever and chronic rheumatic heart disease........	3,281	1.0	0.9	3,372	1.0	0.9
Hypertensive heart disease........	38,721	12.1	10.5	41,688	13.0	11.1
Hypertensive heart and renal disease........	4,403	1.4	1.2	4,974	1.5	1.3
Ischemic heart disease........	364,593	114.3	98.8	366,801	114.1	97.2
Acute myocardial infarction........	114,019	35.8	31.0	114,023	35.5	30.3
Other heart diseases........	203,350	63.8	55.5	217,007	67.5	57.9
Heart failure........	68,626	21.5	18.6	75,251	23.4	19.9
Essential (primary) hypertension and hypertensive renal disease........	30,221	9.5	8.2	32,200	10.0	8.5
Cerebrovascular diseases........	133,103	41.7	36.5	140,323	43.7	37.6
Atherosclerosis........	6,356	2.0	1.7	6,088	1.9	1.6
Malignant neoplasms (cancer) [2]........	591,699	185.6	161.2	595,930	185.4	158.5
Malignant neoplasms of lip, oral cavity, and pharynx........	9,405	2.9	2.5	9,754	3.0	2.5
Malignant neoplasms of esophagus........	14,935	4.7	4.0	15,212	4.7	4.0
Malignant neoplasms of stomach........	11,311	3.5	3.1	11,331	3.5	3.1
Malignant neoplasms of colon, rectum and anus........	52,234	16.4	14.3	53,176	16.5	14.2
Malignant neoplasms of liver and intrahepatic bile ducts........	24,698	7.7	6.5	25,761	8.0	6.6
Malignant neoplasms of pancreas........	40,419	12.7	10.9	41,615	12.9	11.0
Malignant neoplasms of trachea, bronchus and lung........	155,610	48.8	42.1	153,819	47.9	40.5
Malignant melanoma of skin........	9,325	2.9	2.6	8,885	2.8	2.4
Malignant neoplasm of breast........	41,678	13.1	11.4	41,987	13.1	11.2
Malignant neoplasm of ovary........	14,195	4.5	3.9	13,920	4.3	3.7
Malignant neoplasm of prostate........	28,344	8.9	7.8	28,848	9.0	7.7
Malignant neoplasms of kidney and renal pelvis........	13,917	4.4	3.7	14,448	4.5	3.8
Malignant neoplasms of bladder........	15,775	4.9	4.3	16,254	5.1	4.4
Malignant neoplasms of meninges, brain and other parts of central nervous system........	15,998	5.0	4.4	16,268	5.1	4.4
Malignant neoplasms of lymphoid, hematopoietic and related tissue [3]........	57,536	18.0	16.0	56,725	17.6	15.4
Non-Hodgkin's lymphoma........	20,388	6.4	5.6	20,154	6.3	5.4
Leukemia........	23,448	7.4	6.6	22,665	7.1	6.2
Accidents (unintentional injuries)........	136,053	42.7	40.5	146,571	45.6	43.2
Transport accidents [2]........	37,939	11.9	11.6	40,452	12.6	12.2
Motor vehicle accidents........	35,398	11.1	10.8	37,757	11.7	11.4
Nontransport accidents [2]........	98,114	30.8	28.9	106,119	33.0	31.0
Falls........	31,959	10.0	8.8	33,381	10.4	9.0
Accidental discharge of firearms........	586	0.2	0.2	489	0.2	0.2
Accidental drowning and submersion........	3,406	1.1	1.1	3,602	1.1	1.1
Accidental exposure to smoke, fire and flames........	2,701	0.8	0.8	2,646	0.8	0.8
Accidental poisoning and exposure to noxious substances........	42,032	13.2	13.1	47,478	14.8	14.8
Chronic lower respiratory diseases [2]........	147,101	46.1	40.5	155,041	48.2	41.6
Bronchitis, chronic and unspecified........	563	0.2	0.1	617	0.2	0.2
Emphysema........	7,455	2.3	2.1	7,249	2.3	1.9
Asthma........	3,651	1.1	1.1	3,615	1.1	1.0
Pneumonitis due to solids and liquids........	18,792	5.9	5.1	19,803	6.2	5.3
Influenza and pneumonia [2]........	55,227	17.3	15.1	57,062	17.8	15.2
Influenza........	4,605	1.4	1.3	5,251	1.6	1.4
Pneumonia........	50,622	15.9	13.8	51,811	16.1	13.8
Septicemia (blood poisoning)........	38,940	12.2	10.7	40,773	12.7	11.0
Viral hepatitis........	8,081	2.5	2.1	7,461	2.3	1.9
Human immunodeficiency virus (HIV) disease........	6,721	2.1	2.0	6,465	2.0	1.9
Anemias........	5,219	1.6	1.5	5,250	1.6	1.4
Diabetes mellitus........	76,488	24.0	20.9	79,535	24.7	21.3
Nutritional deficiencies........	4,110	1.3	1.1	5,222	1.6	1.4
Malnutrition........	3,933	1.2	1.1	5,010	1.6	1.3
Parkinson's disease........	26,150	8.2	7.4	27,972	8.7	7.7
Alzheimer's disease........	93,541	29.3	25.4	110,561	34.4	29.4
Chronic liver disease and cirrhosis........	38,170	12.0	10.4	40,326	12.5	10.8
Alcoholic liver disease........	19,388	6.1	5.4	21,028	6.5	5.7
Nephritis, nephrotic syndrome, and nephrosis [2]........	48,146	15.1	13.2	49,959	15.5	13.4
Renal failure........	47,364	14.9	13.0	49,113	15.3	13.2
Intentional self-harm (suicide)........	42,773	13.4	13.0	44,193	13.7	13.3
Intentional self-harm (suicide) by discharge of firearms........	21,334	6.7	6.4	22,018	6.9	6.5
Assault (homicide)........	15,809	5.0	5.1	17,793	5.5	5.7
Assault (homicide) by discharge of firearms........	10,945	3.4	3.5	12,979	4.0	4.2
Events of undetermined intent........	4,592	1.4	1.4	4,915	1.5	1.5
Complications of medical and surgical care........	2,540	0.8	0.7	2,686	0.8	0.7
Enterocolitis due to Clostridium difficile [3]........	7,130	2.2	1.9	7,410	2.3	2.0
Injury by firearms [3]........	33,599	10.5	10.3	36,252	11.3	11.1
Drug-induced deaths [3]........	49,714	15.6	15.5	55,403	17.2	17.2
Alcohol-induced deaths [3]........	30,722	9.6	8.5	33,171	10.3	9.1

[1] See text, this section. [2] Includes other causes, not shown separately. [3] Also included in selected other categories.

Source: U.S. National Center for Health Statistics, National Vital Statistics Reports, *Deaths: Final Data for 2014*, Vol. 65, No. 4, June 2016 and earlier reports; and CDC WONDER Online database, "Multiple Cause of Death, 1999-2015," <http://wonder.cdc.gov/>, accessed August 2017. See also <http://www.cdc.gov/nchs/nvss/deaths.htm>.

Table 126. Deaths by Age and Selected Cause: 2015

[Deaths are classified according to the International Classification of Diseases, Tenth Revision (ICD-10). See Appendix III]

Cause of death	All ages [1]	Under 1 year	1 to 4 years	5 to 14 years	15 to 24 years	25 to 34 years	35 to 44 years	45 to 54 years	55 to 64 years	65 to 74 years	75 to 84 years	85 years and over
All causes [2]	2,712,630	23,455	3,965	5,411	30,494	51,517	73,088	174,494	357,785	495,016	637,566	859,701
Septicemia	40,773	180	54	64	130	379	829	2,542	5,774	8,655	10,481	11,681
Human immunodeficiency virus (HIV) disease	6,465	2	–	1	100	529	1,055	2,027	1,824	710	184	31
Malignant neoplasms (cancer) [2]	595,930	53	354	865	1,469	3,704	10,909	43,054	116,122	163,728	153,268	102,393
Malignant neoplasm of esophagus	15,212	–	–	–	4	32	230	1,239	3,813	4,734	3,475	1,684
Malignant neoplasms of colon, rectum, and anus	53,176	–	–	–	41	368	1,407	4,972	10,225	12,586	12,572	11,004
Malignant neoplasms of liver and intrahepatic bile ducts	25,761	2	–	19	31	100	335	2,090	7,979	7,289	5,265	2,636
Malignant neoplasms of pancreas	41,615	–	–	–	14	62	446	2,704	8,307	12,438	11,030	6,614
Malignant neoplasms of trachea, bronchus, and lung	153,819	–	2	5	26	133	1,015	8,837	31,413	49,855	42,655	19,874
Malignant neoplasm of breast	41,987	–	–	–	9	390	1,842	5,220	9,255	9,931	8,156	7,183
Malignant neoplasm of ovary	13,920	–	–	4	29	89	302	1,272	2,959	3,902	3,385	1,978
Malignant neoplasm of prostate	28,848	–	–	–	–	4	18	394	2,715	6,487	9,611	9,619
Malignant neoplasms of kidney and renal pelvis	14,448	5	11	20	28	65	227	1,068	3,077	4,072	3,537	2,338
Malignant neoplasm of bladder	16,254	–	–	–	2	15	68	497	1,817	3,620	5,147	5,088
Malignant neoplasms of meninges, brain and other parts of central nervous system	16,268	9	94	327	230	405	839	1,966	3,748	4,355	2,963	1,332
Malignant neoplasms of lymphoid, hematopoietic and related tissue [2]	56,725	22	118	243	457	689	1,014	2,963	7,672	14,092	17,271	12,184
Non-Hodgkins lymphoma	20,154	–	3	32	86	186	340	1,032	2,795	4,899	6,189	4,592
Leukemia	22,665	22	115	206	335	419	495	1,180	2,795	5,338	6,724	5,036
Diabetes mellitus	79,535	3	5	23	196	798	1,986	6,216	14,166	19,453	19,904	16,785
Parkinson's disease	27,972	–	–	–	3	–	6	66	628	3,813	11,473	11,983
Alzheimer's disease	110,561	–	–	–	–	–	11	87	968	6,167	29,503	73,825
Major cardiovascular diseases [2]	832,024	404	196	300	1,226	4,383	13,104	42,106	95,347	107,805	201,515	335,601
Diseases of heart [2]	633,842	292	147	210	997	3,522	10,387	34,248	76,872	107,303	149,199	250,636
Hypertensive heart disease	41,688	1	–	1	48	461	1,610	4,362	7,436	6,646	7,174	13,946
Ischemic heart diseases	366,801	8	–	12	133	977	4,866	20,119	48,891	68,618	89,224	133,925
Acute myocardial infarction	114,023	4	10	4	54	363	1,875	7,590	17,966	24,187	27,619	34,354
Heart failure	75,251	8	3	11	41	129	374	1,397	4,114	8,769	18,243	42,157
Essential (primary) hypertension and hypertensive renal disease	32,200	3	8	–	15	121	470	1,477	3,595	4,979	7,533	14,003
Cerebrovascular diseases	140,323	89	42	84	166	567	1,788	5,307	12,116	20,793	38,012	61,351
Influenza and pneumonia	57,062	174	88	83	184	397	708	2,050	4,601	8,131	14,149	26,494
Influenza	5,251	18	31	32	29	48	62	153	340	602	1,216	2,720
Pneumonia	51,811	156	57	51	155	349	646	1,897	4,261	7,529	12,933	23,774
Chronic lower respiratory diseases [2]	155,041	26	40	173	202	288	702	4,345	17,457	37,642	49,832	44,330
Emphysema	7,249	1	–	1	1	5	48	264	1,005	2,010	2,299	1,615
Pneumonitis due to solids and liquids	19,803	8	10	6	43	87	171	536	1,468	2,586	5,152	9,736
Chronic liver disease and cirrhosis	40,326	3	2	1	28	844	2,861	8,874	13,278	8,409	4,446	1,577
Alcoholic liver disease	21,028	–	–	–	19	681	2,147	5,997	7,574	3,413	1,012	183
Nephritis, nephrotic syndrome, and nephrosis [2]	49,959	85	16	17	57	262	686	2,124	5,452	9,662	13,881	17,715
Renal failure	49,113	83	15	10	51	247	662	2,076	5,351	9,511	13,653	17,452
Accidents (unintentional injuries) [2]	146,571	1,291	1,235	1,518	12,514	19,795	17,818	21,499	19,488	12,961	15,518	22,916
Transport accidents	40,452	71	440	920	7,244	6,836	5,223	6,087	5,752	3,874	2,570	1,429
Motor vehicle accidents	37,757	70	416	860	6,977	6,504	4,849	5,539	5,209	3,524	2,437	1,367
Nontransport accidents	106,119	1,220	795	598	5,270	12,959	12,595	15,412	13,736	9,087	12,948	21,487
Falls	33,381	4	30	25	217	324	492	1,298	2,504	4,091	8,668	15,727
Accidental poisoning and exposure to noxious substances	47,478	9	29	53	3,920	11,231	10,580	11,670	7,782	1,596	386	216
Intentional self-harm (suicide)	44,193	–	–	413	5,491	6,947	6,936	8,751	7,739	4,201	2,489	1,222
Assault (homicide)	17,793	263	369	298	4,733	4,863	2,895	2,106	1,309	550	294	109
Assault (homicide) by discharge of firearms	12,979	8	50	190	4,140	3,996	2,197	1,299	681	258	119	40
Enterocolitis due to clostridium difficile	7,410	2	–	3	8	22	67	214	650	1,272	2,256	2,913

– Represents zero. [1] Includes persons with age not stated, not shown separately. [2] Includes other causes, not shown separately.

Source: U.S. National Center for Health Statistics, National Vital Statistics Reports (NVSR), Deaths: Final Data for 2014, Vol. 65, No. 4, June 2016; and CDC WONDER Online Database, "Multiple Cause of Death, 1999-2015," <https://wonder.cdc.gov/>, accessed August 2017. See also <http://www.cdc.gov/nchs/nvss/deaths.htm>.

Table 127. Deaths and Death Rates by Leading Cause and Age: 2015

[Rates per 100,000 population in specified group. Data are based on the International Classification of Diseases, Tenth Revision (ICD-10)]

Age and cause of death	Number	Rate	Age and cause of death	Number	Rate
ALL AGES [1]			**25 TO 34 YEARS (continued)**		
All causes	2,712,630	844.0	Diseases of heart	3,522	8.0
Diseases of heart	633,842	197.2	Chronic liver disease and cirrhosis	844	1.9
Malignant neoplasms	595,930	185.4	Diabetes mellitus	798	1.8
Chronic lower respiratory diseases	155,041	48.2	Cerebrovascular diseases	567	1.3
Accidents (unintentional injuries)	146,571	45.6	Human immunodeficiency virus (HIV)	529	1.2
Cerebrovascular diseases	140,323	43.7	Congenital malformations [2]	443	1.0
Alzheimer's disease	110,561	34.4	**35 TO 44 YEARS**		
Diabetes mellitus	79,535	24.7	All causes	73,088	180.1
Influenza and pneumonia	57,062	17.8	Accidents (unintentional injuries)	17,818	43.9
Nephritis, nephrotic syndrome and nephrosis	49,959	15.5	Malignant neoplasms	10,909	26.9
Intentional self-harm (suicide)	44,193	13.7	Diseases of heart	10,387	25.6
1 TO 4 YEARS			Intentional self-harm (suicide)	6,936	17.1
All causes	3,965	24.9	Assault (homicide)	2,895	7.1
Accidents (unintentional injuries)	1,235	7.8	Chronic liver disease and cirrhosis	2,861	7.0
Congenital malformations [2]	435	2.7	Diabetes mellitus	1,986	4.9
Assault (homicide)	369	2.3	Cerebrovascular diseases	1,788	4.4
Malignant neoplasms	354	2.2	Human immunodeficiency virus (HIV)	1,055	2.6
Diseases of heart	147	0.9	Septicemia	829	2.0
Influenza and pneumonia	88	0.6	**45 TO 54 YEARS**		
Septicemia	54	0.3	All causes	174,494	404.0
Conditions originating in the perinatal period	50	0.3	Malignant neoplasms	43,054	99.7
Cerebrovascular diseases	42	0.3	Diseases of heart	34,248	79.3
Chronic lower respiratory diseases	40	0.3	Accidents (unintentional injuries)	21,499	49.8
5 TO 9 YEARS			Chronic liver disease and cirrhosis	8,874	20.5
All causes	2,402	11.7	Intentional self-harm (suicide)	8,751	20.3
Accidents (unintentional injuries)	755	3.7	Diabetes mellitus	6,212	14.4
Malignant neoplasms	437	2.1	Cerebrovascular diseases	5,307	12.3
Congenital malformations [2]	181	0.9	Chronic lower respiratory diseases	4,345	10.1
Assault (homicide)	140	0.7	Septicemia	2,542	5.9
Diseases of heart	85	0.4	Nephritis, nephrotic syndrome and nephrosis	2,124	4.9
Chronic lower respiratory diseases	80	0.4			
Influenza and pneumonia	44	0.2	**55 TO 64 YEARS**		
Cerebrovascular diseases	42	0.2	All causes	357,785	875.3
In situ and benign neoplasms and neoplasms of uncertain or unknown behavior	39	0.2	Malignant neoplasms	116,122	284.1
Septicemia	31	0.2	Diseases of heart	76,872	188.1
10 TO 14 YEARS			Accidents (unintentional injuries)	19,488	47.7
			Chronic lower respiratory diseases	17,457	42.7
All causes	3,009	14.6	Diabetes mellitus	14,166	34.7
Accidents (unintentional injuries)	763	3.7	Chronic liver disease and cirrhosis	13,278	32.5
Malignant neoplasms	428	2.1	Cerebrovascular diseases	12,116	29.6
Intentional self-harm (suicide)	409	2.0	Intentional self-harm (suicide)	7,739	18.9
Assault (homicide)	158	0.8	Septicemia	5,774	14.1
Congenital malformations [2]	156	0.8	Nephritis, nephrotic syndrome and nephrosis	5,452	13.3
Diseases of heart	125	0.6	**65 to 74 YEARS**		
Chronic lower respiratory diseases	93	0.5	All causes	495,016	1,796.8
Cerebrovascular diseases	42	0.2	Malignant neoplasms	163,728	594.3
Influenza and pneumonia	39	0.2	Diseases of heart	107,303	389.5
In situ and benign neoplasms and neoplasms of uncertain or unknown behavior	33	0.2	Chronic lower respiratory diseases	37,642	136.6
15 TO 19 YEARS			Cerebrovascular diseases	20,793	75.5
			Diabetes mellitus	19,453	70.6
All causes	10,186	48.3	Accidents (unintentional injuries)	12,961	47.0
Accidents (unintentional injuries)	3,919	18.6	Nephritis, nephrotic syndrome and nephrosis	9,662	35.1
Intentional self-harm (suicide)	2,061	9.8	Septicemia	8,655	31.4
Assault (homicide)	1,587	7.5	Chronic liver disease and cirrhosis	8,409	30.5
Malignant neoplasms	583	2.8	Influenza and pneumonia	8,131	29.5
Diseases of heart	306	1.4	**75 TO 84 YEARS**		
Congenital malformations [2]	195	0.9	All causes	637,566	4,579.2
Influenza and pneumonia	72	0.3	Malignant neoplasms	153,268	1,100.8
Chronic lower respiratory diseases	63	0.3	Diseases of heart	149,199	1,071.6
Cerebrovascular diseases	61	0.3	Chronic lower respiratory diseases	49,832	357.9
Diabetes mellitus	52	0.2	Cerebrovascular diseases	38,012	273.0
20 TO 24 YEARS			Alzheimer's disease	29,503	211.9
All causes	20,308	89.3	Diabetes mellitus	19,904	143.0
Accidents (unintentional injuries)	8,595	37.8	Accidents (unintentional injuries)	15,518	111.5
Intentional self-harm (suicide)	3,430	15.1	Influenza and pneumonia	14,149	101.6
Assault (homicide)	3,146	13.8	Nephritis, nephrotic syndrome and nephrosis	13,881	99.7
Malignant neoplasms	886	3.9	Parkinson's disease	11,473	82.4
Diseases of heart	691	3.0	**85 YEARS AND OVER**		
Congenital malformations [2]	191	0.8	All causes	859,701	13,673.9
Diabetes mellitus	144	0.6	Diseases of heart	250,636	3,986.5
Chronic lower respiratory diseases	139	0.6	Malignant neoplasms	102,393	1,628.6
Pregnancy, childbirth and the puerperium	120	0.5	Alzheimer's disease	73,825	1,174.2
Influenza and pneumonia	112	0.5	Cerebrovascular diseases	61,351	975.8
			Chronic lower respiratory diseases	44,330	705.1
25 TO 34 YEARS			Influenza and pneumonia	26,494	421.4
All causes	51,517	116.7	Accidents (unintentional injuries)	22,916	364.5
Accidents (unintentional injuries)	19,795	44.8	Nephritis, nephrotic syndrome and nephrosis	17,715	281.8
Intentional self-harm (suicide)	6,947	15.7	Diabetes mellitus	16,785	267.0
Assault (homicide)	4,863	11.0	Essential hypertension and hypertensive renal disease	14,003	222.7
Malignant neoplasms	3,704	8.4			

[1] Includes deaths under 1 year of age. [2] Congenital malformations, deformations and chromosomal abnormalities.

Source: U.S. National Center for Health Statistics, CDC WONDER Online Database, "Multiple Cause of Death, 1999-2015," <https://wonder.cdc.gov/>, accessed August 2017.

Table 128. Age-Adjusted Death Rates for Major Causes of Death by State: 2015

[Age-adjusted rates per 100,000 resident population as of July 1. Excludes nonresidents of the United States. Causes of death classified according to the International Classification of Diseases, Tenth Revision (ICD-10)]

State and Island Areas	All causes of death	Diseases of heart	Malignant neoplasms (cancer)	Accidents Total	Motor vehicle accidents	Chronic lower respiratory disease	Cerebrovascular diseases	Alzheimer's disease	Diabetes mellitus	Influenza and pneumonia	Intentional self-harm (suicide)
U.S............	733.1	168.5	158.5	43.2	11.4	41.6	37.6	29.4	21.3	15.2	13.3
AL.............	924.5	229.7	175.6	50.9	19.4	56.4	52.2	41.8	21.7	19.5	14.9
AK.............	747.4	154.1	159.8	57.9	10.6	37.8	36.8	16.7	23.9	8.4	26.9
AZ.............	671.8	138.8	141.3	49.2	13.4	43.8	30.7	35.8	25.3	9.5	18.2
AR.............	901.8	223.2	185.4	49.6	19.6	62.4	46.8	41.5	24.7	20.0	19.1
CA.............	621.6	145.6	142.8	30.6	9.2	33.1	36.2	35.7	21.2	14.8	10.3
CO.............	665.0	128.4	134.4	49.7	10.4	47.8	34.9	31.3	15.9	12.3	19.5
CT.............	656.1	147.8	146.2	44.8	7.6	29.7	28.5	19.0	13.9	13.6	9.9
DE.............	741.5	165.2	165.6	46.0	13.2	42.5	39.4	22.6	18.1	16.1	12.6
DC.............	748.6	187.6	167.5	40.2	6.6	23.4	38.3	19.2	25.7	16.2	4.9
FL.............	662.9	149.8	150.6	46.2	14.3	38.4	37.1	21.8	18.6	8.9	14.4
GA.............	808.1	180.2	163.0	43.2	14.3	46.7	45.3	42.4	21.4	15.5	12.7
HI.............	588.2	135.6	135.3	32.2	6.9	17.3	38.2	19.5	14.5	27.4	13.5
ID.............	727.8	156.4	153.6	44.7	14.9	46.3	36.3	31.6	22.1	12.4	22.1
IL.............	728.3	171.5	167.6	35.8	8.3	38.2	38.4	24.4	19.2	15.7	10.3
IN.............	833.9	182.3	176.3	47.7	12.6	55.4	39.1	33.1	26.9	13.9	14.4
IA.............	724.6	160.9	164.1	42.1	10.6	49.1	33.2	29.9	26.7	14.2	13.9
KS.............	774.1	158.5	164.6	47.2	13.4	49.7	38.6	23.5	20.2	18.9	16.3
KY.............	924.7	197.8	195.9	66.0	18.6	64.3	40.8	34.9	28.2	19.3	17.1
LA.............	874.2	212.1	180.2	54.7	17.0	43.2	46.0	42.5	23.5	15.3	15.2
ME.............	783.5	157.3	178.0	53.8	11.3	53.6	32.6	28.4	21.9	17.6	16.0
MD.............	705.7	169.3	155.0	29.7	8.3	30.7	37.8	16.4	18.3	17.7	8.8
MA.............	684.8	138.5	152.9	44.0	5.4	33.0	28.4	20.2	16.7	17.1	8.9
MI.............	784.4	198.9	168.0	43.9	8.6	47.5	37.6	30.1	22.5	15.2	13.8
MN.............	653.8	116.6	153.0	42.0	8.3	36.4	33.5	26.0	18.6	10.9	13.2
MS.............	963.7	240.5	188.4	59.8	25.7	57.1	52.6	44.1	32.4	24.0	14.0
MO.............	816.9	197.9	173.4	50.9	14.8	52.8	40.8	28.7	19.7	17.9	17.1
MT.............	762.7	155.8	156.9	56.3	21.1	50.2	33.8	20.7	24.5	13.7	25.3
NE.............	739.2	154.5	157.8	38.9	13.9	52.2	33.4	24.8	24.8	16.9	11.7
NV.............	757.2	200.9	157.2	45.4	12.6	54.1	37.0	32.9	13.4	21.3	18.4
NH.............	720.6	149.0	161.3	59.0	7.5	41.9	26.9	25.5	17.9	16.1	16.5
NJ.............	666.0	166.7	150.8	33.7	6.3	29.6	31.1	19.8	17.9	12.5	8.3
NM.............	741.5	142.4	143.3	67.3	16.5	44.7	32.5	19.9	24.9	13.6	23.7
NY.............	644.0	181.6	148.4	30.2	5.7	29.9	26.0	12.6	17.1	20.0	7.8
NC.............	789.9	162.4	164.7	47.9	14.7	45.5	44.7	34.8	23.6	18.7	13.4
ND.............	696.8	142.4	152.9	44.1	17.2	40.0	33.4	36.7	22.6	17.7	17.5
OH.............	828.4	191.7	175.1	55.9	10.5	49.6	40.7	31.1	25.3	16.6	13.9
OK.............	904.3	234.0	184.3	60.1	17.1	65.8	43.0	34.7	32.4	16.5	20.3
OR.............	722.3	136.1	160.2	44.5	11.9	42.4	37.5	33.0	22.9	9.0	17.8
PA.............	768.3	177.8	167.2	52.0	9.6	38.1	38.8	21.0	22.1	15.9	14.0
RI.............	721.9	160.4	163.1	53.1	5.0	36.9	27.1	28.8	20.2	16.2	11.2
SC.............	840.0	177.8	166.6	54.0	19.8	49.9	46.7	46.2	23.4	15.3	14.8
SD.............	715.4	150.9	154.0	49.5	16.2	45.3	33.2	34.8	26.3	18.2	20.4
TN.............	886.4	207.3	180.5	56.4	14.6	54.9	46.0	43.4	23.4	23.3	15.7
TX.............	745.0	171.6	149.2	37.4	13.6	41.3	42.7	38.2	21.2	13.0	12.5
UT.............	712.1	152.9	125.2	45.6	9.9	33.9	38.4	40.7	24.6	15.7	22.4
VT.............	714.7	152.5	165.3	48.4	8.0	42.3	36.4	35.1	19.8	10.0	14.8
VA.............	721.6	154.2	159.5	39.6	9.1	37.1	38.0	25.6	21.9	15.7	12.7
WA.............	687.4	137.6	156.4	41.9	8.7	39.7	34.2	44.4	22.4	10.7	15.4
WV.............	943.4	191.3	190.4	77.9	16.3	64.6	43.8	30.0	31.7	21.2	17.4
WI.............	715.9	156.0	159.3	49.3	10.1	39.3	35.6	27.5	19.4	14.2	14.7
WY.............	748.3	159.4	139.4	65.8	23.1	57.1	31.4	24.2	20.8	16.0	28.0

Source: U.S. National Center for Health Statistics, National Vital Statistics Reports (NVSR), *Deaths: Final Data for 2014*, Vol. 65, No. 4, June 2016; and CDC WONDER Online database, "Multiple Cause of Death, 1999-2015," <https://wonder.cdc.gov/>, accessed September 2017. See also <http://www.cdc.gov/nchs/nvss/deaths.htm>.

Table 129. Death Rates From Heart Disease by Selected Characteristics: 1980 to 2015

[Rates per 100,000 population. Excludes deaths of nonresidents of the United States. Beginning 1999, deaths classified according to the International Classification of Diseases, Tenth Revision (ICD-10); for earlier years, causes of death were classified according to the revisions then in use. Changes in classification of causes of death due to these revisions may result in discontinuities in cause-of-death trends. See Appendix III]

Characteristics	1980	1990	2000	2005	2010	2012	2013	2014	2015
All ages, age-adjusted [1]	**412.1**	**321.8**	**257.6**	**216.8**	**179.1**	**170.5**	**169.8**	**167.0**	**168.5**
All ages, crude rate	**336.0**	**289.5**	**252.6**	**220.7**	**193.6**	**191.0**	**193.3**	**192.7**	**197.2**
Under 1 year	22.8	20.1	13.0	8.9	8.3	8.5	7.8	8.0	7.3
1 to 4 years	2.6	1.9	1.2	0.9	1.0	1.0	1.1	0.9	0.9
5 to 14 years	0.9	0.9	0.7	0.6	0.5	0.4	0.4	0.5	0.5
15 to 24 years	2.9	2.5	2.6	2.6	2.4	2.2	2.1	2.2	2.3
25 to 34 years	8.3	7.6	7.4	8.3	7.8	7.6	7.6	7.7	8.0
35 to 44 years	44.6	31.4	29.2	29.2	25.8	25.9	25.6	25.6	25.6
45 to 54 years	180.2	120.5	94.2	89.7	81.6	79.7	80.3	80.1	79.3
55 to 64 years	494.1	367.3	261.2	212.8	186.6	184.6	184.6	185.8	188.1
65 to 74 years	1,218.6	894.3	665.6	512.3	409.2	388.3	390.3	385.2	389.5
75 to 84 years	2,993.1	2,295.7	1,780.3	1,458.5	1,172.0	1,103.7	1,095.1	1,070.2	1,071.6
85 years and over	7,777.1	6,739.9	5,926.1	5,188.3	4,285.2	4,046.1	4,013.9	3,920.9	3,986.5
MALE									
All ages, age-adjusted [1]	**538.9**	**412.4**	**320.0**	**268.2**	**225.1**	**214.7**	**214.5**	**210.9**	**211.8**
White	539.6	409.2	316.7	264.8	222.9	213.1	213.1	210.0	211.2
Black	561.4	485.4	392.5	338.8	280.6	265.3	262.8	259.5	258.6
American Indian, Alaska Native	320.5	264.1	222.2	191.7	158.7	152.5	152.3	149.7	148.0
Asian, Pacific Islander	286.9	220.7	185.5	149.4	127.2	116.1	118.4	109.1	109.7
Hispanic origin [2]	(NA)	270.0	238.2	210.5	165.1	151.6	151.5	145.7	146.4
Non-Hispanic, White [2]	(NA)	413.6	319.9	267.9	226.9	217.7	217.9	215.2	216.3
All ages, crude rate	**368.6**	**297.6**	**249.8**	**222.3**	**202.5**	**202.3**	**206.5**	**207.1**	**211.7**
Under 1 year	25.5	21.9	13.3	9.6	9.8	9.6	8.7	8.6	7.5
1 to 4 years	2.8	1.9	1.4	1.0	1.1	1.0	1.2	0.9	1.0
5 to 14 years	1.0	0.9	0.8	0.6	0.5	0.5	0.4	0.5	0.5
15 to 24 years	3.7	3.1	3.2	3.5	3.2	2.9	2.8	2.7	3.0
25 to 34 years	11.4	10.3	9.6	11.2	10.7	10.4	10.2	10.3	10.3
35 to 44 years	68.7	48.1	41.4	41.3	36.0	35.8	35.5	34.8	35.1
45 to 54 years	282.6	183.0	140.2	131.6	117.8	114.3	115.1	113.5	112.1
55 to 64 years	746.8	537.3	371.7	303.9	269.5	266.4	267.3	268.1	269.4
65 to 74 years	1,728.0	1,250.0	898.3	680.1	553.0	527.7	530.9	525.7	529.7
75 to 84 years	3,834.3	2,968.2	2,248.1	1,815.1	1,475.7	1,388.1	1,382.4	1,354.8	1,354.4
85 years and over	8,752.7	7,418.4	6,430.0	5,713.2	4,833.6	4,582.7	4,564.2	4,453.4	4,495.1
FEMALE									
All ages, age-adjusted [1]	**320.8**	**257.0**	**210.9**	**177.5**	**143.3**	**135.5**	**134.3**	**131.8**	**133.6**
White	315.9	250.9	205.6	173.2	140.4	133.4	132.0	130.0	132.4
Black	378.6	327.5	277.6	234.5	185.3	172.7	172.1	167.7	165.7
American Indian, Alaska Native	175.4	153.1	143.6	129.3	103.5	92.9	93.9	94.0	94.0
Asian, Pacific Islander	132.3	149.2	115.7	97.5	81.2	74.0	73.3	68.2	68.5
Hispanic origin [2]	(NA)	177.2	163.7	139.9	107.8	98.6	97.0	92.4	93.0
Non-Hispanic, White [2]	(NA)	252.6	206.8	174.8	142.5	135.8	134.6	133.0	135.6
All ages, crude rate	**305.1**	**281.8**	**255.3**	**219.0**	**184.9**	**180.2**	**180.6**	**178.6**	**183.1**
Under 1 year	20.0	18.3	12.5	8.2	6.8	7.3	6.9	7.4	7.2
1 to 4 years	2.5	1.9	1.0	0.9	0.9	0.9	0.9	0.9	0.9
5 to 14 years	0.9	0.8	0.5	0.6	0.4	0.4	0.4	0.4	0.5
15 to 24 years	2.1	1.8	2.1	1.7	1.5	1.5	1.5	1.6	1.5
25 to 34 years	5.3	5.0	5.2	5.3	4.9	4.8	4.9	5.0	5.6
35 to 44 years	21.4	15.1	17.2	17.2	15.6	16.0	15.7	16.4	16.2
45 to 54 years	84.5	61.0	49.8	49.1	46.5	46.0	46.6	47.5	47.4
55 to 64 years	272.1	215.7	159.3	128.0	109.3	108.4	107.5	109.3	112.3
65 to 74 years	828.6	616.8	474.0	369.5	284.2	266.2	266.8	261.7	266.2
75 to 84 years	2,497.0	1,893.8	1,475.1	1,213.8	952.7	893.0	879.8	854.8	855.9
85 years and over	7,350.5	6,478.1	5,720.9	4,955.1	4,020.3	3,777.5	3,732.9	3,643.8	3,717.6

NA Not available. [1] Age-adjusted death rates were prepared using the direct method, in which age-specific death rates for a population of interest are applied to a standard population distributed by age. Age adjustment eliminates the differences in observed rates between points in time or among compared population groups that result from age differences in population composition. [2] Persons of Hispanic origin may be of any race. Prior to 1997, excludes data from states lacking a Hispanic-origin item on their death certificates. See text, this section.

Source: U.S. National Center for Health Statistics, *Health, United States, 2016*, May 2017. See also <http://www.cdc.gov/nchs/hus.htm>.

Table 130. Death Rates From Cerebrovascular Diseases (Stroke) by Sex and Age: 1990 to 2015

[Rates per 100,000 population. Excludes deaths of nonresidents of the United States. Beginning 1999, deaths classified according to tenth revision of International Classification of Diseases (ICD-10); for earlier years, causes of death were classified according to the revisions then in use. Changes in classification of causes of death due to these revisions may result in discontinuities in cause-of-death trends. For explanation of age adjustment, see text, this section]

Characteristics	Total				Male				Female			
	1990	2000	2010	2015	1990	2000	2010	2015	1990	2000	2010	2015
All ages, age-adjusted [1]	65.3	60.9	39.1	37.6	68.5	62.4	39.3	37.8	62.6	59.1	38.3	36.9
All ages, crude rate	57.8	59.6	41.9	43.7	46.7	46.9	34.5	36.8	68.4	71.8	49.1	50.3
Under 1 year	3.8	3.3	3.3	2.2	4.4	3.8	3.2	2.6	3.1	2.7	3.4	1.9
1 to 4 years	0.3	0.3	0.3	0.3	0.3	(B)	0.3	0.3	0.3	0.4	0.3	(B)
5 to 14 years	0.2	0.2	0.2	0.2	0.2	0.2	0.3	0.2	0.2	0.2	0.2	0.2
15 to 24 years	0.6	0.5	0.4	0.4	0.7	0.5	0.5	0.4	0.6	0.5	0.4	0.4
25 to 34 years	2.2	1.5	1.3	1.3	2.1	1.5	1.3	1.4	2.2	1.5	1.2	1.1
35 to 44 years	6.4	5.8	4.6	4.4	6.8	5.8	5.0	4.9	6.1	5.7	4.2	3.9
45 to 54 years	18.7	16.0	13.1	12.3	20.5	17.5	14.9	13.6	17.0	14.5	11.4	11.0
55 to 64 years	47.9	41.0	29.3	29.6	54.3	47.2	34.7	35.4	42.2	35.3	24.3	24.3
65 to 74 years	144.2	128.6	81.7	75.5	166.6	145.0	92.0	86.3	126.7	115.1	72.8	66.0
75 to 84 years	498.0	461.3	288.3	273.0	551.1	490.8	295.2	282.2	466.2	442.1	283.4	266.0
85 years and over	1,628.9	1,589.2	993.8	975.8	1,528.5	1,484.3	892.0	863.3	1,667.6	1,632.0	1,043.0	1,035.3

B Figure too small to meet statistical standards for reliability. [1] See footnote 1, Table 129.

Source: U.S. National Center for Health Statistics, *Health, United States, 2016*, May 2017. See also <http://www.cdc.gov/nchs/hus.htm>.

Table 131. Death Rates From All and Selected Types of Malignant Neoplasms (Cancer) by Age: 1990 to 2015

[Rates per 100,000 population. Excludes deaths of nonresidents of the United States. Beginning 1999, deaths classified according to tenth revision of International Classification of Diseases (ICD-10); for earlier years, causes of death were classified according to the revisions then in use. Changes in classification of causes of death due to these revisions may result in discontinuities in cause-of-death trends. For explanation of age adjustment, see text, this section. See Appendix III]

Characteristic	1990	2000	2005	2010	2012	2013	2014	2015
All ages, age-adjusted [1]	216.0	199.6	185.1	172.8	166.5	163.2	161.2	158.5
All ages, crude rate	203.2	196.5	189.3	186.2	185.6	185.0	185.6	185.4
Under 1 year	2.3	2.4	1.9	1.6	1.6	1.6	1.3	1.3
1 to 4 years	3.5	2.7	2.4	2.1	2.4	2.1	2.0	2.2
5 to 14 years	3.1	2.5	2.5	2.2	2.2	2.2	2.1	2.1
15 to 24 years	4.9	4.4	4.0	3.7	3.6	3.4	3.6	3.4
25 to 34 years	12.6	9.8	9.2	8.8	8.7	8.6	8.3	8.4
35 to 44 years	43.3	36.6	33.5	28.8	28.0	28.1	27.8	26.9
45 to 54 years	158.9	127.5	118.6	111.6	108.5	105.5	103.2	99.7
55 to 64 years	449.6	366.7	323.9	300.1	293.2	288.2	287.6	284.1
65 to 74 years	872.3	816.3	733.2	666.1	632.2	616.9	603.1	594.3
75 to 84 years	1,348.5	1,335.6	1,272.8	1,202.2	1,161.7	1,139.4	1,125.9	1,100.8
85 years old and over	1,752.9	1,819.4	1,778.2	1,729.5	1,658.9	1,635.4	1,632.9	1,628.6
DEATH RATES FOR MALIGNANT NEOPLASM OF BREASTS FOR FEMALES								
All ages, age-adjusted [1]	33.3	26.8	24.2	22.1	21.3	20.8	20.6	20.3
All ages, crude rate	34.0	29.2	27.4	26.1	25.8	25.5	25.5	25.4
Under 25 years	(B)	(B)	(B)	(B)	(B)	(B)	(B)	(B)
25 to 34 years	2.9	2.3	1.8	1.6	1.7	1.6	1.6	1.8
35 to 44 years	17.8	12.4	11.4	9.8	9.7	9.6	9.7	9.0
45 to 54 years	45.4	33.0	28.7	25.7	25.2	24.6	23.8	23.7
55 to 64 years	78.6	59.3	54.0	47.7	45.4	44.1	43.3	43.3
65 to 74 years	111.7	88.3	78.5	73.9	70.0	68.4	67.5	66.7
75 to 84 years	146.3	128.9	119.6	109.1	106.9	104.4	104.2	101.7
85 years old and over	196.8	205.7	191.2	185.8	177.3	173.0	174.0	173.3
DEATH RATES FOR MALIGNANT NEOPLASM OF TRACHEA, BRONCHUS, AND LUNG								
All ages, age-adjusted [1]	59.3	56.1	52.7	47.6	44.9	43.4	42.1	40.5
All ages, crude rate	56.8	55.3	53.9	51.3	50.2	49.4	48.8	47.9
Under 25 years	(Z)	(Z)	(Z)	(Z)	(Z)	(Z)	(Z)	(Z)
25 to 34 years	0.7	0.5	0.3	0.4	0.4	0.3	0.3	0.3
35 to 44 years	6.8	6.1	5.3	3.3	2.9	2.8	2.7	2.5
45 to 54 years	46.8	31.6	29.7	26.9	25.1	23.9	22.4	20.5
55 to 64 years	160.6	122.4	102.4	85.4	81.5	79.9	78.5	76.8
65 to 74 years	288.4	284.2	256.3	223.9	206.1	196.6	189.4	181.0
75 to 84 years	333.3	370.8	375.0	357.2	339.6	328.5	321.2	306.4
85 years old and over	242.5	302.1	328.2	332.4	323.7	320.0	311.7	316.1

B Base figure too small to meet statistical standards for reliability of a derived figure. Z Less than 0.05. [1] Age-adjusted death rates were prepared using the direct method, in which age specific death rates for a population of interest are applied to a standard population distributed by age. Age adjustment eliminates the differences in observed rates between points in time or among compared population groups that result from age differences in population composition.

Source: U.S. National Center for Health Statistics, *Health, United States, 2016*, May 2017. See also <http://www.cdc.gov/nchs/hus.htm>.

Table 132. Death Rates From Suicide by Selected Characteristics: 1990 to 2015

[Rates per 100,000 population. Excludes deaths of nonresidents of the United States. Beginning 1999, deaths classified according to the International Classification of Diseases, Tenth Revision (ICD-10). See Appendix III]

Characteristic	1990	2000	2005	2010	2011	2012	2013	2014	2015
All ages, age-adjusted [1]	**12.5**	**10.4**	**10.9**	**12.1**	**12.3**	**12.6**	**12.6**	**13.0**	**13.3**
All ages, crude rate	**12.4**	**10.4**	**11.0**	**12.4**	**12.7**	**12.9**	**13.0**	**13.4**	**13.7**
5 to 14 years	0.8	0.7	0.7	0.7	0.7	0.8	1.0	1.0	1.0
15 to 24 years	13.2	10.2	9.9	10.5	11.0	11.1	11.1	11.6	12.5
25 to 34 years	15.2	12.0	12.7	14.0	14.6	14.7	14.8	15.1	15.7
35 to 44 years	15.3	14.5	15.1	16.0	16.2	16.7	16.2	16.6	17.1
45 to 54 years	14.8	14.4	16.5	19.6	19.8	20.0	19.7	20.2	20.3
55 to 64 years	16.0	12.1	13.7	17.5	17.1	18.0	18.1	18.8	18.9
65 to 74 years	17.9	12.5	12.4	13.7	14.1	14.0	15.0	15.6	15.2
75 to 84 years	24.9	17.6	16.8	15.7	16.5	16.8	17.1	17.5	17.9
85 years and over	22.2	19.6	18.3	17.6	16.9	17.8	18.6	19.3	19.4
AGE-ADJUSTED RATES [1]									
Male	21.5	17.7	18.1	19.8	20.0	20.4	20.3	20.7	21.1
Female	4.8	4.0	4.4	5.0	5.2	5.4	5.5	5.8	6.0
White male	22.8	19.1	19.8	22.0	22.3	22.6	22.6	23.3	23.6
Black male	12.8	10.0	9.2	9.1	9.3	9.6	9.3	9.5	9.6
American Indian, Alaska Native male	20.1	16.0	17.3	15.5	16.4	17.4	18.1	16.4	18.8
Asian, Pacific Islander male	9.6	8.6	7.3	9.5	8.7	9.4	9.1	8.9	9.1
Hispanic male [2]	13.7	10.3	9.6	9.9	9.4	9.5	9.3	10.3	9.9
Non-Hispanic, White male [2]	23.5	20.2	21.4	24.2	24.8	25.2	25.3	25.9	26.6
White female	5.2	4.3	4.9	5.6	5.9	6.1	6.3	6.6	6.9
Black female	2.4	1.8	1.8	1.8	1.9	2.0	2.0	2.1	2.0
American Indian, Alaska Native female	3.6	3.8	4.2	6.1	5.0	4.3	5.3	5.5	6.5
Asian, Pacific Islander female	4.1	2.8	3.2	3.4	3.4	3.6	3.0	3.4	4.0
Hispanic female [2]	2.3	1.7	1.8	2.1	2.0	2.2	2.3	2.5	2.6
Non-Hispanic, White female [2]	5.4	4.7	5.3	6.2	6.7	6.9	7.1	7.5	7.8

[1] Age-adjusted death rates were prepared using the direct method, in which age-specific death rates for a population of interest are applied to a standard population distributed by age. Age adjustment eliminates the differences in observed rates between points in time or among compared population groups that result from age differences in population composition. [2] Persons of Hispanic origin may be of any race. Excludes data from states lacking a Hispanic-origin item on their death certificates.

Source: U.S. National Center for Health Statistics, *Health, United States, 2016*, May 2017. See also <http://www.cdc.gov/nchs/hus.htm>.

Table 133. Death Rates From Human Immunodeficiency Virus (HIV/AIDS) Disease by Sex, Age, and Race/Ethnicity: 1990 to 2015

[Rates per 100,000 population. Excludes deaths of nonresidents of the United States. Beginning 2000, deaths classified according to the International Classification of Diseases, Tenth Revision (ICD-10). See Appendix III]

Characteristic	1990	1995	2000	2005	2010	2013	2014	2015
All ages, age-adjusted [1]	**10.2**	**16.2**	**5.2**	**4.2**	**2.6**	**2.1**	**2.0**	**1.9**
All ages, crude	**10.1**	**16.2**	**5.1**	**4.2**	**2.7**	**2.2**	**2.1**	**2.0**
Under 1 year	2.7	1.5	(B)	(B)	(B)	(B)	(B)	(B)
1 to 4 years	0.8	1.3	(B)	(B)	(B)	(B)	(B)	(B)
5 to 14 years	0.2	0.5	0.1	(B)	(B)	(B)	(B)	(B)
15 to 24 years	1.5	1.7	0.5	0.4	0.3	0.2	0.3	0.2
25 to 34 years	19.7	28.3	6.1	3.4	1.8	1.5	1.3	1.2
35 to 44 years	27.4	44.2	13.1	10.0	4.6	3.1	2.9	2.6
45 to 54 years	15.2	26.0	11.0	10.6	6.9	5.4	5.1	4.7
55 to 64 years	6.2	10.9	5.1	5.3	5.0	4.6	4.5	4.5
65 to 74 years	2.0	3.6	2.2	2.3	2.2	2.3	2.3	2.6
75 to 84 years	0.7	0.7	0.7	0.8	0.9	1.2	1.1	1.3
85 years and over	(B)	(B)	(B)	(B)	0.4	(B)	0.5	0.5
AGE-ADJUSTED RATES								
Male	18.5	27.3	7.9	6.3	3.8	3.1	3.0	2.8
Female	2.2	5.3	2.5	2.3	1.4	1.1	1.1	1.0
White male	15.7	20.4	4.6	3.7	2.3	1.9	1.8	1.8
Black male	46.3	89.0	35.1	27.7	16.5	12.7	11.9	11.2
American Indian, Alaska Native male	3.3	10.5	3.5	3.7	2.6	2.1	1.6	1.8
Asian, Pacific Islander male	4.3	6.0	1.2	1.0	0.7	0.7	0.6	0.7
Hispanic male [2]	28.8	40.8	10.6	7.7	4.6	3.4	3.3	3.1
Non-Hispanic, White male [2]	14.1	17.9	3.8	3.0	1.8	1.6	1.5	1.4
White female	1.1	2.5	1.0	0.8	0.5	0.4	0.4	0.3
Black female	10.1	24.4	13.2	11.9	7.5	5.7	5.4	5.1
American Indian, Alaska Native female	(B)	2.5	(B)	1.3	(B)	(B)	(B)	1.0
Asian, Pacific Islander female	(B)	0.6	(B)	(B)	(B)	(B)	(B)	(B)
Hispanic female [2]	3.8	8.8	2.9	1.9	1.1	0.9	0.8	0.6
Non-Hispanic, White female [2]	0.7	1.7	0.7	0.6	0.4	0.3	0.3	0.3

B Base figure too small to meet statistical standards. [1] Age-adjusted death rates were prepared using the direct method, in which age-specific death rates for a population of interest are applied to a standard population distributed by age. Age adjustment eliminates the differences in observed rates between points in time or among compared population groups that result from age differences in population composition. [2] Persons of Hispanic origin may be of any race. Excludes data from states lacking a Hispanic-origin item on their death certificates.

Source: U.S. National Center for Health Statistics, *Health, United States*, annual; *Deaths: Final Data 2014*, Vol. 65, No. 4, June 2016; and CDC WONDER Online database, "Multiple Cause of Death, 1999-2015," <http://wonder.cdc.gov/>, accessed September 2017.

Table 134. Suicide Deaths by Age, Sex, and Method: 2015

[It is generally accepted that children under 5 years of age cannot commit suicide. Deaths based on the International Classification of Diseases, Tenth Revision (ICD-10)]

Method	Total	5-14 years	15-24 years	25-34 years	35-44 years	45-54 years	55-64 years	65-74 years	75-84 years	85+ years
Total [1]	**44,193**	**413**	**5,491**	**6,947**	**6,936**	**8,751**	**7,739**	**4,201**	**2,489**	**1,222**
MEN										
Total [1]	**33,994**	**255**	**4,359**	**5,503**	**5,223**	**6,411**	**5,696**	**3,372**	**2,123**	**1,048**
Knife or other sharp object	606	0	24	59	110	145	163	60	29	16
Drowning	316	1	54	44	46	55	62	29	13	12
Jumping from a high place [2]	729	1	148	119	140	128	100	47	32	14
Fire/flame	130	0	15	20	17	32	32	9	5	0
Firearm	18,910	111	2,170	2,658	2,446	3,180	3,303	2,490	1,728	821
Poisoning	3,407	4	234	445	578	891	764	282	130	78
Hanging/suffocation/strangulation	9,134	137	1,570	1,972	1,745	1,853	1,170	417	170	100
WOMEN										
Total [1]	**10,199**	**158**	**1,132**	**1,444**	**1,713**	**2,340**	**2,043**	**829**	**366**	**174**
Knife or other sharp object	157	1	4	12	19	39	45	18	10	9
Drowning	193	3	21	18	20	46	47	21	8	9
Jumping from a high place [2]	279	2	31	47	34	59	54	33	14	5
Fire/flame	53	0	4	3	12	17	9	7	1	0
Firearm	3,108	29	291	460	506	702	648	289	144	39
Poisoning	3,409	19	175	324	603	944	829	321	120	74
Hanging/suffocation,strangulation	2,721	100	549	532	474	480	365	124	62	35

[1] Includes other methods not shown separately and deaths with age not stated. [2] Includes other fall.

Source: U.S. National Center for Health Statistics, CDC WONDER Online database, "Multiple Cause of Death, 1999-2015," <https://wonder.cdc.gov/>, accessed September 2017.

Table 135. Firearm Deaths and Death Rates by Sex and Race/Ethnicity: 2010 to 2015

[Rates are on an annual basis per 100,000 population and are based on populations enumerated as of April 1 for census years and as of July 1 for all other years. Deaths are those attributable to injury by firearms; see source for details]

Sex and race/ethnicity	Number of deaths					Death rates per 100,000 population				
	2010	2012	2013	2014	2015	2010	2012	2013	2014	2015
Total	**31,672**	**33,563**	**33,636**	**33,594**	**36,252**	**10.3**	**10.7**	**10.6**	**10.5**	**11.3**
By sex:										
Male	27,356	28,838	28,794	28,715	31,032	18.0	18.7	18.5	18.3	19.6
Female	4,316	4,725	4,842	4,879	5,220	2.7	3.0	3.0	3.0	3.2
By race/ethnicity:										
White	23,490	24,727	25,044	25,089	26,288	9.6	10.0	10.0	10.0	10.4
Male	20,014	20,955	21,116	21,092	22,061	16.5	17.0	17.1	17.0	17.7
Female	3,476	3,772	3,928	3,997	4,227	2.8	3.0	3.1	3.2	3.3
Black	7,454	8,021	7,797	7,735	9,047	17.7	18.6	17.8	17.5	20.2
Male	6,721	7,191	7,016	6,986	8,194	33.4	34.8	33.5	32.9	38.1
Female	733	830	781	749	853	3.3	3.7	3.4	3.2	3.7
Hispanic [1]	3,008	3,061	2,951	3,010	3,332	6.0	5.8	5.5	5.4	5.9
Male	2,694	2,724	2,595	2,630	2,912	10.5	10.1	9.4	9.4	10.2
Female	314	337	356	380	420	1.3	1.3	1.3	1.4	1.5

[1] Persons of Hispanic origin may be of any race. Data for Hispanic persons are not tabulated separately by race.

Source: U.S. National Center for Health Statistics, *Deaths: Final Data for 2014, Supplemental Tables*, Vol. 65, No. 4, June 2016; and CDC WONDER Online database, "Multiple Cause of Death, 1999-2015," <https://wonder.cdc.gov/>, accessed September 2017.

Table 136. Drug Overdose/Poisoning Deaths and Those Involving Opioid Analgesics and Heroin: 2000 to 2015

[Rates are age-adjusted and per 100,000 population. Deaths are classified according to the International Classification of Diseases, Tenth Revision (ICD-10)]

Year	Total [1]		Opioid analgesics		Heroin	
	Number	Rate	Number	Rate	Number	Rate
2000	17,415	6.2	4,400	1.5	1,842	0.7
2001	19,394	6.8	5,528	1.9	1,779	0.6
2002	23,518	8.2	7,456	2.6	2,089	0.7
2003	25,785	8.9	8,517	2.9	2,080	0.7
2004	27,424	9.4	9,857	3.4	1,878	0.6
2005	29,813	10.1	10,928	3.7	2,009	0.7
2006	34,425	11.5	13,723	4.6	2,088	0.7
2007	36,010	11.9	14,408	4.8	2,399	0.8
2008	36,450	11.9	14,800	4.8	3,041	1.0
2009	37,004	11.9	15,597	5.0	3,278	1.1
2010	38,329	12.3	16,651	5.4	3,036	1.0
2011	41,340	13.2	16,917	5.4	4,397	1.4
2012	41,502	13.1	16,007	5.1	5,925	1.9
2013	43,982	13.8	16,235	5.1	8,257	2.7
2014	47,055	14.7	18,893	5.9	10,574	3.4
2015	52,404	16.3	22,598	7.0	12,989	4.1

[1] Includes deaths due to other drug types not shown separately.

Source: U.S. National Center for Health Statistics, *Health, United States, 2016*, May 2017; and CDC WONDER Online database, "Multiple Cause of Death, 1999-2015," <http://wonder.cdc.gov/>, accessed July 2017.

Table 137. People Who Got Married and Divorced in the Past 12 Months by State: 2015

[For 12-month period prior to interview date, which occurred for each month in calendar year. For example, a person interviewed in January 2015 could report they got married between January 2014 and January 2015. Data shown for persons 15 years old and over. Vital event is counted in state in which respondent lived at the time of survey. Based on 2015 American Community Survey (ACS). The ACS universe includes the household population and the group quarters population. Based on a sample and subject to sampling variability. See Appendix III]

| State | People who got married in the past 12 months | | | | People who got divorced in the past 12 months | | | |
	Males	Marriage rate per 1,000 men	Females	Marriage rate per 1,000 women	Males	Divorce rate per 1,000 men	Females	Divorce rate per 1,000 women
United States............	2,348,113	18.5	2,298,977	17.2	1,008,778	7.9	1,110,579	8.3
Alabama...................	33,087	17.5	33,454	16.2	20,124	10.7	19,416	9.4
Alaska....................	7,844	25.5	8,434	30.7	2,765	9.0	3,222	11.7
Arizona...................	49,134	18.2	47,964	17.3	22,414	8.3	25,894	9.3
Arkansas..................	24,111	20.7	24,758	20.2	12,435	10.7	16,169	13.2
California................	286,456	18.4	270,420	16.9	94,509	6.1	111,013	6.9
Colorado..................	44,191	20.0	44,013	20.0	17,937	8.1	19,391	8.8
Connecticut...............	22,336	15.6	20,320	13.2	10,097	7.0	11,710	7.6
Delaware..................	6,887	18.5	7,455	18.4	2,282	6.1	2,471	6.1
District of Columbia......	7,120	26.6	6,299	20.9	1,829	6.8	2,721	9.0
Florida...................	148,075	18.1	140,523	16.1	66,393	8.1	75,834	8.7
Georgia...................	79,174	20.2	80,672	19.1	38,228	9.8	34,259	8.1
Hawaii....................	15,076	25.5	12,609	21.8	4,029	6.8	3,243	5.6
Idaho.....................	14,656	22.8	13,574	20.8	7,863	12.2	6,788	10.4
Illinois..................	83,494	16.5	81,462	15.2	34,427	6.8	37,920	7.1
Indiana...................	48,146	18.6	49,811	18.3	25,762	10.0	29,009	10.6
Iowa......................	25,759	20.8	25,497	19.9	9,154	7.4	9,860	7.7
Kansas....................	20,800	18.2	22,039	18.9	13,400	11.7	10,475	9.0
Kentucky..................	38,022	21.8	37,938	20.6	18,889	10.8	20,217	11.0
Louisiana.................	33,602	18.6	32,061	16.6	15,901	8.8	14,903	7.7
Maine.....................	8,867	16.3	9,188	15.9	6,209	11.4	4,424	7.7
Maryland..................	40,109	17.1	39,497	15.5	17,665	7.5	18,829	7.4
Massachusetts.............	43,368	16.0	41,181	14.0	17,280	6.4	23,014	7.8
Michigan..................	61,506	15.6	60,470	14.5	31,415	7.9	31,939	7.7
Minnesota.................	37,825	17.3	38,820	17.3	13,955	6.4	17,493	7.8
Mississippi...............	20,072	17.6	20,205	16.2	10,318	9.0	12,333	9.9
Missouri..................	43,685	18.2	43,654	17.2	20,854	8.7	23,773	9.4
Montana...................	7,635	18.0	7,841	18.6	3,004	7.1	3,963	9.4
Nebraska..................	13,803	18.6	13,075	17.2	6,034	8.1	7,276	9.6
Nevada....................	24,851	21.4	22,691	19.4	14,625	12.6	14,352	12.3
New Hampshire.............	8,276	15.1	8,149	14.3	3,945	7.2	4,385	7.7
New Jersey................	50,796	14.4	48,402	12.8	21,362	6.0	24,139	6.4
New Mexico................	14,341	17.5	15,129	17.9	6,532	8.0	7,887	9.3
New York..................	127,600	16.3	122,700	14.5	43,830	5.6	56,573	6.7
North Carolina...........	78,664	20.0	75,551	17.9	33,701	8.6	33,197	7.9
North Dakota.............	7,084	22.5	6,655	22.4	2,487	7.9	2,116	7.1
Ohio......................	77,465	16.9	77,458	15.9	42,509	9.3	40,742	8.4
Oklahoma..................	31,484	20.6	34,041	21.5	17,849	11.7	18,328	11.6
Oregon....................	30,209	18.5	30,667	18.2	13,276	8.1	15,787	9.4
Pennsylvania..............	88,319	17.2	86,266	15.8	35,486	6.9	39,881	7.3
Rhode Island..............	6,694	15.8	5,739	12.5	1,883	4.5	2,520	5.5
South Carolina...........	36,864	19.1	35,024	16.9	17,155	8.9	18,025	8.7
South Dakota.............	6,370	18.7	7,219	21.1	1,921	5.6	3,139	9.2
Tennessee.................	52,118	20.2	52,028	18.7	23,189	9.0	25,696	9.3
Texas.....................	226,679	21.5	222,389	20.4	91,974	8.7	106,445	9.8
Utah......................	29,629	26.6	31,568	28.3	8,993	8.1	11,611	10.4
Vermont...................	4,189	16.2	4,170	15.4	2,220	8.6	2,230	8.2
Virginia..................	67,237	20.2	65,536	18.7	26,538	8.0	30,819	8.8
Washington................	58,352	20.1	55,864	19.1	26,322	9.1	27,952	9.5
West Virginia............	13,091	17.4	15,241	19.5	8,995	12.0	8,317	10.6
Wisconsin.................	37,471	16.1	38,207	16.0	16,408	7.1	15,253	6.4
Wyoming...................	5,490	23.4	5,049	21.7	2,406	10.2	3,626	15.5

Source: U.S. Census Bureau, 2015 American Community Survey, B12501, "Marriage in the Last Year by Sex by Marital Status for the Population 15 Years and Over," and B12503, "Divorces in the Last Year by Sex by Marital Status for the Population 15 Years and Over"; <http://factfinder.census.gov>, accessed December 2016.

Table 138. Marriage and Divorce Rates by State: 1990 to 2015

[Rate per 1,000 population residing in area. Population enumerated as of April 1 for 1990, 2000, and 2010; estimated as of July 1 for all other years. Rates are based on provisional counts by state of occurrence. See Appendix III]

State	Marriage rates						Divorce rates [1]					
	1990	2000	2005	2010	2014	2015	1990	2000	2005	2010	2014	2015
United States [2]........	**9.8**	**8.2**	**7.6**	**6.8**	**6.9**	**6.9**	**4.7**	**4.0**	**3.6**	**3.6**	**3.2**	**3.1**
Alabama..................	10.6	10.1	9.2	8.2	7.8	7.4	6.1	5.5	4.9	4.4	3.8	3.9
Alaska...................	10.2	8.9	8.2	8.0	7.5	7.4	5.5	3.9	4.3	4.7	4.0	4.1
Arizona..................	10.0	7.5	6.6	5.9	5.8	5.9	6.9	4.6	4.2	3.5	3.9	3.6
Arkansas.................	15.3	15.4	12.9	10.8	10.1	10.0	6.9	6.4	6.0	5.7	4.8	4.8
California [3]...........	7.9	5.8	6.4	5.8	6.4	6.2	4.3	(NA)	(NA)	(NA)	(NA)	(NA)
Colorado.................	9.8	8.3	7.6	6.9	7.1	6.8	5.5	4.7	4.4	4.3	3.9	3.7
Connecticut..............	7.9	5.7	5.8	5.6	5.4	5.3	3.2	3.3	3.0	2.9	2.6	3.1
Delaware.................	8.4	6.5	5.9	5.2	6.0	5.7	4.4	3.9	3.8	3.5	3.3	3.1
District of Columbia......	8.2	4.9	4.1	7.6	11.8	8.2	4.5	3.2	2.0	2.8	2.6	2.8
Florida..................	10.9	8.9	8.9	7.3	7.3	8.2	6.3	5.1	4.6	4.4	4.0	4.0
Georgia..................	10.3	6.8	7.0	7.3	(NA)	6.2	5.5	3.3	(NA)	(NA)	(NA)	(NA)
Hawaii...................	16.4	20.6	22.6	17.6	17.7	15.9	4.6	3.9	(NA)	(NA)	(NA)	(NA)
Idaho....................	13.9	10.8	10.5	8.8	8.4	8.2	6.5	5.5	5.0	5.2	4.2	4.1
Illinois.................	8.8	6.9	5.9	5.7	6.2	5.9	3.8	3.2	2.6	2.6	2.2	2.2
Indiana..................	9.6	7.9	6.9	6.3	7.1	6.9	(NA)	(NA)	(NA)	(NA)	(NA)	(NA)
Iowa.....................	9.0	6.9	6.9	6.9	6.9	6.3	3.9	3.3	2.7	2.4	1.5	1.2
Kansas...................	9.2	8.3	6.8	6.4	6.1	5.9	5.0	3.6	3.1	3.7	3.0	2.8
Kentucky.................	13.5	9.8	8.7	7.4	6.9	7.2	5.8	5.1	4.6	4.5	3.8	3.7
Louisiana................	9.6	9.1	8.0	6.9	6.9	6.8	(NA)	(NA)	(NA)	(NA)	2.3	2.8
Maine....................	9.7	8.8	8.2	7.1	7.7	7.6	4.3	5.0	4.1	4.2	3.6	3.4
Maryland.................	9.7	7.5	6.9	5.7	6.5	6.2	3.4	3.3	3.1	2.8	2.5	2.6
Massachusetts............	7.9	5.8	6.2	5.6	5.6	5.5	2.8	2.5	2.2	2.5	2.7	2.6
Michigan.................	8.2	6.7	6.1	5.5	5.8	6.0	4.3	3.9	3.4	3.5	3.0	3.0
Minnesota................	7.7	6.8	6.0	5.3	5.9	5.6	3.5	3.2	(NA)	(NA)	(NA)	(NA)
Mississippi..............	9.4	6.9	5.8	4.9	6.9	7.0	5.5	5.0	4.4	4.3	3.4	3.4
Missouri.................	9.6	7.8	7.0	6.5	6.7	6.2	5.1	4.5	3.6	3.9	3.3	3.2
Montana..................	8.6	7.3	7.4	7.4	7.9	8.0	5.1	4.2	4.5	3.9	3.4	3.4
Nebraska.................	8.0	7.6	7.0	6.6	6.4	6.4	4.0	3.7	3.3	3.6	3.1	3.2
Nevada...................	99.0	72.2	57.4	38.3	31.9	31.0	11.4	9.9	7.4	5.9	5.3	4.6
New Hampshire............	9.5	9.4	7.3	7.3	7.2	6.9	4.7	4.8	3.9	3.8	3.5	3.3
New Jersey...............	7.6	6.0	5.7	5.1	5.4	5.6	3.0	3.0	2.9	3.0	2.8	2.8
New Mexico...............	8.8	8.0	6.6	7.7	8.1	6.2	4.9	5.1	4.6	4.0	3.6	3.3
New York.................	8.6	7.1	6.8	6.5	6.7	7.1	3.2	3.0	2.9	2.9	2.8	2.7
North Carolina...........	7.8	8.2	7.3	6.6	6.9	7.0	5.1	4.5	4.1	3.8	3.4	3.1
North Dakota.............	7.5	7.2	6.8	6.5	6.3	6.2	3.6	3.4	2.9	3.1	2.8	2.8
Ohio.....................	9.0	7.8	6.5	5.8	5.8	5.9	4.7	4.2	3.5	3.4	3.2	3.1
Oklahoma.................	10.6	(NA)	7.3	7.2	7.1	7.4	7.7	(NA)	5.6	5.2	4.5	4.4
Oregon...................	8.9	7.6	7.3	6.5	6.8	6.9	5.5	4.8	4.2	4.0	3.4	3.4
Pennsylvania.............	7.1	6.0	5.8	5.3	5.8	5.7	3.3	3.1	2.3	2.7	2.7	2.6
Rhode Island.............	8.1	7.6	7.0	5.8	6.7	6.4	3.7	2.9	3.0	3.2	2.8	3.0
South Carolina...........	15.9	10.6	8.3	7.4	7.6	7.5	4.5	3.8	2.9	3.1	2.9	2.8
South Dakota.............	11.1	9.4	8.4	7.3	7.1	7.2	3.7	3.5	2.8	3.4	2.8	2.6
Tennessee................	13.9	15.5	10.9	8.8	8.4	8.5	6.5	5.9	4.6	4.2	3.8	3.7
Texas....................	10.5	9.4	7.8	7.1	6.9	7.2	5.5	4.0	3.3	3.3	2.7	2.6
Utah.....................	11.2	10.8	9.8	8.5	7.3	8.1	5.1	4.3	4.1	3.7	3.1	3.6
Vermont..................	10.9	10.0	8.9	9.3	8.7	8.1	4.5	4.1	3.6	3.8	3.5	3.1
Virginia.................	11.4	8.8	8.2	6.8	6.7	7.0	4.4	4.3	4.0	3.8	3.5	3.3
Washington...............	9.5	6.9	6.5	6.0	7.0	6.2	5.9	4.6	4.3	4.2	3.6	3.4
West Virginia............	7.2	8.7	7.4	6.7	6.7	6.6	5.3	5.1	5.1	5.1	4.2	4.0
Wisconsin................	7.9	6.7	6.1	5.3	5.7	5.6	3.6	3.2	2.9	3.0	2.7	2.6
Wyoming..................	10.7	10.0	9.3	7.6	7.7	7.3	6.6	5.8	5.2	5.1	4.6	4.1

NA Not available. [1] Includes annulments. Includes divorce petitions filed or legal separations for some counties or States. [2] Beginning 2000, rates based solely on the combined counts and populations for reporting states and the District of Columbia. [3] Marriage data includes nonlicensed marriages registered.

Source: U.S. National Center for Health Statistics, National Vital Statistics System, "Marriages and Divorces, Detailed State Tables," <https://www.cdc.gov/nchs/nvss/marriage-divorce.htm>, accessed February 2017.

Table 139. People Who Got Married or Divorced in the Past 12 Months by Selected Characteristics: 2015

[In units, as indicated (260,415 represents 260,415,000). For 12-month period prior to interview date, which occurred for each month in calendar year. For example, a person interviewed in January 2015 could report they got married between January 2014 and January 2015. Persons 15 years and over. Based on 2015 American Community Survey (ACS). The ACS universe includes the household population and the group quarters population. Based on a sample and subject to sampling variability. See Appendix III]

Characteristic	Total population	Married in the past 12 months		Divorced in the past 12 months	
		Males	Females	Males	Females
Population 15 years old and over (1,000)........................	**260,415**	**2,348**	**2,299**	**1,009**	**1,111**
AGE					
Median age..	45.3	32.4	30.5	44.9	43.3
EDUCATIONAL ATTAINMENT					
Population 18 years and over (1,000)............................	247,789	2,318	2,272	1,007	1,109
Bachelor's degree or higher (percent)............................	28.0	32.0	37.4	24.1	28.2
LABOR FORCE PARTICIPATION					
Population 16 years and over (1,000)............................	256,168	2,332	2,286	1,009	1,111
In labor force (percent)............................	63.1	88.2	77.2	78.4	76.8
Not in labor force (percent)............................	36.9	11.8	22.8	21.6	23.2
POVERTY STATUS IN PAST 12 MONTHS					
Population for whom poverty status is determined (1,000)..........	253,528	2,312	2,289	976	1,103
Below poverty (percent)............................	13.2	8.1	9.6	11.4	21.4
PRESENCE OF OWN CHILD UNDER 18 YEARS					
Population in households (1,000)............................	252,416	2,308	2,285	971	1,101
With an own child under 18 years (percent)........................	23.9	31.2	33.9	18.4	38.3
HOUSING TENURE					
Population 15 years and over in occupied housing units (1,000). ..	252,416	2,308	2,285	971	1,101
Owner-occupied housing units (percent)............................	66.2	50.2	50.4	55.2	51.1
Renter-occupied housing units (percent)............................	33.8	49.8	49.6	44.8	48.9

Source: U.S. Census Bureau, 2015 American Community Survey, S1251, "Characteristics of People with a Marital Event in the Last 12 Months," <http://factfinder.census.gov>, accessed December 2016.

Table 140. Marital Status of Population and Number of Times Married by Sex and Median Duration of Marriage: 2009 to 2015

[245,156 represents 245,156,000. Data shown are for the population age 15 years and over. Based on the American Community Survey (ACS). The ACS universe includes the household population and the group quarters population. Based on a sample and subject to sampling variability. See Appendix III]

Characteristic	2009	2010	2011	2012	2013	2014	2015
NUMBER (1,000)							
Population aged 15 years and over.........	**245,156**	**248,056**	**250,393**	**252,745**	**255,017**	**257,771**	**260,415**
Male..	119,716	120,743	121,988	123,175	124,380	125,665	127,013
Never married..	42,158	42,741	43,675	44,292	45,175	45,865	46,677
Ever married..	77,558	78,001	78,313	78,883	79,205	79,800	80,336
Once..	58,438	58,734	58,865	59,349	59,667	60,106	60,648
Two times..	15,021	15,183	15,332	15,382	15,284	15,406	15,381
Three or more times............................	4,098	4,085	4,116	4,152	4,253	4,287	4,307
Female..	125,440	127,313	128,405	129,571	130,637	132,106	133,402
Never married..	35,853	36,899	37,709	38,367	39,145	39,944	40,667
Ever married..	89,587	90,414	90,696	91,203	91,492	92,162	92,734
Once..	67,660	68,330	68,426	68,939	69,185	69,723	70,088
Two times..	17,312	17,449	17,665	17,620	17,533	17,642	17,776
Three or more times............................	4,616	4,636	4,605	4,644	4,774	4,796	4,871
PERCENT DISTRIBUTION							
Male:							
Never married..	35.2	35.4	35.8	36.0	36.3	36.5	36.7
Ever married..	64.8	64.6	64.2	64.0	63.7	63.5	63.3
Once..	48.8	48.6	48.3	48.2	48.0	47.8	47.7
Two times..	12.5	12.6	12.6	12.5	12.3	12.3	12.1
Three or more times............................	3.4	3.4	3.4	3.4	3.4	3.4	3.4
Female:							
Never married..	28.6	29.0	29.4	29.6	30.0	30.2	30.5
Ever married..	71.4	71.0	70.6	70.4	70.0	69.8	69.5
Once..	53.9	53.7	53.3	53.2	53.0	52.8	52.5
Two times..	13.8	13.7	13.8	13.6	13.4	13.4	13.3
Three or more times............................	3.7	3.6	3.6	3.6	3.7	3.6	3.7
Median duration of marriage (years) [1]............	18.6	19.0	19.2	19.3	19.5	19.5	19.6

[1] Data shown for current marriage.

Source: U.S. Census Bureau, American Community Survey, B12504, "Median Duration of Current Marriage in Years By Sex By Marital Status for the Married Population 15 years and Over," and B12505, "Number of Times Married by Sex By Marital Status for the Population 15 Years and Over"; <http://factfinder.census.gov>, accessed December 2016.

Health and Nutrition

This section presents statistics on numerous indicators of the nation's health care system, the health care industry and its institutions, and the health of its population. Data in this section cover national and personal health expenditures, health insurance coverage, Medicare and Medicaid, medical personnel, hospitals, nursing homes and other health care facilities, injuries, diseases, disability status, substance use (including alcohol, tobacco, and illicit drug use), exercise, the nutritional intake of the population, and food consumption. This section also includes data on selected conditions among children.

Data on national health expenditures, medical costs, and insurance coverage are compiled by the U.S. Centers for Medicare & Medicaid Services (CMS) and appear on the CMS website at <http://www.cms.gov/NationalHealthExpendData/>. In the past, Medicare and Medicaid data came from the annual *Medicare and Medicaid Statistical Supplement,* but this report was discontinued after the 2013 release, and has been replaced with "CMS Program Statistics." Internet users can use the online CMS Program Statistics tool to obtain data on Medicare enrollment, utilization, and expenditures, and also data on Medicare-certified institutional and noninstitutional providers. Another key source of information on Medicare is the annual report to Congress from the Boards of Trustees for Medicare. The Trustees' report covers the financial operations and actuarial status of Medicare. Medicaid data had been available from CMS's Medicaid Statistical Information System (MSIS), but this system is no longer being updated, and a new system is currently in development, and will be known as the Transformed MSIS (T-MSIS). CMS is working to transition all states into the T-MSIS. Selected data on Medicaid and the Children's Health Insurance Program (CHIP) continue to be available from other sources, including the U.S. National Center for Health Statistics (NCHS), and the Medicaid and CHIP Payment and Access Commission, a nonpartisan legislative branch agency that provides analysis to the states, Congress, and the Secretary of the Department of Health and Human Services.

Summary statistics showing recent trends in health care and health indicators of the population, and discussions of selected health issues are published annually by the NCHS in *Health, United States.* Statistics on health insurance are collected by surveys conducted by the Census Bureau. The NCHS also collects health insurance data and other detailed data on the population's health status annually in its National Health Interview Survey, the results of which are released in brief reports under the Early Release Program, and in online summary tables. After issuing reports covering the 2012 NHIS, the NCHS discontinued issuing NHIS data in *Vital and Health Statistics* Series 10 reports. NCHS also operates other programs to track various health indicators such as food and nutrition, exercise, body weight, and incidence of high blood cholesterol and blood pressure (hypertension).

Statistics on hospitals are published annually by the Health Forum, LLC, an affiliate of the American Hospital Association (AHA), in *AHA Hospital Statistics.* Data on food consumption and nutrition are available from the U.S. Department of Agriculture's Economic Research Service, online at <https://www.ers.usda.gov/data-products/food-availability-per-capita-data-system/>.

National health expenditures—CMS compiles estimates of national health expenditures (NHE) to measure spending for health care in the United States. The NHE accounts are structured to show spending by type of expenditure: hospital care, physician and clinical care, dental care, and other professional care; home health care; retail sales of prescription drugs; other medical nondurable goods; nursing home care and other personal health expenditures; other health expenditures such as public health activities, administration, and the net cost of private health insurance; and medical sector investment, which is the sum of noncommercial medical research and capital formation in medical sector structures and equipment. The NHE also shows spending by source of funding (e.g., private health insurance, Medicare, Medicaid, out-of-pocket payments, and other third party payers and programs).

Data used to estimate health expenditures come from existing sources, which are tabulated for other purposes. The expenditure type estimates rely upon statistics produced by such groups as the AHA, the Census Bureau, and the U.S. Department of Health and Human Services (HHS). Funding source estimates are constructed using administrative and statistical records from the Medicare and Medicaid programs, the U.S. Department of Defense and Veterans Affairs medical programs, the Social Security Administration, Census Bureau's *Governmental Finances,* state and local governments, other HHS agencies, and other nongovernment sources.

The Health Care Satellite Account (HCSA), developed by the Bureau of Economic Analysis, is a tool that measures health care spending as the cost to treat specific diseases and medical conditions (such as cancer, or diseases of the circulatory system), as opposed to spending on specific types of health care services (physician services, or prescription drugs). The HCSA can help answer questions regarding whether changes in medical expenditures are due to changes in costs of treatments or changes in number of persons receiving care, which medical conditions account for larger portions of spending, and which medical conditions experience the greatest changes in treatment costs. The BEA presents two versions of the HCSA. One version, the "MEPS Account," uses data from the Medical Expenditure Panel Survey; the other version, the "Blended Account," combines data from multiple sources, including large claims databases that cover millions of health insurance enrollees and billions of claims. The table in this section presents data from the Blended Account. See <http://bea.gov/national/health_care_satellite_account.htm> for detailed information about how the Health Care Satellite Account is constructed.

Medicare, Medicaid, and Children's Health Insurance Program (CHIP)—The Original Medicare program has two components. Hospital Insurance (HI), also known as Medicare Part A, helps pay for in-patient hospital stays, care in a skilled nursing facility, hospice care, and some home health care. Supplementary Medical Insurance (SMI) consists of Medicare Part B and Part D. Part B coverage is optional, and helps pay for physician and outpatient hospital care services, medical supplies, and preventive services. Part D provides subsidized access to drug insurance coverage on a voluntary basis for all beneficiaries and premium and cost-sharing subsidies for low-income enrollees. Participants in Parts B and D pay monthly premiums. In addition to covering persons age 65 and older, Medicare covers persons under age 65 with a disability and who have been receiving for the past 24 months disability benefits from Social Security or the Railroad Retirement Board; persons of any age with ALS (Amyotrophic Lateral Sclerosis, also known as Lou Gehrig's disease); and persons of any age with end-stage renal disease. Medicare's HI and SMI have separate trust funds, sources of revenue, and categories of expenditures.

Medicare also has an alternative to Original Medicare coverage, the Medicare Advantage Plan (also known as Part C). Medicare Advantage plans are offered by private companies and organizations, are required to provide at least services covered by Medicare Parts A and B (except hospice services), and are financed from both Medicare's Hospital Insurance (HI) trust fund and the Part B account within the Supplementary Medical Insurance (SMI) trust fund in proportion to the relative weights of Part A and Part B benefits to the total benefits paid by the Medicare program.

Medicaid is a health insurance program for certain low-income people, families and children, pregnant women, the elderly, and people with disabilities. There are special rules for those who live in nursing homes and for disabled children living at home. Medicaid is funded and administered through a federal-state partnership. Although there are broad federal requirements for Medicaid, states have a wide degree of flexibility to design their programs.

The Children's Health Insurance Program Reauthorization Act of 2009 (CHIPRA or Public Law 111-3) reauthorized CHIP, which was originally signed into law in 1997. The program went into effect on April 1, 2009. CHIP replaces the State Children's Health Insurance Program (SCHIP). It preserves coverage for the millions of children who rely on CHIP, and provides the resources for states to reach millions of additional children who would otherwise be without health insurance coverage. CHIP is a federal-state partnership, similar to Medicaid, that expands health insurance to children whose families earn too much money to be eligible for Medicaid, but not enough money to purchase private health insurance. CHIPRA also gives states the option to provide prenatal, delivery, and postpartum care to low-income pregnant women without health insurance. Under CHIP, states can operate their programs as an expansion of Medicaid, a program entirely separate from Medicaid, or a combination of both approaches. Most states have either expanded Medicaid or run a combination of both types of programs. Only two states, Connecticut and Washington, run separate programs without Medicaid expansions.

Health care resources and utilization—Hospital statistics based on data from AHA's yearly survey are published annually in *AHA Hospital Statistics* and cover all hospitals accepted for registration by the Association. To be accepted for registration, hospitals may provide proof of accreditation by the Joint

Commission on Accreditation of Healthcare Organizations or certification under Title 18 of the Social Security Act; or meet certain requirements relating to number of beds, construction, equipment, medical and nursing staff, patient care and services, clinical records, and other factors. The NCHS has replaced the National Hospital Discharge Survey (last conducted in 2010) with the National Hospital Care Survey and the National Hospital Ambulatory Medical Care Survey (NHAMCS). The National Hospital Care Survey is currently underway and data are not yet available. Ambulatory care data, including emergency room visits, are presented here from the NHAMCS. Data on physicians generally come from the professional organizations that collect data on medical school graduates and physicians. Statistics on patient visits to health care providers come from the National Health Interview Survey, and the National Ambulatory Medical Care Survey.

Disability and illness, mental health, and substance use—General health statistics, including morbidity, disability, injuries, preventive care, and findings from physiological testing are collected by NCHS in its National Health Interview Survey and its National Health and Nutrition Examination Surveys. The Centers for Disease Control and Prevention in Atlanta, Georgia is responsible for collecting and publishing data on nationally notifiable diseases. Data are collected from State health departments and territories under the National Notifiable Diseases Surveillance System (NNDSS), which is operated by the CDC in collaboration with the Council of State and Territorial Epidemiologists. The list of diseases is revised annually. The Substance Abuse and Mental Health Services Administration, an agency within HHS, studies and provides data regarding mental illness and substance use.

Statistical reliability—For discussion of statistical collection, estimation, and sampling procedures and measures of reliability applicable to data from NCHS and CMS, see Appendix III.

Table 141. National Health Expenditures by Type of Service—Summary: 1960 to 2015

[In billions of dollars (27.2 represents $27,200,000,000). Excludes Puerto Rico and Island Areas. For definitions, methodology, and related information, see <http://www.cms.gov/NationalHealthExpendData/Downloads/DSM-15.pdf>]

Year	Total expenditures [1]	Health consumption expenditures, total [2]	Personal health care expenditures									
			Total [3]	Hospital care	Physician and clinical services	Dental services	Other professional services [4]	Home health care [5]	Nursing care facilities [6]	Prescription drugs	Durable medical equipment [7]	Nondurable medical equipment [8]
1960....	27.2	24.7	23.3	9.0	5.6	2.0	0.4	0.1	0.8	2.7	0.7	1.6
1961....	29.1	26.3	24.8	9.8	5.8	2.1	0.4	0.1	0.8	2.7	0.8	1.8
1962....	31.8	28.4	26.7	10.4	6.3	2.2	0.4	0.1	0.9	3.0	0.9	1.9
1963....	34.6	30.9	29.1	11.5	7.1	2.4	0.5	0.1	1.0	3.2	0.9	1.9
1964....	38.4	34.1	32.0	12.5	8.1	2.6	0.5	0.1	1.2	3.3	1.0	2.1
1965....	41.9	37.2	34.7	13.5	8.6	2.8	0.5	0.1	1.4	3.7	1.1	2.2
1966....	46.1	41.2	38.4	15.3	9.3	3.0	0.6	0.1	1.7	4.0	1.2	2.4
1967....	51.6	46.5	43.5	17.8	10.4	3.4	0.6	0.2	2.2	4.2	1.1	2.5
1968....	58.4	52.7	49.1	20.5	11.3	3.7	0.6	0.2	2.9	4.7	1.3	2.7
1969....	65.9	59.1	55.5	23.4	12.7	4.2	0.7	0.3	3.4	5.1	1.5	3.0
1970....	74.6	67.0	63.1	27.2	14.3	4.7	0.7	0.2	4.0	5.5	1.7	3.3
1971....	82.7	74.3	69.4	30.2	15.9	5.2	0.8	0.2	4.6	5.9	1.8	3.5
1972....	92.7	83.4	77.2	33.8	17.7	5.6	0.9	0.2	5.2	6.3	2.0	3.7
1973....	102.8	93.1	86.2	37.9	19.6	6.4	1.0	0.3	6.0	6.8	2.2	4.0
1974....	116.5	105.9	98.8	44.1	22.2	7.1	1.2	0.4	6.9	7.4	2.5	4.5
1975....	133.3	121.1	113.2	51.2	25.3	8.0	1.3	0.6	8.0	8.1	2.8	4.9
1976....	152.7	139.3	129.3	59.4	28.7	9.0	1.6	0.9	9.1	8.7	3.0	5.4
1977....	173.9	159.9	146.7	67.0	33.1	10.1	2.1	1.1	10.3	9.2	3.2	6.1
1978....	195.3	180.0	164.2	75.6	35.8	11.0	2.4	1.6	11.8	9.9	3.4	7.1
1979....	221.5	204.6	187.1	86.2	41.2	12.0	2.8	1.9	13.3	10.7	3.8	8.5
1980....	255.3	235.5	217.0	100.5	47.7	13.3	3.5	2.4	15.3	12.0	4.1	9.8
1981....	296.2	273.4	251.8	117.5	55.6	15.7	4.3	2.9	17.3	13.4	4.3	11.3
1982....	334.0	308.0	283.1	133.6	61.6	17.0	4.9	3.5	19.5	15.0	4.6	12.6
1983....	367.8	339.5	311.7	144.7	68.6	18.3	5.7	4.2	21.7	17.3	5.3	13.8
1984....	405.0	375.1	341.6	154.4	77.4	19.9	7.3	5.1	23.7	19.6	6.1	15.0
1985....	442.9	412.8	376.4	164.6	90.9	21.7	8.1	5.6	26.2	21.8	7.1	16.0
1986....	474.7	443.7	408.8	175.6	100.7	23.2	9.3	6.4	28.6	24.3	8.1	17.1
1987....	516.5	482.3	447.7	189.5	112.8	25.3	11.3	6.6	30.6	26.9	9.5	18.3
1988....	579.3	540.5	498.5	206.5	128.4	27.4	13.7	8.4	34.2	30.6	11.1	19.4
1989....	644.8	602.3	550.4	226.0	142.9	29.4	14.5	10.2	38.6	34.8	11.9	20.8
1990....	721.4	674.1	615.3	250.4	158.4	31.6	17.3	12.5	44.7	40.3	13.8	22.4
1991....	788.1	737.7	675.9	275.8	175.8	33.4	18.6	15.1	49.2	44.4	13.1	23.2
1992....	854.1	798.7	731.5	298.5	190.2	37.1	20.9	18.7	52.8	47.0	13.5	23.2
1993....	916.6	857.7	778.7	315.7	201.4	39.0	23.0	22.7	55.8	49.6	14.1	23.7
1994....	967.2	905.7	820.2	328.4	210.5	41.6	24.0	27.3	58.4	53.0	15.3	24.3
1995....	1,021.6	958.2	869.6	339.3	220.3	44.6	26.7	32.3	64.2	59.8	15.9	25.1
1996....	1,074.4	1,009.6	917.5	350.8	228.4	46.9	28.9	35.7	69.2	68.1	17.4	26.0
1997....	1,135.5	1,065.1	969.5	363.4	239.1	50.3	31.3	36.9	74.1	77.6	19.2	27.6
1998....	1,202.0	1,126.8	1,026.1	374.9	256.9	53.6	33.4	34.1	79.1	88.5	21.4	28.6
1999....	1,278.3	1,197.5	1,086.3	393.6	270.0	57.3	34.6	32.8	80.6	104.6	23.0	30.6
2000....	1,369.7	1,286.4	1,162.0	415.5	288.7	62.1	36.6	32.3	85.0	121.0	25.2	31.6
2001....	1,486.8	1,399.4	1,261.9	449.4	313.3	67.6	40.3	34.3	90.8	139.0	25.1	32.3
2002....	1,629.2	1,532.4	1,367.6	486.5	338.4	73.4	43.3	36.5	94.5	157.9	27.1	33.3
2003....	1,768.2	1,664.4	1,477.7	525.9	365.1	76.0	46.5	40.2	100.1	176.7	28.5	36.2
2004....	1,896.3	1,784.9	1,588.0	565.4	390.3	81.7	50.2	44.6	105.1	192.8	30.4	38.1
2005....	2,024.2	1,904.5	1,696.2	608.6	414.1	86.7	52.8	49.3	111.4	205.1	32.4	40.8
2006....	2,156.5	2,031.4	1,804.7	651.2	435.8	91.1	55.3	52.1	115.9	224.1	34.4	43.7
2007....	2,295.7	2,157.3	1,918.8	692.0	458.6	97.0	60.1	57.5	124.9	235.6	37.1	47.8
2008....	2,399.1	2,251.1	2,010.7	725.7	482.9	101.9	64.5	62.2	130.3	241.4	37.7	49.5
2009....	2,494.7	2,355.7	2,114.2	779.7	498.7	102.3	67.2	67.3	134.9	252.7	37.8	50.3
2010....	2,596.4	2,453.7	2,194.6	822.4	513.1	105.0	69.8	71.0	140.0	253.0	39.9	51.2
2011....	2,687.9	2,538.4	2,272.6	852.0	536.4	107.1	72.7	73.8	145.0	258.7	42.3	52.8
2012....	2,795.4	2,642.2	2,365.9	902.7	558.0	108.8	76.4	77.1	147.4	259.1	43.7	53.7
2013....	2,877.6	2,724.5	2,435.6	937.9	569.5	110.1	78.8	80.0	149.2	265.1	45.1	55.7
2014....	3,029.3	2,878.4	2,562.8	981.0	597.1	112.8	82.8	83.6	152.6	297.9	46.6	56.9
2015....	3,205.6	3,050.8	2,717.2	1,036.1	634.9	117.5	87.7	88.8	156.8	324.6	48.5	59.0

[1] Includes Health Consumption Expenditures plus medical research, and medical structures and equipment. [2] Includes Personal Health Expenditures plus, not shown, government administration, net cost of health insurance, and government public health activities. [3] Includes items shown here, and also other health, residential, and personal services. [4] Includes health practitioners other than physicians and dentists, such as, but not limited to, chiropractors, optometrists, physical, occupational, and speech therapists, podiatrists, and private-duty nurses. [5] Services delivered by freestanding home health care facilities only. [6] Care provided in nursing care facilities (NAICS 6231), continuing care retirement communities (623311), state and local government nursing facilities, and nursing facilities operated by the Department of Veterans Affairs. [7] Retail sales of items such as contact lenses, eyeglasses and other ophthalmic products, surgical and orthopedic products, medical equipment rental, oxygen, and hearing aids. Durable products generally last over 3 years. [8] Non-prescription drugs and sundry medical items.

Source: U.S. Centers for Medicare and Medicaid Services, Office of the Actuary, National Health Statistics Group, "National Health Expenditure Data, Historical," <http://cms.gov/nationalhealthexpenddata>, accessed January 2017.

Table 142. National Health Expenditures by Source of Funds: 1990 to 2015

[In billions of dollars (721.4 represents $721,400,000,000), except percent. Excludes Puerto Rico and Island Areas. For definitions and related information, see <http://www.cms.gov/NationalHealthExpendData/Downloads/DSM-15.pdf>]

Source of funds	1990	2000	2005	2010	2012	2013	2014	2015
National health expenditure, total.........	**721.4**	**1,369.7**	**2,024.2**	**2,596.4**	**2,795.4**	**2,877.6**	**3,029.3**	**3,205.6**
Annual percent change [1]......................	11.9	7.1	6.7	4.1	4.0	2.9	5.3	5.8
Percent of gross domestic product............	12.1	13.3	15.5	17.4	17.3	17.2	17.4	17.8
Consumer out of pocket.........................	137.9	199.0	263.8	298.7	317.6	325.1	329.7	338.2
Health insurance...............................	439.1	919.4	1,414.6	1,875.1	2,019.6	2,086.3	2,228.2	2,384.5
Private health insurance......................	233.9	458.5	701.7	863.1	925.1	944.9	1,000.0	1,072.1
Medicare....................................	110.2	224.8	339.8	519.3	569.5	590.4	618.5	646.2
Medicaid (Title XIX)...........................	73.7	200.3	309.2	397.2	422.7	445.4	497.2	545.1
CHIP (Title XIX and Title XXI).................	(X)	3.0	7.6	11.5	12.6	13.5	13.2	14.6
Department of Defense........................	10.4	13.7	26.5	38.3	39.8	39.2	41.5	41.8
Department of Veterans Affairs................	10.9	19.1	29.8	45.7	49.8	52.8	57.9	64.7
Other third party payers and programs.........	77.1	124.9	168.9	204.3	227.7	235.2	241.5	247.2
Worksite health care........................	2.2	3.5	4.3	4.7	5.2	5.4	5.7	6.1
Other private revenues [2].....................	29.2	57.2	70.7	100.4	116.0	119.3	123.2	124.3
Indian health services.......................	1.0	1.9	2.4	3.5	3.7	3.6	3.7	3.8
Workers' compensation.......................	17.5	26.5	41.5	36.2	42.4	44.2	46.5	49.4
General assistance..........................	5.0	3.9	6.2	7.1	6.4	6.7	7.1	6.8
Maternal and Child health....................	1.7	3.2	3.4	3.9	3.4	3.6	3.7	3.7
Vocational rehabilitation.....................	0.3	0.4	0.5	0.6	0.5	0.5	0.5	0.5
Other federal programs [3].....................	1.6	4.5	6.4	7.7	11.6	13.0	12.2	12.3
Substance Abuse and Mental Health Services Administration....................	1.4	2.6	3.2	3.4	3.4	3.3	3.5	3.5
Other state and local programs [4]............	15.9	18.8	26.9	32.6	30.8	31.2	31.0	32.3
School health...............................	1.3	2.5	3.4	4.3	4.3	4.4	4.5	4.6
Public health activity [5].......................	20.0	43.1	57.2	75.5	77.2	77.9	79.0	80.9
Investment..................................	**47.3**	**83.3**	**119.7**	**142.7**	**153.2**	**153.0**	**150.9**	**154.7**
Research [6].................................	12.7	25.5	40.3	49.2	48.4	46.7	45.9	46.7
Structures & equipment [7]....................	34.6	57.8	79.4	93.5	104.8	106.4	105.0	108.0

X Not applicable. [1] Average percent change from prior year. [2] Most common source is philanthropy; support can come from individuals or through philanthropic fund-raising organizations, and also from foundations or corporations. [3] Includes federal general hospital/medical, and pre-existing conditions insurance plans. [4] Includes temporary disability insurance, state and local subsidies to providers, and non-XIX state and local. [5] Governments provide health services such as epidemiological surveillance, inoculations, immunization/vaccination services, disease prevention programs, and public health laboratories. In the National Health Expenditure Accounts, spending for these activities is reported in government public health activity. [6] Non-profit or government entities. Excludes R&D expenditures by drug and medical supply and equipment manufacturers. [7] Structures are defined as the value of new construction by the medical sector. Equipment includes the value of new capital equipment (including software). Includes establishments that provide health care, and excludes retail establishments that sell non-durable or durable medical goods. Excludes maintenance and repairs.

Source: U. S. Centers for Medicare and Medicaid Services, Office of the Actuary, National Health Statistics Group, "National Health Expenditure Data, Historical," <http://cms.gov/nationalhealthexpenddata>, accessed January 2017.

Table 143. National Health Expenditure Projections by Source of Funds and Type of Expenditure: 2016 to 2024

[In billions of dollars (3,350.7 represents $3,350,700,000,000). For calendar years. Projections are based on the 2014 version of the National Health Expenditures (NHE) released in December 2015; projections as of July 2016. Methodology available at <https://www.cms.gov/NationalHealthExpendData/Downloads/ProjectionsMethodology.pdf>. Excludes Puerto Rico and Island areas]

Funding source and expenditure type	2016	2017	2018	2019	2020	2021	2022	2023	2024
Total......................................	**3,350.7**	**3,521.6**	**3,731.4**	**3,958.6**	**4,198.3**	**4,457.5**	**4,732.8**	**5,022.0**	**5,321.7**
SOURCE OF FUNDS									
Consumer out-of-pocket.....................	350.1	364.6	383.2	402.9	427.5	451.3	476.0	501.5	528.1
Health insurance............................	2,473.7	2,604.6	2,765.4	2,939.8	3,119.6	3,317.0	3,527.5	3,749.8	3,979.6
Private health insurance [1].................	1,092.7	1,149.0	1,217.0	1,286.3	1,350.1	1,425.4	1,505.1	1,587.2	1,671.1
Medicare.................................	681.3	721.1	770.2	827.6	893.1	961.6	1,036.3	1,117.2	1,199.9
Medicaid..................................	577.7	605.7	641.5	680.8	722.0	766.2	812.7	862.1	915.4
Other health insurance programs [2].........	122.0	128.9	136.7	145.1	154.4	163.8	173.4	183.3	193.2
Other third party payers and programs.........	526.9	552.5	582.8	615.8	651.2	689.2	729.2	770.7	814.0
TYPE OF EXPENDITURE									
Health consumption expenditures [3]..........	3,185.5	3,348.9	3,549.1	3,766.0	3,994.7	4,242.1	4,504.8	4,780.9	5,066.8
Personal health care........................	2,830.4	2,975.1	3,150.8	3,341.1	3,543.3	3,761.0	3,992.0	4,234.5	4,485.4
Hospital care.............................	1,067.3	1,122.1	1,185.7	1,259.0	1,336.0	1,420.0	1,509.6	1,603.6	1,700.7
Physician and clinical services............	664.9	697.3	735.8	779.9	825.1	874.7	927.3	981.8	1,037.2
Dental services..........................	123.6	129.1	136.0	143.7	152.6	161.5	170.8	179.8	189.2
Other professional services [4]............	93.3	97.9	103.6	110.0	116.8	123.9	131.5	139.3	147.4
Home health care [5]......................	92.2	97.2	102.8	109.2	116.3	123.9	132.1	140.7	149.9
Nondurable medical products..............	61.1	63.6	66.8	70.3	74.3	78.5	82.8	87.2	91.7
Prescription drugs........................	342.1	362.7	393.6	418.6	445.9	474.6	505.1	539.3	575.4
Durable medical equipment................	50.4	52.8	55.6	58.9	62.9	67.2	71.8	76.2	80.8
Nursing care facilities and continuing care retirement communities [6]..............	169.5	178.3	187.7	198.2	209.7	221.8	234.7	248.0	262.0
Other health, residential, and personal care [7]......	166.0	174.2	183.3	193.2	203.6	214.8	226.5	238.6	251.3
Public health activity [8]....................	87.4	92.0	97.5	103.5	109.9	116.7	124.0	131.7	139.6
Research [9]..............................	47.3	49.1	51.3	53.8	56.4	59.2	62.1	65.1	68.2
Structures & equipment [10]...............	117.8	123.6	130.9	138.9	147.2	156.3	165.9	176.0	186.7

[1] Includes employer sponsored insurance and other private insurance, which includes marketplace plans. [2] Children's Health Insurance Program (Titles XIX and XXI), Department of Defense, and Department of Veterans' Affairs. [3] See footnote 2, Table 141. [4] See footnote 4, Table 141. [5] See footnote 5, Table 141. [6] See footnote 6, Table 141. [7] See footnote 6, Table 144. [8] See footnote 5, Table 142. [9] See footnote 6, Table 142. [10] See footnote 7, Table 142.

Source: U.S. Centers for Medicare and Medicaid Services, Office of the Actuary, National Health Statistics Group, "National Health Expenditure Data, Projected," <http://cms.gov/nationalhealthexpenddata>, accessed January 2017.

Table 144. Health Consumption Expenditures—Per Capita Spending by Type of Expenditure: 2000 to 2015

[In dollars, except percent. Based on U.S. Census Bureau estimates of total U.S. resident population. Health consumption expenditures include all personal health care spending, government administration and the net cost of private health insurance, and public health activities. Excludes research and structures and equipment. Excludes Puerto Rico and Island Areas]

Type of expenditure	2000	2005	2009	2010	2011	2012	2013	2014	2015
Total [1]	**4,562**	**6,450**	**7,687**	**7,942**	**8,158**	**8,427**	**8,625**	**9,041**	**9,508**
Annual percent change [2]	(NA)	5.7	3.7	3.3	2.7	3.3	2.3	4.8	5.2
Hospital care	1,474	2,061	2,544	2,662	2,738	2,879	2,969	3,081	3,229
Physician and clinical services	1,024	1,402	1,628	1,661	1,724	1,780	1,803	1,876	1,979
Dental services	220	294	334	340	344	347	349	354	366
Other professional services [3]	130	179	219	226	234	244	249	260	273
Home health care	115	167	220	230	237	246	253	262	277
Other nondurable medical products [4]	112	138	164	166	170	171	176	179	184
Prescription drugs	429	695	825	819	831	826	839	936	1,011
Durable medical equipment [5]	89	110	123	129	136	139	143	146	151
Nursing care facilities and continuing care retirement communities	302	377	440	453	466	470	472	479	489
Other health, residential, and personal care [6]	227	322	403	418	423	444	457	476	509
Public health activities [7]	153	194	242	244	238	246	247	248	252

NA Not available. [1] Includes other items, not shown separately. [2] Average annual growth from previous year. [3] See footnote 4, Table 141. [4] See footnote 8, Table 141. [5] See footnote 7, Table 141. [6] Includes expenditures for residential care facilities (NAICS 623210 and 623220), ambulance providers (NAICS 621910), medical care delivered in non-traditional settings (such as community centers, senior citizens centers, schools, and military field stations), and expenditures for Home and Community Waiver programs under Medicaid. [7] See footnote 5, Table 142.

Source: U. S. Centers for Medicare and Medicaid Services, Office of the Actuary, National Health Statistics Group, "National Health Expenditure Data, Historical," <http://cms.gov/nationalhealthexpenddata>, accessed January 2017.

Table 145. Health Consumption Expenditures by Type of Expenditure and Source of Funds: 2015

[In billions of dollars (3,050.8 represents $3,050,800,000,000). Excludes Puerto Rico and Island Areas. Excludes research, structures, and equipment]

Type of expenditure	Total	Out-of-pocket	Health insurance Total	Private health insurance	Medicare	Medicaid	Other health insurance programs [1]	Other third party payers and programs [2]
Total	**3,050.8**	**338.1**	**2,384.5**	**1,072.1**	**646.2**	**545.1**	**121.1**	**247.2**
Personal health care [3]	2,717.2	338.1	2,151.2	944.7	605.0	486.5	115.1	227.8
Hospital care	1,036.1	32.1	909.1	403.6	257.0	185.1	63.3	94.9
Physician and clinical services	634.9	56.6	514.7	272.3	144.3	69.7	28.5	63.6
Dental services	117.5	46.9	70.2	54.7	0.5	11.5	3.5	0.4
Other health, residential, and personal care [4]	163.3	6.2	112.0	12.3	5.0	92.4	2.3	45.1
Home health care	88.8	8.8	77.3	9.4	35.1	32.0	0.7	2.7
Nursing care facilities and continuing care retirement communities	156.8	40.1	105.7	13.4	37.6	49.7	5.0	11.0
Prescription drugs	324.6	45.5	277.0	139.8	94.1	31.8	11.4	2.0
Durable medical equipment [5]	48.5	23.3	24.3	9.0	7.9	7.3	0.1	0.8
Government administration [5]	42.6	(X)	38.0	(X)	9.6	23.6	4.8	4.6
Net cost of health insurance [5]	210.1	(X)	195.3	127.4	31.6	35.1	1.3	14.8
Public health activities [6]	80.9	(X)	(X)	(X)	(X)	(X)	(X)	(X)

X Not applicable. [1] Includes Children's Health Insurance Program (CHIP) Titles XIX and XXI, Department of Defense, and Department of Veterans Affairs. [2] Includes worksite health care, other private revenues, Indian Health Service, workers' compensation, general assistance, maternal and child health, vocational rehabilitation, other federal programs, Substance Abuse and Mental Health Services Administration, other state and local programs, and school health. [3] Comprises all medical goods and services that are rendered to treat or prevent a specific disease or condition in a specific person. Includes expenditures for other items, not shown separately. [4] See footnote 6, Table 144. [5] See source for definitions. [6] See footnote 5, Table 142.

Source: U. S. Centers for Medicare and Medicaid Services, Office of the Actuary, National Health Statistics Group, "National Health Expenditure Data, Historical," <http://cms.gov/nationalhealthexpenddata>, accessed January 2017.

Table 146. Personal Health Care Expenditures by Source of Funds: 2000 to 2015

[In billions of dollars (1,162.0 represents $1,162,000,000,000). Excludes Puerto Rico and Island Areas]

Item	2000	2005	2009	2010	2011	2012	2013	2014	2015
Personal health care expenditures	**1,162.0**	**1,696.2**	**2,114.2**	**2,194.6**	**2,272.6**	**2,365.9**	**2,435.6**	**2,562.8**	**2,717.2**
Out-of-pocket	199.0	263.8	293.1	298.7	308.5	317.6	325.1	329.7	338.2
Health insurance	844.2	1,279.2	1,636.7	1,699.3	1,766.1	1,833.1	1,891.0	2,009.4	2,151.2
Private health insurance	406.1	604.9	734.4	754.8	784.1	812.5	829.3	875.2	944.7
Medicare	216.3	326.3	470.3	488.5	513.5	535.1	555.1	580.6	605.0
Medicaid	186.9	287.6	346.2	365.8	373.9	388.5	406.4	446.7	486.5
Other health insurance [1]	34.9	60.5	85.7	90.2	94.6	97.1	100.2	107.0	115.1
Other third party payers and programs [2]	118.9	153.2	184.4	196.6	198.0	215.2	219.5	223.7	227.8

[1] Includes Children's Health Insurance Program (Titles XIX and XXI), Department of Defense, and Department of Veterans Affairs. [2] See footnote 2, Table 148.

Source: U.S. Centers for Medicare and Medicaid Services, Office of the Actuary, National Health Statistics Group, "National Health Expenditure Data, Historical," <http://cms.gov/nationalhealthexpenddata>, accessed January 2017.

Table 147. National Health Expenditures by Sponsor: 2000 to 2015

[In billions of dollars (1,369.7 represents $1,369,700,000,000). Excludes Puerto Rico and Island Areas. Type of sponsor is defined as the entity that is ultimately responsible for financing the health care bill. These sponsors pay health insurance premiums and out-of-pocket costs, or finance health care through dedicated taxes and/or general revenues]

Type of sponsor	2000	2005	2010	2011	2012	2013	2014	2015
Total	1,369.7	2,024.2	2,596.4	2,687.9	2,795.4	2,877.6	3,029.3	3,205.6
Business, households and other private revenues	883.0	1,225.7	1,444.6	1,496.4	1,576.2	1,611.1	1,662.8	1,739.4
Private business [1]	335.2	469.5	518.0	541.9	567.0	578.5	605.6	637.5
Household [2]	443.5	618.9	750.2	773.6	807.2	824.9	846.6	886.8
Other private revenues	104.2	137.2	176.3	181.0	201.9	207.7	210.5	215.1
Governments	486.7	798.6	1,151.8	1,191.5	1,219.2	1,266.5	1,366.5	1,466.2
Federal government [3]	260.7	450.4	730.3	731.4	731.2	759.4	843.1	918.5
State and local government [4]	226.0	348.2	421.6	460.0	488.1	507.1	523.4	547.7

[1] Excludes Medicare Retiree Drug Subsidy (RDS) payments to private plans as of 2006, small business tax credits as of 2010, and Early Retirement Reinsurance Program (ERRP) Payments for 2010-2011. Includes one-half of self employment contribution to Medicare Hospital Insurance (HI) Trust Fund. [2] Excludes government-subsidized COBRA payments for 2009-2011, and Affordable Care Act health insurance premium tax credits and cost-sharing subsidies as of 2014. Includes one-half self-employment contribution to the Medicare HI Trust Fund, and trust fund revenues from taxation of social security benefits. Beginning in 2010, also includes premiums paid for the Pre-Existing Condition Insurance Plan (PCIP). [3] Includes employer contributions to private health insurance premiums and Medicare HI Trust Fund, adjusted Medicare expenditures, and health program expenditures (excluding Medicare); see source for details. [4] Includes employer contributions to private health insurance premiums and Medicare HI Trust Fund, and expenditures for Medicaid and other programs; see source for details.

Source: U.S. Centers for Medicare and Medicaid Services, Office of the Actuary, National Health Statistics Group, "National Health Expenditure Data, Historical," <http://cms.gov/nationalhealthexpenddata>, accessed January 2017.

Table 148. Hospital Care, Physician and Clinical Services, Nursing Care Facilities and Continuing Care Retirement Communities, and Prescription Drug Expenditures by Source of Funds: 2000 to 2015

[In billions of dollars (415.5 represents $415,500,000,000). Excludes Puerto Rico and Island Areas]

Source of payment	2000	2005	2010	2011	2012	2013	2014	2015
Hospital care, total	**415.5**	**608.6**	**822.4**	**852.0**	**902.7**	**937.9**	**981.0**	**1,036.1**
Out-of-pocket	13.4	19.7	27.8	29.2	31.8	33.9	33.1	32.1
Health insurance	358.2	531.6	714.1	741.5	780.3	808.6	851.9	909.1
Private health insurance	141.1	215.9	301.1	315.7	337.6	350.0	369.8	403.6
Medicare	123.4	176.4	219.8	228.4	238.4	246.2	252.8	257.0
Medicaid	70.9	103.8	141.8	143.9	149.8	155.7	169.1	185.1
CHIP [1]	0.9	2.7	3.2	3.3	3.4	3.5	3.4	3.7
Dept. of Defense	7.6	12.1	16.6	17.2	16.8	16.3	16.1	15.2
Veterans Affairs	14.3	20.8	31.7	33.0	34.3	36.9	40.7	44.5
Other third party payers and programs [2]	43.9	57.3	80.5	81.3	90.6	95.4	96.0	94.9
Physician and clinical services, total	**288.7**	**414.1**	**513.1**	**536.4**	**558.0**	**569.5**	**597.1**	**634.9**
Out-of-pocket	32.0	41.8	48.6	51.3	51.7	53.3	54.0	56.6
Health insurance	220.6	326.4	410.4	430.3	446.7	457.8	483.4	514.7
Private health insurance	135.9	198.6	230.2	240.3	248.0	249.2	255.6	272.3
Medicare	58.7	85.6	115.8	122.2	128.1	132.1	137.9	144.3
Medicaid	19.3	30.1	43.3	45.2	47.0	52.0	63.6	69.7
CHIP [1]	0.7	1.7	3.1	3.0	3.2	3.5	3.2	3.4
Dept. of Defense	4.7	8.1	12.3	13.2	13.8	13.8	15.2	15.1
Veterans Affairs	1.3	2.5	5.8	6.4	6.6	7.2	7.9	9.9
Other third party payers and programs [2]	36.1	45.8	54.2	54.8	59.6	58.4	59.7	63.6
Nursing care facilities and continuing care retirement communities, total	**85.0**	**111.4**	**140.0**	**145.0**	**147.4**	**149.2**	**152.6**	**156.8**
Out-of-pocket	27.1	32.5	37.2	36.8	39.1	39.4	39.7	40.1
Health insurance	52.0	71.8	93.3	98.8	97.7	99.0	101.8	105.7
Private health insurance	7.5	7.1	10.6	10.9	11.5	11.7	12.3	13.4
Medicare	10.8	20.5	32.3	35.9	34.0	34.7	35.6	37.6
Medicaid	31.9	41.3	46.3	47.7	47.8	48.1	49.1	49.7
Veterans Affairs	1.9	2.8	4.0	4.3	4.4	4.5	4.7	5.0
Other third party payers and programs [2]	5.9	7.1	9.6	9.5	10.6	10.8	11.2	11.0
Prescription drugs, total	**121.0**	**205.1**	**253.0**	**258.7**	**259.1**	**265.1**	**297.9**	**324.6**
Out-of-pocket	33.6	51.3	45.2	45.2	45.1	43.6	44.8	45.5
Health insurance	85.1	150.0	204.4	210.6	211.4	219.1	251.0	277.0
Private health insurance	61.1	102.1	116.0	116.9	112.8	113.5	128.2	139.8
Medicare	2.1	3.9	58.9	63.3	67.5	74.1	84.8	94.1
Medicaid	19.8	36.5	20.4	21.0	21.6	22.4	28.0	31.8
CHIP [1]	0.3	1.1	1.4	1.4	1.5	1.5	1.4	1.5
Dept. of Defense	0.7	3.6	4.7	4.8	4.8	4.8	5.7	6.6
Veterans Affairs	1.1	2.7	3.0	3.2	3.1	2.8	3.0	3.3
Other third party payers and programs [2]	2.3	3.9	3.4	2.8	2.6	2.4	2.0	2.0

[1] Children's Health Insurance Program (Titles XIX and XXI), signed into law in 1997. [2] Includes worksite health care, other private revenues, Indian Health Service, workers' compensation, general assistance, maternal and child health, vocational rehabilitation, other federal programs, Substance Abuse and Mental Health Services Administration, other state and local programs, and school health.

Source: U.S. Centers for Medicare and Medicaid Services, Office of the Actuary, National Health Statistics Group, "National Health Expenditure Data, Historical," <http://cms.gov/nationalhealthexpenddata>, accessed January 2017.

Table 149. Medical Care Consumer Price Indexes: 1980 to 2016

[Indexes with base of 1982-1984=100. Indexes are annual averages of monthly data based on components of consumer price index for all urban consumers; for explanation, see text, Section 14 and Appendix III]

Year	Medical care, total	Medical care services				Hospital and related services	Medical care commodities		Annual percent change [3]		
		Total [1]	Professional services				Total [2]	Pre-scription drugs	Medical care, total	Medical care services	Medical care com-modities
			Total [1]	Physi-cians	Dental						
1980.......	74.9	74.8	77.9	76.5	78.9	69.2	75.4	72.5	11.0	11.3	9.3
1990.......	162.8	162.7	156.1	160.8	155.8	178.0	163.4	181.7	9.0	9.3	8.4
1995.......	220.5	224.2	201.0	208.8	206.8	257.8	204.5	235.0	4.5	5.1	1.9
2000.......	260.8	266.0	237.7	244.7	258.5	317.3	238.1	285.4	4.1	4.3	3.2
2005.......	323.2	336.7	281.7	287.5	324.0	439.9	276.0	349.0	4.2	4.8	2.5
2010.......	388.4	411.2	328.2	331.3	398.8	607.7	314.7	407.8	3.4	3.5	3.1
2011.......	400.3	423.8	335.7	340.3	408.0	641.5	324.1	425.0	3.0	3.1	3.0
2012.......	414.9	440.3	342.0	347.3	417.5	672.1	333.6	440.1	3.7	3.9	2.9
2013.......	425.1	454.0	349.5	354.2	431.8	701.3	335.1	442.6	2.5	3.1	0.4
2014.......	435.3	464.8	355.2	359.1	441.0	733.8	343.4	458.3	2.4	2.4	2.5
2015.......	446.8	476.2	361.5	366.1	452.2	761.9	354.6	479.3	2.6	2.4	3.3
2016.......	463.7	494.8	371.5	378.1	465.0	795.1	366.8	502.5	3.8	3.9	3.4

[1] Includes other services not shown separately. [2] Includes other commodities not shown separately. [3] Percent change from the immediate prior year.

Source: U.S. Bureau of Labor Statistics, Consumer Price Index Databases, <http://www.bls.gov/cpi/data.htm>, accessed January 2017. See also <http://www.bls.gov/cpi/>.

Table 150. Average Annual Expenditures Per Consumer Unit for Health Care: 2015

[In dollars, except percent. Expenditures are direct out-of-pocket expenditures. Consumers units may be all members in a housing unit (families), a person living alone or sharing a household with others and financially independent, or 2 or more unrelated persons living together who share expenses. See also text for Section 13, and source. For composition of regions, see map, inside front cover]

Item	Health care, total		Health insur-ance	Medical services	Drugs and medical sup-plies [1]	Percent distribution		
	Amount	Percent of total expendi-tures				Health insur-ance	Medical services	Drugs and medical sup-plies [1]
Total...............................	4,342	7.8	2,977	791	574	68.6	18.2	13.2
Age of reference person:								
Under 25 years old...................	978	3.0	575	237	166	58.8	24.2	17.0
25 to 34 years old...................	2,770	5.3	1,999	481	289	72.2	17.4	10.4
35 to 44 years old...................	3,873	5.9	2,726	732	415	70.4	18.9	10.7
45 to 54 years old...................	4,669	6.7	3,215	879	575	68.9	18.8	12.3
55 to 64 years old...................	5,112	8.7	3,436	983	693	67.2	19.2	13.6
65 years old and older................	5,756	12.9	3,893	967	896	67.6	16.8	15.6
Race of reference person:								
White and other [2]....................	4,686	8.1	3,173	884	628	67.7	18.9	13.4
Asian...............................	3,876	6.1	2,777	677	422	71.6	17.5	10.9
Black...............................	2,305	5.7	1,795	238	272	77.9	10.3	11.8
Origin of reference person:								
Hispanic............................	2,632	5.5	1,868	454	309	71.0	17.2	11.7
Non-Hispanic........................	4,598	8.0	3,143	842	613	68.4	18.3	13.3
Region of residence:								
Northeast...........................	4,328	7.3	3,112	682	534	71.9	15.8	12.3
Midwest............................	4,616	8.4	3,022	982	613	65.5	21.3	13.3
South..............................	4,264	8.2	2,971	714	580	69.7	16.7	13.6
West...............................	4,221	6.9	2,834	830	557	67.1	19.7	13.2
Size of consumer unit:								
One person.........................	2,638	7.9	1,783	465	390	67.6	17.6	14.8
Two or more persons.................	5,044	7.7	3,469	926	649	68.8	18.4	12.9
Two persons.....................	5,406	9.2	3,713	933	761	68.7	17.3	14.1
Three persons...................	4,728	7.0	3,318	831	579	70.2	17.6	12.2
Four persons....................	4,943	6.6	3,374	1,026	543	68.3	20.8	11.0
Five persons or more.............	4,406	6.2	2,979	918	510	67.6	20.8	11.6
Income before taxes, by quintile:								
Lowest 20 percent...................	1,930	7.9	1,299	326	305	67.3	16.9	15.8
Second 20 percent..................	3,423	9.8	2,312	611	500	67.5	17.8	14.6
Third 20 percent....................	3,965	8.6	2,786	645	534	70.3	16.3	13.5
Fourth 20 percent...................	5,327	8.4	3,742	939	647	70.2	17.6	12.1
Highest 20 percent..................	7,048	6.4	4,738	1,432	879	67.2	20.3	12.5
Education:								
Less than a high school graduate............	2,358	8.8	1,351	628	379	57.3	26.6	16.1
High school graduate.....................	3,203	8.8	2,306	451	447	72.0	14.1	14.0
High school graduate with some college....	3,600	7.8	2,507	611	482	69.6	17.0	13.4
Associate's degree.....................	4,269	8.0	2,935	772	562	68.8	18.1	13.2
Bachelor's degree.....................	5,097	7.3	3,565	894	638	69.9	17.5	12.5
Master's, professional, or doctoral degree...	6,560	7.5	4,334	1,388	837	66.1	21.2	12.8

[1] Includes prescription and nonprescription drugs. [2] All other races includes Native Hawaiian or other Pacific Islander, American Indian or Alaska Native, and approximately 1 percent reporting more than one race.

Source: U.S. Bureau of Labor Statistics, "Consumer Expenditure Survey, Annual Calendar Year Tables, 2015," <http://www.bls.gov/cex/tables.htm>, accessed January 2017.

Table 151. Medical Expenditures by Health Condition in Current and Chained (2009) Dollars and Per Capita: 2000 to 2013

[In billions of dollars (1,109.59 represents $1,109,590,000,000), except as noted. Health conditions are classified according to the International Classification of Diseases, 9th revision (ICD-9). Based on Bureau of Economic Analysis' Health Care Satellite Account, Blended Account. The Blended Account blends data from multiple sources, including large claims databases. The BEA also has available health expenditure data based on the Medical Expenditure Panel Survey. See source for details]

Health expense item	Current dollars (billions)			Chained (2009) billion dollars			Per capita (dollars)		
	2000	2010	2013	2000	2010	2013	2000	2010	2013
Total health	**1,109.59**	**2,080.44**	**2,322.99**	**1,671.01**	**2,016.86**	**2,119.77**	**3,932.45**	**6,725.27**	**7,341.30**
Health services	1,052.23	1,979.18	2,208.35	1,609.82	1,915.12	2,006.18	3,729.16	6,397.93	6,979.01
Medical services by disease	900.75	1,722.41	1,934.97	1,389.20	1,664.09	1,754.21	3,192.31	5,567.89	6,115.05
Infectious and parasitic diseases	24.15	58.29	70.45	43.43	54.26	63.25	85.59	188.43	222.64
Neoplasms	59.62	115.50	126.88	99.85	114.79	120.18	211.30	373.37	400.98
Endocrine, nutritional, and metabolic diseases and immunity disorders	53.45	126.28	141.87	79.25	125.33	134.66	189.43	408.21	448.35
Mental illness	43.07	78.88	89.33	59.36	78.02	87.68	152.64	254.99	282.31
Diseases of the nervous system and sense organs	60.77	119.43	135.55	100.03	112.42	118.65	215.37	386.07	428.38
Diseases of the circulatory system	153.47	235.23	236.34	205.25	227.67	229.13	543.91	760.41	746.90
Diseases of the respiratory system	92.45	144.48	160.99	133.62	136.62	138.63	327.65	467.05	508.77
Diseases of the digestive system	56.31	100.51	114.32	88.01	95.45	94.42	199.57	324.91	361.28
Diseases of the genitourinary system	53.15	104.66	114.36	88.09	105.19	110.85	188.37	338.33	361.41
Complications of pregnancy, childbirth, and the puerperium	24.22	38.80	46.96	35.51	35.95	39.15	85.84	125.43	148.41
Diseases of the skin and subcutaneous organs	21.31	38.44	45.24	34.34	38.16	39.98	75.52	124.26	142.97
Diseases of the musculoskeletal system and connective tissue	76.96	170.13	190.48	121.92	159.75	169.89	272.75	549.97	601.97
Injury and poisoning	65.53	110.24	118.49	105.65	104.77	107.47	232.24	356.36	374.46
Symptoms, signs, and ill-defined conditions	83.29	212.16	254.32	135.79	203.15	225.48	295.18	685.83	803.72
Other diseases	33.01	69.38	89.39	59.83	72.71	75.34	116.99	224.28	282.50
Diseases of blood and blood-forming organs	8.55	20.64	32.51	18.34	22.41	22.00	30.30	66.72	102.74
Congenital anomalies	5.51	7.63	7.64	9.65	8.84	8.46	19.53	24.66	24.14
Conditions originating in perinatal period	5.16	6.35	9.15	8.45	7.47	7.68	18.29	20.53	28.92
Residual codes, unclassified, all E codes [1]	13.78	34.77	40.10	23.85	33.90	37.49	48.84	112.40	126.73
Medical services by provider	151.48	256.78	273.38	220.78	251.04	251.82	536.85	830.07	863.96
Dental services	63.57	104.48	109.94	95.42	101.69	98.87	225.30	337.74	347.44
Nursing homes	87.91	152.29	163.43	125.35	149.35	153.01	311.56	492.30	516.48
Proprietary and government nursing homes	56.85	100.22	109.62	81.06	98.28	102.62	201.48	323.97	346.43
Nonprofit nursing homes services to households	31.06	52.07	53.81	44.29	51.08	50.38	110.08	168.32	170.05
Medical products, appliances and equipment	57.36	101.26	114.64	63.43	101.83	114.13	203.29	327.33	362.29
Pharmaceutical and other medical products	25.19	45.64	51.88	27.40	45.86	52.31	89.27	147.54	163.96
Pharmaceutical products (excludes prescription drugs) [2]	23.24	41.66	47.24	25.35	41.79	47.67	82.36	134.67	149.29
Nonprescription drugs	23.24	41.66	47.24	25.35	41.79	47.67	82.36	134.67	149.29
Other medical products	1.95	3.99	4.64	2.06	4.07	4.65	6.91	12.90	14.66
Therapeutic appliances and equipment	32.17	55.61	62.77	36.05	55.97	61.83	114.01	179.77	198.37
Corrective eyeglasses and contact lenses	19.91	29.71	32.90	23.34	29.51	31.94	70.56	96.04	103.97
Therapeutic medical equipment	12.26	25.91	29.86	12.95	26.46	29.92	43.45	83.76	94.37

[1] E codes cover external causes of injury or poisoning. [2] Excludes prescription drugs; prescription drug expenses have been allocated by health condition.

Source: U.S. Bureau of Economic Analysis, Health Care Satellite Account, "Blended Account, 2000-2013," <http://www.bea.gov/national/health_care_satellite_account.htm>, accessed February 2017.

Table 152. Children's Health Insurance Program (CHIP)—Enrollment and Expenditures by State: 2015 and 2016

[Expenditures in millions of dollars (13,461.4 represents $13,461,400,000). For fiscal years. Enrollment data are subject to revision. Components may not add to total due to rounding. CHIP is a federal-state program that provides health benefits coverage to children without health insurance and living in families whose incomes are too high to qualify for Medicaid. States may create CHIP programs as an expansion of Medicaid, a program separate from Medicaid, or a combination of both approaches. As of July 2016, Connecticut and Washington have separate CHIP programs; all other states use either Medicaid expansion or a combination of the two approaches. Based on analysis of CHIP data from the Centers for Medicare & Medicaid Services; see source for details]

	Children enrolled [1]		Expenditures, 2015			Expenditures, 2016		
	2015 [2]	2016	Total	Federal	State [3]	Total	Federal	State [3]
United States..............	8,439,933	8,900,074	13,461.4	9,528.0	3,933.4	15,386.5	14,231.4	1,155.2
Alabama [4]....................	133,043	150,040	267.4	209.0	58.4	281.5	290.1	-8.6
Alaska.......................	10,182	15,662	22.1	14.3	7.7	33.4	29.6	3.9
Arizona [4]...................	38,811	88,224	118.3	92.1	26.2	188.0	187.0	0.9
Arkansas....................	112,071	120,863	170.0	135.4	34.6	176.8	176.4	0.4
California [1]................	1,912,128	2,022,213	2,216.3	1,440.6	775.7	2,956.0	2,421.9	534.1
Colorado....................	138,903	167,227	239.4	157.3	82.0	256.4	229.5	26.9
Connecticut.................	24,884	25,551	36.6	34.4	2.2	41.2	70.2	-29.0
Delaware....................	16,341	17,784	42.2	28.6	13.6	35.2	32.0	3.2
District of Columbia [4].......	10,676	13,943	23.7	18.7	5.0	37.8	37.8	-(Z)
Florida......................	428,094	374,884	581.6	417.9	163.7	648.2	616.6	31.6
Georgia [4]..................	230,815	232,050	403.0	309.6	93.4	364.4	365.7	-1.3
Hawaii......................	27,239	25,780	49.2	32.7	16.5	54.0	47.2	6.7
Idaho [4]....................	34,513	35,964	61.7	49.5	12.2	75.0	75.0	(Z)
Illinois......................	330,571	325,990	437.8	286.8	151.0	564.1	496.8	67.3
Indiana [4]..................	100,560	114,927	157.6	120.7	37.0	172.0	173.4	-1.4
Iowa........................	82,657	84,989	153.3	105.7	47.6	144.7	132.0	12.7
Kansas.....................	77,139	79,319	116.0	80.8	35.2	122.8	113.1	9.7
Kentucky [4]................	86,976	92,728	222.0	174.8	47.2	243.3	243.4	-0.1
Louisiana...................	135,614	161,565	237.4	174.3	63.1	344.0	325.6	18.4
Maine.......................	22,310	23,257	31.8	23.4	8.5	33.4	32.4	1.0
Maryland....................	142,327	137,592	313.2	203.6	109.6	305.9	268.6	37.4
Massachusetts..............	172,190	185,578	581.3	377.9	203.5	696.1	609.3	86.8
Michigan....................	119,699	82,693	327.5	248.9	78.6	244.2	240.3	3.9
Minnesota..................	3,835	3,876	32.5	46.8	-14.3	27.2	104.4	-77.2
Mississippi.................	87,105	88,531	235.0	191.5	43.4	287.8	287.5	0.3
Missouri....................	78,344	87,790	171.8	127.7	44.1	164.8	159.0	5.8
Montana....................	45,261	44,688	91.7	69.8	21.9	94.8	93.5	1.3
Nebraska...................	62,218	55,041	82.5	55.5	27.0	73.7	65.4	8.3
Nevada.....................	61,908	68,951	61.2	45.9	15.3	64.1	63.0	1.1
New Hampshire.............	16,651	17,946	29.0	24.8	4.2	26.4	34.7	-8.3
New Jersey.................	215,191	230,960	441.9	287.6	154.3	481.2	420.1	61.1
New Mexico [4]..............	17,195	15,100	116.1	91.5	24.7	123.6	123.5	0.1
New York....................	630,732	684,625	1,165.4	757.7	407.8	1,275.2	1,119.5	155.7
North Carolina..............	234,654	256,446	430.3	327.6	102.8	436.9	434.9	2.1
North Dakota................	4,955	(NA)	22.3	14.5	7.8	22.0	19.3	2.7
Ohio........................	181,100	223,583	349.2	257.9	91.3	384.1	371.5	12.6
Oklahoma...................	190,858	187,971	179.6	131.8	47.8	244.5	224.8	19.8
Oregon.....................	121,869	140,786	206.3	154.4	51.9	231.7	225.7	6.0
Pennsylvania...............	294,342	342,268	388.8	257.7	131.1	535.1	478.6	56.5
Rhode Island...............	31,324	36,262	72.8	47.3	25.5	75.6	66.1	9.5
South Carolina..............	98,336	81,574	154.4	122.4	31.9	139.2	139.2	–
South Dakota...............	16,216	18,507	24.7	16.3	8.4	27.1	24.4	2.7
Tennessee..................	106,215	105,990	205.5	155.1	50.4	471.8	421.8	49.9
Texas.......................	1,049,623	1,075,212	1,354.1	956.4	397.7	1,334.9	1,241.1	93.7
Utah [4].....................	55,285	58,410	147.5	117.0	30.4	118.6	118.6	-(Z)
Vermont.....................	4,766	5,305	9.5	13.6	-4.1	9.8	27.4	-17.7
West Virginia [4].............	189,366	192,831	287.7	187.0	100.7	300.6	263.9	36.7
Washington.................	46,037	66,517	117.9	125.3	-7.4	161.9	218.9	-57.0
West Virginia...............	33,579	48,187	62.1	49.7	12.5	55.4	55.4	-(Z)
Wisconsin..................	168,576	171,552	200.4	150.5	49.8	187.4	203.7	-16.4
Wyoming....................	6,649	7,387	12.0	7.8	4.2	13.1	11.5	1.6

– Represents zero. Z Less than $50,000. [1] Due to reporting system updates, CHIP enrollment totals are estimates as a result of the exclusion of certain unborn CHIP enrollees in reporting. [2] Several states experienced challenges in their reporting systems, resulting in artificially high or low enrollment numbers. For details, see <https://www.medicaid.gov/chip/downloads/fy-2015-childrens-enrollment-report.pdf> and <https://www.medicaid.gov/chip/downloads/fy-2016-childrens-enrollment-report.pdf>. [3] Section 2105(g) of the Social Security Act permits 11 qualifying states to use CHIP funds to pay the difference between the regular Medicaid matching rate and the enhanced CHIP matching rate for Medicaid-enrolled, Medicaid-financed children whose family income exceeds 133 percent of the federal poverty level. Although these are CHIP funds, they effectively reduce state spending on children in Medicaid and do not require a state match within the CHIP program. In cases where the sum of 2105(g) federal CHIP spending (for Medicaid enrollees) and regular federal CHIP spending (for CHIP enrollees) exceeds total spending for CHIP enrollees, states are shown in this table as having negative state CHIP spending. [4] State reports negative state CHIP spending for benefits or state program administration due to federal CHIP spending exceeding total CHIP spending. Federal CHIP spending exceeds total CHIP spending due to negative prior period adjustments and the 23 percentage point increase in the enhanced federal medical assistance percentage (E-FMAP) that went into effect in FY2016. Because these prior period adjustments apply to periods before the 23 percentage point increase to the E-FMAP, these negative adjustments decrease total spending to a greater extent than federal spending.

Source: Medicaid and CHIP Payment and Access Commission, "MACStats: Program Enrollment and Spending, CHIP," <http://www.macpac.gov/macstats>, accessed August 2017.

Table 153. Medicare Enrollment by State: 2015 and 2016

[In thousands (55,584.1 represents 55,584,100). Covers Medicare beneficiaries enrolled in either Hospital Insurance and/or Supplementary Medical Insurance. Enrollment counts are determined by using a person-year methodology; for each calendar year, total person-year counts are determined by summing the total number of months that each beneficiary is enrolled during the year and dividing by 12 (see source for more information). Numbers may not add to totals because of rounding]

State	2015			2016		
	Total Medicare	Original Medicare [1]	Medicare Advantage [2]	Total Medicare	Original Medicare [1]	Medicare Advantage [2]
Total	**55,584.1**	**37,785.5**	**17,798.6**	**57,049.7**	**38,310.9**	**18,738.8**
United States [3]	**54,347.7**	**37,114.6**	**17,233.1**	**55,791.4**	**37,627.5**	**18,163.9**
Alabama	969.2	721.4	247.8	989.4	723.7	265.7
Alaska	84.1	83.2	0.8	88.2	87.3	0.9
Arizona	1,136.4	700.8	435.6	1,178.7	726.0	452.7
Arkansas	595.2	472.8	122.4	605.8	476.7	129.1
California	5,655.9	3,301.6	2,354.4	5,812.6	3,339.7	2,472.9
Colorado	786.5	495.1	291.4	816.7	513.9	302.8
Connecticut	631.3	469.0	162.3	642.3	470.8	171.5
Delaware	180.7	165.3	15.5	187.0	168.7	18.3
District of Columbia	88.7	76.8	11.8	90.3	77.1	13.2
Florida	4,029.2	2,415.0	1,614.3	4,159.8	2,451.1	1,708.6
Georgia	1,521.9	1,037.5	484.4	1,572.0	1,041.6	530.4
Hawaii	244.8	132.6	112.2	251.7	137.0	114.7
Idaho	282.3	189.8	92.5	294.3	199.0	95.2
Illinois	2,069.3	1,599.6	469.7	2,110.5	1,612.1	498.4
Indiana	1,152.0	875.9	276.0	1,178.7	882.8	295.9
Iowa	572.5	485.3	87.1	585.7	481.3	104.4
Kansas	487.6	419.6	68.0	498.9	424.4	74.5
Kentucky	864.0	635.9	228.1	880.7	635.9	244.8
Louisiana	794.1	552.8	241.3	814.9	556.8	258.1
Maine	306.8	236.2	70.6	314.5	234.9	79.6
Maryland	932.0	849.8	82.2	959.0	863.1	95.9
Massachusetts	1,219.9	959.0	261.0	1,248.7	976.2	272.6
Michigan	1,897.5	1,258.1	639.4	1,940.5	1,245.7	694.8
Minnesota	913.4	421.7	491.7	940.3	417.1	523.2
Mississippi	560.9	475.5	85.4	571.2	477.8	93.3
Missouri	1,137.5	811.5	326.0	1,161.2	809.0	352.2
Montana	201.5	164.3	37.2	208.6	166.8	41.8
Nebraska	314.1	274.7	39.4	322.0	280.3	41.6
Nevada	453.7	302.4	151.4	472.3	310.3	161.9
New Hampshire	266.5	246.1	20.4	274.8	250.5	24.3
New Jersey	1,494.4	1,260.0	234.4	1,523.6	1,264.3	259.3
New Mexico	373.4	254.7	118.7	385.2	260.3	124.9
New York	3,349.5	2,099.4	1,250.1	3,413.2	2,121.0	1,292.2
North Carolina	1,771.2	1,237.4	533.7	1,822.9	1,254.5	568.4
North Dakota	119.0	98.8	20.2	121.8	97.8	24.0
Ohio	2,157.0	1,257.8	899.2	2,203.6	1,364.3	839.3
Oklahoma	679.6	562.5	117.2	693.0	570.4	122.6
Oregon	755.5	423.1	332.4	782.6	435.0	347.6
Pennsylvania	2,536.8	1,518.2	1,018.6	2,583.8	1,541.7	1,042.1
Rhode Island	203.5	131.6	71.9	207.6	132.3	75.3
South Carolina	942.2	720.1	222.1	974.4	732.9	241.5
South Dakota	156.3	126.5	29.8	160.8	126.2	34.6
Tennessee	1,237.1	808.1	429.0	1,267.1	811.8	455.3
Texas	3,638.8	2,465.4	1,173.4	3,760.1	2,482.7	1,277.4
Utah	346.0	228.1	117.8	358.8	234.0	124.8
Vermont	131.6	121.4	10.2	135.5	124.6	10.9
Virginia	1,351.0	1,093.1	257.9	1,389.2	1,116.5	272.7
Washington	1,192.0	832.1	359.9	1,235.3	861.1	374.1
West Virginia	417.3	304.2	113.0	422.8	305.6	117.2
Wisconsin	1,051.2	651.6	399.6	1,080.6	658.4	422.2
Wyoming	95.2	91.4	3.8	98.5	94.6	3.9

[1] Original Medicare consists of Part A (Hospital Insurance) and Part B (Supplementary Medical Insurance). Enrollment in Original Medicare includes beneficiaries enrolled in either Part A and/or Part B. [2] Medicare Advantage and other health plans are also known as Medicare Part C. Medicare Part C includes both Part A and Part B coverage. Medicare Advantage and other health plan enrollees are Medicare beneficiaries who are enrolled in health plans offered by private companies approved by Medicare. [3] U.S. total excludes territories, possessions, foreign countries or outlying areas, and unknown.

Source: U.S. Centers for Medicare and Medicaid Services, CMS Program Statistics, "Medicare Enrollment Dashboard," <https://www.cms.gov/Research-Statistics-Data-and-Systems/Statistics-Trends-and-Reports/CMSProgramStatistics/index.html>, accessed May 2017.

Table 154. Medicare Enrollment by Type: 2008 to 2014

[In thousands (45,472 represents 45,472,000), except as noted. Based on person-year methodology; see source for details. Medicare Advantage is an alternative to traditional Medicare. Medicare Advantage plans are offered by private companies and organizations, are required to provide at least services covered by Medicare Parts A and B (except hospice services), and are financed from both Medicare's Hospital Insurance (HI) trust fund and the Part B account within the Supplementary Medical Insurance (SMI) trust fund in proportion to the relative weights of Part A and Part B benefits to the total benefits paid by the Medicare program. Numbers and percentages may not add to totals because of rounding]

Enrollment by type	2008	2009	2010	2011	2012	2013	2014
Total Medicare enrollment [1]	**45,472**	**46,573**	**47,703**	**48,944**	**50,828**	**52,507**	**54,096**
Aged	38,064	38,941	39,804	40,762	42,390	43,853	45,312
Disabled [2]	7,408	7,632	7,899	8,182	8,438	8,654	8,783
Part A, Hospital insurance	45,121	46,231	47,346	48,596	50,490	52,167	53,754
Aged	37,714	38,599	39,449	40,416	42,054	43,516	44,976
Disabled [2]	7,407	7,631	7,897	8,180	8,435	8,651	8,779
Part B, Medical insurance	42,252	43,259	44,325	45,459	47,127	48,676	50,235
Aged	35,643	36,393	37,151	37,976	39,371	40,676	42,056
Disabled [2]	6,609	6,867	7,174	7,483	7,756	8,001	8,179
Original Medicare enrollment [1]	**35,406**	**35,395**	**35,922**	**36,467**	**37,126**	**37,532**	**37,665**
Percent of total	77.9	76.0	75.3	74.5	73.0	71.5	69.6
Aged	29,113	29,044	29,397	29,786	30,394	30,801	31,038
Disabled [2]	6,293	6,352	6,524	6,681	6,732	6,731	6,627
Part A, Hospital insurance	35,061	35,060	35,575	36,131	36,809	37,216	37,349
Aged	28,769	28,709	29,052	29,451	30,080	30,489	30,726
Disabled [2]	6,292	6,351	6,523	6,680	6,729	6,727	6,622
Part B, Medical insurance	32,187	32,083	32,545	32,983	33,426	33,704	33,807
Aged	26,692	26,496	26,745	27,000	27,376	27,626	27,783
Disabled [2]	5,494	5,586	5,800	5,983	6,051	6,078	6,024
Medicare Advantage enrollment [1]	**10,067**	**11,178**	**11,781**	**12,477**	**13,702**	**14,975**	**16,430**
Percent of total	22.1	24.0	24.7	25.5	27.0	28.5	30.4
Part A, Hospital insurance	10,060	11,171	11,771	12,465	13,680	14,951	16,406
Aged	8,944	9,890	10,396	10,964	11,974	13,028	14,249
Disabled [2]	1,115	1,281	1,374	1,501	1,706	1,923	2,156
Part B, Medical insurance	10,065	11,177	11,780	12,476	13,701	14,973	16,428
Aged	8,950	9,896	10,406	10,976	11,995	13,050	14,273
Disabled [2]	1,115	1,280	1,374	1,500	1,706	1,922	2,155

[1] Enrollment in Medicare Part A and/or Part B. [2] Persons enrolled due to end stage renal disease-only are included in the disabled enrollee counts.

Source: U.S. Centers for Medicare & Medicaid Services, "CMS Program Statistics, Medicare," <https://www.cms.gov/Research-Statistics-Data-and-Systems/Statistics-Trends-and-Reports/CMSProgramStatistics/index.html>, accessed March 2017.

Table 155. Medicare Utilization—Persons Utilizing Medicare, Program Payments, and Cost Sharing: 2010 to 2014

[35,922 represents 35,922,000. Covers all Original Medicare (also known as "fee-for-service"), which consists of Part A (Hospital Insurance), and Part B (Medical Insurance). Persons utilizing Medicare do not include beneficiaries who received services but for whom no program payments were reported. Amounts do not sum to totals because beneficiaries may have used more than one type of service during a year; and, for payments and costs, due to rounding]

Item	2010	2011	2012	2013	2014
ORIGINAL MEDICARE ENROLLEES (1,000):					
Part A and/or Part B	**35,922**	**36,467**	**37,126**	**37,532**	**37,665**
Part A	35,575	36,131	36,809	37,216	37,349
Part B	32,545	32,983	33,426	33,704	33,807
UTILIZATION (1,000)					
Medicare Part A and/or Part B	**32,898**	**33,346**	**33,775**	**34,102**	**34,283**
Part A	7,953	7,969	7,894	7,761	7,602
Inpatient hospital services	7,133	7,109	6,985	6,808	6,626
Skilled nursing facility services	1,844	1,870	1,847	1,846	1,832
Hospice services [1]	1,164	1,225	1,279	1,320	1,333
Home health agency services	1,728	1,725	1,706	1,709	1,650
Part B	32,414	32,853	33,262	33,570	33,741
Physician and other medical services	32,081	32,490	32,883	33,141	33,271
Outpatient services	23,660	24,151	24,628	24,885	25,012
Home health agency services	1,874	1,894	1,911	1,933	1,934
PAYMENTS AND COSTS (mil. dol.)					
Medicare Part A and/or Part B	**330,636**	**341,420**	**344,811**	**346,447**	**350,101**
Part A	175,142	180,155	178,265	179,334	178,754
Inpatient hospital services	127,627	128,942	128,598	129,157	128,455
Skilled nursing facility services	27,283	30,483	27,745	28,270	28,614
Hospice services [1]	12,966	13,851	15,136	15,122	15,070
Home health agency services	7,266	6,879	6,786	6,786	6,615
Part B	155,494	161,265	166,546	167,113	171,347
Physician and other medical services	95,737	98,423	100,142	98,618	99,073
Outpatient services	47,549	51,238	55,097	57,260	61,158
Home health agency services	12,208	11,605	11,307	11,235	11,116
Beneficiary cost sharing (mil. dol.): [2]					
Medicare Part A and/or Part B	**55,760**	**57,506**	**57,999**	**58,835**	**59,967**
Part A	15,507	15,889	15,744	15,850	15,892
Part B	40,253	41,617	42,256	42,985	44,075

[1] The total Medicare Part A enrollee counts are based on enrollees in Original Medicare and Medicare Advantage/Other Health Plans (also known as Part C), combined, because once a beneficiary enrolled in a Medicare Advantage/Other Health Plan elects the hospice benefit, his or her Medicare benefits revert to fee-for-service. [2] Includes costs for copayments, coinsurance, deductibles, and out-of-pocket payments for balanced billing (the difference between Medicare allowed charges and physicians' submitted charges). Excludes monthly premium for Part B coverage, Part D coverage, voluntary hospital insurance coverage, and supplemental insurance.

Source: Centers for Medicare and Medicaid Services, "CMS Program Statistics," <https://www.cms.gov/Research-Statistics-Data-and-Systems/Statistics-Trends-and-Reports/CMSProgramStatistics/index.html>, accessed May 2017.

Table 156. Medicare and Medicaid Dual Enrollment by Type of Eligibility: 2009 to 2014

[In thousands (8,144.9 represents 8,144,900). Covers Medicare beneficiaries who have low incomes and limited resources who also receive Medicaid program benefits. Services that are covered by Medicare are paid for by the Medicare program first before any payments are made by Medicaid. Based on person-year methodology; see source for details. See headnote, Table 154. Numbers may not sum to totals due to rounding]

Year	Total Medicare-Medicaid dual enrollment	Type of eligibility							
		Full benefit enrollment				Partial benefit enrollment			
		Total	Qualified Medicare beneficiary plus [1]	Specified low-income Medicare beneficiary plus [2]	Other full-benefit enrollees with Medicaid	Total	Qualified Medicare benefi-ciary [1]	Specified low-income Medicare benefi-ciary [2]	Qualified disabled & working individ-uals [3]
Total Medicare:									
2009................	8,144.9	6,220.1	4,510.1	211.3	1,498.6	1,924.8	888.7	673.0	363.2
2010................	8,537.1	6,397.0	4,702.7	222.4	1,471.9	2,140.1	986.7	751.0	402.4
2011................	8,920.0	6,561.7	4,818.1	229.9	1,513.7	2,358.3	1,094.7	816.3	447.3
2012................	9,251.3	6,719.3	4,944.3	241.7	1,533.3	2,532.0	1,179.6	870.2	482.2
2013................	9,510.3	6,854.9	5,067.6	242.7	1,544.5	2,655.5	1,252.6	906.5	496.4
2014................	9,850.5	7,082.9	5,172.0	249.8	1,661.1	2,767.6	1,323.6	916.6	527.3
Original Medicare:									
2009................	6,605.1	5,251.3	3,802.4	181.1	1,267.8	1,353.8	689.3	445.1	219.4
2010................	6,889.9	5,399.0	3,956.1	189.9	1,253.0	1,490.9	756.1	492.4	242.5
2011................	7,090.3	5,469.0	3,993.4	194.6	1,281.0	1,621.3	823.0	529.7	268.6
2012................	7,161.6	5,479.1	4,002.8	200.4	1,275.9	1,682.6	854.1	546.5	281.9
2013................	7,122.1	5,427.5	3,972.1	197.2	1,258.2	1,694.6	867.2	548.2	279.2
2014................	7,057.4	5,357.4	3,856.8	197.8	1,302.7	1,700.0	879.2	532.3	288.5
Medicare Advantage:									
2009................	1,539.8	968.8	707.7	30.2	230.8	571.0	199.4	227.9	143.8
2010................	1,647.2	998.0	746.6	32.5	218.8	649.1	230.6	258.6	159.9
2011................	1,829.7	1,092.7	824.8	35.2	232.7	737.0	271.7	286.6	178.7
2012................	2,089.6	1,240.2	941.6	41.3	257.3	849.5	325.5	323.7	200.3
2013................	2,388.2	1,427.3	1,095.4	45.5	286.4	960.9	385.4	358.3	217.2
2014................	2,793.1	1,725.6	1,315.2	52.0	358.3	1,067.5	444.4	384.4	238.7

[1] A qualified Medicare beneficiary (QMB) has Medicare Part A, income less than or equal to 100 percent of the Federal poverty level, and resources below twice the value allowed under supplemental security income (SSI). For those who qualify, the Medicaid program pays Medicare Part A premiums (if applicable), Part B premiums, and Medicare deductibles and coinsurance amounts for Medicare covered services depending on the Medicaid state plan. An individual qualifying for full Medicaid benefits is sometimes referred to as "QMB plus." [2] A specified low-income Medicare beneficiary (SLMB) has Medicare Part A, income above 100 percent but less than 120 percent of the Federal poverty level, and resources below twice the value allowed under SSI. For those who qualify, the Medicaid program pays only the Medicare Part B premium. An individual who qualifies for full Medicaid benefits is sometimes referred to as "SLMB plus". [3] Data are combined for qualified disabled and working individuals (QDWIs) and qualifying individuals; total counts for QDWIs are less than 100. For QDWIs, Medicaid pays Medicare Part A premiums for certain disabled individuals who lost Medicare coverage because they returned to work. These individuals have incomes below 200 percent of the Federal Poverty Level, resources not more than twice the value allowed under SSI, and are not otherwise eligible for Medicaid. Qualifying individuals are entitled to Medicare Part A, have income of at least 120% but less than 135% of the Federal Poverty Level, resources that do not exceed twice the limit for SSI eligibility, and are not otherwise eligible for Medicaid. Medicaid pays their Medicare Part B premiums only. There is an annual cap on the amount of money available, which may limit the number of individuals in the group.

Source: U.S. Centers for Medicare and Medicaid Services, CMS Program Statistics, "2014 Medicare Enrollment," <https://www.cms.gov/Research-Statistics-Data-and-Systems/Statistics-Trends-and-Reports/CMSProgramStatistics/>, accessed March 2017.

Table 157. Medicare Hospital Insurance and Supplementary Medical Insurance—Average Costs per Beneficiary: 1976 to 2017

[In dollars. See headnote, Table 158]

Year	Total	Hospital Insurance	SMI Part B	SMI Part D	Year	Total	Hospital Insurance	SMI Part B	SMI Part D
1976........	788	548	240	(X)	1997........	5,635	3,616	2,033	(X)
1977........	891	618	273	(X)	1998........	5,562	3,468	2,134	(X)
1978........	1,010	697	314	(X)	1999........	5,614	3,306	2,255	(X)
1979........	1,147	786	361	(X)	2000........	5,844	3,383	2,496	(X)
1980........	1,352	929	423	(X)	2001........	6,370	3,656	2,760	(X)
1981........	1,583	1,093	490	(X)	2002........	6,788	3,839	2,975	(X)
1982........	1,819	1,249	570	(X)	2003........	7,144	3,922	3,221	(X)
1983........	2,025	1,367	658	(X)	2004........	7,723	4,162	3,560	(X)
1984........	2,236	1,512	724	(X)	2005........	8,278	4,439	3,839	(X)
1985........	2,373	1,579	795	(X)	2006........	10,179	4,601	4,116	1,461
1986........	2,504	1,596	907	(X)	2007........	10,703	4,759	4,313	1,630
1987........	2,661	1,636	1,024	(X)	2008........	11,232	4,996	4,574	1,662
1988........	2,781	1,646	1,135	(X)	2009........	11,702	5,174	4,798	1,730
1989........	3,097	1,860	1,237	(X)	2010........	11,908	5,193	4,907	1,808
1990........	3,334	1,979	1,355	(X)	2011........	12,167	5,271	5,038	1,858
1991........	3,569	2,125	1,443	(X)	2012........	12,229	5,217	5,173	1,839
1992........	3,941	2,411	1,530	(X)	2013........	12,224	5,175	5,175	1,874
1993........	4,259	2,648	1,611	(X)	2014........	12,461	5,034	5,396	2,031
1994........	4,678	2,948	1,730	(X)	2015........	12,741	5,036	5,550	2,154
1995........	5,061	3,194	1,867	(X)	2016........	12,872	5,053	5,689	2,130
1996........	5,378	3,424	1,954	(X)	2017, proj...	13,068	5,077	5,865	2,126

X Not applicable.

Source: U.S. Centers for Medicare and Medicaid Services, Trustees Report & Trust Funds, "2017 Expanded and Supplementary Tables and Figures," <https://www.cms.gov/Research-Statistics-Data-and-Systems/Statistics-Trends-and-Reports/ReportsTrustFunds/index.html>, accessed July 2017.

Table 158. Medicare Insurance Trust Funds: 1990 to 2016

[In billions of dollars (126.3 represents $126,300,000,000), on cash basis, for calendar years. Medicare has two components: Hospital Insurance (HI), also known as Medicare Part A; and Supplementary Medical Insurance (SMI), consisting of Medicare Part B (medical insurance) and Part D (prescription drug coverage). See text, this section, for details]

Type of trust fund	1990	2000	2005	2010	2012	2013	2014	2015	2016
TOTAL MEDICARE									
Total income [1]	126.3	257.1	357.5	486.1	536.9	575.8	599.3	644.4	710.2
Total expenditures	111.0	221.8	336.4	522.9	574.2	582.9	613.3	647.6	678.7
Assets, end of year	114.4	221.5	309.8	344.0	287.6	280.5	266.4	263.2	294.7
HOSPITAL INSURANCE, PART A									
Net contribution income [2]	71.9	155.5	183.3	199.5	228.6	239.3	249.6	265.3	280.6
Interest and other income [3, 4]	8.5	11.7	16.1	16.1	14.5	11.8	11.7	10.1	10.1
Benefit payments [4, 5]	66.2	128.5	180.0	244.5	262.9	261.9	264.9	273.4	280.5
Trust fund balance, end of year	98.9	177.5	285.8	271.9	220.4	205.4	197.3	193.8	199.1
SMI, PART B									
Premiums from enrollees [1]	11.3	20.6	37.5	52.0	58.0	63.1	65.6	69.4	72.1
Government contributions [6]	33.0	65.9	118.1	153.5	163.8	185.8	188.5	203.9	235.6
Interest and other income [3, 4]	1.6	3.5	1.4	3.3	5.2	6.1	5.7	5.7	5.5
Benefit payments [1, 4, 5]	42.5	88.9	149.2	209.7	236.5	243.8	261.9	275.8	289.5
Trust fund balance, end of year	15.5	44.0	24.0	71.4	66.2	74.1	68.1	68.2	88.0
SMI, PART D									
Premiums from enrollees [7]	(X)	(X)	–	6.5	8.3	9.9	11.4	12.8	13.8
Government contributions [8]	(X)	(X)	1.1	51.1	50.1	51.0	58.1	68.4	82.4
Interest and other income	(X)	(X)	–	(Z)	(Z)	(Z)	(Z)	(Z)	(Z)
Benefit payments [9]	(X)	(X)	1.1	61.7	66.5	69.3	77.7	89.5	99.5
Trust fund balance, end of year	(X)	(X)	–	0.7	1.0	1.0	1.1	1.3	7.6

– Represents zero. X Not applicable. Z Less than $50 million. [1] Includes adjustments for benefit checks issued at the end of the year instead of the following January; see source for details on this and other adjustments. [2] Includes income from payroll taxes, taxation of benefits, railroad retirement account transfers, reimbursement for uninsured persons, premiums from voluntary enrollees, and payments for military wage credits. [3] Includes recoveries of amounts reimbursed from the trust fund, receipts from fraud and abuse control program, and other miscellaneous income. [4] Values after 2005 include additional premiums for Medicare Advantage (MA) plans that are deducted from beneficiaries' Social Security checks; see source for details. [5] Includes monies transferred to the SMI trust fund in 1998-2003 for home health agency costs. In 2008 benefit payments were $223,815 million and include a transfer of $8,484 million to the general fund of the Treasury for HI hospice costs that were misallocated to, and paid from, the Part B account of the SMI trust fund from May 2005 to September 2007. (The general fund, in turn, transferred $8,484 million to the Part B account.) [6] Matching payments from the general fund, plus certain interest-adjustment items. See also footnote 1. [7] Premiums include both amounts withheld from Social Security benefit checks (and other certain Federal benefit payments) and amounts paid directly to Part D plans. [8] Includes, net of transfers from States, all government transfers required to fund benefit payments, administrative expenses, and State expenses for making low-income eligibility determinations. [9] Includes payments to plans, subsidies to employer-sponsored retiree prescription drug plans, payments to States for making low-income eligibility determinations, Part D drug premiums collected from beneficiaries and transferred to Medicare Advantage plans and private drug plans, and premium amounts paid directly by enrollees to plans. (The last item is on an estimated basis; see note 7.) Includes amounts for transitional assistance benefits in 2004-2007.

Source: U.S. Centers for Medicare and Medicaid Services, Trustees Report & Trust Funds, "2017 Expanded and Supplementary Tables and Figures," <https://www.cms.gov/Research-Statistics-Data-and-Systems/Statistics-Trends-and-Reports/ReportsTrustFunds/index.html>, accessed July 2017.

Table 159. Medicaid Enrollment by Race/Ethnicity, Age, and Poverty Status: 2015

[In thousands, except percent (62,068 represents 62,068,000). Based on the 2016 Current Population Survey Annual Social and Economic Supplement (CPS ASEC). Represents number of persons who were enrolled at any time in year shown. Excludes unrelated individuals under age 15. Persons did not have to receive medical care paid for by Medicaid in order to be counted. For explanation of poverty level, see text, Section 13. For methodology, see source report, and also <http://www2.census.gov/library/publications/2016/demo/p60-257sa.pdf>. See source regarding changes in and comparability of CPS ASEC health insurance data]

Poverty status	Total [1]	White alone [2]	Black alone [2]	Asian alone [2]	His-panic [3]	Under 18 years	18–44 years	45–64 years	65 years and over
Persons covered, total	**62,068**	**42,768**	**12,441**	**2,869**	**18,710**	**28,860**	**19,285**	**10,660**	**3,263**
Below poverty level	22,055	14,117	5,743	677	7,165	11,128	6,468	3,425	1,035
Above poverty level	40,013	28,650	6,698	2,192	11,545	17,732	12,817	7,235	2,229
Percent of population covered by Medicaid:									
All persons	**19.5**	**17.4**	**29.9**	**15.7**	**33.0**	**39.2**	**17.0**	**12.7**	**6.9**
Persons in poverty	51.1	49.4	57.3	32.6	59.1	76.7	40.1	41.3	24.6
Persons not in poverty	14.5	13.2	21.2	13.6	25.9	30.0	13.2	9.6	5.1

[1] Includes other races, not shown separately. [2] Refers to people who reported specified race and did not report any other race category. [3] Persons of Hispanic origin may be of any race.

Source: U.S. Census Bureau, 2016 Current Population Survey Annual Social and Economic Supplement, CPS Table Creator, <http://www.census.gov/cps/data/cpstablecreator.html>, accessed January 2017. See also Health Insurance Coverage in the United States: 2015, Current Population Reports, P60-P257(RV), <http://www.census.gov/topics/health/health-insurance.html>.

Table 160. Medicaid and Children's Health Insurance Program (CHIP)—Summary by State: 2010 to 2013

[65,700 represents 65,700,000. For years ending September 30. Beneficiaries include those who are enrolled or received services through Medicaid or the Children's Health Insurance Program (CHIP), including beneficiaries of separate CHIP programs. Beginning 2011, a new tabular methodology was used, therefore estimates may not be comparable to earlier data]

State	Beneficiaries (1,000)				Payments per beneficiary (dollars)			
	2010	2011	2012	2013	2010 [1]	2011	2012	2013
United States.............	65,700	71,449	71,604	73,669	5,160	5,159	5,082	5,094
Alabama.....................	931	945	964	972	4,342	4,427	4,261	4,297
Alaska.......................	127	137	138	147	9,520	9,578	9,638	9,260
Arizona......................	1,805	2,005	1,698	1,629	5,270	4,707	4,843	5,050
Arkansas....................	773	803	810	821	4,916	4,548	4,425	4,406
California...................	11,212	11,798	10,987	12,329	3,094	3,184	3,232	3,418
Colorado....................	682	757	(NA)	(NA)	4,840	4,597	(NA)	(NA)
Connecticut................	664	749	774	770	8,120	7,796	7,603	8,104
Delaware...................	210	234	246	253	6,380	6,298	6,383	6,558
District of Columbia........	211	239	250	(NA)	8,577	8,895	6,509	(NA)
Florida......................	3,656	3,949	4,052	4,292	4,412	4,893	4,657	4,731
Georgia.....................	1,875	2,194	2,296	2,266	3,717	3,817	3,963	4,109
Hawaii......................	288	328	335	338	4,692	4,475	4,466	4,459
Idaho.......................	430	263	(NA)	(NA)	2,871	5,493	(NA)	(NA)
Illinois......................	2,758	2,940	3,089	3,184	4,222	4,041	4,349	4,379
Indiana.....................	1,177	1,278	1,342	1,332	4,889	4,509	4,882	5,032
Iowa........................	508	548	562	577	5,920	5,970	6,093	6,209
Kansas.....................	364	481	435	(NA)	6,309	5,335	5,883	(NA)
Kentucky...................	959	1,124	1,108	1,030	5,532	5,014	5,114	5,542
Louisiana...................	1,237	1,327	1,343	1,389	4,439	4,149	4,318	4,109
Maine.......................	330	339	370	359	4,451	4,669	5,248	5,732
Maryland....................	940	1,073	1,127	1,206	7,273	6,694	6,611	6,162
Massachusetts..............	1,637	1,733	1,542	1,586	6,760	6,537	7,009	7,178
Michigan....................	2,219	2,390	2,355	2,382	5,127	4,867	4,996	4,849
Minnesota..................	851	1,036	1,106	1,195	8,390	7,673	7,825	7,166
Mississippi.................	801	834	897	779	4,197	4,398	4,160	4,932
Missouri....................	1,141	1,207	1,206	1,204	5,429	5,212	5,466	6,045
Montana....................	126	137	141	147	6,023	5,818	5,856	6,038
Nebraska...................	269	304	311	312	5,890	5,306	5,441	5,845
Nevada.....................	334	376	390	408	3,899	3,716	3,526	3,621
New Hampshire.............	148	155	165	162	6,805	6,676	6,387	6,605
New Jersey.................	1,229	1,410	1,596	1,633	6,963	6,306	5,896	6,020
New Mexico................	557	636	633	648	4,971	4,058	4,009	4,062
New York...................	5,011	5,758	6,076	6,542	8,526	8,893	7,954	7,779
North Carolina.............	1,876	1,911	2,071	2,023	5,111	5,033	4,829	3,843
North Dakota...............	83	89	92	93	8,261	8,222	8,474	8,823
Ohio........................	2,319	2,537	2,574	2,685	6,231	6,237	6,289	6,114
Oklahoma..................	853	972	997	1,072	4,355	3,891	3,894	3,814
Oregon.....................	644	771	787	798	4,948	4,642	4,776	5,006
Pennsylvania...............	2,326	2,544	2,578	2,590	6,834	6,958	6,901	7,239
Rhode Island...............	214	229	234	(NA)	7,367	7,005	6,769	(NA)
South Carolina.............	953	983	1,005	1,058	5,339	5,241	4,739	4,721
South Dakota..............	142	135	136	136	5,479	5,670	5,626	5,732
Tennessee..................	1,532	1,548	1,683	1,545	5,914	7,240	7,305	8,833
Texas.......................	4,745	5,266	6,021	6,294	4,367	4,257	3,673	3,509
Utah........................	369	448	443	434	5,404	4,805	5,344	6,079
Vermont....................	181	188	189	191	5,525	5,592	5,690	5,945
Virginia.....................	969	1,057	1,077	1,134	6,045	5,781	5,605	5,636
Washington.................	1,330	1,431	1,487	1,474	4,744	4,382	4,208	4,534
West Virginia...............	397	420	411	417	6,774	6,965	7,426	7,712
Wisconsin..................	1,230	1,356	1,398	1,390	4,393	4,185	4,070	4,128
Wyoming...................	76	78	78	78	7,540	7,380	7,425	7,770

NA Not available. [1] Medicaid payment data for 2010 and earlier exclude disproportionate share hospital (DSH) payments ($14.7 billion in FY2010) and DSH mental health facility payments ($2.9 billion in FY2010).

Source: U.S. National Center for Health Statistics, *Health, United States, 2016,* May 2017. See also <https://www.cdc.gov/nchs/hus/index.htm>.

Table 161. Medicaid and Children's Health Insurance Program—Beneficiaries and Payments by Basis of Eligibility and Service Category: 2000 to 2013

[In units, as indicated (42.8 represents 42,800,000). For years ending September 30. See headnote, Table 160]

Basis of eligibility and type of service	2000	2005	2008	2009	2010	2011	2012	2013
Total beneficiaries (millions)	**42.8**	**57.7**	**58.8**	**62.6**	**65.7**	**71.4**	**71.6**	**73.7**
Total payments (billion dollars)	**168.3**	**274.9**	**296.8**	**326.0**	**339.0**	**368.6**	**363.9**	**375.3**
Payments per beneficiary (dollars)	3,936	4,768	5,051	5,209	5,160	5,159	5,082	5,094
PERCENT OF BENEFICIARIES								
By basis of eligibility:								
Age 65 and over	8.7	7.6	7.1	6.7	6.5	5.7	5.7	5.6
Blind and disabled	16.1	14.2	14.8	14.4	14.3	13.1	13.2	13.0
Adults in families with dependent children [1]	20.5	21.8	22.0	23.1	23.7	18.9	19.5	19.0
Children under age 21 [2]	46.1	47.2	47.8	47.7	48.3	40.5	40.6	40.4
Other Title XIX [3]	8.6	9.1	8.4	8.1	7.2	9.6	8.7	9.8
Separate CHIP [4]	(NA)	(NA)	(NA)	(NA)	(NA)	12.2	12.3	12.1
By service category:								
Inpatient hospital	11.5	9.5	8.9	8.7	6.9	11.4	11.8	12.5
Mental health facility	0.2	0.2	0.2	0.2	0.2	0.2	0.2	0.2
Intermediate care facility for individuals with intellectual disabilities	0.3	0.2	0.2	0.2	0.2	0.1	0.1	0.1
Nursing facility	4.0	3.0	2.7	2.6	2.4	2.5	2.3	2.3
Physician	44.7	42.0	36.9	36.9	36.9	62.6	64.4	65.5
Dental	13.8	16.2	16.7	17.8	19.1	26.6	27.4	28.3
Other practitioner	11.1	10.2	8.8	8.8	9.2	13.6	14.2	14.3
Outpatient hospital	30.9	28.2	25.2	26.4	24.2	38.8	39.5	40.1
Clinic	17.9	20.7	20.2	20.6	20.7	24.4	23.6	23.9
Laboratory and radiological	26.6	27.7	26.6	26.2	25.8	41.6	42.0	42.5
Home health	2.3	2.1	1.9	1.7	1.7	2.4	2.5	2.4
Prescribed drugs	48.0	49.2	41.8	42.6	44.7	56.8	57.2	57.5
Capitated care	49.7	58.1	64.9	66.6	70.8	93.6	86.9	88.4
Primary care case management	13.0	15.1	14.9	13.1	13.3	13.3	13.6	11.4
Personal support	10.6	11.8	10.8	10.7	11.0	1.7	1.7	1.6
Other care	21.4	21.9	21.3	20.6	19.9	47.6	47.9	49.3
PAYMENTS PER BENEFICIARY (dollars) [5]								
By basis of eligibility:								
Age 65 and over	11,929	14,427	14,742	15,337	15,286	15,073	14,862	15,194
Blind and disabled	10,559	14,531	14,843	15,670	15,695	16,104	15,825	16,115
Adults in families with dependent children [1]	2,030	2,583	2,912	3,144	3,095	3,443	3,460	3,503
Children under age 21 [2]	1,358	1,732	2,035	2,145	2,122	2,300	2,281	2,315
Other Title XIX [3]	1,778	2,380	2,407	2,104	2,219	2,402	2,030	1,803
Separate CHIP [4]	(NA)	(NA)	(NA)	(NA)	(NA)	3,125	2,979	3,083
By service category:								
Inpatient hospital	4,919	6,411	7,083	7,070	7,347	4,858	4,437	3,885
Mental health facility	17,800	19,252	21,975	21,404	20,782	14,557	13,221	12,691
Intermediate care facility for individuals with intellectual disabilities	79,330	107,028	123,053	127,837	125,851	129,806	119,903	120,995
Nursing facility	20,220	26,185	29,533	29,551	31,617	26,995	28,060	27,808
Physician	356	465	485	496	492	271	238	219
Dental	238	326	389	423	432	301	245	181
Other practitioner	139	200	171	171	190	186	183	173
Outpatient hospital	533	617	736	735	803	470	454	424
Clinic	805	749	772	792	791	712	680	709
Laboratory and radiological	113	183	188	198	205	119	102	91
Home health	3,135	4,487	5,789	6,628	6,375	4,286	3,565	3,581
Prescribed drugs	975	1,509	957	951	926	719	540	432
Capitated care	1,148	1,386	1,786	1,991	1,983	1,627	1,964	2,178
Primary care case management	30	27	32	41	49	45	47	50
Personal support	2,543	3,035	3,852	3,903	3,593	9,959	9,619	9,588
Other care	1,600	2,228	2,856	3,015	3,289	1,724	1,653	1,554

NA Not available. [1] Includes adults in the Temporary Assistance for Needy Families (TANF) program. Beginning 2001, also includes women in the Breast and Cervical Cancer Prevention and Treatment Program, and unemployed adults. [2] Includes children (including those in the foster care system) in the TANF program. [3] Includes participants in the Supplemental Security Income program, and other people deemed medically needy in participating states. Excludes foster care children. Includes unknown eligibility. Prior to 2001, includes unemployed adults. [4] Children's Health Insurance Program (CHIP) provides federal funds for states to provide health care coverage to eligible low-income, uninsured children who do not qualify for Medicaid. Some states use CHIP funds to expand Medicaid. For 2012 data, all states except Colorado and Idaho had separate CHIP beneficiaries. [5] Medicaid payment data for 2010 and earlier excluded disproportionate share hospital (DSH) payments and DSH mental health facility payments.

Source: U.S. National Center for Health Statistics, *Health, United States, 2016,* May 2017. See also <https://www.cdc.gov/nchs/hus/index.htm>.

Table 162. Medicaid Managed Care Enrollment by State and Other Areas: 1995 to 2014

[In thousands except as noted (33,373 represents 33,373,000). Through 2011, for year ending June 30; beginning with 2013, as of July 1. Medicaid managed care provides Medicaid health benefits and additional services through contracted arrangements between state Medicaid agencies and managed care entities. The unduplicated Medicaid enrollment figures include individuals in state health care reform programs that expand eligibility beyond traditional Medicaid eligibility standards. The unduplicated managed care enrollment figures include enrollees in any Medicaid managed care program, including comprehensive managed care organizations (MCOs), limited benefit MCOs, and primary care case management programs]

State and other areas	Total enrollment	Managed care enrollment Number	Managed care enrollment Percent of total	State and other areas	Total enrollment	Managed care enrollment Number	Managed care enrollment Percent of total	State and other areas	Total enrollment	Managed care enrollment Number	Managed care enrollment Percent of total
1995.......	33,373	9,800	29.4	GA.........	1,961	1,353	69.0	NM........	727	580	79.8
2000.......	33,690	18,786	55.8	HI.........	321	318	99.1	NY.........	5,846	4,413	75.5
2005.......	45,392	28,576	63.0	ID.........	266	266	100.0	NC.........	1,718	1,718	100.0
2009.......	50,472	36,202	71.7	IL.........	3,250	2,163	66.6	ND........	79	46	58.4
2010.......	54,612	39,020	71.5	IN.........	1,176	774	65.8	OH........	2,796	2,028	72.5
2011.......	57,107	42,385	74.2	IA.........	594	533	89.9	OK........	826	737	89.2
2012.......	(NA)	(NA)	(NA)	KS........	399	357	89.3	OR........	1,052	971	92.3
2013.......	62,507	45,923	73.5	KY........	1,210	1,082	89.4	PA........	2,153	1,979	91.9
2014				LA.........	1,306	1,045	80.0	RI.........	264	224	84.9
Total [1]...	71,705	55,208	77.0	ME......	262	161	61.5	SC........	1,090	721	66.1
U.S........	70,246	53,749	76.5	MD.......	1,309	1,084	82.8	SD........	122	91	74.6
AL........	1,055	641	60.8	MA.......	1,878	1,110	59.1	TN........	1,289	1,289	100.0
AK........	133	–	–	MI.........	3,872	3,775	97.5	TX........	4,137	3,232	78.1
AZ........	1,548	1,317	85.1	MN.......	1,112	791	71.1	UT [3]......	288	283	98.3
AR........	596	515	86.5	MS........	699	155	22.2	VT [3]......	188	80	42.3
CA........	11,523	7,841	68.0	MO........	826	798	96.6	VA.........	962	708	73.6
CO........	1,080	1,030	95.4	MT........	132	91	69.0	WA........	1,245	1,245	100.0
CT........	725	–	–	NE........	243	230	94.7	WV........	487	203	41.8
DE........	228	196	86.2	NV........	534	464	86.9	WI.........	1,200	701	58.5
DC........	257	186	72.2	NH........	142	121	85.1	WY........	68	–	0.1
FL [2].......	3,532	2,684	76.0	NJ.........	1,542	1,418	92.0	PR.......	1,459	1,459	100.0

– Represents or rounds to zero. NA Not available. [1] Includes enrollment for U.S. territories not shown separately. [2] Florida reports enrollment as of August 1, 2014. [3] The Department of Vermont Health Access, a state agency, acts as Vermont's single managed care organization entity.

Source: U.S. Centers for Medicare and Medicaid Services, Data and System Group, *Medicaid Managed Care Enrollment and Program Characteristics, 2014*, Spring 2016. See also <https://www.medicaid.gov/medicaid-chip-program-information/by-topics/data-and-systems/medicaid-managed-care/medicaid-managed-care-enrollment-report.html>.

Table 163. Medicare Hospital Insurance and Supplemental Medical Insurance Expenditures, Total and as a Percent of GDP: 1980 to 2030

[In millions of dollars (2,862,475 represents $2,862,475,000,000), except percent. Incurred amounts relate to expenditures for services performed in a given year, even if payment for those expenditures occurs in a later year. The Medicare program has two components: Medicare Part A Hospital Insurance (HI); and Supplementary Medical Insurance (SMI), consisting of Part B Medical Insurance, and Part D Prescription Drug Coverage. See text in this section for details]

Year	GDP	Medicare expenditures Total	Medicare expenditures HI Part A	Medicare expenditures SMI Part B	Medicare expenditures SMI Part D	Medicare expenditures as percent of GDP Total	Medicare expenditures as percent of GDP HI Part A	Medicare expenditures as percent of GDP SMI Part B	Medicare expenditures as percent of GDP SMI Part D
ACTUAL									
1980.............	2,862,475	37,556	26,008	11,548	(X)	1.31	0.91	0.40	(X)
1990.............	5,979,575	110,903	66,785	44,118	(X)	1.85	1.12	0.74	(X)
2000.............	10,284,750	225,983	132,803	93,180	(X)	2.20	1.29	0.91	(X)
2005.............	13,093,700	342,106	187,456	153,553	1,098	2.61	1.43	1.17	0.01
2006.............	13,855,900	413,274	198,164	170,460	44,649	2.98	1.43	1.23	0.32
2007.............	14,477,625	444,316	209,466	183,678	51,173	3.07	1.45	1.27	0.35
2008.............	14,718,575	463,250	225,568	183,514	54,168	3.15	1.53	1.25	0.37
2009.............	14,418,725	503,386	239,336	205,857	58,193	3.49	1.66	1.43	0.40
2010.............	14,964,400	524,164	245,981	215,326	62,857	3.50	1.64	1.44	0.42
2011.............	15,517,925	548,553	255,896	226,277	66,379	3.53	1.65	1.46	0.43
2012.............	16,155,250	572,974	263,643	240,446	68,885	3.55	1.63	1.49	0.43
2013.............	16,691,500	591,391	269,955	248,143	73,294	3.54	1.62	1.49	0.44
2014.............	17,393,100	619,582	270,691	266,637	82,254	3.56	1.56	1.53	0.47
2015.............	18,036,650	649,715	278,013	281,640	90,062	3.60	1.54	1.56	0.50
PROJECTED [1]									
2016.............	18,568,401	673,640	285,299	296,326	92,015	3.63	1.54	1.60	0.50
2017.............	19,455,287	704,384	295,946	313,918	94,521	3.62	1.52	1.61	0.49
2018.............	20,530,798	747,668	308,462	334,893	104,312	3.64	1.50	1.63	0.51
2019.............	21,617,519	811,275	329,355	366,320	115,600	3.75	1.52	1.69	0.53
2020.............	22,733,698	875,297	353,213	396,578	125,506	3.85	1.55	1.74	0.55
2025.............	28,457,799	1,254,298	491,326	582,859	180,113	4.41	1.73	2.05	0.63
2030.............	35,313,962	1,770,025	672,444	845,337	252,245	5.01	1.90	2.39	0.71

X Not applicable. [1] Projections are a projected baseline, and are based on current law; that is, they assume that laws on the books will be implemented and adhered to with respect to scheduled taxes, premium revenues, and payments to providers and health plans. The one exception is that the projections disregard payment reductions that would result from the projected depletion of the Medicare Hospital Insurance trust fund (Part A). To date, Congress has not allowed the assets of the Medicare Hospital Insurance trust fund to become depleted.

Source: U.S. Centers for Medicare and Medicaid Services, Trustees Report & Trust Funds, "2017 Expanded and Supplementary Tables and Figures," <https://www.cms.gov/Research-Statistics-Data-and-Systems/Statistics-Trends-and-Reports/ReportsTrustFunds/index.html>, accessed July 2017.

Table 164. Health Insurance Coverage Status by Selected Characteristics: 2015

[318,869 represents 318,869,000. Data for coverage during all or part of 2015; people not covered had no health insurance for the entire year. Based on the 2016 Current Population Survey, Annual Social and Economic Supplement (CPS ASEC); see text, Section 1, and Appendix III. The CPS ASEC defines private health insurance as a plan provided through an employer or a union, and coverage purchased directly by an individual from an insurance company or through an exchange. Government health insurance includes Medicare, Medicaid, the Children's Health Insurance Program (CHIP), individual state health plans, TRICARE, CHAMPVA (Civilian Health and Medical Program of the Department of Veterans Affairs), as well as care provided by the Department of Veterans Affairs and the military. People covered only through the Indian Health Service were considered uninsured]

Characteristic	Number (1,000)							Percent			
	Total persons	Not covered by health insur-ance	Covered by private or government health insurance					Not covered by health insur-ance	Covered by private or government health insurance		
			Total [1]	Private		Government			Total [1]	Private	Medic-aid
				Total	Employer based	Medic-aid	Medi-care				
Total.................	318,869	28,966	289,903	214,238	177,540	62,385	51,865	9.1	90.9	67.2	19.6
Age:											
Under 18 years......	74,062	3,866	70,196	46,138	40,908	29,176	321	5.2	94.8	62.3	39.4
18 to 24 years.......	29,791	3,915	25,876	20,684	17,496	6,546	272	13.1	86.9	69.4	22.0
25 to 34 years......	43,763	7,128	36,634	30,523	26,259	6,790	592	16.3	83.7	69.7	15.5
35 to 44 years......	40,005	5,489	34,517	29,099	25,919	5,950	930	13.7	86.3	72.7	14.9
45 to 54 years......	42,566	4,449	38,116	32,541	28,218	5,311	1,804	10.5	89.5	76.4	12.5
55 to 64 years......	41,135	3,613	37,522	30,484	25,405	5,349	3,588	8.8	91.2	74.1	13.0
65 years and over...	47,547	506	47,041	24,771	13,334	3,263	44,358	1.1	98.9	52.1	6.9
Sex:											
Male.................	156,205	15,512	140,693	105,830	88,678	29,180	23,147	9.9	90.1	67.8	18.7
Female..............	162,664	13,454	149,210	108,409	88,861	33,205	28,718	8.3	91.7	66.6	20.4
Race:											
White alone [2]........	245,805	21,454	224,351	169,565	139,863	42,962	43,135	8.7	91.3	69.0	17.5
Black alone [2]........	41,704	4,627	37,076	23,330	20,012	12,511	5,617	11.1	88.9	55.9	30.0
Asian alone [2].......	18,249	1,360	16,890	13,775	11,209	2,869	2,034	7.5	92.5	75.5	15.7
Hispanic origin [3].....	56,873	9,235	47,637	29,352	24,472	18,779	4,343	16.2	83.8	51.6	33.0
Household income:											
Less than $25,000...	51,999	7,713	44,286	16,009	8,696	21,869	14,736	14.8	85.2	30.8	42.1
$25,000–$49,999. ..	65,289	8,143	57,146	34,739	25,071	17,867	14,854	12.5	87.5	53.2	27.4
$50,000–$74,999. ..	55,131	5,318	49,813	38,802	31,914	9,703	8,007	9.6	90.4	70.4	17.6
$75,000 or more.....	146,451	7,793	138,658	124,688	111,858	12,946	14,268	5.3	94.7	85.1	8.8
Persons below poverty..............	43,123	7,489	35,634	12,352	7,378	22,055	5,822	17.4	82.6	28.6	51.1

[1] Includes other private and government insurance, not shown separately. Persons with coverage counted only once in total, even though they may have been covered by more than one type of policy. [2] Refers to people who reported specified race and did not report any other race category. [3] Persons of Hispanic origin may be of any race.

Source: U.S. Census Bureau, *Health Insurance Coverage in the United States: 2015*, Current Population Reports, P60-257(RV), September 2016; and "Current Population Survey Tables for Health Insurance Coverage: HI01. Health Insurance Coverage Status and Type of Coverage by Selected Characteristics" and "HI03. Health Insurance Coverage Status and Type of Coverage by Selected Characteristics for Poor People Below Poverty in the Poverty Universe," <http://www.census.gov/topics/health/health-insurance/data/tables.html>, accessed January 2017.

Table 165. Persons With and Without Health Insurance Coverage by State: 2015

[286,693 represents 286,693,000. Data are from the American Community Survey (ACS), and measures population without health insurance coverage at the time of the interview. See source for more information]

State	Total persons covered (1,000)	Total persons not covered		Children not covered		State	Total persons covered (1,000)	Total persons not covered		Children not covered	
		Number (1,000)	Percent of total	Number (1,000)	Percent of total			Number (1,000)	Percent of total	Number (1,000)	Percent of total
U.S.........	286,693	29,758	9.4	3,534	4.8	MO.........	5,386	583	9.8	80	5.7
AL..........	4,297	484	10.1	34	3.1	MT.........	899	119	11.6	17	7.6
AK..........	607	106	14.9	20	10.6	NE.........	1,713	154	8.2	25	5.3
AZ..........	5,991	728	10.8	134	8.3	NV.........	2,505	351	12.3	50	7.6
AR..........	2,647	278	9.5	35	4.9	NH.........	1,231	83	6.3	7	2.7
CA..........	35,332	3,317	8.6	302	3.3	NJ.........	8,079	771	8.7	75	3.7
CO..........	4,935	433	8.1	52	4.2	NM.........	1,826	224	10.9	22	4.5
CT..........	3,327	211	6.0	25	3.3	NY.........	18,176	1,381	7.1	104	2.5
DE..........	877	54	5.9	6	3.0	NC.........	8,753	1,103	11.2	99	4.4
DC..........	636	25	3.8	2	1.5	ND.........	683	57	7.8	13	7.9
FL..........	17,299	2,662	13.3	284	6.9	OH.........	10,696	746	6.5	115	4.4
GA..........	8,636	1,388	13.9	166	6.7	OK.........	3,298	533	13.9	71	7.4
HI..........	1,321	55	4.0	5	1.6	OR.........	3,711	280	7.0	31	3.6
ID..........	1,452	180	11.0	25	5.8	PA.........	11,797	802	6.4	111	4.1
IL..........	11,780	900	7.1	75	2.5	RI.........	982	59	5.7	7	3.4
IN..........	5,893	628	9.6	106	6.7	SC.........	4,278	523	10.9	44	4.1
IA..........	2,925	155	5.0	26	3.5	SD.........	755	86	10.2	14	6.7
KS..........	2,590	261	9.1	37	5.1	TN.........	5,829	667	10.3	62	4.2
KY..........	4,081	261	6.0	43	4.2	TX.........	22,375	4,615	17.1	682	9.5
LA..........	4,022	546	11.9	40	3.6	UT.........	2,660	311	10.5	65	7.2
ME..........	1,204	111	8.4	14	5.7	VT.........	596	24	3.8	1	1.0
MD..........	5,519	389	6.6	52	3.9	VA.........	7,416	746	9.1	91	4.9
MA..........	6,529	189	2.8	16	1.1	WA.........	6,599	468	6.6	43	2.6
MI..........	9,214	597	6.1	68	3.1	WV.........	1,707	108	6.0	11	2.8
MN..........	5,187	245	4.5	39	3.1	WI.........	5,376	323	5.7	46	3.6
MS..........	2,556	372	12.7	29	4.0	WY.........	510	66	11.5	11	7.8

Source: U.S. Census Bureau, 2015 American Community Survey, S2701 "Selected Characteristics of Health Insurance Coverage in the United States," <http://factfinder.census.gov>, accessed January 2017.

Table 166. Health Insurance Coverage—Public, Private, and Exchange-Based Coverage by Selected Characteristics: 2010 to 2016

[In percent, except as noted (5.9 represents 5,900,000). Covers persons under age 65. Based on the National Health Interview Survey. Data are estimates that have been released prior to final data editing and final weighting; see source for details. Data are based on a sample of the civilian noninstitutionalized population and are subject to sampling error]

Year and characteristics	No insurance [1]	Private health insurance [2]	Public health plan [3]	Exchange-based private health insurance [4] Total (millions)	Percent
Total:					
2010................................	18.2	61.2	22.0	(NA)	(NA)
2014................................	13.3	63.6	24.5	5.9	2.2
2015................................	10.5	65.6	25.3	10.2	3.8
2016................................	10.4	65.0	26.3	11.2	4.1
Age 17 and under:					
2010................................	7.8	53.8	39.8	(NA)	(NA)
2014................................	5.5	53.7	42.2	0.7	0.9
2015................................	4.5	54.7	42.2	1.4	2.0
2016................................	5.1	53.8	43.0	1.8	2.5
Age 18 to 64:					
2010................................	22.3	64.1	15.0	(NA)	(NA)
2014................................	16.3	67.3	17.7	5.2	2.7
2015................................	12.8	69.7	18.9	8.8	4.5
2016................................	12.4	69.2	20.0	9.4	4.7
Male:					
2010................................	25.3	63.4	12.5	(NA)	(NA)
2014................................	18.3	67.7	15.2	2.3	2.4
2015................................	14.9	69.9	16.6	4.0	4.1
2016................................	14.4	69.8	17.4	4.5	4.7
Female:					
2010................................	19.3	64.7	17.4	(NA)	(NA)
2014................................	14.3	66.9	20.1	2.9	2.9
2015................................	10.8	69.6	21.2	4.8	4.8
2016................................	10.5	68.6	22.5	4.9	4.8
White only, non-Hispanic:					
2010................................	16.4	72.2	12.8	(NA)	(NA)
2014................................	11.6	75.3	14.6	3.0	2.5
2015................................	8.7	77.3	15.7	5.2	4.3
2016................................	8.6	76.6	16.6	5.6	4.6
Black only, non-Hispanic:					
2010................................	27.2	49.3	25.3	(NA)	(NA)
2014................................	17.7	53.4	30.5	0.7	2.9
2015................................	14.4	57.8	29.7	1.0	4.0
2016................................	15.0	56.7	29.9	1.0	4.1
Hispanic or Latino: [5]					
2010................................	43.2	41.1	16.3	(NA)	(NA)
2014................................	33.7	46.4	20.6	0.9	2.6
2015................................	27.7	50.0	23.0	1.7	5.1
2016................................	25.0	51.4	24.9	1.8	5.2
Poor: [6]					
2010................................	42.2	19.6	38.8	(NA)	(NA)
2014................................	32.3	21.9	46.6	0.6	2.2
2015................................	25.2	24.3	51.7	0.9	3.8
2016................................	26.2	21.6	53.7	0.7	2.9
Near poor: [6]					
2010................................	43.0	34.7	23.7	(NA)	(NA)
2014................................	30.9	41.2	29.6	1.6	4.5
2015................................	24.1	43.8	34.2	2.7	7.9
2016................................	23.2	40.3	38.5	2.5	7.5
Not poor: [6]					
2010................................	12.6	80.8	8.1	(NA)	(NA)
2014................................	8.9	83.9	8.5	3.1	2.3
2015................................	7.6	84.7	9.1	5.1	3.8
2016................................	7.2	84.6	9.6	6.0	4.3

NA Not available. [1] Also includes persons who had only Indian Health Service coverage or only a private plan that paid for one type of service, such as accidents or dental care. [2] Includes plans obtained through an employer, purchased directly, purchased through local or community programs, or purchased through the Health Insurance Marketplace or a state-based exchange. Excludes plans that pay for only one type of service, such as accidents or dental care. A small number of persons covered by both public and private plans are included in both categories. [3] Includes Medicaid, Children's Health Insurance Program (CHIP), state-sponsored or other government-sponsored health plan, Medicare, and military plans. A small number of persons covered by both public and private plans are included in both categories. [4] Covers persons who purchased a private health insurance plan through the Health Insurance Marketplace or state-based exchanges that were established under the Affordable Care Act of 2010 (P.L. 111-148, P.L. 111-152). These persons are also included under "private health insurance." [5] Persons of Hispanic or Latino origin may be of any race or combination of races. [6] Based on family income and family size, using the U.S. Census Bureau's poverty thresholds. "Poor" persons have incomes below the poverty threshold; "Near poor" persons have incomes of 100% to less than 200% of the poverty threshold; and "Not poor" persons have incomes of 200% of the poverty threshold or greater. Excludes persons with unknown poverty status.

Source: U.S. National Center for Health Statistics, "Early Release Reports and Tabulations on Special Topics," *Health Insurance Coverage: Early Release of Quarterly Estimates from the National Health Interview Survey, January 2010-December 2016,* May 2017. See also <https://www.cdc.gov/nchs/nhis/releases.htm>.

Table 167. Health Insurance Coverage Status and Plan Type: 1970 to 2016

[142.3 represents 142,300,000. Based on the National Health Interview Survey. Covers persons under age 65. Persons may report more than one type of health insurance coverage]

Year	Private insurance, any [1]	Private, employer based	Private, other [2]	Medicaid	Medicare	Other public	No health insurance [3]
NUMBER (mil.)							
1970	142.3	124.1	18.0	(NA)	(NA)	(NA)	(NA)
1974	148.7	131.5	17.9	8.7	(NA)	4.6	24.4
1976	148.9	129.4	19.5	9.3	0.5	4.9	26.6
1978	151.6	134.0	17.5	12.8	2.4	4.3	23.0
1980	154.1	138.5	15.6	13.8	2.7	3.9	23.3
1982	157.5	141.8	16.0	12.2	2.5	7.5	28.0
1984	156.7	139.4	17.7	13.9	2.3	7.3	29.7
1986	157.5	141.7	15.7	13.9	2.4	7.6	29.8
1989	160.4	144.6	15.8	13.4	2.5	6.9	31.3
1990	162.7	146.3	16.3	15.4	3.0	6.1	33.4
1991	160.5	143.7	16.8	15.4	2.8	6.5	37.2
1992	160.8	137.1	23.7	18.6	3.0	6.4	35.8
1993	158.9	143.2	15.8	21.6	3.2	6.4	37.1
1994	158.8	145.9	12.9	23.9	3.0	6.1	38.8
1995	159.8	146.2	13.5	25.6	3.1	6.4	40.6
1996	164.4	151.3	13.1	26.6	3.7	5.9	37.7
1997	165.5	151.4	14.2	25.8	3.7	6.0	38.9
1998	165.8	155.9	9.8	22.9	3.8	6.4	41.0
1999	170.8	159.8	10.8	21.1	4.1	6.3	39.2
2000	174.2	163.4	10.5	21.9	4.1	5.2	38.5
2001	173.0	162.5	10.1	22.9	4.0	5.4	40.5
2002	174.1	163.8	10.0	25.2	4.3	5.1	39.2
2003	173.6	162.1	10.1	30.9	4.5	6.1	41.6
2004	174.5	162.3	11.6	31.6	4.5	6.1	41.6
2005	174.7	162.9	11.1	33.2	4.5	6.4	42.1
2006	171.2	158.8	11.8	36.2	5.4	6.5	43.9
2007	174.1	160.7	12.7	36.2	5.4	7.0	43.3
2008	171.9	158.6	12.6	38.4	5.9	7.0	44.1
2009	166.7	152.8	13.1	42.4	6.2	7.7	46.2
2010	163.9	150.2	12.7	44.8	6.0	8.1	48.3
2011	164.5	150.1	12.7	47.4	6.4	7.9	45.8
2012	164.9	151.8	11.8	48.1	6.5	8.1	45.2
2013	165.3	151.5	12.5	48.5	7.1	8.1	44.6
2014	170.7	151.3	17.2	52.6	6.7	8.4	35.7
2015	176.6	154.7	20.8	55.4	7.0	8.1	28.7
2016	176.7	154.8	20.9	57.6	7.6	7.9	28.0
PERCENT							
1970	78.7	68.6	10.0	(NA)	(NA)	(NA)	(NA)
1974	79.7	70.5	9.6	4.7	(NA)	2.5	13.1
1976	78.9	68.5	10.3	4.9	0.2	2.6	14.1
1978	79.3	70.2	9.2	6.7	1.2	2.3	12.0
1980	79.4	71.4	8.0	7.1	1.4	2.0	12.0
1982	78.1	70.3	7.9	6.1	1.2	3.7	13.9
1984	76.9	68.4	8.7	6.8	1.1	3.6	14.6
1986	76.7	69.1	7.7	6.8	1.2	3.7	14.5
1989	76.8	69.3	7.6	6.4	1.2	3.3	15.0
1990	75.9	68.3	7.6	7.2	1.4	2.9	15.6
1991	74.2	66.4	7.8	7.1	1.3	3.0	17.2
1992	73.6	62.8	10.8	8.5	1.4	2.9	16.4
1993	72.0	64.9	7.1	9.8	1.4	2.9	16.8
1994	69.9	64.0	5.9	11.2	1.4	2.8	17.8
1995	71.3	65.6	5.7	11.5	1.6	2.6	16.3
1996	71.2	65.1	6.1	11.1	1.6	2.6	16.7
1997	70.7	66.4	4.2	9.7	1.6	2.7	17.5
1998	72.1	67.5	4.6	8.9	1.7	2.7	16.6
1999	72.8	68.3	4.4	9.1	1.7	2.2	16.1
2000	71.7	67.3	4.2	9.5	1.7	2.2	16.8
2001	71.5	67.2	4.1	10.4	1.8	2.1	16.1
2002	69.7	65.6	3.9	11.8	1.7	2.3	16.5
2003	68.9	64.4	4.0	12.3	1.8	2.4	16.5
2004	68.8	64.0	4.6	12.5	1.8	2.4	16.4
2005	68.2	63.6	4.4	12.9	1.8	2.5	16.4
2006	66.3	61.5	4.6	14.0	2.1	2.5	17.0
2007	66.8	61.6	4.9	13.9	2.1	2.7	16.6
2008	65.6	60.5	4.8	14.7	2.3	2.7	16.8
2009	63.3	58.0	5.0	16.1	2.3	2.9	17.5
2010	61.7	56.6	4.8	16.9	2.3	3.1	18.2
2011	61.8	56.4	4.8	17.8	2.4	3.0	17.2
2012	61.8	56.9	4.4	18.0	2.4	3.0	16.9
2013	61.8	56.6	4.7	18.1	2.6	3.0	16.7
2014	63.7	56.4	6.4	19.6	2.5	3.1	13.3
2015	65.5	57.4	7.7	20.6	2.6	3.0	10.6
2016	65.3	57.2	7.7	21.3	2.8	2.9	10.3

NA Not available. [1] Private health insurance coverage obtained through an employer, purchased directly, or obtained through any other means. Beginning in 2014, also includes plans purchased through the Health Insurance Marketplace or a state-based exchange under the Affordable Care Act of 2010. Excludes plans that cover only one type of service such as accidents or dental care. [2] Private insurance that is directly purchased as well as plans obtained through school or other means. Beginning in 2014, also includes plans purchased through the Health Insurance Marketplace or a state-based exchange. [3] Includes persons who did not have any private or government-sponsored health plan, or military-related coverage. Persons with only Indian Health Service coverage or a private plan that covers only one type of service are considered uninsured.

Source: U.S. National Center for Health Statistics, "Long-term Trends in Health Insurance: Estimates from the National Health Interview Survey, United States, 1968-2016," <https://www.cdc.gov/nchs/health_policy/coverage_and_access.htm>, accessed August 2017.

Table 168. People Without Health Insurance for the Entire Year by Age, Sex, Race/Ethnicity, and Family Type: 2014 and 2015

[In thousands, except as noted (316,168 represents 316,168,000). Based on the Current Population Survey, Annual Social and Economic Supplement (CPS ASEC); see text, Section 1 and Appendix III]

Characteristic	2014			2015		
		Uninsured persons			Uninsured persons	
	Total persons	Number	Percent of total persons	Total persons	Number	Percent of total persons
Total [1]	**316,168**	**32,968**	**10.4**	**318,869**	**28,966**	**9.1**
Under 18 years	73,920	4,472	6.0	74,062	3,866	5.2
18 to 24 years	30,116	4,712	15.6	29,791	3,915	13.1
25 to 34 years	43,006	7,877	18.3	43,763	7,128	16.3
35 to 44 years	39,919	6,163	15.4	40,005	5,489	13.7
45 to 54 years	42,796	5,054	11.8	42,566	4,449	10.5
55 to 64 years	40,417	4,061	10.0	41,135	3,613	8.8
65 years and over	45,994	629	1.4	47,547	506	1.1
Male	154,815	17,537	11.3	156,205	15,512	9.9
Female	161,353	15,431	9.6	162,664	13,454	8.3
White alone [2]	244,468	24,759	10.1	245,805	21,454	8.7
Black alone [2]	41,227	4,847	11.8	41,704	4,627	11.1
Asian alone [2]	17,796	1,659	9.3	18,249	1,360	7.5
Hispanic [3]	55,614	11,059	19.9	56,873	9,235	16.2
In families	256,308	24,451	9.5	258,121	21,546	8.3
In married-couple families	190,855	14,779	7.7	191,337	12,843	6.7
In families with male householders, no spouse present	17,435	3,176	18.2	18,287	3,027	16.6
In families with female householders, no spouse present	48,019	6,496	13.5	48,497	5,676	11.7

[1] Includes other races not shown separately. [2] Refers to people who reported specified race and did not report any other race category. [3] Persons of Hispanic origin may be of any race.

Source: U.S. Census Bureau, *Health Insurance Coverage in the United States: 2015*, Current Population Reports, P60-257(RV), September 2016, and earlier reports; and "Current Population Survey Tables for Health Insurance Coverage: HI-01, Health Insurance Coverage Status and Type of Coverage by Selected Characteristics," <http://www.census.gov/topics/health/health-insurance/data/tables.html>, accessed January 2017.

Table 169. Worker Participation in Employer-Sponsored Health Insurance and Benefit Programs, and Participant Contributions: 2016

[Based on the March 2016 National Compensation Survey; survey drew responses from approximately 6,880 private industry establishments of all sizes, representing about 114.2 million workers. Excludes federal government workers, the military, agricultural workers, private household workers, and the self-employed. For more information, see Appendix III, and the Bureau of Labor Statistics (BLS) Handbook of Methods, Chapter 8, at <http://www.bls.gov/opub/hom/pdf/homch8.pdf>]

Characteristic	Percent of workers participating—				Single coverage medical plans		Family coverage medical plans	
	Medical care	Dental care	Vision care	Out-patient prescription drug coverage	Percent of employees required to contribute to premiums	Average monthly contribution [1] (dol.)	Percent of employees required to contribute to premiums	Average monthly contribution [1] (dol.)
Total	**49**	**33**	**18**	**48**	**84**	**126.68**	**92**	**511.47**
WORKER CHARACTERISTICS								
Management, professional, and related	66	49	27	65	84	124.23	94	498.90
Management, business, and financial	73	53	29	72	87	120.51	96	474.13
Professional and related	62	47	25	61	83	126.62	93	514.63
Service	23	15	10	22	81	128.62	89	578.68
Sales and office	47	29	15	46	89	127.87	96	521.14
Sales and related	37	20	12	36	93	131.91	96	531.19
Office and administrative support	54	36	18	53	87	125.86	96	516.45
Natural resources, construction, and maintenance	58	32	21	57	76	136.27	84	551.94
Production, transportation, and material moving	55	36	20	54	83	124.11	90	467.37
Production	61	38	19	60	85	124.53	92	442.23
Transportation, and material moving	49	34	21	49	81	123.58	87	499.00
Full-time [2]	63	42	24	62	84	126.24	92	509.51
Part-time [2]	11	8	4	11	84	133.30	89	541.64
Union [3]	78	63	45	78	61	129.40	66	418.40
Nonunion	46	30	16	45	88	126.37	96	522.15
Average hourly wage: [4]								
Less than $12.00	19	10	6	18	87	133.75	94	555.30
Less than $9.37	11	6	4	10	89	143.60	96	575.10
$12.00 to $17.72	50	31	17	49	85	128.60	94	542.47
$17.73 to $28.59	65	42	23	64	83	126.26	92	509.37
$28.60 or more	72	54	31	71	83	123.07	91	474.14
$44.33 or more	72	57	33	72	85	122.21	92	452.80

[1] The average is presented for all workers with medical care benefits. Averages are for plans stating a flat monthly cost. [2] Employees are classified as working either a full-time or part-time schedule based on the definition used by each establishment. [3] Union workers are those whose wages are determined through collective bargaining. [4] The National Compensation Survey - Benefits program presents wage data in percentiles rather than dollar amounts; see "Technical Note" in source, <https://www.bls.gov/ncs/ebs/benefits/2016/tech_note.htm>.

Source: U.S. Bureau of Labor Statistics, Annual Bulletin on Benefit Coverage, *National Compensation Survey: Employee Benefits in the United States, March 2016*, Bulletin 2785, September 2016. See also <https://www.bls.gov/ncs/ebs/benefits/2016/home.htm>.

Table 170. Employer-Sponsored Health Insurance Enrollment by Type of Plan and Employer Size: 2014

[In millions (175.0 represents 175,000,000). Based on the Current Population Survey, Annual and Social Economic Supplement, and Agency for Healthcare Research and Quality's Medical Expenditure Panel Surveys. For persons and their dependents covered by health insurance sponsored by a current or former employer. Abbreviations: HMO = health maintenance organization; PPO = preferred provider organization; POS = point-of-service plan; and HDED = high deductible health plan (including but not limited to IRS-qualified high deductible health plans)]

Employer sector and size	Total					Self-insured plans [1]					Fully insured plans [2]				
	Total	HMO	PPO	POS	HDED	Total	HMO	PPO	POS	HDED	Total	HMO	PPO	POS	HDED
TOTAL															
Total................	**175.0**	**24.0**	**106.2**	**12.2**	**32.6**	**98.1**	**6.8**	**68.8**	**3.7**	**18.8**	**76.9**	**17.2**	**37.4**	**8.5**	**13.8**
Less than 50 employees..............	27.7	3.2	13.0	4.5	7.1	3.8	(Z)	2.5	0.3	1.0	23.8	3.2	10.5	4.1	6.1
50 to 99 employees.......	11.8	1.2	5.6	2.1	2.9	2.1	(Z)	1.4	0.2	0.5	9.7	1.2	4.2	1.9	2.3
100 to 499 employees....	24.3	3.9	14.0	1.9	4.6	10.4	0.6	7.7	0.4	1.7	13.9	3.3	6.3	1.5	2.9
500 to 999 employees....	12.8	1.8	7.6	0.9	2.5	6.6	0.4	4.8	0.3	1.1	6.2	1.5	2.8	0.6	1.3
1,000 or more employees..............	98.4	13.9	66.0	2.9	15.6	75.1	5.8	52.4	2.5	14.4	23.3	8.1	13.6	0.5	1.2
PRIVATE SECTOR [3]															
Total................	**134.0**	**16.1**	**79.9**	**10.9**	**27.2**	**82.2**	**5.8**	**57.4**	**3.3**	**15.7**	**51.9**	**10.3**	**22.5**	**7.6**	**11.5**
Less than 50 employees..............	26.4	3.1	12.3	4.3	6.7	3.7	(Z)	2.4	0.3	1.0	22.7	3.0	9.9	4.0	5.8
50 to 99 employees.......	10.6	1.2	5.0	1.9	2.6	1.9	(Z)	1.3	0.2	0.5	8.7	1.1	3.7	1.7	2.1
100 to 499 employees....	20.6	3.2	11.9	1.6	3.9	9.5	0.5	7.0	0.4	1.6	11.1	2.7	4.9	1.3	2.3
500 to 999 employees....	10.2	1.4	6.2	0.8	1.9	5.8	0.3	4.2	0.3	0.9	4.4	1.1	2.0	0.5	0.9
1,000 or more employees..............	66.2	7.3	44.5	2.3	12.1	61.2	4.9	42.5	2.1	11.7	5.0	2.3	2.0	0.2	0.4

Z Less than 50,000 persons. [1] Self-insured plans are those in which the employer directly assumes some or all medical claim and administrative costs. [2] Fully insured plans are those in which the employer contracts with another organization to assume financial responsibility for the enrollees' medical claims and administrative costs. [3] Private sector includes the self-employed.

Source: U.S. Department of Labor, Employee Benefits Security Administration, *Health Insurance Coverage Bulletin: Abstract of Auxiliary Data for the March 2015 Annual Social and Economic Supplement to the Current Population Survey*, June 2016. See also <https://www.dol.gov/agencies/ebsa/researchers/data/auxiliary-data>.

Table 171. Health Insurance Enrollment in High Deductible Health Plans (HDHP) and Health Spending Accounts: 2010 to 2016

[In percent. Covers persons under age 65 with private health insurance coverage. In 2016, an HDHP is a private health plan with an annual deductible of at least $1,300 for self-only coverage or $2,600 for family coverage. The deductible is adjusted annually for inflation. For deductibles for earlier years, see Technical Notes in source. Components of HDHP may not sum due to rounding. Based on the National Health Interview Survey. Data are based on a sample of the civilian noninstitutionalized population and are subject to sampling error]

Year	HDHP enrollment					In a family with a flexible spending account [5]
	Total	HDHP without health savings account [1]	CDHP [2]	By source		
				Employment based [3]	Directly purchased [4]	
2010..........	25.3	17.6	7.7	23.3	48.0	20.4
2011..........	29.0	19.9	9.2	26.9	52.4	21.4
2012..........	31.1	20.3	10.8	29.2	54.7	21.6
2013..........	33.9	22.2	11.7	32.0	56.4	21.6
2014..........	36.9	23.6	13.3	36.2	54.1	21.2
2015..........	36.7	23.4	13.3	36.6	50.9	21.7
2016 (P).......	39.4	23.9	15.5	39.6	51.9	22.1

P Preliminary [1] Health savings accounts are tax-favored accounts available only to persons with an HDHP to pay for current and future medical expenses. Funds contributed are not subject to federal income tax at the time of deposit and may be used to cover qualified medical expenses without federal tax liability. HSA funds are rolled over annually and accumulate year to year. [2] A Consumer Driven Health Plan (CDHP) is an HDHP coupled with a health savings account. [3] Private insurance originally obtained through a current or former employer, union, or professional association. [4] Private insurance originally obtained through direct purchase or other means not related to employment. [5] A flexible spending account (FSA) allows employees to set aside pretax dollars to cover out-of-pocket medical expenses. FSAs are typically available to persons who do not have an HDHP and thus are not eligible for an HSA. Any money not used during the year is lost to the employee.

Source: U.S. National Center for Health Statistics, *Health Insurance Coverage: Early Release of Estimates From the National Health Interview Survey, 2016*, May 2017. See also <https://www.cdc.gov/nchs/nhis/releases.htm>.

Table 172. Annual Revenue for Health Care Industries: 2010 to 2015

[In millions of dollars (1,890,085 represents $1,890,085,000,000). For all employer firms, and taxable employer firms. Estimates have been adjusted to the results of the 2012 Economic Census. Based on the Service Annual Survey and administrative data; see Appendix III]

Kind of business	2007 NAICS code [1]	Total, all firms [2]			Taxable employer firms		
		2010	2014	2015	2010	2014	2015
Health care and social assistance [3]	**62**	**1,890,085**	**2,181,843**	**2,304,000**	**928,158**	**1,074,590**	**1,138,936**
Ambulatory health care services [3]	**621**	**753,036**	**863,818**	**912,343**	**680,746**	**780,929**	**824,835**
Offices of physicians (except mental health specialists)	621111	367,040	418,853	442,965	367,040	418,853	442,965
Offices of physicians, mental health specialists	621112	4,554	5,266	5,295	4,554	5,266	5,295
Offices of dentists	6212	101,313	109,278	113,855	101,313	109,278	113,855
Offices of chiropractors	62131	10,594	11,933	12,334	10,594	11,933	12,334
Offices of optometrists	62132	11,440	13,359	13,912	11,440	13,359	13,912
Offices of mental health practitioners, (except physicians)	62133	6,285	8,341	9,092	6,285	8,341	9,092
Offices of PT/OT/speech therapists and audiologists [4]	62134	22,239	26,170	28,365	22,239	26,170	28,365
Offices of podiatrists	621391	4,087	4,400	4,410	4,087	4,400	4,410
Family planning centers	62141	1,933	2,291	2,417	735	994	1,065
Outpatient mental health and substance abuse centers	62142	13,110	16,547	18,089	3,394	4,923	5,705
HMO medical centers [5]	621491	6,007	7,496	8,080	(S)	682	749
Kidney dialysis centers	621492	15,739	19,198	20,947	14,363	17,825	19,452
Freestanding ambulatory surgical and emergency centers	621493	18,417	22,067	23,843	15,639	19,480	21,092
All other outpatient care centers	621498	32,467	41,394	44,666	9,618	12,991	13,780
Medical laboratories	621511	27,597	30,745	31,695	27,597	30,745	31,695
Diagnostic imaging centers	621512	16,992	16,054	16,280	16,992	16,054	16,280
Home health care services	6216	58,809	70,776	74,447	41,878	52,273	55,730
Ambulance services	62191	11,855	14,237	14,932	9,164	11,218	11,779
Blood and organ banks	621991	10,263	9,986	9,994	2,331	(S)	(S)
Hospitals	**622**	**802,760**	**946,303**	**1,003,499**	**95,824**	**113,773**	**123,916**
General medical and surgical hospitals, government	622118	146,945	167,795	174,697	(X)	(X)	(X)
General medical and surgical hospitals, private	622119	601,076	713,829	760,060	77,783	92,380	101,190
Psychiatric and substance abuse hospitals, government	622218	10,526	12,754	13,077	(X)	(X)	(X)
Psychiatric and substance abuse hospitals, private	622219	8,913	9,962	10,724	5,063	5,656	6,215
Specialty hospitals, government	622318	5,974	6,952	7,309	(X)	(X)	(X)
Specialty hospitals, private	622319	29,326	35,011	37,632	12,978	15,737	16,511
Nursing and residential care facilities [3]	**623**	**190,850**	**214,810**	**223,345**	**117,184**	**136,092**	**143,163**
Nursing care facilities (skilled nursing facilities) [6]	6231	104,959	114,329	117,714	81,080	90,472	94,406
Residential intellectual/developmental disability facilities [6]	62321	21,232	23,393	24,142	6,046	6,766	6,952
Residential mental health and substance abuse facilities	62322	10,724	12,915	14,297	3,974	5,200	6,099
Continuing care retirement communities	623311	26,303	29,382	30,373	8,806	10,076	10,477
Homes for the elderly	623312	19,683	26,375	28,115	16,154	22,277	23,808

X Not applicable. S Figure does not meet publication standards. [1] North American Industry Classification System (NAICS), 2007; see text, Section 15. [2] Includes taxable and tax-exempt employer firms. [3] Includes other kinds of business, not shown separately. See Table 600, for data on NAICS 624 Social assistance industries. [4] Offices of physical, occupational, and speech therapists, and audiologists. [5] HMO is health maintenance organization. [6] The industry name and description have been changed to reflect the 2012 NAICS manual in order to be consistent with industry nomenclature.

Source: U.S. Census Bureau, Annual & Quarterly Services, "2015 Service Annual Survey," <http://www.census.gov/services/index.html>, accessed January 2017.

Table 173. Employment in the Health Service Industries: 2000 to 2016

[In thousands (12,861 represents 12,861,000). See headnote, Table 654. Based on the 2012 North American Industry Classification System (NAICS); see text, Section 15]

Industry	2012 NAICS code	2000	2005	2010	2012	2013	2014	2015	2016 (P)
Health care and social assistance [1]	**62**	**12,861**	**14,840**	**16,820**	**17,428**	**17,731**	**18,022**	**18,590**	**19,152**
Ambulatory health care services [1]	621	4,320	5,114	5,975	6,307	6,477	6,632	6,872	7,130
Offices of physicians	6211	1,840	2,094	2,313	2,390	2,429	2,463	2,533	2,611
Office of mental health physicians	621112	37	43	46	48	49	50	51	(NA)
Offices of dentists	6212	688	774	828	854	870	887	909	938
Offices of other health practitioners	6213	438	549	671	727	752	780	813	859
Outpatient care centers	6214	386	473	600	649	680	712	746	781
Medical and diagnostic laboratories	6215	162	198	228	236	243	249	259	259
Home health care services	6216	633	821	1,085	1,185	1,230	1,262	1,324	1,390
Hospitals	622	3,954	4,345	4,679	4,779	4,786	4,787	4,913	5,081
General medical and surgical hospitals	6221	3,745	4,096	4,357	4,416	4,442	4,433	4,514	(NA)
Psychiatric and substance abuse hospitals	6222	86	93	109	121	121	126	138	(NA)
Other hospitals	6223	123	156	213	242	223	228	261	(NA)
Nursing and residential care facilities [1]	623	2,583	2,855	3,124	3,196	3,229	3,258	3,295	3,326
Nursing care facilities	6231	1,514	1,577	1,657	1,663	1,654	1,650	1,653	1,657

NA Not available. P Data are preliminary. [1] Includes other industries, not shown separately.

Source: U.S. Bureau of Labor Statistics, Current Employment Statistics, "Employment, Hours, and Earnings—National," <http://www.bls.gov/ces/data.htm>, accessed January 2017.

Table 174. Revenue for Selected Health Care Industries by Source of Revenue: 2015

[In millions of dollars (448,260 represents $448,260,000,000). For all employer firms regardless of tax status. Estimates are adjusted to the results of the 2012 Economic Census, and are shown by industry classification based on the 2007 North American Industry Classification System (NAICS). Based on Service Annual Survey and administrative data; see Appendix III]

Source of revenue	Offices of physicians (NAICS 6211)	Offices of dentists (NAICS 6212)	Offices of mental health practitioners (NAICS 62133)	Home health care services (NAICS 6216)	Hospitals (NAICS 622)	Nursing and residential care facilities (NAICS 623) [1]
Total	**448,260**	**113,855**	**9,092**	**74,447**	**1,003,499**	**223,345**
Government [2]	121,133	10,167	3,341	52,111	383,152	130,230
Private insurance	203,226	51,036	2,648	13,014	453,225	17,563
Patient out-of-pocket from patients and families	38,373	43,611	1,607	5,657	34,716	51,886
Patient out-of-pocket from Social Security benefits	1,339	257	(S)	13	994	(NA)
Other patient care revenue	56,470	7,990	671	2,122	60,704	7,806
Contributions, gifts, grants	2,550	(S)	357	818	16,385	3,764
Investment, property income	768	59	(S)	(S)	6,214	1,511
All other non-patient revenue	24,401	(S)	304	586	48,109	7,102

NA Not available. S Figure does not meet publication standards. [1] Includes NAICS 6231 Nursing care facilities (skilled); NAICS 6232 Residential intellectual and developmental disability, mental health, and substance abuse facilities; NAICS 6233 Community care facilities for the elderly; and NAICS 6239 Other residential care facilities. [2] Includes Medicare, Medicaid, other government, and workers compensation.

Source: U.S. Census Bureau, Annual & Quarterly Services, "2015 Service Annual Survey," <http://www.census.gov/services/index.html>, accessed January 2017.

Table 175. Physicians by Sex and Specialty: 2000 to 2013

[In thousands (813.8 represents 813,800). As of Dec. 31. Office-based physicians work in patient care. Includes Puerto Rico and Island Areas]

Item	2000 Total	2000 Office-based	2010 Total	2010 Office-based	2012 Total	2012 Office-based	2013 Total	2013 Office-based
Doctors of medicine, total	**813.8**	**490.4**	**985.4**	**565.0**	**1,026.8**	**585.9**	**1,045.9**	**600.9**
Place of medical education:								
U.S. medical graduates [1]	616.8	376.5	719.1	424.8	743.3	(NA)	754.8	(NA)
Canadian medical graduates	(NA)	(NA)	11.9	(NA)	11.8	(NA)	11.7	(NA)
International medical graduates [2]	197.0	113.9	254.4	140.2	271.7	147.2	278.5	151.7
Sex:								
Male	618.2	382.3	688.5	399.4	705.0	402.1	712.6	406.9
Female	195.5	108.1	296.9	165.6	321.8	183.8	333.3	193.9
Specialty:								
Allergy/immunology	4.0	3.1	4.3	3.4	4.4	3.5	4.6	3.6
Anesthesiology	35.7	27.6	43.4	31.8	44.6	32.6	46.2	33.2
Cardiovascular diseases	21.0	16.3	22.9	17.5	28.1	17.5	23.6	17.7
Child and adolescent psychiatry	6.2	4.3	7.4	5.4	7.9	5.8	8.3	6.1
Dermatology	9.7	8.0	11.3	9.3	11.8	9.7	12.1	9.9
Diagnostic radiology	21.1	14.6	26.1	17.5	26.4	17.9	27.2	18.2
Emergency medicine	23.1	14.5	33.3	20.7	35.9	22.2	38.4	23.4
Family practice	71.6	54.2	87.6	69.9	91.4	73.1	93.7	74.7
Gastroenterology	10.6	8.5	13.2	10.5	13.8	11.0	14.4	11.3
General practice	15.2	13.0	8.6	7.2	7.0	5.9	6.7	5.6
General surgery	36.7	24.5	37.1	24.3	37.7	24.4	39.2	25.0
Internal medicine	134.5	89.7	161.3	110.6	170.7	116.9	177.1	120.4
Neurological surgery	5.0	3.7	5.8	4.0	6.0	4.1	6.3	4.2
Neurology	12.3	8.6	15.9	10.5	16.8	11.2	17.9	11.8
Obstetrics and gynecology	40.2	31.7	42.8	34.1	43.5	34.6	44.3	34.8
Ophthalmology	18.1	15.6	18.5	15.7	18.8	16.0	19.4	16.3
Orthopedic surgery	22.3	17.4	25.2	19.3	25.7	19.6	26.5	20.0
Otolaryngology	9.4	7.6	10.3	8.0	10.5	8.0	10.8	8.1
Pathology	18.8	10.6	19.0	10.7	18.9	10.6	19.2	10.5
Pediatrics	63.9	43.2	76.4	53.1	80.8	56.7	84.6	58.2
Physical medicine/rehabilitation	6.5	4.3	9.0	6.5	9.8	7.1	10.5	7.7
Plastic surgery	6.2	5.3	7.4	6.2	7.7	6.3	8.0	6.4
Psychiatry	39.5	25.0	39.7	25.7	39.9	26.2	40.7	26.7
Pulmonary diseases	8.7	5.9	11.1	7.8	11.8	8.4	12.6	8.9
Radiology	8.7	6.7	9.4	7.0	9.6	7.2	10.2	7.5
Urological surgery	10.3	8.5	10.7	8.6	10.8	8.6	11.1	8.6
Unspecified	8.3	3.8	9.5	3.6	12.4	4.1	11.8	4.1
Not classified	45.1	(X)	64.2	(X)	57.6	(X)	43.5	(X)
Other categories [3]	75.2	(X)	126.4	(X)	143.1	(X)	147.7	(X)

NA Not available. X Not applicable. [1] Includes other categories not shown, including graduates from inactive schools. [2] International medical graduates received their medical education in schools outside the United States and Canada. [3] Includes inactive and address unknown.

Source: American Medical Association, Chicago, IL, *Physician Characteristics and Distribution in the U.S., 2015 edition* ©, and previous reports.

Table 176. Registered Nurses, Nurse Practitioners, and Licensed Practical and Vocational Nurses by State: 2016

[Covers nurses working in the health care and social assistance industry (North American Industry Classification System code 62), as of May. Rates per 100,000 resident population; based on U.S. Census Bureau estimates as of July 1 for year shown]

State	Registered nurses (RNs)		Nurse practitioners		Licensed practical and vocational nurses (LPNs, VPNs)	
	Total	Rate	Total	Rate	Total	Rate
United States [1]	2,510,840	777.0	137,350	42.5	605,380	187.4
Alabama	41,560	854.6	2,390	49.1	10,960	225.4
Alaska	4,610	621.4	420	56.6	340	45.8
Arizona	46,190	666.4	2,210	31.9	4,890	70.6
Arkansas	20,450	684.3	1,480	49.5	10,660	356.7
California	248,660	633.5	11,340	28.9	55,650	141.8
Colorado	42,150	760.8	2,460	44.4	4,280	77.2
Connecticut	27,760	776.2	1,940	54.2	7,040	196.8
Delaware	10,130	1,064.0	550	57.8	1,960	205.9
District of Columbia	9,030	1,325.7	530	77.8	1,500	220.2
Florida	158,680	769.8	8,430	40.9	40,510	196.5
Georgia	64,020	620.9	3,900	37.8	21,480	208.3
Hawaii	9,710	679.7	310	21.7	1,040	72.8
Idaho	11,030	655.3	540	32.1	2,090	124.2
Illinois	107,340	838.5	3,690	28.8	17,980	140.5
Indiana	58,010	874.6	3,840	57.9	15,070	227.2
Iowa	28,980	924.5	1,370	43.7	5,770	184.1
Kansas	24,010	825.9	1,610	55.4	6,510	223.9
Kentucky	40,580	914.6	2,840	64.0	9,410	212.1
Louisiana	40,680	868.9	1,600	34.2	18,680	399.0
Maine	12,580	944.8	1,100	82.6	1,130	84.9
Maryland	45,100	749.6	2,630	43.7	10,180	169.2
Massachusetts	74,730	1,097.1	5,750	84.4	13,290	195.1
Michigan	84,760	853.7	3,390	34.1	13,200	133.0
Minnesota	55,580	1,006.9	3,270	59.2	15,600	282.6
Mississippi	25,550	854.9	2,110	70.6	8,040	269.0
Missouri	59,520	976.9	3,290	54.0	13,010	213.5
Montana	8,580	823.0	450	43.2	2,090	200.5
Nebraska	18,190	953.8	980	51.4	4,240	222.3
Nevada	17,680	601.3	600	20.4	1,840	62.6
New Hampshire	11,480	860.1	930	69.7	1,840	137.8
New Jersey	68,610	767.1	3,640	40.7	13,960	156.1
New Mexico	13,570	652.1	800	38.4	1,800	86.5
New York	151,950	769.6	12,000	60.8	39,830	201.7
North Carolina	86,950	856.9	3,930	38.7	15,560	153.3
North Dakota	7,560	997.4	400	52.8	2,400	316.6
Ohio	115,160	991.5	6,380	54.9	35,810	308.3
Oklahoma	23,750	605.3	1,040	26.5	9,410	239.8
Oregon	26,950	658.4	1,390	34.0	2,210	54.0
Pennsylvania	123,560	966.5	4,750	37.2	33,200	259.7
Rhode Island	10,840	1,026.1	590	55.8	940	89.0
South Carolina	35,030	706.1	1,710	34.5	7,480	150.8
South Dakota	10,380	1,199.4	440	50.8	1,540	177.9
Tennessee	53,120	798.7	4,790	72.0	20,200	303.7
Texas	179,750	645.1	7,880	28.3	61,220	219.7
Utah	19,230	630.2	1,260	41.3	1,650	54.1
Vermont	4,980	797.3	490	78.5	1,220	195.3
Virginia	53,970	641.6	4,270	50.8	18,290	217.4
Washington	47,680	654.2	2,390	32.8	5,890	80.8
West Virginia	18,520	1,011.4	930	50.8	5,380	293.8
Wisconsin	48,000	830.6	2,120	36.7	6,550	113.3
Wyoming	3,950	674.6	200	34.2	560	95.6
Puerto Rico	13,180	386.4	1,820	53.4	3,010	88.2

[1] U.S. total excludes Puerto Rico.

Source: U.S. Bureau of Labor Statistics, Occupational Employment Statistics, "OES Data: Research Estimates by State and Industry," <https://www.bls.gov/oes/home.htm>, accessed June 2017.

Table 177. Medical Record Confidentiality Breaches Reported: Incidents and Persons Affected by Type and Location of Breach: 2013 to 2016

[6,939 represents 6,939,000. Data for breaches by date of submission to the Secretary of Health and Human Services (HHS), affecting 500 or more individuals. As required by section 13402(e)(4) of the Health Information Technology for Economic and Clinical Health (HITECH) Act, the Secretary of HHS must post a list of breaches of unsecured protected health information affecting 500 or more individuals. The Privacy Rule of the Health Insurance Portability and Accountability Act of 1996 (HIPAA) provides federal protections for individually identifiable health information held by covered entities and their business associates. Covered entities include health care providers, health plans, and health care clearinghouses]

Item	2013 Incidents (number)	2013 Individuals affected (1,000)	2014 Incidents (number)	2014 Individuals affected (1,000)	2015 Incidents (number)	2015 Individuals affected (1,000)	2016 Incidents (number)	2016 Individuals affected (1,000)
Total	277	6,939	312	12,682	269	113,267	327	16,655
TYPE OF BREACH [1]								
Hacking/information technology incident	24	238	34	1,797	57	111,812	113	13,427
Improper disposal	13	527	12	106	6	82	7	126
Loss	23	133	28	213	23	50	16	558
Theft	127	5,404	115	7,124	81	749	62	904
Unauthorized access/disclosure	63	384	75	3,028	101	574	129	1,640
Other/unknown	27	254	48	415	1	(NA)	0	0
LOCATION OF INFORMATION BREACHED [2]								
Desktop computer	39	4,348	28	2,322	29	316	27	139
Electronic medical record	14	40	14	122	18	3,951	31	433
E-mail	20	59	36	520	37	584	46	996
Laptop computer	70	1,029	43	1,315	38	392	26	813
Network server	30	320	49	7,259	41	107,252	82	13,175
Other portable electronic device	19	145	24	195	16	218	14	24
Paper/films	53	575	65	607	68	233	73	839
Other/unknown [3]	32	422	53	343	22	321	28	236

NA Not available. [1] Types of breaches can include a combination of other types of breaches within the categories specified. For example, incidents of improper disposal can also involve loss and/or theft. Incidents are categorized according to the first type of breach as given in the source. [2] Locations of information breached can include a combination of other locations within the categories specified. For example, incidents involving desktop computers can also involve breaches of information via laptop computer, network server, paper, and other locations. Incidents are categorized according to the first type as given in the source. [3] Other locations of information breaches can include incidents involving hard drives, computer disks, safes, websites, and other miscellaneous materials or locations. Also includes unknown locations of breaches.

Source: U.S. Department of Health and Human Services, Office for Civil Rights, HIPAA for Professionals—Breach Notification Rule, "Breaches Affecting 500 or More Individuals," <http://www.hhs.gov/hipaa/for-professionals/breach-notification/index.html>, accessed May 2017.

Table 178. Nursing Homes, Beds, Residents, and Occupancy Rate by State: 2015

[Based on a census of certified nursing facilities. Annual numbers of nursing homes, beds, and residents are based on the Centers for Medicare & Medicaid Services' reporting cycle. Starting with 2013 data, a new editing rule was used for number of beds. For the U.S., the number of beds decreased by less than 1%. For most states, this caused little or no change in the data. The change in the number of beds also caused a change in some occupancy rates. Because of the methodology change, interpret trends with caution]

State	Nursing homes	Beds	Residents	Occupancy rate [1]	State	Nursing homes	Beds	Residents	Occupancy rate [1]
U.S.	15,656	1,694,777	1,360,970	80.3	MO	512	55,245	38,418	69.5
AL	227	26,506	22,721	85.7	MT	80	6,693	4,466	66.7
AK	18	693	626	90.3	NE	217	15,961	11,938	74.8
AZ	145	16,523	11,588	70.1	NV	54	6,256	4,827	77.2
AR	228	24,463	17,655	72.2	NH	76	7,525	6,706	89.1
CA	1,213	119,046	102,674	86.2	NJ	365	52,538	44,998	85.6
CO	217	20,560	16,290	79.2	NM	73	7,070	5,502	77.8
CT	229	27,608	24,018	87.0	NY	626	116,666	104,684	89.7
DE	45	4,791	4,253	88.8	NC	423	45,221	36,612	81.0
DC	19	2,766	2,540	91.8	ND	80	6,009	5,571	92.7
FL	689	83,668	73,492	87.8	OH	959	90,667	75,523	83.3
GA	358	39,857	33,399	83.8	OK	305	28,580	18,854	66.0
HI	46	4,313	3,568	82.7	OR	137	12,274	7,379	60.1
ID	79	5,977	3,881	64.9	PA	699	88,133	78,822	89.4
IL	762	98,489	71,952	73.1	RI	84	8,720	7,966	91.4
IN	541	61,048	39,267	64.3	SC	187	19,758	16,830	85.2
IA	442	31,843	24,585	77.2	SD	111	6,893	6,301	91.4
KS	344	25,756	18,204	70.7	TN	319	36,719	28,246	76.9
KY	289	27,060	23,453	86.7	TX	1,222	137,396	93,316	67.9
LA	279	34,537	25,722	74.5	UT	100	8,639	5,518	63.9
ME	103	6,904	6,199	89.8	VT	37	3,174	2,628	82.8
MD	228	28,013	24,572	87.7	VA	286	32,447	27,874	85.9
MA	413	47,990	40,794	85.0	WA	220	21,145	16,969	80.3
MI	437	46,669	39,275	84.2	WV	126	10,858	9,471	87.2
MN	377	29,934	25,725	85.9	WI	388	33,800	26,804	79.3
MS	204	18,426	16,026	87.0	WY	38	2,950	2,268	76.9

[1] Percentage of beds occupied (number of nursing home residents per 100 nursing home beds).

Source: U.S. National Center for Health Statistics, *Health, United States, 2016,* May 2017. See also <http://www.cdc.gov/nchs/hus.htm>.

Table 179. Long-Term Care Facilities, Staff, and Clients by Provider Type and Selected Characteristics: 2014

[Data for 2014 except as noted. Based on the National Study of Long-Term Care Providers. Long-term care services assist the needs of frail older people and other adults with limited capacity for self-care due to chronic illness, injury, disability, or other health-related conditions]

Item	Facilities by provider type				
	Adult day services center	Home health agency	Hospice	Nursing home	Residential care community
Number of providers	**4,800**	**12,400**	**4,000**	**15,600**	**30,200**
Number of beds or licensed maximum capacity [1]	289,400	(X)	(X)	1,663,300	1,000,000
Average capacity [1]	62	(X)	(X)	106	33
Average number of people served [2]	39	427	355	88	28
Provider ownership type (percent):					
For profit	44.2	80.0	60.2	69.8	81.8
Not for profit	50.5	15.0	25.9	24.1	16.9
Government and other	5.4	5.0	13.9	6.1	1.4
Services provided (percent):					
Social work	51.7	82.4	99.9	89.2	48.0
Mental health or counseling	33.5	(NA)	97.2	87.1	52.1
Therapy [3]	48.8	96.6	98.1	99.4	69.0
Skilled nursing or nursing	66.1	100.0	100.0	100.0	59.0
Pharmacy or pharmacist	27.3	4.8	(NA)	97.4	82.4
Hospice	12.4	5.4	(X)	79.5	61.6
Total nursing employee FTEs [4]	**23,100**	**143,900**	**73,200**	**971,100**	**332,400**
Percent of total nursing employee FTEs:					
Registered nurse	17.8	53.1	48.1	12.0	6.5
Licensed practical nurse or licensed vocational nurse	10.9	18.8	8.5	22.3	10.7
Aide	59.2	25.6	31.5	63.9	82.0
Clients [2]	**282,200**	**4,934,600**	**1,340,700**	**1,369,700**	**835,200**
By age (percent):					
Under 65	36.4	17.5	5.6	15.1	7.2
65 and over	63.7	82.6	94.4	84.9	92.9
65 to 74	20.0	25.5	17.1	16.1	10.4
75 to 84	27.5	31.1	30.0	27.2	29.9
85 and over	16.2	26.0	47.3	41.6	52.6
By sex (percent):					
Men	41.1	37.9	40.9	33.2	29.8
Women	58.9	62.1	59.1	66.8	70.2
Selected conditions (percent):					
Diagnosed with Alzheimer's or other dementia	29.9	31.4	44.7	50.4	39.6
Diagnosed with depression	25.5	37.9	22.9	48.7	23.2

NA Not available. X Not applicable. [1] For adult day services, capacity is based on licensed maximum capacity. For nursing homes and residential care communities, capacity is based on number of licensed or certified beds. [2] Includes adult day services center participants in 2014; home health patients who ended care in 2013 (i.e., discharges); hospice patients who received care at any time in 2013; nursing home residents in 2014; and residential care community residents in 2014. [3] Physical, occupational, or speech therapy. [4] FTE is full-time equivalent.

Source: U.S. Centers for Disease Control and Prevention, National Center for Health Statistics, *Long-Term Care Providers and Services Users in the United States: Data From the National Study of Long-Term Care Providers, 2013-2014*, Series 3, No. 38, February 2016. See also <http://www.cdc.gov/nchs/nsltcp.htm>.

Table 180. Mental Health Treatment Facilities by Type: 2014

[Covers facilities in the 50 states, District of Columbia, American Samoa, Guam, Puerto Rico, and the U.S. Virgin Islands. Excludes: (1) Department of Defense (DoD) military treatment facilities, (2) individual private practitioners or small group practices not licensed as a mental health clinic or center, and (3) jails or prisons. Based on the National Mental Health Services Survey]

Characteristic	Total	Psychiatric hospitals	General hospitals [1]	RTCs, total [2]	RTCs for children [2]	Veterans Affairs medical centers	Outpatient clinics [3]	Multi-setting facilities [4]	Other
Total (number)	**13,176**	**667**	**1,149**	**2,484**	**675**	**354**	**7,689**	**572**	**261**
Percent	100.0	5.1	8.7	18.9	5.1	2.7	58.4	4.3	2.0
SERVICE SETTING [5]									
24-hour hospital inpatient	2,032	652	1,137	45	10	94	57	36	11
24-hour residential	2,573	131	32	2,026	671	67	65	246	6
Less than 24-hour day treatment or partial hospitalization	2,282	238	298	284	67	70	1,000	340	52
Less than 24-hour outpatient	9,677	238	378	537	70	339	7,507	458	220
FACILITY CONTROL									
Private for-profit	2,293	269	218	440	155	5	1,214	118	29
Private non-profit	8,462	183	791	1,816	500	22	5,060	386	204
Public [6]	2,421	215	140	228	20	327	1,415	68	28
AGE OF PATIENTS ACCEPTED [5]									
All ages	5,358	176	192	128	(X)	14	4,585	194	69
Children age 12 and younger	7,424	234	219	766	455	19	5,686	346	154
Children age 13 to 17	8,146	317	307	1,024	636	20	5,919	390	169
Young adults age 18 to 25	11,320	570	934	1,599	6	347	7,146	503	221
Adults age 26 to 64	10,887	592	1,017	1,549	(X)	347	6,793	420	169
Senior adults age 65 and older	10,346	581	1,084	1,344	(X)	348	6,452	379	158

X Not applicable. [1] Nonfederal general hospitals with separate psychiatric units. [2] RTC is residential treatment center. [3] Includes community mental health centers, and outpatient or day treatment or partial hospitalization facilities. [4] Facilities providing mental health services in two or more service settings (residential and outpatient and/or day treatment/partial hospitalization) and not classified as psychiatric or general hospitals, medical centers, or residential treatment centers. [5] Sums to more than the total because a facility could offer mental health treatment in more than one service setting and to more than one age group. [6] Includes facilities operated by state mental health and other state government agencies, local/county/municipal governments, tribal governments, Indian Health Service, and Department of Veterans Affairs.

Source: U.S. Substance Abuse and Mental Health Services Administration, *National Mental Health Services Survey (N-MHSS): 2014 Data on Mental Health Treatment Facilities*, December 2016. See also <http://www.samhsa.gov/data/mental-health-facilities-data-nmhss>.

Table 181. Medicare-Certified Hospitals, Institutions, and Physicians by Provider Type: 2009 to 2014

[Inpatient hospitals and other institutional providers are active and Medicare-certified in the reporting year. Physician provider counts originate from Medicare fee-for-service Part B claims, and reflect services provided by participating and non-participating physicians]

Providers by type	2009	2010	2011	2012	2013	2014
INPATIENT HOSPITALS						
Total hospitals [1]	**6,172**	**6,169**	**6,172**	**6,170**	**6,164**	**6,142**
Beds (1,000)	926,388	927,535	925,951	931,458	934,874	931,057
Beds per 1,000 enrollees [2]	20.0	19.6	19.1	18.4	17.9	17.3
Short stay	3,606	3,566	3,549	3,521	3,506	3,466
Psychiatric units	1,211	1,180	1,156	1,135	1,128	1,114
Rehabilitation units	963	938	927	918	914	915
Swing bed hospitals	545	510	522	515	513	502
Psychiatric	506	511	509	527	541	551
Rehabilitation	227	235	235	241	245	255
Children's	78	77	93	97	98	98
Long term care	427	438	437	437	430	423
Critical access	1,311	1,325	1,331	1,331	1,329	1,334
OTHER INSTITUTIONAL PROVIDERS [1]						
Skilled nursing facilities [1]	15,071	15,084	15,132	15,143	15,156	15,179
Beds (1,000)	1,561,299	1,572,511	1,581,549	1,586,378	1,588,797	1,594,927
Beds per 1,000 enrollees [2]	33.8	33.2	32.5	31.4	30.5	29.7
Home health agencies	10,184	10,914	11,930	12,253	12,459	12,268
Hospices	3,405	3,509	3,630	3,782	3,941	4,140
Independent and clinical labs	218,145	224,684	229,611	235,408	244,427	250,247
Outpatient physical therapy and/or speech pathology	2,640	2,536	2,351	2,248	2,172	2,102
End stage renal disease	5,476	5,631	5,766	5,916	6,145	6,374
Rural health clinics	3,752	3,845	3,940	4,001	4,026	4,062
Ambulatory surgical centers	5,260	5,316	5,335	5,349	5,368	5,444
Community mental health centers	652	644	606	545	524	(NA)
Federally qualified health centers	4,143	4,308	5,082	5,534	5,882	6,451
PHYSICIAN PROVIDERS						
All physician specialties [1,3]	**582,417**	**595,783**	**614,024**	**628,330**	**640,241**	**649,291**
Primary care	205,599	212,849	216,573	219,095	222,237	226,180
Family practice	81,978	84,982	86,903	88,631	90,208	91,832
General practice	13,731	13,401	12,235	11,403	10,820	10,558
Internal medicine	102,282	106,343	108,310	109,659	111,452	113,567
Pediatric medicine	7,608	8,123	9,125	9,402	9,757	10,223
Surgical specialties	105,544	108,093	109,169	109,773	110,748	111,444
Radiology	35,744	36,656	37,004	37,350	37,704	38,020
Obstetrics/gynecology	32,044	32,881	33,673	34,256	34,681	34,996
Psychiatry	27,475	27,550	27,887	28,208	28,321	28,396

NA Not available. [1] Includes other provider types not shown separately. [2] Beds per 1,000 enrollees based on Medicare Part A enrollee counts. [3] Physicians may be counted in more than one specialty.

Source: U.S. Centers for Medicare & Medicaid Services, "CMS Program Statistics, Medicare," <https://www.cms.gov/Research-Statistics-Data-and-Systems/Statistics-Trends-and-Reports/CMSProgramStatistics/index.html>, accessed May 2017.

Table 182. Hospital Outpatient Department Visits by Leading Reason for Visit and Primary Diagnosis: 2011

[125,721 represents 125,721,000. Based on the 2011 National Hospital Ambulatory Medical Care Survey (NHAMCS). NHAMCS is an annual nationally representative sample survey of visits to emergency departments, hospital outpatient departments, ambulatory surgical centers (ASCs) of nonfederal short-stay and general hospitals, and freestanding ASCs. Data are subject to sampling and nonsampling errors]

Leading Reason for Visit	Visits (1,000)	Percent distri-bution	Leading Diagnosis for Visit	Visits (1,000)	Percent distri-bution
All visits	**125,721**	**100.0**	**All Visits**	**125,721**	**100.0**
Progress visit, not otherwise specified	16,695	13.3	Malignant neoplasms	5,196	4.1
General medical examination	7,736	6.2	Diabetes mellitus	4,997	4.0
Postoperative visit	3,337	2.7	Routine infant or child health check	4,307	3.4
Medication, other and unspecified kinds	2,711	2.2	Arthropathies and related disorders	4,107	3.3
Counseling, not otherwise specified	2,698	2.1	Essential hypertension	3,743	3.0
Cough	2,631	2.1	Spinal disorders	3,434	2.7
Prenatal examination, routine	2,398	1.9	Acute upper respiratory infections, excluding pharyngitis	3,255	2.6
Diabetes mellitus	2,339	1.9	Normal pregnancy	3,246	2.6
Symptoms referable to throat	2,106	1.7	Psychoses, excl. major depressive disorder	2,778	2.2
Well-baby examination	1,915	1.5	General medical examination	2,546	2.0
Preoperative visit for specified and unspecified types of surgery	1,689	1.3	Heart disease, excluding ischemic	1,900	1.5
Earache, or ear infection	1,658	1.3	Follow up examination	1,830	1.5
Stomach and abdominal pain, cramps and spasms	1,559	1.2	Otitis media and eustachian tube disorders	1,815	1.4
Fever	1,532	1.2	Specific procedures and aftercare	1,724	1.4
Psychotherapy	[1] 1,525	[1] 1.2	Rheumatism, excluding back	1,710	1.4
Knee symptoms	1,508	1.2	Complications of pregnancy, childbirth, and the puerperium	1,705	1.4
Gynecological examination	1,489	1.2	Attention deficit disorder	1,439	1.1
Skin rash	1,381	1.1	Major depressive disorder	1,417	1.1
Hypertension	1,369	1.1	Gynecological examination	1,297	1.0
Back symptoms	1,332	1.1	Potential health hazards related to personal and family history	1,245	1.0
All other reasons	66,115	52.6	All other diagnoses	72,031	57.3

[1] Figure does not meet standards of reliability or precision.

Source: U.S. National Center for Health Statistics, *National Hospital Ambulatory Medical Care Survey: 2011 Outpatient Department Summary Tables*. See also <http://www.cdc.gov/nchs/ahcd/web_tables.htm>.

Table 183. Health Care Sources Used Most Often—Percent Distribution of Persons Age 18 and Over by Selected Characteristics: 2015

[In percent, except as noted (242,501 represents 242,501,000). Data are age-adjusted, unless otherwise noted. Based on a survey question that asked, "Is there a place that you usually go to when you are sick or need advice about your health?" If there was at least one such place, a follow-up question was asked: "What kind of place [is it/do you go to most often]—a clinic, a doctor's office, an emergency room, or some other place?" From the National Health Interview Survey, a sample survey of the civilian noninstitutionalized population; see Appendix III]

Characteristic	Adults age 18 and over, number (1,000)	Without a usual place for health care	With a usual place for health care	Usual place of health care			
				Physician office or Health Maintenance Organization (HMO)	Clinic or health center	Hospital emergency room or outpatient department	Other place
Total [1]	242,501	14.7	85.3	72.5	23.9	2.3	1.1
SEX							
Male	116,875	18.8	81.2	71.0	24.7	2.9	1.4
Female	125,625	10.7	89.3	73.9	23.3	2.0	0.9
AGE [2]							
18 to 44 years old	112,760	21.5	78.5	67.5	28.2	2.9	1.4
45 to 64 years old	83,239	9.2	90.8	76.6	20.5	2.2	0.8
65 to 74 years old	27,297	4.0	96.0	79.9	18.0	[9] 0.9	1.1
75 and over	19,204	2.4	97.6	82.3	15.5	[9] 1.7	0.6
RACE							
Single race [3]	238,301	14.6	85.4	72.6	23.9	2.4	1.1
White	191,218	14.8	85.2	73.2	23.8	1.8	1.2
Black or African American	29,796	13.1	86.9	69.4	24.3	5.5	0.9
American Indian or Alaska Native	2,307	16.1	83.9	42.0	45.7	(NA)	(B)
Asian	14,360	15.4	84.6	77.6	20.7	[9] 1.2	[9] 0.5
Native Hawaiian or Other Pacific Islander	619	24.6	75.4	44.9	45.4	(NA)	(B)
Two or more races [4]	4,200	19.2	80.8	67.4	26.2	[9] 4.1	[9] 2.3
Black or African American, white	851	18.8	81.2	86.6	[9] 11.9	(NA)	(B)
American Indian or Alaska Native, white	1,647	15.9	84.1	58.9	32.3	(NA)	[9] 3.7
HISPANIC ORIGIN AND RACE [5]							
Hispanic or Latino	37,755	20.5	79.5	57.4	38.3	3.2	1.0
Mexican or Mexican American	22,992	21.6	78.4	53.7	41.8	3.5	0.9
Not Hispanic or Latino	204,746	13.5	86.5	75.2	21.3	2.2	1.2
White, single race	157,410	13.3	86.7	76.5	20.6	1.7	1.3
Black or African American, single race	28,418	13.2	86.8	69.7	23.8	5.7	0.8
EDUCATION [6]							
Less than high school diploma	26,648	20.2	79.8	56.0	38.6	5.4	[9] 1.1
High school diploma or GED [7]	50,847	16.8	83.2	70.6	25.8	3.5	0.9
Some college	61,605	12.3	87.7	74.7	23.2	2.1	1.2
Bachelor's degree or higher	72,373	10.0	90.0	82.4	16.7	1.0	1.2
FAMILY INCOME							
Less than $35,000	66,342	20.1	79.9	58.8	35.0	5.0	1.1
$35,000 to $49,999	25,114	18.0	82.0	71.8	24.7	2.3	1.3
$50,000 to $74,999	37,018	15.4	84.6	73.5	23.5	[9] 1.8	1.1
$75,000 to $99,999	27,607	12.2	87.8	76.8	20.8	(NA)	1.1
$100,000 or more	58,917	8.2	91.8	82.3	16.0	[9] 0.7	0.9
HEALTH INSURANCE COVERAGE [8]							
Under age 65:							
Private	135,220	12.1	87.9	77.9	19.9	1.1	1.2
Medicaid	25,313	12.3	87.7	56.0	38.4	5.1	0.6
Other	9,086	9.1	90.9	54.2	38.8	(NA)	2.1
Uninsured	24,896	49.1	50.9	40.8	47.4	9.8	2.0
Age 65 and over:							
Private	19,581	2.3	97.7	85.3	13.6	[9] 0.4	0.6
Medicare and Medicaid	3,267	[9] 3.0	97.0	71.9	25.7	(NA)	[9] 0.6
Medicare Advantage	11,634	2.4	97.6	84.2	14.3	[9] 1.1	[9] 0.4
Medicare only	7,890	5.8	94.2	79.7	17.1	[9] 2.1	[9] 1.1
Other	3,808	3.2	96.8	62.3	31.1	(NA)	3.0
Uninsured	249	37.1	62.9	51.7	45.3	–	(B)

– Represents zero. NA Not available. B Figure too small to meet statistical standards for reliability of a derived figure. [1] Includes other races not shown separately and persons with unknown education, family income, and health insurance characteristics. [2] Estimates for age groups are not age adjusted. [3] Persons who indicated only a single race group. [4] Persons who indicated more than one race group. [5] Persons of Hispanic or Latino origin may be of any race or combination of races. [6] Shown only for adults age 25 and over. [7] GED is General Educational Development high school equivalency diploma. [8] Based on a hierarchy of mutually exclusive categories. Persons with more than one type of health insurance were assigned to the first appropriate category in the hierarchy. [9] Figure has a relative standard error greater than 30% and less than or equal to 50%, and does not meet standards of reliability or precision.

Source: U.S. National Center for Health Statistics, 2015 National Health Interview Survey, "Tables of Summary Health Statistics," <https://www.cdc.gov/nchs/nhis/SHS.htm>, accessed January 2017.

Table 184. Percent Distribution of Health Care Visits by Selected Patient Characteristics: 2010 and 2015

[Covers visits to hospital emergency departments, home health care visits, and visits to doctor's offices, clinics, or some other place during a 12-month period. Excludes dental visits. Based on the National Health Interview Survey. See source, and Appendix III]

Characteristic	Percent distribution of health care visits							
	None		1–3 visits		4–9 visits		10 or more visits	
	2010	2015	2010	2015	2010	2015	2010	2015
All persons [1,2]	**15.6**	**15.0**	**45.4**	**48.4**	**25.8**	**23.7**	**13.2**	**12.8**
SEX [2]								
Male	20.4	19.5	46.4	49.8	22.7	20.3	10.5	10.5
Female	10.9	10.8	44.4	47.1	28.8	26.9	15.9	15.2
AGE								
Under 18 years	8.1	7.9	55.6	59.7	28.2	25.7	8.2	6.7
Under 6 years	3.7	4.7	48.9	52.2	36.8	35.7	10.6	7.5
6 to 17 years	10.4	9.5	59.1	63.3	23.6	20.9	6.9	6.4
18 to 44 years	24.2	23.3	43.9	46.9	20.6	18.7	11.3	11.1
45 to 64 years	14.8	13.7	42.8	45.5	26.1	24.5	16.4	16.3
65 years and over	5.3	5.5	33.8	35.5	36.7	33.9	24.2	25.1
75 years and over	4.1	4.2	31.0	32.0	38.0	34.2	27.0	29.6
RACE [2,3]								
White	15.3	14.8	44.9	47.8	26.1	24.0	13.7	13.4
Black or African American	15.7	14.5	47.2	50.2	24.7	24.1	12.4	11.2
American Indian or Alaska Native	19.4	20.6	40.3	39.0	28.1	23.3	12.2	17.1
Asian	20.4	18.2	49.9	54.7	22.1	18.7	7.6	8.5
Two or more races	13.9	17.3	42.3	41.5	25.2	25.0	18.6	16.2
HISPANIC ORIGIN AND RACE [2,3,4]								
Hispanic or Latino	23.5	22.3	43.2	45.9	22.6	21.9	10.7	9.9
Mexican	25.2	24.8	43.3	44.8	21.4	20.7	10.1	9.7
Not Hispanic or Latino	14.0	13.4	45.8	49.0	26.5	24.1	13.7	13.5
White, non-Hispanic	13.2	12.7	45.3	48.1	27.1	24.7	14.4	14.5
Black, non-Hispanic	15.6	14.7	47.3	50.5	24.9	23.8	12.2	11.0
HEALTH INSURANCE STATUS [5,6]								
Insured	12.3	13.3	48.5	51.7	26.1	23.3	13.1	11.7
Private	12.4	13.7	51.0	53.8	25.5	22.7	11.1	9.9
Medicaid	10.9	12.4	38.2	43.4	28.0	25.4	23.0	18.8
Uninsured	37.2	39.8	42.2	41.4	15.2	13.7	5.4	5.1
Insured continuously 12 months prior to interview	12.1	12.9	48.6	52.0	26.2	23.4	13.0	11.7
Uninsured for any period up to 12 months prior to interview	18.5	21.5	47.8	46.9	22.0	20.0	11.6	11.6
Uninsured more than 12 months prior to interview	43.8	48.7	39.7	37.8	12.6	10.4	3.9	3.1

[1] Includes other categories not shown separately. [2] Age adjusted to the year 2000 standard population. [3] Race groups include persons of Hispanic and non-Hispanic origin. Race-specific estimates are for persons reporting one race only. [4] Persons of Hispanic or Latino origin may be of any race. [5] For persons under age 65, at time of interview. Estimates are age-adjusted to the year 2000 standard population. [6] Health insurance categories are mutually exclusive. Persons who reported both Medicaid and private coverage are classified as having private coverage. Medicaid coverage includes State-sponsored health plans and the Children's Health Insurance Program (CHIP). The insured category also includes military plans, other government-sponsored health plans, and Medicare, not shown separately. Persons not covered by private insurance, Medicaid, CHIP, state-sponsored or other government-sponsored health plans, Medicare, or military plans are considered to have no health insurance coverage. Persons with only Indian Health Service coverage are considered to have no health insurance coverage.

Source: U.S. National Center for Health Statistics, *Health, United States, 2016*, May 2017. See also <http://www.cdc.gov/nchs/hus.htm>.

Table 185. Emergency Room Visits by Wait Time and Total Time Spent: 2012 and 2013

[130,870 represents 130,870,000. See headnote, Table 182]

Visit characteristic	2012		2013	
	Number of visits (1,000)	Percent	Number of visits (1,000)	Percent
Total visits [1]	**130,870**	**100.0**	**130,353**	**100.0**
TIME SPENT WAITING TO SEE MEDICAL PROFESSIONAL [2]				
Fewer than 15 minutes	39,242	30.0	38,885	29.8
15 to 59 minutes	43,946	33.6	48,137	36.9
1 hour, but less than 2 hours	14,160	10.8	14,448	11.1
2 hours, but less than 3 hours	4,526	3.5	4,774	3.7
3 hours, but less than 4 hours	1,871	1.4	1,903	1.5
4 hours, but less than 6 hours	1,156	0.9	1,184	0.9
6 hours or more	725	0.6	675	0.5
TIME SPENT IN EMERGENCY DEPARTMENT				
Less than 1 hour	15,448	11.8	15,972	12.3
1 hour, but less than 2 hours	29,866	22.8	32,623	25.0
2 hours, but less than 4 hours	43,924	33.6	44,036	33.8
4 hours, but less than 6 hours	19,811	15.1	18,008	13.8
6 hours, but less than 10 hours	10,064	7.7	8,358	6.4
10 hours, but less than 14 hours	2,312	1.8	1,957	1.5
14 hours, but less than 24 hours	1,611	1.2	1,683	1.3
24 hours or more	1,024	0.8	1,035	0.8

[1] Totals include nonresponse and nonapplicable categories. [2] Medical professional may be a medical doctor, doctor of osteopathy, physician assistant, or nurse practitioner.

Source: U.S. National Center for Health Statistics, *National Hospital Ambulatory Medical Care Survey: 2013 Emergency Department Summary Tables*, December 2016 and earlier reports. See also <https://www.cdc.gov/nchs/ahcd/index.htm>.

Table 186. Physician Office Visits by Sex and Leading Reason for Visit and Primary Diagnosis: 2014

[884,707 represents 884,707,000. Based on the 2014 National Ambulatory Medical Care Survey (NAMCS). NAMCS is an annual nationally representative sample survey of visits to nonfederal office-based patient care physicians, excluding anesthesiologists, radiologists, and pathologists. The sampling frame for the 2014 NAMCS was composed of all physicians contained in the master files maintained by the American Medical Association and the American Osteopathic Association. Data are subject to sampling and nonsampling errors]

Leading reason for visit	Number of visits (1,000)	Percent distribution Male [1]	Percent distribution Female [2]	Leading diagnosis for visit	Number of visits (1,000)	Percent distribution Male [1]	Percent distribution Female [2]
All visits [3]	884,707	100.0	100.0	All visits [3]	884,707	100.0	100.0
Progress visit [4]	118,655	14.3	12.8	Essential hypertension	40,323	5.0	4.2
General medical examination	62,485	7.9	6.4	Arthropathies and related disorders	34,024	3.3	4.2
Postoperative visit	25,497	2.6	3.1	Spinal disorders	33,199	3.8	3.7
Medication, other and unspecified kinds	20,898	2.4	2.3	General medical examination	32,479	4.2	3.3
Counseling, not otherwise specified	18,748	2.1	2.1	Routine infant/child health check	31,659	4.5	2.9
Cough	18,353	2.3	1.9	Diabetes mellitus	30,297	4.2	2.9
Other and unspecified test results	14,682	1.5	1.8	Acute upper respiratory infections, excluding pharyngitis	23,946	2.9	2.5
Knee symptoms	12,545	1.5	1.4	Malignant neoplasms	19,960	2.6	2.0
Hypertension	12,387	1.7	1.2	Rheumatism, excluding back	17,379	1.7	2.2
Diabetes mellitus	11,976	1.6	1.1	Specific procedures and aftercare	15,786	1.7	1.9
Gynecological examination	11,434	(X)	2.2	Heart disease, excluding ischemic	15,309	2.0	1.6
Stomach and abdominal pain, cramps and spasms	10,705	1.1	1.3	Disorders of lipid metabolism	13,408	1.7	1.4
Low back symptoms	10,501	1.3	1.1	Follow up examination	13,188	1.1	1.7
Well baby examination	10,213	1.3	1.1	Psychoses, excluding major depressive disorder	12,731	1.5	1.4
Prenatal examination, routine	9,860	(X)	1.9	Ischemic heart disease	11,534	2.1	0.7
Back symptoms	9,859	1.1	1.1	Benign neoplasms	11,388	1.3	1.3
Skin rash	9,550	1.2	1.0	Attention deficit disorder	11,351	1.7	0.9
Preoperative visit for surgery	8,808	0.9	1.1	Asthma	11,029	1.3	1.2
Symptoms referable to throat	8,181	1.0	0.9	Normal pregnancy	10,449	(X)	2.1
Depression	7,820	0.6	1.1	Gynecological examination	10,420	(X)	2.0
All other reasons	471,551	53.6	53.0	All other diagnoses [5]	484,850	53.3	55.9

X Not applicable. [1] Based on 375,947,000 visits made by males. [2] Based on 508,760,000 visits made by females. [3] Numbers may not sum to totals due to rounding. [4] Not otherwise specified. [5] Includes all other diagnoses not listed above, as well as unknown and blank diagnoses.

Source: U.S. National Center for Health Statistics, *National Ambulatory Medical Care Survey: 2014 State and National Summary Tables*, June 2017. See also <https://www.cdc.gov/nchs/ahcd/web_tables.htm>.

Table 187. Ambulatory Care Visits by Patient and Other Characteristics: Physician Offices, 2014, and Emergency Departments, 2013

[884,707 represents 884,707,000. Based on the annual National Ambulatory Medical Care Survey and National Hospital Ambulatory Medical Care Survey, and subject to sampling error; see source for details]

Characteristic	Physician office visits, 2014 Number (1,000)	Physician office visits, 2014 Per 100 persons [1]	Emergency department visits, 2013 Number (1,000)	Emergency department visits, 2013 Per 100 persons [1]
Total	884,707	282.0	130,353	41.9
AGE				
Under 15 years old	118,264	193.8	23,726	38.9
15 to 24 years old	60,414	140.5	19,709	45.9
25 to 44 years old	168,087	205.1	35,808	44.1
45 to 64 years old	273,423	330.4	30,358	36.9
65 years and over	264,518	588.5	20,752	47.8
65 to 74 years old	143,355	547.8	9,354	37.4
75 years old and over	121,164	645.4	11,398	61.9
PATIENT SEX				
Male	375,947	245.4	57,301	37.7
Female	508,760	317.1	73,052	45.9
PATIENT RACE/ETHNICITY [2]				
White	753,215	309.8	96,569	39.9
Black or African American	81,038	198.7	29,071	72.2
Other	50,455	169.4	4,713	16.4
Hispanic or Latino	117,776	215.2	19,916	37.3
EXPECTED PAYMENT SOURCE [3]				
Private insurance	530,288	(X)	46,969	(X)
Medicare	236,832	(X)	25,593	(X)
Medicaid/CHIP [4]	114,334	(X)	39,115	(X)
No insurance: [5]	44,554	(X)	19,623	(X)
Self pay	42,912	(X)	18,628	(X)
No charge/charity	1,710	(X)	1,196	(X)
Worker's compensation	8,517	(X)	1,421	(X)

X Not applicable. [1] Rates are based on Census Bureau July 1, 2014 estimates of the civilian noninstitutional population. [2] Race groups White, Black or African American, and Other include persons of Hispanic origin. Persons of Hispanic origin may be of any race. See source for information on missing and imputed data. [3] Estimates include all expected sources of payment reported at the visit. Other and unknown not shown separately. [4] Children's Health Insurance Program. [5] "No insurance" is defined as having only "self-pay" or "no charge/charity" as payment sources.

Source: U.S. National Center for Health Statistics, Ambulatory Health Care Data, "NAMCS and NHAMCS Web Tables: 2013 and 2014," <http://www.cdc.gov/nchs/ahcd/web_tables.htm>, accessed August 2017.

Table 188. Hospital Emergency Department Visits by Sex and Diagnosis: 2014

[Number in thousands (64,004 represents 64,004,000). Based on the National Hospital Ambulatory Medical Care Survey]

Leading diagnosis	Number (1,000)	Rate per 1,000 persons [1]	Leading diagnosis	Number (1,000)	Rate per 1,000 persons [1]
MALE			**FEMALE**		
All ages	**64,004**	**418**	**All ages**	**77,416**	**482**
Under 15 years old [2]	**14,572**	**468**	**Under 15 years old** [2]	**13,167**	**441**
Acute upper respiratory infections [3]	1,302	42	Acute upper respiratory infections [3]	1,522	51
Pyrexia (fever) of unknown origin	919	30	Pyrexia (fever) of unknown origin	818	27
Otitis media (ear infection) and eustachian tube disorders	785	25	Otitis media (ear infection) and eustachian tube disorders	734	25
Contusion with intact skin surface	552	18	Abdominal pain	460	15
Asthma	528	17	Contusion with intact skin surface	438	15
15 to 64 years old [2]	**40,227**	**394**	**15 to 64 years old** [2]	**51,676**	**489**
Abdominal pain	2,184	21	Abdominal pain	4,211	40
Chest pain	2,010	20	Chest pain	2,125	20
Spinal disorders	1,719	17	Complications of pregnancy, childbirth, and the puerperium	1,974	19
Open wound, excluding head	1,699	17	Spinal disorders	1,954	19
Cellulitis and abscess	1,606	16	Urinary tract infection, site not specified	1,691	16
65 years old and over [2]	**9,205**	**461**	**65 years old and over** [2]	**12,573**	**503**
Heart disease, excluding ischemic	421	21	Chest pain	664	27
Chest pain	409	20	Heart disease, excluding ischemic	527	21
Spinal disorders	[5] 334	17	Contusion with intact skin surface	480	19
Dyspnea and respiratory abnormalities [4]	297	15	Urinary tract infection, site not specified	451	18
Abdominal pain	244	12	Spinal disorders	425	17

[1] Based on the Census Bureau's July 1 estimates of the civilian noninstitutional population. [2] Includes other first-listed diagnoses, not shown separately. [3] Excluding pharyngitis. [4] Dyspnea is shortness of breath. [5] Estimate is considered unreliable.

Source: U.S. National Center for Health Statistics, National Hospital Ambulatory Medical Care Survey, unpublished data. See also <http://www.cdc.gov/nchs/ahcd/web_tables.htm>.

Table 189. Hospital Utilization Rates by Type of Hospital: 1990 to 2015

[In units, as indicated (21.9 represents 21,900,000)]

Type of hospital	1990	2000	2005	2010	2012	2013	2014	2015
COMMUNITY HOSPITALS [1]								
Admissions per 1,000 population [2]	125	117	119	114	110	106	104	104
Admissions per bed	34	40	44	44	43	42	42	43
Average length of stay (days) [3]	7.2	5.8	5.6	5.4	5.4	5.4	5.5	5.5
Outpatient visits per admission	9.7	15.8	16.6	18.5	19.6	20.2	21.0	21.7
Outpatient visits per 1,000 population [2]	1,207	1,852	1,976	2,108	2,150	2,145	2,174	2,247
Surgical operations (million)	21.9	26.1	27.5	27.3	26.8	26.6	26.4	26.5
Number per admission	0.7	0.8	0.8	0.8	0.8	0.8	0.8	0.8
NONFEDERAL PSYCHIATRIC								
Admissions per 1,000 population [2]	2.9	2.4	2.5	2.5	2.5	2.6	2.5	2.6
Days in hospital per 1,000 population [2]	190	93	89	77	69	67	65	67

[1] Nonfederal, short-term general, and other specialty hospitals. Other specialty hospitals include obstetrics and gynecology; eye, ear, nose, and throat; rehabilitation; orthopedic; and other individually described specialty services. Includes academic medical centers or other teaching hospitals if they are nonfederal short-term hospitals. Excluded are hospitals not accessible by the general public, such as prison hospitals or college infirmaries. [2] Based on Census Bureau estimated resident population as of July 1. Data for 1990, 2000, and 2010 based on enumerated resident population as of April 1. Other years are estimates, which reflect revisions based on the preceding decennial Census of Population. [3] Number of inpatient days divided by number of admissions.

Source: Health Forum LLC, an affiliate of the American Hospital Association, Chicago, IL, *AHA Hospital Statistics 2017 Edition* ©, and previous editions. See also <http://www.ahadata.com/>.

Table 190. Hospitals—Summary Characteristics: 2000 to 2015

[In units indicated (for beds, 984 represents 984,000). Covers hospitals accepted for registration by the American Hospital Association; see text, this section. Short-term hospitals have an average patient stay of less than 30 days; long-term, an average stay of longer duration. Special hospitals include obstetrics and gynecology; eye, ear, nose, and throat; rehabilitation; orthopedic; chronic; and other special hospitals except psychiatric, tuberculosis, alcoholism, and chemical dependency hospitals]

Item	2000	2005	2009	2010	2011	2012	2013	2014	2015
NUMBER									
All hospitals	**5,810**	**5,756**	**5,795**	**5,754**	**5,724**	**5,723**	**5,686**	**5,627**	**5,564**
With 100 beds or more	3,102	2,942	2,861	2,832	2,790	2,772	2,740	2,709	2,682
Nonfederal [1]	5,565	5,530	5,584	5,541	5,516	5,512	5,473	5,414	5,352
Community hospitals [2]	4,915	4,936	5,008	4,985	4,973	4,999	4,974	4,926	4,862
Nongovernmental nonprofit	3,003	2,958	2,918	2,904	2,903	2,894	2,904	2,870	2,845
For profit	749	868	998	1,013	1,025	1,068	1,060	1,053	1,034
State and local government	1,163	1,110	1,092	1,068	1,045	1,037	1,010	1,003	983
Long term general and special	131	115	115	109	110	88	80	74	77
Psychiatric	496	456	444	435	421	413	406	403	401
Tuberculosis	4	3	2	2	2	1	1	1	2
Federal	245	226	211	213	208	211	213	213	212
BEDS (1,000) [3]									
All hospitals	**984**	**947**	**944**	**942**	**924**	**921**	**915**	**902**	**898**
Rate per 1,000 population [4]	3.5	3.2	3.1	3.0	3.0	2.9	2.9	2.8	2.8
Beds per hospital	169	165	163	164	161	161	161	160	160
Nonfederal [1]	931	901	900	897	886	882	876	863	859
Community hospitals [2]	824	802	806	805	797	801	796	787	782
Rate per 1,000 population [4]	2.9	2.7	2.6	2.6	2.6	2.6	2.5	2.5	2.4
Nongovernmental nonprofit	583	561	556	556	548	545	544	535	531
For profit	110	114	122	125	128	135	135	136	135
State and local government	131	128	127	125	121	120	117	116	117
Long term general and special	18	15	16	15	15	11	10	8	8
Psychiatric	87	82	76	76	73	70	69	68	68
Tuberculosis	(Z)	(Z)	(Z)	(Z)	(Z)	(Z)	(Z)	(Z)	(Z)
Federal	53	46	45	45	38	39	39	39	39
AVERAGE DAILY CENSUS (1,000) [5]									
All hospitals	**650**	**656**	**641**	**627**	**615**	**600**	**592**	**584**	**588**
Community hospitals [2]	526	540	528	520	513	507	500	494	497
Nongovernmental nonprofit	382	388	375	368	362	354	351	344	346
For profit	61	68	70	71	73	77	76	77	77
State and local government	83	85	83	80	78	77	74	73	74
EXPENSES (bil. dol.) [6]									
All hospitals	**395.4**	**570.5**	**726.7**	**750.6**	**773.5**	**829.7**	**859.4**	**892.7**	**936.5**
Nonfederal [1]	371.5	533.7	676.6	698.2	722.3	775.4	801.5	828.4	872.0
Community hospitals [2]	356.6	515.7	656.2	678.0	702.1	756.9	782.0	808.9	851.5
Nongovernmental nonprofit	267.1	386.0	492.9	510.7	528.3	564.0	585.5	602.6	636.0
For profit	35.0	51.8	64.4	67.2	70.3	79.1	81.6	85.4	88.8
State and local government	54.5	77.9	98.9	100.1	103.4	113.8	115.0	120.9	126.7
Long term general and special	2.8	3.6	4.2	4.2	3.9	2.8	3.0	3.0	3.2
Psychiatric	11.9	13.9	15.1	15.8	15.6	15.4	16.1	16.3	16.8
Tuberculosis	(Z)	(Z)	(Z)	(Z)	(Z)	(Z)	(Z)	(Z)	(Z)
Federal	23.9	36.8	50.1	52.4	51.2	54.3	57.9	64.3	64.5
PERSONNEL (1,000) [7]									
All hospitals	**4,454**	**4,790**	**5,178**	**5,184**	**5,196**	**5,258**	**5,342**	**5,314**	**5,397**
Nonfederal [1]	4,157	4,479	4,814	4,825	4,864	4,927	4,984	4,945	5,056
Community hospitals [2]	3,911	4,260	4,585	4,600	4,650	4,731	4,786	4,755	4,859
Nongovernmental nonprofit	2,919	3,154	3,369	3,388	3,427	3,477	3,500	3,494	3,562
For profit	378	421	464	474	485	515	553	522	534
State and local government	614	681	751	738	738	739	734	739	762
Long term general and special	41	38	37	39	35	26	25	22	23
Psychiatric	200	182	183	182	175	169	171	167	172
Tuberculosis	1	1	(Z)	(Z)	(Z)	(Z)	(Z)	(Z)	(Z)
Federal	297	311	364	359	331	331	358	369	341
OUTPATIENT VISITS (mil.)									
Total	**592.7**	**673.7**	**742.0**	**750.4**	**754.5**	**778.0**	**787.4**	**802.7**	**832.3**
Emergency visits	106.9	118.9	131.4	131.5	133.4	137.3	137.5	140.2	145.3

Z Less than 500 or $50 million. [1] Includes hospital units of institutions. [2] Short-term (average length of stay less than 30 days) general and special (e.g., obstetrics and gynecology; eye, ear, nose and throat; rehabilitation, etc. except psychiatric, tuberculosis, alcoholism, and chemical dependency). Excludes hospital units of institutions. [3] Number of beds at end of reporting period. [4] Based on Census Bureau estimated resident population as of July 1. Data for 2000 and 2010 based on enumerated resident population as of April 1. Other years are estimates, which reflect revisions based on the preceding decennial Census of Population. [5] The average number of people served on an inpatient basis on a single day during the reporting period. [6] Excludes new construction. [7] Includes full-time equivalents of part-time personnel.

Source: Health Forum LLC, an affiliate of the American Hospital Association, Chicago, IL, *AHA Hospital Statistics 2017 Edition* ©, and previous editions. See also <http://www.ahadata.com/>.

Table 191. Community Hospital Summary Data by State: 2010 and 2015

[In units indicated (804.9 represents 804,900). Community hospitals are defined as all nonfederal, short-term general, and other special hospitals. Other special hospitals include obstetrics and gynecology; eye, ear, nose, and throat; rehabilitation; orthopedic; and other individually described specialty services. Community hospitals include academic medical centers or other teaching hospitals if they are nonfederal short-term hospitals. Excluded are hospitals not accessible by the general public, such as prison hospitals or college infirmaries]

State	Number of hospitals		Beds (1,000)		Patients admitted (1,000)		Average daily census [1] (1,000)		Outpatient visits (mil.)		Average cost per day (dol.)	
	2010	2015	2010	2015	2010	2015	2010	2015	2010	2015	2010	2015
United States	**4,985**	**4,862**	**804.9**	**782.2**	**35,149**	**33,260**	**519.5**	**494.4**	**651.4**	**722.1**	**1,910**	**2,271**
Alabama	105	95	15.1	14.7	642	617	9.2	9.4	8.8	8.7	1,372	1,491
Alaska	22	21	1.5	1.6	57	53	0.9	1.0	1.8	2.0	2,020	2,161
Arizona	73	71	13.4	13.5	712	620	8.7	8.0	8.1	8.8	2,173	2,485
Arkansas	85	80	9.5	9.4	370	351	5.2	5.0	5.0	5.6	1,477	1,625
California	343	342	70.4	70.1	3,424	3,261	47.8	45.7	51.7	57.0	2,566	3,341
Colorado	80	81	10.2	10.5	449	424	6.1	5.9	8.3	8.8	2,190	2,721
Connecticut	34	32	8.1	7.5	407	377	6.3	5.5	8.3	8.9	2,154	2,601
Delaware	7	7	2.2	2.1	102	106	1.6	1.6	1.8	2.3	2,227	2,814
District of Columbia	11	11	3.5	3.6	132	129	2.5	2.6	2.3	2.7	2,434	2,609
Florida	210	210	53.3	53.0	2,452	2,512	33.4	34.4	24.2	26.2	1,837	2,087
Georgia	154	141	25.5	24.5	961	968	16.8	16.8	14.3	16.7	1,338	1,665
Hawaii	26	24	3.1	2.6	111	110	2.3	2.0	2.2	2.5	1,755	2,349
Idaho	41	40	3.4	3.3	131	129	1.7	1.7	3.2	5.8	1,748	2,659
Illinois	189	188	33.3	31.8	1,543	1,386	20.7	18.7	32.6	37.6	1,983	2,394
Indiana	125	120	17.8	17.3	718	672	10.3	9.8	18.7	19.5	1,964	2,280
Iowa	118	118	10.1	9.6	342	325	5.7	5.4	11.0	11.1	1,288	1,472
Kansas	130	131	10.0	9.8	305	297	5.4	5.2	6.7	7.3	1,304	1,537
Kentucky	106	103	14.2	14.1	609	550	8.6	8.4	10.4	13.0	1,546	1,668
Louisiana	126	120	15.4	14.2	625	552	9.2	8.4	12.4	12.1	1,561	1,782
Maine	37	34	3.6	3.5	146	138	2.2	2.2	6.0	7.2	2,077	2,327
Maryland	47	50	11.7	11.8	708	594	8.7	8.3	8.4	9.4	2,383	2,514
Massachusetts	79	76	15.7	15.5	823	761	11.4	11.1	21.8	22.8	2,419	2,783
Michigan	156	147	25.6	24.7	1,208	1,168	17.0	16.1	30.3	35.7	1,959	2,159
Minnesota	133	130	15.3	14.4	592	547	9.9	9.2	11.1	12.2	1,731	2,113
Mississippi	96	95	12.9	12.2	403	359	7.0	6.8	4.6	5.5	1,154	1,343
Missouri	122	121	18.7	18.6	821	784	11.5	11.3	19.8	23.1	1,981	2,179
Montana	48	50	3.7	3.8	97	94	2.3	2.3	3.5	3.6	1,190	1,284
Nebraska	88	88	7.2	6.6	209	193	4.0	3.6	4.6	4.7	1,516	1,758
Nevada	36	36	5.2	5.5	241	261	3.6	4.1	2.7	3.0	1,885	1,887
New Hampshire	28	28	2.9	2.8	120	120	1.7	1.8	4.8	5.4	2,164	2,322
New Jersey	73	75	21.1	20.6	1,067	963	14.9	13.6	16.0	16.0	2,179	2,555
New Mexico	36	36	4.0	3.9	186	177	2.3	2.3	4.6	6.0	2,058	2,442
New York	185	170	59.5	52.8	2,510	2,216	47.2	41.3	53.7	57.5	1,883	2,475
North Carolina	117	113	23.0	21.6	1,038	1,005	16.0	15.0	18.3	19.9	1,633	2,010
North Dakota	41	40	3.3	3.2	94	92	2.0	1.8	3.1	2.7	1,342	1,726
Ohio	183	179	34.3	33.5	1,517	1,420	20.8	19.6	35.8	39.8	2,138	2,608
Oklahoma	113	110	11.2	11.1	429	393	6.4	5.9	5.7	6.2	1,499	1,798
Oregon	58	59	6.4	6.8	321	342	3.8	4.1	9.2	10.9	2,818	3,368
Pennsylvania	196	186	39.9	37.3	1,810	1,575	26.8	23.7	38.6	39.1	1,906	2,307
Rhode Island	11	11	2.5	2.3	123	115	1.7	1.6	2.7	2.3	2,325	2,759
South Carolina	67	68	12.5	12.3	523	522	8.2	7.7	6.4	8.3	1,788	1,938
South Dakota	53	53	4.1	4.0	101	100	2.6	2.8	2.0	2.4	1,113	1,218
Tennessee	134	121	20.8	19.8	833	827	12.5	12.5	11.4	12.3	1,462	1,704
Texas	426	404	61.4	62.7	2,580	2,549	36.5	37.4	38.3	41.8	1,943	2,292
Utah	44	47	5.1	5.3	224	236	2.7	2.8	5.5	7.8	2,233	2,612
Vermont	14	14	1.3	1.2	49	48	0.8	0.8	3.4	3.2	1,656	2,162
Virginia	89	92	17.7	17.8	777	787	11.8	12.1	13.8	17.0	1,736	1,933
Washington	86	90	11.5	12.0	589	593	7.2	7.7	11.8	13.5	2,810	3,248
West Virginia	56	54	7.3	6.9	278	255	4.4	4.1	6.7	7.5	1,323	1,570
Wisconsin	124	127	13.5	12.5	589	538	8.1	7.5	14.6	17.7	1,953	2,280
Wyoming	24	23	2.0	1.8	50	43	1.1	1.0	1.0	1.3	1,103	1,538

[1] The average number of people served on an inpatient basis on a single day during the reporting period.

Source: Health Forum LLC, an affiliate of the American Hospital Association, Chicago, IL, *AHA Hospital Statistics 2017 Edition* ©, and previous editions. See also <http://www.ahadata.com/>.

Table 192. Average Cost to Community Hospitals Per Patient: 1990 to 2015

[In dollars, except percent. Covers non-federal short-term general or specialty hospitals (excluding psychiatric or tuberculosis hospitals and hospital units of institutions). Total cost per patient based on total hospital expenses (payroll, employee benefits, professional fees, supplies, etc.). Data have been adjusted for outpatient visits]

Type of expense and hospital	1990	2000	2005	2009	2010	2011	2012	2013	2014	2015
Average cost per day, total	**687**	**1,149**	**1,522**	**1,853**	**1,910**	**1,960**	**2,090**	**2,157**	**2,212**	**2,271**
Annual percent change [1]	7.8	4.2	5.0	4.0	3.1	2.6	6.6	3.2	2.5	2.7
Nongovernmental nonprofit	692	1,182	1,585	1,957	2,025	2,088	2,214	2,289	2,346	2,413
For profit	752	1,057	1,412	1,574	1,629	1,628	1,747	1,791	1,798	1,831
State and local government	635	1,064	1,329	1,611	1,625	1,667	1,831	1,878	1,974	2,013
Average cost per stay, total	**4,947**	**6,649**	**8,793**	**10,043**	**10,313**	**10,533**	**11,221**	**11,651**	**12,015**	**12,359**
Nongovernmental nonprofit	5,001	6,717	8,670	10,379	10,652	10,933	11,563	12,000	12,385	12,755
For profit	4,727	5,642	7,351	8,037	8,336	8,263	8,861	9,296	9,414	9,510
State and local government	4,838	7,106	8,793	10,068	10,283	10,532	11,668	12,028	12,601	13,070

[1] Change from immediate prior year.

Source: Health Forum LLC, an affiliate of the American Hospital Association, Chicago, IL, *AHA Hospital Statistics 2017 Edition* ©, and previous editions. See also <http://www.ahadata.com/>.

Table 193. Selected Cosmetic Plastic Surgery and Nonsurgical Procedures: 2005 to 2016

[In thousands (11,428.8 represents 11,428,800). As of December 31. The final data are projected to reflect nationwide statistics and are based on a survey of doctors who have been certified by the American Board of Medical Specialties recognized boards, including but not limited to the American Board of Plastic Surgery. Data for the procedures include but are not limited to those performed by American Society for Aesthetic Plastic Surgery (ASAPS) members. ASAPS members are plastic surgeons certified by the American Board of Plastic Surgery who specialize in cosmetic surgery of the face and the entire body]

Procedure	2005	2010	2012	2013	2014	2015	2016
Total all procedures	**11,428.8**	**9,183.2**	**10,105.2**	**11,248.7**	**10,578.4**	**12,792.4**	**13,654.3**
Total surgical procedures [1]	**2,131.0**	**1,624.3**	**1,688.7**	**1,792.7**	**1,688.8**	**1,912.5**	**1,979.6**
Liposuction	455.5	289.0	313.0	363.9	342.5	396.0	414.3
Breast augmentation	364.6	318.1	330.6	313.3	286.7	305.9	310.4
Abdominoplasty (tummy tuck)	169.3	144.9	156.5	160.1	164.0	180.7	181.5
Blepharoplasty (eyelid surgery)	231.5	152.1	153.2	161.4	165.7	169.7	173.9
Breast lift	121.0	121.4	127.8	137.2	132.9	149.0	161.4
Total nonsurgical procedures [1]	**9,297.7**	**7,558.9**	**8,416.5**	**9,456.0**	**8,898.7**	**10,879.9**	**11,674.8**
Botulinum toxin injection [2]	3,294.8	2,437.2	3,257.9	3,766.1	3,588.2	4,267.0	4,597.9
Hyaluronic acid [3]	1,194.2	1,315.1	1,423.7	1,872.2	1,696.6	2,148.3	2,494.8
Hair removal (laser or pulsed light)	1,566.9	936.3	883.9	901.6	828.5	1,136.8	1,035.8
Photorejuvenation [4]	(X)	381.5	337.5	456.6	370.5	482.8	657.2
Chemical peel	556.2	493.9	443.8	444.3	484.1	603.3	616.2
Total female procedures	**10,443.8**	**8,586.7**	**9,136.7**	**10,349.2**	**9,591.8**	**11,572.4**	**12,433.5**
Total surgical procedures [1]	**1,918.1**	**1,479.7**	**1,528.2**	**1,694.3**	**1,593.6**	**1,715.8**	**1,795.1**
Liposuction	402.9	251.8	271.4	312.2	302.0	344.7	369.3
Breast augmentation	364.6	318.1	330.6	313.3	286.7	305.9	310.4
Abdominoplasty (tummy tuck)	164.1	137.9	149.0	151.2	156.4	172.6	173.5
Breast lift	121.0	121.4	127.8	137.2	132.9	149.0	161.4
Blepharoplasty (eyelid surgery)	198.1	131.4	129.9	133.2	137.9	139.0	145.9
Breast reduction	160.5	138.2	112.8	122.8	114.5	103.1	112.1
Total nonsurgical procedures [1]	**8,525.7**	**7,107.1**	**7,608.5**	**8,654.9**	**7,998.1**	**9,856.6**	**10,638.4**
Botulinum toxin injection [2]	2,990.7	2,211.9	2,915.9	3,381.5	3,174.9	3,828.5	4,144.6
Hyaluronic acid [3]	1,149.2	1,245.3	1,318.2	1,739.0	1,561.0	1,989.3	2,326.0
Hair removal (laser or pulsed light)	1,334.7	817.4	757.5	773.3	721.9	1,006.7	910.2
Photorejuvenation [4]	(X)	345.5	308.8	413.2	318.8	418.3	596.4
Chemical peel	533.0	469.6	418.8	412.9	452.9	561.4	574.1
Microdermabrasion [5]	939.5	416.3	454.1	452.4	372.2	519.2	547.9
Laser skin resurfacing (full field ablative)	432.6	518.3	401.9	334.0	381.9	309.2	287.7
Sclerotherapy [6]	548.0	435.0	283.2	367.4	305.4	314.6	265.0
Total male procedures	**984.9**	**750.1**	**968.5**	**1,070.4**	**1,071.8**	**1,219.9**	**1,220.8**
Total surgical procedures [1]	**212.9**	**142.6**	**160.5**	**188.8**	**171.3**	**196.6**	**184.5**
Liposuction	52.5	37.2	41.6	51.7	40.5	51.4	45.0
Male breast reduction (to treat gynecomastia)	17.7	18.3	22.7	22.6	24.2	30.5	31.4
Blepharoplasty (eyelid surgery)	33.4	20.7	23.3	28.2	27.8	30.7	28.0
Rhinoplasty (nose reshaping)	45.9	30.1	30.0	26.8	32.6	30.9	26.2
Facelift	13.0	10.4	11.4	12.3	15.0	13.7	13.7
Otoplasty (ear surgery)	11.4	10.8	12.1	15.9	11.7	11.8	10.5
Total nonsurgical procedures [1]	**772.0**	**607.4**	**808.0**	**881.7**	**900.5**	**1,023.3**	**1,036.3**
Botulinum toxin injection [2]	304.1	225.2	342.0	384.7	413.4	438.5	453.3
Hyaluronic acid [3]	45.0	69.8	105.5	133.2	135.7	159.1	168.8
Hair removal (laser or pulsed light)	232.2	118.9	126.4	128.3	106.6	130.1	125.6
Photorejuvenation [4]	(X)	35.9	28.7	43.4	51.7	64.5	60.7
Chemical peel	23.2	24.3	25.1	31.4	31.2	41.9	42.1
Microdermabrasion [5]	84.4	34.4	44.8	27.5	44.8	38.5	40.2

X Not applicable. [1] Totals include procedures not shown separately. [2] Includes Botox, Dysport, and Xeomin. [3] In 2003, the FDA approved hyaluronic acid injections for filling soft tissue defects such as facial wrinkles. [4] Intense pulse light (IPL) laser treatment for facial rejuvenation, and addressing pigmentation issues and wrinkles. [5] Procedure for reducing fine lines, "crow's feet," age spots, and acne scars. [6] Treatment of varicose and spider veins.

Source: The American Society for Aesthetic Plastic Surgery, 2016 Cosmetic Surgery National Data Bank–Statistics ©, and earlier reports. See also <http://www.surgery.org/media/statistics>.

Table 194. Organ Transplants: 2000 to 2016

[As of end of year. Based on Organ Procurement and Transplantation Network data; data are from work supported in part by Health Resources and Services Administration contract 234-2005-37011C. The content is the responsibility of the authors alone and does not necessarily reflect the views or policies of the Department of Health and Human Services, nor does mention of trade names, commercial products, or organizations imply endorsement by the U.S. Government]

Procedure	Number of procedures					Number of people waiting				
	2000	2005	2010	2015	2016	2000	2005	2010	2015	2016
Transplant: [1]										
Heart....................	2,199	2,125	2,332	2,804	3,191	4,164	3,004	3,202	4,199	4,047
Heart-lung..............	48	35	42	15	18	209	143	70	49	48
Lung.....................	959	1,406	1,769	2,057	2,327	3,679	3,192	1,824	1,553	1,430
Liver....................	5,001	6,444	6,291	7,127	7,841	17,132	17,831	16,857	15,287	14,859
Kidney..................	13,631	16,485	16,900	17,879	19,060	50,426	68,429	93,486	108,846	106,895
Kidney-pancreas.......	915	903	828	719	798	2,553	2,571	2,293	2,033	1,841
Pancreas...............	439	542	349	228	215	1,032	1,706	1,431	1,040	965
Intestine...............	82	178	151	141	147	151	205	265	264	275
Multi-organ............	222	522	560	891	985	(NA)	(NA)	(NA)	(NA)	(NA)

NA Not available. [1] Kidney-pancreas and heart-lung transplants are each counted as one procedure. All other multiorgan transplants are included in the multi-organ row.

Source: U.S. Department of Health and Human Services, Health Resources and Services Administration, Organ Procurement and Transplantation Network (OPTN), <https://optn.transplant.hrsa.gov/data/view-data-reports/>, accessed July 2017; and unpublished data, based on OPTN data as of January 31, 2017.

Table 195. Cancer Survival Rates by Race and Type/Body Site and Year of Diagnosis: 1993 to 2013

[For invasive cancer, unless otherwise noted. For top 15 cancers ranked by incidence rates per 100,000 persons for 2010-2014 period. Based on follow-up of patients into 2014. The 5-year relative survival rate represents the proportion of patients alive 5 years after their cancer diagnosis, compared to similar persons among the general population without cancer. Data are based on information collected as part of the National Cancer Institute's Surveillance, Epidemiology and End Results (SEER) program, a collection of population-based registries in 9 areas]

Cancer type	5-year relative survival rates by year of diagnosis (percent)									
	White					Black				
	1993 to 1995	1996 to 1998	1999 to 2001	2003 to 2006	2007 to 2013	1993 to 1995	1996 to 1998	1999 to 2001	2003 to 2006	2007 to 2013
All types [1].....................	**62.4**	**64.4**	**67.2**	**68.8**	**70.1**	**52.8**	**55.2**	**58.0**	**59.9**	**63.3**
Female breast...................	87.6	89.4	90.8	91.7	92.2	72.7	76.2	78.9	77.9	82.7
Lung and bronchus..............	14.5	14.8	15.5	17.1	19.6	12.8	12.3	12.6	13.4	17.3
Prostate...........................	95.9	97.9	99.7	99.8	99.6	91.7	94.9	97.3	97.8	97.4
Colon and rectum................	60.5	63.0	66.5	67.0	67.1	51.7	53.9	54.1	57.0	58.8
Melanoma of skin................	89.6	90.9	92.2	93.2	93.6	[4] 69.5	[4] 73.9	[4] 73.2	[4] 72.9	[4] 69.0
Urinary bladder [2]................	81.0	79.8	81.0	80.9	78.6	60.6	62.7	67.5	63.8	65.4
Non-Hodgkin's lymphoma [3].....	53.2	59.4	64.9	71.6	74.2	42.1	54.6	55.7	62.4	67.1
Kidney and renal pelvis..........	62.0	62.0	64.9	71.6	74.8	57.4	66.9	63.9	68.1	76.3
Thyroid...........................	95.6	95.9	96.9	97.8	98.4	93.2	95.0	92.0	96.6	96.9
Leukemia [3].......................	48.6	49.6	52.0	60.4	64.8	41.3	38.6	43.3	53.3	57.8
Corpus and uterus...............	84.9	85.1	85.9	85.5	85.3	58.5	61.4	61.4	61.3	64.7
Pancreas........................	3.9	4.1	5.0	6.2	8.9	3.7	3.4	5.6	5.0	7.5
Oral cavity and pharynx.........	60.1	59.9	62.2	66.1	69.2	37.9	36.1	44.6	45.1	49.3
Liver and intrahepatic bile duct.............................	5.2	8.4	10.3	15.2	17.7	4.0	4.6	7.6	10.5	14.0
Stomach........................	20.0	20.3	22.3	26.9	29.9	19.3	22.6	23.2	28.6	31.4

[1] Includes other sites, not shown separately. [2] Invasive and in situ. [3] All types combined. [4] The standard error is between 5 and 10 percentage points.

Source: U.S. National Institutes of Health, National Cancer Institute, Surveillance Epidemiology and End Results Program, "SEER Cancer Statistics Review (CSR), 1975-2014," <https://seer.cancer.gov/statistics/summaries.html>, accessed April 2017.

Table 196. Top 15 Cancers Among Men and Women by Race/Ethnicity: 2010 to 2014

[Rates per 100,000 population, age-adjusted to the 2000 U.S. standard population. Cancer incidence measures the number of newly diagnosed cancers occurring during a year. Data are for 2010 to 2014 period, based on cancer registries in 18 areas monitored by the Surveillance, Epidemiology, and End Results (SEER) Program, covering about 30 percent of the U.S. population. See source for more information]

Cancer by site, and sex	All race/ethnicities		White		Black		Hispanic [1]	
	Rank	Rate	Rank	Rate	Rank	Rate	Rank	Rate
TOTAL								
All Sites.........................	(X)	442.7	(X)	451.8	(X)	459.3	(X)	340.6
Breast..........................	1	67.0	1	67.8	2	71.1	1	49.8
Lung and bronchus.....................	2	55.8	2	57.3	3	63.0	4	28.8
Prostate [2]........................	3	54.7	3	52.1	1	80.7	2	43.7
Colon and rectum...................	4	40.1	4	39.3	4	48.7	3	33.9
Melanoma of the skin..............	5	22.3	5	26.6	(X)	(X)	(X)	(X)
Urinary bladder....................	6	19.8	6	21.7	10	12.5	11	11.0
Non-Hodgkin lymphoma..............	7	19.5	7	20.4	7	14.6	5	17.8
Kidney and renal pelvis................	8	15.6	8	16.1	5	18.0	6	15.4
Thyroid..........................	9	14.2	9	14.9	15	8.7	8	12.3
Leukemia........................	10	13.7	10	14.5	11	10.9	12	10.6
Corpus and uterus, NOS [2,6]........	11	13.6	11	13.8	8	14.0	9	11.6
Pancreas........................	12	12.5	12	12.5	6	15.5	10	11.1
Oral cavity and pharynx................	13	11.2	13	11.7	14	9.1	14	6.6
Liver and IBD [3]...................	14	8.6	14	7.8	13	10.1	7	13.2
Stomach.........................	15	7.3	(X)	(X)	12	10.2	13	10.5
Myeloma.........................	(X)	(X)	(X)	(X)	9	13.2	15	6.1
Brain and ONS [4]...................	(X)	(X)	15	7.0	(X)	(X)	(X)	(X)
MEN								
All Sites.........................	(X)	492.4	(X)	497.1	(X)	549.7	(X)	372.2
Prostate.........................	1	119.8	1	112.8	1	188.7	1	98.3
Lung and bronchus.....................	2	65.7	2	65.9	2	83.7	3	35.3
Colon and rectum...................	3	46.0	3	45.0	3	56.4	2	40.0
Urinary bladder....................	4	34.9	4	38.1	5	21.0	7	19.3
Melanoma of the skin..............	5	29.2	5	34.4	(X)	(X)	(X)	(X)
Non-Hodgkin lymphoma..............	6	23.7	6	24.8	6	17.6	4	20.7
Kidney and renal pelvis................	7	21.4	7	21.9	4	25.0	5	20.2
Leukemia........................	8	17.6	8	18.5	11	14.0	9	12.9
Oral cavity and pharynx................	9	16.9	9	17.6	10	14.2	11	9.8
Pancreas........................	10	14.2	10	14.2	7	17.0	10	11.8
Liver and IBD [3]...................	11	13.3	11	11.9	8	16.7	6	19.7
Stomach.........................	12	9.9	12	9.0	12	13.6	8	13.0
Myeloma.........................	13	8.3	14	7.8	9	15.9	12	7.7
Brain and ONS [4]...................	14	7.5	13	8.3	15	4.8	13	5.7
Esophagus.......................	15	7.3	15	7.7	14	6.9	(X)	(X)
Larynx..........................	(X)	(X)	(X)	(X)	13	8.5	(X)	(X)
Thyroid..........................	(X)	(X)	(X)	(X)	(X)	(X)	14	5.2
Testis...........................	(X)	(X)	(X)	(X)	(X)	(X)	15	5.1
WOMEN								
All Sites.........................	(X)	408.7	(X)	421.5	(X)	397.4	(X)	323.3
Breast..........................	1	124.9	1	127.7	1	125.1	1	93.1
Lung and bronchus.....................	2	48.4	2	50.8	2	49.0	3	24.2
Colon and rectum...................	3	35.1	3	34.4	3	43.2	2	29.1
Corpus and uterus, NOS [6]............	4	25.7	4	26.3	4	24.8	4	21.9
Thyroid..........................	5	21.0	5	22.4	6	13.0	5	19.3
Melanoma of the skin..............	6	17.3	6	20.9	(X)	(X)	(X)	(X)
Non-Hodgkin lymphoma..............	7	16.0	7	16.9	8	12.2	6	15.4
Ovary [5]........................	8	11.7	8	12.2	10	9.4	8	10.6
Pancreas........................	9	11.1	11	11.0	5	14.3	9	10.5
Kidney and renal pelvis................	10	10.7	10	11.0	7	12.6	7	11.5
Leukemia........................	11	10.7	9	11.3	11	8.8	11	8.8
Urinary bladder....................	12	8.4	12	9.1	14	6.8	15	4.9
Cervix uteri......................	13	7.4	13	7.4	12	8.7	10	9.1
Oral cavity and pharynx................	14	6.2	14	6.4	15	5.1	(X)	(X)
Brain and ONS [4]...................	15	5.3	15	5.9	(X)	(X)	(X)	(X)
Myeloma.........................	(X)	(X)	(X)	(X)	9	11.4	14	4.9
Stomach.........................	(X)	(X)	(X)	(X)	13	7.8	12	8.5
Liver and IBD [3]...................	(X)	(X)	(X)	(X)	(X)	(X)	13	7.6

X Not applicable. [1] Persons of Hispanic origin may be of any race. [2] Rates for sex-specific cancer sites are calculated using the population for both sexes combined. [3] IBD, intrahepatic bile duct. [4] ONS, other nervous system. [5] Ovary excludes borderline cases or histologies 8442, 8451, 8462, 8472, and 8473. [6] NOS, not otherwise specified.

Source: National Institutes of Health, National Cancer Institute, Surveillance, Epidemiology, and End Results Program, "SEER Cancer Statistics Review, 1975-2014," <http://seer.cancer.gov/statistics/summaries.html>, accessed April 2017.

Table 197. Selected Notifiable Diseases—Cases Reported: 1990 to 2014

[In thousands only where indicated (690.2 represents 690,200). Interpret figures with caution. Although reporting of some of these diseases is incomplete, the figures are of value in indicating trends of disease incidence. Includes cases imported from outside the U.S.]

Disease	1990	1995	2000	2005	2010	2011	2012	2013	2014
AIDS/HIV [1]	41,595	71,547	40,758	41,120	35,741	35,266	35,361	34,969	35,606
Botulism [2]	92	97	138	135	112	153	168	152	161
Brucellosis (undulant fever)	82	98	87	120	115	79	114	99	92
Coccidoidomycosis	([11])	1,212	2,867	6,542	([11])	22,634	17,802	9,438	8,232
Cryptosporidiosis	([11])	2,970	3,128	5,659	8,944	9,250	7,956	9,056	8,682
Dengue fever and dengue hemorrhagic fever [3]	([11])	([11])	([11])	([11])	700	254	547	843	680
Giardiasis	([11])	([11])	([11])	19,733	19,811	16,747	15,178	15,106	14,554
Haemophilus influenza	([11])	1,180	1,398	2,304	3,151	3,539	3,418	3,792	3,541
Hansen disease (Leprosy)	198	144	91	87	98	82	82	81	88
Hepatitis virus, acute: A	31,441	31,582	13,397	4,488	1,670	1,398	1,562	1,781	1,239
Hepatitis virus, acute: B	21,102	10,805	8,036	5,119	3,374	2,903	2,895	3,050	2,791
Hepatitis virus, acute: C	2,553	4,576	3,197	652	849	1,229	1,782	2,138	2,204
Invasive pneumococcal disease [4]	(X)	(X)	(X)	(X)	16,569	17,138	15,635	17,193	15,356
Legionellosis	1,370	1,241	1,127	2,301	3,346	4,202	3,688	4,954	5,166
Listeriosis	([11])	([11])	755	896	821	870	727	735	769
Lyme disease	([11])	11,700	17,730	23,305	30,158	33,097	30,831	36,307	33,461
Malaria	1,292	1,419	1,560	1,494	1,773	1,724	1,503	1,594	1,653
Measles	27,786	309	86	66	63	220	55	187	667
Meningococcal infections	2,451	3,243	2,256	1,245	833	759	551	556	433
Mumps	5,292	906	338	314	2,612	404	229	584	1,223
Pertussis (whooping cough)	4,570	5,137	7,867	25,616	27,550	18,719	48,277	28,639	32,971
Rabies, animal	4,826	7,811	6,934	5,915	4,331	4,357	4,541	4,248	5,988
Rubella [5]	1,125	128	176	11	5	4	9	9	6
Salmonellosis [6]	48,603	45,970	39,574	45,322	54,424	51,887	53,800	50,634	51,455
Shiga toxin-producing E. coli (STEC)	([11])	([11])	([11])	([11])	5,476	6,047	6,463	6,663	6,179
Shigellosis [7]	27,077	32,080	22,922	16,168	14,786	13,352	15,283	12,729	20,745
Spotted fever rickettsiosis (including Rocky Mountain spotted fever) [8]	([11])	([11])	495	1,936	1,985	2,802	4,470	3,359	3,757
Streptococcal toxic-shock syndrome	([11])	10	83	129	142	168	194	224	259
Tetanus	64	41	35	27	26	36	37	26	25
Toxic-shock syndrome	322	191	135	90	82	78	65	71	59
Tuberculosis [9]	25,701	22,860	16,377	14,097	11,182	10,528	9,945	9,582	9,421
Typhoid fever	552	369	377	324	467	390	354	338	349
Varicella (chickenpox) [10]	173,099	120,624	27,382	32,242	15,427	14,513	13,447	11,362	10,176
West Nile virus, neuroinvasive [3]	([11])	([11])	([11])	1,309	629	486	2,872	1,267	1,347
West Nile virus, nonneuroinvasive [3]	([11])	([11])	([11])	1,691	392	226	2,801	1,202	858
Sexually transmitted diseases:									
Chlamydia (1,000)	([11])	477.6	702.1	976.4	1,307.9	1,412.8	1,423.0	1,401.9	1,441.8
Gonorrhea (1,000)	690.2	392.8	359.0	339.6	309.3	321.8	334.8	333.0	350.1
Syphilis (1,000)	134.3	69.0	31.6	33.3	45.8	46.0	49.9	56.5	63.5

X Not applicable. [1] Acquired immunodeficiency syndrome/Human immunodeficiency virus. Includes all cases reported to the Division of HIV/AIDS Prevention, National Center for HIV/AIDS, Viral Hepatitis, STD, and TB Prevention. In 2008 CDC published a revised HIV case definition which combined definitions for HIV infection and AIDS into a single case definition for HIV infection that includes AIDS. [2] Includes foodborne, infant, wound, and unspecified cases. [3] Totals reported to the Division of Vector-Borne Diseases (DVBD), National Center for Emerging and Zoonotic Infectious Diseases (NCEZID) (ArboNET Surveillance). [4] Data for 2010 and 2011 reported as Streptococcus pneumoniae invasive disease. [5] German measles. Excludes congenital syndrome. [6] Excludes typhoid fever. [7] Bacillary dysentery. [8] Data for Rocky Mountain spotted fever are now reported under a new category called Spotted fever rickettsiosis (including Rocky Mountain spotted fever). [9] Totals reported to the Division of Tuberculosis Elimination, NCHHSTP. [10] Varicella (chickenpox) was removed from the nationally notifiable disease list in 1981; it became nationally notifiable again in 2003. [11] Disease was not notifiable.

Source: U.S. Centers for Disease Control and Prevention, "Summary of Notifiable Infectious Diseases and Conditions—United States, 2014," *Morbidity and Mortality Weekly Report,* 63:54, October 14, 2016, and earlier reports. See also <http://www.cdc.gov/mmwr/mmwr_nd/index.html>.

Table 198. HIV Diagnoses and Chlamydia and Lyme Disease Cases Reported by State: 2014

State	HIV diagnoses [1]	Chlamydia [2]	Lyme disease	State	HIV diagnoses [1]	Chlamydia [2]	Lyme disease	State	HIV diagnoses [1]	Chlamydia [2]	Lyme disease
U.S.	35,606	1,441,789	33,461	IA	98	11,804	194	NC	1,378	47,147	170
				KS	112	11,116	20	ND	24	3,451	14
				KY	235	17,664	44	OH	932	54,858	119
AL	517	29,010	64	LA	1,400	28,955	2	OK	276	20,662	–
AK	41	5,789	8	ME	40	3,530	1,401	OR	215	15,508	45
AZ	705	32,397	21	MD	778	27,424	1,373	PA	1,094	50,536	7,487
AR	283	15,605	–	MA	474	21,271	5,304	RI	82	4,349	904
CA	3,988	176,308	73	MI	703	44,256	127	SC	741	28,087	37
CO	361	21,863	–	MN	245	19,907	1,416	SD	25	4,166	2
CT	248	13,382	2,360	MS	463	19,605	2	TN	729	30,793	17
DE	105	4,473	417	MO	468	27,981	10	TX	3,690	131,219	40
DC	242	5,293	40	MT	15	4,193	7	UT	37	8,223	13
FL	5,257	84,194	155	NE	81	7,499	7	VT	14	2,237	599
GA	1,401	51,945	4	NV	388	11,841	6	VA	912	36,048	1,346
HI	82	6,419	([3])	NH	29	3,586	724	WA	437	26,577	15
ID	12	5,442	9	NJ	1,029	29,904	3,286	WV	81	4,719	136
IL	1,171	66,536	233	NM	124	11,558	–	WI	212	23,154	1,361
IN	431	28,519	110	NY	3,192	98,814	3,736	WY	9	1,972	3

– Represents zero. [1] Total number of HIV diagnoses reported to the Division of HIV/AIDS Prevention, National Center for HIV/AIDS, Viral Hepatitis, STD, and TB Prevention, as of December 31, 2014. [2] As of June 10, 2015. [3] Not reportable.

Source: U.S. Centers for Disease Control and Prevention, "Summary of Notifiable Infectious Diseases and Conditions—United States, 2014," *Morbidity and Mortality Weekly Report,* 63:54, October 14, 2016. See also <https://www.cdc.gov/mmwr/mmwr_nd/index.html>.

Table 199. Estimated Number of Persons with Stage 3 HIV Infection (AIDS) by Year of Diagnosis, Sex and Transmission Category: 2010 to 2015

[Data reported to the CDC as of June 30, 2016. HIV infection is classified as stage 3 (AIDS) when the immune system of a person infected with human immunodeficiency virus becomes severely compromised (measured by CD4 lymphocyte count or percentages) and/or the person becomes ill with an AIDS-defining opportunistic illness. Data cover the 50 states, the District of Columbia, and 6 U.S. dependent areas (American Samoa, Guam, Northern Mariana Islands, Puerto Rico, Republic of Palau, and the U.S. Virgin Islands). As of April 2008, all jurisdictions had implemented confidential name-based HIV infection reporting. Beginning with the 2015 *HIV Surveillance Report,* data are presented without statistical adjustments for delays in reporting cases to the CDC. Data may not be representative of all persons with HIV; completeness of HIV infection reporting is estimated at more than 80%. See source for more information]

Transmission category and sex	2010	2011	2012	2013	2014	2015	Cumulative through 2015 [1]
Total, all ages [2]	28,187	26,377	25,372	24,202	19,883	18,538	1,252,890
Males age 13 and over, total	21,053	19,736	19,027	18,334	14,887	13,996	985,835
Male-to-male sexual contact	14,190	13,619	13,332	13,121	10,582	10,133	596,000
Injection drug use	2,158	1,797	1,676	1,436	1,243	1,058	199,956
Male-to-male sexual contact and injection drug use	1,429	1,257	1,180	994	770	770	88,910
Heterosexual contact [3]	3,153	2,939	2,724	2,655	2,215	1,936	89,121
Other [4]	123	124	115	128	77	99	11,848
Females age 13 and over, total	7,113	6,623	6,334	5,859	4,918	4,513	257,166
Injection drug use	1,472	1,320	1,202	1,060	888	792	93,805
Heterosexual contact [3]	5,507	5,171	5,026	4,663	3,936	3,639	157,229
Other [4]	133	132	106	136	94	82	6,132

[1] From the beginning of the epidemic through 2015. [2] Because column totals for estimated numbers were calculated independently of the values for the subpopulations, the values in each column may not sum to the column total. [3] Heterosexual contact with a person known to have, or to be at high risk for, HIV infection. [4] Includes hemophilia, blood transfusion, perinatal exposure, and risk factor not reported or not identified.

Source: U.S. Centers for Disease Control and Prevention, *HIV Surveillance Report: Diagnoses of HIV Infection in the United States and Dependent Areas, 2015,* Vol. 27, November 2016. See also <https://www.cdc.gov/hiv/library/reports/hiv-surveillance.html>.

Table 200. Estimated Number of Persons Living with HIV Infection Ever Classified as Stage 3 (AIDS) Diagnosis by Selected Characteristics: 2010 to 2014

[See headnote, Table 199]

Characteristic and transmission category	2010	2011	2012	2013	2014
Total persons [1]	488,288	500,732	512,558	523,715	530,931
AGE AS OF END OF YEAR					
Less than 13 years [2]	470	387	329	282	311
13 and 14 years	327	257	198	161	137
15 to 19 years	2,587	2,336	2,011	1,738	1,335
20 to 24 years	7,633	8,125	8,373	8,376	7,628
25 to 34 years	44,100	44,814	45,449	46,190	46,066
35 to 44 years	124,292	116,937	110,977	105,493	99,881
45 to 54 years	195,105	200,067	202,262	202,908	200,827
55 to 64 years	90,075	100,519	111,215	121,774	132,368
65 years and over	23,699	27,290	31,744	36,793	42,378
RACE/ETHNICITY					
American Indian/Alaska Native	1,322	1,374	1,431	1,470	1,516
Asian [3]	4,997	5,290	5,589	5,891	6,181
Black/African American	197,187	203,207	209,096	214,547	218,210
Hispanic/Latino [4]	112,986	116,041	119,107	121,979	123,897
Native Hawaiian/Other Pacific Islander	398	420	440	455	468
White	151,589	154,102	156,239	158,410	159,641
Multiple races	19,809	20,298	20,656	20,963	21,018
TRANSMISSION CATEGORY [5]					
Males age 13 and over, total	371,686	381,144	390,157	398,786	404,280
Male-to-male sexual contact	232,911	241,224	249,361	257,345	262,924
Injection drug use	57,859	57,311	56,731	56,064	55,270
Male-to-male sexual contact and injection drug use	34,369	34,490	34,557	34,471	34,186
Heterosexual contact [6]	42,083	43,599	44,951	46,279	47,246
Other [7]	4,465	4,520	4,557	4,627	4,655
Females age 13 and over, total	116,132	119,201	122,072	124,647	126,340
Injection drug use	33,199	33,151	33,084	32,898	32,613
Heterosexual contact [6]	79,360	82,360	85,228	87,884	89,791
Other [7]	3,574	3,690	3,760	3,866	3,936
Children under age 13 at end of year [2]	470	387	329	282	311
Perinatal	450	363	306	260	278
Other [7]	20	24	23	22	33

[1] Because column totals were calculated independently of the values for the subpopulations, the values in each column may not sum to the column total. [2] The criteria for HIV Stage 3 (AIDS) classification among pediatric cases were expanded in 2014; see Technical Notes in source. [3] Includes Asian/Pacific Islander legacy cases. See Technical Notes in source. [4] Hispanics/Latinos may be of any race. [5] Data are statistically adjusted to account for missing transmission category information. [6] Heterosexual contact with a person known to have, or to be at high risk for, HIV infection. [7] Includes hemophilia, blood transfusion, perinatal for persons age 13 and over, and risk factor not reported or not identified.

Source: U.S. Centers for Disease Control and Prevention, *HIV Surveillance Report: Diagnoses of HIV Infection in the United States and Dependent Areas, 2015,* Vol. 27, November 2016. See also <https://www.cdc.gov/hiv/library/reports/hiv-surveillance.html>.

Table 201. Population With a Disability by Age Group and by State: 2010 and 2015

[In thousands (36,355 represents 36,355,000). Disability data limited to civilian noninstitutionalized population. For children under age 5, covers children with a hearing or vision difficulty. For children age 5 to 17, covers children with a hearing, vision, cognitive, ambulatory, or self-care difficulty. For adults age 18 to 64 and age 65 and over, covers individuals with a hearing, vision, cognitive, ambulatory, self-care, or independent living difficulty. American Community Survey (ACS) disability data should not be compared with disability estimates from Census 2000, and more detailed measures of disability from sources such as the National Health Interview Survey and the Survey of Income and Program Participation. Based on a sample and subject to sampling variability; see text, Section 1 and Appendix III]

State	2010				2015			
	Total [1]	5 to 17 years	18 to 64 years	65 years and over	Total [1]	5 to 17 years	18 to 64 years	65 years and over
United States	**36,355**	**2,799**	**19,048**	**14,352**	**39,906**	**2,885**	**20,412**	**16,461**
Alabama	760	54	423	281	797	51	436	308
Alaska	75	6	48	20	83	7	47	28
Arizona	706	52	364	287	864	55	418	387
Arkansas	468	37	255	173	500	39	265	195
California	3,640	263	1,818	1,539	4,097	265	2,018	1,799
Colorado	499	38	273	185	553	37	286	228
Connecticut	368	28	179	159	390	29	191	168
Delaware	108	8	60	39	114	9	55	49
District of Columbia	66	6	37	23	76	5	45	25
Florida	2,367	148	1,115	1,096	2,669	171	1,187	1,301
Georgia	1,113	96	615	397	1,224	97	658	464
Hawaii	141	11	66	63	148	7	64	77
Idaho	196	17	103	74	225	18	118	88
Illinois	1,291	101	640	544	1,355	88	668	594
Indiana	800	66	435	295	899	69	478	351
Iowa	337	25	172	138	368	30	180	156
Kansas	341	26	178	136	366	31	185	149
Kentucky	711	51	423	233	738	49	422	265
Louisiana	672	58	378	232	681	55	372	252
Maine	198	15	104	78	215	16	115	83
Maryland	581	48	298	231	644	52	329	262
Massachusetts	699	57	354	285	785	59	393	330
Michigan	1,325	109	715	496	1,413	105	760	543
Minnesota	523	45	266	209	594	46	298	248
Mississippi	473	36	267	168	474	32	259	182
Missouri	814	60	440	311	868	62	463	339
Montana	125	8	64	52	140	7	72	60
Nebraska	206	16	104	85	209	17	102	90
Nevada	283	19	152	110	383	30	203	147
New Hampshire	146	14	77	54	170	11	90	69
New Jersey	845	69	398	375	921	64	429	424
New Mexico	269	16	140	112	307	17	156	132
New York	2,020	142	1,012	858	2,223	157	1,098	959
North Carolina	1,235	95	673	460	1,369	98	729	538
North Dakota	69	4	32	32	79	4	38	36
Ohio	1,506	128	804	569	1,593	130	848	612
Oklahoma	577	39	323	212	597	43	320	230
Oregon	525	37	287	198	605	38	321	245
Pennsylvania	1,638	132	824	677	1,747	134	885	723
Rhode Island	140	12	75	53	140	9	74	56
South Carolina	629	37	352	237	713	50	371	290
South Dakota	90	6	43	40	101	8	51	42
Tennessee	947	66	530	348	1,009	62	551	392
Texas	2,864	273	1,549	1,029	3,126	281	1,624	1,208
Utah	234	22	124	85	293	28	156	107
Vermont	82	7	45	30	92	8	48	36
Virginia	845	59	447	336	935	71	479	381
Washington	792	56	425	307	909	59	483	364
West Virginia	345	21	197	126	352	22	187	143
Wisconsin	606	51	306	246	681	50	352	277
Wyoming	66	5	36	25	71	4	38	29

[1] Total population with a disability includes population under age 5, not shown separately.

Source: U.S. Census Bureau, 2010 and 2015 American Community Survey, S1810, "Disability Characteristics," <http://factfinder.census.gov>, accessed January 2017.

Table 202. Use of Complementary and Alternative Health Practices Among Adults Age 18 and Over, in the Past 12 Months by Type of Therapy: 2007 and 2012

[3,141 represents 3,141,000. Percentages are age-adjusted. Based on the National Health Interview Survey of civilian noninstitutional population. The denominators for percent calculations exclude persons with unknown complementary health approach use. Estimates are age-adjusted using the projected 2000 U.S. population as the standard population, using age groups 18-24, 25-44, 45-64 and 65/over]

Therapy	2007 Number (1,000)	2007 Percent	2012 Number (1,000)	2012 Percent
Acupuncture	3,141	1.4	3,484	1.5
Ayurveda	214	0.1	241	0.1
Biofeedback	362	0.2	281	0.1
Chiropractic or osteopathic manipulation	18,740	8.6	19,369	8.4
Deep-breathing exercises [1]	27,794	12.7	24,218	10.9
Energy healing therapy	1,216	0.5	1,077	0.5
Guided imagery	4,866	2.2	3,846	1.7
Homeopathic treatment [2]	3,909	1.8	5,046	2.2
Hypnosis	561	0.2	347	0.1
Massage therapy	18,068	8.3	15,411	6.9
Meditation [3]	20,541	9.4	17,948	8.0
Naturopathy	729	0.3	957	0.4
Nonvitamin, nonmineral dietary supplements [4]	38,797	17.7	40,579	17.7
Progressive relaxation	6,454	2.9	4,766	2.1
Special diets [5]	6,040	2.8	6,853	3.0
Yoga, tai chi, and qi gong	14,436	6.7	22,281	10.1

[1] In 2012, deep-breathing exercises included deep-breathing exercises as part of hypnosis, biofeedback, Mantra meditation, mindfulness meditation, spiritual meditation, guided imagery, progressive relaxation, yoga, tai chi, or qi gong. In 2007, the use of deep-breathing exercises was asked broadly and not if used as part of other complementary health approaches. [2] No distinction was made between persons who sought treatment from a homeopathic practitioner and those who self-medicated. [3] In 2012, meditation included Mantra, mindfulness, and spiritual meditation; and meditation used as part of other practices. In 2007, the use of meditation was asked broadly and not if practiced as part of other complementary health approaches. [4] While questions were asked about nonvitamin, nonmineral dietary supplements in 2007 and 2012, the data should be interpreted with caution due to question order and the specific nonvitamin, nonmineral dietary supplements covered. [5] Respondents used one or more named special diets for 2 weeks or more in the past 12 months. Special diets included vegetarian (including vegan), macrobiotic, Atkins, Pritikin, and Ornish diets.

Source: U.S. National Center for Health Statistics, *Trends in the Use of Complementary Health Approaches Among Adults: United States, 2002–2012*, National Health Statistics Reports, Number 79, February 10, 2015. See also <https://nccih.nih.gov/research/statistics/NHIS/bibliography> or <http://www.cdc.gov/nchs/products/nhsr.htm>.

Table 203. Respiratory Diseases Among Persons Age 18 and Over by Selected Characteristics: 2015

[In thousands (242,501 represents 242,501,000). Respondents were asked in two separate questions if they had ever been told by a doctor or other health professional that they had emphysema or asthma. Respondents who had been told they had asthma were asked if they still had asthma. Respondents were asked in separate questions if they had been told by a doctor or other health professional in the past 12 months that they had hay fever, sinusitis, or bronchitis. Based on the National Health Interview Survey, a sample survey of the civilian noninstitutionalized population; see Appendix III]

Selected characteristic	Total persons	Emphysema	Asthma Ever	Asthma Still	Hay fever	Sinusitis	Chronic bronchitis
Total [2]	**242,501**	**3,515**	**30,606**	**18,445**	**19,976**	**29,367**	**9,274**
SEX							
Male	116,875	1,892	12,643	6,293	7,704	10,287	3,123
Female	125,625	1,624	17,963	12,151	12,272	19,080	6,152
AGE							
18 to 44 years	112,760	194	15,266	8,415	6,602	9,947	2,528
45 to 64 years	83,239	1,374	10,560	6,951	9,245	12,668	3,982
65 to 74 years	27,297	1,074	3,018	1,891	2,723	4,434	1,641
75 years and over	19,204	873	1,762	1,188	1,405	2,318	1,123
RACE							
Single race [3]	238,301	3,410	29,699	17,884	19,613	28,792	8,981
White	191,218	3,061	23,945	14,305	16,809	24,347	7,529
Black or African American	29,796	277	4,199	2,728	1,822	3,377	1,244
American Indian or Alaska Native	2,307	(B)	412	240	120	233	45
Asian	14,360	[6] 64	1,071	574	835	798	163
Native Hawaiian or other Pacific Islander	619	(B)	[6] 73	(B)	(B)	(B)	–
Two or more races [4]	4,200	[6] 105	907	561	362	575	294
HISPANIC ORIGIN AND RACE [5]							
Hispanic or Latino	37,755	136	3,920	2,227	1,730	2,832	823
Mexican or Mexican American	22,992	[6] 59	2,013	1,226	998	1,570	334
Not Hispanic or Latino	204,746	3,379	26,687	16,217	18,246	26,535	8,451
White	157,410	2,940	20,647	12,435	15,238	21,782	6,853
Black or African American	28,418	267	3,970	2,595	1,758	3,237	1,165

– Represents zero. B Figure too small to meet statistical standards for reliability of a derived figure. [1] A person may be represented in more than one column. [2] Total includes other races not shown separately. [3] Refers to persons who indicated only a single race group, including those of Hispanic and Latino origin. [4] Refers to all persons who indicated more than one race group. [5] Persons of Hispanic or Latino origin may be of any race or combination of races. [6] Data have a relative standard error (RSE) greater than 30% and less than or equal to 50%, and should be used with caution.

Source: U.S. National Center for Health Statistics, 2015 National Health Interview Survey, "Tables of Summary Statistics," <https://www.cdc.gov/nchs/nhis/SHS.htm>, accessed February 2017.

Table 204. Selected Diseases and Conditions Among Persons Age 18 and Over by Selected Characteristics: 2015

[In thousands (242,501 represents 242,501,000). Persons with selected diseases and conditions may be represented in more than one column. Based on National Health Interview Survey, a sample survey of the civilian noninstitutionalized population; see Appendix III]

Selected characteristic	Total persons	Persons with selected diseases and conditions					
		Diabetes[1,2]	Ulcers[1]	Kidney disease[3,4]	Liver disease[3]	Arthritis diagnosis[5]	Chronic joint symptoms[5]
Total[6]	**242,501**	**23,161**	**14,765**	**4,850**	**3,934**	**55,386**	**72,532**
SEX							
Male	116,875	11,538	6,836	2,481	1,836	23,054	33,063
Female	125,625	11,623	7,930	2,369	2,098	32,332	39,469
AGE							
18 to 44 years	112,760	2,469	3,955	613	1,003	7,846	18,886
45 to 64 years	83,239	10,603	6,342	1,754	2,008	24,054	31,179
65 to 74 years	27,297	6,016	2,529	1,130	683	13,244	12,913
75 years and over	19,204	4,073	1,938	1,353	241	10,243	9,555
RACE							
Single race[7]	238,301	22,729	14,457	4,698	3,799	54,543	71,199
White	191,218	17,342	12,029	3,746	3,186	45,908	59,706
Black or African American	29,796	3,732	1,481	658	271	6,558	8,023
American Indian or Alaska Native	2,307	424	229	[10]99	82	483	698
Asian	14,360	1,190	704	193	259	1,541	2,596
Native Hawaiian or other Pacific Islander	619	[10]42	(B)	(B)	–	[10]53	176
Two or more races[8]	4,200	431	309	151	[10]135	843	1,334
HISPANIC ORIGIN[9]							
Hispanic or Latino	37,755	3,616	1,683	643	625	4,437	7,765
Mexican or Mexican American	22,992	2,293	937	449	385	2,426	4,684

– Represents zero. B Does not meet statistical standards for reliability (relative standard error greater than 50%). [1] Respondents who had ever been told by a health professional that they had an ulcer or diabetes. [2] Excludes borderline and pregnancy-related diabetes. [3] Respondents who had been told in the last 12 months by a health professional that they had weak or failing kidneys or any kind of liver condition. [4] Excludes kidney stones, bladder infections, or incontinence. [5] Respondents with an arthritis diagnosis had ever been told by a health professional that they had some form of arthritis, rheumatoid arthritis, gout, lupus or fibromyalgia. Respondents with joint symptoms (excluding back and neck) that began more than 3 months prior to interview were classified as having chronic joint symptoms. [6] Total includes other races not shown separately. [7] Refers to persons who indicated only a single race group, including Hispanic or Latino origin. [8] Refers to all persons who indicated more than one race group. [9] Persons of Hispanic or Latino origin may be of any race or combination of races. [10] Figure does not meet standard of reliability or precision.

Source: U.S. National Center for Health Statistics, 2015 National Health Interview Survey, "Tables of Summary Health Statistics," <https://www.cdc.gov/nchs/nhis/SHS.htm>, accessed February 2017.

Table 205. Circulatory Diseases Among Persons Age 18 and Over by Selected Characteristics: 2015

[In thousands (242,501 represents 242,501,000). In separate questions, respondents were asked if they had ever been told by a doctor or other health professional that they had: hypertension (or high blood pressure), coronary heart disease, angina (or angina pectoris), heart attack (or myocardial infarction), any other heart condition or disease not already mentioned, or a stroke. A person may be represented in more than one column. Based on National Health Interview Survey, a sample survey of the civilian noninstitutionalized population; see Appendix III]

Characteristic	Total adults	Selected circulatory diseases			
		Heart disease		Hypertension[3]	Stroke
		All types[1]	Coronary[2]		
Total[4]	**242,501**	**28,406**	**14,876**	**65,428**	**6,520**
SEX					
Male	116,875	14,705	8,809	32,251	3,219
Female	125,625	13,702	6,067	33,176	3,300
AGE					
18 to 44 years	112,760	4,880	885	10,320	617
45 to 64 years	83,239	9,849	5,100	28,352	2,243
65 to 74 years	27,297	7,073	4,458	14,895	1,516
75 years and over	19,204	6,604	4,432	11,860	2,143
RACE					
Single race[5]	238,301	27,763	14,539	64,377	6,372
White	191,218	23,826	12,372	50,822	5,132
Black or African American	29,796	2,722	1,524	10,086	1,018
American Indian or Alaska Native	2,307	264	165	603	[8]51
Asian	14,360	911	448	2,766	169
Native Hawaiian or Other Pacific Islander	619	(B)	(B)	[8]100	(B)
Two or more races[6]	4,200	644	337	1,050	147
HISPANIC ORIGIN[7]					
Hispanic or Latino	37,755	2,476	1,432	7,141	675
Mexican or Mexican American	22,992	1,323	790	4,105	430

B Figure too small to meet statistical standards for reliability of a derived figure. [1] Heart disease includes coronary heart disease, angina pectoris, heart attack, or any other heart condition or disease. [2] Coronary heart disease includes coronary heart disease, angina pectoris, or heart attack. [3] Persons told on two or more different visits that they had hypertension, or high blood pressure, are classified as hypertensive. [4] Includes other races not shown separately. [5] Refers to persons who indicated only a single race group, including Hispanic or Latino origin. [6] Refers to all persons who indicated more than one race group. [7] Persons of Hispanic or Latino origin may be of any race or combination of races. [8] Figure does not meet standard of reliability or precision.

Source: U.S. National Center for Health Statistics, 2015 National Health Interview Survey, "Tables of Summary Health Statistics," <https://www.cdc.gov/nchs/nhis/SHS.htm>, accessed February 2017.

Table 206. Migraine Headaches and Pain in the Neck, Lower Back, Face or Jaw Among Persons Age 18 and Over by Selected Characteristics: 2015

[In thousands (242,501 represents 242,501,000). Based on National Health Interview Survey, a sample survey of the civilian noninstitutionalized population. See Appendix III]

Selected characteristic	Total persons	Migraine and pain [1]			
		Migraine or severe headache [2]	Pain in neck [2]	Pain in lower back [2]	Pain in face or jaw [2]
Total [3]	**242,501**	**36,413**	**38,968**	**72,268**	**10,063**
SEX					
Male	116,875	11,309	16,627	33,043	3,209
Female	125,625	25,104	22,341	39,224	6,854
AGE					
18 to 44 years	112,760	20,177	14,554	26,943	4,696
45 to 64 years	83,239	13,254	16,711	29,377	3,774
65 to 74 years	27,297	2,000	4,603	9,258	959
75 years and over	19,204	982	3,100	6,690	634
RACE					
Single race [4]	238,301	35,528	38,202	70,889	9,758
White	191,218	28,421	31,911	58,788	8,269
Black or African American	29,796	4,940	4,149	8,481	1,027
American Indian or Alaska Native	2,307	443	449	764	[7] 129
Asian	14,360	1,598	1,635	2,713	311
Native Hawaiian or other Pacific Islander	619	[7] 126	[7] 57	142	[7] 22
Two or more races [5]	4,200	885	767	1,379	305
HISPANIC ORIGIN AND RACE [6]					
Hispanic or Latino	37,755	5,806	5,012	10,008	1,463
Mexican or Mexican American	22,992	3,355	2,655	5,790	918
Not Hispanic or Latino	204,746	30,606	33,956	62,260	8,600
White, single race	157,410	23,373	27,511	49,853	7,062
Black or African American, single race	28,418	4,653	3,936	8,070	930

[1] A person may be represented in more than one column. [2] Respondents were asked, in separate questions, "During the past 3 months, did you have a severe headache or migraine [or neck pain; or low back pain; or facial ache or pain in the jaw muscles or the joint in front of the ear]?" Respondents were instructed to report pain that had lasted a whole day or more and, conversely, not to report fleeting or minor aches or pains. [3] Total includes other races not shown separately. [4] Refers to persons who indicated only a single race group. [5] Refers to all persons who indicated more than one race group. [6] Persons of Hispanic or Latino origin may be of any race or combination of races. [7] Figure does not meet standard of reliability or precision.

Source: U.S. National Center for Health Statistics, 2015 National Health Interview Survey, "Tables of Summary Health Statistics," <https://www.cdc.gov/nchs/nhis/SHS.htm>, accessed February 2017.

Table 207. Injury and Poisoning Episodes by Age and Sex: 2014

[In thousands (39,549 represents 39,549,000), except as noted. Covers all medically attended injuries and poisonings occurring during the 5–week period prior to the survey interview. Age adjustment is used to adjust for differences in the age distribution of populations being compared. There may be more than one condition per episode. Based on the National Health Interview Survey, a sample survey of the civilian noninstitutionalized population; see Appendix III]

External cause and nature of injury	Total	Rate, age adjusted [1]	By age						By sex	
			Under age 12	12-17	18-44	45-64	65-74	75 and over	Male	Female
EPISODES										
Number (1,000) [2]	**39,549**	(X)	**4,782**	**4,972**	**12,192**	**10,140**	**3,551**	**3,913**	**20,091**	**19,459**
Annual rate per 1,000 population, total [3]	(X)	125.7	98.7	199.2	108.7	122.8	135.5	208.98	131.8	119.7
BY CAUSE										
Fall	14,963	46.9	2,269	1,723	2,928	3,728	1,865	2,450	6,542	8,421
Struck by a person or an object	4,228	13.6	729	658	1,144	994	[6] 263	[6] 439	2,733	1,495
Transportation [4]	3,293	10.6	[6] 172	531	1,429	809	[6] 205	(B)	1,624	1,669
Overexertion	3,699	11.8	(B)	[6] 458	1,538	1,104	[6] 202	[6] 252	1,698	2,001
Cutting, piercing instruments	3,191	10.3	[6] 168	[6] 172	1,705	746	[6] 312	(B)	2,003	1,189
Poisoning [5]	629	2.0	(B)	(B)	[6] 201	(B)	(B)	–	[6] 247	[6] 382

– Represents zero. X Not applicable. B Base figure too small to meet statistical standards for reliability of a derived figure. [1] Total annual rate per 1,000 population. Age-adjusted using the 2000 standard population. [2] Includes other items not shown separately. [3] Rates by age group are not age adjusted. [4] Includes motor vehicle, bicycle, motorcycle, pedestrian, train, boat, and airplane. [5] Excludes food poisoning and allergic reaction. [6] Figure has relative standard error (RSE) greater than 30% and less than or equal to 50% and should be used with caution.

Source: U.S. National Center for Health Statistics, 2014 National Health Interview Survey, "Tables of Summary Health Statistics," <http://www.cdc.gov/nchs/nhis/SHS/tables.htm>, accessed February 2016.

Table 208. Injuries Associated With Selected Consumer Products: 2015

[Estimates are based on a national probability sample of hospitals in the U.S. and its territories. Patient information is collected from each participating hospital for every emergency visit involving an injury associated with consumer products. From this sample, the total number of product-related injuries treated in hospital emergency rooms nationwide is estimated. A person's injury may be represented in up to two product groups]

Product type	Number	Product type	Number
Items for infants/children:		**Housewares:**	
All nursery equipment	94,524	Cans, other containers	294,604
Baby strollers	14,808	Cleaning agents (excludes soaps)	38,548
High chairs	10,250	Cleaning equipment, noncaustic detergents	53,129
Playground equipment (excluding swings)	242,844	Soaps, detergents	50,414
Swings or swings sets	56,937	Glass bottles, jars	41,992
Toys	244,181	**Tools & garden equipment:**	
Sports & recreational equipment:		Chain saws	24,917
All terrain vehicles, mopeds, minibikes, etc.	212,030	Hand garden tools	64,595
Baseball, softball	215,248	Lawn mowers	81,938
Basketball	493,011	Power home tools (excluding saws)	27,543
Bicycles & accessories	497,134	Power home workshop saws	78,939
Exercise, exercise equipment	464,363	Workshop manual tools	129,677
Football	399,873	**Household appliances:**	
Lacrosse, rugby, misc. ball games	84,617	Cooking ranges, ovens, etc.	48,966
Skateboards	125,145	Heating stoves, space heaters	24,899
Skating (excluding in-line)	74,906	Refrigerators, freezers	48,938
Soccer	227,732	Small kitchen appliances	56,076
Swimming, pools, equipment	192,458	**Home furnishings & fixtures:**	
Trampolines	107,123	Bathroom structures & fixtures	482,988
Home entertainment equipment:		Beds, mattresses, pillows	773,256
Computers (equipment and electronic games)	24,525	Carpets, rugs	181,810
Television sets & stands	59,981	Chairs, sofas, sofa beds	590,808
Personal use items:		Desks, cabinets, shelves, racks	293,423
Grooming devices	48,220	Glass doors, windows, panels	135,774
Mobility carts, electric [1]	16,026	Ladders, stools	256,279
Razors, shavers, razor blades	49,580	Tables [2]	343,810

[1] Motorized vehicles, not elsewhere classified (three or more wheels). [2] Excludes baby-changing tables, billiard or pool tables, and television tables or stands.

Source: Consumer Product Safety Commission, National Electronic Injury Surveillance System (NEISS), *2015 NEISS Data Highlights;* and "NEISS Estimates Query Builder," <http://www.cpsc.gov/en/Research--Statistics/NEISS-Injury-Data/>, accessed April 2017.

Table 209. Food Security Status of Households and Households with Children: 2005 to 2015

[114,437 represents 114,437,000. Food security status of households is measured through a series of questions about experiences and behaviors known to characterize households that are having difficulty meeting basic food needs. All questions refer to the previous 12 months and include a qualifying phrase reminding respondents to report only conditions resulting from inadequate financial resources; restrictions to food intake due to dieting and voluntary fasting are excluded. *Food-secure* households report 0-2 food-insecure conditions. *Food-insecure* households report 3 or more conditions. Low and very low food security differ in the extent and character of the adjustments the household makes to its eating patterns and food intake. Households classified as having *low food security* report multiple indications of food access problems, but typically report few, if any, indications of reduced food intake. Households classified as having *very low food security* report multiple indications of reduced food intake and disrupted eating patterns due to inadequate resources for food. Prior to 2006, households with low and very low food security were described as "food insecure with hunger." The omission of homeless persons may be a cause of underreporting. Data are from the Food Security Supplement to the Current Population Survey (CPS); for details about the CPS, see text, Section 1 and Appendix III]

Household status	Number (1,000)					Percent distribution				
	2005	2010	2013	2014	2015	2005	2010	2013	2014	2015
Households, total [1]	**114,437**	**118,756**	**122,579**	**124,044**	**125,164**	**100.0**	**100.0**	**100.0**	**100.0**	**100.0**
Food-secure	101,851	101,527	105,070	106,618	109,315	89.0	85.5	85.7	86.0	87.3
Food-insecure	12,586	17,229	17,509	17,426	15,849	11.0	14.5	14.3	14.0	12.7
With low food security	8,158	10,872	10,664	10,488	9,540	7.1	9.1	8.7	8.4	7.7
With very low food security	4,428	6,357	6,845	6,938	6,309	3.9	5.4	5.6	5.6	5.0
Adult members [2]	**217,897**	**229,129**	**237,219**	**239,937**	**242,706**	**100.0**	**100.0**	**100.0**	**100.0**	**100.0**
In food-secure households	195,172	196,505	203,913	207,125	213,586	89.6	85.8	86.0	86.3	88.0
In food-insecure households	22,725	32,624	33,306	32,812	29,120	10.4	14.2	14.0	13.7	12.0
With low food security	15,146	21,357	21,115	20,425	18,235	7.0	9.3	8.9	8.5	7.5
With very low food security	7,579	11,267	12,191	12,387	10,885	3.5	4.9	5.1	5.2	4.5
Child members [2, 3]	**73,604**	**74,905**	**73,634**	**73,368**	**73,455**	**100.0**	**100.0**	**100.0**	**100.0**	**100.0**
In food-secure households	61,201	58,697	57,862	58,045	60,337	83.1	78.4	78.6	79.1	82.1
In food-insecure households	12,403	16,208	15,772	15,323	13,118	16.9	21.6	21.4	20.9	17.9
With very low food security among children	606	976	765	914	541	0.8	1.3	1.0	1.2	0.7

[1] Total excludes households for which food security status is unknown. [2] The food security survey measures food security status at the household level. Not all individuals and children residing in food-insecure households were directly affected by the households' food insecurity. Similarly, not all individuals and children in households classified as having very low food security were subject to the reductions in food intake and disruptions in eating patterns that characterize this condition. Young children, in particular, are often protected from effects of the households' food insecurity. [3] Percents among only households with children.

Source: U.S. Department of Agriculture, Economic Research Service, *Household Food Security in the United States in 2015*, Economic Research Report Number 215, September 2016. See also <https://www.ers.usda.gov/topics/food-nutrition-assistance/food-security-in-the-us.aspx>.

Table 210. Mammography Use Among Women Age 40 and Over by Patient Characteristics: 2000 to 2015

[Percent of women having a mammogram within the past 2 years. Covers civilian noninstitutional population. Based on National Health Interview Survey; see Appendix III]

Characteristic	2000	2003	2005	2008	2010	2013	2015
Women age 40 and over, total [1]	70.4	69.7	66.8	67.6	67.1	66.8	65.3
AGE							
40 to 49 years	64.3	64.4	63.5	61.5	62.3	59.6	58.3
50 to 64 years	78.7	76.2	71.8	74.2	72.6	71.4	71.3
65 years and over	67.9	67.7	63.8	65.5	64.4	66.9	63.3
RACE AND ETHNICITY							
White, non-Hispanic	72.2	70.5	68.3	68.7	67.8	67.6	65.8
Black, non-Hispanic	67.9	70.5	65.2	68.3	67.4	67.2	69.7
Hispanic origin [2]	61.2	65.0	58.8	61.2	64.2	61.4	60.9
HEALTH INSURANCE STATUS [3]							
Insured	76.0	75.1	72.5	73.4	74.1	72.1	69.7
Private insurance	77.1	76.3	74.5	74.2	75.6	73.4	72.2
Medicaid	61.7	63.5	55.6	64.2	64.4	63.5	57.7
Uninsured	40.7	41.5	38.1	39.7	36.0	37.3	30.0
EDUCATION							
No high school diploma nor GED [4]	57.7	58.1	52.8	53.8	53.0	53.6	51.7
High school diploma or GED	69.7	67.8	64.9	65.2	64.4	63.4	60.1
Some college or more	76.2	75.1	72.7	73.4	72.1	71.6	70.5
POVERTY STATUS [5]							
Below 100% poverty	54.8	55.4	48.5	51.4	51.4	49.9	52.2
100% to 199% poverty	58.1	60.8	55.3	55.8	53.8	56.7	54.9
200% to 399% poverty	68.8	69.9	67.2	64.4	66.2	66.0	63.4
400% and over poverty	81.5	77.7	76.6	79.0	78.1	77.2	74.7

[1] Includes other races not shown separately and unknown education level and poverty status. [2] Persons of Hispanic origin may be of any race or combination of races. [3] Health insurance status at time of interview, only for women age 40 to 64. Health insurance categories are mutually exclusive. Persons who reported both Medicaid and private coverage are classified as having private coverage. Persons with only Indian Health Service coverage are considered to have no health insurance coverage. [4] GED is General Educational Development high school equivalency diploma. [5] Poverty as percent of Federal poverty level based on family income and family size and composition using U.S. Census Bureau poverty thresholds.

Source: U.S. National Center for Health Statistics, *Health, United States, 2016*, May 2017. See also <http://www.cdc.gov/nchs/hus.htm>.

Table 211. Current Cigarette Smoking Among Adults: 2000 to 2015

[In percent. A current smoker is a person who has smoked at least 100 cigarettes and who now smokes every day or some days. Excludes unknown smoking status. Race groups White and Black include persons of Hispanic and non-Hispanic origin. For definition of age adjustment, see text, Section 2. Based on National Health Interview Survey; for details, see Appendix III]

Sex, age, and race	2000	2005	2010	2015	Sex, age, and race	2000	2005	2010	2015
Total smokers, age-adjusted [1]	23.1	20.8	19.3	15.3	Black, total	26.2	26.5	24.3	20.6
Male	25.2	23.4	21.2	16.8	18 to 24 years	20.9	21.6	18.8	[3] 15.9
Female	21.1	18.3	17.5	13.8	25 to 34 years	23.2	29.8	25.7	26.0
					35 to 44 years	30.7	23.3	22.6	17.9
White male	25.4	23.3	21.4	16.8	45 to 64 years	32.2	32.4	31.8	22.8
Black male	25.7	25.9	23.3	20.3	65 years and over	14.2	16.8	10.0	16.0
					Female, total	20.9	18.1	17.3	13.6
White female	22.0	19.1	18.3	14.8	18 to 24 years	24.9	20.7	17.4	11.0
Black female	20.7	17.1	16.6	13.2	25 to 34 years	22.3	21.5	20.6	15.0
					35 to 44 years	26.2	21.3	19.0	16.5
Total smokers [2]	23.2	20.9	19.3	15.1	45 to 64 years	21.7	18.8	19.1	16.1
Male, total	25.6	23.9	21.5	16.7	65 years and over	9.3	8.3	9.3	7.3
18 to 24 years	28.1	28.0	22.8	15.0	White, total	21.4	18.7	17.9	14.3
25 to 34 years	28.9	27.7	26.1	21.3	18 to 24 years	28.5	22.6	18.4	11.2
35 to 44 years	30.2	26.0	22.5	18.3	25 to 34 years	24.9	23.1	22.0	16.3
45 to 64 years	26.4	25.2	23.2	17.9	35 to 44 years	26.6	22.2	20.5	18.3
65 years and over	10.2	8.9	9.7	9.7	45 to 64 years	21.4	18.9	19.5	17.1
White, total	25.7	23.6	21.4	16.5	65 years and over	9.1	8.4	9.4	7.5
18 to 24 years	30.4	29.7	23.8	15.6	Black, total	20.8	17.3	17.0	13.1
25 to 34 years	29.7	27.7	26.6	20.9	18 to 24 years	14.2	14.2	14.2	[3] 8.6
35 to 44 years	30.6	26.3	23.1	19.1	25 to 34 years	15.5	16.9	19.3	14.9
45 to 64 years	25.8	24.5	22.5	17.3	35 to 44 years	30.2	19.0	17.2	15.4
65 years and over	9.8	7.9	9.6	9.3	45 to 64 years	25.6	21.0	19.8	14.5
					65 years and over	10.2	10.0	9.4	9.7

[1] Data are age-adjusted to the year 2000 standard population using five age groups: 18–24 years, 25–34 years, 35–44 years, 45–64 years, 65 years and over. [2] Crude, not age-adjusted. [3] Figure does not meet standard of reliability or precision.

Source: U.S. National Center for Health Statistics, *Health, United States, 2016,* May 2017. See also <http://www.cdc.gov/nchs/hus.htm>.

Table 212. Current Cigarette Smoking by Sex and State: 2015

[In percent. Current cigarette smoking is defined as persons age 18 and older who reported having smoked 100 or more cigarettes during their lifetime and who currently smoke every day or some days. Based on the Behavioral Risk Factor Surveillance System (BRFSS), a telephone survey of health behaviors of the civilian, noninstitutionalized U.S. population, age 18 and over. New methods, including surveying cellular telephone-only households, and a new weighting method, were implemented for the 2011 BRFSS and prior data cannot accurately be compared to current survey results; for details, see source]

State	Total	Male	Female	State	Total	Male	Female	State	Total	Male	Female
U.S. [1]	**17.5**	**19.3**	**15.8**	KY	26.0	26.4	25.5	OH	21.6	23.1	20.2
AL	21.4	23.8	19.2	LA	21.9	24.7	19.3	OK	22.2	24.0	20.4
AK	19.1	19.6	18.6	ME	19.5	21.0	18.1	OR	17.1	18.0	16.3
AZ	14.0	16.2	12.0	MD	15.1	16.9	13.4	PA	18.1	19.8	16.6
AR	24.9	27.8	22.1	MA	14.0	16.4	11.9	RI	15.5	18.5	12.8
CA	11.7	15.2	8.3	MI	20.7	22.4	19.1	SC	19.7	23.4	16.2
CO	15.7	17.1	14.2	MN	16.2	17.6	14.8	SD	20.1	19.6	20.6
CT	13.5	16.3	10.9	MS	22.6	27.0	18.4	TN	21.9	22.8	21.1
DE	17.4	20.9	14.2	MO	22.3	23.6	21.0	TX	15.2	18.2	12.4
DC	16.0	15.8	16.1	MT	18.9	19.3	18.5	UT	9.1	11.2	7.0
FL	15.8	17.4	14.3	NE	17.1	18.4	15.8	VT	16.0	18.0	14.0
GA	17.7	20.0	15.5	NV	17.6	20.5	14.6	VA	16.5	18.8	14.4
HI	14.1	17.3	10.8	NH	15.9	16.5	15.4	WA	15.0	16.6	13.4
ID	13.8	14.7	13.0	NJ	13.5	15.7	11.5	WV	25.7	25.8	25.7
IL	15.1	17.6	12.8	NM	17.5	19.1	16.0	WI	17.3	19.8	14.9
IN	20.6	21.9	19.3	NY	15.2	17.7	12.9	WY	19.1	20.6	17.5
IA	18.1	19.5	16.7	NC	19.0	21.9	16.3	Guam	27.4	32.5	22.3
KS	17.7	19.3	16.1	ND	18.7	21.9	15.4	PR [2]	10.8	14.6	7.4

[1] Represents median value among the states and DC. For definition of median, see Guide to Tabular Presentation. [2] Puerto Rico.

Source: U.S. Centers for Disease Control and Prevention, Chronic Disease and Health Promotion Data & Indicators, Tobacco Use Data, "Behavioral Risk Factor Data: Tobacco Use (2011 to present)," <https://chronicdata.cdc.gov/health-area/tobacco-use>, accessed February 2017.

Table 213. Substance Abuse Treatment Facilities and Clients: 2010 to 2014

[As of the end of March. Based on the National Survey of Substance Abuse Treatment Services, a census of all known public and private facilities that provide substance abuse treatment in the United States and associated jurisdictions. Selected missing data for responding facilities were imputed]

Facility characteristic	Number of facilities			Number of clients		
	2010	2013	2014	2010	2013	2014
Total	**13,339**	**14,148**	**14,152**	**1,175,462**	**1,249,629**	**(NA)**
FACILITY OPERATIONAL STRUCTURE						
Private non-profit	7,683	7,820	7,817	625,321	638,858	(NA)
Private for-profit	3,985	4,575	4,664	372,525	430,362	(NA)
Local, county, or community government	751	739	713	70,963	72,949	(NA)
State government	380	351	344	47,203	35,812	(NA)
Federal government	348	370	337	47,676	53,695	(NA)
Dept. of Veterans Affairs	218	228	211	39,157	44,180	(NA)
Dept. of Defense	91	88	85	7,035	6,685	(NA)
Indian Health Service	36	42	32	1,431	1,368	(NA)
Other	3	12	9	53	1,462	(NA)
Tribal government	192	293	277	11,774	17,953	(NA)
TYPE OF CARE OFFERED/RECEIVED [1]						
Outpatient	10,753	11,542	11,618	1,056,532	1,127,235	(NA)
Regular	9,914	10,771	10,826	593,077	603,315	(NA)
Intensive	5,990	6,363	6,409	138,188	147,162	(NA)
Detoxification	1,227	1,362	1,422	13,216	13,839	(NA)
Day treatment/partial hospitalization	1,678	1,742	1,759	22,458	22,828	(NA)
Methadone maintenance [2]	1,137	1,848	2,498	289,593	340,091	(NA)
Residential (non-hospital)	3,452	3,450	3,473	103,692	107,727	(NA)
Detoxification	893	861	914	7,549	10,244	(NA)
Short-term treatment (30 days or fewer)	1,691	1,736	1,785	26,014	27,184	(NA)
Long-term treatment (more than 30 days)	2,801	2,858	2,845	70,129	70,299	(NA)
Hospital inpatient	748	753	762	15,238	14,667	(NA)
Detoxification	666	660	664	6,476	5,768	(NA)
Treatment	548	547	550	8,762	8,899	(NA)
TREATMENT FOR SUBSTANCE ABUSE PROBLEM						
Both alcohol and drug	(NA)	12,911	(NA)	498,671	534,078	(NA)
Drug abuse only	(NA)	11,691	(NA)	459,069	491,903	(NA)
Alcohol abuse only	(NA)	11,153	(NA)	215,101	216,856	(NA)
Both substance abuse and mental health disorders	(NA)	12,465	(NA)	479,699	563,071	(NA)

NA Not available. [1] Number of facilities can sum to more than the total because a facility could provide more than 1 type of care. [2] Methadone/buprenorphine maintenance or injectable naltrexone treatment.

Source: U.S. Substance Abuse and Mental Health Services Administration, *National Survey of Substance Abuse Treatment Services (N-SSATS): 2014 Data on Substance Abuse Treatment Facilities,* March 2016, and earlier reports. See also <http://www.samhsa.gov/data/substance-abuse-facilities-data-nssats>.

Table 214. Drug Use by Type of Drug and Age Group: 2010 to 2015

[In percent. Data comes from the National Survey on Drug Use and Health (NSDUH). Based on a representative sample of the U.S. population age 12 and older, including persons living in households, in noninstitutional group quarters such as dormitories and homeless shelters, and civilians on military bases. Estimates are based on computer-assisted interviews of approximately 68,000 respondents. Please note that the NSDUH was redesigned in 2015, and therefore data from previous surveys for several survey items are not comparable to data from the 2015 NSDUH; see source for more information. Subject to sampling variability]

Age and type of drug	Lifetime (ever) use			Past year use			Past month use		
	2010	2014	2015	2010	2014	2015	2010	2014	2015
12 YEARS OLD AND OVER									
Any illicit drug [1]	(NA)	(NA)	48.8	(NA)	(NA)	17.8	(NA)	(NA)	10.1
Marijuana	42.0	44.2	44.0	11.6	13.2	13.5	6.9	8.4	8.3
Cocaine	14.7	14.8	14.5	1.8	1.7	1.8	0.6	0.6	0.7
Crack	3.6	3.6	3.4	0.3	0.3	0.3	0.1	0.1	0.1
Heroin	1.6	1.8	1.9	0.2	0.3	0.3	0.1	0.2	0.1
Hallucinogens	(NA)	(NA)	15.3	(NA)	(NA)	1.8	(NA)	(NA)	0.5
LSD	9.2	9.4	9.5	0.3	0.5	0.6	0.1	0.1	0.1
PCP	2.5	2.4	2.4	0.0	0.0	0.0	0.0	(B)	0.0
Ecstasy	(NA)	(NA)	6.8	(NA)	(NA)	1.0	(NA)	(NA)	0.2
Inhalants	(NA)	(NA)	9.6	(NA)	(NA)	0.7	(NA)	(NA)	0.2
Methamphetamine [2]	(NA)	(NA)	5.4	(NA)	(NA)	0.6	(NA)	(NA)	0.3
Illicit drugs except marijuana	(NA)	(NA)	28.8	(NA)	(NA)	9.2	(NA)	(NA)	3.5
Tobacco products [3]	68.8	66.2	63.9	(NA)	30.6	29.2	27.5	25.2	23.9
Cigarettes	64.2	61.0	58.5	(NA)	24.8	23.1	23.0	20.8	19.4
Smokeless tobacco	(NA)	(NA)	16.3	(NA)	(NA)	4.7	(NA)	(NA)	3.4
Cigars	35.0	33.7	32.8	(NA)	9.0	9.1	5.2	4.5	4.7
Pipe tobacco	13.6	12.7	12.5	(NA)	(NA)	(NA)	0.8	0.8	0.8
Alcohol	82.5	82.1	81.0	(NA)	66.6	65.7	51.8	52.7	51.7
"Binge" alcohol use [4]	(NA)	(NA)	(NA)	(NA)	(NA)	(NA)	(NA)	(NA)	24.9
12 TO 17 YEARS OLD									
Any illicit drug [1]	(NA)	(NA)	25.3	(NA)	(NA)	17.5	(NA)	(NA)	8.8
Marijuana	17.1	16.4	15.7	14.0	13.1	12.6	7.4	7.4	7.0
Cocaine	1.5	0.9	0.8	1.0	0.7	0.6	0.2	0.2	0.2
Hallucinogens	(NA)	(NA)	3.1	(NA)	(NA)	2.1	(NA)	(NA)	0.5
Inhalants	(NA)	(NA)	9.1	(NA)	(NA)	2.7	(NA)	(NA)	0.7
Methamphetamine [2]	(NA)	(NA)	0.3	(NA)	(NA)	0.2	(NA)	(NA)	0.1
Illicit drugs except marijuana	(NA)	(NA)	15.9	(NA)	(NA)	9.1	(NA)	(NA)	3.0
Tobacco products [3]	25.1	18.5	17.3	(NA)	12.7	11.6	10.7	7.0	6.0
Cigarettes	20.5	14.2	13.2	(NA)	8.9	8.1	8.4	4.9	4.2
Smokeless tobacco	(NA)	(NA)	5.5	(NA)	(NA)	3.5	(NA)	(NA)	1.5
Cigars	11.1	8.0	7.2	(NA)	5.7	5.1	3.2	2.1	2.1
Alcohol	35.4	29.6	28.4	(NA)	24.0	22.7	13.6	11.5	9.6
"Binge" alcohol use [4]	(NA)	(NA)	(NA)	(NA)	(NA)	(NA)	(NA)	(NA)	5.8
18 TO 25 YEARS OLD									
Any illicit drug [1]	(NA)	(NA)	57.5	(NA)	(NA)	37.5	(NA)	(NA)	22.3
Marijuana	51.4	52.6	52.7	30.0	31.9	32.2	18.5	19.6	19.8
Cocaine	13.4	11.1	11.7	4.7	4.6	5.4	1.5	1.4	1.7
Crack	2.6	1.6	1.5	0.5	0.4	0.3	0.2	0.1	0.1
Heroin	1.8	2.0	1.8	0.6	0.8	0.6	0.3	0.2	0.3
Hallucinogens	(NA)	(NA)	18.6	(NA)	(NA)	7.0	(NA)	(NA)	1.8
Inhalants	(NA)	(NA)	9.9	(NA)	(NA)	1.4	(NA)	(NA)	0.4
Methamphetamine [2]	(NA)	(NA)	3.3	(NA)	(NA)	0.9	(NA)	(NA)	0.4
Illicit drugs except marijuana	(NA)	(NA)	33.2	(NA)	(NA)	20.2	(NA)	(NA)	7.6
Tobacco products [3]	68.8	63.8	61.7	(NA)	46.0	43.8	40.9	35.0	33.0
Cigarettes	62.3	56.1	53.3	(NA)	37.7	35.0	34.3	28.4	26.7
Smokeless tobacco	(NA)	(NA)	19.6	(NA)	(NA)	9.0	(NA)	(NA)	5.4
Cigars	41.1	37.7	36.3	(NA)	20.0	19.5	11.3	9.7	8.9
Alcohol	85.7	83.4	82.4	(NA)	76.5	75.5	61.4	59.6	58.3
"Binge" alcohol use [4]	(NA)	(NA)	(NA)	(NA)	(NA)	(NA)	(NA)	(NA)	39.0
26 YEARS OLD AND OVER									
Any illicit drug [1]	(NA)	(NA)	50.1	(NA)	(NA)	14.6	(NA)	(NA)	8.2
Marijuana	43.5	46.1	46.0	8.0	10.1	10.4	4.8	6.6	6.5
Cocaine	16.6	17.1	16.6	1.4	1.4	1.3	0.5	0.5	0.6
Crack	4.2	4.3	4.1	0.4	0.3	0.3	0.2	0.2	0.2
Heroin	1.8	2.0	2.1	0.2	0.3	0.3	0.1	0.2	0.1
Hallucinogens	(NA)	(NA)	16.2	(NA)	(NA)	0.8	(NA)	(NA)	0.2
Inhalants	(NA)	(NA)	9.6	(NA)	(NA)	0.3	(NA)	(NA)	0.1
Methamphetamine [2]	(NA)	(NA)	6.4	(NA)	(NA)	0.6	(NA)	(NA)	0.4
Illicit drugs except marijuana	(NA)	(NA)	29.6	(NA)	(NA)	7.3	(NA)	(NA)	2.8
Tobacco products [3]	74.2	72.3	69.9	(NA)	30.1	28.9	27.2	25.8	24.5
Cigarettes	70.0	67.5	64.7	(NA)	24.6	22.9	22.8	21.5	20.0
Smokeless tobacco	(NA)	(NA)	17.0	(NA)	(NA)	4.1	(NA)	(NA)	3.2
Cigars	36.9	36.1	35.3	(NA)	7.5	7.8	4.4	3.9	4.3
Alcohol	87.8	88.3	87.1	(NA)	70.1	69.2	54.9	56.5	55.6
"Binge" alcohol use [4]	(NA)	(NA)	(NA)	(NA)	(NA)	(NA)	(NA)	(NA)	24.8

NA Not available. [1] Illicit drugs include marijuana, cocaine (including crack), heroin, hallucinogens, inhalants, and the misuse of prescription psychotherapeutic drugs. Beginning with 2015, methamphetamine was reallocated from prescription psychotherapeutics to the illicit drugs category. [2] Beginning with 2015, methamphetamine is included with illicit drugs. [3] Includes other products not shown separately. Tobacco product use in the past year excludes past year pipe tobacco use, but includes past month pipe tobacco use. [4] Binge alcohol use is defined as drinking five or more drinks (for males) or four or more drinks (for females) on the same occasion (i.e., at the same time or within a couple of hours of each other) on at least 1 day in the past 30 days. In 2015, the definition for females changed from five to four drinks.

Source: U.S. Substance Abuse and Mental Health Services Administration, *Results from the 2015 National Survey on Drug Use and Health: Detailed Tables,* September 2016, and earlier reports. See also <http://www.samhsa.gov/data/population-data-nsduh/reports>.

Table 215. Estimated Use of Drugs and Alcohol by State: 2014 to 2015

[35,584 represents 35,584,000. Table presents annual averages for a 2-year period. Data are based on the National Survey on Drug Use and Health (NSDUH). Covers persons age 12 years and over who indicated use of a substance within the past year (during the 12 months prior to the interview) and the past month (during the 30 days prior to the interview). Based on a representative sample of the U.S. population, including persons living in households, noninstitutional group quarters such as dormitories and homeless shelters, and civilians on military bases. Data were collected in 2014 and 2015 from over 135,000 persons. State estimates have been developed using small area estimation procedure in which State-level data are combined with county and census block group/tract-level data from the State. For methodology information, see "2014-2015 NSDUH Guide to State Tables and Summary of Small Area Estimation Methodology" at <https://www.samhsa.gov /data/sites/default/files/NSDUHsaeMethodology2015/NSDUHsaeMethodology2015.pdf>]

| State | Past year use | | | | Alcohol use disorder in past year [1] | | Past month use | | | |
| | Marijuana | | Cocaine | | | | Marijuana | | Alcohol use | |
	Number (1,000)	Percent	Number (1,000)	Percent	Number (1,000)	Percent	Number (1,000)	Percent	Number (1,000)	Percent
United States...........	35,584	13.4	4,690	1.8	16,365	6.1	22,207	8.3	139,003	52.2
Alabama...................	389	9.6	50	1.2	188	4.6	217	5.3	1,779	43.9
Alaska.....................	127	21.9	12	2.0	43	7.4	83	14.4	319	55.0
Arizona...................	734	13.1	128	2.3	373	6.7	476	8.5	2,865	51.2
Arkansas.................	284	11.6	26	1.1	120	4.9	176	7.2	1,024	41.8
California.................	4,936	15.2	699	2.2	2,122	6.6	3,133	9.7	16,688	51.5
Colorado.................	1,033	23.1	123	2.8	335	7.5	742	16.6	2,651	59.2
Connecticut.............	479	15.7	74	2.4	211	6.9	293	9.6	1,844	60.3
Delaware.................	103	13.1	17	2.2	46	5.9	64	8.0	425	53.9
District of Columbia......	134	23.5	18	3.2	47	8.2	68	11.9	393	69.1
Florida....................	2,152	12.6	325	1.9	1,009	5.9	1,330	7.8	9,369	54.8
Georgia...................	1,052	12.7	143	1.7	455	5.5	646	7.8	4,058	48.9
Hawaii.....................	147	12.7	22	1.9	62	5.4	92	7.9	538	46.6
Idaho......................	152	11.4	14	1.0	81	6.0	85	6.3	595	44.5
Illinois....................	1,339	12.5	194	1.8	649	6.0	850	7.9	5,826	54.3
Indiana...................	760	13.9	68	1.2	325	5.9	477	8.7	2,761	50.4
Iowa.......................	235	9.1	27	1.1	165	6.4	124	4.8	1,451	56.0
Kansas....................	292	12.4	28	1.2	141	6.0	172	7.3	1,241	52.5
Kentucky.................	449	12.3	58	1.6	206	5.6	258	7.1	1,560	42.6
Louisiana.................	427	11.2	66	1.7	251	6.6	241	6.3	1,906	50.0
Maine.....................	227	19.7	21	1.8	61	5.3	157	13.7	696	60.4
Maryland.................	757	15.1	75	1.5	329	6.6	481	9.6	2,921	58.4
Massachusetts...........	1,058	18.3	142	2.4	388	6.7	677	11.7	3,357	57.9
Michigan.................	1,266	15.1	104	1.2	474	5.7	845	10.1	4,517	53.9
Minnesota...............	579	12.7	69	1.5	289	6.3	346	7.6	2,709	59.4
Mississippi...............	212	8.7	25	1.0	126	5.2	131	5.4	965	39.5
Missouri..................	683	13.5	68	1.3	310	6.1	405	8.0	2,562	50.8
Montana..................	133	15.4	13	1.5	60	7.0	96	11.1	499	57.9
Nebraska.................	166	10.7	21	1.4	106	6.8	97	6.3	886	57.4
Nevada...................	309	13.0	35	1.5	149	6.2	186	7.8	1,259	52.8
New Hampshire..........	199	17.4	35	3.1	82	7.2	138	12.1	729	63.6
New Jersey...............	894	11.9	129	1.7	431	5.7	528	7.0	4,271	56.7
New Mexico..............	253	14.7	33	1.9	117	6.8	174	10.1	807	47.0
New York.................	2,519	15.0	425	2.5	1,073	6.4	1,601	9.6	9,144	54.6
North Carolina...........	975	11.8	148	1.8	437	5.3	603	7.3	3,790	45.8
North Dakota.............	61	9.9	7	1.2	43	7.1	36	5.9	360	58.8
Ohio.......................	1,179	12.1	140	1.4	629	6.5	744	7.7	5,109	52.6
Oklahoma................	358	11.3	35	1.1	196	6.2	198	6.2	1,460	46.0
Oregon...................	659	19.4	73	2.1	235	6.9	432	12.7	1,997	58.8
Pennsylvania............	1,339	12.4	175	1.6	699	6.4	838	7.7	6,130	56.6
Rhode Island............	170	18.8	23	2.5	63	7.0	118	13.0	536	59.4
South Carolina..........	507	12.6	66	1.6	240	5.9	328	8.1	1,865	46.2
South Dakota............	75	10.8	7	1.0	51	7.4	48	6.9	403	58.0
Tennessee...............	606	11.0	83	1.5	290	5.3	347	6.3	2,382	43.4
Texas.....................	2,213	10.1	310	1.4	1,305	6.0	1,336	6.1	10,499	47.9
Utah.......................	211	9.1	20	0.9	111	4.8	117	5.0	728	31.3
Vermont..................	111	20.5	15	2.7	38	7.0	80	14.7	330	60.7
Virginia...................	796	11.5	85	1.2	397	5.8	457	6.6	3,572	51.8
Washington..............	1,037	17.5	109	1.8	337	5.7	665	11.2	3,395	57.3
West Virginia............	174	11.1	24	1.5	86	5.5	109	6.9	648	41.3
Wisconsin................	584	12.1	77	1.6	355	7.3	334	6.9	2,923	60.4
Wyoming.................	52	10.9	5	1.1	31	6.4	30	6.3	261	54.3

[1] Alcohol use disorder is defined as meeting the criteria for alcohol abuse or alcohol dependence, as outlined in the *Diagnostic and Statistical Manual of Mental Disorders,* 4th edition (DSM-IV).

Source: U.S. Substance Abuse and Mental Health Services Administration, "2014-2015 NSDUH State Estimates of Substance Use and Mental Disorders," <https://www.samhsa.gov/data/population-data-nsduh/reports>, accessed March 2017.

Table 216. Prescription Psychotherapeutic Drug Use and Misuse by Drug Type and User Characteristics: 2015

[In percent. Data are from the National Survey on Drug Use and Health, and cover persons age 12 and older. Misuse of prescription drugs is defined as use in any way not directed by a physician, including use without a prescription of one's own medication; use in greater amounts, more often, or longer than instructed to take a drug; or use in any other way not directed by a physician. Excludes over-the-counter drugs. See also headnote, Table 214]

User characteristics	Any use in past year					Past year misuse by drug type				
	Any drug	Pain relievers	Tranquil- izers	Stimu- lants	Seda- tives	Any drug	Pain relievers	Tranquil- izers	Stimu- lants	Seda- tives
Total	**44.5**	**36.4**	**14.7**	**6.4**	**6.9**	**7.1**	**4.7**	**2.3**	**2.0**	**0.6**
SEX										
Male	40.9	33.9	11.3	6.5	5.6	7.8	5.3	2.4	2.3	0.5
Female	47.8	38.8	17.9	6.3	8.2	6.4	4.0	2.1	1.6	0.7
AGE										
12 to 17 years	28.1	22.7	4.3	7.3	2.4	5.9	3.9	1.6	2.0	0.4
18 years and over	46.1	37.8	15.8	6.3	7.4	7.2	4.7	2.3	2.0	0.6
18 to 25 years	44.3	34.8	12.1	14.1	3.8	15.3	8.5	5.4	7.3	0.8
26 years and over	46.4	38.3	16.4	5.0	8.0	5.8	4.1	1.8	1.1	0.5
RACE AND ETHNICITY										
Not Hispanic	46.1	37.6	15.5	6.7	7.5	7.1	4.6	2.3	2.1	0.6
White	48.2	38.7	17.8	7.5	8.3	7.6	4.8	2.6	2.4	0.7
Black or African American	42.7	38.3	9.1	3.9	4.9	5.8	4.4	1.5	0.7	0.2
American Indian or Alaska Native	44.4	38.7	12.1	6.3	5.2	6.8	5.6	2.0	1.8	–
Native Hawaiian or Other Pacific Islander	38.3	32.7	4.7	5.0	3.3	7.0	5.4	2.1	1.8	0.5
Asian	26.7	22.0	4.6	2.9	3.7	3.1	1.8	0.7	1.0	0.1
Two or more races	52.9	44.8	16.4	10.2	7.1	11.7	8.4	3.6	4.1	1.4
Hispanic or Latino	36.3	30.2	10.3	4.9	4.2	7.0	5.0	2.0	1.5	0.4
REGION										
Northeast	42.8	33.6	15.3	6.1	6.7	6.9	4.2	2.3	2.1	0.6
Midwest	43.5	35.9	13.8	6.6	6.1	6.7	4.4	1.9	2.2	0.4
South	46.1	37.8	16.1	7.1	7.6	7.1	4.6	2.6	2.0	0.6
West	44.0	36.8	12.8	5.5	6.9	7.6	5.3	2.1	1.6	0.6
METRO STATUS										
Large metro [1]	42.9	34.7	13.9	6.4	6.6	7.3	4.7	2.2	2.0	0.6
Small metro [2]	46.5	38.6	15.7	6.8	7.4	6.9	4.6	2.4	2.0	0.6
Nonmetro	46.2	38.5	15.7	5.8	7.3	6.4	4.6	2.2	1.7	0.5

–Represents or rounds to zero. [1] Over 1 million population. [2] Less than 1 million population.

Source: U.S. Substance Abuse and Mental Health Services Administration, *Results From the 2015 National Survey on Drug Use and Health: Detailed Tables,* September 2016. See also <https://www.samhsa.gov/data/population-data-nsduh>.

Table 217. Prescription Drug Use in Past 30 Days by Sex, Race/Ethnicity, and Age: 1988 to 2014

[Data shown as percent of population using prescription drugs in past 30 days. Based on the National Health and Nutrition Examination Survey, covering a sample of the civilian noninstitutionalized population]

Sex, race/ethnicity, and age	Use of 1 or more prescription drugs			Use of 3 or more prescription drugs			Use of 5 or more prescription drugs		
	1988- 1994	2007- 2010	2011- 2014	1988- 1994	2007- 2010	2011- 2014	1988- 1994	2007- 2010	2011- 2014
Both sexes, age adjusted [1, 2]	**39.1**	**47.5**	**46.9**	**11.8**	**20.8**	**21.5**	**4.0**	**10.1**	**10.9**
Male	32.7	42.8	42.6	9.4	19.1	19.7	2.9	9.2	9.7
Female	45.0	52.0	51.2	13.9	22.5	23.2	4.9	11.0	12.0
White alone [3]	41.1	52.8	51.9	12.4	22.4	23.1	4.2	10.7	11.5
Male	34.2	47.5	46.8	9.9	20.6	21.0	3.1	9.8	10.2
Female	47.6	57.9	57.0	14.6	24.3	25.1	5.1	11.6	12.8
Black or African American alone [3]	36.9	42.3	44.2	12.6	20.7	22.5	3.8	10.8	12.1
Male	31.1	36.7	38.3	10.2	17.7	19.4	2.9	9.1	10.1
Female	41.4	46.8	49.0	14.3	22.9	24.9	4.5	12.0	13.7
Asian alone [3]	(NA)	(NA)	34.3	(NA)	(NA)	14.3	(NA)	(NA)	6.2
Male	(NA)	(NA)	31.9	(NA)	(NA)	14.1	(NA)	(NA)	6.2
Female	(NA)	(NA)	36.3	(NA)	(NA)	14.6	(NA)	(NA)	6.1
Hispanic or Latino [4]	(NA)	35.2	35.7	(NA)	15.7	16.0	(NA)	8.4	8.4
Male	(NA)	31.7	32.1	(NA)	14.0	15.0	(NA)	7.3	7.9
Female	(NA)	38.8	39.2	(NA)	17.4	17.1	(NA)	9.5	8.8
Both sexes, crude	**37.8**	**48.5**	**48.9**	**11.0**	**21.7**	**23.1**	**3.6**	**10.6**	**11.9**
Male	30.6	43.0	43.7	8.3	19.0	20.4	2.5	9.1	10.0
Under 18 years	20.4	24.5	21.1	2.6	4.4	4.3	(B)	0.8	0.9
18 to 44 years	21.5	29.5	28.8	3.6	7.1	7.5	[5] 0.8	2.1	3.0
45 to 64 years	47.2	61.3	65.6	15.1	30.4	33.0	4.8	14.4	15.7
65 years and over	67.2	88.8	88.7	31.3	66.8	65.2	11.3	39.5	38.4
Female	44.6	53.8	53.9	13.6	24.2	25.8	4.7	12.1	13.6
Under 18 years	20.6	23.5	22.0	2.3	3.1	3.5	(B)	[5] 0.7	(B)
18 to 44 years	40.7	47.6	45.3	7.6	12.2	12.6	1.7	4.0	4.8
45 to 64 years	62.0	70.8	72.1	24.7	38.1	39.4	9.7	19.1	20.7
65 years and over	78.3	90.4	92.1	38.2	66.4	68.1	15.6	39.8	42.6

NA Not available. B Estimate has a relative standard error greater than 30%. [1] Estimates are age-adjusted to the year 2000 standard population using four age groups: under 18 years, 18-44 years, 45-64 years, and 65 years and over. [2] Includes persons of other race/ethnicities, not shown separately. [3] Not Hispanic or Latino. [4] Persons of Hispanic or Latino origin may be of any race. [5] Estimate has a relative standard error (RSE) of 20% to 30% and is considered unreliable.

Source: U.S. National Center for Health Statistics, *Health, United States, 2016,* May 2017. See also <http://www.cdc.gov/nchs/hus.htm>.

Table 218. Height of Population Age 20 and Over by Sex, Age, and Race/Ethnicity: 2011 to 2014

[In inches. Data are for the 2011-2014 period. Based on National Health and Nutrition Examination Survey (NHANES), a sample of the civilian noninstitutional population. Data are collected through household interviews and health examinations. Height was measured without shoes. Survey oversampled persons age 80 and over, Hispanic persons, and non-Hispanic Black and Asian persons; see source for more information]

Age and race/ethnicity	Males, height in inches						Females, height in inches					
	Mean	Percentile					Mean	Percentile				
		10th	25th	50th	75th	90th		10th	25th	50th	75th	90th
Total: [1]												
20 years and over......	69.2	65.4	67.2	69.1	71.2	73.0	63.7	60.1	61.7	63.7	65.5	67.2
20-29 years............	69.4	65.7	67.4	69.4	71.4	73.4	64.1	60.8	62.3	64.1	65.8	67.4
30-39 years............	69.5	65.8	67.5	69.5	71.5	73.5	64.3	60.5	62.3	64.4	66.4	67.9
40-49 years............	69.4	65.7	67.3	69.3	71.2	73.1	64.1	60.5	62.2	64.2	65.9	67.6
50-59 years............	69.3	65.7	67.2	69.1	71.4	73.0	63.7	60.2	61.8	63.9	65.3	67.1
60-69 years............	69.0	65.2	67.1	69.1	71.2	72.5	63.2	60.1	61.5	63.2	64.9	66.5
70-79 years............	68.1	64.7	66.3	67.9	69.8	71.7	62.7	59.2	60.8	63.0	64.5	66.1
80 years and over......	67.6	64.2	65.9	67.7	69.4	71.0	61.3	57.7	59.6	61.3	63.1	64.3
White, non-Hispanic:												
20 years and over......	69.7	66.2	67.7	69.6	71.5	73.3	64.1	60.6	62.3	64.1	65.8	67.5
20-39 years............	70.1	66.6	68.2	70.2	72.1	73.8	64.9	61.7	63.2	64.9	66.6	68.2
40-59 years............	69.9	66.5	68.1	69.9	71.7	73.3	64.4	61.1	62.8	64.4	66.0	67.8
60 years and over......	69.0	65.3	67.0	69.0	70.9	72.4	63.0	59.7	61.1	63.0	64.7	66.3
Black, non-Hispanic:												
20 years and over......	69.5	66.0	67.4	69.3	71.4	73.3	64.2	60.7	62.5	64.2	65.9	67.4
20-39 years............	69.8	66.3	67.6	69.7	71.9	73.6	64.4	60.9	62.9	64.4	66.0	67.5
40-59 years............	69.5	66.1	67.6	69.3	71.4	72.8	64.5	61.1	62.9	64.6	66.1	67.7
60 years and over......	68.5	65.2	66.7	68.4	70.3	72.4	63.1	59.6	61.4	63.2	64.9	66.4
Hispanic:												
20 years and over......	67.4	63.8	65.5	67.3	69.3	71.1	62.0	58.7	60.3	61.9	63.7	65.3
20-39 years............	67.9	64.4	65.9	67.8	69.8	71.5	62.6	59.2	60.8	62.6	64.2	65.5
40-59 years............	67.2	63.6	65.3	67.2	69.1	70.9	61.9	58.7	60.1	61.6	63.5	65.4
60 years and over......	66.0	62.6	64.1	65.9	67.6	69.4	60.6	57.5	59.1	60.6	62.1	63.6

[1] Total includes persons of other race/ethnicities not shown separately.

Source: U.S. Centers for Disease Control and Prevention, National Health and Nutrition Examination Survey, *Anthropometric Reference Data For Children and Adults: United States, 2011-2014*, Series 3, No. 39, August 2016. See also <http://www.cdc.gov/nchs/nhanes.htm>.

Table 219. Weight of Population Age 20 and Over by Age, Sex, and Race/Ethnicity: 2011 to 2014

[In pounds. Data are for 2011-2014 period. Based on National Health and Nutrition Examination Survey (NHANES). Pregnant females are excluded from the tabulations on weight. See headnote, Table 218]

Age and race/ethnicity	Males, weight in pounds						Females, weight in pounds					
	Mean	Percentile					Mean	Percentile				
		10th	25th	50th	75th	90th		10th	25th	50th	75th	90th
Total: [1]												
20 years and over.......	195.7	146.2	165.1	189.3	218.8	249.9	168.5	119.8	136.0	159.1	191.1	229.3
20–29 years............	186.8	137.6	152.9	177.8	208.5	247.2	161.8	113.9	128.8	149.8	184.6	228.7
30–39 years............	198.8	150.2	168.1	190.8	221.2	259.6	172.9	124.0	137.7	160.5	195.9	237.7
40–49 years............	201.7	156.3	171.7	196.4	222.5	249.0	173.1	124.8	138.8	164.0	196.8	237.2
50–59 years............	199.5	152.0	170.2	195.9	222.3	250.4	174.4	124.9	141.0	167.4	197.2	239.4
60–69 years............	199.7	147.0	168.0	195.3	223.1	255.3	168.8	122.5	140.3	164.4	191.2	224.8
70–79 years............	189.3	146.2	166.6	183.6	212.0	236.3	165.8	120.2	138.6	158.5	188.5	216.5
80 years and over.......	174.6	132.6	154.2	171.1	194.5	216.1	141.9	103.8	121.7	141.0	160.6	180.4
White, non-Hispanic:												
20 years and over.......	198.8	151.6	169.1	192.9	221.4	250.5	168.4	122.2	137.4	158.7	190.3	226.5
20–39 years............	193.8	144.9	161.7	183.5	218.5	255.0	167.9	119.8	134.0	155.9	189.0	230.8
40–59 years............	204.6	161.2	175.7	199.3	225.5	250.4	173.4	127.0	140.9	166.1	195.4	237.5
60 years and over.......	196.5	149.0	168.9	190.2	219.3	249.2	162.9	117.0	136.2	157.0	183.4	215.3
Black, non-Hispanic:												
20 years and over.......	199.3	141.4	161.4	191.6	227.2	264.4	190.2	131.6	154.0	183.1	217.8	256.8
20–39 years............	197.7	138.6	157.9	189.0	228.0	264.2	190.0	129.6	151.0	183.1	219.0	263.3
40–59 years............	204.8	147.0	169.8	196.6	231.4	270.3	196.5	140.0	159.2	187.3	223.5	259.6
60 years and over.......	191.4	141.2	158.8	185.5	214.4	251.9	179.9	126.0	147.2	174.7	208.9	235.1
Hispanic:												
20 years and over.......	189.9	143.1	161.6	184.7	209.1	240.0	164.7	121.3	135.5	157.4	186.2	219.2
20–39 years............	192.2	142.3	160.7	186.0	214.1	243.9	163.5	120.7	134.8	152.9	182.5	220.7
40–59 years............	190.1	147.2	166.0	186.8	207.2	232.2	169.1	122.7	138.6	163.6	191.8	221.7
60 years and over.......	179.3	140.1	153.3	175.4	198.3	226.5	158.3	114.4	132.5	154.0	179.9	204.8

[1] Total includes persons of other race/ethnicities not shown separately.

Source: U.S. Centers for Disease Control and Prevention, National Health and Nutrition Examination Survey, *Anthropometric Reference Data For Children and Adults: United States, 2011-2014*, Series 3, No. 39, August 2016. See also <http://www.cdc.gov/nchs/nhanes.htm>.

Table 220. Body Mass Index of Population Age 20 and Over by Age, Sex, and Race/Ethnicity: 2011 to 2014

[Data are for 2011-2014 period. Body Mass Index (BMI) is a measure that adjusts body weight for height, and is calculated as weight in kilograms divided by the square of height in meters. For both men and women, BMI weight categories are: under 18.5 underweight, 18.5-24.9 normal, 25.0-29.9 overweight, and 30.0 and over obese. Data are based on National Health and Nutrition Examination Survey (NHANES), a sample of the civilian noninstitutional population. Data are collected through household interviews and health examinations. Excludes pregnant women. Survey oversampled persons age 80 and over, Hispanic persons, and non-Hispanic Black and Asian persons; see source for more information]

Age and race/ethnicity	Males, BMI						Females, BMI					
	Mean	Percentile					Mean	Percentile				
		10th	25th	50th	75th	90th		10th	25th	50th	75th	90th
Total: [1]												
20 years and over......	28.7	22.2	24.6	27.7	31.6	36.1	29.2	21.0	23.6	27.7	33.2	39.3
20–29 years............	27.2	20.5	22.5	25.5	30.5	35.1	27.6	19.8	21.9	25.6	31.8	38.9
30–39 years............	28.9	22.4	24.8	27.5	31.9	36.5	29.4	21.1	23.3	27.6	33.1	40.0
40–49 years............	29.4	23.4	25.7	28.5	31.9	36.5	29.6	21.5	23.7	28.1	33.4	39.6
50–59 years............	29.1	22.7	25.4	28.3	32.0	35.2	30.2	21.5	24.5	28.6	34.4	40.7
60–69 years............	29.4	22.7	25.3	28.0	32.4	36.9	29.7	21.7	24.5	28.9	33.4	38.7
70–79 years............	28.6	23.2	25.4	27.8	30.9	34.9	29.6	22.1	24.6	28.3	33.4	39.1
80 years and over......	26.7	21.5	24.1	26.3	29.0	32.3	26.6	20.4	23.3	26.1	29.7	32.8
White, non-Hispanic:												
20 years and over......	28.7	22.3	24.8	27.7	31.6	36.0	28.8	20.9	23.4	27.3	32.6	38.8
20–39 years............	27.7	21.1	23.2	26.4	30.6	35.9	28.0	20.4	22.3	25.9	31.8	38.9
40–59 years............	29.4	23.2	25.7	28.5	32.2	36.0	29.4	21.4	23.6	27.9	33.4	40.1
60 years and over......	29.0	22.8	25.3	27.9	31.6	36.0	28.9	21.4	24.2	27.9	32.4	37.5
Black, non-Hispanic:												
20 years and over......	28.9	21.1	24.0	27.9	32.2	37.7	32.5	22.8	26.6	31.3	36.8	43.5
20–39 years............	28.4	20.5	23.3	26.4	32.5	37.2	32.1	21.8	25.9	31.0	36.9	43.4
40–59 years............	29.7	21.9	25.1	28.7	32.4	39.2	33.3	23.5	27.1	31.9	37.2	44.8
60 years and over......	28.6	22.1	24.2	27.7	31.6	36.5	31.7	22.8	26.2	30.9	35.8	41.3
Hispanic:												
20 years and over......	29.3	22.9	25.5	28.6	32.0	36.4	30.0	22.1	25.1	28.9	33.9	38.8
20–39 years............	29.3	22.1	24.9	28.6	32.4	37.3	29.3	21.7	24.4	27.9	32.9	38.6
40–59 years............	29.5	23.8	26.4	28.8	31.7	35.3	31.0	22.7	26.1	30.2	34.9	39.5
60 years and over......	28.8	23.7	25.5	27.9	31.6	34.5	30.3	22.4	25.9	29.5	34.3	38.4

[1] Total includes persons of other race/ethnicities not shown separately.

Source: U.S. Centers for Disease Control and Prevention, National Health and Nutrition Examination Survey, *Anthropometric Reference Data For Children and Adults: United States, 2011-2014*, Series 3, No. 39, August 2016. See also <http://www.cdc.gov/nchs/nhanes.htm>.

Table 221. Leisure-Time Aerobic and Muscle-Strengthening Activity Among Adults Age 18 and Over by Selected Characteristics: 2015

[In percent. Percents are age-adjusted and allow for comparisons to results from earlier surveys and within demographic groups. Covers persons age 18 and over. Based on the National Health Interview Survey (NHIS), a sample survey of the civilian noninstitutionalized population. Measures of physical activity reflect the federal "2008 Physical Activity Guidelines for Americans"; see <https://health.gov/PAGuidelines/>. The guidelines include an aerobic component; the full physical activity guidelines include muscle-strengthening and aerobic activities. NHIS questions ask about frequency and duration of light-to moderate-intensity and vigorous-intensity leisure-time physical activities, and frequency of leisure-time muscle strengthening activities. Questions are phrased in terms of current behavior and lack a specific reference period. For definition of age adjustment, see text, Section 2]

Characteristic	Inactive/ insufficiently active [1]	Sufficiently active [2]	Met muscle strengthening and aerobic guidelines [3]	Characteristic	Inactive/ insufficiently active [1]	Sufficiently active [2]	Met muscle strengthening and aerobic guidelines [3]
Total..................	**50.3**	**49.7**	**21.5**	Native Hawaiian/ Pacific Islander...............	49.5	50.5	32.9
SEX				Two or more races............	51.1	48.9	22.7
Male....................	47.0	52.9	25.3				
Female..................	53.3	46.7	17.9	HISPANIC ORIGIN AND RACE			
				Hispanic or Latino [5]............	56.7	43.3	16.8
AGE [4]				Not Hispanic or Latino..........	48.9	51.1	22.5
18 to 44 years..................	43.6	56.4	26.4	White, non-Hispanic..........	47.1	53.0	23.4
45 to 64 years..................	54.1	45.9	18.1	Black, non-Hispanic...........	58.2	41.8	19.8
65 to 74 years..................	56.7	43.3	15.5				
75 years and over..............	72.8	27.2	8.7	EDUCATION [6]			
				Less than high school diploma......................	70.0	30.0	7.9
RACE				High school diploma or GED [7]......................	61.1	38.9	13.1
Single race.....................	50.2	49.7	21.5	Some college...................	53.2	46.8	19.0
White.........................	49.2	50.9	22.0	Bachelor's degree or higher....	37.2	62.8	30.4
Black or African American.....	58.3	41.7	19.7				
American Indian/ Alaska Native................	52.8	47.2	18.9				
Asian........................	48.6	51.4	19.1				

[1] "Inactive" is having no leisure-time aerobic activity that lasted at least 10 minutes. "Insufficiently active" is having aerobic activities for 10 minutes or more but less than 150 minutes per week. [2] "Sufficiently active," which meets the aerobic component of the 2008 federal physical activity guidelines, is participating in moderate-intensity leisure-time physical activity 150 minutes or more per week, or in vigorous-intensity leisure-time physical activity 75 minutes or more per week, or an equivalent combination. [3] Persons who are sufficiently active, and who engage in muscle strengthening activities at least 2 times a week. [4] Age data are not age-adjusted. [5] Persons of Hispanic or Latino origin may be of any race. [6] For persons age 25 and over. [7] General educational development high school equivalency diploma.

Source: U.S. National Center for Health Statistics, 2015 National Health Interview Survey, "Tables of Summary Health Statistics," <http://www.cdc.gov/nchs/nhis/SHS.htm>, accessed February 2017.

Table 222. Sleep—Percent Distribution of Adults Age 18 and Over by Hours of Sleep by Selected Characteristics: 2011 to 2014

[235,845 represents 235,845,000. Data are annualized over 2011-2014 (4-year) period. Estimates are age-adjusted using the projected 2000 U.S. population as the standard population and using three age groups: 18–44 years, 45–64 years, and 65 years and over. All estimates are based on data from the Sample Adult files, which are derived from the Sample Adult component of the National Health Interview Survey. Survey respondents where asked, "On average, how many hours of sleep do you get in a 24 hour period?" Response options were 1-24 hours]

Characteristic	Adults age 18 and over (1,000)	Hours of sleep (percent distribution)		
		6 or less	7 to 8	9 or more
Total [1]	**235,845**	**29.7**	**61.6**	**8.7**
SEX				
Male	113,760	29.6	62.4	8.0
Female	122,085	29.8	60.9	9.3
AGE [2]				
18 to 24 years old	30,153	22.9	63.6	13.4
25 to 44 years old	81,276	31.8	62.4	5.8
45 to 64 years old	81,945	33.8	60.1	6.2
65 to 74 years old	24,278	25.1	63.6	11.3
75 years old and over	18,194	22.0	57.1	20.9
RACE				
Single race [3]	232,068	29.6	61.7	8.6
White	188,610	28.3	63.0	8.7
Black or African American	28,367	37.8	52.6	9.7
American Indian or Alaska Native	1,954	35.0	55.3	9.6
Asian	12,745	29.6	64.4	6.0
Native Hawaiian or Other Pacific Islander	393	47.5	44.3	8.2
Two or more races [4]	3,776	37.7	53.0	9.2
Black or African American, white	753	40.5	54.3	5.2
American Indian or Alaska Native, white	1,557	40.5	48.7	10.8
HISPANIC ORIGIN AND RACE [5]				
Hispanic or Latino	34,996	28.8	62.2	8.9
Mexican or Mexican American	21,611	26.8	63.5	9.7
Not Hispanic or Latino	200,849	30.1	61.4	8.6
White, single race	156,720	28.5	62.9	8.6
Black or African American, single race	27,201	38.0	52.4	9.6
EDUCATION [6]				
Less than high school graduate	27,998	30.9	57.6	11.4
GED diploma [7]	6,018	37.3	53.2	9.5
High school graduate	46,650	32.1	59.1	8.8
Some college, no degree	35,745	35.2	57.3	7.5
Associate of arts degree	23,771	33.3	59.2	7.5
Bachelor of arts, science degree	40,524	27.0	67.3	5.7
Masters, doctorate, medical degree	23,877	24.5	70.3	5.3
POVERTY STATUS [8]				
Below poverty level	32,666	33.6	55.0	11.4
100% to less than 200% poverty level	45,025	32.2	57.2	10.6
200% to less than 400% poverty level	70,656	30.4	60.9	8.7
400% or more of poverty level	87,498	26.8	66.6	6.5
MARITAL STATUS				
Never married	52,245	28.9	60.5	10.6
Married	124,885	29.0	64.0	7.1
Cohabiting	17,226	32.4	58.6	9.0
Divorced or separated	26,937	38.5	54.0	7.6
Widowed	14,165	38.4	54.0	7.7

[1] Includes persons of other races and unknown race and ethnicity, unknown education, unknown poverty status, and unknown marital status. [2] Estimates for age groups are not age adjusted. [3] Refers to persons who indicated only a single race group, including those of Hispanic or Latino origin. [4] Refers to all persons who indicated more than one race group, including those of Hispanic or Latino origin. [5] Persons of Hispanic or Latino origin may be of any race or combination of races. [6] Shown only for adults age 25 and over. Estimates are age adjusted to the projected 2000 U.S. population as the standard population using three age groups: 25–44, 45–64, and 65 and over. [7] General Educational Development high school equivalency diploma. [8] Based on family income and family size using the U.S. Census Bureau poverty thresholds for 2010, 2011, 2012, and 2013.

Source: U.S. National Center for Health Statistics, National Health Interview Survey, "Tables of Summary Health Statistics," <http://www.cdc.gov/nchs/nhis/SHS.htm>, accessed February 2017.

Table 223. Depression and Receipt of Mental Health Treatment in the Past Year Among Adults Age 18 and Over by Selected Characteristics: 2014 and 2015

[In thousands (15,655 represents 15,655,000), except percent. Based on the National Survey on Drug Use and Health. Covers adults who had a major depressive episode as defined in the 4th edition of the *Diagnostic and Statistical Manual of Mental Disorders* (DSM-IV), which specifies a period of at least 2 weeks when a person experienced a depressed mood or loss of interest or pleasure in daily activities and had a majority of specified depression symptoms. Treatment is defined as seeing or talking to a professional or using prescription medication for depression in the past year; respondents with unknown treatment data were excluded]

Characteristic	Had major depressive episode (MDE)				Those with an MDE who received treatment for depression			
	2014		2015		2014		2015	
	Number (1,000)	Percent of population	Number (1,000)	Percent of population	Number (1,000)	Percent	Number (1,000)	Percent
Total.................	15,655	6.6	16,079	6.7	10,717	68.6	10,801	67.2
AGE								
18 to 25 years old...........	3,200	9.3	3,554	10.3	1,581	49.5	1,662	46.8
26 to 49 years old...........	6,970	7.2	7,329	7.5	4,723	67.9	4,938	67.4
50 years old and older.........	5,485	5.2	5,196	4.8	4,413	80.8	4,201	80.9
SEX AND AGE								
Male.........	5,492	4.8	5,461	4.7	3,422	62.4	3,208	58.8
18 to 25 years old...........	1,198	6.9	1,321	7.6	520	43.6	478	36.2
26 to 49 years old...........	2,441	5.1	2,486	5.2	1,443	59.2	1,518	61.1
50 years old and older.........	1,853	3.7	1,654	3.3	1,459	78.8	1,212	73.3
Female.........	10,163	8.2	10,618	8.5	7,295	72.0	7,593	71.6
18 to 25 years old...........	2,002	11.6	2,233	13.0	1,061	53.0	1,184	53.1
26 to 49 years old...........	4,528	9.2	4,843	9.7	3,280	72.6	3,420	70.7
50 years old and older.........	3,633	6.4	3,542	6.2	2,954	81.8	2,989	84.4
RACE AND HISPANIC ORIGIN								
Not Hispanic or Latino...........	13,605	6.8	14,278	7.0	9,469	69.7	9,721	68.1
White...........	10,979	7.1	11,747	7.5	7,877	71.9	8,297	70.6
Black or African American...........	1,511	5.4	1,380	4.9	879	58.5	799	57.9
American Indian or Alaska Native......	74	6.0	111	8.9	(B)	(B)	(B)	(B)
Native Hawaiian or other Pacific Islander...........	60	6.7	31	5.2	(B)	(B)	(B)	(B)
Asian...........	519	4.2	543	4.1	(B)	(B)	(B)	(B)
Two or more races...........	461	12.7	467	12.2	350	75.9	314	67.9
Hispanic or Latino...........	2,050	5.6	1,801	4.8	1,248	61.2	1,080	60.1

B Low precision; no estimate reported. Does not meet statistical standards for reliability of a derived figure.

Source: U.S. Substance Abuse and Mental Health Services Administration, "Results from the 2015 National Survey on Drug Use and Health: Detailed Tables," accessed February 2017. See also <https://www.samhsa.gov/data/population-data-nsduh/reports>.

Table 224. Dental Care Visit in the Past Year—Percent of Population by Age and Selected Characteristics: 2000 to 2015

[In percent. Covers civilian noninstitutionalized population who had a dental care visit in the past year. Based on National Health Interview Survey; see Appendix III]

Characteristic	Age 2 years and over			Age 2 to 17 years			Age 18 to 64 years			Age 65 years and over		
	2000	2010	2015	2000	2010	2015	2000	2010	2015	2000	2010	2015
Total [1].................	66.2	64.7	68.2	74.1	78.9	84.7	65.1	61.1	64.0	56.6	57.7	62.7
Sex:												
Male.................	63.5	61.7	66.0	73.7	78.3	84.2	60.7	56.8	60.5	56.1	56.2	62.1
Female.................	68.8	67.5	70.3	74.6	79.6	85.2	69.4	65.4	67.3	56.9	58.9	63.2
Race ethnicity: [2]												
White alone.................	67.9	65.6	68.8	75.8	79.2	84.8	67.2	62.4	64.6	58.4	59.3	64.9
Black or African American alone......	59.5	58.8	64.3	70.0	79.0	85.1	57.1	53.1	59.4	38.2	40.6	46.3
American Indian/Alaska Native alone.................	58.6	57.4	61.7	71.3	73.2	82.1	55.0	49.8	57.9	(B)	72.2	[5] 36.1
Asian alone.................	67.1	66.5	71.1	72.8	74.8	82.2	65.6	64.6	69.2	60.6	61.9	62.8
Two or more races.................	65.1	65.2	68.1	71.4	77.9	84.7	60.5	54.7	58.3	57.4	48.1	41.7
Hispanic [3].................	52.3	56.5	62.2	60.6	74.8	83.8	48.6	48.5	53.2	44.5	42.1	52.2
Percent of poverty level: [4]												
Below 100%.................	50.4	50.6	55.8	62.4	73.2	82.2	46.8	41.0	45.0	33.3	32.8	35.9
100% to 199%.................	52.2	51.6	55.4	66.1	73.4	81.2	48.4	44.1	47.1	43.0	43.8	44.0
200% to 399%.................	65.6	63.5	66.4	75.5	79.0	84.1	62.2	59.6	61.8	62.8	57.9	61.3
400% or more.................	79.5	79.3	81.2	85.9	88.0	90.1	78.5	77.5	79.2	73.8	77.2	80.8

B Base figure too small to meet statistical standards of reliability of a derived figure. Data have a relative standard error greater than 30%. [1] Includes persons of other race and ethnic groups, not shown separately. [2] Race groups include persons of Hispanic and non-Hispanic origin. [3] Persons of Hispanic origin may be of any race. [4] Poverty level is based on family income and family size and composition using Census Bureau poverty thresholds. [5] Data have relative standard error of 20% to 30%.

Source: U.S. National Center for Health Statistics, *Health, United States, 2016,* May 2017. See also <http://www.cdc.gov/nchs/hus/>.

Table 225. Overweight and Obesity Prevalence Among Adults Age 20 and Over by Sex, Age, and Race/Ethnicity: 1988 to 2014

[Shown as percent of population age 20 and over. Weight status is determined by body mass index (BMI), which is calculated as weight in kilograms divided by the square of height in meters. Excludes pregnant women. Data are based on the National Health and Nutrition Examination Survey (NHANES); measurements of height and weight of a sample of the civilian noninstitutionalized population were taken without shoes. Percents do not sum to 100 because data for persons with BMI under 18.5 are not shown, and percent of persons with obesity are included with the overweight]

Characteristics	Normal weight [1]			Overweight or obese [2]			Obese [3]		
	1988 to 1994	2001 to 2004	2011 to 2014	1988 to 1994	2001 to 2004	2011 to 2014	1988 to 1994	2001 to 2004	2011 to 2014
Total, age-adjusted [4]	**41.6**	**32.3**	**28.9**	**56.0**	**66.0**	**69.5**	**22.9**	**31.4**	**36.4**
Male	37.9	28.3	26.0	60.9	70.5	73.0	20.2	29.5	34.5
Female	45.0	36.1	31.7	51.4	61.6	66.2	25.5	33.2	38.1
Total, crude	**42.6**	**32.2**	**28.6**	**54.9**	**66.1**	**69.8**	**22.3**	**31.5**	**36.5**
Male	39.4	28.4	26.2	59.4	70.4	72.8	19.5	29.5	34.5
Female	45.7	35.8	31.0	50.7	61.9	67.0	25.0	33.3	38.5
White, non-Hispanic	43.6	33.2	29.0	53.8	65.1	69.6	21.3	30.9	35.3
Male	38.2	27.4	25.1	60.6	71.6	74.2	19.8	30.5	34.3
Female	48.8	38.8	32.8	47.4	58.7	65.2	22.7	31.2	36.2
Black or African American, non-Hispanic	35.9	24.8	21.9	61.8	73.3	76.3	29.5	41.9	48.2
Male	41.5	31.5	29.3	56.7	66.3	69.1	20.7	30.7	37.6
Female	31.2	19.3	15.8	66.0	79.1	82.3	36.7	51.1	56.9
Asian, non-Hispanic	(NA)	(NA)	55.8	(NA)	(NA)	40.0	(NA)	(NA)	11.8
Male	(NA)	(NA)	50.7	(NA)	(NA)	46.3	(NA)	(NA)	11.7
Female	(NA)	(NA)	60.3	(NA)	(NA)	34.5	(NA)	(NA)	11.9
Hispanic [5]	(NA)	(NA)	21.7	(NA)	(NA)	77.5	(NA)	(NA)	42.3
Male	(NA)	(NA)	20.2	(NA)	(NA)	78.8	(NA)	(NA)	39.7
Female	(NA)	(NA)	23.1	(NA)	(NA)	76.3	(NA)	(NA)	45.0
Male by age:									
20 to 34 years	51.1	38.3	37.6	47.5	59.0	60.4	14.1	23.2	28.5
35 to 44 years	33.4	26.5	20.5	65.5	72.9	79.3	21.3	33.8	39.8
45 to 54 years	33.6	21.2	18.7	66.1	78.5	80.8	23.2	31.8	36.6
55 to 64 years	28.6	22.2	22.7	70.5	77.3	76.7	27.2	36.0	38.1
65 to 74 years	30.1	23.1	22.2	68.5	76.1	76.1	24.1	32.1	36.2
75 years and over	40.9	32.1	28.1	56.5	66.8	71.0	13.2	19.9	26.8
Female by age:									
20 to 34 years	57.9	44.2	38.1	37.0	51.6	58.5	18.5	28.6	33.4
35 to 44 years	47.1	38.3	32.5	49.6	60.1	65.6	25.5	33.3	39.1
45 to 54 years	37.2	31.0	27.8	60.3	67.4	71.4	32.4	38.0	41.7
55 to 64 years	31.5	29.2	24.2	66.3	69.9	74.3	33.7	39.0	44.4
65 to 74 years	37.0	27.0	26.9	60.3	71.5	71.2	26.9	37.9	40.7
75 years and over	43.0	34.6	32.9	52.3	63.7	64.6	19.2	23.2	30.5

NA Not available. [1] Normal weight status is a BMI of 18.5 to 24.9. [2] Overweight or obese is a BMI of 25.0 or more. [3] Obese is a BMI of 30.0 or more. [4] Estimates are age-adjusted to the year 2000 standard population using five age groups: 20–34 years, 35–44 years, 45–54 years, 55–64 years, and 65 years and over. [5] Persons of Hispanic origin may be of any race.

Source: U.S. National Center for Health Statistics, *Health, United States, 2016,* May 2017. See also <http://www.cdc.gov/nchs/hus/>.

Table 226. Children With Allergies by Type and Selected Characteristics: 2015

[In percent, except as indicated (73,453 represents 73,453,000). Covers incidence of allergies in the past 12 months among children under age 18. A child may have multiple types of allergies. Based on household interviews of a sample of the civilian noninstitutionalized population, regarding the sample child, not all children in the family. Percent data are age-adjusted, except as indicated. Unknowns for the columns were not included in the denominators when calculating percentages]

Selected characteristic	Total (1,000)	Hay fever	Respiratory allergies	Food allergies	Skin allergies
Total [1]	**73,453**	**8.4**	**10.1**	**5.7**	**12.0**
SEX					
Male	37,485	9.4	11.7	5.6	12.0
Female	35,968	7.3	8.5	5.9	11.9
AGE [2]					
4 years old and under	19,843	4.3	5.6	5.8	13.7
5 to 11 years old	28,776	8.9	11.6	5.5	12.3
12 to 17 years old	24,833	10.9	11.9	5.9	10.2
RACE					
Single race [3]	69,960	8.2	9.8	5.6	11.9
White	54,218	8.4	10.1	5.6	11.1
Black or African American	10,747	7.9	10.3	5.3	16.4
American Indian or Alaska Native	841	[5] 5.5	7.9	[5] 3.1	[5] 6.7
Asian	3,889	6.9	6.2	7.5	11.5
Native Hawaiian or Other Pacific Islander	265	(B)	(B)	(B)	[5] 17.9
Two or more races [3]	3,493	12.3	16.0	8.7	12.5
HISPANIC ORIGIN AND RACE [4]					
Hispanic or Latino	18,091	7.6	8.5	4.6	11.1
Not Hispanic or Latino	55,362	8.6	10.6	6.1	12.2
White only	38,196	8.9	11.0	6.1	11.2
Black or African American only	9,979	7.6	10.0	5.4	16.6

B Estimates are unreliable (relative standard error greater than 50%). [1] Total includes children of other races not shown separately, and children with unknown health status. [2] Estimates for age groups are not age-adjusted. [3] Includes children of Hispanic or Latino origin. [4] Children of Hispanic or Latino origin may be of any race or combination of races. [5] Figure has a relative standard error greater than 30% and less than or equal to 50% and should be used with caution.

Source: U.S. National Center for Health Statistics, 2015 National Health Interview Survey, "Tables of Summary Health Statistics," <http://www.cdc.gov/nchs/nhis/SHS.htm>, accessed February 2017.

Table 227. Learning Disability and Attention Deficit Hyperactivity Disorder Among Children Age 3 to 17 Years by Selected Characteristics: 2015

[In thousands (61,879 represents 61,879,000), except percent. Learning disability is based on the question, "Has a representative from a school or a health professional ever told you that (child's name) had a learning disability?" Attention deficit hyperactivity disorder is based on the question, "Has a doctor or other health professional ever told you that (child's name) had attention hyperactivity disorder or attention deficit disorder?"]

Selected characteristic	Total	Ever told child had—			
		Learning disability		Attention deficit hyperactivity disorder	
		Number [1]	Percent [2]	Number [1]	Percent [2]
Total [3]	**61,879**	**4,608**	**7.5**	**6,050**	**9.8**
SEX					
Male	31,593	2,948	9.3	4,238	13.4
Female	30,286	1,659	5.5	1,812	6.0
AGE [4]					
3 to 4 years	8,269	163	2.0	[8] 67	[8] 0.8
5 to 11 years	28,776	1,915	6.7	2,470	8.6
12 to 17 years	24,833	2,529	10.2	3,513	14.2
RACE					
Single race [5]	59,100	4,349	7.4	5,628	9.5
White	45,749	3,431	7.5	4,519	9.8
Black or African American	9,140	762	8.4	965	10.7
American Indian or Alaska Native	713	[8] 30	[8] 4.3	[8] 57	7.9
Asian	3,254	108	3.3	72	2.2
Native Hawaiian or other Pacific Islander	243	(B)	(B)	(B)	(B)
Two or more races [6]	2,780	258	9.5	422	15.7
Black or African American and White	1,227	116	9.6	227	19.8
American Indian or Alaska Native and White	452	(B)	[8] 13.4	(B)	[8] 16.9
HISPANIC ORIGIN AND RACE [7]					
Hispanic or Latino	14,975	1,030	6.9	891	6.0
Mexican or Mexican American	10,318	686	6.7	546	5.3
Not Hispanic or Latino	46,904	3,577	7.6	5,159	11.0
White, single race	32,442	2,513	7.7	3,787	11.6
Black or African American, single race	8,536	707	8.3	913	10.8
CURRENT HEALTH STATUS					
Excellent or very good	51,949	2,914	5.7	4,465	8.7
Good	8,867	1,252	13.4	1,188	12.6
Fair or poor	1,056	442	39.1	397	32.2

B Base figure too small to meet statistical standards for reliability of a derived figure. [1] Unknowns for the columns are not included in the frequencies, but they are included in the "Total" column. [2] Unknowns for the column variables are not included in the denominators when calculating percentages. Percents are age-adjusted to the 2000 projected U.S. standard population using age groups 3-4 years, 5-11 years, and 12-17 years, except for data shown for each age group. [3] Includes other races not shown separately, and children with unknown health status. [4] Estimates for age groups are not age adjusted. [5] Refers to children of only a single race group, including those of Hispanic or Latino origin. [6] Refers to children of more than once race group, including those of Hispanic or Latino origin. [7] Persons of Hispanic or Latino origin may be of any race. [8] Figure has relative standard error greater than 30% and less than or equal to 50%, and should be used with caution.

Source: U.S. National Center for Health Statistics, 2015 National Health Interview Survey, "Tables of Summary Health Statistics," <http://www.cdc.gov/nchs/nhis/SHS.htm>, accessed February 2017.

Table 228. Children and Youth With Disabilities Receiving Special Education and Related Services by Type of Disability: 2000 to 2015

[In thousands (5,773.9 represents 5,773,900). As of Fall. For children and youth age 6 to 21 receiving special education and related services under the Individuals with Disabilities Education Act (IDEA) Part B. Includes outlying areas]

Disability	2000	2005	2010	2011	2012	2013	2014	2015
Total	**5,773.9**	**6,109.6**	**5,834.9**	**5,789.9**	**5,823.8**	**5,847.6**	**5,944.2**	**6,050.7**
Autism	79.6	193.6	370.6	407.2	444.0	479.0	513.7	550.4
Deaf-blindness	1.3	1.6	1.3	1.4	1.3	1.3	1.2	1.3
Developmental delay [1]	28.6	79.1	109.4	115.6	123.4	133.8	141.9	149.3
Emotional disturbance	474.3	472.4	388.2	371.6	361.3	352.3	347.8	346.5
Hearing impairment	70.8	72.4	69.9	69.3	68.9	68.2	67.9	67.4
Intellectual disability	613.4	545.5	445.8	431.2	424.5	417.6	415.3	418.5
Multiple disabilities	122.9	133.9	123.8	125.2	126.3	125.6	125.5	125.2
Orthopedic impairment	73.0	63.1	55.8	54.4	52.5	50.3	46.3	41.2
Other health impairment	294.0	561.0	706.1	734.3	770.6	809.9	857.5	907.2
Specific learning disability	2,881.6	2,780.2	2,420.0	2,357.5	2,338.3	2,311.1	2,328.5	2,348.9
Speech or language impairment	1,093.4	1,157.2	1,093.7	1,071.6	1,061.8	1,047.7	1,047.6	1,044.3
Traumatic brain injury	14.9	23.5	24.7	24.9	25.1	25.3	25.4	25.5
Visual impairment	26.0	26.0	25.7	25.7	25.7	25.5	25.6	24.9

[1] States had the option of reporting children ages 3 to 9 under developmental delay beginning 1997.

Source: U.S. Department of Education, Office of Special Education Programs, "IDEA Section 618 Data Products: State Level Data Files," <https://www2.ed.gov/programs/osepidea/618-data/index.html>, accessed February 2017.

Table 229. Children Under Age 18 Receiving Special Education or Early Intervention Services: 2014 and 2015

[In thousands (73,406 represents 73,406,000), except percent. Percents are age-adjusted. Receiving special education or early intervention services is based on the question, "Do any of these family members (under 18 years of age) receive special education or early intervention services?" Based on household interviews of a sample of the civilian noninstitutionalized population, and about all children in the family]

Selected characteristic	2014			2015		
	Total	Children receiving special education early intervention services		Total	Children receiving special education early intervention services	
		Number [1]	Percent [2]		Number [1]	Percent [2]
Total [3]	73,406	5,305	7.2	73,452	5,752	7.9
SEX						
Male	37,487	3,535	9.5	37,484	3,734	10.0
Female	35,920	1,770	4.9	35,967	2,018	5.6
AGE [4]						
4 years and younger	19,871	737	3.7	19,886	827	4.2
5 to 11 years	28,572	2,494	8.7	28,891	2,521	8.7
12 to 17 years	24,964	2,074	8.3	24,674	2,405	9.8
RACE						
Single race [5]	70,005	4,999	7.2	70,158	5,456	7.8
White	54,255	3,982	7.3	54,300	4,372	8.1
Black or African American	10,883	815	7.5	10,833	825	7.6
American Indian or Alaska Native	914	62	6.9	865	82	9.6
Asian	3,796	133	3.5	3,893	146	3.7
Native Hawaiian or other Pacific Islander	157	(B)	(B)	266	(B)	(B)
Two or more races [6]	3,401	306	9.2	3,294	296	9.3
HISPANIC ORIGIN AND RACE [7]						
Hispanic or Latino	17,906	982	5.5	18,090	1,166	6.5
Mexican or Mexican American	12,210	588	4.9	12,331	713	5.8
Not Hispanic or Latino	55,500	4,324	7.8	55,361	4,586	8.3
White, single race	38,438	3,120	8.1	38,293	3,405	8.8
Black or African American, single race	10,019	743	7.5	10,029	747	7.5

B Does not meet statistical standards for reliability of a derived figure (relative standard error greater than 50%). [1] Unknowns for the columns are not included in the frequencies, but they are included in the "Total" column. [2] Unknowns for the column variables are not included in the denominators when calculating percentages. Percents are age-adjusted to the 2000 projected U.S. standard population using the age groups shown; data for each age group are not age-adjusted. [3] Includes other races not shown separately. [4] Estimates for the age groups are not age-adjusted. [5] Refers to persons who indicated only a single race group, including those of Hispanic or Latino origin. [6] Refers to all persons who indicated more than one race group, including those of Hispanic or Latino origin. [7] Persons of Hispanic or Latino origin may be of any race.

Source: U.S. National Center for Health Statistics, 2014 and 2015 National Health Interview Surveys, "Tables of Summary Health Statistics," <https://www.cdc.gov/nchs/nhis/shs.htm>, accessed February 2017.

Table 230. Depression and Receipt of Mental Health Treatment in the Past Year Among Youth Age 12-17 by Selected Characteristics: 2005 to 2015

[In percent. Data are from Substance Abuse and Mental Health Services Administration, National Survey on Drug Use and Health. Covers youth age 12 to 17 who had a major depressive episode (MDE) as defined in the 4th edition of the *Diagnostic and Statistical Manual of Mental Disorders* (DSM-IV), which specifies a period of at least 2 weeks when a person experienced a depressed mood or loss of interest or pleasure in daily activities and had a majority of specified depression symptoms. Treatment is defined as seeing or talking to a medical doctor or other professional, or using prescription medication in the past year for depression. Respondents with unknown incidence of major depressive episode and unknown treatment data were excluded]

Item	Youth with major depressive episode (MDE)				Youth with an MDE receiving treatment for depression			
	2005	2010	2014	2015	2005	2010	2014	2015
Total [1]	8.8	8.0	11.4	12.5	37.8	37.8	41.2	39.3
AGE								
12 to 13 years	5.2	4.3	7.2	7.8	32.9	32.5	35.9	31.9
14 to 15 years	9.5	9.0	11.9	13.8	41.1	38.4	40.1	40.6
16 to 17 years	11.5	10.6	14.6	15.5	37.1	39.3	44.4	41.5
SEX								
Male	4.5	4.4	5.7	5.8	34.1	32.0	37.7	36.3
Female	13.3	11.9	17.3	19.5	39.0	40.1	42.4	40.3
RACE ETHNICITY								
White, non-Hispanic	9.1	8.6	12.0	13.4	39.3	41.1	46.1	40.6
Black, non-Hispanic	7.6	6.8	9.1	9.0	39.3	23.0	40.6	42.0
American Indian or Alaska Native	6.1	7.4	6.9	(B)	(NA)	(NA)	(NA)	(NA)
Asian	6.0	5.5	10.4	9.7	(NA)	(NA)	(NA)	(NA)
Two or more races	10.5	9.4	12.5	15.6	(NA)	(NA)	(NA)	(NA)
Hispanic [2]	9.1	7.8	11.5	12.6	31.8	38.4	33.1	35.5
POVERTY STATUS [3]								
Below 100% poverty	8.1	7.2	10.9	11.1	37.3	33.8	40.0	40.4
100-199% poverty	9.6	9.0	12.3	13.3	32.1	39.1	40.9	38.6
200% poverty and above	8.7	7.9	11.2	12.7	40.1	38.4	41.7	39.3

B Data do not meet statistical standards for reliability of a derived figure. NA Not available. [1] Total includes persons of other races, not shown separately. [2] Persons of Hispanic origin may be of any race. [3] Estimates are based on a definition of poverty level that incorporates information on family income, size, and composition and is calculated as a percentage of the U.S. Census Bureau's poverty thresholds.

Source: Federal Interagency Forum on Child and Family Statistics, "America's Children: Key National Indicators of Well-Being, 2017," <http://www.childstats.gov/>, accessed July 2017.

Table 231. Immunization of Children Age 19 to 35 Months by Vaccine Type and State: 2015

[In percent. Covers civilian noninstitutionalized children age 19 months to 35 months; born January 2012 to May 2014. Based on estimates from the National Immunization Survey (NIS). The NIS consists of a household survey, and a survey of health care providers of the children to verify and/or complete vaccination information. Abbreviations: DTaP = diphtheria, tetanus toxoids, and acellular pertussis vaccine (includes children who might have been vaccinated with diphtheria and tetanus toxoids vaccine, or diphtheria, tetanus toxoids, and pertussis vaccine); MMR = measles, mumps, and rubella vaccine; HepB = hepatitis B vaccine; HepA = hepatitis A vaccine; Hib = Haemophilus influenzae type b vaccine; PCV = pneumococcal conjugate vaccine]

State	DTaP, ≥3 doses	DTaP, ≥4 doses	Polio, ≥3 doses	MMR, ≥1 dose	Hib, primary series[1]	Hib, full series[1]	HepB, ≥3 doses	HepB, birth dose[2]	Varicella, ≥1 dose	PCV, ≥3 doses	PCV, ≥4 doses	HepA, ≥2 doses	Rotavirus[3]	Combined series[4]
U.S.[5]..	95.0	84.6	93.7	91.9	94.3	82.7	92.6	72.4	91.8	93.3	84.1	59.6	73.2	72.2
AL......	96.4	82.2	95.1	95.2	96.9	83.3	92.4	83.2	92.9	96.7	85.7	57.6	76.2	70.6
AK.....	92.4	79.7	91.9	89.7	90.9	81.6	90.5	65.7	81.8	89.8	80.3	56.5	72.0	66.3
AZ.....	93.4	83.7	92.4	90.6	92.5	85.5	90.1	78.0	92.7	93.5	81.7	58.6	75.1	72.3
AR.....	94.1	76.4	91.9	90.2	93.0	75.5	94.4	80.6	89.1	91.6	76.1	54.2	68.2	66.6
CA.....	97.4	85.2	96.3	92.8	96.6	85.2	94.3	69.1	93.4	95.4	86.2	60.8	74.6	75.0
CO.....	94.8	86.1	92.7	93.6	93.6	83.6	92.1	73.1	92.5	93.9	87.4	59.7	75.9	75.4
CT.....	98.9	90.8	97.9	97.5	99.5	89.0	97.3	81.8	96.8	97.1	91.5	72.0	77.9	80.6
DE.....	97.4	89.9	97.0	97.2	97.1	85.5	95.1	76.0	95.8	95.3	90.8	67.6	81.5	79.3
DC.....	93.7	86.1	90.9	92.4	92.1	85.4	89.4	72.7	94.4	92.1	89.9	67.9	73.0	76.3
FL......	96.5	86.0	93.9	90.4	97.1	86.0	90.4	56.9	93.0	94.7	85.9	54.6	63.8	66.6
GA.....	92.0	82.3	91.9	90.5	93.0	83.5	94.2	80.5	89.5	92.7	84.8	62.0	73.8	75.6
HI.....	94.4	83.2	93.7	94.7	92.9	82.8	91.8	75.5	91.6	93.6	80.6	51.4	72.5	73.8
ID......	91.1	81.0	88.9	91.2	90.3	81.2	89.8	69.8	88.5	90.3	84.4	58.8	74.5	71.6
IL......	94.5	85.0	93.3	91.6	94.2	82.7	93.2	71.2	91.7	92.1	83.9	57.9	75.4	70.8
IN......	95.2	85.3	94.9	92.0	93.9	83.3	91.7	80.0	94.1	91.4	83.4	65.3	72.6	74.7
IA......	96.6	88.9	95.9	95.5	95.7	90.0	96.3	78.2	92.1	94.5	88.1	64.7	75.1	77.9
KS.....	94.9	86.8	94.9	92.3	95.4	84.6	95.7	83.3	92.8	94.2	86.2	67.9	77.0	75.2
KY.....	95.6	87.0	94.9	91.6	95.8	83.5	92.9	75.3	95.7	94.0	86.1	48.3	65.3	73.0
LA.....	95.3	84.4	94.6	92.6	94.6	77.2	94.8	75.3	93.4	94.6	84.2	59.0	67.7	70.8
ME.....	98.8	92.0	95.0	96.0	96.2	84.5	88.9	68.7	93.8	96.5	84.9	53.8	71.1	71.8
MD.....	95.8	87.6	94.4	95.4	94.1	87.0	94.0	79.0	91.5	94.8	89.5	63.0	76.8	76.8
MA.....	97.6	87.2	96.9	91.8	96.2	86.6	96.0	78.4	92.0	96.9	87.2	65.7	83.5	78.5
MI......	94.3	84.9	92.9	90.6	91.3	79.5	93.5	80.0	89.5	88.5	80.5	64.1	65.5	67.6
MN.....	96.2	85.4	94.5	92.6	95.4	83.2	94.7	67.8	93.4	95.1	86.6	65.4	82.6	73.2
MS.....	91.4	79.6	92.0	89.8	89.4	74.3	92.9	77.0	89.2	91.1	78.0	41.2	65.9	70.6
MO.....	92.7	82.6	90.8	91.6	92.5	82.7	91.4	75.0	92.4	93.4	83.4	57.2	76.1	71.0
MT.....	92.9	78.6	91.1	91.7	92.5	81.2	91.3	73.8	89.1	87.3	75.6	43.9	67.3	68.1
NE.....	98.3	86.9	97.4	95.6	97.7	85.5	93.7	72.5	94.4	97.7	87.1	72.8	73.0	73.8
NV.....	93.8	84.7	92.3	93.7	92.4	81.7	91.4	77.7	92.9	90.7	82.4	61.9	65.5	71.3
NH.....	97.5	88.4	96.9	93.4	98.0	88.7	95.8	72.0	89.6	93.6	86.8	60.2	80.9	74.1
NJ.....	96.1	89.8	93.1	92.8	95.8	87.6	93.9	63.9	93.0	94.5	86.8	58.3	75.2	76.5
NM.....	96.0	84.8	93.7	89.7	92.0	79.0	91.9	67.8	86.4	93.2	82.9	62.7	73.8	70.1
NY.....	96.9	87.4	94.9	92.5	95.4	81.8	93.8	59.0	93.4	93.8	82.7	51.2	73.0	71.9
NC.....	94.1	83.9	94.1	94.3	93.9	83.6	93.4	81.3	92.7	92.8	82.2	56.2	75.9	76.4
ND.....	97.0	85.7	96.7	92.8	96.0	85.6	96.0	87.5	95.3	94.9	91.2	66.3	79.8	80.2
OH.....	93.3	80.9	91.8	88.1	92.4	78.6	92.3	77.9	86.2	91.3	79.1	53.1	71.8	68.3
OK.....	92.6	85.7	92.4	92.6	92.8	83.7	94.0	80.4	93.6	90.2	82.7	71.6	67.2	75.4
OR.....	96.5	85.8	93.4	94.1	96.8	79.1	93.7	72.5	93.0	93.3	81.8	61.8	72.9	67.4
PA.....	95.3	88.7	93.1	90.9	94.6	84.1	91.9	73.2	90.4	92.6	88.6	64.6	74.3	72.8
RI......	98.1	90.5	97.2	94.5	98.2	85.2	96.2	73.2	95.1	98.7	90.4	65.1	87.6	77.2
SC.....	91.9	77.5	91.3	88.5	90.7	76.1	90.2	68.9	91.0	89.9	82.0	54.5	69.8	68.2
SD.....	94.0	83.1	93.6	91.4	94.2	82.0	91.8	71.4	90.3	91.5	84.2	53.0	73.4	75.6
TN.....	94.1	81.2	91.8	90.2	93.8	81.1	91.2	64.7	89.7	93.5	83.0	59.5	70.9	70.1
TX.....	93.0	82.1	92.5	92.5	92.6	80.4	90.7	76.4	92.3	92.3	83.3	64.6	75.7	71.2
UT.....	92.2	82.0	92.2	89.2	91.0	79.3	91.7	79.6	88.8	92.0	78.3	59.8	74.5	68.1
VT.....	97.1	89.2	94.6	95.5	95.3	86.8	93.6	49.4	91.5	94.3	89.7	57.1	72.7	75.6
VA.....	92.7	80.6	90.2	83.4	92.3	73.9	87.8	67.3	84.2	88.5	75.3	54.1	67.1	64.4
WA.....	94.4	87.3	92.9	95.3	95.2	87.2	91.4	71.2	92.9	93.7	86.5	57.5	73.6	77.1
WV.....	93.2	78.6	90.9	86.7	93.2	75.4	92.6	68.3	85.9	93.1	82.9	65.7	69.6	64.9
WI.....	94.3	85.2	93.1	92.4	91.0	77.3	90.1	73.1	90.3	93.5	83.2	58.6	75.3	68.8
WY.....	97.1	83.2	96.2	93.5	97.6	82.1	95.9	67.2	91.2	94.4	83.5	45.8	76.4	73.3

[1] Hib primary series: receipt of ≥2 or ≥3 doses, depending on product type received. Full series: receipt of ≥3 or ≥4 doses, depending on product type received (primary series and booster dose). [2] HepB administered from birth through age 3 days. [3] ≥2 or ≥3 doses of Rotavirus vaccine, depending on product type received. [4] The combined (4:3:1:3*:3:1:4) vaccine series includes ≥4 doses of DTaP, ≥3 doses of poliovirus vaccine, ≥1 dose of measles-containing vaccine, full series of Hib vaccine (≥3 or ≥4 doses, depending on product type), ≥3 doses of HepB, ≥1 dose of varicella vaccine, and ≥4 doses of PCV. [5] U.S. total does not include U.S. territories.

Source: U.S. Centers for Disease Control and Prevention, Immunization Managers, "ChildVaxView," <https://www.cdc.gov/vaccines/imz-managers/coverage/childvaxview/index.html>, accessed February 2017.

Table 232. Child Immunization Rates by Vaccine, Race/Ethnicity, and Poverty Status: 2010 and 2015

[In percent. Covers civilian noninstitutionalized children age 19 months to 35 months. Based on estimates from the National Immunization Survey (NIS). The survey also contacts the health care providers of the children to verify and/or complete vaccination information. Results are based on race/ethnic status of the child as reported by parent or guardian. DTaP = diphtheria, tetanus toxoids, and acellular pertussis vaccine (includes children who might have been vaccinated with diphtheria and tetanus toxoids vaccine, or diphtheria, tetanus toxoids, and pertussis vaccine); MMR = measles, mumps, and rubella vaccine; Hib = Haemophilus influenzae type b vaccine; HepB = hepatitis B vaccine; PCV = pneumococcal conjugate vaccine; HepA = hepatitis A vaccine]

| Vaccination | 2010, total | 2015 [1] | | | | | | | |
		Total	White [2]	Black [2]	His-panic [3]	American Indian/ Alaska Native only [2]	Asian [2]	At or above poverty	Below poverty
DTaP, ≥3 doses	95.0	95.0	94.8	94.3	95.5	92.3	97.3	96.0	93.1
DTaP, ≥4 doses	84.4	84.6	85.2	82.0	84.5	79.6	90.0	87.1	80.2
Poliovirus, ≥3 doses	93.3	93.7	93.1	93.3	94.5	91.8	96.9	94.6	91.8
MMR, ≥1 dose	91.5	91.9	91.8	90.7	92.3	88.5	92.5	92.9	90.3
Hib, Primary series [4]	92.2	94.3	94.4	93.3	95.1	89.8	94.8	95.6	91.9
Hib, Full series [4]	66.8	82.7	83.0	78.9	83.0	81.4	87.0	85.5	78.1
HepB, ≥ 3 doses	91.8	92.6	92.0	93.3	93.2	92.4	95.5	92.7	92.5
HepB, 1 dose within 3 days of birth	64.1	72.4	68.2	74.2	77.8	80.7	76.7	70.2	76.3
Varicella (chickenpox), ≥1 dose [5]	90.4	91.8	91.2	91.8	92.7	87.8	93.4	92.5	90.6
PCV, ≥3 doses	92.6	93.3	93.2	92.5	94.4	89.7	92.4	94.6	91.2
HepA, ≥1 dose	78.3	85.8	(NA)	(NA)	(NA)	(NA)	(NA)	(NA)	(NA)
HepA, ≥2 doses	49.7	59.6	58.7	59.3	60.9	61.3	67.8	61.7	56.0
Rotavirus [6]	59.2	73.2	74.6	69.7	72.9	(NA)	75.6	76.8	66.8
Combined series [7]	56.6	72.2	72.7	69.1	71.7	68.2	77.9	74.7	68.7

NA Not available. [1] 2015 NIS covers children born January 2012 to May 2014. [2] Non-Hispanic. [3] Children of Hispanic origin may be of any race. [4] Hib primary series: receipt of ≥2 or ≥3 doses, depending on product type received. Full series: receipt of ≥3 or ≥4 doses, depending on product type received (primary series and booster dose). [5] At or after child's first birthday, unadjusted for history of varicella illness. [6] Rotavirus vaccine includes ≥2 or ≥3 doses, depending on the product type received (≥2 doses for Rotarix [RV1] or ≥3 doses for RotaTeq [RV5]). [7] The combined (4:3:1:3*:3:1:4) vaccine series includes ≥4 doses of DTaP, ≥3 doses of poliovirus vaccine, ≥1 dose of measles-containing vaccine, full series of Hib vaccine (≥3 or ≥4 doses, depending on product type), ≥3 doses of HepB, ≥1 dose of varicella vaccine, and ≥4 doses of PCV.

Source: U.S. Centers for Disease Control and Prevention, Immunization Managers, "National Immunization Survey – Children (19-35 months)," <https://www.cdc.gov/vaccines/imz-managers/coverage/nis/child/index.html>, accessed February 2017; and Hill, Holly A. et al, "Vaccination Coverage Among Children Aged 19-35 Months—United States, 2015," *Morbidity and Mortality Weekly Report,* 65:39 (2016), <https://www.cdc.gov/mmwr/volumes/65/wr/mm6539a4.htm>.

Table 233. Asthma Incidence Among Children Under Age 18 by Selected Characteristics: 2015

[In thousands (73,453 represents 73,453,000), except percent. Based on the National Health Interview Survey, a sample survey of the civilian noninstitutionalized population; see Appendix III. Survey responses cover the sample child, not all children in the family]

| Characteristic | Total (1,000) | Ever told had asthma | | Still have asthma | |
		Number (1,000) [1]	Percent [2]	Number (1,000) [1]	Percent [2]
Total [3]	73,453	9,546	13.0	6,188	8.4
SEX					
Male	37,485	5,708	15.2	3,705	9.9
Female	35,968	3,839	10.7	2,483	6.9
AGE [4]					
Age 4 and younger	19,843	1,127	5.7	935	4.7
5 to 11 years	28,776	4,130	14.4	2,761	9.6
12 to 17 years	24,833	4,288	17.3	2,492	10.0
RACE					
Single race [5]	69,960	9,056	12.9	5,832	8.3
White	54,218	6,438	11.9	4,065	7.5
Black or African American	10,747	2,020	18.8	1,446	13.5
American Indian or Alaska Native	841	[8] 104	12.5	[8] 95	11.5
Asian	3,889	408	10.6	204	5.3
Native Hawaiian or Other Pacific Islander	265	(B)	[8] 27.4	(B)	(B)
Two or more races [6]	3,493	490	15.0	356	10.9
HISPANIC ORIGIN AND RACE [7]					
Hispanic or Latino	18,091	2,270	12.7	1,438	8.0
Mexican or Mexican American	12,359	1,429	11.7	899	7.3
Not Hispanic or Latino	55,362	7,276	13.1	4,750	8.6
White, single race	38,196	4,485	11.7	2,810	7.3
Black or African American, single race	9,979	1,866	18.6	1,336	13.4

B Figure too small to meet statistical standards for reliability of a derived figure (relative standard error greater than 50%). [1] Unknowns for the columns are not included in the frequencies, but they are included in the "Total" column. [2] Unknowns for the column variables are not included in the denominators when calculating percentages. Percents are age-adjusted to the 2000 projected U.S. standard population using the age groups shown. [3] Includes other races, not shown separately. [4] Estimates for the age groups are not age-adjusted. [5] Refers to persons who indicated only a single race group, including those of Hispanic or Latino origin. [6] Refers to all persons who indicated more than one race group, including those of Hispanic or Latino origin. [7] Persons of Hispanic or Latino origin may be of any race or combination of races. [8] Figure has relative standard error greater than 30% and less than or equal to 50% and should be used with caution.

Source: U.S. National Center for Health Statistics, 2015 National Health Interview Survey, "Tables of Summary Health Statistics," <https://www.cdc.gov/nchs/nhis/shs.htm>, accessed February 2017.

Table 234. Child Obesity by Age, Sex, and Race/Ethnicity: 1976 to 2014

[In percent. For children age 6 to 17. Data are from U.S. National Center for Health Statistics, National Health and Nutrition Examination Surveys, a program of studies that combines interviews and physical examinations to assess the health and nutritional status of adults and children. Children classified as obese have a body mass index (BMI) at or above the 95th percentile]

Selected characteristic	1976 to 1980	1988 to 1994	1999 to 2002	2003 to 2006	2007 to 2010	2011 to 2014
Total [1]...........	**5.7**	**11.2**	**16.0**	**17.3**	**18.6**	**19.5**
RACE AND HISPANIC ORIGIN						
White, non-Hispanic............	4.9	10.5	13.2	15.5	16.0	17.1
Black, non-Hispanic............	8.2	14.0	20.7	21.5	24.0	22.5
Asian, non-Hispanic............	(NA)	(NA)	(NA)	(NA)	(NA)	9.8
Hispanic origin [2,3]...........	(NA)	(NA)	(NA)	(NA)	23.7	24.3
Mexican-American [2,3].......	(NA)	15.4	23.0	22.7	23.8	25.2
SEX AND AGE						
Male............	5.5	11.8	17.2	18.1	20.4	18.9
Female...........	5.8	10.6	14.7	16.3	16.7	20.0
Ages 6 to 11...........	6.5	11.3	15.8	17.0	18.8	17.5
Male............	6.7	11.6	16.9	18.0	20.7	17.6
Female...........	6.4	11.0	14.7	15.8	16.9	17.5
Ages 12 to 17...........	4.9	11.1	16.1	17.5	18.4	21.3
Male............	4.5	12.0	17.5	18.2	20.1	20.1
Female...........	5.4	10.2	14.7	16.8	16.6	22.5

NA Not available. [1] Includes other races not shown separately. [2] Persons of Hispanic and Mexican origin may be of any race. [3] From 1976 to 2006, the survey sample was designed to provide estimates specifically for persons of Mexican origin. Beginning in 2007, the survey allows for reporting of both total Hispanics and Mexican Americans.

Source: Federal Interagency Forum on Child and Family Statistics, "America's Children: Key National Indicators of Well-Being, 2017," <http://www.childstats.gov/index.asp>, accessed July 2017.

Table 235. High School Students Engaged in Physical Activity by Sex: 2015

[In percent. For students in grades 9 to 12. Based on the Youth Risk Behavior Survey, a school-based survey and subject to sampling error; for details, see source]

Characteristic	Participated in 60+ min. of physical activity on 5 of last 7 days [1]	Participated in 60+ min. of physical activity on all 7 days [2]	Did not participate in 60+ min. of physical activity on any day [3]	Attended physical education class		Played on at least one sports team [6]	Used computers 3 or more hours/ day [7]	Watched TV 3 or more hours/ day [8]
				Total [4]	Attended daily [5]			
All students.....	**48.6**	**27.1**	**14.3**	**51.6**	**29.8**	**57.6**	**41.7**	**24.7**
Male..............	**57.8**	**36.0**	**11.1**	**55.3**	**33.8**	**62.2**	**40.6**	**25.0**
Grade 9..........	62.3	40.1	9.5	72.2	44.6	68.1	42.5	26.3
Grade 10.........	58.7	36.7	10.4	61.3	36.1	63.5	43.4	24.6
Grade 11.........	56.3	34.3	12.4	42.2	25.2	62.3	36.1	24.6
Grade 12.........	53.3	32.6	12.4	42.9	27.9	54.6	40.8	24.4
Female..............	**39.1**	**17.7**	**17.5**	**47.8**	**25.5**	**53.0**	**42.8**	**24.4**
Grade 9..........	43.9	20.9	14.7	70.4	39.5	57.6	48.7	25.3
Grade 10.........	41.9	19.0	15.8	53.9	27.0	55.1	43.3	24.1
Grade 11.........	36.6	16.0	18.2	34.6	18.1	51.7	38.1	22.4
Grade 12.........	33.4	14.3	21.4	29.1	16.0	46.9	40.4	25.9

[1] Were physically active doing any kind of physical activity that increased their heart rate and made them breathe hard some of the time for a total of at least 60 minutes/day for at least 5 or more days out of the 7 days preceding the survey. [2] Participated in 60 or more minutes of any kind of physical activity that increased their heart rate and made them breathe hard some of the time on all 7 days before the survey. [3] Did not participate in 60 or more minutes of any kind of physical activity that increased their heart rate and made them breathe hard some of the time on at least 1 day during the 7 days before the survey. [4] On one or more days in an average week when they were in school. [5] Five days in an average week when they were in school. [6] Run by their school or community groups during the 12 months before the survey. [7] Played video or computer games or used computer for something that was not school work on an average school day. [8] On an average school day.

Source: U.S. Centers for Disease Control and Prevention, *Morbidity and Mortality Weekly Report, Surveillance Summaries*, 65:6, June 10, 2016, "Youth Risk Behavior Surveillance—United States, 2015." See also <http://www.cdc.gov/healthyyouth/data/yrbs/index.htm>.

Table 236. High School Student Use of Tobacco and Nicotine Products by Sex and Race/Ethnicity: 2016

[In percent, except as noted (3,050 represents 3,050,000). Data represent current use of tobacco and nicotine products, defined as use within the past 30 days. Data are based on the National Youth Tobacco Survey, administered to students in middle school (grades 6-8) and high school (grades 9-12)]

Tobacco and nicotine products	Total		Sex		Race and ethnicity			
	Number (1,000) [1]	Percent	Male	Female	White, non-Hispanic	Black, non-Hispanic	Other race, non-Hispanic	Hispanic [2]
Use of any tobacco product.........	**3,050**	**20.2**	**23.5**	**17.0**	**23.0**	**16.4**	**11.3**	**18.3**
Electronic cigarettes (vaping) [3]..........	1,680	11.3	13.1	9.5	13.7	6.2	5.4	10.3
Cigarettes.................	1,180	8.0	9.1	6.9	9.9	3.9	4.8	6.4
Cigars.................	1,130	7.7	9.0	5.6	7.9	9.5	3.7	7.2
Smokeless tobacco [4].................	860	5.8	8.3	3.3	7.4	2.1	3.8	4.4
Hookah [5].................	700	4.8	4.5	5.1	4.5	4.1	3.4	6.4
Pipe tobacco.................	190	1.4	1.8	0.9	1.4	1.2	(B)	1.2
Bidis [6].................	70	0.5	0.7	0.3	0.4	–	–	0.6
Two or more tobacco products..........	1,440	9.6	11.4	7.8	11.3	6.1	5.0	8.9

– Represents zero. B Statistically unreliable. Sample size less than 50 or relative standard error greater than 0.3. [1] Estimates are rounded down to nearest 10,000. [2] Persons of Hispanic origin may be of any race. [3] Electronic cigarettes (e-cigarettes) are battery-powered devices that vaporize a nicotine-based liquid for the user to inhale. [4] Includes chewing tobacco, snuff/dip, snus, and dissolvable tobacco. [5] Water pipes used to smoke tobacco, which is often flavored. [6] Small imported cigarettes wrapped in a leaf.

Source: U.S. Centers for Disease Control and Prevention, Jamal, Ahmed et al., "Tobacco Use Among Middle and High School Students—United States, 2011-2016," *Morbidity and Mortality Weekly Report*, 66:23, June 16, 2017. See also <http://www.cdc.gov/tobacco/data_statistics/by_topic/youth_data/index.htm>.

Table 237. Fruit and Vegetable Availability for Consumption Per Capita by Commodity: 1980 to 2014

[In pounds, farm weight. Available supply of fresh fruits and vegetables at the farm level or early stage of processing for domestic consumption after subtracting measurable uses, such as farm inputs (feed and seed), exports, ending stocks, and industrial uses. Food availability is a popular proxy for actual food consumption. Based on Census Bureau estimated resident population plus Armed Forces overseas for most commodities]

Commodity	1980	1990	2000	2005	2010	2011	2012	2013	2014
Fruits and vegetables, total [1]	**603.2**	**649.3**	**710.9**	**684.4**	**648.7**	**627.2**	**641.6**	**643.0**	**644.6**
Fruits, total	**264.9**	**257.9**	**286.7**	**270.5**	**252.2**	**244.8**	**250.3**	**261.4**	**259.3**
Fresh fruits	106.5	117.0	128.8	125.3	128.5	129.3	131.7	136.1	135.9
Noncitrus [2]	80.4	95.6	105.3	103.7	107.0	106.6	108.2	112.2	112.6
Apples	19.4	19.8	17.6	16.8	15.4	15.6	16.1	17.4	18.9
Avocados	2.1	1.4	2.2	3.5	4.0	5.1	5.7	6.2	6.5
Bananas	20.8	24.3	28.4	25.2	25.6	25.5	27.0	28.1	27.9
Blueberries	0.2	0.1	0.3	0.4	1.1	1.3	1.3	1.4	1.5
Cantaloupes	5.8	9.2	11.1	9.6	8.5	8.6	7.5	8.3	7.0
Cherries	0.7	0.4	0.6	0.9	1.3	1.3	1.5	1.0	1.2
Grapes	4.0	7.9	7.5	8.7	8.0	7.4	7.6	7.8	7.7
Honeydew melons	1.4	2.1	2.3	1.9	1.7	1.6	1.5	1.6	1.7
Mangoes	0.2	0.5	1.8	1.9	2.2	2.5	2.5	2.9	2.5
Papayas	0.2	0.2	0.7	0.9	1.2	1.0	1.0	1.1	1.1
Peaches and nectarines	7.1	5.5	5.3	4.8	4.7	4.5	3.9	3.0	3.3
Pears	2.6	3.3	3.4	2.9	2.9	3.2	2.8	2.9	2.9
Pineapples	1.5	2.0	3.2	4.9	5.7	5.7	6.4	6.7	7.2
Plums	1.5	1.5	1.2	1.1	0.8	0.9	0.6	0.5	0.6
Strawberries	2.0	3.2	4.9	5.8	7.2	7.4	8.0	8.0	7.9
Watermelons	10.7	13.3	13.8	13.5	15.7	13.8	13.9	14.5	13.5
Fresh citrus	26.1	21.4	23.5	21.6	21.6	22.8	23.5	23.9	23.3
Oranges and temples	14.3	12.4	11.7	11.4	9.7	10.0	10.5	10.4	9.4
Tangerines and tangelos	2.2	1.3	2.9	2.5	3.8	4.1	4.2	4.4	5.0
Grapefruit	7.3	4.4	5.1	2.6	2.8	2.7	2.4	2.6	2.4
Lemons	1.9	2.6	2.4	2.9	2.8	3.5	3.9	3.5	3.4
Limes	0.4	0.7	1.4	2.1	2.6	2.5	2.6	3.0	3.1
Processed fruit	158.5	141.0	157.9	145.2	123.6	115.5	118.6	125.2	123.4
Canned fruit [3]	23.8	21.1	17.6	16.7	15.0	14.2	13.3	15.1	13.7
Fruit juice [4]	119.3	103.1	124.9	112.6	93.4	85.8	90.9	94.5	93.8
Frozen fruit [5]	3.3	4.3	4.5	5.2	5.1	4.7	4.6	4.8	5.5
Dried fruit [6]	11.3	12.2	10.5	10.1	9.4	9.7	9.3	10.1	9.6
Vegetables, total	**338.3**	**391.3**	**424.2**	**413.9**	**396.5**	**382.4**	**391.3**	**381.6**	**385.4**
Fresh vegetables [7]	151.8	176.4	200.7	196.4	190.0	185.7	188.8	184.1	185.7
Asparagus	0.3	0.6	1.0	1.1	1.4	1.4	1.4	1.4	1.6
Bell peppers (all uses)	2.9	5.9	8.2	9.2	10.3	10.6	10.7	10.0	10.7
Broccoli	1.4	3.4	5.9	5.3	5.6	5.9	6.3	6.9	6.6
Cabbage	8.0	8.3	8.9	7.8	7.5	6.6	6.3	6.9	6.7
Carrots	6.2	8.3	9.2	8.7	7.8	7.5	7.9	8.0	8.5
Cauliflower	1.1	2.2	1.7	1.8	1.3	1.2	1.2	1.3	1.3
Celery (all uses)	7.4	7.2	6.3	5.9	6.1	6.0	6.0	5.5	5.5
Corn, sweet	6.5	6.7	9.0	8.7	9.2	8.2	8.7	8.9	7.6
Cucumbers	3.9	4.7	6.4	6.2	6.7	6.4	7.1	7.3	7.4
Garlic (all uses)	0.9	1.4	2.2	2.4	2.3	2.3	2.3	2.0	1.9
Kale	(NA)	(NA)	0.4	0.4	0.5	0.5	0.5	0.6	0.5
Lettuce, head	25.6	27.7	23.5	20.9	15.9	15.8	15.9	14.1	14.5
Lettuce, Romaine and leaf	(NA)	3.8	8.4	9.7	12.0	11.7	11.9	11.4	10.8
Mushrooms	1.2	2.0	2.6	2.6	2.6	2.8	2.7	2.7	3.0
Onions	11.4	15.1	18.9	20.9	19.6	19.1	19.5	18.5	18.3
Potatoes	51.1	46.7	47.1	41.3	36.8	34.0	34.5	34.5	33.5
Pumpkin (all uses)	(NA)	4.4	4.6	4.8	4.4	4.4	5.0	4.7	5.3
Snap beans	1.3	1.1	2.0	1.8	1.9	1.7	1.6	1.6	1.5
Spinach	0.4	0.8	1.4	2.3	1.7	1.8	1.6	1.6	1.7
Squash (all uses)	2.3	3.5	4.4	4.4	4.3	4.4	4.6	4.4	4.6
Sweet potatoes (all uses)	4.4	4.4	4.2	4.5	6.3	7.1	6.9	6.3	7.5
Tomatoes	12.8	15.5	19.0	20.2	20.6	21.0	20.8	20.2	20.5
Processed vegetables	186.5	214.9	223.6	217.5	206.5	196.7	202.5	197.6	199.7
Canned vegetables [8]	102.3	110.3	103.2	104.8	99.4	91.3	92.8	91.7	93.2
Frozen vegetables [9]	51.6	66.7	79.7	76.4	71.0	70.2	70.3	67.1	66.1
Dehydrated vegetables [10]	10.5	14.9	17.3	13.9	12.5	11.9	15.1	13.9	13.5
Chips, potato	16.5	16.3	15.6	16.0	15.0	16.8	17.6	17.8	19.8
Legumes [11]	5.6	6.8	7.8	6.3	8.6	6.6	6.8	7.2	7.0

NA Not available. [1] Excludes wine grapes. [2] Includes other fruits not shown separately. [3] Canned fruit include apples, apricots, cherries, olives, peaches, pears, pineapples, plums, and prunes. [4] Fruit juice includes apple, cranberry, grape, grapefruit, lemon, lime, orange, pineapple, and prune juice. [5] Frozen fruit include apples, apricots, blackberries, blueberries, boysenberries, cherries, loganberries, peaches, plums, prunes, raspberries, strawberries, and other miscellaneous fruit and berries. [6] Dried fruit include apples, apricots, dates, figs, peaches, pears, prunes, and raisins. [7] Includes other vegetables not shown separately. [8] Canned vegetables include asparagus, lima beans, snap beans, beets, cabbage, carrots, sweet corn, cucumbers, mushrooms, green peas, chile peppers, potatoes, spinach, tomatoes, and other miscellaneous vegetables. [9] Frozen vegetables include asparagus, lima beans, snap beans, broccoli, carrots, cauliflower, sweet corn, green peas, potatoes, spinach and other miscellaneous vegetables. [10] Onions and potatoes. [11] Dry peas, lentils, and dry edible beans.

Source: U.S. Department of Agriculture, Economic Research Service, "Food Availability (Per Capita) Data System," <https://www.ers.usda.gov/data-products/food-availability-per-capita-data-system/>, accessed March 2017.

Table 238. Food Availability for Consumption Per Capita by Major Food Commodity: 1980 to 2014

[In pounds, retail weight, except as indicated. Available supply for domestic consumption after subtracting measurable uses, such as farm inputs (feed and seed), exports, ending stocks, and industrial uses. Food availability is a proxy for actual food consumption. Based on Census Bureau estimated resident population plus Armed Forces overseas for most commodities. For commodities not shipped overseas in substantial amounts, such as fluid milk and cream, the resident population is used]

Commodity	Unit	1980	1990	2000	2005	2010	2013	2014
Red meat, total (boneless, trimmed weight) [1]	Pounds	126.4	112.2	113.7	110.2	102.1	97.9	95.4
Beef	Pounds	72.1	63.9	64.5	62.5	56.7	53.5	51.5
Veal	Pounds	1.3	0.9	0.5	0.4	0.3	0.3	0.2
Pork	Pounds	52.1	46.4	47.8	46.6	44.4	43.4	43.1
Lamb	Pounds	1.0	1.0	0.8	0.8	0.7	0.7	0.7
Poultry (boneless, trimmed weight)	Pounds	40.8	56.2	67.9	73.7	70.6	70.2	71.1
Chicken	Pounds	32.7	42.4	54.2	60.5	58.0	57.6	58.7
Turkey	Pounds	8.1	13.8	13.7	13.2	12.6	12.5	12.4
Fish and shellfish (boneless, trimmed weight)	Pounds	12.4	14.9	15.2	16.2	15.8	14.3	14.5
Eggs	Number	271.1	234.1	254.7	260.1	252.4	258.5	266.5
Shell	Number	236.2	186.2	177.7	176.9	172.1	179.7	186.6
Processed	Number	34.9	47.9	77.1	83.2	80.4	78.8	79.9
Dairy products, total [2]	Pounds	543.1	568.0	589.9	603.4	603.0	605.3	614.3
Fluid milk products [3]	Gallons	27.8	26.1	23.6	22.6	22.1	20.9	20.1
Beverage milks	Gallons	27.5	25.6	22.8	21.4	20.5	19.1	18.4
Plain whole milk	Gallons	16.4	10.2	7.8	6.8	5.5	5.2	5.1
Plain reduced-fat milk (2%)	Gallons	6.3	9.1	7.2	7.0	7.2	6.8	6.5
Plain reduced-fat milk (1%)	Gallons	1.8	2.3	2.6	2.5	2.8	2.8	2.7
Plain skim milk	Gallons	1.3	2.6	3.4	3.2	3.2	2.6	2.3
Flavored whole milk	Gallons	0.5	0.3	0.4	0.3	0.2	0.2	0.2
Flavored milk, low-fat and skim	Gallons	0.6	0.8	1.1	1.4	1.5	1.4	1.4
Buttermilk	Gallons	0.5	0.4	0.3	0.2	0.2	0.2	0.2
Yogurt (excl. frozen)	1/2 pints	4.6	7.2	12.0	19.1	24.8	27.6	27.4
Fluid cream products [4]	1/2 pints	10.5	14.3	18.5	22.4	8.3	8.4	8.5
Cream [5]	1/2 pints	6.3	8.7	11.6	14.9	(NA)	(NA)	(NA)
Sour cream	1/2 pints	3.4	4.7	6.1	6.6	7.5	7.6	7.7
Condensed and evaporated milks	Pounds	7.0	7.9	5.8	6.1	7.2	7.2	6.8
Whole milk	Pounds	3.8	3.1	2.0	2.3	2.0	1.9	1.4
Skim milk	Pounds	3.3	4.8	3.8	3.7	5.2	5.3	5.4
Cheese [6]	Pounds	17.5	24.6	29.5	31.3	32.7	33.4	33.9
American [7]	Pounds	9.6	11.1	12.7	12.7	13.3	13.3	13.5
Cheddar	Pounds	6.8	9.1	9.9	10.2	10.1	9.6	9.7
Italian [7]	Pounds	4.4	8.9	11.4	12.7	13.5	13.8	14.2
Mozzarella	Pounds	3.0	6.9	9.1	9.9	10.6	10.7	11.2
Other [7]	Pounds	3.5	4.6	5.4	6.0	5.9	6.2	6.3
Swiss	Pounds	1.3	1.3	1.0	1.2	1.2	1.0	1.0
Cream and Neufchatel	Pounds	1.0	1.7	2.4	2.4	2.3	2.5	2.4
Cottage cheese, total	Pounds	4.4	3.3	2.6	2.6	2.3	2.1	2.1
Low-fat	Pounds	0.8	1.2	1.3	1.4	1.3	1.2	1.1
Frozen dairy products [8]	Pounds	24.7	27.2	26.7	24.3	23.0	22.3	21.9
Ice cream	Pounds	16.4	14.8	15.6	14.6	13.5	12.7	12.2
Low-fat ice cream	Pounds	5.8	6.3	6.4	5.8	6.3	5.9	6.1
Sherbet	Pounds	1.2	1.2	1.1	1.1	1.0	0.9	0.9
Frozen yogurt	Pounds	(NA)	2.8	2.0	1.3	1.0	1.4	1.2
Fats and oils:								
Total, fat content only	Pounds	55.6	60.6	81.7	85.5	82.2	(NA)	(NA)
Butter (product weight)	Pounds	4.5	4.3	4.5	4.5	4.9	5.5	5.5
Margarine (product weight)	Pounds	11.3	10.9	8.2	4.0	3.5	(NA)	(NA)
Lard, direct use	Pounds	2.3	0.9	0.8	1.6	1.5	(NA)	(NA)
Edible beef tallow, direct use	Pounds	1.1	0.6	4.0	3.8	3.3	(NA)	(NA)
Shortening	Pounds	16.9	20.6	31.5	29.0	15.3	(NA)	(NA)
Salad and cooking oils	Pounds	21.2	25.1	33.7	42.7	53.6	(NA)	(NA)
Other edible fats and oils	Pounds	1.5	1.2	1.5	1.6	1.7	(NA)	(NA)
Flour and cereal products [9]	Pounds	146.4	181.1	199.5	190.9	194.2	174.7	174.4
Wheat flour	Pounds	116.9	135.6	146.3	134.4	134.8	135.0	134.7
Rice, milled	Pounds	11.0	16.2	19.2	19.4	20.4	(NA)	(NA)
Corn products	Pounds	12.9	21.4	28.4	31.4	33.1	33.9	34.0
Oat products	Pounds	3.9	6.5	4.4	4.6	4.7	4.5	4.5
Caloric sweeteners, total [10]	Pounds	120.2	132.3	150.6	143.9	133.7	130.1	131.0
Sugar, refined cane and beet	Pounds	83.6	64.4	65.5	63.0	65.9	67.9	68.3
Corn sweeteners [11]	Pounds	35.3	66.8	83.3	79.2	66.0	60.4	60.7
High-fructose corn syrup	Pounds	19.0	49.6	64.2	60.7	50.5	45.7	45.5
Honey	Pounds	0.8	0.7	1.1	1.1	1.0	1.1	1.2
Other:								
Cocoa, bean equivalent	Pounds	3.4	5.4	5.9	6.5	5.5	5.3	5.1
Coffee, green bean equivalent	Pounds	10.3	10.3	10.3	9.5	9.2	9.9	10.0
Tea, dry leaf equivalent	Pounds	0.8	0.7	0.8	0.8	1.0	0.9	0.9
Peanuts, total	Pounds	5.1	6.1	5.9	6.7	7.0	6.9	7.0
Tree nuts, total	Pounds	1.8	2.5	2.6	2.7	3.9	4.0	4.2

NA Not available. [1] Excludes edible offal. [2] Milk-equivalent. Includes fluid milk and cream, butter, cheese, frozen and dry dairy products, and evaporated and condensed milk. [3] Fluid milk figures are aggregates of commercial sales and milk produced and consumed on farms. [4] Includes eggnog, not shown separately. [5] Heavy cream, light cream, and half-and-half. [6] Excludes full-skim American, cottage, pot, and baker's cheese. [7] Includes other cheeses, not shown separately. [8] Includes mellorine until 1990, and other nonstandardized frozen dairy products. [9] Includes rye flour and barley products, not shown separately. Excludes quantities used in alcoholic beverages and fuel. [10] Dry weight. Includes edible syrups (maple, molasses, etc.), not shown separately. [11] Includes glucose and dextrose, not shown separately.

Source: U.S. Department of Agriculture, Economic Research Service, "Food Availability (Per Capita) Data System," <https://www.ers.usda.gov/data-products/food-availability-per-capita-data-system/>, accessed March 2017.

Table 239. Nutrition—Nutrients in Foods Available for Civilian Consumption Per Capita Per Day: 1970 to 2010

[Computed by the Center for Nutrition Policy and Promotion (CNPP), using food availability data from the Economic Research Service, and nutrient composition of foods data from the Agricultural Research Service. Data represent nutrients in foods available for consumption, not actual nutrient intake, and do not account for nutrient losses from trimming, cooking, plate waste, and spoilage. Includes nutrients added to certain commodities commercially through fortification and enrichment]

Nutrient	Unit	1970	1980	1990	2000	2010
Food energy	Kilocalories	3,300	3,500	3,800	4,200	4,000
Carbohydrate	Grams	401	408	468	505	474
Protein	Grams	98	111	118	124	120
Total fat [1]	Grams	147	162	167	191	190
Saturated	Grams	52	56	56	62	59
Monounsaturated	Grams	58	65	68	83	77
Polyunsaturated	Grams	25	29	32	37	44
Cholesterol	Milligrams	470	490	460	470	460
Fiber	Grams	19	20	24	25	25
Vitamin A	Micrograms RAE [2]	1,040	1,060	1,080	1,100	920
Carotene	Micrograms	480	580	640	670	630
Vitamin E	Milligrams a-TE [3]	13.3	14.4	16.5	20.3	21.9
Vitamin C	Milligrams	104	115	114	125	105
Thiamin	Milligrams	2.0	2.6	2.9	3.1	2.9
Riboflavin	Milligrams	2.4	2.9	3.2	3.2	3
Niacin	Milligrams	22	30	33	35	34
Vitamin B6	Milligrams	2.0	2.4	2.5	2.6	2.5
Folate [4]	Micrograms DFE [5]	301	375	407	916	889
Vitamin B12	Micrograms	9.6	10.6	10.1	10	9.3
Calcium	Milligrams	990	950	1,020	1,030	1,030
Phosphorus	Milligrams	1,580	1,690	1,820	1,860	1,810
Magnesium	Milligrams	340	350	400	410	410
Iron	Milligrams	15.7	18.4	23.8	25.1	24.6
Zinc	Milligrams	12.8	16.8	17.9	18.2	17.6
Copper	Milligrams	1.7	1.9	2.1	2.2	2.1
Potassium	Milligrams	3,610	3,740	3,910	4,030	3,760
Selenium	Micrograms	129	150	162	191	187
Sodium [6]	Milligrams	1,230	1,260	1,310	1,300	1,210

[1] Includes other types of fat not shown separately. [2] Retinol activity equivalents. [3] Alpha-Tocopherol equivalents. [4] Reflects new terminology from Institute of Medicine's Dietary Reference Intakes reports. [5] Dietary Folate Equivalents (DFE). [6] Does not include amount from processed foods; underestimates actual availability.

Source: U.S. Department of Agriculture, Economic Research Service, "Food Availability (Per Capita) Data System, Nutrient Availability," <https://www.ers.usda.gov/data-products/food-availability-per-capita-data-system/>, accessed March 2016.

Table 240. Nutrients Available for Consumption from Major Food Groups Per Capita Per Day: 2010

[In units as indicated. Computed by the Center for Nutrition Policy and Promotion (CNPP), using food availability data from the Economic Research Service, and nutrient composition of foods data from the Agricultural Research Service. Data represent nutrients in foods available for consumption, not actual nutrient intake, and do not account for nutrient losses from trimming, cooking, plate waste, and spoilage. Includes nutrients added to certain commodities commercially through fortification and enrichment. Metric symbols: kcal = kilocalorie. g = gram. mg = milligram. mcg = microgram]

Nutrient	Unit	Meat, poultry, and fish	Dairy products [1]	Eggs	Fats and oils [2]	Fruits	Legumes, nuts, and soy	Vege-tables	Grain products	Sugars, sweet-eners
Food energy	kcal	644.0	398.0	49.4	901.2	112.6	136.5	153.6	937.4	631.7
Percent	(X)	16.1	10.0	1.2	22.5	2.8	3.4	3.8	23.4	15.8
Carbohydrates	g	0.3	28.9	0.3	(Z)	27.7	11.3	35.3	198.6	169.3
Protein	g	49.5	21.7	4.2	0.1	1.3	7.4	5.0	23.8	(Z)
Fat, total	g	44.3	20.7	3.2	96.3	0.9	7.3	0.6	4.2	(Z)
Saturated	g	16.2	12.9	1.0	22.7	0.1	1.3	0.1	0.9	(Z)
Mono-unsaturated	g	22.1	6.2	1.4	43.4	0.6	3.6	0.1	1.0	(Z)
Polyunsaturated	g	4.3	0.7	0.4	27.8	0.1	1.9	0.2	1.4	(Z)
Cholesterol	mg	205.3	67.6	137.3	19.6	–	–	–	0.1	–
Dietary fiber	g	–	0.3	–	–	2.8	4.0	5.7	8.8	–
Vitamin A RAE [3]	mcg	226.6	232.4	56.6	88.4	26.9	0.5	359.9	70.5	–
Carotene	mcg	–	15.5	–	11.8	53.5	0.9	560.7	5.5	–
Vitamin E ATE [4]	mg	0.8	0.4	0.3	15.3	0.6	1.4	1.2	0.9	–
Vitamin C	mg	2.2	1.6	–	(Z)	49.9	0.1	56.4	7.1	(Z)
Thiamin	mg	0.5	0.2	(Z)	(Z)	0.1	0.1	0.2	1.7	(Z)
Riboflavin	mg	0.5	0.8	0.2	(Z)	0.1	(Z)	0.1	1.1	(Z)
Niacin	mg	12.7	0.4	(Z)	(Z)	0.6	1.4	2.6	14.3	(Z)
Vitamin B6 [5]	mg	1.0	0.2	(Z)	(Z)	0.2	0.1	0.5	0.5	(Z)
Folate (DFE) [5]	mcg	29.0	24.7	16.4	0.2	36.6	73.4	72.2	634.4	(Z)
Vitamin B12	mcg	5.9	1.9	0.4	(Z)	–	–	(Z)	(Z)	–
Calcium	mg	34.8	696.5	17.3	2.6	22.6	44.7	61.9	46.3	5.2
Phosphorus	mg	465.3	550.0	63.5	2.3	30.8	116.0	113.1	329.2	2.4
Magnesium	mg	55.5	55.4	4.1	0.2	22.5	58.7	48.6	96.2	2.4
Iron	mg	4.0	0.4	0.6	(Z)	0.5	1.8	1.9	12.0	0.1
Zinc	mg	6.4	2.5	0.3	(Z)	0.2	0.9	0.7	3.8	(Z)
Copper	mg	0.5	0.1	(Z)	–	0.1	0.4	0.2	0.5	(Z)
Potassium	mg	755.3	679.6	47.1	3.3	376.1	387.0	861.2	377.4	17.3
Selenium	mcg	56.9	23.7	11.1	0.1	0.6	13.5	2.8	76.6	1.8
Sodium	mg	235.0	465.5	49.9	80.7	34.5	4.2	313.6	13.8	34.9

– Represents zero. Z Less than 0.05 but more than zero. [1] Excludes butter. [2] Includes butter. [3] Retinal activity equivalent. [4] Alpha-tocopheral equivalent. [5] Dietary folate equivalent.

Source: U.S. Department of Agriculture, Economic Research Service, "Food Availability (Per Capita) Data System, Nutrient Availability," <https://www.ers.usda.gov/data-products/food-availability-per-capita-data-system/>, accessed March 2016.

Table 241. Foodborne Disease Outbreaks and Illnesses by Etiology, Food Category, and Location of Food Preparation: 2014

[Data reported as of February 17, 2016. Foodborne disease outbreaks are a nationally notifiable condition. An outbreak involves 2 or more cases of a similar illness resulting from consuming a common food. Public health agencies in all 50 States, D.C., and the U.S. territories voluntarily submit reports of foodborne disease outbreaks that their agencies investigate. Excludes outbreaks on cruise ships that dock in U.S. and international ports and those in which food was eaten outside the U.S. Not all outbreaks are identified, investigated, or reported. Data are subject to change. See source for other limitations]

Item	Out-breaks	Ill-nesses	Hospital-izations	Item	Out-breaks	Ill-nesses
Total...............	**864**	**13,246**	**712**	**By food category:**		
By etiology (cause): [1]				Aquatic animals.......................	64	338
Bacterial [2]................................	317	5,858	594	Land animals [2].......................	80	1,182
Salmonella...............................	149	2,563	400	Chicken..............................	23	354
Campylobacter..........................	31	353	30	Dairy................................	19	267
Clostridium perfringens...............	30	1,230	1	Beef................................	15	152
Escherichia coli (E. coli) [3].............	24	222	62	Pork................................	9	134
Staphylococcus aureus enterotoxin.....	17	566	10	Turkey..............................	6	235
Shigella.................................	16	389	27	Plant products........................	55	1,092
Chemical and toxin........................	52	171	26	Other [4]..............................	665	10,634
Parasitic.................................	8	46	4	**By location of food preparation:**		
Cryptosporidium..........................	4	24	2	Restaurant............................	485	4,780
Cyclospora..............................	2	16	1	Catering or banquet facility...........	92	3,192
Viral [2]...................................	288	5,390	71	Private home..........................	86	778
Norovirus...............................	284	5,340	64	Institutional location..................	26	1,404
Hepatitis A..............................	2	15	7	Grocery store.........................	13	146
Other [4].................................	199	1,781	17	Other [4]..............................	162	2,946

[1] Includes both confirmed and suspected etiologies. [2] Includes other categories not shown separately. [3] Also includes E. coli that produce shiga toxins, known as Shiga toxin-producing E. coli (STEC). These bacteria are also called verocytotoxic-producing E. coli and enterohemorrhagic E. coli. [4] Other includes incidents that involved multiple categories and unknown or not reported categories.

Source: U.S. Centers for Disease Control and Prevention, *Surveillance for Foodborne Disease Outbreaks, United States, 2014: Annual Report*, 2016. See also <https://www.cdc.gov/foodsafety/fdoss/index.html>.

Section 4
Education

This section presents data primarily concerning formal education as a whole, at various levels, and for public and private schools. Data shown relate to the school-age population and school enrollment, educational attainment, education personnel, and financial aspects of education. In addition, data are shown for charter schools, homeschooling, post-secondary education, security measures used in schools, and academic libraries. The chief sources are the decennial census of population and the Current Population Survey (CPS), both conducted by the U.S. Census Bureau (see text, Section 1, Population); annual, biennial, and other periodic surveys conducted by the National Center for Education Statistics (NCES), a part of the U.S. Department of Education; and surveys conducted by the National Education Association.

The censuses of population have included data on school enrollment since 1840 and on educational attainment since 1940. The CPS has reported on school enrollment annually and on educational attainment periodically since 1947.

The NCES is continuing the pattern of statistical studies and surveys conducted by the U.S. Office of Education since 1870. The annual *Digest of Education Statistics*, found at <http://nces.ed.gov/programs/digest/>, provides summary data on pupils, staff, finances, including government expenditures, and organization at the elementary, secondary, and higher education levels. It is also a primary source for detailed information on federal funds for education, projections of enrollment, graduates, and teachers. The *Condition of Education*, issued annually and found at <http://nces.ed.gov/programs/coe/>, presents a summary of information on education of particular interest to policymakers. NCES also conducts special studies periodically.

The census of governments, conducted by the Census Bureau every 5 years (for the years ending in "2" and "7"), provides data on school district finances and state and local government expenditures for education. Reports published by the Bureau of Labor Statistics contain data relating civilian labor force experience to educational attainment (see also Tables 616, 643, and 650 in Section 12, Labor Force, Employment, and Earnings).

Types and sources of data—The statistics in this section are of two general types. One type, exemplified by data from the Census Bureau, is based on direct interviews with individuals to obtain information about their own and their family members' education. Data of this type relate to school enrollment and level of education attained, classified by age, sex, and other characteristics of the population. The school enrollment statistics reflect attendance or enrollment in any regular school within a given period; educational attainment statistics reflect the highest grade completed by an individual, or beginning 1992, the highest diploma or degree received.

Beginning in 2012, CPS estimates reflect population controls based on Census 2010. From 2000–2011, the CPS used Census 2000 population controls. From 1994 to 2000, the CPS used 1990 census population controls plus adjustment for undercount. Also beginning 1994, the survey is conducted through computer-assisted technology rather than by paper forms. For years 1981 through 1993, 1980 census population controls were used; 1971 through 1980, 1970 census population controls had been used. These changes had little impact on summary measures (e.g., medians) and proportional measures (e.g., enrollment rates); however, use of the controls may have significant impact on absolute numbers.

The second type of data, generally exemplified by data from the NCES and the National Education Association, is based on reports from administrators of educational institutions and of state and local agencies having jurisdiction over education. Data of this type relate to enrollment, attendance, staff, and finances for the nation, individual states, and local areas.

Unlike the NCES, the Census Bureau does not regularly include specialized vocational, trade, business, or correspondence schools in its surveys. The NCES includes nursery schools and kindergartens that are part of regular grade schools in their enrollment figures. The Census Bureau includes all nursery schools and kindergartens. At the higher education level, the statistics of both agencies are concerned with institutions granting degrees or offering work acceptable for degree-credit, such as junior colleges.

School attendance—All states require that children attend school. While state laws vary as to the ages and circumstances of compulsory attendance, generally they require that formal schooling begin by age 6 and continue to age 16.

Schools—The NCES defines a school as "a division of the school system consisting of students composing one or more grade groups or other identifiable groups, organized as one unit with one or more teachers to give instruction of a defined type, and housed in a school plant of one or more buildings. More than one school may be housed in one school plant, as is the case when the elementary and secondary programs are housed in the same school plant."

Regular schools are those which advance a person toward a diploma or degree. They include public and private nursery schools, kindergartens, graded schools, colleges, universities, and professional schools.

Public schools are schools controlled and supported by local, state, or federal governmental agencies.

Private schools are those controlled and supported mainly by religious organizations or by private persons or organizations.

The Census Bureau defines *elementary* schools as including grades 1 through 8; *high* schools as including grades 9 through 12; and *colleges* as including junior or community colleges, regular 4-year colleges, and universities and graduate or professional schools. Statistics reported by the NCES and the National Education Association by type of organization, such as elementary level and secondary level, may not be strictly comparable with those from the Census Bureau because the grades included at the two levels vary, depending on the level assigned to the middle or junior high school by the local school systems.

School year—Except as otherwise indicated in the tables, data refer to the school year which, for elementary and secondary schools, generally begins in August or September of the preceding year and ends in June of the year stated. For the most part, statistics concerning school finances are for a 12-month period, usually July 1 to June 30. Enrollment data generally refer to a specific point in time, such as Fall, as indicated in the tables.

Statistical reliability—For a discussion of statistical collection, estimation, and sampling procedures and measures of statistical reliability applicable to the Census Bureau and the NCES data, see Appendix III.

Table 242. Federal Funds for Education and Related Programs: 2010 to 2015

[In millions of dollars (183,190.0 represents $183,190,000,000), except percent. For fiscal years ending in September. Figures represent on-budget funds]

Level, agency, and program	2010	2014	2015 [1]
Total, all programs	**183,190.0**	**190,498.2**	**196,456.1**
Percent of federal budget outlays	5.3	5.4	5.3
Elementary/secondary education programs	**86,681.8**	**79,411.3**	**77,566.0**
Department of Education [2]	49,621.5	37,772.0	37,394.2
Grants for the disadvantaged	15,864.7	15,552.7	15,536.1
School improvement programs	16,999.9	5,883.4	5,478.1
Indian education	127.3	123.9	123.9
Special education	12,587.0	12,497.3	12,522.4
Vocational and adult education	2,016.4	1,702.7	1,707.7
Department of Agriculture	17,875.6	21,818.5	20,617.1
Child nutrition programs	16,383.4	20,487.3	19,288.0
Agricultural Marketing Service—commodities [3]	1,100.0	888.0	1,029.0
Department of Defense [2]	1,981.3	2,193.9	2,134.7
Overseas dependents schools	1,186.6	1,187.7	1,170.6
Section VI schools [4]	435.1	556.0	582.8
Department of Health and Human Services	8,547.0	9,963.2	9,981.2
Head Start	7,234.0	8,598.0	8,598.0
Social security student benefits	1,313.0	1,365.2	1,383.2
Department of Homeland Security	0.5	0.3	0.3
Department of the Interior [2]	781.1	782.4	807.2
Mineral Leasing Act and other funds	73.0	89.4	76.6
Indian Education	707.1	692.0	730.6
Department of Justice	137.5	151.6	(NA)
Department of Labor	6,826.0	5,463.1	5,314.2
Job Corps	1,850.0	1,691.1	1,688.2
Department of Veterans Affairs	760.5	1,079.7	1,201.5
Vocational rehab for disabled veterans	150.8	186.6	115.6
Higher education programs	**50,188.5**	**69,439.9**	**76,955.2**
Department of Education [2]	36,539.7	51,896.5	57,908.2
Student financial assistance	25,959.5	30,589.5	30,278.1
Federal Family Education Loans	3,933.0	2,269.3	1,362.7
Department of Agriculture	80.7	83.0	83.0
Department of Commerce	(NA)	(NA)	(NA)
Department of Defense	2,550.7	2,314.4	2,204.1
Tuition assistance for military personnel	669.9	580.8	520.8
Service academies [5]	402.6	225.2	227.4
Senior ROTC	885.5	856.9	840.4
Professional development education	592.6	651.5	615.5
Department of Health and Human Services [2]	1,278.9	1,308.2	1,302.9
Health professions training programs	406.0	469.2	438.7
National Health Service Corps scholarships [6]	41.0	43.3	38.5
National Institutes of Health training grants [6]	775.2	753.0	767.0
Department of Homeland Security	45.8	36.1	35.9
Department of the Interior	177.6	116.3	115.2
Shared revenues, Mineral Leasing Act and other receipts—estimated education share	16.3	23.1	19.8
Indian programs	161.4	93.2	95.4
Department of State	657.7	567.8	589.9
Department of Transportation	90.0	96.8	97.7
Department of Veterans Affairs [2]	8,034.5	12,024.4	13,605.3
Post-Vietnam veterans	1.5	0.4	0.4
All-volunteer-force educational assistance	1,854.9	680.3	605.8
Other agencies and programs [2]	732.9	996.2	1,013.1
National Endowment for the Humanities	47.9	39.8	42.9
National Science Foundation	646.0	894.0	893.4
Other education programs [2]	**9,326.4**	**9,443.4**	**9,467.1**
Department of Education [2]	5,073.1	5,420.5	5,457.9
Administration	1,531.2	1,972.0	1,965.7
Rehabilitative services and disability research	3,506.9	3,422.7	3,466.4
Department of Agriculture	567.4	545.7	548.2
Department of Health and Human Services	339.7	327.7	336.9
Department of Homeland Security	341.1	258.7	259.6
Department of Justice	33.6	30.1	30.8
Department of State	120.5	251.2	234.3
Other agencies and programs [2]	2,850.9	2,609.4	2,599.3
Agency for International Development	542.7	576.4	589.6
Library of Congress	516.0	485.8	469.6
National Endowment for the Arts	2.9	4.5	3.7
National Endowment for the Humanities	94.6	77.5	77.1
Research programs at universities and related institutions [2]	**36,993.3**	**32,203.6**	**32,467.9**
Department of Agriculture	737.2	697.9	794.1
Department of Defense	3,154.3	2,788.7	2,940.2
Department of Energy	3,402.6	3,288.7	3,099.4
Department of Health and Human Services	21,796.2	17,305.4	17,416.3
National Aeronautics and Space Administration	1,585.5	2,287.8	2,333.1
National Science Foundation	4,914.7	4,584.3	4,723.4

NA Not available. [1] Data for research programs at universities and related institutions are estimated. [2] Includes other programs and agencies, not shown separately. [3] Purchased under Section 32 of the Act of August 1935 for use in child nutrition programs. [4] Program provides for the education of dependents of federal employees residing on federal property where free public education is unavailable in the nearby community. [5] Instructional costs only including academics, audiovisual, academic computer center, faculty training, military training, physical education, and libraries. [6] Includes alcohol, drug abuse, and mental health training programs.

Source: U.S. National Center for Education Statistics, *Digest of Education Statistics 2015*, December 2016. See also <http://www.nces.ed.gov/programs/digest/>.

Table 243. School Expenditures by Level of Instruction in Current and Constant (2015 to 2016) Dollars: 1980 to 2016

[In millions of dollars (160,075 represents $160,075,000,000). For school years ending in year shown. Data shown reflect historical revisions. Total expenditures for public elementary and secondary schools include current expenditures, interest on school debt, and capital outlay. Based on survey of state education agencies; see source for details]

Year	Current dollars			Constant 2015-16 dollars [1]			
	Total	Elementary and secondary schools	Colleges and universities [2]	Total	Elementary and secondary schools		Colleges and universities [2]
					Total	Public	
1980.................	160,075	103,162	56,914	491,313	316,630	294,531	174,683
1985.................	239,351	149,400	89,951	539,220	336,574	308,639	202,646
1990.................	365,825	231,170	134,656	686,492	433,803	399,275	252,689
1995.................	485,169	302,200	182,969	768,603	478,745	441,992	289,858
1999.................	603,847	384,638	219,209	874,440	557,000	515,295	317,440
2000.................	649,322	412,538	236,784	913,912	580,641	537,432	333,270
2001.................	705,017	444,811	260,206	959,430	605,327	559,057	354,104
2002.................	752,780	472,064	280,715	1,006,607	631,238	582,164	375,369
2003.................	795,691	492,807	302,884	1,041,108	644,805	595,215	396,304
2004.................	830,293	513,542	316,751	1,063,124	657,549	607,229	405,574
2005.................	875,988	540,969	335,019	1,088,866	672,432	620,971	416,434
2006.................	925,246	571,669	353,577	1,107,903	684,525	632,557	423,378
2007.................	984,034	608,495	375,539	1,148,594	710,253	656,211	438,340
2008.................	1,054,904	646,414	408,490	1,187,321	727,555	672,292	459,766
2009.................	1,089,683	658,926	430,757	1,209,577	731,425	677,478	478,152
2010.................	1,100,897	654,418	446,479	1,210,314	719,460	667,349	490,854
2011.................	1,124,352	652,356	471,997	1,211,768	703,075	651,343	508,693
2012.................	1,136,876	648,794	488,083	1,190,387	679,331	630,328	511,056
2013.................	1,153,674	654,813	498,861	1,188,202	674,411	624,974	513,791
2014.................	1,193,083	676,016	517,067	1,209,890	685,539	633,821	524,351
2015 [3].............	1,225,000	689,000	536,000	1,233,000	694,000	642,000	540,000
2016 [4].............	1,254,000	707,000	548,000	1,254,000	707,000	655,000	548,000

[1] Constant dollars based on the Consumer Price Index, prepared by the Bureau of Labor Statistics, U.S. Department of Labor, adjusted to a school-year basis. [2] Postsecondary data through 1996 are for institutions of higher education; thereafter, data are for degree-granting institutions. See source for details. [3] Data for elementary and secondary education are estimated; data for degree-granting institutions are actual. [4] Estimated.

Source: U.S. National Center for Education Statistics, *Digest of Education Statistics*, "Advance Release of Selected 2016 Digest Tables," <http://www.nces.ed.gov/programs/digest/>, accessed July 2017.

Table 244. School Enrollment: 1990 to 2026

[In thousands (60,683 represents 60,683,000). As of Fall]

Year	All levels			Pre-kindergarten through grade 8		Grades 9 through 12		College [3]	
	Total	Public	Private	Public	Private [1,2]	Public	Private [1]	Public	Private
1990.................	60,683	52,061	8,622	29,876	4,512	11,341	1,136	10,845	2,974
1995.................	65,020	55,933	9,087	32,338	4,756	12,502	1,163	11,092	3,169
1996.................	65,911	56,732	9,180	32,762	4,755	12,849	1,178	11,120	3,247
1997.................	66,574	57,323	9,251	33,071	4,759	13,056	1,185	11,196	3,306
1998.................	67,033	57,676	9,357	33,344	4,776	13,195	1,212	11,138	3,369
1999.................	67,725	58,233	9,492	33,486	4,789	13,371	1,229	11,376	3,474
2000.................	68,685	58,956	9,729	33,686	4,906	13,517	1,264	11,753	3,560
2001.................	69,920	59,905	10,014	33,936	5,023	13,736	1,296	12,233	3,695
2002.................	71,015	60,935	10,080	34,114	4,915	14,069	1,306	12,752	3,860
2003.................	71,551	61,399	10,152	34,201	4,788	14,339	1,311	12,859	4,053
2004.................	72,154	61,776	10,379	34,178	4,756	14,618	1,331	12,980	4,292
2005.................	72,674	62,135	10,539	34,204	4,724	14,909	1,349	13,022	4,466
2006.................	73,066	62,496	10,570	34,235	4,631	15,081	1,360	13,180	4,579
2007.................	73,449	62,781	10,668	34,204	4,546	15,086	1,364	13,491	4,757
2008.................	74,076	63,238	10,838	34,286	4,365	14,980	1,342	13,972	5,131
2009.................	75,163	64,172	10,991	34,409	4,179	14,952	1,309	14,811	5,503
2010.................	75,886	64,626	11,260	34,625	4,084	14,860	1,299	15,142	5,877
2011.................	75,800	64,638	11,162	34,773	3,977	14,749	1,291	15,116	5,894
2012.................	75,748	64,656	11,092	35,018	4,031	14,753	1,302	14,885	5,760
2013.................	75,817	64,791	11,026	35,251	4,084	14,794	1,312	14,747	5,630
2014.................	75,843	64,968	10,875	35,370	3,988	14,943	1,334	14,655	5,552
2015, projections [4]........	75,740	65,053	10,687	35,414	3,949	15,070	1,329	14,568	5,409
2016, projections..........	76,044	65,469	10,575	35,514	3,918	15,111	1,316	14,844	5,341
2017, projections..........	76,304	65,712	10,591	35,562	3,879	15,148	1,303	15,003	5,410
2018, projections..........	76,580	65,966	10,614	35,593	3,852	15,166	1,281	15,206	5,481
2019, projections..........	76,957	66,287	10,670	35,657	3,845	15,186	1,259	15,443	5,566
2020, projections..........	77,425	66,681	10,745	35,667	3,849	15,329	1,234	15,684	5,662
2021, projections..........	77,875	67,062	10,813	35,639	3,855	15,513	1,210	15,910	5,749
2022, projections..........	78,244	67,379	10,865	35,660	3,863	15,641	1,192	16,078	5,810
2023, projections..........	78,637	67,706	10,931	35,815	3,882	15,640	1,176	16,251	5,873
2024, projections..........	78,963	67,968	10,995	35,982	3,902	15,579	1,169	16,407	5,924
2025, projections..........	79,218	68,174	11,045	36,156	3,921	15,476	1,161	16,541	5,962
2026, projections..........	79,465	68,379	11,086	36,362	3,942	15,376	1,154	16,642	5,990

[1] Since the biennial Private School Universe Survey (PSS) is collected in the fall of odd numbered years, data for even numbered years are estimated based on data from the PSS. [2] Includes private nursery and pre-kindergarten enrollment in schools that offer kindergarten or higher grades. [3] Data beginning 1996 based on new classification system. See footnote 1, Table 288. [4] Pre-K through 12 are projections; college data are actual.

Source: U.S. National Center for Education Statistics, *Digest of Education Statistics*, "Advance Release of Selected 2016 Digest Tables," <http://www.nces.ed.gov/programs/digest/>, accessed May 2017.

Table 245. School Enrollment, Faculty, Graduates, and Finances—Projections: 2016 to 2022

[55,077 represents 55,077,000. As of Fall, except as indicated]

Item	Unit	2016	2017	2018	2019	2020	2021	2022
ELEMENTARY AND SECONDARY SCHOOLS								
School enrollment, total	1,000	55,077	55,447	55,719	56,031	56,404	56,779	57,151
Pre-kindergarten through grade 8	1,000	39,010	39,363	39,642	39,938	40,205	40,450	40,728
Grades 9 through 12	1,000	16,067	16,084	16,078	16,093	16,199	16,330	16,424
Public	1,000	50,229	50,584	50,871	51,183	51,547	51,910	52,260
Pre-kindergarten through grade 8	1,000	35,282	35,595	35,856	36,125	36,366	36,587	36,839
Grades 9 through 12	1,000	14,947	14,989	15,015	15,058	15,182	15,324	15,421
Private	1,000	4,848	4,863	4,848	4,848	4,856	4,869	4,891
Pre-kindergarten through grade 8	1,000	3,728	3,768	3,786	3,813	3,839	3,863	3,889
Grades 9 through 12	1,000	1,120	1,095	1,063	1,035	1,017	1,006	1,003
Classroom teachers, total FTE [1]	1,000	3,525	3,577	3,617	3,660	3,700	3,743	3,788
Public	1,000	3,138	3,185	3,224	3,264	3,302	3,342	3,383
Private	1,000	387	392	393	395	398	401	405
High school graduates, total [2]	1,000	3,433	3,475	3,462	3,430	3,447	3,464	3,472
Public	1,000	3,168	3,212	3,211	3,186	3,206	3,231	3,246
Public schools: [2]								
Average daily attendance (ADA)	1,000	46,946	47,277	47,546	47,837	48,178	48,517	48,844
Constant (2013–2014) dollars: [3]								
Current school expenditure	Bil. dol.	560	575	587	601	614	626	638
Per pupil in fall enrollment	Dollar	11,150	11,370	11,545	11,737	11,906	12,059	12,212
HIGHER EDUCATION								
Enrollment, total	1,000	20,486	20,925	21,330	21,630	21,859	22,168	22,511
Male	1,000	8,783	8,941	9,105	9,217	9,297	9,423	9,567
Full-time	1,000	5,721	5,811	5,903	5,972	6,021	6,089	6,167
Part-time	1,000	3,063	3,130	3,202	3,245	3,277	3,333	3,400
Female	1,000	11,702	11,984	12,225	12,412	12,561	12,745	12,943
Full-time	1,000	7,062	7,253	7,402	7,495	7,574	7,685	7,805
Part-time	1,000	4,640	4,731	4,823	4,918	4,987	5,061	5,139
Public	1,000	14,820	15,129	15,421	15,639	15,802	16,022	16,267
Four-year institutions	1,000	8,091	8,265	8,421	8,535	8,627	8,750	8,883
Two-year institutions	1,000	6,729	6,865	7,000	7,104	7,175	7,272	7,384
Private	1,000	5,666	5,796	5,909	5,991	6,057	6,146	6,243
Four-year institutions	1,000	5,304	5,425	5,531	5,608	5,671	5,754	5,845
Two-year institutions	1,000	362	371	378	383	387	392	398
Undergraduate	1,000	17,472	17,823	18,156	18,404	18,591	18,843	19,119
Postbaccalaureate	1,000	3,013	3,102	3,173	3,225	3,268	3,325	3,391
Full-time equivalent	1,000	15,566	15,905	16,205	16,417	16,582	16,809	17,059
Public	1,000	10,805	11,035	11,243	11,391	11,503	11,658	11,831
2-year	1,000	4,012	4,098	4,179	4,238	4,277	4,334	4,401
4-year	1,000	6,793	6,937	7,064	7,153	7,226	7,324	7,430
Private	1,000	4,761	4,870	4,962	5,027	5,079	5,150	5,228
2-year	1,000	335	343	350	355	358	363	369
4-year	1,000	4,426	4,527	4,612	4,672	4,721	4,788	4,860
Degrees conferred, total [2]	1,000	3,824	3,876	3,954	4,037	4,113	4,182	4,252
Associate's	1,000	973	991	1,016	1,041	1,062	1,082	1,103
Bachelor's	1,000	1,845	1,847	1,871	1,903	1,933	1,956	1,977
Master's	1,000	824	851	877	899	920	943	969
Doctoral	1,000	182	187	190	194	198	201	203

[1] Full-time equivalent. [2] For school year ending in June the following year. [3] Based on the Consumer Price Index (CPI) for all urban consumers, U.S. Bureau of Labor Statistics. CPI adjusted to a school year basis by NCES.

Source: U.S. National Center for Education Statistics, *Projections of Education Statistics to 2024*, April 2017. See also <http://www.nces.ed.gov/>.

Table 246. School Enrollment by Control and Level: 1980 to 2017

[In thousands (58,305 represents 58,305,000). As of Fall. Data below college level are for regular day schools and exclude subcollegiate departments of colleges, federal schools, and home-schooled children. College data include degree-credit and nondegree-credit enrollment. Based on survey of state education agencies; see source for details. For more projections, see Table 244 and Table 245]

Control of school and level	1980	1990	2000	2005	2010	2013	2014	2015, proj.	2016, proj.	2017, proj.
Total	58,305	60,683	68,685	72,674	75,886	75,817	75,843	75,740	76,044	76,304
Public	50,335	52,061	58,956	62,135	64,626	64,791	64,968	65,053	65,469	65,712
Private	7,971	8,622	9,729	10,539	11,260	11,026	10,875	10,687	10,575	10,591
Pre-kindergarten through 8	31,639	34,388	38,592	38,928	38,708	39,335	39,358	39,363	39,432	39,440
Public	27,647	29,876	33,686	34,204	34,625	35,251	35,370	35,414	35,514	35,562
Private	3,992	[1] 4,512	[1] 4,906	4,724	[1] 4,084	4,084	[1] 3,988	3,949	3,918	3,879
Grades 9 through 12	14,570	12,476	14,781	16,258	16,159	16,106	16,277	16,400	16,427	16,451
Public	13,231	11,341	13,517	14,909	14,860	14,794	14,943	15,070	15,111	15,148
Private [2, 3]	1,339	[1] 1,136	[1] 1,264	1,349	[1] 1,299	1,312	[1] 1,334	1,329	1,316	1,303
College [2, 3]	12,097	13,819	15,312	17,487	21,019	20,377	20,207	19,977	20,185	20,413
Public	9,457	10,845	11,753	13,022	15,142	14,747	14,655	14,568	14,844	15,003
Private	2,640	2,974	3,560	4,466	5,877	5,630	5,552	5,409	5,341	5,410
Not-for-profit	2,528	2,760	3,109	3,455	3,854	3,971	3,996	4,063	(NA)	(NA)
For profit	112	214	450	1,011	2,023	1,658	1,556	1,346	(NA)	(NA)

NA Not available. [1] Estimated. [2] Beginning 2000, reflects new classification system. See footnote 1, Table 288. [3] Data for 2015 are actual.

Source: U.S. National Center for Education Statistics, *Digest of Education Statistics*, "Advance Release of Selected 2016 Digest Tables," <http://www.nces.ed.gov/programs/digest/>, accessed May 2017.

Table 247. School Enrollment by Age: 1970 to 2015

[Enrollment in thousands (60,357 represents 60,357,000); rate as percent of total population in each age group. As of October. Covers civilian noninstitutional population enrolled in nursery school and above. Based on Current Population Survey; see text, Section 1 and Appendix III]

Age	1970	1980	1990	1995	2000	2005	2010	2013	2014	2015
ENROLLMENT (1,000)										
Total, 3 to 34 years old	**60,357**	**57,348**	**60,588**	**66,939**	**69,560**	**72,768**	**75,148**	**74,729**	**74,197**	**77,066**
3 and 4 years old	1,461	2,280	3,292	4,042	4,097	4,383	4,706	4,449	4,426	4,203
5 and 6 years old	7,000	5,853	7,207	7,901	7,648	7,486	7,955	7,780	7,577	7,507
7 to 13 years old	28,943	23,751	25,016	27,003	28,296	27,936	27,984	28,202	28,093	28,250
14 and 15 years old	7,869	7,282	6,555	7,651	7,885	8,375	7,736	8,150	8,178	8,207
16 and 17 years old	6,927	7,129	6,098	6,997	7,341	8,472	7,963	7,731	7,755	7,923
18 and 19 years old	3,322	3,788	4,044	4,274	4,926	5,109	5,904	5,687	5,654	5,591
20 and 21 years old	1,949	2,515	2,852	3,025	3,314	4,069	4,552	4,532	4,384	4,641
22 to 24 years old	1,410	1,931	2,231	2,545	2,731	3,254	3,602	4,007	3,996	3,793
25 to 29 years old	1,011	1,714	2,013	2,216	2,030	2,340	3,088	2,790	2,798	2,880
30 to 34 years old	466	1,105	1,281	1,284	1,292	1,344	1,658	1,401	1,336	1,398
35 years old and over	(NA)	1,290	2,439	2,830	2,653	3,013	3,372	3,042	3,017	2,674
ENROLLMENT RATE										
Total, 3 to 34 years old	**56.4**	**49.7**	**50.2**	**53.7**	**55.9**	**56.5**	**56.5**	**55.8**	**55.2**	**55.2**
3 and 4 years old	20.5	36.7	44.4	48.7	52.1	53.6	53.2	54.9	54.5	52.7
5 and 6 years old	89.5	95.7	96.5	96.0	95.6	95.4	94.5	93.8	93.4	94.2
7 to 13 years old	99.2	99.3	99.6	98.9	98.2	98.6	98.0	98.1	97.6	97.7
14 and 15 years old	98.1	98.2	99.0	98.9	98.7	98.0	98.1	98.4	97.8	98.0
16 and 17 years old	90.0	89.0	92.5	93.6	92.8	92.8	95.1	96.1	93.7	92.9	93.7
18 and 19 years old	47.7	46.4	57.3	59.4	61.2	67.6	69.2	67.1	68.4	68.5
20 and 21 years old	31.9	31.0	39.7	44.9	44.1	48.7	52.4	52.8	51.4	53.3
22 to 24 years old	14.9	16.3	21.0	23.2	24.6	27.3	28.9	29.7	29.6	28.8
25 to 29 years old	7.5	9.3	9.7	11.6	11.4	11.9	14.6	13.3	13.1	13.2
30 to 34 years old	4.2	6.5	5.8	6.0	6.7	6.9	8.3	6.7	6.4	6.6
35 years old and over	(NA)	1.6	2.1	2.2	1.9	2.0	2.1	1.8	1.8	1.6

NA Not available.

Source: U.S. Census Bureau, Current Population Reports, P-20, and earlier reports; and "School Enrollment," <http://www.census.gov/hhes/school/index.html>, accessed November 2016.

Table 248. School Enrollment by Race, Hispanic Origin, and Age: 2000 to 2015

[Enrollment in thousands (54,257 represents 54,257,000); rate as percent of total population in each age group. As of October. See headnote, Table 247]

Age	White [1]			Black [1]			Hispanic [2]		
	2000	2010	2015	2000	2010	2015	2000	2010	2015
ENROLLMENT (1,000)									
Total, 3 to 34 years old	**54,257**	**56,776**	**56,056**	**11,115**	**11,272**	**11,544**	**9,928**	**15,235**	**17,362**
3 and 4 years old	3,091	3,439	2,990	725	776	644	518	1,025	913
5 and 6 years old	5,959	5,956	5,438	1,219	1,207	1,108	1,390	1,961	1,904
7 to 13 years old	22,061	21,201	20,569	4,675	4,108	4,206	4,373	6,241	7,041
14 and 15 years old	6,176	5,907	6,028	1,260	1,157	1,251	1,093	1,555	1,827
16 and 17 years old	5,845	6,059	5,781	1,106	1,245	1,184	959	1,448	1,804
18 and 19 years old	3,924	4,566	4,217	716	837	795	617	1,171	1,148
20 and 21 years old	2,688	3,432	3,405	416	678	598	311	582	958
22 to 24 years old	2,101	2,720	2,711	393	514	560	309	559	692
25 to 29 years old	1,473	2,289	2,074	353	462	415	198	462	496
30 to 34 years old	939	1,207	966	252	288	229	160	231	198
35 years old and over	2,087	2,462	1,876	387	697	553	235	435	381
ENROLLMENT RATE									
Total, 3 to 34 years old	**55.1**	**55.8**	**54.6**	**59.0**	**58.4**	**55.3**	**51.3**	**55.1**	**55.8**
3 and 4 years old	50.2	52.1	52.2	52.1	56.2	52.7	35.9	44.2	44.1
5 and 6 years old	95.3	94.2	94.1	94.2	94.4	93.7	94.3	94.3	93.7
7 to 13 years old	98.2	97.9	97.7	97.9	98.0	97.0	97.5	97.8	97.5
14 and 15 years old	98.4	98.1	97.8	98.0	98.5	98.7	96.2	97.9	96.7
16 and 17 years old	92.8	96.2	93.8	96.2	95.5	94.4	87.0	96.0	92.6
18 and 19 years old	61.3	70.0	68.6	70.0	62.7	64.5	49.5	66.2	65.2
20 and 21 years old	44.9	51.6	53.8	51.6	50.2	43.7	26.1	37.0	48.8
22 to 24 years old	23.7	28.1	27.7	28.1	29.0	27.5	18.2	23.8	25.2
25 to 29 years old	10.4	13.9	12.8	13.9	16.0	13.1	7.4	11.4	11.2
30 to 34 years old	6.0	7.8	6.1	7.8	10.9	8.2	5.6	5.7	4.6
35 years old and over	1.8	1.9	1.4	2.6	4.0	2.8	2.0	2.3	1.7

[1] Beginning 2003, represents persons who selected this race group only. See footnote 4, Table 251. [2] Persons of Hispanic origin may be of any race.

Source: U.S. Census Bureau, Current Population Reports, P-20, and earlier reports; and "School Enrollment," <http://www.census.gov/hhes/school/index.html>, accessed November 2016.

Table 249. Enrollment in Public and Private Schools: 1970 to 2015

[In millions (52.2 represents 52,200,000), except percent. As of October. For civilian noninstitutional population. Prior to 1995, total enrolled does not include the population age 35 and over. For enrollment of population age 35 and over, see Table 247. Based on Current Population Survey]

Year	Public						Private					
	Total	Nursery	Kinder-garten	Elemen-tary	High school	College	Total	Nursery	Kinder-garten	Elemen-tary	High school	College
1970...........	52.2	0.3	2.6	30.0	13.5	5.7	8.1	0.8	0.5	3.9	1.2	1.7
1975...........	52.8	0.6	2.9	27.2	14.5	7.7	8.2	1.2	0.5	3.3	1.2	2.0
1980...........	(NA)	0.6	2.7	24.4	(NA)	(NA)	(NA)	1.4	0.5	3.1	(NA)	(NA)
1985...........	49.0	0.9	3.2	23.8	12.8	8.4	9.0	1.6	0.6	3.1	1.2	2.5
1990 [1]........	53.8	1.2	3.3	26.6	11.9	10.7	9.2	2.2	0.6	2.7	0.9	2.9
1995...........	58.7	2.0	3.2	28.4	13.7	11.4	11.1	2.4	0.7	3.4	1.2	3.3
2000...........	61.2	2.2	3.2	29.4	14.4	12.0	11.0	2.2	0.7	3.5	1.3	3.3
2001...........	62.4	2.2	3.1	29.8	14.8	12.4	10.8	2.1	0.6	3.4	1.2	3.5
2002...........	62.8	2.2	3.0	29.7	15.1	12.8	11.3	2.2	0.6	3.5	1.3	3.7
2003...........	63.8	2.6	3.1	29.2	15.8	13.1	11.1	2.4	0.6	3.4	1.3	3.5
2004...........	64.3	2.5	3.4	29.2	15.5	13.7	11.3	2.3	0.6	3.4	1.3	3.7
2005...........	64.2	2.5	3.3	29.0	15.8	13.4	11.5	2.1	0.6	3.4	1.4	4.0
2006...........	64.1	2.5	3.6	29.0	15.6	13.5	11.1	2.2	0.5	3.1	1.5	3.8
2007...........	65.1	2.6	3.7	29.1	15.8	14.1	10.8	2.1	0.5	3.1	1.3	3.9
2008...........	65.5	2.6	3.6	29.2	15.4	14.7	10.8	2.0	0.5	3.2	1.3	4.0
2009...........	66.9	2.7	3.8	29.4	15.3	15.7	10.4	2.0	0.4	2.9	1.2	4.0
2010...........	67.9	2.8	3.8	29.8	15.3	16.2	10.6	2.1	0.4	2.8	1.2	4.1
2011...........	68.2	2.9	3.7	30.0	15.4	16.1	10.9	2.0	0.5	2.9	1.2	4.3
2012...........	67.8	2.7	3.7	29.9	15.7	15.8	10.7	1.9	0.5	2.8	1.3	4.2
2013...........	67.4	2.6	3.7	30.2	15.5	15.5	10.3	2.1	0.4	2.7	1.1	4.0
2014...........	66.8	2.7	3.6	29.8	15.4	15.3	10.4	2.0	0.5	2.8	1.3	3.9
2015...........	67.0	2.6	3.6	30.2	15.4	15.2	10.1	1.9	0.4	2.7	1.2	3.9
Percent White:												
1970..........	84.5	59.5	84.4	83.1	85.6	90.7	93.4	91.1	88.2	94.1	96.1	92.8
1980..........	(NA)	68.2	80.7	80.9	(NA)	(NA)	(NA)	89.0	87.0	90.7	(NA)	(NA)
1990..........	79.8	71.7	78.3	78.9	79.2	84.1	87.4	89.6	83.2	88.2	89.4	85.0
2000..........	77.0	69.4	77.3	76.7	78.0	78.0	83.5	84.9	82.8	85.9	84.6	79.8
2005 [2].......	75.7	71.3	78.0	75.2	76.0	76.7	81.4	83.6	79.0	83.0	83.6	78.4
2010 [2].......	74.9	71.8	72.9	75.0	75.1	75.4	78.9	81.0	79.4	80.9	84.5	74.7
2011 [2].......	74.7	68.8	75.2	74.8	74.8	75.4	80.2	79.7	81.5	84.1	84.8	76.3
2012 [2].......	73.0	70.5	70.1	73.4	73.2	73.1	77.3	77.4	78.2	80.2	78.9	74.6
2013 [2].......	72.8	68.0	69.5	73.2	72.9	73.3	75.9	75.6	81.2	79.5	78.3	72.4
2014 [2].......	72.7	67.4	70.7	72.7	73.6	73.3	74.6	77.0	68.2	78.4	76.0	70.8
2015 [2].......	72.3	68.1	72.2	72.2	72.9	72.7	75.5	75.5	79.4	78.7	79.4	71.9

NA Not available. [1] Beginning 1990, based on a revised edit and tabulation package. [2] Beginning in 2003, represents persons who selected this race group only. See footnote 4, Table 251.

Source: U.S. Census Bureau, "School Enrollment, Historical Time Series Tables," <http://www.census.gov/hhes/school/data/cps/historical/index.html>, accessed November 2016.

Table 250. School Enrollment by Sex and Level: 1970 to 2015

[In millions (60.4 represents 60,400,000). As of October. For the civilian noninstitutional population. Prior to 1980, persons 3 to 34 years old; beginning 1980, 3 years old and over. Elementary includes kindergarten and grades 1–8; high school, grades 9–12; and college, 2-year and 4-year colleges, universities, and graduate and professional schools. Data for college represent degree-credit enrollment. See headnote, Table 247]

Year	All levels [1]			Elementary			High school			College		
	Total	Male	Female	Total	Male	Female	Total	Male	Female	Total	Male	Female
1970............	60.4	31.4	28.9	37.1	19.0	18.1	14.7	7.4	7.3	7.4	4.4	3.0
1980............	58.6	29.6	29.1	30.6	15.8	14.9	14.6	7.3	7.3	11.4	5.4	6.0
1990 [2].........	63.0	31.5	31.5	33.2	17.1	16.0	12.8	6.5	6.4	13.6	6.2	7.4
1996............	70.3	35.1	35.2	35.5	18.3	17.3	15.3	7.9	7.4	15.2	6.8	8.4
1997............	72.0	35.9	36.2	36.3	18.7	17.6	15.8	8.0	7.7	15.4	6.8	8.6
1998............	72.1	36.0	36.1	36.4	18.7	17.7	15.6	7.9	7.6	15.5	6.9	8.6
1999............	72.4	36.3	36.1	36.7	18.8	17.9	15.9	8.2	7.7	15.2	7.0	8.2
2000............	72.2	35.8	36.4	36.7	18.9	17.9	15.8	8.1	7.7	15.3	6.7	8.6
2001............	73.1	36.3	36.9	36.9	19.0	17.9	16.1	8.2	7.8	15.9	6.9	9.0
2002............	74.0	36.8	37.3	36.7	18.9	17.8	16.4	8.3	8.0	16.5	7.2	9.3
2003............	74.9	37.3	37.6	36.3	18.7	17.6	17.1	8.6	8.4	16.6	7.3	9.3
2004............	75.5	37.4	38.0	36.5	19.0	17.6	16.8	8.4	8.4	17.4	7.6	9.8
2005............	75.8	37.4	38.4	36.4	18.6	17.7	17.4	8.9	8.5	17.5	7.5	9.9
2006............	75.2	37.2	38.0	36.1	18.5	17.6	17.1	8.8	8.4	17.2	7.5	9.7
2007............	76.0	37.6	38.4	36.3	18.6	17.7	17.1	8.8	8.3	18.0	7.8	10.1
2008............	76.4	37.8	38.6	36.4	18.7	17.7	16.7	8.5	8.2	18.6	8.3	10.3
2009............	77.3	38.0	39.3	36.4	18.6	17.7	16.4	8.4	8.1	19.8	8.6	11.1
2010............	78.5	38.7	39.8	36.8	18.8	18.1	16.6	8.5	8.0	20.3	9.0	11.3
2011............	79.0	39.2	39.8	37.1	19.0	18.1	16.6	8.6	8.1	20.4	9.1	11.3
2012............	78.4	38.5	39.9	36.8	19.0	17.9	17.0	8.6	8.5	19.9	8.6	11.3
2013............	77.8	38.3	39.5	37.0	19.0	18.0	16.6	8.4	8.2	19.5	8.5	10.9
2014............	77.2	38.2	39.0	36.7	18.8	17.9	16.7	8.4	8.2	19.2	8.6	10.5
2015............	77.1	38.2	38.9	36.9	18.9	18.0	16.5	8.4	8.1	19.1	8.5	10.6

[1] Includes nursery schools, not shown separately. [2] For data beginning 1990, based on a revised edit and tabulation package.

Source: U.S. Census Bureau, Current Population Reports, P20, and earlier reports; and "School Enrollment," <http://www.census.gov/hhes/school/data/cps/index.html>, accessed November 2016.

Table 251. Educational Attainment by Race and Hispanic Origin: 1970 to 2016

[In percent. For persons 25 years old and over. 1970 and 1980 data as of April 1 and based on sample data from the censuses of population. Other years as of March and based on the Current Population Survey; see text, Section 1 and Appendix III. See Table 252 for data by sex]

Year	High school graduate or more [1]					College graduate or more [2]				
	Total [3]	White [4]	Black [4]	Asian and Pacific Islander [4,5]	His-panic [6]	Total [3]	White [4]	Black [4]	Asian and Pacific Islander [4,5]	His-panic [6]
1970............	52.3	54.5	31.4	62.2	32.1	10.7	11.3	4.4	20.4	4.5
1975............	62.5	64.5	42.5	(NA)	37.9	13.9	14.5	6.4	(NA)	6.3
1980............	66.5	68.8	51.2	74.8	44.0	16.2	17.1	8.4	32.9	7.6
1985............	73.9	75.5	59.8	(NA)	47.9	19.4	20.0	11.1	(NA)	8.5
1990............	77.6	79.1	66.2	80.4	50.8	21.3	22.0	11.3	39.9	9.2
1995............	81.7	83.0	73.8	(NA)	53.4	23.0	24.0	13.2	(NA)	9.3
2000............	84.1	84.9	78.5	85.7	57.0	25.6	26.1	16.5	43.9	10.6
2001............	84.1	84.8	78.8	87.6	56.8	26.2	26.6	15.7	47.5	11.1
2002............	84.1	84.8	78.7	87.4	57.0	26.7	27.2	17.0	47.2	11.1
2003............	84.6	85.1	80.0	87.6	57.0	27.2	27.6	17.3	49.8	11.4
2004............	85.2	85.8	80.6	86.8	58.4	27.7	28.2	17.6	49.4	12.1
2005............	85.2	85.8	81.1	87.6	58.5	27.7	28.1	17.6	50.2	12.0
2006............	85.5	86.1	80.7	87.4	59.3	28.0	28.4	18.5	49.7	12.4
2007............	85.7	86.2	82.3	87.8	60.3	28.7	29.1	18.5	52.1	12.7
2008............	86.6	87.1	83.0	88.7	62.3	29.4	29.8	19.6	52.6	13.3
2009............	86.7	87.1	84.1	88.2	61.9	29.5	29.9	19.3	52.3	13.2
2010............	87.1	87.6	84.2	88.9	62.9	29.9	30.3	19.8	52.4	13.9
2011............	87.6	88.1	84.5	88.6	64.3	30.4	31.0	19.9	50.3	14.1
2012............	87.6	88.1	85.0	88.9	65.0	30.9	31.3	21.2	51.0	14.5
2013............	88.2	88.6	85.1	90.1	66.2	31.7	32.0	21.8	53.2	15.1
2014............	88.3	88.8	85.8	89.5	66.5	32.0	32.3	22.2	52.3	15.2
2015............	88.4	88.8	87.0	89.1	66.7	32.5	32.8	22.5	53.9	15.5
2016............	89.1	89.5	87.1	90.3	68.5	33.4	33.7	23.3	55.9	16.4

NA Not available. [1] Through 1991, completed 4 years of high school or more. [2] Through 1991, completed 4 years of college or more. [3] Includes other races not shown separately. [4] The 2003 Current Population Survey (CPS) allowed respondents to choose more than one race. Beginning 2003, data represent persons who selected this race group only and exclude persons reporting more than one race. The CPS in prior years only allowed respondents to report one race group. See also comments on race in the text for Section 1, Population. [5] Starting in 2003, data are for Asians only; excludes Pacific Islanders. [6] Persons of Hispanic origin may be of any race.

Source: U.S. Census Bureau, U.S. Census of Population,1960, 1970, and 1980, Summary File 3; Current Population Reports, P20-550, and earlier reports; and "Educational Attainment in the United States: Historical Tables," <https://www.census.gov/topics/education/educational-attainment.html>, accessed April 2017.

Table 252. Educational Attainment by Race, Hispanic Origin, and Sex: 1970 to 2016

[In percent. See Table 251 for headnote and totals for both sexes]

Year	All races [1]		White [2]		Black [2]		Asian and Pacific Islander [2,5]		Hispanic [3]	
	Male	Female	Male	Female	Male	Female	Male	Female	Male	Female
HIGH SCHOOL GRADUATE OR MORE [4]										
1970....................	51.9	52.8	54.0	55.0	30.1	32.5	61.3	63.1	37.9	34.2
1980....................	67.3	65.8	69.6	68.1	50.8	51.5	78.8	71.4	45.4	42.7
1990....................	77.7	77.5	79.1	79.0	65.8	66.5	84.0	77.2	50.3	51.3
2000....................	84.2	84.0	84.8	85.0	78.7	78.3	88.2	83.4	56.6	57.5
2005....................	84.9	85.5	85.2	86.2	81.0	81.2	90.4	85.2	57.9	59.1
2010....................	86.6	87.6	86.9	88.2	83.6	84.6	91.2	87.0	61.4	64.4
2011....................	87.1	88.0	87.4	88.6	83.8	85.0	90.4	87.1	63.6	65.1
2012....................	87.3	88.0	87.6	88.5	84.3	85.5	90.4	87.6	64.0	66.0
2013....................	87.6	88.6	88.0	89.2	84.1	86.0	91.5	89.0	64.6	67.9
2014....................	87.7	88.9	88.0	89.6	85.3	86.2	91.9	87.4	65.1	67.9
2015....................	88.0	88.8	88.3	89.3	86.4	87.6	91.0	87.4	65.5	67.8
2016....................	88.5	89.6	88.8	90.1	86.4	87.7	91.9	89.0	67.2	69.7
COLLEGE GRADUATE OR MORE [4]										
1970....................	13.5	8.1	14.4	8.4	4.2	4.6	23.5	17.3	7.8	4.3
1980....................	20.1	12.8	21.3	13.3	8.4	8.3	39.8	27.0	9.4	6.0
1990....................	24.4	18.4	25.3	19.0	11.9	10.8	44.9	35.4	9.8	8.7
2000....................	27.8	23.6	28.5	23.9	16.3	16.7	47.6	40.7	10.7	10.6
2005....................	28.9	26.5	29.4	26.8	16.0	18.8	54.0	46.8	11.8	12.1
2010....................	30.3	29.6	30.8	29.9	17.7	21.4	55.6	49.5	12.9	14.9
2011....................	30.8	30.1	31.5	30.5	18.0	21.4	53.4	47.7	13.1	15.2
2012....................	31.4	30.6	31.9	30.8	19.2	22.9	53.7	48.8	13.3	15.8
2013....................	32.0	31.4	32.4	31.6	19.8	23.3	56.1	50.8	13.9	16.2
2014....................	31.9	32.0	32.3	32.3	20.4	23.7	54.7	50.3	14.2	16.1
2015....................	32.3	32.7	32.6	32.9	20.6	24.0	56.8	51.5	14.3	16.6
2016....................	33.2	33.7	33.4	34.0	21.7	24.6	58.8	53.4	15.4	17.4

[1] Includes other races not shown separately. [2] Beginning 2003, for persons who selected this race group only. See footnote 4, Table 251. [3] Persons of Hispanic origin may be of any race. [4] Through 1990, completed 4 years of high school or more and 4 years of college or more. [5] Starting in 2003, data are for Asians only; excludes Pacific Islanders.

Source: U.S. Census Bureau, U.S. Census of Population, 1960, 1970, and 1980, Summary File 3; Current Population Reports, P20-550, and earlier reports; and "Educational Attainment: CPS Historical Time Series Tables," <https://www.census.gov/topics/education/educational-attainment.html>, accessed April 2017.

Table 253. Educational Attainment by Selected Characteristics: 2016

[215,015 represents 215,015,000. For persons 25 years old and over. As of March. Based on the Current Population Survey; see text, Section 1 and Appendix III]

| Characteristic | Population (1,000) | Percent of population— | | | | | |
		Not a high school graduate	High school graduate	Some college, but no degree	Associate's degree [1]	Bachelor's degree	Advanced degree
Total persons	215,015	10.9	28.8	16.7	10.1	20.8	12.6
Age:							
25 to 34 years old	43,763	8.5	25.6	18.3	10.5	25.4	11.6
35 to 44 years old	40,005	10.5	25.2	15.9	10.6	23.0	14.7
45 to 54 years old	42,566	10.6	28.7	15.8	11.1	21.1	12.7
55 to 64 years old	41,135	9.8	30.8	17.4	10.6	19.1	12.2
65 to 74 years old	27,942	11.7	30.7	17.1	9.0	17.8	13.6
75 years old or over	19,605	18.7	36.8	14.9	6.1	13.4	9.9
Sex:							
Male	103,372	11.5	29.8	16.5	9.1	20.6	12.6
Female	111,643	10.4	28.0	17.0	10.9	21.0	12.6
Race:							
White [2]	170,114	10.5	28.9	16.5	10.4	21.1	12.6
Black [2]	25,976	12.9	33.6	20.7	9.6	14.8	8.5
Asian [2]	12,746	9.7	18.5	9.5	6.4	31.8	24.1
Hispanic origin:							
Hispanic	32,019	31.5	30.6	14.0	7.4	11.1	5.3
Non-Hispanic white	141,414	6.2	28.5	17.1	11.0	23.2	14.1
Marital status:							
Never married	43,435	11.8	29.3	18.1	9.1	21.4	10.3
Married, spouse present	123,140	9.2	27.0	15.2	10.5	23.0	15.1
Married, spouse absent [3]	3,372	19.8	27.5	13.3	8.3	17.1	14.0
Separated	4,894	20.5	33.3	19.8	8.7	11.9	5.9
Widowed	14,857	18.7	38.1	16.5	7.5	12.0	7.2
Divorced	25,318	10.0	31.0	21.8	11.8	16.6	8.9
Civilian labor force status:							
Employed	132,217	7.6	25.3	16.4	11.1	24.4	15.2
Unemployed	5,982	14.4	35.1	19.1	8.9	15.4	7.2
Not in the labor force	76,816	16.4	34.4	17.2	8.4	15.1	8.5

[1] Includes vocational degrees. [2] For persons who selected this race group only. See footnote 4, Table 251. [3] Excludes those separated.

Source: U.S. Census Bureau, "Educational Attainment in the United States: 2016," <https://www.census.gov/topics/education/educational-attainment.html>, accessed April 2017.

Table 254. Mean Earnings by Highest Level of Education or Degree and Selected Characteristics: 2015

[In dollars. Persons as of March 2016. For persons 18 years old and over with earnings. Based on Current Population Survey, 2016 Annual Social and Economic Supplement; see text, Section 1 and Appendix III. For definition of mean, see Guide to Tabular Presentation]

| Characteristic | Mean earnings, total [1] | Mean earnings by highest level of education or degree (dollars) | | | | | | | |
		Ninth to twelfth grade, non-graduate	High school graduate only	Some college, no degree	Associate's	Bachelor's	Master's	Professional	Doctorate
All persons [2]	49,994	24,567	35,615	36,139	44,012	65,482	79,753	142,008	114,235
Age:									
25 to 34 years old	43,934	24,176	34,295	34,627	38,501	54,836	63,046	93,525	74,860
35 to 44 years old	57,960	29,003	40,165	45,012	48,524	71,096	87,318	159,214	116,094
45 to 54 years old	61,081	30,775	42,277	49,104	50,406	77,595	92,763	163,371	143,639
55 to 64 years old	58,145	33,324	40,227	46,942	49,499	75,219	86,580	144,768	129,345
65 years old and over	47,278	28,755	30,867	34,416	40,525	57,099	55,153	148,200	96,131
Sex:									
Male	58,944	29,514	41,942	43,268	51,865	79,927	96,896	167,967	131,569
Female	39,929	16,812	26,832	28,798	37,234	50,856	64,834	103,514	91,254
White [3]	51,183	25,793	37,106	37,165	44,732	66,926	78,613	145,104	116,334
Male	60,652	30,716	43,711	44,946	53,407	82,495	96,580	169,431	137,252
Female	40,112	16,996	27,440	28,813	36,906	50,759	63,349	104,937	88,759
Black [3]	39,394	19,365	29,211	32,747	39,115	55,506	73,542	105,789	112,522
Male	43,781	23,397	33,881	38,759	41,385	63,477	78,067	(B)	122,959
Female	35,521	15,384	24,047	27,719	37,680	48,842	70,684	93,949	101,516
Asian [3]	61,603	23,884	34,215	31,417	46,172	65,558	93,052	150,779	106,154
Male	71,362	27,017	39,038	34,545	48,814	74,452	108,317	178,306	112,334
Female	50,544	20,492	28,748	28,086	44,176	55,956	71,949	111,643	97,384
Hispanic [4]	37,083	26,566	31,647	33,498	40,790	58,152	73,987	122,161	92,606
Male	41,556	30,917	36,549	37,713	47,737	69,600	80,812	152,050	103,606
Female	31,160	18,811	24,151	29,106	34,646	46,372	68,704	82,047	80,589

B Base figure too small to meet statistical standards for reliability of a derived figure. [1] Includes those with less than ninth grade education, not shown separately. [2] Includes other races not shown separately. [3] For persons who selected this race group only. See footnote 4, Table 251. [4] Persons of Hispanic origin may be of any race.

Source: U.S. Census Bureau, *Income and Poverty in the United States: 2015*, Current Population Reports, P60-256(RV), September 2016; and "Current Population Survey Tables for Personal Income: Table PINC-04," <http://www.census.gov/data/tables/time-series/demo/income-poverty/cps-pinc.html>, accessed November 2016.

Table 255. Educational Attainment by State: 2000 to 2015

[In percent. 2000 as of April; 2010 and 2015 represents annual averages for calendar year. For persons 25 years old and over. Based on the 2000 Census of Population, and the American Community Survey, which includes the household population and the population living in institutions, college dormitories, and other group quarters. See text, Section 1 and Appendix III. For margin of error data, see source]

State	2000			2010			2015		
	High school graduate or more	Bachelor's degree or more	Advanced degree or more	High school graduate or more	Bachelor's degree or more	Advanced degree or more	High school graduate or more	Bachelor's degree or more	Advanced degree or more
United States............	80.4	24.4	8.9	85.6	28.2	10.4	87.1	30.6	11.6
Alabama....................	75.3	19.0	6.9	82.1	21.9	8.0	84.9	24.2	8.8
Alaska......................	88.3	24.7	8.6	91.0	27.9	9.4	92.6	29.7	11.0
Arizona....................	81.0	23.5	8.4	85.6	25.9	9.2	86.1	27.7	10.3
Arkansas..................	75.3	16.7	5.7	82.9	19.5	6.3	85.4	21.8	7.8
California..................	76.8	26.6	9.5	80.7	30.1	11.0	82.2	32.3	12.0
Colorado..................	86.9	32.7	11.1	89.7	36.4	13.0	91.2	39.2	14.5
Connecticut..............	84.0	31.4	13.3	88.6	35.5	15.3	90.2	38.3	16.7
Delaware..................	82.6	25.0	9.4	87.7	27.8	11.3	88.9	30.9	12.9
District of Columbia.........	77.8	39.1	21.0	87.4	50.1	26.9	89.8	56.7	32.9
Florida.....................	79.9	22.3	8.1	85.5	25.8	9.2	87.6	28.4	10.2
Georgia....................	78.6	24.3	8.3	84.3	27.3	9.8	86.1	29.9	11.3
Hawaii......................	84.6	26.2	8.4	89.9	29.5	9.6	90.9	31.4	10.6
Idaho.......................	84.7	21.7	6.8	88.3	24.4	7.7	90.0	26.0	8.2
Illinois.....................	81.4	26.1	9.5	86.9	30.8	11.5	88.6	32.9	12.7
Indiana....................	82.1	19.4	7.2	87.0	22.7	8.1	88.2	24.9	9.0
Iowa........................	86.1	21.2	6.5	90.6	24.9	7.9	91.7	26.8	8.7
Kansas.....................	86.0	25.8	8.7	89.2	29.8	10.5	90.3	31.7	11.4
Kentucky..................	74.1	17.1	6.9	81.9	20.5	8.1	85.1	23.3	9.7
Louisiana..................	74.8	18.7	6.5	81.9	21.4	7.0	84.6	23.2	8.0
Maine......................	85.4	22.9	7.9	90.3	26.8	9.5	91.7	30.1	10.6
Maryland..................	83.8	31.4	13.4	88.1	36.1	16.4	89.6	38.8	17.7
Massachusetts............	84.8	33.2	13.7	89.1	39.0	16.7	90.2	41.5	18.4
Michigan..................	83.4	21.8	8.1	88.7	25.2	9.6	90.1	27.8	10.8
Minnesota.................	87.9	27.4	8.3	91.8	31.8	10.3	92.8	34.7	11.8
Mississippi................	72.9	16.9	5.8	81.0	19.5	7.1	83.5	20.8	7.9
Missouri...................	81.3	21.6	7.6	86.9	25.6	9.5	88.9	27.8	10.6
Montana...................	87.2	24.4	7.2	91.7	28.8	9.0	93.5	30.6	10.2
Nebraska..................	86.6	23.7	7.3	90.4	28.6	9.0	91.0	30.2	10.4
Nevada....................	80.7	18.2	6.1	84.7	21.7	7.4	85.6	23.6	8.1
New Hampshire.............	87.4	28.7	10.0	91.5	32.8	12.4	93.1	35.7	13.7
New Jersey................	82.1	29.8	11.0	88.0	35.4	13.3	89.1	37.6	14.3
New Mexico...............	78.9	23.5	9.8	83.3	25.0	10.8	84.6	26.5	12.1
New York..................	79.1	27.4	11.8	84.9	32.5	14.0	86.0	35.0	15.0
North Carolina............	78.1	22.5	7.2	84.7	26.5	8.7	86.6	29.4	10.6
North Dakota..............	83.9	22.0	5.5	90.3	27.6	7.9	92.5	29.1	7.7
Ohio........................	83.0	21.1	7.4	88.1	24.6	8.9	89.7	26.8	10.0
Oklahoma.................	80.6	20.3	6.8	86.2	22.9	7.5	87.3	24.6	8.1
Oregon....................	85.1	25.1	8.7	88.8	28.8	10.5	90.0	32.2	12.0
Pennsylvania..............	81.9	22.4	8.4	88.4	27.1	10.4	89.7	29.7	11.6
Rhode Island..............	78.0	25.6	9.7	83.5	30.2	12.2	87.7	32.7	13.4
South Carolina............	76.3	20.4	6.9	84.1	24.5	8.8	86.3	26.8	9.5
South Dakota..............	84.6	21.5	6.0	89.6	26.3	7.7	91.1	27.5	7.9
Tennessee.................	75.9	19.6	6.8	83.6	23.1	8.5	86.1	25.7	9.6
Texas......................	75.7	23.2	7.6	80.7	25.9	8.6	82.4	28.4	9.7
Utah.......................	87.7	26.1	8.3	90.6	29.3	9.4	91.5	31.8	10.7
Vermont...................	86.4	29.4	11.1	91.0	33.6	13.3	91.7	36.9	14.6
Virginia....................	81.5	29.5	11.6	86.5	34.2	14.2	88.9	37.0	15.7
Washington...............	87.1	27.7	9.3	89.8	31.1	11.1	90.8	34.2	12.5
West Virginia..............	75.2	14.8	5.9	83.2	17.5	6.6	86.0	19.6	7.9
Wisconsin..................	85.1	22.4	7.2	90.1	24.1	9.0	91.4	28.4	9.4
Wyoming..................	87.9	21.9	7.0	92.3	22.3	8.4	92.2	26.2	9.0

Source: U.S. Census Bureau, 2000 Census of Population, P37, "Sex by Educational Attainment for the Population 25 Years and Over"; and American Community Survey, GCT1501, "Percent of People 25 Years and Over Who Have Completed High School (Includes Equivalency)," GCT1502, "Percent of People 25 Years and Over Who Have Completed a Bachelor's Degree," and GCT1503, "Percent of People 25 Years and Over Who Have Completed an Advanced Degree," <http://factfinder.census.gov>, accessed November 2016.

Table 256. Children Who Speak a Language Other Than English at Home by Region: 2015

[In thousands (11,931 represents 11,931,000), except percent. For children 5 to 17 years old. For more on languages spoken at home, see Table 54 and Table 55. Based on the American Community Survey; see text Section 1, and Appendix III. For composition of regions, see map inside front cover]

Characteristic	U.S.	Northeast	Midwest	South	West
Children who speak another language at home...........................	**11,931**	**1,973**	**1,453**	**4,171**	**4,334**
Percent of children 5 to 17 years old......................................	22.2	22.6	12.6	20.2	33.4
Speak Spanish..	8,568	1,074	852	3,293	3,349
Speak English "very well"..	6,930	884	699	2,556	2,791
Speak English less than "very well"...............................	1,639	191	154	736	558
Speak other Indo-European languages...................................	1,528	538	276	415	298
Speak English "very well"..	1,250	427	218	352	253
Speak English less than "very well"...............................	278	111	59	63	45
Speak Asian and Pacific Island languages..............................	1,307	253	184	319	552
Speak English "very well"..	975	189	130	237	419
Speak English less than "very well"...............................	332	64	54	82	132
Speak other languages...	528	107	140	144	135
Speak English "very well"..	423	86	112	114	111
Speak English less than "very well"...............................	104	21	28	30	24
Have difficulty speaking English [1]...................................	2,353	387	294	912	760
Language spoken at home in linguistically isolated households [2]........	2,760	470	316	1,044	929
Speak only English..	196	40	27	69	60
Speak Spanish...	1,942	255	177	825	685
Speak other Indo-European languages...................................	200	81	37	47	35
Speak Asian and Pacific Island languages..............................	323	75	46	77	124
Speak other languages...	99	19	29	27	26

[1] Children aged 5 to 17 who speak English less than "very well." [2] A household in which no person aged 14 or over speaks English at least "very well."

Source: U.S. Census Bureau, 2015 American Community Survey, B16003, "Age by Language Spoken at Home for the Population 5 Years and Over" and B16004, "Age by Language Spoken at Home by Ability to Speak English for the Population 5 Years and Over," <http://factfinder.census.gov>, accessed November 2016.

Table 257. Preprimary School Enrollment—Summary: 1970 to 2015

[10,949 represents 10,949,000. As of October. Civilian noninstitutional population. Includes public and nonpublic preschool (or nursery school) and kindergarten programs. Excludes 5-year-olds enrolled in elementary school. Based on Current Population Survey. See text, Section 1 and Appendix III]

Item	1970	1980	1990	2000	2005	2010	2013	2014	2015
NUMBER OF CHILDREN (1,000)									
Population, 3 to 5 years old..............	**10,949**	**9,284**	**11,207**	**11,858**	**12,134**	**12,949**	**12,165**	**12,191**	**11,958**
Total enrolled [1].......................	**4,104**	**4,878**	**6,659**	**7,592**	**7,801**	**8,493**	**7,879**	**7,891**	**7,683**
Preschool (or nursery school)..............	1,094	1,981	3,378	4,326	4,529	4,797	4,624	4,658	4,475
Public..................................	332	628	1,202	2,146	2,409	2,749	2,522	2,669	2,561
Private.................................	762	1,353	2,177	2,180	2,120	2,048	2,103	1,989	1,914
Kindergarten...............................	3,010	2,897	3,281	3,266	3,272	3,449	3,254	3,233	3,207
Public..................................	2,498	2,438	2,767	2,701	2,804	3,079	2,927	2,874	2,864
Private.................................	511	459	513	565	468	369	327	359	342
White [2]..................................	3,443	3,994	5,389	5,861	6,025	6,160	5,593	5,567	5,515
Black [2]..................................	586	725	964	1,265	1,148	1,301	1,248	1,307	1,193
Hispanic [3]...............................	(NA)	370	642	1,155	1,494	1,874	1,837	1,852	1,810
3 years old...............................	454	857	1,205	1,540	1,715	1,718	1,674	1,721	1,513
4 years old...............................	1,007	1,423	2,086	2,556	2,668	2,988	2,776	2,705	2,691
5 years old...............................	2,643	2,598	3,367	3,496	3,418	3,787	3,429	3,465	3,479
PERCENT ENROLLED									
Total enrolled [1].......................	**37.5**	**52.5**	**59.4**	**64.0**	**64.3**	**63.7**	**64.8**	**64.7**	**64.2**
White [2]..................................	37.8	52.7	59.7	63.2	65.1	63.4	64.2	64.5	63.9
Black [2]..................................	34.9	51.8	57.8	68.5	62.0	64.1	66.7	66.6	65.3
Hispanic [3]...............................	(NA)	43.3	49.0	52.6	56.1	56.0	57.4	58.7	58.7
3 years old...............................	12.9	27.3	32.6	39.2	41.3	38.2	41.9	42.6	38.4
4 years old...............................	27.8	46.3	56.0	64.9	66.2	68.6	67.7	66.3	66.7
5 years old...............................	69.3	84.7	88.8	87.6	86.4	88.1	84.4	85.2	87.3

NA Not available. [1] Includes races not shown separately. [2] Beginning 2003, for persons who selected this race group only. See footnote 4, Table 251. [3] Persons of Hispanic origin may be of any race. The method of identifying Hispanic children was changed in 1980 from allocation based on status of mother to status reported for each child. The number of Hispanic children using the new method is larger.

Source: U.S. Census Bureau, Current Population Reports, P-20 reports and unpublished data; and "School Enrollment," <http://www.census.gov/hhes/school/index.html>, accessed November 2016.

Table 258. Public Elementary and Secondary School Finances by Enrollment-Size Group: 2015

[In millions of dollars (642,638 represents $642,638,000,000), except per pupil. School fiscal year ending in 2015. Enrollment as of Fall 2014. Data are based on the Annual Government Finance Survey. For details, see source. See also Appendix III]

Item	All school systems	\multicolumn{7}{c}{School systems with enrollment of—}						
		50,000 or more	25,000 to 49,999	15,000 to 24,999	7,500 to 14,999	5,000 to 7,499	3,000 to 4,999	Under 3,000
TOTAL								
General revenue	642,638	138,185	78,063	59,656	91,871	57,051	74,833	142,979
From federal sources	53,307	12,747	7,190	5,151	7,110	3,846	5,065	12,196
Through state [1]	48,862	11,816	6,689	4,863	6,450	3,621	4,697	10,727
Child nutrition programs	15,018	3,893	2,169	1,640	2,070	1,179	1,431	2,637
Direct	4,444	931	502	288	660	226	368	1,470
From state sources [1]	302,632	60,370	39,492	31,725	45,323	25,744	32,980	66,998
General formula assistance	209,746	40,188	29,281	23,090	32,802	17,828	21,952	44,605
Compensatory programs	4,729	1,350	664	525	663	297	456	774
Special education	19,077	4,835	2,083	1,564	2,341	1,423	2,353	4,478
From local sources	286,698	65,068	31,380	22,779	39,437	27,461	36,788	63,785
Taxes	196,587	32,848	22,372	16,715	28,945	20,567	27,545	47,595
Contributions from parent government	51,540	24,577	4,576	2,597	5,264	3,725	5,062	5,739
From other local governments	7,968	509	1,161	765	1,141	727	918	2,747
Current charges [1]	14,429	2,334	1,631	1,319	2,049	1,257	1,719	4,120
School lunch	5,597	780	644	542	905	575	745	1,406
Other	16,175	4,800	1,640	1,384	2,039	1,185	1,545	3,582
General expenditure	639,458	140,514	78,281	59,728	90,424	56,237	72,900	141,375
Current spending	567,696	123,721	68,513	52,469	80,656	50,600	65,720	126,018
By function:								
Instruction	344,294	79,358	41,132	31,168	48,730	30,855	39,910	73,141
Support services	194,410	38,073	23,558	18,330	27,724	17,338	22,781	46,606
Other current spending	28,993	6,291	3,823	2,971	4,202	2,406	3,029	6,270
By object:								
Total salaries and wages	322,112	68,983	40,416	30,839	46,539	28,847	37,170	69,318
Total employee benefits	129,817	27,184	14,754	11,681	18,827	12,135	15,875	29,361
Capital outlay	52,142	12,150	7,119	5,335	6,961	4,011	5,189	11,377
Interest on debt	17,357	4,281	2,587	1,858	2,548	1,444	1,774	2,865
Payments to other governments	2,262	362	61	67	258	182	216	1,115
Debt outstanding	433,146	101,611	63,123	46,369	63,064	36,118	46,563	76,300
Long-term	425,186	99,742	62,101	45,955	62,146	35,318	45,503	74,420
Short-term	7,961	1,869	1,022	414	917	799	1,060	1,879
Long-term debt issued	69,461	13,241	11,870	7,501	10,483	6,250	7,239	12,877
Long-term debt retired	56,596	11,125	8,317	6,155	8,267	5,368	6,600	10,764
PER PUPIL								
Fall enrollment (1,000)	48,514	10,578	6,687	5,047	7,274	4,204	5,357	9,367
General revenue	13,246	13,063	11,674	11,819	12,630	13,571	13,968	15,265
From federal sources	1,099	1,205	1,075	1,021	978	915	945	1,302
From state sources [1]	6,238	5,707	5,906	6,285	6,231	6,124	6,156	7,153
General formula assistance	4,323	3,799	4,379	4,574	4,510	4,241	4,098	4,762
Special education	393	457	311	310	322	338	439	478
From local sources [1]	5,910	6,151	4,693	4,513	5,422	6,532	6,867	6,810
Taxes	4,052	3,105	3,346	3,312	3,979	4,892	5,141	5,081
Contributions from parent government	1,062	2,323	684	514	724	886	945	613
Current charges	297	221	244	261	282	299	321	440
School lunch	115	74	96	107	124	137	139	150
General expenditure [1]	12,871	12,828	11,439	11,613	12,174	13,053	13,306	14,831
Current spending	11,392	11,240	9,978	10,174	10,831	11,712	11,966	13,192
By function:								
Instruction	6,903	7,155	5,998	6,074	6,563	7,128	7,258	7,670
Support services	4,007	3,599	3,523	3,632	3,811	4,124	4,252	4,976
By object:								
Total salaries and wages	6,640	6,521	6,044	6,110	6,398	6,862	6,938	7,401
Total employee benefits	2,676	2,570	2,206	2,314	2,588	2,887	2,963	3,135
Capital outlay	1,075	1,149	1,065	1,057	957	954	969	1,215
Interest on debt	358	405	387	368	350	344	331	306
Debt outstanding	8,928	9,606	9,440	9,186	8,670	8,592	8,691	8,146
Long-term	8,764	9,429	9,287	9,105	8,544	8,401	8,493	7,945

[1] Includes other sources not shown separately.

Source: U.S. Census Bureau, *Public Education Finances, 2015*, June 2017. See also <https://www.census.gov/programs-surveys/school-finances.html>.

Table 259. Public Elementary and Secondary School Estimated Finances by State: 2015

[In millions of dollars (642,638 represents $642,638,000,000), except as noted. For the school fiscal year. Includes finances of charter schools whose charters are held directly by a government or government agency]

State	Revenue receipts				Expenditures				
		Source					Current expenditures [3]		
						Per capita [2] (dol.)	Elementary and secondary schools	Average per pupil [4]	
	Total	Federal	State	Local	Total [1]			Amount (dol.) [5]	Rank
Total.............	**642,638**	**53,307**	**302,632**	**286,698**	**639,458**	**2,007**	**567,696**	**11,392**	**(X)**
Alabama................	7,358	795	4,080	2,483	7,493	1,547	6,827	9,128	40
Alaska.................	2,921	344	2,027	550	2,968	4,029	2,646	20,172	2
Arizona................	8,159	1,094	3,232	3,833	7,886	1,174	7,205	7,489	49
Arkansas...............	5,293	581	4,075	636	5,325	1,795	4,683	9,694	35
California.............	75,517	7,556	42,360	25,600	75,165	1,943	66,208	10,467	29
Colorado...............	9,604	715	4,355	4,534	9,512	1,778	8,147	9,245	39
Connecticut............	10,857	444	4,354	6,060	10,256	2,855	9,603	18,377	4
Delaware...............	1,977	138	1,142	697	1,903	2,035	1,779	14,120	13
District of Columbia...	1,382	146	(X)	1,236	1,361	2,065	979	19,396	3
Florida................	26,966	3,118	10,662	13,186	27,277	1,371	24,933	8,881	42
Georgia................	18,581	1,831	8,311	8,439	18,491	1,833	16,402	9,427	38
Hawaii.................	2,704	259	2,382	63	2,521	1,780	2,359	12,855	17
Idaho..................	2,167	232	1,381	554	2,030	1,242	1,903	6,923	50
Illinois...............	31,403	2,262	11,859	17,282	31,544	2,451	28,585	13,755	14
Indiana................	12,215	930	7,676	3,608	11,148	1,690	9,797	9,687	36
Iowa...................	6,453	458	3,461	2,534	6,525	2,100	5,558	10,944	27
Kansas.................	5,990	475	3,968	1,547	6,171	2,128	4,995	10,040	32
Kentucky...............	7,548	849	4,177	2,522	7,553	1,712	6,694	9,630	37
Louisiana..............	8,433	1,236	3,480	3,717	8,174	1,759	7,291	11,010	26
Maine..................	2,670	184	1,061	1,426	2,527	1,899	2,427	13,257	16
Maryland...............	14,488	819	6,268	7,401	13,656	2,289	12,431	14,192	12
Massachusetts..........	16,845	779	6,808	9,258	16,573	2,455	15,316	15,592	8
Michigan...............	18,062	1,583	10,510	5,969	17,462	1,761	15,712	11,482	21
Minnesota..............	11,533	630	7,567	3,336	11,803	2,164	10,085	11,949	18
Mississippi............	4,580	672	2,325	1,583	4,625	1,545	4,161	8,456	47
Missouri...............	10,537	949	4,441	5,147	10,426	1,720	9,270	10,147	31
Montana................	1,788	215	851	722	1,786	1,746	1,603	11,028	25
Nebraska...............	4,156	344	1,350	2,462	4,264	2,267	3,732	11,946	19
Nevada.................	4,344	396	2,745	1,203	4,178	1,475	3,804	8,615	46
New Hampshire..........	2,992	165	1,000	1,827	2,878	2,166	2,711	14,697	11
New Jersey.............	28,254	1,154	11,423	15,676	27,655	3,099	26,025	18,235	5
New Mexico.............	3,790	500	2,596	694	3,839	1,843	3,185	9,752	34
New York...............	63,463	2,870	25,901	34,692	64,799	3,286	59,210	21,206	1
North Carolina.........	13,147	1,590	8,173	3,385	13,995	1,409	12,789	8,687	45
North Dakota...........	1,606	158	943	505	1,749	2,364	1,420	13,320	15
Ohio...................	23,490	1,677	10,170	11,644	22,400	1,932	19,867	11,637	20
Oklahoma...............	6,120	689	2,993	2,438	6,169	1,591	5,456	8,082	48
Oregon.................	7,065	577	3,678	2,810	6,995	1,763	6,173	10,442	30
Pennsylvania...........	28,510	1,858	10,532	16,120	27,977	2,187	25,305	14,717	10
Rhode Island...........	2,344	185	909	1,250	2,301	2,182	2,205	15,179	9
South Carolina.........	8,748	836	4,095	3,817	8,751	1,812	7,463	9,953	33
South Dakota...........	1,412	207	426	780	1,462	1,715	1,206	8,937	41
Tennessee..............	9,433	1,123	4,385	3,925	9,549	1,459	8,766	8,726	44
Texas..................	55,408	5,831	20,967	28,610	56,084	2,081	44,675	8,861	43
Utah...................	4,699	400	2,488	1,811	4,534	1,541	3,806	6,575	51
Vermont................	1,728	105	1,547	77	1,681	2,682	1,612	18,039	6
Virginia...............	15,581	1,012	6,240	8,328	15,869	1,908	14,459	11,237	24
Washington.............	13,610	1,036	8,294	4,279	13,587	1,926	11,567	10,735	28
West Virginia..........	3,465	363	1,979	1,123	3,464	1,874	3,216	11,359	23
Wisconsin..............	11,281	814	5,869	4,597	11,191	1,944	9,929	11,375	22
Wyoming................	1,961	120	1,117	724	1,926	3,301	1,514	16,055	7

X Not applicable. [1] Includes interest on school debt and payments to state and local governments, not shown separately. [2] Based on U.S. Census Bureau estimated resident population, as of July 1, 2014. [3] Includes expenditures for adult education, community services, and other nonelementary-secondary programs. [4] Based on Fall 2014 enrollment, National Center for Education Statistics, Common Core of Data. [5] Excludes expenditures for payments to other school systems, adult education, community services, and other nonelementary-secondary programs.

Source: U.S. Census Bureau, *Public Education Finances: 2015,* June 2017. See also <https://www.census.gov/programs-surveys/school-finances.html>.

Table 260. Students Who Are Homeschooled by Selected Characteristics: 2007 and 2012

[51,135 represents 51,135,000. As of Spring. For students age 5 to 17 with a grade equivalent of K–12. Homeschoolers are students whose parents reported them to be schooled at home instead of a public or private school. Excludes students who were enrolled in school for more than 25 hours a week or were homeschooled due to a temporary illness. Based on the Parent and Family Involvement in Education Survey of the National Household Education Surveys Program; see source and Appendix III for details]

Characteristic	2007			2012		
	Total (1,000)	Home-schooled (1,000)	Percent home-schooled	Total (1,000)	Home-schooled (1,000) [1]	Percent home-schooled
Total.............	**51,135**	**1,520**	**3.0**	**51,657**	**1,773**	**3.4**
Grade equivalent: [2]						
K–5........................	23,529	717	3.0	25,842	423	1.6
Kindergarten..........................	3,669	(S)	(S)	5,295	(S)	(S)
Grades 1 to 3.........................	11,965	406	3.4	12,101	203	1.7
Grades 4 to 5.........................	7,895	197	2.5	8,446	142	1.7
Grades 6 to 8.........................	12,435	371	3.0	12,006	317	2.6
Grades 9 to 12........................	15,161	422	2.8	13,808	341	2.5
Sex:						
Male........................	26,286	639	2.4	26,620	499	1.9
Female.......................	24,849	881	3.5	25,037	583	2.3
Race/ethnicity:						
White, non-Hispanic........................	29,815	1,171	3.9	26,978	893	3.3
Black, non-Hispanic........................	7,523	(S)	(S)	7,191	(S)	(S)
Hispanic [3].........................	9,589	147	1.5	11,814	72	0.6
Asian/Pacific Islander.......................	1,580	(S)	(S)	2,849	(S)	(S)
Other........................	2,629	(S)	(S)	2,825	(S)	(S)
Number of children in the household:						
One child.........................	8,463	197	2.3	10,899	179	1.6
Two children.........................	20,694	414	2.0	20,337	314	1.5
Three or more children..........................	21,979	909	4.1	20,421	589	2.9
Number of parents in the household:						
Two parents.........................	37,219	1,357	3.6	34,252	908	2.7
One parent.........................	11,777	118	1.0	15,436	137	0.9
Nonparental guardians.........................	2,139	(S)	(S)	1,968	(S)	(S)
Parents' participation in the labor force:						
Two parents—both in labor force........................	26,055	518	2.0	22,884	295	1.3
Two parents—one in labor force........................	10,754	808	7.5	11,581	618	5.3
One parent in labor force........................	10,020	127	1.3	13,083	96	0.7
No parent in labor force........................	4,308	(S)	(S)	4,108	74	1.8
Household income:						
$20,000 or less.........................	8,488	186	2.2	7,593	59	0.8
$20,001 to 50,000.........................	13,648	420	3.1	13,973	321	2.3
$50,001 to 75,000.........................	10,289	414	4.0	9,406	278	3.0
$75,001 to 100,000.........................	6,899	264	3.8	6,916	211	3.0
$100,000 or more.........................	11,811	236	2.0	13,769	214	1.6
Parents' highest educational attainment:						
High school diploma or less........................	14,306	208	1.5	16,762	270	1.6
Voc/tech degree or some college........................	14,581	559	3.8	15,621	344	2.2
Bachelor's degree........................	11,448	444	3.9	11,675	275	2.4
Graduate/professional school........................	10,800	309	2.9	7,599	192	2.5

S Figure does not meet publication standards. [1] The National Center for Education Statistics uses a statistical adjustment for estimates of total homeschoolers in 2012; therefore, data will not add to total. All other estimates about homeschoolers do not use a statistical adjustment. [2] Excludes those ungraded. [3] Persons of Hispanic origin may be of any race.

Source: U.S. National Center for Education Statistics, *Digest of Education Statistics 2013*, May 2015. See also <http://www.nces.ed.gov/programs/digest/>.

Table 261. Public Elementary and Secondary Schools by Type and Size of School: 2015

[Enrollment in thousands (50,010 represents 50,010,000), except for average enrollment. For school year ending in 2015. Data reported by schools, rather than school districts. Based on the Common Core of Data Survey; see source for details]

Enrollment size of school	Number of schools					Enrollment [1]				
	Total	Elementary [2]	Secondary [3]	Combined [4]	Other [5]	Total	Elementary [2]	Secondary [3]	Combined [4]	Other [5]
Total.....................	**98,176**	**67,073**	**24,181**	**6,347**	**575**	**50,010**	**32,226**	**15,732**	**2,049**	**3**
PERCENT										
Total......................	100.00	100.00	100.00	100.00	100.00	100.00	100.00	100.00	100.00	100.00
Under 100 students........	10.16	5.29	17.68	36.65	68.00	0.87	0.55	1.08	4.22	13.39
100 to 199 students......	9.01	7.71	11.17	15.58	16.00	2.56	2.42	2.35	6.31	17.16
200 to 299 students......	10.89	11.54	9.14	10.17	4.00	5.23	6.08	3.26	7.09	7.08
300 to 399 students......	13.43	15.74	8.09	7.83	8.00	8.96	11.44	4.06	7.73	20.59
400 to 499 students......	13.93	16.98	6.99	5.93	–	11.90	15.80	4.51	7.51	–
500 to 599 students......	11.83	14.41	5.87	5.45	–	12.32	16.33	4.62	8.40	–
600 to 699 students......	8.61	10.29	4.82	4.15	–	10.61	13.79	4.50	7.61	–
700 to 799 students......	6.10	7.02	4.04	3.54	–	8.66	10.85	4.35	7.48	–
800 to 999 students......	6.82	7.09	6.78	3.94	–	11.50	12.96	8.71	9.98	–
1,000 to 1,499 students...	5.52	3.63	11.45	4.22	4.00	12.55	8.68	20.26	14.21	41.77
1,500 to 1,999 students...	2.04	0.28	7.41	1.40	–	6.73	0.97	18.51	6.78	–
2,000 to 2,999 students...	1.39	0.03	5.59	0.62	–	6.20	0.12	18.91	4.16	–
3,000 or more students...	0.27	–	0.98	0.52	–	1.90	0.01	4.89	8.53	–
Average enrollment [1]...	(X)	(X)	(X)	(X)	(X)	525	483	694	354	131

– Represents or rounds to zero. X Not applicable. [1] Excludes data for schools not reporting enrollment. [2] Includes schools beginning with grade 6 or below and with no grade higher than 8. [3] Includes schools with no grade lower than 7. [4] Includes schools beginning with grade 6 or below and ending with grade 9 or above. [5] Includes special education, alternative, and other schools not classified by grade span.

Source: U.S. National Center for Education Statistics, *Digest of Education Statistics*, "Advance Release of Selected 2016 Digest Tables," <http://www.nces.ed.gov/programs/digest/>, accessed December 2016.

Table 262. Public Elementary and Secondary Schools—Summary: 1990 to 2017

[In units as indicated (44,949 represents 44,949,000). For school year ending in year shown, except as indicated. Data are estimates]

Item	Unit	1990	2000	2005	2010	2015	2016	2017
School districts, total	**Number**	**15,552**	**15,403**	**15,731**	**15,782**	**15,951**	**15,964**	**15,986**
ENROLLMENT								
Population 5-17 years old [1]	1,000	44,949	53,119	53,606	53,980	53,704	53,715	(NA)
Percent of resident population	Percent	18.2	18.9	18.1	17.5	16.7	16.6	(NA)
Fall enrollment [2]	**1,000**	**40,527**	**46,577**	**48,414**	**49,094**	**49,702**	**49,832**	**49,907**
Percent of population 5-17 years old	Percent	90.2	87.7	90.3	90.9	92.5	92.8	(NA)
Elementary [3]	1,000	26,253	29,243	29,630	30,310	30,822	30,922	31,020
Secondary [4]	1,000	14,274	17,334	18,783	18,784	18,880	18,910	18,887
Average daily attendance	1,000	37,573	43,313	45,088	45,998	47,115	47,310	47,574
High school graduates	1,000	2,327	2,544	2,803	3,113	3,310	3,347	3,391
INSTRUCTIONAL STAFF								
Total [5]	**1,000**	**2,685**	**3,273**	**3,509**	**3,645**	**3,614**	**3,601**	**3,606**
Classroom teachers	1,000	2,362	2,891	3,072	3,163	3,144	3,131	3,136
Average salaries:								
Instructional staff	Dollar	32,638	43,837	49,135	57,035	59,377	60,205	60,840
Classroom teachers	Dollar	31,367	41,807	47,516	55,276	57,611	58,353	58,950
REVENUES								
Revenue receipts	**Mil. dol.**	**208,656**	**369,754**	**477,371**	**584,683**	**625,999**	**631,951**	**638,963**
Federal	Mil. dol.	13,184	26,346	42,908	73,747	56,447	56,165	53,933
State	Mil. dol.	100,787	183,986	225,142	258,005	286,979	289,684	293,766
Local	Mil. dol.	94,685	159,421	209,321	252,931	282,572	286,103	291,264
Percent of total:								
Federal	Percent	6.3	7.1	9.0	12.6	9.0	8.9	8.4
State	Percent	48.3	49.8	47.2	44.1	45.8	45.8	46.0
Local/other	Percent	45.4	43.1	43.8	43.3	45.1	45.3	45.6
EXPENDITURES								
Total	**Mil. dol.**	**209,698**	**374,782**	**496,199**	**607,177**	**664,279**	**678,846**	**691,610**
Current expenditures (day schools)	Mil. dol.	186,583	320,954	422,346	522,618	573,675	587,347	598,102
Other current expenditures [6]	Mil. dol.	3,341	6,618	8,710	10,621	11,370	11,378	11,515
Capital outlay	Mil. dol.	16,012	37,552	48,757	49,312	48,959	48,508	48,968
Interest on school debt	Mil. dol.	3,762	9,659	16,385	24,626	30,275	31,614	33,024
Current expenditures per pupil enrolled	Dollar	4,604	6,891	8,724	10,645	11,542	11,787	11,984

NA Not available. [1] Estimated resident population as of July 1 of the previous year, except 1990, 2000, and 2010 population enumerated as of April 1. Estimates reflect revisions based on the 2010 Census of Population. [2] Fall enrollment of the previous year. [3] Kindergarten through grades not higher than 8. [4] Starting from grade 7, 8, or 9, through grade 12. [5] Full-time equivalent. [6] Current expenses for summer schools, adult education, post-high school vocational education, personnel retraining, etc., when operated by local school districts and not part of regular public elementary and secondary day-school program.

Source: National Education Association, Washington, DC. Data from *Rankings of the States 2016 and Estimates of School Statistics 2017*, used with permission of the National Education Association © 2017. All rights reserved.

Table 263. Public Elementary and Secondary School Enrollment by Grade: 1980 to 2014

[In thousands (40,877 represents 40,877,000). As of Fall of year shown. Based on survey of state education agencies; see source for details]

Grade	1980	1990	1995	2000	2005	2009	2010	2011	2012	2013	2014
Pupils enrolled [1]	**40,877**	**41,217**	**44,840**	**47,204**	**49,113**	**49,361**	**49,484**	**49,522**	**49,771**	**50,045**	**50,313**
Pre-kindergarten to 8 [1]	27,647	29,878	32,341	33,688	34,205	34,409	34,625	34,773	35,018	35,251	35,370
Pre-K and kindergarten	2,689	3,610	4,173	4,158	4,656	4,901	4,961	5,037	5,138	5,162	5,142
First	2,894	3,499	3,671	3,636	3,691	3,729	3,754	3,773	3,824	3,885	3,863
Second	2,800	3,327	3,507	3,634	3,606	3,665	3,701	3,713	3,729	3,791	3,857
Third	2,893	3,297	3,445	3,676	3,586	3,707	3,686	3,703	3,719	3,738	3,806
Fourth	3,107	3,248	3,431	3,711	3,578	3,701	3,711	3,672	3,690	3,708	3,719
Fifth	3,130	3,197	3,438	3,707	3,633	3,652	3,718	3,699	3,673	3,697	3,719
Sixth	3,038	3,110	3,395	3,663	3,670	3,644	3,682	3,724	3,723	3,684	3,710
Seventh	3,085	3,067	3,422	3,629	3,777	3,641	3,676	3,696	3,746	3,748	3,710
Eighth	3,086	2,979	3,356	3,538	3,802	3,651	3,659	3,679	3,699	3,753	3,757
Grades 9 to 12 [1]	13,231	11,338	12,500	13,515	14,909	14,952	14,860	14,749	14,753	14,794	14,943
Ninth	3,377	3,169	3,704	3,963	4,287	4,080	4,008	3,957	3,975	3,980	4,033
Tenth	3,368	2,896	3,237	3,491	3,866	3,809	3,800	3,751	3,730	3,761	3,794
Eleventh	3,195	2,612	2,826	3,083	3,455	3,541	3,538	3,546	3,528	3,526	3,568
Twelfth	2,925	2,381	2,487	2,803	3,180	3,432	3,472	3,452	3,477	3,476	3,496

[1] Includes unclassified students not shown separately.

Source: U.S. National Center for Education Statistics, *Digest of Education Statistics*, "Advance Release of Selected 2016 Digest Tables," <http://www.nces.ed.gov/programs/digest/>, accessed March 2017.

Table 264. Selected Statistics for the Largest Public School Districts: 2014

[For the 50 largest districts by enrollment size. For school year ending in 2014. Data from the Common Core Data Program; see source for details. School district boundaries are not necessarily the same as city or county boundaries]

School district	City	County	Number of students [1]	Number of full-time equivalent (FTE) teachers [2]	Number of schools [3]	Total expend-itures per pupil
New York City Public Schools, NY................	New York	(X)	989,012	66,153	1,634	26,299
Los Angeles Unified School District, CA..........	Los Angeles	Los Angeles	653,826	27,748	983	13,054
City of Chicago School District, IL.................	Chicago	Cook	396,641	23,320	595	15,765
Miami-Dade County Public School District, FL....	Miami	Miami-Dade	356,233	20,527	534	10,082
Clark County School District, NV..................	Las Vegas	Clark	320,532	15,321	363	8,841
Broward County School District, FL...............	Fort Lauderdale	Broward	262,666	15,214	349	9,551
Houston Independent School District, TX..........	Houston	Harris	211,552	11,336	283	10,414
Hillsborough County School District, FL...........	Tampa	Hillsborough	203,439	14,266	310	9,870
Orange County Public Schools, FL................	Orlando	Orange	187,092	11,760	249	10,561
Hawaii Department of Education, HI...............	Honolulu	Honolulu	186,825	11,781	288	13,462
Fairfax County Public Schools, VA.................	Falls Church	Fairfax	183,417	14,344	218	15,526
Palm Beach County School District, FL............	West Palm Beach	Palm Beach	182,895	12,694	269	10,814
Gwinnett County School District, GA..............	Suwanee	Gwinnett	169,150	10,357	132	10,577
Dallas Independent School District, TX............	Dallas	Dallas	159,713	9,830	234	10,090
Wake County Schools, NC.........................	Raleigh	Wake	153,534	9,869	170	9,192
Montgomery County Public Schools, MD..........	Rockville	Montgomery	151,295	10,112	207	17,685
Shelby County School District, TN.................	Memphis	Shelby	149,832	9,282	290	10,012
Charlotte-Mecklenburg Schools, NC..............	Charlotte	Mecklenburg	142,991	8,662	160	10,023
Philadelphia City School District, PA..............	Philadelphia	Philadelphia	137,674	7,646	214	19,916
San Diego City Unified School District, CA........	San Diego	San Diego	130,303	5,461	225	11,995
Duval County School District, FL..................	Jacksonville	Duval	127,653	7,751	205	9,454
Prince George's County Public Schools, MD......	Upper Marlboro	Prince George's	125,136	8,326	209	15,806
Cypress-Fairbanks Independent School District, TX...	Houston	Harris	111,440	6,675	84	9,077
Cobb County School District, GA..................	Marietta	Cobb	110,001	6,975	114	9,494
Baltimore County Public Schools, MD.............	Towson	Baltimore	108,191	7,306	173	14,754
Pinellas County School District, FL................	Largo	Pinellas	103,411	6,913	170	10,190
Northside Independent School District, TX........	San Antonio	Bexar	102,129	6,462	113	10,028
Jefferson County School District, KY..............	Louisville	Jefferson	100,529	5,853	174	12,451
DeKalb County School District, GA................	Decatur	DeKalb	99,388	6,316	135	10,074
Polk County School District, FL...................	Bartow	Polk	97,953	6,489	162	9,001
Fulton County, GA..............................	Atlanta	Fulton	95,232	6,330	104	11,583
Albuquerque Public Schools, NM..................	Albuquerque	Bernalillo	93,202	6,185	162	10,976
Lee County School District, FL....................	Fort Myers	Lee	87,425	5,517	120	10,113
Denver School District, CO.......................	Denver	Denver	86,046	5,356	184	15,061
Jefferson County School District, CO..............	Golden	Jefferson	86,011	4,780	164	9,885
Prince William County Public Schools, VA........	Manassas	Prince William	85,451	5,308	89	12,144
Austin Independent School District, TX............	Austin	Travis	85,372	5,899	128	12,710
Baltimore City Public Schools, MD................	Baltimore	Baltimore City	84,730	5,272	189	17,228
Fort Worth Independent School District, TX.......	Fort Worth	Tarrant	84,588	5,217	144	9,447
Nashville Davidson County Schools, TN...........	Nashville	Davidson	82,806	5,497	158	11,689
Long Beach Unified School District, CA...........	Long Beach	Los Angeles	81,155	2,967	86	10,844
Milwaukee School District, WI....................	Milwaukee	Milwaukee	78,516	4,082	165	14,624
Anne Arundel County Public Schools, MD.........	Annapolis	Anne Arundel	78,489	5,337	121	15,309
Greenville County School District, SC.............	Greenville	Greenville	74,475	4,462	96	10,112
Alpine School District, UT........................	American Fork	Utah	73,975	3,078	81	6,894
Fresno Unified School District, CA................	Fresno	Fresno	73,353	3,036	108	10,927
Guilford County Schools, NC.....................	Greensboro	Guilford	72,081	4,976	125	10,627
Brevard County School District, FL................	Viera	Brevard	71,232	4,723	123	8,723
Fort Bend Independent School District, TX........	Sugar Land	Fort Bend	70,931	4,129	73	8,679
Loudoun County Public Schools, VA..............	Ashburn	Loudoun	70,759	5,026	85	14,909

X Not applicable. [1] Number of students receiving educational services from the school district. [2] Full-time equivalent is the amount of time required to perform an assignment stated as a proportion of a full-time position. [3] Totals for number of schools may differ from published estimates since they exclude closed, inactive, and future schools.

Source: U.S. Department of Education, National Center for Education Statistics, "Elementary/Secondary Information System," <http://nces.ed.gov/ccd/elsi/>, accessed April 2017.

Table 265. Public Elementary and Secondary School Enrollment by State: 1990 to 2014

[In thousands (29,876 represents 29,876,000). As of Fall. Includes unclassified students. Based on survey of state education agencies; see source for details]

State	Pre-kindergarten through grade 8					Grades 9 through 12				
	1990	2000	2005	2010	2014	1990	2000	2005	2010	2014
United States...............	29,876	33,686	34,204	34,625	35,370	11,341	13,517	14,909	14,860	14,943
Alabama.......................	527	539	529	534	523	195	201	212	222	221
Alaska........................	85	94	91	92	93	29	39	42	40	38
Arizona.......................	479	641	740	752	780	161	237	355	320	332
Arkansas......................	314	318	336	346	349	123	132	138	136	142
California.....................	3,614	4,407	4,466	4,294	4,360	1,337	1,734	1,972	1,996	1,952
Colorado......................	420	517	550	601	634	154	208	230	242	255
Connecticut...................	347	406	400	387	375	122	156	175	173	168
Delaware......................	73	81	85	90	95	27	34	36	39	39
District of Columbia..........	61	54	56	54	63	19	15	21	18	18
Florida........................	1,370	1,760	1,873	1,858	1,934	492	675	802	785	823
Georgia.......................	849	1,060	1,145	1,202	1,243	303	385	453	475	502
Hawaii........................	123	132	127	128	131	49	52	55	52	51
Idaho.........................	160	170	183	194	205	61	75	79	82	85
Illinois........................	1,310	1,474	1,480	1,455	1,429	512	575	631	637	621
Indiana.......................	676	703	724	729	730	279	286	311	318	316
Iowa..........................	345	334	326	348	359	139	161	157	148	146
Kansas.......................	320	323	321	343	355	117	147	147	141	142
Kentucky.....................	459	471	487	480	492	177	194	192	193	197
Louisiana.....................	586	547	482	512	522	199	197	172	184	195
Maine.........................	155	146	133	129	126	60	61	62	60	56
Maryland......................	527	609	589	588	620	188	244	271	264	254
Massachusetts................	604	703	675	666	667	230	273	297	289	289
Michigan......................	1,145	1,222	1,191	1,076	1,052	440	498	551	511	486
Minnesota....................	546	578	558	570	594	211	277	281	268	263
Mississippi...................	372	364	358	351	353	131	134	137	140	138
Missouri......................	588	645	635	643	649	228	268	283	276	269
Montana......................	111	105	98	98	103	42	50	48	43	42
Nebraska.....................	198	195	195	210	223	76	91	92	88	90
Nevada.......................	150	251	296	307	325	51	90	116	130	135
New Hampshire...............	126	147	139	132	126	46	61	67	63	59
New Jersey...................	783	968	971	981	982	306	346	425	421	418
New Mexico...................	208	225	230	239	241	94	95	97	99	99
New York.....................	1,827	2,029	1,909	1,869	1,889	771	853	907	866	852
North Carolina................	783	945	1,003	1,058	1,092	304	348	413	432	457
North Dakota..................	85	72	66	66	76	33	37	33	30	30
Ohio..........................	1,258	1,294	1,261	1,223	1,205	514	541	578	531	520
Oklahoma.....................	425	445	457	483	504	154	178	178	176	185
Oregon.......................	340	379	380	393	422	132	167	173	178	180
Pennsylvania..................	1,172	1,258	1,228	1,210	1,194	496	556	603	584	549
Rhode Island..................	102	114	104	98	99	37	44	50	46	43
South Carolina................	452	493	498	516	540	170	184	204	210	217
South Dakota.................	95	88	84	88	96	34	41	38	38	37
Tennessee....................	598	668	677	702	707	226	241	277	286	288
Texas.........................	2,511	2,943	3,268	3,587	3,783	872	1,117	1,257	1,349	1,450
Utah..........................	325	333	358	425	457	122	148	151	161	179
Vermont......................	71	70	65	68	61	25	32	32	29	26
Virginia.......................	728	816	841	871	898	270	329	372	380	383
Washington...................	613	694	699	714	740	227	310	333	330	333
West Virginia..................	224	201	197	201	200	98	85	84	81	81
Wisconsin....................	565	595	584	598	607	232	285	291	274	265
Wyoming......................	71	60	57	63	67	27	30	27	26	27

Source: U.S. National Center for Education Statistics, *Digest of Education Statistics*, "Advance Release of Selected 2016 Digest Tables," and earlier releases, <http://www.nces.ed.gov/programs/digest/>, accessed April 2017.

Table 266. Parent Participation in School-Related Activities by Selected School, Student, and Family Characteristics: 2012

[In percent, except as noted (52,215 represents 52,215,000). For school year ending in 2012. Covers parents with children in kindergarten through grade 12. Homeschooled students are excluded]

Characteristic	Number of students in grades K through 12 (1,000)	Participation in school activities by parent or other household member				
		Attended a general school or PTO/PTA meeting [1]	Attended regularly scheduled parent-teacher conference	Attended a school or class event	Volunteered or served on school committee	Participated in school fundraising
Total........................	**52,215**	**87**	**76**	**74**	**42**	**58**
School type: [2]						
Public, assigned....................	40,070	86	74	73	38	56
Public, chosen.....................	7,482	89	76	75	44	57
Private, religious....................	3,276	96	85	88	69	84
Private, nonreligious................	782	95	89	91	65	77
Student's sex:						
Male...............................	26,982	87	76	72	40	57
Female.............................	25,233	88	75	77	44	60
Student's race/ethnicity:						
White, non-Hispanic.................	26,910	89	77	82	50	67
Black, non-Hispanic.................	7,464	85	76	68	31	52
Hispanic [3]........................	12,113	86	73	64	32	46
Asian or Pacific Islander, non-Hispanic............	2,886	84	72	64	37	46
Other, non-Hispanic [4].............	2,842	88	78	77	44	58
Student's grade level: [5]						
K–2nd grade.......................	13,608	93	89	79	56	67
3rd–5th grade......................	12,257	92	89	82	50	69
6th–8th grade......................	11,715	87	71	70	32	53
9th–12th grade.....................	14,635	79	57	66	28	47
Parents' highest education level:						
Less than high school..............	6,335	77	64	48	19	31
High school graduate or equivalent...............	10,570	82	72	62	28	46
Vocational/technical or some college..............	15,804	88	77	77	41	61
Bachelor's degree..................	11,852	92	80	85	55	71
Graduate or professional school..................	7,654	95	82	89	61	75
Parents' language at home:						
Both/only parent(s) speak(s) English..............	44,542	88	77	78	45	63
One of two parents speaks English................	1,862	88	69	62	29	38
No parent speaks English........................	5,812	82	65	50	23	32

[1] Parent Teacher Organization (PTO) or Parent Teacher Association (PTA) meeting. [2] School type classifies the school currently attended as either public or private. Public schools are further classified according to whether the school was chosen or assigned. Private schools are classified as being religious or nonreligious. [3] Persons of Hispanic origin may be of any race. [4] Includes children who were multiracial and not of Hispanic ethnicity, were American Indian or Alaska Native, or were not Hispanic, White, Black, Asian, or Pacific Islander. [5] Students whose parents reported the student's grade equivalent as "ungraded" were excluded from the analyses of grade level.

Source: U.S. Department of Education, National Center for Education Statistics, *Parent and Family Involvement in Education, from the National Household Education Surveys Program of 2012*, May 2015. See also <http://nces.ed.gov/nhes/>.

Table 267. School Enrollment Below Postsecondary—Summary by Sex, Race, and Hispanic Origin: 2015

[In thousands (57,966 represents 57,966,000), except percent. As of October. Covers civilian noninstitutional population enrolled in nursery school through high school. Based on Current Population Survey, see text, Section 1 and Appendix III]

Characteristic	Total			Race and Hispanic origin				
				White [2]				
	Number [1]	Male	Female	Total	Non-Hispanic	Black [2]	Asian [2]	Hispanic [3]
All students.....................	**57,966**	**29,674**	**28,291**	**42,196**	**30,242**	**8,719**	**2,951**	**13,987**
Nursery............................	4,532	2,380	2,152	3,230	2,410	703	244	933
Full day.........................	2,290	(NA)	(NA)	1,519	1,159	473	120	398
Part day.........................	2,242	(NA)	(NA)	1,711	1,251	230	125	535
Public schools....................	2,610	(NA)	(NA)	1,778	1,143	501	102	735
Full day.......................	1,283	(NA)	(NA)	799	535	330	42	298
Part day.......................	1,327	(NA)	(NA)	979	608	170	60	437
Private schools...................	1,922	(NA)	(NA)	1,452	1,268	202	142	198
Full day.......................	1,007	(NA)	(NA)	720	624	143	78	100
Part day.......................	915	(NA)	(NA)	732	644	59	64	98
Kindergarten.......................	4,073	2,052	2,021	2,970	2,022	618	215	1,090
Elementary........................	32,826	16,832	15,994	23,863	16,879	4,883	1,704	8,187
High school........................	16,535	8,410	8,125	12,133	8,931	2,515	787	3,777
Population 18 to 24 years old..........	30,037	15,073	14,963	22,244	16,615	4,635	1,634	6,464
Percent dropouts [4]...............	6.4	6.9	5.9	6.4	4.9	7.5	2.3	10.4
Percent high school graduates.......	87.4	86.5	88.3	87.4	89.1	85.7	92.7	83.0
Percent enrolled in college............	40.5	37.8	43.2	40.3	41.8	35.3	62.8	36.6

NA Not available. [1] Includes other races not shown separately. [2] For persons who selected this race group only. See footnote 4, Table 251. [3] Persons of Hispanic origin may be of any race. [4] For persons not in regular school and who have not completed the 12th grade nor received a general equivalency degree.

Source: U.S. Census Bureau, "School Enrollment, Historical Time Series Tables," <http://www.census.gov/hhes/school/data/cps/historical/index.html>, accessed November 2016.

Table 268. Elementary and Secondary Schools—Teachers, Enrollment, and Pupil-Teacher Ratio: 1970 to 2015

[In thousands (2,292 represents 2,292,000), except ratios. As of Fall. Data are for full-time equivalent teachers. Based on surveys of state education agencies and private schools; see source for details]

Year	Teachers			Enrollment			Pupil-teacher ratio		
	Total	Public	Private	Total	Public	Private	Total	Public	Private
1970	2,292	2,059	233	51,257	45,894	5,363	22.4	22.3	23.0
1980	2,485	2,184	301	46,208	40,877	5,331	18.6	18.7	17.7
1990	2,759	2,398	361	46,864	41,217	5,648	17.0	17.2	15.6
2000 [1]	3,366	2,941	424	53,373	47,204	6,169	15.9	16.0	14.5
2001	3,440	3,000	441	53,992	47,672	6,320	15.7	15.9	14.3
2002 [1]	3,476	3,034	442	54,403	48,183	6,220	15.7	15.9	14.1
2003	3,490	3,049	441	54,639	48,540	6,099	15.7	15.9	13.8
2004 [1]	3,536	3,091	445	54,882	48,795	6,087	15.5	15.8	13.7
2005	3,593	3,143	450	55,187	49,113	6,073	15.4	15.6	13.5
2006 [1]	3,622	3,166	456	55,307	49,316	5,991	15.3	15.6	13.2
2007	3,656	3,200	456	55,201	49,291	5,910	15.1	15.4	13.0
2008 [1]	3,670	3,222	448	54,973	49,266	5,707	15.0	15.3	12.8
2009	3,647	3,210	437	54,849	49,361	5,488	15.0	15.4	12.5
2010 [1]	3,529	3,099	429	54,867	49,484	5,382	15.5	16.0	12.5
2011	3,524	3,103	421	54,790	49,522	5,268	15.5	16.0	12.5
2012 [1]	3,540	3,109	431	55,104	49,771	5,333	15.6	16.0	12.4
2013	3,555	3,114	441	55,440	50,045	5,396	15.6	16.1	12.2
2014	3,568	3,132	436	55,635	50,313	5,323	15.6	16.1	12.2
2015, projected	3,575	3,143	432	55,763	50,485	5,278	15.6	16.1	12.2

[1] Private school numbers are estimated based on data from the Private School Universe Survey.

Source: U.S. National Center for Education Statistics, *Digest of Education Statistics*, "Advance Release of Selected 2016 Digest Tables," <http://www.nces.ed.gov/programs/digest/>, accessed June 2017.

Table 269. Private Schools—Number, Students, and Teachers by School Characteristics: 2014

[In thousands (4,576 represents 4,576,000). For school year ending in year shown. Based on the Private School Survey, conducted every 2 years; see source for details. For composition of regions, see map inside front cover]

Characteristic	Schools				Students (1,000)				Teachers (1,000) [1]			
	Number	Elementary	Secondary	Combined	Total	Elementary	Secondary	Combined	Total	Elementary	Secondary	Combined
Total	**33,619**	**22,509**	**2,701**	**8,409**	**4,576**	**2,155**	**738**	**1,684**	**441**	**194**	**65**	**183**
School type:												
Catholic	6,695	5,290	994	412	1,891	1,198	527	167	139	85	39	15
Parochial	2,712	2,514	126	71	664	585	51	28	47	40	4	2
Diocesan	2,977	2,369	475	132	863	546	252	[2] 65	62	38	18	[2] 5
Private	1,007	407	392	208	364	67	224	74	31	6	17	7
Other religious	16,387	10,235	792	5,360	1,711	632	113	966	171	63	12	97
Conservative Christian	4,255	1,387	140	2,728	614	133	18	462	59	13	2	44
Affiliated	3,035	1,960	284	791	489	214	48	227	52	23	5	24
Unaffiliated	9,098	6,888	368	1,842	608	285	47	277	61	27	5	29
Nonsectarian	10,537	6,984	916	2,637	974	325	98	551	131	46	13	71
Regular	5,229	3,870	354	1,005	667	195	65	407	83	25	9	49
Special emphasis	3,701	2,856	324	521	207	117	24	67	30	19	3	8
Special education	1,607	258	238	1,111	99	13	9	77	18	3	2	14
Program emphasis:												
Regular elem/secondary	23,203	14,909	2,012	6,282	4,118	1,933	691	1,494	373	159	59	155
Montessori	2,754	2,608	(B)	135	101	86	(B)	14	17	15	(B)	2
Special program emphasis	894	489	95	311	118	46	12	60	14	6	2	7
Special education	1,844	302	256	1,286	111	14	10	87	20	3	2	15
Vocational/technical	(B)	(B)	(B)	(B)	(B)	(B)	(B)	(B)	(B)	(B)	(B)	(B)
Alternative	907	215	320	372	64	13	22	29	8	2	2	4
Early childhood	4,009	3,988	(X)	(B)	63	63	(X)	(B)	9	9	(X)	(B)
Size:												
Less than 50	16,237	12,572	819	2,846	320	232	18	71	50	34	4	13
50 to 149	7,730	4,790	521	2,419	706	442	47	217	82	47	6	29
150 to 299	5,350	3,445	461	1,444	1,138	731	100	308	101	58	10	33
300 to 499	2,439	1,297	372	770	937	495	144	298	80	37	13	30
500 to 749	1,119	350	289	480	675	205	177	294	57	13	14	30
750 or more	743	56	239	449	801	50	254	497	71	4	18	49
Region:												
Northeast	7,363	4,787	861	1,715	1,034	470	232	332	111	44	23	44
Midwest	9,523	7,670	569	1,284	1,143	675	202	265	95	54	16	26
South	10,272	5,625	660	3,987	1,540	556	157	827	157	56	14	87
West	6,461	4,427	611	1,423	860	453	146	260	78	40	12	26
Urban/rural status:												
City	10,632	6,977	1,124	2,531	1,976	900	373	703	188	81	31	76
Suburban	12,108	8,229	922	2,958	1,826	917	279	631	175	82	24	69
Town	2,892	1,883	189	819	281	149	25	107	27	13	2	11
Rural	7,987	[2] 5,419	467	2,101	493	190	61	243	52	17	8	27

X Not applicable. B Base figure too small to meet statistical standards. [1] Full-time equivalents. [2] Interpret data with caution.

Source: U.S. National Center for Education Statistics, Private School Universe Survey, "Data Tables," <http://nces.ed.gov/surveys/pss/>, accessed February 2017.

Table 270. Public Elementary and Secondary Schools—Number and Average Salary of Classroom Teachers: 1990 to 2015, and by State, 2016

[2,362 represents 2,362,000. Estimates for school year ending in June of year shown. Elementary includes kindergarten]

Year and state	Teachers [1] (1,000)			Avg. salary ($1,000)		
	Total	Elementary	Secondary	All teachers	Elementary	Secondary
1990	2,362	1,390	972	31.4	30.8	32.0
1995	2,565	1,517	1,048	36.7	36.1	37.5
2000	2,891	1,696	1,195	41.8	41.3	42.5
2005	3,072	1,799	1,273	47.5	47.1	47.7
2010	3,163	1,850	1,313	55.3	(NA)	(NA)
2011	3,131	1,843	1,287	55.6	(NA)	(NA)
2012	3,090	1,870	1,221	55.5	(NA)	(NA)
2013	3,096	1,873	1,229	56.2	(NA)	(NA)
2014	3,124	1,892	1,232	56.8	(NA)	(NA)
2015	3,144	1,918	1,227	57.6	(NA)	(NA)
2016, U.S. total	**3,131**	**1,921**	**1,211**	**58.4**	**58.2**	**58.4**
Alabama	46	25	21	48.5	47.8	49.3
Alaska	9	3	6	67.4	66.7	66.8
Arizona	45	31	14	47.2	47.2	47.2
Arkansas	31	14	17	48.2	46.5	49.6
California	276	188	89	77.2	77.2	77.2
Colorado	55	34	20	46.2	45.3	47.7
Connecticut	42	29	13	72.0	72.0	72.0
Delaware	9	5	4	60.0	60.2	62.2
District of Columbia	5	3	2	75.8	75.8	75.8
Florida	170	91	80	49.2	49.2	49.2
Georgia	112	69	43	54.2	53.6	55.1
Hawaii	11	6	5	57.4	57.4	57.4
Idaho	15	7	8	46.1	45.5	46.7
Illinois	123	99	24	61.3	61.3	61.3
Indiana	60	32	28	50.7	50.7	50.7
Iowa	35	24	11	54.4	54.5	54.3
Kansas	34	17	17	47.8	47.8	47.8
Kentucky	41	29	12	52.1	51.9	52.6
Louisiana	45	30	15	49.7	48.6	49.8
Maine	15	10	5	50.5	50.5	50.5
Maryland	60	37	24	66.5	65.9	67.4
Massachusetts	72	52	20	77.0	77.0	77.0
Michigan	85	47	38	62.0	62.0	62.0
Minnesota	56	39	17	56.9	56.9	56.9
Mississippi	32	18	14	42.7	42.7	42.7
Missouri	73	51	22	48.0	47.4	47.7
Montana	10	7	3	51.0	51.0	51.0
Nebraska	24	16	8	51.4	51.5	51.3
Nevada	17	10	8	56.9	56.9	56.9
New Hampshire	14	10	5	56.6	56.6	56.6
New Jersey	112	75	37	69.3	69.3	68.0
New Mexico	22	15	7	47.2	46.1	47.7
New York	209	102	106	79.2	79.2	79.2
North Carolina	94	66	28	47.9	47.9	47.9
North Dakota	8	5	3	50.5	50.5	50.5
Ohio	112	69	43	56.4	57.7	54.4
Oklahoma	42	30	12	45.3	44.9	46.3
Oregon	29	20	9	60.4	60.0	61.3
Pennsylvania	117	62	55	65.2	65.2	65.2
Rhode Island	9	5	4	66.2	66.2	66.2
South Carolina	50	35	15	48.8	46.8	47.7
South Dakota	9	7	3	42.0	41.9	42.4
Tennessee	66	47	20	48.2	48.2	48.2
Texas	347	178	169	51.9	51.4	52.4
Utah	28	15	13	46.9	46.9	46.9
Vermont	6	3	3	58.9	58.9	58.9
Virginia	102	63	39	50.8	50.8	50.8
Washington	58	32	25	53.7	53.7	53.7
West Virginia	19	14	5	45.6	45.6	45.6
Wisconsin	57	40	17	54.1	53.9	54.7
Wyoming	8	4	3	58.1	57.6	58.8

NA Not available. [1] Full-time equivalent.

Source: National Education Association, Washington, DC. Data from *Rankings of the States 2016 and Estimates of School Statistics 2017*, used with permission of the National Education Association © 2017. All rights reserved.

Table 271. Public School Teachers, Base Salary, and Additional Income by Selected Characteristics: 2012

[3,139.2 represents 3,139,200. For school year ending in 2012. Data shown for regular full-time teachers only; excludes other staff even when they have full-time teaching duties. Based on the 2011-12 Schools and Staffing Survey and subject to sampling error; for details, see <http://nces.ed.gov/surveys/sass/>]

Characteristic	Number of full-time teachers (1,000)	Base teacher salary (dollars)	Total income from school and nonschool sources [1,2] (dollars)	Teachers with additional income					
				Job outside the school system during the school year		Supplemental school system contract during summer [3]		Employed in a non-school job during the summer	
				Percent of teachers	Average income (dollars)	Percent of teachers	Average income (dollars)	Percent of teachers	Average income (dollars)
Total..........................	3,139.2	53,070	56,410	16.1	4,820	17.8	2,510	15.0	3,430
Sex:									
Male...........................	754.6	54,430	60,360	23.3	6,060	21.4	2,880	23.2	4,560
Female........................	2,384.6	52,640	55,160	13.9	4,150	16.6	2,360	12.4	2,770
Race/ethnicity:									
White........................	2,556.2	53,020	56,400	17.0	4,740	16.7	2,410	16.1	3,310
Black........................	221.0	52,370	55,790	15.5	4,740	26.2	2,920	9.5	4,540
Hispanic......................	252.2	53,620	56,240	9.5	4,600	20.7	2,710	9.4	3,640
Asian.........................	57.5	58,850	62,480	7.9	7,000	19.7	3,080	7.0	5,400
Pacific Islander...............	4.4	52,920	57,280	(S)	(S)	(S)	(S)	(S)	(S)
American Indian/Alaska Native......................	15.4	46,630	53,000	22.4	(S)	19.2	2,640	21.5	4,470
Two or more races............	31.2	50,230	53,750	16.0	5,690	14.5	2,610	16.1	3,550
Age:									
Less than 30 years old.......	487.4	41,720	45,160	18.7	3,360	21.5	2,430	24.5	2,980
30 to 39 years old...........	921.9	50,020	53,120	15.7	4,380	18.4	2,420	14.8	3,320
40 to 49 years old...........	783.7	55,420	58,660	16.8	5,070	17.4	2,490	14.6	3,720
50 or more years old.........	946.2	59,940	63,550	14.6	6,000	15.6	2,680	10.6	3,800
Years of full-time teaching experience:									
1 year or less................	144.2	40,540	44,610	16.9	4,380	18.7	2,980	31.2	4,860
2 to 4 years..................	395.9	41,480	44,490	17.3	3,970	20.2	2,260	20.6	2,800
5 to 9 years..................	784.6	47,300	50,370	16.6	4,250	19.4	2,380	14.7	3,110
10 to 14 years................	652.1	54,860	58,040	15.7	4,830	17.2	2,670	12.2	3,450
15 to 19 years................	426.2	58,880	62,050	15.4	5,940	17.2	2,430	13.0	3,390
20 to 24 years................	295.8	60,930	64,210	15.2	5,730	13.4	2,460	13.8	4,220
25 to 29 years................	217.9	63,780	67,440	15.9	5,000	16.8	2,550	12.8	3,010
30 or more years.............	222.5	64,820	69,790	15.6	5,400	16.5	2,920	11.0	3,700
Highest degree held:									
Less than bachelors'.........	118.9	51,330	55,430	20.1	7,340	16.6	2,360	20.9	3,750
Bachelor's....................	1,278.2	46,340	49,410	14.5	4,600	16.8	2,360	16.2	3,400
Master's......................	1,479.3	57,830	61,230	16.6	4,570	18.1	2,600	13.8	3,380
Education specialist..........	228.7	59,680	63,420	17.7	5,330	20.4	2,650	12.2	3,620
Doctorate.....................	34.2	60,230	66,140	30.8	6,610	26.9	2,810	18.8	3,940
Instructional level: [4]									
Elementary...................	1,572.3	52,620	54,820	12.8	4,350	16.6	2,270	12.6	2,930
Secondary....................	1,566.9	53,520	58,000	19.5	5,130	19.0	2,720	17.4	3,790
School locale:									
City..........................	(S)	(S)	(S)	(S)	(S)	(S)	(S)	(S)	(S)
Suburban.....................	1,016.9	58,470	61,610	15.6	4,300	17.4	2,450	13.8	3,350
Town.........................	382.9	47,780	51,050	16.3	4,910	15.6	2,030	16.0	3,520
Rural.........................	853.0	47,130	50,670	16.3	5,340	15.1	2,290	16.9	3,600

S Figure does not meet publication standards. [1] Includes retirement pension funds paid during the school year. [2] Includes types of income not shown separately. [3] Includes teaching summer sessions and other non-teaching jobs at any school. [4] Teachers were classified as elementary or secondary on the basis of the grades they taught, rather than on the level of the school in which they taught. In general, elementary teachers include those teaching pre-kindergarten through grade 5 and those teaching multiple grades, with a preponderance of grades taught being kindergarten through grade 6. In general, secondary teachers include those teaching grades 7 through 12 and those teaching multiple grades, with a preponderance of grades taught being grades 7 through 12 and usually no grade taught being lower than grade 5.

Source: U.S. National Center for Education Statistics, *2013 Digest of Education Statistics*, May 2015. See also <http://http://nces.ed.gov/programs/digest/>.

Table 272. Private School Teachers, Base Salary, and Additional Income by Selected Characteristics: 2012

[368.4 represents 368,400. For school year ending in 2012. Data shown for regular full-time teachers only; excludes other staff even when they have full-time teaching duties. Based on the 2011-12 Schools and Staffing Survey and subject to sampling error; for details, see <http://nces.ed.gov/surveys/sass/>]

Characteristic	Number of full-time teachers (1,000)	Base teacher Salary (dollars)	Total income from school and nonschool income [1,2] (1,000)	Teachers with additional income					
				Job outside the school system during the school year		Supplemental school system contract during summer [3]		Employed in a non-school job during the summer	
				Percent of teachers	Average income (dollars)	Percent of teachers	Average income (dollars)	Percent of teachers	Average income (dollars)
Total [4]	**368.4**	**40,200**	**44,130**	**19.6**	**5,440**	**20.8**	**3,370**	**17.1**	**3,780**
Sex:									
Male	92.9	44,470	51,150	26.9	6,550	29.3	3,600	23.3	4,650
Female	275.5	38,760	41,760	17.1	4,850	17.9	3,240	15.0	3,320
Race/ethnicity:									
White	326.0	40,450	44,390	19.4	5,350	20.2	3,410	17.5	3,710
Black	13.0	37,080	41,790	(S)	(S)	29.6	3,560	(S)	(S)
Hispanic	19.8	39,530	42,550	15.3	6,090	18.0	2,590	(S)	(S)
Asian	6.3	36,720	40,170	(S)	(S)	(S)	(S)	(S)	(S)
Two or more races	2.8	39,640	46,660	(S)	(S)	(S)	(S)	(S)	(S)
Age:									
Less than 30 years old	63.2	31,010	34,340	23.6	4,170	24.0	2,050	32.7	3,460
30 to 39 years old	94.3	38,420	42,110	19.4	4,950	23.9	4,270	15.4	3,590
40 to 49 years old	87.9	42,860	45,740	18.2	4,980	20.2	3,460	12.3	2,690
50 or more years old	123.0	44,420	49,580	18.5	7,000	17.1	3,280	13.9	5,000
Years of full-time teaching experience:									
1 year or less	30.9	29,940	33,980	24.5	5,100	21.4	2,330	30.9	4,390
2 to 4 years	61.5	33,540	36,760	22.0	4,250	23.9	2,540	23.5	2,820
5 to 9 years	85.0	37,220	40,990	19.3	5,760	24.8	4,170	16.1	4,080
10 to 14 years	58.6	40,440	43,570	19.3	5,310	18.6	3,740	14.2	3,340
15 to 19 years	43.9	44,820	47,190	15.1	5,110	20.5	3,180	10.6	2,400
20 to 24 years	27.7	48,170	52,380	20.3	6,230	16.0	1,790	15.4	3,860
25 to 29 years	24.3	47,070	52,040	17.6	5,340	17.6	3,230	(S)	(S)
30 or more years	36.5	50,390	57,950	18.4	7,420	15.1	4,700	14.8	2,410
Highest degree held:									
Less than bachelor's [1]	27.9	27,690	30,160	15.3	3,820	19.5	2,760	15.5	3,750
Bachelor's	180.9	36,270	39,450	18.2	5,420	19.6	2,880	18.7	4,000
Master's	134.3	46,400	50,670	20.7	5,070	21.8	4,160	16.3	3,470
Education specialist	17.7	47,450	55,230	25.2	7,280	24.6	2,820	(S)	(S)
Doctorate	7.7	52,590	64,890	(S)	(S)	(S)	(S)	(S)	(S)
Instructional level: [5]									
Elementary	196.8	36,260	39,310	16.0	5,190	17.1	2,770	15.8	3,730
Secondary	171.6	44,720	49,640	23.7	5,640	25.0	3,840	18.7	3,820

S Figure does not meet publication standards. [1] Includes retirement pension funds paid during the school year. [2] Includes types of income not shown separately. [3] Includes teaching summer sessions and other non-teaching jobs at any school. [4] Includes race/ethnicities not shown separately. [5] Teachers were classified as elementary or secondary on the basis of the grades they taught, rather than on the level of the school in which they taught. In general, elementary teachers include those teaching pre-kindergarten through grade 5 and those teaching multiple grades, with a preponderance of grades taught being kindergarten through grade 6. In general, secondary teachers include those teaching grades 7 through 12 and those teaching multiple grades, with a preponderance of grades taught being grades 7 through 12 and usually no grade taught being lower than grade 5.

Source: U.S. National Center for Education Statistics, *2013 Digest of Education Statistics*, May 2015. See also <http://http://nces.ed.gov/programs/digest/>.

Table 273. Education and Certification Qualifications of Public High School Teachers: 2012

[In percent except where indicated. For school year ending in 2012. Based on the Schools and Staffing Survey (SASS); see source for details]

Teacher and school characteristics	Number of teachers	Certified teachers	Percent of teachers								
			Major in main assignment			Major/minor in main assignment			No major in main assignment [1]		
			Total	Certified	Not certified	Total	Certified	Not certified	Total	Certified	Not certified
Total [2]	**693,400**	**83.2**	**77.8**	**68.4**	**9.4**	**82.6**	**72.3**	**10.3**	**22.2**	**14.8**	**7.4**
Teachers with English main assignment [3]	152,400	82.1	79.4	69.4	9.9	84.0	73.4	10.6	20.6	12.7	8.0
Teachers with mathematics main assignment [4]	144,800	80.9	70.1	61.5	8.7	75.4	65.6	9.8	29.9	19.4	10.4
Teachers with science main assignment [5]	126,300	85.7	79.7	72.3	7.3	84.9	76.5	8.3	20.3	13.4	7.0
Teachers with social science main assignment [6]	120,800	82.9	78.9	67.5	11.4	84.1	71.4	12.7	21.1	15.4	5.7
Years of teaching experience:											
3 or fewer	84,500	75.3	63.2	52.0	11.2	69.0	56.6	12.3	36.8	16.9	19.9
4 to 9	202,700	83.9	74.7	65.9	8.8	79.6	69.7	9.9	25.3	15.5	9.9
10 to 19	240,900	85.6	79.8	71.4	8.4	84.5	75.5	9.1	20.2	15.0	5.2
20 or more	165,300	83.0	79.4	68.3	11.1	84.2	71.9	12.3	20.6	13.8	6.8
Average class size:											
10 or fewer students	33,600	68.9	63.2	52.0	11.2	69.0	56.6	12.3	36.8	16.9	19.9
11-18	146,300	81.3	74.7	65.9	8.8	79.6	69.7	9.9	25.3	15.5	9.9
19-27	313,600	86.4	79.8	71.4	8.4	84.5	75.5	9.1	20.2	15.0	5.2
28 or more students	199,900	82.0	79.4	68.3	11.1	84.2	71.9	12.3	20.6	13.8	6.8
School classification:											
Charter school	25,500	73.0	71.9	57.3	14.6 [7]	77.5	60.4	17.1 [7]	28.1	15.7	12.4 [7]
Traditional public school	667,900	83.6	78.0	68.8	9.2	82.8	72.8	10.1	22.0	14.8	7.2
Community type:											
City	177,600	79.8	78.0	66.7	11.4	83.0	70.6	12.4	22.0	13.1	8.9
Suburban	218,000	85.6	81.2	71.7	9.5	85.4	75.3	10.1	18.8	13.9	4.9
Town	76,500	82.7	76.1	67.0	9.1	81.6	71.3	10.3	23.9	15.7	8.2
Rural	221,300	83.8	74.8	67.0	7.8	80.0	71.1	8.9	25.2	16.8	8.4
Student enrollment:											
Less than 100	14,900	66.9	56.9	47.2	9.7	64.5	53.9	10.7	43.1	19.7	23.4
100-199	25,500	75.7	72.6	60.7	11.9	79.7	66.2	13.5	27.4	15.1	12.4
200-499	101,100	78.7	72.0	62.1	9.9	77.4	66.4	10.9	28.0	16.6	11.4
500-749	81,400	82.7	79.2	68.6	10.6	84.0	71.9	12.0	20.8	14.0	6.8
750-999	66,300	82.9	80.8	69.7	11.0	84.7	73.4	11.3	19.2	13.2	6.0 [7]
1,000-1,499	141,000	85.5	78.7	70.8	7.8	82.3	73.9	8.4	21.3	14.7	6.7
1,500 or more	263,100	85.6	80.1	71.1	9.0	85.2	75.2	10.0	19.9	14.6	5.3
Percent of K-12 students in school who are of a racial/ethnic minority: [8]											
Less than 20	226,000	85.3	81.4	72.6	8.8	85.5	76.1	9.4	18.6	12.7	6.0
20 to 59	229,600	84.2	75.2	67.0	8.1	81.5	72.2	9.3	24.8	17.1	7.7
60 or more	237,800	80.3	76.9	65.7	11.2	81.0	68.8	12.2	23.1	14.6	8.4

[1] No major in main assignment includes teachers with a minor in main assignment. [2] Includes teachers (defined below) who reported a main assignment in English, mathematics, science, social science, French, German, Latin, Spanish, art/arts or crafts, music, or dance/theater. Teachers of art/arts and crafts, music, dance and drama/theater were allowed to report an ungraded or secondary level (grades 9-12) certification. [3] Includes teachers who reported a main assignment in communications, composition, English, journalism, language arts, reading, or speech. [4] Includes teachers who reported a main assignment in algebra, basic and general mathematics, business and applied math, calculus and precalculus, computer science, geometry, prealgebra, statistics and probability, or trigonometry. [5] Includes teachers who reported a main assignment in science (general), biology/life sciences, chemistry, Earth sciences, integrated science, physical science, physics, or engineering. [6] Includes teachers who reported a main assignment in social studies (general), anthropology, economics, geography, government/civics, history, Native American studies, psychology, or sociology. [7] Interpret data with caution. [8] Includes Hispanic or Latino (regardless of race), Black (not of Hispanic or Latino origin), Asian or Pacific Islander, and American Indian or Alaska Native.

Source: U.S. Department of Education, National Center for Education Statistics, *Supplemental Tables to Education and Certification Qualifications of Departmentalized Public High School-Level Teachers of Selected Subjects: Evidence From the 2011-12 Schools and Staffing Survey,* July 2015. See also <http://nces.ed.gov/surveys/npsas/>.

Table 274. Teacher Stayers, Movers, and Leavers by Selected Characteristics: 2013

[2,386.5 represents 2,386,500. For school year ending in year shown. Data compare the teaching status of teacher between one school year and the prior year. Stayers are teachers who were teaching in the same school in both years. Movers are teachers who were still teaching in the current school year but in a different school. Leavers are teachers who left the teaching profession. Based on the School and Staffing Survey; see source for details]

Characteristic	Number of teachers				Percent of teachers		
	Total [1]	Stayers	Movers	Leavers	Stayers	Movers	Leavers
Total................................	**3,377.9**	**2,846.5**	**271.9**	**259.4**	**84.3**	**8.1**	**7.7**
Age:							
Less than 30 years old...............	515.9	406.8	70.7	38.4	78.8	13.7	7.5
30 to 39 years old.....................	982.2	847.4	83.1	51.7	86.3	8.5	5.3
40 to 49 years old.....................	843.3	759.5	49.9	33.9	90.1	5.9	4.0
50 years old and over................	1,036.4	832.8	68.2	135.4	80.4	6.6	13.1
Sex:							
Male....................................	801.2	686.6	63.0	51.6	85.7	7.9	6.4
Female.................................	2,576.6	2,159.9	208.9	207.8	83.8	8.1	8.1
Race/ethnicity:							
White..................................	2,769.7	2,353.4	207.3	209.0	85.0	7.5	7.5
Black...................................	229.4	179.4	[2] 26.9	[2] 23.1	78.2	[2] 11.7	[2] 10.1
Hispanic...............................	261.2	207.4	33.0	[2] 20.8	79.4	12.6	[2] 8.0
Asian..................................	[2] 63.8	[2] 61.2	[2] 1.6	(S)	95.8	(S)	(S)
American Indian/Alaska Native......	[2] 22.3	[2] 17.5	(S)	(S)	78.8	(S)	(S)
Two or more races....................	[2] 31.2	[2] 27.7	[2] 1.8	(S)	88.8	(S)	(S)
Teaching status:							
Full time..............................	3,126.0	2,678.8	234.2	213.0	85.7	7.5	6.8
Part time.............................	251.8	167.7	37.8	46.4	66.6	15.0	18.4
Teaching experience:							
1 year to 3 years.....................	398.5	320.4	49.8	28.2	80.4	12.5	7.1
4 to 9 years...........................	919.5	749.4	107.6	62.5	81.5	11.7	6.8
10 to 19 years........................	1,205.4	1,066.2	68.0	71.2	88.5	5.6	5.9
20 years or more.....................	854.5	710.6	46.5	97.4	83.2	5.4	11.4
Base salary:							
Less than $30,000....................	88.5	61.4	13.9	13.1	69.4	15.7	14.8
$30,000 to $39,999..................	643.7	527.6	74.9	41.2	82.0	11.6	6.4
$40,000 to $49,999..................	970.3	815.3	77.5	77.5	84.0	8.0	8.0
$50,000 or more......................	1,675.3	1,442.2	105.6	127.6	86.1	6.3	7.6
School classification:							
Traditional public.....................	3,264.9	2,754.4	260.4	250.1	84.4	8.0	7.7
Public charter........................	113.0	92.1	[2] 11.6	9.3	81.5	[2] 10.2	8.2
School level:							
Primary................................	1,658.0	1,391.8	143.5	122.7	83.9	8.7	7.4
Middle.................................	539.6	459.7	42.1	37.9	85.2	7.8	7.0
High....................................	987.8	844.8	66.5	76.6	85.5	6.7	7.8
Combined.............................	192.4	150.3	[2] 19.8	[2] 22.2	78.1	[2] 10.3	[2] 11.6
School enrollment:							
Less than 200 students..............	156.8	133.6	13.3	9.9	85.2	8.5	6.3
200 to 499 students..................	1,068.8	899.5	84.8	84.5	84.2	7.9	7.9
500 to 749 students..................	866.1	718.2	79.9	68.0	82.9	9.2	7.8
750 or more students................	1,286.2	1,095.2	94.0	97.1	85.1	7.3	7.5

S Figure does not meet publication standards. [1] Total teachers in base year, which refers to prior school year. [2] Interpret data with caution. The standard error for this estimate is equal to 30 percent or more of the estimate's value.

Source: U.S. National Center for Education Statistics, *Teacher Attrition and Mobility: Results from the 2012-13 Teacher Follow-up Survey*, September 2014. See also <https://nces.ed.gov/pubsearch/pubsinfo.asp?pubid=2014077>.

Table 275. Public School Employment by Occupation, Sex, and Race: 2010 and 2012

[In thousands (4,592 represents 4,592,000). Covers all public elementary-secondary school districts with 100 or more full-time employees]

Occupation	2010					2012				
	Total	Male	Female	White [1]	Black [1]	Total	Male	Female	White [1]	Black [1]
All occupations [2]..............	**4,592**	**1,155**	**3,437**	**3,420**	**579**	**4,646**	**1,170**	**3,476**	**3,419**	**573**
Officials, administrators.............	65	31	34	53	7	80	36	43	62	8
Principals and assistant principals.........................	114	52	62	83	20	124	54	70	89	21
Classroom teachers [3]...............	2,492	594	1,898	2,004	225	2,487	586	1,901	1,987	217
Elementary schools................	1,212	154	1,059	966	101	1,163	136	1,028	925	95
Secondary schools.................	967	375	592	793	85	993	381	612	804	84
Other professional staff.............	353	62	291	275	46	394	70	324	295	49
Teachers' aides [4]....................	538	78	459	359	91	537	79	458	356	91
Clerical, secretarial staff............	317	19	299	221	37	305	12	293	213	34
Service workers [5]...................	712	318	393	426	152	720	333	387	417	152

[1] Excludes individuals of Hispanic origin. [2] 2010 data includes other occupations not shown separately. [3] Includes other classroom teachers not shown separately. [4] Includes technicians. [5] Includes craftworkers and laborers.

Source: U.S. Equal Employment Opportunity Commission, "Equal Employment Opportunity, EEO-5 Statistical File–2012, United States Summary," <http://www.eeoc.gov/eeoc/statistics/employment/jobpat-eeo5/index.cfm>, accessed June 2014.

Table 276. Public Charter and Traditional Schools by Selected Characteristics: 1999 and 2014

[46,689 represents 46,689,000. As of Fall. A public charter school is a public school that, in accordance with an enabling state statute, has been granted a charter exempting it from selected state and local rules and regulations]

Characteristic	1999			2014		
	Total	Traditional	Public charter	Total	Traditional	Public charter
Enrollment (1,000)	**46,689**	**46,350**	**340**	**50,010**	**47,288**	**2,722**
PERCENT DISTRIBUTION OF STUDENTS						
Race/ethnicity	100.0	100.0	100.0	100.0	100.0	100.0
White, non-Hispanic	61.8	61.9	42.5	49.6	50.5	34.0
Black, non-Hispanic	17.1	16.9	33.5	15.5	14.9	27.0
Hispanic	15.9	15.9	19.6	25.4	25.1	30.8
Asian/Pacific Islander	4.1	4.1	2.8	5.3	5.3	4.2
American Indian/Alaska Native	1.2	1.2	1.5	1.0	1.0	0.8
Two or more races	(NA)	(NA)	(NA)	3.2	3.2	3.3
Number of teachers (1,000)	2,636	2,623	14	2,875	2,745	129
Pupil/teacher ratio	16.6	16.6	18.8	16.2	16.1	17.4
Total number of schools	**92,012**	**90,488**	**1,524**	**98,176**	**91,429**	**6,747**
PERCENT DISTRIBUTION OF SCHOOLS						
School level	100.0	100.0	100.0	100.0	100.0	100.0
Elementary [1]	69.7	70.0	54.6	68.3	69.1	57.1
Secondary [2]	24.3	24.3	25.9	24.6	24.7	23.2
Combined [3]	4.4	4.2	18.6	6.5	5.5	19.7
Other	1.6	1.6	0.9	0.6	0.6	–
Size of enrollment	100.0	100.0	100.0	100.0	100.0	100.0
Less than 300 students	31.4	30.7	77.1	30.2	28.7	50.1
300 to 499 students	26.4	26.7	12.0	27.4	27.6	24.7
500 to 999 students	32.6	33.0	8.6	33.2	34.2	20.0
1,000 students or more	9.5	9.7	2.4	9.2	9.5	5.3
Region	100.0	100.0	100.0	100.0	100.0	100.0
Northeast	16.1	16.3	7.2	15.6	16.0	10.1
Midwest	28.9	29.0	24.9	25.8	26.1	21.2
South	33.1	33.2	28.9	34.8	35.0	31.6
West	21.8	21.6	38.9	23.8	22.8	37.1

NA Not available. – Represents or rounds to zero. [1] Includes schools beginning with grade 6 or below and with no grade higher than 8. [2] Includes schools with no grade lower than 7. [3] Includes schools beginning with grade 6 or below and ending with grade 9 or above.

Source: U.S. National Center for Education Statistics, *Digest of Education Statistics,* "Advance Release of Selected 2016 Digest Tables," <http://www.nces.ed.gov/programs/digest/>, accessed January 2017.

Table 277. Public Charter Schools and Enrollment by State: 2014

[2,721.8 represents 2,721,800. As of Fall]

State	Number of charter schools	Number of students (1,000)	Charter schools as a percent of public schools	Charter school enrollment as a percent of public school enrollment	State	Number of charter schools	Number of students (1,000)	Charter schools as a percent of public schools	Charter school enrollment as a percent of public school enrollment
United States	**6,747**	**2,721.8**	**6.9**	**5.4**	Missouri	62	20.0	2.6	2.2
Alabama	–	–	–	–	Montana	–	–	–	–
Alaska	27	6.2	5.3	4.7	Nebraska	–	–	–	–
Arizona	619	206.7	27.1	18.6	Nevada	45	29.0	6.8	6.3
Arkansas	60	20.1	5.5	4.1	New Hampshire	28	2.5	5.7	1.4
California	1,177	544.3	11.4	8.7	New Jersey	87	37.3	3.4	2.7
Colorado	214	101.4	11.6	11.4	New Mexico	97	22.7	11.0	6.7
Connecticut	22	8.0	1.7	1.5	New York	248	106.5	5.1	3.9
Delaware	24	12.2	11.0	9.1	North Carolina	149	70.2	5.7	4.6
Dist. of Columbia	107	34.5	48.2	42.7	North Dakota	–	–	–	–
Florida	651	251.8	15.6	9.1	Ohio	381	122.4	10.5	7.1
Georgia	89	71.6	3.8	4.1	Oklahoma	35	16.6	1.9	2.4
Hawaii	34	10.4	11.8	5.7	Oregon	126	29.9	10.1	5.3
Idaho	52	19.1	7.0	6.6	Pennsylvania	185	132.8	6.1	7.7
Illinois	68	62.4	1.6	3.1	Rhode Island	25	6.4	8.1	4.6
Indiana	80	37.4	4.2	3.6	South Carolina	66	27.1	5.3	3.6
Iowa	3	0.3	0.2	0.1	South Dakota	–	–	–	–
Kansas	11	2.8	0.8	0.6	Tennessee	80	22.1	4.3	2.2
Kentucky	–	–	–	–	Texas	681	262.1	7.7	5.0
Louisiana	135	69.8	9.8	9.7	Utah	110	61.4	10.8	9.7
Maine	6	0.9	1.0	0.5	Vermont	–	–	–	–
Maryland	47	19.3	3.3	2.2	Virginia	7	0.9	0.3	0.1
Massachusetts	80	37.4	4.3	3.9	Washington	1	–	–	–
Michigan	375	142.8	10.7	9.6	West Virginia	–	–	–	–
Minnesota	205	47.7	8.4	5.6	Wisconsin	244	44.1	10.8	5.1
Mississippi	–	–	–	–	Wyoming	4	0.5	1.1	0.5

– Represents or rounds to zero.

Source: U.S. National Center for Education Statistics, *Digest of Education Statistics,* "Advance Release of Selected 2016 Digest Tables," <http://www.nces.ed.gov/programs/digest/>, accessed January 2017.

Table 278. Average Salary and Wages Paid in Public School Systems: 1985 to 2011

[In dollars. For school year ending in year shown. Data reported by a stratified sample of school systems enrolling 300 or more pupils. Data represent unweighted means of average salaries paid school personnel reported by each school system]

Position	1985	1990	1995	2000	2005	2008	2009	2010	2011
ANNUAL SALARY									
Central-office administrators:									
Superintendent (contract salary).......	56,954	75,425	90,198	112,158	128,770	148,387	155,634	159,634	161,992
Deputy/assoc. superintendent..........	52,877	69,623	81,266	97,251	116,186	134,245	136,832	139,463	138,061
Assistant superintendent...............	48,003	62,698	75,236	88,913	103,212	116,833	119,755	123,509	122,333
Administrators for—									
Finance and business.................	40,344	52,354	61,323	73,499	83,678	96,490	98,590	100,306	101,347
Instructional services..................	43,452	56,359	66,767	79,023	88,950	99,748	102,322	103,974	103,025
Public relations/information...........	35,287	44,926	53,263	60,655	70,502	80,534	83,235	86,567	84,629
Staff personnel services..............	44,182	56,344	65,819	76,608	86,966	98,190	100,620	102,269	101,578
Technology..........................	(X)	(X)	(X)	(X)	76,308	86,085	87,898	90,530	90,914
Subject area supervisors..............	34,422	45,929	54,534	63,103	68,714	78,309	80,290	80,964	80,534
School building administrators:									
Principals:									
Elementary..........................	36,452	48,431	58,589	69,407	76,182	85,907	88,062	89,673	89,591
Junior high/middle...................	39,650	52,163	62,311	73,877	81,514	91,334	93,478	95,003	95,426
Senior high..........................	42,094	55,722	66,596	79,839	86,938	97,486	99,365	102,387	102,191
Assistant principals:									
Elementary..........................	30,496	40,916	48,491	56,419	63,140	71,192	71,893	73,181	71,764
Junior high/middle...................	33,793	44,570	52,942	60,842	67,600	76,053	77,476	79,164	78,131
Senior high..........................	35,491	46,486	55,556	64,811	71,401	79,391	81,083	83,074	82,027
Classroom teachers....................	23,587	31,278	37,264	42,213	45,884	51,329	52,900	54,370	54,220
Auxiliary professional personnel:									
Counselors............................	27,593	35,979	42,486	48,195	52,500	57,618	58,775	60,142	60,188
Librarians............................	24,981	33,469	40,418	46,732	50,720	56,933	57,974	59,495	59,093
School nurses........................	19,944	26,090	31,066	35,540	40,520	46,025	46,476	48,032	48,044
Secretarial/clerical personnel:									
Central office:									
Secretaries..........................	15,343	20,238	23,935	28,405	32,716	36,657	37,785	38,601	38,606
Accounting/payroll clerks.............	15,421	20,088	24,042	28,498	33,217	37,732	39,031	39,895	39,790
Typists/data entry clerks.............	12,481	16,125	18,674	22,853	26,214	30,072	31,718	32,555	32,636
School building level:									
Secretaries..........................	12,504	16,184	19,170	22,630	25,381	28,810	29,480	30,474	30,226
Library clerks........................	9,911	12,152	14,381	16,509	18,443	21,004	21,190	21,639	21,142
HOURLY WAGE RATE									
Other support personnel:									
Teacher aides:									
Instructional........................	5.89	7.43	8.77	10.00	11.35	12.86	13.23	13.48	13.55
Noninstructional.....................	5.60	7.08	8.29	9.77	11.23	12.70	13.13	13.59	13.58
Custodians............................	6.90	8.54	10.05	11.35	12.61	14.19	14.59	15.04	14.92
Cafeteria workers.....................	5.42	6.77	7.89	9.02	10.33	11.60	11.94	12.18	12.23
Bus drivers...........................	7.27	9.21	10.69	12.48	14.18	16.56	16.44	16.62	16.61

X Not applicable.

Source: Editorial Projects in Education and Educational Research Service, Bethesda MD, *National Survey of Salaries and Wages in Public Schools*, ©. See also <http://www.edweek.org/ew/marketplace/products/ers/publications.html>.

Table 279. English as a Second Language (ESL)—Public High School Learners, Programs, and Services by District Characteristics: 2016

[In percent, except where noted. For school year ending in year shown. Programs and services only shown for districts with English learners at the high school level. Based on a survey conducted using the Fast Response Survey System]

District characteristics	Number of high school English learners	Percent of districts with high school English learners	Districts with English learners with programs and services					
			Bilingual instruction for English learners only in content classes	English as a Second Language (ESL)		Instructional support by a paraprofessional who—		Sheltered English/ content instruction [2]
				Instruction in scheduled class periods	Push-in or pull-out instruction [1]	Does not speak student's native language	Speaks student's native language	
All public school districts....	**774,500**	**62**	**8**	**68**	**61**	**33**	**31**	**47**
District enrollment size:								
Less than 1,000................	8,200	29	[3] 8	44	58	32	25	34
1,000 to 2,499.................	34,900	69	6	59	60	30	27	38
2,500 to 9,999.................	150,700	95	8	77	64	32	31	52
10,000 or more.................	580,800	100	13	93	62	46	55	76
Community type:								
City...........................	354,400	100	14	89	64	47	55	81
Suburban......................	319,200	90	9	84	62	35	30	53
Town..........................	58,100	74	7	64	61	27	33	50
Rural..........................	42,800	42	5	50	61	32	26	32
Region:								
Northeast......................	115,400	67	8	82	71	25	16	46
Southeast......................	127,000	77	5	59	67	25	24	46
Central........................	116,000	47	9	58	63	41	35	34
West..........................	416,100	71	8	71	51	36	43	62

[1] During push-in instruction the ESL instructor works with students within an ongoing content class; during pull-out instruction students move out of an ongoing class for an ESL session. [2] Regular grade-level instruction in core content areas is provided in English through instructional strategies that make the academic content accessible to English learner students while also assisting them to acquire academic English. [3] Interpret data with caution.

Source: U.S. National Center for Education Statistics, *Programs and Services for High School English Learners in Public School Districts: 2015-16*, September 2016. See also <https://nces.ed.gov/pubsearch/pubsinfo.asp?pubid=2016150>.

Table 280. SAT Scores and Characteristics of College-Bound Seniors: 1980 to 2016

[For school year ending in year shown. Data are for the SAT I: Reasoning Tests. SAT I: Reasoning Test replaced the SAT in March 1994. Scores between the two tests have been equated to the same 200–800 scale and are thus comparable. Scores for 1995 and prior years have been recentered and revised]

Type of test and characteristic	Unit	1980	1990	2000	2005	2010 [2]	2012	2013	2014	2015	2016 [5]
AVERAGE TEST SCORES [1]											
Critical reading, total..............	Point	502	500	505	508	500	496	496	497	495	494
Male................................	Point	506	505	507	513	502	498	499	499	497	495
Female..............................	Point	498	496	504	505	498	493	494	495	493	493
Math, total.........................	Point	492	501	514	520	515	514	514	513	511	508
Male................................	Point	515	521	533	538	533	532	531	530	527	524
Female..............................	Point	473	483	498	504	499	499	499	499	496	494
Writing.............................	Point	(X)	(X)	(X)	(X)	491	488	488	487	484	482
Male................................	Point	(X)	(X)	(X)	(X)	485	481	482	481	478	475
Female..............................	Point	(X)	(X)	(X)	(X)	497	494	493	492	490	487
PARTICIPANTS											
Total [3].........................	**1,000**	**991**	**1,026**	**1,260**	**1,476**	**1,597**	**1,664**	**1,660**	**1,672**	**1,699**	**1,638**
Male................................	Percent	48.3	47.8	46.3	46.5	46.8	46.7	46.8	46.9	46.8	46.5
White [4]............................	Percent	(NA)	73.4	66.4	62.3	56.3	53.0	50.3	49.2	47.1	45.3
Black [4]............................	Percent	(NA)	10.0	11.1	11.6	13.3	13.5	12.7	12.7	12.9	12.2
Obtaining scores of: [1]											
600 or above:											
Critical reading..................	Percent	(NA)	20.3	21.0	22.5	20.3	19.5	19.7	20.2	19.6	19.7
Math..............................	Percent	(NA)	20.4	24.2	26.5	25.2	25.6	25.1	25.3	24.8	24.1
Writing............................	Percent	(X)	(X)	(X)	(X)	18.2	17.8	17.9	17.9	17.6	16.9
Below 400:											
Critical reading..................	Percent	(NA)	17.3	15.9	15.5	17.8	19.0	18.5	19.0	19.4	19.7
Math..............................	Percent	(NA)	15.8	14.7	13.8	15.1	15.5	15.6	15.8	17.0	17.9
Writing............................	Percent	(X)	(X)	(X)	(X)	19.8	20.9	21.0	21.5	22.3	23.2

NA Not available. X Not applicable. [1] Minimum score, 200; maximum score, 800. [2] Beginning in 2007, data reflect examinees who tested through June of senior year. [3] 991 represents 991,000. [4] Non-response excluded from denominator. Non-responders are included in the total/ethnicity portion. [5] Data for 2016 seniors cover students who tested through January 2016.

Source: The College Board, *2016 College-Bound Seniors: Total Group Profile Report*, © 2016, and previous reports. Reproduced with permission. See also <http://www.collegeboard.com>.

Table 281. ACT Program Scores and Characteristics of College-Bound Students: 1990 to 2016

[For academic year ending in year shown. Except as indicated, test scores and characteristics of college-bound students. Through 1980, data based on 10 percent sample; thereafter, based on all ACT tested graduating seniors. Beginning 1990, not comparable with previous years because a new version of the ACT was introduced]

Type of test and characteristic	Unit	1990	1995	2000	2010	2011	2012	2013	2014	2015	2016
TEST SCORES [1]											
Composite.........................	**Point**	**20.6**	**20.8**	**21.0**	**21.0**	**21.1**	**21.1**	**20.9**	**21.0**	**21.0**	**20.8**
Male................................	Point	21.0	21.0	21.2	21.2	21.2	21.2	20.9	21.1	21.1	20.9
Female..............................	Point	20.3	20.7	20.9	20.9	21.0	21.0	20.9	20.9	21.0	20.9
English.............................	Point	20.5	20.2	20.5	20.5	20.6	20.5	20.2	20.3	20.4	20.1
Male................................	Point	20.1	19.8	20.0	20.1	20.2	20.2	19.8	20.0	20.0	19.8
Female..............................	Point	20.9	20.6	20.9	20.8	20.9	20.9	20.6	20.7	20.8	20.6
Math................................	Point	19.9	20.2	20.7	21.0	21.1	21.1	20.9	20.9	20.8	20.6
Male................................	Point	20.7	20.9	21.4	21.6	21.6	21.7	21.4	21.1	21.3	21.0
Female..............................	Point	19.3	19.7	20.2	20.5	20.6	20.6	20.5	20.5	20.4	20.3
Reading [2].........................	Point	(NA)	21.3	21.4	21.3	21.3	21.3	21.1	21.3	21.4	21.3
Male................................	Point	(NA)	21.1	21.2	21.1	21.1	21.2	20.9	21.1	21.2	21.0
Female..............................	Point	(NA)	21.4	21.5	21.4	21.4	21.4	21.4	21.5	21.6	21.6
Science reasoning [3]...............	Point	(NA)	21.0	21.0	20.9	20.9	20.9	20.7	20.8	20.9	20.8
Male................................	Point	(NA)	21.6	21.6	21.4	21.4	21.4	21.2	21.2	21.3	21.1
Female..............................	Point	(NA)	20.5	20.6	20.5	20.5	20.5	20.4	20.5	20.6	20.6
PARTICIPANTS [4]											
Total [5].........................	**1,000**	**817**	**945**	**1,065**	**1,569**	**1,623**	**1,666**	**1,799**	**1,846**	**1,924**	**2,090**
Male................................	Percent	46	44	43	45	46	46	46	46	47	46
White...............................	Percent	73	69	72	62	60	59	58	56	55	54
Black...............................	Percent	9	9	10	14	14	13	13	13	13	13
Obtaining composite scores of: [6]											
27 or above.......................	Percent	12	13	14	16	17	17	16	17	18	14
18 or below.......................	Percent	35	34	32	35	34	34	36	36	37	39

NA Not available. [1] Minimum score, 1; maximum score, 36. [2] Prior to 1990, social studies; data not comparable with previous years. [3] Prior to 1990, natural sciences; data not comparable with previous years. [4] Beginning 1985, data are for seniors who graduated in year shown and had taken the ACT in their sophomore, junior, or senior years. Data by race are for those responding to the race question. [5] 817 represents 817,000. [6] Prior to 1990, 26 or above and 15 or below.

Source: ACT, Inc., Iowa City, IA, Most recent score reported in the *The ACT® Profile Report - National*, annual ©. Reproduced with permission.

Table 282. Proficiency Levels on Selected NAEP Tests for Students in Public Schools by State: 2015

[Represents percent of public school students scoring at or above basic and proficient levels. Basic denotes partial mastery of the knowledge and skills that are fundamental for proficient work at a given grade level. Proficient represents solid academic performance. Students reaching this level demonstrated competency over challenging subject matter. For more detail, see <http://nationsreportcard.gov/>. Based on the National Assessment of Educational Progress (NAEP) tests which are administered to a representative sample of students in public schools, private schools, and Department of Defense schools]

State	Grade 4 Math		Grade 8 Math		Grade 4 Reading		Grade 8 Reading	
	At or above Basic	At or above Proficient	At or above Basic	At or above Proficient	At or above Basic	At or above Proficient	At or above Basic	At or above Proficient
U.S. average	**81**	**39**	**70**	**32**	**68**	**35**	**75**	**33**
Alabama	75	26	56	17	65	29	71	26
Alaska	78	35	71	32	61	30	71	31
Arizona	79	38	72	35	62	30	74	31
Arkansas	79	32	66	25	65	32	70	27
California	72	29	64	27	59	28	70	28
Colorado	82	43	73	37	71	39	78	38
Connecticut	81	41	72	36	74	43	82	43
Delaware	82	37	69	30	70	37	73	31
District of Columbia	69	31	51	19	56	27	56	19
Florida	85	42	64	26	75	39	75	30
Georgia	78	35	67	28	68	34	73	30
Hawaii	79	38	70	30	61	29	68	26
Idaho	80	38	75	34	69	36	81	37
Illinois	77	37	72	32	68	35	77	35
Indiana	89	50	77	39	75	40	80	37
Iowa	84	44	76	37	71	38	81	36
Kansas	83	41	76	33	68	35	79	35
Kentucky	84	40	68	28	75	40	78	36
Louisiana	78	30	57	18	63	29	66	23
Maine	85	41	76	35	71	36	81	36
Maryland	79	40	71	35	68	37	76	37
Massachusetts	90	54	81	51	82	50	83	46
Michigan	77	34	68	29	63	29	76	32
Minnesota	87	53	82	48	71	39	81	40
Mississippi	78	30	60	22	60	26	63	20
Missouri	82	38	71	31	70	36	77	36
Montana	84	41	79	39	72	37	82	37
Nebraska	86	46	77	38	74	40	81	38
Nevada	76	32	65	26	61	29	71	27
New Hampshire	91	51	84	46	79	46	85	45
New Jersey	86	47	79	46	75	43	80	41
New Mexico	73	27	61	21	54	23	65	20
New York	79	35	69	31	68	36	73	33
North Carolina	85	44	69	33	73	38	72	30
North Dakota	88	45	80	39	73	37	80	34
Ohio	85	45	75	35	72	38	76	36
Oklahoma	84	37	67	23	71	33	76	29
Oregon	79	37	73	34	67	34	79	36
Pennsylvania	83	45	72	36	74	41	78	39
Rhode Island	80	37	72	32	72	40	76	35
South Carolina	79	36	65	26	65	33	71	28
South Dakota	83	40	77	34	68	35	80	34
Tennessee	82	40	68	29	66	33	76	33
Texas	86	44	75	32	64	31	72	28
Utah	84	44	76	38	74	40	81	38
Vermont	85	43	79	42	76	45	83	44
Virginia	87	47	76	38	74	43	77	36
Washington	83	47	74	39	71	40	77	37
West Virginia	78	33	62	21	64	30	72	27
Wisconsin	83	45	78	41	71	37	79	39
Wyoming	88	48	78	35	75	41	81	36

Source: U.S. National Center for Education Statistics, "National Assessment of Educational Progress (NAEP), 2015 Mathematics and Reading Assessments," <http://nces.ed.gov/nationsreportcard/naepdata/dataset.aspx>, accessed January 2016.

Table 283. Public High School Graduates by State: 1980 to 2014

[In thousands (2,747.7 represents 2,747,700). For school year ending in year shown. Data include regular diploma recipients, but exclude students receiving a certificate of attendance and persons receiving high school equivalency certificates]

State	1980	1990	2000	2009	2010	2012	2013	2014 (P)
United States...........	2,747.7	[2] 2,320.3	2,553.8	[2] 3,039.0	3,128.0	3,149.2	3,169.3	3,168.5
Alabama.......................	45.2	40.5	37.8	42.1	43.2	45.4	44.2	44.5
Alaska.........................	5.2	5.4	6.6	8.0	8.2	8.0	7.9	7.7
Arizona........................	28.6	32.1	38.3	62.4	61.1	63.2	62.2	66.7
Arkansas......................	29.1	26.5	27.3	28.1	28.3	28.4	28.9	29.6
California.....................	249.2	236.3	309.9	372.3	405.0	418.7	422.1	424.1
Colorado......................	36.8	33.0	38.9	47.5	49.3	50.1	51.0	51.3
Connecticut..................	37.7	27.9	31.6	35.0	34.5	38.7	38.7	37.9
Delaware......................	7.6	5.6	6.1	7.8	8.1	8.2	8.1	8.2
District of Columbia [1].......	5.0	3.6	2.7	3.5	3.6	3.9	4.0	3.9
Florida.........................	87.3	88.9	106.7	153.5	156.1	152.0	158.0	158.4
Georgia........................	61.6	56.6	62.6	88.0	91.6	90.6	92.4	94.4
Hawaii.........................	11.5	10.3	10.4	11.5	11.0	11.4	10.8	11.1
Idaho..........................	13.2	12.0	16.2	16.8	17.8	17.6	17.2	19.1
Illinois.........................	135.6	108.1	111.8	131.7	139.0	139.6	139.2	137.6
Indiana........................	73.1	60.0	57.0	63.7	64.6	65.7	66.6	67.6
Iowa...........................	43.4	31.8	33.9	33.9	34.5	33.2	32.5	32.6
Kansas........................	30.9	25.4	29.1	30.4	31.6	31.9	31.9	32.2
Kentucky......................	41.2	38.0	36.8	41.9	42.7	42.6	42.9	42.4
Louisiana.....................	46.3	36.1	38.4	35.6	36.6	36.7	37.5	38.2
Maine..........................	15.4	13.8	12.2	[3] 14.1	14.1	13.5	13.2	12.7
Maryland......................	54.3	41.6	47.8	58.3	59.1	58.8	58.9	58.1
Massachusetts...............	73.8	55.9	53.0	65.3	64.5	65.2	66.4	65.2
Michigan......................	124.3	93.8	97.7	112.7	110.7	105.4	104.2	102.5
Minnesota....................	64.9	49.1	57.4	59.7	59.7	57.5	58.3	56.4
Mississippi...................	27.6	25.2	24.2	24.5	25.5	26.2	26.5	26.7
Missouri.......................	62.3	49.0	52.8	63.0	64.0	61.3	61.4	60.9
Montana.......................	12.1	9.4	10.9	10.1	10.1	9.8	9.4	9.5
Nebraska......................	22.4	17.7	20.1	19.5	19.4	20.5	20.4	20.6
Nevada........................	8.5	9.5	14.6	19.9	21.0	21.9	23.0	22.7
New Hampshire..............	11.7	10.8	11.8	14.8	15.0	14.4	14.3	13.8
New Jersey...................	94.6	69.8	74.4	95.1	96.2	93.8	96.5	95.2
New Mexico..................	18.4	14.9	18.0	17.9	18.6	20.3	19.2	18.6
New York.....................	204.1	143.3	141.7	180.9	183.8	180.8	180.4	178.8
North Carolina...............	70.9	64.8	62.1	86.7	88.7	94.0	94.3	96.2
North Dakota.................	9.9	7.7	8.6	7.2	7.2	6.9	6.9	7.0
Ohio...........................	144.2	114.5	111.7	122.2	123.4	123.1	122.5	119.5
Oklahoma.....................	39.3	35.6	37.6	37.2	38.5	37.3	37.0	37.3
Oregon........................	29.9	25.5	30.2	35.1	34.7	34.3	33.9	34.4
Pennsylvania.................	146.5	110.5	114.0	130.7	131.2	131.7	129.8	127.2
Rhode Island.................	10.9	7.8	8.5	10.0	9.9	9.8	9.6	9.7
South Carolina...............	38.7	32.5	31.6	39.1	40.4	41.4	42.2	41.7
South Dakota................	10.7	7.7	9.3	8.1	8.2	8.2	8.2	8.0
Tennessee....................	49.8	46.1	41.6	60.4	62.4	62.5	61.3	61.0
Texas..........................	171.4	172.5	212.9	264.3	280.9	292.5	301.4	304.4
Utah...........................	20.0	21.2	32.5	30.5	31.5	31.2	33.2	33.4
Vermont.......................	6.7	6.1	6.7	7.2	7.2	6.9	6.5	6.4
Virginia........................	66.6	60.6	65.6	79.7	81.5	83.3	83.3	83.1
Washington...................	50.4	45.9	57.6	62.8	66.0	65.2	66.1	66.2
West Virginia.................	23.4	21.9	19.4	17.7	17.7	17.6	17.9	17.5
Wisconsin.....................	69.3	52.0	58.5	65.4	64.7	62.7	61.4	60.8
Wyoming......................	6.1	5.8	6.5	5.5	5.7	5.6	5.5	5.6

P Projected. [1] Beginning in 1990, graduates from adult programs are excluded. [2] U.S. total includes estimates for nonreporting states. [3] Includes 1,169 graduates in 2008-09 from private high schools that received a majority of their funding from public sources.

Source: U.S. National Center for Education Statistics, *Digest of Education Statistics*, "Advance Release of Selected 2016 Digest Tables," and earlier releases, <http://www.nces.ed.gov/programs/digest/>, accessed July 2017.

Table 284. High School Dropouts by Race and Hispanic Origin: 1980 to 2015

[In percent. As of October. Dropouts are persons 18 to 24 years old who have not completed high school and are not enrolled, regardless of when they dropped out]

Item	1980	1985	1990 [1]	1995	2000	2005	2010	2012	2013	2014	2015
Total [2]...........................	15.6	13.9	14.4	13.9	12.4	11.3	8.7	7.6	7.3	6.9	6.4
White [3].............................	14.4	13.5	14.1	13.6	12.2	11.3	8.5	7.2	7.1	7.1	6.4
Male...........................	15.7	14.7	15.4	14.3	13.5	13.2	9.7	8.1	7.5	7.6	7.0
Female........................	13.2	12.3	12.8	13.0	10.9	9.4	7.3	6.3	6.7	6.6	5.8
Black [3].............................	23.5	17.6	16.4	14.4	15.3	12.9	10.1	9.9	8.3	7.3	7.5
Male...........................	26.0	18.8	18.6	14.2	17.4	14.8	12.1	11.2	9.6	7.2	7.3
Female........................	21.5	16.6	14.5	14.6	13.5	11.2	8.2	8.5	7.0	7.4	7.7
Hispanic [4].........................	40.3	31.5	37.7	34.7	32.3	27.3	18.5	15.2	13.7	11.8	10.4
Male...........................	42.6	35.8	40.3	34.2	36.8	32.1	21.3	16.9	14.8	12.8	11.1
Female........................	38.1	27.0	35.0	35.4	27.3	21.8	15.4	13.2	12.6	10.9	9.6

[1] Beginning 1990, reflects new editing procedures for cases with missing data on school enrollment. [2] Includes other races, not shown separately. [3] Beginning 2003, for persons who selected this race group only. See footnote 4, Table 251. [4] Persons of Hispanic origin may be of any race.

Source: U.S. Census Bureau, Current Population Reports, P-20, and earlier reports; and "School Enrollment," <http://www.census.gov/hhes/school/index.html>, accessed November 2016.

Table 285. High School Dropouts by Age, Race, and Hispanic Origin: 1980 to 2015

[5,212 represents 5,212,000. As of October. For persons 14 to 24 years old. Dropouts are persons not in regular school and who have not completed the 12th grade nor received a general equivalency degree. Based on Current Population Survey; see text, Section 1 and Appendix III]

Age and race	Number of dropouts (1,000)					Percent of population				
	1980	1990	2000	2010	2015	1980	1990	2000	2010	2015
Total dropouts [1,2]......	**5,212**	**3,854**	**3,883**	**2,952**	**2,409**	**12.0**	**10.1**	**9.1**	**6.4**	**5.1**
16 to 17 years............	709	418	460	227	337	8.8	6.3	5.8	2.7	4.0
18 to 21 years............	2,578	1,921	2,005	1,445	1,135	15.8	13.4	12.9	8.4	6.7
22 to 24 years............	1,798	1,458	1,310	1,144	781	15.2	13.8	11.8	9.2	5.9
White [2,3]...............	4,169	3,127	3,065	2,232	1,802	11.3	10.1	9.1	6.3	5.2
16 to 17 years............	619	334	366	181	243	9.2	6.4	5.8	2.9	4.0
18 to 21 years............	2,032	1,516	1,558	1,048	848	14.7	13.1	12.6	8.0	6.8
22 to 24 years............	1,416	1,235	1,040	893	582	14.0	14.0	11.7	9.2	6.0
Black [2,3].................	934	611	705	498	411	16.0	10.9	10.9	7.2	5.7
16 to 17 years............	80	73	84	30	48	6.9	6.9	7.0	2.3	3.8
18 to 21 years............	486	345	383	283	202	23.0	16.0	16.0	10.5	7.8
22 to 24 years............	346	185	232	167	144	24.0	13.5	14.3	9.4	7.1
Hispanic [2,4].............	919	1,122	1,499	1,122	826	29.5	26.8	23.5	12.8	8.0
16 to 17 years............	92	89	121	40	102	16.6	12.9	11.0	2.7	5.2
18 to 21 years............	470	502	733	506	369	40.3	32.9	30.0	15.2	9.9
22 to 24 years............	323	523	602	543	301	40.6	42.8	35.5	23.2	11.0

[1] Includes other groups not shown separately. [2] Includes persons 14 to 15 years not shown separately. [3] Beginning 2003, for persons who selected this race only. See footnote 4, Table 251. [4] Persons of Hispanic origin may be of any race.

Source: U.S. Census Bureau, Current Population Reports, series PPL and P-20; and "School Enrollment," <http://www.census.gov/hhes/school/data/index.html>, accessed November 2016.

Table 286. School Enrollment Status by Race, Hispanic Origin, and Sex: 2010 and 2015

[17,210 represents 17,210,000. As of October. For persons 18 to 21 years old. For the civilian noninstitutional population. Based on the Current Population Survey; see text, Section 1 and Appendix III]

Characteristic	Total persons 18 to 21 years old (1,000)		Percent distribution							
			Enrolled in high school		High school graduates				Not high school graduates and not enrolled in high school	
					Total		In college			
	2010	2015	2010	2015	2010	2015	2010	2015	2010	2015
Total [1]...........................	**17,210**	**16,860**	**9.9**	**10.1**	**81.5**	**82.9**	**50.6**	**50.3**	**8.4**	**6.7**
White..................................	13,176	12,475	9.7	9.9	82.2	83.1	50.8	51.0	8.0	6.8
Black..................................	2,538	2,602	13.9	11.3	73.0	80.3	41.5	41.7	13.0	7.8
Hispanic [2]...........................	3,339	3,723	13.5	10.7	71.3	79.4	38.9	45.8	15.2	9.9
Male [1]..............................	**8,824**	**8,476**	**11.0**	**11.0**	**79.8**	**81.5**	**46.7**	**46.6**	**9.0**	**7.5**
White..................................	6,867	6,353	10.8	10.6	80.4	81.7	46.6	47.2	8.7	7.6
Black..................................	1,277	1,279	15.5	12.8	69.1	79.0	36.2	37.6	15.4	7.7
Hispanic [2]...........................	1,744	1,833	14.0	11.5	70.0	77.3	35.7	40.2	15.8	11.3
Female [1]...........................	**8,386**	**8,383**	**8.8**	**9.3**	**83.2**	**84.4**	**54.8**	**54.1**	**7.8**	**6.0**
White..................................	6,308	6,121	8.4	9.3	84.1	84.6	55.5	55.0	7.2	5.9
Black..................................	1,261	1,323	12.3	9.8	76.9	81.5	46.9	45.6	10.5	7.9
Hispanic [2]...........................	1,595	1,891	12.9	10.1	72.7	81.4	42.4	51.2	14.4	8.5

[1] Includes other races not shown separately. [2] Persons of Hispanic origin may be of any race.

Source: U.S. Census Bureau, Current Population Reports, P-20, and earlier reports; and "School Enrollment," <http://www.census.gov/hhes/school/index.html>, accessed November 2016.

Table 287. General Educational Development (GED) Credentials Issued: 1980 to 2013

[GEDs issued in thousands (479 represents 479,000). For the 50 states and DC]

Year	GEDs issued	Percent distribution of GED test takers				
		16 to 18 years old [1]	19 to 24 years old [1]	25 to 29 years old	30 to 34 years old	35 years old and over
1980.............................	479	37	27	13	8	15
1985.............................	413	32	26	15	10	16
1990.............................	410	22	39	13	10	15
1995.............................	504	27	36	13	9	15
2000.............................	487	33	37	11	7	13
2005.............................	424	34	37	12	7	11
2006.............................	398	35	36	12	6	11
2007.............................	429	35	35	12	7	11
2008.............................	469	34	35	13	7	11
2009.............................	448	31	36	13	8	12
2010.............................	452	27	37	14	9	14
2011.............................	434	27	37	13	9	14
2012.............................	401	26	37	14	9	13
2013.............................	541	22	35	15	11	17

[1] For 1985 and prior years, 19-year-olds are included with the 16- to 18-year-olds instead of the 19- to 24-year-olds.

Source: U.S. National Center for Education Statistics, 2014 Digest of Education Statistics, April 2016. See also <http://www.nces.ed.gov/programs/digest/>.

Table 288. Higher Education—Institutions and Enrollment: 1990 to 2015

[817 represents 817,000. As of Fall. Covers universities, colleges, professional schools, junior and teachers' colleges, both publicly and privately controlled, regular session. Includes estimates for institutions not reporting. Data for 1990 cover institutions of higher education; beginning 2000, data cover degree-granting institutions. Degree-granting institutions grant associate's or higher degrees and participate in Title IV federal financial aid programs. The degree-granting classification includes more 2-year colleges and excludes a few higher education institutions that did not grant degrees. Data are based on the Integrated Postsecondary Education Data System. See also Appendix III]

Item	Unit	1990	2000	2005	2010	2013	2014	2015
ALL INSTITUTIONS								
Number of institutions [1]	**Number**	**3,559**	**4,182**	**4,276**	**4,599**	**4,724**	**4,627**	**4,583**
4-year	Number	2,141	2,450	2,582	2,870	3,039	3,011	3,004
2-year	Number	1,418	1,732	1,694	1,729	1,685	1,616	1,579
Instructional staff—								
lecturer or above	**1,000**	**817**	**(NA)**	**1,290**	**(NA)**	**1,545**	**(NA)**	**1,551**
Percent full-time	Percent	61	(NA)	52	(NA)	51	(NA)	52
Total enrollment [2]	**1,000**	**13,819**	**15,312**	**17,487**	**21,019**	**20,377**	**20,207**	**19,977**
Male	1,000	6,284	6,722	7,456	9,046	8,861	8,797	8,721
Female	1,000	7,535	8,591	10,032	11,974	11,515	11,410	11,256
4-year institutions	1,000	8,579	9,364	10,999	13,336	13,406	13,493	13,486
2-year institutions	1,000	5,240	5,948	6,488	7,684	6,971	6,714	6,491
Full-time	1,000	7,821	9,010	10,797	13,087	12,597	12,454	12,291
Part-time	1,000	5,998	6,303	6,690	7,932	7,780	7,753	7,686
Public	1,000	10,845	11,753	13,022	15,142	14,747	14,655	14,568
Private	1,000	2,974	3,560	4,466	5,877	5,630	5,552	5,409
Not-for-profit	1,000	2,760	3,109	3,455	3,854	3,971	3,996	4,063
For profit	1,000	214	450	1,011	2,023	1,658	1,556	1,346
Undergraduate	1,000	11,959	13,155	14,964	18,079	17,475	17,293	17,037
Men	1,000	5,380	5,778	6,409	7,835	7,660	7,586	7,500
Women	1,000	6,579	7,377	8,555	10,244	9,815	9,707	9,537
First-time freshmen	1,000	2,257	2,428	2,657	3,157	2,985	2,925	2,881
Postbaccalaureate	1,000	1,860	2,157	2,524	2,937	2,900	2,915	2,940
Men	1,000	904	944	1,047	1,209	1,201	1,211	1,222
Women	1,000	955	1,213	1,476	1,728	1,699	1,703	1,719
2-YEAR INSTITUTIONS								
Number of institutions [1]	Number	1,418	1,732	1,694	1,729	1,685	1,616	1,579
Public	Number	972	1,076	1,053	978	934	920	910
Private	Number	446	656	641	751	751	696	669
Instructional staff—								
lecturer or above	1,000	(NA)	(NA)	373	(NA)	394	(NA)	371
Enrollment [2]	1,000	5,240	5,948	6,488	7,684	6,971	6,714	6,491
Public	1,000	4,996	5,697	6,184	7,218	6,626	6,398	6,216
Private	1,000	244	251	304	466	344	317	275
Male	1,000	2,233	2,559	2,680	3,266	2,998	2,894	2,816
Female	1,000	3,007	3,390	3,808	4,418	3,971	3,821	3,675
4-YEAR INSTITUTIONS								
Number of institutions [1]	Number	2,141	2,450	2,582	2,870	3,039	3,011	3,004
Public	Number	595	622	640	678	691	701	710
Private	Number	1,546	1,828	1,942	2,192	2,348	2,310	2,294
Instructional staff—								
lecturer or above	1,000	(NA)	(NA)	917	(NA)	1,152	(NA)	1,180
Enrollment [2]	1,000	8,579	9,364	10,999	13,336	13,406	13,493	13,486
Public	1,000	5,848	6,055	6,838	7,924	8,120	8,257	8,352
Private	1,000	2,730	3,308	4,162	5,412	5,286	5,236	5,134
Male	1,000	4,051	4,163	4,776	5,780	5,863	5,903	5,905
Female	1,000	4,527	5,201	6,224	7,556	7,544	7,590	7,581

NA Not available. [1] Number of institutions includes count of branch campuses. Includes schools accredited by the National Association of Trade and Technical Schools. [2] Branch campuses counted according to actual status, e.g., 2-year branch in 2-year category. May include unclassified students taking courses for credit but not towards a degree.

Source: U.S. National Center for Education Statistics, *Digest of Education Statistics*, "Advance Release of Selected 2016 Digest Tables," and earlier releases, <http://nces.ed.gov/Programs/digest/>, accessed May 2017.

Table 289. Degree-Granting Higher Education Institutions, Number and Enrollment by State and Selected Characteristics: 2015

[19,977 represents 19,977,000. Number of institutions beginning in academic year. Opening Fall enrollment of resident and extension students attending full-time or part-time. Based on data from the Integrated Postsecondary Education Data System (IPEDS)]

State	Number of institutions [1]	Enrollment (1,000) Total	Male	Female	Public	Private	Full-time	White [2]	Minority Total [3]	Minority Black [2]	Minority Hispanic	Non-resident alien
United States........	**4,583**	**19,977**	**8,721**	**11,256**	**14,568**	**5,409**	**12,291**	**10,937**	**7,398**	**2,675**	**3,292**	**983**
Alabama...............	77	303	131	172	247	56	207	187	102	84	10	8
Alaska................	9	31	13	19	28	3	15	19	9	1	3	1
Arizona...............	86	650	256	394	361	289	408	323	274	91	142	20
Arkansas..............	53	168	71	98	150	18	106	115	42	28	10	6
California.............	448	2,688	1,220	1,468	2,203	485	1,487	800	1,630	183	1,024	138
Colorado..............	87	348	155	193	266	82	199	226	97	25	54	11
Connecticut...........	43	200	86	114	120	80	129	119	64	26	28	11
Delaware..............	9	60	24	36	41	20	38	34	19	13	4	5
District of Columbia....	20	94	38	56	5	89	64	42	39	25	7	10
Florida................	229	1,083	459	625	794	289	613	495	513	200	271	44
Georgia...............	130	531	218	313	418	113	346	260	236	173	35	21
Hawaii................	20	69	29	40	56	14	41	12	36	2	8	4
Idaho.................	19	121	53	68	72	49	61	93	14	1	10	10
Illinois................	185	802	348	454	509	293	464	441	301	110	136	42
Indiana...............	84	426	191	236	322	105	275	309	79	43	23	27
Iowa..................	64	275	119	156	171	104	160	202	55	27	19	13
Kansas...............	75	220	101	119	180	40	133	150	49	21	19	13
Kentucky.............	72	256	109	147	206	50	162	206	36	23	8	7
Louisiana.............	64	245	100	145	211	33	166	136	95	75	12	8
Maine................	31	72	30	42	47	24	45	61	7	3	2	2
Maryland..............	58	364	161	203	304	60	191	171	160	102	30	20
Massachusetts.........	124	510	222	289	222	288	353	301	139	45	54	55
Michigan..............	103	600	271	330	502	98	355	422	127	75	26	33
Minnesota............	115	428	169	259	256	172	232	289	110	63	22	15
Mississippi...........	41	172	69	104	153	19	129	95	71	65	3	3
Missouri..............	125	410	178	232	249	161	255	292	84	51	19	22
Montana..............	22	51	24	27	46	5	37	41	7	0	2	2
Nebraska.............	42	136	61	76	100	36	89	102	25	7	13	6
Nevada...............	26	116	50	66	104	12	63	55	52	9	28	2
New Hampshire........	27	124	50	74	43	81	71	93	25	13	8	3
New Jersey............	72	424	194	230	340	84	277	207	187	61	86	21
New Mexico...........	43	138	59	79	131	7	71	47	84	4	64	4
New York..............	304	1,285	562	723	709	576	901	631	522	179	217	105
North Carolina.........	150	562	235	327	448	114	361	331	196	133	38	20
North Dakota..........	20	54	27	27	48	6	37	43	6	2	2	3
Ohio..................	208	668	295	372	505	163	426	492	123	79	25	34
Oklahoma.............	67	211	93	118	179	32	138	125	58	19	16	11
Oregon...............	63	241	109	132	198	43	149	161	54	8	28	12
Pennsylvania..........	256	737	326	411	409	328	534	498	173	85	48	46
Rhode Island..........	13	82	35	47	41	41	62	54	20	6	10	5
South Carolina........	77	250	104	146	202	47	172	158	80	65	10	5
South Dakota..........	25	54	24	30	44	9	33	44	7	2	2	2
Tennessee............	105	323	138	186	223	100	232	221	83	62	13	10
Texas.................	272	1,571	689	881	1,379	191	837	602	853	200	556	73
Utah.................	36	294	137	156	171	122	208	223	54	12	28	8
Vermont..............	24	44	20	24	25	18	32	36	5	1	2	2
Virginia...............	131	570	247	323	394	176	348	328	203	119	45	18
Washington...........	86	365	165	200	315	51	250	221	97	16	41	23
West Virginia..........	44	151	77	74	86	64	77	113	29	17	8	4
Wisconsin.............	84	350	155	196	282	68	220	272	57	20	21	12
Wyoming..............	10	34	16	18	34	1	19	28	4	(Z)	3	1
U.S. military [4]..........	5	15	11	3	15	(X)	15	10	4	1	2	(Z)

X Not applicable. Z Fewer than 500. [1] Branch campuses counted as separate institutions. [2] Non-Hispanic. [3] Includes other races not shown separately. [4] Service academies.

Source: U.S. National Center for Education Statistics, *Digest of Education Statistics*, "Advance Release of Selected 2016 Digest Tables," <http://www.nces.ed.gov/programs/digest/>, accessed May 2017.

Table 290. College Enrollment of Recent High School Completers: 1970 to 2015

[2,758 represents 2,758,000. For persons 16 to 24 years old who graduated from high school in the preceding 12 months. Includes persons receiving GEDs. Based on sample surveys and subject to sampling error; data not comparable with that in other tables]

Year	Number of high school completers (1,000)						Percent enrolled in college [5]					
	Total [1]	Male	Female	White [2]	Black [2,3]	His-panic [3,4]	Total [1]	Male	Female	White [2]	Black [2,3]	His-panic [3,4]
1970	2,758	1,343	1,415	2,461	(NA)	(NA)	51.7	55.2	48.5	52.0	(NA)	(NA)
1975	3,185	1,513	1,672	2,701	302	132	50.7	52.6	49.0	51.1	41.7	58.0
1980	3,088	1,498	1,589	2,554	350	130	49.3	46.7	51.8	49.8	42.7	52.3
1985	2,668	1,287	1,381	2,104	332	141	57.7	58.6	56.8	60.1	42.2	51.0
1990	2,362	1,173	1,189	1,819	331	121	60.1	58.0	62.2	63.0	46.8	42.7
1991	2,276	1,140	1,136	1,727	310	154	62.5	57.9	67.1	65.4	46.4	57.2
1992	2,397	1,216	1,180	1,724	354	198	61.9	60.0	63.8	64.3	48.2	55.0
1993	2,342	1,120	1,223	1,719	304	201	62.6	59.9	65.2	62.9	55.6	62.2
1994	2,517	1,244	1,273	1,915	316	178	61.9	60.6	63.2	64.5	50.8	49.1
1995	2,599	1,238	1,361	1,861	349	288	61.9	62.6	61.3	64.3	51.2	53.7
1996	2,660	1,297	1,363	1,875	406	227	65.0	60.1	69.7	67.4	56.0	50.8
1997	2,769	1,354	1,415	1,909	384	336	67.0	63.6	70.3	68.2	58.5	65.6
1998	2,810	1,452	1,358	1,980	386	314	65.6	62.4	69.1	68.5	61.9	47.4
1999	2,897	1,474	1,423	1,978	436	329	62.9	61.4	64.4	66.3	58.9	42.3
2000	2,756	1,251	1,505	1,938	393	300	63.3	59.9	66.2	65.7	54.9	52.9
2001	2,549	1,277	1,273	1,834	381	241	61.8	60.1	63.5	64.3	55.0	51.7
2002	2,796	1,412	1,384	1,903	382	344	65.2	62.1	68.4	69.1	59.4	53.6
2003	2,677	1,306	1,372	1,832	327	314	63.9	61.2	66.5	66.2	57.5	58.6
2004	2,752	1,327	1,425	1,854	398	286	66.7	61.4	71.5	68.8	62.5	61.8
2005	2,675	1,262	1,414	1,799	345	390	68.6	66.5	70.4	73.2	55.7	54.0
2006	2,692	1,328	1,363	1,805	318	382	66.0	65.8	66.1	68.5	55.5	57.9
2007	2,955	1,511	1,444	2,043	416	355	67.2	66.1	68.3	69.5	55.7	64.0
2008	3,151	1,640	1,511	2,091	416	458	68.6	65.9	71.6	71.7	55.7	63.9
2009	2,937	1,407	1,531	1,863	415	459	70.1	66.0	73.8	71.3	69.5	59.3
2010	3,160	1,679	1,482	1,937	461	507	68.1	62.8	74.0	70.5	62.0	59.7
2011	3,079	1,611	1,468	1,747	464	623	68.2	64.7	72.2	68.3	67.1	66.6
2012	3,203	1,622	1,581	(NA)	(NA)	(NA)	66.2	61.3	71.3	65.7	56.4	70.3
2013	2,977	1,524	1,453	(NA)	(NA)	(NA)	65.9	63.5	68.4	68.8	56.7	59.8
2014	2,868	1,423	1,445	(NA)	(NA)	(NA)	68.4	64.0	72.6	67.7	70.2	65.2
2015	2,965	1,448	1,516	(NA)	(NA)	(NA)	69.2	65.8	72.5	71.3	55.6	68.9

NA Not available. [1] Includes other races not shown separately. [2] Beginning 2003, for persons of this race group only. See footnote 4, Table 251. [3] Due to small sample size, data are subject to relatively large sampling errors. [4] Persons of Hispanic origin may be of any race. [5] As of October.

Source: U.S. National Center for Education Statistics, *Digest of Education Statistics*, "Advance Release of Selected 2016 Digest Tables," <http://www.nces.ed.gov/programs/digest/>, accessed December 2016.

Table 291. College Enrollment by Sex and Attendance Status: 2005 to 2015

[In thousands (17,487 represents 17,487,000). As of Fall. Includes enrollment at branch campuses, some additional (primarily 2-year) colleges, and excludes a few institutions that did not award degrees. Includes enrollment at institutions that were eligible to participate in Title IV federal financial aid programs. Includes unclassified students (students taking courses for credit, but are not candidates for degrees)]

Sex and age	2005		2010		2013		2014		2015 (P)	
	Total	Part-time	Total	Part-time	Total	Part-time	Total	Part-time	Total	Part-time
Total	**17,487**	**6,690**	**21,019**	**7,932**	**20,376**	**7,779**	**20,207**	**7,753**	**20,264**	**7,779**
Male	7,456	2,653	9,046	3,207	8,861	3,179	8,797	3,178	8,760	3,122
14 to 17 years old	68	15	94	23	125	20	126	20	114	16
18 to 19 years old	1,523	184	1,820	245	1,661	239	1,639	239	1,688	297
20 to 21 years old	1,658	260	1,948	362	1,955	413	1,932	409	2,034	451
22 to 24 years old	1,410	428	1,723	508	1,846	576	1,803	554	1,799	538
25 to 29 years old	1,057	551	1,410	695	1,356	622	1,376	632	1,329	596
30 to 34 years old	591	365	731	430	634	377	621	387	565	350
35 years old and over	1,149	850	1,320	944	1,283	932	1,300	936	1,231	874
Female	10,032	4,038	11,974	4,725	11,515	4,600	11,410	4,576	11,503	4,657
14 to 17 years old	119	21	108	9	131	27	130	28	137	53
18 to 19 years old	1,920	233	2,237	316	2,059	283	2,055	257	2,193	288
20 to 21 years old	1,905	327	2,155	377	2,228	443	2,142	405	2,258	564
22 to 24 years old	1,704	564	2,036	666	2,118	738	2,187	816	2,163	804
25 to 29 years old	1,413	745	1,844	953	1,694	900	1,640	857	1,625	827
30 to 34 years old	847	526	1,074	630	972	564	931	548	906	546
35 years old and over	2,123	1,623	2,520	1,774	2,314	1,646	2,325	1,664	2,221	1,575

P Projected.

Source: U.S. National Center for Education Statistics, *2015 Digest of Education Statistics,* December 2016. See also <http://www.nces.ed.gov/programs/digest/>.

Table 292. College Enrollment by Selected Characteristics: 1990 to 2015

[In thousands (13,818.6 represents 13,818,600). As of Fall. Nonresident alien students are not distributed among racial/ethnic groups. Beginning in 2000, data reflect a new classification of institutions; this classification includes some additional, primarily 2-year, colleges and excludes a few institutions that did not award degrees. Includes institutions that were eligible to participate in Title IV federal financial aid programs and schools accredited by the National Association of Trade and Technical Schools. Based on data from the Integrated Postsecondary Education Data System (IPEDS)]

Characteristic	1990	2000	2005	2010	2013	2014	2015
Total.	13,818.6	15,312.3	17,487.5	21,019.4	20,376.7	20,207.4	19,977.3
Male.	6,283.9	6,721.8	7,455.9	9,045.8	8,861.2	8,797.1	8,721.4
Female.	7,534.7	8,590.5	10,031.6	11,973.7	11,515.5	11,410.3	11,255.9
Public.	10,844.7	11,752.8	13,021.8	15,142.2	14,746.8	14,655.0	14,568.1
Private.	2,973.9	3,559.5	4,465.6	5,877.3	5,629.8	5,552.4	5,409.2
2-year.	5,240.1	5,948.4	6,488.1	7,683.6	6,970.6	6,714.5	6,490.9
4-year.	8,578.6	9,363.9	10,999.4	13,335.8	13,406.0	13,492.9	13,486.3
Undergraduate.	11,959.2	13,155.4	14,964.0	18,082.4	17,476.3	17,292.8	17,036.8
Postbaccalaureate.	1,859.6	2,156.9	2,523.5	2,937.0	2,900.4	2,914.6	2,940.5
White [1]	**10,722.5**	**10,462.1**	**11,495.4**	**12,720.8**	**11,589.4**	**11,237.4**	**10,937.1**
Male.	4,861.0	4,634.6	5,007.2	5,605.8	5,132.4	4,973.7	4,848.0
Female.	5,861.5	5,827.5	6,488.2	7,115.0	6,457.0	6,263.7	6,089.0
Public.	8,385.4	7,963.4	8,518.2	9,182.1	8,363.3	8,119.5	7,913.0
Private.	2,337.0	2,498.7	2,977.3	3,538.7	3,226.1	3,117.9	3,024.0
2-year.	3,954.3	3,804.1	3,998.6	4,321.3	3,635.2	3,409.8	3,225.0
4-year.	6,768.1	6,658.0	7,496.9	8,399.5	7,954.2	7,827.6	7,712.0
Undergraduate.	9,272.6	8,983.5	9,828.6	10,895.9	9,898.1	9,581.5	9,302.4
Postbaccalaureate.	1,449.9	1,478.6	1,666.8	1,824.9	1,691.3	1,655.9	1,634.6
Black [1]	**1,247.0**	**1,730.3**	**2,214.6**	**3,039.0**	**2,872.0**	**2,791.9**	**2,675.4**
Male.	484.7	635.3	774.1	1,089.0	1,064.9	1,034.7	997.7
Female.	762.3	1,095.0	1,440.4	1,949.9	1,807.1	1,757.2	1,677.7
Public.	976.4	1,319.2	1,580.4	1,988.8	1,886.5	1,839.7	1,770.4
Private.	270.6	411.1	634.2	1,050.2	985.6	952.2	904.9
2-year.	524.3	734.9	901.1	1,198.9	1,072.8	1,013.7	935.5
4-year.	722.8	995.4	1,313.4	1,840.0	1,799.2	1,778.2	1,739.8
Undergraduate.	1,147.2	1,548.9	1,955.4	2,677.1	2,504.7	2,425.8	2,311.1
Postbaccalaureate.	99.8	181.4	259.2	361.9	367.3	366.0	364.3
Hispanic.	**782.4**	**1,461.8**	**1,882.0**	**2,748.8**	**3,093.2**	**3,191.7**	**3,292.2**
Male.	353.9	627.1	774.6	1,157.6	1,307.7	1,347.9	1,387.3
Female.	428.5	834.7	1,107.3	1,591.2	1,785.5	1,843.8	1,904.9
Public.	671.4	1,229.3	1,525.6	2,163.8	2,479.4	2,580.4	2,689.4
Private.	111.0	232.5	356.4	585.0	613.8	611.3	602.8
2-year.	424.2	843.9	981.5	1,393.0	1,493.5	1,520.9	1,550.4
4-year.	358.2	617.9	900.5	1,355.9	1,599.6	1,670.8	1,741.8
Undergraduate.	724.6	1,351.0	1,733.6	2,551.0	2,872.2	2,961.9	3,049.6
Postbaccalaureate.	57.9	110.8	148.4	197.8	221.0	229.8	242.6
American Indian/Alaska Native [1]	**102.8**	**151.2**	**176.3**	**196.2**	**162.2**	**152.9**	**146.2**
Male.	43.1	61.4	68.4	78.7	64.7	61.3	58.2
Female.	59.7	89.7	107.9	117.5	97.5	91.6	88.0
Public.	90.4	127.3	143.0	150.8	124.4	117.8	113.8
Private.	12.4	23.9	33.3	45.5	37.8	35.1	32.4
2-year.	54.9	74.7	80.7	87.2	70.8	65.9	62.9
4-year.	47.9	76.5	95.6	109.0	91.4	87.0	83.3
Undergraduate.	95.5	138.5	160.4	179.1	147.4	138.6	132.3
Postbaccalaureate.	7.3	12.6	15.9	17.1	14.8	14.3	13.9
Asian/Pacific Islander [1]	**572.4**	**978.2**	**1,134.4**	**1,281.6**	**1,259.7**	**1,272.4**	**1,283.8**
Male.	294.9	465.9	522.0	600.6	594.3	599.2	602.8
Female.	277.5	512.3	612.4	681.0	665.4	673.2	681.0
Public.	461.0	770.5	881.9	968.7	944.9	956.3	969.3
Private.	111.5	207.7	252.4	312.8	314.8	316.1	314.5
2-year.	215.2	401.9	434.4	463.1	416.0	407.5	401.1
4-year.	357.2	576.3	700.0	818.5	843.7	864.9	882.8
Undergraduate.	500.5	845.5	971.4	1,087.3	1,064.5	1,075.0	1,083.4
Postbaccalaureate.	71.9	132.6	163.0	194.3	195.2	197.4	200.4
Nonresident alien.	**391.5**	**528.7**	**584.8**	**707.7**	**840.2**	**918.9**	**983.1**
Male.	246.3	297.3	309.5	379.6	460.1	510.5	548.9
Female.	145.2	231.4	275.3	328.0	380.1	408.4	434.2
Public.	260.0	343.1	372.8	453.0	534.5	588.2	627.8
Private.	131.4	185.6	212.0	254.7	305.7	330.7	355.3
2-year.	67.1	89.0	91.8	99.3	92.1	96.2	105.0
4-year.	324.3	439.7	493.1	608.3	748.0	822.7	878.1
Undergraduate.	218.7	288.0	314.7	398.4	483.6	530.4	565.8
Postbaccalaureate.	172.7	240.7	270.1	309.3	356.5	388.5	417.3

[1] Non-Hispanic.

Source: U.S. National Center for Education Statistics, *Digest of Education Statistics*, "Advance Release of Selected 2016 Digest Tables," and earlier releases, <http://nces.ed.gov/programs/digest/>, accessed March 2017.

Table 293. College Enrollment by Sex, Age, and Race/Ethnicity: 1980 to 2015

[In thousands (11,387 represents 11,387,000). As of October for the civilian noninstitutional population, 14 years old and over. Based on the Current Population Survey; see text, Section 1 and Appendix III]

Characteristic	1980	1990 [1]	1995	2000	2005	2010	2011	2012	2013	2014	2015
Total [2]	**11,387**	**13,621**	**14,715**	**15,314**	**17,472**	**20,275**	**20,397**	**19,930**	**19,467**	**19,175**	**19,101**
Male [3]	5,430	6,192	6,703	6,682	7,539	9,007	9,132	8,602	8,536	8,629	8,484
18 to 24 years	3,604	3,922	4,089	4,342	4,972	5,698	5,953	5,730	5,629	5,677	5,694
25 to 34 years	1,325	1,412	1,561	1,361	1,486	2,055	1,986	1,770	1,775	1,792	1,803
35 years old and over	405	772	985	918	1,019	1,161	1,084	971	984	1,036	878
Female [3]	5,957	7,429	8,013	8,631	9,933	11,268	11,266	11,327	10,931	10,546	10,617
18 to 24 years	3,625	4,042	4,452	5,109	5,859	6,515	6,618	6,726	6,572	6,455	6,460
25 to 34 years	1,378	1,749	1,788	1,846	2,115	2,569	2,630	2,563	2,291	2,197	2,372
35 years old and over	802	1,546	1,684	1,589	1,838	2,049	1,922	1,899	1,907	1,784	1,672
White [3,4]	9,925	11,488	12,021	11,999	13,467	15,258	15,412	14,628	14,240	13,953	13,859
18 to 24 years	6,334	6,635	7,011	7,566	8,499	9,324	9,813	9,302	9,050	9,077	8,969
25 to 34 years	2,328	2,698	2,686	2,339	2,647	3,414	3,339	3,050	2,849	2,830	2,966
35 years old and over	1,051	2,023	2,208	1,978	2,206	2,365	2,120	2,072	2,107	1,899	1,776
Male	4,804	5,235	5,535	5,311	5,844	6,883	7,054	6,392	6,241	6,398	6,253
Female	5,121	6,253	6,486	6,689	7,624	8,375	8,358	8,236	7,999	7,555	7,607
Black [3,4]	1,163	1,393	1,772	2,164	2,297	3,083	3,146	3,038	2,857	2,934	2,826
18 to 24 years	688	894	988	1,216	1,229	1,692	1,639	1,689	1,599	1,529	1,637
25 to 34 years	289	258	426	567	520	715	818	769	686	656	627
35 years old and over	156	207	334	361	448	642	651	553	540	695	537
Male	476	587	710	815	864	1,185	1,212	1,152	1,116	1,132	1,147
Female	686	807	1,062	1,349	1,435	1,898	1,934	1,886	1,740	1,802	1,679
Asian [3,4]	(NA)	(NA)	(NA)	(NA)	1,184	1,322	1,204	1,447	1,576	1,543	1,616
18 to 24 years	(NA)	(NA)	(NA)	(NA)	696	811	748	914	1,001	1,022	1,026
25 to 34 years	(NA)	(NA)	(NA)	(NA)	341	354	288	363	372	353	426
35 years old and over	(NA)	(NA)	(NA)	(NA)	130	125	147	143	173	148	143
Male	(NA)	(NA)	(NA)	(NA)	605	647	567	700	789	797	752
Female	(NA)	(NA)	(NA)	(NA)	579	676	637	747	787	746	864
Hispanic origin [3,5]	443	748	1,207	1,426	1,942	2,879	2,953	3,400	3,219	3,295	3,374
18 to 24 years	315	435	745	899	1,216	1,814	2,079	2,403	2,192	2,282	2,369
25 to 34 years	118	168	250	309	438	652	582	622	639	630	648
35 years old and over	(NA)	130	193	195	257	372	256	313	345	332	315
Male	222	364	568	619	804	1,302	1,438	1,510	1,438	1,441	1,484
Female	221	384	639	807	1,139	1,576	1,515	1,890	1,781	1,855	1,890

NA Not available. [1] Beginning 1990, based on a revised edit and tabulation package. [2] Includes other races not shown separately. [3] Includes persons 14 to 17 years old not shown separately. [4] Beginning 2003, for persons who selected this race group only. See footnote 4, Table 251. [5] Persons of Hispanic origin may be of any race.

Source: U.S. Census Bureau, Current Population Reports, P-20, and earlier reports; and "School Enrollment," <http://www.census.gov/hhes/school/index.html>, accessed November 2016.

Table 294. College Enrollment by Type of College, Sex, and Selected Characteristics: 2015

[In thousands (19,101 represents 19,101,000). As of October. Covers civilian noninstitutional population 15 years old and over enrolled in colleges and graduate schools. Based on Current Population Survey. See text, Section 1 and Appendix III]

Characteristic	Total				Male		Female	
	Total enrolled	Two-year college	Four-year college	Graduate school	Total enrolled [1]	Four-year college	Total enrolled [1]	Four-year college
Total enrollment [2]	**19,101**	**4,717**	**10,716**	**3,667**	**8,484**	**4,877**	**10,617**	**5,837**
Age:								
15 to 19 years old	4,200	1,432	2,732	35	1,946	1,209	2,254	1,523
20 to 24 years old	8,174	1,736	5,409	1,029	3,856	2,600	4,318	2,808
25 to 34 years old	4,175	912	1,658	1,606	1,803	748	2,372	911
35 years old and over	2,551	637	916	998	878	322	1,673	596
Race/ethnicity:								
White [3]	13,859	3,512	7,779	2,568	6,253	3,568	7,607	4,211
White non-Hispanic [3]	10,904	2,452	6,243	2,208	4,970	2,916	5,934	3,327
Black [3]	2,826	743	1,604	478	1,147	715	1,679	890
Asian [3]	1,616	242	874	500	752	421	864	453
Hispanic [4]	3,374	1,187	1,785	402	1,484	778	1,890	1,008
Control of school:								
Public	15,175	4,344	8,417	2,413	6,708	3,792	8,467	4,625
Private	3,926	372	2,299	1,254	1,776	1,085	2,150	1,213
Employment status:								
Employed full-time	4,769	1,131	2,069	1,570	2,097	988	2,672	1,081
Employed part-time	5,375	1,526	3,104	745	2,168	1,259	3,207	1,846
Not employed	8,956	2,061	5,542	1,353	4,219	2,630	4,737	2,912
Enrollment status:								
Full time students	14,236	3,048	8,867	2,321	6,520	4,098	7,716	4,769
15 to 19 years old	3,786	1,142	2,609	35	1,731	1,136	2,055	1,473
20 to 24 years old	6,872	1,195	4,823	854	3,258	2,349	3,614	2,474
25 to 34 years old	2,475	457	966	1,051	1,121	444	1,354	523
35 years old and over	1,103	254	468	381	410	168	693	300
Part time students	4,865	1,669	1,849	1,347	1,964	780	2,901	1,068
15 to 19 years old	414	291	123	–	215	73	199	51
20 to 24 years old	1,302	541	586	175	598	251	704	334
25 to 34 years old	1,700	454	691	555	682	303	1,018	388
35 years old and over	1,448	383	448	617	469	153	980	295

– Represents or rounds to zero. [1] Includes enrollment in two-year colleges and graduate school not shown separately. [2] Includes other races not shown separately. [3] For persons who selected this race group only. See footnote 4, Table 251. [4] Persons of Hispanic origin may be of any race.

Source: U.S. Census Bureau, "School Enrollment," <http://www.census.gov/hhes/school/index.html>, accessed November 2016.

Table 295. Foreign (Nonimmigrant) Student Enrollment in U.S. Colleges and Universities by World Region and Selected Country of Origin: 1980 to 2016

[In thousands (286 represents 286,000). For Fall of the previous year]

Region of origin	1980	1990	1995	2000	2005	2007	2008	2009	2010	2011	2012	2013	2014	2015	2016
All regions.........	**286**	**387**	**453**	**515**	**565**	**583**	**624**	**672**	**691**	**723**	**764**	**820**	**886**	**975**	**1,044**
Africa [1]............	36	25	21	30	36	36	36	37	37	37	35	36	37	40	43
Nigeria..............	16	4	2	4	6	6	6	6	7	7	7	7	8	9	11
Asia [1,2,3]............	165	245	292	315	356	367	405	444	469	504	547	597	655	724	790
China...............	1	33	39	54	63	68	81	98	128	158	194	236	274	304	329
Taiwan..............	18	31	36	29	26	29	29	28	27	25	23	22	21	21	21
Hong Kong..........	10	11	13	8	7	8	8	8	8	8	8	8	8	8	8
India...............	9	26	34	42	80	84	95	103	105	104	100	97	103	133	166
Indonesia...........	2	9	12	11	8	7	8	8	7	7	7	8	8	8	9
Iran................	51	7	3	2	2	3	3	4	5	6	7	9	10	11	12
Japan...............	12	30	45	47	42	35	34	29	25	21	20	20	19	19	19
Malaysia............	4	14	14	9	6	5	5	6	6	7	7	7	7	7	8
Saudi Arabia........	10	4	4	5	3	8	10	13	16	23	34	45	54	60	61
South Korea........	5	22	34	41	53	62	69	75	72	73	73	71	68	64	61
Thailand............	7	7	11	11	9	9	9	9	9	8	8	7	7	7	7
Europe [4]...........	23	46	65	78	72	83	84	88	85	84	85	86	87	91	92
Latin America [1,5].....	42	48	47	62	68	65	64	68	66	64	64	67	72	86	85
Mexico.............	6	7	9	11	13	14	15	15	13	14	14	14	15	17	17
Venezuela..........	10	3	4	5	5	5	4	5	5	5	6	6	7	8	8
North America [6]......	16	19	23	24	29	29	29	30	29	28	27	27	28	27	27
Canada.............	15	18	23	24	28	28	29	30	28	28	27	27	28	27	27
Oceania.............	4	4	4	5	4	4	5	5	5	6	6	6	6	6	7

[1] Includes countries not shown separately. [2] Includes the Middle East. [3] Beginning 2006, excludes Cyprus and Turkey. [4] Beginning 2006, includes Cyprus and Turkey. [5] Includes Mexico, Central America, Caribbean, and South America. Prior to 2011, excludes Bermuda. [6] Prior to 2011, includes Bermuda.

Source: Institute of International Education, New York, NY, *Open Doors Report on International Educational Exchange* ©, annual (2016). See also <https://www.iie.org/opendoors>.

Table 296. Higher Education Enrollment in Languages Other Than English: 1970 to 2013

[1,153.2 represents 1,153,200. As of Fall. For credit enrollment]

Enrollment	1970	1980	1986	1990	1995	2002	2006	2009	2013
Registrations [1] (1,000)..................	**1,153.2**	**924.3**	**1,003.2**	**1,185.5**	**1,138.8**	**1,395.8**	**1,575.7**	**1,673.5**	**1,562.2**
By selected language (1,000):									
Spanish.........................	386.6	379.0	411.4	534.1	606.3	745.2	822.1	861.0	790.8
French..........................	358.5	248.3	275.1	273.1	205.4	202.0	206.0	215.2	197.8
American Sign Language..................	(NA)	(NA)	(NA)	1.6	4.3	60.8	79.7	92.1	109.6
German.........................	201.8	127.0	120.9	133.6	96.3	91.1	94.1	95.6	86.7
Italian..........................	34.2	34.8	40.9	49.8	43.8	63.9	78.2	80.3	71.3
Japanese........................	6.6	11.5	23.5	45.8	44.7	52.2	65.4	72.4	66.7
Chinese.........................	6.1	11.4	16.9	19.4	26.5	34.2	51.4	59.9	61.1
Arabic..........................	1.3	3.5	3.4	3.7	4.4	10.6	24.0	34.9	32.3
Latin...........................	28.4	25.0	25.0	28.2	25.9	29.8	32.2	32.4	27.2
Russian.........................	36.4	24.0	33.9	44.5	24.7	23.9	24.8	26.8	22.0
Ancient Greek....................	16.5	22.1	17.8	16.4	16.3	20.4	22.8	20.0	12.9
Hebrew.........................	16.6	19.3	15.7	13.0	13.1	22.8	23.8	22.7	19.9
Portuguese......................	5.1	4.9	5.1	6.1	6.5	8.4	10.3	11.3	12.4
Korean..........................	0.1	0.4	0.9	2.4	3.3	5.2	7.1	8.4	12.2
Index (1965=100).....................	111.5	89.3	97.0	114.6	110.1	134.9	152.3	161.7	151.0

NA Not available. [1] Includes other languages, not shown separately.

Source: Modern Language Association, David Goldberg, Dennis Looney, and Natalia Lusin. *Enrollments in Languages Other Than English in United States Institutions of Higher Education, Fall 2013*, February 2015 ©. For 1970 to 2009, consult Association of Departments of Foreign Languages (ADFL) Bulletins.

Table 297. Active Duty Military Personnel and Veterans Enrolled in Higher Education: 2008 and 2012

[20,510.7 represents 20,510,700. For school year ending in year shown. Based on the National Postsecondary Student-Aid Study]

Characteristic	Undergraduate				Graduate			
	2008		2012		2008		2012	
	Number (1,000)	Percent	Number (1,000)	Percent	Number (1,000)	Percent	Number (1,000)	Percent
Total students................	**20,510.7**	**100.0**	**23,055.4**	**100.0**	**3,476.1**	**100.0**	**3,682.2**	**100.0**
Total military students.........	**913.8**	**4.5**	**1,132.9**	**4.9**	**146.5**	**4.2**	**159.7**	**4.3**
Veterans.......................	688.0	3.4	855.9	3.7	106.7	3.1	109.7	3.0
Military service members......	225.8	1.1	277.0	1.1	39.8	1.1	50.0	1.3
Active duty....................	150.4	0.7	170.8	0.7	31.4	0.9	26.3	0.7
Reserves.....................	75.4	0.4	74.3	0.3	8.4	0.2	18.2	0.5
National Guard [1].............	(NA)	(NA)	31.9	0.1	(NA)	(NA)	5.5	0.1
Nonmilitary students.............	19,596.8	95.5	21,922.6	95.1	3,329.5	95.8	3,522.4	95.7

NA Not available. [1] Information on National Guard status was not collected in 2008; students were only considered military students if they were veterans or military service members on active duty or in the reserves.

Source: U.S. National Center for Education Statistics, *After the Post-9/11 GI Bill: A Profile of Military Service Members and Veterans Enrolled in Undergraduate and Graduate Education*, August 2016. See also <https://nces.ed.gov/pubsearch/pubsinfo.asp?pubid=2016435>.

Table 298. College Students Reporting Disability Status by Selected Characteristic: 2011 to 2012

[23,055 represents 23,055,000. Disabled students reported that they had one or more of the following conditions: a specific learning disability, a visual handicap, hard of hearing, deafness, a speech disability, an orthopedic handicap, or a health impairment. Based on the 2011–2012 National Postsecondary Student-Aid Study; see source for details. Includes Puerto Rico. See also Appendix III]

Student characteristic	Undergraduate			Graduate and first-professional		
	All students	Disabled students	Nondisabled students	All students	Disabled students	Nondisabled students
Total students (1,000)...............	23,055	2,563	20,493	3,682	195	3,487
PERCENT DISTRIBUTION						
Total............	100.0	11.1	88.9	100.0	5.3	94.7
Age:						
15 to 23 years old............	56.2	45.3	57.6	11.4	8.4	11.5
24 to 29 years old............	18.4	18.8	18.4	40.3	35.3	40.5
30 years or older............	25.4	35.8	24.0	48.4	56.3	47.9
Sex:						
Male............	43.0	43.7	42.9	39.7	35.7	40.0
Female............	57.0	56.3	57.1	60.3	64.3	60.0
Race/ethnicity of student:						
White, non-Hispanic............	57.9	58.0	57.9	63.6	60.4	63.8
Black, non-Hispanic............	16.1	17.6	15.9	11.8	15.5	11.6
Hispanic............	16.0	14.9	16.2	8.7	10.5	8.6
Asian............	5.6	4.0	5.8	12.9	10.4	13.0
Pacific Islander............	0.5	0.7	0.5	0.6	(S)	0.6
American Indian/Alaska Native............	0.9	1.2	0.9	0.4	(S)	0.4
Two or more races............	3.0	3.6	2.9	2.0	2.5	2.0
Attendance status:						
Full-time, full-year............	38.4	33.0	39.1	37.8	38.2	37.8
Part-time or part-year............	61.6	67.0	60.9	62.2	61.8	62.2
Student housing status:						
On-campus............	12.1	9.4	12.5	(NA)	(NA)	(NA)
Off-campus............	46.1	48.9	45.7	(NA)	(NA)	(NA)
With parents or relatives............	33.5	34.2	33.5	(NA)	(NA)	(NA)
Attended more than one institution............	8.3	7.4	8.4	(NA)	(NA)	(NA)
Dependency status:						
Dependent............	48.7	37.5	50.1	(NA)	(NA)	(NA)
Independent, unmarried............	17.8	22.9	17.2	49.8	53.0	49.6
Independent, married............	6.0	7.1	5.8	15.4	12.3	15.5
Independent with dependents............	27.5	32.5	26.9	34.8	34.7	34.8

NA Not available. S Figure does not meet publication standards.

Source: U.S. National Center for Education Statistics, *2014 Digest of Education Statistics*, April 2016. See also <http://www.nces.ed.gov/programs/digest/>.

Table 299. College Freshmen—Summary Characteristics: 1980 to 2016

[In percent, except family income (24.5 represents $24,500). As of Fall for first-time full-time freshmen in 4-year colleges and universities. Based on sample survey and subject to sampling error; see source]

Characteristic	1980	1990	1995	2000	2005	2010	2014	2015	2016
Sex:									
Male............	48.8	46.9	45.6	45.2	45.0	44.3	43.4	43.8	42.2
Female............	51.2	53.1	54.4	54.8	55.0	55.7	56.6	56.2	57.8
Applied to more than three colleges............	31.5	42.9	44.4	50.5	55.4	64.1	72.5	71.9	71.3
Average grade in high school:									
A- to A+............	26.6	29.4	36.1	42.9	46.6	48.4	53.1	58.7	55.1
B- to B+............	58.2	57.0	54.2	50.5	48.0	47.5	43.9	38.5	42.3
C to C+............	14.9	13.4	9.6	6.5	5.4	4.1	2.9	2.8	2.6
D............	0.2	0.2	0.1	0.1	0.1	0.1	0.0	0.0	0.0
Political orientation:									
Liberal............	21.0	24.6	22.9	24.8	27.1	27.3	28.8	29.6	31.3
Middle of the road............	57.0	51.7	51.3	51.9	45.0	46.4	47.2	44.9	42.3
Conservative............	19.0	20.6	21.8	18.9	22.6	21.7	19.4	19.8	20.2
Probable field of study:									
Biological sciences............	4.5	4.9	8.3	6.6	7.6	10.8	13.8	14.9	15.7
Business............	21.2	21.1	15.4	16.7	17.4	13.7	14.6	13.4	13.8
Education............	8.4	10.3	10.1	11.0	9.9	7.2	5.0	4.2	4.6
Engineering............	11.2	9.7	8.1	8.7	8.3	10.3	11.7	13.1	10.7
Physical science............	3.2	2.8	3.1	2.6	3.1	2.7	2.5	2.7	2.7
Social science............	8.2	11.0	9.9	10.0	10.7	8.9	10.2	10.8	10.7
Data processing/computer programming............	1.7	0.7	0.8	1.5	0.5	0.5	(NA)	(NA)	(NA)
Other [1]............	41.6	39.5	44.3	42.9	42.5	45.9	41.5	40.6	41.5
Communications [2]............	2.4	2.9	1.8	2.7	2.0	1.8	2.2	1.9	2.1
Computer science............	2.6	1.7	2.2	3.7	1.1	1.0	3.5	3.8	3.7
Personal objectives—very important or essential:									
Being very well off financially............	62.5	72.3	72.8	73.4	74.5	77.4	82.4	81.9	82.3
Developing a meaningful philosophy of life............	62.5	45.9	45.4	42.4	45.0	46.9	44.6	46.5	46.8
Keeping up to date with political affairs............	45.2	46.6	32.3	28.1	36.4	33.2	35.0	40.4	46.0
Median family income ($1,000)............	24.5	46.6	54.8	64.4	73.2	76.1	(NA)	(NA)	(NA)

NA Not available. [1] Includes other fields not shown separately. [2] Beginning in 2012, the communications field includes journalism majors.

Source: The Higher Education Research Institute, University of California, Los Angeles, CA, *The American Freshman: National Norms Fall 2016* ©, 2017, and earlier editions. See also <http://www.heri.ucla.edu/tfsPublications.php>.

Table 300. Residence and Migration of College Freshmen by State: 2014

[As of Fall. Includes first-time postsecondary students who had graduated from high school in the previous 12 months and were enrolled at public and private not-for-profit 4-year degree-granting institutions that participated in Title IV federal financial aid programs. Excludes respondents for whom state residence and/or migration are unknown. Also excludes U.S. Service Academies (Air Force Academy, Coast Guard Academy, Merchant Marine Academy, Military Academy, and Naval Academy). Based on data from the Integrated Postsecondary Education Data System (IPEDS). See source for more information]

State	Total freshmen enrollment in institutions located in the state	Ratio of in-state students to freshmen enrollment	Ratio of in-state students to residents enrolled in any state[1]	State	Total freshmen enrollment in institutions located in the state	Ratio of in-state students to freshmen enrollment	Ratio of in-state students to residents enrolled in any state[1]
U.S.......	1,542,436	0.72	0.74	MO.........	30,048	0.66	0.75
AL..........	25,181	0.58	0.83	MT..........	6,115	0.61	0.78
AK..........	2,434	0.89	0.66	NE..........	11,478	0.72	0.80
AZ..........	25,996	0.57	0.77	NV..........	10,290	0.82	0.74
AR..........	17,079	0.70	0.88	NH..........	8,929	0.34	0.40
CA..........	133,112	0.85	0.76	NJ..........	28,740	0.85	0.44
CO..........	24,081	0.70	0.67	NM..........	6,802	0.78	0.76
CT..........	19,450	0.53	0.42	NY..........	106,977	0.69	0.72
DE..........	5,930	0.38	0.53	NC..........	47,250	0.73	0.83
DC..........	8,564	0.05	0.19	ND..........	6,502	0.48	0.79
FL..........	106,116	0.86	0.87	OH..........	68,579	0.76	0.82
GA..........	52,526	0.82	0.80	OK..........	19,469	0.68	0.86
HI..........	4,034	0.61	0.45	OR..........	15,693	0.55	0.70
ID..........	7,321	0.57	0.65	PA..........	82,947	0.63	0.77
IL..........	48,510	0.74	0.55	RI..........	11,205	0.25	0.51
IN..........	45,808	0.70	0.85	SC..........	24,236	0.62	0.84
IA..........	20,223	0.52	0.78	SD..........	5,850	0.58	0.73
KS..........	15,577	0.68	0.78	TN..........	30,051	0.73	0.78
KY..........	24,088	0.72	0.86	TX..........	102,409	0.91	0.82
LA..........	23,470	0.81	0.88	UT..........	18,321	0.65	0.90
ME..........	7,000	0.54	0.59	VT..........	6,273	0.24	0.44
MD..........	18,390	0.65	0.44	VA..........	43,326	0.68	0.74
MA..........	51,799	0.49	0.58	WA..........	26,452	0.76	0.71
MI..........	51,500	0.82	0.85	WV..........	12,119	0.57	0.89
MN..........	25,208	0.71	0.59	WI..........	35,148	0.72	0.78
MS..........	12,342	0.58	0.83	WY..........	1,488	0.52	0.54

[1] Students residing in a particular state when admitted to an institution anywhere, either in their home state or another state.

Source: U.S. National Center for Education Statistics, *Digest of Education Statistics 2015*, December 2016. See also <http://www.nces.ed.gov/programs/digest/>.

Table 301. Average Total Price of Attendance of Undergraduate Education: 2012

[In dollars. For school year ending in 2012. Excludes students attending more than one institution. Price of attendance includes tuition and fees, books and supplies, room and board, transportation, and personal and other expenses allowed for federal cost of attendance budgets. Based on the 2011–2012 National Postsecondary Student-Aid Study; see source for details. Includes Puerto Rico. See also Appendix III]

Student characteristic			Type of institution				
			Public 4-year		Private not-for-profit 4-year		
	All institu- tions[1]	Public 2-year	Non- doctorate granting	Doctorate granting	Non- doctorate granting	Doctorate granting	Private for-profit
Total...	**16,477**	**8,712**	**13,722**	**20,078**	**31,587**	**36,819**	**20,159**
Age:[2]							
18 years or younger..........................	20,826	9,680	16,593	23,139	39,029	44,457	23,664
19 to 23 years................................	18,957	8,957	15,252	21,357	36,364	42,352	21,126
24 to 29 years................................	13,540	8,583	11,584	16,626	23,794	24,432	19,972
30 to 39 years................................	13,174	8,574	11,075	14,732	18,746	21,683	19,490
40 years or older..............................	11,816	7,790	9,805	13,507	16,029	17,200	19,152
Sex:							
Male...	16,533	8,735	13,598	20,363	32,047	37,261	20,326
Female..	16,434	8,693	13,817	19,821	31,246	36,470	20,065
Race:							
One race:							
White...	16,820	8,605	14,238	20,124	31,917	36,529	20,001
Black or African American....................	15,472	8,977	13,018	19,270	26,787	30,585	19,637
Hispanic or Latino[3].........................	14,917	8,424	12,305	19,282	31,762	38,595	21,088
Asian...	20,007	9,506	14,167	22,574	40,032	44,623	20,445
American Indian/Alaska Native..............	14,426	8,844	11,095	18,568	(S)	(S)	18,117
Native Hawaiian or other Pacific Islander.......................	16,082	9,609	(S)	19,552	(S)	(S)	21,719
More than one race...........................	17,815	9,518	15,215	19,786	34,789	36,780	22,090
Attendance pattern:							
Full-time, full-year............................	26,417	15,031	20,141	24,231	40,087	46,476	29,332
Full-time, part-year...........................	13,522	8,107	11,004	15,040	21,727	24,024	16,555
Part-time, full-year...........................	12,769	9,701	12,279	16,773	22,192	22,873	20,363
Part-time, part-year..........................	6,397	4,868	6,272	8,571	10,638	11,359	11,466

S Data do not meet publication standards. [1] Includes public less-than-2-year and private not-for-profit less-than-4-year. [2] As of December 31, 2011. [3] Persons of Hispanic origin may be of any race.

Source: U.S. Department of Education, National Center for Education Statistics, National Postsecondary Student Aid Study (NPSAS), "Datalab," <http://nces.ed.gov/datalab/>, accessed September 2014.

Table 302. Institutions of Higher Education—Average Charges: 1985 to 2016

[In current dollars. Estimated. For the entire academic year ending in year shown. Figures are average charges per full-time equivalent student. Room and board are based on full-time students]

Academic control and year	Tuition and required fees [1]			Board rates [2]			Dormitory room charges		
	All institutions	2-yr. colleges	4-yr. institutions	All institutions	2-yr. colleges	4-yr. institutions	All institutions	2-yr. colleges	4-yr. institutions
Public:									
1985.................	971	584	1,228	1,241	1,302	1,237	1,196	921	1,217
1990.................	1,356	756	1,780	1,635	1,581	1,638	1,513	962	1,557
1995.................	2,057	1,192	2,681	1,949	1,712	1,967	1,959	1,232	2,023
2000.................	2,504	1,348	3,349	2,364	1,834	2,406	2,440	1,549	2,519
2005.................	3,629	1,849	5,027	2,931	2,353	2,981	3,304	2,174	3,418
2010.................	4,763	2,283	6,717	3,655	2,571	3,755	4,401	2,854	4,564
2011.................	5,075	2,441	7,132	3,845	2,683	3,956	4,646	2,955	4,832
2012.................	5,563	2,651	7,713	3,946	2,866	4,042	4,849	3,100	5,031
2013.................	5,899	2,792	8,070	4,061	2,888	4,163	5,062	3,247	5,241
2014.................	6,120	2,881	8,312	4,205	2,955	4,308	5,304	3,448	5,479
2015.................	6,371	2,955	8,543	4,313	3,072	4,412	5,504	3,559	5,677
2016.................	6,613	3,038	8,778	4,457	3,128	4,561	5,688	3,772	5,850
Private:									
1985.................	5,315	3,485	5,556	1,462	1,294	1,469	1,426	1,424	1,426
1990.................	8,147	5,196	8,396	1,948	1,811	1,953	1,923	1,663	1,935
1995.................	11,111	6,914	11,481	2,509	2,023	2,520	2,587	2,233	2,601
2000.................	14,100	8,225	14,616	2,877	2,753	2,879	3,236	3,067	3,242
2005.................	18,154	12,122	18,604	3,485	3,700	3,483	4,178	4,475	4,173
2010.................	21,764	14,862	22,269	4,329	4,390	4,329	5,248	5,211	5,248
2011.................	22,042	13,687	22,677	4,430	4,475	4,430	5,403	4,939	5,410
2012.................	22,850	13,961	23,464	4,586	4,475	4,586	5,622	5,169	5,627
2013.................	23,943	14,149	24,523	4,709	3,977	4,712	5,831	5,228	5,837
2014.................	25,110	14,170	25,707	4,864	4,211	4,866	6,021	5,489	6,026
2015.................	26,184	14,254	26,740	5,019	4,560	5,021	6,221	5,504	6,229
2016.................	27,444	14,524	27,951	5,111	4,177	5,116	6,456	5,666	6,463

[1] For public institutions, data are for in-state students. [2] Beginning 1990, rates reflect 20 meals per week, rather than meals served 7 days a week.

Source: U.S. National Center for Education Statistics, *Digest of Education Statistics*, "Advance Release of Selected 2016 Digest Tables," <http://www.nces.ed.gov/programs/digest/>, accessed May 2017.

Table 303. Average Out-of-Pocket Net Price of Attendance for Undergraduates: 2012

[In dollars. For school year ending in 2012. Excludes students attending more than one institution. Net price of attendance is the price that students pay to receive postsecondary education after taking financial aid into account. Based on net tuition and net price for all students. Based on the 2011–2012 National Postsecondary Student-Aid Study; see source for details. Includes Puerto Rico. See also Appendix III]

Student characteristic		Type of Institution					
	All institutions [1]	Public 2-year	Public 4-year		Private not-for-profit 4-year		Private for-profit
			Non-doctorate granting	Doctorate granting	Non-doctorate granting	Doctorate granting	
Total............................	**8,657**	**6,013**	**7,725**	**10,585**	**13,155**	**16,640**	**10,350**
Age: [2]							
18 years or younger..........................	10,270	6,912	8,396	11,342	14,225	18,800	12,400
19 to 23 years.................................	10,236	6,482	8,889	11,767	15,236	18,999	11,118
24 to 29 years.................................	6,706	5,660	6,450	7,886	10,407	12,430	10,194
30 to 39 years.................................	6,028	5,421	5,610	6,502	8,446	10,337	9,780
40 years or older.............................	5,937	5,315	5,809	7,225	7,681	8,661	9,758
Sex:							
Male...	8,968	6,154	7,800	11,139	13,317	17,453	9,836
Female..	8,404	5,901	7,668	10,084	13,036	15,999	10,638
Race:							
One race:							
White...	9,221	6,058	8,177	11,342	14,214	17,076	10,302
Black or African American...................	6,210	5,413	5,866	6,508	7,688	10,769	10,072
Hispanic or Latino [3].........................	7,370	5,965	7,119	9,071	11,220	13,696	10,733
Asian...	12,752	7,367	9,720	14,612	20,138	25,186	11,871
American Indian/Alaska Native.............	6,292	5,654	5,978	6,275	(S)	(S)	9,105
Native Hawaiian or other Pacific Islander........	8,342	6,804	(S)	10,461	(S)	(S)	10,427
More than one race............................	8,619	6,456	7,564	8,937	11,172	17,020	10,191
Attendance pattern:							
Full-time, full-year.............................	12,834	9,883	10,309	12,274	15,855	20,057	15,023
Full-time, part-year...........................	7,297	5,358	6,706	9,158	10,528	12,536	8,918
Part-time, full-year...........................	7,452	6,716	7,257	8,836	10,781	11,681	9,598
Part-time, part-year..........................	4,195	3,709	4,573	5,646	5,410	7,119	5,485

S Data do not meet publication standards. [1] Includes public less-than-2-year and private not-for-profit less-than-4-year. [2] As of December 2007. [3] Persons of Hispanic origin may be of any race.

Source: U.S. Department of Education, National Center for Education Statistics, National Postsecondary Student Aid Study (NPSAS), "Datalab," <http://nces.ed.gov/datalab/>, accessed September 2014.

Table 304. Average Cost of Attendance for Undergraduate Education by Control of Institution and Type of Cost: 2014 and 2016

[In constant 2016-17 dollars, except percent change. Data are preliminary. For school year beginning in year shown. Data shown are for full-time, first-time degree/certificate-seeking undergraduates at Title IV institutions. Amounts are institutional averages as reported by the institution, not average amounts paid by students. Based on data from the Integrated Postsecondary Education Data System (IPEDS)]

Item	4-year			2-year			Less than 2-year		
	2014	2016	Percent change	2014	2016	Percent change	2014	2016	Percent change
Tuition and required fees:									
Public:									
In-district [1]	7,801	8,148	4.5	3,312	3,479	5.0	6,176	6,367	3.1
In-state	7,824	8,173	4.5	3,875	4,087	5.5	6,188	6,392	3.3
Out-of-state	17,639	18,415	4.4	7,586	7,937	4.6	7,442	7,720	3.7
Private nonprofit [2]	25,916	27,276	5.2	14,088	14,282	1.4	13,578	14,217	4.7
Private for-profit [2]	15,797	16,011	1.4	14,525	14,694	1.2	15,719	16,053	2.1
Books and supplies:									
Public	1,295	1,284	-0.8	1,409	1,422	0.9	1,156	1,000	-13.5
Private nonprofit	1,201	1,190	-0.9	1,371	1,370	-0.1	1,223	1,286	5.2
Private for-profit	1,370	1,316	-4.0	1,502	1,627	8.3	1,370	1,189	-13.2
Room and board:									
Public:									
On campus	9,382	9,814	4.6	6,288	6,568	4.5	4,112	5,748	39.8
Off campus (not with family)	9,393	9,602	2.2	7,961	8,191	2.9	8,142	8,053	-1.1
Private nonprofit:									
On campus	9,698	10,145	4.6	8,273	8,814	6.5	(X)	(X)	(X)
Off campus (not with family)	9,341	9,663	3.5	9,416	9,470	0.6	10,369	9,583	-7.6
Private for-profit:									
On campus	9,847	10,076	2.3	9,773	10,308	5.5	(X)	(X)	(X)
Off campus (not with family)	8,342	8,322	-0.2	8,547	8,466	-0.9	9,131	9,016	-1.3
Other expenses [3]									
Public:									
On campus	3,319	3,332	0.4	3,229	3,270	1.3	1,215	1,200	-1.2
Off campus (not with family)	3,796	3,804	0.2	3,930	3,964	0.9	3,917	3,858	-1.5
Off campus (with family)	3,973	3,940	-0.8	3,928	3,988	1.5	3,832	3,604	-5.9
Private nonprofit:									
On campus	2,831	2,847	0.5	3,409	3,465	1.7	(X)	(X)	(X)
Off campus (not with family)	3,511	3,530	0.6	4,438	4,495	1.3	2,126	4,255	100.2
Off campus (with family)	3,737	3,737	–	4,525	4,335	-4.2	3,316	3,582	8.0
Private for-profit:									
On campus	4,029	4,111	2.0	2,804	3,452	23.1	(X)	(X)	(X)
Off campus (not with family)	4,380	4,278	-2.3	4,882	4,900	0.4	4,846	4,827	-0.4
Off campus (with family)	5,038	3,991	-20.8	4,358	4,344	-0.3	3,660	3,644	-0.4

X Not applicable. – Rounds to zero. [1] For public institutions, "in-district" refers to the charges paid by a student who lives in the locality surrounding the institution, such as county. [2] For private institutions that reported varying tuitions by residency, out-of-state tuition and required fees were used in the averages displayed in this table. [3] Other expenses refers to the amount of money needed by a student to cover expenses such as laundry, transportation, and entertainment.

Source: U.S. National Center for Education Statistics, *Postsecondary Institutions and Cost of Attendance in 2016–17; Degrees and Other Awards Conferred, 2015–16; and 12-Month Enrollment, 2015–16,* July 2017. See also <https://nces.ed.gov/pubsearch/pubsinfo. asp?pubid=2017075>.

Table 305. Bachelor's Degree Recipients with Loans and Amount Borrowed in Constant (2009) Dollars by Selected Characteristics: 1994 to 2009

[Data shown for first-time Bachelor's degree recipients. Based on Baccalaureate and Beyond Longitudinal Studies]

Characteristic	Percent with loans			Average Cumulative Amount Borrowed for Undergraduate Education (2009 Dollars)		
	1994	2001	2009	1994	2001	2009
Total loans	**49.3**	**63.5**	**65.6**	**14,700**	**21,800**	**24,700**
Sex:						
Male	50.1	62.5	62.9	15,000	21,300	23,900
Female	49.4	64.3	67.6	14,400	22,100	25,200
Race/ethnicity: [1]						
White	47.8	62.2	64.6	14,900	21,700	24,500
Black	65.5	79.8	80.3	13,800	25,200	28,700
Hispanic	60.5	66.7	67.0	11,400	19,900	22,800
Asian	43.1	55.5	53.4	16,800	19,100	21,000
Other	63.4	62.8	68.8	14,900	21,500	25,600
Age at receipt of bachelor's degree:						
18-23	43.9	60.0	61.0	15,200	20,800	23,700
24-29	62.9	71.3	76.8	13,800	23,100	24,900
30 and older	55.9	65.7	72.5	13,800	23,000	28,300
Institution type:						
2-Year or less:						
Public 2-year	53.1	67.8	67.5	13,300	21,500	24,500
Other 2-year or less	56.8	64.6	85.0	13,600	24,500	31,600
4-Year:						
Public	45.7	59.5	62.1	12,900	20,100	21,900
Private nonprofit	53.4	69.0	69.4	18,200	24,100	27,900
For-profit	63.4	77.3	87.7	(X)	27,400	36,000

X Not applicable. [1] Black includes African American; Hispanic includes Latino; Asian includes Pacific Islander and Native Hawaiian; other includes American Indian, Alaska Native, and graduates having origins in two or more races or a race not listed. Race categories exclude persons of Hispanic ethnicity unless specified. In 1994, graduates of two or more races were asked to choose one category, in subsequent studies graduates could identify as multiracial.

Source: National Center for Education Statistics, *Trends in Debt for Bachelor's Degree Recipients a Year After Graduation: 1994, 2001, and 2009,* December 2012. See also <http://nces.ed.gov/>.

Table 306. Federal Student Financial Assistance: 1995 to 2015

[35,477 represents $35,477,000,000. For award years July 1 of year shown to the following June 30. Funds utilized exclude operating costs, etc., and represent funds given to students]

Type of assistance	1995	2000	2005	2010	2013	2014	2015
FUNDS UTILIZED (mil. dol.)							
Total	**35,477**	**44,007**	**72,634**	**144,182**	**135,863**	**130,415**	**125,920**
Federal Pell Grants	5,472	7,956	12,693	35,677	31,477	30,626	28,559
Academic Competitiveness Grants[1]	(X)	(X)	(X)	553	(X)	(X)	(X)
SMART Grants[1]	(X)	(X)	(X)	433	(X)	(X)	(X)
TEACH Grants[2]	(X)	(X)	(X)	121	93	94	89
Federal Supplemental Educational Opportunity Grant	764	907	1,084	1,022	926	983	993
Federal Work-Study	764	939	1,050	1,198	1,100	1,100	1,096
Federal Perkins Loan	1,029	1,144	1,593	857	1,011	1,160	1,045
Federal Direct Student Loan (FDSL)	8,296	10,348	12,930	84,704	101,256	96,450	94,137
Federal Family Education Loans (FFEL)[3]	19,152	22,712	43,284	19,618	(X)	(X)	(X)
NUMBER OF AWARDS (1,000)							
Total	**13,667**	**15,044**	**21,318**	**34,895**	**31,636**	**26,676**	**25,028**
Federal Pell Grants	3,612	3,899	5,168	9,308	8,663	8,316	7,660
Academic Competitiveness Grants[1]	(X)	(X)	(X)	729	(X)	(X)	(X)
SMART Grants[1]	(X)	(X)	(X)	140	(X)	(X)	(X)
TEACH Grants[2]	(X)	(X)	(X)	39	32	32	31
Federal Supplemental Educational Opportunity Grant	1,083	1,175	1,419	1,633	1,545	1,619	1,530
Federal Work-Study	702	713	710	718	656	651	635
Federal Perkins Loan	688	639	727	461	500	528	422
Federal Direct Student Loan (FDSL)	2,339	2,739	2,971	16,647	20,240	15,530	14,750
Federal Family Education Loans (FFEL)[3]	5,243	5,878	10,323	5,220	(X)	(X)	(X)
AVERAGE AWARD (dol.)							
Total	**2,596**	**2,925**	**3,407**	**4,132**	**4,295**	**4,889**	**5,031**
Federal Pell Grants	1,515	2,040	2,456	3,833	3,634	3,683	3,728
Academic Competitiveness Grants[1]	(X)	(X)	(X)	759	(X)	(X)	(X)
SMART Grants[1]	(X)	(X)	(X)	3,095	(X)	(X)	(X)
TEACH Grants[2]	(X)	(X)	(X)	3,137	2,873	2,946	2,902
Federal Supplemental Educational Opportunity Grant	705	772	764	620	599	607	649
Federal Work-Study	1,088	1,318	1,478	1,668	1,678	1,689	1,726
Federal Perkins Loan	1,496	1,790	2,190	1,860	2,022	2,198	2,479
Federal Direct Student Loan (FDSL)	3,547	3,778	4,352	5,088	(NA)	2,769	6,382
Federal Family Education Loans (FFEL)[3]	3,653	3,864	4,193	3,758	(X)	(X)	(X)
COHORT DEFAULT RATE[4]							
Federal Perkins Loan	12.6	9.9	8.1	10.5	(NA)	(NA)	(NA)

X Not applicable. NA Not available. [1] National Science and Mathematics Access to Retain Talent (SMART). Funding for Academic Competitiveness Grants and SMART Grants was terminated in 2011. [2] Teacher Education Assistance for College and Higher Education (TEACH) Grant Program. [3] The FFEL Program was terminated effective 2011. [4] As of June 30. Represents the percent of borrowers entering repayment status in year shown who defaulted in the following year.

Source: U.S. Department of Education, Office of Postsecondary Education, unpublished data.

Table 307. Voluntary Financial Support of Higher Education: 1990 to 2016

[9,800 represents $9,800,000,000. For school years ending in years shown. Voluntary support, as defined in Gift Reporting Standards, excludes income from endowment and other invested funds as well as all support received from federal, state, and local governments and their agencies and contract research]

Item	Unit	1990	1995	2000	2005	2010	2014	2015	2016
Estimated support, total	**Mil. dol.**	**9,800**	**12,750**	**23,200**	**25,600**	**28,000**	**37,450**	**40,300**	**41,000**
SOURCES OF SUPPORT									
Individuals, total	Mil. dol.	4,770	6,540	12,220	12,100	12,020	16,350	18,850	17,450
Alumni	Mil. dol.	2,540	3,600	6,800	7,100	7,100	9,850	10,850	9,930
Nonalumni individuals	Mil. dol.	2,230	2,940	5,420	5,000	4,920	6,500	8,000	7,520
Organizations, total	Mil. dol.	5,030	6,210	10,980	13,500	15,675	21,100	21,450	23,550
Corporations	Mil. dol.	2,170	2,560	4,150	4,400	4,730	5,750	5,750	6,600
Foundations	Mil. dol.	1,920	2,460	5,080	7,000	8,400	11,200	11,600	12,450
Other organizations	Mil. dol.	940	1,190	1,750	2,100	2,545	4,150	4,100	4,500
PURPOSES OF SUPPORT									
Current operations, total	Mil. dol.	5,440	7,230	11,270	14,200	17,000	21,800	24,650	25,150
Capital purposes	Mil. dol.	4,360	5,520	11,930	11,400	11,000	15,650	15,650	15,850
Support for institutions reporting support only:									
Institutions reporting support	Number	1,056	1,086	945	997	996	1,019	983	950
Total support reported	Mil. dol.	8,214	10,992	19,419	20,953	23,487	31,658	35,082	33,604
Private 4-year institutions	Mil. dol.	5,072	6,500	11,047	11,011	12,189	16,927	17,944	17,378
Public 4-year institutions	Mil. dol.	3,056	4,382	8,254	9,780	11,114	14,514	14,876	16,039
2-year colleges	Mil. dol.	85	110	117	163	185	217	192	187

Source: Council for Aid to Education, New York, NY, *Voluntary Support of Education* ©, annual. See also <www.cae.org>.

Table 308. Undergraduate Students Who Received a Pell Grant by Selected Characteristics: 2000 to 2012

[In units as indicated. For school year ending in year shown. Data shown for students enrolled in Title IV eligible postsecondary institutions in the 50 States, the District of Columbia, and Puerto Rico. Based on the National Postsecondary Student-Aid Study; see source for details]

Institutional and student characteristics	2000 Percent	2000 Average amount (dollars)	2004 Percent	2004 Average amount (dollars)	2008 Percent	2008 Average amount (dollars)	2012 [1] Percent	2012 [1] Average amount (dollars)
Total..............................	22.6	1,900	27.2	2,400	27.8	2,500	41.3	3,400
AGE								
23 or younger......................	22.4	2,000	25.5	2,600	25.6	2,700	37.8	3,600
24 to 29............................	29.8	1,900	36.6	2,400	36.1	2,400	48.9	3,200
30 or older........................	18.3	1,800	24.8	2,300	26.9	2,300	43.5	3,200
SEX								
Male...............................	18.9	1,900	22.3	2,500	21.9	2,600	36.5	3,400
Female.............................	25.4	1,900	30.8	2,400	32.2	2,500	44.8	3,400
RACE/ETHNICITY								
White..............................	17.2	1,800	20.7	2,300	20.9	2,400	33.5	3,300
Black..............................	39.9	2,000	47.9	2,500	46.0	2,600	61.9	3,400
Hispanic [1].......................	29.5	2,100	37.5	2,600	39.8	2,700	50.0	3,500
Asian/Pacific Islander.............	22.4	2,200	21.9	2,800	23.3	2,800	33.8	3,800
American Indian....................	30.9	1,900	31.9	2,400	36.0	2,500	54.0	3,400
Other or two or more races........	24.6	2,000	29.8	2,500	31.1	2,600	45.2	3,500
DEPENDANT STUDENT FAMILY INCOME [2]								
Lowest 25 percent.................	60.1	2,200	62.1	2,900	65.2	3,200	79.4	4,300
Lower middle 25 percent..........	17.0	1,200	24.0	1,600	25.0	1,700	53.3	3,000
Upper middle 25 percent..........	1.0	900	1.5	1,300	–	(S)	5.5	1,800
Highest 25 percent................	[3] 0.1	(S)	–	(S)	–	(S)	0.4	3,700
INDEPENDENT STUDENT FAMILY INCOME [2]								
Lowest 25 percent.................	58.5	2,000	55.5	2,700	58.5	2,800	65.9	3,600
Lower middle 25 percent..........	31.1	1,900	44.0	2,300	44.5	2,200	65.8	3,200
Upper middle 25 percent..........	13.2	1,200	25.2	1,800	29.6	1,800	40.5	3,200
Highest 25 percent................	0.7	1,100	1.3	1,100	0.7	800	17.9	2,300
ATTENDANCE STATUS								
Full-time, full-year................	29.6	2,300	32.2	3,100	33.6	3,300	47.1	4,400
Part-time or part-year.............	18.3	1,500	23.8	1,900	24.4	1,900	37.6	2,600
TYPE OF INSTITUTION [4]								
Public 4-year......................	24.1	2,000	26.4	2,600	26.2	2,800	38.0	3,800
Private nonprofit 4-year...........	24.1	2,000	27.9	2,600	26.8	2,900	35.8	3,700
Public 2-year......................	16.5	1,700	22.3	2,200	21.1	2,300	37.7	3,000
For profit..........................	54.2	2,000	55.5	2,400	57.5	2,400	64.2	3,400
EMPLOYMENT STATUS [5]								
Not employed......................	27.0	2,100	28.8	2,600	31.0	2,700	44.7	3,500
Employed part-time................	28.5	2,000	28.1	2,500	29.2	2,600	41.4	3,500
Employed full-time................	16.0	1,600	24.5	2,300	23.4	2,200	36.2	3,000

S Does not meet publication standards. – Represents zero. [1] Data for 2012 excludes Puerto Rico. [2] Independent students are age 24 or over and students under 24 who are married, have dependents, are veterans or on active duty, are orphans or wards of the courts, are homeless or at risk of homelessness (in 2011–12 only), or were determined to be independent by a financial aid officer using professional judgment. Other undergraduates under age 24 are considered to be dependent. [3] Interpret data with caution. [4] Students attending private nonprofit less-than-4-year, public less-than-2-year, and multiple institutions are included in the total but not shown separately. For-profit includes less-than-2-year and 2-year or more institutions. [5] Employment includes work-study, assistantships, and traineeships. Full-time work is defined as 35 or more hours per week, and part-time work is defined as less than 35 hours.

Source: U.S. Department of Education, National Center for Education Statistics, *Trends in Pell Grant Receipt and the Characteristics of Pell Grant Recipients: Selected Years, 1999–2000 to 2011–12*, September 2015. See also <http://nces.ed.gov/surveys/npsas/>.

Table 309. Undergraduate Students Who Received Grant and Scholarship Aid by Source and Type of Institution Attended: 2012

[In percent. For school year ending in 2012. Based on the National Postsecondary Student-Aid Study; see source for details. Excludes Puerto Rico]

Type of institution	Total [1]	Source of aid				
		Federal [2]	Non-federal [3]	State [4]	Institu-tional [5]	Employer [6]
Total.................................	**70.7**	**57.2**	**40.4**	**15.4**	**20.5**	**5.6**
Institution attended:						
Public 2-year..............................	57.0	43.6	30.5	12.2	13.4	4.0
Public 4-year..............................	73.9	60.3	46.8	22.7	21.5	5.9
Private nonprofit 4-year.....................	86.1	67.2	72.1	21.1	58.4	9.5
For-profit 2-year or more....................	88.1	78.4	27.4	5.3	4.2	7.0
For-profit less-than-2-year..................	88.5	86.7	20.6	(S)	(S)	2.8
More than one institution or other............	73.6	60.2	41.6	13.8	21.4	5.7

S Does not meet publication standards. [1] Does not include aid from parents, friends, or relatives or federal tax credits for education. Includes Direct PLUS Loans to parents and other types of aid such as Veterans' benefits and job training funds. [2] Includes federal grants, loans, work-study awards, and federal Workforce Investment Act (WIA) job training funds. [3] Includes grants from states, institutions, and private organizations and loans from private sources. [4] Includes all grants and scholarships, loans, and work-study provided by state governments, including vocational rehabilitation and job training grants funded by the federal WIA. [5] Includes all institution need- and merit-based grants, scholarships, tuition waivers, loans, and work-study assistance. [6] Excludes tuition waivers to students holding assistantships.

Source: U.S. Department of Education, National Center for Education Statistics, *Trends in Undergraduate Nonfederal Grant and Scholarship Aid by Demographic and Enrollment Characteristics, Selected Years: 1999–2000 to 2011–12,* September 2015. See also <http://nces.ed.gov/surveys/npsas/>.

Table 310. Financial Aid for Graduate Students by Degree Type and Source of Aid: 2012

[In percent except, unless otherwise noted. For school year ending in 2012. Based on the National Postsecondary Student-Aid Study; see source for details. Excludes Puerto Rico]

Degree type	Total [1]	Source of aid				Average aid received (dollars)	Tuition and fees (dollars)	Price of atten-dance (dollars) [5]	Out-of-pocket net price (dollars) [6]
		Fed-eral [2]	Institu-tional [3]	Em-ployer	Other [4]				
Total.............................	**71.3**	**44.9**	**27.6**	**14.4**	**24.4**	**22,300**	**11,100**	**27,200**	**11,400**
Master's degree program:									
Business administration (M.B.A.)...............	69.2	35.8	18.4	21.9	33.3	16,500	10,200	23,600	12,300
Education (any master's).....................	62.5	47.9	14.6	9.5	17.3	14,300	6,400	18,000	9,400
M.A. (except in education)...................	72.4	45.0	29.3	12.4	23.2	16,900	8,600	21,900	9,900
M.S. (except in education)...................	67.3	38.1	25.0	15.1	24.6	17,100	10,100	24,800	13,400
Other master's [7]........................	75.4	54.2	25.4	15.5	27.5	20,000	11,100	26,000	11,000
Doctor's degree program - research/scholarship:									
Ph.D. (except in education).................	85.3	19.2	72.8	24.1	30.8	35,100	16,800	40,900	10,800
Education (any doctorate)...................	69.9	48.0	20.9	14.6	22.1	18,700	8,400	24,300	11,300
Other doctorate.........................	81.3	47.5	35.9	18.1	29.0	26,600	12,600	32,900	11,600
Doctor's degree program - professional practice:									
Medicine (M.D. or D.O.).....................	86.8	80.4	34.4	5.4	23.0	46,900	23,200	55,300	14,700
Other health science [8]...................	91.0	85.1	27.7	4.3	20.8	38,000	18,400	45,600	11,000
Law (LL.B. or J.D.).........................	88.1	81.3	40.0	2.7	15.4	45,500	24,500	53,300	13,300
Control of institution: [9]									
Public.................................	67.7	38.3	32.7	14.4	23.6	20,700	8,300	23,600	9,600
Private nonprofit.........................	73.4	47.6	27.0	14.4	25.1	26,200	14,900	32,600	13,400
For-profit..............................	75.7	57.9	11.8	14.5	24.3	15,000	9,300	22,700	11,400

[1] Excludes aid from parents, friends, or relatives and federal tax credits for education. Includes graduate PLUS Loans and other types of aid such as veterans' benefits and job training funds. [2] Consists of federal loans, federal grants, and federal work-study. Does not include military benefits. [3] Includes all institution need- and merit-based grants, scholarships, tuition waivers, graduate assistantships, loans, and work-study assistance funded by the institution attended. [4] Primarily includes outside grants, private/commercial loans, and veterans' benefits. [5] Price of attendance is the total budget (attendance intensity-adjusted) at the institution for students who attended only one institution during the academic year. The budget includes tuition, fees, housing, meals, books, supplies, transportation, and personal expenses. Institutions typically use this value as a student's budget for the purpose of awarding federal financial aid. [6] In calculating the out-of-pocket net price, all financial aid received including loans, is subtracted from the price of attendance. Price of attendance includes tuition, fees, books, supplies, housing, meals, transportation, and personal expenses. Federal education tax benefits are not included in the calculation. Averages include students who received no aid. [7] Includes M.S.W. (Master of Social Work), M.P.A. (Master of Public Administration), and M.F.A. (Master of Fine Arts). [8] Includes chiropractic (D.C. or D.C.M.), dentistry (D.D.S. or D.M.D.), optometry (O.D.), pharmacy (D.Pharm.), podiatry (Pod.D. or D.P.M.), and veterinary medicine (D.V.M.). [9] Excludes students attending more than one institution.

Source: U.S. Department of Education, National Center for Education Statistics, *Profile and Financial Aid Estimates of Graduate Students: 2011–12,* November 2014. See also <http://nces.ed.gov/surveys/npsas/>.

Table 311. State and Local Financial Support for Higher Education by State: 2016

[11,074.2 represents 11,074,200. For fiscal year ending in 2016. Educational appropriations include State and local appropriations for general operating expenses of public postsecondary education. Includes state-funded financial aid to students attending in-state public institutions. Excludes appropriations for independent institutions, financial aid for students attending independent institutions, sums for research, and teaching hospitals and medical schools]

State	FTE enroll-ment [1] (1,000)	Educational appropri-ations [2] (million dollars)	Educational appropri-ations per FTE enrollment [2] (dollars)	State	FTE enroll-ment [1] (1,000)	Educational appropri-ations [2] (million dollars)	Educational appropri-ations per FTE enrollment [2] (dollars)
Total U.S......	**11,074.2**	**77,010.3**	**6,954**	MO..............	192.8	1,158.6	6,010
				MT..............	38.0	186.4	4,912
AL..............	197.0	1,080.3	5,483	NE..............	77.2	676.6	8,769
AK..............	19.2	232.6	12,096	NV..............	69.0	450.2	6,528
AZ..............	279.2	1,253.5	4,489	NH..............	36.6	91.2	2,489
AR..............	114.5	817.4	7,138	NJ..............	268.3	1,531.7	5,709
CA..............	1,581.8	11,265.6	7,122	NM..............	93.4	777.0	8,321
CO..............	180.3	679.4	3,769	NY..............	555.6	3,948.4	7,106
CT..............	85.7	685.6	8,000	NC..............	383.9	3,358.9	8,750
DE..............	36.5	165.0	4,525	ND..............	36.5	262.5	7,189
FL..............	599.2	3,411.3	5,693	OH..............	388.8	2,085.8	5,365
GA..............	344.8	2,523.4	7,319	OK..............	135.0	829.7	6,148
HI..............	38.4	302.4	7,873	OR..............	151.5	755.7	4,987
ID..............	52.7	428.5	8,124	PA..............	350.6	1,253.7	3,576
IL [3]..............	376.9	827.7	2,196	RI..............	30.8	144.0	4,681
IN..............	223.5	1,376.5	6,159	SC..............	178.2	861.8	4,836
IA..............	126.2	692.8	5,491	SD..............	33.7	169.4	5,030
KS..............	135.4	768.7	5,679	TN..............	185.5	1,299.0	7,001
KY..............	149.3	1,011.6	6,775	TX..............	1,020.4	7,304.8	7,159
LA..............	167.9	830.2	4,945	UT..............	122.1	750.3	6,147
ME..............	34.6	216.1	6,244	VT..............	20.4	48.4	2,369
MD..............	228.9	1,597.7	6,981	VA..............	310.4	1,419.6	4,574
MA..............	169.2	1,071.6	6,334	WA..............	240.8	1,438.2	5,973
MI..............	379.2	2,121.5	5,595	WV..............	71.0	339.5	4,780
MN..............	193.2	1,210.8	6,267	WI..............	217.9	1,206.3	5,537
MS..............	128.7	885.4	6,878	WY..............	23.8	419.6	17,620

[1] Full-time equivalent. Includes degree enrollment and enrollment in public postsecondary programs resulting in a certificate or other formal recognition. Includes summer sessions. Excludes medical enrollments. [2] State and local appropriations for general operating expenses of public postsecondary education. Includes state-funded financial aid to students attending in-state public institutions. Excludes appropriations for independent institutions, financial aid for students attending independent institutions, sums for research, and teaching hospitals and medical schools. [3] Illinois lawmakers did not pass a budget for FY2016. The funds listed here for FY2016 represent partial stopgap funding for higher education.

Source: State Higher Education Executive Officers, Boulder, CO, *State Higher Education Finance: FY2016* ©, 2017. See also <http://www.sheeo.org>.

Table 312. Higher Education Price Indexes: 2008 to 2016 ©

[1983=100. For years ending June 30. The Higher Education Price Index (HEPI), calculated for the July-June academic fiscal year, reflects prices paid by colleges and universities for the following eight cost factors: faculty salaries, administrative salaries, clerical and service employees, fringe benefits, miscellaneous services, supplies and materials, and utilities. Minus sign (-) indicates decrease]

Item and year	Total	Personnel compensation					Contracted services, supplies, and equipment		
		Faculty salaries [1]	Admin-istrative salaries	Clerical salaries	Service employ-ees salaries	Fringe benefits [1]	Miscel-laneous services	Supplies and materials	Utilities
INDEXES									
2008......................	273.2	268.1	314.0	245.0	220.4	380.7	246.5	180.0	252.0
2009......................	279.3	277.3	330.9	251.6	226.7	394.4	253.1	181.6	213.8
2010......................	281.8	280.6	337.6	255.2	230.0	402.8	255.8	179.3	193.6
2011......................	288.4	284.5	343.2	260.2	233.2	417.6	260.3	193.9	201.5
2012......................	293.2	289.6	352.3	264.8	235.7	425.3	264.6	203.9	191.7
2013......................	297.8	294.6	362.4	269.8	239.4	437.5	269.4	180.0	195.6
2014......................	306.7	301.0	366.4	274.8	242.0	458.3	274.2	200.2	211.4
2015......................	313.3	307.7	381.9	280.4	248.4	484.0	279.8	190.6	183.5
2016......................	319.0	316.0	393.3	289.1	253.3	503.9	285.7	179.5	146.5
ANNUAL PERCENT CHANGE [2]									
2008......................	5.0	4.1	5.0	3.1	3.2	5.5	3.4	8.9	14.2
2009......................	2.3	3.4	5.4	2.7	2.9	3.6	2.7	0.9	-15.1
2010......................	0.9	1.2	2.0	1.4	1.4	2.1	1.1	-1.3	-9.5
2011......................	2.3	1.4	1.7	2.0	1.4	3.7	1.8	8.2	4.1
2012......................	1.7	1.8	2.7	1.7	1.1	1.8	1.7	5.2	-4.9
2013......................	1.6	1.7	2.9	1.9	1.6	2.9	1.8	-11.7	2.0
2014......................	3.0	2.2	1.1	1.9	1.1	4.8	1.8	11.2	8.1
2015......................	2.1	2.2	4.2	2.1	2.6	5.6	2.1	-4.9	-13.2
2016......................	1.8	2.7	3.0	3.1	2.0	4.1	2.1	-5.8	-20.2

[1] Data derived from faculty compensation data published by the American Association of University Professors (AAUP), which in FY2016 began using a new methodology that is not comparable with prior year data. [2] Percent change from the immediate prior year.

Source: The Commonfund Institute, Wilton, CT ©. See also <http://www.commonfund.org>.

Table 313. Average Salaries for College Faculty Members: 2015 to 2017

[In thousands of dollars (83.9 represents $83,900). For academic year ending in year shown. Figures are for 9 months teaching for full-time faculty members in 2-year and 4-year institutions]

Type of control and academic rank	2015	2016	2017	Type of control and academic rank	2015	2016	2017
Public: All ranks	**83.9**	**78.8**	**79.1**	**Private:** [1] **All ranks**	**105.2**	**80.5**	**83.6**
Professor	115.6	100.1	103.0	Professor	148.0	99.5	105.3
Associate professor	82.3	77.6	80.2	Associate professor	92.5	77.1	81.2
Assistant professor	70.8	67.6	69.7	Assistant professor	78.6	66.7	70.4
Instructor	49.2	52.8	54.3	Instructor	59.0	55.4	57.6

[1] Excludes church-related colleges and universities.

Source: American Association of University Professors, Washington, DC, *AAUP Annual Report on the Economic Status of the Profession* © 2017. See also: <http://www.aaup.org/>.

Table 314. Employees in Higher Education Institutions by Employment Status, Sex, and Occupation: 2015

[In thousands (3,915.9 represents 3,915,900). As of Fall. Covers institutions that grant associate's or higher degrees and that participate in Title IV federal financial aid programs. Includes institutions with fewer than 15 full-time employees. Detail may not sum to totals because of rounding. Based on Integrated Postsecondary Education Data System data]

Primary occupation	Full-time and part-time				Full-time		Part-time	
			Female					
	Total	Male	Total	Percent	Male	Female	Male	Female
All institutions	**3,915.9**	**1,777.8**	**2,138.1**	**54.6**	**1,121.8**	**1,385.8**	**656.0**	**752.3**
Faculty	1,551.0	788.8	762.2	49.1	438.8	368.2	350.0	393.9
Instruction	1,436.3	724.9	711.4	49.5	386.3	328.9	338.6	382.5
Research	87.1	50.8	36.4	41.7	43.0	29.8	7.8	6.6
Public service	27.5	13.1	14.4	52.4	9.5	9.5	3.6	4.9
Graduate assistants [1]	369.6	194.6	175.0	47.4	(X)	(X)	194.6	175.0
Librarians, curators, and archivists	42.6	12.5	30.1	70.6	11.0	25.3	1.5	4.8
Student and academic affairs, and other education services	171.6	55.5	116.0	67.6	33.8	79.7	21.7	36.4
Management	256.9	114.1	142.8	55.6	111.1	138.2	3.0	4.6
Business and financial operations	203.9	55.1	148.8	73.0	51.6	138.8	3.5	10.0
Computer, engineering, and science	232.0	140.9	91.1	39.3	131.9	80.2	9.0	10.8
Community, social service, legal, arts, design, entertainment, sports, and media	174.7	78.3	96.4	55.2	62.4	79.3	15.9	17.1
Healthcare practitioners and technicians	121.1	34.2	86.9	71.7	28.8	70.3	5.5	16.6
Service occupations	243.8	141.2	102.7	42.1	118.3	84.0	22.8	18.7
Sales and related occupations	13.9	4.9	9.0	64.9	4.2	7.2	0.6	1.8
Office and administrative support	441.2	73.5	367.7	83.3	51.1	307.0	22.4	60.7
Natural resources, construction, and maintenance	74.0	68.0	6.1	8.2	65.0	4.9	3.0	1.2
Production, transportation, and material moving	19.6	16.3	3.3	17.0	13.7	2.5	2.5	0.8

X Not applicable. [1] By definition, all graduate assistants are part time.

Source: U.S. National Center for Education Statistics, *Digest of Education Statistics*, "Advance Release of Selected 2016 Digest Tables," and earlier releases, <http://nces.ed.gov/programs/digest/>, accessed May 2017.

Table 315. Faculty in Institutions of Higher Education: 1980 to 2015

[In thousands (686 represents 686,000), except percent. As of Fall. Beginning in 1997, data reflect a new classification of institutions; this classification includes some additional, primarily 2-year, colleges and excludes a few institutions that did not award degrees. Includes institutions that were eligible to participate in Title IV federal financial aid programs. Includes schools accredited by the National Association of Trade and Technical Schools. Based on complete census taken every other year; see source]

Year	Total	Employment status		Control		Level		Percent		
		Full-time	Part-time	Public	Private	4-year	2-year or less	Part-time	Public	2-year or less
1980 [1]	686	450	236	495	191	494	192	34	72	28
1985 [1]	715	459	256	503	212	504	211	36	70	30
1991 [2]	826	536	291	581	245	591	235	35	70	28
1995	932	551	381	657	275	647	285	41	70	31
2001	1,113	618	495	771	342	764	349	44	69	31
2003	1,174	630	544	792	382	814	359	46	67	31
2005	1,290	676	615	841	449	917	373	48	65	29
2007 [3]	1,371	703	668	877	494	991	381	49	64	28
2009 [3]	1,439	729	710	914	525	1,038	401	49	63	28
2011 [3]	1,524	762	762	954	570	1,116	409	50	63	27
2013 [3]	1,545	791	754	969	577	1,152	394	49	63	25
2015 [3]	1,551	807	744	970	581	1,180	371	48	63	24

[1] Estimated on the basis of enrollment. [2] Data beginning 1991 not comparable to prior years. [3] Beginning in 2007, data include institutions with fewer than 15 full-time employees; these institutions did not report staff data prior to 2007.

Source: U.S. National Center for Education Statistics, *Digest of Education Statistics*, "Advance Release of Selected 2016 Digest Tables," <http://www.nces.ed.gov/programs/digest/>, accessed May 2017.

Table 316. Starting Salaries for New College Graduates by Degree and Field of Study: 2012 to 2016

[In dollars. Data prior to 2014 are average beginning salaries based on offers made by business, industrial, government, nonprofit, and educational employers to graduating students. Beginning in 2014, data are actual starting salaries. Data from representative colleges throughout the United States]

Field of study	Bachelor's					Master's [1]				
	2012	2013	2014	2015	2016	2012	2013	2014	2015	2016
Accounting....................	50,400	53,800	49,420	51,426	53,539	63,800	62,800	(NA)	54,721	57,429
Business administration/ management [2]..............	52,500	56,300	46,830	49,494	50,962	64,100	70,000	(NA)	73,951	81,757
Marketing....................	53,400	52,200	43,123	43,678	44,858	(NA)	(NA)	(NA)	66,537	67,903
Engineering:										
Civil.........................	57,500	58,500	54,656	57,368	57,091	(NA)	(NA)	(NA)	58,290	62,636
Chemical...................	66,200	67,500	68,061	65,782	68,239	(NA)	(NA)	(NA)	64,140	65,074
Computer..................	71,800	70,900	68,053	68,820	74,439	(NA)	(NA)	(NA)	87,546	81,905
Electrical..................	60,500	63,000	68,778	67,593	70,950	73,000	67,100	(NA)	86,218	91,693
Mechanical...............	61,300	64,500	63,555	[3] 62239	64,241	75,700	68,100	(NA)	66,786	74,321
Nuclear [4].................	(NA)	(NA)	60,164	54,351	[3] 60,121	(NA)	(NA)	(NA)	[3] 56643	[3] 86,594
Petroleum.................	(NA)	97,000	86,255	74,996	78,541	(NA)	(NA)	(NA)	(NA)	[3] 97,985
Engineering technology......	(NA)	61,500	57,090	(NA)	(NA)	(NA)	(NA)	(NA)	(NA)	(NA)
Chemistry..................	44,500	45,300	57,300	41,832	43,622	(NA)	(NA)	(NA)	[3] 51908	[3] 54,775
Mathematics...............	49,500	50,200	53,604	56,440	59,759	48,500	52,800	(NA)	72,976	53,466
Physics.....................	33,600	40,700	55,710	56,403	56,178	(NA)	(NA)	(NA)	[3] 65875	[3] 55,100
Humanities.................	37,300	34,700	41,605	52,990	42,902	(NA)	(NA)	(NA)	[3] 47583	72,271
Social sciences [5].............	38,100	37,800	41,917	40,964	46,749	50,000	48,400	(NA)	50,705	53,760
Computer science.............	62,200	64,700	66,801	75,191	78,199	80,400	73,500	(NA)	90,934	76,934

NA Not available. [1] Candidates with 1 year or less of full-time nonmilitary employment. [2] For master's degree, starting salaries are after nontechnical undergraduate degree. [3] Fewer than 50 salaries reported. [4] Includes engineering physics. [5] Excludes economics.

Source: National Association of Colleges and Employers, Bethlehem, PA ©. Reprinted with permission from Fall 2010, 2011, 2012, 2013, 2014, and Spring 2015 and 2016 Salary Surveys. All rights reserved.

Table 317. Degrees Earned by Level and Sex: 1960 to 2015

[In thousands (477 represents 477,000), except percent. Based on data from the Integrated Postsecondary Education Data System (IPEDS)]

Year ending	All degrees		Associate's		Bachelor's		Master's		Doctoral [1]	
	Total	Percent male	Male	Female	Male	Female	Male	Female	Male	Female
1960...............	477	65.8	(NA)	(NA)	[2] 254	[2] 138	51	24	9	1
1970...............	1,271	59.2	117	89	451	341	131	83	54	6
1975...............	1,666	56.0	191	169	505	418	166	131	71	14
1980...............	1,732	51.1	184	217	474	456	157	148	70	26
1985...............	1,828	49.3	203	252	483	497	149	144	66	35
1986...............	1,830	49.0	196	250	486	502	149	146	65	35
1987...............	1,823	48.4	191	245	481	510	147	149	63	36
1988...............	1,835	48.0	190	245	477	518	150	156	63	36
1989...............	1,873	47.3	186	250	483	535	154	163	63	38
1990...............	1,940	46.6	191	264	492	560	158	172	64	40
1991...............	2,025	45.8	199	283	504	590	161	182	64	41
1992...............	2,108	45.6	207	297	521	616	166	192	67	43
1993...............	2,167	45.5	212	303	533	632	173	202	67	45
1994...............	2,206	45.1	215	315	532	637	181	212	67	46
1995...............	2,218	44.9	218	321	526	634	183	221	67	47
1996...............	2,248	44.2	220	336	522	642	183	229	67	48
1997...............	2,288	43.6	224	347	521	652	185	240	68	50
1998...............	2,298	43.2	218	341	520	664	189	247	67	52
1999...............	2,330	42.7	221	344	520	682	190	256	65	51
2000...............	2,385	42.6	225	340	530	708	196	267	65	54
2001...............	2,416	42.4	232	347	532	712	198	276	64	55
2002...............	2,494	42.2	238	357	550	742	203	285	63	57
2003...............	2,623	42.1	253	381	573	776	215	304	63	59
2004...............	2,755	41.8	260	405	595	804	233	331	64	62
2005...............	2,850	41.6	268	429	613	826	237	343	67	67
2006...............	2,936	41.3	270	443	631	855	242	358	69	69
2007...............	3,007	41.2	275	453	650	875	242	368	71	73
2008...............	3,093	41.2	283	468	668	895	250	380	73	76
2009...............	3,205	41.3	298	489	685	916	264	399	76	79
2010...............	3,351	41.2	323	526	707	943	275	418	77	82
2011...............	3,554	41.3	361	582	734	982	292	439	80	84
2012...............	3,740	41.3	393	628	766	1,026	302	453	83	88
2013...............	3,775	41.4	389	618	787	1,053	302	450	85	90
2014...............	3,807	41.5	391	614	802	1,068	303	452	86	92
2015...............	3,846	41.6	397	617	813	1,082	307	452	85	94

NA Not available. [1] Includes Ph.D., Ed.D., and comparable degrees at the doctoral level. Includes most degrees formerly classified as first-professional, such as M.D., D.D.S., and law degrees. [2] Includes some degrees classified as master's or doctor's degrees in later years.

Source: U.S. National Center for Education Statistics, *Digest of Education Statistics*, "Advance Release of Selected 2016 Digest Tables," <https://nces.ed.gov/programs/digest/index.asp>, accessed November 2016.

Table 318. Degrees Earned by Level and Race/Ethnicity: 1990 to 2015

[For school year ending in year shown. Based on Integrated Postsecondary Education Data System surveys; see Appendix III]

Level of degree and race/ethnicity	Total					Percent distribution		
	1990	2000 [1]	2010	2014	2015	2000 [1]	2010	2015
Associate's degrees, total	**455,102**	**564,933**	**848,856**	**1,005,155**	**1,013,971**	**100.0**	**100.0**	**100.0**
White, non-Hispanic	376,816	408,822	552,376	601,959	590,390	72.4	65.1	58.2
Black, non-Hispanic	34,326	60,208	113,867	134,621	137,892	10.7	13.4	13.6
Hispanic	21,504	51,563	112,403	168,106	180,515	9.1	13.2	17.8
Asian or Pacific Islander	13,066	27,778	44,026	50,368	51,750	4.9	5.2	5.1
American Indian/Alaska Native	3,430	6,474	10,101	10,338	9,993	1.2	1.2	1.0
Two or more races	(NA)	(NA)	(NA)	22,695	25,494	(NA)	(NA)	2.5
Nonresident alien	5,960	10,088	16,083	17,068	17,937	1.8	1.9	1.8
Bachelor's degrees, total	**1,051,344**	**1,237,875**	**1,649,919**	**1,870,150**	**1,894,934**	**100.0**	**100.0**	**100.0**
White, non-Hispanic	887,151	929,102	1,167,322	1,218,998	1,210,523	75.1	70.8	63.9
Black, non-Hispanic	61,046	108,018	164,789	191,437	192,715	8.7	10.0	10.2
Hispanic	32,829	75,063	140,426	202,425	217,718	6.1	8.5	11.5
Asian or Pacific Islander	39,230	77,909	117,391	131,662	133,996	6.3	7.1	7.1
American Indian/Alaska Native	4,390	8,717	12,405	10,784	10,211	0.7	0.8	0.5
Two or more races	(NA)	(NA)	(NA)	45,422	54,201	(NA)	(NA)	2.9
Nonresident alien	26,698	39,066	47,586	69,422	75,570	3.2	2.9	4.0
Master's degrees, total [2]	**(NA)**	**463,185**	**693,313**	**754,582**	**758,708**	**100.0**	**100.0**	**100.0**
White, non-Hispanic	(NA)	324,990	445,158	444,771	433,106	70.2	64.2	57.1
Black, non-Hispanic	(NA)	36,606	76,472	88,606	87,265	7.9	11.0	11.5
Hispanic	(NA)	19,379	43,603	55,962	58,684	4.2	6.3	7.7
Asian or Pacific Islander	(NA)	23,523	42,520	44,533	44,517	5.1	6.1	5.9
American Indian/Alaska Native	(NA)	2,263	3,965	3,512	3,412	0.5	0.6	0.4
Two or more races	(NA)	(NA)	(NA)	13,417	14,622	(NA)	(NA)	1.9
Nonresident alien	(NA)	56,424	81,595	103,781	117,102	12.2	11.8	15.4
Doctoral degrees, total [2,3]	**(NA)**	**118,736**	**158,590**	**177,587**	**178,547**	**100.0**	**100.0**	**100.0**
White, non-Hispanic	(NA)	82,984	104,419	110,157	108,912	69.9	65.8	61.0
Black, non-Hispanic	(NA)	7,078	10,413	12,621	13,278	6.0	6.6	7.4
Hispanic	(NA)	5,042	8,085	10,665	11,257	4.2	5.1	6.3
Asian or Pacific Islander	(NA)	10,682	16,560	19,118	19,193	9.0	10.4	10.7
American Indian/Alaska Native	(NA)	708	952	861	884	0.6	0.6	0.5
Two or more races	(NA)	(NA)	(NA)	2,966	3,671	(NA)	(NA)	2.1
Nonresident alien	(NA)	12,242	18,161	21,199	21,352	10.3	11.5	12.0
First-professional degrees, total	**70,988**	**80,057**	**94,103**	**99,524**	**97,953**	**100.0**	**100.0**	**100.0**
White, non-Hispanic	60,487	59,637	66,172	66,029	63,472	74.5	70.3	64.8
Black, non-Hispanic	3,409	5,555	6,850	7,256	7,512	6.9	7.3	7.7
Hispanic	2,425	3,865	5,430	6,820	6,994	4.8	5.8	7.1
Asian or Pacific Islander	3,362	8,584	12,691	14,267	14,071	10.7	13.5	14.4
American Indian/Alaska Native	257	564	665	528	541	0.7	0.7	0.6
Two or more races	(NA)	(NA)	(NA)	2,014	2,556	(NA)	(NA)	2.6
Nonresident alien	1,048	1,852	2,295	2,610	2,807	2.3	2.4	2.9

NA Not available. [1] Beginning 2000, data reflect the new classification of institutions. See headnote, Table 288. [2] Data prior to 2009 have been revised. Revisions for 1990 not available. [3] Includes Ph.D., Ed.D., and comparable degrees at the doctoral level, as well as M.D., D.D.S., and law degrees that were formerly classified as first-professional degrees.

Source: U.S. National Center for Education Statistics, *Digest of Education Statistics*, "Advance Release of Selected 2016 Digest Tables," <http://www.nces.ed.gov/programs/digest/>, accessed July 2017.

Table 319. Bachelor's Degrees Earned by Field: 1980 to 2015

[For school year ending in year shown. The new Classification of Instructional Programs was introduced in 2009-2010. Data for previous years has been reclassified where necessary to conform to the new classifications. Based on data from the Integrated Postsecondary Education Data System (IPEDS)]

Field of study	1980	1990	2000	2010	2014	2015
Total [1]	**929,417**	**1,051,344**	**1,237,875**	**1,649,919**	**1,870,150**	**1,894,934**
Agriculture and natural resources	22,802	12,900	24,238	26,343	35,125	36,277
Architecture and related services	9,132	9,364	8,462	10,051	9,149	9,090
Area, ethnic, cultural, and gender studies	2,840	4,447	6,212	8,620	8,275	7,782
Biological and biomedical sciences	46,190	37,204	63,005	86,391	104,657	109,896
Business	186,264	248,568	256,070	358,119	358,132	363,799
Communication, journalism, and related programs [2]	28,616	51,572	57,058	86,062	92,603	95,785
Computer and information sciences	11,154	27,347	37,788	39,593	55,271	59,581
Education	118,038	105,112	108,034	101,287	98,838	91,623
Engineering and engineering technologies	69,387	82,480	73,419	88,735	108,976	115,096
English language and literature/letters	32,187	46,803	50,106	53,229	50,464	45,847
Family and consumer sciences/human sciences	18,411	13,514	16,321	21,832	24,689	24,584
Foreign languages, literatures, and linguistics	12,480	13,133	15,886	21,507	20,332	19,493
Health professions and related clinical sciences	63,848	58,983	80,863	129,623	198,777	216,228
Homeland security, law enforcement, and firefighting	15,015	15,354	24,877	43,613	62,416	62,723
Legal professions and studies	683	1,632	1,969	3,886	4,513	4,420
Liberal arts and sciences, general studies, and humanities	23,196	27,985	36,104	46,963	45,281	43,647
Mathematics and statistics	11,378	14,276	11,418	16,029	20,987	21,853
Multi/interdisciplinary studies	11,457	16,557	28,561	37,717	48,392	47,556
Parks, recreation, leisure, and fitness studies	5,753	4,582	17,571	33,332	46,047	49,006
Philosophy and religious studies	7,069	7,034	8,535	12,503	11,999	11,072
Physical sciences and science technologies	23,407	16,056	18,331	23,381	29,307	30,038
Psychology	42,093	53,952	74,194	97,215	117,312	117,557
Public administration and social services	16,644	13,908	20,185	25,421	33,483	34,363
Social sciences and history	103,662	118,083	127,101	172,782	173,132	166,944
Theology and religious vocations	6,170	5,185	6,789	8,719	9,642	9,708
Transportation and materials moving	213	2,387	3,395	4,998	4,588	4,711
Visual and performing arts	40,892	39,934	58,791	91,798	97,414	95,832

[1] Includes other fields of study, not shown separately. [2] Includes communications technologies.

Source: U.S. National Center for Education Statistics, *Digest of Education Statistics*, "Advance Release of Selected 2016 Digest Tables," <https://nces.ed.gov/programs/digest/index.asp>, accessed November 2016.

Table 320. Associate's Degrees and Certificates Below the Associate's Degree Level by Field and Sex: 2015

[For school year ending in 2015. The new Classification of Instructional Programs was introduced in 2009-2010. Covers certificates below the associate's degree level based on postsecondary curriculums of less than 4 years in degree- and nondegree-granting institutions of higher education and associate's degrees conferred by degree-granting institutions. Based on Integrated Postsecondary Education Data System (IPEDS) survey; see Appendix III]

Field of study	Less than 1-year awards			1- to less than 4-year awards			Associate's degree		
	Total	Male	Female	Total	Male	Female	Total	Male	Female
Total [1]	**485,304**	**221,688**	**263,616**	**475,863**	**172,978**	**302,885**	**1,013,971**	**396,613**	**617,358**
Agriculture and natural resources, total	3,534	2,295	1,239	2,457	1,588	869	7,693	4,902	2,791
Architecture and related services	199	119	80	95	71	24	491	342	149
Area, ethnic, cultural, gender, and group studies	435	106	329	164	43	121	382	148	234
Biological and biomedical sciences	565	136	429	239	89	150	4,882	1,634	3,248
Business, management, marketing, and support services [1]	57,684	20,194	37,490	24,799	7,182	17,617	113,670	43,117	70,553
Accounting and related services	11,419	3,588	7,831	5,692	1,415	4,277	16,080	4,439	11,641
Business administration, management, and operations	14,600	5,806	8,794	4,049	1,418	2,631	52,666	23,089	29,577
Communication, journalism, and related programs	1,856	902	954	1,936	1,070	866	6,034	2,576	3,458
Communications technologies	2,553	1,596	957	3,263	2,498	765	4,628	3,159	1,469
Computer and information sciences and support services	24,348	17,303	7,045	10,297	7,831	2,466	36,401	28,782	7,619
Construction trades	12,692	12,016	676	11,663	11,161	502	4,643	4,355	288
Education	6,605	621	5,984	3,821	440	3,381	17,175	1,948	15,227
Engineering	718	620	98	346	292	54	4,875	4,203	672
Engineering technologies and engineering-related fields	18,746	16,231	2,515	13,411	12,029	1,382	31,958	27,886	4,072
English language and literature/letters	1,060	351	709	975	340	635	2,324	802	1,522
Family and consumer sciences	15,875	1,193	14,682	3,641	297	3,344	8,752	405	8,347
Foreign languages, literatures, and linguistics	1,285	237	1,048	676	117	559	2,102	505	1,597
Health professions and related programs	161,193	31,240	129,953	177,386	24,256	153,130	199,991	31,814	168,177
Dental assisting	7,567	610	6,957	14,097	1,232	12,865	7,762	366	7,396
Emergency medical technician (EMT paramedic)	16,483	10,751	5,732	5,318	3,981	1,337	3,456	2,397	1,059
Clinical/medical lab science	9,536	1,328	8,208	2,545	717	1,828	3,143	781	2,362
Medical assisting	14,806	1,309	13,497	53,128	4,570	48,558	36,813	5,068	31,745
Pharmacy assisting	4,798	1,108	3,690	6,897	1,386	5,511	(NA)	(NA)	(NA)
Other allied health assisting	7,046	2,334	4,712	2,508	378	2,130	(NA)	(NA)	(NA)
Nursing and patient care assistant	43,980	5,543	38,437	1,502	210	1,292	50	5	45
Practical nursing	5,853	681	5,176	46,256	4,996	41,260	1,858	174	1,684
Nursing, R.N. and other	1,441	165	1,276	3,229	451	2,778	82,952	11,785	71,167
Health sciences, other	49,683	7,411	42,272	41,906	6,335	35,571	63,957	11,238	52,719
Homeland security, law enforcement, and firefighting	28,880	21,314	7,566	7,910	5,145	2,765	43,039	23,876	19,163
Legal professions and studies	1,868	319	1,549	3,272	553	2,719	9,095	1,362	7,733
Liberal arts and sciences, general studies, and humanities	3,604	1,360	2,244	41,335	16,418	24,917	367,626	141,139	226,487
Library science	217	40	177	54	6	48	170	25	145
Mathematics and statistics	135	108	27	16	7	9	2,697	1,915	782
Mechanic and repair technologies/technicians	35,672	33,526	2,146	47,386	45,413	1,973	19,983	18,933	1,050
Military technologies and applied sciences	28	24	4	29	23	6	1,229	1,015	214
Multi/interdisciplinary studies	1,832	741	1,091	1,216	652	564	29,139	11,998	17,141
Parks, recreation, leisure, and fitness studies	1,632	818	814	900	553	347	4,669	2,941	1,728
Personal and culinary services	38,955	5,328	33,627	86,852	12,249	74,603	18,693	7,423	11,270
Philosophy and religious studies	87	35	52	11	4	7	697	339	358
Physical sciences and science technologies	1,249	618	631	1,096	731	365	7,568	4,497	3,071
Precision production	25,542	24,072	1,470	17,269	16,269	1,000	4,382	4,149	233
Psychology	77	22	55	82	14	68	8,739	2,050	6,689
Public administration and social service professions	1,459	288	1,171	1,012	179	833	8,437	1,254	7,183
Social sciences and history	1,126	638	488	316	176	140	17,885	6,643	11,242
Theology and religious vocations	313	154	159	948	407	541	1,133	551	582
Transportation and materials moving	26,391	24,061	2,330	1,072	994	78	1,801	1,514	287
Visual and performing arts	6,889	3,062	3,827	9,918	3,881	6,037	20,988	8,411	12,577

[1] Includes other fields of study, not shown separately.

Source: U.S. National Center for Education Statistics, *Digest of Education Statistics*, "Advance Release of Selected 2016 Digest Tables," <http://www.nces.ed.gov/programs/digest/>, accessed June 2017.

Table 321. Master's and Doctoral Degrees Earned by Field: 1971 to 2015

[For school years ending in years shown. The new Classification of Instructional Programs was introduced in 2009-2010. Data for previous years has been reclassified where necessary to conform to the new classifications. Based on data from the Integrated Postsecondary Education Data System (IPEDS)]

Field of study	1971	1981	1991	2001	2011	2015
MASTER'S DEGREES						
Total [1]	**235,564**	**302,637**	**342,863**	**473,502**	**730,922**	**758,708**
Agriculture and natural resources	2,457	4,003	3,295	4,272	5,766	6,426
Architecture and related services	1,705	3,153	3,490	4,302	7,788	8,006
Area, ethnic, cultural, gender, and group studies	1,032	802	1,233	1,555	1,913	1,847
Biological and biomedical sciences	5,625	5,766	4,834	7,017	11,324	14,650
Business	26,490	57,888	78,255	115,602	187,178	185,222
Communication, journalism, and related programs	1,770	2,896	4,123	5,218	8,302	9,581
Communications technologies	86	209	204	427	502	554
Computer and information sciences	1,588	4,218	9,324	16,911	19,516	31,474
Education	87,666	96,713	87,352	127,829	185,127	146,561
Engineering	16,813	16,893	24,454	25,174	38,664	46,115
Engineering technologies	134	323	996	2,013	4,515	5,324
English language and literature/letters	10,441	5,742	6,784	6,763	9,475	8,928
Family and consumer sciences/human sciences	1,452	2,570	1,541	1,838	2,918	3,148
Foreign languages, literatures, and linguistics	5,480	2,934	3,049	3,035	3,727	3,566
Health professions and related programs	5,330	16,176	21,354	43,623	75,571	102,897
Homeland security, law enforcement, and firefighting	194	1,538	1,108	2,514	7,433	9,643
Legal professions and studies	955	1,832	2,057	3,829	6,475	7,924
Liberal arts and sciences, general studies, and humanities	885	2,375	2,213	3,193	3,997	2,794
Library science	7,001	4,859	4,763	4,727	7,729	5,259
Mathematics and statistics	5,191	2,567	3,549	3,209	5,866	7,589
Parks, recreation, leisure, and fitness studies	218	643	483	2,354	6,546	7,639
Philosophy and religious studies	1,326	1,231	1,471	1,386	1,839	1,912
Physical sciences and science technologies	6,336	5,246	5,281	5,134	6,386	7,100
Psychology	5,717	10,223	11,349	16,539	25,062	26,773
Public administration and social services	7,785	17,803	17,905	25,268	38,614	46,083
Social sciences and history	16,539	11,945	12,233	13,791	21,085	20,533
Theology and religious vocations	7,747	11,061	10,498	9,876	13,170	14,271
Transportation and materials moving	—	—	406	756	1,390	960
Visual and performing arts	6,675	8,629	8,657	11,404	16,277	17,756
DOCTORAL DEGREES						
Total [1]	**64,998**	**98,016**	**105,547**	**119,585**	**163,827**	**178,547**
Agriculture and natural resources	1,086	1,067	1,185	1,127	1,246	1,561
Architecture and related services	36	93	135	153	205	272
Area, ethnic, cultural, gender, and group studies	143	161	159	216	278	312
Biological and biomedical sciences	3,603	3,640	4,152	5,225	7,693	8,053
Business	774	808	1,185	1,180	2,286	3,116
Communication, journalism, and related programs	145	171	259	368	577	644
Computer and information sciences	128	252	676	768	1,588	1,998
Education	6,041	7,279	6,189	6,284	9,642	11,772
Engineering	3,687	2,598	5,316	5,485	8,369	10,239
English language and literature/letters	1,554	1,040	1,056	1,330	1,344	1,418
Foreign languages, literatures, and linguistics	1,084	931	889	1,078	1,158	1,243
Health professions and related programs	15,988	29,595	29,842	39,019	60,221	71,003
Legal professions and studies	17,441	36,391	38,035	38,190	44,853	40,329
Mathematics and statistics	1,199	728	978	997	1,586	1,801
Philosophy and religious studies	555	411	464	600	804	762
Physical sciences and science technologies	4,324	3,105	4,248	3,968	5,295	5,823
Psychology	2,144	3,576	3,932	5,091	5,851	6,583
Public administration and social services	174	362	430	574	851	1,123
Social sciences and history	3,660	3,122	3,012	3,930	4,390	4,828
Theology and religious vocations	312	1,273	1,076	1,461	2,374	1,927
Visual and performing arts	621	654	838	1,167	1,646	1,793

— Represents zero. [1] Includes other fields of study, not shown separately.

Source: U.S. National Center for Education Statistics, *Digest of Education Statistics*, "Advance Release of Selected 2016 Digest Tables," <http://www.nces.ed.gov/programs/digest/>, accessed November 2016.

Table 322. First Professional Degrees Earned in Selected Professions: 1970 to 2015

[First professional degrees include degrees which require at least 6 years of college work for completion (including at least 2 years of preprofessional training). Based on Integrated Postsecondary Education Data System surveys; see Appendix III]

Type of degree and sex of recipient	1970	1980	1985	1990	1995	2000	2005	2010	2014	2015
Medicine (M.D.):										
Institutions conferring degrees	86	112	120	124	119	118	120	120	124	127
Degrees conferred, total	8,314	14,902	16,041	15,075	15,537	15,286	15,461	16,356	17,604	18,302
Percent to women	8.4	23.4	30.4	34.2	38.8	42.7	47.3	48.2	47.6	47.8
Dentistry (D.D.S. or D.M.D.):										
Institutions conferring degrees	48	58	59	57	53	54	53	55	57	60
Degrees conferred, total	3,718	5,258	5,339	4,100	3,897	4,250	4,454	5,062	5,407	5,816
Percent to women	0.9	13.3	20.7	30.9	36.4	40.1	43.8	45.8	47.5	47.9
Law (LL.B. or J.D.):										
Institutions conferring degrees	145	179	181	182	183	190	198	205	210	212
Degrees conferred, total	14,916	35,647	37,491	36,485	39,349	38,152	43,423	44,346	43,772	40,024
Percent to women	5.4	30.2	38.5	42.2	42.6	45.9	48.7	47.3	46.8	48.0
Theological (B.D., M.Div., M.H.L.):										
Institutions conferring degrees	(NA)	(NA)	(NA)	(NA)	192	198	(NA)	(NA)	(NA)	(NA)
Degrees conferred, total	5,298	7,115	7,221	5,851	5,978	6,129	5,533	5,825	6,339	6,296
Percent to women	2.3	13.8	18.5	24.8	25.7	29.2	35.6	(NA)	33.3	31.4

NA Not available.

Source: U.S. National Center for Education Statistics, *Digest of Education Statistics*, "Advance Release of Selected 2016 Digest Tables," <http://www.nces.ed.gov/programs/digest/>, accessed July 2017.

Table 323. Graduate and Undergraduate Students Taking Online Classes and Degree Programs by Selected Characteristics: 2012

[23,055 represents 23,055,000. For school year ending in 2012]

Student characteristics	Undergraduate students					Graduate students				
	Number of students		Percent of students taking—			Number of students		Percent of students taking—		
	Total enroll-ment	Students taking any online classes	Any online classes	Exclus-ively online classes	Entire degree program is online [1]	Total enroll-ment	Students taking any online classes	Any online classes	Exclus-ively online classes	Entire degree program is online [1]
Total.....................	**23,055**	**7,368**	**32.0**	**8.4**	**6.5**	**3,682**	**1,326**	**36.0**	**20.1**	**18.2**
Sex:										
Male.......................	9,921	2,831	28.5	6.5	4.9	1,463	461	31.5	17.8	15.9
Female....................	13,135	4,537	34.5	9.8	7.7	2,219	865	39.0	21.7	19.8
Race/ethnicity:										
White......................	13,345	4,472	33.5	9.0	6.8	2,341	864	36.9	20.2	18.2
Black......................	3,709	1,214	32.7	10.7	9.1	434	212	48.8	33.0	31.4
Hispanic..................	3,696	1,032	27.9	5.5	4.3	321	111	34.6	19.3	17.9
Asian......................	1,292	336	26.0	[2] 4.2	2.9	474	92	19.4	7.5	6.0
Pacific Islander..........	119	35	29.9	[2] 3.5	[2] 3.1	20	9	44.2	[2] 20.3	(S)
American Indian or Alaska Native............	209	68	32.6	9.1	7.0	16	(S)	55.1	[2] 42.5	[2] 43.4
Two or more races.........	686	210	30.6	8.3	5.5	75	30	40.4	20.9	18.4
Age:										
15 to 23 years old.........	12,956	3,429	26.5	4.5	3.2	419	82	19.5	4.5	4.3
24 to 29 years old.........	4,253	1,551	36.5	10.4	8.0	1,483	456	30.8	15.8	14.4
30 years old and over......	5,846	2,388	40.9	15.6	13.0	1,781	788	44.3	27.4	24.9
Attendance status:										
Exclusively full-time........	11,632	3,346	28.8	7.6	6.5	1,713	543	31.7	18.4	17.4
Exclusively part-time.......	7,308	2,583	35.3	10.7	7.4	1,396	572	41.0	22.7	19.5
Mixed full-time and part-time..................	4,116	1,440	35.0	6.4	5.0	573	212	36.9	19.1	17.9
Field of study:										
Business/management....	3,487	1,371	39.3	13.1	11.4	615	246	40.0	26.8	25.1
Education..................	1,175	397	33.8	8.4	6.4	775	379	48.9	26.1	23.7
Engineering................	1,087	252	23.2	3.8	2.3	(NA)	(NA)	(NA)	(NA)	(NA)
Health.....................	4,271	1,420	33.3	8.5	6.7	679	248	36.5	18.9	16.5
Humanities................	3,817	1,175	30.8	5.8	4.1	290	81	28.1	14.1	12.1
Law........................	(NA)	(NA)	(NA)	(NA)	(NA)	146	15	10.3	2.9	2.5
Social/behavioral sciences.................	1,568	499	31.8	8.9	7.0	223	82	36.6	22.6	21.7
Vocational/technical........	718	160	22.3	4.1	2.8	(NA)	(NA)	(NA)	(NA)	(NA)

S Data do not meet publication standards. NA Not available. [1] Excludes students not in a degree or certificate program. [2] Interpret data with caution. The coefficient of variation (CV) for this estimate is between 30 and 50 percent.

Source: U.S. National Center for Education Statistics, *2014 Digest of Education Statistics*, April 2016. See also <http://www.nces.ed.gov/programs/digest/>.

Table 324. Academic Libraries by Selected Characteristics: 2012

[As of Fall of year shown. For information on public libraries, see Table 1182 and Table 1181]

Institution characteristic	Number of libraries	Circulation (1,000)		Expendi-tures (mil. dol.)	Paid staff [1]			
		General collection	Reserve collection		Total [2]	Librar-ians	Other pro-fessional staff	Student assistants
All U.S. academic libraries............	**3,793**	**116,891**	**37,518**	**7,008**	**85,752**	**26,606**	**7,817**	**20,509**
Control:								
Public.......................	1,560	75,013	24,884	4,078	51,064	15,124	4,477	11,288
Private......................	2,233	41,878	12,634	2,930	34,687	11,482	3,339	9,222
Level: [3]								
Total 4-year and above.................	2,489	100,772	30,312	6,395	74,241	22,504	6,821	18,308
Doctor's...................	894	75,996	20,820	5,216	55,386	16,243	5,337	12,768
Master's..................	842	16,263	6,788	797	12,491	4,066	929	3,688
Bachelor's................	753	8,513	2,705	382	6,364	2,195	555	1,852
Less than 4-year...........	1,304	16,119	7,205	613	11,510	4,102	996	2,202
Size (FTE enrollment): [4]								
Less than 1,000............	1,388	6,407	1,197	309	5,579	2,210	572	1,694
1,000 to 2,999.............	1,108	16,459	6,537	854	12,958	4,390	1,069	3,612
3,000 to 4,999.............	450	9,385	3,023	527	8,006	2,683	682	2,063
5,000 to 9,999.............	443	17,084	6,891	1,086	14,232	4,432	1,146	3,457
10,000 to 19,999...........	268	23,466	9,417	1,646	18,478	5,558	1,619	3,729
20,000 or more............	136	44,091	10,452	2,587	26,498	7,333	2,729	5,955

[1] Full-time equivalent (FTE) staff is calculated by dividing the total number of hours for all part-time positions by the number of hours the library defines as a full-time position. [2] Includes other staff not shown separately. [3] Level refers to the highest level of any degree offered by the institution. Doctoral, master's, and bachelor's level institutions do not sum to total number of 4-year and above institutions because there are 4-year and above institutions that grant "other" degrees and are thus not included in the breakdown. [4] FTE enrollment is calculated by adding one-third of part-time enrollment to full-time enrollment.

Source: U.S. National Center for Education Statistics, *Academic Libraries: 2012, First Look*, January 2014. See also <http://nces.ed.gov/surveys/libraries/academic.asp>.

Table 325. Public Schools Reporting Incidents of Crime by Incident Type and Selected School Characteristics: 2014

[For school year ending in 2014. Includes incidents that happen in school buildings, on school grounds, on school buses, and at places that hold school-sponsored events or activities. Based on sample; see source for details]

School characteristic	Total number of schools	Percent of schools with—		Number of incidents		Rate per 1,000 students	
		Violent incidents[1]	Serious violent incidents[2]	Violent incidents[1]	Serious violent incidents[2]	Violent incidents[1]	Serious violent incidents[2]
All public schools.................	**84,100**	**65.0**	**13.1**	**757,000**	**25,700**	**15.4**	**0.5**
Level:[3]							
Primary............................	49,700	52.8	9.2	318,300	7,700	13.0	0.3
Middle..............................	16,100	87.6	18.3	228,700	7,600	23.3	0.8
High school/combined[4]..........	18,400	78.0	19.3	209,900	10,400	13.9	0.7
Enrollment size:							
Less than 300......................	19,500	54.6	11.3	72,200	(S)	16.0	0.8
300 to 499.........................	25,400	60.7	10.7	202,700	5,000	19.5	0.5
500 to 999.........................	30,700	69.1	12.9	316,200	11,500	14.9	0.5
1,000 or more......................	8,500	86.4	25.3	165,900	6,300	12.7	0.5
Percent minority enrollment:							
Less than 5 percent...............	7,300	59.7	5 5.7	30,500	(S)	11.6	5 0.2
5 to 20 percent....................	22,800	62.1	10.2	111,600	5,400	10.3	0.5
20 to 50 percent..................	22,700	62.1	14.9	173,500	6,800	11.9	0.5
50 percent or more................	31,300	70.4	15.7	441,400	13,000	20.9	0.6

S Figure does not meet publication standards. [1] Violent incidents include rape, sexual battery other than rape, physical attack or fight with or without a weapon, threat of physical attack with or without a weapon, and robbery with or without a weapon. [2] Serious violent incidents include rape, sexual battery other than rape, physical attack or fight with a weapon, threat of physical attack with a weapon, and robbery with or without a weapon. [3] Primary schools are defined as schools in which the lowest grade is not higher than grade 3 and the highest grade is not higher than grade 8. Middle schools are defined as schools in which the lowest grade is not lower than grade 4 and the highest grade is not higher than grade 9. High schools are defined as schools in which the lowest grade is not lower than grade 9 and the highest grade is not higher than grade 12. Combined schools include all other combinations of grades, including K–12 schools. [4] Separate data on high schools and combined schools are not available for 2013-2014 school year. [5] Interpret data with caution.

Source: U.S. National Center for Education Statistics, *Indicators of School Crime and Safety: 2015,* May 2016. See also <http://nces.ed.gov/programs/crimeindicators/>.

Table 326. Percent of Public Schools Reporting Selected Types of Disciplinary Problems Occurring at School by Selected School Characteristics: 2013 to 2014

[In percent. For school year ending in 2014. "At school" includes activities that happen in school buildings, on school grounds, on school buses, and at places that hold school-sponsored events or activities. Based on the "School Safety and Discipline: 2013-14" survey. Respondents to the survey had the option of either completing the survey on paper and mailing it back, or completing the survey online. The online option was not available to respondents in previous years. The change in survey administration may have impacted 2013-14 results. Based on sample; see source for details]

School characteristic	Happens at least once a week					
	Student racial tensions	Student bullying	Student sexual harassment of other students[1]	Student verbal abuse of teachers	Widespread disorder in classrooms	Student acts of disrespect for teachers
All public schools.............................	**1.4**	**15.7**	**1.4**	**5.1**	**2.3**	**8.6**
Level:[2]						
Primary...	3 1.2	12.2	(S)	4.4	3 2.1	6.2
Middle..	3 2.5	24.5	3.4	6.1	3 2.5	11.1
High school/combined.............................	3 1.1	17.2	3 1.8	6.2	2.8	12.8
Enrollment size:						
Less than 300....................................	(S)	13.5	(S)	(S)	(S)	3 5.1
300 to 499.......................................	(S)	14.6	3 1.8	6.1	3 3.7	7.8
500 to 999.......................................	3 2.1	16.1	1.3	5.4	2.4	9.5
1,000 or more....................................	3.7	22.1	3 3.8	8.4	3 2.6	15.6
Percent minority enrollment:						
Less than 5 percent..............................	(S)	3 14.6	(S)	(S)	(S)	(S)
5 to 20 percent..................................	(S)	11.9	(S)	3 1.6	(S)	4.1
20 to 50 percent.................................	3 1.5	18.1	3 2.2	6.0	3 3.6	10.1
50 percent or more...............................	2.5	16.8	1.5	7.8	3.4	11.6

S Figure does not meet publication standards. [1] Sexual harassment was defined as conduct that is unwelcome, sexual in nature, and denies or limits a student's ability to participate in or benefit from a school's education program. The conduct can be carried out by school employees, other students, and non-employee third parties. Both male and female students can be victims of sexual harassment, and the harasser and the victim can be of the same sex. The conduct can be verbal, nonverbal, or physical. [2] Primary schools are defined as schools in which the lowest grade is not higher than grade 3 and the highest grade is not higher than grade 8. Middle schools are defined as schools in which the lowest grade level is not lower than grade 4 and the highest grade is not higher than grade 9. High schools are defined as schools in which the lowest grade is not lower than grade 9 and the highest grade is not higher than grade 12. Combined schools include all other combinations of grades, including K–12 schools. [3] Interpret data with caution.

Source: U.S. National Center for Education Statistics, *2014 Digest of Education Statistics*, April 2016. See also <http://www.nces.ed.gov/programs/digest/>.

Table 327. Students Who Reported Being Threatened or Injured With a Weapon on School Property by Selected Student Characteristics: 2001 to 2015

[In percent. Based on the Centers for Disease Control and Prevention's Youth Risk Behavior Surveillance System, which surveys students in public and private schools, in grades 9 to 12. Data are for previous 12 months. "On school property" was not defined for survey respondents. "Weapon" was defined as a gun, knife, or club for survey respondents]

Characteristic	2001	2003	2005	2007	2009	2011	2013	2015
Total................................	8.9	9.2	7.9	7.8	7.7	7.4	6.9	6.0
Sex:								
Male.............................	11.5	11.6	9.7	10.2	9.6	9.5	7.7	7.0
Female...........................	6.5	6.5	6.1	5.4	5.5	5.2	6.1	4.6
Race/ethnicity: [1]								
White............................	8.5	7.8	7.2	6.9	6.4	6.1	5.8	4.9
Black............................	9.3	10.9	8.1	9.7	9.4	8.9	8.4	7.9
Hispanic.........................	8.9	9.4	9.8	8.7	9.1	9.2	8.5	6.6
Asian............................	11.3	11.5	4.6	[2] 7.6	5.5	7.0	5.3	[2] 3.6
American Indian/Alaska Native.........	[2] 15.2	22.1	9.8	5.9	16.5	8.2	18.5	[2] 8.2
Pacific Islander/Native Hawaiian........	24.8	16.3	[2] 14.5	[2] 8.1	12.5	11.3	[2] 8.7	[2] 20.5
More than one race.....................	10.3	18.7	10.7	13.3	9.2	9.9	7.7	8.0
Grade:								
9th..............................	12.7	12.1	10.5	9.2	8.7	8.3	8.5	7.2
10th.............................	9.1	9.2	8.8	8.4	8.4	7.7	7.0	6.2
11th.............................	6.9	7.3	5.5	6.8	7.9	7.3	6.8	5.5
12th.............................	5.3	6.3	5.8	6.3	5.2	5.9	4.9	4.4

[1] Race categories exclude persons of Hispanic ethnicity. [2] Interpret data with caution.

Source: U.S. National Center for Education Statistics, *Digest of Education Statistics*, "Advance Release of Selected 2016 Digest Tables," <https://nces.ed.gov/programs/digest/index.asp>, accessed December 2016; and *Indicators of School Crime and Safety*, annual. See also <https://nces.ed.gov/surveys/ssocs/>.

Table 328. Public Schools Using Selected Safety and Security Measures by Type: 2000 to 2014

[In percent. For school year ending in year shown. Based on the School Survey on Crime and Safety and subject to sampling error; see source for details]

Measure	2000	2004	2006	2008	2010	2014 [1]
Controlled access during school hours:						
Buildings (locked or monitored doors).......................	74.6	83.0	84.9	89.5	91.7	93.3
Grounds (locked or monitored gates).......................	33.7	36.2	41.1	42.6	46.0	42.7
Visitors required to sign or check in.........................	96.6	98.3	97.6	98.7	99.3	98.6
Campus closed for most students during lunch............................	64.6	66.0	66.1	65.0	66.9	92.6
Student dress, IDs, and school supplies:						
Required students to wear uniforms.........................	11.8	13.8	13.8	17.5	18.9	20.4
Enforced a strict dress code...........................	47.4	55.1	55.3	54.8	56.9	58.5
Required students to wear badges or picture IDs..........................	3.9	6.4	6.2	7.6	6.9	8.9
Required faculty and staff to wear badges or picture IDs..................	25.4	48.0	47.9	58.3	62.9	68.0
Required clear book bags or banned book bags on school grounds......	5.9	6.2	6.4	6.0	5.5	6.3
Provided school lockers to students...........................	46.5	49.5	50.5	48.9	52.1	49.9
Drug testing:						
Athletes..	(NA)	4.2	5.0	6.4	6.0	6.6
Students in non-athletic extracurricular activities....................	(NA)	2.6	3.4	4.5	4.6	4.3
Any other students.............................	(NA)	(NA)	3.0	3.0	3.0	3.5
Metal detectors, dogs, and sweeps:						
Random metal detector checks on students..................................	7.2	5.6	4.9	5.3	5.2	4.2
Students required to pass through metal detectors daily.....................	0.9	1.1	1.1	1.3	1.4	2.0
Random dog sniffs to check for drugs............................	20.6	21.3	23.0	21.5	22.9	24.1
Random sweeps for contraband [2]............................	11.8	12.8	13.1	11.4	12.1	11.4
Communications systems and technology:						
Provided telephones in most classrooms.................................	44.6	60.8	66.9	71.6	74.0	78.7
Provided electronic notification system for school wide emergencies.....	(NA)	(NA)	(NA)	43.2	63.1	81.6
Provided structured anonymous threat reporting system [3].................	(NA)	(NA)	(NA)	31.2	35.9	46.5
Used security cameras to monitor the school.............................	19.4	36.0	42.8	55.0	61.1	75.1
Provided two-way radios to any staff...........................	(NA)	71.2	70.9	73.1	73.3	74.2
Limited access to social networking sites from school computers.........	(NA)	(NA)	(NA)	(NA)	93.4	91.9
Prohibited use of cell phones and text messaging devices................	(NA)	(NA)	(NA)	(NA)	90.9	75.9

NA Not available. [1] Data for 2013-14 were collected using the Fast Response Survey System. The 2013-14 survey was designed to allow comparisons with School Survey on Crime and Safety (SSOCS) data. However, respondents to the 2013-14 survey could choose either to complete the survey by mail or online, whereas respondents to SSOCS did not have the online option. The 2013-14 survey also relied on a smaller sample. These differences may have impacted 2013-14 results. [2] Does not include random dog sniffs. [3] For example, a system for reporting threats through online submission, telephone hotline, or written submission via drop box.

Source: U.S. National Center for Education Statistics, *Indicators of School Crime and Safety: 2015*, May 2016. See also <http://nces.ed.gov/programs/crimeindicators/>.

Table 329. Students Who Reported Being Bullied at School or Cyber-Bullied by Student Characteristics: 2013 and 2015

[In percent. For school year ending in 2015. For students aged 12 through 18. "At school" includes the school building, on school property, on a school bus, or going to and from school. For more information, see Appendix A of source]

Characteristic	Bullied at school, 2015						Cyber-bullying, 2013 [2]
	Total bullying at school [1]	Made fun of, called names, or insulted	Subject of rumors	Pushed, shoved, tripped, spit on	Purposefully excluded from activities	Threatened with harm	
Total	**20.8**	**13.3**	**12.3**	**5.1**	**5.0**	**3.9**	**6.9**
Sex:							
Male	18.8	12.7	9.1	6.0	4.4	4.8	5.2
Female	22.8	13.9	15.5	4.2	5.7	2.9	8.6
Race/ethnicity: [3]							
White	21.6	14.2	12.8	5.3	5.6	3.9	7.6
Black	24.7	17.2	14.3	5.6	4.9	5.2	4.5
Hispanic	17.2	9.5	10.4	3.7	3.4	2.9	5.8
Asian	15.6	[4] 10.1	[4] 4.9	[4] 3.9	(S)	(S)	5.8
Other	25.9	16.4	18.6	[4] 11.2	[4] 9.8	[4] 8.9	13.4
Grade:							
6th	31.0	21.4	17.7	13.1	10.1	7.3	5.9
7th	25.1	18.6	12.9	7.8	6.4	3.8	7.0
8th	22.2	15.6	13.1	7.5	5.1	5.0	6.4
9th	19.0	12.5	10.6	4.4	4.4	[4] 2.8	6.7
10th	21.2	12.6	12.9	[4] 2.2	5.7	[4] 2.9	8.6
11th	15.8	8.8	10.2	[4] 2.1	[4] 3.0	4.2	6.8
12th	14.9	6.2	10.8	[4] 1.6	[4] 2.4	[4] 2.5	5.9

NA Not available. S Reporting standards not met. [1] Bullying types do not sum to total because students could have experienced more than one type of bullying. Total includes other types of bullying not shown separately. [2] Cyber-bullied students includes students who responded that another student had posted hurtful information about them on the internet; purposefully shared private information about them on the internet; harassed them via instant messaging, via Short Message Service (SMS) text messaging, or via email; harassed them while gaming; or excluded them online. [3] Race categories exclude persons of Hispanic ethnicity. Other includes American Indian, Alaska Native, Pacific Islander, and more than one race. [4] Interpret data with caution.

Source: U.S. National Center for Education Statistics, Digest of Education Statistics, "Advance Release of Selected 2016 Digest Tables," <http://nces.ed.gov/programs/digest/index.asp>, accessed October 2017; and Indicators of School Crime and Safety, annual. See also <http://nces.ed.gov/surveys/ssocs/>.

Table 330. Violent Deaths, Homicides, and Suicides Occurring at Schools, Total and for Youth Aged 5 to 18: 1993 to 2014

[For school year ending in year shown. A school-associated violent death is defined as a homicide, suicide, or legal intervention (involving a law enforcement officer) in which the fatal injury occurred on the campus of a functioning elementary or secondary school in the United States, including while the victim was on the way to or from regular sessions at school or while the victim was attending or traveling to or from an official school-sponsored event. Victims include students, staff members, and others who are not students. Based on data from U.S. Centers for Disease Control and Prevention, and Federal Bureau of Investigation and Bureau of Justice Statistics]

Year	School-associated violent deaths				Homicides of youth aged 5 to 18		Suicides of youth aged 5 to 18	
	Total [1]	Homicides	Suicides [2]	Legal inter-ventions	Total	At school	Total	At school
1993	57	47	10	0	2,721	34	1,680	6
1994	48	38	10	0	2,932	29	1,723	7
1995	48	39	8	0	2,696	28	1,767	7
1996	53	46	6	1	2,545	32	1,725	6
1997	48	45	2	1	2,221	28	1,633	1
1998	57	47	9	1	2,100	34	1,626	6
1999	47	38	6	2	1,777	33	1,597	4
2000 [3]	37	26	11	0	1,567	14	1,415	8
2001 [3]	34	26	7	1	1,509	14	1,493	6
2002 [3]	36	27	8	1	1,498	16	1,400	5
2003 [3]	36	25	11	0	1,553	18	1,331	10
2004 [3]	45	37	7	1	1,474	23	1,285	5
2005 [3]	52	40	10	2	1,554	22	1,471	8
2006 [3]	44	37	6	1	1,697	21	1,408	3
2007 [3]	63	48	13	2	1,801	32	1,296	9
2008 [3]	48	39	7	2	1,744	21	1,231	5
2009 [3]	44	29	15	0	1,605	18	1,344	7
2010 [3]	35	27	5	3	1,410	19	1,467	2
2011 [3]	32	26	6	0	1,339	11	1,456	3
2012 [3]	45	26	14	5	1,201	15	1,568	5
2013 [3]	53	41	11	1	1,186	31	1,590	6
2014 [3]	48	26	20	2	1,053	12	1,645	8

[1] Total includes unintentional firearm-related deaths, not shown separately. [2] Total youth suicides are reported for calendar years 1992 through 2013 (instead of school years 1992-1993 through 2013-2014). [3] Data from school year 2000 onward are subject to change until interviews with school and law enforcement officials have been completed. The details learned during interviews can occasionally change the classification of a case.

Source: U.S. National Center for Education Statistics, Digest of Education Statistics, "Advance Release of Selected 2016 Digest Tables," <http://nces.ed.gov/programs/digest/>, accessed December 2016; and Indicators of School Crime and Safety, annual. See also <http://nces.ed.gov/surveys/ssocs/>.

Table 331. College Campus Crime—Incidents and Rates by Type of Crime and Institution: 2001 to 2014

[For school year ending in year shown. Data are from Department of Education's Campus Safety and Security Reporting System. Data are for degree-granting institutions, which are institutions that grant associate's or higher degrees and participate in Title IV federal financial aid programs. Some institutions that report data as mandated by the Clery Act, specifically, non-degree-granting institutions and institutions outside of the 50 states and the District of Columbia, are excluded from this table. Crimes, arrests, and referrals include incidents involving students, staff, and on-campus guests. Excludes off-campus crimes and arrests even if they involve college students or staff]

Control and level of institution and type of crime	Total, in residence halls and other locations						2014		
	2001	2006	2010	2011	2012	2013	Total	In residence halls	At other locations
NUMBER OF INCIDENTS									
Selected crimes against persons and property	**41,596**	**44,492**	**32,097**	**30,407**	**29,766**	**27,416**	**26,954**	**13,486**	**13,468**
Murder[1]	17	8	15	16	12	23	11	4	7
Negligent manslaughter[2]	2	–	1	1	1	–	2	–	2
Sex offenses, forcible[3]	2,201	2,670	2,927	3,375	4,015	5,002	6,723	4,888	1,835
Sex offenses, nonforcible[4]	461	43	33	46	46	47	55	34	21
Robbery	1,663	1,547	1,392	1,285	1,368	1,326	1,061	165	896
Aggravated assault	2,947	2,817	2,221	2,239	2,423	2,059	2,063	709	1,354
Burglary	26,904	31,260	21,335	19,472	18,183	15,358	13,542	7,341	6,201
Motor vehicle theft	6,221	5,231	3,441	3,334	3,013	2,971	2,901	10	2,891
Arson	1,180	916	732	639	705	630	596	335	261
Arrests[5]	**40,348**	**50,187**	**51,519**	**54,285**	**52,325**	**47,291**	**44,732**	**23,906**	**20,826**
Illegal weapons possession	1,073	1,316	1,112	1,023	1,023	1,022	1,011	233	778
Drug law violations	11,854	13,952	18,589	20,729	21,212	19,970	19,236	10,409	8,827
Liquor law violations	27,421	34,919	31,818	32,533	30,090	26,299	24,485	13,264	11,221
Referrals for disciplinary action[5]	**155,201**	**218,040**	**230,269**	**249,694**	**251,402**	**246,685**	**254,175**	**229,304**	**24,871**
Illegal weapons possession	1,277	1,871	1,314	1,282	1,404	1,412	1,429	927	502
Drug law violations	23,900	27,251	42,022	51,562	53,959	53,812	57,403	49,208	8,195
Liquor law violations	130,024	188,918	186,933	196,850	196,039	191,461	195,343	179,169	16,174
INCIDENTS PER 10,000 FTE STUDENTS[6,7]									
Selected crimes against persons and property	**35.6**	**33.3**	**20.9**	**20.0**	**20.0**	**18.4**	**17.9**	**23.8**	**5.4**
By type of crime:									
Murder[1]	(Z)	(Z)	(Z)	(Z)	(Z)	(Z)	(Z)	(Z)	(Z)
Negligent manslaughter[2]	(Z)	(Z)	(Z)	(Z)	(Z)	–	(Z)	(Z)	(Z)
Sex offenses, forcible[3]	1.9	2.0	1.9	2.2	2.7	3.4	4.5	6.3	0.6
Sex offenses, nonforcible[4]	0.4	(Z)	(Z)	(Z)	(Z)	(Z)	(Z)	(Z)	(Z)
Robbery	1.4	1.2	0.9	0.8	0.9	0.9	0.7	0.8	0.4
Aggravated assault	2.5	2.1	1.4	1.5	1.6	1.4	1.4	1.7	0.6
Burglary	23.0	23.4	13.9	12.8	12.2	10.3	9.0	12.2	2.3
Motor vehicle theft	5.3	3.9	2.2	2.2	2.0	2.0	1.9	2.2	1.4
Arson	1.0	0.7	0.5	0.4	0.5	0.4	0.4	0.5	0.1
By type of institution:									
Public 4-year	36.2	35.5	23.4	22.0	21.7	19.5	19.5	20.8	5.8
Nonprofit 4-year	57.4	57.7	35.2	33.2	33.2	31.3	30.1	32.2	8.1
For-profit 4-year	19.1	9.6	6.5	6.0	5.5	8.1	5.5	20.0	2.2
Public 2-year	19.9	15.4	10.2	10.0	9.4	8.0	7.7	15.5	5.8
Nonprofit 2-year	64.0	81.9	48.4	45.5	35.1	25.9	30.9	33.0	29.8
For profit-2-year	25.4	18.2	8.2	7.5	9.3	7.1	5.8	31.1	4.5
Arrests[5]	**34.6**	**37.6**	**33.5**	**35.8**	**35.1**	**31.8**	**29.7**	**42.1**	**3.5**
Illegal weapons possession	0.9	1.0	0.7	0.7	0.7	0.7	0.7	0.8	0.5
Drug law violations	10.2	10.5	12.1	13.7	14.2	13.4	12.8	17.7	2.5
Liquor law violations	23.5	26.2	20.7	21.4	20.2	17.7	16.3	23.7	0.6
By type of institution:									
Public 4-year	60.1	68.7	63.5	67.2	64.4	56.8	53.1	57.9	4.2
Nonprofit 4-year	24.5	21.0	17.2	16.8	16.9	17.1	14.9	16.1	1.9
For-profit 4-year	0.4	0.8	1.9	2.0	1.9	1.3	1.4	6.0	0.4
Public 2-year	7.8	10.9	8.8	9.0	8.7	8.1	8.6	25.2	4.5
Nonprofit 2-year	27.9	22.0	19.8	16.0	17.1	25.5	15.8	33.0	7.3
For profit-2-year	8.8	1.8	1.1	0.7	1.9	2.6	2.3	25.3	1.1
Referrals for disciplinary action[5]	**132.9**	**163.4**	**149.7**	**164.5**	**168.8**	**165.8**	**168.9**	**247.1**	**3.5**
Illegal weapons possession	1.1	1.4	0.9	0.8	0.9	0.9	0.9	1.2	0.3
Drug law violations	20.5	20.4	27.3	34.0	36.2	36.2	38.1	55.4	1.7
Liquor law violations	111.3	141.6	121.5	129.7	131.6	128.6	129.8	190.5	1.5
By type of institution:									
Public 4-year	153.1	184.6	175.5	194.0	197.7	189.8	198.3	217.3	1.3
Nonprofit 4-year	275.5	354.0	329.7	341.4	339.3	332.8	328.3	357.7	19.9
For-profit 4-year	12.0	7.6	8.8	9.7	10.2	17.8	11.3	59.5	0.4
Public 2-year	10.3	16.0	18.6	19.7	19.0	17.6	19.3	83.0	3.4
Nonprofit 2-year	160.9	176.0	152.2	110.8	98.5	123.6	131.2	392.1	1.2
For profit-2-year	15.4	13.9	3.8	4.9	8.2	8.1	9.2	179.0	0.3

– Represents zero. Z Data rounds to less than .05. [1] Excludes suicides, fetal deaths, traffic fatalities, accidental deaths, and justifiable homicide (such as the killing of a felon by a law enforcement officer in the line of duty). [2] Defined as the killing of another person through gross negligence (excludes traffic fatalities). [3] Any sexual act directed against another person forcibly and/or against that person's will. [4] Includes only statutory rape or incest. [5] If an individual is both arrested and referred to college officials for disciplinary action for a single offense, only the arrest is counted. [6] FTE is full-time equivalent. Although crimes, arrests, and referrals include incidents involving students, staff, and campus guests, they are expressed as a ratio to FTE students because comprehensive FTE counts of all these groups are not available. [7] Data on incidents per 10,000 FTE students are shown for institutions with and without residence halls.

Source: U.S. National Center for Education Statistics, *Digest of Education Statistics*, "Advance Release of Selected 2016 Digest Tables," <http://nces.ed.gov/programs/digest/index.asp>, accessed December 2016.

Law Enforcement, Courts, and Prisons

This section presents data on crimes committed, victims of crimes, arrests, and data related to criminal violations and the criminal justice system. The major sources of these data are the Bureau of Justice Statistics (BJS), the Federal Bureau of Investigation (FBI), and the Administrative Office of the U.S. Courts. BJS issues many reports—see our Guide to Sources for a complete listing. The Federal Bureau of Investigation's major annual reports are *Crime in the United States, Law Enforcement Officers Killed and Assaulted,* and *Hate Crimes,* which present data on reported crimes as gathered from state and local law enforcement agencies.

Legal jurisdiction and law enforcement—Law enforcement is, for the most part, a function of state and local officers and agencies. The U.S. Constitution reserves general police powers to the states. By act of Congress, federal offenses include only offenses against the U.S. government and against or by its employees while engaged in their official duties, and offenses which involve the crossing of state lines or an interference with interstate commerce. Excluding the military, there are 52 separate criminal law jurisdictions in the United States: one in each of the 50 states, one in the District of Columbia, and the federal jurisdiction. Each of these has its own criminal law and procedure and its own law enforcement agencies. While the systems of law enforcement are quite similar among the states, there are often substantial differences in the penalties for like offenses.

Law enforcement can be divided into three parts: Investigation of crimes and arrests of persons suspected of committing them; prosecution of those charged with crime; and the punishment or treatment of persons convicted of crime.

Crime—The U.S. Department of Justice administers two statistical programs to measure the magnitude, nature, and impact of crime in the nation: the Uniform Crime Reporting (UCR) Program and the National Crime Victimization Survey (NCVS). Each of these programs produces valuable information about aspects of the nation's crime problem. Because the UCR and NCVS programs are conducted for different purposes, use different methods, and focus on somewhat different aspects of crime, the information they produce together provides a more comprehensive panorama of the nation's crime problem than either could produce alone.

Uniform Crime Reports (UCR)—The FBI's UCR Program, which began in 1929, collects information on the following crimes reported to law enforcement authorities: Part 1 offenses, for which detailed data is reported— murder and nonnegligent manslaughter, rape, robbery, aggravated assault, burglary, larceny-theft, motor vehicle theft, and arson; and Part 2 offenses, 20 additional crime categories for which law enforcement agencies report only arrest data. UCR definitions of criminal offenses (including those listed) can be found at <https://ucr.fbi.gov/crime-in-the-u.s/2015/crime-in-the-u.s.-2015/resource-pages/offense-definitions>.

Beginning in 2013, the UCR program implemented a revised definition of rape. Not all state and local agencies have been able to effect the change in their records management systems and some agencies currently can report the offense based on only the legacy definition. Therefore, rape data collected under both definitions are used in the *Crime in the United States* report. Additionally, the ability to show trend data for rape has been impacted. For details, see <https://ucr.fbi.gov/crime-in-the-u.s/2015/crime-in-the-u.s.-2015/resource-pages/rape-addendum>.

The UCR Program compiles data from monthly law enforcement reports or individual crime incident records transmitted directly to the FBI or to centralized state agencies that then report to the FBI. The Program thoroughly examines each report it receives for reasonableness, accuracy, and deviations that may indicate errors. Large variations in crime levels may indicate modified records procedures, incomplete reporting, or changes in a jurisdiction's boundaries. To identify any unusual fluctuations in an agency's crime counts, the Program compares monthly reports to previous submissions of the agency and with those for similar agencies.

The UCR Program presents crime counts for the nation as a whole, as well as for regions, states, counties, cities, towns, tribal law enforcement, and colleges and universities. This permits studies among neighboring jurisdictions and among those with similar populations and other common characteristics.

The UCR Program annually publishes its findings online in a preliminary release in the spring of the following calendar year, followed by a detailed report, *Crime in the United States,* issued in the fall. In addition to crime counts and trends, this report includes data on crimes cleared, persons arrested (age, sex, and race), law enforcement personnel (including the number of sworn officers killed or assaulted), and the characteristics of homicides (including age, sex, and race of victims and offenders; victim-offender relationships; weapons used; and circumstances surrounding the homicides). Other periodic reports are also available from the UCR Program.

National Crime Victimization Survey (NCVS)—A second perspective on crime is provided by this survey of the Bureau of Justice Statistics (BJS). The NCVS is an annual data collection (interviews of persons aged 12 or older), conducted by the U.S. Census Bureau for the BJS. As an ongoing survey of households, the NCVS measures crimes of violence and property both reported and not reported to police. It produces national rates and levels of personal and property victimization. No attempt is made to validate the information against police records or any other source.

The NCVS measures rape/sexual assault, robbery, assault, pocket-picking, purse snatching, burglary, and motor vehicle theft. The NCVS includes crimes reported to the police, as well as those not reported. Murder and kidnaping are not covered. The so-called victimless crimes, such as drunkenness, drug abuse, and prostitution, also are excluded, as are crimes for which it is difficult to identify knowledgeable respondents or to locate data records.

Crimes of which the victim may not be aware also cannot be measured effectively. Buying stolen property may fall into this category, as may some instances of embezzlement. Attempted crimes of many types probably are under-recorded for this reason. Events in which the victim has shown a willingness to participate in illegal activity also are excluded.

In any encounter involving a personal crime, more than one criminal act can be committed against an individual. For example, a rape may be associated with a robbery, or a household property offense, such as a burglary, can escalate into something more serious in the event of a personal confrontation. In classifying the survey measured crimes, each criminal incident has been counted only once, by the most serious act that took place during the incident, and ranked in accordance with the seriousness classification system used by the FBI. The order of seriousness for crimes against persons is as follows: rape, robbery, assault, and larceny. Personal crimes take precedence over household offenses.

A *victimization*, the basic measure of the occurrence of crime, is a specific criminal act as it affects a single victim. The number of victimizations is determined by the number of victims of such acts. Victimization counts serve as key elements in computing rates of victimization. For crimes against persons, the rates are based on the total number of individuals aged 12 and over or on a portion of that population sharing a particular characteristic or set of traits. As general indicators of the danger of having been victimized during the reference period, the rates are not sufficiently refined to represent true measures of risk for specific individuals or households.

An *incident* is a specific criminal act involving one or more victims; therefore the number of incidents of personal crimes is lower than that of victimizations.

Courts—Statistics on criminal offenses and the outcome of prosecutions are incomplete for the country as a whole, although data are available for many states individually.

From 1986 to 2006, through its National Judicial Reporting Program, the BJS surveyed a nationally representative sample of 300 counties every 2 years and collected detailed information on demographic characteristics of felons, conviction offenses, type of sentences, sentence lengths, and time from arrest to conviction and sentencing.

The bulk of civil and criminal litigation in the country is commenced and determined in the various state courts. Only when the U.S. Constitution and acts of Congress specifically confer jurisdiction upon the federal courts may civil or criminal litigation be heard and decided by them. Generally, the federal courts have jurisdiction over the following types of cases: suits or proceedings by or against the United States; civil actions between private parties arising under the

Constitution, laws, or treaties of the United States; civil actions between private litigants who are citizens of different states; civil cases involving admiralty, maritime, or private jurisdiction; and all matters in bankruptcy.

There are several types of courts with varying degrees of legal jurisdiction. These jurisdictions include original, appellate, general, and limited or special. A court of original jurisdiction is one having the authority initially to try a case and pass judgment on the law and the facts; a court of appellate jurisdiction is one with the legal authority to review cases and hear appeals; a court of general jurisdiction is a trial court of unlimited original jurisdiction in civil and/or criminal cases, also called a "major trial court"; a court of limited or special jurisdiction is a trial court with legal authority over only a particular class of cases, such as probate, juvenile, or traffic cases.

The 94 federal courts of original jurisdiction are known as the U.S. district courts. One or more of these courts is established in every state and one each in the District of Columbia, Puerto Rico, the Virgin Islands, the Northern Mariana Islands, and Guam. Appeals from the district courts are taken to intermediate appellate courts of which there are 13, known as U.S. courts of appeals and the United States Court of Appeals for the Federal Circuit. The Supreme Court of the United States is the final and highest appellate court in the federal system of courts.

Juvenile offenders—For statistical purposes, the FBI and most states classify as juvenile offenders persons under the age of 18 years who have committed a crime or crimes.

Delinquency cases are all cases of youths referred to a juvenile court for violation of a law or ordinance or for seriously "antisocial" conduct. Several types of facilities are available for those adjudicated delinquents, ranging from the short-term physically unrestricted environment to the long-term very restrictive atmosphere.

Prisoners and jail inmates—BJS started to collect annual data in 1979 on prisoners in federal and state prisons and reformatories. Adults convicted of criminal activity may be given a prison or jail sentence. A *prison* is a confinement facility having custodial authority over adults sentenced to confinement of more than 1 year. A *jail* is a facility, usually operated by a local law enforcement agency, holding persons detained pending adjudication and/or persons committed after adjudication to 1 year or less.

Data on inmates in local jails were collected by the BJS for the first time in 1970. Since then, BJS has conducted censuses of facilities and inmates every 5 to 6 years. In 1984, BJS initiated an annual survey of jails conducted in noncensus years.

Statistical reliability—For discussion of statistical collection, estimation and sampling procedures, and measures of statistical reliability pertaining to the National Crime Victimization Survey and Uniform Crime Reporting Program, see Appendix III.

Table 332. Crimes and Crime Rates by Type of Offense: 1980 to 2015

[13,408 represents 13,408,000. Data include offenses reported to law enforcement, and offense estimations for nonreporting and partially reporting agencies within each state. Rates are based on Census Bureau estimated resident population as of July 1, except 1980, 1990, 2000, and 2010, which are enumerated as of April 1. See source for details]

Item and year	All crimes	Violent crime						Property crimes			
		Total	Murder [1]	Forcible rape [2]	Rape [2]	Robbery	Aggra-vated assault	Total	Burglary	Larceny/ theft	Motor vehicle theft
NUMBER OF OFFENSES (1,000)											
1980	13,408	1,345	23.0	83.0	(NA)	566	673	12,064	3,795	7,137	1,132
1985	12,430	1,328	19.0	87.7	(NA)	498	723	11,103	3,073	6,926	1,103
1990	14,476	1,820	23.4	102.6	(NA)	639	1,055	12,655	3,074	7,946	1,636
1995	13,863	1,799	21.6	97.5	(NA)	581	1,099	12,064	2,594	7,998	1,472
2000	11,608	1,425	15.6	90.2	(NA)	408	912	10,183	2,051	6,972	1,160
2001 [3]	11,877	1,439	16.0	90.9	(NA)	424	909	10,437	2,117	7,092	1,228
2002	11,879	1,424	16.2	95.2	(NA)	421	891	10,455	2,151	7,057	1,247
2003	11,827	1,384	16.5	93.9	(NA)	414	859	10,443	2,155	7,027	1,261
2004	11,679	1,360	16.1	95.1	(NA)	401	847	10,319	2,144	6,937	1,238
2005	11,565	1,391	16.7	94.3	(NA)	417	862	10,175	2,155	6,783	1,236
2006	11,455	1,435	17.3	94.5	(NA)	449	874	10,020	2,195	6,626	1,198
2007	11,305	1,423	17.1	92.2	(NA)	447	866	9,882	2,190	6,592	1,100
2008	11,169	1,394	16.5	90.8	(NA)	444	844	9,774	2,229	6,586	959
2009	10,663	1,326	15.4	89.2	(NA)	409	813	9,337	2,203	6,338	796
2010	10,364	1,251	14.7	85.6	(NA)	369	782	9,113	2,168	6,205	740
2011	10,259	1,206	14.7	84.2	(NA)	355	752	9,053	2,185	6,151	717
2012	10,219	1,217	14.9	85.1	(NA)	355	762	9,002	2,110	6,169	723
2013	9,820	1,168	14.3	82.1	113.7	345	727	8,652	1,932	6,019	700
2014	9,362	1,153	14.2	84.9	118.0	323	731	8,209	1,713	5,809	687
2015	9,191	1,198	15.7	90.2	124.0	327	764	7,994	1,580	5,706	708
RATE PER 100,000 POPULATION											
1980	5,950	597	10.2	36.8	(NA)	251	299	5,353	1,684	3,167	502
1985	5,225	558	8.0	36.8	(NA)	209	304	4,666	1,292	2,911	464
1990	5,803	730	9.4	41.1	(NA)	256	423	5,073	1,232	3,185	656
1995	5,276	685	8.2	37.1	(NA)	221	418	4,591	987	3,043	560
2000	4,125	507	5.5	32.0	(NA)	145	324	3,618	729	2,477	412
2001 [3]	4,163	505	5.6	31.8	(NA)	149	319	3,658	742	2,486	431
2002	4,125	494	5.6	33.1	(NA)	146	310	3,631	747	2,451	433
2003	4,067	476	5.7	32.3	(NA)	143	295	3,591	741	2,417	434
2004	3,977	463	5.5	32.4	(NA)	137	289	3,514	730	2,362	422
2005	3,901	469	5.6	31.8	(NA)	141	291	3,432	727	2,288	417
2006	3,826	479	5.8	31.6	(NA)	150	292	3,347	733	2,213	400
2007	3,748	472	5.7	30.6	(NA)	148	287	3,276	726	2,185	365
2008	3,673	459	5.4	29.8	(NA)	146	278	3,215	733	2,166	315
2009	3,473	432	5.0	29.1	(NA)	133	265	3,041	718	2,065	259
2010	3,350	405	4.8	27.7	(NA)	119	253	2,946	701	2,006	239
2011	3,292	387	4.7	27.0	(NA)	114	242	2,905	701	1,974	230
2012	3,256	388	4.7	27.1	(NA)	113	243	2,868	672	1,965	230
2013	3,103	369	4.5	25.9	35.9	109	230	2,734	611	1,902	221
2014	2,936	362	4.4	26.6	37.0	101	229	2,574	537	1,822	215
2015	2,860	373	4.9	28.1	38.6	102	238	2,487	491	1,775	220

NA Not available. [1] Includes nonnegligent manslaughter. [2] Beginning 2013, the FBI introduced a revised definition of rape. For more information, see <https://ucr.fbi.gov/crime-in-the-u.s/2015/crime-in-the-u.s.-2015/resource-pages/rape_addendum-2015-_final>. [3] The murder and non-negligent homicides that occurred as a result of the events of September 11, 2001, were not included in this table.

Source: U.S. Department of Justice, Federal Bureau of Investigation, "Crime in the United States 2015," <https://ucr.fbi.gov/>, accessed November 2016.

Table 333. Crimes and Crime Rates by Offense Type and Metropolitan Status: 2015

[In thousands (1,231.6 represents 1,231,600), except rate. Rate per 100,000 population. See headnote, Table 332]

Type of crime	United States		Metropolitan Statistical Areas [1]		Cities outside metropolitan areas		Nonmetropolitan counties	
	Total	Rate	Total	Rate	Total	Rate	Total	Rate
Violent crime	1,231.6	383.2	1,104.0	401.9	74.0	388.4	53.6	193.9
Murder [2]	15.7	4.9	13.9	5.1	826.0	4.3	960.0	3.5
Rape [3]	124.0	38.6	104.5	38.0	10.0	52.5	9.6	34.6
Robbery	327.4	101.9	314.8	114.6	9.4	49.1	3.2	11.7
Aggravated assault	764.4	237.8	670.8	244.2	53.8	282.4	39.9	144.2
Property crime	7,993.6	2,487.0	7,048.1	2,565.6	591.9	3,107.2	353.7	1,279.0
Burglary	1,579.5	491.4	1,349.5	491.2	118.1	620.2	111.9	404.6
Larceny-theft	5,706.3	1,775.4	5,042.1	1,835.4	448.0	2,352.0	216.3	782
Motor vehicle theft	707.8	220.2	656.5	239	25.7	135.0	25.5	92.3

[1] For definition, see Appendix II. [2] Includes nonnegligent manslaughter. [3] Estimated using the revised FBI Uniform Crime Reporting (UCR) definition of rape. Data are not comparable with those found in previous versions of this table. For more information, see <https://ucr.fbi.gov/crime-in-the-u.s/2015/crime-in-the-u.s.-2015/resource-pages/rape_addendum-2015-_final>.

Source: U.S. Department of Justice, Federal Bureau of Investigation, "Crime in the United States 2015," <https://ucr.fbi.gov/>, accessed November 2016.

Table 334. Crime Rates by State, 2014 and 2015, and by Type, 2015

[For year ending December 31. Rates per 100,000 population. Offenses reported to law enforcement. Based on Census Bureau estimated resident population as of July 1]

State	Violent crime						Property crime				
	2014, total	2015					2014, total	2015			
		Total	Murder	Rape [1]	Robbery	Aggravated assault		Total	Burglary	Larceny/theft	Motor vehicle theft
United States	**372.0**	**383.2**	**4.9**	**38.6**	**101.9**	**237.8**	**2,574.1**	**2,487.0**	**491.4**	**1,775.4**	**220.2**
Alabama	427.7	472.4	7.2	42.0	94.9	328.3	3,179.4	2,978.9	725.6	2,040.7	212.7
Alaska	635.5	730.2	8.0	122.0	103.1	497.1	2,758.9	2,817.6	475.5	2,065.1	277.1
Arizona	392.7	410.2	4.5	45.5	93.1	267.1	3,171.5	3,033.2	555.9	2,231.5	245.8
Arkansas	480.2	521.3	6.1	64.8	70.4	380.0	3,352.1	3,251.5	760.2	2,297.5	193.8
California	396.4	426.3	4.8	32.7	135.0	253.8	2,441.7	2,618.3	504.3	1,677.1	436.8
Colorado	307.8	321.0	3.2	59.7	60.9	197.2	2,535.5	2,641.5	429.8	1,918.5	293.2
Connecticut	238.5	218.5	3.3	21.5	80.5	113.1	1,928.5	1,812.0	280.0	1,355.5	176.5
Delaware	488.1	499.0	6.7	36.0	130.6	325.7	2,982.5	2,691.0	504.6	2,061.6	124.9
District of Columbia [2]	1,242.6	1,269.1	24.1	73.5	556.7	614.8	5,175.1	4,676.2	442.0	3,748.7	485.5
Florida	458.9	461.9	5.1	37.3	104.3	315.2	2,932.7	2,813.2	539.0	2,073.6	200.6
Georgia [3]	385.8	378.3	6.0	31.6	119.9	220.8	3,358.8	3,022.3	649.8	2,113.3	259.2
Hawaii	236.7	293.4	1.3	39.2	84.0	168.9	3,240.4	3,796.2	458.0	2,934.5	403.7
Idaho	210.4	215.6	1.9	41.9	11.6	160.1	1,862.0	1,743.8	370.0	1,260.7	113.1
Illinois	370.9	383.8	5.8	37.5	115.9	224.6	2,093.2	1,988.6	361.1	1,490.2	137.3
Indiana [4]	365.3	387.5	5.6	36.3	107.4	238.2	2,651.0	2,596.0	519.8	1,872.0	204.2
Iowa	272.8	286.1	2.3	37.0	33.5	213.2	2,093.6	2,047.3	476.7	1,431.6	139.0
Kansas	352.6	389.9	4.4	55.5	62.4	267.6	2,757.2	2,720.1	527.6	1,953.5	238.9
Kentucky	215.2	218.7	4.7	33.7	74.7	105.5	2,264.2	2,177.6	503.0	1,498.7	175.9
Louisiana	515.9	539.7	10.3	36.9	118.8	373.7	3,467.2	3,353.4	759.0	2,385.8	208.6
Maine [4]	127.6	130.1	1.7	35.7	23.4	69.3	1,986.6	1,830.0	352.4	1,416.4	61.2
Maryland	448.0	457.2	8.6	27.7	164.2	256.7	2,516.8	2,315.0	427.5	1,668.5	218.9
Massachusetts	395.1	390.9	1.9	30.5	77.8	280.7	1,857.6	1,690.7	322.2	1,249.7	118.8
Michigan	429.1	415.5	5.8	65.0	78.6	266.2	2,044.0	1,885.6	403.5	1,323.2	158.9
Minnesota	229.1	242.6	2.4	42.3	68.7	129.2	2,297.5	2,222.1	351.6	1,725.2	145.4
Mississippi [4]	278.3	275.8	8.7	40.2	76.7	150.3	2,902.6	2,833.6	828.8	1,863.0	141.8
Missouri	443.3	497.4	8.3	42.0	104.8	342.4	2,909.6	2,854.2	559.0	2,015.8	279.4
Montana	328.5	349.6	3.5	53.0	20.3	272.8	2,494.5	2,623.6	371.6	2,017.9	234.1
Nebraska [4]	276.2	274.9	3.3	46.0	52.4	173.1	2,524.0	2,241.1	338.7	1,691.4	211.0
Nevada	635.7	695.9	6.2	58.4	217.5	413.9	2,627.4	2,668.3	773.5	1,502.2	392.7
New Hampshire	197.7	199.3	1.1	47.1	35.2	116.0	1,965.2	1,745.7	260.6	1,418.2	67.0
New Jersey	260.9	255.4	4.1	15.3	108.6	127.4	1,733.4	1,626.5	312.1	1,182.9	131.5
New Mexico	597.7	656.1	5.6	80.2	119.2	451.2	3,542.3	3,697.4	819.4	2,469.1	408.9
New York [4]	384.7	379.7	3.1	30.7	120.9	225.0	1,717.1	1,604.0	223.7	1,303.0	77.4
North Carolina	329.1	347.0	5.1	26.7	87.9	227.3	2,872.1	2,750.1	745.2	1,871.1	133.8
North Dakota	270.4	239.4	2.8	45.6	19.6	171.5	2,142.7	2,116.5	395.9	1,511.4	209.1
Ohio [4]	285.7	291.9	4.3	44.3	108.1	135.1	2,781.0	2,587.7	596.7	1,842.6	148.4
Oklahoma	413.8	422.0	6.0	47.3	76.8	291.9	3,027.2	2,885.9	726.2	1,892.5	267.2
Oregon [4]	259.2	259.8	2.5	39.5	53.3	164.6	3,100.9	2,946.6	455.1	2,229.7	261.8
Pennsylvania	315.0	315.1	5.1	33.6	101.6	174.8	1,930.5	1,812.8	309.8	1,408.2	94.8
Rhode Island [4]	219.9	242.5	2.7	43.5	52.6	143.7	2,178.6	1,897.5	373.7	1,392.3	131.5
South Carolina	497.8	504.5	8.1	46.9	80.3	369.1	3,484.7	3,293.3	705.7	2,322.7	264.9
South Dakota	328.3	383.1	3.7	57.7	25.2	296.6	1,879.3	1,943.0	344.8	1,459.8	138.4
Tennessee	610.7	612.1	6.2	40.5	113.2	452.2	3,068.4	2,936.2	655.2	2,086.0	195.0
Texas	406.7	412.2	4.8	44.6	116.3	246.6	3,015.4	2,831.3	557.2	2,028.5	245.7
Utah [4]	219.5	236.0	1.8	54.9	44.3	135.1	2,902.8	2,980.0	416.2	2,273.2	290.6
Vermont	102.6	118.0	1.6	21.7	16.1	78.6	1,551.0	1,406.6	314.4	1,063.8	28.4
Virginia	198.4	195.6	4.6	27.9	53.0	110.2	1,944.4	1,866.5	254.6	1,515.2	96.8
Washington [4]	285.8	284.4	2.9	37.7	76.0	167.8	3,698.9	3,463.8	711.2	2,378.0	374.7
West Virginia	316.4	337.9	3.8	36.4	41.2	256.4	2,070.7	2,020.0	497.3	1,401.3	121.4
Wisconsin [4]	291.1	305.8	4.2	30.8	90.7	180.1	2,092.8	1,974.0	338.8	1,444.8	190.3
Wyoming	195.4	222.1	2.7	29.5	10.1	179.8	1,964.2	1,902.6	300.6	1,500.9	101.0

[1] Estimated using the revised FBI Uniform Crime Reporting (UCR) definition of rape. Data are not comparable with those found in previous versions of this table. For more information, see <https://ucr.fbi.gov/crime-in-the-u.s/2015/crime-in-the-u.s.-2015/resource-pages/rape_addendum-2015-_final>. [2] Includes offenses reported by the Zoological Police and the Metro Transit Police. [3] Because of changes in the state's reporting practices, figures are not comparable to previous years' data. [4] Agencies within this state submitted rape data according to both the revised UCR definition of rape and the legacy UCR definition of rape.

Source: U.S. Department of Justice, Federal Bureau of Investigation, "Crime in the United States 2015," <https://ucr.fbi.gov/>, accessed November 2016.

Table 335. Crime Rates by Type—Selected Large Cities: 2015

[For year ending December 31. Rates per 100,000 population. Only offenses reported to law enforcement and the FBI]

Cities ranked by population size, 2015	Violent crime					Property crime			
	Total	Murder	Rape (revised definition) [1]	Robbery	Aggravated assault	Total	Burglary	Larceny/ theft	Motor vehicle theft
New York, NY.	586	4.1	26.2	198	357	1,519	165	1,267	86
Los Angeles, CA.	635	7.1	55.7	226	346	2,360	408	1,544	408
Chicago, IL.	904	17.5	52.5	354	480	2,946	482	2,090	375
Houston, TX.	967	13.3	43.3	452	458	4,398	873	2,929	596
Philadelphia, PA.	1,029	17.9	84.3	431	495	3,147	516	2,311	321
Las Vegas, NV.	921	8.1	70.9	321	521	2,995	952	1,537	506
Phoenix, AZ.	594	7.2	65.1	194	328	3,491	821	2,198	473
San Antonio, TX.	587	6.4	71.7	136	373	5,029	795	3,813	422
San Diego, CA.	399	2.6	40.4	98	257	2,082	366	1,352	364
Dallas, TX.	694	10.4	60.1	321	303	3,440	854	2,003	583
San Jose, CA.	330	2.9	36.4	111	180	2,427	475	1,274	679
Honolulu, HI.	244	1.5	31.8	90	121	3,111	429	2,295	387
Austin, TX.	373	2.5	51.9	99	219	3,771	533	2,990	248
Charlotte-Mecklenburg, NC.	678	6.9	[2] 24.6	222	424	3,768	770	2,744	254
Jacksonville, FL.	648	11.2	54.3	161	422	3,673	701	2,705	267
San Francisco, CA.	777	6.1	39.8	418	313	6,138	600	4,737	801
Indianapolis, IN.	1,288	17.1	78.4	440	752	4,791	1,283	2,929	578
Columbus, OH.	546	9.1	95.1	264	178	3,934	852	2,716	367
Fort Worth, TX.	525	6.7	62.2	118	338	3,586	724	2,590	272
El Paso, TX.	367	2.5	46.9	60	257	1,914	207	1,591	116
Seattle, WA.	599	3.4	21.1	224	350	5,522	1,123	3,832	567
Denver, CO.	674	7.8	80.3	180	406	3,530	698	2,192	640
Louisville Metro, KY.	632	11.9	30.1	227	363	4,166	922	2,770	474
Detroit, MI.	1,760	43.8	78.7	513	1,124	4,094	1,162	2,157	775
Washington, DC.	1,203	24.1	73.5	506	599	4,516	442	3,599	475
Boston, MA.	707	5.7	36.1	233	432	2,316	354	1,770	192
Nashville, TN.	1,101	10.9	77.0	281	732	3,806	780	2,806	220
Memphis, TN.	1,740	20.5	80.6	476	1,163	5,631	1,561	3,655	414
Oklahoma City, OK.	766	11.6	76.1	189	489	3,956	923	2,573	459
Baltimore, MD.	1,536	55.4	46.2	694	740	4,980	1,249	2,842	889
Milwaukee, WI.	1,596	24.2	72.6	624	875	4,264	913	2,122	1,229
Albuquerque, NM.	966	7.7	[2] 72.2	301	585	6,073	1,071	4,077	925
Tucson, AZ.	655	5.9	79.7	200	370	6,643	692	5,587	364
Fresno, CA.	551	7.5	32.1	194	317	4,148	850	2,723	575
Sacramento, CA.	737	8.8	21.4	240	467	3,369	758	2,014	597
Long Beach, CA.	581	7.6	37.2	221	315	3,010	650	1,766	594
Kansas City, MO.	1,417	23.0	77.3	360	957	4,441	1,029	2,588	825
Mesa, AZ.	419	3.4	51.2	87	277	2,527	471	1,881	175
Atlanta, GA.	1,120	20.2	[2] 36.6	429	634	5,499	1,029	3,549	921
Virginia Beach, VA.	138	4.2	22.7	60	52	2,206	211	1,898	96
Colorado Springs, CO.	438	5.5	75.4	83	274	3,648	534	2,733	382
Omaha, NE.	515	10.6	38.5	145	321	3,596	478	2,556	562
Miami, FL.	1,021	17.1	18.3	384	602	4,367	710	3,133	525
Oakland, CA.	1,442	20.3	67.9	784	570	5,857	795	3,539	1,523
Minneapolis, MN.	1,063	11.4	98.4	459	495	4,194	860	2,919	415
Tulsa, OK.	904	13.7	90.9	213	586	5,203	1,373	3,170	660
New Orleans, LA.	950	41.7	104.0	380	423	3,874	737	2,498	640
Wichita, KS.	985	6.9	89.5	188	700	5,041	893	3,624	525
Arlington, TX.	502	2.1	53.7	136	310	3,444	560	2,657	227
Bakersfield, CA.	484	5.9	19.0	175	284	4,161	1,037	2,484	640
Tampa, FL.	631	9.3	21.1	184	416	2,296	503	1,629	164
Aurora, CO.	461	6.7	97.7	124	232	2,937	467	2,119	350
Anaheim, CA.	364	5.2	36.9	126	196	2,872	422	1,972	478
Santa Ana, CA.	482	3.6	45.7	155	278	2,155	269	1,332	554
Corpus Christi, TX.	645	5.2	86.9	121	431	3,466	675	2,633	158
Riverside, CA.	446	3.1	42.4	161	240	3,260	505	2,211	543
St. Louis, MO.	1,817	59.3	82.9	564	1,110	6,316	1,325	3,999	992
Lexington, KY.	332	4.8	51.9	163	113	3,950	798	2,834	318
Pittsburgh, PA.	706	18.6	26.7	280	381	3,224	716	2,313	196
Stockton, CA.	1,352	16.1	44.3	375	916	4,263	948	2,663	652
Anchorage, AK.	1,071	8.6	171.6	206	685	3,917	559	2,975	383
St. Paul, MN.	703	5.3	67.8	237	393	3,282	707	1,994	581
Cincinnati, OH.	925	22.1	79.1	423	401	5,510	1,479	3,643	389
Greensboro, NC.	597	9.1	[2] 25.2	185	377	3,568	828	2,551	188
Plano, TX.	153	1.4	32.2	41	78	1,799	260	1,443	96
Henderson, NV.	168	1.4	34.7	64	69	1,893	480	1,226	188
Toledo, OH.	1,129	8.6	81.6	323	716	4,475	1,476	2,677	322
Lincoln, NE.	371	0.4	[2] 69.8	77	223	3,266	480	2,655	131
Orlando, FL.	941	11.9	67.8	194	666	6,016	1,267	4,309	440
Chula Vista, CA.	266	2.3	23.8	90	150	1,742	268	1,166	308
Jersey City, NJ.	522	10.2	36.6	207	268	1,595	368	999	228
Fort Wayne, IN.	379	9.6	37.3	172	160	3,058	570	2,361	128
Chandler, AZ.	189	0.4	30.5	44	114	2,083	297	1,687	99
Irvine, CA.	56	0.8	10.5	22	22	1,498	203	1,218	78
Buffalo, NY.	1,119	15.9	67.0	400	635	4,330	1,076	2,875	379

NA Not available. [1] Beginning in 2013, the FBI has revised the definition of rape as used in Uniform Crime Reporting (UCR) Program. For more information, see <https://ucr.fbi.gov/crime-in-the-u.s/2015/crime-in-the-u.s.-2015/resource-pages/rape_addendum-2015-_final>. [2] City used legacy definition of rape, see source for details.

Source: U.S. Department of Justice, Federal Bureau of Investigation, "Crime in the United States 2015," <https://ucr.fbi.gov/>, accessed December 2016.

Table 336. Murder Victims—Circumstances and Weapons Used or Cause of Death: 2000 to 2015

[For year ending December 31. The FBI's Uniform Crime Reporting (UCR) Program defines murder and nonnegligent manslaughter as the willful (nonnegligent) killing of one human being by another. The classification of this offense is based solely on police investigation as opposed to the determination of a court, medical examiner, coroner, jury, or other judicial body. The UCR Program does not include the following situations in this offense classification: deaths caused by negligence, suicide, or accident; justifiable homicides; and attempts to murder, which are scored as aggravated assaults]

Characteristic	2000	2010	2011	2012	2013	2014	2015
Murders, total [1]	**13,230**	**13,164**	**12,795**	**12,888**	**12,253**	**12,270**	**13,455**
CIRCUMSTANCES							
Felonies, total [1]	2,229	1,974	1,842	1,842	1,909	1,862	2,014
Rape [2]	58	41	16	16	20	26	12
Robbery	1,077	803	750	656	686	586	595
Burglary	76	85	95	91	94	82	102
Larceny-theft	23	21	12	15	16	24	16
Motor vehicle theft	25	35	23	22	27	25	41
Arson	81	35	38	32	37	23	19
Prostitution and commercialized vice	6	5	3	6	13	19	6
Other sex offenses	10	14	10	13	9	3	15
Narcotic drug laws	589	474	397	375	386	386	468
Gambling	12	7	8	7	7	11	5
Suspected felony type	60	68	62	137	122	84	117
Other than felony type [1]	6,871	6,485	6,056	6,320	5,782	5,771	5,958
Romantic triangle	122	90	88	98	69	85	106
Child killed by babysitter	30	36	38	26	30	39	36
Brawl due to influence of alcohol	188	122	113	84	93	100	112
Brawl due to influence of narcotics	99	60	121	65	59	50	75
Argument over money or property	206	187	156	152	133	151	184
Other arguments	3,589	3,280	3,163	3,147	2,889	2,863	2,941
Gangland killings	65	181	149	152	138	144	188
Juvenile gang killings	653	675	526	722	584	578	604
Institutional killings	10	17	22	13	15	18	24
Unknown	4,070	4,637	4,835	4,589	4,440	4,553	5,366
TYPE OF WEAPON OR CAUSE OF DEATH [1]							
Total firearms	8,661	8,874	8,653	8,897	8,454	8,312	9,616
Handguns	6,778	6,115	6,251	6,404	5,782	5,673	6,447
Rifles	411	367	332	298	285	258	252
Shotguns	485	366	362	310	308	264	269
Other guns	53	93	97	116	123	93	171
Firearms, type not stated	934	1,933	1,611	1,769	1,956	2,024	2,477
Knives or cutting instruments	1,782	1,732	1,716	1,604	1,490	1,595	1,544
Blunt objects (club, hammer, etc.)	617	549	502	522	428	446	437
Personal weapons (hands, fists, feet, pushed, etc.)	927	769	751	707	687	682	624
Fire	134	78	76	87	94	71	82
Narcotics	20	45	33	38	53	70	70
Drowning	15	10	15	14	4	14	14
Strangulation	166	122	88	90	85	89	96
Asphyxiation	92	98	92	106	95	102	120

[1] Includes items not shown separately. [2] Rape figures in this table are an aggregate total of data submitted using both the revised and legacy UCR definitions.

Source: U.S. Department of Justice, Federal Bureau of Investigation, "Crime in the United States 2015" and earlier releases, <https://ucr.fbi.gov/>, accessed November 2016.

Table 337. Murder Victims by Age, Sex, and Race/Ethnicity: 2015

[See headnote, Table 336]

Age	Total	Sex [1]		Race [1]			Ethnicity [1,2]	
		Male	Female	White	Black	Other [3]	Hispanic or Latino	Not Hispanic or Latino
Murders, total	**13,455**	**10,608**	**2,818**	**5,854**	**7,039**	**366**	**2,028**	**7,971**
Percent of total [4]	100.0	78.8	20.9	43.5	52.3	2.7	16.6	65.2
Under 18 years old [1]	1,093	761	329	504	544	26	193	611
18 years old and over [1]	12,228	9,773	2,448	5,296	6,451	339	1,823	7,305
Infant (under 1 year old)	168	104	63	89	65	8	24	104
1 to 4 years old	260	153	106	130	117	6	32	160
5 to 8 years old	91	49	42	58	30	1	12	57
9 to 12 years old	56	35	20	30	22	3	9	30
13 to 16 years old	282	218	64	110	167	4	62	141
17 to 19 years old	996	870	126	325	647	16	191	546
20 to 24 years old	2,431	2,102	329	764	1,596	45	414	1,398
25 to 29 years old	2,071	1,733	338	717	1,290	48	321	1,201
30 to 34 years old	1,647	1,340	307	650	927	49	266	974
35 to 39 years old	1,263	1,021	241	539	666	45	200	728
40 to 44 years old	925	701	222	467	428	23	150	545
45 to 49 years old	781	586	194	399	330	33	118	485
50 to 54 years old	737	568	169	428	282	17	84	468
55 to 59 years old	580	425	154	363	183	27	57	389
60 to 64 years old	360	250	109	226	114	12	36	231
65 to 69 years old	235	168	67	166	59	6	14	168
70 to 74 years old	159	93	65	113	33	9	11	100
75 years old and over	279	118	161	226	39	13	15	191
Age unknown	134	74	41	54	44	1	12	55

[1] Does not include unknown victim categories. [2] Not all agencies provide ethnicity data; therefore, data will not sum to total. [3] Includes American Indian or Alaska Native, Asian, and Native Hawaiian or Pacific Islander. [4] Percentages rounded, may not add to 100.

Source: U.S. Department of Justice, Federal Bureau of Investigation, "Crime in the United States 2015," <https://ucr.fbi.gov/>, accessed November 2016.

Table 338. Homicide Trends: 1990 to 2015

[Based on Federal Bureau of Investigation's Uniform Crime Reports Supplementary Homicide Reports. Homicide includes murder and nonnegligent manslaughter, which is the willful killing of one human being by another. Excludes deaths caused by negligence, suicide, or accident; justifiable homicides; and attempts to murder. Justifiable homicides based on the reports of law enforcement agencies are analyzed separately. Deaths from the terrorist attacks of September 11, 2001 are not included. Data based on criminal homicides handled by state and local law enforcement, and as determined solely by police investigation, and not by the determination of a court, medical examiner, coroner, jury, or other non-law enforcement body. Excludes homicides handled by Federal law enforcement]

| Year | Number of victims | | | | | | | Rate [1] | | | | | | |
	Total [2]	Male	Female	White	Black	American Indian/ Alaskan Native	Asian [3]	Total [2]	Male	Female	White	Black	American Indian/ Alaska Native	Asian [3]
1990...	23,438	18,303	5,115	11,278	11,487	150	250	9.4	15.0	4.0	5.4	37.5	7.3	3.3
1991...	24,703	19,273	5,395	11,662	12,227	152	457	9.8	15.6	4.2	5.5	39.1	7.1	5.7
1992...	23,760	18,513	5,217	11,229	11,777	158	415	9.3	14.8	4.0	5.2	36.8	7.2	4.9
1993...	24,526	18,934	5,550	11,276	12,433	141	460	9.4	14.9	4.2	5.2	38.1	6.2	5.2
1994...	23,326	18,291	5,007	10,772	11,854	133	393	8.9	14.2	3.7	4.9	35.6	5.6	4.3
1995...	21,606	16,549	5,021	10,374	10,442	160	421	8.1	12.7	3.7	4.7	30.9	6.6	4.4
1996...	19,645	15,149	4,468	9,480	9,473	134	377	7.3	11.5	3.2	4.3	27.5	5.3	3.8
1997...	18,208	14,055	4,124	8,619	8,841	149	375	6.7	10.5	3.0	3.8	25.3	5.7	3.6
1998...	16,974	12,756	4,140	8,391	7,933	141	252	6.2	9.4	2.9	3.7	22.3	5.2	2.3
1999...	15,522	11,704	3,800	7,777	7,139	160	298	5.6	8.6	2.7	3.4	19.7	5.6	2.6
2000...	15,586	11,818	3,733	7,560	7,425	119	280	5.5	8.6	2.6	3.3	20.3	4.0	2.4
2001...	16,037	12,232	3,775	7,884	7,522	105	319	5.6	8.7	2.6	3.4	20.2	3.4	2.6
2002...	16,229	12,429	3,770	7,796	7,770	130	308	5.6	8.8	2.6	3.3	20.6	4.1	2.4
2003...	16,528	12,792	3,707	7,944	7,883	117	351	5.7	9.0	2.5	3.4	20.6	3.5	2.6
2004...	16,148	12,553	3,555	7,939	7,570	134	282	5.5	8.7	2.4	3.4	19.5	3.9	2.0
2005...	16,740	13,149	3,565	8,045	8,016	131	312	5.7	9.1	2.4	3.4	20.4	3.7	2.2
2006...	17,309	13,605	3,661	8,063	8,548	123	343	5.8	9.3	2.4	3.4	21.4	3.3	2.3
2007...	17,128	13,411	3,678	8,017	8,450	104	302	5.7	9.1	2.4	3.3	20.9	2.7	1.9
2008...	16,465	12,844	3,573	7,953	7,860	124	250	5.4	8.6	2.3	3.3	19.1	3.1	1.6
2009...	15,399	11,846	3,535	7,450	7,374	119	290	5.0	7.9	2.3	3.0	17.7	2.9	1.7
2010...	14,722	11,371	3,328	6,851	7,322	117	260	4.8	7.5	2.1	2.8	17.4	2.7	1.5
2011...	14,661	11,354	3,281	6,786	7,277	111	284	4.7	7.4	2.1	2.7	17.1	2.6	1.6
2012...	14,856	11,534	3,302	6,812	7,502	101	285	4.7	7.5	2.1	2.7	17.4	2.3	1.6
2013...	14,319	11,116	3,178	6,519	7,268	104	257	4.5	7.1	2.0	2.6	16.6	2.3	1.4
2014...	14,164	10,940	3,187	6,427	7,187	121	251	4.4	7.0	2.0	2.6	16.2	2.7	1.3
2015...	15,696	12,352	3,315	6,856	8,195	181	250	4.9	7.8	2.0	2.7	18.3	4.0	1.2

[1] Rate is per 100,000 inhabitants. [2] Includes unknown sex, race, or ethnicity. [3] Includes Native Hawaiian and Pacific Islanders.

Source: U.S. Department of Justice, Office of Justice Programs, "Easy Access to the FBI's Supplementary Homicide Reports (EZASHR)," <http://www.ojjdp.gov/ojstatbb/ezashr/>; and U.S. Centers for Disease Control and Prevention, WONDER Online Database, "Multiple Cause of Death, 1999-2015," <http://wonder.cdc.gov/>; accessed September 2017.

Table 339. Homicide Victims by Race and Sex: 1990 to 2015

[Excludes deaths to nonresidents of United States. Effective with data for 1999, causes of death are classified by the International Classification of Diseases, Tenth Revision (ICD-10), replacing the Ninth Revision (ICD-9) used for 1979–1998 data. In ICD-9, the category Homicide also includes death as a result of legal intervention. ICD-10 differentiates between homicides due to assault and deaths due to legal intervention. Some caution should be used in comparing data. See text, Section 2]

| Year | Homicide victims | | | | | Homicide rate [2] | | | | |
| | Total [1] | White | | Black | | Total [1] | White | | Black | |
		Male	Female	Male	Female		Male	Female	Male	Female
1990............	24,932	9,147	3,006	9,981	2,163	10.0	9.0	2.8	69.2	13.5
1995............	22,895	8,336	3,028	8,847	1,936	8.7	7.8	2.7	56.3	11.1
1996............	20,971	7,570	2,747	8,183	1,800	7.9	7.0	2.5	51.5	10.2
1997............	19,846	7,343	2,570	7,601	1,652	7.4	6.7	2.3	47.1	9.3
1998............	18,272	6,707	2,534	6,873	1,547	6.8	6.1	2.2	42.1	8.6
1999............	16,889	6,162	2,466	6,214	1,434	6.1	5.5	2.1	36.1	7.6
2000............	16,765	5,925	2,414	6,482	1,385	6.0	5.2	2.1	37.2	7.2
2001............	20,308	8,254	3,074	6,780	1,446	7.1	7.2	2.6	38.2	7.4
2002............	17,638	6,282	2,403	6,896	1,391	6.1	5.4	2.0	38.4	7.0
2003............	17,732	6,337	2,372	7,083	1,309	6.1	5.5	2.0	38.9	6.5
2004............	17,357	6,302	2,341	6,839	1,296	5.9	5.4	2.0	37.0	6.4
2005............	18,124	6,457	2,313	7,412	1,257	6.1	5.5	1.9	39.6	6.1
2006............	18,573	6,514	2,346	7,677	1,355	6.2	5.5	1.9	40.4	6.5
2007............	18,361	6,541	2,373	7,584	1,286	6.1	5.5	1.9	39.3	6.1
2008............	17,826	6,556	2,337	7,148	1,187	5.9	5.5	1.9	36.5	5.5
2009............	16,799	5,983	2,340	6,715	1,159	5.5	4.9	1.9	33.8	5.3
2010............	16,259	5,648	2,215	6,704	1,114	5.3	4.7	1.8	33.4	5.1
2011............	16,238	5,569	2,199	6,739	1,119	5.2	4.6	1.8	33.0	5.0
2012............	16,688	5,639	2,197	7,129	1,112	5.3	4.6	1.8	34.5	4.9
2013............	16,121	5,393	2,130	6,937	1,122	5.1	4.4	1.7	33.1	4.9
2014............	15,872	5,304	2,093	6,823	1,080	5.0	4.3	1.7	32.1	4.7
2015............	17,793	5,798	2,209	8,021	1,152	5.5	4.6	1.7	37.3	4.9

[1] Includes other races not shown separately. [2] Rates per 100,000 resident population in specified group. Based on enumerated population figures as of April 1 for 1990, 2000, and 2010; estimated resident population as of July 1 for other years.

Source: U.S. National Center for Health Statistics, CDC WONDER Online Database, "Multiple Cause of Death, 1999-2015," <http://wonder.cdc.gov/>; and National Vital Statistics Reports (NVSR), *Deaths: Final Data for 2014*, Vol. 65, No. 4, June 2016 and earlier reports.

Table 340. Criminal Victimizations and Victimization Rates: 2010 to 2015

[20,348 represents 20,348,000. A victimization refers to a single victim or household that experienced a criminal incident. Criminal incidents or crimes are distinguished from victimizations in that one criminal incident may have multiple victims or victimizations. Based on the National Crime Victimization Survey (NCVS). See source for more information]

Type of crime	Number of victimizations (1,000)				Victimization rates [1]			
	2010	2013	2014	2015	2010	2013	2014	2015
Total............................	20,348	22,901	20,648	19,618	(X)	(X)	(X)	(X)
Violent victimization [2].....................	4,936	6,126	5,360	5,007	19.3	23.2	20.1	18.6
Not injured........................	3,646	4,522	3,984	3,703	14.2	17.1	14.9	13.7
Injured...........................	1,290	1,604	1,376	1,303	5.0	6.1	5.2	4.8
Serious violent victimization [3]................	1,695	1,940	2,041	1,827	6.6	7.3	7.7	6.8
Rape/sexual assault......................	269	300	284	432	1.0	1.1	1.1	1.6
Robbery............................	569	646	664	579	2.2	2.4	2.5	2.1
Not injured........................	370	394	436	370	1.4	1.5	1.6	1.4
Injured...........................	198	252	228	209	0.8	1.0	0.9	0.8
Aggravated assault....................	858	994	1,092	817	3.4	3.8	4.1	3.0
Not injured........................	538	660	758	526	2.1	2.5	2.8	1.9
Injured...........................	320	335	334	291	1.2	1.3	1.3	1.1
Simple assault.......................	3,241	4,186	3,319	3,179	12.7	15.8	12.4	11.8
Not injured........................	2,619	3,322	2,635	2,534	10.2	12.6	9.9	9.4
Injured...........................	622	865	683	645	2.4	3.3	2.6	2.4
Personal theft/larceny [4]..................	138	141	106	89	0.5	0.5	0.4	0.3
Property crimes.......................	15,412	16,774	15,288	14,611	125.4	131.4	118.1	110.7
Household burglary...................	3,176	3,286	2,993	2,905	25.8	25.7	23.1	22.0
Motor vehicle theft..................	607	661	534	564	4.9	5.2	4.1	4.3
Theft [5]............................	11,628	12,827	11,761	11,142	94.6	100.5	90.8	84.4

X Not applicable. [1] Per 1,000 persons age 12 or older for violent victimization and personal theft/larceny; per 1,000 households for property crime. [2] Excludes homicide because the NCVS is based on interviews with victims and therefore cannot measure murder. [3] Includes rape, sexual assault, personal robbery, and aggravated assault, attempted and completed crimes. [4] Includes pocket picking, completed purse snatching, and attempted purse snatching. [5] The taking or attempted unlawful taking of property or cash without personal contact with the victim. Incidents involving theft of property from within a household are classified as theft if the offender has a legal right to be in the house (such as a maid, delivery person, or guest).

Source: U.S. Department of Justice, Bureau of Justice Statistics, "NCVS Victimization Analysis Tool," <http://www.bjs.gov/index.cfm?ty=nvat>, accessed November 2016.

Table 341. Victimization Rates by Type of Crime and Characteristics of the Victim: 2015

[Rate per 1,000 persons age 12 years or older. Based on the National Crime Victimization Survey. See text, this section and Appendix III]

Characteristic of the victim	Violent victimization						Personal theft [1]
	Total	Serious violent victim-ization	Rape/ sexual assault	Robbery	Aggravated assault	Simple assault	
Total...........................	18.6	6.8	1.6	2.1	3.0	11.8	0.3
Male...........................	15.9	5.4	0.5	2.2	2.7	10.5	0.3
Female.........................	21.1	8.1	2.7	2.1	3.3	13.0	0.4
12 to 14 years old..............	42.0	10.0	[3] 1.8	[3] 2.7	5.6	32.0	(Z)
15 to 17 years old..............	20.8	5.7	[3] 0.9	[3] 2.4	[3] 2.3	15.1	(Z)
18 to 20 years old..............	20.7	9.0	3.2	2.4	3.5	11.6	(Z)
21 to 24 years old..............	28.2	11.8	[3] 1.6	5.4	4.8	16.4	[3] 0.3
25 to 34 years old..............	21.8	9.3	3.7	2.7	2.8	12.5	[3] 0.6
35 to 49 years old..............	22.6	7.8	1.2	2.7	3.8	14.8	[3] 0.5
50 to 64 years old..............	14.2	5.7	1.3	1.3	3.0	8.6	[3] 0.2
65 years old and over...........	5.2	1.5	[3] 0.2	[3] 0.4	0.9	3.7	[3] 0.4
White..........................	16.9	6.2	1.6	1.8	2.8	10.7	0.3
Black..........................	22.7	8.5	[3] 0.5	3.6	4.4	14.3	[3] 0.8
Other [2]........................	28.3	9.9	3.3	3.4	3.3	18.3	[3] 0.2
Hispanic.......................	16.8	7.1	1.1	3.0	3.0	9.6	[3] 0.2
Non-Hispanic White.............	17.4	6.0	1.7	1.5	2.8	11.5	0.3
Non-Hispanic Black.............	22.6	8.4	[3] 0.5	3.7	4.3	14.3	[3] 0.8
Household income:							
Less than $7,500...............	45.5	16.7	4.6	4.2	7.9	28.8	[3] 0.9
$7,500 to $14,999..............	47.6	22.6	[3] 4.9	7.0	10.7	25.0	[3] 0.3
$15,000 to $24,999.............	32.5	10.4	2.5	4.4	3.4	22.1	[3] 1.1
$25,000 to $34,999.............	19.7	7.0	[3] 0.7	2.4	3.9	12.7	[3] 0.3
$35,000 to $49,999.............	18.0	5.5	[3] 1.7	1.4	2.4	12.5	[3] 0.2
$50,000 to $74,999.............	17.7	6.4	[3] 1.7	1.4	3.3	11.3	[3] 0.2
$75,000 or more................	12.7	4.4	1.5	1.3	1.6	8.3	[3] 0.2
Unknown.......................	14.3	5.5	0.9	2.0	2.5	8.8	[3] 0.3

Z Rounds to less than .05 victimizations per 1,000. [1] Includes pocket picking, completed purse snatching, and attempted purse snatching. [2] Includes American Indians and Alaska Natives, Asians, Native Hawaiians and other Pacific Islanders, and persons of two or more races. [3] Based on 10 or fewer sample cases.

Source: U.S. Department of Justice, Bureau of Justice Statistics, "NCVS Victimization Analysis Tool," <http://www.bjs.gov/index.cfm?ty=nvat>, accessed November 2016.

Table 342. Criminal Victimizations by Age of Victim and Selected Characteristics: 2003 to 2013

[In percent, unless otherwise noted. Covers period 2003 to 2013. Data are for violent victimizations that are nonfatal. Based on the National Crime Victimization Survey. For details, see source <http://www.bjs.gov/index.cfm?ty=dcdetail&iid=245>]

Item	Age			
	12–24 years old	25–49 years old	50–64 years old	Aged 65 years or older
VIOLENT VICTIMIZATIONS				
Average annual (number)	2,709,260	2,899,310	834,510	136,720
Rate per 1,000 households	49.9	27.6	15.2	3.6
By type of weapon:				
Total	100.0	100.0	100.0	100.0
No weapon used	72.6	70.2	69.9	69.3
Weapon used	21.5	22.4	21.0	19.5
Firearm	6.2	7.7	7.0	7.6
Knife	6.4	5.9	5.6	4.3
Other	7.2	7.1	6.9	6.2
Type unknown	1.6	1.7	1.5	[5] 1.4
Don't know	5.9	7.5	9.0	11.1
By victim-offender relationship:				
Total	100.0	100.0	100.0	100.0
Known to victim	57.2	50.6	52.1	48.8
Domestic	16.4	26.0	19.9	14.3
Intimate partner [1]	9.9	20.4	9.6	6.1
Immediate family	4.2	3.5	7.3	4.6
Other relative	2.2	2.1	3.0	3.6
Well-known/casual acquaintance	40.8	24.6	32.3	34.5
Stranger	34.0	41.2	39.8	43.4
Unknown [2]	8.8	8.1	8.1	7.8
By location of crime:				
Total	100.0	100.0	100.0	100.0
At or near victim's home	25.4	41.1	43.5	59.3
At or near friend, neighbor, or relative's home	11.3	5.9	5.5	6.0
Other location [3]	63.3	53.1	51.0	34.7
Type of crime by whether reported to police:				
Violent crime	38.0	53.5	50.5	56.2
Serious violent crime	48.0	63.9	58.2	64.3
Rape/sexual assault	30.9	43.5	25.4	[1] 28.0
Robbery	52.8	64.8	61.2	76.1
Aggravated assault	50.0	68.2	63.1	64.3
Simple assault	32.9	48.5	47.0	51.8
PROPERTY VICTIMIZATIONS [4]				
Average annual (number)	2,031,930	9,924,460	4,307,210	1,796,740
Rate per 1,000 households	262.0	177.1	134.6	72.3
Type of crime by whether reported to police:				
Property crime	36.9	38.2	36.6	38.3
Household burglary	52.3	56.2	51.7	50.1
Motor vehicle theft	78.6	82.8	79.0	83.5
Theft	29.3	31.1	30.3	31.9

[1] Includes current or former spouses, boyfriends, and girlfriends. [2] Includes unknown victim–offender relationships and unknown number of offenders. [3] Includes commercial places, parking lots or garages, schools, open areas, public transportation, and other locations. [4] Data by age of householder. [5] Interpret with caution.

Source: U.S. Department of Justice, Bureau of Justice Statistics, *Crimes Against the Elderly, 2003–2013*, NCJ 248339, November 2014. See also <http://www.bjs.gov/index.cfm?ty=pbse&sid=21>.

Table 343. Rape and Sexual Assault Rates Among College-Age Females: 1998 to 2013

[Estimated victimization rates per 1,000 females, based on 3-year rolling averages centered on the most recent year. Data from the National Crime Victimization Survey]

Year	Students 18 to 24 years old [1]	Nonstudents 18 to 24 years old [2]	Not college-age females [3]	Year	Students 18 to 24 years old [1]	Nonstudents 18 to 24 years old [2]	Not college-age females [3]
1998	7.8	8.9	3.1	2006	5.4	5.5	1.7
1999	6.0	11.2	3.5	2007	5.5	5.4	1.7
2000	7.1	12.2	2.8	2008	5.2	6.7	1.9
2001	8.8	11.2	3.0	2009	3.7	8.3	1.6
2002	8.9	10.0	2.2	2010	[4] 4.1	8.4	1.6
2003	7.6	8.8	2.2	2011	4.6	7.1	1.4
2004	6.5	7.0	1.8	2012	5.9	4.1	1.3
2005	4.7	5.6	1.6	2013	4.4	4.3	1.4

[1] Includes female victims age 18 to 24 enrolled part time or full time in a post-secondary institution (i.e., college or university, trade school, or vocational school). [2] Includes female victims age 18 to 24 not enrolled in a post-secondary institution. [3] Includes females age 12 to 17 and age 25 or older. [4] Interpret with caution, subject to sampling error.

Source: U.S. Bureau of Justice Statistics, *Rape and Sexual Assault Victimization Among College-Age Females, 1995–2013*, NCJ 248471, December 2014. See also <http://www.bjs.gov/index.cfm?ty=tp&tid=317>.

Table 344. Violent Crime Between Intimate Partners by Sex of Victims: 1994 to 2011

[Intimate partners are defined as current and former spouses, boyfriends, and girlfriends. Estimates based on 2-year rolling averages beginning in 1993. Based on the National Crime Victimization Survey (NCVS); see text this section, and Source]

Year and type of crime	Female victims				Male victims			
	Total intimate partner violence	Rate per 1,000 [1]			Total intimate partner violence	Rate per 1,000 [1]		
		Overall intimate partner violence	Serious violence [3]	Simple assault [4]		Overall intimate partner violence	Serious violence [3]	Simple assault [4]
1994.............	1,766,700	16.1	5.9	10.3	303,460	3.0	1.1	1.9
1995.............	1,785,590	16.1	4.9	11.3	272,450	2.6	0.8	1.8
1996.............	1,676,990	15.0	4.2	10.8	240,280	2.3	0.9	1.4
1997.............	1,644,100	14.6	4.8	9.8	185,650	1.8	0.6	1.1
1998.............	1,499,130	13.2	4.2	8.9	202,720	1.9	0.6	1.3
1999.............	1,250,570	10.9	3.6	7.3	229,510	2.1	0.6	1.6
2000.............	974,160	8.4	2.7	5.7	173,190	1.6	0.3	1.3
2001.............	882,720	7.5	2.4	5.1	112,450	1.0	0.3	0.7
2002.............	889,740	7.5	2.5	5.0	120,350	1.1	0.5	0.6
2003.............	852,220	7.0	2.8	4.2	132,810	1.2	0.5	0.7
2004.............	861,380	7.0	2.9	4.0	174,620	1.5	0.5	1.0
2005.............	718,590	5.8	1.9	3.8	205,270	1.7	0.7	1.0
2006 [2].........	842,410	6.7	2.4	4.3	218,220	1.8	1.0	0.8
2007 [2].........	922,380	7.2	2.6	4.6	183,150	1.5	0.7	0.8
2008.............	847,700	6.6	2.3	4.3	156,900	1.3	0.5	0.8
2009.............	914,480	7.1	2.0	5.0	157,050	1.3	0.5	0.8
2010.............	775,650	5.9	1.6	4.3	130,890	1.1	0.4	0.7
2011.............	620,850	4.7	1.6	3.1	191,540	1.5	0.4	1.1

[1] Rates are per 1,000 persons age 12 and older. [2] Due to methodological changes, use caution when comparing 2006 NCVS criminal victimization estimates to other years. [3] Rape or sexual assault, robbery, and aggravated assault. [4] Attack or attempted attack without a weapon that results in no injury, minor injury, or an undetermined injury requiring less than two days of hospitalization.

Source: U.S. Department of Justice, Bureau of Justice Statistics, *Intimate Partner Victimization: Attributes of Victimization, 1993-2011*, NCJ 243300, November 2013. See also <https://www.bjs.gov/index.cfm?ty=pbse&sid=78>.

Table 345. Fraud and Identity Theft—Consumer Complaints by State: 2016

[Rate per 100,000 population. As of December 31. Rates based on U.S. Census Bureau's 2016 population estimates. The Consumer Sentinel Network is a secure online database of consumer complaints available only to law enforcement. Based on unverified complaints reported by consumers. Excludes complaints from state-specific data contibutors]

State	Fraud and other complaints		Identity theft victims		State	Fraud and other complaints		Identity theft victims	
	Number	Rate	Number	Rate		Number	Rate	Number	Rate
U.S.......	**2,349,973**	**727.3**	**372,526**	**115.3**	MO.......	43,050	706.5	8,292	136.1
AL.........	39,344	809.0	4,007	82.4	MT.......	4,600	441.2	711	68.2
AK.........	2,663	358.9	713	96.1	NE.......	7,855	411.9	1,584	83.1
AZ.........	45,528	656.9	8,748	126.2	NV.......	25,636	872.0	3,993	135.8
AR.........	15,510	519.0	2,308	77.2	NH.......	7,525	563.8	1,352	101.3
CA.........	279,887	713.1	54,744	139.5	NJ.......	56,951	636.7	9,977	111.5
CO.........	33,745	609.1	6,203	112.0	NM.......	13,900	667.9	2,016	96.9
CT.........	21,117	590.4	4,933	137.9	NY.......	112,006	567.3	20,205	102.3
DE.........	7,593	797.5	1,484	155.9	NC.......	65,059	641.2	9,746	96.1
DC.........	10,030	1,474.5	1,352	198.5	ND.......	2,158	284.7	465	61.3
FL.........	269,117	1,305.6	34,384	166.8	OH.......	77,213	664.8	11,009	94.8
GA.........	117,189	1,136.6	12,787	124.0	OK.......	20,350	518.7	3,337	85.1
HI.........	5,768	403.8	789	55.2	OR.......	22,385	546.8	4,312	105.3
ID.........	7,800	463.4	1,348	80.1	PA.......	84,270	659.2	14,030	109.7
IL.........	73,829	576.7	17,660	138.0	RI.......	7,206	682.1	1,216	115.1
IN.........	37,329	562.8	5,091	76.8	SC.......	34,767	700.8	4,438	89.5
IA.........	10,735	342.5	2,135	68.1	SD.......	2,775	320.6	503	58.1
KS.........	14,635	503.4	2,532	87.1	TN.......	51,036	767.3	5,718	86.0
KY.........	23,948	539.7	2,898	65.3	TX.......	265,347	952.3	33,214	119.2
LA.........	32,861	701.9	3,264	69.7	UT.......	12,750	417.9	2,540	83.2
ME.........	5,642	423.7	1,170	87.9	VT.......	2,532	405.4	387	62.0
MD.........	48,594	807.7	8,251	137.1	VA.......	58,991	701.3	8,772	104.3
MA.........	37,271	547.2	7,287	107.0	WA.......	40,423	554.7	8,310	114.0
MI.........	107,557	1,083.3	17,430	175.6	WV.......	9,948	543.3	1,093	59.7
MN.........	25,980	470.7	5,919	107.2	WI.......	26,921	465.9	5,054	87.5
MS.........	18,210	609.3	2,378	79.6	WY.......	2,437	416.2	437	74.6

Source: U.S. Federal Trade Commission, *Consumer Sentinel Network Data Book for January–December 2016*, March 2017. See also <http://www.ftc.gov/sentinel/reports.shtml>.

Table 346. Property Crime by Selected Household Characteristics: 2015

[131,962 represents 131,962,000. For crimes against households (burglary, theft, and motor vehicle theft), each household affected by a crime is counted as a single victimization. Based on National Crime Victimization Survey (NCVS); see text, this section and Appendix III]

Characteristic	Number of house-holds (1,000)	Property crimes							
		Number of victimizations (1,000)				Victimization rate per 1,000 households			
		Total	Burglary	Motor vehicle theft	Theft	Total	Burglary	Motor vehicle theft	Theft
Total..................	131,962	14,611	2,905	564	11,142	110.7	22.0	4.3	84.4
Race:									
White..................	104,986	11,520	2,252	434	8,834	109.7	21.4	4.1	84.1
Black..................	17,745	2,008	429	95	1,484	113.2	24.2	5.4	83.6
Other [1]................	9,231	1,083	224	35	824	117.3	24.2	3.8	89.3
Ethnicity:									
Hispanic................	17,015	2,338	402	132	1,804	137.4	23.7	7.8	106.0
Non-Hispanic..........	114,948	12,273	2,502	432	9,339	106.8	21.8	3.8	81.2
Household income:									
Less than $7,500......	4,204	743	160	[2] 18	565	176.6	38.0	[2] 4.2	134.4
$7,500 to $14,999.....	6,825	1,107	287	33	787	162.3	42.1	4.8	115.4
$15,000 to $24,999....	9,540	1,487	273	47	1,167	155.8	28.7	4.9	122.3
$25,000 to $34,999....	11,297	1,396	305	52	1,038	123.5	27.0	4.6	91.9
$35,000 to $49,999....	13,887	1,689	363	113	1,213	121.6	26.1	8.1	87.3
$50,000 to $74,999....	15,555	1,749	268	64	1,417	112.4	17.2	4.1	91.1
$75,000 or more......	27,862	2,839	454	124	2,260	101.9	16.3	4.4	81.1
Unknown...............	42,793	3,603	794	114	2,695	84.2	18.6	2.7	63.0
Number of persons in household:									
1........................	41,834	3,712	920	123	2,670	88.7	22.0	2.9	63.8
2 or 3...................	65,142	6,934	1,355	280	5,298	106.4	20.8	4.3	81.3
4 or 5...................	21,456	3,136	507	139	2,490	146.2	23.6	6.5	116.1
6 or more...............	3,531	829	122	23	684	234.9	34.6	6.5	193.8

[1] Includes American Indians and Alaska Natives, Asians, Native Hawaiians and other Pacific Islanders, and persons of two or more races. [2] Based on 10 or fewer sample cases or the coefficient of variation is greater than 50%.

Source: U.S. Department of Justice, Bureau of Justice Statistics, "NCVS Victimization Analysis Tool," <http://www.bjs.gov/index.cfm?ty=nvat>, accessed November 2016.

Table 347. Robbery and Property Crimes by Type, Location, and Average Value Lost: 2010 to 2015

[300.3 represents 300,300. Data are from the FBI's Unified Crime Reporting (UCR) Program]

Characteristic of offense	Number of offenses (1,000)				Average value lost (dol.)			
	2010	2013	2014	2015	2010	2013	2014	2015
Robbery, total.........	300.3	301.2	283.8	284.8	1,239	1,170	1,227	1,190
Location of crime:								
Street or highway..............	129.6	127.9	116.3	113.5	908	853	871	1,023
Commercial house.............	39.7	39.9	39.8	41.0	1,858	1,808	1,872	1,416
Gas or service station..........	7.0	7.3	7.1	7.7	939	830	1,026	938
Convenience store.............	15.7	14.9	15.3	16.2	782	1,171	699	623
Residence.....................	51.9	50.1	47.6	47.0	1,491	1,480	1,466	1,545
Bank..........................	6.5	5.7	5.2	4.9	4,410	3,542	3,816	3,884
Miscellaneous.................	49.9	55.4	52.6	54.5	1,115	961	1,235	1,023
Burglary, total.............	1,898.0	1,743.6	1,532.1	1,395.9	2,119	2,322	2,251	2,316
Location and time of burglary:								
Residence (dwelling):..........	1,402.2	1,289.0	1,121.4	999.4	2,137	2,315	2,229	2,296
Night.......................	389.9	357.0	312.5	289.1	1,868	1,736	1,760	1,904
Day.........................	722.2	682.8	598.6	522.9	2,158	2,521	2,311	2,316
Unknown....................	290.1	249.3	210.3	187.5	2,445	2,577	2,691	2,844
Nonresidence (store, office, etc.):..............	495.7	454.5	410.7	396.5	2,070	2,344	2,312	2,366
Night.......................	204.6	185.9	168.1	166.3	1,765	2,356	2,020	2,154
Day.........................	168.9	165.5	150.0	140.0	2,010	1,957	2,144	2,244
Unknown....................	122.2	103.1	92.5	90.2	2,662	2,945	3,114	2,946
Larceny-theft, total [1]............	5,391.6	5,392.2	5,111.5	5,014.3	988	1,259	941	929
Type of larceny:								
Pocket-picking................	21.1	29.0	27.5	27.3	526	514	548	652
Purse-snatching...............	24.5	23.2	20.7	20.3	400	467	508	563
Shoplifting....................	925.1	1,074.2	1,097.4	1,118.4	174	207	204	262
From motor vehicles (except accessories)......	1,423.9	1,259.3	1,172.9	1,203.5	704	937	835	782
Motor vehicle accessories......................	477.8	393.4	359.5	350.0	681	556	553	573
Bicycles......................	179.6	190.7	184.6	180.1	351	420	418	444
From buildings................	607.9	663.0	626.6	582.1	1,406	1,384	1,333	1,394
From coin-operated machines..................	17.6	14.2	11.7	11.4	365	448	480	497
All others....................	1,714.0	1,745.1	1,610.7	1,521.2	1,654	2,372	1,530	1,512
Larceny-theft by value:								
Over $200....................	2,443.1	2,525.7	2,364.9	2,289.5	2,089	2,625	1,972	1,969
$50 to $200..................	1,235.1	1,202.6	1,149.5	1,119.7	111	104	104	106
Under $50....................	1,713.3	1,663.9	1,597.2	1,605.1	17	21	16	20
Motor vehicle theft, total.....................	641.9	652.3	611.6	638.0	6,152	5,972	6,537	7,001

[1] Excludes motor vehicles.

Source: U.S. Department of Justice, Federal Bureau of Investigation, "Crime in the United States 2015," and earlier releases, <https://ucr.fbi.gov/>, accessed November 2016.

Table 348. Hate Crimes—Number of Incidents, Offenses, Victims, and Known Offenders by Bias Motivation: 2000 to 2015

[1,742 law enforcement agencies submitted data on hate crimes. 14,997 law enforcement agencies covering over 283 million people participated in the Hate Crime Statistics Program in 2015. Hate crime offenses cover incidents motivated by race, religion, sexual orientation, ethnicity/national origin, and disability. See source and Appendix III]

Bias motivation	Incidents reported	Offenses	Victims [1]	Known offenders [2]
2000	8,213	9,619	10,117	7,690
2010	6,628	7,699	8,208	6,008
2015, total [3]	**5,850**	**6,885**	**7,173**	**5,493**
Race/ethnicity/ancestry, total	**3,310**	**4,029**	**4,216**	**3,196**
Anti-White	613	734	789	681
Anti-Black or African American	1,745	2,125	2,201	1,605
Anti-American Indian/Alaska native	131	137	141	113
Anti-Asian	111	132	136	108
Anti-Native Hawaiian or Other Pacific Islander	4	6	6	3
Anti-multi-races, group	113	138	160	83
Anti-Arab	37	47	48	35
Anti-Hispanic	299	379	392	325
Anti-other ethnicity (not Hispanic)	257	331	343	243
Religion, total [3]	**1,244**	**1,354**	**1,402**	**809**
Anti-Jewish	664	695	731	387
Anti-Catholic	53	59	60	29
Anti-Protestant	37	47	48	18
Anti-Islamic	257	301	307	228
Anti-other religion	96	104	107	53
Anti-multi-religious group	51	57	58	30
Anti-Eastern Orthodox (Russian, Greek, Other)	48	50	50	36
Sexual orientation, total	**1,053**	**1,219**	**1,263**	**1,221**
Anti-gay (male homosexual)	664	758	786	803
Anti-lesbian (female homosexual)	136	168	170	142
Anti-gay, lesbian, bisexual, transgender	203	235	248	218
Anti-heterosexual	19	23	24	19
Anti-bisexual	31	35	35	39
Disability, total	**74**	**88**	**88**	**73**
Anti-physical	43	52	52	40
Anti-mental	31	36	36	33
Gender identity	**114**	**118**	**122**	**157**
Anti-transgender	73	75	76	114
Anti-gender non-conforming	41	43	46	43
Multiple bias [4]	**32**	**48**	**52**	**18**

[1] The term "victim" may refer to a person, business, institution, or a society as a whole. [2] The term "known offender" does not imply that the identity of the suspect is known, but only that an attribute of the suspect has been identified which distinguishes him/her from an unknown offender. [3] Includes motivation types not shown separately. [4] A "multiple-bias incident" is an incident in which one or more offense types are motivated by two or more biases.

Source: U.S. Department of Justice, Federal Bureau of Investigation, "Hate Crime Statistics 2015," <https://ucr.fbi.gov/>, accessed November 2016.

Table 349. Hate Crimes by Bias Motivation and Location of Incident: 2015

[See headnote, Table 348]

Location	Total incidents	Race/ ethnicity/ ancestry	Religion	Sexual orientation	Disability	Gender	Gender identity	Multiple-bias incidents [1]
Total [2]	**5,850**	**3,310**	**1,244**	**1,053**	**74**	**23**	**114**	**32**
Air/bus/train terminal	82	57	9	15	–	–	–	1
Bar/nightclub	99	55	9	32	–	–	3	–
Church/synagogue/temple/mosque	259	45	199	8	–	–	5	2
Commercial office building	111	56	32	15	3	–	4	1
Community center	15	5	10	–	–	–	–	–
Convenience store	94	67	14	11	1	–	1	–
Department/discount store	68	48	12	5	–	2	1	–
Drug store/doctor's office/hospital	66	50	10	4	–	1	1	–
Field/woods	31	21	4	3	1	–	1	1
Government/public building	104	74	13	12	1	–	3	1
Grocery/supermarket	48	35	5	6	1	–	1	–
Highway/road/alley/street/sidewalk	1,018	588	99	266	16	2	38	9
Hotel/motel/etc.	49	28	9	9	1	1	1	–
Jail/prison/corrections facility	58	38	6	11	2	1	–	–
Liquor store	14	8	3	3	–	–	–	–
Park/playground	88	53	18	13	1	–	3	–
Parking/drop lot/garage	328	212	51	53	3	1	7	1
Residence/home	1,843	1,109	318	345	28	10	27	6
Restaurant	125	83	13	25	1	–	1	2
School/college [3]	149	73	57	19	–	–	–	–
School—college/university	152	85	41	19	2	–	3	2
School—elementary/secondary	184	103	44	25	4	2	4	2
Service/gas station	65	46	11	7	–	–	–	1
Specialty store (TV, fur, etc.)	43	25	8	8	2	–	–	–
Other/unknown	642	269	235	125	5	2	5	1

– Represents zero. [1] See footnote 4, Table 348. [2] Includes locations not shown separately. [3] The location designation school/college has been retained for agencies that have not updated their records to include the new location designations of school, which allow for more specificity in reporting.

Source: U.S. Department of Justice, Federal Bureau of Investigation, "Hate Crime Statistics 2015," <https://ucr.fbi.gov/>, accessed November 2016.

Table 350. Firearm Violence, Homicides and Nonfatal Victimizations: 1993 to 2011

[Detail may not sum to total due to rounding. Data are primarily from the Bureau of Justice Statistics' National Crime Victimization Survey and Centers for Disease Control and Prevention's Injury Statistics Query and Reporting System]

| Year | Fatal and nonfatal firearm violence | | | | Percent | | Rate of nonfatal firearm victimization [3] |
	Total	Firearm homicides	Nonfatal firearm victimizations [1]	Nonfatal firearm incidents [2]	All violence involving firearms	All firearm violence that was homicide	
1993.........	1,548,000	18,253	1,529,700	1,222,700	9.2	1.2	7.3
1994.........	1,585,700	17,527	1,568,200	1,287,200	9.3	1.1	7.4
1995.........	1,208,800	15,551	1,193,200	1,028,900	7.9	1.3	5.5
1996.........	1,114,800	14,037	1,100,800	939,500	7.9	1.3	5.1
1997.........	1,037,300	13,252	1,024,100	882,900	7.7	1.3	4.7
1998.........	847,200	11,798	835,400	673,300	7.0	1.4	3.8
1999.........	651,700	10,828	640,900	523,600	6.1	1.7	2.9
2000.........	621,000	10,801	610,200	483,700	7.3	1.7	2.7
2001.........	574,500	11,348	563,100	507,000	7.7	2.0	2.5
2002.........	551,800	11,829	540,000	450,800	7.4	2.1	2.3
2003.........	479,300	11,920	467,300	385,000	6.2	2.5	2.0
2004.........	468,100	11,624	456,500	405,800	6.9	2.5	1.9
2005.........	515,900	12,352	503,500	446,400	7.4	2.4	2.1
2006.........	627,200	12,791	614,400	552,000	7.4	2.0	2.5
2007.........	567,400	12,632	554,800	448,400	8.3	2.2	2.2
2008.........	383,500	12,179	371,300	331,600	6.0	3.2	1.5
2009.........	421,600	11,493	410,100	383,400	7.4	2.7	1.6
2010.........	426,100	11,078	415,000	378,800	8.6	2.6	1.6
2011 [4].......	478,400	11,101	467,300	414,600	8.2	2.3	1.8

[1] A victimization refers to a single victim that experienced a criminal incident. [2] An incident is a specific criminal act involving one or more victims or victimizations. [3] Per 1,000 persons age 12 or older. [4] Preliminary homicide estimates from Centers for Disease Control, *Deaths: Preliminary Data for 2011*, NVSR Vol. 61, No. 6.

Source: Department of Justice, Bureau of Justice Statistics, *Firearm Violence, 1993-2011,* NCJ 241730, May 2013. See also <http://www.bjs.gov/index.cfm?ty=pbdetail&iid=4616>

Table 351. Nonfatal Firearm and Nonfirearm Violence by Victim-Offender Relationship and Location of Crime: 2007 to 2011

[Data are for victimizations. Detail may not sum to total due to rounding. Data from National Crime Victimization Survey]

| Characteristic | Total nonfatal violence | | Firearm violence | | Nonfirearm violence | |
	Number	Percent [1]	Number	Percent [1]	Number	Percent [1]
RELATIONSHIP TO VICTIM						
Total..	**29,611,300**	**(X)**	**2,218,500**	**7.5**	**27,392,800**	**92.5**
Nonstranger.......................................	15,715,900	(X)	738,000	4.7	14,977,900	95.3
Intimate [2].......................................	4,673,600	(X)	195,700	4.2	4,477,900	95.8
Other relative....................................	2,157,700	(X)	158,100	7.3	1,999,500	92.7
Friend/acquaintance...........................	8,884,600	(X)	384,100	4.3	8,500,500	95.7
Stranger..	10,983,100	(X)	1,177,900	10.7	9,805,200	89.3
Unknown [3]......................................	2,912,300	(X)	302,600	10.4	2,609,600	89.6
LOCATION						
Total..	**29,618,300**	**100.0**	**2,218,500**	**100.0**	**27,399,800**	**100.0**
Victim's home or lodging......................	6,491,400	21.9	427,600	19.3	6,063,800	22.1
Near victim's home.............................	4,804,700	16.2	504,500	22.7	4,300,200	15.7
In, at, or near a friend, neighbor, or relative's home......	2,175,900	7.3	132,600	6.0	2,043,300	7.5
Commercial place...............................	2,878,600	9.7	195,400	8.8	2,683,200	9.8
Parking lot or garage..........................	1,688,400	5.7	340,600	15.4	1,347,900	4.9
School [4]...	3,931,100	13.3	[5] 12,600	[5] 0.6	3,918,500	14.3
Open area, on street, or public transportation.............	4,636,900	15.7	508,400	22.9	4,128,500	15.1
Other location...................................	3,011,200	10.2	96,800	4.4	2,914,400	10.6

X Not applicable. [1] Percent of total violence is shown for data by relationship to victim. Percent distribution of specified type of violence is shown for data by location. [2] Includes current or former spouses, boyfriends, or girlfriends. [3] Includes relationships unknown and number of offenders unknown. [4] Includes inside a school building or on school property. [5] Interpret with caution. Estimate based on 10 or fewer sample cases, or coefficient of variation is greater than 50%.

Source: Department of Justice, Bureau of Justice Statistics, *Firearm Violence, 1993-2011*, NCJ 241730, May 2013. See also <http://www.bjs.gov/index.cfm?ty=pbdetail&iid=4616>.

Table 352. Victims of Identity Theft by Type of Account and Selected Victim Characteristics: 2014

[17,576.2 represents 17,576,200. Data shown are for persons age 16 or older who experienced at least one identity theft incident during the past 12 months. Estimates are based on the most recent identity theft incident. Includes successful and attempted identity theft in which the victim experienced no loss. Based on the National Crime Victimization Survey's Identity Theft Supplement]

Characteristic	Any identity theft		Misuse of existing credit card		Misuse of existing bank account		New account or personal information [1]	
	Number of victims	Percent of all persons	Number of victims	Percent of persons with credit card	Number of victims	Percent of persons with bank account	Number of victims	Percent of all persons
Total.................................	17,576.2	7.0	8,598.6	5.0	8,082.6	3.7	1,732.6	0.7
By sex:								
Male..................................	8,332.9	6.9	4,279.8	5.2	3,696.8	3.5	788.4	0.7
Female................................	9,243.3	7.2	4,318.8	4.8	4,385.8	3.9	944.2	0.7
By age:								
16 to 17 years old [2]...............	38.6	0.5	(Z)	(Z)	5.8	0.2	7.5	0.1
18 to 24 years old.................	1,300.8	4.3	309.4	2.5	843.1	3.7	144.1	0.5
25 to 34 years old.................	3,566.4	8.3	1,488.4	5.1	1,821.6	4.9	392.5	0.9
35 to 49 years old.................	5,012.3	8.2	2,339.9	5.2	2,405.0	4.4	496.3	0.8
50 to 64 years old.................	5,061.1	8.1	2,733.2	5.6	2,191.0	3.8	472.8	0.8
65 years or older..................	2,596.9	5.8	1,727.7	4.8	816.1	2.0	219.5	0.5
By race/Hispanic origin:								
White [3]............................	13,264.1	8.0	7,061.0	5.6	5,804.7	3.8	1,005.4	0.6
Black [3]............................	1,407.7	4.7	389.7	2.6	775.1	3.4	295.5	1.0
Hispanic/Latino....................	1,789.8	4.9	577.1	3.0	1,040.2	3.9	290.1	0.8
Other race [3,4]....................	861.1	6.1	526.3	5.0	322.7	2.6	70.9	0.5
Two or more races [3]..............	253.4	9.0	44.5	2.8	139.9	5.8	70.8	2.5
By household income:								
$24,999 or less....................	1,838.6	4.9	495.8	3.2	991.1	3.7	397.9	1.1
$25,000-$49,999...................	3,010.9	5.9	1,175.2	3.7	1,651.3	3.8	329.5	0.7
$50,000-$74,999..................	2,493.7	7.6	1,146.4	4.4	1,273.0	4.2	188.8	0.6
$75,000 or more...................	6,758.0	10.7	4,137.0	7.6	2,616.9	4.4	423.9	0.7
Unknown............................	3,474.9	5.4	1,644.1	3.7	1,550.3	2.8	392.4	0.6

Z Less than 1 or less than 0.05%. [1] Includes the misuse of personal information to open a new account or to commit other fraud. [2] Interpret with caution; estimates are based on 10 or fewer sample cases or coefficient of variation is greater than 50%. [3] Excludes persons of Hispanic or Latino origin. [4] Includes persons identifying as American Indian, Alaska Native, Asian, Hawaiian, or other Pacific Islander.

Source: U.S. Department of Justice, Bureau of Justice Statistics, *Victims of Identity Theft, 2014*, NCJ 248991, September 2015. See also <http://www.bjs.gov/index.cfm?ty=pbse&sid=60>.

Table 353. Employment by State and Local Law Enforcement Agencies by Type of Agency and Employee: 2008

[As of September 30. Based on census of all state and local law enforcement agencies operating nationwide, conducted every 4 years]

Type of agency	Number of agencies	Number of employees					
		Full-time			Part-time		
		Total	Sworn	Civilian	Total	Sworn	Civilian
Total [1]............................	17,985	1,133,905	765,237	368,668	100,340	44,062	56,278
Local police........................	12,501	593,003	461,054	131,949	58,129	27,810	30,319
Sheriffs' offices....................	3,063	353,461	182,979	170,482	26,052	11,334	14,718
Primary State.......................	50	93,148	60,772	32,376	947	54	893
Special jurisdiction.................	1,733	90,262	56,968	33,294	14,681	4,451	10,230
Constable/marshal.................	638	4,031	3,464	567	531	413	118

[1] Excludes agencies with less than one full-time officer or the equivalent in part-time officers.

Source: U.S. Bureau of Justice Statistics, *Census of State and Local Law Enforcement Agencies, 2008*. See also <https://www.bjs.gov/index.cfm?ty=pbse&sid=73>.

Table 354. Background Checks for Firearm Transfers: 2004 to 2014

[In thousands (8,133 represents 8,133,000), except percent. The Brady Handgun Violence Prevention Act (Brady Act) P.L. 103–159, 1993 requires a background check on an applicant for a firearm purchase from a dealer who is a Federal Firearms Licensee. The period beginning November 30, 1998 is the effective date for the Brady Act. The National Instant Criminal Background Check System (NICS) began operations in 1998. Checks on handgun and long gun transfers are conducted by the FBI, and by state and local agencies. Totals combine Firearm Inquiry Statistics (FIST) estimates for state and local agencies with transactions and denials reported by the FBI]

Inquiries and rejections	2004	2005	2006	2007	2008	2009	2010	2011	2012	2013	2014
Applications received...............	8,133	8,324	8,772	8,836	10,131	11,071	10,643	12,135	15,718	17,602	14,993
Applications denied.................	126	132	135	136	147	150	153	160	192	193	193
Denied (percent)..................	*1.6*	*1.6*	*1.6*	*1.6*	*1.5*	*1.4*	*1.5*	*1.3*	*1.2*	*1.1*	*1.3*
Selected reasons for rejection: [1]											
Felony indictment/conviction......	(NA)	(NA)	(NA)	(NA)	77	67	62	(NA)	82	(NA)	82
Other................................	(NA)	(NA)	(NA)	(NA)	70	83	91	(NA)	110	(NA)	111
Felony denials per 1,000 applications.............	(NA)	(NA)	(NA)	(NA)	7.2	6.2	6.0	(NA)	5.2	(NA)	5.5

NA Not available. [1] Beginning in 2008, the FBI instituted a new classification system; therefore, data prior to 2008 aren't comparable to previously published estimates.

Source: U.S. Department of Justice, Bureau of Justice Statistics, *Background Checks for Firearm Transfers, 2013-14 Statistical Tables*, NCJ 249849, June 2016. See also <https://www.bjs.gov/index.cfm?ty=pbse&sid=13>.

Table 355. Federal Drug Incidents and Seizures by Type of Drug: 2000 to 2012

[For fiscal years ending in year shown. Previously, data for amount of drugs seized at the Federal level was obtained from the Federal-wide Drug Seizure System (FDSS). A new system has been created called the National Seizure System (NSS), which broadens the scope of data collected for the amount of drugs seized (in pounds) at the national level. Data for "Seizure in (pounds)" are from NSS. Includes only information that has been reported to El Paso Intelligence Center (EPIC) by Federal, State, Local, Tribal, and International agencies, who reported seizures and may not necessarily reflect total seizures nationwide. There is no mandatory reporting for local and state agencies]

Drug	2000	2005	2007	2008	2009	2010	2011	2012
Number of incidents, total [1]	**37,201**	**57,127**	**55,064**	**55,593**	**68,541**	**72,612**	**55,046**	**40,271**
Cannabis [2]	21,159	32,735	35,697	36,560	46,362	47,034	31,266	23,708
Methamphetamine	5,233	9,310	6,109	5,667	7,014	8,607	8,119	7,207
Cocaine	8,670	11,927	11,061	10,845	12,067	13,543	11,925	6,675
Heroin	2,135	2,941	1,923	2,274	2,803	3,126	3,504	2,532
MDMA [3]	4	214	274	247	295	302	232	149
Seizure in (pounds), total	**2,447,710**	**3,210,311**	**4,180,386**	**3,665,022**	**4,846,001**	**5,141,789**	**5,359,037**	**4,287,415**
Cannabis [2]	2,339,439	3,062,572	4,025,023	3,539,544	4,705,320	4,990,423	5,173,627	4,133,141
Cocaine	95,231	126,208	133,172	101,364	116,157	115,213	145,078	96,283
Methamphetamine	9,966	14,760	14,067	14,042	14,894	24,571	29,436	47,005
Heroin	2,738	4,297	3,764	4,238	5,122	6,619	8,624	9,904
MDMA [3]	337	2,474	4,361	5,833	4,509	4,964	2,271	1,081

[1] Seizure of drugs, weapons, currency, etc., which can occur without any arrest taking place. [2] Includes hashish. [3] MDMA methylene dioxymethamphetamine, an amphetamine derivative, used illicitly as a hallucinogen and mood-enhancer.

Source: Drug Enforcement Administration, El Paso Intelligence Center, unpublished data from the National Seizure System.

Table 356. Asset Forfeiture Fund—Net Deposits by State: 2014 to 2016

[In thousands of dollars (4,473,669 represents 4,473,669,000). For fiscal years ending September 30. Transactions to or from the Department of Justice's (DOJ) Asset Forfeiture Fund (AFF). Seizure and forfeiture of assets that represent the proceeds of or were used to facilitate federal crimes. These figures represent official accounting transactions. They do not reflect total forfeiture activity for any jurisdiction. See source for more details. Minus sign indicates refunds]

State or territory	2014	2015	2016	State or territory	2014	2015	2016
Total	**4,473,669**	**1,629,262**	**1,921,274**	Montana	3,610	424	422
				Nebraska	4,222	5,452	2,277
Investment income [1]	6,280	6,611	34,336	Nevada	6,366	12,798	6,264
Alabama	3,681	1,428	1,254	New Hampshire	1,827	1,720	1,604
Alaska	1,615	860	584	New Jersey	52,484	37,333	30,059
Arizona	9,353	9,915	7,562	New Mexico	4,843	4,329	5,494
Arkansas	4,691	5,503	14,959	New York	[2] 3,595,164	554,624	1,187,090
California	225,853	170,920	117,545	North Carolina	18,579	20,392	16,242
Colorado	7,176	10,466	9,001	North Dakota	93	197	674
Connecticut	6,150	6,056	5,321	Ohio	20,022	31,702	19,135
Delaware	–	–	–	Oklahoma	4,719	31,436	8,204
District of Columbia	8,997	209,171	35,353	Oregon	3,524	2,734	3,935
Florida	89,757	95,615	74,196	Pennsylvania	97,628	48,221	13,552
Georgia	27,043	18,724	17,933	Rhode Island	2,488	8,416	3,262
Hawaii	5,461	1,892	608	South Carolina	8,753	4,885	5,738
Idaho	799	1,711	1,185	South Dakota	–	4,565	68
Illinois	32,611	40,677	47,495	Tennessee	8,642	7,489	13,012
Indiana	5,988	14,955	12,957	Texas	80,305	60,400	97,832
Iowa	1,895	2,175	643	Utah	7,275	3,353	1,985
Kansas	5,893	4,705	3,412	Vermont	1,378	1,429	1,568
Kentucky	14,263	14,056	14,605	Virginia	25,302	42,896	10,213
Louisiana	4,383	5,301	6,401	Washington	13,030	5,618	6,853
Maine	841	1,157	240	West Virginia	1,986	820	3,413
Maryland	20,554	25,057	10,694	Wisconsin	10,953	5,647	2,308
Massachusetts	11,906	24,232	12,784	Wyoming	124	35	195
Michigan	16,634	10,307	31,268	Guam	136	420	819
Minnesota	10,479	4,100	3,600	Puerto Rico	8,133	7,110	5,078
Mississippi	9,747	5,253	6,446	Virgin Islands	89	51	652
Missouri	9,792	22,726	13,509	Other [3]	-49,848	11,191	-10,563

– Represents or rounds to zero. [1] Idle funds invested in U.S. Treasury Securities. [2] Includes $1.7 billion related to the JP Morgan Chase/Bernard Madoff case and $1.2 billion associated with the Toyota Motor Corporation case. [3] Comprised of transactions made to the AFF where a district has not been identified, where Federal reimbursements were made for services rendered, or summary estimates for financial reporting purposes where details by state were not available.

Source: U.S. Department of Justice, Asset Forfeiture Program, "Annual Reports to Congress," <https://www.justice.gov/afp>, accessed May 2017.

Table 357. Arrests by Offense, Sex, and Age: 2015

[8,305.9 represents 8,305,900. For year ending December 31. Based on Uniform Crime Reporting Program. Arrests reported by 12,706 agencies with an estimated total population of 246,947,242. Some persons may be arrested more than once during a year; therefore, in some cases, the data in this table could represent multiple arrests of the same person]

Offense charged	Total			Male			Female		
	Total	Under 18 years	18 years and over	Total	Under 18 years	18 years and over	Total	Under 18 years	18 years and over
Total..................	8,305.9	709.3	7,596.6	6,067.6	501.5	5,566.1	2,238.3	207.9	2,030.5
Violent crime..................	388.1	39.5	348.6	309.3	32.2	277.0	78.8	7.3	71.5
Murder and nonnegligent manslaughter....	8.5	0.6	7.9	7.5	0.6	7.0	1.0	(Z)	0.9
Rape [1]................	17.5	2.7	14.8	17.0	2.6	14.4	0.5	0.1	0.4
Robbery................	73.2	14.2	59.1	62.7	12.7	50.0	10.5	1.5	9.0
Aggravated assault..............	288.8	22.0	266.8	222.0	16.4	205.6	66.8	5.6	61.2
Property crime..............	1,133.3	161.7	971.6	699.3	106.9	592.4	434.1	54.8	379.2
Burglary................	166.6	27.5	139.1	135.1	23.8	111.3	31.5	3.7	27.9
Larceny-theft..............	900.1	121.0	779.1	511.6	72.1	439.4	388.5	48.8	339.7
Motor vehicle theft.............	59.8	11.2	48.7	47.2	9.2	38.0	12.7	2.0	10.7
Arson................	6.8	2.1	4.7	5.5	1.8	3.7	1.3	0.3	1.0
Other assaults..............	831.7	101.0	730.7	598.0	63.9	534.1	233.7	37.0	196.6
Forgery and counterfeiting..............	42.7	0.8	41.9	27.6	0.6	27.0	15.1	0.2	14.9
Fraud................	102.3	3.5	98.9	62.7	2.3	60.4	39.6	1.2	38.5
Embezzlement..............	12.2	0.5	11.8	6.1	0.3	5.8	6.2	0.2	6.0
Stolen property; buying, receiving, possessing..................	68.3	8.0	60.4	53.6	6.7	46.9	14.7	1.3	13.4
Vandalism................	147.2	32.1	115.0	115.7	26.7	89.0	31.5	5.4	26.1
Weapons; carrying, possessing, etc...........	111.3	14.8	96.5	101.4	13.2	88.2	10.0	1.6	8.3
Prostitution and commercialized vice.........	31.5	0.4	31.1	11.4	0.1	11.2	20.2	0.3	19.8
Sex offenses except rape & prostitution......	39.4	6.7	32.7	36.4	5.8	30.5	3.0	0.9	2.2
Drug abuse violations..............	1,144.0	76.2	1,067.8	886.0	60.0	826.0	258.0	16.2	241.8
Gambling................	3.6	0.4	3.3	2.9	0.3	2.6	0.7	(Z)	0.7
Offenses against family and children........	72.4	2.6	69.8	51.6	1.6	50.0	20.8	1.0	19.8
Driving under the influence..................	833.8	5.1	828.8	625.9	3.8	622.1	207.9	1.3	206.7
Liquor laws................	204.7	33.2	171.5	145.2	19.9	125.3	59.4	13.2	46.2
Drunkenness................	314.9	4.2	310.6	253.6	3.0	250.5	61.3	1.2	60.1
Disorderly conduct..............	298.3	55.1	243.2	214.1	35.7	178.4	84.1	19.4	64.7
Vagrancy................	19.4	0.8	18.6	15.1	0.6	14.5	4.3	0.2	4.1
All other offenses (except traffic)..............	2,471.8	128.8	2,343.0	1,826.7	93.3	1,733.4	645.1	35.5	609.6
Suspicion................	1.0	0.1	0.9	0.8	0.1	0.7	0.2	(Z)	0.2
Curfew and loitering law violations............	33.9	33.9	(X)	24.3	24.3	(X)	9.6	9.6	(X)

Z Less than 50. X Not applicable. [1] The rape figures in this table are an aggregate total of the data submitted using both the revised and legacy Uniform Crime Reporting definitions. For more information, see <https://ucr.fbi.gov/crime-in-the-u.s/2015/crime-in-the-u.s.-2015/resource-pages/rape_addendum-2015-_final>.

Source: U.S. Department of Justice, Federal Bureau of Investigation, "Crime in the United States 2015," <https://ucr.fbi.gov/>, accessed December 2016.

Table 358. Arrests by Offense and Race/Ethnicity: 2015

[8,248.7 represents 8,248,700. Arrests reported by 12,692 agencies with an estimate total population of 246,920,373]

Offense charged	Total	White	Black	Hispanic or Latino [1]	American Indian/ Alaska Native	Asian	Native Hawaiian/ other Pacific Islander
Total..................	8,248.7	5,753.2	2,197.1	1,204.9	174.0	101.1	23.3
Violent crime..................	386.5	232.2	140.5	77.6	6.8	5.7	1.2
Murder and nonnegligent manslaughter......	8.5	3.9	4.3	1.4	0.1	0.1	–
Rape [2]................	17.4	11.8	4.9	3.5	0.3	0.3	0.1
Robbery................	73.0	32.4	39.1	12.8	0.6	0.7	0.3
Aggravated assault..............	287.6	184.0	92.2	59.9	5.8	4.6	0.8
Property crime..............	1,126.0	779.5	312.6	147.0	17.1	13.9	2.8
Burglary................	165.9	113.0	48.9	28.3	1.7	2.0	0.4
Larceny-theft..............	893.7	621.6	244.7	104.7	14.3	11.1	2.0
Motor vehicle theft.............	59.5	40.0	17.5	13.1	0.9	0.8	0.4
Arson................	6.8	5.0	1.5	0.9	0.2	0.1	–
Other assaults..............	826.9	544.9	254.6	118.1	15.0	9.9	2.5
Forgery and counterfeiting..............	42.4	27.4	14.0	5.5	0.3	0.6	0.1
Fraud................	101.6	67.6	31.5	8.8	1.2	1.2	0.1
Embezzlement..............	12.2	7.4	4.5	1.1	0.1	0.2	–
Stolen property; buying, receiving, possessing..................	68.1	44.6	21.8	10.6	0.8	0.8	0.1
Vandalism................	146.1	101.5	39.8	21.5	2.8	1.7	0.3
Weapons—carrying, possessing, etc...........	110.8	64.0	44.3	20.7	1.1	1.2	0.2
Prostitution and commercialized vice...........	31.4	17.1	12.5	5.3	0.1	1.6	0.1
Sex offenses except rape & prostitution........	39.2	28.7	9.1	7.8	0.6	0.7	0.1
Drug abuse violations..............	1,137.0	803.8	307.1	186.8	11.7	12.4	1.8
Gambling................	3.6	1.3	2.0	0.5	–	0.2	–
Offenses against the family and children.......	71.9	47.3	21.4	6.6	2.6	0.5	–
Driving under the influence..................	825.2	681.6	108.6	147.4	16.0	16.4	2.5
Liquor laws................	201.6	160.8	27.7	22.3	9.8	2.7	0.5
Drunkenness................	313.4	239.6	44.7	66.3	25.7	3.0	0.5
Disorderly conduct..............	295.8	189.3	91.7	26.0	11.9	2.3	0.6
Vagrancy................	19.3	13.2	5.1	2.3	0.7	0.2	–
All other offenses (except traffic)..............	2,455.2	1,683.3	688.1	316.7	49.1	25.2	9.5
Suspicion................	1.1	0.5	0.3	–	0.3	–	–
Curfew and loitering law violations.............	33.7	17.8	15.1	6.0	0.4	0.4	0.1

– Represents or rounds to zero. [1] Persons of Hispanic origin may be of any race. [2] See footnote 1, Table 357.

Source: U.S. Department of Justice, Federal Bureau of Investigation, "Crime in the United States 2015," <https://ucr.fbi.gov/>, accessed December 2016.

Table 359. Law Enforcement Officers Killed and Assaulted: 1990 to 2015

[The statistics presented in this table are based on information collected by the staff of the FBI's Law Enforcement Officers Killed and Assaulted Program from law enforcement agencies throughout the U.S. and U.S. Territories. It contains statistics on line-of-duty felonious deaths, accidental deaths, and assaults of duly sworn local, state, tribal, and federal law enforcement officers]

Item	1990	1995	2000	2005	2010	2011	2012	2013	2014	2015
OFFICERS KILLED										
Total killed.....................	**132**	**133**	**134**	**122**	**128**	**125**	**97**	**76**	**96**	**86**
By region and area:										
Northeast............................	13	16	13	12	11	18	15	7	16	9
Midwest.............................	20	19	32	23	24	28	9	8	12	11
South................................	68	63	67	58	61	56	50	46	36	48
West.................................	23	32	19	24	29	20	17	15	27	14
Puerto Rico.........................	8	2	3	5	3	3	5	–	5	4
Island Areas.......................	–	1	–	–	–	–	1	–	–	–
Total feloniously killed...........	**65**	**74**	**51**	**55**	**56**	**72**	**49**	**27**	**51**	**41**
By type of weapon:										
Firearms.............................	56	63	47	50	55	63	44	26	46	38
Handgun.........................	47	44	33	42	38	50	34	18	33	29
Rifle..............................	8	14	10	3	15	7	7	5	10	7
Shotgun.........................	1	5	4	5	2	6	3	3	3	1
Firearm type not reported......	–	–	–	–	–	–	–	–	–	1
Knife/cutting instrument..........	3	1	1	–	–	1	1	–	–	–
Bomb...............................	–	8	–	–	–	–	–	–	–	–
Blunt instrument....................	–	–	–	–	–	–	–	–	–	–
Personal weapons [1].............	2	–	–	–	–	2	2	–	1	–
Vehicle.............................	1	2	3	5	1	6	2	1	4	3
Other...............................	3	–	–	–	–	–	–	–	–	–
Total accidentally killed.........	**67**	**59**	**83**	**67**	**72**	**53**	**48**	**49**	**45**	**45**
OFFICERS ASSAULTED										
Population covered (1,000) [2].....	197,426	191,759	204,599	222,874	248,727	254,535	250,151	256,689	246,681	241,382
Number of—										
Reporting agencies...............	9,343	8,503	8,940	10,119	11,826	12,031	11,794	11,958	11,235	11,961
Officers employed................	410,131	428,379	452,531	489,393	557,884	539,282	525,217	551,893	543,331	507,852
Total assaulted.................	**72,091**	**57,762**	**58,398**	**57,820**	**56,491**	**55,631**	**53,867**	**50,802**	**48,988**	**50,212**
By type of weapon:										
Firearm.............................	3,651	2,354	1,749	2,157	1,925	2,240	2,276	2,299	1,976	2,018
Knife/cutting instrument..........	1,647	1,356	1,015	1,059	918	1,003	909	901	966	917
Other dangerous weapon........	7,423	6,414	8,132	8,379	7,413	7,856	7,435	7,042	6,976	7,597
Personal weapons [1].............	59,370	47,638	47,502	46,225	46,235	44,532	43,247	40,560	39,070	39,680

– Represents zero. [1] Includes hands, fists, feet, etc. [2] Represents the number of persons covered by reporting agencies.

Source: U.S. Department of Justice, Federal Bureau of Investigation, "Law Enforcement Officers Killed and Assaulted, 2015," and previous reports, <https://ucr.fbi.gov/>, accessed December 2016.

Table 360. Presidential Pardons and Commutations: 1961 to 2017

[For fiscal years shown. Not shown are petitions pending at the beginning of the fiscal year, or in the case of a change of administration, the number of cases pending at the time of the new President's inauguration]

Period	President	Petitions received	Petitions granted [1]			Petitions denied or closed without Presidential Action
			Pardon	Commutation	Remission	
1961 to 2017...........	**Total**	**73,008**	**4,475**	**2,240**	**17**	**55,341**
1961 to 1964...........	John F. Kennedy	1,749	472	100	3	831
1964 to 1969...........	Lyndon B. Johnson	4,537	960	226	1	2,830
1969 to 1975...........	Richard M. Nixon	2,591	863	60	3	2,614
1975 to 1977...........	Gerald R. Ford	1,527	382	22	5	900
1977 to 1981...........	Jimmy Carter	2,627	534	29	3	2,056
1981 to 1989...........	Ronald W. Reagan	3,404	393	13	–	2,804
1989 to 1993...........	George H.W. Bush	1,466	74	3	–	1,621
1993 to 2001...........	William J. Clinton	7,489	396	61	2	4,554
2001 to 2009...........	George W. Bush	11,074	189	11	–	11,914
2009 to 2017...........	Barack Obama	36,544	212	1,715	–	25,217

– Represents zero. [1] Petitions granted are taken from a count of clemency warrants maintained by the Office of the Pardon Attorney. Cases in which multiple forms of relief were granted are counted in only one category. Cases in which clemency was granted to a person who did not file an application with the Office of the Pardon Attorney are counted as "petitions granted" but have not been counted as "petitions pending" or "petitions received" since at least FY1990. Excludes individual members of a class of persons granted pardons by proclamation.

Source: U.S. Department of Justice, Office of the Pardon Attorney, "Clemency Statistics," <https://www.justice.gov/pardon/clemency-statistics>, accessed April 2017.

Table 361. State and Local Government Criminal Justice Expenditures Per Capita by State: 2014

[In dollars. Based on Census Bureau's Annual Survey of State and Local Government Finances]

State	Total justice system	Police protec-tion	Judicial and legal	Correc-tions	State	Total justice system	Police protec-tion	Judicial and legal	Correc-tions
Total................	**693**	**320**	**138**	**235**	Missouri................	528	281	87	160
Alabama...............	477	249	82	146	Montana...............	681	288	154	238
Alaska.................	1,300	506	329	465	Nebraska...............	522	220	88	214
Arizona................	671	290	137	244	Nevada.................	807	400	161	245
Arkansas..............	482	221	71	191	New Hampshire.........	534	304	101	130
California..............	1,000	409	221	370	New Jersey.............	775	376	165	234
Colorado..............	697	336	134	227	New Mexico............	798	325	155	317
Connecticut...........	726	323	210	193	New York..............	990	477	200	313
Delaware..............	892	360	218	315	North Carolina.........	561	311	75	175
District of Columbia.....	1,377	896	181	299	North Dakota...........	549	249	128	173
Florida.................	685	370	115	200	Ohio...................	595	282	153	160
Georgia...............	566	239	108	219	Oklahoma..............	556	266	96	194
Hawaii.................	692	320	219	153	Oregon.................	747	305	157	284
Idaho..................	572	252	124	196	Pennsylvania...........	683	276	149	258
Illinois.................	666	388	116	163	Rhode Island...........	695	371	128	196
Indiana................	423	183	83	157	South Carolina.........	450	230	67	153
Iowa...................	490	233	114	143	South Dakota...........	513	212	98	203
Kansas................	542	260	110	172	Tennessee..............	559	276	105	177
Kentucky..............	452	162	122	169	Texas..................	576	263	102	210
Louisiana..............	741	321	159	261	Utah...................	538	229	126	183
Maine..................	417	194	74	149	Vermont................	654	312	119	223
Maryland..............	871	428	143	300	Virginia................	654	271	107	276
Massachusetts.........	690	349	162	179	Washington............	608	253	127	227
Michigan...............	616	242	119	255	West Virginia...........	515	196	127	191
Minnesota.............	614	321	126	166	Wisconsin..............	676	305	109	262
Mississippi............	488	235	84	169	Wyoming...............	942	384	200	359

Source: U.S. Census Bureau, "LF1400A1: State and Local Government Finances by Level of Government and by State: 2014," <http://factfinder.census.gov/>, accessed August 2017; and "Table 1. Annual Estimates of the Resident Population for the United States, Regions, States, and Puerto Rico: April 1, 2010 to July 1, 2016 (NST-EST2016-01)," December 2016, <http://www.census.gov/data/tables/2016/demo/popest/state-total.html>.

Table 362. Denials of Firearm Transfer Applications by Reason and Agency Type: 2012 to 2014

[In percent. Reasons for denials are based on The Brady Handgun Violence Prevention Act, pursuant to 18 U.S.C. 922 and state laws. Denial occurs when an applicant is prohibited from receiving a firearm or a permit that can be used to receive a firearm because a disqualifying factor was found during a background check. Application for firearm transfer is information submitted by a person to a state or local checking agency to purchase a firearm or obtain a permit that can be used for a purchase. Information may be submitted directly to a checking agency or forwarded by a prospective seller. Totals were based on federal and state agencies that reported counts on reasons for denial. Reasons for denial for local agencies were estimated]

Reason for denial	2012			2013			2014		
	FBI	State	Local	FBI	State	Local [1]	FBI	State	Local
Felony indictment/conviction..............	48.2	29.8	17.8	48.5	30.6	(NA)	47.7	31.0	18.8
Felony indictment.........................	5.7	1.2	3.7	5.6	3.5	(NA)	5.5	8.7	2.7
Felony conviction.........................	42.5	28.6	14.1	42.9	27.1	(NA)	42.2	22.3	16.1
Felony arrest with no disposition.........	(X)	6.0	2.4	(X)	7.7	(NA)	(X)	4.4	2.5
Fugitive...................................	18.7	11.6	2.6	18.2	12.9	(NA)	19.1	10.8	3.2
Domestic violence.........................	10.0	13.6	14.5	9.2	11.8	(NA)	9.7	11.0	19.7
Misdemeanor conviction.................	6.3	5.9	11.0	6.1	6.3	(NA)	6.8	6.1	15.0
Restraining order........................	3.7	7.7	3.5	3.1	5.5	(NA)	2.9	4.9	4.7
Drug user/addict..........................	9.9	3.2	5.6	10.4	3.7	(NA)	10.4	5.3	4.6
Mental illness or disability.................	2.6	3.4	5.4	3.3	3.5	(NA)	3.9	5.3	6.9
Illegal alien.................................	1.2	0.4	0.4	1.3	2.4	(NA)	1.6	2.7	1.2
State law prohibition.......................	9.0	20.8	20.0	8.8	23.9	(NA)	7.3	25.7	19.9
Local law prohibition.......................	(X)	(NA)	(NA)	(X)	(NA)	(NA)	(X)	(NA)	2.3
Other prohibitions [2]......................	0.3	11.2	31.2	0.3	3.5	(NA)	0.2	4.0	21.0

NA Not available. X Not applicable. [1] Data not available for local law prohibition, see source. [2] Includes juveniles, persons dishonorably discharged from the Armed Services, persons who have renounced their U.S. citizenship, and other unspecified persons.

Source: U.S. Department of Justice, Bureau of Justice Statistics, *Background Checks For Firearm Transfers, 2013-14 - Statistical Tables*, NCJ 249849, June 2016, and earlier reports. See also <https://www.bjs.gov/index.cfm?ty=pbse&sid=13>.

Table 363. Forensic Services Requests and Backlog by Type of Request: 2014

[Numbers are rounded to the nearest hundred. Census of 409 laboratories, with a 88% return rate. Totals exclude requests outsourced to other laboratories. Request is classified as backlogged if it has been submitted to a crime lab, but has not yet been examined and reported to the submitting agency within 30 days. Estimates based on imputations for labs that did not report backlog data, see source for details]

Type of request	Received		Completed		Backlogged requests	
	Number	Percent	Number	Percent	Number	Percent
All requests	**3,783,000**	**100**	**3,646,000**	**100**	**570,100**	**100**
Controlled substances	1,265,000	33	1,197,000	33	213,700	37
Crime scene	171,000	5	170,000	5	(X)	(X)
Digital evidence	25,000	1	24,000	1	7,800	1
Firearms/toolmarks	154,000	4	142,000	4	51,100	9
Forensic biology:						
Casework [1]	333,000	9	296,000	8	107,800	19
Convicted offender/arrestee samples [1]	908,000	24	904,000	25	64,800	11
Impressions	7,000	(Z)	7,000	(Z)	2,400	(Z)
Latent prints	295,000	8	301,000	8	69,400	12
Questioned documents	9,000	(Z)	9,000	(Z)	800	(Z)
Toxicology	566,000	15	554,000	15	40,000	7
Trace evidence	49,000	1	41,000	1	12,200	2

X Not applicable. Z Less than 0.5%. [1] Includes biology screening and DNA analysis.

Source: U.S. Bureau of Justice Statistics, *Publicly Funded Forensic Crime Laboratories: Resources and Services, 2014*, NCJ 250151, November 2016. See also <https://www.bjs.gov/index.cfm?ty=dcdetail&iid=244>.

Table 364. Freedom of Information Act (FOIA) Requests Received, Processed, Granted and Denied by Federal Department and Selected Agency: 2016

[For year ending September 30. Freedom of Information Act (FOIA) provides the public the right to request access to records from any executive federal agency. Agencies are required to disclose any information requested under the FOIA unless it falls under one of nine exemptions; see <https://www.foia.gov/faq.html#exemptions> for full listing. Each agency is required to file an annual report with the Department of Justice detailing their administration of the FOIA. Data are compiled from those reports]

Department or agency	Requests pending from prior year	Requests received	Requests processed	Requests pending at year end	Disposition		
					Requests granted in full	Requests granted in part	Full denials [2]
Total [1]	**129,716**	**788,769**	**759,842**	**158,643**	**175,309**	**279,602**	**304,931**
Department of Agriculture	3,682	23,870	23,134	4,418	18,884	2,171	2,079
Department of Commerce	576	2,026	2,148	454	600	448	1,100
Department of Defense	12,469	53,544	52,332	13,681	18,247	14,546	19,539
Department of Education	370	2,445	2,307	508	511	1,063	733
Department of Energy	430	1,974	2,008	396	583	462	963
Department of Health and Human Services	7,672	34,232	36,190	5,714	14,811	4,737	16,642
Department of Homeland Security	49,143	325,780	310,549	64,374	17,281	186,054	107,214
Department of Housing and Urban Development	442	2,345	2,281	506	466	431	1,384
Department of Interior	1,057	6,428	6,437	1,048	2,392	1,800	2,245
Department of Justice	14,213	73,103	71,854	15,462	30,147	10,452	31,255
Department of Labor	1,563	16,196	16,466	1,293	1,494	7,161	7,811
Department of State	11,731	27,961	15,482	24,210	884	2,194	12,404
Department of the Treasury	1,465	12,368	12,171	1,662	3,525	3,244	5,402
Department of Transportation	3,056	13,800	11,929	4,927	6,429	2,570	2,930
Department of Veterans Affairs	3,327	34,459	33,313	4,473	14,111	9,769	9,433
Board of Governors of the Federal Reserve System	42	728	701	69	385	85	231
Central Intelligence Agency	1,130	2,547	2,208	1,469	247	218	1,743
Consumer Financial Protection Bureau	16	442	427	31	82	147	198
Court Services and Offender Supervision Agency	65	627	651	41	88	516	47
Environmental Protection Agency	2,149	10,403	10,498	2,054	5,179	767	4,552
Equal Employment Opportunity Commission	1,563	17,680	17,068	2,175	404	12,296	4,368
Federal Communications Commission	107	836	893	50	140	379	374
Federal Deposit Insurance Corporation	38	465	481	22	94	79	308
Federal Trade Commission	26	1,260	1,258	28	326	528	404
General Services Administration	136	957	967	126	186	371	410
National Aeronautics and Space Administration	56	834	847	43	119	176	552
National Archives and Records Administration	4,396	49,966	50,205	4,157	1,013	1,810	47,382
National Labor Relations Board	434	2,679	2,819	294	412	1,721	686
National Science Foundation	186	348	304	230	19	194	91
National Transportation Safety Board	690	471	272	889	31	45	196
Nuclear Regulatory Commission	39	785	753	71	278	189	286
Office of Personnel Management	1,065	10,189	11,104	150	6,700	2,847	1,557
Office of the Director of National Intelligence	303	382	363	322	52	152	159
Pension Benefit Guaranty Corporation	147	3,713	3,779	81	2,260	1,070	449
Securities and Exchange Commission	1,288	14,458	15,196	550	3,969	987	10,240
Small Business Administration	53	1,116	1,075	94	593	177	305
Social Security Administration	2,790	29,631	31,634	787	20,277	5,870	5,487
U.S. Agency for International Development	321	377	354	344	67	106	181
U.S. Consumer Product Safety Commission	199	702	697	204	213	292	192
U.S. Postal Service	197	2,718	2,734	181	567	529	1,638

[1] Includes other agencies not shown below. [2] Denials due to FOIA exemptions and other nonexemption reasons including no records available, incorrect agency, duplicate, and not reasonably descriptive.

Source: U.S. Department of Justice, Office of Information Policy, "Annual FOIA Reports - FY 2016," <https://www.justice.gov/oip/annual-foia-reports-fy-2016>. See also <https://www.foia.gov/>

Table 365. Suspects Arrested by Drug Enforcement Administration by Type of Drug and Arrestee Characteristics: 2014

[For fiscal year ending in year shown. Data are from Drug Enforcement Administration's (DEA) Defendant Statistical System]

Arrestee characteristic	Total arrested	Percent arrested	Cocaine powder	Crack cocaine	Marijuana	Metham-phetamine	Opiates	Other or non drug [2]
Total [1].................	**29,549**	**100.0**	**5,582**	**1,782**	**5,082**	**7,005**	**4,852**	**5,245**
SEX								
Male......................	23,968	81.3	4,871	1,521	4,380	5,394	3,960	3,842
Female....................	5,521	18.7	695	260	695	1,595	882	1,393
RACE								
White.....................	20,280	70.1	3,448	362	3,668	6,170	3,121	3,511
Black/African American..............	7,799	27.0	1,947	1,394	1,080	408	1,563	1,406
American Indian/Alaska Native........	166	0.6	16	1	34	63	14	38
Asian/Pacific Islander..................	667	2.3	31	7	217	210	23	179
HISPANIC ORIGIN								
Hispanic/Latino........................	12,085	42.2	3,082	215	2,313	3,268	2,109	1,098
Non-Hispanic/Latino...................	16,549	57.8	2,309	1,501	2,639	3,572	2,582	3,946
AGE								
18 years old and under................	374	1.3	33	13	128	72	77	51
19 to 20 years old.....................	1,157	3.9	143	69	314	247	206	178
21 to 30 years old.....................	10,431	35.3	1,675	710	2,024	2,336	1,938	1,747
31 to 40 years old.....................	9,726	32.9	2,102	597	1,467	2,441	1,515	1,604
41 years old and older.................	7,861	26.6	1,629	393	1,149	1,909	1,116	1,665

[1] Details may not sum to the total number of arrestees due to missing data. [2] Includes pharmaceutical controlled substances, equipment used to manufacture controlled substances, and drug use paraphernalia.

Source: U.S. Department of Justice, Bureau of Justice Statistics, *Federal Justice Statistics 2014 - Statistical Tables*, NCJ 250183, March 2017. See also <https://www.bjs.gov/index.cfm?ty=pbse&sid=62>.

Table 366. Missing Person Reports by Selected Characteristics: 2014 to 2016

[Data shown are missing person records entered into the National Crime Information Center's (NCIC) Missing Person File during the year shown and does not include records removed (canceled, cleared, and located). The NCIC contained 88,040 active missing person records remaining in the database as of December 31, 2016; this figure includes entries from earlier years. For more information, see source]

Characteristic	2014			2015			2016		
	All ages	Under age 18	Age 18 and older	All ages	Under age 18	Age 18 and older	All ages	Under age 18	Age 18 and older
Total missing person entries...........	**635,155**	**466,949**	**168,206**	**634,908**	**460,699**	**174,209**	**647,435**	**465,676**	**181,759**
By type:									
Juvenile (under age 21) [1]...	449,549	445,045	4,504	442,442	438,229	4,213	447,444	443,053	4,391
Endangered [2]................	44,029	9,770	34,259	44,772	9,326	35,446	45,654	9,046	36,608
Involuntary [3].................	17,631	4,806	12,825	18,687	5,137	13,550	17,505	5,176	12,329
Disability [4]...................	31,501	4,258	27,243	32,706	4,647	28,059	32,991	4,649	28,342
Catastrophe [5]...............	269	91	178	272	103	169	309	121	188
Other (over age 21).........	92,176	2,979	89,197	96,029	3,257	92,772	103,532	3,631	99,901
By sex:									
Female......................	320,086	250,418	69,668	319,655	248,037	71,618	322,263	247,846	74,417
Male.........................	315,025	216,500	98,525	315,199	212,616	102,583	325,129	217,798	107,331
Unknown....................	44	31	13	54	46	8	43	32	11
By race/ethnicity:									
White [6]......................	377,546	267,273	110,273	377,068	262,177	114,891	384,478	264,443	120,035
Black........................	217,684	171,865	45,819	216,055	169,655	46,400	218,818	170,899	47,919
Asian........................	12,547	7,410	5,137	12,659	7,223	5,436	12,903	7,336	5,567
American Indian.............	9,362	7,346	2,016	9,940	7,724	2,216	10,574	8,181	2,393
Unknown....................	18,016	13,055	4,961	19,186	13,920	5,266	20,662	14,817	5,845

[1] A person under the age of 21 who is missing and does not meet any of the entry criteria set forth in the other categories. [2] Indicating that physical safety may be in danger. [3] Disappearance may not have been voluntary, i.e. abduction or kidnapping. [4] Proven physical/mental disability or senile and subjecting themselves or others to personal and immediate danger. [5] Person missing after a catastrophe. [6] Includes Hispanic ethnicity or origin.

Source: U.S. Department of Justice, Federal Bureau of Investigation, "2016 NCIC Missing Person and Unidentified Person Statistics," and earlier releases, <https://www.fbi.gov/services/cjis/ncic>, accessed April 2017.

Table 367. Federal Prosecutions of Public Corruption by Prosecution Status: 2000 to 2015

[As of December 31. Prosecution of persons who have corrupted public office in violation of Federal Criminal Statutes]

Type of official	2000			2010			2014			2015		
	Charged	Con-victed	Await-ing trial	Charged	Con-victed	Await-ing trial	Charged	Con-victed	Await-ing trial	Charged	Con-victed	Await-ing trial
Total....................	**1,000**	**938**	**327**	**1,184**	**1,036**	**554**	**916**	**989**	**350**	**1,102**	**904**	**504**
Federal officials.........	441	422	92	422	397	103	364	364	111	458	402	153
State officials...........	92	91	37	168	108	105	80	109	33	123	97	66
Local officials...........	211	183	89	296	280	146	231	252	100	259	200	135
Others involved [1].......	256	242	109	298	251	200	241	264	106	262	205	150

[1] Includes individuals who are neither public officials nor employees, but were involved with public officials or employees in violating the law.

Source: U.S. Department of Justice, Criminal Division, *Report to Congress on the Activities and Operations of the Public Integrity Section for 2015*, and earlier reports. See also <http://www.justice.gov/criminal/pin/>.

Table 368. U.S. Supreme Court—Cases Filed and Disposition: 1990 to 2015

[Statutory term of court begins first Monday in October. Often the Court grants or denies cases after the Court recesses but before the next statutory term]

Action	1990	2000	2005	2010	2011	2012	2013	2014	2015
Total cases on docket	**6,316**	**8,965**	**9,608**	**9,066**	**8,952**	**8,806**	**8,580**	**8,066**	**7,535**
Appellate paid cases on docket	2,351	2,305	2,025	1,895	1,867	1,806	1,869	1,845	1,839
From prior term	365	351	354	337	324	303	301	301	293
Docketed during present term	1,986	1,954	1,671	1,558	1,552	1,503	1,566	1,544	1,546
Cases acted upon	2,042	2,024	1,703	1,618	(NA)	(NA)	(NA)	(NA)	(NA)
Granted review	114	85	63	76	59	83	68	63	69
Denied, dismissed, or withdrawn	1,802	1,842	1,554	1,461	(NA)	(NA)	(NA)	(NA)	(NA)
Summarily decided	81	63	46	45	(NA)	(NA)	(NA)	(NA)	(NA)
Cases not acted upon	309	281	322	(NA)	(NA)	(NA)	(NA)	(NA)	(NA)
Pauper cases on docket	3,951	6,651	7,575	7,167	7,082	6,997	6,706	6,215	5,688
Cases acted upon [1]	3,436	5,736	6,533	6,250	(NA)	(NA)	(NA)	(NA)	(NA)
Granted review	27	14	15	14	7	10	8	8	12
Denied, dismissed, or withdrawn	3,369	5,658	6,459	6,195	(NA)	(NA)	(NA)	(NA)	(NA)
Summarily decided	28	61	58	37	(NA)	(NA)	(NA)	(NA)	(NA)
Cases not acted upon	515	915	1,042	(NA)	(NA)	(NA)	(NA)	(NA)	(NA)
Original cases on docket	14	9	8	4	3	3	5	6	8
Cases disposed of during term	3	2	4	2	1	0	0	1	1
Total cases available for argument	**201**	**138**	**119**	**131**	**111**	**124**	**122**	**111**	**116**
Cases disposed of	131	89	88	88	80	79	82	78	83
Cases argued	125	86	87	86	79	77	79	75	82
Cases disposed of by full opinion	121	83	82	83	73	76	77	75	70
Cases disposed of by *per curiam* opinion	4	4	5	3	5	1	2	0	12
Cases dismissed or remanded without argument	6	3	1	2	1	2	3	3	1
Cases remaining at start of next term	70	49	31	43	31	45	40	33	33
Number of written opinions	112	77	69	75	64	73	67	66	62

NA Not available. [1] Includes cases granted review and carried over to next term, not shown separately.

Source: Office of the Clerk, Supreme Court of the United States, unpublished data. Beginning 2011, *Journal of the Supreme Court of the United States*, July 2016, and earlier reports. See also <http://www.supremecourt.gov/orders/journal.aspx> and <http://www.uscourts.gov/Statistics.aspx>.

Table 369. Judicial Caseloads for the Federal Judiciary: 2000 to 2016

[For 12-month periods ending June 30]

Judicial caseload	2000	2010	2012	2013	2014	2015	2016
U.S. Courts of Appeals: [1]							
Cases filed	54,642	56,097	57,699	56,360	55,260	53,032	60,099
Cases terminated	56,509	59,343	57,272	58,534	55,803	53,934	56,244
Cases pending	40,815	46,816	44,529	42,485	41,945	40,913	44,768
U.S. District Courts Civil:							
Cases filed	263,049	289,630	286,232	283,087	298,713	280,037	290,430
Cases terminated	260,277	295,908	286,953	257,057	260,352	273,562	258,894
Cases pending	247,973	285,071	269,671	295,780	334,261	340,401	371,937
U.S. District Courts Criminal (includes transfers):							
Cases filed	62,523	78,213	73,455	69,642	64,027	60,866	61,021
Defendants filed	84,147	100,031	96,915	91,812	84,017	79,154	79,968
Cases terminated	57,543	77,633	76,589	69,601	67,115	61,299	60,521
Cases pending	46,796	80,506	76,679	77,207	73,829	72,094	72,041
U.S. Bankruptcy Courts:							
Cases filed	1,276,922	1,572,597	1,311,602	1,137,978	1,000,083	879,736	819,159
Cases terminated	1,271,300	1,441,419	1,354,274	1,215,118	1,124,534	1,024,504	931,085
Cases pending	1,396,916	1,659,399	1,662,461	1,584,972	1,461,132	1,316,672	1,204,717
Post-conviction supervision:							
Persons under supervision	99,577	126,642	132,785	132,362	132,597	133,428	137,882
Pretrial services:							
Total cases activated	86,067	110,666	111,557	107,995	103,640	95,538	93,220
Pretrial services cases activated	84,107	109,711	110,593	107,243	102,949	94,757	92,599
Pretrial diversion cases activated	1,960	955	964	752	691	781	621
Total released on supervision	31,607	29,748	29,971	28,557	26,197	24,429	24,027
Pretrial supervision	31,927	28,440	28,625	27,472	25,183	23,368	23,141
Diversion supervision	2,166	1,308	1,346	1,085	1,014	1,061	886

[1] Excludes the U.S. Court of Appeals for the Federal Circuit.

Source: Administrative Office of the United States Courts, "Statistical Tables for the Federal Judiciary," <http://www.uscourts.gov/statistics-reports/analysis-reports/statistical-tables-federal-judiciary>, accessed April 2017.

Table 370. U.S. District Courts—Civil Cases Filed: by Basis of Jurisdiction and Nature of Suit: 2010 to 2016

[For 12-month periods ending June 30]

Type of case	Cases filed						
	2010	2011	2012	2013	2014	2015	2016
Cases total [1]	285,215	289,630	286,232	283,087	298,713	280,037	290,430
BASIS OF JURISDICTION							
U.S. cases:							
U.S. plaintiff	8,427	10,282	9,707	7,863	6,833	6,182	5,007
U.S. defendant	34,306	36,502	37,569	39,778	39,926	35,651	52,943
Private cases:							
Federal question	137,776	141,334	144,387	146,086	149,380	151,330	149,294
Diversity of citizenship	104,703	101,508	94,568	89,359	102,568	86,865	83,170
NATURE OF SUIT							
Contract actions [1]	31,461	32,366	29,771	28,591	28,631	26,506	24,796
Recovery of overpayments [2]	3,079	4,623	4,041	2,499	2,357	2,307	1,670
Real property actions [1]	6,809	10,078	12,609	11,530	8,454	8,963	9,147
Foreclosure	3,836	6,569	8,194	6,832	4,401	4,043	4,882
Tort actions	87,256	79,394	70,204	67,172	81,024	69,875	62,646
Personal injury	82,057	74,921	65,898	62,715	77,443	62,318	56,452
Personal injury product liability	66,958	60,631	51,850	48,754	63,245	41,607	41,019
Other personal injury [1]	15,099	14,290	14,048	13,961	14,198	20,711	15,433
Medical malpractice	1,120	1,089	1,061	1,034	976	1,097	1,344
Personal property damage	5,199	4,473	4,306	4,457	3,581	7,557	6,194
Actions under statutes [1]	159,683	167,791	173,648	175,794	180,604	174,693	193,841
Bankruptcy suits	2,615	2,597	4,073	2,708	2,708	2,688	2,492
Civil rights [1]	34,427	37,000	37,676	35,965	34,829	37,015	37,477
Employment	14,343	15,255	15,207	13,832	12,035	12,258	11,583
Environmental matters	826	881	696	1,253	749	578	1,784
Prisoner petitions	52,450	53,692	53,606	55,369	62,402	52,844	70,863
Forfeiture and penalty	2,297	2,372	2,297	2,238	1,959	1,620	1,138
Labor laws	18,878	18,025	19,222	17,977	18,702	19,047	19,235
Immigration [3]	1,262	1,097	1,032	1,044	1,134	1,244	1,552
Protected property rights [3]	8,519	9,944	10,985	13,232	13,195	14,145	12,415
Securities commodities and exchanges	1,442	1,394	1,422	1,187	1,000	1,012	1,069
Social security laws	13,725	15,697	17,043	19,121	19,530	19,102	18,407
Tax suits	1,171	1,217	1,208	1,103	969	1,005	973
Freedom of information	315	354	366	367	432	481	516
Cases terminated	295,909	301,773	286,953	257,057	260,352	273,562	258,894
Cases pending	285,071	275,068	269,671	295,780	334,261	340,401	371,937

[1] Includes other types not shown separately. [2] Includes enforcement of judgments in student loan cases, and overpayments of veterans' benefits. [3] Includes copyright, patent, and trademark rights.

Source: Administrative Office of the United States Courts, "Statistical Tables for the Federal Judiciary," <http://www.uscourts.gov/statistics-reports/analysis-reports/statistical-tables-federal-judiciary>, accessed April 2017.

Table 371. U.S. Courts of Appeals—Nature of Suit or Offense in Cases Arising from the U.S. District Courts: 2010 to 2016

[For 12-month periods ending June 30. Excludes data for the U.S. Court of Appeals for the Federal Circuit. Includes appeals reopened, remanded, and reinstated (after being terminated due to procedural defaults) as well as original appeals]

Nature of suit and offense	2010	2011	2012	2013	2014	2015	2016
Total cases	43,880	43,113	44,317	42,227	41,618	40,234	39,506
Criminal cases	12,863	12,412	13,580	11,975	11,340	10,902	11,945
Civil cases	31,017	30,701	30,737	30,252	30,278	29,332	27,561
U.S cases	7,772	7,427	7,589	7,513	7,668	7,471	6,586
U.S. plaintiff	435	364	360	345	292	353	321
U.S. defendant	7,337	7,063	7,229	7,168	7,376	7,118	6,265
Private cases	23,245	23,274	23,148	22,739	22,610	21,861	20,975
Federal question	20,599	20,412	20,004	19,647	19,012	18,821	18,005
Diversity of citizenship	2,646	2,860	3,142	3,092	3,598	3,040	2,969
General local jurisdiction	–	2	2	–	–	–	1
Criminal cases	12,863	12,412	13,580	11,975	11,340	10,902	11,945
Violent offenses	621	658	610	550	563	483	477
Property offenses	1,624	1,630	1,721	1,620	1,606	1,420	1,403
Drug offenses	5,066	4,444	5,653	4,547	3,766	3,843	4,844
Firearms, explosives offenses	1,927	1,749	1,749	1,653	1,620	1,560	1,806
Sex offenses	651	708	755	732	733	786	736
Justice system offenses	142	147	160	151	138	169	129
Immigration offenses	1,787	1,736	1,680	1,551	1,473	1,491	1,342
General offenses	411	369	346	338	348	289	261
Other [1]	634	971	906	833	1,093	861	947

– Represents or rounds to zero. [1] Other includes regulatory, traffic, and unclassified offenses.

Source: Administrative Office of the United States Courts, "Statistical Tables for the Federal Judiciary," <http://www.uscourts.gov/statistics-reports/analysis-reports/statistical-tables-federal-judiciary>, accessed May 2017.

Table 372. Total Incoming Caseloads in State Trial Courts by Case Category: 2015

[States reporting incomplete data or data not conforming to reporting guidelines are not shown. Represents new filings, plus reopened and reactivated cases when provided, as reported to the Court Statistics Project. Since state court caseload statistics should only be viewed in the context of each state's court structure, comparisons of the data reported here should not be made without additional information]

State	Total	Civil [1]	Domestic relations [2]	Criminal [3]	Juvenile [4]	Traffic/other violations [5]
Alaska.................	124,790	23,707	12,783	30,883	2,934	54,483
Arizona.................	2,006,440	288,906	88,751	588,442	16,713	1,023,628
Arkansas.................	1,030,201	85,901	54,377	470,458	18,775	400,690
California.................	7,183,530	848,949	378,589	1,437,324	93,447	4,425,221
Colorado.................	964,878	304,570	36,972	265,730	22,495	335,111
Connecticut...............	760,873	192,443	48,380	116,011	23,959	380,080
Delaware.................	497,710	59,256	35,684	159,667	7,204	235,899
District of Columbia.......	95,611	55,533	12,379	25,288	2,411	([6])
Florida.................	3,419,253	727,816	235,318	739,440	54,793	1,661,886
Georgia.................	3,141,812	711,036	145,666	540,394	71,542	1,673,174
Hawaii.................	525,811	39,448	14,017	73,788	9,271	389,287
Idaho.................	361,984	66,473	22,960	93,771	11,541	167,239
Illinois.................	2,756,515	458,235	145,682	326,192	22,421	1,803,985
Indiana.................	1,404,980	399,805	93,879	269,331	53,497	588,468
Iowa.................	714,140	117,735	34,009	121,835	10,826	429,735
Kansas.................	820,833	141,766	35,329	47,360	15,305	581,073
Kentucky.................	915,171	215,067	64,454	336,778	32,510	266,362
Louisiana.................	1,426,333	183,915	60,745	279,391	36,588	865,694
Maine.................	198,571	29,965	13,089	48,535	2,407	104,575
Maryland.................	2,004,051	988,232	115,255	315,550	19,628	565,386
Massachusetts...........	732,751	297,909	77,917	204,941	20,689	131,295
Michigan.................	3,552,668	622,687	116,732	928,386	37,182	1,847,681
Minnesota.................	1,336,682	168,818	53,347	207,477	38,410	868,630
Missouri.................	2,367,530	243,647	117,012	212,206	12,281	1,782,384
Montana.................	308,069	50,522	15,457	63,888	3,631	174,571
Nebraska.................	466,629	116,910	31,974	139,016	23,097	155,632
Nevada.................	858,867	157,579	51,696	189,549	12,840	447,203
New Hampshire...........	144,862	41,365	14,556	45,763	3,970	39,208
New Jersey...............	6,852,147	783,918	255,800	711,618	39,584	5,061,227
New Mexico...............	360,193	81,805	34,967	106,630	5,128	131,663
New York.................	3,498,540	1,419,459	590,393	604,780	61,716	822,192
Ohio.................	3,275,593	531,198	210,878	763,578	107,467	1,662,472
Pennsylvania...............	3,627,095	440,167	351,256	517,672	42,721	2,275,279
Texas.................	12,534,037	1,595,525	370,794	2,989,073	48,119	7,530,526
Utah.................	673,752	115,214	23,784	122,154	29,760	382,840
Vermont.................	138,641	17,886	19,992	16,092	2,339	82,332
Wisconsin.................	1,309,667	205,213	55,718	111,422	14,419	922,895

[1] Includes tort, contract, real property, small claims, probate/estate, mental health, and civil appeals cases. [2] Includes divorce/dissolution, paternity, custody, support, visitation, adoption, and civil protection/restraining order cases. [3] Includes felony, misdemeanor, and appeals from limited jurisdiction courts. [4] Includes delinquency, dependency, and status offense petitions. [5] Includes non-criminal traffic violations (infractions), parking violations, and ordinance violations. [6] Data are not applicable because the reporting unit does not have jurisdiction over the case type or case category.

Source: National Center for State Courts, Court Statistics Project, DataViewer, "Statewide Incoming Caseloads," <http://www.courtstatistics.org>, accessed January 2017 ©.

Table 373. U.S. District Courts—National Petit and Grand Juror Service: 2010 to 2016

[For years ending September 30. Includes data on jury selection days only. Data on juror service after the selection day are not included]

Juror service	2010	2011	2012	2013	2014	2015	2016
PETIT JUROR SERVICE							
Jurors present for jury selection or orientation..........................	262,376	249,266	237,411	237,251	218,203	195,206	194,211
Percent selected........................	22.7	23.0	23.1	22.2	22.4	22.6	22.5
Percent challenged....................	38.5	39.4	39.5	40.3	40.1	40.6	39.5
Percent not selected or challenged....................	38.7	37.7	37.3	37.5	37.4	36.8	38.0
Voir Dire [1]	24.9	25.0	24.7	23.5	24.3	23.7	25.2
Non-Voir Dire [2]	13.9	12.7	12.7	14.0	13.1	13.1	12.8
Total juries selected....................	5,332	5,565	4,899	4,656	4,278	4,149	3,887
GRAND JUROR SERVICE							
Juries serving..........................	784	799	783	778	763	749	734
Sessions convened....................	9,277	9,083	8,923	8,531	8,230	8,087	8,249
Jurors in session.......................	186,020	182,106	179,076	171,038	164,856	161,493	164,733
Average per session....................	20.1	20.0	20.1	20.0	20.0	20.0	20.0
Hours in session.......................	44,845	43,083	41,477	39,565	36,719	36,098	36,621
Average hours per session............................	4.8	4.7	4.6	4.6	4.5	4.5	4.4
Proceedings filed by indictment:							
Cases....................................	49,654	49,175	(NA)	(NA)	(NA)	(NA)	(NA)
Defendants..............................	70,433	72,505	66,670	64,015	55,890	56,164	55,227
Average defendants indicted per session..............	7.6	8.0	7.5	7.5	6.8	6.9	6.7

NA Not available. [1] Jurors who completed pre-screening questionnaires or were in the courtroom during the conducting of voir dire. [2] Other jurors not selected or challenged who were not called to the courtroom or otherwise did not participate in the actual voir dire.

Source: Administrative Office of the United States Courts, "Judicial Business of the United States Courts 2016," <http://www.uscourts.gov/Statistics/JudicialBusiness.aspx>, accessed August 2017.

Table 374. Problem-Solving Courts—Point of Case Entry and Case Outcomes by Type of Court: 2012

[In percent, except number of courts. Problem-solving courts generally allow participants to agree to follow court guidelines in order to avoid prosecution, incarceration, or other typical criminal justice outcomes. The concept has also been extended to civil and family court. Multiple responses to survey questions were allowed, so detail may sum to more than 100 percent. See source for methodology]

Characteristic	All courts	Drug	Mental health	Family	Youth specialty	Hybrid DWI/drug [1]	DWI	Domestic violence	Veterans	Tribal wellness	Other
Total number of problem-solving courts...........	**3,052**	**1,330**	**337**	**261**	**244**	**217**	**183**	**170**	**133**	**31**	**146**
POINT OF ENTRY INTO PROBLEM-SOLVING COURTS											
Pre-plea or at case filing...............	35.5	27.1	44.1	43.3	49.5	24.0	14.7	72.8	46.3	29.2	49.2
Post-plea.............................	65.1	73.9	73.1	16.1	54.3	85.4	68.4	39.1	81.0	83.3	45.8
Post-sentence or post-release [2].......	35.7	44.5	41.1	12.1	11.7	40.1	41.2	14.6	27.3	54.2	36.7
Judicial order............................	8.5	2.1	3.7	60.7	3.2	1.6	2.3	15.9	2.5	16.7	7.5
Other [3]................................	2.4	0.9	0.7	10.7	6.4	0.5	1.1	2.0	3.3	–	4.2
BENEFITS OF SUCCESSFUL PROGRAM COMPLETION											
Case dismissed........................	61.3	65.2	74.1	45.5	75.5	56.6	13.5	49.3	80.0	78.3	58.7
Sentence suspended...................	39.5	42.6	48.6	10.3	11.7	54.4	49.7	41.3	55.0	65.2	33.0
Record expunged......................	22.4	26.8	22.1	3.6	36.7	24.2	4.3	21.7	22.5	21.7	12.8
Expedited settlement..................	11.1	7.6	12.1	33.5	4.3	13.7	7.4	13.0	11.7	4.3	11.0
Other [4]...............................	34.0	28.8	28.3	57.6	18.6	36.8	49.7	44.9	35.8	8.7	45.9

– Represents zero. [1] DWI is driving while intoxicated. Handles alcohol- or drug-dependent offenders also charged with a driving offense. [2] Includes entry after violation or revocation of parole. [3] Includes acceptance on a case-by-case basis, post-referral from outside agency, entry after child adjudicated dependent, and entry after admitting to impaired ability to care for child. [4] Includes benefits such as case closure, charge reduction, and successful completion of probation.

Source: U.S. Department of Justice, Bureau of Justice Statistics, *Census of Problem-Solving Courts, 2012*, NCJ 249803, September 2016. See also <https://www.bjs.gov/index.cfm?ty=pbdetail&iid=5744>.

Table 375. U.S. Sentencing Commission Summary—Cases Reviewed by Disposition and Primary Offense: 2016

[In numbers, except as noted. For fiscal year ending in year shown. Covers federal felony and Class A misdemeanor cases reported to the U.S. Sentencing Commission by federal courts as required under the Sentencing Reform Act. See source for details]

Characteristic	Total [1]	Robbery	Larceny	Embezzlement	Fraud	Drug trafficking	Counterfeiting	Firearms	Immigration	All other
Total sentenced....................	**[2] 67,742**	**702**	**1,034**	**321**	**6,517**	**19,232**	**450**	**7,305**	**20,051**	**12,130**
CASES INVOLVING PRISON										
Total receiving prison..............	**60,708**	**688**	**414**	**130**	**5,078**	**18,460**	**360**	**6,985**	**19,195**	**9,398**
Prison..	58,832	658	374	112	4,666	17,913	325	6,806	18,986	8,992
Prison/community split................	1,876	30	40	18	412	547	35	179	209	406
Prison term ordered:										
Up to 12 months.....................	16,382	17	168	53	1,175	1,451	92	351	10,220	2,855
13 to 24 months.....................	11,789	47	118	39	1,270	2,909	138	1,018	4,773	1,477
25 to 36 months.....................	6,000	63	32	12	760	1,961	54	838	1,561	719
37 to 60 months.....................	9,720	233	42	14	865	4,198	42	1,707	1,465	1,154
Over 60 months......................	14,400	318	21	5	620	7,370	11	2,962	273	2,820
Mean sentence (in months) [3].........	50	75	20	19	34	71	23	80	15	69
Median sentence (in months) [3].......	27	60	12	12	24	57	18	57	10	29
CASES INVOLVING PROBATION										
Total receiving probation...........	**6,530**	**14**	**573**	**184**	**1,413**	**769**	**89**	**312**	**851**	**2,325**
Probation only..........................	4,876	7	439	145	955	512	63	195	704	1,856
Probation and confinement...........	1,654	7	134	39	458	257	26	117	147	469
CASES INVOLVING FINES AND RESTITUTION										
Total receiving fines and restitution....................	**15,019**	**594**	**863**	**297**	**5,282**	**1,540**	**299**	**1,069**	**406**	**4,669**
Median amount (in dollars)............	11,700	4,841	19,153	33,000	125,750	1,200	3,916	2,846	1,500	5,000

[1] Details may not sum to total due to rounding. [2] 504 cases are excluded due to missing information on type of sentence or cases in which no prison or probation was imposed. [3] Life sentences are included in these calculations as 470 months.

Source: U.S. Sentencing Commission, "2016 Sourcebook of Federal Sentencing Statistics," <https://www.ussc.gov/research/sourcebook-2016>, accessed August 2017.

Table 376. Delinquency Cases Disposed by Juvenile Courts by Type of Offense: 1990 to 2014

[In thousands (1,321 represents 1,321,000), except rate. A delinquency offense is an act committed by a juvenile for which an adult could be prosecuted in a criminal court. Disposition of a case involves taking a definite action such as waiving the case to criminal court, dismissing the case, placing the youth on probation, placing the youth in a facility for delinquents, or actions such as fines, restitution, and community service. Data are developed and maintained by the National Center for Juvenile Justice]

Type of offense	1990	1995	2000	2005	2006	2007	2008	2009	2010	2011	2012	2013	2014
All delinquency offenses.......	**1,321**	**1,825**	**1,715**	**1,675**	**1,618**	**1,624**	**1,600**	**1,468**	**1,342**	**1,227**	**1,126**	**1,031**	**975**
Case rate [1].....................	51.5	63.6	55.7	52.1	50.4	50.8	50.4	46.5	42.6	39.1	36.0	32.9	30.9
Person offenses [2]..................	258	414	404	436	416	411	399	363	342	317	291	271	263
Criminal homicide..................	2	3	2	1	1	1	1	1	1	1	1	1	1
Forcible rape.....................	5	8	10	11	11	10	10	10	9	9	9	9	9
Robbery.........................	27	42	23	27	31	32	33	30	27	23	21	21	21
Aggravated assault...............	44	62	50	50	48	47	45	40	37	33	29	26	27
Simple assault....................	136	236	262	285	267	263	255	234	225	212	193	180	173
Property offenses [2]..............	773	920	709	614	587	600	608	561	495	444	402	355	334
Burglary.........................	145	149	118	102	104	104	106	97	87	80	73	63	60
Larceny-theft....................	346	442	334	278	249	264	282	274	243	218	200	178	167
Motor vehicle theft...............	69	56	37	32	30	27	23	19	16	13	12	11	12
Arson............................	6	10	9	8	8	8	7	7	5	5	5	4	4
Drug law violations................	68	164	186	183	180	182	176	164	161	154	146	137	129
Public order offenses [2]............	223	328	416	442	436	432	418	380	344	312	288	268	250
Obstruction of justice.............	89	135	213	199	194	194	191	180	163	150	141	131	128
Disorderly conduct...............	55	89	103	132	128	129	123	109	99	90	81	73	65
Weapons offenses................	30	47	34	42	43	40	38	32	29	26	23	23	20
Liquor law violations.............	14	12	16	16	18	19	18	15	14	10	8	7	6
Nonviolent sex offenses..........	10	9	14	14	13	12	12	12	12	11	11	10	11

[1] Number of cases disposed per 1,000 juveniles (ages 10 to upper age of juvenile court jurisdiction). The upper age of juvenile court jurisdiction is defined by statute in each state. [2] Total includes other offenses not shown.

Source: U.S. Department of Justice, Office of Juvenile Justice and Delinquency Prevention, "Delinquency Case Rates by Offense, Sex, and Race (1985-2014)," <http://www.ojjdp.gov/ojstatbb/court/data.html>; and "Easy Access to Juvenile Court Statistics, Detailed Offenses," <http://ojjdp.gov/ojstatbb/ezajcs/>; accessed July 2017.

Table 377. Delinquency Cases Disposed by Juvenile Courts by Type of Offense, Sex, and Race: 2005 to 2014

[See headnote, Table 376. Data are developed and maintained by the National Center for Juvenile Justice]

Sex, race, and offense	Number of cases disposed				Case rate [1]			
	2005	2010	2013	2014	2005	2010	2013	2014
Male, total.........................	**1,214,075**	**964,561**	**744,883**	**705,125**	**73.7**	**59.8**	**46.6**	**43.8**
Person.............................	305,300	236,566	185,933	180,785	18.5	14.7	11.6	11.2
Property............................	443,645	347,184	257,082	242,052	26.9	21.5	16.1	15.0
Drugs.............................	147,237	132,037	110,135	102,278	8.9	8.2	6.9	6.4
Public order........................	317,893	248,774	191,733	180,011	19.3	15.4	12.0	11.2
Female, total......................	**461,286**	**377,306**	**285,631**	**269,824**	**29.5**	**24.6**	**18.7**	**17.5**
Person.............................	130,810	105,630	85,070	82,011	8.4	6.9	5.6	5.3
Property............................	170,249	147,455	97,950	91,482	10.9	9.6	6.4	5.9
Drugs.............................	35,864	29,158	26,771	26,616	2.3	1.9	1.7	1.7
Public order........................	124,363	95,063	75,839	69,716	7.9	6.2	5.0	4.5
White, total [2]......................	**806,167**	**608,177**	**455,179**	**422,357**	**41.6**	**33.8**	**26.0**	**24.1**
Person.............................	191,175	143,384	111,436	105,475	9.9	8.0	6.4	6.0
Property............................	323,506	235,520	160,055	146,525	16.7	13.1	9.1	8.4
Drugs.............................	103,538	89,510	75,066	70,539	5.3	5.0	4.3	4.0
Public order........................	187,949	139,763	108,623	99,818	9.7	7.8	6.2	5.7
Black, total [2]......................	**558,772**	**447,797**	**362,630**	**350,121**	**110.8**	**93.7**	**78.0**	**75.1**
Person.............................	177,189	137,954	112,714	111,175	35.1	28.9	24.3	23.8
Property............................	178,874	155,504	124,680	120,809	35.5	32.5	26.8	25.9
Drugs.............................	43,757	32,919	28,076	25,949	8.7	6.9	6.0	5.6
Public order........................	158,952	121,420	97,160	92,189	31.5	25.4	20.9	19.8
Hispanic, total.....................	**264,273**	**249,123**	**184,438**	**175,931**	**45.8**	**37.7**	**26.9**	**25.1**
Person.............................	57,650	52,995	40,620	40,229	10.0	8.0	5.9	5.7
Property............................	91,955	88,324	59,216	55,904	15.9	13.4	8.6	8.0
Drugs.............................	31,179	34,290	29,653	28,350	5.4	5.2	4.3	4.0
Public order........................	83,490	73,514	54,950	51,447	14.5	11.1	8.0	7.3
American Indian, total [3]........	**23,515**	**19,204**	**16,080**	**15,602**	**44.0**	**33.3**	**28.1**	**27.0**
Person.............................	5,295	4,386	3,656	3,615	9.9	7.6	6.4	6.3
Property............................	9,569	7,384	6,090	5,902	17.9	12.8	10.6	10.2
Drugs.............................	2,736	2,544	2,407	2,470	5.1	4.4	4.2	4.3
Public order........................	5,914	4,890	3,927	3,615	11.1	8.5	6.9	6.3
Asian/Native Hawaiian/Pacific Islander, total [2]..............	**22,635**	**17,566**	**12,187**	**10,940**	**16.2**	**11.2**	**7.3**	**6.3**
Person.............................	4,801	3,477	2,577	2,302	3.4	2.2	1.5	1.3
Property............................	9,991	7,907	4,992	4,393	7.1	5.1	3.0	2.5
Drugs.............................	1,892	1,932	1,705	1,586	1.4	1.2	1.0	0.9
Public order........................	5,951	4,250	2,912	2,658	4.3	2.7	1.7	1.5

[1] Cases per 1,000 juveniles (ages 10 to upper age of juvenile court jurisdiction). The upper age of juvenile court jurisdiction is defined by statute in each state. [2] Non-Hispanic. [3] Data did not always allow for identification of Hispanic ethnicity for cases involving American Indian youth. The American Indian group includes an unknown proportion of Hispanic youth.

Source: U.S. Department of Justice, Office of Juvenile Justice and Delinquency Prevention, "Delinquency Case Rates by Offense, Sex, and Race (1985-2014)," <http://www.ojjdp.gov/ojstatbb/court/data.html>; and "Easy Access to Juvenile Court Statistics, Analyze Delinquency Cases," <http://ojjdp.gov/ojstatbb/ezajcs/>; accessed August 2017.

Table 378. Child Victims of Abuse and Neglect—Total and First-Time Victims by State: 2014 and 2015

[For fiscal years ending in year shown. Data are unique counts, which count a child once, regardless of the number of reports concerning that child. Based on available State submissions to National Child Abuse and Neglect Data System (NCANDS) of alleged child abuse and neglect. States reporting 95 percent or more first-time victims are excluded due to potential issues with data quality. NCANDS collects case level data on children who received child protective services response in the form of an investigative or alternative response. Each state has its own definition of child abuse and neglect based on standards set by federal law. Child abuse is defined as any recent act or failure to act on the part of a parent or caretaker which results in death, serious physical or emotional harm, sexual abuse or exploitation; or an act or failure to act which presents an imminent risk or serious harm. See source for details]

State	2014				2015			
			First-time victims				First-time victims	
	Total child population	Victims	Number	Rate per 1,000 children	Total child population	Victims	Number	Rate per 1,000 children
Total..................	74,371,086	675,693	482,707	6.7	74,382,502	683,487	481,925	6.9
Alabama................	1,106,370	8,697	7,186	6.5	1,103,496	8,466	7,003	6.3
Alaska..................	187,079	2,484	1,546	8.3	186,266	2,898	1,966	10.6
Arizona.................	1,619,031	13,885	11,742	7.3	1,622,850	11,955	9,879	6.1
Arkansas...............	706,599	8,971	7,416	10.5	705,300	9,204	7,557	10.7
California..............	9,141,154	75,033	63,126	6.9	9,120,916	72,000	60,903	6.7
Colorado...............	1,247,096	9,979	7,417	5.9	1,257,065	10,100	7,465	5.9
Connecticut............	774,818	7,651	5,346	6.9	764,059	6,970	4,862	6.4
Delaware...............	203,664	1,482	1,167	5.7	204,386	1,538	1,241	6.1
District of Columbia.....	115,233	1,528	1,074	9.3	118,107	1,348	967	8.2
Florida.................	4,057,230	45,738	22,088	5.4	4,105,129	43,775	20,898	5.1
Georgia................	2,493,045	22,163	18,019	7.2	2,504,172	26,952	21,757	8.7
Hawaii..................	309,205	1,331	1,101	3.6	310,833	1,506	1,182	3.8
Idaho...................	430,918	1,595	1,351	3.1	432,837	1,623	1,313	3.0
Illinois.................	2,990,748	25,597	18,681	6.2	2,958,673	29,993	21,832	7.4
Indiana.................	1,582,360	23,334	17,453	11.0	1,579,456	26,397	19,357	12.3
Iowa...................	727,493	8,071	5,506	7.6	728,796	7,877	5,433	7.5
Kansas.................	721,621	1,998	1,802	2.5	719,557	1,992	1,833	2.5
Kentucky...............	1,013,687	17,932	12,597	12.4	1,011,667	18,897	13,263	13.1
Louisiana...............	1,114,600	12,057	9,494	8.5	1,114,813	12,631	9,722	8.7
Maine..................	259,098	3,823	2,585	10.0	256,380	3,372	2,253	8.8
Maryland...............	1,349,676	9,119	6,785	5.0	1,348,226	6,790	4,852	3.6
Massachusetts..........	1,391,634	31,863	19,491	14.0	1,387,087	31,089	18,072	13.0
Michigan...............	2,226,737	30,705	14,819	6.7	2,207,304	34,729	16,998	7.7
Minnesota..............	1,282,412	4,143	3,498	2.7	1,284,387	5,120	4,358	3.4
Mississippi.............	730,975	8,435	7,476	10.2	726,848	8,730	7,802	10.7
Missouri................	1,393,961	5,322	4,582	3.3	1,391,476	5,699	4,876	3.5
Montana................	225,205	1,191	958	4.3	226,420	1,868	1,515	6.7
Nebraska...............	467,484	3,940	2,858	6.1	470,337	3,483	2,604	5.5
Nevada.................	662,672	4,589	2,875	4.3	669,164	4,953	3,096	4.6
New Hampshire.........	267,433	646	552	2.1	263,998	745	612	2.3
New Jersey.............	2,012,281	11,842	9,688	4.8	1,998,821	9,689	7,661	3.8
New Mexico............	501,403	7,606	5,680	11.3	496,908	8,701	6,556	13.2
New York..............	4,228,208	65,042	39,687	9.4	4,210,817	66,676	40,568	9.6
North Carolina..........	2,286,359	8,414	5,795	2.5	2,290,568	7,857	5,464	2.4
North Dakota...........	168,792	1,612	1,236	7.3	173,926	1,760	1,336	7.7
Ohio...................	2,640,764	24,936	17,587	6.7	2,628,477	23,006	16,151	6.1
Oklahoma..............	954,230	13,183	10,524	11.0	961,321	14,449	11,401	11.9
Oregon.................	859,066	10,088	6,805	7.9	862,856	10,428	7,029	8.1
Pennsylvania...........	2,702,674	3,262	3,055	1.1	2,690,274	3,855	(NA)	(NA)
Rhode Island...........	212,694	3,410	2,407	11.3	211,044	3,183	2,213	10.5
South Carolina.........	1,083,879	12,439	9,508	8.8	1,091,588	14,856	11,428	10.5
South Dakota...........	210,502	886	696	3.3	211,324	1,073	861	4.1
Tennessee..............	1,494,788	11,695	9,964	6.7	1,497,611	11,362	9,481	6.3
Texas..................	7,126,227	65,334	52,477	7.4	7,211,771	63,781	50,909	7.1
Utah...................	904,774	9,876	7,104	7.9	912,496	9,569	6,819	7.5
Vermont................	121,627	813	678	5.6	119,923	921	777	6.5
Virginia................	1,868,604	6,464	(NA)	(NA)	1,870,422	6,112	(NA)	(NA)
Washington.............	1,602,064	7,341	4,052	2.5	1,611,842	5,894	3,082	1.9
West Virginia...........	380,721	4,962	3,984	10.5	379,596	4,857	4,118	10.8
Wisconsin..............	1,301,560	4,642	3,987	3.1	1,294,626	4,840	4,149	3.2
Wyoming...............	138,726	861	700	5.0	138,895	968	817	5.9

NA Not available.

Source: U.S. Department of Health and Human Services, Administration for Children and Families, Statistics and Research, *Child Maltreatment 2015*, January 2017. See also <http://www.acf.hhs.gov/programs/cb/research-data-technology/statistics-research/child-maltreatment>.

Table 379. Child Abuse and Neglect Victims by Type of Maltreatment and Age and Sex of Victim: 2009 to 2015

[For fiscal years ending in year shown. Data are unique counts, which count a child once, regardless of the number of reports concerning that child. Based on available State submissions to National Child Abuse and Neglect Data System (NCANDS) of alleged child abuse and neglect. NCANDS collects case level data on children who received child protective services response in the form of an investigative or alternative response. Each state has its own definition of child abuse and neglect based on standards set by federal law. Child abuse is defined as any recent act or failure to act on the part of a parent or caretaker which results in death, serious physical or emotional harm, sexual abuse or exploitation; or an act or failure to act which presents an imminent risk or serious harm]

Item	2009	2010	2011	2012	2013	2014	2015
Victims, total [1]	**693,507**	**688,251**	**676,569**	**678,810**	**678,932**	**702,208**	**683,487**
TYPES OF MALTREATMENT [2,3]							
Neglect	502,417	499,691	531,413	531,241	539,576	526,744	514,500
Physical abuse	120,510	118,502	118,825	124,544	122,159	119,517	117,772
Sexual abuse	64,358	62,057	61,472	62,936	60,956	58,105	57,286
Psychological or emotional	50,466	53,426	60,839	57,880	59,236	42,290	42,549
Medical neglect	16,373	15,711	15,074	15,705	15,450	15,645	15,169
Other and unknown	64,394	68,590	71,217	73,172	68,266	48,256	47,514
SEX OF VICTIM							
Male	334,404	333,864	329,004	330,620	330,914	343,684	332,464
Female	354,677	352,174	345,587	345,823	345,633	355,928	348,087
Unknown	4,426	2,213	1,978	2,367	2,385	2,596	2,936
AGE OF VICTIM							
1 year and younger	136,502	136,910	133,942	134,024	139,360	146,300	144,354
2 to 5 years old	177,126	180,271	181,140	182,845	179,949	180,654	172,337
6 to 9 years old	147,812	145,354	142,412	145,190	147,888	156,232	153,019
10 to 13 years old	120,577	119,555	117,876	118,021	115,125	119,253	115,153
14 to 17 years old	108,633	103,764	98,607	95,734	93,459	96,428	95,134
18 years old and over [4]	638	490	(NA)	(NA)	(NA)	(NA)	(NA)
Unknown [5]	1,327	979	2,592	2,996	3,151	3,341	3,490

NA Not available. [1] Total victims is the sum for states contributing data to the Child File. The number of states not contributing data varies by year. [2] This is a count of the number of distinct victims of the specified types of maltreatment. A child may be a victim of more than one type of maltreatment, so the sum of types is greater than the count of victims. [3] Not all states use this taxonomy, nor do states define the categories in the same way. [4] Beginning in 2011, data included in unknown. [5] Includes unborn, unknown age, and beginning 2011, victims age 18–21.

Source: U.S. Department of Health and Human Services, Administration for Children and Families, Statistics and Research, *Child Maltreatment 2015*, January 2017 and earlier editions, and unpublished data. See also <http://www.acf.hhs.gov/programs/cb/research-data-technology/statistics-research/child-maltreatment>.

Table 380. Prisoners Under Jurisdiction of Federal or State Correctional Authorities—Summary by State: 2000 to 2015

[For years ending December 31. Jurisdiction refers to the legal authority over a prisoner, regardless of where held. Occasionally, states do not submit data in a given year and estimates will be imputed; see source for details]

State	2000	2010	2013	2014	2015	State	2000	2010	2013	2014	2015
U.S.	**1,394,231**	**1,613,803**	**1,576,950**	**1,562,319**	**1,526,792**	MS	20,241	21,067	21,969	18,793	18,911
Federal [1]	145,416	209,771	215,866	210,567	196,455	MO	27,543	30,623	31,537	31,942	32,330
State	1,248,815	1,404,032	1,361,084	1,351,752	1,330,337	MT	3,105	3,716	3,642	3,699	3,685
AL	26,406	31,764	32,381	31,771	30,810	NE	3,895	4,587	5,026	5,441	5,372
AK [2]	4,173	5,391	5,081	5,794	5,338	NV	10,063	12,653	13,056	12,537	13,071
AZ [3]	26,510	40,209	41,177	42,259	42,719	NH	2,257	2,761	3,018	2,963	2,897
AR	11,915	16,204	17,235	17,874	17,707	NJ	29,784	25,007	22,452	21,590	20,489
CA	163,001	165,062	135,981	136,085	129,593	NM	5,342	6,763	6,931	7,021	7,169
CO	16,833	22,815	20,371	20,646	20,168	NY	70,199	56,656	53,550	52,518	51,727
CT [2]	18,355	19,321	17,563	16,636	15,816	NC	31,266	40,382	36,922	37,096	36,617
DE [2,3]	6,921	6,615	7,004	6,955	6,654	ND	1,076	1,487	1,576	1,718	1,795
DC [4]	10,352	(NA)	(NA)	(NA)	(NA)	OH	45,833	51,712	51,729	51,519	52,233
FL	71,319	104,306	103,028	102,870	101,424	OK	23,181	26,252	27,547	27,650	28,547
GA	44,232	56,432	54,004	52,949	52,193	OR	10,580	14,876	15,517	15,075	15,245
HI [2,5]	5,053	5,912	5,632	5,866	5,879	PA [2,5]	36,847	51,264	51,422	50,694	49,858
ID	5,535	7,431	8,242	8,117	8,052	RI [2,5]	3,286	3,357	3,361	3,359	3,248
IL	45,281	48,418	48,653	48,278	46,240	SC	21,778	23,578	22,060	21,401	20,929
IN	20,125	28,028	29,913	29,271	27,355	SD	2,616	3,434	3,682	3,608	3,564
IA [3]	7,955	9,455	8,697	8,838	8,849	TN	22,166	27,451	28,521	28,769	28,172
KS	8,344	9,051	9,763	9,877	9,857	TX	166,719	173,649	168,280	166,043	163,909
KY	14,919	20,544	21,030	21,657	21,701	UT	5,637	6,807	7,077	7,031	6,492
LA	35,207	39,445	39,299	38,030	36,377	VT [2]	1,697	2,079	2,078	1,979	1,750
ME	1,679	2,154	2,173	2,242	2,279	VA	30,168	37,638	36,982	37,544	38,403
MD	23,538	22,645	21,335	21,011	20,764	WA	14,915	18,235	17,984	18,120	18,284
MA	10,722	11,313	10,950	10,713	9,922	WV	3,856	6,681	6,824	6,896	7,118
MI	47,718	44,165	43,759	43,390	42,628	WI	20,754	22,729	22,471	22,597	22,975
MN	6,238	9,796	10,289	10,637	10,798	WY	1,680	2,112	2,310	2,383	2,424

NA Not available. [1] Includes inmates held in nonsecure privately operated community corrections facilities and juveniles held in contract facilities. [2] Data include both total jail and prison population. Prisons and jails form one integrated system. [3] Numbers are for custody rather than jurisdiction counts. [4] As of December 31, 2001, sentenced felons from the District of Columbia are the responsibility of the Federal Bureau of Prisons. [5] Counts include dual jurisdiction cases where the inmate is currently housed in another jurisdiction's facilities.

Source: U.S. Department of Justice, Bureau of Justice Statistics, *Prisoners in 2015*, NCJ 250229, December 2016; and "Corrections Statistical Analysis Tool," <http://www.bjs.gov/index.cfm?ty=nps>, accessed January 2017.

Table 381. Jail Inmates by Sex, Race, and Hispanic Origin: 2000 to 2014

[As of the last week day in June. Data for 2000 and 2010-2014 are based on the Annual Survey of Jails; 2005 from Census of Jail Inmates]

Characteristic	2000	2005	2010	2011 [6]	2012 [6]	2013 [6]	2014 [6]
Total inmates [1, 2]	621,149	747,529	748,728	735,601	744,524	731,208	744,592
Incarceration rate per 100,000							
U.S. residents	220	252	242	236	237	231	234
Rated capacity [3]	677,787	786,954	857,918	870,422	877,396	872,943	890,486
Adult	613,534	740,770	741,168	729,700	739,100	726,600	740,400
Male	543,120	646,807	649,284	636,900	640,900	624,700	631,600
Female	70,414	93,963	91,884	92,800	98,100	101,900	108,800
Juveniles [4]	7,615	6,759	7,560	5,900	5,400	4,600	4,200
White, non-Hispanic	260,500	331,000	331,600	329,400	341,100	344,900	352,800
Black, non-Hispanic	256,300	290,500	283,200	276,400	274,600	261,500	263,800
Hispanic/Latino [5]	94,100	111,900	118,100	113,900	112,700	107,900	110,600
American Indian or Alaska Native non-Hispanic	5,500	7,600	9,900	9,400	9,300	10,200	10,400
Asian or Pacific Islander	4,700	5,400	5,100	5,300	5,400	5,100	6,000
Two or more races	(NA)	1,000	800	1,200	1,500	1,600	1,000

NA Not available. [1] Total does not include offenders who were supervised outside of jail facilities. [2] Prior to 2005, race and Hispanic origin data do not include two or more races. [3] Rated capacity is the number of beds or inmates assigned by a rating official to facilities within each jurisdiction. [4] Juveniles are persons held that are age 17 or younger at midyear. Includes juveniles who were tried or awaiting trial as adults. [5] Persons of Hispanic origin may be of any race. [6] Data adjusted for nonresponse and rounded to the nearest 100. See source methodology.

Source: U.S. Department of Justice, Bureau of Justice Statistics, *Jail Inmates at Midyear 2014*, NCJ 248629, June 2015. See also <https://www.bjs.gov/index.cfm?ty=pbse&sid=38>.

Table 382. Prisoners Under Federal or State Jurisdiction by Sex: 1980 to 2015

[As of December 31. Represents prisoners sentenced to more than one year under jurisdiction of federal or state authorities rather than those in the custody of such authorities. Federal prisoners includes inmates held in nonsecure privately operated community corrections facilities and juveniles held in contract facilities. From the National Prisoner Statistics (NPS) Program]

Year	Total [1]	Rate [2]	Federal	State	Male	Female	White [3, 4]	Black [3, 4]	Hispanic [3]
1980	315,974	139	20,611	295,363	303,643	12,331	(NA)	(NA)	(NA)
1990	739,980	297	50,403	689,577	699,416	40,564	(NA)	(NA)	(NA)
2000	1,334,174	470	125,044	1,209,130	1,249,130	85,044	(NA)	(NA)	(NA)
2010	1,552,669	500	190,641	1,362,028	1,447,766	104,903	519,600	592,000	349,700
2011	1,538,847	492	197,050	1,341,797	1,435,141	103,706	516,200	581,300	349,900
2012	1,511,497	480	196,574	1,314,923	1,410,208	101,289	500,600	551,200	332,200
2013	1,520,403	478	195,098	1,325,305	1,416,102	104,301	505,600	549,100	332,200
2014	1,507,781	471	191,374	1,316,407	1,401,685	106,096	506,600	539,500	326,500
2015 [5]	1,476,847	458	178,688	1,298,159	1,371,879	104,968	499,400	523,000	319,400

NA Not available. [1] Includes prisoners under the legal authority of state or federal correctional officials. [2] Rate per 100,000 estimated population. Based on U.S. Census Bureau estimated resident population. [3] Rounded to the nearest 100. [4] Excludes persons of Hispanic or Latino origin and persons of two or more races. [5] Total and state estimates include imputed counts for Nevada and Oregon, which did not submit 2015 NPS data.

Source: U.S. Department of Justice, Bureau of Justice Statistics, *Prisoners in 2015*, NCJ 250229, December 2016, and earlier reports. See also <https://www.bjs.gov/index.cfm?ty=pbse&sid=40>.

Table 383. Prisoners Under Death Sentence by Characteristic: 1980 to 2015

[As of December 31. Excludes prisoners under sentence of death who remained within local correctional systems pending exhaustion of appellate process or who had not been committed to prison. Data from the National Prisoner Statistics Program]

Characteristic	1980	1990	2000	2007	2008	2009	2010	2011	2012	2013	2014	2015
Total [1, 2]	692	2,346	3,601	3,215	3,210	3,173	3,139	3,065	3,011	2,983	2,942	2,881
White	418	1,368	1,989	1,806	1,795	1,780	1,743	1,721	1,684	1,663	(NA)	(NA)
Black and other [3]	270	978	1,612	1,409	1,415	1,393	1,396	1,274	1,258	1,248	(NA)	(NA)
Under 20 years old	11	8	11	1	–	–	(NA)	–	–	–	(NA)	(NA)
20 to 24 years old	173	168	237	42	44	39	(NA)	28	26	21	(NA)	(NA)
25 to 34 years old	334	1,110	1,103	680	610	564	(NA)	471	401	374	(NA)	(NA)
35 to 54 years old	186	1,006	2,019	2,060	2,076	2,062	(NA)	1,982	1,963	1,903	(NA)	(NA)
55 years old and over	10	64	223	437	477	508	(NA)	601	643	681	(NA)	(NA)
Years of school completed:												
8 years or less	142	364	447	372	361	356	(NA)	347	333	318	(NA)	(NA)
7 years or less	68	178	214	183	176	176	(NA)	(NA)	(NA)	(NA)	(NA)	(NA)
8 years	74	186	233	189	185	180	(NA)	(NA)	(NA)	(NA)	(NA)	(NA)
9 to 11 years	204	775	1,157	989	977	950	(NA)	899	874	847	(NA)	(NA)
12 years	162	729	1,184	1,089	1,094	1,097	(NA)	1,067	1,063	1,042	(NA)	(NA)
More than 12 years	43	209	315	248	247	238	(NA)	235	232	228	(NA)	(NA)
Unknown	163	279	490	522	528	532	(NA)	534	531	544	(NA)	(NA)
Marital status:												
Never married	268	998	1,749	1,558	1,552	1,531	(NA)	1,488	1,469	1,450	(NA)	(NA)
Married	229	632	739	635	630	613	(NA)	608	587	569	(NA)	(NA)
Divorced/other [4]	217	726	1,105	1,027	1,025	1,029	(NA)	986	977	530	(NA)	(NA)

– Represents zero. NA Not available. [1] Revisions to the total number of prisoners were not carried to the characteristics except for race. [2] Includes races not shown separately. [3] Beginning 2011, data are shown only for black. [4] Includes persons married but separated, widows, widowers, and unknown.

Source: U.S. Department of Justice, Bureau of Justice Statistics, *Capital Punishment, 2014-2015*, NCJ 250638, May 2017, and earlier reports. See also <http://www.bjs.gov/index.cfm?ty=pbse&sid=1>.

Table 384. Prisoners Executed Under Civil Authority by Sex and Race: 1930 to 2015

[Excludes executions by military authorities. See source for more information]

Year or period	Total [1]	Male	Female	White [2]	Black [2]	Hispanic	All other races [2,3]
1930 to 1939	1,667	1,656	11	827	816	(NA)	(NA)
1940 to 1949	1,284	1,272	12	490	781	(NA)	(NA)
1950 to 1959	717	709	8	336	376	(NA)	(NA)
1960 to 1967	191	190	1	98	93	(NA)	(NA)
1968 to 1976 [4]	–	–	–	–	–	–	–
1977 to 2013	1,359	1,346	13	770	464	111	14
1990	23	23	–	16	7	–	–
1995	56	56	–	31	22	2	1
1996	45	45	–	29	14	2	–
1997	74	74	–	41	26	5	2
1998	68	66	2	40	18	8	2
1999	98	98	–	53	33	9	3
2000	85	83	2	43	35	6	1
2001	66	63	3	45	17	3	1
2002	71	69	2	47	18	6	–
2003	65	65	–	41	20	3	1
2004	59	59	–	36	19	3	1
2005	60	59	1	38	19	3	–
2006	53	53	–	25	20	8	–
2007	42	42	–	22	14	6	–
2008	37	37	–	17	17	3	–
2009	52	52	–	24	21	7	–
2010	46	45	1	28	13	5	–
2011	43	43	–	22	16	5	–
2012	43	43	–	25	11	7	–
2013	39	38	1	23	13	3	–
2014	35	33	2	(NA)	(NA)	(NA)	(NA)
2015	28	(NA)	(NA)	(NA)	(NA)	(NA)	(NA)

– Represents zero. NA Not available. [1] Prior to 1977, includes races other than White or Black not shown separately. [2] Excludes persons of Hispanic or Latino origin. [3] Includes American Indians, Alaska Natives, Asians, Native Hawaiians, and other Pacific Islanders. [4] In 1972, the U.S. Supreme Court invalidated capital punishment statutes in several states, effecting a moratorium on executions. Executions resumed in 1977 when the Supreme Court found revisions to several state statutes had effectively addressed the issues previously held as unconstitutional.

Source: Through 1978, U.S. Law Enforcement Assistance Administration; thereafter, U.S. Department of Justice, Bureau of Justice Statistics, *Capital Punishment, 2014-2015 - Statistical Brief*, NCJ 250638, May 2017. See also <https://www.bjs.gov/index.cfm?ty=tp&tid=18>.

Table 385. Prisoners Executed Under Civil Authority by State: 1977 to 2015

[Alaska, District of Columbia, Hawaii, Illinois, Iowa, Maine, Massachusetts, Michigan, Minnesota, New Jersey, North Dakota, Rhode Island, Vermont, West Virginia, and Wisconsin are jurisdictions without a death penalty. New Mexico abolished the death penalty for offenses committed after July 1, 2009, Connecticut repealed the death penalty for offenses committed on or after Apr. 25, 2012, and Maryland repealed the death penalty effective Oct. 1, 2013; two men in New Mexico, 11 men in Connecticut, and 4 men in Maryland under previously imposed death sentences are still subject to execution]

State	1977 to 2015	2000	2010	2013	2014	2015	State	1977 to 2015	2000	2010	2013	2014	2015
U.S. [1]	1,422	85	46	39	35	28	Missouri	86	5	–	2	10	6
							Montana	3	–	–	–	–	–
Alabama	56	4	5	1	–	–	Nebraska	3	–	–	–	–	–
Arizona	37	3	1	2	1	–	Nevada	12	–	–	–	–	–
Arkansas	27	2	–	–	–	–	New Mexico	1	–	–	–	–	–
California	13	1	–	–	–	–	North Carolina	43	1	–	–	–	–
Colorado	1	–	–	–	–	–	Ohio	53	–	8	3	1	–
Connecticut	1	–	–	–	–	–	Oklahoma	112	11	3	6	3	1
Delaware	16	1	–	–	–	–	Oregon	2	–	–	–	–	–
Florida	91	6	1	7	8	2	Pennsylvania	3	–	–	–	–	–
Georgia	60	–	2	1	2	5	South Carolina	43	1	–	–	–	–
Idaho	3	–	–	–	–	–	South Dakota	3	–	–	–	–	–
Illinois	12	–	–	–	–	–	Tennessee	6	1	–	–	–	–
Indiana	20	–	–	–	–	–	Texas	531	40	17	16	10	13
Kentucky	3	–	–	–	–	–	Utah	7	–	1	–	–	–
Louisiana	28	1	1	–	–	–	Virginia	111	8	3	1	–	1
Maryland	5	–	–	–	–	–	Washington	5	–	1	–	–	–
Mississippi	21	–	3	–	–	–	Wyoming	1	–	–	–	–	–

– Represents zero. [1] Includes persons executed within the Federal system.

Source: Through 1978, U.S. Law Enforcement Assistance Administration; thereafter, U.S. Department of Justice, Bureau of Justice Statistics, *Capital Punishment, 2014-2015—Statistical Brief*, NCJ 250638, May 2017, and earlier reports. See also <http://bjs.ojp.usdoj.gov/index.cfm?ty=pbse&sid=1>.

Table 386. Adults Under Community Supervision, Probation, and Parole by State: 2015

[As of December 31, 2015, unless otherwise noted. Counts are rounded to nearest hundred. Rates are per 100,000, computed using the estimated U.S. adult resident population in each jurisdiction on January 1, 2016. Counts may not be actual as reporting agencies may provide estimates on some or all detailed data; see source for details. Based on Bureau of Justice Statistics' Annual Survey of Probation and Parole]

Area	Community supervision [1]		Probation		Parole	
	Number	Rate per 100,000	Number	Rate per 100,000	Number	Rate per 100,000
U.S. total..................	**4,650,900**	**1,868**	**3,789,785**	**1,522**	**870,526**	**350**
Federal.........................	132,800	53	18,368	7	114,471	46
States........................	4,518,100	1,814	3,771,417	1,514	756,055	304
Alabama.......................	64,600	1,714	56,700	1,505	8,138	216
Alaska.........................	(NA)	(NA)	(NA)	(NA)	(NA)	(NA)
Arizona........................	83,300	1,589	76,005	1,449	7,379	141
Arkansas......................	51,500	2,256	28,900	1,267	[2] 23,093	1,012
California......................	349,600	1,158	263,531	873	[2] 86,053	285
Colorado [3]...................	89,200	2,102	78,883	1,860	10,269	242
Connecticut...................	45,300	1,598	42,346	1,494	2,939	104
Delaware......................	16,100	2,155	15,646	2,098	425	57
District of Columbia...........	9,900	1,776	5,536	990	4,594	822
Florida [3].....................	225,400	1,381	220,769	1,353	4,611	28
Georgia........................	451,800	5,823	432,235	5,570	24,130	311
Hawaii.........................	22,500	1,996	20,912	1,859	1,540	137
Idaho..........................	37,800	3,071	32,898	2,675	4,875	396
Illinois........................	151,300	1,526	122,125	1,232	29,146	294
Indiana........................	122,500	2,423	113,076	2,236	9,434	187
Iowa..........................	35,600	1,481	29,875	1,243	5,918	246
Kansas........................	20,900	951	16,588	754	4,331	197
Kentucky......................	70,600	2,063	54,049	1,579	16,563	484
Louisiana......................	71,900	2,014	40,764	1,143	31,187	874
Maine.........................	6,700	626	6,708	624	21	2
Maryland......................	87,400	1,870	76,505	1,637	10,887	233
Massachusetts.................	66,900	1,232	64,934	1,195	1,978	36
Michigan [3]....................	193,900	2,507	175,965	2,276	17,909	232
Minnesota.....................	105,100	2,489	98,258	2,328	6,808	161
Mississippi....................	44,800	1,972	36,333	1,601	8,424	371
Missouri.......................	62,600	1,329	44,876	953	17,694	376
Montana.......................	9,700	1,198	8,610	1,063	1,092	135
Nebraska......................	13,700	955	12,626	882	1,043	73
Nevada........................	19,200	858	13,724	612	5,507	246
New Hampshire................	6,300	590	3,861	361	2,451	229
New Jersey....................	151,300	2,167	136,137	1,949	15,180	217
New Mexico....................	16,800	1,054	15,048	946	2,888	182
New York......................	145,600	931	100,996	646	44,562	285
North Carolina.................	97,400	1,249	85,634	1,098	11,744	151
North Dakota..................	6,900	1,179	6,303	1,069	644	109
Ohio [3].......................	262,000	2,908	243,710	2,706	18,284	203
Oklahoma.....................	33,400	1,126	31,281	1,055	2,116	71
Oregon........................	(NA)	(NA)	(NA)	(NA)	(NA)	(NA)
Pennsylvania..................	296,200	2,923	183,868	1,814	112,351	1,109
Rhode Island..................	24,400	2,873	23,920	2,822	433	51
South Carolina.................	38,500	1,006	33,843	883	5,021	131
South Dakota..................	9,800	1,505	7,118	1,096	2,652	408
Tennessee....................	75,400	1,470	62,325	1,215	13,093	255
Texas.........................	488,800	2,390	378,937	1,853	111,892	547
Utah..........................	15,700	746	12,181	579	3,506	167
Vermont.......................	6,300	1,236	5,170	1,021	1,090	215
Virginia........................	57,000	873	55,472	849	1,576	24
Washington [3].................	104,700	1,870	93,535	1,670	11,198	200
West Virginia..................	10,100	692	7,008	478	3,123	213
Wisconsin.....................	65,600	1,462	46,144	1,028	19,453	434
Wyoming......................	5,900	1,323	5,113	1,142	812	181

NA Not known. [1] December 31, 2015 population excludes 9,375 offenders under community supervision who were on both probation and parole. [2] In California, includes post-release community supervision and mandatory supervision parolees. [3] Includes estimates for nonreporting agencies; see source for explanatory notes.

Source: U.S. Department of Justice, Bureau of Justice Statistics, *Probation and Parole in the United States, 2015*, NCJ 250230, February 2017. See also <http://www.bjs.gov/index.cfm?ty=tp&tid=15>.

Table 387. Prisoner Recidivism by Selected Characteristics: 2005 to 2010

[In percent. Prisoners released on community supervision in 2005 who were arrested for a new crime/returned to prison 2005 through 2010. See source for details]

Characteristic	Federal prisoners		State prisoners	
	Arrested	Returned to prison [1]	Arrested [2]	Returned to prison [1,3]
Total, released prisoners	**47.2**	**31.6**	**76.5**	**59.4**
SEX				
Male	49.6	33.4	77.5	56.4
Female	35.4	22.1	68.1	44.9
RACE/HISPANIC ORIGIN				
White alone, non-Hispanic	39.7	26.2	73.1	53.2
Black alone, non-Hispanic	55.1	35.7	80.6	55.6
Hispanic/Latino	48.3	33.1	75.7	57.8
Other [4]	48.5	38.5	74.2	58.8
AGE AT RELEASE				
24 years old and under	64.7	45.8	84.2	62.2
25 to 29 years old	59.3	40.7	80.6	57.3
30 to 34 years old	52.9	34.7	77.0	54.8
35 to 39 years old	48.6	31.9	78.1	56.0
40 to 44 years old	44.5	29.4	74.2	55.0
45 to 49 years old	37.7	24.7	69.0	48.8
50 years old and over	23.5	14.7	58.8	41.9
MOST SERIOUS COMMITMENT OFFENSE				
Violent [5]	58.1	44.3	73.8	51.0
Property	39.5	26.1	82.2	62.5
Drug	44.0	27.1	76.7	53.2
Other public order [6]	57.0	40.2	73.0	54.2
Sex offense [7]	36.7	33.9	61.0	45.4
NUMBER OF PRIOR ARRESTS [8]				
1-2	27.0	16.3	52.4	31.1
3-4	46.4	29.6	67.3	44.3
5-9	59.9	40.8	75.6	53.8
10 or more	72.2	52.4	86.3	65.8

[1] Includes returns to a federal or state prison. [2] Based on prisoners released conditionally in 30 states. [3] Based on prisoners released conditionally in 23 states that provided the necessary prison admission data. [4] Includes American Indian, Alaska Native, Asian, Native Hawaiian, Other Pacific Islander, and persons of two or more races. [5] Excludes rape and sexual assault. [6] Excludes sex offenses. [7] Includes rape, sexual assault, and sexual abuse; possession, distribution, and production of child pornography; and transportation for illegal sexual purposes. [8] Number of times prisoner arrested before release in 2005, including the arrest that led to the 2005 release.

Source: U.S. Department of Justice, Bureau of Justice Statistics, *Recidivism of Offenders Placed on Federal Community Supervision in 2005: Patterns from 2005 to 2010*, NCJ 249743, June 2016. See also <http://www.bjs.gov/index.cfm?ty=pbdetail&iid=5642>.

Table 388. Rate of Adults Under Community Supervision, Probation, and Parole: 2000 to 2015

[Rate per 100,000 population. From Annual Survey of Probation and Parole. Probation is a court-ordered period of correctional supervision in the community, generally as an alternative to incarceration. Probation can be a combined sentence of incarceration followed by a period of community supervision. Parole is a period of conditional supervised release in the community following a prison term. Including parolees released through discretionary or mandatory supervised release from prison, those released through other types of post-custody conditional supervision, and those sentenced to a term of supervised release]

Year	Rate			U.S. residents on—		
	Community supervision [1,2]	Probation	Parole	Community supervision [1]	Probation	Parole
2000	2,162	1,818	344	1 in 46	1 in 55	1 in 291
2005	2,215	1,864	351	1 in 45	1 in 54	1 in 285
2006	2,228	1,875	353	1 in 45	1 in 53	1 in 283
2007	2,239	1,878	361	1 in 45	1 in 53	1 in 277
2008	2,202	1,847	357	1 in 45	1 in 54	1 in 280
2009	2,148	1,797	353	1 in 47	1 in 56	1 in 283
2010	2,067	1,715	356	1 in 48	1 in 58	1 in 281
2011	2,017	1,663	358	1 in 50	1 in 60	1 in 279
2012	1,984	1,634	356	1 in 50	1 in 61	1 in 281
2013	1,946	1,603	348	1 in 51	1 in 62	1 in 287
2014	1,911	1,568	348	1 in 52	1 in 64	1 in 288
2015	1,868	1,522	350	1 in 53	1 in 66	1 in 286

[1] Adults on probation, parole or other post-prison supervision. [2] Beginning 2008, detail does not sum to total because the community supervision rate was adjusted to exclude parolees who were also on probation.

Source: U.S. Department of Justice, Bureau of Justice Statistics, *Probation and Parole in the United States, 2015*, NCJ 250230, February 2017, and earlier reports. See also <http://www.bjs.gov/index.cfm?ty=tp&tid=15>.

Table 389. Fire Losses—Total and Per Capita: 1980 to 2015

[5,579 represents $5,579,000,000. Includes allowances for Fair Access to Insurance Requirements Plan and uninsured losses]

Year	Property loss total, (mil. dol.)	Per capita [1] (dol.)	Year	Property loss total, (mil. dol.)	Per capita [1] (dol.)	Year	Property loss total, (mil. dol.)	Per capita [1] (dol.)
1980	5,579	24.56	2004	17,344	59.23	2010	20,486	66.22
1985	7,753	32.70	2005	20,427	69.12	2011	19,511	62.59
1990	9,495	38.07	2006	20,340	68.17	2012	23,977	76.33
1995	11,887	45.23	2007	24,399	81.00	2013	19,054	60.22
2000	13,457	47.69	2008	24,734	81.34	2014	21,801	68.36
2003	21,129	72.83	2009	22,911	74.68	2015	21,020	65.40

[1] Based on estimated resident population as of July 1, decennial Census years enumerated population as of April 1.

Source: Insurance Information Institute, New York, NY. *The Insurance Fact Book, 2017* ©, and previous reports. See also <http://www.iii.org>.

Table 390. The U.S. Fire Service: Departments, Personnel, and Responses by Type: 1990 to 2015

[In thousands (1,025.7 represents 1,025,700), except where noted. A fire department is a public or private organization that provides fire prevention, fire suppression, and associated emergency and non-emergency services to a jurisdiction such as a county, municipality, or organized fire district]

Items	1990	2000	2005	2010	2011	2012	2013	2014	2015
FIRE DEPARTMENTS (NUMBER)									
Total departments.............	**30,391**	**30,339**	**30,300**	**30,125**	**30,145**	**30,100**	**30,052**	**29,980**	**29,727**
All career........................	1,949	2,178	2,087	2,495	2,550	2,610	2,477	2,440	2,651
Mostly career....................	1,338	1,667	1,766	1,860	1,865	1,995	1,971	2,045	1,893
Mostly volunteer.................	4,000	4,523	4,902	5,290	5,530	5,445	5,797	5,580	5,421
All volunteer.....................	23,104	21,971	21,575	20,480	20,200	20,050	19,807	19,915	19,762
By whether Emergency Medical Service (EMS) provided:									
Provide EMS service only..........	(NA)	(NA)	12,900	13,440	13,555	13,600	13,400	13,665	13,500
Provide EMS service and advance life support..........	(NA)	(NA)	4,260	4,515	4,590	4,550	5,050	4,635	4,617
No EMS service..................	(NA)	(NA)	13,170	12,170	12,000	11,950	11,600	11,680	11,610
FIRE DEPARTMENT PERSONNEL (1,000)									
Total personnel...............	**1,025.7**	**1,064.2**	**1,136.7**	**1,103.3**	**1,100.5**	**1,129.3**	**1,140.8**	**1,134.4**	**1,160.5**
Career [1].......................	253.0	286.8	313.3	335.2	344.1	346.0	354.6	346.2	345.6
Volunteer [2]....................	772.7	777.4	823.4	768.2	756.4	783.3	786.2	788.3	814.9
RESPONSES BY TYPE (1,000)									
Total responses..............	**13,708**	**20,520**	**23,252**	**28,205**	**30,098**	**31,854**	**31,645**	**31,645**	**33,636**
Fires...........................	2,019	1,708	1,602	1,332	1,389	1,375	1,240	1,298	1,346
Medical aid.....................	7,650	12,251	14,375	18,522	19,803	21,706	21,372	20,178	21,500
False alarms....................	1,476	2,127	2,134	2,187	2,383	2,238	2,343	2,488	2,567
Malicious mischievous........	442	300	241	163	183	168	165	162	166
System malfunctions.........	593	884	746	709	748	713	757	820	828
Unintentional calls..........	318	714	838	992	1,062	1,045	1,080	1,166	1,200
Other [3]....................	124	230	310	324	391	314	341	342	374
Mutual aid/assistance..........	487	864	1,091	1,190	1,252	1,327	1,298	1,447	1,493
Hazardous material.............	210	319	375	402	379	360	367	405	442
Other hazardous [4].............	423	544	667	660	720	694	678	615	643
All other [5]...................	1,443	2,708	3,009	3,913	4,172	4,155	4,347	5,214	5,646

NA Not available. [1] Includes full-time uniform firefighters regardless of assignment (i.e., suppression, administrative, prevention/inspection, etc.). Does not include firefighters who work for the state or federal government or in private fire brigades. [2] Volunteer firefighters include any active part-time (call or volunteer) firefighters. [3] Bomb scares, etc. [4] Arcing wires, bomb removal, power line down, biological hazard, etc. [5] Smoke scares, lock-outs, animal rescue, unauthorized burning, severe weather, etc.

Source: National Fire Protection Association, Quincy, MA, *U.S. Fire Department Profile 2015* ©, *Fire Loss in the United States During 2015* ©, and earlier reports. See also <http://www.nfpa.org/News-and-Research>.

Table 391. Fires—Number and Loss by Type and Property Use: 2012 to 2015

[Number of fires in thousands (1,375 represents 1,375,000); property loss in millions of dollars (12,427 represents $12,427,000,000). Based on annual sample survey of fire departments. No adjustments were made for unreported fires and losses]

Type and property use	Number (1,000)				Direct property loss (mil. dol.) [1]			
	2012	2013	2014	2015	2012	2013	2014	2015 [7]
Fires, total....................	**1,375**	**1,240**	**1,298**	**1,346**	**12,427**	**11,525**	**11,605**	**14,298**
Structure.......................	481	488	494	502	9,776	9,526	9,846	10,280
Outside of structure [2].........	83	67	65	76	727	520	141	151
Brush and rubbish..............	529	413	448	460	–	–	–	–
Vehicle [3].....................	203	188	194	205	1,838	1,392	1,522	1,816
Other..........................	80	85	98	104	86	87	96	101
Structure fires by property use:								
Public assembly................	12	13	14	17	281	369	429	323
Educational....................	5	6	5	5	64	66	59	40
Institutional...................	6	6	7	7	35	42	40	51
Stores and offices..............	18	18	18	17	643	611	708	635
Residential....................	381	387	387	388	7,199	6,969	6,992	7,210
1-2 family homes [4].........	268	272	274	271	5,818	5,626	5,844	5,799
Apartments.................	97	98	94	95	1,192	1,166	982	1,161
Other residential [5].........	16	18	19	23	189	177	166	250
Storage.......................	29	26	28	31	751	692	781	1,032
Industry, utility, defense [6]......	9	9	10	9	676	637	626	924
Special structures..............	22	24	27	29	127	140	211	65

– Represents zero. [1] Direct property damage figures do not include indirect losses (such as business interruption and temporary shelter costs) and adjustments for inflation. [2] Includes outside storage, crops, timber, etc. [3] Includes highway and other vehicles (trains, boats, ships, aircraft, and farm and construction vehicles). In 2015, there were 174,000 highway vehicle fires and 30,500 fires in other vehicles. [4] Includes manufactured homes. [5] Includes hotels and motels, college dormitories, boarding houses, etc. [6] Data underreported as some incidents were handled by private fire brigades or fixed suppression systems which do not report. [7] Includes $1,950 million, total property loss for the Valley and Butte Wildfires in California. Loss by specific property type was not available for these fires.

Source: National Fire Protection Association, Quincy, MA, *Fire Loss in the United States During 2015* ©, September 2016, and earlier reports. See also <http://www.nfpa.org/News-and-Research>.

Table 392. Fires and Property Loss for Incendiary and Suspicious Fires and Civilian Fire Deaths and Injuries by Selected Property Type: 2009 to 2015

[In thousands (481 represents 481,000), except as indicated. Based on sample survey of fire departments]

Characteristic	2009	2010	2011	2012	2013	2014	2015
NUMBER (1,000)							
Structure fires, total	481	482	485	481	488	494	502
Structure fires that were intentionally set	27	28	27	26	23	19	23
PROPERTY LOSS (mil. dol.) [1]							
Structure fires, total	10,842	9,716	9,693	9,776	9,526	9,846	10,280
Structure fires that were intentionally set	684	585	601	581	577	613	460
CIVILIAN FIRE DEATHS							
Deaths, total [2]	3,010	3,120	3,005	2,855	3,240	3,275	3,280
Residential property	2,590	2,665	2,550	2,405	2,785	2,795	2,605
One- and two-family dwellings	2,100	2,200	2,105	2,000	2,430	2,345	2,155
Apartments	465	440	415	380	325	400	405
Vehicles [3]	280	310	300	325	320	345	500
CIVILIAN FIRE INJURIES							
Injuries, total [2]	17,050	17,720	17,500	16,500	15,925	15,775	15,700
Residential property	13,050	13,800	14,360	13,175	12,575	12,175	11,575
One- and two-family dwellings	9,300	9,400	9,485	8,825	8,300	8,025	8,050
Apartments	3,350	3,950	4,425	4,050	3,900	3,800	3,025
Vehicles [3]	1,610	1,590	1,190	975	1,050	1,450	1,875

[1] Direct property loss only. [2] Includes injuries from other types of fires, not shown separately. [3] Includes highway vehicles, and trains, boats, ships, farm vehicles, and construction vehicles.

Source: National Fire Protection Association, Quincy, MA, *Fire Loss in the United States During 2015* ©, September 2016, and earlier reports. See also <http://www.nfpa.org/News-and-Research>.

Table 393. Firefighter On-Duty Fatalities and Injuries: 2005 to 2015

[Number, unless otherwise noted. On-duty refers to involvement in operations at the scene of an emergency, whether it is a fire or nonfire incident; responding to or returning from an incident; performing other officially assigned duties including training; and being on call]

Item	2005	2008	2009	2010	2011	2012	2013	2014	2015
Total fatalities	110	123	94	90	87	84	108	94	90
Fatalities per 100,000 fires (rate)	2.81	3.86	2.97	2.33	2.52	2.33	4.84	2.39	(NA)
Emergency duty deaths (percent)	52	64	63	55	54	56	73	46	49
By incident characteristic:									
Wildland related fatalities	19	26	17	12	10	16	31	11	12
Incidents with multiple fatalities	4	5	6	4	3	4	4	2	3
Training fatalities	14	12	10	12	8	8	7	9	7
Cause of fatal injury: [1]									
Stress/overexertion [2]	62	55	52	56	54	48	39	63	60
Vehicle collision	25	28	16	11	5	18	9	9	5
Total nonfatal Injuries [3]	80,100	79,700	78,150	71,875	70,090	69,400	65,880	63,350	68,085
Fireground injuries	41,950	36,595	32,205	32,675	30,505	31,490	29,760	27,015	29,130
Injuries at nonfire emergencies	12,250	15,745	15,455	13,355	14,905	12,760	12,535	14,595	14,320
Nature of injury:									
Burns (fire or chemical)	3,650	2,990	2,965	2,585	2,385	2,220	1,975	1,810	2,020
Smoke or gas inhalation	2,875	2,735	2,340	1,500	1,760	1,685	1,895	1,980	1,645
Other respiratory distress	1,390	1,645	915	940	1,060	910	915	855	1,060
Burns and smoke inhalation	1,120	735	565	635	695	320	195	585	535
Wound, cut, bleeding, bruise	14,165	12,835	11,685	11,110	10,210	9,905	10,530	9,705	10,205
Dislocation, fracture	2,315	1,880	1,950	1,820	1,885	1,695	1,900	1,995	1,685
Heart attack or stroke	765	770	1,140	810	860	780	620	905	920
Strain, sprain, muscular pain	39,740	42,200	42,585	40,385	39,960	39,535	37,565	35,015	37,945
Thermal stress (frostbite, heat exhaustion)	3,565	2,890	2,530	3,195	2,945	2,465	2,080	2,245	2,860
Other	10,515	11,020	11,475	8,895	8,660	9,885	8,205	8,255	9,210
Fire department vehicle collisions	15,885	14,950	15,100	14,200	14,850	14,300	12,350	14,910	16,600
Injuries	1,120	670	820	775	970	725	730	550	1,150
Personal vehicle collisions	1,080	1,000	870	1,000	790	750	830	620	700
Injuries	125	70	100	75	190	70	185	90	50

NA Not available. [1] Includes other categories not shown, such as struck by object, caught/trapped, structural collapse, fall, violence, lost/disoriented, and unknown. [2] Stress/overexertion include all firefighter deaths that are cardiac or cerebrovascular in nature such as heart attacks, strokes, and other events such as extreme climatic thermal exposure (heat exhaustion). [3] Includes other types of nonfatal injuries not shown separately.

Source: Fatalities: U.S. Department of Homeland Security, Federal Emergency Management Agency, *U.S. Fire Administration, Firefighter Fatalities in the United States in 2015*, October 2016, and earlier reports. See also <https://apps.usfa.fema.gov/firefighter-fatalities/>. Nonfatal Injuries: National Fire Protection Association, *U.S. Firefighter Injuries 2015* ©, October 2016, and earlier reports. See also <http://www.nfpa.org/News-and-Research>.

Section 6
Geography and Environment

This section presents a variety of information on the physical environment of the United States, starting with basic area measurement data and ending with climatic data for selected weather stations around the country. The subjects covered between those points are mostly concerned with environmental trends but include related subjects such as land use, water consumption, air pollutant emissions, toxic releases, oil spills, hazardous waste sites, municipal waste and recycling, threatened and endangered wildlife, and the environmental industry.

The information in this section is selected from a wide range of federal agencies that compile the data for various administrative or regulatory purposes, such as the Environmental Protection Agency (EPA), U.S. Geological Survey (USGS), National Oceanic and Atmospheric Administration (NOAA), Natural Resources Conservation Service (NRCS).

Area—2013 area measurements are the latest available. These measurements were calculated by computer based on the information contained in a single, consistent geographic database, the Topologically Integrated Geographic Encoding & Referencing system (TIGER®) database, a national geographic and cartographic database prepared by the Census Bureau. The 2013 area measurements may be found in Table 394.

Geography—The USGS conducts investigations, surveys, and research in the fields of geography, geology, topography, geographic information systems, mineralogy, hydrology, and geothermal energy resources as well as natural hazards. The USGS provides United States cartographic data through the Earth Sciences Information Center and water resources data through the *Water Resources of the United States* at <http://water.usgs.gov/pubs/>. In a joint project with the U.S. Census Bureau, during the 1980s, the USGS provided the basic information on geographic features for input into the TIGER® database. Since then, using a variety of sources, the Census Bureau has updated these features and their related attributes (names, descriptions, etc.) and inserted current information on the boundaries, names, and codes of legal and statistical geographic entities. The 2013 area measures, land and water, including their classifications, reflect base feature updates made in the Master Address File (MAF)/TIGER® database through May 2013. The boundaries of the states and equivalent areas are as of January 1, 2013. Maps prepared by the Census Bureau using the TIGER® database show the names and boundaries of entities and are available on a current basis.

An inventory of the nation's land resources by type of use/cover was conducted by the NRCS every 5 years beginning in 1977 through 1997. Since 2000, data have been gathered annually, though major releases of these data continue to be reported at 5-year intervals. The most recent survey results, which were published for the year 2012, covered all nonfederal land for the contiguous 48 states.

Environment—The principal federal agency responsible for pollution abatement and control activities is the EPA. It is responsible for establishing and monitoring national air quality standards, water quality activities, solid and hazardous waste disposal, and control of toxic substances. Many of these series now appear in the "Envirofacts" portion of the EPA website at <https://www3.epa.gov/enviro/>.

The Clean Air Act, which was last amended in 1990, requires the EPA to set National Ambient Air Quality Standards (NAAQS) (40 CFR part 50) for pollutants considered harmful to public health and the environment. The Clean Air Act established two types of national air quality standards. *Primary standards* set limits to protect public health, including the health of "sensitive" populations such as asthmatics, children, and the elderly. *Secondary standards* set limits to protect public welfare, including protection against decreased visibility, damage to animals, crops vegetation, and buildings. See <https://www.epa.gov/criteria-air-pollutants/naaqs-table> for more information. The EPA Office of Air Quality Planning and Standards (OAQPS) has set National Ambient Air Quality Standards for six principal pollutants, which are called "criteria" pollutants. These pollutants are: carbon monoxide, lead, nitrogen dioxide, particulate matter, ozone, and sulfur dioxide. NAAQS are periodically reviewed and revised to include any additional or new health or welfare data. Table 408 gives some of the health-related standards for the six air pollutants having NAAQS. Data gathered from state networks are periodically submitted to EPA's National Aerometric Information Retrieval System (AIRS) for summarization in annual reports on the nationwide status and trends in air quality. For details, see "Air Trends" on the EPA website at <http://www.epa.gov/airtrends/>.

The Toxics Release Inventory (TRI), a database published by the EPA, is a valuable source of information on approximately 624 chemicals that are being used, manufactured, treated, transported, or released into the environment. Sections 313 of the Emergency Planning and Community Right-to-Know Act (EPCRA) and 6607 of the Pollution Prevention Act (PPA), mandate that a publicly-accessible toxic chemical database be developed and maintained by the EPA. The TRI database contains information concerning waste management activities and the release of toxic chemicals by facilities that manufacture, process, or otherwise use said materials. Data on the release of these chemicals are collected from about 21,000 facilities that have the equivalent of 10 or more full time employees and meet the established thresholds for manufacturing, processing, or "other use" of listed chemicals. Facilities must report their releases and other waste management quantities. Since 1994 federal facilities have been required to report their data regardless of industry classification. In May 1997, EPA added seven new industry sectors that reported to the TRI for the first time in July 1999 for the 1998 reporting year. More current information on this program can be found at <https://www.epa.gov/toxics-release-inventory-tri-program>.

Climate—NOAA, through the National Weather Service and the National Environmental Satellite, Data, and Information Service, is responsible for collecting climate data. NOAA maintains about 8,000 weather stations, of which a portion produce precipitation measurement records, some also take hourly readings of a series of weather elements, and the remainder record data once a day. These data are reported monthly in the *Climatological Data* and *Storm Data*, published monthly and annually in the *Local Climatological Data* (published by location for major cities). Data can be found in tables 423 and 427–431.

Table 394. Land and Water Area of States and Other Entities: 2013

[One square mile = 2.59 square kilometers. The area measurements were derived from the Census Bureau's Master Address File/Topologically Integrated Geographic Encoding and Referencing (MAF/TIGER®) database. The boundaries of the states and equivalent areas are as of January 1, 2013. The land and water areas, including their classifications, reflect base feature updates made in the MAF/TIGER® database through May 2013. For more details, see <http://www.census.gov/geo/maps-data/data/tiger-line.html>]

State and other areas [2]	Total area		Land area [1]		Water area [1]					
					Total		Inland (sq. mi.)	Coastal (sq. mi.)	Great Lakes (sq. mi.)	Territorial (sq. mi.)
	Sq. mi.	Sq. km.	Sq. mi.	Sq. km.	Sq. mi.	Sq. km.				
Total [3]	3,805,972	9,857,423	3,535,952	9,158,072	270,021	699,350	85,747	42,370	60,093	81,811
United States [4]	3,796,787	9,833,634	3,531,925	9,147,643	264,862	685,991	85,631	42,334	60,093	76,804
Alabama	52,420	135,767	50,646	131,172	1,774	4,595	1,057	517	(X)	200
Alaska	665,384	1,723,337	570,601	1,477,849	94,783	245,488	19,346	26,117	(X)	49,320
Arizona	113,990	295,233	113,593	294,205	397	1,028	397	–	(X)	–
Arkansas	53,179	137,732	52,036	134,773	1,142	2,959	1,142	–	(X)	–
California	163,695	423,967	155,786	403,483	7,909	20,484	2,827	245	(X)	4,837
Colorado	104,094	269,603	103,642	268,433	452	1,171	452	–	(X)	–
Connecticut	5,543	14,357	4,842	12,542	701	1,815	171	530	(X)	–
Delaware	2,489	6,446	1,949	5,047	540	1,399	91	355	(X)	94
District of Columbia	68	177	61	158	7	19	7	–	(X)	–
Florida	65,757	170,311	53,629	138,897	12,129	31,414	5,023	1,349	(X)	5,757
Georgia	59,425	153,911	57,515	148,963	1,910	4,948	1,411	46	(X)	454
Hawaii	10,970	28,412	6,423	16,634	4,547	11,778	42	9	(X)	4,496
Idaho	83,569	216,443	82,644	214,046	926	2,398	926	–	(X)	–
Illinois	57,914	149,996	55,519	143,794	2,394	6,202	820	–	1,574	–
Indiana	36,420	94,326	35,826	92,790	593	1,537	361	–	233	–
Iowa	56,273	145,745	55,857	144,669	416	1,076	416	–	(X)	–
Kansas	82,278	213,100	81,758	211,753	520	1,347	520	–	(X)	–
Kentucky	40,408	104,656	39,484	102,262	924	2,393	924	–	(X)	–
Louisiana	52,375	135,651	43,205	111,900	9,170	23,751	4,561	2,876	(X)	1,733
Maine	35,380	91,634	30,843	79,884	4,537	11,750	2,314	591	(X)	1,633
Maryland	12,406	32,131	9,708	25,144	2,698	6,987	768	1,819	(X)	111
Massachusetts	10,554	27,336	7,800	20,203	2,754	7,133	485	1,177	(X)	1,092
Michigan	96,713	250,487	56,547	146,455	40,167	104,031	1,993	–	38,173	–
Minnesota	86,935	225,161	79,628	206,236	7,307	18,924	4,761	–	2,546	–
Mississippi	48,441	125,460	46,924	121,532	1,517	3,928	769	620	(X)	128
Missouri	69,707	180,540	68,741	178,039	966	2,501	966	–	(X)	–
Montana	147,040	380,832	145,546	376,963	1,494	3,868	1,494	–	(X)	–
Nebraska	77,347	200,329	76,824	198,972	524	1,356	524	–	(X)	–
Nevada	110,572	286,380	109,781	284,331	791	2,049	791	–	(X)	–
New Hampshire	9,349	24,214	8,953	23,188	396	1,026	327	–	(X)	69
New Jersey	8,723	22,591	7,355	19,049	1,368	3,543	435	427	(X)	506
New Mexico	121,590	314,917	121,298	314,161	292	756	292	–	(X)	–
New York	54,555	141,297	47,127	122,057	7,428	19,240	1,989	975	3,986	479
North Carolina	53,819	139,391	48,617	125,919	5,202	13,472	4,053	–	(X)	1,149
North Dakota	70,698	183,108	69,000	178,709	1,698	4,399	1,698	–	(X)	–
Ohio	44,826	116,098	40,862	105,831	3,964	10,267	473	–	3,491	–
Oklahoma	69,899	181,037	68,596	177,662	1,303	3,375	1,303	–	(X)	–
Oregon	98,379	254,800	95,988	248,608	2,390	6,191	1,068	72	(X)	1,251
Pennsylvania	46,054	119,280	44,743	115,884	1,311	3,396	563	–	748	–
Rhode Island	1,545	4,001	1,034	2,678	511	1,323	182	64	(X)	266
South Carolina	32,020	82,933	30,061	77,858	1,959	5,075	1,063	110	(X)	786
South Dakota	77,116	199,729	75,811	196,349	1,305	3,380	1,305	–	(X)	–
Tennessee	42,144	109,153	41,236	106,800	908	2,353	908	–	(X)	–
Texas	268,597	695,662	261,236	676,599	7,360	19,063	5,612	401	(X)	1,347
Utah	84,898	219,884	82,194	212,881	2,704	7,003	2,704	–	(X)	–
Vermont	9,616	24,906	9,217	23,872	399	1,034	399	–	(X)	–
Virginia	42,775	110,787	39,491	102,280	3,284	8,506	1,281	1,565	(X)	438
Washington	71,298	184,661	66,456	172,121	4,842	12,540	1,714	2,468	(X)	660
West Virginia	24,230	62,756	24,041	62,267	189	489	189	–	(X)	–
Wisconsin	65,496	169,635	54,158	140,269	11,338	29,366	1,997	–	9,342	–
Wyoming	97,813	253,334	97,094	251,471	719	1,863	719	–	(X)	–
Puerto Rico	5,325	13,791	3,424	8,868	1,901	4,923	76	13	(X)	1,812
Island Areas:	3,860	9,998	603	1,562	3,257	8,436	39	22	(X)	3,196
American Samoa	581	1,505	76	198	505	1,307	8	–	(X)	497
Guam	571	1,478	210	543	361	935	8	1	(X)	352
Northern Mariana Islands	1,976	5,117	182	472	1,793	4,644	6	5	(X)	1,782
U.S. Virgin Islands	733	1,898	134	348	599	1,550	17	16	(X)	565

– Represents or rounds to zero. X Not applicable. [1] Water area calculations in this table include only perennial water. All other water (intermittent, glacier, and marsh/swamp) is included in this table as part of land area calculations. [2] This table does not include area calculations for the U.S. Minor Outlying Islands. [3] Includes all 50 states, the District of Columbia, Puerto Rico, and the Island Areas. [4] Includes all 50 states and the District of Columbia.

Source: U.S. Census Bureau, unpublished data from the MAF/TIGER® database. See <https://www.census.gov/geo/maps-data/data/tiger.html>.

Table 395. Great Lakes Profile

[The Great Lakes contain the largest supply of freshwater in the world, holding about 18% of the world's total freshwater and about 90% of the United States' total freshwater. The Lakes are a series of five interconnecting large lakes, one small lake, four connecting channels, and the St. Lawrence Seaway. Combined, the lakes cover an area of over 94,000 square miles (245,000 square kilometers) and contain over 5,400 cubic miles (23,000 cubic kilometers) of water]

Characteristics	Unit	Lake Superior	Lake Michigan	Lake Huron	Lake Erie	Lake Ontario
Length................................	Miles	350	307	206	241	193
Breadth...............................	Miles	160	118	183	57	53
Depth:						
Average..............................	Feet	489	279	159	62	283
Maximum.............................	Feet	1,333	923	750	210	802
Volume................................	Cubic miles	2,935	1,180	849	116	393
Water surface area [1]...............	Square miles	31,700	22,300	23,000	9,910	7,340
Surface area in U.S................	Square miles	20,598	22,300	9,111	4,977	3,560
Retention/replacement time [2].......	Years	191	99	22	3	6

[1] Includes surface area in both U.S. and Canada. [2] The amount of time it takes for lakes to get rid of pollutants.

Source: Department of Commerce, National Oceanic and Atmospheric Administration, Great Lakes Environmental Research Laboratory, "About Our Great Lakes, Lake by Lake Profiles," June 2004, <https://www.glerl.noaa.gov/education/ourlakes/>.

Table 396. Great Lakes Length of Shoreline in Separate Basin

[In statute miles]

Shorelines	Total	Canada	U.S.	MI	MN	WI	IL	IN	OH	PA	NY
Total...............	**10,368**	**5,127**	**5,241**	**3,288**	**189**	**820**	**63**	**45**	**312**	**51**	**473**
Lake Superior......	2,980	1,549	1,431	917	189	325	–	–	–	–	–
St. Marys River.....	297	206	91	91	–	–	–	–	–	–	–
Lake Michigan......	1,661	–	1,661	1,058	–	495	63	45	–	–	–
Lake Huron.........	3,350	2,416	934	934	–	–	–	–	–	–	–
St. Clair River.......	128	47	81	81	–	–	–	–	–	–	–
Lake St. Clair.......	160	71	89	89	–	–	–	–	–	–	–
Detroit River........	107	43	64	64	–	–	–	–	–	–	–
Lake Erie...........	860	366	494	54	–	–	–	–	312	51	77
Niagara River.......	99	34	65	–	–	–	–	–	–	–	65
Lake Ontario........	726	395	331	–	–	–	–	–	–	–	331

– Represents zero.

Source: State of Michigan, Department of Environment Quality, "Great Lakes, Shorelines of the Great Lakes," and U.S. Lake Survey, File no. 3-3284 corrected to 1952. <http://www.michigan.gov/deq/0,1607,7-135-3313_3677---,00.html>.

Table 397. Largest Lakes in the United States

[The list of lakes include manmade lakes and those that are only partially within the United States]

Lake	Location	Area in sq. mi.	Lake	Location	Area in sq. mi.
Lake Superior..................	MI-MN-WI-Ontario	31,700	Lake Pontchartrain......	Louisiana	631
Lake Huron.....................	MI-Ontario	23,000	Lake Sakakawea [1].......	North Dakota	520
Lake Michigan.................	IL-IN-MI-WI	22,300	Lake Champlain.........	NY-VT-Quebec	490
Lake Erie......................	MI-NY-OH-PA-Ontario	9,910	Becharof Lake...........	Alaska	453
Lake Ontario...................	NY-Ontario	7,340	Lake St. Clair.............	MI-Ontario	430
Great Salt Lake................	Utah	2,117	Red Lake................	Minnesota	427
Lake of the Woods.............	MN-Manitoba-Ontario	1,485	Selawik Lake............	Alaska	404
Iliamna Lake...................	Alaska	1,014	Fort Peck Lake [1].........	Montana	393
Lake Oahe [1]...................	ND-SD	685	Salton Sea..............	California	347
Lake Okeechobee.............	Florida	662	Rainy Lake..............	MN-Ontario	345

[1] Manmade lakes.

Source: U.S. Geological Survey, 2003, and National Oceanic and Atmospheric Administration, "Great Lakes, 2002" and The National Atlas of the United States of America, *Lakes*, <http://nationalmap.gov/small_scale/#ten>.

Table 398. Coastline Counties Most Frequently Hit by Hurricanes: 1960 to 2008

[Hurricane is a type of tropical cyclone, an intense tropical weather system of strong thunderstorms with a well-defined surface circulation and maximum sustained winds of 74 miles per hour or higher]

County and State	Coastline region	Number of hurricanes	Percent change in population 1960 to 2008	Percent change in population 2000 to 2008	Percent change in housing units 1960 to 2008	Percent change in housing units 2000 to 2008
Monroe County, FL..................	Gulf of Mexico	15	50.8	-9.2	221.8	4.3
Lafourche Parish, LA................	Gulf of Mexico	14	67.2	2.9	151.5	8.9
Carteret County, NC.................	Atlantic	14	104.3	6.4	366.4	12.4
Dare County, NC....................	Atlantic	13	465.9	12.1	709.6	22.8
Hyde County, NC....................	Atlantic	13	-10.1	-11.1	83.7	5.8
Jefferson Parish, LA................	Gulf of Mexico	12	108.9	-4.2	201.4	-3.5
Palm Beach County, FL.............	Atlantic	12	454.7	11.9	616.9	15.2
Miami-Dade County, FL.............	Atlantic	11	156.5	6.4	180.6	14.9
St. Bernard Parish, LA..............	Gulf of Mexico	11	17.2	-43.9	-2.6	-67.9
Cameron Parish, LA................	Gulf of Mexico	11	4.8	-27.6	87.7	-8.1
Terrebonne Parish, LA.............	Gulf of Mexico	11	78.7	3.9	179.4	11.0

Source: U.S. National Oceanic and Atmospheric Administration (NOAA), Coastal Services Center, Historical Hurricane Tracks: 1851 to 2008; U.S. Census Bureau, Current Population Reports, P25-1139, Population Estimates and Projections, "Coastline Population Trends in the United States: 1960 to 2008," May 2010. See also <https://www.census.gov/prod/www/population.html>

Table 399. U.S.–Canada and U.S.–Mexico Border Lengths

[In statute miles. Each statute mile equals one mile. For 2016, there were over 49 million personal vehicle passengers entering the United States from Canada, and over 140 million personal vehicle passengers entering the United States from Mexico]

State	Length of international border	State	Length of international border
United States–Canada total	**5,525**	Ohio	146
Alaska	1,538	Pennsylvania	42
Idaho	45	Vermont	90
Maine	611	Washington	427
Michigan	721		
Minnesota	547	**United States–Mexico total**	**1,933**
Montana	545	Arizona	373
New Hampshire	58	California	140
New York	445	New Mexico	180
North Dakota	310	Texas	1,241

Source: U.S.–Canada lengths: International Boundary Commission, 2003; U.S. Mexico lengths: U.S. Geological Survey; and The National Atlas of the United States, 1976, "Borders," <http://nationalatlas.gov/articles/mapping/a_general.html>.

Table 400. Coastline and Shoreline of the United States by State

[In statute miles. Each statute mile equals one mile. The term coastline is United States coastline measurements were made from small-scale maps, and the coastline was generalized. The coastlines of large sounds and used to describe the general outline of the seacoast. For the table below, bays were included. Measurements were made in 1948. Shoreline is the term used to describe a more detailed measure of the seacoast. The tidal shoreline figures in the table below were obtained in 1939–1940 from the largest-scale charts and maps then available. Shoreline of the outer coast, offshore islands, sounds, and bays was included, as well as the tidal portion of rivers and creeks. Only states with coastline or shoreline are included in the following table]

State	General coastline	Tidal shoreline	State	General coastline	Tidal shoreline
United States	**12,383**	**88,633**	Mississippi	44	359
Alabama	53	607	New Hampshire	13	131
Alaska	6,640	33,904	New Jersey	130	1,792
California	840	3,427	New York	127	1,850
Connecticut	–	618	North Carolina	301	3,375
Delaware	28	381	Oregon	296	1,410
Florida	1,350	8,426	Pennsylvania	–	89
Georgia	100	2,344	Rhode Island	40	384
Hawaii	750	1,052	South Carolina	187	2,876
Louisiana	397	7,721	Texas	367	3,359
Maine	228	3,478	Virginia	112	3,315
Maryland	31	3,190	Washington	157	3,026
Massachusetts	192	1,519			

– Represents zero.

Source: National Oceanic Atmospheric Administration, 1975 and The National Atlas of the United States, "Coastline and Shoreline," <http://nationalmap.gov/small_scale/>. See also <http://shoreline.noaa.gov/>.

Table 401. Flows of Largest U.S. Rivers—Length, Discharge, and Drainage Area

[A flow of 1,000 cubic ft. per second is equal to 646 million gallons per day, 724,000 acre-feet per year, or 28.3 cubic meters per second. One acre-foot is the volume of water that would cover 1 acre to a depth of 1 foot]

River	Location of mouth	Source stream (name and location)	Length (miles) [1]	Average discharge at mouth (1,000 cubic feet per second)	Drainage area (1,000 sq. miles)
Missouri	Missouri	Red Rock Creek, MT	[2] 2,540	76.2	[3] 529
Mississippi	Louisiana	Mississippi River, MN	2,340	[4] 593	[3,5] 1,150
Yukon	Alaska	McNeil River, Canada	1,980	225	[3] 328
St. Lawrence	Canada	North River, MN	1,900	348	[3] 396
Rio Grande	Mexico-Texas	Rio Grande, CO	1,900	([6])	336
Arkansas	Arkansas	East Fork Arkansas River, CO	1,460	41	161
Colorado	Mexico	Colorado River, CO	1,450	([6])	246
Atchafalaya [7]	Louisiana	Tierra Blanca Creek, NM	1,420	58	95
Ohio	Illinois-Kentucky	Allegheny River, PA	1,310	281	203
Red [7]	Louisiana	Tierra Blanca Creek, NM	1,290	56	93
Brazos	Texas	Blackwater Draw, NM	1,280	([6])	46
Columbia	Oregon-Washington	Columbia River, Canada	1,240	265	[3] 258
Snake	Washington	Snake River, WY	1,040	56.9	108
Platte	Nebraska	Grizzly Creek, CO	990	([6])	85
Pecos	Texas	Pecos River, NM	926	([6])	44
Canadian	Oklahoma	Canadian River, CO	906	([6])	47
Tennessee	Kentucky	Courthouse Creek, NC	886	68	41

[1] From source to mouth. [2] The length from the source of the Missouri River to the Mississippi River and thence to the Gulf of Mexico is about 3,710 miles. [3] Drainage area includes both the United States and Canada. [4] Includes about 167,000 cubic feet per second diverted from the Mississippi into the Atchafalaya River but excludes the flow of the Red River. [5] Excludes the drainage areas of the Red and Atchafalaya Rivers. [6] Less than 15,000 cubic feet per second. [7] In east-central Louisiana, the Red River flows into the Atchafalaya River, a distributary of the Mississippi River. Data on average discharge, length, and drainage area include the Red River, but exclude all water diverted into the Atchafalaya from the Mississippi River.

Source: U.S. Geological Survey, *Largest Rivers in the United States*, September 2005, <http://pubs.usgs.gov/of/1987/ofr87-242/>.

Table 402. Extreme and Mean Elevations by State and Other Areas

[One foot = .305 meter. There are 2,130 square miles of the United States below sea level (Death Valley is the lowest point). There are 20,230 square miles above 10,000 feet (Mount McKinley is the highest point in the United States). Minus sign (-) indicates below sea level]

State and other areas	Highest point Name	Elevation Feet	Elevation Meters	Lowest point Name	Elevation Feet	Elevation Meters	Approximate mean elevation Feet	Approximate mean elevation Meters
U.S.	**Mt. McKinley (AK)**	**20,310**	**6,190**	**Death Valley (CA)**	**-282**	**-86**	**2,500**	**763**
AL	Cheaha Mountain	2,407	734	Gulf of Mexico	([1])	([1])	500	153
AK	Mount McKinley	20,310	6,190	Pacific Ocean	([1])	([1])	1,900	580
AZ	Humphreys Peak	12,633	3,853	Colorado River	70	21	4,100	1,251
AR	Magazine Mountain	2,753	840	Ouachita River	55	17	650	198
CA	Mount Whitney	14,494	4,419	Death Valley	-282	-86	2,900	885
CO	Mt. Elbert	14,433	4,402	Arikaree River	3,315	1,011	6,800	2,074
CT	Mt. Frissell on south slope	2,380	726	Long Island Sound	([1])	([1])	500	153
DE	Ebright Road [2]	448	137	Atlantic Ocean	([1])	([1])	60	18
DC	Tenleytown at Reno Reservoir	410	125	Potomac River	1	(Z)	150	46
FL	Britton Hill	345	105	Atlantic Ocean	([1])	([1])	100	31
GA	Brasstown Bald	4,784	1,459	Atlantic Ocean	([1])	([1])	600	183
HI	Pu'u Wekiu, Mauna Kea	13,796	4,208	Pacific Ocean	([1])	([1])	3,030	924
ID	Borah Peak	12,662	3,862	Snake River	710	217	5,000	1,525
IL	Charles Mound	1,235	377	Mississippi River	279	85	600	183
IN	Hoosier Hill	1,257	383	Ohio River	320	98	700	214
IA	Hawkeye Point	1,670	509	Mississippi River	480	146	1,100	336
KS	Mount Sunflower	4,039	1,232	Verdigris River	679	207	2,000	610
KY	Black Mountain	4,145	1,264	Mississippi River	257	78	750	229
LA	Driskill Mountain	535	163	New Orleans	-8	-2	100	31
ME	Mount Katahdin	5,268	1,607	Atlantic Ocean	([1])	([1])	600	183
MD	Hoye Crest	3,360	1,025	Atlantic Ocean	([1])	([1])	350	107
MA	Mount Greylock	3,491	1,065	Atlantic Ocean	([1])	([1])	500	153
MI	Mount Arvon	1,979	604	Lake Erie	571	174	900	275
MN	Eagle Mountain	2,301	702	Lake Superior	601	183	1,200	366
MS	Woodall Mountain	806	246	Gulf of Mexico	([1])	([1])	300	92
MO	Taum Sauk Mountain	1,772	540	St. Francis River	230	70	800	244
MT	Granite Peak	12,799	3,904	Kootenai River	1,800	549	3,400	1,037
NE	Panorama Point	5,424	1,654	Missouri River	840	256	2,600	793
NV	Boundary Peak	13,140	4,007	Colorado River	479	146	5,500	1,678
NH	Mount Washington	6,288	1,918	Atlantic Ocean	([1])	([1])	1,000	305
NJ	High Point	1,803	550	Atlantic Ocean	([1])	([1])	250	76
NM	Wheeler Peak	13,161	4,014	Red Bluff Reservoir	2,842	867	5,700	1,739
NY	Mount Marcy	5,344	1,630	Atlantic Ocean	([1])	([1])	1,000	305
NC	Mount Mitchell	6,684	2,039	Atlantic Ocean	([1])	([1])	700	214
ND	White Butte	3,506	1,069	Red River of the North	750	229	1,900	580
OH	Campbell Hill	1,550	473	Ohio River	455	139	850	259
OK	Black Mesa	4,973	1,517	Little River	289	88	1,300	397
OR	Mount Hood	11,239	3,428	Pacific Ocean	([1])	([1])	3,300	1,007
PA	Mount Davis	3,213	980	Delaware River	([1])	([1])	1,100	336
RI	Jerimoth Hill	812	248	Atlantic Ocean	([1])	([1])	200	61
SC	Sassafras Mountain	3,560	1,086	Atlantic Ocean	([1])	([1])	350	107
SD	Harney Peak	7,242	2,209	Big Stone Lake	966	295	2,200	671
TN	Clingmans Dome	6,643	2,026	Mississippi River	178	54	900	275
TX	Guadalupe Peak	8,749	2,668	Gulf of Mexico	([1])	([1])	1,700	519
UT	Kings Peak	13,528	4,126	Beaverdam Wash	2,000	610	6,100	1,861
VT	Mount Mansfield	4,393	1,340	Lake Champlain	95	29	1,000	305
VA	Mount Rogers	5,729	1,747	Atlantic Ocean	([1])	([1])	950	290
WA	Mount Rainier	14,411	4,395	Pacific Ocean	([1])	([1])	1,700	519
WV	Spruce Knob	4,863	1,483	Potomac River	240	73	1,500	458
WI	Timms Hill	1,951	595	Lake Michigan	579	177	1,050	320
WY	Gannett Peak	13,804	4,210	Belle Fourche River	3,099	945	6,700	2,044
Other areas: Puerto Rico	Cerro de Punta	4,390	1,339	Atlantic Ocean	([1])	([1])	1,800	549
American Samoa	Lata Mountain	3,160	964	Pacific Ocean	([1])	([1])	1,300	397
Guam	Mount Lamlam	1,332	406	Pacific Ocean	([1])	([1])	330	101
U.S. Virgin Islands	Crown Mountain	1,556	475	Atlantic Ocean	([1])	([1])	750	229

Z Less than .5 meter. [1] Sea level. [2] At DE–PA state line.

Source: For highest and lowest points, see U.S. Geological Survey, "Elevations and Distances in the United States," <http://egsc.usgs.gov/isb/pubs/booklets/elvadist/elvadist.html>, released April 2005. For mean elevations, see *Elevations and Distances in the United States*, 1983 edition.

Table 403. Acres of Land Cover by Type and Use: 1987 to 2012

[In millions of acres (1,944 represents 1,944,000,000), except percent. Excludes Alaska and District of Columbia. For inventory-specific glossary of key terms, see <http://www.nrcs.usda.gov/wps/portal/nrcs/main/national/technical/nra/nri/>]

| Year | Total surface area | Nonfederal rural land | | | | | | | Developed land | Water areas | Federal land |
		Rural land total	Cropland	CRP land [1]	Pastureland	Rangeland	Forest land	Other rural land			
Land											
1987...........	1,944	1,417	406	14	127	414	412	43	78	51	399
1992...........	1,944	1,407	382	34	126	410	412	43	85	51	401
1997...........	1,944	1,395	376	33	121	408	413	43	96	51	403
2002...........	1,944	1,384	368	32	119	408	414	43	105	52	404
2007...........	1,944	1,376	359	32	120	407	413	45	111	52	405
2012...........	1,944	1,373	363	24	121	406	413	45	114	52	405
Percent of total land											
1987...........	100.0	72.9	20.9	0.7	6.6	21.3	21.2	2.2	4.0	2.6	20.5
1992...........	100.0	72.4	19.6	1.7	6.5	21.1	21.2	2.2	4.4	2.6	20.6
1997...........	100.0	71.7	19.4	1.7	6.2	21.0	21.3	2.2	4.9	2.6	20.7
2002...........	100.0	71.2	18.9	1.6	6.1	21.0	21.3	2.2	5.4	2.7	20.8
2007...........	100.0	70.8	18.5	1.7	6.2	20.9	21.2	2.3	5.7	2.7	20.8
2012...........	100.0	70.6	18.7	1.2	6.2	20.9	21.3	2.3	5.9	2.7	20.8

[1] Conservation Reserve Program (CRP) land. CRP is a federal program established under the Food Security Act of 1985 to assist private landowners to convert highly erodible cropland to vegetative cover for 10 years.

Source: U.S. Department of Agriculture, Natural Resources and Conservation Service, *Summary Report: 2012 National Resources Inventory*, August 2015. See also <http://www.nrcs.usda.gov/technical/NRI/>.

Table 404. Wetlands on Nonfederal Land and Water Areas by Land Cover Type and Farm Production Region: 2012

[In thousands of acres (111,221 represents 111,221,000). Covers both palustrine (nontidal) and estuarine (tidal) wetlands; see source]

Farm production region [1]	Total	Cropland [3]	Forest land	Rangeland	Other rural land	Developed land	Water area
Wetlands, total [2]...............	**111,221**	**17,770**	**65,798**	**7,984**	**14,693**	**1,410**	**3,566**
Southeast........................	22,622	986	16,645	952	3,078	364	597
Lake states......................	22,265	3,386	15,041	–	3,472	166	201
Delta states.....................	17,661	3,021	11,022	188	2,796	176	458
Northeast........................	13,732	1,226	10,636	–	1,422	227	221
Northern plains..................	7,862	3,120	234	2,908	1,150	76	375
Appalachian......................	7,462	401	6,118	–	543	96	304
Southern plains..................	5,697	1,037	2,601	864	426	157	613
Mountain.........................	5,101	1,667	253	2,314	728	15	125
Corn belt........................	4,716	1,371	2,410	–	371	99	465
Pacific..........................	3,981	1,535	788	754	675	34	196

– Represents zero. [1] Ten regions established by USDA, Economic Research Service, that group states according to differences in soils, slope of land, climate, distance to market, and storage and marketing facilities. [2] Total includes Hawaii and Caribbean territories, which are not included in the regions. [3] Cultivated and non-cultivated. Includes pastureland and Conservation Reserve Program (CRP) lands.

Source: U.S. Department of Agriculture, Natural Resources Conservation Service, *Summary Report: 2012 National Resources Inventory*, August 2015. See also <http://www.nrcs.usda.gov/technical/NRI/>.

Table 405. Acres of Federal and Non-Federal Land Cover by Type and State: 2012

[In thousands of acres (1,944,143 represents 1,944,143,000), except percent. Excludes Alaska, District of Columbia, and Island Areas]

| State | Total surface area [1] | Selected nonfederal rural land, percent of total | | | State | Total surface area [1] | Selected nonfederal rural land, percent of total | | |
		Cropland	Rangeland	Forest land			Cropland	Rangeland	Forest land
United States......	**1,944,143**	**18.7**	**20.9**	**21.3**	Montana..........	94,110	15.4	39.2	6.2
Alabama.............	33,424	6.9	0.2	65.1	Nebraska.........	49,510	40.4	46.5	1.7
Arizona.............	72,964	1.2	45.2	6.0	Nevada...........	70,763	0.9	12.4	0.5
Arkansas............	34,037	21.0	0.1	44.3	New Hampshire...	5,941	2.0	–	63.8
California...........	101,510	9.0	18.6	14.0	New Jersey.......	5,216	9.3	–	31.4
Colorado............	66,625	11.9	37.3	5.1	New Mexico.......	77,823	2.0	52.3	7.2
Connecticut.........	3,195	5.4	–	50.2	New York.........	31,409	16.3	–	55.7
Delaware............	1,534	26.8	–	22.2	North Carolina....	33,709	15.3	–	46.4
Florida.............	37,534	7.6	6.8	35.1	North Dakota......	45,251	54.7	23.9	1.0
Georgia.............	37,741	11.1	–	57.8	Ohio.............	26,445	42.0	–	26.8
Hawaii..............	4,123	2.1	25.9	37.0	Oklahoma.........	44,738	19.6	30.6	17.3
Idaho..............	53,488	10.1	12.4	7.7	Oregon...........	62,161	5.6	14.5	19.8
Illinois............	36,059	66.3	–	11.2	Pennsylvania.....	28,995	17.4	–	53.8
Indiana.............	23,158	57.5	–	17.0	Rhode Island......	813	2.1	–	44.4
Iowa...............	36,017	72.1	–	6.5	South Carolina....	19,939	11.0	–	56.0
Kansas..............	52,661	49.1	30.0	3.4	South Dakota.....	49,358	35.7	45.1	1.2
Kentucky............	25,863	21.1	–	41.0	Tennessee........	26,974	16.8	–	44.1
Louisiana...........	31,377	15.8	0.7	41.0	Texas............	171,052	14.0	54.8	8.2
Maine..............	20,966	1.7	–	83.8	Utah.............	54,339	2.7	19.5	4.2
Maryland............	7,870	17.6	–	29.2	Vermont..........	6,154	8.6	–	65.8
Massachusetts......	5,339	4.1	–	47.8	Virginia..........	27,087	10.3	–	49.1
Michigan............	37,349	21.4	–	44.6	Washington.......	44,035	13.2	13.5	27.9
Minnesota...........	54,010	39.0	–	30.3	West Virginia......	15,508	4.6	–	67.2
Mississippi.........	30,527	15.6	–	56.2	Wisconsin........	35,920	28.9	–	40.9
Missouri............	44,614	31.3	0.1	28.2	Wyoming..........	62,603	3.4	43.2	1.7

– Represents or rounds to zero. [1] Total surface area includes both Federal and non-Federal land.

Source: U.S. Department of Agriculture, Natural Resources and Conservation Service, *Summary Report, 2012 National Resources Inventory*, August 2015. See also <http://www.nrcs.usda.gov/technical/NRI/>.

Table 406. U.S. Wetland Resources and Deepwater Habitats by Type: 2004 and 2009

[In thousands of acres (153,121.4 represents 153,121,400). Wetlands and deepwater habitats are defined separately because the term wetland does not include permanent water bodies. Deepwater habitats are permanently flooded land lying below the deepwater boundary of wetlands. Deepwater habitats include environments where surface water is permanent and often deep, so that water, rather than air, is the principal medium within which the dominant organisms live, whether or not they are attached to the substrate. As in wetlands, the dominant plants are hydrophytes; however, the substrates are considered nonsoil because the water is too deep to support emergent vegetation. In general terms, wetlands are lands where saturation with water is the dominant factor determining the nature of soil development and the types of plant and animal communities living in the soil and on its surface. The single feature that most wetlands share is soil or substrate that is at least periodically saturated with or covered by water. Wetlands are lands transitional between terrestrial and aquatic systems where the water table is usually at or near the surface or the land is covered by shallow water. For more information on wetlands, see the "Classification of Wetlands and Deepwater Habitats of the United States" at <http://www.npwrc.usgs.gov/resource/wetlands/classwet/index.htm>]

Wetland or deepwater category	Estimated area, 2004	Estimated area, 2009	Change, 2004 to 2009
All wetlands and deepwater habitats, total	**153,121.4**	**153,206.4**	**85.0**
All deepwater habitats, total	42,999.4	43,146.6	147.2
Lacustrine [1]	16,786.0	16,859.6	73.6
Riverine [2]	7,517.9	7,510.5	-7.4
Estuarine Subtidal [3]	18,695.4	18,776.5	81.1
All wetlands, total	110,122.1	110,059.8	-62.3
Intertidal wetlands [4]	5,869.3	5,785.2	-84.1
Marine intertidal	219.2	227.8	8.5
Estuarine intertidal nonvegetated	999.4	1,017.7	18.3
Estuarine intertidal vegetated	4,650.7	4,539.7	-110.9
Freshwater wetlands	104,252.7	104,274.6	21.9
Freshwater nonvegetated	6,502.1	6,709.3	207.2
Freshwater vegetated	97,750.6	97,565.3	-185.3
Freshwater emergent [5]	27,162.7	27,430.5	267.8
Freshwater forested [6]	52,256.5	51,623.3	-633.1
Freshwater shrub [7]	18,331.4	18,511.5	180.1

[1] The lacustrine system includes deepwater habitats with all of the following characteristics: (1) situated in a topographic depression or a dammed river channel; (2) lacking trees, shrubs, persistent emergents, emergent mosses or lichens with greater than 30 percent coverage; and (3) total area exceeds 20 acres (8 hectares). [2] The riverine system includes deepwater habitats contained within a channel, with the exception of habitats with water containing ocean derived salts in excess of 0.5 parts per thousand. [3] The estuarine system consists of deepwater tidal habitats and adjacent tidal wetlands that are usually semi-enclosed by land but have open, partly obstructed, or sporadic access to the open ocean, and in which ocean water is at least occasionally diluted by freshwater runoff from the land. Subtidal is where the substrate is continuously submerged by marine or estuarine waters. [4] Intertidal is where the substrate is exposed and flooded by tides. Intertidal includes the splash zone of coastal waters. [5] Emergent wetlands are characterized by erect, rooted, herbaceous hydrophytes, excluding mosses and lichens. This vegetation is present for most of the growing season in most years. These wetlands are usually dominated by perennial plants. [6] Forested wetlands are characterized by woody vegetation that is 20 feet tall or taller. [7] Shrub wetlands include areas dominated by woody vegetation less than 20 feet tall. The species include true shrubs, young trees, and trees or shrubs that are small or stunted because of environmental conditions.

Source: U.S. Fish and Wildlife Service, *Status and Trends of Wetlands in the Conterminous United States, 2004 to 2009*, September 2011. See also <http://www.fws.gov/wetlands/Status-And-Trends-2009/index.html>.

Table 407. U.S. Water Withdrawals Per Day by End Use: 1950 to 2010

[In billions (180 represents 180,000,000,000). Includes the District of Columbia, Puerto Rico and U.S. Virgin Islands. Withdrawal signifies water physically withdrawn from a source. Includes fresh and saline water; excludes water used for hydroelectric power. For information on changes in data collection and presentation methods, see 2010 source report]

Year	Total with-drawals	Public supply	Rural domestic and livestock: Self supplied domestic	Rural domestic and livestock: Live-stock	Irri-gation	Thermo electric power	Other: Self supplied industrial	Other: Mining	Other: Com-mercial	Other: Aqua-culture
1950 [1]	180	14	2.1	1.5	89	40	37	(5)	(5)	(5)
1955 [2]	240	17	2.1	1.5	110	72	39	(5)	(5)	(5)
1960 [3]	270	21	2.0	1.6	110	100	38	(5)	(5)	(5)
1965 [4]	310	24	2.3	1.7	120	130	46	(5)	(5)	(5)
1970 [4]	370	27	2.6	1.9	130	170	47	(5)	(5)	(5)
1975 [3]	420	29	2.8	2.1	140	200	45	(5)	(5)	(5)
1980 [3]	430	33	3.4	2.2	150	210	45	(5)	(5)	(5)
1985 [3]	397	37	3.3	2.2	135	187	26	3	1	2
1990 [3]	404	39	3.4	2.3	134	194	23	5	2	2
1995 [3]	398	40	3.4	2.3	130	190	22	4	3	3
2000 [3]	413	43	3.6	2.4	139	195	20	4	(NA)	6
2005 [3]	409	44	3.7	2.2	127	201	18	4	(NA)	9
2010 [3]	355	42	3.6	2.0	115	161	16	5	(NA)	9

NA Not available. [1] Population covered: 48 states, District of Columbia, and Hawaii. [2] Population covered: 48 states. [3] Population covered: 50 states, District of Columbia, Puerto Rico, and the Virgin Islands. [4] Population covered: 50 states, District of Columbia, and Puerto Rico. [5] Included in "self-supplied industrial."

Source: 1950–1960, U.S. Bureau of Domestic Business Development, based principally on committee prints, *Water Resources Activities in the United States*, for the Senate Committee on National Water Resources, U.S. Senate; thereafter, U.S. Geological Survey, *Estimated Use of Water in the United States in 2010*, circular 1405, November 2014. See also <http://pubs.usgs.gov/circ/1405/>.

Table 408. National Ambient Air Pollutant Concentrations by Type of Pollutant: 2009 to 2015

[Data represent composite averages across monitoring stations meeting minimum data completeness requirements for the trend period. Carbon monoxide is based on the second-highest, nonoverlapping, 8-hour average; ozone, the fourth-highest maximum 8-hour value; particulates (PM-10) on the second highest daily 24-hour average; fine particulates (PM2.5) annual average on the weighted annual mean of daily 24-hour averages; and lead on the 'maximum rolling three-month average. Based on data from the Air Quality System. µg/m³ = micrograms of pollutant per cubic meter of air; ppm = parts per million; ppb = parts per billion]

Pollutant	Unit	Monitoring stations, number	Air quality standard [1]	2009	2010	2011	2012	2013	2014	2015
Carbon monoxide	ppm	170	[2] 9	1.7	1.6	1.6	1.5	1.5	1.4	1.4
Ozone	ppm	846	[3] 0.070	0.069	0.072	0.073	0.074	0.067	0.067	0.067
Sulfur dioxide	ppb	227	[4] 75	48	45	37	36	30	29	25
Particulates (PM-10)	µg/m³	374	[5] 150	60.5	63.3	68.4	68.9	66.0	62.9	60.9
Fine particulates (PM2.5) annual average	µg/m³	480	[6] 12	9.8	9.9	9.7	9.1	8.9	8.8	8.5
Nitrogen dioxide	ppb	178	[7] 100	43	44	43	41	41	41	39
Lead	µg/m³	35	[8] 0.15	0.08	0.08	0.10	0.07	0.06	0.03	0.02

[1] Refers to the primary National Ambient Air Quality Standard. [2] Based on 8-hour standard of 9 ppm. [3] Based on 8-hour standard of 0.070 ppm. On December 28, 2015, EPA revised the level of the primary and secondary 8-hour ozone standards to 0.070 ppm. [4] Based on a 1-hour daily maximum concentration of 75 ppb. [5] Based on 24-hour (daily) standard of 150 µg/m³. The particulates (PM-10) standard replaced the previous standard for total suspended particulates in 1987. In 2006, EPA revoked the annual PM-10 standard. [6] Based on annual standard of 12 µg/m³. The PM-2.5 national monitoring network was deployed in 1999. [7] Based on a 1-hour daily maximum concentration of 100 ppb. [8] Based on 3-month rolling average of 0.15 µg/m³.

Source: U.S. Environmental Protection Agency, "Air Trends," <https://www.epa.gov/air-trends>, accessed January 2017.

Table 409. Selected Air Pollutant Emissions: 1990 to 2016

[In thousands of tons (4,320 represents 4,320,000), except as indicated. For documentation regarding the data see <https://www.epa.gov/air-emissions-inventories/national-emissions-inventory-nei>]

Year	Ammonia	Carbon monoxide	Nitrogen oxide	PM-10 [1]	PM-2.5 [1]	Sulfur dioxide	V.O.C. [2]
1990	4,320	154,188	25,529	27,753	7,560	23,077	24,108
2000	4,907	114,467	22,598	23,747	7,288	16,347	17,512
2005	3,932	88,546	20,355	21,302	5,592	14,546	17,753
2010	4,271	73,771	14,846	20,823	5,964	7,732	17,835
2011	4,232	73,762	14,519	20,723	6,100	6,479	18,154
2012	4,232	71,065	13,901	22,074	6,222	6,477	17,752
2013	4,231	68,369	13,283	23,425	6,345	6,476	17,350
2014	3,871	63,299	12,598	24,502	6,220	4,803	16,489
2015	3,864	61,130	11,617	24,472	6,191	3,801	16,172
2016	3,858	58,983	10,489	24,442	6,163	2,709	15,858

[1] PM = Particular Matter; PM-10 is equal to or less than ten microns in diameter; PM-2.5 to or less than 2.5 microns effective diameter. [2] Volatile organic compound.

Source: U.S. Environmental Protection Agency, "National Emissions Inventory (NEI) Air Pollutant Emissions Trends Data, 1970-2016," <https://www.epa.gov/air-emissions-inventories/air-pollutant-emissions-trends-data>, accessed January 2017.

Table 410. Selected Air Pollutant Emissions by Pollutant and Source: 2016

[In thousands of tons (3,858 represents 3,858,000). See headnote, Table 409]

Source	Ammonia	Carbon monoxide	Nitrogen oxide	PM-10 [1]	PM-2.5 [1]	Sulfur dioxide	V.O.C. [2]
Total emissions	3,858	58,983	10,489	24,442	6,163	2,709	15,858
Fuel combustion, stationary sources	110	4,125	2,776	922	781	1,973	532
Electric utilities	26	717	1,053	229	177	1,185	37
Industrial	16	957	1,189	325	240	657	110
Other fuel combustion	68	2,452	534	368	363	131	384
Industrial processes	76	4,373	1,401	1,268	673	538	7,495
Chemical and allied product manufacturing	22	129	47	20	14	115	75
Metals processing	1	609	74	58	45	107	29
Petroleum and related industries	2	859	822	36	32	103	3,220
Other	22	608	337	777	307	172	353
Solvent utilization	1	2	1	4	4	–	2,942
Storage and transport	5	10	6	67	18	3	681
Waste disposal and recycling	23	2,156	114	305	253	37	197
Highway vehicles	90	17,872	3,606	287	133	18	1,765
Off highway [3]	3	12,989	2,415	163	151	31	1,577
Miscellaneous [4]	3,578	19,624	292	21,803	4,425	149	4,488

– Rounds to zero. [1] See footnote 1, Table 409. [2] Volatile organic compound. [3] Includes emissions from farm tractors and other farm machinery, construction equipment, industrial machinery, recreational marine vessels, and small general utility engines such as lawn mowers. [4] Includes emissions from forest fires and other kinds of burning, various agricultural activities, fugitive dust from paved and unpaved roads, other construction and mining activities, and natural sources.

Source: U.S. Environmental Protection Agency, "National Emissions Inventory (NEI) Air Pollutant Emissions Trends Data, 1970-2016," <https://www.epa.gov/air-emissions-inventories/air-pollutant-emissions-trends-data>, accessed January 2017.

Table 411. Greenhouse Gas Emissions by Type and Source: 1990 to 2015

[In millions of metric tons of carbon dioxide equivalent (MMT CO2 Eq.). MMT CO2 Eq. weights each gas by its global warming potential (GWP) value. GWP is a quantified measure of the globally averaged relative radiative forcing impacts of a particular greenhouse gas. The reference gas used is CO2; therefore, GWP-weighted emissions are measured in MMT CO2 Eq. See source for details]

Type and/or source	1990	2011	2012	2013	2014	2015
Total emissions	**6,363.1**	**6,776.7**	**6,538.3**	**6,680.1**	**6,739.7**	**6,586.7**
BY SOURCE						
Energy	5,328.1	5,721.2	5,507.0	5,659.1	5,704.9	5,549.1
Industrial processes and product use [1]	340.4	371.0	360.9	363.7	379.8	375.9
Sulfur hexafluoride (SF6)	28.8	9.2	6.8	6.4	6.6	5.8
Hydrofluorocarbons (HFCs)	46.6	154.3	155.9	159.0	166.7	173.2
Perfluorocarbons (PFCs)	24.3	6.9	6.0	5.8	5.8	5.2
Agriculture	495.3	541.9	525.9	516.9	514.7	522.3
Land use, land-use change, and forestry (LULUCF)	10.6	19.9	26.1	19.2	19.7	19.7
Waste	199.3	142.6	144.4	140.4	140.2	139.4
Net CO2 flux from land use, land use change, and forestry	*-819.6*	*-749.2*	*-753.8*	*-763.0*	*-761.4*	*-758.9*
Net emissions (sources and sinks) [2]	5,543.5	6,027.6	5,784.5	5,917.1	5,978.3	5,827.7
BY TYPE AND SOURCE						
Carbon dioxide (CO2), total	**5,123.0**	**5,569.5**	**5,362.1**	**5,514.0**	**5,565.5**	**5,411.4**
Energy	4,907.2	5,387.2	5,180.9	5,332.7	5,377.8	5,231.9
Fossil fuel combustion	4,740.3	5,227.1	5,024.6	5,156.5	5,202.3	5,049.8
Electricity	1,820.8	2,157.7	2,022.2	2,038.1	2,038.0	1,900.7
Transportation	1,493.8	1,707.6	1,696.8	1,713.0	1,742.8	1,736.4
Industrial	842.5	775.0	782.9	812.2	806.1	805.5
Residential	338.3	325.5	282.5	329.7	345.4	319.6
Commercial	217.4	220.4	196.7	221.0	228.7	246.2
Biomass (wood) [3]	215.2	195.2	194.9	211.6	217.7	198.7
Industrial processes and product use	208.8	174.3	171.0	172.9	179.3	170.7
Land use, land-use change, and forestry (sink)	*-830.2*	*-769.1*	*-779.8*	*-782.2*	*-781.1*	*-778.7*
Methane (CH4), total	**780.8**	**672.1**	**666.1**	**658.8**	**659.1**	**655.7**
Energy	367.3	289.5	284.1	284.6	286.8	278.6
Industrial processes and product use	0.3	0.1	0.1	0.1	0.2	0.2
Agriculture	217.6	246.3	244.0	240.4	238.7	244.3
Land use, land-use change, and forestry	6.7	11.2	14.9	11.0	11.3	11.3
Waste management	195.6	136.2	137.9	133.7	133.5	132.6
Nitrous oxide (N2O), total	**359.5**	**364.0**	**340.7**	**335.5**	**335.5**	**334.8**
Energy	53.6	44.4	42.1	41.7	40.3	38.6
Industrial processes and product use	31.6	25.6	20.4	19.0	20.8	20.3
Agriculture	270.6	287.6	271.7	268.1	267.6	269.1
Land use, land-use change, and forestry	3.9	8.7	11.1	8.2	8.4	8.4
Waste management	3.7	6.4	6.6	6.7	6.8	6.9

[1] Total includes items not shown separately. [2] The net CO2 flux total includes both emissions and sequestration, and constitutes a sink in the United States. Sinks are only included in net emissions total. [3] Emissions from wood biomass and ethanol consumption are not included specifically in summing energy sector totals. Net carbon fluxes from changes in biogenic carbon reservoirs are accounted for in the estimates for land use, land-use change, and forestry.

Source: U.S. Environmental Protection Agency, *Inventory of U.S. Greenhouse Gas Emissions and Sinks, 1990-2015*, April 2017. See also <https://www.epa.gov/ghgemissions/inventory-us-greenhouse-gas-emissions-and-sinks>.

Table 412. Carbon Dioxide Emissions from Fossil Fuel Combustion by Fuel Type and Sector: 1990 to 2015

[In millions of metric tons of carbon dioxide equivalent (MMT CO2 Eq.); 4,740.3 MMT represents 4,740,300,000 million metric tons. See source for details on methodology]

Fuel and sector	1990	2005	2011	2012	2013	2014	2015
Total [1]	**4,740.3**	**5,746.9**	**5,227.1**	**5,024.6**	**5,156.5**	**5,202.3**	**5,049.8**
Coal	**1,718.4**	**2,112.3**	**1,813.9**	**1,592.8**	**1,653.8**	**1,652.6**	**1,423.3**
Residential	3.0	0.8	(2)	(2)	(2)	(2)	(2)
Commercial	12.0	9.3	5.8	4.1	3.9	3.8	2.9
Industrial	155.3	115.3	82.0	74.1	75.7	75.6	65.9
Electricity generation	1,547.6	1,983.8	1,722.7	1,511.2	1,571.3	1,569.1	1,350.5
Natural gas	**1,000.3**	**1,166.7**	**1,291.5**	**1,352.6**	**1,391.2**	**1,422.0**	**1,463.6**
Residential	238.0	262.2	254.7	224.8	266.2	277.9	252.8
Commercial	142.1	162.9	170.5	156.9	179.1	189.3	175.4
Industrial	408.9	388.5	417.3	434.8	451.9	468.4	467.5
Transportation	36.0	33.1	38.9	41.3	47.0	40.3	38.8
Electricity generation	175.3	318.8	408.8	492.2	444.0	443.2	526.1
Petroleum	**2,021.2**	**2,467.6**	**2,121.3**	**2,078.8**	**2,111.1**	**2,127.3**	**2,162.5**
Residential	97.4	94.9	70.9	57.7	63.4	67.5	66.8
Commercial	63.3	51.3	44.1	35.7	38.0	35.6	67.9
Industrial	278.3	324.2	275.7	274.1	284.6	262.1	272.2
Transportation	1,457.7	1,854.0	1,668.8	1,655.4	1,666.0	1,702.5	1,697.6
Electricity generation	97.5	97.9	25.8	18.3	22.4	25.3	23.7

[1] Includes data not shown separately. [2] Not occurring.

Source: U.S. Environmental Protection Agency, *Inventory of U.S. Greenhouse Gas Emissions and Sinks, 1990-2015*, April 2017. See also <https://www.epa.gov/ghgemissions/inventory-us-greenhouse-gas-emissions-and-sinks>.

Table 413. Municipal Solid Waste Generation, Materials Recovery, Combustion With Energy Recovery, and Discards: 1980 to 2014

[In millions of tons (151.6 represents 151,600,000), except as indicated. Covers post-consumer residential, commercial, and institutional solid wastes which comprise the major portion of typical municipal collections. Excludes mining, agricultural and industrial processing, demolition and construction wastes, sewage sludge, junked autos and obsolete equipment wastes. Based on material-flows estimating procedure and wet weight as generated]

Item and material	1980	1990	2000	2010	2012	2013	2014
Waste generated.....	**151.6**	**208.3**	**243.5**	**251.1**	**251.8**	**255.0**	**258.5**
Per person per day (lb.).....	3.7	4.6	4.7	4.5	4.4	4.4	4.4
Total materials recovery.....	**14.5**	**33.2**	**69.5**	**85.4**	**86.9**	**87.6**	**89.4**
Per person per day (lb.).....	0.4	0.7	1.4	1.5	1.5	1.5	1.5
Recovery for recycling.....	14.5	29.0	53.0	65.3	65.6	65.1	66.4
Per person per day (lb.).....	0.4	0.6	1.0	1.2	1.1	1.1	1.1
Recovery for composting [1].....	(Z)	4.2	16.5	20.2	21.3	22.4	23.0
Per person per day (lb.).....	(Z)	0.1	0.3	0.4	0.4	0.4	0.4
Combustion with energy recovery.....	2.8	29.8	33.7	29.3	32.5	33.2	33.1
Per person per day (lb.).....	0.1	0.7	0.7	0.5	0.6	0.6	0.6
Discards to landfill, other disposal.....	134.4	145.3	140.3	136.3	132.5	134.3	135.9
Per person per day (lb.).....	3.2	3.2	2.7	2.4	2.3	2.3	2.3
PERCENT DISTRIBUTION OF GENERATION							
Percent of total generation.....	**71.8**	**70.3**	**73.4**	**70.9**	**70.5**	**70.5**	**70.3**
Paper and paperboard.....	36.4	34.9	36.0	28.4	27.2	26.9	26.5
Glass.....	10.0	6.3	5.2	4.6	4.6	4.5	4.4
Metals.....	10.2	7.9	7.8	8.9	8.9	9.1	9.0
Plastics.....	4.5	8.2	10.5	12.5	12.7	12.8	12.9
Rubber and leather.....	2.8	2.8	2.7	3.1	3.2	3.3	3.2
Textiles.....	1.7	2.8	3.9	5.3	5.8	6.0	6.3
Wood.....	4.6	5.9	5.6	6.3	6.3	6.2	6.2
Other.....	1.7	1.5	1.6	1.9	1.8	1.7	1.7
Total other waste.....	**28.2**	**29.7**	**26.6**	**29.1**	**29.5**	**29.5**	**29.7**
Food waste.....	8.6	11.5	12.6	14.2	14.5	14.5	14.9
Yard trimmings.....	18.1	16.8	12.5	13.3	13.5	13.4	13.3
Miscellaneous inorganic wastes.....	1.5	1.4	1.4	1.5	1.5	1.5	1.5

Z Less than 5,000 tons or 0.05 percent. [1] Composting of yard trimmings, food scraps, and other municipal solid waste organic material. Does not include backyard composting.

Source: U.S. Environmental Protection Agency, *Advancing Sustainable Materials Management: 2014 Tables and Figures*, December 2016. See also <https://www.epa.gov/smm>.

Table 414. Generation and Recovery of Selected Materials in Municipal Solid Waste: 1980 to 2014

[In millions of tons (151.6 represents 151,600,000), except as indicated. Covers post-consumer residential, commercial, and institutional solid wastes which comprise the major portion of typical municipal collections. Excludes mining, agricultural and industrial processing, demolition and construction wastes, sewage sludge, and junked autos and obsolete equipment wastes. Based on material-flows estimating procedure and wet weight as generated. Material recovered includes material recycled and composted]

Item and material	1980	1990	2000	2010	2012	2013	2014
Waste generated, total [1].....	**151.6**	**208.3**	**243.5**	**251.1**	**251.8**	**255.0**	**258.5**
Paper and paperboard.....	55.2	72.7	87.7	71.3	68.6	68.6	68.6
Glass.....	15.1	13.1	12.8	11.5	11.6	11.5	11.5
Metals: Ferrous.....	12.6	12.6	14.2	16.9	16.9	17.7	17.7
Aluminum.....	1.7	2.8	3.2	3.5	3.5	3.5	3.5
Other nonferrous.....	1.2	1.1	1.6	2.0	2.0	2.0	2.0
Plastics.....	6.8	17.1	25.6	31.4	31.9	32.6	33.3
Food waste.....	13.0	23.9	30.7	35.7	36.4	37.1	38.4
Yard trimmings.....	27.5	35.0	30.5	33.4	34.0	34.2	34.5
Materials recovered, total [1].....	**14.5**	**33.2**	**69.5**	**85.4**	**86.9**	**87.6**	**89.4**
Paper and paperboard.....	11.7	20.2	37.6	44.6	44.4	43.4	44.4
Glass.....	0.8	2.6	2.9	3.1	3.2	3.2	3.0
Metals: Ferrous.....	0.4	2.2	4.7	5.8	5.6	5.9	5.8
Aluminum.....	0.3	1.0	0.9	0.7	0.7	0.7	0.7
Other nonferrous.....	0.5	0.7	1.1	1.4	1.4	1.4	1.4
Plastics.....	(Z)	0.4	1.5	2.5	2.8	3.0	3.2
Food waste [2].....	(Z)	(Z)	0.7	1.0	1.7	1.8	1.9
Yard trimmings.....	(Z)	4.2	15.8	19.2	19.6	20.6	21.1
Percent of generation recovered, total [1].....	**9.6**	**16.0**	**28.5**	**34.0**	**34.5**	**34.3**	**34.6**
Paper and paperboard.....	21.3	27.8	42.8	62.5	64.6	63.3	64.7
Glass.....	5.0	20.1	22.6	27.2	27.7	27.3	26.0
Metals: Ferrous.....	2.9	17.6	33.1	34.3	33.0	33.1	33.0
Aluminum.....	17.9	35.9	27.0	19.4	20.2	20.0	19.8
Other nonferrous.....	46.6	66.4	66.3	71.3	70.2	68.2	66.7
Plastics.....	0.3	2.2	5.8	8.0	8.7	9.2	9.5
Food waste [2].....	(Z)	(Z)	2.2	2.7	4.8	5.0	5.1
Yard trimmings.....	(Z)	12.0	51.7	57.5	57.7	60.2	61.1

Z Less than 5,000 tons or 0.05 percent. [1] Includes products not shown separately. [2] Includes recovery of paper and mixed municipal solid waste for composting.

Source: U.S. Environmental Protection Agency, *Advancing Sustainable Materials Management: 2014 Tables and Figures*, December 2016. See also <https://www.epa.gov/smm>.

Table 415. Municipal Solid Waste—Generation, Recycling, and Landfill Disposal by Selected Type of Product: 2014

[68,600 represents 68,600,000. See headnote, Table 414]

Type of product	Generation (1,000 tons)	Recycling		Landfill disposal (1,000 tons)
		Product recycled (1,000 tons)	Percent of generation	
Paper and paperboard products [1]	**68,600**	**44,400**	**64.7**	**19,460**
Nondurable goods	29,470	14,910	50.6	11,710
Newspapers/mechanical papers	7,620	5,200	68.2	1,950
Other paper nondurable goods	21,850	9,710	44.4	9,760
Containers and packaging	39,130	29,490	75.4	7,750
Corrugated boxes	30,490	27,280	89.5	2,580
Other paper and paperboard packaging	8,640	2,210	25.6	5,170
Glass products [1]	**11,480**	**2,990**	**26.0**	**8,390**
Containers and packaging	9,200	2,990	35.5	6,110
Beer and soft drink bottles	5,370	2,120	39.5	3,180
Wine and liquor bottles	1,790	570	31.8	1,140
Other bottles and jars	2,040	300	14.7	1,790
Metal products [1]	**23,260**	**7,900**	**34.0**	**12,820**
Metals in durable goods	19,080	5,620	29.5	11,300
Ferrous	15,520	4,260	27.4	9,360
Aluminum	1,520	(NA)	(NA)	1,310
Other nonferrous	660	(Z)	(Z)	610
Metals in containers and packaging	3,980	2,280	57.3	1,360
Plastics [1]	**33,250**	**3,170**	**9.5**	**25,100**
Plastics in durable goods	12,150	910	7.5	9,960
Plastics in nondurable goods	6,780	140	2.1	5,330
Plastics in containers and packaging	14,320	2,120	14.8	9,810
Rubber and leather [1]	**8,210**	**1,440**	**17.5**	**4,150**
Durable goods	7,120	1,440	20.2	3,270
Rubber in tires	3,550	1,440	40.6	150
Other durables	3,570	(Z)	(Z)	3,120
Nondurable goods	1,090	(Z)	(Z)	880
Clothing and footwear	830	(Z)	(Z)	670
Other nondurables	260	(Z)	(Z)	210

NA Not available. Z Less than 5,000 tons or .05 percent. [1] Includes products not shown separately.

Source: U.S. Environmental Protection Agency, *Advancing Sustainable Materials Management: 2014 Tables and Figures,* December 2016. See also <https://www.epa.gov/smm>.

Table 416. Environmental Industry—Revenues and Employment by Industry Segment: 2000 to 2015

[209.9 represents $209,900,000,000. Covers approximately 30,000 private and public companies engaged in revenue-generating environmental activities]

Industry segment	Revenue (billion dollars)				Employment			
	2000	2010	2014	2015	2000	2010	2014	2015
Industry total	**209.9**	**299.2**	**350.8**	**363.1**	**1,299,300**	**1,616,200**	**1,725,400**	**1,729,100**
SERVICES								
Analytical services [1]	1.8	1.9	1.9	2.0	20,200	19,800	19,300	19,300
Wastewater treatment works [2]	28.7	45.5	55.9	57.6	118,800	170,100	192,800	194,800
Solid waste management [3]	39.4	53.4	57.9	59.0	221,400	278,000	291,400	290,800
Hazardous waste management [4]	8.8	10.0	10.8	10.9	45,100	48,500	49,700	49,400
Remediation/industrial services	10.1	12.7	13.7	13.6	100,200	107,400	106,100	102,100
Consulting and engineering	17.4	26.6	28.8	29.5	184,000	255,900	257,000	260,800
EQUIPMENT								
Water equipment and chemicals	19.8	26.9	30.7	31.3	130,500	160,100	172,800	173,700
Instrument manufacturing	3.8	5.4	6.4	6.7	30,200	37,100	41,300	43,000
Air pollution control equipment [5]	19.0	14.9	16.0	16.3	129,600	96,400	97,900	97,300
Waste management equipment [6]	10.0	10.8	12.2	12.6	75,500	73,800	78,100	79,200
Process and prevention technology	1.2	1.9	2.1	2.2	29,000	28,900	29,700	30,900
RESOURCES								
Water utilities [7]	29.9	43.5	52.0	53.8	130,000	172,100	195,900	200,300
Resource recovery [8]	16.0	28.5	29.1	25.9	61,900	102,600	94,500	83,700
Clean energy systems and power [9]	4.0	17.2	33.4	41.8	22,900	65,500	98,900	103,800

[1] Covers environmental laboratory testing and services. [2] Mostly revenues collected by municipal entities for sewage or wastewater plants. [3] Covers activities such as collection, transportation, transfer stations, disposal, landfill ownership and management for solid waste and recyclables. [4] Transportation and disposal of hazardous, medical, and nuclear waste. [5] Includes stationary and mobile sources. [6] Includes vehicles, containers, liners, processing, and remediation equipment. [7] Revenues generated from the sale of water, majority in public sector. [8] Revenues generated from the sale of recovered metals, paper, plastic, etc. [9] Revenues generated from the sale of equipment and systems and electricity.

Source: Environmental Business International, Inc., San Diego, CA, publisher of *Environmental Business Journal;* © 2017 EBI Inc. See also <http://www.ebionline.org>.

Table 417. Toxic Chemical Releases and Transfers by Media: 2011 to 2015

[In millions of pounds (4,116.1 represents 4,116,100,000), except as indicated. Based on reports filed to the Toxic Release Inventory (TRI) Program, as required by Section 313 of the Emergency Planning and Community Right-to-Know Act (EPCRA). The Pollution Prevention Act (PPA) of 1990 mandates collection of data on toxic chemicals that are treated on-site, recycled, and combusted for energy recovery. Owners and operators of facilities within specific North American Industry Classification System industries that have 10 or more full-time employees, and that manufacture, process, or otherwise use any listed toxic chemical in quantities greater than the established threshold in the course of a calendar year are covered and required to report. For trend analysis, a 2011 core list of must-be-reported chemicals is used. Includes carcinogens; persistent, bioaccumulative, toxic (PBT) chemicals; and dioxin and dioxin-like compounds. Does not include off-site disposal or other releases transferred to other TRI program facilities that reported the amounts as on-site disposal or other releases]

Media	2011	2012	2013	2014	2015
Total facilities reporting	**21,882**	**22,015**	**22,118**	**22,103**	**21,898**
Total on- and off-site disposal or other releases	**4,116.1**	**3,614.4**	**4,125.1**	**3,909.9**	**3,329.6**
On-site releases	3,700.2	3,198.9	3,694.2	3,481.8	2,865.3
Air emissions [1]	807.4	749.4	751.8	732.8	667.4
Surface water discharges	222.6	217.9	213.3	217.0	190.9
Underground injection class I	197.8	203.9	200.2	201.9	209.1
Underground injection class II-V	0.2	0.2	2.1	0.3	0.3
RCRA subtitle C landfills [2]	69.4	94.3	68.1	57.7	74.6
Other landfills	273.6	267.8	294.5	292.9	283.5
Land treatment/application farming	15.0	15.9	13.8	13.9	15.0
Surface impoundments	884.8	724.3	738.1	753.1	754.5
Other land disposal	1,229.5	925.3	1,412.4	1,212.1	670.1
Off-site releases	415.9	415.5	430.9	428.1	464.2
Total transfers offsite for further waste management	**3,668.6**	**3,856.6**	**3,539.7**	**3,580.3**	**3,556.7**
Transfers to recycling	2,316.4	2,425.2	2,123.9	2,138.9	2,055.5
Transfers to energy recovery	354.7	388.2	407.5	422.9	443.3
Transfers to treatment	308.3	346.3	301.9	313.7	314.5
Transfers to POTWs (non metals) [3]	240.5	247.1	236.3	240.0	242.6
Transfers to POTWs (metal and metal compounds) [3]	0.8	0.9	0.7	0.7	0.6
Other off-site transfers	0.2	0.1	–	–	–
Transfers off-site for disposal or other releases	447.7	448.8	469.4	464.1	500.2
Total production-related waste managed	**22,638.6**	**22,494.2**	**23,457.2**	**26,770.3**	**25,885.8**
Recycled on-site	6,294.5	6,539.2	6,826.7	9,948.5	9,766.4
Recycled off-site	2,313.0	2,120.9	2,123.4	2,137.1	2,054.7
Energy recovery on-site	2,109.5	2,309.9	2,307.7	2,666.2	2,477.7
Energy recovery off-site	354.9	387.3	407.0	421.9	442.4
Treated on-site	6,883.1	6,912.0	7,292.9	7,108.2	7,237.9
Treated off-site	522.6	568.6	516.6	526.1	525.9
Quantity disposed or otherwise release of on- and off-site	4,161.1	3,656.4	3,982.9	3,962.2	3,380.8
Non-production-related waste managed	14.7	14.4	203.8	14.4	18.3

– Represents or rounds zero. [1] Air emissions include both fugitive and point source. [2] RCRA=Resource Conservation and Recovery Act. [3] POTW (Publicly Owned Treatment Work) is a wastewater treatment facility that is owned by a state or municipality.

Source: Environmental Protection Agency, Toxic Release Inventory (TRI) Program, "TRI Explorer," <https://iaspub.epa.gov/triexplorer/tri_release.chemical>, accessed June 2017.

Table 418. Industrial Pollution—Toxic Chemical Releases by Industry: 2015

[In millions of pounds (3,329.6 represents 3,329,600,000). Based on 21,898 facilities. See headnote, Table 417]

Industry	NAICS [1] code	Total on- and off-site releases	On-site releases Total [2]	On-site releases Air emissions	On-site releases Other surface impound-ments	Off-site releases/ transfers to disposal [3]
Total [4]	**(X)**	**3,329.6**	**2,865.3**	**667.4**	**752.0**	**464.2**
Coal mining	2121	7.5	7.5	(Z)	0.2	(Z)
Metal mining	2122	1,242.9	1,236.5	2.1	603.2	6.4
Electric utilities	2211	434.8	369.9	132.8	60.5	64.9
Food/beverages/tobacco	311/312	126.1	118.8	45.0	0.4	7.4
Textiles	313/314	2.9	2.5	1.2	(Z)	0.4
Apparel	315	(Z)	(Z)	(Z)	–	(Z)
Leather	316	1.8	0.2	0.2	–	1.6
Wood products	321	9.3	8.9	8.7	(Z)	0.4
Paper	322	162.7	156.8	123.6	1.9	5.9
Printing and publishing	323/51	4.9	4.5	4.5	–	0.4
Petroleum	324	77.5	66.4	38.9	–	11.1
Chemicals	325	499.6	435.8	160.5	21.7	63.9
Plastics and rubber	326	37.4	31.5	31.3	(Z)	5.9
Stone/clay/glass	327	28.9	25.3	20.2	0.1	3.6
Primary metals	331	342.4	191.8	34.8	60.3	150.6
Fabricated metals	332	36.2	19.4	18.4	(Z)	16.7
Machinery	333	6.7	2.5	2.3	(Z)	4.3
Computers/electronic products	334	4.0	2.8	1.1	–	1.2
Electrical equipment	335	4.5	1.3	1.3	(Z)	3.2
Transportation equipment	336	34.4	26.4	26.0	0.1	8.0
Furniture	337	4.9	4.7	4.7	–	0.2
Miscellaneous manufacturing	339	3.3	2.1	2.1	–	1.2
Chemical wholesalers	4246	2.0	0.8	0.8	–	1.2
Petroleum bulk terminals	4247	1.8	1.5	1.5	(Z)	0.3
Hazardous waste	562	208.1	106.1	0.4	0.5	102.1
No codes [4]	(X)	44.8	41.4	–	3.1	3.4

– Represents zero. X Not applicable. Z less than 50,000 lbs. [1] North American Industry Classification System, see text, Section 12. [2] Includes other on-site releases, not shown separately. [3] Includes off-site disposal to underground injection for Class I wells, Class II to V wells, other surface impoundments, land releases, and other releases, not shown separately. [4] Includes industries with no specific industry identified, and uses a double counting algorithm.

Source: Environmental Protection Agency, Toxic Release Inventory (TRI) Program, "TRI Explorer," <https://iaspub.epa.gov/triexplorer/tri_release.chemical>, accessed June 2017.

Table 419. Pollution—Toxic Chemical Releases by State and Outlying Area: 2015

[In millions of pounds (3,329.6 represents 3,329,600,000). Based on reports filed as required by Section 313 of the EPCRA. See headnote, Table 417]

State and outlying areas	Total on- and off-site releases	On-site releases or other disposal			Off-site releases/ transfers to disposal	State and outlying areas	Total on- and off-site releases	On-site releases or other disposal			Off-site releases/ transfers to disposal
		Total[2]	Total air emissions	Other surface impoundments				Total[2]	Total air emissions	Other surface impoundments	
Total[1]	3,329.6	2,865.3	667.4	752.0	464.2	MO	75.5	70.4	10.3	40.4	5.1
U.S. total	3,327.0	2,863.0	665.3	752.0	464.1	MT	38.4	37.3	1.9	6.8	1.1
AL	82.4	69.7	33.6	7.9	12.7	NE	20.8	19.0	5.4	(Z)	1.8
AK	586.4	585.7	0.5	277.6	0.7	NV	323.5	318.7	1.6	186.5	4.8
AZ	85.5	84.0	2.3	32.3	1.5	NH	0.5	0.3	0.3	–	0.1
AR	31.5	28.2	14.4	2.8	3.3	NJ	74.6	6.8	1.9	–	67.8
CA	31.1	26.7	7.8	0.1	4.4	NM	16.3	13.2	0.6	0.6	3.0
CO	27.2	21.7	2.1	6.5	5.5	NY	15.3	11.7	5.4	(Z)	3.5
CT	1.5	0.8	0.7	–	0.7	NC	60.2	38.4	20.4	2.4	21.7
DE	6.2	4.6	0.7	(Z)	1.6	ND	45.5	35.5	21.5	2.9	10.0
DC	(Z)	(Z)	(Z)	(Z)	(Z)	OH	106.3	84.3	37.3	5.6	22.0
FL	59.9	55.2	20.8	0.2	4.8	OK	26.8	24.6	13.8	0.8	2.1
GA	53.9	50.5	34.9	3.7	3.4	OR	15.8	14.6	6.4	(Z)	1.3
HI	2.6	2.4	1.6	–	0.2	PA	65.6	38.3	22.1	0.5	27.3
ID	46.8	46.3	4.6	12.3	0.5	RI	0.5	0.3	0.3	–	0.2
IL	115.3	75.1	25.4	5.0	40.2	SC	38.3	30.3	22.7	0.9	7.9
IN	135.7	86.8	34.7	2.4	48.9	SD	6.4	6.3	1.4	(Z)	0.1
IA	35.1	28.5	19.5	0.4	6.6	TN	84.3	71.4	26.8	10.3	12.9
KS	18.3	15.5	8.7	0.4	2.8	TX	232.0	187.6	56.3	3.9	44.4
KY	62.1	54.2	32.1	4.7	7.9	UT	229.2	227.4	8.4	89.1	1.8
LA	139.1	129.5	50.3	3.3	9.6	VT	0.4	0.2	(Z)	–	0.1
ME	9.0	6.3	2.8	–	2.6	VA	38.3	34.6	19.7	1.1	3.7
MD	7.7	6.0	4.6	(Z)	1.7	WA	25.6	21.5	8.7	0.5	4.0
MA	3.4	1.5	1.4	(Z)	1.9	WV	31.5	25.5	14.9	0.9	5.9
MI	72.7	46.3	14.3	15.0	26.4	WI	31.8	18.9	10.9	0.1	12.9
MN	25.8	21.1	8.8	7.1	4.6	WY	20.5	17.9	2.0	3.1	2.6
MS	64.2	61.0	18.1	14.0	3.2	PR	2.0	1.8	1.8	–	0.2

– Represents zero. Z Less than 50,000 lbs. [1] Total includes all states, Puerto Rico, and other outlying areas not shown separately. [2] Includes other types of release, not shown separately.

Source: Environmental Protection Agency, Toxic Release Inventory (TRI) Program, "TRI Explorer," <https://iaspub.epa.gov/triexplorer/tri_release.chemical>, accessed June 2017.

Table 420. Hazardous Waste Sites on the Superfund National Priority List by State and Outlying Area: 2016

[As of August 2017. Includes both proposed and final sites listed on the National Priorities List for the Superfund program as authorized by the Comprehensive Environmental Response, Compensation, and Liability Act (CERCLA) of 1980 and the Superfund Amendments and Reauthorization Act (SARA) of 1986. For information on CERCLA and SARA, see <http://www.epa.gov/superfund/policy/cercla.htm>]

State and outlying areas	Total sites	Rank	Percent distribution	Federal	Non-federal	State and outlying areas	Total sites	Rank	Percent distribution	Federal	Non-federal
Total[1]	1,392	(X)	(X)	160	1,232	Missouri	33	15	2.4	3	30
United States	1,371	(X)	(X)	158	1,213	Montana	18	23	1.3	–	18
Alabama	14	32	1.0	3	11	Nebraska	17	26	1.2	1	16
Alaska	6	45	0.4	5	1	Nevada	2	48	0.1	–	2
Arizona	9	43	0.7	2	7	New Hampshire	21	20	1.5	1	20
Arkansas	9	43	0.7	–	9	New Jersey	115	1	8.4	6	109
California	99	2	7.2	24	75	New Mexico	16	28	1.2	1	15
Colorado	21	20	1.5	3	18	New York	87	4	6.3	4	83
Connecticut	15	30	1.1	1	14	North Carolina	39	12	2.8	2	37
Delaware	15	30	1.1	1	14	North Dakota	–	51	–	–	–
Dist. of Columbia	1	50	0.1	1	–	Ohio	43	10	3.1	4	39
Florida	55	6	4.0	6	49	Oklahoma	9	43	0.7	1	8
Georgia	17	26	1.2	2	15	Oregon	14	32	1.0	2	12
Hawaii	3	46	0.2	2	1	Pennsylvania	97	3	7.1	6	91
Idaho	9	43	0.7	2	7	Rhode Island	12	38	0.9	2	10
Illinois	49	9	3.6	5	44	South Carolina	25	18	1.8	2	23
Indiana	40	11	2.9	–	40	South Dakota	2	48	0.1	1	1
Iowa	13	35	0.9	1	12	Tennessee	18	23	1.3	3	15
Kansas	13	35	0.9	1	12	Texas	54	7	3.9	4	50
Kentucky	13	35	0.9	1	12	Utah	18	23	1.3	5	13
Louisiana	16	28	1.2	1	15	Vermont	12	38	0.9	–	12
Maine	13	35	0.9	4	9	Virginia	31	16	2.3	11	20
Maryland	21	20	1.5	10	11	Washington	51	8	3.7	13	38
Massachusetts	34	14	2.5	6	28	West Virginia	10	40	0.7	2	8
Michigan	67	5	4.9	–	67	Wisconsin	38	13	2.8	–	38
Minnesota	25	18	1.8	2	23	Wyoming	2	48	0.1	1	1
Mississippi	10	40	0.7	–	10	Puerto Rico	18	(X)	(X)	1	17

– Represents zero. X Not applicable. [1] Total includes areas not shown separately.

Source: U.S. Environmental Protection Agency, "National Priorities List," <http://www.epa.gov/superfund>, accessed August 2017.

Table 421. Hazardous Waste Generated, Shipped, and Received by State and Other Areas: 2015

[In thousands of tons (33,646.7 represents 33,646,700). Covers hazardous waste regulated under the Resource Conservation and Recovery Act (RCRA) of 1976 as amended. See source for data exclusions]

State and other areas	Hazardous waste quantity			State and other areas	Hazardous waste quantity		
	Generated	Shipped	Received		Generated	Shipped	Received
Total	**33,646.7**	**6,643.8**	**6,215.6**	Montana	6.8	3.5	–
United States	**33,625.9**	**6,626.6**	**6,215.3**	Nebraska	26.8	36.4	43.7
Alabama	709.7	187.4	132.1	Nevada	13.1	15.6	71.2
Alaska	4.0	2.7	(Z)	New Hampshire	3.7	3.7	–
Arizona	38.7	34.1	11.3	New Jersey	333.8	342.8	146.0
Arkansas	338.7	209.6	276.7	New Mexico	5.6	7.3	2.1
California	309.1	603.5	174.9	New York	281.3	140.0	58.2
Colorado	40.4	46.4	45.9	North Carolina	81.2	94.5	21.0
Connecticut	35.9	42.5	39.5	North Dakota	265.1	1.6	0.2
Delaware	12.6	12.3	0.1	Ohio	1,711.1	610.7	673.3
District of Columbia	1.1	0.6	–	Oklahoma	105.3	88.6	210.3
Florida	90.8	41.1	12.9	Oregon	52.8	47.6	48.9
Georgia	172.8	60.0	0.6	Pennsylvania	293.9	264.3	389.9
Hawaii	484.6	0.9	0.1	Rhode Island	7.3	11.2	7.2
Idaho	7.0	5.4	20.9	South Carolina	154.6	181.0	294.8
Illinois	601.5	183.9	297.4	South Dakota	1.9	2.0	0.1
Indiana	930.4	424.8	551.9	Tennessee	47.8	40.0	21.2
Iowa	56.9	55.7	0.3	Texas	16,288.7	796.6	647.2
Kansas	1,280.1	91.7	139.4	Utah	33.9	65.1	155.1
Kentucky	135.1	170.2	79.4	Vermont	288.0	19.1	1.8
Louisiana	5,010.2	600.5	490.9	Virginia	62.4	61.0	0.5
Maine	2.6	2.5	0.5	Washington	135.5	74.7	25.8
Maryland	125.8	128.3	43.2	West Virginia	52.2	36.6	10.9
Massachusetts	39.1	44.9	8.2	Wisconsin	172.7	149.5	94.1
Michigan	407.8	344.8	709.1	Wyoming	7.3	7.0	–
Minnesota	120.9	53.2	30.0	Guam	0.1	0.1	(Z)
Mississippi	1,946.3	85.1	20.2	Puerto Rico	20.3	16.7	0.3
Missouri	291.1	94.2	206.4	Virgin Islands	0.3	0.3	–

– Represents zero. Z Less than 50.

Source: U.S. Environmental Protection Agency, Office of Resource Conservation and Recovery, RCRAInfo Web, "Biennial Report," <https://rcrainfo.epa.gov/rcrainfoweb/>, accessed July 2017.

Table 422. Oil Spills in U.S. Water—Number and Volume: 2000 to 2015

[Based on reported discharges of oil and petroleum based products into U.S. navigable waters, including territorial waters (extending 3 to 12 miles from the coastline), tributaries, the contiguous zone, onto shoreline, or into other waters that threaten the marine environment. Data from the U.S. Coast Guard, see also *Pollution Incidents In and Around U.S. Waters, A Spill/Release Compendium: 1969–2011*]

Spill source	Number of spills					Spill volume (gallons)				
	2000	2010	2013	2014	2015	2000	2010	2013	2014	2015
Total	**8,354**	**3,008**	**3,223**	**3,077**	**2,413**	**1,431,370**	**207,712,793**	**497,710**	**668,363**	**304,689**
Vessel sources, total	**5,560**	**1,508**	**1,721**	**1,716**	**1,375**	**1,033,643**	**894,934**	**207,106**	**273,432**	**276,059**
Tankship	111	23	20	18	21	608,176	421,583	711	146	461
Tank barge	229	73	100	89	70	133,540	965	19,568	199,667	144,046
Other vessels [1]	5,220	1,412	1,601	1,609	1,284	291,927	472,386	186,827	73,619	131,553
Nonvessel sources, total	**1,645**	**1,008**	**1,048**	**963**	**681**	**373,761**	**206,809,141**	**284,513**	**386,350**	**26,782**
Offshore pipelines	4	34	35	41	25	17	4,627	6,028	5,267	432
Onshore pipelines	21	–	–	–	–	17,004	–	–	–	–
Other [2]	1,620	974	1,013	922	656	356,740	206,804,514	278,485	381,083	26,350
Mystery [3]	1,149	492	454	398	357	23,966	8,718	6,091	8,581	1,847

– Represents zero. [1] Other vessels include commercial vessels, fishing boats, freight barges, freight ships, industrial vessels, oil recovery vessels, passenger vessels, unclassified public vessels, recreational boats, research vessels, school ships, tow and tug boats, mobile offshore drilling units, offshore supply vessels, publicly owned tank and freight ships, and vessels not fitting any particular class (unclassified). [2] Other nonvessel sources include deepwater ports, designated waterfront facilities, nonmarine land facilities, fixed offshore and inshore platforms, mobile facility, municipal facility, aircraft, land vehicles, railroad equipment, bridges, factories, fleeting areas, industrial facilities, intakes, locks, marinas, MARPOL reception facilities, nonvessel common carrier facilities, outfalls, sewers, drains, permanently moored facilities, shipyards, and ship repair facilities. [3] Mystery spills are spills from unknown or unidentified sources. U.S. Coast Guard investigators are unable to identify the vessel or facility that spilled the oil into U.S. navigable waters.

Source: U.S. Bureau of Transportation Statistics, "National Transportation Statistics," <http://www.bts.gov/publications/national_transportation_statistics>, accessed September 2016.

Table 423. Tornadoes, Floods, Tropical Storms, and Lightning: 2000 to 2016

[424 represents $424,000,000]

Weather type	2000	2005	2009	2010	2011	2012	2013	2014	2015	2016
Tornadoes: [1]										
Number	1,072	1,262	1,305	1,543	1,894	1,119	943	1,057	1,259	1,059
Lives lost	41	38	21	45	553	70	55	47	36	18
Injuries	882	537	351	699	5,483	822	756	641	924	325
Property loss (mil. dol.)	424	422	566	1,107	9,463	1,649	3,642	622	317	181
Floods and flash floods:										
Lives lost	38	43	56	103	113	29	82	40	187	126
Injuries	47	38	27	310	40	25	33	20	50	31
Property loss (mil. dol.)	1,255	1,538	1,050	3,927	7,978	494	2,173	2,626	2,277	10,708
North Atlantic tropical cyclones and hurricanes: [2]	15	27	11	21	20	19	15	9	12	16
Hurricanes	8	15	3	12	7	10	2	6	4	7
Lives lost	–	1,016	2	–	9	4	1	–	14	11
Property loss (mil. dol.)	8	93,064	1	15	344	172	10	3	41	3,054
Lightning:										
Deaths	51	38	34	29	26	28	23	26	27	38
Injuries	364	309	201	182	187	139	145	154	130	120

– Represents zero. [1] Source: U.S. National Weather Service, <http://www.spc.noaa.gov/climo/online/monthly/newm.html>. A violent, rotating column of air descending from a cumulonimbus cloud in the form of a tubular- or funnel-shaped cloud, usually characterized by movements along a narrow path and wind speeds from 100 to over 300 miles per hour. Also known as a "twister" or "waterspout." [2] Tropical cyclones include depressions, storms and hurricanes. Fatalities are assumed to be caused by wind-driven debris or structural failure due to winds. For data on individual hurricanes, see National Hurricane Center (NHC) at <http://www.nhc.noaa.gov/>.

Source: Except as noted, U.S. National Oceanic and Atmospheric Administration (NOAA), National Weather Service (NWS), Office of Climate, Water, and Weather Services, "Natural Hazard Statistics," <http://www.nws.noaa.gov/om/hazstats.shtml>, accessed July 2017.

Table 424. Number of Earthquakes in the United States: 2000 to 2012

[The United States Geological Survey (USGS) detects but does not generally locate mine blasts (explosions) throughout the United States on any given business day. For more information, see "Routine United States Mining Seismicity" at <http://earthquake.usgs.gov/earthquakes/eqarchives/mineblast/>. For information on "Top Earthquake States," see <http://earthquake.usgs.gov/earthquakes/states/top_states.php>]

Magnitude	2000	2004	2005	2006	2007	2008	2009	2010	2011	2012	Top earthquake states	1974–2003 [1]
Total	2,342	3,550	3,685	2,783	2,791	3,618	4,262	8,496	5,237	3,365	Total	21,080
8.0 to 9.9	–	–	–	–	–	–	–	–	–	–	AK	[2] 12,053
7.0 to 7.9	–	–	1	–	1	–	–	1	1	–	CA	4,895
6.0 to 6.9	6	2	4	7	9	9	4	8	3	4	HI	1,533
5.0 to 5.9	63	25	47	51	72	85	58	89	51	25	NV	778
4.0 to 4.9	281	284	345	346	366	432	288	631	347	250	WA	424
3.0 to 3.9	917	1,362	1,475	1,213	1,137	1,486	1,492	3,584	1,838	1,096	ID	404
2.0 to 2.9	660	1,336	1,738	1,145	1,173	1,573	2,379	4,132	2,941	1,951	WY	217
1.0 to 1.9	–	1	2	7	11	13	26	39	47	34	MT	186
0.1 to 0.9	–	–	–	1	–	–	1	–	1	–	UT	139
No magnitude	415	540	73	13	22	20	14	12	8	5	OR	73

– Represents zero. [1] The total number represents earthquakes of a magnitude range of 3.5 and greater. [2] The number of earthquakes is underreported. Events in the magnitude range of 3.5 to 4.0 in the Aleutian Islands are not recorded on enough seismograph stations to be located.

Source: U.S. Geological Survey, *Earthquake Facts and Statistics*, <http://earthquake.usgs.gov/earthquakes>, accessed August 2016.

Table 425. Wildland Fires, Number, and Acres: 1970 to 2016

[Acres in thousands (3,278.6 represents 3,278,600). As of December 31. Wildland fire is any nonstructural fire that occurs in the wildland. Wildland fires include prescribed fires and wildfires (wildfires are unplanned and unwanted, and include unauthorized human-caused fires, and escaped prescribed fire projects)]

Year	Total [1] Fires	Acres (1,000)	Year	Total [1] Fires	Acres (1,000)	State	Wildfire [1] Fires	Acres (1,000)	Prescribed [2] Fires	Acres (1,000)
1970	121,736	3,278.6	2005	66,753	8,689.4	Total	67,743	5,510.0	83,005	4,015.5
1975	134,872	1,791.3	2006	96,385	9,873.7	OK	1,938	767.8	52	7.0
1980	234,892	5,260.8	2007	85,705	9,328.0	CA	7,349	560.8	501	47.0
1985	82,591	2,896.1	2008	78,949	5,292.5	AK	572	496.5	15	33.6
1990	66,481	4,621.6	2009	78,792	5,921.8	ID	630	361.6	271	41.7
1995	82,234	1,840.5	2010	71,971	3,422.7	TX	9,300	356.7	89	98.9
2000	92,250	7,393.5	2011	74,126	8,711.4	KS	75	349.8	38	12.6
2001	84,079	3,570.9	2012	67,774	9,326.2	AZ	2,288	308.2	217	102.0
2002	73,457	7,184.7	2013	47,579	4,319.5	WA	1,272	293.7	86	9.4
2003	63,629	3,960.8	2014	63,612	3,595.6	NV	467	265.2	27	6.7
2004 [3]	65,461	8,097.9	2015	68,151	10,125.1	OR	1,245	219.5	582	84.4

[1] Data are for wildland fires only. Data do not include prescribed fires. [2] Prescribed fire is any fire which is ignited by management action under certain predetermined conditions to meet specific objectives related to hazardous fuels or habitat improvement. [3] 2004 fires and acres do not include state lands for North Carolina.

Source: National Interagency Coordination Center, *Wildland Fire Summary and Statistics Annual Report, 2016*, and earlier reports. See also <http://www.predictiveservices.nifc.gov/intelligence/intelligence.htm>.

ProQuest Statistical Abstract of the United States: 2018

Table 426. Major U.S. Weather and Climate Disasters: 2016

[2.4 represents $2,400,000,000. Cost in CPI-adjusted dollars. Covers only weather and climate related disasters costing $1 billion or more. See source for more information]

Event	Description	Time period	Estimated cost (bil. dol.)	Deaths (number)
Western/Southeast Wildfires..........	Western and Southern states experienced an active wildfire season with over 5.0 million acres burned nationally. Most notable was the firestorm that impacted Gatlinburg, Tennessee with hurricane-force wind gusts in extremely dry conditions creating volatile wildfire behavior. These wildfires destroyed nearly 2,500 structures and caused 14 fatalities. The drought conditions in many areas of the Southeast and California worsened the wildfire potential.	June 1-Dec. 31, 2016	2.4	21
West/Northeast/Southeast Drought......	California's 5-year drought persisted during 2016 while new areas of extreme drought developed in states across the Northeast and Southeast. The long-term impacts of the drought in California have damaged forests where 100+ million trees have perished and are a public safety hazard. The agricultural impacts were reduced in California as water prices and crop fallowing declined. However, agricultural impacts developed in Northeast and Southeast due to stressed water supplies.	Jan. 1-Dec. 31, 2016	3.5	–
Hurricane Matthew......	Hurricane Matthew paralleled the Southeast coast from FL to NC causing widespread damage from wind, storm surge and inland flooding. The most costly impacts were due to historic levels of river flooding in eastern NC where 100,000 homes, businesses and other structures were damaged.	October 8-12, 2016	10.1	49
Louisiana Flooding........	A historic flood devastated a large area of southern Louisiana resulting from 20 to 30 inches of rainfall over several days. Watson, Louisiana received an astounding 31.39 inches of rain from the storm. Two-day rainfall totals in the hardest hit areas have a 0.2% chance of occurring in any given year: a 1 in 500 year event. More than 30,000 people were rescued from the floodwaters that damaged or destroyed over 50,000 homes, 100,000 vehicles and 20,000 businesses.	August 12-15, 2016	10.1	13
Rockies and Northeast Severe Weather...........	Severe storms across the Rockies and Northeastern states (CO, WY, VA, MD, PA, NJ, NY) caused large hail and high wind damage. Storm damage in Colorado was the most costly due to hail.	July 28-30, 2016	1.5	–
West Virginia Flooding and Ohio Valley Tornadoes...........	Torrential rainfall caused destructive flooding in West Virginia, damaging thousands of homes and businesses and causing considerable loss of life. Over 1,500 roads and bridges were damaged or destroyed. The storm system also produced numerous tornadoes causing damage across several Ohio Valley states.	June 22-24, 2016	1.0	23
Rockies/Central Tornadoes and Severe Weather......	Sustained period of severe thunderstorms and tornadoes affecting several states including Montana, Colorado, Kansas, Missouri and Texas. The most concentrated days for tornado development were on May 22 and 24. Additional damage was created by straight-line high wind and hail damage.	May 21-26, 2016	1.2	–
Plains Tornadoes and Central Severe Weather......	Tornadoes and severe storms cause widespread damage across the Plains and Central states (NE, MO, TX, OK, KS, CO, IL, KY, TN) over a multi-day period. The damage from tornadoes and high wind was most costly in Nebraska and Missouri.	May 8-11, 2016	1.7	2
South/Southeast Tornadoes...........	Large outbreak of tornadoes affects numerous states across the South and Southeast. Additional damage also from large hail and straight-line wind during the multi-day thunderstorm event.	April 26-May 2, 2016	2.4	6
Houston Flooding...........	A period of extreme rainfall up to 17 inches created widespread urban flooding in Houston and surrounding suburbs. Thousands of homes and businesses were damaged and more than 1,800 high water rescues were conducted.	April 17-18, 2016	2.7	8
North/Central Texas Hail Storm...........	Widespread severe hail damage across north and central Texas including the cities of Plano, Wylie, Frisco, Allen, and San Antonio. In San Antonio the National Weather Service verified reports of hail size reaching 4.5 inches in diameter.	April 10-12, 2016	3.5	–
North Texas Hail Storm...........	Large hail and strong winds caused considerable damage in heavily populated areas of north Texas. This damage was most notable in the cities of Dallas, Fort Worth and Plano.	March 23-24, 2016	2.1	–
Southern Severe Weather...........	Severe hail impacts the Fort Worth and Arlington metro region in Texas. Additional large hail and high wind damage occurred in other locations of Texas, Louisiana, and Mississippi.	March 17-18, 2016	1.2	1
Texas and Louisiana Flooding...........	Multiple days of heavy rainfall averaging 15 to 20 inches led to widespread flooding along the Sabine River basin on the Texas and Louisiana border. This prompted numerous evacuations, high-water rescues and destruction, as more than 1,000 homes and businesses were damaged or destroyed.	March 8-12, 2016	2.3	5
Southeast and Eastern Tornadoes........	Early outbreak of tornadoes and severe weather across many southern and eastern states including (AL, CT, FL, GA, LA, MA, MD, MS, NC, NJ, NY, PA, SC, TX, VA). There were at least 50 confirmed tornadoes.	February 22-25, 2016	1.1	10

– Represents zero.

Source: U.S. National Oceanic and Atmospheric Administration, National Centers for Environmental Information, "Billion-Dollar Weather and Climate Disasters, 1980-2017," <http://www.ncdc.noaa.gov/billions/events>, accessed May 2017.

Table 427. Highest and Lowest Temperatures by State Through 2016

[Data have been evaluated by the National Oceanic and Atmospheric Administration National Climatic Data Center, and/or by the State Climate Extremes Committee and determined to be valid. The data may come from sources other than official NOAA-supervised weather stations, but are archived, officially recognized observations]

State	Highest temperatures			Lowest temperatures		
	Station	Temperature (°F)	Date	Station	Temperature (°F)	Date
U.S...........	**Greenland Ranch, CA**	**134**	**July 10, 1913**	**Prospect Creek Camp, AK**	**-80**	**Jan. 23, 1971**
AL............	Centerville	112	Sep. 5, 1925	New Market	-27	Jan. 30, 1966
AK............	Fort Yukon	100	June 27, 1915	Prospect Creek Camp	-80	Jan. 23, 1971
AZ............	Lake Havasu City	128	June 29, 1994	Hawley Lake	-40	Jan. 7, 1971
AR............	Ozark	120	Aug. 10, 1936	Gravette	-29	Feb. 13, 1905
CA............	Greenland Ranch	134	July 10, 1913	Boca	-45	Jan. 20, 1937
CO...........	Sedgwick	114	[1] July 11, 1954	Maybell	-61	Feb. 1, 1985
CT............	Danbury	106	[1] July 15, 1995	Coventry	-32	[1] Jan. 22, 1961
DE............	Millsboro	110	July 21, 1930	Millsboro	-17	Jan. 17, 1893
FL............	Monticello	109	June 29, 1931	Tallahassee	-2	Feb. 13, 1899
GA...........	Greenville 2 NNW	112	[1] Aug. 20, 1983	CCC Camp F-16	-17	Jan. 27, 1940
HI............	Pahala	100	Apr. 27, 1931	Mauna Kea Obs. 111.2	12	May 17, 1979
ID............	Orofino	118	July 28, 1934	Island Park Dam	-60	Jan. 18, 1943
IL............	East St. Louis	117	July 14, 1954	Congerville	-36	Jan. 5, 1999
IN............	Collegeville	116	July 14, 1936	New Whiteland	-36	Jan. 19, 1994
IA............	Keokuk	118	July 20, 1934	Elkader	-47	[1] Feb. 3, 1996
KS............	Alton	121	July 24, 1936	Lebanon	-40	Feb. 13, 1905
KY............	Greensburg	114	July 28, 1930	Shelbyville	-37	Jan. 19, 1994
LA............	Plain Dealing	114	Aug. 10, 1936	Minden	-16	Feb. 13, 1899
ME..........	North Bridgton	105	[1] July 10, 1911	Big Black River	-48	Jan. 16, 2009
MD..........	Cumberland & Frederick	109	[1] July 10, 1936	Oakland	-40	Jan. 13, 1912
MA..........	New Bedford & Chester	107	[1] Aug. 2, 1975	Chester	-35	[1] Jan. 12, 1981
MI............	Mio Hydro Plant & Stanwood	112	July 13, 1936	Vanderbilt	-51	Feb. 9, 1934
MN..........	Beardsley	115	July 29, 1917	Tower	-60	Feb. 2, 1996
MS..........	Holly Springs	115	July 29, 1930	Corinth	-19	Jan. 30, 1966
MO..........	Warsaw & Union	118	[1] July 14, 1954	Warsaw	-40	Feb. 13, 1905
MT..........	Medicine Lake	117	[1] July 5, 1937	Rogers Pass	-70	Jan. 20, 1954
NE...........	Minden	118	[1] July 24, 1936	Oshkosh	-47	[1] Dec. 22, 1989
NV...........	Laughlin	125	June 29, 1994	San Jacinto	-50	Jan. 8, 1937
NH...........	Nashua	106	July 4, 1911	Mt. Washington	-47	Jan. 22, 1885
NJ............	Runyon	110	July 10, 1936	River Vale	-34	Jan. 5, 1904
NM...........	Waste Isolat Pilot Plt	122	June 27, 1994	Gavilan	-50	Feb. 1, 1951
NY............	Troy	108	July 22, 1926	Old Forge	-52	Feb. 18, 1979
NC...........	Fayetteville	110	Aug. 21, 1983	Mt. Mitchell	-34	Jan. 21, 1985
ND...........	Steele	121	July 6, 1936	Parshall	-60	Feb. 15, 1936
OH...........	Gallipolis (near)	113	July 21, 1934	Milligan	-39	Feb. 10, 1899
OK...........	Altus Irig Res	120	[1] Aug. 12, 1936	Nowata	-31	Feb. 10, 2011
OR...........	Pendleton.	119	[1] Aug. 10, 1898	Seneca	-54	[1] Feb. 10, 1933
PA...........	Phoenixville	111	July 10, 1936	Smethport	-42	Jan. 5, 1904
RI............	Providence	104	Aug. 2, 1975	Wood River Junction	-25	Jan. 11, 1942
SC...........	Columbis Univ. of SC	113	June 29, 2012	Caesars Head	-19	Jan. 21, 1985
SD...........	Fort Pierre	120	[1] July 15, 2006	McIntosh	-58	Feb. 17, 1936
TN............	Perryville	113	Aug. 9, 1930	Mountain City	-32	Dec. 30, 1917
TX............	Monahans	120	[1] June 28, 1994	Seminole	-23	Feb. 8, 1933
UT............	Saint George	117	July 5, 1985	East Portal	-69	Jan. 5, 1913
VT............	Vernon	107	July 7, 1912	Bloomfield	-50	Dec. 30, 1933
VA...........	Balcony Falls	110	[1] July 15, 1954	Mtn. Lake Bio. Stn.	-30	Jan. 22, 1985
WA..........	Ice Harbor Dam	118	[1] Aug. 5, 1961	Mazama & Winthrop	-48	[1] Dec. 30, 1968
WV...........	Martinsburg	112	[1] July 10, 1936	Lewisburg	-37	Dec. 30, 1917
WI............	Wisconsin Dells	114	July 13, 1936	Couderay	-55	[1] Feb. 4, 1996
WY...........	Diversion Dam	115	[1] July 15, 1988	Riverside R.S.	-66	Feb. 9, 1933

[1] Also on earlier dates at the same or other places.

Source: U.S. National Oceanic and Atmospheric Administration, National Climatic Data Center, State Climate Extremes Committee, "Maximum and Minimum Temperature Records," <http://www.ncdc.noaa.gov/extremes/scec/records>, accessed July 2017.

Table 428. Highest Temperature of Record—Selected Cities

[In degrees Fahrenheit. Airport data, except as noted. Data for each city are shown for varying periods of record; see source for date ranges for each location]

State	Station	Jan.	Feb.	Mar.	Apr.	May	June	July	Aug.	Sept.	Oct.	Nov.	Dec.	Annual [1]
AL.....	Mobile	84	84	89	94	100	103	104	105	99	93	87	81	105
AK.....	Juneau	60	57	61	74	80	86	90	84	78	61	56	54	90
AZ.....	Phoenix	88	92	100	105	113	122	121	117	118	107	96	88	122
AK.....	Little Rock	83	85	91	95	98	107	112	114	106	98	86	81	114
CA. ...	Los Angeles	95	95	98	106	102	112	107	105	113	108	100	92	113
CA. ...	Sacramento	76	76	88	95	105	115	114	110	108	104	87	73	115
CA. ...	San Diego	88	90	93	98	97	101	99	98	111	107	100	88	111
CA. ...	San Francisco	79	81	87	94	93	103	95	98	101	102	86	76	103
CO.....	Denver	74	76	84	90	96	104	104	102	97	89	81	75	104
CT.....	Hartford	72	73	89	96	99	101	103	102	101	91	83	76	103
DE. ...	Wilmington	75	78	86	94	96	100	103	101	100	91	85	75	103
DC. ...	Washington	79	82	89	95	99	104	105	105	101	94	86	79	105
FL.....	Jacksonville	85	88	91	95	102	103	105	102	100	96	89	85	105
FL.....	Miami	88	89	93	96	96	98	98	98	97	95	91	89	98
GA. ...	Atlanta	79	80	89	93	97	106	105	104	99	95	84	79	106
HI.	Honolulu	88	88	89	91	93	92	94	93	95	94	93	89	95
ID.....	Boise	63	71	81	92	99	110	111	110	102	94	78	65	111
IL......	Chicago	65	72	88	91	97	104	104	101	99	91	78	71	104
IL......	Peoria	70	72	86	92	94	105	104	103	100	93	81	71	105
IN.....	Indianapolis	71	76	85	89	93	104	105	102	100	91	81	74	105
IA......	Des Moines	67	73	91	93	98	103	106	108	101	95	81	69	108
KS.....	Wichita	75	87	89	96	102	110	113	111	108	97	86	83	113
KY.....	Louisville	77	77	86	91	95	105	106	105	104	93	84	76	106
LA.....	New Orleans	83	85	89	92	96	101	101	102	101	94	87	84	102
ME....	Portland	67	64	88	92	94	98	100	103	95	88	74	71	103
MD....	Baltimore	75	79	89	94	100	103	106	105	100	99	86	77	106
MA....	Boston	72	70	89	94	96	100	103	102	100	90	83	76	103
MI.....	Detroit	64	70	86	89	95	104	102	100	98	91	77	69	104
MI.....	Sault Ste. Marie	47	49	83	85	89	93	97	98	95	81	74	62	98
MN....	Duluth	48	55	75	88	90	94	97	95	95	86	71	55	97
MN....	Minneapolis-St. Paul	58	61	83	95	98	103	105	102	98	90	77	68	105
MS....	Jackson	83	85	89	94	99	105	106	107	104	96	88	84	107
MO....	Kansas City	74	78	86	93	95	105	107	109	106	95	82	74	109
MO....	St. Louis	77	85	89	93	98	108	115	107	104	94	85	76	115
MT....	Great Falls	67	70	78	89	93	101	105	106	98	91	76	69	106
NE. ...	Omaha	69	78	91	97	101	105	110	107	103	95	83	69	110
NV. ...	Reno	71	75	83	90	97	104	108	105	101	93	77	71	108
NH. ...	Concord	69	67	89	95	97	98	102	101	98	90	80	73	102
NJ.....	Atlantic City	78	75	87	94	99	106	105	103	99	90	81	77	106
NM....	Albuquerque	69	76	85	89	98	107	105	101	100	91	77	72	107
NY. ...	Albany	71	68	89	93	94	99	100	99	100	91	82	72	100
NY. ...	Buffalo	72	71	82	94	91	96	97	99	98	87	80	74	99
NY. ...	Islip	69	67	82	94	98	96	102	100	93	88	78	77	102
NC. ...	Charlotte	79	82	90	93	100	104	104	104	104	98	85	80	104
NC. ...	Raleigh	80	84	92	95	97	105	105	105	104	98	88	81	105
ND. ...	Bismarck	63	69	81	93	96	111	112	107	105	95	79	65	112
OH. ...	Cincinnati	74	75	84	89	93	102	104	102	102	91	81	75	104
OH. ...	Cleveland	73	74	83	88	92	104	103	102	101	90	82	77	104
OH. ...	Columbus	74	75	85	89	93	101	104	101	100	91	80	76	104
OK. ...	Oklahoma City	80	92	93	100	104	105	110	113	108	96	87	86	113
OR. ...	Portland	66	71	80	90	100	102	107	107	105	92	73	65	107
PA.....	Philadelphia	74	74	86	95	97	100	104	101	100	89	84	73	104
PA.....	Pittsburgh	75	76	83	89	91	98	103	100	97	89	82	74	103
RI.....	Providence	69	72	85	98	96	97	102	104	100	88	81	77	104
SC. ...	Columbia	84	84	91	94	101	109	107	107	101	101	90	83	109
SD. ...	Sioux Falls	66	70	88	94	104	110	110	109	104	94	81	63	110
TN.....	Memphis	79	81	86	94	99	104	108	107	103	95	86	81	108
TN.....	Nashville	78	84	86	91	95	109	107	106	105	94	84	79	109
TX.....	Dallas	88	95	97	100	103	112	111	111	110	100	89	89	112
TX.....	El Paso	80	83	90	98	105	114	112	108	104	96	87	80	114
TX.....	Houston	84	91	91	95	99	107	104	109	109	96	89	85	109
UT.....	Salt Lake City	63	69	80	89	99	105	107	106	100	89	75	69	107
VT.....	Burlington	66	62	84	91	93	100	100	101	98	85	75	68	101
VA.....	Norfolk	80	82	88	97	100	101	105	104	99	95	86	82	105
VA.....	Richmond	81	82	91	96	100	104	105	104	103	99	86	81	105
WA....	Seattle	64	70	78	85	93	96	103	99	98	89	74	66	103
WA....	Spokane	62	63	72	90	97	105	108	108	98	87	70	60	108
WV....	Charleston	79	79	89	94	94	103	104	104	102	93	85	80	104
WI.....	Milwaukee	63	68	84	91	93	101	103	103	98	89	77	68	103
WY....	Cheyenne	70	71	76	83	91	100	100	98	95	84	75	69	100
PR. ...	San Juan	92	96	96	97	96	97	95	97	97	98	96	94	98

[1] Represents the highest observed temperature in any month.

Source: U.S. National Oceanic and Atmospheric Administration, *Comparative Climatic Data for the United States Through 2015.* See also <https://www.ncdc.noaa.gov/ghcn/comparative-climatic-data>.

Table 429. Lowest Temperature of Record—Selected Cities

[In degrees Fahrenheit. Airport data, except as noted. Data for each city are shown for varying periods of record; see source for date ranges for each location]

State	Station	Jan.	Feb.	Mar.	Apr.	May	June	July	Aug.	Sept.	Oct.	Nov.	Dec.	Annual [1]
AL......	Mobile	3	11	21	32	43	49	62	59	42	30	22	8	3
AK......	Juneau	-22	-22	-15	6	25	31	36	27	23	11	-5	-21	-22
AZ......	Phoenix	17	22	25	34	40	50	61	60	47	34	25	22	17
AR.....	Little Rock	-4	-5	11	28	38	46	54	52	37	29	17	-1	-5
CA.....	Los Angeles	28	29	35	39	43	49	53	51	50	41	38	30	28
CA.....	Sacramento	20	23	26	31	34	41	48	48	42	35	26	18	18
CA.....	San Diego	29	36	39	41	48	50	55	57	51	43	38	34	29
CA.....	San Francisco	30	31	35	40	43	47	47	48	48	43	39	27	27
CO.....	Denver	-25	-25	-10	-2	22	30	43	41	17	3	-10	-25	-25
CT......	Hartford	-26	-21	-8	9	28	37	44	36	27	17	1	-14	-26
DE.....	Wilmington	-14	-6	2	18	30	41	48	43	36	24	14	-7	-14
DC.....	Washington	-5	4	14	24	34	47	54	49	39	29	16	3	-5
FL......	Jacksonville	7	19	23	31	45	47	61	63	48	33	21	11	7
FL......	Miami	30	35	32	42	55	60	69	68	68	53	39	30	30
GA.....	Atlanta	-8	5	10	26	37	46	53	55	36	28	3	0	-8
HI.......	Honolulu	52	53	55	56	60	65	66	65	66	61	57	54	52
ID.......	Boise	-17	-15	6	19	22	31	35	34	23	11	-3	-25	-25
IL.......	Chicago	-27	-19	-8	7	24	36	40	41	28	17	1	-25	-27
IL.......	Peoria	-25	-19	-10	14	25	39	47	41	29	19	-2	-23	-25
IN......	Indianapolis	-27	-21	-7	18	28	37	48	41	32	20	-2	-23	-27
IA......	Des Moines	-24	-26	-22	9	28	41	47	40	28	14	-4	-22	-26
KS.....	Wichita	-12	-21	-2	15	31	43	51	48	31	18	1	-16	-21
KY.....	Louisville	-22	-19	-1	22	31	42	50	46	33	23	-1	-15	-22
LA......	New Orleans	14	16	25	32	41	50	60	60	42	35	24	11	11
ME.....	Portland	-26	-39	-21	8	23	33	40	33	23	15	3	-21	-39
MD.....	Baltimore	-7	-3	4	20	32	40	50	45	35	25	13	0	-7
MA.....	Boston	-12	-14	1	16	34	41	50	46	37	25	12	-11	-14
MI......	Detroit	-21	-15	-4	10	25	36	41	38	29	17	9	-10	-21
MI......	Sault Ste. Marie	-36	-37	-28	-2	18	26	36	29	25	16	-10	-31	-37
MN.....	Duluth	-39	-39	-29	-5	17	27	35	32	23	8	-23	-34	-39
MN.....	Minneapolis-St. Paul	-34	-32	-32	2	18	34	43	39	26	13	-17	-29	-34
MS.....	Jackson	2	10	15	27	36	47	51	54	35	26	17	4	2
MO.....	Kansas City	-17	-19	-10	12	30	42	51	43	31	17	1	-23	-23
MO.....	St. Louis	-18	-12	-5	22	31	43	51	47	32	22	1	-16	-18
MT.....	Great Falls	-37	-35	-29	-8	12	31	36	30	16	-11	-25	-43	-43
NE.....	Omaha	-23	-21	-16	5	27	38	44	43	25	13	-9	-23	-23
NV.....	Reno	-16	-16	0	13	18	25	33	24	20	8	1	-16	-16
NH.....	Concord	-33	-37	-16	8	21	26	33	29	20	10	-5	-22	-37
NJ.....	Atlantic City	-10	-11	2	12	25	37	42	40	32	20	10	-2	-11
NM.....	Albuquerque	-17	-7	8	18	28	40	52	50	35	21	-7	-7	-17
NY.....	Albany	-28	-22	-21	10	26	35	40	34	24	16	-11	-22	-28
NY.....	Buffalo	-16	-20	-7	12	26	35	43	38	31	20	7	-10	-20
NY.....	Islip	-7	1	5	23	32	42	50	45	38	28	11	5	-7
NC.....	Charlotte	-5	5	4	21	32	45	53	50	39	24	11	2	-5
NC.....	Raleigh	-9	0	11	23	29	38	48	46	37	19	11	4	-9
ND.....	Bismarck	-44	-43	-31	-12	15	30	35	33	11	-10	-30	-43	-44
OH.....	Cincinnati	-25	-15	-11	15	27	39	47	43	31	16	0	-20	-25
OH.....	Cleveland	-20	-17	-5	10	25	31	41	38	32	19	3	-15	-20
OH.....	Columbus	-22	-13	-6	14	25	35	43	39	31	17	-4	-17	-22
OK.....	Oklahoma City	-4	-5	1	20	32	47	53	50	36	16	11	-8	-8
OR.....	Portland	-2	-3	19	29	29	39	43	44	34	26	13	6	-3
PA......	Philadelphia	-7	-4	7	19	28	44	51	44	35	25	15	1	-7
PA......	Pittsburgh	-22	-12	-5	14	26	34	42	39	31	16	-1	-12	-22
RI.......	Providence	-13	-7	1	14	29	41	48	40	32	20	6	-10	-13
SC.....	Columbia	-1	5	4	26	34	44	54	53	40	23	12	4	-1
SD.....	Sioux Falls	-36	-31	-23	4	17	33	38	34	22	9	-17	-28	-36
TN......	Memphis	-4	-11	12	28	36	48	52	48	36	25	9	-13	-13
TN......	Nashville	-17	-13	2	23	34	42	54	49	36	26	-1	-10	-17
TX......	Dallas	0	7	11	31	39	53	60	56	36	27	17	1	0
TX......	El Paso	-8	1	14	23	31	46	57	56	42	25	1	5	-8
TX......	Houston	12	20	22	31	42	52	62	60	48	29	19	7	7
UT......	Salt Lake City	-22	-14	2	15	25	35	40	37	27	16	-14	-15	-22
VT......	Burlington	-30	-30	-20	2	24	33	39	35	25	15	-2	-26	-30
VA.....	Norfolk	-3	8	18	28	36	45	54	49	45	27	20	7	-3
VA.....	Richmond	-12	-8	10	23	31	40	51	47	35	21	14	1	-12
WA.....	Seattle	0	1	11	29	28	38	43	44	35	28	6	6	0
WA.....	Spokane	-24	-24	-10	14	24	33	37	35	22	7	-21	-25	-25
WV.....	Charleston	-16	-12	0	19	26	33	46	41	34	17	6	-12	-16
WI.....	Milwaukee	-26	-26	-10	12	21	33	40	44	28	18	-5	-20	-26
WY.....	Cheyenne	-30	-34	-21	-8	9	25	33	36	8	-1	-21	-28	-34
PR.....	San Juan	61	62	60	64	66	69	69	70	69	67	66	63	60

[1] Represents the lowest observed temperature in any month.

Source: U.S. National Oceanic and Atmospheric Administration, *Comparative Climatic Data for the United States Through 2015.* See also <https://www.ncdc.noaa.gov/ghcn/comparative-climatic-data>.

Table 430. Average Snow, Hail, Ice Pellets, and Sleet—Selected Cities

[Average in inches. Data for each city are shown for varying periods of record; see source for date ranges for each location. T denotes trace. Stations may show snowfall (hail) during the warm months]

State	Station	Jan.	Feb.	Mar.	Apr.	May	June	July	Aug.	Sept.	Oct.	Nov.	Dec.	Annual
AL.....	Mobile	0.1	0.1	0.1	–	–	–	–	–	–	–	–	0.1	0.4
AK....	Juneau	26.1	18.5	13.8	2.6	–	–	–	–	–	1.0	12.6	21.6	96.2
AZ....	Phoenix	–	–	–	–	–	–	–	–	–	–	–	–	–
AR....	Little Rock	2.0	1.6	0.6	–	–	–	–	–	–	–	0.1	0.7	5.0
CA....	Los Angeles	–	–	–	–	–	–	–	–	–	–	–	–	–
CA....	Sacramento	–	–	–	–	–	–	–	–	–	–	–	–	–
CA....	San Diego	–	–	–	–	–	–	–	–	–	–	–	–	–
CA....	San Francisco	–	–	–	–	–	–	–	–	–	–	–	–	–
CO....	Denver	7.5	7.6	11.9	8.0	1.7	–	–	–	1.3	4.0	8.3	7.8	58.1
CT....	Hartford	13.5	12.8	8.8	1.1	–	–	–	–	–	0.2	1.8	9.9	48.1
DE....	Wilmington	6.6	7.3	3.1	0.2	–	–	–	–	–	–	0.7	3.5	21.4
DC....	Washington	5.2	5.6	2.1	–	–	–	–	–	–	–	0.6	2.8	16.3
FL.....	Jacksonville	–	–	–	–	–	–	–	–	–	–	–	–	–
FL.....	Miami	–	–	–	–	–	–	–	–	–	–	–	–	–
GA....	Atlanta	0.9	0.5	0.4	–	–	–	–	–	–	–	–	0.2	2.0
HI.....	Honolulu	–	–	–	–	–	–	–	–	–	–	–	–	–
ID.....	Boise	6.2	3.4	1.6	0.5	0.1	–	–	–	–	0.1	2.2	5.7	19.8
IL......	Chicago	11.6	9.2	6.4	1.4	–	–	–	–	–	0.3	1.8	8.4	39.1
IL......	Peoria	6.9	6.0	3.8	0.7	T	–	–	–	–	–	1.8	6.1	25.3
IN.....	Indianapolis	8.1	6.4	3.5	0.4	–	–	–	–	–	0.2	1.5	5.9	26.0
IA.....	Des Moines	8.5	8.2	5.9	1.7	0.1	–	–	–	–	0.3	2.8	7.4	34.9
KS....	Wichita	4.0	4.3	2.5	0.2	–	–	–	–	–	–	1.1	3.4	15.5
KY....	Louisville	5.1	4.5	2.8	0.1	–	–	–	–	–	0.1	0.8	2.4	15.8
LA.....	New Orleans	–	–	–	–	–	–	–	–	–	–	–	0.1	0.1
ME....	Portland	19.4	17.3	12.7	2.7	0.1	–	–	–	–	0.2	2.8	14.4	69.6
MD....	Baltimore	5.7	7.0	3.4	–	–	–	–	–	–	–	0.6	3.2	19.9
MA....	Boston	13.3	12.5	7.8	1.1	–	–	–	–	–	–	1.2	8.0	43.9
MI.....	Detroit	12.0	10.7	6.7	1.6	–	–	–	–	–	0.1	2.4	9.7	43.2
MI.....	Sault Ste. Marie	30.5	19.5	14.3	5.9	0.4	–	–	–	0.1	2.0	15.4	30.2	118.3
MN....	Duluth	17.4	12.5	14.2	7.6	0.7	–	–	–	0.1	1.7	12.0	16.9	83.1
MN....	Minneapolis-St. Paul	10.3	8.4	10.3	2.7	0.1	–	–	–	–	0.5	7.0	10.1	49.4
MS....	Jackson	0.4	0.3	0.1	–	–	–	–	–	–	–	–	0.2	1.0
MO....	Kansas City	5.3	5.8	2.4	0.5	–	–	–	–	–	0.2	1.1	4.4	19.7
MO....	St. Louis	5.6	4.5	3.8	0.4	–	–	–	–	–	–	1.2	3.7	19.2
MT....	Great Falls	9.7	8.7	10.5	7.9	1.9	0.3	–	0.1	1.1	3.4	7.7	9.1	60.4
NE....	Omaha	7.0	6.8	5.8	0.8	0.1	–	–	–	–	0.3	2.4	5.9	29.1
NV....	Reno	5.2	5.0	3.5	1.1	0.7	–	–	–	–	0.3	1.9	4.7	22.4
NH....	Concord	18.1	15.5	11.5	2.4	0.1	–	–	–	–	0.4	3.4	13.7	65.1
NJ.....	Atlantic City	5.4	6.8	2.2	0.3	–	–	–	–	–	–	0.3	2.9	17.9
NM....	Albuquerque	2.2	1.9	1.5	0.5	–	–	–	–	–	0.1	1.0	2.5	9.7
NY....	Albany	16.7	13.9	11.1	2.3	0.1	–	–	–	–	0.2	3.8	13.7	61.8
NY....	Buffalo	24.7	18.3	12.2	2.8	0.2	–	–	–	–	0.5	10.2	23.0	91.9
NY....	Islip	9.2	8.8	5.4	0.5	–	–	–	–	–	–	0.6	4.9	29.4
NC....	Charlotte	1.9	1.6	0.9	T	–	–	–	–	–	–	0.1	0.4	4.9
NC....	Raleigh	2.5	2.4	1.0	–	–	–	–	–	–	–	0.1	0.7	6.7
ND....	Bismarck	8.3	7.3	8.4	4.1	0.7	–	–	–	0.1	1.5	6.6	8.3	45.3
OH....	Cincinnati	7.3	6.1	4.0	0.5	–	–	–	–	–	0.2	1.6	4.2	23.9
OH....	Cleveland	14.9	13.4	10.6	2.4	–	–	–	–	–	0.4	5.0	12.0	58.7
OH....	Columbus	9.0	6.8	4.5	0.8	–	–	–	–	–	0.1	1.9	5.6	28.7
OK....	Oklahoma City	2.7	2.3	1.3	–	–	–	–	–	–	T	0.6	2.0	8.9
OR....	Portland	3.1	1.2	0.4	–	–	–	–	–	–	–	0.4	1.3	6.4
PA....	Philadelphia	6.9	7.6	3.5	0.4	–	–	–	–	–	–	0.5	3.6	22.5
PA....	Pittsburgh	12.0	10.1	8.0	1.4	0.1	–	–	–	–	0.3	3.5	8.2	43.6
RI.....	Providence	10.2	10.2	6.8	0.5	0.1	–	–	–	–	0.1	1.0	7.1	36.0
SC....	Columbia	0.6	0.7	0.2	–	–	–	–	–	–	–	–	0.2	1.7
SD....	Sioux Falls	7.0	8.3	8.7	2.9	0.1	–	–	–	–	0.7	5.2	7.7	40.6
TN....	Memphis	1.9	1.2	0.7	–	–	–	–	–	–	–	0.1	0.5	4.4
TN....	Nashville	3.6	2.7	1.3	–	–	–	–	–	–	–	0.4	1.1	9.1
TX....	Dallas	0.9	0.8	0.2	–	–	–	–	–	–	–	0.1	0.3	2.3
TX....	El Paso	1.1	0.8	0.3	0.3	–	–	–	–	–	–	1.0	1.9	5.4
TX....	Houston	0.1	0.1	–	–	–	–	–	–	–	–	–	0.1	0.3
UT....	Salt Lake City	13.1	10.1	9.1	5.1	0.6	–	–	–	0.1	1.3	6.8	13.1	59.3
VT....	Burlington	19.8	17.4	13.8	3.9	0.1	–	–	–	T	0.3	6.3	18.8	80.4
VA....	Norfolk	2.9	2.7	0.9	–	–	–	–	–	–	–	–	1.0	7.5
VA....	Richmond	4.8	4.0	2.1	0.1	–	–	–	–	–	–	0.3	1.8	13.1
WA....	Seattle	4.7	1.6	1.2	0.1	–	–	–	–	–	–	0.9	2.5	11.0
WA....	Spokane	13.0	7.6	3.6	0.6	0.1	–	–	–	–	0.2	5.6	11.6	42.3
WV....	Charleston	10.5	9.0	5.4	0.7	–	–	–	–	–	0.3	2.0	5.3	33.2
WI.....	Milwaukee	14.0	10.7	8.2	1.7	0.1	–	–	–	–	0.2	2.9	10.5	48.3
WY....	Cheyenne	5.8	7.3	11.1	10.3	3.2	0.2	–	–	0.8	4.2	7.2	7.1	57.2
PR....	San Juan	–	–	–	–	–	–	–	–	–	–	–	–	–

– Represents zero.

Source: U.S. National Oceanic and Atmospheric Administration, *Comparative Climatic Data for the United States Through 2015*. See also <https://www.ncdc.noaa.gov/ghcn/comparative-climatic-data>.

Geography and Environment 269

Table 431. Cloudiness, Average Wind Speed, and Average Relative Humidity—Selected Cities

[Airport data, except as noted. Data shown for varying periods of record, see source for date ranges for each location, M = morning. A = afternoon]

State	Station	Cloudiness-average percentage of days annually [1]	Average wind speed (miles per hour, m.p.h.)			Average relative humidity (percent)					
			Annual	Jan-uary	July	Annual		Jan.		July	
						M	A	M	A	M	A
AL.........	Mobile	72.1	7.5	8.6	5.8	87	57	83	60	90	61
AK.........	Juneau	87.9	7.5	7.3	6.6	85	74	84	80	84	72
AZ.........	Phoenix	42.3	6.1	4.9	7.2	47	23	62	32	43	21
AR.........	Little Rock	67.5	7.0	7.7	6.0	84	57	80	62	87	56
CA.........	Los Angeles	59.8	1.9	1.4	2.2	61	54	53	47	68	59
CA.........	Sacramento	48.5	6.4	5.0	7.7	79	45	88	69	72	29
CA.........	San Diego	60.0	6.4	5.2	7.1	75	63	70	58	81	66
CA.........	San Francisco	56.2	10.5	6.8	13.0	87	69	87	66	91	71
CO.........	Denver	68.5	8.0	7.8	7.9	53	43	54	53	49	35
CT.........	Hartford	77.5	7.8	8.2	6.6	77	53	73	57	78	51
DE.........	Wilmington	73.4	8.5	9.2	7.4	78	55	75	59	79	54
DC.........	Washington	73.8	9.0	9.5	8.1	74	53	71	55	76	53
FL.........	Jacksonville	74.2	6.7	7.0	5.9	88	56	87	57	89	59
FL.........	Miami	79.7	8.4	8.6	7.3	82	60	84	59	82	63
GA.........	Atlanta	69.9	8.3	9.3	7.2	82	55	79	59	86	58
HI.........	Honolulu	75.3	10.3	8.5	11.9	75	56	80	61	71	53
ID.........	Boise	67.1	7.6	6.5	7.5	66	42	79	70	50	20
IL.........	Chicago	77.0	9.9	11.2	8.2	80	60	78	68	81	56
IL.........	Peoria	73.9	8.4	9.5	6.5	83	61	80	70	86	58
IN.........	Indianapolis	76.0	9.5	10.9	7.6	82	60	81	70	83	58
IA.........	Des Moines	71.3	9.9	10.6	8.3	81	60	78	68	84	58
KS.........	Wichita	64.9	11.5	11.1	10.9	80	55	79	62	80	50
KY.........	Louisville	74.6	7.8	9.0	6.6	80	57	78	64	82	56
LA.........	New Orleans	72.3	8.0	9.1	5.9	87	62	84	65	90	65
ME.........	Portland	72.3	8.0	8.2	6.9	78	59	75	60	79	60
MD.........	Baltimore	71.2	7.3	7.9	6.3	77	53	73	57	79	52
MA.........	Boston	73.2	11.5	12.6	10.3	72	57	69	58	73	56
MI.........	Detroit	79.5	9.5	11.2	8.0	80	59	80	69	80	54
MI.........	Sault Ste. Marie	81.9	7.8	7.9	6.8	84	65	80	73	87	61
MN.........	Duluth	79.0	10.1	10.6	8.6	82	63	78	70	86	60
MN.........	Minneapolis-St. Paul	74.0	9.7	9.7	8.8	79	59	76	68	81	54
MS.........	Jackson	69.6	6.1	7.1	4.5	90	57	85	63	93	59
MO.........	Kansas City	67.1	10.4	11.0	9.0	81	60	77	64	85	59
MO.........	St. Louis	72.4	9.1	10.1	7.6	81	58	79	66	82	55
MT.........	Great Falls	78.4	11.5	14.0	9.1	65	46	65	61	62	30
NE.........	Omaha	69.6	10.0	10.2	8.5	82	59	79	66	85	57
NV.........	Reno	56.7	6.4	4.5	7.2	65	31	76	50	56	18
NH.........	Concord	75.3	6.0	6.5	5.1	80	53	76	59	81	51
NJ.........	Atlantic City	74.2	8.7	9.5	7.4	80	56	78	58	82	57
NM.........	Albuquerque	54.2	8.2	7.3	8.2	54	29	64	40	55	28
NY.........	Albany	81.1	7.9	8.7	6.7	79	57	77	64	79	54
NY.........	Buffalo	85.2	10.3	12.5	9.0	79	62	79	72	78	55
NY.........	Islip [2]	73.8	9.0	9.9	7.8	76	58	75	59	77	59
NC.........	Charlotte	70.2	6.4	6.6	5.7	81	53	78	54	85	55
NC.........	Raleigh	69.7	6.6	7.0	6.1	83	53	79	54	87	56
ND.........	Bismarck	74.5	9.4	9.3	8.6	81	58	77	70	85	49
OH.........	Cincinnati	77.8	8.3	9.7	6.6	81	59	80	68	84	56
OH.........	Cleveland	81.9	9.6	11.3	7.9	79	61	79	71	80	56
OH.........	Columbus	80.3	7.6	9.2	6.1	80	58	78	68	82	55
OK.........	Oklahoma City	61.9	11.3	11.6	9.9	80	55	78	59	82	51
OR.........	Portland	81.3	7.5	9.1	7.1	83	59	85	76	78	44
PA.........	Philadelphia	74.5	9.3	9.9	8.4	76	54	74	59	78	53
PA.........	Pittsburgh	83.8	7.9	9.3	6.3	79	57	77	66	82	54
RI.........	Providence	73.2	9.3	9.7	8.5	75	55	71	57	77	56
SC.........	Columbia	68.5	6.2	6.7	5.7	85	50	82	53	86	53
SD.........	Sioux Falls	71.2	10.3	10.4	9.2	82	60	77	68	84	55
TN.........	Memphis	67.7	8.1	9.0	6.9	80	56	77	62	84	57
TN.........	Nashville	72.0	7.1	8.1	5.9	84	57	80	64	87	56
TX.........	Dallas	63.0	9.5	8.8	8.9	78	54	76	58	77	50
TX.........	El Paso	47.1	8.1	7.3	7.6	51	27	59	34	57	29
TX.........	Houston	75.3	7.5	7.9	6.2	89	59	85	62	93	57
UT.........	Salt Lake City	65.8	8.4	6.6	9.2	64	43	78	70	48	21
VT.........	Burlington	84.1	8.3	9.3	7.1	77	58	74	65	77	53
VA.........	Norfolk	71.0	9.6	10.1	8.5	78	57	75	59	80	59
VA.........	Richmond	72.7	7.7	8.2	6.9	81	53	78	55	83	55
WA.........	Seattle-Tacoma	84.2	7.9	8.4	7.4	83	63	83	76	81	49
WA.........	Spokane	76.4	8.8	8.3	8.7	75	52	86	80	61	27
WV.........	Charleston	82.2	4.5	5.7	3.5	83	56	78	62	90	58
WI.........	Milwaukee	75.3	10.2	11.1	8.9	80	63	76	69	81	60
WY.........	Cheyenne	71.0	12.3	14.6	10.0	62	45	56	51	65	38
PR.........	San Juan	80.0	7.8	7.7	9.4	79	66	81	65	78	67

[1] Percent of days that are either partly cloudy or cloudy. [2] La Guardia data for cloudiness.

Source: U.S. National Oceanic and Atmospheric Administration, *Comparative Climatic Data For the United States Through 2015*. See also <https://www.ncdc.noaa.gov/ghcn/comparative-climatic-data>.

Table 432. Drought Conditions—Area and Population Impacted by Level of Drought: 2016

[In percent. For continental United States. Data shown for the last week of each month, as of Tuesday. Drought classifications are measured in four intensity levels—D0: Abnormally dry, D1: Moderate drought, D2: Severe drought, D3: Extreme drought, and D4: Exceptional drought. Data are categorical statistics showing percent of the area or population that is in a certain drought category. See source for details, <http://droughtmonitor.unl.edu/AboutUSDM.aspx>. The U.S. Drought Monitor is jointly produced by the National Drought Mitigation Center at the University of Nebraska-Lincoln, the United States Department of Agriculture, and the National Oceanic and Atmospheric Administration]

Week	Area (percent of continental U.S. square miles)						Population (percent of continental U.S. population)					
	None	D0	D1	D2	D3	D4	None	D0	D1	D2	D3	D4
1/26/2016....	71.99	12.53	6.96	3.90	2.32	2.29	73.82	10.93	3.32	2.17	3.17	6.60
2/23/2016....	70.10	15.29	6.85	3.72	1.86	2.19	76.31	8.66	3.32	2.03	3.18	6.49
3/29/2016....	61.10	23.81	9.24	2.09	1.89	1.87	75.02	10.48	3.96	1.61	2.63	6.30
4/26/2016....	60.36	24.26	9.49	2.46	2.33	1.11	56.79	27.44	4.97	2.15	4.01	4.65
5/31/2016....	68.18	19.09	8.55	1.72	1.35	1.11	61.86	20.41	7.40	2.59	3.10	4.65
6/28/2016....	56.61	27.21	10.75	3.07	1.25	1.11	48.11	25.24	13.96	4.89	3.16	4.65
7/26/2016....	49.07	30.19	13.61	4.21	1.81	1.11	44.60	21.85	17.71	7.17	4.01	4.65
8/30/2016....	54.92	25.57	12.25	4.56	1.60	1.11	49.21	20.81	13.59	6.85	4.89	4.65
9/27/2016....	53.60	27.44	10.86	4.90	2.04	1.16	44.07	22.88	14.13	7.89	6.23	4.80
10/25/2016...	55.68	20.40	13.67	6.17	2.54	1.54	47.35	13.44	14.24	12.57	6.99	5.41
11/29/2016...	43.69	24.86	14.85	7.94	5.98	2.68	36.34	15.04	18.63	13.21	9.82	6.95
12/27/2016...	49.19	26.77	13.95	5.56	2.72	1.81	34.67	23.87	19.05	10.39	7.73	4.29

Source: National Drought Mitigation Center, "United States Drought Monitor," <http://droughtmonitor.unl.edu/>, accessed January 2017.

Table 433. Top 20 Significant Flood Event Losses Covered by the National Flood Insurance Program, as of Dec. 31, 2016

[In nominal dollars. Covers period beginning in 1978. A significant event is one with 1,500 or more paid losses, or occasionally one added for other reasons]

Event	Date	Number of paid losses	Amount paid ($)	Average paid loss ($)
Hurricane Katrina............................	Aug. 2005	167,985	16,318,241,618	97,141
Superstorm Sandy............................	Oct. 2012	130,772	8,440,862,275	64,546
Hurricane Ike................................	Sept. 2008	46,668	2,697,504,554	57,802
Louisiana severe storms and flooding..........	Aug. 2016	24,920	2,101,507,447	84,330
Hurricane Ivan...............................	Sept. 2004	28,297	1,612,192,606	56,974
Hurricane Irene..............................	Aug. 2011	44,285	1,342,000,336	30,304
Tropical Storm Allison.......................	June 2001	30,671	1,105,003,344	36,028
Louisiana flood..............................	May 1995	31,343	585,071,593	18,667
Tropical Storm Isaac.........................	Aug. 2012	12,052	555,884,012	46,124
Hurricane Isabel.............................	Sept. 2003	19,939	500,274,351	25,090
Hurricane Rita...............................	Sept. 2005	9,529	474,740,062	49,821
Hurricane Floyd..............................	Sept. 1999	20,439	462,326,389	22,620
Tropical Storm Lee...........................	Sept. 2011	9,896	461,188,144	46,603
Texas flooding...............................	May 2015	6,740	459,675,311	68,201
Torrential Rain – Texas......................	Apr. 2016	7,322	452,569,547	61,810
Hurricane Opal...............................	Oct. 1995	10,343	405,527,543	39,208
Hurricane Hugo...............................	Sept. 1989	12,840	376,433,739	29,317
Hurricane Wilma..............................	Oct. 2005	9,618	365,830,186	38,036
Nor'Easter...................................	Dec. 1992	25,142	346,150,356	13,768
Hurricane Matthew............................	Oct. 2016	9,714	294,575,379	30,325

Source: U.S. Department of Homeland Security, Federal Emergency Management Agency, National Flood Insurance Program Statistics, "Significant Flood Events [since 1978], as of December 31, 2016," <http://www.fema.gov/significant-flood-events>, accessed February 2017.

Table 434. Threatened and Endangered Wildlife and Plant Species: 2017

[As of July 2017. Endangered species: one in danger of becoming extinct throughout all or a significant part of its natural range. Threatened species: one likely to become endangered in the foreseeable future]

Item	Mammals	Birds	Reptiles	Amphibians	Fishes	Snails	Clams	Crustaceans	Insects	Arachnids	Plants
Total listings..............	376	336	139	44	192	53	91	28	88	12	945
Endangered species, total......................	327	298	87	28	114	41	77	24	77	12	775
United States...............	68	81	16	20	92	40	75	24	73	12	774
Foreign.....................	259	217	71	8	22	1	2	–	4	–	1
Threatened species, total......................	49	38	52	16	78	12	14	4	11	–	170
United States...............	27	20	28	15	72	12	14	4	11	–	168
Foreign.....................	22	18	24	1	6	–	–	–	–	–	2

– Represents zero.

Source: U.S. Fish and Wildlife Service, Environmental Conservation Online System, Threatened & Endangered Species, "Listed Species Summary," <http://ecos.fws.gov/ecp/>, accessed July 2017.

Section 7
Elections

This section relates primarily to presidential, congressional, and gubernatorial elections. Also presented are summary tables on congressional legislation; state legislatures; minority and female officeholders; population of voting age; voter participation; and campaign finances.

Official statistics on federal elections, collected by the Clerk of the House, are published biennially in *Statistics of the Presidential and Congressional Election* and *Statistics of the Congressional Election*. Federal elections data also appear in the *Congressional Directory* and in official state documents. Data on reported registration and voting for social and economic groups are obtained by the U.S. Census Bureau as part of the Current Population Survey (CPS) and are published in *Current Population Reports*, Series P20 (see text, Section 1).

Almost all federal, state, and local governmental units in the United States conduct elections for political offices and other purposes. The conduct of elections is regulated by state laws or, in some cities and counties, by local charter. An exception is that the U.S. Constitution prescribes the basis of representation in Congress and the manner of electing the president and grants to Congress the right to regulate the times, places, and manner of electing federal officers. Amendments to the Constitution have prescribed national criteria for voting eligibility. The 15th Amendment, adopted in 1870, gave all male citizens the right to vote regardless of race, color, or previous condition of servitude. The 19th Amendment, adopted in 1920, further extended the right to vote to all citizens regardless of sex. The payment of poll taxes as a prerequisite to voting in federal elections was banned by the 24th Amendment in 1964. In 1971, as a result of the 26th Amendment, eligibility to vote in national elections was extended to all citizens, 18 years old and over.

Presidential election—The Constitution specifies how the president and vice president are selected. Each state elects, by popular vote, a group of electors equal in number to its total of members of Congress. The 23rd Amendment, adopted in 1961, grants the District of Columbia three presidential electors, a number equal to that of the least populous state. Subsequent to the election, the electors meet in their respective states to vote for president and vice president. Usually, each elector votes for the candidate receiving the most popular votes in his or her state. A majority vote of all electors is necessary to elect the president and vice president. If no candidate receives a majority, the House of Representatives, with each state having one vote, is empowered to elect the president and vice president, again, with a majority of votes required.

The 22nd Amendment to the Constitution, adopted in 1951, limits presidential tenure to two elective terms of 4 years each or to one elective term for any person who, upon succession to the presidency, has held the office or acted as President for more than 2 years.

Congressional election—The Constitution provides that representatives be apportioned among the states according to their population, that a census of population be taken every 10 years as a basis for apportionment, and that each state have at least one representative. At the time of each apportionment, Congress decides what the total number of representatives will be. Since 1912, the total has been 435, except during 1960 to 1962 when it increased to 437, adding one representative each for Alaska and Hawaii. The total reverted to 435 after reapportionment following the 1960 census. Members are elected for 2-year terms, all terms covering the same period. The District of Columbia, American Samoa, Guam, and the Virgin Islands each elect one nonvoting delegate, and Puerto Rico elects a nonvoting resident commissioner.

The Senate is composed of 100 members, two from each state, who are elected to serve for a term of 6 years. One-third of the Senate is elected every 2 years. Senators were originally chosen by the state legislatures. The 17th Amendment to the Constitution, adopted in 1913, prescribed that senators be elected by popular vote.

Voter eligibility and participation—The Census Bureau publishes estimates of the population of voting age and the percent casting votes in each state for presidential and congressional election years. These voting-age estimates include a number of persons who meet the age requirement but are not eligible to vote, (e.g. aliens and some institutionalized persons). In addition, since 1964, voter participation and voter characteristics data have been collected during November of election years as part of the CPS. Survey data on voting age population estimates includes non-citizens but excludes members of the Armed Forces and institutionalized populations. Data on percent casting votes excludes institutionalized populations, members of the Armed forces and citizens residing outside the U.S. casting absentee ballots.

Statistical reliability—For a discussion of statistical collection and estimation, sampling procedures, and measures of statistical reliability applicable to Census Bureau data, see Appendix III.

Table 435. Participation in Elections for President and U.S. Representatives: 1934 to 2016

[77,997 represents 77,997,000. As of November, except as noted. Estimated resident population 21 years old and over, 1934-70, except as noted, and 18 years old and over thereafter; includes Armed Forces stationed in the U.S. Prior to 1958, excludes Alaska and prior to 1960, excludes Hawaii. District of Columbia is included in votes cast for President beginning 1964]

Year	Resident population (includes aliens) of voting age [1] (1,000)	Votes cast			
		For President (1,000)	Percent of voting-age population	For U.S. Representatives (1,000)	Percent of voting-age population
1934...............	77,997	(X)	(X)	32,804	42.1
1936...............	80,174	45,647	56.9	(NA)	(NA)
1938...............	82,354	(X)	(X)	(NA)	(NA)
1940...............	84,728	49,815	58.8	(NA)	(NA)
1942...............	86,465	(X)	(X)	28,074	32.5
1944...............	85,654	48,026	56.1	45,110	52.7
1946...............	92,659	(X)	(X)	34,410	37.1
1948...............	95,573	48,834	51.1	46,220	48.4
1950...............	98,134	(X)	(X)	40,430	41.2
1952...............	99,929	61,552	61.6	57,571	57.6
1954...............	102,075	(X)	(X)	42,583	41.7
1956...............	104,515	62,027	59.3	58,886	56.3
1958...............	106,447	(X)	(X)	45,719	43.0
1960...............	109,672	68,836	62.8	64,124	58.5
1962...............	112,952	(X)	(X)	51,242	45.4
1964...............	114,090	70,098	61.4	65,879	57.7
1966...............	116,638	(X)	(X)	52,902	45.4
1968...............	120,285	73,027	60.7	66,109	55.0
1970...............	124,498	(X)	(X)	54,259	43.6
1972...............	140,777	77,625	55.1	71,188	50.6
1974...............	146,338	(X)	(X)	52,313	35.7
1976...............	152,308	81,603	53.6	74,259	48.8
1978...............	158,369	(X)	(X)	54,584	34.5
1980...............	163,945	86,497	52.8	77,874	47.5
1982...............	169,643	(X)	(X)	63,881	37.7
1984...............	173,995	92,655	53.3	82,422	47.4
1986...............	177,922	(X)	(X)	59,758	33.6
1988...............	181,956	91,587	50.3	81,682	44.9
1990...............	185,812	(X)	(X)	62,355	33.6
1992...............	189,493	104,600	55.2	97,198	51.3
1994...............	193,010	(X)	(X)	70,494	36.5
1996...............	196,789	96,390	49.0	90,233	45.9
1998...............	201,270	(X)	(X)	66,605	33.1
2000...............	[2] 209,786	105,594	61.6	98,800	47.1
2002...............	[2] 214,689	(X)	(X)	74,707	34.8
2004...............	[2] 219,508	122,349	55.7	113,192	51.6
2006...............	[2] 224,622	(X)	(X)	80,976	36.0
2008...............	[2] 229,989	131,407	57.1	122,586	53.3
2010...............	[2] 235,225	(X)	(X)	86,785	36.9
2012...............	[2] 240,291	129,140	53.7	122,346	50.9
2014...............	[2] 244,986	(X)	(X)	78,813	32.2
2016...............	[2] 249,485	136,787	54.8	129,833	52.0

X Not applicable. NA Not available. [1] Population 18 and over in Georgia, 1944-70, and in Kentucky, 1956–70; and 20 and over in Alaska and Hawaii, 1960–70. Source: Through 1990, U.S. Census Bureau, "Table 4. Participation in Elections for President and U.S. Representatives: 1930 to 1992," May 1994, <http://www.census.gov/population/socdemo/voting/p25-1117/tab03-04.pdf>. For 1992–1998, "Estimates and Projections of the Voting-Age Population, 1992 to 2000, and Percent Casting Votes for President, by State: November 1992 and 1996," July 2000, <http://www.census.gov/population/socdemo/voting/proj00/tab03.txt>. For 2000-2009, "Annual Estimates of the Resident Population for Selected Age Groups by Sex for the United States, States, Counties, and Puerto Rico Commonwealth and Municipios: April 1, 2000 to July 1, 2009," <https://www.census.gov/topics/population.html>, accessed June 2015. Starting 2010, "Annual estimates of the resident population by single year of age and sex for the United States: April 1, 2010 to July 1, 2016," <https://www.census.gov/data/datasets/2016/demo/popest/nation-detail.html>, accessed April 2017. [2] As of July 1.

Source: Except as noted, U.S. House of Representatives, Office of the Clerk, *Statistics of the Presidential and Congressional Election*, February 2017, and earlier reports. See also <http://clerk.house.gov/member_info/election.aspx>.

Table 436. Resident Population of Voting-Age, Total Votes Cast, and Percent Casting Votes—States: 2014 to 2016

[245,273 represents 245,273,000. As of November. Estimated population, 18 years old and over. Includes Armed Forces stationed in each state, aliens, and institutional population]

State	Voting-age population (1,000) [1]		Total votes cast (1,000)			Percent casting votes for—		
			Presidential electors	U.S. Representatives		Presidential electors	U.S. Representatives	
	2014	2016	2016	2014	2016	2016	2014	2016
U.S.	245,273	249,485	136,787	78,813	129,833	54.8	32.1	52.0
AL.	3,742	3,766	2,123	1,081	1,890	56.4	28.9	50.2
AK.	550	555	319	280	308	57.5	50.8	55.6
AZ.	5,110	5,300	2,573	1,468	2,412	48.6	28.7	45.5
AR.	2,259	2,283	1,131	831	1,069	49.5	36.8	46.8
CA.	29,649	30,157	14,182	7,132	13,414	47.0	24.1	44.5
CO.	4,109	4,279	2,780	2,001	2,701	65.0	48.7	63.1
CT.	2,821	2,823	1,645	1,068	1,575	58.3	37.9	55.8
DE.	731	748	442	232	421	59.1	31.7	56.2
DC.	544	560	313	(X)	(X)	55.8	(X)	(X)
FL.	15,840	16,466	9,420	4,999	8,837	57.2	31.6	53.7
GA.	7,604	7,799	4,115	2,306	3,773	52.8	30.3	48.4
HI.	1,111	1,121	438	370	438	39.1	33.3	39.1
ID.	1,203	1,246	690	435	682	55.4	36.2	54.7
IL.	9,892	9,875	5,536	3,568	5,242	56.1	36.1	53.1
IN.	5,015	5,058	2,735	1,342	2,658	54.1	26.8	52.6
IA.	2,381	2,404	1,566	1,120	1,516	65.1	47.0	63.0
KS.	2,181	2,192	1,184	862	1,174	54.0	39.5	53.5
KY.	3,401	3,426	1,924	1,398	1,765	56.2	41.1	51.5
LA.	3,536	3,568	2,029	1,569	1,749	56.9	44.4	49.0
ME.	1,071	1,077	772	617	772	71.7	57.6	71.7
MD.	4,626	4,668	2,781	1,703	2,708	59.6	36.8	58.0
MA.	5,355	5,434	3,379	2,187	3,379	62.2	40.8	62.2
MI.	7,686	7,737	4,799	3,089	4,671	62.0	40.2	60.4
MN.	4,175	4,232	2,945	1,964	2,860	69.6	47.0	67.6
MS.	2,263	2,267	1,209	626	1,182	53.3	27.7	52.1
MO.	4,671	4,706	2,809	1,426	2,750	59.7	30.5	58.4
MT.	799	815	495	368	508	60.7	46.1	62.3
NE.	1,415	1,434	844	536	788	58.9	37.8	55.0
NV.	2,176	2,263	1,125	543	1,078	49.7	25.0	47.7
NH.	1,060	1,074	744	481	716	69.3	45.4	66.7
NJ.	6,926	6,960	3,874	1,821	3,463	55.7	26.3	49.8
NM.	1,584	1,590	798	512	780	50.2	32.3	49.1
NY.	15,517	15,565	7,802	3,935	7,800	50.1	25.4	50.1
NC.	7,656	7,848	4,742	2,808	4,598	60.4	36.7	58.6
ND.	571	582	344	249	338	59.2	43.6	58.2
OH.	8,956	9,002	5,496	3,000	5,218	61.1	33.5	58.0
OK.	2,925	2,962	1,453	653	1,133	49.1	22.3	38.3
OR.	3,112	3,225	2,001	1,451	1,912	62.1	46.6	59.3
PA.	10,086	10,109	6,115	3,324	5,744	60.5	33.0	56.8
RI.	842	848	464	316	432	54.7	37.5	50.9
SC.	3,748	3,863	2,103	1,156	2,012	54.4	30.8	52.1
SD.	643	652	370	276	370	56.7	43.0	56.7
TN.	5,055	5,149	2,508	1,371	2,391	48.7	27.1	46.4
TX.	19,841	20,568	8,969	4,453	8,529	43.6	22.4	41.5
UT.	2,039	2,129	1,131	566	1,114	53.1	27.8	52.3
VT.	505	506	320	192	320	63.3	37.9	63.3
VA.	6,457	6,542	3,983	2,135	3,782	60.9	33.1	57.8
WA.	5,459	5,659	3,317	2,030	3,141	58.6	37.2	55.5
WV.	1,470	1,456	713	439	686	49.0	29.9	47.1
WI.	4,457	4,491	2,976	2,356	2,774	66.3	52.8	61.8
WY.	446	447	259	171	259	57.9	38.4	57.9

X Not applicable. [1] As of July 1. Source: U.S. Census Bureau, "Annual Estimates of the Resident Population for Selected Age Groups by Sex for the United States, States, Counties, and Puerto Rico Commonwealth and Municipios: April 1, 2010 to July 1, 2016," <http://factfinder.census.gov>, accessed June 2017.

Source: Except as noted, U.S. House of Representatives, Office of the Clerk, *Statistics of the Presidential and Congressional Election*, February 2017, and earlier reports. See also <http://history.house.gov/Institution/Election-Statistics/Election-Statistics/>.

Table 437. Voting-Age Population—Reported Registration and Voting by Selected Characteristics: 2004 to 2016

[215.7 represents 215,700,000. As of November. Covers civilian noninstitutional population 18 years old and over. Includes aliens. Figures are based on Current Population Survey (see text, Section 1 and Appendix III) and differ from those in Table 435 based on population estimates and official vote counts]

Characteristic	Voting-age population (mil.)							Percent reporting they registered							Percent reporting they voted						
								Presidential election years				Congressional election years			Presidential election years				Congressional election years		
	2004	2006	2008	2010	2012	2014	2016	2004	2008	2012	2016	2006	2010	2014	2004	2008	2012	2016	2006	2010	2014
Total [1]	**215.7**	**220.6**	**225.5**	**229.7**	**235.2**	**239.9**	**245.5**	**65.9**	**64.9**	**65.1**	**64.2**	**61.6**	**59.8**	**59.3**	**58.3**	**58.2**	**56.5**	**56.0**	**43.6**	**41.8**	**38.5**
AGE																					
18 to 20 years old	11.5	11.6	11.7	12.2	12.3	11.9	11.7	50.7	49.3	44.2	46.7	37.0	34.4	32.6	41.0	41.0	35.1	36.4	17.1	16.4	14.1
21 to 24 years old	16.4	16.2	16.6	16.7	17.6	17.8	13.2	52.1	56.2	53.1	71.4	44.9	47.2	43.6	42.5	46.6	40.0	55.2	21.9	22.0	17.1
25 to 34 years old	39.0	39.4	40.2	41.2	41.1	42.3	43.8	55.6	56.5	57.0	56.4	50.3	49.8	49.4	46.9	48.5	46.1	46.4	28.3	26.9	24.2
35 to 44 years old	43.1	42.6	41.5	39.9	39.6	39.6	39.9	64.2	61.4	61.7	60.0	59.3	57.3	56.3	56.6	55.2	52.9	51.8	40.1	37.7	32.8
45 to 64 years old	71.0	75.0	78.1	80.7	82.1	82.8	83.8	72.7	70.4	70.4	68.5	69.6	66.3	65.4	66.6	65.0	63.4	61.7	54.3	51.1	46.0
65 years old and over	34.7	35.8	37.5	39.0	42.5	45.6	48.7	76.9	75.0	76.9	75.3	75.4	72.5	73.0	68.9	68.1	69.7	68.4	60.5	58.9	57.5
SEX																					
Male	103.8	106.5	109.0	111.1	113.2	115.6	118.5	64.0	62.6	63.1	62.3	59.5	57.9	57.2	56.3	55.7	54.4	53.8	42.4	40.9	37.2
Female	111.9	114.1	116.5	118.6	122.0	124.2	127.0	67.6	67.0	67.0	66.0	63.5	61.5	61.2	60.1	60.4	58.5	58.1	44.7	42.7	39.6
RACE/ETHNICITY																					
White [2]	176.6	179.9	183.5	185.8	187.1	189.3	192.1	67.9	66.6	66.7	66.3	64.0	61.6	61.3	60.3	59.6	57.6	58.2	45.8	43.4	40.3
Black [2, 3]	24.9	25.7	26.5	27.4	28.7	29.7	30.6	64.4	65.5	68.5	65.3	57.4	58.8	59.7	56.3	60.8	62.0	55.9	38.6	40.7	37.3
Asian [2, 3]	9.3	9.9	10.5	11.0	12.5	13.5	14.9	34.9	37.3	37.2	38.9	32.9	34.1	34.4	29.8	32.1	31.3	33.9	21.8	21.3	19.1
Hispanic [4]	27.1	29.0	30.9	32.5	35.2	36.8	39.0	34.3	37.6	38.9	39.2	32.1	33.8	34.9	28.0	31.6	31.8	32.5	19.3	20.5	18.4
REGION [5]																					
Northeast	41.0	41.2	41.5	42.3	42.9	43.5	43.9	65.3	63.7	65.2	64.0	60.3	59.7	58.3	58.6	57.4	56.6	56.2	42.8	41.6	36.3
Midwest	48.4	49.1	49.4	50.1	50.6	51.0	51.6	72.8	70.6	71.4	70.2	68.3	65.0	65.0	65.0	63.4	62.3	61.4	50.7	45.1	42.3
South	77.2	80.0	82.4	84.2	87.1	89.2	92.0	65.5	65.5	65.3	64.0	62.0	59.4	60.0	56.4	57.7	55.7	54.9	40.3	39.3	38.4
West	49.1	50.4	52.2	53.2	54.6	56.1	58.0	60.1	59.4	58.9	59.3	55.4	55.5	53.7	54.4	54.6	52.3	52.9	42.4	42.7	36.8
EDUCATIONAL ATTAINMENT																					
8 years or less	12.6	12.1	11.1	11.1	10.5	9.9	9.8	32.5	30.1	28.7	24.5	29.5	27.0	24.5	23.6	23.4	21.6	18.3	17.1	15.8	13.2
High school:																					
Less than high school graduate	20.7	20.2	19.1	18.8	18.7	18.6	17.7	45.8	43.2	42.6	39.0	39.6	37.8	37.5	34.6	33.7	32.2	29.3	22.8	20.8	18.2
High school graduate or GED [6]	68.5	70.0	70.4	71.0	70.6	70.6	71.3	61.5	59.5	59.0	57.5	57.5	54.0	53.5	52.4	50.9	48.7	47.4	37.6	35.2	31.5
College:																					
Some college or Associate's degree	58.9	60.2	63.8	65.3	67.7	68.8	69.9	73.7	72.0	71.2	69.8	68.3	65.5	64.0	66.1	65.0	61.5	60.5	47.3	44.4	40.0
Bachelor's or advanced degree	54.9	58.2	61.1	63.5	67.8	72.0	76.8	78.1	76.8	77.2	76.2	73.9	72.5	70.8	74.2	73.3	71.7	71.0	59.5	57.1	52.5
EMPLOYMENT STATUS																					
Employed	138.8	143.8	143.2	138.3	142.6	146.2	150.9	67.1	66.4	67.1	65.9	62.7	61.5	60.4	60.0	60.1	58.6	57.8	43.9	42.5	38.2
Unemployed	7.3	6.2	9.5	13.9	11.1	8.4	6.9	56.3	57.2	56.9	57.0	48.5	52.3	50.7	46.4	48.8	46.1	44.8	28.0	31.6	26.9
Not in labor force	69.6	70.5	72.8	77.5	81.6	85.2	87.8	64.4	62.9	62.8	61.8	60.7	58.0	58.2	56.2	55.5	54.3	53.8	44.3	42.3	40.1

[1] Includes other races, not shown separately. [2] Beginning with the 2003 Current Population Survey (CPS), respondents could choose more than one race. As of 2004, data represent persons who selected this race group only and exclude persons reporting more than one race. The CPS in prior years only allowed respondents to report one race group. See also comment on race in the text for Section 1. [3] Prior to 2004, this category was "Asian and Pacific Islanders," therefore rates are not comparable with prior years. [4] Persons of Hispanic origin may be of any race. [5] For composition of regions, see map, inside cover. [6] The General Educational Development (GED) Test measures how well a non-high school graduate has mastered the skills and general knowledge that are acquired in a 4-year high school education. Successfully passing the exam is a credential generally considered to be equivalent to a high school diploma.

Source: U.S. Census Bureau, "Voting and Registration in the Election of November 2016 - Detailed Tables," <https://www.census.gov/topics/public-sector/voting.html>, accessed May 2017, and earlier releases.

Table 438. Persons Reporting Voter Registration and Whether Voted by State: 2016

[245,502 represents 245,502,000. As of November. See headnote, Table 437]

State	Voting-age population (1,000)	Percent of voting-age population Registered	Percent of voting-age population Voted	State	Voting-age population (1,000)	Percent of voting-age population Registered	Percent of voting-age population Voted
U.S.	**245,502**	**64.2**	**56.0**	Missouri	4,626	72.1	62.8
Alabama	3,717	68.0	56.4	Montana	798	72.8	65.2
Alaska	518	69.1	59.4	Nebraska	1,407	71.7	63.4
Arizona	5,196	60.5	53.3	Nevada	2,234	61.4	53.5
Arkansas	2,216	65.7	56.0	New Hampshire	1,044	73.1	66.9
California	29,894	53.8	48.2	New Jersey	6,862	60.7	53.4
Colorado	4,242	68.2	63.8	New Mexico	1,547	59.2	49.4
Connecticut	2,759	63.9	57.5	New York	15,506	59.0	50.7
Delaware	729	66.8	57.2	North Carolina	7,631	68.1	61.6
District of Columbia	553	75.9	68.7	North Dakota	583	72.8	62.1
Florida	16,202	59.3	52.9	Ohio	8,811	69.5	61.4
Georgia	7,626	64.1	55.7	Oklahoma	2,923	63.7	53.2
Hawaii	1,064	49.8	43.3	Oregon	3,185	67.4	61.0
Idaho	1,224	64.5	58.3	Pennsylvania	9,980	69.2	60.2
Illinois	9,723	68.5	58.8	Rhode Island	836	64.4	55.5
Indiana	4,988	66.1	56.0	South Carolina	3,733	69.0	59.8
Iowa	2,394	69.2	60.7	South Dakota	631	69.3	57.3
Kansas	2,142	67.1	58.0	Tennessee	5,057	64.3	52.0
Kentucky	3,348	67.3	55.3	Texas	20,172	58.1	47.7
Louisiana	3,463	70.6	59.7	Utah	2,096	66.7	58.9
Maine	1,058	78.5	71.3	Vermont	500	70.2	61.0
Maryland	4,623	67.3	59.2	Virginia	6,343	69.4	62.6
Massachusetts	5,374	68.1	61.7	Washington	5,592	69.9	60.5
Michigan	7,624	71.3	61.8	West Virginia	1,434	63.6	50.4
Minnesota	4,190	72.9	65.3	Wisconsin	4,465	74.4	68.7
Mississippi	2,203	78.3	66.7	Wyoming	436	69.7	63.5

Source: U.S. Census Bureau, "Voting and Registration in the Election of November 2016 - Detailed Tables," <https://www.census.gov/data/tables/time-series/demo/voting-and-registration/p20-580.html>, accessed May 2017.

Table 439. Reported Voting and Registration Among Native and Naturalized Citizens by Race and Hispanic Origin: 2016

[In thousands, except percent, (224,059 represents 224,059,000). Data shown for population aged 18 years and over. As of November]

Nativity status, race, and Hispanic origin	Total citizen population (1,000)	U.S. citizen Reported registered Number (1,000)	Percent	Not registered Number (1,000)	Percent	Reported voted Number (1,000)	Percent	Did not vote Number (1,000)	Percent
Total:									
All races [1]	224,059	157,596	70.3	32,622	14.6	137,537	61.4	53,860	24.0
White alone [2]	177,865	127,463	71.7	24,822	14.0	111,891	62.9	41,356	23.3
White alone, non-Hispanic	154,450	114,151	73.9	19,210	12.4	100,849	65.3	33,310	21.6
Black alone [2]	28,808	19,984	69.4	3,732	13.0	17,119	59.4	6,674	23.2
Asian alone [2]	10,283	5,785	56.3	2,467	24.0	5,043	49.0	3,315	32.2
Hispanic [3]	26,662	15,267	57.3	6,394	24.0	12,682	47.6	9,118	34.2
Native citizen:									
All races [1]	204,212	145,351	71.2	28,134	13.8	126,763	62.1	47,782	23.4
White alone [2]	167,069	120,760	72.3	22,458	13.4	106,047	63.5	38,057	22.8
White alone, non-Hispanic	149,815	111,095	74.2	18,356	12.3	98,255	65.6	31,946	21.3
Black alone [2]	26,597	18,512	69.6	3,363	12.6	15,756	59.2	6,197	23.3
Asian alone [2]	3,976	2,046	51.5	830	20.9	1,778	44.7	1,159	29.2
Hispanic [3]	19,848	11,198	56.4	4,754	24.0	9,040	45.5	7,023	35.4
White alone or in combination [4]	170,288	122,837	72.1	23,079	13.6	107,748	63.3	39,095	23.0
Black alone or in combination [4]	28,037	19,428	69.3	3,632	13.0	16,477	58.8	6,665	23.8
Asian alone or in combination [4]	4,750	2,586	54.4	964	20.3	2,238	47.1	1,386	29.2
Naturalized citizen:									
All races [1]	19,847	12,245	61.7	4,488	22.6	10,774	54.3	6,079	30.6
White alone [2]	10,796	6,704	62.1	2,365	21.9	5,844	54.1	3,300	30.6
White alone, non-Hispanic	4,635	3,056	65.9	854	18.4	2,594	56.0	1,365	29.4
Black alone [2]	2,210	1,472	66.6	369	16.7	1,363	61.7	477	21.6
Asian alone [2]	6,307	3,738	59.3	1,637	26.0	3,265	51.8	2,156	34.2
Hispanic [3]	6,815	4,070	59.7	1,641	24.1	3,642	53.4	2,095	30.7
White alone or in combination [4]	10,981	6,827	62.2	2,393	21.8	5,959	54.3	3,336	30.4
Black alone or in combination [4]	2,290	1,507	65.8	396	17.3	1,398	61.1	504	22.0
Asian alone or in combination [4]	6,367	3,783	59.4	1,641	25.8	3,305	51.9	2,164	34.0

[1] Includes other races, not shown separately. [2] Beginning with the 2003 Current Population Survey (CPS), respondents could choose more than one race. Data shown represent persons who selected this race group only and exclude persons reporting more than one race. [3] Persons of Hispanic origin may be of any race. [4] In combination with one or more races.

Source: U.S. Census Bureau, "Voting and Registration in the Election of November 2016 - Detailed Tables," <https://www.census.gov/data/tables/time-series/demo/voting-and-registration/p20-580.html>, accessed May 2017.

Table 440. Vote Cast for President by Major Political Party: 1948 to 2016

[In thousands (48,834 represents 48,834,000), except percent and electoral vote. Prior to 1960, excludes Alaska and Hawaii; prior to 1964, excludes DC. Vote cast for major party candidates includes the votes of minor parties cast for those candidates]

Year	Candidates for President		Vote cast for President						
				Democratic			Republican		
			Total popular vote [1] (1,000)	Popular vote		Electoral vote	Popular vote		Electoral vote
	Democratic	Republican		Number (1,000)	Percent		Number (1,000)	Percent	
1948..........	Truman	Dewey	48,834	24,106	49.4	303	21,969	45.0	189
1952..........	Stevenson	Eisenhower	61,552	27,315	44.4	89	33,779	54.9	442
1956..........	Stevenson	Eisenhower	62,027	26,739	43.1	73	35,581	57.4	457
1960..........	Kennedy	Nixon	68,836	34,227	49.7	303	34,108	49.5	219
1964..........	Johnson	Goldwater	70,098	42,825	61.1	486	27,147	38.7	52
1968..........	Humphrey	Nixon	73,027	30,989	42.4	191	31,710	43.4	301
1972..........	McGovern	Nixon	77,625	28,902	37.2	17	46,740	60.2	520
1976..........	Carter	Ford	81,603	40,826	50.0	297	39,148	48.0	240
1980..........	Carter	Reagan	86,497	35,481	41.0	49	43,643	50.5	489
1984..........	Mondale	Reagan	92,655	37,450	40.4	13	54,167	58.5	525
1988..........	Dukakis	Bush	91,587	41,717	45.5	111	48,643	53.1	426
1992..........	Clinton	Bush	104,600	44,858	42.9	370	38,799	37.1	168
1996..........	Clinton	Dole	96,390	47,402	49.2	379	39,198	40.7	159
2000..........	Gore	Bush	105,594	50,996	48.3	266	50,465	47.8	271
2004..........	Kerry	Bush	122,349	58,895	48.1	251	61,873	50.6	286
2008..........	Obama	McCain	131,407	69,498	52.9	365	59,948	45.6	173
2012..........	Obama	Romney	129,140	65,752	50.9	332	60,670	47.0	206
2016..........	Clinton	Trump	136,787	65,677	48.0	227	62,692	45.8	304

[1] Include votes for minor party candidates, independents, unpledged electors, and scattered write-in votes.

Source: U.S. House of Representatives, Office of the Clerk, *Statistics of the Presidential and Congressional Election*, February 2017, and earlier reports. See also <http://clerk.house.gov/member_info/election.html>.

Table 441. Vote Cast for Leading Minority Party Candidates for President: 1948 to 2016

[In thousands (1,169 represents 1,169,000). See headnote, Table 440. Data do not include write-ins, scatterings, or votes for candidates who ran on party tickets not shown, unless otherwise noted]

Year	Candidate	Party	Popular vote (1,000)	Candidate	Party	Popular vote (1,000)
1948..........	Strom Thurmond	States' Rights	1,169	Henry Wallace	Progressive	1,156
1952..........	Vincent Hallinan	Progressive	135	Stuart Hamblen	Prohibition	73
1956 [1]........	T. Coleman Andrews	States' Rights	91	Eric Hass	Socialist Labor	41
1960..........	Eric Hass	Socialist Labor	46	Rutherford Decker	Prohibition	46
1964..........	Eric Hass	Socialist Labor	43	Clifton DeBerry	Socialist Workers	22
1968..........	George Wallace	American Independent	9,446	Henning Blomen	Socialist Labor	52
1972 [1]........	John Schmitz	American Independent	993	Benjamin Spock	People's	9
1976..........	Eugene McCarthy	Independent	680	Roger McBride	Libertarian	172
1980..........	John Anderson	Independent	5,251	Ed Clark	Libertarian	920
1984..........	David Bergland	Libertarian	227	Lyndon H. LaRouche	Independent	79
1988..........	Ron Paul	Libertarian	410	Lenora B. Fulani	New Alliance	129
1992..........	H. Ross Perot	Independent	19,722	Andre Marrou	Libertarian	281
1996..........	H. Ross Perot	Reform	7,137	Ralph Nader	Green	527
2000..........	Ralph Nader	Green	2,530	Pat Buchanan	Reform	324
2004..........	Michael Badnarik	Libertarian	369	Ralph Nader	Independent	156
2008..........	Ralph Nader	Independent	739	Bob Barr	Libertarian	515
2012..........	Gary Johnson	Libertarian	1,216	Jill Stein	Green	401
2016..........	Gary Johnson	Libertarian	4,081	Jill Stein	Green	1,351

[1] Data include write-ins, scatterings, and/or votes for candidates who ran on party tickets not shown.

Source: U.S. House of Representatives, Office of the Clerk, *Statistics of the Presidential and Congressional Election*, February 2017, and earlier reports. See also <http://clerk.house.gov/member_info/election.html/>.

Table 442. Electoral Vote Cast for President by Major Political Party—States: 1976 to 2016

[D = Democratic, R = Republican. For composition of regions, see map, inside front cover]

State	1976 [1]	1980	1984	1988 [2]	1992	1996	2000 [3]	2004 [4]	2008 [5]	2012	2016 [6]
Democratic	**297**	**49**	**13**	**111**	**370**	**379**	**266**	**251**	**365**	**332**	**227**
Republican	**240**	**489**	**525**	**426**	**168**	**159**	**271**	**286**	**173**	**206**	**304**
Northeast:											
Democratic	86	4	–	53	106	106	102	101	101	96	75
Republican	36	118	113	60	–	–	4	–	–	–	21
Midwest:											
Democratic	58	10	10	29	100	100	68	57	97	80	30
Republican	87	135	127	108	29	29	61	66	27	38	88
South:											
Democratic	149	31	3	8	68	80	15	16	71	58	29
Republican	20	138	174	168	116	104	168	173	118	138	165
West:											
Democratic	4	4	–	21	96	93	81	77	96	98	93
Republican	97	98	111	90	23	26	38	47	28	30	30
Alabama	D-9	R-9	R-9	R-9	R-9	R-9	R-9	R-9	R-9	R-9	R-9
Alaska	R-3	R-3	R-3	R-3	R-3	R-3	R-3	R-3	R-3	R-3	R-3
Arizona	R-6	R-6	R-7	R-7	R-8	R-8	R-8	R-10	R-10	R-11	R-11
Arkansas	D-6	R-6	R-6	R-6	D-6	D-6	R-6	R-6	R-6	R-6	R-6
California	R-45	R-45	R-47	R-47	D-54	D-54	D-54	D-55	D-55	D-55	D-55
Colorado	R-7	R-7	R-8	R-8	D-8	R-8	R-8	R-9	D-9	D-9	D-9
Connecticut	R-8	R-8	R-8	R-8	D-8	D-8	D-8	D-7	D-7	D-7	D-7
Delaware	D-3	R-3	R-3	R-3	D-3	D-3	D-3	D-3	D-3	D-3	D-3
District of Columbia	D-3	D-3	D-3	D-3	D-3	D-3	D-2	D-3	D-3	D-3	D-3
Florida	D-17	R-17	R-21	R-21	R-25	D-25	R-25	R-27	D-27	D-29	R-29
Georgia	D-12	D-12	R-12	R-12	D-13	R-13	R-13	R-15	R-15	R-16	R-16
Hawaii	D-4	D-4	D-4	D-4	D-4	D-4	D-4	D-4	D-4	D-4	D-3
Idaho	R-4	R-4	R-4	R-4	R-4	R-4	R-4	R-4	R-4	R-4	R-4
Illinois	R-26	R-26	R-24	R-24	D-22	D-22	D-22	D-21	D-21	D-20	D-20
Indiana	R-13	R-13	R-12	R-12	R-12	R-12	R-12	R-11	D-11	R-11	R-11
Iowa	R-8	R-8	R-8	D-8	D-7	D-7	D-7	R-7	D-7	D-6	R-6
Kansas	R-7	R-7	R-7	R-7	R-6	R-6	R-6	R-6	R-6	R-6	R-6
Kentucky	D-9	R-9	R-9	R-9	D-8	D-8	R-8	R-8	R-8	R-8	R-8
Louisiana	D-10	R-10	R-10	R-10	D-9	D-9	R-9	R-9	R-9	R-8	R-8
Maine	R-4	R-4	R-4	R-4	D-4	D-4	D-4	D-4	D-4	D-4	D-3
Maryland	D-10	D-10	R-10	R-10	D-10	D-10	D-10	D-10	D-10	D-10	D-10
Massachusetts	D-14	R-14	R-13	D-13	D-12	D-12	D-12	D-12	D-12	D-11	D-11
Michigan	R-21	R-21	R-20	R-20	D-18	D-18	D-18	D-17	D-17	D-16	R-16
Minnesota	D-10	D-10	D-10	D-10	D-10	D-10	D-10	D-9	D-10	D-10	D-10
Mississippi	D-7	R-7	R-7	R-7	R-7	R-7	R-7	R-6	R-6	R-6	R-6
Missouri	D-12	R-12	R-11	R-11	D-11	D-11	R-11	R-11	R-11	R-10	R-10
Montana	R-4	R-4	R-4	R-4	D-3	R-3	R-3	R-3	R-3	R-3	R-3
Nebraska	R-5	R-5	R-5	R-5	R-5	R-5	R-5	R-5	R-4	R-5	R-5
Nevada	R-3	R-3	R-4	R-4	D-4	D-4	R-4	R-5	D-5	D-6	D-6
New Hampshire	R-4	R-4	R-4	R-4	D-4	D-4	R-4	D-4	D-4	D-4	D-4
New Jersey	R-17	R-17	R-16	R-16	D-15	D-15	D-15	D-15	D-15	D-14	D-14
New Mexico	R-4	R-4	R-5	R-5	D-5	D-5	D-5	R-5	D-5	D-5	D-5
New York	D-41	R-41	R-36	D-36	D-33	D-33	D-33	D-31	D-31	D-29	D-29
North Carolina	D-13	R-13	R-13	R-13	R-14	R-14	R-14	R-15	D-15	R-15	R-15
North Dakota	R-3	R-3	R-3	R-3	R-3	R-3	R-3	R-3	R-3	R-3	R-3
Ohio	D-25	R-25	R-23	R-23	D-21	D-21	R-21	R-20	D-20	D-18	R-18
Oklahoma	R-8	R-8	R-8	R-8	R-8	R-8	R-8	R-7	R-7	R-7	R-7
Oregon	R-6	R-6	R-7	D-7	D-7	D-7	D-7	D-7	D-7	D-7	D-7
Pennsylvania	D-27	R-27	R-25	R-25	D-23	D-23	D-23	D-21	D-21	D-20	R-20
Rhode Island	D-4	D-4	R-4	D-4	D-4	D-4	D-4	D-4	D-4	D-4	D-4
South Carolina	D-8	R-8	R-8	R-8	R-8	R-8	R-8	R-8	R-8	R-9	R-9
South Dakota	R-4	R-4	R-3	R-3	R-3	R-3	R-3	R-3	R-3	R-3	R-3
Tennessee	D-10	R-10	R-11	R-11	D-11	D-11	R-11	R-11	R-11	R-11	R-11
Texas	D-26	R-26	R-29	R-29	R-32	R-32	R-32	R-34	R-34	R-38	R-36
Utah	R-4	R-4	R-5	R-5	R-5	R-5	R-5	R-5	R-5	R-6	R-6
Vermont	R-3	R-3	R-3	R-3	D-3	D-3	D-3	D-3	D-3	D-3	D-3
Virginia	R-12	R-12	R-12	R-12	R-13	R-13	R-13	R-13	D-13	D-13	D-13
Washington	R-8	R-9	R-10	D-10	D-11	D-11	D-11	D-11	D-11	D-12	D-8
West Virginia	D-6	D-6	R-6	D-5	D-5	D-5	R-5	R-5	R-5	R-5	R-5
Wisconsin	D-11	R-11	R-11	D-11	D-11	D-11	D-11	D-10	D-10	D-10	R-10
Wyoming	R-3	R-3	R-3	R-3	R-3	R-3	R-3	R-3	R-3	R-3	R-3

– Represents zero. [1] Excludes one electoral vote cast for Ronald Reagan in Washington. [2] Excludes one electoral vote cast for Lloyd Bentsen for President in West Virginia. [3] Excludes one electoral vote left blank by a Democratic elector in the District of Columbia. [4] Excludes one electoral vote cast for Democratic vice presidential nominee John Edwards in Minnesota. [5] Excludes one electoral vote cast for Barack Obama in Nebraska. [6] Excludes one electoral vote cast for Bernie Sanders in Hawaii, one electoral vote cast for Donald J. Trump in Maine, one electoral vote each cast for John Kasich and Ron Paul in Texas, and three electoral votes for Colin Powell and one electoral vote for Faith Spotted Eagle in Washington.

Source: U.S. House of Representatives, Office of the Clerk, *Statistics of the Presidential and Congressional Election*, February 2017, and earlier reports. See also <http://clerk.house.gov/member_info/election.html>.

Table 443. Popular Vote Cast for President by Political Party—States: 2012 and 2016

[In thousands (129,140 represents 129,140,000), except percent]

State	2012					2016				
	Total [1]	Demo-cratic party	Republi-can party	Percent of total vote Demo-cratic party	Percent of total vote Republi-can party	Total [1]	Demo-cratic party	Republi-can party	Percent of total vote Demo-cratic party	Percent of total vote Republi-can party
United States.........	**129,140**	**65,752**	**60,670**	**50.9**	**47.0**	**136,787**	**65,677**	**62,692**	**48.0**	**45.8**
Alabama..............	2,074	796	1,256	38.4	60.5	2,123	730	1,318	34.4	62.1
Alaska................	300	123	165	40.8	54.8	319	116	163	36.6	51.3
Arizona...............	2,299	1,025	1,234	44.6	53.7	2,573	1,161	1,252	45.1	48.7
Arkansas.............	1,069	394	648	36.9	60.6	1,131	380	685	33.7	60.6
California.............	13,039	7,854	4,840	60.2	37.1	14,182	8,754	4,484	61.7	31.6
Colorado..............	2,570	1,323	1,185	51.5	46.1	2,780	1,339	1,202	48.2	43.3
Connecticut...........	1,558	905	635	58.1	40.7	1,645	898	673	54.6	40.9
Delaware..............	414	243	165	58.6	40.0	442	236	185	53.4	41.9
District of Columbia.....	294	267	21	90.9	7.3	313	283	13	90.5	4.1
Florida................	8,474	4,238	4,163	50.0	49.1	9,420	4,505	4,618	47.8	49.0
Georgia...............	3,898	1,774	2,079	45.5	53.3	4,115	1,878	2,089	45.6	50.8
Hawaii................	437	307	121	70.1	27.7	438	267	129	61.0	29.4
Idaho.................	652	213	421	32.6	64.5	690	190	409	27.5	59.3
Illinois................	5,242	3,020	2,135	57.6	40.7	5,536	3,091	2,146	55.8	38.8
Indiana...............	2,625	1,153	1,421	43.9	54.1	2,735	1,033	1,557	37.8	56.9
Iowa..................	1,582	823	731	52.0	46.2	1,566	654	801	41.8	51.2
Kansas...............	1,160	441	693	38.0	59.7	1,184	427	671	36.1	56.7
Kentucky..............	1,797	679	1,087	37.8	60.5	1,924	629	1,203	32.7	62.5
Louisiana.............	1,994	809	1,152	40.6	57.8	2,029	780	1,179	38.4	58.1
Maine.................	725	401	292	55.4	40.3	772	358	336	46.3	43.5
Maryland..............	2,707	1,678	972	62.0	35.9	2,781	1,678	943	60.3	33.9
Massachusetts..........	3,184	1,921	1,188	60.3	37.3	3,379	1,995	1,091	59.1	32.3
Michigan..............	4,731	2,565	2,115	54.2	44.7	4,799	2,269	2,280	47.3	47.5
Minnesota.............	2,937	1,546	1,320	52.7	45.0	2,945	1,368	1,323	46.4	44.9
Mississippi............	1,286	563	711	43.8	55.3	1,209	485	701	40.1	57.9
Missouri..............	2,757	1,224	1,482	44.4	53.8	2,809	1,071	1,595	38.1	56.8
Montana..............	484	202	268	41.7	55.4	495	178	279	35.9	56.5
Nebraska.............	794	302	475	38.0	59.8	844	284	496	33.7	58.7
Nevada...............	1,015	531	464	52.4	45.7	1,125	539	512	47.9	45.5
New Hampshire..........	711	370	330	52.0	46.4	744	349	346	46.8	46.5
New Jersey............	3,638	2,123	1,478	58.3	40.6	3,874	2,148	1,602	55.5	41.4
New Mexico...........	784	415	336	53.0	42.8	798	385	320	48.3	40.0
New York..............	7,117	4,324	2,223	60.8	31.2	7,802	4,380	2,527	56.1	32.4
North Carolina..........	4,505	2,178	2,270	48.4	50.4	4,742	2,189	2,363	46.2	49.8
North Dakota...........	323	125	188	38.7	58.3	344	94	217	27.2	63.0
Ohio..................	5,581	2,828	2,661	50.7	47.7	5,496	2,394	2,841	43.6	51.7
Oklahoma.............	1,335	444	891	33.2	66.8	1,453	420	949	28.9	65.3
Oregon................	1,789	970	754	54.2	42.1	2,001	1,002	782	50.1	39.1
Pennsylvania..........	5,742	2,990	2,680	52.1	46.7	6,115	2,926	2,971	47.9	48.6
Rhode Island..........	446	280	157	62.7	35.2	464	253	181	54.4	38.9
South Carolina..........	1,964	866	1,072	44.1	54.6	2,103	855	1,155	40.7	54.9
South Dakota...........	364	145	211	39.9	57.9	370	117	228	31.7	61.5
Tennessee............	2,459	961	1,462	39.1	59.5	2,508	871	1,523	34.7	60.7
Texas................	7,994	3,308	4,570	41.4	57.2	8,969	3,878	4,685	43.2	52.2
Utah..................	1,017	252	741	24.7	72.8	1,131	311	515	27.5	45.5
Vermont...............	299	199	93	66.6	31.0	320	179	95	55.7	29.8
Virginia...............	3,854	1,972	1,823	51.2	47.3	3,983	1,981	1,769	49.8	44.4
Washington............	3,126	1,755	1,291	56.2	41.3	3,317	1,743	1,222	52.5	36.8
West Virginia..........	670	238	418	35.5	62.3	713	189	489	26.5	68.6
Wisconsin.............	3,071	1,621	1,411	52.8	45.9	2,976	1,383	1,405	46.5	47.2
Wyoming..............	251	69	171	27.6	68.2	259	56	174	21.6	67.4

[1] Includes other parties.

Source: U.S. House of Representatives, Office of the Clerk, *Statistics of the Presidential and Congressional Election*, February 2017, and earlier reports. See also <http://clerk.house.gov/member_info/election.html>.

Table 444. Vote Cast for U.S. Senators, 2014 and 2016, and Incumbent Senators, 2017—States

[818 represents 818,000. D = Democrat, R = Republican, I = Independent]

State	2014 Total [2] (1,000)	2014 Percent for leading party	2016 Total [2] (1,000)	2016 Percent for leading party	Incumbent senators and year term expires [1] — Name, party, and year	Incumbent senators and year term expires [1] — Name, party, and year
Alabama............	818	R-97.3	2,087	R-64.0	Luther Strange [3] (R) 2019	Richard C. Shelby (R) 2023
Alaska..............	282	R-48.0	311	R-44.4	Lisa Murkowski (R) 2023	Dan Sullivan (R) 2021
Arizona.............	(X)	(X)	2,531	R-53.7	Jeff Flake (R) 2019	John McCain (R) 2023
Arkansas...........	848	R-56.5	1,108	R-59.8	John Boozman (R) 2023	Tom Cotton (R) 2021
California...........	(X)	(X)	12,244	[4] D-100.0	Kamala D. Harris (D) 2023	Dianne Feinstein (D) 2019
Colorado............	2,041	R-48.2	2,743	D-50.0	Cory Gardner (R) 2021	Michael F. Bennett (D) 2023
Connecticut.........	(X)	(X)	1,596	D-57.7	Richard Blumenthal (D) 2023	Christopher Murphy (D) 2019
Delaware............	234	D-55.8	(X)	(X)	Christopher Coons (D) 2021	Thomas R. Carper (D) 2019
Florida..............	(X)	(X)	9,302	R-52.0	Marco Rubio (R) 2023	Bill Nelson (D) 2019
Georgia.............	2,568	R-52.9	3,899	R-54.8	David A. Perdue (R) 2021	Johnny Isakson (R) 2023
Hawaii..............	370	D-66.8	438	D-70.1	Brian Schatz (D) 2023	Mazie Hirono (D) 2019
Idaho...............	437	R-65.3	679	R-66.1	James E. Risch (R) 2021	Mike Crapo (R) 2023
Illinois..............	3,604	D-53.5	5,492	D-54.9	Richard J. Durbin (D) 2021	Tammy Duckworth (D) 2023
Indiana.............	(X)	(X)	2,733	R-52.1	Todd C. Young (R) 2023	Joe Donnelly (D) 2019
Iowa................	1,130	R-52.1	1,541	R-60.1	Chuck Grassley (R) 2023	Joni Ernst (R) 2021
Kansas.............	866	R-53.1	1,178	R-62.2	Jerry Moran (R) 2023	Pat Roberts (R) 2021
Kentucky...........	1,436	R-56.2	1,903	R-57.3	Rand Paul (R) 2023	Mitch McConnell (R) 2021
Louisiana [5]........	1,273	R-55.9	820	R-58.8	Bill Cassidy (R) 2021	John Kennedy (R) 2023
Maine...............	617	R-67.0	(X)	(X)	Susan M. Collins (R) 2021	Angus King (I) 2019
Maryland............	(X)	(X)	2,726	D-60.9	Chris Van Hollen (D) 2023	Benjamin L. Cardin (D) 2019
Massachusetts......	2,187	D-59.0	(X)	(X)	Elizabeth Warren (D) 2019	Ed Markey (D) 2021
Michigan............	3,122	D-54.6	(X)	(X)	Gary C. Peters (D) 2021	Debbie Stabenow (D) 2019
Minnesota..........	1,982	D-53.2	(X)	(X)	Al Franken (D) 2021	Amy Klobuchar (D) 2019
Mississippi.........	632	R-59.9	(X)	(X)	Thad Cochran (R) 2021	Roger F. Wicker (R) 2019
Missouri............	(X)	(X)	2,803	R-49.2	Roy Blunt (R) 2023	Claire McCaskill (D) 2019
Montana............	370	R-57.8	(X)	(X)	Steve Daines (R) 2021	John Tester (D) 2019
Nebraska...........	540	R-64.3	(X)	(X)	Ben Sasse (R) 2021	Deb Fischer (R) 2019
Nevada.............	(X)	(X)	1,108	D-47.1	Dean Heller (R) 2019	Catherine Cortez Masto (D) 2023
New Hampshire.....	488	D-51.5	739	D-48.0	Maggie Hassan (D) 2023	Jeanne Shaheen (D) 2021
New Jersey.........	1,870	D-55.8	(X)	(X)	Robert Menendez (D) 2019	Cory A. Booker (D) 2021
New Mexico........	516	D-55.6	(X)	(X)	Martin Heinrich (D) 2019	Tom Udall (D) 2021
New York...........	(X)	(X)	7,801	D-61.3	Kirsten E. Gillibrand (D) 2019	Charles E. Schumer (D) 2023
North Carolina......	2,915	R-48.8	4,691	R-51.1	Richard Burr (R) 2023	Thom Tillis (R) 2021
North Dakota.......	(X)	(X)	343	R-78.5	Heidi Heitkamp (D) 2019	John Hoeven (R) 2023
Ohio................	(X)	(X)	5,374	R-58.0	Sherrod Brown (D) 2019	Rob Portman (R) 2023
Oklahoma..........	821	R-68.0	1,448	R-67.7	James Lankford (R) 2023	James M. Inhofe (R) 2021
Oregon.............	1,462	D-55.7	1,952	D-56.6	Jeff Merkley (D) 2021	Ron Wyden (D) 2023
Pennsylvania.......	(X)	(X)	6,052	R-48.8	Robert P. Casey Jr. (D) 2019	Patrick J. Toomey (R) 2023
Rhode Island.......	317	D-70.6	(X)	(X)	Sheldon Whitehouse (D) 2019	Jack Reed (D) 2021
South Carolina......	1,240	R-54.3	2,050	R-60.6	Tim Scott (R) 2023	Lindsey Graham (R) 2021
South Dakota.......	279	R-50.4	370	R-71.8	Mike Rounds (R) 2021	John Thune (R) 2023
Tennessee..........	1,374	R-61.9	(X)	(X)	Lamar Alexander (R) 2021	Bob Corker (R) 2019
Texas..............	4,648	R-61.6	(X)	(X)	John Cornyn (R) 2021	Ted Cruz (R) 2019
Utah................	(X)	(X)	1,116	R-68.1	Mike Lee (R) 2023	Orrin G. Hatch (R) 2019
Vermont............	(X)	(X)	320	D-60.0	Bernard Sanders (I) 2019	Patrick J. Leahy (D) 2023
Virginia.............	2,184	D-49.1	(X)	(X)	Tim Kaine (D) 2019	Mark R. Warner (D) 2021
Washington.........	(X)	(X)	3,243	D-59.0	Maria Cantwell (D) 2019	Patty Murray (D) 2023
West Virginia.......	454	R-62.1	(X)	(X)	Joe Manchin III (D) 2019	Shelley Moore Capito (R) 2021
Wisconsin..........	(X)	(X)	2,949	R-50.2	Ronald H. Johnson (R) 2023	Tammy Baldwin (D) 2019
Wyoming............	171	R-71.0	(X)	(X)	Michael B. Enzi (R) 2021	John Barrasso (R) 2019

X Not applicable. [1] As of March 16, 2017, see <http://www.senate.gov/pagelayout/reference/three_column_table/Senators.htm>. [2] Includes vote cast for minor parties. [3] Appointed February 9, 2017 to fill the vacancy caused by the resignation of Jeff Sessions. [4] Two Democrats ran for Senate; no Republican challenger. [5] Louisiana holds an open-primary election with candidates from all parties running on the same ballot. Any candidate who receives a majority is elected. No candidate received a majority in the 2016 open-primary and a runoff election was held on Dec. 10, 2016. Data shown are runoff election totals.

Source: U.S. House of Representatives, Office of the Clerk, *Statistics of the Congressional Election*, February 2017, and earlier reports; and ProQuest research. See also <http://clerk.house.gov/member_info/election.html>.

Table 445. Vote Cast for U.S. Representatives by Major Political Party—States: 2012 to 2016

[In thousands (122,346 represents 122,346,000), except percent. R = Republican, D = Democrat, and I = Independent. In each state, totals represent the sum of votes cast in each Congressional District or votes cast for Representative-at-Large in states where only one member is elected. In all years there are numerous districts within the state where either the Republican or Democratic party had no candidate. In some states the Republican and Democratic vote includes votes cast for the party candidate by endorsing parties]

State	2012 Total [1]	2012 Democratic	2012 Republican	2012 Percent for leading party	2014 Total [1]	2014 Democratic	2014 Republican	2014 Percent for leading party	2016 Total [1]	2016 Democratic	2016 Republican	2016 Percent for leading party
U.S......	122,346	59,215	57,623	D-48.4	78,813	35,369	39,927	R-50.7	129,833	61,417	62,772	R-48.3
AL.........	1,934	693	1,234	R-63.8	1,081	332	705	R-65.2	1,890	622	1,222	R-64.7
AK.........	290	83	185	R-63.9	280	115	143	R-51.0	308	111	155	R-50.3
AZ.........	2,173	947	1,132	R-52.1	1,468	578	817	R-55.7	2,412	1,035	1,264	R-52.4
AR.........	1,038	305	638	R-61.4	831	255	510	R-61.4	1,069	111	760	R-71.2
CA.........	12,204	7,393	4,530	D-60.6	7,132	4,068	2,951	D-57.0	13,414	8,624	4,682	D-64.3
CO.........	2,450	1,080	1,144	R-46.7	2,001	936	1,000	R-50.0	2,701	1,264	1,289	R-47.7
CT.........	1,467	884	491	D-60.3	1,068	596	410	D-55.8	1,575	917	558	D-58.2
DE.........	388	250	130	D-64.4	232	137	85	D-59.3	421	234	172	D-55.5
FL [2]......	7,514	3,392	3,827	R-50.9	4,999	2,131	2,713	R-54.3	8,837	3,985	4,734	R-53.6
GA.........	3,553	1,449	2,104	R-59.2	2,306	956	1,349	R-58.5	3,773	1,498	2,272	R-60.2
HI.........	437	285	138	D-65.2	370	235	120	D-63.7	438	316	86	D-72.3
ID.........	635	208	407	R-64.0	435	160	275	R-63.2	682	209	448	R-65.7
IL.........	5,058	2,744	2,208	D-54.2	3,568	1,823	1,722	D-51.1	5,242	2,811	2,397	D-53.6
IN.........	2,554	1,143	1,352	R-52.9	1,342	502	789	R-58.8	2,658	1,053	1,443	R-54.3
IA.........	1,537	772	727	D-50.3	1,120	509	596	R-53.2	1,516	674	813	R-53.7
KS.........	1,058	196	741	R-70.1	862	312	541	R-62.7	1,174	318	694	R-59.1
KY.........	1,745	685	1,028	R-58.9	1,398	508	887	R-63.5	1,765	517	1,248	R-70.7
LA [2]......	1,706	359	1,143	R-67.0	1,569	406	1,031	R-65.7	1,749	530	1,178	R-67.3
ME.........	725	428	266	D-59.0	617	305	228	D-49.5	772	387	357	D-50.1
MD.........	2,586	1,627	858	D-62.9	1,703	978	704	D-57.4	2,708	1,636	962	D-60.4
MA.........	3,184	2,081	698	D-65.3	2,187	1,475	309	D-67.5	3,379	2,345	451	D-69.4
MI.........	4,575	2,328	2,087	D-50.9	3,089	1,519	1,467	D-49.2	4,671	2,194	2,243	R-48.0
MN.........	2,813	1,561	1,210	D-55.5	1,964	986	914	D-50.2	2,860	1,435	1,335	D-50.2
MS.........	1,208	411	704	R-58.2	626	230	329	R-52.6	1,182	450	681	R-57.6
MO.........	2,676	1,120	1,464	R-54.7	1,426	514	838	R-58.8	2,750	1,041	1,601	R-58.2
MT.........	480	205	255	R-53.3	368	149	204	R-55.4	508	206	285	R-56.2
NE.........	773	276	496	R-64.2	536	185	341	R-63.6	788	221	558	R-70.7
NV.........	974	453	457	R-47.0	543	210	305	R-56.1	1,078	508	498	D-47.1
NH.........	682	341	312	D-50.0	481	247	232	D-51.5	716	336	316	D-47.0
NJ.........	3,282	1,794	1,430	D-54.7	1,821	914	877	D-50.2	3,463	1,822	1,542	D-52.6
NM.........	766	422	343	D-55.1	512	271	241	D-53.0	780	437	343	D-56.0
NY.........	7,116	3,898	1,733	D-54.8	3,935	1,788	1,257	D-45.4	7,800	4,202	2,141	D-53.9
NC.........	4,384	2,218	2,137	D-50.6	2,808	1,234	1,555	R-55.4	4,598	2,143	2,447	R-53.2
ND.........	316	132	174	R-54.9	249	96	138	R-55.5	338	80	234	R-69.1
OH.........	5,142	2,412	2,620	R-51.0	3,000	1,180	1,771	R-59.0	5,218	2,155	2,996	R-57.4
OK [2]......	1,326	410	857	R-64.6	653	174	458	R-70.0	1,133	305	782	R-69.0
OR.........	1,708	853	547	D-49.9	1,451	778	583	D-53.6	1,912	1,027	731	D-53.7
PA.........	5,556	2,794	2,710	D-50.3	3,324	1,468	1,833	R-55.2	5,744	2,625	3,097	R-53.9
RI.........	428	233	162	D-54.4	316	193	123	D-61.0	432	264	141	D-61.1
SC.........	1,803	714	1,026	R-56.9	1,156	377	734	R-63.5	2,012	768	1,177	R-58.5
SD.........	361	154	208	R-57.4	276	92	184	R-66.5	370	133	237	R-64.1
TN.........	2,284	797	1,370	R-60.0	1,371	448	849	R-61.9	2,391	814	1,494	R-62.5
TX.........	7,664	2,950	4,429	R-57.8	4,453	1,474	2,685	R-60.3	8,529	3,161	4,878	R-57.2
UT.........	999	324	648	R-64.9	566	183	351	R-62.0	1,114	356	711	R-63.8
VT.........	290	209	68	D-71.9	192	123	59	D-64.4	320	264	(X)	D-82.5
VA.........	3,740	1,806	1,877	R-50.2	2,135	846	1,144	R-53.6	3,782	1,859	1,843	D-49.2
WA.........	3,006	1,637	1,370	D-54.4	2,030	1,048	982	D-51.6	3,141	1,736	1,405	D-55.3
WV.........	641	257	384	R-59.9	439	182	243	R-55.3	686	224	445	R-64.8
WI.........	2,866	1,445	1,402	D-50.4	2,356	1,103	1,233	R-52.4	2,774	1,380	1,270	D-49.8
WY.........	251	58	166	R-66.4	171	38	113	R-66.0	259	75	156	R-60.3

X Not applicable. [1] Includes votes cast for minor parties. [2] State law does not require tabulation of votes for unopposed candidates.

Source: U.S. House of Representatives, Office of the Clerk, *Statistics of the Congressional Election*, February 2017, and earlier reports. See also <http://clerk.house.gov/member_info/election.html>.

Table 446. Vote Cast for U.S. Representatives by Major Political Party—Congressional Districts: 2016

[As of February 2017. Does not include special elections or votes received from endorsing parties. If multiple candidates from the same party ran in the general election, only the candidate with the leading number of votes is shown]

State and district	Democratic candidate Name	Percent of total	Republican candidate Name	Percent of total	State and district	Democratic candidate Name	Percent of total	Republican candidate Name	Percent of total
AL.....	(X)	(X)	(X)	(X)	2d.....	Polis	56.9	Morse	37.2
1st....	[1]	[1]	Byrne	96.4	3d.....	Schwartz	40.3	Tipton	54.6
2d.....	Mathis	40.5	Roby	48.8	4th....	Seay	31.7	Buck	63.5
3d.....	Smith	32.9	Rogers	66.9	5th....	Plowright	30.9	Lamborn	62.3
4th....	[1]	[1]	Aderholt	98.5	6th....	Carroll	42.6	Coffman	50.9
5th....	Boyd	33.2	Brooks	66.7	7th....	Perlmutter	55.2	Athanasopoulos	39.8
6th....	Putman	25.4	Palmer	74.5	**CT**.....	(X)	(X)	(X)	(X)
7th....	Sewell	98.4	[1]	[1]	1st....	Larson	59.8	Corey	33.8
AK.....	Lindbeck	36.0	Young	50.3	2d.....	Courtney	56.4	Novak	33.7
AZ.....	(X)	(X)	(X)	(X)	3d.....	DeLauro	62.1	Cadena	31.0
1st.....	O'Halleran	50.7	Babeu	43.4	4th....	Himes	59.9	Shaban	38.5
2d.....	Heinz	43.0	McSally	57.0	5th....	Esty	52.9	Cope	40.4
3d.....	Grijalva	98.6	[1]	[1]	**DC**.....	[1]	[1]	[1]	[1]
4th....	Weisser	28.5	Gosar	71.5	**DE**.....	Rochester	55.5	Reigle	41.0
5th....	Fuentes	35.9	Biggs	64.1	**FL**.....	(X)	(X)	(X)	(X)
6th....	Williamson	37.9	Schweikert	62.1	1st...	Specht	30.9	Gaetz	69.1
7th....	Gallego	75.2	Nunez	24.7	2d.....	Dartland	29.9	Dunn	67.3
8th....	[1]	[1]	Franks	68.5	3d.....	McGurn	39.8	Yoho	56.6
9th....	Sinema	60.9	Giles	39.0	4th....	Bruderly	27.6	Rutherford	70.2
AR.....	(X)	(X)	(X)	(X)	5th....	Lawson	64.2	Smith	35.8
1st.....	[1]	[1]	Crawford	76.3	6th....	McCullough	41.4	DeSantis	58.6
2d.....	Curry	36.8	Hill	58.3	7th....	Murphy	51.5	Mica	48.5
3d.....	[1]	[1]	Womack	77.3	8th....	Westbrook	32.5	Posey	63.1
4th....	[1]	[1]	Westerman	74.9	9th....	Soto	57.5	Liebnitzky	42.5
CA.....	(X)	(X)	(X)	(X)	10th...	Demings	64.9	Lowe	35.1
1st....	Reed	40.9	LaMalfa	59.1	11th...	Koller	31.6	Webster	65.4
2d.....	Huffman	76.9	Mensing	23.1	12th...	Tager	31.4	Bilirakis	68.6
3d.....	Garamendi	59.4	Cleek	40.6	13th...	Crist	51.9	Jolly	48.1
4th....	Derlet	37.3	McClintock	62.7	14th...	Castor	61.8	Quinn	38.2
5th....	Thompson	76.9	Santamaria	23.1	15th...	Lange	42.5	Ross	57.5
6th....	Matsui	75.4	Evans	24.6	16th...	Schneider	40.2	Buchanan	59.8
7th....	Bera	51.2	Jones	48.8	17th...	Freeman	34.2	Rooney	61.8
8th....	Ramirez	37.7	Cook	62.3	18th...	Perkins	43.1	Mast	53.6
9th....	McNerney	57.4	Amador	42.6	19th...	Neeld	34.1	Rooney	65.9
10th...	Eggman	48.3	Denham	51.7	20th...	Hastings	80.3	Stein	19.7
11th...	DeSaulnier	72.1	Petersen	27.9	21st...	Frankel	62.7	Spain	35.1
12th...	Pelosi	80.9	[1]	[1]	22d..	Deutch	58.9	McGee	41.1
13th...	Lee	90.8	Caro	9.2	23d...	Wasserman Schultz	56.7	Kaufman	40.5
14th...	Speier	80.9	Cardenas	19.1	24th...	Wilson	[2]		[1]
15th...	Swalwell	73.8	Turner	26.2	25th...	Valdes	37.6	Diaz-Balart	62.4
16th...	Costa	58.0	Tacherra	42.0	26th...	Garcia	41.2	Curbelo	53.0
17th...	Khanna	61.0	[1]	[1]	27th...	Fuhrman	45.1	Ros-Lehtinen	54.9
18th...	Eshoo	71.1	Fox	28.9	**GA**.....	(X)	(X)	(X)	(X)
19th...	Lofgren	73.9	Lancaster	26.1	1st....	[1]	[1]	Carter	99.6
20th...	Panetta	70.8	Lucius	29.2	2d.....	Bishop Jr.	61.2	Duke	38.8
21st...	Huerta	43.3	Valadao	56.7	3d.....	Pendley	31.7	Ferguson	68.3
22d..	Campos	32.4	Nunes	67.6	4th....	Johnson Jr.	75.7	Armendariz	24.3
23d...	Reed	30.8	McCarthy	69.2	5th....	Lewis	84.4	Bell	15.6
24th...	Carbajal	53.4	Fareed	46.6	6th....	Stooksbury	38.3	Price	61.7
25th...	Caforio	46.9	Knight	53.1	7th....	Malik	39.6	Woodall	60.4
26th...	Brownley	60.4	Dagnesses	39.6	8th....	Harris	32.4	Scott	67.6
27th...	Chu	67.4	Orswell	32.6	9th....	[1]	[1]	Collins	100.0
28th...	Schiff	78.0	Solis	22.0	10th...	[1]	[1]	Hice	99.6
29th...	Cárdenas	74.7	[1]	[1]	11th...	Wilson	32.6	Loudermilk	67.4
30th...	Sherman	72.6	Reed	27.4	12th...	McCracken	38.4	Allen	61.6
31st...	Aguilar	56.1	Chabot	43.9	13th...	Scott	100.0	[1]	[1]
32d..	Napolitano	61.6	[1]	[1]	14th...	[1]	[1]	Graves	100.0
33d..	Lieu	66.4	Wright	33.6	**HI**......	(X)	(X)	(X)	(X)
34th...	Becerra	77.2	[1]	[1]	1st....	Hanabusa	68.1	Ostrov	21.5
35th...	Torres	72.4	Fischella	27.6	2d.....	Gabbard	76.2	Kaaihue	17.7
36th...	Ruiz	62.1	Stone	37.9	**ID**......	(X)	(X)	(X)	(X)
37th...	Bass	81.1	[1]	[1]	1st....	Piotrowski,	31.8	Labrador	68.2
38th...	Sánchez	70.5	Downing	29.5	2d.....	Martinez	29.4	Simpson	62.9
39th...	Murdock	42.8	Royce	57.2	**IL**.......	(X)	(X)	(X)	(X)
40th...	Roybal-Allard	71.4	[1]	[1]	1st....	Rush	74.1	Deuser	25.9
41st...	Takano	65.0	Sheperd	35.0	2d.....	Kelly	79.8	Morrow	20.2
42d..	Sheridan	41.2	Calvert	58.8	3d.....	Lipinski	100.0	[1]	[1]
43d..	Waters	76.1	Navarro	23.9	4th....	Gutiérrez	100.0	[1]	[1]
44th...	Diaz Barragán	52.2	[1]	[1]	5th....	Quigley	67.8	Kolber	27.5
45th...	Varasteh	41.4	Walters	58.6	6th....	Howland	40.8	Roskam	59.2
46th...	Correa	70.0	[1]	[1]	7th....	Davis	84.2	Leef	15.8
47th...	Lowenthal	63.7	Whallon	36.3	8th....	Krishnamoorthi	58.3	DiCianni	41.7
48th...	Savary	41.7	Rohrabacher	58.3	9th....	Schakowsky,	66.5	McCarthy Lasonde	33.5
49th...	Applegate	49.7	Issa	50.3	10th...	Schneider	52.6	Dold	47.4
50th...	Malloy	36.5	Hunter	63.5	11th...	Foster	60.4	Khouri	39.6
51st...	Vargas	72.8	Hidalgo Jr.	27.2	12th...	Baricevic	39.7	Bost	54.3
52d..	Peters	56.5	Gitsham	43.5	13th...	Wicklund	40.3	Davis	59.7
53d..	Davis	67.0	Veltmeyer	33.0	14th...	Walz	40.7	Hultgren	59.3
CO.....	(X)	(X)	(X)	(X)	15th...	[1]	[1]	Shimkus	100.0
1st....	DeGette	67.9	Stockham	27.7	16th...	[1]	[1]	Kinzinger	99.9

See footnotes at end of table.

Table 446. Vote Cast for U.S. Representatives by Major Political Party— Congressional Districts: 2016-Continued.

See headnote on page 283.

State and district	Democratic candidate Name	Percent of total	Republican candidate Name	Percent of total
17th...	Bustos	60.3	Harlan	39.7
18th...	Rodriguez	27.9	LaHood	72.1
IN.....	(X)	(X)	(X)	(X)
1st...	Visclosky	81.5	[1]	[1]
2d.....	Coleman	36.9	Walorski	59.3
3d.....	Schrader	23.0	Banks	70.1
4th...	Dale	30.5	Rokita	64.6
5th...	Demaree	34.3	Brooks	61.5
6th...	Welsh	26.7	Messer	69.1
7th...	Carson	60.0	Ping	35.7
8th...	Drake	31.7	Bucshon	63.7
9th...	Yoder	40.5	Hollingsworth	54.1
IA.....	(X)	(X)	(X)	(X)
1st...	Vernon	46.1	Blum	53.7
2d.....	Loebsack	53.7	Peters	46.2
3d.....	Mowrer	39.7	Young	53.4
4th...	Weaver	38.6	King	61.2
KS.....	(X)	(X)	(X)	(X)
1st...	[1]	[1]	Marshall	65.9
2d.....	Potter	32.6	Jenkins	60.9
3d.....	Sidie	40.6	Yoder	51.3
4th...	Giroux	29.6	Pompeo	60.7
KY.....	(X)	(X)	(X)	(X)
1st...	Gaskins	27.3	Comer	72.6
2d.....	[1]	[1]	Guthrie	100.0
3d.....	Yarmuth	63.5	Bratcher	36.5
4th...	Sidle	28.7	Massie	71.3
5th...	[1]	[1]	Rogers	100.0
6th...	Kemper	38.9	Barr	61.1
LA.....	(X)	(X)	(X)	(X)
1st...	Dugas	12.8	Scalise	74.6
2d.....	Richmond	69.8	[1]	[1]
3d.....	Hebert	10.0	Higgins	27.5
4th...	Jones	17.3	Johnson	32.5
5th...	[1]	[1]	Abraham	81.6
6th...	Lieberman	14.9	Graves	62.7
ME.....	(X)	(X)	(X)	(X)
1st...	Pingree	55.9	Holbrook	40.4
2d.....	Cain	43.6	Poliquin	52.9
MD.....	(X)	(X)	(X)	(X)
1st...	Werner	28.6	Harris	67.0
2d.....	Ruppersberger	62.1	McDonough	33.1
3d.....	Sarbanes	63.2	Plaster	33.9
4th...	Brown	74.1	McDermott	21.4
5th...	Hoyer	67.4	Arness	29.4
6th...	Delaney	56.0	Hoeber	40.1
7th...	Cummings	74.9	Vaughn	21.8
8th...	Raskin	60.6	Cox	34.2
MA.....	(X)	(X)	(X)	(X)
1st...	Neal	67.4	[1]	[1]
2d.....	McGovern	75.9	[1]	[1]
3d.....	Tsongas	65.7	Wofford	29.9
4th...	Kennedy III	67.2	Rosa	28.6
5th...	Clark	74.1	[1]	[1]
6th...	Moulton	74.3	[1]	[1]
7th...	Capuano	81.8	[1]	[1]
8th...	Lynch	68.4	Burke	25.9
9th...	Keating	52.5	Alliegro	31.7
MI.....	(X)	(X)	(X)	(X)
1st...	Johnson	40.1	Bergmann	54.9
2d.....	Murphy	32.5	Huizenga	62.6
3d.....	Smith	37.5	Amash	59.5
4th...	Wirth	32.1	Moolenaar	61.6
5th...	Kildee	61.2	Hardwick	35.1
6th...	Clements	36.4	Upton	58.6
7th...	Driskell	40.0	Walberg	55.1
8th...	Shkreli	39.2	Bishop	56.0
9th...	Levin	57.9	Morse	37.4
10th...	Accavitti, Jr.	32.3	Mitchell	63.1
11th...	Kumar	40.2	Trott	52.9
12th...	Dingell	64.3	Jones	29.3
13th...	Conyers, Jr.	77.1	Gorman	15.7
14th...	Lawrence	78.5	Klausner	18.7
MN.....	(X)	(X)	(X)	(X)
1st...	Walz	50.3	Hagedorn	49.6
2d.....	Craig	45.2	Lewis	47.0
3d.....	Bonoff	43.0	Paulsen	56.7
4th...	McCollum	57.8	Ryan	34.4
5th...	Ellison	69.1	Drake	22.3
6th...	Snyder	34.3	Emmer	65.6
7th...	Peterson	52.5	Hughes	47.4
8th...	Nolan	50.2	Mills	49.6
MS.....	(X)	(X)	(X)	(X)
1st...	Owens	27.9	Kelly	68.7
2d.....	Thompson	67.1	Bouie II	29.1
3d.....	Quinn	30.4	Harper	66.2
4th...	Gladney	27.8	Palazzo	65.0
MO.....	(X)	(X)	(X)	(X)
1st...	Clay	75.5	Bailey	20.0
2d.....	Otto	37.7	Wagner	58.5
3d.....	Miller	27.9	Luetkemeyer	67.8
4th...	Christensen	27.8	Hartzler	67.8
5th...	Cleaver	58.8	Turk	38.2
6th...	Blackwell	28.4	Graves	68.0
7th...	Williams	27.4	Long	67.5
8th...	Cowell	22.7	Smith	74.4
MT.....	Juneau	40.5	Zinke	56.2
NE.....	(X)	(X)	(X)	(X)
1st...	Wik	30.5	Fortenberry	69.5
2d.....	Ashford	47.7	Bacon	50.0
3d.....	[1]	[1]	Smith	100.0
NV.....	(X)	(X)	(X)	(X)
1st...	Titus	61.9	Perry	28.8
2d.....	Evans	36.9	Amodei	58.3
3d.....	Rosen	47.2	Tarkanian	46.0
4th...	Kihuen	48.5	Hardy	44.5
NH.....	(X)	(X)	(X)	(X)
1st...	Shea-Porter	44.3	Guinta	42.9
2d.....	Kuster	49.7	Lawrence	45.3
NJ.....	(X)	(X)	(X)	(X)
1st...	Norcross	60.0	Patterson	36.8
2d.....	Cole	37.2	LoBiondo	59.2
3d.....	Lavergne	38.9	MacArthur	59.3
4th...	Phillipson	33.5	Smith	63.7
5th...	Gottheimer	51.1	Garrett	46.7
6th...	Pallone, Jr.	63.7	Sonnek-Schmelz	34.9
7th...	Jacob	43.1	Lance	54.1
8th...	Sires	77.0	Khan	18.5
9th...	Pascrell, Jr.	69.7	Castillo	28.0
10th...	Payne, Jr.	85.7	Pinckney	11.9
11th...	Wenzel	38.9	Frelinghuysen	58.0
12th...	Coleman	62.9	Uccio	32.0
NM.....	(X)	(X)	(X)	(X)
1st...	Grisham	65.1	Priem	34.9
2d.....	Soules	37.2	Pearce	62.7
3d.....	Luján	62.4	Romero	37.6
NY.....	(X)	(X)	(X)	(X)
1st...	Throne-Holst	37.1	Zeldin	46.4
2d.....	Gregory	32.2	King	49.6
3d.....	Suozzi	48.9	Martins	38.2
4th...	Rice	53.0	Gurfein	32.4
5th...	Meeks	79.4	O'Reilly	10.7
6th...	Meng	62.5	Maio	20.8
7th...	Velázquez	80.1	Romaguera	7.2
8th...	Jefferies	78.9	[1]	[1]
9th...	Clarke	77.4	[1]	[1]
10th...	Nadler	67.6	Rosenthal	17.4
11th...	Reichard	33.9	Donovan, Jr.	48.7
12th...	Maloney	73.7	Ardini	15.8
13th...	Espaillat	81.2	Evans, Jr.	5.1
14th...	Crowley	70.1	Spotorno	13.6
15th...	Serrano	85.5	Vega	3.2
16th...	Engel	69.1	[1]	[1]
17th...	Lowey	59.5	[1]	[1]
18th...	Maloney	44.2	Oliva	34.8
19th...	Teachout	38.6	Faso	41.6
20th...	Tonko	56.7	Vitollo	25.1
21st...	Derrick	26.3	Stefanik	52.9
22d...	Myers	34.7	Tenney	38.3
23d...	Plumb	36.0	Reed	46.2
24th...	Deacon	35.0	Katko	47.7
25th...	McIntosh Slaughter	50.1	Assini	33.8
26th...	Higgins	62.8	Schratz	18.3
27th...	Kastenbaum	30.4	Collins	49.5
NC.....	(X)	(X)	(X)	(X)
1st...	Butterfield	68.6	Dew, Jr.	29.0
2d.....	McNeil	43.3	Holding	56.7
3d.....	Reeves	32.8	Jones	67.2
4th...	Price	68.2	Googe	31.8
5th...	Brannon	41.6	Foxx	58.4
6th...	Glidewell	40.8	Walker	59.2
7th...	Casteen	39.1	Rouzer	60.9
8th...	Mills	41.2	Hudson	58.8
9th...	Cano	41.8	Pittenger	58.2

See footnotes at end of table.

Table 446. Vote Cast for U.S. Representatives by Major Political Party—Congressional Districts: 2016-Continued.

See headnote on page 283.

State and district	Democratic candidate Name	Percent of total	Republican candidate Name	Percent of total
10th...	Millard	36.9	McHenry	63.1
11th...	Bryson	35.9	Meadows	64.1
12th...	Adams	67.0	Threatt	33.0
13th...	Davis	43.9	Budd	56.1
ND.....	Iron Eyes	23.7	Cramer	69.1
OH.....	(X)	(X)	(X)	(X)
1st....	Young	40.8	Chabot	59.2
2d.....	Smith	32.8	Wenstrup	65.0
3d.....	Beatty	68.6	Adams	31.4
4th....	Garrett	32.0	Jordan	68.0
5th....	Neu, Jr.	29.1	Latta	70.9
6th....	Lorentz	29.3	Johnson	70.7
7th....	Rich	29.0	Gibbs	64.0
8th....	Fought	27.0	Davidson	68.8
9th....	Kaptur	68.7	Larson	31.3
10th...	Klepinger	32.7	Turner	64.1
11th...	Fudge	80.3	Goldstein	19.7
12th...	Albertson	29.8	Tiberi	66.6
13th...	Ryan	67.7	Morckel	32.3
14th...	Wager	37.4	Joyce	62.6
15th...	Wharton	33.8	Stivers	66.2
16th...	Mundy	34.7	Renacci	65.3
OK.....	(X)	(X)	(X)	(X)
1st....	([1])	([1])	Bridenstine	([2])
2d.....	Harris-Till	23.2	Mullin	70.6
3d.....	Robbins	21.7	Lucas	78.3
4th....	Owen	26.1	Cole	69.6
5th....	McAffrey	36.8	Russell	57.1
OR.....	(X)	(X)	(X)	(X)
1st....	Bonamici	59.6	Heinrich	37.0
2d.....	Crary	28.0	Walden	71.7
3d.....	([1])	([1])	Blumenauer	71.8
4th....	DeFazio	55.5	Robinson	39.7
5th....	Schrader	53.5	Willis	43.0
PA.....	(X)	(X)	(X)	(X)
1st....	Brady	82.2	Williams	17.8
2d.....	Evans	90.2	Jones	9.8
3d.....	([1])	([1])	Kelly	100.0
4th....	Burkholder	33.9	Perry	66.1
5th....	Strano Taylor	32.8	Thompson	67.2
6th....	Parrish	42.8	Costello	57.2
7th....	Balchunis	40.5	Meehan	59.5
8th....	Santarsiero	45.6	Fitzpatrick	54.4
9th....	Halvorson	36.7	Shuster	63.3
10th...	Molesevich	29.8	Marino	70.2
11th...	Marsicano	36.3	Barletta	63.7
12th...	McClelland	38.2	Rothfus	61.8
13th...	Boyle	100.0	([1])	([1])
14th...	Doyle	74.4	McAllister	25.6
15th...	Daugherty	38.0	Dent	58.4
16th...	Hartman	42.9	Smucker	53.8
17th...	Cartwright	53.8	Connolly	46.2
18th...	([1])	([1])	Murphy	100.0
RI.....	(X)	(X)	(X)	(X)
1st....	Cicilline	64.5	Taub	35.1
2d.....	Langevin	58.1	Reis	30.7
SC.....	(X)	(X)	(X)	(X)
1st....	Cherny	34.0	Sanford	58.6
2d.....	Bjorn	34.5	Wilson	60.2
3d.....	Cleveland	27.1	Duncan	72.8
4th....	Fedalei	31.0	Gowdy	67.2
5th....	Person	38.7	Mulvaney	59.2
6th....	Clyburn	70.1	Sterling	27.6
7th....	Hyman	35.7	Rice	61.0
SD.....	Hawks	35.9	Noem	64.2
TN.....	(X)	(X)	(X)	(X)
1st....	Bohms	15.4	Roe	78.4
2d.....	Starr	24.4	Duncan, Jr.	75.6
3d.....	Shekari	28.8	Fleischmann	66.4
4th....	Reynolds	35.0	DesJarlais	65.0
5th....	Cooper	62.6	Snyder	37.4
6th....	Kent	21.8	Black	71.1
7th....	Chandler	23.5	Blackburn	72.2
8th....	Hobson	25.1	Kustoff	68.8
9th....	Cohen	78.7	Alberson	18.9
TX.....	(X)	(X)	(X)	(X)
1st....	McKellar	24.1	Gohmert	73.9
2d.....	Bryan	36.0	Poe	60.6
3d.....	Bell	34.6	Johnson	61.2
4th....	([1])	([1])	Ratcliffe	88.0
5th....	([1])	([1])	Hensarling	80.6
6th....	Woolridge	39.0	Barton	58.3
7th....	Cargas	43.8	Culberson	56.2
8th....	([1])	([1])	Brady	100.0
9th....	Green	80.6	Martin	19.4
10th...	Cadien	38.4	McCaul	57.3
11th...	([1])	([1])	Conaway	89.5
12th...	Bradshaw	26.9	Granger	69.4
13th...	([1])	([1])	Thornberry	90.0
14th...	Cole	38.1	Weber, Sr.	61.9
15th...	Gonzalez	57.3	Westley	37.7
16th...	O'Rourke	85.7	([1])	([1])
17th...	Matta	35.2	Flores	60.8
18th...	Jackson Lee	73.5	Bartley	23.6
19th...	([1])	([1])	Arrington	86.7
20th...	Castro	79.7	([1])	([1])
21st...	Wakely	36.4	Smith	57.0
22d...	Gibson	40.5	Olson	59.5
23d...	Gallego	47.0	Hurd	48.3
24th...	McDowell	39.3	Marchant	56.2
25th...	Thomas	37.7	Williams	58.3
26th...	Mauck	29.6	Burgess	66.4
27th...	Barrera	38.3	Farenthold	61.7
28th...	Cuellar	66.2	Hardin	31.3
29th...	Green	72.5	Garza	24.0
30th...	Johnson	77.9	Lingerfelt	19.0
31st...	Clark	36.5	Carter	58.4
32d...	([1])	([1])	Sessions	71.1
33d...	Veasey	73.7	Mitchell	26.3
34th...	Vela	62.7	Gonzalez, Jr.	37.3
35th...	Doggett	63.1	Narvaiz	31.6
36th...	([1])	([1])	Babin	88.6
UT.....	(X)	(X)	(X)	(X)
1st....	Clemens	26.4	Bishop	65.9
2d.....	Albarran	33.9	Stewart	61.6
3d.....	Tryon	26.5	Chaffetz	73.5
4th....	Owens	41.3	Love	53.8
VT.....	Welch	82.5	([1])	([1])
VA.....	(X)	(X)	(X)	(X)
1st....	Rowe	36.6	Wittman	59.9
2d.....	Brown	38.5	Taylor	61.3
3d.....	Scott	66.7	Williams	33.1
4th....	McEachin	57.7	Wade	42.0
5th....	Dittmar	41.6	Garrett, Jr.	58.2
6th....	Degner	33.1	Goodlatte	66.6
7th....	Bedell	42.2	Brat	57.5
8th....	Beyer, Jr.	68.4	Hernick	27.3
9th....	Kitts	28.3	Griffith	68.6
10th...	Bennett	46.9	Comstock	52.7
11th...	Connolly	87.9	([1])	([1])
WA.....	(X)	(X)	(X)	(X)
1st....	DelBene	55.4	Sutherland	44.6
2d.....	Larsen	64.0	Hennemann	36.0
3d.....	Moeller	38.2	Herrera Beutler	61.8
4th....	([1])	([1])	Newhouse	57.6
5th....	Pakootas	40.4	McMorris Rodgers	59.6
6th....	Kilmer	61.5	Bloom	38.5
7th....	Jayapal	56.0	([1])	([1])
8th....	Ventrella	39.8	Reichert	60.2
9th....	Smith	72.9	Basler	27.1
10th...	Heck	58.7	Postma	41.3
WV.....	(X)	(X)	(X)	(X)
1st....	Manypenny	31.0	McKinley	69.0
2d.....	Hunt	41.8	Mooney	58.2
3d.....	Detch	24.0	Jenkins	67.9
WI.....	(X)	(X)	(X)	(X)
1st....	Solen	30.2	Ryan	64.9
2d.....	Pocan	68.7	Theron	31.2
3d.....	Kind	98.9	([1])	([1])
4th....	Moore	76.7	([1])	([1])
5th....	Penebaker	29.3	Sensenbrenner, Jr.	66.7
6th....	Lloyd	37.3	Grothman	57.2
7th....	Hoeft	38.3	Duffy	61.7
8th....	Nelson	37.3	Gallagher	62.6
WY.....	Greene	29.2	Cheney	60.3

X Not applicable. [1] No candidate. [2] Unopposed candidate; state law either doesn't require name to appear on the ballot or vote tabulation.

Source: U.S. House of Representatives, Office of the Clerk, *Statistics of the Congressional Election,* February 2017, and earlier reports. See also <http://clerk.house.gov/member_info/election.html>.

Table 447. Apportionment of Membership in House of Representatives by State: 1800 to 2010

[Total membership includes Representatives assigned to newly admitted States after the apportionment acts. Population figures used for apportionment purposes are those determined for States by each decennial census. No reapportionment based on 1920 population census. For method of calculating apportionment and a short history of apportionment, see House Report 91-1314, 91st Congress, 2d session, The Decennial Population Census and Congressional Apportionment]

State	Membership based on Census of—																				
	1800	1820	1830	1840	1850	1860	1870	1880	1890	1900	1910	1920	1930	1940	1950	1960	1970	1980	1990	2000	2010
U.S.	**142**	**213**	**242**	**232**	**237**	**243**	**293**	**332**	**357**	**391**	**435**	**435**	**435**	**435**	**437**	**435**	**435**	**435**	**435**	**435**	**435**
AL	(X)	3	5	7	7	6	8	8	9	9	10	10	9	9	9	8	7	7	7	7	7
AK	(X)	(X)	(X)	(X)	(X)	(X)	(X)	(X)	(X)	(X)	(X)	(X)	(X)	(X)	¹1	1	1	1	1	1	1
AZ	(X)	(X)	(X)	(X)	(X)	(X)	(X)	(X)	(X)	(X)	²2	1	1	2	2	3	4	5	6	8	9
AR	(X)	(X)	¹1	1	2	3	4	5	6	7	7	7	7	7	6	4	4	4	4	4	4
CA	(X)	(X)	(X)	¹2	2	3	4	6	7	8	11	11	20	23	30	38	43	45	52	53	53
CO	(X)	(X)	(X)	(X)	(X)	(X)	¹1	1	2	3	4	4	4	4	4	4	5	6	6	7	7
CT	7	6	6	4	4	4	4	4	4	5	5	5	6	6	6	6	6	6	6	5	5
DE	1	1	1	1	1	1	1	1	1	1	1	1	1	1	1	1	1	1	1	1	1
FL	(X)	(X)	(X)	¹1	1	1	2	2	2	3	4	4	5	6	8	12	15	19	23	25	27
GA	4	7	9	8	8	7	9	10	11	11	12	12	10	10	10	10	10	10	11	13	14
HI	(X)	(X)	(X)	(X)	(X)	(X)	(X)	(X)	(X)	(X)	(X)	(X)	(X)	(X)	¹1	2	2	2	2	2	2
ID	(X)	(X)	(X)	(X)	(X)	(X)	(X)	¹1	1	1	2	2	2	2	2	2	2	2	2	2	2
IL	(X)	1	3	7	9	14	19	20	22	25	27	27	27	26	25	24	24	22	20	19	18
IN	(X)	3	7	10	11	11	13	13	13	13	13	13	12	11	11	11	11	10	10	9	9
IA	(X)	(X)	(X)	¹2	2	6	9	11	11	11	11	11	9	8	8	7	6	6	5	5	4
KS	(X)	(X)	(X)	(X)	(X)	1	3	7	8	8	8	8	7	6	6	5	5	5	4	4	4
KY	6	12	13	10	10	9	10	11	11	11	11	11	9	9	8	7	7	7	6	6	6
LA	(X)	3	3	4	4	5	6	6	6	7	8	8	8	8	8	8	8	8	7	7	6
ME	(X)	7	8	7	6	5	5	4	4	4	4	4	3	3	3	2	2	2	2	2	2
MD	9	9	8	6	6	5	6	6	6	6	6	6	6	6	7	8	8	8	8	8	8
MA	17	13	12	10	11	10	11	12	13	14	16	16	15	14	14	12	12	11	10	10	9
MI	(X)	(X)	¹1	3	4	6	9	11	12	12	13	13	17	17	18	19	19	18	16	15	14
MN	(X)	(X)	(X)	(X)	¹2	2	3	5	7	9	10	10	9	9	9	8	8	8	8	8	8
MS	(X)	1	2	4	5	5	6	7	7	8	8	8	7	7	6	5	5	5	5	4	4
MO	(X)	1	2	5	7	9	13	14	15	16	16	16	13	13	11	10	10	9	9	9	8
MT	(X)	(X)	(X)	(X)	(X)	(X)	(X)	¹1	1	1	2	2	2	2	2	2	2	2	1	1	1
NE	(X)	(X)	(X)	(X)	(X)	¹1	1	3	6	6	6	6	5	4	4	3	3	3	3	3	3
NV	(X)	(X)	(X)	(X)	(X)	¹1	1	1	1	1	1	1	1	1	1	1	1	2	2	3	4
NH	5	6	5	4	3	3	3	2	2	2	2	2	2	2	2	2	2	2	2	2	2
NJ	6	6	6	5	5	5	7	7	8	10	12	12	14	14	14	15	15	14	13	13	12
NM	(X)	(X)	(X)	(X)	(X)	(X)	(X)	(X)	(X)	(X)	²1	1	1	2	2	2	2	3	3	3	3
NY	17	34	40	34	33	31	33	34	34	37	43	43	45	45	43	41	39	34	31	29	27
NC	12	13	13	9	8	7	8	9	9	10	10	10	11	12	12	11	11	11	12	13	13
ND	(X)	(X)	(X)	(X)	(X)	(X)	(X)	¹1	1	2	3	3	2	2	2	2	1	1	1	1	1
OH	¹1	14	19	21	21	19	20	21	21	21	22	22	24	23	23	24	23	21	19	18	16
OK	(X)	(X)	(X)	(X)	(X)	(X)	(X)	(X)	(X)	¹5	8	8	9	8	6	6	6	6	6	5	5
OR	(X)	(X)	(X)	(X)	¹1	1	1	1	2	2	3	3	3	4	4	4	4	5	5	5	5
PA	18	26	28	24	25	24	27	28	30	32	36	36	34	33	30	27	25	23	21	19	18
RI	2	2	2	2	2	2	2	2	2	2	3	3	2	2	2	2	2	2	2	2	2
SC	8	9	9	7	6	4	5	7	7	7	7	7	6	6	6	6	6	6	6	6	7
SD	(X)	(X)	(X)	(X)	(X)	(X)	(X)	¹2	2	2	3	3	2	2	2	2	2	1	1	1	1
TN	3	9	13	11	10	8	10	10	10	10	10	10	9	10	9	9	8	9	9	9	9
TX	(X)	(X)	(X)	¹2	2	4	6	11	13	16	18	18	21	21	22	23	24	27	30	32	36
UT	(X)	(X)	(X)	(X)	(X)	(X)	(X)	(X)	¹1	1	2	2	2	2	2	2	2	3	3	3	4
VT	4	5	5	4	3	3	3	2	2	2	2	2	1	1	1	1	1	1	1	1	1
VA	22	22	21	15	13	11	9	10	10	10	10	10	9	9	10	10	10	10	11	11	11
WA	(X)	(X)	(X)	(X)	(X)	(X)	(X)	¹1	2	3	5	5	6	6	7	7	7	8	9	9	10
WV	(X)	(X)	(X)	(X)	(X)	(X)	3	4	4	4	5	6	6	6	6	5	4	4	3	3	3
WI	(X)	(X)	(X)	¹2	3	6	8	9	10	11	11	11	10	10	10	10	9	9	9	8	8
WY	(X)	(X)	(X)	(X)	(X)	(X)	(X)	¹1	1	1	1	1	1	1	1	1	1	1	1	1	1

X Not applicable. ¹ Assigned after apportionment. ² Included in apportionment in anticipation of statehood.

Source: U.S. Census Bureau, Congressional Apportionment, Census 2010, <http://www.census.gov/population/apportionment/>.

Table 448. Composition of Congress by Political Party Affiliation—States: 2011 to 2017

[Figures are for the beginning of the first session, except as noted. Dem. = Democratic; Rep. = Republican]

State	Representatives								Senators							
	112th Cong., 2011		113th Cong.,[1] 2013		114th Cong.,[2] 2015		115th Cong., 2017		112th Cong.,[3] 2011		113th Cong.,[4] 2013		114th Cong.,[4] 2015		115th Cong.,[4] 2017	
	Dem.	Rep.	Dem.	Rep.	Dem.	Rep.	Dem.	Rep.	Dem.	Rep.	Dem.	Rep.	Dem.	Rep.	Dem.	Rep.
U.S.	193	242	201	232	188	245	194	241	51	47	53	45	44	54	46	52
AL	1	6	1	6	1	6	1	6	–	2	–	2	–	2	–	2
AK	–	1	–	1	–	1	–	1	1	1	1	1	–	2	–	2
AZ	3	5	5	4	4	5	4	5	–	2	–	2	–	2	–	2
AR	1	3	–	4	–	4	–	4	1	1	1	1	–	2	–	2
CA	34	19	38	15	39	14	39	14	2	–	2	–	2	–	2	–
CO	3	4	3	4	3	4	3	4	2	–	2	–	1	1	1	1
CT	5	–	5	–	5	–	5	–	1	–	2	–	2	–	2	–
DE	1	–	1	–	1	–	1	–	2	–	2	–	2	–	2	–
FL	6	19	10	17	10	17	11	16	1	1	1	1	1	1	1	1
GA	5	8	5	9	4	10	4	10	–	2	–	2	–	2	–	2
HI	2	–	2	–	2	–	2	–	2	–	2	–	2	–	2	–
ID	–	2	–	2	–	2	–	2	–	2	–	2	–	2	–	2
IL	8	11	12	6	10	8	11	7	1	1	1	1	1	1	2	–
IN	3	6	2	7	2	7	2	7	–	2	1	1	1	1	1	1
IA	3	2	2	2	1	3	1	3	1	1	1	1	–	2	–	2
KS	–	4	–	4	–	4	–	4	–	2	–	2	–	2	–	2
KY	2	4	1	5	1	5	1	5	–	2	–	2	–	2	–	2
LA	1	6	1	5	1	5	1	5	1	1	1	1	–	2	–	2
ME	2	–	2	–	1	1	1	1	–	2	–	1	–	1	–	1
MD	6	2	7	1	7	1	7	1	2	–	2	–	2	–	2	–
MA	10	–	9	–	9	–	9	–	1	1	2	–	2	–	2	–
MI	6	9	5	9	5	9	5	9	2	–	2	–	2	–	2	–
MN	4	4	5	3	5	3	5	3	2	–	2	–	2	–	2	–
MS	1	3	1	3	1	2	1	3	–	2	–	2	–	2	–	2
MO	3	6	2	5	2	6	2	6	1	1	1	1	1	1	1	1
MT	–	1	–	1	–	1	–	1	2	–	2	–	1	1	1	1
NE	–	3	–	3	1	2	–	3	1	1	–	2	–	2	–	2
NV	1	2	2	2	1	3	3	1	1	1	1	1	1	1	1	1
NH	–	2	2	–	1	1	2	–	1	1	1	1	1	1	2	–
NJ	7	6	6	6	6	6	7	5	2	–	2	–	2	–	2	–
NM	2	1	2	1	2	1	2	1	2	–	2	–	2	–	2	–
NY	21	8	21	6	18	8	18	9	2	–	2	–	2	–	2	–
NC	7	6	4	9	3	10	3	10	1	1	1	1	–	2	–	2
ND	–	1	–	1	–	1	–	1	1	1	1	1	1	1	1	1
OH	5	13	4	12	4	12	4	12	1	1	1	1	1	1	1	1
OK	1	4	–	5	–	5	–	5	–	2	–	2	–	2	–	2
OR	4	1	4	1	4	1	4	1	2	–	2	–	2	–	2	–
PA	7	12	5	13	5	13	5	13	1	1	1	1	1	1	1	1
RI	2	–	2	–	2	–	2	–	2	–	2	–	2	–	2	–
SC	1	5	1	5	1	6	1	6	–	2	–	2	–	2	–	2
SD	–	1	–	1	–	1	–	1	1	1	1	1	–	2	–	2
TN	2	7	2	7	2	7	2	7	–	2	–	2	–	2	–	2
TX	9	23	12	24	11	25	11	25	–	2	–	2	–	2	–	2
UT	1	2	1	3	–	4	–	4	–	2	–	2	–	2	–	2
VT	1	–	1	–	1	–	1	–	1	–	1	–	1	–	1	–
VA	3	8	3	8	3	8	4	7	2	–	2	–	2	–	2	–
WA	5	4	6	4	6	4	6	4	2	–	2	–	2	–	2	–
WV	1	2	1	2	–	3	–	3	2	–	2	–	1	1	1	1
WI	3	5	3	5	3	5	3	5	1	1	1	1	1	1	1	1
WY	–	1	–	1	–	1	–	1	–	2	–	2	–	2	–	2

– Represents zero. [1] Two vacancies—one in Missouri due to the resignation of Jo Ann Emerson, January 22, 2013, and one in South Carolina due to the resignation of Tim Scott, January 2, 2013. [2] Two vacancies—one in Mississippi due to the death of Alan Nunnelee, February 6, 2015, and one in New York due to the resignation of Michael G. Grimm, January 5, 2015. [3] Vermont and Connecticut had one Independent senator each. [4] Vermont and Maine had one Independent senator each.

Source: U.S. House of Representatives, Office of the Clerk, *Official List of Members*, January 2017, and earlier editions. See also <http://clerk.house.gov/member_info/>.

Table 449. Members of Congress—Seniority of Senators and Representatives: 1959 to 2015

[Represents the makeup of Congress on the 1st day of the session]

Congress	Senators					Representatives				
	Number by length of service				Mean years of service	Number by terms served				Mean terms of service
	6 years or less [1]	7-12 years	13-18 years	19 or more years		1-3 terms	4-6 terms	7-9 terms	10+ terms	
86th (1959)	42 (20)	30	14	12	9.4	176	136	64	57	5.2
87th (1961)	42 (7)	25	22	11	9.7	163	131	76	67	5.5
88th (1963)	42 (12)	26	18	14	9.9	182	106	78	68	5.5
89th (1965)	29 (8)	36	16	19	11.1	198	97	73	67	5.1
90th (1967)	28 (7)	34	19	19	11.6	183	108	69	73	5.3
91st (1969)	32 (14)	32	17	19	11.2	171	126	65	73	5.6
92nd (1971)	25 (10)	24	29	22	11.5	162	122	68	83	5.8
93rd (1973)	40 (13)	20	20	20	11.2	162	128	66	76	5.5
94th (1975)	[2] 36 (12)	22	23	19	11.5	196	100	78	61	5.2
95th (1977)	42 (17)	25	13	20	10.6	219	87	70	59	4.9
96th (1979)	48 (20)	24	10	18	9.6	219	95	65	54	4.8
97th (1981)	55 (18)	20	10	15	8.5	209	121	56	49	4.7
98th (1983)	43 (5)	28	16	13	9.6	210	125	45	54	4.7
99th (1985)	32 (7)	38	18	12	10.1	184	138	58	54	5.1
100th (1987)	26 (13)	44	16	14	9.6	163	143	64	65	5.5
101st (1989)	31 (10)	26	29	14	9.8	120	167	86	60	5.8
102nd (1991)	30 (5)	23	28	19	11.1	133	137	91	74	6.1
103rd (1993)	30 (13)	17	32	21	11.3	192	109	69	65	5.2
104th (1995)	29 (11)	26	20	25	12.3	220	78	78	59	4.9
105th (1997)	40 (15)	24	13	23	11.2	243	71	65	56	4.8
106th (1999)	35 (8)	24	16	25	11.2	185	127	58	65	4.8
107th (2001)	37 (11)	21	19	23	11.5	149	155	54	76	5.6
108th (2003)	30 (10)	29	16	25	12.7	149	158	60	68	5.5
109th (2005)	29 (9)	27	15	29	12.5	137	128	97	72	5.9
110th (2007)	29 (10)	26	14	31	13.1	149	116	99	71	6.0
111th (2009)	[3] 32 (11)	19	20	29	14.0	147	102	106	79	6.2
112th (2011)	42 (13)	17	14	27	12.3	170	97	69	97	6.0
113th (2013)	43 (13)	23	15	19	10.2	196	91	72	74	5.7
114th (2015)	45 (13)	24	11	20	9.4	205	91	51	88	5.5

[1] Numbers in parenthesis are number of freshman senators. Senators who are currently in their first full term are listed under "6 years or less." [2] Total includes John Durkin (D-NH). After a contested election in 1974, the Senate declared the seat vacant as of August 8, 1975. He was then elected by special election, September 16, 1975, to fill the vacancy. [3] Total includes Al Franken (D-MN), who was declared elected after a challenge in court to the vote count by his Republican challenger on June 30, 2009; and Roland Burris (D-IL) who was appointed to fill the seat vacated by Barack Obama on December 31, 2008. Total also includes Joe Biden (D-DE), who resigned his seat on January 15, 2009, but was present on the first day of the session.

Source: The Brookings Institution, "Vital Statistics on Congress" ©, January 2017, <http://www.brookings.edu/vitalstats>.

Table 450. Women, Black, Asian, and Hispanic Members of Congress by Party Affiliation: 1997 to 2015

[As of beginning of first session of each Congress]

Characteristic	Congress									
	105th (1997)	106th (1999)	107th (2001)	108th (2003)	109th (2005)	110th (2007)	111th (2009) [1]	112th (2011)	113th (2013) [2]	114th (2015)
Women, total	60	65	72	73	79	87	91	93	96	104
Representatives	51	56	59	59	65	71	74	76	76	84
Democrat	35	40	41	38	42	50	57	52	56	62
Republican	16	16	18	21	23	21	17	24	20	22
Senators	9	9	13	14	14	16	17	17	20	20
Democrat	6	6	10	9	9	11	13	12	16	14
Republican	3	3	3	5	5	5	4	5	4	6
Black, total	38	37	36	37	41	41	39	42	42	46
Representatives	37	37	36	37	40	40	39	42	41	44
Democrat	36	36	35	37	40	40	39	40	41	42
Republican	1	1	1	0	0	0	0	2	0	2
Senators	1	0	0	0	1	1	0	0	1	2
Democrat	1	0	0	0	1	1	0	0	0	1
Republican	0	0	0	0	0	0	0	0	1	1
Asian, total	7	6	7	6	7	8	7	10	11	12
Representatives	5	4	5	4	5	6	5	8	10	11
Democrat	4	4	5	4	4	5	4	7	10	11
Republican	1	0	0	0	1	1	1	1	0	0
Senators	2	2	2	2	2	2	2	2	1	1
Democrat	2	2	2	2	2	2	2	2	1	1
Republican	0	0	0	0	0	0	0	0	0	0
Hispanic, total	17	19	19	22	25	26	26	29	31	35
Representatives	17	19	19	22	23	23	24	27	28	32
Democrat	14	16	16	18	19	20	21	19	23	23
Republican	3	3	3	4	4	3	3	8	5	9
Senators	0	0	0	0	2	3	2	2	3	3
Democrat	0	0	0	0	1	2	1	1	1	1
Republican	0	0	0	0	1	1	1	1	2	2

[1] Roland Burris was not seated on the first day of the 111th session. [2] Tim Scott, who was appointed on December 17th to replace outgoing Senator Jim DeMint, is included in the Senate totals.

Source: The Brookings Institution, "Vital Statistics on Congress" ©, January 2017, <http://www.brookings.edu/vitalstats>.

Table 451. Composition of Congress by Political Party: 1977 to 2017

[D = Democratic, R = Republican. As of beginning of first session of each Congress. Data reflect immediate result of elections. Vacancies and third party candidates are noted]

Year	Party and president	Congress	House Majority party	House Minority party	House Other	Senate Majority party	Senate Minority party	Senate Other
1977 [1]	D (Carter)	95th	D-292	R-143	–	D-61	R-38	1
1979 [1]	D (Carter)	96th	D-277	R-158	–	D-58	R-41	1
1981 [2]	R (Reagan)	97th	D-242	R-192	1	R-53	D-46	1
1983	R (Reagan)	98th	D-269	R-166	–	R-54	D-46	1
1985	R (Reagan)	99th	D-253	R-182	–	R-53	D-47	–
1987	R (Reagan)	100th	D-258	R-177	–	D-55	R-45	–
1989	R (Bush)	101st	D-260	R-175	–	D-55	R-45	–
1991 [3]	R (Bush)	102nd	D-267	R-167	1	D-56	R-44	–
1993 [3]	D (Clinton)	103rd	D-258	R-176	1	D-57	R-43	–
1995 [3]	D (Clinton)	104th	R-230	D-204	1	R-52	D-48	–
1997 [4]	D (Clinton)	105th	R-226	D-207	2	R-55	D-45	–
1999 [3]	D (Clinton)	106th	R-223	D-211	1	R-55	D-45	–
2001 [4]	R (Bush)	107th	R-221	D-212	2	R-50	R-50	–
2003 [2, 5]	R (Bush)	108th	R-229	D-204	1	R-51	D-48	1
2005 [2]	R (Bush)	109th	R-232	D-202	1	R-55	D-44	1
2007 [6]	R (Bush)	110th	D-233	R-202	–	D-49	R-49	2
2009 [5, 6, 7]	D (Obama)	111th	D-256	R-178	–	D-55	R-41	2
2011 [6]	D (Obama)	112th	R-242	D-193	–	D-51	R-47	2
2013 [5, 6]	D (Obama)	113th	R-234	D-200	–	D-53	R-45	2
2015 [6]	D (Obama)	114th	R-247	D-188	–	R-54	D-44	2
2017 [6]	R (Trump)	115th	R-241	D-194	–	R-52	D-46	2

– Represents zero. [1] Senate had one Independent. [2] House and Senate each had one Independent. [3] House had one Independent-Socialist. [4] House had one Independent-Socialist and one Independent. [5] House had one vacancy. [6] Senate had two Independents. [7] Senate had two vacancies.

Source: U.S. House of Representatives, Office of the Clerk, *Official List of Members*, January 2017, and earlier editions. See also <http://clerk.house.gov/member_info/>.

Table 452. U.S. Congress—Measures Introduced and Enacted and Time in Session: 1999 to 2016

[Excludes simple and concurrent resolutions]

Item	106th Cong., 1999–00	107th Cong., 2001–02	108th Cong., 2003–04	109th Cong., 2005–06	110th Cong., 2007–08	111th Cong., 2009–10	112th Cong., 2011-12	113th Cong., 2013-14	114th Cong., 2015-16
Measures introduced	9,158	9,130	8,625	10,703	11,228	10,778	10,612	9,097	10,223
Bills	8,968	8,953	8,468	10,560	11,081	10,629	10,439	8,919	10,074
Joint resolutions	190	177	157	143	147	149	173	178	149
Measures enacted	604	337	504	590	460	385	239	296	329
Public [1]	580	331	498	589	460	383	238	296	329
Private [2]	24	6	6	1	0	2	1	0	0
HOUSE OF REPRESENTATIVES									
Number of days	272	265	243	241	283	286	327	295	288
Number of hours	2,179	1,694	1,894	1,917	2,138	2,126	1,718	1,471	1,438
Number of hours per day	8.0	6.4	7.8	8.0	7.6	7.4	5.3	5.0	5.0
SENATE									
Number of days	303	322	300	297	374	349	323	292	333
Number of hours	2,200	2,279	2,486	2,250	2,364	2,495	2,032	2,003	1,855
Number of hours per day	7.3	7.1	8.3	7.6	6.3	7.1	6.3	6.9	5.6

[1] Laws on public matters that apply to all persons. [2] Laws designed to provide legal relief to specified persons or entities adversely affected by laws of general applicability.

Source: U.S. Congress, *Résumé of Congressional Activity*, March 2017, and earlier reports. See also <http://www.senate.gov/pagelayout/reference/two_column_table/Resumes.htm>.

Table 453. Congressional Bills Vetoed: 1961 to 2017

Period	President	Total vetoes	Regular vetoes	Pocket vetoes	Vetoes sustained	Bills passed over veto
1961–1963	John F. Kennedy	21	12	9	21	–
1963–1969	Lyndon B. Johnson	30	16	14	30	–
1969–1974	Richard M. Nixon	43	26	17	36	7
1974–1977	Gerald R. Ford	66	48	18	54	12
1977–1981	Jimmy Carter	31	13	18	29	2
1981–1989	Ronald W. Reagan	78	39	39	69	9
1989–1993	George Bush	44	29	15	43	1
1993–2001	William J. Clinton	37	36	1	35	2
2001–2009	George W. Bush	12	12	–	8	4
2009–2017	Barack Obama	12	12	–	11	1
2017 [1]	Donald J. Trump	–	–	–	–	–

– Represents zero. [1] For the period January 20, 2017 through August 8, 2017.

Source: Congressional Research Service, *Regular Vetoes and Pocket Vetoes: In Brief*, August 2016; and U.S. Senate, "Summary of Bills Vetoed," <http://www.senate.gov/reference/Legislation/Vetoes/vetoCounts.htm>, accessed August 2017.

Table 454. Number of Governors by Political Party Affiliation: 1975 to 2017

[Reflects figures after inaugurations for each year. State governors only]

Year	Demo-cratic	Republi-can	Inde-pendent/other	Year	Demo-cratic	Republi-can	Inde-pendent/other	Year	Demo-cratic	Republi-can	Inde-pendent/other
1975.........	36	13	1	2005.........	22	28	–	2012.........	20	29	1
1980.........	31	19	–	2007.........	28	22	–	2013.........	20	30	–
1985.........	34	16	–	2008.........	28	22	–	2014.........	21	29	–
1990.........	29	21	–	2009.........	28	22	–	2015.........	18	31	1
1995.........	19	30	1	2010.........	26	24	–	2016.........	18	31	1
2000.........	18	30	2	2011.........	20	29	1	2017.........	16	33	1

– Represents zero.

Source: ProQuest research.

Table 455. Vote Cast for and Governor Elected by State: 2012 to 2015

[D = Democratic, R = Republican, I = Independent]

State	Current governor [1]	Year of election	Total vote [2]	Republican	Democratic	Percent leading party
Alabama.................	Robert Bentley	2014	1,180,413	750,231	427,787	R-63.6
Alaska..................	Bill Walker	2014	279,958	128,435	8,985	I-48.4
Arizona.................	Doug Ducey	2014	1,506,416	805,062	626,921	R-53.4
Arkansas................	Asa Hutchinson	2014	848,952	470,429	352,115	R-55.4
California...............	Jerry Brown	2014	7,317,581	2,929,213	4,388,368	D-60.0
Colorado................	John Hickenlooper	2014	2,041,574	938,195	1,006,433	D-49.3
Connecticut..............	Dan Malloy	2014	1,092,773	526,295	554,314	D-50.7
Delaware................	Jack Markell	2012	398,155	113,793	275,993	D-69.3
Florida..................	Rick Scott	2014	5,951,561	2,865,343	2,801,198	R-48.1
Georgia.................	Nathan Deal	2014	2,550,648	1,345,237	1,144,794	R-52.7
Hawaii..................	David Ige	2014	366,210	135,775	181,106	D-49.5
Idaho...................	C.L. "Butch" Otter	2014	442,268	235,378	169,595	R-53.2
Illinois..................	Bruce Rauner	2014	3,637,690	1,833,627	1,681,343	R-50.4
Indiana.................	Mike Pence	2012	2,577,329	1,275,424	1,200,016	R-49.5
Iowa....................	Terry Branstad	2014	1,129,034	666,023	420,778	R-59.0
Kansas..................	Sam Brownback	2014	869,502	433,196	401,100	R-49.8
Kentucky................	Matt Bevin	2015	973,692	511,374	426,620	R-52.5
Louisiana...............	John Bel Edwards	2015	1,152,864	505,940	646,924	D-56.1
Maine...................	Paul LePage	2014	611,227	294,519	265,114	R-48.2
Maryland................	Larry Hogan	2014	1,728,975	884,400	818,890	R-51.2
Massachusetts...........	Charlie Baker	2014	2,158,326	1,044,573	1,004,408	R-48.4
Michigan................	Rick Snyder	2014	3,156,531	1,607,399	1,479,057	R-50.9
Minnesota...............	Mark Dayton	2014	1,975,406	879,257	989,113	D-50.1
Mississippi..............	Phil Bryant	2015	718,185	476,697	231,643	R-66.4
Missouri.................	Jay Nixon	2012	2,727,883	1,160,265	1,494,056	D-54.8
Montana................	Steve Bullock	2012	483,489	228,879	236,450	D-48.9
Nebraska................	Pete Ricketts	2014	539,657	308,751	211,905	R-57.2
Nevada.................	Brian Sandoval	2014	547,349	386,340	130,722	R-70.6
New Hampshire..........	Maggie Hassan	2014	486,183	230,610	254,666	D-52.4
New Jersey..............	Christopher Christie	2013	2,120,866	1,278,932	809,978	R-60.3
New Mexico.............	Susana Martinez	2014	512,805	293,443	219,362	R-57.2
New York...............	Andrew Cuomo	2014	3,819,427	1,536,879	2,069,480	D-54.2
North Carolina..........	Pat McCrory	2012	4,468,295	2,440,707	1,931,580	R-54.6
North Dakota............	Jack Dalrymple	2012	317,814	200,525	109,048	R-63.1
Ohio....................	John Kasich	2014	3,055,913	1,944,848	1,009,359	R-63.6
Oklahoma...............	Mary Fallin	2014	824,831	460,298	338,239	R-55.8
Oregon.................	Kate Brown	2014	1,469,724	648,542	733,230	D-49.9
Pennsylvania............	Tom Wolf	2014	3,495,866	1,575,511	1,920,355	D-54.9
Rhode Island............	Gina Raimondo	2014	324,055	117,428	131,899	D-40.7
South Carolina..........	Nikki Haley	2014	1,246,303	696,645	516,166	R-55.9
South Dakota............	Dennis Daugaard	2014	277,403	195,477	70,549	R-70.5
Tennessee..............	Bill Haslam	2014	1,353,728	951,796	309,237	R-70.3
Texas...................	Greg Abbot	2014	4,718,268	2,796,547	1,835,596	R-59.3
Utah....................	Gary Hebert	2012	1,006,524	688,592	277,622	R-68.4
Vermont................	Peter Shumlin	2014	193,087	87,075	89,509	D-46.4
Virginia.................	Terry McAuliffe	2013	2,240,314	1,013,354	1,069,789	D-47.8
Washington.............	Jay Inslee	2012	3,071,047	1,488,245	1,582,802	D-51.5
West Virginia............	Earl Ray Tomblin	2012	664,455	303,291	335,468	D-50.5
Wisconsin...............	Scott Walker	2014	2,410,314	1,259,706	1,122,913	R-52.3
Wyoming................	Matt Mead	2014	167,877	99,700	45,752	R-59.4

[1] As of January 2016. [2] Includes minor party and scattered votes.

Source: The Council of State Governments, Lexington, KY, *The Book of the States 2016*, and earlier reports ©. See also <http://www.csg.org/>.

Table 456. Political Party Control of State Legislatures by Party: 1990 to 2017

[As of beginning of year. Nebraska has a nonpartisan legislature]

Year	Democratic control	Split control or tie	Republican control	Year	Democratic control	Split control or tie	Republican control	Year	Democratic control	Split control or tie	Republican control
1990	29	11	9	2004	17	11	21	2011	15	8	26
1995	18	12	19	2005	19	10	20	2012	15	8	26
1998	20	12	17	2006	19	10	20	2013	19	4	26
2000	16	15	18	2007	22	12	15	2014	19	3	27
2001	16	15	18	2008	23	14	12	2015	11	8	30
2002	17	15	17	2009	27	8	14	2016	11	8	30
2003	16	12	21	2010	27	8	14	2017	14	3	32

Source: National Conference of State Legislatures, Denver, CO, *State Legislatures* ©. See also <ncsl.org>.

Table 457. Composition of State Legislatures by Political Party Affiliation: 2015 and 2016

[Data as of January. Figures reflect immediate results of elections, including holdover members in state houses which do not have all of their members running for reelection. Dem. = Democrat, Rep. = Republican, Vac. = Vacancies. In general, Lower House refers to body consisting of state representatives and Upper House of state senators]

State	Lower House 2015 Dem.	Rep.	Other	Vac.	Lower House 2016 Dem.	Rep.	Other	Vac.	Upper House 2015 Dem.	Rep.	Other	Vac.	Upper House 2016 Dem.	Rep.	Other	Vac.
U.S.	2,350	3,036	21	4	2,335	3,031	25	20	833	1,082	4	4	827	1,085	4	7
AL [1]	33	72	–	–	33	70	–	2	8	26	1	–	8	26	1	–
AK [2]	16	23	–	1	16	23	1	–	6	14	–	–	6	14	–	–
AZ [3]	24	36	–	–	24	36	–	–	13	17	–	–	12	18	–	–
AR [2]	36	64	–	–	35	64	1	–	11	23	–	1	11	24	–	–
CA [2]	52	28	–	–	51	28	–	1	26	14	–	–	26	14	–	–
CO [2]	34	31	–	–	34	31	–	–	17	18	–	–	17	18	–	–
CT [3]	87	64	–	–	86	64	–	1	21	15	–	–	21	15	–	–
DE [2]	25	16	–	–	25	16	–	–	12	9	–	–	12	9	–	–
FL [2]	38	80	–	2	39	81	–	–	14	25	–	1	14	26	–	–
GA [3]	59	120	1	–	61	117	1	1	18	38	–	–	17	39	–	–
HI [2]	43	8	–	–	44	7	–	–	24	1	–	–	24	1	–	–
ID [3]	14	56	–	–	14	56	–	–	7	28	–	–	7	28	–	–
IL [4]	71	47	–	–	71	47	–	–	39	20	–	–	39	20	–	–
IN [2]	29	71	–	–	29	71	–	–	10	40	–	–	10	40	–	–
IA [2]	43	57	–	–	43	57	–	–	26	23	–	1	26	24	–	–
KS [2]	28	97	–	–	28	97	–	–	8	32	–	–	8	32	–	–
KY [2]	54	46	–	–	50	46	–	4	11	26	–	1	11	27	–	–
LA [1]	44	59	2	–	42	61	2	–	13	26	–	–	14	25	–	–
ME [3]	79	68	4	–	78	69	4	–	14	21	–	–	15	20	–	–
MD [1]	91	50	–	–	91	50	–	–	33	14	–	–	32	14	–	1
MA [3]	125	35	–	–	123	34	–	3	34	6	–	–	34	5	–	1
MI [2]	47	63	–	–	46	61	–	3	12	26	–	–	11	27	–	–
MN [2]	62	72	–	–	61	72	–	1	39	28	–	–	39	28	–	–
MS [1]	56	66	–	–	48	74	–	–	20	32	–	–	20	32	–	–
MO [2]	44	118	–	1	45	117	1	–	9	25	–	–	8	24	–	2
MT [2]	41	59	–	–	41	59	–	–	21	29	–	–	21	29	–	–
NE [5]	(5)	(5)	(5)	(5)	(5)	(5)	(5)	(5)	(5)	(5)	(5)	(5)	(5)	(5)	(5)	(5)
NV [2]	17	25	–	–	17	25	–	–	10	11	–	–	10	11	–	–
NH [3]	160	239	1	–	160	239	1	–	14	10	–	–	14	10	–	–
NJ [2]	48	32	–	–	52	28	–	–	24	16	–	–	24	16	–	–
NM [2]	33	37	–	–	33	37	–	–	25	17	–	–	25	17	–	–
NY [3]	106	44	–	–	104	43	–	3	31	32	–	–	31	32	–	–
NC [3]	46	74	–	–	45	74	1	–	16	34	–	–	16	34	–	–
ND [1]	23	71	–	–	23	71	–	–	15	32	–	–	15	32	–	–
OH [2]	34	65	–	–	34	65	–	–	10	23	–	–	10	23	–	–
OK [2]	29	72	–	–	30	71	–	–	8	40	–	–	8	39	–	1
OR [2]	35	25	–	–	35	25	–	–	18	12	–	–	18	12	–	–
PA [2]	84	119	–	–	84	119	–	–	20	30	–	–	19	31	–	–
RI [3]	63	11	1	–	63	11	1	–	32	5	1	–	32	4	1	1
SC [2]	46	78	–	–	46	78	–	–	18	28	–	–	17	28	–	1
SD [3]	12	58	–	–	12	58	–	–	8	27	–	–	8	27	–	–
TN [2]	26	73	–	–	26	73	–	–	6	27	–	–	5	28	–	–
TX [2]	52	98	–	–	51	98	–	1	11	20	–	–	11	20	–	–
UT [2]	12	63	–	–	12	63	–	–	5	24	–	–	5	24	–	–
VT [3]	85	53	12	–	85	53	12	–	19	9	2	–	19	9	2	–
VA [2]	32	68	–	–	34	66	–	–	19	21	–	–	19	21	–	–
WA [2]	51	47	–	–	50	48	–	–	24	25	–	–	24	25	–	–
WV [2]	36	64	–	–	36	64	–	–	16	18	–	–	16	18	–	–
WI [2]	36	63	–	–	36	63	–	–	14	19	–	–	14	19	–	–
WY [2]	9	51	–	–	9	51	–	–	4	26	–	–	4	26	–	–

– Represents zero. [1] Members of both houses serve 4-year terms. [2] Upper House members serve 4-year terms and Lower House members serve 2-year terms. [3] Members of both houses serve 2-year terms. [4] Illinois–4- and 2-year term depending on district. [5] Nebraska–4-year term and only state to have a nonpartisan unicameral legislature. For 2015 and 2016, Nebraska legislature has 49 members.

Source: The Council of State Governments, Lexington, KY, *The Book of the States 2016*, and earlier reports ©. See also <http://www.csg.org/>.

Table 458. Women Holding State Public Offices by Office and State: 2017

[As of January]

State	Total	Statewide elective executive office [1]	State legislature Total	Percent	State	Total	Statewide elective executive office [1]	State legislature Total	Percent
U.S.	**1,918**	**75**	**1,843**	**25**	MO	45	1	44	22
					MT	46	3	43	29
AL	23	2	21	15	NE	13	–	13	27
AK	18	–	18	30	NV	26	1	25	40
AZ	37	2	35	39	NH	123	–	123	29
AR	27	2	25	19	NJ	37	1	36	30
CA	27	1	26	22	NM	36	2	34	30
CO	41	2	39	39	NY	60	1	59	28
CT	55	3	52	28	NC	46	4	42	25
DE	15	2	13	21	ND	29	3	26	18
FL	42	1	41	26	OH	31	1	30	23
GA	62	–	62	26	OK	22	3	19	13
HI	21	–	21	28	OR	33	3	30	33
ID	33	1	32	30	PA	47	–	47	19
IL	67	3	64	36	RI	36	2	34	30
IN	34	5	29	19	SC	24	1	23	14
IA	36	2	34	23	SD	23	2	21	20
KS	47	–	47	28	TN	22	–	22	17
KY	26	3	23	17	TX	38	1	37	20
LA	22	–	22	15	UT	20	–	20	19
ME	64	–	64	34	VT	72	1	71	39
MD	60	–	60	32	VA	27	–	27	19
MA	56	4	52	26	WA	57	3	54	37
MI	36	1	35	24	WV	18	–	18	13
MN	68	3	65	32	WI	32	1	31	23
MS	26	2	24	14	WY	12	2	10	11

– Represents zero. [1] Excludes women elected to the judiciary, women appointed to state cabinet-level positions, women elected to executive posts by the legislature, and elected members of university Board of Trustees or Board of Education.

Source: Center for American Women and Politics, Eagleton Institute of Politics, Rutgers University, New Brunswick, NJ, "Women in Elective Office," <http://www.cawp.rutgers.edu/> ©, accessed June 2017.

Table 459. Hispanic Public Elected Officials by Office, 2009 to 2016, and by State, 2016

[As of January of year shown. For states not shown, no Hispanic public officials had been identified]

State	Total [1]	State executives and legislators [2]	County and municipal officials	Judicial and law enforcement	Education and school boards	State	Total [1]	State executives and legislators [2]	County and municipal officials	Judicial and law enforcement	Education and school boards
2009	5,695	277	2,264	842	2,037	MD	18	6	10	0	2
2010	5,763	275	2,270	874	2,072	MA	51	6	26	1	18
2011	5,876	286	2,282	864	2,173	MI	22	6	4	5	7
2012	5,954	292	2,293	881	2,225	MN	15	5	2	6	2
2013	6,042	320	2,285	878	2,287	MO	2	2	0	0	0
2014	6,115	334	2,313	878	2,322	MT	3	0	1	1	1
2015	6,124	349	2,334	860	2,342	NE	2	0	0	0	2
						NV	18	10	4	3	1
2016	**6,176**	**347**	**2,388**	**859**	**2,344**	NH	2	2	0	0	0
AK	2	1	1	0	0	NJ	145	12	86	1	46
AZ	349	22	129	48	145	NM	683	52	327	117	147
AR	1	0	0	0	1	NY	170	25	59	46	40
CA	1,426	34	442	76	752	NC	1	0	1	0	0
CO	163	11	89	16	39	OH	15	2	9	1	3
CT	56	13	29	0	14	OK	1	1	0	0	0
DE	5	2	2	1	0	OR	23	3	7	7	6
FL	179	26	93	51	7	PA	21	2	8	5	6
GA	11	2	5	2	2	RI	18	6	11	0	1
HI	4	4	0	0	0	TN	5	1	3	1	0
ID	7	1	5	1	0	TX	2,498	49	898	448	1,050
IL	115	15	66	12	14	UT	10	5	4	0	1
IN	24	1	12	3	8	VT	1	1	0	0	0
IA	16	0	7	0	9	VA	8	2	3	0	3
KS	13	6	5	1	1	WA	46	4	28	0	14
KY	1	1	0	0	0	WI	9	2	3	4	0
LA	4	1	1	2	0	WV	1	1	0	0	0
ME	2	0	1	0	1	WY	10	2	7	0	1

[1] Includes special district officials, not shown separately. [2] Includes U.S. Senators and Representatives, not shown separately.

Source: National Association of Latino Elected and Appointed Officials (NALEO) Educational Fund, Washington, DC, *National Directory of Latino Elected Officials* ©, and earlier reports. See also <http://www.naleo.org/>.

Table 460. Political Action Committees—Financial Activity Summary by Committee Type: 2011 to 2016

[In millions of dollars (2,259.1 represents $2,259,100,000). Covers financial activity during 2-year calendar period indicated]

Committee type	Receipts			Disbursements [1]			Contributions to candidates		
	2011-12	2013-14	2015-16	2011-12	2013-14	2015-16	2011-12	2013-14	2015-16
Total..........	2,259.1	2,368.6	4,046.3	2,198.4	2,304.8	3,973.3	446.3	435.9	444.0
Corporate..........	361.1	384.8	405.5	343.0	370.7	385.7	181.1	178.1	182.8
Labor..........	282.6	305.7	342.4	279.4	289.2	331.5	57.5	50.6	46.7
Trade..........	136.4	146.3	159.9	132.3	140.4	148.2	79.1	79.2	82.8
Membership..........	134.0	156.4	159.8	132.2	150.1	152.0	42.2	40.1	40.3
Cooperative..........	7.3	7.7	8.0	6.7	7.0	7.0	5.3	4.9	4.7
Corporation without stock..........	17.3	19.7	15.7	16.2	19.4	14.5	7.5	7.0	7.5
Nonconnected..........	1,320.4	1,347.9	2,954.9	1,288.5	1,327.9	2,934.3	73.5	76.0	79.2

[1] Comprises contributions to candidates, independent expenditures, and other disbursements.

Source: U.S. Federal Election Commission, "Campaign Finance Statistics—Public Action Committee (PAC) Data Summary Tables," <http://www.fec.gov/press/campaign_finance_statistics.shtml>, accessed April 2017.

Table 461. Congressional Campaign Finances—Receipts and Disbursements: 2007 to 2016

[In millions of dollars (983.3 represents $983,300,000). Covers all campaign finance activity during 2-year calendar period indicated for primary, general, run-off, and special elections. Data have been adjusted to eliminate transfers between all committees within a campaign. For further information on legal limits of contributions, see Federal Election Campaign Act of 1971, as amended]

Item	House of Representatives					Senate				
	2007–08	2009–10	2011–12	2013–14	2015–16	2007–08	2009–10	2011–12	2013–14	2015–16
Total receipts [1]..........	983.3	1,103.2	1,136.5	1,033.9	1,049.8	433.7	757.2	742.3	635.4	594.5
Individual contributions..........	529.5	640.6	637.0	557.0	546.4	268.7	468.0	466.1	439.4	424.2
Other committees..........	315.0	326.2	351.0	341.9	354.5	78.8	87.6	80.9	98.4	92.8
Candidate contributions & loans..........	103.1	109.6	108.2	96.4	107.0	30.5	149.6	167.3	51.2	31.6
Democrats..........	536.8	510.3	486.8	446.4	476.4	237.2	314.7	307.9	299.6	313.4
Incumbents..........	326.9	393.0	249.1	286.1	249.9	83.8	139.5	172.1	204.1	67.0
Challengers..........	120.2	64.4	174.8	82.9	126.7	115.5	38.8	71.4	41.3	176.2
Open seats [2]..........	89.6	52.9	62.9	77.3	99.7	37.9	136.5	64.4	54.1	70.1
Republicans..........	435.1	587.5	632.7	583.7	559.4	196.0	427.4	416.1	327.9	278.8
Incumbents..........	246.6	231.7	436.2	355.5	406.7	150.3	109.5	77.8	90.2	201.3
Challengers..........	103.4	266.0	125.7	119.7	51.5	26.1	148.9	143.1	144.1	29.1
Open seats [2]..........	85.1	89.8	70.7	108.5	101.2	19.6	169.1	195.3	93.5	48.5
Others..........	11.4	5.4	17.0	3.9	14.0	0.5	15.0	18.3	8.0	2.3
Incumbents..........	5.7	1.7	2.2	0.1	4.4	–	–	6.3	–	–
Challengers..........	3.0	3.2	13.5	1.3	5.0	0.4	0.5	8.7	6.4	2.1
Open seats [2]..........	2.7	0.5	1.3	2.5	4.6	0.1	14.5	3.3	1.5	0.2
Total disbursements..........	941.0	1,096.3	1,099.3	960.8	971.7	442.9	737.3	747.9	654.2	625.3
Democrats..........	495.5	534.7	479.1	422.3	425.1	230.6	319.3	315.7	311.5	316.0
Republicans..........	434.6	556.6	604.3	534.5	533.5	211.9	403.2	417.7	334.8	306.8
Others..........	10.9	5.1	15.9	3.9	13.1	0.5	14.9	14.5	8.0	2.5

– Represents or rounds to zero. [1] Includes other types of receipts, not shown separately. [2] Elections in which an incumbent did not seek reelection.

Source: U.S. Federal Election Commission, "Campaign Finance Statistics," <http://www.fec.gov/press/campaign_finance_statistics.shtml>, accessed April 2017.

Table 462. Contributions to Congressional Campaigns by Political Action Committees (PAC) by Type of Committee: 2013 to 2016

[In millions of dollars (193.4 represents $193,400,000). Covers amounts given to candidates in primary, general, run-off, and special elections during the 2-year calendar period indicated]

Type of committee	Total [1]	Democrats	Republicans	Incumbents	Challengers	Open seats [2]
HOUSE OF REPRESENTATIVES						
2013–14..........	341.6	149.3	192.3	298.9	17.6	25.1
2015–16, total [3]..........	**351.5**	**145.1**	**203.6**	**313.8**	**17.7**	**20.0**
Corporate..........	144.5	49.3	94.0	139.2	1.3	4.0
Trade association [4]..........	100.6	35.6	64.0	93.1	2.6	4.9
Labor..........	40.9	34.8	6.0	30.6	6.4	3.9
Nonconnected [5]..........	54.9	21.2	33.4	40.9	7.2	6.8
Cooperative..........	4.1	1.8	2.3	3.8	0.1	0.2
Corporation without stock..........	6.5	2.6	3.9	6.2	0.1	0.2
SENATE						
2013–14..........	94.3	41.8	52.5	63.6	14.8	15.9
2015–16, total [3]..........	**89.8**	**29.4**	**60.4**	**68.4**	**9.4**	**12.0**
Corporate..........	37.3	8.9	28.4	32.3	1.0	4.0
Trade association [4]..........	22.1	5.9	16.2	18.0	1.4	2.7
Labor..........	5.6	4.9	0.7	1.7	2.6	1.3
Nonconnected [5]..........	23.1	9.2	13.9	15.0	4.3	3.8
Cooperative..........	0.6	0.2	0.4	0.5	0.1	0.1
Corporation without stock..........	1.1	0.3	0.7	0.9	0.1	0.1

[1] Includes other parties, not shown separately. [2] Elections in which an incumbent did not seek reelection. [3] Includes other types of political action committees, not shown separately. [4] Includes membership organizations and health organizations. [5] Represents "ideological" groups as well as other issue groups not necessarily ideological in nature.

Source: U.S. Federal Election Commission, "Campaign Finance Statistics—Political Action Committees (PAC) Data Summary Tables," <http://www.fec.gov/press/campaign_finance_statistics.shtml>, accessed April 2017.

State and Local Government Finances and Employment

This section presents data on revenues, expenditures, debt, and employment of state and local governments. Nationwide statistics relating to state and local governments, their numbers, finances, and employment are compiled primarily by the U.S. Census Bureau through a program of censuses and surveys. Every fifth year (for years ending in "2" and "7"), the Census Bureau conducts a census of governments involving collection of data for all governmental units in the United States. In addition, the Census Bureau conducts annual surveys which cover all the state governments and a sample of local governments.

Annually, the Census Bureau releases information on financial data for the federal government, nationwide totals for state and local governments, and state-local data by states. Also released annually is a series on state, city, county, and school finances and on state and local public employment. There is also a series of quarterly data releases covering tax revenue and finances of major public employee retirement systems.

Basic information for Census Bureau statistics on governments is obtained by mail canvass from state and local officials; however, financial data for each state government and for many of the large local governments are compiled from their official records and reports by Census Bureau personnel. In over two-thirds of the states, all or part of local government financial data are obtained through central collection arrangements with state governments. Financial data on the federal government are primarily based on the *Budget of the United States Government* published by the Office of Management and Budget.

Governmental units—The governmental structure of the United States includes, in addition to the federal government and the states, thousands of local governments—counties, municipalities, townships, school districts, and many "special districts." In 2012, 90,056 local governments were identified by the census of governments (see table 463 and table 464). As defined by the census, governmental units include all agencies or bodies having an organized existence, governmental character, and substantial autonomy. While most of these governments can impose taxes, many of the special districts—such as independent public housing authorities and numerous local irrigation, power, and other types of districts—are financed from rentals, charges for services, benefit assessments, grants from other governments, and other non-tax sources. The count of governments excludes semi-autonomous agencies through which states, cities, and counties sometimes provide for certain functions—for example, "dependent" school systems, state institutions of higher education, and certain other "authorities" and special agencies which are under the administrative or fiscal control of an established governmental unit.

Finances—The financial statistics relate to government fiscal years ending June 30 or at some date within the 12 previous months. The following governments are exceptions and are included as though they were part of the June 30 group: the state governments of Alabama and Michigan, and the city government of The District of Columbia, with fiscal years ending September 30; the state government of Texas ending August 31; and New York State ending its fiscal year on March 31. The federal government ended the fiscal year June 30 until 1976 when its fiscal year, by an act of Congress, was revised to extend from Oct. 1 to Sept. 30. A 3-month quarter (July 1 to Sept. 30, 1976) bridged the transition.

Nationwide government finance statistics have been classified and presented in terms of uniform concepts and categories, rather than according to the highly diverse terminology, organization, and fund structure utilized by individual governments.

Statistics on governmental finances distinguish among general government, utilities, liquor stores, and insurance trusts. *General government* comprises all activities except utilities, liquor stores, and insurance trusts. *Utilities* include government water supply, electric light and power, gas supply, and transit systems. *Liquor stores* and dispensaries are operated by 17 states and by local governments in 4 states. *Insurance trusts* relate to employee retirement, unemployment compensation, and other social insurance systems administered by the federal, state, and local governments.

Data for cities or counties relate only to municipal or county and their dependent agencies and do not include amounts for other local governments in the same geographic location. Therefore, expenditure figures for "education" do not include spending by the separate school districts which administer public schools within most municipal or county areas. Variations in the assignment of governmental responsibility for public assistance, health, hospitals, public housing, and other functions to a lesser degree also have an important effect upon reported amounts of city or county expenditure, revenue, and debt.

Employment and payrolls—These data are based mainly on mail canvassing of state and local governments. Payroll includes all salaries, wages, and individual fee payments for the month specified. Employment relates to all persons on governmental payrolls during a pay period of the month covered, including paid officials, temporary help, and (unless otherwise specified) part-time as well as full-time personnel. Effective with the 1997 Census of Governments, the reference period for measuring government employment was changed from October of the calendar year to March of the calendar year. As a result, there was no annual survey of government employment covering the October 1996 period. The prior reference month of October was used from 1958 to 1995. Figures shown for individual governments cover major dependent agencies such as institutions of higher education, as well as the basic central departments and agencies of the government.

Statistical reliability—For a discussion of statistical collection and estimation, sampling procedures, and measures of statistical reliability applicable to Census Bureau data, see Appendix III.

Table 463. Number of Governmental Units by Type: 1967 to 2012

Type of government	1967	1972	1977	1982	1987	1992	1997	2002	2007	2012
Total units....................	**81,299**	**78,269**	**79,913**	**81,831**	**83,237**	**85,006**	**87,504**	**87,576**	**89,527**	**90,107**
U.S. government..............	1	1	1	1	1	1	1	1	1	1
State governments............	50	50	50	50	50	50	50	50	50	50
Local governments............	81,248	78,218	79,862	81,780	83,186	84,955	87,453	87,525	89,476	90,056
County......................	3,049	3,044	3,042	3,041	3,042	3,043	3,043	3,034	3,033	3,031
Municipal..................	18,048	18,517	18,862	19,076	19,200	19,279	19,372	19,429	19,492	19,519
Township and town..........	17,105	16,991	16,822	16,734	16,691	16,656	16,629	16,504	16,519	16,360
School district................	21,782	15,781	15,174	14,851	14,721	14,422	13,726	13,506	13,051	12,880
Special district...............	21,264	23,885	25,962	28,078	29,532	31,555	34,683	35,052	37,381	38,266

Source: U.S. Census Bureau, Census of Governments, "2012 Census of Governments Organization Tables: Final," <http://www.census.gov/govs/cog/>, accessed November 2013.

Table 464. Number of Local Governments by Type—States: 2012

[Governments in existence in January. Excludes, therefore, a few counties and numerous townships and incorporated places existing as areas for which statistics can be presented as to population and other subjects, but lacking any separate organized county, township, or municipal government. See Appendix III]

State	All govern-mental units [1]	County	Municipal	Township [1]	School district	Special district [2] Total [3]	Natural resources	Fire protection	Housing [4]
United States...........	**90,056**	**3,031**	**19,519**	**16,360**	**12,880**	**38,266**	**7,335**	**5,865**	**3,438**
Alabama....................	1,208	67	461	–	132	548	68	12	148
Alaska.....................	177	14	148	–	–	15	–	–	14
Arizona....................	674	15	91	–	242	326	92	156	–
Arkansas...................	1,556	75	502	–	239	740	260	73	119
California..................	4,425	57	482	–	1,025	2,861	479	360	67
Colorado...................	2,905	62	271	–	180	2,392	168	260	93
Connecticut................	643	–	30	149	17	447	1	72	114
Delaware...................	339	3	57	–	19	260	238	–	4
District of Columbia........	2	–	1	–	–	1	–	–	–
Florida.....................	1,650	66	410	–	95	1,079	126	57	95
Georgia....................	1,378	153	535	–	180	510	37	–	191
Hawaii.....................	21	3	1	–	–	17	16	–	–
Idaho......................	1,168	44	200	–	118	806	176	158	11
Illinois.....................	6,963	102	1,298	1,431	905	3,227	1,026	837	114
Indiana....................	2,709	91	569	1,006	291	752	143	2	70
Iowa.......................	1,947	99	947	–	366	535	241	60	28
Kansas....................	3,826	103	626	1,268	306	1,523	262	1	184
Kentucky...................	1,338	118	418	–	174	628	126	155	18
Louisiana..................	529	60	304	–	69	96	10	2	–
Maine......................	840	16	22	466	99	237	16	–	32
Maryland...................	347	23	157	–	–	167	130	–	20
Massachusetts.............	857	5	53	298	84	417	20	12	251
Michigan...................	2,875	83	533	1,240	576	443	78	24	–
Minnesota.................	3,672	87	853	1,784	338	610	152	9	157
Mississippi................	983	82	298	–	164	439	237	30	55
Missouri...................	3,768	114	954	312	534	1,854	329	375	125
Montana...................	1,265	54	129	–	319	763	134	219	13
Nebraska..................	2,581	93	530	417	272	1,269	84	414	166
Nevada....................	191	16	19	–	17	139	34	15	3
New Hampshire............	541	10	13	221	166	131	11	14	21
New Jersey................	1,344	21	324	242	523	234	15	184	–
New Mexico................	863	33	103	–	96	631	564	–	4
New York..................	3,453	57	614	929	679	1,174	3	876	–
North Carolina.............	973	100	553	–	–	320	138	–	95
North Dakota..............	2,685	53	357	1,313	183	779	78	279	38
Ohio.......................	3,842	88	937	1,308	668	841	104	100	78
Oklahoma..................	1,852	77	590	–	550	635	106	27	129
Oregon....................	1,542	36	241	–	230	1,035	187	271	19
Pennsylvania..............	4,897	66	1,015	1,546	514	1,756	6	–	90
Rhode Island..............	133	–	8	31	4	90	4	35	26
South Carolina.............	678	46	270	–	83	279	45	65	42
South Dakota..............	1,983	66	311	907	152	547	105	83	46
Tennessee.................	916	92	345	–	14	465	106	1	96
Texas.....................	5,147	254	1,214	–	1,079	2,600	435	155	387
Utah.......................	622	29	245	–	41	307	81	12	19
Vermont...................	738	14	43	237	291	153	14	16	9
Virginia....................	518	95	229	–	1	193	47	–	–
Washington................	1,900	39	281	–	295	1,285	179	372	44
West Virginia..............	659	55	232	–	55	317	14	–	35
Wisconsin.................	3,128	72	596	1,255	440	765	274	1	168
Wyoming..................	805	23	99	–	55	628	136	71	–

– Represents zero. [1] Includes town governments in the six New England States and in Minnesota, New York, and Wisconsin. [2] Single function districts. [3] Includes other special districts not shown separately. [4] Includes community development.

Source: U.S. Census Bureau, Census of Governments, "2012 Census of Governments Organization Tables: Final," <http://www.census.gov/govs/cog/>, accessed November 2013.

Table 465. State and Local Government Current Receipts and Expenditures in the National Income and Product Accounts: 1990 to 2016

[In billions of dollars (729.6 represents $729,600,000,000). For explanation of national income, see text, Section 13. Minus sign (-) indicates net loss]

Item	1990	2000	2005	2010	2012	2013	2014	2015	2016
Current receipts	**729.6**	**1,303.1**	**1,708.8**	**1,998.5**	**2,057.2**	**2,136.8**	**2,227.7**	**2,331.5**	**2,372.9**
Current tax receipts	519.1	893.2	1,166.5	1,305.6	1,416.1	1,481.4	1,518.9	1,564.6	1,590.8
Personal current taxes	122.6	236.7	276.4	297.6	346.7	375.9	384.6	406.1	412.5
Income taxes	109.6	217.4	251.5	267.1	314.3	342.8	350.9	371.4	376.8
Other	13.0	19.4	24.9	30.5	32.4	33.0	33.7	34.6	35.6
Taxes on production and imports	374.1	621.3	835.1	960.4	1,016.9	1,050.1	1,075.7	1,098.3	1,118.2
Sales taxes	184.3	316.8	402.5	446.0	482.8	505.1	523.8	542.7	556.4
Property taxes	161.5	254.7	351.3	435.0	442.2	448.8	453.6	456.6	461.7
Other	28.3	49.8	81.4	79.4	92.0	96.2	98.3	98.9	100.1
Taxes on corporate income	22.5	35.2	54.9	47.7	52.5	55.5	58.6	60.3	60.0
Contributions for government social insurance	10.0	10.8	24.6	18.1	18.0	18.5	19.1	19.0	19.3
Income receipts on assets	68.5	93.9	88.6	82.6	75.4	75.4	77.2	79.6	82.4
Interest receipts	64.1	86.3	76.8	69.1	59.8	58.9	59.6	60.7	62.1
Dividends	0.2	1.4	2.0	2.3	3.3	3.6	3.8	4.2	4.7
Rents and royalties	4.2	6.3	9.8	11.2	12.3	12.9	13.9	14.7	15.6
Current transfer receipts	126.4	299.7	436.4	612.0	558.0	571.3	624.5	679.6	691.9
Federal grants-in-aid	104.4	233.1	343.4	505.3	444.0	450.0	494.8	531.2	551.1
From business (net)	7.1	28.6	36.5	43.4	44.0	49.5	49.5	67.8	57.0
From persons	14.9	38.0	56.5	63.2	70.1	71.7	75.0	80.1	83.8
Current surplus of government enterprises	5.6	5.4	-7.3	-19.8	-10.4	-9.8	-11.9	-11.4	-11.4
Current expenditures	**736.0**	**1,293.2**	**1,775.4**	**2,235.8**	**2,277.9**	**2,327.3**	**2,397.6**	**2,492.8**	**2,565.1**
Consumption expenditures	546.2	969.1	1,256.6	1,518.3	1,536.3	1,562.7	1,601.6	1,641.2	1,677.1
Government social benefit payments to persons	127.7	271.4	406.6	523.8	540.0	563.4	612.9	666.0	695.2
Interest payments	61.8	52.1	111.8	192.1	201.2	200.7	182.6	185.2	192.3
Subsidies	0.4	0.5	0.4	1.6	0.5	0.5	0.5	0.5	0.5
Net state and local government saving	**-6.5**	**9.9**	**-66.6**	**-237.3**	**-220.8**	**-190.5**	**-169.8**	**-161.3**	**-192.2**
Social insurance funds	2.0	2.0	7.2	3.2	4.2	4.3	4.7	4.7	4.8
Other	-8.4	7.9	-73.8	-240.5	-225.0	-194.8	-174.5	-165.9	-197.0

Source: U.S. Bureau of Economic Analysis, National Income and Product Accounts Tables, "Table 3.3. State and Local Government Current Receipts and Expenditures," <http://www.bea.gov/itable/>, accessed April 2017.

Table 466. Federal Grants–in–Aid to State and Local Governments: 1990 to 2017

[135,325 represents $135,325,000,000, except as indicated. For fiscal year ending Sept. 30. Minus sign (-) indicates decrease]

Year	Current dollars							Constant (2009) dollars	
			Grants to individuals		Grants as percent of—				
	Total grants (mil. dol.)	Annual percent change [1]	Total (mil. dol.)	Percent of total grants	State & local government expenditures from own sources [2]	Federal outlays	Gross domestic product	Total grants (bil. dol.)	Annual percent change [1]
1990	135,325	11.0	77,431	57.2	25.2	10.8	2.3	224.5	6.0
1995	224,991	6.8	145,652	64.7	31.5	14.8	3.0	318.6	4.0
2000	285,874	6.7	186,534	65.3	27.4	16.0	2.8	366.4	3.8
2001	318,542	11.4	208,008	65.3	28.4	17.1	3.0	397.7	8.5
2002	352,895	10.8	231,854	65.7	29.5	17.5	3.2	433.9	9.1
2003	388,542	10.1	251,235	64.7	30.5	18.0	3.4	467.1	7.7
2004	407,512	4.9	267,046	65.5	30.9	17.8	3.4	475.7	1.8
2005	428,018	5.0	278,764	65.1	30.8	17.3	3.3	480.6	1.0
2006	434,099	1.4	277,559	63.9	29.7	16.3	3.2	469.9	-2.2
2007	443,797	2.2	289,460	65.2	28.4	16.3	3.1	464.8	-1.1
2008	461,317	3.9	306,123	66.4	27.4	15.5	3.1	464.4	-0.1
2009	537,991	16.6	362,031	67.3	33.1	15.3	3.7	538.0	15.8
2010	608,390	13.1	391,427	64.3	37.5	17.6	4.1	599.1	11.4
2011	606,766	-0.3	392,713	64.7	(NA)	16.8	3.9	583.7	-2.6
2012	544,569	-10.3	364,095	66.9	(NA)	15.4	3.4	512.4	-12.2
2013	546,171	0.3	379,008	69.4	(NA)	15.8	3.3	505.6	-1.3
2014	576,967	5.6	412,466	71.5	(NA)	16.5	3.4	525.4	3.9
2015	624,354	8.2	463,392	74.2	(NA)	16.9	3.5	565.1	7.6
2016	660,818	5.8	495,711	75.0	(NA)	17.2	3.6	593.5	5.0
2017, estimate	686,303	3.9	515,688	75.1	(NA)	16.9	3.6	601.7	1.4

NA Not available. [1] Average annual percent change from previous year. [2] Expenditures from own sources as defined in the national income and product accounts.

Source: U.S. Office of Management and Budget, *Budget of the U.S. Government, Fiscal Year 2018: Historical Tables*, May 2017. See also <http://www.whitehouse.gov/omb/budget>.

Table 467. Federal Outlays for Grants to State and Local Governments—Selected Agencies and Programs: 1990 to 2017

[In millions of dollars (135,325 represents $135,325,000,000). For fiscal year ending September. 30. Includes trust funds]

Agency and program	1990	1995	2000	2005	2010	2013	2014	2015	2016	2017 est.
Total outlays for grants	**135,325**	**224,991**	**285,874**	**428,018**	**608,390**	**546,171**	**576,967**	**624,354**	**660,818**	**686,303**
Energy	461	492	433	636	2,656	936	759	577	764	736
Natural resources and environment	3,745	3,985	4,595	5,858	9,132	7,298	6,700	7,044	7,154	7,227
Environmental Protection Agency [1]	2,874	2,912	3,490	3,734	6,883	5,006	4,382	4,571	4,270	4,279
Agriculture	1,118	780	724	933	843	670	701	707	806	849
Transportation	19,174	25,787	32,222	43,370	60,981	60,518	62,260	60,831	63,861	63,914
Grants for airports [1]	1,220	1,859	1,624	3,530	3,156	3,519	3,100	2,988	2,963	3,266
Federal-aid highways [2]	13,854	18,945	24,711	30,915	30,385	41,388	41,626	41,205	43,035	41,593
Urban mass transportation [1]	3,728	4,353	5,262	8,114	12,939	11,506	12,135	11,784	12,271	12,316
Community and regional development	4,965	7,230	8,665	20,167	18,908	16,781	13,232	14,357	15,298	14,079
Rural Community Advancement Program	139	333	479	814	–	–	–	–	–	–
Community Development Fund	2,818	4,333	4,955	4,985	7,043	5,768	6,369	6,548	6,013	6,554
Homeland Security	1,184	1,772	2,439	13,541	8,483	7,798	4,759	5,924	7,951	6,119
State and local programs	–	–	–	2,116	3,337	4,444	3,510	2,918	2,683	2,404
Firefighter assistance grants	–	–	–	1,185	–	–	–	–	–	–
Operations and support, FEMA	11	79	192	132	–	–	–	–	–	–
Predisaster mitigation grants	–	–	13	39	–	–	–	–	–	–
Disaster relief fund	1,173	1,693	2,234	10,069	5,141	3,281	1,156	2,919	5,155	3,483
Education, training, employment, social services	21,780	30,881	36,672	57,247	97,586	62,690	60,485	60,527	60,867	64,175
Education for the disadvantaged [3]	4,437	6,785	8,511	14,539	19,515	16,742	15,729	15,199	15,570	16,406
School improvement programs	1,080	1,288	2,394	6,569	5,184	4,637	4,281	4,138	4,224	4,234
Special education	1,485	2,938	4,696	10,661	17,075	12,165	12,410	12,077	12,357	12,088
Social Services block grant	2,749	2,797	1,827	1,822	2,035	1,877	1,748	1,832	1,780	1,699
Children and family services programs	2,618	4,463	5,843	8,490	10,473	9,342	9,004	9,608	10,026	11,277
Training and employment services	3,042	3,620	2,957	3,372	4,592	2,891	2,641	2,639	2,673	3,177
Health	43,890	93,587	124,843	197,848	290,168	283,036	320,022	368,026	396,666	411,445
Substance abuse and mental health services [4]	1,241	2,444	1,931	3,203	2,846	2,891	2,713	2,671	2,927	3,143
Grants to states for Medicaid [4]	41,103	89,070	117,921	181,720	272,771	265,392	301,472	349,762	368,280	378,455
State children's health insurance fund [4]	–	–	1,220	5,129	7,887	9,469	9,314	9,233	14,305	16,655
Income security	36,935	58,366	68,653	90,885	115,156	102,190	100,869	101,082	104,769	110,262
Supplemental Nutrition Assistance Program (SNAP) (formerly Food Stamp Program) [4]	2,130	2,740	3,508	4,385	5,739	6,072	5,791	5,100	6,406	7,123
Child nutrition programs [4]	4,871	7,387	9,060	11,726	16,259	19,304	19,468	20,999	21,952	23,738
Temporary Assistance for Needy Families (TANF) [4]	–	–	15,464	17,357	17,513	17,107	16,266	15,940	15,620	16,502
Veterans benefits and services [4]	134	253	434	552	836	1,087	1,223	1,821	1,829	2,072
Administration of justice	574	1,222	5,263	4,784	5,086	4,550	4,262	3,664	3,536	6,323

– Represents zero. [1] Grants include trust funds. [2] Trust funds. [3] Formerly Accelerating Achievement and Ensuring Equity. [4] Includes grants for payments to individuals.

Source: U.S. Office of Management and Budget, *Budget of the U.S. Government, Fiscal Year 2018: Historical Tables,* May 2017. See also <http://www.whitehouse.gov/omb/budget>.

Table 468. State and Local Governments—Summary of Finances: 1990 to 2014

[In millions of dollars (1,032,115 represents $1,032,115,000,000). For fiscal year ending in year shown; see text, this section. Local government amounts are estimates subject to sampling variation; see Appendix III and source]

Item	1990	2000	2005	2010	2013	2014
Revenue [1]	**1,032,115**	**1,942,328**	**2,528,546**	**3,180,023**	**3,404,546**	**3,633,774**
From federal government	136,802	291,950	438,558	623,801	582,970	602,230
Public welfare	59,961	148,549	(NA)	(NA)	(NA)	(NA)
Highways	14,368	24,414	(NA)	(NA)	(NA)	(NA)
Education	23,233	45,873	(NA)	(NA)	(NA)	(NA)
Health and hospitals	5,904	15,611	(NA)	(NA)	(NA)	(NA)
Housing and community development	9,655	17,690	(NA)	(NA)	(NA)	(NA)
Other and unallocable	23,683	39,812	(NA)	(NA)	(NA)	(NA)
From state and local sources	**895,313**	**1,650,379**	**2,089,988**	**2,556,222**	**2,821,576**	**3,031,544**
General, net intergovernmental	712,700	1,249,373	1,587,476	1,887,045	2,096,842	2,155,885
Taxes	501,619	872,351	1,098,513	1,278,847	1,451,399	1,490,816
Property	155,613	249,178	335,779	443,947	453,053	466,392
Sales and gross receipts	177,885	309,290	384,266	435,571	495,238	517,368
Individual income	105,640	211,661	242,273	261,510	338,710	341,136
Corporation net income	23,566	36,059	43,256	44,108	52,909	54,560
Other	38,915	66,164	92,939	93,710	111,490	111,361
Charges and miscellaneous	211,081	377,022	488,963	608,198	645,443	665,069
Utility and liquor stores	58,642	89,546	119,608	154,758	162,795	169,089
Water supply system	17,674	30,515	37,378	49,327	57,484	59,378
Electric power system	29,268	42,436	59,157	76,492	75,663	78,257
Gas supply system	5,216	8,049	6,937	8,219	6,521	7,154
Transit system	3,043	3,954	10,146	13,003	14,986	15,798
Liquor stores	3,441	4,592	5,990	7,716	8,141	8,503
Insurance trust revenue [2]	123,970	311,460	382,904	514,420	561,939	706,570
Employee retirement	94,268	273,881	316,576	416,536	465,909	621,480
Unemployment compensation	18,441	23,366	35,367	75,191	74,421	62,298
Direct expenditure	**972,695**	**1,742,914**	**2,363,696**	**3,110,833**	**3,174,127**	**3,258,190**
By function:						
Direct general expenditure [2]	831,573	1,502,768	2,007,490	2,537,892	2,621,156	2,706,935
Education [2]	288,148	521,612	688,314	860,118	876,252	904,310
Elementary and secondary	202,009	365,181	473,843	573,641	568,525	586,107
Higher education	73,418	134,352	182,003	243,515	260,887	268,977
Highways	61,057	101,336	126,350	155,912	157,544	162,152
Public welfare	107,287	233,350	360,730	456,200	515,674	542,569
Health	24,223	51,366	66,637	81,383	86,511	89,734
Hospitals	50,412	75,976	103,555	145,902	158,075	165,589
Police protection	30,577	56,798	74,131	95,772	98,982	101,945
Fire protection	13,186	23,102	30,830	41,335	42,551	44,140
Natural resources	12,330	20,235	23,519	28,433	28,424	27,724
Parks and recreation	14,326	25,038	31,925	40,247	36,803	37,401
Housing and community development	15,479	26,590	40,014	53,923	50,165	49,945
Sanitation and sewerage	28,453	45,261	57,940	75,620	74,775	74,501
Financial administration	16,217	29,300	36,695	40,241	39,785	41,162
Interest on general debt [3]	49,739	69,814	81,122	105,715	108,722	107,401
Utility and liquor stores [3]	77,801	114,916	160,470	213,914	217,846	226,463
Water supply system	22,101	35,789	45,695	60,655	63,478	65,373
Electric power system	30,997	39,719	58,612	78,478	76,143	77,347
Gas supply system	2,989	3,724	7,075	8,273	6,915	7,364
Transit system	18,788	31,883	44,203	60,149	65,011	69,496
Liquor stores	2,926	3,801	4,885	6,359	6,298	6,884
Insurance trust expenditure [2]	63,321	125,230	195,735	359,027	335,125	324,792
Employee retirement	38,355	95,679	145,796	204,803	246,416	259,586
Unemployment compensation	16,499	18,648	29,849	135,367	71,450	48,234
By character and object:						
Current operation	700,131	1,288,746	1,760,283	2,228,794	2,341,200	2,433,795
Capital outlay	123,102	217,063	278,063	355,437	320,416	321,379
Construction	89,144	161,694	218,691	284,213	255,656	255,498
Equipment, land, and existing structures	33,958	55,369	59,372	71,224	64,760	65,882
Assistance and subsidies	27,227	31,375	37,755	47,636	52,344	54,441
Interest on debt (general and utility)	58,914	80,499	91,859	119,939	125,042	123,784
Insurance benefits and repayments	63,321	125,230	195,735	359,027	335,125	324,792
Expenditure for salaries and wages [4]	340,654	548,796	694,583	844,650	856,856	877,411
Debt outstanding, year end	**858,006**	**1,451,815**	**2,085,026**	**2,844,190**	**2,956,197**	**2,974,441**
Long-term	838,700	1,427,524	2,054,268	2,799,101	2,924,119	2,940,196
Short-term	19,306	24,291	30,758	45,088	32,078	34,245
Long-term debt:						
Issued	108,468	184,831	323,739	398,962	363,507	302,026
Retired	64,831	121,897	224,639	275,810	363,832	309,168

NA Not available. [1] Aggregates exclude duplicative transactions between state and local governments; see source. [2] Includes amounts not shown separately. [3] Interest on utility debt included in "utility and liquor stores expenditure." For total interest on debt, see "Interest on debt (general and utility)." [4] Included in items above.

Source: U.S. Census Bureau, Federal, State, and Local Governments, Government Finance Statistics, "Annual Surveys of State and Local Government Finances," <http://www.census.gov/govs/local/>, accessed February 2017.

Table 469. State and Local Governments—Revenue and Expenditures by Function: 2010 and 2014

[In millions of dollars (3,180,023 represents $3,180,023,000,000). For fiscal year ending in year shown; see text, this section. Local government amounts are estimates subject to sampling variation; see Appendix III and source]

Item	2010			2014		
	Total	State	Local	Total	State	Local
Revenue [1]	**3,180,023**	**2,039,927**	**1,635,634**	**3,633,774**	**2,361,474**	**1,772,053**
Intergovernmental revenue [1]	623,801	575,372	543,967	602,230	550,561	551,422
Total revenue from own sources [1]	2,556,222	1,464,555	1,091,667	3,031,544	1,810,913	1,220,631
General revenue from own sources	1,887,045	991,835	895,210	2,155,885	1,189,181	966,704
Taxes [2]	1,278,847	705,929	572,917	1,490,816	867,177	623,638
Property	443,947	14,454	429,494	466,392	14,241	452,150
Individual income	261,510	236,987	24,524	341,136	311,508	29,628
Corporation income	44,108	38,006	6,102	54,560	46,436	8,124
Sales and gross receipts	435,571	344,522	91,048	517,368	411,872	105,496
General sales	288,499	224,314	64,185	347,183	271,863	75,320
Selective sales [2]	147,072	120,208	26,864	170,185	140,009	30,176
Motor fuel	37,922	36,632	1,291	42,723	41,491	1,233
Alcoholic beverages	6,021	5,511	511	6,726	6,162	564
Tobacco products	17,303	16,858	444	17,410	16,989	421
Public utilities	28,487	14,653	13,834	28,315	14,038	14,277
Motor vehicle and operators' licenses	22,459	20,861	1,598	25,654	23,810	1,844
Charges and miscellaneous [2]	608,198	285,906	322,293	665,069	322,003	343,066
Current charges [2]	411,200	169,855	241,345	453,830	190,846	262,983
Education [2]	121,138	94,530	26,608	120,745	97,323	23,423
School lunch sales	6,600	34	6,567	5,880	39	5,840
Higher education	105,515	93,081	12,434	104,867	95,926	8,942
Hospitals	113,339	42,938	70,401	133,385	56,033	77,352
Highways	12,001	6,885	5,116	16,212	8,997	7,215
Airports	18,067	1,327	16,740	21,091	1,519	19,572
Sea and inland port facilities	3,881	1,038	2,843	4,739	1,472	3,267
Natural resources	4,633	2,788	1,845	4,884	2,790	2,094
Parks and recreation	9,329	1,516	7,813	9,966	1,486	8,480
Housing and community development	5,789	622	5,167	6,451	736	5,715
Sewerage	43,472	612	42,860	51,866	887	50,979
Solid waste management	15,738	420	15,317	16,776	409	16,366
Interest earnings	59,828	34,523	25,305	50,447	33,240	17,206
Special assessments	7,001	165	6,836	7,782	28	7,754
Sale of property	2,829	692	2,137	4,310	1,091	3,219
Utility and liquor store revenue	154,758	21,617	133,141	169,089	21,490	147,599
Insurance trust revenue	514,420	451,103	63,316	706,570	600,242	106,328
Expenditures [1]	**3,115,172**	**1,943,523**	**1,666,796**	**3,261,580**	**2,048,406**	**1,722,749**
Intergovernmental expenditure [1]	4,339	485,557	13,929	3,389	496,879	16,086
Direct expenditure [1]	3,110,833	1,457,965	1,652,867	3,258,190	1,551,527	1,706,663
General expenditure [2]	2,537,892	1,108,137	1,429,755	2,706,935	1,241,213	1,465,723
Education [1]	860,118	253,758	606,360	904,310	283,726	620,584
Elementary and secondary education	573,641	7,832	565,809	586,107	6,955	579,151
Higher education	243,515	202,964	40,551	268,977	227,544	41,433
Public welfare	456,200	403,572	52,627	542,569	489,994	52,575
Hospitals	145,902	58,752	87,150	165,589	70,199	95,389
Health	81,383	39,971	41,412	89,734	44,260	45,474
Highways	155,912	93,127	62,786	162,152	96,441	65,711
Police protection	95,772	12,376	83,395	101,945	14,052	87,893
Fire protection	41,335	–	41,335	44,140	–	44,140
Corrections	73,100	46,095	27,005	74,750	47,820	26,930
Natural resources	28,433	19,336	9,097	27,724	18,971	8,753
Parks and recreation	40,247	4,912	35,335	37,401	4,878	32,523
Housing and community development	53,923	11,487	42,437	49,945	8,976	40,969
Sewerage	51,991	1,118	50,873	51,400	909	50,491
Solid waste management	23,629	2,281	21,348	23,101	1,053	22,048
Governmental administration	126,719	52,147	74,572	128,590	53,425	75,164
Interest on general debt	105,715	45,260	60,455	107,401	45,487	61,914
Utility	207,555	23,864	183,691	219,579	26,285	193,294
Liquor store expenditure	6,359	5,244	1,115	6,884	5,705	1,179
Insurance trust expenditure	359,027	320,721	38,306	324,792	278,324	46,468
By character and object:						
Current operation	2,228,794	934,322	1,294,473	2,433,795	1,064,765	1,369,030
Capital outlay	355,437	118,011	237,426	321,379	116,599	204,780
Construction	284,213	100,962	183,251	255,498	98,307	157,191
Equipment, land, and existing structures	71,224	17,048	54,175	65,882	18,293	47,589
Assistance and subsidies	47,636	37,562	10,074	54,441	43,920	10,521
Interest on debt (general and utility)	119,939	47,351	72,588	123,784	47,919	75,865
Insurance benefits and repayments	359,027	320,721	38,306	324,792	278,324	46,468
Expenditure for salaries and wages [3]	844,650	244,952	599,698	877,411	253,420	623,990

– Represents or rounds to zero. [1] Aggregates exclude duplicative transactions between levels of government; see source. [2] Includes other items, not shown separately. [3] Included in items shown above.

Source: U.S. Census Bureau, Federal, State, and Local Governments, Government Finance Statistics, "Annual Surveys of State and Local Government Finances," <http://www.census.gov/govs/local/>, accessed February 2017.

Table 470. State and Local Governments—Capital Outlays: 1990 to 2014

[In millions of dollars (123,102 represents $123,102,000,000), except percent. For fiscal year ending in year shown; see text, this section. Local government amounts are subject to sampling variation; see Appendix III and source]

Level and function	1990	2000	2005	2010	2011	2012	2013	2014
State & local governments: Total	**123,102**	**217,063**	**278,063**	**355,437**	**336,340**	**333,228**	**320,416**	**321,379**
Percent of direct expenditure	12.7	12.5	11.8	11.4	10.7	10.6	10.1	9.9
By function:								
Education [1]	25,997	60,968	77,780	93,562	86,760	84,660	80,600	80,240
Elementary and secondary	18,057	45,150	54,563	60,240	52,989	51,202	47,906	48,702
Higher education	7,441	15,257	22,735	31,644	32,216	32,670	31,869	30,700
Highways	33,867	56,439	70,689	89,895	86,281	90,809	87,728	86,703
Health and hospitals [2]	3,848	5,502	6,100	8,553	8,494	9,500	9,345	10,194
Natural resources	2,545	4,347	4,541	5,214	5,368	5,460	4,912	4,360
Parks and recreation	3,877	6,916	8,136	10,711	9,012	8,297	7,632	7,318
Sewerage	8,356	10,093	14,081	21,915	22,921	20,640	18,388	17,980
Utilities	16,601	24,847	34,790	49,258	47,490	47,174	49,685	50,958
State governments: Total	**45,524**	**76,233**	**95,155**	**118,011**	**115,571**	**119,668**	**114,840**	**116,599**
Percent of direct expenditure	11.5	10.1	8.9	8.1	7.7	8.0	7.6	7.5
By function:								
Education [1]	7,253	14,077	20,585	28,643	29,037	28,651	28,620	27,421
Elementary and secondary	388	521	447	1,066	747	600	658	728
Higher education	6,366	12,995	19,656	25,899	26,734	27,262	27,137	25,855
Highways	24,850	41,651	52,607	64,755	62,626	67,342	63,249	63,513
Health and hospitals [2]	1,531	2,228	2,363	2,654	2,738	3,298	3,062	3,302
Natural resources	1,593	2,758	2,667	2,337	2,411	2,303	2,266	2,080
Parks and recreation	601	1,044	915	910	889	732	754	709
Sewerage	333	403	486	488	83	188	134	123
Utilities	2,605	4,232	4,319	5,318	5,351	4,700	6,082	7,038
Local governments: Total	**77,578**	**140,830**	**182,908**	**237,426**	**220,770**	**213,560**	**205,576**	**204,780**
Percent of direct expenditure	13.5	14.3	14.1	14.4	13.4	12.9	12.4	12.0
By function:								
Education [1]	18,744	46,890	57,195	64,919	57,723	56,009	51,980	52,820
Elementary and secondary	17,669	44,629	54,116	59,174	52,242	50,602	47,249	47,974
Higher education	1,076	2,261	3,079	5,745	5,481	5,407	4,732	4,846
Highways	9,017	14,789	18,083	25,140	23,655	23,467	24,479	23,191
Health and hospitals [2]	2,316	3,274	3,737	5,899	5,755	6,202	6,283	6,891
Natural resources	952	1,589	1,873	2,878	2,957	3,157	2,647	2,280
Parks and recreation	3,276	5,872	7,221	9,802	8,123	7,565	6,879	6,609
Sewerage	8,023	9,690	13,595	21,426	22,839	20,452	18,254	17,857
Utilities	13,996	20,615	30,471	43,940	42,139	42,475	43,603	43,921

[1] Includes other education, not shown separately. [2] After 2003, includes only hospital outlays.

Source: U.S. Census Bureau, Federal, State, and Local Governments, Government Finance Statistics, "Annual Surveys of State and Local Government Finances," <http://www.census.gov/govs/local/>, accessed February 2017.

Table 471. State and Local Governments—Expenditures for Public Works: 2000 to 2014

[In millions of dollars (230,569 represents $230,569,000,000), except percent. Represents direct expenditures excluding intergovernmental grants]

Item	Total	Highways	Air trans-portation	Sea and inland port facilities	Sewerage	Solid waste manage-ment	Water supply	Mass transit
2000, total	**230,569**	**101,336**	**13,160**	**3,141**	**28,052**	**17,208**	**35,789**	**31,883**
State	74,974	61,942	1,106	863	955	2,347	354	7,407
Local	155,595	39,394	12,054	2,277	27,098	14,861	35,435	24,476
Capital expenditures (percent)	41.9	55.7	51.0	51.5	36.0	8.9	29.5	30.5
2010, total	**381,808**	**155,912**	**24,209**	**5,263**	**51,991**	**23,629**	**60,655**	**60,149**
State	111,280	93,127	1,724	1,245	1,118	2,281	378	11,407
Local	270,529	62,786	22,485	4,019	50,873	21,348	60,277	48,742
Capital expenditures (percent)	(NA)	57.7	(NA)	(NA)	42.2	8.9	(NA)	(NA)
2013, total	**387,584**	**157,544**	**21,459**	**5,317**	**50,549**	**24,226**	**63,478**	**65,011**
State	114,478	94,016	1,848	1,568	721	2,386	371	13,569
Local	273,106	63,529	19,611	3,749	49,828	21,840	63,108	51,442
Capital expenditures (percent)	(NA)	55.7	(NA)	(NA)	36.4	7.8	(NA)	(NA)
2014, total	**399,186**	**162,152**	**21,654**	**6,010**	**51,400**	**23,101**	**65,373**	**69,496**
State	118,419	96,441	1,980	1,654	909	1,053	398	15,984
Local	280,767	65,711	19,674	4,356	50,491	22,048	64,975	53,512
Capital expenditures (percent)	(NA)	53.5	(NA)	(NA)	35.0	7.7	(NA)	(NA)

NA Not available.

Source: U.S. Census Bureau, Federal, State, and Local Governments, Government Finance Statistics, "Annual Surveys of State and Local Government Finances," <http://www.census.gov/govs/local/>, accessed January 2017, and unpublished data.

Table 472. State and Local Governments—Indebtedness: 1990 to 2014

[In billions of dollars (858.0 represents $858,000,000,000). For fiscal year ending in year shown; see text, this section. Local government amounts are estimates subject to sampling variation; see Appendix III and source]

Item	Debt outstanding						Long-term		
		Cash and security holdings	Long-term			Short-term	Net long-term [1]	Debt issued	Debt retired
	Total		Total	Public debt for private purposes	All other				
1990: Total.......	858.0	1,490.8	838.7	294.1	544.6	19.3	474.4	108.5	64.8
State...........	318.3	963.3	315.5	154.4	161.1	2.8	125.5	43.5	22.9
Local...........	539.8	527.5	523.2	139.7	383.5	16.5	348.9	65.0	42.0
1995: Total.......	1,115.4	2,058.5	1,088.3	300.6	787.7	27.0	697.3	129.3	95.1
State...........	427.2	1,393.9	421.1	176.8	244.4	6.1	205.3	52.6	37.5
Local...........	688.1	664.6	667.2	123.9	543.3	20.9	491.9	76.8	57.6
2000: Total.......	1,451.8	3,503.7	1,427.5	372.6	1,054.9	24.3	959.6	184.8	121.9
State...........	547.9	2,518.9	541.5	227.3	314.2	6.4	266.9	75.0	44.4
Local...........	903.9	984.8	886.0	145.3	740.7	17.9	692.7	109.8	77.5
2002: Total.......	1,681.4	3,650.7	1,638.1	417.7	1,220.5	43.2	1,121.0	262.7	161.9
State...........	636.8	2,555.4	618.2	258.5	359.6	18.6	311.8	104.2	64.9
Local...........	1,044.6	1,095.3	1,020.0	159.2	860.8	24.6	809.2	158.5	97.0
2003: Total.......	1,812.7	3,696.1	1,772.2	431.4	1,340.8	40.5	1,242.7	345.8	215.2
State...........	697.9	2,594.2	681.8	267.3	414.5	16.1	366.2	148.8	85.9
Local...........	1,114.7	1,101.9	1,090.4	164.1	926.3	24.3	876.5	196.9	129.3
2004: Total.......	1,976.6	4,137.8	1,938.3	459.3	1,479.0	38.3	(NA)	359.8	242.1
State...........	779.5	2,944.9	766.0	279.1	486.9	13.6	(NA)	170.8	107.4
Local...........	1,197.0	1,192.9	1,172.3	180.2	992.1	24.7	(NA)	189.0	134.7
2005: Total.......	2,085.0	4,439.2	2,054.3	483.3	1,571.0	30.8	(NA)	323.7	224.6
State...........	810.9	3,153.8	805.3	297.4	507.9	5.6	(NA)	131.6	93.6
Local...........	1,274.2	1,285.4	1,249.0	185.9	1,063.0	25.2	(NA)	192.2	131.1
2006: Total.......	2,204.0	4,818.1	2,170.8	509.6	1,661.3	33.2	(NA)	341.9	229.5
State...........	870.0	3,443.2	859.4	318.0	541.5	10.6	(NA)	148.2	95.9
Local...........	1,334.0	1,374.8	1,311.4	191.6	1,119.8	22.6	(NA)	193.7	133.6
2007: Total.......	2,404.7	5,457.7	2,373.3	553.3	1,820.0	31.4	(NA)	381.8	228.4
State...........	936.0	3,918.8	929.4	353.9	575.6	6.6	(NA)	161.6	93.4
Local...........	1,468.7	1,538.9	1,443.9	199.5	1,244.4	24.8	(NA)	220.3	135.0
2008: Total.......	2,564.4	5,310.8	2,518.7	602.9	1,915.8	45.7	(NA)	373.6	243.5
State...........	1,006.4	3,755.7	992.2	379.0	613.2	14.2	(NA)	151.7	93.4
Local...........	1,558.0	1,555.2	1,526.5	223.9	1,302.6	31.6	(NA)	221.9	150.1
2009: Total.......	2,713.2	4,537.4	2,676.3	627.8	2,048.6	36.9	(NA)	371.3	256.5
State...........	1,048.7	3,082.5	1,041.3	395.1	646.2	7.3	(NA)	154.2	109.0
Local...........	1,664.6	1,454.9	1,635.0	232.7	1,402.3	29.6	(NA)	217.1	147.6
2010: Total.......	2,844.2	4,826.0	2,799.1	625.9	2,173.2	45.1	(NA)	399.0	275.8
State...........	1,115.5	3,323.0	1,100.8	397.1	703.6	14.7	(NA)	183.7	125.1
Local...........	1,728.7	1,503.0	1,698.3	228.8	1,469.6	30.4	(NA)	215.2	150.7
2011: Total.......	2,923.1	5,265.1	2,888.4	616.1	2,272.3	34.7	(NA)	364.6	275.1
State...........	1,139.7	3,681.4	1,134.2	389.1	745.1	5.4	(NA)	138.1	112.4
Local...........	1,783.5	1,583.7	1,754.2	227.0	1,527.2	29.3	(NA)	226.5	162.7
2012: Total.......	2,948.4	5,280.7	2,904.6	597.3	2,307.4	43.8	(NA)	339.4	335.6
State...........	1,148.9	3,699.2	1,133.5	375.6	757.8	15.5	(NA)	136.2	140.9
Local...........	1,799.5	1,581.5	1,771.2	221.6	1,549.5	28.3	(NA)	203.2	194.7
2013: Total.......	2,956.2	5,590.4	2,924.1	575.1	2,349.1	32.1	(NA)	363.5	363.8
State...........	1,137.9	3,918.6	1,132.3	354.3	778.0	5.7	(NA)	147.5	155.2
Local...........	1,818.3	1,671.8	1,791.9	220.8	1,571.1	26.4	(NA)	216.0	208.6
2014: Total.......	2,974.4	6,050.6	2,940.2	549.1	2,391.0	34.2	(NA)	302.0	309.2
State...........	1,149.1	4,303.7	1,140.4	341.1	799.3	8.7	(NA)	128.3	125.0
Local...........	1,825.3	1,746.9	1,799.8	208.0	1,591.8	25.5	(NA)	173.7	184.2

NA Not available. [1] Net long-term debt outstanding is the amount of long-term debt held by a government for which no funds have been set aside for its repayment.

Source: U.S. Census Bureau, Federal, State, and Local Governments, Government Finance Statistics, "Annual Surveys of State and Local Government Finances," <http://www.census.gov/govs/local/>, accessed February 2017.

Table 473. New Security Issues—State and Local Governments: 1990 to 2016

[In billions of dollars (122.9 represents $122,900,000,000)]

Type of issue, issuer, or use	1990	1995	2000	2005	2010	2012	2013	2014	2015	2016
All issues, new and refunding [1].........	**122.9**	**145.7**	**180.4**	**409.6**	**460.8**	**390.4**	**313.9**	**318.5**	**399.6**	**431.0**
By type of issue:										
General obligation...........................	39.5	57.0	64.5	145.8	137.5	126.6	116.2	126.4	161.1	161.4
Revenue..................................	83.3	88.7	115.9	263.8	323.2	263.8	197.7	192.1	238.7	269.9
By type of issuer:										
State....................................	15.0	14.7	19.9	31.6	55.2	(NA)	(NA)	(NA)	(NA)	(NA)
Special district or statutory authority [2]....	75.9	93.5	121.2	298.6	294.9	(NA)	(NA)	(NA)	(NA)	(NA)
Municipality, county, or township..........	32.0	37.5	39.3	79.4	86.6	(NA)	(NA)	(NA)	(NA)	(NA)
Issues for new capital....................	**97.9**	**102.4**	**154.3**	**223.8**	**278.5**	**159.5**	**156.0**	**140.8**	**169.5**	**168.4**
By use of proceeds:										
Education.................................	17.1	24.0	38.7	71.0	60.4	34.1	37.1	36.2	46.5	50.4
Transportation............................	11.8	11.9	19.7	25.4	32.3	20.5	23.3	16.0	13.9	19.6
Utilities and conservation...................	10.0	9.6	11.9	9.9	22.3	11.5	6.4	5.0	8.5	3.9
Industrial aid.............................	6.6	6.6	7.1	18.6	35.7	21.3	11.9	12.6	14.7	14.1
Other purposes...........................	31.7	30.8	47.3	60.6	92.4	48.3	60.1	54.5	56.0	56.7

NA Not available. [1] Par amounts of long-term issues based on date of sale. [2] Includes school districts.

Source: Board of Governors of the Federal Reserve System, Business Finance, "New Security Issues, State and Local Governments," <http://www.federalreserve.gov/econresdata/statisticsdata.htm>, accessed June 2017.

Table 474. State and Local Governments—Total Revenue and Expenditures by State: 2000 to 2014

[In millions of dollars (1,942,328 represents $1,942,328,000,000). For fiscal year ending in year shown; see text, this section. These data cannot be used to compute the deficit or surplus for any single government, as these are estimates for all state and local governments within a state area. For further information, see the *2006 Government Finance and Employment Classification Manual* at <http://www.census.gov/govs/classification/>]

State	Revenue				Expenditures			
	2000	2005	2010	2014	2000	2005	2010	2014
United States.............	1,942,328	2,528,546	3,180,023	3,633,774	1,746,943	2,368,316	3,115,172	3,261,580
Alabama....................	25,726	33,377	42,189	43,222	25,319	31,752	42,255	42,869
Alaska.....................	10,525	11,404	15,643	17,148	8,628	10,027	14,450	16,774
Arizona....................	27,778	41,057	54,099	59,744	27,293	39,458	53,432	52,970
Arkansas...................	13,833	18,866	24,539	28,599	12,245	16,682	22,798	25,137
California..................	270,380	381,059	453,354	552,480	236,645	342,546	432,363	473,516
Colorado...................	29,603	38,915	49,260	57,556	26,173	35,063	48,630	53,460
Connecticut................	25,828	30,490	39,427	45,562	24,011	29,631	39,311	42,674
Delaware...................	6,224	7,637	9,831	11,385	5,153	7,595	9,745	10,906
District of Columbia........	6,383	10,046	11,644	14,713	6,527	8,947	13,682	15,349
Florida....................	92,402	135,491	166,817	179,242	84,301	130,860	163,536	159,919
Georgia....................	49,310	60,297	76,370	87,384	43,517	60,730	78,158	78,806
Hawaii.....................	8,488	11,000	14,666	18,638	8,254	10,534	14,340	15,930
Idaho......................	7,590	10,004	12,490	13,970	6,404	8,915	12,054	11,699
Illinois...................	80,695	99,670	126,384	148,451	74,727	97,723	129,518	137,446
Indiana....................	32,716	44,302	54,803	58,166	31,250	42,164	53,247	53,625
Iowa.......................	17,220	23,204	31,055	36,183	17,275	21,486	29,537	32,741
Kansas.....................	16,235	19,990	26,330	29,575	14,419	18,948	26,536	27,300
Kentucky...................	25,200	28,069	37,560	41,252	21,473	27,308	38,595	39,631
Louisiana..................	27,109	35,858	47,078	48,711	25,018	32,578	48,755	47,217
Maine......................	8,554	11,383	12,557	13,996	7,652	10,207	12,286	12,760
Maryland...................	33,949	45,076	57,493	67,902	30,598	41,373	57,485	63,622
Massachusetts..............	46,103	62,019	76,100	88,328	44,362	57,862	76,679	82,164
Michigan...................	70,112	81,138	93,819	99,462	61,506	76,063	90,935	89,218
Minnesota..................	38,785	45,465	57,410	68,056	35,424	42,936	55,975	59,994
Mississippi................	16,672	21,113	28,690	31,218	15,379	20,041	27,216	27,842
Missouri...................	31,635	41,340	51,592	58,177	27,953	37,186	50,040	50,587
Montana....................	5,643	7,438	9,784	11,409	4,983	6,412	9,296	9,688
Nebraska...................	11,650	15,905	20,121	23,920	10,831	14,332	19,315	20,901
Nevada.....................	11,885	18,953	22,838	27,425	11,230	17,405	23,856	22,247
New Hampshire..............	6,948	8,911	11,581	12,489	6,222	8,679	11,439	11,462
New Jersey.................	62,331	79,126	99,751	101,861	54,590	78,522	102,667	105,425
New Mexico.................	13,073	16,656	21,998	25,064	11,195	15,427	22,372	21,710
New York...................	188,907	234,689	313,781	364,433	171,858	226,867	295,467	308,861
North Carolina.............	50,542	64,813	86,699	94,287	46,135	60,080	79,955	83,435
North Dakota...............	4,495	5,239	7,890	12,294	4,041	4,794	6,746	9,107
Ohio.......................	80,074	102,498	123,289	134,167	68,418	91,972	113,844	117,214
Oklahoma...................	18,760	24,552	32,939	38,227	15,962	22,044	31,338	33,210
Oregon.....................	28,644	32,406	41,031	50,783	24,086	29,084	39,506	42,974
Pennsylvania...............	80,546	103,692	124,379	135,043	75,624	101,484	130,085	131,870
Rhode Island...............	7,427	9,731	11,726	12,481	6,432	9,226	11,303	11,571
South Carolina.............	23,467	33,278	42,509	46,895	23,436	33,012	42,800	43,892
South Dakota...............	4,277	5,857	6,941	8,873	3,760	4,973	6,845	7,261
Tennessee..................	33,625	44,888	54,297	57,297	32,010	42,800	53,554	56,125
Texas......................	120,666	162,806	209,930	259,268	109,634	151,960	218,807	231,604
Utah.......................	14,954	19,183	24,149	28,207	13,044	17,247	24,552	25,202
Vermont....................	4,019	5,393	7,016	7,723	3,766	5,172	6,781	7,442
Virginia...................	44,175	56,658	71,093	81,666	38,092	51,529	67,673	75,615
Washington.................	46,372	57,510	71,623	86,258	41,794	55,800	75,167	77,627
West Virginia..............	10,760	14,587	16,993	19,013	9,990	12,110	15,685	16,757
Wisconsin..................	43,003	48,235	66,291	65,259	34,559	43,146	55,839	57,429
Wyoming....................	7,030	7,269	10,176	10,314	3,743	5,619	8,720	8,794

Source: U.S. Census Bureau, Federal, State, and Local Governments, Government Finance Statistics, "Annual Surveys of State and Local Government Finances," <http://factfinder.census.gov/>, accessed January 2017.

Table 475. State and Local Governments—Revenue by State: 2014

[In millions of dollars (3,663,774 represents $3,663,774,000,000). For fiscal year ending in year shown; see text, this section]

State	Total revenue	General revenue Total	Intergovernmental from federal government	General revenue from own sources	Select taxes Total	Property	Sales and gross receipt	Individual income	Corporation income	Total [1]	Current charges Total [1]	Education	Hospitals	Sewerage	Miscellaneous revenue Total [1]	Interest earnings	Special assessments	Utility and liquor stores	Insurance trust revenue
U.S.	3,633,774	2,758,115	602,230	2,155,885	1,490,816	466,392	517,368	341,136	54,560	665,069	453,830	120,745	133,385	51,866	211,239	50,447	7,782	169,089	706,570
AL	43,222	34,637	8,975	25,662	14,548	2,530	7,027	3,307	406	11,114	8,925	2,608	4,661	467	2,189	416	16	3,125	5,461
AK	17,148	14,267	3,094	11,173	5,568	1,945	574	–	409	5,605	1,428	213	335	139	4,176	854	6	408	2,472
AZ	59,744	44,772	11,589	33,183	22,512	6,635	10,945	3,462	575	10,671	7,430	2,498	1,938	878	3,241	861	77	4,714	10,258
AR	28,599	22,173	6,354	15,819	11,143	2,001	5,573	2,602	398	4,676	3,322	1,115	1,194	285	1,354	300	28	996	5,431
CA	552,480	370,790	71,594	299,196	211,365	53,731	66,407	67,996	8,858	87,832	64,857	9,841	20,177	7,071	22,974	4,584	1,709	27,759	153,932
CO	57,556	44,620	8,377	36,242	23,379	7,311	8,285	5,658	718	12,864	8,928	3,014	2,237	888	3,936	1,094	127	2,656	10,280
CT	45,562	38,070	6,914	31,156	26,058	9,971	6,782	7,773	627	5,098	3,067	1,332	340	418	2,030	675	56	809	6,683
DE	11,385	9,112	2,095	7,017	4,125	775	495	1,096	284	2,892	1,529	798	8	157	1,364	144	24	456	1,817
DC	14,713	11,931	3,790	8,141	6,378	2,071	1,600	1,679	416	1,762	734	33	119	280	1,028	71	–	1,005	1,777
FL	179,242	138,496	29,634	108,862	66,132	23,578	34,394	–	2,044	42,730	29,476	4,429	6,865	3,302	13,254	1,725	2,419	9,221	31,525
GA	87,384	65,878	15,501	50,377	34,096	10,980	12,176	8,966	944	16,281	12,016	3,112	4,082	1,277	4,265	637	54	4,878	16,628
HI	18,638	14,498	3,127	11,371	8,103	1,392	4,300	1,745	126	3,268	2,354	410	622	456	914	47	36	388	3,751
ID	13,970	10,661	2,662	7,999	5,288	1,517	1,852	1,338	190	2,711	2,036	486	595	214	675	156	28	368	2,941
IL	148,451	112,175	21,334	90,841	70,821	25,851	20,017	16,642	4,440	20,020	12,726	4,198	1,605	1,361	7,294	1,835	445	4,960	31,316
IN	58,166	49,235	11,384	37,851	24,727	6,401	10,589	6,044	867	13,124	9,916	3,601	3,726	1,498	3,208	1,107	20	2,571	6,360
IA	36,183	28,709	6,682	22,028	13,756	4,743	4,318	3,312	389	8,272	6,395	1,866	3,052	551	1,877	288	20	1,425	6,048
KS	29,575	24,231	4,207	20,024	12,706	4,166	5,060	2,514	330	7,318	5,248	1,420	2,454	422	2,070	524	125	1,420	3,924
KY	41,252	33,179	10,210	22,969	15,917	3,253	6,003	4,988	818	7,051	5,128	1,554	1,860	585	1,923	637	20	1,713	6,360
LA	48,711	39,305	11,064	28,240	18,079	3,898	9,448	2,754	481	10,162	6,688	1,430	3,302	400	3,474	838	19	1,144	8,262
ME	13,996	11,528	3,123	8,405	6,395	2,552	1,921	1,414	183	2,010	1,340	383	153	162	670	206	7	142	2,327
MD	67,902	56,013	11,997	44,016	33,470	8,911	8,857	12,531	983	10,546	6,953	2,481	188	1,171	3,593	658	47	1,243	10,646
MA	88,328	69,184	15,098	54,086	40,623	14,732	8,285	13,246	2,195	13,463	7,829	2,821	303	1,647	5,634	1,701	20	3,554	15,590
MI	99,462	78,372	19,289	59,083	37,426	13,241	12,874	8,335	881	21,657	15,336	5,637	3,746	1,929	6,322	1,498	172	3,692	17,397
MN	68,056	52,292	9,774	42,518	30,781	7,700	10,135	9,624	1,326	11,737	7,718	2,405	1,932	1,010	4,019	970	321	2,695	13,069
MS	31,218	24,568	7,622	16,947	10,482	2,743	4,811	1,667	526	6,464	5,376	1,209	3,271	222	1,089	166	9	1,172	5,478
MO	58,177	42,726	10,925	31,801	21,061	5,822	7,855	5,694	431	10,740	6,958	2,442	2,247	838	3,782	1,012	82	2,496	12,955
MT	11,409	8,311	2,565	5,746	3,929	1,499	558	1,063	150	1,817	1,161	484	96	103	656	205	72	214	2,884
NE	23,920	16,682	3,381	13,301	9,185	3,308	2,818	2,124	307	4,115	2,906	933	868	203	1,210	231	32	4,376	2,862
NV	27,425	18,907	3,363	15,544	10,998	2,704	6,778	–	–	4,546	3,203	530	590	460	1,343	225	78	1,010	7,507
NH	12,489	9,980	1,806	8,174	5,747	3,799	880	93	543	2,427	1,370	642	8	140	1,058	399	1	736	1,774
NJ	101,861	91,658	16,440	75,219	57,638	27,395	12,929	11,974	2,368	17,581	11,122	3,764	1,316	1,685	6,459	1,573	7	2,119	8,083
NM	25,064	19,624	5,741	13,883	8,274	1,525	3,841	1,297	206	5,609	2,335	642	927	177	3,274	777	15	607	4,833
NY	364,433	270,016	54,612	215,404	166,087	50,981	40,674	53,308	11,536	49,317	28,871	4,150	8,886	2,806	20,445	5,211	139	15,899	78,517

See footnotes at end of table.

Table 475. State and Local Governments—Revenue by State: 2014-Continued.

See headnote on page 304.

State	Total revenue	Intergovernmental from federal government — Total	General revenue from own sources	Select taxes — Total[1]	Property	Sales and gross receipt	Individual income	Corporation income	Total	Current charges — Total[1]	Education	Hospitals	Sewerage	Miscellaneous revenue — Total[1]	Interest earnings	Special assessments	Utility and liquor stores	Insurance trust revenue
NC...	94,287	17,653	56,385	36,008	9,457	12,701	10,391	1,361	20,377	15,864	3,643	8,181	1,322	4,513	888	17	5,291	14,958
ND...	12,294	1,719	9,215	7,212	830	2,071	499	250	2,003	1,204	467	4	58	799	282	107	201	1,159
OH...	134,167	23,865	72,679	48,789	13,954	17,802	13,019	281	23,890	16,193	6,010	4,250	2,152	7,698	1,967	263	3,901	33,722
OK...	38,227	7,701	21,977	13,832	2,418	6,189	2,962	397	8,146	5,019	2,165	1,240	392	3,127	574	18	1,863	6,686
OR...	50,783	9,673	26,255	16,281	5,360	1,890	6,649	557	9,974	7,189	1,899	2,091	1,001	2,785	528	71	1,981	12,873
PA...	135,043	24,080	85,101	60,217	17,971	18,707	15,614	2,771	24,884	17,520	6,454	3,001	2,730	7,364	2,081	90	4,703	21,158
RI...	12,481	2,628	7,627	5,454	2,434	1,591	1,088	120	2,173	1,168	484	6	210	1,005	375	7	227	1,998
SC...	46,895	7,486	28,914	15,550	5,215	5,280	3,423	328	13,364	10,290	2,300	6,008	630	3,074	608	31	3,498	6,997
SD...	8,873	1,712	4,725	3,143	1,111	1,684	–	25	1,582	842	366	60	100	740	238	12	391	2,045
TN...	57,297	11,295	30,753	20,243	5,433	11,323	239	1,177	10,510	7,595	2,093	2,696	874	2,915	542	42	9,191	6,057
TX...	259,268	42,936	159,965	109,121	44,109	54,548	–	–	50,844	32,278	9,208	10,095	3,747	18,566	6,293	297	13,386	42,982
UT...	28,207	4,742	16,949	10,315	2,853	3,689	2,890	308	6,634	4,847	1,611	1,627	408	1,786	453	50	2,368	4,148
VT...	7,723	2,013	4,663	3,473	1,466	1,035	675	106	1,189	755	508	(Z)	72	434	120	3	292	755
VA...	81,666	11,297	54,001	35,009	12,133	8,690	10,878	741	18,992	13,682	4,276	3,910	1,488	5,310	1,181	49	2,601	13,767
WA...	86,258	12,865	49,452	32,187	9,633	19,447	–	–	17,265	13,263	3,188	3,627	2,273	4,002	796	360	6,548	17,393
WV...	19,013	4,449	11,123	7,314	1,576	2,694	1,770	204	3,808	2,389	879	403	278	1,420	236	35	342	3,099
WI...	65,259	9,608	37,588	26,398	9,544	7,811	6,793	981	11,190	7,580	2,533	1,547	860	3,609	872	85	2,006	16,058
WY...	10,314	2,184	6,236	3,473	1,232	1,151	–	–	2,764	1,469	184	934	69	1,295	788	12	327	1,566

– Represents or rounds to zero. Z Less than 50,000. [1] Includes items not shown separately.

Source: U.S. Census Bureau, Federal, State, and Local Governments, Government Finance Statistics, "Annual Surveys of State and Local Government Finances," <http://www.census.gov/govs/local/>, accessed January 2017.

Table 476. State and Local Governments—Expenditures and Debt by State: 2014

[In millions of dollars (3,261,580 represents $3,261,580,000,000). For fiscal year ending in year shown; see text, this section]

State	Total expenditures	Total [1]	General expenditures Total [1]	Direct general expenditures: Education	Public welfare	Health	Hospitals	Highways	Police protection	Corrections	Natural resources	Parks and recreation	Housing and community development	Sewerage	Solid waste	Governmental administration	Interest on general debt	Utility and liquor store expenditures	Insurance trust expenditures	Total debt outstanding
U.S.	3,261,580	2,710,325	2,706,935	904,310	542,569	89,734	165,589	162,152	101,945	74,750	27,724	37,401	49,945	51,400	23,101	128,590	107,401	226,463	324,792	2,974,441
AL	42,869	36,170	36,170	13,141	6,523	812	4,998	2,250	1,204	706	267	407	467	352	242	1,518	1,105	3,137	3,562	31,076
AK	16,774	14,587	14,587	3,575	2,095	279	392	1,576	373	342	370	108	391	117	132	1,164	424	890	1,297	9,051
AZ	52,970	42,845	42,845	15,076	8,898	2,148	1,712	1,943	1,951	1,639	532	610	528	661	365	2,088	1,529	5,685	4,440	48,737
AR	25,137	22,241	22,241	8,136	5,730	353	1,136	1,634	656	565	280	235	178	351	218	1,038	488	996	1,901	15,997
CA	473,516	373,837	371,051	111,037	75,051	15,944	24,622	18,049	15,806	14,307	4,777	5,271	8,183	7,232	2,704	19,782	16,667	40,499	59,180	425,878
CO	53,460	43,531	43,527	14,563	6,751	1,320	2,690	2,754	1,800	1,213	430	1,127	795	976	110	2,461	2,173	4,216	5,713	54,072
CT	42,674	35,852	35,852	12,568	6,983	869	1,311	1,711	1,161	694	176	251	1,101	601	334	1,920	1,794	1,615	5,207	44,623
DE	10,906	9,583	9,582	3,517	2,133	468	45	671	336	294	92	70	140	163	64	641	427	586	736	7,870
DC	15,349	11,960	11,960	2,624	3,111	454	307	767	591	197	57	238	691	664	110	502	533	2,819	570	13,087
FL	159,919	138,467	138,467	39,038	25,605	5,131	7,896	9,050	7,356	3,975	2,924	2,734	2,375	3,176	2,410	6,778	4,882	10,676	10,776	155,142
GA	78,806	65,499	65,499	25,440	11,625	2,084	4,832	3,481	2,407	2,214	484	787	1,264	1,235	654	3,359	1,422	6,263	7,044	56,865
HI	15,930	13,682	13,682	3,389	2,619	542	822	717	453	217	120	280	280	359	233	814	586	919	1,329	14,296
ID	11,699	10,354	10,354	3,144	2,261	250	615	892	412	320	262	140	126	194	138	590	241	330	1,015	6,230
IL	137,446	109,229	109,220	37,261	19,422	2,839	2,878	7,664	4,987	2,098	659	2,558	2,089	1,847	518	5,371	6,427	8,695	19,523	149,256
IN	53,625	47,820	47,816	16,572	10,615	949	4,899	2,516	1,206	1,033	389	445	800	946	219	1,886	1,892	2,750	3,056	49,082
IA	32,741	28,849	28,849	10,432	5,522	428	3,348	2,427	726	444	493	314	207	578	262	1,093	621	1,454	2,438	18,832
KS	27,300	24,021	24,019	8,778	3,822	680	2,435	1,779	754	500	288	306	278	365	153	1,060	935	1,340	1,940	25,948
KY	39,631	33,418	33,418	11,541	8,286	853	1,789	2,794	713	745	358	283	399	520	208	1,457	1,617	1,953	4,259	40,201
LA	47,217	41,308	41,308	12,242	8,000	699	4,100	2,186	1,491	1,215	949	1,005	919	825	315	2,162	1,530	1,414	4,495	39,908
ME	12,760	11,551	11,545	3,313	3,396	492	207	875	258	199	170	111	296	187	115	493	326	205	1,005	8,448
MD	63,622	55,581	55,581	19,400	11,014	1,786	560	3,100	2,552	1,791	492	893	1,481	1,085	654	3,484	2,032	2,601	5,440	49,972
MA	82,164	67,912	67,713	21,477	16,444	1,238	1,294	3,058	2,353	1,206	336	419	2,769	1,210	389	2,942	3,192	5,020	9,233	91,398
MI	89,218	76,025	76,012	28,559	13,888	4,364	4,108	3,410	2,401	2,525	395	885	1,066	2,069	463	3,052	3,185	3,891	9,302	76,671
MN	59,994	51,382	51,382	16,497	13,369	1,130	2,089	4,155	1,751	908	830	1,014	941	814	351	2,334	1,610	3,304	5,308	48,996
MS	27,842	24,184	24,184	7,602	5,441	416	3,549	1,582	705	505	288	224	276	362	178	1,046	514	1,150	2,508	14,244
MO	50,587	42,867	42,803	14,606	8,214	1,965	3,244	2,463	1,704	967	398	662	611	984	160	1,610	1,569	2,791	4,929	46,433
MT	9,688	8,522	8,522	2,738	1,524	277	151	954	295	244	285	82	113	137	79	560	182	248	918	5,349
NE	20,901	15,727	15,683	6,255	2,707	476	951	1,265	414	402	385	212	165	266	96	599	320	4,172	1,001	15,124
NV	22,247	18,469	18,464	5,546	2,931	480	1,036	1,125	1,134	693	290	548	304	401	119	1,155	880	1,408	2,370	26,214
NH	11,462	10,100	10,100	3,784	1,878	135	54	767	403	172	78	91	207	173	144	555	464	617	745	10,727
NJ	105,425	88,134	88,115	34,205	15,263	1,796	2,590	4,723	3,357	2,084	469	757	1,366	1,504	1,028	3,381	3,371	3,916	13,374	99,306
NM	21,710	18,749	18,749	6,291	4,324	580	1,230	1,092	677	661	275	317	155	195	211	1,189	481	735	2,226	15,706
NY	308,861	245,642	245,642	73,297	55,681	6,796	14,854	10,483	9,402	6,174	551	2,754	5,460	3,435	2,866	9,767	12,034	30,487	32,732	344,923

See footnotes at end of table.

Table 476. State and Local Governments—Expenditures and Debt by State: 2014-Continued.

See headnote on page 306.

State	Total expenditures	General expenditures Total¹	Direct general expenditures Total¹	Education	Public welfare	Health	Hospitals	Highways	Police protection	Corrections	Natural resources	Parks and recreation	Housing and community development	Sewerage	Solid waste	Governmental administration	Interest on general debt	Utility and liquor store expenditures	Insurance trust expenditures	Total debt outstanding
NC....	83,435	71,858	71,858	23,522	12,786	3,603	9,059	4,142	3,093	1,738	625	944	1,477	970	747	2,941	2,110	5,655	5,922	50,072
ND....	9,107	8,178	8,178	2,639	1,121	175	57	1,674	184	128	286	259	76	73	57	329	175	232	697	5,289
OH....	117,214	95,758	95,744	32,820	22,269	4,189	4,697	5,415	3,270	1,860	417	1,144	2,162	2,205	562	5,097	3,302	4,342	17,114	85,865
OK....	33,210	28,608	28,553	10,115	6,514	1,103	1,256	2,373	1,032	751	241	445	492	315	205	1,422	633	1,966	2,637	18,646
OR....	42,974	35,055	35,055	10,988	7,561	1,242	2,430	1,814	1,212	1,128	620	612	633	835	131	2,083	1,180	2,779	5,141	35,739
PA....	131,870	110,955	110,814	37,900	26,513	4,788	3,520	8,505	3,532	3,299	719	883	1,701	2,704	997	6,093	4,227	6,231	14,684	127,847
RI....	11,571	9,697	9,716	3,230	2,475	184	68	449	391	207	63	78	232	148	98	521	593	366	1,489	12,065
SC....	43,892	37,017	37,017	13,178	6,611	1,204	5,761	1,518	1,113	737	256	476	456	559	354	1,538	1,151	3,348	3,526	42,915
SD....	7,261	6,371	6,371	2,115	994	219	90	939	181	173	173	215	98	120	58	362	187	389	502	5,693
TN....	56,125	43,381	43,380	14,048	10,251	966	3,159	2,453	1,810	1,160	329	532	873	725	363	2,289	1,078	9,676	3,068	34,771
TX....	231,604	196,493	196,493	76,678	32,514	4,772	15,411	12,645	7,083	5,670	1,706	2,238	2,007	3,740	1,348	7,157	9,624	17,333	17,779	268,793
UT....	25,202	20,959	20,959	8,374	3,266	466	1,390	1,072	675	540	243	450	312	374	164	1,309	520	2,558	1,686	20,274
VT....	7,442	6,733	6,733	2,505	1,676	343	3	699	196	140	106	53	150	69	36	296	120	312	397	4,559
VA....	75,615	67,313	67,312	24,425	11,059	2,175	4,156	4,423	2,256	2,296	250	1,058	1,084	1,518	631	3,428	2,397	2,932	5,371	65,491
WA....	77,627	61,959	61,955	20,622	9,959	3,011	4,770	4,060	1,786	1,604	1,244	939	1,282	1,772	582	2,609	2,577	8,509	7,159	80,189
WV..	16,757	14,795	14,795	5,426	3,708	337	455	1,217	363	354	200	171	133	274	79	842	295	434	1,529	11,489
WI....	57,429	49,403	49,403	17,463	11,346	1,607	1,598	4,132	1,757	1,508	788	610	338	944	371	1,891	1,723	2,244	5,783	43,103
WY..	8,794	7,680	7,677	2,619	819	317	963	708	224	209	307	159	16	70	76	531	58	377	737	1,978

¹ Includes items not shown separately.

Source: U.S. Census Bureau, Federal, State, and Local Governments, Government Finance Statistics, "Annual Surveys of State and Local Government Finances," <http://www.census.gov/govs/local/>, accessed February 2017.

Table 477. Estimated State and Local Taxes Paid by a Family of Three for Largest City in Selected States: 2015

[Data based on average family of three (two wage earners and one school age child) owning their own home and living in a city where taxes apply. Comprises state and local sales, income, auto, and real estate taxes. For definition of median, see Guide to Tabular Presentation]

City	Total taxes paid by gross family income level (dollars)					Total taxes paid as percent of income				
	$25,000	$50,000	$75,000	$100,000	$150,000	$25,000	$50,000	$75,000	$100,000	$150,000
Albuquerque, NM	1,817	3,735	6,248	8,647	13,222	7.3	7.5	8.3	8.6	8.8
Anchorage, AK	2,293	1,794	2,856	3,795	5,658	9.2	3.6	3.8	3.8	3.8
Atlanta, GA	3,116	4,402	6,595	9,257	14,280	12.5	8.8	8.8	9.3	9.5
Baltimore, MD	2,333	6,168	9,593	13,248	19,950	9.3	12.3	12.8	13.2	13.3
Boston, MA	3,824	5,249	8,123	11,122	16,931	15.3	10.5	10.8	11.1	11.3
Charlotte, NC	3,264	4,571	7,323	9,672	14,367	13.1	9.1	9.8	9.7	9.6
Chicago, IL	3,596	4,712	7,432	9,940	14,340	14.4	9.4	9.9	9.9	9.6
Columbus, OH	2,800	5,515	8,332	11,670	17,469	11.2	11.0	11.1	11.7	11.6
Denver, CO	2,508	3,374	5,526	7,470	10,839	10.0	6.7	7.4	7.5	7.2
Detroit, MI	2,848	6,830	10,652	14,385	21,296	11.4	13.7	14.2	14.4	14.2
Honolulu, HI	4,427	3,059	5,160	7,332	11,263	17.7	6.1	6.9	7.3	7.5
Houston, TX	2,716	3,113	4,681	6,068	8,378	10.9	6.2	6.2	6.1	5.6
Indianapolis, IN	3,064	4,359	6,988	9,659	15,618	12.3	8.7	9.3	9.7	10.4
Jacksonville, FL	2,659	2,681	4,325	5,880	8,452	10.6	5.4	5.8	5.9	5.6
Kansas City, MO	3,230	4,893	7,553	10,315	15,528	12.9	9.8	10.1	10.3	10.4
Las Vegas, NV	2,923	3,252	4,906	6,309	9,038	11.7	6.5	6.5	6.3	6.0
Los Angeles, CA	3,767	4,574	7,312	10,257	16,429	15.1	9.1	9.7	10.3	11.0
Memphis, TN	3,306	3,841	5,593	7,171	9,736	13.2	7.7	7.5	7.2	6.5
Milwaukee, WI	2,175	5,468	8,569	12,566	19,014	8.7	10.9	11.4	12.6	12.7
New Orleans, LA	3,325	3,824	6,111	8,406	12,158	13.3	7.6	8.1	8.4	8.1
New York City, NY	3,325	4,520	7,840	11,148	18,143	13.3	9.0	10.5	11.1	12.1
Oklahoma City, OK	2,460	5,280	8,342	11,165	16,644	9.8	10.6	11.1	11.2	11.1
Omaha, NE	2,027	4,010	6,743	9,676	15,438	8.1	8.0	9.0	9.7	10.3
Philadelphia, PA	4,461	6,148	9,217	12,365	17,705	17.8	12.3	12.3	12.4	11.8
Phoenix, AZ	2,932	4,193	6,407	8,617	12,969	11.7	8.4	8.5	8.6	8.6
Portland, OR	2,415	4,409	6,975	9,675	15,122	9.7	8.8	9.3	9.7	10.1
Seattle, WA	3,879	3,104	4,395	5,670	7,716	15.5	6.2	5.9	5.7	5.1
Virginia Beach, VA	3,213	4,267	6,623	9,171	14,141	12.9	8.5	8.8	9.2	9.4
Washington, DC	3,142	3,731	5,926	9,020	14,206	12.6	7.5	7.9	9.0	9.5
Wichita, KS	2,415	4,010	6,594	8,866	13,343	9.7	8.0	8.8	8.9	8.9
Average [1]	2,772	4,315	6,822	9,409	14,297	11.1	8.6	9.1	9.4	9.5
Median [1]	2,800	4,279	6,732	9,474	14,318	11.2	8.6	9.0	9.5	9.5

[1] Based on selected cities and District of Columbia. For complete list of cities, see Table 478.

Source: Government of the District of Columbia, Office of the Chief Financial Officer, *Tax Rates and Tax Burdens in the District of Columbia – A Nationwide Comparison 2015*, December 2016, and earlier reports. See also <http://cfo.dc.gov/>.

Table 478. Residential Property Tax Rates for Largest City in Each State: 2015

[The real property tax is a function of housing values, real estate tax rates, assessment levels, homeowner exemptions and credits. Effective rate is the amount each jurisdiction considers based upon assessment level used. Assessment level is ratio of assessed value to assumed market value. Nominal rates represent the "announced" rates levied by the jurisdiction]

City	Effective tax rate per $100		Assessment level (percent)	Nominal rate per $100	City	Effective tax rate per $100		Assessment level (percent)	Nominal rate per $100
	Rank	Rate				Rank	Rate		
Detroit, MI	1	3.46	50.0	6.91	Anchorage, AK	28	1.32	100.0	1.32
Indianapolis, IN	2	3.03	100.0	3.03	Boston, MA	29	1.31	100.0	1.31
Bridgeport, CT	3	2.95	70.0	4.22	Phoenix, AZ	30	1.31	10.0	13.11
Newark, NJ	4	2.90	93.1	3.31	Minneapolis, MN	31	1.31	91.3	1.43
Milwaukee, WI	5	2.85	100.0	2.85	Portland, OR	32	1.26	59.4	2.09
Des Moines, IA	6	2.65	55.4	4.77	Fargo, ND	33	1.24	3.9	31.73
Oklahoma City, OK	7	2.61	11.0	23.72	Louisville, KY	34	1.18	100.0	1.18
Houston, TX	8	2.54	100.0	2.54	Charlotte, NC	35	1.16	89.8	1.29
Manchester, NH	9	2.31	98.4	2.35	Kansas City, MO	36	1.16	19.0	6.11
Baltimore, MD	10	2.25	97.5	2.31	Las Vegas, NV	37	1.15	35.0	3.28
Columbus, OH	11	2.15	31.3	6.87	Los Angeles, CA	38	1.14	100.0	1.14
Burlington, VT	12	2.15	87.5	2.45	Virginia Beach, VA	39	0.99	100.0	0.99
Columbia, SC	13	2.11	4.0	52.82	Salt Lake City, UT	40	0.93	55.0	1.68
Omaha, NE	14	2.10	94.0	2.23	Billings, MT	41	0.92	1.4	67.00
Portland, ME	15	2.06	100.0	2.06	Seattle, WA	42	0.88	92.5	0.95
Memphis, TN	16	1.95	25.0	7.78	New York, NY	43	0.86	4.5	19.08
Providence, RI	17	1.93	100.0	1.93	Washington, DC	44	0.85	100.0	0.85
Jacksonville, FL	18	1.85	97.9	1.89	Charleston, WV	45	0.84	60.0	1.4
Atlanta, GA	19	1.78	40.0	4.45	Cheyenne, WY	46	0.84	9.5	8.82
Boise, ID	20	1.63	96.7	1.69	Birmingham, AL	47	0.73	10.0	7.25
Albuquerque, NM	21	1.57	33.3	4.70	Chicago, IL	48	0.68	10.0	6.81
New Orleans, LA	22	1.52	10.0	15.18	Denver, CO	49	0.66	8.0	8.23
Sioux Falls, SD	23	1.48	85.0	1.74	Honolulu, HI	50	0.35	100.0	0.35
Little Rock, AR	24	1.40	20.0	7.01	Jackson, MS	51	0.02	10.0	0.18
Wichita, KS	25	1.38	11.5	11.98					
Philadelphia, PA	26	1.34	100.0	1.34	**Unweighted average**	(X)	1.58	59.1	7.33
Wilmington, DE	27	1.32	31.1	4.25	**Median**	(X)	1.34	60.0	2.85

X Not applicable.

Source: Government of the District of Columbia, Office of the Chief Financial Officer, *Tax Rates and Tax Burdens in the District of Columbia—A Nationwide Comparison 2015*, December 2016. See also <http://cfo.dc.gov/>.

Table 479. Gross Revenue From Parimutuel and Amusement Taxes and Lotteries by State: 2013 to 2015

[In millions of dollars (69,388.5 represents $69,388,500,000). For fiscal years; see text, this section]

State	2013, total gross revenue	2014, total gross revenue	2015 Total gross revenue	2015 Amusement taxes [1]	2015 Pari-mutuel taxes [2]	Lottery revenue Total [3]	Apportionment of funds Prizes	Administration	Proceeds available from ticket sales
United States.........	69,388.5	71,938.3	74,213.9	7,303.8	122.0	66,788.0	42,278.9	3,180.2	21,362.8
Alabama................	1.7	1.6	1.5	–	1.5	(X)	(X)	(X)	(X)
Alaska.................	8.4	9.2	9.1	9.1	(X)	(X)	(X)	(X)	(X)
Arizona................	646.6	675.5	699.7	0.6	0.2	699.0	486.6	42.0	170.3
Arkansas...............	453.8	429.8	435.7	47.5	2.8	385.4	280.5	33.0	72.0
California..............	4,460.0	5,048.6	5,538.9	–	14.0	5,524.9	3,501.7	270.6	1,752.5
Colorado...............	629.0	610.8	608.9	110.1	0.6	498.2	331.5	40.0	126.7
Connecticut............	1,449.2	1,404.8	1,394.4	307.8	6.9	1,079.7	707.7	44.1	327.9
Delaware...............	453.0	405.3	400.7	–	0.1	400.6	109.0	50.9	240.7
Florida................	4,916.5	5,274.1	5,483.2	198.1	7.4	5,277.7	3,627.9	156.9	1,492.9
Georgia................	3,407.0	3,515.1	3,674.0	(X)	–	3,674.0	2,528.9	164.7	980.5
Hawaii.................				(X)	–	(X)	(X)	(X)	(X)
Idaho..................	183.4	194.0	197.3	–	3.5	193.8	136.8	11.1	45.9
Illinois...............	3,437.4	3,471.4	3,591.0	746.8	6.4	2,837.8	1,817.5	308.7	711.6
Indiana................	1,627.3	1,608.7	1,591.3	618.6	2.2	970.5	671.0	143.3	156.2
Iowa...................	613.9	600.7	616.7	288.1	3.9	324.8	196.9	51.5	76.4
Kansas.................	230.9	231.6	231.6	0.3	–	231.3	138.7	23.4	69.1
Kentucky...............	763.7	793.1	834.2	0.2	3.0	831.1	556.3	41.4	233.4
Louisiana..............	1,102.5	1,103.7	1,145.3	713.8	4.4	427.2	239.2	25.8	162.2
Maine..................	266.1	267.5	289.6	51.6	1.9	236.2	166.7	14.2	89.1
Maryland...............	2,047.6	2,442.2	2,549.1	416.5	1.1	2,131.5	1,051.5	85.6	994.4
Massachusetts..........	4,569.7	4,858.8	5,011.3	4.5	1.2	5,005.6	3,641.4	100.6	1,263.7
Michigan...............	2,376.2	2,480.9	2,640.4	110.8	3.9	2,525.7	1,697.0	73.1	755.6
Minnesota..............	566.9	543.4	563.6	49.1	0.5	514.0	351.7	25.0	137.3
Mississippi............	139.6	127.8	131.3	131.3	–	(X)	(X)	(X)	(X)
Missouri...............	1,496.8	1,496.7	1,473.4	366.4	–	1,107.0	755.4	46.7	304.8
Montana................	117.5	113.1	115.3	59.8	–	55.5	29.3	8.2	18.0
Nebraska...............	175.3	153.3	156.2	6.3	0.2	149.7	94.7	18.4	36.7
Nevada.................	921.9	947.3	952.6	952.6	–	(X)	(X)	(X)	(X)
New Hampshire..........	264.9	261.3	282.5	0.4	0.9	281.1	176.4	16.0	88.7
New Jersey.............	2,878.4	2,958.5	3,037.2	206.1	–	2,831.1	1,873.3	119.3	838.4
New Mexico.............	207.6	206.8	210.0	72.1	0.9	137.0	75.6	20.4	41.0
New York...............	7,721.0	7,958.7	7,893.9	1.1	19.0	7,873.8	4,396.9	374.3	3,102.7
North Carolina.........	1,585.6	1,724.0	1,836.3	1.8	(X)	1,834.5	1,231.2	81.4	521.8
North Dakota...........	32.9	30.3	30.8	3.6	1.4	25.8	14.0	5.0	6.9
Ohio...................	2,762.7	2,851.7	2,988.6	270.0	5.8	2,712.8	1,875.3	122.2	715.3
Oklahoma...............	222.2	213.1	193.6	20.8	1.2	171.6	87.8	24.1	59.8
Oregon.................	866.4	851.5	904.0	–	2.3	901.7	211.4	78.0	612.3
Pennsylvania...........	4,901.6	4,945.7	4,964.9	1,408.0	10.3	3,546.6	2,411.7	40.0	1,095.0
Rhode Island...........	540.2	536.5	543.8	–	1.1	542.7	150.1	10.1	382.6
South Carolina.........	1,153.6	1,213.7	1,345.6	42.8	–	1,302.8	924.1	38.8	339.9
South Dakota...........	156.4	153.1	157.3	9.0	0.4	147.9	29.7	7.8	110.4
Tennessee..............	1,278.3	1,324.4	1,379.0	–	–	1,379.0	774.3	59.1	545.6
Texas..................	4,176.0	4,184.1	4,319.2	31.0	7.1	4,281.1	2,858.3	191.1	1,231.7
Utah...................	–	–	–	–	–	(X)	(X)	(X)	(X)
Vermont................	96.1	96.2	104.9	–	–	104.9	72.7	9.2	22.9
Virginia...............	1,594.3	1,709.4	1,740.1	0.1	–	1,740.0	1,116.6	87.6	535.7
Washington.............	535.6	633.4	660.3	–	1.5	658.9	432.9	45.1	180.8
West Virginia..........	786.4	707.3	708.0	46.9	2.3	658.8	106.5	32.3	520.0
Wisconsin..............	566.3	569.1	574.9	0.2	–	574.6	342.4	38.9	193.3
Wyoming................	0.1	0.4	2.5	–	2.5	(X)	(X)	(X)	(X)

– Represents or rounds to zero. X Not applicable. [1] Represents nonlicense taxes. [2] Represents legalized gambling taxes. [3] Excludes commissions.

Source: U.S. Census Bureau, "2015 Annual Survey of State Government Finances," <http://factfinder.census.gov>, accessed June 2017. See also <http://www.census.gov/govs/state>.

Table 480. Lottery Sales—Type of Game and Proceeds: 1990 to 2016

[In millions of dollars (20,137 represents $20,137,000,000). For fiscal years]

Game	1990	1995	2000	2005	2010	2014	2015	2016
Total ticket sales......................	20,137	32,147	37,201	52,055	60,846	70,653	66,715	73,058
Instant [1].............................	5,204	11,511	15,387	26,006	30,665	38,740	41,653	44,775
Three-digit [2].........................	4,572	5,738	5,780	5,858	5,861	5,819	5,925	6,098
Four-digit [2]..........................	1,302	1,918	2,273	2,869	3,424	3,665	3,865	4,025
Lotto [3]...............................	8,563	10,594	9,339	9,828	10,879	12,169	10,820	13,188
Other [4]...............................	497	2,388	4,423	7,493	10,017	10,260	4,452	4,972
State proceeds (net income) [5]..........	7,703	11,100	11,871	15,792	17,957	20,084	21,154	22,829

[1] Player scratches a latex section on ticket which reveals instantly whether ticket is a winner. [2] Players choose and bet on three or four digits, depending on game, with various payoffs for different straight order or mixed combination bets. [3] Players typically select six digits out of a large field of numbers. Varying prizes are offered for matching three through six numbers drawn by lottery. [4] Includes break-open tickets, spiel, keno, video lottery, etc. [5] Sales minus prizes and expenses equal net government income.

Source: TLF Publications, Inc. © 2017. All Rights Reserved.

Table 481. State Financial Resources, Expenditures, and Balances: 2015 and 2016

[In millions of dollars (1,853,859 represents $1,853,859,000,000). For fiscal year ending in year shown; see text, this section. General funds exclude special funds earmarked for particular purposes, such as highway trust funds and federal funds; they support most on-going broad-based state services, and are available for appropriation to support any governmental activity. Minus sign (-) indicates deficit]

| State | Expenditures by fund source | | | | State general fund | | | | | |
| | Total, 2015 actual | 2016 estimated | | | Resources [2,3] | | Expenditures [3] | | Balance [4] | |
		Total [1]	General fund	Federal fund	2015	2016 (P)	2015	2016 (P)	2015	2016 (P)
United States......	**1,853,859**	**1,927,892**	**779,375**	**602,424**	**804,473**	**824,928**	**757,736**	**785,723**	**41,597**	**34,822**
Alabama..............	25,291	26,474	7,975	10,135	7,952	8,213	7,770	7,817	215	255
Alaska...............	13,423	10,602	5,729	3,302	2,328	1,293	6,014	5,440	-2,679	-3,921
Arizona..............	38,821	40,629	9,161	15,809	9,581	9,740	9,269	9,515	312	224
Arkansas............	23,796	23,832	5,120	7,301	5,058	5,190	5,058	5,190	–	–
California............	250,344	265,894	115,571	96,129	116,943	120,446	113,448	115,571	3,445	4,875
Colorado.............	34,439	36,003	9,863	9,486	10,303	10,631	9,594	10,159	709	472
Connecticut..........	29,531	31,086	17,990	6,122	17,282	17,781	17,420	17,921	-113	-171
Delaware............	9,769	10,240	3,914	2,151	4,370	4,482	3,833	3,914	537	568
Florida..............	71,043	78,397	28,869	24,921	30,547	31,068	28,008	29,292	2,540	1,777
Georgia.............	45,009	47,496	21,917	13,394	21,579	24,037	20,050	21,935	1,529	2,102
Hawaii..............	12,873	13,835	6,881	2,563	7,242	7,910	6,413	6,882	828	1,028
Idaho...............	7,183	7,944	3,058	2,905	2,944	3,078	2,936	3,072	45	50
Illinois.............	63,510	55,978	25,115	16,810	36,451	30,994	30,763	26,801	621	246
Indiana.............	29,342	31,406	15,168	12,448	16,196	15,945	14,935	14,991	887	776
Iowa................	21,948	22,694	7,247	6,349	7,467	7,315	7,056	7,168	411	75
Kansas..............	15,089	15,528	6,203	4,023	6,309	6,152	6,237	6,115	72	37
Kentucky............	30,811	32,703	10,230	12,182	10,433	10,894	10,108	10,320	221	334
Louisiana...........	27,754	29,603	8,659	10,338	8,477	8,667	8,588	8,652	-117	–
Maine...............	7,726	8,055	3,271	2,536	3,242	3,412	3,166	3,272	26	71
Maryland............	39,916	41,183	16,641	11,549	16,231	16,541	15,995	16,642	320	385
Massachusetts.......	58,371	60,403	30,561	9,751	39,687	42,015	38,116	40,573	1,571	1,442
Michigan............	53,200	54,672	10,250	22,728	9,897	9,885	9,203	9,750	695	135
Minnesota...........	35,792	38,209	20,405	11,494	22,396	23,004	20,293	20,405	2,103	2,599
Mississippi..........	19,637	22,320	5,693	9,592	5,578	5,706	5,529	5,699	48	7
Missouri.............	24,098	24,628	9,018	7,677	9,022	9,182	8,744	9,029	278	153
Montana.............	6,383	6,384	2,237	2,370	2,625	2,573	2,171	2,318	455	255
Nebraska............	10,980	11,610	4,196	2,989	4,763	4,727	4,030	4,196	732	532
Nevada..............	11,629	11,527	3,558	3,984	3,649	4,003	3,400	3,596	242	398
New Hampshire......	5,450	5,785	1,383	2,162	1,420	1,610	1,278	1,383	49	130
New Jersey..........	57,028	59,838	33,526	17,440	33,611	34,237	32,794	33,686	817	551
New Mexico.........	17,078	18,076	6,220	7,375	6,939	6,665	6,326	6,307	613	133
New York............	143,891	150,708	68,042	49,476	70,156	76,976	62,856	68,042	7,300	8,934
North Carolina.......	43,796	44,367	21,205	13,007	20,931	21,910	20,666	21,735	265	176
North Dakota........	7,923	8,054	3,097	1,779	4,147	3,420	3,270	3,152	877	391
Ohio................	65,096	67,450	33,591	12,450	33,173	35,642	31,462	34,449	1,712	1,193
Oklahoma...........	22,388	22,719	6,555	7,656	6,452	6,115	6,403	6,115	49	–
Oregon..............	37,208	37,126	8,992	10,317	8,665	9,232	8,136	8,754	529	478
Pennsylvania........	73,502	78,011	30,558	27,153	29,427	30,590	29,153	30,559	206	31
Rhode Island........	9,792	9,662	3,541	3,065	3,629	3,724	3,454	3,549	168	167
South Carolina.......	22,615	23,074	7,319	7,710	8,124	8,530	6,815	7,181	1,182	1,131
South Dakota........	3,932	4,050	1,473	1,364	1,418	1,497	1,386	1,461	22	14
Tennessee...........	30,840	32,949	13,801	12,793	13,454	13,982	12,330	12,920	873	746
Texas...............	119,308	127,283	59,140	44,956	57,650	57,120	49,308	53,430	8,342	3,691
Utah................	12,866	13,707	6,196	3,815	6,216	6,458	5,774	6,308	442	150
Vermont.............	5,433	5,562	1,465	2,016	1,449	1,484	1,429	1,479	–	–
Virginia.............	47,051	49,152	19,672	9,901	18,917	19,367	18,240	19,102	677	265
Washington..........	40,082	41,251	17,918	11,507	17,662	19,442	16,671	18,190	991	1,252
West Virginia........	15,949	16,172	4,195	3,340	4,653	4,552	4,234	4,175	420	371
Wisconsin...........	46,083	45,670	15,323	10,796	15,730	15,830	15,504	15,853	136	314
Wyoming............	8,840	7,891	1,663	1,308	2,101	1,663	2,101	1,663	–	–

P Preliminary. – Represents zero. [1] Includes bonds and other state funds, not shown separately. [2] Includes funds budgeted, adjustments, and balances from previous year. [3] May or may not include budget stabilization fund transfers, depending on state accounting practices. [4] Resources less expenditures, minus adjustments.

Source: National Association of State Budget Officers, Washington, DC, *State Expenditure Report: Examining Fiscal 2014-2016 State Spending* ©, 2016; and *Fiscal Survey of the States, Fall 2016* ©, 2016. See also <http://www.nasbo.org>.

Table 482. State Governments—Summary of Finances: 2000 to 2015

[In millions of dollars (1,260,829 represents $1,260,829,000,000). For fiscal year ending in year shown; see text, this section]

Item	2000	2005	2010	2013	2014	2015
Total revenue	**1,260,829**	**1,642,468**	**2,039,927**	**2,196,211**	**2,365,591**	**2,203,631**
General revenue	984,783	1,286,899	1,567,207	1,688,574	1,743,353	1,854,018
Intergovernmental revenue	274,382	407,792	575,372	526,670	550,738	604,860
From federal	259,114	386,314	555,592	(NA)	(NA)	(NA)
From local	15,268	21,478	19,779	(NA)	(NA)	(NA)
Total taxes	539,655	650,612	705,929	850,842	870,437	911,698
General sales and gross receipts taxes	174,461	212,921	224,314	261,709	273,899	286,383
Selective sales and gross receipts taxes	77,685	99,663	120,208	139,650	141,007	144,933
License taxes	32,598	42,584	50,429	51,030	51,318	52,032
Individual income taxes	194,573	221,597	236,987	309,881	311,562	336,173
Corporation net income taxes	32,522	38,691	38,006	44,871	46,492	48,685
All other taxes	27,815	35,155	35,985	43,700	46,159	43,491
Current charges	86,467	123,129	169,855	183,412	191,021	200,890
Miscellaneous general revenue	84,279	105,367	116,051	127,650	131,157	136,571
Utility revenue	4,513	14,628	15,122	13,575	14,311	14,715
Liquor stores revenue	3,895	5,118	6,495	6,868	7,179	7,609
Insurance trust revenue [1]	267,639	335,822	451,103	487,195	600,748	327,288
Unemployment compensation systems	23,260	35,243	75,038	(NA)	(NA)	(NA)
State-administered pension systems	230,166	269,617	353,374	(NA)	(NA)	(NA)
Workers' compensation systems	11,845	23,353	15,311	(NA)	(NA)	(NA)
Other insurance trust systems	2,368	7,609	7,381	(NA)	(NA)	(NA)
Total expenditure	**1,084,097**	**1,472,542**	**1,943,523**	**2,005,863**	**2,048,927**	**2,192,440**
Direct expenditure	757,027	1,066,617	1,457,965	1,516,418	1,550,341	1,677,137
Current operations	523,114	738,886	934,322	1,019,820	1,063,718	1,143,374
Capital outlay	76,233	95,155	118,011	114,816	116,583	124,524
Insurance benefits and repayments	105,456	168,200	320,721	291,069	278,190	316,628
Assistance and subsidies	22,136	28,403	37,562	42,175	43,934	45,216
Interest on debt	30,089	35,974	47,351	48,538	47,916	47,395
Exhibit: salaries and wages	154,504	194,907	244,952	245,673	253,420	259,095
General expenditure	964,723	1,278,434	1,593,694	1,685,103	1,738,746	1,840,821
Intergovernmental general expenditure	327,070	405,925	485,557	489,445	498,586	515,304
Direct general expenditure	637,653	872,508	1,108,137	1,195,658	1,240,160	1,325,517
General expenditure, by function:						
Education	346,465	454,348	571,147	599,080	613,748	637,520
Public welfare	238,890	368,765	462,431	519,127	544,711	608,988
Hospitals	32,578	43,623	64,509	67,433	71,712	76,050
Health	42,066	48,634	58,245	63,253	64,207	62,865
Highways	74,415	92,816	111,170	112,174	117,322	120,941
Police protection	9,788	11,395	13,828	15,107	15,669	16,144
Correction	35,129	40,562	48,550	48,605	50,219	51,770
Natural resources	15,967	18,822	21,515	21,344	21,391	22,475
Parks and recreation	4,676	5,334	5,720	5,658	5,765	6,169
Governmental administration	35,527	46,464	53,976	52,992	54,807	55,887
Interest on general debt	29,187	34,242	45,260	46,148	45,485	44,906
Other and unallocable	100,034	113,427	137,344	134,180	133,710	137,107
Utility expenditure	10,723	21,827	23,864	24,522	26,285	28,892
Liquor store expenditure	3,195	4,082	5,244	5,169	5,705	6,099
Insurance trust expenditure [1]	105,456	168,200	320,721	291,069	278,190	316,628
Unemployment compensation systems	18,583	29,776	134,908	(NA)	(NA)	(NA)
State-administered pension systems	75,971	118,333	166,956	(NA)	(NA)	(NA)
Workers' compensation systems	8,317	12,740	12,025	(NA)	(NA)	(NA)
Other insurance trust systems	2,585	7,351	6,831	(NA)	(NA)	(NA)
Debt outstanding, long term and short term [2]	**547,876**	**810,852**	**1,115,463**	**1,137,965**	**1,148,779**	**1,149,926**
Cash and security holdings	**2,518,936**	**3,153,795**	**3,323,047**	**3,828,644**	**4,190,108**	**4,764,323**

NA Not available. [1] Within insurance trust revenue, net earnings of state-administered pension systems is a calculated statistic, and thus can be positive or negative. Net earnings is the sum of earnings on investments plus gains on investments minus losses on investments. [2] As of fiscal year 2005 the Census Bureau no longer collects government debt information by the character of long-term debt. For further information see the 2006 Government Finance and Employment Classification Manual at <http://www.census.gov/govs/pubs/>.

Source: U.S. Census Bureau, "State and Local Government Finances," <http://www.census.gov/govs/local/>; and SG1500A1, "State Government Finances," <http://factfinder.census.gov/>; accessed July 2017.

Table 483. State Government Tax Collections by State: 2016

[In millions of dollars (927,991 represents $927,991,000,000)]

State	All taxes	Total property taxes	Selective sales and gross receipts: Total [1]	Total general sales and gross receipts: Total	Selective sales tax: Total [1]	Alcoholic beverage sales	Insurance premiums	Motor fuels sales	Public utilities	Tobacco products	Other	License taxes: Total [1]	Corporation	Motor vehicle operators	Occupancy and business n.e.c. [2]	Income taxes: Total	Individual income	Corporation net income	Other taxes: Total [1]	Death and gift	Severance
U.S.	927,991	18,364	440,637	290,543	150,094	6,620	20,495	43,757	13,256	18,012	47,954	52,164	5,615	2,598	12,962	392,287	345,529	46,758	24,538	5,133	7,650
AL	9,920	346	5,106	2,596	2,510	211	318	527	696	180	579	507	162	34	56	3,870	3,493	377	90	(X)	47
AK	1,042	112	261	(X)	261	42	64	49	4	68	33	121	(X)	(X)	47	212	(X)	212	337	(X)	337
AZ	14,676	943	8,680	6,661	2,019	72	545	898	22	317	164	482	18	31	159	4,538	3,968	571	33	–	15
AR	9,453	1,120	4,590	3,314	1,276	55	192	480	(X)	231	318	397	27	22	143	3,232	2,781	450	114	–	48
CA	155,231	2,513	53,366	39,189	14,177	369	2,562	5,001	715	840	4,691	8,551	75	296	3,304	90,656	80,753	9,902	145	(X)	69
CO	12,795	(X)	4,897	2,840	2,057	43	278	667	12	201	856	702	20	37	40	7,112	6,486	626	84	(X)	84
CT	15,245	(X)	6,150	3,753	2,397	56	209	468	299	351	1,014	455	29	49	133	8,277	7,557	719	363	195	(X)
DE	3,522	(X)	539	(X)	539	20	96	125	55	112	130	1,453	1,275	7	106	1,431	1,112	318	100	9	(X)
DC	7,405	2,417	1,784	1,343	441	6	107	25	186	30	85	180	33	5	49	2,464	1,908	556	559	54	(X)
FL	37,640	–	30,429	22,291	8,138	396	705	2,611	2,408	1,223	794	2,241	315	117	177	2,272	(X)	2,272	2,697	–	35
GA	21,454	962	8,408	5,480	2,928	191	429	1,655	220	220	434	664	51	108	82	11,421	10,440	981	–	–	(X)
HI	6,919	(X)	4,316	3,206	1,110	51	158	93	153	125	531	263	2	–	42	2,224	2,116	108	116	50	(X)
ID	4,210	(X)	2,121	1,559	562	9	88	337	2	51	75	373	3	11	79	1,710	1,521	189	5	(X)	5
IL	36,635	61	16,252	9,072	7,180	288	425	1,354	1,586	845	2,682	2,746	363	116	469	17,174	13,807	3,367	402	325	(X)
IN	17,588	11	10,608	7,306	3,302	48	235	845	215	443	1,515	715	8	237	55	6,253	5,218	1,034	2	1	1
IA	9,559	1	4,591	3,163	1,429	22	120	690	29	228	340	926	47	17	153	3,930	3,553	377	110	89	(X)
KS	8,059	664	4,325	3,240	1,085	134	306	451	–	147	48	397	27	20	82	2,624	2,232	392	50	–	50
KY	11,779	578	5,603	3,463	2,140	139	145	750	65	246	796	505	109	17	131	4,889	4,282	607	204	51	149
LA	9,310	62	5,353	3,187	2,166	63	519	622	9	121	832	400	106	14	100	3,038	2,866	172	456	(X)	456
ME	4,130	35	2,078	1,359	719	19	103	245	22	141	189	272	10	11	111	1,689	1,552	137	56	27	(X)
MD	20,894	748	8,939	4,504	4,435	32	553	1,018	138	395	2,300	884	104	37	229	9,647	8,518	1,129	675	262	(X)
MA	27,283	6	8,684	6,090	2,594	83	407	767	25	641	671	1,122	27	99	324	16,764	14,430	2,334	707	399	(X)
MI	27,437	2,034	13,239	9,164	4,076	157	328	1,029	28	947	1,586	1,661	24	59	163	10,202	9,304	898	301	–	24
MN	25,189	850	10,121	5,584	4,537	88	458	901	–	650	2,439	1,426	8	47	499	12,248	10,733	1,516	544	182	50
MS	7,660	27	4,778	3,298	1,480	42	318	444	2	146	529	554	144	15	130	2,263	1,800	463	39	–	39
MO	12,245	31	5,302	3,536	1,766	37	401	717	102	102	509	547	13	17	143	6,352	6,024	329	12	–	–
MT	2,628	278	562	(X)	562	32	98	186	44	86	116	319	4	9	107	1,300	1,181	119	168	(X)	164
NE	5,117	–	2,363	1,783	579	31	65	342	49	61	31	185	16	11	36	2,552	2,245	308	17	(X)	3
NV	8,025	280	6,348	4,266	2,082	45	310	316	23	175	1,212	651	76	31	243	(X)	(X)	(X)	746	(X)	103
NH	2,642	406	983	(X)	983	13	113	145	58	226	427	330	59	6	100	788	88	700	135	(X)	(X)
NJ	31,547	5	13,173	9,268	3,906	139	605	554	965	677	965	1,500	248	56	485	15,585	13,356	2,229	1,283	770	(X)
NM	5,462	107	2,930	2,085	845	37	215	245	30	83	235	343	26	12	42	1,524	1,410	114	559	–	559
NY	81,354	(X)	24,790	13,534	11,256	300	1,539	1,612	914	1,247	5,643	1,795	24	159	127	50,690	46,509	4,182	4,079	1,364	(X)

See footnotes at end of table.

Table 483. State Government Tax Collections by State: 2016-Continued.

See headnote on page 312.

State	All taxes	Total property taxes	Selective sales and gross receipts — Total general sales and gross receipts: Total	Selective sales tax: Total[1]	Alcoholic beverage sales	Insurance premiums	Motor fuels sales	Public utilities	Tobacco products	Other	License taxes — Selected license taxes: Total[1]	Corporation	Motor vehicle operators	Occupancy and oper-business n.e.c.[2]	Income taxes: Total	Individual income	Corporation net income	Other taxes — Selected other taxes: Total[1]	Death and gift	Severance
NC	26,202	(X)	7,188	3,961	379	503	1,936	–	286	857	1,869	609	134	307	13,109	12,043	1,067	74	4	2
ND	3,709	4	1,017	480	9	65	197	46	31	131	204	(X)	4	60	454	351	103	1,550	(X)	1,550
OH	28,695	(X)	12,227	6,005	101	579	1,856	1,157	1,009	1,303	2,224	237	79	944	8,202	8,169	33	38	2	35
OK	8,491	(X)	2,471	1,307	120	323	464	46	316	38	1,039	55	27	58	3,325	2,997	328	349	–	331
OR	11,043	21	(X)	1,532	18	86	518	97	269	544	1,049	35	38	353	8,300	7,690	610	142	126	14
PA	37,395	43	10,222	9,063	373	821	2,972	1,310	962	2,625	2,159	81	72	901	14,388	11,932	2,456	1,519	933	(X)
RI	3,266	3	974	692	20	114	90	104	144	219	121	5	5	59	1,380	1,236	144	96	75	(X)
SC	9,551	33	3,268	1,352	173	246	565	29	27	311	499	89	9	100	4,310	3,869	440	89	(X)	(X)
SD	1,748	(X)	969	471	17	87	187	4	63	114	268	5	5	108	33	(X)	33	7	(X)	6
TN	13,386	(X)	7,006	2,698	174	885	898	8	264	469	1,517	773	56	330	1,863	324	1,539	302	62	1
TX	52,133	(X)	32,131	14,239	1,192	2,171	3,500	605	1,480	5,291	3,414	137	137	517	(X)	(X)	(X)	2,348	(X)	2,348
UT	7,083	(X)	2,084	948	52	133	420	24	120	200	290	1	15	53	3,708	3,375	333	53	(X)	53
VT	3,086	1,056	371	660	25	59	77	9	80	409	117	3	10	21	828	730	98	53	13	(X)
VA	21,220	30	3,932	2,955	269	491	896	122	179	998	826	61	41	202	12,991	12,238	753	486	–	2
WA	22,280	2,062	13,560	4,076	348	535	1,458	489	451	795	1,461	36	120	324	(X)	(X)	(X)	1,121	136	40
WV	5,128	7	1,287	1,280	18	158	396	120	100	487	128	1	95	10	1,990	1,846	145	435	(X)	425
WI	17,608	171	5,059	2,663	59	197	1,043	327	650	388	1,152	20	40	438	8,473	7,487	987	90	2	11
WY	1,914	339	641	179	2	28	115	5	24	5	157	14	2	31	(X)	(X)	(X)	598	(X)	594

X Not applicable. – Represents zero or rounds to zero. [1] Includes other items not shown separately. [2] N.e.c. means not elsewhere classified.

Source: U.S. Census Bureau, Census of Governments, "2016 Annual Survey of State Government Tax Collections," <http://factfinder.census.gov>, accessed May 2017. See also <http://www.census.gov/govs/statetax>.

Table 484. State Governments—Expenditures and Debt by State: 2014

[In millions of dollars (2,048,406 represents $2,048,406,000,000) except as indicated. For fiscal year ending in year shown; see text, this section]

State	Total expenditures	Intergovernmental	Direct expenditures Total	Direct general expenditures Total [1]	Education	Public welfare	Health	Hospitals	Highways	Police protection	Correction	Parks and recreation	Housing and community development	Sewerage	Solid waste management	Governmental administration	Interest on general debt	Other	Utility and liquor store	Insurance trust	Cash and security holdings	Total debt outstanding
U.S...	2,048,406	496,879	1,551,527	1,241,213	283,726	489,994	44,260	70,199	96,441	14,052	47,820	4,878	8,976	909	1,053	53,425	45,487	79,992	31,990	278,324	4,303,657	1,149,148
AL...	28,417	6,474	21,943	18,315	5,608	6,492	487	1,630	1,526	146	511	20	17	–	2	589	454	833	269	3,359	43,515	8,908
AK...	13,043	2,059	10,984	9,489	1,584	2,089	199	54	1,278	136	337	23	206	–	–	683	250	2,649	228	1,267	84,390	6,049
AZ...	33,433	7,448	25,985	21,847	5,799	8,796	1,962	855	1,105	236	1,029	63	76	–	2	660	519	745	30	4,107	57,816	14,316
AR...	20,476	5,199	15,277	13,425	3,259	5,712	304	950	1,149	119	393	64	16	–	13	632	140	674	–	1,852	34,234	4,533
CA...	285,493	91,869	193,624	143,899	31,410	57,577	1,776	9,961	7,797	1,681	8,837	453	247	245	247	7,930	7,206	8,533	1,937	47,788	639,186	156,808
CO...	30,832	6,750	24,082	18,636	5,623	5,856	987	809	1,229	170	837	88	98	3	1	838	833	1,264	16	5,430	74,147	16,929
CT...	29,658	4,899	24,759	19,471	3,668	6,884	733	1,311	1,055	239	694	30	205	–	122	1,310	1,422	1,798	771	4,517	46,444	33,230
DE...	8,871	1,391	7,481	6,641	1,609	2,132	430	45	540	127	294	39	69	–	37	496	356	467	160	680	15,881	5,354
FL...	83,572	18,708	64,865	56,065	10,231	24,373	3,860	905	6,116	532	2,196	116	204	–	136	2,243	1,185	3,967	185	8,615	223,236	36,348
GA...	45,680	10,558	35,122	28,715	8,031	11,368	964	1,151	2,098	298	1,438	191	255	7	26	841	660	1,388	33	6,374	95,877	13,380
HI...	12,549	256	12,293	10,959	3,389	2,585	515	822	422	37	217	93	181	–	–	496	383	1,818	5	1,329	19,177	8,427
ID...	8,523	2,015	6,508	5,388	1,060	2,228	175	53	569	55	249	28	81	–	–	309	152	428	107	1,014	22,071	3,606
IL...	77,580	16,924	60,656	46,716	8,506	18,774	2,020	1,191	4,418	458	1,412	88	363	12	26	1,473	3,390	4,586	–	13,939	155,147	65,832
IN...	36,141	9,315	26,826	23,854	6,950	10,553	471	168	1,699	222	632	62	406	1	6	579	971	1,133	–	2,972	60,140	21,120
IA...	21,385	4,964	16,421	13,805	3,320	5,438	136	1,621	1,347	96	294	28	57	1	2	560	235	671	182	2,434	43,411	6,343
KS...	17,030	4,108	12,922	11,077	2,562	3,789	392	1,597	994	92	309	38	93	–	–	417	226	567	–	1,845	22,579	6,743
KY...	30,117	4,649	25,468	21,241	5,397	8,243	594	1,275	2,280	161	504	92	224	–	23	885	674	889	28	4,199	40,862	14,830
LA...	32,078	6,053	26,025	21,709	4,541	7,922	501	1,852	1,468	280	537	314	292	–	–	955	801	2,247	5	4,310	63,886	18,996
ME...	9,316	1,285	8,031	7,006	1,023	3,344	460	114	577	72	128	8	167	–	–	285	218	611	20	1,005	19,037	5,474
MD...	41,436	8,734	32,702	27,429	5,503	10,835	1,302	524	2,009	489	1,408	127	383	111	22	1,890	1,142	1,684	1,072	4,201	66,549	26,379
MA...	58,517	9,812	48,705	38,705	6,411	16,351	1,102	521	2,031	793	1,206	147	1,216	285	9	1,859	2,683	4,090	2,403	7,597	96,067	74,235
MI...	64,209	19,779	44,430	35,856	10,589	12,786	1,172	3,222	1,341	406	1,846	117	615	–	5	899	1,509	1,348	779	7,794	94,682	31,528
MN...	42,141	12,621	29,520	24,124	5,744	11,813	379	304	1,851	312	481	215	112	123	17	995	478	1,301	366	5,030	77,010	15,818
MS...	20,115	4,920	15,195	12,454	2,499	5,412	317	1,180	948	110	323	56	37	–	–	432	278	861	233	2,508	32,921	7,104
MO...	30,650	5,785	24,865	20,559	3,986	8,074	1,637	1,730	1,350	217	788	47	192	–	3	530	753	1,252	–	4,306	80,864	19,042
MT...	7,276	1,387	5,889	4,881	970	1,465	143	52	731	49	199	18	56	1	1	342	125	730	90	918	18,069	3,402
NE...	10,121	2,202	7,919	7,225	1,964	2,596	419	263	749	70	282	44	2	4	9	206	62	555	–	694	19,246	1,909
NV...	13,306	4,169	9,136	6,699	1,696	2,592	351	254	422	103	267	20	24	–	7	273	165	526	67	2,370	38,337	3,521
NH...	7,402	1,269	6,134	4,913	1,025	1,656	107	54	487	61	99	22	105	1	20	245	343	689	489	731	14,345	8,099
NJ...	70,030	12,104	57,926	41,709	9,672	14,185	1,445	2,231	3,504	536	1,380	195	451	2	44	1,711	2,103	4,249	2,850	13,367	122,220	66,090
NM...	17,805	4,605	13,200	10,974	2,439	4,225	492	1,021	696	123	440	55	52	–	–	659	287	486	–	2,226	49,743	6,887
NY...	179,741	58,135	121,607	87,027	12,232	45,020	3,009	4,985	4,316	766	3,106	613	415	–	46	4,878	4,302	3,340	13,140	21,439	350,043	136,441
NC...	51,448	13,173	38,275	32,278	8,690	11,119	1,114	1,737	3,575	656	1,187	140	292	1	10	1,377	605	1,773	120	5,877	100,606	17,853

See footnotes at end of table.

ProQuest Statistical Abstract of the United States: 2018

Table 484. State Governments—Expenditures and Debt by State: 2014-Continued.

See headnote on page 314.

State	Total expend-itures	Inter-govern-mental	Total (Direct expenditures)	Total [1] (Direct general)	Educa-tion	Public welfare	Health	Hospi-tals	High-ways	Police protec-tion	Correc-tions	Parks and recre-ation	Hous-ing and com-munity devel-opment	Sewer-age	Solid waste man-age-ment	Govern-men-tal admin-istra-tion	Inter-est on gen-eral debt	Other	Utility and liquor store	Insur-ance trust	Cash and security holdings	Total debt out-stand-ing
ND...	7,541	2,262	5,279	4,607	1,117	1,044	133	57	1,065	35	88	29	26	–	–	162	79	771	–	672	23,595	1,887
OH...	79,625	16,648	62,977	45,356	10,693	19,858	1,939	3,202	3,066	304	1,371	74	304	–	34	1,713	1,368	1,431	703	16,918	250,405	33,662
OK...	23,632	4,279	19,354	16,102	4,185	6,484	867	241	1,572	220	581	82	169	–	1	753	404	545	716	2,536	45,383	9,047
OR...	29,616	6,007	23,609	18,337	3,782	7,330	536	2,133	882	180	667	67	128	3	6	1,186	397	1,039	277	4,994	83,640	14,583
PA...	87,464	18,836	68,628	54,521	10,635	22,554	1,978	3,513	6,227	934	1,912	246	70	12	39	3,002	1,460	1,939	1,644	12,464	133,011	47,573
RI...	8,367	1,198	7,169	5,675	995	2,468	167	68	326	77	187	31	51	50	51	366	484	353	156	1,338	17,088	9,388
SC...	29,013	5,581	23,432	18,175	5,261	6,575	1,023	1,520	1,085	162	502	92	148	–	–	563	362	882	1,735	3,522	42,818	15,089
SD...	4,567	746	3,821	3,339	719	979	182	23	584	39	123	49	40	–	–	179	108	314	–	482	15,655	3,239
TN...	30,675	7,222	23,453	21,017	4,898	10,101	580	408	1,531	242	715	84	245	–	6	878	255	1,074	–	2,436	46,889	6,049
TX...	131,322	29,192	102,130	86,201	24,788	32,113	2,568	5,491	8,063	926	3,680	135	43	5	46	1,785	1,628	4,928	–	15,930	331,456	41,855
UT...	17,250	3,266	13,984	12,092	4,103	3,125	331	1,340	686	144	325	45	83	–	–	613	263	1,034	219	1,673	33,019	7,327
VT...	6,325	1,571	4,754	4,315	946	1,673	333	3	476	93	140	14	91	2	4	190	90	259	55	385	7,894	3,291
VA...	48,703	11,793	36,910	31,917	8,250	9,614	935	3,850	3,340	345	1,219	116	164	40	1	1,225	1,123	1,695	539	4,454	85,491	27,739
WA...	47,858	10,441	37,417	30,373	8,170	9,785	1,811	2,259	2,331	256	975	65	157	–	10	982	1,364	2,209	145	6,899	100,563	31,601
WV...	13,311	2,414	10,897	9,335	2,243	3,702	278	134	1,122	82	303	49	18	–	10	425	193	775	80	1,483	23,644	7,987
WI...	38,826	9,891	28,935	23,587	5,385	9,509	379	1,512	1,906	120	1,029	19	20	–	7	695	965	2,039	42	5,306	111,263	22,368
WY...	5,916	1,913	4,002	3,173	561	793	263	4	502	46	144	28	9	–	4	229	35	554	92	737	30,103	930

– Represents or rounds to zero. [1] Includes other direct general expenditures not shown separately.

Source: U.S. Census Bureau, Federal, State, and Local Governments, Government Finance Statistics, "Annual Surveys of State and Local Government Finances," <http://www.census.gov/govs/local/>, accessed February 2017.

Table 485. Local Governments—Revenue by State: 2014

[In millions of dollars (1,772,053 represents $1,772,053,000,000). For fiscal year ending in year shown; see text, this section. Minus sign (-) indicates decrease]

State	Total revenue	General revenue, total	Inter-governmental revenue	General revenue from own sources — Total	Taxes — Total[1]	Property	Sales and gross receipt	Individual income	Corporation income	Other taxes	Current charges and miscellaneous general revenue	Current charges — Total[1]	Education	Hospitals	Sewerage	Miscellaneous general revenue — Total[1]	Interest earnings	Special assessment	Utility revenue	Liquor store revenue	Insurance trust revenue
U.S.	1,772,053	1,518,125	551,422	966,704	623,638	452,150	105,496	29,628	8,124	28,240	343,066	262,983	23,423	77,352	50,979	80,082	17,206	7,754	146,276	1,324	106,328
AL	20,747	17,493	6,644	10,848	5,254	2,200	2,214	100	–	740	5,594	4,669	343	3,012	467	925	160	16	2,836	–	419
AK	6,304	5,858	2,311	3,547	2,176	1,817	316	–	–	42	1,371	801	25	331	139	571	208	6	387	4	55
AZ	28,531	23,263	8,819	14,444	9,087	5,812	2,863	–	–	412	5,356	3,748	472	642	878	1,608	458	77	4,685	–	583
AR	9,965	8,928	5,070	3,857	2,206	924	1,248	–	–	34	1,651	1,121	154	171	285	530	182	28	996	–	41
CA	294,217	235,154	103,182	131,971	73,295	51,555	16,405	–	–	5,335	58,677	45,486	2,168	12,107	7,071	13,191	2,403	1,709	26,765	–	32,299
CO	29,418	26,130	7,349	18,781	11,623	7,311	3,811	–	–	502	7,157	5,511	487	1,582	888	1,646	256	127	2,656	–	632
CT	18,727	16,690	5,015	11,675	10,120	9,971	–	–	–	149	1,555	1,169	124	–	418	386	65	56	773	–	1,264
DE	3,501	2,921	1,407	1,513	948	775	14	56	6	98	565	388	13	–	157	177	24	24	438	–	143
DC	14,713	11,931	3,790	8,141	6,378	2,071	1,600	1,679	416	612	1,762	734	33	119	280	1,028	71	–	1,005	–	1,777
FL	94,686	81,241	23,405	57,837	30,748	23,578	5,347	–	–	1,823	27,089	20,131	1,889	6,100	3,302	6,958	1,113	2,419	9,197	–	4,248
GA	44,053	37,747	11,766	25,981	15,467	10,192	4,866	–	–	409	10,514	8,426	497	3,873	1,277	2,088	396	54	4,872	–	1,434
HI	3,812	3,424	547	2,877	2,070	1,392	453	–	–	225	808	689	–	–	456	119	9	33	388	–	–
ID	5,469	5,235	2,138	3,097	1,619	1,517	33	–	–	69	1,478	1,279	80	541	214	199	34	28	232	–	2
IL	76,280	63,902	22,210	41,692	30,898	25,796	4,259	–	–	843	10,793	7,921	1,252	912	1,361	2,873	280	445	4,960	–	7,419
IN	28,821	26,160	10,513	15,647	7,880	6,393	194	1,148	–	145	7,767	6,436	325	3,726	1,498	1,331	195	20	2,571	–	90
IA	16,037	14,871	5,514	9,357	5,484	4,743	546	115	–	80	3,873	3,299	485	1,587	551	574	105	20	1,159	–	6
KS	14,619	12,897	4,289	8,608	5,372	4,085	1,169	2	–	116	3,237	2,206	393	794	422	1,031	363	125	1,420	–	303
KY	14,173	12,339	4,869	7,469	4,814	2,691	649	1,239	144	92	2,655	2,000	110	508	585	655	396	20	1,713	–	121
LA	21,222	19,740	6,636	13,103	8,383	3,843	4,332	–	–	208	4,720	3,656	63	2,037	400	1,064	379	19	1,136	–	347
ME	4,805	4,673	1,433	3,240	2,547	2,516	9	–	–	22	693	574	41	83	162	119	26	7	132	–	–
MD	31,253	27,782	9,009	18,773	14,541	8,185	835	4,757	–	764	4,233	3,375	531	18	1,056	858	143	47	818	286	2,366
MA	35,851	29,409	10,205	19,204	15,386	14,728	352	–	–	307	3,818	2,966	360	302	1,215	852	59	20	2,747	–	3,695
MI	49,296	42,507	20,625	21,882	12,325	11,321	267	460	–	276	9,557	7,583	1,082	745	1,929	1,973	301	172	2,735	–	4,054
MN	29,955	26,966	12,372	14,593	7,535	6,862	425	–	–	247	7,059	5,205	513	1,768	789	1,854	514	321	2,270	326	394
MS	12,373	11,494	4,746	6,748	2,908	2,718	106	–	–	84	3,840	3,392	356	2,334	222	448	66	9	879	–	–
MO	25,929	22,309	6,791	15,518	9,820	5,792	2,940	332	73	682	5,698	4,203	621	1,505	838	1,496	307	82	2,496	–	1,124
MT	3,777	3,648	1,538	2,110	1,273	1,231	7	–	–	35	837	611	77	90	103	226	40	72	129	–	–
NE	14,060	9,156	2,550	6,606	4,298	3,308	515	–	–	475	2,309	1,836	238	623	203	473	87	32	4,376	–	528
NV	13,473	12,525	5,439	7,086	3,855	2,445	1,064	–	–	346	3,231	2,504	41	577	460	727	102	73	948	–	–
NH	5,910	5,750	1,639	4,111	3,461	3,416	–	–	–	45	650	487	48	–	139	163	30	1	124	–	36
NJ	49,003	47,899	13,190	34,709	27,958	27,388	178	–	–	393	6,751	4,852	1,155	326	1,664	1,899	270	7	1,090	–	14
NM	8,637	8,030	4,179	3,851	2,517	1,420	1,041	–	–	56	1,334	935	96	166	177	399	106	15	607	–	–
NY	209,513	174,032	56,370	117,663	89,108	50,981	17,129	10,343	6,674	3,981	28,555	19,923	1,274	4,972	2,806	8,632	1,531	139	7,343	–	28,138

See footnotes at end of table.

ProQuest Statistical Abstract of the United States: 2018

Table 485. Local Governments—Revenue by State: 2014-Continued.

See headnote on page 316.

State	Total revenue	General revenue, total	Inter-govern-mental revenue	Taxes Total	Property	Sales and gross receipt	Indi-vidual income	Corpo-ration income	Other taxes	Current charges and miscel-laneous general revenue	Current charges Total [1]	Educa-tion	Hospi-tals	Sewer-age	Misc. Total [1]	Interest earn-ings	Special assess-ment	Utility re-venue	Liquor store re-venue	Insur-ance trust re-venue
NC...	45,611	40,202	15,157	25,045	9,457	2,720	–	–	360	12,508	10,994	565	7,126	1,322	1,513	242	17	4,609	682	118
ND...	4,092	3,849	1,949	1,900	827	222	–	–	43	808	451	62	–	58	356	47	107	201	–	42
OH...	55,240	51,941	19,013	32,928	13,954	2,184	4,594	281	755	11,160	8,011	1,220	1,442	2,152	3,149	984	263	2,892	–	407
OK...	13,764	12,308	4,362	7,946	2,418	2,200	–	–	110	3,217	2,444	307	999	392	773	108	18	1,229	–	228
OR...	19,048	17,503	6,812	10,690	5,338	446	–	62	752	4,093	3,217	563	277	1,001	876	234	71	1,463	–	82
PA...	65,964	59,285	22,674	36,611	17,926	1,288	4,804	469	1,537	10,586	7,628	902	32	2,730	2,958	1,168	90	2,917	–	3,762
RI...	4,653	4,307	1,286	3,020	2,431	24	–	–	33	532	407	37	–	117	125	17	7	194	–	153
SC...	20,662	18,961	5,484	13,478	5,193	652	–	–	773	6,860	5,840	248	4,109	630	1,020	289	31	1,694	–	6
SD...	3,512	3,038	901	2,137	1,111	387	–	–	37	602	488	97	60	100	114	22	12	364	27	83
TN...	33,011	22,560	7,654	14,905	5,433	2,565	–	–	439	6,468	5,482	475	2,677	874	986	336	42	9,191	–	1,260
TX...	131,246	113,343	34,381	78,961	44,109	8,915	–	–	950	24,987	18,980	2,145	4,968	3,747	6,006	2,300	297	13,386	–	4,517
UT...	11,817	9,741	3,560	6,181	2,853	1,007	–	–	142	2,178	1,476	94	47	408	703	121	49	2,058	–	18
VT...	2,824	2,551	1,717	834	480	20	–	–	10	323	223	27	–	72	100	11	3	239	–	34
VA...	39,689	35,584	13,024	22,560	12,097	2,627	–	–	1,336	6,501	5,046	339	334	1,488	1,454	277	49	1,932	–	2,173
WA...	42,464	35,299	12,667	22,632	7,659	4,237	–	–	843	9,893	8,338	357	2,369	2,273	1,555	180	360	6,548	–	617
WV...	5,541	5,235	2,015	3,220	1,569	133	–	–	226	1,292	995	33	333	275	297	41	35	249	–	57
WI...	29,023	25,778	11,330	14,448	9,385	452	–	–	196	4,415	3,578	534	94	860	838	117	66	2,006	–	1,239
WY...	4,764	4,542	1,878	2,664	932	225	–	–	52	1,455	1,269	72	933	69	186	35	12	222	–	–

– Represents or rounds to zero. [1] Includes items not shown separately.

Source: U.S. Census Bureau, Federal, State, and Local Governments, Government Finance Statistics, "Annual Surveys of State and Local Government Finances," <http://www.census.gov/govs/local/>, accessed February 2017.

Table 486. Local Governments—Expenditures and Debt by State: 2014

[In millions of dollars (1,722,749 represents $1,722,749,000,000). For fiscal year ending in year shown; see text, this section]

State	Total expenditures [1]	Direct expenditures Total [1]	Direct general expenditures Total	Education	Public welfare	Hospitals	Health	Highways	Police protection	Corrections	Parks and recreation	Housing and community development	Sewerage	Solid Waste Management	Governmental administration	Interest on general debt	Other	Utility expenditures	Insurance trust expenditures	Debt outstanding
U.S.	1,722,749	1,706,663	1,465,723	620,584	52,575	95,389	45,474	65,711	87,893	26,930	32,523	40,969	50,491	22,048	75,164	61,914	188,058	193,294	46,468	1,825,294
AL	20,948	20,927	17,856	7,533	31	3,368	325	724	1,058	196	387	450	352	240	929	651	1,612	2,868	203	22,168
AK	5,790	5,790	5,098	1,992	5	337	80	299	237	6	85	185	117	132	481	173	970	659	30	3,003
AZ	27,158	26,985	20,997	9,276	101	857	186	837	1,716	609	548	452	661	363	1,428	1,009	2,954	5,655	332	34,421
AR	9,879	9,860	8,816	4,877	18	187	49	485	538	173	171	162	350	205	406	347	849	996	49	11,463
CA	277,318	277,106	227,152	79,627	17,475	14,661	14,168	10,253	14,124	5,470	4,818	7,935	6,988	2,457	11,852	9,461	27,864	38,562	11,392	269,070
CO	29,407	29,374	24,892	8,940	895	1,882	333	1,525	1,630	377	1,039	697	972	110	1,624	1,340	3,529	4,200	282	37,142
CT	17,920	17,914	16,381	8,900	99	–	135	656	923	–	222	896	601	212	610	372	2,757	844	690	11,394
DE	3,426	3,424	2,941	1,908	1	–	38	132	209	–	31	71	163	27	145	71	144	427	57	2,516
DC	15,349	15,349	11,960	2,624	3,111	307	454	767	591	197	238	691	664	110	502	533	1,171	2,819	570	13,087
FL	95,328	95,054	82,402	28,807	1,232	6,991	1,271	2,935	6,824	1,778	2,618	2,171	3,176	2,274	4,535	3,696	14,093	10,491	2,161	118,794
GA	43,726	43,684	36,783	17,409	257	3,682	1,120	1,383	2,109	776	596	1,010	1,228	629	2,518	762	3,306	6,230	671	43,485
HI	3,637	3,637	2,723	–	34	–	27	295	416	–	187	99	359	233	318	203	553	914	–	5,870
ID	5,193	5,191	4,967	2,084	33	562	75	324	357	71	112	46	194	138	281	89	603	223	2	2,624
IL	76,782	76,782	62,504	28,755	648	1,687	820	3,246	4,529	685	2,470	1,726	1,836	492	3,898	3,037	8,673	8,695	5,583	83,424
IN	26,811	26,795	23,962	9,622	62	4,732	477	817	984	401	383	394	944	214	1,307	921	2,705	2,750	83	27,962
IA	16,362	16,320	15,044	7,113	85	1,727	292	1,080	630	150	286	150	577	259	533	386	1,776	1,272	4	12,488
KS	14,384	14,377	12,943	6,216	33	838	288	785	661	190	267	185	365	153	643	709	1,610	1,340	95	19,205
KY	14,171	14,163	12,177	6,144	43	514	259	514	551	241	191	176	520	185	573	943	1,325	1,925	60	25,371
LA	21,218	21,192	19,599	7,701	78	2,248	198	719	1,211	678	691	627	825	315	1,207	729	2,373	1,409	184	20,912
ME	4,726	4,724	4,539	2,291	52	94	32	298	186	71	103	129	187	115	207	108	666	185	–	2,974
MD	31,024	30,920	28,152	13,897	179	37	484	1,091	2,062	383	767	1,097	973	632	1,594	890	4,066	1,278	1,239	23,593
MA	34,037	33,261	29,008	15,065	93	773	136	1,027	1,560	–	272	1,553	926	380	1,083	509	5,631	2,617	1,635	17,163
MI	45,035	44,775	40,156	17,970	1,102	886	3,192	2,069	1,994	679	768	451	2,069	458	2,153	1,675	4,689	3,112	1,507	45,143
MN	30,540	30,474	27,258	10,753	1,555	1,785	751	2,304	1,438	427	799	829	691	334	1,338	1,132	3,120	2,620	278	33,178
MS	12,649	12,647	11,730	5,102	29	2,369	99	634	594	182	168	239	362	178	613	236	923	917	–	7,140
MO	25,659	25,658	22,245	10,620	140	1,514	328	1,113	1,487	179	616	419	984	157	1,080	817	2,791	2,791	622	27,392
MT	3,799	3,798	3,641	1,767	59	100	135	224	246	45	64	57	136	78	218	57	455	157	–	1,947
NE	12,941	12,937	8,458	4,291	112	687	57	516	344	121	168	164	262	87	392	258	1,000	4,172	307	13,215
NV	13,117	13,107	11,766	3,851	340	782	129	704	1,032	427	528	280	401	112	882	715	1,586	1,341	–	22,693
NH	5,399	5,328	5,187	2,759	222	–	28	280	343	74	69	103	172	124	309	120	585	127	14	2,628
NJ	47,925	47,480	46,406	24,533	1,078	359	350	1,219	2,822	704	561	914	1,502	984	1,670	1,269	8,442	1,066	7	33,216
NM	8,526	8,510	7,775	3,852	100	210	88	397	554	222	262	103	195	211	530	194	858	735	–	8,819
NY	198,547	187,254	158,614	61,065	10,662	9,869	3,787	6,167	8,636	3,068	2,141	5,045	3,435	2,820	4,889	7,732	29,298	17,347	11,294	208,483

See footnotes at end of table.

Table 486. Local Governments—Expenditures and Debt by State: 2014-Continued.

See headnote on page 318.

State	Total expendi- tures [1]	Direct expenditures Total [1]	Direct general expenditures Total	Educa- tion	Public welfare	Hospi- tals	Health	High- ways	Police protec- tion	Correc- tions	Parks and recre- ation	Housing and com- munity devel- opment	Sewer- age	Solid Waste Manage- ment	Gov- ern- mental admini- stration	Interest on general debt	Other	Utility expen- ditures	Insur- ance trust expen- ditures	Debt out- stand- ing
NC...	45,312	45,161	39,580	14,832	1,667	7,322	2,489	566	2,437	551	804	1,185	969	737	1,564	1,505	2,953	4,951	45	32,219
ND...	3,838	3,828	3,571	1,522	78	–	42	609	149	39	229	50	73	57	167	96	459	232	26	3,402
OH...	54,747	54,223	50,388	22,127	2,411	1,495	2,251	2,348	2,967	489	1,069	1,858	2,205	529	3,384	1,934	5,321	3,640	195	52,203
OK...	13,805	13,801	12,450	5,930	30	1,016	236	801	813	171	363	323	315	205	670	229	1,350	1,250	101	9,599
OR...	19,368	19,366	16,718	7,206	232	296	706	932	1,032	461	545	505	832	125	897	783	2,167	2,501	147	21,156
PA...	63,116	63,101	56,293	27,265	3,958	8	2,810	2,278	2,599	1,386	637	1,632	2,692	958	3,092	2,766	4,213	4,587	2,221	80,275
RI...	4,384	4,384	4,023	2,235	7	–	17	123	314	20	47	181	98	47	154	109	671	210	151	2,677
SC...	20,504	20,460	18,842	7,917	36	4,241	181	433	951	235	383	308	559	354	975	789	1,482	1,613	4	27,825
SD...	3,441	3,440	3,032	1,396	15	67	36	355	143	50	166	57	120	58	183	79	307	366	20	2,454
TN...	32,673	32,671	22,363	9,150	150	2,750	386	922	1,568	445	449	629	725	357	1,410	822	2,599	9,676	632	28,722
TX...	130,720	129,474	110,292	51,889	400	9,920	2,204	4,582	6,157	1,990	2,104	1,963	3,735	1,302	5,372	7,996	10,679	17,333	1,849	226,938
UT...	11,227	11,218	8,867	4,270	141	50	135	386	530	215	404	229	374	164	697	257	1,016	2,338	12	12,947
VT...	2,688	2,688	2,418	1,559	3	–	10	222	103	–	39	58	68	32	106	31	188	257	12	1,268
VA...	38,723	38,704	35,395	16,175	1,445	306	1,240	1,083	1,911	1,077	942	920	1,478	630	2,203	1,275	4,709	2,392	917	37,752
WA...	40,281	40,206	31,582	12,452	174	2,511	1,200	1,729	1,531	629	874	1,125	1,772	572	1,627	1,214	4,171	8,364	260	48,588
WV...	5,864	5,860	5,460	3,182	6	321	59	95	281	50	121	115	274	69	417	102	368	354	46	3,502
WI...	28,539	28,495	25,816	12,078	1,837	86	1,228	2,226	1,637	478	590	318	944	364	1,195	758	2,076	2,202	477	20,735
WY...	4,789	4,788	4,503	2,058	26	959	54	206	178	66	131	7	70	72	302	23	–	285	–	1,048

– Represents or rounds to zero. [1] Includes other items not shown separately.

Source: U.S. Census Bureau, Federal, State, and Local Governments, Government Finance Statistics, "Annual Surveys of State and Local Government Finances," <http://www.census.gov/govs/local/>, accessed February 2017.

State and Local Government Finances and Employment

Table 487. State Governments—Revenue by State: 2014

[In millions of dollars (2,361,474 represents $2,361,474,000,000). For fiscal year ending in year shown. See text, this section. Includes local shares of state imposed taxes]

State	Total revenue [1,2]	General revenue							Utilities and liquor store revenue	Insurance trust revenue
		Total	Intergovernmental revenue		General revenue from own sources					
			Total [1]	From federal govern-ment	Total	Total taxes	Current charges	Miscel-laneous general revenue		
United States.........	**2,361,474**	**1,739,742**	**550,561**	**535,678**	**1,189,181**	**867,177**	**190,846**	**131,157**	**21,490**	**600,242**
Alabama...............	28,280	22,948	8,135	8,005	14,813	9,294	4,255	1,264	289	5,043
Alaska................	12,871	10,436	2,810	2,803	7,626	3,393	628	3,606	18	2,417
Arizona...............	39,394	29,690	10,951	10,549	18,739	13,424	3,682	1,633	29	9,675
Arkansas..............	23,448	18,058	6,097	6,055	11,961	8,937	2,200	824	–	5,390
California.............	353,368	230,742	63,517	59,926	167,225	138,070	19,371	9,784	994	121,633
Colorado..............	34,388	24,739	7,278	7,188	17,462	11,755	3,416	2,290	–	9,648
Connecticut...........	31,301	25,845	6,365	6,350	19,481	15,938	1,899	1,644	36	5,419
Delaware..............	9,298	7,605	2,102	2,031	5,504	3,176	1,141	1,186	19	1,674
Florida................	104,128	76,827	25,802	25,469	51,026	35,384	9,345	6,296	24	27,276
Georgia...............	54,207	39,007	14,612	14,327	24,395	18,629	3,590	2,177	6	15,194
Hawaii................	15,056	11,304	2,811	2,804	8,494	6,033	1,665	796	–	3,751
Idaho.................	10,509	7,433	2,531	2,516	4,902	3,669	757	476	136	2,939
Illinois................	91,274	67,376	18,227	17,852	49,149	39,923	4,805	4,421	–	23,897
Indiana...............	39,529	33,260	11,056	10,975	22,204	16,847	3,480	1,877	–	6,270
Iowa..................	25,197	18,889	6,219	6,165	12,670	8,272	3,096	1,302	266	6,042
Kansas................	19,013	15,391	3,976	3,923	11,416	7,334	3,042	1,039	–	3,621
Kentucky..............	31,508	25,268	9,769	9,732	15,499	11,104	3,128	1,268	–	6,239
Louisiana.............	33,276	25,352	10,215	10,170	15,137	9,695	3,032	2,410	9	7,915
Maine.................	10,529	8,193	3,028	2,997	5,164	3,847	766	551	10	2,327
Maryland..............	44,700	36,281	11,038	10,671	25,242	18,929	3,578	2,735	139	8,280
Massachusetts.........	61,750	49,048	14,166	13,659	34,882	25,237	4,863	4,782	808	11,895
Michigan..............	69,431	55,131	17,930	17,723	37,201	25,101	7,752	4,349	957	13,343
Minnesota.............	49,809	37,036	9,111	8,877	27,925	23,246	2,513	2,165	99	12,675
Mississippi............	23,347	17,576	7,378	7,194	10,199	7,575	1,984	640	293	5,478
Missouri...............	38,508	26,677	10,395	10,128	16,282	11,241	2,755	2,286	–	11,831
Montana...............	8,946	5,977	2,342	2,336	3,635	2,656	550	430	85	2,884
Nebraska..............	12,123	9,789	3,095	3,034	6,694	4,888	1,070	737	–	2,334
Nevada................	19,049	11,480	3,021	2,842	8,459	7,143	699	616	62	7,507
New Hampshire........	8,265	5,916	1,853	1,659	4,063	2,286	883	895	611	1,738
New Jersey............	65,658	56,559	16,049	15,439	40,510	29,679	6,271	4,560	1,029	8,070
New Mexico............	20,423	15,591	5,558	5,371	10,032	5,757	1,400	2,875	–	4,833
New York..............	205,806	146,869	49,128	48,169	97,741	76,979	8,948	11,813	8,557	50,380
North Carolina.........	61,823	46,983	15,643	15,356	31,340	23,470	4,869	3,000	–	14,840
North Dakota..........	9,967	8,850	1,534	1,484	7,316	6,120	753	443	–	1,117
Ohio..................	96,425	62,101	22,350	21,761	39,751	27,021	8,182	4,549	1,008	33,315
Oklahoma.............	28,534	21,441	7,410	7,290	14,032	9,103	2,575	2,353	634	6,458
Oregon................	37,665	24,356	8,791	8,776	15,565	9,684	3,973	1,909	519	12,791
Pennsylvania..........	89,542	70,360	21,869	21,647	48,491	34,193	9,892	4,406	1,787	17,396
Rhode Island..........	8,996	7,117	2,510	2,468	4,607	2,966	762	880	33	1,846
South Carolina........	31,871	23,076	7,640	7,089	15,436	8,933	4,450	2,054	1,804	6,991
South Dakota..........	6,124	4,162	1,574	1,547	2,588	1,608	354	626	–	1,962
Tennessee.............	31,291	26,493	10,645	10,561	15,848	11,806	2,113	1,928	–	4,798
Texas.................	160,030	121,565	40,561	38,637	81,004	55,147	13,298	12,559	–	38,465
Utah..................	19,419	14,979	4,211	4,206	10,768	6,312	3,372	1,083	310	4,129
Vermont...............	6,545	5,772	1,943	1,938	3,829	2,963	532	334	53	721
Virginia...............	53,731	41,469	10,028	9,461	31,441	18,949	8,636	3,856	669	11,594
Washington............	55,072	38,296	11,475	11,191	26,821	19,448	4,925	2,448	–	16,776
West Virginia..........	15,388	12,253	4,350	4,261	7,903	5,387	1,393	1,123	93	3,042
Wisconsin.............	47,214	32,395	9,256	9,015	23,139	16,365	4,003	2,772	–	14,819
Wyoming..............	7,451	5,780	2,208	2,050	3,572	2,263	200	1,108	105	1,566

– Represents or rounds to zero. [1] Includes amounts for categories not shown separately. [2] Duplicate intergovernmental transactions are excluded.

Source: U.S. Census Bureau, Federal, State, and Local Governments, Government Finance Statistics, "Annual Surveys of State and Local Government Finances," <http://www.census.gov/govs/local/>, accessed February 2017.

Table 488. Government Employment and Payrolls by Level of Government: 1982 to 2015

[Employees in thousands (15,841 represents 15,841,000); payroll in millions of dollars (23,173 represents $23,173,000,000). Data through 1992 are for the month of October. Beginning with the 1997 survey, data are for the month of March. Covers both full-time and part-time employees. Local government data are estimates subject to sampling variation; see Appendix III and source]

Type of government	1982	1987	1992	1997	2000	2005	2010	2013	2014	2015
EMPLOYEES (1,000)										
Total	**15,841**	**17,212**	**18,745**	**19,540**	**20,876**	**21,725**	**22,607**	**21,831**	**21,931**	**(NA)**
Federal (civilian) [1]	2,848	3,091	3,047	2,807	2,899	2,720	3,008	2,745	2,700	(NA)
State and local	12,993	14,121	15,698	16,733	17,976	19,004	19,599	19,086	19,230	19,298
Percent of total	82	82	84	86	86	87	87	87	88	88
State	3,744	4,116	4,595	4,733	4,877	5,078	5,326	5,282	5,336	(NA)
Local	9,249	10,005	11,103	12,000	13,099	13,926	14,274	13,804	13,895	13,945
PAYROLLS (mil. dol.)										
Total	**23,173**	**32,669**	**43,120**	**49,156**	**58,166**	**71,599**	**86,643**	**87,940**	**90,113**	**(NA)**
Federal (civilian) [1]	5,959	7,924	9,937	9,744	11,485	13,475	16,238	16,503	16,996	(NA)
State and local	17,214	24,745	33,183	39,412	46,681	58,123	70,404	71,437	73,118	74,988
Percent of total	74	76	77	80	80	81	81	81	81	(NA)
State	5,022	7,263	9,828	11,413	13,279	16,062	19,579	20,502	21,118	21,591
Local	12,192	17,482	23,355	27,999	33,402	42,062	50,825	50,936	51,999	53,397

NA Not available. [1] Includes employees outside the United States.

Source: U.S. Census Bureau, Census of Governments, "2015 Annual Survey of Public Employment and Payroll," <http://www.census.gov/govs/apes/>, accessed August 2017.

Table 489. State and Local Government Employment and Payroll by Function: 2015

[Employees in thousands (19,298 represents 19,298,000); payroll in millions of dollars (74,988.5 represents $74,988,500,000). See headnote, Table 488]

Function	Employees (1,000)			Payrolls (mil. dol.)		
	Total	State	Local	Total	State	Local
Total	**19,298**	**5,353**	**13,945**	**74,988.5**	**21,591.2**	**53,397.3**
Financial administration	430	175	255	1,903.9	826.3	1,077.5
Other government administration	414	58	356	1,243.0	257.5	985.5
Judicial & legal	435	178	257	2,156.0	972.3	1,183.8
National defense [1]	(X)	(X)	(X)	(X)	(X)	(X)
Police protection	974	104	870	5,263.0	609.1	4,653.8
Fire protection	433	–	433	2,153.2	–	2,153.2
Corrections	719	450	269	3,209.6	2,011.1	1,198.4
Streets & highways	509	219	290	2,233.5	1,042.9	1,190.5
Air transportation	50	3	47	260.4	18.4	242.1
Water transport/terminals	14	5	9	79.8	26.2	53.6
Public welfare	532	246	287	2,081.7	966.0	1,115.6
Health	467	191	275	1,953.1	857.9	1,095.3
Hospitals	1,068	429	639	5,035.5	1,993.5	3,042.0
Social insurance administration	75	74	–	327.8	324.8	3.0
Solid waste management	114	2	111	435.2	14.0	421.2
Sewerage	134	2	132	619.4	11.0	608.5
Parks and recreation	412	41	371	929.9	125.2	804.7
Housing and community development	113	1	112	487.1	3.6	483.5
Natural resources	191	147	44	778.1	611.3	166.8
Water supply	181	1	181	842.9	4.2	838.7
Electric power	79	4	75	555.5	29.8	525.7
Gas supply	11	–	11	52.9	–	52.9
Transit	247	34	213	1,362.8	211.4	1,151.4
Elementary and secondary education	7,683	60	7,624	27,268.2	236.7	27,031.5
Higher education	3,231	2,643	588	10,824.3	9,132.9	1,691.3
Other education	92	92	–	395.9	395.9	–
Libraries	184	1	183	449.1	2.2	446.9
Space research and technology	(X)	(X)	(X)	(X)	(X)	(X)
Postal Service	(X)	(X)	(X)	(X)	(X)	(X)
State liquor stores	12	12	–	29.3	29.3	–
Other and unallocable	493	183	311	2,057.6	877.7	1,179.9

– Represents or rounds to zero. X Not applicable. [1] Includes international relations.

Source: U.S. Census Bureau, Census of Governments, "2015 Annual Survey of Public Employment and Payroll," <http://www.census.gov/govs/apes/>, accessed August 2017.

Table 490. State and Local Government—Employer Costs Per Hour Worked: 2017

[In dollars. As of March. Based on a sample; see source for details]

Occupation and industry	Total compen- sation	Wages and salaries	Benefit cost					
			Total	Paid leave	Supple- mental pay	Insur- ance	Retire- ment and savings	Legally required benefits
Total workers	**48.24**	**30.34**	**17.90**	**3.62**	**0.48**	**5.72**	**5.40**	**2.68**
OCCUPATIONAL GROUP								
Management, professional, and related	57.99	37.68	20.31	4.09	0.39	6.34	6.47	3.01
Professional and related	56.43	36.95	19.48	3.64	0.36	6.35	6.23	2.90
Teachers [1]	63.80	42.84	20.96	3.25	0.25	7.00	7.38	3.09
Primary, secondary, and special education school teachers	63.41	42.14	21.26	2.99	0.23	7.26	7.84	2.95
Sales and office	33.26	19.44	13.82	2.93	0.29	5.25	3.34	2.02
Office and administrative support	33.43	19.50	13.93	2.94	0.29	5.32	3.36	2.02
Service	34.87	20.26	14.61	2.94	0.72	4.45	4.31	2.18
INDUSTRY GROUP								
Education and health services	50.59	32.90	17.68	3.35	0.33	5.96	5.44	2.61
Educational services	51.84	33.92	17.92	3.23	0.25	6.08	5.73	2.63
Elementary and secondary schools	50.18	32.94	17.24	2.67	0.21	6.00	5.89	2.48
Junior colleges, colleges, and universities	56.71	36.81	19.91	4.92	0.34	6.34	5.24	3.06
Health care and social assistance	42.64	26.47	16.17	4.08	0.81	5.17	3.58	2.53
Hospitals	45.15	28.57	16.58	4.33	0.95	5.15	3.48	2.67
Public administration	46.31	27.09	19.22	4.33	0.73	5.56	5.73	2.88

[1] Includes postsecondary teachers; primary, secondary, and special education teachers; and other teachers and instructors.

Source: U.S. Bureau of Labor Statistics, National Compensation Survey, *Employer Costs for Employee Compensation–March 2017*, June 2017. See also <http://www.bls.gov/ncs/ect/>.

Table 491. State and Local Government—Full-Time Employment and Salary by Sex and Race/Ethnicity: 1980 to 2015

[2,350 represents 2,350,000. As of June 30. Excludes school systems and educational institutions. Based on reports from state governments (42 in 1980; 49 in 1984 through 1987; and 50 in 1989 through 1991) and a sample of county, municipal, township, and special district jurisdictions employing 15 or more nonelected, nonappointed full-time employees. Beginning 1993, only for state and local governments with 100 or more employees. For definition of median, see Guide to Tabular Presentation]

Year and occupation	Employment (1,000)						Median annual salary ($1,000)				
				Minority						Minority	
	Male	Female	White [1]	Total [2]	Black [1]	His- panic [3]	Male	Female	White [1]	Black [1]	His- panic [3]
1980	2,350	1,637	3,146	842	619	163	15.2	11.4	13.8	11.5	12.3
1984	2,700	1,880	3,458	1,121	799	233	21.4	16.2	19.6	16.5	18.4
1985	2,789	1,952	3,563	1,179	835	248	22.3	17.3	20.6	17.5	19.2
1986	2,797	1,982	3,549	1,230	865	259	23.4	18.1	21.5	18.7	20.2
1987	2,818	2,031	3,600	1,249	872	268	24.2	18.9	22.4	19.3	21.1
1989	3,030	2,227	3,863	1,394	961	308	26.1	20.6	24.1	20.7	22.7
1990	3,071	2,302	3,918	1,456	994	327	27.3	21.8	25.2	22.0	23.8
1991	3,110	2,349	3,965	1,494	1,011	340	28.4	22.7	26.4	22.7	24.5
1993	2,820	2,204	3,588	1,436	948	341	30.6	24.3	28.5	24.2	26.8
1995	2,960	2,355	3,781	1,534	993	379	33.5	27.0	31.4	26.8	28.6
1997	2,898	2,307	3,676	1,529	973	392	34.6	27.9	32.2	27.4	29.5
1999	2,939	2,393	3,723	1,609	1,012	417	37.0	29.9	34.8	29.6	31.2
2001	3,080	2,554	3,888	1,746	1,077	471	39.8	32.1	37.5	31.5	33.8
2003	3,134	2,610	3,919	1,826	1,097	508	42.2	34.7	40.0	33.6	36.6
2005	3,185	2,644	3,973	1,856	1,100	532	44.1	36.4	41.5	35.3	38.9
2007	3,383	2,823	4,156	(NA)	(NA)	(NA)	(NA)	(NA)	(NA)	(NA)	(NA)
2009	3,239	2,742	3,976	2,004	1,145	601	50.3	41.5	47.6	40.3	44.8
2011	2,924	2,477	3,561	1,839	1,015	570	51.8	43.1	49.1	41.7	47.0
2013	3,055	2,568	3,671	1,952	1,057	634	52.5	43.8	49.9	42.0	46.8
2015, total	**2,969**	**2,492**	**3,536**	**1,926**	**1,011**	**634**	**54.9**	**46.5**	**52.2**	**44.1**	**49.8**
Officials/administrators	209	155	279	86	45	26	72.7	71.3	72.1	71.8	72.1
Professionals	626	902	1,024	396	253	131	67.8	58.4	62.4	54.5	61.8
Technicians	244	186	280	149	69	53	53.6	44.0	50.4	42.2	48.7
Protective service	933	223	784	371	194	144	56.4	45.1	54.8	45.6	60.7
Paraprofessionals	96	249	188	158	96	46	39.3	37.1	38.7	34.1	38.9
Administrative support	117	643	458	302	151	114	49.6	42.9	38.3	46.8	51.2
Skilled craft	369	20	273	117	58	44	40.8	33.1	31.2	38.5	40.1
Service/maintenance	375	113	250	238	145	75	40.2	38.3	38.2	38.0	39.5

NA Not available. [1] Non-Hispanic. [2] Includes other minority groups, not shown separately. [3] Persons of Hispanic origin may be of any race.

Source: U.S. Equal Employment Opportunity Commission, "Job Patterns for Minorities and Women in State and Local Government," <www.eeoc.gov>, accessed August 2017.

Table 492. State and Local Government Full-Time Equivalent Employment by Selected Function and State: 2015

[In thousands (1,890.4 represents 1,890,400). For March. Local government amounts are estimates subject to sampling variation; see Appendix III and <http://www.census.gov/govs/apes/>]

State	Total [1] State	Total [1] Local	Education Elementary/secondary State	Education Elementary/secondary Local	Education Higher education State	Education Higher education Local	Public welfare State	Public welfare Local	Health State	Health Local	Hospitals State	Hospitals Local	Highways State	Highways Local	Police protection State	Police protection Local	Fire protection State	Fire protection Local	Corrections State	Corrections Local	Parks and recreation State	Parks and recreation Local
U.S.	1,890.4	6,949.1	49.0	6,612.6	1,756.4	336.5	241.5	269.3	183.1	246.4	395.6	585.9	213.6	275.6	102.1	814.4	(X)	348.7	440.2	262.1	35.7	230.1
AL	45.4	96.1	–	96.1	42.4	0.1	4.0	1.1	4.3	6.6	12.1	26.8	4.3	6.3	1.4	12.9	(X)	6.1	4.8	3.5	0.5	3.9
AK	8.3	16.8	3.1	16.7	5.0	–	1.9	0.2	0.7	0.3	0.3	0.9	3.2	0.8	0.7	1.3	(X)	0.8	2.3	0.1	0.1	0.6
AZ	36.5	119.4	–	107.4	33.5	12.0	6.1	1.1	2.3	3.9	7.0	2.7	2.8	3.9	1.9	17.6	(X)	9.1	9.6	5.4	0.4	4.4
AR	27.4	70.2	–	69.8	26.0	0.4	4.2	0.1	3.7	0.6	6.7	1.4	3.5	3.9	1.2	7.5	(X)	3.0	5.5	2.6	1.0	1.3
CA	164.1	715.3	–	647.6	159.8	67.7	3.8	74.1	15.3	46.4	43.9	68.6	19.0	22.3	11.3	88.7	(X)	33.4	55.2	32.2	3.4	31.5
CO	46.2	105.5	–	104.3	44.6	1.2	2.4	6.7	1.3	5.2	6.0	9.9	3.1	5.1	1.3	14.0	(X)	6.8	7.2	3.9	1.0	7.4
CT	22.0	94.1	–	94.1	18.9	0.1	5.7	1.5	3.9	1.3	6.5	9.9	3.3	3.2	1.9	8.0	(X)	4.6	5.8	3.9	0.2	1.9
DE	8.3	17.2	–	17.2	7.9	–	1.6	–	2.1	0.3	1.3	–	1.5	0.5	1.2	1.5	(X)	0.2	2.9	–	0.3	0.3
DC	(X)	8.0	(X)	7.1	(X)	–	(X)	–	(X)	0.7	(X)	1.4	(X)	0.8	(X)	4.5	(X)	1.8	(X)	1.4	(X)	0.8
FL	68.0	379.9	–	351.9	65.0	0.9	9.2	2.3	16.7	5.7	4.0	50.3	6.4	12.9	4.1	57.7	(X)	28.4	23.5	16.7	1.3	17.8
GA	62.2	228.7	–	228.7	59.8	28.0	6.6	3.9	4.0	8.2	7.6	20.2	4.5	7.3	2.8	25.4	(X)	13.2	19.2	10.0	3.5	5.3
HI	37.2	–	26.1	–	10.9	–	0.4	1.8	1.9	0.3	4.7	–	0.9	0.9	–	4.0	(X)	1.5	–	–	0.2	2.1
ID	8.9	33.7	–	31.8	8.5	–	1.8	0.1	1.7	0.9	0.6	3.7	1.4	1.8	0.5	3.5	(X)	1.5	2.4	1.7	0.5	1.0
IL	58.8	302.7	–	277.6	56.9	1.8	9.5	5.4	2.4	5.6	10.9	11.3	6.7	10.6	3.2	38.0	(X)	17.5	11.3	10.4	0.1	18.7
IN	58.0	130.6	–	130.6	57.0	25.1	5.4	1.1	1.6	2.9	1.8	24.7	3.4	5.5	1.8	13.8	(X)	7.8	6.0	6.3	0.6	3.3
IA	24.1	84.4	–	77.3	23.1	–	2.7	1.2	0.4	1.8	7.9	11.5	2.2	5.2	0.9	6.2	(X)	2.0	2.9	1.6	1.1	2.0
KS	23.0	92.8	–	85.0	22.3	7.2	2.2	0.5	1.0	3.1	7.9	8.4	2.8	4.7	1.0	7.9	(X)	3.4	3.5	2.9	0.9	2.4
KY	40.0	105.2	–	105.2	37.8	7.8	8.3	0.4	3.5	5.0	6.2	5.0	4.6	3.0	2.1	7.6	(X)	4.3	4.2	3.9	0.2	1.8
LA	29.6	98.8	0.1	98.8	27.1	–	4.4	0.8	3.2	1.5	9.9	18.7	4.4	1.7	1.7	15.6	(X)	5.0	5.8	6.6	0.4	4.0
ME	7.5	34.1	–	34.1	7.2	–	2.8	0.1	1.0	0.3	0.5	1.1	2.0	4.7	0.5	2.4	(X)	1.7	1.7	0.7	1.0	0.7
MD	30.5	139.1	–	126.8	28.4	12.3	6.7	0.1	6.1	5.1	3.7	0.3	4.5	5.6	2.3	16.6	(X)	7.0	12.6	3.7	0.6	6.6
MA	37.0	159.2	–	159.1	33.6	0.1	7.4	2.5	7.6	3.0	5.5	2.9	2.5	7.7	2.9	17.3	(X)	12.7	12.5	–	0.6	2.2
MI	75.4	179.0	2.3	165.5	74.8	13.5	11.2	3.7	5.5	9.9	16.4	8.0	2.5	6.7	2.8	18.1	(X)	11.2	12.0	–	0.3	3.7
MN	40.4	122.1	–	122.1	36.5	–	3.0	11.0	3.4	3.4	4.6	5.6	4.5	4.3	0.9	11.2	(X)	2.9	4.2	5.4	0.5	4.7
MS	21.2	79.8	–	73.7	19.8	6.2	4.5	0.5	3.3	0.2	10.1	18.5	3.2	6.3	1.2	8.3	(X)	3.5	3.0	5.3	0.6	1.4
MO	32.5	139.1	–	133.0	30.9	6.2	6.9	3.0	2.8	3.9	10.1	12.5	5.5	1.3	2.6	16.2	(X)	7.3	12.2	2.2	0.3	4.3
MT	7.7	23.1	–	22.6	7.3	0.5	1.8	0.5	0.9	1.1	0.7	0.9	2.1	3.0	0.5	2.1	(X)	0.8	1.3	3.0	0.2	0.5
NE	13.1	50.2	–	46.8	12.5	3.4	2.6	1.6	0.6	0.5	3.7	4.7	2.1	1.0	0.8	4.2	(X)	1.5	2.9	0.7	0.3	1.0
NV	10.0	44.7	–	44.7	9.9	–	2.3	0.9	1.4	0.3	1.3	4.1	1.7	8.5	0.8	6.8	(X)	2.7	2.9	1.5	0.3	2.5
NH	7.5	35.7	–	35.7	7.2	–	1.9	2.3	0.8	0.3	0.6	–	1.6	2.0	0.5	3.4	(X)	2.7	1.1	2.2	0.2	0.5
NJ	54.6	217.9	16.9	206.7	35.1	11.3	9.0	8.5	4.0	4.0	14.0	1.5	5.7	26.7	4.1	30.0	(X)	8.1	8.5	6.2	0.3	5.6
NM	19.2	50.0	–	46.8	18.3	3.2	1.8	0.3	2.4	0.6	7.5	1.2	2.2	4.0	0.5	5.4	(X)	2.5	3.8	2.4	0.9	2.0
NY	62.6	487.0	–	461.1	58.7	25.9	4.8	42.6	8.1	15.3	40.4	50.8	10.6	1.3	6.2	79.5	(X)	24.5	29.0	23.9	0.6	12.4
NC	63.4	218.8	–	197.7	60.3	21.1	1.1	15.7	2.3	14.7	18.3	51.3	10.0	12.3	3.2	24.5	(X)	9.2	19.0	5.7	2.7	5.7
ND	9.2	17.3	–	17.3	8.8	–	0.5	1.0	1.7	0.6	0.9	–	1.0	5.0	0.2	1.6	(X)	0.4	0.9	0.6	1.6	0.2
OH	76.2	243.2	–	238.5	74.1	4.7	2.8	20.8	2.8	14.9	14.9	11.4	6.1	12.3	2.6	28.7	(X)	17.3	13.0	8.5	0.2	8.6
OK	31.6	94.8	–	94.8	30.0	–	8.0	0.2	5.5	1.7	1.6	10.6	2.9	5.0	2.1	9.5	(X)	4.4	4.5	2.0	0.5	1.6
OR	24.9	71.6	–	63.1	24.0	8.5	7.7	1.2	2.3	4.9	7.0	2.3	3.7	3.3	1.4	7.4	(X)	4.1	5.2	3.4	0.7	3.7
PA	64.3	246.5	–	236.3	59.1	10.1	11.3	16.5	1.7	5.5	11.3	–	13.5	10.5	6.7	25.4	(X)	5.3	18.5	13.1	0.4	3.2
RI	6.1	19.8	–	19.8	5.2	–	1.3	0.1	1.0	2.4	0.8	–	0.7	0.8	0.3	3.4	(X)	2.2	1.5	–	2.6	0.4
SC	35.0	101.6	–	101.6	31.9	–	5.1	0.4	5.3	0.4	7.0	23.9	4.4	2.6	2.1	12.0	(X)	5.8	8.1	3.4	0.8	3.7
SD	5.9	21.1	0.4	20.5	5.6	0.6	1.7	0.3	0.6	4.3	0.4	0.5	1.0	1.4	0.3	1.7	(X)	0.5	0.9	0.7	0.1	0.7
TN	36.1	133.0	–	133.0	34.2	–	7.4	1.7	4.2	–	3.7	21.5	3.2	6.5	1.8	19.2	(X)	7.5	6.9	5.5	1.0	4.1
TX	139.9	758.6	–	715.3	135.5	43.3	23.9	3.9	19.2	27.6	23.3	56.8	12.8	19.7	6.8	68.3	(X)	27.1	39.3	29.0	1.2	17.0
UT	27.2	51.3	–	51.3	25.3	21.1	2.5	0.6	1.9	3.4	9.3	0.4	1.5	1.6	0.9	5.3	(X)	2.7	3.1	2.2	0.3	3.3
VT	5.3	20.5	–	20.5	4.9	–	1.6	–	0.5	0.1	0.3	–	1.0	1.1	0.6	0.9	(X)	0.3	1.1	–	0.3	0.1
VA	59.5	197.5	–	196.2	56.8	1.3	3.0	8.6	5.5	6.9	15.3	2.2	7.6	4.1	3.2	18.6	(X)	10.8	13.2	11.3	1.0	8.1
WA	58.5	100.7	–	100.7	56.3	–	10.5	1.1	6.7	3.7	10.1	17.1	6.5	6.5	2.2	12.1	(X)	9.5	8.4	4.8	1.0	5.5
WV	15.0	42.5	–	42.5	13.7	–	3.4	–	0.8	1.2	10.7	2.3	5.1	0.9	1.1	3.0	(X)	4.9	3.5	0.2	0.5	0.8
WI	40.8	129.3	–	119.4	39.6	9.9	2.2	13.1	1.8	5.0	3.7	1.0	1.5	8.5	0.9	15.0	(X)	0.5	9.5	3.9	0.6	2.0
WY	4.3	20.6	–	18.5	4.0	2.1	0.6	0.2	0.9	0.4	0.7	6.9	1.8	0.8	0.3	1.7	(X)	0.5	1.3	0.7	0.2	0.8

– Represents or rounds to zero. X Not applicable. [1] Includes other categories, not shown separately.

Source: U.S. Census Bureau, Census of Governments, "2015 Annual Survey of Public Employment and Payroll," <http://www.census.gov/govs/apes/>, accessed April 2017.

Table 493. State and Local Government Employment and Average Monthly Earnings by State: 2000 to 2015

[4,083 represents 4,083,000. As of March. Full-time equivalent is a computed statistic representing the number of full-time employees that could have been employed if the reported number of hours worked by part-time employees had been worked by full-time employees. This statistic is calculated separately for each function of a government by dividing the "part-time hours paid" by the standard number of hours for full-time employees in the particular government and then adding the resulting quotient to the number of full-time employees]

| State | Full-time equivalent employment (1,000) | | | | | | Average monthly earnings [2] (dol.) | | | | | |
| | State | | | Local [1] | | | State | | | Local [1] | | |
	2000	2010	2015	2000	2010	2015	2000	2010	2015	2000	2010	2015
United States...	4,083	4,378	4,342	10,995	12,171	11,937	3,374	4,620	5,159	3,169	4,310	4,646
Alabama...........	80	90	89	182	198	193	2,841	4,099	4,498	2,431	3,240	3,523
Alaska.............	23	27	26	25	28	28	3,842	5,176	5,709	3,818	4,935	5,352
Arizona...........	65	67	79	182	225	207	3,055	4,365	4,852	2,942	4,163	4,300
Arkansas.........	49	63	63	96	106	107	2,842	3,795	4,001	2,175	3,208	3,148
California.........	355	411	404	1,322	1,381	1,371	4,451	5,740	6,877	4,062	5,787	6,314
Colorado.........	66	71	81	164	199	202	3,779	5,033	5,489	3,076	4,230	4,622
Connecticut......	66	63	64	111	123	128	3,909	5,632	6,288	3,856	5,063	5,345
Delaware.........	24	26	26	21	23	23	3,222	4,113	4,593	3,163	4,484	4,919
District of Columbia......	(X)	(X)	(X)	45	44	47	(X)	(X)	(X)	3,923	5,900	6,839
Florida.............	185	184	179	580	727	698	3,149	3,861	4,337	2,865	3,986	4,144
Georgia...........	120	124	128	334	392	378	2,899	3,795	4,104	2,677	3,439	3,610
Hawaii.............	55	58	58	14	15	17	2,926	3,943	4,631	3,352	5,040	5,151
Idaho..............	23	22	23	51	55	57	3,022	4,280	4,877	2,478	3,341	3,488
Illinois............	128	131	124	493	513	504	3,441	5,324	5,764	3,307	4,716	5,162
Indiana............	83	90	88	232	254	233	2,990	4,023	4,413	2,711	3,547	3,775
Iowa...............	55	51	50	121	124	132	3,656	5,326	6,260	2,727	3,831	4,266
Kansas............	43	44	50	128	156	145	3,071	4,178	4,489	2,491	3,361	3,692
Kentucky..........	74	81	86	149	161	157	3,051	3,940	4,313	2,339	3,101	3,396
Louisiana.........	95	89	74	185	187	185	2,807	4,282	4,592	2,278	3,397	3,460
Maine.............	21	21	21	51	51	49	2,983	4,063	4,322	2,609	3,545	3,796
Maryland..........	91	88	88	182	215	216	3,312	4,650	5,213	3,535	5,190	5,398
Massachusetts. ..	96	95	102	232	233	236	3,683	4,973	5,762	3,403	4,800	5,226
Michigan..........	142	146	142	351	329	295	3,934	5,208	5,753	3,518	4,618	4,628
Minnesota........	73	80	82	206	201	203	3,892	5,338	5,733	3,255	4,447	4,828
Mississippi........	56	57	57	133	136	134	2,752	3,537	3,788	2,121	2,985	3,181
Missouri..........	91	89	88	208	234	229	2,678	3,518	3,835	2,678	3,502	3,659
Montana..........	18	20	21	34	38	37	2,931	4,016	4,542	2,546	3,476	3,764
Nebraska.........	30	33	32	78	88	86	2,514	4,013	4,248	2,779	3,785	4,384
Nevada...........	22	28	28	61	86	80	3,444	4,891	4,818	3,817	5,149	5,552
New Hampshire...	19	19	19	46	53	52	3,079	4,584	5,101	2,830	3,813	4,313
New Jersey.......	133	152	141	316	356	337	4,075	5,767	6,243	3,967	5,449	6,011
New Mexico.......	48	48	46	70	80	79	2,811	3,978	4,593	2,494	3,440	3,702
New York..........	251	251	243	924	975	931	3,859	5,484	6,136	3,961	5,315	5,893
North Carolina....	123	146	140	328	402	400	3,012	3,886	4,748	2,708	3,690	3,913
North Dakota......	16	18	19	23	26	28	2,826	4,103	4,753	2,778	3,550	4,142
Ohio...............	136	140	138	459	466	446	3,369	4,995	5,252	3,118	4,101	4,290
Oklahoma.........	64	71	69	134	146	149	2,821	3,864	4,187	2,280	3,119	3,309
Oregon...........	53	65	67	124	133	125	3,269	4,452	4,924	3,332	4,348	5,016
Pennsylvania.....	150	168	163	388	429	404	3,436	4,564	5,040	3,296	4,290	4,809
Rhode Island......	20	19	18	36	31	30	3,772	5,298	5,771	3,550	4,953	5,334
South Carolina....	79	77	80	155	171	182	2,741	3,810	4,162	2,474	3,557	3,702
South Dakota.....	13	14	14	28	31	32	2,777	3,938	4,386	2,359	3,149	3,458
Tennessee........	81	83	78	218	247	246	2,786	3,822	4,249	2,631	3,358	3,590
Texas.............	269	318	304	909	1,134	1,154	3,095	4,280	4,952	2,643	3,604	3,927
Utah...............	49	51	55	73	90	87	2,880	4,409	4,808	2,836	3,706	4,098
Vermont...........	14	14	15	23	26	26	3,153	4,645	5,015	2,534	3,589	4,105
Virginia...........	119	125	127	269	319	319	3,229	4,384	4,907	2,928	3,905	4,217
Washington.......	112	123	122	193	226	221	3,551	4,913	5,213	3,835	5,416	6,032
West Virginia......	32	39	40	61	62	62	2,694	3,554	3,789	2,517	3,219	3,397
Wisconsin.........	64	72	74	220	211	212	3,710	4,901	5,219	3,210	4,239	4,527
Wyoming..........	11	14	13	29	37	37	2,589	4,240	4,475	2,660	4,068	4,658

X Not applicable. [1] Estimates subject to sampling variation; see Appendix III and source. [2] For full-time employees.

Source: U.S. Census Bureau, Census of Governments, "2015 Annual Survey of Public Employment and Payroll," <http://www.census.gov/govs/apes/>, accessed April 2017.

Table 494. City Government Employment and Payroll—Largest Cities: 2000 to 2015

[In thousands (458.1 represents 458,100), except as noted. As of March. Individual government data has not been reviewed as a separate time series; therefore, caution should be exercised in use and interpretation of data over time. Full-time equivalent is a computed statistic; see headnote, Table 493 for details]

Cities ranked by 2015 population [1]	Total employment (1,000)			Full-time equivalent employment total (1,000)			Payroll (mil. dol.)			Average monthly earnings for full-time employees (dol.)		
	2000	2010	2015	2000	2010	2015	2000	2010	2015	2000	2010	2015
New York, NY	458.1	444.0	433.8	429.3	413.0	416.6	1,708.8	2,407.5	2,540.2	4,150	5,918	6,194
Los Angeles, CA	49.4	55.1	58.2	48.4	51.0	53.3	230.1	385.2	434.5	4,793	7,850	8,502
Chicago, IL	41.3	35.8	32.1	40.7	35.8	31.8	171.3	216.5	210.6	4,239	6,052	6,669
Houston, TX	25.2	22.8	21.7	24.9	22.6	21.6	75.2	99.0	106.0	3,037	4,389	4,958
Philadelphia, PA	31.1	30.8	30.3	30.0	29.9	29.6	109.2	144.7	160.3	3,637	4,867	5,444
Phoenix, AZ	13.0	14.9	13.5	12.7	14.4	13.0	50.3	80.7	71.6	4,024	5,718	5,618
San Antonio, TX	16.9	16.5	15.8	15.7	15.4	15.2	48.0	64.9	85.7	3,160	4,293	5,706
San Diego, CA	12.3	10.8	10.8	11.4	10.2	9.8	46.9	63.0	68.5	4,201	6,288	7,153
Dallas, TX	15.6	15.5	14.8	15.2	15.1	14.7	50.4	72.8	77.3	3,332	4,884	5,307
San Jose, CA	7.6	7.6	5.7	6.9	6.7	4.9	36.3	52.5	36.5	5,569	8,401	7,973
Austin, TX	10.6	12.6	13.5	10.1	12.3	13.2	31.2	59.5	76.8	3,128	4,863	5,946
Jacksonville, FL	10.1	9.7	10.4	9.7	9.4	10.0	35.6	41.8	46.7	3,815	4,487	4,697
San Francisco, CA	27.7	30.7	32.8	27.7	27.3	31.4	141.6	207.2	230.5	5,112	7,666	7,664
Indianapolis, IN	12.4	14.2	15.4	12.0	13.7	14.9	36.7	54.8	68.4	3,115	4,050	4,664
Columbus, OH	9.1	8.2	8.7	8.8	7.9	8.3	30.1	40.6	48.3	3,478	5,210	5,896
Ft Worth, TX	6.1	6.3	6.5	5.7	6.2	6.2	18.9	28.7	32.7	3,394	4,618	5,345
Charlotte, NC	5.2	7.4	7.9	5.1	6.9	7.5	17.1	31.2	39.6	3,408	4,570	5,349
Seattle, WA	11.4	13.9	12.2	10.3	12.5	11.5	48.3	72.4	86.7	4,726	5,948	8,005
Denver, CO	14.5	13.0	13.7	13.7	12.3	12.7	47.3	65.2	75.2	3,534	5,388	6,099
El Paso, TX	5.9	5.9	6.6	5.8	5.6	6.5	15.6	21.2	23.6	2,701	3,836	3,688
Detroit, MI	40.7	13.1	11.7	36.1	12.9	11.6	132.1	58.4	55.4	3,693	4,570	4,819
Washington, DC	37.7	35.2	35.8	36.5	34.0	35.3	139.4	197.8	230.5	3,863	5,893	6,849
Boston, MA	23.3	19.9	20.8	22.0	19.3	20.1	80.2	104.0	126.6	3,734	5,452	6,509
Memphis, TN	28.2	24.5	10.7	26.9	23.5	10.3	80.3	87.1	47.8	3,024	3,746	4,848
Nashville, TN	20.6	23.9	22.9	19.6	21.7	21.1	62.3	91.4	94.5	3,235	4,311	4,573
Portland, OR	6.2	6.8	6.7	5.4	5.8	5.8	23.4	35.1	39.0	4,416	6,253	6,929
Oklahoma City, OK	5.1	4.7	4.9	4.8	4.4	4.6	16.0	21.0	27.1	3,457	4,858	5,980
Las Vegas, NV	2.6	3.2	3.1	2.5	2.9	2.7	11.2	19.3	19.0	4,681	7,162	7,504
Baltimore, MD	30.8	27.9	26.6	29.2	26.7	25.5	95.3	121.8	131.7	3,361	4,597	5,284
Louisville, KY	4.6	8.9	8.1	4.3	8.6	7.9	11.8	33.9	33.9	2,844	4,028	4,371
Milwaukee, WI	7.9	6.9	6.7	7.7	6.7	6.5	28.5	33.3	34.3	3,706	5,020	5,375
Albuquerque, NM	7.1	7.0	7.1	6.6	6.5	6.5	18.3	22.9	35.9	2,868	3,654	5,750
Tucson, AZ	7.1	5.6	5.2	5.8	5.3	4.9	16.0	23.5	23.5	2,787	4,545	4,970
Fresno, CA	3.2	4.1	3.4	3.1	4.0	3.2	12.7	20.2	19.1	4,073	5,260	6,174
Sacramento, CA	4.4	5.7	4.4	4.0	5.0	4.0	17.0	28.1	27.8	4,400	6,061	7,168
Kansas City, MO	6.8	6.4	6.4	6.6	6.3	6.4	21.3	27.3	18.7	3,246	4,324	2,945
Long Beach, CA	6.1	6.6	5.7	5.7	6.1	5.3	25.7	35.0	37.4	4,855	5,982	7,510
Mesa, AZ	3.5	3.6	3.8	3.3	3.5	3.7	13.4	19.2	21.5	4,072	5,532	5,954
Atlanta, GA	8.8	8.1	8.0	8.6	8.1	8.0	25.6	31.5	35.8	2,974	3,872	4,500
Colorado Springs, CO	7.4	8.3	7.1	6.9	7.6	6.6	25.3	39.8	37.5	3,747	5,307	5,749
Virginia Beach, VA	19.7	19.2	19.8	17.4	17.7	18.0	43.4	61.1	66.3	2,679	3,775	3,989
Raleigh, NC	3.2	5.1	5.1	2.9	4.2	4.3	8.9	16.3	17.7	3,114	4,166	4,323
Omaha, NE	3.4	3.1	3.1	2.9	2.9	2.8	10.6	14.8	16.3	3,874	5,491	6,127
Miami, FL	3.8	4.3	4.1	3.6	4.1	3.8	15.1	21.2	20.3	4,276	5,378	5,444
Oakland, CA	4.2	4.1	4.7	4.2	3.6	4.1	24.8	28.4	34.8	5,861	8,702	9,282
Minneapolis, MN	6.3	5.5	5.6	5.8	5.1	5.1	21.3	25.7	28.0	3,866	5,159	5,600
Tulsa, OK	4.5	4.0	3.8	4.5	3.9	3.7	13.7	16.8	18.3	3,126	4,376	4,954
Wichita, KS	3.6	3.1	3.2	3.1	3.1	2.9	9.3	13.0	13.2	3,072	4,198	4,646
New Orleans, LA	(NA)	6.9	6.4	(NA)	6.8	6.2	(NA)	25.9	25.8	(NA)	3,815	4,191
Arlington, TX	3.0	2.9	2.9	2.4	2.6	2.5	7.1	12.1	13.0	3,090	4,878	5,355
Cleveland, OH	10.1	8.4	7.6	9.4	7.9	7.1	27.8	35.2	35.7	2,989	4,462	5,041
Bakersfield, CA	1.3	1.5	1.6	1.2	1.5	1.5	5.3	8.2	9.8	4,469	5,691	6,453
Tampa, FL	4.3	4.5	4.2	4.2	4.4	4.1	14.1	23.2	22.9	3,370	5,376	5,722
Aurora, CO	2.5	2.6	2.7	2.5	2.6	2.7	9.0	13.8	16.1	3,682	5,374	5,984
Honolulu, HI	9.8	9.5	12.0	9.1	8.8	10.3	30.9	45.8	51.2	3,435	5,266	5,041
Anaheim, CA	3.2	3.2	2.7	2.5	2.6	2.2	11.5	17.4	17.0	5,267	7,982	9,144
Santa Ana, CA	2.5	1.7	1.3	2.2	1.5	1.1	10.1	12.1	8.4	5,606	8,623	8,479
Corpus Christi, TX	3.5	2.8	2.8	3.3	2.8	2.7	8.6	10.5	12.7	2,675	3,848	4,800
Riverside, CA	2.1	2.4	2.8	1.9	2.2	2.4	8.0	13.8	15.0	4,625	6,536	6,652
St Louis, MO	8.0	6.9	6.2	7.6	6.8	6.2	24.1	26.8	31.7	3,176	3,973	5,158
Lexington, KY	4.0	4.1	3.8	3.6	3.8	3.5	10.2	16.6	15.3	2,910	4,575	4,596
Stockton, CA	2.3	1.8	1.7	1.9	1.6	1.5	7.1	9.4	10.2	4,054	6,160	7,232
Pittsburgh, PA	4.4	3.3	3.2	4.3	3.3	3.0	15.3	13.8	17.8	3,593	4,210	6,001
St Paul, MN	4.2	3.2	3.3	3.2	3.0	2.9	13.3	16.4	16.7	4,189	5,751	5,976
Anchorage, AK	10.1	11.1	10.3	9.0	9.9	9.3	34.6	50.6	51.1	3,973	5,142	5,589
Cincinnati, OH	6.5	5.9	5.5	6.4	5.6	5.3	21.3	27.9	28.2	3,504	5,122	5,553
Henderson, NV	(NA)	2.7	2.6	(NA)	2.2	2.2	(NA)	13.7	14.7	(NA)	7,007	7,491
Greensboro, NC	(NA)	3.4	3.4	(NA)	3.1	3.1	(NA)	11.6	12.0	(NA)	3,837	3,966
Plano, TX	2.0	2.5	2.6	1.8	2.2	2.3	6.4	10.2	11.7	3,702	4,927	5,485
Newark, NJ	5.5	4.7	3.9	5.2	4.5	3.8	22.3	26.6	15.9	4,371	6,061	4,271
Toledo, OH	2.8	2.6	2.7	2.8	2.6	2.7	10.0	11.7	13.2	3,628	4,551	4,852
Lincoln, NE	2.7	2.9	2.8	2.5	2.6	2.7	8.2	12.4	14.0	3,382	4,982	5,584
Orlando, FL	(NA)	3.0	2.8	(NA)	3.0	2.7	(NA)	14.8	16.7	(NA)	4,959	6,099
Chula Vista, CA	(NA)	1.4	1.2	(NA)	1.3	1.0	(NA)	7.9	6.9	(NA)	6,314	7,228
Jersey City, NJ	(NA)	3.6	3.2	(NA)	3.4	3.0	(NA)	20.2	21.2	(NA)	6,122	7,446

NA Not available. [1] Based on estimated resident population as of July 1.

Source: U.S. Census Bureau, Census of Governments, "2015 Annual Survey of Public Employment and Payroll," <http://www.census.gov/govs/apes/>, accessed July 2017.

Table 495. County Government Employment and Payroll—Largest Counties: 2010 to 2015

[In units as indicated (107.5 represents 107,500). As of March. Individual government data has not been reviewed as a separate time series; therefore, caution should be exercised in use and interpretation of data over time. Full-time equivalent employment is a derived statistic that provides an estimate of a government's total full-time employment by converting part-time employees to a full-time amount; see headnote, Table 493 for details]

Counties ranked by 2015 population [1]	Total employment (1,000)			Total full-time equivalent employment (1,000)		Payroll (mil. dol.)			Average monthly earnings for full-time employees (dol.)	
	2010	2014	2015	2010	2015	2010	2014	2015	2010	2015
Los Angeles, CA..........	107.5	103.5	103.8	103.9	102.0	610.3	658.6	655.9	5,925	6,519
Cook, IL.................	22.8	21.0	20.6	22.8	20.6	120.7	128.6	128.2	5,305	6,230
Harris, TX...............	27.8	28.2	27.3	26.4	25.9	119.8	127.9	129.2	4,537	5,076
Maricopa, AZ.............	13.7	13.1	13.2	13.1	13.0	54.2	59.1	61.4	4,188	4,753
San Diego, CA............	20.9	21.3	21.7	19.5	20.4	101.1	104.2	107.7	5,201	5,301
Orange, CA..............	17.7	20.4	20.3	16.9	19.2	102.9	71.9	61.0	6,103	3,134
Miami-Dade, FL...........	51.1	37.3	38.7	49.9	37.8	285.0	217.5	237.1	5,794	6,429
Dallas, TX...............	18.1	19.8	19.9	16.8	18.6	76.6	90.7	94.3	4,536	5,071
Riverside, CA............	21.0	22.0	22.6	20.1	22.2	110.8	128.2	141.0	5,517	6,420
San Bernardino, CA......	21.2	20.6	20.6	19.9	19.5	101.7	103.5	103.4	5,269	5,408
King, WA.................	14.1	13.9	13.7	13.4	12.9	82.3	89.9	89.7	6,321	7,051
Clark, NV................	22.4	17.8	17.9	20.3	17.3	121.5	112.3	117.4	6,155	6,897
Tarrant, TX..............	11.0	13.1	13.5	10.7	12.8	46.0	53.9	56.1	4,307	4,376
Santa Clara, CA.........	19.0	18.9	19.5	18.2	18.7	129.6	138.3	146.8	7,297	8,007
Bexar, TX................	11.0	12.2	13.4	10.6	12.9	41.3	49.9	55.9	3,865	4,303
Broward, FL..............	12.1	11.3	11.3	11.7	10.9	61.4	52.7	58.0	5,313	5,419
Wayne, MI...............	4.7	4.2	3.9	4.7	3.8	21.5	20.0	19.3	4,645	5,168
Alameda, CA.............	12.1	13.1	14.1	11.5	13.3	77.2	93.4	100.9	6,885	7,634
Suffolk, NY..............	15.0	14.9	15.0	13.2	12.8	74.7	81.4	83.1	5,813	6,616
Sacramento, CA..........	13.1	12.7	12.6	12.7	11.9	72.5	76.4	79.6	5,736	6,744
Palm Beach, FL..........	11.3	11.5	10.9	10.9	10.3	60.7	63.3	63.0	5,634	6,232
Nassau, NY..............	18.0	16.1	15.8	16.0	13.6	88.5	79.6	79.2	5,748	5,988
Hillsborough, FL..........	10.5	9.8	9.7	10.1	9.3	45.7	44.8	46.4	4,583	5,009
Orange, FL..............	11.3	10.7	11.1	10.4	10.5	43.8	43.2	45.9	4,235	4,476
Cuyahoga, OH............	14.6	13.9	14.4	14.2	14.1	62.1	67.8	71.1	4,305	5,085
Franklin, OH.............	6.7	6.4	6.4	6.4	6.3	25.3	27.3	28.1	3,957	4,568
Oakland, MI.............	4.3	4.1	4.3	4.0	3.9	18.8	18.1	18.9	4,764	4,948
Allegheny, PA...........	7.1	7.5	7.0	7.0	6.8	26.3	30.1	28.8	3,853	4,251
Hennepin, MN...........	7.7	7.7	7.7	7.6	7.5	40.3	43.2	44.3	5,449	6,078
Travis, TX...............	5.3	6.8	7.2	5.2	7.2	22.0	29.6	29.9	4,228	4,160
Fairfax, VA..............	47.6	51.4	49.6	39.2	44.2	200.7	223.7	224.6	5,170	5,227
Contra Costa, CA........	8.6	8.4	8.6	7.9	7.9	49.8	51.0	51.4	6,337	6,574
Salt Lake, UT...........	7.1	7.6	7.6	5.4	5.4	20.8	20.8	21.1	4,198	4,289
Montgomery, MD........	43.3	42.6	42.4	36.3	36.0	232.5	234.3	240.5	6,859	7,143
Mecklenburg, NC........	28.3	26.6	29.3	26.2	27.1	104.4	100.8	106.1	4,040	3,953
Wake, NC...............	25.5	27.3	27.3	21.9	23.7	88.1	92.4	99.9	4,018	4,179
Pima, AZ................	7.7	6.9	6.8	7.2	6.5	28.3	26.6	27.2	4,056	4,268
Fulton, GA..............	6.0	4.8	5.3	6.0	5.2	23.1	20.4	20.0	3,890	3,887
St. Louis, MO...........	4.1	4.0	4.1	4.0	4.0	15.9	15.4	17.2	4,042	4,341
Westchester, NY..........	11.6	10.6	10.7	10.3	9.6	66.5	66.2	66.4	6,463	7,102
Fresno, CA..............	9.0	8.2	8.5	8.4	8.0	37.6	34.8	35.6	4,513	4,517
Milwaukee, WI...........	7.3	7.2	7.1	6.8	6.7	30.1	31.5	32.1	4,436	4,830
Pinellas, FL..............	6.2	5.6	5.7	6.1	5.5	26.9	25.8	27.0	4,430	4,885
Shelby, TN..............	13.9	27.4	25.0	13.4	24.0	48.5	102.1	88.5	3,641	3,863
Bergen, NJ..............	6.0	6.0	5.8	4.9	4.8	26.8	27.8	27.8	5,674	6,162
Du Page, IL..............	3.0	2.5	2.7	2.9	2.7	12.5	10.8	11.6	4,403	4,449
Erie, NY.................	11.2	10.0	9.9	10.0	8.7	44.2	40.6	42.6	4,583	5,061
Collin, TX...............	2.0	1.9	1.9	2.0	1.9	7.6	7.8	7.9	3,875	4,311
Prince Georges, MD.....	35.7	34.4	35.9	29.4	31.1	155.6	149.0	157.2	5,489	5,393
Gwinnett, GA............	5.3	5.1	5.3	4.9	4.9	20.4	20.7	21.5	4,200	4,419
Kern, CA................	11.3	10.0	10.0	10.7	9.6	55.6	54.5	55.3	5,263	5,916
Macomb, MI.............	3.1	2.9	2.6	2.9	2.5	11.7	11.3	10.9	4,241	4,586
Ventura, CA.............	9.3	9.6	9.7	8.9	9.2	57.0	60.2	64.9	6,584	7,253
Pierce, WA..............	3.5	3.3	3.3	3.3	3.1	20.2	20.1	20.9	6,108	6,715
Hidalgo, TX.............	2.9	2.8	2.9	2.9	2.9	9.1	9.2	9.5	3,140	3,280
Middlesex, NJ...........	4.6	4.1	4.2	3.7	3.5	19.5	20.2	20.3	5,448	6,045
El Paso, TX.............	5.1	5.7	5.6	5.0	5.5	20.4	24.7	24.5	4,173	4,537
Baltimore, MD...........	30.6	31.6	31.2	26.2	26.6	122.2	126.3	127.9	4,979	5,196
Montgomery, PA.........	3.6	3.4	3.5	3.5	3.4	13.0	12.5	13.3	3,824	4,110
Hamilton, OH............	5.1	4.9	4.9	5.0	4.8	19.0	19.0	19.6	3,838	4,121
Essex, NJ...............	5.2	5.4	5.0	4.6	4.5	24.3	27.7	25.8	5,351	5,950
Multnomah, OR..........	4.9	5.1	5.3	4.6	4.9	22.4	23.2	25.6	4,998	5,262
Denton, TX..............	1.9	2.0	2.1	1.9	2.0	7.0	7.7	8.2	3,763	4,061
Oklahoma, OK...........	2.4	2.3	2.5	2.2	2.4	6.5	7.2	6.9	2,977	2,958
Snohomish, WA..........	2.7	2.7	2.7	2.7	2.7	14.9	15.3	15.8	5,481	5,957
San Mateo, CA..........	7.3	6.4	6.5	6.9	5.6	41.7	38.8	40.2	7,042	7,316
Monroe, NY.............	7.1	6.8	6.8	6.2	5.8	25.6	25.4	25.4	4,279	4,553
Cobb, GA...............	5.0	4.7	4.8	4.5	4.5	18.7	18.6	19.5	4,235	4,475
Dekalb, GA..............	7.5	6.3	6.4	7.4	6.3	27.9	23.7	24.7	3,827	3,954
San Joaquin, CA.........	8.3	7.7	7.9	7.2	7.0	37.6	40.4	42.2	5,334	6,251
Fort Bend, TX...........	2.3	2.3	2.4	2.2	2.4	8.1	8.8	9.4	3,652	4,001
Lake, IL.................	3.3	2.8	2.8	3.0	2.6	14.2	12.5	12.6	4,809	5,013
Lee, FL..................	4.8	4.6	4.6	4.7	4.6	19.4	19.8	20.1	4,142	4,439
Will, IL..................	2.4	2.4	2.3	2.3	2.2	9.7	10.8	10.7	4,259	4,848
Jackson, MO.............	2.0	1.3	1.3	2.0	1.3	6.7	4.5	4.9	3,417	3,892

NA Not available. [1] Based on estimated resident population as of July 1.

Source: U.S. Census Bureau, Census of Governments, "2015 Annual Survey of Public Employment and Payroll," <http://www.census.gov/govs/apes/>, accessed July 2017.

Federal Government Finances and Employment

This section presents statistics relating to the financial structure and civilian employment of the federal government. The fiscal data cover taxes, other receipts, outlays, and debt. The principal sources of fiscal data are the *Budget of the United States Government* and related documents, published annually by the Office of Management and Budget (OMB), and the U.S. Department of the Treasury's *Combined Statement of Receipts, Outlays, and Balances of the United States Government*. Detailed data on tax returns and collections are published annually by the Internal Revenue Service. The personnel data relate to staffing, payrolls, and retirements are published by the Office of Personnel Management. Data on federally owned land and real property are collected by the General Services Administration and presented in its annual *Federal Real Property Report*.

Budget concept—Under the unified budget concept, all federal monies are included in one comprehensive budget. These monies comprise both federal funds and trust funds. Federal funds are derived mainly from taxes and borrowing and are not restricted by law to any specific government purpose. Trust funds, such as the Unemployment Trust Fund, collect certain taxes and other receipts for use in carrying out specific purposes or programs in accordance with the terms of the trust agreement or statute. Fund balances include both cash balances with the Treasury and investments in U.S. securities. Part of the balance is obligated, part unobligated. Prior to 1985, the budget totals, under provisions of law, excluded some federal activities—including the Federal Financing Bank, the Postal Service, the Synthetic Fuels Corporation, and the lending activities of the Rural Electrification Administration. The Balanced Budget and Emergency Deficit Control Act of 1985 (P.L.99-177) repealed the off-budget status of these entities and placed Social Security (Federal Old-Age and Survivors Insurance and the Federal Disability Insurance Trust Funds) off-budget. Though Social Security is now off-budget and, by law excluded from coverage of the congressional budget resolutions, it continues to be a federal program.

Receipts arising from the government's sovereign powers are reported as governmental receipts and all other receipts, i.e., from business or market-oriented activities, are offset against outlays. Outlays are reported on a checks-issued (net) basis (i.e., outlays are recorded at the time the checks to pay bills are issued).

Debt concept—For most of U.S. history, the total debt consisted of debt borrowed by the Treasury (i.e., public debt). The present debt series includes both public debt and agency debt. The *gross federal debt* includes money borrowed by the Treasury and by various federal agencies; it is the broadest generally used measure of the federal debt. *Total public debt* is covered by a statutory debt limitation and includes only borrowing by the Treasury.

Treasury receipts and outlays—All receipts of the government, with a few exceptions, are deposited to the credit of the U.S. Treasury regardless of ultimate disposition. Under the Constitution, no money may be withdrawn from the Treasury unless appropriated by the Congress.

The day-to-day cash operations of the federal government clearing through the accounts of the U.S. Treasury are reported in the *Daily Treasury Statement*. Extensive detail on the public debt is published in the *Monthly Statement of the Public Debt of the United States*.

Budget receipts such as taxes, customs duties, and miscellaneous receipts, which are collected by government agencies, and outlays represented by checks issued and cash payments made by disbursing officers as well as government agencies are reported in the *Monthly Treasury Statement of Receipts and Outlays of the United States Government* and in the Treasury's *Combined Statement of Receipts, Outlays, and Balances of the United States Government*. These deposits in and payments from accounts maintained by government agencies are on the same basis as the unified budget.

The quarterly *Treasury Bulletin* contains data on fiscal operations and related Treasury activities, including financial statements of government corporations and other business-type activities.

Income tax returns and tax collections—Tax data are compiled by the Internal Revenue Service of the Treasury Department. The annual *Internal Revenue Service Data Book* gives a detailed account of tax collections by kind of tax. The agency's annual *Statistics of Income* reports present detailed data from individual income tax returns and corporation income tax returns as well as historical tax data. The quarterly *Statistics of Income Bulletin* presents data on such diverse subjects as tax-exempt organizations, unincorporated businesses, fiduciary income tax and estate tax returns, sales of capital assets by individuals, international income and taxes reported by corporations and individuals, and estate tax wealth.

Employment and payrolls—The Office of Personnel Management collects employment, payroll, and retirement data from all departments and agencies of the federal government, except the Central Intelligence Agency, the National Security Agency, the National Geospatial-Intelligence Agency, and the Defense Intelligence Agency. Employment figures represent the number of persons who occupied civilian positions at the end of the report month shown and who are paid for services rendered to the federal government, regardless of the nature of appointment or method of payment. Federal payrolls include all payments for personnel services rendered during the report month and payments for accumulated annual leave of employees who separate from the service. Since most federal employees are paid on a biweekly basis, the calendar month earnings are partially estimated on the basis of the number of work days in each month where payroll periods overlap.

Federal employment and payroll figures are published by the Office of Personnel Management in its *Federal Civilian Workforce Statistics—Employment and Trends* and the FedScope database system. It also publishes employment data on minority groups, white- and blue-collar workers, employment by geographic area, and salary and wage distribution of federal employees. General schedule is primarily white-collar; wage system primarily blue-collar. Data on federal employment are also issued by the Bureau of Labor Statistics in its *Monthly Labor Review* and *Employment and Earnings Online* and by the U.S. Census Bureau in its annual report series *Federal, State, and Local Governments: Public Employment and Payroll Data.*

Table 496. Federal Budget—Receipts and Outlays: 1960 to 2017

[92.5 represents $92,500,000,000. For fiscal years ending in year shown; See text, Section 8. See also headnote, Table 498]

Fiscal year	In current dollars (bil. dol.)			In constant (2009) dollars (bil. dol.)			As percentage of GDP [1]		
	Receipts	Outlays	Surplus or deficit (-)	Receipts	Outlays	Surplus or deficit (-)	Receipts	Outlays	Surplus or deficit (-)
1960	92.5	92.2	0.3	655.5	653.4	2.1	17.3	17.2	0.1
1970	192.8	195.6	-2.8	1,015.3	1,030.3	-15.0	18.4	18.6	-0.3
1980	517.1	590.9	-73.8	1,308.8	1,495.7	-186.9	18.5	21.1	-2.6
1990	1,032.0	1,253.0	-221.0	1,654.6	2,009.0	-354.4	17.4	21.2	-3.7
1995	1,351.8	1,515.7	-164.0	1,850.2	2,074.7	-224.4	17.8	20.0	-2.2
1996	1,453.1	1,560.5	-107.4	1,948.1	2,092.1	-144.0	18.2	19.6	-1.3
1997	1,579.2	1,601.1	-21.9	2,074.7	2,103.4	-28.7	18.6	18.9	-0.3
1998	1,721.7	1,652.5	69.3	2,242.1	2,151.9	90.2	19.2	18.5	0.8
1999	1,827.5	1,701.8	125.6	2,349.8	2,188.3	161.5	19.2	17.9	1.3
2000	2,025.2	1,789.0	236.2	2,541.0	2,244.6	296.4	20.0	17.6	2.3
2001	1,991.1	1,862.8	128.2	2,433.2	2,276.5	156.7	18.8	17.6	1.2
2002	1,853.1	2,010.9	-157.8	2,227.6	2,417.2	-189.6	17.0	18.5	-1.5
2003	1,782.3	2,159.9	-377.6	2,083.6	2,525.0	-441.4	15.7	19.1	-3.3
2004	1,880.1	2,292.8	-412.7	2,141.8	2,612.0	-470.2	15.6	19.0	-3.4
2005	2,153.6	2,472.0	-318.3	2,371.6	2,722.1	-350.6	16.7	19.2	-2.5
2006	2,406.9	2,655.0	-248.2	2,561.9	2,826.0	-264.2	17.6	19.4	-1.8
2007	2,568.0	2,728.7	-160.7	2,663.1	2,829.7	-166.7	17.9	19.1	-1.1
2008	2,524.0	2,982.5	-458.6	2,529.0	2,988.5	-459.5	17.1	20.2	-3.1
2009	2,105.0	3,517.7	-1,412.7	2,105.0	3,517.7	-1,412.7	14.6	24.4	-9.8
2010	2,162.7	3,457.1	-1,294.4	2,129.3	3,403.6	-1,274.4	14.6	23.4	-8.7
2011	2,303.5	3,603.1	-1,299.6	2,215.9	3,466.2	-1,250.2	15.0	23.4	-8.5
2012	2,450.0	3,536.9	-1,087.0	2,310.7	3,335.8	-1,025.1	15.3	22.1	-6.8
2013	2,775.1	3,454.6	-679.5	2,583.9	3,216.6	-632.7	16.8	20.9	-4.1
2014	3,021.5	3,506.1	-484.6	2,770.5	3,214.8	-444.3	17.5	20.4	-2.8
2015	3,249.9	3,688.4	-438.5	2,960.9	3,360.4	-399.5	18.2	20.6	-2.4
2016	3,268.0	3,852.6	-584.7	2,953.2	3,481.5	-528.3	17.8	20.9	-3.2
2017, estimate	3,459.7	4,062.2	-602.5	3,056.0	3,588.2	-532.2	18.1	21.2	-3.1

[1] Gross domestic product; see text, Section 13.

Source: U.S. Office of Management and Budget, *Budget of the U.S. Government, Fiscal Year 2018: Historical Tables*, May 2017. See also <http://www.whitehouse.gov/omb/budget>.

Table 497. Federal Budget Debt: 1960 to 2017

[290.5 represents $290,500,000,000. As of the end of the fiscal year. See text, Section 8]

Fiscal year	Total (bil. dol.)					As percentages of GDP [1]				
	Gross federal debt	Federal government accounts	Held by the public			Gross federal debt	Federal government accounts	Held by the public		
			Total	Federal Reserve System	Other			Total	Federal Reserve System	Other
1960	290.5	53.7	236.8	26.5	210.3	54.3	10.0	44.3	5.0	39.3
1970	380.9	97.7	283.2	57.7	225.5	36.3	9.3	27.0	5.5	21.5
1980	909.0	197.1	711.9	120.8	591.1	32.5	7.0	25.5	4.3	21.1
1985	1,817.4	310.2	1,507.3	169.8	1,337.5	42.6	7.3	35.3	4.0	31.3
1990	3,206.3	794.7	2,411.6	234.4	2,177.1	54.2	13.4	40.8	4.0	36.8
1991	3,598.2	909.2	2,689.0	258.6	2,430.4	58.9	14.9	44.0	4.2	39.8
1992	4,001.8	1,002.1	2,999.7	296.4	2,703.3	62.2	15.6	46.6	4.6	42.0
1993	4,351.0	1,102.6	3,248.4	325.7	2,922.7	64.0	16.2	47.8	4.8	43.0
1994	4,643.3	1,210.2	3,433.1	355.2	3,077.9	64.5	16.8	47.7	4.9	42.8
1995	4,920.6	1,316.2	3,604.4	374.1	3,230.3	64.9	17.4	47.5	4.9	42.6
1996	5,181.5	1,447.4	3,734.1	390.9	3,343.1	64.9	18.1	46.8	4.9	41.9
1997	5,369.2	1,596.9	3,772.3	424.5	3,347.8	63.3	18.8	44.5	5.0	39.5
1998	5,478.2	1,757.1	3,721.1	458.2	3,262.9	61.2	19.6	41.6	5.1	36.4
1999	5,605.5	1,973.2	3,632.4	496.6	3,135.7	58.9	20.7	38.2	5.2	33.0
2000	5,628.7	2,218.9	3,409.8	511.4	2,898.4	55.5	21.9	33.6	5.0	28.6
2001	5,769.9	2,450.3	3,319.6	534.1	2,785.5	54.6	23.2	31.4	5.1	26.4
2002	6,198.4	2,658.0	3,540.4	604.2	2,936.2	57.0	24.4	32.5	5.6	27.0
2003	6,760.0	2,846.6	3,913.4	656.1	3,257.3	59.7	25.1	34.5	5.8	28.7
2004	7,354.7	3,059.1	4,295.5	700.3	3,595.2	60.8	25.3	35.5	5.8	29.7
2005	7,905.3	3,313.1	4,592.2	736.4	3,855.9	61.3	25.7	35.6	5.7	29.9
2006	8,451.4	3,622.4	4,829.0	768.9	4,060.0	61.8	26.5	35.3	5.6	29.7
2007	8,950.7	3,915.6	5,035.1	779.6	4,255.5	62.5	27.3	35.2	5.4	29.7
2008	9,986.1	4,183.0	5,803.1	491.1	5,311.9	67.7	28.4	39.3	3.3	36.0
2009	11,875.9	4,331.1	7,544.7	769.2	6,775.5	82.4	30.0	52.3	5.3	47.0
2010	13,528.8	4,509.9	9,018.9	811.7	8,207.2	91.4	30.5	60.9	5.5	55.5
2011	14,764.2	4,636.0	10,128.2	1,664.7	8,463.5	96.0	30.1	65.9	10.8	55.0
2012	16,050.9	4,769.8	11,281.1	1,645.3	9,635.8	100.1	29.8	70.4	10.3	60.1
2013	16,719.4	4,736.7	11,982.7	2,072.3	9,910.4	101.2	28.7	72.6	12.5	60.0
2014	17,794.5	5,014.6	12,779.9	2,451.7	10,328.2	103.3	29.1	74.2	14.2	60.0
2015	18,120.1	5,003.4	13,116.7	2,461.9	10,654.7	101.2	27.9	73.3	13.8	59.5
2016	19,539.4	5,371.7	14,167.7	2,463.5	11,704.3	106.1	29.2	77.0	13.4	63.6
2017, estimate	20,354.4	5,530.6	14,823.8	(NA)	(NA)	106.2	28.9	77.4	(NA)	(NA)

NA Not available. [1] Gross domestic product; see text, Section 13.

Source: U.S. Office of Management and Budget, *Budget of the U.S. Government, Fiscal Year 2018: Historical Tables*, May 2017. See also <http://www.whitehouse.gov/omb/budget>.

Table 498. Federal Budget Outlays by Type: 1990 to 2017

[1,253.0 represents $1,253,000,000,000. For fiscal years ending September 30. Given the inherent imprecision in adjusting outlays for inflation, the data shown in constant dollars present a reasonable perspective, not precision. The deflators and the categories that are deflated are as comparable over time as feasible. Minus sign (-) indicates offset]

Type	Unit	1990	2000	2005	2010	2015	2016	2017, est.
Current dollar outlays	**Bil. dol.**	**1,253.0**	**1,789.0**	**2,472.0**	**3,457.1**	**3,688.4**	**3,852.6**	**4,062.2**
National defense [1]	Bil. dol.	299.3	294.4	495.3	693.5	589.7	593.4	602.8
Nondefense, total	Bil. dol.	953.7	1,494.6	1,976.7	2,763.6	3,098.7	3,259.2	3,459.4
Payments for individuals	Bil. dol.	592.4	1,067.4	1,511.9	2,305.9	2,653.8	2,776.7	2,886.9
Direct payments [2]	Bil. dol.	513.5	876.6	1,229.0	1,906.7	2,186.3	2,276.8	2,367.6
Grants to state and local governments	Bil. dol.	78.9	190.7	282.9	399.2	467.5	499.9	519.3
All other grants	Bil. dol.	56.2	95.1	145.1	209.2	156.9	160.9	167.0
Net interest [2]	Bil. dol.	184.3	222.9	184.0	196.2	223.2	240.0	276.2
All other [2]	Bil. dol.	157.4	151.7	200.9	134.4	180.7	176.9	222.7
Undistributed offsetting receipts [2]	Bil. dol.	-36.6	-42.6	-65.2	-82.1	-115.8	-95.3	-93.4
Constant (2009) dollar outlays	**Bil. dol.**	**2,009.0**	**2,244.6**	**2,722.1**	**3,403.6**	**3,360.4**	**3,481.5**	**3,588.2**
National defense [1]	Bil. dol.	512.2	406.9	552.6	681.0	539.1	540.0	538.6
Nondefense, total	Bil. dol.	1,496.9	1,837.7	2,169.5	2,722.5	2,821.4	2,941.6	3,049.6
Payments for individuals	Bil. dol.	886.6	1,288.6	1,647.0	2,269.1	2,418.2	2,509.1	2,547.8
Direct payments [2]	Bil. dol.	768.3	1,057.6	1,338.3	1,876.1	1,992.3	2,057.4	2,089.5
Grants to state and local governments	Bil. dol.	118.3	231.0	308.7	393.0	426.0	451.7	458.3
All other grants	Bil. dol.	105.2	134.5	171.5	206.1	139.2	141.8	143.5
Net interest [2]	Bil. dol.	278.2	273.7	201.5	194.5	203.2	216.0	244.1
All other [2]	Bil. dol.	303.2	200.9	223.1	132.4	161.9	156.8	193.4
Undistributed offsetting receipts [2]	Bil. dol.	-76.3	-60.0	-73.6	-79.6	-101.3	-82.3	-79.2
Outlays as percent of GDP [3]	**Percent**	**21.2**	**17.6**	**19.2**	**23.4**	**20.6**	**20.9**	**21.2**
National defense [1]	Percent	5.1	2.9	3.8	4.7	3.3	3.2	3.1
Nondefense, total	Percent	16.1	14.7	15.3	18.7	17.3	17.7	18.1
Payments for individuals	Percent	10.0	10.5	11.7	15.6	14.8	15.1	15.1
Direct payments [2]	Percent	8.7	8.6	9.5	12.9	12.2	12.4	12.4
Grants to state and local governments	Percent	1.3	1.9	2.2	2.7	2.6	2.7	2.7
All other grants	Percent	1.0	0.9	1.1	1.4	0.9	0.9	0.9
Net interest [2]	Percent	3.1	2.2	1.4	1.3	1.2	1.3	1.4
All other [2]	Percent	2.7	1.5	1.6	0.9	1.0	1.0	1.2
Undistributed offsetting receipts [2]	Percent	-0.6	-0.4	-0.5	-0.6	-0.6	-0.5	-0.5

[1] Includes a small amount of grants to state and local governments and direct payments for individuals. [2] Includes some off-budget amounts; most of the off-budget amounts are direct payments for individuals (social security benefits). [3] Gross domestic product; see text, Section 13.

Source: U.S. Office of Management and Budget, *Budget of the U.S. Government, Fiscal Year 2018: Historical Tables*, May 2017. See also <http://www.whitehouse.gov/omb/budget>.

Table 499. Federal Budget Outlays by Agency: 1990 to 2017

[In billions of dollars (1,253.0 represents $1,253,000,000,000). For fiscal years ending September 30]

Department or other unit	1990	2000	2005	2010	2015	2016	2017, est.
Outlays, total [1]	**1,253.0**	**1,789.0**	**2,472.0**	**3,457.1**	**3,688.4**	**3,852.6**	**4,062.2**
Legislative branch	2.2	2.9	4.0	5.8	4.3	4.3	5.2
Judicial branch	1.6	4.1	5.5	7.2	7.1	7.5	8.1
Agriculture	45.9	75.1	85.3	129.5	139.1	138.2	133.0
Commerce	3.7	7.8	6.1	13.2	9.0	9.2	10.7
Defense—Military	289.7	281.0	474.4	666.7	562.5	565.4	573.0
Education	23.0	33.5	72.9	93.7	90.0	77.0	111.8
Energy	12.1	15.0	21.3	30.8	25.4	25.9	27.0
Health and Human Services	175.5	382.3	581.4	854.1	1,027.5	1,103.0	1,130.7
Homeland Security	7.2	13.2	38.7	44.5	42.6	45.2	51.4
Housing and Urban Development	20.2	30.8	42.5	60.1	35.5	26.4	56.8
Interior	5.8	8.0	9.3	13.2	12.3	12.6	13.5
Justice	5.9	16.8	22.4	29.6	26.9	29.5	38.2
Labor	26.1	31.9	46.9	173.1	45.2	41.4	45.1
State	4.8	6.7	12.7	23.8	26.5	29.4	30.1
Transportation	25.6	41.6	56.6	77.8	75.4	78.4	79.4
Treasury	253.9	390.5	410.2	444.3	485.6	526.1	567.0
Veterans Affairs	29.0	47.0	69.8	108.3	159.2	174.0	174.4
Corps of Engineers—Civil Works	3.3	4.2	4.7	9.9	6.7	6.4	6.9
Other Defense—Civil Programs	21.7	32.8	43.5	54.0	63.0	64.5	58.0
Environmental Protection Agency	5.1	7.2	7.9	11.0	7.0	8.7	8.6
Executive Office of the President	0.2	0.3	7.7	0.6	0.4	0.4	0.4
International Assistance Programs	10.1	12.1	15.0	20.0	21.0	16.2	26.3
National Aeronautics and Space Administration	12.4	13.4	15.6	18.9	18.3	18.8	19.1
National Science Foundation	1.8	3.4	5.4	6.7	6.8	6.9	7.0
Office of Personnel Management	31.9	48.7	59.5	69.9	91.7	91.3	93.6
Social Security Administration (on-budget)	17.3	45.1	54.6	70.8	87.4	93.2	94.6
Social Security Administration (off-budget)	245.0	396.2	506.8	683.4	856.8	883.5	914.3
Undistributed offsetting receipts [2]	-98.9	-173.0	-226.2	-267.9	-257.6	-241.4	-243.3

[1] Includes other agencies, not shown separately. [2] Includes some off-budget amounts; most of the off-budget amounts are direct payments to individuals (social security benefits).

Source: U.S. Office of Management and Budget, *Budget of the U.S. Government, Fiscal Year 2018: Historical Tables*, May 2017. See also <http://www.whitehouse.gov/omb/budget>.

Table 500. Federal Budget Outlays by Detailed Function: 1990 to 2017

[In billions of dollars (1,253.0 represents $1,253,000,000,000). For fiscal years ending September 30. Minus sign (-) indicates decrease]

Superfunction and function	1990	2000	2005	2010	2013	2014	2015	2016	2017, est.
Total outlays	**1,253.0**	**1,789.0**	**2,472.0**	**3,457.1**	**3,454.6**	**3,506.1**	**3,688.4**	**3,852.6**	**4,062.2**
National defense [1]	299.3	294.4	495.3	693.5	633.4	603.5	589.7	593.4	602.8
Department of Defense—Military	289.7	281.0	474.1	666.7	607.8	577.9	562.5	565.4	573.0
Military personnel	75.6	76.0	127.5	155.7	150.8	148.9	145.2	147.9	145.7
Operation and maintenance	88.3	105.8	188.1	276.0	259.7	244.5	247.2	243.2	244.6
Procurement	81.0	51.7	82.3	133.6	114.9	107.5	101.3	102.7	105.0
Research, development, test, and evaluation	37.5	37.6	65.7	77.0	66.9	64.9	64.1	64.9	66.4
Military construction	5.1	5.1	5.3	21.2	12.3	9.8	8.1	6.7	7.2
Atomic energy defense activities	9.0	12.1	18.0	19.3	17.6	17.4	18.7	19.4	20.0
International affairs [1]	13.8	17.2	34.6	45.2	46.2	46.7	48.6	45.3	56.4
International development and humanitarian assistance	5.5	6.5	17.7	19.0	22.6	23.5	24.1	24.1	25.7
International security assistance	8.7	6.4	7.9	11.4	10.0	11.4	12.9	11.3	13.3
Conduct of foreign affairs	3.0	4.7	9.1	13.6	13.0	12.9	13.2	13.9	14.7
General science, space, and technology	14.4	18.6	23.6	30.1	28.9	28.6	29.4	30.2	31.1
General science and basic research	2.8	6.2	8.8	11.7	12.5	12.0	11.7	12.0	12.6
Space flight, research, and supporting activities	11.6	12.4	14.8	18.4	16.4	16.6	17.7	18.2	18.5
Energy [1]	3.3	-0.8	0.4	11.6	11.0	5.3	6.8	3.7	6.0
Energy supply	2.0	-1.8	-0.9	5.8	9.0	4.1	4.7	2.0	4.9
Natural resources and environment [1]	17.1	25.0	28.0	43.7	38.1	36.2	36.0	39.5	40.6
Water resources	4.4	5.1	5.7	11.7	7.7	7.9	7.8	7.4	8.6
Conservation and land management	4.0	6.8	6.2	10.8	10.7	9.7	10.5	12.3	12.0
Recreational resources	1.4	2.5	3.0	3.9	3.5	3.4	3.5	3.7	4.0
Pollution control and abatement	5.2	7.4	8.1	10.8	9.6	8.6	7.2	8.6	8.7
Agriculture	11.6	36.5	26.6	21.4	29.7	24.4	18.5	18.3	21.1
Farm income stabilization	9.6	33.4	22.0	16.5	25.2	20.0	13.4	13.4	15.8
Agricultural research and services	2.1	3.0	4.5	4.9	4.5	4.4	5.1	4.9	5.3
Commerce and housing credit [1]	67.6	3.2	7.6	-82.3	-83.2	-94.9	-37.9	-34.1	-17.7
Mortgage credit	3.8	-3.3	-0.9	35.8	-87.9	-84.3	-35.7	-34.7	-27.3
Postal service	2.1	2.1	-1.2	-0.7	-1.8	-2.5	-1.6	-1.3	1.3
Deposit insurance	57.9	-3.1	-1.4	-32.0	4.3	-13.8	-12.8	-13.1	-11.4
Transportation [1]	29.5	46.9	67.9	92.0	91.7	91.9	89.5	92.6	93.8
Ground transportation	19.0	31.7	42.3	60.8	60.0	60.8	59.1	62.1	62.0
Air transportation	7.2	10.6	18.8	21.4	21.5	20.9	20.0	20.0	21.5
Water transportation	3.2	4.4	6.4	9.4	9.8	9.8	10.0	10.1	9.6
Community and regional development [1]	8.5	10.6	26.3	23.9	32.3	20.7	20.7	20.1	22.1
Community development	3.5	5.5	5.9	9.9	7.8	7.9	7.8	7.1	7.8
Disaster relief and insurance	2.1	2.6	17.7	10.7	23.0	9.7	9.0	10.6	11.3
Education, training, employment, and social services [1]	37.2	53.8	97.6	128.6	72.8	90.6	122.1	109.7	147.0
Elementary, secondary, and vocational education	9.9	20.6	38.3	73.3	42.4	40.8	40.0	39.8	41.0
Higher education	11.1	10.1	31.4	20.9	-0.5	20.1	51.3	38.8	72.0
Research and general education aids	1.6	2.5	3.1	3.6	3.7	3.6	3.5	3.5	3.5
Training and employment	5.6	6.8	6.9	9.9	7.3	7.0	7.1	7.0	7.6
Social services	8.1	12.6	16.3	19.2	18.1	17.3	18.3	18.8	20.9
Health	57.7	154.5	250.5	369.1	358.3	409.4	482.2	511.3	545.7
Health care services	47.6	136.2	219.6	330.7	321.8	374.6	446.4	474.8	504.7
Health research and training	8.6	16.0	28.1	34.2	32.9	30.9	31.4	31.9	36.1
Consumer and occupational health and safety	1.5	2.3	2.9	4.1	3.6	4.0	4.5	4.7	4.8
Medicare	98.1	197.1	298.6	451.6	497.8	511.7	546.2	594.5	599.7
Income security [1]	148.8	253.7	345.8	622.2	536.5	513.6	508.8	514.1	513.9
General retirement and disability insurance (excluding social security)	5.1	5.2	7.0	6.6	7.0	8.8	7.8	3.8	7.3
Federal employee retirement and disability	52.0	77.2	93.4	119.9	131.7	134.6	139.2	144.8	140.8
Unemployment compensation	18.9	23.0	35.4	160.1	70.7	45.7	35.0	35.2	35.9
Housing assistance	15.9	28.9	37.9	58.7	46.7	47.6	47.8	49.1	49.1
Food and nutrition assistance	24.1	32.5	50.8	95.1	109.7	102.9	104.8	102.3	102.8
Social security	248.6	409.4	523.3	706.7	813.6	850.5	887.8	916.1	951.9
Veterans' benefits and services [1]	29.0	47.0	70.1	108.4	138.9	149.6	159.7	174.5	175.0
Income security for veterans	15.3	24.9	35.8	49.2	65.9	70.9	76.4	86.8	85.3
Veterans education, training, and rehabilitation	0.2	1.3	2.8	8.1	12.9	13.5	13.4	14.4	14.6
Hospital and medical care for veterans	12.1	19.5	28.8	45.7	52.5	56.2	61.9	65.2	68.0
Veterans housing	0.5	0.4	0.9	0.5	1.3	2.1	0.7	0.8	-0.7
Administration of justice	10.2	28.5	40.0	54.4	52.6	50.5	51.9	55.8	67.8
Federal law enforcement activities	4.8	12.1	19.9	28.7	27.3	26.1	26.9	28.9	34.0
Federal litigative and judicial activities	3.6	7.8	10.7	14.5	14.8	14.2	14.7	14.9	18.4
Federal correctional activities	1.3	3.7	4.8	6.3	6.8	6.8	7.0	7.0	7.0
Criminal justice assistance	0.5	4.9	4.6	4.8	3.8	3.4	3.2	5.0	8.4
General government	10.5	13.0	17.0	23.0	27.7	26.9	21.0	22.7	26.3
Net interest [1]	184.3	222.9	184.0	196.2	220.9	229.0	223.2	240.0	276.2
Interest on Treasury debt securities (gross)	264.7	361.9	352.3	413.9	415.7	429.5	402.4	430.0	474.5
Interest received by on-budget trust funds	-46.3	-69.3	-69.2	-67.3	-51.0	-57.8	-45.8	-55.5	-63.4
Interest received by off-budget trust funds	-16.0	-59.8	-91.8	-118.5	-105.7	-100.3	-96.0	-90.6	-86.5
Allowances	–	–	–	–	–	–	–	–	-3.9
Undistributed offsetting receipts [2]	-36.6	-42.6	-65.2	-82.1	-92.8	-88.0	-115.8	-95.3	-93.4

– Represents or rounds to zero. [1] Includes functions not shown separately. [2] Includes some off-budget amounts; most of the off-budget amounts are direct payments for individuals (social security benefits).

Source: U.S. Office of Management and Budget, *Budget of the U.S. Government, Fiscal Year 2018: Historical Tables*, May 2017. See also <http://www.whitehouse.gov/omb/budget>.

Table 501. Federal Budget Outlays for Payments for Individuals by Category and Major Program: 1990 to 2017

[In billions of dollars (592.4 represents $592,400,000,000). For fiscal years ending September 30]

Category and program	1990	2000	2005	2010	2013	2014	2015	2016	2017, est.
Total, payments for individuals	**592.4**	**1,067.4**	**1,512.6**	**2,307.0**	**2,406.3**	**2,508.8**	**2,654.9**	**2,777.8**	**2,888.0**
Social security and railroad retirement	253.3	410.7	523.5	706.6	814.5	853.2	890.2	919.1	956.7
Social security:									
Old age and survivors insurance	221.9	351.4	434.0	576.6	667.2	702.5	738.0	766.4	801.5
Disability insurance	24.4	54.4	84.2	123.5	140.1	141.9	143.4	143.5	144.4
Railroad retirement (excl. social security)	7.0	4.8	5.4	6.5	7.3	8.8	8.9	9.3	10.8
Federal employees' retirement and insurance	64.2	100.4	127.0	166.8	194.2	202.7	212.0	228.3	222.7
Military retirement	21.6	32.9	39.0	50.7	54.4	55.4	56.8	61.6	57.7
Civil service retirement	31.0	45.1	54.7	69.5	77.2	79.5	81.8	82.9	82.9
Veterans service-connected compensation	10.7	20.8	30.9	43.5	59.4	64.4	69.7	79.9	78.3
Other	0.8	1.7	2.4	3.2	3.2	3.4	3.7	3.9	3.8
Unemployment assistance	17.5	21.1	33.1	158.3	68.3	43.5	32.7	32.9	33.5
Medical care [1]	167.4	368.6	575.4	876.8	935.8	1,006.2	1,111.0	1,197.2	1,240.1
Medicare:									
Hospital insurance	65.9	127.9	181.3	245.6	262.4	262.6	273.5	286.0	287.7
Supplementary medical insurance	41.5	87.2	150.0	264.9	305.5	322.4	348.6	391.5	401.6
State children's health insurance	–	1.2	5.1	7.9	9.5	9.3	9.2	14.4	16.9
Medicaid	41.1	117.9	181.7	272.8	265.4	301.5	349.8	368.3	378.5
Indian health	1.1	2.4	3.1	4.4	4.3	4.5	4.6	4.1	4.4
Hospital and medical care for veterans	12.3	20.1	30.7	48.5	55.1	58.9	63.7	65.8	68.4
Health resources and services	1.4	3.9	5.9	7.1	7.3	7.6	7.7	8.8	8.8
Substance abuse and mental health services	1.2	2.5	3.2	3.3	3.2	3.2	3.1	3.4	3.7
Uniformed Services retiree health care fund	–	–	6.3	8.4	8.2	9.3	10.0	9.8	11.1
Other	2.9	5.4	8.2	14.0	14.2	12.8	12.7	13.3	14.2
Assistance to students	11.2	10.9	32.1	55.5	58.1	70.1	74.7	60.2	96.2
Veterans' education benefits	0.8	1.6	3.3	8.8	13.2	13.7	13.6	14.6	14.8
Student assistance, Department of Education and other	10.4	9.2	28.9	46.8	44.9	56.3	61.1	45.6	81.4
Housing assistance	15.9	28.6	37.5	57.6	45.6	46.6	46.7	48.0	47.8
Food and nutrition assistance	24.0	32.4	50.7	95.0	109.6	102.8	104.6	102.1	102.6
SNAP (including Puerto Rico) [2]	15.9	18.3	32.6	70.5	82.5	76.2	76.1	73.1	71.9
Child nutrition and special milk programs	5.0	9.2	11.9	16.4	19.3	19.5	21.0	22.0	23.8
Supplemental feeding programs (WIC and CSFP [3])	2.1	4.0	5.0	6.5	6.6	6.3	6.3	6.0	5.8
Commodity donations and other	1.0	0.9	1.2	1.6	1.1	0.8	1.1	1.1	1.2
Public assistance and related programs [1]	34.9	88.5	123.4	183.2	172.5	175.2	175.3	180.2	177.5
Supplemental security income program	11.5	29.7	35.4	44.0	50.3	51.5	52.3	56.7	52.2
Family support payments to states and TANF [4]	12.2	18.4	21.3	21.9	21.2	20.4	20.0	19.7	20.8
Low income home energy assistance	1.3	1.5	2.1	4.6	3.5	3.5	3.4	3.3	3.1
Earned income tax credit	4.4	26.1	34.6	54.7	57.5	60.1	60.1	60.6	60.9
Payments to states for daycare assistance	–	3.3	4.9	5.9	5.0	5.1	5.1	5.3	5.7
Veterans' non-service-connected pensions	3.6	3.0	3.7	4.4	5.2	5.3	5.3	5.8	5.6
Payments to states for foster care/adoption assistance	1.6	5.5	6.4	7.0	6.8	6.9	7.3	7.7	8.0
Payment where child credit exceeds tax liability	–	0.8	14.6	22.7	21.6	21.5	20.6	20.2	20.2
Other public assistance	0.3	0.3	0.4	18.1	1.4	1.1	1.2	1.0	1.0
All other payments for individuals	4.0	6.2	9.8	7.2	7.8	8.6	7.7	9.8	11.1
Coal miners and black lung benefits	1.5	1.5	1.4	0.5	0.4	0.4	0.4	0.4	0.5
Veterans' insurance and burial benefits	1.4	1.4	1.4	1.3	1.2	1.2	1.2	0.9	1.1
Aging services programs	–	0.9	1.4	1.5	1.4	1.5	1.7	2.0	2.0
Energy employees compensation fund	–	–	0.6	1.1	1.2	1.1	1.0	1.1	1.0
September 11th victim compensation	–	–	(Z)	–	(Z)	(Z)	0.1	1.7	(Z)
Refugee assistance and other	1.1	2.4	5.0	2.8	3.4	4.4	3.2	3.7	6.5

– Represents zero. Z Less than $50,000,000. [1] Includes other items not shown separately. [2] Supplemental Nutrition Assistance Program, formerly known as food stamps. [3] WIC is Women, Infants, and Children. CSFP is Commodity Supplemental Food Program. [4] TANF is Temporary Assistance for Needy Families.

Source: U.S. Office of Management and Budget, *Budget of the U.S. Government, Fiscal Year 2018: Historical Tables*, May 2017. See also <http://www.whitehouse.gov/omb/budget>.

Table 502. Federal Budget Receipts by Source: 1990 to 2017

[In billions of dollars (1,032.0 represents $1,032,000,000,000). For fiscal years ending September 30. Receipts reflect collections. Covers both federal funds and trust funds; see text, this section. Minus sign (-) indicates decrease]

Source	1990	2000	2005	2010	2013	2014	2015	2016	2017, est.
Total federal receipts	**1,032.0**	**2,025.2**	**2,153.6**	**2,162.7**	**2,775.1**	**3,021.5**	**3,249.9**	**3,268.0**	**3,459.7**
(On-budget)	750.3	1,544.6	1,576.1	1,531.0	2,101.8	2,285.9	2,479.5	2,457.8	2,602.3
(Off-budget)	281.7	480.6	577.5	631.7	673.3	735.6	770.4	810.2	857.4
Individual income taxes	466.9	1,004.5	927.2	898.5	1,316.4	1,394.6	1,540.8	1,546.1	1,659.9
Corporation income taxes	93.5	207.3	278.3	191.4	273.5	320.7	343.8	299.6	323.6
Social insurance and retirement receipts	380.0	652.9	794.1	864.8	947.8	1,023.5	1,065.3	1,115.1	1,174.7
Excise taxes	35.3	68.9	73.1	66.9	84.0	93.4	98.3	95.0	87.0
Other	56.2	91.7	80.9	141.0	153.4	189.4	201.8	212.2	214.5
Social insurance and retirement receipts	**380.0**	**652.9**	**794.1**	**864.8**	**947.8**	**1,023.5**	**1,065.3**	**1,115.1**	**1,174.7**
Employment and general retirement, total	353.9	620.5	747.7	815.9	887.4	965.0	1,010.4	1,062.3	1,121.2
Old–age and survivors insurance (off–budget)	255.0	411.7	493.6	540.0	575.6	628.8	658.5	665.7	693.5
Disability insurance (off–budget)	26.6	68.9	83.8	91.7	97.7	106.8	111.8	144.5	163.9
Hospital insurance	68.6	135.5	166.1	180.1	209.3	224.1	234.2	246.8	258.2
Railroad retirement/pension fund	2.3	2.7	2.3	2.3	2.8	3.0	3.3	3.1	3.2
Unemployment insurance funds	21.6	27.6	42.0	44.8	56.8	55.0	51.2	48.9	49.3
Other retirement	4.5	4.8	4.5	4.1	3.6	3.5	3.7	3.9	4.2
Federal employees retirement—employee share	4.4	4.7	4.4	4.1	3.5	3.4	3.6	3.9	4.2
Excise taxes, total	**35.3**	**68.9**	**73.1**	**66.9**	**84.0**	**93.4**	**98.3**	**95.0**	**87.0**
Federal funds [1]	15.6	22.7	22.5	18.3	28.3	34.2	37.8	34.0	24.0
Alcohol	5.7	8.1	8.1	9.2	9.3	9.8	9.6	9.8	9.9
Tobacco	4.1	7.2	7.9	17.2	15.1	15.6	14.5	14.1	14.0
Telephone	3.0	5.7	6.0	1.0	0.7	0.6	0.6	0.5	0.6
Ozone–depleting chemicals/products	0.4	0.1	–	–	–	–	–	–	–
Transportation fuels	–	0.8	-0.8	-11.0	-2.7	-3.5	-3.4	-4.8	-3.5
Indoor tanning services	–	–	–	–	0.1	0.1	0.1	0.1	0.1
Trust funds [1]	19.8	46.2	50.5	48.7	55.7	59.1	60.5	61.0	63.0
Transportation	13.9	35.0	37.9	35.0	36.5	39.0	40.8	41.3	41.6
Airport and airway	3.7	9.7	10.3	10.6	12.9	13.5	14.3	14.4	14.9
Black lung disability	0.7	0.5	0.6	0.6	0.5	0.6	0.6	0.4	0.4
Inland waterway	0.1	0.1	0.1	0.1	0.1	0.1	0.1	0.1	0.1
Hazardous substance superfund	0.8	(Z)	–	–	–	–	–	–	–
Oil spill liability	0.1	0.2	–	0.5	0.4	0.4	0.5	0.5	0.6
Aquatic resources	0.2	0.3	0.4	0.6	0.5	0.6	0.6	0.6	0.5
Leaking underground storage tank	0.1	0.2	0.2	0.2	0.2	0.2	0.2	0.2	0.2
Tobacco assessments	–	–	0.9	0.9	0.9	1.1	(Z)	(Z)	
Vaccine injury compensation	0.2	0.1	0.1	0.2	0.2	0.2	0.3	0.3	0.3

– Represents zero. Z Less than $50,000,000. [1] Includes other funds, not shown separately.

Source: U.S. Office of Management and Budget, *Budget of the U.S. Government, Fiscal Year 2018: Historical Tables*, May 2017. See also <http://www.whitehouse.gov/omb/budget>.

Table 503. Federal Trust Fund Income, Outlays, and Balances: 2016 to 2018

[In billions of dollars (14.8 represents $14,800,000,000). For fiscal years ending September 30. Income reflects receipts deposited. Outlays are on a checks-issued basis less refunds collected. Balances reflect funds that have not been spent. See text, this section, for discussion of the budget concept and trust funds]

Description	Income			Outlays			Balances [1]		
	2016	2017, est.	2018, est.	2016	2017, est.	2018, est.	2016	2017, est.	2018, est.
Airport and airway trust fund	14.8	15.3	15.8	-14.0	-14.6	-14.8	14.8	15.4	16.5
Civil service retirement and disability fund	98.2	98.2	99.8	-83.0	-83.0	-85.2	887.2	902.4	916.9
Federal employees' health benefits fund	50.7	53.5	56.6	-50.1	-52.6	-55.9	23.7	24.6	25.2
Foreign military sales trust fund	32.1	37.4	36.0	-28.2	-39.6	-38.7	29.6	27.4	24.7
Highway trust fund	111.8	42.3	42.6	-54.5	-53.4	-54.2	69.2	58.1	46.5
Medicare:									
Hospital insurance (HI) trust fund	295.4	307.2	323.5	-298.9	-300.5	-304.5	192.5	199.2	218.2
Supplemental medical insurance trust fund	393.4	415.1	441.7	-399.7	-410.0	-413.6	62.8	67.9	96.0
Military retirement fund	120.1	131.8	131.4	-61.6	-57.6	-54.4	584.5	658.7	735.7
Railroad retirement trust funds	12.9	12.2	12.2	-12.7	-13.9	-13.4	22.0	20.3	19.2
Social security:									
Disability insurance trust fund	150.4	170.9	178.5	-146.3	-147.2	-151.8	45.7	69.4	96.1
Old-age and survivors trust fund	799.9	828.2	857.6	-769.8	-804.7	-858.6	2,796.6	2,820.1	2,819.2
Unemployment trust funds	50.6	51.4	52.2	-36.6	-37.2	-38.3	45.7	59.9	73.8
Veterans' life insurance trust funds	0.4	0.4	0.3	-1.2	-1.2	-1.1	6.0	5.2	4.5
Other trust funds	37.3	30.1	38.6	-26.6	-28.1	-27.0	99.1	101.1	112.6

[1] Balances available on a cash basis (rather than an authorization basis) at the end of the year. Balances are primarily invested in federal debt securities.

Source: U.S. Office of Management and Budget, *Budget of the U.S. Government, Fiscal Year 2018: Analytical Perspectives*, May 2017. See also <http://www.whitehouse.gov/omb/budget>.

Table 504. Internal Revenue Gross Collections by Type of Tax: 2005 to 2016

[2,269 represents $2,269,000,000,000, except percent. For fiscal years ending September 30. See text, this section, for information on taxes]

Type of tax	Gross collections (bil. dol.)						Percent of total					
	2005	2010	2013	2014	2015	2016	2005	2010	2013	2014	2015	2016
United States, total............	**2,269**	**2,345**	**2,855**	**3,064**	**3,303**	**3,333**	**100.0**	**100.0**	**100.0**	**100.0**	**100.0**	**100.0**
Individual income taxes............	1,108	1,164	1,540	1,614	1,760	1,786	48.8	49.7	53.9	52.7	53.3	53.6
Withheld by employers...........	787	900	1,123	1,170	1,241	1,267	34.7	38.4	39.3	38.2	37.6	38.0
Tax payments [1]...................	321	264	416	444	519	519	14.1	11.3	14.6	14.5	15.7	15.6
Estate and trust income tax.......	(NA)	12	25	29	33	30	(NA)	0.5	0.9	1.0	1.0	0.9
Employment taxes.................	771	824	898	976	1,022	1,074	34.0	35.1	31.4	31.9	31.0	32.2
Old-age and disability insurance........................	760	813	884	962	1,007	1,060	33.5	34.7	31.0	31.4	30.5	31.8
Unemployment insurance........	7	7	8	9	9	8	0.3	0.3	0.3	0.3	0.3	0.3
Railroad retirement..............	5	5	6	6	6	6	0.2	0.2	0.2	0.2	0.2	0.2
Business income taxes [2].........	307	278	312	353	390	346	13.5	11.9	10.9	11.5	11.8	10.4
Estate and gift taxes..............	26	20	20	20	20	22	1.1	0.8	0.7	0.7	0.6	0.7
Excise taxes.....................	57	47	61	71	77	76	2.5	2.0	2.1	2.3	2.3	2.3

NA Not available. [1] Includes estimated income tax collections and payments made with tax filings. Also includes estate and trust income tax for 2005. [2] Includes corporate income tax and tax-exempt organization unrelated business income tax.

Source: U.S. Internal Revenue Service, *IRS Data Book 2016*, March 2017, and earlier editions. See also <http://www.irs.gov/uac/SOI-Tax-Stats-IRS-Data-Book>.

Table 505. Individual Income Tax Returns Filed—Audits Coverage: 1995 to 2016

[114,683 represents 114,683,000, except percent. See the annual *IRS Data Book* (Publication 55B) for a detailed explanation. An IRS audit is a review/examination of an organization's or individual's tax return]

Year	Returns filed [1] (1,000)	Returns examined		Total recommended additional tax [3] ($1,000)	Average recommended additional tax per return (dol.) [3]
		Total [2] (1,000)	Percent coverage		
1995........................	114,683	1,919	1.7	7,756,954	4,041
1996........................	116,060	1,942	1.7	7,600,191	3,915
1997........................	118,363	1,519	1.3	8,363,918	5,505
1998........................	120,342	1,193	1.0	6,095,698	5,110
1999........................	122,547	1,100	0.9	4,458,474	4,052
2000........................	124,887	618	0.5	3,388,905	5,486
2001........................	127,097	732	0.6	3,301,860	4,512
2002........................	129,445	744	0.6	3,636,486	4,889
2003........................	130,341	849	0.7	4,559,902	5,369
2004........................	130,134	997	0.8	6,201,693	6,220
2005........................	130,577	1,199	0.9	13,355,087	11,138
2006........................	132,276	1,284	1.0	13,045,221	10,160
2007........................	134,543	1,385	1.0	15,705,155	11,343
2008........................	137,850	1,392	1.0	12,462,770	8,956
2009 [4].....................	138,950	1,426	1.0	14,940,892	10,478
2010........................	142,823	1,581	1.1	15,066,486	9,527
2011........................	140,837	1,565	1.1	14,652,239	9,364
2012........................	143,400	1,482	1.0	15,310,908	10,331
2013........................	145,819	1,405	1.0	14,049,657	10,000
2014........................	145,236	1,242	0.9	11,885,411	9,566
2015........................	146,861	1,228	0.8	12,308,319	10,022
2016........................	147,967	1,035	0.7	9,864,674	9,532

[1] Returns generally filed in previous calendar year. [2] Includes taxpayer examinations by correspondence. [3] For 1995, amount includes associated penalties. [4] Excludes returns filed by individuals only to receive an economic stimulus payment and who had no other reason to file.

Source: U.S. Internal Revenue Service, *IRS Data Book, 2016*, March 2017, and earlier editions. See also <http://www.irs.gov/uac/SOI-Tax-Stats-IRS-Data-Book>.

Table 506. Federal Individual Income Tax Returns—Adjusted Gross Income, Taxable Income, and Total Income Tax: 2010 to 2014

[142,892 represents 142,892,000. For tax years. Based on a sample of returns; see source and Appendix III]

Year	2010		2013		2014		Percent change in amount, 2013-14
	Number of returns (1,000)	Amount (mil. dol.)	Number of returns (1,000)	Amount (mil. dol.)	Number of returns (1,000)	Amount (mil. dol.)	
Adjusted gross income (less deficit).....	**142,892**	**8,089,142**	**147,351**	**9,093,629**	**148,607**	**9,771,035**	**7.4**
Exemptions [1]................................	287,679	1,049,272	289,929	1,107,723	290,412	1,121,603	1.3
Taxable income................................	107,304	5,502,001	110,503	6,387,828	112,658	6,997,856	9.5
Total income tax...............................	84,476	951,674	94,532	1,235,040	96,544	1,377,797	11.6
Alternative minimum tax....................	4,020	27,461	3,940	27,426	4,278	28,646	4.4

[1] The number of returns represent the number of exemptions.

Source: U.S. Internal Revenue Service, Statistics of Income Bulletin, "Historical Tables," <http://www.irs.gov/uac/SOI-Tax-Stats-SOI-Bulletin-Historical-Tables-and-Appendix>, accessed May 2017.

Table 507. Federal Individual Income Tax Returns—Adjusted Gross Income (AGI) by Selected Source of Income and Income Class: 2014

[In millions of dollars (9,771,035 represents $9,771,035,000,000), except as indicated. For the tax year. Minus sign (-) indicates net loss was greater than net income. Based on sample; see Appendix III]

Item	Total [1]	Adjusted gross income class						
		Under $10,000 [1]	$10,000 to $19,999	$20,000 to $29,999	$30,000 to $39,999	$40,000 to $49,999	$50,000 to $99,999	$100,000 and over
Number of taxable returns (1,000)......	**96,544**	**2,093**	**9,585**	**10,701**	**10,305**	**9,568**	**30,699**	**23,593**
Adjusted gross income (AGI) [2].........	**9,102,640**	**2,157**	**146,824**	**267,363**	**360,118**	**429,685**	**2,207,667**	**5,688,827**
Salaries and wages.......................	6,083,517	14,423	117,215	211,360	288,213	344,906	1,684,541	3,422,859
Percent of AGI...........................	67	669	80	79	80	80	76	60
Interest received........................	139,509	822	863	1,978	2,308	2,504	15,985	115,049
Dividends in AGI........................	412,608	1,284	1,201	2,845	4,026	5,687	41,716	355,848
Business, profession, net profit less loss.......................	251,234	[5] 103	5,541	7,822	8,706	9,180	48,738	171,144
Sales of property, net gain less loss [3].....................	679,685	[5] 4,407	[5] 448	655	921	2,015	25,549	648,605
Pensions and annuities in AGI...........	613,795	172	15,499	28,478	35,843	39,955	217,013	276,835
Rents and royalties, net income less loss [4]..................	69,358	[5] 84	321	973	892	915	3,557	62,617
Number of all returns (1,000)...........	**148,607**	**24,087**	**23,621**	**18,881**	**14,600**	**11,473**	**32,220**	**23,725**
Adjusted gross income [2]...............	**9,771,035**	**-81,593**	**351,605**	**467,812**	**507,486**	**513,960**	**2,303,583**	**5,708,182**
Salaries and wages.......................	6,784,948	114,321	261,996	381,260	418,568	418,380	1,757,200	3,433,224
Interest received........................	156,368	8,543	3,143	3,404	3,288	3,091	18,325	116,573
Dividends in AGI........................	447,150	11,749	5,950	6,337	6,911	7,670	48,555	359,979
Business, profession, net profit less loss.......................	317,259	6,540	36,688	19,616	15,957	13,333	53,073	172,052
Sales of property, net gain less loss [3].....................	696,360	6,804	1,592	2,151	2,581	3,659	28,015	651,559
Pensions and annuities in AGI...........	663,223	11,885	33,658	37,426	39,279	41,938	221,209	277,827
Rents and royalties, net income less loss [4]..................	65,800	-3,775	893	909	860	739	3,413	62,760

[1] Includes a small number of returns with no adjusted gross income. [2] Includes other sources, not shown separately. [3] Includes sales of capital assets and other property. [4] Excludes rental passive losses disallowed in the computation of AGI. [5] Estimate should be used with caution because of the small number of returns on which it is based.

Source: U.S. Internal Revenue Service, *Statistics of Income—Individual Income Tax Returns 2014*, Publication 1304, August 2016. See also <http://www.irs.gov/uac/Tax-Stats-2>.

Table 508. Federal Individual Income Tax Returns—Total and Selected Sources of Adjusted Gross Income: 2013 and 2014

[147,351 represents 147,351,000. For tax years. Based on a sample of returns; see source and Appendix III. Minus sign (-) indicates decrease]

Item	2013		2014		Change in amount, 2013-2014	
	Number of returns (1,000)	Amount (mil. dol.)	Number of returns (1,000)	Amount (mil. dol.)	Net change (mil. dol.)	Percent change
Adjusted gross income (less deficit) [1].....................	**147,351**	**9,093,629**	**148,607**	**9,771,035**	**677,407**	**7.4**
Salaries and wages..............................	122,189	6,475,381	123,140	6,784,948	309,567	4.8
Taxable interest.................................	44,921	100,649	43,334	93,894	-6,754	-6.7
Ordinary dividends..............................	27,688	214,973	27,652	254,702	39,730	18.5
Qualified dividends............................	25,494	158,069	25,702	192,448	34,379	21.7
Business or profession net income (less loss)...................	23,530	302,073	24,073	317,259	15,186	5.0
Net capital gain................................	23,993	489,621	24,268	698,649	209,028	42.7
Capital gain distributions [2].....................	12,845	44,774	13,665	79,059	34,285	76.6
Sales of property other than capital assets, net gain (less loss)......................	2,139	1,029	2,289	8,973	7,943	771.7
Sales of property other than capital assets, net gain.........	982	26,292	1,087	31,473	5,181	19.7
Taxable social security benefits....................	18,507	243,327	19,019	261,156	17,828	7.3
Total rental and royalty net income (less net loss) [3].............	11,544	57,505	11,571	65,800	8,295	14.4
Partnership and S corporation net income (less loss)...........	8,460	531,614	8,679	583,791	52,178	9.8
Estate and trust net income (less loss)................	649	24,423	634	29,792	5,369	22.0
Farm net income (less loss).......................	1,813	-7,798	1,784	-8,276	-478	6.1
Farm net income................................	589	17,343	591	16,296	-1,047	-6.0
Unemployment compensation.....................	9,287	51,923	7,451	33,289	-18,634	-35.9
Taxable pensions and annuities....................	27,756	638,659	28,144	663,223	24,564	3.8
Taxable Individual Retirement Account (IRA) distributions......	13,331	213,602	13,654	235,005	21,403	10.0
Other net income (less loss) [4].....................	6,810	37,172	6,377	39,156	1,983	5.3
Gambling earnings..............................	1,918	29,978	1,871	29,496	-482	-1.6

[1] Includes other sources of income, not shown separately. [2] Includes both Schedule D and Form 1040 or 1040A capital gain distributions. [3] Includes farm rental net income (less loss). [4] Other net income (less loss) represents data reported on Form 1040, line 21, except net operating losses, foreign-earned income exclusions, cancellation of debt, taxable health savings account distributions, and gambling earnings.

Source: U.S. Internal Revenue Service, Statistics of Income, "SOI Tax Stats - Individual Statistical Tables by Size of Adjusted Gross Income," <https://www.irs.gov/uac/soi-tax-stats-individual-statistical-tables-by-size-of-adjusted-gross-income>, accessed September 2016.

Table 509. Federal Individual Income Tax Returns—Net Capital Gains and Capital Gain Distributions From Mutual Funds: 1990 to 2014

[14,288 represents 14,288,000. For tax years. Based on a sample of returns; see source and Appendix III. Minus sign (-) indicates decrease]

Tax year	Net capital gain (less loss)				Capital gain distributions [2]			
	Number of returns (1,000)	Current dollars (mil. dol.)	Constant (1982–1984) dollars [1]		Number of returns (1,000)	Current dollars (mil. dol.)	Constant (1982–1984) dollars [1]	
			Amount (mil. dol.)	Percent change			Amount (mil. dol.)	Percent change
1990	14,288	114,231	87,399	-25.6	5,069	3,905	2,988	-32.4
1991	15,009	102,776	75,460	-13.7	5,796	4,665	3,425	14.6
1992	16,491	118,230	84,269	11.7	5,917	7,426	5,293	54.5
1993	18,409	144,172	99,773	18.4	9,998	11,995	8,301	56.8
1994	18,823	142,288	96,011	-3.8	9,803	11,322	7,640	-8.0
1995	19,963	170,415	111,821	16.5	10,744	14,391	9,443	23.6
1996	22,065	251,817	160,495	43.5	12,778	24,722	15,757	66.9
1997	24,240	356,083	221,859	38.2	14,969	45,132	28,120	78.5
1998	25,690	446,084	273,671	23.4	16,070	46,147	28,311	0.7
1999	27,701	542,758	325,785	19.0	17,012	59,473	35,698	26.1
2000	29,521	630,542	366,168	12.4	17,546	79,079	45,923	28.6
2001	25,956	326,527	184,374	-49.6	12,216	13,609	7,684	-83.3
2002	24,189	238,789	132,734	-28.0	7,567	5,343	2,970	-61.4
2003	22,985	294,354	159,975	20.5	7,265	4,695	2,552	-14.1
2004	25,267	473,662	250,747	56.7	10,733	15,336	8,119	218.2
2005	26,196	668,015	342,046	36.4	13,393	35,581	18,219	124.4
2006	26,668	779,462	386,638	13.0	14,511	59,417	29,473	61.8
2007	27,156	907,656	437,758	13.2	15,714	86,397	41,669	41.4
2008	23,731	469,273	217,959	-50.2	11,544	21,954	10,197	-75.5
2009	20,291	231,548	107,929	-50.5	4,191	2,411	1,124	-89.0
2010	21,315	364,410	167,118	54.8	6,567	6,270	2,875	155.9
2011	22,154	377,037	167,617	0.3	8,859	14,171	6,300	119.1
2012	22,721	622,887	271,299	61.9	10,412	17,829	7,766	23.3
2013	23,993	489,621	210,176	-22.5	12,845	44,774	19,220	147.5
2014	24,268	698,649	295,117	40.4	13,665	79,059	33,396	73.8

[1] Constant dollars were calculated using the U.S. Bureau of Labor Statistics consumer price index for urban consumers (CPI-U, 1982–84 = 100). See Table 749. [2] Capital gain distributions are included in net capital gain (less loss). For 1991–1996, and 1999 and later years, capital gain distributions from mutual funds are the sum of the amounts reported on the Form 1040 and Schedule D. For 1997 and 1998, capital gain distributions were reported entirely on the Schedule D.

Source: U.S. Internal Revenue Service, Statistics of Income, "SOI Tax Stats - Individual Statistical Tables by Size of Adjusted Gross Income," <https://www.irs.gov/uac/soi-tax-stats-individual-statistical-tables-by-size-of-adjusted-gross-income>, accessed September 2016.

Table 510. Alternative Minimum Tax: 1987 to 2014

[140 represents 140,000. For tax years. Based on a sample of returns; see source and Appendix III]

Tax year	Highest statutory alternative minimum tax rate (percent)	Alternative minimum tax		Tax year	Highest statutory alternative minimum tax rate (percent)	Alternative minimum tax	
		Number of returns (1,000)	Amount (mil. dol.)			Number of returns (1,000)	Amount (mil. dol.)
1987	21	140	1,675	2001	[1] 28	1,120	6,757
1988	21	114	1,028	2002	[1] 28	1,911	6,854
1989	21	117	831	2003	[1] 28	2,358	9,470
1990	21	132	830	2004	[1] 28	3,096	13,029
1991	24	244	1,213	2005	[1] 28	4,005	17,421
1992	24	287	1,357	2006	[1] 28	3,967	21,565
1993	28	335	2,053	2007	[1] 28	4,109	24,110
1994	28	369	2,212	2008	[1] 28	3,935	25,649
1995	28	414	2,291	2009	[1] 28	3,828	22,580
1996	28	478	2,813	2010	[1] 28	4,020	27,461
1997	[1] 28	618	4,005	2011	[1] 28	4,248	30,479
1998	[1] 28	853	5,015	2012	[1] 28	4,225	32,770
1999	[1] 28	1,018	6,478	2013	[1] 28	3,940	27,426
2000	[1] 28	1,304	9,601	2014	[1] 28	4,278	28,646

[1] Top rate on most long-term capital gains was 20 percent; beginning 2003, the rate was 15 percent.

Source: U.S. Internal Revenue Service, Statistics of Income, "SOI Tax Stats - Individual Statistical Tables by Size of Adjusted Gross Income," <https://www.irs.gov/uac/soi-tax-stats-individual-statistical-tables-by-size-of-adjusted-gross-income>, accessed September 2016.

Table 511. Federal Individual Income Tax Returns—Sources of Net Losses Included in Adjusted Gross Income: 2013 and 2014

[25,930 represents 25,930,000. For tax years. Based on a sample of returns; see source and Appendix III]

Item	2013 Number of returns (1,000)	2013 Amount (mil. dol.)	2014 Number of returns (1,000)	2014 Amount (mil. dol.)	Percent change in amount, 2013–2014
Total net losses	**25,930**	**488,765**	**24,725**	**491,577**	**0.6**
Business or profession net loss	5,561	55,291	5,776	57,400	3.8
Net capital loss [1]	9,009	20,909	7,595	17,620	-15.7
Net loss, sales of property other than capital assets	1,156	25,262	1,202	22,500	-10.9
Total rental and royalty net loss [2]	4,752	46,536	4,660	46,614	0.2
Partnership and S corporation net loss	2,689	116,349	2,743	117,322	0.8
Estate and trust net loss	59	4,286	54	3,012	-29.7
Farm net loss	1,224	25,141	1,193	24,572	-2.3
Net operating loss [3]	1,212	189,041	1,201	196,187	3.8
Other net loss [4]	269	5,949	301	6,350	6.8

[1] As reported on Form 1040, Schedule D. Includes only the portion of capital losses allowable in the calculation of adjusted gross income. Only $3,000 of net capital loss per return ($1,500 for married filing separately) are allowed to be included in negative total income. Any excess is carried forward to future years. [2] Includes farm rental net loss. [3] Net operating loss is a carryover of the loss from a business when taxable income from a prior year was less than zero. [4] Other net loss represents losses reported on Form 1040, line 21, except net operating loss and the foreign-earned income exclusion.

Source: U.S. Internal Revenue Service, Statistics of Income, "SOI Tax Stats - Individual Statistical Tables by Size of Adjusted Gross Income," <https://www.irs.gov/uac/soi-tax-stats-individual-statistical-tables-by-size-of-adjusted-gross-income>, accessed September 2016.

Table 512. Federal Individual Income Tax Returns—Number, Income Tax, and Average Tax by Size of Adjusted Gross Income: 2013 and 2014

[147,351 represents 147,351,000. Based on sample of returns; see Appendix III. Minus sign (-) indicates net loss was greater than net income]

Size of adjusted gross income	Number of returns (1,000) 2013	Number of returns (1,000) 2014	Adjusted gross income (AGI) (bil. dol.) 2013	Adjusted gross income (AGI) (bil. dol.) 2014	Income tax total [1] (bil. dol.) 2013	Income tax total [1] (bil. dol.) 2014	Taxes as percent of AGI (for taxable returns only) 2013	Taxes as percent of AGI (for taxable returns only) 2014	Average tax (for taxable returns only) (dol.) 2013	Average tax (for taxable returns only) (dol.) 2014
Total	**147,351**	**148,607**	**9,094**	**9,771**	**1,235**	**1,378**	**14.7**	**15.1**	**13,065**	**14,271**
No AGI [2]	2,113	2,034	-199	-198	–	–	(X)	(X)	28,477	27,132
$1 to $999	1,827	1,834	1	1	–	–	–	–	–	–
$1,000 to $2,999	4,270	4,126	9	8	–	–	4.7	3.4	99	73
$3,000 to $4,999	4,511	4,302	18	17	–	–	4.6	5.7	184	225
$5,000 to $6,999	4,503	4,463	27	27	–	–	1.3	1.4	85	93
$7,000 to $8,999	4,636	4,550	37	36	–	–	2.7	2.4	212	191
$9,000 to $10,999	5,505	5,254	55	52	–	–	2.8	2.7	284	279
$11,000 to $12,999	4,755	4,713	57	57	–	–	2.1	2.2	250	264
$13,000 to $14,999	5,134	5,101	72	71	1	1	3.0	2.7	414	380
$15,000 to $16,999	4,848	4,651	78	74	1	1	3.6	3.6	578	574
$17,000 to $18,999	4,599	4,557	83	82	2	1	4.1	4.1	733	735
$19,000 to $21,999	6,396	6,198	131	127	3	3	4.7	4.8	964	979
$22,000 to $24,999	5,903	5,987	139	141	4	4	5.3	5.3	1,241	1,238
$25,000 to $29,999	8,810	8,819	242	242	9	9	6.1	6.0	1,678	1,659
$30,000 to $39,999	14,474	14,600	504	507	24	25	6.7	6.8	2,360	2,383
$40,000 to $49,999	11,279	11,473	505	514	31	32	7.4	7.4	3,316	3,330
$50,000 to $74,999	19,229	19,395	1,184	1,192	96	96	8.6	8.6	5,309	5,290
$75,000 to $99,999	12,574	12,826	1,089	1,112	103	106	9.6	9.7	8,331	8,390
$100,000 to $199,999	16,425	17,501	2,209	2,362	279	297	12.7	12.7	17,067	17,095
$200,000 to $499,999	4,488	4,979	1,277	1,420	251	276	19.7	19.5	55,978	55,641
$500,000 to $999,999	724	835	487	563	126	145	25.9	25.8	174,001	173,901
$1,000,000 to $1,499,999	156	180	188	217	53	61	28.3	28.3	340,539	340,500
$1,500,000 to $1,999,999	64	77	110	132	32	38	29.2	29.0	501,907	498,242
$2,000,000 to $4,999,999	91	109	270	327	80	96	29.5	29.5	875,431	878,995
$5,000,000 to $9,999,999	21	27	146	182	43	53	29.3	29.1	1,996,766	1,993,206
$10,000,000 or more	13	17	375	506	98	132	26.2	26.1	7,653,970	7,890,396

– Represents or rounds to zero. X Not applicable. [1] Consists of income tax after credits (including alternative minimum tax). [2] In addition to low-income taxpayers, this size class (and others) includes taxpayers with "tax preferences," not reflected in adjusted gross income or taxable income, which are subject to the "alternative minimum tax" (included in total income tax).

Source: U.S. Internal Revenue Service, Statistics of Income Bulletin, "Historical Tables," <http://www.irs.gov/uac/Tax-Stats-2>, accessed May 2017.

Table 513. Federal Individual Income Tax Returns—Selected Itemized Deductions and the Standard Deduction: 2013 and 2014

[44,330 represents 44,330,000. For tax years. Based on a sample of returns; see source and Appendix III. Minus sign (-) indicates decrease]

Item	2013		2014		Percent change, 2013–2014	
	Number of returns [1] (1,000)	Amount (mil. dol.)	Number of returns [1] (1,000)	Amount (mil. dol.)	Number of returns [1] (1,000)	Amount (percent)
Total itemized deductions........................	**44,330**	**1,188,595**	**43,965**	**1,206,705**	**-0.8**	**1.5**
Medical and dental expenses after Adjusted Gross Income (AGI) limitation.....................	8,998	84,507	8,606	83,812	-4.3	-0.8
Taxes paid [2]......................................	43,977	506,191	43,613	520,449	-0.8	2.8
State and local income taxes.....................	32,590	304,274	32,456	311,222	-0.4	2.3
State and local general sales taxes..............	10,077	16,597	9,804	17,081	-2.7	2.9
Interest paid [3]......................................	33,898	317,317	33,332	307,962	-1.7	-2.9
Home mortgage interest..........................	33,279	296,186	32,729	286,749	-1.7	-3.2
Charitable contributions...........................	36,431	194,664	36,221	210,599	-0.6	8.2
Other than cash contributions....................	22,176	51,591	22,163	65,330	-0.1	26.6
Casualty and theft losses..........................	97	2,463	90	2,204	-7.1	-10.5
Total limited miscellaneous deductions after 2% AGI limitation...........................	12,302	98,383	12,332	104,902	0.2	6.6
Total unlimited miscellaneous deductions.....................	1,205	21,498	1,172	21,476	-2.8	-0.1
Itemized deductions in excess of limitation...................	2,517	36,428	2,794	44,699	11.0	22.7
Basic standard deduction.......................	**100,899**	**823,063**	**102,595**	**849,368**	**1.7**	**3.2**
Additional standard deduction..................	**14,287**	**25,583**	**14,810**	**26,869**	**3.7**	**5.0**

[1] Returns with no adjusted gross income are excluded from the deduction counts. For this reason, the sum of the number of returns with total itemized deductions and the number of returns with total standard deduction is less than the total number of returns for all filers. [2] Includes real estate taxes, personal property taxes, and other taxes, not shown separately. [3] Includes investment interest, deductible mortgage "points," and qualified mortgage interest premiums, not shown separately.

Source: U.S. Internal Revenue Service, Statistics of Income, "SOI Tax Stats - Individual Statistical Tables by Size of Adjusted Gross Income," <https://www.irs.gov/uac/soi-tax-stats-individual-statistical-tables-by-size-of-adjusted-gross-income>, accessed September 2016.

Table 514. Federal Individual Income Tax Returns—Statutory Adjustments: 2013 and 2014

[37,666 represents 37,666,000. For tax years. Based on a sample of returns; see source and Appendix III. Minus sign (-) indicates decrease]

Item	2013		2014		Percent change in amount, 2013-2014
	Number of returns (1,000)	Amount (mil. dol.)	Number of returns (1,000)	Amount (mil. dol.)	
Total statutory adjustments...........................	**37,666**	**139,882**	**38,387**	**145,184**	**3.8**
Payments to an Individual Retirement Account (IRA).................	2,713	12,973	2,708	13,229	2.0
Educator expenses deduction............................	3,838	964	3,768	959	-0.5
Certain business expenses of reservists, performing artists, etc.....	157	587	152	537	-8.5
Moving expenses adjustment...........................	1,244	3,561	1,128	3,445	-3.3
Student loan interest deduction.........................	11,460	11,618	12,083	12,813	10.3
Tuition and fees deduction.............................	1,893	4,341	1,747	3,872	-10.8
Health savings account deduction.......................	1,195	3,716	1,361	4,106	10.5
Self-employment tax deduction.........................	18,875	27,912	19,351	29,287	4.9
Self-employment health insurance deduction..........................	3,996	27,139	4,185	28,113	3.6
Payments to a self-employed retirement (Keogh) plan.................	955	22,408	990	23,215	3.6
Early withdrawal of savings penalty.......................	691	221	612	140	-36.7
Alimony paid..	652	11,761	608	11,808	0.4
Domestic production activities deduction............................	717	11,229	699	11,976	6.7
Other adjustments [1]................................	150	1,452	135	1,684	16.0

[1] Includes foreign housing adjustment, medical savings accounts deduction, and other adjustments.

Source: U.S. Internal Revenue Service, Statistics of Income, "SOI Tax Stats - Individual Statistical Tables by Size of Adjusted Gross Income," <https://www.irs.gov/uac/soi-tax-stats-individual-statistical-tables-by-size-of-adjusted-gross-income>, accessed September 2016.

Table 515. Federal Individual Income Tax Returns—Itemized Deductions and Statutory Adjustments by Size of Adjusted Gross Income: 2014

[43,965 represents 43,965,000. Based on a sample of returns; see Appendix III]

Item	Unit	Total [1]	Under $10,000 [1]	$10,000 to $19,999	$20,000 to $29,999	$30,000 to $39,999	$40,000 to $49,999	$50,000 to $99,999	$100,000 and over
Returns with itemized deductions:									
Number of returns [2]	1,000	43,965	721	1,445	2,092	2,637	3,071	14,760	19,238
Amount [2,3]	Mil. dol.	1,206,705	11,645	22,691	32,221	41,001	48,792	283,211	767,144
Medical and dental expenses: [4]									
Returns	1,000	8,606	509	909	1,013	962	842	3,024	1,349
Amount	Mil. dol.	83,812	4,938	8,016	8,036	7,558	7,279	29,783	18,202
Taxes paid:									
Returns	1,000	43,613	675	1,392	2,035	2,591	3,027	14,683	19,210
Amount	Mil. dol.	520,449	2,761	4,796	6,793	9,585	12,993	92,942	390,578
State and local taxes: [5]									
Returns	1,000	42,260	565	1,268	1,896	2,468	2,898	14,277	18,890
Amount	Mil. dol.	328,304	524	1,071	1,996	3,644	5,351	45,917	269,799
Real estate taxes:									
Returns	1,000	37,321	516	988	1,383	1,888	2,369	12,528	17,648
Amount	Mil. dol.	181,036	2,144	3,537	4,422	5,460	7,032	43,771	114,671
Interest paid:									
Returns	1,000	33,332	390	768	1,136	1,677	2,135	11,376	15,849
Amount	Mil. dol.	307,962	2,795	5,338	7,522	11,138	13,990	86,786	180,393
Home mortgage interest:									
Returns	1,000	32,729	376	748	1,113	1,653	2,108	11,258	15,472
Amount	Mil. dol.	286,749	2,717	5,095	7,165	10,533	13,185	82,139	165,915
Charitable contributions:									
Returns	1,000	36,221	406	943	1,501	1,917	2,294	11,969	17,191
Amount	Mil. dol.	210,599	476	1,787	3,661	4,727	6,218	37,843	155,888
Unreimbursed employee business expenses:									
Returns	1,000	14,532	79	306	722	989	1,162	5,474	5,800
Amount	Mil. dol.	90,653	392	1,974	5,244	6,963	7,543	33,092	35,445
Returns with statutory adjustments:									
Number of returns [1]	1,000	38,387	4,339	5,176	3,642	3,363	2,998	9,826	9,044
Amount of adjustments [3]	Mil. dol.	145,184	6,204	6,577	6,329	6,902	6,712	28,443	84,016
Payments to IRAs: [6]									
Returns	1,000	2,708	65	136	207	284	235	960	820
Amount	Mil. dol.	13,229	257	391	700	1,096	929	4,692	5,164
Deduction for self-employment tax:									
Returns	1,000	19,351	3,353	3,832	1,797	1,334	1,088	3,642	4,305
Amount	Mil. dol.	29,287	1,589	3,114	1,946	1,611	1,379	5,471	14,178
Self-employment health insurance:									
Returns	1,000	4,185	356	312	293	298	266	973	1,687
Amount	Mil. dol.	28,113	1,416	1,112	1,051	1,361	1,224	5,678	16,271
Payments to Keogh plans:									
Returns	1,000	990	[7] 8	[7] 13	15	20	23	157	755
Amount	Mil. dol.	23,215	[7] 120	[7] 43	78	198	258	1,752	20,764

[1] For returns with statutory adjustments, includes a small number of taxable returns with no adjusted gross income. [2] After limitations. [3] Includes other deductions and adjustments, not shown separately. [4] Before limitation. [5] State and local taxes include income taxes and sales taxes. [6] Individual Retirement Accounts. [7] Includes estimates that should be used with caution due to the small number of sample returns on which they are based.

Source: U.S. Internal Revenue Service, Statistics of Income, "SOI Tax Stats - Individual Statistical Tables by Size of Adjusted Gross Income," <https://www.irs.gov/uac/soi-tax-stats-individual-statistical-tables-by-size-of-adjusted-gross-income>, accessed September 2016.

Table 516. Federal Individual Income Tax Returns—Selected Tax Credits: 2013 and 2014

[48,104 represents 48,104,000. For tax years. Based on a sample of returns; see source and Appendix III]

Item	2013 Number of returns (1,000)	2013 Amount (mil. dol.)	2014 Number of returns (1,000)	2014 Amount (mil. dol.)	Percent change, 2013-2014 Number of returns (1,000)	Percent change, 2013-2014 Amount (mil. dol.)
Total tax credits [1]	**48,104**	**74,614**	**48,773**	**76,243**	**1.4**	**2.2**
Child care credit	6,316	3,459	6,341	3,505	0.4	1.3
Earned income credit [2]	4,241	1,294	4,465	1,387	5.3	7.2
Foreign tax credit	7,488	20,238	7,958	21,648	6.3	7.0
General business credit	462	3,065	348	3,137	-24.6	2.4
Minimum tax credit	322	1,005	316	964	-1.9	-4.0
Child tax credit	22,563	27,233	22,395	27,202	-0.7	-0.1
Education credit [3]	10,197	10,646	9,910	10,445	-2.8	-1.9
Retirement savings contribution credit	7,412	1,317	7,918	1,381	6.8	4.8
Residential energy credit	3,036	1,614	2,664	1,638	-12.3	1.5

[1] Includes credits not shown separately. [2] Represents portion of credit used to offset income tax before credits. [3] Excludes refundable portion.

Source: U.S. Internal Revenue Service, Statistics of Income, "SOI Tax Stats - Individual Statistical Tables by Size of Adjusted Gross Income," <https://www.irs.gov/uac/soi-tax-stats-individual-statistical-tables-by-size-of-adjusted-gross-income>, accessed September 2016.

Table 517. Federal Individual Income Tax Returns by State: 2015

[In units as indicated (149,727 represents 149,727,000). For tax year. Data may not agree with data in other tables due to differing survey methodology used to derive state data]

State	Total number of returns (1,000)	Adjusted gross income (mil. dol.)			Itemized deductions (mil. dol.)				Income tax (mil. dol.)
		Total [1]	Salaries and wages	Net capital gain [2]	Total [1]	State and local income tax	Real estate taxes	Home mortgage interest paid	
United States......	**149,727**	**10,149,347**	**7,070,643**	**694,509**	**1,258,541**	**334,386**	**187,386**	**277,835**	**1,444,099**
Alabama.............	2,054	111,843	80,344	4,338	12,032	2,228	618	2,773	13,224
Alaska...............	362	25,061	17,647	827	1,690	25	319	638	3,559
Arizona..............	2,905	171,481	120,496	9,288	20,167	3,460	1,946	5,612	21,994
Arkansas............	1,229	66,570	46,044	2,562	7,306	1,886	437	1,266	7,860
California............	17,760	1,381,947	950,335	118,550	225,225	79,922	28,313	52,563	209,860
Colorado............	2,617	188,899	130,372	14,627	21,764	5,243	1,992	6,629	26,907
Connecticut..........	1,761	167,477	111,715	14,696	24,558	8,752	5,029	4,612	28,920
Delaware............	453	28,796	20,033	1,172	3,411	960	339	1,011	3,686
District of Columbia..	345	32,135	22,125	3,206	4,784	1,831	394	983	5,558
Florida...............	9,627	613,537	377,516	64,977	60,731	3,557	9,098	13,497	93,793
Georgia..............	4,443	266,463	195,305	12,847	37,828	8,889	3,680	8,143	34,547
Hawaii...............	689	41,845	29,217	2,146	5,304	1,564	355	1,811	4,998
Idaho................	722	39,165	27,219	2,356	4,867	1,244	470	1,190	4,503
Illinois...............	6,162	441,642	307,575	31,743	50,820	11,615	11,617	11,048	65,537
Indiana..............	3,105	173,427	126,996	6,286	15,680	4,424	1,463	3,483	21,076
Iowa.................	1,454	88,048	62,286	3,620	9,658	2,736	1,395	1,774	10,557
Kansas..............	1,339	83,669	58,433	4,500	8,315	1,806	1,100	1,625	10,905
Kentucky............	1,910	102,643	74,375	4,360	11,111	3,632	1,050	2,347	11,905
Louisiana............	1,994	112,188	81,797	4,709	11,092	2,101	720	2,319	14,409
Maine................	646	35,559	24,948	1,620	4,112	1,219	726	939	4,054
Maryland............	2,964	222,249	161,221	9,643	38,740	12,498	4,750	9,408	30,533
Massachusetts.......	3,397	298,525	204,469	25,991	37,507	12,003	6,974	8,627	48,926
Michigan.............	4,718	277,631	194,038	11,120	28,427	6,914	4,593	6,247	36,005
Minnesota...........	2,725	193,029	137,712	10,617	24,789	8,751	3,131	5,690	26,313
Mississippi...........	1,245	59,015	43,630	1,710	6,642	1,129	448	1,200	6,302
Missouri.............	2,788	162,877	114,572	7,827	17,536	4,726	1,986	3,654	20,735
Montana.............	499	27,848	17,857	1,866	3,301	911	359	776	3,343
Nebraska............	899	55,307	39,140	3,122	6,065	1,684	898	1,083	6,843
Nevada..............	1,351	82,484	55,084	7,157	9,233	490	815	2,320	11,747
New Hampshire......	693	49,676	35,925	2,831	5,057	549	1,500	1,406	7,014
New Jersey..........	4,386	366,858	265,682	18,317	56,472	16,772	14,880	11,312	58,070
New Mexico.........	917	46,682	32,356	1,895	4,715	927	473	1,241	5,357
New York...........	9,615	782,601	516,839	81,429	122,176	51,700	20,906	17,163	130,110
North Carolina.......	4,457	262,137	188,279	13,321	32,027	8,464	3,406	7,526	32,927
North Dakota........	369	25,516	17,226	1,333	1,651	261	182	358	3,629
Ohio.................	5,592	323,081	230,861	12,690	32,350	9,471	5,439	6,758	40,638
Oklahoma...........	1,642	96,748	67,200	5,501	10,555	2,227	860	1,821	12,127
Oregon..............	1,874	118,011	79,901	7,172	17,891	5,949	2,472	4,276	14,696
Pennsylvania.........	6,201	405,142	284,404	23,347	43,066	11,323	8,228	9,658	55,856
Rhode Island.........	528	33,254	23,999	1,524	4,253	1,159	863	1,033	4,394
South Carolina.......	2,170	119,054	83,009	5,441	14,278	3,650	1,141	3,391	14,063
South Dakota........	415	25,539	16,086	1,817	1,779	66	240	360	3,416
Tennessee...........	2,970	168,595	122,109	8,702	13,832	595	1,428	3,500	22,096
Texas................	12,152	813,802	587,955	54,942	74,746	1,425	14,824	15,722	120,495
Utah.................	1,264	79,254	57,846	4,246	11,697	2,605	976	2,921	9,388
Vermont.............	326	19,008	13,014	1,269	2,189	592	496	474	2,253
Virginia..............	3,912	289,310	208,641	14,089	39,746	10,472	5,156	11,464	40,491
Washington..........	3,433	261,164	180,583	20,863	26,789	765	4,458	8,610	38,148
West Virginia.........	781	39,662	28,516	1,183	2,989	988	201	669	4,363
Wisconsin............	2,841	174,433	123,864	8,386	20,319	6,221	3,784	4,137	22,155
Wyoming.............	279	20,838	12,710	2,604	1,813	121	145	411	3,119
Other [3].............	751	77,622	61,139	14,129	5,457	1,885	312	358	10,694

[1] Includes other items, not shown separately. [2] Less loss. [3] Includes returns filed from Army Post Office and Fleet Post Office addresses by members of the armed forces stationed overseas; returns filed by other U.S. citizens abroad; and returns filed by residents of Puerto Rico with income from sources outside of Puerto Rico or with income earned as U.S. government employees.

Source: U.S. Internal Revenue Service, Statistics of Income Bulletin, "Historical Data Tables," <https://www.irs.gov/statistics/soi-tax-stats-historical-data-tables>, accessed September 2017.

Table 518. Federal Civilian Employment and Annual Payroll by Branch: 1970 to 2014

[2,997 represents 2,997,000. For fiscal year ending in year shown. See text, Section 8. Includes employees in U.S. territories and foreign countries. Data represent employees in active-duty status, including intermittent employees. Annual employment figures are averages of monthly figures. Excludes Central Intelligence Agency; National Security Agency; as of November 1984, Defense Intelligence Agency; and, as of October 1996, National Geospatial-Intelligence Agency]

Year	Employment						Payroll (mil. dol.)				
	Total (1,000)	Percent of U.S. employed [1]	Executive (1,000)		Legis- lative (1,000)	Judicial (1,000)	Total	Executive		Legis- lative	Judicial
			Total	Defense				Total	Defense		
1970	[2] 2,997	3.81	2,961	1,263	29	7	27,322	26,894	11,264	338	89
1975	2,877	3.35	2,830	1,044	37	10	39,126	38,423	13,418	549	154
1980	[2] 2,987	3.01	2,933	971	40	14	58,012	56,841	18,795	883	288
1985	3,001	2.80	2,944	1,080	39	18	80,599	78,992	28,330	1,098	509
1990	[2] 3,233	2.72	3,173	1,060	38	23	99,138	97,022	31,990	1,329	787
1995	2,943	2.36	2,880	852	34	28	118,304	115,328	31,753	1,598	1,379
2000	[2] 2,879	2.10	2,816	681	31	32	130,832	127,472	29,607	1,619	1,741
2005	2,701	1.91	2,636	671	31	34	152,222	148,275	29,331	2,048	1,900
2006	2,700	1.87	2,637	676	29	34	160,570	156,543	29,580	2,109	1,918
2007	2,699	1.85	2,636	673	30	33	161,394	157,010	29,025	2,119	2,265
2008	2,758	1.90	2,694	694	30	34	167,166	162,675	29,749	2,162	2,328
2009	2,838	2.03	2,774	737	31	34	174,804	170,349	30,995	2,203	2,252
2010	2,841	2.04	2,777	773	31	34	152,321	147,554	32,377	2,515	2,251
2011	2,820	2.02	2,756	774	30	34	166,508	161,897	33,075	2,359	2,255
2012	2,761	1.94	2,697	730	30	34	182,030	177,332	32,670	2,442	2,255
2013	2,731	1.90	2,668	729	29	34	165,697	161,004	32,810	2,438	2,256
2014	2,726	1.86	2,663	723	29	34	154,777	150,172	28,639	2,350	2,256

[1] Civilian employment only. See Table 609, Section 12. [2] Includes temporary census workers.

Source: U.S. Office of Personnel Management, "Federal Civilian Workforce Statistics—Employment and Trends," <http://www.opm.gov/policy-data-oversight/data-analysis-documentation/federal-employment-reports/#url=Employment-Trends>; and unpublished data.

Table 519. Full-Time Federal Civilian Employment—Employees and Average Pay by Pay System: 2010 to 2016

[1,950 represents 1,950,000. As of September 30. Data are shown for all full-time nonseasonal employees. Includes employees in U.S., U.S. territories, foreign countries, and unspecified locations. Excludes postal employees and other selected agencies; see <http://www.fedscope.opm.gov/datadefn/aboutehri_sdm.asp> for details. See text, this section, for explanation of general schedule and wage system]

Pay system	Employees (1,000)				Average annual pay (dol.)			
	2010	2014	2015	2016	2010	2014	2015	2016
Total, excluding postal	**1,950**	**1,912**	**1,940**	**1,962**	**75,704**	**79,853**	**80,903**	**82,252**
General schedule and equivalently graded	1,410	1,418	1,430	1,428	73,656	78,061	78,873	79,826
Prevailing rate pay plans (blue collar)	195	183	185	185	52,051	53,225	53,573	54,411
Other white collar pay plans	344	311	325	349	97,459	103,679	105,479	106,985

Source: U.S. Office of Personnel Management, "FedScope," <http://www.fedscope.opm.gov/>, accessed March 2017.

Table 520. Federal Government Civilian Employment by State: 2010 to 2016

[In thousands (2,061.3 represents 2,061,300). As of September 30. For agencies excluded from total, see <http://www.fedscope.opm.gov/datadefn/aboutehri_sdm.asp>]

State	2010	2015	2016	State	2010	2015	2016	State	2010	2015	2016
U.S. [1]	**2,061.3**	**2,029.2**	**2,053.2**	IA	9.2	8.6	8.7	NC	43.7	43.1	43.6
				KS	17.8	16.0	16.0	ND	6.7	5.5	5.6
				KY	26.5	22.5	22.7	OH	53.0	48.3	49.4
AL	42.3	38.0	38.4	LA	21.1	18.0	18.1	OK	39.5	36.9	38.1
AK	14.1	11.6	11.6	ME	11.1	10.3	10.6	OR	22.5	20.2	20.5
AZ	42.4	32.0	32.3	MD	128.3	129.0	130.2	PA	69.8	59.2	59.8
AR	14.7	13.2	13.0	MA	29.2	25.2	24.9	RI	7.1	7.2	7.3
CA	172.5	141.7	143.3	MI	30.0	25.7	25.7	SC	21.7	20.6	20.7
CO	40.7	37.2	37.8	MN	18.6	16.2	16.4	SD	8.8	8.2	8.5
CT	8.7	8.0	8.0	MS	19.4	18.0	17.9	TN	28.8	26.2	26.1
DE	3.4	3.1	3.1	MO	38.4	33.8	34.3	TX	140.3	111.7	113.0
DC	167.9	169.4	172.6	MT	12.0	10.4	10.5	UT	31.1	27.6	28.7
FL	88.9	76.9	78.6	NE	10.7	9.6	9.8	VT	4.5	3.3	3.4
GA	80.2	70.5	71.7	NV	11.5	11.0	11.1	VA	145.4	134.7	136.3
HI	25.4	21.9	22.3	NH	4.4	4.4	4.4	WA	57.9	54.3	54.9
ID	10.5	9.7	9.6	NJ	30.1	20.7	20.6	WV	16.3	15.1	15.2
IL	51.1	41.5	41.4	NM	27.7	22.2	22.2	WI	15.8	15.3	15.4
IN	24.7	22.6	23.1	NY	68.2	52.1	52.1	WY	6.6	6.3	6.4

[1] Total includes data that has been suppressed for security purposes; see source for details.

Source: U.S. Office of Personnel Management, "FedScope," <http://www.fedscope.opm.gov/>, accessed March 2017.

Table 521. Federal Civilian Employment by Branch and Agency: 1990 to 2014

[For years ending September 30. Annual averages of monthly figures. Excludes Central Intelligence Agency, National Security Agency, Defense Intelligence Agency, and as of October 1996, National Geospatial-Intelligence Agency]

Agency	1990	2000	2005	2010	2013	2014
Total, all agencies [1]	3,128,267	2,708,101	2,700,965	2,841,143	[6] 2,730,551	2,725,590
Legislative branch	37,495	31,157	30,816	30,643	28,672	28,910
Judicial branch	23,605	32,186	34,064	33,756	[6] 33,776	33,766
Executive branch	3,067,167	2,644,758	2,636,085	2,776,744	2,668,103	2,662,914
Executive Office of the President	1,731	1,658	1,693	1,965	[6] 1,828	[6] 1,823
Executive departments	2,065,542	1,592,200	1,685,211	1,937,291	1,898,443	1,894,472
State	25,288	27,983	33,948	39,016	41,768	[6] 41,768
Treasury	158,655	143,508	107,950	110,099	[6] 112,461	[6] 112,461
Defense	1,034,152	676,268	671,364	772,601	728,823	723,175
Justice	83,932	125,970	105,458	117,916	115,616	114,055
Interior	77,679	73,818	75,973	70,231	71,543	69,807
Agriculture [2]	122,594	104,466	107,852	106,867	95,223	94,083
Commerce [2]	69,920	47,652	39,836	56,856	45,035	43,182
Labor	17,727	16,040	15,383	17,592	17,187	[6] 16,796
Health & Human Services [3]	123,959	62,605	60,736	69,839	72,703	71,862
Housing & Urban Development	13,596	10,319	9,941	9,585	8,136	7,795
Transportation [4]	67,364	63,598	55,559	57,972	55,288	54,790
Energy	17,731	15,692	15,010	16,145	15,213	14,802
Education	4,771	4,734	4,321	4,452	4,166	4,123
Veterans Affairs	248,174	219,547	235,210	304,665	323,208	[6] 339,903
Homeland Security [4]	(X)	(X)	146,670	183,455	192,073	[6] 185,870
Independent agencies [1]	999,894	1,050,900	949,181	837,488	[6] 767,832	766,619
Board of Governors Federal Reserve System	1,525	2,372	1,860	1,873	[6] 1,873	[6] 1,873
Environmental Protection Agency	17,123	18,036	17,824	18,740	17,002	[6] 16,871
Equal Employment Opportunity Commission	2,880	2,780	2,360	2,543	[6] 2,219	[6] 2,219
Federal Communications Commission	1,778	1,965	1,885	1,838	1,759	1,720
Federal Deposit Insurance Corporation	17,641	6,958	4,635	6,436	[6] 7,587	7,094
Federal Trade Commission	988	1,019	1,007	1,131	[6] 1,131	[6] 1,131
General Services Administration	20,277	14,334	12,769	12,820	11,819	11,482
National Archives & Records Administration	3,120	2,702	3,029	3,523	[6] 3,201	3,041
National Aeronautics & Space Administration	24,872	18,819	18,752	18,664	18,001	17,685
National Labor Relations Board	2,263	2,054	1,869	1,715	1,588	1,589
National Science Foundation	1,318	1,247	1,305	1,474	[6] 1,491	1,420
Nuclear Regulatory Commission	3,353	2,858	3,242	4,240	3,863	3,863
Office of Personnel Management	6,636	3,780	4,939	5,892	[6] 5,558	[6] 5,558
Peace Corps	1,178	1,065	1,072	1,082	1,068	[6] 1,069
Securities & Exchange Commission	2,302	2,955	3,907	3,917	4,136	4,136
Small Business Administration	5,128	4,150	4,343	4,037	[6] 4,037	[6] 4,037
Smithsonian Institution	5,092	5,065	4,901	4,984	[6] 4,900	[6] 4,676
Social Security Administration [3]	(X)	64,474	66,144	69,975	62,549	64,689
Tennessee Valley Authority	28,392	13,145	12,703	12,457	12,612	[6] 11,843
Broadcasting Board of Governors [5]	8,555	2,436	2,175	1,953	[6] 1,845	1,728
U.S. Agency for International Development	4,698	2,552	2,493	2,515	[6] 2,515	[6] 2,515
U.S. Postal Service	816,886	860,726	764,165	643,420	584,027	583,400

X Not applicable. [1] Includes agencies not shown separately. [2] Includes enumerators for the 1990 and 2000 censuses. [3] The Social Security Administration was separated from the Department of Health and Human Services to become an independent agency effective April 1995. [4] See text, Section 10, National Security and Veteran Affairs, concerning the development of the Department of Homeland Security. [5] Prior to 1999, data for U.S. Information Agency. [6] Preliminary employment totals were used.

Source: U.S. Office of Personnel Management, "Federal Civilian Workforce Statistics--Employment and Trends," <http://www.opm.gov/policy-data-oversight/data-analysis-documentation/federal-employment-reports/#url=Employment-Trends>, accessed July 2015; and unpublished data.

Table 522. Federal Employees—Summary Characteristics: 1990 to 2015

[In percent, except as indicated. As of September 30. For civilian employees of executive branch agencies participating in Office of Personnel Management's Central Personnel Data File (CPDF)]

Characteristics	1990	1995	2000	2005	2010	2012	2013	2014 [3]	2015
Average age (years) [1]	42.3	44.3	46.3	46.9	46.8	47.0	47.3	(NA)	47.4
Average length of service (years)	13.4	15.5	17.1	16.4	14.3	13.7	13.9	(NA)	13.7
Retirement eligible: [2]									
Civil Service Retirement System	8.0	10.0	17.0	33.0	57.0	67.0	72.0	(NA)	81.1
Bachelor's degree or higher	35.0	39.0	41.0	43.0	46.0	48.1	49.3	(NA)	51.0
Sex: Male	57.0	56.0	55.0	56.0	55.9	56.4	56.5	(NA)	56.8
Female	43.0	44.0	45.0	44.0	44.1	43.6	43.5	(NA)	43.2
Race and national origin:									
Total minorities	27.4	28.9	30.4	31.7	33.3	34.0	34.4	(NA)	35.3
Black	16.7	16.8	17.1	17.0	17.5	17.7	17.9	(NA)	17.7
Hispanic	5.4	5.9	6.6	7.4	7.7	8.0	8.1	(NA)	8.4
Asian/Pacific Islander	3.5	4.2	4.5	5.1	5.6	5.8	6.5	(NA)	6.2
American Indian/Alaska Native	1.8	2.0	2.2	2.1	2.1	2.1	2.0	(NA)	1.7
Disabled	7.0	7.0	7.0	7.0	7.0	7.9	8.7	(NA)	12.5
Veterans preference	30.0	26.0	24.0	22.0	23.1	24.5	24.9	(NA)	25.9
Vietnam era veterans	17.0	17.0	14.0	11.0	8.0	5.0	4.4	(NA)	3.2
Retired military	4.9	4.2	3.9	5.4	7.0	7.7	7.9	(NA)	8.3
Retired officers	0.5	0.5	0.5	0.5	1.0	1.7	1.8	(NA)	1.9
Average base salary (dollar) [1]	32,026	41,557	51,618	64,175	76,231	78,061	79,030	(NA)	81,249

NA Not available. [1] For full-time permanent employees. [2] Represents full-time permanent employees under the Civil Service Retirement System (excluding hires since January 1984), and the Federal Employees Retirement System (since January 1984). [3] Data for 2014 were not made available.

Source: U.S. Office of Personnel Management, Office of Workforce Information, *The Fact Book, Federal Civilian Workforce Statistics*, annual. Beginning 2008, Central Personnel Data File, "Profile of Federal Civilian Non-Seasonal Full-Time Employees," <http://www.opm.gov/policy-data-oversight/data-analysis-documentation/federal-employment-reports/reports-publications/profile-of-federal-civilian-non-postal-employees/>, accessed December 2016.

Table 523. Federal Executive Branch Retirements: 2005 to 2015

[For fiscal years ending September 30. Covers non-postal, executive branch federal civilian employees with personnel records in the Enterprise Human Resources Integration-Statistical Data Mart (EHRI-SDM) and Central Personnel Data File (CPDF). Retiring employees must satisfy the minimum years of service requirement; for more information, see source]

Characteristic	2005	2009	2010	2011	2012	2013	2014	2015
Total retirements	**61,860**	**46,100**	**52,660**	**64,238**	**69,320**	**65,264**	**68,735**	**65,107**
Sex:								
Male	37,241	27,401	30,481	36,402	38,493	36,787	38,110	35,994
Female	24,619	18,699	22,179	27,836	30,827	28,477	30,625	29,113
Race:								
White	46,687	34,401	38,947	47,506	50,259	46,816	49,447	46,084
Black	8,970	6,449	7,547	9,460	10,621	9,664	10,579	10,172
Hispanic	3,438	2,608	3,008	3,479	4,149	3,953	4,261	4,210
Other	2,757	2,559	3,070	3,756	4,259	4,805	4,440	4,622
Retirement type:								
Mandatory	557	585	755	834	941	965	1,024	958
Disability	5,606	4,456	3,925	3,919	3,743	3,254	3,664	4,224
Voluntary	47,155	38,983	45,758	54,900	59,812	58,295	61,011	58,097
Early out	7,511	1,241	1,456	2,815	4,124	2,184	2,468	1,289
Other	1,031	835	766	1,770	700	566	568	539
Occupational category:								
Administrative	24,711	18,915	21,673	27,304	29,460	27,153	28,627	26,898
Professional	12,434	9,285	10,906	13,583	14,322	14,410	16,089	15,141
Technical	11,514	8,247	9,539	11,188	12,237	11,416	11,825	11,740
Blue collar	8,232	5,959	6,489	7,379	8,097	7,296	7,064	6,508
Other	4,934	3,679	4,033	4,772	5,194	4,982	5,120	4,812
Veteran status:								
Veteran	23,828	16,635	18,686	21,173	22,738	21,276	21,750	20,434
Exempt	1,770	1,211	1,130	1,155	923	611	548	532
Non-veteran	36,262	28,254	32,844	41,910	45,659	43,377	46,437	44,141
Average retirement age (years)	58.9	59.8	60.3	60.6	60.8	61.3	61.4	61.5
Average length of service (years)	27.9	27.8	27.7	28.0	27.9	27.5	26.9	26.3

Source: U.S. Office of Personnel Management, *Executive Branch Retirement Statistics: Fiscal Years 2006-2015*, March 2016. See also <http://www.opm.gov/policy-data-oversight/data-analysis-documentation/federal-employment-reports/>.

Table 524. Area of Federally Owned Buildings by State: 2015

[2,804.1 represents 2,804,100,000. As of September 30. For executive branch departments and agencies subject to the Chief Financial Officers Act of 1990]

State	Total building area (mil. sq. ft.)	Owned building area (mil. sq. ft.) [2]	Leased building area (mil. sq. ft.)	State	Total building area (mil. sq. ft.)	Owned building area (mil. sq. ft.) [2]	Leased building area (mil. sq. ft.)
U.S. [1]	**2,804.1**	**2,521.0**	**283.1**	Missouri	55.7	44.8	10.8
Alabama	55.0	51.0	4.0	Montana	16.1	13.9	2.3
Alaska	41.6	40.1	1.5	Nebraska	15.0	13.5	1.5
Arizona	55.1	50.8	4.3	Nevada	27.9	25.7	2.1
Arkansas	23.0	21.7	1.4	New Hampshire	5.0	4.3	0.6
California	288.8	268.8	20.0	New Jersey	43.6	38.8	4.8
Colorado	59.2	52.2	7.0	New Mexico	56.9	53.5	3.3
Connecticut	13.8	12.8	1.0	New York	90.2	81.6	8.6
Delaware	6.3	5.9	0.4	North Carolina	92.6	87.8	4.8
Dist. of Columbia	96.6	71.9	24.6	North Dakota	16.5	15.4	1.1
Florida	114.4	102.6	11.9	Ohio	67.4	62.0	5.4
Georgia	122.5	112.2	10.3	Oklahoma	55.2	49.9	5.3
Hawaii	48.9	47.2	1.7	Oregon	22.9	20.1	2.8
Idaho	18.2	16.5	1.8	Pennsylvania	79.8	70.2	9.6
Illinois	67.1	61.3	5.8	Rhode Island	11.8	11.2	0.6
Indiana	29.4	26.6	2.8	South Carolina	52.4	50.2	2.2
Iowa	16.8	15.0	1.9	South Dakota	16.3	15.5	0.9
Kansas	32.5	29.6	2.9	Tennessee	51.4	48.1	3.2
Kentucky	46.5	43.4	3.0	Texas	189.9	167.1	22.8
Louisiana	41.5	37.9	3.6	Utah	30.8	27.9	2.9
Maine	11.4	10.5	0.9	Vermont	4.5	3.3	1.2
Maryland	133.5	113.0	20.4	Virginia	179.3	150.9	28.4
Massachusetts	34.0	31.3	2.7	Washington	83.3	77.9	5.4
Michigan	28.6	23.6	5.0	West Virginia	24.2	21.5	2.6
Minnesota	21.7	19.4	2.3	Wisconsin	22.8	20.2	2.6
Mississippi	42.0	39.8	2.3	Wyoming	14.1	13.3	0.8

[1] Includes property in U.S. territories, not shown separately. [2] Includes Federal Government owned, foreign government owned, museum trust, and state government owned. Non-federal government entities hold title to the real property asset but rights for use have been granted to the Federal Government in a method other than a leasehold arrangement; in the case of a museum trust, the trust holds title but Federal funds may be received to cover operational and maintenance costs.

Source: U.S. General Services Administration, "Real Property Management Policy—Asset Management, FRPP Summary Report Library," <http://www.gsa.gov/portal/content/102880>, accessed November 2016.

National Security and Veterans Affairs

This section displays data for national security (national defense and homeland security) and benefits for veterans. Data are presented on national defense and its human and financial costs; active and reserve military personnel; federally sponsored programs and benefits for veterans; and funding, budget and selected agencies for homeland security. The principal sources of these data are the *Annual Report of Secretary of Veterans Affairs*, U.S. Department of Veterans Affairs; *Budget in Brief*, U.S. Department of Homeland Security; and *The Budget of the United States Government*, Office of Management and Budget. For data on international expenditures and personnel, see Table 1415, Section 30.

Department of Defense (DoD)—The U.S. Department of Defense is responsible for providing the military forces of the United States. It includes the Office of the Secretary of Defense, the Joint Chiefs of Staff, the Army, the Navy, the Air Force, and the defense agencies. The President serves as Commander-in-Chief of the Armed Forces; from him, the authority flows to the Secretary of Defense and through the Joint Chiefs of Staff to the commanders of unified and specified commands (e.g., U.S. Strategic Command).

Reserve components—The Reserve components of the Armed Forces consist of the Army National Guard of the United States, Army Reserve, Naval Reserve, Marine Corps Reserve, Air National Guard, Air Force Reserve, and Coast Guard Reserve. They provide trained personnel and units available for active duty in the Armed Forces during times of war or national emergency, and at such other times as national security may require. The National Guard has dual federal/state responsibilities and uses jointly provided equipment, facilities, and budget support. The President is empowered to mobilize the National Guard and to use such of the Armed Forces as he considers necessary to enforce federal authority in any state. There is in each Armed Force a ready reserve, a standby reserve, and a retired reserve. The Ready Reserve includes the Selected Reserve, which provides trained and ready units and individuals to augment the active forces during times of war or national emergency, or at other times when required; and the Individual Ready Reserve, which is a manpower pool that can be called to active duty during times of war or national emergency and would normally be used as individual fillers for active, guard, and reserve units, and as a source of combat replacements. Most of the Ready Reserve serves in an active status.

Department of Veterans Affairs (VA)—A veteran is someone 18 years and older (there are a few 17-year-old veterans) who is not currently on active duty, but who once served on active duty in the United States Army, Navy, Air Force, Marine Corps, or Coast Guard, or who served in the Merchant Marine during World War II. There are many groups whose active service makes them veterans including: those who incurred a service-connected disability during active duty for training in the Reserves or National Guard even though that service would not otherwise have counted for veteran status and members of a national guard or reserve component who have been ordered to active duty by order of the President or those who have a full-time military job. The latter are called AGRs (Active Guard and Reserve). No one who has received a dishonorable discharge is a veteran.

The VA administers laws authorizing benefits for eligible former and present members of the Armed Forces and for the beneficiaries of deceased members. Veterans' benefits available under various acts of Congress include compensation for service-connected disability or death; pensions for non-service-connected disability or death; vocational rehabilitation, education and training; home loan insurance; life insurance; health care; special housing and automobiles or other conveyances for certain disabled veterans; burial and plot allowances; and educational assistance to families of deceased or totally disabled veterans, servicemen missing in action, or prisoners of war. Since these benefits are legislated by Congress, the dates they were enacted and the dates they apply to veterans may be different from the actual dates the conflicts occurred. VA estimates of veterans cover all persons discharged from active U.S. military service under conditions other than dishonorable.

Department of Homeland Security (DHS)—The creation of DHS, which began operations in March 2003, represents a fusion of 22 federal agencies from different legacy agencies (the Coast Guard and Secret Service remained intact) to coordinate and centralize the leadership of many homeland security activities under a single department. The largest organizations under DHS include: Customs and Border Protection (CBP), Immigration and Customs Enforcement (ICE), Transportation Security Administration (TSA), Federal Emergency Management Agency (FEMA), and the Coast Guard.

Coast Guard—With more than 218 years of service to the Nation, the Coast Guard is a military, multi-mission, maritime organization that promotes safety and safeguards U.S. economic and security interests throughout the maritime environment. As one of the five Armed Services of the United States, it is the only military organization within the DHS. Unlike its sister services in the Department of Defense (DoD), the Coast Guard is also a law enforcement and regulatory agency with broad domestic authorities.

Federal Emergency Management Agency (FEMA)—FEMA manages and coordinates the federal response to and recovery from major domestic disasters and emergencies of all types in accordance with the Robert T. Stafford Disaster Relief and Emergency Assistance Act. The agency ensures the effectiveness of emergency response providers at all levels of government in responding to terrorist attacks, major disasters, and other emergencies. Through the Disaster Relief Fund, FEMA provides individual and public assistance to help families and communities impacted by declared disasters rebuild and recover. FEMA is also the principal component for preparing state and local governments to prevent or respond to threats or incidents of terrorism and other catastrophic events, through their state and local programs.

The Customs and Border Protection (CBP)—CBP is responsible for managing, securing, and controlling U.S. borders. This includes carrying out traditional border-related responsibilities, such as stemming the tide of illegal drugs and illegal aliens; securing and facilitating legitimate global trade and travel; and protecting the food supply and agriculture industry from pests and disease. CBP is composed of the Border Patrol and Inspections (both moved from INS) along with Customs (absorbed from the U.S. Department of Treasury) and Animal and Plant Health Inspections Services (absorbed from the U.S. Department of Agriculture).

The Immigration and Customs Enforcement

(ICE)—ICE's mission is to protect America and uphold public safety by targeting the people, money, and materials crossing the nation's borders that support terrorist and criminal activities. ICE is the largest investigation arm of DHS. ICE is composed of five law enforcement divisions: Investigations, Intelligence, Federal Protective Service, International Affairs, and Detention and Removal Operations. ICE investigates a wide range of national security, financial, and smuggling violations including drug smuggling, human trafficking, illegal arms exports, financial crimes, commercial fraud, human smuggling, document fraud, money laundering, child pornography/exploitation, and immigration fraud.

The Transportation Security Administration

(TSA)—TSA was created as part of the Aviation and Transportation Security Act on November 19, 2001. TSA was originally part of the U.S. Department of Transportation, but was moved to DHS. TSA's mission is to provide security to our nation's transportation systems with a primary focus on aviation security.

Table 525. National Defense Outlays and Veterans' Benefits: 1960 to 2018

[In billions of dollars (53.6 represents $53,600,000,000), except percent. For fiscal year ending in year shown, see text, Section 8. Includes outlays of Department of Defense, Department of Veterans Affairs, and other agencies for activities primarily related to national defense and veterans programs. For explanation of average annual percent change, see Guide to Tabular Presentation. Minus sign (-) indicates decrease]

Year	National defense and veterans' outlays				Annual percent change [1]			Defense outlays, percent of—	
		Defense outlays							
	Total outlays	Current dollars	Constant (2009) dollars	Veterans' outlays	Total outlays	Defense outlays	Veterans' outlays	Federal outlays	Gross domestic product [2]
1960.................	53.6	48.1	(NA)	5.4	-1.63	-1.81	-0.04	52.2	9.0
1970.................	90.4	81.7	468.9	8.7	0.26	-0.98	13.60	41.8	7.8
1980.................	155.2	134.0	361.3	21.2	13.88	15.17	6.30	22.7	4.8
1990.................	328.4	299.3	512.2	29.0	-1.56	-1.39	-3.23	23.9	5.1
2000.................	341.4	294.4	406.9	47.0	7.37	7.13	8.88	16.5	2.9
2001.................	349.7	304.7	406.6	45.0	2.45	3.52	-4.29	16.4	2.9
2002.................	399.4	348.5	449.0	50.9	14.21	14.35	13.24	17.3	3.2
2003.................	461.7	404.7	491.2	57.0	15.61	16.15	11.89	18.7	3.6
2004.................	515.6	455.8	533.0	59.7	11.66	12.62	4.85	19.9	3.8
2005.................	565.4	495.3	552.6	70.1	9.67	8.66	17.36	20.0	3.8
2006.................	591.6	521.8	558.1	69.8	4.64	5.36	-0.44	19.7	3.8
2007.................	624.1	551.3	571.4	72.8	5.48	5.64	4.31	20.2	3.8
2008.................	700.7	616.1	614.9	84.7	12.28	11.76	16.25	20.7	4.2
2009.................	756.4	661.0	661.0	95.4	7.95	7.30	12.73	18.8	4.6
2010.................	801.9	693.5	681.0	108.4	6.01	4.91	13.58	20.1	4.7
2011.................	832.7	705.6	672.2	127.2	3.85	1.74	17.35	19.6	4.6
2012.................	802.4	677.9	636.7	124.6	-3.64	-3.93	-2.04	19.2	4.2
2013.................	772.4	633.4	591.1	138.9	-3.75	-6.55	11.51	18.3	3.8
2014.................	753.1	603.5	553.7	149.6	-2.50	-4.73	7.69	17.2	3.5
2015.................	749.4	589.7	539.1	159.7	-0.49	-2.29	6.77	16.0	3.3
2016.................	**767.9**	**593.4**	**540.0**	**174.5**	**2.47**	**0.63**	**9.25**	**15.4**	**3.2**
2017 estimate.......	777.7	602.8	538.6	175.0	1.28	1.59	0.25	14.8	3.1
2018 estimate.......	830.5	652.6	572.7	177.9	6.78	8.26	1.68	15.9	3.3

NA Not available. [1] Change from immediate prior year. [2] Represents fiscal year GDP; for definition, see text, Section 13.

Source: U.S. Office of Management and Budget, *Budget of the U.S. Government, Fiscal Year 2018: Historical Tables*, May 2017. See also <http://www.whitehouse.gov/omb/budget/>.

Table 526. National Defense Budget Authority and Outlays for Defense Functions: 2000 to 2018

[In billions of dollars (304.0 represents $304,000,000,000). For year ending September 30. Data includes defense budget authority and outlays by other departments. Minus sign (-) indicates decrease]

Function	2000	2005	2010	2011	2012	2013	2014	2015	2016	2017 est.	2018 est.
Total budget authority..........	**304.0**	**505.7**	**721.2**	**717.0**	**681.4**	**610.2**	**622.3**	**598.4**	**624.1**	**655.1**	**677.1**
Department of Defense—Military...	290.3	483.8	695.6	691.5	655.4	585.2	595.7	570.9	595.7	626.2	646.9
Military personnel...................	73.8	121.3	157.1	158.4	158.4	153.5	150.2	145.9	145.4	145.7	153.5
Operation and maintenance.......	108.7	179.2	293.6	305.2	286.8	258.3	262.5	246.6	245.1	249.9	273.0
Procurement.........................	55.0	96.6	135.8	131.9	118.3	97.8	100.4	102.1	118.9	119.7	125.4
Research, development, test, and evaluation....................	38.7	68.8	80.2	76.7	72.0	63.3	63.5	63.9	69.5	70.5	83.7
Military construction................	5.1	7.3	22.6	16.0	11.4	8.1	8.4	5.7	6.9	6.6	9.0
Family housing......................	3.5	4.1	2.3	1.8	1.7	1.5	1.4	1.1	1.3	1.3	1.4
Other.................................	5.4	6.6	4.0	1.4	6.9	2.8	9.4	5.7	8.5	32.5	1.0
Atomic energy defense activities. ..	12.4	17.9	18.2	18.5	18.3	17.5	18.4	19.0	20.1	20.1	21.8
Defense-related activities...........	1.3	4.0	7.3	7.0	7.7	7.4	8.2	8.5	8.3	8.8	8.4
Total outlays.....................	**294.4**	**495.3**	**693.5**	**705.6**	**677.9**	**633.4**	**603.5**	**589.7**	**593.4**	**602.8**	**652.6**
Department of Defense—Military...	281.0	474.1	666.7	678.1	650.9	607.8	577.9	562.5	565.4	573.0	621.7
Military personnel...................	76.0	127.5	155.7	161.6	152.3	150.8	148.9	145.2	147.9	145.7	152.5
Operation and maintenance.......	105.8	188.1	276.0	291.0	282.3	259.7	244.5	247.2	243.2	244.6	253.0
Procurement.........................	51.7	82.3	133.6	128.0	124.7	114.9	107.5	101.3	102.7	105.0	113.5
Research, development, test, and evaluation....................	37.6	65.7	77.0	74.9	70.4	66.9	64.9	64.1	64.9	66.4	76.5
Military construction................	5.1	5.3	21.2	19.9	14.6	12.3	9.8	8.1	6.7	7.2	8.2
Family housing......................	3.4	3.7	3.2	3.4	2.3	1.8	1.4	1.2	1.3	1.2	1.2
Other.................................	1.4	1.5	0.1	-0.8	4.3	1.4	0.9	-4.7	-1.2	2.8	16.8
Atomic energy defense activities. ..	12.1	18.0	19.3	20.4	19.2	17.6	17.4	18.7	19.4	20.0	22.8
Defense-related activities...........	1.2	3.2	7.5	7.1	7.8	8.0	8.1	8.5	8.6	9.8	8.1

Source: U.S. Office of Management and Budget, *Budget of the U.S. Government, Fiscal Year 2018: Historical Tables*, May 2017. See also <http://www.whitehouse.gov/omb/budget/>.

Table 527. Department of Defense Property—Sites, Land, and Assets: 2015

[In units, as indicated (879.37 represents $879,370,000,000). For fiscal year ending September 30. A site is a physical location owned by, leased to, or otherwise possessed by a DoD component]

Assets	Unit	Total	Army	Navy	Air Force	Marine Corps	WHS [1]
DoD sites, total............................	**Number**	**4,855**	**1,858**	**995**	**1,726**	**182**	**94**
United States...........................	Number	4,154	1,562	803	1,535	160	94
Territories..............................	Number	114	41	64	9	–	–
Overseas..............................	Number	587	255	128	182	22	–
Acres of land, total.....................	**Number**	**24,911,696**	**11,236,168**	**2,199,082**	**9,122,702**	**2,352,796**	**948**
Owned................................	Number	14,477,496	7,219,008	579,823	1,751,798	835,617	948
Leased...............................	Number	329,335	171,315	58,711	103,814	404	–
Other [2]..............................	Number	9,890,374	3,845,846	1,560,548	7,267,090	1,516,775	–
Assets, total [3]...........................	**Number**	**561,975**	**272,810**	**111,371**	**127,880**	**49,128**	**786**
Buildings.............................	Number	276,770	138,545	61,109	50,766	26,156	194
Structures............................	Number	178,113	78,902	34,788	46,743	17,253	427
Linear structures......................	Number	107,092	55,363	15,474	30,371	5,719	165
Plant replacement value of assets, total [4]...	**Bil. dol.**	**879.37**	**301.80**	**223.38**	**275.85**	**71.37**	**6.97**
Buildings.............................	Bil. dol.	585.07	216.20	136.74	174.33	51.04	6.76
Structures............................	Bil. dol.	131.22	35.85	50.33	35.29	9.60	0.15
Linear structures......................	Bil. dol.	163.08	49.75	36.31	66.23	10.73	0.06

– Represents zero. [1] Washington Headquarters Service. [2] Includes buildings that have been privatized or are operated by private entities in direct support of the DoD mission. [3] Buildings (roofed and floored facilities enclosed by exterior walls); structures (facilities other than buildings or linear structures constructed on or in the land such as towers, storage tanks, wharfs, and piers); and linear structures (facilities that traverse land such as runways, roads, rail lines, pipelines, fences, pavements, and electrical distribution line and are reported by a linear unit of measure). [4] Calculated cost to replace the current physical plant (facilities and supporting infrastructure) using today's construction costs (labor and materials) and standards (methodologies and codes).

Source: Department of Defense, Office of the Assistant Secretary of Defense for Energy, Installations, and Environment, *Base Structure Report Fiscal Year 2015 Baseline, A Summary of the Real Property Inventory*, 2016. See also <http://www.acq.osd.mil/eie/Library.html#BSR>.

Table 528. Military Personnel and Families by Selected Characteristics: 2005 to 2015

[In units, as indicated. Reserve and National Guard includes Selected Reserve only, unless otherwise noted. Personnel data primarily from Defense Manpower Data Center (DMDC). Family member data is from the Defense Enrollment and Eligibility Reporting System]

Characteristic	2005 Active Duty	2005 Reserve and Guard	2010 Active Duty	2010 Reserve and Guard	2014 Active Duty	2014 Reserve and Guard	2015 Active Duty	2015 Reserve and Guard
MILITARY PERSONNEL								
Total (number).......................	**1,373,534**	**829,005**	**1,417,370**	**857,261**	**1,326,273**	**831,992**	**1,301,443**	**826,106**
Ratio of officers to enlisted members......	1 to 5.1	1 to 5.6	1 to 5.0	1 to 5.7	1 to 4.6	1 to 5.4	1 to 4.6	1 to 5.3
Separations from duty (number)...........	217,598	160,882	176,248	133,223	204,556	135,804	188,276	125,895
Retired personnel (number) [1]..............	1,522,532	627,424	1,540,830	716,228	1,562,163	755,024	1,573,562	766,658
PERCENT								
Male...................................	85.4	82.8	85.6	82.1	84.9	81.2	84.5	81.0
Female.................................	14.6	17.2	14.4	17.9	15.1	18.8	15.5	19.0
Minority race/ethnicity [2]....................	35.9	30.4	30.0	24.1	31.2	25.6	31.3	26.0
Duty location in the U.S. and U.S. territories.............................	85.3	96.9	86.4	99.1	87.1	99.1	87.5	99.2
25 years old and under....................	46.6	31.2	44.2	33.3	43.2	34.3	43.8	34.0
With bachelor's degree or higher..........	17.7	19.7	17.7	19.4	20.7	22.1	21.1	22.7
Married................................	54.6	51.4	56.4	48.2	55.3	45.3	54.3	44.7
In dual-military marriages.................	6.9	2.6	6.7	2.6	6.4	2.6	6.4	2.7
MILITARY FAMILIES								
Family members (number)...............	**1,865,058**	**1,141,735**	**1,983,236**	**1,161,631**	**1,802,615**	**1,084,069**	**1,728,710**	**1,064,795**
Spouses (number).......................	679,738	415,548	725,877	413,295	665,619	381,773	641,639	374,621
Adult dependents (number)..............	8,130	1,762	9,485	1,961	10,670	1,811	10,268	1,708
PERCENT								
With children...........................	43.2	43.0	44.1	43.2	42.2	42.0	41.1	41.5
With children age 5 and under...........	39.8	24.8	42.3	27.9	41.9	30.1	42.0	30.5
Single parents..........................	5.4	8.2	5.4	9.3	4.7	9.2	4.5	9.1
Average age at birth of first child..........	24.8	27.3	24.9	26.6	25.7	27.8	25.8	28.0

[1] Retired Reserve and Guard includes ready reserve. [2] Black or African American, Asian, American Indian or Alaska Native, Native Hawaiian or Other Pacific Islander, multi-racial, or other/unknown.

Source: Department of Defense, Office of the Deputy Assistant Secretary of Defense, Military Community and Family Policy, *2015 Demographics Profile of the Military Community*, and earlier reports. See also <http://www.militaryonesource.mil/>

Table 529. Military Personnel on Active Duty by Location: 1980 to 2016

[In thousands (2,051 represents 2,051,000). As of September 30. Prior to 2012, data from DOD Statistical Information Analysis Division (SIAD). Beginning 2012, data from Defense Manpower Data Center (DMDC)]

Location	1980	1990	2000	2010	2011	2012	2013	2014	2015	2016
Total.............................	**2,051**	**2,046**	**1,384**	**1,431**	**1,425**	**1,388**	**1,370**	**1,326**	**1,301**	**1,328**
Shore-based [1]....................	1,840	1,794	1,237	1,328	1,325	(NA)	(NA)	(NA)	(NA)	(NA)
Afloat [2]........................	211	252	147	103	101	(NA)	(NA)	(NA)	(NA)	(NA)
United States [3].................	1,562	1,437	1,127	1,134	1,220	1,214	1,209	1,168	1,146	1,130
Foreign countries................	489	609	258	297	205	174	161	159	156	199

NA Not available. [1] Includes Navy personnel temporarily on shore. [2] Includes Marine Corps. [3] Includes Puerto Rico and Island Areas.

Source: U.S. Department of Defense, DoD Personnel and Procurement Statistics, data prior to 2016, "Active Duty Military Personnel By Service By Region/Country," November 2015 and earlier reports. Beginning 2016, "Counts of Active Duty and Reserve Service Members and APF Civilians," <https://www.dmdc.osd.mil/appj/dwp>, accessed August 2017.

Table 530. Department of Defense Personnel by Service Branch and Sex: 1960 to 2016

[In thousands (2,475 represents 2,475,000). As of end of fiscal year; see text, Section 8. Includes National Guard, Reserve, and retired regular personnel on extended or continuous active duty. Excludes Coast Guard. Other officer candidates are included under enlisted personnel]

Year	Total¹,²	Army					Navy²					Marine Corps					Air Force				
		Total¹	Male Officers	Male Enlisted	Female Officers	Female Enlisted	Total¹	Male Officers	Male Enlisted	Female Officers	Female Enlisted	Total¹	Male Officers	Male Enlisted	Female Officers	Female Enlisted	Total¹	Male Officers	Male Enlisted	Female Officers	Female Enlisted
1960	2,475	873	97	762	4.3	8.3	617	67	540	2.7	5.4	171	16	153	0.1	1.5	815	126	677	3.7	5.7
1965	2,654	969	108	846	3.8	8.5	670	75	583	2.6	5.3	190	17	172	0.1	1.4	825	128	685	4.1	4.7
1970	3,065	1,323	162	1,142	5.2	11.5	691	78	600	2.9	5.8	260	25	233	0.3	2.1	791	125	648	4.7	9.0
1975	2,128	784	98	640	4.6	37.7	535	62	449	3.7	17.5	196	19	174	0.3	2.8	613	100	478	5.0	25.2
1980	2,051	777	91	612	7.6	61.7	527	58	430	4.9	30.1	189	18	164	0.5	6.2	558	90	404	8.5	51.9
1985	2,151	781	99	599	10.8	68.4	571	64	449	6.9	45.7	198	19	169	0.7	9.0	602	96	431	11.9	58.1
1986	2,169	781	99	597	11.3	69.7	581	65	457	7.3	47.2	200	19	170	0.6	9.2	608	97	434	12.4	61.2
1987	2,174	781	96	596	11.6	71.6	587	65	462	7.2	47.7	200	19	170	0.6	9.1	607	94	432	12.6	63.2
1988	2,138	772	95	588	11.8	72.0	593	65	466	7.3	49.7	197	19	168	0.6	9.1	576	92	405	12.9	61.5
1989	2,130	770	95	584	12.2	74.3	593	65	464	7.5	52.1	197	19	168	0.7	9.0	571	91	399	13.4	63.7
1990	2,044	732	92	553	12.4	71.2	579	64	451	7.8	52.1	197	19	168	0.7	8.7	535	87	370	13.3	60.8
1991	1,986	711	91	535	12.5	67.8	570	63	444	8.0	51.4	194	19	166	0.7	8.3	510	84	350	13.3	59.1
1992	1,807	610	83	449	11.7	61.7	542	61	417	8.3	51.0	185	18	157	0.6	7.9	470	77	320	12.7	56.1
1993	1,705	572	77	420	11.1	60.2	510	58	390	8.3	49.3	178	17	153	0.6	7.2	444	72	302	12.3	54.5
1994	1,610	541	74	394	10.9	59.0	469	54	355	8.0	47.9	174	17	149	0.6	7.0	426	69	287	12.3	54.0
1995	1,518	509	72	365	10.8	57.3	435	51	324	7.9	47.9	175	17	150	0.7	7.4	400	66	266	12.1	52.1
1996	1,439	491	70	347	10.6	59.0	417	50	308	7.8	46.9	175	17	149	0.8	7.8	389	64	256	12.0	52.8
1997	1,407	492	69	346	10.4	62.4	396	48	290	7.8	44.8	174	17	148	0.8	8.5	377	62	246	12.0	53.8
1998	1,434	484	68	340	10.4	61.4	382	47	280	7.8	42.9	173	17	146	0.9	8.9	368	60	237	12.0	54.2
1999	1,427	479	67	337	10.5	61.5	373	46	271	7.7	43.9	173	17	145	0.9	9.3	361	58	232	11.8	54.6
2000	1,384	482	66	339	10.8	62.9	373	46	272	7.8	43.8	173	17	146	0.9	9.5	356	57	227	11.8	55.0
2001	1,385	481	65	337	11.0	63.4	378	46	273	8.0	46.6	173	17	145	1.0	9.6	354	57	224	12.0	55.6
2002	1,414	487	66	341	11.5	63.3	385	47	279	8.2	47.3	174	17	146	1.0	9.5	368	59	233	12.9	58.6
2003	1,434	499	68	352	12.0	63.5	382	47	276	8.2	47.3	178	18	149	1.1	9.6	375	61	237	13.5	60.0
2004	1,427	500	69	358	12.3	61.0	373	46	273	8.1	46.1	178	18	149	1.1	9.7	377	61	242	13.6	60.2
2005	1,389	493	69	353	12.4	57.9	363	45	266	7.8	44.5	180	18	151	1.0	9.8	354	60	225	13.4	55.6
2006	1,385	505	69	365	12.5	58.5	350	44	255	7.6	43.2	180	18	151	1.1	10.0	349	58	223	12.8	55.8
2007	1,380	522	71	379	13.0	58.8	338	44	244	7.6	42.2	186	18	156	1.1	10.5	333	54	214	11.8	53.4
2008	1,402	544	74	392	13.5	59.7	332	44	235	7.7	41.4	199	19	167	1.2	11.1	327	53	207	11.9	51.4
2009	1,419	553	76	399	14.3	59.4	329	44	231	7.9	42.2	203	19	170	1.2	11.7	333	53	211	12.1	52.0
2010	1,431	566	79	407	15.1	60.3	328	44	228	8.2	43.4	202	18	169	1.3	12.2	334	54	212	12.4	50.9
2011	1,425	565	82	403	15.7	60.2	325	44	224	8.5	44.0	201	21	167	1.3	12.4	333	53	213	12.3	50.3
2012	1,400	550	82	390	16.0	57.4	318	44	217	8.6	44.3	198	20	164	1.3	12.6	333	53	214	12.5	49.8
2013	1,383	532	82	373	16.2	55.7	324	45	219	9.0	47.0	196	20	162	1.4	12.8	330	52	213	12.7	49.1
2014	1,338	508	81	353	16.2	53.8	326	45	219	9.2	48.1	188	19	154	1.4	12.8	316	50	203	12.4	46.7
2015	1,314	491	79	339	15.9	53.4	328	45	219	9.4	49.9	183	19	150	1.5	12.6	311	49	200	12.4	46.3
2016	1,301	475	76	326	15.7	53.2	325	45	216	9.8	50.2	184	19	149	1.5	13.3	318	48	204	12.6	48.3

¹ Includes cadets, midshipmen, and others, not shown separately. ² Beginning 1980, excludes Navy Reserve personnel on active duty for Training and Administration of Reserves (TARS).

Source: U.S. Department of Defense, Statistical Information Analysis Division, *Selected Manpower Statistics*, discontinued; and Defense Manpower Data Center, "Active Duty Military Personnel by Service by Rank/Grade," <https://www.dmdc.osd.mil/appj/dwp/dwp_reports.jsp>, accessed January 2017.

Table 531. Military Personnel on Active Duty by Rank or Grade: 2000 to 2016

[As of September 30]

Rank/grade	2000	2010	2012	2013	2014	2015	2016
Total	**1,384,338**	**1,430,985**	**1,399,622**	**1,382,684**	**1,338,487**	**1,313,940**	**1,301,308**
Total officers	**217,178**	**234,000**	**238,074**	**238,531**	**235,000**	**230,468**	**228,148**
General – Admiral	34	39	40	37	38	38	39
Lieutenant General – Vice Admiral	119	150	155	158	145	141	137
Major General – Rear Admiral (U)	282	310	316	312	304	310	307
Brigadier General – Rear Admiral (L)	436	482	433	436	424	420	420
Colonel – Captain	11,304	12,160	11,913	11,955	11,591	11,240	11,253
Lieutenant Colonel – Commander	27,461	28,773	28,655	28,888	27,932	27,221	27,079
Major – LT Commander	43,229	45,295	46,461	46,155	45,624	43,609	42,958
Captain – Lieutenant	68,106	74,997	74,769	75,632	76,207	75,525	74,633
1st Lieutenant – Lieutenant (JG)	24,713	25,523	30,765	31,133	29,863	29,484	28,303
2nd Lieutenant – Ensign	26,405	27,128	25,008	24,454	23,639	23,724	24,745
Chief Warrant Officer W-5	473	746	813	830	836	797	769
Chief Warrant Officer W-4	2,029	3,233	3,205	3,047	2,937	2,782	2,631
Chief Warrant Officer W-3	3,824	4,795	5,071	5,128	5,269	5,424	5,348
Chief Warrant Officer W-2	6,674	7,489	8,069	8,143	7,952	7,694	7,393
Warrant Officer W-1	2,089	2,880	2,401	2,223	2,239	2,059	2,133
Total enlisted	**1,154,624**	**1,183,200**	**1,148,481**	**1,131,285**	**1,090,759**	**1,070,546**	**1,060,084**
E-9	10,240	10,192	10,316	10,495	10,238	9,991	9,979
E-8	26,035	27,331	27,111	27,459	27,296	26,443	25,965
E-7	97,717	97,070	96,578	96,397	94,076	89,580	89,428
E-6	164,857	170,856	165,673	163,907	159,711	156,786	154,408
E-5	229,492	249,981	237,193	234,745	227,369	219,613	214,296
E-4	250,999	279,315	293,089	277,403	268,701	277,371	262,254
E-3	196,276	228,152	206,584	196,218	190,482	174,695	183,762
E-2	98,983	75,177	64,862	70,043	65,878	66,744	67,996
E-1	80,025	45,126	47,075	54,618	47,008	49,323	51,996
Cadets and Midshipmen	**12,536**	**13,785**	**13,067**	**12,868**	**12,728**	**12,926**	**13,076**

Source: U.S. Department of Defense, Statistical Information Analysis Division, *Atlas/Data Abstract for the United States and Selected Areas*, annual, discontinued; and "Active Duty Military Personnel by Rank/Grade," <https://www.dmdc.osd.mil/appj/dwp/dwp_reports.jsp>, accessed November 2016.

Table 532. Military Retirement System—Disabled and Non-Disabled Personnel and Payments: 2016

[Payment in thousands of dollars (4,431,106 represents $4,431,106,000). As of September 30. The data published in the source report are produced from files maintained by the Defense Manpower Data Center. This report compiles data primarily from the "Retiree Pay and Survivor Pay" files. Any grouping of members by address reflects mailing, not necessarily residence, address. Only those members in plans administered by the Department of Defense (DoD) are included in this table. The data are preliminary because of reporting delays about members who retired or died within one month of the September 30 reporting date. These data were not processed in time to be included in this report. For more information, see Introduction and Overview, source]

State	Retired military personnel [1]			Monthly payment ($1,000)	State	Retired military personnel [1]			Monthly payment ($1,000)
	Total	Disabled [2]	Non-disabled			Total	Disabled [2]	Non-disabled	
Total [3]	**2,143,677**	**252,988**	**1,890,689**	**4,431,106**	MS	27,813	2,961	24,852	49,824
					MO	38,635	5,365	33,270	69,138
U.S.	**2,102,142**	**248,246**	**1,853,896**	**4,352,561**	MT	9,395	1,100	8,295	18,081
AL	60,837	6,370	54,467	124,966	NE	14,660	1,416	13,244	31,079
AK	10,730	1,304	9,426	22,006	NV	29,322	2,571	26,751	61,503
AZ	56,629	5,977	50,652	119,063	NH	9,572	1,063	8,509	19,744
AR	25,616	3,159	22,457	46,281	NJ	19,434	3,021	16,413	31,984
CA	159,004	18,300	140,704	330,680	NM	21,276	2,165	19,111	46,141
CO	53,160	6,441	46,719	126,626	NY	40,004	7,365	32,639	60,697
CT	10,282	1,478	8,804	18,619	NC	96,184	11,660	84,524	204,318
DE	9,034	735	8,299	17,155	ND	5,430	498	4,932	9,396
DC	2,465	368	2,097	5,878	OH	47,180	7,194	39,986	86,181
FL	198,016	19,987	178,029	440,578	OK	36,448	4,430	32,018	68,545
GA	97,451	12,231	85,220	195,771	OR	21,139	3,161	17,978	38,836
HI	17,739	1,608	16,131	40,310	PA	51,760	6,996	44,764	92,320
ID	14,163	1,616	12,547	27,688	RI	5,361	629	4,732	10,938
IL	37,058	5,473	31,585	70,092	SC	59,988	6,039	53,949	121,389
IN	26,291	4,360	21,931	42,545	SD	8,425	758	7,667	16,078
IA	13,157	1,846	11,311	21,306	TN	56,058	6,913	49,145	108,409
KS	22,112	2,734	19,378	44,981	TX	209,327	27,854	181,473	448,962
KY	28,790	4,274	24,516	53,340	UT	17,216	1,703	15,513	34,118
LA	26,824	3,837	22,987	50,319	VT	3,902	513	3,389	6,493
ME	11,935	1,372	10,563	21,611	VA	156,513	10,673	145,840	437,825
MD	55,173	4,939	50,234	128,057	WA	74,188	7,511	66,677	158,388
MA	18,544	2,813	15,731	31,425	WV	11,033	1,600	9,433	18,648
MI	30,403	5,638	24,765	48,091	WI	21,807	3,104	18,703	35,255
MN	19,107	2,575	16,532	30,198	WY	5,552	548	5,004	10,685

[1] Represents military personnel (officers and enlisted) receiving and not receiving pay from DoD. [2] A disabled military member is entitled to disability retired pay if the disability is not the result of the member's intentional misconduct or willful neglect, was not incurred during a period of unauthorized absence, and either: (1) the member has at least 20 years of service; or (2) at the time of determination, the disability is at least 30 percent (under a standard schedule of rating disabilities by the Veterans Administration) and one of four additional conditions are met. For details on these conditions and additional information, see Overview, source. [3] Includes states, U.S. territories, and retirees living in foreign countries.

Source: U.S. Department of Defense, Office of the Actuary, *Statistical Report on the Military Retirement System, Fiscal Year 2016*, August 2017. See also <http://actuary.defense.gov>.

Table 533. U.S. Active Duty Military Deaths by Manner of Death: 1980 to 2012

[As of December 11, 2013]

Manner of death	1980	1990	1995	2000	2004	2005	2006	2007	2008	2009	2010	2011	2012
Deaths, total	2,392	1,507	1,040	832	1,874	1,929	1,882	1,953	1,440	1,515	1,485	1,446	1,307
Accident	1,556	880	538	429	605	646	561	561	506	467	424	423	396
Hostile action	–	–	–	–	735	739	769	847	352	346	456	393	239
Homicide	174	74	67	37	46	54	47	52	47	77	39	41	44
Illness	419	277	174	180	256	280	257	237	244	277	238	246	244
Pending	–	–	–	–	–	1	8	22	6	19	22	17	31
Self-inflicted	231	232	250	153	197	182	213	211	259	302	289	292	336
Terrorist attack	1	1	7	17	–	–	–	–	1	–	–	2	–
Undetermined	11	43	4	16	8	27	27	23	25	27	17	32	17
Deaths per 100,000 of personnel strength	110.8	66.7	62.6	54.4	107.9	115.9	116.8	121.4	85.6	92.3	88.1	87.4	80.4
Accident	72.0	39.0	32.4	28.0	35.3	38.8	34.8	34.9	30.1	28.5	25.2	25.6	24.4
Hostile action	–	–	–	–	42.9	44.4	47.7	52.7	20.9	21.1	27.1	23.8	14.7
Homicide	8.1	3.3	4.0	2.4	2.7	3.2	2.9	3.2	2.8	4.7	2.3	2.5	2.7
Illness	19.4	12.3	10.5	11.8	15.0	16.8	15.9	14.7	14.5	16.9	14.1	14.9	15.0
Pending	–	–	–	–	–	0.1	0.5	1.4	0.4	1.2	1.3	1.0	1.9
Self-inflicted	10.7	10.3	15.0	10.0	11.5	10.9	13.2	13.1	15.4	18.4	17.1	17.7	20.7
Terrorist attack	–	–	0.4	1.1	–	–	–	–	0.1	–	–	0.1	–
Undetermined	0.5	1.9	0.2	1.0	0.5	1.6	1.7	1.4	1.5	1.6	1.0	1.9	1.0

– Represents zero.

Source: Defense Manpower Data Center, data prior to 2010, "Defense Casualty Analysis System," <https://www.dmdc.osd.mil/dcas/pages/main.xhtml>; and 2010 to 2012, unpublished data obtained via Freedom of Information Act request.

Table 534. U.S. Military Personnel on Active Duty in Selected Foreign Countries: 2000 to 2015

[As of September 30. Prior to 2012, data from Statistical Information Analysis Division (SIAD). Beginning 2012, data from Defense Manpower Data Center (DMDC)]

Country	2000	2005	2010	2011	2012	2013	2014	2015
Total in foreign countries [1]	257,817	290,997	297,286	205,118	173,929	161,194	158,650	155,511
Ashore	212,858	268,214	277,151	186,476	(NA)	(NA)	(NA)	(NA)
Afloat	44,959	22,783	20,135	18,642	(NA)	(NA)	(NA)	(NA)
Australia	175	196	130	198	346	170	173	175
Bahrain	949	1,641	1,349	2,142	2,713	2,992	3,372	3,419
Belgium	1,554	1,366	1,252	1,205	1,174	1,157	1,211	1,210
Bosnia and Herzegovina	5,708	263	8	9	9	2	2	2
Canada	156	150	127	130	147	135	131	133
Colombia	224	52	62	63	73	47	47	52
Cuba (Guantanamo)	688	950	913	929	996	836	732	668
Diego Garcia [2]	625	683	238	292	529	517	528	488
Djibouti	2	622	1,379	335	168	5	5	1
Egypt	499	410	275	251	280	237	283	250
Germany	69,203	66,418	53,951	53,766	47,761	41,007	38,826	36,691
Greece	678	428	338	382	351	353	386	373
Greenland	125	146	133	142	139	140	142	145
Honduras	351	438	403	354	408	367	360	395
Italy	11,190	11,841	9,646	10,801	10,922	10,790	11,317	11,799
Japan	40,159	35,571	34,385	39,222	50,937	50,104	49,503	52,060
Korea, South	36,565	30,983	(NA)	(NA)	(NA)	(NA)	(NA)	24,899
Kuwait	4,602	(3)	(3)	(3)	(NA)	(NA)	(NA)	(NA)
Netherlands	659	583	442	405	374	348	371	362
Portugal	1,005	970	703	723	743	702	647	457
Qatar	52	463	555	621	806	611	600	593
Saudi Arabia	7,053	258	239	274	284	299	324	315
Senegal	10	42	9	13	15	7	7	12
Singapore	411	169	132	163	154	171	188	189
Spain	2,007	1,660	1,240	1,479	1,727	1,475	2,177	2,503
Turkey	2,006	1,780	1,530	1,491	1,505	1,471	1,524	1,581
United Kingdom	11,207	10,752	9,229	9,382	9,317	9,450	9,231	8,920
DEPLOYMENTS								
Operation Enduring Freedom (OEF) [4]	(X)	19,500	105,900	109,200	78,055	66,732	33,427	(NA)
Operation Iraqi Freedom (OIF) and Operation New Dawn (OND) [5]	(X)	192,600	96,200	92,200	1,171	342	494	(NA)

X Not applicable. NA Not available. [1] Includes items not shown separately, and also personnel in unknown and classified locations. [2] British Indian Ocean Territory. [3] Military personnel data for Kuwait are included with the Operation New Dawn (OND) data. [4] Total (in/around Afghanistan as of September 30) includes Reserve/National Guard. [5] Total (in/around Iraq as of September 30) includes Reserve/National Guard. Prior to 2010, operations in/around Iraq were known as Operation Iraqi Freedom (OIF).

Source: U.S. Department of Defense, DoD Personnel and Procurement Statistics, "Active Duty Military Personnel By Service By Region/Country," November 2015 and earlier reports, <https://www.dmdc.osd.mil/>, accessed March 2016.

Table 535. Suicides and Attempted Suicides of Military Personnel by Selected Characteristics: 2010 to 2015

[Data are shown for suicides reported in Department of Defense Suicide Event Report (DoDSER). Covers all service members in active status at time of event, including Reserve component service members in active status. DoDSER standardizes suicide surveillance efforts across the military services to support the DoD's suicide prevention mission. Confirmed suicides are those that have been confirmed by the Armed Forces Medical Examiner System (AFMES)]

Characteristics	Suicides						Suicide attempts reported [2]					
	2010	2011	2012	2013 [1]	2014 [1]	2015 [1]	2010	2011	2012	2013	2014	2015
Suicide attempts reported...........	(X)	(X)	(X)	(X)	(X)	(X)	863	935	869	1,080	1,126	1,199
Suicides confirmed/pending confirmation [1]......................	295	301	319	256	276	266	(X)	(X)	(X)	(X)	(X)	(X)
By sex:												
Male................................	281	285	295	241	256	252	653	687	663	796	824	847
Female..............................	14	16	24	15	20	14	210	248	206	284	302	352
By race/ethnicity: [3]												
White...............................	235	231	244	192	199	186	587	600	589	799	788	837
Black or African American.........	36	37	44	32	42	45	133	172	165	171	233	237
Asian or Pacific Islander..........	16	17	13	8	8	12	23	36	28	50	38	51
American Indian or Alaska Native...............................	6	6	4	8	3	4	11	13	11	17	20	18
By Hispanic origin:												
Hispanic or Latino.................	(NA)	18	27	21	34	29	(NA)	99	102	122	134	166
Non-Hispanic or Latino............	(NA)	283	287	232	240	229	(NA)	836	641	953	990	1,031
Unknown...........................	(NA)	(NA)	(NA)	3	2	8	(NA)	(NA)	(NA)	(NA)	(NA)	2
By age: [3]												
Under 25 years old.................	140	114	130	108	102	109	514	535	506	616	620	748
25-29 years old....................	76	91	89	72	73	61	190	220	201	236	261	254
30-39 years old....................	63	68	81	57	82	76	122	141	121	169	194	158
40 years old and over.............	16	28	19	19	19	20	37	39	40	55	51	39
By marital status: [3]												
Never married......................	125	107	134	106	105	116	364	390	385	510	518	589
Married.............................	147	167	171	126	145	132	364	406	364	499	526	513
Legally separated..................	1	–	–	2	–	–	41	28	21	5	5	10
Divorced...........................	20	23	14	22	25	17	73	80	59	62	74	86
Widowed...........................	–	4	–	–	1	1	1	1	2	1	2	1

– Represents zero. X Not applicable. NA Not available. [1] Data for 2013-2015 do not include selected reserve members in active status. [2] Data are for DoDSERS submitted for suicides, which may include more than one report per individual. [3] Includes other or unknown, not shown separately.

Source: U.S. Department of Defense, National Center for Telehealth and Technology, *Department of Defense Suicide Event Report, Calendar Year 2015 Annual Report*, 2017, and earlier reports. See also <http://t2health.dcoe.mil/programs/dodser>.

Table 536. Sexual Assault in the Military—Incident Reports and Victims by Type of Report and Selected Characteristics: 2010 to 2016

[Data are for fiscal years. Reports of sexual assault (rape, aggravated sexual assault, sexual assault, aggravated sexual contact, abusive sexual contact, wrongful sexual contact, non-consensual sodomy, and attempts to commit these offenses) by or against Service Members. Restricted Reporting allows victim confidential access to medical care and advocacy services. When a victim makes an Unrestricted Report, the report is also referred to a Military Criminal Investigation Organization for investigation and command is notified]

Item	Unrestricted				Restricted [1]			
	2010	2014	2015	2016	2010	2014	2015	2016
REPORTS [2]								
Total......................	**2,410**	**4,611**	**4,510**	**4,499**	**882**	**1,471**	**1,499**	**1,581**
Service member on service member....................	1,358	2,502	2,379	2,232	352	577	711	720
Service member on non-service member..............	691	712	779	739	(NA)	33	25	39
Non-service member on service member..............	104	206	196	157	115	397	323	407
Unidentified subject on service member.................	257	555	592	785	415	226	355	345
VICTIMS IN COMPLETED INVESTIGATIONS [3]								
Total......................	**1,741**	**4,241**	**4,303**	**4,409**	(X)	(X)	(X)	(X)
Service member victims.....................	1,303	3,357	3,422	3,551	(X)	(X)	(X)	(X)
Non-service member victims................	438	884	881	858	(X)	(X)	(X)	(X)
VICTIMS [4, 5]								
By sex:								
Male................................	180	735	807	824	114	243	313	312
Female..............................	1,561	3,310	3,457	3,558	739	1,224	1,178	1,266
By age:								
0-15 years old.......................	(NA)	19	37	45	(NA)	192	157	182
16-19 years old......................	324	851	967	1,028	191	339	346	359
20-24 years old......................	864	1,820	1,815	1,858	392	577	590	616
25-34 years old......................	402	770	845	842	188	251	295	307
35-49 years old......................	96	195	213	193	49	59	61	68
50-64 years old......................	8	18	10	17	–	1	6	4
65 years and older...................	–	1	2	21	–	–	–	–
SERVICE MEMBER VICTIMS [5]								
By service branch:								
Army................................	681	1,402	1,569	1,567	327	400	470	485
Navy................................	302	914	848	951	169	287	361	355
Marines.............................	134	428	392	424	51	354	277	303
Air Force............................	183	611	608	607	287	391	355	392
Coast Guard.........................	3	1	3	1	4	1	–	1

– Represents zero. X Not applicable. NA Not available. [1] For 2010 service member victims only. Beginning in 2011, data shown for all victims. [2] Reports of sexual assault during the fiscal year. [3] Victims in investigations completed during the fiscal year. [4] For unrestricted reports, data shown for victims in investigations completed during the fiscal year. [5] Includes other and unknown, not shown separately.

Source: U.S. Department of Defense, *Annual Report on Sexual Assault in the Military, Fiscal Year 2016*, May 2017, and earlier reports. See also <http://sapr.mil/index.php/reports>.

Table 537. U.S. Military Sales and Assistance to Foreign Governments: 1990 to 2015

[In millions of dollars (14,588 represents $14,588,000,000). For year ending September 30. Department of Defense (DoD) sales deliveries cover deliveries against sales orders authorized under Arms Export Control Act, as well as earlier and applicable legislation. For details regarding individual programs, see source]

Item	1990	2000	2005	2010	2011	2012	2013	2014	2015
Military sales agreements	14,588	11,403	9,019	22,926	27,453	68,698	24,535	33,278	40,629
Military construction sales agreements	628	284	300	900	496	890	340	1,418	440
Military sales deliveries [1]	8,360	10,939	11,322	13,476	13,757	14,312	15,743	15,381	17,178
Military construction sales deliveries	348	183	349	459	511	488	497	389	493
Military financing program	4,354	4,333	4,956	5,016	5,320	5,929	4,874	4,601	5,212
Commercial exports licensed under Arms Export Control Act [2]	6,216	478	30,146	–	–	–	–	–	–
Military assistance program delivery [3]	125	5	71	–	15	–	60	111	101
IMET program/deliveries [4]	43	50	86	108	106	105	99	103	104

– Represents or rounds to zero. [1] Includes military construction sales deliveries. [2] The total dollar value of deliveries made for purchases of munitions-controlled items by foreign governments directly from U.S. manufacturers. [3] Includes Military Assistance Service Funded (MASF) program data and Section 506(a) drawdown authority. [4] International Military Education and Training. Includes military assistance services and emergency drawdowns.

Source: U.S. Department of Defense, Defense Security Cooperation Agency, DSCA Data & Statistics, *DSCA Fiscal Year Series, as of September 30, 2015*. See also <http://dsca.mil/publications>.

Table 538. U.S. Military Sales Deliveries by Selected Country: 2000 to 2015

[In millions of dollars (10,939 represents $10,939,000,000). For year ending September 30. Represents Department of Defense military sales]

Country	2000	2005	2009	2010	2011	2012	2013	2014	2015
Total [1]	10,939	11,322	16,433	13,476	13,757	14,312	15,743	15,381	17,178
International organizations	61	62	4,022	86	147	116	166	167	124
Afghanistan	–	340	11	18	17	4	8	34	87
Argentina	10	4	10	26	12	14	13	16	85
Australia	332	350	374	914	731	632	634	804	2,313
Bahrain	55	63	101	111	51	98	69	56	40
Belgium	61	49	39	26	27	57	22	49	67
Brazil	61	10	44	29	36	133	54	52	73
Canada	84	150	518	381	395	287	289	243	180
Colombia	14	41	112	428	149	122	146	91	77
Denmark	43	40	43	43	67	45	91	51	85
Ecuador	1	4	1	3	1	1	2	1	–
Egypt	1,186	1,454	922	956	917	846	1,552	949	480
El Salvador	14	3	10	6	5	6	4	2	2
Finland	690	38	82	127	94	82	103	62	135
France	217	69	58	112	132	125	184	143	295
Georgia	3	12	18	10	28	18	36	14	9
Germany	136	207	162	296	160	141	148	163	139
Greece	389	466	1,249	265	149	163	61	94	120
India	–	100	15	31	57	167	194	370	704
Iraq	–	–	720	400	765	610	520	1,119	1,658
Israel	550	1,612	779	938	789	925	937	897	661
Italy	51	126	92	179	101	87	69	78	86
Japan	432	410	857	779	435	498	352	526	1,325
Jordan	52	140	182	173	212	377	337	282	194
Kenya	2	7	6	2	16	29	3	4	3
Korea, South	1,399	581	475	594	712	723	605	637	505
Kuwait	321	291	252	242	434	262	303	554	374
Malaysia	411	49	23	45	29	35	41	46	95
Mexico	9	4	4	59	38	8	20	195	19
Morocco	8	17	10	28	981	434	213	79	43
Netherlands	278	177	248	200	184	177	134	145	199
Nigeria	–	7	3	5	13	8	14	10	34
Norway	64	106	281	127	147	94	170	143	138
Pakistan	–	61	117	1,129	549	382	277	339	176
Poland	13	84	133	74	190	162	154	87	130
Portugal	20	84	94	29	36	46	16	18	21
Saudi Arabia	1,988	872	1,722	1,679	1,485	1,607	3,318	2,331	2,890
Singapore	131	229	188	296	250	241	211	223	141
Spain	141	125	173	152	98	67	98	113	89
Taiwan	784	1,399	639	863	767	975	784	1,681	1,103
Thailand	114	91	47	41	89	62	82	100	80
Turkey	216	185	306	251	876	1,240	664	195	427
Ukraine	1	2	5	21	8	4	4	10	19
United Arab Emirates	3	149	119	583	639	1,355	767	804	454
United Kingdom	347	380	753	265	343	311	1,295	403	309

– Represents or rounds to zero. [1] Includes countries not shown.

Source: U.S. Department of Defense, Defense Security Cooperation Agency, DSCA Historical Facts Book & Fiscal Year Series, *DSCA Fiscal Year Series, as of September 30, 2015*. See also <http://dsca.mil/resources/dsca-historical-facts-book-fiscal-year-series>.

National Security and Veterans Affairs

Table 539. Arms Transfer Agreements with Developing Nations by Supplier Country: 2008 to 2015

[In millions of constant 2015 U.S. dollars (57,475 is $57,475,000,000). Developing nations category excludes the United States, Europe, Canada, Japan, Australia, and New Zealand. All data are for the calendar year given except for U.S. MAP (Military Assistance Program), IMET (International Military Education and Training), and Excess Defense Article data, which are included for the particular fiscal year. All amounts given include the values of all categories of weapons, spare parts, construction, all associated services, military assistance, excess defense articles, and training programs. Statistics for foreign countries are based upon estimated selling prices. All foreign data are rounded to the nearest $100 million]

Supplier	2008	2009	2010	2011	2012	2013	2014	2015 [1]	2008-2015
Total	57,475	59,841	35,029	82,700	58,276	58,234	80,699	65,243	497,496
United States	30,714	14,614	15,988	59,873	11,891	18,404	30,246	26,743	208,473
Russia	6,098	16,598	7,399	6,080	17,525	11,041	10,375	11,000	86,116
France	6,323	10,360	2,067	5,013	3,253	3,921	5,696	15,200	51,834
United Kingdom	0	1,225	1,306	533	5,982	3,715	407	700	13,868
China	2,484	3,342	2,176	3,413	3,673	4,437	3,357	6,000	28,882
Germany	3,388	2,451	109	107	5,142	7,223	407	700	19,526
Italy	1,581	1,448	1,306	1,173	1,574	929	1,119	1,000	10,130
All other European	4,630	5,124	3,046	3,093	6,087	3,715	24,819	2,900	53,415
All others	2,258	4,679	1,632	3,413	3,148	4,850	4,272	1,000	25,253

[1] Data are rounded to the nearest $100 million.

Source: Congressional Research Service, *Conventional Arms Transfers to Developing Nations, 2008-2015*, R44716, December 2016.

Table 540. Veterans by Selected Period of Service and State and Other Areas: 2015

[In thousands (21,681 represents 21,681,000). As of September 30. The Veteran Population Projection Model 2014 (VetPop2014) is the Department of Veterans Affairs (VA) latest official estimate and projection of the veteran population. It is based on tabulations prepared for the VA Office of the Actuary; recent American Community Survey, Internal Revenue Service, and Social Security Administration data; administrative data and projections of service member separations from active duty provided by the Department of Defense, Defense Manpower Data Center and the Office of the Actuary; and VA data on veterans benefits]

State/Area	Total [1,2]	Gulf War era [3]	Vietnam era [4]	State/Area	Total [1,2]	Gulf War era [3]	Vietnam era [4]
United States	21,681	7,252	7,103	Montana	99	32	35
Alabama	412	161	132	Nebraska	141	51	46
Alaska	73	38	20	Nevada	225	73	79
Arizona	528	166	184	New Hampshire	111	32	37
Arkansas	248	88	82	New Jersey	413	103	138
California	1,802	566	604	New Mexico	170	55	61
Colorado	409	156	138	New York	863	227	270
Connecticut	207	52	69	North Carolina	774	301	246
Delaware	77	25	25	North Dakota	57	23	17
District of Columbia	29	11	8	Ohio	848	243	288
Florida	1,558	474	506	Oklahoma	336	122	112
Georgia	752	305	232	Oregon	326	88	122
Hawaii	120	54	37	Pennsylvania	917	242	303
Idaho	132	46	48	Rhode Island	70	20	22
Illinois	706	212	236	South Carolina	418	153	140
Indiana	469	144	147	South Dakota	72	26	22
Iowa	228	68	77	Tennessee	504	172	166
Kansas	218	80	72	Texas	1,675	679	533
Kentucky	328	114	110	Utah	151	59	46
Louisiana	326	128	104	Vermont	48	14	16
Maine	125	36	44	Virginia	783	398	218
Maryland	430	171	124	Washington	598	216	204
Massachusetts	368	88	122	West Virginia	166	50	59
Michigan	641	158	233	Wisconsin	406	114	138
Minnesota	361	100	127	Wyoming	50	20	17
Mississippi	219	86	67	Puerto Rico	90	22	29
Missouri	488	152	165	Island Areas & Foreign	111	36	32

[1] Veterans serving in more than one period of service are counted only once in the total. [2] Current civilians discharged from active duty, other than for training only without service-connected disability. [3] Service from August 2, 1990 to the present. [4] Service from August 5, 1964 to May 7, 1975.

Source: U.S. Department of Veterans Affairs, National Center for Veterans Analysis and Statistics, "The Veteran Population Projection Model 2014 (VetPop2014)," <http://www.va.gov/vetdata/veteran_population.asp>, accessed January 2015.

Table 541. Veterans Benefits—Expenditures by Program and Compensation for Service-Connected Disabilities: 2000 to 2016

[In millions of dollars (47,086 represents $47,086,000,000). For years ending September 30]

Program	2000	2005	2010	2011	2012	2013	2014	2015	2016
Total expenditures	**47,086**	**69,667**	**108,635**	**122,859**	**120,405**	**142,822**	**161,229**	**167,210**	**173,686**
Medical programs	19,637	29,433	42,372	43,085	45,521	55,994	59,424	65,561	63,473
Construction	466	483	1,618	1,813	1,538	1,330	1,536	1,828	1,708
General operating expenses	1,016	1,294	6,101	6,655	6,445	6,890	7,602	8,056	7,898
Compensation and pension	22,012	34,694	47,785	57,596	53,243	63,575	75,265	75,787	84,028
Vocational rehabilitation and education	1,610	2,937	8,260	10,630	10,425	11,949	13,681	13,408	13,838
All other [1]	2,345	826	2,499	3,079	3,233	3,085	3,721	2,570	2,740
Compensation for service-connected disabilities	15,511	24,515	36,486	39,374	44,359	49,150	54,230	60,210	64,710

[1] Includes insurance, indemnities, and miscellaneous funds and expenditures and offsets from public receipts. (Excludes expenditures from personal funds of patients.)

Source: U.S. Department of Veterans Affairs, "Summary of Expenditures By State," <http://www.va.gov/vetdata/Expenditures.asp>, accessed July 2017; and *Annual Benefits Report*, July 2017, and earlier reports. See also <http://www.benefits.va.gov/REPORTS/annual_benefits_report.asp>.

Table 542. Veterans Compensation and Pension Benefits—Number on Rolls by Period of Service and Status: 1990 to 2016

[In thousands (3,584 represents 3,584,000). As of September 30. Living veterans refers to veterans receiving compensation for disability incurred or aggravated while on active duty, and war veterans receiving pension benefits for non-service connected disabilities and/or who are age 65 and older. Survivors include veterans' spouses, dependent children, and (based on need) dependent parents of veterans]

Period of service and veteran status	1990	2000	2005	2010	2011	2012	2013	2014	2015	2016
Total	**3,584**	**3,236**	**3,503**	**4,070**	**4,226**	**4,425**	**4,639**	**4,848**	**5,061**	**5,247**
Living veterans	2,746	2,672	2,973	3,524	3,668	3,852	4,051	4,254	4,464	4,645
Compensation [1]	2,184	2,308	2,637	3,210	3,355	3,537	3,743	3,949	4,169	4,356
Pension [2]	562	364	336	314	314	315	308	305	295	289
Survivors of veterans	838	564	530	546	557	574	587	594	597	602
Compensation [1]	320	307	323	347	355	366	377	382	390	399
Pension [2]	518	257	207	199	202	207	210	212	206	203
World War I and earlier	198	34	13	6	5	5	4	4	3	3
Living veterans	18	(Z)	(Z)	(Z)	(Z)	(Z)	(Z)	(Z)	(Z)	(Z)
World War II	1,723	968	718	529	498	469	434	399	357	320
Living veterans	1,294	676	466	298	271	245	215	189	160	135
Korean conflict [3]	390	323	295	275	275	274	271	268	262	256
Living veterans	305	255	231	209	207	204	199	194	186	178
Vietnam era [4]	774	969	1,218	1,447	1,524	1,594	1,660	1,716	1,765	1,803
Living veterans	685	848	1,068	1,261	1,326	1,381	1,433	1,477	1,514	1,538
Gulf War era [5]	(X)	334	630	1,140	1,239	1,383	1,561	1,723	1,915	2,090
Living veterans	(X)	326	617	1,117	1,215	1,357	1,523	1,694	1,883	2,057
Peacetime	495	607	627	673	685	701	709	738	759	775
Living veterans	444	567	591	638	650	665	683	700	720	737

X Not applicable. Z Fewer than 500. [1] Compensation is based on military service-connected disability and death. [2] Pension is based on need and includes coverage for veterans with disabilities not connected to military service. [3] Service during period June 27, 1950 to January 31, 1955. [4] Service from August 5, 1964 to May 7, 1975. [5] Service from August 2, 1990 to the present.

Source: U.S. Department of Veterans Affairs, 1990 to 1995, *Annual Report of the Secretary of Veterans Affairs*; 1996 to 2010, *Annual Accountability Report* and unpublished data; and beginning 2011, *Annual Benefits Report, Fiscal Year 2016*, June 2017 and earlier reports. See also <https://www.benefits.va.gov/REPORTS/>.

Table 543. Veterans Living by Period of Service, Age, and Sex: 2015

[20,784 represents 20,784,000. As of September 30. Includes veterans living outside the United States. Based on a projection model]

Period of service and age	Total	Male	Female	Period of service and age	Total	Male	Female
Total	**20,784**	**18,948**	**1,836**	30 to 34 years old	981	797	184
PERIOD OF SERVICE				35 to 39 years old	968	787	181
Wartime vets [1]	15,987	14,582	1,405	40 to 44 years old	1,064	896	168
Gulf War Era [2]	6,882	5,784	1,098	45 to 49 years old	1,438	1,242	196
Vietnam Era [3]	7,013	6,773	241	50 to 54 years old	1,694	1,475	219
Korean conflict [4]	1,803	1,753	51	55 to 59 years old	1,929	1,708	221
World War II	939	896	43	60 to 64 years old	1,937	1,771	166
Peacetime	4,796	4,365	431	65 to 69 years old	2,928	2,832	96
AGE				70 to 74 years old	2,168	2,106	61
Under 20 years old	12	8	3	75 to 79 years old	1,525	1,482	43
20 to 24 years old	281	224	57	80 to 84 years old	1,459	1,420	39
25 to 29 years old	748	612	136	85 years & over	1,651	1,585	66

[1] Veterans who served in more than one wartime period are counted only once in the total. [2] Service from August 2, 1990 to the present. [3] Service from August 5, 1964 to May 7, 1975. [4] Service during period June 27, 1950 to January 31, 1955.

Source: U.S. Department of Veterans Affairs, National Center for Veterans Analysis and Statistics, "Veteran Population 2016," <https://www.va.gov/vetdata/Veteran_Population.asp>, accessed August 2017.

Table 544. Veteran Income, Education, Poverty, and Disability Status Compared to Nonveteran Population: 2014 and 2015

[244,299 represents 244,299,000. Data are based on American Community Survey (ACS). The ACS universe includes the civilian household and group quarters population. Based on a sample and subject to sampling variability]

Characteristic	2014			2015		
	Total	Veterans	Nonveterans	Total	Veterans	Nonveterans
Population 18 years old and over (1,000)...............	**244,299**	**19,260**	**225,039**	**246,780**	**18,830**	**227,950**
INCOME						
Median income in past 12 months (dollars) [1]...............	27,168	36,927	26,398	28,385	38,334	27,248
Male..	(NA)	37,307	32,433	(NA)	38,978	34,168
Female...	(NA)	31,810	21,804	(NA)	32,446	22,505
EDUCATIONAL ATTAINMENT						
Population 25 years old and over.............................	213,128	18,982	194,146	215,829	18,572	197,256
Less than high school graduate (percent)...................	13.1	6.9	13.7	12.9	6.6	13.5
High school graduate or equivalency (percent)............	27.8	29.0	27.6	27.6	28.6	27.5
Some college or associate's degree (percent).............	29.1	36.9	28.3	28.9	37.1	28.2
Bachelor's degree or higher (percent)......................	30.0	27.2	30.3	30.6	27.7	30.8
POVERTY AND DISABILITY STATUS						
Population for whom poverty status is determined..........	237,845	18,906	218,939	240,326	18,496	221,830
Below poverty in the past 12 months (percent)............	13.7	7.2	14.2	13.0	6.9	13.5
With any disability (percent)................................	15.4	28.7	14.2	15.3	28.9	14.2

NA Not available. [1] For population with income.

Source: U.S. Census Bureau, American Community Survey, S2101, "Veteran Status," <http://factfinder.census.gov>, accessed December 2016.

Table 545. Veterans by Sex, Race, and Hispanic Origin: 2014 and 2015

[See headnote, Table 544]

Characteristic	2014			2015		
	Total veterans	18 to 64 years	65 years and over	Total veterans	18 to 64 years	65 years and over
Total....................................	**19,259,717**	**9,899,301**	**9,360,416**	**18,830,450**	**9,514,621**	**9,315,829**
Male..	17,681,070	8,602,870	9,078,200	17,254,563	8,223,644	9,030,919
Female.....................................	1,578,647	1,296,431	282,216	1,575,887	1,290,977	284,910
White alone...............................	16,039,351	7,621,253	8,418,098	15,618,397	7,262,194	8,356,203
Male..	14,888,808	6,716,842	8,171,966	14,477,088	6,367,071	8,110,017
Female.....................................	1,150,543	904,411	246,132	1,141,309	895,123	246,186
Black or African American alone........	2,196,289	1,562,848	633,441	2,183,616	1,539,890	643,726
Male..	1,900,499	1,289,711	610,788	1,876,513	1,258,398	618,115
Female.....................................	295,790	273,137	22,653	307,103	281,492	25,611
American Indian/Alaska Native alone..	140,556	94,141	46,415	130,802	81,855	48,947
Male..	123,144	79,333	43,811	116,361	68,931	47,430
Female.....................................	17,412	14,808	2,604	14,441	12,924	1,517
Asian alone...............................	286,926	175,425	111,501	283,827	173,146	110,681
Male..	254,801	147,854	106,947	251,969	146,113	105,856
Female.....................................	32,125	27,571	4,554	31,858	27,033	4,825
Native Hawaiian and other Pacific Islander alone..........................	30,990	22,974	8,016	29,833	21,197	8,636
Male..	27,060	19,652	7,408	24,261	16,307	7,954
Female.....................................	3,930	3,322	608	5,572	4,890	682
Some other race alone..................	225,165	174,426	50,739	235,405	179,347	56,058
Male..	198,666	149,302	49,364	209,302	154,647	54,655
Female.....................................	26,499	25,124	1,375	26,103	24,700	1,403
Two or more races.......................	340,440	248,234	92,206	348,570	256,992	91,578
Male..	288,092	200,176	87,916	299,069	212,177	86,892
Female.....................................	52,348	48,058	4,290	49,501	44,815	4,686
Hispanic or Latino origin [1]...............	1,171,596	825,471	346,125	1,206,698	849,684	357,014
Male..	1,049,168	714,750	334,418	1,070,627	727,265	343,362
Female.....................................	122,428	110,721	11,707	136,071	122,419	13,652

[1] Persons of Hispanic or Latino origin may be of any race.

Source: U.S. Census Bureau, American Community Survey, Tables B21001, B21001A, B21001B, B21001C, B21001D, B21001E, B21001F, B21001G, and B21001I, <http://factfinder.census.gov>, accessed December 2016.

Table 546. Homeland Security Funding by Agency: Fiscal Years 2010 to 2016

[In millions of dollars (70,009 represents 70,009,000,000). A total of 29 agencies comprise federal homeland security funding. Department of Homeland Security (DHS) is the designated department to coordinate and centralize the leadership of many homeland security activities under a single department. In addition to DHS, the Departments of Defense (DoD), Justice (DoJ), Health and Human Services (HHS), State Department and Energy (DOE) account for 94% of the total government-wide homeland security funding. Data reflect the Executive Branch's homeland security activities, and do not include the activities of the Legislative or Judicial branches]

Agency	2010	2011	2012	2013	2014	2015 [1]	2016 [1]
Total budget authority [2]	**70,009**	**66,983**	**68,586**	**66,037**	**66,244**	**71,760**	**71,679**
Department of Agriculture	614	580	435	431	509	452	577
Department of Commerce [3]	284	262	338	613	2,104	5,389	1,374
Department of Defense	19,054	16,994	17,780	16,527	11,908	12,363	13,708
Department of Education	29	30	31	31	37	36	52
Department of Energy	2,016	1,994	1,938	1,991	1,910	1,931	2,048
Department of Health and Human Services	7,196	4,182	4,118	4,016	4,784	4,753	5,328
Department of Homeland Security [4]	32,609	34,901	35,088	33,715	35,763	36,635	37,601
Department of Housing and Urban Development	5	3	2	2	3	1	1
Department of the Interior	52	58	58	57	55	54	58
Department of Justice	4,094	3,966	4,039	3,685	4,018	4,081	4,149
Department of Labor	40	43	46	37	36	29	29
Department of State	1,793	1,949	2,674	2,929	3,029	3,642	4,345
Department of Transportation	228	243	245	249	207	308	343
Department of the Treasury	125	126	122	119	112	122	122
Department of Veterans Affairs	427	413	381	368	312	368	335
Corps of Engineers	36	36	15	16	8	11	11
Environmental Protection Agency	154	108	102	96	94	91	91
Executive Office of the President	12	9	10	9	8	9	10
General Services Administration	214	19	38	36	225	371	321
National Aeronautics and Space Administration	218	228	225	209	226	231	251
National Science Foundation	390	386	444	434	443	431	439
Office of Personnel Management	2	2	1	1	(NA)	(NA)	(NA)
Social Security Administration	190	213	212	231	207	231	256
District of Columbia	15	15	15	23	24	13	13
Federal Communications Commission	1	3	3	1	1	2	2
Intelligence Community Management Account [5]	14	13	9	(X)	(X)	(X)	(X)
National Archives and Records Administration	20	22	23	23	27	26	25
Nuclear Regulatory Commission	65	73	79	74	76	61	64
Securities and Exchange Commission	6	6	8	8	8	7	9
Smithsonian Institution	99	98	97	97	101	102	107
United States Holocaust Memorial Museum	10	10	11	11	11	11	12

X Not applicable. NA Not available. [1] In addition, Homeland Security Budget Authority includes $1,088.1 million in FY2015 supplemental emergency funding. [2] The Department of Homeland Security Appropriations Act, 2004, provided $5.6 billion for Project BioShield, to remain available through 2013. Including this uneven funding stream can distort year-over-year comparisons. [3] Funding increases for FY2014-FY2016 reflect non-recurrence of authority to build a nationwide interoperable public safety broadband network for first responders and related programs. [4] Not all activities carried out by DHS constitute homeland security funding (e.g. response to natural disasters and Coast Guard search and rescue activities). DHS estimates in this table do not represent the entire DHS budget. See Table 547. [5] Funding for Intelligence Community Management Account was moved under DoD beginning in 2013.

Source: U.S. Office of Management and Budget, *Budget of the U.S. Government, Fiscal Year 2017: Analytical Perspectives*, February 2016, and earlier reports. See also <http://www.whitehouse.gov/omb/budget/>.

Table 547. Department of Homeland Security Total Budget Authority and Personnel by Organization: 2016 and 2017

[65,674,835 represents $65,674,835,000. For the fiscal year ending September 30. Not all activities carried out by the Department of Homeland Security (DHS) constitute homeland security funding (e.g., Coast Guard search and rescue activities)]

Organization or activity	Budget authority (thousand dollars)		Full-time employees (number)	
	2016 [1]	2017	2016 [1]	2017
Total	**65,674,835**	**65,978,997**	**217,150**	**218,403**
Departmental management and operations [2]	1,082,413	1,095,607	2,041	2,399
Analysis and operations	260,224	254,303	818	818
Office of the Inspector General	161,467	137,151	796	796
U.S. Customs & Border Protection	13,295,208	13,474,495	58,677	58,677
U.S. Immigration & Customs Enforcement	6,177,578	6,139,917	19,908	19,987
Transportation Security Administration	7,543,364	7,425,805	51,833	51,309
U.S. Coast Guard	10,893,631	10,940,660	46,555	47,927
U.S. Secret Service	2,191,808	2,190,481	6,481	6,481
National Protection and Programs Directorate	3,075,838	3,081,428	3,178	3,299
Office of Health Affairs	125,333	122,747	96	96
Federal Emergency Management Agency (FEMA)	15,712,464	16,151,751	9,673	9,838
FEMA Grants [3]	2,752,652	2,747,992	([4])	([4])
U.S. Citizenship & Immigration Services	3,787,338	3,606,909	15,371	15,091
Federal Law Enforcement Training Center	244,480	243,994	1,106	1,068
Science & Technology Directorate (S&T)	776,653	771,690	480	480
Domestic Nuclear Detection Office	347,036	342,059	137	137
CBRNE [5]	(NA)	501,445	233	276

NA Not available. [1] Revised enacted. [2] Comprised of the Office of the Secretary & Executive Management, the Under Secretary for Management, the Office of the Chief Financial Officer, the Office of the Chief Information Officer, and DHS Headquarters Consolidation. [3] Includes State and Local Programs and Emergency Management Performance Grants, and Assistance to Firefighters Grants. [4] Employee data are included among FEMA full-time employees. [5] The Chemical, Biological, Radiological, Nuclear, and Explosives Office (CBRNE) is established as of FY2017.

Source: U.S. Department of Homeland Security, *Budget-in-Brief, Fiscal Year 2018*, 2017. See also <http://www.dhs.gov/dhs-budget>.

Table 548. Homeland Security Grants by State and Outlying Area: 2016 and 2017

[In thousands of dollars (1,037,000 represents $1,037,000,000). For years ending September 30. The Homeland Security Grant Program consists of the following: State Homeland Security Program (SHSP), Urban Areas Security Initiative (UASI), and Operation Stonegarden]

State/territory	2016	2017	State/territory	2016	2017	State/territory	2016	2017
Total........	1,037,000	1,037,000	KS...........	3,735	3,752	OK...........	3,735	3,752
			KY...........	3,978	3,962	OR...........	6,799	6,659
U.S............	1,028,540	1,028,693	LA...........	4,323	4,182	PA...........	31,389	30,768
			ME...........	4,535	4,652	RI...........	3,735	3,752
AL............	3,885	3,872	MD...........	9,116	10,349	SC...........	3,735	3,752
AK............	3,735	3,752	MA...........	23,415	22,898	SD...........	3,735	3,752
AZ............	21,798	21,531	MI...........	12,827	12,714	TN...........	3,978	3,962
AR............	3,735	3,752	MN...........	9,880	9,652	TX...........	80,593	80,206
CA............	194,237	192,018	MS...........	3,915	3,902	UT...........	3,735	4,752
CO............	6,941	6,800	MO...........	6,940	6,799	VT...........	3,985	4,087
CT............	3,978	3,962	MT...........	4,612	4,810	VA...........	7,446	8,429
DE............	3,735	3,752	NE...........	3,735	3,752	WA...........	13,273	13,205
DC............	57,451	56,934	NV...........	6,697	6,589	WV...........	3,735	3,752
FL............	20,748	20,176	NH...........	3,858	3,912	WI...........	3,978	3,962
GA............	12,237	15,220	NJ...........	28,888	28,371	WY...........	3,735	3,752
HI............	3,735	3,752	NM...........	6,435	6,472	AS [1]........	854	858
ID............	3,760	3,787	NY...........	257,237	256,875	GU [1]........	854	858
IL............	85,019	84,502	NC...........	8,451	8,309	MP [1]........	854	858
IN............	3,978	4,962	ND...........	4,321	4,405	PR [1]........	4,915	4,757
IA............	3,735	3,752	OH...........	11,361	11,273	VI [1]........	984	978

[1] AS—American Samoa, GU—Guam, MP—Northern Mariana Islands, PR—Puerto Rico, VI—Virgin Islands.

Source: U.S. Department of Homeland Security, *Grant Programs Directorate Information Bulletin*, No. 422, September 2017, and earlier reports. See also <http://www.fema.gov/preparedness-non-disaster-grants>.

Table 549. Urban Areas Security Initiative (UASI) Grant Program: 2017

[In thousands of dollars (580,000 represents $580,000,000). For year ending September 30. The UASI Program provides financial assistance to address the unique multi-disciplinary planning, operations, equipment, training, and exercise needs of high-threat, high-density urban areas. A total of 33 high-threat, high-density urban areas were eligible for funding under the FY2017 UASI program. For a listing of all grant programs and their descriptions, see <http://www.fema.gov/preparedness-non-disaster-grants>]

State	Urban area	Amount	State	Urban area	Amount
Total...........	(X)	580,000	MI..............	Detroit	5,180
AZ.............	Phoenix	5,180	MN.............	Minneapolis-Saint Paul (Twin Cities)	5,180
CA.............	Anaheim/Santa Ana	5,180	MO.............	St. Louis	2,837
CA.............	San Francisco Bay Area	27,536	NV.............	Las Vegas	2,837
CA.............	Los Angeles/Long Beach	68,110	NJ.............	Jersey City/Newark	20,034
CA.............	Riverside	2,837	NY.............	New York City	178,123
CA.............	Sacramento	2,837	NC.............	Charlotte	2,837
CA.............	San Diego	16,158	OH.............	Cleveland	2,837
CO.............	Denver	2,837	OR.............	Portland	2,837
DC.............	National Capital Region	52,809	PA.............	Philadelphia	17,763
FL.............	Miami/Fort Lauderdale	5,180	PA.............	Pittsburgh	2,837
FL.............	Tampa	2,837	TX.............	Dallas/Fort Worth/Arlington	14,802
GA.............	Atlanta	8,430	TX.............	Houston	23,193
IL.............	Chicago	68,110	TX.............	San Antonio Area	1,000
IN.............	Indianapolis	1,000	UT.............	Salt Lake City Area	1,000
MD.............	Baltimore	4,212	VA.............	Hampton Roads Area	1,000
MA.............	Boston	17,270	WA.............	Seattle	5,180

X Not applicable.

Source: U.S. Department of Homeland Security, *Grant Programs Directorate Information Bulletin*, No. 422, September 2017, and earlier reports. See also <http://www.fema.gov/preparedness-non-disaster-grants>.

Table 550. Preparedness Grant Programs: 2010 to 2017

[In millions of dollars (2,968 represents $2,968,000,000. For years ending September 30]

Program	2010	2011	2012	2013	2014	2015	2016	2017
Total [1].................	2,968	2,191	1,381	1,507	1,616	1,617	[2] 1,617	1,622
Homeland Security Grant Program [1]...............	1,786	1,289	831	968	1,043	1,044	1,037	1,037
State Homeland Security Program...............	842	527	294	355	401	402	402	402
Urban Areas Security Initiative..............	833	663	490	559	587	587	580	580
Operation Stonegarden................	60	55	47	55	55	55	55	55
Emergency Management Performance Grants Program...............	330	329	340	332	350	350	350	350
Tribal Homeland Security Grant Program..............	10	10	6	10	10	10	10	10
Nonprofit Security Grant Program..............	19	19	10	10	13	13	20	25
Transit Security Grant Program [1]...............	253	200	88	84	90	87	87	88
Port Security Grant Program..............	288	235	98	93	100	100	100	100
Intercity Bus Security Grant Program..............	12	5	(NA)	(NA)	(NA)	3	3	2

NA Not available. [1] Includes programs not listed separately. [2] Awarded separately: Countering Violent Extremism Grants ($10,000,000), Complex Coordinated Attack Grants ($39,000,000), Assistance to Firefighters Grants ($310,500,000), Staffing for Adequate Fire and Emergency Response Grants ($345,000,000), and Fire Prevention and Safety Grants ($34,500,000).

Source: U.S. Department of Homeland Security, Federal Emergency Management Agency, Information Bulletin No. 415, *FY2017 DHS Preparedness Grant Programs Allocation Announcement,* June 2017, and earlier reports. See also <http://www.fema.gov/preparedness-non-disaster-grants>.

Table 551. Deportable Aliens Apprehended or Arrested by Program and Border Patrol Sector: 2000 to 2015

[As of the end of September. Deportable aliens located refer to Border Patrol apprehensions and Immigration and Customs Enforcement (ICE) administrative arrests]

Program and sector	2000	2010	2012	2013	2014	2015
Total	1,814,729	796,587	671,327	662,483	679,996	462,388
Investigations	138,291	18,290	15,937	11,996	11,626	7,288
Enforcement and Removal Operations (ERO)[1]	(X)	314,915	290,622	229,698	181,719	117,983
Border Patrol (apprehensions)	1,676,438	463,382	364,768	420,789	486,651	337,117
All southwest sectors	1,643,679	447,731	356,873	414,397	479,371	331,333
Rio Grande Valley, TX	133,243	59,766	97,762	154,453	256,393	147,257
Tucson, AZ	616,346	212,202	120,000	120,939	87,915	63,397
Laredo, TX	108,973	35,287	44,872	50,749	44,049	35,888
San Diego, CA	151,681	68,565	28,461	27,496	29,911	35,888
Del Rio, TX	157,178	14,694	21,720	23,510	24,255	26,290
El Paso, TX	115,696	12,251	9,678	11,154	12,339	19,013
El Centro, CA	238,126	32,562	23,916	16,306	14,511	14,495
Yuma, AZ	108,747	7,116	6,500	6,106	5,902	12,820
Big Bend, TX[2]	13,689	5,288	3,964	3,684	4,096	7,142
All other sectors	32,759	15,651	7,895	6,392	7,280	5,031
Miami, FL	6,237	4,651	2,509	1,738	2,034	5,784
New Orleans, LA	6,478	3,171	474	500	950	1,752
Grand Forks, ND	562	543	418	469	767	849
Detroit, MI	2,057	1,669	950	650	647	789
Ramey, Puerto Rico	1,731	398	702	924	958	637
Swanton, VT	1,957	1,422	702	531	506	557
Buffalo, NY	1,570	2,422	1,143	796	741	341
Blaine, WA	2,581	673	537	360	272	291
Spokane, WA	1,324	356	317	299	269	282
Havre, MT	1,568	290	102	88	91	190
Houlton, ME	489	56	41	37	45	64
Livermore, CA[3]	6,205	(X)	(X)	(X)	(X)	32

X Not applicable. [1] Includes arrests of fugitive and nonfugitive aliens under the Office of Detention and Removal Operations (DRO), National Fugitive Operations Program. Beginning in 2008, includes all administrative arrests conducted by ICE ERO. [2] Formerly known as Marfa, TX. [3] Livermore sector closed August 31, 2004.

Source: U.S. Department of Homeland Security, Office of Immigration Statistics, "2015 Yearbook of Immigration Statistics," and earlier reports, <https://www.dhs.gov/immigration-statistics/yearbook>, accessed January 2017.

Table 552. Deportable Aliens Apprehended or Arrested: 1925 to 2015

[As of the end of September. Prior to 1952, data refer to Border Patrol Apprehensions. Detention and Removal Operations data are included beginning in 2006. Beginning in 2008, includes all administrative arrests conducted by the ICE, Office of Enforcement and Removal Operations. Beginning in 2009, data also include administrative arrests conducted under the 287(g) program (Delegation of Immigration Authority)]

Year	Number	Year	Number	Year	Number	Year	Number
1925	22,199	1956	87,696	1976 [1]	1,097,739	1996	1,649,986
1930	20,880	1957	59,918	1977	1,042,215	1997	1,536,520
1935	11,016	1958	53,474	1978	1,057,977	1998	1,679,439
1939	12,037	1959	45,336	1979	1,076,418	1999	1,714,035
1940	10,492	1960	70,684	1980	910,361	2000	1,814,729
1941	11,294	1961	88,823	1981	975,780	2001	1,387,486
1942	11,784	1962	92,758	1982	970,246	2002	1,062,270
1943	11,175	1963	88,712	1983	1,251,357	2003	1,046,422
1944	31,174	1964	86,597	1984	1,246,981	2004	1,264,232
1945	69,164	1965	110,371	1985	1,348,749	2005	1,291,065
1946	99,591	1966	138,520	1986	1,767,400	2006	1,206,408
1947	193,657	1967	161,608	1987	1,190,488	2007	960,673
1948	192,779	1968	212,057	1988	1,008,145	2008	1,043,759
1949	288,253	1969	283,557	1989	954,243	2009	889,212
1950	468,339	1970	345,353	1990	1,169,939	2010	796,587
1951	509,040	1971	420,126	1991	1,197,875	2011	678,606
1952	543,535	1972	505,949	1992	1,258,481	2012	671,327
1953	885,587	1973	655,968	1993	1,327,261	2013	662,483
1954	1,089,583	1974	788,145	1994	1,094,719	2014	679,996
1955	254,096	1975	766,600	1995	1,394,554	2015	462,388

[1] Includes the 15 months from July 1, 1975 to September 30, 1976 because the end date of fiscal years was changed from June 30 to September 30.

Source: U.S. Department of Homeland Security, Office of Immigration Statistics, "2015 Yearbook of Immigration Statistics," <https://www.dhs.gov/immigration-statistics/yearbook>, accessed January 2017.

Table 553. Aliens Returned or Removed by Leading Crime Category and Country of Nationality: 2010 to 2015

[For year ending September 30. For definitions of immigration enforcement terms, see source. "Crime categories" and "Countries of nationality" are ranked by data for most recent year]

Crime category and country of nationality	2010	2011	2012	2013	2014	2015
Total aliens returned or removed:..............................	855,933	708,118	646,684	612,706	570,320	462,463
Returns [1]...	474,195	322,098	230,360	178,691	163,245	129,122
Removals [2]...	381,738	386,020	416,324	434,015	407,075	333,341
Noncriminal..	212,082	197,056	216,181	235,034	237,822	193,391
Criminal [3]..	169,656	188,964	200,143	198,981	169,253	139,950
Leading crime category:						
Immigration.......................................	31,828	37,606	47,616	62,364	53,087	(NA)
Dangerous drugs.................................	42,890	43,378	42,679	30,688	27,581	(NA)
Criminal traffic offenses.......................	31,062	43,154	46,162	29,945	23,754	(NA)
Assault...	12,175	12,783	13,045	20,244	17,283	(NA)
Burglary..	4,213	3,808	3,569	5,521	4,623	(NA)
Weapon offenses................................	(NA)	2,730	2,513	5,310	4,511	(NA)
Larceny..	5,459	5,728	5,428	5,303	4,273	(NA)
Fraudulent activities.............................	3,889	4,232	3,879	5,196	3,860	(NA)
Sexual assault....................................	3,268	3,576	3,353	3,176	2,924	(NA)
Forgery...	(NA)	(NA)	2,430	3,045	2,304	(NA)
Robbery..	3646	3,757	(NA)	(NA)	(NA)	(NA)
Public peace (including disorderly conduct).....................	2,240	2,493	(NA)	(NA)	(NA)	(NA)
Other, including unknown.......................	28,986	25,719	29,469	28,189	23,540	(NA)
Leading country of nationality of criminals removed:						
Mexico...	128,396	145,133	151,444	146,769	123,024	106,193
Guatemala...	9,432	11,718	13,494	15,373	13,732	10,478
Honduras...	10,420	10,825	13,815	16,625	14,011	8,526
El Salvador..	8,368	8,507	8,674	9,451	9,021	7,115
Dominican Republic..............................	2,241	2,142	2,182	1,811	1,640	1,512
Colombia...	1,241	1,048	1,055	961	859	763
Jamaica..	1,169	1,225	1,150	997	828	630
Ecuador..	692	704	706	585	565	481
Nicaragua..	804	696	731	695	637	436
Brazil...	487	550	424	368	284	282
Haiti...	126	251	568	453	350	265
Canada...	457	417	383	380	300	258

NA Not available. [1] Returns are the confirmed movement of an inadmissible or deportable alien out of the U.S. not based on an order of removal. Most voluntary departures are of Mexican nationals who have been apprehended by the U.S. Border Patrol and are returned to Mexico. [2] Removals are the compulsory and confirmed movement of an inadmissible or deportable alien out of the U.S. based on an order of removal. An alien who is removed has administrative or criminal consequences placed on subsequent reentry. [3] Persons removed based on a criminal charge or those with a criminal conviction.

Source: U.S. Department of Homeland Security, Office of Immigration Statistics, "2015 Yearbook of Immigration Statistics," <https://www.dhs.gov/immigration-statistics/yearbook>, accessed January 2017; and *Immigration Enforcement Actions: 2014*, and previous editions.

Table 554. Coast Guard Migrant Interdictions by Nationality of Alien: 1990 to 2015

[For the year ending September 30]

Year	Total	Haiti	Dominican Republic	China	Cuba	Mexico	Ecuador	Other
1990.......................	2,836	871	1,426	–	443	1	–	95
1991.......................	4,990	2,065	1,007	138	1,722	–	–	58
1992.......................	40,627	37,618	588	181	2,066	–	–	174
1993.......................	10,584	4,270	873	2,511	2,882	–	–	48
1994.......................	64,443	25,302	232	291	38,560	–	–	58
1995.......................	5,367	909	3,388	509	525	–	–	36
1996.......................	9,080	2,295	6,273	61	411	–	2	38
1997.......................	2,194	288	1,200	240	421	–	–	45
1998.......................	3,648	1,369	1,097	212	903	30	–	37
1999.......................	4,826	1,039	583	1,092	1,619	171	298	24
2000.......................	4,210	1,113	499	261	1,000	49	1,244	44
2001.......................	3,948	1,391	659	53	777	17	1,020	31
2002.......................	4,104	1,486	177	80	666	32	1,608	55
2003.......................	6,068	2,013	1,748	15	1,555	–	703	34
2004.......................	10,899	3,229	5,014	68	1,225	86	1,189	88
2005.......................	9,455	1,850	3,612	32	2,712	55	1,149	45
2006.......................	7,886	1,198	3,011	31	2,810	52	693	91
2007.......................	6,338	1,610	1,469	73	2,868	26	125	167
2008.......................	4,825	1,583	688	1	2,216	47	220	65
2009.......................	3,467	1,782	727	35	799	77	6	41
2010.......................	2,088	1,377	140	–	422	61	–	88
2011.......................	2,474	1,137	222	11	985	68	1	50
2012.......................	2,955	977	456	23	1,275	79	7	138
2013.......................	2,094	508	110	5	1,357	31	1	82
2014.......................	3,587	1,103	293	–	2,111	48	–	32
2015.......................	3,828	561	257	10	2,927	27	3	43

– Represents zero.

Source: U.S. Department of Homeland Security, United States Coast Guard, "Alien Migrant Interdiction," <http://www.uscg.mil/hq/cg5/cg531/AMIO/amio.asp>, accessed March 2016.

Table 555. Foreign Visitor Overstays by Country of Citizenship: 2016

[Data shown for foreign nationals entering the U.S. as nonimmigrant visitors for business or pleasure through an air or sea point of entry. For fiscal year ending Sept. 30. An overstay is a nonimmigrant who was lawfully admitted to the U.S. for an authorized period but stayed or remains in the U.S. beyond the lawful admission period. The Visa Waiver Program (VWP) allows citizens of specific countries to travel to the U.S. for tourism, business, or while in transit for up to 90 days without obtaining a visa. Data are generated from Department of Homeland Security's Arrival and Departure Information System (ADIS). Data shown for countries with more than 50,000 expected departures]

Country of citizenship	Expected departures	Overstays (number)			Overstay rates	
		Total	Out-of-country [1]	Suspected in-country [2]	Total	Suspected in-country [2]
Total	50,437,278	739,478	110,679	628,799	1.47	1.25
North American, total	**12,088,020**	**182,269**	**16,193**	**166,076**	**1.51**	**1.37**
Canada	9,008,496	129,311	9,893	119,418	1.44	1.33
Mexico	3,079,524	52,958	6,300	46,658	1.72	1.52
VISA WAIVER PROGRAM						
Total	21,616,034	147,282	18,476	128,806	0.68	0.60
United Kingdom	4,709,633	23,472	2,802	20,670	0.50	0.44
Japan	3,007,800	4,842	441	4,401	0.16	0.15
Germany	2,061,112	20,196	1,416	18,780	0.98	0.91
France	1,751,536	11,987	1,629	10,358	0.68	0.59
Australia	1,362,199	7,563	980	6,583	0.56	0.48
Korea, South	1,266,839	5,875	1,368	4,507	0.46	0.36
Italy	1,207,242	16,376	1,480	14,896	1.36	1.23
Spain	940,218	13,685	1,969	11,716	1.46	1.25
Netherlands	721,977	4,592	511	4,081	0.64	0.57
Sweden	560,320	2,971	370	2,601	0.53	0.46
Ireland	483,613	2,569	392	2,177	0.53	0.45
Switzerland	434,189	2,546	289	2,257	0.59	0.52
Taiwan	388,713	2,203	681	1,522	0.57	0.39
Chile	363,570	6,229	813	5,416	1.71	1.49
Denmark	329,981	1,663	158	1,505	0.50	0.46
New Zealand	308,703	1,799	273	1,526	0.58	0.49
Belgium	288,117	1,547	178	1,369	0.54	0.48
Norway	281,559	1,150	158	992	0.41	0.35
Austria	211,224	2,900	116	2,784	1.37	1.32
Portugal	164,662	3,986	621	3,365	2.42	2.04
Finland	156,057	716	112	604	0.46	0.39
Singapore	127,149	617	146	471	0.49	0.37
Czech Republic	103,158	1,141	214	927	1.11	0.90
Hungary	82,533	2,272	431	1,841	2.75	2.23
Greece	77,562	1,701	421	1,280	2.19	1.65
Iceland	54,806	182	28	154	0.33	0.28
NON-VISA WAIVER PROGRAM						
Total	13,848,480	287,107	23,637	263,470	2.07	1.90
Brazil	2,074,363	39,455	2,526	36,929	1.90	1.78
China	2,058,311	19,601	2,493	17,108	0.95	0.83
India	1,004,245	17,763	2,040	15,723	1.77	1.57
Colombia	863,417	19,466	1,062	18,404	2.26	2.13
Argentina	840,739	7,070	318	6,752	0.84	0.80
Venezuela	551,048	23,821	915	22,906	4.32	4.16
Ecuador	392,521	7,743	387	7,356	1.97	1.87
Israel	374,404	4,035	451	3,584	1.08	0.96
Dominican Republic	341,628	9,653	442	9,211	2.83	2.70
Peru	296,684	5,764	454	5,310	1.94	1.79
Jamaica	281,797	9,621	444	9,177	3.41	3.26
Costa Rica	260,245	2,761	231	2,530	1.06	0.97
Russia	256,280	3,678	334	3,344	1.44	1.31
Philippines	250,753	5,000	562	4,438	1.99	1.77
Guatemala	247,084	5,804	362	5,442	2.35	2.20
Bahamas, The	233,902	4,220	344	3,876	1.80	1.66
Nigeria	189,883	12,043	582	11,461	6.34	6.04
El Salvador	183,255	5,079	308	4,771	2.77	2.60
Honduras	182,601	5,357	272	5,085	2.93	2.79
Trinidad and Tobago	181,218	997	129	868	0.55	0.48
Turkey	176,695	2,843	312	2,531	1.61	1.43
Poland	176,495	3,121	334	2,787	1.77	1.58
Panama	158,076	948	143	805	0.60	0.51
Saudi Arabia	135,108	2,419	990	1,429	1.79	1.06
Haiti	129,617	5,669	669	5,000	4.37	3.86
South Africa	121,072	1,015	178	837	0.84	0.69
Pakistan	87,871	2,641	226	2,415	3.01	2.75
Thailand	84,785	2,122	168	1,954	2.50	2.31
Ukraine	83,401	2,950	243	2,707	3.54	3.25
Indonesia	80,936	1,311	115	1,196	1.62	1.48
Egypt	80,716	1,916	201	1,715	2.37	2.13
Vietnam	79,097	3,082	393	2,689	3.90	3.40
Malaysia	77,827	1,377	93	1,284	1.77	1.65
Uruguay	77,164	1,429	76	1,353	1.85	1.75
Romania	66,451	1,238	186	1,052	1.86	1.58
Nicaragua	66,206	1,444	105	1,339	2.18	2.02
Bolivia	63,071	1,239	110	1,129	1.96	1.79
Barbados	59,316	1,695	74	1,621	2.86	2.73
Guyana	54,471	1,924	113	1,811	3.53	3.33

[1] Individuals whose departure was recorded after their lawful admission period expired. [2] Individuals for whom no departure has been recorded.

Source: Department of Homeland Security, *Fiscal Year 2016 Entry/Exit Overstay Report*, May 2017. See also <https://www.dhs.gov/publication/entryexit-overstay-report>.

Table 556. Terrorism Related Deaths, Injuries, and Kidnappings of Private U.S. Citizens by Selected Country: 2010 to 2016

[Private U.S. citizen refers to any U.S. citizen overseas not acting in an official capacity on behalf of the U.S. government. This includes U.S. government employees' households and U.S. citizens working for contractors hired by the U.S. government. Figures do not include U.S. military personnel while on active duty or employees of the Department of State and other federal agencies while overseas on U.S. government orders]

Incident type and location	2010	2011	2012	2013	2014	2015	2016
DEATHS							
Total.................................	15	17	10	16	24	20	16
Afghanistan.........................	13	15	10	12	10	8	1
Algeria..............................	–	–	–	3	–	–	–
Bangladesh.........................	–	–	–	–	–	1	1
Belgium.............................	–	–	–	–	–	–	4
Burkina Faso.......................	–	–	–	–	–	–	1
Egypt...............................	–	–	–	–	1	–	–
France..............................	–	–	–	–	–	1	3
Iraq.................................	1	1	–	–	–	–	–
Israel, Jerusalem, West Bank, Gaza.........	–	1	–	–	5	3	3
Jordan..............................	–	–	–	–	–	2	–
Lebanon............................	–	–	–	1	–	–	–
Libya................................	–	–	–	–	–	1	–
Mali.................................	–	–	–	–	–	1	–
Pakistan............................	–	–	–	–	–	1	1
Somalia.............................	–	–	–	–	3	1	–
Syria................................	–	–	–	–	4	1	–
Turkey..............................	–	–	–	–	–	–	2
Uganda.............................	1	–	–	–	–	–	–
United Arab Emirates...............	–	–	–	–	1	–	–
INJURIES							
Total.................................	9	14	2	[1] 7	8	22	34
Afghanistan.........................	–	10	1	1	2	2	5
Bangladesh.........................	–	–	–	–	–	1	–
Belgium.............................	–	–	–	–	–	–	17
Burkina Faso.......................	–	–	–	–	–	–	1
France..............................	–	–	–	–	–	6	3
Germany............................	1	–	–	–	–	–	2
Iraq.................................	–	1	1	–	–	1	–
Israel, Jerusalem, West Bank, Gaza.........	–	3	–	–	5	6	6
Jordan..............................	–	–	–	–	–	2	–
Kenya...............................	–	–	–	6	–	–	–
Pakistan............................	–	–	–	–	–	1	–
Philippines..........................	1	–	–	–	–	–	–
Saudi Arabia........................	–	–	–	–	1	2	–
Somalia.............................	–	–	–	–	–	1	–
Uganda.............................	7	–	–	–	–	–	–
KIDNAPPINGS							
Total.................................	–	3	3	13	3	–	6
Afghanistan.........................	–	–	–	–	2	–	1
Colombia...........................	–	–	–	1	–	–	–
Iraq.................................	–	1	–	–	–	–	3
Libya................................	–	–	–	1	–	–	–
Niger................................	–	–	–	–	–	–	1
Nigeria..............................	–	–	1	3	1	–	–
Pakistan............................	–	1	–	–	–	–	–
Somalia.............................	–	1	1	–	–	–	–
Syria................................	–	–	–	7	–	–	1
Yemen..............................	–	–	1	1	–	–	–

– Represents zero. [1] Does not include 2 citizens held hostage in Algeria and 48 citizens present, but not medically injured, at the Westgate Mall attack in Kenya.

Source: U.S. State Department, Bureau of Counterterrorism, "Country Reports on Terrorism," <http://www.state.gov/j/ct/rls/crt/index.htm>, accessed August 2017.

Table 557. Customs and Border Protection (CBP)—Processed and Cleared Passengers, Planes, Vehicles, and Containers: 2008 to 2015

[In thousands (93,768 represents 93,768,000). For year ending September 30]

Characteristic	2008	2009	2010	2011	2012	2013	2014	2015
AIR								
Passengers..........................	93,768	87,749	91,488	94,605	98,367	10,221	107,049	112,505
Commercial aircraft [1].............	696	638	657	662	675	870	900	941
Private aircraft......................	138	109	115	121	116	116	117	116
LAND								
Passengers [2,3]....................	290,146	257,476	244,322	227,965	234,898	242,064	247,813	250,449
Privately owned vehicles [2]........	109,548	99,017	93,966	92,673	94,952	98,460	100,909	103,022
Truck containers [4]................	11,013	9,238	10,003	10,117	10,419	10,473	10,851	10,937
Rail containers......................	2,747	2,179	2,431	2,634	2,936	3,061	3,272	3,290
SEA								
Passengers [5]......................	16,636	15,967	17,170	17,796	18,335	17,883	19,713	19,796
Vessels [6]..........................	148	146	152	141	139	133	133	136
Vessel containers [7]...............	10,886	9,300	10,282	10,721	10,975	11,044	11,549	12,119

[1] A commercial aircraft is any aircraft transporting passengers and/or cargo for some payment or other consideration, including money or services rendered. [2] See Table 1288 for more details. [3] Includes pedestrians. [4] Truck containers—number of trucks entering the U.S. [5] Does not include passengers on ferries. [6] Includes every description of water craft or other contrivance used or capable of being used as a means of transportation on water; does not include aircraft. [7] Number of vessel containers.

Source: U.S. Department of Homeland Security, Customs and Border Protection, ProQuest Freedom of Information Act request, received March 2016. See also <http://www.cbp.gov>.

Table 558. Value of Counterfeit Goods Seized for Intellectual Property Rights Violations by Commodity and Country of Origin: 2015 and 2016

[In thousands of dollars (1,352,495 represents $1,352,495,000), except as indicated. Customs and Border Protection enforces Intellectual Property Rights (IPR), most visibly by seizing products that infringe IPR such as trademarks, copyrights, and patents. Value of goods seized represent Manufacturer's Suggested Retail Price (MSRP), which is the price at which merchandise is sold at retail to the consumer or what the value of the counterfeit goods would have been at retail had they been genuine]

Commodity	2015	2016	Country of origin	2015	2016
Number of IPR Seizures	**28,865**	**31,560**	China	697,084	616,881
			Hong Kong	472,331	599,785
			India	6,409	14,668
Total MSRP value of IPR seizures	**1,352,495**	**1,382,903**	Singapore	10,267	7,706
Jewelry, watches, and parts	580,792	653,590	Cambodia	(NA)	7,015
Handbags/wallets/backpacks	208,379	234,079	Pakistan	(NA)	4,776
Consumer electronics/parts	132,479	122,892	Bangladesh	(NA)	4,592
Wearing apparel/accessories	157,196	110,806	Colombia	(NA)	4,221
Pharmaceuticals/personal care	75,062	73,716	Korea, South	3,789	3,585
Transportation/parts	(NA)	55,199	Mexico	(NA)	3,539
Footwear	64,967	51,231	United Kingdom / Great Britain	4,358	(NA)
Computers/technology components	38,393	19,319	United Arab Emirates	3,433	(NA)
Labels/tags	33,336	17,053	Italy	2,849	(NA)
Optical media	32,504	8,166	Malaysia	2,345	(NA)
Toys	9,757	(NA)	Canada	1,974	(NA)
All other commodities	19,630	36,851	All other countries	147,656	116,135

NA Not available.

Source: U.S. Department of Homeland Security, Customs and Border Protection, *Intellectual Property Rights Seizure Statistics FY2016*, January 2017, and earlier reports. See also <http://www.cbp.gov/trade/priority-issues/ipr/statistics>.

Social Insurance and Human Services

This section presents data related to government expenditures for social insurance and human services; population receiving government assistance; government programs for Old-Age, Survivors, and Disability Insurance (OASDI), commonly known as Social Security; government employee retirement; private retirement plans; government unemployment and disability insurance; federal supplemental security income payments and aid to the needy; child and other welfare services; and federal food programs. Also included here are selected data on workers' compensation, child support, child care, homelessness, social assistance organizations, charitable contributions, and philanthropic foundations.

A principal source for these data is the Social Security Administration's *Annual Statistical Supplement to the Social Security Bulletin* which presents current data on many of the programs. Additional sources of data include the Census Bureau's Annual Social and Economic Supplement of the Current Population Survey, and the Survey of Income and Program Participation (conducted as a series of surveys over a period of time spanning several years); and the Department of Health and Human Services' Administration for Children and Families.

Social insurance under the Social Security Act
—Programs established by the Social Security Act provide protection against wage loss resulting from retirement, prolonged disability, death, or unemployment, and protection against the cost of medical care during old age and disability. The federal OASDI program provides monthly benefits to retired or disabled insured workers and their dependents, and to survivors of insured workers. To be eligible, a worker must have had a specified period of employment in which OASDI taxes were paid. The age of eligibility for full retirement benefits had been 65 for many years. For persons born in 1938 or later, however, that age gradually increases until it reaches age 67 for those born in 1960 and later. Reduced benefits may be obtained as early as age 62. The worker's spouse is under the same limitations. Survivor benefits are payable to dependents of deceased insured workers. Disability benefits are payable to an insured worker under full retirement age with a prolonged disability, and to the disabled worker's dependents on the same basis as dependents of retired workers. Disability benefits are provided at age 50 to the disabled widow or widower of a deceased worker who was fully insured at the time of death. Disabled children, age 18 or older, of retired, disabled, or deceased workers are also eligible for benefits. A special lump sum benefit may be payable on the death of an insured worker to a spouse or minor children. For information on the Medicare program, see Section 3, Health and Nutrition.

Retirement, survivors, and disability insurance benefits are funded by a payroll tax on annual earnings (up to a maximum share of earnings set by law) of workers, employers, and the self-employed. The maximum taxable earnings are adjusted annually to reflect increasing wage levels (see Table 565). Tax receipts and benefit payments are administered through federal trust funds. Special benefits for

uninsured persons; hospital benefits for persons age 65 and over with specified amounts of social security coverage less than that required for cash benefit eligibility; and that part of the cost of supplementary medical insurance not financed by contributions from participants are all financed from federal general revenues.

Unemployment insurance is presently administered by the U.S. Employment and Training Administration and each state's employment security agency. By agreement with the U.S. Secretary of Labor, state agencies also administer unemployment compensation for eligible former military personnel and federal employees. Under state unemployment insurance laws, benefits related to an individual's past earnings are paid to unemployed eligible workers. State laws vary concerning the length of time benefits are paid and their amount. In most states, benefits are payable for 26 weeks and, during periods of high unemployment, extended benefits are payable under a federal-state program to those who have exhausted their regular state benefits. Some states also supplement the basic benefit with allowances for dependents. Unemployment insurance is financed through Federal and state employer payroll taxes. Generally, employers pay both Federal and state unemployment taxes for workers paid $1,500 or more during any quarter of a calendar year, or if they had at least 1 employee during any day of the week during 20 weeks in a calendar year (weeks need not be consecutive).

Retirement programs for government employees
—The Civil Service Retirement System (CSRS) and the Federal Employees' Retirement System (FERS) are the two major programs providing old-age, disability, and survivor annuities for federal civilian employees. The FERS replaced the CSRS for federal employees who first entered covered service on or after January 1, 1987. CSRS employees were offered the option of transferring to FERS during 1987 and 1998. There are separate retirement systems for the uniformed services (supplementing OASDI) and for certain special groups of federal employees. State and local government employees are covered for the most part by state and local retirement systems similar to the federal programs. In many jurisdictions, these benefits supplement OASDI coverage.

Workers' compensation
—All states provide protection against work-connected injuries and deaths, although some states exclude certain workers (e.g., domestic workers). Federal laws cover federal employees, private employees in the District of Columbia, and longshoremen and harbor workers. In addition, the Department of Labor administers "black lung" benefit programs for coal miners disabled by pneumoconiosis and for specified dependents and survivors. Specified occupational diseases are compensable to some extent. In most states, benefits are related to the worker's salary. The benefits may or may not be augmented by dependents' allowances or automatically adjusted to prevailing wage levels.

Income support
—Income support programs are designed to provide benefits for persons with limited income and resources. The Supplemental Security

Income (SSI) program and Temporary Assistance for Needy Families (TANF) program are the major programs providing monthly payments. In addition, a number of programs provide money payments or in-kind benefits for special needs or purposes. Several programs offer food and nutritional services. Also, various federal-state programs provide energy assistance, public housing, and subsidized housing to individuals and families with low incomes. General assistance may also be available at the state or local level.

The SSI program, administered by the Social Security Administration, provides income support to persons age 65 and older and to blind or disabled adults and children. Unlike social security, SSI benefits are not based on a person's work history, and the program is financed by general funds of the U.S. Treasury. Eligibility requirements and federal payment standards are nationally uniform. Most states supplement the basic SSI payment for all or selected categories of persons.

The Personal Responsibility and Work Opportunity Reconciliation Act of 1996 contained provisions that replaced the Aid to Families With Dependent Children (AFDC), Job Opportunities and Basic Skills (JOBS), and Emergency Assistance programs with the TANF block grant program. This law contains strong work requirements, comprehensive child support enforcement, support for families moving from welfare to work, and other features. The TANF program became effective as soon as each state submitted a complete implementation plan, but no later than July 1, 1997. The older AFDC program provided cash assistance based on need, income, resources, and family size.

Federal nutrition assistance—Under the Supplemental Nutrition Assistance Program (SNAP), formerly known as the food stamp program, single persons and those living in households meeting nationwide standards for income and assets may receive benefit payments redeemable for food at most retail food stores through electronic benefits transfer. The monthly amount of benefits, also known as allotments, is determined by household size and income. Households without income receive the determined monthly cost of a nutritionally adequate diet for their household size. This amount is updated to account for food price increases. Households with income receive the difference between the amount of a nutritionally adequate diet and 30 percent of their income, after certain allowable deductions.

For the fiscal year ending 2018, a household qualifying for SNAP may have no more than $2,250 in disposable assets ($3,500 if one member is age 60 or older, or is disabled), gross income below 130 percent of the official poverty guidelines for the household size, and net income below 100 percent of the poverty guidelines. Households with a person age 60 or older or a disabled person receiving SSI, social security, state general assistance, or veterans' disability benefits may have gross income exceeding 130 percent of the poverty guidelines. All households in which all members receive TANF or SSI are categorically eligible for SNAP without meeting these income or resource criteria. Households are certified for varying lengths of time, depending on their income sources and individual circumstances.

Health and welfare services—Programs providing health and welfare services are aided through federal grants to states for child welfare services, vocational rehabilitation, activities for the elderly, maternal and child health services, maternity and infant care projects, comprehensive health services, and a variety of public health activities. For information about the Medicaid program, see Section 3, Health and Nutrition.

Noncash benefits—The U.S. Census Bureau annually collects data on the characteristics of recipients of noncash (in-kind) benefits to supplement the collection of annual money income data in the Current Population Survey (see text, Section 1, Population, and Section 13, Income, Expenditures, Poverty, and Wealth). Noncash benefits are those benefits received in a form other than money which serve to enhance or improve the economic well-being of the recipient. As for money income, the data for noncash benefits are for the calendar year prior to the date of the interview. The major categories of noncash benefits covered are public transfers (e.g., SNAP, school lunch, public housing, and Medicaid) and employer or union-provided benefits to employees.

Statistical reliability—For discussion of statistical collection, estimation, and sampling procedures and measures of statistical reliability applicable to Social Security Administration and Census Bureau data, see Appendix III.

Table 559. Government Transfer Payments to Individuals—Summary: 1990 to 2015

[In billions of current dollars (568.1 represents $568,100,000,000)]

Year	Government transfer payments to individuals, total	Retirement and disability insurance benefits	Medical payments	Income maintenance benefits	Unemployment insurance benefits	Veterans benefits	Education and training assistance payments [1]	Other [2]
1990	568.1	263.9	188.8	65.4	18.2	17.7	12.3	1.7
2000	1,032.4	424.5	427.2	110.6	21.0	25.0	21.9	2.3
2001	1,131.5	449.8	480.8	113.8	32.1	26.6	25.4	3.0
2002	1,234.8	474.5	521.9	125.0	53.7	29.5	27.8	2.4
2003	1,304.3	493.4	556.5	137.7	53.6	31.8	28.3	3.0
2004	1,387.2	517.0	611.4	149.1	37.1	34.0	30.8	3.0
2005	1,473.6	545.5	655.6	166.0	32.3	36.4	33.0	7.7
2006	1,575.4	577.2	720.5	170.1	30.9	38.9	34.8	4.9
2007	1,679.9	608.8	776.8	179.9	33.4	41.7	36.8	3.1
2008	1,901.2	639.0	826.8	195.3	52.0	45.0	42.5	2.6
2009	2,088.5	698.4	891.7	230.8	132.0	51.5	53.5	100.4
2010	2,260.6	724.9	938.7	255.9	139.7	58.0	64.5	30.7
2011	2,288.8	747.7	970.2	263.7	107.9	63.3	65.0	78.9
2012	2,301.2	796.7	1,003.1	267.1	84.6	70.1	63.1	71.0
2013	2,364.3	833.2	1,042.5	270.6	62.9	79.1	63.1	16.5
2014	2,472.0	870.9	1,115.8	269.5	35.8	83.7	64.1	12.9
2015	2,604.9	909.2	1,195.0	268.9	32.5	89.8	63.6	46.0

[1] See footnote 9, Table 560. [2] See footnote 10, Table 560.

Source: U.S. Bureau of Economic Analysis, Regional Economic Accounts, Annual State Personal Income and Employment, "Personal Current Transfer Receipts (SA35)," <http://www.bea.gov/regional/index.htm>, accessed February 2017.

Table 560. Government Transfer Payments to Individuals by Type: 1990 to 2015

[In millions of current dollars (568,060 represents $568,060,000,000)]

Item	1990	2000	2005	2010	2013	2014	2015
Total	**568,060**	**1,032,404**	**1,473,620**	**2,260,644**	**2,364,261**	**2,472,018**	**2,604,945**
Retirement & disability insurance benefits	263,888	424,461	545,484	724,934	833,246	870,929	909,191
Social security	244,135	401,393	512,728	690,174	799,044	834,640	871,793
Railroad retirement and disability	7,221	8,267	9,194	10,779	11,676	11,955	12,228
Workers' compensation (federal & state)	8,618	10,898	15,863	15,544	14,804	14,851	14,707
Other government disability insurance & retirement [1]	3,914	3,903	7,699	8,437	7,722	9,483	10,463
Medical payments	188,808	427,194	655,613	938,709	1,042,502	1,115,767	1,195,026
Medicare	107,638	219,117	332,161	513,820	575,013	601,085	628,220
Public assistance medical care [2]	78,176	205,021	315,197	410,834	453,465	500,029	551,843
Military medical insurance [3]	2,994	3,056	8,255	14,055	14,024	14,653	14,963
Income maintenance benefits	65,441	110,582	165,972	255,941	270,561	269,532	268,869
Supplemental Security Income (SSI)	16,670	31,675	38,261	49,159	54,851	55,794	56,661
Earned income tax credit	6,313	30,243	39,237	59,778	65,482	68,920	69,118
Supplemental Nutrition Assistance Program	14,741	14,565	29,492	66,515	74,657	69,411	68,737
Family assistance [4]	19,187	18,440	18,355	22,421	19,728	19,805	19,944
Other, excluding family assistance [5]	8,530	15,479	40,627	58,068	55,843	55,602	54,409
Unemployment insurance compensation	18,208	20,989	32,276	139,712	62,880	35,775	32,490
State unemployment insurance compensation	17,644	20,223	31,001	137,015	60,945	34,561	31,460
Unemployment compensation for federal civilian employees	215	226	224	535	402	257	204
Unemployment compensation for railroad employees	89	81	72	114	82	90	90
Unemployment compensation for veterans	144	181	446	1,155	870	510	389
Other unemployment compensation [6]	116	278	533	893	581	357	347
Veterans benefits	17,687	25,004	36,382	57,961	79,056	83,710	89,828
Veterans pension and disability	15,550	21,966	32,505	48,455	65,789	70,327	75,856
Veterans readjustment [7]	257	1,322	2,256	7,976	11,894	12,060	12,691
Veterans life insurance benefits	1,868	1,706	1,596	1,442	1,280	1,228	1,185
Other assistance to veterans [8]	12	10	25	88	93	95	96
Federal education & training assistance payments [9]	12,286	21,851	33,017	64,513	63,139	64,080	63,589
Other payments to individuals [10]	1,742	2,323	4,876	78,874	12,877	32,225	45,952

[1] Mostly temporary disability, pension benefit guaranty, black lung, and Panama Canal construction annuity payments. [2] Medicaid and other medical vendor payments. [3] Payments made under TriCare Management Program (formerly called CHAMPUS) for medical care of dependents of active duty and retired military personnel and their dependents at nonmilitary medical facilities. [4] Through 1995, consists of Emergency Assistance and Aid to Families with Dependent Children. Beginning with 1998, consists of Temporary Assistance for Needy Families benefits. [5] Mostly general assistance; food expenditures for Special Supplemental Nutrition Program for Women, Infants, and Children (WIC); Other Needs Assistance; refugee assistance; foster home care and adoption assistance; 2008 Economic Stimulus Act Rebates; Child Tax Credits; American Recovery and Reinvestment Act of 2009 (ARRA) funded tax credits; other tax credits; and energy assistance. [6] Trade readjustment allowance, Redwood Park benefit, public service employment benefit, and transitional benefit. [7] Mostly veterans' readjustment benefit payments, educational assistance to spouses and children of disabled or deceased veterans, and payments to paraplegics and for autos and conveyances for disabled veterans. [8] Mostly state and local government payments to veterans. [9] Mostly federal fellowship payments (National Science Foundation fellowships and traineeships, subsistence payments to state maritime academy cadets, and other fellowships), interest subsidy on higher education loans, Pell Grants, Job Corps payments, education exchange payments, and state education assistance payments. [10] Mostly Bureau of Indian Affairs payments; Alaska Permanent Fund dividend payments; compensation of survivors of public safety officers; compensation of crime victims; disaster relief payments; compensation for Japanese internment; ARRA funded Federal Additional Compensation for unemployment, COBRA premium reduction, and Economic Recovery lump sum payment; and other special payments to individuals.

Source: U.S. Bureau of Economic Analysis, Regional Economic Accounts, Annual State Personal Income and Employment, "Personal Current Transfer Receipts (SA35)," <http://www.bea.gov/regional/index.htm>, accessed February 2017.

Table 561. Government Transfer Payments to Individuals by State: 2010 to 2015

[In millions of current dollars not adjusted for inflation (2,260,644 represents $2,260,644,000,000)]

State	2010, total	2014, total	2015							
			Total	Retirement and disability insurance benefits	Medical payments	Income maintenance benefits	Unemployment insurance benefits	Veterans benefits	Education and training assistance payments [1]	Other [2]
United States........	2,260,644	2,472,018	2,604,945	909,191	1,195,026	268,869	32,490	89,828	63,589	45,952
Alabama...............	36,858	40,265	41,783	16,335	16,553	4,709	231	2,104	1,150	700
Alaska.................	5,145	6,292	6,442	1,313	2,395	843	95	322	64	1,409
Arizona................	46,996	51,920	54,735	19,220	24,275	4,910	351	2,089	3,268	622
Arkansas..............	23,013	25,518	26,629	9,762	11,867	2,518	270	1,146	800	265
California..............	259,181	291,629	314,779	91,111	158,738	35,918	5,274	8,452	8,879	6,408
Colorado..............	28,490	32,998	35,626	12,827	16,171	2,939	519	1,908	880	381
Connecticut...........	28,318	29,852	30,873	10,953	15,028	2,600	617	559	623	493
Delaware..............	7,037	8,269	8,791	3,215	4,145	689	83	245	310	104
District of Columbia....	5,336	5,880	6,108	1,152	3,615	987	56	120	151	27
Florida................	147,510	167,085	175,659	65,293	75,549	17,262	639	6,764	4,009	6,143
Georgia...............	59,897	67,672	70,600	25,630	27,592	9,337	445	3,680	1,959	1,958
Hawaii................	8,981	10,212	10,546	3,855	4,382	1,301	144	583	196	85
Idaho.................	9,916	10,857	11,430	4,788	4,443	1,019	127	471	272	310
Illinois................	90,575	91,944	96,449	34,462	43,385	11,079	1,790	2,067	2,455	1,212
Indiana...............	45,978	50,322	53,021	20,744	22,990	4,943	362	1,411	1,743	828
Iowa..................	21,087	22,833	23,967	9,564	10,389	1,969	402	675	747	220
Kansas...............	18,588	19,731	20,590	8,439	8,519	1,894	260	758	413	307
Kentucky..............	34,514	39,065	41,191	14,193	19,556	4,125	319	1,393	1,287	318
Louisiana.............	33,368	35,972	39,747	12,319	19,433	4,552	262	1,381	1,076	723
Maine.................	11,062	12,051	12,529	4,644	5,638	1,005	129	574	209	331
Maryland..............	37,982	43,682	45,294	15,468	21,648	4,397	670	1,654	914	543
Massachusetts.........	54,841	57,634	61,491	18,933	32,159	5,985	1,425	1,387	945	656
Michigan..............	80,643	84,538	89,160	34,419	39,974	8,419	924	2,221	1,944	1,259
Minnesota............	37,937	41,713	42,976	15,437	20,177	3,950	741	1,306	1,119	246
Mississippi............	23,406	25,686	26,651	9,136	12,138	3,236	131	904	636	471
Missouri...............	44,380	47,935	50,270	18,967	22,713	4,303	394	1,862	1,098	934
Montana..............	6,855	7,492	7,852	3,345	3,048	624	120	372	167	175
Nebraska.............	11,491	12,436	13,018	5,267	5,324	1,143	94	624	303	264
Nevada...............	16,276	18,423	20,042	7,410	8,480	2,069	384	940	454	305
New Hampshire........	8,863	9,738	10,424	4,525	4,403	628	89	380	249	150
New Jersey............	68,875	71,703	74,159	27,327	33,879	6,841	2,000	1,284	1,645	1,182
New Mexico...........	15,442	17,228	18,608	5,797	8,978	2,126	183	874	414	235
New York..............	178,477	186,360	196,522	57,256	106,012	22,096	2,315	3,015	3,960	1,868
North Carolina.........	68,597	76,058	79,821	29,768	33,410	8,474	316	3,971	1,659	2,223
North Dakota...........	4,410	4,908	5,155	2,120	2,116	427	115	197	91	89
Ohio..................	88,375	95,480	99,274	35,996	47,095	9,668	948	2,553	2,058	955
Oklahoma.............	26,910	29,431	30,360	11,360	12,522	3,033	351	1,996	705	391
Oregon...............	28,512	32,695	34,775	12,782	15,740	3,245	554	1,456	645	354
Pennsylvania..........	108,425	114,418	119,321	43,910	55,936	10,894	2,229	2,830	1,991	1,533
Rhode Island..........	9,322	10,110	10,431	3,475	5,001	1,135	166	268	248	139
South Carolina.........	35,378	39,143	41,560	16,157	16,652	4,232	204	2,209	1,340	766
South Dakota..........	5,213	5,670	5,894	2,426	2,354	545	31	272	134	132
Tennessee.............	49,111	53,009	55,641	20,728	24,090	6,215	320	2,348	1,215	723
Texas.................	153,287	172,814	183,708	57,952	84,667	21,580	2,835	8,964	3,920	3,790
Utah..................	13,196	14,509	15,321	5,939	5,704	1,836	177	576	672	418
Vermont...............	5,220	5,919	6,207	2,127	3,003	586	71	157	163	99
Virginia...............	47,763	54,275	57,391	22,376	22,763	5,294	404	3,697	1,531	1,326
Washington............	48,751	53,908	54,743	21,709	21,830	5,347	1,023	2,578	1,564	691
West Virginia...........	16,453	17,998	18,695	7,269	8,133	1,714	245	766	418	150
Wisconsin.............	40,871	42,959	44,683	18,182	18,920	3,988	567	1,287	811	928
Wyoming..............	3,531	3,779	4,004	1,812	1,494	240	89	177	81	111

[1] Mostly federal fellowship payments (National Science Foundation fellowships and traineeships, subsistence payments to state maritime academy cadets, and other federal fellowships), interest subsidy on higher education loans, Pell Grants, Job Corps payments, education exchange payments, and state education assistance payments. [2] Mostly Bureau of Indian Affairs payments; Alaska Permanent Fund dividend payments; compensation of survivors of public safety officers; compensation of victims of crime; disaster relief payments; compensation for Japanese internment; the American Recovery and Reinvestment Act of 2009 funded Federal Additional Compensation for unemployment, COBRA premium reduction, and the Economic Recovery lump sum payment; and other special payments to individuals.

Source: U.S. Bureau of Economic Analysis, Regional Economic Accounts, Annual State Personal Income and Employment, "Personal Current Transfer Receipts (SA35)," <http://www.bea.gov/regional/index.htm>, accessed February 2017.

Table 562. Number of Persons With Income by Source of Income: 2015

[In thousands (226,762 represents 226,762,000). Persons 15 years old and over as of March of following year. Based on Current Population Survey, 2016 Annual Social and Economic Supplement (CPS ASEC); see text, Sections 1 and 13, and Appendix III. See source for information regarding the 2015 CPS ASEC use of a redesigned questionnaire]

Source of income	Total persons with income	Under 65 years	65 years and over	Men	Women	White[1]	Black[1]	Hispanic origin[2]
Total.....................	**226,762**	**180,840**	**45,922**	**112,322**	**114,440**	**179,910**	**27,225**	**32,964**
Earnings..........................	163,409	152,474	10,935	86,435	76,974	129,172	19,382	26,595
Wages and salary..................	154,115	144,746	9,368	80,623	73,492	121,230	18,760	25,103
Nonfarm self-employment...........	12,060	10,413	1,646	7,225	4,835	10,165	912	1,821
Farm self-employment..............	2,063	1,741	322	1,273	791	1,801	133	167
Unemployment compensation.........	4,214	3,966	248	2,424	1,790	3,336	597	684
State or local only...............	3,975	3,746	229	2,277	1,698	3,147	565	632
Combinations......................	239	220	19	146	92	189	32	52
Workers' compensation.............	1,478	1,311	167	789	689	1,179	212	238
State payments....................	347	308	38	195	152	266	53	48
Employment insurance..............	638	591	47	366	272	517	89	130
Own insurance.....................	20	19	1	17	3	19	1	6
Other.............................	780	682	99	399	381	616	117	121
Social Security...................	50,693	11,661	39,032	22,517	28,175	42,546	5,375	4,039
SSI (Supplemental Security Income)	6,414	5,111	1,303	2,894	3,520	4,185	1,650	1,079
Public assistance, total..........	1,767	1,644	123	391	1,375	1,111	467	416
TANF only[3]......................	1,050	1,011	40	166	884	631	314	267
Other assistance only.............	681	598	83	222	459	455	146	143
Both..............................	35	35	0	3	32	25	7	6
Veterans' benefits................	3,858	2,037	1,821	3,188	670	3,135	532	281
Disability only...................	2,456	1,371	1,084	2,200	256	2,006	336	176
Survivors only....................	273	85	188	7	265	223	39	9
Pension only......................	627	244	382	569	58	499	93	45
Education only....................	122	122	0	84	38	93	17	23
Other only........................	164	78	86	151	14	133	22	17
Combinations......................	216	136	80	176	40	182	25	12
Means-tested......................	717	383	335	590	127	550	134	50
Nonmeans-tested...................	3,141	1,654	1,486	2,597	543	2,585	398	230
Survivors benefits[4].............	3,265	994	2,270	697	2,568	2,888	223	168
Company or union..................	1,267	198	1,069	177	1,089	1,144	78	68
Federal government................	314	48	266	41	273	270	23	14
Military retirement...............	200	51	149	9	192	163	23	9
Disability benefits[4]............	2,814	2,437	376	1,468	1,346	2,170	472	384
Workers' compensation.............	363	332	31	216	147	279	59	88
Company or union..................	586	488	98	302	284	457	100	52
Federal government................	146	125	22	83	63	116	29	22
Military retirement...............	191	157	34	157	35	157	26	12
State or local government.........	498	418	80	218	281	378	82	105
Pension income[4].................	19,076	4,725	14,351	10,303	8,772	16,667	1,533	822
Company or union retirement.......	13,276	3,155	10,121	7,195	6,081	11,502	1,165	635
Federal government retirement.....	2,213	729	1,484	1,311	903	1,860	242	131
Military retirement...............	1,157	521	636	848	309	978	126	52
State or local government retirement	6,158	1,974	4,183	2,569	3,588	5,309	561	367
Property income[5]................	132,001	102,320	29,681	64,793	67,208	109,941	10,996	12,060
Interest..........................	129,110	100,383	28,727	63,235	65,875	107,552	10,752	11,782
Dividends.........................	30,396	21,242	9,153	16,280	14,116	26,521	1,400	1,433
Rents, royalties, estates or trusts	12,842	8,392	4,451	6,798	6,044	10,960	731	894
Educational assistance[4].........	9,070	9,014	57	3,885	5,185	6,415	1,553	1,451
Pell grant only...................	2,746	2,732	14	1,023	1,724	1,734	712	515
Other government only.............	1,105	1,099	6	568	536	785	160	225
Scholarships only.................	2,733	2,715	18	1,198	1,535	2,057	307	357
Child support.....................	4,697	4,634	63	375	4,322	3,446	950	809
Financial assistance from outside the household..........................	2,885	2,628	256	1,157	1,728	2,046	452	366
Other income, not elsewhere classified..........	1,886	1,478	408	826	1,060	1,494	210	136
Combinations of income types:								
Government transfer payments...................	68,990	28,107	40,883	31,679	37,310	55,727	8,952	6,977
Public assistance or SSI or both............	7,954	6,559	1,395	3,235	4,719	5,165	2,038	1,472

[1] Refers to people who reported specified race only and no other race category. [2] Persons of Hispanic origin may be of any race. [3] TANF is Temporary Assistance for Needy Families Program. [4] Includes other sources not shown separately. [5] Includes estates and trusts reported as survivor benefits.

Source: U.S. Census Bureau, *Income and Poverty in the United States: 2015*, Current Population Reports, P60-256(RV), September 2016; and "Current Population Survey Tables for Personal Income: Table PINC-09," <http://www.census.gov/topics/income-poverty/income/data/tables.html>, accessed November 2016.

Table 563. Participation in Means-Tested Government Assistance Programs by Selected Participant Characteristics and Program: 2010 and 2012

[As percent of total population, except as noted (48,304 represents 48,304,000). Data are average monthly participation rates. Means-tested programs, which provide cash and noncash assistance, are those that require the income and/or assets of an individual or family to fall below specific thresholds in order to qualify for benefits. There may be additional eligibility requirements. Based on Census Bureau's Survey of Income and Program Participation (SIPP), 2008 Panel, Waves 2-14]

Characteristic	All programs		Medicaid		SNAP[1]		Housing assistance		SSI[2]		TANF or GA[3]	
	2010	2012	2010	2012	2010	2012	2010	2012	2010	2012	2010	2012
Total number of recipients (1,000s)	**48,304**	**52,249**	**35,558**	**37,520**	**28,970**	**33,032**	**10,110**	**10,248**	**6,655**	**7,465**	**2,759**	**2,377**
As percent of the population	20.2	21.3	14.9	15.3	12.1	13.4	4.2	4.2	2.8	3.0	1.2	1.0
Age:												
Under 18 years	37.3	39.2	33.3	34.9	21.1	22.9	6.2	6.1	1.6	1.8	3.2	2.6
18 to 64 years	15.1	16.6	9.2	9.7	10.0	11.5	3.3	3.4	2.9	3.2	0.6	0.5
65 years and over	13.3	12.6	8.3	7.8	6.1	6.9	5.1	4.2	4.4	4.3	0.2	0.1
Sex:												
Male	18.3	19.3	13.5	13.9	10.6	11.8	3.3	3.3	2.5	2.9	1.0	0.8
Female	22.1	23.2	16.2	16.6	13.5	15.0	5.2	5.0	3.0	3.2	1.3	1.1
Race and Hispanic origin:[4]												
White	16.7	17.6	12.3	12.6	9.4	10.6	2.5	2.4	2.2	2.3	0.8	0.7
White, non-Hispanic	12.7	13.2	9.3	9.3	7.3	8.1	2.0	1.9	2.0	2.1	0.5	0.4
Black	40.9	41.6	29.1	29.3	29.0	30.1	15.4	14.5	6.4	7.0	3.4	2.5
Asian or Pacific Islander	18.0	17.8	14.5	14.2	7.5	7.9	3.3	3.9	3.5	3.6	0.6	0.3
Hispanic	35.7	36.4	27.1	26.9	20.8	22.0	5.9	5.3	3.2	3.4	2.3	1.9
Non-Hispanic	17.2	18.1	12.5	12.9	10.5	11.7	3.9	3.9	2.7	3.0	0.9	0.8
Family status:												
In families	20.8	21.8	15.7	16.0	12.6	13.8	3.8	3.7	2.2	2.5	1.3	1.1
Married-couple families	13.9	14.7	10.4	10.7	7.1	8.1	1.2	1.3	1.4	1.5	0.5	0.4
Male householder[5]	28.1	29.5	20.6	21.1	17.2	18.8	2.5	2.3	3.4	3.8	1.6	1.2
Female householder[5]	48.5	50.0	37.5	37.3	34.8	36.7	15.2	14.7	5.6	6.1	4.9	3.7
Unrelated individuals	17.5	18.6	10.8	11.4	10.0	11.7	6.6	6.5	5.5	5.8	0.3	0.5
Marital status:[6]												
Married	9.1	9.8	5.1	5.2	5.7	6.6	1.2	1.2	1.4	1.7	0.2	0.2
Separated, divorced, or widowed	21.2	22.0	12.9	13.1	13.4	14.8	6.6	6.1	6.1	6.2	0.5	0.5
Never married	22.5	24.0	14.8	15.3	14.0	15.7	6.7	6.7	4.9	5.0	1.1	0.9
Educational attainment:[6]												
Less than high school graduate	35.9	37.3	22.7	22.7	23.6	26.4	9.4	8.9	10.0	10.1	1.2	1.2
High school graduate, no college	19.4	21.6	11.8	12.8	12.0	14.4	4.6	4.8	3.9	4.4	0.7	0.6
One or more years of college	8.7	9.6	5.2	5.5	5.3	6.1	2.1	2.1	1.5	1.8	0.3	0.3
Employment or labor force status:[6]												
Employed full-time[7]	5.9	6.7	2.6	2.7	3.8	4.5	1.1	1.2	0.2	0.3	0.1	0.1
Employed part-time[7]	16.0	17.6	9.2	9.6	10.1	12.0	3.3	3.5	1.4	1.7	0.4	0.5
Unemployed	29.0	33.5	15.9	16.4	22.3	26.8	6.3	7.7	1.6	1.6	1.5	1.6
Not in labor force	24.4	25.3	16.8	17.2	14.5	16.1	6.8	6.3	8.3	8.4	0.9	0.9
Disability status:[8]												
With a work disability	42.3	44.7	31.7	33.1	25.9	28.7	10.6	10.7	19.1	20.2	1.6	1.5
With no work disability	11.9	13.0	7.0	7.3	7.7	8.8	2.4	2.4	0.5	0.6	0.5	0.5

[1] Supplemental Nutrition Assistance Program. [2] Supplemental Security Income. [3] Temporary Assistance for Needy Families, or General Assistance. [4] Persons of Hispanic origin may be of any race. [5] No spouse present. [6] For persons age 18 and older. [7] Full-time and part-time employment reflect monthly employment status. [8] For persons age 15 to 64.

Source: U.S. Census Bureau, *Dynamics of Economic Well-Being: Participation in Government Programs, 2009–2012: Who Gets Assistance?*, Current Population Report, P70-141, May 2015. See also <http://www.census.gov/sipp/>.

Table 564. Persons Living in Households Receiving Selected Benefits by Selected Characteristics: 2015

[318,454 represents 318,454,000, except percent. Based on Current Population Survey, 2016 Annual Social and Economic Supplement (CPS ASEC); see text of Section 1 and Appendix III. Persons who lived with someone (a nonrelative or a relative) who received aid. Not every person tallied here received the aid themselves. Persons living in households receiving more than one type of aid are counted only once. Excludes members of the Armed Forces except those living off post or with their families on post. Population controls are based on Census 2010. SNAP = Supplemental Nutrition Assistance Program. See source for information regarding the 2015 CPS ASEC use of a redesigned questionnaire]

Characteristic	Total (1,000)	In household receiving means-tested assistance [1] (1,000)	Percent	In household receiving means-tested cash assistance (1,000)	Percent	In household receiving food stamps (SNAP) (1,000)	Percent	In household in which one or more persons are covered by Medicaid (1,000)	Percent	Living in public or authorized housing (1,000)	Percent
Total.	318,454	115,222	36.2	20,448	6.4	41,098	12.9	92,798	29.1	11,993	3.8
Under 18 years.	73,647	38,722	52.6	5,028	6.8	15,210	20.7	31,669	43.0	3,749	5.1
18 to 24 years.	29,791	12,454	41.8	1,946	6.5	3,960	13.3	10,263	34.5	1,436	4.8
25 to 34 years.	43,763	16,238	37.1	2,328	5.3	5,898	13.5	13,412	30.6	1,562	3.6
35 to 44 years.	40,005	15,167	37.9	2,328	5.8	4,822	12.1	12,131	30.3	1,209	3.0
45 to 54 years.	42,565	12,987	30.5	2,784	6.5	3,915	9.2	10,462	24.6	1,108	2.6
55 to 59 years.	21,835	5,595	25.6	1,745	8.0	2,041	9.3	4,634	21.2	571	2.6
60 to 64 years.	19,300	4,879	25.3	1,503	7.8	1,717	8.9	3,972	20.6	574	3.0
65 years and over.	47,547	9,180	19.3	2,787	5.9	3,535	7.4	6,254	13.2	1,786	3.8
Male.	156,009	54,668	35.0	9,681	6.2	18,250	11.7	44,027	28.2	4,855	3.1
Female.	162,445	60,554	37.3	10,768	6.6	22,848	14.1	48,771	30.0	7,139	4.4
White alone [2].	245,536	79,607	32.4	13,318	5.4	26,185	10.7	64,789	26.4	6,002	2.4
Black alone [2].	41,625	22,910	55.0	4,985	12.0	10,822	26.0	17,770	42.7	4,597	11.0
Asian alone [2].	18,241	5,820	31.9	826	4.5	1,257	6.9	4,781	26.2	450	2.5
Hispanic [3].	56,780	33,527	59.0	4,223	7.4	11,707	20.6	27,801	49.0	2,836	5.0
In married couple families.	191,337	56,594	29.6	8,130	4.2	13,583	7.1	45,685	23.9	2,513	1.3
In families with male householder, no spouse present.	18,287	9,663	52.8	1,376	7.5	3,337	18.2	8,153	44.6	570	3.1
In families with female householder, no spouse present.	48,497	33,040	68.1	6,991	14.4	16,911	34.9	27,558	56.8	5,306	10.9

[1] Means-tested assistance includes means-tested cash assistance, food stamps, Medicaid, and public or authorized housing. [2] Refers to people who reported specific race and did not report any other race category. [3] People of Hispanic origin may be of any race.

Source: U.S. Census Bureau, *Income and Poverty in the United States: 2015*, Current Population Reports, P60-256(RV), September 2016; and "Current Population Survey Detailed Tables for Poverty: Table POV-26," <http://www.census.gov/topics/income-poverty/poverty/data/tables.html>, accessed November 2016.

Table 565. Social Security—Covered Employment, Earnings, and Contribution Rates: 1990 to 2016

[164.5 represents 164,500,000. Includes the Island areas of the U.S. Represents all reported employment. Data are estimated. OASDI is Old-age, survivors, and disability insurance; SMI is Supplementary medical insurance. All data are subject to revision by source]

Item	Unit	1990	2000	2010	2011	2012	2013	2014	2015	2016
Workers with insured status [1]	**Million**	**164.5**	**185.2**	**204.2**	**205.6**	**207.4**	**209.5**	**211.9**	**214.3**	**216.6**
Male.	Million	86.8	95.5	103.4	104.0	104.9	105.8	106.9	108.0	109.0
Female.	Million	77.7	89.7	100.7	101.6	102.6	103.7	105.0	106.3	107.6
Under 20 years old.	Million	4.8	4.9	2.5	2.1	2.1	2.1	2.2	2.3	2.4
Age 20 to 24.	Million	16.6	16.0	16.0	15.7	15.6	15.6	15.7	15.5	15.1
Age 25 to 29.	Million	20.6	17.5	19.3	19.3	19.3	19.5	19.8	20.4	20.8
Age 30 to 34.	Million	21.3	19.2	18.7	19.0	19.4	19.6	19.7	19.7	19.8
Age 35 to 39.	Million	19.3	21.2	18.2	17.9	17.9	18.1	18.3	18.8	19.2
Age 40 to 44.	Million	17.0	21.4	19.6	19.6	19.5	19.1	18.8	18.3	18.0
Age 45 to 49.	Million	12.8	19.2	21.2	20.7	20.2	19.7	19.4	19.5	19.5
Age 50 to 54.	Million	10.1	16.6	20.9	21.1	21.1	21.2	21.1	20.8	20.3
Age 55 to 59.	Million	8.8	12.2	18.3	18.8	19.3	19.6	19.9	20.3	20.4
Age 60 to 64.	Million	8.6	9.3	15.5	15.9	16.2	16.5	17.1	17.6	18.0
Age 65 to 69.	Million	8.0	7.8	11.1	11.9	12.7	13.3	14.0	14.7	15.2
Age 70 to 74.	Million	6.5	7.0	8.0	8.4	8.9	9.4	9.9	10.2	10.9
Age 75 and older.	Million	10.1	12.8	14.8	15.1	15.3	15.7	16.0	16.4	16.9
Workers reported with—										
Taxable earnings [2].	Million	133.0	154.6	157.0	158.6	160.8	163.1	165.6	168.4	170.8
Maximum earnings [2].	Million	7.6	9.6	9.0	9.8	9.9	9.8	10.0	10.2	11.0
Earnings in covered employment [2].	Bil. dol.	2,716	4,832	6,294	6,563	6,894	7,065	7,437	7,834	8,157
Reported taxable [2].	Bil. dol.	2,359	4,008	5,307	5,486	5,707	5,908	6,187	6,499	6,757
Percent of total.	Percent	86.9	82.9	84.3	83.6	82.8	83.6	83.2	83.0	82.8
Average per worker:										
Total earnings [2].	Dollars	20,424	31,256	40,081	41,389	42,882	43,309	44,914	46,512	47,751
Taxable earnings [2].	Dollars	17,739	25,926	33,794	34,594	35,494	36,218	37,363	38,587	39,555
Annual maximum taxable earnings [3].	Dollars	51,300	76,200	106,800	106,800	110,100	113,700	117,000	118,500	118,500
Contribution rates for OASDI: [4]										
Each employer and employee.	Percent	7.65	7.65	7.65	7.65	7.65	7.65	7.65	7.65	7.65
Self-employed [5].	Percent	15.30	15.30	15.30	15.30	15.30	15.30	15.30	15.30	15.30
SMI, monthly premium (as of Jan. 1).	Dollars	28.60	45.50	110.50	115.40	99.90	104.90	104.90	104.90	121.80

[1] Estimated number fully insured for retirement and/or survivor benefits as of end of year. [2] Includes self-employment. Averages per worker computed with unrounded earnings and worker amounts, and may not agree with rounded table amounts. [3] Beginning in 1994, the upper limit on earnings subject to HI taxes was removed. [4] OASDI tax rates for employees and self-employed workers were reduced by 2 percent for 2011 and 2012. This reduction is being made up by transfers from the General Fund of the Treasury to the OASI and DI trust funds. [5] Half of self-employment tax is deductible for income tax purposes and for computing self-employment income subject to social security tax.

Source: U.S. Social Security Administration, *Annual Statistical Supplement to the Social Security Bulletin,* May 2017, and unpublished data. See also <https://www.ssa.gov/policy/docs/statcomps/supplement/2016/>.

Table 566. Social Security (OASDI)—Benefits by Type of Beneficiary: 1990 to 2016

[39,832 represents 39,832,000. A person eligible to receive more than one type of benefit is generally classified or counted only once as a retired-worker beneficiary. OASDI = Old-age, survivors, and disability insurance. See also headnote, Table 567]

Type of beneficiary	1990	2000	2005	2010	2011	2012	2013	2014	2015	2016
Number of benefits [1] (1,000)	**39,832**	**45,415**	**48,434**	**54,032**	**55,404**	**56,758**	**57,979**	**59,007**	**59,963**	**60,907**
Retired workers [2]	24,838	28,499	30,461	34,593	35,600	36,720	37,893	39,009	43,073	44,266
Disabled workers [3]	3,011	5,042	6,519	8,204	8,576	8,827	8,941	8,955	8,909	8,809
Wives and husbands [2,4]	3,367	2,963	2,680	2,477	2,456	2,443	2,442	2,452	2,478	2,506
Children	3,187	3,803	4,025	4,313	4,375	4,419	4,413	4,355	4,297	4,222
Under age 18	2,497	2,976	3,130	3,209	3,245	3,258	3,237	3,166	3,096	3,007
Disabled children [5]	600	729	769	949	977	1,007	1,030	1,049	1,068	1,085
Students [6]	89	98	127	155	153	154	146	140	133	129
Of retired workers	422	459	488	580	594	612	625	635	649	662
Of deceased workers	1,776	1,878	1,903	1,913	1,907	1,907	1,899	1,892	1,893	1,893
Of disabled workers	989	1,466	1,633	1,820	1,874	1,900	1,888	1,828	1,755	1,667
Widowed mothers and fathers [7]	304	203	178	158	158	154	150	143	140	133
Widows and widowers [2,8]	5,111	4,901	4,569	4,286	4,239	4,193	4,139	4,092	4,050	4,004
Parents [2]	6	3	2	2	2	1	1	1	1	1
Special benefits [9]	7	(Z)	(Z)	(Z)	(Z)	(NA)	(NA)	(NA)	(NA)	(NA)
AVERAGE MONTHLY BENEFIT, CURRENT DOLLARS										
Retired workers [2]	603	844	1,002	1,176	1,229	1,262	1,294	1,329	1,342	1,360
Retired worker and wife [2]	1,027	1,420	1,660	1,930	2,019	2,078	2,140	2,209	2,249	2,296
Disabled workers [3]	587	786	938	1,068	1,111	1,130	1,146	1,165	1,166	1,171
Wives and husbands [2,4]	298	416	485	561	587	605	626	651	669	687
Children of retired workers	259	395	493	577	603	617	632	647	651	657
Children of deceased workers	406	550	656	752	783	799	814	831	832	837
Children of disabled workers	164	228	279	318	330	336	341	349	351	355
Widowed mothers and fathers [7]	409	595	725	849	884	900	918	935	940	947
Widows and widowers, nondisabled [2]	556	810	967	1,134	1,185	1,215	1,244	1,276	1,286	1,301
Parents [2]	482	704	851	998	1,045	1,073	1,094	1,121	1,133	1,154
Special benefits [9]	167	217	247	276	286	(NA)	(NA)	(NA)	(NA)	(NA)
AVERAGE MONTHLY BENEFIT, CONSTANT (2016) DOLLARS [10]										
Retired workers [2]	1,088	1,172	1,229	1,295	1,314	1,327	1,341	1,380	1,388	1,360
Retired worker and wife [2]	1,853	1,970	2,037	2,126	2,160	2,185	2,218	2,313	2,343	2,296
Disabled workers [3]	1,059	1,091	1,151	1,176	1,188	1,189	1,188	1,199	1,195	1,171
Wives and husbands [2,4]	538	578	594	618	628	636	649	688	701	687
Children of deceased workers	733	763	805	828	838	840	843	856	855	837
Widowed mothers and fathers [7]	738	826	889	935	945	947	951	966	967	947
Widows and widowers, nondisabled [2]	1,003	1,124	1,186	1,249	1,267	1,278	1,289	1,323	1,328	1,301
Number of benefits awarded (1,000)	**3,717**	**4,290**	**4,672**	**5,697**	**5,567**	**5,655**	**5,533**	**5,361**	**5,440**	**5,456**
Retired workers [2]	1,665	1,961	2,000	2,634	2,578	2,735	2,794	2,772	2,839	2,911
Disabled workers [3]	468	622	830	1,027	999	960	869	779	741	706
Wives and husbands [2,4]	379	385	379	409	399	420	420	428	463	476
Children	695	777	908	1,045	1,017	959	877	810	798	776
Widowed mothers and fathers [7]	58	40	38	32	30	29	27	25	25	24
Widows and widowers [2,8]	452	505	517	550	545	552	546	547	573	563
Parents [2]	(Z)	(Z)	(Z)	(Z)	(Z)	(Z)	(Z)	(Z)	(Z)	(Z)
Special benefits [9]	(Z)	(Z)	(Z)	(Z)	(Z)	(NA)	(NA)	(NA)	(NA)	(NA)
BENEFIT PAYMENTS DURING YEAR (bil. dol.)										
Total [11]	**247.8**	**407.6**	**520.8**	**701.6**	**725.1**	**774.8**	**812.2**	**848.4**	**886.2**	**911.3**
Monthly benefits [12]	247.8	407.6	520.6	701.4	724.9	774.6	812.0	848.2	886.0	911.1
Retired workers [2]	156.8	253.5	321.7	443.4	461.2	497.5	528.9	560.1	592.4	616.0
Disabled workers [3]	22.1	49.8	78.4	115.1	119.6	127.2	130.4	132.2	133.9	143.0
Wives and husbands [2,4]	14.5	19.4	20.5	24.6	24.8	26.0	26.9	28.1	29.3	30.0
Children	12.0	19.3	24.5	30.7	31.2	32.4	33	33.0	33.5	33.5
Under age 18	9.0	14.1	17.9	21.4	21.2	22.2	22.2	22.2	22.3	22.1
Disabled children [5]	2.5	4.6	5.8	8.0	8.7	8.9	9.2	9.6	10.0	10.3
Students [6]	0.5	0.7	0.8	1.3	1.3	1.3	1.3	1.3	1.2	1.2
Of retired workers	1.3	2.1	2.9	4.1	4.3	4.6	4.8	5.0	5.2	5.4
Of deceased workers	8.6	12.5	15.1	18.0	18.1	18.8	18.9	19.2	19.6	19.8
Of disabled workers	2.2	4.7	6.5	8.5	8.8	9.1	9.0	8.9	8.7	8.5
Widowed mothers and fathers [7]	1.4	1.4	1.5	1.6	1.6	1.7	1.7	1.6	1.6	1.6
Widows and widowers [2,8]	40.7	63.9	73.4	86.0	86.5	89.9	91.4	93.2	95.1	95.8
Parents [2]	(Z)	(Z)	(Z)	(Z)	(Z)	(Z)	(Z)	(Z)	(Z)	(Z)
Special benefits [9]	(Z)	(Z)	(Z)	(Z)	(Z)	(NA)	(NA)	(NA)	(NA)	(NA)
Lump sum	0.2	0.2	0.2	0.2	0.2	0.2	0.2	0.2	0.2	0.2

NA Not available. Z Fewer than 500 or less than $50 million. [1] Number of benefit payments in current-payment status, i.e., actually being made at a specified time with no deductions or with deductions amounting to less than a month's benefit. [2] Age 62 and over. [3] Disabled workers under age 65. [4] Includes wife beneficiaries with entitled children in their care and entitled divorced wives. [5] Age 18 and over. Disability began before age 22. [6] Full-time students age 18 and 19. [7] Also includes surviving divorced mothers with entitled children in their care. [8] Includes widows and widowers age 60–61, surviving divorced wives age 60 and over, and disabled widows and widowers age 50 and over. [9] Benefits for persons age 72 and over not insured under regular or transitional provisions of Social Security Act. [10] Constant dollar figures are based on the consumer price index (CPI-U) for December as published by the U.S. Bureau of Labor Statistics. [11] Represents total disbursements of benefit checks by the U.S. Department of the Treasury during the years specified. [12] Distribution by type estimated.

Source: U.S. Social Security Administration, *Annual Statistical Supplement to the Social Security Bulletin, 2016*, May 2017 and earlier reports. See also <http://www.ssa.gov/policy/index.html>.

Table 567. Social Security—Beneficiaries, Annual Payments, and Average Monthly Benefit, 2000 to 2015, and by State and Other Areas, 2016

[45,417 represents 45,417,000. Number of beneficiaries in current-payment status, and annual and average monthly benefit as of December. Data for 2000 are based on 10-percent sample of administrative records. All other years are 100 percent data. See also headnote, Table 566]

Year, state, and other area	Number of beneficiaries (1,000)				Annual payments[2] (mil. dol.)				Average monthly benefit (dol.)		
	Total	Retired workers and dependents[1]	Survivors	Disabled workers and dependents	Total	Retired workers and dependents[1]	Survivors	Disabled workers and dependents	Retired workers[3]	Disabled workers	Widows and widowers[4]
2000	45,417	31,761	6,981	6,675	407,431	274,645	77,848	54,938	845	787	810
2010	54,032	37,489	6,358	10,184	701,436	471,505	105,740	124,191	1,176	1,068	1,134
2011	55,404	38,486	6,305	10,613	724,943	489,698	106,310	128,935	1,229	1,111	1,185
2012	56,758	39,613	6,256	10,889	774,626	527,402	110,346	136,878	1,262	1,130	1,215
2013	57,979	40,804	6,189	10,988	812,050	559,946	112,032	140,072	1,294	1,146	1,244
2014	59,007	41,918	6,790	10,931	848,228	592,616	114,037	141,620	1,329	1,165	1,276
2015	59,963	43,073	6,084	10,806	886,012	626,378	116,352	143,282	1,342	1,166	1,286
Total, 2016[5,6]	60,907	44,266	6,031	10,610	911,132	651,280	117,149	142,703	1,360	1,171	1,301
United States	59,373	43,180	5,812	10,381	896,577	642,279	114,309	139,989	1,360	1,171	1,301
Alabama	1,120	714	125	281	16,336	10,376	2,265	3,695	(NA)	(NA)	(NA)
Alaska	96	70	10	15	1,352	975	177	200	1,337	1,150	1,257
Arizona	1,275	977	113	185	19,462	14,642	2,233	2,587	1,299	1,157	1,261
Arkansas	685	444	72	170	9,669	6,259	1,264	2,146	1,388	1,216	1,343
California	5,755	4,417	529	808	85,057	63,173	10,483	11,401	1,293	1,115	1,229
Colorado	831	632	75	123	12,512	9,294	1,508	1,710	1,335	1,203	1,291
Connecticut	665	511	57	97	11,008	8,394	1,245	1,369	1,358	1,190	1,336
Delaware	202	152	18	32	3,255	2,423	365	467	1,498	1,221	1,459
District of Columbia	81	58	8	16	1,140	812	126	202	1,466	1,248	1,425
Florida	4,431	3,381	381	669	66,293	49,614	7,525	9,154	1,288	1,032	1,153
Georgia	1,751	1,225	181	345	25,782	17,852	3,320	4,610	1,353	1,186	1,325
Hawaii	262	214	21	27	3,911	3,126	413	372	1,340	1,174	1,280
Idaho	325	242	29	54	4,728	3,462	571	695	1,347	1,199	1,267
Illinois	2,196	1,630	225	341	34,026	24,684	4,644	4,698	1,326	1,144	1,337
Indiana	1,318	930	137	251	20,594	14,433	2,787	3,374	1,391	1,192	1,377
Iowa	630	476	62	92	9,543	7,095	1,261	1,187	1,421	1,177	1,406
Kansas	536	394	53	89	8,266	6,027	1,070	1,169	1,363	1,114	1,348
Kentucky	972	610	115	248	13,865	8,568	2,057	3,240	1,404	1,148	1,390
Louisiana	882	560	129	193	12,343	7,585	2,307	2,451	1,299	1,145	1,227
Maine	334	235	29	71	4,676	3,250	547	879	1,272	1,127	1,208
Maryland	967	722	91	153	15,286	11,270	1,845	2,171	1,270	1,095	1,259
Massachusetts	1,247	894	106	247	19,077	13,596	2,168	3,313	1,431	1,215	1,365
Michigan	2,162	1,525	216	421	34,440	24,087	4,528	5,825	1,394	1,175	1,357
Minnesota	995	760	85	149	15,418	11,653	1,766	1,999	1,450	1,212	1,420
Mississippi	653	418	78	158	9,139	5,819	1,312	2,008	1,407	1,162	1,371
Missouri	1,270	881	128	260	18,795	12,927	2,441	3,427	1,280	1,117	1,195
Montana	223	170	21	32	3,188	2,367	404	417	1,341	1,141	1,324
Nebraska	335	252	33	50	5,035	3,738	663	634	1,288	1,104	1,301
Nevada	506	387	42	77	7,561	5,630	830	1,101	1,360	1,104	1,338
New Hampshire	294	212	22	60	4,611	3,339	465	807	1,339	1,232	1,331
New Jersey	1,597	1,215	142	241	26,632	19,941	3,107	3,584	1,445	1,203	1,421
New Mexico	417	297	42	78	5,824	4,094	741	989	1,505	1,289	1,440
New York	3,547	2,622	316	608	55,182	40,267	6,497	8,418	1,280	1,110	1,210
North Carolina	2,020	1,450	182	388	30,225	21,572	3,392	5,261	1,415	1,204	1,353
North Dakota	128	96	15	16	1,852	1,354	290	208	1,360	1,170	1,293
Ohio	2,312	1,623	267	422	34,540	23,746	5,292	5,502	1,297	1,095	1,255
Oklahoma	769	530	86	152	11,206	7,633	1,611	1,962	1,345	1,131	1,331
Oregon	836	639	70	127	12,632	9,437	1,454	1,741	1,325	1,126	1,289
Pennsylvania	2,769	2,006	277	485	43,178	30,886	5,744	6,548	1,361	1,168	1,365
Rhode Island	220	158	18	45	3,339	2,395	354	590	1,409	1,175	1,371
South Carolina	1,090	775	104	211	16,371	11,560	1,909	2,902	1,384	1,146	1,363
South Dakota	172	132	17	23	2,453	1,849	319	285	1,371	1,189	1,282
Tennessee	1,412	966	147	299	20,823	14,207	2,699	3,917	1,289	1,090	1,239
Texas	4,025	2,864	465	696	58,394	40,642	8,726	9,026	1,350	1,141	1,283
Utah	386	288	39	59	5,826	4,279	774	773	1,332	1,152	1,260
Vermont	145	106	12	27	2,157	1,579	237	341	1,388	1,169	1,401
Virginia	1,471	1,077	140	254	22,497	16,302	2,744	3,451	1,371	1,102	1,325
Washington	1,291	971	109	211	20,129	14,919	2,300	2,910	1,395	1,182	1,313
West Virginia	470	301	60	109	6,966	4,326	1,155	1,485	1,423	1,189	1,397
Wisconsin	1,189	891	105	194	18,358	13,615	2,167	2,576	1,343	1,183	1,276
Wyoming	107	81	10	16	1,625	1,206	207	212	1,398	1,163	1,385
American Samoa	6	3	1	2	56	25	14	17	1,379	1,170	1,372
Guam	17	12	3	2	174	114	35	25	877	872	792
Northern Mariana Islands	3	2	1	(Z)	23	14	6	3	916	1,048	870
Puerto Rico	841	529	103	209	8,792	5,002	1,321	2,469	721	790	674
U.S. Virgin Islands	22	18	2	2	290	229	33	28	907	1,040	798
Abroad	642	520	108	14	5,182	3,588	1,422	172	1,191	1,180	1,040
									708	1,124	764

NA Not available. Z Less than 500. [1] Data for 1990-2006 include special benefits for persons age 72 years and over not insured under regular or transitional provisions of Social Security Act. [2] Unnegotiated checks not deducted. [3] Excludes persons with special benefits. [4] Nondisabled only. [5] Includes those with state or area unknown. [6] 2016 data are preliminary.

Source: U.S. Social Security Administration, *Annual Statistical Supplement to the Social Security Bulletin, 2016*, May 2017 and earlier reports. See also <http://www.ssa.gov/policy/index.html>.

Table 568. Social Security Trust Funds: 1990 to 2016

[In billions of dollars (286.7 represents $286,700,000,000)]

Type of trust fund	1990	2000	2010	2011	2012	2013	2014	2015	2016
OLD-AGE AND SURVIVORS INSURANCE (OASI)									
Total income [1]	286.7	490.5	677.1	698.8	731.1	743.8	769.4	801.6	797.5
Net payroll tax contributions	266.1	421.4	544.8	482.4	503.9	620.8	646.2	679.5	678.8
Taxation of benefits	4.8	11.6	22.1	22.2	26.7	20.7	28.0	30.6	31.6
Interest received [2]	16.4	57.5	108.2	106.5	102.8	98.1	94.8	91.2	87.0
Total expenditures [1]	227.5	358.3	584.9	603.8	645.5	679.5	714.2	750.5	776.4
Benefit payments [3]	223.0	352.7	577.4	596.2	637.9	672.1	706.8	742.9	768.6
Assets, end of year	214.2	931.0	2,429.0	2,524.1	2,609.7	2,674.0	2,729.2	2,780.3	2,801.3
DISABILITY INSURANCE (DI)									
Total income [1]	28.8	77.9	104.0	106.3	109.1	111.2	114.9	118.6	160.0
Net payroll tax contributions	28.4	71.1	92.5	81.9	85.6	105.4	109.7	115.4	157.4
Taxation of benefits	0.1	0.7	1.9	1.6	0.6	0.4	1.7	1.1	1.2
Interest received [2]	0.9	6.9	9.3	7.9	6.4	4.7	3.4	2.1	1.4
Total expenditures [1]	25.6	56.8	127.7	132.3	140.3	143.5	145.1	146.6	145.9
Benefit payments [3]	24.8	55.0	124.2	128.9	136.9	140.1	141.7	143.4	142.8
Assets, end of year	11.1	118.5	179.9	153.9	122.7	90.4	60.2	32.3	46.3

[1] Includes other income or expenses not shown separately. [2] Includes relatively small amounts of gifts to the fund. [3] Includes payments for vocational rehabilitation services furnished to disabled persons receiving benefits because of their disabilities. Amounts reflect deductions for unnegotiated benefit checks.

Source: U.S. Social Security Administration, Office of the Chief Actuary, "Statistical Tables," <https://www.ssa.gov/oact/STATS/index.html>, accessed April 2017.

Table 569. Retirement Employee Benefit Participation by Worker Characteristics: 2010 to 2016

[In percent. Based on National Compensation Survey (NCS). The March 2016 NCS obtained data from approximately 6,886 private industry establishments, representing about 114.2 million workers; see Appendix III. Defined benefit plans provide retirement benefits based on employer benefit formulas that may take into account salary, years of service, and age. Defined contribution plans provide benefits based on employer and employee contributions to individual employee accounts and the rate of return on money invested; the retirement benefit depends on the account balance at retirement. See source for more information]

Characteristic	Total [1]				Defined benefit				Defined contribution			
	2010	2014	2015	2016	2010	2014	2015	2016	2010	2014	2015	2016
All workers	**50**	**48**	**49**	**49**	**19**	**16**	**15**	**15**	**41**	**42**	**43**	**44**
Management, professional, and related	68	67	67	69	25	23	21	21	60	61	62	63
Service	23	21	22	23	7	6	6	6	18	17	18	19
Sales and office	53	49	49	50	16	13	13	11	46	45	45	46
Natural resources, construction, and maintenance	51	53	52	49	26	23	24	21	40	44	44	41
Production, transportation, and material moving	51	53	53	53	24	20	19	19	38	42	44	44
Full-time	59	58	59	60	22	19	19	18	50	52	53	54
Part-time	21	19	19	21	8	6	6	5	15	15	15	17
Union	82	83	82	81	67	66	67	65	44	45	45	44
Nonunion	46	45	46	46	13	11	10	10	41	42	43	44

[1] Total is less than the sum of the individual retirement items because many employees participate in both types of plans.

Source: U.S. Bureau of Labor Statistics, *National Compensation Survey: Employee Benefits in the United States, March 2016*, Bulletin 2785, September 2016, and earlier editions. See also <https://www.bls.gov/ncs/ebs/benefits/2016/home.htm>.

Table 570. Percent of U.S. Households Owning Individual Retirement Accounts (IRAs): 2000 to 2016

[Prior to 2014, incidence of individual retirement account (IRA) ownership is based on an annual tracking survey of approximately 4,000 randomly selected, representative U.S. households conducted via landline telephones only. Beginning in 2014, the survey was expanded and is based on a dual frame sample of landline and cell phone numbers, for a total of approximately 6,000 U.S. households. See source for details]

Year and characteristic	Any type of IRA [1]	Tradi- tional IRA	Roth IRA	Employer- spon- sored IRA [2]	Year and characteristic	Any type of IRA [1]	Tradi- tional IRA	Roth IRA	Employer- spon- sored IRA [2]
2000	35.7	28.7	9.2	6.8	2014 [3]	33.7	25.3	15.6	6.0
2005	37.9	30.0	12.8	7.4	2015 [3]	32.3	24.4	16.3	5.4
2007	39.8	32.5	14.9	7.9					
2008	40.5	32.1	15.9	8.6	**2016, total [3, 4]**	**33.8**	**25.5**	**17.4**	**5.7**
2009	39.3	31.2	14.5	8.2	Under 35 years	24.0	14.0	15.0	5.0
2010	41.4	32.8	16.6	8.0	35 to 44 years	33.0	20.0	21.0	6.0
2011	38.8	31.2	15.7	7.5	45 to 54 years	35.0	28.0	21.0	7.0
2012	40.4	32.5	16.8	7.6	55 to 64 years	40.0	33.0	18.0	7.0
2013	37.6	29.4	15.6	7.5	65 years and over	37.0	32.0	14.0	4.0

[1] Excludes ownership of Coverdell Education Savings Accounts, which were referred to as Education IRAs before July 2001. [2] Employer-sponsored IRAs include SEP IRAs, SARSEP IRAs, and SIMPLE IRAs. [3] Lower incidence in 2014, 2015, and 2016 likely results in part from a revised sampling methodology. See source for details. [4] Age is based on the age of the sole or co-decision maker for household saving and investing.

Source: Investment Company Institute, Washington, DC, Holden, Sarah, and Daniel Schrass, "Appendix: Additional Data on IRA Ownership in 2016," ICI Research Perspective 23, No. 1A, January 2017 ©. See also <www.ici.org/pdf/per23-01a.pdf>.

Table 571. State and Local Government Retirement Systems—Beneficiaries and Finances: 1990 to 2016

[In billions of dollars (111.3 represents $111,300,000,000), except as indicated. For fiscal years closed during the 12 months ending June 30. Minus sign (-) indicates negative earnings on investment. Based on the Annual Survey of Public Pensions]

Year and level of government	Number of beneficiaries (1,000)	Receipts					Benefits and withdrawals			Cash and security holdings
		Total [1]	Employee contributions	Government contributions		Earnings on investments	Total [1]	Benefits	Withdrawals	
				State	Local					
1990: All systems.............	4,026	111.3	13.9	14.0	18.6	64.9	38.4	36.0	2.4	721
State-administered............	3,232	89.2	11.6	14.0	11.5	52.0	29.6	27.6	2.0	575
Locally administered..........	794	22.2	2.2	(Z)	7.0	12.9	8.8	8.4	0.4	145
2000: All systems.............	6,292	297.0	25.0	17.5	22.6	231.9	95.7	91.3	4.4	2,169
State-administered............	4,786	247.4	20.7	17.2	16.7	192.8	76.0	72.2	3.8	1,798
Locally administered..........	1,506	49.7	4.3	0.4	5.9	39.1	19.8	19.1	0.7	371
2010: All systems.............	8,271	125.8	39.3	36.2	50.3	347.5	216.5	200.6	4.2	2,671
State-administered............	7,020	98.0	33.2	35.6	29.2	291.1	176.5	163.4	3.5	2,218
Locally administered..........	1,252	27.9	6.1	0.6	21.2	56.5	40.0	37.2	0.7	453
2016: All systems [2]........	10,319	191.6	51.0	60.6	80.0	49.9	303.6	282.9	6.1	3,739
State-administered............	8,791	150.4	43.2	59.8	47.5	44.0	248.1	231.9	5.1	3,055
Locally administered..........	1,528	41.2	7.9	0.8	32.5	5.8	55.5	51.0	1.1	684

Z Less than $50 million. [1] May include items not shown separately. [2] Beginning 2015: 1) the universe of local pension systems was enhanced compared to prior survey years, and 2) data for state systems refer to funds rather than entire systems; changes to accounting standards provide actuarial data on a fund basis and not a system basis.

Source: U.S. Census Bureau, through 1995, *Finances of Employee-Retirement Systems of State and Local Governments*, Series GF, No. 2, annual; and, beginning 2000, "Federal, State, and Local Governments—Survey of Public Pensions: State & Local Data," <http://www.census.gov/govs/retire/>, accessed July 2017.

Table 572. Defined Benefit Retirement Plan Participation Among Workers by Plan Status: 2016

[In percent. All workers participating in defined benefit plans = 100 percent. Based on the March 2016 National Compensation Survey; survey drew responses from approximately 6,886 private industry establishments of all sizes, representing about 114.2 million workers. Excludes farm and private households, the self-employed, Federal government, and establishments with no workers in the survey scope. For more information, see Appendix III, and source <http://www.bls.gov/ncs/ebs/home.htm>]

Characteristics	Open plans [1]	Frozen plans [2]			
		No participants accrue benefits [3]	All participants accrue benefits	Some participants accrue benefits	Workers in plans frozen over 5 years
All workers.................	**62**	**12**	**23**	**3**	**77**
OCCUPATION					
Management, professional, and related..........................	55	15	27	3	75
Management, business, and financial........................	55	19	23	3	80
Professional and related........................	55	13	29	4	71
Service....................	76	(S)	13	(S)	61
Sales and office....................	59	15	24	2	80
Sales and related....................	58	20	20	2	91
Office and administrative support....................	59	14	25	2	76
Natural resources, construction, and maintenance...............	76	4	17	2	70
Construction, extraction, farming, fishing, and forestry..........	92	(S)	5	(S)	65
Installation, maintenance, and repair..........................	59	6	31	4	71
Production, transportation, and material moving.................	62	11	24	3	86
Production....................	48	16	32	3	83
Transportation and material moving....................	74	6	17	2	93
WORK STATUS					
Full time....................	60	13	24	3	77
Part time....................	75	(S)	18	(S)	80
UNION STATUS					
Union....................	79	(S)	18	(S)	66
Nonunion....................	50	19	27	4	80
AVERAGE WAGE PERCENTILE [4]					
Lowest 25 percent....................	65	(S)	23	(S)	81
Lowest 10 percent....................	79	5	16	(S)	61
Second 25 percent....................	64	16	18	2	79
Third 25 percent....................	63	13	22	3	79
Highest 25 percent....................	59	11	27	3	75
Highest 10 percent....................	57	(S)	26	(S)	77
INDUSTRY					
Goods-producing industries....................	56	13	28	3	77
Manufacturing....................	42	18	36	4	76
Service-providing industries....................	64	12	22	2	77
Trade, transportation, and utilities....................	69	6	24	1	90
Information....................	30	(S)	56	(S)	80
Financial activities....................	55	23	19	3	74
Professional and business services....................	70	10	(S)	(S)	99
Education and health services....................	62	(S)	22	(S)	57

S No workers in this category or data do not meet publication standards. [1] Plans open to new participants. [2] New employees are not allowed in the plan. Benefit accruals may continue for existing participants. [3] Participants in these plans stopped accruing benefits on the date the plan was frozen. The benefit the employee receives is calculated as of the day the plan was frozen. [4] The percentiles were computed using earnings and scheduled hours of work reported for individual workers in sampled establishment jobs. For more information, and values, see "Technical Note" in source.

Source: U.S. Bureau of Labor Statistics, *National Compensation Survey: Employee Benefits in the United States, March 2016*, Bulletin 2785, September 2016. See also <http://www.bls.gov/ncs/ebs/>.

Table 573. Defined Benefit Retirement Plans—Distribution of Workers by Primary Formula: 2015

[In percent. All workers participating in defined benefit plans = 100 percent. As of March. Covers full-time employees in private industry. Based on approximately 2,400 private industry establishments participating in the 2015 National Compensation Survey, representing approximately 111.8 million workers; see Appendix III. For definitions of retirement benefit formulas, see source <http://www.bls.gov/ncs/ebs/glossary20152016.htm>. For definition of defined benefit, see headnote, Table 574]

| Characteristics | Tradi- tional | Traditional plan formula | | | | Non- traditional | Non-traditional plan formula | |
		Percent of terminal earnings	Percent of career earnings	Dollar times years [1]	Percent of employer contri- bution		Cash balance	Pension equity
WORKER CHARACTERISTICS								
All workers..........................	**67**	**37**	**7**	**17**	**6**	**33**	**33**	**(S)**
Management, professional, and related........	54	44	9	(S)	(S)	46	45	(S)
Service........................	78	38	(S)	(S)	(S)	22	22	(S)
Sales and office...................	62	40	(S)	10	(S)	38	38	(S)
Natural resources, construction, and maintenance..................	84	23	(S)	40	(S)	16	16	(S)
Production, transportation, and material moving.......................	81	27	(S)	37	(S)	19	19	(S)
Full time.............................	65	38	7	15	5	35	34	(S)
Part time............................	81	21	(S)	41	(S)	19	19	(S)
Union...............................	89	29	(S)	42	(S)	11	11	(S)
Nonunion...........................	54	41	10	(S)	(S)	46	46	(S)
ESTABLISHMENT CHARACTERISTICS								
Goods producing industries..................	77	35	(S)	26	(S)	23	23	(S)
Service providing industries..................	64	37	7	15	5	36	36	(S)
1 to 99 workers.........................	80	47	(S)	21	(S)	20	20	(S)
100 workers or more.........................	62	33	7	16	7	38	38	(S)

S No data were reported or data do not meet publication criteria. [1] Benefits are based on a dollar amount per month for each year of service recognized by the plan.

Source: U.S. Bureau of Labor Statistics, *National Compensation Survey: Health and Retirement Plan Provisions in Private Industry in the United States, 2015,* April 2016, Bulletin 2784. See also <http://www.bls.gov/ncs/ebs/detailedprovisions/2015/ownership/private/home.htm>.

Table 574. Private Pension Plans—Summary by Type of Plan: 2000 to 2014

[In units as indicated (735.7 represents 735,700). Pension plans include defined benefit plans, and defined contribution plans. A defined benefit plan, funded by the employer, promises a specific monthly benefit at retirement, often determined by a formula that includes factors such as salary, age, and job tenure. A defined contribution plan requires the employee to make contributions to an individual account; employers may add contributions to accounts for each employee. The retirement benefit is dependent upon the account balance at retirement, which will reflect contributions, investment gains or losses, and fees charged to the account. Employee Stock Ownership Plans (ESOP) and 401(k) plans are included among defined contribution plans. Data are based on Form 5500 series reports filed with the Department of Labor and exclude (1) selected pension plans qualified under sections 403(b), 457(b) and 457(f) of the Internal Revenue Code, (2) most SARSEP, SEP and SIMPLE IRA plans, (3) unfunded excess benefit plans, (4) selected church plans, (5) unfunded pension plan for select group of management or highly compensated employees, (6) individual retirement accounts (IRAs), and (7) governmental plans]

| Item | Unit | Total | | | | Defined contribution plan | | | | Defined benefit plan | | | |
		2000	2005	2010	2014	2000	2005	2010	2014	2000	2005	2010	2014
Number of plans [1].........	1,000	735.7	679.1	701.0	685.2	686.9	631.5	654.5	640.3	48.8	47.6	46.5	44.9
Total participants [2]........	Million	103.3	117.4	129.7	132.4	61.7	75.5	88.3	94.7	41.6	41.9	41.4	37.7
Active participants [3].....	Million	73.1	82.7	90.6	89.9	50.9	62.4	73.4	75.4	22.2	20.3	17.2	14.5
Assets [4]....................	Bil. dol.	4,203	5,062	6,282	8,307	2,216	2,808	3,833	5,322	1,986	2,254	2,448	2,985
Contributions [5].............	Bil. dol.	231.9	341.4	445.3	501.4	198.5	248.8	314.3	403.5	33.4	92.7	131.1	97.9
Benefits [6]..................	Bil. dol.	341.0	354.5	456.9	650.0	213.5	218.0	287.3	428.4	127.5	136.6	169.6	221.6

[1] Excludes all plans covering only one participant. [2] Includes active, retired, and separated vested participants not yet in pay status. Also includes double counting of workers in more than one plan. [3] Includes any workers currently in employment covered by a plan and who are earning or retaining credited service under a plan. Also includes any nonvested former employees who have not yet incurred breaks in service. [4] Asset amounts shown exclude funds held by life insurance companies under allocated group insurance contracts for payment of retirement benefits. [5] Includes both employer and employee contributions. [6] Includes benefits paid directly from trust funds and premium payments made from plans to insurance carriers. Excludes benefits paid directly by insurance carriers.

Source: U.S. Department of Labor, Employee Benefits Security Administration, "Retirement Bulletins: Private Pension Plans," <https://www.dol.gov/agencies/ebsa/researchers/statistics/retirement-bulletins>, accessed December 2016.

Table 575. Characteristics of U.S. Households Owning Individual Retirement Accounts (IRAs): 2016

[Prior to 2014, incidence of individual retirement account (IRA) ownership is based on an annual tracking survey of approximately 4,000 randomly selected, representative U.S. households conducted via landline telephones only. Beginning in 2014, the survey was expanded and is based on a dual frame sample of landline and cell phone numbers. The 2016 survey is based on a sample of 5,500 U.S. households]

| Characteristic | Unit | Households owning IRAs | | | | House-holds not own-ing IRAs |
		Total	Tradi-tional IRA	Roth IRA	Employer-spon-sored [1]	
MEDIAN PER HOUSEHOLD						
Age of household sole or co-decision maker for investing..........	Years	54	58	52	52	49
Household income [2]...............................	Dollars	90,000	92,500	112,500	100,000	40,000
Household financial assets [3]........................	Dollars	250,000	310,000	300,000	200,000	40,000
Household financial assets in all types of IRAs...................	Dollars	70,000	90,000	77,300	(X)	(X)
Share of household financial assets in type of IRA indicated.......	Percent	33	28	14	(X)	(X)
PERCENT OF HOUSEHOLDS						
Household has defined contribution account or defined benefit plan coverage (total) [4]	Percent	84	83	86	82	42
Defined contribution retirement plan account......................	Percent	76	71	79	75	33
Defined benefit plan coverage..	Percent	40	49	47	38	19
Types of IRAs owned: [4]						
Traditional IRA...	Percent	76	100	64	52	(X)
Roth IRA...	Percent	52	43	100	42	(X)
Employer-sponsored IRA [1]..	Percent	17	12	14	100	(X)

X Not applicable. [1] Employer-sponsored IRAs include SEP IRAs, SAR-SEP IRAs, and SIMPLE IRAs. [2] Total reported is household income before taxes in 2016. [3] Household financial assets include assets in employer-sponsored retirement plans but exclude the household's primary residence. [4] Multiple responses are included.

Source: Investment Company Institute, Washington, DC. Holden, Sarah, and Daniel Schrass, "Appendix: Additional Data on IRA Ownership in 2016," ICI Research Perspective 23, No. 1A, January 2017 ©. See also <www.ici.org/pdf/per23-01a.pdf>.

Table 576. Households with Assets in Individual Retirement Accounts (IRAs) by Type of IRA: 2015 and 2016

[Shown as percent of households with assets in IRAs, by household asset size group. Prior to 2014, incidence of individual retirement account (IRA) ownership is based on an annual tracking survey of approximately 4,000 randomly selected, representative U.S. households conducted via landline telephones only. Beginning in 2014, the survey was expanded and is based on a dual frame sample of landline and cell phone numbers; see source for details. The 2016 survey is based on a sample of 5,500 U.S. households]

| Size of assets | Unit | 2015 | | | 2016 | | |
| | | Total assets in IRAs | Type of IRA owned | | Total assets in IRAs | Type of IRA owned | |
			Traditional IRAs	Roth IRAs		Traditional IRAs	Roth IRAs
PERCENT DISTRIBUTION OF HOUSEHOLDS							
Less than $10,000............................	Percent	15	14	26	14	15	25
$10,000 to $24,999...........................	Percent	19	15	28	14	14	21
$25,000 to $49,999...........................	Percent	13	14	12	12	14	16
$50,000 to $99,999...........................	Percent	16	17	18	17	16	19
$100,000 to $249,999........................	Percent	19	20	11	19	19	14
$250,000 or more............................	Percent	18	20	5	24	22	5
TOTAL ASSETS IN IRAs							
Mean......................................	Dollars	140,800	149,800	61,800	175,200	164,000	66,900
Median....................................	Dollars	50,000	62,500	20,000	70,000	62,500	30,000

Source: Investment Company Institute, Washington, DC. Holden, Sarah, and Daniel Schrass, "Appendix: Additional Data on IRA Ownership in 2016," ICI Research Perspective 23, No. 1A, January 2017 ©. See also <www.ici.org/pdf/per23-01a.pdf>.

Table 577. Defined Contribution 401(k) Type Plans, Active Participants, Assets, Contributions, Benefits, and Return Rates: 1990 to 2014

[Participants in thousands (19,466 represents 19,466,000); values in millions of dollars (384,854 represents $384,854,000,000). Excludes "one-participant plans." Based on Form 5500 filings with Department of Labor. See source for methodology]

Year	Number of 401(k) type plans	Active participants (1,000) [1]	Total assets (mil. dol.) [2]	Total contributions (mil. dol.) [3]	Total benefits (mil. dol.) [4]	Investment rates of return [5]
1990.................	97,614	19,466	384,854	48,998	32,028	(NA)
2000.................	348,053	39,847	1,724,549	169,238	172,211	-3.8
2005.................	436,207	54,623	2,395,792	223,533	189,822	6.3
2010.................	518,675	60,510	3,142,141	267,584	245,474	12.0
2011.................	513,496	61,371	3,146,851	285,679	252,692	2.8
2012.................	516,293	63,088	3,530,122	306,092	284,677	11.1
2013.................	527,047	64,495	4,179,351	327,886	328,680	18.1
2014.................	533,769	62,651	4,399,891	349,216	365,657	6.5

NA Not available. [1] Since 2005, active participants include any workers currently in employment covered by a plan and earning or retaining credited service under a plan. Also includes any nonvested former employees who have not yet incurred a break in service and individuals who are eligible to elect to have the employer make payments to a Code section 401(k) plan. Prior to 2005, active participants were adjusted to exclude individuals who were not contributing to the retirement plan and not entitled to receive benefits. Between 2009 and 2013, all participants reported on the Form 5500-SF were assumed to be active. Since 2014, active participants are separately reported on the Form 5500-SF. [2] Excludes funds held by life insurance companies under allocated group insurance contracts for payment of retirement benefits. [3] Includes both employer and employee contributions. [4] Includes both benefits paid directly from trust funds and premium payments made by plans to insurance carriers. Amounts exclude benefits paid directly by insurance carriers. [5] For plans with 100 or more participants.

Source: U.S. Department of Labor, Employee Benefits Security Administration, Retirement Bulletins, *Private Pension Plan Bulletin Historical Tables and Graphs, 1975-2014*, September 2016. See also <https://www.dol.gov/agencies/ebsa/researchers/statistics>.

Table 578. State Unemployment Insurance—Summary: 2000 to 2015

[In units as indicated (2,110 represents 2,110,000). Includes unemployment compensation for state and local government employees where covered by state law]

Item	Unit	2000	2005	2009	2010	2011	2012	2013	2014	2015
Insured unemployment, average weekly	1,000	2,110	2,661	5,724	4,487	3,681	3,297	2,947	2,574	2,238
Percent of covered employment [1]	Percent	1.7	2.1	4.5	3.6	2.9	2.5	2.2	1.9	1.6
Percent of civilian unemployed	Percent	37.1	35.1	40.1	30.3	26.8	26.4	25.7	26.8	27.0
Unemployment benefits, average weekly	Dollars	221	267	309	299	296	303	310	315	329
Percent of weekly wage	Percent	32.9	34.6	35.8	33.7	32.4	32.4	32.8	32.2	32.6
Weeks compensated	Million	96.0	121.2	266.0	203.1	165.5	147.6	132.2	115.1	100.7
Beneficiaries, first payments [2]	1,000	7,033	7,917	14,173	10,727	9,475	8,662	7,819	7,006	6,501
Average duration of benefits [2]	Weeks	13.7	15.3	18.8	18.9	17.5	17.0	16.9	16.4	15.5
Claimants exhausting benefits	1,000	2,144	2,856	7,530	6,365	4,837	4,228	3,689	3,035	2,508
Percent of first payment [3]	Percent	31.8	35.9	55.3	53.4	48.8	47.2	44.6	40.5	37.6
Contributions collected [4]	Bil. dol.	19.9	34.8	28.2	35.9	44.1	50.5	47.4	43.9	41.8
Benefits paid	Bil. dol.	19.4	29.3	75.9	53.8	43.2	39.8	36.5	32.4	29.8
Unemployment trust fund reserves [5]	Bil. dol.	54.1	29.0	11.1	9.5	11.3	16.7	23.0	30.4	38.8
Average employer tax rate [6]	Percent	1.75	2.86	2.29	3.00	3.40	3.50	3.26	2.90	2.70

[1] Insured unemployment as percent of average covered employment. [2] Weeks compensated during the year divided by the number of first payments. May include more than one period of continuous unemployment. [3] Based on first payments for 12-month period ending June 30. [4] Contributions collected through unemployment taxes paid by employers and by employees in states that tax workers. [5] Reserves as of December 31 are the funds on deposit in a State's account, as reported by the U.S. Treasury. Trust fund balances are the major portion of reserves. The reserves for all States have been adjusted to contain amounts loaned or advanced from the Federal Unemployment Account. These advances, which can be used only for the payment of unemployment benefits, must be repaid. [6] As percent of taxable wages.

Source: U.S. Department of Labor, Employment and Training Administration, "Benefits and Claims: Annual Program & Financial Data (Handbook 394)," <http://www.ows.doleta.gov/unemploy/DataDashboard.asp>, accessed December 2016.

Table 579. State Unemployment Insurance by State and Island Area: 2015

[In units, as indicated (6,501 represents 6,501,000). See headnote, Table 578. For state data on insured unemployment, see Table 652]

State and Island Areas	Beneficiaries, first payments (1,000)	Benefits paid (mil. dol.)	Avg. weekly unemployment benefits (dol.)	Average duration of benefits (weeks)	State and Island Areas	Beneficiaries, first payments (1,000)	Benefits paid (mil. dol.)	Avg. weekly unemployment benefits (dol.)	Average duration of benefits (weeks)
Total	6,501	29,753	329	15.5	MT	24	94	314	14.8
AL	65	193	216	14.5	NE	24	81	300	12.3
AK	27	105	266	17.3	NV	71	343	321	16.1
AZ	83	275	223	15.7	NH	17	67	304	13.2
AR	58	200	303	14.1	NJ	294	1,864	410	18.0
CA	1,012	5,002	306	17.5	NM	33	156	321	17.2
CO	92	498	390	14.4	NY	459	2,156	317	17.3
CT	120	611	356	17.7	NC	108	266	236	11.0
DE	16	70	253	19.1	ND	28	171	498	12.3
DC	21	102	298	17.9	OH	196	898	342	14.6
FL	194	506	235	11.4	OK	60	330	369	15.7
GA	165	382	276	9.3	OR	94	510	348	15.7
HI	23	135	442	15.2	PA	392	1,993	376	16.1
ID	30	95	298	11.9	RI	32	154	334	15.3
IL	326	1,668	339	16.7	SC	56	167	252	11.0
IN	97	324	259	13.9	SD	6	25	302	13.7
IA	93	383	369	12.7	TN	94	284	226	13.1
KS	60	183	365	12.0	TX	483	2,565	385	15.4
KY	60	279	306	18.3	UT	38	153	370	12.1
LA	57	223	215	16.7	VT	17	64	329	13.9
ME	30	109	300	13.2	VA	86	376	299	15.4
MD	107	523	329	16.5	WA	163	892	417	14.9
MA	190	1,337	453	18.0	WV	52	222	301	14.9
MI	242	865	287	12.4	WI	153	528	296	14.1
MN	123	665	409	15.8	WY	16	86	402	14.4
MS	36	94	203	13.9	PR	70	151	118	18.7
MO	104	316	247	13.1	VI	2	10	329	17.3

Source: U.S. Department of Labor, Employment and Training Administration, "Benefits and Claims: Annual Program & Financial Data (Handbook 394)," <http://www.ows.doleta.gov/unemploy/DataDashboard.asp>, accessed December 2016.

Table 580. Workers' Compensation Payments: 2000 to 2014

[In units as indicated (127.1 represents 127,100,000). See headnote, Table 581]

Item	2000	2005	2007	2008	2009	2010	2011	2012	2013	2014
Workers covered (mil.)...................	127.1	128.2	131.7	130.6	124.9	124.6	126.0	128.1	130.2	132.7
Covered wages (bil. dol.).................	4,495.0	5,213.0	5,857.0	5,954.0	5,675.0	5,834.0	6,063.0	6,322.0	6,466.0	6,820.0
Employer costs [1] (bil. dol.)............	**60.7**	**89.8**	**86.5**	**80.6**	**73.9**	**72.8**	**77.8**	**84.4**	**87.6**	**91.8**
Private carriers [1].........................	36.0	51.0	52.3	47.3	43.0	42.8	46.2	51.7	54.3	56.6
State funds........................	8.9	18.2	13.9	12.2	10.6	9.6	9.9	10.6	11.7	12.8
Federal programs [2]....................	3.6	4.1	4.2	4.3	4.1	4.2	4.4	4.5	4.5	4.7
Self-insured employers.................	12.1	16.5	16.1	16.7	16.3	16.2	17.2	17.6	17.1	17.7
Benefits paid [3] (bil. dol.).............	**47.7**	**57.1**	**56.4**	**58.8**	**58.8**	**58.9**	**61.0**	**63.1**	**62.5**	**62.3**
By private carriers.......................	26.9	29.0	29.4	30.7	31.3	31.7	32.7	34.4	34.6	34.4
From state funds........................	7.4	11.1	10.2	10.3	9.9	9.8	9.8	10.0	9.5	9.2
Federal programs [2]....................	3.0	3.3	3.3	3.4	3.5	3.7	3.8	3.8	3.7	3.7
Self-insured employers.................	10.5	13.7	13.5	14.3	14.0	13.9	14.6	14.9	14.7	15.1
Type of benefit:										
Medical..............................	20.9	26.4	27.1	29.0	27.6	29.3	30.5	31.5	31.4	31.4
Cash................................	26.8	30.7	29.3	29.8	31.2	29.7	30.4	31.6	31.1	30.9
Per $100 of covered wages: (dol.)										
Employer costs........................	1.35	1.72	1.48	1.35	1.30	1.25	1.28	1.33	1.35	1.35
Benefits paid.........................	1.06	1.09	0.96	0.99	1.04	1.01	1.01	1.00	0.97	0.91

[1] Costs are employer expenditures in the calendar year for workers' compensation benefits, administrative costs, and/or insurance premiums; for private carriers, includes benefit payments made under deductible provisions. [2] Federal costs and benefits include costs to the federal government and benefits paid, under the Federal Employees' Compensation Act, and costs associated with and benefits paid via the Federal Black Lung Disability Trust Fund. Beginning 1997, data also account for the Longshore and Harbor Workers' Compensation Act. [3] Benefits are payments in the calendar year to injured workers and to providers of their medical care, including benefits paid by employers under deductible provisions in their workers' compensation insurance.

Source: National Academy of Social Insurance, Washington, DC, *Workers' Compensation: Benefits, Coverage, and Costs, 2014*, October 2016, and earlier reports ©. See also <http://www.nasi.org>.

Table 581. Workers' Compensation Payments by State: 2000 to 2014

[In millions of dollars (47,699 represents $47,699,000,000). Calendar-year data. Workers' compensation provides medical care, rehabilitation, and cash benefits for workers who are injured on the job or who contract work-related illnesses. It also pays benefits to families of workers who die of work-related causes. Workers' compensation benefits are paid by private insurance carriers, by state or federal workers' compensation funds, or by self-insured employers. See source for data estimation methodology]

State	2000	2005	2010	2013	2014	State	2000	2005	2010	2013	2014
Total.................	**47,699**	**57,067**	**58,939**	**62,510**	**62,307**	Missouri..................	780	892	801	838	853
						Montana..................	155	227	266	248	246
Alabama................	529	620	629	639	637	Nebraska.................	230	306	316	307	325
Alaska..................	139	183	222	253	215	Nevada...................	347	457	430	370	369
Arizona.................	498	571	702	716	737	New Hampshire.........	177	229	252	221	210
Arkansas...............	214	227	214	208	212	New Jersey..............	1,378	1,702	2,067	2,233	2,269
California...............	9,449	10,868	10,099	12,125	12,093	New Mexico.............	144	259	276	273	262
Colorado................	810	932	800	827	799	New York................	2,761	3,378	4,617	5,544	5,581
Connecticut.............	638	720	795	917	886	North Carolina...........	865	1,382	1,357	1,427	1,311
Delaware................	118	215	212	240	249	North Dakota............	70	82	120	194	191
District of Columbia.....	78	92	105	110	101	Ohio.....................	2,099	2,447	2,209	2,070	2,028
Florida..................	2,577	3,474	2,777	3,131	3,148	Oklahoma...............	485	638	843	813	714
Georgia.................	965	1,409	1,459	1,418	1,433	Oregon..................	425	555	681	669	656
Hawaii..................	231	251	242	260	271	Pennsylvania...........	2,379	2,741	2,935	2,992	3,011
Idaho...................	114	243	240	247	254	Rhode Island............	127	137	160	169	164
Illinois..................	1,944	2,419	3,003	2,624	2,752	South Carolina..........	515	925	891	878	889
Indiana.................	545	569	599	644	589	South Dakota...........	63	86	100	100	98
Iowa....................	343	487	564	639	650	Tennessee..............	774	862	781	761	710
Kansas.................	323	390	405	384	379	Texas...................	2,160	1,597	1,491	1,622	1,549
Kentucky................	584	703	663	676	657	Utah....................	172	257	275	282	272
Louisiana...............	547	705	802	821	795	Vermont.................	101	122	137	150	153
Maine...................	245	281	252	253	253	Virginia..................	597	852	786	897	933
Maryland................	641	784	954	945	955	Washington.............	1,527	1,848	2,309	2,332	2,393
Massachusetts..........	801	922	1,016	1,062	1,148	West Virginia...........	661	765	543	438	424
Michigan................	1,474	1,474	1,272	1,134	1,035	Wisconsin...............	765	1,170	1,072	1,126	1,163
Minnesota..............	798	949	1,035	1,065	1,079	Wyoming................	89	117	154	192	184
Mississippi..............	293	290	338	333	337	**Federal, total [1]**........	**2,957**	**3,258**	**3,672**	**3,691**	**3,681**

[1] Federal benefits include: those paid under the Federal Employees' Compensation Act for civilian employees; the portion of the black lung benefit program that is financed by employers; and a portion of benefits under the Longshore and Harbor Workers' Compensation Act (LHWCA) that are not reflected in state data, namely, benefits paid by self-insured employers and by special funds under the LHWCA. See Appendix H in source for more information about federal programs.

Source: National Academy of Social Insurance, Washington, DC, *Workers' Compensation: Benefits, Coverage, and Costs, 2014*, October 2016, and earlier reports ©. See also <http://www.nasi.org>.

Table 582. Supplemental Security Income—Recipients and Payments: 1990 to 2015

[In units as indicated (4,817 represents 4,817,000). Recipients and monthly payment as of December. Payments are federally administered, for the calendar year. Includes persons with a federal SSI payment and/or state supplementation]

Program	Unit	1990	2000	2005	2010	2011	2012	2013	2014	2015
Recipients, total	**1,000**	**4,817**	**6,602**	**7,114**	**7,912**	**8,113**	**8,263**	**8,363**	**8,336**	**8,310**
Aged	1,000	1,454	1,289	1,214	1,184	1,182	1,156	1,157	1,152	1,157
Blind	1,000	84	79	75	69	69	68	68	67	68
Disabled	1,000	3,279	5,234	5,825	6,659	6,862	7,039	7,139	7,116	7,084
Payments, total [1]	**Mil. dol.**	**16,133**	**30,672**	**37,236**	**48,195**	**49,520**	**52,075**	**53,900**	**54,693**	**54,966**
Aged	Mil. dol.	3,559	4,540	4,965	5,454	5,431	5,486	5,592	5,688	5,729
Blind	Mil. dol.	329	386	414	423	422	427	432	440	448
Disabled	Mil. dol.	12,245	25,746	31,857	42,317	43,667	46,162	47,875	48,565	48,788
Average monthly payment, total	**Dollars**	**276**	**379**	**439**	**501**	**502**	**519**	**529**	**532**	**541**
Aged	Dollars	208	300	360	400	398	409	417	420	428
Blind	Dollars	319	413	475	522	520	532	542	548	558
Disabled	Dollars	303	398	455	518	519	537	547	550	560

[1] Totals for Aged, Blind, and Disabled are derived. The derivation creates slight discrepancies between the sum of the group totals and total payments.

Source: U.S. Social Security Administration, *Annual Statistical Supplement to the Social Security Bulletin, 2016,* May 2017. See also <http://www.ssa.gov/policy/index.html>.

Table 583. Supplemental Security Income (SSI)—Recipients and Payments by State and Other Area: 2010 to 2015

[In units as indicated (7,912 represents 7,912,000). Recipients as of December; payments for calendar year. Data cover federal SSI payments and/or federally administered state supplementation]

State and other area	Recipients (1,000) 2010	Recipients (1,000) 2015	Payments for the year (mil. dol.) 2010	Payments for the year (mil. dol.) 2014	Payments for the year (mil. dol.) 2015	State and other area	Recipients (1,000) 2010	Recipients (1,000) 2015	Payments for the year (mil. dol.) 2010	Payments for the year (mil. dol.) 2014	Payments for the year (mil. dol.) 2015
Total [1]	**7,912**	**8,310**	**48,195**	**54,693**	**54,966**	MO	134	140	785	898	902
U.S.	**7,911**	**8,309**	**48,189**	**54,685**	**54,959**	MT	18	18	98	112	113
AL	172	171	996	1,087	1,085	NE	26	28	144	169	174
AK	12	13	70	76	77	NV	41	53	241	327	349
AZ	110	120	644	764	782	NH	18	20	103	121	123
AR	107	110	603	703	706	NJ	169	182	1,001	1,152	1,174
CA	1,269	1,293	8,870	9,572	9,626	NM	60	64	340	392	402
CO	66	73	377	461	466	NY	681	649	4,445	4,665	4,193
CT	58	64	340	405	417	NC	219	236	1,243	1,461	1,492
DE	16	17	91	107	109	ND	8	8	43	47	48
DC	24	27	153	187	191	OH	286	312	1,784	2,074	2,103
FL	484	571	2,760	3,491	3,612	OK	94	97	541	617	624
GA	228	258	1,317	1,625	1,677	OR	75	86	439	549	563
HI	25	25	157	170	170	PA	358	368	2,229	2,509	2,510
ID	27	31	155	190	195	RI	33	33	201	210	214
IL	273	275	1,662	1,811	1,830	SC	112	118	635	733	747
IN	118	129	716	833	861	SD	14	15	75	88	90
IA	48	51	266	310	316	TN	175	182	1,023	1,160	1,181
KS	46	48	269	307	313	TX	617	666	3,316	4,000	4,070
KY	192	184	1,116	1,174	1,173	UT	28	31	160	195	202
LA	175	179	989	1,140	1,147	VT	15	16	87	98	99
ME	35	37	196	227	230	VA	148	156	832	968	995
MD	107	120	658	792	818	WA	137	151	881	1,009	1,022
MA	193	188	1,211	1,183	1,197	WV	80	76	472	494	493
MI	254	276	1,581	1,854	1,875	WI	107	118	625	747	768
MN	86	94	516	614	624	WY	6	7	35	41	41
MS	126	123	699	766	771	MP [2]	1	1	6	8	7

[1] Includes Northern Mariana Islands and recipients whose residence was "unknown." Total may not equal sum due to rounding. [2] Northern Marianas.

Source: U.S. Social Security Administration, *Annual Statistical Supplement to the Social Security Bulletin, 2016*, May 2017. See also <http://www.ssa.gov/policy/>.

Table 584. Temporary Assistance for Needy Families (TANF)—Families and Recipients: 1980 to 2016

[In thousands (3,712 represents 3,712,000). Average monthly families and recipients for calendar year. Prior to TANF, the cash assistance program to families was called Aid to Families with Dependent Children (1980–1996). Under the Personal Responsibility and Work Opportunity Reconciliation Act of 1996, the program became TANF. See text, this section. Includes Puerto Rico, Guam, and Virgin Islands]

Year	Families	Recipients	Year	Families	Recipients	Year	Families	Recipients
1980	3,712	10,774	2001	2,104	5,359	2009	1,769	4,154
1990	4,057	11,695	2002	2,048	5,069	2010	1,858	4,403
1995	4,791	13,418	2003	2,024	4,929	2011	1,846	4,363
1996	4,434	12,321	2004	1,979	4,748	2012	1,723	4,017
1997	3,740	10,376	2005	1,894	4,469	2013	1,612	3,713
1998	3,050	8,347	2006	1,777	4,148	2014	1,476	3,407
1999	2,554	6,824	2007	1,674	3,897	2015	1,300	3,010
2000	2,215	5,778	2008	1,633	3,795	2016	1,174	2,678

Source: U.S. Department of Health and Human Services, Administration for Children and Families, "Temporary Assistance for Needy Families, Caseload Data," <http://www.acf.hhs.gov/programs/ofa/programs/tanf>, accessed July 2017.

Table 585. Temporary Assistance for Needy Families (TANF)—Recipients by State and Other Areas: 2010 to 2016

[In thousands (1,858 represents 1,858,000). Average monthly families and recipients for calendar year. See headnote, Table 584]

State or other area	Families 2010	2015	2016	Recipients 2010	2015	2016	State or other area	Families 2010	2015	2016	Recipients 2010	2015	2016
Total [1]	1,858	1,300	1,174	4,403	3,010	2,678	MT	4	3	3	9	7	8
U.S.	1,843	1,289	1,165	4,361	2,981	2,652	NE	8	5	5	18	10	11
AL	22	13	11	53	30	25	NV	11	11	10	27	27	24
AK	3	3	3	9	8	8	NH	5	3	2	11	5	5
AZ	28	11	10	60	24	20	NJ	34	23	17	81	53	39
AR	8	5	4	19	10	8	NM	20	12	12	54	30	29
CA	584	436	390	1,437	1,094	955	NY	122	110	105	272	255	240
CO	11	17	17	29	44	44	NC	24	14	17	46	26	31
CT	17	13	11	34	25	21	ND	2	1	1	5	3	3
DE	5	4	4	15	13	12	OH	104	59	57	238	112	107
DC	8	6	5	19	15	12	OK	9	7	7	21	16	16
FL	58	49	47	105	83	78	OR	28	19	17	72	44	37
GA	20	13	13	38	26	24	PA	54	63	56	130	158	140
HI	9	7	6	26	21	17	RI	7	5	5	17	11	10
ID	2	2	2	3	3	3	SC	19	10	9	44	23	21
IL	23	18	15	66	40	33	SD	3	3	3	7	6	6
IN	35	9	8	86	17	16	TN	61	36	30	157	81	67
IA	18	11	10	46	28	26	TX	51	31	29	117	68	64
KS	15	6	5	38	14	12	UT	6	4	4	18	9	9
KY	30	24	23	62	48	49	VT	3	3	3	6	6	6
LA	11	5	6	24	12	14	VA	35	23	21	79	50	44
ME	11	5	4	26	10	8	WA	67	33	30	162	73	65
MD	25	20	21	60	48	51	WV	10	7	7	23	16	15
MA	50	35	31	97	65	57	WI	23	22	18	53	50	39
MI	68	20	16	179	49	39	WY	(Z)	(Z)	(Z)	1	1	1
MN	23	19	19	50	44	45	GU	1	1	1	3	2	2
MS	12	7	6	25	13	11	PR	14	10	8	37	28	23
MO	36	24	14	86	57	32	VI	1	(Z)	(Z)	2	1	1

Z Less than 500. [1] Includes Puerto Rico (PR), Guam (GU), and the Virgin Islands (VI).

Source: U.S. Department of Health and Human Services, Administration for Children and Families, "Temporary Assistance for Needy Families, Caseload Data," <http://www.acf.hhs.gov/programs/ofa/programs/tanf/data-reports>, accessed July 2017.

Table 586. Household Use of Food Pantries and Emergency (Soup) Kitchens: 2015

[In thousands (124,593 represents 124,593,000), except percent. Based on the 2015 Current Population Survey Food Security Supplement that asked questions about use of food pantries and emergency kitchens among households with incomes below 185 percent of the Federal poverty level, and households above this level that indicated difficulty in meeting food needs. Covers the use of food pantries and emergency kitchens at least once during the 12-month period ended December 2015, for persons occupying housing units; survey excludes homeless persons, and may also miss persons in tenuous housing arrangements (such as temporarily living with another family)]

Category	Food pantries Total households [1]	Number of users	Percent using	Emergency (soup) kitchens Total households [1]	Number of users	Percent using
All households	**124,593**	**6,514**	**5.2**	**124,589**	**727**	**0.6**
All persons in households	314,558	17,638	5.6	314,551	1,456	0.5
Adults in households	241,629	12,231	5.1	241,653	1,123	0.5
Children in households	72,929	5,407	7.4	72,898	333	0.5
Households by food security status: [2]						
Food-secure households	108,933	2,095	1.9	108,931	177	0.2
Food-insecure households	15,631	4,404	28.2	15,633	550	3.5
Households with low food security	9,418	2,160	22.9	9,423	192	2.0
Households with very low food security	6,213	2,244	36.1	6,210	358	5.8

[1] Totals exclude households that did not answer questions about using food pantries and emergency kitchens, and also households that did not answer questions about food security. [2] Food secure households report zero or 1-2 indications, typically anxiety over food sufficiency or supply, with little or no indication of changes in diets or food intake. Households with low food security report reduced quality, variety, or desirability of diet, with little or no indication of reduced food intake. Households with very low food security report multiple indications of disrupted eating patterns and reduced food intake. See also headnote, Table 209.

Source: U.S. Department of Agriculture, Economic Research Service, *Statistical Supplement to Household Food Security in the United States in 2015*, No. 072, September 2016. See also <http://www.ers.usda.gov/topics/food-nutrition-assistance/food-security-in-the-us.aspx>.

Table 587. Temporary Assistance for Needy Families (TANF)—Expenditures by State: Fiscal Years 2000 to 2015

[In millions of dollars (24,781 represents $24,781,000,000). Represents federal and state funds expended in fiscal year. Negative values occur when contracted obligations are fulfilled or terminated and the actual cost for the service is less than the obligated amount. Expenditures on assistance includes cash, payments, vouchers, and other forms of benefits designed to meet a family's ongoing basic needs (food, clothing, shelter, utilities, household goods, personal care items, and general incidental expenses)]

State	2000, Total	2010, Total	2015 Total [1]	2015 Expenditures on assistance	State	2000, Total	2010, Total	2015 Total [1]	2015 Expenditures on assistance
U.S.	24,781	33,255	29,204	7,797	MO	321	405	398	77
AL	96	191	161	32	MT	44	47	41	17
AK	93	62	74	46	NE	79	98	92	24
AZ	261	350	449	27	NV	69	108	91	46
AR	139	233	144	9	NH	73	86	42	15
CA	6,481	7,239	6,273	2,839	NJ	321	1,446	1,089	191
CO	205	323	301	77	NM	149	237	205	53
CT	436	500	479	70	NY	3,512	5,347	4,972	1,574
DE	55	75	95	20	NC	440	563	483	52
DC	157	251	263	70	ND	33	37	39	5
FL	781	901	823	177	OH	995	1,331	1,007	271
GA	386	563	533	64	OK	130	179	171	28
HI	162	378	264	52	OR	169	392	348	126
ID	43	35	35	8	PA	1,327	964	889	215
IL	879	1,255	1,374	68	RI	172	149	148	20
IN	342	344	233	20	SC	245	180	180	41
IA	163	194	179	40	SD	21	31	27	14
KS	151	207	141	20	TN	293	338	247	81
KY	203	281	254	140	TX	727	908	965	58
LA	118	264	213	19	UT	100	132	79	22
ME	108	141	85	40	VT	62	78	83	18
MD	336	564	579	111	VA	418	299	241	83
MA	690	1,022	974	266	WA	535	1,494	935	154
MI	1,264	1,703	1,295	150	WV	134	199	117	24
MN	381	475	491	85	WI	382	524	505	120
MS	62	106	68	11	WY	34	29	28	5

[1] Includes other items not shown separately.

Source: U.S. Department of Health and Human Services, Administration for Children and Families, "Temporary Assistance for Needy Families, Expenditure Data," <http://www.acf.hhs.gov/programs/ofa/programs/tanf/data-reports>, accessed May 2017.

Table 588. Federal Food Programs: Fiscal Years 1990 to 2016

[20.0 represents 20,000,000, except as noted. For fiscal years ending September 30. Program data include Puerto Rico, Virgin Islands, Guam, American Samoa, Northern Marianas, and the former Trust Territory when a federal food program was operated in these areas. Participation data are average monthly figures except as noted. Participants are not reported for The Emergency Assistance Program (TEFAP)]

Program	Unit	1990	2000	2005	2010	2013	2014	2015	2016 (P)
Supplemental nutrition assistance program: [1]									
Participants	Million	20.0	17.2	25.6	40.3	47.6	46.7	45.8	44.2
Value of benefits	Mil. dol.	14,143	14,983	28,568	64,702	76,066	69,999	69,645	66,597
Average monthly benefit value per recipient	Dollars	59	73	93	134	133	125	127	126
Nutrition assistance program for Puerto Rico: [2]									
Federal grant	Mil. dol.	937	1,268	1,495	2,001	2,001	1,903	1,951	1,959
National school lunch program (NSLP):									
Children participating [3]	Million	24.1	27.3	29.6	31.8	30.7	30.5	30.5	30.4
Free lunches served	Million	1,662	2,205	2,477	2,948	3,168	3,191	3,274	3,365
Reduced-price lunches served	Million	273	409	479	498	425	403	360	336
Federal cost (cash payments)	Mil. dol.	3,214	5,493	7,055	9,752	11,058	11,356	11,697	12,256
School breakfast (SB):									
Children participating [3]	Million	4.1	7.6	9.4	11.7	13.2	13.6	14.0	14.8
Federal cash payments	Mil. dol.	599	1,393	1,927	2,859	3,514	3,685	3,892	4,212
Special supplemental food program (WIC): [4]									
Participants	Million	4.5	7.2	8.0	9.2	8.7	8.3	8.0	7.7
Federal cost for food	Mil. dol.	1,637	2,853	3,603	4,562	4,497	4,324	4,176	3,949
Child and adult care (CACFP): [5]									
Participants [6]	Million	1.5	2.7	3.1	3.4	3.7	3.9	4.2	4.4
Federal cash payments	Mil. dol.	719	1,500	1,904	2,398	2,721	2,850	3,010	3,220
Federal cost of food commodities for: [7]									
School food programs [8]	Mil. dol.	617	655	975	1,128	1,163	1,302	1,307	1,311
TEFAP [9]	Mil. dol.	329	225	372	566	629	560	452	586

P Preliminary. [1] The program name was changed from Food Stamp to Supplemental Nutrition Assistance (SNAP) in October 2008. [2] Puerto Rico receives a grant in lieu of SNAP benefits. [3] Average participation per day are 9-month averages (excludes summer months). Includes children in public and nonprofit private elementary and secondary schools and in residential child care institutions. [4] WIC serves pregnant and postpartum women, infants, and children up to age 5. [5] CACFP provides year-round subsidies to feed preschool children and elderly and disabled adults in day care centers, and children and youth in emergency shelters for the homeless and eligible afterschool care programs. [6] Average quarterly daily attendance at participating institutions. [7] Includes the federal cost of commodity entitlements, cash-in-lieu of commodities, and bonus foods. [8] National school lunch and breakfast programs, and special milk program. [9] The Emergency Food Assistance Program distributes foods through nonprofit local emergency feeding organizations. Data for 1990 includes soup kitchens/food banks program.

Source: U.S. Department of Agriculture, Food and Nutrition Service, "Program Data, Overview," <https://www.fns.usda.gov/pd/overview>, accessed March 2017.

Table 589. Federal Supplemental Nutrition Assistance Program (SNAP) by State: 2000 to 2016

[17,194 represents 17,194,000; 14,983 represents $14,983,000,000. Participation data are average monthly number participating in fiscal year ending September 30]

State	Persons (1,000)			Benefits (mil. dol.)			State	Persons (1,000)			Benefits (mil. dol.)		
	2000	2010	2016	2000	2010	2016		2000	2010	2016	2000	2010	2016
Total [1]	17,194	40,302	44,219	14,983	64,702	66,597	MS..........	276	576	583	226	847	814
							MO..........	423	901	811	358	1,361	1,183
U.S.........	17,156	40,245	44,145	14,927	64,562	66,434	MT..........	59	114	117	51	177	166
AL..........	396	805	851	344	1,226	1,255	NE..........	82	163	176	61	238	241
AK..........	38	76	82	46	159	175	NV..........	61	278	440	57	415	630
AZ..........	259	1,018	960	240	1,588	1,402	NH..........	36	104	98	28	152	121
AR..........	247	467	426	206	686	578	NJ..........	345	622	880	304	1,030	1,223
CA..........	1,831	3,239	4,340	1,639	5,692	7,238	NM..........	169	357	471	140	542	693
CO..........	156	405	476	127	688	728	NY..........	1,439	2,758	2,968	1,361	4,985	4,922
CT..........	165	336	432	138	570	686	NC..........	488	1,346	1,568	403	2,072	2,249
DE..........	32	113	148	31	171	221	ND..........	32	60	54	25	95	79
DC..........	81	118	135	77	196	210	OH..........	610	1,607	1,609	520	2,734	2,396
FL..........	882	2,603	3,455	771	4,417	5,221	OK..........	253	582	613	208	900	886
GA..........	559	1,591	1,733	489	2,565	2,663	OR..........	234	705	735	198	1,067	1,073
HI..........	118	138	177	166	358	484	PA..........	777	1,575	1,864	656	2,333	2,729
ID..........	58	194	185	46	300	255	RI..........	74	139	171	59	238	273
IL..........	817	1,646	1,914	777	2,784	3,041	SC..........	295	797	805	249	1,256	1,222
IN..........	300	813	742	268	1,291	1,068	SD..........	43	95	96	37	153	145
IA..........	123	340	381	100	526	508	TN..........	496	1,224	1,113	415	1,966	1,672
KS..........	117	270	254	83	403	342	TX..........	1,333	3,552	3,768	1,215	5,447	5,309
KY..........	403	778	666	337	1,186	981	UT..........	82	247	220	68	367	302
LA..........	500	826	927	448	1,286	1,547	VT..........	41	86	80	32	124	116
ME..........	102	230	189	81	356	255	VA..........	336	786	826	263	1,213	1,169
MD..........	219	561	744	199	878	1,079	WA..........	295	956	1,011	241	1,387	1,453
MA..........	232	749	779	182	1,166	1,190	WV..........	227	341	358	185	487	499
MI..........	603	1,776	1,474	457	2,809	2,168	WI..........	193	715	728	129	1,000	923
MN..........	196	430	479	165	625	603	WY..........	22	35	34	19	52	49

[1] Includes Guam and the Virgin Islands. Puerto Rico, American Samoa, and the Northern Marianas receive nutrition assistance grants in lieu of SNAP.

Source: U.S. Department of Agriculture, Food and Nutrition Service, Supplemental Nutrition Assistance Program (SNAP), "National and/or State Level Monthly and/or Annual Data," <https://www.fns.usda.gov/pd/supplemental-nutrition-assistance-program-snap>, accessed March 2017.

Table 590. Selected Characteristics of Supplemental Nutrition Assistance Program (SNAP) Households and Participants: 1990 to 2015

[7,811 represents 7,811,000. For fiscal years ending September 30. Data for 1990 exclude Guam and the Virgin Islands. Based on a sample of households from the SNAP Quality Control System]

Fiscal Year	Households				Participants		
	Total [1] (1,000)	Percent of total			Total (1,000)	Percent of total	
		With children	With elderly [2]	With disabled [3]		Children	Elderly [2]
1990................	7,811	60.3	18.1	8.9	20,440	49.6	7.7
1995................	10,883	59.7	16.0	18.9	26,955	51.5	7.1
1996................	10,552	59.5	16.2	20.2	25,926	51.0	7.3
1997................	9,452	58.3	17.6	22.3	23,117	51.4	7.9
1998................	8,246	58.3	18.2	24.4	19,969	52.8	8.2
1999................	7,670	55.7	20.1	26.4	18,149	51.5	9.4
2000................	7,335	53.9	21.0	27.5	17,091	51.3	10.0
2001................	7,450	53.6	20.4	27.7	17,297	51.1	9.6
2002................	8,201	54.1	18.7	27.0	19,041	51.0	8.9
2003................	8,971	55.1	17.1	22.1	20,764	50.8	8.1
2004................	10,069	54.3	17.3	22.7	23,279	50.0	8.2
2005................	10,852	53.7	17.1	23.0	24,794	49.9	8.3
2006................	11,313	52.0	17.9	23.1	25,472	49.1	8.7
2007................	11,561	51.0	17.8	23.8	25,775	48.9	8.8
2008................	12,464	50.6	18.5	22.6	27,607	48.4	9.1
2009................	14,981	49.9	16.6	21.2	32,889	47.5	8.3
2010................	18,369	48.7	15.5	19.8	39,759	46.6	7.9
2011................	20,803	47.1	16.5	20.2	44,148	45.1	8.5
2012................	22,046	45.3	17.2	20.0	46,022	44.5	9.0
2013................	22,802	44.8	17.4	20.3	47,098	44.4	9.3
2014................	22,445	43.6	19.0	20.4	45,874	44.2	10.1
2015................	22,293	42.7	19.6	20.2	45,184	44.0	10.6

[1] Total does not include those who are ineligible or those receiving disaster benefits. [2] Persons 60 years old and over. [3] The substantial increase in 1995 and decrease in 2003 are due in part to the changes in definition of a household with an individual with a disability. Prior to 1995, disabled households were defined as households with SSI income but no members over age 59. In 1995, that definition changed to households with at least one member under age 65 who received SSI, or at least one member age 18-61 who received Social Security, veterans' benefits, or other government benefits as a result of a disability. In 2003, the definition changed to households with either SSI income, or a medical expense deduction and without an elderly person, or containing a nonelderly adult working fewer than 30 hours per week and receiving Social Security, veterans' benefits, or workers' compensation. In 2015, the definition of individuals with disabilities was expanded to include also non-elderly adults in single-person SNAP households who receive Social Security income.

Source: U.S. Department of Agriculture, Food and Nutrition Service, *Characteristics of Supplemental Nutrition Assistance Program Households: Fiscal Year 2015*, Report No. SNAP-16-CHAR, November 2016. See also <http://www.fns.usda.gov/ops/supplemental-nutrition-assistance-program-snap-research>.

Table 591. Supplemental Nutrition Assistance Program (SNAP) Households and Participants—Summary: 2015

[22,293 represents 22,293,000. For fiscal year ending September 30. Based on a sample of households from the Supplemental Nutrition Assistance Program Quality Control (QC) System. Figures are lower than official participation counts because they do not include ineligible participants or those receiving disaster food stamp assistance]

Household type and income source	Households Number (1,000)	Households Percent	Age, sex, race, and ethnicity	Participants Number (1,000)	Participants Percent
Total	**22,293**	**100.0**	**Total**	**45,184**	**100.0**
With children	9,510	42.7	Children	19,891	44.0
Single-parent households	5,587	25.1	Under 5 years old	6,119	13.5
Married-couple households	1,610	7.2	5 to 17 years old	13,772	30.5
Other [1]	2,313	10.4	Nonelderly adults	20,494	45.4
With elderly	4,361	19.6	18 to 35 years old	10,159	22.5
Living alone	3,495	15.7	36 to 59 years old	10,335	22.9
Not living alone	865	3.8	Elderly (60 years old and over)	4,799	10.6
Disabled nonelderly	4,498	20.2			
Living alone	2,761	12.4	Male	19,547	43.3
Not living alone	1,737	7.8	Female	25,637	56.7
With earned income	7,081	31.8	White, non-Hispanic	16,574	36.7
Wages and salaries	6,221	27.9	Black, non-Hispanic	11,772	26.1
Unearned income	12,378	55.5	Hispanic	7,730	17.1
TANF [2]	1,293	5.8	Asian	1,301	2.9
Supplemental security income	4,559	20.5	Native American	560	1.2
Social security	5,451	24.5	Multiracial, non-Hispanic	431	1.0
No income	4,943	22.2	Race unknown	6,816	15.1

[1] Other households with children include other multiple-adult households and children-only households. [2] Temporary Assistance for Needy Families (TANF) program.

Source: U.S. Department of Agriculture, Food and Nutrition Service, *Characteristics of Supplemental Nutrition Assistance Program Households: Fiscal Year 2015*, Report No. SNAP-16-CHAR, November 2016. See also <https://www.fns.usda.gov/ops/supplemental-nutrition-assistance-program-snap-research>.

Table 592. Primary Child Care Arrangements for Children Under Age 5, by Selected Characteristics: Spring 2011

[In percent, except as indicated (10,859 represents 10,859,000). For children with employed mothers. The primary child care arrangement is defined as the arrangement used the most hours per week. The numbers for all arrangements may exceed the total number of children because of ties among arrangements in the greatest number of hours per week. Based on Survey of Income and Program Participation (SIPP), 2008 Panel, Wave 8, January-April 2011. Estimates are based on responses from a sample of the population, and may differ from the actual values because of sampling variability and other factors. Apparent differences between the estimates of two or more groups may not be statistically different]

Characteristic	Children Number (1,000)	Type of arrangement [1] (percent) In relative care	In non-relative care	In day care center	No child care arrange-ment
Total	**10,859**	**51.7**	**40.0**	**19.8**	**11.0**
MARITAL STATUS OF MOTHER					
Married	7,692	51.0	40.0	19.6	11.7
Widowed, separated, divorced	816	47.5	39.0	20.1	11.5
Never married	2,352	55.2	40.3	20.6	8.6
RACE AND HISPANIC ORIGIN OF MOTHER					
White alone	8,391	51.7	39.8	19.3	11.9
Non-Hispanic	6,945	48.9	42.7	21.3	12.5
Black alone	1,539	52.2	38.5	21.2	8.6
Asian alone	497	52.1	41.4	19.0	9.3
Hispanic (of any race)	1,604	65.6	25.6	9.7	8.3
AGE OF MOTHER					
15-24 years	1,413	64.5	30.2	18.2	9.4
25-34 years	5,830	51.5	41.0	20.7	10.8
35+ years	3,616	47.0	42.1	19.2	12.0
EDUCATION OF MOTHER					
Less than high school	751	58.1	22.1	6.5	19.3
High school graduate	2,091	59.7	31.9	16.1	10.8
Some college	3,690	57.3	36.3	17.2	9.3
Bachelor's degree or higher	4,327	42.0	50.1	26.3	11.1
WORK STATUS OF MOTHER					
Employed full-time	7,264	48.0	45.4	24.1	9.7
Employed part-time	2,808	62.2	28.6	12.5	11.6
Self-employed	787	48.2	30.4	6.9	20.3
FAMILY INCOME (monthly)					
Less than $1,500	1,150	58.4	31.8	12.5	12.2
$1,500 - $2,999	1,788	56.4	35.4	19.2	11.0
$3,000 - $4,499	1,668	59.8	36.0	17.5	8.7
$4,500 and over	6,068	46.7	44.4	22.5	11.2
AGE OF CHILD					
Less than 1 year	1,870	58.0	20.3	14.4	13.4
1-2 years	4,682	54.2	23.3	23.4	10.5
3-4 years	4,307	46.3	48.3	18.3	10.5

[1] Columns do not add to 100.0 because some children participated in more than one type of arrangement.

Source: U.S. Census Bureau, Survey of Income and Program Participation (SIPP), 2008 Panel, Wave 8, *Who's Minding the Kids? Child Care Arrangements: Spring 2011*; and "Detailed Tables," <http://www.census.gov/topics/families/child-care.html>, accessed June 2013.

Table 593. Child Support—Award and Recipient Status of Custodial Parents: 2013

[In thousands (13,418 represents 13,418,000), except as noted. Income and support received in 2013 dollars. Based on the Child Support Supplement to the April 2014 Current Population Survey. Custodial parents 15 years and older with own children under 21 years of age living with them, and receiving support from noncustodial parents living elsewhere. Covers civilian noninstitutional population]

Award and recipient status	All custodial parents				Custodial parents below poverty level			
	Total				Total			
	Number	Percent distri- bution	Mothers	Fathers	Number	Percent distri- bution	Mothers	Fathers
Total................................	**13,418**	(X)	**11,069**	**2,350**	**3,859**	(X)	**3,451**	**409**
With child support agreement or award [1].........	6,528	(X)	5,789	739	1,737	(X)	1,590	147
Supposed to receive payments in 2013.........	5,697	100.0	5,049	648	1,474	100.0	1,344	130
Actually received payments in 2013...........	4,222	74.1	3,743	479	978	66.4	906	73
Received full amount...........................	2,595	45.6	2,331	264	513	34.8	477	36
Received partial payments.....................	1,627	28.6	1,412	214	465	31.5	429	37
Did not receive payments in 2013..............	1,475	25.9	1,305	169	495	33.6	438	57
Child support not awarded........................	6,891	(X)	5,280	1,610	2,122	(X)	1,860	262
MEAN INCOME AND CHILD SUPPORT								
Received child support payments in 2013:								
Mean total money income (dol.)..................	37,367	(X)	33,096	70,758	8,927	(X)	8,860	9,753
Mean child support received (dol.)...............	5,333	(X)	5,181	6,526	4,396	(X)	4,125	(B)
Received the full amount due:								
Mean total money income (dol.)..............	40,094	(X)	36,970	67,633	9,264	(X)	9,411	(B)
Mean child support received (dol.)...........	7,080	(X)	6,829	9,293	6,515	(X)	6,022	(B)
Received partial payments:								
Mean total money income (dol.)..............	33,017	(X)	26,703	74,612	8,555	(X)	8,249	(B)
Mean child support received (dol.)...........	2,547	(X)	2,460	3,114	2,062	(X)	2,016	(B)
Received no payments in 2013:								
Mean total money income (dol.).................	30,460	(X)	29,360	38,937	8,116	(X)	8,180	7,627
Without child support agreement or award:								
Mean total money income (dol.).................	30,343	(X)	23,268	53,539	7,897	(X)	7,796	8,614

X Not applicable. B Base figure too small to meet statistical standards for reliability of a derived figure. [1] Child support award status as of April 2014.

Source: U.S. Census Bureau, *Custodial Mothers and Fathers and Their Child Support: 2013* and *Detailed Tables, 2013*, Current Population Report P60-255, January 2016. See also <http://www.census.gov/people/childsupport/>.

Table 594. Child Support Enforcement Program—Caseload and Finances: 2010 to 2016

[In units as indicated (15,859 represents 15,859,000). For fiscal years ending September 30. Includes Puerto Rico, Guam, and the Virgin Islands. The Child Support Program is a federal/state/tribal/local partnership that operates under Title IV-D of the Social Security Act. The Office of Child Support (OCSE) locates absent parents, establishes paternity of children, and establishes and enforces support orders. The OCSE does not assist families directly but rather helps child support agencies in the states and tribes to develop, manage and operate their programs. Case types include IV-A cases in which children are eligible for Temporary Assistance for Needy Families (TANF); and IV-E cases in which children are entitled to foster care maintenance; case types reflect Social Security Act Titles IV-A and IV-E. Child support collected for families not receiving TANF goes to the family to help it remain self-sufficient. Most child support collected on behalf of TANF and foster care families goes to Federal and State governments to offset program payments. Some States pass-through a portion of their collections to help families become self-sufficient. Based on data reported by state agencies. Minus sign (-) indicates net outlay]

Item	Unit	2010	2013	2014	2015	2016 (P)
Total cases..............................	1,000	**15,859**	**15,589**	**15,124**	**14,745**	**14,522**
Number of children.........................	1,000	17,509	16,900	16,338	15,899	15,562
Paternities established or acknowledged, total.........	1,000	1,734	1,595	1,542	1,484	1,479
Support orders established, total......................	1,000	1,297	1,142	1,069	1,016	981
FINANCES						
Total distributed collections......................	Mil. dol.	**26,556**	**28,007**	**28,199**	**28,559**	**28,834**
Total payments to families or foster care................	Mil. dol.	24,474	25,950	26,211	26,592	26,880
Total medical support.....................................	Mil. dol.	303	464	483	511	540
Total passed through......................................	Mil. dol.	135	123	118	112	105
Total fees withheld by state..............................	Mil. dol.	37	51	52	53	53
Total assistance reimbursement [1]......................	Mil. dol.	1,607	1,418	1,335	1,292	1,256
State share...	Mil. dol.	704	627	592	574	559
Federal share..	Mil. dol.	903	791	743	717	697
Current Assistance Collections [2].......................	Mil. dol.	1,015	908	847	808	771
Former Assistance Collections [3].......................	Mil. dol.	8,971	8,772	8,819	8,959	8,868
Medicaid Never Assistance Collections [4]................	Mil. dol.	4,729	6,945	7,072	7,368	7,904
Never Assistance Collections [5].........................	Mil. dol.	11,840	11,381	11,461	11,425	11,291
Total administrative expenditures.......................	Mil. dol.	5,776	5,588	5,690	5,749	5,728
Federal share..	Mil. dol.	3,811	3,344	3,446	3,474	3,444
State share...	Mil. dol.	1,964	2,244	2,244	2,275	2,284
Cost effectiveness ratio..................................	Dol.	4.88	5.31	5.25	5.26	5.33

P Preliminary. [1] Equals collections that will be divided between State and Federal governments to reimburse their respective shares of either Title IV-A (TANF) payments or Title IV-E (foster care) maintenance payments. [2] Made on behalf of families currently receiving Title IV-A (TANF) or Title IV-E (foster care) assistance. [3] Made on behalf of families formerly receiving Title IV-A (TANF) or Title IV-E (foster care) assistance. [4] Collections received and distributed on behalf of children who are receiving Child Support Enforcement services under Title IV-D of the Social Security Act, and who are either currently receiving or who have formerly received Medicaid payments, but who were not currently receiving and who have never formerly received assistance under either Title IV-A (TANF or AFDC) or Title IV-E (Foster Care) of the Social Security Act. [5] Made on behalf of families never receiving public assistance under TANF or Foster Care.

Source: U.S. Department of Health and Human Services, Administration for Children & Families, Office of Child Support Enforcement, *Preliminary Report FY2016,* April 2017, and earlier editions. See also <http://www.acf.hhs.gov/css/data>.

Table 595. Support Provided on Behalf of Children Under Age 21 Living in Another Household by Gender of Provider: 2010

[Numbers in thousands (4,547 represents 4,547,000), except as noted. Data are for whole year. Based on Survey of Income and Program Participation (SIPP), 2008 Panel, Wave 6, May-August 2010. Estimates are based on responses from a sample of the population, and may differ from the actual values because of sampling variability and other factors. Apparent differences between the estimates of two or more groups may not be statistically different]

Characteristics	Providers on behalf of children under age 21								
	Total			Male providers			Female providers		
	Total provid- ers	Percent of provid- ers	Median support pro- vided (dollars)	Total	Percent of provid- ers	Median support pro- vided (dollars)	Total	Percent of provid- ers	Median support pro- vided (dollars)
Total [1]	4,547	100.0	3,600	3,881	100.0	3,900	666	100.0	2,400
NUMBER OF CHILDREN SUPPORTED									
One child	2,658	58.5	3,000	2,197	56.6	3,200	461	69.2	2,200
Two children	1,416	31.1	5,460	1,290	33.2	5,700	127	19.1	4,416
Three or more children	473	10.4	5,200	395	10.2	5,200	78	11.7	2,892
BASIS FOR SUPPORT									
Child support agreement or court order	3,375	74.2	3,880	3,056	78.7	4,160	319	47.9	2,400
Voluntary and ratified by the court	747	16.4	4,000	702	18.1	4,300	45	6.8	(B)
Court-ordered agreement	2,377	52.3	3,720	2,125	54.8	4,140	252	37.8	2,400
Other written agreement	68	1.5	(B)	60	1.5	(B)	7	1.1	(B)
Non-written agreement	183	4.0	3,600	168	4.3	3,100	15	2.3	(B)
Not result of agreement or court order	1,173	25.8	3,000	826	21.3	3,500	347	52.1	2,500
PAYMENT METHOD									
Wage withholding	1,075	23.6	4,320	991	25.5	4,680	85	12.8	2,500
Directly to other parent	1,011	22.2	4,800	911	23.5	4,800	100	15.0	3,000
Directly to court	454	10.0	2,496	414	10.7	2,600	39	5.9	(B)
Directly to child support agency	702	15.4	3,120	630	16.2	3,600	72	10.8	(B)
Other method	133	2.9	2,400	110	2.8	2,400	23	3.5	(B)
HEALTH INSURANCE PROVISIONS									
Non-custodial parent provides	1,325	29.1	5,000	1,222	31.5	5,184	103	15.5	2,400
Custodial parent provides	839	18.5	4,200	764	19.7	4,200	75	11.3	2,544
Non-custodial parent pays bills	186	4.1	4,800	169	4.4	4,800	17	2.6	(B)
Included in child support payments	138	3.0	3,000	134	3.5	3,000	3	0.5	(B)
Other provision	280	6.2	3,600	253	6.5	3,600	28	4.2	(B)
No provision	845	18.6	2,712	740	19.1	3,000	104	15.6	1,800
CUSTODY ARRANGEMENTS									
Joint legal and physical custody	660	14.5	3,600	587	15.1	4,200	74	11.1	(B)
Joint legal with mother physical custody	1,053	23.2	5,160	1,031	26.6	5,160	22	3.3	(B)
Joint legal with father physical custody	130	2.9	2,544	17	0.4	(B)	113	17.0	2,400
Mother legal and physical custody	971	21.4	3,120	967	24.9	3,120	3	0.5	(B)
Father legal and physical custody	64	1.4	(B)	19	0.5	(B)	45	6.8	(B)
Split custody	230	5.1	4,613	224	5.8	4,800	6	0.9	(B)
Other custody arrangements	268	5.9	2,400	211	5.4	2,400	57	8.6	(B)

B Base figure too small to meet statistical standards for reliability of a derived figure. [1] Excludes 208,000 providers who also provided support for other adult nonhousehold members.

Source: U.S. Census Bureau, People and Households, Child Support, "Support Providers: 2010," <https://www.census.gov/topics/families/child-support.Tables.html>, accessed July 2013.

Table 596. Children in Foster Care and Awaiting Adoption: 2015

[Data cover fiscal year ending September 30 of year shown, and are current as of June 2016. Data are preliminary. States may resubmit data, and therefore estimates may change. Due to missing data for some characteristics, data may not sum to totals]

Characteristic	In foster care [1]	Entered foster care	Exited foster care	Waiting to be adopted [1,2]	Adopted [3]
Total	427,910	269,509	243,060	111,820	53,549
SEX					
Male	222,849	(NA)	(NA)	58,746	27,237
Female	204,999	(NA)	(NA)	53,069	26,307
AGE					
Under 1 year	29,684	47,219	10,967	3,980	1,096
1 to 5 years	142,053	82,080	84,664	45,460	29,124
6 to 10 years	99,573	57,592	56,905	31,059	14,888
11 to 15 years	89,294	55,988	43,141	23,668	6,732
16 to 17 years	52,337	25,201	23,551	7,653	1,538
18 to 20 years	13,768	1,404	22,994	(X)	163
Mean age, years	8.6	7.3	8.9	7.6	6.2
Median age, years	7.8	6.3	7.9	6.8	5.2
RACE/ETHNICITY [4]					
White	182,711	122,088	109,132	48,195	25,870
Black	103,376	60,733	54,795	25,510	9,764
Asian	2,232	1,653	1,598	462	203
American Indian/Alaska Native	10,130	6,350	5,249	2,112	898
Hispanic origin [5]	91,105	54,001	51,667	25,093	11,683
Two or more races	28,751	17,264	15,596	8,600	4,316
TIME IN CARE					
Mean months	20.4	(X)	19.0	31.7	(NA)
Median months	12.6	(X)	13.5	25.0	(NA)

NA Not available. X Not applicable. [1] As of September 30. [2] Includes children whose goal is adoption and/or whose parents' parental rights have been terminated. Excludes children age 16 and older whose parents' parental rights have been terminated and whose goal is emancipation. [3] Children adopted with public agency involvement. Data are from the Adoption and Foster Care Analysis and Reporting System (AFCARS) Adoption file; the number of adoptions reported here may not equal the number reported as discharges to adoption from foster care. [4] All races exclude children of Hispanic origin. [5] Children of Hispanic origin may be of any race.

Source: U.S. Department of Health and Human Services, Administration for Children and Families, *The Adoption and Foster Care Analysis and Reporting System Report, Preliminary FY2015 Estimates as of June 2016,* No. 23. See also <http://www.acf.hhs.gov/cb>.

Table 597. Child Care Expenditures for Children Under Age 5 for Families with Employed Mothers by Selected Characteristics: 2011

[In units as indicated (3,863 represents 3,863,000). Covers families making child care payments. Based on Survey of Income and Program Participation (SIPP), 2008 Panel, Wave 8, January-April 2011. Estimates are based on responses from a sample of the population, and may differ from the actual values because of sampling variability and other factors]

Characteristic	Number (1,000)	Income		Expenditures		
		Average monthly family income (dollars)	Average monthly mother's income (dollars)	Average weekly child care expenditures (dollars)	Percent of family monthly income spent on child care [1]	Ratio of child care expenditures to mother's income [2]
Families with children under age 5	**3,863**	**8,783**	**3,477**	**181**	**8.9**	**22.5**
MARITAL STATUS OF MOTHER						
Married	2,845	10,675	3,894	199	8.1	22.2
Widowed, separated, divorced	273	3,742	2,831	130	15.0	19.9
Never married	745	3,406	2,120	128	16.2	26.1
RACE/HISPANIC ORIGIN OF MOTHER						
White alone	3,052	9,406	3,580	186	8.6	22.6
Non-Hispanic	2,570	10,206	3,815	195	8.3	22.2
Black alone	501	4,388	2,382	121	11.9	22.0
Asian alone	183	12,342	5,094	270	9.5	23.0
Hispanic (of any race)	519	5,035	2,318	137	11.8	25.6
AGE OF MOTHER						
15 to 24 years	367	3,580	1,471	112	13.5	33.0
25 to 34 years	2,064	6,903	3,305	169	10.6	22.2
35 or more years	1,432	12,826	4,239	214	7.2	21.9
EDUCATION OF MOTHER						
Less than high school	174	3,302	1,657	131	17.2	34.2
High school graduate	520	4,652	2,090	140	13.0	29.0
Some college	1,295	5,368	2,454	131	10.6	23.2
Bachelor's degree or higher	1,874	12,798	4,738	231	7.8	21.1
WORK STATUS OF MOTHER						
Employed full-time	2,954	7,541	3,865	186	10.7	20.9
Employed part-time	707	6,705	2,128	150	9.7	30.5
Self-employed	201	34,289	2,521	208	2.6	35.8
MONTHLY FAMILY INCOME						
Less than $1,500	258	976	966	104	46.1	46.6
$1,500 to $2,999	552	2,182	1,695	109	21.7	27.9
$3,000 to $4,499	556	3,740	2,091	143	16.6	29.7
$4,500 and over	2,497	12,172	4,439	213	7.6	20.8
FAMILY POVERTY LEVEL						
Below poverty level	330	1,239	1,044	103	35.9	42.6
At or above poverty level	3,532	9,488	3,705	188	8.6	22.0

[1] Percent is a ratio of average monthly child care payments (prorated from weekly averages) to average family monthly income. [2] Ratio is of average monthly child care payments (prorated from weekly averages) to mother's average monthly income, shown as a percentage.

Source: U.S. Census Bureau, "Who's Minding the Kids? Child Care Arrangements: 2011: Detailed Tables," <http://www.census.gov/topics/families/child-care/data.html>, accessed July 2013.

Table 598. Head Start—Summary: 2010 to 2016

[Funding data in millions of dollars (7,234.8 represents $7,234,800,000); all other data in thousands (904.1 represents 904,100). For fiscal years. The Head Start program serves children, families, and pregnant women in all 50 states, DC, and six territories. Data on cumulative enrollment, staff, and volunteers are submitted by Head Start grantees and delegates. Federal funding covers all Head Start programs, including American Indian and Alaska Native and Migrant and Seasonal Programs, and support activities]

Item	2010	2011	2012	2013	2014	2015	2016
Federal funding (million dollars)	7,234.8	7,559.6	7,968.5	7,573.1	[3] 8,598.1	8,285.5	8,727.2
Funded enrollment slots [1]	904.1	964.4	956.5	903.7	927.3	944.6	915.6
Cumulative enrollment [2]	**1,117.7**	**1,141.9**	**1,146.5**	**1,129.8**	**1,076.1**	**1,100.1**	**1,097.4**
Children age 2 and under	146.3	174.0	176.4	177.0	173.2	193.2	230.3
Children age 3	386.7	389.4	388.2	392.4	375.9	399.4	383.9
Children age 4	548.0	542.1	547.1	531.9	497.1	480.0	455.9
Children age 5 and older	23.2	19.8	18.5	12.9	15.3	12.2	11.9
Hispanic/Latino	405.4	420.3	423.8	419.9	406.6	413.9	411.4
Non-Hispanic/non-Latino	712.3	721.6	722.0	709.8	669.5	686.2	686.0
American Indian/Alaska Native	41.7	44.7	44.2	44.1	45.2	45.4	42.1
Asian	19.0	19.4	20.2	19.9	19.8	21.8	22.6
Black/African American	326.5	325.0	331.0	326.5	309.9	318.3	319.9
Native Hawaiian/Pacific Islander	6.9	7.3	7.2	6.5	7.0	9.8	7.4
White	450.3	468.6	473.5	476.4	458.0	473.4	477.8
Biracial/multiracial	83.9	90.5	97.9	104.4	102.2	107.2	107.5
Other/unspecified	189.4	186.4	172.5	100.7	134.1	124.3	120.1
Total staff	228.3	233.4	230.6	236.7	226.0	230.0	241.5
Total volunteers	1,335.9	1,324.0	1,315.7	1,234.6	1,167.1	1,140.7	1,118.8
Parent volunteers	881.1	873.2	867.4	817.8	800.2	782.0	783.6

[1] Funded enrollment is the number of children and pregnant women supported by federal Head Start funds at any one time during the year. Data are derived from the annual Administration for Children and Families budget and congressional documents, and do not reflect changes made during the year. [2] Cumulative enrollment refers to actual number of children and pregnant women served, including enrollees who left during the year and enrollees who filled those empty slots. More children and families may receive Head Start services cumulatively throughout the year than indicated by funded enrollment numbers. [3] Represents funding available after Congress restored funds in the amount of the previous year's fiscal sequestration.

Source: U.S. Department of Health and Human Services, Administration for Children and Families, Early Childhood Learning & Knowledge Center, "Head Start Program Facts Sheets," <https://eclkc.ohs.acf.hhs.gov/hslc/data/factsheets>; and "Office of Head Start Enterprise System," <https://hses.ohs.acf.hhs.gov/pir/home>; accessed June 2017.

Table 599. Social Assistance Services—Nonemployer Establishments and Receipts: 2010 to 2015

[Receipts in millions of dollars (12,753 represents $12,753,000,000). Includes only firms subject to federal income tax. Nonemployers are businesses with no paid employees. Nonemployer firm receipts may include commissions or earnings]

Kind of business	NAICS code [1]	Establishments			Receipts (mil. dol.)		
		2010	2014	2015	2010	2014	2015
Social assistance, total.....................................	624	912,247	850,786	822,350	12,753	13,114	13,238
Individual and family services.............................	6241	141,971	160,562	163,337	2,599	3,275	3,492
Community/emergency and other relief services..........	6242	6,080	6,399	6,355	96	106	111
Vocational rehabilitation services...........................	6243	11,984	12,938	12,916	287	318	341
Child day care services......................................	6244	752,212	670,887	639,742	9,772	9,415	9,294

[1] North American Industry Classification System; see text, Section 15. Data for 2010 based on NAICS 2007; and data begining 2012 based on NAICS 2012.

Source: U.S. Census Bureau, Nonemployer Statistics, "Geographic Area Series: Nonemployer Statistics for the U.S., States, Metropolitan Areas, and Counties: 2015," <http://factfinder.census.gov/>, accessed May 2017. See also <http://www.census.gov/econ/nonemployer/index.html>.

Table 600. Social Assistance Services—Revenue for Employer Firms: 2010 and 2015

[In millions of dollars (143,439 represents $143,439,000,000). Based on Census Bureau's Service Annual Survey and administrative data. Estimates have been adjusted to the results of the 2012 Economic Census. Based on the 2007 North American Industry Classification System (NAICS); see text, Section 15. See Appendix III]

Kind of business	2007 NAICS code	2010			2015		
		Total	Taxable firms	Tax-exempt firms	Total	Taxable firms	Tax-exempt firms
Social assistance, total...........................	624	143,439	34,404	109,035	164,813	47,022	117,791
Child and youth services............................	62411	11,923	1,065	10,858	13,457	1,143	12,314
Services for elderly and disabled persons.........	62412	30,737	9,497	21,240	40,735	16,501	24,234
Other individual and family services...............	62419	29,013	3,282	25,731	30,628	4,003	26,625
Community food services...........................	62421	6,917	80	6,837	10,172	54	10,118
Community housing services.......................	62422	11,126	123	11,003	11,970	95	11,875
Emergency and other relief services...............	62423	9,795	38	9,757	9,240	110	9,130
Vocational rehabilitation services..................	6243	12,847	2,196	10,651	13,222	2,264	10,958
Child day care services.............................	6244	31,081	18,123	12,958	35,389	22,852	12,537

Source: U.S. Census Bureau, Annual & Quarterly Services, "2015 Service Annual Survey," <http://www.census.gov/services/index.html>, accessed December 2016.

Table 601. Number of Emergency and Transitional Beds in Homeless Assistance Systems Nationwide: 2016

[Data include beds located in Puerto Rico, Guam, and the Virgin Islands. Data were reported by 403 Continuums of Care, and were collected for a point-in-time during the last week in January 2016. Data were not independently verified by Department of Housing and Urban Development (HUD)]

Homeless programs	Total year-round beds	Year-round units/beds [1]				Other beds	
		Family units	Family beds	Adult-only beds	Child-only beds	Seasonal beds [2]	Overflow/ voucher [3]
Total......................................	867,102	132,654	413,226	449,853	4,023	21,358	17,446
Emergency, safe haven, and transitional housing.................	411,285	63,870	209,122	198,247	3,916	21,358	17,446
Emergency shelters......................	264,629	39,603	133,523	128,315	2,791	21,358	17,446
Safe haven [4].............................	1,907	(X)	(X)	1,907	(X)	(X)	(X)
Transitional housing [5]....................	144,749	24,267	75,599	68,025	1,125	(X)	(X)
Permanent housing.........................	455,817	68,784	204,104	251,606	107	(X)	(X)
Permanent supportive housing [6]........	340,906	43,007	122,978	217,841	87	(X)	(X)
Rapid re-housing.........................	77,141	18,312	56,589	20,541	11	(X)	(X)
Other permanent housing...............	37,770	7,465	24,537	13,224	9	(X)	(X)

X Not applicable. [1] Year-round beds are available for use throughout the year and are considered part of the stable inventory of beds for homeless persons. [2] Seasonal beds are typically available during particularly high-demand seasons of the year (e.g. winter months in the North or summer months in the South) to accommodate increased need for emergency shelters to prevent illness or death due to the weather. [3] Overflow beds are typically used during unanticipated emergencies (e.g., precipitous temperature drops or a natural disaster that displaces residents). Voucher beds are made available in a hotel or motel, and often function like overflow beds. [4] Private or semi-private long-term housing for people with severe mental illness. [5] Provides a place to stay with supportive services for up to 24 months. [6] Provides long-term housing with supportive services for formerly homeless people with disabilities, and often also those with chronic homelessness.

Source: U.S. Department of Housing and Urban Development, 2016 Continuum of Care Homeless Assistance Programs: Housing Inventory Count Report, December 2016. See also <https://www.hudexchange.info/manage-a-program/coc-housing-inventory-count-reports/>.

Table 602. Homeless Population by Type and Shelter Status: 2010 to 2016

[Data are point-in-time (PIT) counts made on a single night in January by Continuums of Care (CoCs) in all States, DC, Puerto Rico, Guam, and Virgin Islands. Data are not independently verified by the Department of Housing and Urban Development (HUD). CoCs are required to provide an unduplicated count of homeless persons according to HUD standards. See HUD's guide to conducting point-in-time counts of homeless people at <https://www.hudexchange.info/resource/4036/point-in-time-count-methodology-guide/>. Sheltered homeless people may be staying in emergency shelters, hotels/motels paid for by charities or government programs, transitional housing programs, or safe havens (long-term housing for people with severe mental illness). People staying in places not designed for use as regular accommodations, including cars, abandoned buildings, transit stations, and campgrounds, are considered unsheltered]

Homeless population by type	2010	2011	2012	2013	2014	2015	2016
Total	**637,077**	**623,788**	**621,553**	**591,768**	**576,450**	**564,708**	**549,928**
Sheltered	403,543	392,316	390,155	394,698	401,051	391,440	373,571
Unsheltered	233,534	231,472	231,398	197,070	175,399	173,268	176,357
Individuals [1]	395,140	387,613	382,156	369,571	360,189	358,422	355,212
Sheltered	212,218	205,834	199,159	203,127	209,148	205,616	198,008
Unsheltered	182,922	181,779	182,997	166,444	151,041	152,806	157,204
Persons in families with children	241,937	236,175	239,397	222,197	216,261	206,286	194,716
Sheltered	191,325	186,482	190,996	191,571	191,903	185,824	175,563
Unsheltered	50,612	49,693	48,401	30,626	24,358	20,462	19,153
Chronically homeless individuals [2]	106,062	103,522	96,268	86,455	83,989	83,170	77,486
Sheltered	43,329	38,971	32,647	29,418	31,203	28,355	24,596
Unsheltered	62,733	64,551	63,621	57,037	52,786	54,815	52,890
Chronically homeless people in families [2]	(NA)	15,511	15,769	16,539	15,143	13,105	8,646
Sheltered	(NA)	7,198	6,913	8,150	9,362	8,412	5,512
Unsheltered	(NA)	8,313	8,856	8,389	5,781	4,693	3,134
Veterans	74,087	65,455	60,579	55,779	49,689	47,725	39,471
Sheltered	43,437	40,033	35,143	34,909	32,119	31,505	26,404
Unsheltered	30,650	25,422	25,436	20,870	17,570	16,220	13,067
Children under age 18, unaccompanied	8,153	6,826	6,632	(NA)	(NA)	4,667	3,824
Sheltered	4,349	2,981	2,746	(NA)	(NA)	2,287	2,218
Unsheltered	3,804	3,845	3,886	(NA)	(NA)	2,380	1,606
Severely mentally ill	107,539	111,749	108,378	117,764	116,363	104,083	107,801
Sheltered	71,989	70,884	65,443	69,005	70,253	59,394	61,846
Unsheltered	35,550	40,865	42,935	48,759	46,110	44,689	45,955
Chronic substance abuse	139,853	140,360	127,477	127,275	116,516	103,888	94,496
Sheltered	95,049	87,630	75,581	76,021	70,500	60,071	52,290
Unsheltered	44,804	52,730	51,896	51,254	46,016	43,817	42,206
Persons with HIV/AIDS	14,498	12,970	11,471	11,856	12,223	9,294	9,240
Sheltered	10,590	9,698	8,300	8,847	9,638	6,532	6,860
Unsheltered	3,908	3,272	3,171	3,009	2,585	2,762	2,380
Domestic violence victims	66,878	72,133	73,343	63,689	59,352	67,690	68,464
Sheltered	49,709	53,055	54,142	44,900	42,893	41,015	41,779
Unsheltered	17,169	19,078	19,201	18,789	16,459	26,675	26,685

NA Not available. [1] People who are not part of a family. Includes homeless single adults, unaccompanied youth, or individuals in multiple-adult or multiple-child households. [2] An individual or household head of a family with a disability, and continuously homeless for a year or more, or with at least four episodes of homelessness in the last 3 years.

Source: U.S. Department of Housing and Urban Development, HUD Exchange, "PIT and HIC Data Since 2007: 2007 - 2016 PIT Counts by State," November 2016, <https://www.hudexchange.info/resource/3031/pit-and-hic-data-since-2007/>, accessed February 2017; and 2016 CoC (Continuum of Care) Homeless Populations and Subpopulations Report, March 2017 and earlier reports. See also <https://www.hudexchange.info/manage-a-program/coc-homeless-populations-and-subpopulations-reports/>.

Table 603. Volunteers by Selected Characteristics: 2015

[In percent, except as noted (62,623 represents 62,623,000). Based on a Current Population Survey supplement. Data on volunteers relate to persons who performed unpaid work (except for expenses) for an organization at any point from September 2014 through September 2015. Data represent the percent of the population involved in the activity]

Type of main organization [1]	Total, both sexes	Sex		Educational attainment [2]			
		Male	Female	Less than a high school diploma	High school graduate, no college [3]	Less than a bachelor's degree [4]	College graduates
Total volunteers (1,000)	**62,623**	**26,498**	**36,126**	**1,900**	**9,576**	**15,102**	**27,629**
Percent of population	24.9	21.8	27.8	8.1	15.6	26.5	38.8
Median annual hours [5]	52	52	50	52	52	52	52
Civic and political [6]	4.8	5.9	4.0	2.3	4.5	5.1	5.3
Educational or youth service	25.2	23.9	26.2	19.9	21.7	23.3	26.3
Environmental or animal care	2.9	2.7	3.0	1.0	2.1	2.4	3.2
Hospital or other health	6.6	5.3	7.6	2.7	5.1	5.9	7.2
Public safety	1.1	1.7	0.6	1.1	2.2	1.2	0.6
Religious	33.1	32.6	33.5	52.7	40.3	36.3	29.9
Social or community service	14.6	15.6	14.0	12.1	13.8	15.3	14.8
Sport and hobby [7]	3.7	4.0	3.4	1.6	3.4	3.1	4.3

[1] Main organization is defined as the organization for which the volunteer worked the most hours during the year. [2] Data refer to persons age 25 and over. [3] Includes high school diploma or equivalent. [4] Includes the categories "some college, no degree" and "associate degree." [5] At all organizations. For those reporting annual hours. [6] Includes professional and/or international activities. [7] Includes cultural and/or arts activities.

Source: U.S. Bureau of Labor Statistics, Volunteering in the United States—2015, News Release USDL-16-0363, February 2016. See also <http://www.bls.gov/news.release/volun.toc.htm>.

Table 604. Charitable Giving by Source and Type of Recipient Organization: 1990 to 2016

[In billions of dollars (98.5 represents $98,500,000,000). Individual giving is estimated using Internal Revenue Service information from individual tax returns, and from a study of approximately 8,000 to 9,000 households participating in the Philanthropy Panel Study conducted by Indiana University Lilly Family School of Philanthropy. Data on foundation giving are provided by the Foundation Center. Corporate giving data are based on itemized contributions claimed on federal tax returns, and also from the Foundation Center. Data on contributions by bequest are primarily based on data from the Council for Aid to Education, with additional calculations performed by Giving USA using IRS tax data on charitable bequest deductions. Giving to recipient organizations are from various research organizations, including the Evangelical Council for Financial Accountability, and Urban Institute's National Center for Charitable Statistics]

Source and allocation	1990	2000	2005	2008	2009	2010	2011	2012	2013	2014	2015	2016
Total charitable giving	98.5	229.7	292.4	299.6	274.8	288.2	298.5	332.6	332.5	365.2	379.9	390.1
Individuals	79.0	174.1	220.8	213.8	200.8	208.0	213.9	244.4	242.4	261.1	271.3	281.9
Foundations[1]	7.2	24.6	32.4	42.2	41.1	41.0	43.8	46.4	49.9	54.9	57.3	59.3
Corporations	5.5	10.7	15.2	12.4	13.8	15.8	15.6	17.2	15.9	18.1	17.9	18.6
Charitable bequests	6.8	20.3	24.0	31.2	19.1	23.4	25.2	24.6	24.4	31.1	33.4	30.4
Giving by recipient organization:												
Religion	49.8	77.0	90.9	98.2	99.6	97.5	101.8	105.8	110.4	116.0	119.4	122.9
Health	7.8	15.3	20.3	24.1	26.1	27.7	25.9	26.2	29.1	31.2	31.4	33.1
Education	11.8	28.8	35.0	35.9	35.0	42.2	42.9	46.9	48.1	53.2	57.7	59.8
Human services	6.7	20.8	30.4	35.4	36.0	36.8	37.4	41.1	40.5	43.3	45.0	46.8
Arts, culture, and humanities	3.7	10.6	12.4	12.3	12.6	13.4	12.8	13.9	14.1	16.2	17.1	18.2
Public/societal benefit	6.6	15.0	20.8	18.0	17.3	19.2	21.4	22.9	26.0	27.2	28.8	29.9
Environment/animals	1.3	4.9	6.5	7.7	7.3	7.9	8.2	8.9	8.6	9.7	10.3	11.1
International affairs	2.1	6.3	12.7	20.6	16.4	13.9	15.2	16.0	16.8	18.3	20.8	22.0
Gifts to individuals	(NA)	(NA)	3.1	3.6	4.2	4.9	6.1	5.8	7.2	6.8	7.3	7.1
Gifts to foundations[1]	3.8	24.7	24.5	30.1	32.4	26.1	30.2	40.1	40.8	43.8	39.4	40.6
Unallocated[2]	5.0	26.4	36.0	13.7	-12.0	-1.4	-3.3	5.0	-9.0	-0.4	2.7	-1.5

NA Not available. [1] Data are from the Foundation Center. [2] Money deducted as a charitable contribution by donors but not allocated to sources. May include gifts to governmental entities, in-kind giving, or gifts to new charities.

Source: Giving USA Foundation, Chicago, IL, *Giving USA 2017: The Annual Report on Philanthropy for the Year 2016* ©, researched and written at the Indiana University Lilly Family School of Philanthropy. See also <https://givingusa.org/>.

Table 605. Domestic Private Foundations—Financial Information: 1990 to 2013

[Financial data in billions of dollars (122.4 represents $122,400,000,000). Minus sign (-) indicates loss]

Item	1990	2000	2005	2006	2007	2008	2009	2010	2011	2012	2013
Number of tax returns	40,105	66,738	79,535	81,850	84,613	90,850	92,624	93,436	92,990	93,542	95,121
Nonoperating foundations[1]	36,880	61,501	72,800	74,364	77,457	83,024	84,660	86,254	85,500	85,447	86,584
Operating foundations[2]	3,226	5,238	6,734	7,486	7,156	7,826	7,964	7,181	7,490	8,095	8,537
Total assets, book value[3]	122.4	409.5	481.8	569.3	591.2	531.4	550.9	584.2	594.3	633.1	693.3
Total assets, fair market value[3]	151.0	471.6	545.9	645.8	652.4	526.5	588.5	641.0	641.3	698.6	791.0
Investments in securities	115.0	361.4	373.1	403.7	400.3	287.6	324.7	353.3	344.8	373.3	430.9
Total revenue	19.0	72.8	76.4	94.1	107.3	49.7	52.2	72.5	79.4	95.3	106.1
Total expenses	11.3	37.4	42.8	48.8	58.8	60.3	56.2	60.1	64.3	64.8	73.7
Contributions, gifts, and grants paid	8.6	27.6	31.9	34.9	42.6	42.8	40.9	44.7	46.9	48.6	54.2
Excess of revenue over expenses (net)	7.7	35.3	33.5	45.3	48.6	-10.6	-4.0	12.3	15.1	30.5	32.4
Net investment income[4]	11.9	48.8	44.3	54.2	62.8	23.1	17.6	29.8	34.2	38.4	50.4

[1] Generally provide charitable support through grants and other financial means to charitable organizations; the majority of foundations are nonoperating. [2] Generally conduct their own charitable activities, e.g., museums. [3] Data for book and fair market assets were reduced to avoid overstating the joint assets of the Bill and Melinda Gates Foundation and the Bill and Melinda Gates Foundation Trust, by tax year as follows: 2007, $38.7 billion; 2008, $29.6 billion; 2009, $33.4 billion; 2010, $36.7 billion; 2011, $33.8 billion; 2012, $36.4 billion; and 2013, $40.5 billion. [4] This equals gross investment income less allowable deductions. Represents income not considered related to a foundation's charitable purpose, e.g., interest, dividends, and capital gains. Foundations could be subject to an excise tax on such income.

Source: Internal Revenue Service, *Statistics of Income Bulletin*, "SOI Tax Stats – Domestic Private Foundation and Charitable Trust Statistics," <https://www.irs.gov/uac/tax-stats>, accessed April 2017.

Table 606. Foundations—Number and Finances by Foundation Type: 1990 to 2014

[In millions of dollars (142,480 represents $142,480,000,000), except number of foundations. Figures are for fiscal years, and cover foundations that reported giving. Covers nongovernmental nonprofit organizations with funds and programs managed by their own trustees or directors, whose goals were to maintain or aid social, educational, religious, or other activities deemed to serve the common good. Excludes organizations that make general appeals to the public for funds, act as trade associations for industrial or other special groups, or do not currently award grants]

Year	Number	Assets (million dollars)	Gifts received (million dollars)	Total giving[1] (million dollars)
1990	32,401	142,480	5,000	8,680
2000	56,582	486,085	27,614	24,563
2005	71,097	550,553	31,465	36,402
2010	76,610	643,974	37,961	45,858
2013	87,142	798,176	56,241	55,263
Total, 2014	**86,726**	**865,250**	**56,700**	**60,244**
Independent	79,729	712,446	34,860	41,268
Operating	3,687	44,059	8,057	7,349
Corporate	2,521	26,710	4,585	5,118
Community	789	82,034	9,198	6,509
Family[2]	42,008	400,919	27,989	25,948

[1] Includes grants, scholarships, and employee matching gifts; excludes set-asides, loans, program-related investments (PRIs), and program expenses. [2] Family foundations are a subset of independent foundations; data are included in independent foundation data.

Source: The Foundation Center, New York, NY ©, "Foundation Stats," <http://foundationcenter.org/>, accessed April 2017.

Table 607. Nonprofit Charitable Organizations—Financial Information: 2000 to 2014

[In billions of dollars (1,562.5 represents $1,562,500,000,000), except as indicated. Includes data reported by organizations described in Internal Revenue Code, Section 501(c)(3), excluding private foundations and most religious organizations. Prior to 2010, organizations with receipts under $25,000 were not required to file. Beginning with 2010, organizations with receipts under $50,000 were not required to file]

Year	Number of tax returns (1,000)	Total assets	Net assets	Revenue			Total expenses	Excess of revenue over expenses (net)
				Total	Program service revenue [1]	Contributions, gifts, and grants		
2000..............	230.2	1,562.5	1,023.2	866.2	579.1	199.1	796.4	69.8
2001..............	240.6	1,631.7	1,020.3	897.0	630.8	212.4	862.7	34.3
2002..............	251.7	1,733.9	1,040.3	955.3	691.8	214.5	934.7	20.6
2003..............	263.4	1,899.9	1,164.3	1,072.2	754.6	230.0	1,009.7	62.5
2004..............	276.2	2,058.6	1,276.1	1,153.0	801.2	248.6	1,058.5	94.5
2005..............	286.6	2,241.9	1,411.3	1,252.9	852.6	276.3	1,137.9	115.0
2006..............	301.2	2,549.7	1,617.7	1,370.9	920.2	303.2	1,230.4	140.5
2007..............	313.1	2,683.4	1,674.4	1,445.9	980.3	324.5	1,317.2	128.7
2008..............	315.2	2,521.2	1,434.7	1,378.3	1,038.0	320.7	1,396.4	-18.1
2009..............	320.8	2,697.1	1,564.2	1,481.1	1,085.9	327.4	1,433.9	47.2
2010..............	269.5	2,946.5	1,772.4	1,593.0	1,147.3	344.9	1,497.2	95.8
2011..............	274.3	3,030.1	1,781.9	1,647.9	1,194.2	357.4	1,558.4	89.5
2012..............	279.4	3,274.0	1,970.4	1,734.2	1,248.2	371.1	1,624.1	110.1
2013..............	285.9	3,507.6	2,184.0	1,828.2	1,296.1	394.1	1,700.4	127.8
2014..............	201.8	3,703.1	2,280.9	1,941.5	1,382.2	417.6	1,793.3	148.2

[1] Represents fees collected by organizations in support of their tax-exempt purposes, such as tuition and fees at educational institutions, hospital patient charges, and admission and activity fees collected by museums and other nonprofit organizations or institutions.

Source: U.S. Internal Revenue Service, Statistics of Income, "SOI Tax Stats – Charities & Other Tax-Exempt Organizations Statistics," <https://www.irs.gov/uac/tax-stats>, accessed August 2017.

Table 608. Individual Charitable Contributions by State: 2015

[In units, as indicated (222,230 represents $222,230,000,000). Covers returns primarily for 2015 tax year that were filed during 2016, but may also include a limited number of returns for tax years prior to 2015 that were also received during 2016. Data will not agree with data in other tables due to differing survey methodology used to derive state data. Data for 2015 are preliminary]

State	Charitable contributions		State	Charitable contributions		State	Charitable contributions		State	Charitable contributions	
	Number of returns (1,000)	Amount (mil. dol.)		Number of returns (1,000)	Amount (mil. dol.)		Number of returns (1,000)	Amount (mil. dol.)		Number of returns (1,000)	Amount (mil. dol.)
Total [1].....	36,682	222,230	ID........	166	1,045	MO.......	588	3,442	PA.......	1,449	6,903
AL..........	466	3,387	IL.........	1,607	8,659	MT.......	110	585	RI........	144	466
AK..........	58	336	IN.........	567	3,201	NE.......	209	1,186	SC......	508	3,107
AZ..........	701	3,416	IA........	348	1,657	NV.......	278	1,600	SD......	56	551
AR..........	223	2,162	KS.......	282	1,902	NH.......	167	617	TN......	491	4,123
CA..........	5,055	31,546	KY.......	404	2,081	NJ.......	1,534	6,050	TX......	2,241	17,482
CO..........	694	3,882	LA........	361	2,251	NM.......	159	791	UT.......	390	3,711
CT..........	608	3,475	ME......	135	464	NY.......	2,787	19,214	VT.......	65	289
DE..........	119	519	MD......	1,140	5,892	NC.......	1,103	6,563	VA.......	1,205	6,314
DC..........	113	993	MA......	1,036	5,507	ND.......	50	364	WA......	832	5,768
FL..........	1,815	13,316	MI.......	1,054	5,478	OH.......	1,151	5,527	WV......	96	507
GA..........	1,257	9,412	MN......	799	3,724	OK.......	314	2,427	WI........	711	2,964
HI..........	161	656	MS......	246	1,681	OR.......	543	2,624	WY......	42	562

[1] Total includes data for U.S. outlying areas, not shown separately.

Source: U.S. Internal Revenue Service, Statistics of Income, Individual Income Tax Return (Form 1040) Statistics: State Data, "SOI Tax Stats - Historic Table 2," <https://www.irs.gov/uac/soi-tax-stats-individual-income-tax-return-form-1040-statistics>, accessed August 2017.

Section 12
Labor Force, Employment, and Earnings

This section presents statistics on the labor force; its distribution by occupation and industry affiliation; and the supply of, demand for, and conditions of labor. The chief source of these data is the Current Population Survey (CPS) conducted by the U.S. Census Bureau for the Bureau of Labor Statistics (BLS). Comprehensive historical and current data are available from the BLS internet site at <http://www.bls.gov/cps/>. These data are published on a current basis in the BLS monthly publication *Employment and Earnings Online*. Detailed data on the labor force are also available from the Census Bureau's decennial census of population.

Types of data—Most statistics in this section are obtained by two methods: household interviews or questionnaires and reports of establishment payroll records. Each method provides data that the other cannot suitably supply. Population characteristics, for example, are readily obtainable only from the household survey, while detailed industrial classifications can be readily derived only from establishment records.

CPS data are obtained from a monthly sample survey of the population. The CPS is used to gather data for the calendar week, generally the week including the 12th of the month, and provides current comprehensive data on the labor force (see text, Section 1, Population). The CPS provides information on the work status of the population without duplication since each person is classified as employed, unemployed, or not in the labor force. Employed persons holding more than one job are counted only once, according to the job at which they worked the most hours during the survey week.

Employment and Earnings Online presents data including national totals of the number of persons in the civilian labor force by sex, disability status, race, Hispanic origin, and age; the number employed; hours of work; industry and occupational groups; usual weekly earnings; and the number unemployed, as well as reasons for and duration of unemployment. Annual data shown in this section are averages of monthly figures for each calendar year, unless otherwise specified. Historical national CPS data are available at <http://www.bls.gov/cps/>.

The CPS also produces annual estimates of employment and unemployment for each state, 50 large metropolitan statistical areas, and selected cities. These estimates are published annually in *Geographic Profile of Employment and Unemployment* available at <http://www.bls.gov/gps/>.

Data based on establishment records are compiled by the BLS and cooperating state agencies as part of an ongoing Current Employment Statistics (CES) program. The BLS collects survey data monthly from a probability-based sample of nonfarm, business establishments through internet electronic data interchange, touchtone data entry, and computer-assisted telephone interviews, internet, other electronic media, fax, transcript, or mail. CES data are adjusted annually to data from government unemployment insurance administrative records, which are supplemented by data from other government agencies. The estimates exclude self-employed persons, private household workers, unpaid family workers, agricultural workers, and members of the Armed Forces.

The establishment survey counts workers each time they appear on a payroll during the reference period (the payroll period that includes the 12th of the month). Thus, unlike the CPS, a person with two jobs is counted twice. The establishment survey is designed to provide estimates of nonfarm wage and salary employment, average weekly hours, and average hourly and weekly earnings by detailed industry for the nation, states, and selected metropolitan areas. Establishment survey data also are published in *Employment and Earnings Online*. Historical national data are available at <http://www.bls.gov/ces/>. Historical data for states and metropolitan areas are available at <http://www.bls.gov/sae/>. CES estimates are currently classified by the 2012 North American Industry Classification System (NAICS). All published series for the nation have a NAICS-based history extending back to at least 1990. Employment series for total nonfarm and other high-level aggregates start in 1939.

For more information on data concepts, sample design, and estimating methods for the CES Survey, see the BLS Handbook of Methods, Chapter 2 <http://www.bls.gov/opub/hom/>. For information regarding revisions and collection rates see <http://www.bls.gov/ces/cesrevinfo.htm>.

Labor force—According to the CPS definitions, the civilian labor force comprises all civilians in the noninstitutionalized population 16 years and over classified as "employed" or "unemployed" according to specific criteria. *Employed* civilians comprise (a) all civilians, who, during the reference week, did any work for pay or profit (minimum of an hour's work) or worked 15 hours or more as unpaid workers in a family enterprise and (b) all civilians who were not working but who had jobs or businesses from which they were temporarily absent for noneconomic reasons (illness, weather conditions, vacation, labor-management dispute, etc.) whether they were paid for the time off or were seeking other jobs. *Unemployed* persons comprise all civilians who had no employment during the reference week, who made specific efforts to find a job within the previous 4 weeks (such as applying directly to an employer or to a public employment service or checking with friends) and who were available for work during that week, except for temporary illness. Persons on layoff from a job and expecting recall also are classified as unemployed. All other civilian persons, 16 years old and over, are classified as "not in the labor force."

Various breaks in the CPS data series have occurred over time due to the introduction of population adjustments and other changes. For details on these breaks in series and the effect that they had on the CPS data, see the BLS website at <www.bls.gov/cps/documentation.htm#concepts>.

Beginning in January of each year, the CPS data reflect the introduction of revised population controls. For additional information on the effects of revised population controls on estimates from the CPS, see <www.bls.gov/cps/documentation.htm#pop>.

Hours and earnings—Average hourly earnings, based on establishment data, are gross earnings (i.e., earnings before payroll deductions) and include overtime premiums; they exclude irregular bonuses and value of payments in kind. Hours are those for which pay was received. Annual wages and salaries from the CPS consist of total monies received for work performed by an employee during the income year. It includes wages, salaries, commissions, tips, piece-rate payments, and cash bonuses earned before deductions were made for taxes, bonds, union dues, etc. Persons who worked 35 hours or more are classified as working full-time.

Industry and occupational groups—Industry data derived from the CPS for 1983-91 utilize the 1980 census industrial classification developed from the 1972 Standard Industrial Classification (SIC). CPS data from 1971 to 1982 were based on the 1970 census classification system, which was developed from the 1967 SIC. Most of the industry categories were not affected by the change in classification.

The occupational classification system used in the 1980 census and in the CPS for 1983-91, evolved from the 1980 Standard Occupational Classification (SOC) system, first introduced in 1977. Occupational categories used in the 1980 census classification system are so radically different from the 1970 census system used in the CPS through 1982 that their implementation represented a break in historical data series.

Beginning in January 1992, the occupational and industrial classification systems used in the 1990 census were introduced into the CPS. (These systems were largely based on the 1980 SOC and the 1987 SIC systems, respectively.)

Beginning in 2003, the 2002 occupational and industrial classification systems were introduced into the CPS. These systems were derived from the 2000 SOC and the 2002 NAICS. The composition of detailed occupational and industrial classifications in the new classification systems was substantially changed from the previous systems in use, as was the structure for aggregating them into broad groups. Consequently, the use of the new classification systems created breaks in existing data series at all levels of aggregation. CPS data using the new classification systems are available for data from 2000. Additional information on the occupational and industrial classifications systems used in the CPS, including changes over time, appear on the BLS website at <www.bls.gov/cps/documentation.htm#oi>. Establishments responding to the establishment survey are classified according to the 2012 NAICS. Previously they were classified according to the SIC manual. See text, Section 15, Business Enterprise, for information about the SIC manual and NAICS.

Productivity—BLS publishes data on output per hour (labor productivity), output per combined unit of labor and capital input (multifactor productivity), and, for industry groups and industries, output per combined

unit of capital, labor, energy, materials, and purchased service inputs. Labor productivity and related indexes are published for the business sector as a whole and its major subsectors: nonfarm business, manufacturing, and nonfinancial corporations, and for over 200 detailed industries. Productivity indexes that take into account capital, labor, energy, materials, and service inputs are published for 18 major manufacturing industry groups, 86 detailed manufacturing industries, utility services, and air and railroad transportation. The major sector data are published in the BLS quarterly news release *Productivity and Costs* and in the annual *Multifactor Productivity Trends* release. Industry productivity measures are updated and published annually in the news releases *Productivity and Costs by Industry* and *Multifactor Productivity Trends by Industry*. The latest data are available at the Labor Productivity and Costs website at <http://www.bls.gov/lpc/> and the Multifactor Productivity website at <http://www.bls.gov/mfp>. Detailed information on methods, limitations, and data sources appears in the BLS *Handbook of Methods*, Chapters 10 and 11 at <http://www.bls.gov/opub/hom/home.htm> and <http://www.bls.gov/lpc/lpcmethods.htm>.

Unions—As defined here, unions include traditional labor unions and employee associations similar to labor unions. Data on union membership status provided by BLS are for employed wage and salary workers and relate to their principal job. Earnings by union membership status are usual weekly earnings of full-time wage and salary workers. The information is collected through the Current Population Survey.

Work stoppages—Work stoppages include all strikes and lockouts known to BLS that last for at least 1 full day or shift and involve 1,000 or more workers. All stoppages, whether or not authorized by a union, legal or illegal, are counted. Excluded are work slowdowns and instances where employees report to work late or leave early to attend meetings or rallies.

Seasonal adjustment—Many economic statistics reflect a regularly recurring seasonal movement that can be estimated on the basis of past experience. By eliminating that part of the change which can be ascribed to usual seasonal variation (e.g., climate or school openings and closings), it is possible to observe the cyclical and other nonseasonal movements in the series. However, in evaluating deviations from the seasonal pattern—that is, changes in a seasonally adjusted series—it is important to note that seasonal adjustment is merely an approximation based on past experience. Seasonally adjusted estimates have a broader margin of possible error than the original data on which they are based, since they are subject not only to sampling and other errors, but also are affected by the uncertainties of the adjustment process itself. Consistent with BLS practices, annual estimates will be published only for not seasonally-adjusted data.

Statistical reliability—For discussion of statistical collection, estimation, sampling procedures, and measures of statistical reliability applicable to Census Bureau and BLS data, see Appendix III.

Table 609. Civilian Population—Employment Status: 1970 to 2016

[In thousands (137,085 represents 137,085,000), except as indicated. Annual averages of monthly figures. Civilian noninstitutionalized population 16 years old and over. Data not strictly comparable with data for earlier years; see BLS Handbook of Methods, <http://www.bls.gov/opub/hom/>. Based on Current Population Survey; see text, Section 1 and Appendix III]

Year	Civilian noninstitutional population	Civilian labor force				Unemployed		Not in labor force	
		Total	Percent of population	Employed	Employment/population ratio [1]	Number	Percent of labor force	Number	Percent of population
1970	137,085	82,771	60.4	78,678	57.4	4,093	4.9	54,315	39.6
1980	167,745	106,940	63.8	99,303	59.2	7,637	7.1	60,806	36.2
1990	189,164	125,840	66.5	118,793	62.8	7,047	5.6	63,324	33.5
1995	198,584	132,304	66.6	124,900	62.9	7,404	5.6	66,280	33.4
2000	212,577	142,583	67.1	136,891	64.4	5,692	4.0	69,994	32.9
2001	215,092	143,734	66.8	136,933	63.7	6,801	4.7	71,359	33.2
2002	217,570	144,863	66.6	136,485	62.7	8,378	5.8	72,707	33.4
2003	221,168	146,510	66.2	137,736	62.3	8,774	6.0	74,658	33.8
2004	223,357	147,401	66.0	139,252	62.3	8,149	5.5	75,956	34.0
2005	226,082	149,320	66.0	141,730	62.7	7,591	5.1	76,762	34.0
2006	228,815	151,428	66.2	144,427	63.1	7,001	4.6	77,387	33.8
2007	231,867	153,124	66.0	146,047	63.0	7,078	4.6	78,743	34.0
2008	233,788	154,287	66.0	145,362	62.2	8,924	5.8	79,501	34.0
2009	235,801	154,142	65.4	139,877	59.3	14,265	9.3	81,659	34.6
2010	237,830	153,889	64.7	139,064	58.5	14,825	9.6	83,941	35.3
2011	239,618	153,617	64.1	139,869	58.4	13,747	8.9	86,001	35.9
2012	243,284	154,975	63.7	142,469	58.6	12,506	8.1	88,310	36.3
2013	245,679	155,389	63.2	143,929	58.6	11,460	7.4	90,290	36.8
2014	247,947	155,922	62.9	146,305	59.0	9,617	6.2	92,025	37.1
2015	250,801	157,130	62.7	148,834	59.3	8,296	5.3	93,671	37.3
2016	253,538	159,187	62.8	151,436	59.7	7,751	4.9	94,351	37.2

[1] Civilian employed as a percent of the civilian noninstitutional population.

Source: U.S. Bureau of Labor Statistics, "Employment and Earnings Online," <www.bls.gov/opub/ee/home.htm>, accessed February 2017.

Table 610. Civilian Labor Force and Participation Rates Projections: 2014 to 2024

[155.9 represents 155,900,000. Civilian noninstitutionalized population 16 years old and over. Based on Current Population Survey; see text, Section 1 and Appendix III]

Race, Hispanic origin, sex, and age	Civilian labor force (mil.)						Participation rate (percent) [1]					
	2014 [2]	2020	2021	2022	2023	2024	2014 [2]	2020	2021	2022	2023	2024
Total [3]	155.9	160.7	161.5	162.3	163.0	163.8	62.9	61.7	61.5	61.3	61.1	60.9
White	123.3	125.2	125.5	125.7	125.9	126.1	63.1	61.7	61.5	61.2	61.0	60.8
Male	66.7	67.5	67.6	67.7	67.8	67.8	69.8	67.8	67.5	67.2	66.8	66.5
Female	56.6	57.8	57.9	58.0	58.2	58.3	56.7	55.9	55.7	55.5	55.4	55.2
Black	18.9	20.1	20.2	20.4	20.6	20.8	61.2	60.4	60.3	60.1	59.9	59.7
Male	8.9	9.4	9.5	9.5	9.6	9.7	63.6	61.9	61.6	61.3	61.0	60.7
Female	10.0	10.7	10.8	10.9	11.0	11.1	59.2	59.2	59.1	59.1	59.0	58.9
Asian	8.8	10.0	10.2	10.4	10.6	10.8	63.6	63.2	63.1	63.1	63.0	63.0
Male	4.6	5.3	5.4	5.5	5.6	5.7	72.4	71.8	71.7	71.6	71.4	71.3
Female	4.1	4.7	4.8	4.9	5.0	5.1	55.8	55.7	55.7	55.7	55.7	55.7
Hispanic [4]	25.4	29.5	30.2	31.0	31.7	32.5	66.1	66.1	66.0	66.0	66.0	65.9
Male	14.7	16.9	17.3	17.7	18.1	18.5	76.1	75.1	74.9	74.7	74.5	74.3
Female	10.7	12.6	12.9	13.3	13.6	14.0	56.0	56.9	57.0	57.1	57.3	57.4
Male	82.9	85.1	85.5	85.8	86.2	86.5	69.2	67.4	67.1	66.8	66.5	66.2
16 to 19 years	2.8	2.4	2.4	2.3	2.3	2.2	33.5	29.4	28.6	28.1	27.4	26.8
20 to 24 years	8.2	7.4	7.4	7.3	7.3	7.3	73.9	71.1	70.7	70.5	70.2	69.8
25 to 34 years	18.5	19.8	19.9	20.0	20.0	20.0	88.7	87.9	87.9	87.8	87.7	87.6
35 to 44 years	17.5	18.5	18.8	19.0	19.3	19.6	90.5	89.9	89.8	89.7	89.6	89.5
45 to 54 years	17.9	16.6	16.4	16.4	16.3	16.3	85.6	84.8	84.6	84.5	84.3	84.2
55 to 64 years	13.4	14.3	14.2	14.1	14.0	13.9	69.9	69.9	69.9	69.8	69.8	69.9
65 years and over	4.6	6.1	6.4	6.7	6.9	7.2	23.0	24.9	25.2	25.4	25.5	25.7
Female	73.0	75.6	76.0	76.4	76.8	77.2	57.0	56.3	56.2	56.1	56.0	55.8
16 to 19 years	2.8	2.3	2.2	2.2	2.2	2.1	34.5	28.9	28.0	27.3	26.6	25.9
20 to 24 years	7.5	6.9	6.9	6.9	6.9	6.9	67.7	66.7	66.6	66.6	66.6	66.5
25 to 34 years	15.7	16.7	16.8	16.8	16.9	16.9	73.8	74.6	74.6	74.7	74.8	74.9
35 to 44 years	15.0	15.6	15.8	16.0	16.1	16.4	74.1	74.0	74.0	74.0	73.9	73.9
45 to 54 years	16.2	15.4	15.4	15.4	15.5	15.5	73.8	75.8	76.1	76.4	76.7	77.0
55 to 64 years	12.1	13.5	13.5	13.4	13.3	13.3	58.8	61.4	61.8	62.1	62.5	62.9
65 years and over	3.8	5.2	5.5	5.7	6.0	6.2	15.1	17.3	17.7	17.9	18.1	18.4

[1] Civilian labor force as a percent of the civilian noninstitutional population projections. [2] Data for 2014 is actual. [3] Includes other races, not shown separately. [4] Persons of Hispanic origin may be of any race.

Source: U.S. Bureau of Labor Statistics, "Employment Projections Program," <http://www.bls.gov/emp/ep_data_labor_force.htm>, accessed July 2016.

Table 611. Civilian Population—Employment Status by Sex, Race, and Ethnicity: 1980 to 2016

[In thousands (79,398 represents 79,398,000), except as indicated. Annual averages of monthly figures. Data not strictly comparable with data for earlier years, see BLS Handbook of Methods, <http://www.bls.gov/opub/hom/>; see Table 609 for U.S. totals and coverage]

Year, sex, race, and Hispanic origin	Civilian noninstitu- tionalized population	Civilian labor force			Employ- ment/ population ratio [1]	Unemployed		Not in labor force	
		Total	Percent of population	Employed		Number	Percent of labor force	Number	Percent of population
Male:									
1980................	79,398	61,453	77.4	57,186	72.0	4,267	6.9	17,945	22.6
1990................	90,377	69,011	76.4	65,104	72.0	3,906	5.7	21,367	23.6
2000................	101,964	76,280	74.8	73,305	71.9	2,975	3.9	25,684	25.2
2010................	115,174	81,985	71.2	73,359	63.7	8,626	10.5	33,189	28.8
2014................	119,748	82,882	69.2	77,692	64.9	5,190	6.3	36,865	30.8
2015................	121,101	83,620	69.1	79,131	65.3	4,490	5.4	37,481	31.0
2016................	122,497	84,755	69.2	80,568	65.8	4,187	4.9	37,743	30.8
Female:									
1980................	88,348	45,487	51.5	42,117	47.7	3,370	7.4	42,861	48.5
1990................	98,787	56,829	57.5	53,689	54.3	3,140	5.5	41,957	42.5
2000................	110,613	66,303	59.9	63,586	57.5	2,717	4.1	44,310	40.1
2010................	122,656	71,904	58.6	65,705	53.6	6,199	8.6	50,752	41.4
2014................	128,199	73,039	57.0	68,613	53.5	4,426	6.1	55,159	43.0
2015................	129,700	73,510	56.7	69,703	53.7	3,807	5.2	56,190	43.3
2016................	131,040	74,432	56.8	70,868	54.1	3,564	4.8	56,608	43.2
White: [2]									
1980................	146,122	93,600	64.1	87,715	60.0	5,884	6.3	52,523	35.9
1990................	160,625	107,447	66.9	102,261	63.7	5,186	4.8	53,178	33.1
2000................	176,220	118,545	67.3	114,424	64.9	4,121	3.5	57,675	32.7
2005................	184,446	122,299	66.3	116,949	63.4	5,350	4.4	62,148	33.7
2010................	192,075	125,084	65.1	114,168	59.4	10,916	8.7	66,991	34.9
2014................	195,498	123,327	63.1	116,788	59.7	6,540	5.3	72,170	36.9
2015................	196,868	123,607	62.8	117,944	59.9	5,662	4.6	73,261	37.2
2016................ [2]	198,215	124,658	62.9	119,313	60.2	5,345	4.3	73,557	37.1
Black: [2]									
1980................	17,824	10,865	61.0	9,313	52.2	1,553	14.3	6,959	39.0
1990................	21,477	13,740	64.0	12,175	56.7	1,565	11.4	7,737	36.0
2000................	24,902	16,397	65.8	15,156	60.9	1,241	7.6	8,505	34.2
2010................	28,708	17,862	62.2	15,010	52.3	2,852	16.0	10,846	37.8
2014................	30,843	18,873	61.2	16,732	54.3	2,141	11.3	11,970	38.8
2015................	31,386	19,318	61.5	17,472	55.7	1,846	9.6	12,068	38.5
2016................ [2,3]	31,889	19,637	61.6	17,982	56.4	1,655	8.4	12,252	38.4
Asian: [2,3]									
2000................	9,330	6,270	67.2	6,043	64.8	227	3.6	3,060	32.8
2010................	11,199	7,248	64.7	6,705	59.9	543	7.5	3,951	35.3
2014................	13,785	8,760	63.6	8,325	60.4	436	5.0	5,024	36.4
2015................	14,420	9,053	62.8	8,706	60.4	347	3.8	5,366	37.2
2016................	15,121	9,562	63.2	9,213	60.9	349	3.6	5,559	36.8
Hispanic: [4]									
1980................	9,598	6,146	64.0	5,527	57.6	620	10.1	3,451	36.0
1990................	15,904	10,720	67.4	9,845	61.9	876	8.2	5,184	32.6
2000................	23,938	16,689	69.7	15,735	65.7	954	5.7	7,249	30.3
2010................	33,713	22,748	67.5	19,906	59.0	2,843	12.5	10,964	32.5
2014................	38,400	25,370	66.1	23,492	61.2	1,878	7.4	13,030	33.9
2015................	39,617	26,126	65.9	24,400	61.6	1,726	6.6	13,491	34.1
2016................	40,697	26,797	65.8	25,249	62.0	1,548	5.8	13,900	34.2
Mexican:									
1990................	9,752	6,707	68.8	6,146	63.0	561	8.4	3,045	31.2
2000................	15,333	10,783	70.3	10,144	66.2	639	5.9	4,550	29.7
2010................	21,267	14,403	67.7	12,622	59.4	1,781	12.4	6,864	32.3
2014................	23,829	15,768	66.2	14,629	61.4	1,139	7.2	8,061	33.8
2015................	24,711	16,392	66.3	15,342	62.1	1,050	6.4	8,319	33.7
2016................	24,960	16,458	65.9	15,502	62.1	955	5.8	8,503	34.1
Puerto Rican:									
1990................	1,718	960	55.9	870	50.6	91	9.5	758	44.1
2000................	2,193	1,411	64.3	1,318	60.1	92	6.6	783	35.7
2010................	3,110	1,906	61.3	1,612	51.8	293	15.4	1,204	38.7
2014................	3,515	2,114	60.1	1,891	53.8	224	10.6	1,401	39.9
2015................	3,679	2,220	60.4	2,022	55.0	198	8.9	1,459	39.7
2016................	3,835	2,305	60.1	2,146	56.0	159	6.9	1,530	39.9
Cuban:									
1990................	918	603	65.7	559	60.9	44	7.2	315	34.3
2000................	1,174	740	63.1	707	60.3	33	4.5	434	37.0
2010................	1,549	970	62.6	850	54.9	120	12.4	579	37.4
2014................	1,659	1,009	60.8	950	57.3	59	5.8	650	39.2
2015................	1,760	1,079	61.3	1,010	57.4	69	6.4	681	38.7
2016................	1,819	1,149	63.2	1,088	59.8	61	5.3	670	36.8

[1] Civilian employed as a percent of the civilian noninstitutional population. [2] Beginning with the 2003 CPS, respondents could choose more than one race. Beginning in 2003, data represent persons who selected this race group only and exclude persons reporting more than one race. The CPS in prior years allowed respondents to report only one race group. See also comments on race in text for section 1. [3] Prior to 2003, includes Pacific Islanders. [4] Persons of Hispanic origin may be of any race. Includes persons of other Hispanic or Latino ethnicity, not shown separately.

Source: U.S. Bureau of Labor Statistics, Employment & Earnings Online, "Employment status of the civilian noninstitutional population by age, sex, and race" and "Employment status of the Hispanic or Latino population by sex, age, and detailed ethnic group," February 2017, and earlier releases, <www.bls.gov/opub/ee/home.htm>.

Table 612. Foreign-Born and Native-Born Populations—Employment Status by Selected Characteristics: 2016

[253,538 represents 253,538,000. For civilian noninstitutional population 16 years old and over, except as indicated. The foreign born are persons who reside in the United States but who were born outside the country or in one of its outlying areas to parents who were not U.S. citizens. The foreign born include legally admitted immigrants, refugees, temporary residents such as students and temporary workers, and undocumented immigrants. Annual averages of monthly figures. Based on Current Population Survey; see text, Section 1 and Appendix III]

Characteristic	Civilian noninstitutionalized population (1,000)	Civilian labor force					Not in the labor force (1,000)
		Total (1,000)	Participation rate[1]	Employed (1,000)	Unemployed		
					Number (1,000)	Unemployment rate	
Total	**253,538**	**159,187**	**62.8**	**151,436**	**7,751**	**4.9**	**94,351**
Male	122,497	84,755	69.2	80,568	4,187	4.9	37,742
Female	131,040	74,432	56.8	70,868	3,564	4.8	56,608
FOREIGN BORN							
Total[2]	**41,321**	**26,951**	**65.2**	**25,779**	**1,172**	**4.3**	**14,370**
Male	20,057	15,595	77.8	15,007	588	3.8	4,462
Female	21,264	11,356	53.4	10,772	584	5.1	9,908
Age:							
16 to 24 years old	3,702	1,886	50.9	1,726	160	8.5	1,816
25 to 34 years old	7,785	5,836	75.0	5,589	247	4.2	1,949
35 to 44 years old	9,218	7,259	78.8	6,990	269	3.7	1,959
45 to 54 years old	8,369	6,690	79.9	6,430	259	3.9	1,679
55 to 64 years old	6,019	4,044	67.2	3,863	180	4.5	1,975
65 years old and over	6,228	1,235	19.8	1,180	55	4.5	4,993
Race and Hispanic ethnicity:							
White non-Hispanic	7,415	4,375	59.0	4,213	162	3.7	3,040
Black non-Hispanic	3,576	2,508	70.1	2,356	152	6.1	1,068
Asian non-Hispanic	10,697	6,747	63.1	6,516	231	3.4	3,950
Hispanic[3]	19,175	13,014	67.9	12,404	610	4.7	6,161
Educational attainment:							
Total, 25 years old and over	37,619	25,064	66.6	24,053	1,011	4.0	12,555
Less than a high school diploma	9,696	5,625	58.0	5,333	291	5.2	4,071
High school graduates, no college[4]	9,509	6,187	65.1	5,911	276	4.5	3,322
Some college or associate's degree	6,109	4,259	69.7	4,090	169	4.0	1,850
Bachelor's degree and higher[5]	12,305	8,994	73.1	8,718	275	3.1	3,311
NATIVE BORN							
Total[2]	**212,217**	**132,236**	**62.3**	**125,657**	**6,580**	**5.0**	**79,981**
Male	102,441	69,160	67.5	65,561	3,599	5.2	33,281
Female	109,776	63,076	57.5	60,096	2,981	4.7	46,700
Age:							
16 to 24 years old	34,733	19,316	55.6	17,266	2,050	10.6	15,417
25 to 34 years old	35,762	29,683	83.0	28,133	1,550	5.2	6,079
35 to 44 years old	30,599	25,560	83.5	24,572	988	3.9	5,039
45 to 54 years old	34,028	27,219	80.0	26,289	929	3.4	6,809
55 to 64 years old	35,289	22,422	63.5	21,661	761	3.4	12,867
65 years old and over	41,807	8,036	19.2	7,736	300	3.7	33,771
Race and Hispanic ethnicity:							
White non-Hispanic	154,543	96,503	62.4	92,671	3,832	4.0	58,040
Black non-Hispanic	26,538	15,947	60.1	14,536	1,411	8.8	10,591
Asian non-Hispanic	4,004	2,508	62.6	2,401	107	4.2	1,496
Hispanic[3]	21,522	13,783	64.0	12,845	938	6.8	7,739
Educational attainment:							
Total, 25 years and over	177,484	112,920	63.6	108,391	4,529	4.0	64,564
Less than a high school diploma	13,672	5,054	37.0	4,551	504	10.0	8,618
High school graduates, no college[4]	52,513	29,461	56.1	27,890	1,571	5.3	23,052
Some college or associate's degree	51,075	33,675	65.9	32,295	1,380	4.1	17,400
Bachelor's degree and higher[5]	60,224	44,729	74.3	43,655	1,074	2.4	15,495

[1] Civilian labor force as a percent of the civilian noninstitutionalized population. [2] Includes other races, not shown separately. [3] Persons of Hispanic origin may be of any race. [4] Includes persons with a high school diploma or equivalent. [5] Includes persons with bachelor's, master's, professional, and doctoral degrees.

Source: U.S. Bureau of Labor Statistics, *Foreign-Born Workers: Labor Force Characteristics—2016*, News Release, USDL 17-0618, May 2017. See also <http://www.bls.gov/news.release/forbrn.toc.htm>.

Table 613. Employment Status of Veterans by Period of Service and Sex: 2016

[In thousands (244,544 represents 244,544,000). For civilian noninstitutional population 18 years old and over. Veterans are defined as men and women who have previously served on active duty in the U.S. Armed Forces and who were civilians at the time they were surveyed. Veterans are counted in only one period of service, their most recent wartime period; veterans who served in both a wartime period and any other service period are classified in the wartime period. See text, Section 10. Annual averages of monthly figures. Beginning with 2014, estimates for veterans incorporate updated weighting procedures. The primary impact of the change was an increase in the "Gulf War-era I" veteran population and a decrease in the number of veterans in the "Other service periods" category. For more information, see <http://www.bls.gov/cps/vetsweights2014.pdf>. Based on Current Population Survey; see text, Section 1 and Appendix III]

Veteran status, period of service, and sex	Civilian non-institutionalized population	Civilian labor force							Not in labor force
		Total	Percent of population	Employed		Unemployed			
				Total	Percent of population	Total	Percent of labor force		
Total, 18 years and over..................	244,544	157,060	64.2	149,689	61.2	7,371	4.7		87,484
Veterans.........................	**20,895**	**10,581**	**50.6**	**10,129**	**48.5**	**453**	**4.3**		**10,314**
Gulf War era, total............................	7,250	5,869	81.0	5,610	77.4	259	4.4		1,381
Gulf War era II [1]............................	3,896	3,174	81.5	3,013	77.3	161	5.1		722
Gulf War era I [2]............................	3,354	2,695	80.4	2,597	77.4	98	3.6		659
WWII, Korean War, and Vietnam era [3]......	8,490	2,108	24.8	2,025	23.8	83	3.9		6,382
Other service periods [4]......................	5,156	2,604	50.5	2,494	48.4	110	4.2		2,551
Nonveterans [5]............................	223,649	146,479	65.5	139,560	62.4	6,919	4.7		77,170
Male, 18 years and over..................	117,989	83,727	71.0	79,743	67.6	3,984	4.8		34,262
Veterans.........................	**18,881**	**9,334**	**49.4**	**8,944**	**47.4**	**390**	**4.2**		**9,547**
Gulf War era, total............................	6,052	4,981	82.3	4,766	78.8	215	4.3		1,070
Gulf War era II [1]............................	3,207	2,666	83.1	2,533	79.0	133	5.0		541
Gulf War era I [2]............................	2,845	2,315	81.4	2,233	78.5	82	3.5		530
WWII, Korean War, and Vietnam era [3]......	8,186	2,033	24.8	1,955	23.9	78	3.9		6,153
Other service periods [4]......................	4,644	2,320	50.0	2,224	47.9	96	4.1		2,324
Nonveterans [5]............................	99,107	74,393	75.1	70,799	71.4	3,594	4.8		24,714
Female, 18 years and over.................	126,555	73,333	57.9	69,946	55.3	3,388	4.6		53,222
Veterans.........................	**2,014**	**1,247**	**61.9**	**1,184**	**58.8**	**63**	**5.0**		**767**
Gulf War era, total............................	1,198	888	74.1	844	70.4	44	5.0		310
Gulf War era II [1]............................	689	508	73.7	480	69.6	28	5.6		181
Gulf War era I [2]............................	509	379	74.6	364	71.5	16	4.2		129
WWII, Korean War, and Vietnam era [3]......	304	75	24.6	70	23.1	5	6.4		229
Other service periods [4]......................	512	285	55.6	271	52.9	14	4.9		227
Nonveterans [5]............................	124,541	72,086	57.9	68,761	55.2	3,325	4.6		52,455

[1] Gulf War era II: September 2001–present. [2] Gulf War era I: August 1990–August 2001. [3] World War II: December 1941–December 1946. Korean War: July 1950–January 1955. Vietnam era: August 1964–April 1975. [4] Other service periods; all other time periods. [5] Nonveterans are men and women who never served on active duty in the U.S. Armed Forces.

Source: U.S. Bureau of Labor Statistics, *Employment Situation of Veterans—2016*, USDL 17-0354, March 2017. See also <http://www.bls.gov/news.release/vet.nr0.htm>.

Table 614. Labor Force Status of Persons With and Without a Disability: 2016

[29,971 represents 29,971,000. For civilian noninstitutionalized population 16 years old and over. Persons with a disability are those who have a physical, mental, or emotional condition that causes serious difficulty with their daily activities. Annual averages of monthly figures. Based on Current Population Survey; see text, Section 1 and Appendix III]

Characteristic	Civilian non-institutionalized population (1,000)	Civilian labor force					Not in the labor force (1,000)
		Total (1,000)	Participation rate [1]	Employed (1,000)	Unemployed		
					Number (1,000)	Unemployment rate	
WITH DISABILITY							
Total....................	**29,971**	**6,005**	**20.0**	**5,372**	**633**	**10.5**	**23,965**
Sex:							
Male..............................	13,898	3,295	23.7	2,961	334	10.1	10,603
Female...........................	16,073	2,710	16.9	2,411	299	11.0	13,363
Age:							
16 to 64 years....................	15,746	4,919	31.2	4,356	564	11.5	10,827
16 to 19 years...................	654	161	24.6	103	58	35.8	493
20 to 24 years...................	913	399	43.7	321	78	19.5	514
25 to 34 years...................	1,824	770	42.2	657	113	14.6	1,054
35 to 44 years...................	2,161	827	38.3	745	82	9.9	1,333
45 to 54 years...................	3,807	1,159	30.4	1,049	110	9.5	2,648
55 to 64 years...................	6,387	1,603	25.1	1,480	123	7.7	4,784
65 years and over................	14,225	1,086	7.6	1,016	70	6.4	13,139
WITHOUT DISABILITY							
Total....................	**223,567**	**153,182**	**68.5**	**146,064**	**7,118**	**4.6**	**70,385**
Sex:							
Male..............................	108,599	81,459	75.0	77,607	3,852	4.7	27,140
Female...........................	114,968	71,722	62.4	68,457	3,266	4.6	43,245
Age:							
16 to 64 years....................	189,757	144,996	76.4	138,164	6,832	4.7	44,761
16 to 19 years...................	16,060	5,728	35.7	4,861	867	15.1	10,331
20 to 24 years...................	20,808	14,914	71.7	13,706	1,208	8.1	5,893
25 to 34 years...................	41,723	34,750	83.3	33,065	1,685	4.8	6,973
35 to 44 years...................	37,656	31,992	85.0	30,817	1,175	3.7	5,663
45 to 54 years...................	38,590	32,750	84.9	31,671	1,079	3.3	5,841
55 to 64 years...................	34,921	24,862	71.2	24,044	818	3.3	10,059
65 years and over................	33,810	8,185	24.2	7,900	285	3.5	25,624

[1] Civilian labor force as a percent of the civilian noninstitutional population.

Source: U.S. Bureau of Labor Statistics, "Persons with A Disability: Labor Force Characteristics—2016," USDL 17-0857, <http://www.bls.gov/cps/demographics.htm#disability>, accessed June 2017.

Table 615. Civilian Labor Force—Percent Distribution by Sex and Age: 1980 to 2016

[106,940 represents 106,940,000. Civilian noninstitutionalized population 16 years old and over. Annual averages of monthly figures. Data not strictly comparable with data for earlier years, see BLS Handbook of Methods, <http://www.bls.gov/opub/hom/>. Based on Current Population Survey; see text, Section 1 and Appendix III]

Year and sex	Civilian labor force (1,000)	Percent distribution						
		16 to 19 years	20 to 24 years	25 to 34 years	35 to 44 years	45 to 54 years	55 to 64 years	65 years and over
Total:								
1980....................	106,940	8.8	14.9	27.3	19.1	15.8	11.2	2.9
1990....................	125,840	6.2	11.7	28.6	25.5	16.1	9.2	2.7
2000....................	142,583	5.8	10.0	23.0	26.3	21.8	10.1	3.0
2010....................	153,889	3.8	9.8	21.8	21.7	23.4	15.1	4.4
2016....................	159,187	3.7	9.6	22.3	20.6	21.3	16.6	5.8
Male:								
1980....................	61,453	8.1	14.0	27.6	19.3	16.1	11.8	3.1
1990....................	69,011	5.9	11.4	28.8	25.3	16.1	9.6	2.9
2000....................	76,280	5.6	9.9	23.4	26.3	21.3	10.2	3.3
2010....................	81,985	3.6	9.6	22.4	22.1	23.0	14.8	4.5
2016....................	84,755	3.5	9.4	22.6	20.9	21.1	16.4	6.1
Female:								
1980....................	45,487	9.6	16.1	26.9	19.0	15.4	10.4	2.6
1990....................	56,829	6.5	12.0	28.3	25.8	16.1	8.7	2.6
2000....................	66,303	6.0	10.2	22.5	26.4	22.3	9.9	2.7
2010....................	71,904	4.1	10.0	21.2	21.2	23.8	15.6	4.2
2016....................	74,432	3.9	9.9	22.0	20.3	21.5	16.8	5.5

Source: U.S. Bureau of Labor Statistics, Employment & Earnings Online, "Employment status of the civilian noninstitutional population by age, sex, and race," February 2017, and earlier releases, <www.bls.gov/opub/ee/home.htm>.

Table 616. Civilian Labor Force and Participation Rates by Educational Attainment, Sex, Race, and Hispanic Origin: 2000 to 2016

[120,061 represents 120,061,000. Civilian noninstitutional population 25 years old and over. Annual averages of monthly figures. Revisions to population controls and other changes can affect the comparability of data over time; see BLS Handbook of Methods, <http://www.bls.gov/opub/hom/>. See Table 650 for unemployment data. Rates are based on annual average civilian noninstitutional population of each specified group and represent proportion of each specified group in the civilian labor force]

Year, sex, and race/ethnicity	Civilian labor force					Participation rate (percent) [1]				
		Percent distribution								
	Total (1,000)	Less than a high school diploma	High school graduate, no college	Less than a bachelor's degree	College graduate	Total	Less than a high school diploma	High school graduate, no college	Less than a bachelor's degree	College graduate
Total: [2]										
2000..............	120,061	10.4	31.4	27.7	30.5	67.3	43.5	64.4	73.9	79.4
2005..............	127,030	10.0	30.1	27.5	32.4	67.1	45.5	63.2	72.5	77.9
2010..............	132,955	8.9	28.8	27.7	34.6	66.5	46.3	61.6	70.5	76.7
2016..............	137,985	7.7	25.8	27.5	38.9	64.1	45.7	57.5	66.3	74.1
Male:										
2000..............	64,490	11.8	31.1	25.9	31.2	76.1	56.0	75.1	80.9	84.4
2005..............	68,389	11.7	30.9	25.4	32.1	75.4	58.6	73.6	79.3	82.9
2010..............	71,129	10.6	30.4	25.6	33.4	74.1	59.1	71.4	76.7	81.3
2016..............	73,805	9.2	28.1	25.7	36.9	71.6	58.1	67.6	72.8	78.6
Female:										
2000..............	55,572	8.8	31.8	29.7	29.7	59.4	32.3	55.5	68.0	74.0
2005..............	58,641	8.0	29.2	30.0	32.8	59.4	32.9	53.8	66.8	72.9
2010..............	61,825	7.0	26.9	30.1	36.0	59.5	33.5	52.4	65.4	72.4
2016..............	64,179	6.0	23.2	29.5	41.3	57.3	33.3	47.5	60.9	69.9
White: [3]										
2000..............	99,964	10.1	31.4	27.5	31.0	67.0	44.1	63.6	73.1	79.0
2005..............	104,240	9.8	29.9	27.6	32.7	66.9	46.4	62.5	72.0	77.5
2010..............	108,274	8.9	28.7	27.5	34.9	66.5	47.7	61.2	70.1	76.5
2016..............	108,487	7.8	25.7	27.4	39.1	63.8	47.2	56.9	65.6	73.6
Black: [3]										
2000..............	13,582	12.4	36.0	31.2	20.5	68.2	39.3	69.9	79.3	84.4
2005..............	14,252	11.2	36.4	30.2	22.2	67.2	39.8	67.9	75.6	82.0
2010..............	15,114	9.4	33.3	32.8	24.5	65.8	38.8	63.8	73.5	79.5
2016..............	16,648	7.5	31.1	32.6	28.8	63.9	37.8	59.2	69.4	77.7
Asian: [3, 4]										
2000..............	5,402	9.1	20.7	20.2	50.1	70.9	46.0	65.6	76.4	79.1
2005..............	5,805	8.0	17.7	17.3	57.0	69.4	45.3	61.8	71.6	77.5
2010..............	6,601	7.3	18.8	17.1	56.7	68.7	44.1	62.8	70.6	75.9
2016..............	8,665	6.0	16.8	16.3	60.8	67.1	40.6	60.1	68.5	73.8
Hispanic: [5]										
2000..............	12,975	36.7	29.3	20.6	13.4	71.5	61.9	75.0	80.8	83.5
2005..............	16,135	35.5	29.4	20.9	14.2	70.8	61.4	74.3	78.8	81.7
2010..............	18,987	31.4	30.8	21.7	16.0	71.4	61.9	73.9	77.8	81.7
2016..............	22,233	26.2	30.3	23.7	19.8	69.0	59.0	68.9	74.8	79.8

[1] Civilian labor force as a percent of the civilian noninstitutional population. [2] Includes other races, not shown separately. [3] Beginning in 2003, data represent persons who selected this race group only and exclude persons reporting more than one race. See footnote 3, Table 611. [4] 2000 data include Pacific Islanders. [5] Persons of Hispanic origin may be of any race.

Source: U.S. Bureau of Labor Statistics, Employment & Earnings Online, "Employment status of the civilian noninstitutional population 25 years and over by educational attainment, sex, race, and Hispanic or Latino ethnicity," February 2017 and earlier releases, <https://www.bls.gov/opub/ee/home.htm>.

Table 617. Civilian Labor Force by Employment Status and Sex, by State: 2016

[In thousands (159,187 represents 159,187,000), except ratio and rate. Preliminary data. Civilian noninstitutionalized population 16 years old and over. Annual averages of monthly figures. Data for states may not sum to national totals due to rounding]

State	Total		Employed		Employ-ment/ population ratio [1]	Unemployed					Participation rate [3]	
						Total		Rate [2]				
	Num-ber	Female	Total	Female		Num-ber	Female	Total	Male	Female	Male	Female
United States	**159,187**	**74,432**	**151,436**	**70,868**	**59.7**	**7,751**	**3,564**	**4.9**	**4.9**	**4.8**	**69.2**	**56.8**
Alabama	2,172	1,024	2,041	968	53.4	131	56	6.0	6.6	5.4	63.5	50.8
Alaska	357	165	334	155	61.5	24	10	6.6	7.2	6.0	68.8	62.5
Arizona	3,236	1,473	3,068	1,396	57.2	167	77	5.2	5.1	5.2	67.6	53.5
Arkansas	1,351	634	1,299	608	56.1	53	27	3.9	3.6	4.2	64.3	52.8
California	19,193	8,612	18,159	8,131	58.8	1,034	481	5.4	5.2	5.6	70.2	54.6
Colorado	2,904	1,304	2,809	1,256	64.9	95	48	3.3	3.0	3.6	74.7	59.7
Connecticut	1,906	919	1,806	873	62.6	100	47	5.2	5.4	5.1	71.2	61.3
Delaware	475	231	454	221	59.9	21	10	4.3	4.2	4.4	67.7	57.9
District of Columbia	395	201	371	189	65.8	24	12	6.1	6.2	5.9	74.0	66.6
Florida	9,759	4,636	9,283	4,414	55.8	476	222	4.9	5.0	4.8	64.4	53.5
Georgia	4,936	2,364	4,671	2,226	59.2	265	139	5.4	4.9	5.9	68.9	56.9
Hawaii	691	326	670	316	60.9	21	10	3.0	2.9	3.2	67.7	58.0
Idaho	809	366	777	352	61.4	32	14	3.9	3.9	3.9	70.9	57.2
Illinois	6,578	3,100	6,192	2,919	61.4	386	182	5.9	5.9	5.9	71.4	59.5
Indiana	3,348	1,584	3,199	1,512	62.0	150	73	4.5	4.4	4.6	70.5	59.6
Iowa	1,714	815	1,647	787	67.2	67	28	3.9	4.3	3.4	74.4	65.5
Kansas	1,490	694	1,428	668	64.3	63	26	4.2	4.6	3.8	73.2	61.3
Kentucky	2,004	948	1,905	905	55.1	99	42	4.9	5.4	4.4	63.3	52.9
Louisiana	2,132	1,036	2,000	976	55.6	132	60	6.2	6.6	5.8	64.3	54.8
Maine	693	329	666	317	60.9	27	12	3.9	4.1	3.7	68.9	58.3
Maryland	3,187	1,557	3,052	1,484	64.3	135	73	4.2	3.8	4.7	72.6	62.3
Massachusetts	3,599	1,733	3,466	1,675	62.5	133	58	3.7	4.0	3.3	70.3	59.9
Michigan	4,853	2,287	4,616	2,173	58.4	238	114	4.9	4.8	5.0	67.1	56.1
Minnesota	2,985	1,415	2,870	1,369	66.4	116	46	3.9	4.5	3.2	73.7	64.7
Mississippi	1,281	627	1,208	593	52.8	74	34	5.7	6.0	5.5	60.8	51.6
Missouri	3,142	1,502	3,002	1,434	62.9	140	68	4.4	4.4	4.5	71.2	60.8
Montana	522	245	500	236	60.8	22	9	4.2	4.6	3.8	67.4	59.3
Nebraska	1,014	481	980	468	67.2	34	13	3.4	4.0	2.6	74.3	65.1
Nevada	1,417	630	1,333	594	58.0	84	36	5.9	6.1	5.7	69.3	54.2
New Hampshire	751	354	730	345	67.0	21	9	2.8	3.1	2.5	74.2	63.8
New Jersey	4,553	2,109	4,328	1,997	60.7	225	111	4.9	4.6	5.3	71.3	56.9
New Mexico	933	437	870	410	54.0	63	27	6.8	7.3	6.1	63.4	52.7
New York	9,625	4,603	9,161	4,386	57.5	463	218	4.8	4.9	4.7	66.1	55.3
North Carolina	4,873	2,323	4,628	2,199	58.6	245	124	5.0	4.8	5.3	68.2	55.9
North Dakota	429	194	414	189	69.5	14	6	3.3	3.7	2.8	76.7	66.7
Ohio	5,737	2,725	5,453	2,598	59.5	284	127	4.9	5.2	4.7	68.2	57.4
Oklahoma	1,836	830	1,743	791	58.0	93	39	5.1	5.4	4.7	69.1	53.5
Oregon	2,061	969	1,960	920	59.9	101	49	4.9	4.8	5.1	68.3	57.9
Pennsylvania	6,507	3,120	6,144	2,953	59.8	362	167	5.6	5.8	5.3	68.5	58.6
Rhode Island	551	269	522	258	60.8	30	11	5.4	6.5	4.1	68.8	59.9
South Carolina	2,316	1,127	2,203	1,081	56.8	113	47	4.9	5.6	4.2	64.8	55.0
South Dakota	452	210	440	204	67.1	13	5	2.8	3.0	2.6	74.5	63.6
Tennessee	3,147	1,467	3,000	1,394	57.5	147	73	4.7	4.4	5.0	67.4	53.8
Texas	13,344	5,937	12,735	5,681	60.8	609	256	4.6	4.8	4.3	72.8	55.2
Utah	1,509	654	1,455	632	66.3	54	22	3.6	3.7	3.4	78.5	59.2
Vermont	346	167	335	162	64.9	11	5	3.3	3.7	2.8	71.4	63.3
Virginia	4,218	1,992	4,047	1,912	61.7	171	80	4.1	4.1	4.0	70.7	58.4
Washington	3,639	1,710	3,441	1,624	60.3	199	86	5.5	5.8	5.0	68.7	59.0
West Virginia	787	366	740	347	50.0	48	19	6.1	6.8	5.2	58.5	48.2
Wisconsin	3,129	1497	2,999	1,444	65.6	129	53	4.1	4.7	3.5	72.6	64.3
Wyoming	303	136	286	130	63.1	17	6	5.4	6.4	4.3	72.9	60.7

[1] Civilian employment as a percent of civilian noninstitutionalized population. [2] Percent unemployed of the civilian labor force. [3] Percent of civilian noninstitutionalized population of each specified group in the civilian labor force.

Source: U.S. Bureau of Labor Statistics, CPS Tables, "Employment status of the civilian noninstitutional population by sex, age, and race," <http://www.bls.gov/cps/tables.htm>, and "Local Area Unemployment Statistics," <http://www.bls.gov/lau/>; accessed August 2017.

Table 618. Civilian Labor Force Status by Selected Metropolitan Area: 2016

[159,187 represents 159,187,000. Civilian noninstitutional population 16 years old and over. Annual averages of monthly figures. Data are derived from the Local Area Unemployment Statistics program, a Federal-State cooperative effort in which monthly estimates of total employment and unemployment are prepared for approximately 7,300 areas. For definitions of metropolitan areas, see Appendix II]

Metropolitan area ranked by 2010 population	Civilian labor force (1,000)	Unemployment rate [1]	Metropolitan area ranked by 2010 population	Civilian labor force (1,000)	Unemployment rate [1]
U.S. total	159,187	4.9	San Antonio-New Braunfels, TX	1,136	3.7
New York-Newark-Jersey City, NY-NJ-PA	10,003	4.8	Orlando-Kissimmee-Sanford, FL	1,255	4.5
Los Angeles-Long Beach-Anaheim, CA	6,646	4.9	Cincinnati, OH-KY-IN	1,083	4.3
Chicago-Naperville-Elgin, IL-IN-WI	4,926	5.8	Cleveland-Elyria, OH	1,028	5.3
Dallas-Fort Worth-Arlington, TX	3,685	3.8	Kansas City, MO-KS	1,128	4.3
Philadelphia-Camden-Wilmington, PA-NJ-DE-MD	3,092	5.1	Las Vegas-Henderson-Paradise, NV	1,048	5.8
Houston-The Woodlands-Sugar Land, TX	3,288	5.2	Columbus, OH	1,051	4.1
Washington-Arlington-Alexandria, DC-VA-MD-WV	3,313	3.8	Indianapolis-Carmel-Anderson, IN	1,037	4.0
Miami-Fort Lauderdale-West Palm Beach, FL	3,056	5.0	San Jose-Sunnyvale-Santa Clara, CA	1,056	3.8
Atlanta-Sandy Springs-Roswell, GA	2,939	5.1	Austin-Round Rock, TX	1,110	3.2
Boston-Cambridge-Nashua, MA-NH NECTA [2]	2,648	3.4	Virginia Beach-Norfolk-Newport News, VA-NC	835	4.6
San Francisco-Oakland-Hayward, CA	2,544	3.8	Nashville-Davidson-Murfreesboro-Franklin, TN	973	3.8
Detroit-Warren-Dearborn, MI	2,067	5.4	Providence-Warwick, RI-MA NECTA [2]	679	5.1
Riverside-San Bernardino-Ontario, CA	1,987	5.9	Milwaukee-Waukesha-West Allis, WI	828	4.5
Phoenix-Mesa-Scottsdale, AZ	2,239	4.6	Jacksonville, FL	734	4.7
Seattle-Tacoma-Bellevue, WA	2,026	4.5	Memphis, TN-MS-AR	624	5.3
Minneapolis-St. Paul-Bloomington, MN-WI	1,939	3.6	Oklahoma City, OK	666	4.2
San Diego-Carlsbad, CA	1,570	4.7	Louisville-Jefferson County, KY-IN	642	4.2
St. Louis, MO-IL	1,483	4.6	Hartford-W. Hartford-E. Hartford, CT NECTA [2]	616	5.1
Tampa-St. Petersburg-Clearwater, FL	1,476	4.6	Richmond, VA	663	4.1
Baltimore-Columbia-Towson, MD	1,484	4.4	New Orleans-Metairie, LA	599	5.5
Denver-Aurora-Lakewood, CO	1,541	3.1	Buffalo-Cheektowaga-Niagara Falls, NY	547	5.0
Pittsburgh, PA	1,218	5.7	Raleigh, NC	680	4.3
Portland-Vancouver-Hillsboro, OR-WA	1,276	4.7	Birmingham-Hoover, AL	536	5.6
Charlotte-Concord-Gastonia, NC-SC	1,283	4.7	Salt Lake City, UT	636	3.2
Sacramento-Roseville-Arden-Arcade, CA	1,073	5.2	Rochester, NY	524	4.7

[1] Percent of the civilian labor force unemployed. [2] New England City and Town Areas. See Appendix II.

Source: U.S. Bureau of Labor Statistics, "Local Area Unemployment Statistics," <http://www.bls.gov/lau/>, accessed May 2017.

Table 619. School Enrollment and Labor Force Status of Teenagers and Young Adults: 2016

[In thousands (38,367 represents 38,367,000), except percent rate. As of October. Covers civilian noninstitutional population age 16 to 24. Based on Current Population Survey; see text, Section 1 and Appendix III]

Characteristic	Population	Civilian labor force	Employed	Unemployed Total	Unemployed Rate [1]	Not in labor force
Total, 16 to 24 years [2]	38,367	20,951	18,820	2,130	10.2	17,417
Enrolled in school [2]	22,058	7,947	7,276	671	8.4	14,111
Enrolled in high school	9,521	1,971	1,650	321	16.3	7,550
Male	4,962	900	731	169	18.8	4,061
Female	4,560	1,071	919	152	14.2	3,489
Enrolled in college	12,536	5,976	5,626	350	5.9	6,561
Male	5,876	2,761	2,538	223	8.1	3,116
Female	6,660	3,215	3,088	127	3.9	3,445
Enrolled in two-year college	3,070	1,792	1,656	136	7.6	1,278
Enrolled in four-year college	9,466	4,184	3,970	214	5.1	5,282
By race/ethnicity:						
White:						
Enrolled in high school	6,847	1,546	1,329	217	14.0	5,301
Enrolled in college	9,259	4,611	4,348	263	5.7	4,648
Black or African American:						
Enrolled in high school	1,557	196	127	69	35.2	1,362
Enrolled in college	1,674	753	696	57	7.6	921
Asian:						
Enrolled in high school	504	75	60	15	20.1	429
Enrolled in college	1,017	318	295	23	7.1	699
Hispanic: [3]						
Enrolled in high school	2,179	384	307	76	19.9	1,796
Enrolled in college	2,647	1,258	1,145	113	9.0	1,389
Not enrolled in school [2]	16,309	13,004	11,544	1,460	11.2	3,306
White	12,118	9,709	8,793	915	9.4	2,409
Black	2,592	2,068	1,646	422	20.4	524
Asian	706	533	492	41	7.7	173
Hispanic [3]	3,686	2,844	2,545	298	10.5	842

[1] Percent unemployed of civilian labor force in each category. [2] Includes other races, not shown separately. [3] Persons of Hispanic origin may be of any race.

Source: U.S. Bureau of Labor Statistics, *College Enrollment and Work Activity of 2016 High School Graduates*, News Release, USDL 17-0477, April 2017. See also <http://www.bls.gov/news.release/hsgec.toc.htm>.

Table 620. Labor Force Participation Rates by Marital Status, Sex, and Age: 1970 to 2016

[In percent. For the civilian noninstitutional population 16 years old and over. Annual averages of monthly figures. Participation rate is the civilian labor force as a percent of the civilian noninstitutional population. Based on Current Population Survey; see text, Section 1 and Appendix III]

Marital status and year	Male participation rate							Female participation rate						
	Total	16–19 years	20–24 years	25–34 years	35–44 years	45–64 years	65 years and over	Total	16–19 years	20–24 years	25–34 years	35–44 years	45–64 years	65 years and over
Single: [1]														
1970	65.5	54.6	73.8	87.9	86.2	75.7	25.2	56.8	44.7	73.0	81.4	78.6	73.0	19.7
1980	72.6	59.9	81.3	89.2	82.2	66.9	16.8	64.4	53.6	75.2	83.3	76.9	65.6	13.9
1990	74.8	55.1	81.6	89.9	84.5	67.3	15.7	66.7	51.7	74.5	80.9	80.8	66.2	12.1
2000	73.6	52.5	80.5	89.4	82.9	69.7	17.3	68.9	51.1	76.1	83.9	80.9	69.9	10.8
2008	69.9	39.8	77.1	87.9	84.3	69.5	24.7	65.3	40.3	71.9	82.6	79.6	70.4	20.5
2009	68.3	37.1	74.6	86.5	83.7	68.5	26.1	64.2	37.5	71.4	81.6	79.5	69.3	19.7
2010	67.3	34.6	73.1	85.8	83.7	67.6	25.0	63.3	34.9	69.8	81.3	78.2	69.4	20.1
2011	67.0	33.4	73.3	85.4	82.6	67.4	23.8	62.8	34.3	69.1	79.9	77.8	67.8	21.7
2012	66.8	33.7	72.9	85.8	81.7	67.1	23.6	62.8	34.5	68.5	79.8	78.1	68.2	20.5
2013	66.9	34.0	72.5	85.4	82.2	66.9	24.5	63.0	34.5	69.2	79.2	77.5	67.3	22.7
2014	66.7	33.3	72.5	85.1	82.4	64.4	25.9	62.9	34.4	69.1	79.9	77.6	65.5	21.3
2015	66.8	33.9	71.7	85.6	81.2	64.6	26.6	62.9	34.1	69.3	79.7	77.6	65.8	20.9
2016	67.3	35.1	71.8	85.5	82.5	65.2	26.1	63.4	35.0	69.2	80.9	77.3	65.4	22.6
Married: [2]														
1970	86.1	92.3	94.7	98.0	98.1	91.2	29.9	40.5	37.8	47.9	38.8	46.8	44.0	7.3
1980	80.9	91.3	96.9	97.5	97.2	84.3	20.5	49.8	49.3	61.4	58.8	61.8	46.9	7.3
1990	78.6	92.1	95.6	96.9	96.7	82.6	17.5	58.4	49.5	66.1	69.6	74.0	56.5	8.5
2000	77.3	79.5	94.1	96.7	95.8	83.0	19.2	61.1	53.2	63.8	70.3	74.8	65.4	10.1
2008	76.8	83.4	92.0	95.3	95.2	84.0	22.8	61.4	38.0	62.3	69.5	73.8	68.3	14.1
2009	76.3	75.8	91.2	94.7	94.8	83.8	23.3	61.4	44.7	61.8	69.4	73.7	68.6	14.9
2010	75.8	78.2	89.3	94.3	94.5	83.6	23.5	61.0	40.2	60.9	68.8	72.8	68.8	15.2
2011	74.9	75.9	90.2	93.9	94.3	82.8	24.5	60.2	44.7	60.6	68.2	72.5	68.0	15.3
2012	74.6	83.7	91.3	94.2	94.3	83.0	25.6	59.5	42.1	60.5	68.5	72.3	67.3	15.9
2013	74.2	81.7	90.1	94.0	94.1	83.0	25.7	58.9	46.3	58.4	67.8	71.3	67.1	16.5
2014	73.5	76.8	92.0	93.4	94.0	82.9	24.9	58.4	45.1	58.9	67.7	71.3	66.6	16.8
2015	73.4	75.9	89.7	93.5	94.2	83.1	25.2	58.1	47.1	61.6	67.1	71.9	66.0	16.8
2016	73.1	71.5	89.3	93.7	94.2	83.2	25.5	57.9	43.8	59.9	67.9	71.8	66.3	16.6
Other: [3]														
1970	60.7	(B)	90.4	93.7	91.1	78.5	19.3	40.3	48.6	60.3	64.6	68.8	61.9	10.0
1980	67.5	(B)	92.6	94.1	91.9	73.3	13.7	43.6	50.0	68.4	76.5	77.1	60.2	8.2
1990	68.9	(B)	93.1	93.0	90.7	74.9	12.0	47.2	53.9	65.4	77.0	82.1	65.0	8.4
2000	66.8	60.5	88.1	93.2	89.9	73.9	12.9	49.0	46.0	74.0	83.1	82.9	69.8	8.7
2008	65.0	43.2	84.9	90.7	89.4	73.2	16.8	49.2	39.7	64.9	77.4	81.4	69.1	12.1
2009	63.7	42.6	78.6	88.5	88.5	71.8	17.0	49.3	39.0	68.3	78.2	80.5	68.8	12.1
2010	63.0	37.6	78.8	89.0	88.5	71.8	17.2	48.8	35.2	66.3	77.7	80.7	68.8	12.1
2011	62.4	39.7	76.2	88.3	87.2	71.1	17.8	48.8	39.9	65.6	77.1	79.2	68.3	12.3
2012	61.7	35.1	78.3	88.5	87.4	70.9	17.6	48.3	34.9	68.4	77.4	79.8	67.6	12.6
2013	60.2	29.2	74.1	89.4	88.3	69.4	16.8	47.3	36.6	63.8	76.4	79.7	66.6	12.8
2014	59.6	31.2	80.3	88.8	87.1	70.4	16.9	47.3	38.2	66.3	77.2	80.1	66.8	13.0
2015	58.8	36.6	73.0	87.0	86.8	70.3	17.7	46.7	42.9	67.0	75.4	79.0	66.4	13.4
2016	59.6	37.7	71.0	88.2	87.1	71.0	19.1	46.9	40.4	67.5	76.1	80.6	66.4	13.8

B Percentage not shown where base is less than 50,000. [1] Never married. [2] Spouse present. [3] Widowed, divorced, and separated (married, spouse absent).

Source: U.S. Bureau of Labor Statistics, unpublished data. See also <http://www.bls.gov/cps/home.htm>.

Table 621. Marital Status of Women in the Civilian Labor Force: 1970 to 2016

[31,543 represents 31,543,000. For civilian noninstitutional population 16 years and over. Annual averages of monthly figures. Based on the Current Population Survey; see text, Section 1 and Appendix III]

Year	Female civilian labor force (1,000)				Female participation rate (percent) [3]			
	Total	Never married	Married [1]	Other [2]	Total	Never married	Married [1]	Other [2]
1970	31,543	7,265	18,475	5,804	43.3	56.8	40.5	40.3
1980	45,487	11,865	24,980	8,643	51.5	64.4	49.8	43.6
1990	56,829	14,612	30,901	11,315	57.5	66.7	58.4	47.2
2000	66,303	17,849	35,146	13,308	59.9	68.9	61.1	49.0
2005	69,288	19,183	35,941	14,163	59.3	66.0	60.7	49.4
2010	71,904	20,592	36,742	14,570	58.6	63.3	61.0	48.8
2011	71,642	20,878	36,141	14,623	58.1	62.8	60.2	48.8
2012	72,648	21,506	36,436	14,706	57.7	62.8	59.5	48.3
2013	72,722	22,070	36,137	14,515	57.2	63.0	58.9	47.3
2014	73,039	22,320	36,082	14,637	57.0	62.9	58.4	47.3
2015	73,510	22,738	36,135	14,637	56.7	62.9	58.1	46.7
2016	74,433	23,321	36,387	14,725	56.8	63.4	57.9	46.9

[1] Spouse present. [2] Widowed, divorced, and separated (married, spouse absent). [3] Civilian labor force as a percent of the civilian noninstitutional population.

Source: U.S. Bureau of Labor Statistics, unpublished data. See also <http://www.bls.gov/cps/home.htm>.

Table 622. Employment Status of Women by Marital Status and Presence and Age of Children: 1970 to 2016

[7.0 represents 7,000,000. As of March. Data are from the Current Population Survey, Annual Social and Economic Supplement (ASEC), which includes civilian noninstitutionalized population, age 16 years old and over. For more information; see text, Section 1 and Appendix III]

Item	Total			With any children under age 18								
				Total			Children 6 to 17 years			Children under 6 years		
	Single [1]	Married [2]	Other [3]	Single [1]	Married [2]	Other [3]	Single [1]	Married [2]	Other [3]	Single [1]	Married [2]	Other [3]
IN LABOR FORCE (mil.)												
1970	7.0	18.4	5.9	(NA)	10.2	1.9	(NA)	6.3	1.3	(NA)	3.9	0.6
1980	11.2	24.9	8.8	0.6	13.7	3.6	0.2	8.4	2.6	0.3	5.2	1.0
1990	14.0	31.0	11.2	1.5	16.5	4.2	0.6	9.3	3.0	0.9	7.2	1.2
2000	17.8	35.0	13.2	3.1	18.2	4.5	1.2	10.8	3.4	1.8	7.3	1.1
2010	20.0	37.2	14.7	3.6	17.6	4.5	1.6	10.4	3.3	2.1	7.2	1.2
2015	22.4	36.4	14.6	4.2	16.8	4.1	1.9	10.1	3.1	2.3	6.7	1.1
2016	23.2	36.9	14.7	4.1	16.9	4.1	1.9	10.2	3.0	2.2	6.7	1.1
PARTICIPATION RATE [4]												
1970	53.0	40.8	39.1	(NA)	39.7	60.7	(NA)	49.2	66.9	(NA)	30.3	52.2
1980	61.5	50.1	44.0	52.0	54.1	69.4	67.6	61.7	74.6	44.1	45.1	60.3
1990	66.4	58.2	46.8	55.2	66.3	74.2	69.7	73.6	79.7	48.7	58.9	63.6
2000	68.6	62.0	50.2	73.9	70.6	82.7	79.7	77.2	84.9	70.5	62.8	76.6
2010	62.3	61.7	49.2	70.1	69.7	79.2	77.0	75.9	81.8	65.6	62.5	73.1
2015	62.1	58.5	46.9	72.2	67.6	78.2	77.6	72.4	80.5	68.5	61.3	72.3
2016	62.7	58.9	47.2	72.8	68.6	79.3	78.3	73.0	80.6	68.6	62.9	75.5
EMPLOYMENT (mil.)												
1970	6.5	17.5	5.6	(NA)	9.6	1.8	(NA)	6.0	1.2	(NA)	3.6	0.6
1980	10.1	23.6	8.2	0.4	12.8	3.3	0.2	8.1	2.4	0.2	4.8	0.9
1990	12.9	29.9	10.5	1.2	15.8	3.8	0.5	8.9	2.7	0.7	6.9	1.1
2000	16.4	34.0	12.7	2.7	17.6	4.3	1.1	10.6	3.2	1.6	7.1	1.1
2010	17.5	35.0	13.3	3.0	16.5	4.0	1.3	9.8	2.9	1.6	6.7	1.1
2015	20.5	35.3	13.8	3.7	16.3	3.9	1.7	9.9	2.9	2.0	6.5	1.0
2016	21.4	35.7	14.0	3.7	16.3	3.9	1.8	9.9	2.9	1.9	6.5	1.0
UNEMPLOYMENT RATE [5]												
1970	7.1	4.8	4.8	(NA)	6.0	7.2	(NA)	4.8	5.9	(NA)	7.9	9.8
1980	10.3	5.3	6.4	23.2	5.9	9.2	15.6	4.4	7.9	29.2	8.3	12.8
1990	8.2	3.5	5.7	18.4	4.2	8.5	14.5	3.8	7.7	20.8	4.8	10.2
2000	7.3	2.7	4.3	11.0	2.9	5.1	8.7	2.6	4.8	12.6	3.5	5.9
2010	12.3	6.0	9.7	18.1	6.3	11.1	14.4	6.0	10.3	20.9	6.7	13.4
2015	8.3	3.0	5.6	12.6	2.8	6.3	10.2	2.7	5.1	14.6	3.0	9.9
2016	8.0	3.1	4.7	10.4	3.2	5.5	8.7	3.1	4.5	11.9	3.4	8.2

NA Not available. [1] Never married. [2] Spouse present. [3] Widowed, divorced, or separated (married, spouse absent). [4] Percent of women in each specific category in the labor force. [5] Unemployed as a percent of civilian labor force in specified group.

Source: U.S. Bureau of Labor Statistics, unpublished data. See also <http://www.bls.gov/cps/home.htm>

Table 623. Labor Force Participation Rates for Wives, Spouse Present, by Age of Own Youngest Child: 1990 to 2016

[In percent. As of March. Base on Current Population Survey, Annual Social and Economic Supplement (ASEC), which includes civilian noninstitutionalized population, 16 years old and over, and military personnel who live in households with at least one other civilian adult. Armed Forces includes only those Armed Forces members living on or off post with their families; all other members of the Armed Forces are excluded. Data refer to persons in primary families. For more information; see text, Section 1 and Appendix III]

Presence and age of child	1990	2000	2010	2014	2015	2016				
						Total	White [1]	Black [1]	Asian [1,2]	Hispanic [3]
Wives, total	**58.3**	**62.2**	**61.9**	**58.8**	**58.7**	**59.1**	**58.8**	**62.5**	**58.8**	**53.5**
No children under 18 years	51.1	54.8	56.0	52.3	52.6	52.7	52.6	53.8	53.3	51.6
With children under 18 years	66.5	70.9	70.1	68.5	67.8	68.9	68.9	75.1	63.9	54.9
Under 6 years, total	59.1	63.1	62.9	61.8	61.6	63.1	63.4	71.0	54.7	48.0
Under 3 years	55.9	59.4	59.5	60.4	59.8	62.3	62.9	69.7	52.7	46.2
under 1 year	53.9	58.4	59.0	59.9	57.2	60.0	61.5	66.1	45.6	39.3
1 year	(NA)	(NA)	57.6	61.1	61.3	62.3	63.4	63.7	49.5	48.4
2 years	60.9	61.9	62.4	60.1	61.0	64.9	63.8	80.4	62.7	50.2
3 to 5 years	64.1	68.6	67.7	63.6	63.9	64.2	64.1	72.7	57.6	50.1
3 years	63.0	66.0	66.4	62.3	60.0	61.2	61.3	66.1	55.6	49.2
4 years	65.0	69.6	68.9	63.0	66.5	65.7	65.3	78.1	59.0	49.0
5 years	64.4	70.7	68.1	65.5	66.0	66.2	66.1	74.4	59.1	52.4
6 to 13 years	73.1	76.0	74.8	72.4	71.2	72.2	71.7	79.1	71.0	59.2
14 to 17 years	75.0	80.8	79.0	76.6	75.8	75.8	76.3	75.1	74.4	65.0

NA Not available. [1] Persons in this race group only. See footnote 2, Table 611. [2] Excludes Pacific Islanders. [3] Persons of Hispanic origin may be of any race.

Source: U.S. Bureau of Labor Statistics, unpublished data. See also <http://www.bls.gov/cps/home.htm>

Table 624. Married Couples by Labor Force Status of Spouses: 1990 to 2016

[52,317 represents 52,317,000. As of March. Based on the Annual Social and Economic Supplement (ASEC) to the Current Population Survey; for details see source and Appendix III]

Year	Number (1,000)					Percent distribution				
	All married couples	In labor force			Husband and wife not in labor force	All married couples	In labor force			Husband and wife not in labor force
		Husband and wife	Husband only	Wife only			Husband and wife	Husband only	Wife only	
TOTAL										
1990.........................	52,317	28,056	13,013	2,453	8,794	100.0	53.6	24.9	4.7	16.8
2000.........................	55,311	31,095	11,815	3,301	9,098	100.0	56.2	21.4	6.0	16.4
2009.........................	60,844	33,249	13,207	4,314	10,074	100.0	54.6	21.7	7.1	16.6
2010.........................	60,384	32,731	13,074	4,526	10,053	100.0	54.2	21.7	7.5	16.6
2011.........................	60,840	32,231	13,455	4,516	10,636	100.0	53.0	22.1	7.4	17.5
2012.........................	61,047	31,803	13,820	4,595	10,830	100.0	52.1	22.6	7.5	17.7
2013.........................	61,295	31,673	13,901	4,656	11,065	100.0	51.7	22.7	7.6	18.1
2014.........................	61,850	31,666	13,913	4,708	11,563	100.0	51.2	22.5	7.6	18.7
2015.........................	62,230	31,688	14,164	4,757	11,622	100.0	50.9	22.8	7.6	18.7
2016.........................	62,628	32,120	13,885	4,790	11,833	100.0	51.3	22.2	7.6	18.9
WITH CHILDREN UNDER AGE 18										
1990.........................	24,537	15,768	7,667	558	544	100.0	64.3	31.2	2.3	2.2
2000.........................	25,248	17,116	6,950	795	387	100.0	67.8	27.5	3.1	1.5
2009.........................	25,799	17,054	7,284	963	501	100.0	66.1	28.2	3.7	1.9
2010.........................	25,317	16,710	7,220	962	425	100.0	66.0	28.5	3.8	1.7
2011.........................	24,936	16,189	7,270	1,007	469	100.0	64.9	29.2	4.0	1.9
2012.........................	24,445	15,752	7,226	1,009	457	100.0	64.4	29.6	4.1	1.9
2013.........................	24,677	15,755	7,408	1,051	462	100.0	63.8	30.0	4.3	1.9
2014.........................	24,775	15,945	7,336	949	545	100.0	64.4	29.6	3.8	2.2
2015.........................	24,857	15,828	7,454	987	589	100.0	63.7	30.0	4.0	2.4
2016.........................	24,638	15,873	7,176	1,042	546	100.0	64.4	29.1	4.2	2.2
WITH CHILDREN UNDER AGE 6										
1990.........................	12,051	6,932	4,692	192	235	100.0	57.5	38.9	1.6	2.0
2000.........................	11,393	6,984	4,077	211	121	100.0	61.3	35.8	1.9	1.1
2009.........................	11,760	6,917	4,330	329	185	100.0	58.8	36.8	2.8	1.6
2010.........................	11,599	6,924	4,181	335	159	100.0	59.7	36.0	2.9	1.4
2011.........................	11,416	6,720	4,152	368	177	100.0	58.9	36.4	3.2	1.6
2012.........................	11,055	6,509	3,986	383	176	100.0	58.9	36.1	3.5	1.6
2013.........................	10,867	6,347	3,951	403	166	100.0	58.4	36.4	3.7	1.5
2014.........................	10,887	6,378	3,965	340	204	100.0	58.6	36.4	3.1	1.9
2015.........................	10,862	6,351	3,969	320	222	100.0	58.5	36.5	2.9	2.0
2016.........................	10,688	6,349	3,759	383	197	100.0	59.4	35.2	3.6	1.8

Source: U.S. Census Bureau, Families and Living Arrangements, Detailed Table MC-1, "Married Couples by Labor Force Status of Spouses: 1986 to Present," <http://www.census.gov/hhes/families/data/families.html>, accessed January 2017.

Table 625. Employed Civilians and Weekly Hours: 1990 to 2016

[In thousands (118,793 represents 118,793,000), except as indicated. Annual averages of monthly figures. Civilian noninstitutionalized population 16 years old and over. Based on Current Population Survey; see text, Section 1 and Appendix III]

Item	1990	2000	2010	2012	2013	2014	2015	2016
Total employed............................	**118,793**	**136,891**	**139,064**	**142,469**	**143,929**	**146,305**	**148,834**	**151,436**
Age:								
16 to 19 years old...........................	6,581	7,189	4,378	4,426	4,458	4,548	4,734	4,965
20 to 24 years old...........................	13,401	13,229	12,699	13,408	13,599	13,894	14,022	14,027
25 to 34 years old...........................	33,935	31,549	30,229	30,701	31,242	31,975	32,742	33,722
35 to 44 years old...........................	30,817	36,433	30,663	30,576	30,650	30,966	31,252	31,562
45 to 54 years old...........................	19,525	30,310	33,191	32,874	32,523	32,556	32,643	32,720
55 to 64 years old...........................	11,189	14,002	21,636	23,239	23,776	24,395	24,975	25,524
65 years old and over.......................	3,346	4,179	6,268	7,245	7,681	7,971	8,465	8,916
Sex:								
Male...	65,104	73,305	73,359	75,555	76,353	77,692	79,131	80,568
Female..	53,689	63,586	65,705	66,914	67,577	68,613	69,703	70,868
Class of worker:								
Nonagricultural industries..................	115,570	134,427	136,858	140,283	141,799	144,068	146,411	148,976
Wage and salary worker [1]..............	106,598	125,114	127,914	131,452	133,111	135,402	137,678	140,161
Self-employed.............................	8,719	9,205	8,860	8,749	8,619	8,602	8,665	8,751
Unpaid family workers...................	253	108	84	81	70	64	68	65
Agriculture and related industries..........	3,223	2,464	2,206	2,186	2,130	2,237	2,422	2,460
Wage and salary worker [1]..............	1,740	1,421	1,353	1,377	1,310	1,459	1,547	1,583
Self-employed.............................	1,378	1,010	821	780	789	756	844	853
Unpaid family workers...................	105	33	33	29	31	22	32	23
Weekly hours:								
Nonagricultural industries:								
Wage and salary workers [1]..............	39.2	39.6	38.3	38.6	38.7	38.7	38.7	38.8
Self-employed.............................	40.8	39.7	35.6	36.0	35.9	35.9	36.1	36.1
Unpaid family workers...................	34.0	32.5	33.3	33.2	32.1	33.3	28.9	30.6
Agriculture and related industries:								
Wage and salary workers [1]..............	41.2	43.2	41.6	(NA)	(NA)	(NA)	(NA)	(NA)
Self-employed.............................	46.8	45.3	42.0	(NA)	(NA)	(NA)	(NA)	(NA)
Unpaid family workers...................	38.5	38.3	42.1	(NA)	(NA)	(NA)	(NA)	(NA)

NA Not available. [1] Includes the incorporated self-employed.

Source: U.S. Bureau of Labor Statistics, "Labor Force Statistics from the Current Population Survey," <http://www.bls.gov/cps>, accessed April 2017.

Table 626. Persons at Work by Hours Worked: 2016

[In thousands (146,152 represents 146,152,000), except as indicated. Annual averages of monthly figures. Persons "at work" are a subgroup of employed persons. This subgroup excludes those absent from their jobs during reference period for reasons such as vacation, illness, or industrial dispute. Civilian noninstitutionalized population 16 years old and over. Based on Current Population Survey; see text, Section 1, and Appendix III]

Hours of work	Persons at work (1,000)			Percent distribution		
	Total	Agriculture and related industries	Non-agricultural industries	Total	Agriculture and related industries	Non-agricultural industries
Total.............................	**146,152**	**2,369**	**143,783**	**100.0**	**100.0**	**100.0**
1 to 34 hours..........................	34,632	575	34,058	23.7	24.3	23.7
1 to 4 hours..........................	1,421	37	1,385	1.0	1.6	1.0
5 to 14 hours.........................	5,257	133	5,124	3.6	5.6	3.6
15 to 29 hours........................	17,362	261	17,101	11.9	11.0	11.9
30 to 34 hours........................	10,593	144	10,448	7.2	6.1	7.3
35 hours and over.....................	111,519	1,794	109,726	76.3	75.7	76.3
35 to 39 hours........................	9,564	104	9,460	6.5	4.4	6.6
40 hours.............................	65,184	729	64,455	44.6	30.8	44.8
41 hours and over.....................	36,771	961	35,810	25.2	40.6	24.9
41 to 48 hours........................	12,747	186	12,561	8.7	7.9	8.7
49 to 59 hours........................	14,300	274	14,026	9.8	11.6	9.8
60 hours and over.....................	9,724	501	9,223	6.7	21.2	6.4
Average weekly hours of:						
Total persons at work................	38.7	43.0	38.7	(X)	(X)	(X)
Persons usually working full-time [1].....	42.5	48.2	42.4	(X)	(X)	(X)

X Not applicable. [1] Full-time workers are those who usually worked 35 hours or more (at all jobs).

Source: U.S. Bureau of Labor Statistics, CPS Tables, "Persons at Work in Agriculture and Nonagricultural Industries by Hours of Work," <http://www.bls.gov/cps/tables.htm>, accessed March 2017.

Table 627. Persons With a Job, But Not at Work by Reason: 1980 to 2016

[In thousands (5,881 represents 5,881,000), except percent. For civilian noninstitutionalized population 16 years old and over. Annual averages of monthly figures. Based on Current Population Survey; see text, Section 1 and Appendix III]

Reason for not working	1980	1990	2000	2009	2010	2011	2012	2013	2014	2015	2016
All industries, number..............	**5,881**	**6,160**	**5,681**	**5,434**	**5,060**	**4,990**	**5,132**	**5,003**	**5,029**	**5,066**	**5,284**
Percent of employed................	5.9	5.2	4.2	3.9	3.6	3.6	3.6	3.5	3.4	3.4	3.5
Reason for not working:											
Vacation...........................	3,320	3,529	3,109	2,806	2,487	2,500	2,633	2,501	2,512	2,563	2,671
Illness.............................	1,426	1,341	1,156	993	942	921	906	940	953	907	1,001
Child care problems.................	(NA)	(NA)	(NA)	(NA)	(NA)	23	20	22	28	32	29
Other family/personal obligations..	(NA)	(NA)	(NA)	(NA)	(NA)	229	253	245	258	259	284
Labor/industrial dispute............	105	24	14	6	8	9	6	6	3	5	5
Bad weather........................	155	90	89	126	172	169	107	112	138	119	130
Maternity or paternity leave........	(NA)	(NA)	(NA)	(NA)	(NA)	254	286	279	288	322	303
School/training.....................	(NA)	(NA)	(NA)	(NA)	(NA)	114	119	113	120	134	125
Civic/military duty..................	(NA)	(NA)	(NA)	(NA)	(NA)	6	11	9	7	8	7
All other...........................	876	1,177	1,313	1,503	1,451	766	792	775	721	718	729

NA Not available.

Source: U.S. Bureau of Labor Statistics, Current Population Survey, unpublished data. See also <http://www.bls.gov/cps/>.

Table 628. Class of Worker by Sex and Selected Characteristics: 2016

[In percent, except as indicated (9,604 represents 9,604,000). Civilian noninstitutionalized population 16 years old and over. Annual averages of monthly figures. Based on Current Population Survey; see text, Section 1 and Appendix III]

Characteristic	Unincorporated self-employed			Incorporated self-employed			Wage and salary workers [1]		
	Total	Male	Female	Total	Male	Female	Total	Male	Female
Total (1,000)......................	**9,604**	**5,980**	**3,624**	**5,643**	**3,963**	**1,680**	**136,111**	**70,600**	**65,511**
PERCENT DISTRIBUTION........	100.0	100.0	100.0	100.0	100.0	100.0	100.0	100.0	100.0
Age:									
16 to 19 years old.................	0.8	0.8	0.9	0.2	0.1	0.3	3.6	3.4	3.7
20 to 24 years old.................	2.8	2.9	2.5	1.0	1.1	1.0	10.1	9.9	10.2
25 to 34 years old.................	14.2	14.1	14.4	10.6	10.3	11.1	23.3	24.0	22.6
35 to 44 years old.................	19.8	19.5	20.4	20.1	19.6	21.5	21.0	21.4	20.5
45 to 54 years old.................	23.6	23.1	24.3	29.0	28.5	30.1	21.2	20.9	21.4
55 to 64 years old.................	23.6	23.7	23.5	26.0	26.0	25.9	16.0	15.5	16.5
65 years old and over.............	15.2	16.0	14.0	13.2	14.5	10.2	4.9	4.8	5.0
Race/ethnicity:									
White [2]............................	85.4	85.4	85.3	85.1	86.4	82.0	78.1	79.4	76.6
Black [2]............................	6.8	6.8	6.7	5.5	5.3	6.1	12.5	11.1	14.0
Asian [2]............................	5.1	5.0	5.4	7.3	6.4	9.4	6.1	6.2	6.0
Hispanic [3].........................	16.3	17.7	14.0	9.5	9.6	9.3	17.0	18.6	15.3
Country of birth:									
U.S. born...........................	80.1	78.7	82.3	82.1	82.4	81.4	83.2	81.6	85.0
Foreign-born.......................	19.9	21.3	17.7	17.9	17.6	18.6	16.8	18.4	15.0

[1] Excludes the incorporated self-employed. [2] For persons in this race group only. [3] Persons of Hispanic origin may be of any race.

Source: U.S. Bureau of Labor Statistics, Current Population Survey, unpublished data. See also <http://www.bls.gov/cps>.

Table 629. Self-Employed Workers by Industry and Occupation: 2000 to 2016

[In thousands (10,214 represents 10,214,000). Civilian noninstitutionalized population 16 years old and over. Annual averages of monthly figures. Data represent the unincorporated self-employed; the incorporated self-employed are considered wage and salary workers. Based on the occupational and industrial classification derived from those used in the 2000 census. See text, this section. Based on the Current Population Survey (CPS); see text, Section 1 and Appendix III]

Item	2000	2010	2011	2012	2013	2014	2015	2016
Total self-employed...............................	**10,214**	**9,681**	**9,449**	**9,529**	**9,408**	**9,358**	**9,509**	**9,604**
INDUSTRY								
Agriculture and related industries............................	1,010	821	846	780	789	756	844	853
Mining..	12	20	20	20	16	20	21	17
Construction...	1,728	1,699	1,585	1,518	1,530	1,595	1,603	1,628
Manufacturing...	334	304	273	308	275	278	288	267
Wholesale and retail trade.....................................	1,221	962	949	872	825	851	870	888
Transportation and utilities...................................	348	360	352	355	340	368	397	417
Information..	139	139	131	141	126	132	161	120
Financial activities...	735	641	615	651	651	628	625	687
Professional and business services..........................	1,927	1,999	2,011	2,109	2,057	1,984	1,944	2,073
Education and health services................................	1,107	1,100	1,077	1,101	1,072	1,074	1,069	1,037
Leisure and hospitality...	660	610	636	659	671	658	698	668
Other services...	993	1,028	956	1,016	1,055	1,014	988	949
OCCUPATION								
Management, professional, and related occupations.....	4,169	3,928	3,857	4,009	3,963	3,878	3,958	3,953
Service occupations..	1,775	1,885	1,872	1,984	2,030	1,969	1,948	1,943
Sales and office occupations..................................	1,982	1,586	1,520	1,494	1,449	1,438	1,470	1,463
Natural resources, construction, and maintenance occupations..	1,591	1,635	1,572	1,395	1,365	1,462	1,482	1,548
Production, transportation, and material moving occupations..	698	647	628	648	602	610	650	697

Source: U.S. Bureau of Labor Statistics, "Labor Force Statistics from the Current Population Survey," <http://www.bls.gov/cps/tables.htm>, accessed June 2017; and unpublished CPS data.

Table 630. Type of Work Flexibility Provided to Employees: 2016

[In percent. The National Study of Employers does not ask employers to report on whether they have "written policies," but rather whether their organization "allows employees to" or "provides the following benefits or programs." The wording is used for two reasons. First, employers may have written policies, but not allow employees to use them. Second, smaller employers are less likely to have written policies than larger ones. For methodology, see source]

Type of work flexibility provided to employees	Organizations allowing flexibility to all or most employees		
	Total employers	Employers with 50 to 99 employees	Employers with 1,000 or more employees
FLEX TIME AND PLACE			
Periodically change starting and quitting times within some range of hours......................	32	36	17
Change starting and quitting times on a daily basis...	11	12	4
Compress workweek by working longer hours on fewer days for at least part of the year......	9	10	4
Work some regular paid hours at home occasionally...	8	9	1
Work some regular paid hours at home on regular basis..	2	2	3
CHOICES IN MANAGING TIME			
Have control over when to take breaks..	59	63	47
Have choices about and control over which shifts to work...	10	10	14
Have control over paid and unpaid overtime hours...	21	22	11
REDUCED TIME			
Move from full time to part time and back again while remaining in same position or level...	8	8	10
Work part year (work reduced time on annual basis)..	2	2	3
CAREGIVING LEAVE			
Return to work gradually after childbirth or adoption..	52	57	42
TIME OFF			
Family or personal time off without loss of pay...	47	51	33
Do volunteer work during regular work hours...	23	26	21
FLEX CAREERS			
Phase into retirement by working reduced hours over time prior to full retirement...............	21	25	17
Take sabbaticals (paid or unpaid for six months or more)...	11	12	10
Take extended career breaks for caregiving or other personal or family reasons................	35	42	27
Receive special consideration when returning to the organization after an extended career break...	13	18	10

Source: Society for Human Resource Management, Families and Work Institute, *2016 National Study of Employers* ©. See also <http://www.whenworkworks.org/be-effective/guides-tools/2016-national-study-of-employers>.

Table 631. Multiple Jobholders: 2016

[7,531 represents 7,531,000. Annual average of monthly figures. Civilian noninstitutionalized population 16 years old and over. Multiple jobholders are employed persons who either had jobs as wage or salary workers with two employers or more; were self-employed and also held a wage and salary job; or were unpaid family workers and also held a wage and salary job. Based on the Current Population Survey; see text, Section 1 and Appendix III]

Characteristic	Total Number (1,000)	Total Percent of employed	Male Number (1,000)	Male Percent of employed	Female Number (1,000)	Female Percent of employed
Total [1,2]	**7,531**	**5.0**	**3,645**	**4.5**	**3,887**	**5.5**
Age:						
16 to 19 years old	205	4.1	81	3.3	124	5.0
20 to 24 years old	848	6.0	335	4.6	514	7.5
25 to 54 years old	4,961	5.1	2,460	4.7	2,501	5.5
55 to 64 years old	1,161	4.5	571	4.3	589	4.9
65 years old and over	356	4.0	198	4.0	158	4.0
Race and ethnicity:						
White	5,999	5.0	2,926	4.5	3,072	5.6
Black	958	5.3	449	5.3	510	5.4
Asian	308	3.3	143	2.9	165	3.8
Hispanic [3]	820	3.2	433	3.0	387	3.6
Marital status:						
Married, spouse present	3,761	4.7	2,114	4.7	1,647	4.7
Widowed, divorced, or separated	1,307	5.4	442	4.4	865	6.2
Single, never married	2,463	5.3	1,089	4.3	1,374	6.4
Full- or part-time status: [4]						
Primary job full-time, secondary job part-time	4,084	(X)	2,235	(X)	1,849	(X)
Both jobs part-time	2,075	(X)	703	(X)	1,372	(X)
Both jobs full-time	278	(X)	167	(X)	112	(X)
Hours vary on primary or secondary job	1,038	(X)	512	(X)	526	(X)

X Not applicable. [1] Includes a small number of persons who work part-time on their primary job and full-time on their secondary job(s), not shown separately. [2] Includes other races, not shown separately. [3] Persons of Hispanic origin may be of any race. [4] Full-time work is 35 or more hours per week; part-time work is less than 35 hours per week.

Source: U.S. Bureau of Labor Statistics, CPS Tables, "Multiple Jobholders by Selected Characteristics," <http://www.bls.gov/cps/tables.htm>, accessed March 2017.

Table 632. Average Number of Jobs Held From Ages 18 to 48 during 1978 to 2012

[For persons ages 47 to 56 in 2012-13 (and who were ages 14 to 22 when first interviewed in 1979). A job is an uninterrupted period of work with a particular employer. Educational attainment as of 2012-13. Based on the National Longitudinal Survey of Youth 1979; see source for details]

Sex, race, ethnicity and educational attainment	Total [1]	18 to 24 years	25 to 29 years	30 to 34 years	35 to 39 years	40 to 46 years
Total [2]	**11.7**	**5.5**	**3.0**	**2.4**	**2.1**	**2.4**
Less than a high school diploma	11.5	5.0	2.9	2.4	2.0	2.1
High school graduates, no college	11.2	5.1	2.8	2.4	2.1	2.3
Some college or associate's degree	12.3	5.8	3.1	2.5	2.1	2.5
Bachelor's degree or more	11.8	6.1	3.0	2.4	2.1	2.3
Male	11.8	5.7	3.1	2.5	2.1	2.4
Less than a high school diploma	12.9	5.7	3.5	2.6	2.1	2.5
High school graduate, no college	11.7	5.5	3.1	2.6	2.1	2.3
Some college or associate's degree	12.4	6.0	3.2	2.7	2.1	2.5
Bachelor's degree or more	11.2	5.8	2.8	2.4	2.2	2.3
Female	11.5	5.3	2.8	2.3	2.1	2.4
Less than a high school diploma	9.6	4.0	2.2	2.1	1.9	1.7
High school graduate, no college	10.7	4.6	2.5	2.2	2.1	2.3
Some college or associate's degree	12.3	5.6	3.0	2.4	2.2	2.6
Bachelor's degree or more	12.5	6.4	3.2	2.3	2.0	2.4
White, non-Hispanic	11.7	5.7	3.0	2.4	2.1	2.3
Less than a high school diploma	12.1	5.4	3.1	2.6	2.1	2.2
High school graduate, no college	11.4	5.3	2.9	2.4	2.1	2.3
Some college or associate's degree	12.3	5.9	3.1	2.5	2.1	2.5
Bachelor's degree or more	11.8	6.2	3.0	2.3	2.0	2.3
Black, non-Hispanic	11.4	4.6	2.9	2.5	2.1	2.5
Less than a high school diploma	10.1	3.7	2.6	2.2	1.7	1.9
High school graduate, no college	10.9	4.4	2.8	2.5	2.2	2.4
Some college or associate's degree	12.6	5.1	3.1	2.6	2.4	2.8
Bachelor's degree or more	11.9	5.6	3.0	2.6	2.1	2.8
Hispanic [3]	11.4	4.9	2.8	2.3	2.1	2.4
Less than a high school diploma	10.9	4.3	2.8	2.1	1.9	2.3
High school graduate, no college	10.9	4.9	2.7	2.3	2.1	2.4
Some college or associate's degree	12.5	5.2	3.1	2.5	2.3	2.8
Bachelor's degree or more	11.6	5.5	2.8	2.5	2.2	2.1

[1] Jobs held in more than one age category were counted in each category, but only once in the total. [2] Includes other races, not shown separately. [3] Persons of Hispanic origin may be of any race.

Source: U.S. Bureau of Labor Statistics, *Number of Jobs Held, Labor Market Activity, and Earnings Growth Among the Youngest Baby Boomers: Results from a Longitudinal Survey,* USDL 15-0528, March 2015. See also <http://www.bls.gov/news.release/nlsoy.nr0.htm>.

Table 633. Distribution of Workers by Tenure With Current Employer by Selected Characteristics: 2016

[134,167 represents 134,167,000. As of January. From the 2016 Displaced Worker Supplement to the Current Population Survey. For employed wage and salary workers 16 years old and over. Data exclude the incorporated and unincorporated self-employed; see source and Appendix III]

Characteristic	Number employed (1,000)	Percent distribution by tenure with current employer								Median years [1]
		12 months or less	13-23 months	2 years	3-4 years	5-9 years	10-14 years	15-19 years	20 years or more	
Total [2]	**134,167**	**22.6**	**7.0**	**5.5**	**17.1**	**19.0**	**11.5**	**7.1**	**10.3**	**4.2**
AGE AND SEX										
16 to 19 years old	4,432	73.7	11.7	7.5	7.0	0.1	–	–	–	(NA)
20 years old and over	129,735	20.9	6.9	5.4	17.4	19.6	11.9	7.3	10.6	(NA)
20 to 24 years old	13,396	50.8	14.2	10.8	19.1	5.0	0.1	–	–	1.3
25 to 34 years old	31,304	28.9	9.4	7.8	24.9	21.7	6.7	0.7	(Z)	2.8
35 to 44 years old	28,272	17.1	6.1	4.8	18.4	24.4	16.5	9.4	3.4	4.9
45 to 54 years old	28,737	12.4	5.0	3.4	13.7	20.6	15.7	11.9	17.3	7.9
55 to 64 years old	21,601	10.2	3.5	2.9	11.7	18.1	14.4	11.3	28.0	10.1
65 years old and over	6,425	9.9	2.9	2.3	9.8	19.9	15.6	11.6	28.1	10.3
Male	**69,068**	**22.0**	**7.0**	**5.3**	**17.0**	**19.3**	**11.4**	**7.0**	**11.0**	**4.3**
16 to 19 years old	2,113	72.7	13.3	6.4	7.6	0.1	–	–	–	(NA)
20 years old and over	66,955	20.4	6.8	5.3	17.3	19.9	11.7	7.3	11.4	(NA)
20 to 24 years old	6,754	49.7	14.1	11.8	18.4	5.9	0.1	–	–	1.3
25 to 34 years old	16,665	27.5	9.1	7.6	24.9	22.7	7.3	0.9	(Z)	2.9
35 to 44 years old	14,922	17.1	5.8	4.5	18.1	24.8	16.3	9.6	3.8	5.0
45 to 54 years old	14,626	11.7	5.1	3.2	13.0	19.6	15.4	12.5	19.4	8.4
55 to 64 years old	10,809	10.6	3.5	2.7	11.7	17.4	13.7	10.1	30.3	10.2
65 years old and over	3,179	9.3	2.7	2.0	9.1	22.3	14.2	11.0	29.4	10.2
Female	**65,099**	**23.3**	**7.1**	**5.6**	**17.2**	**18.6**	**11.6**	**7.1**	**9.5**	**4.0**
16 to 19 years old	2,319	74.6	10.3	8.6	6.4	0.1	–	–	–	(NA)
20 years old and over	62,780	21.4	7.0	5.4	17.6	19.3	12.0	7.3	9.8	(NA)
20 to 24 years old	6,642	52.0	14.3	9.7	19.7	4.2	0.1	–	–	1.2
25 to 34 years old	14,640	30.4	9.8	7.9	24.8	20.5	6.0	0.6	–	2.6
35 to 44 years old	13,350	17.2	6.4	5.0	18.8	23.9	16.6	9.1	3.0	4.8
45 to 54 years old	14,111	13.0	4.8	3.7	14.5	21.6	16.1	11.2	15.1	7.5
55 to 64 years old	10,791	9.8	3.5	3.1	11.7	18.8	15.1	12.4	25.6	10.0
65 years old and over	3,246	10.5	3.0	2.7	10.4	17.5	17.0	12.1	26.8	10.4
RACE AND HISPANIC ORIGIN										
White [3]	105,057	21.7	7.0	5.2	16.9	19.0	11.7	7.4	11.1	(NA)
Male	54,917	21.1	6.9	5.2	16.4	19.6	11.5	7.4	12.0	(NA)
Female	50,140	22.4	7.2	5.3	17.4	18.4	12.0	7.4	10.0	(NA)
Black [3]	16,509	25.8	6.7	6.5	17.8	18.3	10.3	6.4	8.2	(NA)
Male	7,522	26.8	6.7	6.0	18.3	17.2	10.2	6.6	8.2	(NA)
Female	8,987	25.0	6.8	6.8	17.4	19.3	10.4	6.2	8.2	(NA)
Asian [3]	7,843	21.4	7.5	6.4	18.1	21.5	12.4	5.7	7.0	(NA)
Male	4,170	18.9	8.3	6.7	19.2	21.2	13.5	5.5	6.9	(NA)
Female	3,673	24.3	6.7	6.1	16.8	21.8	11.2	5.9	7.2	(NA)
Hispanic [4]	22,637	25.1	6.4	7.8	19.2	19.6	11.0	5.3	5.6	(NA)
Male	12,709	24.5	6.1	7.2	19.1	20.8	11.4	5.2	5.7	(NA)
Female	9,928	25.9	6.9	8.6	19.4	18.1	10.5	5.3	5.3	(NA)

– Represents zero. NA Not available. Z Less than 0.05 percent. [1] Median definition, see Guide to Tabular Presentation. [2] Includes other races, not shown separately. [3] For persons in this race group only. See footnote 2, Table 611. [4] Persons of Hispanic origin may be of any race.

Source: U.S. Bureau of Labor Statistics, "Employee Tenure in 2016," USDL 16-1867, September 2016, <http://www.bls.gov/news.release/tenure.toc.htm>.

Table 634. Part-Time Workers by Reason: 2016

[34,632 represents 34,632,000, except hours. For persons working 1 to 34 hours per week. For civilian noninstitutionalized population 16 years old and over. Annual average of monthly figures. Based on the Current Population Survey; see text, Section 1 and Appendix III]

Reason	All industries			Nonagricultural industries		
	Total	Usually work—		Total	Usually work—	
		Full-time	Part-time		Full-time	Part-time
Total working fewer than 35 hours	**34,632**	**9,507**	**25,125**	**34,058**	**9,341**	**24,717**
Economic reasons	5,943	1,498	4,445	5,841	1,444	4,398
Slack work or business conditions	3,595	1,258	2,338	3,526	1,219	2,307
Could find only part time work	2,015	(S)	2,015	2,004	(S)	2,004
Seasonal work	228	135	93	207	120	87
Job started or ended during the week	105	105	(S)	105	105	(S)
Non-economic reasons	28,689	8,009	20,680	28,216	7,897	20,319
Child-care problems	1,038	83	956	1,031	82	949
Other family or personal obligations	4,912	662	4,250	4,828	649	4,180
Health or medical limitations	1,023	(S)	1,023	1,005	(S)	1,005
In school or training	6,093	86	6,007	6,041	85	5,956
Retired or social security limit on earnings	2,633	(S)	2,633	2,516	(S)	2,516
Vacation or personal day	3,555	3,555	(S)	3,520	3,520	(S)
Holiday, legal, or religious	1,016	1,016	(S)	1,009	1,009	(S)
Weather-related curtailment	357	357	(S)	336	336	(S)
Other	8,061	2,250	5,811	7,929	2,216	5,713
Average hours per week:						
Economic reasons	23.2	24.0	22.9	23.2	24.1	22.9
Noneconomic reasons	21.4	25.2	20.0	21.5	25.2	20.0

S No data or data do not meet publication standards.

Source: U.S. Bureau of Labor Statistics, CPS Tables, "Persons at work 1 to 34 hours in all and in nonagricultural industries by reason for working less than 35 hours and usual full- or part-time status," <http://www.bls.gov/cps/tables.htm>, accessed March 2017.

Table 635. Displaced Workers by Selected Characteristics: 2016

[In percent, except total (3,191 represents 3,191,000). As of January 2016. For persons 20 years old and over with job tenure of 3 years or more who lost or left a job between January 2013 and December 2015 because of plant closings or moves, insufficient work for workers to do, or the abolishment of their positions. Based on Current Population Survey; see source and Appendix III]

Characteristic	Total (1,000)	Employment status in January 2016			Reason for job loss, 2013-2015		
		Employed	Unemployed	Not in the labor force	Plant or company closed down or moved	Insufficient work	Position or shift abolished
Total [1]	3,191	65.5	15.9	18.6	37.4	25.6	37.1
20 to 24 years old	71	(2)	(2)	(2)	(2)	(2)	(2)
25 to 54 years old	2,023	72.5	17.1	10.4	37.4	27.4	35.2
55 to 64 years old	853	60.0	15.0	24.9	36.4	22.8	40.8
65 years old and over	245	26.5	10.7	62.8	33.9	23.7	42.4
Males	1,773	66.5	15.7	17.8	37.2	29.0	33.8
20 to 24 years old	33	(2)	(2)	(2)	(2)	(2)	(2)
25 to 54 years old	1,151	72.7	17.2	10.1	36.9	31.3	31.8
55 to 64 years old	469	62.6	15.1	22.3	38.4	24.3	37.3
65 years old and over	119	24.0	7.9	68.1	25.9	31.7	42.4
Females	1,419	64.1	16.3	19.6	37.5	21.3	41.1
20 to 24 years old	38	(2)	(2)	(2)	(2)	(2)	(2)
25 to 54 years old	872	72.3	17.0	10.7	38.1	22.2	39.7
55 to 64 years old	383	56.8	15.0	28.2	33.9	20.9	45.2
65 years old and over	125	28.9	13.3	57.8	41.6	16.0	42.4
White only	2,573	66.5	14.8	18.6	37.2	25.9	36.9
Male	1,450	67.7	14.8	17.5	37.1	30.6	32.3
Female	1,123	65.0	14.9	20.1	37.4	19.7	42.9
Black only	394	61.5	20.3	18.2	35.4	27.7	36.9
Male	170	60.1	19.6	20.3	33.4	23.7	42.9
Female	224	62.5	20.9	16.6	36.9	30.7	32.4
Asian only	145	54.9	24.7	20.3	45.9	21.3	32.8
Male	96	59.4	20.3	20.3	46.7	19.8	33.5
Female	49	(2)	(2)	(2)	(2)	(2)	(2)
Hispanic [3]	423	69.4	14.3	16.3	45.3	24.4	30.3
Male	236	75.4	11.0	13.7	43.5	27.2	29.3
Female	187	61.9	18.4	19.6	47.4	20.9	31.7

[1] Includes other races, not shown separately. [2] Data not shown where base is less than 75,000. [3] Persons of Hispanic or Latino origin may be of any race.

Source: U.S. Bureau of Labor Statistics, *Worker Displacement: 2013-2015*, USDL 16-1731, August 2016. See also <http://www.bls.gov/news.release/disp.toc.htm>.

Table 636. Persons Not in the Labor Force By Age, Sex, and Reason: 2016

[In thousands (94,351 represents 94,351,000). For civilian noninstitutional population 16 years old and over. Persons who are neither employed nor unemployed are not in the labor force. This includes retired persons, students, those taking care of children or other family members, and others who are neither working nor seeking work. Annual average of monthly figures. Based on the Current Population Survey; see text, Section 1, and Appendix III]

Status and reason	Total	Age			Sex	
		16 to 24 years old	25 to 54 years old	55 years old and over	Male	Female
Total not in the labor force	94,351	17,232	23,513	53,606	37,743	56,608
Do not want a job now [1]	88,502	15,452	21,032	52,018	35,009	53,492
Want a job now	5,849	1,780	2,481	1,587	2,733	3,116
In the previous year:						
Did not search for a job	3,415	994	1,353	1,069	1,522	1,894
Did search for a job, but not in past 4 weeks [2]	2,434	787	1,128	519	1,211	1,222
Not available for work now	630	257	287	86	251	379
Available for work now, but not looking for work [3]	1,804	530	841	433	960	843
Reason for not currently looking for work:						
Discouraged over job prospects [4]	553	130	267	156	345	208
Family responsibilities	199	26	127	46	61	138
In school or training	224	171	47	7	120	105
Ill health or disability	144	16	67	62	77	67
Other [5]	682	187	333	162	356	326

[1] Includes some persons who are not asked if they want a job. [2] Persons who had a job in previous 12 months must have searched since the end of that job. [3] Persons who have searched for work in previous 12 months and are available to work now also are referred to as "marginally attached to the labor force." [4] Includes such things as believes no work available, could not find work, lacks necessary schooling or training, employer thinks too young or old, and other types of discrimination. [5] Includes such things as child care and transportation problems.

Source: U.S. Bureau of Labor Statistics, CPS Tables, "Persons not in the labor force by desire and availability for work, age, and sex," <http://www.bls.gov/cps/tables.htm>, accessed March 2017.

Table 637. Employment Status of Parents by Age of Youngest Child and Family Type: 2013 to 2016

[In thousands (34,392 represents 34,392,000), except percent distribution. Annual average of monthly figures. For families with own children (sons, daughters, step-children, and adopted children). Based on the Current Population Survey, see text, Section 1, and Appendix III]

Characteristic	Number				Percent distribution			
	2013	2014	2015	2016	2013	2014	2015	2016
WITH OWN CHILDREN UNDER 18 YEARS OLD								
Total families	**34,392**	**34,434**	**34,363**	**34,206**	**100.0**	**100.0**	**100.0**	**100.0**
Parent(s) employed	30,336	30,545	30,672	30,671	88.2	88.7	89.3	89.7
No parent employed	4,056	3,889	3,692	3,534	11.8	11.3	10.7	10.3
Married-couple families	23,259	23,330	23,401	23,125	100.0	100.0	100.0	100.0
Parent(s) employed	22,408	22,528	22,631	22,379	96.3	96.6	96.7	96.8
Mother employed	15,200	15,347	15,420	15,377	65.4	65.8	65.9	66.5
Both parents employed	13,746	14,033	14,174	14,123	59.1	60.2	60.6	61.1
Mother employed, not father	1,454	1,314	1,246	1,254	6.3	5.6	5.3	5.4
Father employed, not mother	7,208	7,181	7,211	7,001	31.0	30.8	30.8	30.3
Neither parent employed	851	801	771	746	3.7	3.4	3.3	3.2
Families maintained by women [1]	8,575	8,589	8,505	8,538	100.0	100.0	100.0	100.0
Mother employed	5,851	5,958	6,024	6,191	68.2	69.4	70.8	72.5
Mother not employed	2,724	2,632	2,481	2,347	31.8	30.6	29.2	27.5
Families maintained by men [1]	2,558	2,515	2,457	2,544	100.0	100.0	100.0	100.0
Father employed	2,077	2,059	2,017	2,102	81.2	81.9	82.1	82.6
Father not employed	481	456	440	442	18.8	18.1	17.9	17.4
WITH OWN CHILDREN 6 to 17 YEARS OLD								
Total families	**19,767**	**19,850**	**19,774**	**19,774**	**100.0**	**100.0**	**100.0**	**100.0**
Parent(s) employed	17,592	17,768	17,762	17,814	89.0	89.5	89.8	90.1
No parent employed	2,175	2,082	2,012	1,960	11.0	10.5	10.2	9.9
Married-couple families	13,183	13,239	13,306	13,105	100.0	100.0	100.0	100.0
Parent(s) employed	12,676	12,753	12,842	12,649	96.2	96.3	96.5	96.5
Mother employed	9,213	9,321	9,363	9,284	69.9	70.4	70.4	70.8
Both parents employed	8,291	8,453	8,565	8,483	62.9	63.9	64.4	64.7
Mother employed, not father	922	868	798	801	7.0	6.6	6.0	6.1
Father employed, not mother	3,463	3,432	3,479	3,365	26.3	25.9	26.1	25.7
Neither parent employed	507	486	464	456	3.8	3.7	3.5	3.5
Families maintained by women [1]	5,125	5,130	5,080	5,189	100.0	100.0	100.0	100.0
Mother employed	3,727	3,811	3,790	3,955	72.7	74.3	74.6	76.2
Mother not employed	1,398	1,319	1,290	1,234	27.3	25.7	25.4	23.8
Families maintained by men [1]	1,459	1,481	1,388	1,481	100.0	100.0	100.0	100.0
Father employed	1,188	1,204	1,130	1,211	81.4	81.3	81.4	81.8
Father not employed	271	277	258	270	18.6	18.7	18.6	18.2
WITH OWN CHILDREN UNDER 6 YEARS OLD								
Total families	**14,625**	**14,584**	**14,589**	**14,432**	**100.0**	**100.0**	**100.0**	**100.0**
Parent(s) employed	12,745	12,777	12,910	12,857	87.1	87.6	88.5	89.1
No parent employed	1,880	1,807	1,680	1,575	12.9	12.4	11.5	10.9
Married-couple families	10,076	10,091	10,096	10,020	100.0	100.0	100.0	100.0
Parent(s) employed	9,732	9,775	9,789	9,730	96.6	96.9	97.0	97.1
Mother employed	5,987	6,027	6,057	6,093	59.4	59.7	60.0	60.8
Both parents employed	5,455	5,580	5,609	5,640	54.1	55.3	55.6	56.3
Mother employed, not father	532	447	448	453	5.3	4.4	4.4	4.5
Father employed, not mother	3,745	3,749	3,732	3,637	37.2	37.1	37.0	36.3
Neither parent employed	344	315	307	290	3.4	3.1	3.0	2.9
Families maintained by women [1]	3,450	3,460	3,425	3,349	100.0	100.0	100.0	100.0
Mother employed	2,124	2,147	2,234	2,236	61.6	62.1	65.2	66.8
Mother not employed	1,326	1,313	1,191	1,113	38.4	37.9	34.8	33.2
Families maintained by men [1]	1,100	1,034	1,069	1,063	100.0	100.0	100.0	100.0
Father employed	889	854	887	891	80.9	82.7	83.0	83.8
Father not employed	210	179	182	172	19.1	17.3	17.0	16.2

[1] No spouse present.

Source: U.S. Bureau of Labor Statistics, *Employment Characteristics of Families—2016*, USDL 17-0444, April 2017, and earlier releases. See also <http://www.bls.gov/news.release/famee.toc.htm>.

Table 638. Employed Civilians by Occupation, Sex, Race, and Hispanic Origin: 2016

[151,436 represents 151,436,000. Civilian noninstitutionalized population 16 years old and over. Annual average of monthly figures. Based on Current Population Survey; see text, Section 1 and Appendix III. Occupational classifications are those used in the 2010 Census]

Occupation	Total employed (1,000)	Percent of total			
		Female	Black [1]	Asian [1]	Hispanic [2]
Total, 16 years and over................................	**151,436**	**46.8**	**11.9**	**6.1**	**16.7**
Management, professional and related occupations........................	**59,438**	**51.5**	**9.1**	**8.1**	**9.3**
Management, business, and financial operations occupations...............	24,941	43.8	8.2	6.6	9.8
Management occupations [3]................................	17,418	39.1	7.5	6.1	9.9
Chief executives................................	1,649	27.3	3.4	6.0	5.6
General and operations managers................	949	29.8	7.1	5.6	11.3
Marketing and sales managers..................	1,066	45.3	5.3	6.0	9.9
Administrative services managers..............	181	42.6	13.2	3.4	10.0
Computer and information systems managers......	597	25.5	6.2	15.2	6.7
Financial managers............................	1,197	52.5	6.9	8.3	10.3
Human resources managers......................	287	74.2	13.5	4.9	11.2
Industrial production managers................	275	23.2	4.9	9.2	7.4
Purchasing managers...........................	203	47.4	9.1	2.9	10.6
Transportation, storage, and distribution managers...	299	17.1	11.4	4.8	18.4
Farmers, ranchers, and other agricultural managers....	1,042	24.8	1.0	1.0	4.7
Construction managers.........................	812	7.4	3.8	2.0	11.0
Education administrators......................	954	65.1	14.3	2.2	8.8
Architectural and engineering managers........	136	5.3	4.2	10.6	3.8
Food service managers.........................	1,157	45.9	10.2	12.0	17.7
Lodging managers..............................	166	52.2	9.7	15.8	9.0
Medical and health services managers..........	593	72.3	13.2	5.4	10.2
Property, real estate, and community association managers....	709	46.5	9.0	3.6	11.3
Social and community service managers.........	421	70.5	15.4	4.8	11.0
Business and financial operations occupations [3]...	7,523	54.7	9.7	7.8	9.8
Wholesale and retail buyers, except farm products....	207	53.1	6.4	4.4	11.8
Purchasing agents, except wholesale, retail, and farm products....	272	48.0	9.9	6.2	11.6
Claims adjusters, appraisers, examiners, and investigators....	349	62.2	15.1	1.6	12.7
Compliance officers...........................	270	57.1	12.4	7.9	10.0
Cost estimators...............................	113	12.0	2.9	3.2	8.3
Human resources workers.......................	693	74.6	12.8	5.2	11.3
Management analysts...........................	902	41.7	9.0	10.7	7.9
Accountants and auditors......................	1,777	61.3	8.5	10.9	9.0
Appraisers and assessors of real estate.......	73	35.6	5.5	2.2	9.5
Financial analysts............................	307	36.9	6.5	12.8	10.9
Personal financial advisors...................	513	31.6	6.0	7.7	7.1
Insurance underwriters........................	104	62.5	9.6	6.3	4.9
Credit counselors and loan officers...........	367	57.7	11.5	5.6	10.9
Tax preparers.................................	108	63.2	8.5	5.3	14.9
Professional and related occupations..........	34,498	57.0	9.8	9.2	9.0
Computer and mathematical occupations [3]......	4,601	25.5	7.9	21.3	6.8
Computer systems analysts.....................	526	35.7	10.8	17.6	6.7
Computer programmers..........................	466	22.6	7.6	19.8	6.7
Software developers, applications and systems software....	1,483	20.0	4.1	35.7	4.8
Computer support specialists..................	570	25.5	9.8	12.6	7.8
Database administrators.......................	90	46.2	4.4	16.2	2.9
Network and computer systems administrators....	218	17.1	9.6	10.8	9.4
Operations research analysts..................	129	55.4	11.2	12.9	10.4
Architecture and engineering occupations [3]....	3,106	14.2	5.6	11.6	8.8
Architects, except naval......................	246	26.0	3.0	11.1	8.0
Aerospace engineers...........................	130	7.8	2.6	9.3	7.3
Civil engineers...............................	425	10.8	3.6	7.7	10.4
Computer hardware engineers...................	69	24.7	5.3	29.2	12.0
Electrical and electronics engineers..........	293	10.8	7.5	15.1	9.3
Industrial engineers, including health and safety....	220	20.3	2.7	6.6	11.2
Mechanical engineers..........................	350	6.4	4.2	10.5	5.5
Drafters......................................	109	15.0	4.9	4.9	22.7
Engineering technicians, except drafters......	385	19.8	11.2	8.8	10.6
Life, physical, and social science occupations [3]...	1,367	44.0	6.4	16.0	8.2
Biological scientists.........................	96	43.4	6.5	17.2	7.0
Medical scientists............................	154	46.9	3.7	37.3	4.6
Chemists and materials scientists.............	95	34.6	10.6	18.4	2.7
Environmental scientists and geoscientists....	89	30.0	3.4	8.0	5.6
Psychologists.................................	161	67.5	5.8	4.2	6.9
Community and social services occupations [3]....	2,612	65.5	18.6	3.4	12.1
Counselors....................................	869	73.0	19.6	2.7	11.6
Social workers................................	781	81.5	22.7	3.0	13.8
Miscellaneous community and social service specialists....	89	74.9	20.4	2.5	16.1
Clergy..	436	17.6	11.8	5.9	9.1
Legal occupations.............................	1,808	51.8	6.3	4.1	8.4
Lawyers.......................................	1,133	35.7	4.4	4.7	5.6
Judges, magistrates, and other judicial workers....	59	34.2	11.0	1.2	3.5
Paralegals and legal assistants...............	433	86.7	10.2	3.5	16.2
Miscellaneous legal support workers...........	168	77.0	8.4	1.9	8.7
Education, training, and library occupations [3]....	8,948	73.1	10.0	4.7	10.0
Postsecondary teachers........................	1,420	48.3	7.0	12.3	6.9
Preschool and kindergarten teachers...........	692	97.5	12.5	3.4	13.3
Elementary and middle school teachers.........	3,186	78.5	10.3	2.4	9.8
Secondary school teachers.....................	1,078	60.5	8.0	2.0	7.9
Special education teachers....................	353	85.2	8.6	2.2	6.5
Other teachers and instructors................	868	65.3	10.3	7.2	10.6

See footnotes at end of table.

Labor Force, Employment, and Earnings

Occupation	Total employed (1,000)	Percent of total			
		Female	Black [1]	Asian [1]	Hispanic [2]
Librarians	190	83.8	7.5	5.8	7.1
Teacher assistants	950	89.3	14.8	3.4	17.3
Arts, design, entertainment, sports, and media occupations [3]	3,097	48.5	6.6	5.5	10.6
Artists and related workers	232	56.6	3.6	3.6	9.9
Designers	878	54.8	5.1	8.4	10.6
Producers and directors	173	38.5	3.6	4.6	6.3
Athletes, coaches, umpires, and related workers	312	34.2	8.4	2.2	11.7
Musicians, singers, and related workers	192	40.4	14.6	3.7	9.3
News analysts, reporters and correspondents	73	48.8	3.6	9.6	10.5
Public relations specialists	121	58.9	8.2	1.7	7.3
Editors	167	52.4	1.9	6.6	6.0
Writers and authors	229	62.8	3.4	2.5	5.6
Miscellaneous media and communication workers	116	68.7	11.3	13.0	37.8
Broadcast and sound engineering technicians and radio operators	111	15.2	13.1	2.4	12.1
Photographers	205	47.7	5.7	5.7	8.4
Healthcare practitioner and technical occupations [3]	8,960	75.6	11.8	9.6	7.8
Dentists	163	34.4	3.2	20.2	9.5
Dietitians and nutritionists	120	89.4	15.9	6.1	4.9
Pharmacists	306	59.9	10.1	18.1	4.6
Physicians and surgeons	1,061	38.2	7.5	19.3	5.9
Physician assistants	92	70.0	3.2	11.5	6.0
Occupational therapists	118	89.2	7.5	8.2	6.3
Physical therapists	290	69.3	5.2	9.5	5.3
Speech-language pathologists	162	97.5	2.9	3.2	9.0
Veterinarians	101	63.2	2.1	3.7	0.3
Registered nurses	3,102	90.0	11.9	9.0	6.6
Clinical laboratory technologists and technicians	361	68.5	16.5	10.6	13.0
Dental hygienists	169	97.1	5.2	2.7	9.2
Diagnostic-related technologists and technicians	311	73.0	9.8	5.4	8.8
Emergency medical technicians and paramedics	194	35.7	12.4	2.3	12.1
Health practitioner support technologists and technicians	610	79.5	12.7	8.8	12.2
Licensed practical and licensed vocational nurses	653	90.0	30.3	4.2	10.1
Medical records and health information technicians	184	92.1	10.7	5.3	6.4
Service occupations	**26,811**	**56.6**	**16.8**	**5.5**	**23.9**
Healthcare support occupations [3]	3,554	87.7	27.3	5.5	16.9
Nursing, psychiatric, and home health aides	2,058	88.1	37.5	5.8	14.6
Massage therapists	170	80.7	6.8	7.7	9.6
Dental assistants	294	93.3	11.4	6.5	24.1
Medical assistants	570	92.9	14.3	4.1	28.6
Protective service occupations [3]	3,117	22.3	19.0	2.8	14.1
First-line supervisors of police and detectives	114	18.3	12.3	0.2	10.6
Firefighters	252	3.5	6.8	1.4	7.7
Bailiffs, correctional officers, and jailers	383	28.2	25.5	1.9	12.9
Detectives and criminal investigators	130	23.6	6.9	4.0	7.6
Police and sheriff's patrol officers	708	14.1	12.0	2.7	16.0
Private detectives and investigators	94	44.0	11.5	4.5	6.7
Security guards and gaming surveillance officers	923	22.0	30.4	4.0	17.6
Lifeguards and other protective service workers	149	44.2	8.7	1.2	11.4
Food preparation and serving related occupations	8,542	53.5	13.8	5.8	25.8
Chefs and head cooks	460	21.4	14.7	11.6	23.0
First-line supervisors of food preparation and serving workers	543	57.7	15.5	5.3	17.6
Cooks	2,179	38.7	17.3	4.8	35.0
Food-preparation workers	1,000	58.2	14.9	6.7	29.3
Bartenders	454	56.1	7.4	2.5	17.0
Combined food preparation and serving workers, including fast food	420	63.5	18.0	3.3	20.2
Counter attendants, cafeteria, food concession, and coffee shop	214	67.2	11.4	5.7	18.0
Waiters and waitresses	2,085	70.0	9.4	6.6	20.9
Food servers, nonrestaurant	213	71.3	16.3	5.7	22.5
Dining room and cafeteria attendants and bartender helpers	331	42.9	15.3	6.4	27.8
Dishwashers	319	18.0	16.3	5.9	35.4
Hosts and hostesses, restaurant, lounge, and coffee shop	319	80.8	8.8	3.8	16.3
Building and grounds cleaning and maintenance occupations	5,804	40.1	14.6	2.9	38.2
First-line supervisors of housekeeping and janitorial workers	323	39.9	16.0	1.2	28.4
First-line supervisors of landscaping, lawn service, and groundskeeping workers	231	4.6	5.1	1.0	24.6
Janitors and building cleaners	2,276	34.2	17.9	3.4	32.8
Maids and housekeeping cleaners	1,485	89.6	17.3	4.2	47.3
Pest control workers	79	2.6	6.2	0.2	14.6
Grounds maintenance workers	1,411	5.4	8.1	1.4	43.1
Personal care and service occupations [3]	5,795	77.3	15.9	9.3	16.3
First-line supervisors of gaming workers	206	46.4	4.8	4.1	11.6
First-line supervisors of personal service workers	191	70.5	9.2	15.5	10.6
Nonfarm animal caretakers	233	76.9	4.7	2.4	11.7
Gaming services workers	92	47.9	8.0	28.2	9.8
Barbers	126	11.7	39.9	3.3	19.6
Hairdressers, hairstylists, and cosmetologists	806	92.4	12.4	5.2	16.5
Miscellaneous personal appearance workers	364	86.1	9.5	57.8	9.2
Baggage porters, bellhops, and concierges	66	17.5	18.4	8.1	31.8
Child care workers	1,280	94.4	17.1	2.8	20.9
Personal care aides	1,396	84.9	24.4	10.2	20.6

See footnotes at end of table.

Table 638. Employed Civilians by Occupation, Sex, Race, and Hispanic Origin: 2016-Continued.

See headnote on page 411.

Occupation	Total employed (1,000)	Percent of total			
		Female	Black [1]	Asian [1]	Hispanic [2]
Recreation and fitness workers	440	62.2	10.0	1.0	7.8
Sales and office occupations	**33,539**	**61.2**	**12.6**	**5.2**	**15.6**
Sales and related occupations [3]	15,848	61.2	12.6	5.2	15.6
First-line supervisors of retail sales workers	3,282	49.0	11.0	5.7	15.7
First-line supervisors of non-retail sales workers	1,180	44.1	8.9	6.1	14.7
Cashiers	3,260	26.8	6.8	6.7	13.6
Counter and rental clerks	105	73.2	17.8	7.2	20.7
Parts salespersons	117	46.6	14.0	3.2	22.6
Retail salespersons	3,312	13.8	7.5	3.1	17.9
Advertising sales agents	222	48.4	12.3	5.3	18.2
Insurance sales agents	630	45.5	12.0	4.0	11.7
Securities, commodities, and financial services sales agents	263	46.5	11.0	4.6	11.7
Travel agents	83	30.4	7.1	7.2	8.9
Sales representatives, services, all other	512	84.7	2.6	10.3	11.3
Sales representatives, wholesale and manufacturing	1,308	31.8	8.5	3.9	11.3
Real estate brokers and sales agents	977	29.1	4.8	4.3	10.7
Telemarketers	61	55.5	6.9	4.6	10.2
Door-to-door sales workers, news and street vendors, and related workers	160	64.0	34.9	4.8	19.7
		62.5	9.1	3.4	22.3
Office and administrative support occupations [3]	17,691	72.1	14.1	4.7	15.6
First-line supervisors of office and administrative support workers	1,352	68.5	11.1	4.6	13.6
Bill and account collectors	152	67.4	25.1	2.0	19.3
Billing and posting clerks	452	89.0	14.0	4.6	15.8
Bookkeeping, accounting, and auditing clerks	1,137	88.5	7.7	4.9	11.9
Payroll and timekeeping clerks	129	90.7	10.4	8.1	13.2
Tellers	342	81.7	12.5	5.3	17.5
Court, municipal, and license clerks	80	71.1	18.9	2.4	19.6
Customer service representatives	2,388	65.0	16.9	4.5	18.3
File clerks	183	82.7	21.2	5.7	11.6
Hotel, motel, and resort desk clerks	138	66.1	17.2	9.7	21.5
Interviewers, except eligibility and loan	152	88.1	20.7	5.2	11.6
Library assistants, clerical	87	86.2	12.5	1.4	10.5
Loan interviewers and clerks	132	79.0	10.8	5.4	13.8
Order clerks	105	57.3	8.1	4.1	21.5
Receptionists and information clerks	1,331	90.1	13.0	3.7	18.4
Reservation and transportation ticket agents and travel clerks	144	55.1	24.8	8.2	20.0
Couriers and messengers	227	18.4	22.1	6.0	19.3
Dispatchers	292	55.7	12.8	3.1	16.6
Postal service clerks	121	53.7	23.9	12.1	8.7
Postal service mail carriers	320	38.9	18.6	8.3	12.3
Postal service mail sorters, processors, and processing machine operators	60	42.4	34.3	7.5	9.7
Production, planning, and expediting clerks	245	51.5	8.6	4.2	9.1
Shipping, receiving, and traffic clerks	546	33.9	16.1	2.2	21.7
Stock clerks and order fillers	1,530	37.0	18.8	4.8	19.5
Weighers, measurers, checkers, and samplers, recordkeeping	51	52.0	17.8	1.7	19.2
Secretaries and administrative assistants	2,744	94.6	8.6	3.2	11.8
Computer operators	91	50.8	13.8	4.1	14.3
Data entry keyers	272	77.6	13.4	9.1	20.9
Word processors and typists	82	88.9	14.3	4.1	11.2
Insurance claims and policy processing clerks	273	85.2	17.9	6.7	11.4
Mail clerks and mail machine operators, except postal service	77	43.5	21.7	1.0	21.2
Office clerks, general	1,295	82.8	14.6	6.9	16.9
Natural resources, construction, and maintenance occupations	**13,904**	**4.7**	**7.3**	**2.2**	**29.6**
Farming, fishing, and forestry occupations [3]	1,096	22.3	4.9	1.8	45.0
Construction and extraction occupations [3]	7,929	3.0	6.8	1.7	34.0
First-line supervisors of construction trades and extraction workers	680	2.6	5.5	1.5	22.5
Brickmasons, blockmasons, and stonemasons	160	0.5	6.4	0.5	45.5
Carpenters	1,359	2.1	5.4	1.2	33.9
Carpet, floor, and tile installers and finishers	168	1.9	3.5	0.9	50.8
Cement masons, concrete finishers, and terrazzo workers	56	2.2	10.5	1.6	48.8
Construction laborers	1,801	3.5	8.1	2.2	45.5
Operating engineers and other construction equipment operators	351	2.3	8.7	0.2	19.3
Drywall installers, ceiling tile installers, and tapers	180	1.1	6.7	0.5	62.7
Electricians	774	3.0	5.9	3.1	16.8
Painters, construction and maintenance	612	6.2	5.7	3.6	50.7
Pipelayers, plumbers, pipefitters, and steamfitters	583	1.4	7.5	0.9	21.2
Roofers	230	1.7	4.9	1.1	51.7
Sheet metal workers	126	2.9	6.7	2.1	16.7
Construction and building inspectors	93	6.4	11.8	2.4	9.9
Highway maintenance workers	92	3.2	9.6	0.2	15.1
Installation, maintenance, and repair occupations [3]	4,879	3.6	8.8	3.2	19.0
First-line supervisors of mechanics, installers, and repairers	264	10.1	10.2	2.0	10.4
Computer, automated teller, and office machine repairers	212	9.6	13.0	10.0	12.0
Radio and telecommunications equipment installers and repairers	143	16.1	16.3	5.3	15.8
Aircraft mechanics and service technicians	140	1.7	3.3	6.0	18.5
Automotive body and related repairers	147	3.6	5.2	3.0	24.1
Automotive service technicians and mechanics	879	1.7	9.6	4.3	23.3
Bus and truck mechanics and diesel engine specialists	342	0.8	7.0	1.9	16.1
Heavy vehicle and mobile equip. service technicians and mechanics	203	0.5	3.8	1.9	16.9

See footnotes at end of table.

Table 638. **Employed Civilians by Occupation, Sex, Race, and Hispanic Origin:**
2016-Continued.
See headnote on page 411.

Occupation	Total employed (1,000)	Percent of total			
		Female	Black [1]	Asian [1]	Hispanic [2]
Heating, air conditioning, and refrigeration mechanics and installers..............	427	1.4	7.0	1.3	21.9
Industrial and refractory machinery mechanics..........................	393	3.3	8.5	1.9	15.0
Maintenance and repair workers, general...........................	552	3.0	10.6	2.2	19.8
Electrical power-line installers and repairers...............................	136	0.6	7.7	0.9	10.5
Telecommunications line installers and repairers.........................	171	2.5	16.1	5.2	20.9
Production, transportation, and material moving occupations.........	**17,743**	**22.1**	**15.8**	**4.8**	**22.2**
Production occupations [3].................................	8,459	28.2	12.9	5.9	22.3
First-line supervisors of production and operating workers................	763	18.7	9.7	3.9	15.0
Electrical, electronics, and electromechanical assemblers.................	117	49.3	14.1	16.9	22.5
Bakers..	224	64.8	13.9	7.2	27.3
Butchers and other meat, poultry, and fish processing workers............	277	26.9	19.8	9.9	34.6
Food batchmakers...	107	58.7	14.2	3.1	30.6
Cutting, punching, and press machine setters, operators, and tenders, metal and plastic................................	83	18.3	5.8	0.6	22.3
Machinists...	356	3.4	5.4	6.8	13.0
Welding, soldering, and brazing workers........................	603	4.1	10.0	2.8	23.6
Printing press operators.....................................	205	20.3	6.7	4.7	15.9
Laundry and dry-cleaning workers............................	188	58.1	21.4	7.9	34.0
Sewing machine operators..................................	208	71.5	8.0	12.1	46.9
Tailors, dressmakers, and sewers.............................	79	79.7	7.8	22.6	19.3
Stationary engineers and boiler operators........................	78	4.7	9.6	5.0	14.1
Water and wastewater treatment plant and system operators..............	77	5.2	13.9	2.1	6.8
Crushing, grinding, polishing, mixing, and blending workers..............	94	11.9	12.2	1.5	35.3
Inspectors, testers, sorters, samplers, and weighers......................	734	37.9	12.8	7.4	17.7
Medical, dental, and ophthalmic laboratory technicians....................	85	51.4	8.4	11.8	11.3
Packaging and filling machine operators and tenders......................	236	50.5	16.1	6.2	43.1
Painting workers..	173	8.9	8.8	1.8	28.4
Transportation and material-moving occupations [3].........................	9,284	16.5	18.4	3.8	22.1
Supervisors, transportation and material-moving workers.................	190	21.4	13.4	3.2	21.2
Aircraft pilots and flight engineers.............................	141	5.2	3.0	0.5	7.7
Bus drivers..	553	48.7	29.4	3.3	11.8
Driver/sales workers and truck drivers..........................	3,542	6.0	14.8	2.6	21.3
Taxi drivers and chauffeurs..................................	500	14.3	28.7	16.0	12.6
Parking lot attendants......................................	89	10.7	24.3	7.3	28.5
Automotive and water craft service attendants.....................	97	8.6	9.9	6.4	18.1
Industrial truck and tractor operators............................	605	9.6	26.0	2.3	28.0
Cleaners of vehicles and equipment............................	328	13.0	18.0	2.5	29.4
Laborers and freight, stock, and material movers, hand..................	1,900	18.1	19.9	3.2	23.4
Packers and packagers, hand.................................	550	54.5	18.9	7.1	43.6
Refuse and recyclable material collectors........................	101	8.6	16.4	0.5	23.5

– Represents or rounds to zero. [1] The Current Population Survey (CPS) allows respondents to choose more than one race. Data represent persons who selected this race group only and exclude persons reporting more than one race. The CPS in prior years only allowed respondents to report one race group. See also comments on race in the text for Section 1. [2] Persons of Hispanic origin may be of any race. [3] Includes other occupations, not shown separately.

Source: U.S. Bureau of Labor Statistics, CPS Tables, "Employed persons by detailed occupation, sex, race, and Hispanic or Latino ethnicity," <http://www.bls.gov/cps/tables.htm>, accessed March 2017.

Table 639. Employment and Annual and Hourly Wages by Occupation: 2016

[In dollars, except employment. As of May. Data shown for occupations with over 1,500,000 employees. Data from the Occupational Employment Statistics survey. For definition of mean and median, see Guide to Tabular Presentation]

Occupation	Employment (number)	Mean hourly wage	Annual wages [1]	Median hourly wage
All occupations [2]	**140,400,040**	**23.86**	**49,630**	**17.81**
Management occupations	7,090,790	56.74	118,020	48.46
Top executives	2,465,800	61.03	126,950	49.19
General and operations managers	2,188,870	58.70	122,090	47.74
Operations specialties managers	1,693,430	60.32	125,470	53.88
Other management occupations	2,267,610	46.86	97,480	42.03
Business and financial operations occupations	7,281,190	36.09	75,070	31.99
Business operations specialists	4,629,810	34.54	71,840	31.37
Financial specialists	2,651,370	38.80	80,700	33.07
Computer and mathematical occupations	4,165,140	42.25	87,880	39.82
Computer occupations	3,997,370	42.24	87,870	39.84
Software developers and programmers	1,604,570	48.11	100,080	46.07
Architecture and engineering occupations	2,499,050	40.53	84,300	37.45
Engineers	1,635,420	46.37	96,440	43.75
Community and social service occupations	2,019,250	22.69	47,200	20.67
Counselors, social workers, and other community and social service specialists	1,941,090	22.70	47,220	20.68
Education, training, and library occupations	8,636,430	26.21	54,520	23.08
Postsecondary teachers	1,530,010	([3])	81,880	([3])
Preschool, primary, secondary, and special education school teachers	4,133,490	([3])	57,470	([3])
Elementary and middle school teachers	2,031,700	([3])	59,270	([3])
Arts, design, entertainment, sports, and media occupations	1,902,970	28.07	58,390	22.69
Healthcare practitioners and technical occupations	8,318,500	38.06	79,160	30.49
Health diagnosing and treating practitioners	5,143,640	47.51	98,830	37.49
Registered nurses	2,857,180	34.70	72,180	32.91
Health technologists and technicians	3,018,820	22.34	46,460	20.55
Healthcare support occupations	4,043,480	14.65	30,470	13.42
Nursing, psychiatric, and home health aides	2,377,790	12.65	26,320	11.93
Protective service occupations	3,386,340	22.03	45,810	18.59
Food preparation and serving related occupations	12,981,720	11.47	23,850	10.01
Cooks and food preparation workers	3,190,940	11.53	23,990	10.80
Cooks	2,340,280	11.72	24,370	10.99
Food and beverage serving workers	7,355,090	10.78	22,430	9.50
Fast food and counter workers	3,925,640	9.89	20,580	9.38
Combined food preparation and serving workers, including fast food	3,426,090	9.84	20,460	9.35
Waiters and waitresses	2,564,610	11.73	24,410	9.61
Building and grounds cleaning and maintenance occupations	4,426,090	13.47	28,010	11.87
Building cleaning and pest control workers	3,174,220	12.64	26,300	11.33
Building cleaning workers	3,101,400	12.55	26,090	11.26
Janitors and cleaners, except maids and housekeeping cleaners	2,161,740	12.99	27,030	11.63
Personal care and service occupations	4,514,960	12.74	26,510	10.92
Other personal care and service workers	2,820,750	12.22	25,410	10.83
Sales and related occupations	14,536,530	19.50	40,560	12.78
Retail sales workers	8,791,750	12.14	25,250	10.37
Cashiers	3,564,130	10.44	21,710	9.71
Retail salespersons	4,528,550	13.07	27,180	10.90
Sales representatives, services	1,903,140	33.90	70,510	25.29
Sales representatives, wholesale and manufacturing	1,732,420	35.12	73,060	29.10
Office and administrative support occupations	22,026,080	17.91	37,260	16.37
Financial clerks	3,133,030	18.17	37,790	17.23
Bookkeeping, accounting, and auditing clerks	1,566,960	19.34	40,220	18.46
Information and record clerks	5,630,810	16.53	34,370	15.24
Customer service representatives	2,707,040	16.91	35,170	15.53
Material recording, scheduling, dispatching, and distributing workers	4,101,520	16.42	34,150	14.63
Stock clerks and order fillers	2,016,340	12.82	26,670	11.46
Secretaries and administrative assistants	3,675,140	19.39	40,330	17.90
Secretaries and administrative assistants, except legal, medical, and executive	2,295,510	17.38	36,140	16.74
Other office and administrative support workers	3,940,510	16.31	33,930	15.19
Office clerks, general	2,955,550	15.87	33,010	14.70
Construction and extraction occupations	5,585,420	23.51	48,900	20.96
Construction trades workers	4,216,890	22.88	47,580	20.34
Installation, maintenance, and repair occupations	5,456,640	22.45	46,690	20.89
Vehicle and mobile equipment mechanics, installers, and repairers	1,578,250	21.02	43,710	19.68
Other installation, maintenance, and repair occupations	2,836,540	21.28	44,270	19.68
Production occupations	9,105,650	17.88	37,190	15.93
Assemblers and fabricators	1,798,860	16.16	33,610	14.87
Metal workers and plastic workers	1,924,170	19.15	39,830	18.06
Other production occupations	2,582,350	16.80	34,950	15.15
Transportation and material moving occupations	9,731,790	17.34	36,070	14.78
Motor vehicle operators	3,934,070	17.93	37,280	16.82
Driver/sales workers and truck drivers	2,989,540	18.70	38,900	17.63
Heavy and tractor-trailer truck drivers	1,704,520	20.96	43,590	19.87
Material moving workers	4,580,950	14.11	29,360	12.62
Laborers and material movers, hand	3,730,410	13.25	27,570	11.88
Laborers and freight, stock, and material movers, hand	2,587,900	13.81	28,720	12.49

[1] Annual wages have been calculated by multiplying the hourly mean wage by a "year-round, full-time" hours figure of 2,080 hours; for those occupations where there is not an hourly mean wage published, the annual wage has been directly calculated from the reported survey data. [2] Includes occupations not shown separately. [3] Wages for some occupations that do not generally work year-round full-time are reported as either hourly wages or as annual salaries, depending on how they are typically paid.

Source: U.S. Bureau of Labor Statistics, Occupational Employment Statistics, *Occupational Employment and Wages—May 2016*, USDL 17-0376, March 2017. See also <http://www.bls.gov/oes/>.

Table 640. Employed Civilians by Occupation—States: 2014

[In thousands (146,305 represents 146,305,000). Excludes persons with no previous work experience. Based on the Current Population Survey see text, Section 1 and Appendix III]

State	Total employed	Management, professional, and related occupations			Sales and office occupations		Natural resources, construction, and maintenance occupations			Production, transportation, and material-moving occupations	
		Management, business, and financial operations	Professional and related occupations	Service occupations	Sales and related occupations	Office and administrative occupations	Farming, fishing, and forestry occupations	Construction and extraction occupations	Installation, maintenance, and repair occupations	Production occupations	Transportation and material-moving occupations
Total U.S...	146,305	23,171	32,879	25,854	15,646	17,771	1,022	7,637	4,879	8,438	9,010
AL............	2,011	263	406	322	219	247	(S)	113	84	190	159
AK............	342	53	73	62	31	46	(S)	22	17	12	22
AZ............	2,888	415	615	554	368	384	(S)	143	95	128	167
AR............	1,216	154	240	207	133	151	(S)	66	46	112	86
CA............	17,391	2,876	3,992	3,204	1,877	2,026	210	872	491	843	1,001
CO............	2,683	530	632	455	253	316	(S)	168	89	103	129
CT............	1,769	329	474	298	188	183	(S)	82	46	87	80
DE............	427	71	98	79	42	58	(S)	19	15	17	26
DC............	348	92	134	51	22	28	(S)	6	3	3	10
FL............	9,073	1,386	1,916	1,782	1,196	1,169	50	482	315	294	484
GA............	4,392	720	970	686	506	536	39	211	160	248	317
HI............	642	88	128	148	75	83	(S)	31	21	21	41
ID............	738	110	157	126	77	89	24	39	22	42	51
IL............	6,056	991	1,361	1,050	665	727	(S)	237	188	401	415
IN............	3,041	387	592	530	300	383	(S)	165	115	317	233
IA............	1,630	282	333	253	167	202	(S)	75	47	129	122
KS............	1,434	226	320	244	135	172	(S)	87	61	99	80
KY............	1,877	243	397	313	179	276	(S)	88	76	154	136
LA............	2,021	249	421	344	229	243	(S)	177	75	129	140
ME............	656	101	156	115	69	79	11	34	24	36	31
MD............	2,918	564	825	487	278	327	(S)	146	100	67	119
MA............	3,353	603	939	609	329	383	(S)	140	75	140	129
MI............	4,406	653	1,013	755	479	492	36	164	148	399	266
MN............	2,853	529	650	457	299	344	(S)	132	86	178	154
MS............	1,137	145	244	184	110	130	(S)	74	40	108	91
MO............	2,855	469	575	506	292	394	(S)	149	125	144	190
MT............	500	83	98	98	53	56	(S)	36	19	19	30
NE............	983	153	210	171	98	115	(S)	49	28	86	56
NV............	1,288	167	207	346	154	174	(S)	73	42	45	77
NH............	708	120	170	114	79	81	(S)	37	27	44	34
NJ............	4,221	725	1,021	721	455	554	(S)	198	113	131	295
NM............	852	123	204	169	77	117	(S)	53	22	35	43
NY............	8,946	1,441	2,254	1,758	942	1,052	(S)	392	242	355	490
NC............	4,360	622	982	715	469	525	44	251	168	304	280
ND............	405	72	80	68	44	46	(S)	28	13	19	26
OH............	5,390	776	1,180	921	536	705	(S)	221	182	454	398
OK............	1,688	240	340	269	172	219	(S)	124	80	135	97
OR............	1,807	303	398	310	200	218	34	77	57	95	114
PA............	6,005	959	1,325	1,042	612	766	(S)	271	187	384	428
RI............	511	87	124	94	52	64	(S)	19	13	31	26
SC............	2,070	263	444	359	245	255	(S)	101	86	175	123
SD............	433	78	83	67	41	59	(S)	23	17	31	26
TN............	2,826	372	599	516	316	361	(S)	133	108	197	212
TX............	12,453	1,885	2,511	2,216	1,345	1,473	63	936	447	719	857
UT............	1,372	217	294	172	169	196	(S)	96	52	84	86
VT............	333	57	86	55	29	36	(S)	18	11	20	17
VA............	4,055	806	1,032	698	376	410	(S)	207	138	153	211
WA............	3,269	561	782	530	322	375	51	176	129	176	169
WV............	739	87	171	135	71	94	(S)	55	27	39	58
WI............	2,918	445	629	492	279	350	(S)	127	103	304	176
WY............	294	41	57	48	24	34	(S)	30	16	15	24

S Data are not shown when the labor force base does not meet publication standard of reliability for the particular area, as determined by the sample size.

Source: U.S. Bureau of Labor Statistics, *Geographic Profile of Employment and Unemployment, 2014*, Bulletin 2873, September 2015. See also <http://www.bls.gov/gps/>.

Table 641. Fastest Growing and Largest Occupations Projected with Education Needed and Median Wages: 2014 to 2024

[In thousands (4.4 represents 4,400), except percent and wage. Estimates based on the Current Employment Statistics Program, the Occupational Employment Statistics Survey, and the Current Population Survey. See source for methodological assumptions. Occupations based on the 2010 Standard Occupational Classification system. Additional occupation information in the Occupational Outlook Handbook <http://www.bls.gov/ooh>]

Occupation	Employment (1,000)		Change, 2014–2024		Median annual wage (in dollars), 2015	Typical education needed for entry [1]
	2014	2024	Number (1,000)	Percent		
FASTEST GROWING						
Wind turbine service technicians	4.4	9.2	4.8	108.0	51,050	Some college, no degree
Occupational therapy assistants	33.0	47.1	14.1	42.7	57,870	Associate's degree
Physical therapist assistants	78.7	110.7	31.9	40.6	55,170	Associate's degree
Physical therapist aides	50.0	69.5	19.5	39.0	25,120	High school diploma or equivalent
Home health aides	913.5	1,261.9	348.4	38.1	21,920	No formal educational credential
Commercial divers	4.4	6.0	1.6	36.9	50,470	Postsecondary nondegree award
Nurse practitioners	126.9	171.7	44.7	35.2	98,190	Master's degree
Physical therapists	210.9	282.7	71.8	34.0	84,020	Doctoral or professional degree
Statisticians	30.0	40.1	10.1	33.8	80,110	Master's degree
Ambulance drivers and attendants, except emergency medical technicians	19.6	26.1	6.5	33.0	23,740	High school diploma or equivalent
Occupational therapy aides	8.8	11.6	2.7	30.6	27,800	High school diploma or equivalent
Physician assistants	94.4	123.2	28.7	30.4	98,180	Master's degree
Operations research analysts	91.3	118.9	27.6	30.2	78,630	Bachelor's degree
Personal financial advisors	249.4	323.2	73.9	29.6	89,160	Bachelor's degree
Cartographers and photogrammetrists	12.3	15.9	3.6	29.3	61,880	Bachelor's degree
Genetic counselors	2.4	3.1	0.7	28.8	72,090	Master's degree
Interpreters and translators	61.0	78.5	17.5	28.7	44,190	Bachelor's degree
Audiologists	13.2	16.9	3.8	28.6	74,890	Doctoral or professional degree
Hearing aid specialists	5.9	7.5	1.6	27.2	49,600	High school diploma or equivalent
Optometrists	40.6	51.6	11.0	27.0	103,900	Doctoral or professional degree
Forensic science technicians	14.4	18.2	3.8	26.6	56,320	Bachelor's degree
Web developers	148.5	188.0	39.5	26.6	64,970	Associate's degree
Occupational therapists	114.6	145.1	30.4	26.5	80,150	Master's degree
Diagnostic medical sonographers	60.7	76.7	16.0	26.4	68,970	Associate's degree
Personal care aides	1,768.4	2,226.5	458.1	25.9	20,980	No formal educational credential
Phlebotomists	112.7	140.8	28.1	24.9	31,630	Postsecondary nondegree award
Ophthalmic medical technicians	37.0	46.1	9.1	24.7	35,350	Postsecondary nondegree award
Nurse midwives	5.3	6.6	1.3	24.6	92,510	Master's degree
Solar photovoltaic installers	5.9	7.4	1.4	24.3	37,830	High school diploma or equivalent
Emergency medical technicians and paramedics	241.2	299.6	58.5	24.2	31,980	Postsecondary nondegree award
LARGEST JOB GROWTH						
Personal care aides	1,768.4	2,226.5	458.1	25.9	20,980	No formal educational credential
Registered nurses	2,751.0	3,190.3	439.3	16.0	67,490	Bachelor's degree
Home health aides	913.5	1,261.9	348.4	38.1	21,920	No formal educational credential
Combined food preparation and serving workers, including fast food	3,159.7	3,503.2	343.5	10.9	18,910	No formal educational credential
Retail salespersons	4,624.9	4,939.1	314.2	6.8	21,780	No formal educational credential
Nursing assistants	1,492.1	1,754.1	262.0	17.6	25,710	Postsecondary nondegree award
Customer service representatives	2,581.8	2,834.8	252.9	9.8	31,720	High school diploma or equivalent
Cooks, restaurant	1,109.7	1,268.7	158.9	14.3	23,100	No formal educational credential
General and operations managers	2,124.1	2,275.2	151.1	7.1	97,730	Bachelor's degree
Construction laborers	1,159.1	1,306.5	147.4	12.7	31,910	No formal educational credential
Accountants and auditors	1,332.7	1,475.1	142.4	10.7	67,190	Bachelor's degree
Medical assistants	591.3	730.2	138.9	23.5	30,590	Postsecondary nondegree award
Janitors and cleaners, except maids and housekeeping cleaners	2,360.6	2,496.9	136.3	5.8	23,440	No formal educational credential
Software developers, applications	718.4	853.7	135.3	18.8	98,260	Bachelor's degree
Laborers and freight, stock, and material movers, hand	2,441.3	2,566.4	125.1	5.1	25,010	No formal educational credential
First-line supervisors of office and administrative support workers	1,466.1	1,587.3	121.2	8.3	52,630	High school diploma or equivalent
Computer systems analysts	567.8	686.3	118.6	20.9	85,800	Bachelor's degree
Licensed practical and licensed vocational nurses	719.9	837.2	117.3	16.3	43,170	Postsecondary nondegree award
Maids and housekeeping cleaners	1,457.7	1,569.4	111.7	7.7	20,740	No formal educational credential
Medical secretaries	527.6	635.8	108.2	20.5	33,040	High school diploma or equivalent
Management analysts	758.0	861.4	103.4	13.6	81,320	Bachelor's degree
Heavy and tractor-trailer truck drivers	1,797.7	1,896.4	98.8	5.5	40,260	Postsecondary nondegree award
Receptionists and information clerks	1,028.6	1,126.3	97.8	9.5	27,300	High school diploma or equivalent
Office clerks, general	3,062.5	3,158.2	95.8	3.1	29,580	High school diploma or equivalent
Sales representatives, wholesale and manufacturing, except technical and scientific products	1,453.1	1,546.5	93.4	6.4	55,730	High school diploma or equivalent
Stock clerks and order fillers	1,878.1	1,971.1	92.9	4.9	23,220	No formal educational credential
Market research analysts and marketing specialists	495.5	587.8	92.3	18.6	62,150	Bachelor's degree
First-line supervisors of food preparation and serving workers	890.1	978.6	88.5	9.9	30,340	High school diploma or equivalent
Electricians	628.8	714.7	85.9	13.7	51,880	High school diploma or equivalent
Maintenance and repair workers, general	1,374.7	1,458.1	83.5	6.1	36,630	High school diploma or equivalent

[1] An occupation is placed into 1 of 8 categories that best describe the typical education needed by most workers to enter that occupation. For more information, see "Measures of Education and Training" at <http://www.bls.gov/emp/ep_education_tech.htm>.

Source: U.S. Bureau of Labor Statistics, "Occupational employment projections to 2024," *Monthly Labor Review*, December 2015. See also <http://www.bls.gov/emp/ep_pub_occ_projections.htm>.

Table 642. Employment Projections by Industry: 2014 to 2024

[6,138.4 represents 6,138,400. Estimates based on the Current Employment Statistics program. See source for methodological assumptions. Minus sign (-) indicates decline]

Industry	2012 NAICS code [1]	Employment (1,000) 2014	Employment (1,000) 2024	Change, 2014– 2024 (1,000)	Average annual rate of change 2014– 2024
LARGEST GROWTH					
Construction	23	6,138.4	6,928.8	790.4	1.2
Home health care services	6216	1,262.2	2,022.6	760.4	4.8
Nursing and residential care facilities	623	3,261.0	3,996.7	735.7	2.1
Food services and drinking places	722	10,717.0	11,375.0	658.0	0.6
Offices of physicians	6211	2,470.2	2,992.9	522.7	1.9
Local government educational services compensation	(X)	7,791.2	8,217.6	426.4	0.5
Employment services	5613	3,421.0	3,845.8	424.8	1.2
Computer systems design and related services	5415	1,777.7	2,186.6	408.9	2.1
Hospitals; private	622	4,784.3	5,179.2	394.9	0.8
Offices of other health practitioners	6213	784.2	1,136.5	352.3	3.8
Outpatient care centers	6214	711.1	1,059.2	348.1	4.1
Management, scientific, and technical consulting services	5416	1,244.4	1,573.7	329.3	2.4
Wholesale trade	42	5,826.0	6,151.4	325.4	0.5
Individual and family services	6241	2,032.5	2,318.8	286.3	1.3
General Merchandise stores	452	3,113.6	3,376.8	263.2	0.8
Retail trade [2]	([3])	7,395.6	7,646.6	251.0	0.3
Junior colleges, colleges, universities, and professional schools [4]	6112, 6113	1,777.2	1,997.2	220.0	1.2
Securities, commodity contracts, and other financial investments and related activities	523	877.6	1,074.2	196.6	2.0
Offices of dentists	6212	891.1	1,050.9	159.8	1.7
Motor vehicle and parts dealers	441	1,861.3	2,017.2	155.9	0.8
FASTEST GROWTH					
Home health care services	6216	1,262.2	2,022.6	760.4	4.8
Outpatient care centers	6214	711.1	1,059.2	348.1	4.1
Offices of other health practitioners	6213	784.2	1,136.5	352.3	3.8
Other ambulatory health care services	6219	278.6	389.0	110.4	3.4
Medical and diagnostic laboratories	6215	247.4	327.1	79.7	2.8
Management, scientific, and technical consulting services	5416	1,244.4	1,573.7	329.3	2.4
Software publishers	5112	312.5	393.2	80.7	2.3
Facilities support services	5612	131.4	163.2	31.8	2.2
Computer systems design and related services	5415	1,777.7	2,186.6	408.9	2.1
Nursing and residential care facilities	623	3,261.0	3,996.7	735.7	2.1
Securities, commodity contracts, and other financial investments and related activities	523	877.6	1,074.2	196.6	2.0
Offices of physicians	6211	2,470.2	2,992.9	522.7	1.9
Offices of dentists	6212	891.1	1,050.9	159.8	1.7
Funds, trusts, and other financial vehicles	525	3.7	4.4	0.7	1.7
Local government passenger transit	(X)	277.6	322.0	44.4	1.5
Other information services	519	217.8	251.0	33.2	1.4
Office administrative services	5611	461.7	530.0	68.3	1.4
Support activities for mining	213	438.5	501.7	63.2	1.4
Individual and family services	6241	2,032.5	2,318.8	286.3	1.3
Wireless telecommunications carriers (except satellite)	5172	155.3	176.5	21.2	1.3
MOST RAPIDLY DECLINING					
Apparel, leather, and allied manufacturing	315, 316	168.5	91.7	-76.8	-5.9
Tobacco manufacturing	3122	13.6	9.2	-4.4	-3.9
Postal Service	(X)	593.0	427.9	-165.1	-3.2
Federal enterprises except the Postal Service and electric utilities	(X)	81.1	58.9	-22.2	-3.1
Manufacturing and reproducing magnetic and optical media	3346	18.9	14.0	-4.9	-2.9
Communications equipment manufacturing	3342	93.5	69.5	-24.0	-2.9
Newspaper, periodical, book, and directory publishers	5111	412.3	309.0	-103.3	-2.8
Textile mills and textile product mills	313, 314	232.1	174.2	-57.9	-2.8
Audio and video equipment manufacturing	3343	18.9	14.6	-4.3	-2.6
Glass and glass product manufacturing	3272	85.8	67.3	-18.5	-2.4
Pulp, paper, and paperboard mills	3221	104.2	83.0	-21.2	-2.2
Other miscellaneous manufacturing	3399	275.2	219.3	-55.9	-2.2
Hardware manufacturing	3325	24.3	19.6	-4.7	-2.1
Federal electric utilities	(X)	17.9	14.5	-3.4	-2.1
Printing and related support activities	323	452.7	371.3	-81.4	-2.0
Spring and wire product manufacturing	3326	43.8	36.1	-7.7	-1.9
Foundries	3315	127.0	105.2	-21.8	-1.9
Computer and peripheral equipment manufacturing	3341	162.8	135.5	-27.3	-1.8
Clay product and refractory manufacturing	3271	39.5	33.0	-6.5	-1.8
Wired telecommunications carriers	111	607.0	509.2	-97.8	-1.7

X Not applicable. [1] Based on the North American Industry Classification System, 2012; see text, Section 15. [2] Except motor vehicle and parts dealers, food and beverage stores, and general merchandise stores. [3] 2012 NAICS 442-444, 446-448, 451, and 453-454. [4] Private institutions.

Source: U.S. Bureau of Labor Statistics, "Industry employment and output projections to 2024," *Monthly Labor Review*, December 2015. See also <http://www.bls.gov/opub/mlr/2015/>.

Table 643. Occupations of the Employed by Race/Ethnicity and Educational Attainment: 2016

[In thousands (132,444 represents 132,444,000). Annual averages of monthly figures. Civilian noninstitutional population 25 years old and over. Based on Current Population Survey; see text, Section 1 and Appendix III]

Race and educational attainment	Total employed	Managerial, professional, and related	Service	Sales and office	Natural resources, construction, and maintenance	Production, transportation, and material-moving
Total [1]	**132,444**	**55,924**	**20,734**	**27,805**	**12,425**	**15,556**
Less than a high school diploma	9,884	714	3,180	1,158	2,429	2,403
High school graduate, no college	33,801	5,486	7,590	8,376	5,217	7,133
Some college or associate degree	36,386	11,844	6,717	9,857	3,654	4,313
Bachelor's degree or higher	52,374	37,881	3,247	8,414	1,126	1,706
White [2]	104,624	44,971	14,949	22,143	10,794	11,768
Less than a high school diploma	7,879	602	2,386	874	2,152	1,865
High school graduate, no college	26,623	4,610	5,253	6,734	4,575	5,450
Some college or associate degree	28,668	9,695	4,841	7,833	3,116	3,182
Bachelor's degree or higher	41,454	30,063	2,468	6,702	951	1,270
Black [2]	15,517	5,081	3,699	3,346	931	2,460
Less than a high school diploma	1,069	52	451	165	108	292
High school graduate, no college	4,737	534	1,577	1,046	415	1,166
Some college or associate degree	5,099	1,365	1,284	1,319	329	801
Bachelor's degree or higher	4,612	3,130	387	815	79	202
Asian [2]	8,386	4,543	1,276	1,478	288	800
Less than a high school diploma	500	41	201	72	55	131
High school graduate, no college	1,400	186	465	335	86	328
Some college or associate degree	1,359	416	323	381	84	155
Bachelor's degree or higher	5,127	3,900	287	690	62	187
Hispanic [3]	21,186	4,987	5,168	3,922	3,688	3,420
Less than a high school diploma	5,472	223	1,889	459	1,647	1,253
High school graduate, no college	6,398	726	1,728	1,332	1,267	1,344
Some college or associate degree	5,053	1,349	1,117	1,413	574	601
Bachelor's degree or higher	4,263	2,689	434	719	200	222

[1] Includes other races, not shown separately. [2] For persons in this race group only. See footnote 2, Table 611. [3] Persons of Hispanic origin may be of any race.

Source: U.S. Bureau of Labor Statistics, Current Population Survey, unpublished data. See also <http://www.bls.gov/cps/>.

Table 644. Employment by Industry, Sex, and Race/Ethnicity: 2000 to 2016

[In thousands (136,891 represents 136,891,000), except percent. Civilian noninstitutional population 16 years old and over. Annual average of monthly figures. Based on Current Population Survey; see text, Section 1, Population, and Appendix III]

Industry	Total				2016, percent			
	2000	2005	2010	2016	Female	Black [1]	Asian [1]	Hispanic [2]
Total employed	**136,891**	**141,730**	**139,064**	**151,436**	**46.8**	**11.9**	**6.1**	**16.7**
Agriculture and related industries	2,464	2,197	2,206	2,460	25.3	2.7	1.1	24.5
Mining and related industries	475	624	731	792	13.4	6.4	2.3	17.8
Construction	9,931	11,197	9,077	10,328	9.1	5.8	1.9	28.9
Manufacturing	19,644	16,253	14,081	15,408	28.9	10.0	6.8	16.1
Durable goods	12,519	10,333	8,789	9,704	24.9	8.9	7.1	14.1
Nondurable goods	7,125	5,919	5,293	5,704	35.8	11.7	6.2	19.5
Wholesale trade	4,216	4,579	3,805	3,641	29.5	8.4	6.0	17.6
Retail trade	15,763	16,825	15,934	16,577	47.8	12.0	5.9	17.0
Transportation and utilities	7,380	7,360	7,134	8,012	23.5	18.0	5.3	17.3
Transportation and warehousing	6,096	6,184	5,880	6,693	23.8	19.4	5.6	18.6
Utilities	1,284	1,176	1,253	1,319	22.0	10.9	3.8	10.8
Information	4,059	3,402	3,149	2,855	40.6	11.1	7.6	11.3
Financial activities	9,374	10,203	9,350	10,404	52.3	10.4	7.0	12.2
Finance and insurance	6,641	7,035	6,605	7,241	55.1	10.4	8.3	10.6
Real estate and rental and leasing	2,734	3,168	2,745	3,163	45.6	10.4	4.1	15.7
Professional and business services	13,649	14,294	15,253	18,325	41.4	9.7	8.3	16.6
Professional and technical services	8,266	8,584	9,115	11,228	42.2	6.5	11.2	8.8
Management, administrative, and waste services	5,383	5,709	6,138	7,097	40.0	14.9	3.6	28.9
Education and health services	26,188	29,174	32,062	34,263	74.6	14.9	6.0	12.1
Educational services	11,255	12,264	13,155	13,674	68.4	11.1	4.6	11.2
Health care and social assistance	14,933	16,910	18,907	20,589	78.7	17.4	6.9	12.7
Hospitals	5,202	5,719	6,249	6,990	76.7	15.3	8.8	10.0
Health services, except hospitals	7,009	8,332	9,406	10,220	78.4	18.2	6.7	13.1
Social assistance	2,722	2,860	3,252	3,379	84.1	19.6	4.0	16.9
Leisure and hospitality	11,186	12,071	12,530	14,193	50.6	12.6	6.5	22.9
Arts, entertainment, and recreation	2,539	2,765	2,966	3,241	45.2	10.3	4.4	13.2
Accommodation and food services	8,647	9,306	9,564	10,952	52.3	13.3	7.1	25.8
Other services	6,450	7,020	6,769	7,320	52.2	10.6	7.7	18.1
Other services, except private households	5,731	6,208	6,102	6,596	47.9	11.0	8.1	15.9
Private households	718	812	667	724	91.7	7.6	4.1	38.5
Public administration	6,113	6,530	6,983	6,857	45.1	16.7	4.5	12.2

[1] Persons in this race group only. See footnote 2, Table 611. [2] Persons of Hispanic origin may be of any race.

Source: U.S. Bureau of Labor Statistics, Labor Force Statistics from the Current Population Survey, "Employed persons by detailed industry, sex, race, and Hispanic or Latino ethnicity," February 2017, and earlier releases, <http://www.bls.gov/cps/tables.htm>.

Table 645. Unemployed Workers—Summary: 1990 to 2016

[In thousands (7,047 represents 7,047,000), except as indicated. For civilian noninstitutionalized population 16 years old and over. Annual averages of monthly figures. Revisions to population controls and other changes can affect the comparability of data over time. Based on the Current Population Survey; see text, Section 1 and Appendix III]

Item	1990	2000	2010	2011	2012	2013	2014	2015	2016
UNEMPLOYED									
Total [1]	7,047	5,692	14,825	13,747	12,506	11,460	9,617	8,296	7,751
16 to 19 years old	1,212	1,081	1,528	1,400	1,397	1,327	1,106	966	925
20 to 24 years old	1,299	1,022	2,329	2,234	2,054	1,997	1,747	1,501	1,286
25 to 34 years old	1,995	1,207	3,386	3,187	2,764	2,504	2,224	1,905	1,797
35 to 44 years old	1,328	1,133	2,703	2,389	2,158	1,913	1,539	1,351	1,258
45 to 54 years old	723	762	2769	2,493	2,181	1,945	1,507	1,259	1,189
55 to 64 years old	386	355	1660	1579	1,470	1,340	1,107	978	941
65 years and over	105	132	449	465	482	435	387	337	355
Male	3,906	2,975	8,626	7,684	6,771	6,314	5,190	4,490	4,187
16 to 19 years old	667	599	863	786	787	746	605	531	512
20 to 24 years old	715	547	1398	1275	1,163	1,143	996	865	742
25 to 34 years old	1,092	602	1993	1795	1,476	1,381	1,185	1,030	966
35 to 44 years old	711	557	1534	1316	1,124	1,015	813	695	644
45 to 54 years old	413	398	1614	1370	1,142	1,039	782	649	602
55 to 64 years old	249	189	962	882	811	741	600	536	528
65 years and over	59	83	262	261	268	250	210	184	193
Female	3,140	2,717	6,199	6,063	5,734	5,146	4,426	3,807	3,564
16 to 19 years old	544	483	665	613	609	581	501	435	413
20 to 24 years old	584	475	931	960	891	854	751	636	545
25 to 34 years old	902	604	1392	1392	1,288	1,123	1,039	874	832
35 to 44 years old	617	577	1169	1073	1,034	898	726	656	614
45 to 54 years old	310	364	1156	1123	1,039	906	725	610	586
55 to 64 years old	137	165	698	697	659	600	507	442	413
65 years and over	46	50	187	204	214	185	177	153	162
White [2]	5,186	4,121	10,916	9,889	8,915	8,033	6,540	5,662	5,345
Black [2]	1,565	1,241	2,852	2,831	2,544	2,429	2,141	1,846	1,655
Asian [2, 3]	(NA)	227	543	518	483	448	436	347	349
Hispanic [4]	876	954	2843	2,629	2,514	2,257	1,878	1,726	1,548
UNEMPLOYMENT RATE [5] (percent)									
Total [1]	5.6	4.0	9.6	8.9	8.1	7.4	6.2	5.3	4.9
16 to 19 years old	15.5	13.1	25.9	24.4	24.0	22.9	19.6	16.9	15.7
20 to 24 years old	8.8	7.2	15.5	14.6	13.3	12.8	11.2	9.7	8.4
25 to 34 years old	5.6	3.7	10.1	9.5	8.3	7.4	6.5	5.5	5.1
35 to 44 years old	4.1	3.0	8.1	7.3	6.6	5.9	4.7	4.1	3.8
45 to 54 years old	3.6	2.5	7.7	7.1	6.2	5.6	4.4	3.7	3.5
55 to 64 years old	3.3	2.5	7.1	6.6	5.9	5.3	4.3	3.8	3.6
65 years and over	3.0	3.1	6.7	6.5	6.2	5.4	4.6	3.8	3.8
Male	5.7	3.9	10.5	9.4	8.2	7.6	6.3	5.4	4.9
16 to 19 years old	16.3	14.0	28.8	27.2	26.8	25.5	21.4	18.4	17.1
20 to 24 years old	9.1	7.3	17.8	15.7	14.3	14.0	12.2	10.8	9.3
25 to 34 years old	5.5	3.4	10.9	9.7	8.2	7.6	6.4	5.5	5.0
35 to 44 years old	4.1	2.8	8.5	7.4	6.4	5.8	4.6	4.0	3.6
45 to 54 years old	3.7	2.4	8.6	7.4	6.2	5.7	4.4	3.6	3.4
55 to 64 years old	3.8	2.4	8.0	7.1	6.3	5.6	4.5	3.9	3.8
65 years and over	3.0	3.3	7.1	6.5	6.2	5.5	4.6	3.8	3.8
Female	5.5	4.1	8.6	8.5	7.9	7.1	6.1	5.2	4.8
16 to 19 years old	14.7	12.1	22.8	21.7	21.1	20.3	17.7	15.5	14.3
20 to 24 years old	8.5	7.1	13.0	13.4	12.1	11.5	10.1	8.5	7.4
25 to 34 years old	5.6	4.1	9.1	9.1	8.4	7.3	6.6	5.5	5.1
35 to 44 years old	4.2	3.3	7.7	7.2	6.8	6.0	4.9	4.4	4.1
45 to 54 years old	3.4	2.5	6.8	6.7	6.2	5.5	4.5	3.8	3.7
55 to 64 years old	2.8	2.5	6.2	6.1	5.6	5.0	4.2	3.6	3.3
65 years and over	3.1	2.7	6.2	6.5	6.3	5.1	4.7	3.9	3.9
White [2]	4.8	3.5	8.7	7.9	7.2	6.5	5.3	4.6	4.3
Black [2]	11.4	7.6	16.0	15.8	13.8	13.1	11.3	9.6	8.4
Asian [2, 3]	(NA)	3.6	7.5	7.0	5.9	5.2	5.0	3.8	3.6
Hispanic [4]	8.2	5.7	12.5	11.5	10.3	9.1	7.4	6.6	5.8
PERCENT WITHOUT WORK FOR—									
Fewer than 5 weeks	46.3	44.9	18.7	19.5	21.1	22.5	25.7	28.9	30.5
5 to 14 weeks	32.0	31.9	22.0	21.8	22.9	24.1	25.3	27.7	28.7
15 weeks and over	21.6	23.2	59.3	58.8	55.9	53.4	49.0	43.3	40.8
15 to 26 weeks	11.7	11.8	16.0	15.0	14.9	15.8	15.6	15.3	14.9
27 weeks and over	10.0	11.4	43.3	43.8	41.1	37.6	33.5	28.1	25.9
Unemployment duration, average (weeks) [6]	12.0	12.6	33.0	39.3	39.4	36.5	33.7	29.2	27.5

NA Not available. [1] Includes other races not shown separately. [2] For persons reporting this race group only. [3] Prior to 2003, includes Pacific Islanders. [4] Persons of Hispanic or Latino origin may be of any race. [5] Unemployed as percent of civilian labor force in specified group. [6] Beginning 2011, the CPS increased the maximum duration of unemployment that respondents could report from 2 years to 5 years. For more information, see <http://www.bls.gov/cps/duration.htm>.

Source: U.S. Bureau of Labor Statistics, "Labor Force Statistics from the Current Population Survey," <http://www.bls.gov/cps>, accessed June 2017.

Table 646. Unemployed Jobseekers' Job Search Methods: 2016

[7,751 represents 7,751,000. For the civilian noninstitutionalized population 16 years old and over. Annual averages of monthly data. Based on the Current Population Survey; see text, Section 1 and Appendix III]

Characteristic	Population (1,000)		Jobseekers' job search methods (percent)							Average number of methods used
	Total unemployed	Total jobseekers[1]	Contact employer directly	Sent out a resume or filled out applications	Placed or answered ads	Friends or relatives	Public employment agency	Private employment agency	Other activities	
Total, 16 years and over[2]...	7,751	6,785	50.6	57.7	15.4	25.8	15.9	8.0	13.6	1.9
AGE										
16 to 19 years old............	925	880	48.9	62.1	12.2	18.4	6.9	2.3	8.8	1.6
20 to 24 years old............	1,286	1,196	52.3	58.6	14.3	23.1	14.6	6.3	12.8	1.8
25 to 34 years old............	1,797	1,605	51.9	60.2	15.8	25.7	17.3	9.1	13.0	1.9
35 to 44 years old............	1,258	1,071	51.8	57.3	15.3	26.6	16.7	8.8	14.0	1.9
45 to 54 years old............	1,189	1,001	50.1	55.9	17.5	30.6	20.2	10.6	15.3	2.0
55 to 64 years old............	941	764	49.6	54.1	17.9	30.2	20.4	10.7	16.4	2.0
65 years old and over........	355	269	41.0	42.2	13.2	28.2	12.0	6.8	19.4	1.6
SEX										
Male, total..................	4,187	3,625	52.2	55.7	15.0	26.8	16.4	8.4	13.6	1.9
16 to 19 years old............	512	487	50.8	61.6	11.0	18.8	7.5	2.5	8.9	1.6
20 to 24 years old............	742	684	53.0	55.2	13.6	24.2	15.7	7.6	13.3	1.8
25 to 34 years old............	966	850	52.6	57.5	15.7	27.1	17.9	9.6	12.2	1.9
35 to 44 years old............	644	535	54.9	55.6	15.0	27.6	16.2	9.0	13.9	1.9
45 to 54 years old............	602	492	52.6	53.2	17.8	32.0	20.7	11.5	16.5	2.0
55 to 64 years old............	528	429	51.1	53.9	18.3	31.8	21.6	10.9	16.1	2.0
65 years old and over........	193	148	42.5	41.4	13.2	28.5	12.4	6.1	19.9	1.6
Female, total................	3,564	3,160	48.8	60.0	15.8	24.6	15.4	7.4	13.5	1.9
16 to 19 years old............	413	392	46.5	62.8	13.6	17.9	6.1	2.0	8.7	1.6
20 to 24 years old............	545	513	51.2	63.1	15.3	21.7	13.1	4.5	12.1	1.8
25 to 34 years old............	832	755	51.2	63.3	16.0	24.2	16.6	8.5	13.8	1.9
35 to 44 years old............	614	536	48.6	58.9	15.7	25.7	17.2	8.5	14.1	1.9
45 to 54 years old............	586	509	47.7	58.4	17.3	29.1	19.8	9.7	14.2	2.0
55 to 64 years old............	413	335	47.7	54.5	17.3	28.2	18.8	10.6	16.9	2.0
65 years old and over........	162	120	39.3	43.3	13.3	27.8	11.6	7.7	18.9	1.6
RACE/ETHNICITY										
White[3].....................	5,345	4,574	51.2	56.9	15.9	25.9	14.9	7.7	14.2	1.9
Male........................	2,952	2,501	52.7	55.3	15.4	26.5	15.0	8.2	14.3	1.9
Female......................	2,393	2,073	49.4	58.9	16.6	25.1	14.6	7.0	14.1	1.9
Black[3].....................	1,655	1,532	48.9	59.2	14.1	24.3	19.6	8.7	11.0	1.9
Male........................	845	776	50.0	57.4	13.9	25.7	20.7	9.1	10.4	1.9
Female......................	810	756	47.8	61.0	14.3	22.8	18.4	8.4	11.5	1.8
Asian[3].....................	349	323	50.9	56.3	16.1	32.7	15.8	10.3	17.5	2.0
Male........................	176	166	52.8	53.5	16.8	34.5	18.1	11.5	18.4	2.1
Female......................	172	157	48.9	59.3	15.5	30.9	13.3	9.0	16.5	1.9
Hispanic[4]..................	1,548	1,314	50.9	53.6	12.7	29.3	15.9	8.1	12.3	1.8
Male........................	833	690	52.8	51.4	12.6	29.7	16.7	8.5	11.9	1.8
Female......................	715	624	48.8	56.1	12.9	29.0	15.1	7.7	12.7	1.8

[1] Excludes persons on temporary layoff. [2] Includes other races not shown separately. [3] Data for this race group only. [4] Persons of Hispanic or Latino origin may be of any race.

Source: U.S. Bureau of Labor Statistics, CPS Tables, "Unemployed jobseekers by sex, age, race, Hispanic or Latino ethnicity, and active jobsearch methods used," February 2017, <http://www.bls.gov/cps/tables.htm>.

Table 647. Unemployed Persons by Sex and Reason: 2000 to 2016

[In thousands (2,975 represents 2,975,000). For civilian noninstitutionalized population 16 years old and over. Annual averages of monthly figures. Revisions to population controls and other changes affect comparability of data over time. Based on Current Population Survey; see text, Section 1 and Appendix III]

Sex and reason	2000	2006	2007	2008	2009	2010	2011	2012	2013	2014	2015	2016
Male, total.............	**2,975**	**3,753**	**3,882**	**5,033**	**8,453**	**8,626**	**7,684**	**6,771**	**6,314**	**5,190**	**4,490**	**4,187**
Job losers[1]...............	1,516	2,021	2,175	3,055	5,967	5,919	4,968	4,103	3,690	2,926	2,441	2,232
Job leavers...............	387	406	408	458	438	457	494	487	465	416	397	414
Reentrants...............	854	1,015	956	1128	1,504	1,608	1,545	1481	1,491	1,279	1,178	1108
New entrants.............	217	312	343	393	545	641	678	699	668	569	474	433
Female, total...........	**2,717**	**3,247**	**3,196**	**3,891**	**5,811**	**6,199**	**6,063**	**5,734**	**5,146**	**4,426**	**3,807**	**3,564**
Job losers[1]...............	1,001	1,300	1,340	1,735	3,193	3,331	3,139	2,774	2,383	1,952	1,622	1,508
Job leavers...............	393	421	385	438	444	432	463	480	467	408	423	444
Reentrants...............	1,107	1,223	1,186	1,345	1,683	1,858	1,857	1,864	1,716	1,550	1,357	1,222
New entrants.............	217	304	285	374	491	579	605	617	579	517	405	390

[1] Persons who completed temporary jobs are identified separately and are included as job losers.

Source: U.S. Bureau of Labor Statistics, CPS Tables, "Unemployed jobseekers by sex, reason for unemployment, and active jobsearch methods used," March 2017, and earlier releases, <http://www.bls.gov/cps/tables.htm>.

Table 648. Unemployment Rates by Industry and by Sex: 2010 to 2016

[In percent. Civilian noninstitutionalized population 16 years old and over. Annual averages of monthly figures. Rate represents unemployment as a percent of labor force in each specified group. Based on Current Population Survey; see text, Section 1 and Appendix III. See also headnote, Table 629, regarding industries]

Industry	Total				Male		Female	
	2010	2014	2015	2016	2015	2016	2015	2016
All employed [1]	**9.6**	**6.2**	**5.3**	**4.9**	**5.4**	**4.9**	**5.2**	**4.8**
Wage and salary workers:								
Agriculture and related industries	13.9	9.4	9.4	8.3	8.7	7.5	11.7	11.0
Mining, quarrying, and oil and gas extraction	9.4	4.7	8.6	8.0	9.1	8.3	5.4	5.6
Construction	20.6	8.9	7.3	6.3	7.5	6.4	5.4	4.6
Manufacturing	10.6	4.9	4.3	4.3	4.0	4.0	5.1	4.8
Wholesale trade	7.3	4.4	3.8	3.6	3.4	3.4	4.5	4.0
Retail trade	10.0	6.5	5.9	5.3	5.5	4.9	6.4	5.7
Transportation and utilities	8.4	5.7	4.4	4.2	3.8	4.1	6.4	4.7
Transportation and warehousing	9.4	6.3	4.8	4.4	4.2	4.3	6.7	4.8
Utilities	3.4	2.1	2.2	3.1	1.3	2.8	4.9	4.1
Information	9.7	5.2	3.9	4.6	3.3	4.3	4.8	5.0
Telecommunications	9.2	4.0	3.1	3.3	2.9	3.2	3.4	3.4
Financial activities	6.9	4.0	2.6	2.7	2.7	2.6	2.5	2.8
Finance and insurance	6.6	3.8	2.3	2.4	2.3	2.3	2.4	2.5
Real estate and rental and leasing	7.6	4.5	3.3	3.6	3.5	3.3	3.0	3.9
Professional and business services	10.8	6.9	5.6	5.1	5.5	4.9	5.8	5.3
Professional and technical services	6.5	4.1	3.2	2.8	2.9	2.5	3.7	3.2
Management, administrative, and waste services	16.8	11.2	9.3	8.6	9.3	8.5	9.2	8.8
Education and health services	5.8	4.2	3.6	3.3	3.3	3.2	3.7	3.3
Educational services	6.4	4.9	4.4	4.1	4.5	4.3	4.4	3.9
Health care and social assistance	5.6	4.0	3.4	3.1	2.8	2.7	3.5	3.2
Leisure and hospitality	12.2	8.6	7.9	6.8	7.8	6.6	8.0	6.9
Arts, entertainment, and recreation	11.6	8.4	7.4	6.3	7.8	6.7	6.9	5.9
Accommodation and food services	12.3	8.6	8.0	6.9	7.8	6.5	8.2	7.1
Other services	8.5	5.7	5.2	4.4	4.9	4.0	5.4	4.8
Government workers	4.4	3.2	2.7	2.7	2.8	2.7	2.6	2.7

[1] Includes a small amount of persons whose last job was in the Armed Forces.

Source: U.S. Bureau of Labor Statistics, CPS Tables, "Unemployed persons by industry, class of worker, and sex," February 2017, and earlier releases, <http://www.bls.gov/cps/tables.htm>.

Table 649. Unemployment by Occupation: 2010 to 2016

[14,825 represents 14,825,000. Civilian noninstitutionalized population 16 years old and over. Annual averages of monthly data. Rate represents unemployment as a percent of the labor force for each specified group. Based on Current Population Survey; see text, Section 1 and Appendix III. See also headnote, Table 629, regarding occupations]

Occupation	Number unemployed (1,000)				Unemployment rate				
							2016		
	2010	2014	2015	2016	2010	2015	Total	Male	Female
Total [1]	**14,825**	**9,617**	**8,296**	**7,751**	**9.6**	**5.3**	**4.9**	**4.9**	**4.8**
Management, professional, and related occupations	2,566	1,777	1,504	1,513	4.7	2.5	2.5	2.4	2.6
Management, business, and financial operations	1,117	704	602	629	5.1	2.4	2.5	2.3	2.7
Management	762	440	386	404	4.8	2.2	2.3	2.1	2.5
Business and financial operations	355	263	217	225	5.6	3.0	2.9	2.7	3.0
Professional and related occupations	1,449	1,073	902	884	4.5	2.6	2.5	2.5	2.5
Computer and mathematical	195	120	115	120	5.2	2.6	2.5	2.3	3.1
Architecture and engineering	173	91	80	78	6.2	2.6	2.5	2.5	2.2
Life, physical, and social science	69	54	41	34	4.6	2.8	2.4	2.6	2.3
Community and social services	114	79	59	70	4.6	2.2	2.6	2.2	2.8
Legal	48	44	31	23	2.7	1.7	1.2	0.9	1.5
Education, training, and library	379	306	276	271	4.2	3.0	2.9	2.9	3.0
Arts, design, entertainment, sports, and media	269	193	145	155	8.9	4.5	4.8	5.0	4.5
Healthcare practitioner and technical	203	186	154	133	2.5	1.7	1.5	1.1	1.6
Service occupations	2,819	2,048	1,855	1,655	10.3	6.7	5.8	5.9	5.7
Healthcare support	276	197	185	168	7.6	5.0	4.5	4.1	4.6
Protective service	207	145	129	119	5.9	4.0	3.7	3.2	5.4
Food preparation and serving-related	1,079	758	702	627	12.4	7.9	6.8	7.0	6.7
Building and grounds cleaning and maintenance	780	550	484	430	12.8	7.8	6.9	7.1	6.6
Personal care and service	477	397	354	312	8.7	6.1	5.1	4.8	5.2
Sales and office occupations	3,315	2,119	1,792	1,623	9.0	5.1	4.6	4.3	4.8
Sales and related	1,596	1,022	909	799	9.4	5.5	4.8	3.8	5.8
Office and administrative support	1,719	1,096	883	825	8.7	4.7	4.5	5.2	4.2
Natural resources, construction, and maintenance	2,504	1,171	1,058	953	16.1	7.2	6.4	6.1	11.4
Farming, fishing, and forestry	193	134	132	127	16.3	10.9	10.4	8.2	17.2
Construction and extraction	1,809	813	701	618	20.1	8.4	7.2	7.1	9.9
Installation, maintenance, and repair	503	224	225	207	9.3	4.3	4.1	4.1	4.3
Production, transportation, and material moving	2,365	1,385	1,182	1,160	12.8	6.3	6.1	5.7	7.6
Production	1,206	632	513	516	13.1	5.7	5.7	5.1	7.2
Transportation and material moving	1,159	754	668	644	12.4	6.8	6.5	6.2	8.0

[1] Includes a small amount of persons whose last job was in the Armed Forces.

Source: U.S. Bureau of Labor Statistics, CPS Tables, "Unemployed persons by occupation and sex," February 2017, and earlier releases, <http://www.bls.gov/cps/tables.htm>.

Table 650. Unemployed and Unemployment Rates by Educational Attainment, Sex, Race, and Hispanic Origin: 2000 to 2016

[3,589 represents 3,589,000. Annual averages of monthly figures. Civilian noninstitutionalized population 25 years old and over. See Table 616 for civilian labor force and participation rate data. Revisions to population controls and other changes can affect the comparability of data over time. Based on Current Population Survey; see text, Section 1 and Appendix III]

Year, sex, and race/ethnicity	Unemployed (1,000)					Unemployment rate [1]				
	Total	Less than a high school diploma	High school graduate, no college	Some college or associate's degree	Bachelor's degree or higher	Total	Less than a high school diploma	High school graduate, no college	Some college or associate's degree	Bachelor's degree or higher
Total: [2]										
2000	3,589	791	1,298	890	610	3.0	6.3	3.4	2.7	1.7
2010	10,968	1,765	3,943	3,093	2,167	8.2	14.9	10.3	8.4	4.7
2016	5,540	795	1,847	1,549	1,349	4.0	7.4	5.2	4.1	2.5
Male:										
2000	1,829	411	682	427	309	2.8	5.4	3.4	2.6	1.5
2010	6,365	1,137	2,452	1,646	1,130	8.9	15.0	11.3	9.0	4.8
2016	2,933	448	1,069	755	661	4.0	6.6	5.1	4.0	2.4
Female:										
2000	1,760	380	616	463	301	3.2	7.8	3.5	2.8	1.8
2010	4,603	628	1,492	1,447	1,037	7.4	14.6	9.0	7.8	4.7
2016	2,606	346	778	794	688	4.1	8.9	5.2	4.2	2.6
White: [3]										
2000	2,644	564	924	667	489	2.6	5.6	2.9	2.4	1.6
2010	8,174	1,337	2,937	2,278	1,622	7.5	13.9	9.5	7.6	4.3
2016	3,863	549	1,251	1,078	985	3.6	6.5	4.5	3.6	2.3
Black: [3]										
2000	731	179	315	169	68	5.4	10.7	6.4	4.0	2.5
2010	2,022	321	795	614	292	13.4	22.5	15.8	12.4	7.9
2016	1,131	175	448	332	176	6.8	14.1	8.6	6.1	3.7
Asian: [3, 4]										
2000	146	28	34	35	49	2.7	5.7	3.0	3.2	1.8
2010	446	54	95	92	205	6.8	11.1	7.6	8.1	5.5
2016	279	20	59	55	145	3.2	3.9	4.0	3.9	2.8
Hispanic: [5]										
2000	569	297	150	85	38	4.4	6.2	3.9	3.2	2.2
2010	2,041	787	674	399	182	10.8	13.2	11.5	9.7	6.0
2016	1,049	344	346	224	135	4.7	5.9	5.1	4.3	3.1

[1] Unemployed as percent of the civilian labor force. [2] Includes other races, not shown separately. [3] Beginning 2003, data are for persons in this race group only; 2000 data reflect the primary race persons identified with. [4] 2000 data include Pacific Islanders. [5] Persons of Hispanic origin may be of any race.

Source: U.S. Bureau of Labor Statistics, CPS Tables, "Employment status of the civilian noninstitutional population 25 years and over by educational attainment, sex, race, and Hispanic or Latino ethnicity," February 2017, and earlier releases, <http://www.bls.gov/cps/tables.htm>.

Table 651. Unemployed Persons by Reason for Unemployment and Duration: 2016

[7,751 represents 7,751,000. Annual averages of monthly data. Based on Current Population Survey; see text, Section 1 and Appendix III]

Age, sex, and reason	Total unemployed (1,000)	Less than 5 weeks	5 to 14 weeks	Percent distribution by duration		
				15 weeks and over		
				Total	15 to 26 weeks	27 weeks or longer
Total 16 years old and over	7,751	30.5	28.7	40.8	14.9	25.9
16 to 19 years old	925	41.7	32.4	25.9	12.7	13.2
Total 20 years old and over	6,826	(NA)	(NA)	(NA)	(NA)	(NA)
Males, 20 years old and over	3,675	28.4	27.4	44.2	15.3	28.9
Job losers and persons who completed temporary jobs	2,165	31.5	28.4	40.1	15.7	24.4
On temporary layoff	537	52.5	32.4	15.1	10.7	4.4
Not on temporary layoff	1,628	24.6	27.1	48.3	17.3	31.0
Permanent job losers	1,148	22.5	25.9	51.6	17.9	33.6
Persons who completed temporary jobs	480	29.6	29.8	40.6	15.8	24.8
Job leavers	388	31.2	31.3	37.5	14.5	23.0
Reentrants	936	22.5	24.6	52.9	14.8	38.1
New entrants	185	15.9	22.1	62.0	14.9	47.1
Females, 20 years old and over	3,151	29.6	29.2	41.2	15.2	26.0
Job losers and persons who completed temporary jobs	1,461	32.8	29.6	37.6	14.6	22.9
On temporary layoff	383	55.5	33.6	11.0	7.4	3.6
Not on temporary layoff	1,078	24.8	28.1	47.1	17.2	29.8
Permanent job losers	780	23.2	28.4	48.4	17.8	30.6
Persons who completed temporary jobs	298	29.1	27.3	43.6	15.7	27.8
Job leavers	417	32.6	33.6	33.8	14.9	18.8
Reentrants	1,087	25.6	27.7	46.7	16.1	30.7
New entrants	186	20.5	24.9	54.6	15.5	39.1

NA Not available.

Source: U.S. Bureau of Labor Statistics, CPS Tables, "Unemployed persons by reason for unemployment, sex, age, and duration of unemployment," February 2017, <http://www.bls.gov/cps/tables.htm>.

Table 652. Total Unemployed and Insured Unemployed by State: 2000 to 2016

[5,692 represents 5,692,000. Civilian noninstitutionalized population 16 years old and over. Annual averages of monthly figures. State total unemployment estimates come from the Local Area Unemployment Statistics program, while U.S. totals come from the Current Population Survey; see text, Section 1 and Appendix III. U.S. totals derived by independent population controls; therefore state data may not add to U.S. totals. Unemployment data are based on population controls from Census 2010]

| State | Total unemployed | | | | | | | | Insured unemployed [2,4] | | | |
| | Number (1,000) | | | | Percent [1] | | | | Number (1,000) | | Percent [3] | |
	2000	2010	2015	2016	2000	2010	2015	2016	2010	2016	2010	2016
United States	5,692	14,825	8,296	7,751	4.0	9.6	5.3	4.9	4,487	2,099	3.6	1.5
Alabama	98	231	132	130	4.6	10.5	6.1	6.0	53	22	3.0	1.2
Alaska	20	28	23	24	6.4	7.9	6.4	6.6	14	9	4.6	3.0
Arizona	99	320	191	172	4.0	10.4	6.0	5.3	79	30	3.5	1.2
Arkansas	54	111	67	54	4.3	8.2	5.1	4.0	44	17	4.0	1.5
California	835	2,244	1,170	1,038	4.9	12.2	6.2	5.4	655	362	4.6	2.2
Colorado	65	238	111	96	2.8	8.7	3.9	3.3	64	28	3.0	1.1
Connecticut	42	174	108	96	2.4	9.1	5.7	5.1	67	39	4.3	2.4
Delaware	15	37	23	21	3.7	8.4	4.8	4.4	13	6	3.4	1.5
District of Columbia	17	33	27	24	5.6	9.4	6.9	6.0	5	4	1.1	0.7
Florida	291	1,018	521	480	3.7	11.1	5.4	4.9	225	48	3.2	0.6
Georgia	151	495	285	264	3.6	10.5	6.0	5.4	117	33	3.2	0.8
Hawaii	26	45	24	21	4.2	6.9	3.6	3.0	17	7	3.1	1.1
Idaho	31	68	34	31	4.7	9.0	4.2	3.8	26	8	4.5	1.2
Illinois	282	688	386	384	4.3	10.4	5.9	5.9	220	116	4.1	2.0
Indiana	97	330	158	147	3.1	10.4	4.8	4.4	79	27	3.0	0.9
Iowa	42	101	65	62	2.6	6.0	3.8	3.7	40	22	2.9	1.5
Kansas	50	106	62	62	3.6	7.1	4.2	4.2	37	14	2.9	1.0
Kentucky	82	210	104	100	4.2	10.2	5.3	5.0	50	23	3.0	1.2
Louisiana	108	166	137	129	5.3	8.0	6.3	6.1	55	16	3.1	0.8
Maine	23	57	30	27	3.4	8.1	4.4	3.9	18	8	3.2	1.3
Maryland	100	235	161	136	3.6	7.7	5.1	4.3	73	38	3.1	1.5
Massachusetts	90	289	174	133	2.7	8.3	4.9	3.7	116	68	3.7	2.0
Michigan	186	605	257	238	3.6	12.6	5.4	4.9	160	64	4.3	1.5
Minnesota	89	218	111	117	3.2	7.4	3.7	3.9	81	45	3.2	1.6
Mississippi	71	136	81	75	5.4	10.4	6.4	5.8	36	13	3.4	1.2
Missouri	106	293	155	141	3.6	9.6	5.0	4.5	75	28	3.0	1.1
Montana	23	37	22	22	5.0	7.3	4.2	4.1	17	8	4.2	1.9
Nebraska	27	46	31	32	2.8	4.6	3.0	3.2	19	6	2.1	0.6
Nevada	45	184	96	81	4.2	13.5	6.8	5.7	54	23	4.9	1.9
New Hampshire	18	43	25	21	2.7	5.8	3.4	2.8	18	4	3.1	0.7
New Jersey	158	434	263	224	3.7	9.5	5.8	5.0	166	104	4.5	2.7
New Mexico	42	76	61	62	4.9	8.1	6.6	6.7	25	13	3.4	1.6
New York	415	826	507	463	4.5	8.6	5.3	4.8	290	161	3.5	1.8
North Carolina	152	501	274	246	3.7	10.9	5.8	5.1	156	27	4.2	0.6
North Dakota	10	14	12	13	3.0	3.8	2.8	3.2	5	6	1.5	1.4
Ohio	231	600	279	282	4.0	10.3	4.9	4.9	144	63	3.0	1.2
Oklahoma	50	120	80	89	3.0	6.8	4.4	4.9	34	21	2.4	1.4
Oregon	93	211	111	100	5.1	10.6	5.6	4.9	83	30	5.3	1.7
Pennsylvania	252	540	341	352	4.1	8.5	5.3	5.4	265	136	4.9	2.4
Rhode Island	22	63	33	29	4.1	11.2	6.0	5.3	18	10	4.1	2.1
South Carolina	75	241	136	111	3.8	11.2	6.0	4.8	71	16	4.1	0.8
South Dakota	10	22	14	13	2.5	5.0	3.1	2.8	4	2	1.2	0.5
Tennessee	110	299	172	151	3.9	9.7	5.6	4.8	68	20	2.7	0.7
Texas	445	997	581	613	4.3	8.1	4.5	4.6	216	173	2.2	1.5
Utah	38	106	53	52	3.3	7.8	3.6	3.4	28	11	2.5	0.8
Vermont	9	22	12	11	2.8	6.1	3.6	3.3	10	5	3.6	1.6
Virginia	83	297	188	170	2.3	7.1	4.5	4.0	62	28	1.8	0.8
Washington	158	351	200	198	5.2	10.0	5.6	5.4	109	50	4.0	1.6
West Virginia	44	70	53	47	5.5	8.7	6.8	6.0	21	16	3.2	2.5
Wisconsin	105	267	141	129	3.5	8.7	4.6	4.1	122	41	4.7	1.5
Wyoming	10	20	13	16	3.9	6.4	4.2	5.3	7	5	2.6	2.0

[1] Total unemployment as percent of civilian labor force. [2] Number of jobless workers who are receiving state unemployment benefits. Source: U.S. Employment and Training Administration, "Unemployment Insurance, Financial Data Handbook 394," <https://workforcesecurity.doleta.gov/unemploy/hb394.asp>, accessed August 2017. [3] Those currently collecting unemployment insurance as a percent of the total number of eligible workers. [4] U.S. totals include Puerto Rico and the Virgin Islands.

Source: Except as noted, U.S. Bureau of Labor Statistics, "Local Area Unemployment Statistics," <http://www.bls.gov/lau/>, accessed August 2017.

Table 653. Nonfarm Establishments—Employees, Hours, and Earnings by Industry: 1990 to 2016

[109,527 represents 109,527,000. Annual averages of monthly data. Based on data from establishment reports. Includes all full- and part-time employees who worked during, or received pay for, any part of the pay period including the 12th of the month. Excludes proprietors, the self-employed, farm workers, unpaid family workers, private household workers, and Armed Forces. Establishment data shown here conform to industry definitions in the 2012 North American Industry Classification System (NAICS) and are adjusted to March employment benchmarks. Based on the Current Employment Statistics Program; see source and Appendix III]

Item and year	Total nonfarm	Total[1]	Construction	Manufacturing	Wholesale trade	Retail trade	Transportation and warehousing	Utilities	Information	Finance and insurance	Real estate and rental and leasing	Professional, scientific, and technical services	Administrative and waste services	Educational services	Health care and social assistance	Arts entertainment and recreation	Accommodations and food services	Government
EMPLOYEES (1,000)																		
1990	109,527	91,112	5,263	17,695	5,268	13,182	3,476	740	2,688	4,976	1,637	4,538	4,643	1,688	9,336	1,132	8,156	18,415
2000	132,024	111,235	6,787	17,263	5,933	15,280	4,410	601	3,630	5,773	2,011	6,702	8,168	2,390	12,861	1,788	10,074	20,790
2005	134,051	112,247	7,336	14,227	5,764	15,280	4,361	554	3,061	6,063	2,134	7,025	8,170	2,836	14,840	1,892	10,923	21,804
2010	130,361	107,871	5,518	11,528	5,452	14,440	4,191	553	2,707	5,761	1,934	7,441	7,414	3,155	16,820	1,913	11,135	22,490
2012	134,175	112,255	5,646	11,927	5,667	14,841	4,416	553	2,676	5,828	1,955	7,892	8,016	3,341	17,428	1,969	11,800	21,920
2013	136,381	114,529	5,856	12,020	5,733	15,079	4,498	552	2,706	5,886	2,000	8,121	8,291	3,354	17,731	2,030	12,224	21,853
2014	138,958	117,076	6,151	12,185	5,813	15,357	4,661	552	2,726	5,931	2,046	8,336	8,558	3,417	18,022	2,103	12,593	21,882
2015	141,843	119,814	6,461	12,336	5,855	15,605	4,871	556	2,750	6,035	2,088	8,608	8,818	3,472	18,557	2,166	12,994	22,029
2016	144,306	122,083	6,711	12,348	5,867	15,820	4,989	556	2,772	6,142	2,143	8,877	9,018	3,560	19,056	2,235	13,386	22,223
WEEKLY EARNINGS[2] (dol.)																		
1990	(NA)	349.63	513.43	436.13	444.48	235.56	471.82	670.80	479.50	(NA)	(NA)	504.83	273.60	(NA)	319.26	219.02	147.92	(NA)
2000	(NA)	480.99	685.78	591.04	631.24	333.41	562.56	955.09	700.92	(NA)	(NA)	745.94	387.59	(NA)	447.45	273.79	207.44	(NA)
2005	(NA)	544.00	750.37	673.34	685.00	377.58	618.55	1,095.91	805.11	(NA)	(NA)	862.76	431.92	(NA)	555.82	330.31	226.48	(NA)
2010	(NA)	636.19	891.83	765.18	816.50	400.07	710.85	1,262.89	939.85	(NA)	(NA)	1,073.92	535.79	(NA)	652.07	363.91	266.78	(NA)
2012	(NA)	665.65	942.14	794.63	860.70	422.10	742.22	1,298.23	973.52	(NA)	(NA)	1,108.50	550.84	(NA)	687.56	377.92	276.19	(NA)
2013	(NA)	677.70	958.72	807.37	875.79	423.07	762.06	1,344.70	1,003.65	(NA)	(NA)	1,129.48	557.81	(NA)	696.05	379.58	280.48	(NA)
2014	(NA)	694.85	977.11	822.03	897.73	431.82	788.77	1,388.91	1,030.17	(NA)	(NA)	1,173.59	568.23	(NA)	706.15	388.40	290.05	(NA)
2015	(NA)	708.90	998.02	832.05	911.41	445.52	804.49	1,444.03	1,038.10	(NA)	(NA)	1,201.16	568.75	(NA)	722.49	379.22	300.17	(NA)
2016	(NA)	723.69	1,031.16	855.69	933.16	447.62	811.02	1,501.50	1,068.25	(NA)	(NA)	1,224.52	585.56	(NA)	737.90	380.39	309.92	(NA)
WEEKLY HOURS[2]																		
1990	(NA)	34.3	38.3	40.5	38.4	30.6	37.7	41.6	35.8	(NA)	(NA)	36.1	32.3	(NA)	31.8	26.1	25.9	(NA)
2000	(NA)	34.3	39.2	41.3	38.8	30.7	37.4	42.0	36.8	(NA)	(NA)	36.2	33.1	(NA)	32.1	25.6	26.2	(NA)
2005	(NA)	33.8	38.6	40.7	37.7	30.6	37.0	41.1	36.5	(NA)	(NA)	35.7	32.8	(NA)	32.8	25.7	25.7	(NA)
2010	(NA)	33.4	38.4	41.1	37.9	30.2	37.1	42.0	36.3	(NA)	(NA)	35.9	33.9	(NA)	32.2	23.8	25.0	(NA)
2012	(NA)	33.7	39.3	41.7	38.7	30.6	38.0	41.1	36.0	(NA)	(NA)	36.0	34.2	(NA)	32.4	23.7	25.2	(NA)
2013	(NA)	33.7	39.6	41.8	38.7	30.2	38.5	41.7	35.9	(NA)	(NA)	36.1	34.3	(NA)	32.2	23.9	25.1	(NA)
2014	(NA)	33.7	39.6	42.0	38.6	30.0	38.4	42.3	35.9	(NA)	(NA)	36.4	34.5	(NA)	32.2	24.1	25.3	(NA)
2015	(NA)	33.7	39.6	41.8	38.6	30.1	38.8	42.4	35.7	(NA)	(NA)	36.4	34.0	(NA)	32.2	23.7	25.3	(NA)
2016	(NA)	33.6	39.7	41.9	38.6	29.7	38.8	42.5	35.6	(NA)	(NA)	36.3	33.9	(NA)	32.3	23.3	25.1	(NA)
HOURLY EARNINGS[2] (dol.)																		
1990	(NA)	10.20	13.42	10.78	11.58	7.71	12.50	16.14	13.40	(NA)	(NA)	13.99	8.48	(NA)	10.03	8.41	5.70	(NA)
2000	(NA)	14.02	17.48	14.32	16.28	10.87	15.05	22.75	19.07	(NA)	(NA)	20.61	11.69	(NA)	13.93	10.68	7.92	(NA)
2005	(NA)	16.12	19.46	16.56	18.16	12.36	16.70	26.68	22.06	(NA)	(NA)	24.14	13.16	(NA)	16.94	12.85	8.80	(NA)
2010	(NA)	19.05	23.22	18.61	21.54	13.25	19.16	30.04	25.87	(NA)	(NA)	29.94	15.80	(NA)	20.23	15.27	10.68	(NA)
2012	(NA)	19.74	23.97	19.08	22.24	13.82	19.54	31.61	27.04	(NA)	(NA)	30.76	16.10	(NA)	21.19	15.96	10.96	(NA)
2013	(NA)	20.13	24.22	19.30	22.62	14.02	19.81	32.27	27.98	(NA)	(NA)	31.32	16.28	(NA)	21.59	15.88	11.16	(NA)
2014	(NA)	20.61	24.67	19.56	23.24	14.40	20.51	32.86	28.70	(NA)	(NA)	32.23	16.48	(NA)	21.96	16.14	11.47	(NA)
2015	(NA)	21.03	25.20	19.91	23.63	14.82	20.75	34.02	29.05	(NA)	(NA)	32.96	16.72	(NA)	22.41	15.97	11.87	(NA)
2016	(NA)	21.54	25.97	20.43	24.18	15.05	20.92	35.31	30.04	(NA)	(NA)	33.73	17.27	(NA)	22.84	16.35	12.32	(NA)

NA Not available. [1] Includes other industries not shown separately. [2] Average hours and earnings of production and nonsupervisory employees.

Source: U.S. Bureau of Labor Statistics, Current Employment Statistics, "Employment, Hours, and Earnings—National," <http://www.bls.gov/ces/home.htm>, accessed March 2017.

Table 654. Employees in Nonfarm Establishments by State and Industry: 2016

[In thousands (144,593.2 represents 144,593,200). Includes all full- and part-time employees who worked during, or received pay for, any part of the pay period reported. Excludes proprietors, the self-employed, farm workers, unpaid family workers, private household workers, and Armed Forces. Compiled from data supplied by cooperating state agencies. Based on North American Industry Classification System, 2012; see text, section 15]

State	Total [1]	Construction	Manufacturing	Trade, transportation and utilities	Information	Financial activities [2]	Professional and business services [3]	Education and health services [4]	Leisure and hospitality [5]	Other services [6]	Government
U.S.	144,593.2	6,705.6	12,329.4	27,284.4	2,811.6	8,222.1	20,087.3	22,664.3	15,595.9	5,665.3	22,563.3
AL	1,975.8	84.3	260.7	380.3	20.6	96.5	234.0	232.8	197.7	80.1	379.3
AK	332.4	16.3	13.4	65.3	6.3	12.1	28.2	48.6	35.4	11.1	81.2
AZ	2,704.1	134.5	160.0	516.4	45.3	202.1	413.3	411.1	310.0	89.1	410.8
AR	1,227.5	50.3	154.8	252.2	13.5	51.2	142.5	181.4	115.4	47.4	212.4
CA	16,477.4	774.1	1,305.6	2,990.2	523.1	822.9	2,530.8	2,537.4	1,897.3	556.9	2,514.6
CO	2,598.3	154.6	142.2	454.4	71.7	163.3	405.7	327.2	323.6	105.7	426.4
CT	1,679.1	59.0	156.3	298.4	32.3	130.0	217.7	329.5	154.0	65.0	236.3
DE	452.8	20.8	25.8	82.5	4.6	47.1	61.1	77.1	49.8	18.7	65.3
DC	782.2	15.2	1.2	32.5	17.0	30.0	165.6	134.3	75.1	72.1	239.4
FL	8,383.4	473.4	355.4	1,718.1	137.0	546.7	1,284.8	1,243.4	1,174.6	349.8	1,094.5
GA	4,378.0	176.1	388.2	926.0	111.4	238.9	653.4	561.7	469.4	157.6	685.9
HI	647.6	37.8	14.0	119.9	8.8	28.5	83.5	83.4	118.2	27.2	126.3
ID	696.2	41.7	64.7	137.7	9.0	34.1	86.3	101.0	72.2	24.3	121.5
IL	6,012.8	217.0	574.1	1,208.8	98.7	383.2	934.6	914.3	594.0	250.7	829.3
IN	3,082.8	130.6	522.7	595.1	32.5	133.8	334.8	464.1	307.2	126.8	428.9
IA	1,570.4	80.7	213.3	316.0	22.5	108.5	138.7	228.6	142.5	59.3	258.0
KS	1,409.9	61.2	160.4	266.9	20.7	85.6	178.3	196.3	127.3	50.5	255.9
KY	1,914.2	77.0	248.7	397.2	22.9	93.6	218.5	268.9	192.9	65.3	318.6
LA	1,971.3	140.6	135.8	387.9	23.6	92.2	210.7	310.2	231.5	75.5	325.4
ME	617.3	27.4	50.7	120.5	7.7	30.9	65.5	125.3	65.2	21.7	100.1
MD	2,707.8	160.6	103.8	466.6	37.7	149.0	441.4	458.7	271.3	113.6	504.0
MA	3,561.5	145.8	245.5	573.7	89.0	223.7	549.0	781.9	360.1	136.3	455.5
MI	4,325.6	155.6	600.2	781.6	57.5	212.9	650.0	664.8	425.7	169.6	600.7
MN	2,895.6	116.2	317.9	532.1	50.6	175.6	372.3	521.9	263.2	115.6	424.0
MS	1,144.6	44.2	142.9	229.3	12.1	43.8	107.2	140.2	133.4	40.1	244.4
MO	2,842.3	120.6	262.8	545.6	53.2	169.0	378.8	457.1	300.7	116.4	434.1
MT	467.7	27.2	19.5	95.2	6.4	23.8	40.7	74.1	64.4	18.2	91.3
NE	1,015.0	50.6	96.8	205.1	18.5	73.4	117.9	152.6	90.3	36.8	172.1
NV	1,299.9	76.3	43.6	241.8	14.4	62.7	176.6	127.5	345.7	40.1	157.5
NH	668.3	25.6	68.1	140.0	12.5	37.0	77.8	121.0	70.3	24.3	90.8
NJ	4,075.5	153.0	241.7	866.0	73.1	248.4	662.4	675.4	369.7	170.1	614.2
NM	830.6	43.4	26.9	138.9	12.8	33.5	101.2	138.7	95.6	28.6	191.4
NY	9,395.9	372.9	451.3	1,573.0	267.1	712.4	1,296.5	1,951.3	914.2	405.7	1,446.5
NC	4,339.9	200.6	465.0	813.9	78.5	226.4	607.4	584.9	480.3	150.7	726.6
ND	434.8	32.1	24.6	96.5	6.7	24.1	34.8	62.0	39.4	16.0	83.3
OH	5,480.9	205.7	685.5	1,020.6	72.3	299.8	722.2	923.8	550.8	212.6	776.5
OK	1,651.7	77.1	128.7	306.7	21.3	78.8	180.5	233.9	164.4	62.7	353.6
OR	1,832.7	90.6	187.8	341.5	33.5	96.8	238.3	266.7	199.0	63.7	307.0
PA	5,883.6	238.5	558.1	1,127.7	84.6	316.7	792.7	1,221.1	558.0	257.7	703.9
RI	490.0	18.2	40.4	76.4	8.0	33.4	65.7	106.4	57.8	23.1	60.5
SC	2,053.9	94.8	238.4	394.5	27.1	100.0	268.0	241.9	246.9	74.4	363.9
SD	432.7	22.9	42.0	88.4	5.8	29.3	31.3	70.4	46.8	16.1	78.7
TN	2,965.8	115.2	343.3	617.0	45.5	152.8	405.6	424.3	320.3	110.3	427.5
TX	12,028.4	701.6	847.1	2,421.7	201.9	732.5	1,627.4	1,632.9	1,291.8	425.7	1,923.7
UT	1,427.4	91.7	125.9	272.1	36.8	81.8	202.9	191.9	138.4	39.5	238.1
VT	313.1	15.3	29.9	55.5	4.6	12.0	27.7	64.4	36.5	10.5	55.9
VA	3,917.6	187.5	232.5	662.3	68.0	200.5	715.3	531.2	398.2	199.6	714.4
WA	3,244.1	186.1	290.0	607.6	120.7	150.7	402.9	464.1	324.7	117.9	573.1
WV	747.8	30.1	46.7	133.3	9.7	27.6	65.4	129.9	74.7	54.0	156.1
WI	2,924.2	111.8	465.3	539.7	48.8	151.7	321.7	445.1	274.6	149.4	412.5
WY	280.8	21.2	9.2	53.8	3.7	10.8	17.7	27.6	35.4	11.2	71.4

[1] Includes mining and logging, not shown separately. [2] Finance and insurance; and real estate and rental and leasing. [3] Professional, scientific, and technical services; management of companies and enterprises; and administrative and support, and waste management and remediation services. [4] Education services; and health care and social assistance. [5] Arts, entertainment, and recreation; and accommodations and food services. [6] Includes repair and maintenance; personal and laundry services; and membership associations and organizations.

Source: U.S. Bureau of Labor Statistics, State and Metro Area Employment, Hours, and Earnings, "Employees on nonfarm payrolls in States and selected areas by major industry," <http://www.bls.gov/sae/tables.htm>, accessed April 2017.

Table 655. Nonfarm Industries—Employees and Earnings: 1990 to 2016

[Annual averages of monthly figures (109,527 represents 109,527,000). Covers all full- and part-time employees who worked during, or received pay for, any part of the pay period including the 12th of the month. See also headnote, Table 653]

Industry	2012 NAICS code [1]	All employees (1,000)					Average hourly earnings [2] (dol.)		
		1990	2000	2010	2015	2016	2000	2010	2016
Total nonfarm	(X)	**109,527**	**132,024**	**130,361**	**141,843**	**144,306**	**(NA)**	**(NA)**	**(NA)**
Goods-producing [3]	(X)	23,723	24,649	17,751	19,610	19,736	15.27	20.28	22.58
Service-providing [4]	(X)	85,804	107,375	112,610	122,233	124,569	(NA)	(NA)	(NA)
Total private	(X)	**91,112**	**111,235**	**107,871**	**119,814**	**122,083**	**14.02**	**19.05**	**21.54**
Mining and logging	(X)	**765**	**599**	**705**	**813**	**677**	**16.55**	**23.82**	**27.05**
Logging	1133	85	79	50	52	51	13.70	18.85	21.29
Mining	21	**680**	**520**	**655**	**760**	**626**	**16.94**	**24.24**	**27.56**
Oil and gas extraction	211	190	125	159	193	180	19.43	27.36	33.76
Mining, except oil and gas	212	302	225	205	198	181	18.07	24.63	26.46
Support activities for mining	213	188	171	292	369	265	14.55	22.95	25.64
Construction	23	**5,263**	**6,787**	**5,518**	**6,461**	**6,711**	**17.48**	**23.22**	**25.97**
Construction of buildings	236	1,413	1,633	1,230	1,424	1,490	16.74	22.73	25.50
Residential building	2361	673	823	572	694	736	15.18	19.80	22.81
Nonresidential building	2362	741	809	658	730	755	18.18	25.13	27.85
Heavy and civil engineering construction	237	813	937	825	938	944	16.80	23.76	27.49
Highway, street, and bridge construction	2373	289	340	287	310	322	18.17	23.76	27.00
Specialty trade contractors	238	3,037	4,217	3,463	4,100	4,277	17.91	23.22	25.74
Building foundation and exterior contractors	2381	703	919	680	804	847	16.93	21.20	23.89
Building equipment contractors	2382	1,282	1,897	1,634	1,932	2,021	19.52	24.89	27.69
Building finishing contractors	2383	665	857	634	744	773	16.44	22.06	24.09
Manufacturing	31-33	**17,695**	**17,263**	**11,528**	**12,336**	**12,348**	**14.32**	**18.61**	**20.43**
Durable goods	(X)	**10,737**	**10,877**	**7,064**	**7,765**	**7,719**	**14.93**	**19.80**	**21.48**
Wood products	321	543	615	342	383	392	11.63	14.85	16.81
Nonmetallic mineral products	327	528	554	371	398	408	14.53	17.48	20.30
Cement and concrete products	3273	195	234	170	185	191	14.64	17.84	21.01
Primary metals	331	689	622	362	394	378	16.64	20.13	23.11
Iron and steel mills and ferroalloy production	3311	187	135	87	88	84	(NA)	(NA)	(NA)
Foundries	3315	214	217	112	125	118	14.72	18.22	20.27
Fabricated metal products	332	1,610	1,753	1,282	1,458	1,425	13.77	17.94	19.67
Architectural and structural metals	3323	357	428	321	368	367	13.43	17.47	18.74
Machine shops and threaded products	3327	309	365	313	368	353	14.53	18.68	20.27
Machinery	333	1,410	1,457	996	1,121	1,080	15.21	18.96	21.81
Agricultural, construction, and mining machinery	3331	229	222	208	239	209	14.21	18.95	20.45
Heating, ventilation and air conditioning, and commercial refrigeration equipment	3334	165	194	125	129	129	13.10	16.16	18.53
Metalworking machinery	3335	267	274	155	184	180	16.66	20.00	22.48
Computer and electronic products	334	1,903	1,820	1,095	1,053	1,048	14.73	22.78	24.27
Computer and peripheral equipment	3341	367	302	158	160	164	(NA)	(NA)	(NA)
Communications equipment	3342	223	239	117	88	86	14.39	23.88	20.01
Semiconductors and electronic components	3344	574	676	369	370	367	13.46	20.35	21.43
Electronic instruments	3345	635	488	406	399	396	15.80	24.82	28.21
Electrical equipment and appliances	335	633	591	360	384	383	13.23	16.87	19.29
Household appliances	3352	114	106	60	62	64	(NA)	(NA)	(NA)
Electrical equipment	3353	244	210	136	144	139	13.28	16.51	19.71
Transportation equipment	336	2,135	2,057	1,333	1,605	1,625	18.89	25.23	25.05
Motor vehicles	3361	271	291	153	201	209	24.45	29.05	28.61
Motor vehicle parts	3363	653	840	419	565	580	17.95	20.66	19.94
Aerospace products and parts	3364	841	517	478	490	489	20.52	33.65	36.47
Ship and boat building	3366	174	154	125	138	135	(NA)	(NA)	(NA)
Furniture and related products	337	602	680	357	381	389	11.73	15.06	16.82
Household and institutional furniture	3371	398	441	223	239	245	11.39	14.75	16.54
Miscellaneous durable goods manufacturing	339	686	728	567	590	591	11.93	16.56	18.44
Medical equipment and supplies	3391	283	305	303	309	308	12.70	17.56	19.18
Nondurable goods	(X)	**6,958**	**6,386**	**4,464**	**4,571**	**4,629**	**13.31**	**16.80**	**18.74**
Food manufacturing	311	1,507	1,553	1,451	1,512	1,554	11.77	14.41	16.51
Fruit and vegetable preserving	3114	218	197	173	170	173	11.90	14.56	16.78
Dairy products	3115	145	136	130	136	141	14.85	18.92	22.07
Animal slaughtering and processing	3116	427	507	489	486	495	10.27	12.69	14.47
Bakeries and tortilla manufacturing	3118	292	306	277	297	304	11.45	14.44	16.12
Textile mills	313	492	378	119	117	114	11.23	13.56	15.71
Textile product mills	314	236	230	119	116	115	10.31	11.79	13.64
Apparel	315	903	484	157	137	131	8.61	11.43	13.73
Cut and sew apparel	3152	750	380	124	111	106	(NA)	(NA)	(NA)
Leather and allied products	316	(NA)	(NA)	(NA)	(NA)	(NA)	(NA)	(NA)	(NA)
Paper and paper products	322	647	605	395	373	371	15.91	20.04	21.71
Pulp, paper, and paperboard mills	3221	238	191	112	102	100	20.62	25.12	27.82
Converted paper products	3222	409	413	282	271	271	13.58	17.81	19.26
Printing and related support activities	323	809	807	488	450	447	14.09	16.91	18.59
Petroleum and coal products	324	153	123	114	113	112	22.80	31.31	38.84
Chemicals	325	1,036	980	787	807	811	17.09	21.07	22.71
Basic chemicals	3251	249	188	142	149	148	21.06	24.93	28.09
Resin, rubber, and artificial fibers	3252	158	136	89	94	93	17.09	21.11	24.59
Pharmaceuticals and medicines	3254	207	274	277	282	287	17.27	21.95	22.78
Plastics and rubber products	326	825	951	625	689	699	12.70	15.71	17.17
Plastics products	3261	618	737	502	556	566	12.04	15.47	17.09
Rubber products	3262	207	214	123	133	133	14.83	16.64	17.47
Trade, transportation, and utilities	(X)	**22,666**	**26,225**	**24,636**	**26,887**	**27,233**	**13.31**	**16.82**	**18.99**
Wholesale trade	42	**5,268**	**5,933**	**5,452**	**5,855**	**5,867**	**16.28**	**21.54**	**24.18**
Durable goods	423	2,834	3,251	2,714	2,929	2,930	16.71	20.95	24.09
Motor vehicles and parts	4231	309	356	309	330	332	14.27	17.61	20.25
Lumber and construction supplies	4233	181	227	188	208	217	13.61	18.45	21.26
Commercial equipment	4234	597	722	604	615	621	20.29	25.03	29.20

See footnotes at end of table.

Table 655. Nonfarm Industries—Employees and Earnings: 1990 to 2016-Continued.

See headnote on page 427.

Industry	2012 NAICS code [1]	All employees (1,000)					Average hourly earnings [2] (dol.)		
		1990	2000	2010	2015	2016	2000	2010	2016
Electric goods........................	4236	357	425	309	325	329	19.43	23.12	26.13
Hardware and plumbing................	4237	216	247	218	242	247	15.07	19.82	23.14
Machinery and supplies...............	4238	690	725	608	681	669	16.47	21.03	24.29
Nondurable goods....................	424	1,900	2,065	1,928	2,028	2,041	14.33	19.62	20.83
Paper and paper products.............	4241	162	177	124	122	121	15.65	22.48	22.39
Druggists' goods.....................	4242	136	192	190	200	202	18.98	23.39	26.29
Apparel and piece goods..............	4243	152	163	137	149	152	14.58	21.34	20.36
Grocery and related products..........	4244	623	689	704	742	753	13.57	19.07	19.86
Alcoholic beverages..................	4248	115	128	163	188	194	15.72	20.01	21.50
Electronic markets and agents and brokers. . .	425	535	618	811	898	896	20.79	28.32	33.00
Retail trade.......................	**44,45**	**13,182**	**15,280**	**14,440**	**15,605**	**15,820**	**10.87**	**13.25**	**15.05**
Motor vehicle and parts dealers...........	441	1,494	1,847	1,629	1,929	1,982	14.94	17.06	19.01
Automobile dealers.................	4411	983	1,217	1,012	1,239	1,282	16.95	18.22	20.31
Auto parts, accessories, and tire stores.....	4413	418	499	489	545	550	11.04	14.54	16.05
Furniture and home furnishings stores........	442	432	544	438	467	474	12.33	15.25	17.55
Furniture stores.....................	4421	244	289	217	220	227	13.37	16.17	18.64
Home furnishings stores..............	4422	188	254	221	247	247	11.06	14.03	16.30
Electronics and appliance stores.............	443	451	647	522	522	522	13.16	16.83	22.70
Building material and garden supply stores. ..	444	891	1,142	1,132	1,234	1,272	11.25	14.11	15.53
Building material and supplies dealers.......	4441	753	982	1,005	1,085	1,115	11.30	14.13	15.58
Food and beverage stores..................	445	2,779	2,993	2,808	3,062	3,089	9.76	12.03	12.71
Grocery stores.....................	4451	2,406	2,582	2,461	2,682	2,703	9.71	12.12	12.76
Specialty food stores................	4452	232	270	211	227	230	9.97	11.13	12.32
Beer, wine, and liquor stores.........	4453	141	141	136	153	156	10.40	11.89	12.27
Health and personal care stores.........	446	792	928	981	1,034	1,050	11.68	16.99	17.45
Gasoline stations......................	447	910	936	819	905	926	8.05	10.25	11.31
Clothing & clothing accessories stores........	448	1,313	1,322	1,353	1,354	1,346	9.96	11.59	13.49
Clothing stores.....................	4481	930	954	1,040	1,006	996	9.88	10.91	12.72
Shoe stores........................	4482	216	193	182	212	214	8.96	11.80	14.77
Jewelry, luggage, and leather goods stores..	4483	167	175	131	136	137	11.48	15.56	15.86
Sporting goods, hobby, book, and music stores...	451	464	603	579	623	621	9.38	11.69	14.15
Sporting goods and musical instrument stores...	4511	352	437	459	538	536	9.55	11.82	14.23
Book stores and news dealers........	4512	111	166	120	86	85	8.91	11.10	13.57
General merchandise stores..............	452	2,500	2,820	2,998	3,131	3,171	9.22	10.98	12.28
Department stores..................	4521	1,494	1,755	1,502	1,327	1,310	(NA)	(NA)	(NA)
Miscellaneous store retailers.............	453	738	1,007	762	828	833	10.20	12.50	13.64
Florists............................	4531	121	130	69	63	62	8.95	11.05	11.61
Office supplies, stationery, and gift stores....	4532	358	471	303	281	272	10.46	13.06	14.56
Used merchandise stores............	4533	56	107	125	171	175	8.07	10.72	11.82
Nonstore retailers......................	454	419	492	421	515	536	13.22	17.73	21.90
Electronic shopping and mail-order houses..	4541	157	257	247	343	362	13.38	18.22	22.92
Transportation and warehousing.............	**48,49**	**3,476**	**4,410**	**4,191**	**4,871**	**4,989**	**15.05**	**19.16**	**20.92**
Air transportation......................	481	529	614	458	459	476	13.57	24.56	32.18
Scheduled air transportation..........	4811	503	570	417	419	434	(NA)	(NA)	(NA)
Rail transportation.....................	482	272	232	216	241	215	(NA)	(NA)	(NA)
Water transportation...................	483	57	56	62	66	66	(NA)	(NA)	(NA)
Truck transportation....................	484	1,122	1,406	1,250	1,452	1,454	15.86	18.62	21.20
General freight trucking..............	4841	807	1,013	868	995	1,003	16.37	18.51	21.49
Specialized freight trucking..........	4842	315	393	383	457	451	14.51	18.88	20.55
Transit and ground passenger transport.......	485	274	372	430	478	478	11.88	14.98	16.66
Urban, interurban, rural, and charter bus transportation....................	4851, 2,5	72	97	94	100	100	(NA)	(NA)	(NA)
Taxi and limousine service............	4853	57	72	68	80	80	(NA)	(NA)	(NA)
School and employee bus transportation. . .	4854	114	152	186	196	195	11.42	14.90	17.15
Pipeline transportation..............	486	60	46	42	50	50	19.86	29.54	39.46
Scenic and sightseeing transportation........	487	16	28	27	33	35	(NA)	(NA)	(NA)
Support activities for transportation.........	488	364	537	543	652	660	14.57	21.09	21.38
Support activities for air transportation......	4881	96	141	154	187	196	13.42	17.04	18.46
Support activities for water transportation....	4883	91	97	91	98	91	19.57	35.16	35.29
Support activities for road transportation.....	4884	35	66	80	95	98	13.98	15.68	16.14
Freight transportation arrangement..........	4885	111	178	169	206	210	13.46	21.24	21.82
Couriers and messengers.....................	492	375	605	528	613	642	13.51	17.67	17.51
Couriers and express delivery services......	4921	340	546	480	551	574	(NA)	(NA)	(NA)
Warehousing and storage......................	493	407	514	633	829	915	14.46	15.50	15.83
Utilities.............................	**22**	**740**	**601**	**553**	**556**	**556**	**22.75**	**30.04**	**35.31**
Power generation and supply.................	2211	550	434	398	394	394	23.13	31.25	37.12
Natural gas distribution..............	2212	155	121	108	113	113	23.41	28.36	33.14
Water, sewage and other systems..........	2213	35	46	47	49	50	16.93	23.73	24.48
Information........................	**51**	**2,688**	**3,630**	**2,707**	**2,750**	**2,772**	**19.07**	**25.87**	**30.04**
Publishing industries, except internet.........	511	871	1,035	759	727	730	(NA)	26.78	34.41
Newspaper, book, and directory publishers. ..	5111	773	774	498	392	374	(NA)	20.98	23.71
Software publishers.................	5112	98	261	261	334	356	28.48	36.41	45.34
Motion picture and sound recording............	512	255	383	370	398	420	21.25	22.11	23.22
Broadcasting, except internet..............	515	284	344	290	277	269	16.74	24.01	28.50
Radio and television broadcasting......	5151	232	253	210	217	216	(NA)	(NA)	(NA)
Cable and other subscription programming. ..	5152	52	91	80	59	53	(NA)	(NA)	(NA)
Telecommunications....................	517	1,009	1,397	903	811	795	18.59	26.24	28.10
Wired telecommunications carriers.......	5171	760	922	603	593	589	18.62	25.99	27.76
Wireless telecommunications carriers (except satellite)...............	5172	36	186	170	128	121	(NA)	(NA)	(NA)
Data processing, hosting and related services........................	518	211	316	243	296	300	16.97	27.03	30.65
Financial activities.................	**(X)**	**6,614**	**7,783**	**7,695**	**8,123**	**8,285**	**15.04**	**21.55**	**26.11**

See footnotes at end of table.

ProQuest Statistical Abstract of the United States: 2018

Industry	2012 NAICS code [1]	All employees (1,000)					Average hourly earnings [2] (dol.)		
		1990	2000	2010	2015	2016	2000	2010	2016
Finance and insurance............	**52**	**4,976**	**5,773**	**5,761**	**6,035**	**6,142**	**(NA)**	**(NA)**	**(NA)**
Monetary authorities—central bank..........	521	24	23	20	18	19	(NA)	(NA)	(NA)
Credit intermediation and related activities....	522	2,425	2,548	2,550	2,571	2,612	13.14	18.25	22.37
Depository credit intermediation..............	5221	1,909	1,681	1,729	1,684	1,699	11.97	17.55	20.25
Commercial banking...................	52211	1,362	1,251	1,306	1,285	1,307	11.83	17.56	20.35
Nondepository credit intermediation.........	5222	398	644	562	595	612	15.30	20.14	26.53
Activities related to credit intermediation.....	5223	119	222	259	292	302	15.39	18.29	24.79
Securities, commodity contracts, and investments..........	523	489	851	850	908	928	20.04	31.21	40.83
Securities and commodity contracts brokerage and exchanges..................	5231,2	341	569	471	452	453	20.05	31.72	42.38
Other financial investment activities, incl. funds trusts........................	5239, 525	148	282	379	456	476	20.03	30.51	39.28
Insurance carriers and related activities.......	524	2,039	2,351	2,341	2,538	2,583	17.47	24.58	28.70
Insurance carriers..........	5241	1,349	1,544	1,445	1,467	1,485	18.03	25.95	30.38
Insurance agencies, brokerages, and related services..........	5242	690	807	896	1,072	1,098	16.32	22.18	26.17
Real estate and rental and leasing...........	**53**	**1,637**	**2,011**	**1,934**	**2,088**	**2,143**	**(NA)**	**(NA)**	**(NA)**
Real estate........................	531	1,109	1,316	1,396	1,517	1,559	12.26	17.37	20.69
Lessors of real estate.....................	5311	566	610	565	582	586	11.19	16.52	19.03
Offices of real estate agents and brokers....	5312	217	281	286	294	304	12.57	17.10	21.45
Activities related to real estate............	5313	327	424	544	642	669	13.60	18.37	21.77
Rental and leasing services................	532	514	667	514	548	560	11.69	15.96	18.75
Automotive equipment rental and leasing....	5321	163	208	161	201	206	(NA)	(NA)	(NA)
Consumer goods rental......................	5322	220	292	198	163	169	(NA)	(NA)	(NA)
Machinery/equipment rental and leasing....	5324	84	103	114	145	145	14.95	19.83	24.81
Lessors of nonfinancial intangible assets.....	533	14	28	25	24	24	(NA)	(NA)	(NA)
Professional and business services...........	**(X)**	**10,848**	**16,666**	**16,728**	**19,633**	**20,136**	**15.52**	**22.78**	**25.42**
Professional and technical services..........	**54**	**4,538**	**6,702**	**7,441**	**8,608**	**8,877**	**20.61**	**29.94**	**33.73**
Legal services..........	5411	944	1,066	1,114	1,119	1,121	21.38	31.04	33.96
Accounting and bookkeeping services........	5412	664	866	887	969	986	14.42	21.02	24.30
Architectural and engineering services.......	5413	942	1,238	1,275	1,401	1,411	20.49	30.22	32.69
Specialized design services................	5414	82	132	113	134	140	15.32	22.36	26.62
Computer systems design and related........	5415	410	1,254	1,449	1,909	1,991	27.13	37.16	41.29
Management and technical consulting........	5416	305	673	999	1,282	1,373	20.83	28.52	33.13
Scientific research and development.........	5417	494	515	621	659	682	21.39	35.67	38.88
Advertising and related services...........	5418	382	497	408	482	490	16.99	24.61	29.45
Management of companies and enterprises..	**55**	**1,667**	**1,796**	**1,872**	**2,207**	**2,241**	**15.28**	**23.79**	**27.46**
Administrative and waste services............	**56**	**4,643**	**8,168**	**7,414**	**8,818**	**9,018**	**11.69**	**15.80**	**17.27**
Administrative and support services...........	561	4,413	7,855	7,057	8,421	8,613	11.53	15.59	17.03
Office administrative services.............	5611	211	264	407	471	495	14.68	23.56	26.77
Facilities support services.................	5612	58	97	133	140	141	16.73	20.97	19.86
Employment services.....................	5613	1,512	3,849	2,723	3,527	3,567	11.89	16.19	16.98
Temporary help services..............	56132	1,156	2,636	2,094	2,877	2,916	11.79	14.23	16.18
Business support services.................	5614	505	787	809	894	912	11.08	14.49	16.64
Travel arrangement and reservation........	5615	250	299	186	205	216	12.72	17.10	22.20
Investigation and security services..........	5616	507	689	781	871	899	9.78	14.14	15.32
Services to buildings and dwellings.........	5617	1,175	1,571	1,745	2,007	2,070	10.02	12.97	14.71
Waste management and remediation services..........	562	229	313	357	397	405	15.29	19.32	21.78
Waste collection..........	5621	82	100	141	164	170	12.97	17.50	19.40
Waste treatment and disposal..............	5622	77	119	96	95	96	15.02	20.29	25.37
Education and health services.............	**(X)**	**11,024**	**15,252**	**19,975**	**22,029**	**22,616**	**13.91**	**19.95**	**22.53**
Educational services.............	**61**	**1,688**	**2,390**	**3,155**	**3,472**	**3,560**	**(NA)**	**(NA)**	**(NA)**
Elementary and secondary schools...........	6111	461	716	849	967	1,011	(NA)	(NA)	(NA)
Junior colleges..........	6112	44	79	99	67	69	(NA)	(NA)	(NA)
Colleges and universities................	6113	939	1,196	1,591	1,728	1,750	(NA)	(NA)	(NA)
Business, computer, and management training..........	6114	60	86	78	75	70	(NA)	(NA)	(NA)
Technical and trade schools...............	6115	72	91	126	116	115	(NA)	(NA)	(NA)
Other schools and instruction..............	6116	96	184	309	387	404	(NA)	(NA)	(NA)
Educational support services..............	6117	17	39	103	132	142	(NA)	(NA)	(NA)
Health care and social assistance.............	**62**	**9,336**	**12,861**	**16,820**	**18,557**	**19,056**	**13.93**	**20.23**	**22.84**
Health care..........	621,2,3	8,211	10,858	13,777	15,042	15,420	14.63	21.71	24.67
Ambulatory health care services..............	621	2,842	4,320	5,975	6,856	7,082	15.00	21.68	24.83
Offices of physicians......................	6211	1,251	1,801	2,264	2,471	2,528	15.65	24.03	29.64
Offices of dentists.....................	6212	513	688	828	905	926	15.96	22.65	24.73
Offices of other health practitioners.......	6213	276	438	671	813	859	14.24	20.48	22.32
Outpatient care centers.................	6214	287	425	649	806	856	15.36	22.81	24.82
Medical and diagnostic laboratories.........	6215	129	162	228	260	263	15.74	23.48	24.62
Home health care services..............	6216	288	633	1,085	1,315	1,362	12.86	16.64	17.96
Hospitals..........	622	3,513	3,954	4,679	4,896	5,025	16.71	26.11	29.82
General medical and surgical hospitals......	6221	3,305	3,745	4,357	4,498	4,612	16.75	26.33	30.18
Psychiatric and substance abuse hospitals...	6222	113	86	109	138	145	(NA)	(NA)	(NA)
Nursing and residential care facilities.......	623	1,856	2,583	3,124	3,291	3,314	10.67	14.21	15.36
Nursing care facilities...................	6231	1,170	1,514	1,657	1,648	1,644	11.08	15.26	16.41
Residential mental health facilities..........	6232	269	437	565	607	614	9.96	13.06	14.21
Community care facilities for the elderly......	6233	330	478	741	873	892	9.83	12.89	14.20
Social assistance..........	624	1,125	2,003	3,043	3,515	3,636	9.72	12.75	13.99
Individual and family services...............	6241	429	821	1,664	2,144	2,229	10.30	13.07	14.34
Emergency and other relief services..........	6242	67	117	143	156	162	10.95	14.41	16.79
Vocational rehabilitation services...........	6243	242	370	388	337	338	9.57	12.47	13.80
Child day care services..................	6244	388	696	848	878	906	8.88	11.99	12.77
Leisure and hospitality.............	**(X)**	**9,288**	**11,862**	**13,049**	**15,160**	**15,620**	**8.32**	**11.31**	**12.85**
Arts, entertainment, and recreation...........	**71**	**1,132**	**1,788**	**1,913**	**2,166**	**2,235**	**10.68**	**15.27**	**16.35**

See footnotes at end of table.

See headnote on page 427.

Industry	2012 NAICS code [1]	All employees (1,000)					Average hourly earnings [2] (dol.)		
		1990	2000	2010	2015	2016	2000	2010	2016
Performing arts and spectator sports...........	711	273	382	406	450	456	13.11	21.01	23.41
Museums, historical sites, zoos, and parks....	712	68	110	128	153	160	12.20	15.60	17.47
Amusements, gambling, and recreation.......	713	791	1,296	1,379	1,563	1,619	9.86	13.38	14.13
Accommodation and food services........	**72**	**8,156**	**10,074**	**11,135**	**12,994**	**13,386**	**7.92**	**10.68**	**12.32**
Accommodation.............................	721	1,616	1,884	1,760	1,923	1,947	9.48	13.02	14.11
Traveler accommodation..................	7211	1,582	1,837	1,703	1,861	1,881	9.49	13.07	14.15
Food services and drinking places.............	722	6,540	8,189	9,376	11,071	11,439	7.49	10.15	11.96
Full-service restaurants...................	722511	3,070	3,845	4,482	5,215	5,373	7.78	10.93	13.18
Limited-service restaurants..................	722513	2,429	3,042	3,418	4,109	4,261	6.80	8.86	10.09
Special food services....................	7223	392	491	543	650	666	9.45	11.83	14.11
Drinking places, alcoholic beverages.........	7224	312	391	341	374	381	7.24	10.15	13.13
Other services........................	**81**	**4,261**	**5,168**	**5,331**	**5,622**	**5,685**	**12.73**	**17.06**	**19.36**
Repair and maintenance.....................	811	1,009	1,242	1,139	1,277	1,289	13.28	16.82	19.05
Automotive repair and maintenance............	8111	659	888	801	896	913	12.45	15.55	17.77
Electronic equipment repair and maintenance.................	8112	100	107	98	103	101	16.31	19.41	21.91
Commercial machinery repair and maintenance.................	8113	161	161	172	204	200	15.53	21.03	23.45
Personal and laundry services..................	812	1,120	1,243	1,265	1,405	1,445	10.18	13.42	15.16
Personal care services......................	8121	430	490	601	669	689	10.18	13.97	16.44
Death care services.......................	8122	123	136	131	136	137	13.04	17.46	18.95
Dry-cleaning and laundry services............	8123	371	388	302	298	300	9.17	11.80	12.76
Dry-cleaning and laundry services, except coin-operated.........................	81232	215	211	146	137	135	8.14	10.56	11.43
Other personal services....................	8129	196	229	232	302	320	10.52	12.43	13.80
Pet care services, except veterinary..........	81291	23	31	63	95	105	12.12	12.83	13.88
Parking lots and garages..................	81293	68	93	111	137	141	8.81	11.18	12.21
Membership associations & organizations......	813	2,132	2,683	2,926	2,940	2,950	13.66	18.76	21.50
Grantmaking and giving services..............	8132	113	116	178	174	182	14.65	23.51	29.85
Social advocacy organizations.................	8133	126	143	202	212	218	12.08	17.36	20.41
Civic and social organizations................	8134	377	404	392	388	389	9.85	12.16	14.15
Professional and similar organizations.........	8139	379	473	477	470	476	15.98	22.67	25.62
Government........................	**(X)**	**18,415**	**20,790**	**22,490**	**22,029**	**22,223**	**(NA)**	**(NA)**	**(NA)**
Federal.....................................	(X)	3,196	2,865	2,977	2,757	2,795	(NA)	(NA)	(NA)
Federal, except U.S. Postal Service.............	(X)	2,371	1,985	2,318	2,160	2,186	(NA)	(NA)	(NA)
U.S. Postal Service........................	(X)	825	880	659	597	609	(NA)	(NA)	(NA)
State.......................................	(X)	4,305	4,786	5,137	5,077	5,089	(NA)	(NA)	(NA)
Local.......................................	(X)	10,914	13,139	14,376	14,195	14,339	(NA)	(NA)	(NA)

NA Not available. X Not applicable. [1] Based on the North American Industry Classification System, 2012. See text, Section 15. [2] Production employees in the goods-producing industries and nonsupervisory employees in service-providing industries. [3] Mining and logging, construction, and manufacturing. [4] Trade, transportation and utilities, information, financial activities, professional and business services, education and health services, leisure and hospitality, other services, and government.

Source: U.S. Bureau of Labor Statistics, Current Employment Statistics, "Employment, Hours, and Earnings—National," <http://www.bls.gov/ces/data.htm>, accessed June 2017.

Table 656. **Women Employed by Nonfarm Industry: 1990 to 2016**

[51,619 represents 51,619,000. Annual averages of monthly data. For coverage, see headnote, Table 653]

Industry	Women employees (1,000)				Percent of total employees			
	1990	2000	2010	2016	1990	2000	2010	2016
Total nonfarm.................................	**51,619**	**63,399**	**65,087**	**71,492**	**47.1**	**48.0**	**49.9**	**49.5**
Total private.................................	**41,764**	**51,629**	**52,258**	**58,747**	**45.8**	**46.4**	**48.4**	**48.1**
Construction.................................	656	846	723	839	12.5	12.5	13.1	12.5
Manufacturing...............................	5,702	5,359	3,268	3,382	32.2	31.0	28.3	27.4
Trade, transportation, and utilities................	9,363	10,859	10,007	11,063	41.3	41.4	40.6	40.6
Wholesale trade............................	1,611	1,827	1,641	1,735	30.6	30.8	30.1	29.6
Retail trade.................................	6,696	7,680	7,226	7,981	50.8	50.3	50.0	50.4
Transportation and warehousing................	879	1,202	1,002	1,216	25.3	27.3	23.9	24.4
Utilities....................................	177	151	139	131	24.0	25.1	25.1	23.5
Information.................................	1,324	1,697	1,104	1,108	49.3	46.7	40.8	40.0
Financial activities...........................	4,055	4,697	4,530	4,713	61.3	60.3	58.9	56.9
Professional and business services.............	5,105	7,680	7,454	9,022	47.1	46.1	44.6	44.8
Professional and technical services............	2,209	3,146	3,522	4,123	48.7	46.9	47.3	46.4
Management of companies and enterprises......	849	924	939	1,079	50.9	51.4	50.1	48.2
Administrative and waste services..............	2,048	3,610	2,993	3,820	44.1	44.2	40.4	42.4
Education and health services..................	8,455	11,703	15,435	17,427	76.7	76.7	77.3	77.1
Educational services........................	958	1,417	1,929	2,183	56.8	59.3	61.2	61.3
Health care and social assistance................	7,496	10,286	13,505	15,244	80.3	80.0	80.3	80.0
Leisure and hospitality........................	4,829	6,082	6,819	8,113	52.0	51.3	52.3	51.9
Arts, entertainment, and recreation..............	516	815	886	1,051	45.6	45.6	46.3	47.0
Other services..............................	2,164	2,614	2,820	2,981	50.8	50.6	52.9	52.4
Government................................	**9,855**	**11,771**	**12,829**	**12,745**	**53.5**	**56.6**	**57.0**	**57.4**
Federal.....................................	1,378	1,231	1,326	1,236	43.1	43.0	44.5	44.2
State government............................	2,137	2,464	2,639	2,728	49.6	51.5	51.4	53.6
Local government............................	6,340	8,076	8,864	8,781	58.1	61.5	61.7	61.2

[1] Includes other industries, not shown separately.

Source: U.S. Bureau of Labor Statistics, Current Employment Statistics, "Employment, Hours, and Earnings–National," <http://www.bls.gov/ces/data.htm>, accessed March 2017.

Table 657. Job Gains and Job Losses of Private Sector Establishments by Industry Sector: 2000 to 2016

[In thousands (16,145 represents 16,145,000). For year ending in March. Based on the Quarterly Census of Employment and Wages (QCEW). Excludes self-employed and certain nonprofit organizations. Minus sign (-) indicates a decrease in employment and comes from either closing establishments or contracting establishments. For more information, see source]

Year and industry	Gross job gains			Gross job losses			Net change [1]
	Total	Expanding establishments	Opening establishments	Total	Contracting establishments	Closing establishments	
2000	16,145	10,620	5,525	13,160	8,291	4,869	2,985
2005	13,829	9,406	4,423	11,826	7,675	4,151	2,003
2006	14,096	9,629	4,467	11,494	7,715	3,779	2,602
2007	13,517	9,243	4,274	12,002	8,249	3,753	1,515
2008	12,786	8,718	4,068	12,674	8,776	3,898	112
2009	10,149	6,668	3,481	15,969	11,706	4,263	-5,820
2010	10,075	6,839	3,236	12,760	9,142	3,618	-2,685
2011	11,629	8,295	3,334	9,721	6,623	3,098	1,908
2012	12,216	8,662	3,554	9,546	6,508	3,038	2,670
2013	12,045	8,553	3,492	9,924	6,829	3,095	2,121
2014	12,282	8,700	3,582	10,008	6,945	3,063	2,274
2015	12,834	9,143	3,691	10,115	6,940	3,175	2,719
2016, Total private	**13,104**	**9,385**	**3,719**	**10,633**	**7,416**	**3,217**	**2,471**
Goods producing	2,240	1,776	464	2,100	1,619	481	140
Natural resources and mining	207	149	58	381	306	75	-174
Construction	1,204	909	295	875	613	262	329
Manufacturing	829	718	111	844	700	144	-15
Service providing	10,863	7,608	3,255	8,534	5,797	2,737	2,329
Wholesale trade	576	447	129	527	354	173	49
Retail trade	1,444	1,029	415	1,183	823	360	261
Transportation and warehousing	500	388	112	369	261	108	131
Utilities	24	20	4	23	19	4	1
Information	309	244	65	272	200	72	37
Financial activities	806	600	206	668	455	213	138
Professional and business services	2,656	1,979	677	2,244	1,591	653	412
Education and health services	1,897	1,406	491	1,344	895	449	553
Leisure and hospitality	1,902	1,138	764	1,430	920	510	472
Other services	498	339	159	426	270	156	72

[1] Net change is the difference between total gross job gains and total gross job losses.

Source: U.S. Bureau of Labor Statistics, Business Employment Dynamics, "Annual Business Employment Dynamics Data," <http://www.bls.gov/bdm/bdmann.htm#TOTAL>, accessed May 2017.

Table 658. Private Sector Gross Job Gains and Job Losses by State: 2016

[In thousands (13,104 represents 13,104,000). For year ending in March. Based on the Quarterly Census of Employment and Wages (QCEW). Excludes self-employed and certain nonprofit organizations. Minus sign (-) indicates a decrease in employment and comes from either closing establishments or contracting establishments. For more information, see source]

State	Gross job gains			Gross job losses			Net change [1]	State	Gross job gains			Gross job losses			Net change [1]
	Total	Expanding establishments	Opening establishments	Total	Contracting establishments	Closing establishments			Total	Expanding establishments	Opening establishments	Total	Contracting establishments	Closing establishments	
U.S.	**13,104**	**9,385**	**3,719**	**10,633**	**7,416**	**3,217**	**2,471**	MO	233	167	66	181	128	53	53
AL	167	117	50	137	99	38	30	MT	40	29	11	34	24	10	6
AK	23	18	6	27	21	6	-4	NE	78	57	21	66	48	18	12
AZ	270	192	77	196	131	65	74	NV	130	94	37	96	68	28	34
AR	104	75	29	79	58	22	25	NH	54	39	14	42	30	12	12
CA	1,764	1,226	538	1,406	903	503	358	NJ	387	266	120	305	204	101	82
CO	250	177	73	202	140	63	48	NM	68	46	22	66	48	18	2
CT	127	94	33	114	89	26	13	NY	847	606	241	676	442	234	171
DE	45	32	14	33	22	11	13	NC	399	289	111	291	199	91	109
DC	61	42	19	48	32	17	12	ND	32	21	11	61	46	14	-29
FL	962	624	338	695	427	268	267	OH	431	328	103	346	269	78	85
GA	449	315	134	333	222	111	116	OK	134	91	43	151	109	41	-17
HI	50	36	14	41	28	13	9	OR	171	126	45	121	86	35	50
ID	71	50	21	50	33	18	21	PA	453	340	113	388	286	102	65
IL	510	360	151	437	295	142	73	RI	39	28	11	31	21	10	8
IN	247	188	59	195	149	46	52	SC	187	132	55	135	100	35	52
IA	121	89	32	109	83	25	12	SD	30	22	8	27	21	6	3
KS	115	80	35	109	76	33	6	TN	267	204	63	183	137	47	83
KY	165	122	43	129	95	34	36	TX	1,076	822	253	1,035	770	265	40
LA	180	124	56	192	144	47	-12	UT	148	108	40	100	71	30	47
ME	49	36	13	39	25	13	10	VT	23	17	6	22	16	7	1
MD	242	172	70	192	131	61	50	VA	363	237	126	276	193	83	87
MA	291	215	76	220	155	66	71	WA	304	225	79	216	159	57	88
MI	344	261	83	266	194	72	78	WV	54	39	15	64	46	18	-10
MN	217	160	57	183	131	52	34	WI	213	160	53	174	132	42	39
MS	98	72	27	79	57	23	19	WY	22	15	7	32	24	8	-11

[1] Net change is the difference between total gross job gains and total gross job losses.

Source: U.S. Bureau of Labor Statistics, Business Employment Dynamics, "Annual Business Employment Dynamics Data," <http://www.bls.gov/bdm/bdmann.htm>, accessed May 2017.

Table 659. Hires and Separations Affecting Establishment Payrolls By Industry: 2013 to 2016

[54,320 represents 54,320,000. Hires represent any additions to payrolls, including new and rehired employees, full- and part-time workers, short-term and seasonal workers, etc. Separations represent terminations of employment, including quits, layoffs, and discharges, etc. Based on a monthly survey of private nonfarm establishments and governmental entities]

Industry	Annual hires (1,000)				Annual separations (1,000)			
	2013	2014	2015	2016	2013	2014	2015	2016
Total................	**54,320**	**58,657**	**62,050**	**62,719**	**51,932**	**55,587**	**59,275**	**60,419**
Total private industry............	50,882	55,001	57,909	58,385	48,421	52,056	55,331	56,305
Mining and logging............	355	398	299	299	337	362	451	377
Construction..................	3,867	3,755	3,931	3,953	3,641	3,432	3,587	3,841
Manufacturing................	2,893	3,129	3,214	3,314	2,774	2,921	3,147	3,341
Durable goods...............	1,743	1,830	1,876	1,934	1,650	1,669	1,879	1,975
Nondurable goods...........	1,152	1,299	1,334	1,381	1,122	1,253	1,271	1,366
Trade, transportation, and utilities.........	11,151	12,811	13,012	12,667	10,568	12,193	12,599	12,276
Wholesale trade.............	1,427	1,744	1,662	1,686	1,367	1,668	1,650	1,642
Retail trade.................	7,802	8,853	9,026	8,660	7,389	8,551	8,829	8,440
Transportation, warehousing, and utilities.................	1,919	2,211	2,328	2,320	1,811	1,972	2,121	2,193
Information....................	845	894	952	919	801	882	928	919
Financial activities...........	2,415	2,318	2,366	2,316	2,332	2,202	2,218	2,130
Finance and insurance........	1,584	1,510	1,586	1,519	1,546	1,458	1,479	1,398
Real estate and rental and leasing........	830	805	779	795	788	745	740	730
Professional and business services.......	11,047	12,058	12,590	13,209	10,502	11,433	12,084	12,695
Education and health services..............	6,429	6,876	7,434	7,599	6,166	6,354	6,791	7,064
Educational services........	902	989	1,062	1,093	862	892	983	1,033
Health care and social assistance........	5,525	5,885	6,373	6,505	5,304	5,462	5,807	6,031
Leisure and hospitality.........	9,632	10,530	11,624	11,912	9,130	10,096	11,098	11,526
Arts, entertainment, and recreation.......	1,569	1,769	1,811	1,833	1,493	1,708	1,717	1,767
Accommodation and food services.......	8,062	8,761	9,813	10,078	7,637	8,387	9,383	9,759
Other services................	2,249	2,238	2,488	2,201	2,163	2,181	2,432	2,132
Government workers..........	3,439	3,658	4,139	4,335	3,512	3,531	3,943	4,114
Federal.....................	370	389	487	496	439	381	452	455
State and local...............	3,067	3,267	3,650	3,840	3,070	3,148	3,489	3,656

Source: U.S. Bureau of Labor Statistics, *Job Openings and Labor Turnover—January 2017*, USDL 17-0320, March 2017. See also <http://www.bls.gov/jlt/news.htm>.

Table 660. Type of Separations Affecting Establishment Payrolls: 2016

[36,091 represents 36,091,000. Covers all private nonfarm establishments. Separations are the total number of terminations of employment occurring at any time during the reference month, and are reported by type of separation—quits, layoffs and discharges, and other separations. Annual rate estimates are computed by dividing annual levels by the Current Employment Statistics (CES) annual average employment level and multiplying that quotient by 100]

Industry	Number (1,000)			Rate (percent) [1]		
	Annual quits level [2]	Annual layoffs and discharge levels [3]	Annual other separations [4]	Annual quits level [2]	Annual layoffs and discharge levels [3]	Annual other separations [4]
Total............	**36,091**	**19,911**	**4,418**	**25.0**	**13.8**	**3.1**
Total private industry............	34,051	18,585	3,670	27.9	15.2	3.0
Mining and logging............	160	170	48	23.6	25.1	7.1
Construction..................	1,469	2,188	184	21.9	32.6	2.7
Manufacturing................	1,799	1,254	289	14.6	10.2	2.3
Durable goods...............	1,000	792	182	13.0	10.3	2.4
Nondurable goods...........	801	459	107	17.3	9.9	2.3
Trade, transportation, and utilities............	7,758	3,418	1,099	28.5	12.6	4.0
Wholesale trade.............	1,012	487	144	17.2	8.3	2.5
Retail trade.................	5,568	2,105	768	35.2	13.3	4.9
Transportation, warehousing, and utilities.................	1,181	824	186	21.3	14.9	3.4
Information....................	483	304	132	17.4	11.0	4.8
Financial activities...........	1,192	650	287	14.4	7.8	3.5
Finance and insurance........	797	369	237	13.0	6.0	3.9
Real estate and rental and leasing..........	396	281	52	18.5	13.1	2.4
Professional and business services..........	7,234	4,780	681	35.9	23.7	3.4
Education and health services................	4,680	1,915	468	20.7	8.5	2.1
Educational services........	567	400	66	15.9	11.2	1.9
Health care and social assistance..........	4,113	1,514	401	21.6	7.9	2.1
Leisure and hospitality.........	7,993	3,142	393	51.2	20.1	2.5
Arts, entertainment, and recreation.......	826	909	35	37.0	40.7	1.6
Accommodation and food services..........	7,168	2,231	358	53.5	16.7	2.7
Other services................	1,280	766	88	22.5	13.5	1.5
Government workers............	2,038	1,326	748	9.2	6.0	3.4
Federal.....................	161	153	140	5.8	5.5	5.0
State and local...............	1,877	1,173	607	9.7	6.0	3.1

[1] As a percent of total employment. [2] Quits are voluntary separations by employees (except for retirements, which are reported as other separations). [3] Layoffs and discharges are involuntary separations initiated by the employer and include layoffs with no intent to rehire; formal layoffs lasting or expected to last more than seven days; discharges resulting from mergers, downsizing, or closings, firings or other discharges for cause; terminations of permanent or short term employees; and terminations of seasonal employees. [4] Other separations include retirements, transfers to other locations, deaths, and separations due to disability.

Source: U.S. Bureau of Labor Statistics, *Job Openings and Labor Turnover—January 2017*, USDL 17-0320, March 2017. See also <https://www.bls.gov/jlt/news.htm>.

Table 661. Productivity and Related Measures for Selected NAICS Industries: 1987 to 2016 and 2015 to 2016

[For a discussion of productivity measures and methodology, see text, this section and BLS Handbook of Methods, Chapter 11, <http://www.bls.gov/opub/hom/homch11.htm>. Minus sign (-) indicates decrease]

Industry	2012 NAICS code [1]	Average annual percent change [2]							
		1987-2016 [3]				2015-2016			
		Output per hour	Unit labor costs	Output	Hours	Output per hour	Unit labor costs	Output	Hours
Mining	21	1.1	2.8	1.0	-0.1	17.5	-15.2	-4.4	-18.6
Oil and gas extraction	211	1.4	3.6	1.1	-0.3	5.4	-6.2	-4.2	-9.1
Mining, except oil and gas	212	1.5	1.3	–	-1.5	4.3	-6.2	-4.9	-8.8
Coal mining	2121	1.9	0.8	-1.7	-3.5	9.5	-10.3	-19.6	-26.6
Utilities:									
Power generation and supply	2211	3.1	0.5	2.1	-1.0	-1.0	4.0	-0.7	0.3
Natural gas distribution	2212	0.6	3.8	-0.3	-1.0	1.0	1.7	-0.8	-1.8
Water, sewage and other systems	2213	-1.6	4.5	0.8	2.5	-5.2	9.3	-3.3	2.1
Manufacturing:									
Food	311	1.0	1.6	1.4	0.4	-3.5	6.3	-0.3	3.3
Fruit and vegetable preserving and specialty	3114	1.3	1.6	1.1	-0.2	-8.0	4.9	-1.5	7.1
Dairy products	3115	1.7	1.7	1.4	-0.3	-1.2	7.0	-1.9	-0.7
Animal slaughtering and processing	3116	0.6	1.6	1.7	1.1	-2.6	5.1	1.0	3.7
Bakeries and tortilla manufacturing	3118	0.2	1.8	0.3	0.1	-0.9	9.7	-2.9	-2.0
Beverages and tobacco products	312	-0.1	2.3	-0.1	–	-10.2	13.4	-4.1	6.8
Textile mills	313	3.1	-0.2	-2.2	-5.1	6.6	2.7	-1.9	-8.0
Apparel	315	-0.7	1.9	-6.8	-6.2	-1.0	13.9	-11.4	-10.6
Leather and allied products	316	0.8	1.8	-4.2	-5.0	-5.0	5.8	-7.2	-2.3
Wood products	321	1.4	1.6	0.2	-1.2	-0.8	4.7	2.1	2.9
Paper and paper products	322	2.0	1.1	–	-1.9	-0.4	2.7	-1.8	-1.4
Converted paper products	3222	1.4	1.7	0.1	-1.3	-2.4	4.2	-2.1	0.3
Printing and related support activities	323	1.3	1.2	-0.6	-1.8	2.2	2.8	-0.3	-2.5
Petroleum and coal products	324	2.4	2.3	1.3	-1.1	4.3	-3.1	4.3	–
Chemicals	325	1.6	1.8	1.0	-0.6	1.0	-0.8	-0.7	-1.7
Pharmaceuticals and medicines	3254	–	3.3	1.6	1.6	-4.0	-2.1	-3.3	0.8
Plastics and rubber products	326	1.6	1.4	1.3	-0.3	-2.6	7.9	-2.2	0.4
Plastics products	3261	1.5	1.5	1.5	–	-2.9	8.8	-2.3	0.7
Nonmetallic mineral products	327	1.0	1.6	0.2	-0.8	-2.4	6.6	-0.3	2.2
Primary metals	331	2.6	0.2	0.6	-1.9	4.1	-3.9	-0.2	-4.1
Fabricated metal products	332	1.0	1.7	0.7	-0.2	-2.0	4.5	-4.3	-2.3
Forging and stamping	3321	2.2	0.7	1.2	-0.9	-0.1	0.8	-1.9	-1.8
Cutlery and hand tools	3322	1.3	1.4	-1.0	-2.3	-6.2	3.1	-3.5	2.9
Architectural and structural metals	3323	0.4	2.4	0.7	0.3	-5.8	9.9	-6.2	-0.4
Machine shops and threaded products	3327	1.4	1.4	2.1	0.6	-2.1	4.0	-6.3	-4.3
Other fabricated metal products	3329	0.5	2.0	-0.1	-0.5	-2.4	4.4	-4.4	-2.0
Machinery	333	1.9	0.8	1.1	-0.8	-0.7	0.1	-3.7	-3.0
Agriculture, construction, and mining machinery	3331	2.0	0.6	1.9	-0.2	5.0	-5.1	-9.0	-13.4
Industrial machinery	3332	1.4	1.1	0.7	-0.7	-1.4	1.3	1.9	3.4
Computer and electronic products	334	9.0	-5.3	6.7	-2.1	-3.7	8.9	-3.6	0.1
Semiconductors and electronic components	3344	12.6	-8.4	11.0	-1.5	-4.9	13.3	-5.4	-0.6
Electronic instruments	3345	3.0	0.6	1.2	-1.7	-4.3	7.9	-4.8	-0.5
Electrical equipment and appliances	335	1.9	1.2	0.1	-1.8	-1.5	2.4	-0.5	1.0
Transportation equipment	336	2.8	-0.3	2.0	-0.8	-3.9	6.1	-2.0	2.0
Motor vehicles	3361	3.1	-0.3	2.1	-1.0	-9.6	14.4	-2.1	8.3
Motor vehicle parts	3363	3.0	-1.5	2.9	-0.1	-1.0	3.4	2.5	3.5
Aerospace products and parts	3364	2.5	0.6	0.7	-1.7	-5.0	6.3	-4.6	0.4
Ship and boat building	3366	1.7	1.9	0.6	-1.1	-0.8	5.2	-6.0	-5.2
Furniture and related products	337	1.4	1.6	-0.1	-1.5	-2.3	8.8	-1.5	0.8
Household and institutional furniture	3371	1.2	1.8	-0.5	-1.8	-1.0	6.7	0.2	1.2
Miscellaneous manufacturing	339	1.8	1.4	1.7	-0.1	-3.6	2.9	-1.3	2.3
Medical equipment and supplies	3391	2.2	0.9	3.4	1.2	-2.5	-0.5	0.8	3.4
Wholesale trade	42	2.8	0.9	3.2	0.3	1.2	-0.7	1.6	0.4
Durable goods	423	4.4	-0.5	4.5	0.1	0.5	1.0	0.7	0.2
Nondurable goods	424	1.2	2.7	1.4	0.2	1.0	-2.4	2.6	1.6
Electronic markets and agents and brokers	425	1.5	0.8	3.7	2.1	3.9	-2.3	1.7	-2.1
Retail trade	44-45	2.9	–	3.4	0.5	4.6	-1.5	4.6	0.1
Motor vehicle and parts dealers	441	2.2	0.6	3.0	0.8	3.2	-1.3	4.8	1.6
Automobile dealers	4411	2.2	0.6	3.1	0.9	3.0	-0.9	5.2	2.1
Other motor vehicle dealers	4412	2.6	0.9	3.7	1.1	7.1	-4.0	4.5	-2.5
Auto parts, accessories, and tire stores	4413	1.1	1.3	1.8	0.8	-0.1	0.6	1.3	1.4
Furniture and home furnishings stores	442	3.7	-1.0	3.8	0.1	5.5	-4.4	5.4	-0.1
Furniture stores	4421	3.2	-0.7	3.2	–	3.6	-1.8	4.3	0.7
Home furnishings stores	4422	4.4	-1.4	4.5	0.1	7.6	-7.2	6.6	-0.9
Electronics and appliance stores	443	10.8	-7.3	11.5	0.7	8.0	-6.4	3.9	-3.8
Building material and garden supply stores	444	2.7	-0.1	3.4	0.6	5.3	-2.5	6.7	1.3
Building material and supplies dealers	4441	2.6	0.1	3.4	0.7	5.9	-2.7	7.4	1.4
Lawn and garden equipment and supplies stores	4442	3.3	-0.8	3.2	–	1.4	-2.0	2.0	0.6
Food and beverage stores	445	0.6	2.4	0.5	–	4.7	-1.1	3.2	-1.4
Grocery stores	4451	0.4	2.6	0.5	0.1	5.5	-1.7	3.2	-2.1
Specialty food stores	4452	0.3	2.2	-0.4	-0.6	3.4	0.2	2.6	-0.7
Beer, wine and liquor stores	4453	2.1	0.7	1.3	-0.8	-5.4	7.4	3.2	9.1
Health and personal care stores	446	2.0	1.3	3.1	1.1	-1.1	1.6	1.4	2.5
Gasoline stations	447	1.6	1.2	1.3	-0.3	4.2	-1.2	4.8	0.6
Clothing and clothing accessories stores	448	4.1	-1.2	3.7	-0.4	2.0	-0.3	0.7	-1.2
Clothing stores	4481	4.5	-1.4	4.2	-0.3	1.7	0.5	0.2	-1.5
Shoe stores	4482	2.7	-0.7	2.6	-0.1	3.5	-3.7	4.4	0.9
Jewelry, luggage, and leather goods stores	4483	3.5	-0.3	2.7	-0.7	2.2	-0.4	–	-2.2
Sporting goods, hobby, book, and music stores	451	3.5	-0.8	4.1	0.6	2.6	-6.1	3.5	0.8

See footnotes at end of table.

Table 661. Productivity and Related Measures for Selected NAICS Industries: 1987 to 2016 and 2015 to 2016-Continued.

See headnote on page 433.

| Industry | 2012 NAICS code [1] | Average annual percent change [2] | | | | | | | |
| | | 1987-2016 [3] | | | | 2015-2016 | | | |
		Output per hour	Unit labor costs	Output	Hours	Output per hour	Unit labor costs	Output	Hours
Sporting goods and musical instrument stores..	4511	4.1	-1.3	4.9	0.8	3.0	-6.6	3.8	0.8
Book, periodical, and music stores.............	4512	1.5	0.9	0.7	-0.8	0.6	-3.5	1.2	0.7
General merchandise stores.....................	452	3.0	-0.8	4.4	1.3	1.3	1.9	1.7	0.4
Department stores............................	4521	0.6	1.0	0.7	0.1	-1.9	2.8	-4.7	-2.8
Other general merchandise stores............	4529	5.3	-2.0	7.7	2.2	1.3	3.3	3.8	2.4
Miscellaneous store retailers...................	453	3.3	-1.0	3.3	-0.1	9.8	-3.6	5.3	-4.1
Florists......................................	4531	3.3	-0.3	0.2	-2.9	26.9	-14.1	10.8	-12.7
Office supplies, stationery and gift stores.......	4532	5.5	-2.4	4.0	-1.4	14.4	-3.2	0.6	-12.0
Used merchandise stores....................	4533	4.4	-2.1	6.0	1.5	2.0	0.6	1.1	-0.9
Other miscellaneous store retailers..........	4539	1.2	0.3	2.5	1.4	6.3	-2.7	8.1	1.7
Nonstore retailers.............................	454	8.1	-4.0	8.9	0.8	7.7	-0.4	12.6	4.5
Electronic shopping and mail-order houses.....	4541	10.0	-5.1	14.3	3.9	11.4	1.9	14.1	2.4
Vending machine operators...................	4542	0.4	2.9	-2.4	-2.8	-5.6	-0.4	-3.6	2.1
Direct selling establishments.................	4543	2.3	0.3	1.0	-1.3	-4.4	-0.2	4.5	9.4
Transportation and warehousing:									
Air transportation.............................	481	3.1	0.6	2.6	-0.4	0.4	5.7	3.4	2.9
Line-haul railroads............................	482111	3.6	-0.3	2.0	-1.5	9.6	-7.0	-0.1	-8.9
Truck transportation...........................	484	0.6	0.9	2.1	1.5	0.5	1.8	–	-0.5
General freight trucking......................	4841	1.1	1.0	2.4	1.3	-2.3	5.1	-1.9	0.5
Used household and office goods moving.......	48421	-0.7	2.6	-0.2	0.5	(NA)	(NA)	(NA)	(NA)
Postal service.................................	491	0.5	3.2	-0.7	-1.2	1.3	3.1	1.2	-0.2
Couriers and messengers......................	492	-1.9	3.3	0.4	2.4	-1.5	3.4	3.6	5.2
Warehousing and storage......................	493	2.2	–	5.8	3.5	-8.8	5.6	5.1	15.2
General warehousing and storage.............	49311	3.4	-0.9	7.2	3.6	(NA)	(NA)	(NA)	(NA)
Refrigerated warehousing and storage.........	49312	-0.3	1.7	2.8	3.1	(NA)	(NA)	(NA)	(NA)
Information:									
Publishing....................................	511	3.7	1.5	3.4	-0.3	2.3	7.3	-0.4	-2.6
Newspaper, book, and directory publishers.....	5111	-0.4	4.4	-2.6	-2.2	(NA)	(NA)	(NA)	(NA)
Software publishers..........................	5112	11.6	-6.0	18.1	5.9	-2.1	10.4	1.8	4.0
Motion picture and video exhibition............	51213	1.9	1.8	1.8	-0.1	(NA)	(NA)	(NA)	(NA)
Broadcasting, except internet..................	515	2.9	1.8	3.0	0.1	7.7	-2.7	4.3	-3.2
Radio and television broadcasting..............	5151	1.9	2.1	1.6	-0.3	2.3	2.0	1.3	-0.9
Cable and other subscription programming.....	5152	5.1	2.7	6.9	1.7	19.1	-9.6	6.6	-10.5
Wired telecommunications carriers.............	5171	3.7	-0.8	2.8	-0.9	3.0	4.6	1.4	-1.6
Wireless telecommunications carriers...........	5172	11.7	-6.7	19.1	6.6	12.7	-10.4	8.5	-3.8
Finance and insurance:									
Commercial banking...........................	52211	3.4	1.8	3.2	-0.2	-3.5	3.8	-0.6	3.1
Real estate and rental and leasing:									
Passenger car rental..........................	532111	1.8	2.0	2.7	0.9	(NA)	(NA)	(NA)	(NA)
Truck, trailer and RV rental and leasing..........	53212	2.2	1.1	2.5	0.4	-1.4	3.8	4.2	5.7
Video tape and disc rental.....................	53223	6.8	-2.1	-1.2	-7.4	(NA)	(NA)	(NA)	(NA)
Professional and technical services:									
Accounting and bookkeeping services..........	5412	2.6	1.2	3.4	0.7	8.8	-3.3	8.1	-0.6
Architectural services.........................	54131	1.5	1.9	2.4	0.9	(NA)	(NA)	(NA)	(NA)
Engineering services..........................	54133	1.2	3.0	2.8	1.6	-0.2	0.4	0.2	0.4
Advertising agencies..........................	54181	1.6	2.5	2.2	0.6	(NA)	(NA)	(NA)	(NA)
Photography studios, portrait..................	541921	0.2	1.8	1.2	1.0	(NA)	(NA)	(NA)	(NA)
Administrative and waste services:									
Employment placement agencies...............	56131	4.1	0.3	5.1	1.0	(NA)	(NA)	(NA)	(NA)
Travel arrangement and reservation services....	5615	6.2	-1.2	3.6	-2.4	0.3	3.4	6.6	6.2
Janitorial services.............................	56172	1.9	1.5	3.5	1.6	(NA)	(NA)	(NA)	(NA)
Health care and social assistance:									
Medical and diagnostic laboratories..............	6215	2.0	0.5	5.1	3.1	2.1	2.1	2.2	0.1
Arts, entertainment, and recreation:									
Amusement parks and arcades.................	7131	-2.7	6.2	-0.9	1.9	3.4	3.9	2.7	-0.7
Fitness and recreational sports centers...........	71394	3.7	-0.8	4.0	0.3	(NA)	(NA)	(NA)	(NA)
Accommodation and food services...............	72	0.8	2.7	2.3	1.5	(NA)	(NA)	(NA)	(NA)
Accommodation...............................	721	2.1	1.7	2.8	0.7	(NA)	(NA)	(NA)	(NA)
Traveler accommodation......................	7211	2.1	1.7	2.8	0.7	(NA)	(NA)	(NA)	(NA)
Food services and drinking places...............	722	0.4	3.1	2.1	1.7	1.3	2.5	3.5	2.2
Special food services.........................	7223	1.0	1.6	2.4	1.4	12.4	-1.7	3.2	-8.2
Drinking places, alcoholic beverages..........	7224	-0.5	3.5	-0.6	-0.1	1.4	1.8	3.9	2.5
Restaurants and other eating places...........	7225	0.5	3.3	2.3	1.8	0.3	3.1	3.5	3.2
Other services:									
Automotive repair and maintenance..............	8111	1.0	2.3	1.4	0.4	-0.8	7.1	-0.5	0.3
Reupholstery and furniture repair................	81142	-0.5	3.4	-2.7	-2.2	(NA)	(NA)	(NA)	(NA)
Personal care services.........................	8121	2.4	1.6	3.4	1.0	(NA)	(NA)	(NA)	(NA)
Funeral homes and funeral services.............	81221	-0.4	4.1	-0.3	0.1	(NA)	(NA)	(NA)	(NA)
Dry cleaning and laundry services..............	8123	2.0	1.5	1.0	-0.9	1.3	1.3	2.4	1.0
Coin-operated laundries and drycleaners.........	81231	2.5	1.7	0.5	-2.0	(NA)	(NA)	(NA)	(NA)
Dry cleaning and laundry services..............	81232	0.8	2.1	-1.1	-1.9	(NA)	(NA)	(NA)	(NA)
Photofinishing.................................	81292	2.6	2.0	-4.3	-6.7	(NA)	(NA)	(NA)	(NA)

NA Not available. – Represents zero or rounds to less than half the unit of measurement shown. [1] North American Industry Classification System, 2012 (NAICS); see text, Section 15. [2] Average annual percent changes based on compound rate formula. Rates of change are calculated using index numbers to three decimal places. [3] For NAICS industries 22 and 48-81 average annual percent changes are for 1987-2015. For NAICS industries 484, 4841, 493, 49311, and 49312, annual percent changes are for 1992-2015. For NAICS industries 48421, 71391 and 71394, average annual percent changes are for 2002-2015. For NAICS industries 5412, and 5615 average annual percent changes are for 1997-2015. For NAICS industries 56131, and 6215 average annual percent changes are for 1994-2015. For NAICS industry 7131 average annual percent change is for 2007-2015.

Source: U.S. Bureau of Labor Statistics. Labor Productivity and Costs, "Productivity and Costs by Industry," <http://www.bls.gov/lpc/data.htm>, accessed September 2017.

Table 662. Productivity and Related Measures: 1980 to 2016

[See text, this section. Minus sign (-) indicates decrease]

Item	1980	1990	2000	2010	2012	2013	2014	2015	2016
INDEXES (2009=100)									
Output per hour, business sector...................	53.5	64.1	80.0	103.3	104.0	104.8	105.4	106.2	106.6
Nonfarm business...............................	54.9	64.6	80.3	103.3	104.3	104.7	105.5	106.4	106.7
Manufacturing................................	(NA)	50.6	75.0	110.7	119.0	119.1	119.3	118.5	118.7
Output [1], business sector........................	41.9	59.3	87.3	103.2	108.4	110.8	114.1	117.6	119.8
Nonfarm business...............................	42.1	59.4	87.5	103.2	108.8	110.9	114.3	117.8	119.8
Manufacturing................................	(NA)	75.6	111.4	110.7	124.1	125.3	127.4	127.8	128.1
Hours [2], business sector.........................	78.2	92.5	109.2	99.9	104.2	105.8	108.3	110.7	112.4
Nonfarm business...............................	76.7	91.9	109.0	99.9	104.2	106.0	108.4	110.7	112.3
Manufacturing................................	(NA)	149.4	148.7	100.0	104.3	105.2	106.8	107.8	107.8
Compensation per hour [3], business sector.......	29.2	49.7	73.9	101.8	106.8	108.3	111.1	114.2	117.0
Nonfarm business...............................	29.5	49.9	74.1	101.9	106.9	108.2	111.2	114.5	117.3
Manufacturing................................	(NA)	50.5	73.3	101.3	104.9	105.1	108.0	110.6	113.5
Real hourly compensation [3], business sector....	72.4	79.1	92.1	100.2	99.8	99.7	100.7	103.4	104.6
Nonfarm business...............................	73.1	79.5	92.4	100.3	99.9	99.6	100.8	103.6	104.8
Manufacturing................................	(NA)	80.4	91.4	99.6	98.0	96.8	97.9	100.1	101.4
Unit labor costs [4], business sector..............	54.5	77.6	92.5	98.6	102.7	103.4	105.4	107.5	109.8
Nonfarm business...............................	53.7	77.2	92.3	98.7	102.5	103.3	105.4	107.5	109.9
Manufacturing................................	(NA)	99.7	97.8	91.5	88.2	88.2	90.5	93.3	95.6
ANNUAL PERCENT CHANGE [5]									
Output per hour, business sector...................	-0.1	2.0	3.1	3.3	0.7	0.7	0.6	0.8	0.3
Nonfarm business...............................	-0.1	1.7	3.0	3.3	0.9	0.3	0.8	0.9	0.2
Manufacturing................................	(NA)	3.6	6.6	10.7	1.7	0.1	0.1	-0.6	0.2
Output [1], business sector........................	-0.9	1.6	4.5	3.2	2.9	2.2	3.0	3.1	1.8
Nonfarm business...............................	-0.9	1.5	4.4	3.2	3.1	2.0	3.0	3.1	1.7
Manufacturing................................	(NA)	0.5	5.7	10.7	4.1	1.0	1.7	0.3	0.2
Hours [2], business sector.........................	-0.9	-0.4	1.4	-0.1	2.2	1.5	2.3	2.3	1.5
Nonfarm business...............................	-0.8	-0.2	1.4	-0.1	2.2	1.7	2.2	2.1	1.5
Manufacturing................................	(NA)	-3.0	-0.8	–	2.3	0.8	1.5	1.0	–
Compensation per hour [3], business sector.......	10.7	6.2	7.0	1.8	2.7	1.3	2.6	2.8	2.4
Nonfarm business...............................	10.7	6.0	7.0	1.9	2.6	1.2	2.8	3.0	2.5
Manufacturing................................	(NA)	5.5	7.0	1.3	1.7	0.2	2.8	2.4	2.6
Real hourly compensation [3], business sector....	-0.4	1.2	3.4	0.2	0.7	-0.1	1.0	2.7	1.2
Nonfarm business...............................	-0.4	1.0	3.5	0.3	0.6	-0.3	1.1	2.8	1.2
Manufacturing................................	(NA)	0.6	3.5	-0.4	-0.3	-1.3	1.1	2.3	1.3
Unit labor costs [4], business sector..............	10.8	4.1	3.7	-1.4	2.0	0.6	2.0	2.0	2.1
Nonfarm business...............................	10.8	4.2	4.0	-1.3	1.7	0.9	2.0	2.0	2.2
Manufacturing................................	(NA)	1.9	0.4	-8.5	–	–	2.7	3.0	2.4

– Represents or rounds to zero. NA Not available. [1] Refers to gross sectoral product, a chain–type, current–weighted index. [2] Hours at work of all persons engaged in the business and nonfarm business sectors (employees, proprietors, and unpaid family workers), and employees' and proprietors' hours in manufacturing. [3] Wages and salaries of employees plus employers' contributions for social insurance and private benefit plans. Also includes an estimate of same for self-employed. Real compensation deflated by the Consumer Price Index research series; see text, Section 14. [4] Hourly compensation divided by output per hour. [5] All changes are from the immediate prior year.

Source: U.S. Bureau of Labor Statistics, Labor Productivity and Costs, "Major Sector Productivity and Costs," <http://www.bls.gov/lpc/home.htm>, accessed June 2017.

Table 663. Employed Persons and Average Hours Worked Per Day at Workplace and at Home: 2016

[161,767 represents 161,767,000. Civilian noninstitutionalized population 15 years old and over, except as indicated. Includes work at main job and any other jobs. Excludes travel related to work. Based on the American Time Use Survey]

Characteristic	Total employed (1,000)	Employed persons who worked on an average day [1]								
		Total			Worked at workplace			Worked at home [2]		
		Number (1,000)	Percent of employed	Hours of work	Number (1,000)	Percent of those who worked	Hours of work	Number (1,000)	Percent of those who worked	Hours of work
Total......................	**161,767**	**110,592**	**68.4**	**7.63**	**92,045**	**83.2**	**7.88**	**24,703**	**22.3**	**3.13**
Work status: [3]										
Full-time workers [4]........	124,574	90,275	72.5	8.15	75,881	84.1	8.33	20,214	22.4	3.31
Part-time workers [4].......	37,193	20,318	54.6	5.34	16,164	79.6	5.78	4,489	22.1	2.31
Male [3].....................	86,113	61,666	71.6	8.04	51,823	84.0	8.23	13,146	21.3	3.28
Full-time workers [4]........	72,970	54,468	74.6	8.35	45,704	83.9	8.55	11,899	21.8	3.32
Part-time workers [4].......	13,143	7,198	54.8	5.73	6,119	85.0	5.90	1,246	17.3	2.93
Female [3]....................	75,654	48,927	64.7	7.11	40,222	82.2	7.43	11,557	23.6	2.95
Full-time workers [4]........	51,604	35,807	69.4	7.84	30,177	84.3	8.00	8,314	23.2	3.30
Part-time workers [4].......	24,050	13,119	54.5	5.12	10,045	76.6	5.70	3,243	24.7	2.08
Jobholding status:										
Single jobholders.........	145,543	97,319	66.9	7.59	81,430	83.7	7.87	20,439	21.0	3.05
Multiple jobholders........	16,224	13,273	81.8	7.90	10,616	80.0	7.95	4,264	32.1	3.49
Educational attainment: [5]										
Less than high school....	9,693	6,546	67.5	8.00	5,599	85.5	7.85	577	8.8	5.14
High school diploma [6]....	34,377	23,076	67.1	7.87	20,714	89.8	8.08	2,780	12.0	2.89
Some college..............	34,655	23,846	68.8	7.92	20,361	85.4	7.98	4,914	20.6	3.60
Bachelor's degree or higher...................	59,417	42,719	71.9	7.47	31,855	74.6	7.98	15,476	36.2	2.99

[1] Individuals may have worked at more than one location. [2] "Working at home" includes any time persons did work at home and is not restricted to persons whose usual workplace is their home. [3] Includes workers whose hours vary. [4] Full-time workers usually worked 35 or more hours per week at all jobs combined; part-time workers worked fewer than 35 hours per week. [5] For persons 25 years old and over. [6] Includes persons with a high school diploma or equivalent.

Source: U.S. Bureau of Labor Statistics, *American Time Use Survey—2016 Results*, USDL 17-0880, June 2017. See also <http://www.bls.gov/tus/home.htm#news>.

Table 664. Annual Total Compensation and Wages and Salary Accruals Per Full-Time Equivalent Employee by Industry: 2000 to 2016

[In dollars. Compensation is equal to the sum of wages and salaries and of supplements to wages and salaries; supplements are made on behalf of employees but are not included in regular wage payments to employees, such as contributions for employee pension and insurance funds, and employer contributions for government social insurance. Wages and salaries consist of cash remuneration of labor, including sick or vacation pay, severance pay, commissions, tips, and bonuses. Based on the 2002 North American Industry Classification System (NAICS); see text, Section 15]

Industry	Total annual compensation				Annual salary and wages			
	2000	2010	2015	2016	2000	2010	2015	2016
Compensation of employees..................	**47,619**	**66,472**	**74,060**	**75,168**	**39,238**	**53,247**	**59,952**	**60,905**
Domestic industries...................................	47,520	66,085	73,405	74,407	39,166	52,951	59,439	60,308
Private industries....................................	46,136	62,414	69,958	70,764	38,862	51,906	58,708	59,458
Agriculture, forestry, fishing, and hunting........	25,875	37,525	41,719	44,399	22,146	31,058	34,691	37,136
Mining...	70,434	107,698	124,511	125,975	58,134	91,870	105,536	105,178
Utilities...	84,821	123,870	140,598	145,781	64,772	89,595	104,901	105,897
Construction.......................................	46,190	63,590	71,644	73,119	38,551	52,753	59,679	61,353
Manufacturing......................................	54,167	75,493	83,119	84,045	43,957	60,018	66,821	67,607
Wholesale trade...................................	59,068	78,047	89,718	90,107	50,896	67,163	77,164	77,670
Retail trade..	31,224	38,457	42,171	42,690	26,589	32,029	35,417	35,880
Transportation and warehousing..................	48,462	62,399	68,589	70,192	39,055	49,710	55,738	56,824
Information..	72,135	98,949	123,589	124,809	62,571	81,295	103,708	106,713
Finance and insurance............................	76,234	104,096	121,011	122,705	64,574	88,166	103,644	104,782
Real estate and rental and leasing...............	43,235	57,905	69,890	70,377	37,150	49,081	59,918	60,583
Professional, scientific, and technical services..	71,592	95,328	110,175	110,571	62,472	82,524	95,481	96,451
Management of companies and enterprises [1]...	90,766	126,733	145,641	142,610	74,253	103,874	125,502	122,552
Administrative and waste management services..	28,921	44,875	48,644	49,289	25,035	37,369	41,291	42,183
Educational services..............................	34,164	50,674	56,673	58,263	29,244	41,324	45,189	45,959
Health care and social assistance...............	42,009	59,635	64,278	65,530	35,249	48,993	53,005	53,843
Arts, entertainment, and recreation...............	37,384	49,764	55,883	57,489	32,482	42,715	48,163	49,020
Accommodation and food services..............	20,819	27,955	32,169	32,731	18,045	24,133	27,640	28,290
Other services, except government..............	30,412	41,703	47,671	49,016	25,990	35,857	41,036	42,172
Government...	55,070	83,990	92,688	95,140	40,824	58,045	63,524	65,146
Federal...	61,449	105,049	114,145	114,977	46,749	74,665	79,879	80,384
State and local....................................	53,288	78,242	87,120	89,914	39,169	53,509	59,280	61,132

[1] Consists of offices of bank and other holding companies and of corporate, subsidiary, and regional managing offices.

Source: U.S. Bureau of Economic Analysis, National Income and Product Accounts Tables, "Table 6.2D. Compensation of Employees by Industry," "Table 6.5D. Full-Time Equivalent Employees by Industry," and "Table 6.6D. Wages and Salaries Per Full-Time Equivalent Employee by Industry," <http://www.bea.gov/itable/>, accessed August 2017.

Table 665. Average Hourly and Weekly Earnings by Private Industry Group: 2000 to 2016

[In dollars. Average earnings include overtime. Data are for production and nonsupervisory employees. See headnote, Table 653]

Private industry group	Current dollars					Constant (1982–84) dollars [1]				
	2000	2010	2014	2015	2016	2000	2010	2014	2015	2016
AVERAGE HOURLY EARNINGS										
Total private...............................	**14.02**	**19.05**	**20.61**	**21.03**	**21.54**	**8.30**	**8.90**	**8.85**	**9.07**	**9.20**
Mining and logging...........................	16.55	23.82	26.84	26.48	27.05	9.80	11.13	11.53	11.42	11.56
Construction..................................	17.48	23.22	24.67	25.20	25.97	10.35	10.85	10.60	10.87	11.09
Manufacturing.................................	14.32	18.61	19.56	19.91	20.43	8.48	8.70	8.40	8.59	8.73
Trade, transportation, and utilities [2]........	13.31	16.82	18.27	18.67	18.99	7.88	7.86	7.85	8.05	8.11
Information.....................................	19.07	25.87	28.70	29.05	30.04	11.29	12.09	12.33	12.53	12.83
Financial activities [2].........................	15.04	21.55	24.71	25.34	26.11	8.90	10.07	10.62	10.93	11.15
Professional and business services [2].....	15.52	22.78	24.29	24.79	25.42	9.19	10.65	10.44	10.69	10.86
Education and health services [2]...........	13.91	19.95	21.64	22.09	22.53	8.24	9.32	9.30	9.53	9.63
Leisure and hospitality [2]....................	8.32	11.31	12.09	12.41	12.85	4.93	5.29	5.19	5.35	5.49
Other services.................................	12.73	17.06	18.51	19.01	19.36	7.54	7.97	7.95	8.20	8.27
AVERAGE WEEKLY EARNINGS										
Total private...............................	**481**	**636**	**695**	**709**	**724**	**285**	**297**	**299**	**306**	**309**
Mining and logging...........................	735	1,063	1,271	1,212	1,224	435	497	546	523	523
Construction..................................	686	892	977	998	1,031	406	417	420	431	441
Manufacturing.................................	591	765	822	832	856	350	358	353	359	366
Trade, transportation, and utilities.........	450	560	614	629	637	266	262	264	271	272
Information.....................................	701	940	1,030	1,038	1,068	415	439	443	448	456
Financial activities [2].........................	540	780	908	939	963	320	365	390	405	411
Professional and business services [2].....	535	799	864	879	899	317	373	371	379	384
Education and health services [2]...........	448	639	693	709	724	265	299	298	306	309
Leisure and hospitality [2]....................	217	281	304	311	320	129	131	131	134	137
Other services.................................	413	524	569	584	596	245	245	244	252	255

[1] Earnings in current dollars divided by the Consumer Price Index (CPI-W) on a 1982–84 base; see text, Section 14. [2] For composition of industries, see Table 655.

Source: U.S. Bureau of Labor Statistics, Current Employment Statistics, "Employment, Hours, and Earnings—National," <http://www.bls.gov/ces/data.htm>, accessed March 2017.

Table 666. Employment and Wages of Private Sector and Government Employees: 2000 to 2016

[7,879 represents 7,879,000. Based on federal-state cooperative program, The Quarterly Census of Employment and Wages (QCEW), also referenced as ES-202. Includes workers covered by state unemployment insurance laws and federal civilian workers covered by unemployment compensation for federal employees. Excludes most agricultural workers on small farms, all Armed Forces, elected officials in most states, railroad employees, most domestic workers, most student workers at school, value of meals and lodging, and tips and other gratuities]

Employment and wages	Unit	2000	2010	2012	2013	2014	2015	2016
Establishments:								
Total	**1,000**	**7,879**	**8,993**	**9,122**	**9,206**	**9,361**	**9,523**	**9,717**
Excluding federal	1,000	7,829	8,926	9,057	9,144	9,300	9,462	9,656
Private	1,000	7,622	8,696	8,826	8,912	9,067	9,224	9,418
State government	1,000	65	67	66	66	68	69	69
Local governments	1,000	141	164	164	165	165	169	169
Federal government	1,000	50	67	65	62	61	61	60
Average annual employment:								
Total	**1,000**	**129,877**	**127,820**	**131,696**	**133,968**	**136,614**	**139,492**	**141,870**
Excluding federal	1,000	127,006	124,840	128,876	131,198	133,884	136,735	139,077
Private	1,000	110,015	106,201	110,646	112,958	115,569	118,308	120,505
State government	1,000	4,370	4,606	4,524	4,525	4,545	4,567	4,570
Local governments	1,000	12,620	14,032	13,706	13,714	13,770	13,861	14,003
Federal government	1,000	2,871	2,981	2,821	2,771	2,730	2,756	2,793
Annual wages:								
Total	**Bil. dol.**	**4,588**	**5,976**	**6,491**	**6,673**	**7,017**	**7,385**	**7,607**
Excluding federal	Bil. dol.	4,455	5,769	6,284	6,471	6,810	7,170	7,388
Private	Bil. dol.	3,888	4,934	5,444	5,614	5,928	6,256	6,449
State government	Bil. dol.	159	226	232	238	246	255	261
Local governments	Bil. dol.	409	610	608	619	636	659	678
Federal government	Bil. dol.	133	206	207	202	207	215	219
Average annual wage per employee:								
Total	**Dol.**	**35,323**	**46,751**	**49,289**	**49,808**	**51,364**	**52,942**	**53,621**
Excluding federal	Dol.	35,077	46,215	48,763	49,320	50,866	52,439	53,124
Private	Dol.	35,337	46,455	49,200	49,701	51,296	52,876	53,515
State government	Dol.	36,296	48,960	51,366	52,544	54,179	55,878	57,168
Local governments	Dol.	32,387	43,493	44,373	45,115	46,155	47,573	48,440
Federal government	Dol.	46,228	69,198	73,340	72,903	75,797	77,900	78,379
Average weekly wage per employee:								
Total	**Dol.**	**679**	**899**	**948**	**958**	**988**	**1,018**	**1,031**
Excluding federal	Dol.	675	889	938	948	978	1,008	1,022
Private	Dol.	680	893	946	956	986	1,017	1,029
State government	Dol.	698	942	988	1,010	1,042	1,075	1,099
Local governments	Dol.	623	836	853	868	888	915	932
Federal government	Dol.	889	1,331	1,410	1,402	1,458	1,498	1,507

Source: U.S. Bureau of Labor Statistics, Quarterly Census of Employment and Wages, "QCEW Data Viewer," and earlier releases <http://www.bls.gov/cew/>, accessed September 2017.

Table 667. Average Annual Wage by State: 2015 and 2016

[In dollars, except percent change. See headnote, Table 666]

State/area	Average wage per employee 2015	2016	Percent change, 2015-16	State/area	Average wage per employee 2015	2016	Percent change, 2015-16
United States	**52,942**	**53,621**	**1.3**	Montana	40,056	40,716	1.6
Alabama	44,273	44,832	1.3	Nebraska	42,854	43,597	1.7
Alaska	54,755	53,605	-2.1	Nevada	45,739	47,114	3.0
Arizona	47,933	48,523	1.2	New Hampshire	52,553	53,563	1.9
Arkansas	40,895	41,571	1.7	New Jersey	62,365	62,777	0.7
California	61,698	62,964	2.1	New Mexico	42,555	42,599	0.1
Colorado	54,182	54,664	0.9	New York	67,521	67,940	0.6
Connecticut	65,530	65,870	0.5	North Carolina	46,530	47,269	1.6
Delaware	53,991	53,765	-0.4	North Dakota	50,696	48,873	-3.6
District of Columbia	88,159	89,481	1.5	Ohio	47,146	47,700	1.2
Florida	46,260	47,035	1.7	Oklahoma	44,306	43,906	-0.9
Georgia	49,551	50,676	2.3	Oregon	48,328	49,474	2.4
Hawaii	46,919	48,178	2.7	Pennsylvania	52,187	52,460	0.5
Idaho	38,857	39,637	2.0	Rhode Island	50,651	51,453	1.6
Illinois	55,989	56,447	0.8	South Carolina	42,002	42,881	2.1
Indiana	43,903	44,590	1.6	South Dakota	40,181	41,178	2.5
Iowa	44,095	44,910	1.8	Tennessee	46,742	47,403	1.4
Kansas	43,878	44,142	0.6	Texas	54,281	54,333	0.1
Kentucky	43,365	44,099	1.7	Utah	44,318	45,255	2.1
Louisiana	45,928	45,622	-0.7	Vermont	44,234	45,030	1.8
Maine	41,791	42,596	1.9	Virginia	54,276	54,836	1.0
Maryland	57,176	58,106	1.6	Washington	56,661	59,024	4.2
Massachusetts	66,692	67,432	1.1	West Virginia	41,727	41,665	-0.1
Michigan	50,063	50,943	1.8	Wisconsin	45,365	46,008	1.4
Minnesota	53,527	54,297	1.4	Wyoming	46,306	44,974	-2.9
Mississippi	37,642	38,144	1.3	Puerto Rico	27,457	27,415	-0.2
Missouri	45,565	46,122	1.2	Virgin Islands	39,154	39,807	1.7

Source: U.S. Bureau of Labor Statistics, Quarterly Census of Employment and Wages, "Employment and Wages Online Annual Averages, 2016," and earlier editions, <http://www.bls.gov/cew/home.htm>, accessed September 2017.

Table 668. Full-Time Wage and Salary Workers—Number and Earnings: 2010 to 2016

[99,531 represents 99,531,000. Earnings shown in current dollars; data represent annual averages of usual weekly earnings. Full time workers are those who usually worked 35 hours or more at all jobs combined. Based on the Current Population Survey; see text, Section 1 and Appendix III. For definition of median, see Guide to Tabular Presentation]

Characteristic	Number of workers (1,000)			Median weekly earnings (dollars)		
	2010	2015	2016	2010	2015	2016
All workers [1]	99,531	109,080	111,091	747	809	832
Male	55,059	60,746	61,930	824	895	915
Female	44,472	48,334	49,161	669	726	749
White [2]	80,656	85,443	86,474	765	835	862
Black [2]	11,658	13,587	13,963	611	641	678
Asian [2]	4,946	6,638	7,030	855	993	1,021
Hispanic [3]	14,837	18,311	18,950	535	604	624
OCCUPATION						
Management, professional and related occupations	39,145	44,844	45,930	1,063	1,158	1,188
Management, business, and financial operations	15,648	18,422	19,023	1,155	1,258	1,284
Professional and related occupations	23,497	26,423	26,907	1,008	1,112	1,141
Computer and mathematical occupations	3,202	4,009	4,104	1,289	1,428	1,443
Architecture and engineering occupations	2,366	2,656	2,835	1,255	1,424	1,482
Life, physical, and social science occupations	1,127	1,176	1,151	1,062	1,206	1,209
Community and social services occupations	1,909	2,143	2,136	802	889	919
Legal occupations	1,248	1,346	1,294	1,213	1,391	1,431
Education, training, and library occupations	6,535	6,884	6,859	913	956	984
Arts, design, entertainment, sports, and media	1,431	1,643	1,671	920	1,001	1,040
Healthcare practitioner and technical occupations	5,678	6,566	6,857	986	1,041	1,104
Service occupations	14,424	15,279	15,908	479	509	523
Healthcare support occupations	2,219	2,395	2,423	471	498	525
Protective service occupations	2,872	2,729	2,697	747	796	809
Food preparation and serving-related occupations	3,823	4,124	4,619	406	441	465
Building and grounds cleaning and maintenance	3,310	3,605	3,602	446	486	510
Personal care and service occupations	2,199	2,427	2,568	455	498	505
Sales and office occupations	23,060	23,620	23,625	631	673	698
Sales and related occupations	9,121	9,725	9,759	666	716	744
Office and administrative support occupations	13,939	13,894	13,866	619	656	679
Natural resources, construction, and maintenance	9,869	10,834	11,022	719	761	786
Farming, fishing, and forestry occupations	729	810	842	416	464	520
Construction and extraction occupations	5,020	5,722	5,979	709	749	784
Installation, maintenance, and repair occupations	4,120	4,301	4,201	794	839	861
Production, transportation, and material-moving	13,034	14,504	14,606	599	656	665
Production occupations	6,861	7,551	7,513	599	663	668
Transportation and material-moving occupations	6,172	6,953	7,093	599	646	662

[1] Includes other races, not shown separately. [2] For persons in this race group only. See footnote 3, Table 611. [3] Persons of Hispanic origin may be of any race.

Source: U.S. Bureau of Labor Statistics, CPS Tables, "Median weekly earnings of full-time wage and salary workers by selected characteristics" and "Median weekly earnings of full-time wage and salary workers by detailed occupation and sex," February 2017, and earlier releases, <http://www.bls.gov/cps/tables.htm>.

Table 669. Median Usual Weekly Earnings of Full-Time Wage and Salary Workers by Sex and Education: 1980 to 2016

[In current dollars. For wage and salary workers 25 years old and over. Based on Current Population Survey; see text, Section 1 and Appendix III. Wages and salaries are collected before taxes and other deductions and include overtime pay, commissions, or tips usually received at principal job. Earnings reported on basis other than weekly are converted to a weekly equivalent. Excludes all incorporated and unincorporated self employed. Data not strictly comparable to data for earlier years. See text this section and <http://www.bls.gov/cps/eetech_methods.pdf>]

Year and sex	Total	Less than a high school diploma	High school, no college [1]	Some college or associate's degree	Bachelor's degree and higher [2]
CURRENT DOLLARS					
Male:					
1980	339	267	327	358	427
1990	512	349	459	542	741
2000	693	406	591	691	1,020
2010	874	486	710	845	1,330
2015	947	520	759	883	1,420
2016	969	551	769	896	1,464
Female:					
1980	213	164	201	231	290
1990	369	240	315	395	535
2000	516	304	420	505	756
2010	704	388	543	638	986
2015	761	418	586	664	1,064
2016	784	423	599	688	1,101
WOMEN'S EARNINGS AS PERCENT OF MEN'S					
1980	62.8	61.4	61.5	64.5	67.9
1990	72.1	68.8	68.6	72.9	72.2
2000	74.5	74.9	71.1	73.1	74.1
2010	80.5	79.8	76.5	75.5	74.1
2015	80.4	80.4	77.2	75.2	74.9
2016	80.9	76.8	77.9	76.8	75.2

[1] Includes persons with a high school diploma or equivalent. [2] Includes persons with a bachelor's, master's, professional, or doctoral degree.

Source: U.S. Bureau of Labor Statistics, "Labor Force Statistics," <http://www.bls.gov/cps/data.htm>, accessed February 2017.

Table 670. Workers With Earnings by Occupation of Longest Held Job and Sex: 2015

[76,974 represents 76,974,000. As of March. For definition of median, see Guide to Tabular Presentation. Based on Annual Social and Economic Supplement (ASEC) of Current Population Survey; includes civilian noninstitutional population 15 years old and over, and military personnel who live in households with at least one other civilian adult. See text, Section 1, and Appendix III]

Major occupation group of longest job held in 2015	All workers				Full-time, year-round			
	Female		Male		Female		Male	
	Number (1,000)	Median earnings (dol.)	Number (1,000)	Median earnings (dol.)	Number (1,000)	Median earnings (dol.)	Number (1,000)	Median earnings (dol.)
Total	**76,974**	**30,246**	**86,435**	**41,615**	**47,211**	**40,742**	**63,887**	**51,212**
Management, business, and financial occupations	11,640	51,089	14,220	71,597	9,249	57,403	12,266	76,983
Professional and related occupations	21,108	44,221	15,462	65,508	13,512	51,855	12,022	75,510
Service occupations	16,378	17,009	12,777	23,878	7,720	26,025	7,694	32,074
Sales and office occupations	22,588	26,250	13,926	36,006	13,599	35,411	9,773	48,237
Natural resources, construction, and maintenance	828	20,204	14,317	36,352	408	31,127	10,372	41,710
Production, transportation, and material-moving occupations	4,358	22,247	15,043	34,671	2,662	29,697	11,140	40,873
Armed Forces	74	(B)	690	49,421	61	(B)	620	51,058

B Base less than 75,000.

Source: U.S. Census Bureau, *Income and Poverty in the United States: 2015*, September 2016, Current Population Reports, P60-256(RV); and "Detailed Tables: Person Table PINC-06," <http://www.census.gov/data/tables/time-series/demo/income-poverty/cps-pinc.html>, accessed January 2017.

Table 671. Employment Cost Index (ECI) for Total Compensation by Occupation and Industry: 2010 to 2016

[As of December (2005 = 100). The ECI is a measure of the rate of change in compensation (wages, salaries, and employer costs for employee benefits). Data are not seasonally adjusted. Industry classifications based on North American Industry Classification System (NAICS); occupation classifications based on the 2010 Standard Occupational Classification (SOC)]

Occupational group and industry	Indexes (December 2005 = 100)				Percent change for 12 months ending December			
	2010	2014	2015	2016	2010	2014	2015	2016
Civilian workers [1]	**113.2**	**122.7**	**125.1**	**127.9**	**2.0**	**2.2**	**2.0**	**2.2**
State and local government	**116.2**	**124.7**	**127.8**	**130.9**	**1.8**	**2.0**	**2.5**	**2.4**
Workers, by occupational group:								
Management, professional and related occupations	115.5	123.7	126.8	129.8	1.5	2.1	2.5	2.4
Sales and office occupations	116.6	126.4	129.2	132.4	1.9	2.4	2.2	2.5
Service occupations	118.0	127.1	130.0	133.5	2.3	2.3	2.3	2.7
Workers, by industry division:								
Service-providing industries: [2]								
Education and health services [2]	115.6	123.4	126.7	129.8	1.5	1.9	2.7	2.4
Schools	115.3	123.0	126.2	129.4	1.4	2.0	2.6	2.5
Health care and social assistance [2]	117.9	126.8	129.9	132.8	2.2	1.4	2.4	2.2
Hospitals	117.0	125.0	127.4	130.5	2.4	1.1	1.9	2.4
Public administration	116.8	126.4	129.1	132.0	1.9	2.4	2.1	2.2
Private industry workers [3]	**112.5**	**122.2**	**124.5**	**127.2**	**2.1**	**2.3**	**1.9**	**2.2**
Workers, by occupational group:								
Management, professional, and related occupations	113.0	123.0	125.3	127.4	2.1	2.3	1.9	1.7
Sales and office occupations	111.6	121.9	123.9	126.8	2.2	2.4	1.6	2.3
Natural resources, construction, and maintenance occupations	113.3	123.2	124.9	127.7	1.9	2.6	1.4	2.2
Production, transportation, and material moving occupations	111.5	120.6	123.7	127.0	2.4	2.2	2.6	2.7
Service occupations	113.5	121.1	123.2	127.2	1.5	1.8	1.7	3.2
Workers, by industry division:								
Goods-producing industries [2]	111.1	120.3	123.2	125.8	2.3	2.2	2.4	2.1
Construction	112.7	120.7	123.4	125.8	0.9	1.8	2.2	1.9
Manufacturing	110.0	119.8	122.8	125.5	2.8	2.4	2.5	2.2
Service-providing industries [2]	113.0	122.8	124.9	127.7	2.0	2.3	1.7	2.2
Trade, transportation, and utilities	111.4	122.6	125.0	128.5	2.4	2.6	2.0	2.8
Information	110.0	124.4	122.7	125.4	1.6	5.6	-1.4	2.2
Financial activities	111.4	121.0	123.8	127.4	2.6	1.8	2.3	2.9
Professional and business services	114.6	124.2	126.5	128.0	2.0	2.5	1.9	1.2
Education and health services	114.7	123.3	125.4	127.8	1.7	1.7	1.7	1.9
Leisure and hospitality	114.1	119.6	121.8	125.8	1.2	1.7	1.8	3.3
Bargaining status:								
Union	114.8	126.7	128.7	130.6	3.3	3.3	1.6	1.5
Nonunion	112.1	121.5	123.8	126.6	1.8	2.1	1.9	2.3

[1] Includes workers in the private nonfarm economy except those in private households, and workers in the public sector, except the federal government. [2] Includes all other items not shown separately. [3] Excludes farm and household workers.

Source: U.S. Bureau of Labor Statistics, Employment Cost Trends, "Employment Cost Index," <http://www.bls.gov/ncs/ect/home.htm#data>, accessed January 2017.

Table 672. Federal and State Minimum Wage Rates: 1940 to 2017

[In current dollars. Wage rates are as of January 1, except Maine (January 7). Where an employee is subject to both the state and federal minimum wage laws, the employee is entitled to the higher minimum wage rate]

Year	Federal minimum wage rates per hour	State	2017 minimum wage rates per hour	State	2017 minimum wage rates per hour	State	2017 minimum wage rates per hour
1940................	0.30	AL.........	(X)	KY.........	7.25	ND.........	7.25
1945 (as of Oct. 24).....	0.40	AK.........	9.80	LA.........	(X)	OH.........	[7] 7.25/8.15
1950 (as of Jan. 25).....	0.75	AZ.........	8.05	ME.........	9.00	OK.........	[8] 2.00/7.25
1960................	1.00	AR.........	[2] 8.50	MD.........	8.75	OR.........	9.75
1965 (as of Sept. 3).....	1.25	CA.........	[9] 10.00/10.50	MA.........	11.00	PA.........	7.25
1970 (as of Feb. 1)......	1.45	CO.........	9.30	MI.........	[1] 8.90	RI.........	9.60
1975................	2.10	CT.........	10.10	MN.........	[4] 7.75/9.50	SC.........	(X)
1980................	3.10	DE.........	8.25	MS.........	(X)	SD.........	8.65
1985................	3.35	DC.........	11.50	MO........	[5] 7.70	TN.........	(X)
1990 (as of Apr. 1)......	3.80	FL.........	8.10	MT.........	[5] 4.00/8.15	TX.........	7.25
1995................	4.25	GA.........	[3] 5.15	NE.........	[2] 9.00	UT.........	7.25
2000................	5.15	HI.........	9.25	NV.........	[6] 7.25/8.25	VT.........	[1] 10.00
2005................	5.15	ID.........	7.25	NH.........	7.25	VA.........	[2] 7.25
2007 (as of Jul. 24).....	5.85	IL.........	[2] 8.25	NJ.........	8.44	WA.........	11.00
2008 (as of Jul. 24).....	6.55	IN.........	[1] 7.25	NM........	7.50	WV.........	[3] 8.75
2009 (as of Jul. 24).....	7.25	IA.........	7.25	NY.........	9.70	WI.........	7.25
2017................	7.25	KS.........	7.25	NC.........	7.25	WY.......	5.15

X Not applicable. [1] Employers of 2 or more. [2] Employers of 4 or more. [3] Employers of 6 or more. [4] Large employer (receipts of $500,000 or more) and small employer (with annual receipts of less than $500,000). [5] Lower rate for businesses with gross annual sales of $110,000 or less. [6] Nevada: $8.25 with no health insurance benefits provided by employer. $7.25 with health insurance provided by employer and received by employee. [7] Ohio: $7.25 for those employers grossing $297,000 or less. [8] Oklahoma: employers of 10 or more full time employees at any one location, and employers with gross sales over $100,000 regardless of number of full-time employees. All other employers $2.00. [9] California $10.00 minimum wage for employers with 25 or fewer employees, and $10.50 minimum wage for employers with 26 or more employees.

Source: U.S. Department of Labor, Wage and Hour Division, "History of Federal Minimum Wage Rates Under the Fair Labor Standards Act," and "Minimum Wage Laws in the States—January 1, 2017," <https://www.dol.gov/whd/minwage/america.htm>, accessed May 2017.

Table 673. Workers Paid Hourly Rates At or Below Federal Minimum Wage by Selected Characteristics: 2016

[79,883 represents 79,883,000. Data are annual averages. For employed wage and salary workers, excluding the incorporated self-employed. Based on the Current Population Survey; see text, Section 1 and Appendix III]

Characteristic	Number of workers paid hourly rates (1,000)				Percent of workers paid hourly rates			
		At or below federal minimum wage				At or below federal minimum wage		
	Total	Total	At prevailing federal minimum wage	Below prevailing federal minimum wage	Total	Total	At prevailing federal minimum wage	Below prevailing federal minimum wage
Total, 16 years and over [1]..........	79,883	2,153	701	1,451	2.7	0.9	1.8	
16 to 24 years.....................	15,856	976	383	594	6.2	2.4	3.7	
25 years and over...................	64,026	1,176	319	857	1.8	0.5	1.3	
Male, 16 years old and over...........	39,568	769	270	499	1.9	0.7	1.3	
16 to 24 years.....................	7,967	357	147	210	4.5	1.8	2.6	
25 years and over...................	30,601	412	122	289	1.3	0.4	0.9	
Female, 16 years old and over........	40,315	1,384	432	952	3.4	1.1	2.4	
16 to 24 years.....................	7,890	619	235	384	7.8	3.0	4.9	
25 years and over...................	32,425	764	196	568	2.4	0.6	1.8	
White [2]............................	61,080	1,597	469	1,127	2.6	0.8	1.8	
Men...............................	30,823	554	190	364	1.8	0.6	1.2	
Women.............................	30,256	1,043	280	763	3.4	0.9	2.5	
Black [2]............................	11,681	390	193	197	3.3	1.7	1.7	
Men...............................	5,297	156	62	93	2.9	1.2	1.8	
Women.............................	6,385	234	131	103	3.7	2.1	1.6	
Asian [2]............................	3,692	96	21	75	2.4	0.5	1.9	
Men...............................	1,841	35	10	25	1.9	0.5	1.4	
Women.............................	2,121	61	11	50	2.9	0.5	2.3	
Hispanic [3].........................	16,241	366	103	264	2.3	0.6	1.6	
Men...............................	9,044	137	44	93	1.5	0.5	1.0	
Women.............................	7,197	229	59	171	3.2	0.8	2.4	
Full-time workers....................	59,198	884	183	702	1.5	0.3	1.2	
Men...............................	32,418	334	66	268	1.0	0.2	0.8	
Women.............................	26,780	550	116	434	2.1	0.4	1.6	
Part-time workers [4].................	20,582	1,267	519	748	6.2	2.5	3.6	
Men...............................	7,108	434	203	231	6.1	2.9	3.3	
Women.............................	13,474	833	316	517	6.2	2.3	3.8	
Private sector industries..............	70,396	2,035	647	1,388	2.9	0.9	2.0	
Public sector industries..............	9,486	118	54	63	1.2	0.6	0.7	

[1] Includes other races, not shown separately. Also includes a small number of multiple jobholders whose full- or part-time status cannot be determined for their principal job. [2] For persons in this race group only. See footnote 3, Table 611. [3] Persons of Hispanic or Latino origin may be of any race. [4] Working fewer than 35 hours per week.

Source: U.S. Bureau of Labor Statistics, *Characteristics of Minimum Wage Workers: 2016*, April 2017. See also <https://www.bls.gov/cps/earnings.htm#minwage>.

Table 674. Earnings by Sex and Women's Earnings as a Percent of Men's Earnings by Occupation: 2015

[Median earnings in 2015 inflation-adjusted dollars for the full-time, year round civilian employed population age 16 years and over. Estimates subject to sampling variability. Based on the American Community Survey]

Occupation	Median earnings		Women's earnings as a percent of men's earnings
	Female	Male	
Total:	**40,022**	**50,119**	**79.9**
Management, business, science, and arts	53,521	75,407	71.0
Management, business, and financial	58,401	77,975	74.9
Management	61,138	80,809	75.7
Business and financial operations	55,043	71,816	76.6
Computer, engineering, and science	68,236	81,089	84.1
Computer and mathematical	71,378	82,130	86.9
Architecture and engineering	70,435	81,198	86.7
Life, physical, and social science	59,905	70,726	84.7
Education, legal, community service, arts, and media	46,386	57,809	80.2
Community and social service	41,893	45,658	91.8
Legal	64,121	120,270	53.3
Education, training, and library	45,789	55,772	82.1
Arts, design, entertainment, sports, and media	47,131	55,746	84.5
Healthcare practitioners and technical	56,629	80,084	70.7
Health diagnosing and treating practitioners and other technical	66,517	102,084	65.2
Health technologists and technicians	38,906	45,956	84.7
Service	23,924	31,254	76.5
Healthcare support	27,170	30,921	87.9
Protective service	40,787	52,118	78.3
Fire fighting and prevention, and other protective service workers including supervisors	32,959	42,027	78.4
Law enforcement workers including supervisors	48,388	61,190	79.1
Food preparation and serving related	20,620	23,729	86.9
Building and grounds cleaning and maintenance	21,421	28,980	73.9
Personal care and service	22,718	29,220	77.7
Sales and office	34,506	45,469	75.9
Sales and related	32,588	50,928	64.0
Office and administrative support	34,962	39,077	89.5
Natural resources, construction, and maintenance	31,210	41,124	75.9
Farming, fishing, and forestry	20,606	26,962	76.4
Construction and extraction	35,673	40,300	88.5
Installation, maintenance, and repair	41,070	45,515	90.2
Production, transportation, and material moving	27,200	39,401	69.0
Production	27,256	40,435	67.4
Transportation	31,533	42,204	74.7
Material moving	24,835	31,092	79.9

Source: U.S. Census Bureau, 2015 American Community Survey, B24022, "Sex by Occupation and Median Earnings in the Past 12 Months (in 2015 Inflation-Adjusted Dollars) for the Full-time, Year-Round Civilian Employed Population 16 Years and Over," <http://factfinder.census.gov/>, accessed December 2016.

Table 675. Workers' Earnings by Certification and License Status and Selected Characteristics: 2016

[In dollars, unless otherwise noted. Data shown for wage and salary workers aged 16 years old and over, unless otherwise noted. Excludes self-employed workers. Certifications are issued by a non-governmental certification body and convey that an individual has the knowledge or skill to perform a specific job. A license is awarded by a government agency and conveys a legal authority to work in an occupation. For definition of median, see Guide to Tabular Presentation]

Characteristic	Full-time wage and salary workers (1,000)	Median weekly earnings				
		Total	With a certification or license [1]			Without a certification or license
			Total	Certification only	With a license [2]	
Total workers, 16 years old and over	**111,091**	**832**	**1,032**	**1,089**	**1,026**	**765**
AGE						
16 to 24 years old	10,076	501	588	577	590	492
25 to 54 years old	78,392	871	1,035	1,127	1,025	804
55 years old and over	22,624	939	1,167	1,199	1,165	864
SEX						
Men	61,930	915	1,144	1,197	1,137	848
Women	49,161	749	945	928	947	684
RACE/ETHNICITY						
White	86,474	862	1,062	1,118	1,057	785
Black or African American	13,963	678	797	806	796	642
Asian	7,030	1,021	1,250	1,469	1,222	962
Hispanic or Latino ethnicity	18,950	624	884	917	880	600
EDUCATIONAL ATTAINMENT						
Workers, 25 years old and over	101,015	885	1,064	1,137	1,056	816
Less than a high school diploma	7,108	504	620	686	617	498
High school graduates, no college [3]	25,475	692	795	869	786	676
Some college or associate degree	27,307	779	849	910	838	760
Bachelor's degree and higher	41,125	1,259	1,296	1,480	1,272	1,242

[1] A person may have more than one certification or license. [2] Persons with a license may also have a certification. [3] Includes persons with a high school diploma or equivalent.

Source: U.S. Bureau of Labor Statistics, "Labor Force Statistics from the Current Population Survey," <http://www.bls.gov/cps/certifications-and-licenses.htm>, accessed July 2017.

Table 676. Average Hours Spent Per Day on Primary Activities by Married Mothers and Fathers by Employment Status: 2011 to 2015

[Data are shown for households with own children under age 18. Data are averages for 2011-2015 and cover an individual's main activity. Does not include secondary activities done simultaneously]

Activity	Both spouses work full time		Mother employed part time and father employed full time		Mother not employed and father employed full time	
	Mothers	Fathers	Mothers	Fathers	Mothers	Fathers
Total, all activities	24.00	24.00	24.00	24.00	24.00	24.00
Personal care activities	9.06	8.62	9.19	8.63	9.65	8.88
Sleeping	8.22	8.03	8.43	8.00	8.96	8.26
Household activities	1.87	1.29	2.70	1.22	3.62	0.98
Housework	0.74	0.27	1.14	0.22	1.56	0.18
Food preparation and cleanup	0.80	0.40	1.09	0.36	1.60	0.28
Lawn and garden care	0.06	0.24	0.13	0.22	0.13	0.16
Purchasing goods and services	0.51	0.31	0.62	0.30	0.66	0.35
Grocery shopping	0.13	0.07	0.19	0.05	0.21	0.07
Consumer goods purchases, except grocery shopping	0.31	0.20	0.33	0.20	0.34	0.23
Caring for and helping household members	1.36	0.92	1.79	0.87	2.58	0.81
Caring for and helping household children	1.35	0.89	1.76	0.86	2.56	0.79
Physical care	0.56	0.28	0.65	0.24	0.96	0.24
Education-related activities	0.11	0.09	0.20	0.08	0.31	0.06
Reading to/with children	0.04	0.03	0.07	0.03	0.09	0.03
Playing/doing hobbies with children	0.28	0.28	0.34	0.28	0.62	0.30
Working and work-related activities [1]	5.25	6.17	2.79	6.15	0.10	6.42
Working [1]	5.22	6.14	2.75	6.11	0.04	6.40
Leisure and sports	2.94	3.59	3.30	3.64	3.94	3.42
Socializing and communicating	0.63	0.59	0.71	0.61	0.82	0.62
Watching television	1.48	2.04	1.56	2.00	2.00	1.88
Participating in sports, exercise, and recreation	0.19	0.26	0.24	0.31	0.25	0.27
Travel	1.34	1.43	1.48	1.44	1.16	1.37
Travel related to caring for/helping household children	0.24	0.15	0.32	0.11	0.32	0.10
Other activities, not elsewhere classified	1.67	1.66	2.12	1.75	2.30	1.77

[1] Estimates include a small amount of work time done by persons who do not meet the American Time Use Survey definition of employed.

Source: U.S. Bureau of Labor Statistics, "American Time Use Survey," <http://www.bls.gov/tus/#tables>, accessed February 2017.

Table 677. Workers in Private Industry with Access to Domestic Partner Benefits for Same or Opposite Sex Partners by Selected Characteristics: 2011 and 2016

[In percent. As of March. Based on National Compensation Survey (NCS). See headnote, Table 680, and Appendix III. See Table 169 for data on health benefit program participation]

Characteristic	Defined benefit retirement survivor benefits				Healthcare benefits			
	Same sex		Opposite sex		Same sex		Opposite sex	
	2011	2016	2011	2016	2011	2016	2011	2016
Total	7	11	7	10	29	39	25	35
WORKER CHARACTERISTICS								
Management, professional, and related occupations	11	17	10	17	46	57	38	51
Service occupations	3	4	3	5	17	21	14	19
Sales and office occupations	8	10	7	10	30	41	26	38
Natural resources, construction, and maintenance occupations	8	9	7	7	22	28	18	24
Production, transportation, and material moving occupations	8	10	7	10	25	33	21	30
Full-time [1]	9	13	8	12	36	47	31	42
Part-time [1]	4	5	4	5	9	17	8	16
Union [2]	25	33	22	28	46	58	31	44
Nonunion [2]	6	8	5	9	28	37	24	34
AVERAGE HOURLY WAGE [3]								
Lowest 25 percent (under $12.00)	2	3	2	4	11	18	9	18
Lowest 10 percent (under $9.37)	1	1	1	2	6	8	4	8
Second 25 percent ($12.00 to $17.73)	5	8	5	8	26	37	23	34
Third 25 percent ($17.73 to $28.60)	9	12	8	12	35	45	30	40
Highest 25 percent ($28.60 and over)	15	22	14	20	50	61	41	53
Highest 10 percent ($44.33 and over)	16	24	15	23	59	69	49	61
ESTABLISHMENT CHARACTERISTICS								
1 to 99 workers	3	5	3	5	18	26	16	25
100 or more workers	12	17	12	17	42	55	34	47
Goods producing [4]	6	10	6	9	27	35	24	32
Service producing [4]	8	11	7	11	30	40	25	35

[1] Employees are classified as working either a full-time or part-time schedule based on the definition used by each establishment. [2] See footnote 6, Table 680. [3] The National Compensation Survey—Benefits program presents wage data in percentiles rather than dollar amounts; for calculation detail, see "Technical Note" in source. [4] See Table 655 for composition of goods- and service-producing industries.

Source: U.S. Bureau of Labor Statistics, *National Compensation Survey: Employee Benefits in the United States, March 2016*, Bulletin 2785, September 2016, and earlier reports. See also <https://www.bls.gov/ncs/ebs/benefits/2016/home.htm>.

Table 678. Employer Costs for Employee Compensation Per Hour Worked: 2016

[In dollars. As of December. Based on the National Compensation Survey (NCS). See Appendix III]

Compensation component	Total civilian workers	State and local government workers	Private industry workers						
			Total	Goods producing[1]	Service providing[2]	Union workers	Non-union workers	1–99 workers	100 workers or more
Total compensation	**34.90**	**47.85**	**32.76**	**39.03**	**31.50**	**47.82**	**31.31**	**27.71**	**38.80**
Wages and salaries	23.87	30.14	22.83	25.94	22.20	28.61	22.27	20.11	26.08
Total benefits	11.03	17.71	9.93	13.09	9.29	19.21	9.04	7.60	12.71
Paid leave	2.46	3.59	2.28	2.54	2.22	3.47	2.16	1.62	3.06
Vacation	1.20	1.36	1.17	1.31	1.15	1.75	1.12	0.83	1.59
Holiday	0.74	1.03	0.69	0.88	0.65	1.02	0.65	0.51	0.90
Sick	0.37	0.92	0.28	0.26	0.29	0.52	0.26	0.20	0.38
Supplemental pay	1.05	0.46	1.15	1.51	1.08	1.40	1.12	0.99	1.33
Overtime[3]	0.25	0.20	0.26	0.58	0.19	0.78	0.21	0.19	0.34
Insurance	3.06	5.66	2.63	3.64	2.43	6.34	2.28	1.85	3.57
Health insurance	2.91	5.51	2.48	3.45	2.29	5.98	2.15	1.76	3.35
Retirement and savings	1.88	5.33	1.31	2.14	1.15	4.36	1.02	0.80	1.93
Defined benefit	1.20	4.94	0.58	1.16	0.46	3.09	0.34	0.31	0.90
Defined contributions	0.68	0.39	0.73	0.98	0.68	1.27	0.68	0.49	1.02
Legally required	2.58	2.66	2.56	3.26	2.42	3.64	2.46	2.33	2.83
Social Security and Medicare	1.91	2.07	1.89	2.19	1.83	2.36	1.84	1.64	2.19
Social Security[4]	1.52	1.58	1.51	1.76	1.46	1.87	1.47	1.31	1.75
Medicare	0.40	0.49	0.38	0.43	0.37	0.48	0.37	0.33	0.44
Federal unemployment	0.03	(5)	0.04	0.03	0.04	0.03	0.04	0.04	0.03
State unemployment	0.16	0.07	0.18	0.23	0.17	0.23	0.17	0.18	0.17
Workers' compensation	0.47	0.51	0.46	0.81	0.39	1.02	0.40	0.47	0.44

[1] Based on the North American Industry Classification System, 2002 (NAICS). See text, this section. Includes mining, construction, and manufacturing. The agriculture, forestry, farming, and hunting sector is excluded. [2] Based on the 2002 NAICS. Includes utilities; wholesale and retail trade; transportation and warehousing; information; finance and insurance; real estate and rental and leasing; professional and technical services; management of companies and enterprises, administrative and waste services; education services; health care and social assistance; arts, entertainment, and recreation; accommodations and food services; and other services, except public administration. [3] Includes premium pay for work in addition to regular work schedule, such as, overtime, weekends, and holidays. [4] Comprises the Old-Age, Survivors, and Disability Insurance Program (OASDI). [5] Cost per hour worked is $0.01 or less.

Source: U.S. Bureau of Labor Statistics, *Employer Costs for Employee Compensation—December 2016*, USDL 17-0321, March 2017. See also <http://www.bls.gov/ncs/ect/home.htm>.

Table 679. Workers in Private Industry With Access to Retirement and Health Care Benefits by Selected Characteristics: 2016

[In percent (all workers = 100 percent). As of March. Based on National Compensation Survey (NCS). See headnote, Table 680, and Appendix III. See Table 169 for data on health benefit program participation]

Characteristic	Retirement benefits			Healthcare benefits			
	All plans[1]	Defined benefit[2]	Defined contribution[2]	Medical care	Dental care	Vision care	Outpatient prescription drug coverage
Total	**66**	**18**	**62**	**67**	**42**	**24**	**66**
WORKER CHARACTERISTICS							
Management, professional, and related occupations	81	25	77	86	60	34	85
Service occupations	41	7	38	39	22	13	37
Sales and office occupations	69	16	66	66	38	20	65
Natural resources, construction, and maintenance occupations	62	22	56	72	38	25	71
Production, transportation, and material moving occupations	70	22	63	74	45	26	73
Full-time[3]	77	21	72	86	53	30	84
Part-time[3]	37	8	33	19	12	7	19
Union[4]	91	70	55	93	73	54	92
Nonunion[4]	64	13	62	65	39	20	64
AVERAGE HOURLY WAGE[5]							
Lowest 25 percent (under $12.00)	42	6	39	33	16	9	32
Lowest 10 percent (under $9.37)	33	4	30	22	10	6	22
Second 25 percent ($12.00 to $17.73)	65	13	61	71	40	21	69
Third 25 percent ($17.73 to $28.60)	78	23	72	85	53	29	84
Highest 25 percent ($28.60 and over)	87	34	82	92	67	39	91
Highest 10 percent ($44.33 and over)	88	35	84	93	70	42	92
ESTABLISHMENT CHARACTERISTICS							
1 to 99 workers	52	9	49	55	29	17	54
100 or more workers	83	29	77	82	57	32	82
Goods producing[6]	74	25	70	84	52	31	83
Service producing[6]	64	16	60	64	40	22	63

[1] Employees may have access to defined benefit and/or defined contribution plans. Total excludes duplication. [2] A defined benefit plan is a retirement plan that uses a specific, predetermined formula to calculate the amount of an employee's guaranteed future benefit. A defined contribution plan provides benefits based on employer and employee contributions to individual employee accounts and the rate of return on money invested; the retirement benefit depends on the account balance at retirement. [3] Employees are classified as working either a full-time or part-time schedule based on the definition used by each establishment. [4] See footnote 6, Table 680. [5] The National Compensation Survey—Benefits program presents wage data in percentiles rather than dollar amounts; for calculation detail, see "Technical Note" in source. [6] See Table 655 for composition of goods- and service-producing industries.

Source: U.S. Bureau of Labor Statistics, *National Compensation Survey: Employee Benefits in the United States, March 2016*, Bulletin 2785, September 2016. See also <http://www.bls.gov/ncs/ebs/benefits/2016/home.htm>.

Table 680. Percent of Workers In Private Industry With Access to Selected Employee Benefits: 2016

[As of March. Based on National Compensation Survey (NCS). The NCS benefits survey obtained data from 6,886 private industry establishments of all sizes, representing approximately 114 million workers. Excludes agricultural establishments, private households, and the self-employed. An employee has access to a benefit plan if the plan is made available by the employer, regardless of whether the employee participates in the plan. See Appendix III. See also <https://www.bls.gov/ncs/ebs/glossary20152016.htm> for glossary of terms]

| Characteristic | Leave benefits | | | | | | Quality of life benefits | | | Nonproduction bonuses | |
	Paid holidays	Paid sick leave	Paid vacation	Paid jury duty leave	Family leave [1] Paid	Unpaid	Employer assistance for child care [2]	Flexible work-place [3]	Subsidized commuting	All non-production bonuses [4]	End of year bonus
Total	**77**	**64**	**76**	**57**	**13**	**87**	**10**	**7**	**6**	**38**	**10**
WORKER CHARACTERISTIC											
Management, professional, and related occupations	89	82	88	79	24	93	19	15	13	47	14
Service occupations	50	42	52	33	7	79	8	(Z)	4	23	5
Sales and office occupations	81	69	79	58	13	88	8	7	5	40	11
Natural resources, construction, and maintenance occupations	79	56	77	48	8	83	7	1	3	39	12
Production, transportation, and material moving occupations	83	59	81	59	6	88	4	3	1	40	9
Full-time [5]	90	76	91	69	16	90	12	8	7	44	13
Part-time [5]	40	30	36	26	5	79	4	2	3	21	4
Union [6]	89	76	88	77	11	91	17	3	6	33	4
Nonunion [6]	76	63	75	55	13	86	10	7	6	39	11
AVERAGE HOURLY WAGE [7]											
Lowest 25 percent (under $12.00)	52	39	50	30	6	80	4	1	2	23	5
Lowest 10 percent (under $9.37)	40	27	41	22	4	76	2	1	2	16	5
Second 25 percent ($12.00 to $17.73)	82	65	81	59	11	87	8	3	4	39	11
Third 25 percent ($17.73 to $28.60)	89	75	88	69	14	90	10	7	7	45	14
Highest 25 percent ($28.60 and over)	92	84	91	80	24	92	21	17	13	50	14
Highest 10 percent ($44.33 and over)	93	87	92	83	24	94	23	24	16	51	15
ESTABLISHMENT CHARACTERISTICS											
1 to 99 workers	69	55	68	45	9	81	5	5	3	34	13
100 or more workers	87	75	85	73	18	94	17	9	10	43	8
Goods producing [8]	89	63	87	62	9	88	8	6	2	47	14
Service producing [8]	74	64	74	56	14	87	11	7	7	36	10
GEOGRAPHIC AREA [9]											
New England	73	65	73	71	13	89	16	12	12	35	14
Middle Atlantic	78	68	77	69	18	84	14	9	9	38	14
South Atlantic	79	61	78	60	12	88	11	6	5	42	10
East South Central	79	62	81	59	9	83	7	3	1	42	11
West South Central	79	63	78	60	14	82	9	6	5	43	11
East North Central	76	60	77	55	12	88	9	6	4	39	10
West North Central	75	60	76	57	10	91	6	6	4	37	9
Mountain	73	58	71	51	14	86	10	6	7	37	12
Pacific	75	73	71	42	13	88	9	5	8	31	6

Z Less than 0.5 percent. [1] Some workers may have access to both types of plans. [2] A workplace program that provides for either the full or partial cost of caring for an employee's children in a nursery, day care center, or a babysitter in facilities either on or off the employer's premises. [3] Permits employees to work an agreed-upon portion of their work schedule at home or at some other approved location. [4] Includes cash profit-sharing, employee recognition, end-of-year, holiday, longevity, referral, and all other bonuses. [5] Employees are classified as working either a full-time or part-time schedule based on the definition used by each establishment. [6] Union workers are those whose wages are determined through collective bargaining. [7] The National Compensation Survey—Benefits program presents wage data in percentiles rather than dollar amounts; see "Technical Note" in source. [8] See Table 655, for composition of goods- and service-producing industries. [9] For composition of census divisions, see inside front cover.

Source: U.S. Bureau of Labor Statistics, *National Compensation Survey: Employee Benefits in the United States, March 2016*, Bulletin 2785, September 2016. See also <http://www.bls.gov/ncs/ebs/benefits/2016/home.htm>.

Table 681. Industries With the Highest Total Case Incidence Rates for Nonfatal Injuries and Illnesses: 2015

[Rates per 100 full-time employees. Private industry unless otherwise noted. Incidence rates refer to any Occupational Safety & Health Administration (OSHA)-recordable occupational injury or illness, whether or not it resulted in days away from work, job transfer, or restriction. Incidence rates were calculated as: number of injuries and illnesses divided by total hours worked by all employees during the year multiplied by 200,000 as base for 100 full-time equivalent workers (working 40 hours per week, 50 weeks per year)]

Industry	2012 NAICS code [1]	Incidence rate	Industry	2012 NAICS code [1]	Incidence rate
All industries, including State and local government [2]	(X)	3.3	Travel trailer and camper manufacturing	336214	8.6
Aquaculture	1125	13.6	Truck trailer manufacturing	336212	8.3
Nursing and residential care facilities [3]	623	12.0	Correctional institutions [3]	92214	8.3
Police protection [4]	92212	11.3	Hospitals [3]	622	8.1
Household furniture manufacturing [5]	337125	10.8	Psychiatric and substance abuse hospitals	6222	8.1
Manufactured (mobile) manufacturing	321991	10.2	Hog and pig farming	1122	8.0
Fire protection [4]	92216	10.2	Heavy and civil engineering construction [4]	237	8.0
Veterinary services	54194	10.0	Prefabricated wood building manufacturing	321992	7.9
Motor home manufacturing	336213	9.5	Pet and pet supplies stores	45391	7.7
Steel foundries (except investment)	331513	9.1	Mattress manufacturing	33791	7.6

X Not applicable [1] Based on the North American Industry Classification System, 2012 (NAICS). See text, this section. [2] Excludes farms with fewer than 11 employees. [3] State government. [4] Local government. [5] Except wood and metal.

Source: U.S. Bureau of Labor Statistics, Industry Injury and Illness Data, "Supplemental News Release Tables," <http://www.bls.gov/iif/oshsum.htm>, accessed February 2017.

Table 682. Nonfatal Occupational Injuries and Illnesses by Industry: 2014 and 2015

[3,675.8 represents 3,675,800. Rates per 100 full-time employees. Except as noted, data refer to any Occupational Safety and Health Administration (OSHA) recordable occupational injury or illness, whether or not it resulted in days away from work, job transfer, or restriction. Incidence rates were calculated as: number of injuries and illnesses divided by total hours worked by all employees during the year multiplied by 200,000 as base for 100 full-time equivalent workers (working 40 hours, per week, 50 weeks per year)]

Industry	2012 NAICS code [1]	Number of cases (1,000) 2014	Number of cases (1,000) 2015	Incidence rate of cases 2014	Incidence rate of cases 2015
Total	(X)	3,675.8	3,658.5	3.4	3.3
Private industry [2]	(X)	2,953.5	2,905.9	3.2	3.0
Agriculture, forestry, fishing, hunting [2]	11	52.4	56.1	5.5	5.7
Mining [3]	21	17.9	12.8	2.0	1.4
Construction	23	200.9	204.7	3.6	3.5
Manufacturing	31–33	483.3	466.5	4.0	3.8
Wholesale trade	42	163.1	174.6	2.9	3.1
Retail trade	44–45	416.1	410.4	3.6	3.5
Transportation and warehousing [4]	48–49	201.5	201.6	4.8	4.5
Utilities	22	13.4	12.0	2.4	2.2
Information	51	35.3	32.9	1.4	1.3
Finance and insurance	52	34.8	29.1	0.7	0.5
Real estate and rental and leasing	53	51.1	49.9	2.9	2.7
Professional, scientific, and technical services	54	69.9	68.9	0.9	0.9
Management of companies and enterprises	55	21.1	20.7	1.0	1.0
Administrative and support & waste management and remediation services	56	129.3	124.0	2.6	2.4
Educational services	61	38.5	38.5	2.1	2.1
Health care and social assistance	62	612.5	598.3	4.5	4.3
Arts, entertainment, and recreation	71	54.7	55.3	4.2	4.1
Accommodation and food services	72	282.8	277.4	3.5	3.3
Other services, except public administration	81	74.8	72.2	2.5	2.3
State and local government [2]	(X)	722.3	752.6	5.0	5.1
State government	(X)	162.3	148.5	4.1	3.7
Local government	(X)	560.0	604.1	5.4	5.6

X Not applicable. [1] North American Industry Classification System, 2012; see text, this section. [2] Excludes farms with fewer than 11 employees. [3] Data for Mining (2012 NAICS Sector 21) include establishments not governed by the Mine Safety and Health Administration rules and reporting, such as those in Oil and Gas Extraction and related support activities. Data for mining operators in coal, metal, and nonmetal mining are provided to BLS by the Mine Safety and Health Administration, U.S. Department of Labor. Independent mining contractors are excluded from the coal, metal, and nonmetal mining industries. These data do not reflect the changes the Occupational Safety and Health Administration made to its recordkeeping requirements effective January 1, 2002; therefore, estimates for these industries are not comparable to estimates in other industries. [4] Data for employers in railroad transportation are provided to BLS by the Federal Railroad Administration, U.S. Department of Transportation.

Source: U.S. Bureau of Labor Statistics, *Employer-Reported Workplace Injuries and Illnesses – 2015*, News Release, USDL 16-2056, October 2016, and earlier releases. See also <http://www.bls.gov/iif/home.htm>.

Table 683. Fatal Work Injuries by Event or Exposure: 2015

[For the 50 states and the District of Columbia. Based on the Census of Fatal Occupational Injuries. For details, see source]

Event or exposure	Number of fatalities	Percent distribution	Event or exposure	Number of fatalities	Percent distribution
Total [1]	**4,836**	**100**	Contacts with objects and equipment [1]	722	15
Transportation incidents [1]	2,054	42	Struck by object or equipment [1]	519	11
Roadway incident [1]	1,264	26	Struck by falling object or equipment	247	5
Collision between motor vehicles [2]	660	14	Struck by flying object	22	(Z)
Noncollision incidents	240	5	Caught in or compressed by equipment		
Nonroadway incident	253	5	or objects	99	2
Aircraft accidents	139	3	Caught in or crushed in collapsing materials	90	2
Pedestrians struck by a vehicle [2]	289	6	Falls	800	17
Water vehicle accidents	44	1	Exposure to harmful substances or		
Railway accidents	50	1	environments [1]	424	9
Assaults and violent acts [1]	703	15	Contact with electric current	134	3
Homicides [1]	417	9	Exposure to caustic, noxious or allergenic		
Shooting	354	7	substances	215	4
Stabbing	28	1	Oxygen deficiency	35	1
Self-inflicted injury	229	5	Fires and explosions	121	3

Z Less than 0.5 percent. [1] Includes other causes, not shown separately. [2] Including mobile equipment.

Source: U.S. Bureau of Labor Statistics, "Census of Fatal Occupational Injuries—Current and Revised Data," <http://www.bls.gov/iif/oshcfoi1.htm>, accessed May 2017.

Table 684. Workers Killed on the Job by Industry and Occupation: 2015

[Excludes homicides and suicides]

Industry group	Deaths Number	Deaths Rate [1]	Occupations with highest fatal work injury rates	Deaths Number	Deaths Rate [1]
Total	**4,836**	**3.4**	Logging workers	67	132.7
			Fishers and related fishing workers	23	54.8
			Aircraft pilots and flight engineers	57	40.4
Agriculture [2]	570	22.8	Roofers	75	39.7
Mining [3]	120	11.4	Refuse and recyclable material collectors	33	38.8
Construction	937	10.1	Structural iron and steel workers	17	29.8
Manufacturing	353	2.3	Farming, fishing, and forestry occupations	284	25.3
Wholesale trade	175	4.7	Driver/sales workers and truck drivers	885	24.3
Retail trade	269	1.8	Farmers, ranchers, and other agricultural managers	252	22.0
Transportation and warehousing	765	13.8	Miscellaneous agricultural workers	174	20.6
Utilities	22	2.2	Electrical power-line installers and repairers	26	20.5
Information	42	1.5	First-line supervisors of landscaping,		
Financial activities [4]	83	0.9	lawn service, and groundskeeping workers	38	18.1
Professional & business services [4]	477	3.0	First-line supervisors/managers of		
Educational & health services	139	0.7	construction trades and extraction workers	123	16.1
Leisure & hospitality [4]	225	2.0	Construction laborers	235	15.6
Other services [5]	202	3.0	Grounds maintenance workers	183	15.0
Government	457	1.9	Transportation and material moving occupations	1,301	14.7

[1] The rate represents the number of fatal occupational injuries per 100,000 full-time equivalent workers. [2] Includes forestry, fishing, and hunting. [3] Includes oil and gas extraction. [4] For composition of industry, see Table 655. [5] Excludes public service administration.

Source: U.S. Bureau of Labor Statistics, Census of Fatal Occupational Injuries, "Fatal Injury Rates," <http://stats.bls.gov/iif/oshcfoi1.htm#rates>, accessed August 2017.

Table 685. Nonfatal Occupational Injury and Illness Cases in Private Industry by Type of Injury or Illness and Days Away from Work: 2015

[902.2 represents 902,200. Covers work-related injuries and illnesses involving one or more days of missed work]

Type of work-related injury or illness	Number of injury or illness cases (1,000)								Median number of days away from work
	All cases	1 day	2 days	3-5 days	6-10 days	11-20 days	21-30 days	31 days or more	
Total [1]	**902.2**	**127.6**	**100.5**	**156.4**	**104.9**	**96.6**	**57.8**	**258.3**	**8**
Traumatic injuries and disorders	874.3	123.6	97.0	152.4	101.8	93.7	55.5	250.3	8
Fractures	81.2	5.0	3.3	8.1	7.2	9.2	7.2	41.2	32
Sprains, strains, tears	324.7	33.4	31.8	57.4	41.7	37.2	21.5	101.7	10
Concussions	13.7	1.7	1.9	2.8	1.8	1.5	0.6	3.4	7
Hernia	11.3	0.3	0.2	0.6	0.7	2.4	2.6	4.4	27
Soreness, pain, hurt-nonspecified injury	136.3	20.0	16.3	24.8	15.2	13.3	8.4	38.3	7
Disease and disorders of body systems	17.7	2.1	2.2	2.2	1.8	1.9	1.7	5.8	14
Carpal tunnel syndrome	4.9	0.3	0.3	0.4	0.5	0.6	0.6	2.3	28
Disorders of the eye, adnexa, vision	0.7	0.3	0.1	0.2	–	–	(S)	–	2
Infectious and parasitic diseases	2.1	0.4	0.2	0.6	0.4	0.3	–	0.1	5
Mental disorders or syndromes	2.5	0.2	0.2	0.2	0.2	0.2	0.2	1.3	33

– Represents or rounds to zero. S Data do not meet publication guidelines. [1] Total includes unclassified and ill-defined conditions.

Source: U.S. Bureau of Labor Statistics, Survey of Occupational Injuries and Illnesses, 2015 Resource Tables, "R.67. Detailed nature by number of days away from work," <http://stats.bls.gov/iif/oshcdnew2015.htm>, accessed February 2017.

Table 686. Labor Union Membership by Sector: 1990 to 2016

[16,740 represents 16,740,000. Annual averages of monthly figures. For wage and salary workers in agriculture and non-agriculture. Data represent union members by place of residence. Based on the Current Population Survey and subject to sampling error. For methodological details, see source]

Sector	1990	2000	2005	2010	2011	2012	2013	2014	2015	2016
TOTAL (1,000)										
Wage and salary workers:										
Union members...............	16,740	16,258	15,685	14,715	14,755	14,349	14,516	14,570	14,786	14,550
Covered by unions............	19,058	17,944	17,223	16,290	16,281	15,906	16,016	16,142	16,433	16,265
Public sector workers:										
Union members...............	6,485	7,111	7,430	7,623	7,550	7,319	7,203	7,214	7,234	7,113
Covered by unions............	7,691	7,976	8,262	8,406	8,309	8,062	7,894	7,923	8,023	7,827
Private sector workers:										
Union members...............	10,255	9,148	8,255	7,092	7,204	7,030	7,313	7,356	7,552	7,436
Covered by unions............	11,366	9,969	8,962	7,884	7,972	7,844	8,122	8,219	8,410	8,438
PERCENT										
Wage and salary workers:										
Union members...............	16.1	13.5	12.5	11.9	11.8	11.2	11.2	11.1	11.1	10.7
Covered by unions............	18.3	14.9	13.7	13.1	13.0	12.5	12.4	12.3	12.3	11.9
Public sector workers:										
Union members...............	36.5	37.5	36.5	36.2	37.0	35.9	35.3	35.7	35.2	34.4
Covered by unions............	43.3	42.0	40.5	40.0	40.7	39.6	38.7	39.2	39.0	37.9
Private sector workers:										
Union members...............	11.9	9.0	7.8	6.9	6.9	6.6	6.7	6.6	6.7	6.4
Covered by unions............	13.2	9.8	8.5	7.7	7.6	7.3	7.5	7.4	7.4	7.3

Source: Bloomberg BNA, *Union Membership and Earnings Data Book: Compilations from the Current Population Survey* (2017 edition), authored by Barry Hirsch of Georgia State University and David Macpherson of Trinity University. See also <http://www.bna.com/data-book> and <http://unionstats.gsu.edu>. © 2017 by The Bureau of National Affairs, Inc., Research & Custom Solutions, (800-372-1033) <http://www.bna.com>.

Table 687. Labor Union Members by Selected Characteristics: 2016

[In units as indicated (136,101 represents 136,101,000). Annual averages of monthly data. Covers employed wage and salary workers 16 years old and over. Excludes self-employed workers whose businesses are incorporated and not incorporated. Based on Current Population Survey, see text, Section 1 and Appendix III]

Characteristic	Employed wage and salary workers			Median usual weekly earnings [3] (dollars)			
		Percent					
	Total (1,000)	Union members [1]	Represented by union [2]	Total	Union members [1]	Represented by union [2]	Not represented by union
Total [4]............................	**136,101**	**10.7**	**12.0**	**832**	**1,004**	**995**	**802**
SEX							
Men...........................	70,589	11.2	12.3	915	1,050	1,042	890
Women........................	65,512	10.2	11.6	749	955	942	723
AGE							
16 to 24 years old............	18,556	4.4	5.3	501	600	599	497
25 to 34 years old............	31,750	9.2	10.4	751	893	890	734
35 to 44 years old............	28,515	12.0	13.3	934	1,071	1,059	908
45 to 54 years old............	28,807	13.3	14.8	955	1,084	1,069	930
55 to 64 years old............	21,778	13.3	14.7	952	1,072	1,069	930
65 years and over............	6,696	9.6	10.8	866	984	988	846
RACE/ETHNICITY							
White [5]......................	106,160	10.5	11.7	862	1,050	1,034	827
Men...........................	56,007	11.0	12.1	942	1,111	1,099	915
Women........................	50,153	9.9	11.3	766	989	975	738
Black [5]......................	17,014	13.0	14.5	678	808	807	646
Men...........................	7,852	14.1	15.7	718	818	826	690
Women........................	9,163	12.1	13.6	641	799	790	616
Asian [5]......................	8,340	9.0	10.1	1,021	1,020	1,017	1,022
Men...........................	4,368	8.1	9.3	1,151	1,061	1,076	1,160
Women........................	3,972	10.0	10.9	902	985	975	892
Hispanic [6]..................	23,085	8.8	10.0	624	886	876	608
Men...........................	13,125	9.2	10.3	663	908	901	637
Women........................	9,960	8.3	9.6	586	844	829	565
INDUSTRY [7]							
Private sector.................	115,417	6.4	7.3	801	937	932	789
Mining........................	765	5.6	6.3	1,197	(B)	(B)	1,190
Construction..................	7,488	13.9	14.6	822	1,168	1,146	780
Manufacturing................	14,783	8.8	9.6	857	885	884	852
Wholesale and retail trade...	18,515	4.2	4.8	676	701	700	675
Transportation and utilities...	6,048	18.9	20.5	860	1,033	1,023	808
Information...................	2,473	9.0	10.1	1,143	1,238	1,257	1,133
Financial activities...........	8,963	2.3	3.1	977	896	916	981
Professional and business services.......	14,257	2.4	3.3	992	887	935	995
Education and health services............	22,152	8.2	9.5	817	944	937	799
Leisure and hospitality........	12,687	3.0	3.5	528	670	667	522
Other services................	5,973	2.6	3.1	686	959	869	681
Public sector..................	20,684	34.4	37.9	967	1,070	1,055	900

B Base is less than 50,000. [1] Members of a labor union or an employee association similar to a labor union. [2] Members of a labor union or an employee association similar to a union as well as workers who report no union affiliation but whose jobs are covered by a union or an employee association contract. [3] For full-time employed wage and salary workers. [4] Includes races not shown separately. Also includes a small number of multiple jobholders whose full- and part-time status cannot be determined for their principal job. [5] For persons in this race group only. [6] Persons of Hispanic origin may be of any race. [7] For composition of industries, see Table 655.

Source: U.S. Bureau of Labor Statistics, *Union Members—2016*, USDL 17-0107, January 2017. See also <http://www.bls.gov/news.release/union2.toc.htm>.

Table 688. Labor Union Membership by State: 2000 and 2016

[Annual averages of monthly figures (16,258.2 represents 16,258,200). For wage and salary workers in agriculture and non-agriculture. Data represent union members by place of residence. Based on the Current Population Survey and subject to sampling error. For methodological details, see source]

State	Union members (1,000)		Workers covered by unions (1,000)		Percent of workers					
					Union members		Covered by unions		Private sector union members	
	2000	2016	2000	2016	2000	2016	2000	2016	2000	2016
United States	**16,258.2**	**14,549.6**	**17,944.1**	**16,264.6**	**13.5**	**10.7**	**14.9**	**11.9**	**9.0**	**6.4**
Alabama [1]	180.8	153.9	197.6	170.3	9.6	8.1	10.5	9.0	5.8	5.3
Alaska	56.8	54.9	64.3	59.0	21.9	18.5	24.8	19.9	12.8	9.9
Arizona [1]	129.7	121.8	147.8	150.6	6.4	4.5	7.3	5.5	4.2	2.6
Arkansas [1]	61.5	46.9	70.9	59.5	5.8	4.0	6.7	5.0	4.0	2.7
California	2,295.1	2,549.6	2,546.0	2,795.4	16.0	15.9	17.7	17.5	9.7	8.8
Colorado	173.2	238.2	193.0	263.2	9.0	9.8	10.0	10.8	6.0	6.9
Connecticut	245.8	274.8	262.5	288.1	16.3	17.5	17.4	18.4	9.4	8.9
Delaware	46.9	47.9	51.7	55.7	13.3	11.4	14.6	13.3	8.9	5.8
District of Columbia	35.9	32.7	40.2	37.1	14.7	9.5	16.5	10.8	9.5	6.2
Florida [1]	433.6	456.1	553.6	574.1	6.8	5.6	8.7	7.1	3.3	2.5
Georgia [1]	228.1	164.4	267.0	209.8	6.3	3.9	7.4	4.9	4.6	2.6
Hawaii	123.5	118.3	129.1	124.3	24.8	19.8	26.0	20.8	14.4	13.2
Idaho [1]	40.7	42.1	48.0	46.5	7.6	6.1	9.0	6.7	5.5	3.9
Illinois	1,046.3	812.4	1,100.6	856.6	18.6	14.5	19.5	15.3	14.1	9.7
Indiana [3]	418.4	303.4	460.6	334.2	15.6	10.4	17.1	11.4	13.1	7.9
Iowa [1]	181.8	128.5	215.1	152.7	13.6	8.8	16.1	10.5	10.5	5.1
Kansas [1]	108.5	109.2	134.5	131.8	9.0	8.6	11.2	10.3	8.0	5.9
Kentucky [6]	208.0	189.7	234.6	228.3	12.0	11.1	13.6	13.4	10.1	9.2
Louisiana [1]	121.9	75.2	154.8	88.1	7.1	4.2	9.0	4.9	5.5	2.3
Maine	78.1	64.7	92.2	76.8	14.0	11.4	16.6	13.5	8.0	4.5
Maryland	353.3	309.4	405.5	346.8	14.6	11.0	16.7	12.3	7.8	5.6
Massachusetts	406.3	381.9	444.9	406.9	14.3	12.1	15.7	12.9	7.9	6.4
Michigan [3]	938.3	606.9	985.3	651.4	20.8	14.5	21.8	15.5	15.7	10.1
Minnesota	419.0	364.1	434.3	387.7	18.2	14.2	18.8	15.1	12.3	8.3
Mississippi [1]	67.7	73.4	104.3	89.5	6.0	6.6	9.3	8.1	5.4	4.9
Missouri [6]	337.9	261.8	365.3	289.9	13.2	9.6	14.2	10.7	12.1	7.6
Montana	51.2	49.6	57.8	58.1	13.9	11.9	15.7	13.9	8.2	6.4
Nebraska [1]	64.9	64.4	89.4	74.4	8.4	7.4	11.5	8.5	4.6	3.7
Nevada [1]	150.9	146.2	165.3	181.8	17.1	12.0	18.8	15.0	13.8	9.7
New Hampshire	59.8	62.9	66.7	73.8	10.4	9.4	11.6	11.0	6.3	3.5
New Jersey	762.0	643.2	800.7	666.1	20.8	16.1	21.8	16.6	13.1	8.3
New Mexico	56.2	49.3	69.7	64.3	8.1	6.3	10.1	8.2	5.5	2.8
New York	1,958.0	1,941.3	2,036.4	2,074.8	25.5	23.6	26.5	25.2	15.3	14.8
North Carolina [1]	124.1	128.8	148.4	174.1	3.6	3.0	4.4	4.1	2.4	1.7
North Dakota [1]	17.6	20.1	21.1	25.1	6.5	5.5	7.8	6.9	3.7	3.3
Ohio	879.0	616.3	955.1	701.1	17.3	12.4	18.8	14.1	12.3	7.6
Oklahoma [2]	93.8	79.5	108.0	97.0	6.8	5.4	7.8	6.5	4.4	3.3
Oregon	234.4	227.7	251.0	266.6	16.1	13.5	17.2	15.8	9.8	7.6
Pennsylvania	869.6	686.6	925.7	725.4	16.9	12.1	18.0	12.7	11.2	7.4
Rhode Island	79.6	74.4	82.5	81.5	18.2	15.4	18.8	16.9	9.9	8.1
South Carolina [1]	70.3	32.2	88.8	51.8	4.0	1.6	5.1	2.6	2.8	0.8
South Dakota [1]	18.2	19.6	22.2	26.3	5.5	5.2	6.7	7.0	2.5	2.5
Tennessee [1]	211.5	157.4	238.8	173.9	8.9	5.7	10.0	6.3	6.7	4.3
Texas [1]	505.4	461.7	645.1	605.6	5.8	4.0	7.4	5.3	3.8	2.1
Utah [1]	69.3	62.0	84.9	79.2	7.3	4.7	9.0	6.0	4.5	2.4
Vermont	28.2	33.2	33.9	37.2	10.3	11.5	12.4	12.8	5.1	5.5
Virginia [1]	179.1	160.1	227.0	226.4	5.6	4.3	7.1	6.0	3.9	2.7
Washington	470.8	538.4	516.1	576.4	18.2	17.4	19.9	18.6	11.8	10.0
West Virginia [5]	102.9	78.7	111.4	87.9	14.3	11.8	15.5	13.2	12.4	8.9
Wisconsin [4]	446.0	218.2	473.1	243.4	17.6	8.1	18.7	9.0	11.7	5.5
Wyoming [1]	17.9	15.7	21.6	18.2	8.3	6.3	10.0	7.3	5.5	4.7

[1] Right to work state as of 2000. [2] Passed right to work law in 2001. [3] Passed right to work law in 2012. [4] Passed right to work law in 2015. [5] Passed right to work law in 2016. [6] Passed right to work law in 2017.

Source: Bloomberg BNA, *Union Membership and Earnings Data Book: Compilations from the Current Population Survey* (2017 edition), authored by Barry Hirsch of Georgia State University and David Macpherson of Trinity University. Internet sites: <http://www.bna.com/data-book> and <http://www.unionstats.com>. © 2017 by The Bureau of National Affairs, Inc., Research and Customs Solutions (800-372-1033), <http://www.bna.com>.

Table 689. Work Stoppages: 1960 to 2016

[896 represents 896,000. Excludes work stoppages involving fewer than 1,000 workers and lasting less than 1 day. The term "major work stoppage" includes both worker-initiated strikes and employer-initiated lockouts that involve 1,000 workers or more. Information is based on reports of labor disputes appearing in daily newspapers, trade journals, and other public sources]

Year	Number of work stoppages [1]	Workers involved [2] (1,000)	Days idle total Number [3] (1,000)	Days idle total Percent estimated working time [4]	Year	Number of work stoppages [1]	Workers involved [2] (1,000)	Days idle total Number [3] (1,000)	Days idle total Percent estimated working time [4]
1960	222	896	13,260	0.09	1998	34	387	5,116	0.02
1970	381	2,468	52,761	0.29	1999	17	73	1,996	0.01
1980	187	795	20,844	0.09	2000	39	394	20,419	0.06
1982	96	656	9,061	0.04	2001	29	99	1,151	(Z)
1983	81	909	17,461	0.08	2002	19	46	660	(Z)
1984	62	376	8,499	0.04	2003	14	129	4,091	0.01
1985	54	324	7,079	0.03	2004	17	171	3,344	0.01
1986	69	533	11,861	0.05	2005	22	100	1,736	0.01
1987	46	174	4,481	0.02	2006	20	70	2,688	0.01
1988	40	118	4,381	0.02	2007	21	189	1,265	(Z)
1989	51	452	16,996	0.07	2008	15	72	1,954	0.01
1990	44	185	5,926	0.02	2009	5	13	124	(Z)
1991	40	392	4,584	0.02	2010	11	45	302	(Z)
1992	35	364	3,989	0.01	2011	19	113	1,020	(Z)
1993	35	182	3,981	0.01	2012	19	148	1,131	(Z)
1994	45	322	5,021	0.02	2013	15	55	290	(Z)
1995	31	192	5,771	0.02	2014	11	34	200	(Z)
1996	37	273	4,889	0.02	2015	12	47	740	(Z)
1997	29	339	4,497	0.01	2016	15	99	1,543	(Z)

Z Less than 0.005 percent. [1] Beginning in year indicated. [2] Workers counted more than once if involved in more than one stoppage during the year. [3] Resulting from all stoppages in effect in a year, including those that began in an earlier year. [4] Agricultural and government employees are included in the total working time; private household and forestry and fishery employees are excluded.

Source: U.S. Bureau of Labor Statistics, *Major Work Stoppages in 2016*, USDL 17-0180, February 2017. See also <http://www.bls.gov/wsp>.

Labor Force, Employment, and Earnings   449

Income, Expenditures, Poverty, and Wealth

This section presents data on gross domestic product (GDP), gross national product (GNP), national and personal income, savings and investment, money income, poverty, and national and personal wealth. The data on income and expenditures measure two aspects of the U.S. economy. One aspect relates to the National Income and Product Accounts (NIPA), a summation reflecting the entire complex of the nation's economic income and output and the interaction of its major components; the other relates to personal and household income and wealth, and consumer expenditures.

The primary source for data on GDP, GNP, national and personal income, gross saving and investment, and fixed assets and consumer durables is the *Survey of Current Business*, issued monthly by the Bureau of Economic Analysis (BEA). These data are also available in tables accessible through an interactive tool on the BEA's website, <http://www.bea.gov/iTable/index.cfm>. Revisions occur annually. The BEA conducts a comprehensive revision approximately every 5 years. The most recent comprehensive revision to the NIPA was released beginning in July 2013. Discussions of the revision are available at the BEA's website.

Sources of income distribution data are the decennial censuses of population, the Annual Social and Economic Supplement of the Current Population Survey (CPS), and the American Community Survey, all products of the U.S. Census Bureau (see text, Section 1). Annual data on income of families, individuals, and households are presented in *Current Population Reports, Income and Poverty in the United States,* in print and online. Detailed statistics and historical data are available on the Census Bureau's website at <http://www.census.gov/topics/income-poverty.html>.

Data on the household sector's savings and assets are published by the Board of Governors of the Federal Reserve System in the quarterly statistical release *Financial Accounts of the United States.* The Federal Reserve Board also periodically conducts the *Survey of Consumer Finances,* which presents financial information on family assets and net worth. The most recent survey is available online at <http://www.federalreserve.gov/econresdata/scf/scfindex.htm>. Detailed information on personal wealth is published periodically by the Internal Revenue Service (IRS) in the *SOI (Statistics of Income) Bulletin.*

National income and product—*GDP* is the total output of goods and services produced by labor and property located in the United States, valued at market prices. GDP can be viewed in terms of the expenditure categories that comprise its major components: personal consumption expenditures, gross private domestic investment, net exports of goods and services, and government consumption expenditures and gross investment. The goods and services included are largely those bought for final use (excluding illegal transactions) in the market economy. A number of inclusions, however, represent imputed values, the most important of which is the rental value of owner-occupied housing. GDP, in this broad context, measures the output attributable to the factors of production located in the United States. GDP

by state is the gross market value of the goods and services attributable to labor and property located in a state. It is the state counterpart of the nation's GDP.

The featured measure of real GDP is an index based on chain-type annual weights. Changes in this measure of real output and prices are calculated as the average of changes based on weights for the current and preceding years. (Components of real output are weighted by price, and components of prices are weighted by output.) These annual changes are "chained" (multiplied) together to form a time series that allows for the effects of changes in relative prices and changes in the composition of output over time. Quarterly and monthly changes are based on quarterly and monthly weights, respectively.

The output indexes are expressed as 2009 = 100, and in 2009 dollars. Price indexes are based to 1982-84 = 100. For more information on chained-dollar indexes, see the article on this subject in the November 2003 issue of the *Survey of Current Business.*

Chained (2009) dollar estimates of most components of GDP are not published for periods prior to 1990, because during periods far from the base period, the levels of the components may provide misleading information about their contributions to an aggregate. Values are published in index form (2009 = 100) for 1929 to the present to allow users to calculate the percent changes for all components, which are accurate for all periods. In addition, BEA publishes estimates of contributions of major components to the percent change in GDP for all periods.

Gross national product measures the output attributable to all labor and property supplied by United States residents, including residents working abroad. The GNP takes into account net income payments to the rest of the world. In brief, the GNP is the result of subtracting net income payments to the rest of the world from GDP.

National income includes all net incomes, net of consumption of fixed capital (CFC), earned in production. National income is also the sum of compensation of employees, proprietors' income with inventory valuation adjustment (IVA) and capital consumption adjustment (CCAdj), rental income of persons with CCAdj, corporate profits with IVA and CCAdj, net interest and miscellaneous payments, taxes on production and imports less subsidies, business current transfer payments (net), and current surplus of government enterprises, less subsidies.

Capital consumption adjustment for corporations and for nonfarm sole proprietorships and partnerships is the difference between capital consumption based on income tax returns and capital consumption measured using empirical evidence on prices of used equipment and structures in resale markets, which have shown that depreciation for most types of assets approximates a geometric pattern. The tax return data are valued at historical costs and reflect changes over time in service lives and depreciation patterns as permitted by tax regulations. Inventory valuation adjustment represents the difference between the book value of inventories used up in production and the cost of replacing them.

Personal income is the current income that persons receive in return for their provision of labor, land, and capital used in current production, plus current transfer receipts less contributions for government social insurance (domestic). Classified as "persons" are individuals (including owners of unincorporated firms), nonprofit institutions that primarily serve individuals, private trust funds, and private noninsured welfare funds. Personal income includes personal current transfer receipts (payments not resulting from current production) from government and business such as social security benefits, public assistance, etc., but excludes transfers among persons. Also included are certain nonmonetary types of income; chiefly, estimated net rental value to owner-occupants of their homes and the value of services furnished without payment by financial intermediaries. Capital gains (and losses) are excluded.

Disposable personal income is personal income less personal current taxes. It is the income available to persons for spending or saving. Personal current taxes are tax payments (net of refunds) by persons (except personal contributions for government social insurance) that are not chargeable to business expense. Personal taxes include income taxes, personal property taxes, motor vehicle licenses, and other miscellaneous taxes.

Gross domestic product by industry—The BEA also prepares estimates of value added by industry. *Value added* is a measure of the contribution of each private industry and of government to the nation's GDP. It is defined as an industry's gross output (which consists of sales or receipts and other operating income, commodity taxes, and inventory change) minus its intermediate inputs (which consist of energy, raw materials, semi-finished goods, and purchased services). These estimates of value added are produced for approximately 60 private industries and for 4 government classifications—federal general government and government enterprises, and state and local general government and government enterprises. Industries are classified according to the North American Industry Classification System.

The estimates by industry are available in current dollars and are derived from the estimates of gross domestic income, which consists of three components—the compensation of employees, gross operating surplus, and taxes on production and imports, less subsidies. Real, or inflation-adjusted, estimates are also available.

Regional Economic Accounts—These accounts consist of estimates of state and local area personal income and of gross domestic product by state and are consistent with estimates of personal income and gross domestic product in the BEA's national economic accounts. BEA's estimates of state and local area personal income provide a framework for analyzing individual state and local economies, and they show how the economies compare with each other. The *personal income* of a state and/or local area is the income received by, or on behalf of, the residents of that state or area. Estimates of labor and proprietors' earnings by place of work indicate the economic activity of business and government within that area, and estimates of personal income by place of residence indicate the income within the area that is available for spending. BEA prepares estimates for states, counties, metropolitan areas, and BEA economic areas.

Gross domestic product by state estimates measure the value added to the nation's production by the labor and property in each state. GDP by state is often considered the state counterpart of the nation's GDP. The GDP by state estimates provide the basis for analyzing the regional impacts of national economic trends. GDP by state is measured as the sum of the distributions by industry and state of the components of gross domestic income; that is, the sum of the costs incurred and incomes earned in the production of GDP by state. The GDP estimates are presented in current dollars and in real (chained dollars) for approximately 60 industries.

Consumer Expenditure Survey—The Consumer Expenditure Survey program began in 1980. The principal objective of the survey is to collect current consumer expenditure data, which provide a continuous flow of data on the buying habits of American consumers. The data are necessary for future revisions of the Consumer Price Index.

The survey conducted by the Census Bureau for the Bureau of Labor Statistics consists of two components: (1) an interview panel survey in which the expenditures of consumer units are obtained over 4 quarters, and (2) a diary or recordkeeping survey completed by participating households for two consecutive 1-week periods. See Appendix III for more information.

Money income of households, families, and individuals—Money income statistics are based on data collected in various field surveys of income conducted since 1936. Since 1947, the Census Bureau has collected the data on an annual basis and published them in *Current Population Reports*, P60 Series. In each of the surveys, field representatives interview samples of the population with respect to income received during the previous year. *Money income* as defined by the Census Bureau differs from the BEA concept of "personal income." Data on consumer income collected in the CPS by the Census Bureau cover money income received (exclusive of certain money receipts such as capital gains) before payments for personal income taxes, social security, union dues, Medicare deductions, etc. Money income does not reflect the fact that some families receive part of their income in the form of noncash benefits (see Section 11) such as food stamps, health benefits, and subsidized housing; that some farm families receive noncash benefits in the form of goods produced and consumed on the farm; or that noncash benefits are also received by some nonfarm residents, which often take the form of the use of business transportation and facilities, full or partial payments by business for retirement programs, medical and educational expenses, etc. These elements should be considered when comparing income levels. None of the aggregate income concepts (GDP, national income, or personal income) is exactly comparable with money income, although personal income is the closest. For a definition of families and households, see text, Section 1.

Poverty—Families and unrelated individuals are classified as being above or below poverty following the Office of Management and Budget's Statistical Policy Directive 14. The Census Bureau uses a set of thresholds that vary by family size and composition.

The official poverty thresholds do not vary geographically, but they are updated for inflation using the consumer price index (CPI-U). The official poverty definition uses money income before taxes and does not include capital gains or noncash benefits (such as public housing, Medicaid, and food stamps).

The original thresholds were based on the U.S. Department of Agriculture's 1961 Economy Food Plan and reflected the different consumption requirements of families. The poverty thresholds are updated every year to reflect changes in the Consumer Price Index. The following technical changes to the thresholds were made in 1981: (1) distinctions based on sex of householder were eliminated, (2) separate thresholds for farm families were dropped, and (3) the matrix was expanded to families of nine or more persons from the old cutoff of seven or more persons. These changes were incorporated in the calculation of poverty data beginning with data for 1981. Besides the Census Bureau website at <http://www.census.gov/topics/income-poverty/poverty.html>, information on poverty guidelines and research may be found at the U.S. Department of Human Services website at <http://aspe.hhs.gov/poverty-research>.

Statistical reliability—For a discussion of statistical collection and estimation, sampling procedures, and measures of statistical reliability pertaining to Census Bureau data, see Appendix III.

Table 690. Gross Domestic Product in Current and Chained (2009) Dollars: 1990 to 2016

[In billions of dollars (5,980 represents $5,980,000,000,000). For explanation of gross domestic product and chained dollars, see text, this section. Minus sign (-) indicates decline in inventories or net imports]

Item	1990	2000	2002	2003	2004	2005	2006	2007	2008	2009	2010	2011	2012	2013	2014	2015	2016
CURRENT DOLLARS																	
Gross domestic product	5,980	10,285	10,978	11,511	12,275	13,094	13,856	14,478	14,719	14,419	14,964	15,518	16,155	16,692	17,428	18,121	18,625
Personal consumption expenditures	3,826	6,792	7,384	7,766	8,260	8,794	9,304	9,751	10,014	9,847	10,202	10,689	11,051	11,361	11,864	12,332	12,821
Durable goods	497	913	985	1,018	1,080	1,127	1,156	1,185	1,102	1,023	1,071	1,125	1,192	1,242	1,296	1,367	1,411
Nondurable goods	994	1,540	1,613	1,704	1,820	1,953	2,080	2,177	2,273	2,175	2,292	2,471	2,547	2,593	2,674	2,666	2,710
Services	2,334	4,340	4,786	5,044	5,360	5,714	6,068	6,389	6,638	6,649	6,839	7,093	7,312	7,527	7,893	8,299	8,699
Gross private domestic investment	994	2,034	1,925	2,028	2,277	2,527	2,681	2,644	2,425	1,878	2,101	2,240	2,512	2,706	2,916	3,094	3,057
Fixed investment	979	1,979	1,907	2,009	2,213	2,468	2,614	2,609	2,457	2,026	2,039	2,198	2,450	2,614	2,838	2,982	3,022
Nonresidential	739	1,494	1,349	1,372	1,463	1,612	1,776	1,921	1,941	1,633	1,658	1,812	2,008	2,094	2,268	2,336	2,316
Residential	240	485	558	637	750	856	837	689	516	392	381	386	442	520	570	645	706
Change in private inventories	15	55	19	19	64	60	67	35	-32	-148	62	42	62	92	78	112	35
Net exports of goods and services	-78	-376	-427	-504	-619	-721	-771	-719	-723	-395	-513	-580	-566	-492	-510	-524	-521
Exports	552	1,097	1,003	1,040	1,182	1,309	1,476	1,665	1,842	1,588	1,852	2,106	2,198	2,277	2,374	2,265	2,215
Imports	630	1,473	1,429	1,544	1,801	2,030	2,247	2,383	2,565	1,983	2,365	2,686	2,764	2,769	2,883	2,789	2,736
Government consumption expenditures and gross investment	1,238	1,834	2,095	2,221	2,357	2,494	2,642	2,802	3,003	3,089	3,174	3,169	3,159	3,116	3,157	3,219	3,268
Federal	560	632	741	825	892	946	1,002	1,050	1,156	1,218	1,304	1,304	1,293	1,230	1,218	1,224	1,232
National defense	403	392	457	520	570	608	642	679	754	788	833	837	818	767	746	732	729
Nondefense	157	241	284	305	322	338	360	371	402	429	471	467	475	463	473	492	503
State and local	678	1,202	1,354	1,396	1,465	1,547	1,640	1,752	1,848	1,871	1,870	1,865	1,866	1,887	1,939	1,995	2,036
CHAINED (2009) DOLLARS [1]																	
Gross domestic product	8,955	12,560	12,909	13,271	13,774	14,234	14,614	14,874	14,830	14,419	14,784	15,021	15,355	15,612	16,013	16,472	16,716
Personal consumption expenditures	5,673	8,171	8,599	8,868	9,208	9,532	9,822	10,042	10,007	9,847	10,036	10,264	10,413	10,565	10,868	11,264	11,572
Durable goods	(NA)	758	857	918	993	1,047	1,092	1,142	1,083	1,023	1,086	1,152	1,236	1,313	1,403	1,512	1,595
Nondurable goods	(NA)	1,864	1,931	1,999	2,064	2,132	2,202	2,239	2,215	2,175	2,224	2,263	2,278	2,316	2,373	2,447	2,514
Services	(NA)	5,599	5,838	5,967	6,157	6,353	6,527	6,656	6,709	6,649	6,728	6,851	6,908	6,951	7,116	7,340	7,507
Gross private domestic investment	1,241	2,376	2,218	2,309	2,511	2,673	2,730	2,644	2,396	1,878	2,120	2,230	2,466	2,617	2,762	2,905	2,858
Fixed investment	(NA)	2,316	2,201	2,290	2,444	2,611	2,663	2,610	2,433	2,026	2,056	2,187	2,400	2,521	2,677	2,783	2,803
Nonresidential	(NA)	1,648	1,498	1,526	1,605	1,717	1,840	1,948	1,934	1,633	1,674	1,802	1,964	2,033	2,173	2,224	2,210
Residential	(NA)	638	683	745	819	873	807	655	498	392	382	385	437	488	505	557	587
Change in private inventories	(NA)	66	23	23	71	64	72	36	-34	-148	58	38	55	79	68	101	33
Net exports of goods and services	(NA)	-478	-584	-642	-735	-782	-794	-713	-558	-395	-459	-459	-447	-405	-428	-545	-586
Exports	(NA)	1,258	1,165	1,185	1,301	1,382	1,507	1,646	1,741	1,588	1,777	1,898	1,963	2,032	2,118	2,127	2,120
Imports	(NA)	1,736	1,749	1,827	2,035	2,164	2,301	2,359	2,299	1,983	2,235	2,358	2,410	2,436	2,546	2,672	2,706
Government consumption expenditures and gross investment	2,224	2,498	2,706	2,764	2,808	2,826	2,869	2,914	2,995	3,089	3,091	2,997	2,942	2,858	2,839	2,879	2,900
Federal	(NA)	818	911	973	1,017	1,035	1,061	1,079	1,152	1,218	1,271	1,236	1,214	1,143	1,115	1,114	1,115
National defense	(NA)	512	567	615	653	666	679	696	748	788	814	795	768	716	687	672	667
Nondefense	(NA)	305	343	358	365	369	382	383	404	429	457	441	445	427	428	442	447
State and local	(NA)	1,689	1,802	1,795	1,793	1,792	1,809	1,836	1,842	1,871	1,821	1,761	1,728	1,714	1,723	1,763	1,784
Residual	-106	-84	-71	-46	-20	-2	-4	-10	-14	(Z)	-1	-11	-20	-24	-38	-45	-50

NA Not available. Z Less than $500 million. [1] Chained (2009) dollar series are calculated as the product of the chain-type quantity index and the 2009 current-dollar value of the corresponding series, divided by 100. Because the formula for the chain-type quantity indexes uses weights of more than one period, the corresponding chained-dollar estimates are usually not additive. The residual line is the difference between the first line and the sum of the most detailed lines.

Source: U.S. Bureau of Economic Analysis, National Income and Product Accounts Tables, "Table 1.1.5. Gross Domestic Product," and "Table 1.1.6. Real Gross Domestic Product, Chained Dollars," <http://www.bea.gov/iTable/>, accessed July 2017.

Table 691. Real Gross Domestic Product, Chained (2009) Dollars—Annual Percent Change: 1990 to 2016

[Percent change from immediate previous year; for example, 1990, change from 1989. Minus sign (-) indicates decrease]

Component	1990	2000	2005	2010	2011	2012	2013	2014	2015	2016
Gross domestic product (GDP)	**1.9**	**4.1**	**3.3**	**2.5**	**1.6**	**2.2**	**1.7**	**2.6**	**2.9**	**1.5**
Personal consumption expenditures	2.1	5.1	3.5	1.9	2.3	1.5	1.5	2.9	3.6	2.7
Durable goods	-0.4	8.6	5.4	6.1	6.1	7.4	6.2	6.9	7.7	5.5
Nondurable goods	1.2	3.2	3.3	2.2	1.8	0.6	1.7	2.5	3.1	2.8
Services	3.0	5.0	3.2	1.2	1.8	0.8	0.6	2.4	3.2	2.3
Gross private domestic investment	-2.6	6.5	6.4	12.9	5.2	10.6	6.1	5.5	5.2	-1.6
Fixed investment	-1.4	6.9	6.8	1.5	6.3	9.8	5.0	6.2	3.9	0.7
Nonresidential	1.1	9.1	7.0	2.5	7.7	9.0	3.5	6.9	2.3	-0.6
Structures	1.5	7.8	1.7	-16.4	2.3	12.9	1.4	10.5	-1.8	-4.1
Equipment	-2.1	9.7	9.6	15.9	13.6	10.8	4.6	6.6	3.5	-3.4
Intellectual property products	8.4	8.9	6.5	1.9	3.6	3.9	3.4	4.6	3.8	6.3
Residential	-8.5	0.7	6.6	-2.5	0.5	13.5	11.9	3.5	10.2	5.5
Exports	8.8	8.6	6.3	11.9	6.9	3.4	3.5	4.3	0.4	-0.3
Goods	8.6	10.1	7.3	14.4	6.5	3.6	3.1	4.6	-0.4	0.3
Services	9.5	4.7	3.8	6.8	7.6	3.0	4.4	3.6	2.1	-1.5
Imports	3.6	13.0	6.3	12.7	5.5	2.2	1.1	4.5	5.0	1.3
Goods	2.9	13.1	6.7	14.9	5.8	2.1	1.2	4.9	5.2	0.9
Services	6.5	12.6	4.5	3.8	4.0	3.0	0.6	2.6	4.0	3.1
Government consumption expenditures and gross investment	3.2	1.9	0.6	0.1	-3.0	-1.9	-2.9	-0.6	1.4	0.8
Federal	2.1	0.3	1.7	4.4	-2.7	-1.9	-5.8	-2.4	-0.1	—
National defense	0.3	-0.9	2.0	3.2	-2.3	-3.4	-6.8	-4.0	-2.2	-0.7
Nondefense	7.3	2.3	1.3	6.4	-3.4	0.9	-4.1	0.2	3.2	1.2
State and local	4.1	2.8	—	-2.7	-3.3	-1.9	-0.8	0.5	2.3	1.2

– Represents or rounds to zero.

Source: U.S. Bureau of Economic Analysis, National Income and Product Accounts Tables, "Table 1.1.1. Percent Change From Preceding Period in Real Gross Domestic Product," <http://www.bea.gov/iTable/index_nipa.cfm>, accessed July 2017.

Table 692. Gross Domestic Product in Current and Chained (2009) Dollars by Type of Product and Sector: 1990 to 2016

[In billions of dollars (5,980 represents $5,980,000,000,000). For explanation of chained dollars, see text, this section]

Type of product and sector	1990	2000	2005	2010	2012	2013	2014	2015	2016
CURRENT DOLLARS									
Gross domestic product	**5,980**	**10,285**	**13,094**	**14,964**	**16,155**	**16,692**	**17,428**	**18,121**	**18,625**
Product:									
Goods	2,121	3,437	3,889	4,397	4,922	5,151	5,331	5,484	5,517
Durable goods	1,176	2,083	2,316	2,447	2,761	2,857	2,949	3,006	3,021
Nondurable goods	946	1,355	1,574	1,950	2,161	2,294	2,382	2,478	2,496
Services [1]	3,309	5,862	7,766	9,519	10,070	10,297	10,725	11,179	11,614
Structures	549	986	1,439	1,048	1,164	1,243	1,372	1,458	1,493
Sector:									
Business [2]	4,553	7,892	9,920	11,060	12,097	12,554	13,164	13,709	14,070
Nonfarm [3]	4,475	7,816	9,815	10,930	11,946	12,367	12,997	13,563	13,933
Farm	78	76	105	130	152	187	168	146	137
Households and institutions	643	1,203	1,600	1,929	2,029	2,084	2,165	2,261	2,355
General government [4]	785	1,191	1,574	1,976	2,029	2,053	2,099	2,151	2,200
Federal	304	359	488	644	669	663	670	676	686
State and local	480	832	1,087	1,332	1,360	1,390	1,429	1,475	1,514
CHAINED (2009) DOLLARS									
Gross domestic product	**8,955**	**12,560**	**14,234**	**14,784**	**15,355**	**15,612**	**16,013**	**16,472**	**16,716**
Product:									
Goods	2,205	3,431	3,953	4,410	4,805	5,020	5,201	5,360	5,434
Durable goods	(NA)	1,903	2,261	2,468	2,769	2,866	2,971	3,023	3,061
Nondurable goods	(NA)	1,532	1,691	1,943	2,040	2,156	2,232	2,336	2,372
Services [1]	5,778	7,675	8,658	9,323	9,447	9,459	9,624	9,875	10,041
Structures	1,090	1,457	1,627	1,052	1,111	1,149	1,208	1,257	1,262
Sector:									
Business [2]	6,282	9,253	10,612	10,934	11,489	11,745	12,123	12,544	12,744
Nonfarm [3]	6,228	9,173	10,513	10,823	11,406	11,633	12,015	12,426	12,611
Farm	56	84	102	112	94	114	112	121	136
Households and institutions	1,200	1,634	1,829	1,931	1,962	1,977	2,004	2,038	2,068
General government [4]	1,573	1,681	1,794	1,920	1,904	1,891	1,889	1,893	1,908
Federal	576	501	541	624	630	618	613	608	610
State and local	993	1,181	1,254	1,295	1,274	1,273	1,276	1,285	1,298

NA Not available. [1] Includes government consumption expenditures, which are for services (such as education and national defense) produced by government. In current dollars, these services are valued at their cost of production. [2] Equals gross domestic product excluding gross value added of households and institutions and of general government. [3] Equals gross domestic business value added excluding gross farm value added. [4] Equals compensation of general government employees plus general government consumption of fixed capital.

Source: U.S. Bureau of Economic Analysis, "National Income and Product Accounts Tables," <http://www.bea.gov/iTable/index_nipa.cfm>, accessed July 2017.

Table 693. Gross Domestic Product in Current and Chained (2009) Dollars by Industry: 2000 to 2016

[In billions of dollars (10,285 represents $10,285,000,000,000). Based on 2007 North American Industry Classification System (NAICS); see text, Section 15. Value added GDP is the contribution of each industry's labor and capital to its gross output and to the overall gross domestic product (GDP) of the United States. Value added is equal to an industry's gross output (sales or receipts and other operating income, commodity taxes, and inventory change) minus its intermediate inputs (the value of goods and services used up in production). Current-dollar value added is calculated as the sum of distributions by an industry to its labor and capital which are derived from the components of gross domestic income]

Industry	Current dollars				Chained (2009) dollars [1]			
	2000	2010	2015	2016 [2]	2000	2010	2015	2016 [2]
Gross domestic product	**10,285**	**14,964**	**18,037**	**18,569**	**12,560**	**14,784**	**16,397**	**16,662**
Private industries	8,956	12,827	15,699	16,178	10,826	12,650	14,144	14,382
Agriculture, forestry, fishing, and hunting	99	160	175	160	106	140	147	158
Farms	76	130	137	121	84	112	115	127
Forestry, fishing, and related activities	23	31	39	39	23	29	32	32
Mining	111	332	328	265	211	273	392	349
Oil and gas extraction	68	209	206	170	119	159	282	271
Mining, except oil and gas	29	77	66	59	75	70	60	53
Mining support activities	14	45	56	35	25	46	52	35
Utilities	180	267	284	288	304	274	264	277
Construction	462	542	732	784	769	552	624	646
Manufacturing	1,555	1,831	2,170	2,175	1,603	1,818	1,912	1,909
Durable goods	927	957	1,176	1,185	806	976	1,110	1,110
Wood products	28	22	30	32	25	21	24	24
Nonmetallic mineral products	43	36	48	50	51	37	43	42
Primary metals	47	48	56	54	47	38	55	61
Fabricated metal products	122	120	149	149	162	129	140	137
Machinery	113	122	153	148	130	128	134	126
Computer and electronic products	226	249	278	282	92	256	296	302
Electrical equipment, appliances, and components	46	50	56	56	54	51	52	51
Motor vehicles, bodies & trailers, & parts	138	93	163	176	107	100	154	163
Other transportation equipment	71	112	131	126	92	112	116	109
Furniture and related products	34	22	28	29	41	23	26	27
Miscellaneous manufacturing	59	81	83	83	62	82	77	76
Nondurable goods	628	874	994	991	807	844	814	811
Food & beverage & tobacco	164	230	258	263	210	233	220	211
Textile mills and textile product mills	28	16	18	18	30	16	16	16
Apparel and leather and allied products	22	11	10	10	20	11	9	9
Paper products	62	55	60	59	73	53	51	51
Printing and related support activities	44	39	39	39	41	40	39	39
Petroleum and coal products	53	130	162	140	76	99	110	114
Chemical products	189	331	377	388	263	330	302	303
Plastics and rubber products	66	63	71	73	79	65	63	64
Wholesale trade	625	869	1,093	1,098	741	848	984	990
Retail trade	696	869	1,057	1,087	783	862	969	990
Transportation and warehousing	306	425	543	563	380	421	446	455
Air transportation	56	72	96	105	69	70	69	74
Rail transportation	23	35	46	42	35	34	36	33
Water transportation	8	16	19	19	5	14	16	16
Truck transportation	98	113	146	150	121	120	126	127
Transit & ground passenger transport	18	28	34	37	28	27	27	28
Pipeline transportation	9	19	27	27	11	17	21	20
Other transportation & support	66	96	118	123	86	91	90	92
Warehousing and storage	27	46	57	60	31	48	65	69
Information	472	730	840	886	445	735	855	909
Publishing industries (except internet, includes software)	116	182	205	219	130	185	203	215
Motion picture and sound recording	54	108	115	124	61	107	111	116
Broadcasting and telecommunications	278	371	413	426	230	373	428	453
Data processing, internet publishing, & related services	24	70	107	118	24	70	114	127
Finance and insurance	750	1,006	1,293	1,356	783	969	1,028	1,042
Real estate and rental and leasing	1,242	1,946	2,363	2,462	1,540	1,957	2,165	2,188
Professional, scientific, and technical services	656	1,022	1,293	1,356	818	1,009	1,175	1,215
Legal services	134	206	242	258	211	198	190	197
Computer systems design, related services	114	190	266	278	107	193	276	290
Miscellaneous services	409	626	785	820	504	619	717	737
Management of companies & enterprises	173	268	356	368	273	266	346	351
Administrative and waste management services	282	440	558	585	328	443	519	528
Educational services	86	169	202	207	125	165	168	167
Health care and social assistance	595	1,079	1,299	1,369	798	1,056	1,187	1,223
Ambulatory health care services	288	518	630	664	361	505	595	622
Hospitals	182	346	412	438	262	339	366	377
Nursing and residential care facilities	73	124	140	144	106	122	128	127
Social assistance	53	92	117	122	70	90	99	100
Arts, entertainment, and recreation	99	144	186	198	129	145	169	173
Performing arts, spectator sports, museums, & related	49	79	102	110	68	78	90	93
Amusements, gambling, & recreation	50	66	84	88	61	67	79	80
Accommodation and food services	287	396	524	552	392	396	455	458
Accommodation	93	111	149	153	118	112	130	130
Food services and drinking places	194	286	375	398	273	285	325	328
Other services, except government	280	332	402	420	404	324	340	346
Government	1,329	2,138	2,338	2,392	1,876	2,080	2,053	2,066
Federal	422	701	729	740	587	680	653	654
State and local	907	1,437	1,609	1,652	1,289	1,399	1,400	1,412

[1] Chained (2009) dollar series are the product of the chain-type quantity index and the 2009 current-dollar value of the corresponding series, divided by 100. The formula uses weights of more than one period, and the corresponding chained-dollar estimates are usually not additive. [2] Data for 2016 are averages of quarterly estimates. For industry subsectors, quarterly statistics on which these estimates rely are of lower quality and pass through a less rigorous review process than the higher level industry sector aggregates in which they are included.

Source: U.S. Bureau of Economic Analysis, Industry Economic Accounts, "GDP by Industry Data," <http://www.bea.gov/industry/index.htm>, accessed May 2017.

Table 694. Gross Domestic Product by State in Current and Chained (2009) Dollars: 2005 to 2016

[In billions of dollars (13,015.2 represents $13,015,200,000,000). For definition of gross domestic product by state or chained dollars, see text, this section]

State	Current dollars					Chained (2009) dollars				
	2005	2010	2014	2015	2016	2005	2010	2014	2015	2016
United States [1]	**13,015.2**	**14,859.8**	**17,277.5**	**17,925.1**	**18,456.3**	**14,203.2**	**14,628.2**	**15,690.3**	**16,094.5**	**16,342.9**
Alabama	156.8	174.7	194.4	200.0	204.9	171.7	171.9	177.0	178.9	181.2
Alaska	40.1	54.1	58.3	53.4	50.7	40.8	49.7	49.7	49.9	47.5
Arizona	227.4	245.7	280.8	291.4	303.0	251.2	243.1	258.2	261.9	267.5
Arkansas	90.3	103.0	117.9	118.7	120.7	99.1	101.3	107.5	107.8	108.7
California	1,766.7	1,965.9	2,349.3	2,491.6	2,602.7	1,910.3	1,936.5	2,141.9	2,235.4	2,300.8
Colorado	220.5	253.4	305.3	313.3	323.7	238.4	248.7	278.3	286.7	292.5
Connecticut	210.2	234.5	244.8	256.3	263.4	231.6	232.4	223.5	228.5	230.7
Delaware	53.2	57.5	65.9	68.9	70.4	57.1	56.5	59.2	60.5	60.6
District of Columbia	83.6	103.8	116.3	121.1	126.8	92.5	101.7	105.0	106.7	109.3
Florida	700.3	735.1	832.3	883.9	926.8	773.0	727.7	763.7	791.4	815.1
Georgia	388.3	412.5	477.5	501.5	525.4	425.0	408.2	436.9	447.9	461.1
Hawaii	58.6	68.2	76.8	80.6	83.9	64.8	67.4	70.1	71.7	73.3
Idaho	47.2	55.3	63.3	65.5	67.3	51.3	54.4	57.3	58.6	59.7
Illinois	586.4	653.5	747.6	772.2	791.6	646.1	646.0	679.3	686.0	692.5
Indiana	245.2	282.3	324.4	333.4	341.9	268.9	279.1	294.0	296.2	300.6
Iowa	123.4	141.7	169.8	175.8	178.8	135.0	140.0	153.0	156.4	157.7
Kansas	104.9	128.5	147.6	151.8	153.3	114.6	126.5	133.4	136.3	136.6
Kentucky	143.9	166.0	185.7	191.9	197.0	159.8	163.4	169.0	170.8	173.0
Louisiana	199.7	232.6	242.1	238.1	235.1	215.1	220.9	205.7	206.8	205.6
Maine	46.3	51.5	55.3	57.3	59.3	51.4	50.9	50.6	51.1	51.8
Maryland	263.8	314.0	350.4	366.2	378.3	290.6	310.7	322.3	329.1	333.3
Massachusetts	345.1	402.7	459.1	488.1	507.9	376.4	399.2	421.9	437.6	446.5
Michigan	395.2	385.0	445.2	470.6	487.2	431.4	382.9	411.6	422.8	430.6
Minnesota	243.9	269.9	317.0	326.8	335.1	267.5	266.3	289.0	292.7	296.4
Mississippi	81.7	95.8	104.3	105.9	107.7	89.5	94.1	94.3	94.6	95.3
Missouri	224.1	255.9	282.0	292.7	300.9	247.9	253.1	257.2	260.9	263.9
Montana	30.6	38.4	45.1	45.8	46.0	34.0	37.4	40.1	41.0	41.0
Nebraska	73.5	92.2	112.1	113.5	115.3	81.1	90.7	99.9	100.1	101.3
Nevada	118.8	121.7	132.7	141.1	147.5	133.3	120.5	121.6	125.9	128.8
New Hampshire	57.3	64.2	71.1	74.3	77.9	62.8	63.7	65.7	67.1	69.1
New Jersey	443.1	489.1	542.5	564.4	581.1	491.2	484.4	496.5	504.6	510.6
New Mexico	74.4	86.1	94.7	93.2	93.3	79.6	83.2	85.1	86.5	86.0
New York	1,023.4	1,204.7	1,391.1	1,445.6	1,488.0	1,119.3	1,188.7	1,250.5	1,265.6	1,275.1
North Carolina	357.2	416.0	474.5	499.7	517.9	392.1	412.4	430.9	442.5	449.8
North Dakota	24.6	36.2	59.6	55.9	52.1	26.7	35.2	52.6	50.9	47.6
Ohio	467.4	499.0	591.5	607.3	625.7	512.2	492.4	537.8	543.4	552.5
Oklahoma	125.2	149.9	196.8	188.0	182.9	133.6	144.0	174.5	179.2	175.1
Oregon	147.5	191.1	203.3	216.5	226.8	153.8	190.4	191.8	200.4	207.1
Pennsylvania	506.5	596.7	684.8	708.4	724.9	560.7	589.7	628.7	644.9	652.0
Rhode Island	45.7	49.4	53.7	55.7	57.4	50.4	48.8	49.2	49.7	50.3
South Carolina	143.6	164.1	191.2	201.8	209.7	159.7	162.8	175.2	180.1	183.9
South Dakota	31.4	38.2	45.5	47.1	48.1	33.2	37.2	39.9	40.9	41.6
Tennessee	227.5	252.5	298.9	316.7	328.8	250.8	250.3	273.7	282.3	287.8
Texas	990.1	1,243.4	1,614.1	1,611.2	1,616.8	1,047.0	1,197.0	1,427.9	1,492.8	1,498.9
Utah	94.5	117.7	140.5	149.1	156.4	102.4	115.2	126.7	132.2	136.2
Vermont	23.5	26.6	29.4	30.3	31.1	25.8	26.4	27.0	27.2	27.4
Virginia	359.3	420.9	459.1	481.7	494.3	396.3	416.9	422.5	432.7	435.2
Washington	296.4	359.7	425.1	446.4	469.7	325.1	355.2	388.0	399.4	414.2
West Virginia	53.5	67.3	74.0	73.4	73.4	61.2	65.6	66.8	67.1	66.5
Wisconsin	226.3	252.9	290.9	301.6	309.5	250.3	251.1	266.8	270.3	273.1
Wyoming	27.5	39.1	41.8	39.4	37.9	29.6	36.5	35.8	35.7	34.4

[1] For chained (2009) dollar estimates, states will not add to U.S. total.

Source: U.S. Bureau of Economic Analysis, Regional Economic Accounts, "Gross Domestic Product by State," <http://www.bea.gov/iTable/index_regional.cfm>, accessed May 2017.

Table 695. Gross Domestic Product by Selected Industry and State: 2016

[In billions of dollars (18,456.3 represents $18,456,300,000,000). Data are subject to revision. For definition of gross domestic product by state, see text, this section. Industries based on 2007 North American Industry Classification System; see text, Section 15]

State	Total [1]	Manu-facturing	Whole-sale trade	Retail trade	Infor-mation	Finance and insur-ance	Real estate, rental, and leasing	Profes-sional and technical services	Health care and social assist-ance	Govern-ment [2]
United States	**18,456.3**	**2,175.2**	**1,098.0**	**1,087.1**	**886.0**	**1,355.5**	**2,461.8**	**1,355.7**	**1,368.7**	**2,278.8**
Alabama	204.9	35.7	11.5	15.1	4.4	10.6	22.4	11.9	15.1	34.2
Alaska	50.7	1.6	1.3	2.3	1.4	1.2	5.2	1.9	3.7	10.6
Arizona	303.0	24.4	17.0	23.7	9.5	21.3	47.2	17.2	25.7	40.7
Arkansas	120.7	17.3	8.7	8.8	4.4	5.4	12.7	4.3	10.2	15.8
California	2,602.7	289.0	138.8	144.9	217.6	127.2	437.8	224.3	164.5	318.0
Colorado	323.7	22.6	17.9	18.1	19.3	18.8	46.2	30.0	20.8	39.9
Connecticut	263.4	28.5	16.8	14.4	13.0	34.1	38.5	17.9	21.2	27.1
Delaware	70.4	3.9	2.3	3.0	1.0	21.0	11.2	4.5	5.1	6.9
District of Columbia	126.8	0.3	1.1	1.6	6.0	5.0	11.9	27.0	5.7	42.8
Florida	926.8	47.1	62.1	69.8	37.8	56.6	146.8	67.9	79.9	110.4
Georgia	525.4	56.5	40.2	31.0	37.2	43.3	62.6	36.0	34.0	62.4
Hawaii	83.9	1.8	2.6	5.7	1.9	2.9	16.0	3.4	5.6	17.7
Idaho	67.3	7.8	4.0	5.9	1.3	3.0	9.0	3.8	5.5	8.9
Illinois	791.6	100.4	59.9	40.3	25.3	76.6	104.1	65.4	56.6	76.5
Indiana	341.9	98.4	18.4	20.4	6.2	18.3	33.5	13.8	27.4	31.4
Iowa	178.8	32.7	10.2	9.9	3.9	22.4	18.2	5.8	12.3	20.7
Kansas	153.3	23.8	10.2	10.0	5.7	8.7	16.9	8.5	11.6	21.0
Kentucky	197.0	37.2	13.1	11.9	4.2	10.2	20.8	7.9	16.5	27.8
Louisiana	235.1	49.9	11.9	15.5	5.6	8.8	23.3	11.4	17.3	26.3
Maine	59.3	5.3	3.3	4.9	1.1	3.5	9.1	3.1	7.0	8.3
Maryland	378.3	20.7	16.0	19.9	15.0	22.0	62.8	36.9	28.3	78.6
Massachusetts	507.9	48.7	25.2	21.4	26.0	47.8	73.1	59.1	47.6	53.3
Michigan	487.2	93.5	31.6	31.9	12.2	27.1	57.6	38.1	40.3	51.3
Minnesota	335.1	48.2	22.4	19.0	11.5	25.6	38.9	23.5	31.7	33.9
Mississippi	107.7	17.1	5.5	9.1	2.2	4.8	11.1	3.5	8.3	19.1
Missouri	300.9	39.4	19.9	19.2	10.9	22.2	34.6	19.9	25.8	35.7
Montana	46.0	3.6	2.6	3.1	1.0	2.0	6.2	2.2	4.5	7.0
Nebraska	115.3	13.2	7.7	6.4	3.0	11.3	11.3	4.8	8.6	14.6
Nevada	147.5	6.1	5.9	11.0	3.5	8.1	22.0	7.1	8.9	16.8
New Hampshire	77.9	8.5	5.0	5.5	3.0	7.2	11.4	5.5	7.0	8.9
New Jersey	581.1	45.4	46.9	33.8	23.3	39.5	98.2	52.9	45.7	62.4
New Mexico	93.3	3.9	3.0	5.6	3.4	3.4	12.4	6.8	7.1	22.4
New York	1,488.0	71.3	68.9	71.3	114.2	259.1	217.8	128.0	104.9	166.5
North Carolina	517.9	99.8	29.4	27.9	17.2	41.2	58.4	30.0	35.1	68.7
North Dakota	52.1	3.7	4.3	3.2	1.2	2.7	6.0	1.8	3.9	5.9
Ohio	625.7	106.0	37.9	38.1	17.1	54.5	68.6	32.3	53.4	69.2
Oklahoma	182.9	17.7	10.2	11.5	4.3	6.9	18.2	7.9	13.4	29.4
Oregon	226.8	49.4	11.5	11.2	7.3	10.3	30.5	11.7	18.0	26.1
Pennsylvania	724.9	85.0	41.0	36.8	46.6	46.3	91.2	52.6	69.7	72.0
Rhode Island	57.4	4.6	3.3	3.2	1.6	5.4	8.7	3.1	5.8	7.8
South Carolina	209.7	35.2	11.9	14.8	5.2	9.3	26.4	11.1	14.0	32.4
South Dakota	48.1	4.4	3.5	3.6	1.2	7.2	4.5	1.6	4.4	5.6
Tennessee	328.8	53.2	22.6	23.0	9.2	17.5	36.6	18.2	31.7	37.3
Texas	1,616.8	225.8	132.8	97.4	54.7	87.1	150.7	109.1	96.0	172.7
Utah	156.4	17.5	7.7	11.0	6.7	15.6	19.8	10.1	9.0	20.1
Vermont	31.1	2.8	1.6	2.4	0.8	1.9	4.4	2.0	3.3	4.6
Virginia	494.3	42.1	20.2	26.1	17.5	25.6	71.4	62.4	31.2	91.8
Washington	469.7	58.4	25.2	37.2	47.0	17.3	66.1	30.4	29.5	64.1
West Virginia	73.4	7.5	3.3	5.1	1.6	2.5	7.3	2.9	7.5	11.8
Wisconsin	309.5	56.4	18.4	18.3	10.1	23.9	37.9	13.5	26.9	35.2
Wyoming	37.9	2.2	1.6	2.2	0.6	1.2	4.3	1.1	1.7	6.3

[1] Includes industries not shown separately. [2] Includes federal civilian and military, and state and local government.

Source: U.S. Bureau of Economic Analysis, Regional Economic Accounts, "Gross Domestic Product by State," <http://www.bea.gov/regional/index.htm>, accessed May 2017.

Table 696. Relation of GDP, GNP, Net National Product, National Income, Personal Income, Disposable Personal Income, and Personal Saving: 2000 to 2016

[In billions of dollars (10,285 represents $10,285,000,000,000). For definitions, see text, this section. Minus sign (-) indicates deficit or net disbursement]

Item	2000	2005	2010	2012	2013	2014	2015	2016
Gross domestic product (GDP)..............	**10,285**	**13,094**	**14,964**	**16,155**	**16,692**	**17,428**	**18,121**	**18,625**
Plus: Income receipts from the rest of the world..	383	576	720	802	826	847	813	844
Less: Income payments to the rest of the world..	346	483	514	564	581	613	608	647
Equals: Gross national product (GNP).........	**10,322**	**13,186**	**15,170**	**16,393**	**16,936**	**17,662**	**18,325**	**18,822**
Less: Consumption of fixed capital................	1,514	1,982	2,382	2,534	2,629	2,748	2,842	2,917
Equals: Net national product.....................	**8,808**	**11,204**	**12,789**	**13,859**	**14,307**	**14,914**	**15,484**	**15,905**
Less: Statistical discrepancy......................	-100	-36	49	-203	-138	-230	-256	-147
Equals: National income.........................	**8,907**	**11,240**	**12,740**	**14,062**	**14,445**	**15,144**	**15,740**	**16,052**
Less: Corporate profits [1].......................	781	1,478	1,746	1,998	2,033	2,141	2,118	2,074
Taxes on production and imports less subsidies...................................	663	874	1,001	1,074	1,116	1,164	1,199	1,226
Contributions for government social insurance..	706	873	984	952	1,105	1,155	1,208	1,245
Net interest and miscellaneous payments on assets......................................	565	497	489	528	505	535	583	571
Business current transfer payments (net)......	85	94	129	105	118	139	165	164
Current surplus of government enterprises......	11	-6	-23	-19	-21	-18	-14	-10
Plus: Personal income receipts on assets........	1,454	1,667	1,740	2,124	2,056	2,245	2,387	2,378
Personal current transfer receipts.............	1,087	1,517	2,325	2,366	2,428	2,544	2,684	2,768
Equals: Personal income.........................	**8,637**	**10,614**	**12,477**	**13,915**	**14,074**	**14,818**	**15,553**	**15,929**
Less: Personal current taxes......................	1,237	1,213	1,239	1,511	1,678	1,786	1,938	1,960
Equals: Disposable personal income...........	**7,401**	**9,401**	**11,238**	**12,404**	**12,396**	**13,033**	**13,615**	**13,969**
Less: Personal outlays............................	7,093	9,158	10,608	11,457	11,776	12,294	12,787	13,288
Equals: Personal saving.........................	**308**	**243**	**630**	**947**	**620**	**739**	**828**	**681**

[1] Corporate profits with inventory valuation and capital consumption adjustments.

Source: U.S. Bureau of Economic Analysis, National Income and Product Accounts Tables, "Table 1.7.5. Relation of Gross Domestic Product, Gross National Product, Net National Product, National Income, and Personal Income," and "Table 2.1. Personal Income and Its Disposition," <http://www.bea.gov/iTable/index_nipa.cfm>, accessed July 2017.

Table 697. Gross Saving and Investment: 2000 to 2016

[In billions of dollars (2,120 represents $2,120,000,000,000), except as noted. Minus (-) sign indicates deficit]

Item	2000	2005	2010	2012	2013	2014	2015	2016
Gross saving.........................	**2,120**	**2,339**	**2,258**	**2,861**	**3,051**	**3,357**	**3,507**	**3,353**
Net saving................................	606	357	-124	327	422	609	666	437
Net private saving....................	439	728	1,442	1,638	1,256	1,388	1,399	1,301
Domestic business..................	131	485	812	691	636	649	570	621
Undistributed corporate profits....	97	660	906	824	759	757	611	706
Inventory valuation adjustment, corporate.......	-17	-32	-41	-14	3	4	52	3
Capital consumption adjustment, corporate.....	51	-144	-53	-119	-127	-113	-94	-88
Households and institutions........................	308	243	630	947	620	739	828	681
Personal saving...............................	308	243	630	947	620	739	828	681
Net government saving...........................	166	-371	-1,566	-1,311	-834	-779	-733	-865
Federal....................................	157	-305	-1,329	-1,090	-644	-610	-587	-697
State and local...........................	10	-67	-237	-221	-191	-169	-146	-167
Consumption of fixed capital......................	1,514	1,982	2,382	2,534	2,629	2,748	2,842	2,917
Private....................................	1,237	1,635	1,924	2,038	2,122	2,231	2,320	2,391
Domestic business.......................	1,007	1,273	1,523	1,633	1,695	1,775	1,847	1,895
Households and institutions...............	230	362	401	405	428	456	473	495
Government...............................	278	347	458	496	507	517	522	526
Federal...................................	162	189	245	264	268	271	271	271
State and local...........................	116	157	213	232	239	246	251	255
Gross domestic investment, capital account transactions, and net lending.......	**2,020**	**2,303**	**2,307**	**2,658**	**2,913**	**3,127**	**3,251**	**3,206**
Gross domestic investment..................	2,424	3,041	2,753	3,126	3,299	3,511	3,702	3,667
Gross private domestic investment.............	2,034	2,527	2,101	2,512	2,706	2,916	3,094	3,057
Gross government investment.................	390	514	652	614	592	594	608	610
Capital account transactions (net) [1]...........	(Z)	-13	1	-7	1	(Z)	(Z)	(Z)
Net lending or net borrowing...................	-404	-725	-447	-462	-387	-384	-451	-461
Statistical discrepancy...........................	-100	-36	49	-203	-138	-230	-256	-147
Addenda:								
Gross private saving..........................	1,676	2,363	3,365	3,676	3,378	3,619	3,718	3,692
Gross government saving.......................	444	-25	-1,108	-815	-328	-262	-211	-339
Federal..	318	-115	-1,083	-826	-376	-339	-315	-426
State and local................................	126	91	-25	11	48	77	104	88
Net domestic investment.......................	910	1,059	371	592	670	763	860	750
Gross saving as a percentage of gross national income........................	20.3	17.7	14.9	17.2	17.9	18.8	18.9	17.7
Net saving as a percentage of gross national income........................	5.8	2.7	-0.8	2.0	2.5	3.4	3.6	2.3
Disaster losses [2].............................	–	110	–	46	–	–	–	–

– Represents or rounds to zero. Z Less than $500 million. [1] Consists of capital transfers and the acquisition and disposal of nonproduced nonfinancial assets. [2] Consists of damages to fixed assets.

Source: U.S. Bureau of Economic Analysis, National Income and Product Accounts Tables, "Table 5.1 Saving and Investment by Sector," <http://www.bea.gov/iTable/index_nipa.cfm>, accessed July 2017.

Table 698. Financial Accounts of the United States—Composition of Individuals' Savings: 1990 to 2016

[In billions of dollars (642.2 represents $642,200,000,000). Combined statement for households, nonprofit organizations, and nonfinancial noncorporate business. Minus sign (-) indicates decrease]

Composition of savings	1990	2000	2010	2012	2013	2014	2015	2016
Net acquisition of financial assets	**642.2**	**633.9**	**739.8**	**1,427.2**	**1,251.0**	**1,684.6**	**1,590.9**	**1,439.3**
Foreign deposits	1.4	7.6	4.5	-7.9	2.6	-6.4	-14.1	-2.1
Checkable deposits and currency	-9.3	-95.1	36.3	239.0	144.9	142.5	184.7	60.5
Time and savings deposits	52.9	355.0	167.7	422.3	222.2	454.0	527.4	738.5
Money market fund shares	39.8	170.3	-180.3	4.9	32.4	-22.6	-38.4	-39.3
Debt securities	216.3	-49.8	-90.6	-66.6	-422.1	-40.3	149.7	-55.5
Treasury securities	96.9	-203.4	320.4	226.6	-25.8	-224.6	220.8	209.4
Agency and GSE-backed securities [1]	35.6	29.9	4.0	-68.2	-29.8	105.3	194.3	-120.1
Municipal securities	35.9	17.7	70.9	-121.6	-55.7	-59.3	-60.7	11.5
Corporate and foreign bonds	47.9	106.0	-485.8	-103.5	-310.8	138.3	-204.7	-156.4
Loans	16.4	111.4	21.3	15.2	56.5	45.2	-59.3	-5.0
Corporate equities [2]	-56.8	-554.8	-225.1	-182.7	137.6	167.9	18.1	-38.5
Mutual fund shares	28.9	77.4	214.3	304.3	230.9	241.7	58.3	27.2
Trade receivables	5.9	10.1	6.3	9.0	5.6	6.9	6.9	6.9
Life insurance reserves	27.0	42.9	7.3	-30.5	12.0	35.1	35.6	39.7
Pension entitlements	300.9	393.6	626.9	496.0	507.5	297.5	446.5	388.0
Miscellaneous and other assets	18.8	165.4	151.2	224.2	320.9	363.2	275.4	318.8
Gross investment in nonfinancial assets	**825.1**	**1,590.6**	**1,694.1**	**1,935.6**	**2,089.7**	**2,195.8**	**2,349.5**	**2,435.2**
Minus: Consumption of fixed capital	617.8	1,009.9	1,580.9	1,640.0	1,697.5	1,760.0	1,814.0	1,848.8
Equals: Net investment in nonfinancial assets	**207.3**	**580.7**	**113.2**	**295.5**	**392.2**	**435.8**	**535.5**	**586.4**
Net increase in liabilities	**239.1**	**919.0**	**-131.6**	**527.7**	**426.6**	**796.8**	**780.4**	**911.8**
Home mortgages	206.9	423.0	-133.4	-76.9	2.1	38.9	140.9	264.7
Other mortgages	-4.4	106.3	-33.4	122.1	92.5	188.0	194.1	217.5
Consumer credit	15.1	176.5	-28.1	164.1	175.8	221.8	232.7	229.0
Other loans and advances	3.6	8.6	77.6	66.1	37.5	33.2	-76.5	-10.5
Other liabilities	18.0	204.6	-14.3	252.3	118.7	315.0	289.2	211.2
Personal saving, FOF concept (FOF) [3]	625.9	331.2	956.3	1,185.1	1,236.6	1,333.2	1,367.5	1,129.3
Personal saving, NIPA concept (FOF) [3]	549.1	87.9	877.6	1,025.1	1,058.2	1,127.0	1,132.9	855.5
Personal saving, NIPA concept (NIPA) [4]	335.4	307.7	630.0	946.7	620.1	726.0	783.6	824.2

[1] GSE = government-sponsored enterprises. [2] Only directly held and those in closed-end and exchange-traded funds. Other equities are included in mutual funds, life insurance reserves, and pension entitlements. [3] Flow of Funds measure. [4] National Income and Product Accounts measure.

Source: Board of Governors of the Federal Reserve System, "Z.1 Financial Accounts of the United States: Summary Table F.6 Derivation of Measures of Personal Saving," March 2017, <https://www.federalreserve.gov/releases/Z1/current/default.htm>, accessed March 2017.

Table 699. Government Consumption Expenditures and Gross Investment by Level of Government and Type: 2000 to 2016

[In billions of dollars (1,834 represents $1,834,000,000,000). Government consumption expenditures are services (such as education and national defense) produced by government that are valued at their cost of production; excludes government sales to other sectors and government own-account investment (construction, software, and research and development). Gross government investment consists of general government and government enterprise expenditures for fixed assets; inventory investment is included in government consumption expenditures. For explanation of national income and chained dollars, see text, Section 13]

Item	Current dollars				Chained (2009) dollars			
	2000	2010	2015	2016	2000	2010	2015	2016
Government consumption expenditures and gross investment, total	**1,834**	**3,174**	**3,219**	**3,268**	**2,498**	**3,091**	**2,879**	**2,900**
Consumption expenditures	1,444	2,522	2,611	2,658	1,998	2,445	2,323	2,345
Gross investment	390	652	608	610	501	647	555	554
Structures	190	313	285	281	305	312	250	244
Equipment	87	151	132	133	80	151	130	131
Intellectual property products	113	187	191	196	127	183	175	179
Federal	**632**	**1,304**	**1,224**	**1,232**	**818**	**1,271**	**1,114**	**1,115**
Consumption expenditures	475	1,004	960	965	646	975	868	866
Gross investment	157	300	264	267	174	295	246	249
Structures	14	33	17	17	21	33	15	14
Equipment	49	109	92	91	47	109	89	89
Intellectual property products	95	158	156	159	108	154	142	145
National defense	**392**	**833**	**732**	**729**	**512**	**814**	**672**	**667**
Consumption expenditures	308	653	588	585	423	636	537	532
Gross investment	83	180	143	144	91	178	135	135
Structures	5	17	4	3	8	17	4	3
Equipment	38	90	73	72	38	90	71	71
Intellectual property products	40	73	67	68	46	71	60	62
Nondefense	**241**	**471**	**492**	**503**	**305**	**457**	**442**	**447**
Consumption expenditures	167	351	372	379	223	339	330	334
Gross investment	74	120	121	123	82	118	111	113
Structures	8	16	13	13	13	16	11	12
Equipment	11	19	19	19	9	19	19	19
Intellectual property products	55	85	89	91	62	83	82	83
State and local	**1,202**	**1,870**	**1,995**	**2,036**	**1,689**	**1,821**	**1,763**	**1,784**
Consumption expenditures	969	1,518	1,651	1,694	1,356	1,470	1,454	1,478
Gross investment	233	352	344	343	334	351	308	304
Structures	176	281	268	264	285	280	234	229
Equipment	39	42	41	42	33	42	41	42
Intellectual property products	18	30	36	36	19	29	34	34

Source: U.S. Bureau of Economic Analysis, National Income and Product Accounts Tables, "Table 3.9.5. Government Consumption Expenditures and Gross Investment" and "Table 3.9.6. Real Government Consumption Expenditures and Gross Investment, Chained Dollars," <http://www.bea.gov/iTable/index_nipa.cfm>, accessed July 2017.

Table 700. Personal Consumption Expenditures by Function: 2000 to 2016

[In billions of dollars (6,792 represents $6,792,000,000,000). In current and chained (2009) dollars. For definition of chained dollars, see text, this section. Minus sign (-) indicates decrease]

Function	Current dollars				Chained (2009) dollars			
	2000	2010	2015	2016	2000	2010	2015	2016
Personal consumption expenditures [1]	**6,792**	**10,202**	**12,332**	**12,821**	**8,171**	**10,036**	**11,264**	**11,572**
Food and nonalcoholic beverages purchased for off-premises consumption	463	676	765	776	591	674	682	701
Alcoholic beverages purchased for off-premises consumption	77	113	134	139	93	112	128	132
Clothing, footwear, and related services	298	336	403	411	276	338	385	393
Clothing	251	274	326	331	227	277	313	319
Footwear [2]	47	62	77	80	48	61	71	74
Housing [1]	1,011	1,610	1,921	2,020	1,321	1,609	1,714	1,742
Rental of tenant-occupied nonfarm housing [3]	228	373	490	519	306	372	429	438
Imputed rental of owner-occupied nonfarm housing [4]	769	1,215	1,410	1,478	993	1,215	1,266	1,285
Household utilities and fuels	204	326	336	331	311	318	305	303
Water supply and sanitation	50	78	89	91	77	73	67	66
Electricity, gas, and other fuels	154	248	247	239	234	244	239	238
Furnishings, household equipment, and routine household maintenance [1]	343	417	513	534	336	429	558	588
Furniture, furnishings, and floor coverings [5]	115	138	173	181	101	144	201	214
Household appliances [6]	38	46	54	55	40	48	60	64
Tools and equipment for house and garden	17	18	22	23	17	18	22	24
Medical products, appliances, and equipment	191	390	534	561	247	378	459	465
Pharmaceutical and other medical products [7]	159	334	467	490	211	322	392	396
Outpatient services	437	768	920	966	541	751	861	897
Physician services [8]	229	403	480	503	270	393	457	479
Dental services	64	105	118	125	95	102	101	104
Paramedical services [9]	144	261	322	338	178	257	303	315
Hospital and nursing home services	482	923	1,142	1,197	680	898	1,018	1,053
Transportation	795	942	1,130	1,129	930	870	1,020	1,047
Motor vehicles	321	287	403	410	293	269	362	373
New motor vehicles	211	182	277	273	198	179	254	249
Net purchases of used motor vehicles	111	104	126	136	95	91	112	126
Motor vehicle operation [1]	400	575	621	611	567	525	572	589
Motor vehicle parts and accessories	42	56	69	71	53	54	64	66
Motor vehicle fuels, lubricants, and fluids	169	307	284	255	266	260	265	268
Motor vehicle maintenance and repair	127	152	182	193	175	150	164	171
Public transportation	74	81	107	107	84	77	90	91
Telephone and facsimile equipment	6	13	19	18	3	13	28	30
Postal and delivery services	10	12	11	10	14	11	8	8
Telecommunication services	126	152	166	166	126	153	177	177
Internet access	16	63	104	115	13	63	103	115
Recreation [1]	634	888	1,086	1,138	569	911	1,185	1,256
Video and audio equipment	80	100	103	103	34	115	194	215
Information processing equipment	44	90	111	116	12	97	170	192
Services related to video/audio goods and computers	57	87	100	100	74	86	88	85
Sports and recreational goods and related services	146	174	227	237	130	179	263	282
Magazines, newspapers, books, and stationery	81	90	113	124	91	90	105	115
Pets, pet products, and related services	40	76	99	107	57	76	91	96
Education [1]	134	245	286	295	237	234	225	226
Higher education	77	158	183	188	140	150	142	141
Food services	354	532	690	727	470	525	601	617
Accommodations [10]	55	86	118	122	65	84	102	103
Financial services	360	473	598	626	386	453	439	427
Insurance [1]	206	290	349	359	276	281	305	305
Life insurance	65	88	93	92	85	86	82	79
Net health insurance	94	136	178	185	131	130	157	160
Net motor vehicle and other transportation insurance	43	59	66	68	54	57	56	54
Personal care [11]	132	204	259	274	157	203	243	256
Personal items [12]	64	88	115	120	66	87	113	115
Social services and religious activities [13]	81	139	171	179	104	136	151	155
Professional and other services [1]	113	163	186	191	163	158	159	159
Legal services	65	91	102	105	95	88	88	87
Accounting and other business services	17	27	33	35	25	26	27	27
Funeral and burial services	16	25	29	29	23	24	25	25
Tobacco	69	106	108	107	119	96	84	81
Net foreign travel and expenditures abroad by: U.S. residents [1]	-26	-27	-59	-49	-20	-28	-44	-30
Foreign travel by U.S. residents	72	107	145	156	102	102	132	146
Less: Expenditures in the United States by nonresidents	102	140	208	209	129	135	182	181
Final consumption expenditures of nonprofit institutions serving households (NPISHs) [14]	158	275	329	359	163	278	300	317

[1] Includes other expenditures not shown separately. [2] Also includes repair and hire of footwear. [3] Rent for space (see footnote 4) and rent for appliances, furnishings, and furniture. [4] Rent for space and for heating and plumbing facilities, water heaters, lighting fixtures, kitchen cabinets, linoleum, storm windows and doors, window screens, and screen doors; excludes rent for appliances and furniture and purchases of fuel and electricity. [5] Includes clocks, lamps, lighting fixtures, other household decorative items, and repair of furniture, furnishings, and floor coverings. [6] Major and small electric household appliances, and repair of appliances. [7] Excludes drug preparations and related products dispensed by physicians, hospitals, and other medical services. [8] Offices of physicians, HMO medical centers, and freestanding ambulatory surgical and emergency centers. [9] Includes home health care, medical laboratories, and other health professionals (except physicians) and services. [10] Hotels, motels, other traveler accommodations, clubs, and housing at schools. [11] Cosmetics and toiletries, and personal care appliances and services. [12] Jewelry, watches, luggage, and similar items. [13] Household purchases from business, government, and nonprofit institutions providing social services and religious activities. Purchases from nonprofit establishments exclude unrelated sales, secondary sales, and sales to businesses, government, and the rest of the world, but include membership dues and fees. [14] Net expenses of NPISHs, defined as their gross operating expenses less primary sales to households.

Source: U.S. Bureau of Economic Analysis, National Income and Product Accounts, "2.5.5 Personal Consumption Expenditures by Function," and "2.5.6 Real Personal Consumption Expenditures by Function, Chained Dollars," <https://www.bea.gov/iTable/index_nipa.cfm>, accessed August 2017.

Table 701. Personal Income By Source and Disposition: 2000 to 2016

[In billions of dollars (8,637 represents $8,637,000,000,000), except as indicated. For definition of personal income and chained dollars, see text, this section]

Item	2000	2005	2010	2012	2013	2014	2015	2016
Personal income	**8,637**	**10,614**	**12,477**	**13,915**	**14,074**	**14,818**	**15,553**	**15,929**
Compensation of employees, received	5,857	7,087	7,961	8,610	8,842	9,257	9,708	9,979
Wages and salaries	4,826	5,692	6,378	6,930	7,117	7,477	7,859	8,085
Supplements to wages and salaries	1,031	1,395	1,584	1,680	1,726	1,780	1,849	1,893
Proprietors' income [1]	758	979	1,033	1,241	1,285	1,316	1,319	1,342
Farm	32	46	46	62	88	68	54	43
Nonfarm	726	933	987	1,180	1,197	1,248	1,265	1,299
Rental income of persons [2]	188	238	403	525	567	612	663	707
Personal income receipts on assets	1,454	1,667	1,740	2,124	2,056	2,245	2,387	2,378
Personal interest income	1,070	1,088	1,195	1,289	1,262	1,303	1,367	1,415
Personal dividend income	383	578	545	835	794	942	1,020	963
Personal current transfer receipts	1,087	1,517	2,325	2,366	2,428	2,544	2,684	2,768
Government social benefits to persons [3]	1,045	1,491	2,282	2,324	2,387	2,499	2,631	2,711
Social security [4]	401	513	690	762	799	835	872	897
Unemployment insurance	21	32	139	84	62	35	32	32
Veterans' benefits	25	36	58	70	79	84	90	93
Other current transfer receipts, from business (net)	42	26	43	43	41	46	53	57
Less: Contributions for government social insurance	706	873	984	952	1,105	1,155	1,208	1,245
Less: Personal current taxes	1,237	1,213	1,239	1,511	1,678	1,786	1,938	1,960
Equals: Disposable personal income	**7,401**	**9,401**	**11,238**	**12,404**	**12,396**	**13,033**	**13,615**	**13,969**
Less: Personal outlays	7,093	9,158	10,608	11,457	11,776	12,294	12,787	13,288
Personal consumption expenditures	6,792	8,794	10,202	11,051	11,361	11,864	12,332	12,821
Personal interest payments [5]	218	249	251	241	244	254	269	278
Personal current transfer payments	83	115	155	166	171	177	186	189
Equals: Personal saving	**308**	**243**	**630**	**947**	**620**	**739**	**828**	**681**
Personal saving as a percentage of disposable personal income	4.2	2.6	5.6	7.6	5.0	5.7	6.1	4.9
Addenda:								
Disposable personal income:								
Total, billions of chained (2009) dollars [6]	8,902	10,189	11,055	11,688	11,528	11,939	12,436	12,608
Per capita:								
Current dollars	26,206	31,760	36,274	39,455	39,157	40,869	42,392	43,194
Chained (2009) dollars	31,524	34,424	35,685	37,179	36,414	37,441	38,720	38,988

[1] With inventory valuation and capital consumption adjustments. [2] Includes capital consumption adjustment. [3] Includes other benefits not shown separately. [4] Social security benefits include benefits distributed from the Old-Age and Survivors Insurance Trust Fund and the Disability Insurance Trust Fund. [5] Consists of nonmortgage interest paid by households. [6] The current-dollar measure is deflated by the implicit price deflator for personal consumption expenditures.

Source: U.S. Bureau of Economic Analysis, National Income and Product Accounts Tables, "Table 2.1 Personal Income and Its Disposition," <http://www.bea.gov/iTable/index_nipa.cfm>, accessed July 2017.

Table 702. Selected Per Capita Income and Product Measures in Current and Chained (2009) Dollars: 1980 to 2016

[In dollars. Based on U.S. Census Bureau estimated population including Armed Forces abroad, and institutionalized population; based on monthly averages. For explanation of chained dollars, see text, this section]

Year	Current dollars					Chained (2009) dollars			
	Gross domestic product	Gross national product	Personal income	Disposable personal income	Personal consumption expenditures	Gross domestic product	Gross national product	Disposable personal income	Personal consumption expenditures
1980	12,570	12,720	10,177	8,861	7,705	28,325	28,707	20,158	17,528
1985	18,225	18,331	14,743	12,991	11,416	31,839	32,068	22,960	20,175
1990	23,901	24,040	19,611	17,235	15,291	35,794	36,024	25,555	22,674
1995	28,749	28,857	23,561	20,753	18,696	38,167	38,326	27,180	24,486
1996	30,033	30,150	24,719	21,615	19,532	39,156	39,325	27,719	25,047
1997	31,538	31,626	25,941	22,527	20,372	40,427	40,556	28,397	25,681
1998	32,913	32,979	27,498	23,759	21,376	41,737	41,836	29,723	26,741
1999	34,585	34,682	28,599	24,617	22,579	43,196	43,330	30,350	27,838
2000	36,419	36,550	30,585	26,206	24,053	44,475	44,649	31,524	28,933
2001	37,240	37,422	31,525	27,179	24,904	44,464	44,694	32,075	29,390
2002	38,122	38,291	31,789	28,127	25,643	44,829	45,041	32,754	29,862
2003	39,606	39,837	32,657	29,198	26,720	45,664	45,943	33,342	30,512
2004	41,857	42,160	34,280	30,697	28,166	46,967	47,321	34,221	31,399
2005	44,237	44,549	35,859	31,760	29,711	48,090	48,442	34,424	32,203
2006	46,369	46,595	38,130	33,589	31,136	48,905	49,156	35,458	32,868
2007	47,987	48,404	39,776	34,826	32,319	49,300	49,738	35,866	33,284
2008	48,330	48,895	41,052	36,101	32,881	48,697	49,270	36,078	32,860
2009	46,930	47,422	39,366	35,616	32,050	46,930	47,422	35,616	32,050
2010	48,303	48,968	40,275	36,274	32,931	47,720	48,324	35,685	32,396
2011	49,719	50,509	42,467	37,811	34,248	48,125	48,831	36,305	32,884
2012	51,388	52,144	44,263	39,455	35,151	48,841	49,501	37,179	33,123
2013	52,726	53,498	44,457	39,157	35,888	49,317	49,980	36,414	33,375
2014	54,651	55,387	46,469	40,869	37,203	50,216	50,838	37,441	34,082
2015	56,420	57,057	48,426	42,392	38,398	51,286	51,819	38,720	35,072
2016	57,591	58,201	49,255	43,194	39,645	51,690	52,194	38,988	35,784

Source: U.S. Bureau of Economic Analysis, National Income and Product Accounts Tables, "Table 7.1. Selected Per Capita Product and Income Series in Current and Chained Dollars," <http://www.bea.gov/iTable/index_nipa.cfm>, accessed July 2017.

Table 703. Personal Income in Current and Constant (2009) Dollars by State: 2000 to 2016

[In billions of dollars (8,634.8 represents $8,634,800,000,000). Represents a measure of income received from all sources during the calendar year by residents of each state. Data exclude federal employees overseas and U.S. residents employed by private U.S. firms on temporary foreign assignment. Totals may differ from those in Table 696, Table 701, and Table 702]

State	Current dollars					Constant (2009) dollars [1]				
	2000	2005	2010	2015	2016	2000	2005	2010	2015	2016
United States.............	8,634.8	10,610.3	12,459.6	15,464.0	16,017.8	10,387.0	11,500.3	12,257.0	14,118.2	14,466.4
Alabama....................	108.0	136.2	161.3	184.8	190.8	129.9	147.6	158.6	168.7	172.3
Alaska.....................	19.9	25.9	34.7	41.5	41.0	23.9	28.1	34.1	37.9	37.1
Arizona....................	135.4	188.5	215.1	267.4	278.9	162.8	204.3	211.6	244.1	251.9
Arkansas...................	61.0	77.7	92.9	113.9	117.6	73.4	84.3	91.4	104.0	106.2
California.................	1,124.8	1,415.9	1,617.1	2,103.7	2,197.5	1,353.1	1,534.7	1,590.8	1,920.6	1,984.7
Colorado...................	147.2	176.1	201.6	277.7	288.4	177.1	190.9	198.3	253.6	260.5
Connecticut................	147.7	176.1	222.4	246.7	254.0	177.7	190.9	218.8	225.2	229.4
Delaware...................	27.1	33.4	37.0	45.1	46.4	32.6	36.2	36.4	41.1	41.9
District of Columbia.......	24.5	30.6	37.4	49.3	51.5	29.5	33.1	36.8	45.0	46.5
Florida....................	477.3	647.1	728.1	900.6	944.4	574.2	701.4	716.2	822.3	853.0
Georgia....................	236.5	296.9	336.5	411.7	431.3	284.4	321.8	331.0	375.9	389.6
Hawaii.....................	35.7	47.2	56.9	69.1	72.2	42.9	51.2	56.0	63.1	65.2
Idaho......................	32.6	41.9	49.8	63.5	65.8	39.2	45.4	49.0	58.0	59.4
Illinois...................	412.8	474.7	535.5	646.8	666.9	496.6	514.6	526.8	590.5	602.3
Indiana....................	171.5	195.1	227.7	277.6	288.5	206.3	211.5	224.0	253.5	260.5
Iowa.......................	80.6	96.7	115.8	143.4	146.7	96.9	104.8	113.9	130.9	132.5
Kansas.....................	76.5	88.6	112.1	137.3	141.1	92.0	96.0	110.3	125.4	127.4
Kentucky...................	100.5	121.4	143.6	170.8	175.3	120.9	131.5	141.3	155.9	158.3
Louisiana..................	105.9	134.7	169.2	200.6	203.6	127.4	145.9	166.4	183.1	183.9
Maine......................	34.9	43.1	49.8	56.9	59.0	42.0	46.7	49.0	51.9	53.3
Maryland...................	188.5	242.2	288.7	336.2	348.6	226.7	262.5	284.0	306.9	314.8
Massachusetts..............	245.2	287.1	348.3	425.4	443.7	295.0	311.2	342.7	388.3	400.7
Michigan...................	302.5	329.8	347.7	424.8	440.3	363.8	357.5	342.1	387.8	397.6
Minnesota..................	159.1	193.4	223.7	279.3	287.7	191.4	209.6	220.1	255.0	259.8
Mississippi................	61.3	77.2	90.8	104.0	107.4	73.8	83.7	89.3	95.0	97.0
Missouri...................	156.9	187.8	220.3	257.3	266.4	188.7	203.5	216.7	234.9	240.6
Montana....................	21.1	28.0	35.1	43.2	44.2	25.3	30.3	34.6	39.4	39.9
Nebraska...................	49.5	60.1	74.1	92.0	94.7	59.6	65.2	72.9	84.0	85.5
Nevada.....................	64.4	94.0	99.5	121.1	128.3	77.5	101.9	97.9	110.6	115.9
New Hampshire..............	44.0	53.1	62.1	74.4	77.8	52.9	57.6	61.1	67.9	70.3
New Jersey.................	332.3	392.4	451.9	537.0	554.3	399.7	425.3	444.5	490.3	500.6
New Mexico.................	41.8	55.6	68.4	79.1	80.8	50.3	60.2	67.3	72.2	72.9
New York...................	682.6	793.2	934.3	1,161.4	1,195.3	821.1	859.7	919.1	1,060.3	1,079.5
North Carolina.............	221.2	280.6	337.7	409.3	426.2	266.1	304.2	332.2	373.7	384.9
North Dakota...............	16.7	20.4	29.5	42.3	41.7	20.1	22.1	29.0	38.7	37.7
Ohio.......................	324.0	372.8	419.6	506.0	521.2	389.7	404.1	412.7	461.9	470.7
Oklahoma...................	82.8	110.2	135.0	178.3	179.2	99.7	119.5	132.8	162.7	161.9
Oregon.....................	98.1	117.1	137.0	176.4	184.4	118.0	127.0	134.8	161.0	166.5
Pennsylvania...............	373.2	451.3	533.9	636.9	655.5	448.9	489.1	525.2	581.4	592.0
Rhode Island...............	31.8	39.4	45.0	52.8	54.5	38.3	42.7	44.3	48.2	49.2
South Carolina.............	100.3	123.7	149.1	187.5	195.8	120.6	134.0	146.7	171.2	176.8
South Dakota...............	20.3	26.2	33.5	41.1	41.6	24.4	28.4	33.0	37.5	37.6
Tennessee..................	154.9	188.4	226.6	277.8	288.5	186.3	204.2	222.9	253.7	260.6
Texas......................	589.5	747.0	956.6	1,289.6	1,327.3	709.1	809.6	941.0	1,177.4	1,198.7
Utah.......................	54.2	70.7	87.9	117.8	124.3	65.2	76.6	86.5	107.5	112.3
Vermont....................	17.6	21.5	25.6	30.4	31.4	21.2	23.3	25.2	27.8	28.4
Virginia...................	232.5	305.5	363.9	436.3	451.9	279.6	331.1	358.0	398.4	408.1
Washington.................	194.1	236.3	284.5	372.1	389.9	233.5	256.1	279.9	339.7	352.1
West Virginia..............	40.3	48.4	59.5	67.8	68.5	48.4	52.5	58.5	61.9	61.8
Wisconsin..................	159.5	189.5	219.6	265.0	273.2	191.9	205.4	216.1	241.9	246.7
Wyoming....................	14.3	19.7	25.7	32.9	32.3	17.2	21.3	25.2	30.0	29.2

[1] Constant dollar estimates are computed by ProQuest using the national implicit price deflator for personal consumption expenditures from the Bureau of Economic Analysis' National Income and Product Accounts Tables. Any regional differences in the rate of inflation are not reflected in these constant dollar estimates.

Source: Except as noted, U.S. Bureau of Economic Analysis, Regional Economic Accounts, State Annual Personal Income and Employment, "Table SA1 Personal Income Summary," <http://www.bea.gov/regional/index.htm>, accessed March 2017.

Table 704. Personal Income Per Capita in Current and Constant (2009) Dollars by State: 2000 to 2016

[In dollars, except as indicated. Represents a measure of income received from all sources during the calendar year by residents of each state. Data exclude federal employees overseas and U.S. residents employed by private U.S. firms on temporary foreign assignment. Totals may differ from those in Table 696, Table 701, and Table 702]

State	Current dollars				Constant (2009) dollars [1]				Income rank [2]	
	2000	2010	2015	2016	2000	2010	2015	2016	2010	2016
United States..................	**30,602**	**40,277**	**48,190**	**49,571**	**36,812**	**39,622**	**43,996**	**44,770**	**(X)**	**(X)**
Alabama.........................	24,258	33,697	38,070	39,231	29,180	33,149	34,757	35,431	42	47
Alaska...........................	31,651	48,613	56,202	55,307	38,074	47,822	51,311	49,950	6	9
Arizona.........................	26,232	33,558	39,217	40,243	31,555	33,012	35,804	36,345	43	43
Arkansas.......................	22,784	31,798	38,257	39,345	27,407	31,281	34,928	35,534	48	46
California.......................	33,095	43,317	53,949	55,987	39,811	42,613	49,254	50,564	12	8
Colorado........................	34,026	39,926	50,971	52,059	40,931	39,277	46,535	47,017	23	16
Connecticut....................	43,287	62,126	68,822	71,033	52,071	61,116	62,833	64,153	1	2
Delaware.......................	34,430	41,088	47,727	48,697	41,417	40,420	43,574	43,981	19	22
District of Columbia..........	42,903	61,860	73,505	75,596	51,609	60,854	67,108	68,274	2	1
Florida..........................	29,744	38,626	44,487	45,819	35,780	37,998	40,616	41,381	25	28
Georgia.........................	28,740	34,643	40,367	41,835	34,572	34,080	36,854	37,783	41	41
Hawaii..........................	29,403	41,724	48,506	50,551	35,369	41,046	44,285	45,655	17	19
Idaho...........................	25,087	31,726	38,440	39,107	30,178	31,210	35,095	35,319	49	48
Illinois..........................	33,202	41,698	50,377	52,098	39,939	41,020	45,993	47,052	18	15
Indiana.........................	28,159	35,081	41,984	43,492	33,873	34,511	38,330	39,280	40	36
Iowa............................	27,512	37,946	45,930	46,794	33,095	37,329	41,933	42,262	27	27
Kansas.........................	28,404	39,206	47,241	48,537	34,168	38,568	43,130	43,836	24	23
Kentucky.......................	24,819	33,026	38,592	39,499	29,855	32,489	35,234	35,673	45	44
Louisiana.......................	23,692	37,226	42,963	43,487	28,500	36,621	39,224	39,275	30	37
Maine...........................	27,345	37,528	42,795	44,316	32,894	36,918	39,071	40,024	29	33
Maryland........................	35,487	49,880	56,078	57,936	42,688	49,069	51,198	52,325	5	7
Massachusetts.................	38,547	53,054	62,697	65,137	46,369	52,191	57,241	58,828	3	3
Michigan........................	30,391	35,204	42,833	44,347	36,558	34,632	39,105	40,052	39	32
Minnesota......................	32,247	42,119	50,938	52,117	38,791	41,434	46,505	47,069	15	14
Mississippi.....................	21,535	30,569	34,805	35,936	25,905	30,072	31,776	32,455	51	51
Missouri........................	27,982	36,732	42,352	43,723	33,660	36,135	38,666	39,488	32	34
Montana........................	23,315	35,458	41,845	42,386	28,046	34,881	38,203	38,281	37	39
Nebraska.......................	28,890	40,518	48,606	49,636	34,752	39,859	44,376	44,829	22	21
Nevada.........................	31,903	36,820	41,992	43,637	38,377	36,221	38,338	39,411	31	35
New Hampshire.................	35,460	47,148	55,926	58,322	42,656	46,381	51,059	52,673	8	6
New Jersey.....................	39,411	51,330	60,101	61,968	47,408	50,495	54,871	55,966	4	4
New Mexico.....................	22,973	33,109	38,025	38,807	27,635	32,571	34,716	35,048	44	49
New York.......................	35,924	48,152	58,814	60,534	43,214	47,369	53,696	54,671	7	5
North Carolina..................	27,373	35,331	40,790	42,002	32,928	34,756	37,240	37,934	38	40
North Dakota...................	26,004	43,661	55,956	55,038	31,281	42,951	51,086	49,707	11	11
Ohio............................	28,509	36,355	43,597	44,876	34,294	35,764	39,803	40,530	33	31
Oklahoma.......................	23,983	35,911	45,619	45,682	28,850	35,327	41,649	41,258	34	29
Oregon..........................	28,596	35,692	43,830	45,049	34,399	35,112	40,016	40,686	35	30
Pennsylvania...................	30,381	42,001	49,786	51,275	36,546	41,318	45,453	46,309	16	18
Rhode Island....................	30,284	42,744	50,050	51,576	36,429	42,049	45,694	46,581	13	17
South Carolina..................	24,921	32,160	38,312	39,465	29,978	31,637	34,978	35,643	46	45
South Dakota...................	26,808	41,063	47,912	48,049	32,248	40,395	43,742	43,395	20	24
Tennessee......................	27,154	35,653	42,127	43,380	32,664	35,073	38,461	39,178	36	38
Texas...........................	28,145	37,892	47,015	47,636	33,856	37,276	42,924	43,022	28	25
Utah............................	24,138	31,683	39,378	40,744	29,036	31,168	35,951	36,798	50	42
Vermont........................	28,904	40,916	48,584	50,321	34,769	40,251	44,356	45,447	21	20
Virginia.........................	32,713	45,340	52,148	53,723	39,351	44,603	47,610	48,520	10	12
Washington.....................	32,839	42,194	51,971	53,493	39,503	41,508	47,448	48,312	14	13
West Virginia...................	22,280	32,082	36,820	37,386	26,801	31,560	33,616	33,765	47	50
Wisconsin.......................	29,682	38,597	45,942	47,275	35,705	37,969	41,944	42,696	26	26
Wyoming........................	28,966	45,450	56,038	55,212	34,844	44,711	51,161	49,865	9	10

X Not applicable. [1] Constant dollar estimates are computed by ProQuest using the national implicit price deflator for personal consumption expenditures from the Bureau of Economic Analysis' National Income and Product Accounts tables. Any regional differences in the rate of inflation are not reflected in these constant dollar estimates. [2] Ranking based on current dollar income.

Source: Except as noted, U.S. Bureau of Economic Analysis, Regional Economic Accounts, State Annual Personal Income and Employment, "Table SA1 Personal Income Summary," <http://www.bea.gov/regional/index.htm>, accessed March 2017.

Table 705. Disposable Personal Income Per Capita in Current and Constant (2009) Dollars by State: 2000 to 2016

[In dollars, except as indicated. Per capita disposable personal income is total disposable personal income divided by total midyear population. Disposable personal income is total personal income minus personal current taxes. It is the portion of personal income that is available for consumption expenditures, interest payments, current transfer payments, or saving. The estimate of personal income in the United States is derived as the sum of the state estimates and the estimate for the District of Columbia; it differs from the estimate of personal income in the national income and product accounts (NIPAs) because of differences in coverage, in the methodologies used to prepare the estimates, and in the timing of the availability of source data. See text, Section 13. For methodology, see <https://www.bea.gov/regional/methods.cfm>]

State	Current dollars				Constant (2009) dollars [1]				Index, compared to U.S. average [2]	
	2000	2010	2015	2016	2000	2010	2015	2016	2010	2016
United States.........	26,224	36,275	42,154	43,536	31,545	35,685	38,486	39,319	100.0	100.0
Alabama.................	21,526	30,933	34,413	35,574	25,894	30,430	31,418	32,129	85.3	81.7
Alaska...................	28,212	44,863	51,029	50,432	33,937	44,133	46,588	45,547	123.7	115.8
Arizona..................	22,891	30,841	35,222	36,247	27,536	30,339	32,157	32,736	85.0	83.3
Arkansas................	20,220	29,135	34,371	35,452	24,323	28,661	31,380	32,018	80.3	81.4
California...............	27,344	38,536	46,080	47,989	32,893	37,909	42,070	43,341	106.2	110.2
Colorado................	28,892	35,616	44,295	45,427	34,755	35,037	40,440	41,027	98.2	104.3
Connecticut............	35,195	54,339	57,517	59,777	42,337	53,455	52,512	53,987	149.8	137.3
Delaware...............	29,837	37,017	42,322	43,409	35,892	36,415	38,639	39,205	102.0	99.7
District of Columbia......	35,865	54,179	62,380	64,504	43,143	53,298	56,951	58,257	149.4	148.2
Florida..................	26,036	35,526	39,531	40,824	31,319	34,948	36,091	36,870	97.9	93.8
Georgia.................	24,794	31,436	35,718	37,130	29,825	30,925	32,610	33,534	86.7	85.3
Hawaii..................	25,821	38,219	43,309	45,296	31,061	37,598	39,540	40,909	105.4	104.0
Idaho...................	21,962	29,173	34,600	35,227	26,419	28,699	31,589	31,815	80.4	80.9
Illinois..................	28,429	37,401	43,600	45,342	34,198	36,793	39,806	40,950	103.1	104.1
Indiana..................	24,670	31,914	37,551	39,044	29,676	31,395	34,283	35,262	88.0	89.7
Iowa....................	24,344	34,559	40,963	41,834	29,284	33,997	37,398	37,782	95.3	96.1
Kansas..................	24,757	35,516	42,174	43,536	29,781	34,938	38,504	39,319	97.9	100.0
Kentucky...............	21,742	30,049	34,485	35,381	26,154	29,560	31,484	31,954	82.8	81.3
Louisiana...............	21,177	34,278	38,717	39,414	25,474	33,721	35,348	35,597	94.5	90.5
Maine...................	23,859	34,232	38,296	39,778	28,700	33,675	34,963	35,925	94.4	91.4
Maryland................	30,025	44,188	48,331	50,181	36,118	43,469	44,125	45,321	121.8	115.3
Massachusetts..........	31,111	46,510	52,603	54,960	37,424	45,754	48,025	49,637	128.2	126.2
Michigan................	26,271	32,044	37,888	39,344	31,602	31,523	34,591	35,533	88.3	90.4
Minnesota...............	27,419	37,444	43,767	44,939	32,983	36,835	39,958	40,587	103.2	103.2
Mississippi..............	19,447	28,245	31,844	32,980	23,393	27,786	29,073	29,786	77.9	75.8
Missouri.................	24,412	33,458	37,567	38,927	29,366	32,914	34,298	35,157	92.2	89.4
Montana................	20,609	32,387	36,919	37,507	24,791	31,860	33,706	33,874	89.3	86.2
Nebraska...............	25,350	36,926	43,139	44,207	30,494	36,326	39,385	39,925	101.8	101.5
Nevada.................	27,787	33,729	37,592	39,166	33,426	33,181	34,321	35,373	93.0	90.0
New Hampshire.........	30,632	43,308	50,171	52,464	36,848	42,604	45,805	47,383	119.4	120.5
New Jersey.............	33,066	45,454	51,636	53,495	39,776	44,715	47,142	48,314	125.3	122.9
New Mexico.............	20,488	30,581	34,475	35,331	24,645	30,084	31,475	31,909	84.3	81.2
New York...............	29,898	41,432	48,870	50,622	35,965	40,758	44,617	45,719	114.2	116.3
North Carolina..........	23,696	32,084	36,173	37,367	28,504	31,562	33,025	33,748	88.4	85.8
North Dakota............	23,491	39,835	49,340	49,054	28,258	39,187	45,046	44,303	109.8	112.7
Ohio....................	24,559	32,821	38,596	39,875	29,543	32,287	35,237	36,013	90.5	91.6
Oklahoma...............	21,083	32,956	41,135	41,367	25,361	32,420	37,555	37,360	90.9	95.0
Oregon.................	24,399	31,989	38,117	39,282	29,350	31,469	34,800	35,477	88.2	90.2
Pennsylvania............	26,258	37,818	43,828	45,355	31,586	37,203	40,014	40,962	104.3	104.2
Rhode Island............	26,126	38,754	44,179	45,677	31,428	38,124	40,334	41,253	106.8	104.9
South Carolina..........	21,988	29,540	34,481	35,620	26,450	29,060	31,480	32,170	81.4	81.8
South Dakota...........	24,248	38,301	43,388	43,525	29,168	37,678	39,612	39,309	105.6	100.0
Tennessee..............	24,455	33,294	38,481	39,725	29,417	32,753	35,132	35,877	91.8	91.2
Texas...................	24,785	34,808	41,984	42,724	29,814	34,242	38,330	38,586	96.0	98.1
Utah....................	21,064	28,858	34,937	36,244	25,338	28,389	31,897	32,734	79.6	83.3
Vermont................	25,227	37,448	43,380	45,085	30,346	36,839	39,605	40,718	103.2	103.6
Virginia.................	27,841	40,436	45,422	47,040	33,491	39,778	41,469	42,484	111.5	108.0
Washington.............	28,371	38,745	46,282	47,735	34,128	38,115	42,254	43,112	106.8	109.6
West Virginia...........	19,908	29,325	33,123	33,799	23,948	28,848	30,240	30,525	80.8	77.6
Wisconsin...............	25,610	34,825	40,589	41,904	30,807	34,259	37,057	37,845	96.0	96.3
Wyoming................	25,004	41,303	49,717	49,404	30,078	40,631	45,390	44,619	113.9	113.5

[1] Constant dollar estimates are computed by ProQuest using the national implicit price deflator for personal consumption expenditures from the Bureau of Economic Analysis' National Income and Product Accounts Tables. Any regional differences in the rate of inflation are not reflected in these constant dollar estimates. [2] Indexes calculated using disposable personal income per capita in current dollars.

Source: Except as noted, U.S. Bureau of Economic Analysis, Regional Economic Accounts, State Annual Personal Income & Employment, "Table SA51 Disposable Personal Income Summary," <http://www.bea.gov/regional/index.htm>, accessed April 2017.

Table 706. Personal Income by Selected Large Metropolitan Area: 2000 to 2015

[7,623,475 represents $7,623,475,000,000. MSA = Metropolitan Statistical Area. The MSAs used by the Bureau of Economic Analysis are county-based areas developed by the Office of Management and Budget (OMB); see OMB Bulletin No. 15-01, July 15, 2015. Per capita personal income was computed using Census Bureau midyear population estimates. Estimates for 2010-2015 reflect county population estimates available as of March 2016]

Metropolitan statistical areas ranked by 2015 population	Personal income			Personal income per capita			Index (U.S.= 100), 2015
	2000 (mil. dol.)	2010 (mil. dol.)	2015 (mil. dol.)	2000 (dol.)	2010 (dol.)	2015 (dol.)	
United States, metro portion........................	7,623,475	10,984,545	13,718,236	32,110	41,750	49,827	100.0
New York-Newark-Jersey City, NY-NJ-PA MSA.........	771,821	1,045,891	1,303,530	40,665	53,359	64,588	129.6
Los Angeles-Long Beach-Anaheim, CA MSA...........	391,911	574,299	727,377	31,624	44,714	54,526	109.4
Chicago-Naperville-Elgin, IL-IN-WI MSA................	328,951	414,871	514,662	36,096	43,803	53,886	108.1
Dallas-Fort Worth-Arlington, TX MSA..................	176,437	262,061	362,948	33,701	40,613	51,099	102.6
Houston-The Woodlands-Sugar Land, TX MSA........	156,709	264,687	361,777	33,219	44,498	54,346	109.1
Washington-Arlington-Alexandria, DC-VA-MD-WV MSA......................................	206,821	329,497	395,632	42,526	58,148	64,882	130.2
Philadelphia-Camden-Wilmington, PA-NJ-DE-MD MSA....................................	200,929	288,083	347,032	35,300	48,243	57,173	114.7
Miami-Fort Lauderdale-West Palm Beach, FL MSA...	165,082	240,662	299,528	32,846	43,086	49,819	100.0
Atlanta-Sandy Springs-Roswell, GA MSA...............	145,375	205,462	257,510	33,860	38,739	45,092	90.5
Boston-Cambridge-Newton, MA-NH MSA..............	187,187	265,544	326,046	42,530	58,164	68,292	137.1
San Francisco-Oakland-Hayward, CA MSA............	203,143	264,061	368,795	49,117	60,768	79,206	159.0
Phoenix-Mesa-Scottsdale, AZ MSA...................	94,431	146,616	186,693	28,847	34,867	40,811	81.9
Riverside-San Bernardino-Ontario, CA MSA...........	76,375	126,656	159,429	23,306	29,844	35,514	71.3
Detroit-Warren-Dearborn, MI MSA.....................	154,782	162,372	201,741	34,740	37,837	46,894	94.1
Seattle-Tacoma-Bellevue, WA MSA....................	119,112	166,156	227,827	39,025	48,180	61,021	122.5
Minneapolis-St. Paul-Bloomington, MN-WI MSA.......	111,992	153,074	194,372	36,786	45,618	55,148	110.7
San Diego-Carlsbad, CA MSA..........................	94,885	136,576	175,859	33,560	43,995	53,298	107.0
Tampa-St. Petersburg-Clearwater, FL MSA...........	70,833	107,636	127,958	29,464	38,597	43,008	86.3
Denver-Aurora-Lakewood, CO MSA....................	82,628	109,387	157,532	38,060	42,822	55,975	112.3
St. Louis, MO-IL MSA..................................	85,828	118,065	137,702	32,039	42,317	48,977	98.3
Baltimore-Columbia-Towson, MD MSA.................	88,091	131,896	154,626	34,438	48,570	55,275	110.9
Charlotte-Concord-Gastonia, NC-SC MSA.............	52,812	84,662	109,028	30,552	38,073	44,935	90.2
Portland-Vancouver-Hillsboro, OR-WA MSA...........	63,147	88,151	115,691	32,638	39,486	48,422	97.2
Orlando-Kissimmee-Sanford, FL MSA..................	46,164	71,097	92,221	27,862	33,230	38,632	77.5
San Antonio-New Braunfels, TX MSA..................	46,101	76,786	103,790	26,803	35,661	43,535	87.4
Pittsburgh, PA MSA....................................	74,537	100,644	119,432	30,695	42,700	50,756	101.9
Sacramento-Roseville-Arden Arcade, CA MSA........	56,089	87,912	112,889	31,023	40,804	49,639	99.6
Cincinnati, OH-KY-IN MSA..............................	61,977	85,152	101,960	30,996	40,207	47,254	94.8
Las Vegas-Henderson-Paradise, NV MSA..............	43,235	69,292	85,970	31,017	35,473	40,652	81.6
Kansas City, MO-KS MSA..............................	58,559	82,309	100,316	32,212	40,874	48,056	96.4
Cleveland-Elyria, OH MSA..............................	68,290	81,783	98,472	31,799	39,401	47,783	95.9
Columbus, OH MSA....................................	51,755	73,062	94,148	30,769	38,324	46,570	93.5
Austin-Round Rock, TX MSA...........................	41,626	69,239	102,072	32,908	40,078	51,014	102.4
Indianapolis-Carmel-Anderson, IN MSA...............	54,617	77,224	96,004	32,823	40,803	48,272	96.9
San Jose-Sunnyvale-Santa Clara, CA MSA............	93,416	111,306	161,295	53,727	60,414	81,592	163.8
Nashville-Davidson-Murfreesboro-Franklin, TN MSA..	44,307	69,687	92,680	31,935	41,580	50,635	101.6
Virginia Beach-Norfolk-Newport News, VA-NC MSA....	44,380	68,253	80,034	28,004	40,627	46,400	93.1
Providence-Warwick, RI-MA MSA.......................	47,202	67,310	79,722	29,760	42,006	49,423	99.2
Milwaukee-Waukesha-West Allis, WI MSA..............	50,816	67,189	79,861	33,823	43,161	50,681	101.7
Jacksonville, FL MSA..................................	34,534	52,177	64,095	30,662	38,676	44,219	88.7
Oklahoma City, OK MSA................................	29,010	48,744	62,592	26,417	38,749	46,076	92.5
Memphis, TN-MS-AR MSA..............................	35,857	48,938	56,856	29,481	36,895	42,300	84.9
Louisville/Jefferson County, KY-IN MSA................	33,753	46,329	56,960	30,027	37,428	44,556	89.4
Raleigh, NC MSA.......................................	27,449	48,483	61,655	34,133	42,624	48,411	97.2
Richmond, VA MSA.....................................	34,047	51,533	64,152	32,151	42,580	50,460	101.3
New Orleans-Metairie, LA MSA.........................	36,003	50,308	60,404	26,882	42,077	47,830	96.0
Hartford-West Hartford-East Hartford, CT MSA........	43,781	60,861	71,227	38,041	50,127	58,801	118.0
Salt Lake City, UT MSA................................	25,880	38,770	51,558	27,458	35,513	44,057	88.4
Birmingham-Hoover, AL MSA...........................	30,515	43,972	51,059	28,970	38,952	44,568	89.4
Buffalo-Cheektowaga-Niagara Falls, NY MSA..........	32,688	43,954	51,958	27,961	38,706	45,769	91.9
Rochester, NY MSA....................................	31,864	42,717	49,852	29,878	39,542	46,076	92.5
Grand Rapids-Wyoming, MI MSA.......................	28,226	35,829	47,121	30,215	36,208	45,371	91.1
Tucson, AZ MSA.......................................	21,030	33,362	38,922	24,799	33,978	38,536	77.3
Honolulu, HI MSA......................................	27,574	43,244	52,055	31,454	45,216	52,122	104.6
Tulsa, OK MSA...	23,637	37,105	56,631	27,446	39,474	57,727	115.9

Source: U.S. Bureau of Economic Analysis, Regional Economic Accounts, Local Area Personal Income and Employment, "Table CA1. Personal Income, Population, Per Capita Personal Income," <http://www.bea.gov/regional/index.htm>, accessed April 2017.

Table 707. Household Income—Distribution by Income Level and State: 2015

[In thousands (118,208 represents 118,208,000), except as indicated. The American Community Survey universe includes the household population and the population living in institutions, college dormitories, and other group quarters. Based on a sample and subject to sampling variability; see text, Section 1 and Appendix III. For definition of median, see Guide to Tabular Presentation]

State	Number of households (1,000)								Median income (dollars)
	Total	Under $25,000	$25,000 to $49,999	$50,000 to $74,999	$75,000 to $99,999	$100,000 to $149,999	$150,000 to $199,999	$200,000 or more	
United States........	118,208	26,055	27,245	21,068	14,471	16,031	6,485	6,852	55,775
Alabama...............	1,846	537	463	329	198	194	67	58	44,765
Alaska.................	250	35	49	44	38	47	21	17	73,355
Arizona................	2,463	570	621	464	296	297	111	103	51,492
Arkansas..............	1,145	338	316	203	119	106	29	34	41,995
California.............	12,896	2,503	2,615	2,119	1,579	1,970	963	1,148	64,500
Colorado...............	2,075	359	451	379	279	334	136	136	63,909
Connecticut...........	1,344	236	249	213	167	228	111	139	71,346
Delaware..............	353	64	79	66	52	51	22	18	61,255
District of Columbia. ..	282	57	46	36	31	45	24	41	75,628
Florida.................	7,463	1,820	1,944	1,380	849	829	311	329	49,426
Georgia................	3,656	889	887	667	420	455	171	168	51,244
Hawaii.................	446	68	79	80	65	84	38	33	73,486
Idaho..................	597	147	161	113	72	70	19	16	48,275
Illinois.................	4,795	1,000	1,043	839	607	703	293	309	59,588
Indiana................	2,515	575	667	484	314	300	91	84	50,532
Iowa....................	1,247	263	302	255	173	163	49	42	54,736
Kansas................	1,112	237	273	215	140	154	46	46	53,906
Kentucky..............	1,716	483	447	311	191	177	56	50	45,215
Louisiana.............	1,738	516	409	283	190	202	75	63	45,727
Maine..................	545	132	132	107	71	64	22	17	51,494
Maryland..............	2,178	318	386	372	292	393	207	209	75,847
Massachusetts.........	2,560	483	454	403	310	441	213	256	70,628
Michigan..............	3,859	918	964	723	464	471	169	150	51,084
Minnesota.............	2,147	380	460	405	301	342	137	122	63,488
Mississippi............	1,104	361	287	183	120	104	27	23	40,593
Missouri...............	2,374	567	614	443	285	284	93	87	50,238
Montana...............	415	103	106	82	49	48	13	14	49,509
Nebraska..............	744	157	181	143	98	104	33	29	54,996
Nevada................	1,042	223	271	199	136	129	45	40	52,431
New Hampshire.......	518	81	101	92	76	90	40	38	70,303
New Jersey............	3,188	556	581	497	388	543	276	346	72,222
New Mexico...........	762	221	191	130	84	84	29	23	45,382
New York..............	7,234	1,610	1,448	1,178	853	1,063	496	585	60,850
North Carolina........	3,844	976	1,010	683	439	431	150	155	47,830
North Dakota...........	313	61	73	54	42	50	18	16	60,557
Ohio...................	4,607	1,102	1,147	854	564	573	196	171	51,075
Oklahoma.............	1,466	373	377	277	170	163	54	52	48,568
Oregon................	1,553	342	376	291	196	203	72	73	54,148
Pennsylvania..........	4,956	1,082	1,149	912	636	667	257	253	55,702
Rhode Island..........	407	93	85	67	53	60	25	23	58,073
South Carolina........	1,858	489	479	348	217	200	66	60	47,238
South Dakota.........	339	74	86	67	48	41	11	12	53,017
Tennessee.............	2,530	660	664	468	282	272	89	94	47,275
Texas..................	9,421	2,032	2,222	1,694	1,127	1,273	510	563	55,653
Utah...................	931	146	211	194	140	143	53	44	62,912
Vermont...............	255	54	57	49	36	36	12	11	56,990
Virginia...............	3,107	549	632	541	399	497	230	260	66,262
Washington...........	2,729	477	586	496	376	432	177	185	64,129
West Virginia..........	735	221	202	127	80	70	19	16	42,019
Wisconsin.............	2,320	472	563	462	325	314	97	85	55,638
Wyoming..............	229	43	52	43	33	39	11	8	60,214

Source: U.S. Census Bureau, 2015 American Community Survey, B19001, "Household Income in the Past 12 Months (In 2015 Inflation-Adjusted Dollars)"; and B19013, "Median Household Income in the Past 12 Months (In 2015 Inflation-Adjusted Dollars)"; <http://factfinder.census.gov/>, accessed December 2016.

Table 708. Family Income—Distribution by Income Level and State: 2015

[In thousands (77,531 represents 77,531,000), except as indicated. The American Community Survey universe includes the household population and the population living in institutions, college dormitories, and other group quarters. Based on a sample and subject to sampling variability; see text, Section 1 and Appendix III. For definition of median, see Guide to Tabular Presentation]

State	Number of families (1,000)								Median income (dollars)
	Total	Less than $25,000	$25,000 to $49,999	$50,000 to $74,999	$75,000 to $99,999	$100,000 to $149,999	$150,000 to $199,999	$200,000 and over	
United States	**77,531**	**11,406**	**16,382**	**14,453**	**10,975**	**12,988**	**5,474**	**5,853**	**68,260**
Alabama	1,214	236	288	245	163	170	60	52	57,160
Alaska	164	15	27	29	24	37	18	14	86,376
Arizona	1,598	259	382	323	219	237	94	85	61,042
Arkansas	761	151	209	153	99	94	26	31	52,449
California	8,836	1,299	1,722	1,457	1,147	1,504	768	940	73,581
Colorado	1,332	141	248	241	203	266	116	118	78,384
Connecticut	876	92	132	132	118	182	95	124	91,388
Delaware	235	29	44	44	39	43	20	15	74,931
District of Columbia	125	22	19	13	12	18	14	28	94,846
Florida	4,807	818	1,197	945	645	665	261	277	59,339
Georgia	2,466	438	562	466	324	377	150	148	61,250
Hawaii	309	28	48	57	48	69	31	27	83,823
Idaho	400	61	101	87	59	61	17	14	60,081
Illinois	3,099	412	602	553	450	563	251	267	73,884
Indiana	1,634	232	385	345	256	260	80	75	63,165
Iowa	797	91	167	178	140	141	44	36	69,382
Kansas	721	88	153	150	114	132	41	42	69,401
Kentucky	1,132	221	278	226	157	155	50	45	56,187
Louisiana	1,109	228	249	199	147	167	64	55	58,964
Maine	343	48	75	77	56	54	19	14	64,651
Maryland	1,455	134	217	235	206	306	173	183	91,567
Massachusetts	1,613	182	244	244	215	334	175	219	90,590
Michigan	2,480	378	560	501	362	398	150	131	63,893
Minnesota	1,384	130	248	264	230	282	121	108	79,893
Mississippi	743	179	192	139	97	91	24	20	50,069
Missouri	1,519	223	358	315	226	240	82	75	62,989
Montana	253	35	59	56	39	41	11	12	64,061
Nebraska	470	55	95	98	77	89	29	26	71,039
Nevada	659	101	152	135	101	102	36	32	63,206
New Hampshire	341	29	53	60	58	74	35	32	85,873
New Jersey	2,206	245	348	328	290	442	242	311	90,245
New Mexico	485	98	118	92	65	67	26	19	56,207
New York	4,561	697	847	763	597	806	391	462	73,854
North Carolina	2,506	428	610	487	348	366	129	137	60,074
North Dakota	188	20	34	34	32	41	15	13	79,642
Ohio	2,922	441	644	589	439	482	175	152	65,176
Oklahoma	970	163	233	202	137	142	46	46	60,215
Oregon	978	138	218	195	145	162	60	60	66,287
Pennsylvania	3,204	417	670	628	489	556	221	222	70,194
Rhode Island	250	34	47	41	39	48	22	19	76,623
South Carolina	1,221	214	294	252	176	172	59	53	59,282
South Dakota	217	28	47	46	39	36	10	11	67,643
Tennessee	1,676	293	424	341	226	234	77	81	57,830
Texas	6,521	1,055	1,445	1,177	864	1,049	440	491	65,316
Utah	693	73	141	150	118	124	47	40	71,594
Vermont	152	17	28	30	28	30	10	9	75,595
Virginia	2,055	226	375	360	291	384	191	228	80,403
Washington	1,761	188	332	330	273	333	146	157	76,954
West Virginia	472	95	125	95	66	60	16	14	53,463
Wisconsin	1,470	167	306	312	255	269	86	75	70,870
Wyoming	145	14	27	30	27	32	9	6	75,540

Source: U.S. Census Bureau, 2015 American Community Survey, B19101, "Family Income in the Past 12 Months (In 2015 Inflation-Adjusted Dollars)"; and B19113, "Median Family Income in the Past 12 Months (In 2015 Inflation-Adjusted Dollars)"; <http://factfinder.census.gov/>, accessed December 2016.

Table 709. Average Annual Expenditures of All Consumer Units by Major Type of Expenditure: 1990 to 2015

[Consumer units in thousands (96,968 represents 96,968,000); expenditures in dollars. Based on Consumer Expenditure Survey. Data are averages for the noninstitutional population. Expenditures are direct out-of-pocket expenditures. Consumers units may be all members in a housing unit (families), a person living alone or sharing a household with others and financially independent, or 2 or more unrelated persons living together who share expenses]

Type of expenditure	1990	2000	2005	2010	2012	2013	2014	2015
Number of consumer units (1,000)............	96,968	109,367	117,356	121,107	124,416	125,670	127,006	127,006
Expenditures, avg. (dol.) [1].................	**28,381**	**38,045**	**46,409**	**48,109**	**51,442**	**51,100**	**53,495**	**55,978**
Food..	4,296	5,158	5,931	6,129	6,599	6,602	6,759	7,023
Food at home [1]...........................	2,485	3,021	3,297	3,624	3,921	3,977	3,971	4,015
Cereals and bakery products............	368	453	445	502	538	544	519	518
Meats, poultry, fish, and eggs...........	668	795	764	784	852	856	892	896
Dairy products...........................	295	325	378	380	419	414	423	413
Fruits and vegetables....................	408	521	552	679	731	751	756	769
Other food at home......................	746	927	1,158	1,278	1,380	1,412	1,382	1,419
Food away from home......................	1,811	2,137	2,634	2,505	2,678	2,625	2,787	3,008
Alcoholic beverages.........................	293	372	426	412	451	445	463	515
Housing [1].................................	8,703	12,319	15,167	16,557	16,887	17,148	17,798	18,409
Shelter...................................	4,836	7,114	8,805	9,812	9,891	10,080	10,491	10,742
Utilities, fuels, and public services...........	1,890	2,489	3,183	3,660	3,648	3,737	3,921	3,885
Apparel and services.........................	1,618	1,856	1,886	1,700	1,736	1,604	1,786	1,846
Transportation [1]...........................	5,120	7,417	8,344	7,677	8,998	9,004	9,073	9,503
Vehicle purchases........................	2,129	3,418	3,544	2,588	3,210	3,271	3,301	3,997
Gasoline and motor oil....................	1,047	1,291	2,013	2,132	2,756	2,611	2,468	2,090
Other vehicle expenses...................	1,642	2,281	2,339	2,464	2,490	2,584	2,723	2,756
Public transportation.....................	302	427	448	493	542	537	581	661
Health care [2].............................	1,480	2,066	2,664	3,157	3,556	3,631	[2] 4,290	[2] 4,342
Entertainment..............................	1,422	1,863	2,388	2,504	2,605	2,482	2,728	2,842
Personal care products and services..........	364	564	541	582	628	608	645	683
Reading....................................	153	146	126	100	109	102	103	114
Education..................................	406	632	940	1,074	1,207	1,138	1,236	1,315
Tobacco products, smoking supplies..........	274	319	319	362	332	330	319	349
Personal insurance and pensions..............	2,592	3,365	5,204	5,373	5,591	5,528	5,726	6,349
Life and other personal insurance.............	345	399	381	318	353	319	327	333
Pensions and Social Security.................	2,248	2,966	4,823	5,054	5,238	5,209	5,399	6,016

[1] Includes expenditures not shown separately. [2] Due to changes implemented with the 2014 questionnaire on health insurance, 2014 and subsequent data are not directly comparable to data from previous years.

Source: U.S. Bureau of Labor Statistics, Consumer Expenditure Survey program, "Annual Calendar Year Tables, 2015," <http://www.bls.gov/cex/tables.htm>, accessed November 2016; and previous releases.

Table 710. Average Annual Expenditures of All Consumer Units by Metropolitan Statistical Area: 2014 to 2015

[In dollars. Covers 2-year period, 2014 to 2015. MSA = Metropolitan Statistical Area. See text, Section 1 and Appendix II. See headnote, Table 709]

Metropolitan statistical area	Total expenditures [1]	Food	Housing Total [1]	Housing Shelter	Housing Utility, fuels [2]	Transportation Total [1]	Transportation Vehicle purchases	Transportation Gasoline and motor oil	Health care
Atlanta, Georgia MSA........................	53,195	5,892	17,684	10,482	4,231	8,586	3,010	2,535	4,098
Baltimore, Maryland MSA....................	68,441	7,780	23,908	14,796	4,290	10,783	3,712	2,389	4,683
Chicago, Illinois MSA........................	63,697	7,926	21,964	14,063	3,894	9,908	3,910	2,276	4,843
Dallas-Fort Worth, Texas MSA..............	63,976	8,240	20,976	11,415	4,557	11,306	5,082	2,606	4,935
Detroit, Michigan MSA.......................	60,485	7,356	18,356	10,308	4,305	11,357	2,926	2,643	4,334
Houston, Texas MSA.........................	67,161	8,408	21,672	12,235	4,625	13,462	6,468	2,892	4,296
Los Angeles, California MSA................	58,388	7,235	21,854	14,716	3,508	8,827	2,434	2,651	3,615
Miami, Florida MSA..........................	48,967	6,755	17,750	11,878	3,362	8,884	2,538	2,282	2,929
Minneapolis-St. Paul, Minnesota MSA.....	69,967	7,843	22,526	14,219	3,702	11,652	5,003	2,502	5,672
New York City MSA..........................	62,872	6,943	24,879	16,835	4,318	8,002	1,903	1,796	4,146
Philadelphia, Pennsylvania MSA...........	60,480	6,788	21,195	12,805	4,673	9,588	3,236	2,070	4,901
Phoenix, Arizona MSA.......................	55,118	7,167	18,328	10,908	4,217	8,981	3,290	2,352	4,474
San Diego, California MSA..................	71,039	7,440	25,464	17,030	3,603	11,020	3,358	2,902	4,732
San Francisco, California MSA..............	71,433	8,612	26,483	18,724	3,493	9,911	2,677	2,219	4,685
Seattle, Washington MSA...................	69,017	8,929	23,768	14,913	3,690	9,767	2,835	2,230	4,635
Washington, DC MSA........................	81,293	7,840	29,753	19,813	4,537	12,744	5,498	2,386	5,556

[1] Includes expenditures not shown separately. [2] Includes public services.

Source: U.S. Bureau of Labor Statistics, Consumer Expenditure Survey program, "Metropolitan Statistical Area Tables," <http://www.bls.gov/cex/tables.htm>, accessed November 2016.

Table 711. Personal Consumption Expenditures—Total and Per Capita by State: 2000 to 2015

[Total in millions of dollars (6,789,177 represents $6,789,177,000,000); per capita amounts in dollars. Per capita data reflect Census Bureau midyear population estimates available as of December 2015. Estimates for 2015 based on unpublished Census Bureau data last updated on March 24, 2016]

State	Total personal consumption expenditures (million dollars)					Per capita personal consumption expenditures (dollars)				
	2000	2010	2013	2014	2015	2000	2010	2013	2014	2015
United States......	**6,789,177**	**10,196,850**	**11,355,529**	**11,857,620**	**12,278,861**	**24,061**	**32,962**	**35,879**	**37,188**	**38,196**
Alabama..............	87,604	129,660	140,835	144,697	148,022	19,677	27,093	29,134	29,838	30,459
Alaska...............	17,251	29,663	33,533	34,666	35,941	27,471	41,553	45,484	47,054	48,666
Arizona..............	115,586	193,977	214,601	224,772	232,614	22,398	30,252	32,344	33,391	34,061
Arkansas............	50,927	76,932	84,737	86,948	88,737	19,013	26,326	28,639	29,311	29,791
California............	845,268	1,271,844	1,421,045	1,487,932	1,554,880	24,870	34,065	36,976	38,346	39,715
Colorado............	119,329	175,799	198,955	211,361	221,708	27,578	34,822	37,738	39,463	40,625
Connecticut.........	100,823	147,262	158,498	165,027	168,787	29,551	41,142	44,035	45,883	46,998
Delaware............	20,579	33,111	36,645	38,355	39,819	26,170	36,801	39,605	40,995	42,088
Dist. of Columbia....	18,941	29,338	33,432	35,207	37,032	33,111	48,475	51,505	53,433	55,078
Florida..............	380,491	602,273	678,158	714,791	750,615	23,710	31,947	34,599	35,931	37,020
Georgia.............	186,136	279,840	314,823	329,065	340,740	22,624	28,807	31,499	32,589	33,353
Hawaii..............	30,051	49,604	56,076	58,877	61,250	24,763	36,368	39,799	41,475	42,778
Idaho...............	26,867	43,983	49,074	51,465	53,340	20,676	28,003	30,427	31,487	32,226
Illinois...............	315,060	439,765	479,416	497,918	512,654	25,338	34,249	37,191	38,657	39,859
Indiana..............	136,854	195,055	214,221	220,360	225,744	22,465	30,053	32,602	33,404	34,098
Iowa................	65,752	95,308	105,501	109,080	111,289	22,448	31,246	34,117	35,106	35,621
Kansas.............	59,589	86,066	95,250	98,676	101,455	22,122	30,104	32,892	33,979	34,840
Kentucky............	83,304	122,973	134,150	137,527	141,286	20,574	28,271	30,491	31,161	31,925
Louisiana............	87,777	131,051	146,164	152,500	157,031	19,629	28,830	31,574	32,798	33,616
Maine...............	31,824	48,924	52,504	54,146	55,207	24,919	36,858	39,516	40,709	41,525
Maryland............	139,299	219,329	240,904	249,726	258,294	26,228	37,893	40,565	41,785	42,997
Massachusetts......	193,428	282,173	310,617	325,120	337,835	30,408	42,987	46,299	48,199	49,717
Michigan............	241,942	316,577	347,817	362,062	374,871	24,310	32,054	35,139	36,536	37,775
Minnesota...........	136,079	191,522	214,193	222,993	230,798	27,582	36,065	39,504	40,862	42,038
Mississippi..........	50,986	76,844	84,086	86,138	87,777	17,900	25,866	28,102	28,769	29,330
Missouri.............	132,466	190,136	209,664	214,591	220,159	23,624	31,710	34,684	35,390	36,184
Montana.............	19,585	33,038	37,595	39,476	41,034	21,670	33,353	37,044	38,567	39,718
Nebraska............	38,961	59,245	66,445	68,985	70,996	22,733	32,377	35,551	36,665	37,437
Nevada..............	47,004	83,481	92,817	97,244	101,052	23,284	30,879	33,250	34,252	34,949
New Hampshire.....	35,228	53,797	58,850	61,301	63,132	28,412	40,863	44,495	46,202	47,441
New Jersey..........	242,535	363,716	395,886	410,536	423,383	28,768	41,315	44,424	45,931	47,256
New Mexico........	37,752	61,619	67,889	70,380	72,022	20,729	29,841	32,531	33,746	34,535
New York............	496,495	738,393	820,647	865,135	896,329	26,129	38,060	41,666	43,813	45,272
North Carolina......	173,664	268,474	301,342	315,735	326,451	21,489	28,085	30,596	31,751	32,501
North Dakota........	14,591	24,779	33,003	35,551	36,236	22,727	36,745	45,593	48,076	47,864
Ohio................	265,807	360,663	397,768	411,526	423,481	23,391	31,253	34,373	35,494	36,460
Oklahoma...........	67,300	104,324	118,850	123,823	126,736	19,483	27,750	30,845	31,929	32,397
Oregon..............	83,356	124,289	139,084	146,284	153,488	24,304	32,392	35,408	36,845	38,090
Pennsylvania........	296,305	438,184	477,942	492,903	505,738	24,121	34,473	37,394	38,547	39,498
Rhode Island........	25,581	37,911	40,374	42,026	43,486	24,357	36,000	38,329	39,829	41,163
South Carolina......	83,889	133,139	145,830	152,120	156,868	20,846	28,717	30,560	31,479	32,033
South Dakota........	16,437	27,057	30,720	31,951	32,699	21,747	33,151	36,333	37,449	38,085
Tennessee..........	125,886	183,003	202,730	210,891	218,250	22,071	28,789	31,202	32,200	33,062
Texas...............	474,657	755,482	884,927	939,783	976,073	22,663	29,925	33,386	34,862	35,527
Utah................	47,896	78,975	90,714	95,566	100,044	21,339	28,466	31,251	32,473	33,389
Vermont.............	15,911	24,564	27,214	28,342	29,133	26,100	39,252	43,414	45,235	46,531
Virginia..............	176,516	285,437	316,384	327,567	336,993	24,841	35,567	38,255	39,341	40,195
Washington..........	156,488	239,027	269,907	283,755	296,800	26,476	35,454	38,703	40,183	41,386
West Virginia........	34,969	53,285	58,533	60,015	61,385	19,352	28,738	31,578	32,435	33,282
Wisconsin...........	126,777	186,413	203,201	209,736	215,823	23,591	32,766	35,383	36,428	37,391
Wyoming............	11,364	19,546	21,979	22,990	23,345	22,990	34,633	37,686	39,356	39,825

Source: U.S. Bureau of Economic Analysis, Regional Economic Accounts, "Personal Consumption Expenditures (PCE) by State," <http://bea.gov/regional/index.htm>, accessed November 2016.

Table 712. Average Annual Expenditures of All Consumer Units by Race, Hispanic Origin, and Age of Householder: 2015

[In dollars. See headnote, Table 709. See source for definitions, standard errors, and other information]

Type	All consumer units [1]	White and all other races [2]	Asian	Black or African American	Hispanic [3]	Age of householder Under 25 years	Age of householder 65 years old and over
Expenditures, total	**55,978**	**57,997**	**63,672**	**40,372**	**47,663**	**32,797**	**44,664**
Food	7,023	7,302	8,515	4,644	6,929	4,890	5,506
Food at home	4,015	4,180	4,375	2,792	4,182	2,543	3,398
Cereals and bakery products	518	536	574	376	526	335	470
Cereals and cereal products	172	172	241	146	193	127	134
Bakery products	346	364	333	230	333	208	337
Meats, poultry, fish, and eggs [4]	896	913	977	752	1,080	599	715
Beef	245	260	220	157	293	168	191
Pork	165	167	173	151	206	108	144
Poultry	172	173	175	170	221	138	116
Fish and seafood	126	120	223	125	145	62	115
Eggs	63	64	83	54	86	44	55
Dairy products [4]	413	441	403	230	396	243	360
Fresh milk and cream	140	146	172	87	161	87	117
Fruits and vegetables [4]	769	789	1,117	510	857	462	678
Fresh fruits	284	292	442	172	326	175	255
Fresh vegetables	247	252	428	150	284	143	215
Processed fruits	108	109	129	90	114	64	97
Other food at home [4]	1,419	1,501	1,303	923	1,323	904	1,174
Sugar and other sweets	155	167	111	91	107	78	139
Nonalcoholic beverages	374	395	325	257	419	261	322
Food away from home	3,008	3,122	4,140	1,851	2,747	2,347	2,108
Alcoholic beverages	515	573	362	193	354	250	362
Housing	18,409	18,711	22,170	15,213	16,855	11,328	15,529
Shelter	10,742	10,795	14,856	9,024	10,257	7,410	8,570
Owned dwellings	6,210	6,525	8,386	3,476	4,256	1,150	5,457
Mortgage interest and charges	2,859	2,950	4,467	1,739	2,282	531	1,298
Property taxes	1,913	2,031	2,693	906	1,150	358	2,131
Maintenance, repair, insurance, other expenses	1,438	1,544	1,226	832	824	261	2,027
Rented dwellings	3,802	3,485	5,694	5,189	5,695	6,026	2,218
Other lodging	730	786	776	358	305	233	895
Utilities, fuels, and public services	3,885	3,934	3,567	3,678	3,567	2,058	3,624
Natural gas	421	412	467	462	322	162	428
Electricity	1,460	1,479	1,195	1,429	1,345	826	1,412
Fuel oil and other fuels	116	131	33	54	28	36	179
Telephone	1,347	1,363	1,301	1,261	1,386	795	1,063
Water and other public services	540	550	570	472	486	240	542
Household operations	1,309	1,371	1,612	811	1,000	472	1,122
Personal services	427	441	712	242	361	115	156
Other household expenses	882	930	899	569	639	357	965
Housekeeping supplies [4]	655	697	505	429	575	270	722
Laundry and cleaning supplies	156	159	114	149	187	89	129
Postage and stationery	131	142	84	77	97	49	167
Household furnishings and equipment [4]	1,818	1,913	1,631	1,271	1,457	1,119	1,492
Household textiles	115	115	93	121	89	38	102
Furniture	502	513	455	447	478	407	308
Major appliances	268	286	234	168	223	155	268
Miscellaneous household equipment	798	853	717	467	543	443	692
Apparel and services [4]	1,846	1,889	2,149	1,453	2,035	1,271	1,060
Men and boys	422	425	529	359	540	264	211
Women and girls	697	719	850	497	696	464	477
Footwear	354	357	359	330	452	250	187
Other apparel products and services	291	303	298	210	235	202	163
Transportation	9,503	9,790	10,174	7,436	9,101	6,320	6,846
Vehicle purchases (net outlay) [4]	3,997	4,158	3,723	3,065	3,718	3,085	2,567
Cars and trucks, new	1,956	2,071	2,252	1,127	1,771	873	1,568
Cars and trucks, used	1,982	2,019	1,471	1,918	1,924	2,098	988
Gasoline and motor oil	2,090	2,151	2,097	1,694	2,208	1,432	1,445
Other vehicle expenses	2,756	2,822	3,003	2,244	2,700	1,479	2,268
Vehicle finance charges	216	221	141	210	212	127	98
Maintenance and repair	837	872	868	601	674	517	709
Vehicle insurance	1,079	1,091	1,155	966	1,237	554	1,002
Vehicle rental, leases, licenses, other charges	624	638	839	467	577	280	459
Public transportation	661	660	1,351	432	475	324	566
Health care [5]	4,342	4,686	3,876	2,305	2,632	978	5,756
Entertainment [6]	2,842	3,075	2,371	1,500	1,771	1,354	2,464
Personal care products and services	683	698	696	574	604	406	573
Reading	114	125	97	48	48	38	175
Education	1,315	1,347	2,380	747	825	2,572	263
Tobacco products and smoking supplies	349	374	146	260	154	230	209
Miscellaneous	871	932	718	530	619	198	900
Cash contributions	1,819	1,926	1,245	1,328	923	397	2,287
Personal insurance and pensions	6,349	6,567	8,773	4,142	4,814	2,564	2,733
Life and other personal insurance	333	346	334	247	157	24	332
Pensions and social security	6,016	6,221	8,440	3,895	4,657	2,540	2,401
Personal taxes	**9,178**	**9,659**	**14,774**	**4,240**	**4,118**	**1,995**	**3,668**

[1] Includes other races not shown separately. [2] All other races includes Native Hawaiian/Pacific Islander, Native American/Alaskan, and about 1 percent reporting more than one race. [3] People of Hispanic origin may be of any race. [4] Includes other types, not shown separately. [5] Due to changes in the questionnaire on health insurance, 2014 and subsequent data are not directly comparable to data from prior years. For additional health care expenditures, see Table 150. [6] For additional recreation expenditures, see Section 26.

Source: U.S. Bureau of Labor Statistics, Consumer Expenditure Survey Program, "Annual Calendar Year Tables, 2015," <http://www.bls.gov/cex/tables.htm>, accessed November 2016.

Table 713. Average Annual Expenditures of All Consumer Units by Region and Size of Unit: 2015

[In dollars. For composition of regions, see map, inside front cover. See headnote, Table 709. See source for definitions, standard errors, and other information]

Type	Region				Size of consumer unit				
	North-east	Mid-west	South	West	One person	Two persons	Three persons	Four persons	Five or more
Expenditures, total....................	**58,976**	**55,071**	**52,020**	**61,244**	**33,508**	**58,668**	**67,702**	**75,276**	**70,972**
Food........................	6,882	7,090	6,613	7,776	3,989	7,085	8,526	9,771	10,015
Food at home................	3,939	4,152	3,756	4,387	2,185	3,964	4,929	5,624	6,180
Cereals and bakery products...........	542	533	481	546	266	506	628	741	858
Cereals and cereal products...........	194	175	155	182	85	154	215	265	307
Bakery products..................	348	358	327	365	181	351	412	475	551
Meats, poultry, fish, and eggs [1].........	879	946	869	907	459	884	1,094	1,274	1,450
Beef............................	207	302	239	233	111	257	290	327	430
Pork...........................	153	173	170	158	83	166	203	234	260
Poultry.........................	185	166	167	177	90	159	219	269	270
Fish and seafood................	135	113	116	146	77	126	154	165	177
Dairy products...................	426	439	365	458	216	409	493	616	626
Fresh milk and cream...........	144	143	129	151	73	129	166	214	242
Other dairy products............	282	296	236	306	143	280	328	401	384
Fruits and vegetables [1].............	823	757	690	870	435	752	950	1,077	1,151
Fresh fruits....................	307	286	241	336	162	279	328	410	432
Fresh vegetables...............	273	237	212	295	138	250	305	339	355
Processed fruits................	121	102	98	118	64	99	145	145	165
Other food at home [1].............	1,268	1,478	1,351	1,607	810	1,414	1,763	1,917	2,096
Sugar and other sweets...........	124	155	142	204	115	153	175	182	219
Nonalcoholic beverages...........	345	367	386	386	218	371	467	495	554
Food away from home....................	2,943	2,938	2,857	3,389	1,805	3,121	3,597	4,148	3,835
Alcoholic beverages....................	562	523	421	630	393	648	569	511	343
Housing.........................	20,817	17,370	16,518	20,716	12,393	19,059	21,268	24,044	22,504
Shelter.........................	12,814	9,886	8,939	12,999	8,069	10,903	12,026	13,615	12,495
Owned dwellings................	7,684	6,115	5,224	6,796	3,321	6,699	7,405	8,999	7,723
Mortgage interest and charges...........	2,778	2,684	2,512	3,701	1,198	2,615	3,880	4,968	4,365
Property taxes..................	3,394	1,931	1,284	1,762	1,098	2,195	2,164	2,559	2,163
Maintenance, repair, insurance, other expenses..................	1,512	1,500	1,428	1,332	1,024	1,889	1,361	1,472	1,196
Rented dwellings................	4,277	3,076	3,032	5,460	4,382	3,111	3,943	3,865	4,146
Other lodging...................	853	695	683	744	366	1,093	678	751	626
Utilities, fuels, and public services...........	4,210	3,775	3,954	3,604	2,348	4,062	4,580	5,026	5,353
Natural gas....................	687	599	250	324	286	432	489	513	567
Electricity......................	1,345	1,282	1,759	1,209	926	1,537	1,657	1,868	1,972
Fuel oil and other fuels............	352	103	55	41	76	150	117	115	120
Telephone services...............	1,430	1,295	1,346	1,331	752	1,375	1,688	1,820	1,902
Water and other public services...........	396	495	543	699	308	568	628	709	792
Household operations....................	1,575	1,121	1,176	1,503	650	1,156	1,796	2,371	1,667
Personal services...............	651	367	353	428	79	142	841	1,251	731
Other household expenses................	925	753	823	1,075	571	1,014	955	1,120	936
Housekeeping supplies [1].............	594	702	662	648	375	754	764	749	857
Laundry and cleaning supplies...........	140	162	163	151	88	154	184	206	259
Postage and stationery............	126	133	130	136	87	153	160	132	142
Household furnishings and equipment [1]....	1,624	1,887	1,789	1,962	951	2,184	2,103	2,283	2,131
Household textiles...............	107	119	97	148	57	129	144	165	130
Furniture......................	448	555	503	495	282	620	439	680	628
Major appliances................	194	320	290	241	126	333	284	330	369
Miscellaneous household equipment......	734	747	787	919	408	937	1,076	967	844
Apparel and services [1].....................	1,792	1,716	1,656	2,343	957	1,596	2,230	3,390	2,766
Men and boys...................	418	466	373	467	204	360	568	663	757
Women and girls.................	692	628	614	910	405	656	853	1,109	937
Footwear......................	334	316	351	412	159	286	424	683	630
Other apparel products and services.......	289	198	232	481	172	253	241	734	261
Transportation........................	9,026	9,597	9,598	9,640	4,960	9,669	12,216	13,687	12,951
Vehicle purchases (net outlay) [1].............	3,570	3,996	4,527	3,431	1,851	3,877	5,407	6,238	5,763
Cars and trucks, new.............	1,707	1,901	2,240	1,725	998	2,145	2,388	2,965	2,193
Cars and trucks, used.............	1,849	2,006	2,246	1,608	816	1,670	2,973	3,165	3,496
Gasoline and motor oil.............	1,827	2,058	2,123	2,279	1,085	2,085	2,589	3,043	3,121
Other vehicle expenses.............	2,656	2,965	2,495	3,086	1,632	2,896	3,474	3,672	3,353
Vehicle finance charges...........	171	221	249	192	90	213	287	342	335
Maintenance and repair............	774	830	805	951	512	910	930	1,087	1,095
Vehicle insurance................	897	1,252	970	1,248	663	1,095	1,452	1,411	1,266
Vehicle rental, leases, licenses, other charges..................	815	662	471	695	367	678	806	832	657
Public transportation....................	972	578	453	844	393	812	746	735	714
Health care [2]...........................	4,328	4,616	4,264	4,221	2,638	5,406	4,728	4,943	4,406
Entertainment [3]........................	2,754	2,859	2,682	3,177	1,711	3,312	3,219	3,468	3,229
Personal care products and services.........	699	673	615	794	417	729	839	887	814
Reading...........................	130	117	89	142	80	151	101	124	94
Education..........................	2,021	1,343	973	1,295	735	991	2,102	2,074	1,963
Tobacco products/smoking supplies..........	318	418	388	240	253	321	449	449	455
Miscellaneous.......................	877	926	698	1,113	685	870	1,003	998	1,069
Cash contributions...................	1,667	1,563	1,896	2,059	1,400	2,238	1,791	1,517	2,076
Personal insurance and pensions..........	7,103	6,260	5,608	7,098	2,897	6,594	8,662	9,413	8,288
Life and other personal insurance..........	409	323	291	353	127	404	438	408	443
Pensions and social security..............	6,694	5,937	5,317	6,746	2,770	6,190	8,223	9,005	7,844
Personal taxes............................	**12,303**	**8,581**	**7,092**	**10,799**	**5,129**	**10,306**	**12,488**	**12,180**	**8,317**

[1] Includes other types not shown separately. [2] See footnote 5, Table 712. For additional health care expenditures, see Table 150. [3] For additional recreation expenditures, see Section 26.

Source: U.S. Bureau of Labor Statistics, Consumer Expenditure Survey Program, "Annual Calendar Year Tables, 2015," <http://stats.bls.gov/cex/home.htm>, accessed November 2016.

Table 714. Average Annual Expenditures of All Consumer Units by Income Level: 2015

[In dollars. See headnote, Table 709. See source for definitions, standard errors, and other information]

Income level	Total expenditures [1]	Food	Housing Total [1]	Shelter	Utilities, fuels [2]	Transportation Total [1]	Vehicle purchases	Gasoline and motor oil	Health care [3]	Pensions and social security
All consumer units	**55,978**	**7,023**	**18,409**	**10,742**	**3,885**	**9,503**	**3,997**	**2,090**	**4,342**	**6,016**
BY INCOME										
Less than $15,000	23,479	3,751	9,507	5,875	2,191	3,407	1,048	896	1,724	404
$15,000 to $29,999	30,974	4,394	11,821	6,840	2,953	5,069	1,864	1,291	3,019	1,073
$30,000 to $39,999	38,634	5,550	13,714	7,772	3,447	6,494	2,421	1,757	3,587	2,368
$40,000 to $49,999	42,529	5,219	15,082	8,603	3,618	8,221	3,652	2,003	3,761	3,050
$50,000 to $69,999	51,394	6,595	17,213	9,798	4,041	9,809	4,155	2,315	4,444	4,871
$70,000 to $99,999	66,008	8,506	20,871	12,105	4,489	11,857	5,289	2,661	5,436	7,522
$100,000 to $149,999	86,140	10,349	26,032	14,992	5,172	15,745	7,217	3,126	6,308	11,519
$150,000 to $199,999	113,272	13,433	33,244	19,390	5,813	16,835	6,715	3,201	7,351	17,550
$200,000 and over	158,731	15,210	47,927	29,557	6,382	22,003	9,509	3,378	8,185	28,027

[1] Includes expenditures not shown separately. [2] Includes public services. [3] Due to changes in the questionnaire on health insurance, 2014 and subsequent data are not directly comparable to data from prior years.

Source: U.S. Bureau of Labor Statistics, Consumer Expenditure Survey, "Annual Calendar Year Tables, 2015," <http://stats.bls.gov/cex/tables.htm>, accessed December 2016.

Table 715. Annual Expenditures Per Child by Married-Couple Families by Family Income and Expenditure Type: 2015

[In dollars. Excludes expenses for college. Estimates are based on 2011-2015 Consumer Expenditure Survey data updated to 2015 dollars by using the Consumer Price Index. Data are for the younger child in a two-child family. Estimates are about the same for the older child, so to calculate expenses for two children, figures should be summed for the appropriate age categories. To estimate expenses for an only child, multiply the total expense for the appropriate age category by 1.27. To estimate expenses for each child in a family with three or more children, multiply the total expense for each appropriate age category by 0.76; for expenses on all children in a family, these totals should be summed. Please note that estimates for 2015 are not directly comparable to estimates published for 2013 due to the change in using base data from the 2005-2006 vs. 2011-2015 Consumer Expenditure surveys. For methodology, see source]

Family income and age of child	Total	Housing	Food	Transportation	Clothing	Health care	Child care and education [1]	Miscellaneous [2]
INCOME: LESS THAN $59,200 (Average = $36,300)								
Less than 2 years old	9,690	3,160	1,310	1,200	670	820	2,080	450
3 to 5 years old	9,700	3,160	1,350	1,250	540	760	2,080	560
6 to 8 years old	9,330	3,160	1,930	1,310	540	790	920	680
9 to 11 years old	9,960	3,160	2,200	1,350	690	900	920	740
12 to 14 years old	9,570	3,160	2,290	1,500	740	860	440	580
15 to 17 years old	9,980	3,160	2,300	1,690	720	910	640	560
INCOME: $59,200 to $107,400 (Average = $81,700)								
Less than 2 years old	12,680	3,680	1,580	1,790	750	1,180	2,870	830
3 to 5 years old	12,730	3,680	1,690	1,840	600	1,110	2,870	940
6 to 8 years old	12,350	3,680	2,280	1,900	600	1,130	1,710	1,050
9 to 11 years old	13,180	3,680	2,680	1,940	780	1,280	1,710	1,110
12 to 14 years old	13,030	3,680	2,780	2,090	860	1,240	1,430	950
15 to 17 years old	13,900	3,680	2,790	2,270	830	1,300	2,090	940
INCOME: MORE THAN $107,400 (Average = $185,400)								
Less than 2 years old	19,770	5,460	2,210	2,590	1,110	1,580	5,170	1,650
3 to 5 years old	19,790	5,460	2,320	2,640	940	1,490	5,170	1,770
6 to 8 years old	19,380	5,460	2,960	2,690	940	1,440	4,010	1,880
9 to 11 years old	20,700	5,460	3,570	2,740	1,180	1,800	4,010	1,940
12 to 14 years old	21,050	5,460	3,560	2,890	1,310	1,740	4,310	1,780
15 to 17 years old	23,380	5,460	3,720	3,070	1,280	1,820	6,270	1,760

[1] Includes only families with child care and education expenses. [2] Expenses include personal care items, entertainment, and reading materials.

Source: U.S. Department of Agriculture, Center for Nutrition Policy and Promotion, *Expenditures on Children by Families, 2015*, March 2017 (revised). See also <https://www.cnpp.usda.gov/ExpendituresonChildrenbyFamilies>.

Table 716. Money Income of Households—Percent Distribution by Income Level, Race, and Hispanic Origin, in Constant (2015) Dollars: 2000 to 2015

[In percent except as noted (108,209 represents 108,209,000). Households as of March of following year. Constant dollars based on CPI-U-RS deflator. Based on Current Population Survey, Annual Social and Economic Supplement (CPS ASEC); see text, this section and Section 1, and Appendix III. For definition of median, see Guide to Tabular Presentation. A household consists of all the persons who occupy a housing unit. Household count excludes persons living in group quarters and institutions. Beginning with the 2003 CPS covering data for 2002, refers to respondents reporting only one race. Two basic ways of defining a race group are possible: a group such as Asian may be defined as 1) those who reported Asian and no other race (the race-alone concept), or 2) those who reported Asian regardless of whether they also reported another race (the race-alone-or-in-combination concept). For 2001 data and earlier, the CPS allowed respondents to report only one race group. Please note that the 2014 CPS ASEC covering data for 2013 included redesigned questions for income; use caution when comparing 2013 and subsequent data to data for previous years. See source for more information]

Year	Number of house- holds (1,000)	Percent distribution							Median income (dollars)
		Under $15,000	$15,000 to $24,999	$25,000 to $34,999	$35,000 to $49,999	$50,000 to $74,999	$75,000 to $99,999	$100,000 and over	
ALL HOUSEHOLDS [1]									
2000 [4]	108,209	10.4	10.1	9.8	13.5	18.0	13.1	25.0	57,790
2010 [5]	119,927	12.4	11.3	10.6	13.1	17.2	12.2	23.2	53,568
2014 [6]	124,587	12.6	10.9	10.1	13.1	17.0	11.5	24.7	53,718
2015 [6]	125,819	11.6	10.5	10.0	12.7	16.7	12.1	26.4	56,516
WHITE [2]									
2000 [4]	90,030	9.2	9.8	9.5	13.5	18.2	13.6	26.4	60,441
2010 [5]	96,306	10.6	11.0	10.4	13.2	17.5	12.7	24.7	56,213
2014 [6]	98,679	10.9	10.5	9.8	13.1	17.5	12.1	26.1	56,931
2015 [6]	99,313	9.9	10.1	9.9	12.7	16.9	12.6	28.0	60,109
BLACK [2]									
2000 [4]	13,174	19.0	12.9	12.7	14.6	17.7	9.8	13.2	40,830
2010 [5]	15,265	23.9	14.0	12.4	14.3	15.0	9.3	11.1	34,922
2014 [6]	16,437	22.4	14.4	12.7	14.4	15.1	8.2	12.8	35,439
2015 [6]	16,539	21.7	14.2	11.9	13.6	15.9	8.9	13.9	36,898
ASIAN AND PACIFIC ISLANDER [2]									
2000 [4]	3,963	8.1	6.8	7.4	10.9	15.8	14.4	36.5	76,737
2010 [5]	5,212	10.1	8.4	7.8	9.5	17.7	11.7	34.8	69,856
2014 [6]	6,040	10.3	7.0	7.7	9.7	15.6	11.8	37.9	74,382
2015 [6]	6,328	9.7	6.7	6.2	10.2	15.5	12.2	39.4	77,166
HISPANIC [3]									
2000 [4]	10,034	12.3	13.4	12.1	16.7	19.5	11.5	14.3	45,649
2010 [5]	14,435	15.8	13.9	14.1	14.8	17.6	10.2	13.6	40,909
2014 [6]	16,239	14.6	14.1	12.4	15.6	18.0	10.7	14.7	42,540
2015 [6]	16,667	13.6	13.0	12.7	15.1	18.1	10.8	16.6	45,148

[1] Includes other races not shown separately. [2] Beginning with 2002, data represent White alone, Black alone, or Asian alone. [3] People of Hispanic origin may be of any race. [4] Data reflect implementation of Census 2000-based population controls and a 28,000 household sample expansion to 78,000 households. [5] Median income is calculated using $2,500 income intervals. Beginning with 2009 income data, the Census Bureau expanded the upper income intervals used to calculate medians to $250,000 or more. Medians falling in the upper open-ended interval are plugged with "$250,000." Before 2009, the upper open-ended interval was $100,000 and a plug of "$100,000" was used. Data reflect implementation of Census 2010-based population controls. [6] Beginning with 2013, data are based on redesigned questions on income.

Source: U.S. Census Bureau, *Income and Poverty in the United States: 2015,* Current Population Reports, P60-256(RV), September 2016; and "Historical Income Tables: Households, Table H-17," <http://www.census.gov/topics/income-poverty/income/data/tables.html>, accessed November 2016.

Table 717. Money Income of Households—Median Income by Race and Hispanic Origin, in Current and Constant (2015) Dollars: 1990 to 2015

[In dollars. See headnote, Table 716]

Year	Median income in current dollars					Median income in constant (2015) dollars				
	All house- holds [1]	White [2]	Black [2]	Asian, Pacific Islander [2]	His- panic [3]	All house- holds [1]	White [2]	Black [2]	Asian, Pacific Islander [2]	His- panic [3]
1990	29,943	31,231	18,676	38,450	22,330	52,684	54,950	32,860	67,652	39,289
1995 [4]	34,076	35,766	22,393	40,614	22,860	52,664	55,276	34,608	62,769	35,330
2000 [5,6]	41,990	43,916	29,667	55,757	33,168	57,790	60,441	40,830	76,737	45,649
2005	46,326	48,554	30,858	61,094	35,967	56,224	58,928	37,451	74,148	43,652
2010 [7]	49,276	51,709	32,124	64,259	37,631	53,568	56,213	34,922	69,856	40,909
2011 [8]	50,054	52,214	32,229	65,129	38,624	52,751	55,027	33,965	68,638	40,705
2012	51,017	53,706	33,321	68,636	39,005	52,666	55,442	34,398	70,854	40,265
2013 [9]	53,585	56,745	35,324	72,383	39,687	54,525	57,740	35,943	73,652	40,383
2014 [9]	53,657	56,866	35,398	74,297	42,491	53,719	56,931	35,439	74,382	42,540
2015 [9]	56,516	60,109	36,898	77,166	45,148	56,516	60,109	36,898	77,166	45,148

[1] Includes other races, not shown separately. [2] Beginning with 2002, refers to people who reported specified race and did not report any other race category; for "Asian, Pacific Islander," refers to people who reported "Asian alone." [3] People of Hispanic origin may be of any race. [4] Data reflect full implementation of the 1990 Census-based sample design and metropolitan definitions, 7,000 household sample reduction, and revised race edits. [5] Implementation of Census 2000-based population controls. [6] Implementation of a 28,000 household sample expansion. [7] Median income is calculated using $2,500 income intervals. Beginning with 2009 income data, the Census Bureau expanded the upper income intervals used to calculate medians to $250,000 or more. Before 2009, the upper open-ended interval was $100,000 and a plug of "$100,000" was used. [8] Implementation of Census 2010-based population controls. [9] Beginning with 2013, data are based on redesigned questions on income.

Source: U.S. Census Bureau, *Income and Poverty in the United States: 2015,* Current Population Reports, P60-256(RV), September 2016; and "Historical Income Tables: Households, Table H-5," <http://www.census.gov/topics/income-poverty/income/data/tables.html>, accessed November 2016.

Table 718. Money Income of Households—Distribution by Income Level and Selected Characteristics: 2015

[125,819 represents 125,819,000. Households as of March of the following year. Based on Current Population Survey, Annual Social and Economic Supplement (CPS ASEC); see text, this section and Section 1, and Appendix III. For definition of median, see Guide to Tabular Presentation. See headnote, Table 716]

Characteristic	Number of households (1,000)								Median house-hold income (dollars) [1]
	Total house-holds	Under $15,000	$15,000 to $24,999	$25,000 to $34,999	$35,000 to $49,999	$50,000 to $74,999	$75,000 to $99,999	$100,000 and over	
Total..........................	125,819	14,630	13,235	12,576	15,948	21,001	15,199	33,228	56,516
Region: [2]									
Northeast.....................	22,347	2,516	2,206	2,055	2,525	3,460	2,672	6,913	62,182
Midwest......................	27,455	2,949	2,745	2,798	3,603	4,849	3,442	7,067	57,082
South.........................	47,822	6,302	5,636	5,157	6,206	7,905	5,445	11,170	51,174
West..........................	28,195	2,862	2,649	2,568	3,615	4,786	3,641	8,078	61,442
Age of householder:									
15 to 24 years...............	6,361	1,296	907	889	959	1,115	566	631	36,108
25 to 34 years...............	20,047	1,843	1,733	2,150	2,869	4,005	2,777	4,671	57,366
35 to 44 years...............	21,222	1,693	1,551	1,750	2,395	3,681	2,994	7,159	71,417
45 to 54 years...............	23,294	2,040	1,576	1,641	2,561	3,958	3,168	8,352	73,857
55 to 64 years...............	23,896	2,993	2,098	2,049	2,667	3,747	2,934	7,409	62,802
65 years and over...........	30,998	4,766	5,371	4,099	4,497	4,496	2,757	5,011	38,515
Type of household:									
Family household.............	82,184	5,188	5,930	7,014	9,835	14,500	11,728	27,989	72,165
Married-couple.............	60,251	1,895	2,982	4,273	6,452	10,474	9,450	24,721	84,626
Male householder, spouse absent.............	6,310	495	644	649	1,004	1,317	852	1,345	55,861
Female householder, spouse absent.............	15,622	2,798	2,305	2,092	2,379	2,708	1,427	1,918	37,797
Nonfamily household.........	43,635	9,442	7,305	5,562	6,113	6,500	3,470	5,241	33,805
Male householder...........	20,542	3,693	2,918	2,449	2,861	3,631	1,872	3,116	40,762
Female householder........	23,093	5,748	4,386	3,113	3,253	2,869	1,597	2,123	29,022
Size of household:									
One person...................	35,388	8,903	6,770	4,949	5,073	4,704	2,192	2,799	28,800
Two people...................	42,785	3,025	3,485	4,299	5,723	8,065	6,106	12,081	63,850
Three people.................	19,423	1,279	1,387	1,413	2,223	3,524	2,764	6,837	73,990
Four people..................	16,267	796	811	1,039	1,601	2,511	2,458	7,049	87,739
Five people..................	7,548	392	506	536	823	1,331	1,078	2,879	78,622
Six people...................	2,813	154	184	214	299	520	372	1,070	77,343
Seven or more people.......	1,596	81	94	126	207	346	227	519	70,514
Number of earners:									
No earners...................	29,694	10,428	6,453	4,021	3,485	2,680	1,246	1,381	21,519
One earner...................	46,356	3,806	5,829	6,763	8,284	8,986	4,961	7,726	46,763
Two earners and more.......	49,769	398	954	1,793	4,180	9,333	8,992	24,118	97,231
Two earners...............	39,648	377	883	1,657	3,692	7,920	7,289	17,829	92,023
Three earners..............	7,608	20	66	121	439	1,205	1,316	4,441	111,416
Four earners or more.......	2,513	–	5	16	48	209	387	1,846	136,308
Work experience of householder:									
Total........................	125,819	14,630	13,235	12,576	15,948	21,001	15,199	33,228	56,516
Worked........................	82,861	3,567	5,737	7,041	10,308	15,580	12,053	28,577	73,182
Worked at full-time jobs....	68,874	1,576	3,879	5,559	8,423	13,456	10,511	25,469	77,554
50 weeks or more..........	59,702	687	2,810	4,575	7,270	11,725	9,417	23,217	81,224
27 to 49 weeks...........	5,884	286	626	660	747	1,158	783	1,626	61,879
26 weeks or less..........	3,287	604	442	324	405	572	313	627	43,786
Worked at part-time jobs. ..	13,988	1,990	1,858	1,483	1,884	2,123	1,540	3,108	48,145
50 weeks or more..........	7,852	772	1,032	856	1,094	1,247	923	1,928	52,214
27 to 49 weeks...........	2,887	417	382	307	418	416	331	615	47,344
26 weeks or less..........	3,249	800	445	320	372	460	289	561	37,592
Did not work.................	42,957	11,064	7,498	5,535	5,641	5,420	3,146	4,650	29,915
Educational attainment of householder: [3]									
Total........................	119,457	13,334	12,330	11,689	14,989	19,887	14,632	32,600	58,044
Less than 9th grade..........	4,671	1,300	928	615	649	593	283	302	26,252
9th to 12th grade (no diploma)................	7,640	2,203	1,467	1,020	1,066	1,026	388	470	26,356
High school graduate.........	32,349	4,607	4,692	4,290	4,829	5,716	3,354	4,858	42,047
Some college, no degree.....	21,477	2,342	2,385	2,376	3,148	4,138	2,759	4,331	51,906
Associate's degree..........	12,298	980	1,097	1,217	1,588	2,358	1,887	3,172	62,485
Bachelor's degree or more....	41,022	1,902	1,760	2,171	3,709	6,055	5,960	19,465	94,934
Bachelor's degree...........	25,063	1,289	1,180	1,481	2,496	3,947	3,812	10,858	87,991
Master's degree.............	11,714	460	431	569	967	1,606	1,702	5,982	101,323
Professional degree.........	1,842	72	52	47	114	205	176	1,177	136,640
Doctoral degree..............	2,402	82	97	74	131	297	270	1,449	121,244
Housing tenure:									
Owner occupied..............	79,903	5,716	6,599	6,805	9,240	13,477	10,973	27,094	71,018
Renter occupied..............	44,265	8,405	6,359	5,597	6,492	7,334	4,111	5,968	38,318
Occupier paid no cash rent..	1,650	508	278	175	217	190	114	165	26,427

– Represents zero. [1] Median income calculated using $2,500 income intervals. Medians falling in the upper open-ended interval are plugged with "$250,000." [2] For composition of regions, see map, inside front cover. [3] People age 25 and over.

Source: U.S. Census Bureau, *Income and Poverty in the United States: 2015*, Current Population Reports, P60-256(RV), September 2016; and "Current Population Survey Tables for Household Income: Table HINC-01," <http://www.census.gov/topics/income-poverty/income/data/tables.html>, accessed November 2016.

Table 719. Money Income of Households—Number and Distribution by Race and Hispanic Origin: 2015

[125,819 represents 125,819,000. Households as of March of the following year. Based on Current Population Survey, 2016 Annual Social and Economic Supplement (ASEC); see text, this section and Section 1, and Appendix III. Data shown for persons reporting specified race only. Please note that beginning with the 2015 CPS ASEC covering data for 2014, data are based on a redesigned questionnaire. See source for more information. Use caution when comparing 2014 and subsequent data to data for previous years]

Income interval	Number of households (1,000)					Percent distribution				
	All races	White alone	Black alone	Asian alone	His-panic [1]	All races	White alone	Black alone	Asian alone	His-panic [1]
All households.............	**125,819**	**99,313**	**16,539**	**6,328**	**16,667**	**100.0**	**100.0**	**100.0**	**100.0**	**100.0**
Under $10,000.................	8,306	5,278	2,233	403	1,326	6.6	5.3	13.5	6.4	8.0
$10,000 to $14,999...........	6,324	4,561	1,354	210	944	5.0	4.6	8.2	3.3	5.7
$15,000 to $19,999...........	6,470	4,813	1,205	209	992	5.1	4.8	7.3	3.3	6.0
$20,000 to $24,999...........	6,765	5,202	1,141	218	1,175	5.4	5.2	6.9	3.4	7.0
$25,000 to $29,999...........	6,222	4,877	965	203	1,028	4.9	4.9	5.8	3.2	6.2
$30,000 to $34,999...........	6,354	4,949	998	190	1,083	5.1	5.0	6.0	3.0	6.5
$35,000 to $39,999...........	5,743	4,531	820	214	924	4.6	4.6	5.0	3.4	5.5
$40,000 to $44,999...........	5,203	4,132	729	215	836	4.1	4.2	4.4	3.4	5.0
$45,000 to $49,999...........	5,002	3,924	698	215	758	4.0	4.0	4.2	3.4	4.5
$50,000 to $59,999...........	9,218	7,299	1,180	414	1,345	7.3	7.3	7.1	6.5	8.1
$60,000 to $74,999...........	11,783	9,451	1,444	566	1,677	9.4	9.5	8.7	8.9	10.1
$75,000 to $84,999...........	7,004	5,770	689	354	884	5.6	5.8	4.2	5.6	5.3
$85,000 to $99,999...........	8,195	6,774	785	421	920	6.5	6.8	4.7	6.7	5.5
$100,000 to $149,999........	17,777	14,897	1,450	1,062	1,620	14.1	15.0	8.8	16.8	9.7
$150,000 to $199,999........	7,811	6,519	463	665	620	6.2	6.6	2.8	10.5	3.7
$200,000 to $249,999........	3,456	2,875	182	331	231	2.7	2.9	1.1	5.2	1.4
$250,000 and above..........	4,184	3,464	204	437	305	3.3	3.5	1.2	6.9	1.8

[1] Persons of Hispanic origin may be of any race.

Source: U.S. Census Bureau, *Income and Poverty in the United States: 2015*, Current Population Reports, P60-256(RV), September 2016; and "Current Population Survey Tables for Household Income: Table HINC-06," <http://www.census.gov/topics/income-poverty/income/data/tables.html>, accessed November 2016.

Table 720. Share of Aggregate Income Received by Each Fifth and Top 5 Percent of Households: 1990 to 2015

[In units as indicated (94,312 represents 94,312,000). Households as of March of the following year. Income in constant 2015 CPI-U-RS-adjusted dollars. The shares method ranks households from highest to lowest on the basis of income and then divides them into groups of equal population size, typically quintiles. The aggregate income of each group is then divided by the overall aggregate income to derive shares. Based on the Current Population Survey, Annual Social and Economic Supplement (CPS ASEC); see text, this section and Section 1, and Appendix III. For data collection changes over time, see source. See also headnote, Table 716]

Year	Number of house-holds (1,000)	Income at selected positions in constant (2015) dollars				Top 5 percent, lower limit	Percent distribution of aggregate income					
		Upper limit of each fifth					Lowest 5th	Second 5th	Third 5th	Fourth 5th	Highest 5th	Top 5 percent
		Lowest	Second	Third	Fourth							
1990...........	94,312	21,993	41,633	63,693	97,132	166,707	3.8	9.6	15.9	24.0	46.6	18.5
1995 [1].......	99,627	22,255	41,595	64,914	100,649	174,641	3.7	9.1	15.2	23.3	48.7	21.0
2000 [2, 3]......	108,209	24,663	45,417	71,806	112,533	199,864	3.6	8.9	14.8	23.0	49.8	22.1
2005...........	114,384	23,276	43,692	69,980	111,299	201,468	3.4	8.6	14.6	23.0	50.4	22.2
2006...........	116,011	23,552	44,405	70,533	114,067	204,561	3.4	8.6	14.5	22.9	50.5	22.3
2007...........	116,783	23,195	44,697	70,875	114,314	202,336	3.4	8.7	14.8	23.4	49.7	21.2
2008...........	117,181	22,801	42,933	69,051	110,350	198,154	3.4	8.6	14.7	23.3	50.0	21.5
2009 [4].........	117,538	22,594	42,586	68,271	110,470	198,846	3.4	8.6	14.6	23.2	50.3	21.7
2010 [5].........	119,927	21,742	41,310	66,857	108,742	196,206	3.3	8.5	14.6	23.4	50.3	21.3
2011...........	121,084	21,354	40,595	65,798	107,055	196,021	3.2	8.4	14.3	23.0	51.1	22.3
2012...........	122,459	21,265	41,049	66,669	107,460	197,333	3.2	8.3	14.4	23.0	51.0	22.3
2013 [6].........	123,931	21,368	41,754	68,378	112,165	208,725	3.1	8.2	14.3	23.0	51.4	22.2
2014 [6].........	124,587	21,457	41,233	68,290	112,391	206,806	3.1	8.2	14.3	23.2	51.2	21.9
2015 [6].........	125,819	22,800	43,511	72,001	117,002	214,462	3.1	8.2	14.3	23.2	51.1	22.1

[1] Data reflect full implementation of the 1990 Census-based sample design and metropolitan definitions, 7,000 household sample reduction, and revised race edits. [2] Implementation of Census 2000-based population controls. [3] Implementation of a 28,000 household sample expansion. [4] Beginning with 2009 income data, the Census Bureau expanded the upper income interval used to calculate medians and Gini indexes to $250,000 or more. Medians falling in the upper open-ended interval are plugged with "$250,000." [5] Implementation of Census 2010-based population controls. [6] Beginning with 2013, data are based on redesigned questions on income. See source for more information.

Source: U.S. Census Bureau, *Income and Poverty in the United States: 2015,* Current Population Reports, P60-252(RV), September 2016; and "Historical Income Tables: Households, Tables H1 and H2," <http://www.census.gov/topics/income-poverty/income/data/tables.html>, accessed November 2016.

Table 721. Money Income of Families—Number and Distribution by Race and Hispanic Origin: 2015

[82,199 represents 82,199,000. Families as of March of the following year. Based on Current Population Survey, Annual Social and Economic Supplement (CPS ASEC); see text, this section, Section 1, and Appendix III. A family is a group of persons residing together and related by birth, marriage, or adoption. See also headnote in Table 716 regarding changes in the CPS ASEC]

Income interval	Number of families (1,000)					Percent distribution				
	All races	White alone	Black alone	Asian alone	His-panic [1]	All races	White alone	Black alone	Asian alone	His-panic [1]
All families	**82,199**	**65,272**	**9,848**	**4,697**	**12,761**	**100.0**	**100.0**	**100.0**	**100.0**	**100.0**
Under $10,000	3,659	2,345	957	160	890	4.5	3.6	9.7	3.4	7.0
$10,000 to $14,999	2,247	1,516	561	80	534	2.7	2.3	5.7	1.7	4.2
$15,000 to $19,999	2,816	1,972	576	150	713	3.4	3.0	5.8	3.2	5.6
$20,000 to $24,999	3,375	2,520	633	126	891	4.1	3.9	6.4	2.7	7.0
$25,000 to $29,999	3,599	2,782	588	133	802	4.4	4.3	6.0	2.8	6.3
$30,000 to $34,999	3,596	2,764	562	119	809	4.4	4.2	5.7	2.5	6.3
$35,000 to $39,999	3,455	2,643	547	134	720	4.2	4.0	5.6	2.9	5.6
$40,000 to $44,999	3,265	2,592	432	150	691	4.0	4.0	4.4	3.2	5.4
$45,000 to $49,999	3,156	2,489	403	154	591	3.8	3.8	4.1	3.3	4.6
$50,000 to $59,999	6,021	4,757	730	302	1,059	7.3	7.3	7.4	6.4	8.3
$60,000 to $74,999	8,160	6,510	963	441	1,283	9.9	10.0	9.8	9.4	10.1
$75,000 to $84,999	5,165	4,272	492	269	716	6.3	6.5	5.0	5.7	5.6
$85,000 to $99,999	6,261	5,189	568	348	736	7.6	7.9	5.8	7.4	5.8
$100,000 to $149,999	14,376	12,068	1,151	869	1,382	17.5	18.5	11.7	18.5	10.8
$150,000 to $199,999	6,485	5,410	372	570	492	7.9	8.3	3.8	12.1	3.9
$200,000 to $249,999	2,931	2,433	144	299	194	3.6	3.7	1.5	6.4	1.5
$250,000 and above	3,630	3,008	167	391	253	4.4	4.6	1.7	8.3	2.0

[1] Persons of Hispanic origin may be of any race.

Source: U.S. Census Bureau, *Income and Poverty in the United States: 2015,* Current Population Reports, P60-256(RV), September 2016; and "Current Population Survey Tables for Family Income: Table FINC-07," <http://www.census.gov/topics/income-poverty/income/data/tables.html>, accessed November 2016.

Table 722. Money Income of Families—Percent Distribution by Income Level in Constant (2015) Dollars: 2000 to 2015

[73,778 represents 73,778,000. Income in 2015 Consumer Price Index Research Series Using Current Methods (CPI-U-RS) adjusted dollars. Families as of March of the following year. Based on Current Population Survey, Annual Social and Economic Supplement (CPS ASEC); see text, this section and Section 1, and Appendix III. For data collection changes over time, see "Changes in Methodology for the March Current Population Survey" at <http://www.census.gov/topics/income-poverty/income/guidance/cps-methodology-changes.html>. For definition of median, see Guide to Tabular Presentation. For comments on race, see headnote, Table 716, and also text for Section 1, Population. Beginning with 2013, data are based on redesigned questions on income. Use caution in comparing 2014 and subsequent data with data for previous years; see source for more information]

Year	Number of families (1,000)	Percent distribution							Median income (dollars)
		Under $15,000	$15,000 to $24,999	$25,000 to $34,999	$35,000 to $49,999	$50,000 to $74,999	$75,000 to $99,999	$100,000 and over	
ALL FAMILIES [1]									
2000 [4]	73,778	5.9	7.4	8.5	13.1	18.9	15.2	31.0	69,822
2010 [5]	79,559	8.1	8.2	9.4	12.8	18.1	14.2	29.4	65,483
2014 [6]	81,730	8.0	8.0	8.9	12.5	17.8	13.5	31.3	66,709
2015 [6]	82,199	7.2	7.5	8.8	12.0	17.3	13.9	33.4	70,697
WHITE [2]									
2000 [4]	61,330	4.8	6.7	8.0	12.9	19.1	15.8	32.8	72,983
2010 [5]	63,976	6.6	7.5	9.0	12.7	18.4	14.7	31.1	68,394
2014 [6]	64,945	6.7	7.3	8.4	12.3	18.2	14.2	33.0	70,690
2015 [6]	65,272	5.9	6.9	8.5	11.8	17.3	14.5	35.1	74,291
BLACK [2]									
2000 [4]	8,731	13.7	12.3	12.4	15.3	18.6	11.4	16.2	46,348
2010 [5]	9,571	17.7	12.8	12.5	14.7	16.6	11.1	14.5	41,956
2014 [6]	9,909	16.2	13.3	11.9	14.7	16.6	10.2	17.2	43,201
2015 [6]	9,848	15.4	12.3	11.7	14.0	17.2	10.8	18.7	45,781
ASIAN AND PACIFIC ISLANDER [2]									
2000 [4]	2,982	4.9	5.7	6.4	9.9	16.1	15.1	41.8	86,179
2010 [5]	3,879	6.2	7.1	6.7	9.8	16.7	13.0	40.6	81,769
2014 [6]	4,499	5.9	5.7	8.2	9.3	15.9	12.3	42.6	82,827
2015 [6]	4,697	5.1	5.9	5.4	9.3	15.9	13.1	45.3	90,847
HISPANIC ORIGIN [3]									
2000 [4]	8,017	10.4	12.9	12.5	17.5	19.6	11.9	15.2	47,402
2010 [5]	11,284	14.4	13.7	14.1	14.8	18.4	10.4	14.3	42,723
2014 [6]	12,464	12.6	13.7	12.6	15.8	18.4	10.9	16.1	45,166
2015 [6]	12,761	11.2	12.6	12.6	15.7	18.4	11.4	18.2	47,328

[1] Includes other races not shown separately. [2] Beginning with data for 2002, represents White alone, Black alone, or Asian alone. [3] People of Hispanic origin may be of any race. [4] Data reflect implementation of Census 2000-based population controls and a 28,000 household sample expansion to 78,000 households. [5] Median income is calculated using $2,500 income intervals. Beginning with 2009 income data, the Census Bureau expanded the upper income intervals used to calculate medians to $250,000 or more. Medians falling in the upper open-ended interval are plugged with "$250,000." Before 2009, the upper open-ended interval was $100,000 and a plug of "$100,000" was used. Implementation of Census 2010-based population controls. [6] Beginning with 2013, data are based on redesigned questions on income. See source for more information.

Source: U.S. Census Bureau, *Income and Poverty in the United States: 2015,* Current Population Reports, P60-256(RV), September 2016; and "Historical Income Tables: Families, Table F-23," <http://www.census.gov/topics/income-poverty/income/data/tables.html>, accessed November 2016.

Table 723. Money Income of Families—Median Income by Race and Hispanic Origin in Current and Constant (2015) Dollars: 1990 to 2015

[In dollars. Beginning with the 2003 CPS covering data for 2002, respondents were allowed to choose more than one race. Two basic ways of defining a race group are possible. A group such as Asian may be defined as those who reported Asian and no other race (the race-alone or single-race concept), or as those who reported Asian regardless of whether they also reported another race (the race-alone-or-in-combination concept). For 2001 data and earlier, the CPS allowed respondents to report only one race group. See also comments on race in the text for Section 1, Population. See also headnote, Table 722]

Year	Median income in current dollars					Median income in constant (2015) dollars				
	All races [1]	White [2]	Black [2]	Asian, Pacific Islander [2]	His-panic [3]	All races [1]	White [2]	Black [2]	Asian, Pacific Islander [2]	His-panic [3]
1990.............	35,353	36,915	21,423	42,246	23,431	62,203	64,951	37,693	74,331	41,226
2000 [4].............	50,732	53,029	33,676	62,617	34,442	69,822	72,983	46,348	86,179	47,402
2005.............	56,194	59,317	35,464	68,957	37,867	68,201	71,991	43,041	83,691	45,958
2010 [5].............	60,236	62,914	38,594	75,217	39,300	65,483	68,394	41,956	81,769	42,723
2011.............	60,974	64,081	40,495	72,996	40,061	64,259	67,533	42,677	76,929	42,219
2012.............	62,241	65,880	40,517	77,864	40,764	64,252	68,009	41,826	80,380	42,081
2013 [6].............	65,471	68,802	41,890	82,793	40,939	66,619	70,008	42,624	84,245	41,657
2014 [6].............	66,632	70,609	43,151	82,732	45,114	66,709	70,690	43,201	82,827	45,166
2015 [6].............	70,697	74,291	45,781	90,847	47,328	70,697	74,291	45,781	90,847	47,328

[1] Includes other races not shown separately. [2] Beginning with 2002, data represent White alone, Black alone, or Asian alone. [3] People of Hispanic origin may be of any race. [4] Implementation of Census 2000-based population controls, and 28,000 household sample expansion. [5] Median income calculated using $2,500 income intervals. Beginning 2009, Census Bureau expanded upper income intervals used to calculate medians to $250,000 or more. Medians falling in the upper open-ended interval are plugged with "$250,000." Before 2009, the upper open-ended interval was $100,000 and a plug of "$100,000" was used. Implementation of Census 2010-based population controls. [6] Based on redesigned questions on income.

Source: U.S. Census Bureau, *Income and Poverty in the United States: 2015*, Current Population Reports, P60-256(RV), September 2016; and "Historical Income Tables: Families, Table F-05," <http://www.census.gov/topics/income-poverty/income/data/tables.html>, accessed November 2016.

Table 724. Money Income of Families—Distribution by Family Characteristics and Income Level: 2015

[82,199 represents 82,199,000. See headnote, Table 722. Median income is calculated using $2,500 income intervals. Medians falling in the upper open-ended interval are plugged with "$250,000." For composition of regions, see map inside front cover]

Characteristic	Number of families (1,000)								Median income (dollars)
	Total	Under $15,000	$15,000 to $24,999	$25,000 to $34,999	$35,000 to $49,999	$50,000 to $74,999	$75,000 to $99,999	$100,000 and over	
All families........................	**82,199**	**5,907**	**6,192**	**7,195**	**9,876**	**14,181**	**11,427**	**27,423**	**70,697**
Region:									
Northeast...........................	14,255	901	987	1,110	1,421	2,223	1,954	5,660	80,482
Midwest.............................	17,456	1,050	1,078	1,342	2,131	3,289	2,578	5,990	73,535
South................................	31,505	2,683	2,791	3,147	3,996	5,433	4,153	9,300	62,544
West.................................	18,983	1,274	1,336	1,595	2,326	3,238	2,741	6,475	72,399
Type of family:									
Married-couple families............	60,258	1,906	3,011	4,279	6,494	10,498	9,427	24,642	84,324
Male householder, no spouse present................	6,311	668	710	758	1,033	1,208	782	1,151	49,772
Female householder, no spouse present................	15,630	3,333	2,470	2,158	2,348	2,475	1,217	1,629	34,126
Unrelated subfamilies..............	563	214	98	82	85	44	24	18	21,716
Age of householder:									
15 to 24 years old.................	3,187	665	374	457	483	563	291	355	37,759
25 to 34 years old.................	12,911	1,426	1,238	1,334	1,741	2,239	1,836	3,101	56,775
35 to 44 years old.................	16,915	1,231	1,231	1,255	1,736	2,767	2,427	6,267	76,780
45 to 54 years old.................	17,093	910	888	1,013	1,673	2,861	2,456	7,289	85,748
55 to 64 years old.................	15,496	792	897	1,032	1,533	2,578	2,275	6,387	83,813
65 years old and over..............	16,597	882	1,562	2,106	2,709	3,174	2,141	4,022	57,360
Number of earners:									
No earners..........................	13,080	3,287	2,093	2,093	2,008	1,717	869	1,013	30,118
One earner..........................	27,174	2,309	3,379	3,707	4,541	5,026	3,069	5,145	48,626
Two earners or more................	41,945	312	720	1,395	3,329	7,437	7,488	21,268	100,874
Educational attainment of householder:									
Persons 25 years old and over, total..........................	**79,012**	**5,242**	**5,817**	**6,739**	**9,393**	**13,618**	**11,135**	**27,068**	**72,135**
Less than 9th grade.................	3,099	443	603	477	581	509	228	260	35,542
9th to 12th grade (no diploma).....	4,808	914	867	714	830	771	315	396	32,906
High school graduate (includes equivalency)........................	21,010	1,808	2,156	2,485	3,350	4,268	2,738	4,206	52,906
Some college, no degree...........	13,983	1,006	1,035	1,344	1,846	2,960	2,155	3,639	64,043
Associate's degree.................	8,366	381	511	713	961	1,590	1,506	2,706	75,399
Bachelor's degree or more.........	27,746	690	646	1,006	1,827	3,522	4,193	15,863	111,270
Bachelor's degree.................	16,840	466	434	705	1,279	2,383	2,718	8,855	103,224
Master's degree...................	7,991	156	166	233	438	898	1,176	4,926	120,489
Professional degree...............	1,290	33	22	36	49	90	119	942	162,488
Doctoral degree...................	1,624	36	24	34	59	152	181	1,139	143,776

Source: U.S. Census Bureau, *Income and Poverty in the United States: 2015*, Current Population Reports, P60-256(RV), September 2016; and "Current Population Survey Tables for Family Income: Table FINC-01," <http://www.census.gov/topics/income-poverty/income/data/tables.html>, accessed November 2016.

Table 725. Median Income of Families by Type of Family in Current and Constant (2015) Dollars: 1990 to 2015

[In dollars. See headnote, Table 722. For definition of median, see Guide to Tabular Presentation]

Year	Current dollars						Constant (2015) dollars					
		Married-couple families			Male house-holder, no spouse present	Female house-holder, no spouse present		Married-couple families			Male house-holder, no spouse present	Female house-holder, no spouse present
	All families	Total	Wife in paid labor force	Wife not in paid labor force			All families	Total	Wife in paid labor force	Wife not in paid labor force		
1990..........	35,353	39,895	46,777	30,265	29,046	16,932	62,203	70,194	82,303	53,250	51,106	29,791
2000 [1]......	50,732	59,099	69,235	39,982	37,727	25,716	69,822	81,337	95,287	55,027	51,923	35,393
2005..........	56,194	65,906	78,755	44,457	41,111	27,244	68,201	79,988	95,582	53,956	49,895	33,065
2010 [2]......	60,236	72,241	87,397	48,733	43,206	29,155	65,483	78,534	95,010	52,978	46,969	31,695
2011..........	60,974	73,790	89,017	50,414	43,069	30,259	64,259	77,765	93,813	53,130	45,389	31,889
2012..........	62,241	75,535	91,779	50,881	42,358	30,686	64,252	77,976	94,745	52,525	43,727	31,678
2013 [3]......	65,471	78,614	96,062	54,231	47,191	31,131	66,619	79,992	97,746	55,182	48,018	31,677
2014 [3]......	66,632	80,814	99,983	54,779	47,597	31,770	66,709	80,907	100,098	54,842	47,652	31,807
2015 [3]......	70,697	84,324	103,699	56,010	49,772	34,126	70,697	84,324	103,699	56,010	49,772	34,126

[1] Implementation of Census 2000-based population controls, and of a 28,000 household sample expansion. [2] Median income calculated using $2,500 income intervals. Beginning with 2009 income data, the Census Bureau expanded from $100,000 the upper income intervals used to calculate medians to $250,000 or more. Implementation of Census 2010-based population controls. [3] Based on redesigned income questions; see source for details.

Source: U.S. Census Bureau, *Income and Poverty in the United States: 2015,* Current Population Reports, P60-256(RV), September 2016; and "Historical Income Tables: Families, Table F-7," <http://www.census.gov/topics/income-poverty/income/data/tables.html>, accessed November 2016.

Table 726. Married-Couple Families—Number and Median Income by Work Experience of Husbands and Wives and Presence of Related Children: 2015

[60,258 represents 60,258,000. Based on the 2016 Current Population Survey, Annual Social and Economic Supplement; see text, Sections 1 and 13, and Appendix III. See headnote, Table 728]

Work experience of husband or wife	Number (1,000)					Median income (dollars)				
	All married-couple families	With no related children	One or more related children under 18 years old			All married-couple families	With no related children	One or more related children under 18 years old		
			Total	One child	Two children or more			Total	One child	Two children or more
All married-couple families........	**60,258**	**35,141**	**25,117**	**9,710**	**15,407**	**84,324**	**79,881**	**91,097**	**93,325**	**89,399**
Husband worked [1].....................	45,469	22,227	23,243	8,824	14,419	98,210	101,196	95,306	98,660	92,530
Wife worked............................	32,341	15,983	16,358	6,582	9,776	108,727	110,667	107,184	107,777	106,806
Wife did not work....................	13,129	6,244	6,885	2,242	768	69,187	76,360	61,328	65,225	56,626
Husband worked year-round, full-time [1]...........................	37,452	17,228	20,224	7,577	12,647	103,516	107,923	100,255	102,935	97,386
Wife worked............................	27,196	12,940	14,255	5,669	8,587	113,454	115,910	111,255	111,817	110,900
Wife did not work....................	10,256	4,288	5,969	1,908	4,060	74,032	81,983	66,156	70,427	64,614
Husband did not work [1].............	14,788	12,914	1,874	886	988	46,342	46,476	44,773	48,598	41,188
Wife worked............................	4,485	3,362	1,123	504	619	64,618	66,911	57,964	60,607	53,838
Wife did not work....................	10,303	9,553	751	382	369	39,636	40,390	25,948	30,998	20,562

[1] Spouse has any work status.

Source: U.S. Census Bureau, *Income and Poverty in the United States: 2015*, Current Population Reports, P60-256(RV), September 2016; and "Current Population Survey Tables for Family Income: Table FINC-04," <http://www.census.gov/topics/income-poverty/income/data/tables.html>, accessed November 2016.

Table 727. Median Income of People in Constant (2015) Dollars by Sex, Race, and Hispanic Origin: 2000 to 2015

[In dollars. People as of March of following year. People age 15 and over. Constant dollars based on CPI-U-RS deflator. Based on the Current Population Survey, Annual Social and Economic Supplement (CPS ASEC); see text, this section and Section 1 and Appendix III. Beginning with the 2003 CPS covering data for 2002, respondents were allowed to choose more than one race. Two basic ways of defining a race group are possible. A group such as Asian may be defined as 1) those who reported Asian and no other race (the race-alone or single-race concept), or 2) those who reported Asian regardless of whether they also reported another race (the race-alone-or-in-combination concept). For 2001 data and earlier, the CPS allowed respondents to report only one race group. See also headnote, Table 722]

Race and Hispanic origin	Male					Female				
	2000 [1]	2005	2010 [2]	2014 [3]	2015 [3]	2000 [1]	2005	2010 [2]	2014 [3]	2015 [3]
All races [4]...................	**39,008**	**37,957**	**35,010**	**36,344**	**37,138**	**22,107**	**22,545**	**22,585**	**22,266**	**23,769**
White [5]..........................	41,009	39,054	37,368	37,617	39,491	22,129	22,658	22,716	22,505	24,278
Black [5]..........................	29,374	27,493	25,325	26,600	27,404	21,857	21,398	21,357	20,990	21,613
Asian [5]..........................	42,435	41,525	38,943	40,948	43,705	23,887	26,265	25,615	25,420	26,532
Hispanic [6]......................	26,835	26,809	24,373	26,706	28,110	16,857	18,249	17,711	17,605	18,905
White non-Hispanic...........	43,364	42,897	40,390	41,119	42,207	22,936	23,607	23,607	24,033	25,629

[1] Implementation of Census 2000-based population controls and sample expanded by 28,000 households. [2] See footnote 2, Table 725. [3] Based on redesigned questions on income. [4] Includes other races not shown separately. [5] Data for 2002 and later refer to people reporting White alone, Black alone, or Asian alone ("Asian alone" replaced "Asian and Pacific Islander"). [6] People of Hispanic origin may be of any race.

Source: U.S. Census Bureau, *Income and Poverty in the United States: 2015*, Current Population Reports, P60-256(RV), September 2016; and "Historical Income Tables: People, Table P-2 and P-5," <http://www.census.gov/topics/income-poverty/income/data/tables.html>, accessed November 2016.

Table 728. Money Income of People—Selected Characteristics by Income Level: 2015

[125,091 represents 125,091,000. People age 15 and over as of March of following year. Based on the 2016 Current Population Survey, Annual Social and Economic Supplement (CPS ASEC), see text, this section and Section 1, and Appendix III. Median income is calculated using $2,500 income intervals. Medians falling in the upper open-ended interval are plugged with "$250,000." For definition of median, see Guide to Tabular Presentation. Please note that beginning with the 2015 CPS ASEC covering data for 2014, data are based on a redesigned questionnaire; users should exercise caution when comparing 2014 and subsequent data to data for previous years]

Characteristic	All persons (1,000)	People with income Total (1,000)	Under $5,000 or loss	$5,000 to $9,999	$10,000 to $14,999	$15,000 to $24,999	$25,000 to $34,999	$35,000 to $49,999	$50,000 to $74,999	$75,000 and over	Median income (current dollars)
MALE											
Total	125,091	112,322	7,215	6,443	8,005	16,490	14,499	16,643	18,669	24,356	37,138
15 to 24 years old	21,719	13,956	3,891	2,274	1,767	2,665	1,573	945	596	245	11,702
25 to 34 years old	21,845	20,332	868	907	1,053	2,987	3,377	4,059	3,827	3,254	37,225
35 to 44 years old	19,700	18,733	517	645	839	1,917	2,367	3,099	3,831	5,516	49,845
45 to 54 years old	20,839	19,788	603	686	863	2,013	2,338	3,017	3,938	6,332	51,067
55 to 64 years old	19,778	18,858	795	817	1,185	2,417	2,018	2,614	3,584	5,426	46,698
65 years old and over	21,209	20,656	542	1,115	2,299	4,490	2,826	2,909	2,893	3,583	31,372
Educational attainment of householder: [1]											
Total	103,372	98,367	3,324	4,170	6,238	13,824	12,927	15,699	18,074	24,112	41,886
Less than 9th grade	4,696	4,328	198	438	723	1,273	789	525	253	128	20,877
9th to 12th grade [2]	7,144	6,420	354	758	884	1,537	1,102	944	581	258	22,214
High school graduate [3]	30,780	28,760	1,061	1,452	2,433	5,244	5,019	5,287	4,967	3,299	32,307
Some college, no degree	17,011	16,218	691	593	982	2,348	2,424	3,047	3,269	2,868	39,823
Associate's degree	9,457	9,171	302	311	392	1,152	1,302	1,672	2,119	1,918	43,785
Bachelor's degree or more	34,283	33,470	717	617	823	2,270	2,293	4,224	6,885	15,639	70,437
Bachelor's degree	21,281	20,772	507	438	624	1,575	1,619	3,067	4,489	8,453	62,304
Master's degree	8,829	8,594	134	135	144	510	471	857	1,742	4,602	78,222
Professional degree	1,841	1,824	22	11	28	73	94	113	250	1,234	111,881
Doctoral degree	2,332	2,281	54	34	28	111	109	187	407	1,353	91,604
Housing tenure:											
Owner-occupied	84,513	76,783	4,968	3,732	4,701	10,041	8,780	10,995	13,680	19,886	42,044
Renter-occupied	39,082	34,292	2,110	2,601	3,189	6,177	5,538	5,475	4,839	4,364	30,250
Occupier paid no cash rent	1,495	1,247	137	111	114	273	183	174	149	105	24,046
Region:											
Northeast	22,265	20,128	1,325	1,153	1,407	2,708	2,211	2,750	3,579	4,995	40,943
Midwest	26,411	24,405	1,635	1,324	1,523	3,252	3,333	3,879	4,433	5,029	39,018
South	46,412	41,089	2,601	2,440	3,204	6,582	5,401	6,139	6,355	8,367	35,505
West	30,003	26,701	1,654	1,528	1,871	3,948	3,555	3,877	4,299	5,966	37,044
FEMALE											
Total	132,812	114,440	13,736	11,763	13,463	20,106	15,487	15,404	13,207	11,274	23,769
15 to 24 years old	21,169	13,434	4,210	2,319	2,016	2,325	1,319	761	346	140	10,342
25 to 34 years old	21,918	18,859	2,042	1,274	1,525	3,227	3,208	3,321	2,647	1,612	28,825
35 to 44 years old	20,305	17,921	2,110	1,225	1,294	2,578	2,372	2,987	2,811	2,544	31,621
45 to 54 years old	21,726	19,484	2,004	1,359	1,494	2,837	2,712	3,237	3,064	2,776	31,846
55 to 64 years old	21,357	19,476	2,121	1,719	1,962	3,010	2,709	2,704	2,621	2,627	27,877
65 years old and over	26,337	25,266	1,249	3,866	5,173	6,127	3,166	2,394	1,717	1,577	18,250
Educational attainment of householder: [1]											
Total	111,643	101,006	9,526	9,445	11,448	17,781	14,168	14,643	12,862	11,135	26,282
Less than 9th grade	4,796	3,569	456	906	903	848	274	117	43	23	11,863
9th to 12th grade [2]	6,817	5,508	727	1,250	1,179	1,329	592	278	97	53	12,768
High school graduate [3]	31,221	27,607	2,809	3,488	4,340	6,372	4,731	3,331	1,792	742	19,810
Some college, no degree	18,992	17,437	1,611	1,597	2,088	3,567	2,911	2,849	1,773	1,042	24,512
Associate's degree	12,200	11,409	973	782	1,078	2,079	1,891	2,049	1,618	939	28,664
Bachelor's degree or more	37,617	35,477	2,948	1,423	1,859	3,587	3,767	6,019	7,540	8,335	45,170
Bachelor's degree	23,497	22,045	2,116	970	1,341	2,470	2,704	4,042	4,385	4,016	40,115
Master's degree	11,129	10,558	687	373	438	927	851	1,676	2,567	3,037	51,494
Professional degree	1,337	1,278	77	39	44	93	93	135	233	566	65,012
Doctoral degree	1,654	1,595	68	39	37	97	121	168	355	714	68,887
Housing tenure:											
Owner-occupied	88,551	77,758	9,411	7,321	8,520	12,806	10,129	10,700	9,895	8,977	25,638
Renter-occupied	42,807	35,501	4,157	4,282	4,735	7,049	5,217	4,571	3,235	2,256	21,150
Occupier paid no cash rent	1,454	1,180	169	161	209	251	139	133	79	41	16,608
Region:											
Northeast	23,881	20,915	2,377	2,098	2,314	3,528	2,721	2,567	2,792	2,519	25,387
Midwest	27,815	25,051	2,915	2,430	2,928	4,556	3,607	3,612	2,816	2,187	24,216
South	50,211	42,363	5,070	4,503	5,278	7,545	5,730	5,809	4,729	3,701	22,652
West	30,905	26,110	3,375	2,733	2,944	4,478	3,429	3,417	2,869	2,868	23,579

[1] Population age 25 and over. [2] No diploma attained. [3] Includes high school equivalency.

Source: U.S. Census Bureau, *Income and Poverty in the United States: 2015*, Current Population Reports, P60-256(RV), September 2016; and "Current Population Survey Tables for Personal Income: Table PINC-01," <http://www.census.gov/topics/income-poverty/income/data/tables.html>, accessed November 2016.

Table 729. Average Earnings of Year-Round, Full-Time Workers by Educational Attainment: 2015

[In dollars. For people 18 years old and over, as of March of the following year. Based on the Current Population Survey, Annual Social and Economic Supplement (ASEC); see text, this section and Section 1, and Appendix III. See headnote, Table 728]

Sex and age	All workers	Less than 9th grade	High school 9th to 12th grade (no diploma)	High school graduate [1]	College Some college, no degree	Associate degree	Bachelor's degree or more
Male, total	**69,513**	**36,392**	**39,640**	**48,027**	**55,391**	**59,481**	**102,101**
18 to 24 years old	32,305	(B)	27,303	28,609	29,589	31,234	56,716
25 to 34 years old	55,997	29,601	34,790	44,639	47,220	51,745	73,971
35 to 44 years old	75,031	35,143	40,691	51,560	61,000	62,176	107,828
45 to 54 years old	77,879	34,765	40,533	51,843	64,232	64,202	116,124
55 to 64 years old	79,044	37,271	48,230	53,672	62,596	65,019	116,427
65 years old and over	80,904	72,601	50,731	51,292	58,937	65,109	107,153
Female, total	**51,634**	**22,710**	**26,009**	**34,682**	**40,315**	**45,999**	**70,320**
18 to 24 years old	27,713	(B)	21,208	23,195	23,662	24,657	41,027
25 to 34 years old	46,535	21,223	24,084	30,567	35,110	40,137	59,329
35 to 44 years old	54,901	21,537	24,740	34,778	39,766	47,260	73,495
45 to 54 years old	56,125	23,821	25,441	38,432	46,276	47,856	77,825
55 to 64 years old	55,601	21,767	29,165	37,696	47,356	52,383	78,079
65 years old and over	55,760	(B)	36,024	37,946	46,699	58,496	76,922

B Base figure too small to meet statistical standards for reliability of derived figure. [1] Includes general educational development equivalency.

Source: U.S. Census Bureau, *Income and Poverty in the United States: 2015*, Current Population Reports, P60-256(RV), September 2016; and "Current Population Survey Tables for Personal Income: Table PINC-04," <http://www.census.gov/topics/income-poverty/income/data/tables.html>, accessed November 2016.

Table 730. Per Capita Money Income in Current and Constant (2015) Dollars by Race and Hispanic Origin: 1990 to 2015

[In dollars. Constant dollars based on 2015 CPI-U-RS deflator. People as of March of following year. Based on the Current Population Survey, Annual Social and Economic Supplement (ASEC); see text, this section, Section 1, and Appendix III. For data collection changes over time, see "Changes in Methodology for the March Current Population Survey," <http://www.census.gov/topics/income-poverty/income/guidance/cps-methodology-changes.html>. See headnote, Table 722]

Year	Current dollars All races [1]	White [2]	Black [2]	Asian [2]	His-panic [3]	Constant (2015) dollars All races [1]	White [2]	Black [2]	Asian [2]	His-panic [3]
1990	14,387	15,265	9,017	(NA)	8,424	25,314	26,858	15,865	(NA)	14,822
2000 [4]	22,346	23,582	14,796	23,350	12,651	30,754	32,456	20,364	32,136	17,411
2005 [5]	25,036	26,496	16,874	27,331	14,483	30,385	32,157	20,479	33,171	17,577
2010 [6]	26,558	28,356	18,019	28,673	15,044	28,871	30,826	19,589	31,171	16,354
2011	27,554	29,401	18,988	29,235	15,479	29,038	30,985	20,011	30,810	16,313
2012	28,281	30,114	19,267	31,905	16,125	29,195	31,087	19,890	32,936	16,646
2013 [7]	30,027	31,759	20,658	34,843	17,354	30,553	32,316	21,020	35,454	17,658
2014 [7]	30,176	32,089	21,066	34,096	17,699	30,211	32,126	21,090	34,135	17,719
2015 [7]	31,653	33,564	22,452	36,280	19,457	31,653	33,564	22,452	36,280	19,457

NA Not available. [1] Includes other races, not shown separately. [2] As of 2002, data refer to people reporting specified race alone ("Asian alone" replaced "Asian and Pacific Islander"). [3] People of Hispanic origin may be of any race. [4] Implementation of Census 2000-based population controls, and of a 28,000 household sample expansion. [5] Data have been revised to reflect a correction to the weights in the 2005 ASEC. [6] Implementation of Census 2010-based population controls. [7] Beginning 2013, data based on redesigned income questions.

Source: U.S. Census Bureau, *Income and Poverty in the United States: 2015*, Current Population Reports, P60-256(RV), September 2016; and "Historical Income Tables: People, Table P-1," <http://www.census.gov/topics/income-poverty/income/data/tables.html>, accessed November 2016.

Table 731. Money Income of People—Number by Income Level and by Sex, Race, and Hispanic Origin: 2015

[In thousands (125,091 represents 125,091,000). People age 15 years and over as of March of the following year. Based on Current Population Survey, Annual Social and Economic Supplement (ASEC); see text, this section, Section 1, and Appendix III. See headnote, Table 719]

Income interval	Male All races [1]	White alone	Black alone	Asian alone	His-panic [2]	Female All races [1]	White alone	Black alone	Asian alone	His-panic [2]
Total	**125,091**	**98,949**	**14,885**	**7,109**	**20,740**	**132,812**	**102,744**	**17,635**	**8,000**	**20,766**
Under $10,000 [3]	26,427	18,559	4,914	1,653	5,501	43,872	32,709	6,198	3,163	9,600
$10,000 to $19,999	16,264	12,437	2,401	751	3,354	23,807	18,538	3,397	1,098	3,728
$20,000 to $29,999	15,447	12,364	1,797	761	3,501	17,704	13,880	2,429	798	2,767
$30,000 to $39,999	13,214	10,707	1,485	567	2,689	13,518	10,611	1,864	631	1,683
$40,000 to $49,999	10,712	8,685	1,203	518	1,728	9,431	7,313	1,324	516	1,007
$50,000 to $59,999	8,835	7,366	785	445	1,184	6,682	5,371	796	345	613
$60,000 to $74,999	9,834	8,252	887	499	1,012	6,525	5,263	692	407	543
$75,000 to $84,999	5,004	4,217	353	331	415	2,971	2,463	256	198	221
$85,000 to $99,999	4,482	3,722	315	360	356	2,419	1,914	209	232	184
$100,000 to $149,999	8,536	7,214	470	716	551	3,906	3,110	333	381	267
$150,000 to $199,999	3,188	2,707	148	267	223	1,064	851	55	126	82
$200,000 to $249,999	1,237	1,060	34	111	85	446	358	55	57	24
$250,000 and above	1,909	1,659	93	134	140	468	365	50	43	47

[1] Includes races not shown separately. [2] Persons of Hispanic origin may be of any race. [3] Includes persons without income.

Source: U.S. Census Bureau, *Income and Poverty in the United States: 2015*, Current Population Reports, P60-256(RV), September 2016; and "Current Population Survey Tables for Personal Income: Table PINC-11," <http://www.census.gov/topics/income-poverty/income/data/tables.html>, accessed November 2016.

Table 732. Household, Family, and Per Capita Income, and Individuals and Families Below Poverty Level, by City: 2015

[The American Community Survey universe includes the household population and the population living in institutions, college dormitories, and other group quarters. Based on a sample and subject to sampling variability; see text, Section 1 and Appendix III. For definition of median, see Guide to Tabular Presentation. CDP is Census designated place]

City	Median household income (dol.)	Median family income (dol.)	Per capita income (dol.)	Number below poverty level [1] Individuals [1]	Families	Percent below poverty level Individuals [1]	Families
Albuquerque, NM	47,096	60,670	26,897	110,402	18,197	20.0	14.2
Anaheim, CA	63,104	66,777	24,612	52,668	8,581	15.2	11.8
Anchorage, AK	78,662	94,419	39,389	24,405	4,431	8.4	6.6
Arlington, TX	53,487	61,153	25,417	65,067	11,928	17.0	12.9
Atlanta, GA	50,210	64,825	39,660	97,650	14,993	22.5	19.2
Aurora, CO	58,445	67,142	27,345	44,264	7,541	12.5	9.1
Austin, TX	62,250	76,629	36,949	131,796	18,501	14.5	9.8
Bakersfield, CA	61,039	66,992	25,810	64,117	12,232	17.3	14.3
Baltimore, MD	44,165	53,340	27,035	136,746	22,486	22.9	18.2
Boston, MA	58,263	65,083	37,842	128,385	21,225	20.5	17.0
Charlotte, NC	53,919	69,001	32,953	129,143	22,270	15.8	11.8
Chicago, IL	50,702	59,134	31,641	556,134	93,551	20.9	16.5
Cincinnati, OH	35,001	45,594	26,684	78,894	13,012	27.4	21.1
Cleveland, OH	28,831	33,302	17,739	130,811	25,194	34.7	30.6
Colorado Springs, CO	56,079	71,934	29,959	55,114	10,295	12.3	8.9
Columbus, OH	47,401	56,511	25,755	171,009	28,190	20.7	15.6
Corpus Christi, TX	51,255	61,675	25,778	59,155	10,729	18.7	13.7
Dallas, TX	45,918	49,088	30,569	288,715	52,919	22.5	18.6
Denver, CO	58,003	72,455	36,792	104,385	15,829	15.6	11.0
Detroit, MI	25,980	30,209	15,611	265,097	50,109	39.8	35.5
El Paso, TX	45,069	50,447	20,376	123,877	23,812	18.4	14.8
Fort Worth, TX	55,888	64,786	26,463	133,496	24,226	16.3	12.7
Fresno, CA	43,494	49,835	20,116	144,807	26,287	28.4	23.4
Greensboro, NC	44,934	53,250	27,047	44,445	8,324	16.2	12.6
Henderson, NV	64,035	77,289	34,436	24,103	4,985	8.5	6.9
Honolulu, Urban CDP, HI	64,658	79,393	32,697	41,242	5,278	12.1	7.2
Houston, TX	48,064	52,024	29,310	480,534	97,264	21.2	18.5
Indianapolis, IN	41,278	55,177	24,696	171,019	26,284	20.6	15.2
Jacksonville, FL	48,239	59,678	26,077	139,428	25,292	16.4	12.5
Kansas City, MO	50,259	65,356	29,261	83,641	13,040	17.9	12.4
Las Vegas, NV	49,676	60,270	26,534	100,069	16,543	16.3	12.3
Lexington-Fayette, KY	51,948	67,855	31,120	58,992	10,400	19.5	13.6
Long Beach, CA	54,971	62,042	28,205	89,600	13,592	19.2	13.5
Los Angeles, CA	52,024	58,824	30,136	800,902	128,016	20.5	15.8
Louisville/Jefferson County, KY [2]	48,100	62,424	27,618	100,849	16,907	16.7	11.5
Memphis, TN	36,908	42,879	22,702	167,723	30,488	26.2	20.8
Mesa, AZ	49,177	61,260	25,711	80,447	14,249	17.2	12.7
Miami, FL	29,989	35,604	23,328	115,076	19,403	26.6	21.7
Milwaukee, WI	37,495	43,146	21,089	156,573	28,683	26.8	23.1
Minneapolis, MN	54,571	77,427	34,763	77,057	9,896	19.5	12.8
Nashville-Davidson, TN [2]	51,393	61,167	30,138	108,982	19,419	17.2	13.1
New Orleans, LA	39,077	55,450	28,669	88,852	13,037	23.4	17.5
New York, NY	55,752	61,413	34,396	1,680,857	314,027	20.0	16.8
Oakland, CA	58,807	62,838	34,587	81,919	14,168	19.8	15.6
Oklahoma City, OK	50,739	62,614	27,727	102,933	18,572	16.6	12.5
Omaha, NE	51,407	68,470	29,432	72,864	12,957	16.8	12.7
Philadelphia, PA	41,233	49,309	23,961	393,203	66,858	25.8	20.9
Phoenix, AZ	48,452	55,175	25,222	344,455	58,315	22.3	17.3
Pittsburgh, PA	41,293	58,677	29,876	64,769	8,568	23.0	14.7
Plano, TX	83,769	101,953	42,522	24,459	5,010	8.7	6.7
Portland, OR	60,892	78,527	34,345	97,777	11,584	15.8	9.0
Raleigh, NC	56,910	71,192	32,941	67,665	11,469	15.6	11.3
Riverside, CA	61,279	69,153	23,887	49,682	7,002	16.0	10.5
Sacramento, CA	52,151	60,802	26,240	98,204	17,513	20.3	16.4
San Antonio, TX	48,869	55,713	23,748	257,770	45,034	17.8	14.1
San Diego, CA	67,871	78,520	34,733	212,994	31,008	15.6	10.5
San Francisco, CA	92,094	105,924	57,917	105,206	11,807	12.3	7.2
San Jose, CA	91,451	101,150	38,466	96,229	15,205	9.5	6.4
San Juan, Puerto Rico	18,887	25,712	17,299	154,837	32,295	45.8	41.2
Santa Ana, CA	54,392	51,954	16,391	69,778	10,998	21.2	18.3
Seattle, WA	80,349	113,273	50,290	79,728	6,832	12.0	4.9
St. Louis, MO	38,397	49,992	26,606	76,506	13,394	24.9	21.0
St. Paul, MN	50,267	63,173	27,225	62,061	9,281	21.2	15.3
Stockton, CA	46,795	51,501	20,542	65,239	12,482	21.8	18.6
Tampa, FL	44,432	54,889	30,224	74,848	13,685	20.9	16.9
Tucson, AZ	38,155	46,848	20,595	127,626	20,814	25.2	18.5
Tulsa, OK	43,322	53,831	28,756	83,136	16,132	21.0	16.6
Virginia Beach, VA	67,281	77,264	32,056	34,702	6,522	7.9	5.8
Washington, DC	75,628	94,846	50,187	110,500	17,494	17.3	14.0
Wichita, KS	46,894	60,995	25,462	65,862	10,584	17.1	11.9

[1] Poverty status was determined for all people except institutionalized people, people in military group quarters, people in college dormitories, and unrelated individuals under 15 years old. [2] Represents metropolitan government (balance) of locality.

Source: U.S. Census Bureau, 2015 American Community Survey, 2015 ACS 1-year estimates: DP03, B01003, B17001, and B17019, <http://factfinder.census.gov>, accessed December 2016. See also <http://www.census.gov/programs-surveys/acs/>.

Table 733. Individuals and Families Below Poverty Level—Number and Rate by State: 2005 and 2015

[In thousands (38,231 represents 38,231,000), except as indicated. Represents number and percent below poverty in the past 12 months. Poverty status was determined for all people except institutionalized people, people in military group quarters, people in college dormitories, and unrelated individuals under 15 years old. These groups were excluded from the numerator and denominator when calculating poverty rates. Based on a sample and subject to sampling variability; see Appendix III]

State	Number below poverty (1,000)				Percent below poverty			
	Individuals		Families		Individuals		Families	
	2005	2015	2005	2015	2005	2015	2005	2015
United States	**38,231**	**46,153**	**7,605**	**8,233**	**13.3**	**14.7**	**10.2**	**10.6**
Alabama	754	876	168	167	17.0	18.5	13.7	13.7
Alaska	71	75	13	12	11.2	10.3	8.3	7.0
Arizona	824	1,159	159	199	14.2	17.4	10.9	12.5
Arkansas	462	551	100	105	17.2	19.1	13.4	13.7
California	4,673	5,892	850	999	13.3	15.3	10.3	11.3
Colorado	504	614	97	101	11.1	11.5	8.3	7.6
Connecticut	281	367	55	65	8.3	10.5	6.2	7.4
Delaware	85	114	17	20	10.4	12.4	7.6	8.7
District of Columbia	98	111	18	17	19.0	17.3	16.7	14.0
Florida	2,214	3,117	445	541	12.8	15.7	9.7	11.3
Georgia	1,266	1,695	264	322	14.4	17.0	11.6	13.0
Hawaii	121	148	23	21	9.8	10.6	7.7	6.9
Idaho	192	246	38	44	13.9	15.1	10.3	10.9
Illinois	1,484	1,703	287	304	12.0	13.6	9.2	9.8
Indiana	740	933	148	166	12.2	14.5	9.0	10.2
Iowa	310	367	59	61	10.9	12.2	7.5	7.7
Kansas	310	369	60	61	11.7	13.0	8.4	8.4
Kentucky	680	794	150	158	16.8	18.5	13.4	14.0
Louisiana	864	890	183	163	19.8	19.6	16.1	14.7
Maine	161	173	32	31	12.6	13.4	9.0	8.9
Maryland	448	571	84	98	8.2	9.7	6.0	6.7
Massachusetts	637	752	119	128	10.3	11.5	7.6	7.9
Michigan	1,300	1,530	257	276	13.2	15.8	9.9	11.1
Minnesota	457	546	81	87	9.2	10.2	6.1	6.3
Mississippi	600	637	127	126	21.3	22.0	16.8	17.0
Missouri	748	875	152	155	13.3	14.8	10.0	10.2
Montana	130	147	25	23	14.4	14.6	10.5	9.3
Nebraska	186	231	37	40	10.9	12.6	8.2	8.5
Nevada	262	418	52	72	11.1	14.7	8.9	10.9
New Hampshire	95	106	18	17	7.5	8.2	5.3	5.0
New Jersey	739	946	147	178	8.7	10.8	6.8	8.1
New Mexico	348	418	69	72	18.5	20.4	14.3	14.8
New York	2,566	2,970	513	529	13.8	15.4	11.1	11.6
North Carolina	1,263	1,608	269	295	15.1	16.4	11.7	11.8
North Dakota	68	80	12	13	11.2	11.0	7.5	6.9
Ohio	1,451	1,674	297	314	13.0	14.8	9.9	10.7
Oklahoma	565	611	122	114	16.5	16.1	13.1	11.7
Oregon	499	607	91	97	14.1	15.4	10.1	9.9
Pennsylvania	1,420	1,630	274	290	11.9	13.2	8.6	9.1
Rhode Island	126	141	25	25	12.3	13.9	9.5	10.1
South Carolina	639	791	138	148	15.6	16.6	12.5	12.1
South Dakota	101	114	20	18	13.6	13.7	9.7	8.3
Tennessee	900	1,078	200	207	15.5	16.7	12.5	12.3
Texas	3,905	4,256	796	798	17.6	15.9	14.2	12.2
Utah	246	332	47	57	10.2	11.3	8.0	8.3
Vermont	69	61	12	9	11.5	10.2	7.7	5.8
Virginia	729	909	143	160	10.0	11.2	7.4	7.8
Washington	729	858	133	139	11.9	12.2	8.4	7.9
West Virginia	317	322	70	64	18.0	17.9	14.0	13.5
Wisconsin	546	678	100	116	10.2	12.1	7.0	7.9
Wyoming	47	63	8	10	9.5	11.1	6.3	6.7

Source: U.S. Census Bureau, 2015 American Community Survey: B17001, "Poverty Status in the Past 12 Months by Sex By Age"; and B17019, "Poverty Status in the Past 12 Months of Families by Household Type by Tenure"; <http://factfinder.census.gov>, accessed December 2016. See also <http://www.census.gov/programs-surveys/acs/>.

Table 734. Poverty Thresholds by Size of Family Unit: 1980 to 2015

[In dollars per year. The official poverty definition uses money income before taxes and does not include capital gains and noncash benefits (such as public housing and food stamps). For information on the official poverty thresholds, see text, this section. For more on poverty, see <http://www.census.gov/topics/income-poverty/poverty.html>. See also headnote, Table 735]

Size of family unit	1980	1990	1995	2000 [2]	2005	2010 [3]	2013 [4]	2014 [4]	2015 [4]
One person (unrelated individual) [1]......	4,190	6,652	7,763	8,791	9,973	11,137	11,880	12,071	12,082
Under 65 years old......................	4,290	6,800	7,929	8,959	10,160	11,344	12,119	12,316	12,331
65 years old and over...................	3,949	6,268	7,309	8,259	9,367	10,458	11,173	11,354	11,367
Two persons...............................	5,363	8,509	9,933	11,235	12,755	14,216	15,139	15,379	15,391
Householder under 65 years old.........	5,537	8,794	10,259	11,589	13,145	14,676	15,678	15,934	15,952
Householder 65 years old and over.....	4,983	7,905	9,219	10,418	11,815	13,194	14,097	14,326	14,342
Three persons............................	6,565	10,419	12,158	13,740	15,577	17,373	18,554	18,850	18,871
Four persons..............................	8,414	13,359	15,569	17,604	19,971	22,315	23,844	24,230	24,257
Five persons..............................	9,966	15,792	18,408	20,815	23,613	26,442	28,234	28,695	28,741
Six persons...............................	11,269	17,839	20,804	23,533	26,683	29,904	31,887	32,473	32,542
Seven persons............................	12,761	20,241	23,552	26,750	30,249	34,019	36,239	36,927	36,998
Eight persons.............................	14,199	22,582	26,237	29,701	33,610	37,953	39,930	40,968	41,029
Nine or more persons.....................	16,896	26,848	31,280	35,150	40,288	45,224	48,343	49,021	49,177

[1] A person living alone or with non-relatives. [2] Implementation of Census 2000-based population controls and sample expanded by 28,000 households. [3] Implementation of Census 2010-based population controls. [4] Based on redesigned questions on income; see source for more information.

Source: U.S. Census Bureau, *Income and Poverty in the United States: 2015,* Current Population Reports, P60-256(RV), September 2016; and "Poverty Thresholds," <http://www.census.gov/topics/income-poverty/poverty/data/tables.html>, accessed November 2016.

Table 735. People Below Poverty Level by Race and Hispanic Origin, and Below 125 Percent of Poverty Level: 1990 to 2015

[33,585 represents 33,585,000. People as of March of the following year. Based on Current Population Survey, Annual Social and Economic Supplement (ASEC); see text, this section, Section 1, and Appendix III. Beginning with 2003 CPS ASEC covering data for 2002, refers to persons of specified race only and who did not report any other race category; "Asian" replaced "Asian Pacific Islander." For information on measuring poverty, see <http://www.census.gov/topics/income-poverty/poverty/guidance/poverty-measures.html>. Please note that beginning with the 2015 CPS ASEC covering data for 2014, data are based on a redesigned questionnaire, and data for 2013 not previously released was issued based on new income questions given to a portion of the sample in the 2014 CPS ASEC. See source for more information. Use caution when comparing 2013 and subsequent data to data for previous years]

Year	Number of persons below poverty (1,000)					Percent of persons below poverty					Below 125 percent of poverty level [1]	
	All races [2]	White	Black	Asian	His-panic [3]	All races [2]	White	Black	Asian	His-panic [3]	Number (1,000)	Percent of total pop-ulation
1990.........	33,585	22,326	9,837	858	6,006	13.5	10.7	31.9	12.2	28.1	44,837	18.0
1991.........	35,708	23,747	10,242	996	6,339	14.2	11.3	32.7	13.8	28.7	47,527	18.9
1992 [4].......	38,014	25,259	10,827	985	7,592	14.8	11.9	33.4	12.7	29.6	50,592	19.7
1993 [5].......	39,265	26,226	10,877	1,134	8,126	15.1	12.2	33.1	15.3	30.6	51,801	20.0
1994.........	38,059	25,379	10,196	974	8,416	14.5	11.7	30.6	14.6	30.7	50,401	19.3
1995.........	36,425	24,423	9,872	1,411	8,574	13.8	11.2	29.3	14.6	30.3	48,761	18.5
1996.........	36,529	24,650	9,694	1,454	8,697	13.7	11.2	28.4	14.5	29.4	49,310	18.5
1997.........	35,574	24,396	9,116	1,468	8,308	13.3	11.0	26.5	14.0	27.1	47,853	17.8
1998.........	34,476	23,454	9,091	1,360	8,070	12.7	10.5	26.1	12.5	25.6	46,036	17.0
1999 [6].......	32,791	22,169	8,441	1,285	7,876	11.9	9.8	23.6	10.7	22.7	45,030	16.3
2000 [7].......	31,581	21,645	7,982	1,258	7,747	11.3	9.5	22.5	9.9	21.5	43,612	15.6
2001.........	32,907	22,739	8,136	1,275	7,997	11.7	9.9	22.7	10.2	21.4	45,320	16.1
2002.........	34,570	23,466	8,602	1,161	8,555	12.1	10.2	24.1	10.1	21.8	47,084	16.5
2003.........	35,861	24,272	8,781	1,401	9,051	12.5	10.5	24.4	11.8	22.5	48,687	16.9
2004 [8].......	37,040	25,327	9,014	1,201	9,122	12.7	10.8	24.7	9.8	21.9	49,693	17.1
2005.........	36,950	24,872	9,168	1,402	9,368	12.6	10.6	24.9	11.1	21.8	49,327	16.8
2006.........	36,460	24,416	9,048	1,353	9,243	12.3	10.3	24.3	10.3	20.6	49,688	16.8
2007.........	37,276	25,120	9,237	1,349	9,890	12.5	10.5	24.5	10.2	21.5	50,876	17.0
2008.........	39,829	26,990	9,379	1,576	10,987	13.2	11.2	24.7	11.8	23.2	53,805	17.9
2009.........	43,569	29,830	9,944	1,746	12,350	14.3	12.3	25.8	12.5	25.3	56,840	18.7
2010 [9].......	46,343	31,083	10,746	1,899	13,522	15.1	13.0	27.4	12.2	26.5	60,669	19.8
2011.........	46,247	30,849	10,929	1,973	13,244	15.0	12.8	27.6	12.3	25.3	60,949	19.8
2012.........	46,496	30,816	10,911	1,921	13,616	15.0	12.7	27.2	11.7	25.6	61,202	19.7
2013 [10].......	46,269	31,287	10,186	2,255	13,356	14.8	12.9	25.2	13.1	24.7	60,396	19.3
2014 [10]......	46,657	31,089	10,755	2,137	13,104	14.8	12.7	26.2	12.0	23.6	61,339	19.4
2015 [10].......	43,123	28,566	10,020	2,078	12,133	13.5	11.6	24.1	11.4	21.4	56,912	17.9

[1] People in poverty, plus people with income above poverty but less than 1.25 times their poverty threshold. [2] Includes other races, not shown separately. [3] People of Hispanic origin may be of any race. [4] Implementation of 1990 Census population controls. [5] The March 1994 income supplement was revised to allow for the coding of different income amounts on selected questionnaire items. Limits either increased or decreased in the following categories: earnings increased to $999,999; Social Security increased to $49,999; Supplemental Security Income and public assistance increased to $24,999; veterans' benefits increased to $99,999; child support and alimony decreased to $49,999. [6] Implementation of Census-2000-based population controls. [7] Implementation of sample expansion by 28,000 households. [8] Data have been revised to reflect a correction to the weights in the 2005 ASEC. [9] Implementation of Census 2010-based population controls. [10] Data based on redesigned income questions. See source for more information.

Source: U.S. Census Bureau, *Income and Poverty in the United States: 2015,* Current Population Reports, P60-256(RV), September 2016; and "Historical Poverty Tables: People and Families, Tables 2 and 6," <http://www.census.gov/topics/income-poverty/poverty/data/tables.html>, accessed November 2016.

Table 736. Children Below Poverty Level by Race and Hispanic Origin: 1990 to 2015

[12,715 represents 12,715,000. Persons as of March of the following year. Covers only related children under age 18, in families. Based on Current Population Survey, Annual Social and Economic Supplement (CPS ASEC); see text, this section, Section 1, and Appendix III. See headnote, Table 735]

Year	Number of children below poverty level (1,000)					Percent of children below poverty level				
	All races [1]	White	Black	Asian	His-panic [2]	All races [1]	White	Black	Asian	His-panic [2]
1990............	12,715	7,696	4,412	356	2,750	19.9	15.1	44.2	17.0	37.7
1991............	13,658	8,316	4,637	348	2,977	21.1	16.1	45.6	17.1	39.8
1992 [3].........	14,521	8,752	5,015	352	3,440	21.6	16.5	46.3	16.0	39.0
1993 [4].........	14,961	9,123	5,030	358	3,666	22.0	17.0	45.9	17.6	39.9
1994............	14,610	8,826	4,787	308	3,956	21.2	16.3	43.3	17.9	41.1
1995............	13,999	8,474	4,644	532	3,938	20.2	15.5	41.5	18.6	39.3
1996............	13,764	8,488	4,411	553	4,090	19.8	15.5	39.5	19.1	39.9
1997............	13,422	8,441	4,116	608	3,865	19.2	15.4	36.8	19.9	36.4
1998............	12,845	7,935	4,073	542	3,670	18.3	14.4	36.4	17.5	33.6
1999 [5].........	11,678	7,194	3,698	367	3,561	16.6	13.1	32.8	11.5	29.9
2000 [6].........	11,005	6,834	3,495	407	3,342	15.6	12.4	30.9	12.5	27.6
2001............	11,175	7,086	3,423	353	3,433	15.8	12.8	30.0	11.1	27.4
2002............	11,646	7,203	3,570	302	3,653	16.3	13.1	32.1	11.4	28.2
2003............	12,340	7,624	3,750	331	3,982	17.2	13.9	33.6	12.1	29.5
2004 [7].........	12,473	7,876	3,702	265	3,985	17.3	14.3	33.4	9.4	28.6
2005............	12,335	7,652	3,743	312	3,977	17.1	13.9	34.2	11.0	27.7
2006............	12,299	7,522	3,690	351	3,959	16.9	13.6	33.0	12.0	26.6
2007............	12,802	8,002	3,838	345	4,348	17.6	14.4	34.3	11.8	28.3
2008............	13,507	8,441	3,781	430	4,888	18.5	15.3	34.4	14.2	30.3
2009............	14,774	9,440	3,919	444	5,419	20.1	17.0	35.3	13.6	32.5
2010 [8].........	15,598	9,590	4,271	477	5,815	21.5	17.9	39.0	14.0	34.3
2011............	15,539	9,643	4,247	466	5,820	21.4	18.1	38.6	13.0	33.7
2012............	15,437	9,547	4,097	470	5,773	21.3	17.9	37.5	13.3	33.3
2013 [9].........	15,116	9,702	3,678	538	5,638	20.9	18.4	33.8	14.4	32.2
2014 [9].........	14,987	9,172	4,036	492	5,522	20.7	17.4	37.1	13.4	31.3
2015 [9].........	13,962	8,838	3,571	420	5,139	19.2	16.7	32.7	11.4	28.6

[1] Includes other races, not shown separately. [2] People of Hispanic origin may be of any race. [3] Implementation of 1990 Census population controls. [4] See Table 735, footnote 5. [5] Implementation of Census 2000-based population controls. [6] Sample expanded to 28,000 households. [7] Data have been revised to reflect a correction to the weights in the 2005 ASEC. [8] Implementation of Census 2010-based population controls. [9] Data based on redesigned income questions. See source for more information.

Source: U.S. Census Bureau, *Income and Poverty in the United States: 2015,* Current Population Reports, P60-256(RV), September 2016; and "Historical Poverty Tables: People and Families, Table 3," <http://www.census.gov/topics/income-poverty/poverty/data/tables.html>, accessed November 2016.

Table 737. People Below Poverty Level by Selected Characteristics: 2015

[43,123 represents 43,123,000. People as of March of the following year. Based on 2016 Current Population Survey, Annual Social and Economic and Supplement (CPS ASEC). Data by education are for people age 25 and older. Data by nativity or citizenship are for people age 15 and older. See headnote, Table 735]

Sex, age, education, region, nativity	Number below poverty level (1,000)					Percent below poverty level				
	All races [1]	White alone	Black alone	Asian alone	His-panic [2]	All races [1]	White alone	Black alone	Asian alone	His-panic [2]
Total............	43,123	28,566	10,020	2,078	12,133	13.5	11.6	24.1	11.4	21.4
Male.............	19,037	12,580	4,388	967	5,464	12.2	10.4	22.5	11.1	19.2
Female...........	24,086	15,985	5,633	1,111	6,669	14.8	12.9	25.5	11.6	23.6
Under 18 years old..........	14,509	9,204	3,651	466	5,269	19.7	17.2	32.9	12.3	28.9
18 to 24 years old..........	5,658	3,637	1,270	394	1,362	19.0	16.6	27.9	23.0	20.9
25 to 34 years old..........	5,666	3,683	1,337	402	1,619	12.9	11.3	21.8	12.6	18.1
35 to 44 years old..........	4,801	3,294	1,065	223	1,538	12.0	10.9	20.1	7.6	18.8
45 to 54 years old..........	4,045	2,780	861	223	963	9.5	8.3	16.0	9.2	14.6
55 to 59 years old..........	2,162	1,492	541	53	352	9.9	8.5	20.6	4.7	14.1
60 to 64 years old..........	2,081	1,440	493	65	355	10.8	9.1	22.6	7.0	18.4
65 years old and over........	4,201	3,037	801	252	676	8.8	7.5	18.4	11.8	17.5
65 to 74 years old........	2,233	1,583	465	119	390	8.0	6.8	17.3	8.9	16.4
75 years old and over.......	1,968	1,454	336	133	286	10.0	8.6	20.2	16.7	19.2
No high school diploma.......	9,768	6,661	2,216	403	3,926	23.6	21.4	35.8	19.8	27.2
High school, no college........	9,819	6,401	2,610	333	2,065	13.8	11.5	25.2	12.9	17.1
Some college, less than 4-year degree.......	7,662	5,232	1,647	385	1,216	10.9	9.5	17.1	13.0	12.9
College, 4-year degree or higher.......	3,666	2,510	471	602	430	4.9	4.2	7.5	8.0	7.7
Northeast....................	6,891	4,497	1,596	465	1,862	12.4	10.4	21.9	12.3	24.3
Midwest.....................	7,849	5,328	1,872	264	1,140	11.7	9.5	26.7	12.4	20.6
South.......................	18,305	11,165	5,840	575	4,524	15.3	12.7	24.8	13.6	21.4
West.......................	10,079	7,576	713	774	4,607	13.3	13.0	18.6	9.6	20.5
Native......................	35,973	23,871	9,201	681	7,962	13.1	10.9	24.7	9.7	21.6
Foreign born................	7,150	4,694	820	1,397	4,171	16.6	18.1	18.6	12.4	20.9
Naturalized citizen............	2,255	1,346	318	542	983	11.2	12.2	13.5	8.8	14.2
Not a citizen.................	4,895	3,348	501	856	3,188	21.3	22.4	24.5	16.8	24.5

[1] Includes other races, not shown separately. [2] Persons of Hispanic origin may be of any race.

Source: U.S. Census Bureau, *Income and Poverty in the United States: 2015,* Current Population Reports, P60-256(RV), September 2016; and "Current Population Survey Detailed Tables for Poverty: Tables POV01, POV29, and POV41," <http://www.census.gov/topics/income-poverty/poverty/data/tables.html>, accessed November 2016.

Table 738. Work Experience of People During Year by Poverty Status by Sex and Age: 2015

[111,079 represents 111,079,000. Covers persons age 16 and over. Based on Current Population Survey, 2016 Annual Social and Economic Supplement (ASEC); see text, this section, Section 1, and Appendix III. Beginning with the 2015 ASEC covering data for 2014, data are based on a redesigned questionnaire. Use caution when comparing 2014 and subsequent data to data for previous years]

Sex and age	Worked full-time year-round			Did not work full-time year-round			Did not work		
		Below poverty level			Below poverty level			Below poverty level	
	Number (1,000)	Number (1,000)	Percent	Number (1,000)	Number (1,000)	Percent	Number (1,000)	Number (1,000)	Percent
BOTH SEXES									
Total.................	**111,079**	**2,576**	**2.3**	**52,090**	**7,220**	**13.9**	**90,511**	**20,328**	**22.5**
16 to 17 years old........	113	–	0.2	1,874	163	8.7	6,887	1,346	19.5
18 to 64 years old........	105,695	2,537	2.4	44,534	6,920	15.5	47,031	14,957	31.8
18 to 24 years old......	7,244	367	5.1	12,228	2,125	17.4	10,319	3,166	30.7
25 to 34 years old......	25,833	739	2.9	9,928	1,793	18.1	8,002	3,134	39.2
35 to 54 years old......	52,163	1,208	2.3	14,861	2,281	15.4	15,547	5,356	34.4
55 to 64 years old......	20,456	222	1.1	7,518	721	9.6	13,162	3,301	25.1
65 years old and over....	5,271	39	0.7	5,682	137	2.4	36,594	4,025	11.0
MALE									
Total.................	**63,869**	**1,438**	**2.3**	**22,401**	**2,936**	**13.1**	**36,656**	**8,049**	**22.0**
16 to 17 years old........	72	–	(B)	917	75	8.2	3,471	638	18.4
18 to 64 years old........	60,588	1,411	2.3	18,655	2,799	15.0	18,015	6,013	33.4
18 to 24 years old......	4,107	173	4.2	5,907	868	14.7	5,081	1,433	28.2
25 to 34 years old......	14,960	397	2.7	4,211	680	16.2	2,674	1,086	40.6
35 to 54 years old......	30,123	730	2.4	5,446	930	17.1	4,970	2,035	41.0
55 to 64 years old......	11,398	111	1.0	3,092	322	10.4	5,289	1,458	27.6
65 years old and over....	3,210	27	0.8	2,829	61	2.2	15,170	1,399	9.2
FEMALE									
Total.................	**47,210**	**1,138**	**2.4**	**29,689**	**4,284**	**14.4**	**53,855**	**12,279**	**22.8**
16 to 17 years old........	41	–	(B)	958	88	9.1	3,416	708	20.7
18 to 64 years old........	45,108	1,125	2.5	25,879	4,121	15.9	29,016	8,944	30.8
18 to 24 years old......	3,137	193	6.2	6,321	1,258	19.9	5,238	1,733	33.1
25 to 34 years old......	10,873	343	3.2	5,717	1,113	19.5	5,328	2,048	38.4
35 to 54 years old......	22,040	478	2.2	9,415	1,352	14.4	10,577	3,320	31.4
55 to 64 years old......	9,058	111	1.2	4,426	399	9.0	7,873	1,844	23.4
65 years old and over....	2,061	12	0.6	2,852	76	2.7	21,424	2,626	12.3

– Represents zero. B Base figure too small to meet statistical standards for reliability of a derived figure.

Source: U.S. Census Bureau, *Income and Poverty in the United States: 2015*, Current Population Reports, P60-256(RV), September 2016; and "Current Population Survey Detailed Tables for Poverty: Table POV22," <http://www.census.gov/topics/income-poverty/poverty/data/tables.html>, accessed November 2016.

Table 739. Families Below Poverty Level by Race and Hispanic Origin, and Below 125 Percent of Poverty Level: 1990 to 2015

[7,098 represents 7,098,000. Families as of March of the following year. Based on Current Population Survey, Annual Social and Economic Supplement (ASEC); see text, this section and Section 1, and Appendix III. For data collection changes over time, see "Changes in Methodology for the March Current Population Survey" at <http://www.census.gov/topics/income-poverty/income/guidance/cps-methodology-changes.html>. Beginning with the 2003 CPS covering data for 2002, respondents were allowed to choose more than one race. Two basic ways of defining a race group are possible: a group such as Asian may be defined as those who reported Asian and no other race (the race-alone concept), or as those who reported Asian regardless of whether they also reported another race (the race-alone-or-in-combination concept). For 2001 data and earlier, the CPS allowed respondents to report only one race group. See also comments on race in the text for Section 1, Population. See comments on changes to the CPS ASEC in headnote, Table 735]

Year	Number of families below poverty (1,000)					Percent of families below poverty					Below 125 percent of poverty level	
	All races [1]	White [2]	Black [2]	Asian and Pacific Islander [2]	His-panic [3]	All races [1]	White [2]	Black [2]	Asian and Pacific Islander [2]	His-panic [3]	Number (1,000)	Percent
1990........	7,098	4,622	2,193	169	1,244	10.7	8.1	29.3	11.0	25.0	9,564	14.4
1995........	7,532	4,994	2,127	264	1,695	10.8	8.5	26.4	12.4	27.0	10,223	14.7
2000 [4]......	6,400	4,333	1,686	233	1,540	8.7	7.1	19.3	7.8	19.2	9,032	12.2
2005........	7,657	5,068	1,997	289	1,948	9.9	8.0	22.1	9.0	19.7	10,442	13.5
2006........	7,668	5,118	2,007	260	1,922	9.8	8.0	21.6	7.8	18.9	10,531	13.4
2007........	7,623	5,046	2,045	261	2,045	9.8	7.9	22.1	7.9	19.7	10,551	13.5
2008........	8,147	5,414	2,055	341	2,239	10.3	8.4	22.0	9.8	21.3	11,164	14.2
2009........	8,792	5,994	2,125	337	2,369	11.1	9.3	22.7	9.4	22.7	11,620	14.7
2010 [5]......	9,400	6,305	2,311	362	2,739	11.8	9.9	24.1	9.3	24.3	12,448	15.6
2011........	9,497	6,334	2,334	401	2,651	11.8	9.8	24.2	9.7	22.9	12,500	15.5
2012........	9,520	6,299	2,327	387	2,807	11.8	9.7	23.7	9.4	23.5	12,669	15.7
2013 [6]......	9,645	6,526	2,204	448	2,865	11.7	9.9	22.4	10.2	23.1	12,605	15.3
2014 [6]......	9,467	6,310	2,265	401	2,684	11.6	9.7	22.9	8.9	21.5	12,635	15.5
2015 [6]......	8,589	5,743	2,082	374	2,502	10.4	8.8	21.1	8.0	19.6	11,603	14.1

[1] Includes other races, not shown separately. [2] Beginning 2002, data refer to persons who reported specified race only and no other race category; for Asian and Pacific Islander, data refer to persons who reported Asian only. [3] People of Hispanic origin may be of any race. [4] Implementation of Census 2000 based population controls and sample expanded by 28,000 households. [5] Implementation of Census 2010-based population controls. [6] Data are based on redesigned income questions. See source for more information.

Source: U.S. Census Bureau, *Income and Poverty in the United States: 2015*, Current Population Reports, P60-256(RV), September 2016; and "Historical Poverty Tables: People and Families, Table 4," and "Current Population Survey Detailed Tables for Poverty: Table POV04," <http://www.census.gov/topics/income-poverty/poverty/data/tables.html>, accessed November 2016.

Table 740. Families Below Poverty Level by Selected Characteristics: 2015

[In thousands (8,589 represents 8,589,000), except as noted. All families as of March of the following year. Based on the 2016 Current Population Survey (CPS), Annual Social and Economic Supplement (ASEC); see text, this section and Section 1, and Appendix III. Data below represent persons who selected each race group only and exclude persons reporting more than one race. See also comments on race in the text for Section 1. For composition of regions, see map, inside front cover]

Characteristic	Number below poverty level (1,000)					Percent below poverty level				
	All races [1]	White alone	Black alone	Asian alone	His-panic [2]	All races [1]	White alone	Black alone	Asian alone	His-panic [2]
Total families	**8,589**	**5,743**	**2,082**	**374**	**2,502**	**10.4**	**8.8**	**21.1**	**8.0**	**19.6**
Age of householder:										
18 to 24 years old	801	500	243	7	231	26.8	23.7	42.3	5.1	24.6
25 to 34 years old	2,254	1,435	613	98	721	17.5	14.9	31.4	11.6	26.0
35 to 44 years old	2,137	1,457	502	82	749	12.6	11.3	22.4	6.7	22.1
45 to 54 years old	1,355	927	287	82	389	7.9	6.8	14.0	8.4	15.0
55 to 64 years old	1,041	723	248	35	219	6.7	5.7	15.1	4.6	13.4
65 years old and over	939	664	176	63	167	5.7	4.7	13.0	9.0	12.3
Region:										
Northeast	1,347	877	332	82	413	9.5	7.8	19.3	8.4	23.6
Midwest	1,495	1,014	386	41	203	8.6	6.8	23.9	7.7	17.7
South	3,792	2,359	1,208	113	946	12.0	9.8	21.5	10.0	19.1
West	1,954	1,494	157	137	940	10.3	9.9	17.6	6.7	19.2
Type of family:										
Married couple	3,245	2,539	354	250	1,077	5.4	5.0	8.0	6.5	13.5
Male householder, no spouse present	939	610	241	42	259	14.9	13.1	23.5	12.1	17.6
Female householder, no spouse present	4,404	2,594	1,487	82	1,166	28.2	25.8	33.9	16.2	35.5

[1] Includes other races, not shown separately. [2] Hispanic persons may be of any race.

Source: U.S. Census Bureau, *Income and Poverty in the United States: 2015*, Current Population Reports, P60-256(RV), September 2016; and "Current Population Survey Detailed Tables for Poverty: Tables POV04 and POV44," <http://www.census.gov/topics/income-poverty/poverty/data/tables.html>, accessed December 2016.

Table 741. Top Wealth Holders With Gross Assets of $5 Million or More—Debts, Mortgages, and Net Worth: 2013

[7,289,626 represents $7,289,626,000,000. Figures are estimates from the Personal Wealth Study, based on a sample of Federal estate tax returns (Form 706). Covers the segment of the population for whom personal wealth is at least equal to the estate tax filing threshold in effect for the estimation period. Based on the estate multiplier technique; for more information on this methodology, see source]

Sex and net worth	Total assets [1]		Debts and mortgages		Net worth [2]	
	Number of top wealth holders	Amount (mil. dol.)	Number of top wealth holders	Amount (mil. dol.)	Number of top wealth holders	Amount (mil. dol.)
Both sexes, total	**584,194**	**7,289,626**	**442,290**	**432,333**	**584,194**	**6,857,292**
Size of net worth:						
Under $5 million [3]	102,954	437,172	88,466	122,350	102,954	314,823
$5 million to under $10 million	325,371	2,358,888	232,032	115,554	325,371	2,243,334
$10 million to under $20 million	103,903	1,458,237	80,269	69,199	103,903	1,389,038
$20 million to under $50 million	37,596	1,163,133	28,766	59,877	37,596	1,103,255
$50 million or more	14,369	1,872,193	12,756	65,352	14,369	1,806,841
Males, total	**356,549**	**4,540,744**	**268,058**	**327,470**	**356,549**	**4,213,273**
Size of net worth:						
Under $5 million [3]	73,415	321,029	61,536	104,926	73,415	216,102
$5 million to under $10 million	189,343	1,359,306	132,853	78,395	189,343	1,280,911
$10 million to under $20 million	60,875	851,278	47,186	47,931	60,875	803,346
$20 million to under $50 million	24,132	756,426	18,744	49,080	24,132	707,345
$50 million or more	8,784	1,252,704	7,739	47,136	8,784	1,205,567
Females, total	**227,645**	**2,748,882**	**174,232**	**104,865**	**227,645**	**2,644,019**
Size of net worth:						
Under $5 million [3]	29,540	116,144	26,930	17,424	29,540	98,720
$5 million to under $10 million	136,028	999,582	99,178	37,159	136,028	962,423
$10 million to under $20 million	43,029	606,959	33,084	21,267	43,029	585,692
$20 million to under $50 million	13,463	406,708	10,022	10,800	13,463	395,910
$50 million or more	5,586	619,489	5,017	18,216	5,586	601,274

[1] Total assets is the sum of all assets owned by the individual before subtracting debts, mortgages, and liens owed to others. It differs from gross assets, which is a Federal estate tax concept of wealth, in that it includes the cash value of life insurance instead of the full face value of life insurance minus indebtedness. [2] Net worth is defined as total assets minus debts and mortgages. [3] Includes individuals with zero net worth.

Source: U.S. Internal Revenue Service, Statistics of Income Division, "SOI Tax Stats - Personal Wealth Statistics," August 2017. See also <https://www.irs.gov/uac/soi-tax-stats-personal-wealth-statistics>.

Table 742. Top Wealth Holders With Gross Assets of $5 Million or More by Type of Property, Sex, and Size of Net Worth: 2013

[7,289,626 represents $7,289,626,000,000. Figures are estimates from the Personal Wealth Study, based on a sample of Federal estate tax returns (Form 706). Covers the segment of the population for whom personal wealth is at least equal to the estate tax filing threshold in effect for the estimation period. Based on the estate multiplier technique; for more information on this methodology, see source]

Sex and net worth	Number of top wealth holders	Assets (mil. dol.)				
		Total [1]	Personal residences	Other real estate	Closely held stock	Publicly traded stock
Both sexes, total	**584,194**	**7,289,626**	**458,121**	**618,807**	**888,688**	**1,348,302**
Size of net worth:						
Under $5 million [2]	102,954	437,172	55,285	51,141	27,611	46,999
$5 million to under $10 million	325,371	2,358,888	215,480	255,585	173,468	389,202
$10 million to under $20 million	103,903	1,458,237	94,574	138,159	169,026	267,517
$20 million to under $50 million	37,596	1,163,133	54,624	88,287	184,229	235,082
$50 million or more	14,369	1,872,193	38,156	85,633	334,353	409,499
Males, total	**356,549**	**4,540,744**	**238,165**	**369,694**	**659,317**	**742,460**
Size of net worth:						
Under $5 million [2]	73,415	321,029	33,892	39,347	20,802	31,674
$5 million to under $10 million	189,343	1,359,306	97,826	136,043	121,452	202,227
$10 million to under $20 million	60,875	851,278	50,755	77,898	120,811	137,956
$20 million to under $50 million	24,132	756,426	33,883	57,061	146,894	133,897
$50 million or more	8,784	1,252,704	21,809	59,343	249,356	236,705
Females, total	**227,645**	**2,748,882**	**219,956**	**249,113**	**229,371**	**605,842**
Size of net worth:						
Under $5 million [2]	29,540	116,144	21,393	11,794	6,809	15,325
$5 million to under $10 million	136,028	999,582	117,655	119,542	52,015	186,976
$10 million to under $20 million	43,029	606,959	43,819	60,261	48,214	129,562
$20 million to under $50 million	13,463	406,708	20,742	31,226	37,335	101,185
$50 million or more	5,586	619,489	16,347	26,290	84,997	172,794

[1] Total assets is the sum of all assets owned by the individual before subtracting debts, mortgages, and liens owed to others. Includes other types of assets, not shown separately. [2] Includes individuals with zero or negative net worth.

Source: U.S. Internal Revenue Service, Statistics of Income Division, "SOI Tax Stats - Personal Wealth Statistics," August 2017. See also <https://www.irs.gov/uac/soi-tax-stats-personal-wealth-statistics>.

Table 743. Top Wealth Holders With Net Worth of $5 Million or More—Number and Net Worth by State: 2013

[6,542,469 represents $6,542,469,000,000. Estimates based on a sample of federal estate tax returns (Form 706). Estimates of wealth by state can be subject to significant year-to-year fluctuations, especially for individuals at the extreme tail of the net worth distribution and for states with relatively small decedent populations. Based on the estate multiplier technique; for more information on this methodology, see source]

State	Number of top wealth holders	Net worth (mil. dol.)	State	Number of top wealth holders	Net worth (mil. dol.)
Total [1]	**481,239**	**6,542,469**	Missouri	3,899	113,689
			Montana	1,073	45,527
Alabama	4,115	55,864	Nebraska	3,299	59,527
Alaska	2,648	19,056	Nevada	3,383	78,822
Arizona	5,345	65,383	New Hampshire	1,684	20,798
Arkansas	1,342	19,783	New Jersey	13,957	200,859
California	78,413	1,123,895	New Mexico	4,763	34,411
Colorado	4,962	92,484	New York	53,038	712,276
Connecticut	12,316	207,003	North Carolina	11,931	113,321
Delaware	350	3,571	North Dakota	2,877	22,144
District of Columbia	4,993	46,716	Ohio	10,861	116,394
Florida	36,703	617,817	Oklahoma	9,960	80,432
Georgia	10,149	108,776	Oregon	3,115	33,312
Hawaii	826	13,066	Pennsylvania	13,428	194,665
Idaho	2,660	28,187	Rhode Island	2,322	21,151
Illinois	17,597	240,630	South Carolina	7,889	91,076
Indiana	5,416	66,877	South Dakota	1,165	14,388
Iowa	4,448	75,025	Tennessee	4,716	48,567
Kansas	5,643	61,054	Texas	41,736	530,581
Kentucky	3,288	55,828	Utah	1,701	27,181
Louisiana	3,611	40,627	Vermont	2,287	26,514
Maine	4,335	37,156	Virginia	11,208	137,868
Maryland	7,792	118,316	Washington	10,303	128,356
Massachusetts	12,383	158,892	West Virginia	613	6,653
Michigan	8,535	98,191	Wisconsin	4,722	63,550
Minnesota	11,323	145,541	Wyoming	1,412	21,746
Mississippi	2,340	32,678	Other areas [1]	2,365	66,245

[1] Includes U.S. territories and possessions.

Source: U.S. Internal Revenue Service, Statistics of Income Division, "SOI Tax Stats - Personal Wealth Statistics," August 2017, <https://www.irs.gov/uac/soi-tax-stats-personal-wealth-statistics>.

Table 744. Nonfinancial Assets Held by Families by Type of Asset: 2013

[Value of assets in thousands of constant (2013) dollars (177.9 represents $177,900). Families include one-person units and, as used in this table, are comparable to the U.S. Census Bureau's household concept. Based on internal data from the Survey of Consumer Finances; see Appendix III. For definition of median, see Guide to Tabular Presentation. For data on financial assets, see Table 1195]

Family characteristic	Any financial or non-financial asset	Any non-financial asset	Vehicles	Primary residence	Other resi-dential property	Equity in nonresi-dential property	Bus-iness equity	Other asset
PERCENT OF FAMILIES HOLDING ASSET								
All families, total	**97.9**	**91.0**	**86.3**	**65.2**	**13.2**	**7.2**	**11.7**	**7.3**
Age of family head:								
Under 35 years old	97.1	84.9	82.7	35.6	4.7	1.8	6.5	5.2
35 to 44 years old	97.5	92.8	89.9	61.7	9.2	5.7	15.6	4.7
45 to 54 years old	97.9	91.8	87.7	69.1	15.8	7.0	14.6	7.9
55 to 64 years old	98.1	92.9	89.2	74.2	18.4	8.9	15.5	8.2
65 to 74 years old	98.9	95.9	89.4	85.8	21.3	14.1	11.0	11.3
75 years old and over	99.0	89.6	76.0	80.2	12.8	8.9	4.4	7.8
Race or ethnicity of respondent:								
White non-Hispanic	99.3	94.9	90.3	73.8	15.9	8.7	13.9	8.5
Non-White or Hispanic	95.2	83.2	78.1	47.4	7.8	4.0	7.2	4.8
Tenure:								
Owner occupied	100.0	100.0	93.6	100.0	17.8	10.0	15.4	8.6
Renter occupied or other	94.1	74.3	72.6	(B)	4.8	1.8	4.7	4.7
MEDIAN VALUE [1] ($1,000)								
All families, total	**177.9**	**148.4**	**15.8**	**170.0**	**123.8**	**60.0**	**67.5**	**13.0**
Age of family head:								
Under 35 years old	29.6	22.0	12.5	140.0	102.5	45.0	23.8	5.0
35 to 44 years old	163.0	135.8	16.8	170.0	107.0	54.2	50.0	16.0
45 to 54 years old	214.9	174.9	19.2	180.0	100.0	37.0	93.2	15.0
55 to 64 years old	261.0	189.6	17.1	185.0	150.0	96.0	110.0	19.0
65 to 74 years old	304.0	206.8	16.4	175.0	137.0	96.5	100.0	20.0
75 years old and over	217.0	158.1	10.5	145.0	120.0	55.0	157.5	10.0
Race or ethnicity of respondent:								
White non-Hispanic	236.8	178.7	17.5	180.0	135.0	72.0	90.0	15.0
Non-White or Hispanic	57.4	60.6	12.3	143.0	80.0	30.0	30.0	10.0
Tenure:								
Owner occupied	298.9	213.4	19.5	170.0	122.0	65.0	100.0	15.0
Renter occupied or other	13.5	10.3	9.3	(B)	132.0	20.0	17.8	6.5

B Base too small to meet statistical standards for reliability of derived figure. [1] Median value of asset for families holding such assets.

Source: Board of Governors of the Federal Reserve System, 2013 Survey of Consumer Finances, *Changes in U.S. Family Finances From 2010 to 2013: Evidence from the Survey of Consumer Finances,* Federal Reserve Bulletin, Vol. 100, No. 4, September 2014. See also <http://www.federalreserve.gov/econresdata/scf/scfindex.htm>.

Table 745. Family Net Worth—Median and Mean Net Worth in Constant (2013) Dollars by Selected Family Characteristics: 2004 to 2013

[Net worth in thousands of constant (2013) dollars (114.8 represents $114,800). Constant dollar figures are based on Consumer Price Index for all urban consumers published by U.S. Bureau of Labor Statistics. Families include one-person units and as used in this table are comparable to the U.S. Census Bureau's household concept. Based on internal data from the Survey of Consumer Finances; see Appendix III. For definition of mean and median, see Guide to Tabular Presentation]

Family characteristic	2004 Median	2004 Mean	2007 Median	2007 Mean	2010 Median	2010 Mean	2013 Median	2013 Mean
All families	**114.8**	**554.2**	**135.4**	**626.3**	**82.8**	**534.5**	**81.2**	**534.6**
Age of family head:								
Under 35 years old	17.5	90.7	13.2	119.0	10.0	70.0	10.4	75.5
35 to 44 years old	85.6	369.9	99.1	366.4	45.2	233.0	46.7	347.2
45 to 54 years old	179.1	670.7	207.6	743.5	126.3	614.1	105.3	530.1
55 to 64 years old	310.8	1,046.4	285.3	1,057.5	192.3	943.6	165.9	798.4
65 to 74 years old	234.5	852.1	268.8	1,140.4	221.5	909.2	232.1	1,057.0
75 years old and over	201.1	651.2	239.7	716.7	232.3	726.5	194.8	645.2
Race or ethnicity of respondent:								
White non-Hispanic	173.8	694.7	192.3	779.2	139.9	701.4	142.0	705.9
Non-white or Hispanic	30.6	188.9	31.8	257.5	21.9	188.5	18.1	183.9
Tenure:								
Owner occupied	227.8	772.6	263.7	875.9	187.0	764.6	195.4	783.0
Renter occupied or other	4.9	66.7	5.8	80.0	5.4	61.3	5.4	70.3

Source: Board of Governors of the Federal Reserve System, 2013 Survey of Consumer Finances, *Changes in U.S. Family Finances From 2010 to 2013: Evidence from the Survey of Consumer Finances,* Federal Reserve Bulletin, Vol. 100, No. 4, September 2014. See also <http://www.federalreserve.gov/econresdata/scf/scfindex.htm>.

Table 746. Household and Nonprofit Organization Sector Balance Sheet: 1990 to 2016

[In billions of dollars (25,665 represents $25,665,000,000,000), unless otherwise noted. As of December 31. Sector includes domestic hedge funds, private equity funds, and personal trusts. For details of financial assets and liabilities, see Table 1194 and Table 1196]

Item	1990	2000	2005	2010	2013	2014	2015	2016
Assets	**25,665**	**50,878**	**74,075**	**75,963**	**92,820**	**98,172**	**101,918**	**107,909**
Nonfinancial assets [1]	9,747	16,915	28,684	23,071	27,244	28,719	30,497	32,431
Real estate	7,604	13,524	24,291	18,103	21,865	23,213	24,790	26,528
Households [2, 3]	6,811	12,205	22,187	16,135	19,210	20,289	21,568	23,102
Consumer durable goods [4]	2,039	3,202	4,108	4,587	4,941	5,053	5,237	5,418
Financial assets [1]	15,918	33,962	45,391	52,892	65,576	69,453	71,421	75,478
Time and savings deposits	2,674	3,068	4,962	6,442	7,390	7,891	8,391	9,102
Money market fund shares	389	933	941	1,127	1,138	1,113	1,068	1,023
Debt securities [1]	1,536	2,258	3,377	4,836	4,311	3,979	4,423	4,246
Treasury securities	509	589	419	1,099	1,140	838	1,132	1,379
Municipal securities	655	488	1,637	2,069	1,827	1,689	1,633	1,644
Corporate and foreign bonds	249	562	762	1,394	1,078	1,153	1,135	816
Corporate equities [2]	1,981	7,975	8,237	8,793	12,847	14,357	14,190	15,874
Mutual fund shares	466	2,466	3,279	4,473	6,250	6,726	6,504	6,851
Life insurance reserves	392	819	1,083	1,137	1,233	1,283	1,311	1,368
Pension entitlements [5]	4,435	9,971	13,305	16,882	19,869	20,667	21,256	22,259
Equity in noncorporate business [6]	3,057	4,959	8,336	6,764	9,330	10,103	10,834	11,249
Liabilities [1]	**3,692**	**7,359**	**12,179**	**13,863**	**13,917**	**14,288**	**14,631**	**15,104**
Loans [1]	3,517	7,054	11,736	13,292	13,356	13,726	14,069	14,538
Home mortgages [7]	2,489	4,814	8,913	9,971	9,467	9,455	9,536	9,754
Consumer credit	824	1,741	2,321	2,647	3,096	3,318	3,536	3,765
Net worth	**21,972**	**43,519**	**61,896**	**62,100**	**78,904**	**83,884**	**87,287**	**92,805**
Replacement cost value of structures:								
Residential [1]	4,287	7,732	12,244	12,730	14,257	15,098	15,374	16,306
Households	4,184	7,596	12,052	12,527	14,033	14,863	15,135	16,054
Nonresidential (nonprofits)	469	808	1,183	1,421	1,576	1,627	1,663	1,688
Disposable personal income	4,312	7,400	9,401	11,238	12,396	13,023	13,520	14,045
Owners' equity in real estate	4,322	7,391	13,275	6,164	9,743	10,834	12,031	13,349
Owners' equity as percent of real estate	63.5	60.6	59.8	38.2	50.7	53.4	55.8	57.8

[1] Includes types of assets and/or liabilities not shown separately. [2] At market value. [3] Includes all types of owner-occupied housing, including farm houses, mobile homes, second homes that are not rented, vacant homes for sale, and vacant land. [4] At replacement (current) cost. [5] Includes public and private defined benefit and defined contribution pension plans and annuities, including those in IRAs (individual retirement accounts) and at life insurance companies. Excludes social security. [6] Net worth of nonfinancial noncorporate business and owners' equity in unincorporated security brokers and dealers. [7] Includes loans made under home equity lines of credit and home equity loans secured by junior liens.

Source: Board of Governors of the Federal Reserve System, "Z.1 Financial Accounts of the United States: B.101 Balance Sheet of Households and Nonprofit Organizations," March 2017, <https://www.federalreserve.gov/releases/Z1/Current/>, accessed March 2017.

Table 747. Net Stock of Fixed Assets and Consumer Durable Goods in Current and Chained (2009) Dollars: 1990 to 2016

[In billions of dollars (18,868 represents $18,868,000,000,000)]

Item	1990	2000	2005	2010	2013	2014	2015	2016
CURRENT DOLLARS								
Net stock, total	**18,868**	**30,897**	**43,403**	**50,446**	**56,095**	**58,468**	**59,733**	**62,081**
Fixed assets	16,829	27,695	39,295	45,860	51,154	53,413	54,497	56,692
Private	12,772	21,398	30,609	34,345	38,227	40,184	41,130	42,933
Nonresidential	7,070	11,588	15,461	18,562	20,693	21,577	22,039	22,571
Equipment	2,424	3,806	4,482	5,268	5,896	6,040	6,214	6,375
Structures	4,055	6,471	9,320	11,189	12,376	13,008	13,188	13,477
Intellectual property products	591	1,311	1,659	2,105	2,422	2,529	2,637	2,720
Residential	5,702	9,810	15,148	15,783	17,533	18,607	19,092	20,361
Government	4,057	6,298	8,686	11,515	12,927	13,230	13,367	13,760
Nonresidential	3,908	6,066	8,350	11,183	12,554	12,835	12,969	13,335
Equipment	514	646	728	926	982	996	994	999
Structures	2,897	4,767	6,818	9,228	10,450	10,706	10,829	11,179
Intellectual property products	496	653	805	1,029	1,122	1,134	1,145	1,157
Residential	149	232	335	332	374	394	398	424
Consumer durable goods	2,039	3,202	4,108	4,587	4,941	5,055	5,237	5,388
Motor vehicles and parts	650	1,051	1,313	1,288	1,400	1,454	1,514	1,556
Furnishings and durable household equipment	649	977	1,259	1,412	1,498	1,516	1,561	1,595
Recreational goods and vehicles	419	724	963	1,084	1,150	1,176	1,225	1,248
Other	322	449	573	802	894	908	937	989
CHAINED (2009) DOLLARS								
Net stock, total	**(NA)**	**40,217**	**46,305**	**50,332**	**52,139**	**52,943**	**53,814**	**54,659**
Fixed assets	(NA)	37,595	42,340	45,622	46,965	47,562	48,199	48,806
Private	(NA)	28,341	32,044	34,302	35,312	35,843	36,405	36,939
Nonresidential	(NA)	15,402	17,062	18,513	19,359	19,770	20,164	20,505
Equipment	(NA)	4,037	4,717	5,205	5,660	5,869	6,082	6,244
Structures	(NA)	10,053	10,624	11,240	11,431	11,561	11,676	11,770
Intellectual property products	(NA)	1,417	1,730	2,067	2,269	2,347	2,424	2,517
Residential	(NA)	12,958	14,976	15,789	15,951	16,076	16,249	16,446
Government	(NA)	9,273	10,301	11,319	11,651	11,719	11,795	11,868
Nonresidential	(NA)	8,967	9,977	10,984	11,311	11,379	11,454	11,527
Equipment	(NA)	698	763	910	941	941	942	945
Structures	(NA)	7,527	8,362	9,090	9,346	9,409	9,477	9,540
Intellectual property products	(NA)	745	855	983	1,024	1,028	1,033	1,041
Residential	(NA)	302	322	336	340	340	341	341
Consumer durable goods	(NA)	2,840	3,977	4,711	5,198	5,427	5,693	5,972

NA Not available.

Source: U.S. Bureau of Economic Analysis, National Data, "Fixed Assets Accounts Tables," <https://www.bea.gov/iTable/index_FA.cfm>, accessed August 2017.

Prices

The Prices section contains producer and consumer price indexes and actual prices for selected commodities. The primary sources of the data are monthly publications of the U.S. Department of Labor, Bureau of Labor Statistics (BLS), which include *Consumer Price Index Detailed Report*, *Producer Price Index Detailed Report*, and *U.S. Import and Export Price Indexes*. Additionally, BLS provides comprehensive databases for the respective price indexes at <www.bls.gov/data/>. The Bureau of Economic Analysis (BEA) is the source for gross domestic product measures. Table 752 on housing price indexes contains data from the Federal Housing Finance Agency's Housing Price Index. Other commodity, housing, and energy prices may be found in the Energy and Utilities; Forestry, Fishing and Mining; and Construction and Housing sections.

Most price data is measured by an index. An index is a tool that simplifies the measurement of movements in a numerical series. An index allows you to properly compare two or more values in different time periods or places by comparing both to a base year. An index of 110, for example, means there has been a 10-percent increase in price since the reference period; similarly, an index of 90 means a 10-percent decrease. Movements of the index from one date to another can be expressed as changes in index points (simply, the difference between index levels), but it is more useful to express the movements as percent changes. This is because index points are affected by the level of the index in relation to its reference period, while percent changes are not.

Consumer price indexes (CPI)—The CPI is a measure of the average change in prices over time in a "market basket" of goods and services purchased either by urban wage earners and clerical workers or by all urban consumers. The all urban consumer group represents approximately 89 percent of the total U.S. population and is based on the expenditures of residents of urban or metropolitan areas, including professionals, the self-employed, the poor, the unemployed, and retired people, as well as urban wage earners and clerical workers. Not included in the CPI are the spending patterns of people living in rural nonmetropolitan areas, farm families, people in the Armed Forces, and those in institutions, such as prisons and mental hospitals. Consumer inflation for all urban consumers is measured by two indexes, the Consumer Price Index for All Urban Consumers (CPI-U) and the Chained Consumer Price Index for All Urban Consumers (C-CPI-U). The broadest and most comprehensive CPI is called the All Items Consumer Price Index for All Urban Consumers (CPI-U) for the U.S. City Average. CPIs in this section generally have a base of 1982–84 = 100.

The CPI is a product of a series of interrelated samples. Data from the 1990 Census of Population determines the urban areas from which data on prices are collected and the housing units within each area that are eligible for use in the shelter component of the CPI. The Census of Population also provides data on the number of consumers represented by each area selected as a CPI price collection area. A sample (of about 14,500 families each year) serves as the basis for a Point-of-Purchase Survey that identified the places where households purchased various types of goods and services. The CPI market basket is developed from detailed expenditure information provided by families and individuals on what they actually bought. In calculating the index, each item is assigned a weight to account for its relative importance in consumers' budgets. Price changes for the various items in each location are then averaged and local data are combined to obtain a U.S. city average. For the current CPI, this information was collected from the Consumer Expenditure Surveys for 2013 and 2014. In each of those years, about 7,000 families from around the country provided information each quarter on their spending habits in the interview survey. To collect information on frequently purchased items, such as food and personal care products, another 7,000 families in each of these years kept diaries listing everything they bought during a 2-week period. Over the 2 year period, expenditure information came from approximately 28,000 weekly diaries and 60,000 quarterly interviews used to determine the importance, or weight, of the more than 200 item categories in the CPI index structure.

The CPI represents all goods and services purchased for consumption by the reference population. BLS has classified all expenditure items into more than 200 categories, arranged into eight major groups which are food and beverages, housing, apparel, transportation, medical care, recreation, education and communication, and other goods and services. The CPI does not include investment items, such as stocks, bonds, real estate, and life insurance, as these items relate to savings and not to day-to-day consumption expenses.

Producer price index (PPI)— Dating from 1890, the PPI is the oldest continuous statistical series published by BLS. The PPI is a family of indexes that measures the average change over time in the selling prices received by domestic producers of goods and services. Imports are excluded. The target set of goods and services included in the PPI is the entire marketed output of U.S. producers. The set includes both goods and services purchased by other producers as inputs to their operations or as capital investment, as well as goods and services purchased by consumers either directly from the service producer or indirectly from a retailer. About 10,000 PPIs for individual products and groups of products are released each month.

PPIs are published for the output of almost all industries in the goods-producing sectors of the U.S. economy, and, while more indexes are gradually being introduced, are currently available for approximately 72 percent of the service sector. For any given industry, producers are usually selected for the PPI survey using a systematic sampling from a listing of all firms that file with the Unemployment Insurance System. Establishments are asked to report their prices as of Tuesday of the week containing the 13th of the month. Each month over 100,000 prices are solicited from roughly 25,000 reporters. Currently, some PPIs have an index base set at 1982 = 100, while the remainder have an index base that corresponds with the month prior to the month that the index was introduced. For further detail regarding the PPI, see the *BLS Handbook of Methods*, Chapter 14, <http://www.bls.gov/opub/hom/homch14.htm>.

In January 2014, PPI transitioned from the Stage of Processing (SOP) system to the Final Demand–Intermediate Demand (FD-ID) system as its primary index aggregation structure. The transition to the FD-ID system is the culmination of a long-standing PPI objective to improve the SOP system (domestically produced goods for domestic, nongovernment consumption) by incorporating PPIs for services, construction, government purchases, and exports. The FD portion of the FD-ID system expands coverage relative to the finished goods stage of the SOP system by including indexes that examine inflation from the producer perspective for goods, services, and construction sold as personal consumption, capital investment, government purchase, and export. The ID portion of the system allows data users to examine inflation from the producer perspective for goods, services, and construction sold to businesses as inputs to production, excluding capital investment.

BEA price indexes—BEA chain-weighted price indexes are weighted averages of the detailed price indexes used in the deflation of the goods and services that make up the gross domestic product (GDP) and its major components. Growth rates are constructed for years and quarters using quantity weights for the current and preceding year or quarter; these growth rates are used to move the index for the preceding period forward a year or quarter at a time. All chain-weighted price indexes are expressed in terms of the reference year value 2009 = 100.

Personal consumption expenditures (PCE) price and quantity indexes are based on market transactions for which there are corresponding price measures. The price index provides a measure of the prices paid by persons for domestic purchases of goods and services. PCEs are defined as market value of spending by individuals and not-for-profit institutions on all goods and services. Personal consumption expenditures also include the value of certain imputed goods and services—such as the rental value of owner-occupied homes and compensation paid in kind—such as employer-paid health and life insurance premiums. More information on this index may be found at <http://www.bea.gov/national/index.htm>.

Measures of inflation—Inflation is a period of rising price levels for goods and factors of production. Inflation results in a decline in the purchasing power of the dollar. It is suggested that changes in price levels be compared from the same month of the prior year and not as a change from the prior month. The BLS offers several indexes that measure different aspects of inflation, three of which are included in this section. The CPI measures inflation as experienced by consumers in their day-to-day living expenses. The PPI measures prices at the producer level only. The International Price Program measures change in the prices of imports and exports of nonmilitary goods between the United States and other countries.

Whereas the CPI and PPI measure a benchmark approach to price levels, the BEA's Personal Consumption Expenditures uses a chain-weight approach which links weighted averages from adjoining years.

Other measures of inflation include the futures price and spot market price indexes from the Commodity Research Bureau and the employment cost, hourly compensation, and unit labor cost indexes from the BLS. Found in Section 12, Labor Force, Employment, and Earnings, these BLS indexes are used as a measure of the change in cost of the labor factor of production and changes in long-term interest rates that are often used to measure changes in the cost of the capital factor of production.

International price indexes—The BLS International Price Program produces Import/Export Price Indexes (MXP) for nonmilitary goods traded between the United States and the rest of the world.

The U.S. Import and U.S. Export Price Indexes measure the change over time in the prices of goods or services purchased from abroad by U.S. residents (imports) or sold to foreign buyers by U.S. residents (exports). The reference period for the indexes is 2000 = 100, unless otherwise indicated. The product universe for both the import and export indexes includes raw materials, agricultural products, semifinished manufactures, and finished manufactures, including both capital and consumer goods. Price data for these items are collected primarily by mail questionnaire. In nearly all cases, the data are collected directly from the exporter or importer.

To the extent possible, the data gathered refer to prices at the U.S. border for exports and at either the foreign border or the U.S. border for imports. For nearly all products, the prices refer to transactions completed during the first week of the month. Survey respondents are asked to indicate all discounts, allowances, and rebates applicable to the reported prices, so that the price used in the calculation of the indexes is the actual price for which the product was bought or sold.

Table 748. Purchasing Power of the Dollar: 1950 to 2016

[Indexes: PPI, 1982=$1.00; CPI, 1982-84=$1.00. Producer prices prior to 1961 and consumer prices prior to 1964 exclude Alaska and Hawaii. Producer prices based on final demand, finished goods index. Data is obtained by dividing the average price index for the 1982=100, PPI and the 1982-84=100, CPI base periods (100.0) by the price index for a given period and expressing the result in dollars and cents. Annual figures are based on average of monthly data]

Year	Annual average as measured by—		Year	Annual average as measured by—	
	Producer prices	Consumer prices		Producer prices	Consumer prices
1950	3.546	4.149	1987	0.949	0.880
1955	3.279	3.731	1988	0.926	0.845
1959	3.021	3.436	1989	0.880	0.806
1960	2.994	3.378	1990	0.839	0.765
1961	2.994	3.344	1991	0.822	0.734
1962	2.985	3.311	1992	0.812	0.713
1963	2.994	3.268	1993	0.802	0.692
1964	2.985	3.226	1994	0.797	0.675
1965	2.933	3.175	1995	0.782	0.656
1966	2.841	3.086	1996	0.762	0.637
1967	2.809	2.994	1997	0.759	0.623
1968	2.732	2.874	1998	0.765	0.613
1969	2.632	2.725	1999	0.752	0.600
1970	2.545	2.577	2000	0.725	0.581
1971	2.469	2.469	2001	0.711	0.565
1972	2.392	2.392	2002	0.720	0.556
1973	2.193	2.252	2003	0.698	0.543
1974	1.901	2.028	2004	0.673	0.529
1975	1.718	1.859	2005	0.642	0.512
1976	1.645	1.757	2006	0.623	0.496
1977	1.546	1.650	2007	0.600	0.482
1978	1.433	1.534	2008	0.565	0.464
1979	1.289	1.377	2009	0.580	0.466
1980	1.136	1.214	2010	0.556	0.459
1981	1.041	1.100	2011	0.524	0.445
1982	1.000	1.036	2012	0.515	0.436
1983	0.984	1.004	2013	0.508	0.429
1984	0.964	0.962	2014	0.499	0.422
1985	0.955	0.929	2015	0.516	0.422
1986	0.969	0.912	2016	0.521	0.417

Source: U.S. Bureau of Labor Statistics, "CPI Databases," <http://www.bls.gov/cpi/#data>, and "PPI Databases," <http://www.bls.gov/ppi/#data>; accessed June 2017.

Table 749. Consumer Price Indexes (CPI-U) by Major Group: 1990 to 2016

[1982-84 = 100, except as indicated. Represents annual averages of monthly figures. Reflects buying patterns of all urban consumers. Minus sign (-) indicates decrease. See text, this section]

Year	All items	Com-modities	Ser-vices	Food	Energy	All items less food and energy	Food and bever-ages	Hous-ing	Apparel	Trans-porta-tion	Medical care	Educa-tion and com-munica-tion [1]
1990	130.7	122.8	139.2	132.4	102.1	135.5	132.1	128.5	124.1	120.5	162.8	(NA)
1995	152.4	136.4	168.7	148.4	105.2	161.2	148.9	148.5	132.0	139.1	220.5	92.2
2000	172.2	149.2	195.3	167.8	124.6	181.3	168.4	169.6	129.6	153.3	260.8	102.5
2005	195.3	160.2	230.1	190.7	177.1	200.9	191.2	195.7	119.5	173.9	323.2	113.7
2006	201.6	164.0	238.9	195.2	196.9	205.9	195.7	203.2	119.5	180.9	336.2	116.8
2007	207.3	167.5	246.8	202.9	207.7	210.7	203.3	209.6	119.0	184.7	351.1	119.6
2008	215.3	174.8	255.5	214.1	236.7	215.6	214.2	216.3	118.9	195.5	364.1	123.6
2009	214.5	169.7	259.2	218.0	193.1	219.2	218.2	217.1	120.1	179.3	375.6	127.4
2010	218.1	174.6	261.3	219.6	211.4	221.3	220.0	216.3	119.5	193.4	388.4	129.9
2011	224.9	183.9	265.8	227.8	243.9	225.0	227.9	219.1	122.1	212.4	400.3	131.5
2012	229.6	187.6	271.4	233.8	246.1	229.8	233.7	222.7	126.3	217.3	414.9	133.8
2013	233.0	187.7	277.9	237.0	244.4	233.8	237.0	227.4	127.4	217.4	425.1	135.9
2014	236.7	187.9	285.1	242.7	243.6	237.9	242.4	233.2	127.5	215.9	435.3	137.5
2015	237.0	181.7	291.7	247.2	202.9	242.2	246.8	238.1	125.9	199.1	446.8	138.2
2016	240.0	179.2	299.9	247.9	189.5	247.6	247.7	244.0	126.0	194.9	463.7	139.1
PERCENT CHANGE [2]												
1990	5.4	5.2	5.5	5.8	8.3	5.0	5.8	4.5	4.6	5.6	9.0	(NA)
1995	2.8	1.9	3.4	2.8	0.6	3.0	2.8	2.6	-1.0	3.6	4.5	3.8
2000	3.4	3.3	3.4	2.3	16.9	2.4	2.3	3.5	-1.3	6.2	4.1	1.3
2005	3.4	3.6	3.3	2.4	17.0	2.2	2.5	3.3	-0.7	6.6	4.2	1.9
2006	3.2	2.4	3.8	2.4	11.2	2.5	2.4	3.8	–	4.0	4.0	2.7
2007	2.8	2.1	3.3	4.0	5.5	2.3	3.9	3.1	-0.4	2.1	4.4	2.4
2008	3.8	4.3	3.5	5.5	13.9	2.3	5.4	3.2	-0.1	5.9	3.7	3.4
2009	-0.4	-2.9	1.4	1.8	-18.4	1.7	1.9	0.4	1.0	-8.3	3.2	3.0
2010	1.6	2.9	0.8	0.8	9.5	1.0	0.8	-0.4	-0.5	7.9	3.4	2.0
2011	3.2	5.3	1.7	3.7	15.4	1.7	3.6	1.3	2.2	9.8	3.0	1.2
2012	2.1	2.0	2.1	2.6	0.9	2.1	2.5	1.6	3.4	2.3	3.7	1.8
2013	1.5	–	2.4	1.4	-0.7	1.8	1.4	2.1	0.9	–	2.5	1.5
2014	1.6	0.1	2.6	2.4	-0.3	1.7	2.3	2.6	0.1	-0.7	2.4	1.2
2015	0.1	-3.3	2.3	1.9	-16.7	1.8	1.8	2.1	-1.3	-7.8	2.6	0.5
2016	1.3	-1.4	2.8	0.3	-6.6	2.2	0.3	2.5	0.1	-2.1	3.8	0.7

– Represents or rounds to zero. NA Not available. [1] Dec. 1997 = 100. [2] Change from immediate prior year. 1990 change from 1989.

Source: U.S. Bureau of Labor Statistics, "CPI Databases," <http://www.bls.gov/cpi/#data>, April 2017.

Table 750. Consumer Price Indexes (CPI-U) and Annual Percent Change From Prior Year—Selected Areas: 2016

[Percent changes computed from annual averages of monthly figures published by source. Local area CPI indexes are by-products of the national CPI program. Each local index has a smaller sample size than the national index and is therefore subject to substantially more sampling and other measurement error. As a result, local area indexes show greater volatility than the national index, although their long-term trends are similar. Minus sign (-) indicates decrease. See also text, this section and Appendix III]

Area	Consumer Price Index							
	All items	Food and bever- age	Food	Hous- ing	Ap- parel	Trans- por- tation	Medi- cal care	Fuel and other utilities
U.S. city average	**240.0**	**247.7**	**247.9**	**244.0**	**126.0**	**194.9**	**463.7**	**228.9**
Anchorage, AK	217.8	208.7	214.2	202.7	163.4	206.9	530.6	298.8
Atlanta, GA	225.5	249.2	259.9	223.9	141.3	187.1	435.7	287.5
Boston-Brockton-Nashua, MA-NH-ME-CT	260.5	258.0	259.0	263.6	142.2	183.2	633.7	248.9
Chicago-Gary-Kenosha, IL-IN-WI	229.3	242.9	242.8	236.3	88.1	178.1	478.3	194.4
Cincinnati-Hamilton, OH-KY-IN	226.4	220.0	216.5	210.9	147.5	197.7	500.0	228.5
Cleveland-Akron, OH	220.9	249.7	254.5	205.6	136.2	191.1	426.7	185.4
Dallas-Fort Worth, TX	220.7	250.7	245.4	205.2	108.2	195.3	432.2	219.1
Denver-Boulder-Greeley, CO	246.6	224.3	227.5	243.2	104.6	236.7	536.1	224.9
Detroit-Ann Arbor-Flint, MI	222.2	221.8	221.4	205.4	113.7	225.1	418.0	240.1
Honolulu, HI	265.3	272.1	273.0	283.6	111.7	211.6	400.4	318.3
Houston-Galveston-Brazoria, TX	216.4	224.4	224.1	210.0	177.2	173.3	458.9	154.2
Kansas City, MO-KS	224.1	257.1	262.3	216.1	111.8	188.1	361.3	234.3
Los Angeles-Riverside-Orange County, CA	249.2	251.6	251.6	277.4	111.1	191.3	459.7	301.2
Miami-Fort Lauderdale, FL	249.8	258.8	261.2	255.4	138.6	213.3	468.6	164.7
Milwaukee-Racine, WI	227.9	250.1	254.1	217.1	143.6	179.0	496.9	209.8
Minneapolis-St. Paul, MN-WI	234.1	272.5	261.4	214.8	129.1	192.6	517.7	205.2
New York-Northern New Jersey-Long Island, NY-NJ-CT-PA	263.4	257.2	257.1	284.6	127.5	208.6	464.3	178.9
Philadelphia-Wilmington-Atlantic City, PA-NJ-DE-MD	245.3	231.7	231.5	251.4	110.9	200.0	507.1	200.0
Phoenix-Mesa, AZ	130.1	142.6	143.9	130.0	141.3	112.5	165.5	165.3
Pittsburgh, PA	244.6	255.2	254.8	246.5	175.0	180.0	474.7	242.9
Portland-Salem, OR-WA	249.4	232.6	234.6	258.3	126.5	216.3	533.7	260.2
San Diego, CA	274.7	250.4	247.6	314.8	150.7	205.3	(NA)	290.9
San Francisco-Oakland-San Jose, CA	266.3	266.3	266.8	309.3	116.2	183.9	(NA)	369.2
Seattle-Tacoma-Bremerton, WA	254.9	259.9	262.6	286.5	130.3	209.6	394.4	256.5
St. Louis, MO-IL	221.1	246.9	246.2	214.0	153.4	181.4	420.8	208.2
Tampa-St. Petersburg-Clearwater, FL	214.0	219.3	219.5	207.3	165.5	184.3	(NA)	205.4
Washington-Baltimore, DC-MD-VA-WV	157.2	156.6	158.0	170.6	102.2	138.2	183.9	190.4
PERCENT CHANGE, 2015-2016								
U.S. city average	**1.3**	**0.3**	**0.3**	**2.5**	**0.1**	**-2.1**	**3.8**	**-0.6**
Anchorage, AK	0.4	-0.7	-0.9	0.9	2.6	-1.7	4.5	1.4
Atlanta, GA	1.7	-0.5	-0.6	3.0	2.6	-1.3	6.2	-1.1
Boston-Brockton-Nashua, MA-NH-ME-CT	1.5	1.0	1.1	2.6	-4.4	-1.9	4.4	-0.3
Chicago-Gary-Kenosha, IL-IN-WI	0.7	0.6	0.6	1.8	-1.6	-3.1	3.1	-1.7
Cincinnati-Hamilton, OH-KY-IN	1.4	-0.3	-0.4	2.1	3.3	-0.8	6.3	4.5
Cleveland-Akron, OH	0.2	-0.3	-0.5	0.9	2.2	-3.2	3.8	-4.8
Dallas-Fort Worth, TX	1.5	0.5	0.5	3.3	-2.9	-2.3	4.4	-2.8
Denver-Boulder-Greeley, CO	2.8	0.3	0.2	5.9	1.4	-1.8	1.5	0.8
Detroit-Ann Arbor-Flint, MI	1.6	0.5	0.3	2.4	-0.7	-1.6	4.8	1.5
Honolulu, HI	2.0	1.9	2.0	2.7	2.6	-2.4	5.7	-3.3
Houston-Galveston-Brazoria, TX	1.6	0.2	0.2	4.0	-0.9	-1.1	2.5	-1.4
Kansas City, MO-KS	0.8	0.3	0.3	2.0	-2.7	-2.6	4.0	2.9
Los Angeles-Riverside-Orange County, CA	1.9	0.9	0.9	3.9	1.1	-4.2	7.6	2.1
Miami-Fort Lauderdale, FL	1.8	0.6	0.5	3.2	-4.4	0.4	4.0	-4.4
Milwaukee-Racine, WI	0.6	1.0	0.8	2.1	1.4	-4.8	1.9	-0.2
Minneapolis-St. Paul, MN-WI	1.6	0.6	0.5	3.0	-4.8	-2.6	4.9	3.3
New York-Northern New Jersey-Long Island, NY-NJ-CT-PA	1.1	0.4	0.4	1.9	-1.6	-2.1	3.7	-4.0
Philadelphia-Wilmington-Atlantic City, PA-NJ-DE-MD	0.6	-0.2	-0.4	0.6	3.3	-1.4	3.5	-2.2
Phoenix-Mesa, AZ	1.6	1.5	1.5	3.2	5.0	-1.9	0.9	-0.3
Pittsburgh, PA	1.6	0.2	0.2	1.7	12.8	-1.5	2.1	-0.9
Portland-Salem, OR-WA	2.1	-0.1	-0.4	5.5	-0.4	-1.2	-0.3	-0.6
San Diego, CA	2.0	1.2	1.3	3.8	5.0	-4.3	(NA)	4.2
San Francisco-Oakland-San Jose, CA	3.0	2.0	2.0	5.6	1.0	-2.2	(NA)	5.9
Seattle-Tacoma-Bremerton, WA	2.2	0.8	0.6	4.8	0.8	-1.6	2.8	2.2
St. Louis, MO-IL	0.8	-0.3	-0.4	1.8	0.7	-2.2	5.1	-3.6
Tampa-St. Petersburg-Clearwater, FL	1.2	-0.2	–	2.1	0.4	-1.7	(NA)	-3.2
Washington-Baltimore, DC-MD-VA-WV	1.2	0.6	0.7	1.8	7.7	-2.3	3.0	3.3

– Represents or rounds to zero. NA Not available.

Source: U.S. Bureau of Labor Statistics, CPI Databases, "All Urban Consumers (Current Series)," <https://www.bls.gov/cpi/data.htm>, accessed April 2017.

Table 751. Consumer Price Indexes for All Urban Consumers (CPI-U) for Selected Items and Groups: 2000 to 2016

[1982-1984=100, unless otherwise noted. Annual averages of monthly figures. Reflects buying patterns of all urban consumers. For information about the CPI methodology, see the U.S. Bureau of Labor Statistics Handbook of Methods, Chapter 17, Consumer Price Index at <http://www.bls.gov/opub/hom/pdf/homch17.pdf>]

Item	2000	2010	2011	2012	2013	2014	2015	2016
All items	**172.2**	**218.1**	**224.9**	**229.6**	**233.0**	**236.7**	**237.0**	**240.0**
Food and beverages	**168.4**	**220.0**	**227.9**	**233.7**	**237.0**	**242.4**	**246.8**	**247.7**
Food	167.8	219.6	227.8	233.8	237.0	242.7	247.2	247.9
Food at home	167.9	215.8	226.2	231.8	233.9	239.5	242.3	239.1
Cereals and bakery products	188.3	250.4	260.3	267.7	270.4	271.1	274.1	273.1
Cereals and cereal products	175.9	217.6	227.2	232.9	232.7	232.9	234.1	231.2
Rice, pasta, and cornmeal	150.7	224.4	234.1	239.4	239.4	238.1	241.6	239.1
Rice [1,2]	99.3	156.9	163.9	167.3	170.2	170.7	167.2	163.1
Bakery products	194.1	268.0	278.0	286.6	291.5	292.5	296.6	296.9
Bread [2]	107.4	159.8	168.7	173.4	176.8	176.4	178.7	178.5
Cakes, cupcakes, and cookies	187.9	251.7	256.0	266.2	271.0	273.5	278.8	281.6
Other bakery products	191.5	247.1	253.1	260.4	263.5	264.8	266.4	265.4
Meats, poultry, fish and eggs	154.5	207.7	223.2	231.0	236.0	253.0	260.3	247.7
Meats, poultry, and fish	155.5	208.6	223.9	231.9	236.7	253.7	258.5	249.4
Meats	150.7	206.2	224.4	232.0	234.8	256.5	264.2	252.5
Beef and veal	148.1	224.5	247.4	263.1	268.3	300.7	322.5	302.1
Uncooked ground beef	125.2	203.6	226.7	242.7	246.8	276.0	295.3	268.2
Uncooked beef steaks [2]	109.1	153.3	166.5	177.0	179.9	199.9	214.6	206.2
Pork	156.5	190.0	206.1	206.6	208.6	227.6	218.7	209.9
Poultry	159.8	204.0	209.9	221.4	231.7	236.3	237.3	230.9
Chicken [2]	102.5	131.8	134.3	140.8	148.2	151.7	152.1	147.5
Fish and seafood	190.4	243.2	260.5	266.7	273.3	289.0	286.3	284.2
Eggs	131.9	192.8	210.5	217.1	224.2	243.0	286.2	226.0
Dairy products	160.7	199.2	212.7	217.3	217.6	225.3	222.4	217.3
Milk [2]	107.8	133.6	145.8	147.4	149.2	156.6	147.5	140.7
Cheese and related products	162.8	204.8	217.5	222.4	221.9	234.1	233.6	228.0
Ice cream and related products	164.4	195.0	209.1	215.5	215.5	215.4	219.2	219.4
Fruits and vegetables	204.6	273.5	284.7	282.8	290.0	294.4	293.8	296.3
Fresh fruits and vegetables	238.8	314.8	328.9	322.3	332.8	339.2	337.7	341.7
Fresh fruits	258.3	323.3	333.1	336.6	343.2	359.7	352.0	359.8
Fresh vegetables	219.4	305.5	322.5	306.1	320.5	316.3	321.4	321.5
Processed fruits and vegetables [2]	105.6	146.6	150.9	156.7	157.2	157.3	158.5	157.9
Nonalcoholic beverages and beverage materials	137.8	161.6	166.8	168.6	166.9	166.0	167.9	167.3
Juices and nonalcoholic drinks [2]	105.6	124.5	126.7	128.2	127.8	127.1	128.5	128.6
Carbonated drinks	123.4	154.7	158.8	161.0	159.5	158.8	159.6	161.1
Nonfrozen noncarbonated juices and drinks [2]	104.2	114.8	116.0	116.9	117.0	116.2	117.9	117.4
Beverage materials including coffee and tea [2]	97.9	114.0	122.5	123.7	119.8	118.9	120.4	118.3
Coffee	154.0	186.4	213.8	217.4	204.7	201.0	205.5	199.3
Other food at home	155.6	191.1	197.4	204.8	204.8	206.2	209.3	209.5
Sugar and sweets	154.0	201.2	207.8	214.7	211.0	209.3	216.1	215.3
Candy and chewing gum [2]	103.8	132.5	136.0	140.9	139.6	139.7	145.4	145.1
Fats and oils	147.4	200.6	219.2	232.6	229.3	229.7	227.3	225.9
Other foods	172.2	204.6	209.3	216.6	217.7	219.9	223.4	224.1
Frozen and freeze dried prepared food	148.5	165.3	167.8	169.8	167.8	168.7	170.9	169.7
Snacks	166.3	216.6	224.3	238.8	242.8	244.3	250.6	252.2
Spices, seasonings, condiments, sauces	175.6	214.4	219.9	225.9	226.4	229.7	235.6	237.7
Other miscellaneous food [2]	107.5	121.7	124.0	128.3	129.2	130.4	131.8	131.6
Food away from home	169.0	226.1	231.4	238.0	243.1	249.0	256.1	262.7
Full service meals and snacks [2]	106.8	141.1	144.4	148.1	151.5	155.3	159.4	163.1
Limited service meals and snacks [2]	106.3	143.9	147.1	151.7	154.6	158.4	163.3	167.7
At employee sites and schools [2]	104.4	141.0	145.7	150.2	155.3	158.2	161.7	170.0
From vending machines and mobile vendors [2]	102.4	133.1	135.8	140.2	143.3	143.1	146.3	150.8
Other food away from home [2]	109.0	159.3	162.8	166.5	169.6	173.8	179.6	182.7
Alcoholic beverages	174.7	223.3	226.7	230.8	234.6	237.3	239.5	242.5
Alcoholic beverages at home	158.1	191.0	191.8	193.4	195.7	197.0	197.3	199.0
Beer, ale, and other malt beverages at home	156.8	201.0	203.9	207.6	211.1	213.8	215.0	218.9
Distilled spirits at home	162.3	188.8	189.0	188.9	191.0	192.4	192.6	193.3
Wine at home	151.6	169.7	168.5	168.2	169.2	169.0	168.5	168.4
Alcoholic beverages away from home	207.1	291.9	300.5	310.5	317.9	323.8	330.5	336.6
Housing	**169.6**	**216.3**	**219.1**	**222.7**	**227.4**	**233.2**	**238.1**	**244.0**
Shelter	193.4	248.4	251.6	257.1	263.1	270.5	278.8	288.2
Rent of primary residence	183.9	249.4	253.6	260.4	267.7	276.2	286.0	296.8
Lodging away from home [2]	117.5	133.7	137.4	140.5	142.4	148.5	153.0	158.1
Other lodging away from home including hotels and motels	252.4	280.4	287.4	292.6	294.8	307.8	317.4	325.3
Owners' equivalent rent of primary residence [3]	198.7	256.6	259.6	264.8	270.7	277.8	285.9	295.3
Tenants' and household insurance [2]	103.7	125.7	127.4	131.3	135.4	141.9	146.4	147.7
Fuels and utilities	137.9	214.2	220.4	219.0	225.2	234.6	230.1	228.9
Household energy	122.8	189.3	193.6	189.3	193.8	202.2	194.7	191.1
Fuel oil and other fuels	129.7	275.1	337.1	335.9	332.0	338.9	256.2	226.3
Fuel oil	130.3	282.9	367.8	376.1	370.2	365.0	254.3	209.2
Propane, kerosene, and firewood [4]	155.5	320.6	348.1	328.4	327.6	358.4	305.9	295.5
Energy services	128.0	192.9	194.4	189.7	194.8	203.4	198.7	196.1
Electricity	128.5	193.1	196.7	196.6	200.8	208.0	209.2	207.0
Utility (piped) gas service	132.0	189.7	184.3	166.6	174.5	186.8	164.6	160.6
Water and sewer and trash collection services [2]	106.5	170.9	179.6	189.3	197.6	204.9	214.0	221.7
Water and sewerage maintenance	227.5	380.7	402.9	428.6	449.7	468.1	492.9	513.7
Garbage and trash collection [5]	269.8	384.4	395.1	404.7	416.2	425.8	432.0	439.4
Household furnishings and operations	**128.2**	**125.5**	**124.9**	**125.7**	**124.8**	**123.1**	**122.6**	**121.6**
Furniture and bedding	134.4	119.7	118.6	120.2	118.7	115.5	114.7	112.1
Living room, kitchen, and dining room furniture [2]	102.4	88.9	88.9	90.8	90.1	87.1	86.8	85.3
Appliances	96.3	86.9	85.9	88.1	86.3	82.5	79.3	76.6
Other household equipment and furnishings [2]	98.0	70.8	68.5	65.7	63.5	60.7	59.1	57.1
Clocks, lamps, and decorator items	111.7	62.9	59.5	56.1	52.8	49.4	47.1	44.8

See footnotes at end of table.

Table 751. Consumer Price Indexes for All Urban Consumers (CPI-U) for Selected Items and Groups: 2000 to 2016-Continued.

See headnote on page 495.

Item	2000	2010	2011	2012	2013	2014	2015	2016
Nonelectric cookware and tableware [2]...............	98.4	96.6	97.9	97.7	97.2	93.3	90.4	88.7
Tools, hardware, outdoor equipment and supplies [2]....	97.0	91.6	91.6	92.0	92.0	91.3	91.1	90.1
Tools, hardware, and supplies [2]......................	97.3	96.5	98.1	99.6	100.7	100.2	100.1	98.3
Outdoor equipment and supplies [2]....................	96.8	88.9	88.3	88.2	87.9	87.0	86.8	86.2
Housekeeping supplies........................	153.4	183.3	185.4	189.8	189.1	187.6	186.8	186.3
Household cleaning products [2]......................	105.1	120.6	121.4	123.0	121.3	119.1	118.9	119.4
Household paper products [2].........................	113.8	158.0	161.7	167.8	170.3	170.3	169.2	169.2
Miscellaneous household products [2].................	104.3	116.9	117.9	120.8	120.1	119.8	119.0	117.5
Household operations [2]...............................	110.5	150.3	151.8	155.2	157.6	161.6	166.9	171.6
Domestic services [2]................................	109.7	144.4	145.4	147.4	150.1	153.7	155.6	157.2
Gardening and lawncare services [2].................	111.4	155.3	156.9	159.7	160.6	165.0	171.8	174.4
Apparel..	**129.6**	**119.5**	**122.1**	**126.3**	**127.4**	**127.5**	**125.9**	**126.0**
Men's and boy's apparel............................	129.7	111.9	114.7	119.5	121.6	120.6	119.6	118.8
Men's apparel...................................	133.1	117.5	119.8	124.3	126.7	125.0	124.0	122.6
Men's shirts and sweaters [2]...................	98.3	78.6	79.6	82.2	82.9	81.0	79.5	79.5
Boys' apparel..................................	116.2	91.5	95.9	101.5	102.6	103.9	103.0	103.8
Women's and girl's apparel........................	121.5	107.1	109.2	113.0	113.3	114.4	111.2	111.2
Women's apparel................................	121.9	109.5	111.3	115.0	116.2	117.6	114.4	114.6
Women's suits and separates [2]................	98.2	83.9	84.2	86.6	86.7	85.3	81.8	81.5
Women's underwear, nightwear, sportswear, and accessories [2]	101.8	96.0	98.6	101.7	103.2	106.3	105.2	106.4
Girls' apparel..................................	119.7	95.4	98.5	103.2	99.6	99.0	96.0	95.6
Footwear..	123.8	128.0	128.5	131.8	135.0	135.5	136.8	137.3
Men's footwear..................................	129.5	127.6	129.2	133.4	136.8	138.0	137.9	138.8
Women's footwear...............................	119.6	125.3	123.7	127.2	130.4	128.0	128.9	128.6
Jewelry and watches [4]...........................	137.0	152.4	165.2	167.3	168.2	163.6	160.0	169.1
Jewelry [4]......................................	141.2	161.2	176.6	178.2	177.6	170.6	165.5	175.8
Transportation....................................	**153.3**	**193.4**	**212.4**	**217.3**	**217.4**	**215.9**	**199.1**	**194.9**
Private transportation..............................	149.1	188.7	207.6	212.8	212.4	211.0	193.7	189.5
New and used motor vehicles [2].................	100.8	97.1	99.8	100.6	100.9	100.8	100.8	100.2
New vehicles...................................	142.8	138.0	141.9	144.2	145.8	146.3	147.1	147.4
Used cars and trucks..........................	155.8	143.1	149.0	150.3	149.9	149.1	147.1	143.5
Leased cars and trucks [6].....................	(NA)	97.0	94.4	89.5	86.7	84.8	84.2	84.5
Motor fuel.......................................	129.3	239.2	302.6	312.7	303.9	292.4	213.1	188.4
Gasoline (all types)............................	128.6	238.6	301.7	311.5	302.6	290.9	212.0	187.6
Motor vehicle parts and equipment..................	101.5	137.0	143.9	148.6	146.4	144.8	144.2	143.6
Motor vehicle maintenance and repair...............	177.3	248.0	253.1	257.6	261.6	266.0	270.7	275.4
Motor vehicle insurance............................	256.7	375.2	388.7	402.5	419.4	437.2	460.6	489.1
Motor vehicle fees [2].............................	107.3	165.5	167.3	172.1	174.8	176.5	178.9	182.6
Public transportation..............................	209.6	251.4	269.4	271.4	278.9	276.4	268.7	265.4
Airline fare....................................	239.4	278.2	304.0	305.0	312.7	307.7	292.2	282.6
Medical care......................................	**260.8**	**388.4**	**400.3**	**414.9**	**425.1**	**435.3**	**446.8**	**463.7**
Medical care commodities..........................	238.1	314.7	324.1	333.6	335.1	343.4	354.6	366.8
Prescription drugs...............................	285.4	407.8	425.0	440.1	442.6	458.3	479.3	502.5
Nonprescription drugs [10].......................	(NA)	100.0	98.6	99.3	99.4	98.5	97.8	96.6
Medical care services.............................	266.0	411.2	423.8	440.3	454.0	464.8	476.2	494.8
Professional medical services....................	237.7	328.2	335.7	342.0	349.5	355.2	361.5	371.5
Physicians' services..........................	244.7	331.3	340.3	347.3	354.2	359.1	366.1	378.1
Dental services...............................	258.5	398.8	408.0	417.5	431.8	441.0	452.2	465.0
Eyeglasses and eye care [4]..................	149.7	176.7	178.3	179.9	180.8	183.9	184.0	187.0
Services by other medical professionals [4]...	161.9	214.4	217.4	219.6	223.3	226.4	228.2	231.0
Hospital and related services....................	317.3	607.7	641.5	672.1	701.3	733.8	761.9	795.1
Hospital services [7].........................	115.9	227.2	241.2	253.6	265.4	278.8	290.1	303.3
Nursing homes and adult day services [7].....	117.0	177.0	182.2	188.8	194.5	200.1	206.4	213.7
Health insurance [9]..............................	(NA)	106.6	105.5	118.3	123.0	122.1	123.6	131.8
Recreation [2]......................................	**103.3**	**113.3**	**113.4**	**114.7**	**115.3**	**115.5**	**115.9**	**117.0**
Video and audio [2]................................	101.0	99.1	98.4	99.4	99.7	99.8	99.6	100.9
Cable and satellite television and radio service [5]......	266.8	372.4	379.0	395.6	406.5	416.1	422.8	438.3
Pets, pet products and services [2].................	106.1	154.4	158.7	162.4	164.6	165.7	167.3	169.6
Sporting goods....................................	119.0	118.8	118.5	118.7	118.1	116.5	114.6	113.1
Other recreational goods [2].......................	87.8	57.8	55.9	54.0	51.9	49.4	47.0	43.9
Other recreation services [2]......................	111.7	145.1	145.3	148.4	150.5	152.7	156.2	159.9
Club membership dues and fees for participant sports and group exercises [2]...................	108.9	123.5	122.1	125.5	127.5	129.3	130.1	132.2
Admissions.......................................	230.5	322.8	325.0	332.1	336.2	341.9	354.1	365.8
Recreational reading materials.....................	188.3	220.7	219.6	223.9	232.0	236.7	240.7	240.7
Education and communication [2]...................	**102.5**	**129.9**	**131.5**	**133.8**	**135.9**	**137.5**	**138.2**	**139.1**
Education [2]......................................	112.5	199.3	207.8	216.3	224.5	231.9	240.5	247.5
Educational books and supplies....................	279.9	505.6	529.5	562.6	594.7	615.4	648.2	678.8
Tuition, other school fees, and childcare............	324.0	573.2	597.2	621.0	643.7	664.8	688.8	708.1
College tuition and fees.........................	331.9	638.2	670.3	702.8	732.4	759.5	785.9	807.0
Child care and nursery school [11]...............	156.3	240.4	247.1	253.1	259.4	264.9	275.4	283.1
Communication [2].................................	93.6	84.7	83.3	83.1	82.6	82.1	80.2	79.2
Postage and delivery services [2].................	103.2	145.9	152.2	157.7	167.3	174.2	174.6	175.6
Information and information processing [2].........	92.8	81.5	80.0	79.5	78.9	78.2	76.4	75.4
Telephone services [2].........................	98.5	102.4	101.2	101.7	101.6	101.1	99.3	98.8
Wireless telephone services [2]..............	76.0	62.4	60.1	59.7	58.6	57.4	55.2	54.7
Land-line telephone services [10]............	(NA)	101.6	103.3	105.6	108.1	111.1	113.4	114.5
Information technology, hardware, and services [8].......	25.9	9.4	9.0	8.7	8.5	8.4	8.1	7.8
Other goods and services........................	**271.1**	**381.3**	**387.2**	**394.4**	**401.0**	**408.1**	**414.9**	**423.1**
Tobacco and smoking products.....................	394.6	807.3	834.8	853.5	876.8	903.3	930.8	963.4
Cigarettes [2]....................................	159.9	329.0	340.0	347.5	357.1	368.4	380.0	393.5
Personal care.....................................	165.6	206.6	208.6	212.1	215.0	218.0	220.8	224.3
Personal care products.........................	153.7	161.1	160.5	162.2	161.8	163.4	163.3	163.1
Hair, dental, shaving, and miscellaneous personal care products [2].....................	103.3	104.3	102.4	103.1	102.8	103.4	103.7	103.1

See footnotes at end of table.

Item	2000	2010	2011	2012	2013	2014	2015	2016
Cosmetics, perfume, bath, nail preparations and implements...	166.8	182.2	184.3	186.7	186.4	189.3	188.2	188.8
Personal care services...	178.1	229.6	230.8	234.2	238.8	242.0	247.2	252.9
Haircuts and other personal care services [2]...	108.7	140.1	140.8	142.9	145.7	147.7	150.8	154.3
Miscellaneous personal services...	252.3	354.1	362.9	372.7	381.9	389.7	399.3	411.8
Legal services [4]...	189.3	288.1	297.4	303.5	311.8	318.5	323.6	334.5
Funeral expenses [4]...	187.8	282.0	288.3	293.8	301.6	307.1	313.7	319.4
SPECIAL AGGREGATE INDEXES								
Commodities...	149.2	174.6	183.9	187.6	187.7	187.9	181.7	179.2
Commodities less food and beverages...	137.7	150.4	159.9	162.7	161.5	159.6	149.2	145.4
Nondurables less food and beverages...	147.4	189.9	208.4	213.8	212.2	210.0	189.4	183.8
Nondurables less food, beverages, and apparel...	162.5	238.1	267.0	273.2	269.8	266.2	233.3	223.9
Durables...	125.4	111.3	112.6	112.8	111.9	110.3	109.1	107.3
Services [3]...	195.3	261.3	265.8	271.4	277.9	285.1	291.7	299.9
Rent of shelter [3]...	201.3	258.8	262.2	267.8	274.0	281.8	290.4	300.3
Transportation services...	196.1	259.8	268.0	272.9	280.0	285.3	291.0	299.4
Other services...	229.9	309.6	314.4	322.3	328.7	334.4	339.4	346.0
All items less food...	173.0	217.8	224.5	229.0	232.3	235.8	235.4	238.8
All items less shelter...	165.7	208.6	217.0	221.4	223.8	226.2	223.3	223.8
All items less medical care...	167.3	209.7	216.3	220.6	223.6	227.1	226.9	229.3
Commodities less food...	139.2	153.0	162.4	165.3	164.1	162.3	152.2	148.6
Nondurables less food...	149.1	191.9	209.6	215.0	213.6	211.7	192.3	187.2
Nondurables less food and apparel...	162.9	235.6	262.1	268.2	265.4	262.3	232.7	224.5
Nondurables...	158.2	205.3	219.0	224.6	225.3	226.7	217.6	215.0
Apparel less footwear [3]...	126.2	113.3	116.2	120.4	121.1	121.1	118.8	118.9
Services less rent of shelter [3]...	202.9	284.4	290.6	296.6	304.1	311.2	315.8	322.8
Services less medical care services...	188.9	249.6	253.6	258.5	264.5	271.5	277.7	285.2
Energy...	124.6	211.4	243.9	246.1	244.4	243.6	202.9	189.5
All items less energy...	178.6	220.5	224.8	229.7	233.6	238.0	242.3	247.0
All items less food and energy...	181.3	221.3	225.0	229.8	233.8	237.9	242.2	247.6
Commodities less food and energy commodities...	144.9	143.6	145.5	147.3	147.3	146.8	146.1	145.4
Energy commodities...	129.5	242.6	306.4	316.0	307.4	296.9	216.7	191.6
Services less energy services...	202.1	268.3	273.1	279.7	286.4	293.5	301.1	310.4
Domestically produced farm food...	170.1	221.6	232.5	238.7	241.4	247.9	251.0	247.3
Utilities and public transportation...	152.6	203.1	206.5	207.5	212.1	216.7	214.8	215.2

NA Not available. [1] Special indexes based on a substantially smaller sample. [2] December 1997=100. [3] December 1982=100. [4] December 1986=100. [5] December 1983=100. [6] December 2001=100. [7] December 1996=100. [8] December 1988=100. [9] December 2005=100. [10] December 2009=100. [11] December 1990=100.

Source: U.S. Bureau of Labor Statistics, CPI Databases, "All Urban Consumers (Current Series)," <https://www.bls.gov/cpi/data.htm>, accessed April 2017.

Table 752. Single-Family Housing Price Indexes by State: 2000 to 2016

[Data are for the fourth quarter of the year shown. Index 1991, 1st quarter = 100. Purchase only indexes. Data are seasonally adjusted. The index reflects average price changes in repeat sales or refinancings on the same properties. The information is obtained by reviewing repeat mortgage transactions on single-family properties whose mortgages have been purchased or securitized by either Fannie Mae or Freddie Mac; for more information on methodology, see source]

State	2000	2005	2010	2015	2016	State	2000	2005	2010	2015	2016
U.S.	144.0	216.8	183.2	224.3	238.1	MO	150.3	197.6	178.8	206.6	219.3
AL	143.0	183.0	175.8	195.3	206.6	MT	179.0	275.4	280.4	339.6	368.0
AK	137.1	208.2	220.7	249.4	247.9	NE	162.3	193.8	187.6	225.8	234.8
AZ	155.9	304.7	171.7	260.0	279.2	NV	128.3	270.3	125.3	197.2	214.9
AR	141.2	185.6	175.7	199.2	205.3	NH	146.5	238.3	195.3	216.7	226.3
CA	123.8	284.3	160.2	235.4	251.0	NJ	133.5	253.7	215.9	220.2	227.1
CO	217.1	270.3	260.6	366.3	405.2	NM	145.6	214.7	209.5	216.1	226.1
CT	117.9	194.8	166.9	166.1	167.7	NY	128.6	213.0	204.4	215.6	224.9
DE	121.8	209.1	188.1	193.6	192.4	NC	146.3	182.7	182.5	206.5	221.1
DC	133.9	322.3	321.3	473.9	493.1	ND	138.7	192.4	224.7	304.8	309.5
FL	139.9	300.4	173.1	246.1	271.7	OH	148.3	174.7	151.8	174.7	184.5
GA	151.8	191.2	153.4	201.7	215.4	OK	143.9	177.6	192.3	224.9	227.3
HI	92.5	204.6	176.9	227.7	237.2	OR	184.3	297.0	254.6	345.9	383.9
ID	154.5	228.9	190.4	254.9	273.7	PA	121.3	189.6	185.9	201.9	210.0
IL	145.7	203.5	173.9	185.4	196.1	RI	119.9	235.9	182.9	197.7	209.3
IN	142.5	165.7	156.5	179.6	189.5	SC	145.1	185.8	179.4	211.0	225.5
IA	157.4	190.9	194.0	220.3	229.7	SD	159.7	207.7	214.9	258.5	270.5
KS	154.3	188.3	188.7	214.3	227.7	TN	147.1	185.5	180.9	219.8	235.0
KY	150.9	184.6	187.3	210.9	218.9	TX	143.1	172.4	185.1	244.5	263.3
LA	157.0	212.9	225.0	258.9	270.8	UT	194.2	256.2	249.4	323.4	350.7
ME	132.9	220.0	200.9	217.0	232.5	VT	126.4	206.4	200.8	215.1	219.2
MD	122.1	254.9	207.2	227.9	239.9	VA	131.3	234.7	208.0	234.5	243.5
MA	157.0	252.4	214.6	246.8	262.2	WA	154.6	242.7	220.4	280.6	309.1
MI	173.6	200.9	144.5	190.8	202.9	WV	138.3	180.8	188.5	217.3	209.9
MN	172.5	253.0	206.2	246.4	260.3	WI	166.6	222.7	205.0	223.3	236.6
MS	142.7	177.8	172.9	191.7	199.5	WY	169.3	257.5	278.3	327.9	322.7

Source: Federal Housing Finance Agency, "House Price Index Datasets, Quarterly Data, Purchase-Only Indexes," <https://www.fhfa.gov/DataTools/Downloads/Pages/House-Price-Index-Datasets.aspx#qpo>, accessed April 2017.

Table 753. Average Prices of Selected Fuels and Electricity: 1990 to 2016

[Fuels in dollars per unit; electricity in cents per kWh. Represents price to end-users, except as noted]

Item	Unit	1990	2000	2010	2011	2012	2013	2014	2015	2016
Crude oil, composite [1]	Barrel	22.22	28.26	76.69	101.87	100.93	100.49	92.02	48.39	40.66
Motor gasoline: [2]										
Unleaded regular	Gallon	1.16	1.51	2.79	3.53	3.64	3.53	3.37	2.45	2.14
Unleaded premium	Gallon	1.35	1.69	3.05	3.79	3.92	3.84	3.71	2.87	2.61
No. 2 fuel oil (heating oil)	Gallon	0.73	0.93	2.46	3.19	3.36	3.34	3.33	2.02	1.72
No. 2 diesel fuel	Gallon	0.73	0.94	2.31	3.12	3.20	3.12	2.92	1.82	1.51
Propane, consumer grade	Gallon	0.75	0.60	1.48	1.71	1.14	1.03	1.10	0.48	0.50
Residual fuel oil	Gallon	0.44	0.60	1.71	2.40	2.59	2.48	2.33	1.29	0.95
Natural gas, residential	1,000 cu/ft	5.80	7.76	11.39	11.03	10.65	10.32	10.97	10.38	10.06
Electricity, residential	kWh	7.83	8.24	11.54	11.72	11.88	12.13	12.52	12.65	12.55

[1] Refiner acquisition cost. [2] Average, all service.

Source: U.S. Energy Information Administration, *Monthly Energy Review*, April 2017. See also <http://www.eia.gov/totalenergy/data/monthly/>.

Table 754. Retail Gasoline Prices—Selected Areas: 2013 to 2016

[In dollars per gallon. Prices are annual averages]

Area	Regular				Midgrade				Premium			
	2013	2014	2015	2016	2013	2014	2015	2016	2013	2014	2015	2016
U.S. total	**3.51**	**3.36**	**2.43**	**2.14**	**3.66**	**3.54**	**2.65**	**2.40**	**3.82**	**3.71**	**2.83**	**2.62**
Boston, MA	3.53	3.39	2.36	2.11	3.73	3.59	2.59	2.36	3.85	3.72	2.75	2.57
Chicago, IL	3.75	3.57	2.62	2.24	3.92	3.77	2.90	2.57	4.10	3.97	3.17	2.91
Cleveland, OH	3.49	3.35	2.33	2.07	3.61	3.50	2.54	2.36	3.74	3.65	2.76	2.65
Denver, CO	3.41	3.32	2.32	2.02	3.55	3.49	2.54	2.30	3.68	3.63	2.74	2.56
Houston, TX	3.29	3.13	2.13	1.87	3.50	3.37	2.40	2.16	3.66	3.56	2.65	2.44
Los Angeles, CA	3.95	3.78	3.29	2.80	4.05	3.89	3.40	2.91	4.15	3.99	3.50	3.01
Miami, FL	3.63	3.47	2.56	2.31	3.88	3.73	2.84	2.62	4.03	3.90	3.05	2.90
New York, NY	3.60	3.44	2.40	2.12	3.81	3.67	2.67	2.43	3.95	3.81	2.85	2.62
San Francisco, CA	3.90	3.78	3.14	2.75	4.01	3.90	3.26	2.89	4.11	4.00	3.37	3.01
Seattle, WA	3.68	3.60	2.77	2.50	3.82	3.73	2.90	2.66	3.93	3.84	3.01	2.77

Source: U.S. Energy Information Administration, "Weekly Retail Gasoline and Diesel Prices," <http://www.eia.gov/petroleum/data.cfm#prices>, accessed February 2017.

Table 755. Weekly Food Cost of a Nutritious Diet by Type of Family and Individual: 2010 and 2016

[In dollars. As of December. Assumes that food for all meals and snacks is purchased at the store and prepared at home. All four Food Plans are based on 2001-02 data and updated to current dollars by using the Consumer Price Index for specific food items. See source for details]

Family type	Thrifty plan		Low-cost plan		Moderate plan		Liberal plan	
	2010	2016	2010	2016	2010	2016	2010	2016
FAMILIES								
Family of two:								
19 to 50 years	81.10	87.70	103.40	112.20	128.40	139.70	160.80	175.00
51 to 70 years	76.90	83.10	99.20	107.40	122.60	133.70	148.00	161.60
Family of four:								
Couple, 19 to 50 years and children—								
2 to 3 and 4 to 5 years	118.10	128.00	150.20	163.10	185.50	201.80	229.90	250.40
6 to 8 and 9 to 11 years	135.60	146.60	176.60	192.80	221.00	240.80	268.50	292.70
INDIVIDUALS [1]								
Child:								
1 year	20.10	21.50	26.80	28.70	30.60	32.60	37.10	39.80
2 to 3 years	21.70	23.60	27.50	30.10	33.30	36.30	40.50	44.20
4 to 5 years	22.70	24.70	28.70	31.10	35.50	38.60	43.30	47.20
6 to 8 years	28.80	31.40	39.20	43.60	48.20	52.70	56.90	62.50
9 to 11 years	33.00	35.40	43.40	47.20	56.10	61.10	65.50	71.10
Male:								
12 to 13 years	35.10	38.20	49.50	54.20	61.70	68.00	72.70	79.70
14 to 18 years	36.20	39.30	50.80	54.90	63.80	70.00	73.40	80.20
19 to 50 years	39.00	42.20	50.30	54.60	62.90	68.50	77.10	84.30
51 to 70 years	35.60	38.50	47.60	51.50	58.60	64.00	71.10	77.50
71 years and over	35.80	38.80	47.00	50.90	58.50	63.20	71.90	78.20
Female:								
12 to 13 years	35.30	38.20	42.90	46.60	51.90	56.30	63.00	68.90
14 to 18 years	34.80	37.50	43.10	46.60	52.00	56.50	63.90	69.60
19 to 50 years	34.70	37.50	43.70	47.30	53.80	58.50	69.00	74.80
51 to 70 years	34.30	37.10	42.50	46.10	52.90	57.50	63.50	69.40
71 years and over	33.80	36.10	42.10	45.60	52.50	56.60	63.40	68.40

[1] The costs given are for individuals in 4-person families. For individuals in other size families, the following adjustments are suggested: 1-person, add 20 percent; 2-person, add 10 percent; 3-person, add 5 percent; 5- or 6-person, subtract 5 percent; and 7-or-more person, subtract 10 percent.

Source: U.S. Department of Agriculture, Center for Nutrition Policy and Promotion, *Official USDA Food Plans: Cost of Food at Home at Four Levels, U.S. Average, December 2016*, January 2017, and earlier reports. See also <https://www.cnpp.usda.gov/USDAFoodPlansCostofFood/reports>.

Table 756. Food—Retail Prices of Selected Items: 1990 to 2016

[In dollars per pound, except as indicated. As of December. See Appendix III]

Food	1990	2000	2005	2010	2012	2013	2014	2015	2016
Cereals and bakery products:									
Flour, white, all purpose	0.24	0.28	0.30	0.44	0.50	0.51	0.51	0.50	0.50
Rice, white, long grain, raw	0.49	(NA)	0.52	0.73	0.71	0.74	0.70	0.71	0.69
Spaghetti and macaroni	0.85	0.88	0.87	1.19	1.31	1.26	1.16	1.29	1.29
Bread, white, pan	0.70	0.99	1.05	1.39	1.44	1.39	1.47	1.43	1.36
Bread, whole wheat	(NA)	1.36	1.29	1.88	1.93	2.08	1.99	1.95	1.96
Beef:									
Ground beef, 100% beef	1.63	1.63	2.30	2.38	3.08	3.46	4.16	4.06	3.56
Ground chuck, 100% beef	2.02	1.98	2.61	2.93	3.46	3.59	4.22	4.03	3.62
Ground beef, lean and extra lean	(NA)	2.33	2.91	3.49	4.21	5.06	6.08	5.89	5.54
Beef roasts (all, uncooked)	(NA)	2.93	3.73	4.15	4.74	4.91	5.85	5.48	5.16
Beef steaks (all, uncooked)	(NA)	4.09	5.03	5.60	6.30	6.34	7.54	7.51	7.12
Round steak, USDA Choice	3.42	3.28	4.12	4.30	4.70	5.01	6.26	5.93	5.56
Sirloin steak, boneless	4.24	4.81	5.93	6.07	6.78	6.78	8.15	8.29	7.91
Pork:									
Bacon, sliced	2.28	3.03	3.33	4.16	4.64	5.54	5.53	5.73	5.10
Chops, center cut, bone-in	3.32	3.46	3.28	3.58	3.57	3.92	4.26	4.09	3.63
Ham, boneless, excluding canned	(NA)	2.75	3.09	3.47	3.74	4.06	4.35	4.03	3.93
Poultry, fish, and eggs:									
Chicken, fresh, whole	0.86	1.08	1.06	1.28	1.48	1.52	1.54	1.44	1.46
Chicken breast, boneless	(NA)	(NA)	(NA)	3.32	3.27	3.46	3.48	3.28	3.20
Chicken legs, bone-in	1.17	1.26	1.33	1.48	1.65	1.59	1.61	1.57	1.43
Turkey, frozen, whole	0.96	0.99	1.07	1.38	1.43	1.65	1.33	1.45	1.50
Tuna, light, chunk, canned	2.11	1.92	(NA)	(NA)	(NA)	(NA)	(NA)	3.26	3.15
Eggs, grade A, large, (dozen)	1.00	0.96	1.35	1.79	2.01	2.03	2.21	2.75	1.38
Dairy products:									
Milk, fresh, whole, fortified (per gal.)	(NA)	2.79	3.24	3.32	3.58	3.50	3.82	3.31	3.29
Butter, salted, grade AA, stick	1.92	2.80	2.98	3.42	(NA)	(NA)	(NA)	(NA)	(NA)
American processed cheese	(NA)	3.69	3.92	3.80	4.24	4.35	4.71	4.35	4.21
Cheddar cheese, natural	(NA)	3.76	4.43	4.93	5.87	5.39	5.44	5.33	4.90
Ice cream, prepack., bulk, reg. (1/2 gal.)	2.54	3.66	3.69	4.58	5.10	4.98	5.04	4.73	4.68
Fresh fruits and vegetables:									
Apples, Red Delicious	0.77	0.82	0.97	1.20	1.42	1.34	1.29	1.40	1.31
Bananas	0.43	0.49	0.48	0.59	0.61	0.59	0.59	0.58	0.58
Oranges, navel	0.56	0.62	0.89	1.02	1.04	1.13	1.25	1.23	1.17
Grapefruit	0.56	0.58	1.10	0.99	1.07	1.07	1.10	1.09	1.25
Grapes, Thompson seedless	(NA)	2.36	2.76	2.87	3.09	2.57	2.96	2.83	2.88
Lemons	0.97	1.11	1.51	1.60	1.53	1.63	1.97	1.98	1.99
Pears, Anjou	0.79	(NA)	1.00	1.42	(NA)	(NA)	(NA)	(NA)	1.63
Strawberries	(NA)	(NA)	2.67	3.07	2.88	2.87	3.56	3.50	3.28
Lettuce, iceberg	0.58	0.85	0.85	0.99	0.87	0.99	1.11	1.48	1.02
Tomatoes, field grown	0.86	1.57	1.85	1.59	1.59	1.73	2.19	1.93	1.97
Peppers, sweet	(NA)	(NA)	(NA)	2.40	2.36	2.67	2.62	(NA)	2.20
Potatoes, white	0.32	0.35	0.50	0.58	0.62	0.67	0.64	0.64	0.69
Sugar and fats and oils:									
Sugar, white, all sizes	0.43	0.41	0.45	0.64	0.68	0.59	0.61	0.64	0.61
Margarine, tubs, soft	(NA)	0.84	0.91	1.62	2.08	2.07	1.96	1.86	1.78
Peanut butter, creamy, all sizes	2.07	1.96	1.70	1.99	2.90	2.60	2.70	2.68	2.62
Nonalcoholic beverages:									
Coffee, 100% ground roast, all sizes	2.94	3.21	3.24	4.15	5.92	4.95	4.59	4.49	4.28
Prepared foods:									
Potato chips, per 16 ounces	2.97	3.44	3.46	4.74	4.71	4.54	4.27	4.41	4.35

NA Not available.

Source: U.S. Bureau of Labor Statistics, *CPI Detailed Report*, December 2016; and CPI Databases, "Average Price Indexes," <http://www.bls.gov/cpi/data.htm>, accessed February 2017. See also <http://www.bls.gov/cpi/cpi_dr.htm>.

Table 757. Employment Cost Index for Total Compensation, Wages and Salaries, and Benefits: 2006 to 2016

[As of December (2005=100). Data are not seasonally adjusted. For data by industry, see Table 671]

Compensation type and occupation	2006	2007	2008	2009	2010	2011	2012	2013	2014	2015	2016
Total compensation:											
All civilian workers [1]	103.3	106.7	109.5	111.0	113.2	115.5	117.7	120.0	122.7	125.1	127.9
Private industry workers	103.2	106.3	108.9	110.2	112.5	115.0	117.1	119.4	122.2	124.5	127.2
State and local government workers	104.1	108.4	111.6	114.2	116.2	117.7	119.9	122.2	124.7	127.8	130.9
Wages and salaries:											
All civilian workers [1]	103.2	106.7	109.6	111.2	113.0	114.6	116.5	118.7	121.2	123.7	126.6
Private industry workers	103.2	106.6	109.4	110.8	112.8	114.6	116.6	119.0	121.6	124.2	127.1
State and local government workers	103.5	107.1	110.4	112.5	113.8	114.9	116.2	117.5	119.4	121.6	124.1
Benefits:											
All civilian workers [1]	103.6	106.8	109.1	110.7	113.9	117.5	120.3	123.0	126.2	128.4	131.1
Private industry workers	103.1	105.6	107.7	108.7	111.9	115.9	118.2	120.5	123.5	125.1	127.3
State and local government workers	105.2	111.0	114.2	117.7	121.1	123.6	127.8	132.0	135.8	140.6	145.0

[1] Includes workers in the private nonfarm economy except those in private households and workers in the public sector except the federal government.

Source: U.S. Bureau of Labor Statistics, Employment Cost Trends, "Employment Cost Index," <http://www.bls.gov/ncs/ect/#data>, accessed February 2017.

Table 758. Indexes of Spot Primary Market Prices: 1990 to 2016

[1967=100. Represents unweighted geometric average of price quotations of 23 commodities. Computed daily and therefore much more sensitive to changes in market conditions than a monthly producer price index]

Items and number	1990	1995	2000	2005	2009	2010	2011	2012	2013	2014	2015	2016
All commodities (23).....	**258.1**	**289.1**	**224.0**	**303.3**	**424.2**	**520.3**	**481.8**	**482.1**	**456.2**	**438.0**	**374.8**	**423.1**
Foodstuffs (10)...............	206.4	236.4	184.7	241.7	344.7	440.3	435.5	423.9	364.7	369.4	335.0	338.8
Raw industrials (13).........	301.2	332.2	255.8	354.7	489.4	583.8	516.5	526.8	532.4	492.6	404.9	493.2
Livestock and products (5)..	292.7	307.4	265.5	326.6	407.6	528.0	575.4	599.7	547.8	556.2	392.2	446.2
Metals (5)......................	283.2	300.6	214.0	440.9	809.1	1,006.2	837.8	918.7	935.2	824.4	556.0	803.9
Textiles and fibers (4).......	257.6	274.3	245.7	252.5	294.0	342.1	290.2	276.8	278.2	257.7	271.9	287.3
Fats and oils (4)..............	188.7	226.7	163.6	223.4	339.7	478.3	497.7	471.5	387.3	364.0	315.2	393.3

Source: Commodity Research Bureau, Chicago, IL, *CRB Commodity Index Report*, weekly ©. See also <http://www.crbtrader.com>.

Table 759. Producer Price Indexes—Final and Intermediate Demand: 2010 to 2016

[November 2009=100. Minus sign (-) indicates decrease. For information on producer prices, see Bureau of Labor Statistics, <http://www.bls.gov/ppi/>]

Commodity type	Index						
	2010	2011	2012	2013	2014	2015	2016
FINAL DEMAND							
Total............	**101.8**	**105.7**	**107.7**	**109.1**	**110.9**	**109.9**	**110.4**
Final demand goods................	102.8	109.9	111.7	112.6	114.0	109.1	107.6
Final demand foods..............	103.7	112.5	115.9	117.8	121.6	118.4	115.1
Final demand energy.............	107.2	126.2	126.3	125.3	124.2	98.6	90.4
Other final demand goods.......	101.4	104.9	106.8	107.9	109.5	109.9	110.7
Final demand services............	101.3	103.4	105.4	107.1	109.0	110.0	111.5
Final demand trade services.....	101.7	104.0	106.7	108.2	110.2	111.6	113.1
Final demand transportation and warehousing services.........	103.2	110.0	114.2	115.3	117.7	115.3	113.5
Other final demand services......	100.9	102.5	103.9	105.8	107.5	108.7	110.6
INTERMEDIATE DEMAND							
Processed goods for intermediate demand....................	183.4	199.9	200.7	200.8	201.9	188.0	182.2
Processed foods and feeds...........	171.7	192.2	201.4	204.3	210.8	197.7	188.4
Processed energy goods.............	187.8	219.9	218.4	213.7	211.5	168.9	152.6
Other processed materials..........	180.8	192.0	192.6	193.8	195.2	189.4	186.9
Unprocessed goods for intermediate demand.................	212.2	249.4	241.4	246.7	249.3	189.1	173.4
Unprocessed foodstuffs and feedstuffs....................	152.4	188.4	196.4	200.2	210.1	181.4	162.4
Unprocessed energy materials............	216.7	240.3	218.4	234.7	233.1	141.1	128.1
Unprocessed nonfood materials less energy..................	329.1	390.4	369.6	351.2	345.7	296.0	288.0
Services for intermediate demand..........	101.1	103.2	105.3	107.2	108.9	110.2	112.1
Trade services for intermediate demand................	100.8	103.1	106.8	109.2	110.4	113.1	112.1
Transportation and warehousing services for intermediate demand.........	103.3	109.3	113.3	116.1	119.4	119.1	118.2
Other services for intermediate demand.........................	100.7	102.1	103.4	105.0	106.5	107.8	110.9
PERCENT CHANGE [1]							
FINAL DEMAND							
Total........	**(NA)**	**3.8**	**1.9**	**1.3**	**1.6**	**-0.9**	**0.5**
Final demand goods................	(NA)	6.9	1.6	0.8	1.2	-4.3	-1.4
Final demand foods..............	(NA)	8.5	3.0	1.6	3.2	-2.6	-2.8
Final demand energy.............	(NA)	17.7	0.1	-0.8	-0.9	-20.6	-8.3
Other final demand goods.......	(NA)	3.5	1.8	1.0	1.5	0.4	0.7
Final demand services............	(NA)	2.1	1.9	1.6	1.8	0.9	1.4
Final demand trade services.....	(NA)	2.3	2.6	1.4	1.8	1.3	1.3
Final demand transportation and warehousing services.........	(NA)	6.6	3.8	1.0	2.1	-2.0	-1.6
Other final demand services......	(NA)	1.6	1.4	1.8	1.6	1.1	1.7
INTERMEDIATE DEMAND							
Processed goods for intermediate demand....................	6.3	9.0	0.4	(Z)	0.5	-6.9	-3.1
Processed foods and feeds...........	3.4	11.9	4.8	1.4	3.2	-6.2	-4.7
Processed energy goods.............	15.6	17.1	-0.7	-2.2	-1.0	-20.1	-9.7
Other processed materials..........	4.3	6.2	0.3	0.6	0.7	-3.0	-1.3
Unprocessed goods for intermediate demand.................	21.1	17.5	-3.2	2.2	1.1	-24.1	-8.3
Unprocessed foodstuffs and feedstuffs....................	13.3	23.6	4.2	1.9	4.9	-13.7	-10.5
Unprocessed energy materials............	22.6	10.9	-9.1	7.5	-0.7	-39.5	-9.2
Unprocessed nonfood materials less energy..................	32.5	18.6	-5.3	-5.0	-1.6	-14.4	-2.7
Services for intermediate demand..........	(NA)	2.1	2.0	1.8	1.6	1.2	1.7
Trade services for intermediate demand................	(NA)	2.3	3.6	2.2	1.1	2.4	-0.9
Transportation and warehousing services for intermediate demand.........	(NA)	5.8	3.7	2.5	2.8	-0.3	-0.8
Other services for intermediate demand............	(NA)	1.4	1.3	1.5	1.4	1.2	2.9

NA Not available. Z less than 0.05 percent. [1] Change from immediate prior year. 2010, change from 2009.

Source: U.S. Bureau of Labor Statistics, PPI Databases, "Commodity Data including "headline" FD-ID Indexes," <http://www.bls.gov/ppi/data.htm>, accessed June 2017.

[1982=100, unless otherwise noted. For information on producer prices, see Bureau of Labor Statistics, <http://www.bls.gov/ppi/>]

Item	2000	2005	2010	2013	2014	2015	2016
Final demand (Nov. 2009=100)	(NA)	(NA)	101.8	109.1	110.9	109.9	110.4
Final demand goods (Nov. 2009=100)	(NA)	(NA)	102.8	112.6	114.0	109.1	107.6
Final demand foods (Nov. 2009=100)	(NA)	(NA)	103.7	117.8	121.6	118.4	115.1
Fresh fruits & melons	91.4	102.8	123.8	121.2	124.5	124.2	138.7
Fresh & dry vegetables	126.7	142.6	178.5	197.8	194.0	200.2	202.2
Grains	78.3	83.4	160.2	234.5	171.5	151.9	135.1
Eggs for fresh use (Dec. 1991=100)	84.9	79.6	123.4	147.7	169.6	219.3	107.5
Oilseeds	93.8	113.4	191.0	262.1	230.0	176.6	180.5
Bakery products	182.3	201.1	244.8	267.1	270.9	275.0	277.7
Milled rice	101.2	120.1	183.6	209.9	216.8	199.0	189.2
Pasta products (June 1985=100)	121.6	127.9	170.7	203.6	201.3	216.2	207.2
Beef & veal	113.7	147.4	157.1	198.8	236.7	243.6	202.9
Pork	113.4	131.9	142.6	159.3	190.5	145.6	142.6
Processed young chickens	110.4	136.2	149.0	172.8	178.3	174.0	168.7
Processed turkeys	98.7	105.1	132.1	149.1	170.7	164.3	147.2
Finfish & shellfish	198.1	222.6	272.4	299.4	322.4	322.0	327.6
Dairy products	133.7	154.5	174.0	199.7	221.7	193.6	190.4
Processed fruits & vegetables	128.6	140.4	176.6	193.3	193.7	197.7	198.7
Confectionery end products	170.6	205.1	236.4	267.1	275.5	282.8	277.7
Soft drinks	144.1	159.1	183.9	193.5	194.6	196.7	205.5
Roasted coffee	133.5	151.1	190.2	198.0	198.9	204.7	196.3
Shortening & cooking oils	132.4	176.7	233.6	276.3	256.1	243.3	242.3
Frozen specialty food	143.5	152.7	176.4	186.1	188.9	189.5	187.4
Final demand energy (Nov. 2009=100)	(NA)	(NA)	107.2	125.3	124.2	98.6	90.4
Liquefied petroleum gas	127.1	244.7	301.8	269.7	258.5	109.8	106.0
Residential electric power (Dec. 1990=100)	110.8	126.4	154.7	163.8	169.5	172.2	172.2
Residential natural gas (Dec. 1990=100)	135.5	216.8	201.7	193.0	210.4	184.4	182.1
Gasoline	94.6	168.6	225.3	292.6	276.2	177.2	145.2
Home heating oil & distillates	93.5	178.4	207.5	275.9	259.0	160.9	122.9
No. 2 diesel fuel	93.3	189.1	232.9	317.7	299.6	181.4	143.5
Other final demand goods (Nov. 2009=100)	(NA)	(NA)	101.4	107.9	109.5	109.9	110.7
Alcoholic beverages	140.6	158.5	175.1	190.2	191.7	192.6	193.4
Women's, girls', & infants' apparel (Dec. 2003=100)	(NA)	100.3	101.6	105.6	104.7	105.2	106.0
Men's & boys' apparel (Dec. 2003=100)	(NA)	98.7	101.5	114.2	114.5	113.0	113.1
Textile house furnishings	122.0	122.9	131.7	143.7	160.3	162.8	164.6
Footwear	144.9	148.1	162.4	185.1	191.1	196.0	199.5
Soaps & synthetic detergents	128.2	134.6	161.2	176.3	174.4	175.7	177.0
Cosmetics & other toilet preparations	137.4	143.0	149.9	155.3	160.3	161.4	162.4
Tires, tubes, & tread	93.0	108.1	138.1	156.3	152.5	149.3	147.1
Agricultural machinery & equipment	153.7	174.7	203.5	215.9	220.4	222.2	224.4
Construction machinery & equipment	148.6	168.3	191.4	210.7	214.3	217.0	219.0
Metal cutting machine tools	161.9	155.1	174.6	193.6	195.9	198.4	199.0
Pumps, compressors, & equipment	154.1	178.5	215.1	235.2	240.5	244.8	247.1
Industrial material handling equipment	134.7	150.6	183.1	197.9	202.4	207.0	209.2
Electronic computers (Dec. 2004=100)	261.6	85.5	30.3	22.5	21.3	20.4	19.5
Textile machinery	156.2	160.5	165.9	172.8	175.4	176.1	173.0
Paper industries machinery (June 1982=100)	164.7	178.1	197.2	208.6	213.0	216.2	219.8
Printing trades machinery	142.1	144.3	155.4	161.1	160.2	162.3	163.8
Transformers & power regulators	135.8	150.3	223.1	224.0	224.0	212.8	208.0
Oil field & gas field machinery	128.2	155.9	200.7	213.1	216.5	216.5	214.9
Mining machinery & equipment	146.1	175.9	221.5	253.0	256.1	260.6	263.9
Office & store machines & equipment	112.7	115.1	121.0	117.6	118.8	122.7	123.1
Household furniture	152.7	166.5	187.4	199.3	200.8	203.9	205.3
Household appliances	107.3	103.3	110.5	117.0	117.2	116.8	115.8
Home electronic equipment	71.8	62.6	52.9	51.0	51.2	51.3	51.5
Lawn & garden equipment, except tractors	132.0	134.5	141.7	142.7	143.5	143.7	143.8
Passenger cars	132.8	131.8	129.0	130.3	131.2	133.4	133.5
Light motor trucks	157.6	148.4	153.3	162.9	166.9	171.4	173.1
Heavy motor trucks	148.0	162.4	195.7	209.3	213.5	218.1	222.6
Truck trailers	139.4	157.1	181.5	195.2	197.0	201.0	201.5
Aircraft	184.2	223.5	263.0	283.0	287.7	290.8	292.5
Ships (Dec. 1985=100)	146.9	176.6	215.1	220.7	223.5	225.2	224.0
Railroad equipment	135.7	160.4	184.4	195.7	197.7	201.9	203.3
Final demand services (Nov. 2009=100)	(NA)	(NA)	101.3	107.1	109.0	110.0	111.5
Final demand trade services (Nov. 2009=100)	(NA)	(NA)	101.7	108.2	110.2	111.6	113.1
Machinery & equipment wholesaling (Mar. 2009=100)	(NA)	(NA)	101.2	110.3	112.0	110.7	117.9
Furnishings wholesaling (Mar. 2009=100)	(NA)	(NA)	78.5	82.1	90.4	89.1	93.4
Apparel wholesaling (Mar. 2009=100)	(NA)	(NA)	97.3	115.2	116.4	117.9	117.6
Food & alcohol wholesaling (June 2009=100)	(NA)	(NA)	105.7	98.5	99.9	105.2	106.5
Food & alcohol retailing (Mar. 2009=100)	(NA)	(NA)	98.9	115.1	120.1	126.4	129.5
Health, beauty, & optical goods retailing (Mar. 2009=100)	(NA)	(NA)	107.8	121.0	121.1	118.9	119.1
Apparel, jewelry, footwear, & accessories retailing (June 2009=100)	(NA)	(NA)	104.2	111.7	111.2	113.9	114.0
Automobiles & automobile parts retailing (June 2009=100)	(NA)	(NA)	105.9	102.7	103.4	101.2	95.8
Sporting goods, including boats, retailing (Mar. 2009=100)	(NA)	(NA)	96.6	104.1	109.6	108.9	112.2
Furniture retailing (Mar. 2009=100)	(NA)	(NA)	99.7	100.2	100.8	102.2	105.1
Major household appliances retailing (Mar. 2009=100)	(NA)	(NA)	97.3	88.4	80.4	80.5	78.2
Book retailing (Mar. 2009=100)	(NA)	(NA)	104.8	123.1	120.8	110.3	108.7
Final demand transportation & warehousing services (Nov. 2009=100)	(NA)	(NA)	103.2	115.3	117.7	115.3	113.5
Rail transportation of freight & mail (Dec. 2008=100)	(NA)	(NA)	101.6	118.8	121.1	116.5	113.7
Truck transportation of freight (June 2009=100)	(NA)	(NA)	102.0	113.3	115.5	113.4	112.2
Air transportation of freight (Dec. 2008=100)	(NA)	(NA)	100.1	114.9	115.8	112.5	110.7
Courier, messenger, & U.S. postal services (June 2009=100)	(NA)	(NA)	105.5	122.8	128.8	131.5	131.2

See footnotes at end of table.

See headnote on page 501.

Item	2000	2005	2010	2013	2014	2015	2016
Rail transportation of passengers (Dec. 2008=100)	(NA)	(NA)	100.7	112.5	113.3	115.2	117.1
Airline passenger services (Dec. 2008=100)	(NA)	(NA)	102.8	114.7	116.9	112.3	109.3
Other final demand services (Nov. 2009=100)	**(NA)**	**(NA)**	**100.9**	**105.8**	**107.5**	**108.7**	**110.6**
Sales of books	218.2	264.0	317.1	345.1	353.3	363.9	370.6
Cellphone & other wireless telecom services (Mar. 2009=100)	(NA)	(NA)	94.4	87.7	85.1	77.6	71.6
Cable & satellite subscriber services (Dec. 2008=100)	(NA)	(NA)	103.7	109.8	111.2	112.7	118.3
Internet access services (Mar. 2009=100)	(NA)	(NA)	98.3	97.7	97.9	98.2	97.8
Processed goods for intermediate demand	**129.2**	**154.0**	**183.4**	**200.8**	**201.9**	**188.0**	**182.2**
Processed materials less foods & feeds	**130.1**	**155.1**	**184.4**	**200.7**	**201.3**	**187.2**	**181.8**
Synthetic fibers	107.2	112.3	111.6	124.0	125.3	121.3	118.9
Processed yarns & threads	107.9	111.7	130.0	141.5	141.5	135.6	133.2
Finished fabrics	122.5	124.1	137.1	151.4	154.3	154.0	153.7
Commercial electric power	131.5	149.8	182.5	188.7	194.3	195.8	193.9
Industrial electric power	131.5	156.2	193.1	203.7	218.0	223.7	213.6
Commercial natural gas (Dec. 1990=100)	134.7	232.5	208.0	186.4	200.8	176.6	172.0
Industrial natural gas (Dec. 1990=100)	139.0	249.4	202.0	176.5	190.8	158.6	146.7
Natural gas to electric utilities (Dec. 1990=100)	120.7	204.0	174.8	164.4	180.1	159.6	157.7
Jet fuels	88.5	169.6	225.5	295.5	282.3	171.3	134.4
Prepared paint	160.8	187.9	237.1	273.7	276.3	273.0	271.6
Medicinal & botanical chemicals	146.2	136.0	175.2	176.0	176.8	177.1	176.0
Biological products, including diagnostics	172.2	195.1	223.7	245.5	252.5	256.4	263.7
Fats & oils, inedible	70.1	146.9	244.3	302.6	252.8	204.9	209.1
Plastic resins & materials	141.6	193.0	210.1	245.3	257.0	228.0	218.5
Synthetic rubber	119.1	151.3	215.5	231.6	224.8	197.6	193.5
Plastic construction products	135.8	158.8	190.9	208.1	211.1	213.1	211.9
Softwood lumber	178.6	203.6	160.8	199.8	205.6	192.7	198.8
Hardwood lumber	185.9	196.6	187.3	208.4	241.9	221.1	218.1
Millwork	176.4	197.2	207.0	225.8	232.3	237.2	240.6
Plywood	157.6	186.8	176.7	199.6	204.1	198.9	192.3
Paper	149.8	159.6	182.1	190.8	192.7	189.8	186.7
Paperboard	176.7	175.5	224.9	243.7	248.6	243.1	233.4
Paper boxes & containers	172.6	183.7	219.4	240.1	245.8	247.3	248.1
Foundry & forge shop products	136.5	156.2	191.2	208.7	210.4	209.2	207.0
Steel mill products	108.4	159.7	191.7	195.0	200.2	177.1	167.8
Primary nonferrous metals	113.6	158.2	210.3	200.3	192.0	170.7	167.1
Aluminum mill shapes	149.0	161.1	171.9	173.2	179.6	172.4	164.5
Copper & brass mill shapes	162.3	235.8	421.3	412.0	397.3	356.9	331.0
Nonferrous wire & cable	143.7	169.4	258.1	258.4	253.2	238.2	224.1
Hardware	151.2	168.0	194.0	204.6	207.6	209.7	210.6
Plumbing fixtures & brass fittings	180.4	197.6	231.4	245.7	252.6	257.1	257.8
Heating equipment	155.6	179.9	221.5	239.8	243.6	248.2	253.1
Fabricated structural metal products	144.9	175.1	201.1	213.2	215.6	215.6	214.0
Air conditioning & refrigeration equipment	135.3	146.2	163.8	174.4	177.7	179.2	180.9
Motors, generators, motor generator sets	146.2	157.8	190.6	208.5	211.6	211.6	209.4
Electronic components & accessories	97.1	87.0	73.5	69.0	68.6	68.2	67.2
Internal combustion engines	143.8	147.7	161.7	166.2	167.2	168.4	164.3
Machine shop products	138.0	151.0	174.7	183.3	183.6	184.0	184.4
Cement	150.1	176.4	193.5	199.3	208.1	223.4	235.2
Concrete products	147.8	177.2	210.6	221.0	230.3	239.4	247.0
Motor vehicle parts	113.6	113.1	121.8	125.7	125.8	125.9	124.9
Aircraft engines & engine parts (Dec. 1985=100)	141.0	165.9	197.4	215.7	220.2	221.2	224.1
Aircraft parts & auxiliary equipment (June 1985=100)	145.7	155.3	167.7	177.3	181.2	183.3	184.7
Medical/surgical/personal aid devices	146.0	159.2	169.0	174.7	174.7	176.2	177.4
Unprocessed goods for intermediate demand	**120.6**	**182.2**	**212.2**	**246.7**	**249.3**	**189.1**	**173.4**
Unprocessed foodstuffs & feedstuffs	**100.2**	**122.7**	**152.4**	**200.2**	**210.1**	**181.4**	**162.4**
Wheat	80.3	102.7	157.2	204.2	190.6	153.3	122.1
Corn	76.4	75.9	160.8	243.9	163.2	149.6	137.7
Slaughter cattle	104.1	131.5	139.8	187.9	230.7	225.6	181.9
Slaughter hogs	72.7	82.7	92.6	113.2	130.5	80.6	81.0
Slaughter chickens	127.6	181.0	221.3	280.9	298.2	246.8	228.5
Slaughter turkeys	120.7	131.1	173.0	193.6	213.0	234.3	242.4
Raw milk	92.0	113.5	121.9	149.6	179.2	127.7	123.9
Alfalfa hay	156.3	190.1	214.3	381.4	368.8	309.2	253.4
Raw cane sugar & byproducts	100.2	124.9	179.9	150.4	144.0	149.4	158.0
Unprocessed nonfood materials	**130.4**	**223.4**	**249.3**	**269.2**	**265.7**	**183.7**	**171.6**
Raw cotton	95.2	78.9	117.9	126.3	122.7	101.6	103.2
Hides & skins	174.0	189.9	224.9	305.7	326.6	258.8	213.2
Coal	87.9	116.8	189.5	208.1	199.9	194.0	189.6
Natural gas	155.5	335.4	185.8	153.9	182.4	105.4	96.2
Crude petroleum	85.2	150.1	218.6	281.2	259.2	129.5	111.2
Logs & timber	196.4	197.4	213.4	237.3	242.4	241.9	239.2
Wastepaper	282.5	230.9	421.5	363.6	342.0	291.8	312.5
Iron ore	94.8	116.9	147.1	127.0	135.4	132.0	124.3
Iron & steel scrap	142.1	289.8	541.1	526.7	543.1	342.8	328.5
Nonferrous metal ores (Dec. 1983=100)	68.0	150.0	298.6	330.6	313.8	272.6	262.4
Copper base scrap	123.7	258.6	548.2	582.3	532.3	427.6	369.0
Aluminum base scrap	177.0	210.1	241.6	226.1	242.5	208.7	186.2
Construction sand, gravel, & crushed stone	163.1	195.8	262.2	278.8	289.3	299.9	312.6

NA Not available.

Source: U.S. Bureau of Labor Statistics, PPI Databases, "Commodity Data including "headline" FD-ID Indexes," <http://www.bls.gov/ppi/data.htm>, accessed June 2017.

Table 761. Chain-Type Price Indexes for Personal Consumption Expenditures by Type of Expenditure: 1990 to 2016

[2009 = 100. For explanation of "chain-type," see text, Section 13. See also Table 700]

Type of Expenditure	1990	2000	2005	2010	2013	2014	2015	2016
Personal consumption expenditures	**67.4**	**83.1**	**92.3**	**101.7**	**107.5**	**109.2**	**109.5**	**110.8**
Household consumption expenditures [1]	66.8	82.8	92.1	101.7	107.7	109.3	109.5	110.7
Food and beverages purchased for off-premises consumption	65.2	79.0	88.2	100.3	107.8	109.8	111.0	109.9
Food and nonalcoholic beverages purchased for off-premises consumption	65.1	78.3	87.8	100.3	108.6	110.7	112.1	110.7
Alcoholic beverages purchased for off-premises consumption	65.7	83.1	90.7	100.4	103.3	104.0	104.2	105.2
Food produced and consumed on farms	101.9	85.4	104.6	113.1	140.5	154.5	136.3	119.5
Clothing, footwear, and related services	114.4	107.9	100.5	99.5	105.6	105.8	104.7	104.5
Clothing	117.4	110.2	101.4	99.2	105.4	105.6	103.9	103.6
Garments	122.9	113.2	102.4	98.9	105.1	105.2	103.3	102.9
Women's and girls' clothing	128.5	112.4	102.5	99.1	104.4	105.1	102.2	102.2
Men's and boys' clothing	115.7	114.2	102.2	98.5	107.0	105.9	105.1	104.4
Children's and infants' clothing	116.2	114.0	101.9	99.7	102.3	103.3	105.2	101.8
Footwear [2]	100.6	97.3	96.6	100.9	106.5	106.8	107.9	108.3
Housing, utilities, and fuels	56.6	74.5	88.5	100.5	106.5	109.5	111.9	114.9
Housing	57.3	76.5	89.2	100.1	106.0	108.8	112.1	115.9
Rental of tenant-occupied nonfarm housing [3]	56.2	74.4	87.5	100.1	107.4	110.6	114.4	118.5
Imputed rental of owner-occupied nonfarm housing [4]	57.9	77.4	89.7	100.0	105.5	108.3	111.4	115.1
Household utilities and fuels	52.9	65.6	85.4	102.5	109.2	113.4	110.2	109.0
Water supply and sanitation	43.5	65.8	80.7	106.3	123.3	127.9	133.7	138.6
Electricity, gas, and other fuels	55.7	65.6	86.9	101.3	104.9	109.0	103.3	100.4
Electricity	61.0	66.7	78.3	100.2	104.0	107.8	108.5	107.3
Natural gas	50.3	69.0	111.0	98.0	90.1	96.2	85.0	82.7
Fuel oil and other fuels	40.9	54.1	88.6	117.0	148.9	148.2	105.3	87.7
Furnishings, household equipment, and routine household maintenance	94.5	102.1	99.1	97.2	95.3	93.3	92.0	90.8
Furniture, furnishings, and floor coverings [5]	106.5	113.4	105.2	95.5	90.6	87.7	86.4	84.4
Household textiles	159.6	144.1	119.7	94.7	85.6	83.3	79.3	77.1
Household appliances [6]	97.1	94.3	91.9	96.4	98.2	93.5	89.6	85.9
Glassware, tableware, and household utensils [7]	116.0	116.1	103.7	97.4	90.5	86.8	85.1	82.9
Health	52.1	75.7	89.1	102.6	108.2	109.8	111.0	112.9
Medical products, appliances, and equipment	56.6	77.4	90.5	103.0	109.8	112.7	116.4	120.6
Pharmaceutical and other medical products [8]	54.1	75.5	89.8	103.6	111.2	114.5	118.9	123.8
Pharmaceutical products	53.9	75.3	89.7	103.7	111.4	114.7	119.2	124.1
Other medical products	75.9	94.7	96.0	97.9	99.8	99.3	98.6	98.1
Therapeutic appliances and equipment	70.8	89.2	94.4	99.4	101.5	102.2	101.8	102.4
Outpatient services	56.9	80.7	90.6	102.2	105.8	106.8	106.8	107.8
Physician services [9]	60.4	84.9	92.0	102.4	105.5	106.1	104.9	105.2
Dental services	40.4	66.6	83.5	102.7	111.2	113.5	116.4	119.7
Paramedical services	60.2	80.9	91.5	101.6	104.2	105.3	106.2	107.4
Hospital and nursing home services	47.1	70.8	87.1	102.8	109.6	111.0	112.2	113.7
Hospitals [10]	47.7	71.0	87.3	102.9	110.1	111.6	112.5	113.9
Nursing homes	45.0	70.1	86.4	102.0	106.8	108.1	110.3	113.3
Transportation	69.8	85.5	95.7	108.2	121.5	120.8	110.9	107.8
Motor vehicles	87.8	109.6	105.8	106.5	111.2	111.3	111.3	109.9
New motor vehicles	89.4	106.2	102.2	102.1	107.7	108.4	109.3	109.6
Net purchases of used motor vehicles	83.5	116.7	113.0	114.5	116.5	115.2	112.9	107.9
Motor vehicle operation	57.4	70.5	90.8	109.5	127.1	125.6	108.4	103.8
Motor vehicle parts and accessories	80.0	78.4	84.9	101.9	108.5	108.2	108.5	108.4
Motor vehicle fuels, lubricants, and fluids	49.7	63.4	95.8	118.2	149.7	145.5	107.0	95.3
Public transportation	77.2	88.8	88.9	105.8	119.5	120.8	118.4	118.3
Ground transportation [11]	55.4	70.5	85.9	104.3	119.1	118.9	117.7	120.1
Air transportation	91.0	99.6	90.2	107.2	121.3	124.1	120.6	117.9
Water transportation	127.9	142.4	113.0	101.1	97.0	96.3	97.1	104.3
Communication	106.2	106.2	100.9	99.7	98.1	97.7	95.5	94.5
Telecommunication services	103.4	100.0	95.1	99.3	97.1	96.3	94.1	93.7
Internet access	180.6	125.8	125.1	100.7	100.3	101.4	100.7	100.5
Recreation	115.0	111.4	104.4	97.5	93.6	92.7	91.7	90.5
Video and audio equipment, computers, and related services	338.9	184.0	132.7	92.9	78.5	75.4	72.5	69.0
Video and audio equipment	348.2	235.1	165.1	86.4	62.4	57.7	53.2	48.0
Sports and recreational goods and related services	116.0	112.7	103.0	97.1	90.9	88.4	86.2	83.9
Sports and recreational vehicles	81.4	94.2	96.3	100.4	104.9	104.6	104.7	106.2
Other sporting and recreational goods	131.2	120.5	105.8	96.1	87.2	84.2	81.4	78.2
Magazines, newspapers, books, and stationery	66.7	89.2	93.3	100.3	104.9	106.9	107.6	107.6
Education	31.9	56.7	79.5	104.7	119.1	123.1	127.1	130.5
Higher education	28.8	54.7	78.3	105.2	120.6	125.1	129.4	132.9
Net foreign travel and expenditures abroad by U.S. residents:								
Foreign travel by U.S. residents	56.7	70.6	88.6	105.2	113.3	115.0	109.6	106.7
Less: Expenditures in the United States by nonresidents	60.7	78.9	90.0	103.4	113.2	115.6	114.6	115.6

[1] Consists of household purchases of goods and services from business, government, nonprofit institutions, and the rest of the world. [2] Consists of shoes and other footwear, and of repair and hire of footwear. [3] Consists of rent for space (see footnote 4) and rent for appliances, furnishings, and furniture. [4] Consists of rent for space and for heating and plumbing facilities, water heaters, lighting fixtures, kitchen cabinets, linoleum, storm windows and doors, window screens, and screen doors, but excludes rent for appliances and furniture and purchases of fuel and electricity. [5] Includes clocks, lamps, lighting fixtures, and other household decorative items; also includes repair of furniture, furnishings, and floor coverings. [6] Consists of major household appliances, small electric household appliances, and repair of household appliances. [7] Consists of dishes, flatware, and non-electric cookware and tableware. [8] Excludes drug preparations and related products dispensed by physicians, hospitals, and other medical services. [9] Consists of offices of physicians, health maintenance organization medical centers, and freestanding ambulatory surgical and emergency centers. [10] Consists of nonprofit hospitals, proprietary hospitals, and government hospitals. Consists of primary sales of these hospitals for personal consumption. [11] Includes railway transportation, taxicab services, school and employee services, limousine services, and airport bus fares.

Source: U.S. Bureau of Economic Analysis, National Income and Product Accounts Tables, "Table 2.5.4. Price Indexes for Personal Consumption Expenditures by Function," <http://www.bea.gov/itable/>, accessed August 2017.

Table 762. Chain-Type Price Indexes for Gross Domestic Product: 1990 to 2016

[2010=100. For explanation of "chain-type," see text, Section 13]

Component	1990	2000	2005	2010	2013	2014	2015	2016
Gross domestic product	66.8	81.9	92.0	101.2	106.9	108.8	110.0	111.4
Personal consumption expenditures	67.4	83.1	92.3	101.7	107.5	109.2	109.5	110.8
Goods	87.2	94.8	97.0	101.6	106.1	105.8	102.7	101.2
Durable goods	126.3	120.3	107.7	98.6	94.6	92.4	90.4	88.5
Nondurable goods	70.5	82.7	91.6	103.1	111.9	112.7	109.0	107.8
Services	58.5	77.5	89.9	101.7	108.3	110.9	113.1	115.9
Gross private domestic investment	80.1	85.6	94.5	99.1	103.5	105.6	106.5	107.0
Fixed investment	79.3	85.5	94.5	99.2	103.7	106.0	107.1	107.8
Nonresidential	90.4	90.7	93.8	99.1	103.0	104.4	105.1	104.8
Structures	44.2	59.6	82.1	98.8	108.1	113.4	115.5	115.6
Equipment	124.6	105.4	98.6	98.0	100.0	99.9	99.8	99.6
Intellectual property products	86.5	96.1	96.0	100.5	103.8	104.8	105.8	105.0
Residential	57.1	76.1	98.1	99.6	106.4	112.9	115.9	120.2
Net exports of goods and services:								
Exports	87.5	87.2	94.7	104.3	112.1	112.1	106.5	104.5
Goods	94.7	88.4	95.5	105.0	112.8	111.7	103.7	99.9
Services	71.3	84.5	93.2	102.6	110.6	112.9	112.4	114.2
Imports	88.1	84.8	93.8	105.8	113.6	113.2	104.4	101.1
Goods	93.1	86.0	94.6	106.7	115.3	114.5	104.1	100.2
Services	68.6	80.0	91.1	101.8	106.2	108.0	106.2	105.7
Government consumption expenditures and gross investment	55.7	73.4	88.2	102.7	109.0	111.2	111.8	112.7
Federal	60.8	77.3	91.4	102.6	107.6	109.3	109.9	110.5
National defense	60.9	76.5	91.4	102.4	107.2	108.6	108.9	109.3
Nondefense	60.3	78.8	91.5	103.1	108.3	110.4	111.5	112.4
State and local	52.8	71.2	86.3	102.7	110.1	112.5	113.2	114.2

Source: U.S. Bureau of Economic Analysis, National Income and Product Accounts Tables, "Table 1.1.4. Price Indexes for Gross Domestic Product," <http://www.bea.gov/itable/>, accessed July 2017.

Table 763. Import and Export Price Indexes by End-Use Category: 1990 to 2017

[As of June. Import indexes are weighted by the 2000 Tariff Schedule of the United States Annotated, a scheme for describing and reporting product composition and value of U.S. imports. Import prices are based on U.S. dollar prices paid by importer. Export indexes are weighted by 2000 export values according to the Schedule B classification system of the U.S. Census Bureau. Prices used in these indexes were collected from a sample of U.S. manufacturers of exports and are factory transaction prices, except as noted. Minus sign (-) indicates decrease]

Year	Index (2000 = 100)						Percent change [1]					
	Imports			Exports			Imports			Exports		
	Total	Petroleum imports	Non–petroleum imports	Total	Agricultural exports	Non–agricultural exports	Total	Petroleum imports	Non–petroleum imports	Total	Agricultural exports	Non–agricultural exports
1990	90.8	55.4	96.4	95.1	107.7	93.5	-0.8	-13.4	0.5	-0.1	-4.0	0.5
1991	93.4	63.2	98.3	96.1	104.3	95.3	2.9	14.1	2.0	1.1	-3.2	1.9
1992	94.8	66.0	99.5	96.5	104.0	95.8	1.5	4.4	1.2	0.4	-0.3	0.5
1993	95.0	60.4	100.5	96.9	100.3	96.7	0.2	-8.5	1.0	0.4	-3.6	0.9
1994	96.3	57.6	102.6	98.5	109.3	97.5	1.4	-4.6	2.1	1.7	9.0	0.8
1995	101.4	62.9	107.6	104.5	117.0	103.3	5.3	9.2	4.9	6.1	7.0	5.9
1996	100.7	66.4	106.2	105.4	140.8	101.7	-0.7	5.6	-1.3	0.9	20.3	-1.5
1997	98.8	62.5	104.3	103.2	120.5	101.5	-1.9	-5.9	-1.8	-2.1	-14.4	-0.2
1998	93.1	44.3	100.5	99.9	110.8	98.8	-5.8	-29.1	-3.6	-3.2	-8.0	-2.7
1999	92.9	54.5	98.8	98.2	101.1	97.9	-0.2	23.0	-1.7	-1.7	-8.8	-0.9
2000	100.2	101.9	99.9	100.1	100.5	100.0	7.9	87.0	1.1	1.9	-0.6	2.1
2001	97.6	89.4	98.9	99.4	100.9	99.3	-2.6	-12.3	-1.0	-0.7	0.4	-0.7
2002	94.1	85.3	96.2	98.0	100.7	97.8	-3.6	-4.6	-2.7	-1.4	-0.2	-1.5
2003	96.2	96.4	97.3	99.5	110.0	98.7	2.2	13.0	1.1	1.5	9.2	0.9
2004	101.7	129.7	99.7	103.4	127.4	101.5	5.7	34.5	2.5	3.9	15.8	2.8
2005	109.2	181.5	102.0	106.7	123.9	105.4	7.4	39.9	2.3	3.2	-2.7	3.8
2006	117.3	242.6	104.2	111.2	124.1	110.3	7.4	33.7	2.2	4.2	0.2	4.6
2007	120.0	245.6	107.1	116.0	146.7	113.8	2.3	1.2	2.8	4.3	18.2	3.2
2008	145.5	450.3	114.9	126.1	195.2	121.2	21.3	83.3	7.3	8.7	33.1	6.5
2009	120.0	241.5	107.4	117.8	169.7	114.1	-17.5	-46.4	-6.5	-6.6	-13.1	-5.9
2010	125.2	267.4	110.7	122.2	165.3	119.1	4.3	10.7	3.1	3.7	-2.6	4.4
2011	142.2	397.8	116.4	134.5	217.2	128.6	13.6	48.8	5.1	10.1	31.4	8.0
2012	138.7	357.2	116.3	131.7	204.5	126.5	-2.5	-10.2	-0.1	-2.1	-5.8	-1.6
2013	138.8	364.9	115.7	132.8	224.2	126.2	0.1	2.2	-0.5	0.8	9.6	-0.2
2014	140.5	387.9	115.8	133.0	221.4	126.6	1.2	6.3	0.1	0.2	-1.2	0.3
2015	126.6	229.7	112.8	125.3	184.3	120.9	-9.9	-40.8	-2.6	-5.8	-16.8	-4.5
2016	120.7	173.1	110.5	120.9	181.9	116.3	-4.7	-24.6	-2.0	-3.5	-1.3	-3.8
2017	122.5	180.9	112.0	121.6	174.8	117.6	1.5	4.5	1.4	0.6	-3.9	1.1

[1] Percent change from immediate prior year.

Source: U.S. Bureau of Labor Statistics, U.S. Import and Export Price Indexes, "History Tables: Complete Historical Index Information," <http://www.bls.gov/mxp/>, accessed July 2017.

Table 764. Export Price Indexes—Selected Commodities: 2000 to 2017

[2000=100. As of June. Indexes are weighted by 2000 export values according to the Schedule B commodity classification system of the U.S. Census Bureau. Prices used in these indexes were collected from a sample of U.S. manufacturers of exports and are factory transaction prices; see source]

Commodity	2000 [1]	2005	2010	2013	2014	2015	2016	2017
All commodities	100.1	106.7	122.2	132.8	133.0	125.3	120.9	121.6
Live animals and animal products	102.2	130.9	172.2	214.9	242.3	193.5	186.3	206.6
Vegetable products	100.0	130.3	177.5	271.7	252.6	206.1	208.0	187.1
Fruit and nuts	94.8	126.5	131.0	155.0	173.9	175.1	158.2	133.4
Cereals	100.0	118.1	171.4	307.0	246.5	194.4	192.4	177.4
Wheat and meslin	99.4	130.0	151.6	272.2	243.0	198.3	174.2	169.9
Corn (maize)	101.0	111.8	174.3	324.4	227.9	181.1	197.1	175.6
Oilseeds	102.8	136.2	196.2	299.5	293.9	204.7	220.2	190.7
Prepared foodstuffs, beverages, and tobacco	100.0	110.3	139.3	167.1	169.5	153.2	150.0	147.3
Mineral products	97.8	182.3	247.9	292.8	295.9	211.3	167.6	191.7
Fuels	97.4	172.8	239.2	289.7	292.7	205.0	160.1	183.3
Petroleum oils	97.4	184.8	231.5	326.6	333.6	228.8	179.3	181.2
Chemicals and related products	100.3	115.3	144.5	153.9	149.7	143.9	136.3	132.7
Plastics and rubber products	101.5	118.4	136.8	149.9	150.5	143.0	136.3	138.0
Hides, skins, and leather products	95.7	113.0	121.2	146.6	159.2	140.0	119.3	121.1
Woodpulp and paper products	101.6	101.9	117.6	122.7	123.8	123.7	121.2	126.7
Textiles	100.2	100.8	115.7	131.4	132.5	122.2	119.5	120.3
Stone and glass products	100.7	103.5	115.9	118.2	120.2	122.4	122.8	123.0
Gems and precious metals	98.1	106.5	211.0	253.9	245.7	233.8	229.6	233.5
Base metals	100.5	131.8	160.4	165.8	163.2	153.1	143.3	151.2
Iron and steel	101.7	164.0	194.3	186.7	191.8	165.5	144.7	153.4
Copper	98.7	143.1	217.0	236.9	225.0	191.3	150.1	167.8
Aluminum	98.4	113.2	117.8	122.5	119.8	115.5	104.7	111.3
Machinery	99.9	94.9	95.5	97.2	97.6	97.1	95.9	96.1
Nonelectrical machinery	100.0	100.5	106.8	111.5	112.9	113.5	112.9	113.8
Computer equipment	99.9	76.6	53.1	49.3	48.4	43.8	40.6	37.6
Electrical machinery	99.8	88.6	83.2	81.7	81.0	79.3	77.5	77.0
Transportation equipment	100.0	108.8	121.4	127.9	130.0	130.8	131.7	132.7
Motor vehicles and their parts	100.0	103.2	108.5	113.7	115.2	115.0	114.9	115.1
Instruments	100.0	101.3	106.2	107.1	107.7	107.8	106.1	106.7
Miscellaneous manufactured articles	100.4	100.6	108.1	110.5	110.5	111.3	111.6	112.4

[1] June 2000 may not equal 100 because indexes were reweighted to an "average" trade value in 2000.

Source: U.S. Bureau of Labor Statistics, U.S. Import and Export Price Indexes, "History Tables: Complete Historical Index Information," <http://www.bls.gov/mxp/>, accessed July 2017.

Table 765. Import Price Indexes—Selected Commodities: 2000 to 2017

[2000=100. As of June. Indexes are weighted by the 2000 Tariff Schedule of the United States Annotated, a scheme for describing and reporting product composition and value of U.S. imports. Import prices are based on U.S. dollar prices paid by importer]

Commodity	2000 [1]	2005	2010	2013	2014	2015	2016	2017
All commodities	100.2	109.2	125.2	138.8	140.5	126.6	120.7	122.5
Live animals and animal products	99.9	112.7	143.0	179.3	195.8	185.2	189.4	198.7
Meat	100.5	138.7	183.2	219.8	251.6	234.5	236.0	254.8
Fish	100.2	88.3	107.1	134.6	140.3	127.3	139.8	144.3
Vegetable products	97.1	116.9	169.5	204.2	196.4	201.8	185.9	221.8
Vegetables	93.9	136.8	326.2	347.5	354.0	459.9	406.7	469.8
Fruit and nuts	96.9	89.7	106.8	110.4	101.1	95.5	82.1	133.5
Prepared foodstuffs, beverages and tobacco	100.0	114.0	141.2	156.6	161.6	160.7	163.6	160.7
Mineral products	101.3	178.1	248.5	332.2	353.1	210.9	157.9	168.7
Fuels	101.3	177.5	244.9	329.0	350.3	208.1	155.5	165.9
Chemicals and related products	99.8	111.3	139.3	150.1	152.6	148.3	146.8	151.8
Organic chemicals	100.6	109.6	133.8	135.2	135.1	123.7	120.3	124.1
Pharmaceutical products	99.8	111.0	117.9	125.0	134.1	136.7	142.4	148.9
Plastics and rubber products	99.9	113.5	136.7	152.1	148.0	142.1	136.6	139.2
Hides, skins, and leather products	100.2	104.0	114.5	125.4	127.7	128.1	123.5	123.6
Wood products	100.5	124.2	134.3	150.6	146.4	138.6	140.6	154.4
Woodpulp and paper products	100.0	102.3	112.5	113.6	113.7	111.9	109.9	110.6
Textiles	99.7	100.4	103.1	114.1	114.1	114.5	113.2	113.1
Footwear	99.6	100.3	106.1	120.4	121.4	122.3	122.0	121.4
Stone and glass products	99.5	105.4	123.8	132.3	133.2	132.8	131.7	129.1
Gems and precious metals	99.3	98.3	161.5	186.2	180.2	170.8	167.6	170.6
Gold	98.3	150.7	430.5	504.8	446.7	424.4	437.0	458.8
Platinum	(NA)	125.7	292.6	272.7	283.8	249.7	185.7	245.4
Base metals	101.5	132.1	180.2	181.3	183.0	168.1	155.1	166.0
Iron and steel	104.1	170.6	238.8	215.6	222.4	181.6	169.5	195.5
Articles of iron and steel	100.6	122.7	149.9	155.4	154.0	148.2	138.0	142.0
Copper	97.2	142.7	313.8	339.8	327.2	299.8	241.1	266.2
Aluminum	97.9	113.2	132.8	137.6	140.8	131.5	120.9	128.4
Machinery	100.2	89.7	86.5	85.0	84.6	82.5	80.8	80.4
Nonelectrical machinery	99.8	90.1	87.9	89.7	89.7	87.7	85.8	85.8
Electrical machinery	100.5	89.4	85.2	80.6	79.8	77.6	76.0	75.3
Transportation equipment	100.0	104.4	109.7	116.2	116.1	114.6	114.2	114.2
Motor vehicles and their parts	100.1	103.8	108.8	115.0	114.9	113.2	112.9	113.2
Instruments	99.8	100.1	100.8	103.8	104.9	103.7	103.4	101.4
Miscellaneous manufactured articles	99.7	99.4	106.5	113.0	113.5	112.8	112.2	110.9
Furniture	99.5	103.4	109.4	116.8	117.7	117.3	116.8	116.4

NA Not available. [1] June 2000 may not equal 100 because indexes were reweighted to an "average" trade value in 2000.

Source: U.S. Bureau of Labor Statistics, U.S. Import and Export Price Indexes, "History Tables: Complete Historical Index Information," <http://www.bls.gov/mxp/>, accessed July 2017.

Business Enterprise

This section relates to the place and behavior of the business firm and to business initiative in the American economy. It includes data on the number, type, and size of businesses; financial data of domestic and multinational U.S. corporations; business investments, expenditures, and profits; and sales and inventories.

The principal sources of these data are the *Survey of Current Business*, published online by the Bureau of Economic Analysis (BEA); the website of the Board of Governors of the Federal Reserve System at <http://www.federalreserve.gov/econresdata/statisticsdata.htm>; the annual *Statistics of Income (SOI)* reports of the Internal Revenue Service (IRS); and the U.S. Census Bureau's Economic Census, *County Business Patterns, Quarterly Financial Report for Manufacturing, Mining, and Trade Corporations (QFR), Annual Survey of Entrepreneurs, Survey of Business Owners*, and *Annual Capital Expenditures Survey*. See also BEA Interactive Tables <http://www.bea.gov/iTable/index.cfm>.

Business firms—A firm is generally defined as a business organization or entity consisting of one or more domestic establishment locations under common ownership or control. The terms firm, business, company, and enterprise are used interchangeably throughout this section. A firm doing business in more than one industry is classified by industry according to the major activity of the firm as a whole.

The IRS concept of a business firm relates primarily to the legal entity used for tax reporting purposes. A sole proprietorship is an unincorporated business owned by one person and may include large enterprises with many employees and hired managers and part-time operators. A partnership is an unincorporated business owned by two or more persons, each of whom has a financial interest in the business. A corporation is a business that is legally incorporated under state laws. While many corporations file consolidated tax returns, most corporate tax returns represent individual corporations, some of which are affiliated through common ownership or control with other corporations filing separate returns.

Economic Census—The Economic Census is the major source of facts about the structure and functioning of the nation's economy. It provides essential information for government, business, industry, and the general public. It establishes benchmarks for economic indicators such as the gross domestic product estimates, production and price indexes, business sales, and other statistical series that measure short-term changes in economic conditions. The Census Bureau takes the Economic Census every 5 years, covering years ending in "2" and "7."

The Economic Census is collected on an establishment basis. A company operating at more than one location is required to file a separate report for each store, factory, shop, or other location. Companies engaged in distinctly different lines of activity at one location are requested to submit separate reports, if the business records permit such a separation, and if the activities are substantial in size. Each establishment is assigned a separate industry classification based on its primary activity and not that of its parent company. Establishments responding to the establishment survey are classified into industries on the basis of their principal product or activity (determined by self-reporting, annual sales volume, or products manufactured by a plant). The statistics issued by industry in the 2012 Economic Census are classified primarily on the 2012 North American Industry Classification System (NAICS).

Data from the 2012 Economic Census have been fully released as of September 2016 through the Census Bureau's American FactFinder® service on the Census Bureau website at <factfinder.census.gov>. More detailed information about the scope, coverage, methodology, classification system, data items, and publications for the Economic Censuses and related surveys is available at <https://www.census.gov/EconomicCensus>.

Survey of Business Owners—The Survey of Business Owners (SBO) provides statistics that describe the composition of U.S. businesses by gender, ethnicity, race and veteran status. Data from SBO are published in a series of releases: *American Indian- and Alaska Native-Owned Firms, Asian-Owned Firms, Black-Owned Firms, Hispanic-Owned Firms, Native Hawaiian- and Other Pacific Islander-Owned Firms, Women-Owned Firms, Veteran-Owned Firms, Characteristics of Business Owners*, and *Company Summary*. Data are presented by industry classifications, geographic area, and size of firm (employment and receipts). Each owner had the option of selecting more than one race and therefore is included in each race selected. For more information, see <http://www.census.gov/programs-surveys/sbo.html>.

Annual Survey of Entrepreneurs— The Annual Survey of Entrepreneurs provides statistics that describe the economic and demographic characteristics of employer businesses and their owners by gender, ethnicity, race and veteran status. Data from ASE is published in a series of releases: Company Summary Tables, Characteristics of Businesses, and Characteristics of Business Owners. For more information see <https://www.census.gov/programs-surveys/ase.html>.

North American Industry Classification System (NAICS)—NAICS is the standard used by federal statistical agencies in classifying business establishments for the purpose of collecting, analyzing, and publishing statistical data related to the U.S. business economy. NAICS was developed under the auspices of the Office of Management and Budget (OMB), and adopted in 1997 to replace the Standard Industrial Classification (SIC) system. The official *2012 U.S. NAICS Manual* includes definitions for each industry, background information, tables showing changes between 2007 and 2012, and a comprehensive index. For more information, see <http://www.census.gov/eos/www/naics/>.

Noticeable changes were made to six of the twenty NAICS sectors during the 2012 revision of NAICS. Those sectors are 22 (utilities), 23 (construction),

31-33 (manufacturing), 42 (wholesale trade), 44-45 (retail trade) and 72 (accommodation and food services).

Quarterly Financial Report—The Quarterly Financial Report (QFR) program publishes quarterly aggregate statistics on the financial conditions of U.S. corporations. The QFR requests companies to report estimates from their statements of income and retained earnings, and balance sheets. The statistical data are classified and aggregated by type of industry and asset size. The QFR sample includes corporations that have a plurality of business activity in manufacturing industries with domestic assets of $250,000 and above, and mining, wholesale, retail, and selected service industries with assets of $50 million and above. The data are available quarterly in the *Quarterly Financial Report for Manufacturing, Mining, and Trade Corporations* at <https://www.census.gov/econ/qfr/>.

Multinational enterprises—BEA collects financial and operating data on U.S. multinational enterprises. These data provide a picture of the overall activities of foreign affiliates and U.S. parent enterprises, using a variety of indicators of their financial structure and operations. The data on foreign affiliates cover the entire operations of the affiliate, irrespective of the percentage of U.S. ownership. These data cover items such as sales, value added, employment and compensation of employees, capital expenditures, exports and imports, and research and development expenditures. Separate tabulations are available for all affiliates and for affiliates that are majority-owned by their U.S. parent(s). More information is available at <http://www.bea.gov/international/index.htm#omc>.

Statistical reliability—For a discussion of statistical collection, estimation, and sampling procedures and measures of reliability applicable to data from the Census Bureau and the Internal Revenue Service, see Appendix III.

Table 766. Number of Tax Returns, Receipts, and Net Income by Type of Business: 1990 to 2013

[14,783 represents 14,783,000. Covers active enterprises only. Nonfarm sole proprietorship and partnership data are for tax year shown which covers returns processed by the IRS during the following calendar year. Corporation data are for tax year shown which covers (a) corporate returns with accounting periods for the calendar year ending December of year shown and (b) those returns with accounting periods for the noncalendar year ending between July of year shown and June of the following year. Figures are estimates based on sample of unaudited tax returns; see Appendix III]

Item	Number of returns (1,000)			Business receipts [2] (bil. dol.)			Net income (less loss) [3] (bil. dol.)		
	Nonfarm proprietor- ships [1]	Partner- ships	Corpora- tions	Nonfarm proprietor- ships [1]	Partner- ships	Corpora- tions	Nonfarm proprietor- ships [1]	Partner- ships	Corpora- tions
1990...........	14,783	1,554	3,717	731	483	9,860	141	17	383
1991...........	15,181	1,515	3,803	713	483	9,966	142	21	361
1992...........	15,495	1,485	3,869	737	515	10,360	154	43	414
1993...........	15,848	1,468	3,965	757	561	10,866	156	67	510
1994...........	16,154	1,494	4,342	791	656	11,884	167	82	595
1995...........	16,424	1,581	4,474	807	761	12,786	169	107	736
1996...........	16,955	1,654	4,631	843	916	13,659	177	145	839
1997...........	17,176	1,759	4,710	870	1,142	14,461	187	168	957
1998...........	17,409	1,855	4,849	918	1,357	15,010	202	187	895
1999...........	17,576	1,937	4,936	969	1,616	16,314	208	228	985
2000...........	17,905	2,058	5,045	1,021	2,062	17,637	215	269	987
2001...........	18,338	2,132	5,136	1,017	2,278	17,504	217	276	649
2002...........	18,926	2,242	5,267	1,030	2,414	17,297	221	271	597
2003...........	19,710	2,375	5,401	1,050	2,546	18,264	230	301	822
2004...........	20,591	2,547	5,558	1,140	2,819	19,976	248	385	1,170
2005...........	21,468	2,764	5,671	1,223	3,280	21,800	270	546	2,027
2006...........	22,075	2,947	5,841	1,278	3,571	23,310	278	667	2,024
2007...........	23,123	3,096	5,869	1,324	3,847	24,217	281	683	1,950
2008...........	22,614	3,146	5,847	1,317	4,344	24,718	265	458	1,061
2009...........	22,660	3,169	5,825	1,178	3,562	21,585	245	410	971
2010...........	23,004	3,248	5,814	1,196	3,946	23,058	268	594	1,422
2011...........	23,427	3,285	5,823	1,266	4,455	25,198	283	581	1,406
2012...........	23,554	3,389	5,841	1,302	4,690	26,029	305	778	1,872
2013...........	24,075	3,461	5,888	1,342	5,069	26,850	302	769	(NA)

NA Not available. [1] Number of returns represents returns with nonfarm business net income or deficit. [2] Excludes investment income for S corporations; for definition, see footnote 1, Table 775. [3] Net income (less loss) is defined differently by form of organization, basically as follows: (a) Proprietorships: Total taxable receipts less total business deductions, including cost of sales and operations, depletion, and certain capital expensing, excluding charitable contributions and owners' salaries; (b) Partnerships: Total taxable receipts (including investment income except capital gains) less deductions, including cost of sales and operations and certain payments to partners, excluding charitable contributions, oil and gas depletion, and certain capital expensing; and (c) Corporations: Includes "Total net income (less deficit)" from S Corporations and is more comprehensive than what Statistics of Income generally publishes; net income is before income tax.

Source: U.S. Internal Revenue Service, "Tax Statistics," <http://www.irs.gov/uac/Tax-Stats-2>, accessed September 2016.

Table 767. Number of Business Tax Returns by Size of Receipts: 2000 to 2013

[In thousands (5,045 represents 5,045,000). Covers active enterprises only. Figures are estimates based on sample of unaudited tax returns; see Appendix III]

Size-class of receipts	2000	2005	2006	2007	2008	2009	2010	2011	2012	2013
Corporations, total..............	**5,045**	**5,671**	**5,841**	**5,869**	**5,847**	**5,825**	**5,814**	**5,823**	**5,841**	**5,888**
Under $25,000 [1].....................	1,220	1,300	1,363	1,391	1,444	1,501	1,484	1,449	1,409	1,419
$25,000 to $49,999.................	305	340	341	356	368	399	385	379	396	(NA)
$50,000 to $99,999.................	477	544	554	571	556	576	592	582	556	(NA)
$100,000 to $499,999..............	1,515	1,755	1,780	1,766	1,734	1,714	739	1,743	1,761	1,800
$500,000 to $999,999..............	582	644	668	657	663	641	618	624	646	644
$1,000,000 or more................	946	1,088	1,135	1,129	1,084	994	1,005	1,047	1,073	1,103
Partnerships, total..............	**2,058**	**2,764**	**2,947**	**3,096**	**3,146**	**3,169**	**3,249**	**3,285**	**3,389**	**3,461**
Under $25,000 [1].....................	1,105	1,465	1,568	1,650	1,705	1,746	1,788	1,774	1,815	1,845
$25,000 to $49,999.................	183	218	240	233	230	241	238	254	272	297
$50,000 to $99,999.................	187	233	245	275	266	279	289	289	293	274
$100,000 to $499,999..............	353	489	498	530	537	511	531	556	565	580
$500,000 to $999,999..............	92	131	149	149	147	148	151	150	164	171
$1,000,000 or more................	137	227	248	261	260	244	252	262	280	294
Nonfarm proprietorships, total.................................	**17,903**	**21,468**	**22,075**	**23,123**	**22,614**	**22,660**	**23,004**	**23,427**	**23,554**	**24,075**
Under $25,000 [1].....................	11,997	14,456	14,867	15,752	15,532	15,951	16,258	16,468	16,450	16,843
$25,000 to $49,999.................	2,247	2,587	2,721	2,796	2,729	2,722	2,652	2,740	2,838	2,816
$50,000 to $99,999.................	1,645	1,981	1,983	2,027	1,936	1,825	1,892	1,869	1,899	1,969
$100,000 to $499,999..............	1,733	2,091	2,139	2,173	2,051	1,834	1,869	2,002	1,999	2,067
$500,000 to $999,999..............	190	235	236	242	229	211	219	222	234	239
$1,000,000 or more................	92	117	128	132	137	116	114	126	134	140

NA Not available. [1] Includes firms with no receipts.

Source: U.S. Internal Revenue Service, "Statistics of Income Bulletin, Historical Table 12," <http://www.irs.gov/uac/SOI-Tax-Stats-Historical-Table-12>, accessed August 2016; and Statistics of Income 2013, Corporation Income Tax Returns, 2016. See also <https://www.irs.gov/uac/soi-tax-stats-corporation-complete-report>.

Table 768. Number of Tax Returns, Receipts, and Net Income by Type of Business and Industry: 2013

[Tax returns in thousands (24,075 represents 24,075,000); receipts and income in billions of dollars (1,342 represents $1,342,000,000,000). Covers active enterprises only. Nonfarm sole proprietorship and partnership data are for tax year shown which covers returns processed by the IRS during 2014. Corporation data are for tax year shown which covers (a) corporate returns with accounting periods for the calendar year ending December 2013 and (b) those returns with accounting periods for the noncalendar year ending between July 2013 and June 2014. Figures are estimates based on sample of unaudited tax returns; see Appendix III. Based on the North American Industry Classification System (NAICS), 2012; see text, this section. Minus sign (-) indicates net loss]

Industry	2012 NAICS code	Number of returns (1,000)			Business receipts [1] (bil. dol.)			Net income (less loss) [2] (bil. dol.)		
		Non-farm proprietorships	Partnerships	Corporations	Non-farm proprietorships	Partnerships	Corporations	Non-farm proprietorships	Partnerships	Corporations
Total........................	(X)	24,075	3,461	5,888	1,342	5,069	26,850	302	769	1,929
Agriculture, forestry, fishing, and hunting [3]................	11	295	135	136	20	33	184	1	5	9
Mining..........................	21	128	34	36	14	185	472	2	59	18
Utilities.........................	22	16	3	8	1	191	543	(Z)	-9	-7
Construction....................	23	2,700	153	695	201	233	1,322	34	11	45
Special trade contractors........	238	2,150	65	435	141	66	596	27	4	26
Manufacturing...................	31–33	367	69	243	31	1,105	7,934	4	59	527
Wholesale and retail trade [4]..........	(X)	2,726	237	961	247	1,326	8,540	15	27	264
Wholesale trade................	42	346	72	387	55	856	4,539	5	17	131
Retail trade [5]...................	44–45	2,380	165	574	192	470	4,001	11	11	133
Motor vehicle and parts dealers........	441	135	20	83	39	164	840	1	3	16
Food and beverage stores..........	445	108	22	97	26	70	671	1	1	18
Gasoline stations..........	447	15	7	45	23	93	364	(Z)	1	3
Transportation and warehousing........	48–49	1,180	43	220	96	214	827	13	1	31
Information [5]...................	51	373	35	127	12	330	1,011	3	58	92
Broadcasting (except internet)..........	515	105	4	7	4	58	103	1	8	13
Telecommunications..............	517	([6])	7	16	([6])	213	442	([6])	45	35
Finance and insurance........	52	618	317	244	79	218	2,249	19	316	564
Real estate and rental and leasing........	53	1,163	1,722	642	68	145	261	24	82	70
Professional, scientific, and technical services [5]....................	54	3,275	252	902	174	441	1,222	73	90	50
Legal services..................	5411	343	34	120	40	149	103	17	53	12
Accounting, tax preparation, bookkeeping, and payroll services......	5412	407	27	90	13	81	50	6	17	7
Management, scientific, and technical consulting services......................	5416	874	76	236	45	83	259	25	12	22
Management of companies and enterprises....................	55	(NA)	23	59	(NA)	17	185	(NA)	23	160
Administrative and support and waste management and remediation services....................	56	2,602	67	283	72	108	527	22	8	21
Educational services....................	61	758	23	56	11	6	65	4	-(Z)	3
Health care and social assistance........	62	2,116	85	458	119	237	698	48	33	39
Arts, entertainment, and recreation.......	71	1,512	56	126	38	61	116	9	3	5
Accommodation and food services.......	72	454	124	309	55	189	485	2	2	29
Accommodation....................	721	54	36	33	5	72	91	(Z)	(Z)	7
Food services and drinking places......	722	400	89	276	50	117	394	2	1	22
Other services [5]...................	81	3,175	82	384	98	30	208	26	1	9
Auto repair and maintenance............	8111	384	31	112	27	11	74	3	(Z)	4
Personal and laundry services...........	812	2,133	38	172	53	13	80	18	1	4
Religious, grantmaking, civic, professional, and similar organizations....................	813	269	(Z)	43	4	(Z)	9	2	(Z)	(Z)
Unclassified................................	(X)	616	(Z)	–	7	–	–	3	–	(Z)

– Represents zero. NA Not available. X Not applicable. Z Less than 500 or $500 million. [1] Excludes investment income for S corporations; for definition, see footnote 1, Table 775. [2] Net income (less loss) is defined differently by form of organization, basically as follows: (a) Proprietorships: Total taxable receipts less total business deductions, including cost of sales and operations, depletion, and certain capital expensing, excluding charitable contributions and owners' salaries; (b) Partnerships: Total taxable receipts (including investment income except capital gains) less deductions, including cost of sales and operations and certain payments to partners, excluding charitable contributions, oil and gas depletion, and certain capital expensing; and (c) Corporations: Total taxable receipts (including investment income, capital gains, and income from foreign subsidiaries deemed received for tax purposes, except for S corporations) less business deductions, including cost of sales and operations, depletion, certain capital expensing, and officers' compensation excluding S corporation charitable contributions and investment expenses; net income is before income tax. [3] For corporations, represents agricultural services only. [4] For corporations, includes trade business not identified as wholesale or retail. [5] Includes other industries, not shown separately. [6] Broadcasting includes telecommunications.

Source: U.S. Internal Revenue Service, "SOI Tax Stats - Business Tax Statistics," <http://www.irs.gov/uac/SOI-Tax-Stats-Business-Tax-Statistics>, accessed June 2016.

Table 769. Nonfarm Sole Proprietorships—Selected Income and Deduction Items: 2000 to 2014

[In billions of dollars (1,021 represents $1,021,000,000,000), except as indicated. Data are for tax year shown which covers returns processed by the IRS during the following calendar year. All figures are estimates based on samples. Tax law changes have affected the comparability of the data over time; see Statistics of Income reports for a description. See Appendix III]

Item	2000	2005	2008	2009	2010	2011	2012	2013	2014
Number of returns (1,000)	17,905	21,468	22,614	22,660	23,004	23,427	23,554	24,075	24,632
Returns with net income (1,000)	13,308	15,750	16,434	16,528	17,007	17,360	17,571	17,972	18,294
Business receipts	1,021	1,223	1,317	1,178	1,196	1,266	1,302	1,342	1,394
Income from sales and operations	1,008	1,205	1,296	1,159	1,176	1,246	1,281	1,323	1,375
Business deductions [1]	806	953	1,054	935	929	984	998	1,040	1,078
Cost of sales and operations [1]	387	397	435	366	367	394	390	406	417
Purchases	269	253	281	239	240	256	251	260	256
Labor costs	29	32	31	28	27	28	31	33	33
Materials and supplies	43	56	57	45	45	49	50	52	57
Advertising	10	14	15	14	13	13	14	15	15
Car and truck expenses	46	71	85	75	73	83	86	89	92
Commissions	12	15	13	12	12	13	14	14	14
Contract labor	(NA)	28	35	32	34	38	42	48	54
Depreciation	32	39	41	35	35	36	34	35	37
Insurance	14	19	18	17	16	17	17	18	19
Interest paid [2]	12	12	15	13	11	10	9	9	9
Legal and professional services	7	10	11	10	10	11	11	12	12
Office expenses	10	13	13	12	12	12	12	12	13
Rent paid [3]	33	39	44	41	42	43	43	45	47
Repairs	12	15	15	14	15	16	17	18	18
Salaries and wages (net)	63	75	79	75	74	78	80	83	87
Supplies	22	29	32	30	30	32	34	35	37
Taxes paid	14	17	18	17	18	18	18	19	19
Travel	8	11	13	11	12	13	13	14	15
Utilities	19	23	25	24	24	27	28	31	32
Net income (less loss) [4]	215	270	265	245	268	283	305	302	317
Net income [4]	245	315	325	309	323	337	357	357	375
Constant (2009) Dollars [5]									
Business receipts	1,247	1,330	1,327	1,178	1,181	1,225	1,237	1,255	1,283
Business deductions	985	1,037	1,062	935	918	953	948	973	992
Net income (less loss)	262	294	267	245	265	274	290	283	292
Net income	300	342	328	309	319	326	339	334	345

NA Not available. [1] Includes other amounts not shown separately. [2] Interest paid includes "mortgage interest" and "other interest paid on business indebtedness." [3] Rent paid includes "Rent on machinery and equipment" and "Rent on other business property." [4] After adjustment for the passive loss carryover from prior years. Therefore, "business receipts" minus "total deductions" do not equal "net income." [5] Based on the overall implicit price deflator for gross domestic product.

Source: U.S. Internal Revenue Service, "SOI Tax Stats - Nonfarm Sole Proprietorship Statistics," <http://www.irs.gov/uac/SOI-Tax-Stats-Nonfarm-Sole-Proprietorship-Statistics>, accessed February 2017.

Table 770. Partnerships—Selected Income and Balance Sheet Items: 2000 to 2014

[In billions of dollars (6,694 represents $6,694,000,000,000), except as indicated. Covers active partnerships only. Data are for tax year shown which covers returns processed by the IRS during the following calendar year. All figures are estimates based on samples. See Appendix III]

Item	2000	2005	2008	2009	2010	2011	2012	2013	2014
Number of returns (1,000)	2,058	2,764	3,146	3,169	3,248	3,285	3,389	3,461	3,611
Returns with net income (1,000)	1,261	1,580	1,609	1,608	1,635	1,725	1,869	1,944	2,019
Number of partners (1,000)	13,660	16,212	19,300	21,142	22,428	24,390	25,334	27,491	27,714
Assets [1, 2]	6,694	13,734	19,260	18,798	19,820	20,574	22,015	24,163	26,129
Depreciable assets (net)	1,487	2,176	3,254	3,181	3,263	3,337	3,570	3,798	4,093
Inventories, end of year	150	315	431	277	277	285	304	313	331
Land	359	607	885	892	913	922	957	1,001	1,069
Liabilities [1, 2]	3,696	7,483	10,167	9,085	8,994	8,939	9,277	9,841	10,625
Accounts payable	230	400	513	444	492	504	509	533	537
Short-term debt [3]	252	373	582	432	481	394	326	306	328
Long-term debt [4]	1,132	1,772	2,767	2,737	2,693	2,559	2,706	2,717	2,993
Nonrecourse loans	639	914	1,283	1,282	1,225	1,213	1,212	1,225	1,254
Partners' capital accounts [2]	2,999	6,251	9,092	9,713	10,826	11,636	12,738	14,322	15,504
Total receipts [1]	2,405	3,863	5,169	4,265	4,721	5,212	5,557	5,921	6,100
Business receipts	2,062	3,280	4,344	3,562	3,946	4,455	4,690	5,069	5,186
Deductions from a trade or business [1]	2,136	3,317	4,711	3,855	4,128	4,631	4,779	5,152	5,263
Cost of goods sold/operations	1,226	1,976	2,717	2,055	2,336	2,732	2,828	3,087	3,066
Salaries and wages	201	293	403	390	405	436	463	502	541
Taxes paid	31	47	63	62	63	69	73	79	83
Interest paid	93	103	143	94	86	81	81	78	83
Depreciation	59	71	130	125	130	172	137	158	168
Net income (less loss)	269	546	458	410	594	581	778	769	837
Net income	410	724	929	796	904	913	1,068	1,080	1,156

[1] Includes items not shown separately. [2] Assets, liabilities, and partners' capital accounts are understated because not all partnerships file complete balance sheets. [3] Mortgages, notes, and bonds payable in less than 1 year. [4] Mortgages, notes, and bonds payable in 1 year or more.

Source: U.S. Internal Revenue Service, "SOI Tax Stats - Partnership Statistics," <http://www.irs.gov/uac/SOI-Tax-Stats-Partnership-Statistics>, accessed September 2017.

Table 771. Partnerships—Selected Items by Industry: 2014

[In billions of dollars (26,129 represents 26,129,000,000,000), except as indicated. Covers active partnerships only. Data are for tax year shown which covers returns processed by the IRS during 2015. Figures are estimates based on samples. Based on the North American Industry Classification System (NAICS), 2012; see text, this section. Minus sign (-) indicates net loss]

Industry and year	2012 NAICS code	Number of partnerships (1,000)			Total assets [1]	Business receipts	Total deductions	Net income less loss	Net income	Net loss
		Total	With net income	With net loss						
Total [2]	(X)	3,611	2,019	1,593	26,129	5,186	5,163	837.4	1,156.1	318.7
Agriculture, forestry, fishing, and hunting	11	144	83	61	219	33	42	8.5	16.2	7.8
Mining	21	31	19	12	639	209	171	64.9	83.2	18.3
Utilities	22	5	2	3	399	202	213	-4.9	10.7	15.6
Construction	23	143	75	68	215	266	260	12.9	19.0	6.1
Manufacturing	31–33	67	24	42	837	1,142	1,116	61.7	80.9	19.2
Wholesale trade	42	82	37	45	280	668	658	18.4	24.7	6.3
Retail trade	44–45	169	87	82	212	557	559	11.8	18.7	6.9
Transportation and warehousing	48–49	47	28	19	572	238	248	4.6	22.9	18.3
Information	51	42	19	23	764	339	308	55.5	67.4	12.0
Finance and insurance	52	335	229	106	14,737	236	334	346.4	395.6	49.3
Real estate and rental and leasing	53	1,817	1,001	816	5,637	150	169	91.4	199.7	108.3
Professional, scientific, and technical services	54	220	126	93	254	457	383	94.0	105.8	11.8
Management of companies and enterprises	55	33	16	16	700	19	32	23.2	31.3	8.1
Administrative and support & waste management and remediation services	56	66	42	24	91	111	117	7.2	11.0	3.8
Educational services	61	29	13	16	6	7	7	-0.1	0.8	0.8
Health care and social assistance	62	85	54	31	163	253	237	33.6	40.2	6.6
Arts, entertainment, and recreation	71	74	35	39	128	69	77	2.8	10.0	7.2
Accommodation and food services	72	138	74	65	252	197	200	4.0	14.8	10.8
Other services	81	86	53	33	25	33	32	1.6	3.3	1.6

X Not applicable. [1] Total assets are understated because not all partnerships file complete balance sheets. [2] Includes businesses not allocable to individual industries.

Source: U.S. Internal Revenue Service, "SOI Tax Stats - Partnership Statistics," <http://www.irs.gov/uac/SOI-Tax-Stats-Partnership-Statistics-by-Sector-or-Industry>, accessed September 2017.

Table 772. Nonfinancial Noncorporate Business-Sector Balance Sheet: 2000 to 2016

[In billions of dollars (7,743 represents $7,743,000,000,000), except as noted. Represents year-end (4th quarter) outstandings]

Item	2000	2005	2010	2011	2012	2013	2014	2015	2016
Assets	7,743	12,505	12,420	13,050	14,045	15,382	16,532	17,652	18,449
Nonfinancial assets	6,271	9,908	8,692	9,125	9,819	10,852	11,559	12,359	12,820
Real estate [1]	5,536	8,968	7,536	7,896	8,552	9,540	10,191	10,986	11,549
Residential	3,275	5,729	4,281	4,498	4,845	5,366	5,653	6,164	6,533
Nonresidential	2,261	3,239	3,255	3,399	3,707	4,174	4,538	4,821	5,016
Equipment [2]	453	574	709	741	773	811	849	880	876
Residential [3]	35	42	42	44	44	44	43	43	43
Nonresidential	418	533	667	697	728	767	806	836	833
Intellectual property products [2]	96	148	190	197	205	214	223	233	152
Inventories [2]	185	218	257	291	289	287	296	261	243
Financial assets	1,473	2,597	3,728	3,925	4,226	4,531	4,973	5,293	5,629
Checkable deposits and currency	181	374	532	556	616	627	697	737	783
Time and savings deposits	248	324	356	362	372	384	400	427	455
Money market fund shares	49	69	77	78	81	83	86	92	97
Debt securities [4]	43	61	54	55	59	60	61	65	70
Treasury securities	40	56	48	49	53	55	57	61	65
Municipal securities	2	4	6	6	6	4	4	4	5
Loans [4]	23	36	42	36	34	35	34	37	39
Mortgages	23	36	42	36	34	35	34	37	39
Trade receivables	342	431	533	594	599	648	669	715	761
Miscellaneous assets	587	1,302	2,134	2,244	2,466	2,695	3,027	3,220	3,424
Insurance receivables	77	99	132	127	142	116	129	119	121
Equity investment in GSEs [5]	3	4	7	7	7	8	8	9	10
Other	506	1,198	1,996	2,110	2,316	2,571	2,889	3,092	3,294
Liabilities	2,796	4,180	5,672	5,643	5,885	6,069	6,447	6,832	7,214
Loans	1,912	2,898	3,951	3,887	4,057	4,162	4,443	4,744	5,047
Depository institution loans n.e.c. [6]	402	671	927	901	968	990	1,077	1,175	1,247
Other loans and advances	129	135	171	171	181	187	196	202	205
Mortgages	1,381	2,093	2,853	2,814	2,909	2,985	3,170	3,368	3,595
Trade payables	267	335	428	483	494	528	537	588	646
Taxes payable	65	87	99	100	107	111	117	121	124
Miscellaneous liabilities	549	858	1,189	1,168	1,220	1,262	1,339	1,368	1,385
Net worth	4,947	8,325	6,748	7,407	8,160	9,314	10,085	10,820	11,234
Debt/net worth (percent)	39	35	59	53	50	44	44	44	45

[1] At market value. [2] At replacement (current) cost. [3] Durable goods in rental properties. [4] Includes other items not shown separately. [5] Government-sponsored enterprises (GSEs). Equity in the Farm Credit System. [6] Not elsewhere classified.

Source: Board of Governors of the Federal Reserve System, "Z.1, Financial Accounts of the United States," March 2017, <http://www.federalreserve.gov/releases/z1/>, accessed March 2017.

Table 773. Nonfinancial Corporate Business-Sector Balance Sheet: 2000 to 2016

[In billions of dollars (20,433 represents $20,433,000,000,000). Represents year-end (4th quarter) outstandings]

Item	2000	2005	2010	2011	2012	2013	2014	2015	2016
Assets	**20,433**	**26,065**	**28,952**	**30,502**	**31,941**	**34,829**	**37,311**	**39,568**	**41,759**
Nonfinancial assets	10,673	14,164	14,935	15,993	16,853	18,568	20,036	21,395	22,535
Real estate [1]	5,363	7,920	7,540	8,228	8,794	10,199	11,378	12,523	13,319
Equipment [2]	2,889	3,298	3,854	4,008	4,139	4,287	4,447	4,584	4,709
Intellectual property products [2]	1,081	1,322	1,669	1,747	1,819	1,917	2,007	2,105	2,227
Inventories [2]	1,340	1,624	1,873	2,010	2,100	2,164	2,204	2,184	2,280
Financial assets [3]	9,761	11,901	14,017	14,509	15,088	16,261	17,274	18,173	19,224
Checkable deposits and currency	226	268	234	265	220	283	347	334	401
Time and savings deposits	272	450	549	562	595	631	613	582	616
Money market fund shares	214	352	498	462	519	559	558	577	583
Debt securities	123	213	156	147	135	122	133	126	146
Mutual fund shares [1]	118	134	187	166	180	211	235	236	256
Trade receivables	1,939	2,108	2,157	2,241	2,293	2,555	2,659	2,638	2,757
U.S. direct investment abroad	1,352	2,206	3,403	3,759	4,135	4,390	4,616	4,807	5,090
Liabilities [3]	**9,632**	**11,182**	**13,227**	**13,878**	**14,696**	**15,397**	**16,572**	**17,355**	**18,064**
Debt securities	2,710	3,007	3,962	4,166	4,519	4,812	5,122	5,530	5,825
Commercial paper	278	90	83	116	130	145	182	177	183
Municipal securities [4]	154	242	506	514	527	529	529	544	561
Corporate bonds	2,278	2,674	3,373	3,536	3,861	4,138	4,411	4,809	5,081
Loans	1,955	2,258	2,090	2,211	2,197	2,280	2,377	2,479	2,599
Depository institution loans n.e.c. [5]	901	591	477	629	712	786	856	936	985
Other loans and advances	701	903	948	1,008	1,037	1,063	1,126	1,109	1,140
Mortgages	353	763	665	573	448	431	395	435	474
Trade payables	1,542	1,701	1,746	1,772	1,837	1,938	2,088	2,048	2,146
Taxes payable	78	86	45	52	54	45	43	42	29
Foreign direct investment in U.S.	1,180	1,549	2,129	2,231	2,400	2,580	2,741	2,965	3,313
Net worth (market value)	**10,801**	**14,883**	**15,725**	**16,623**	**17,246**	**19,432**	**20,738**	**22,213**	**23,694**
Debt/net worth (percent)	60.6	53.5	51.4	52.8	54.3	53.2	54.5	55.6	55.3

[1] At market value. [2] At replacement (current) cost. [3] Includes items not shown separately. [4] Industrial revenue bonds. Issued by state and local governments to finance private investment and secured in interest and principal by the industrial user of the funds. [5] Not elsewhere classified.

Source: Board of Governors of the Federal Reserve System, "Z.1, Financial Accounts of the United States," March 2017 <http://www.federalreserve.gov/releases/z1/>, accessed March 2017.

Table 774. Corporate Funds—Sources and Uses: 2000 to 2016

[In billions of dollars (451 represents $451,000,000,000)]

Item	2000	2005	2010	2011	2012	2013	2014	2015	2016
Profits before tax	451	1,005	1,039	1,009	1,241	1,315	1,372	1,259	1,274
- Taxes on corporate income	170	272	221	229	267	284	314	308	322
- Net dividends	251	171	375	441	518	532	580	608	622
+ Capital consumption allowance [1]	786	808	1,077	1,236	1,107	1,139	1,204	1,266	1,306
= U.S. internal funds, book	816	1,370	1,520	1,575	1,564	1,638	1,682	1,609	1,635
+ Foreign earnings retained abroad	103	-18	218	215	190	226	228	216	213
+ Inventory valuation adjustment (IVA)	-17	-32	-41	-68	-14	3	3	55	-2
- Net capital transfers	(Z)	-16	21	-6	-17	-6	-7	-3	3
= Internal funds + IVA	902	1,335	1,677	1,729	1,756	1,873	1,920	1,883	1,843
Gross investment	1,108	1,171	1,381	934	1,022	1,628	1,219	1,798	1,805
Capital expenditures [2]	1,142	1,192	1,235	1,332	1,501	1,565	1,677	1,766	1,667
Fixed investment [3]	1,093	1,138	1,179	1,297	1,435	1,490	1,618	1,655	1,639
Inventory change + IVA	50	53	58	35	66	74	58	81	21
Net lending (+) or net borrowing (-) [2]	-34	-21	145	-398	-479	63	-458	32	138
Net acquisition of financial assets [2]	1,204	944	633	497	506	990	924	911	959
Foreign deposits	-7	10	9	-6	1	42	-8	-21	3
Checkable deposits and currency	35	61	80	31	-46	64	64	-13	67
Time and savings deposits [2]	35	50	60	13	33	36	-18	-31	34
Debt securities [2]	19	40	16	-8	-12	-13	12	-7	20
Municipal securities	7	(Z)	-3	-2	1	-2	(Z)	3	4
Loans	8	2	-4	2	-1	-3	3	1	1
Mutual fund shares	(Z)	1	11	-13	-2	1	15	7	7
Trade receivables	282	278	97	83	53	262	104	-21	119
U.S. direct investment abroad	138	25	303	404	319	299	293	297	261
Miscellaneous assets [2]	679	418	215	26	107	264	447	674	442
Insurance receivables	(Z)	21	12	12	8	-6	10	2	14
Investment in finance company subsidiaries	65	64	27	27	3	15	14	-4	-14
Net increase in liabilities [2]	1,238	965	488	894	986	927	1,382	879	821
Debt securities [2]	201	-7	236	204	353	293	310	408	296
Commercial paper	48	-8	25	33	14	14	37	-5	6
Corporate bonds	151	-41	178	162	325	277	273	399	272
Loans	157	265	-286	121	-57	98	97	100	124
Depository institution loans n.e.c [4]	55	-27	-87	152	101	74	70	78	49
Other loans and advances [5]	78	110	-90	60	-34	42	63	-17	31
Mortgages	24	182	-108	-91	-125	-17	-36	39	44
Corporate equities	-118	-300	-251	-455	-345	-353	-394	-561	-566
Trade payables	313	199	156	25	66	101	150	-41	98
Foreign direct investment in U.S.	249	99	157	193	182	176	152	320	339
Miscellaneous liabilities [2]	430	711	467	797	785	621	1,068	655	543
Claims of pension fund on sponsor	118	93	-25	-16	-3	109	85	67	5

Z Less than $500 million. [1] Consumption of fixed capital plus capital consumption adjustment. [2] Includes other items not shown separately. [3] Nonresidential fixed investment plus residential fixed investment. [4] Not elsewhere classified. [5] Loans from rest of the world, U.S. government, and nonbank financial institutions.

Source: Board of Governors of the Federal Reserve System, "Z.1, Financial Accounts of the United States," March 2017, <http://www.federalreserve.gov/releases/z1/>, accessed March 2017.

Table 775. Corporations—Selected Financial Items: 2000 to 2013

[In billions of dollars (47,027 represents $47,027,000,000,000), except as noted. Covers active corporations only. Corporation data are for tax year shown which covers (a) corporate returns with accounting periods for the calendar year ending December of year shown and (b) those returns with accounting periods for the noncalendar year ending between July of year shown and June of the following year. All corporations are required to file returns except those specifically exempt. See source for changes in law affecting comparability of historical data. Based on samples; see Appendix III]

Item	2000	2005	2007	2008	2009	2010	2011	2012	2013
Number of returns (1,000)	5,045	5,671	5,869	5,847	5,825	5,814	5,823	5,841	5,888
Number with net income (1,000)	2,819	3,324	3,368	3,184	3,149	3,265	3,385	3,549	3,581
S Corporation returns [1] (1,000)	2,860	3,684	3,990	4,050	4,095	4,128	4,159	4,205	4,258
Assets [2]	47,027	66,445	81,486	76,799	75,965	79,905	81,280	84,952	88,214
Cash	1,820	2,823	3,625	4,384	4,853	3,893	4,196	4,404	4,871
Notes and accounts receivable	8,754	11,962	15,315	13,855	12,544	12,718	13,089	13,016	12,714
Inventories	1,272	1,505	1,656	1,619	1,474	1,544	1,653	1,750	1,836
Investments in government obligations	1,236	1,613	1,785	2,193	2,501	2,730	2,859	3,002	2,958
Mortgage and real estate	2,822	4,777	5,177	5,450	4,847	7,914	7,615	7,579	7,533
Other investments	17,874	25,162	30,939	27,169	27,574	29,389	29,745	32,158	34,758
Depreciable assets	7,292	8,416	9,222	9,467	9,613	9,875	10,226	10,672	11,210
Depletable assets	191	310	497	587	629	661	757	855	922
Land	303	407	493	509	517	584	567	584	601
Liabilities [2]	47,027	66,445	81,486	76,799	75,965	79,905	81,280	84,952	88,214
Accounts payable	3,758	6,029	7,724	6,822	5,694	5,768	5,343	5,288	5,063
Short-term debt [3]	4,020	4,192	4,735	4,726	4,542	3,752	3,839	3,557	3,682
Long-term debt [4]	6,184	8,332	10,786	11,062	10,718	14,680	14,489	14,473	13,579
Net worth [5]	17,349	23,525	28,812	25,469	24,567	28,938	29,250	31,804	35,079
Capital stock	3,966	2,482	2,775	3,184	3,019	3,064	2,983	3,067	2,982
Paid-in or capital surplus	12,265	17,828	21,792	23,574	24,110	24,283	24,859	26,243	27,642
Retained earnings [6]	3,627	4,331	5,970	613	2,024	3,534	3,586	4,804	6,969
Receipts [2,7]	20,606	25,505	28,763	28,590	24,773	26,199	28,336	29,404	30,192
Business receipts [7,8]	17,637	21,800	24,217	24,718	21,585	23,058	25,198	26,029	26,850
Interest [9]	1,628	1,773	2,640	2,179	1,540	1,366	1,344	1,209	1,109
Rents and royalties	254	290	314	317	296	307	315	332	355
Deductions [2,7]	19,692	23,613	26,974	27,687	23,944	24,944	27,093	27,713	28,357
Cost of goods sold [8]	11,135	13,816	15,513	16,080	13,286	14,502	16,180	16,579	17,141
Compensation of officers	401	445	479	467	428	435	454	479	479
Rent paid on business property	380	439	477	491	476	467	471	484	495
Taxes paid	390	473	509	469	473	493	519	546	564
Interest paid	1,272	1,287	2,085	1,659	1,070	888	860	814	711
Depreciation	614	531	599	759	712	728	874	709	730
Advertising	234	253	277	267	241	256	264	275	285
Net income (less loss) [7,10]	928	1,949	1,837	984	919	1,356	1,323	1,774	1,929
Net income	1,337	2,235	2,253	1,807	1,615	1,836	1,829	2,175	2,329
Deficit	409	286	416	823	696	480	506	401	401
Income subject to tax	760	1,201	1,248	978	895	1,022	994	1,150	1,258
Income tax before credits [11]	266	419	437	342	313	358	349	403	442
Tax credits	62	107	106	114	108	135	128	135	148
Foreign tax credit	49	82	87	100	94	118	107	110	118
Income tax after credits [12]	204	312	331	229	205	223	221	268	293

[1] Represents certain small corporations with a limit on the number of shareholders, mostly individuals, electing to be taxed at the shareholder level. [2] Includes items not shown separately. [3] Payable in less than 1 year. [4] Payable in 1 year or more. [5] Net worth is the sum of "capital stock," "additional paid-in capital," "retained earnings, appropriated," "retained earnings, unappropriated," "adjustments to shareholders' equity," minus "cost of treasury stock." [6] Appropriated and unappropriated and "adjustments to shareholders' equity." [7] Receipts, deductions, and net income of S corporations are limited to those from trade or business. Those from investments are excluded. [8] Includes gross sales and cost of sales of securities, commodities, and real estate by exchanges, brokers, or dealers selling on their own accounts. Excludes investment income. [9] Includes tax-exempt interest income. [10] Includes tax-exempt interest in state and local government obligations. [11] Excludes regulated investment companies. [11] Consists of regular (and alternative tax) only. [12] Includes minimum tax, alternative minimum tax, adjustments for prior year credits, and other income-related taxes.

Source: U.S. Internal Revenue Service, "SOI Tax Stats - Corporation Complete Report," <http://www.irs.gov/uac/SOI-Tax-Stats-Corporation-Complete-Report>, accessed August 2016.

Table 776. Corporations by Receipt-Size Class and Industry: 2013

[Number of returns in thousands (5,888 represents 5,888,000); receipts and net income in billions of dollars (26,850 represents $26,850,000,000,000). Data are for tax year shown which covers (a) corporate returns with accounting periods for the calendar year ending December 2013, and (b) those returns with accounting periods for the noncalendar year ending between July 2013 and June 2014. Covers active enterprises only. Figures are estimates based on a sample of unaudited tax returns; see Appendix III. Numbers in parentheses represent North American Industry Classification System (NAICS) 2012 codes; see text, this section]

Industry	Total	Receipt-size class				
		Under $1 mil. [1]	$1 to $4.9 mil.	$5 to $9.9 mil.	$10 to $49.9 mil.	$50 mil. or more
All industries: [2]						
Number of returns	5,888	4,785	798	139	130	36
Business receipts [3]	26,850	958	1,678	939	2,523	20,752
Net income (less loss)	1,929	77	83	42	137	1,590
Agriculture, forestry, fishing, and hunting (11):						
Returns	136	114	17	2	2	(Z)
Business receipts	184	20	35	17	35	77
Mining (21):						
Returns	36	25	7	1	1	(Z)
Business receipts	472	4	16	11	25	417
Utilities (22):						
Returns	8	7	1	(Z)	(Z)	(Z)
Business receipts	543	1	1	1	3	537
Construction (23):						
Returns	695	546	110	20	16	3
Business receipts	1,322	132	239	134	325	492
Manufacturing (31–33):						
Returns	243	143	57	16	20	7
Business receipts	7,934	35	132	110	413	7,244
Wholesale and retail trade (42, 44–45):						
Returns	961	644	208	47	48	14
Business receipts	8,540	164	465	328	1,000	6,583
Transportation and warehousing (48–49):						
Returns	220	179	28	6	5	1
Business receipts	827	35	63	41	100	589
Information (51):						
Returns	127	111	11	2	3	1
Business receipts	1,011	18	25	15	64	890
Finance and insurance (52):						
Returns	244	206	24	4	7	4
Business receipts [3]	2,249	35	36	14	47	2,118
Real estate and rental and leasing (53):						
Returns	642	619	20	2	2	(Z)
Business receipts	261	52	45	12	33	120
Professional, scientific, and technical services (54):						
Returns	902	785	92	13	10	2
Business receipts	1,222	133	191	91	199	607
Management of companies (holding companies) (55):						
Returns	59	51	4	2	2	1
Business receipts [3]	185	(Z)	1	2	8	174
Administrative and support and waste management and remediation services (56):						
Returns	283	238	35	5	4	1
Business receipts	527	49	76	32	75	295
Educational services (61):						
Returns	56	51	4	1	1	(Z)
Business receipts	65	7	9	5	12	32
Health care and social assistance (62):						
Returns	458	361	81	9	6	1
Business receipts	698	105	156	62	103	272
Arts, entertainment, and recreation (71):						
Returns	126	111	11	3	1	(Z)
Business receipts	116	19	25	17	12	43
Accommodation and food services (72):						
Returns	309	247	55	4	2	(Z)
Business receipts	485	79	105	29	48	223
Other services (81):						
Returns	384	347	33	3	1	(Z)
Business receipts	208	71	59	17	22	40

Z Less than 500 returns or $500 million in receipts. [1] Includes businesses without receipts. [2] Includes businesses not allocable to individual industries. [3] Size of total receipts was used instead of size of business receipts to classify data for "Finance and insurance" and "Management of companies and enterprises."

Source: U.S. Internal Revenue Service, "SOI Tax Stats - Corporation Complete Report," <http://www.irs.gov/uac/SOI-Tax-Stats-Corporation-Complete-Report>, accessed June 2016.

Table 777. Corporations by Asset-Size Class and Industry: 2013

[In billions of dollars (30,192 represents $30,192,000,000,000), except number of returns. Data are for tax year shown which covers (a) corporate returns with accounting periods for the calendar year ending December 2013, and (b) those returns with accounting periods for the noncalendar year ending between July 2013 and June 2014. Covers active corporations only. Excludes corporations not allocable by industry. Numbers in parentheses represent North American Industry Classification System (NAICS) 2012 codes; see text, this section]

Industry	Total	Under $10 mil. [1]	$10 to $24.9 mil.	$25 to $49.9 mil.	$50 to $99.9 mil.	$100 to $249.9 mil.	$250 mil. and over
All industries:							
Number of returns	5,887,804	5,781,957	48,639	19,031	11,674	10,344	16,158
Total receipts	30,192	5,890	1,364	937	878	1,174	19,949
Net income (less deficit)	1,929	267	38	26	24	37	1,536
Agriculture, forestry, fishing, and hunting (11):							
Returns	136,493	135,009	911	302	147	81	41
Total receipts	212	126	18	10	11	16	31
Mining (21):							
Returns	35,603	33,733	808	358	246	158	300
Total receipts	519	49	11	9	10	13	427
Utilities (22):							
Returns	7,845	7,383	113	73	53	50	173
Total receipts	570	10	2	1	3	9	545
Construction (23):							
Returns	695,261	688,174	4,746	1,300	555	301	184
Total receipts	1,340	742	146	83	68	71	230
Manufacturing (31–33):							
Returns	242,755	226,437	7,745	3,306	1,880	1,430	1,958
Total receipts	8,432	534	224	189	197	293	6,995
Wholesale and retail trade (42, 44–45):							
Returns	960,846	938,891	13,451	4,311	1,997	1,158	1,038
Total receipts	8,718	1,935	679	439	378	453	4,834
Transportation and warehousing (48–49):							
Returns	219,600	217,278	1,218	468	256	170	211
Total receipts	854	239	41	30	28	34	482
Information (51):							
Returns	127,105	124,168	1,297	557	362	296	425
Total receipts	1,197	118	24	17	20	31	987
Finance and insurance (52):							
Returns	243,961	222,352	4,603	3,121	2,548	3,273	8,065
Total receipts	3,654	159	25	26	31	65	3,347
Real estate and rental and leasing (53):							
Returns	642,008	632,768	5,170	1,634	993	675	767
Total receipts	428	148	20	11	14	18	216
Professional, scientific, and technical services (54):							
Returns	901,715	895,977	3,088	1,158	624	458	410
Total receipts	1,266	590	78	54	47	68	428
Management of companies (holding companies) (55):							
Returns	58,604	50,163	2,031	1,271	1,296	1,836	2,007
Total receipts	800	40	4	5	5	15	731
Administrative and support and waste management and remediation services (56):							
Returns	283,361	281,660	863	330	206	128	173
Total receipts	542	237	30	22	21	22	208
Educational services (61):							
Returns	56,494	56,190	144	50	47	35	27
Total receipts	66	29	3	3	3	5	22
Health care and social assistance (62):							
Returns	457,620	456,279	655	252	192	107	135
Total receipts	731	444	24	17	20	28	198
Arts, entertainment, and recreation (71):							
Returns	125,763	125,002	415	149	75	51	70
Total receipts	124	69	5	3	3	5	38
Accommodation and food services (72):							
Returns	309,204	307,573	965	288	140	103	135
Total receipts	522	251	19	11	14	23	204
Other services (81):							
Returns	383,567	382,919	417	103	57	32	39
Total receipts	216	168	9	5	4	4	25

[1] Includes returns with zero assets.

Source: U.S. Internal Revenue Service, "SOI Tax Stats - Corporation Complete Report," <http://www.irs.gov/uac/SOI-Tax-Stats-Corporation-Complete-Report>, accessed June 2016.

Table 778. Economic Census Summary (NAICS 2007 Basis): 2007 and 2012

[23 represents 23,000. Covers establishments with payroll. Data are based on the 2007 and 2012 Economic Censuses which are subject to nonsampling error. Data for the construction sector are also subject to sampling errors. For details on survey methodology and nonsampling and sampling errors, see Appendix III]

Kind of business	2007 NAICS code [1]	Establishments (1,000)		Sales, receipts, or shipments (bil. dol.)		Annual payroll (bil. dol.)		Paid employees [2] (1,000)	
		2007	2012	2007	2012	2007	2012	2007	2012
Mining, quarrying, and oil and gas extraction....	21	23	25	414	529	41	59	730	848
Oil & gas extraction...................	211	6	7	255	311	10	15	150	176
Mining (except oil & gas)...............	212	6	6	86	98	12	14	211	212
Support activities for mining............	213	10	13	73	120	19	30	369	460
Utilities...........................	22	17	18	584	532	52	59	637	651
Construction........................	23	729	598	1,732	1,366	331	273	7,316	5,670
Construction of buildings............	236	212	164	748	508	78	55	1,541	1,085
Heavy and civil engineering construction.......	237	39	33	260	256	54	55	1,044	961
Specialty trade contractors............	238	478	401	723	603	199	163	4,731	3,623
Manufacturing......................	31-33	333	297	5,319	5,697	614	593	13,396	11,214
Wholesale trade....................	42	435	419	6,516	7,900	336	362	6,227	5,882
Merchant wholesalers, durable goods..........	423	255	245	2,898	3,152	207	217	3,619	3,355
Merchant wholesalers, nondurable goods......	424	135	131	2,991	4,108	116	132	2,320	2,244
Wholesale electronic markets and agents and brokers...................	425	45	43	627	639	13	14	289	283
Retail trade.......................	44–45	1,128	1,062	3,918	4,220	363	369	15,515	14,704
Motor vehicle & parts dealers.............	441	127	116	891	869	73	70	1,914	1,710
Furniture & home furnishings stores.............	442	65	52	108	89	15	11	557	425
Electronics & appliance stores............	443	51	47	109	101	11	10	486	416
Building material & garden equipment & supplies dealers..........	444	91	78	318	279	38	34	1331.3	1,145
Food & beverage stores...............	445	146	148	539	620	55	61	2,827	2,865
Health & personal care stores............	446	88	91	234	270	28	31	1,068	1,002
Gasoline stations...................	447	119	114	450	554	15	16	891	857
Clothing & clothing accessories stores..........	448	156	148	216	234	27	28	1,644	1,664
Sporting goods, hobby, musical instrument, and book stores....................	451	57	48	81	79	9	9	619	535
General merchandise stores............	452	46	49	577	641	54	58	2,763	2,773
Miscellaneous store retailers............	453	122	107	104	98	14	14	792	713
Nonstore retailers...................	454	59	64	290	386	23	27	621	600
Transportation & warehousing [3]...........	48-49	220	214	640	731	173	184	4,454	4,305
Truck transportation...............	484	120	112	218	238	58	58	1,508	1,363
Information........................	51	142	138	1,072	1,238	229	269	3,497	3,321
Publishing industries (except internet)..........	511	31	28	282	272	81	80	1,093	876
Motion picture & sound recording industries....	512	24	25	95	92	18	16	336	304
Broadcasting (except internet)............	515	10	10	100	127	18	20	295	278
Telecommunications.................	517	52	51	491	546	75	76	1,251	1,134
Data processing, hosting, and related services........	518	17	15	67	108	26	41	394	497
Other information services.............	519	7	11	37	94	10	35	128	231
Finance & insurance [4].................	52	502	468	3,669	3,636	502	524	6,608	6,041
Credit intermediation & related activities........	522	231	196	1,343	1,095	181	184	3,280	2,815
Insurance carriers & related activities........	524	185	176	1,669	1,925	154	169	2,423	2,304
Real estate & rental & leasing [4]..............	53	384	354	485	488	85	85	2,188	1,924
Professional, scientific, & technical services....	54	847	856	1,251	1,480	502	581	7,870	8,204
Management of companies & enterprises........	55	51	54	104	116	250	309	2,664	3,082
Admin/support waste management/remediation services........	56	395	386	631	673	301	329	10,251	9,774
Administrative & support services...............	561	374	363	556	594	285	311	9,865	9,406
Waste management & remediation services....	562	22	23	75	79	17	18	386	368
Educational services.................	61	61	68	45	53	14	17	540	642
Health care and social assistance...............	62	785	831	1,668	2,040	663	801	16,792	18,415
Ambulatory health care services.............	621	548	583	668	814	275	340	5,703	6,475
Hospitals........................	622	7	6	703	877	265	317	5,529	5,751
Nursing & residential care facilities..............	623	76	81	169	203	75	87	3,071	3,364
Social assistance...................	624	154	161	128	146	48	58	2,489	2,824
Arts, entertainment, & recreation.............	71	125	125	189	201	58	64	2,061	2,082
Performing arts, spectator sports, & related industries.................	711	44	46	78	86	28	32	438	434
Museums, historical sites, & like institutions....	712	7	7	13	14	4	4	130	135
Amusement, gambling, & recreation industries.................	713	74	72	98	101	27	28	1,494	1,513
Accommodation & food services.................	72	634	662	614	708	171	196	11,601	12,008
Accommodation....................	721	63	64	180	196	46	50	1,971	1,950
Food services & drinking places.............	722	572	599	433	512	124	146	9,630	10,058
Other services (except public administration)....	81	540	530	405	427	99	108	3,479	3,431
Repair & maintenance.............	811	222	210	138	144	40	41	1,261	1,194
Personal and laundry services..................	812	210	213	82	87	27	29	1,338	1,349
Religious, grantmaking, civic, professional, and similar organizations........	813	108	107	185	196	32	38	880	887

[1] Based on North American Industry Classification System, 2007; see text, this section. [2] For pay period including March 12. [3] For detailed industries, see Table 1083. [4] For detailed industries, see Table 1187.

Source: U.S. Census Bureau, 2012 Economic Census, Table EC1200CCOMP1, "All sectors: Core Business Statistics Series: Comparative Statistics for the U.S. (2007 NAICS Basis): 2012 and 2007," <http://factfinder.census.gov>, accessed September 2016.

Table 779. Nonemployer Establishments and Receipts by Industry: 2000 to 2015

[16,530 represents 16,530,000. Includes only firms subject to federal income tax. Nonemployers are businesses with no paid employees. Data originate chiefly from administrative records of the Internal Revenue Service; see Appendix III. Data for 2000 based on the North American Industry Classification System (NAICS), 1997; data for 2010 based on NAICS 2007; and data for 2015 based on NAICS 2012]

Kind of business	NAICS code	Establishments (1,000)			Receipts (mil. dol.)		
		2000	2010	2015	2000	2010	2015
All industries............................	(X)	**16,530**	**22,111**	**24,331**	**709,379**	**950,814**	**1,148,716**
Agriculture, forestry, fishing and hunting..............	11	223	237	236	9,196	10,115	11,014
Mining, quarrying, and oil and gas extraction...........	21	86	106	98	5,227	6,923	6,111
Utilities...	22	14	17	20	504	698	981
Construction..	23	2,014	2,424	2,430	107,538	120,151	146,341
Manufacturing......................................	31–33	285	318	355	13,022	14,572	17,473
Wholesale trade....................................	42	388	393	417	31,684	34,082	37,946
Retail trade..	44–45	1,743	1,822	1,986	73,810	75,720	87,352
Transportation & warehousing........................	48–49	747	1,021	1,528	37,824	60,746	83,890
Information..	51	238	311	329	7,620	10,739	12,762
Finance & insurance................................	52	692	717	718	49,058	50,626	55,329
Real estate & rental & leasing.......................	53	1,696	2,343	2,636	133,398	209,549	259,768
Professional, scientific, & technical services...........	54	2,420	3,121	3,411	90,272	130,613	157,584
Admin/support waste mgmt/remediation services......	56	1,032	1,937	2,069	23,754	39,111	46,393
Educational services................................	61	283	567	710	3,736	7,703	9,893
Health care & social assistance......................	62	1,317	1,935	1,979	36,550	57,686	64,702
Arts, entertainment, & recreation....................	71	782	1,154	1,342	17,713	26,756	34,549
Accommodation & food services.....................	72	218	329	371	13,418	14,355	17,658
Other services (except public administration)...........	81	2,350	3,358	3,695	55,056	80,669	98,971

X Not applicable.

Source: U.S. Census Bureau, Nonemployer Statistics, "Geographic Area Series: Nonemployer Statistics for the U.S., States, Metropolitan Areas, and Counties," <http://factfinder.census.gov>, accessed June 2017. See also <http://www.census.gov/econ/nonemployer/>.

Table 780. Establishments, Employees, and Payroll by Employment-Size Class: 1990 to 2015

[In units as noted (6,176 represents 6,176,000). Excludes most government employees, railroad employees, and self-employed persons. Employees are for the week including March 12. Covers establishments with payroll. An establishment is a single physical location where business is conducted or where services or industrial operations are performed. For statement on methodology, see Appendix III]

Employment-size class	Unit	1990	2000	2005	2010	2012	2013	2014	2015
Establishments, total............	1,000	**6,176**	**7,070**	**7,500**	**7,397**	**7,432**	**7,488**	**7,563**	**7,664**
Under 20 employees................	1,000	5,354	6,069	6,468	6,408	6,407	6,440	6,492	6,559
20 to 99 employees................	1,000	684	826	856	824	854	873	891	919
100 to 499 employees..............	1,000	122	157	157	148	153	156	161	166
500 to 999 employees..............	1,000	10	12	12	11	11	12	12	13
1,000 or more employees..........	1,000	6	7	7	7	7	7	7	7
Employees, total.................	1,000	**93,476**	**114,065**	**116,317**	**111,970**	**115,938**	**118,266**	**121,080**	**124,086**
Under 20 employees................	1,000	24,373	27,569	28,874	28,958	29,060	29,128	29,379	29,406
20 to 99 employees................	1,000	27,414	33,147	34,302	32,730	33,995	34,799	35,494	36,640
100 to 499 employees..............	1,000	22,926	29,736	29,591	27,718	28,930	29,545	30,460	31,416
500 to 999 employees..............	1,000	6,551	8,291	8,053	7,331	7,847	8,063	8,270	8,550
1,000 or more employees..........	1,000	12,212	15,322	15,497	15,233	16,106	16,732	17,477	18,074
Annual payroll, total.............	Bil. dol.	**2,104**	**3,879**	**4,483**	**4,941**	**5,414**	**5,622**	**5,940**	**6,253**
Under 20 employees................	Bil. dol.	485	818	970	1,057	1,121	1,142	1,187	1,235
20 to 99 employees................	Bil. dol.	547	1,006	1,177	1,281	1,391	1,435	1,505	1,584
100 to 499 employees..............	Bil. dol.	518	1,031	1,176	1,280	1,409	1,469	1,565	1,651
500 to 999 employees..............	Bil. dol.	174	336	376	410	464	486	516	550
1,000 or more employees..........	Bil. dol.	381	690	784	913	1,029	1,090	1,167	1,235

Source: U.S. Census Bureau, County Business Patterns, "Geographic Area Series: County Business Patterns by Employment Size Class," <http://factfinder.census.gov>, accessed April 2017. See also <https://www.census.gov/programs-surveys/cbp.html>.

Table 781. Employer Firms by Industry and Whether Family-Owned and Owner's Education and Age: 2015

[In thousands, (5,531 represents 5,531,000). Includes all U.S. firms with paid employees operating during 2015 with receipts of $1,000 or more and classified in the 2012 North American Industry Classification System (NAICS) sectors 11 through 99, except for NAICS 111, 112, 482, 491, 521, 525, 813, 814, and 92. Firms with more than one domestic establishment are counted in each industry in which they operate, but only once in the total. Additionally, detail may not add to total due to nonresponse on selected survey items and because the survey asked for information for up to four persons owning the largest percentage(s) of the business. Based on the 2015 Annual Survey of Entrepreneurs]

Industry	NAICS code	Total firms	Owner's highest level of education					Age of owner			Family owned firms
			High school or less	Some college, no degree	Associates or technical degree	Bachelor's degree	Advanced degree	Under 35	35 to 64	65 or over	
All industries	(X)	5,531	1,171	795	605	1,560	1,219	314	4,029	1,008	1,001
Agriculture, forestry, fishing and hunting	11	27	11	5	4	7	2	2	20	7	7
Mining, quarrying, and oil and gas extraction	21	23	8	4	3	8	3	2	17	7	6
Utilities	22	6	(Z)	(Z)	(Z)	1	1	(Z)	2	1	(Z)
Construction	23	653	235	130	123	130	30	38	518	91	136
Manufacturing	31-33	251	72	49	39	93	34	13	204	70	64
Wholesale trade	42	309	69	55	31	133	39	13	237	77	65
Retail trade	44-45	650	190	119	74	198	68	41	478	129	147
Transportation & warehousing	48-49	177	68	30	22	33	10	10	124	28	35
Information	51	72	7	9	5	33	16	6	51	14	11
Finance & insurance	52	235	22	34	16	111	42	12	164	51	34
Real estate & rental & leasing	53	282	44	46	26	118	52	15	187	85	59
Professional, scientific, & technical services	54	787	40	67	44	287	384	38	625	159	112
Management of companies & enterprises	55	26	3	2	1	10	4	1	14	6	4
Administrative & support and waste management & remediation services	56	330	87	62	39	88	34	23	236	52	61
Educational services	61	89	6	8	5	23	18	5	46	9	11
Health care & social assistance	62	641	19	22	23	60	410	26	419	88	60
Arts, entertainment, & recreation	71	119	16	14	8	38	15	8	66	17	16
Accommodation & food services	72	508	161	82	50	141	44	39	368	71	103
Other services (except public administration)	81	378	114	59	91	66	20	23	273	54	73

X Not applicable. Z Less than 500.

Source: U.S. Census Bureau, 2015 Annual Survey of Entrepreneurs, Tables "SE1400CSA01," "SE1400CSCB02," "SE1400CSCBO07," and "SE1400CSCBO08," <http://factfinder.census.gov>, accessed August 2017.

Table 782. Employer Firms by Industry and Whether Franchised: 2015

[In thousands, except as noted (5,531.2 represents 5,531,200). Includes all U.S. firms with paid employees operating during 2015 with receipts of $1,000 or more and classified in the 2012 North American Industry Classification System (NAICS) sectors 11 through 99, except for NAICS 111, 112, 482, 491, 521, 525, 813, 814, and 92. Firms with more than one domestic establishment are counted in each industry in which they operate, but only once in the U.S. industries total. Based on the 2015 Annual Survey of Entrepreneurs]

Industry	NAICS code	Total Firms [1]	All or part of the business operated as a franchise			Did not operate as a franchise		
			Firms	Paid employees [2]	Payroll (mil. dol.)	Firms	Paid employees [2]	Payroll (mil. dol.)
All industries	(X)	5,531.2	185.6	6,466	190,279	3,400.3	52,524	2,679,733
Agriculture, forestry, fishing and hunting	11	27.2	0.2	2	51	17.2	144	4,941
Mining, quarrying, and oil and gas extraction	21	22.9	0.4	3	145	14.9	340	27,201
Utilities	22	5.9	0.1	1	43	1.8	65	5,904
Construction	23	652.6	8.0	77	3,496	429.3	3,911	222,936
Manufacturing	31-33	250.7	3.7	90	4,736	165.5	5,829	306,590
Wholesale trade	42	308.9	5.2	122	6,157	204.3	3,234	202,801
Retail trade	44-45	649.9	38.1	1,137	39,790	373.8	6,061	165,517
Transportation & warehousing	48-49	177.1	4.3	372	18,611	105.3	1,921	86,041
Information	51	71.8	0.7	257	20,209	43.6	992	81,031
Finance & insurance	52	235.0	9.2	53	3,433	154.4	2,917	265,641
Real estate & rental & leasing	53	281.6	8.1	129	4,975	172.9	1,060	52,772
Professional, scientific, & technical services	54	787.4	8.4	208	6,215	567.3	4,803	374,612
Management of companies and enterprises	55	25.5	1.9	124	11,611	12.5	1,150	120,784
Administrative & support and waste management & remediation services	56	330.5	12.0	313	10,240	204.0	5,256	215,291
Educational services	61	88.6	3.9	41	674	38.7	561	19,921
Health care & social assistance	62	640.7	9.7	245	5,369	395.1	7,643	366,492
Arts, entertainment, & recreation	71	118.7	5.5	74	4,075	55.7	733	25,799
Accommodation & food services	72	507.9	57.4	3,059	46,517	229.9	4,368	87,137
Other services (except public administration)	81	378.2	12.0	159	3,924	229.9	1,501	47,789

X Not applicable. [1] Includes firms that did not indicate franchise status. [2] For pay period ending March 12.

Source: U.S. Census Bureau, 2015 Annual Survey of Entrepreneurs, Table "SE1500CSCB06," <http://factfinder.census.gov>, accessed August 2017.

Table 783. Franchised Businesses by Type of Business: 2012

[129,242 represents $129,242,000,000. Data shown for franchisor- and franchisee-owned establishments with paid employees. Covers franchised businesses with over 3,500 establishments. Data are based on the 2012 Economic Census, for details see Appendix III]

Kind of business	2012 NAICS code [1]	Number of establish-ments	Revenue (mil. dol.)	Annual payroll (mil. dol.)	Paid employees (number)
Limited-service restaurants................................	722513	122,042	129,242	31,726	2,630,074
Gasoline stations with convenience stores............................	447110	32,845	158,109	4,267	251,960
Full-service restaurants................................	722511	28,940	36,070	11,828	879,771
Hotels (except casino hotels) and motels..........................	721110	23,305	51,556	11,645	601,424
New car dealers................................	441110	21,292	672,550	47,524	973,745
Snack and nonalcoholic beverage bars................................	722515	16,494	9,614	2,275	195,342
Offices of real estate agents and brokers........................	531210	14,588	16,241	1,406	41,156
Fitness and recreational sports centers................................	713940	7,340	2,584	729	60,957
Beauty salons................................	812112	6,326	1,873	839	49,174
Janitorial services................................	561720	6,194	3,987	1,457	81,833
Optical goods stores................................	446130	5,982	5,492	928	40,343
Tax preparation services................................	541213	5,702	1,331	395	55,215
Other gasoline stations................................	447190	5,212	32,855	918	45,866
General automotive repair................................	811111	3,956	2,961	797	23,484
Convenience stores................................	445120	3,894	5,713	507	27,599

[1] Based on the 2012 North American Industry Classification System (NAICS); see text, this section.

Source: U.S. Census Bureau, 2012 Economic Census, Table "EC1200CFRA1: Economic Census: Core Business Statistics Series, 2012: Franchise Status for Selected Industries and States: 2012," <http://factfinder.census.gov>, accessed February 2016.

Table 784. Employer Firms by Industry and Amount and Source of Capital to Start or Acquire Business: 2015

[In thousands (5,531 represents 5,531,000). Includes all U.S. firms with paid employees operating during 2015 with receipts of $1,000 or more and classified in the 2012 North American Industry Classification System (NAICS) sectors 11 through 99, except for NAICS 111, 112, 482, 491, 521, 525, 813, 814, and 92. Firms with more than one domestic establishment are counted in each industry in which they operate, but only once in the U.S. industries total. Based on the 2015 Annual Survey of Entrepreneurs]

Industry	NAICS code	Total firms [2]	Source of capital [1]			Amount of capital				
			Personal savings, assets, or home equity loan	Credit cards [3]	Busi-ness loan [4]	Under $10,000	$10,000 to $49,000	$50,000 to $249,999	$250,000 to $999,999	$1 mil-lion & over
All industries............................	(X)	5,531	2,957	564	894	843	768	722	244	78
Agriculture, forestry, fishing and hunting................................	11	27	14	2	6	3	3	4	2	1
Mining, quarrying, and oil & gas extraction............................	21	23	10	1	4	3	2	3	1	1
Utilities................................	22	6	1	(Z)	(Z)	(Z)	(Z)	(Z)	(Z)	(Z)
Construction................................	23	653	362	80	72	141	102	54	11	3
Manufacturing................................	31-33	251	138	25	52	27	33	34	14	7
Wholesale trade................................	42	309	165	27	43	39	40	42	15	7
Retail trade................................	44-45	650	360	68	135	58	91	116	38	10
Transportation & warehousing.............	48-49	177	87	19	33	20	30	22	5	2
Information................................	51	72	36	8	7	11	8	8	3	2
Finance & insurance......................	52	235	133	25	28	38	36	31	10	4
Real estate & rental & leasing..............	53	282	141	17	33	45	29	27	13	9
Professional, scientific, & technical services........................	54	787	477	88	78	214	123	72	17	7
Management of companies and enterprises................................	55	26	7	1	3	1	1	2	1	2
Administrative & support and waste management & remediation services....	56	330	177	38	39	75	49	30	6	2
Educational services........................	61	89	37	8	8	12	11	8	2	(Z)
Health care & social assistance............	62	641	288	60	159	69	80	104	46	7
Arts, entertainment, & recreation..........	71	119	50	9	14	15	9	11	6	3
Accommodation & food services...........	72	508	267	46	106	22	56	99	40	12
Other services (except public administration)......................	81	378	209	42	72	48	65	57	15	3

X Not applicable. Z Less than 500. [1] Not all sources of capital are shown separately. [2] Includes firms that did not respond to survey questions regarding amount and source of capital. [3] Includes personal and business credit cards carrying balances. [4] Includes loans and investments from family and friends.

Source: U.S. Census Bureau, 2015 Annual Survey of Entrepreneurs, Tables "SE1500CSCB07," and "SE1500CSCB08," <http://factfinder.census.gov>, accessed August 2017.

Table 785. Establishments, Employees, and Payroll by Employment-Size Class and Industry: 2000 to 2015

[Establishments and employees in thousands (7,070.0 represents 7,070,000); payroll in billions of dollars (3,879 represents $3,879,000,000,000). See headnote, Table 780. Svcs = services. Data for 2000 based on the North American Industry Classification System (NAICS), 1997; 2010 data based on NAICS 2007; and 2015 data based on NAICS 2012. See text, this section]

Industry	NAICS code	2000, total	2010, total	2015					
				Total	Under 20 employees	20 to 99 employees	100 to 499 employees	500 to 999 or employees	1,000 more employees
Establishments, total [1]	(X)	7,070.0	7,396.6	7,663.9	6,559.4	918.7	165.8	12.5	7.5
Agriculture, forestry, fishing & hunting	113–115	26.1	21.7	22.4	20.9	1.3	0.2	(Z)	(Z)
Mining, quarrying, & oil and gas extraction	21	23.7	27.1	29.2	22.9	5.0	1.2	0.1	0.1
Utilities	22	17.3	17.6	18.0	12.6	4.1	1.1	0.1	0.1
Construction	23	709.6	682.7	682.4	623.2	52.0	6.7	0.4	0.1
Manufacturing	31–33	354.5	300.0	292.8	203.0	65.0	21.9	2.1	0.9
Wholesale trade	42	446.2	414.6	413.4	350.9	53.6	8.2	0.5	0.2
Retail trade	44–45	1,113.6	1,068.0	1,070.2	911.3	129.2	29.4	0.3	(Z)
Transportation and warehousing	48–49	190.0	208.5	228.4	190.6	29.6	7.1	0.7	0.3
Information	51	133.6	135.4	139.5	113.2	20.3	5.1	0.6	0.3
Finance and insurance	52	423.7	473.5	470.1	431.0	31.1	6.4	0.9	0.6
Real estate and rental and leasing	53	300.2	347.3	377.6	361.3	14.5	1.7	0.1	(Z)
Professional, scientific, & technical services	54	722.7	851.5	896.0	826.3	58.0	10.3	0.9	0.5
Management of companies and enterprises	55	47.4	50.9	53.9	34.7	13.1	4.9	0.8	0.5
Admin/support waste mgt/remediation svcs	56	351.5	381.8	404.3	341.1	45.4	15.0	1.7	1.1
Educational services	61	68.0	90.1	102.0	78.7	18.7	3.7	0.4	0.5
Health care and social assistance	62	658.6	812.9	876.1	732.9	113.4	25.7	2.0	2.0
Arts, entertainment, and recreation	71	103.8	123.2	133.6	112.2	17.5	3.5	0.2	0.1
Accommodation and food services	72	542.4	644.0	687.6	475.3	201.7	10.0	0.5	0.2
Other services [2]	81	723.3	725.5	746.0	697.0	45.0	3.8	0.2	0.1
Unclassified establishments	99	99.0	20.5	20.4	20.3	(Z)	(Z)	–	–
Employees, total [1]	(X)	114,065	111,970	124,085.9	29,405.6	36,640.0	31,416.5	8,549.8	18,074.1
Agriculture, forestry, fishing & hunting	113–115	184	156	160.1	71.4	51.1	28.9	3.0	5.8
Mining, quarrying, & oil and gas extraction	21	456	582	743.7	108.1	207.9	232.5	84.1	111.1
Utilities	22	655	638	639.2	69.2	180.3	213.2	90.8	85.7
Construction	23	6,573	5,389	6,008.3	2,253.7	2,015.7	1,209.8	233.9	295.1
Manufacturing	31–33	16,474	10,863	11,605.5	1,145.6	2,863.2	4,411.2	1,402.7	1,782.8
Wholesale trade	42	6,112	5,599	6,076.1	1,696.4	2,118.4	1,528.2	364.2	368.9
Retail trade	44–45	14,841	14,497	15,704.2	5,014.9	5,087.5	5,349.7	178.7	73.5
Transportation and warehousing	48–49	3,790	4,012	4,616.6	764.9	1,232.2	1,371.8	514.6	733.0
Information	51	3,546	3,124	3,394.3	489.9	848.6	1,020.2	405.7	630.0
Finance and insurance	52	5,963	5,929	6,135.9	1,797.0	1,211.2	1,322.4	640.6	1,164.7
Real estate and rental and leasing	53	1,942	1,946	2,065.4	1,120.3	542.4	301.0	55.6	46.1
Professional, scientific, & technical services	54	6,816	7,822	8,798.3	2,714.3	2,293.1	1,969.2	587.9	1,233.9
Management of companies and enterprises	55	2,874	2,833	3,308.8	188.2	591.7	1,046.4	517.9	964.6
Admin/support waste mgt/remediation svcs	56	9,138	8,977	11,112.5	1,284.0	1,972.0	3,051.0	1,168.6	3,636.9
Educational services	61	2,532	3,274	3,642.0	381.3	791.8	708.0	317.1	1,443.9
Health care and social assistance	62	14,109	17,788	19,221.9	3,818.5	4,579.4	4,764.9	1,406.9	4,652.2
Arts, entertainment, and recreation	71	1,741	2,004	2,230.8	408.4	743.5	658.5	164.8	255.6
Accommodation and food services	72	9,881	11,312	13,196.9	3,169.7	7,668.0	1,588.9	312.2	458.1
Other services [2]	81	5,293	5,204	5,401.2	2,886.7	1,641.4	640.3	100.7	132.1
Unclassified establishments	99	144	(NA)	24.2	23.2	0.9	([3])	–	–
Annual payroll, total [1]	(X)	3,879	4,941	6,253.5	1,234.6	1,584.0	1,650.7	549.6	1,234.6
Agriculture, forestry, fishing & hunting	113–115	5	5	6.5	3.0	2.2	1.1	0.1	0.1
Mining, quarrying, & oil and gas extraction	21	22	46	61.6	7.1	15.5	20.7	7.6	10.9
Utilities	22	41	55	64.2	5.6	16.5	21.2	10.9	10.1
Construction	23	240	261	348.6	106.4	122.4	83.9	16.8	19.1
Manufacturing	31–33	644	550	656.8	49.7	143.1	243.8	85.6	134.5
Wholesale trade	42	270	339	423.1	98.8	134.2	109.2	32.3	48.7
Retail trade	44–45	303	359	428.2	128.7	139.1	149.6	7.0	3.8
Transportation and warehousing	48–49	126	167	222.0	34.2	56.7	63.3	24.0	43.8
Information	51	209	224	309.3	34.4	61.1	97.0	41.8	75.0
Finance and insurance	52	347	472	595.8	121.2	128.5	146.6	63.2	136.3
Real estate and rental and leasing	53	59	80	106.3	51.5	30.3	18.5	3.4	2.7
Professional, scientific, & technical services	54	362	543	704.4	170.5	187.9	183.9	57.5	104.5
Management of companies and enterprises	55	211	282	367.0	21.8	57.3	113.5	59.1	115.4
Admin/support waste mgt/remediation svcs	56	210	304	428.2	56.4	78.3	101.1	36.6	155.8
Educational services	61	62	110	134.7	10.3	24.9	27.5	9.8	62.1
Health care and social assistance	62	431	753	905.4	179.3	189.2	182.8	70.2	284.0
Arts, entertainment, and recreation	71	43	62	76.8	18.2	17.3	24.0	9.9	7.3
Accommodation and food services	72	126	186	245.2	56.5	127.3	37.2	9.1	15.2
Other services [2]	81	110	140	168.7	80.6	52.2	25.9	4.7	5.3
Unclassified establishments	99	4	(Z)	0.5	0.5	(Z)	(D)	–	–

– Represents zero. D Data withheld to avoid disclosure. NA Not available. X Not applicable. Z Less than 50 establishments, 500 employees, or $500 million. [1] Totals for 2000 include auxiliaries. Beginning 2010, cases previously classified under NAICS code 95 (auxiliaries) are coded in the operating NAICS sector of the establishment. [2] Except public administration. [3] 20 to 99 employees.

Source: U.S. Census Bureau, County Business Patterns, "Geographic Area Series: County Business Patterns by Employment Size Class," <http://factfinder.census.gov>, accessed April 2017. See also <https://www.census.gov/programs-surveys/cbp.html>.

Table 786. Employer Firms, Employment, and Annual Payroll by Employment Size of Firm and Industry: 2014

[5,825 represents 5,825,000. A firm is an aggregation of all establishments owned by a parent company (within a geographic location and/or industry) with some annual payroll. A firm may be a single location or it can include multiple locations. Employment is measured in March and payroll is annual leading to some firms with zero employment. Numbers in parentheses represent North American Industry Classification System codes, 2007; see text, this section]

Industry and data type	Unit	Total	All industries—employment size of firm						
			0 to 4	5 to 9	10 to 19	20 to 99	100 to 499	Less than 500	500 or more
Total [1]:									
Firms..........................	1,000	5,825	3,598	999	609	513	88	5,806	19
Employment..................	1,000	121,070	5,940	6,571	8,177	20,122	17,085	57,895	63,175
Annual payroll...............	Bil. dol.	5,940	252	236	310	838	804	2,439	3,501
Construction (23):									
Firms..........................	1,000	655	443	102	59	44	5	654	1
Employment..................	1,000	5,705	690	671	783	1,667	914	4,726	979
Annual payroll...............	Bil. dol.	319	29	28	38	95	59	250	70
Manufacturing (31–33):									
Firms..........................	1,000	252	104	46	38	47	12	248	4
Employment..................	1,000	11,424	194	310	519	1,941	2,152	5,116	6,309
Annual payroll...............	Bil. dol.	640	8	12	22	92	109	242	398
Wholesale trade (42):									
Firms..........................	1,000	310	177	52	36	34	8	307	3
Employment..................	1,000	5,967	301	341	482	1,267	1,081	3,473	2,494
Annual payroll...............	Bil. dol.	405	16	18	26	74	67	201	204
Retail trade (44–45):									
Firms..........................	1,000	651	392	133	69	47	8	649	2
Employment..................	1,000	15,373	735	873	909	1,774	1,154	5,445	9,928
Annual payroll...............	Bil. dol.	407	19	22	25	61	44	170	236
Transportation & warehousing (48–49):									
Firms..........................	1,000	174	112	25	16	15	4	171	2
Employment..................	1,000	4,407	166	162	219	560	505	1,610	2,796
Annual payroll...............	Bil. dol.	207	6	6	8	23	22	66	141
Information (51):									
Firms..........................	1,000	73	45	10	7	8	2	72	1
Employment..................	1,000	3,365	65	67	98	301	364	895	2,469
Annual payroll...............	Bil. dol.	294	5	3	5	20	30	64	230
Finance & insurance (52):									
Firms..........................	1,000	236	170	34	13	13	4	234	2
Employment..................	1,000	6,079	298	217	178	532	704	1,930	4,148
Annual payroll...............	Bil. dol.	567	15	13	14	46	62	149	418
Professional, scientific and technical services (54):									
Firms..........................	1,000	790	582	101	56	40	7	787	3
Employment..................	1,000	8,620	862	662	744	1,514	1,193	4,976	3,644
Annual payroll...............	Bil. dol.	665	49	37	47	114	98	344	321
Management of companies and enterprises (55):									
Firms..........................	1,000	27	3	1	1	6	9	19	8
Employment..................	1,000	3,236	3	3	7	73	300	387	2,849
Annual payroll...............	Bil. dol.	350	1	(Z)	1	5	24	30	320
Administrative & support and waste management & remediation services (56):									
Firms..........................	1,000	332	213	48	30	28	8	328	4
Employment..................	1,000	10,579	319	317	400	1,118	1,428	3,582	6,997
Annual payroll...............	Bil. dol.	395	14	11	14	42	47	128	268
Educational services (61):									
Firms..........................	1,000	88	43	14	11	15	4	87	1
Employment..................	1,000	3,562	68	93	155	614	635	1,565	1,998
Annual payroll...............	Bil. dol.	130	2	2	3	18	23	50	80
Health care and social assistance (62):									
Firms..........................	1,000	651	338	144	83	64	17	647	4
Employment..................	1,000	18,852	609	952	1,112	2,576	3,336	8,586	10,266
Annual payroll...............	Bil. dol.	860	32	39	47	103	117	338	522
Accommodation and food services (72):									
Firms..........................	1,000	509	199	101	98	100	9	507	2
Employment..................	1,000	12,792	335	673	1,335	3,680	1,690	7,713	5,079
Annual payroll...............	Bil. dol.	228	9	10	20	61	29	128	101
Other services (except public administration) (81):									
Firms..........................	1,000	676	433	134	63	40	4	675	1
Employment..................	1,000	5,347	812	873	830	1,429	640	4,584	763
Annual payroll...............	Bil. dol.	161	21	22	23	42	24	131	30

Z Less than $500 million. [1] Includes other industries, not shown separately.

Source: U.S. Small Business Administration, Office of Advocacy, Firm Size Data, "Statistics of U.S. Businesses," <https://www.sba.gov/advocacy/firm-size-data>, accessed August 2017.

Table 787. Employer Firms, Employment, and Payroll by Employment Size of Firm and State: 2010 and 2013

[5,735 represents 5,735,000. A firm is an aggregation of all establishments owned by a parent company (within a state) with some annual payroll. A firm may be a single location or it can include multiple locations. Employment is measured in March and payroll is annual leading to some firms with zero employment]

| State | Employer firms (1,000) | | | | | Employment, 2013 (1,000) | | | Annual payroll, 2013 (bil. dol.) | | |
| | 2010 | | 2013 | | | | | | | | |
	Total	Less than 20 employees	Total	Less than 20 employees	Less than 500 employees	Total	Less than 20 employees	Less than 500 employees	Total	Less than 20 employees	Less than 500 employees
U.S.	5,735	5,160	5,775	5,168	5,756	118,266	20,508	56,823	5,621.7	766.7	2,318.2
AL	76	64	73	62	71	1,603	273	765	62.4	8.8	27.2
AK	16	14	17	15	16	267	57	141	14.6	2.7	6.9
AZ	102	88	102	88	99	2,173	335	979	92.8	12.1	36.3
AR	51	44	50	43	49	978	178	476	36.8	5.4	15.0
CA	690	616	711	631	705	13,402	2,452	6,651	742.5	105.0	304.7
CO	126	111	128	113	125	2,091	399	1,021	102.2	15.5	42.8
CT	73	62	72	61	70	1,474	257	721	85.9	11.4	35.3
DE	20	16	19	16	18	382	62	174	19.5	2.5	7.5
DC	17	12	17	13	16	491	56	234	35.1	3.8	14.8
FL	401	367	417	380	413	7,135	1,282	3,084	294.1	45.6	115.4
GA	170	149	170	147	166	3,458	557	1,522	154.6	19.9	58.1
HI	25	22	25	21	24	503	90	263	19.9	3.2	9.5
ID	37	32	36	32	35	510	120	285	18.6	3.6	9.1
IL	254	221	254	221	249	5,209	833	2,417	262.3	33.5	106.7
IN	111	95	109	91	105	2,556	395	1,169	103.1	12.5	41.0
IA	63	54	62	53	61	1,305	219	633	50.3	6.8	22.0
KS	59	50	58	49	56	1,150	202	596	47.7	6.6	21.6
KY	70	59	69	58	66	1,507	246	689	57.5	7.5	23.0
LA	81	69	81	68	79	1,688	299	903	72.1	10.4	34.4
ME	34	30	33	29	32	487	108	279	18.7	3.6	9.7
MD	108	93	108	92	105	2,182	378	1,102	108.8	15.4	49.5
MA	137	119	139	120	136	3,071	490	1,424	178.6	22.0	71.6
MI	174	153	172	149	169	3,536	623	1,775	156.8	22.3	69.3
MN	118	102	118	101	115	2,518	391	1,207	120.9	14.2	47.5
MS	46	39	45	38	43	903	163	426	31.7	4.7	13.4
MO	118	102	117	101	114	2,355	392	1,110	98.5	12.5	39.4
MT	31	28	32	28	31	350	104	236	12.4	3.2	7.6
NE	42	36	42	36	41	830	143	394	33.1	4.5	13.7
NV	47	40	48	40	46	1,048	155	428	41.6	6.1	16.3
NH	31	26	30	26	29	552	107	287	24.9	4.2	12.0
NJ	194	171	194	171	191	3,492	659	1,749	195.1	27.4	81.0
NM	36	30	35	29	33	598	123	332	22.9	4.0	11.4
NY	445	401	456	410	451	7,688	1,482	3,894	466.8	63.2	189.9
NC	169	147	168	145	164	3,421	581	1,574	143.3	19.1	55.4
ND	18	15	20	17	19	343	68	200	15.6	2.5	8.0
OH	190	163	186	157	182	4,587	703	2,119	195.6	23.9	78.5
OK	72	62	73	62	70	1,326	253	700	54.7	8.5	25.4
OR	88	77	89	77	87	1,397	312	778	61.1	10.0	28.1
PA	231	200	229	197	225	5,181	846	2,429	237.6	29.5	94.5
RI	25	21	24	20	23	408	81	224	17.8	3.1	8.9
SC	79	68	78	67	76	1,583	277	743	59.3	8.6	24.3
SD	22	19	22	19	21	340	75	200	12.4	2.3	6.5
TN	98	83	96	81	93	2,394	356	1,037	99.0	12.1	39.1
TX	394	343	412	355	406	9,664	1,492	4,407	468.4	58.5	184.2
UT	58	50	60	52	58	1,102	189	520	45.2	6.4	19.4
VT	19	16	18	16	17	262	62	155	10.1	2.1	5.7
VA	149	129	149	128	145	3,132	527	1,468	154.5	19.9	64.4
WA	144	128	145	127	142	2,444	497	1,264	130.8	18.3	53.6
WV	30	25	28	23	27	576	107	291	21.5	3.0	9.3
WI	110	94	108	91	106	2,401	392	1,216	102.1	12.9	44.0
WY	18	15	18	15	17	213	59	132	9.8	2.1	5.1

Source: U.S. Small Business Administration, Office of Advocacy, Research and Statistics, Firm Size Data, "Statistics of U.S. Businesses," <https://www.sba.gov/advocacy/firm-size-data>, accessed August 2017.

Table 788. Employer Firms, Establishments, Employment, and Annual Payroll by Firm Size: 1990 to 2014

[In thousands except as noted (5,074 represents 5,074,000). Firms are an aggregation of all establishments owned by a parent company with some annual payroll. Establishments are locations with active payroll in any quarter. This table illustrates the changing importance of enterprise sizes over time, not job growth, as enterprises can grow or decline and change enterprise size cells over time]

| Item | Total | Employment size of firm | | | | | | |
		0 to 4 [1]	5 to 9	10 to 19	20 to 99	100 to 499	Less than 500	500 or more
Firms:								
1990	5,074	3,021	952	563	454	70	5,060	14
2000	5,653	3,397	1,021	617	516	84	5,635	17
2005	5,984	3,678	1,050	630	521	87	5,966	17
2010	5,735	3,575	968	617	475	82	5,717	17
2011	5,684	3,532	979	593	481	81	5,667	18
2012	5,726	3,544	993	594	494	83	5,708	18
2013	5,775	3,575	992	601	503	85	5,756	19
2014	5,825	3,598	999	609	513	88	5,806	19
Establishments:								
1990	6,176	3,032	971	600	590	255	5,448	728
2000	7,070	3,406	1,035	652	674	312	6,080	990
2005	7,500	3,684	1,063	662	679	332	6,421	1,079
2010	7,397	3,583	982	653	648	354	6,220	1,176
2011	7,354	3,540	993	627	652	350	6,162	1,192
2012	7,432	3,549	1,005	631	687	360	6,232	1,199
2013	7,488	3,581	1,004	634	685	361	6,264	1,224
2014	7,563	3,604	1,010	641	691	361	6,307	1,256
Employment:								
1990	93,469	5,117	6,252	7,543	17,710	13,545	50,167	43,302
2000	114,065	5,593	6,709	8,286	20,277	16,260	57,124	56,941
2005	116,317	5,937	6,898	8,454	20,444	16,911	58,645	57,672
2010	111,970	5,926	6,359	8,288	18,554	15,869	54,997	56,973
2011	113,426	5,858	6,432	7,961	18,880	15,867	54,998	58,428
2012	115,938	5,907	6,528	7,974	19,387	16,267	56,063	59,876
2013	118,266	5,927	6,524	8,058	19,698	16,617	56,823	61,443
2014	121,070	5,940	6,571	8,177	20,122	17,085	57,895	63,175
Annual payroll (bil. dol.):								
1990	2,104	117	114	144	352	279	1,007	1,097
2000	3,879	186	174	231	608	528	1,727	2,152
2005	4,483	220	206	269	700	617	2,013	2,470
2010	4,941	227	212	283	719	666	2,107	2,834
2011	5,165	230	218	284	746	691	2,169	2,996
2012	5,414	238	224	291	784	731	2,268	3,147
2013	5,622	241	228	297	799	752	2,318	3,304
2014	5,940	252	236	310	838	804	2,439	3,501

[1] Employment is measured in March, thus some firms (start-ups after March, closures before March, and seasonal firms) will have zero employment and some annual payroll.

Source: U.S. Small Business Administration, Office of Advocacy, Research and Statistics, Firm Size Data, "Statistics of U.S. Businesses," <https://www.sba.gov/advocacy/firm-size-data>, accessed August 2017.

Table 789. Number of Active Establishments by Firm Age and Size: 2014

[In thousands (2,836 represents 2,836,000), except as indicated. An establishment is a fixed physical location where economic activity occurs. A firm may have one establishment (a single unit establishment) or many establishments (a multi-unit firm). Firms are defined at the enterprise level such that all establishments under the operational control of the enterprise are considered part of the firm. Data cover nonfarm private establishments with paid employees; major exclusions are self-employed individuals, employees of private households, railroad employees, agricultural production employees, and most government employees. Establishments are used in the tabulation of Business Dynamics Statistics (BDS) statistics. Although the BDS program is based on the same basic source data as the Census Bureau's County Business Patterns and Statistics of U.S. Business programs, differences in how the source data are processed lead to differences in published statistics. For more information about concepts and methodology, see <http://www.census.gov/ces/dataproducts/bds/>]

| Firm age [1] | By firm size | | | | | | | Percent of employment | Percent of job creation | Percent of job destruction |
	1 to 4 employees	5 to 9 employees	10 to 19 employees	20 to 99 employees	100 to 499 employees	Less than 500 employees	500 or more employees			
Total	**2,836**	**1,031**	**637**	**671**	**349**	**5,523**	**1,198**	**100.0**	**100.0**	**100.0**
Startups	353	30	13	11	3	410	(Z)	2.1	15.4	0.0
1 to 5 years	781	236	127	95	19	1,258	9	8.8	12.9	17.1
6 to 10 years	544	200	116	96	27	982	14	8.3	8.8	11.0
11 to 20 years	607	254	157	146	51	1,215	64	13.8	12.3	15.6
21 years and over	440	226	151	183	119	1,120	282	24.5	19.3	21.6
Born before 1976	111	84	74	139	131	538	830	42.6	31.3	34.7
Percent of employment	5.0	5.6	6.9	16.7	14.0	48.3	51.7	(X)	(X)	(X)
Percent of job creation	10.4	7.7	7.8	15.9	12.5	54.3	45.7	(X)	(X)	(X)

X Not applicable. Z Less than 500. [1] Establishment age is computed by taking the difference between the current year of operation and the birth year. Firm age is computed from the age of the establishments belonging to that particular firm.

Source: U.S. Census Bureau, Center for Economic Studies, "Business Dynamics Statistics," <http://www.census.gov/ces/dataproducts/bds/data_firm.html>, accessed May 2017.

Table 790. Firm Births and Deaths by Employment Size of Enterprise: 1990 to 2011

[In thousands (541.1 represents 541,100). Data represent activity from March of the beginning year to March of the ending year. Establishments with no employment in the first quarter of the beginning year were excluded. New firms represent new original establishments and deaths represent closed original establishments. Because of the methodology in determining new and closed original establishments, the U.S. Census Bureau considers these figures to be estimates]

Item	Births (initial locations)				Deaths (initial locations)			
	Total	Less than 20 employees	Less than 500 employees	500 employees or more	Total	Less than 20 employees	Less than 500 employees	500 employees or more
Firms:								
1990 to 1991	541.1	515.9	540.9	0.3	546.5	517.0	546.1	0.4
2000 to 2001	585.1	558.0	584.8	0.3	553.3	524.0	552.8	0.5
2005 to 2006	670.1	640.7	669.8	0.2	599.3	573.3	599.1	0.3
2006 to 2007	668.4	639.1	668.2	0.2	592.4	564.3	592.1	0.3
2007 to 2008	597.1	570.3	596.8	0.2	641.4	613.8	641.2	0.2
2008 to 2009 [1]	518.5	497.5	518.4	0.1	680.7	655.9	680.5	0.2
2009 to 2010 [1]	533.9	514.4	533.8	0.1	593.3	572.9	593.2	0.2
2010 to 2011 [1]	534.9	515.1	534.8	0.1	575.7	557.2	575.6	0.1
Employment:								
1990 to 1991	3,105	1,713	2,907	198	3,208	1,723	3,044	164
2000 to 2001	3,418	1,821	3,109	310	3,262	1,701	3,050	212
2005 to 2006	3,682	1,999	3,412	270	3,220	1,711	2,964	256
2006 to 2007	3,554	1,945	3,325	229	3,482	1,734	3,126	356
2007 to 2008	3,376	1,784	3,058	318	3,413	1,846	3,174	240
2008 to 2009 [1]	2,697	1,545	2,523	173	3,459	1,928	3,195	264
2009 to 2010 [1]	2,697	1,613	2,550	147	2,857	1,664	2,602	256
2010 to 2011 [1]	2,619	1,570	2,469	150	2,614	1,631	2,496	118

[1] Methodology from 2008 forward is defining firm births/deaths as establishment births/deaths for single location firms.

Source: U.S. Small Business Administration, Office of Advocacy, Research and Statistics, Firm Size Data, "Statistics of U.S. Businesses," <http://www.sba.gov/advocacy/firm-size-data>, accessed August 2014.

Table 791. Establishments and Employment Changes from Births, Deaths, Expansions, and Contractions by Employment Size of Enterprise: 2013 to 2014

[In thousands (6,731 represents 6,731,000), except percent. See headnote, Table 790. An establishment is a single physical location at which business is conducted or where services or industrial operations are performed. An enterprise is a business organization consisting of one or more domestic establishments under common ownership or control. Minus sign (-) indicates decrease]

Employment size of firm	Establishments			Employment		Percent change in employment due to—			
	Number in initial year	Births [1]	Deaths [2]	Number in initial year	Change in employment	Births [1]	Deaths [2]	Births and expansions [3]	Deaths and contractions [4]
Total	**6,731**	**671**	**607**	**118,246**	**2,811**	**4.4**	**-3.8**	**13.5**	**-11.2**
1 to 4	2,861	432	399	5,922	766	12.9	-11.7	31.0	-18.1
5 to 9	1,003	62	57	6,519	180	6.2	-5.6	17.9	-15.1
10 to 19	634	31	30	8,054	156	5.0	-4.7	15.1	-13.2
20 to 99	684	28	28	19,692	366	4.2	-3.7	12.7	-10.9
100 to 499	357	19	14	16,616	403	3.6	-2.9	11.9	-9.4
Less than 500	5,539	572	527	56,803	1,871	5.3	-4.7	15.3	-12.0
500 or more	1,192	99	80	61,443	940	3.5	-2.9	11.9	-10.4

[1] Births are establishments that have zero employment in the first quarter of the initial year and positive employment in the first quarter of the subsequent year. [2] Deaths are establishments that have positive employment in the first quarter of the initial year and zero employment in the first quarter of the subsequent year. [3] Expansions are establishments that have positive first quarter employment in both the initial and subsequent years and increase employment during the time period between the first quarter of the initial year and the first quarter of the subsequent year. [4] Contractions are establishments that have positive first quarter employment in both the initial and subsequent years and decrease employment during the time period between the first quarter of the initial year and the first quarter of the subsequent year.

Source: U.S. Census Bureau, "Statistics of U.S. Businesses," <https://www.census.gov/programs-surveys/susb.html>, accessed July 2017.

Table 792. Small Business Administration Loans to Minority-Owned Small Businesses: 2000 to 2016

[3,675 represents $3,675,000,000. For year ending September 30. A small business must be independently owned and operated, must not be dominant in its particular industry, and must meet standards set by the Small Business Administration as to its annual receipts or number of employees]

Minority group	Number of loans					Amount (mil. dol.)				
	2000	2010	2014	2015	2016	2000	2010	2014	2015	2016
Total minority loans [1]	**12,041**	**11,235**	**13,625**	**16,979**	**17,994**	**3,675**	**3,982**	**6,563**	**7,934**	**8,649**
Black	2,183	1,707	1,650	2,175	2,458	415	345	403	538	595
Asian or Pacific Islander	5,827	5,942	7,338	8,797	9,130	2,390	2,743	4,806	5,607	6,270
Hispanic (incl. Puerto Rican)	3,491	3,192	4,255	5,549	5,978	767	806	1,251	1,642	1,642
American Indian	540	387	382	458	428	102	86	103	147	142

[1] Beginning 2010, includes other minority loans not shown separately.

Source: U.S. Small Business Administration, "SBA Lending Statistics for Major Programs (as of 9/30/2016)," <https://www.sba.gov/about-sba/sba-newsroom/weekly-lending-report/archive>, accessed June 2017.

Table 793. U.S. Firms—Ownership by Gender, Ethnicity, Race, and Veteran Status: 2012

[27,626 represents 27,626,000. Based on the 2012 Survey of Business Owners; see text, this section and Appendix III. Firm ownership type is determined by the group owning 51 percent or more of the equity, interest, or stock of the business. A minority-owned firm is one in which Black or African Americans, American Indians and Alaska Natives, Asians, Native Hawaiians and Other Pacific Islanders, and/or Hispanics own 51 percent or more of the interest or stock of the business. Detail may not add to total due to rounding, because a Hispanic firm may be of any race, and because each owner had the option of selecting more than one race and is therefore included in each race selected]

Firm ownership type	All firms [1]		Firms with paid employees			
	Firms (1,000)	Sales and receipts (bil. dol.)	Firms (1,000)	Sales and receipts (bil. dol.)	Employees (1,000)	Annual payroll (bil. dol.)
All firms............................	**27,626**	**33,537**	**5,424**	**32,495**	**115,249**	**5,236**
Female............................	9,878	1,420	1,036	1,191	8,432	264
Male............................	14,845	9,466	3,336	8,813	41,132	1,644
Equally male/female............................	2,456	1,078	765	961	6,495	189
Hispanic [2]............................	3,306	474	288	380	2,330	71
Equally Hispanic/non-Hispanic [2].............	130	54	39	48	360	10
Non-Hispanic............................	23,743	11,436	4,810	10,537	53,369	2,015
Minority............................	7,952	1,380	909	1,161	7,165	219
Equally minority/nonminority.............	239	101	71	89	638	21
Nonminority............................	18,988	10,483	4,157	9,714	48,256	1,856
Veteran............................	2,522	1,141	442	1,049	5,026	195
Equally veteran/nonveteran.............	587	306	174	276	1,681	55
Nonveteran............................	24,071	10,517	4,519	9,640	49,352	1,847
White............................	21,540	10,951	4,438	10,105	50,568	1,929
Black or African American.............	2,584	150	109	103	975	28
American Indian and Alaska Native.........	273	39	26	32	208	7
Asian............................	1,918	699	481	628	3,573	111
Native Hawaiian and Other Pacific Islander........	55	8	5	6	39	1
Some other race............................	1,174	110	79	77	596	16

[1] Both firms with paid employees and firms with no paid employees. [2] A Hispanic firm may be of any race and therefore may be included in more than one race group.

Source: U.S. Census Bureau, 2012 Economic Census, Survey of Business Owners, Tables "SB1200CSA01" and "SB1200CSA02," <http://factfinder.census.gov/>, accessed January 2016. See also <https://www.census.gov/programs-surveys/sbo.html>.

Table 794. Women-Owned Firms by Kind of Business: 2012

[9,878 represents 9,878,000. See headnote, Table 793]

Kind of business	2012 NAICS code [1]	All firms [2]		Firms with paid employees			
		Firms (1,000)	Sales and receipts (mil. dol.)	Firms (1,000)	Sales and receipts (mil. dol.)	Employees (1,000)	Annual payroll (mil. dol.)
Total [3]............................	(X)	**9,878**	**1,419,834**	**1,036**	**1,190,586**	**8,432**	**263,720**
Forestry, fishing and hunting, and agricultural support services............	113–115	37	2,918	2	2,055	20	438
Mining, quarrying, and oil & gas extraction...............	21	22	12,689	2	11,674	27	1,763
Utilities............................	22	4	1,173	(Z)	1,105	2	97
Construction............................	23	266	93,002	55	85,116	436	20,265
Manufacturing............................	31–33	139	123,984	36	121,094	559	23,741
Wholesale trade............................	42	155	275,903	42	269,336	374	18,091
Retail trade............................	44–45	1,045	208,976	132	185,476	792	18,813
Transportation and warehousing [4]............	48–49	159	44,216	22	38,671	250	8,971
Information............................	51	114	28,816	10	26,499	124	6,663
Finance and insurance [5]............	52	218	36,136	34	28,379	159	7,932
Real estate and rental and leasing............	53	712	72,714	58	33,392	194	7,026
Professional, scientific, and technical services.........	54	1,335	138,670	165	102,552	775	38,060
Management of companies and enterprises............	55	2	4,854	2	4,854	51	3,874
Administrative and support and waste management and remediation services............	56	1,080	80,329	68	65,147	1,142	29,982
Educational services............................	61	367	14,168	23	10,128	170	3,606
Health care and social assistance............	62	1,603	131,361	171	101,370	1,581	43,478
Arts, entertainment, and recreation............	71	471	20,383	19	12,447	134	4,394
Accommodation and food services............	72	266	69,029	103	63,856	1,203	17,432
Other services (except public administration) [6]............	81	1,885	60,246	93	27,207	437	9,051
Industries not classified............................	99	3	268	3	227	2	45

X Not applicable. Z Less than 500. [1] Based on the 2012 North American Industry Classification System (NAICS); see text, this section. [2] Both firms with paid employees and firms with no paid employees. [3] Firms with more than one establishment are counted in each industry in which they operate, but only once in the total. [4] Excludes rail transportation (NAICS 482), and the postal service (NAICS 491). [5] Excludes monetary authorities-central banks (NAICS 521) and funds, trusts, and other financial vehicles (NAICS 525). [6] Excludes religious, grantmaking, civic, professional, and similar organizations (NAICS 813) and private households (NAICS 814).

Source: U.S. Census Bureau, 2012 Economic Census, Survey of Business Owners, Table "SB1200CSA01," <http://factfinder.census.gov/>, accessed January 2016. See also <https://www.census.gov/programs-surveys/sbo.html>.

Table 795. Minority-Owned Firms by Kind of Business: 2012

[1,380,149 represents $1,380,149,000,000. See headnote, Table 793]

Kind of business	2012 NAICS code [1]	All firms [2] Firms	All firms [2] Sales and receipts (mil. dol.)	Firms with paid employees Firms	Firms with paid employees Sales and receipts (mil. dol.)	Firms with paid employees Employ-ees	Firms with paid employees Annual payroll (mil. dol.)
Total [3]	(X)	**7,952,386**	**1,380,149**	**908,800**	**1,161,431**	**7,165,151**	**219,298**
Forestry, fishing and hunting, and agricultural support services	113–115	36,552	2,326	1,140	1,218	14,187	321
Mining, quarrying, and oil & gas extraction	21	8,450	4,193	1,190	3,487	16,334	875
Utilities	22	5,461	1,281	205	1,179	961	98
Construction	23	712,348	90,342	61,694	67,131	349,466	14,116
Manufacturing	31–33	106,357	80,011	25,304	77,132	331,920	13,315
Wholesale trade	42	160,511	296,999	54,863	286,906	403,154	18,177
Retail trade	44–45	650,346	277,901	138,487	255,949	750,432	16,849
Transportation and warehousing [4]	48–49	525,734	59,169	29,561	31,014	208,569	6,818
Information	51	83,915	17,540	6,931	15,525	71,880	4,962
Finance and insurance [5]	52	152,062	22,059	21,609	15,626	85,680	4,522
Real estate and rental and leasing	53	383,081	38,409	25,911	15,269	81,701	2,810
Professional, scientific, and technical services	54	783,716	121,409	98,528	99,072	625,797	37,609
Management of companies and enterprises	55	1,138	3,829	1,138	3,829	47,854	3,771
Administrative and support and waste management and remediation services	56	920,463	57,283	48,614	43,553	733,549	18,838
Educational services	61	167,585	6,875	9,539	5,110	78,984	1,789
Health care and social assistance	62	1,049,683	118,039	135,899	98,415	1,139,737	38,180
Arts, entertainment, and recreation	71	289,684	11,309	7,091	6,180	46,407	2,063
Accommodation and food services	72	320,808	115,475	163,160	109,428	1,857,539	27,407
Other services (except public administration) [6]	81	1,595,222	55,542	78,925	25,307	319,741	6,760
Industries not classified	99	1,567	159	1,303	101	1,256	20

X Not applicable. [1] Based on the 2012 North American Industry Classification System (NAICS); see text, this section. [2] Both firms with paid employees and firms with no paid employees. [3] Firms with more than one establishment are counted in each industry in which they operate, but only once in the total. [4] Excludes rail transportation (NAICS 482), and the postal service (NAICS 491). [5] Excludes monetary authorities-central banks (NAICS 521) and funds, trusts, and other financial vehicles (NAICS 525). [6] Excludes religious, grantmaking, civic, professional, and similar organizations (NAICS 813) and private households (NAICS 814).

Source: U.S. Census Bureau, 2012 Economic Census, Survey of Business Owners, Table "SB1200CSA01," <http://factfinder.census.gov/>, accessed January 2016. See also <https://www.census.gov/programs-surveys/sbo.html>.

Table 796. Hispanic-Owned Firms by Kind of Business: 2012

[473,636 represents $473,636,000,000. See headnote, Table 793]

Kind of business	2012 NAICS code [1]	All firms [2] Firms	All firms [2] Sales and receipts (mil. dol.)	Firms with paid employees Firms	Firms with paid employees Sales and receipts (mil. dol.)	Firms with paid employees Employ-ees	Firms with paid employees Annual payroll (mil. dol.)
Total [3]	(X)	**3,305,873**	**473,636**	**287,501**	**379,995**	**2,329,553**	**70,856**
Forestry, fishing and hunting, and agricultural support services	113–115	17,590	1,137	631	659	11,214	213
Mining, quarrying, and oil & gas extraction	21	4,849	2,395	700	1,876	10,297	515
Utilities	22	3,188	305	135	236	559	18
Construction	23	475,472	55,830	38,704	38,901	222,161	8,437
Manufacturing	31–33	51,380	25,269	10,475	23,737	122,302	4,630
Wholesale trade	42	64,063	96,238	17,036	92,525	126,660	5,450
Retail trade	44–45	255,837	91,683	33,136	83,644	202,134	5,250
Transportation and warehousing [4]	48–49	243,123	31,178	15,291	16,924	111,642	3,814
Information	51	30,315	4,085	2,312	3,360	20,353	1,028
Finance and insurance [5]	52	55,392	7,680	8,529	5,553	33,547	1,480
Real estate and rental and leasing	53	142,696	12,542	9,995	5,052	30,005	1,015
Professional, scientific, and technical services	54	278,066	33,525	29,582	25,584	170,953	8,858
Management of companies and enterprises	55	376	1,713	376	1,713	20,529	2,018
Administrative and support and waste management and remediation services	56	527,608	26,545	25,243	18,171	326,767	7,721
Educational services	61	53,510	1,964	2,142	1,423	21,222	539
Health care and social assistance	62	347,955	28,937	30,335	23,210	302,521	9,407
Arts, entertainment, and recreation	71	101,624	3,891	2,350	2,097	16,986	701
Accommodation and food services	72	100,176	28,424	37,825	26,423	484,750	7,331
Other services (except public administration) [6]	81	553,065	20,250	23,214	8,885	94,671	2,430
Industries not classified	99	366	44	269	23	278	4

X Not applicable. [1] Based on the 2012 North American Industry Classification System (NAICS); see text, this section. [2] Both firms with paid employees and firms with no paid employees. [3] Firms with more than one establishment are counted in each industry in which they operate, but only once in the total. [4] Excludes rail transportation (NAICS 482), and the postal service (NAICS 491). [5] Excludes monetary authorities-central banks (NAICS 521) and funds, trusts, and other financial vehicles (NAICS 525). [6] Excludes religious, grantmaking, civic, professional, and similar organizations (NAICS 813) and private households (NAICS 814).

Source: U.S. Census Bureau, 2012 Economic Census, Survey of Business Owners, Table "SB1200CSA01," <http://factfinder.census.gov/>, accessed January 2016. See also <https://www.census.gov/programs-surveys/sbo.html>.

Table 797. Black-Owned Firms by Kind of Business: 2012

[150,203 represents $150,203,000,000. See headnote, Table 793]

Kind of business	2012 NAICS code [1]	All firms [2] Firms	All firms [2] Sales and receipts (mil. dol.)	Firms with paid employees Firms	Firms with paid employees Sales and receipts (mil. dol.)	Firms with paid employees Employ-ees	Firms with paid employees Annual payroll (mil. dol.)
Total [3]	(X)	2,584,403	150,203	109,137	103,452	975,052	27,690
Forestry, fishing and hunting, and agricultural support services	113–115	5,465	234	126	114	655	20
Mining	21	1,026	64	40	37	223	8
Utilities	22	1,646	29	5	7	14	1
Construction	23	136,729	11,142	7,594	8,326	39,883	1,708
Manufacturing	31–33	22,649	8,217	1,299	7,797	18,917	725
Wholesale trade	42	24,465	12,938	2,338	12,003	18,486	876
Retail trade	44–45	160,276	17,188	8,274	14,090	43,154	1,167
Transportation and warehousing [4]	48–49	184,777	12,248	6,467	4,099	38,917	1,025
Information	51	28,459	2,497	976	2,024	10,556	619
Finance and insurance [5]	52	43,649	3,665	4,295	2,661	16,423	889
Real estate and rental and leasing	53	78,011	4,468	2,812	1,858	10,845	373
Professional, scientific, and technical services	54	206,942	15,683	13,822	11,282	81,170	4,457
Management of companies and enterprises	55	196	453	196	453	7,957	395
Administrative and support and waste management and remediation services	56	294,977	12,349	10,485	8,979	169,660	4,476
Educational services	61	67,399	1,582	1,586	940	14,360	345
Health care and social assistance	62	492,983	24,244	32,055	16,904	309,855	7,311
Arts, entertainment, and recreation	71	124,286	3,713	1,890	1,704	8,666	549
Accommodation and food services	72	60,329	8,538	6,938	7,657	153,306	2,085
Other services (except public administration) [6]	81	649,896	10,906	7,769	2,490	31,543	656
Industries not classified	99	606	46	536	28	462	5

X Not applicable. [1] Based on the 2012 North American Industry Classification System (NAICS); see text, this section. [2] Both firms with paid employees and firms with no paid employees. [3] Firms with more than one establishment are counted in each industry in which they operate, but only once in the total. [4] Excludes rail transportation (NAICS 482), and the postal service (NAICS 491). [5] Excludes monetary authorities-central banks (NAICS 521) and funds, trusts, and other financial vehicles (NAICS 525). [6] Excludes religious, grantmaking, civic, professional, and similar organizations (NAICS 813) and private households (NAICS 814).

Source: U.S. Census Bureau, 2012 Economic Census, Survey of Business Owners, Table "SB1200CSA01," <http://factfinder.census.gov/>, accessed January 2016. See also <https://www.census.gov/programs-surveys/sbo.html>.

Table 798. Asian–Owned Firms by Kind of Business: 2012

[699,492 represents $699,492,000,000. See headnote, Table 793]

Kind of business	2012 NAICS code [1]	All firms [2] Firms	All firms [2] Sales and receipts (mil. dol.)	Firms with paid employees Firms	Firms with paid employees Sales and receipts (mil. dol.)	Firms with paid employees Employ-ees	Firms with paid employees Annual payroll (mil. dol.)
Total [3]	(X)	1,917,902	699,492	481,026	627,532	3,572,577	110,544
Forestry, fishing and hunting, and agricultural support services	113–115	6,385	500	129	177	736	28
Mining, quarrying, and oil & gas extraction	21	1,144	995	135	934	2,663	177
Utilities	22	525	756	32	746	194	67
Construction	23	76,883	15,362	10,567	12,919	54,404	2,473
Manufacturing	31–33	27,590	42,596	12,212	41,801	172,485	7,148
Wholesale trade	42	67,062	177,956	34,152	172,843	244,854	11,131
Retail trade	44–45	218,054	156,835	93,021	146,868	477,684	9,688
Transportation and warehousing [4]	48–49	93,554	14,157	6,767	8,726	48,424	1,663
Information	51	23,031	10,260	3,207	9,490	38,095	3,135
Finance and insurance [5]	52	48,148	9,700	7,634	6,719	30,511	1,908
Real estate and rental and leasing	53	149,452	19,868	11,975	7,766	36,762	1,257
Professional, scientific, and technical services	54	276,960	67,766	50,834	58,666	345,376	23,067
Management of companies and enterprises	55	481	1,494	481	1,494	17,446	1,249
Administrative and support and waste management and remediation services	56	86,064	15,386	10,891	13,724	191,550	5,378
Educational services	61	42,744	3,047	5,440	2,508	40,051	785
Health care and social assistance	62	203,471	60,879	69,953	54,631	497,812	20,162
Arts, entertainment, and recreation	71	54,857	2,962	2,403	1,817	17,351	537
Accommodation and food services	72	156,391	76,004	115,634	72,950	1,176,725	17,400
Other services (except public administration) [6]	81	385,583	22,903	46,128	12,705	178,974	3,281
Industries not classified	99	549	66	455	48	480	9

X Not applicable. [1] Based on the 2012 North American Industry Classification System (NAICS); see text, this section. [2] Both firms with paid employees and firms with no paid employees. [3] Firms with more than one establishment are counted in each industry in which they operate, but only once in the total. [4] Excludes rail transportation (NAICS 482), and the postal service (NAICS 491). [5] Excludes monetary authorities-central banks (NAICS 521) and funds, trusts, and other financial vehicles (NAICS 525). [6] Excludes religious, grantmaking, civic, professional, and similar organizations (NAICS 813) and private households (NAICS 814).

Source: U.S. Census Bureau, 2012 Economic Census, Survey of Business Owners, Table "SB1200CSA01," <http://factfinder.census.gov/>, accessed January 2016. See also <https://www.census.gov/programs-surveys/sbo.html>.

Table 799. Native Hawaiian- and Other Pacific Islander-Owned Firms by Kind of Business: 2012

[8,136 represents $8,136,000,000. See headnote, Table 793]

Kind of business	2012 NAICS code[1]	All firms[2]		Firms with paid employees			
		Firms	Sales and receipts (mil. dol.)	Firms	Sales and receipts (mil. dol.)	Employees	Annual payroll (mil. dol.)
Total[3]	(X)	54,749	8,136	4,706	6,470	39,001	1,431
Forestry, fishing and hunting, and agricultural support services	113–115	632	17	1	(S)	{4}	(S)
Mining, quarrying, and oil & gas extraction	21	44	(S)	24	(S)	{5}	(S)
Utilities	22	23	(Z)	1	(S)	{4}	(S)
Construction	23	5,551	1,508	724	1,254	4,803	240
Manufacturing	31–33	962	535	249	517	2,645	102
Wholesale trade	42	1,283	1,080	151	1,023	1,696	81
Retail trade	44–45	4,702	816	485	698	2,894	72
Transportation and warehousing[6]	48–49	2,566	545	226	(S)	{5}	(S)
Information	51	626	107	54	91	328	17
Finance and insurance[8]	52	1,227	160	127	70	382	24
Real estate and rental and leasing	53	2,791	196	168	69	564	20
Professional, scientific, and technical services	54	6,292	932	600	765	3,680	255
Management of companies and enterprises	55	8	12	8	12	183	13
Administrative and support and waste management and remediation services	56	6,435	449	283	331	5,968	151
Educational services	61	1,316	38	89	(S)	{9}	(S)
Health care and social assistance	62	6,635	457	548	319	2,788	92
Arts, entertainment, and recreation	71	3,541	285	169	218	1,174	72
Accommodation and food services	72	1,454	351	448	307	5,327	80
Other services (except public administration)[10]	81	8,674	458	367	(S)	{7}	(S)
Industries not classified	99	11	(Z)	11	1	13	(Z)

X Not applicable. S Withheld because estimate did not meet publication standards. Z Less than $500,000. [1] Based on the 2012 North American Industry Classification System (NAICS); see text, this section. [2] Both firms with paid employees and firms with no paid employees. [3] Firms with more than one establishment are counted in each industry in which they operate, but only once in the total. [4] 0 to 19 employees. [5] 1,000 to 2,499 employees. [6] Excludes rail transportation (NAICS 482), and the postal service (NAICS 491). [7] 2,500 to 4,999 employees. [8] Excludes monetary authorities-central banks (NAICS 521) and funds, trusts, and other financial vehicles (NAICS 525). [9] 100 to 249 employees. [10] Excludes religious, grantmaking, civic, professional, and similar organizations (NAICS 813) and private households (NAICS 814).

Source: U.S. Census Bureau, 2012 Economic Census, Survey of Business Owners, Table "SB1200CSA01," <http://factfinder.census.gov/>, accessed January 2016. See also <https://www.census.gov/programs-surveys/sbo.html>.

Table 800. American Indian- and Alaska Native-Owned Firms by Kind of Business: 2012

[38,838 represents $38,838,000,000. See headnote, Table 793]

Kind of business	2012 NAICS code[1]	All firms[2]		Firms with paid employees			
		Firms	Sales and receipts (mil. dol.)	Firms	Sales and receipts (mil. dol.)	Employees	Annual payroll (mil. dol.)
Total[3]	(X)	272,919	38,838	26,179	31,654	208,178	6,995
Forestry, fishing and hunting, and agricultural support services	113–115	6,998	399	250	229	1,590	53
Mining, quarrying, and oil & gas extraction	21	1,407	532	289	434	1,953	103
Utilities	22	296	195	14	187	154	8
Construction	23	35,969	7,401	4,836	6,124	29,700	1,329
Manufacturing	31–33	5,991	2,513	1,146	2,349	13,133	519
Wholesale trade	42	5,946	5,645	1,022	5,281	8,270	419
Retail trade	44–45	22,433	6,535	2,655	5,962	18,524	476
Transportation and warehousing[4]	48–49	11,370	1,467	939	884	5,692	190
Information	51	3,457	445	286	380	2,931	108
Finance and insurance[5]	52	6,199	889	1,225	602	4,901	200
Real estate and rental and leasing	53	10,925	918	873	440	2,678	123
Professional, scientific, and technical services	54	30,966	3,168	3,627	2,193	17,882	787
Management of companies and enterprises	55	56	152	56	152	1,173	75
Administrative and support and waste management and remediation services	56	29,100	2,681	2,035	2,263	39,133	1,096
Educational services	61	7,437	264	266	196	2,813	109
Health care and social assistance	62	29,099	2,200	3,010	1,712	27,822	675
Arts, entertainment, and recreation	71	15,980	679	281	428	2,112	208
Accommodation and food services	72	5,770	1,048	1,462	934	18,591	250
Other services (except public administration)[6]	81	43,573	1,704	1,963	902	9,096	266
Industries not classified	99	37	2	35	2	32	(Z)

X Not applicable. Z Less than $500,000. [1] Based on the 2012 North American Industry Classification System (NAICS); see text, this section. [2] Both firms with paid employees and firms with no paid employees. [3] Firms with more than one establishment are counted in each industry in which they operate, but only once in the total. [4] Excludes rail transportation (NAICS 482), and the postal service (NAICS 491). [5] Excludes monetary authorities-central banks (NAICS 521) and funds, trusts, and other financial vehicles (NAICS 525). [6] Excludes religious, grantmaking, civic, professional, and similar organizations (NAICS 813) and private households (NAICS 814).

Source: U.S. Census Bureau, 2012 Economic Census, Survey of Business Owners, Table "SBO1200CSA01," <http://factfinder.census.gov/>, accessed January 2016. See also <https://www.census.gov/programs-surveys/sbo.html>.

Table 801. Employer Firm Ownership by Industry and Sex, Race/Ethnicity, and Veteran Status: 2015

[In thousands (3,387.2 represents 3,387,200). Includes all U.S. firms with paid employees operating during 2015 with receipts of $1,000 or more and classified in the 2012 North American Industry Classification System (NAICS) sectors 11 through 99, except for NAICS 111, 112, 482, 491, 521, 525, 813, 814, and 92. Firms with more than one domestic establishment are counted in each industry in which they operate, but only once in the U.S. industries total. Additionally, each owner had the option of selecting more than one race and is therefore included in each race selected. Based on the 2015 Annual Survey of Entrepreneurs]

Industry	NAICS code	Sex		Race/ethnicity [1]						Veteran owned
		Male	Female	White	Black	American Indian and Alaska Native	Asian	Native Hawaiian and other Pacific Islander	Hispanic [2]	
All industries.....................	(X)	**3,387.2**	**1,088.5**	**4,483.1**	**113.6**	**27.6**	**530.4**	**4.7**	**312.7**	**398.5**
Agriculture, forestry, fishing and hunting........	11	16.8	3.1	25.1	0.2	0.2	0.3	(Z)	1.3	2.0
Mining, quarrying, and oil and gas extraction..	21	15.4	2.0	20.6	0.1	0.2	0.1	(Z)	0.7	2.0
Utilities..	22	1.7	0.3	2.2	–	(Z)	0.1	–	0.1	0.3
Construction......................................	23	507.1	57.6	609.5	8.0	5.8	13.3	0.8	44.6	54.3
Manufacturing.....................................	31-33	164.6	35.6	216.0	1.5	1.1	12.4	0.1	11.9	22.2
Wholesale trade...................................	42	209.8	43.7	247.8	2.4	0.7	35.5	0.2	16.5	23.5
Retail trade.......................................	44-45	382.0	133.6	511.1	8.4	2.7	102.3	0.5	33.2	38.9
Transportation & warehousing...................	48-49	118.6	24.3	149.1	6.9	1.2	8.6	0.1	18.6	13.9
Information.......................................	51	44.8	10.5	56.7	1.6	0.3	3.7	(Z)	2.4	4.4
Finance & insurance.............................	52	155.4	37.1	199.4	5.2	1.4	7.8	0.1	10.3	22.9
Real estate & rental & leasing..................	53	152.6	61.8	241.9	3.1	0.7	13.1	0.2	10.3	20.7
Professional, scientific, & technical services...	54	511.6	172.3	679.9	16.0	4.4	58.0	0.5	33.1	67.7
Management of companies and enterprises...	55	11.1	1.9	13.7	0.1	0.1	0.5	(Z)	0.2	1.3
Administrative & support and waste management & remediation services..........	56	202.0	68.6	285.9	9.9	2.3	11.7	0.5	26.8	23.8
Educational services.............................	61	23.4	25.4	49.2	2.1	0.2	6.4	(Z)	2.4	3.0
Health care & social assistance................	62	329.7	182.5	448.8	31.9	2.6	74.6	0.7	32.0	46.7
Arts, entertainment, & recreation...............	71	55.8	20.2	85.1	1.7	0.3	2.8	0.2	2.4	5.5
Accommodation & food services...............	72	291.2	105.3	343.8	6.6	1.4	125.3	0.3	40.1	20.9
Other services (except public administration)..	81	205.4	100.0	298.7	7.5	1.9	54.3	0.3	25.6	24.8

X Not applicable. – Represents zero. Z Less than 50. [1] Includes other, not shown separately. [2] A Hispanic firm may be of any race and therefore may be included in more than one race group.

Source: U.S. Census Bureau, 2015 Annual Survey of Entrepreneurs, Table "SE1500CSA01," <http://factfinder.census.gov>, accessed August 2017.

Table 802. Bankruptcy Petitions Filed and Pending by Type and Chapter: 2000 to 2016

[For years ending June 30. Covers only bankruptcy cases filed under the Bankruptcy Reform Act of 1978. Bankruptcy: legal recognition that a company or individual is insolvent and must restructure or liquidate. Section 101 of the U.S. Bankruptcy Code defines consumer (nonbusiness) debt as that incurred by an individual primarily for a personal, family, or household purpose. If the debtor is a corporation or partnership, or if debt related to operation of a business predominates, the nature of the debt is business. Petitions "filed" means the commencement of a proceeding through the presentation of a petition to the clerk of the court; "pending" is a proceeding in which the administration has not been completed]

Item	2000	2005	2010	2011	2012	2013	2014	2015	2016
Total filed..................	**1,276,922**	**1,637,254**	**1,572,597**	**1,529,560**	**1,311,602**	**1,137,978**	**1,000,083**	**879,736**	**819,159**
Chapter 7 [1]...............	885,447	1,196,212	1,133,320	1,083,671	914,015	778,845	669,976	568,679	509,769
Chapter 9 [2]...............	8	6	12	7	17	16	13	7	5
Chapter 11 [3]...............	9,947	6,703	14,272	12,714	10,921	9,633	8,347	6,672	7,928
Chapter 12 [4]...............	732	290	660	717	582	426	394	357	459
Chapter 13 [5]...............	380,770	433,945	424,242	432,333	385,949	348,994	321,278	303,945	300,858
Section 304 [6].............	18	98	(X)	(X)	(X)	(X)	(X)	(X)	(X)
Chapter 15 [7]...............	(X)	(X)	91	118	118	64	74	76	140
Business [8]..................	**36,910**	**32,406**	**59,608**	**52,134**	**44,435**	**36,061**	**30,113**	**25,046**	**25,227**
Nonbusiness [9]............	**1,240,012**	**1,604,848**	**1,512,989**	**1,477,426**	**1,267,167**	**1,101,917**	**969,970**	**854,690**	**793,932**
Chapter 7 [1]...............	864,183	1,174,681	1,091,322	1,047,131	883,119	754,391	649,975	551,808	494,218
Chapter 11 [3]...............	722	847	1,827	1,884	1,636	1,417	1,211	1,078	1,146
Chapter 13 [5]...............	375,107	429,315	419,836	428,410	382,409	346,105	318,781	301,802	298,566
Total pending..............	**1,400,416**	**1,750,562**	**1,659,399**	**1,704,548**	**1,662,461**	**1,584,972**	**1,461,132**	**1,316,672**	**1,204,717**

X Not applicable. [1] Chapter 7, liquidation of nonexempt assets of businesses or individuals. [2] Chapter 9, adjustment of debts of a municipality. [3] Chapter 11, individual or business reorganization. [4] Chapter 12, adjustment of debts of a family farmer with regular income, effective November 26, 1986. [5] Chapter 13, adjustment of debts of an individual with regular income. [6] Chapter 11, U.S.C., Section 304, cases ancillary to foreign proceedings. [7] Chapter 15 was added and Section 304 was terminated by changes in Bankruptcy Laws effective October 2005. [8] Business bankruptcies include those filed under Chapters 7, 9, 11, 12, 13, or 15. [9] Includes other petitions, not shown separately.

Source: Administrative Office of the United States Courts, "Bankruptcy Statistics," <http://www.uscourts.gov/Statistics/BankruptcyStatistics.aspx>, accessed February 2017.

Table 803. Bankruptcy Cases Filed by State: 2000 to 2016

[In thousands (1,276.9 represents 1,276,900). For years ending June 30. See headnote, Table 802]

State	2000	2005	2010	2011	2012	2013	2014	2015	2016
Total [1]	**1,276.9**	**1,637.3**	**1,572.6**	**1,529.6**	**1,311.6**	**1,138.0**	**1,000.1**	**879.7**	**819.2**
Alabama	31.4	42.6	34.9	32.3	29.2	27.7	26.1	25.2	26.1
Alaska	1.4	1.6	1.1	1.1	0.9	0.7	0.5	0.4	0.5
Arizona	21.7	32.4	40.7	41.4	32.1	25.1	21.9	18.0	16.5
Arkansas	16.3	25.5	16.9	15.9	13.6	12.6	11.8	10.4	10.4
California	160.6	122.6	242.0	260.6	213.5	161.2	116.7	91.9	77.8
Colorado	15.6	30.2	31.9	32.1	28.6	24.3	20.3	16.0	13.8
Connecticut	11.4	11.8	11.3	10.8	8.9	7.5	7.1	6.6	6.1
Delaware	4.9	3.6	4.5	4.2	4.1	3.5	3.4	2.7	2.9
District of Columbia	2.6	1.9	1.9	1.1	1.0	0.8	0.8	0.8	0.7
Florida	74.0	85.8	107.4	105.0	87.7	78.5	73.3	62.4	50.3
Georgia	57.9	77.3	77.8	77.7	69.3	61.6	55.2	51.1	49.4
Hawaii	5.0	3.2	3.7	3.8	2.9	2.4	1.9	1.6	1.5
Idaho	7.3	9.7	8.3	8.2	7.0	5.9	5.1	4.4	3.9
Illinois	62.3	83.6	80.8	78.8	70.7	69.1	62.9	58.8	55.8
Indiana	37.5	55.9	49.3	43.4	37.3	35.1	31.2	28.0	25.1
Iowa	8.2	14.3	10.4	8.9	7.2	5.9	5.5	4.7	4.4
Kansas	11.4	17.3	11.4	10.7	9.6	8.7	8.0	7.2	6.5
Kentucky	20.8	29.2	26.0	23.5	21.1	18.9	17.9	15.8	15.4
Louisiana	23.1	31.1	19.5	18.5	16.9	15.9	15.6	14.3	14.0
Maine	4.1	4.7	4.1	4.0	3.3	2.7	2.2	2.0	1.7
Maryland	31.1	28.5	29.1	28.5	24.3	23.2	21.9	19.0	17.9
Massachusetts	16.7	19.6	22.9	22.2	18.8	14.0	11.4	9.6	8.9
Michigan	36.4	68.5	71.0	63.4	53.5	45.4	38.6	33.6	32.1
Minnesota	15.4	19.4	22.6	21.1	18.2	15.4	13.4	11.3	10.1
Mississippi	17.9	21.8	14.8	14.0	13.2	15.4	13.4	10.9	11.1
Missouri	26.3	39.2	32.9	31.6	27.7	27.1	22.3	19.9	18.8
Montana	3.3	4.4	3.1	2.8	2.3	2.0	1.7	1.4	1.4
Nebraska	5.6	9.6	7.9	7.4	6.0	5.6	4.9	4.3	4.2
Nevada	14.3	16.3	31.0	28.0	21.0	15.7	12.3	10.2	9.2
New Hampshire	3.9	4.9	5.7	5.4	4.4	3.6	2.9	2.3	2.0
New Jersey	38.7	40.7	39.7	41.1	34.8	29.3	28.4	26.1	25.7
New Mexico	7.1	10.1	6.6	6.3	5.1	4.6	4.0	3.6	3.3
New York	61.7	81.7	58.2	53.2	45.7	38.3	34.6	30.9	30.2
North Carolina	25.8	37.5	27.7	25.4	22.7	20.0	17.6	16.2	15.4
North Dakota	2.0	2.5	1.6	1.5	1.1	0.9	0.7	0.6	0.6
Ohio	53.6	95.8	72.9	65.3	53.8	49.8	43.6	39.9	37.7
Oklahoma	19.3	28.2	15.1	14.0	12.7	11.3	10.2	9.4	9.1
Oregon	18.1	25.3	20.1	19.0	16.7	14.0	13.1	11.5	9.9
Pennsylvania	43.8	62.3	38.8	37.5	31.1	27.5	25.9	22.7	22.2
Rhode Island	4.8	4.4	5.4	5.4	4.5	3.6	3.3	2.7	2.4
South Carolina	11.7	15.2	9.7	8.9	8.0	7.7	7.6	7.1	6.7
South Dakota	2.1	2.9	2.0	2.0	1.7	1.4	1.3	1.2	1.1
Tennessee	47.1	60.8	52.5	49.1	45.6	43.3	40.7	37.3	36.5
Texas	62.9	97.5	57.8	56.1	50.3	44.0	38.9	34.7	33.7
Utah	14.4	20.5	17.0	19.2	17.1	15.2	14.0	13.0	11.8
Vermont	1.6	1.7	1.7	1.4	1.1	0.9	0.8	0.7	0.6
Virginia	37.1	38.8	37.8	35.6	31.8	27.2	25.1	23.2	23.3
Washington	31.2	37.7	33.5	33.8	30.0	26.5	22.9	19.7	17.4
West Virginia	8.2	12.6	6.6	5.5	4.3	3.8	3.5	3.3	3.3
Wisconsin	18.0	29.0	30.0	29.1	26.5	23.9	22.0	19.9	17.7
Wyoming	2.0	2.5	1.5	1.5	1.3	1.3	1.1	0.9	0.9

[1] Includes Island Areas, not shown separately.

Source: Administrative Office of the United States Courts, "Bankruptcy Statistics," <http://www.uscourts.gov/Statistics/BankruptcyStatistics.aspx>, accessed February 2017.

Table 804. Patents and Trademarks: 2000 to 2016

[In thousands (176.0 represents 176,000), unless otherwise noted. Calendar year data. Covers U.S. patents issued to citizens of the United States and residents of foreign countries. For data on foreign countries, see Table 1405]

Type	2000	2005	2010	2011	2012	2013	2014	2015	2016
Patents issued............................	**176.0**	**157.7**	**244.3**	**247.7**	**276.8**	**302.9**	**326.0**	**326.0**	**333.6**
Inventions..................................	157.5	143.8	219.6	224.5	253.2	277.8	300.7	298.4	303.0
Individuals...............................	22.4	14.7	16.6	15.6	17.2	18.7	19.3	18.9	18.7
Corporations:									
United States........................	70.9	65.2	97.8	99.5	111.8	124.7	136.4	133.4	136.8
Foreign [1]............................	63.3	63.2	104.3	108.5	123.2	133.4	144.0	145.1	146.7
U.S. government........................	0.9	0.7	0.9	0.9	1.0	1.0	1.0	1.0	0.9
Designs..................................	17.4	13.0	22.8	21.4	22.0	23.5	23.7	26.0	28.9
Botanical plants.........................	0.5	0.7	1.0	0.8	0.9	0.8	1.1	1.1	1.2
Reissues.................................	0.5	0.2	0.9	1.0	0.8	0.8	0.6	0.5	0.4
U.S. residents............................	96.9	82.6	121.2	121.3	134.2	147.7	158.7	156.0	160.5
Foreign country residents...............	79.1	75.2	123.2	126.5	142.6	155.3	167.3	170.0	173.0
Percent of total..........................	44.9	47.6	50.4	51.1	51.5	51.3	51.3	52.1	51.9
Trademarks:									
Applications filed........................	361.8	334.7	368.9	398.7	415.0	433.7	455.0	503.9	530.3

[1] Includes patents to foreign governments.

Source: U.S. Patent and Trademark Office, "General Patent Statistics Reports Available for Viewing," <http://www.uspto.gov/web/offices/ac/ido/oeip/taf/reports_stco.htm>, accessed September 2017; and unpublished data.

Table 805. Patents by State and Island Areas: 2016

[Includes only U.S. patents granted to residents of the United States and U.S. territories]

State	Total	Inven-tions	De-signs	Botani-cal plants	Reis-sues	State	Total	Inven-tions	De-signs	Botani-cal plants	Reis-sues
Total [1]..................	**160,540**	**143,724**	**16,139**	**474**	**203**	Missouri............	1,389	1,218	167	0	4
						Montana............	176	152	24	0	0
Alabama................	549	491	55	3	0	Nebraska...........	366	334	32	0	0
Alaska..................	59	54	5	0	0	Nevada.............	892	799	93	0	0
Arizona.................	2,963	2,715	242	1	5	New Hampshire. ..	1,019	926	92	0	1
Arkansas...............	305	243	53	7	2	New Jersey........	4,864	4,363	494	2	5
California...............	44,832	40,815	3,816	151	50	New Mexico........	521	489	31	1	0
Colorado................	3,444	3,035	401	2	6	New York...........	9,902	8,716	1,174	1	11
Connecticut.............	2,513	2,316	192	1	4	North Carolina.....	3,814	3,510	286	13	5
Delaware...............	341	322	18	0	1	North Dakota.......	107	97	10	0	0
District of Columbia. ..	172	141	31	0	0	Ohio................	4,190	3,493	687	3	7
Florida..................	5,069	4,243	759	57	10	Oklahoma..........	578	521	53	2	2
Georgia.................	2,909	2,481	398	27	3	Oregon.............	3,345	2,790	516	37	2
Hawaii..................	178	139	33	5	1	Pennsylvania......	4,319	3,864	436	18	1
Idaho...................	824	765	56	1	2	Rhode Island.......	414	334	80	0	0
Illinois..................	5,832	4,963	851	10	8	South Carolina.....	1,151	1,024	123	2	2
Indiana.................	2,295	2,052	240	2	1	South Dakota.....	156	145	11	0	0
Iowa....................	990	932	58	0	0	Tennessee........	1,222	1,044	169	3	6
Kansas.................	945	844	100	0	1	Texas..............	10,794	10,113	648	12	21
Kentucky................	784	703	78	3	0	Utah................	1,551	1,319	229	0	3
Louisiana...............	517	448	55	14	0	Vermont............	470	447	23	0	0
Maine...................	177	161	13	2	1	Virginia............	2,229	2,055	172	1	1
Maryland................	2,069	1,933	132	1	3	Washington........	7,541	6,665	858	12	6
Massachusetts........	7,426	6,946	460	7	13	West Virginia.......	103	95	8	0	0
Michigan................	6,544	5,800	682	56	6	Wisconsin..........	2,670	2,148	509	9	4
Minnesota..............	4,669	4,218	441	5	5	Wyoming...........	115	104	11	0	0
Mississippi.............	176	149	25	2	0	Island areas........	58	50	7	1	0

[1] Includes unspecified areas.

Source: U.S. Patent and Trademark Office, "General Patent Statistics Reports Available for Viewing," <http://www.uspto.gov/web/offices/ac/ido/oeip/taf/reports_stco.htm>, accessed September 2017; and unpublished data.

Table 806. Copyright Registration by Subject Matter: 1990 to 2015

[In thousands (590.7 represents 590,700). For years ending September 30. Comprises claims to copyrights registered for both U.S. and foreign works. Semiconductor chips and renewals are not considered copyright registration claims]

Subject matter	1990	2000	2005	2009	2010	2011	2012	2013	2014	2015
Total copyright claims...............	**590.7**	**497.6**	**515.2**	**381.3**	**636.0**	**669.5**	**508.7**	**496.2**	**476.0**	**443.0**
Monographs [1]..............................	179.7	169.7	191.4	133.3	245.8	265.8	198.5	180.6	175.4	175.5
Serials....................................	111.5	69.0	57.7	37.5	90.5	58.0	48.2	44.2	43.2	55.1
Sound recordings..........................	37.5	34.2	49.9	42.0	77.9	107.7	74.3	72.4	65.5	43.0
Performing arts [2]........................	185.3	138.9	133.7	93.3	124.5	146.8	114.8	116.1	103.3	80.1
Works of the visual arts [3]................	76.7	85.8	82.5	75.2	97.2	91.2	72.8	82.9	88.7	89.2
Renewals.................................	51.8	16.8	15.8	0.5	0.1	0.2	0.2	0.2	0.1	0.8
Mask work (semiconductor chip products)...............................	1.0	0.7	0.5	0.3	0.3	0.3	2.6	0.3	0.1	0.1

[1] Includes computer software and machine readable works. [2] Includes musical works, dramatic works, choreography, pantomimes, motion pictures, and filmstrips. [3] Two-dimensional works of fine and graphic art, including prints and art reproductions; sculptural works; technical drawings and models; photographs; commercial prints and labels; and works of applied arts, cartographic works, and multimedia works.

Source: The Library of Congress, *Annual Report of the Librarian of Congress, For the Fiscal Year Ending September 30, 2015*, 2016. See also <http://www.loc.gov/about/reports-and-budgets/annual-reports/>.

Table 807. Net Stock of Private Fixed Assets by Industry: 2000 to 2015

[In billions of dollars (21,398 represents $21,398,000,000,000). Estimates as of Dec. 31. Fixed assets are assets that are used repeatedly, or continuously, in processes of production for more than a year. Net stock estimates are presented in terms of current-cost, and cover equipment, structures, and intellectual property products. (pt) = part]

Industry	NAICS code [1]	2000	2005	2010	2014	2015
Private fixed assets.............................	(X)	**21,398**	**30,609**	**34,345**	**39,914**	**40,679**
Agriculture, forestry, fishing, and hunting...................................	11	338	431	490	630	655
Farms [2]...	111, 112	311	395	440	568	590
Forestry, fishing, and related activities.............................	113-115	27	37	49	62	64
Mining...	21	574	1,223	1,483	1,804	1,690
Oil and gas extraction.................................	211	440	1,052	1,241	1,475	1,359
Mining, except oil and gas.............................	212	90	104	136	187	191
Support activities for mining.........................	213	44	67	105	142	141
Utilities...	22	1,042	1,381	1,842	2,205	2,212
Construction...	23	174	228	257	285	296
Manufacturing...	31-33	2,268	2,643	3,130	3,596	3,708
Durable goods...	(X)	1,267	1,431	1,614	1,806	1,850
Wood products...	321	32	36	39	43	44
Nonmetallic mineral products.........................	327	60	71	82	87	89
Primary metals...	331	130	135	155	166	165
Fabricated metal products.............................	332	123	137	156	175	179
Machinery...	333	166	179	206	234	240
Computer and electronic products.....................	334	345	399	456	506	518
Electrical equipment, appliances, and components.....................	335	64	65	68	74	74
Motor vehicles, bodies and trailers, and parts.....................	3361-3363	153	182	185	222	234
Other transportation equipment........................	3364, 3365, 3369	108	118	144	161	166
Furniture and related products........................	337	17	21	22	23	23
Miscellaneous manufacturing.............................	339	68	87	101	115	117
Nondurable goods...	(X)	1,001	1,213	1,516	1,790	1,858
Food and beverage and tobacco products.................	311, 312	197	239	288	336	346
Textile mills and textile product mills..................	313, 314	45	43	41	40	40
Apparel and leather and allied products..................	315, 316	18	19	18	18	17
Paper products...	322	109	112	115	121	121
Printing and related support activities..................	323	44	50	51	49	49
Petroleum and coal products.............................	324	107	128	175	221	237
Chemical products...	325	406	535	735	900	941
Plastics and rubber products.............................	326	77	87	93	104	108
Wholesale trade...	42	347	438	502	590	617
Retail trade...	44-45	655	957	1,126	1,236	1,258
Transportation and warehousing [3]......................	48-49	822	962	1,099	1,295	1,352
Air transportation...	481	185	208	220	249	262
Railroad transportation.............................	482	288	318	360	406	420
Water transportation.............................	483	37	38	41	46	47
Truck transportation.............................	484	71	96	108	144	159
Transit and ground passenger transportation....................	485	37	40	43	45	45
Pipeline transportation.............................	486	74	113	165	227	235
Warehousing and storage.............................	493	21	30	40	46	49
Information...	51	1,187	1,459	1,792	2,005	2,082
Publishing industries (includes software)............	511, 516 (pt)	112	148	180	197	203
Motion picture and sound recording industries............	512	186	235	267	288	295
Broadcasting and telecommunications..................	515, 517	853	1,010	1,247	1,353	1,391
Information and data processing services..............	516 (pt), 518, 519	36	66	97	168	193
Finance and insurance...	52	772	1,025	1,157	1,301	1,351
Federal Reserve banks.............................	521	9	10	11	11	11
Credit intermediation and related activities............	522	483	644	717	834	877
Securities, commodity contracts, and investments............	523	90	118	152	155	157
Insurance carriers and related activities............	524	173	222	238	256	261
Funds, trusts, and other financial vehicles............	525	18	31	40	45	45
Real estate and rental and leasing....................	53	10,736	16,379	17,224	20,143	20,505
Real estate...	531	10,510	16,083	16,885	19,722	20,060
Rental and leasing services and lessors of intangible assets [4]..........	532, 533	227	296	338	421	445
Professional, scientific, and technical services [3]...........................	54	301	427	536	595	608
Legal services...	5411	23	36	42	43	43
Computer systems design and related services..............	5415	54	61	75	74	75
Management of companies and enterprises [5]..........	55	269	327	371	401	405
Administrative and support and waste management......................	56	154	210	253	292	300
Administrative and support services.................	561	87	130	161	189	198
Waste management and remediation services...........	562	66	80	92	102	102
Educational services...	61	218	334	474	558	574
Health care and social assistance....................	62	693	999	1,232	1,428	1,470
Ambulatory health care services......................	621	206	273	319	352	362
Hospitals...	622	428	627	783	916	940
Nursing and residential care facilities..............	623	33	57	76	95	99
Social assistance...	624	26	41	54	65	68
Arts, entertainment, and recreation....................	71	164	241	284	324	337
Performing arts, spectator sports, museums, and related activities....	711, 712	83	118	141	160	167
Amusements, gambling, and recreation industries......................	713	80	123	143	164	171
Accommodation and food services......................	72	341	455	538	608	628
Accommodation...	721	187	262	323	359	370
Food services and drinking places....................	722	154	193	215	249	258
Other services, except government....................	81	345	491	557	620	632

X Not applicable. [1] Based on North American Industry Classification System; see text this section. [2] NAICS crop and animal production. [3] Includes other activities, not shown separately. [4] Intangible assets include patents, trademarks, and franchise agreements, but not copyrights. [5] Consists of bank and other holding companies.

Source: U.S. Bureau of Economic Analysis, National Economic Accounts, "Table 3.1ESI. Current-Cost Net Stock of Private Fixed Assets by Industry," <http://www.bea.gov/itable/>, accessed November 2016.

Table 808. Capital Expenditures: 2000 to 2015

[In billions of dollars (1,161 represents $1,161,000,000,000). Based on a sample survey and subject to sampling error; see source for details]

Item	All companies				Companies with employees				Companies without employees			
	2000	2010	2014	2015	2000	2010	2014	2015	2000	2010	2014	2015
Capital expenditures, total	**1,161**	**1,106**	**1,598**	**1,639**	**1,090**	**1,036**	**1,507**	**1,545**	**71**	**70**	**91**	**94**
Structures	364	430	644	646	338	396	609	604	26	33	35	42
New	329	395	607	592	309	368	578	560	20	28	29	32
Used	35	34	37	53	29	29	31	43	6	6	6	10
Equipment	797	676	954	993	752	640	898	941	45	36	56	52
New	751	638	899	935	718	612	854	894	32	27	45	41
Used	46	38	56	58	34	28	44	47	12	10	12	11
Capitalized computer software [1]	(NA)	(NA)	(NA)	(NA)	(NA)	(NA)	90	94	(NA)	(NA)	(NA)	(NA)
Capital leases [1]	20	16	31	35	19	15	30	35	(Z)	1	1	1

NA Not available. Z Less than $500 million. [1] Included in structures and equipment data shown above.

Source: U.S. Census Bureau, "2015 Annual Capital Expenditures Survey," February 2017 and earlier reports, <http://www.census.gov/programs-surveys/aces.html>, accessed February 2017.

Table 809. Capital Expenditures by Industry: 2000 to 2015

[In billions of dollars (1,090 represents $1,090,000,000,000). Covers only companies with employees. Data from 2000 based on the North American Industry Classification System (NAICS), 1997; 2005 data based on North American Industry Classification System (NAICS), 2002; 2010 through 2013 based on NAICS, 2007; 2014 through 2015 data based on NAICS, 2012; see text this section. Based on a sample survey and subject to sampling error; see source for details]

Industry	NAICS code	2000	2005	2010	2011	2012	2013	2014	2015
Total expenditures	(X)	**1,090**	**1,063**	**1,036**	**1,170**	**1,334**	**1,401**	**1,507**	**1,545**
Forestry, fishing, and agricultural services	113–115	1	3	3	3	3	3	4	3
Mining	21	43	67	116	166	197	202	231	175
Utilities	22	61	58	94	98	125	111	119	130
Construction	23	25	30	18	22	24	28	30	33
Manufacturing	31–33	215	166	161	192	203	221	231	240
Durable goods	321, 327, 33	134	92	87	110	113	121	125	123
Nondurable goods	31, 322–326	81	73	74	82	90	100	106	117
Wholesale trade	42	34	41	31	36	41	38	45	43
Retail trade	44–45	70	74	65	68	78	78	82	86
Transportation and warehousing	48–49	60	57	59	73	82	93	111	117
Information	51	160	91	97	100	107	124	132	136
Finance and insurance	52	134	161	103	109	130	138	153	165
Real estate and rental and leasing	53	92	103	81	91	116	114	122	152
Professional, scientific, & technical services	54	34	33	28	28	32	36	30	34
Management of companies and enterprises	55	5	3	5	5	7	6	5	5
Administrative & support and waste management & remediation services	56	18	18	17	18	19	22	23	26
Educational services	61	18	17	23	21	22	23	26	31
Health care and social assistance	62	52	74	78	83	89	94	89	94
Arts, entertainment, and recreation	71	19	14	12	11	13	15	20	16
Accommodation and food services	72	26	31	20	25	29	35	30	33
Other services (except public administration)	81	21	20	21	16	17	19	20	23
Structure and equipment expenditures serving multiple industry categories	(X)	2	2	2	3	4	3	3	3

X Not applicable.

Source: U.S. Census Bureau, "2015 Annual Capital Expenditures Survey," February 2017 and earlier reports, <http://www.census.gov/programs-surveys/aces.html>, accessed February 2017.

Table 810. Private Domestic Investment in Current and Chained (2009) Dollars: 2000 to 2015

[In billions of dollars (2,034 represents $2,034,000,000,000). Covers equipment, structures, and intellectual property products. Minus sign (-) indicates decrease. For explanation of chained dollars; see text, Section 13]

Item	2000	2005	2010	2011	2012	2013	2014	2015
CURRENT DOLLARS								
Gross private domestic investment	**2,034**	**2,527**	**2,101**	**2,240**	**2,512**	**2,706**	**2,887**	**3,057**
Less: Consumption of fixed capital	1,237	1,635	1,924	1,971	2,038	2,122	2,228	2,308
Equals: Net private domestic investment	797	892	177	269	474	584	659	748
Fixed investment	1,979	2,468	2,039	2,198	2,450	2,614	2,821	2,963
Less: Consumption of fixed capital	1,237	1,635	1,924	1,971	2,038	2,122	2,228	2,308
Equals: Net fixed investment	743	832	116	227	412	492	593	655
Nonresidential	1,494	1,612	1,658	1,812	2,008	2,094	2,251	2,311
Residential	485	856	381	386	442	520	570	652
Change in private inventories	55	60	62	42	62	92	65	93
CHAINED (2009) DOLLARS								
Gross private domestic investment	**2,376**	**2,673**	**2,120**	**2,230**	**2,466**	**2,617**	**2,734**	**2,869**
Less: Consumption of fixed capital	1,414	1,721	1,928	1,949	1,988	2,039	2,094	2,155
Equals: Net private domestic investment	962	951	192	281	478	578	640	714
Fixed investment	2,316	2,611	2,056	2,187	2,400	2,521	2,661	2,768
Nonresidential	1,648	1,717	1,674	1,802	1,964	2,033	2,156	2,200
Residential	638	873	382	385	437	488	505	565
Change in private inventories	66	64	58	38	55	79	58	84

Source: U.S. Bureau of Economic Analysis, National Economic Accounts, "Table 5.2.5. Gross and Net Domestic Investment by Major Type" and "Table 5.2.6. Real Gross and Net Domestic Investment by Major Type, Chained Dollars," <http://www.bea.gov/itable/>, accessed November 2016.

Table 811. Business Cycle Expansions and Contractions—Months of Duration: 1945 to 2009

[A trough is the low point of a business cycle; a peak is the high point. Contraction, or recession, is the period from peak to subsequent trough; expansion is the period from trough to subsequent peak. Business cycle reference dates are determined by the National Bureau of Economic Research, Inc]

Business cycle reference date				Contraction (Peak to trough)	Expansion (Previous trough to peak)	Length of cycle	
Peak		Trough				Trough from previous trough	Peak from previous peak
Month	Year	Month	Year				
February.................	1945	October	1945	8	[1] 80	[1] 88	[2] 93
November.................	1948	October	1949	11	37	48	45
July.....................	1953	May	1954	10	45	55	56
August...................	1957	April	1958	8	39	47	49
April....................	1960	February	1961	10	24	34	32
December.................	1969	November	1970	11	106	117	116
November.................	1973	March	1975	16	36	52	47
January..................	1980	July	1980	6	58	64	74
July.....................	1981	November	1982	16	12	28	18
July.....................	1990	March	1991	8	92	100	108
March....................	2001	November	2001	8	120	128	128
December.................	2007	June	2009	18	73	91	81
Average, all cycles:							
1945 to 2009 (11 cycles)...	(X)	(X)	(X)	11.1	59.4	69.5	68.5

X Not applicable. [1] Previous trough: June 1938. [2] Previous peak: May 1937.

Source: National Bureau of Economic Research, Inc., Cambridge, MA, "US Business Cycle Expansions and Contractions," <http://www.nber.org/cycles.html>, accessed September 2017 ©.

Table 812. The Conference Board Leading, Coincident, and Lagging Economic Indexes®: 2000 to 2016

[299.4 represents 299,400]

Item	Unit	2000	2005	2010	2015	2016
The Conference Board Leading Economic Index®						
(LEI) for the U.S., composite...................	2010=100	110.9	123.2	100.0	121.8	123.3
Average weekly hours, manufacturing...........................	Hours	41.2	40.6	41.1	41.8	41.9
Average weekly initial claims for unemployment insurance....................	1,000	299.4	330.6	458.5	277.4	262.9
Manufacturers' new orders, consumer goods and materials (1982 dollars)...................	Mil. dol.	152,070	150,528	122,234	135,699	137,077
Manufacturers' new orders, nondefense capital goods excluding aircraft (1982 dollars).............	Mil. dol.	45,991	40,541	36,359	38,194	36,286
Building permits, new private housing units...................	1,000	1,598	2,160	604	1,178	1,207
Leading Credit Index™ (standard deviation from the mean)....	Std. dev.	1.4	-0.7	-1.0	-0.6	-0.2
Interest rate spread, 10-year Treasury bonds less federal funds..................	Percent	-0.21	1.08	3.04	2.00	1.45
The Conference Board Coincident Economic Index®						
(CEI) for the U.S., composite....................	2010=100	98.4	102.7	100.0	111.6	113.4
Employees on nonagricultural payrolls...........................	1,000	132,033	134,042	130,353	141,813	144,306
Index of industrial production...........................	2010=100	95.6	99.8	94.2	104.4	103.1
Personal income less transfer payments (2009 dollars).........	Bil. dol.	9,081	9,861	9,987	11,754	11,879
Manufacturing and trade sales (2009 dollars)....................	Mil. dol.	986,249	1,090,827	1,036,756	1,196,331	1,224,463
Composite index of 7 lagging indicators	2010=100	91.1	95.3	100.0	117.6	121.6
Inventories to sales ratio, manufacturing and trade..............	Ratio	1.4	1.4	1.4	1.5	1.5
Average duration of unemployment.........................	Weeks	12.7	18.4	33.1	29.1	27.5
Consumer installment credit to personal income ratio...........	Percent	18.8	21.2	20.3	22.1	23.0
Commercial and industrial loans outstanding (2009 dollars).......................	Mil. dol.	1,053,916	730,001	732,616	1,155,662	1,239,999
Change in labor cost per unit of output, manufacturing..........	Percent	2.5	-1.7	-1.5	3.6	0.7
Change in consumer price index for services....................	Percent	3.8	3.5	0.9	2.4	3.0
Average prime rate....................	Percent	9.2	6.2	3.3	3.3	3.5

Source: The Conference Board, New York, NY 10022-6601, *Business Cycle Indicators*, monthly. Reproduced with permission from The Conference Board, Inc. © 2017, The Conference Board, Inc. For more information, see <http://www.conference-board.org/data/>.

Table 813. Manufacturing and Trade—Sales and Inventories: 1992 to 2016

[In billions of dollars (540 represents $540,000,000,000), except ratios. Based on North American Industry Classification System (NAICS), 2007; see text, this section]

Year	Sales, average monthly [1]				Inventories [2]				Inventory-sales ratio [3]			
	Total	Manufac-turing	Retail trade	Mer-chant whole-salers	Total	Manufac-turing	Retail trade	Mer-chant whole-salers	Total	Manufac-turing	Retail trade	Mer-chant whole-salers
1992......	540	242	151	147	836	379	260	197	1.53	1.57	1.67	1.31
1993......	567	252	161	154	863	380	278	205	1.50	1.50	1.68	1.30
1994......	610	270	175	165	926	400	305	222	1.46	1.44	1.66	1.29
1995......	655	290	185	180	985	425	322	238	1.48	1.44	1.72	1.29
1996......	687	300	197	190	1,005	430	333	241	1.45	1.44	1.67	1.27
1997......	723	320	206	198	1,046	443	344	258	1.42	1.37	1.64	1.26
1998......	742	325	215	202	1,077	448	357	272	1.44	1.39	1.62	1.32
1999......	786	336	234	217	1,137	463	384	290	1.40	1.35	1.59	1.30
2000......	834	351	249	235	1,196	481	406	309	1.41	1.35	1.59	1.29
2001......	818	331	255	232	1,119	427	394	298	1.42	1.38	1.58	1.32
2002......	823	326	261	236	1,139	423	415	301	1.36	1.29	1.55	1.26
2003......	855	335	272	248	1,148	408	431	308	1.34	1.24	1.56	1.22
2004......	926	359	289	278	1,241	441	460	340	1.30	1.19	1.56	1.17
2005......	1,006	395	307	303	1,313	474	472	368	1.27	1.17	1.51	1.17
2006......	1,069	418	323	328	1,408	522	486	399	1.28	1.20	1.50	1.17
2007......	1,128	443	333	352	1,486	561	500	424	1.28	1.22	1.49	1.17
2008......	1,161	456	328	377	1,464	542	477	445	1.31	1.26	1.52	1.20
2009......	989	369	301	319	1,329	504	429	396	1.38	1.39	1.47	1.28
2010......	1,089	409	318	361	1,448	553	455	440	1.27	1.28	1.39	1.14
2011......	1,207	458	342	407	1,561	606	470	485	1.26	1.29	1.35	1.14
2012......	1,267	475	359	434	1,649	624	505	520	1.27	1.30	1.38	1.17
2013......	1,303	484	372	448	1,713	630	542	541	1.29	1.30	1.41	1.18
2014......	1,341	491	387	464	1,771	640	559	572	1.31	1.31	1.43	1.21
2015......	1,297	462	394	441	1,803	640	585	579	1.38	1.39	1.45	1.32
2016......	1,299	454	405	439	1,844	644	607	593	1.40	1.41	1.48	1.33

[1] Averages of monthly not-seasonally-adjusted figures. [2] Seasonally adjusted end-of-year data. [3] Averages of seasonally adjusted monthly ratios.

Source: U.S. Council of Economic Advisors, *Economic Indicators*, June 2017. See also <http://www.gpo.gov/fdsys/browse/collection.action?collectionCode=ECONI>.

Table 814. Industrial Production Indexes by Industry: 2000 to 2016

[2012 = 100]

Industry	NAICS code [1]	2000	2005	2010	2012	2013	2014	2015	2016
Total index...............................	([2])	**95.6**	**99.8**	**94.2**	**100.0**	**102.0**	**105.1**	**104.4**	**103.1**
Manufacturing (SIC) [3]......................	([4])	**98.7**	**103.7**	**94.8**	**100.0**	**100.9**	**102.1**	**102.2**	**102.2**
Manufacturing (NAICS).......................	31–33	95.6	101.4	94.2	100.0	101.1	102.4	102.6	102.8
Durable goods...............................	([5])	85.8	93.8	89.3	100.0	102.2	105.1	104.3	104.1
Wood products..........................	321	138.3	147.6	94.1	100.0	105.8	108.4	112.1	116.5
Nonmetallic mineral products.............	327	132.8	138.6	95.9	100.0	105.2	109.1	109.6	112.3
Primary metals...........................	331	104.9	99.0	95.0	100.0	103.3	104.1	96.8	93.7
Fabricated metal products.................	332	110.7	104.4	90.7	100.0	101.8	103.6	100.6	97.6
Machinery................................	333	94.8	88.9	82.1	100.0	95.4	96.7	90.6	87.6
Computers and electronic products.......................	334	39.5	61.0	86.0	100.0	103.2	107.8	109.0	110.5
Electrical equipment, appliances, and components...............	335	134.9	112.9	93.1	100.0	100.0	101.7	101.8	103.9
Motor vehicles and parts..................	3361–3363	103.3	108.7	82.7	100.0	107.3	117.2	123.3	128.3
Aerospace and other misc. transportation equipment..................	3364–3369	73.2	77.3	90.6	100.0	102.9	106.8	107.0	104.8
Furniture and related products.............	337	147.2	149.8	91.9	100.0	100.8	101.3	105.9	105.8
Miscellaneous products...................	339	91.6	105.3	103.4	100.0	103.2	100.0	99.8	100.5
Nondurable goods..........................	([6])	107.8	110.5	99.8	100.0	100.0	99.3	100.7	101.3
Food, beverage, and tobacco products................................	311–312	98.1	102.7	99.8	100.0	101.7	101.6	104.3	105.6
Textile and product mills.................	313–314	204.2	176.7	105.4	100.0	103.7	105.8	105.0	105.4
Apparel and leather......................	315–316	408.0	225.7	107.8	100.0	92.7	88.8	87.6	79.0
Paper....................................	322	120.0	112.4	97.3	100.0	100.2	99.3	98.3	95.8
Printing and related support..............	323	144.2	131.0	103.5	100.0	100.3	98.5	99.6	98.6
Petroleum and coal products..............	324	89.2	100.1	97.9	100.0	104.0	100.2	98.0	100.9
Chemical.................................	325	96.2	109.3	101.3	100.0	96.6	95.6	97.3	97.9
Plastics and rubber products..............	326	116.5	116.6	94.2	100.0	101.2	103.9	105.6	106.1
Other manufacturing (non-NAICS) [7]..........	1133, 5111	192.9	169.9	111.4	100.0	95.0	94.0	90.3	84.3
Mining..................................	21	**89.1**	**84.3**	**87.6**	**100.0**	**106.0**	**117.3**	**112.2**	**102.2**
Electric and gas utilities......................	2211–2212	**91.8**	**99.2**	**102.6**	**100.0**	**102.3**	**103.7**	**103.1**	**102.8**
Electric power generation, transmission, and distribution.................	2211	90.1	98.8	102.1	100.0	101.1	102.3	102.2	102.2
Natural gas distribution....................	2212	103.6	102.0	106.2	100.0	112.0	115.7	109.6	106.7

[1] Except as noted, based on North American Industry Classification System, 2012; see text, this section. [2] Includes NAICS codes 31–33, 1133, 5111, 21, 2211, and 2212. [3] Standard Industrial Classification (SIC); see text, this section. [4] Includes NAICS codes 31–33, 1133, and 5111. [5] Includes NAICS codes 321, 327, and 331–339. [6] Includes NAICS codes 311–316, and 322–326. [7] Those industries—logging and newspaper, periodical, book, and directory publishing—that have traditionally been considered to be manufacturing.

Source: Board of Governors of the Federal Reserve System, "Industrial Production and Capacity Utilization, G.17," <http://www.federalreserve.gov/econresdata/default.htm>, accessed April 2017.

Table 815. Index of Industrial Capacity and Utilization Rate: 1990 to 2016

[2012 output = 100. Annual figures are averages of monthly data. The capacity index is an indicator of the maximum sustainable output a plant can maintain under realistic circumstances; capacity here is expressed as a proportion of 2012 actual output. Capacity utilization rate is a measure of output as a proportion of capacity; this is the output index divided by the capacity index]

| Year | Index of capacity | | Utilization rate | | | | |
| | Total industry | Manufacturing [1] | Total industry | Stage of process | | | Manufacturing [1] |
				Crude [2]	Primary and semifinished [3]	Finished [4]	
1990...........	78.2	77.8	82.5	87.7	82.7	80.6	81.6
1995...........	88.6	89.4	83.9	89.1	86.3	79.7	83.1
2000...........	117.5	123.9	81.4	88.5	83.9	76.8	79.7
2005...........	124.7	132.4	80.0	86.7	81.7	75.5	78.3
2008...........	129.8	139.1	77.7	87.3	76.7	74.1	74.7
2009...........	130.3	136.7	68.5	77.8	65.7	68.3	65.5
2010...........	128.1	134.0	73.6	83.3	71.8	71.4	70.7
2011...........	127.3	132.4	76.3	84.8	74.3	74.1	73.7
2012...........	129.6	133.6	77.2	86.0	74.6	75.3	74.8
2013...........	131.9	135.1	77.3	85.9	75.5	74.3	74.7
2014...........	133.7	135.4	78.6	88.3	76.7	74.8	75.4
2015...........	135.9	135.3	76.8	81.8	76.2	75.4	75.5
2016...........	136.1	136.0	75.8	78.7	75.4	75.0	75.1

[1] Manufacturing consists of those industries included in the North American Industry Classification System (NAICS) definition of manufacturing plus those industries—logging and newspaper, periodical, book, and directory publishing—that have traditionally been considered to be a part of manufacturing and are included in the industrial sector. [2] Crude processing covers a relatively small portion of total industrial capacity and consists of logging (NAICS 1133), much of mining (excluding stone, sand, and gravel mining, and oil and gas drilling, NAICS 21231, 21221–2, and 213111) and some basic manufacturing industries, including basic chemicals (NAICS 3251); fertilizers, pesticides, and other agricultural chemicals (NAICS 32531, 2); pulp, paper, and paperboard mills (NAICS 3221); and alumina, aluminum, and other nonferrous production and processing mills (NAICS 3313, 4). [3] Primary and semifinished processing loosely corresponds to the previously published aggregate, primary processing. Includes utilities and portions of several 2-digit SIC industries included in the former advanced processing group. These include printing and related support activities (NAICS 3231); paints and adhesives (NAICS 3255); and newspaper, periodical, book, and directory publishers (NAICS 5111). [4] Finished processing generally corresponds to the previously published aggregate, advanced processing. Includes oil and gas well drilling and carpet and rug mills.

Source: Board of Governors of the Federal Reserve System, "Industrial Production and Capacity Utilization, G.17," <http://www.federalreserve.gov/econresdata/default.htm>, accessed April 2017.

Table 816. Corporate Profits, Taxes, and Dividends: 2000 to 2016

[In billions of dollars (781 represents $781,000,000,000). Covers corporations organized for profit and other entities treated as corporations. Represents profits to U.S. residents, without deduction of depletion charges and exclusive of capital gains and losses; intercorporate dividends from profits of domestic corporations are eliminated; and net receipts of dividends, reinvested earnings of incorporated foreign affiliates, and earnings of unincorporated foreign affiliates are added. Minus (-) sign indicates loss]

Item	2000	2005	2010	2011	2012	2013	2014	2015	2016
Corporate profits with IVA and CCA [1].....................	781	1,478	1,746	1,817	1,998	2,033	2,152	2,088	2,086
Taxes on corporate income.........................	265	412	371	379	448	468	533	554	543
Profits after tax with IVA and CCA [1].....................	516	1,065	1,376	1,438	1,551	1,565	1,619	1,534	1,543
Net dividends..........................	385	581	564	704	859	929	971	971	968
Undistributed profits with IVA and CCA [1].............	131	485	812	734	691	636	649	563	575
Addenda for corporate cash flow:									
Net cash flow with IVA and CCA [1].............	976	1,524	2,095	2,072	2,050	2,042	2,108	2,083	2,132
Undistributed profits with IVA and CCA [1].............	131	485	812	734	691	636	649	563	575
Consumption of fixed capital.........................	845	1,052	1,263	1,299	1,351	1,401	1,463	1,517	1,562
Less: Capital transfers paid (net)...................	–	12	-21	-39	-7	-6	3	-3	4

– Represents or rounds to zero. [1] Inventory valuation adjustment (IVA) and capital consumption adjustment (CCA).

Source: U.S. Bureau of Economic Analysis, National Income and Product Accounts Tables, "Table 1.12. National Income by Type of Income," <http://www.bea.gov/itable/>, accessed April 2017.

Table 817. Corporate Profits With Inventory Valuation and Capital Consumption Adjustments—Financial and Nonfinancial Industries: 2000 to 2016

[In billions of dollars (781 represents $781,000,000,000). Based on the North American Industry Classification System, 2002; see text, this section. Minus sign (-) indicates loss. See headnote, Table 816]

Industry group	2000	2005	2010	2013	2014	2015	2016
Corporate profits with IVA/CCA [1].....................	**781**	**1,478**	**1,746**	**2,033**	**2,152**	**2,088**	**2,086**
Domestic industries.............................	635	1,239	1,351	1,621	1,741	1,702	1,676
Rest of the world.............................	146	239	395	412	411	386	410
Corporate profits with IVA [1].........................	**730**	**1,621**	**1,800**	**2,159**	**2,266**	**2,192**	**2,190**
Domestic industries.............................	584	1,382	1,405	1,748	1,855	1,807	1,780
Financial [2]..............................	150	410	406	429	480	493	515
Nonfinancial................................	434	972	998	1,318	1,375	1,313	1,265
Utilities.................................	24	31	30	27	33	7	6
Manufacturing...........................	176	278	288	430	450	413	383
Wholesale trade.........................	60	96	102	143	147	150	132
Retail trade.............................	51	122	119	155	168	179	187
Transportation and warehousing.........................	10	28	45	51	59	68	63
Information.............................	-12	91	95	125	117	120	133
Other nonfinancial [3]..........................	126	327	320	389	400	377	362
Rest of the world.............................	146	239	395	412	411	386	410

[1] Inventory valuation adjustment (IVA) and capital consumption adjustment (CCA). [2] Consists of finance and insurance and bank and other holding companies. [3] Consists of agriculture, forestry, fishing, and hunting; mining; construction; real estate and rental and leasing; professional, scientific, and technical services; administrative and waste management services; educational services; health care and social assistance; arts, entertainment, and recreation; accommodation and food services; and other services, except government.

Source: U.S. Bureau of Economic Analysis, National Income and Product Accounts Tables, "Table 6.16D. Corporate Profits by Industry," <http://www.bea.gov/itable/>, accessed April 2017.

Table 818. Corporate Profits Before Taxes by Industry: 2000 to 2016

[In billions of dollars (747 represents $747,000,000,000). Profits are without inventory valuation and capital consumption adjustments. Minus sign (-) indicates loss. See headnote, Table 816]

Industry	2002 NAICS code [1]	2000	2005	2010	2014	2015	2016
Corporate profits before tax	(X)	**747**	**1,653**	**1,841**	**2,249**	**2,159**	**2,159**
Domestic industries	(X)	601	1,414	1,446	1,852	1,774	1,764
Agriculture, forestry, fishing, and hunting	11	1	5	8	14	12	10
Mining	21	15	45	32	38	-11	-42
Utilities	221	25	32	30	32	21	20
Construction	23	36	82	27	64	79	90
Manufacturing	31-33	186	293	304	450	385	390
Wholesale trade	42	63	103	117	146	133	124
Retail trade	44–45	53	127	125	161	170	179
Transportation and warehousing	48–49	10	28	45	59	60	56
Information	51	-12	91	95	115	138	138
Finance and insurance	52	63	248	220	336	332	323
Real estate and rental and leasing	53	9	27	13	22	18	18
Professional, scientific, and technical services	54	9	47	83	78	71	63
Management of companies and enterprises [2]	551111, 2	87	162	186	148	166	179
Administrative and waste management services	56	9	24	28	35	34	36
Educational services	61	2	5	11	6	5	7
Health care and social assistance	62	23	54	78	82	86	91
Arts, entertainment, and recreation	71	3	8	8	13	14	15
Accommodation and food services	72	14	22	18	34	40	46
Other services, except public administration	81	6	11	15	20	21	22
Rest of the world [3]	(X)	146	239	395	398	385	395

X Not applicable. [1] Based on North American Industry Classification System, 2002; see text, this section. [2] Consists of bank and other holding companies. [3] Consists of receipts by all U.S. residents, including both corporations and persons, of dividends from foreign corporations, and, for U.S. corporations, their share of reinvested earnings of their incorporated foreign affiliates, and earnings of unincorporated foreign affiliates, net of corresponding payments.

Source: U.S. Bureau of Economic Analysis, National Income and Product Accounts Tables, "Table 6.17D. Corporate Profits Before Tax by Industry," <http://www.bea.gov/itable/>, accessed August 2017.

Table 819. Manufacturing, Mining, and Trade Corporations—Profits and Stockholders' Equity by Industry: 2015 and 2016

[Averages of quarterly figures at annual rates. Manufacturing data exclude estimates for corporations with less than $250,000 in assets at time of sample selection. Mining, and wholesale and retail trade data excludes estimates for corporations with less than $50 million in assets at time of sample selection. Based on sample; see source for discussion of methodology. Based on North American Industry Classification System (NAICS), 2012; see text, this section]

Industry	2012 NAICS code	Ratio of profits after taxes to stockholders' equity (percent)		Profits after taxes per dollar of sales (cents)		Ratio of stockholders' equity to debt	
		2015	2016	2015	2016	2015	2016
Manufacturing	31–33	**12.6**	**13.5**	**7.9**	**8.8**	**1.5**	**1.4**
Nondurable manufacturing	(X)	12.0	13.1	7.9	9.3	1.3	1.3
Food	311	12.9	13.3	5.7	6.6	1.3	1.4
Beverage and tobacco products	312	19.9	25.9	17.8	24.8	1.0	1.0
Textile mills and textile product mills	313, 314	13.3	11.8	5.8	6.4	1.7	2.2
Apparel and leather products	315, 316	22.2	22.8	10.1	9.8	2.2	1.9
Paper	322	10.4	17.8	4.1	6.8	0.9	0.8
Printing and related support activities	323	12.2	15.3	2.4	3.0	0.5	0.5
Petroleum and coal products	324	4.4	2.2	2.8	1.6	2.6	2.3
Chemicals	325	14.0	16.1	13.4	15.3	1.1	1.0
Plastics and rubber products	326	16.6	15.7	6.1	7.3	1.2	1.2
Durable manufacturing	(X)	13.3	13.8	7.8	8.3	1.7	1.5
Wood products	321	8.3	16.7	2.5	5.7	1.1	1.2
Nonmetallic mineral products	327	7.6	12.1	5.0	8.8	1.9	2.0
Primary metals	331	-11.9	1.0	-6.4	0.6	1.3	1.6
Fabricated metal products	332	18.1	16.7	7.0	7.0	1.4	1.3
Machinery	333	9.8	6.4	5.2	3.4	1.6	1.4
Computer and electronic products	334	16.6	14.8	19.3	17.3	2.0	1.6
Electrical equipment, appliances, & components	335	1.5	11.0	0.8	8.7	2.8	1.6
Transportation equipment	336	24.9	20.6	6.9	5.9	1.6	1.5
Furniture and related products	337	22.3	27.1	5.7	7.0	1.3	1.3
Miscellaneous manufacturing	339	12.2	14.2	10.8	12.9	1.4	1.5
All mining	21	**-47.0**	**-18.2**	**-87.5**	**-35.7**	**1.3**	**1.0**
All wholesale trade	42	**10.2**	**10.7**	**1.6**	**1.7**	**1.3**	**1.3**
Durable goods	423	8.2	9.6	1.7	2.0	1.6	1.6
Nondurable goods	424, 425	13.6	12.7	1.4	1.4	1.0	1.0
All retail trade	44–45	**18.0**	**19.5**	**3.3**	**3.4**	**1.2**	**1.1**
Food and beverage stores	445	14.4	12.5	1.7	1.6	1.2	1.2
Clothing and general merchandise stores	448, 452	17.5	17.5	3.6	3.4	1.3	1.3
All other retail trade	(X)	19.2	22.6	3.6	3.9	1.2	1.0

X Not applicable.

Source: U.S. Census Bureau, *Quarterly Financial Report for Manufacturing, Mining, Trade, and Selected Service Industries*, <http://www.census.gov/econ/qfr/index.html>.

Table 820. U.S. Multinational Enterprises—Value Added, Employment, and Capital Expenditures: 1989 to 2014

[Value added and capital expenditures in billions of dollars (1,401 represents $1,401,000,000,000); employees in thousands. Data for 2014 are preliminary. For the years shown prior to 2010, the data items needed to calculate value added and capital expenditures for individual U.S. parents and foreign affiliates were collected for nonbank businesses only. The value added and capital expenditures statistics for bank parents and affiliates for those years are estimates. See headnote, Table 821. MNE = Multinational enterprise. MOFA = Majority-owned foreign affiliate]

Item	1989	1994	1999	2004	2010	2012	2013	2014
VALUE ADDED								
MNEs worldwide:								
Parents and MOFAs..................	1,401	1,773	2,645	3,221	4,191	4,664	4,882	5,297
Parents....................................	1,077	1,362	2,064	2,366	2,949	3,249	3,487	3,810
MOFAs....................................	324	411	580	854	1,242	1,415	1,395	1,487
EMPLOYEES								
MNEs worldwide:								
Parents and all affiliates..............	26,370	26,571	33,398	32,892	36,287	37,175	37,657	42,396
Parents and MOFAs..................	24,826	25,142	31,913	31,466	34,105	35,220	35,768	40,362
Parents...................................	19,617	19,330	23,985	22,446	22,791	23,092	23,349	26,560
Affiliates, total..........................	6,753	7,241	9,412	10,445	13,496	14,084	14,308	15,837
MOFAs....................................	5,209	5,812	7,928	9,020	11,313	12,128	12,419	13,802
Other.....................................	1,544	1,429	1,484	1,426	2,182	1,956	1,889	2,035
CAPITAL EXPENDITURES								
MNEs worldwide:								
Parents and all affiliates..............	279	331	563	500	(NA)	(NA)	(NA)	(NA)
Parents and MOFAs..................	263	306	531	476	607	802	817	952
Parents...................................	204	235	417	351	441	584	594	714
Affiliates, total..........................	75	96	146	149	(NA)	(NA)	(NA)	(NA)
MOFAs....................................	59	72	115	125	166	218	223	239
Other.....................................	16	25	31	24	(NA)	(NA)	(NA)	(NA)

NA Not available.

Source: U.S. Bureau of Economic Analysis, *Survey of Current Business*, December 2016. See also <http://www.bea.gov/scb/date_guide.asp>.

Table 821. U.S. Multinational Enterprises—Selected Characteristics: 2014

[In billions of dollars (37,902 represents $37,902,000,000,000), except as indicated. Data for 2014 are preliminary. Consists of U.S. parent enterprises and their foreign affiliates. U.S. parent comprises the domestic operations of a multinational and is a U.S. person that owns or controls, directly or indirectly, 10 percent or more of the voting securities of an incorporated foreign business enterprise, or an equivalent interest in an unincorporated foreign business enterprise. A U.S. person can be an incorporated business enterprise. A majority-owned foreign affiliate (MOFA) is a foreign business enterprise in which a U.S. parent enterprise owns or controls more than 50 percent of the voting securities]

Industry	2007 NAICS code [1]	U.S. parents [2]				Majority-owned foreign affiliates [3]		
		Total assets	Capital expenditures	Value added	Employment (1,000)	Capital expenditures	Value added	Employment (1,000)
All industries.....................................	(X)	**37,902**	**714**	**3,810**	**26,560**	**239**	**1,487**	**13,802**
Mining [4]...	21	693	97	130	288	82	186	263
Oil and gas extraction...........................	211	399	64	75	59	65	149	64
Manufacturing [4].................................	31-33	7,545	229	1,364	7,217	71	581	5,398
Food..	311	577	13	105	826	6	36	479
Beverages and tobacco products.................	312	314	4	57	149	2	60	256
Petroleum and coal products.....................	324	1,118	63	161	281	3	47	17
Chemicals [4]..	325	1,561	32	246	828	13	119	672
Pharmaceuticals and medicines...............	3254	1,003	13	137	403	4	55	265
Machinery...	333	405	11	74	518	5	52	502
Computers and electronic products [4]...........	334	986	22	215	936	17	96	892
Computers and peripheral equipment.........	3341	284	7	70	202	6	42	269
Transportation equipment [4]......................	336	1,406	57	242	1,580	12	64	1,106
Motor vehicles, bodies and trailers, and parts..	3361-3363	590	41	91	623	11	54	1,015
Wholesale trade.....................................	42	1,322	47	234	1,705	9	191	939
Retail trade [4].......................................	44, 45	840	38	342	5,395	8	85	1,454
General merchandise stores.....................	452	274	12	135	2,250	(D)	38	(5)
Information [4].......................................	51	2,137	86	446	1,878	13	79	585
Publishing industries.............................	511	364	6	82	400	2	34	167
Broadcasting (except internet)..................	515	437	11	90	383	(D)	8	21
Telecommunications..............................	517	787	53	177	608	(D)	15	102
Finance and insurance [4].........................	52	22,058	59	481	2,807	6	105	718
Insurance carriers and related activities........	524	6,484	13	111	1,071	1	27	217
Professional, scientific, and technical services [4]............................	54	657	11	239	1,576	5	111	1,289
Computer systems design and related services..	5415	312	5	86	455	3	49	716
Other industries [4].................................	(X)	2,651	147	575	5,696	45	149	3,156
Transportation and warehousing...............	48-49	586	43	177	1,268	5	24	316
Administration, support, and waste management................................	56	202	5	71	1,090	1	37	1,094

X Not applicable. D Data withheld to avoid disclosure. [1] Based on North American Industry Classification System, 2007; see text, this section. [2] Data are by industry of U.S. parent. [3] Data are by industry of foreign affiliate. [4] Includes other industries, not shown separately. [5] 100,000 or more employees.

Source: U.S. Bureau of Economic Analysis, International Economic Accounts, "Direct Investment and Multinational Enterprises," <http://www.bea.gov/iTable/index_MNC.cfm>, accessed January 2017.

Table 822. U.S. Multinational Enterprises—Value Added: 2010 and 2014

[In billions of dollars (4,191 represents $4,191,000,000,000). See headnote, Table 821. Data are by industry of U.S. parent]

Industry	2007 NAICS [1] code	U.S. multinationals		U.S. parents		Majority-owned foreign affiliates	
		2010	2014	2010	2014	2010	2014
All industries..	(X)	**4,191**	**5,297**	**2,949**	**3,810**	**1,242**	**1,487**
Mining [2]..	21	118	180	75	130	43	50
Oil and gas extraction.....................................	211	58	105	41	75	18	29
Manufacturing [2]...	31-33	1,900	2,181	1,147	1,364	753	817
Food...	311	145	153	96	105	49	48
Beverages and tobacco products.......................	312	67	77	49	57	18	20
Petroleum and coal products............................	324	383	368	135	161	248	207
Chemicals [2]..	325	337	402	197	246	140	156
Pharmaceuticals and medicines......................	3254	187	226	113	137	74	89
Machinery.......................................	333	104	123	69	74	35	49
Computers and electronic products [2]...................	334	235	346	155	215	80	130
Computers and peripheral equipment.................	3341	68	131	38	70	31	61
Semiconductors and other electronic components.....	3344	79	83	51	52	28	31
Transportation equipment [2].............................	336	314	347	229	242	85	105
Motor vehicles, bodies and trailers, and parts..........	3361-3363	133	153	83	91	49	62
Wholesale trade...	42	174	279	143	234	32	45
Retail trade [2]...	44, 45	303	400	257	342	46	58
General merchandise stores.............................	452	(NA)	(NA)	122	135	(D)	(D)
Information [2]..	51	392	526	333	446	58	79
Publishing industries..................................	511	100	120	72	82	27	38
Broadcasting (except internet).........................	515	49	96	41	90	8	6
Telecommunications..................................	517	172	189	162	177	10	12
Finance and insurance [2].................................	52	480	660	357	481	123	178
Depository credit intermediation (banking)................	5221	157	207	139	190	18	18
Insurance carriers and related activities.................	524	101	140	84	111	17	29
Professional, scientific, and technical services [2]........	54	275	336	196	239	79	98
Computer systems design and related services..........	5415	133	145	80	86	53	60
Other industries [2]..	(X)	548	736	440	575	108	162
Utilities..	22	66	95	61	88	5	7
Transportation and warehousing..........................	48-49	132	198	116	177	17	21
Real estate and rental and leasing.......................	53	44	76	35	61	9	15
Administration, support, and waste management........	56	99	99	73	71	26	28
Accommodation and food services......................	72	75	90	54	56	22	34

X Not applicable. NA Not available. D Data withheld to avoid disclosure. [1] Based on North American Industry Classification System, 2007; see text, this section. [2] Includes other industries, not shown separately.

Source: U.S. Bureau of Economic Analysis, "Direct Investment and Multinational Enterprises," <http://www.bea.gov/iTable/index_MNC.cfm>, accessed January 2017.

Table 823. U.S. Majority-Owned Foreign Affiliates—Value Added by Industry of Affiliate and Country: 2014

[In millions of dollars (1,487,038 represents $1,487,038,000,000). Data are preliminary. See headnote, Table 821. Numbers in parentheses represent North American Industry Classification System 2007 codes; see text, this section]

Country	All industries [1]	Mining (21)	Manufacturing (31-33)		Wholesale trade (42)	Finance and insurance (52)	Professional, scientific, and technical services (54)
			Total [1]	Chemicals (325)			
All countries [2]...............	**1,487,038**	**186,494**	**581,242**	**118,610**	**190,913**	**104,907**	**110,648**
United Kingdom................	172,466	6,981	61,122	6,925	12,983	28,201	19,125
Canada.........................	151,294	17,390	59,712	10,359	14,962	6,189	9,823
Germany.......................	95,886	1,504	46,992	7,227	17,295	2,520	6,055
Ireland.........................	79,648	(D)	42,475	14,735	1,176	4,208	2,935
China..........................	66,144	2,075	39,146	8,767	11,244	999	3,937
Australia.......................	59,569	9,068	15,391	1,764	8,329	3,472	5,819
Switzerland.....................	55,527	(D)	13,773	5,495	23,585	2,008	2,057
France..........................	55,179	92	27,473	5,862	9,360	3,260	3,854
Mexico.........................	51,232	2,806	25,987	3,458	2,687	2,664	1,678
Japan..........................	47,911	0	16,524	6,096	7,825	6,792	7,103
Singapore......................	46,423	678	18,718	4,476	9,938	6,872	2,085
Brazil..........................	44,076	1,997	27,587	7,241	2,833	2,739	2,755
Netherlands....................	34,642	493	18,680	5,358	4,747	3,242	3,121
Italy...........................	33,516	129	12,197	3,389	3,227	1,327	2,714
Norway.........................	28,661	18,944	5,789	271	1,302	243	410
Belgium........................	27,067	(D)	12,024	5,498	7,225	2,395	1,364
India...........................	26,163	151	6,066	1,959	2,073	3,021	10,274
Hong Kong.....................	19,733	(D)	5,486	565	4,823	5,447	1,882
Argentina......................	17,938	4,852	7,740	1,888	609	1,160	373

D Data withheld to avoid disclosure. [1] Includes other industries, not shown separately. [2] Includes other countries, not shown separately.

Source: U.S. Bureau of Economic Analysis, International Economic Accounts, "Activities of U.S. Multinational Enterprises, Majority-owned Foreign Affiliates, Value Added by Country and Industry 2009-2014," <http://www.bea.gov/international/di1usdop.htm>, accessed January 2017.

Section 16
Science and Technology

This section presents statistics on scientific, engineering, and technological resources, with emphasis on patterns of research and development (R&D) funding and on scientific, engineering, and technical personnel; education; and employment.

The National Science Foundation (NSF) gathers data chiefly through recurring surveys and report the data via detailed statistical tables; info briefs; and annual, biennial, and special reports; see <http://www.nsf.gov/statistics>. Areas of coverage include R&D expenditures; Federal R&D funding; scientific employment; graduate enrollment and support in academic science and engineering; characteristics of doctoral scientists and engineers and of recent graduates in the United States. Report titles include: *Science and Engineering Indicators; National Patterns of R&D Resources; Federal Funds for Research and Development; Federal R&D Funding by Budget Function; Federal Support for S&E to Universities, Colleges, and Selected Nonprofit Institutions*; and *Business Research and Development and Innovation*. Statistical surveys in these areas pose problems of concept and definition and the data should therefore be regarded as broad estimates rather than precise, quantitative statements. See sources for methodological and technical details.

The National Science Board's biennial *Science and Engineering Indicators* at <http://www.nsf.gov/statistics/seind/> contains data and analysis of international and domestic science and technology, including education and workforce statistics.

Research and development outlays—NSF defines research as "systematic study directed toward fuller scientific knowledge of the subject studied" and development as "the systematic use of scientific knowledge directed toward the production of useful materials, devices, systems, or methods, including design and development of prototypes and processes."

National coverage of R&D expenditures is developed primarily from periodic surveys in four principal economic sectors: (1) *government*, made up primarily of federal executive agencies; (2) *industry*, consisting of manufacturing and nonmanufacturing firms and the federally funded research and development centers (FFRDCs) they administer; (3) *universities and colleges*, composed of universities, colleges, and their affiliated institutions, agricultural experiment stations, and associated schools of agriculture and of medicine, and FFRDCs administered by educational institutions; and (4) *other nonprofit institutions*, consisting of such organizations as private philanthropic foundations, nonprofit research institutes, voluntary health agencies, and FFRDCs administered by nonprofit organizations.

The R&D funds reported consist of current operating costs, including planning and administration costs, except as otherwise noted. They exclude funds for routine testing, mapping and surveying, collection of general purpose data, dissemination of scientific information, and training of scientific personnel.

Scientists, engineers, and technicians—Scientists and engineers are defined as persons engaged in scientific and engineering work at a level requiring a knowledge of sciences equivalent at least to that acquired through completion of a 4-year college course. Technicians are defined as persons engaged in technical work at a level requiring knowledge acquired through a technical institute, junior college, or other type of training less extensive than 4-year college training. Craftsmen and skilled workers are excluded.

Table 824. Research and Development (R&D) Expenditures by Source of Funding: 1960 to 2015

[In millions of dollars (13,711 represents $13,711,000,000), except percent]

Year	Total	Sources of funds Federal govern- ment	Industry	Univer- sities/ colleges [1]	Non- profit	Non- federal govern- ment [2]	Percent of total Federal govern- ment	Industry	Univer- sities/ colleges [1]	Non- profit	Non- federal govern- ment [2]
1960	13,711	8,915	4,516	67	123	90	65.0	33.0	0.0	1.0	1.0
1970	26,271	14,984	10,449	259	343	237	57.0	40.0	1.0	1.0	1.0
1980	63,224	29,986	30,929	920	871	519	47.0	49.0	1.0	1.0	1.0
1985	114,671	52,641	57,962	1,743	1,491	834	46.0	51.0	2.0	1.0	1.0
1986	120,249	54,622	60,991	2,019	1,647	969	45.0	51.0	2.0	1.0	1.0
1987	126,360	58,609	62,576	2,262	1,849	1,065	46.0	50.0	2.0	1.0	1.0
1988	133,881	60,131	67,977	2,527	2,081	1,165	45.0	51.0	2.0	2.0	1.0
1989	141,891	60,465	74,966	2,852	2,333	1,274	43.0	53.0	2.0	2.0	1.0
1990	151,993	61,610	83,208	3,187	2,589	1,399	41.0	55.0	2.0	2.0	1.0
1991	160,876	60,783	92,300	3,458	2,852	1,483	38.0	57.0	2.0	2.0	1.0
1992	165,350	60,915	96,229	3,569	3,113	1,525	37.0	58.0	2.0	2.0	1.0
1993	165,730	60,528	96,549	3,709	3,388	1,557	37.0	58.0	2.0	2.0	1.0
1994	169,207	60,777	99,204	3,938	3,665	1,623	36.0	59.0	2.0	2.0	1.0
1995	183,625	62,969	110,871	4,110	3,925	1,751	34.0	60.0	2.0	2.0	1.0
1996	197,346	63,394	123,417	4,436	4,239	1,861	32.0	63.0	2.0	2.0	1.0
1997	212,152	64,574	136,228	4,838	4,590	1,922	30.0	64.0	2.0	2.0	1.0
1998	226,457	66,383	147,825	5,163	5,114	1,972	29.0	65.0	2.0	2.0	1.0
1999	245,319	67,367	164,606	5,619	5,628	2,098	27.0	67.0	2.0	2.0	1.0
2000	268,904	67,861	186,037	6,231	6,528	2,246	25.0	69.0	2.0	2.0	1.0
2001	279,716	74,584	188,478	6,826	7,410	2,418	27.0	67.0	2.0	3.0	1.0
2002	279,387	79,873	180,778	7,617	8,478	2,642	29.0	65.0	3.0	3.0	1.0
2003	293,060	86,293	186,247	8,226	9,405	2,888	29.0	64.0	3.0	3.0	1.0
2004	304,547	92,043	191,429	8,562	9,474	3,038	30.0	63.0	3.0	3.0	1.0
2005	327,184	96,689	207,864	9,265	10,275	3,092	30.0	64.0	3.0	3.0	1.0
2006	352,875	101,261	227,281	10,076	10,841	3,417	29.0	64.0	3.0	3.0	1.0
2007	380,019	106,549	246,921	10,833	12,026	3,689	28.0	65.0	3.0	3.0	1.0
2008	406,952	119,113	258,131	11,640	13,811	4,257	29.0	63.0	3.0	3.0	1.0
2009	405,343	127,395	246,770	11,916	14,976	4,286	31.0	61.0	3.0	4.0	1.0
2010	409,037	128,426	248,315	12,103	15,906	4,287	31.0	61.0	3.0	4.0	1.0
2011	428,675	128,917	266,605	12,949	15,849	4,355	30.0	62.0	3.0	4.0	1.0
2012	436,151	125,796	275,896	14,140	16,215	4,103	29.0	63.0	3.0	4.0	1.0
2013	456,584	122,068	297,368	15,197	17,713	4,239	27.0	65.0	3.0	4.0	1.0
2014	477,708	119,826	318,598	16,040	19,004	4,240	25.0	67.0	3.0	4.0	1.0
2015 (P)	499,299	113,114	344,977	17,109	19,909	4,190	23.0	69.0	3.0	4.0	1.0

P Preliminary. [1] Figures for university and college (U&C) R&D prior to 2003 cover only science and engineering (S&E) fields; in 2003 and later years, R&D in non-S&E fields is also included. Also, adjustments have been made to U&C R&D for 1998 and later years to eliminate double counting of funds passed through from one academic institution to another. [2] Nonfederal R&D expenditures to university and college performers.

Source: U.S. National Science Foundation, *National Patterns of R&D Resources, 2014-2015 Data Update*, NSF 17-311, March 2017. See also <http://www.nsf.gov/statistics/natlpatterns/>.

Table 825. National Research and Development (R&D) Expenditures as a Percent of Gross Domestic Product by Country: 1990 to 2015

Year	United States	Japan [1]	Ger- many [2]	France	United Kingdom	Italy	Canada	South Korea	OECD total [3]	Russia	China
1990	[4]2.55	[8]2.70	[8]2.61	2.26	1.95	[9]1.21	1.48	(NA)	[8]2.16	[7]1.91	(NA)
1995	[4]2.40	[8]2.61	[8]2.13	2.23	1.68	0.94	1.66	[10]2.20	[8]1.96	[7]0.80	[11]0.57
2000	[4]2.62	2.91	2.39	[5]2.08	1.64	1.01	1.86	[10]2.18	[5,8]2.12	[7]0.99	[5]0.89
2004	[4]2.49	3.03	2.42	[5]2.09	1.55	1.05	2.00	[10]2.53	[8]2.11	[7]1.08	1.21
2005	[4]2.51	3.18	2.42	2.04	1.57	1.05	1.98	[10]2.63	[8]2.14	[7]1.00	1.31
2006	[4]2.55	3.28	2.46	2.05	1.59	1.09	1.95	[10]2.83	[8]2.17	[7]1.01	1.37
2007	[4]2.63	3.34	2.45	2.02	1.63	1.13	1.91	[5]3.00	[8]2.21	[7]1.05	1.37
2008	[4]2.77	[5]3.34	2.60	2.06	[8]1.64	1.16	1.86	3.12	[8]2.28	[7]0.98	1.44
2009	[4]2.82	3.23	2.73	2.21	[8]1.70	1.22	1.92	3.29	[8]2.33	[7]1.17	[5]1.66
2010	[4]2.74	3.14	2.71	[5]2.18	[8]1.68	1.22	1.83	3.47	[8]2.29	[7]1.06	1.71
2011	[4]2.77	3.24	2.80	2.19	1.68	1.21	1.79	3.74	[8]2.32	[7]1.02	1.78
2012	[4]2.71	3.21	2.87	2.23	[8]1.61	1.27	[5]1.79	4.03	[8]2.32	[7]1.05	1.91
2013	[4]2.74	[5]3.31	2.82	2.24	1.66	1.31	1.71	4.15	[8]2.35	1.06	1.99
2014	[4]2.76	3.40	2.88	2.23	[8]1.68	[8]1.37	1.74	4.29	[8]2.38	1.07	2.02
2015	[4,6]2.79	3.29	2.93	[6]2.22	[6,8]1.70	[6]1.33	1.71	4.23	[8]2.38	1.10	2.07

NA Not available. [1] Data on Japanese research and development after 1996 may not be consistent with data in earlier years because of changes in methodology. [2] Data for 1990 are for West Germany only. [3] Organization for Economic Cooperation and Development. [4] Excludes most or all capital expenditure. [5] Time series break. [6] Provisional. [7] Compiled according to the System of National Accounts 1993. [8] Estimated value. [9] Excluding extramural R&D expenditure. [10] Excluding R&D in the social sciences and humanities. [11] Underestimated or based on underestimated data.

Source: Organisation for Economic Co-operation and Development (OECD), 2017, "Main Science and Technology Indicators," OECD Science, Technology and R&D Statistics (database) ©, <http://dx.doi.org/10.1787/data-00182-en>, accessed September 2017.

Table 826. Research and Development (R&D) Expenditures By Performing Sector and Source of Funds: 1990 to 2015

[In millions of dollars (151,993 represents $151,993,000,000). For calendar year. FFRDCs are federally funded research and development centers]

Year	Total[1]	Federal government	Industry — Total	Industry — Funded by Federal government	Industry — Funded by Industry[2]	Industry FFRDCs	Universities and colleges — Total	U&C — Funded by Federal government	U&C — Funded by Non-federal government[3]	U&C — Funded by Industry	U&C — Funded by Universities & colleges	U&C — Funded by Non-profits	University & college FFRDCs[4]	Other nonprofit institutions — Total	Other nonprofit — Funded by Federal government	Other nonprofit — Funded by Industry	Other nonprofit — Funded by Non-profits
RESEARCH AND DEVELOPMENT TOTAL																	
1990	151,993	23,524	107,404	25,802	81,602	2,323	16,939	9,939	1,399	1,166	3,187	1,249	4,894	4,126	2,346	440	1,340
2000	268,904	28,516	199,961	17,117	182,844	2,001	30,693	17,719	2,246	2,174	6,231	2,324	5,742	9,734	4,510	1,020	4,204
2009	405,343	47,572	282,393	39,573	221,104	6,646	56,971	33,433	3,808	3,193	11,916	4,621	5,052	18,002	7,097	1,258	9,647
2010	409,037	50,798	278,977	34,199	218,187	7,214	60,369	36,563	3,787	3,144	12,103	4,772	5,315	18,403	7,093	1,265	10,045
2011	428,675	53,524	294,092	31,309	235,426	6,956	62,435	37,717	3,712	3,182	12,949	4,875	5,246	18,132	6,564	1,333	10,234
2012	436,151	52,144	302,251	30,621	242,674	6,808	63,264	36,998	3,631	3,349	14,140	5,146	(NA)	18,024	6,239	1,366	10,420
2013	456,584	51,086	322,528	29,362	259,908	(NA)	63,928	35,845	3,719	3,575	15,197	5,592	(NA)	18,573	5,970	1,444	11,158
2014	477,708	52,299	340,728	26,554	277,272	(NA)	64,704	35,051	3,788	3,817	16,040	6,006	(NA)	19,498	6,111	1,520	11,867
2015[5]	499,299	52,655	359,652	19,512	304,844	(NA)	66,373	35,015	3,752	4,069	17,109	6,428	(NA)	20,134	6,105	1,611	12,418
BASIC RESEARCH																	
1990	23,029	5,352	4,629	869	3,760	499	11,126	6,889	847	705	1,929	756	2,470	1,922	947	245	730
2000	42,729	7,801	7,040	925	6,115	547	22,887	13,960	1,545	1,495	4,287	1,599	2,874	5,000	2,099	566	2,334
2009	74,349	10,012	14,784	1,340	11,999	2,629	39,899	24,112	2,554	2,143	7,997	3,094	1,902	9,553	3,498	698	5,357
2010	77,336	11,748	16,371	1,406	13,239	2,848	39,400	24,579	2,358	1,957	7,535	2,971	2,203	9,694	3,414	702	5,577
2011	74,262	11,522	13,020	677	10,585	2,673	40,093	24,858	2,289	1,962	7,980	3,005	2,213	9,503	3,081	740	5,683
2012	74,643	11,150	13,294	644	10,955	2,446	40,446	24,168	2,249	2,075	8,764	3,189	2,160	9,636	3,092	758	5,785
2013	80,146	9,519	19,508	1,196	14,986	(NA)	40,974	23,464	2,319	2,229	9,475	3,486	(NA)	10,029	3,031	802	6,195
2014	84,012	10,047	21,936	2,044	15,805	(NA)	41,349	22,935	2,353	2,371	9,961	3,730	(NA)	10,560	3,127	844	6,589
2015[5]	86,705	10,598	22,618	1,502	17,377	(NA)	42,417	22,911	2,334	2,531	10,643	3,999	(NA)	10,951	3,161	895	6,895
APPLIED RESEARCH																	
1990	34,897	4,808	24,399	5,967	18,432	386	4,406	2,140	453	377	1,031	404	689	1,284	780	120	384
2000	56,699	7,856	39,176	2,682	36,494	269	6,513	3,194	575	556	1,594	595	1,291	3,155	1,831	258	1,066
2009	75,187	14,063	41,055	7,797	29,264	2,010	14,053	7,697	1,028	861	3,214	1,252	1,282	5,813	3,049	319	2,445
2010	81,003	13,203	44,906	4,705	34,912	2,249	16,742	9,374	1,172	973	3,746	1,477	1,274	5,907	3,041	321	2,546
2011	84,112	13,251	47,186	4,404	37,047	2,256	17,805	10,029	1,167	1,001	4,074	1,533	1,318	5,625	2,693	338	2,594
2012	89,063	14,328	50,755	4,137	38,891	2,387	18,131	9,940	1,133	1,044	4,409	1,605	1,386	5,616	2,629	346	2,641
2013	90,265	15,132	51,013	6,028	37,385	(NA)	18,226	9,556	1,148	1,104	4,692	1,727	(NA)	5,659	2,465	366	2,828
2014	93,631	15,519	53,415	6,445	38,281	(NA)	18,543	9,327	1,177	1,186	4,985	1,867	(NA)	5,915	2,522	385	3,008
2015[5]	96,297	15,896	55,022	4,736	42,087	(NA)	19,037	9,318	1,163	1,261	5,303	1,992	(NA)	6,099	2,544	408	3,147
DEVELOPMENT																	
1990	94,067	13,363	78,376	18,966	59,410	1,438	1,407	910	99	83	226	89	1,735	920	619	75	226
2000	169,476	12,859	153,745	13,510	140,235	1,185	1,293	565	126	122	350	131	1,577	1,579	580	195	804
2009	255,808	23,497	226,554	30,435	179,841	2,008	3,019	1,624	226	189	706	275	1,868	2,636	550	241	1,846
2010	250,698	25,847	217,700	28,089	170,036	2,118	4,227	2,610	257	214	822	324	1,838	2,802	638	242	1,922
2011	270,301	28,751	233,886	26,228	187,794	2,027	4,537	2,831	256	220	894	337	1,715	3,004	790	255	1,958
2012	272,445	26,666	238,202	25,840	192,828	1,975	4,687	2,889	249	229	968	352	1,628	2,773	518	261	1,994
2013	286,173	26,436	252,007	22,137	207,537	(NA)	4,728	2,825	252	242	1,030	379	(NA)	2,885	474	276	2,135
2014	300,065	26,734	265,377	18,065	223,186	(NA)	4,812	2,789	258	260	1,094	410	(NA)	3,022	461	291	2,270
2015[5]	316,298	26,161	282,012	13,274	245,380	(NA)	4,920	2,786	255	277	1,164	437	(NA)	3,084	399	308	2,376

NA Not available. [1] Total includes nonprofit FFRDCs, not shown separately. [2] Includes all nonfederal sources of industry R&D expenditures. [3] Includes all nonfederal sources. [4] Includes all R&D expenditures of FFRDCs administered by academic institutions and funded by the federal government. [5] Preliminary.

Source: National Science Foundation, National Center for Science and Engineering Statistics, *National Patterns of R&D Resources: 2014-15 Data Update*, NSF 17-311, March 2017. See also <http://www.nsf.gov/statistics/natlpatterns/>.

Table 827. Federal Obligations for Research in Current and Constant (2009) Dollars by Field of Science: 2010 to 2016

[In millions of dollars (63,728 represents $63,728,000,000). For years ending September 30. Excludes research and development (R&D) plant (facilities and fixed equipment)]

Field of science	Current dollars				Constant (2009) dollars [1]			
	2010	2014	2015	2016 (P)	2010	2014	2015	2016 (P)
Research, total...............................	**63,728**	**62,909**	**63,645**	**67,761**	**62,959**	**57,806**	**57,860**	**60,802**
Basic...	31,795	31,588	31,527	33,227	31,412	29,026	28,661	29,815
Applied..	31,933	31,321	32,118	34,533	31,547	28,780	29,199	30,987
Life sciences.................................	33,909	30,668	30,473	32,042	33,500	28,180	27,703	28,751
Psychology....................................	2,156	1,968	1,995	2,120	2,130	1,808	1,814	1,902
Physical sciences............................	5,871	6,483	6,510	6,757	5,800	5,957	5,919	6,063
Environmental sciences......................	3,339	4,366	4,414	4,678	3,299	4,012	4,013	4,197
Mathematics and computer sciences........	3,412	3,883	3,863	4,208	3,371	3,568	3,512	3,776
Engineering...................................	11,081	11,888	11,956	13,114	10,948	10,923	10,869	11,767
Social sciences...............................	1,197	1,435	1,136	1,287	1,183	1,319	1,033	1,155
Other sciences, n.e.c. [2].....................	2,763	2,218	3,299	3,555	2,730	2,038	2,999	3,190

P Data are preliminary. [1] Based on gross domestic product implicit price deflator (updated April 2017). [2] Not elsewhere classified.

Source: U.S. National Science Foundation, *Federal Funds for Research and Development, Fiscal Years 2015-17; Data Tables*, April 2017, and earlier reports. See also <http://www.nsf.gov/statistics/fedfunds/>.

Table 828. Federal Budget Authority for Research and Development (R&D) in Current and Constant (2009) Dollars by Selected Budget Function: 2013 to 2016

[In millions of dollars (130,861 represents $130,861,000,000). For year ending September 30. Excludes R&D plant. Represents budget authority. Functions shown are those for which $1 billion or more was authorized since 2001]

Function	Current dollars				Constant (2009) dollars [1]			
	2013	2014	2015	2016 (P)	2013	2014	2015	2016 (P)
Total [2]......................................	**130,861**	**133,547**	**136,090**	**146,425**	**122,400**	**122,714**	**123,720**	**131,387**
National defense.............................	70,620	70,611	72,560	78,362	66,054	64,883	65,965	70,314
Health...	30,044	30,927	30,331	32,182	28,101	28,418	27,574	28,877
Space research and technology..........	10,476	11,055	10,875	12,789	9,799	10,158	9,887	11,476
Energy...	2,269	2,387	3,153	3,436	2,122	2,193	2,866	3,083
General science..............................	8,802	9,482	10,068	10,198	8,233	8,713	9,153	9,151
Natural resources and environment......	2,020	2,172	2,161	2,340	1,889	1,996	1,965	2,100
Transportation...............................	1,337	1,261	1,363	1,369	1,251	1,159	1,239	1,228
Agriculture...................................	1,753	1,967	1,989	2,008	1,640	1,807	1,808	1,802

P Preliminary [1] Based on gross domestic product implicit price deflator. [2] Includes other functions, not shown separately.

Source: U.S. National Science Foundation, *Federal R&D Funding by Budget Function: Fiscal Years 2015-17*, NSF 17-305, December 2016, and earlier reports. See also <http://www.nsf.gov/statistics/fedbudget/>.

Table 829. Federal Research and Development (R&D) by Federal Agency: 2010 to 2018

[In millions of dollars (149,595 represents $149,595,000,000). For fiscal years ending September 30. R&D refers to actual research and development activities as well as R&D facilities. R&D facilities (also known as R&D plants) includes construction, repair, or alteration of physical plant used in the conduct of R&D. Based on Office of Management and Budget data]

Federal agency	2010	2012	2013	2014	2015	2016	2017 [2]	2018 [3]
Total research and development [1]..........	**149,595**	**142,522**	**131,483**	**136,565**	**138,959**	**149,520**	**156,834**	**149,606**
Defense R&D..................................	86,756	78,717	69,766	71,469	72,344	79,109	83,752	92,477
Nondefense R&D..............................	62,840	63,805	61,716	65,096	66,615	70,411	73,082	57,129
Department of Defense.......................	82,902	74,460	65,540	66,505	66,146	72,801	76,653	85,171
NASA..	9,262	11,315	10,999	11,754	12,145	13,273	13,586	10,332
Department of Energy........................	10,836	10,811	10,705	11,994	14,385	15,007	15,958	13,436
Office of Science...........................	4,528	4,463	4,291	4,724	5,099	5,305	5,344	4,433
Health and Human Services..................	31,758	31,375	29,802	30,669	30,453	32,243	34,122	26,144
National Institutes of Health.............	30,189	30,010	28,341	29,251	29,026	30,843	32,802	25,093
National Science Foundation.................	5,392	5,705	5,329	5,800	5,990	6,022	6,051	5,370
Department of Agriculture...................	2,611	2,331	2,116	2,380	2,454	2,657	2,590	2,102
Department of Interior.......................	776	820	785	840	864	973	1,006	798
Department of Transportation...............	1,073	919	818	797	887	948	974	945
Environmental Protection Agency............	597	568	530	538	521	513	496	277
Department of Commerce....................	1,337	1,254	1,297	1,552	1,527	1,675	1,813	1,563
NIST [4].......................................	588	557	596	655	669	762	775	652
Department of Homeland Security............	887	481	684	1,032	919	582	623	564
Department of Veterans Affairs..............	1,034	1,160	1,164	1,101	1,178	1,222	1,346	1,357
All other......................................	1,131	1,322	1,714	1,604	1,491	1,604	1,616	1,547

[1] Includes data for agencies not shown. [2] Estimated. [3] Proposed budget outlays. [4] National Institute of Standards and Technology.

Source: American Association for the Advancement of Science (AAAS), *Guide to the President's Budget: Research and Development FY 2018* ©, July 2017, and earlier reports. See also <http://www.aaas.org/program/rd-budget-and-policy-program/>.

Table 830. Funds for Domestic Business Research and Development (R&D) Performed by Companies by Industry: 2013

[In millions of dollars (365,630 represents $365,630,000,000), except percent. For calendar years. The data represents for-profit companies that have five or more paid employees in the United States, have at least one establishment that is in business during the survey year and is located in the United States. Covers basic research, applied research, and development performed by the company and others. Based on the Business R&D Innovation Survey. For information, see <http://www.nsf.gov/statistics/srvyindustry/>]

Industry	NAICS [1] code	Domestic R&D paid for by the company and others		Domestic R&D paid for by the company		Domestic sales for companies that performed or funded R&D (million dollars)
		Value (million dollars)	As a percent of domestic sales [2]	Value (million dollars)	As a percent of domestic sales [2]	
All industries, total [3]	(X)	365,630	3.8	298,077	3.1	9,654,952
All manufacturing industries, total [3]	(X)	259,254	4.4	211,144	3.6	5,902,677
Chemicals	325	86,503	6.4	75,490	5.5	1,361,379
Pharmaceuticals and medicines	3254	76,653	15.0	66,505	13.0	511,393
Machinery	333	13,216	3.6	12,619	3.4	370,969
Semiconductor machinery	333295	3,214	28.6	3,114	27.7	11,240
Computer and electronic products	334	69,253	10.9	58,877	9.3	634,383
Electrical equipment, appliances, and components	335	4,253	3.0	3,767	2.6	142,537
Transportation equipment	336	53,655	4.8	29,434	2.6	1,113,141
Aerospace products and parts	3364	32,182	9.0	11,872	3.3	355,687
All nonmanufacturing industries, total [3]	(X)	106,376	2.8	86,933	2.3	3,752,275
Mining, extraction, and support activities	21	4,631	1.0	3,992	0.9	467,247
Information	51	58,742	5.6	57,538	5.5	1,048,039
Software publishing	5112	36,403	9.2	35,337	9.0	394,356
Professional, scientific, and technical services	54	33,605	9.1	16,403	4.4	371,322
Computer systems design and related services	5415	9,545	8.6	8,273	7.5	110,779
Scientific research and development services	5417	16,074	22.8	3,308	4.7	70,480

X Not applicable. [1] North American Industry Classification System (NAICS); see text, Section 15. [2] Includes companies located in the United States that performed or funded R&D. [3] Includes industries not shown separately.

Source: U.S. National Science Foundation, National Center for Science and Engineering Statistics, *Business Research and Development and Innovation: 2013*, NSF 16-313, August 2016. See also <http://www.nsf.gov/statistics/industry/>.

Table 831. Domestic Business Research and Development (R&D) Funding in Current and Constant (2009) Dollars for Selected Industries: 2009 to 2013

[In millions of dollars (282,505 represents $282,505,000,000). For calendar years. The data represents for-profit companies that have five or more paid employees in the United States, have at least one establishment that is in business during the survey year and is located in the United States. Covers basic research, applied research, and development. Based on the Business R&D and Innovation Survey, sponsored by National Science Foundation; for information about the survey and methodology, see <http://www.nsf.gov/statistics/srvyindustry/>]

Industry	NAICS [1] code	2009	2010	2011	2012	2013
CURRENT DOLLARS						
All industries	(X)	282,505	279,289	290,240	302,759	322,528
Manufacturing industries	31–33	196,441	199,147	202,363	208,577	221,476
Chemicals and allied products	325	54,753	58,343	55,853	56,748	61,664
Pharmaceuticals and medicines	3254	46,415	49,469	46,308	47,851	52,426
Computer and electronic products	334	55856	61,623	62,438	66,290	67,205
Navigational, measuring, electromedical, and control instruments	3345	14,318	15747	15852	15918	14478
Electrical equipment, appliances, and components	335	3,317	3,320	3,624	3,078	4,136
Transportation equipment	336	48209	42,940	41,094	42,340	45,972
Aerospace products and parts	3364	34,563	29,857	26,086	24,874	27,114
Nonmanufacturing industries	21–23, 42–81	86,064	80,142	87,877	94,183	101,052
Information	51	35,953	37,088	42,697	46,900	57,207
Software publishers	5112	(NA)	26,187	28,039	28,848	35,333
Professional, scientific, and technical services	54	42,380	31,798	33,307	34,121	31,017
Computer systems design and related services	5415	13,351	10,359	10,938	11,006	9,268
Scientific R&D services	5417	16,402	13,712	15,713	16,415	14,201
CONSTANT (2009) DOLLARS [2]						
All industries	(X)	282,505	275,920	280,938	287,755	301,673
Manufacturing industries	31–33	196,441	197,175	196,469	198,645	206,987
Chemicals and allied products	325	54,753	57,639	54,063	53,936	57,677
Pharmaceuticals and medicines	3254	46,415	48,872	44,824	45,480	49,036
Computer and electronic products	334	55,856	60,880	60,437	63,005	62,860
Navigational, measuring, electromedical, and control instruments	3345	14,318	15,557	15,344	15,129	13,542
Electrical equipment, appliances, and components	335	3,317	3,280	3,508	2,925	3,869
Transportation equipment	336	48,209	42,422	39,777	40,242	42,999
Aerospace products and parts	3364	34,563	29,497	25,250	23,641	25,361
Nonmanufacturing industries	21–23, 42–81	86,064	79,349	85,317	89,698	94,441
Information	51	35,953	36,641	41,329	44,576	53,508
Software publishers	5112	(NA)	25,871	27,140	27,418	33,048
Professional, scientific, and technical services	54	42,380	31,414	32,240	32,430	29,011
Computer systems design and related services	5415	13,351	10,234	10,587	10,461	8,669
Scientific R&D services	5417	16,402	13,547	15,209	15,602	13,283

X Not applicable. NA Not available. [1] North American Industry Classification System; see text, Section 15. [2] Based on gross domestic product implicit price deflator, update from August 6, 2016.

Source: U.S. National Science Foundation, National Center for Science and Engineering Statistics, *Business Research and Development and Innovation: 2013*, NSF 16-313, August 2016. See also <http://www.nsf.gov/statistics/industry/>.

Table 832. Academic and Industrial Research and Development (R&D) Performed by State: 2014

[In millions of dollars (64,704 represents 64,704,000,000). Industry R&D data refer to calendar years; other R&D data refer to fiscal years but are used here as approximations to calendar year data. For definition of research and development see text this section]

State	Academic R&D [2] (mil. dol.)	Academic R&D per $1,000 of state GDP	Industry-performed R&D (mil. dol.)	Industry R&D per $1,000 of state GDP	State	Academic R&D [2] (mil. dol.)	Academic R&D per $1,000 of state GDP	Industry-performed R&D (mil. dol.)	Industry R&D per $1,000 of state GDP
U.S. [1]	64,704	3.73	340,728	19.64	MO	1,051	3.58	6,720	22.91
AL	816	4.00	1,961	9.60	MT	181	3.94	205	4.46
AK	174	3.30	57	1.08	NE	455	3.99	590	5.18
AZ	1,047	3.60	5,499	18.92	NV	154	1.09	631	4.47
AR	282	2.29	317	2.57	NH	341	4.70	2,041	28.12
CA	8,400	3.42	98,488	40.06	NJ	1,130	1.99	13,743	24.19
CO	1,232	3.91	4,551	14.45	NM	412	4.47	499	5.41
CT	1,063	4.11	9,093	35.17	NY	5,639	3.91	13,818	9.59
DE	193	2.84	2,520	37.02	NC	2,815	5.64	8,091	16.20
DC	543	4.43	338	2.76	ND	222	4.05	271	4.94
FL	2,273	2.57	5,783	6.55	OH	2,159	3.55	8,945	14.71
GA	1,951	3.94	4,635	9.35	OK	420	2.33	607	3.36
HI	331	4.15	196	2.46	OR	706	3.28	6,434	29.88
ID	143	2.19	1,448	22.19	PA	3,329	4.83	10,816	15.69
IL	2,327	3.00	12,371	15.96	RI	446	7.82	542	9.50
IN	1,309	3.89	5,901	17.54	SC	656	3.30	1,089	5.48
IA	775	4.45	2,098	12.05	SD	105	2.25	135	2.89
KS	548	3.71	1,934	13.09	TN	1,133	3.61	1,586	5.05
KY	534	2.74	1,158	5.95	TX	4,899	3.09	16,373	10.32
LA	666	2.74	386	1.59	UT	689	4.68	2,809	19.09
ME	127	2.24	373	6.59	VT	115	3.78	302	9.93
MD	3,573	9.82	5,124	14.08	VA	1,381	2.88	4,994	10.41
MA	3,501	7.34	21,105	44.27	WA	1,537	3.46	15,699	35.38
MI	2,243	4.81	17,077	36.60	WV	196	2.66	279	3.78
MN	919	2.76	6,975	20.93	WI	1,411	4.61	4,287	14.02
MS	411	3.84	269	2.51	WY	51	1.32	59	1.53

[1] U.S. totals will not equal state totals because the U.S. totals include data for outlying areas (Puerto Rico, Guam, and Virgin Islands), R&D expenditures that can not be allocated to specific states, and double counting of U&C (universities and colleges) data (see footnote 2). [2] State level university R&D data have not been adjusted to eliminate double counting of funds passed through from one academic institution to another. See source for more information.

Source: National Science Foundation, *National Patterns of R&D Resources: 2014-15 Data Update*, NSF 17-311, March 2017. See also <http://www.nsf.gov/statistics/natlpatterns/>.

Table 833. Research and Development (R&D) Expenditures in Science and Engineering at Universities and Colleges in Current and Constant (2009) Dollars: 2005 to 2015

[In millions of dollars (45,774 represents $45,774,000,000). Totals may not add due to rounding. Reference period is the fiscal year of the surveyed institutions. Data are based on the Higher Education R&D (HERD) Survey, which in 2010 succeeded the Survey of Research and Development Expenditures at Colleges and Universities; see source for details]

Characteristic	Current dollars				Constant (2009) dollars [1]			
	2005	2010	2014	2015	2005	2010	2014	2015
Expenditures, total.................	**45,774**	**58,357**	**63,771**	**65,044**	**49,761**	**57,653**	**58,598**	**59,132**
Source of funds:								
Federal government......................	29,187	36,508	36,825	36,805	31,729	36,068	33,838	33,460
State and local government.............	2,940	3,604	3,589	3,526	3,196	3,561	3,298	3,205
Institutions' own funds..................	8,265	10,674	14,305	15,039	8,985	10,545	13,145	13,672
Industry.................................	2,291	3,117	3,630	3,895	2,490	3,079	3,336	3,541
Other....................................	3,092	4,454	5,422	5,778	3,362	4,400	4,982	5,253
Field:								
Computer sciences......................	1,404	1,639	1,927	1,964	1,526	1,619	1,771	1,785
Environmental sciences.................	2,554	2,992	3,230	3,249	2,777	2,956	2,968	2,954
Life sciences...........................	27,604	34,948	37,961	38,820	30,008	34,527	34,882	35,292
Mathematical sciences..................	494	594	658	642	537	587	605	583
Physical sciences.......................	3,703	4,623	4,617	4,711	4,025	4,567	4,242	4,283
Psychology..............................	825	1,078	1,142	1,184	897	1,065	1,049	1,076
Social sciences.........................	1,685	1,997	2,216	2,322	1,831	1,973	2,036	2,111
Other sciences..........................	761	1,161	1,045	1,082	827	1,147	960	984
Engineering.............................	6,743	9,325	10,976	11,070	7,331	9,212	10,086	10,064

[1] Based on gross domestic product implicit price deflator (updated December 2016).

Source: U.S. National Science Foundation, "Higher Education Research and Development: Fiscal Year 2015, Data Tables," and earlier editions, <http://www.nsf.gov/statistics/herd/>, accessed January 2017.

Table 834. Federal Research and Development (R&D) Obligations to Selected Universities and Colleges: 1990 to 2015

[In millions of dollars (9,065.2 represents $9,065,200,000). For fiscal years ending September 30. For the top 40 institutions receiving federal R&D funds in 2015. Awards to the administrative offices of university systems are excluded from totals for individual institutions because the allocation of those funds is unknown, but those awards are included in "total all institutions"]

Major institution ranked by total 2015 federal R&D obligations	1990	2000	2010 [2]	2013	2014	2015
Total, all institutions [1]...........	**9,065.2**	**17,329.3**	**30,806.8**	**26,105.6**	**27,590.6**	**27,040.6**
Johns Hopkins University................	469.5	795.5	1,515.8	1,266.8	1,402.1	1,340.7
University of Washington—Seattle.......	217.2	396.1	734.7	605.2	658.8	611.9
University of Michigan, all campuses....	176.4	346.7	685.8	575.0	860.8	606.1
University of California—San Diego......	164.8	314.4	613.2	510.9	580.8	536.6
University of California—San Francisco..	167.3	289.2	531.3	524.1	546.3	528.5
Stanford University......................	248.0	355.0	516.8	461.1	478.3	504.0
University of Pennsylvania...............	142.5	348.5	609.0	498.3	542.4	494.6
University of California—Los Angeles....	176.7	372.4	548.8	452.5	487.2	481.8
Columbia University in the City of New York...	154.1	284.6	497.6	454.3	465.5	476.1
University of Pittsburgh, all campuses...	116.6	246.2	497.1	425.9	470.6	450.0
Duke University..........................	116.1	232.2	496.8	424.5	440.8	428.5
Harvard University.......................	148.1	299.9	527.5	425.7	460.6	425.5
University of North Carolina at Chapel Hill...	100.2	232.7	429.7	419.5	450.7	416.8
University of Colorado—Boulder.........	116.4	272.3	427.0	390.0	385.6	416.7
Washington University...................	117.9	287.3	445.5	348.1	394.3	391.6
University of Wisconsin—Madison.......	155.2	263.4	458.8	386.2	397.5	386.6
Yale University...........................	142.5	260.0	470.5	383.4	398.8	370.8
Pennsylvania State University, all campuses...	136.4	230.1	411.2	350.0	384.7	362.9
University of Minnesota, all campuses...	137.5	276.8	417.2	373.4	378.9	359.3
Massachusetts Institute of Technology...	218.3	248.9	338.3	310.0	334.0	350.5
Northwestern University.................	61.1	151.5	281.7	296.8	296.9	337.0
Vanderbilt University.....................	70.6	138.4	399.1	347.5	336.8	329.3
Emory University.........................	49.6	145.6	303.1	289.8	293.7	324.2
University of California—Davis...........	68.9	148.5	312.9	294.9	307.8	315.4
Cornell University, all campuses.........	144.7	240.1	359.8	321.8	329.6	296.4
University of California—Berkeley........	121.7	196.2	304.8	260.8	279.1	294.6
University of Southern California.........	122.7	203.9	378.1	276.9	285.6	289.2
Georgia Institute of Technology—Atlanta..	54.3	58.4	234.0	292.0	241.7	286.6
Case Western Reserve University........	71.3	179.4	287.0	276.7	257.8	273.3
New York University......................	75.7	127.0	251.1	236.2	284.2	263.8
Mount Sinai School of Medicine.........	44.0	119.5	216.5	207.1	247.7	263.1
University of Alabama at Birmingham....	74.5	182.9	235.4	208.9	238.8	254.2
University of Florida......................	55.5	129.2	227.3	199.0	203.2	239.0
University of Rochester...................	102.5	153.2	293.8	226.6	234.4	232.2
Ohio State University, all campuses.....	80.1	140.7	311.6	222.8	221.2	231.9
Baylor College of Medicine..............	72.3	172.3	251.3	215.4	226.5	227.5
University of Chicago.....................	88.5	144.5	252.8	198.8	212.0	224.2
University of Illinois at Urbana-Champaign.....	99.7	156.1	230.3	241.8	280.1	216.5
University of Maryland at College Park...	64.7	120.7	179.1	202.7	215.8	206.3
University of Texas at Austin.............	91.8	135.0	192.9	165.1	186.3	203.4

[1] Includes other institutions, not shown separately. Total also includes a small amount of obligations to independent nonprofit institutions. [2] Includes American Recovery and Reinvestment Act of 2009 obligations.

Source: U.S. National Science Foundation, National Center for Science and Engineering Statistics, "Integrated Science and Engineering Resources Data System (WebCASPAR)," <https://webcaspar.nsf.gov/>, accessed September 2017. See also <http://www.nsf.gov/statistics/fedsupport/>.

Table 835. Graduate Science and Engineering Students in Doctorate-Granting Colleges by Characteristic and Field: 2000 to 2015

[In thousands (443.5 represents 443,500). As of Fall. Includes outlying areas. Based on the Survey of Graduate Students and Postdoctorates in Science and Engineering; for information on methodology, see National Science Foundation (NSF) website <https://ncsesdata.nsf.gov/datatables/gradpostdoc/2015/gss_2015_tech_notes.pdf>]

Field of science or engineering	Total			Characteristic								
				Female			Foreign [1]			Part-time		
	2000	2010	2015	2000	2010	2015	2000	2010	2015	2000	2010	2015
Total, all surveyed fields........................	**443.5**	**575.8**	**604.9**	**201.8**	**265.0**	**266.2**	**123.3**	**165.9**	**224.1**	**123.6**	**142.5**	**140.25**
Science/engineering.........	374.8	508.1	548.7	150.3	215.3	225.3	118.0	158.3	216.4	99.3	121.7	123.5
Engineering, total...........	98.8	141.8	160.4	19.7	32.9	38.5	46.3	64.2	90.8	28.2	35.4	37.3
Sciences, total [2]............	275.9	366.3	388.3	130.7	182.4	186.8	71.7	94.1	125.6	71.1	86.4	86.2
Physical sciences.........	29.6	37.9	39.3	8.8	12.4	12.7	11.5	15.0	15.6	3.5	3.6	3.5
Earth related sciences [3]..	13.0	14.8	14.4	5.3	6.7	6.6	2.6	2.9	3.4	2.8	2.9	2.6
Math sciences.............	14.4	21.3	24.4	5.2	7.4	8.7	5.9	8.4	12.0	3.0	4.4	4.0
Computer sciences.......	40.3	45.9	68.2	11.7	11.2	18.5	19.7	22.6	44.7	16.7	15.8	19.1
Agricultural sciences......	11.3	14.6	17.2	4.8	7.2	8.8	2.4	3.2	4.1	2.4	4.1	4.9
Biological sciences........	53.1	69.5	73.0	27.8	39.3	41.1	11.6	16.9	17.0	7.6	9.5	10.5
Psychology [4]...............	40.3	45.2	38.9	29.0	33.8	28.5	2.1	2.9	2.8	10.8	11.7	9.9
Social sciences...........	73.9	95.9	87.7	38.1	51.0	46.6	15.8	18.8	21.0	24.3	28.1	24.5
Health fields, total [4].........	68.8	67.7	56.3	51.5	49.7	40.9	5.4	7.6	7.7	24.3	20.8	16.8

[1] Temporary residents. [2] Beginning in 2010, total includes newly eligible fields (communication, family and consumer science/human science, and multidisciplinary/interdisciplinary studies) and neuroscience, previously reported under health field "neurology," not shown separately. [3] Earth, atmospheric, and ocean sciences. [4] Beginning in 2010, the numbers for psychology and health reflect more rigorous follow-up with institutions regarding the exclusion of practitioner-oriented graduate degree programs and may not reflect changes in actual enrollments.

Source: U.S. National Science Foundation, National Center for Science and Engineering Statistics, "Integrated Science and Engineering Resources Data System (WebCASPAR)," <https://webcaspar.nsf.gov/>, accessed April 2017. See also <http://www.nsf.gov/statistics/gradpostdoc/>

Table 836. Temporary Visa Holders Awarded Doctorates in Science and Engineering For Top 10 Countries of Origin: 2005 to 2015

[Based on the Survey of Earned Doctorates; for information, see <http://www.nsf.gov/statistics/srvydoctorates/>]

Country of origin	2005	2006	2007	2008	2009	2010	2011	2012	2013	2014	2015
All temporary visa holders [1]...............	**12,832**	**14,198**	**15,123**	**15,261**	**14,737**	**13,636**	**14,235**	**14,784**	**15,674**	**15,842**	**16,155**
Science....................	7,005	7,646	8,171	8,553	8,350	7,809	8,021	8,374	8,676	8,765	8,915
Engineering...............	3,756	4,295	4,591	4,492	4,221	3,866	4,164	4,355	4,759	4,963	5,122
COUNTRY											
China [2].....................	3,347	4,123	4,320	4,148	3,753	3,457	3,652	3,906	4,443	4,651	4,979
India.......................	1,093	1,496	1,923	2,158	2,112	1,994	2,036	2,142	2,074	2,208	2,121
South Korea...............	1,136	1,198	1,129	1,153	1,179	1,076	1,085	1,132	1,012	928	923
Taiwan.....................	443	452	478	462	544	501	570	581	571	558	515
Canada....................	330	327	353	370	387	339	307	299	332	321	317
Turkey.....................	321	321	410	467	445	405	422	352	391	360	387
Thailand...................	281	218	236	291	220	182	235	240	227	200	194
Iran........................	113	125	131	132	139	144	193	278	380	463	611
Japan......................	190	194	211	209	193	173	179	179	166	129	119
Mexico.....................	196	173	172	161	171	169	159	185	146	161	155

[1] Total includes doctorates awarded to temporary visa holders from other countries, not shown separately. [2] Includes Hong Kong.

Source: U.S. National Science Foundation, National Center for Science and Engineering Statistics, "Doctorate Recipients from U.S. Universities: 2015, Data Tables," <https://www.nsf.gov/statistics/2017/nsf17306/data.cfm>, accessed January 2017.

Table 837. Science and Engineering (S&E) Degrees Awarded by Degree Level and Sex of Recipient: 1990 to 2012

[For a description of science and engineering degree categories, see source, Appendix B, <http://www.nsf.gov/statistics/nsf13327/>]

Academic year ending	Bachelor's degree				Master's degree				Doctoral degree			
	Total S&E	Men	Women	Percent women	Total S&E	Men	Women	Percent women	Total S&E [1]	Men	Women	Percent women [2]
1990...........	329,094	189,082	140,012	42.5	77,788	51,230	26,558	34.1	22,868	16,498	6,370	27.9
2000...........	398,602	197,650	200,952	50.4	96,230	54,560	41,670	43.3	25,966	16,518	9,394	36.3
2005...........	470,214	233,924	236,290	50.3	120,870	67,244	53,626	44.4	27,985	17,405	10,539	37.7
2006...........	478,858	238,029	240,829	50.3	120,999	66,249	54,750	45.2	29,873	18,375	11,479	38.5
2007...........	485,772	241,697	244,075	50.2	120,278	65,353	54,925	45.7	31,836	19,542	12,282	38.6
2008...........	496,168	246,719	249,449	50.3	126,404	68,810	57,594	45.6	32,837	19,857	12,973	39.5
2009...........	505,435	250,742	254,693	50.4	134,517	73,489	61,028	45.4	33,463	19,840	13,595	40.7
2010...........	525,374	261,091	264,283	50.3	139,926	76,266	63,660	45.5	33,120	19,570	13,540	40.9
2011...........	554,365	275,258	279,107	50.3	150,653	82,451	68,202	45.3	34,474	20,380	14,077	40.9
2012...........	589,330	291,791	297,539	50.5	161,371	87,810	73,561	45.6	35,809	21,233	14,534	40.6

[1] Total includes degree holders who did not report sex. [2] Percentages of women doctoral degree recipients are calculated based on the total of men plus women, not on the total number of degrees.

Source: U.S. National Science Foundation, *Science and Engineering Degrees: 1966–2012*, NSF-15-326, June 2015. See also <http://www.nsf.gov/statistics/degrees/>.

Table 838. Science, Engineering, and Technology (SET) Degrees as Percent of Higher Education Degrees Conferred by State: 2013

[SET fields include the physical, life, earth, ocean, atmospheric, computer, and social sciences; mathematics; engineering; psychology; science technologies; and engineering technologies. Data reflect location of the degree-granting institution]

State	S&E degrees conferred [1]	All higher education degrees [1]	S&E higher education degrees (percent)	State	S&E degrees conferred [1]	All higher education degrees [1]	S&E higher education degrees (percent)	State	S&E degrees conferred [1]	All higher education degrees [1]	S&E higher education degrees (percent)
U.S.........	833,032	2,656,634	31.4								
AL...........	11,362	42,020	27.0	KY.........	8,314	32,274	25.8	ND.......	2,001	7,812	25.6
AK...........	962	2,673	36.0	LA.........	8,529	30,497	28.0	OH.......	25,542	92,227	27.7
AZ...........	26,044	105,950	24.6	ME.........	3,296	9,329	35.3	OK.......	7,430	27,063	27.5
AR...........	4,722	19,834	23.8	MD.........	20,830	52,730	39.5	OR.......	10,422	30,139	34.6
CA...........	100,282	252,512	39.7	MA.........	32,666	95,482	34.2	PA.......	41,719	131,576	31.7
CO...........	17,735	49,247	36.0	MI.........	26,355	81,309	32.4	RI........	4,657	14,382	32.4
CT...........	10,809	32,046	33.7	MN.........	18,001	61,149	29.4	SC.......	9,220	30,840	29.9
DE...........	2,764	9,187	30.1	MS.........	4,843	19,372	25.0	SD.......	2,381	7,373	32.3
DC...........	9,362	23,078	40.6	MO.......	16,058	62,896	25.5	TN.......	11,678	46,961	24.9
FL...........	37,687	129,934	29.0	MT.........	2,521	7,022	35.9	TX.......	48,403	165,921	29.2
GA...........	20,401	66,763	30.6	NE.........	5,055	19,522	25.9	UT.......	10,272	37,036	27.7
HI...........	2,870	8,195	35.0	NV.........	2,964	10,010	29.6	VT.......	3,988	9,484	42.0
ID...........	3,713	12,538	29.6	NH.........	4,304	13,566	31.7	VA.......	27,132	77,649	34.9
IL...........	33,872	123,037	27.5	NJ.........	19,328	55,683	34.7	WA.......	16,644	43,118	38.6
IN...........	18,350	62,807	29.2	NM.........	3,594	11,381	31.6	WV.......	6,243	20,940	29.8
IA...........	14,600	54,481	26.8	NY.........	65,793	209,000	31.5	WI.......	15,302	47,678	32.1
KS...........	6,834	27,176	25.1	NC.........	24,136	71,111	33.9	WY.......	1,042	2,624	39.7

[1] Includes bachelor's, master's, and doctorate degrees.

Source: National Science Foundation, *Science and Engineering Indicators, 2016*, NSB-2016-1, January 2016. See also <http://www.nsf.gov/statistics/seind/>.

Table 839. Doctorates Conferred in Science and Engineering by Field, Sex, Race, and Hispanic Origin: 2015

[In percent, except as indicated. Based on the Survey of Earned Doctorates. For description of methodology, see <http://www.nsf.gov/statistics/srvydoctorates/>]

Characteristic	Total	Life sciences			Physical sciences			Social sciences			Engineering
		Total [1]	Biological sciences	Health sciences	Total [1]	Chemistry	Physics [2]	Total [1]	Psychology	Economics [3]	Engineering
Total conferred (number)...................	**55,006**	**12,520**	**8,801**	**2,280**	**9,749**	**2,675**	**2,192**	**9,095**	**3,782**	**1,256**	**9,897**
SEX											
Male..........................	53.8	44.6	46.7	31.5	69.9	59.7	79.2	41.4	28.0	65.3	76.8
Female........................	46.2	55.4	53.3	68.5	30.1	40.3	20.7	58.6	72.0	34.7	23.2
RACE/ETHNICITY [4]											
Total conferred (number)...................	**35,117**	**8,484**	**6,043**	**1,667**	**5,142**	**1,574**	**1,203**	**6,698**	**3,107**	**552**	**4,223**
Non-Hispanic (number):											
White........................	72.3	71.3	71.1	68.6	77.2	75.1	81.7	71.9	72.7	71.7	67.9
Asian [5].....................	8.7	10.9	12.1	8.5	9.3	9.2	8.6	6.6	6.1	13.2	15.4
Black........................	6.5	5.3	3.7	11.9	3.0	4.6	1.2	8.0	7.8	2.7	3.9
American Indian/Alaska Native.....................	0.4	0.3	0.2	0.5	0.2	0.3	0.2	0.5	0.4	0.4	0.2
Two or more races..........	2.6	2.8	3.1	1.9	2.4	2.9	2.2	2.9	2.6	2.7	2.6
Hispanic [6]..................	7.0	7.4	8.0	5.9	5.0	5.5	4.2	7.4	7.9	6.2	7.0
Other/unknown [7]...........	2.5	2.0	1.8	2.6	3.0	2.4	1.8	2.7	2.5	3.1	3.1

[1] Includes other fields, not shown separately. [2] Includes astronomy. [3] Includes econometrics and natural resource/environmental economics. [4] Excludes those with temporary visas and those who did not report citizenship. [5] Excludes Native Hawaiians or Other Pacific Islanders. [6] Persons reporting Hispanic ethnicity may be of any race or combination of races. [7] Includes other non-Hispanic race, and individuals who did not report race nor ethnicity.

Source: U.S. National Science Foundation, National Center for Science and Engineering Statistics, "Doctorate Recipients from U.S. Universities: 2015, Data Tables," <https://www.nsf.gov/statistics/2017/nsf17306/data.cfm>, accessed January 2017.

Table 840. Doctorates Awarded by Field of Study and Year of Doctorate: 2009 to 2015

[Based on the Survey of Earned Doctorates. For description of methodology, see <http://www.nsf.gov/statistics/srvydoctorates/>]

Field of study	2009	2010	2011	2012	2013	2014	2015
Total, all fields..........................	**49,553**	**48,031**	**48,914**	**50,951**	**52,707**	**54,003**	**55,006**
Science and engineering, total........................	**35,314**	**34,998**	**36,334**	**37,852**	**39,034**	**40,644**	**41,261**
Science, total................................	27,672	27,420	28,302	29,382	30,033	31,011	31,364
Life sciences.............................	11,403	11,319	11,536	11,965	12,209	12,484	12,520
Agricultural sciences.....................	1,283	1,100	1,206	1,255	1,324	1,338	1,439
Biological/biomedical sciences.......................	8,025	8,046	8,153	8,323	8,356	8,867	8,801
Health sciences.........................	2,095	2,173	2,177	2,387	2,529	2,279	2,280
Physical sciences, total......................	8,324	8,218	8,544	8,916	9,244	9,775	9,749
Chemistry............................	2,392	2,304	2,432	2,416	2,484	2,673	2,675
Computer and information sciences.............	1,610	1,633	1,667	1,793	1,843	1,989	2,005
Earth, atmospheric, and ocean sciences...............	877	862	852	941	989	1,099	1,057
Mathematics...........................	1,553	1,590	1,606	1,703	1,817	1,874	1,820
Physics and astronomy....................	1,892	1,829	1,987	2,063	2,111	2,140	2,192
Social sciences, total......................	7,945	7,883	8,222	8,501	8,580	8,752	9,095
Anthropology..........................	503	507	553	547	550	524	493
Economics............................	1,118	1,073	1,121	1,243	1,183	1,196	1,256
Political science.......................	682	728	685	724	803	777	859
Psychology............................	3,472	3,421	3,577	3,601	3,592	3,724	3,782
Sociology.............................	662	639	657	633	636	679	745
Other social sciences....................	1,508	1,515	1,629	1,753	1,816	1,852	1,960
Engineering, total...........................	7,642	7,578	8,032	8,470	9,001	9,633	9,897
Aeronautical/astronautical................	297	252	262	307	348	386	361
Bioengineering/biomedical..................	834	824	898	943	1,039	1,046	1129
Chemical................................	807	822	823	840	824	973	1002
Civil....................................	707	643	634	495	542	622	633
Electrical/electronics/communications....................	1,693	1,778	1,886	1,939	1,897	1,953	2,004
Industrial/manufacturing....................	251	215	258	226	241	298	244
Materials science........................	625	670	662	743	815	833	874
Mechanical..............................	1,095	983	1,084	1,220	1,277	1,331	1,467
Other...................................	1,333	1,391	1,525	1,757	2,018	2,191	2,183
Non-science and engineering, total.......................	**14,239**	**13,033**	**12,580**	**13,099**	**13,673**	**13,359**	**13,745**
Education................................	6,528	5,288	4,670	4,803	4,935	4,791	5,117
Humanities..............................	4,904	5,016	5,227	5,562	5,715	5,526	5,600
Professional/other/unknown................	2,807	2,729	2,683	2,734	3,023	3,042	3,028

Source: U.S. National Science Foundation, National Center for Science and Engineering Statistics, "Doctorate Recipients from U.S. Universities: 2015, Data Tables," <https://www.nsf.gov/statistics/2017/nsf17306/data.cfm>, accessed January 2017.

Table 841. Employed Scientists and Engineers by Sex, Race/Ethnicity, and Selected Characteristics: 2015

[In thousands (25,306 represents 25,306,000). Scientists and engineers are individuals who have a bachelor's or higher degree, and have an S&E (Science and Engineering) or S&E-related degree or occupation. Data is based on various National Science Foundation (NSF) and non-NSF surveys; see <https://www.nsf.gov/statistics/2017/nsf17310/technical-notes.cfm> for details]

Characteristic	Total [1]	Female	Male	Hispanic or Latino [2]	Asian [3]	Black or African American [3]	White [3]	More than one race [3]
All employed scientists and engineers................	**25,306**	**11,897**	**13,409**	**2,029**	**3,123**	**1,716**	**17,842**	**443**
Age:								
Under 30 years..........................	3,896	2,164	1,731	420	609	239	2,501	109
30-39 years.............................	6,402	3,222	3,181	622	991	503	4,077	173
40-49 years.............................	5,997	2,789	3,208	491	788	450	4,148	84
50-75 years.............................	9,010	3,721	5,289	496	736	524	7,118	76
Employment status:								
Employed, full-time......................	21,302	9,217	12,085	1,719	2,639	1,499	14,945	369
Employed, part-time......................	4,004	2,680	1,324	310	484	217	2,898	73
Highest degree attained:								
Bachelor's..............................	13,998	6,468	7,531	1,218	1,452	1,000	9,974	257
Master's................................	7,718	4,012	3,706	558	1,132	545	5,296	141
Doctorate...............................	1,361	514	847	64	280	66	930	16
Professional............................	2,229	903	1,325	189	259	105	1,642	29
By occupation:								
S&E occupations........................	6,407	1,818	4,590	387	1,321	308	4,267	103
Science occupations....................	4,688	1,568	3,120	268	1,042	234	3,054	76
Engineering occupations................	1,719	250	1,469	120	279	74	1,213	27
S&E related occupations.................	7,867	4,558	3,309	629	871	515	5,676	128
Non-S&E related occupations............	11,031	5,521	5,510	1,012	931	894	7,900	211
By employment sector:								
Business or industry.....................	13,593	5,088	8,505	1,019	2,016	762	9,526	205
Federal government......................	1,157	460	698	132	90	151	749	24
Nonprofit...............................	2,741	1,854	886	213	258	187	2,014	49
Self-employed...........................	1,561	771	790	136	129	70	1,190	27
State or local government................	1,571	754	817	149	121	206	1,039	39
Universities and 4-year colleges.........	1,981	1,078	903	132	388	115	1,297	37
Other educational institutions.............	2,701	1,891	810	249	122	225	2,028	61

[1] Total includes other races, not shown separately. [2] Persons of Hispanic origin may be of any race. [3] Non-Hispanic.

Source: U.S. National Science Foundation, National Center for Science and Engineering Statistics, "Women, Minorities, and Persons with Disabilities in Science and Engineering - Data Tables," <https://www.nsf.gov/statistics/2017/nsf17310/data.cfm>, accessed January 2017.

Table 842. Science and Engineering (S&E) Degree Holders by Occupation: 2013

[In thousands (18,226 represents 18,226,000). Data represents all workers who attained their highest degree (bachelor's or higher) in an S&E or S&E-related field. Detail may not add to total due to rounding]

Occupation	Total	Employees by field of highest degree [1]						
		Total S&E fields	Computer and mathematical sciences	Biological, agricultural, and environmental life sciences [2]	Physical and related sciences [3]	Social and related sciences [4]	Engineering	S&E related fields [5]
All occupations	**18,226**	**12,446**	**2,197**	**1,896**	**731**	**4,764**	**2,859**	**5,780**
S&E occupations	**4,660**	**4,341**	**1,190**	**586**	**358**	**587**	**1,620**	**319**
Computer & mathematical scientists	1,928	1,796	1,120	64	45	153	414	132
Computer & information scientists [6]	1,741	1,633	1,005	53	41	134	401	108
Computer engineers—software	445	427	246	7	8	10	157	18
Software developers	372	348	220	9	9	21	88	24
Computer system analysts	229	207	138	11	3	16	39	22
Computer support specialists	124	116	67	3	4	21	20	8
Network/computer systems administrators	138	129	85	3	3	10	28	9
Mathematical scientists	89	82	44	10	3	17	8	7
Biological, agricultural, & environmental life scientists [6]	583	519	4	437	43	20	16	64
Biological & medical scientists [6]	412	357	4	297	32	13	13	55
Biological scientists [7]	121	114	1	107	3	2	1	7
Medical scientists (excluding practitioners)	131	99	1	77	8	9	4	32
Physical & related scientists [6]	304	294	4	46	215	7	23	10
Chemists, except biochemists	99	95	(S)	14	72	1	6	4
Physicists & astronomers	36	35	(S)	(S)	29	(S)	4	1
Social & related scientists [6]	442	408	7	11	6	380	3	34
Psychologists, including clinical	183	179	(S)	1	(S)	178	(S)	4
Postsecondary teachers—social sciences	123	116	2	3	(S)	110	(S)	7
Engineers [6]	1,404	1,325	54	30	49	27	1,165	79
Electrical or computer hardware engineers	319	304	22	3	10	(S)	267	15
Mechanical engineers	271	257	3	1	2	1	249	14
Civil, architectural, or sanitary engineers	213	206	1	1	2	3	198	7
S&E-related occupations	**5,870**	**1,760**	**336**	**467**	**127**	**378**	**453**	**4,110**
Health-related occupations [6]	3,999	558	20	270	31	217	21	3,441
Diagnosing/treating practitioners [8]	1,099	50	(S)	41	(S)	(S)	2	1,049
Registered nurses, pharmacists, dieticians, therapists, physician assistants, & nurse practitioners	2,026	144	3	66	4	70	(S)	1,882
S&E managers	677	450	98	43	30	62	216	227
Medical & health services managers	243	55	(S)	18	3	33	(S)	188
Engineering managers	253	229	16	4	11	5	192	24
Computer & information systems managers	133	126	81	(S)	(S)	19	21	7
S&E precollege teachers [9]	412	219	71	57	28	51	13	193
S&E technicians & technologists [6]	591	501	130	94	37	42	198	90
Computer programmers	146	136	95	(S)	7	6	24	10
Electrical, electronic, industrial, & mechanical technicians	173	138	13	7	7	12	98	35
Other S&E-related occupations [6]	190	31	17	(S)	(S)	5	4	159
Architects	162	15	4	(S)	(S)	2	4	147
Non-S&E occupations	**7,696**	**6,345**	**671**	**842**	**246**	**3,799**	**787**	**1,351**
Non-S&E managers	1,216	987	115	127	48	445	251	229
Management-related occupations [6]	1,390	1,173	176	131	38	659	169	217
Accountants, auditors, & other financial specialists	473	413	76	31	11	268	26	60
Personnel, training, & labor relations specialists	175	155	13	13	2	116	11	20
Non-S&E precollege teachers [6]	498	353	34	39	13	255	12	145
Elementary	201	134	21	8	10	91	(S)	67
Secondary—other subjects	87	56	1	5	(S)	45	5	31
Special education—primary & secondary	104	72	1	6	(S)	62	(S)	32
Non-S&E postsecondary teachers	88	68	8	5	3	44	9	20
Social services & related occupations [6]	557	457	14	14	4	422	3	100
Counselors [10]	288	228	(S)	8	(S)	214	(S)	60
Social workers	227	191	6	4	(S)	180	(S)	36
Sales & marketing occupations	1,235	1,075	116	152	47	656	103	160
Arts, humanities, & related occupations	253	219	27	28	6	150	9	34
Other non-S&E occupations [6]	2,461	2,014	182	345	88	1,169	230	447

S Data suppressed for reasons of confidentiality and/or reliability. [1] Includes bachelor's, master's, and doctorate degrees. [2] Biological sciences include biology, ecology, nutritional sciences, pharmacology, zoology, and related fields. [3] Physical sciences include chemistry; earth, atmospheric, and ocean sciences; physics and astronomy; and related fields. [4] Social sciences include economics, political science, psychology, sociology and anthropology, linguistics, geography, history and philosophy of science, and related fields. [5] S&E-related fields include health fields, science and math teacher education, technology and technical fields, architecture, and actuarial science. [6] Includes other occupations not shown separately. [7] Includes botanists, ecologists, zoologists, etc. [8] Includes dentists, optometrists, physicians, psychiatrists, podiatrists, surgeons, and veterinarians. [9] Secondary teachers in computer, mathematics, sciences, and social sciences. [10] Includes educational, vocational, mental health, substance abuse, etc.

Source: National Science Foundation, *Science and Engineering Indicators, 2016*, NSB-2016-1, January 2016. See also <http://www.nsf.gov/statistics/seind/>.

Table 843. Civilian Employment of Scientists, Engineers, and Related Occupations by Occupation and Industry: 2014

[In thousands (348.5 represents 348,500). Standard Occupational Classification (SOC) system classifies workers into 840 detailed occupations. Industry classifications correspond to 2012 North American Industry Classification (NAICS) industrial groups]

Occupation	Total employment, all workers	Mining (NAICS 21)[1]	Construction (NAICS 23)	Manufacturing (NAICS 31–33)	Information (NAICS 51)	Professional, scientific and technical services (NAICS 54)	Government	Self employed[2]
Computer and information systems..............	348.5	0.8	0.7	31.0	36.7	101.7	23.5	4.5
Architectural and engineering managers........	182.1	3.5	4.2	66.1	3.5	63.6	17.3	0.2
Natural science managers......................	55.1	0.3	(NA)	6.9	(NA)	21.9	16.0	(NA)
Computer and mathematical scientists[3]........	4,068.3	12.4	12.0	282.9	507.5	1,373.3	264.5	104.9
Computer occupations........................	3,916.1	12.3	12.0	271.7	502.1	1,338.4	244.7	103.5
Mathematical science occupations.............	152.2	0.1	(NA)	11.1	5.4	34.8	19.7	1.3
Surveyors, cartographers, and photogrammetrists.................	56.6	1.3	3.6	0.2	0.1	37.6	9.5	1.8
Engineers[3]...........................	1,636.2	38.6	44.5	567.8	36.2	505.8	198.2	35.8
Aerospace engineers...........................	72.5	(NA)	(NA)	33.1	(NA)	22.9	9.7	2.5
Civil engineers...............................	281.4	1.3	25.9	3.5	0.4	146.0	76.8	11.1
Computer hardware engineers.................	77.7	(NA)	0.1	32.4	4.0	28.0	4.9	0.3
Electrical and electronics engineers............	315.9	0.7	5.4	101.6	29.3	93.4	27.7	3.8
Industrial engineers[4].........................	266.3	4.6	(NA)	178.9	1.1	31.0	5.5	2.7
Mechanical engineers........................	277.5	2.4	3.7	136.8	0.4	87.4	(NA)	3.4
Drafters, engineering, and mapping technicians[3]...................	704.7	9.6	24.2	217.7	8.2	256.9	92.7	10.2
Engineering technicians, except drafters.......	443.0	7.2	5.0	164.5	6.5	118.3	78.5	2.2
Surveying and mapping technicians............	57.3	1.9	1.9	0.2	0.3	32.0	10.2	5.3
Life, physical, and social science occupations...	1,310.4	25.2	0.7	115.8	1.6	341.8	316.8	76.6
Life scientists...............................	310.9	0.1	(NA)	29.2	0.1	89.1	69.2	5.0
Physical scientists............................	296.8	12.3	0.3	40.2	0.9	102.3	77.7	7.6
Social scientists and related occupations......	307.1	0.2	0.1	0.3	(NA)	42.7	86.4	56.1
Life, physical, & social science technicians....	395.6	12.6	0.3	46.1	0.2	107.7	83.5	7.9

NA Not available. [1] Includes oil and gas extraction. [2] Includes unpaid family workers. [3] Includes other occupations not shown separately. [4] Includes health and safety engineers.

Source: U.S. Bureau of Labor Statistics, National Employment Matrix, "Employment Projections," <http://www.bls.gov/emp/tables.htm>, accessed February 2016.

Table 844. Top 20 Metropolitan Areas with the Largest Proportion of Workers in Science and Engineering Occupations: 2012 and 2014

[As of May. Ranked by top 20 metro areas in 2014. Data are from U.S. Bureau of Labor Statistics' Occupational Employment Statistics Survey. Excludes metropolitan statistical areas where S&E (science and engineering) proportions were suppressed. Differences among employment estimates may not be statistically significant; see source for details]

Metropolitan statistical area	2012 Workers employed All occupations	2012 Workers employed S&E occupations	2012 Percent of area workforce in S&E occupations	2014 Workers employed All occupations	2014 Workers employed S&E occupations	2014 Percent of area workforce in S&E occupations
U.S. total...........	130,287,700	5,968,240	4.6	135,128,260	6,318,580	4.7
San Jose-Sunnyvale-Santa Clara, CA...................	898,610	142,430	15.9	973,480	163,460	16.8
Boulder, CO..........................	159,440	21,160	13.3	167,200	22,620	13.5
Huntsville, AL........................	203,400	26,590	13.1	208,480	27,820	13.3
Framingham, MA NECTA[1]................................	157,290	19,550	12.4	162,170	21,010	13.0
Corvallis, OR.........................	33,310	4,170	12.5	33,450	3,920	11.7
Durham-Chapel Hill, NC.................	272,250	32,690	12.0	284,480	33,020	11.6
Washington-Arlington-Alexandria, DC-VA-MD-WV......	2,343,510	265,370	11.3	2,378,260	259,080	10.9
Seattle-Bellevue-Everett, WA,	1,409,500	148,670	10.5	1,492,650	154,480	10.3
Bethesda-Rockville-Frederick, MD,	560,000	54,380	9.7	566,300	55,860	9.9
San Francisco-San Mateo-Redwood City, CA,..........	1,000,430	89,480	8.9	1,086,660	105,430	9.7
Ithaca, NY...........................	(X)	(X)	(X)	49,430	4,380	8.9
Ames, IA.............................	40,270	3,280	8.1	42,250	3,740	8.9
Boston-Cambridge-Quincy, MA, NECTA[1]...............	1,711,350	154,470	9.0	1,795,230	157,300	8.8
Lowell-Billerica-Chelmsford, MA-NH, NECTA[1]........	116,620	12,830	11.0	118,980	10,420	8.8
Ann Arbor, MI........................	193,760	16,870	8.7	204,840	17,810	8.7
Columbus, IN.........................	(X)	(X)	(X)	48,120	4,090	8.5
Fort Collins-Loveland, CO..............	132,630	11,060	8.3	139,530	11,810	8.5
Austin-Round Rock-San Marcos, TX.....................	812,600	64,780	8.0	886,620	72,820	8.2
State College, PA.....................	(X)	(X)	(X)	66,660	5,420	8.1
Madison, WI..........................	(X)	(X)	(X)	347,750	27,250	7.8
Bloomington-Normal, IL...............	86,920	8,280	9.5	(X)	(X)	(X)
Kennewick-Pasco-Richland, WA.........	97,300	8,850	9.1	(X)	(X)	(X)
Olympia, WA.........................	93,850	7,520	8.0	(X)	(X)	(X)
College Station-Bryan, TX..............	92,990	7,370	7.9	(X)	(X)	(X)

X Not applicable. [1] NECTA = New England City and Town Area.

Source: National Science Foundation, *Science and Engineering Indicators, 2016*, January 2016, and earlier reports. See also <http://www.nsf.gov/statistics/seind/>.

Table 845. High-Technology Establishments, Business Formations, and Employment by State: 2012

[Employment in thousands (115,914 represents 115,914,000). High-technology industries are those industries for which employment in technology-oriented occupations accounts for a proportion of that industry's total employment that is at least twice the 4.9% average for all industries. Includes only private-sector businesses. For a complete list of included industries, see source. Minus sign (-) indicates loss]

State	All establishments		High technology establishments					
			Establishments		Net business formations		Employment	
	Total	Employment (1,000)	Total	Percent of all establishments	Total	Percent of all establishments	Total (1,000)	Percent of total employment
United States	**7,417,313**	**115,914**	**662,832**	**8.9**	**9,299**	**0.1**	**13,997**	**12.1**
Alabama	97,786	1,585	6,753	6.9	-19	–	162	10.3
Alaska	20,372	258	1,654	8.1	-4	–	35	13.6
Arizona	131,168	2,134	11,884	9.1	33	–	225	10.5
Arkansas	64,715	978	4,890	7.6	-10	–	99	10.1
California	862,879	12,951	89,168	10.3	2,169	0.3	1,797	13.9
Colorado	152,878	2,036	18,928	12.4	462	0.3	322	15.8
Connecticut	88,027	1,463	7,391	8.4	-42	-0.1	198	13.5
Delaware	23,826	364	3,012	12.6	-39	-0.2	41	11.2
District of Columbia	21,567	483	3,628	16.8	15	0.1	72	14.8
Florida	501,512	6,932	46,868	9.4	1,407	0.3	615	8.9
Georgia	215,953	3,390	21,769	10.1	321	0.2	454	13.4
Hawaii	31,465	492	2,226	7.1	-45	-0.1	33	6.8
Idaho	42,827	493	3,061	7.2	-6	–	54	10.9
Illinois	313,598	5,120	29,192	9.3	327	0.1	644	12.6
Indiana	143,712	2,511	10,183	7.1	30	–	225	9.0
Iowa	80,464	1,291	4,738	5.9	4	–	110	8.6
Kansas	73,791	1,134	6,160	8.4	-39	-0.1	149	13.1
Kentucky	89,682	1,481	5,947	6.6	48	0.1	124	8.4
Louisiana	103,924	1,645	8,167	7.9	155	0.2	153	9.3
Maine	40,052	487	2,755	6.9	83	0.2	39	8.0
Maryland	134,090	2,152	15,919	11.9	318	0.2	347	16.1
Massachusetts	170,944	3,034	17,539	10.3	158	0.1	463	15.3
Michigan	217,060	3,467	16,643	7.7	-136	-0.1	410	11.8
Minnesota	145,566	2,480	13,314	9.2	107	0.1	355	14.3
Mississippi	58,538	895	3,566	6.1	6	–	65	7.3
Missouri	146,300	2,319	9,852	6.7	-63	–	257	11.1
Montana	36,144	344	2,658	7.4	80	0.2	25	7.1
Nebraska	52,203	818	3,435	6.6	108	0.2	68	8.3
Nevada	59,324	1,015	6,134	10.3	175	0.3	67	6.6
New Hampshire	37,158	549	3,506	9.4	74	0.2	67	12.2
New Jersey	227,948	3,440	23,352	10.2	-72	–	516	15.0
New Mexico	43,799	602	3,548	8.1	-46	-0.1	66	11.0
New York	525,298	7,554	39,331	7.5	602	0.1	772	10.2
North Carolina	217,012	3,353	18,524	8.5	356	0.2	379	11.3
North Dakota	23,503	331	1,373	5.8	128	0.5	26	7.9
Ohio	250,441	4,549	20,003	8.0	-42	–	517	11.4
Oklahoma	90,792	1,305	7,748	8.5	52	0.1	153	11.7
Oregon	107,284	1,363	8,673	8.1	133	0.1	160	11.8
Pennsylvania	296,478	5,168	24,044	8.1	71	–	601	11.6
Rhode Island	27,989	403	2,090	7.5	-14	-0.1	40	9.9
South Carolina	101,053	1,549	7,036	7.0	5	–	164	10.6
South Dakota	25,733	336	1,469	5.7	35	0.1	24	7.1
Tennessee	130,319	2,343	8,870	6.8	67	0.1	224	9.6
Texas	536,771	9,349	52,966	9.9	1,645	0.3	1,250	13.4
Utah	70,343	1,071	7,468	10.6	176	0.3	130	12.1
Vermont	21,123	265	1,578	7.5	25	0.1	24	9.2
Virginia	192,428	3,089	24,334	12.7	272	0.1	553	17.9
Washington	175,061	2,361	15,494	8.9	239	0.1	393	16.7
West Virginia	37,838	580	2,417	6.4	-71	-0.2	47	8.1
Wisconsin	137,988	2,387	9,719	7.0	-15	–	262	11.0
Wyoming	20,587	214	1,855	9.0	76	0.4	20	9.2

– Represents or rounds to zero.

Source: National Science Foundation, *Science and Engineering Indicators, 2016*, January 2016. See <http://www.nsf.gov/statistics/seind/>.

Table 846. Employment and Median Salary of Worker With Highest Degree in Science and Engineering (S&E) Field, by Sex and Occupation: 2013

[Rounded to the nearest 1,000. Data are for full-time workers who typically work 35 or more hours weekly in their principal job. Data are from National Science Foundation's Scientists and Engineers Statistical Data System (SESTAT)]

Occupation	Total		Female			Male		
	Number	Median salary (dollars)	Number	Percent	Median salary (dollars)	Number	Percent	Median salary (dollars)
All occupations............................	**10,546,000**	**72,000**	**3,639,000**	**34.5**	**55,000**	**6,906,000**	**65.5**	**80,000**
S&E..	3,929,000	85,000	978,000	24.9	70,000	2,951,000	75.1	90,000
Engineers.............................	1,250,000	90,000	179,000	14.3	82,000	1,071,000	85.7	92,000
Computer and mathematical scientists..	1,677,000	90,000	347,000	20.7	80,000	1,330,000	79.3	92,000
Biological, agricultural, and other life scientists.......................	455,000	60,000	210,000	46.2	52,000	245,000	53.8	69,000
Physical scientists........................	259,000	72,000	75,000	29.0	62,000	184,000	71.0	78,000
Social scientists...........................	289,000	67,000	167,000	57.8	62,000	121,000	41.9	80,000
S&E related occupations....................	1,537,000	70,000	580,000	37.7	54,000	957,000	62.3	85,000
Health-related occupations...............	414,000	50,000	275,000	66.4	49,000	138,000	33.3	50,000
Non-S&E related occupations...............	5,079,000	60,000	2,081,000	41.0	50,000	2,998,000	59.0	70,000

Source: National Science Foundation, National Center for Science and Engineering Statistics, *Science and Engineering Indicators 2016*, NSB-2016-1, January 2016. See also <http://www.nsf.gov/statistics/seind/>.

Table 847. Federal Discretionary Outlays for General Science and Space and Other Technology, 1970 to 2016, and Projections for 2017 and 2018

[In billions of dollars (4.5 represents $4,500,000,000). For fiscal years ending in year shown; see text, Section 8]

Year	Current dollars			Constant (2009) dollars		
	Total	General science and research	Space/other technologies	Total	General science and research	Space/other technologies
1970............	4.5	0.9	3.6	24.3	5.1	19.2
1980............	5.8	1.4	4.5	15.8	3.7	12.1
1990............	14.4	2.8	11.6	27.8	5.4	22.4
1995 [1]...........	16.7	4.1	12.6	24.4	6.0	18.4
2000............	18.6	6.2	12.4	24.6	8.2	16.5
2005............	23.6	8.8	14.8	26.2	9.8	16.4
2006............	23.5	9.0	14.5	25.2	9.7	15.5
2007............	24.4	9.1	15.3	25.3	9.5	15.8
2008............	26.7	9.5	17.2	27.0	9.6	17.4
2009............	28.3	9.9	18.4	28.3	9.9	18.4
2010............	30.0	11.6	18.4	29.5	11.4	18.1
2011............	29.4	12.3	17.0	28.1	11.8	16.3
2012............	28.9	12.3	16.6	27.1	11.6	15.5
2013............	28.8	12.4	16.4	27.0	11.6	15.4
2014............	28.5	11.9	16.6	26.3	11.0	15.3
2015............	29.4	11.7	17.7	26.3	10.4	15.9
2016............	30.1	11.9	18.2	26.7	10.5	16.2
2017, proj......	31.0	12.4	18.5	26.9	10.8	16.1
2018, proj......	30.5	11.7	18.8	26.0	9.9	16.0

[1] Due to the effects of the Credit Reform Act of 1990 on the measurement and classification of Federal credit activities, the discretionary outlays for years prior to 1992 are not strictly comparable to those for 1992 and beyond.

Source: U.S. Office of Management and Budget, *Budget of the U.S. Government, Fiscal Year 2018: Historical Tables*, May 2017. See also <http://www.whitehouse.gov/omb/budget>.

Table 848. Space Launch Events Worldwide: 2000 to 2016

[2,729 represents $2,729,000,000.) Data show all U.S. and international orbital launches. Launch data includes launch failures; launch failures happen when the payload does not reach a usable orbit or is destroyed as the result of a launch vehicle malfunction. In 2016 there were 2 launch failures: both were non-commercial launches]

Country/region	Non-commercial launches				Commercial launches				Launch revenues for commercial launch events (mil. dol.)			
	2000	2010	2015	2016	2000	2010	2015	2016	2000	2010	2015	2016
Total..............	**50**	**51**	**64**	**64**	**35**	**23**	**22**	**21**	**2,729**	**2,453**	**2,150**	**2,467**
United States......	21	11	12	11	7	4	8	11	370	307	617	1,185
Russia..............	23	18	21	15	13	13	5	2	671	826	289	130
Europe.............	–	–	5	3	12	6	6	8	1,433	1,320	1,066	1,152
China..............	5	15	19	22	–	–	–	–	(X)	(X)	(X)	(X)
India..............	–	3	3	7	–	–	2	–	(X)	(X)	66	(X)
Japan..............	1	2	3	4	–	–	1	–	(X)	(X)	113	(X)
Israel..............	–	1	–	1	–	–	–	–	(X)	(X)	(X)	(X)
Iran...............	–	–	1	–	–	–	–	–	(X)	(X)	(X)	(X)
Korea, North.......	–	–	–	1	–	–	–	–	(X)	(X)	(X)	(X)
Korea, South......	–	1	–	–	–	–	–	–	(X)	(X)	(X)	(X)
Multinational.......	–	–	–	–	3	–	–	–	255	(X)	(X)	(X)

– Represents zero. X Not applicable.

Source: Federal Aviation Administration, *Commercial Space Transportation: 2014 Year in Review*, February 2015, and earlier editions; and *The Annual Compendium of Commercial Space Transportation: 2017*, January 2017, and earlier editions. See also <http://www.faa.gov/about/office_org/headquarters_offices/ast/reports_studies/>.

Agriculture

This section presents statistics on farms and farm operators; farm income, expenditures, and debt; farm output, productivity, and marketings; foreign trade in agricultural products; specific crops; livestock, poultry, and their products; and direct marketing to consumers and farm to school programs.

The principal sources are the data collected by the National Agricultural Statistics Service (NASS), the Economic Research Service (ERS), and the Foreign Agricultural Service (FAS) of the U.S. Department of Agriculture (USDA) and published in reports or databases. The ERS publishes data on farm assets, debt, and income on the internet at <http://www.ers.usda.gov/data-products/farm-income-and-wealth-statistics>. The ERS also provides data on commodity supply and disappearance via commodity outlook reports, yearbooks, and databases, available on the ERS site at <http://www.ers.usda.gov/data-products.aspx>. Sources of current data on agricultural exports and imports include the Global Agricultural Trade System database provided by the FAS at <http://www.fas.usda.gov/gats> and the "Foreign Agricultural Trade of the United States (FATUS)" data, published by the ERS, available on the ERS site at <https://www.ers.usda.gov/data-products/foreign-agricultural-trade-of-the-united-states-fatus/>.

The field offices of the NASS collect data on crops, livestock and products, agricultural prices, farm employment, and other related subjects mainly through sample surveys. Information is obtained on crops, livestock, and products pertaining to agricultural production and marketing. State estimates and supporting information are sent to the Agricultural Statistics Board of NASS, which reviews the estimates and issues reports containing state and national data. Among these reports are annual summaries such as *Crop Production, Crop Values, Agricultural Prices,* and *Meat Animals Production, Disposition and Income.* The NASS also provides data through the QuickStats database at <http://quickstats.nass.usda.gov>.

The USDA conducts the Census of Agriculture every 5 years and collects information concerning all areas of farming and ranching operations, including production expenses, market value of products, and operator characteristics. The information from the 2012 Census of Agriculture is available in print form in the Volume 1, Geographic Area Series; and on the internet at <http://www.agcensus.usda.gov/Publications/2012/>. An evaluation of coverage has been conducted for each census of agriculture since 1945 to provide estimates of the completeness of census farm counts. Beginning with the 1997 Census of Agriculture, census farm counts and totals were statistically adjusted for coverage and reported at the county level. The size of the adjustments varies considerably by state. In general, farms not on the census mail list tended to be small in acreage, production, and sales of farm products. The response rate for the 2012 Census of Agriculture was 80.1 percent as compared with a response rate of 85.2 for the 2007 Census of Agriculture, 88.0 for the 2002 Census of Agriculture, and 86.2 percent for the 1997 Census of Agriculture.

For more explanation about census mail list compilation, collection methods, coverage measurement, and adjustments, see Appendix A, *2012 Census of Agriculture,* Volume 1 reports <http://www.agcensus.usda.gov/Publications/2012/>.

Farms and farmland—The definitions of a farm have varied through time. Since 1850, when minimum criteria defining a farm for census purposes first were established, the farm definition has changed nine times. The current definition, first used for the 1974 census, is any place from which $1,000 or more of agricultural products were produced and sold, or normally would have been sold, during the census year.

Acreage designated as "land in farms" consists primarily of agricultural land used for crops, pasture, or grazing. It also includes woodland and wasteland not actually under cultivation or used for pasture or grazing, provided it was part of the farm operator's total operation. Land in farms includes acres set aside under annual commodity acreage programs as well as acres idled by federal conservation programs for places meeting the farm definition. Land in farms is an operating unit concept and includes land owned and operated as well as land rented from others. All grazing land, except land used under government permits on a per-head basis, was included as "land in farms" provided it was part of a farm or ranch.

Farm income—The final agricultural sector output comprises cash receipts from farm marketings of crops and livestock, federal government payments made directly to farmers for farm-related activities, rental value of farm homes, value of farm products consumed in farm homes, and other farm-related income such as machine hire and custom work. Farm marketings represent quantities of agricultural products sold by farmers multiplied by prices received per unit of production at the local market. Information on prices received for farm products is generally obtained by the NASS Agricultural Statistics Board from surveys of firms (such as grain elevators, packers, and processors) purchasing agricultural commodities directly from producers. In some cases, the price information is obtained directly from the producers.

Crops—Estimates of crop acreage and production by the NASS are based on current sample survey data obtained from individual producers and objective yield counts, reports of carlot shipments, market records, personal field observations by field statisticians, and reports from other sources.

Prices received by farmers are marketing year average prices and do not include allowances for outstanding loans, government purchases, deficiency payments or disaster payments. These averages are based on monthly prices weighted by monthly sales during specific periods. All state marketing year average prices are based on individual state marketing years, while U.S. marketing year average prices are based on standard U.S. marketing years for each crop. For a description of how U.S. prices are computed as well as a listing of the crop marketing years, see *Crop Values Annual Summary.*

Value of production is computed by multiplying state prices by each state's production. The U.S. value of production is the sum of state values for all states. Value of production figures should not be confused with cash receipts from farm marketings which relate to sales during a calendar year, irrespective of the year of production.

Livestock—Annual inventory numbers of livestock and estimates of livestock, dairy, and poultry production prepared by the Department of Agriculture are based on information from farmers and ranchers obtained by probability survey sampling methods.

Statistical reliability—For a discussion of statistical collection and estimation, sampling procedures, and measures of statistical reliability pertaining to Department of Agriculture data, see Appendix III.

Table 849. Selected Characteristics of Farms by North American Industry Classification System (NAICS): 2012

[394,644,481 represents $394,644,481,000. See text this section and Appendix III]

Industry	2012 NAICS code [1]	Farms	Land in farms (acres)	Harvested cropland (acres)	Market value of agricultural products sold (1,000)		
					Total	Crops	Livestock [2]
Total............................	(X)	**2,109,303**	**914,527,657**	**314,964,600**	**394,644,481**	**212,397,074**	**182,247,407**
Crop production..........................	111	1,054,987	454,064,220	262,297,534	209,421,055	200,168,398	9,252,657
Oilseed and grain farming..............	1111	369,332	289,765,872	213,227,680	127,712,682	120,552,373	7,160,309
Soybean farming.....................	11111	89,946	39,465,959	32,408,918	16,070,358	15,835,107	235,251
Oilseed (except soybean) farming.........	11112	1,079	1,501,942	1,103,482	356,573	351,653	4,920
Dry pea and bean farming.................	11113	1,000	735,057	533,503	258,432	255,631	2,802
Wheat farming.......................	11114	38,542	56,835,727	29,831,424	8,815,719	8,368,777	446,942
Corn farming.........................	11115	167,043	107,075,030	88,821,359	65,231,965	63,396,809	1,835,157
Rice farming.........................	11116	3,170	3,342,921	2,607,924	2,448,145	2,419,709	28,436
Other grain farming..................	11119	68,552	80,809,236	57,921,070	34,531,489	29,924,687	4,606,802
Vegetable and melon farming..............	11121	43,021	8,206,468	5,333,376	16,726,256	16,624,257	101,998
Potato farming......................	111211	2,529	2,630,696	1,999,092	4,010,500	3,995,512	14,989
Other vegetable (except potato) and melon farming.............................	111219	40,492	5,575,772	3,334,284	12,715,756	12,628,746	87,010
Fruit and tree nut farming.................	1113	93,020	13,162,702	5,641,474	25,481,636	25,346,460	135,177
Orange groves........................	11131	6,141	1,268,406	672,041	1,981,134	1,955,556	25,579
Citrus (except orange) groves.............	11132	2,839	357,519	175,912	639,232	632,859	6,373
Noncitrus fruit and tree nut farming.........	11133	84,040	11,536,777	4,793,521	22,861,271	22,758,045	103,225
Apple orchards.......................	111331	8,921	2,133,711	418,403	2,757,137	2,750,702	6,435
Grape vineyards.....................	111332	17,580	2,683,393	1,205,918	6,836,734	6,816,072	20,661
Strawberry farming..................	111333	1,545	109,972	67,848	1,860,850	1,860,428	422
Berry (except strawberry) farming..........	111334	9,928	1,041,594	240,168	1,342,637	1,339,096	3,541
Tree nut farming....................	111335	23,414	3,841,338	2,101,087	6,990,605	6,942,604	48,001
Fruit and tree nut combination farming.............................	111336	979	247,633	112,660	468,648	456,220	12,428
Other noncitrus fruit farming...............	111339	21,673	1,479,136	647,437	2,604,659	2,592,922	11,737
Greenhouse, nursery, and floriculture production..............................	1114	52,777	4,502,514	1,483,765	14,736,375	14,694,443	41,932
Food crops grown under cover.............	11141	3,138	135,425	23,943	1,695,262	1,693,031	2,231
Nursery and floriculture production..........	11142	49,639	4,367,089	1,459,822	13,041,113	13,001,412	39,702
Nursery and tree production..............	111421	32,048	3,796,386	1,306,906	7,071,426	7,040,218	31,207
Floriculture production....................	111422	17,591	570,703	152,916	5,969,688	5,961,193	8,494
Other crop farming.......................	1119	496,837	138,426,664	36,611,239	24,764,106	22,950,865	1,813,241
Tobacco farming.....................	11191	5,132	1,574,110	803,519	1,262,097	1,210,614	51,482
Cotton farming.......................	11192	8,915	11,157,031	7,232,673	4,661,521	4,610,462	51,059
Sugarcane farming...................	11193	526	1,326,957	934,255	1,361,015	1,356,475	4,540
Hay farming.........................	11194	252,382	53,007,901	15,859,037	5,924,002	5,468,044	455,959
All other crop farming..................	11199	229,882	71,360,665	11,781,755	11,555,470	10,305,269	1,250,201
Animal production.........................	112	1,054,316	460,463,437	52,667,066	185,223,427	12,228,676	172,994,750
Cattle ranching and farming..............	1121	678,911	367,223,798	44,311,752	112,182,806	8,365,288	103,817,518
Beef cattle ranching and farming including feedlots.....................	11211	632,906	348,596,036	32,125,853	71,150,505	5,500,152	65,650,353
Beef cattle ranching and farming.........	112111	619,172	336,701,440	28,456,003	32,966,557	3,856,930	29,109,627
Cattle feedlots....................	112112	13,734	11,894,596	3,669,850	38,183,948	1,643,222	36,540,726
Dairy cattle and milk production............	11212	46,005	18,627,762	12,185,899	41,032,301	2,865,136	38,167,165
Hog and pig farming.....................	1122	21,687	5,207,594	3,617,583	22,645,102	2,239,182	20,405,920
Poultry and egg production................	1123	52,849	6,352,747	1,951,105	43,703,626	943,395	42,760,231
Chicken egg production................	11231	27,995	1,861,307	389,376	8,932,413	174,297	8,758,115
Broilers and other meat-type chicken production..........................	11232	16,324	3,137,705	1,058,726	25,115,569	489,383	24,626,186
Turkey production....................	11233	2,521	779,300	380,638	5,732,622	218,157	5,514,465
Poultry hatcheries....................	11234	291	23,238	1,774	3,120,868	1,375	3,119,492
Other poultry production..................	11239	5,718	551,197	120,591	802,155	60,182	741,973
Sheep and goat farming..................	1124	73,272	11,729,223	344,163	766,044	47,781	718,263
Sheep farming.......................	11241	31,316	7,911,730	240,007	572,472	39,717	532,755
Goat farming.........................	11242	41,956	3,817,493	104,156	193,572	8,063	185,509
Animal aquaculture.......................	1125	4,095	1,082,639	27,109	1,530,706	11,142	1,519,564
Other animal production...................	1129	223,502	68,867,436	2,415,354	4,395,143	621,890	3,773,253
Apiculture.............................	11291	7,358	373,819	14,540	257,109	3,814	253,295
Horse and other equine production.........	11292	172,043	27,504,660	888,078	1,333,258	19,888	1,313,370
Fur-bearing animal and rabbit production..........................	11293	633	22,524	2,286	13,491	199	13,292
All other animal production.................	11299	43,468	40,966,433	1,510,450	2,791,285	597,989	2,193,295

X Not applicable. [1] Based on the North American Industry Classification System (NAICS) 2012; see text, Section 15. [2] Includes poultry and poultry products sold.

Source: U.S. Department of Agriculture, National Agricultural Statistics Service, *2012 Census of Agriculture*, Vol. 1, May 2014. See also <http://www.agcensus.usda.gov/Publications/index.php>.

Table 850. Farms—Number and Acreage: 2000 to 2016

[As of June (2,167 represents 2,167,000). Based on 1974 census definition; for definition of farms and farmland, see text, this section. Data for census years have been adjusted for underenumeration]

Year	Unit	2000	2005	2010	2011	2012	2013	2014	2015	2016
Number of farms.........	1,000	2,167	2,099	2,150	2,131	2,110	2,102	2,085	2,068	2,060
Land in farms............	Million acres	945	928	916	914	915	914	913	912	911
Average per farm........	Acres	436	442	426	429	433	435	438	441	442

Source: U.S. Department of Agriculture, National Agricultural Statistics Service, *Farm Numbers and Land in Farms, Final Estimates, 2008–2012* and earlier reports; and *Farms and Land in Farms 2016 Summary*, February 2017. See also <http://www.nass.usda.gov/Publications/index.asp>.

Table 851. Farms—Number and Acreage by State: 2010 and 2016

[2,150 represents 2,150,000. As of June 1. See headnote, Table 850]

State	Farms (1,000) 2010	Farms (1,000) 2016	Land in farms (mil. acres) 2010	Land in farms (mil. acres) 2016	Acreage per farm 2010	Acreage per farm 2016	State	Farms (1,000) 2010	Farms (1,000) 2016	Land in farms (mil. acres) 2010	Land in farms (mil. acres) 2016	Acreage per farm 2010	Acreage per farm 2016
United States.....	**2,150**	**2,060**	**915.7**	**911.0**	**426**	**442**	Missouri............	103	97	28.7	28.5	279	294
							Montana............	29	27	60.6	59.7	2,082	2,179
Alabama...........	46	44	8.9	8.9	193	202	Nebraska...........	50	48	45.4	45.2	917	934
Alaska.............	1	1	0.9	0.8	1,181	1,092	Nevada............	4	4	5.9	6.0	1,579	1,490
Arizona............	18	20	24.8	25.9	1,378	1,321	New Hampshire....	4	4	(Z)	(Z)	109	107
Arkansas..........	47	43	13.7	13.7	291	319	New Jersey........	10	9	0.7	0.7	74	79
California..........	79	77	25.5	25.4	322	331	New Mexico........	22	25	43.4	43.2	1,973	1,756
Colorado..........	36	34	31.5	31.7	868	938	New York..........	36	36	7.1	7.3	197	206
Connecticut........	6	6	(Z)	(Z)	75	73	North Carolina......	52	48	8.4	8.2	163	171
Delaware..........	3	3	0.5	0.5	200	200	North Dakota.......	31	30	39.5	39.1	1,262	1,312
Florida.............	48	47	9.4	9.4	197	200	Ohio..............	75	75	13.8	14.0	184	188
Georgia............	44	42	9.7	9.5	219	227	Oklahoma..........	83	78	34.7	34.2	417	438
Hawaii.............	7	7	1.1	1.1	153	160	Oregon............	37	34	16.2	16.3	439	474
Idaho.............	25	24	11.5	11.8	453	486	Pennsylvania......	61	58	7.7	7.6	126	131
Illinois.............	76	72	26.9	26.7	354	370	Rhode Island.......	1	1	(Z)	(Z)	56	56
Indiana............	61	58	14.8	14.7	242	256	South Carolina......	26	25	5.0	5.0	192	204
Iowa..............	89	87	30.6	30.5	343	351	South Dakota......	32	31	43.4	43.3	1,361	1,397
Kansas............	63	60	46.2	45.9	732	770	Tennessee.........	73	67	10.8	10.8	148	162
Kentucky..........	80	76	13.4	12.9	167	170	Texas.............	249	242	131.6	129.8	530	537
Louisiana..........	29	27	8.0	7.8	274	288	Utah..............	18	18	11.0	11.0	629	608
Maine.............	8	8	1.4	1.5	173	177	Vermont...........	7	7	1.2	1.3	172	171
Maryland..........	13	12	2.1	2.0	164	165	Virginia...........	47	45	8.2	8.1	176	181
Massachusetts.....	8	8	0.5	0.5	69	67	Washington........	38	36	14.6	14.7	382	409
Michigan...........	53	51	10.0	10.0	187	194	West Virginia.......	22	21	3.6	3.6	161	175
Minnesota..........	77	73	26.3	25.9	342	353	Wisconsin..........	73	69	14.7	14.4	201	210
Mississippi.........	40	36	10.9	10.7	275	296	Wyoming...........	12	12	30.0	30.3	2,586	2,612

Z Less than 500,000 acres.

Source: U.S. Department of Agriculture, National Agricultural Statistics Service, "Quick Stats," <http://quickstats.nass.usda.gov/>, accessed February 2017. See also <http://www.nass.usda.gov/Statistics_by_Subject/>.

Table 852. Farms by Size and Type of Organization: 1982 to 2012

[2,241 represents 2,241,000. For comments on adjustment, see text, this section]

Size and type of organization	Unit	Not adjusted for coverage 1982	Not adjusted for coverage 1987	Not adjusted for coverage 1992	Not adjusted for coverage 1997	Adjusted for coverage [1] 1997	Adjusted for coverage [1] 2002	Adjusted for coverage [1] 2007	Adjusted for coverage [1] 2012
Farms.................................	1,000	2,241	2,088	1,925	1,912	2,216	2,129	2,205	2,109
Land in farms........................	Mil. acres	987	964	946	932	955	938	922	915
Average size of farm....................	Acres	440	462	491	487	431	441	418	434
Farms by size:									
1 to 9 acres...........................	1,000	188	183	166	154	205	179	233	224
10 to 49 acres.........................	1,000	449	412	388	411	531	564	620	590
50 to 179 acres........................	1,000	712	645	584	593	694	659	661	634
180 to 499 acres.......................	1,000	527	478	428	403	428	389	368	346
500 to 999 acres.......................	1,000	204	200	186	176	179	162	150	143
1,000 to 1,999 acres....................	1,000	97	102	102	101	103	99	93	91
2,000 acres or more....................	1,000	65	67	71	75	74	78	80	82
Farms by type of organization:									
Family or individual....................	1,000	1,946	1,809	1,653	1,643	1,923	1,910	1,906	1,829
Partnership............................	1,000	223	200	187	169	186	130	174	138
Corporation...........................	1,000	60	67	73	84	90	74	96	107
Other [2]................................	1,000	12	12	12	15	17	16	28	36

[1] Data have been adjusted for coverage; see text, this section. [2] Cooperative, estate or trust, institutional, etc.

Source: U.S. Department of Agriculture, National Agricultural Statistics Service, *2012 Census of Agriculture*, Vol. 1, May 2014, and earlier reports. See also <http://www.agcensus.usda.gov/Publications/index.php>.

Table 853. Farms—Number and Acreage by Size of Farm: 2007 and 2012

[2,205 represents 2,205,000. Data have been adjusted for coverage; see text, this section]

Size of farm	Number of farms (1,000)		Land in farms (mil. acres)		Cropland harvested (mil. acres)		Percent distribution, 2012		
	2007	2012	2007	2012	2007	2012	Number of farms	All land in farms	Cropland harvested
Total	2,205	2,109	922.1	914.5	309.6	315.0	100.0	100.0	100.0
Under 10 acres	233	224	1.1	1.0	0.3	0.3	10.6	0.1	0.1
10 to 49 acres	620	590	15.9	15.1	4.3	4.1	27.9	1.7	1.3
50 to 69 acres	154	154	8.9	8.9	2.5	2.5	7.3	1.0	0.8
70 to 99 acres	192	185	15.8	15.2	4.5	4.4	8.8	1.7	1.4
100 to 139 acres	175	166	20.3	19.3	5.8	5.7	7.9	2.1	1.8
140 to 179 acres	139	129	22.0	20.3	6.6	6.3	6.1	2.2	2.0
180 to 219 acres	88	84	17.3	16.7	5.6	5.6	4.0	1.8	1.8
220 to 259 acres	68	64	16.3	15.1	5.7	5.5	3.0	1.7	1.8
260 to 499 acres	213	198	75.9	70.6	30.4	28.8	9.4	7.7	9.1
500 to 999 acres	150	143	104.1	99.0	51.6	49.5	6.8	10.8	15.7
1,000 to 1,999 acres	93	91	127.6	125.1	69.8	68.7	4.3	13.7	21.8
2,000 acres or more	80	82	496.9	508.2	122.5	133.6	3.9	55.6	42.4

Source: U.S. Department of Agriculture, National Agricultural Statistics Service, *2012 Census of Agriculture*, Vol. 1, May 2014. See also <http://www.agcensus.usda.gov/Publications/index.php>.

Table 854. Farms—Number, Acreage, and Value by Tenure of Principal Operator and Type of Organization: 2007 and 2012

[2,205 represents 2,205,000. Full owners own all the land they operate. Part owners own a part and rent from others the rest of the land they operate. A principal operator is the person primarily responsible for the on-site, day-to-day operation of the farm or ranch business. Data have been adjusted for coverage; see text, this section]

Item and year	Unit	Total [1]	Tenure of operator			Type of organization		
			Full owner	Part owner	Tenant	Family or individual	Partner-ship	Corpora-tion
NUMBER OF FARMS								
2007	1,000	2,205	1,522	542	141	1,906	174	96
2012	1,000	2,109	1,428	533	148	1,829	138	107
Under 50 acres	1,000	813	699	64	51	738	33	30
50 to 179 acres	1,000	634	465	130	39	568	34	21
180 to 499 acres	1,000	346	179	141	26	296	27	17
500 to 999 acres	1,000	143	46	83	14	113	15	12
1,000 acres or more	1,000	173	40	115	19	115	30	26
LAND IN FARMS								
2007	Mil. acres	922	344	496	82	574	161	125
2012	Mil. acres	915	336	491	87	562	156	131
Value of land and buildings, 2012	Bil. dol.	2,269	795	1,270	203	1,535	355	318
Value of farm products sold, 2012	Bil. dol.	395	141	210	43	197	86	105

[1] Includes other types, not shown separately.

Source: U.S. Department of Agriculture, National Agricultural Statistics Service, *2012 Census of Agriculture*, Vol. 1, May 2014, and earlier reports. See also <http://www.agcensus.usda.gov/Publications/index.php>.

Table 855. Corporate Farms—Characteristics by Type: 2002 to 2012

[131.3 represents 131,300,000. Data have been adjusted for coverage; see text, this section and Appendix III]

Item	Unit	All corpora-tions	Family held corporations			Other corporations		
			Total	1 to 10 stock-holders	11 or more stock-holders	Total	1 to 10 stock-holders	11 or more stock-holders
Farms:								
2002	Number	73,752	66,667	65,017	1,650	7,085	6,010	1,075
2007	Number	96,074	85,837	83,796	2,041	10,237	9,330	907
2012								
Farms	Number	106,716	95,142	92,834	2,308	11,574	10,438	1,136
Percent distribution	Percent	100.0	89.2	87.0	2.2	10.8	9.8	1.1
Land in farms	Mil. acres	131.3	118.8	110.8	8.0	12.5	8.8	3.7
Average per farm	Acres	1,230	1,249	1,194	3,454	1,078	843	3,241
Value of—								
Land and buildings	Bil. dol.	318.3	283.9	269.0	15.0	34.4	24.4	10.0
Average per farm	$1,000	2,983	2,984	2,897	6,487	2,969	2,334	8,807
Farm products sold	Bil. dol.	104.9	83.7	75.7	7.9	21.2	12.4	8.8
Average per farm	$1,000	983	879	816	3,431	1,833	1,188	7,756

Source: U.S. Department of Agriculture, National Agricultural Statistics Service, *2012 Census of Agriculture*, Vol. 1, May 2014, and earlier reports. See also <http://www.agcensus.usda.gov/Publications/index.php>.

Table 856. Farms—Number, Acreage, and Value by State: 2007 and 2012

[2,205 represents 2,205,000. Data have been adjusted for coverage; see text, this section and Appendix III]

State	Number of farms (1,000)		Land in farms (mil. acres)		Average size of farm (acres)		Total value of land and buildings (bil. dol.)		Market value of agricultural products sold and government payments, 2012 (mil. dol.)	Total number of operators, 2012 (1,000)
	2007	2012	2007	2012	2007	2012	2007	2012		
U.S.............	2,205	2,109	922.1	914.5	418	434	1,744.3	2,268.5	402,698	3,233
AL................	49	43	9.0	8.9	185	206	20.7	23.7	5,659	64
AK................	1	1	0.9	0.8	1,285	1,094	0.3	0.5	61	1
AZ................	16	20	26.1	26.2	1,670	1,312	19.5	16.9	3,763	34
AR................	49	45	13.9	13.8	281	306	32.5	36.4	10,039	70
CA................	81	78	25.4	25.6	313	328	162.5	160.5	42,774	126
CO................	37	36	31.6	31.9	853	881	33.1	40.8	7,946	59
CT................	5	6	0.4	0.4	83	73	5.1	4.8	555	10
DE................	3	2	0.5	0.5	200	208	5.3	4.2	1,284	4
FL................	47	48	9.2	9.5	195	200	52.1	49.7	7,742	75
GA................	48	42	10.2	9.6	212	228	31.6	29.7	9,397	62
HI................	8	7	1.1	1.1	149	161	8.6	10.2	667	11
ID................	25	25	11.5	11.8	454	474	22.7	26.1	7,901	41
IL................	77	75	26.8	26.9	348	359	101.5	169.8	17,740	109
IN................	61	59	14.8	14.7	242	251	52.9	78.8	11,478	90
IA................	93	89	30.7	30.6	331	345	104.2	195.6	31,604	132
KS................	66	62	46.3	46.1	707	747	42.2	75.3	18,903	93
KY................	85	77	14.0	13.0	164	169	37.5	39.5	5,237	114
LA................	30	28	8.1	7.9	269	281	16.7	20.2	3,948	42
ME................	8	8	1.3	1.5	166	178	3.0	3.4	773	13
MD................	13	12	2.1	2.0	160	166	14.4	14.1	2,307	19
MA................	8	8	0.5	0.5	67	68	6.4	5.5	500	13
MI................	56	52	10.0	9.9	179	191	34.2	40.0	8,834	80
MN................	81	75	26.9	26.0	332	349	69.2	109.9	21,748	111
MS................	42	38	11.5	10.9	273	287	21.4	24.8	6,622	56
MO................	108	99	29.0	28.3	269	285	63.2	78.9	9,489	153
MT................	30	28	61.4	59.8	2,079	2,134	47.6	46.9	4,440	45
NE................	48	50	45.5	45.3	953	907	52.7	107.9	23,461	76
NV................	3	4	5.9	5.9	1,873	1,429	3.6	5.5	767	7
NH................	4	4	0.5	0.5	113	108	2.3	2.0	194	7
NJ................	10	9	0.7	0.7	71	79	11.3	9.1	1,015	15
NM................	21	25	43.2	43.2	2,066	1,748	14.6	18.7	2,621	38
NY................	36	36	7.2	7.2	197	202	16.3	18.7	5,490	57
NC................	53	50	8.5	8.4	160	168	34.7	36.5	12,708	74
ND................	32	31	39.7	39.3	1,241	1,268	30.6	56.0	11,332	45
OH................	76	75	14.0	14.0	184	185	49.2	67.5	10,293	116
OK................	87	80	35.1	34.4	405	428	40.6	46.0	7,386	122
OR................	39	35	16.4	16.3	425	460	31.0	30.7	4,970	59
PA................	63	59	7.8	7.7	124	130	37.3	41.8	7,487	92
RI................	1	1	0.1	0.1	56	56	1.1	1.0	62	2
SC................	26	25	4.9	5.0	189	197	14.0	14.8	3,087	37
SD................	31	32	43.7	43.3	1,401	1,352	39.1	73.0	10,454	49
TN................	79	68	11.0	10.9	138	160	37.1	38.7	3,679	102
TX................	247	249	130.4	130.2	527	523	165.6	218.1	26,020	376
UT................	17	18	11.1	11.0	664	609	13.9	16.0	1,840	29
VT................	7	7	1.2	1.3	177	171	3.6	4.0	790	12
VA................	47	46	8.1	8.3	171	180	34.1	35.8	3,836	70
WA................	39	37	15.0	14.7	381	396	29.8	33.9	9,280	61
WV................	24	21	3.7	3.6	157	168	8.8	8.9	814	32
WI................	78	70	15.2	14.6	194	209	49.0	57.2	11,982	111
WY................	11	12	30.2	30.4	2,726	2,587	15.5	20.6	1,718	20

Source: U.S. Department of Agriculture, National Agricultural Statistics Service, *2012 Census of Agriculture*, Vol. 1, May 2014. See also <http://www.agcensus.usda.gov/Publications/index.php>.

Table 857. Farms—Number, Acreage, and Value of Sales by Size of Sales: 2007 and 2012

[2,205 represents 2,205,000. Data have been adjusted for coverage; see text, this section and Appendix III]

Market value of agricultural products sold	Farms (1,000)	Acreage		Value of sales		Percent distribution		
		Total (mil.)	Average per farm	Total (mil. dol.)	Average per farm (dol.)	Farms	Acreage	Value of sales
2007								
Total..........................	2,205	922.1	418	297,220	134,807	100.0	100.0	100.0
Less than $2,500......................	900	121.5	135	435	483	40.8	13.2	0.1
$2,500 to $4,999.....................	200	17.5	87	718	3,585	9.1	1.9	0.2
$5,000 to $9,999.....................	219	27.6	126	1,553	7,104	9.9	3.0	0.5
$10,000 to $24,999...................	248	65.8	265	3,960	15,949	11.3	7.1	1.3
$25,000 to $49,999...................	155	59.8	386	5,480	35,419	7.0	6.5	1.8
$50,000 to $99,999...................	125	78.2	623	8,961	71,429	5.7	8.5	3.0
$100,000 to $249,999...............	148	147.6	1,000	24,213	164,156	6.7	16.0	8.1
$250,000 to $499,999...............	93	140.7	1,507	33,410	357,811	4.2	15.3	11.2
$500,000 to $999,999...............	61	119.4	1,965	42,691	702,417	2.8	13.0	14.4
$1,000,000 or more.................	56	144.0	2,593	175,800	3,167,050	2.5	15.6	59.1
2012								
Total..........................	2,109	914.5	434	394,644	187,097	100.0	100.0	100.0
Less than $2,500......................	788	118.4	150	380	483	37.4	12.9	0.1
$2,500 to $4,999.....................	191	19.6	102	688	3,592	9.1	2.1	0.2
$5,000 to $9,999.....................	214	25.4	119	1,522	7,104	10.2	2.8	0.4
$10,000 to $24,999...................	245	59.4	243	3,908	15,954	11.6	6.5	1.0
$25,000 to $49,999...................	153	48.4	316	5,418	35,440	7.2	5.3	1.4
$50,000 to $99,999...................	129	64.0	495	9,251	71,507	6.1	7.0	2.3
$100,000 to $249,999...............	139	115.9	835	22,822	164,328	6.6	12.7	5.8
$250,000 to $499,999...............	94	121.1	1,288	33,964	361,045	4.5	13.2	8.6
$500,000 to $999,999...............	76	129.4	1,704	54,686	719,996	3.6	14.2	13.9
$1,000,000 or more.................	79	212.9	2,687	262,006	3,307,109	3.8	23.3	66.4

Source: U.S. Department of Agriculture, National Agricultural Statistics Service, *2012 Census of Agriculture*, Vol. 1, May 2014, and earlier reports. See also <http://www.agcensus.usda.gov/Publications/index.php>.

Table 858. Farms—Number, Value of Sales, and Government Payments by Economic Class of Farm: 2007 and 2012

[2,205 represents 2,205,000. Economic class of farm is a combination of market value of agricultural products sold and federal farm program payments. Data have been adjusted for coverage; see text, this section and Appendix III]

Economic class	Number of farms (1,000)			Market value of agricultural products sold and government payments (mil. dol.)			
	2007, total	2012		2007, total	2012		
		Total	Receiving government payments		Total	Agricultural products sold	Government payments
Total..............................	2,205	2,109	811	305,204	402,698	394,644	8,053
Less than $1,000...................	500	429	36	96	80	64	16
$1,000 to $2,499....................	271	237	72	448	393	291	101
$2,500 to $4,999....................	246	231	69	884	832	652	180
$5,000 to $9,999....................	255	249	78	1,811	1,769	1,459	310
$10,000 to $24,999.................	274	272	102	4,364	4,323	3,768	555
$25,000 to $49,999.................	164	162	80	5,795	5,736	5,225	510
$50,000 to $99,999.................	129	134	83	9,219	9,575	8,988	586
$100,000 to $249,999..............	149	142	102	24,401	23,196	22,221	975
$250,000 to $499,999..............	96	96	75	34,367	34,463	33,338	1,125
$500,000 to $999,999..............	64	78	60	44,578	55,663	54,256	1,408
$1,000,000 to $2,499,999.........	42	58	42	62,751	90,534	89,003	1,531
$2,500,000 to $4,999,999.........	10	15	10	33,190	50,511	50,002	509
$5 million or more..................	6	9	4	83,300	125,624	125,376	248

Source: U.S. Department of Agriculture, National Agricultural Statistics Service, *2012 Census of Agriculture*, Vol. 1, May 2014. See also <http://www.agcensus.usda.gov/Publications/index.php>.

Table 859. Family Farm Household Income and Wealth, 2011 to 2015, and by Farm Type, 2015

[In dollars, except for number of farms. Based on Agricultural Resource Management Survey (ARMS) Phase III. A family farm is defined as one in which the majority of the ownership of the farm business is held by related individuals. Nearly all farms (99 percent in 2015) are family farms. The farm operator is the person who runs the farm, making the day-to-day management decisions. The operator could be an owner, hired manager, cash tenant, share tenant, and/or a partner. If land is rented or worked on shares, the tenant or renter is the operator. For multiple-operator farms, a principal operator is identified as the individual making most of the day-to-day decisions about the operation. In 2015, 39 percent of farms had more than one operator, and 65 percent of secondary operators were the spouses of principal operators; for these, both operators are considered part of the principal operator household. Minus sign (-) indicates loss]

Item	2011	2012	2013	2014	2015 Total	2015 ERS farm typology Rural residence farms [1]	2015 ERS farm typology Intermediate farms [2]	2015 ERS farm typology Commercial farms [3]
Number of family farms	**2,114,668**	**2,043,483**	**2,045,352**	**2,053,008**	**2,032,300**	**1,215,011**	**631,942**	**185,346**
INCOME PER FAMILY FARM HOUSEHOLD								
Net earnings from farming activities	14,625	25,038	30,639	31,025	24,740	-634	6,218	254,220
Off-farm income of the household	72,665	86,486	90,481	103,140	95,140	115,337	64,120	68,511
Earned income	51,376	63,783	66,053	71,754	65,814	84,659	36,510	42,193
Unearned income	21,289	22,703	24,428	31,386	29,326	30,678	27,610	26,318
Total household income, mean [4]	87,290	111,524	121,120	134,164	119,880	114,703	70,338	322,731
WEALTH PER FAMILY FARM HOUSEHOLD								
Assets, mean [4]	1,131,522	1,464,467	1,466,569	1,674,467	1,590,217	1,206,746	1,385,303	4,802,667
Farm assets	856,589	950,818	948,116	998,082	1,003,551	554,188	946,703	4,143,121
Non-farm assets	274,933	513,649	518,453	676,385	586,666	652,558	438,601	659,546
Debt, mean [4]	120,213	175,241	153,593	205,024	190,885	123,044	151,098	771,259
Farm debt	69,387	78,333	80,655	100,288	101,430	31,431	78,974	636,864
Non-farm debt	50,827	96,908	72,938	104,736	89,454	91,612	72,124	134,395
Net worth, mean [4]	1,011,309	1,289,226	1,312,976	1,469,443	1,399,332	1,083,703	1,234,205	4,031,408
Farm net worth	787,203	872,485	867,461	897,794	902,121	522,757	867,729	3,506,257
Non-farm net worth	224,106	416,741	445,515	571,649	497,211	560,946	366,476	525,151

[1] Farms in which the principal operator is retired or has a major occupation other than farming. [2] Beginning in 2012, farms with farming as the operator's major occupation, but with less than $350,000 in gross sales. [3] Beginning in 2012, farms with more than $350,000 in gross sales. [4] For definition of mean see Guide to Tabular Presentation.

Source: U.S. Department of Agriculture, Economic Research Service, *Agricultural Income and Finance Situation and Outlook*, December 2011; and "Farm Household Income and Characteristics," <http://www.ers.usda.gov/data-products/farm-household-income-and-characteristics.aspx>, accessed January 2017.

Table 860. Farm Type, Acreage, and Production: 2000 to 2015

[2,166 represents 2,166,000. Based on Agricultural Resource Management Survey (ARMS). The farm typology used by the Economic Research Service was revised in 2013, and has been applied to data beginning in 2011. For more information, see <https://www.ers.usda.gov/publications/pub-details/?pubid=43744>]

Type of farm	Unit	2000	2005	2009	2010	2011	2012	2013	2014	2015
Total farms:										
Number of farms	1,000	2,166	2,095	2,192	2,193	2,173	2,102	2,095	2,076	2,059
Total value of production	Mil. dol.	177,286	215,295	278,067	286,792	335,259	372,545	383,407	420,251	368,144
Total acres operated	Mil.	995	916	913	912	902	870	897	933	850
Acres operated per farm	Acres	459	437	417	416	415	414	428	449	413
Commercial farms: [1]										
Number of farms	1,000	178	216	271	264	224	243	241	220	212
Total value of production	Mil. dol.	121,202	166,566	230,717	240,751	249,696	288,342	296,218	329,903	279,081
Total acres operated	Mil.	392	418	443	482	432	410	468	510	439
Acres operated per farm	Acres	2,205	1,939	1,635	1,829	1,931	1,691	1,947	2,319	2,066
Intermediate farms: [2]										
Number of farms	1,000	668	550	577	618	685	701	695	632	632
Total value of production	Mil. dol.	41,813	33,872	30,830	30,325	63,250	64,403	62,494	62,630	61,283
Total acres operated	Mil.	392	307	270	242	279	278	257	229	232
Acres operated per farm	Acres	587	558	469	392	407	397	370	363	367
Residence farms: [3]										
Number of farms	1,000	1,320	1,329	1,344	1,311	1,264	1,158	1,160	1,225	1,215
Total value of production	Mil. dol.	14,272	14,856	16,521	15,716	22,313	19,801	24,695	27,717	27,780
Total acres operated	Mil.	211	191	200	187	191	182	172	194	179
Acres operated per farm	Acres	160	144	149	143	151	157	148	158	147

[1] Data for 2010 and earlier include farms with sales of $250,000 or more. Beginning in 2011, data are for farms with $350,000 or more gross cash farm income and nonfamily farms. [2] Data for 2010 and earlier include small family farms whose operators report farming as their major occupation. Beginning in 2011, data are for farms with less than $350,000 in gross cash farm income and a principal operator whose primary occupation is farming. [3] Data for 2010 and earlier include retirement and residential farms. Beginning in 2011, data are for farms with less than $350,000 in gross cash farm income and where the principal operator is either retired or has a primary occupation other than farming.

Source: U.S. Department of Agriculture, Economic Research Service, "ARMS Farm Financial and Crop Production Practices," <http://www.ers.usda.gov/data-products/arms-farm-financial-and-crop-production-practices.aspx>, accessed June 2017.

Table 861. Farms with Renewable Energy Systems by Type of Farm: 2012

[Farms reporting renewable energy systems on their operation. Based on the 1974 definition of farms and farmland, see text, this section. Farm types are based on the USDA's Economic Research Service typology. Family farms, farms in which the majority of the business is owned by the operator and individuals related to the operator, are classified based on the gross cash farm income (GCFI). GCFI includes sales of crops and livestock, fees for delivering commodities under production contracts, government payments, and farm-related income]

Energy system	All farms	Small family farms (GCFI less than $350,000)					Mid-sized family farms (GCFI $350,000 to $999,999)	Large-scale family farms (GCFI greater than $1,000,000)	Non-family farms [3]
		Total small family farms	Retirement or off-farm occupation [1]	Farm-occupation farms [2]				
				Low sales (GCFI less than $150,000)	Moderate sales (GCFI $350,00 to $999,999)			
Number of farms, total..............	2,109,303	1,861,216	1,423,432	342,440	95,344	118,340	59,537	70,210
Number of farms with any renewable energy system......	**57,299**	**48,307**	**34,473**	**10,476**	**3,358**	**4,391**	**2,281**	**2,320**
Percent of all farms....................	2.7	2.6	2.4	3.1	3.5	3.7	3.8	3.3
By type of system:								
Solar panels............................	36,331	32,217	23,005	7,464	1,748	1,742	802	1,570
Wind turbines..........................	9,054	6,646	4,460	1,485	701	1,253	713	442
Methane digesters.....................	537	344	258	68	18	32	111	50
Geoexchange systems................	9,403	7,809	6,122	1,107	580	906	446	242
Small hydro systems..................	1,323	1,168	843	275	50	51	21	83
Biodiesel................................	4,099	3,061	1,958	734	369	547	283	208
Ethanol..................................	2,364	1,623	1,021	338	264	443	211	87
Other.....................................	1243	1121	755	305	61	47	9	66
Wind rights leased to others...........	10,181	6,851	4,402	1,372	1,077	1,893	939	498

[1] Farms in which the principal operator is retired or has a major occupation other than farming. [2] Small family farms with farming as the operator's major occupation. [3] Any farm where the operator and persons related to the operator do not own a majority of the business.

Source: U.S. Department of Agriculture, National Agricultural Statistics Service, *2012 Census of Agriculture, Farm Typology*, Volume 2, January 2015. See also <http://www.agcensus.usda.gov/Publications/index.php>.

Table 862. Sales of Agricultural Products Direct to Consumers: 2002 to 2012

[812,204 represents $812,204,000. Farm operations who sell directly to consumers for human consumption at roadside stands, farmers' markets, pick-your-own, on-farm stores, and community support agricultural arrangements. Excludes non-edible products such as nursery crops, cut flowers, and wool, but includes livestock sales. Sales of agricultural products by vertically integrated operations through their own processing and marketing operations are also excluded]

Size of farm	Number of farms			Value of direct sales ($1,000)		
	2002	2007	2012	2002	2007	2012
Total, all farms with direct sales................	**116,733**	**136,817**	**144,530**	**812,204**	**1,211,270**	**1,309,827**
Percent of all farms................................	5.5	6.2	6.9	0.4	0.4	0.3
BY VALUE OF SALES						
$1 to $499..	32,420	35,440	37,398	6,645	7,217	7,770
$500 to $999...	19,145	20,547	20,170	13,124	14,013	13,685
$1,000 to $4,999....................................	42,660	49,957	52,750	93,611	113,960	121,750
$5,000 to $9,999....................................	9,598	13,060	14,452	64,517	88,174	97,308
$10,000 to $24,999.................................	7,256	10,032	11,045	108,766	151,063	164,774
$25,000 to $49,999.................................	2,831	3,903	4,244	96,322	133,328	143,722
$50,000 or more....................................	2,823	3,878	4,471	429,220	703,515	760,819
BY PRIMARY ACTIVITY OF FARM [1, 2]						
Oilseed and grains.................................	5,443	7,052	8,715	30,629	37,930	63,321
Vegetables and melons............................	14,487	17,961	23,218	198,175	335,311	420,466
Fruit and tree nuts.................................	14,381	17,161	18,399	196,508	343,878	319,523
Greenhouse and nursery [3]......................	4,711	3,834	6,031	74,524	50,169	59,845
Beef cattle ranching and farming...................	27,133	35,984	35,980	76,955	141,427	147,315
Dairy cattle and milk production...................	3,180	3,221	2,982	41,602	52,594	43,546
Hog and pig farming...............................	4,745	5,227	3,897	16,085	18,970	15,970
Poultry and egg production........................	5,585	8,833	9,999	24,345	54,898	36,782
Sheep and goat farming...........................	7,653	9,127	10,198	10,993	16,613	19,647

[1] Based on the farms' North American Industry Classification (NAICS) codes, indicating main commodity type produced. [2] Includes other types, not shown separately. [3] Includes floriculture.

Source: U.S. Department of Agriculture, National Agricultural Statistics Service, *2012 Census of Agriculture*, Vol. 1, May 2014, and earlier reports. See also <http://www.agcensus.usda.gov/Publications/index.php>.

Table 863. Organic Agriculture—Number of Farms, Acreage, and Value of Sales, 2008 and 2014, and for Leading States, 2014

[3,164,995 represents $3,164,995,000. Includes all known organic producers that are either certified organic or exempt from certification in the United States (those grossing less than $5,000 annually from organic sales). Organic food must be produced without the use of conventional pesticides, petroleum-based or sewage sludge-based fertilizers, herbicides, pesticides, genetic engineering (biotechnology), antibiotics, growth hormones, or irradiation. Animals raised on an organic operation must be fed organic feed and given access to the outdoors. Land must have no prohibited substances applied to it for at least 3 years before the harvest of an organic crop]

Year and leading states	Organic farms (number)	Organic land (acres)	Value of sales ($1,000)[1]			
			Total product sales	Crops[2]	Livestock and poultry	Livestock and poultry products
2008	14,540	4,077,337	3,164,995	1,942,317	316,470	906,207
2014, total[3]	14,093	3,670,560	5,454,979	3,290,188	660,340	1,504,452
California	2,805	687,168	2,231,241	1,659,305	271,354	300,582
Washington	716	73,841	514,897	386,701	(D)	(D)
Pennsylvania	679	97,617	313,456	91,362	112,467	109,627
Oregon	525	204,166	237,121	127,568	17,630	91,923
Wisconsin	1,228	228,605	200,800	48,513	24,908	127,379
Texas	234	126,639	199,094	78,169	17,680	103,245
New York	917	212,701	164,203	52,698	16,011	95,494
Colorado	157	115,116	146,799	52,198	(D)	(D)
Michigan	332	58,085	124,612	(D)	(D)	70,698
Iowa	612	97,448	102,626	50,741	(D)	(D)

D Data withheld to limit disclosure. [1] Value of sales of commodities; excludes value-added organic products. [2] Includes nursery and greenhouse. [3] Includes other states, not shown separately.

Source: U.S. Department of Agriculture, National Agricultural Statistics Service, *2012 Census of Agriculture: Organic Survey (2014)*, Vol. 3, Special Studies, Part 4, September 2015, and earlier reports. See also <http://www.agcensus.usda.gov/Publications/Organic_Survey/>.

Table 864. Adoption of Genetically Engineered Crops: 2000 to 2017

[As percent of all crops planted. As of June. Based on June Agricultural Survey conducted by National Agricultural Statistical Services (NASS). Excludes conventionally bred herbicide tolerant varieties. Insect resistant varieties include only those containing bacillus thuringiensis (Bt). The Bt varieties include those that contain more than one gene that can resist different types of insects. Stacked gene varieties include only those varieties containing biotech traits for both herbicide tolerance and insect resistance]

Genetically engineered crop	2000	2005	2009	2010	2011	2012	2013	2014	2015	2016	2017
Corn	25	52	85	86	88	88	90	93	92	92	92
Insect resistant	18	26	17	16	16	15	5	4	4	3	3
Herbicide tolerant	6	17	22	23	23	21	14	13	12	13	12
Stacked gene	1	9	46	47	49	52	71	76	77	76	77
Cotton	61	79	88	93	90	94	90	96	94	93	96
Insect resistant	15	18	17	15	17	14	8	5	5	4	5
Herbicide tolerant	26	27	23	20	15	17	15	12	10	9	11
Stacked gene	20	34	48	58	58	63	67	79	79	80	80
Soybean	54	87	91	93	94	93	93	94	94	94	94
Insect resistant	(X)	(X)	(X)	(X)	(X)	(X)	(X)	(X)	(X)	(X)	(X)
Herbicide tolerant	54	87	91	93	94	93	93	94	94	94	94
Stacked gene	(X)	(X)	(X)	(X)	(X)	(X)	(X)	(X)	(X)	(X)	(X)

X Not applicable.

Source: U.S. Department of Agriculture, Economic Research Service, "Adoption of Genetically Engineered Crops in the U.S.," <http://www.ers.usda.gov/data-products/adoption-of-genetically-engineered-crops-in-the-us.aspx>, accessed July 2017.

Table 865. Farm Production Expenses: 2007 and 2012

[2,205 represents 2,205,000. Data have been adjusted for coverage; see text, this section and Appendix III]

Production expenses	2007			2012		
	Farms (1,000)	Expenses (mil. dol.)	Percent of total	Farms (1,000)	Expenses (mil. dol.)	Percent of total
Total	2,205	241,114	100.0	2,109	328,939	100.0
Fertilizer	1,148	18,107	7.5	1,012	28,533	8.7
Chemicals	919	10,075	4.2	1,000	16,460	5.0
Seeds, plants, vines, and trees	776	11,741	4.9	829	19,493	5.9
Livestock and poultry	491	38,004	15.8	545	41,586	12.6
Feed	1,136	49,095	20.4	1,256	75,706	23.0
Gasoline and fuel	2,149	12,912	5.4	1,988	16,573	5.0
Utilities	1,103	5,918	2.5	1,353	8,262	2.5
Supplies, repairs, and maintenance	1,992	15,897	6.6	1,663	18,868	5.7
Farm labor[1]	665	26,392	11.0	784	33,461	10.2
Customwork and custom hauling	362	4,091	1.7	462	6,611	2.0
Cash rent for land, buildings and grazing fees	490	13,275	5.5	560	21,001	6.4
Rent and lease for machinery, equipment, and farm share	109	1,385	0.6	133	2,332	0.7
Interest expense	667	10,881	4.5	784	12,124	3.7
Property taxes	1,996	6,223	2.6	1,980	7,429	2.3
Other production expenses	1,116	17,119	7.1	1,135	20,501	6.2

[1] Includes hired and contract labor.

Source: U.S. Department of Agriculture, National Agricultural Statistics Service, *2012 Census of Agriculture*, Vol. 1, May 2014. See also <http://www.agcensus.usda.gov/Publications/index.php>.

Table 866. Participation in Farm to School Programs by State: 2014

[Percent, except total. For school year ending in 2014. Farm to School programs include a variety of programs that connect schools with local producers and teaches children about farms and where their food comes from. Data shown for respondents to the Farm to School Census, which collected data on farm to school activities from public school districts, private schools, and charter schools]

| State | Number of school districts, charter schools, and private schools | Percent partici- in farm to school programs | Percent of respondents that participate in any farm to school activity— | | | | | | Spending on local food costs as a percent of total food costs [2] |
| | | | Participation in specific activity | | | | | | |
			Served local foods [1]	Edible school garden or orchard activities	Served products from school based gardens or farms	Organized field trips to farms	Had farmers visit cafeteria or classroom	Integrated farm to school concepts into educational curriculum	
United States....	**18,104**	**37.5**	**76.5**	**18.2**	**23.5**	**31.5**	**17.2**	**14.2**	**11.4**
Alabama...........	153	27.8	81.1	16.2	16.2	27.0	16.2	–	2.8
Alaska.............	47	76.3	86.2	20.7	31.0	20.7	0.0	17.2	5.8
Arizona...........	467	21.5	75.4	19.3	8.8	28.1	14.0	12.3	20.2
Arkansas..........	253	18.0	60.5	21.1	28.9	23.7	23.7	21.1	2.0
California.........	1,045	49.5	75.0	26.8	25.3	31.3	17.3	17.6	14.5
Colorado..........	186	39.9	88.5	23.0	34.4	32.8	29.5	19.7	4.8
Connecticut.......	187	63.8	87.5	15.9	19.3	25.0	19.3	12.5	4.7
Delaware..........	43	60.0	91.7	25.0	25.0	29.2	29.2	16.7	25.4
District of Columbia........	65	63.8	76.7	23.3	20.0	43.3	10.0	10.0	28.6
Florida.............	257	40.6	76.7	26.0	23.3	21.9	20.5	21.9	19.6
Georgia...........	180	54.3	78.0	29.3	25.6	30.5	35.4	30.5	16.9
Hawaii.............	25	47.4	88.9	77.8	33.3	55.6	44.4	44.4	24.2
Idaho..............	142	40.7	84.0	20.0	30.0	34.0	30.0	6.0	10.3
Illinois.............	1,355	22.0	46.4	13.8	11.0	32.6	17.7	12.7	5.9
Indiana............	550	27.0	67.3	10.3	10.3	35.5	9.3	9.3	18.4
Iowa...............	449	26.5	70.8	21.3	39.3	42.7	10.1	9.0	1.7
Kansas............	409	29.8	55.2	11.5	22.9	36.5	15.6	13.5	7.1
Kentucky..........	184	45.6	86.3	16.4	26.0	47.9	28.8	11.0	3.2
Louisiana..........	131	28.0	38.5	19.2	11.5	23.1	7.7	23.1	33.0
Maine.............	177	78.6	82.5	39.8	55.3	55.3	24.3	30.1	16.0
Maryland..........	44	65.9	92.6	7.4	11.1	29.6	33.3	11.1	26.1
Massachusetts.....	419	63.6	84.9	23.3	41.5	30.2	14.5	19.5	21.2
Michigan...........	869	39.7	78.4	9.3	13.6	27.1	11.0	6.8	20.1
Minnesota.........	689	47.0	82.3	14.5	25.7	28.1	18.9	11.2	13.1
Mississippi.........	158	49.1	62.3	1.9	13.2	24.5	7.5	5.7	4.8
Missouri...........	704	23.8	74.2	12.9	15.3	29.8	13.7	7.3	2.7
Montana...........	258	34.9	75.8	21.2	27.3	43.9	15.2	21.2	23.1
Nebraska..........	364	24.0	76.3	8.5	10.2	23.7	15.3	8.5	16.5
Nevada............	22	16.7	66.7	33.3	66.7	33.3	0.0	33.3	14.2
New Hampshire....	107	72.8	76.0	20.0	33.3	25.3	14.7	13.3	6.7
New Jersey........	679	38.8	76.7	18.2	19.5	17.0	10.7	15.7	18.1
New Mexico........	204	25.9	66.7	16.7	16.7	23.3	16.7	23.3	12.1
New York..........	649	56.8	82.1	14.0	23.7	33.0	16.5	10.0	10.7
North Carolina.....	171	61.5	81.9	14.5	4.8	32.5	19.3	20.5	6.9
North Dakota.......	195	29.2	71.4	14.3	26.2	31.0	26.2	9.5	18.5
Ohio...............	1,258	22.8	74.8	12.9	17.2	33.1	13.5	12.3	16.8
Oklahoma..........	539	19.3	73.7	10.5	14.0	14.0	15.8	7.0	14.9
Oregon............	234	51.2	84.4	32.1	38.5	46.8	22.0	30.3	26.9
Pennsylvania.......	940	37.3	74.3	17.7	20.4	34.5	14.6	11.9	16.1
Rhode Island.......	44	88.1	97.3	13.5	5.4	16.2	27.0	10.8	9.3
South Carolina.....	110	45.1	85.4	12.2	17.1	46.3	12.2	19.5	34.8
South Dakota......	149	28.4	84.8	18.2	24.2	27.3	9.1	3.0	3.0
Tennessee.........	190	40.9	83.1	4.6	23.1	36.9	21.5	6.2	20.2
Texas..............	1,238	24.2	63.4	12.4	10.3	11.9	7.2	10.8	22.1
Utah...............	102	33.7	89.7	17.2	17.2	31.0	13.8	6.9	15.6
Vermont...........	81	77.8	79.6	49.0	63.3	51.0	32.7	46.9	18.0
Virginia............	132	50.0	91.7	16.7	26.7	36.7	45.0	3.3	2.6
Washington........	308	43.6	81.0	20.0	17.1	23.8	23.8	15.2	9.1
West Virginia.......	69	73.7	92.9	23.8	40.5	35.7	23.8	16.7	12.3
Wisconsin..........	775	43.7	81.0	21.0	37.5	41.1	15.7	15.7	9.5
Wyoming...........	56	27.5	71.4	21.4	7.1	21.4	14.3	21.4	15.9
Guam..............	2	100.0	–	100.0	–	100.0	–	–	1.0
Puerto Rico.........	38	42.9	55.6	33.3	22.2	22.2	–	11.1	38.2
Virgin Islands.......	2	100.0	100.0	–	100.0	–	–	–	–

– Represents or rounds to zero. [1] The definition of "local" is determined by individual respondents. The Census questionnaire asked respondents how they defined "local" as it relates to their food procurement. Respondents could choose from one of seven options or specify a different definition: (a) produced within a 50 mile radius, (b) produced within a 100 mile radius, (c) produced within a 200 mile radius, (d) produced within a day's drive, (e) produced within the state, (f) produced within the region, and (g) geographic along with other restrictions. [2] For public school districts, charter schools, and private schools participating in farm to school programs. Costs include milk.

Source: U.S. Department of Agriculture, Food and Nutrition Service, "The Farm to School Census," <https://farmtoschoolcensus.fns.usda.gov/>, accessed September 2016. See also <http://www.fns.usda.gov/farmtoschool/>.

Table 867. Balance Sheet of the Farming Sector: 1990 to 2016

[In billions of dollars, except as indicated (841 represents $841,000,000,000). As of December 31. Balance sheet estimates exclude the personal portion of farm households' assets and debts]

Item	1990	2000	2008	2009	2010	2011	2012	2013	2014	2015	2016
Assets............................	**841**	**1,203**	**2,006**	**1,977**	**2,171**	**2,319**	**2,638**	**2,776**	**2,949**	**2,910**	**2,957**
Investments and other financial assets.....	38	57	84	72	135	107	139	86	111	88	78
Investment in cooperatives.................	(NA)	(NA)	5	5	6	6	7	8	8	7	7
Financial assets and net accounts receivable......................	(NA)	(NA)	79	67	130	102	132	78	103	80	71
Inventories......................................	97	110	164	152	168	185	182	192	210	187	180
Crops......................................	23	28	59	53	57	62	65	60	62	53	56
Livestock and poultry........................	71	77	86	80	91	101	96	111	128	118	109
Purchased inputs [1].........................	3	5	19	19	20	21	21	21	20	16	15
Real estate [2]................................	619	946	1,569	1,561	1,660	1,803	2,074	2,251	2,383	2,395	2,443
Value of machinery and motor vehicles [3]...	86	90	189	192	208	224	244	247	246	240	255
Debt [4]...........................	**131**	**164**	**261**	**268**	**279**	**294**	**298**	**315**	**345**	**357**	**373**
Real estate.............................	68	85	148	146	154	167	173	185	197	209	226
Commercial banks [5]........................	15	30	46	44	51	53	65	69	73	79	84
Farm Credit System........................	23	30	63	69	72	75	80	85	89	97	104
Farm Service Agency.......................	7	3	2	3	3	3	4	4	4	5	5
Farmer Mac [6]...............................	(NA)	(NA)	2	2	4	4	4	4	5	5	5
Individuals and others [5]...................	14	11	20	14	10	18	9	10	13	10	12
Storage facility loans.......................	–	(NA)	–	–	1	1	1	1	1	1	1
Life insurance companies...................	9	11	14	13	12	13	11	12	12	13	13
Nonreal estate.............................	63	79	113	122	125	127	124	130	148	148	148
Commercial banks [5]........................	31	45	56	57	56	59	60	64	71	73	73
Farm Credit System........................	10	17	36	39	39	41	43	44	48	48	49
Farm Service Agency........................	10	4	3	3	4	4	3	3	4	4	4
Individuals and others [5]...................	12	13	18	23	26	23	18	20	26	23	22
Equity....................................	**709**	**1,039**	**1,745**	**1,709**	**1,892**	**2,024**	**2,341**	**2,461**	**2,604**	**2,553**	**2,583**
FINANCIAL RATIOS (percent)											
Farm debt/asset ratio........................	15.6	13.6	13.0	13.6	12.9	12.7	11.3	11.4	11.7	12.3	12.6
Farm debt/equity ratio........................	18.5	15.8	15.0	15.7	14.7	14.6	12.7	12.8	13.3	14.0	14.5

– Represents or rounds to zero. NA Not available. [1] Purchased inputs represent value of prepaid expenses on supplies such as fertilizer and lime applied, seed, feed and other inputs purchased for next year's production. It also includes the seed, fertilizer, fuel, and other expenses already invested in crops. [2] Includes farmland, buildings and other service structures. Includes farm real estate assets leased from non-operator landlords. [3] Includes automobiles, trucks and farm machinery leased to farm operators. [4] Reflects outstanding agricultural sector debt where it is held rather than where it originated. Excludes debt on operator dwellings and for nonfarm purposes. Sector-level estimates of farm debt report aggregate data by lender type and therefore does not identify who owes the debt. [5] Beginning with 2012, farm sector debt held by savings associations is reported with the commercial bank lender group instead of the individuals and others grouping. [6] The Federal Agricultural Mortgage Corporation (known as Farmer Mac) operates as a federally sponsored enterprise providing a secondary market for agricultural real estate mortgage loans, rural housing mortgage loans, and rural utility cooperative loans.

Source: U.S. Department of Agriculture, Economic Research Service, "U.S. and State Farm Income and Wealth Statistics," <http://www.ers.usda.gov/data-products/farm-income-and-wealth-statistics.aspx>, accessed September 2017.

Table 868. Farm Sector Output and Value Added: 1990 to 2016

[In billions of dollars (179.9 represents $179,900,000,000). For definition of value added and explanation of chained dollars, see text, Section 13. Minus sign (-) indicates decrease]

Item	1990	2000	2005	2009	2010	2011	2012	2013	2014	2015	2016
CURRENT DOLLARS											
Farm output.............................	**179.9**	**204.3**	**253.0**	**301.2**	**328.2**	**387.0**	**400.9**	**432.9**	**438.9**	**395.3**	**375.7**
Cash receipts from farm marketings....	171.9	197.6	241.4	289.8	322.2	369.1	404.7	406.3	427.0	378.3	359.0
Farm products consumed on farms.....	0.6	0.3	0.4	0.4	0.4	0.4	0.4	0.5	0.6	0.6	0.6
Other farm income......................	4.9	8.4	11.3	12.7	12.5	15.0	14.9	15.5	15.6	15.0	16.4
Change in farm finished goods inventories.............................	2.4	-2.0	-0.1	-1.7	-6.8	2.5	-19.1	10.6	-4.3	1.3	-0.3
Less: Intermediate goods and services consumed..............................	102.1	128.3	148.5	191.4	198.5	220.7	249.4	246.0	271.2	249.9	239.0
Equals: Gross farm value added.......	**77.8**	**76.0**	**104.5**	**109.8**	**129.7**	**166.2**	**151.5**	**187.0**	**167.7**	**145.5**	**136.7**
Less: Consumption of fixed capital.......	17.9	22.8	27.8	34.2	35.0	35.1	37.8	41.4	45.8	48.6	50.1
Equals: Net farm value added..........	**59.8**	**53.2**	**76.7**	**75.6**	**94.7**	**131.2**	**113.7**	**145.6**	**122.0**	**96.8**	**86.6**
Compensation of employees.............	13.4	19.7	22.0	25.6	24.2	22.8	27.6	28.0	28.6	27.1	29.4
Taxes on production and imports........	3.8	4.6	5.3	6.7	6.9	7.3	7.5	7.8	9.3	8.7	9.6
Less: Subsidies to operators.............	7.6	20.0	20.9	10.4	10.5	8.8	8.9	9.1	8.3	9.4	11.6
Net operating surplus....................	50.3	48.8	70.2	53.7	74.2	109.9	87.5	118.9	92.3	70.4	59.2
CHAINED (2009) DOLLARS											
Farm output, total......................	**(NA)**	**276.2**	**290.5**	**301.2**	**304.5**	**292.3**	**289.4**	**307.5**	**315.0**	**319.2**	**342.3**
Cash receipts from farm marketings....	(NA)	268.0	275.8	289.8	298.4	278.0	291.2	287.3	302.0	300.9	322.4
Farm products consumed on farms.....	(NA)	0.4	0.4	0.4	0.4	0.3	0.3	0.3	0.4	0.5	0.5
Other farm income......................	(NA)	12.5	15.2	12.7	12.3	12.3	11.4	12.2	14.6	16.1	18.8
Change in farm finished goods inventories.............................	(NA)	-2.9	-0.1	-1.7	-6.5	1.6	-12.2	6.2	-2.9	0.8	-0.3
Less: Intermediate goods and services consumed..............................	(NA)	197.6	188.0	191.4	193.0	186.8	199.4	193.7	203.5	198.7	207.4
Equals: Gross farm value added.......	**(NA)**	**83.9**	**101.6**	**109.8**	**111.5**	**105.7**	**93.7**	**113.5**	**112.1**	**120.8**	**135.8**
Less: Consumption of fixed capital.......	(NA)	28.7	31.2	34.2	35.1	34.4	36.4	39.3	42.5	44.7	45.4
Equals: Net farm value added..........	**(NA)**	**56.1**	**70.5**	**75.6**	**76.4**	**71.7**	**60.3**	**75.7**	**72.5**	**79.0**	**94.0**

NA Not available.

Source: U.S. Bureau of Economic Analysis, National Income and Product Accounts, "Table 7.3.5 Farm Sector Output, Gross Value Added, and Net Value Added," and "Table 7.3.6 Real Farm Sector Output, Real Gross Value Added, and Real Net Value Added, Chained Dollars," <http://www.bea.gov/itable/>, accessed September 2017.

Table 869. Value Added to Economy by Agricultural Sector: 1990 to 2016

[In billions of dollars (188.5 represents $188,500,000,000). Value of agricultural sector production is the gross value of the commodities and services produced within a year. Net value-added is the sector's contribution to the national economy and is the value of farm sector production minus the value of intermediate goods used. Net farm income is the farm operators' share of income from the sector's production activities. Minus sign (-) indicates decrease]

Item	1990	2000	2008	2009	2010	2011	2012	2013	2014	2015	2016
Value of agricultural production	**188.5**	**218.4**	**352.3**	**324.4**	**344.1**	**410.0**	**439.2**	**472.8**	**473.3**	**429.6**	**399.0**
Value of crop production	83.2	95.0	173.8	164.7	168.1	199.3	212.9	233.6	206.0	183.9	189.0
Cotton	5.5	2.9	5.3	4.3	7.5	7.3	8.2	6.5	7.1	4.8	5.9
Feed crops	18.7	20.5	58.4	51.1	55.1	71.7	82.1	70.8	65.9	56.9	54.8
Food grains	7.5	6.5	17.7	15.3	14.3	16.5	19.3	17.2	16.1	12.3	11.3
Fruits and tree nuts	9.4	12.3	18.6	19.2	21.6	24.2	28.1	29.9	31.9	28.4	28.7
Oil crops	12.3	13.5	28.3	36.3	36.5	35.3	46.9	47.3	42.6	35.5	40.2
Tobacco	2.7	2.3	1.4	1.5	1.3	1.1	1.3	1.5	1.7	1.6	1.3
Vegetables and melons	11.3	15.8	17.0	17.8	17.4	17.6	17.4	19.4	18.9	20.2	19.1
All other crops	12.9	18.6	27.1	26.2	26.5	27.2	28.2	28.1	27.2	27.8	28.1
Home consumption	0.1	0.2	0.1	0.1	0.1	0.1	0.1	0.2	0.2	0.3	0.2
Value of inventory adjustment [1]	2.8	2.2	-0.2	-7.0	-12.3	-1.8	-18.8	12.6	-5.6	-3.9	-0.8
Value of livestock production	90.0	99.1	139.4	119.6	140.2	163.8	169.1	181.0	214.4	194.1	165.5
Milk	20.2	20.6	34.8	24.3	31.4	39.5	37.1	40.3	49.4	35.7	34.5
Meat animals	51.1	53.0	64.4	58.4	69.1	84.0	88.2	91.2	108.0	98.8	82.8
Miscellaneous livestock	2.5	4.1	5.2	5.7	5.7	6.0	6.3	6.8	7.1	6.8	6.8
Poultry and eggs	15.3	21.9	36.0	31.7	34.7	35.4	38.3	44.4	48.4	48.1	38.7
Home consumption	0.5	0.1	0.3	0.3	0.3	0.3	0.3	0.3	0.3	0.4	0.3
Value of inventory adjustment [1]	0.4	-0.6	-1.4	-0.7	-0.9	-1.4	-1.0	-2.1	1.3	4.3	2.3
Farm-related income	15.3	24.4	39.1	40.2	35.8	46.9	57.1	58.2	52.9	51.5	44.5
Forest products sold	1.8	0.8	0.7	0.4	0.5	0.5	0.5	0.6	0.6	0.7	0.7
Gross imputed rental value of farm dwellings	7.2	12.7	16.3	16.6	15.8	16.2	17.9	17.2	16.3	17.1	16.6
Machine hire and custom work	1.8	2.2	3.0	4.0	3.8	4.0	3.9	4.4	4.4	4.7	3.6
Other farm income	4.5	8.7	19.1	19.1	15.7	26.3	34.9	36.0	31.5	29.0	23.6
Less: Intermediate product expenses [2]	90.7	119.1	198.5	186.9	189.1	215.9	237.4	239.9	255.5	235.8	222.0
Farm origin	39.5	47.9	80.9	78.4	82.2	96.2	106.3	109.9	117.0	110.2	99.9
Feed purchased	20.4	24.5	46.9	45.0	45.4	54.6	60.5	62.4	63.7	58.5	55.6
Livestock and poultry purchased	14.6	15.9	18.9	17.9	20.4	23.7	24.8	25.5	31.2	30.4	22.4
Seed purchased	4.5	7.5	15.1	15.5	16.3	17.8	20.9	21.9	22.1	21.3	21.8
Manufactured inputs	22.0	28.7	55.7	49.4	50.1	58.1	64.8	65.8	67.5	59.1	56.5
Electricity	2.6	3.0	4.6	4.6	4.6	4.9	5.4	5.5	5.9	5.7	5.6
Fertilizers, lime, and soil conditioners	8.2	10.0	22.5	20.1	21.0	25.1	28.9	28.3	28.1	25.5	23.5
Pesticides	5.4	8.5	11.7	11.5	10.7	11.8	14.0	14.6	15.8	14.6	15.2
Petroleum fuel and oils	5.8	7.2	16.9	13.2	13.8	16.2	16.5	17.3	17.7	13.2	12.2
Other intermediate expenses [2]	29.2	42.5	61.8	59.1	56.8	61.7	66.3	64.2	70.9	66.5	65.6
Machine hire and custom work	3.0	4.1	4.1	4.1	4.3	4.0	4.9	4.6	5.9	4.8	4.4
Marketing, storage, and transportation expenses	4.2	7.5	8.7	8.9	9.0	9.0	9.2	8.0	10.8	9.2	9.7
Repair and maintenance of capital items	8.6	10.9	14.6	14.5	14.6	15.3	16.5	17.2	17.8	16.6	15.9
Miscellaneous expenses [2]	13.4	19.9	34.5	31.6	29.0	33.4	35.7	34.5	36.5	35.9	35.5
Total insurance premiums [3]	3.4	4.8	9.6	8.0	7.5	9.9	10.4	10.6	10.6	10.0	9.6
Less: Contract labor	1.6	2.7	4.7	3.9	3.9	4.4	4.8	4.6	6.4	5.7	6.0
Plus: Net government transactions [4]	3.1	15.8	0.9	1.1	0.9	-1.6	-1.5	-1.4	-4.6	-2.7	0.3
Direct government payments [5]	9.3	23.2	12.2	12.2	12.4	10.4	10.6	11.0	9.8	10.8	13.0
Property taxes [2]	6.2	7.4	11.3	11.1	11.5	12.0	12.2	12.4	14.3	13.5	12.6
Motor vehicle registration and licensing fees	0.4	0.5	0.6	0.6	0.6	0.7	0.7	0.7	0.7	0.7	0.7
Equals: Gross value added	**99.3**	**112.5**	**150.0**	**134.7**	**152.1**	**188.1**	**195.5**	**227.0**	**206.9**	**185.3**	**171.3**
Less: Capital consumption [2]	18.1	20.1	17.0	16.2	17.6	18.5	34.2	37.7	49.9	41.1	44.7
Equals: Net value added	**81.2**	**92.4**	**133.1**	**118.6**	**134.6**	**169.6**	**161.3**	**189.2**	**156.9**	**144.2**	**126.7**
Less: Factor payments to stakeholders [6]	35.0	41.7	55.1	56.3	57.4	56.0	64.8	65.5	64.5	62.8	65.2
Employee compensation [7]	12.4	17.9	25.2	25.2	23.6	22.6	27.4	27.7	28.1	26.4	28.4
Net rent paid to operator landlords	(X)	(X)	1.6	1.7	2.1	2.1	2.6	2.8	4.7	4.7	4.5
Net rent paid to nonoperator landlords	9.0	9.2	11.4	11.9	14.8	15.3	18.0	20.0	15.9	15.4	14.9
Total interest expenses	13.5	14.6	16.8	17.6	16.9	16.0	16.9	14.9	15.7	16.4	17.3
Equals: Net farm income	**46.3**	**50.7**	**78.0**	**62.2**	**77.1**	**113.6**	**96.5**	**123.8**	**92.4**	**81.4**	**61.5**

X Not applicable. [1] A positive value of inventory change represents current-year production not sold by December 31. A negative value is an offset to production from prior years included in current-year sales. [2] Including expenses associated with operator dwellings. [3] Includes federal and private crop and livestock insurance premiums as well as casualty, hail, motor vehicle and all other insurance premiums. [4] Direct government payments minus motor vehicle registration and licensing fees and property taxes. [5] Government payments reflect payments made directly to all recipients in the farm sector, including landlords. The nonoperator landlords share is offset by its inclusion in rental expenses paid to these landlords and thus is not reflected in net farm income or net cash income. [6] Prior to 2008, factor payments to stakeholders only includes net rent paid to nonoperator landlords. [7] Includes hired labor and non-cash employee compensation.

Source: U.S. Department of Agriculture, Economic Research Service, "U.S. and State Farm Income and Wealth Statistics," <http://www.ers.usda.gov/data-products/farm-income-and-wealth-statistics.aspx>, accessed September 2017.

Table 870. Value of Agricultural Production, Income, and Government Payments by State: 2014 and 2015

[In millions of dollars (473,288 represents $473,288,000,000). See headnote, Table 869. Minus sign (-) indicates decrease]

State	Value of agricultural production 2014	2015	Net farm income 2014	2015	Government payments, 2015	State	Value of agricultural production 2014	2015	Net farm income 2014	2015	Government payments, 2015
U.S.........	473,288	428,890	92,594	80,875	10,804	MO........	12,878	11,047	3,472	1,353	209
						MT........	5,101	4,744	680	958	131
AL..........	7,234	6,481	1,743	1,601	97	NE........	26,448	25,073	5,823	4,885	795
AK..........	51	48	-10	-6	11	NV........	978	831	170	126	37
AZ..........	4,592	4,441	713	1,109	44	NH........	325	321	44	63	7
AR..........	10,808	9,726	2,121	1,303	379	NJ........	1,309	1,270	172	268	8
CA..........	58,662	50,244	18,186	14,631	235	NM........	3,999	3,373	1,130	789	80
CO..........	8,801	8,583	1,143	1,500	219	NY........	7,043	5,934	1,691	1,000	70
CT..........	735	714	44	100	5	NC........	14,569	12,754	3,858	2,924	91
DE..........	1,671	1,437	583	408	8	ND........	9,958	9,186	326	185	363
FL..........	9,297	9,097	2,172	3,014	69	OH........	11,296	10,562	1,730	1,167	306
GA..........	10,829	10,410	2,323	2,529	305	OK........	9,836	8,449	2,755	2,166	534
HI..........	885	867	67	151	25	OR........	5,922	5,601	765	1,214	145
ID..........	9,291	8,294	2,006	1,868	86	PA........	9,925	8,717	2,658	1,895	64
IL..........	21,082	17,424	2,772	-87	417	RI........	103	105	12	28	4
IN..........	13,700	11,558	2,835	1,248	221	SC........	3,170	2,757	238	105	63
IA..........	35,654	31,402	5,242	5,590	1,408	SD........	12,131	11,126	2,134	2,067	426
KS..........	18,263	18,146	2,494	1,757	532	TN........	4,885	4,582	693	730	64
KY..........	7,446	7,110	1,750	1,665	128	TX........	29,539	28,567	4,224	6,512	945
LA..........	4,154	3,591	859	594	176	UT........	2,554	2,311	551	586	52
ME..........	902	848	155	160	12	VT........	1,120	941	320	197	10
MD..........	2,950	2,662	623	508	27	VA........	4,989	4,615	763	716	62
MA..........	636	593	-23	3	4	WA........	11,082	11,483	1,960	3,289	208
MI..........	9,412	8,904	668	767	187	WV........	1,022	976	56	75	17
MN..........	22,151	19,938	3,282	3,421	977	WI........	14,729	12,822	2,765	2,549	306
MS..........	6,957	6,182	1,542	847	174	WY........	2,212	2,043	317	351	60

Source: U.S. Department of Agriculture, Economic Research Service, "U.S. and State Farm Income and Wealth Statistics," <http://www.ers.usda.gov/data-products/farm-income-and-wealth-statistics.aspx>, accessed February 2017.

Table 871. Farm Income—Cash Receipts From Farm Marketings: 2010 to 2016

[In millions of dollars (321,237 represents $321,237,000,000). Represents gross receipts from commercial market sales as well as net Commodity Credit Corporation loans. The source estimates and publishes individual cash receipt values only for major commodities and major producing states. The U.S. receipts for individual commodities, computed as the sum of the reported states, may understate the value of sales for some commodities, with the balance included in the appropriate category labeled "other" or "miscellaneous." The degree of underestimation in some of the minor commodities can be substantial]

Commodities	2010	2014	2015	2016	Commodities	2010	2014	2015	2016
Total [1]........................	321,237	424,217	376,949	352,437	Broccoli...................	727	825	1,059	851
Animals and products...........	140,871	212,799	189,460	162,858	Carrots...................	647	726	820	818
Meat animals.....................	69,144	107,996	98,753	82,801	Corn, sweet.............	952	998	1,043	897
Cattle and calves................	51,246	81,478	78,129	63,945	Lettuce...................	2,213	2,375	3,150	2,881
Hogs...........................	17,898	26,518	20,624	18,857	Lettuce, head..........	1,058	1,120	1,253	1,320
Dairy products, milk..............	31,372	49,353	35,733	34,543	Onions...................	1,050	892	1,039	1,039
Poultry/eggs [1].....................	34,690	48,387	48,136	38,688	Peppers, bell...........	592	626	733	736
Broilers........................	23,692	32,728	28,716	25,936	Tomatoes...............	2,281	2,586	2,603	2,056
Chicken eggs..................	6,553	10,258	13,608	6,483	Tomatoes, fresh.......	1,355	1,133	1,221	963
Turkeys........................	4,372	5,305	5,708	6,184	Cantaloupes............	305	301	264	207
Miscellaneous animals [1]........	5,664	7,063	6,839	6,825	Watermelons...........	499	450	488	579
Aquaculture......................	474	455	468	491	Fruits/nuts [1]...............	21,613	31,931	28,418	28,715
Honey..........................	282	390	329	332	Grapefruit...............	291	242	216	251
Crops...........................	180,366	211,418	187,489	189,579	Lemons..................	395	641	697	734
Food grains [1].....................	14,314	16,050	12,282	11,337	Oranges.................	1,997	2,254	1,963	1,711
Rice...........................	3,263	3,461	2,803	2,425	Apples...................	2,311	2,871	3,350	3,462
Wheat.........................	11,021	12,545	9,427	8,856	Cherries.................	756	873	838	862
Feed crops [1].....................	55,143	65,874	56,919	54,827	Grapes..................	4,024	5,822	5,914	6,257
Corn...........................	47,540	54,473	47,019	46,059	Peaches.................	617	630	606	629
Hay...........................	5,217	8,491	6,955	6,226	Pears....................	387	467	494	475
Sorghum grain...................	1,487	1,733	1,837	1,475	Blueberries..............	644	889	873	748
Cotton.............................	7,465	7,111	4,756	5,922	Cranberries.............	299	254	262	292
Tobacco...........................	1,336	1,716	1,605	1,336	Raspberries.............	259	527	670	458
Oil crops [1]........................	36,544	42,621	35,509	40,229	Strawberries............	2,261	2,822	2,239	2,336
Peanuts........................	824	805	1,275	1,129	Almonds.................	2,903	7,388	5,869	5,158
Soybeans......................	34,665	40,838	33,112	37,970	Pistachios...............	1,159	1,835	888	1,506
Sunflower......................	507	455	567	511	Walnuts..................	1,028	1,907	1,012	1,242
Vegetables and melons [1]........	17,405	18,871	20,230	19,143	All other crops [1].........	26,546	27,244	27,769	28,070
Beans, dry.....................	780	990	915	859	Sugarcane...............	1,075	978	1,016	962
Potatoes.......................	3,336	3,802	3,581	3,478	Sugar beets.............	1,734	1,479	1,503	1,642
Sweet potatoes..................	472	707	676	706	Floriculture..............	4,149	4,203	4,374	(NA)
Beans, snap.....................	434	394	414	441	Mushrooms.............	924	1,116	1,191	1,191

NA Not available. [1] Includes commodities not shown separately.

Source: U.S. Department of Agriculture, Economic Research Service, "U.S. and State Farm Income and Wealth Statistics," <http://www.ers.usda.gov/data-products/farm-income-and-wealth-statistics.aspx>, accessed September 2017.

Table 872. Cash Receipts for Cattle, Corn, Soybeans, and Milk—Total and for Leading States: 2016

[In millions of dollars (63,945 represents $63,945,000,000). See headnote Table 871]

State	Value	State	Value	State	Value	State	Value
Cattle and calves. . .	**63,945**	**Corn.............**	**46,059**	**Soybeans...........**	**37,970**	**Milk...........**	**34,543**
Nebraska..............	10,976	Iowa................	8,133	Illinois..................	5,332	California..............	6,066
Texas.................	8,470	Illinois..............	7,256	Iowa................	5,180	Wisconsin............	5,017
Kansas...............	7,864	Nebraska............	5,414	Minnesota.............	3,497	New York.............	2,501
Iowa.................	3,859	Minnesota............	4,465	Indiana................	2,838	Idaho.................	2,356
Colorado.............	3,088	Indiana..............	3,156	Nebraska.............	2,765	Pennsylvania..........	1,849

Source: U.S. Department of Agriculture, Economic Research Service, "U.S. and State Farm Income and Wealth Statistics," <http://www.ers.usda.gov/data-products/farm-income-and-wealth-statistics.aspx>, accessed September 2017.

Table 873. Farm Marketings: 2015 and 2016; and Principal Commodities, 2016, by State

[In millions of dollars (376,949 represents $376,949,000,000). See headnote Table 871]

State	2015 Total	2015 Animals and products	2015 Crops	2016 Total	2016 Animals and products	2016 Crops	State rank for total farm marketings and three principal commodities in order of marketing receipts
U.S.........	**376,949**	**189,460**	**187,489**	**352,437**	**162,858**	**189,579**	**Cattle and calves, corn, soybeans**
AL...........	5,554	4,516	1,038	4,950	3,881	1,069	27—Broilers, cattle and calves, chicken eggs
AK...........	34	6	28	34	6	28	50—Hay, mushrooms, cattle and calves
AZ...........	4,192	1,788	2,404	4,143	1,518	2,625	29—Lettuce, milk, cattle and calves
AR...........	8,845	5,220	3,625	8,048	4,715	3,334	16—Broilers, soybeans, rice
CA...........	49,114	11,851	37,262	45,325	10,449	34,876	1—Milk, grapes, almonds
CO...........	7,318	5,248	2,070	6,265	4,160	2,105	22—Cattle and calves, milk, corn
CT...........	571	197	374	515	167	347	46—Milk, turkeys, cattle and calves
DE...........	1,289	1,020	269	1,201	929	272	39—Broilers, corn, soybeans
FL...........	8,391	2,275	6,116	7,530	1,662	5,868	18—Oranges, sugarcane, cattle and calves
GA...........	9,088	6,037	3,051	8,399	5,290	3,108	14—Broilers, cotton lint, peanuts
HI...........	671	176	495	649	152	496	43—Coffee, sugarcane for sugar, cattle and calves
ID...........	7,376	4,562	2,815	7,077	4,300	2,776	20—Milk, cattle and calves, potatoes
IL...........	15,666	2,535	13,130	15,722	2,289	13,433	6—Corn, soybeans, hogs
IN...........	11,010	4,204	6,806	9,936	3,379	6,557	11—Corn, soybeans, hogs
IA...........	27,014	14,359	12,654	25,666	12,100	13,566	2—Corn, hogs, soybeans
KS...........	15,553	10,030	5,524	15,000	8,980	6,020	7—Cattle and calves, corn, soybeans
KY...........	5,797	3,339	2,457	5,375	2,948	2,427	24—Broilers, soybeans, corn
LA...........	3,297	1,281	2,016	2,810	1,030	1,780	34—Soybeans, broilers, rice
ME...........	694	360	334	527	297	230	45—Milk, turkeys, chicken eggs
MD...........	2,223	1,365	858	2,107	1,226	881	36—Broilers, corn, soybeans
MA...........	412	128	284	387	116	271	47—Cranberries, milk, turkeys
MI...........	7,838	3,434	4,404	7,294	2,909	4,385	19—Milk, corn, soybeans
MN...........	16,288	7,694	8,594	16,835	7,087	9,748	5—Corn, soybeans, hogs
MS...........	5,385	3,327	2,057	5,093	3,018	2,075	25—Broilers, soybeans, corn
MO...........	9,701	5,010	4,691	8,806	4,157	4,649	13—Soybeans, corn, cattle and calves
MT...........	3,758	1,870	1,888	3,673	1,631	2,041	30—Cattle and calves, wheat, hay
NE...........	22,980	13,951	9,028	21,138	12,147	8,991	4—Cattle and calves, corn, soybeans
NV...........	761	571	190	596	445	151	44—Cattle and calves, milk, hay
NH...........	254	144	110	210	114	96	48—Milk, turkeys, chicken eggs
NJ...........	1,088	162	926	1,018	118	900	40—Tomatoes, blueberries, apples
NM...........	3,061	2,324	737	2,862	2,151	711	33—Milk, cattle and calves, pecans
NY...........	5,334	3,370	1,964	4,990	3,088	1,902	26—Milk, apples, corn
NC...........	11,648	7,944	3,704	10,609	7,214	3,396	9—Broilers, hogs, turkeys
ND...........	7,091	1,320	5,771	7,733	1,111	6,622	17—Soybeans, wheat, corn
OH...........	9,209	4,117	5,092	8,167	3,032	5,135	15—Soybeans, corn, milk
OK...........	7,051	5,847	1,203	6,189	4,839	1,350	23—Cattle and calves, hogs, broilers
OR...........	4,948	1,770	3,178	4,639	1,478	3,161	28—Cattle and calves, milk, hay
PA...........	7,399	4,920	2,479	6,315	3,913	2,402	21—Milk, cattle and calves, mushrooms
RI...........	82	32	50	72	24	49	49—Turkeys, chicken eggs, milk
SC...........	2,423	1,466	956	2,112	1,269	844	35—Broilers, cattle and calves, corn
SD...........	9,187	3,929	5,257	9,057	3,634	5,423	12—Cattle and calves, corn, soybeans
TN...........	3,657	1,557	2,100	3,304	1,317	1,988	32—Soybeans, cattle and calves, broilers
TX...........	23,492	16,674	6,817	21,174	13,155	8,019	3—Cattle and calves, cotton lint, milk
UT...........	1,974	1,522	452	1,658	1,245	413	37—Cattle and calves, milk, hay
VT...........	824	641	184	786	584	202	41—Milk, maple products, cattle and calves
VA...........	3,731	2,546	1,185	3,320	2,200	1,120	31—Broilers, cattle and calves, turkeys
WA...........	10,042	2,928	7,114	10,315	2,477	7,838	10—Apples, milk, cattle and calves
WV...........	740	597	143	689	549	141	42—Cattle and calves, broilers, turkeys
WI...........	11,290	8,029	3,261	10,726	7,309	3,417	8—Milk, cattle and calves, corn
WY...........	1,609	1,266	343	1,391	1,051	340	38—Cattle and calves, hay, hogs

Source: U.S. Department of Agriculture, Economic Research Service, "U.S. and State Farm Income and Wealth Statistics," <http://www.ers.usda.gov/data-products/farm-income-and-wealth-statistics.aspx>, accessed September 2017.

Table 874. Indexes of Prices Received and Paid by Farmers: 2000 to 2016

[2011=100]

Item	2000	2010	2015	2016	Item	2000	2010	2015	2016
Prices received, all products....	**59**	**87**	**99**	**91**	Livestock and poultry............	71	86	147	105
Crops.............................	54	87	87	86	Seed and plants..................	37	93	114	112
Food grains......................	36	74	76	62	Fertilizer [2]......................	34	77	87	72
Feed grains......................	35	66	63	59	Agricultural chemicals..........	83	100	107	108
Cotton...........................	57	81	(NA)	(NA)	Fuels............................	36	78	64	56
Tobacco..........................	99	99	(NA)	(NA)	Supplies and repairs............	73	96	106	106
Oil-bearing crops................	40	81	76	75	Autos and trucks................	103	97	106	106
Fruits and nuts..................	59	89	138	139	Farm machinery.................	57	94	115	115
Commercial vegetables.........	77	104	109	104	Building materials...............	71	97	107	108
Potatoes and dry beans.........	55	82	(NA)	(NA)	Farm services...................	72	98	114	116
Animals and products............	64	86	113	95	Rent.............................	54	93	121	117
Livestock........................	62	82	120	98					
Dairy products...................	61	81	85	81	Interest..........................	78	92	99	105
Poultry and eggs.................	71	102	128	100	Taxes............................	55	96	124	123
Prices paid, total [1].............	**59**	**90**	**110**	**105**	Wage rates.......................	73	99	112	116
Production........................	54	88	110	103					
Feed.............................	45	80	106	102	Parity ratio [3]....................	101	96	90	85

NA Not available. [1] Includes production items, interest, taxes, wage rates, and a family living component. The family living component is the Consumer Price Index for all urban consumers from the Bureau of Labor Statistics. See text, Section 14 and Table 748. [2] Includes lime and soil conditioners. [3] Ratio of prices received by farmers to prices paid.

Source: U.S. Department of Agriculture, National Agricultural Statistics Service, "Quick Stats," <http://quickstats.nass.usda.gov/>, accessed August 2017.

Table 875. Farm and Marketing Bill Share of the U.S. Food Dollar (Nominal) by Selected Characteristics: 1995 to 2015

[In percent. The food dollar series measures annual expenditures by U.S. consumers on domestically produced food; a food dollar represents the average $1 expenditure. Farm share is measured as the average payment from each food dollar expenditure that farmers receive for their raw food dollar commodities. The food marketing bill is measured as the average value added to the raw food dollar from each consumer food dollar expenditure. Based on input-output data from the Bureau of Labor Statistics and Bureau of Economic Analysis]

Item	1995	2000	2005	2010	2011	2012	2013	2014	2015
SHARE OF FOOD DOLLAR									
Food dollar, total:									
Farm share..........................	17.7	15.8	15.8	16.4	17.6	17.4	17.3	17.2	15.6
Marketing bill share................	82.3	84.2	84.2	83.6	82.4	82.6	82.7	82.8	84.4
Food at home dollar:									
Farm share..........................	23.9	22.5	23.6	24.2	25.9	26.1	25.8	26.2	24.1
Marketing bill share................	76.1	77.5	76.4	75.8	74.1	73.9	74.2	73.8	75.9
Food away from home dollar:									
Farm share..........................	9.2	6.2	5.1	5.5	6.0	5.9	6.1	5.8	5.3
Marketing bill share................	90.8	93.8	94.9	94.5	94.0	94.1	93.9	94.2	94.7
Food and beverage dollar: [1]									
Farm share..........................	15.2	13.1	13.2	13.6	14.7	14.6	14.5	14.5	13.1
Marketing bill share................	84.8	86.9	86.8	86.4	85.3	85.4	85.5	85.5	86.9
Home food and beverage dollar: [1]									
Farm share..........................	19.6	18.0	18.9	19.4	21.0	21.1	20.8	21.2	19.4
Marketing bill share................	80.4	82.0	81.1	80.6	79.0	78.9	79.2	78.8	80.6
Away food and beverage dollar: [1]									
Farm share..........................	8.4	5.4	4.5	4.7	5.1	5.1	5.2	5.1	4.7
Marketing bill share................	91.6	94.6	95.5	95.3	94.9	94.9	94.8	94.9	95.3
MARKETING BILL COST COMPONENTS									
Primary factors:									
Salary and benefits [2].................	(NA)	52.9	50.4	49.0	48.8	48.9	48.6	48.7	50.1
Output taxes [3].......................	(NA)	7.3	8.0	9.3	9.0	8.9	8.8	8.8	8.6
Property income [4]....................	(NA)	34.6	35.6	35.9	35.5	35.8	36.7	36.6	35.9
Imports [5]............................	4.2	5.1	6.0	5.8	6.7	6.4	5.9	5.9	5.1
Industry groups: [6]									
Farm and agribusiness [7].............	12.2	10.6	10.9	11.6	12.2	12.1	12.5	12.4	10.8
Food processing.....................	19.0	18.2	15.8	16.7	15.8	15.8	15.8	15.3	15.6
Packaging...........................	4.2	4.2	3.6	2.8	2.8	2.7	2.6	2.5	2.5
Transportation.......................	3.9	3.8	3.6	3.3	3.4	3.3	3.3	3.2	3.5
Wholesale trade.....................	10.2	9.4	9.2	9.4	9.7	9.3	9.3	9.1	9.3
Retail trade..........................	12.6	13.0	13.7	13.9	13.3	13.0	13.1	12.9	12.7
Food services.......................	26.7	28.4	30.6	30.2	30.0	31.1	31.2	32.7	34.4
Energy..............................	3.5	4.7	5.5	5.0	5.6	5.6	5.2	5.1	4.0
Finance and insurance..............	3.6	3.8	3.3	3.4	3.3	3.3	3.3	3.1	3.4
Advertising..........................	2.7	2.5	2.5	2.4	2.5	2.5	2.5	2.5	2.6
Legal and accounting................	1.3	1.5	1.5	1.4	1.4	1.3	1.3	1.2	1.3

NA Not available. [1] Includes alcoholic beverages and soft drinks. [2] Pre-tax employee wages plus employer and employee costs for employee benefits. [3] Value of excise, sales, property, and severance taxes (less subsidies), customs duties, and other non-tax government fees levied on establishments. [4] Allocated compensation to various owners for services on behalf of a domestic establishment that directs sales to the U.S. food supply. Includes machinery, equipment, structures, natural resources, product inventory, and other tangible or intangible assets. [5] Food and non-food commodities imported from international sources and used by U.S. food supply chain industries producing for the U.S. market. [6] For each industry group the amount shown excludes value-added contributions to the food dollar that trace back to other supply chain industry groups. For example, the value of energy used by the transportation and packaging industries is deducted from those groups and included with the energy group. [7] Farm and agribusiness value-added contributions from non-farm supply chain industry groups, such as energy, transportation, and financial services, are deducted from the farm share and therefore the industry group series value for farms and agribusiness is smaller than the farm share value of the marketing bill series.

Source: U.S. Department of Agriculture, Economic Research Service, "Food Dollar Series," <http://www.ers.usda.gov/data-products/food-dollar-series.aspx>, accessed June 2017.

Table 876. Agricultural Exports and Imports—Volume by Principal Commodity: 2000 to 2016

[In thousands (1,436 represents 1,436,000). 1 kiloliter equals 264.17 gallons. Includes Puerto Rico, U.S. territories, and shipments under foreign aid programs. Commodity and commodity grouping definitions used are Foreign Agricultural Trade of the United States (FATUS) groupings. See source for details]

Commodity	Unit	2000	2005	2010	2013	2014	2015	2016
EXPORTS								
Fruit juices and wine	Kiloliters	1,436	1,398	1,498	1,532	1,451	1,286	1,082
Beef, pork, lamb, and poultry meats [1]	Metric tons	4,431	4,343	6,366	7,107	7,141	6,457	6,932
Wheat, unmilled	Metric tons	27,568	27,040	27,608	32,877	25,415	21,258	23,907
Wheat products	Metric tons	844	313	446	386	394	440	461
Rice, paddy, milled	Metric tons	3,241	4,388	4,464	3,753	3,347	3,880	3,921
Feed grains	Metric tons	54,946	50,865	54,504	26,150	57,049	54,604	62,713
Feed grain products	Metric tons	657	3,442	1,081	850	917	851	889
Feeds and fodders [2]	Metric tons	13,065	11,422	19,024	20,316	26,550	22,726	22,308
Fresh fruits and nuts	Metric tons	3,452	3,675	4,308	4,930	4,562	4,575	4,757
Fruit products	Metric tons	387	394	570	572	598	570	525
Vegetables, fresh	Metric tons	2,100	2,077	2,140	2,335	2,273	2,236	2,435
Vegetables, frozen and canned	Metric tons	1,110	1,086	1,410	1,864	1,967	1,889	1,976
Oilcake and meal	Metric tons	6,760	6,905	10,004	10,544	10,611	11,688	10,824
Oilseeds	Metric tons	27,715	26,462	43,282	40,216	50,464	48,910	58,702
Vegetable oils	Metric tons	2,043	1,937	3,544	2,667	2,607	2,646	2,643
Tobacco, unmanufactured	Metric tons	180	154	179	159	150	156	164
Cotton, excluding linters	Metric tons	1,485	3,405	2,956	2,790	2,167	2,396	2,469
IMPORTS								
Fruit juices	Kiloliters	3,114	4,149	4,274	4,425	4,371	4,477	4,627
Wine	Kiloliters	458	726	959	1,128	1,104	1,157	1,166
Malt beverages	Kiloliters	2,346	2,995	3,161	3,225	3,459	3,675	3,915
Coffee, including products	Metric tons	1,370	1,307	1,390	1,541	1,573	1,584	1,647
Rubber and allied gums, crude	Metric tons	1,232	1,169	945	928	947	950	946
Beef, pork, lamb, and poultry meats [1]	Metric tons	1,564	1,778	1,351	1,379	1,698	1,919	1,800
Grains [3]	Metric tons	4,622	3,726	5,166	8,889	7,087	6,328	6,203
Biscuits, pasta, and noodles	Metric tons	711	1,001	1,097	1,246	1,312	1,444	1,643
Feeds and fodders [2]	Metric tons	1,224	963	1,423	1,863	2,000	2,221	1,894
Fruits, nuts, and preparations [4]	Metric tons	8,357	9,570	10,934	12,753	13,065	13,893	14,257
Vegetables, fresh and frozen	Metric tons	3,804	5,183	6,861	7,657	8,074	8,222	9,051
Tobacco, unmanufactured	Metric tons	216	233	164	196	171	154	172
Oilseeds and oilnuts	Metric tons	951	818	1,223	2,084	3,402	1,643	1,418
Vegetable oils and waxes	Metric tons	1,846	2,386	3,730	4,533	4,673	4,890	5,316
Oilcake and meal	Metric tons	1,254	1,541	1,504	3,348	3,747	4,020	3,969

[1] Includes variety meats. [2] Excluding oilcake and meal. [3] Includes wheat, corn, oats, barley, and rice. [4] Includes bananas and plantains.

Source: U.S. Department of Agriculture, Foreign Agricultural Service, "Global Agricultural Trade System," <http://www.fas.usda.gov/gats/>, accessed August 2017.

Table 877. Agricultural Chemical and Fertilizer Exports and General Imports by Type: 2000 to 2016

[In thousands of metric tons (21,480 represents 21,480,000). Metric ton = 1.102 short tons or .984 long tons. Includes Puerto Rico, U.S. territories, and shipments under foreign aid programs. Commodity and commodity grouping definitions used are Foreign Agricultural Trade of the United States (FATUS) groupings. See source for details]

Commodity	2000	2005	2010	2011	2012	2013	2014	2015	2016
GENERAL IMPORTS [1]									
Fertilizers, total	**21,480**	**30,397**	**43,657**	**34,844**	**32,698**	**33,663**	**35,612**	**35,665**	**31,936**
Nitrogen	10,552	17,901	17,171	17,722	18,021	17,374	17,914	18,304	16,178
Potassium	9,324	10,215	10,230	10,650	8,400	9,685	10,646	10,275	8,879
Phosphate	1,592	2,243	16,200	6,435	6,185	6,538	6,965	6,963	6,796
Mixed/organic fertilizer	13	37	56	38	93	65	87	122	83
Agricultural chemicals, total	**58**	**80**	**90**	**97**	**116**	**116**	**100**	**115**	**125**
Herbicides	12	23	15	18	22	19	14	19	28
Fungicides	17	21	25	25	26	26	28	33	35
Insecticides	10	7	1	1	1	1	1	1	1
Other pesticides	19	29	49	54	68	70	57	61	60
EXPORTS									
Fertilizers, total	**21**	**32**	**10,310**	**10,885**	**10,668**	**11,165**	**10,598**	**9,933**	**11,095**
Nitrogen	19	26	1,741	1,719	2,187	2,588	2,564	2,345	2,856
Potassium	–	–	333	147	224	320	96	54	61
Phosphate	2	6	7,820	8,634	7,749	7,580	7,119	6,484	7,169
Mixed/organic fertilizer	–	–	416	386	508	678	819	1,049	1,009
Agricultural chemicals, total	**154**	**127**	**146**	**151**	**160**	**170**	**159**	**150**	**156**
Herbicides	60	56	83	84	91	95	84	81	91
Fungicides	14	18	15	18	17	22	24	19	18
Insecticides	62	23	27	27	29	27	27	24	20
Other pesticides	19	29	22	23	23	25	23	26	27

– Represents or rounds to zero. [1] Total shipments arriving in the U.S., including both merchandise that enters consumption channels immediately and merchandise entered into bonded warehouses or Foreign Trade Zones under Customs custody.

Source: U.S. Department of Agriculture, Foreign Agricultural Service, "Global Agricultural Trade System," <http://www.fas.usda.gov/gats>, accessed May 2017.

Table 878. Agricultural Exports and Imports—Value: 1990 to 2016

[In billions of dollars, except percent (16.6 represents $16,600,000,000). Includes Puerto Rico, U.S. territories, and shipments under foreign aid programs. Excludes fish, forest products, distilled liquors, manufactured tobacco, and products made from cotton; but includes raw tobacco, raw cotton, rubber, beer and wine, and processed agricultural products]

Year	Trade balance	Exports, domestic products	Percent of all exports	Imports for con-sumption	Percent of all imports	Year	Trade balance	Exports, domestic products	Percent of all exports	Imports for con-sumption	Percent of all imports
1990.........	16.6	39.5	11	22.9	5	2010.........	34.0	115.8	10	81.9	4
2000.........	12.3	51.3	7	39.0	3	2011.........	37.5	136.4	11	99.0	5
2005.........	3.9	63.2	8	59.3	4	2012.........	38.6	141.6	10	102.9	5
2006.........	5.6	71.0	8	65.3	4	2013.........	40.1	144.4	11	104.2	5
2007.........	18.1	90.0	9	71.9	4	2014.........	38.1	150.0	11	111.8	5
2008.........	34.3	114.8	10	80.5	4	2015.........	19.4	133.1	10	113.6	5
2009.........	26.8	98.5	10	71.7	5	2016.........	20.3	134.9	11	114.6	5

Source: U.S. Department of Agriculture, Economic Research Service, "Foreign Agricultural Trade of the United States (FATUS)," <https://www.ers.usda.gov/data-products/foreign-agricultural-trade-of-the-united-states-fatus/>, accessed May 2017.

Table 879. Agricultural Imports—Value by Selected Commodity: 2000 to 2016

[In millions of dollars (38,974 represents $38,974,000,000). For calendar year. Includes Puerto Rico, U.S. territories, and shipments under foreign aid programs. Excludes fish, forest products, distilled liquors, manufactured tobacco, and products made from cotton; but includes raw tobacco, raw cotton, rubber, beer and wine, and processed agricultural products]

Commodity [1]	Value (mil. dol.)							Percent distribution		
	2000	2005	2010	2013	2014	2015	2016	2000	2010	2016
Total [2]........................	38,974	59,291	81,863	104,233	111,836	113,635	114,559	100.0	100.0	100.0
Cattle, live....................	1,152	1,039	1,575	1,784	2,495	2,195	1,620	3.0	1.9	1.4
Beef and veal..................	2,399	3,651	2,830	3,755	5,617	6,654	5,263	6.2	3.5	4.6
Pork..........................	997	1,281	1,185	1,428	1,760	1,621	1,626	2.6	1.4	1.4
Dairy products................	1,671	2,686	2,619	3,193	3,524	3,492	3,449	4.3	3.2	3.0
Grains and feeds..............	3,075	4,527	7,788	11,318	11,061	11,080	11,111	7.9	9.5	9.7
Fruits and preparations.......	3,851	5,842	9,168	11,651	12,803	14,046	15,254	9.9	11.2	13.3
Vegetables and preparations [3]...........	3,958	6,410	9,318	11,371	11,629	12,064	13,274	10.2	11.4	11.6
Sugar and related products...............	1,555	2,494	4,047	4,274	4,472	4,600	4,636	4.0	4.9	4.0
Wine..........................	2,207	3,762	4,279	5,296	5,406	5,479	5,647	5.7	5.2	4.9
Malt beverages................	2,179	3,096	3,506	3,699	4,145	4,547	4,868	5.6	4.3	4.2
Oilseeds and products........	1,773	2,998	5,390	8,639	9,601	8,321	8,473	4.5	6.6	7.4
Coffee and products..........	2,700	2,976	4,943	5,809	6,332	6,303	6,004	6.9	6.0	5.2
Cocoa and products...........	1,404	2,751	4,295	4,159	4,728	4,860	5,081	3.6	5.2	4.4
Rubber, crude natural........	842	1,552	2,820	2,559	1,955	1,499	1,308	2.2	3.4	1.1

[1] Commodity and commodity grouping definitions used are the Foreign Agricultural Trade of the United States (FATUS) commodity code groupings. See source for more details. [2] Includes other commodities, not shown separately. [3] Includes pulses.

Source: U.S. Department of Agriculture, Foreign Agricultural Service, "Global Agricultural Trade System (GATS)," <http://www.fas.usda.gov/gats>, accessed April 2017.

Table 880. Agricultural Imports—Value by Selected Country of Origin: 2000 to 2016

[In millions of dollars (38,974 represents $38,974,000,000). Totals include transshipments through Canada, but transshipments are not distributed by country after 1998. See headnote Table 878]

Country	Value (mil. dol.)							Percent distribution		
	2000	2005	2010	2013	2014	2015	2016	2000	2010	2016
Total......................	38,974	59,291	81,863	104,233	111,836	113,635	114,559	100.0	100.0	100.0
Mexico.....................	5,077	8,331	13,578	17,679	19,293	21,034	22,951	13.0	16.6	20.0
Canada.....................	8,661	12,270	16,244	21,759	23,180	21,824	21,569	22.2	19.8	18.8
European Union [1].........	8,312	13,426	14,370	17,580	18,981	20,001	20,588	21.3	17.6	18.0
China......................	812	1,872	3,367	4,420	4,278	4,355	4,319	2.1	4.1	3.8
Brazil.....................	1,144	1,952	2,894	3,398	3,883	3,482	3,396	2.9	3.5	3.0
Australia [2]..............	1,592	2,421	2,307	2,751	3,900	4,274	3,186	4.1	2.8	2.8
Chile......................	1,026	1,521	2,293	2,871	2,756	2,854	3,130	2.6	2.8	2.7
Indonesia..................	998	1,702	2,887	3,118	3,018	2,882	2,882	2.6	3.5	2.5
New Zealand [2]............	1,132	1,712	1,666	2,179	2,608	2,883	2,598	2.9	2.0	2.3
Colombia...................	1,123	1,437	1,977	2,196	2,432	2,428	2,347	2.9	2.4	2.0
Thailand...................	779	1,094	2,034	2,235	2,230	2,274	2,343	2.0	2.5	2.0
Vietnam....................	200	422	970	1,476	1,776	1,841	2,153	0.5	1.2	1.9
India......................	826	923	1,592	3,518	3,181	2,670	2,109	2.1	1.9	1.8
Guatemala..................	710	920	1,387	1,816	1,893	1,928	1,913	1.8	1.7	1.7
Peru.......................	196	448	974	1,270	1,624	1,678	1,830	0.5	1.2	1.6
Costa Rica.................	812	916	1,295	1,475	1,585	1,484	1,624	2.1	1.6	1.4
Argentina..................	672	831	1,159	1,781	1,514	1,536	1,397	1.7	1.4	1.2
Ecuador....................	451	596	869	988	1,095	1,226	1,202	1.2	1.1	1.0
Philippines................	468	568	884	994	1,143	1,146	1,129	1.2	1.1	1.0
Malaysia...................	353	666	1,729	1,597	1,494	1,169	1,019	0.9	2.1	0.9
Rest of world..............	3,627	5,264	7,390	9,131	9,972	10,664	10,873	9.3	9.0	9.5

[1] For consistency, data for all years are shown on the basis of 28 countries in the European Union; see footnote 2, Table 1383. [2] Data is a summarization of component countries.

Source: U.S. Department of Agriculture, Foreign Agricultural Service, "Global Agricultural Trade System (GATS)," <http://www.fas.usda.gov/gats>, accessed April 2017.

Table 881. Selected Farm Products—U.S. and World Production and Exports: 2010 to 2016

[58.9 represents 58,900,000. Metric ton = 1.102 short tons or .984 long tons]

Commodity	Unit	Amount						United States as percent of world		
		United States			World					
		2010	2015	2016	2010	2015	2016	2010	2015	2016
PRODUCTION [1]										
Wheat......................	Mil. metric tons	58.9	56.1	62.9	649.5	737.0	755.0	9.1	7.6	8.3
Corn for grain..............	Mil. metric tons	315.6	345.5	384.8	837.3	969.5	1,070.5	37.7	35.6	35.9
Soybeans..................	Mil. metric tons	90.7	106.9	117.2	264.4	312.9	351.7	34.3	34.2	33.3
Rice, milled................	Mil. metric tons	7.6	6.1	7.1	450.0	471.9	483.9	1.7	1.3	1.5
Cotton [2].................	Million bales [3]	18.1	12.9	17.2	117.6	96.8	106.5	15.4	13.3	16.1
EXPORTS [4]										
Wheat [5].....................	Mil. metric tons	35.1	21.2	28.7	133.0	172.9	182.3	26.4	12.2	15.8
Corn......................	Mil. metric tons	46.5	48.3	56.5	91.6	119.6	162.4	50.8	40.4	34.8
Soybeans..................	Mil. metric tons	41.0	52.9	57.2	91.7	132.5	145.0	44.7	39.9	39.4
Rice, milled basis..........	Mil. metric tons	3.5	3.4	3.7	35.1	40.5	43.1	10.0	8.4	8.5
Cotton [2].................	Million bales [3]	14.4	9.2	14.5	34.9	35.3	37.4	41.2	25.9	38.8

[1] Production years vary by commodity. In most cases, includes harvests from July 1 of the year shown through June 30 of the following year. [2] For production and trade years ending in year shown. [3] Bales of 480 lb. net weight. [4] Trade years may vary by commodity. Wheat, corn, and soybean data are for trade year beginning in year shown. Rice data are for calendar year. [5] Includes wheat flour on a grain equivalent.

Source: U.S. Department of Agriculture, Foreign Agricultural Service, "Production, Supply and Distribution Online," <http://www.fas.usda.gov/psdonline/>, accessed August 2017.

Table 882. Percent of U.S. Agricultural Commodity Output Exported: 2000 to 2013

[In percent. All export shares are estimated from export and production volumes]

Commodity group	2000	2005	2008	2009	2010	2011	2012	2013
Total agriculture [1]....................	**19.4**	**19.3**	**19.7**	**19.7**	**21.7**	**20.4**	**18.8**	**22.2**
Livestock [2]................................	5.3	4.9	8.7	7.1	8.3	9.1	8.9	10.0
Red meat..........................	8.1	7.4	13.2	12.2	13.3	16.2	15.8	15.4
Poultry/eggs........................	12.1	11.5	14.4	14.4	14.0	14.9	15.6	15.6
Dairy.............................	1.5	1.6	4.6	2.6	4.5	4.8	4.4	6.1
Crops [3].................................	21.7	21.7	21.6	21.8	24.0	22.5	20.8	24.3
Food grains........................	47.3	48.0	40.9	40.8	57.6	53.2	45.2	54.6
Feed grains........................	20.7	20.0	15.7	15.7	15.3	12.7	7.2	14.8
Oilseeds...........................	33.0	27.8	40.0	42.1	41.8	40.9	39.8	46.0
Fruit and nuts......................	17.4	20.3	21.2	21.0	23.8	25.9	24.4	24.9
Vegetables.........................	11.6	13.1	16.3	14.9	15.6	17.9	17.9	19.6
Sweeteners........................	4.4	5.5	9.1	8.5	14.1	15.5	16.1	14.1
Wine and beer......................	6.6	8.0	11.3	8.6	9.3	9.9	9.2	9.4

[1] All export shares are computed from physical weights or weight equivalents. [2] Excludes animal fats, live farm animals, fish/shellfish. [3] Exports include vegetable oils and oilseed meal. Excludes nursery crops.

Source: U.S. Department of Agriculture, Economic Research Service, "U.S. Agricultural Trade," <https://www.ers.usda.gov/topics/international-markets-trade/us-agricultural-trade/>, accessed April 2016.

Table 883. Top 10 U.S. Export Markets for Corn, Wheat, Soybeans, and Poultry: 2016

[In thousands of metric tons (55,755 represents 55,755,000). Commodity and commodity grouping definitions used are the Foreign Agricultural Trade of the United States (FATUS) commodity code groupings. See source for details]

Corn		Wheat [1]		Soybeans		Poultry meat	
Country	Amount	Country	Amount	Country	Amount	Country	Amount
World, total.........	**55,755**	**World, total**...........	**23,907**	**World, total**...........	**57,715**	**World, total**...........	**3,448**
Mexico.................	13,793	Mexico..................	2,764	China.....................	35,969	Mexico..................	849
Japan..................	11,880	Japan...................	2,723	Mexico..................	3,631	Canada..................	185
Korea, South...........	4,839	Philippines..............	2,679	Indonesia................	2,564	Hong Kong..............	178
Colombia...............	4,558	Brazil...................	1,255	Japan....................	2,358	Cuba....................	157
Peru...................	2,690	Taiwan..................	1,099	Netherlands.............	1,961	Taiwan..................	155
Taiwan.................	2,659	Korea, South...........	1,088	Taiwan.................	1,503	Guatemala..............	122
Saudi Arabia...........	1,953	Nigeria..................	1,076	Germany................	1,256	Angola.................	114
Venezuela..............	1,116	Indonesia...............	961	Thailand.................	902	Vietnam.................	97
Guatemala.............	987	China...................	901	Spain....................	895	Philippines..............	93
Egypt..................	908	Colombia................	838	Vietnam.................	842	Chile...................	85
Rest of world..........	10,371	Rest of world..........	8,522	Rest of world...........	5,832	Rest of world...........	1,414

[1] Unmilled.

Source: U.S. Department of Agriculture, Foreign Agricultural Service, "Global Agricultural Trade System (GATS)," <http://www.fas.usda.gov/gats/>, accessed August 2017.

Table 884. Agricultural Exports—Value by Principal Commodity: 2000 to 2016

[In millions of dollars (51,265 represents $51,265,000,000). Includes Puerto Rico, U.S. territories, and shipments under foreign aid programs. Excludes fish, forest products, distilled liquors, manufactured tobacco, and products made from cotton; but includes raw tobacco, raw cotton, rubber, beer and wine, and processed agricultural products. Commodity and commodity grouping definitions used are the Foreign Agricultural Trade of the United States (FATUS) commodity code groupings. See source for more details]

Commodity	Value (mil. dol.)							Percent distribution		
	2000	2005	2010	2013	2014	2015	2016	2000	2010	2016
Total agricultural exports......	**51,265**	**63,182**	**115,820**	**144,356**	**149,990**	**133,070**	**134,714**	**100.0**	**100.0**	**100.0**
Animals and animal products [1]....	11,600	12,227	22,340	31,236	32,849	26,718	25,845	22.6	19.3	19.2
Meat and meat products..........	5,276	4,299	9,336	12,805	14,346	12,406	12,860	10.3	8.1	9.5
Poultry and poultry products......	2,235	3,139	4,806	6,459	6,458	4,915	4,653	4.4	4.1	3.5
Grains and feeds [1]................	13,620	16,364	29,224	33,133	35,420	31,278	30,439	26.6	25.2	22.6
Wheat and products..............	3,578	4,520	7,061	10,768	8,027	5,977	5,671	7.0	6.1	4.2
Corn.............................	4,469	4,789	9,792	6,386	10,582	8,271	9,891	8.7	8.5	7.3
Fruits and preparations............	2,743	3,468	5,262	6,700	6,680	6,285	6,181	5.4	4.5	4.6
Nuts and preparations.............	1,322	2,992	4,795	8,229	8,603	9,058	8,585	2.6	4.1	6.4
Vegetables and preparations [2].....	3,112	3,571	5,375	6,722	7,017	6,995	7,207	6.1	4.6	5.4
Oilseeds and products [1]...........	8,584	10,229	27,265	32,248	34,387	28,332	31,555	16.7	23.5	23.4
Soybeans......................	5,258	6,274	18,611	21,570	23,866	18,875	22,820	10.3	16.1	16.9
Vegetable oils and waxes........	1,259	1,656	3,903	3,546	3,230	3,128	3,029	2.5	3.4	2.2
Tobacco, unmanufactured..........	1,204	990	1,168	1,138	1,086	1,109	1,085	2.3	1.0	0.8
Cotton, excluding linters..........	1,873	3,921	5,734	5,592	4,396	3,889	3,959	3.7	5.0	2.9
Other.............................	7,207	9,421	14,658	19,359	19,552	19,408	19,857	14.1	12.7	14.7

[1] Includes commodities not shown separately. [2] Includes pulses.

Source: U.S. Department of Agriculture, Foreign Agricultural Service, "Global Agricultural Trade System (GATS)," <http://www.fas.usda.gov/gats>, accessed August 2017.

Table 885. Agricultural Exports—Value by World Region and Selected Country of Destination: 2000 to 2016

[51,265 represents $51,265,000,000. Includes Puerto Rico, U.S. territories, and shipments under foreign aid programs. Excludes fish, forest products, distilled liquors, manufactured tobacco, and products made from cotton; but includes raw tobacco, raw cotton, rubber, beer and wine, and processed agricultural products]

Country	Value (mil. dol.)							Percent distribution		
	2000	2005	2010	2013	2014	2015	2016	2000	2010	2016
Total agricultural exports [1]......	**51,265**	**63,182**	**115,820**	**144,356**	**149,990**	**133,070**	**134,714**	**100.0**	**100.0**	**100.0**
Canada................................	7,643	10,619	16,897	21,375	21,963	20,988	20,309	14.9	14.6	15.1
Mexico.................................	6,410	9,429	14,585	18,099	19,364	17,695	17,833	12.5	12.6	13.2
Caribbean.............................	1,408	1,913	3,172	3,535	3,675	3,294	3,382	2.7	2.7	2.5
Central America.......................	1,121	1,589	2,904	3,373	3,824	3,734	3,868	2.2	2.5	2.9
South America........................	1,704	1,943	4,240	7,443	8,093	6,404	6,606	3.3	3.7	4.9
Asia, excluding Middle East [2]........	19,877	22,543	49,766	62,319	65,043	56,491	59,406	38.8	43.0	44.1
Japan.................................	9,292	7,931	11,784	12,231	13,158	11,136	11,036	18.1	10.2	8.2
Korea, South.........................	2,546	2,233	5,307	5,257	6,884	6,028	6,186	5.0	4.6	4.6
Taiwan................................	1,996	2,301	3,190	3,081	3,490	3,150	3,227	3.9	2.8	2.4
China [3].............................	1,716	5,233	17,564	25,499	24,219	20,243	21,401	3.3	15.2	15.9
Indonesia.............................	668	958	2,246	2,823	2,912	2,190	2,680	1.3	1.9	2.0
Europe/Eurasia [2]....................	7,654	8,361	11,365	14,697	15,235	14,096	13,461	14.9	9.8	10.0
European Union [4]....................	6,516	7,059	8,925	11,902	12,565	12,133	11,523	12.7	7.7	8.6
Russia...............................	580	972	1,132	1,208	900	426	250	1.1	1.0	0.2
Middle East...........................	2,323	2,844	5,993	6,477	6,573	5,516	5,625	4.5	5.2	4.2
Africa [2].............................	2,308	2,773	5,725	5,347	4,944	3,553	3,356	4.5	4.9	2.5
Egypt.................................	1,050	819	2,095	1,648	1,723	1,052	741	2.0	1.8	0.6
Oceania..............................	490	742	1,389	1,938	2,155	1,996	1,799	1.0	1.2	1.3

[1] Totals include transshipments through Canada, but transshipments are not distributed by country after 2000. [2] Includes areas not shown separately. [3] China includes Macao; however, Hong Kong remains separate economically until 2050 and is not included. [4] For consistency, data for all years are shown on the basis of 28 countries in the European Union; see footnote 3, Table 1390.

Source: U.S. Department of Agriculture, Foreign Agricultural Service, "Global Agricultural Trade System (GATS)," <http://www.fas.usda.gov/gats>, accessed August 2017.

Table 886. Cropland Used for Crops and Acres Harvested: 1990 to 2016

[In millions of acres, except as indicated (341 represents 341,000,000)]

Item	1990	2000	2005	2010	2011	2012	2013	2014	2015	2016 (P)
Cropland used for crops....................	**341**	**345**	**336**	**335**	**328**	**340**	**336**	**341**	**337**	**337**
Index (1977 = 100)...........................	90	91	89	89	87	90	89	90	(NA)	(NA)
Cropland harvested [1].......................	310	314	314	315	302	315	311	318	316	318
Crop failure.................................	6	11	7	5	13	11	12	10	7	7
Cultivated summer fallow......................	25	20	16	14	14	13	13	14	13	12
Cropland idled by all federal programs [2, 3]...	62	31	35	31	31	30	27	25	24	24
Acres of crops harvested [4]................	**322**	**325**	**321**	**322**	**311**	**324**	**321**	**325**	**323**	**325**

NA Not available. P Preliminary. [1] Land supporting one or more harvested crops. [2] Beginning in 2000, includes only the Conservation Reserve Program; all other federal acreage reduction programs were eliminated by the Federal Agricultural Improvement Act of 1996. [3] Data are for fiscal years. [4] Area in principal crops harvested plus acreages in fruits, vegetables for sale, tree nuts, and other minor crops. Acres are counted twice for land that is double cropped.

Source: U.S. Department of Agriculture, Economic Research Service, *Agricultural Resources and Environmental Indicators*, 2006, and earlier reports; "Major Land Uses," <http://www.ers.usda.gov/data-products/major-land-uses.aspx>, accessed September 2017; and Farm Service Agency, "CRP Enrollment and Rental Payments by State, 1986-2016," <http://www.fsa.usda.gov/programs-and-services/conservation-programs/reports-and-statistics/index>, accessed September 2017.

Table 887. Crops—Supply and Use: 2000 to 2016

[72 represents 72,000,000. Marketing year beginning January 1 for potatoes, May 1 for hay, June 1 for wheat, August 1 for cotton, and September 1 for soybeans and corn. Acreage, production, and yield of all crops periodically revised on basis of census data]

Item	Unit	2000	2005	2010	2013	2014	2015	2016
CORN								
Acreage harvested	Million	72	75	81	87	83	81	87
Yield per acre	Bushel	137	148	153	158	171	168	175
Production	Mil. bu.	9,915	11,112	12,425	13,829	14,216	13,602	15,148
Imports	Mil. bu.	7	9	28	36	32	68	55
Total supply [1]	Mil. bu.	11,639	13,235	14,161	14,686	15,479	15,401	16,940
Ethanol	Mil. bu.	630	1,603	5,019	5,124	5,200	5,224	5,435
Exports	Mil. bu.	1,941	2,134	1,831	1,921	1,867	1,901	2,295
Total use [2]	Mil. bu.	9,740	11,268	13,033	13,454	13,748	13,664	14,590
Ending stocks	Mil. bu.	1,899	1,967	1,128	1,232	1,731	1,737	2,350
Price per unit [3]	Dol./bu.	1.85	2.00	5.18	4.46	3.70	3.61	3.35
Value of production	Mil. dol.	18,499	22,194	64,530	61,928	52,952	49,339	51,704
SOYBEANS								
Acreage harvested	Million	72	71	77	76	83	82	83
Yield per acre	Bushel	38	43	44	44	48	48	52
Production	Mil. bu.	2,758	3,068	3,331	3,358	3,927	3,926	4,307
Imports	Mil. bu.	4	3	14	72	33	24	[9] 25
Total supply [1]	Mil. bu.	3,052	3,327	3,497	3,570	4,052	4,140	[9] 4,528
Crushings	Mil. bu.	1,640	1,739	1,648	1,734	1,873	1,886	[9] 1,940
Exports	Mil. bu.	996	940	1,505	1,639	1,842	1,936	[9] 2,025
Total use [2]	Mil. bu.	2,804	2,878	3,282	3,478	3,862	3,944	[9] 4,093
Ending stocks	Mil. bu.	248	449	215	92	191	197	[9] 435
Price per unit [3]	Dol./bu.	4.54	5.66	11.30	13.00	10.10	8.95	9.50
Value of production	Mil. dol.	12,467	17,297	37,571	43,583	39,475	35,192	40,944
WHEAT								
Acreage harvested	Million	53	50	47	45	46	47	44
Yield per acre	Bushel	42	42	46	47	44	44	53
Production	Mil. bu.	2,228	2,103	2,163	2,135	2,026	2,062	2,310
Imports [4]	Mil. bu.	90	81	97	172	151	113	118
Total supply [1]	Mil. bu.	3,268	2,725	3,236	3,025	2,768	2,927	3,403
Exports	Mil. bu.	1,062	1,003	1,291	1,176	864	778	1,055
Total use [2]	Mil. bu.	2,392	2,154	2,373	2,435	2,015	1,951	2,219
Ending stocks	Mil. bu.	876	571	863	590	752	976	1184
Price per unit [3]	Dol./bu.	2.62	3.42	5.70	6.87	5.99	4.89	3.89
Value of production	Mil. dol.	5,772	7,167	12,579	14,604	11,915	10,018	9,104
COTTON								
Acreage harvested	Million	13	14	11	8	9	8	10
Yield per acre	Pounds	632	831	812	821	838	766	867
Production	Mil. bales [5]	17	24	18	13	16	13	16
Imports	Mil. bales [5]	–	–	–	–	–	–	–
Total supply [1]	Mil. bales [5]	21	29	21	17	19	17	20
Exports	Mil. bales [5]	7	18	14	11	11	9	12
Total use [2]	Mil. bales [5]	16	24	18	14	15	13	16
Ending stocks	Mil. bales [5]	6	6	3	2	4	4	5
Price per unit [3]	Cents/lb.	51.6	49.7	84.6	83.8	65.7	64.5	69.7
Value of production	Mil. dol.	4,260	5,695	7,347	5,192	5,147	3,989	5,672
HAY								
Acreage harvested	Million	60	62	60	58	57	54	53
Yield per acre	Sh. tons	3	2	2	2	2	2	3
Production	Mil. sh. tons	154	150	145	135	140	135	135
Price per unit [6,7]	Dol./ton	84.60	98.20	114.00	176.00	172.00	145.00	129.00
Value of production	Mil. dol.	11,557	12,534	14,607	19,815	19,099	16,549	15,626
POTATOES								
Acreage harvested	Million	1	1	1	1	1	1	1
Yield per acre	Cwt. [8]	381	390	401	414	421	418	433
Production	Mil. cwt. [8]	514	424	405	435	442	441	441
Price per unit [3]	Dol./cwt. [8]	5.08	7.04	9.20	9.75	8.88	8.76	9.08
Value of production	Mil. dol.	2,590	2,982	3,725	4,237	3,928	3,866	4,009

– Represents zero or rounds to less than half the unit of measurement shown. [1] Comprises production, imports, and beginning stocks. [2] Includes feed, residual, and other domestic uses not shown separately. [3] Marketing year average price. U.S. prices are computed by weighting U.S. monthly prices by estimated monthly marketings and do not include an allowance for outstanding loans and government purchases and payments. [4] Includes flour and selected other products expressed in grain-equivalent bushels. [5] Bales of 480 pounds, net weight. [6] Prices are for hay sold baled. [7] Season average prices received by farmers. U.S. prices are computed by weighting state prices by estimated sales. [8] Cwt = hundredweight (100 pounds). [9] Forecast.

Source: U.S. Department of Agriculture, National Agricultural Statistics Service, "Quick Stats," <http://quickstats.nass.usda.gov/>; and U.S. Department of Agriculture, Economic Research Service, "Feed Grains Database," "Oil Crops Yearbook," "Wheat Data," and "Cotton and Wool Yearbook," <http://www.ers.usda.gov/data-products.aspx>, accessed September 2017.

Table 888. Corn—Acreage, Production, and Value by Leading States: 2014 to 2016

[83,136 represents 83,136,000. One bushel of corn (bu.) = 56 pounds. State value of production is computed by multiplying the state price by its production; acreage harvested and production value for the United States is the sum of state values]

State	Acreage harvested (1,000 acres)			Yield per acre (bu.)			Production (mil. bu.)			Price per unit ($/bu.)			Value of production (mil. dol.)		
	2014	2015	2016	2014	2015	2016	2014	2015	2016	2014	2015	2016	2014	2015	2016
U.S. [1]...	83,136	80,753	86,748	171	168	175	14,216	13,602	15,148	3.70	3.61	3.40	52,952	49,339	51,704
IA.........	13,300	13,050	13,500	178	192	203	2,367	2,506	2,741	3.71	3.52	3.35	8,783	8,820	9,181
IL.........	11,750	11,500	11,450	200	175	197	2,350	2,013	2,256	3.71	3.69	3.45	8,719	7,426	7,782
NE........	8,950	9,150	9,550	179	185	178	1,602	1,693	1,700	3.77	3.57	3.35	6,040	6,043	5,695
MN.......	7,550	7,600	8,000	156	188	193	1,178	1,429	1,544	3.58	3.37	3.30	4,217	4,815	5,095
IN.........	5,770	5,480	5,470	188	150	173	1,085	822	946	3.75	3.92	3.55	4,068	3,222	3,359
SD........	5,320	5,030	5,130	148	159	161	787	800	826	3.34	3.30	3.20	2,630	2,639	2,643
KS........	3,800	3,920	4,920	149	148	142	566	580	699	3.78	3.69	3.20	2,140	2,141	2,236
MO.......	3,380	3,080	3,500	186	142	163	629	437	571	3.54	3.69	3.35	2,226	1,614	1,911
OH........	3,470	3,260	3,300	176	153	159	611	499	525	3.78	3.89	3.60	2,309	1,940	1,889
ND........	2,530	2,560	3,270	124	128	158	314	328	517	3.34	3.28	3.15	1,048	1,075	1,627
WI.........	3,110	3,000	3,220	156	164	178	485	492	573	3.67	3.46	3.30	1,781	1,702	1,891
TX.........	1,990	1,970	2,550	148	135	127	295	266	324	4.42	4.20	3.75	1,302	1,117	1,214
MI.........	2,210	2,070	2,040	161	162	157	356	335	320	3.65	3.63	3.45	1,299	1,217	1,105
KY........	1,430	1,310	1,400	158	172	159	226	225	223	3.94	3.88	3.70	890	874	824
CO........	1,010	950	1,170	146	142	137	147	135	160	3.95	3.69	3.55	582	498	569
PA........	1,030	940	950	154	147	129	159	138	123	3.90	3.97	4.05	619	549	496
NC........	780	730	940	132	113	129	103	82	121	4.19	4.32	4.05	431	356	491
TN........	840	730	830	168	160	151	141	117	125	3.81	3.92	3.65	538	458	457
AK........	530	445	745	187	181	171	99	81	127	4.13	4.11	3.70	409	331	471
MS........	485	490	720	185	175	166	90	86	120	4.24	4.01	3.75	380	344	448

[1] Includes other states, not shown separately.

Source: U.S. Department of Agriculture, National Agricultural Statistics Service, "Quick Stats," <http://quickstats.nass.usda.gov/>, accessed March 2017. See also <http://www.nass.usda.gov/Publications>.

Table 889. Soybeans—Acreage, Production, and Value by Leading States: 2014 to 2016

[82,591 represents 82,591,000. One bushel of soybeans (bu.) = 60 pounds. State value of production is computed by multiplying the state price by its production; value for the United States is the sum of state values]

State	Acreage harvested (1,000 acres)			Yield per acre (bu.)			Production (mil. bu.)			Price per unit ($/bu.)			Value of production (mil. dol.)		
	2014	2015	2016	2014	2015	2016	2014	2015	2016	2014	2015	2016	2014	2015	2016
U.S. [1]...	82,591	81,732	82,736	48	48	52	3,927	3,926	4,307	10.10	8.95	9.50	39,475	35,192	40,944
IL.........	9,770	9,720	10,050	56	56	59	547	544	593	10.20	9.19	9.85	5,581	5,002	5,841
IA........	9,770	9,800	9,450	51	57	61	498	554	572	9.96	8.91	9.40	4,963	4,933	5,374
MN.......	7,270	7,550	7,500	42	50	53	302	378	394	9.96	8.75	9.25	3,005	3,303	3,642
ND........	5,870	5,720	6,000	35	33	42	203	186	249	9.49	8.49	9.05	1,922	1,578	2,253
IN........	5,440	5,500	5,640	56	50	58	302	275	324	10.20	9.16	9.70	3,080	2,519	3,146
MO......	5,590	4,470	5,540	47	41	49	260	181	271	9.99	9.16	9.60	2,597	1,658	2,606
SD.......	5,110	5,120	5,170	45	46	50	230	236	256	9.37	8.54	9.10	2,155	2,011	2,329
NE.......	5,330	5,270	5,150	54	58	61	288	306	314	9.73	8.66	9.25	2,800	2,647	2,906
OH.......	4,690	4,740	4,840	53	50	55	246	237	264	10.30	9.16	9.65	2,536	2,171	2,545
KS.......	3,960	3,860	4,010	36	39	48	141	149	192	9.63	8.56	9.35	1,354	1,272	1,800
AR.......	3,200	3,170	3,100	50	49	47	158	155	146	10.60	9.46	9.85	1,679	1,469	1,435
MI.......	2,040	2,020	2,060	43	49	51	87	99	104	10.10	8.82	9.45	876	873	983
MS.......	2,190	2,270	2,020	52	46	48	114	104	97	11.00	9.72	9.95	1,253	1,015	965
WI.......	1,790	1,870	1,950	44	50	55	79	93	107	10.00	8.73	9.35	788	808	1,003

[1] Includes other states, not shown separately.

Source: U.S. Department of Agriculture, National Agricultural Statistics Service, "Quick Stats," <http://quickstats.nass.usda.gov/>, accessed March 2017. See also <http://www.nass.usda.gov/Publications>.

Table 890. Wheat—Acreage, Production, and Value by Leading States: 2014 to 2016

[46,385 represents 46,385,000. One bushel of wheat (bu.) = 60 pounds. State value of production is computed by multiplying the price per unit by total production, for each state; value for the United States is the sum of production values for all states]

State	Acreage harvested (1,000 acres)			Yield per acre (bu.)			Production (mil. bu.)			Price per unit ($/bu.)			Value of production (mil. dol.)		
	2014	2015	2016	2014	2015	2016	2014	2015	2016	2014	2015	2016	2014	2015	2016
U.S. [1]...	46,385	47,318	43,890	44	44	53	2,026	2,062	2,310	5.99	4.89	3.85	11,950	10,018	9,071
KS.........	8,800	8,700	8,200	28	37	57	246	322	467	6.07	4.74	3.20	1,496	1,526	1,496
ND.........	7,490	7,915	7,410	46	47	45	347	370	333	5.74	4.80	4.55	1,992	1,776	1,516
MT.........	5,650	5,365	5,025	37	35	42	209	189	213	6.23	4.83	4.40	1,305	911	936
OK.........	2,800	3,800	3,500	17	26	39	48	99	137	6.34	4.77	3.45	302	471	471
TX.........	2,250	3,550	2,800	30	30	32	68	107	90	6.40	4.71	3.55	432	502	318
CO.........	2,358	2,197	2,200	38	37	48	90	81	106	5.88	4.29	3.10	528	350	329
WA.........	2,250	2,225	2,200	48	50	72	108	112	157	6.55	5.35	4.20	710	599	661
SD.........	2,364	2,236	2,157	56	46	52	131	103	111	5.54	4.58	4.00	727	474	445
NE.........	1,450	1,210	1,310	49	38	54	71	46	71	5.77	4.45	3.10	410	205	219

[1] Includes other states, not shown separately.

Source: U.S. Department of Agriculture, National Agricultural Statistics Service, "Quick Stats," <http://quickstats.nass.usda.gov/>, accessed March 2017. See also <http://www.nass.usda.gov/Publications>.

Table 891. Commercial Vegetable and Other Specified Crops—Area, Production, and Value: 2014 to 2016

[228 represents 228,000. Except as noted, relates to commercial production for fresh market and processing combined. Includes market garden areas but excludes minor producing acreage in minor producing states. Excludes production for home use in farm and nonfarm gardens. Value is for season or crop year and should not be confused with calendar-year income. Hundredweight (cwt.) is the unit used for fresh market yield and production and is equal to one hundred pounds]

Crop	Area harvested (1,000 acres)			Production (1,000 cwt.)			Value of production (mil. dol.) [1]		
	2014	2015	2016	2014	2015	2016 [2]	2014	2015	2016
Beans, snap.................	228	230	236	17,345	19,250	20,005	394	414	441
Fresh market...............	69	71	(NA)	3,720	3,952	4,168	224	235	283
Processed.................	159	159	(NA)	13,625	15,298	15,838	170	179	159
Beans, dry edible.............	1,649	1,708	(NA)	28,910	30,057	28,712	981	866	871
Broccoli....................	126	124	131	20,600	21,888	22,466	825	1,059	851
Cabbage [3].................	60	56	(NA)	21,141	20,178	18,449	416	389	402
Cantaloupes [3].............	58	52	(NA)	13,612	13,552	13,764	301	264	207
Carrots.....................	86	86	84	31,815	31,620	30,306	726	820	818
Cauliflower..................	35	37	37	6,361	6,559	6,660	317	402	389
Celery......................	29	28	29	18,393	17,110	17,062	314	425	359
Corn, sweet.................	523	537	483	76,005	77,714	73,926	998	1,043	897
Fresh market...............	211	229	(NA)	24,649	27,952	23,593	708	788	666
Processed.................	312	308	(NA)	51,356	49,762	50,333	290	255	231
Cucumbers..................	122	123	119	17,633	17,394	17,687	371	348	346
Lettuce, head [3].............	126	119	(NA)	45,918	43,108	47,601	1,120	1,253	1,320
Lettuce, leaf [3].............	54	55	(NA)	12,984	14,233	13,264	492	850	659
Lettuce, Romaine [3].........	85	87	(NA)	24,679	26,335	28,946	764	1,047	902
Onions......................	140	134	133	69,815	67,184	66,709	892	1,039	926
Peas, green [4]..............	188	166	(NA)	7,257	8,226	6,810	133	132	88
Peppers, bell................	44	41	46	15,536	15,155	15,615	626	733	736
Spinach.....................	47	48	48	7,725	7,580	7,135	271	354	292
Squash.....................	39	39	36	6,017	6,016	6,131	188	174	164
Tomatoes...................	404	403	357	320,026	321,462	287,464	2,586	2,603	2,056
Fresh market...............	98	92	(NA)	27,280	26,375	23,668	1,133	1,221	963
Processed.................	306	311	(NA)	292,746	295,087	263,796	1,453	1,382	1,093
Watermelons [3].............	111	116	(NA)	33,263	35,475	40,125	450	488	579

NA Not available. [1] Fresh market vegetables valued at f.o.b. (free on board) shipping point. Processing vegetables are equivalent returns at packinghouse door. [2] Beginning 2016, data is for utilized production only. [3] Fresh market only. [4] Processed only.

Source: U.S. Department of Agriculture, National Agricultural Statistics Service, "Quick Stats," <http://quickstats.nass.usda.gov/>, accessed September 2017.

Table 892. Fruits and Nuts: Utilized Production and Value, 2010 to 2016; and Leading Producing States, 2016

[4,603 represents 4,603,000]

Fruits and nuts	Utilized production [1] (1,000 tons)				Value of utilized production (mil. dol.)				Leading states in order of production, 2016
	2010	2014	2015	2016	2010	2014	2015	2016	
FRUITS									
Apples [2].....................	4,603	5,585	4,983	5,415	2,311	2,871	3,350	3,462	WA, MI, NY
Avocados.....................	174	173	229	171	479	327	433	316	CA, FL, HI
Blackberries, cultivated (OR)....	22	23	26	29	33	50	38	26	OR
Blueberries...................	247	335	330	345	644	889	873	748	WA, OR, MI
Cherries, sweet...............	308	359	334	343	716	767	751	773	WA, OR, CA
Cranberries...................	340	412	423	477	299	254	262	292	WI, MA, NJ
Dates (CA)...................	29	33	39	38	37	50	61	68	CA, AZ
Figs (fresh) (CA).............	41	33	32	32	22	24	25	29	CA
Grapefruit....................	1,238	1,047	910	803	291	242	216	254	FL, TX, CA
Grapes (13 states).............	7,430	7,872	7,621	7,667	4,024	5,822	5,914	6,257	CA, WA, NY
Kiwifruit (CA)................	33	28	21	28	25	33	31	44	CA
Lemons.......................	882	824	904	904	395	641	697	755	CA, AZ
Nectarines....................	233	205	173	168	129	178	158	148	CA, WA
Olives (CA)...................	206	95	179	160	137	74	160	138	CA
Oranges......................	8,243	6,768	6,353	6,088	1,997	2,254	1,963	1,927	FL, CA, TX
Peaches......................	1,130	838	825	779	617	630	606	629	CA, SC, GA
Pears........................	813	831	803	736	387	467	494	475	WA, OR, CA
Plums (CA)...................	142	113	105	135	79	103	105	109	CA
Prunes (dried basis) (CA)......	390	324	319	157	176	267	226	86	CA
Raspberries..................	75	112	145	152	259	527	670	458	CA, WA, OR
Strawberries.................	1,426	1,512	1,533	1,566	2,261	2,822	2,239	2,336	CA, FL, NC
Tangelos (FL)................	41	40	30	18	7	10	9	9	FL
Tangerines and mandarins......	596	732	863	935	275	557	468	490	CA, FL
NUTS [3]									
Almonds (CA).................	1,414	1,548	1,630	1,798	2,903	7,388	5,869	5,158	CA
Hazelnuts (OR)..............	28	36	31	44	67	130	87	119	OR
Macadamia nuts (HI)...........	20	23	24	21	30	40	46	42	HI
Pecans (11 states)..............	147	132	127	134	675	517	560	697	GA, NM, TX
Pistachios (CA)................	261	257	135	448	1,159	1,835	888	1,506	CA
Walnuts (CA).................	504	571	606	686	1,028	1,907	1,012	1,242	CA

NA Not available. [1] Excludes quantities not harvested or not marketed. Utilized production is the amount sold plus the quantities used at home or held in storage. [2] Production in commercial orchards with 100 or more bearing-age trees. [3] In-shell equivalent.

Source: U.S. Department of Agriculture, National Agricultural Statistics Service, *Noncitrus Fruits and Nuts Final Estimates 2007-2012*, October 2014; *Citrus Fruits Final Estimates, 2008-2012*, August 2014; *Citrus Fruits 2017 Summary*, August 2017; and *Noncitrus Fruits and Nuts 2016 Summary*, June 2017. See also <https://www.nass.usda.gov/Data_and_Statistics/index.php>.

Table 893. Nuts—Supply and Use: 2000 to 2015

[In thousands of pounds (shelled) (331,466 represents 331,466,000). Season begins in July for hazelnuts, August for almonds, September for pistachios, and October for pecans. For walnuts, season began in August through 2007; as of 2008, season begins September 1]

Year	Beginning stocks	Marketable production [1]	Imports	Supply, total	Consumption	Exports	Ending stocks
Total nuts: [2]							
2000.........................	331,466	1,127,940	293,172	1,752,577	733,921	780,988	237,669
2010.........................	422,217	2,482,242	487,969	3,392,428	1,199,062	1,786,058	407,308
2013.........................	462,065	2,806,741	582,051	3,850,857	1,270,208	2,075,233	505,416
2014.........................	505,416	2,738,442	657,432	3,901,290	1,285,164	2,030,707	585,419
2015, total [2, 3]............	585,419	2,694,286	679,232	3,958,938	1,341,629	2,056,824	560,484
Almonds....................	376,614	1,856,506	31,812	2,264,932	580,630	1,272,300	412,001
Pecans.....................	54,323	(NA)	114,842	273,678	142,203	80,277	51,198
Pistachios..................	79,032	135,000	1,151	215,183	66,103	98,369	50,711
Hazelnuts..................	1,459	47,270	9,224	57,954	21,588	36,162	203
Walnuts....................	73,991	529,644	10,782	614,417	139,939	428,107	46,371

NA Not available. [1] Utilized production minus inedibles and noncommercial usage. [2] Includes macadamia nuts, Brazil nuts, cashew nuts, pine nuts, chestnuts, and mixed nuts, not shown separately. [3] Data are preliminary.

Source: U.S. Department of Agriculture, Economic Research Service, "Fruit and Tree Nut Yearbook Tables," <http://www.ers.usda.gov/data-products/fruit-and-tree-nut-data/yearbook-tables.aspx>, accessed November 2016. See also <http://www.ers.usda.gov/topics/crops/fruit-tree-nuts.aspx>.

Table 894. Honey—Number of Bee Colonies, Yield, and Production: 1990 to 2016

[3,220 represents 3,220,000. Includes only beekeepers with five or more colonies. Colonies were not included if honey was not harvested]

Year	Honey-producing colonies [1] (1,000)	Yield per colony (pounds)	Production (1,000 pounds)	Average price per pound (cents)	Value of production (1,000 dollars)
1990.......................	3,220	61.7	198,674	54	106,688
1995.......................	2,655	79.5	211,073	69	144,585
2000.......................	2,622	84.0	220,286	60	132,865
2005.......................	2,409	72.5	174,614	92	160,994
2010.......................	2,692	65.6	176,462	162	285,692
2013.......................	2,640	56.6	149,499	214	320,077
2014.......................	2,740	65.1	178,270	217	387,381
2015.......................	2,660	58.9	156,544	208	326,081
2016.......................	2,775	58.3	161,882	208	335,905

[1] Honey producing colonies are the maximum number of colonies from which honey was taken during the year. It is possible to take honey from colonies which did not survive the entire year.

Source: U.S. Department of Agriculture, National Agricultural Statistics Service, *Honey–Final Estimates 2008-2012*, September 2014, and earlier editions; and *Honey*, March 2017. See also <http://www.nass.usda.gov/Surveys/Guide_to_NASS_Surveys/Bee_and_Honey>.

Table 895. Vegetables and Dry Edible Beans—Supply and Utilization: 2000 to 2016

[40,556 represents 40,556,000,000. Data for calendar year except where noted. Vegetable data excludes melons]

Item	Unit	2000	2005	2010	2013	2014	2015	2016 (P)
VEGETABLES, FRESH MARKET								
Production...........................	Mil. lbs.	40,556	40,332	37,921	36,906	36,897	35,780	36,507
Imports..............................	Mil. lbs.	5,492	7,773	10,924	11,974	12,735	13,134	14,569
Total supply..........................	Mil. lbs.	47,393	49,597	50,414	50,351	51,157	50,661	52,552
Exports..............................	Mil. lbs.	3,709	3,712	3,382	3,484	3,380	3,015	3,265
Ending stocks [1].....................	Mil. lbs.	1,266	1,280	1,488	1,524	1,747	1,475	1,655
Domestic consumption...............	Mil. lbs.	41,461	43,864	44,710	44,625	45,357	45,522	46,904
Per capita consumption.............	Lbs.	146.8	148.1	144.3	140.9	142.1	141.8	145.1
VEGETABLES, PROCESSED MARKET [2]								
Production...........................	Mil. lbs.	35,369	33,265	36,570	35,824	40,031	40,248	37,352
Imports..............................	Mil. lbs.	3,581	5,555	6,263	6,482	6,616	7,196	7,632
Total supply..........................	Mil. lbs.	62,174	62,646	71,191	70,104	72,285	73,393	75,655
Exports..............................	Mil. lbs.	4,479	4,889	6,627	9,716	10,645	10,211	10,230
Ending stocks.......................	Mil. lbs.	23,291	20,838	27,999	25,638	25,935	30,671	30,983
Domestic consumption...............	Mil. lbs.	34,404	36,919	36,565	34,750	35,705	32,510	34,443
Per capita consumption.............	Lbs.	121.8	124.6	118.0	109.7	111.9	101.2	106.5
POTATOES, FRESH MARKET								
Utilized production [3].................	Mil. lbs.	13,185	12,076	11,342	11,129	10,596	10,982	10,717
Imports..............................	Mil. lbs.	806	788	916	861	1,028	882	1,094
Total supply..........................	Mil. lbs.	13,990	12,863	12,258	11,990	11,624	11,864	11,811
Exports..............................	Mil. lbs.	677	639	856	1,056	922	905	1,074
Domestic consumption...............	Mil. lbs.	13,314	12,224	11,402	10,935	10,702	10,959	10,737
Per capita consumption.............	Lbs.	47.2	41.3	36.8	34.5	33.5	34.1	33.2
DRY EDIBLE BEANS								
Production...........................	Mil. lbs.	2,654	2,658	3,180	2,460	2,891	3,006	2,871
Imports..............................	Mil. lbs.	128	216	288	261	329	342	325
Exports..............................	Mil. lbs.	782	560	909	1,027	1,105	925	1,009
Domestic consumption...............	Mil. lbs.	2,175	1,809	2,175	1,900	1,865	2,331	2,235
Per capita consumption.............	Lbs.	7.7	6.1	7.0	6.0	5.8	7.2	6.9

P Preliminary. [1] Applies only to brussel sprouts, onions, and okra. [2] Includes vegetables for canning and freezing. Excludes potatoes and mushrooms. [3] Crop year utilization for the past season and the current season distributed on a calendar year basis using National Agricultural Statistics Service potato marketing distributions.

Source: U.S. Department of Agriculture, Economic Research Service, *Vegetable and Pulses Yearbook*, April 2017. See also <http://www.ers.usda.gov/data-products/vegetables-and-pulses-data.aspx>.

Table 896. Organic Vegetable, Fruit, and Field Crops—Farms, Production, and Value of Sales: 2015

[Unit column indicates quantity harvested and sales. Includes certified organic producers who have been certified by state or private agencies accredited by the USDA. Organic food must be produced without the use of conventional pesticides, petroleum-based or sewage sludge-based fertilizers, herbicides, pesticides, genetic engineering (biotechnology), antibiotics, growth hormones, or irradiation. Land must have no prohibited substances applied to it for at least 3 years before the harvest of an organic crop. Cwt = hundredweight (100 pounds)]

Commodity	Unit	Farms (number)	Acres harvested (number)[1]	Quantity harvested	Sales Quantity	Value of sales (1,000 dollars)
Vegetables, potatoes, and melons[2]						
Grown in the open	(X)	2,999	185,325	(X)	(X)	1,361,747
Beans, snap, fresh	Cwt	595	1,211	90,536	86,993	10,207
Cabbage, all	Cwt	650	1,803	329,008	312,946	15,643
Carrots	Cwt	636	9,072	2,060,833	1,952,550	83,191
Garlic	Cwt	629	608	37,547	33,153	8,727
Lettuce	Cwt	806	37,916	3,566,770	3,514,404	262,246
Onions	Cwt	554	1,317	481,808	448,620	19,732
Peppers, bell	Cwt	614	1,153	227,407	214,409	25,760
Potatoes	Cwt	688	13,281	3,983,505	3,206,755	66,306
Squash	Cwt	1,316	6,773	956,917	891,861	39,114
Tomatoes, fresh	Cwt	1,184	3,301	446,169	432,266	67,938
Grown under protection[3]	(X)	1,059	14,751,343	(X)	(X)	73,202
Carrots	Cwt	63	101,534	796	738	144
Herbs, fresh cut	Pounds	109	2,668,680	1,862,307	1,715,266	18,072
Lettuce	Cwt	220	1,020,407	13,153	12,682	3,942
Peppers, bell	Cwt	168	453,166	4,508	3,987	724
Spinach	Cwt	139	229,909	4,508	784	413
Tomatoes	Cwt	753	6,314,503	123,492	90,797	18,746
Apples, all	Pounds	699	15,763	468,115,749	455,668,996	302,404
Grapes, all	Tons	714	27,912	138,533	134,501	209,568
Other fruits, tree nuts, and berries[2]	(X)	2,993	63,397	(X)	(X)	691,410
Avocado	Tons	321	3,880	9,035	9,009	24,875
Oranges, all	Tons	279	5,174	46,994	45,741	31,176
Peaches	Tons	243	2,790	18,986	18,245	30,882
Pears	Tons	270	2,286	23,604	22,018	23,216
Almonds	Pounds	81	6,209	7,437,236	7,316,789	40,600
Walnuts, English	Tons	196	6,151	4,429	3,705	18,174
Blueberries, cultivated, all	Pounds	587	5,706	38,847,325	37,069,941	124,488
Strawberries	Cwt	603	4,031	908,293	765,447	151,318
Field crops[2]	(X)	6,403	1,458,706	(X)	(X)	660,044
Barley for grain or seed	Bushels	505	50,826	2,719,286	2,193,883	19,272
Corn for grain or seed	Bushels	2,720	166,841	18,468,287	11,688,523	129,067
Corn for silage or greenchop	Tons	947	35,149	552,324	59,730	4,310
Hay, all dry	Tons	3,451	430,331	1,211,668	579,766	116,768
Oats for grain or seed	Bushels	1,000	39,647	2,467,515	1,623,185	10,451
Soybeans for beans	Bushels	1,420	94,841	3,183,364	2,580,732	62,543
Wheat, all	Bushels	1,035	301,950	9,016,548	7,866,708	108,625

X Not applicable. [1] For crops grown under protection, data are shown in square feet under glass or other protection. [2] Includes commodities not shown separately. [3] Includes vegetables grown in greenhouses under glass, rigid plastic, and plastic film, including tunnel protection and hoop houses.

Source: U.S. Department of Agriculture, National Agricultural Statistics Service, *Certified Organic Survey, 2015 Summary*, September 2016. See also <https://www.nass.usda.gov/Surveys/Guide_to_NASS_Surveys/Organic_Production/index.php>.

Table 897. Organic Livestock and Poultry—Farms, Inventory, and Value of Sales: 2015

[Includes all known organic producers that are certified organic. Animals raised on an organic operation must be fed organic feed and given access to the outdoors]

Type of livestock and poultry	Farms (number)	Inventory[1] (number)	Value of sales (dollars)
Milk cows	2,282	229,197	65,361,338
Beef cows	455	37,719	8,982,291
Other cattle[2]	2,753	193,254	158,251,289
Hogs and pigs	135	8,366	5,112,388
Sheep and lambs	72	7,814	1,117,592
Goats and kids	52	3,972	278,873
Other livestock[3]	23	(X)	135,800
Chickens, layers	730	12,916,545	1,461,403
Chickens, broilers	187	7,920,677	420,312,003
Turkeys	74	235,857	70,020,593
Other poultry[4]	80	(X)	12,193,694

X Not applicable. [1] As of December 31, 2015. [2] Includes organic bulls, beef calves, replacement milk heifers, etc. [3] Includes organic livestock not listed separately on the report form, such as farm raised bison, deer, rabbits, and fish. [4] Includes organic poultry not listed separately on the report form, including ducks, quail, etc.

Source: U.S. Department of Agriculture, National Agricultural Statistics Service, *Certified Organic Survey, 2015 Summary*, September 2016. See also <https://www.nass.usda.gov/Surveys/Guide_to_NASS_Surveys/Organic_Production/index.php>.

Table 898. Horticultural Specialty Crop Operations, Value of Sales, and Total Land Area Used to Grow Horticultural Crops: 2014

[Horticultural specialty operation is defined as any place that produced and sold $10,000 or more of horticultural specialty products. Excludes mushrooms as well as grass seeds, vegetables, and fruits grown in the open. See source for more information]

| Item | Operations | Value of sales (1,000) | Total land area [1] | | | Area in open (acres) [2] |
			Green-houses (1,000 square feet)	Shade structures (1,000 square feet)	Natural shade (acres)	
Horticultural specialty crops, total	**23,221**	**13,789,048**	**894,907**	**429,708**	**5,404**	**497,339**
Annual bedding/garden plants	7,964	2,567,534	282,790	17,537	195	7,294
Herbaceous perennial plants	6,291	944,850	31,262	8,857	292	5,397
Potted flowering plants for indoor or patio use	4,059	1,084,274	63,039	21,576	16	1,794
Foliage plants for indoor or patio use	2,644	721,889	40,164	104,013	47	1,828
Cut flowers	1,998	462,098	57,514	11,378	97	15,931
Cut cultivated greens	728	99,040	3,269	3,269	2,159	2,295
Nursery stock sold	8,226	4,266,631	203,861	166,717	2,224	302,202
Propagative material [3]	1,067	695,126	29,492	83,640	94	12,346
Sod, sprigs, or plugs	1,289	1,138,465	707	2,459	13	55,019
Dried bulbs, corms, rhizomes, and tubers	204	74,014	359	36	8	5,309
Food crops grown under protection	2,521	796,664	84,507	186	75	5,330
Transplants for commercial vegetable production [4]	693	371,817	26,638	2,366	(D)	7,618
Vegetable seeds	385	135,122	510	(D)	(D)	32,620
Flower seeds	169	31,607	172	14	(D)	4,869
Aquatic plants	345	20,205	878	45	2	1,274
Cut Christmas trees	3,352	366,632	516	170	29	26,500
Short rotation woody crops [5]	49	1,845	(NA)	(NA)	(NA)	(NA)
Tobacco transplants	183	11,236	(NA)	(NA)	(NA)	(NA)

D Withheld to avoid disclosure. NA Not available. [1] Total land area represents the land utilized on the operation as the area used for horticultural production. Includes volume of stacked benches and stacked pots and the area used to produce multiple crop types. [2] Excludes acres in production for Christmas trees or sod, sprigs, or plugs. [3] Includes cuttings, plug seedlings, liners, tissue cultured plantlets, and prefinished plants. As of 2014, this data includes seedlings for reforestation and may not be comparable to 2009 data. [4] Includes strawberries. [5] Includes transplants grown for sale; excludes transplants for the farmer's own use.

Source: U.S. Department of Agriculture, National Agricultural Statistics Service, *2014 Census of Horticultural Specialties*, Vol. 3, December 2015. See also <http://www.agcensus.usda.gov/Publications/Census_of_Horticulture_Specialties/>.

Table 899. Meat Supply and Consumption: 2000 to 2016

[In millions of pounds, carcass weight equivalent (82,372 represents 82,372,000,000). Carcass weight equivalent is the weight of the animal minus entrails, head, hide, and internal organs; includes fat and bone. Covers federal and state inspected, and farm slaughtered]

Year and type of meat	Production	Imports	Supply [1]	Exports	Consumption [2]	Ending stocks
RED MEAT AND POULTRY						
2000	82,372	4,144	88,460	9,343	77,073	2,044
2005	86,783	4,856	93,787	9,274	82,328	2,185
2010	91,769	3,459	97,222	13,961	81,147	2,113
2013	92,949	3,447	98,604	15,776	80,687	2,142
2014	91,864	4,299	98,305	15,853	80,385	2,066
2015	94,289	4,877	101,233	14,276	84,596	2,361
2016 [3]	97,269	4,506	104,137	15,173	86,595	2,369
RED MEATS, TOTAL						
2000	46,299	4,127	51,313	3,760	46,556	996
2005	45,849	4,803	51,805	3,373	47,367	1,066
2010	49,180	3,323	53,617	6,538	45,934	1,145
2013	49,271	3,302	53,833	7,582	45,022	1,230
2014	47,435	4,153	52,817	7,672	43,955	1,190
2015	48,520	4,700	54,410	7,282	45,808	1,320
2016 [3]	50,481	4,322	56,123	7,801	47,019	1,304
Beef:						
2000	26,888	3,032	30,332	2,468	27,338	525
2005	24,787	3,599	29,022	697	27,754	571
2010	26,412	2,298	29,275	2,300	26,390	585
2013	25,790	2,250	28,648	2,588	25,476	584
2014	24,316	2,947	27,846	2,574	24,682	591
2015	23,760	3,371	27,722	2,267	24,771	683
2016 [3]	25,288	3,015	28,986	2,556	25,673	757
Pork:						
2000	18,952	965	20,378	1,287	18,639	453
2005	20,705	1,024	22,239	2,666	19,093	480
2010	22,456	859	23,840	4,223	19,077	541
2013	23,203	880	24,707	4,986	19,104	618
2014	22,858	1,011	24,487	5,092	18,836	559
2015	24,517	1,116	26,191	5,010	20,592	590
2016 [3]	24,957	1,091	26,638	5,239	20,891	507
Veal:						
2000	225	(NA)	230	(NA)	225	5
2005	165	(NA)	169	(NA)	164	5
2010	145	(NA)	154	(NA)	150	4
2013	117	(NA)	123	(NA)	119	4
2014	100	(NA)	104	(NA)	98	6
2015	88	(NA)	94	(NA)	88	6
2016 [3]	81	(NA)	87	(NA)	73	14
Lamb and mutton:						
2000	234	130	372	5	354	13
2005	191	180	375	9	356	10
2010	168	166	348	16	317	15
2013	161	173	355	7	324	25
2014	161	195	380	7	340	34
2015	155	214	403	4	357	41
2016 [3]	155	216	412	5	381	26
POULTRY, TOTAL						
2000	36,073	16	37,147	5,583	30,516	1,048
2005	40,935	54	41,981	5,902	34,961	1,119
2010	42,589	136	43,605	7,423	35,214	968
2013	43,678	145	44,771	8,194	35,665	912
2014	44,429	147	45,487	8,181	36,429	877
2015	45,769	177	46,823	6,994	38,788	1,041
2016 [3]	46,789	184	48,014	7,372	39,577	1,065
Broilers:						
2000	30,209	13	31,017	4,918	25,302	798
2005	34,986	42	35,730	5,203	29,617	910
2010	36,515	107	37,238	6,762	29,703	773
2013	37,425	122	38,198	7,345	30,184	669
2014	38,153	117	38,938	7,297	30,961	680
2015	39,620	131	40,431	6,321	33,278	832
2016 [3]	40,260	131	41,223	6,644	33,800	778
Mature chicken:						
2000	531	2	541	220	312	9
2005	516	3	522	130	390	2
2010	504	4	510	79	427	4
2013	523	2	526	108	412	6
2014	521	2	529	109	417	3
2015	522	2	527	145	374	8
2016 [3]	548	3	559	158	392	8
Turkeys:						
2000	5,333	1	5,589	445	4,902	241
2005	5,432	9	5,730	570	4,954	206
2010	5,570	25	5,857	581	5,084	192
2013	5,729	20	6,046	741	5,068	237
2014	5,756	27	6,020	775	5,052	193
2015	5,627	45	5,866	529	5,136	201
2016 [3]	5,981	50	6,232	569	5,384	279

NA Not available. [1] Total supply equals production plus imports plus ending stocks of previous year. [2] Includes shipments to territories. [3] Preliminary data.

Source: U.S. Department of Agriculture, Economic Research Service, "Livestock and Meat Domestic Data," <http://www.ers.usda.gov/data-products/livestock-meat-domestic-data.aspx>, accessed July 2017.

Table 900. Livestock Inventory and Production: 1990 to 2016

[95.8 represents 95,800,000. Production in live weight; includes animals-for-slaughter market, younger animals shipped to other states for feeding or breeding purposes, farm slaughter and custom slaughter consumed on farms where produced, minus livestock shipped into states for feeding or breeding with an adjustment for changes in inventory]

Type of livestock	Unit	1990	2000	2005	2010	2011	2012	2013	2014	2015	2016
ALL CATTLE [1]											
Inventory (number on farms): [2]	Mil.	95.8	98.2	95.0	94.1	92.9	91.2	90.1	88.5	89.1	91.9
Total value	Bil. dol.	59.0	67.1	87.0	78.3	88.0	101.3	102.6	108.3	141.2	129.6
Value per head	Dol.	616	683	916	833	947	1,111	1,139	1,223	1,584	1,410
Production: Quantity	Bil. lb.	39.2	43.0	41.2	41.4	41.5	40.9	40.7	40.2	41.3	42.7
Cattle, price per 100 pounds [3]	Dol.	(NA)	68.4	89.6	92.0	113.0	122.0	125.0	153.0	148.0	120.0
Calves, price per 100 pounds	Dol.	95.6	104.0	135.0	121.0	142.0	173.0	174.0	255.0	263.0	166.0
Value of production	Bil. dol.	29.3	28.5	36.3	36.9	45.1	48.1	48.5	59.9	59.8	48.6
HOGS AND PIGS											
Inventory (number on farms): [4]	Mil.	53.8	59.3	61.0	64.7	64.7	66.3	66.2	64.8	67.8	68.9
Total value	Bil. dol.	4.3	4.3	6.3	5.4	6.9	8.1	7.7	8.9	9.8	6.6
Value per head	Dol.	79	72	103	83	106	123	116	138	144	96
Production: Quantity	Bil. lb.	21.3	25.7	27.4	30.3	30.8	32.1	32.6	32.2	34.9	35.6
Price per 100 pounds	Dol.	53.7	42.3	49.6	55.1	66.5	64.2	67.2	77.1	53.5	49.6
Value of production	Bil. dol.	11.3	10.8	13.6	16.0	20.0	20.3	21.7	24.2	18.9	17.2
SHEEP AND LAMBS											
Inventory (number on farms): [2]	Mil.	11.4	7.0	6.1	5.6	5.5	5.4	5.4	5.2	5.3	5.3
Total value	Mil. dol.	901	670	798	761	929	1,188	951	984	1,129	1,072
Value per head	Dol.	79	95	130	135	170	221	177	188	214	202
Production: Quantity	Mil. lb.	781	512	472	405	(NA)	(NA)	(NA)	(NA)	(NA)	(NA)
Value of production	Mil. dol.	374	365	451	443	(NA)	(NA)	(NA)	(NA)	(NA)	(NA)

NA Not available. [1] Includes milk cows. [2] As of January 1. [3] Cattle weighing 500 pounds or more. [4] As of December 1 of preceding year.

Source: U.S. Department of Agriculture, National Agricultural Statistics Service, "Quick Stats," <http://quickstats.nass.usda.gov/>, accessed May 2017. See also *Meat Animals Production, Disposition, and Income Annual Summary*, <http://www.nass.usda.gov/Publications>.

Table 901. Livestock Operations by Size of Herd: 2000 to 2012

[In thousands (1,076 represents 1,076,000). An operation is any place having one or more head on hand at any time during the year]

Size of herd	2000	2010	2011	2012	Size of herd	2000	2010	2011	2012
CATTLE [1]					MILK COWS [2]				
Total operations	1,076	935	922	913	Total operations	105	63	60	64
1 to 49 head	671	635	627	637	1 to 49 head	53	31	30	34
50 to 99 head	186	129	127	118	50 to 99 head	31	16	15	15
100 to 499 head	192	142	139	130	100 head or more	21	16	16	14
500 to 999 head	19	19	19	17					
1,000 head or more	10	11	11	11	HOGS AND PIGS				
					Total operations	87	69	69	63
BEEF COWS [2]					1 to 99 head	50	49	49	47
Total operations	831	742	734	728	100 to 499 head	17	5	5	4
1 to 49 head	655	588	583	594	500 to 999 head	8	3	2	2
50 to 99 head	100	82	81	71	1,000 to 1,999 head	6	4	3	3
100 to 499 head	71	66	64	57	2,000 to 4,999 head	5	5	6	5
500 head or more	6	6	6	6	5,000 head or more	2	3	3	3

[1] Includes calves. [2] Included in operations with cattle.

Source: U.S. Department of Agriculture, National Agricultural Statistics Service, *Livestock Operations Final Estimates 2003–2007*, March 2009; and *Farms, Land in Farms, and Livestock Operations 2012 Summary*, February 2013. Beginning with 2012 data, *2012 Census of Agriculture*, Vol. 1, May 2014. See also <http://www.agcensus.usda.gov/Publications/index.php>.

Table 902. Hogs and Pigs—Number, Production, and Slaughter by Leading States: 2014 to 2016

[67,776 represents 67,776,000. Production in live weight. See headnote Table 900]

State	Number on farms [1] (1,000)			Quantity produced (mil. lb.)			Value of production (mil. dol.)			Commercial slaughter [2] (mil. lb.)	
	2014	2015	2016	2014	2015	2016	2014	2015	2016	2015	2016
U.S. [3]	67,776	68,919	71,500	32,182	34,856	35,611	24,222	18,877	17,215	32,675	33,302
IA	21,300	20,900	22,400	11,519	12,318	12,388	7,995	6,222	5,516	8,802	9,101
NC	8,800	8,900	9,300	3,538	3,925	4,147	2,822	2,210	2,074	(D)	(D)
MN	8,100	8,100	8,300	4,011	4,124	4,239	2,923	2,177	1,974	2,905	2,932
IL	4,700	5,100	5,100	1,937	2,077	2,122	1,601	1,213	1,134	3,358	3,444
IN	3,700	3,850	4,100	1,632	1,826	1,966	1,194	951	916	2,375	2,392
NE	3,200	3,300	3,400	1,192	1,303	1,326	1,006	780	720	2,216	2,234
MO	2,850	3,050	3,100	1,498	1,557	1,628	1,214	892	831	2,555	2,628

D Data withheld to limit disclosure. [1] As of December 1. [2] Includes slaughter in federally inspected and other slaughter plants; excludes animals slaughtered on farms. [3] Includes other states, not shown separately.

Source: U.S. Department of Agriculture, National Agricultural Statistics Service, "Quick Stats," <http://quickstats.nass.usda.gov/>, accessed May 2017. See also *Meat Animals Production, Disposition, and Income Annual Summary* and *Livestock Slaughter Annual Summary*, <http://www.nass.usda.gov/Publications>.

Table 903. Cattle and Calves—Number, Production, and Value by Leading States: 2014 to 2017

[89,143 represents 89,143,000. Includes milk cows. See headnote, Table 900]

State	Number on farms [1] (1,000)			Production (mil. lb.)			Value of production (mil. dol.)			Commercial slaughter [2] (mil. lb.)	
	2015	2016	2017	2014	2015	2016	2014	2015	2016	2015	2016
U.S. [3]......	89,143	91,918	93,585	40,171	41,340	42,725	59,922	59,836	48,626	39,030	41,576
TX............	11,700	11,800	12,300	5,962	6,299	6,111	9,041	9,237	7,243	6,578	7,089
NE............	6,250	6,450	6,450	5,093	5,344	5,696	7,284	7,394	6,331	9,394	10,266
KS............	5,900	6,250	6,400	3,700	3,854	4,234	4,614	4,712	4,590	7,760	8,364
CA............	5,100	5,150	5,150	1,880	1,880	1,815	2,582	2,461	1,973	1,592	1,637
OK............	4,550	4,800	5,000	2,031	2,043	2,073	3,308	3,173	2,557	27	29
MO............	4,000	4,100	4,350	1,137	1,202	1,293	2,051	2,035	1,673	46	45
IA............	3,850	3,950	3,850	1,924	1,904	2,083	2,841	2,829	2,487	(D)	(D)
SD............	3,700	3,900	3,850	1,514	1,476	1,520	2,500	2,381	1,909	(D)	(D)
WI............	3,500	3,500	3,550	1,271	1,366	1,394	1,911	2,085	1,609	1,586	1,687
CO............	2,550	2,700	2,850	1,595	1,687	1,653	2,398	2,474	1,901	3,265	3,437
MT............	2,500	2,650	2,650	1,108	1,120	1,140	1,751	1,660	1,315	23	25

D Data withheld to limit disclosure. [1] As of January 1. [2] Data cover cattle only. Includes slaughter in federally inspected and other slaughter plants; excludes animals slaughtered on farms. [3] Includes other states, not shown separately.

Source: U.S. Department of Agriculture, National Agricultural Statistics Service, "Quick Stats," <http://quickstats.nass.usda.gov/>, accessed May 2017. See also *Meat Animals Production, Disposition, and Income Annual Summary* and *Livestock Slaughter Annual Summary*, <http://www.nass.usda.gov/Publications>.

Table 904. Milk Cows—Number, Production, and Value by Leading States: 2014 to 2016

[9,257 represents 9,257,000]

State	Number on farms [1] (1,000)			Milk produced on farms [2] (mil. lb.)			Milk produced per milk cow (pounds) [2]			Value of production [3] (mil. dol.)		
	2014	2015	2016	2014	2015	2016	2014	2015	2016	2014	2015	2016
U.S. [4]......	9,257	9,314	9,328	206,054	208,597	212,436	22,259	22,396	22,774	49,589	35,904	34,710
CA............	1,780	1,776	1,762	42,339	40,897	40,469	23,786	23,028	22,968	9,365	6,298	6,070
WI............	1,271	1,279	1,279	27,795	29,030	30,123	21,869	22,697	23,552	6,810	5,167	5,061
NY............	615	618	620	13,730	14,094	14,765	22,325	22,806	23,815	3,487	2,565	2,510
ID............	575	585	595	13,873	14,114	14,665	24,127	24,126	24,647	3,205	2,357	2,361
PA............	530	530	529	10,664	10,800	10,820	20,121	20,377	20,454	2,741	1,998	1,861
TX............	463	463	475	10,310	10,301	10,773	22,268	22,248	22,680	2,536	1,823	1,853
MN............	460	460	461	9,127	9,462	9,666	19,841	20,570	20,967	2,263	1,665	1,624
MI............	390	408	419	9,609	10,261	10,876	24,638	25,150	25,957	2,316	1,703	1,642
NM............	323	323	315	8,105	7,831	7,711	25,093	24,245	24,479	1,807	1,261	1,203

[1] Average number during year. Represents cows and heifers that have calved, kept for milk; excluding heifers not yet fresh. [2] Excludes milk sucked by calves. [3] Valued at average returns per 100 pounds of milk in combined marketings of milk and cream. Includes value of milk fed to calves. [4] Includes other states, not shown separately.

Source: U.S. Department of Agriculture, National Agricultural Statistics Service, "Quick Stats," <http://quickstats.nass.usda.gov/>, accessed May 2017. See also *Milk: Production, Disposition, and Income Annual Summary*, <http://www.nass.usda.gov/Publications>.

Table 905. Milk Production and Manufactured Dairy Products: 2000 to 2016

[105 represents 105,000]

Item	Unit	2000	2005	2010	2011	2012	2013	2014	2015	2016
Number of farms with milk cows..............	**1,000**	**105**	**78**	**63**	**60**	**58**	**(NA)**	**(NA)**	**(NA)**	**(NA)**
Cows and heifers that have calved, kept for milk [1]........................	Mil. head	9.2	9.1	9.1	9.2	9.2	9.2	9.3	9.3	9.3
Milk produced on farms.........................	Bil. lb.	167	177	193	196	201	201	206	209	212
Production per cow.............................	1,000 lb.	18.2	19.6	21.1	21.3	21.7	21.8	22.3	22.4	22.8
Milk marketed by producers [2]..................	Bil. lb.	166	176	192	195	200	200	205	208	211
Value of milk produced.........................	Bil. dol.	20.7	26.9	31.5	39.7	37.2	40.5	49.6	35.9	34.7
Cash receipts from marketing of milk and cream [2]................................	Bil. dol.	20.6	26.7	31.4	39.5	37.1	40.3	49.4	35.7	34.5
Number of dairy manufacturing plants.......	**Number**	**1,164**	**1,088**	**1,250**	**1,278**	**1,281**	**1,265**	**1,269**	**1,273**	**1,272**
Manufactured dairy products:										
Butter (including whey butter)...................	Mil. lb.	1,256	1,347	1,564	1,810	1,860	1,863	1,855	1,850	1,839
Cheese, total [3]................................	Mil. lb.	8,258	9,149	10,443	10,595	10,886	11,102	11,512	11,831	12,158
American (excl. full-skim American)..........	Mil. lb.	3,642	3,808	4,289	4,227	4,355	4,420	4,588	4,694	4,756
Cream and Neufchatel.......................	Mil. lb.	687	715	745	715	808	842	852	876	909
All Italian varieties..........................	Mil. lb.	3,289	3,803	4,416	4,585	4,633	4,735	4,950	5,082	5,293
Cottage cheese—creamed and lowfat.........	Mil. lb.	735	785	719	704	709	678	668	681	697
Nonfat dry milk [4].............................	Mil. lb.	1,457	1,210	1,563	1,499	1,764	1,478	1,765	1,822	1,754
Dry whey [5]..................................	Mil. lb.	1,188	1,041	1,013	1,010	999	953	870	978	955
Yogurt, plain and fruit-flavored..................	Mil. lb.	1,837	3,058	4,181	4,271	4,417	4,715	4,757	4,646	4,456
Ice cream, regular.............................	Mil. gal.	980	960	929	888	894	897	866	897	919
Ice cream, lowfat [6]...........................	Mil. gal.	373	360	415	415	457	401	412	439	435

NA Not available. [1] Average number during year, excluding heifers not yet fresh. [2] Comprises sales to plants and dealers, and retail sales by farmers direct to consumers. [3] Includes varieties not shown separately. [4] Data for 2000 includes dry skim milk for animal feed. [5] Includes animal but excludes modified whey production. [6] Includes freezer-made milkshake in most states.

Source: U.S. Department of Agriculture, National Agricultural Statistics Service, "Quick Stats," <http://quickstats.nass.usda.gov/>, accessed May 2017; *Dairy Products Annual Summary*; *Milk Production, Disposition, and Income Annual Summary*; and *Farms, Land in Farms, And Livestock Operations, Summary*, annual. See also <http://www.nass.usda.gov/Publications/index.asp>.

Table 906. Milk Production and Commercial Use in All Products: 2000 to 2016

[In billions of pounds milkfat basis (167.4 represents 167,400,000,000) except as noted. Changes have been made to conversion factors used for dairy stocks, trade, and commercial use estimates; data have been revised and are not comparable to data previously shown. See <https://www.ers.usda.gov/data-products/dairy-data/documentation>]

| Year | Farm milk supply use | | | Begin-ning stocks | Imports | Com-mercial supply, total | Commercial use | | Ending stocks [1] | Milk price per 100 pounds [2] (dollars) |
	Produc-tion	Farm use	Farm market-ings				USDA net removals	Disap-pear-ance		
2000......	167.4	1.3	166.1	5.8	4.5	176.3	0.3	168.0	6.4	12.30
2005......	176.9	1.1	175.8	6.8	7.4	190.0	–	180.0	7.5	15.10
2010......	192.9	1.0	191.9	10.7	4.0	206.6	0.2	188.2	10.1	16.30
2011.......	196.3	1.0	195.3	10.1	3.5	208.9	–	189.6	10.2	20.10
2012......	200.6	1.0	199.7	10.2	4.1	214.0	–	194.1	11.4	18.50
2013......	201.2	1.0	200.3	11.4	3.7	215.4	–	193.0	10.3	20.10
2014......	206.1	1.0	205.1	10.3	4.3	219.7	–	197.1	10.5	24.00
2015......	208.6	1.0	207.6	10.5	5.7	223.8	–	203.0	12.3	17.10
2016......	212.4	1.0	211.4	12.3	7.0	230.8	–	209.2	12.7	16.20

– Represents or rounds to zero. [1] Includes commercial stocks of butter, cheese, canned milk, dry milk products, whey products, and lactose. [2] Wholesale price received by farmers for all milk delivered to plants and dealers.

Source: U.S. Department of Agriculture, Economic Research Service, "Dairy Data," <http://www.ers.usda.gov/data-products/dairy-data.aspx>, accessed June 2017.

Table 907. Broiler Chicken, Turkey, and Egg Production: 1990 to 2016

[353 represents 353,000,000. For years ending November 30, except as noted]

Item	Unit	1990	1995	2000	2005	2010	2012	2013	2014	2015	2016
Chickens: [1]											
Number [2]................	Million	353	388	437	456	457	467	475	484	477	495
Value per head [2]........	Dollars	2.29	2.41	2.44	2.52	3.58	4.04	4.15	4.11	4.37	4.20
Value, total [2]...........	Mil. dol.	808	935	1,064	1,150	1,637	1,886	1,972	1,989	2,085	2,075
Number sold............	Million	208	180	218	194	173	179	186	191	197	206
Value of sales...........	Mil. dol.	94	60	64	65	73	79	88	96	103	85
PRODUCTION											
Broilers: [3]											
Number..................	Million	5,864	7,326	8,284	8,872	8,624	8,463	8,534	8,545	8,689	8,777
Weight...................	Bil. lb.	25.6	34.2	41.6	47.9	49.2	49.7	50.7	51.4	53.4	54.3
Production value........	Mil. dol.	8,366	11,762	13,989	20,878	23,692	24,828	30,762	32,728	28,716	25,936
Turkeys: [4]											
Number..................	Million	282	292	270	250	244	254	240	238	233	244
Weight...................	Bil. lb.	6.0	6.8	7.0	7.0	7.1	7.6	7.3	7.2	7.0	7.5
Production value........	Mil. dol.	2,393	2,769	2,828	3,108	4,372	5,452	4,840	5,305	5,708	6,184
Eggs:											
Average number of layers...............	Thousand	270,946	294,350	329,067	345,027	341,505	344,844	354,844	364,707	352,411	365,336
Eggs per layer..........	Number	251	254	257	262	269	274	275	277	276	279
Total production.........	Billion	68.1	74.8	84.7	90.3	91.8	94.4	97.6	100.9	97.2	102.0
in dozens.............	Million	(NA)	(NA)	(NA)	(NA)	(NA)	(NA)	(NA)	8,404	8,101	8,496
Production value........	Mil. dol.	4,021	3,893	4,359	4,067	6,553	7,929	8,679	10,258	13,608	6,483

NA Not available. [1] Excludes commercial broilers. [2] As of December 1. [3] Young chickens of the heavy breeds and other meat-type birds, to be marketed at 2-5 lbs. live weight and from which no pullets are kept for egg production. Not included in sales of chickens. [4] Data for turkeys are for year ending August 31.

Source: U.S. Department of Agriculture, National Agricultural Statistics Service, "Quick Stats," <http://quickstats.nass.usda.gov/>, accessed May 2017; and *Poultry Production and Value Final Estimates 2008-2012*, October 2014, and earlier reports; *Chickens and Eggs Final Estimates 2008-2012*, September 2014, and earlier reports; *Poultry—Production and Value*, annual; and *Chickens and Eggs*, annual. See also <http://www.nass.usda.gov/Publications>.

Table 908. Broiler Chicken and Turkey Production by Leading States: 2014 to 2016

[In millions of pounds, live weight production (51,379 represents 51,379,000,000)]

| State | Broiler chickens | | | Turkeys | | | State | Broiler chickens | | | Turkeys | | |
	2014	2015	2016	2014	2015	2016		2014	2015	2016	2014	2015	2016
U.S. [1].....	51,379	53,376	54,259	7,217	7,038	7,487	MO......	1,385	1,414	1,436	546	600	626
AL.........	6,051	6,173	5,993	(NA)	(NA)	(NA)	NC......	6,044	6,417	6,468	998	1,091	1,203
AR.........	6,015	6,157	6,561	612	561	525	OH......	431	450	475	209	209	237
CA.........	(NA)	(NA)	(NA)	310	338	324	OK......	1,338	1,432	1,363	(NA)	(NA)	(NA)
DE.........	1,733	1,759	1,843	(NA)	(NA)	(NA)	PA......	997	1,066	1,040	173	163	190
FL.........	387	378	367	(NA)	(NA)	(NA)	SC......	1,651	1,747	1,811	(NA)	(NA)	(NA)
GA.........	7,548	7,904	8,066	(NA)	(NA)	(NA)	SD......	(NA)	(NA)	(NA)	188	181	180
IN.........	(NA)	(NA)	(NA)	754	753	759	TN......	939	982	929	(NA)	(NA)	(NA)
KY.........	1,725	1,785	1,832	(NA)	(NA)	(NA)	TX......	3,551	3,774	3,840	(NA)	(NA)	(NA)
MD........	1,555	1,730	1,851	(NA)	(NA)	(NA)	UT......	(NA)	(NA)	(NA)	97	95	122
MI.........	(NA)	(NA)	(NA)	206	205	217	VA......	1,441	1,472	1,534	444	461	468
MN........	281	278	295	1,178	976	1,104	WV......	372	356	352	82	91	111
MS.........	4,509	4,552	4,658	(NA)	(NA)	(NA)	WI......	224	226	227	(NA)	(NA)	(NA)

NA Not available. [1] Includes other states, not shown separately.

Source: U.S. Department of Agriculture, National Agricultural Statistics Service, "Quick Stats," <http://quickstats.nass.usda.gov/>, accessed May 2017. See also *Poultry—Production and Value*, <http://www.nass.usda.gov/Publications>.

Forestry, Fishing, and Mining

This section presents data on the area, ownership, production, trade, reserves, and disposition of natural resources, defined here as including forestry, fisheries, and mining and mineral products.

Forestry—This section presents data on the area, ownership, and timber resource of commercial timberland; forestry statistics covering the National Forests and Forest Service cooperative programs; product data for lumber, pulpwood, woodpulp, paper and paperboard; and similar data.

The principal sources of data relating to forests and forest products are *Forest Resources of the United States, 2017; Timber Demand and Technology Assessment; U.S. Timber Production, Trade, Consumption, and Price Statistics, 1965 to 2013; Land Areas of the National Forest System*, issued annually by the Forest Service of the U.S. Department of Agriculture; *Agricultural Statistics*, issued by the Department of Agriculture; and reports of the Annual Survey of Manufactures issued by the U.S. Census Bureau, see <http://www.census.gov/programs-surveys/asm.html>. Further sources used in this section and issued by the U.S. Census Bureau include the annual *County Business Patterns* reports, and the 2012 Economic Census. Additional information is published in the annual *Wood Pulp and Fiber Statistics* and *The Annual Statistics of Paper, Paperboard, and Wood Pulp* of the American Forest and Paper Association, Washington, DC.

The completeness and reliability of statistics on forests and forest products vary considerably. The data for forest land area and stand volumes are much more reliable for areas that have been recently surveyed than for those for which only estimates are available. In general, more data are available for lumber and other manufactured products such as particle board and softwood panels, etc., than for the primary forest products such as poles and piling and fuelwood.

Fisheries—The principal source of data relating to fisheries is data issued annually by the National Marine Fisheries Service (NMFS), National Oceanic and Atmospheric Administration (NOAA). The NMFS collects and disseminates data on commercial landings of fish and shellfish. Annual reports include quantity and value of commercial landings of fish and shellfish, disposition of landings, and number and kinds of fishing vessels and fishing gear. Reports for the fish-processing industry include annual output for wholesaling, and fish processing establishments and annual and seasonal employment. The principal source for these data is the annual *Fisheries of the United States*. Additional government sources include *Agricultural Statistics*, issued annually by the Department of Agriculture; and *Trout Production* and *Catfish Production*, issued by the National Agricultural Statistics service of the U.S. Department of Agriculture.

Mining and mineral products—This section presents data relating to mineral industries and their products, summary measures of production and employment, and more detailed data on production, prices, imports and exports, consumption, and distribution for specific industries and products. Data on mining and mineral products may also be found in Sections 19, 21, 28, and 30 of this *Abstract*; data on mining employment may be found in Section 12.

Mining comprises the extraction of minerals occurring naturally (coal, ores, crude petroleum, natural gas) and quarrying, well operation, milling, refining and processing, and other preparation customarily done at the mine or well site or as a part of extraction activity. (Mineral preparation plants are usually operated together with mines or quarries.) Exploration for minerals is included as is the development of mineral properties.

The principal governmental sources of these data are the *Minerals Yearbook* and *Mineral Commodity Summaries*, published by the U.S. Geological Survey, U.S. Department of the Interior, and various monthly and annual publications of the Energy Information Administration, U.S. Department of Energy. See text, Section 19, for a list of Department of Energy publications.

Mineral statistics, with principal emphasis on commodity detail, have been collected by the U.S. Geological Survey and the former Bureau of Mines since 1880. Current data in U.S. Geological Survey publications include quantity and value of nonfuel minerals produced, sold, or used by producers, or shipped; quantity of minerals stocked; crude materials treated and prepared minerals recovered; and consumption of mineral raw materials.

The Economic Census, conducted by the Census Bureau at various intervals since 1840, collects data on mineral industries. Beginning with the 1967 census, legislation provides for a census to be conducted every 5 years for years ending in "2" and "7."Data from the 2012 Economic Census have been fully released as of September 2016 through the Census Bureau's American FactFinder® service on the Census Bureau website at <factfinder.census.gov>. Economic Census data are based on the North American Industry Classification System (NAICS). The Census provides, for the various types of mineral establishments, information on operating costs, capital expenditures, labor, equipment, and energy requirements in relation to their value of shipments and other receipts.

Table 909. Natural Resource–Related Industries—Establishments, Employees, and Annual Payroll by Industry: 2014 and 2015

[In units as indicated (1,632.7 represents 1,632,700; 112.19 represents $112,190,000,000). Excludes most government employees, railroad employees, and self-employed persons. See source for definitions and statement on reliability of data. An establishment is a single physical location where business is conducted or where services or industrial operations are performed. See Appendix III]

Industry	2012 NAICS Code [1]	Establishments (number)		Number of employees [2] (1,000)		Annual payroll (bil. dol.)	
		2014	2015	2014	2015	2014	2015
Natural resource–related industries, total............	(X)	**69,578**	**69,881**	**1,632.7**	**1,633.3**	**112.19**	**104.90**
Forestry, fishing, hunting, and agriculture support.....	**11**	**21,844**	**22,368**	**156.4**	**160.1**	**6.18**	**6.53**
Forestry and logging...............................	113	8,557	8,754	54.2	56.2	2.34	2.54
Timber tract operations.......................	1131	473	473	3.0	3.7	0.18	0.23
Forest nurseries and gathering forest products..........	1132	176	183	1.5	1.4	0.05	0.06
Logging...	1133	7,908	8,098	49.6	51.1	2.11	2.24
Fishing, hunting and trapping............................	114	2,636	2,688	7.5	7.5	0.38	0.40
Fishing...	1141	2,306	2,343	6.0	5.9	0.34	0.35
Hunting and trapping........................	1142	330	345	1.5	1.6	0.05	0.05
Agriculture and forestry support activities................	115	10,651	10,926	94.7	96.5	3.45	3.59
Crop production support activities........................	1151	4,683	4,761	65.1	65.3	2.41	2.46
Animal production support activities.....................	1152	4,339	4,485	19.1	19.5	0.61	0.65
Forestry support activities....................	1153	1,629	1,680	10.5	11.7	0.43	0.49
Mining, quarrying and oil, and gas extraction............	**21**	**29,754**	**29,225**	**759.0**	**743.7**	**70.65**	**61.65**
Oil and gas extraction.....................................	211	8,256	7,906	137.8	135.5	18.86	17.28
Mining (except oil and gas)................................	212	6,384	6,324	197.9	191.9	14.72	13.99
Coal mining.......................................	2121	916	881	76.6	69.9	6.17	5.40
Metal ore mining...............................	2122	370	330	41.9	40.2	3.65	3.56
Nonmetallic mineral mining and quarrying................	2123	5,098	5,113	79.4	81.8	4.89	5.03
Mining support activities..................................	213	15,114	14,995	423.3	416.2	37.07	30.37
Timber–related manufacturing............................	**(X)**	**17,980**	**18,288**	**717.4**	**729.5**	**35.37**	**36.72**
Wood product manufacturing...............................	321	13,719	14,071	365.4	378.5	14.37	15.24
Sawmills and wood preservation...........................	3211	3,153	3,165	79.9	84.1	3.40	3.57
Veneer, plywood and engineered wood product manufacturing..................................	3212	1,407	1,407	68.3	69.8	3.07	3.22
Other wood product manufacturing........................	3219	9,159	9,499	217.2	224.6	7.90	8.45
Paper manufacturing......................................	322	4,261	4,217	352.0	351.0	21.00	21.48
Pulp, paper and paperboard mills.........................	3221	451	460	106.6	105.7	7.99	8.07
Converted paper product manufacturing..................	3222	3,810	3,757	245.4	245.3	13.01	13.41

X Not applicable. [1] Data based on North American Industry Classification System (NAICS), 2012. [2] Covers full- and part-time employees who are on the payroll in the pay period including March 12.

Source: U.S. Census Bureau, County Business Patterns, "Geography Area Series: County Business Patterns," <http://factfinder.census.gov>, accessed April 2017. See also <https://www.census.gov/programs-surveys/cbp.html>.

Table 910. Natural Resource–Related Industries—Establishments, Sales, Payroll, and Employees by Industry: 2007 and 2012

[414 represents $414,000,000,000. Includes only establishments with payroll. Data are based on the 2007 and 2012 economic censuses, which are subject to nonsampling error. For details on methodology and nonsampling and sampling errors, see Appendix III]

Industry	2007 NAICS code [1]	Establishments (number)		Value of shipments (bil. dol.)		Annual payroll (bil. dol.)		Paid employees [2] (1,000)	
		2007	2012	2007	2012	2007	2012	2007	2012
Mining...	21	22,667	25,417	414	529	41	59	730	848
Oil & gas extraction............................	211	6,260	6,735	255	311	10	15	150	176
Mining (except oil & gas).....................	212	6,472	6,091	86	98	12	14	211	212
Mining support activities......................	213	9,935	12,591	73	120	19	30	369	460
Manufacturing [3]................................	31–33	332,536	297,191	5,319	5,697	614	593	13,396	11,214
Wood product manufacturing................	321	16,868	13,579	102	78	17	12	524	337
Paper manufacturing..........................	322	4,988	4,425	177	181	21	20	418	350
Petroleum & coal products manufacturing...	324	2,283	2,193	615	851	9	9	106	101

[1] Data based on North American Industry Classification System (NAICS), 2007. [2] For pay period including March 12. [3] Includes other industries, not shown separately.

Source: U.S. Census Bureau, 2012 Economic Census, "EC1200CCOMP1: All sectors: Core Business Statistics Series: Comparative Statistics for the U.S. (2007 NAICS Basis): 2012 and 2007," <http://factfinder.census.gov>, accessed September 2016.

Table 911. Gross Domestic Product of Natural Resource-Related Industries in Current and Real (2009) Dollars by Industry: 2010 to 2016

[In billions of dollars (14,964.4 represents $14,964,400,000,000). Data are based on the 2007 North American Industry Classification System (NAICS); see text, Section 15. Data include nonfactor charges (capital consumption allowances, indirect business taxes, etc.) as well as factor charges against gross product; corporate profits and capital consumption allowances have been shifted from a company to an establishment basis]

Industry	Current dollars				Chained (2009) dollars			
	2010	2014	2015	2016	2010	2014	2015	2016
All industries, total [1].............	**14,964.4**	**17,393.1**	**18,036.6**	**18,569.1**	**14,783.8**	**15,982.3**	**16,397.2**	**16,662.1**
Industries covered [2]....................	569.3	771.6	592.8	515.4	487.8	592.6	613.4	582.1
Percent of all industries..............	3.8	4.4	3.3	2.8	3.3	3.7	3.7	3.5
Private industries......................	12,826.5	15,115.8	15,698.7	16,177.5	12,650.2	13,754.4	14,144.3	14,381.9
Agriculture, forestry, fishing, and hunting......	160.2	203.2	175.2	159.9	140.3	143.0	146.5	158.1
Farms.................................	129.7	166.2	136.7	[3] 121.2	111.5	111.4	114.9	[3] 127.1
Forestry, fishing, and related activities.......	30.5	36.9	38.5	[3] 38.8	28.8	32.3	32.3	[3] 32.0
Mining.................................	331.7	482.7	327.8	264.6	272.7	376.2	392.0	348.8
Oil and gas extraction................	209.3	338.2	206.2	[3] 169.9	158.6	243.2	281.7	[3] 270.6
Mining, except oil and gas...........	77.3	72.7	65.8	[3] 59.2	70.1	66.5	59.6	[3] 52.9
Support activities for mining...........	45.1	71.7	55.9	[3] 35.4	46.0	64.8	52.0	[3] 34.9
Timber-related manufacturing.............	77.4	85.7	89.8	90.9	74.8	73.4	74.9	75.2
Wood products........................	22.1	29.1	30.2	[3] 31.6	21.4	22.0	23.5	[3] 24.4
Paper products.......................	55.3	56.6	59.6	[3] 59.3	53.4	51.4	51.4	[3] 50.8

[1] Includes industries not shown separately. [2] Sum of agriculture/forestry/fishing/hunting, mining, and timber-related manufacturing. [3] All statistics for 2016 are prepared by taking the average of the corresponding quarterly series. For annual series marked as underlying detail, the quarterly statistics on which these estimates rely are of lower quality and pass through a less rigorous review process than the higher level aggregates in which they are included.

Source: U.S. Bureau of Economic Analysis, Industry Economic Data, GDP-by-Industry, "Value Added by Industry" and "Real Value Added by Industry," <http://www.bea.gov/itable/>, accessed April 2017.

Table 912. Timber–Based Manufacturing Industries—Establishments, Shipments, Payroll, and Employees: 2012

[78,123,546 represents $78,123,546,000. Includes only establishments or firms with payroll. Data for industries with NAICS codes less than 6-digits were derived by summing values with the corresponding 6-digit NAICS codes. See Appendix III]

Industry	2012 NAICS code [1]	Establish-ments (number)	Value of shipments ($1,000)	Annual payroll ($1,000)	Paid employees [2]
Wood product manufacturing...............	**321**	**13,741**	**78,123,546**	**12,520,235**	**338,773**
Saw mills............................	321113	2,928	18,785,567	2,629,715	64,743
Wood preservation...................	321114	421	4,285,259	367,257	8,061
Hardwood veneer and plywood manufacturing.........	321211	240	2,532,796	439,647	11,734
Softwood veneer and plywood manufacturing.........	321212	100	4,221,047	623,881	13,739
Engineered wood member (except truss) manufacturing.....	321213	107	901,798	120,672	2,854
Truss manufacturing.................	321214	772	3,084,288	696,224	18,828
Reconstituted wood product manufacturing..............	321219	218	6,365,849	661,850	13,531
Wood window and door manufacturing..........	321911	1,139	9,196,661	1,815,229	46,713
Cut stock, resawing lumber, and planing..........	321912	989	5,979,132	838,090	24,358
Other millwork (including flooring)............	321918	1,502	4,994,874	920,332	26,738
Wood container and pallet manufacturing..........	321920	2,687	6,889,954	1,438,803	49,003
Manufactured home (mobile home) manufacturing..........	321991	271	3,492,514	686,290	20,912
Prefabricated wood building manufacturing..........	321992	615	2,323,210	441,883	12,012
All other miscellaneous wood product manufacturing.........	321999	1,752	5,070,597	840,362	25,547
Paper manufacturing.......................	**322**	**4,425**	**180,610,366**	**19,910,069**	**350,185**
Pulp mills...........................	322110	32	5,985,071	590,813	7,728
Paper (except newsprint) mills............	322121	166	44,026,857	4,193,576	60,217
Newsprint mills......................	322122	17	2,720,026	255,201	3,573
Paperboard mills.....................	322130	156	28,441,347	2,612,294	34,910
Corrugated and solid fiber box manufacturing..............	322211	1,264	33,604,124	4,146,346	76,372
Folding paperboard box manufacturing...........	322212	507	12,596,499	1,991,529	39,456
Other paperboard container manufacturing..........	322219	344	7,604,741	909,918	21,047
Paper bag and coated and treated paper manufacturing.....	322220	816	21,304,814	2,601,905	50,481
Stationery product manufacturing.............	322230	460	6,944,097	913,180	21,876
Sanitary paper product manufacturing.............	322291	142	12,175,509	949,647	18,071
All other converted paper product manufacturing..............	322299	521	5,207,281	745,660	16,455

[1] North American Industry Classification System, 2012. [2] For pay period including March 12.

Source: U.S. Census Bureau, 2012 Economic Census, "EC1200A1: All sectors: Geographic Area Series: Economy-Wide Key Statistics: 2012," <http://factfinder.census.gov>, accessed September 2016.

Table 913. Timber-Based Manufacturing Industries—Employees, Payroll, and Shipments: 2015

[In thousands (11,167 represents 11,167,000). Based on the Annual Survey of Manufactures, see Appendix III]

Selected industry	2012 NAICS code [1]	All employees — Number (1,000)	All employees — Payroll Total (mil. dol.)	All employees — Payroll Per employee (dol.)	Production workers, total (1,000)	Value added by manufactures Total (mil. dol.)	Value added by manufactures Per production worker (dol.)	Value of shipments (mil. dol.)
Manufacturing, all industries [2]	31–33	11,167	636,504	56,999	7,808	2,430,098	311,233	5,546,998
Timber-based manufacturing, total	321–322	702	35,772	50,950	554	126,632	228,378	282,704
Percent of total manufacturing	(X)	6.3	5.6	(X)	7.1	5.2	(X)	5.1
Wood product manufacturing	321	367	15,035	41,015	294	40,780	138,857	97,193
Sawmills and wood preservation	3211	76	3,595	47,032	64	10,650	165,754	28,974
Veneer, plywood, and engineered wood product	3212	72	3,169	44,280	57	8,586	151,073	20,948
Other wood product	3219	219	8,271	37,841	173	21,544	124,823	47,272
Millwork	32191	102	4,128	40,319	81	11,348	139,275	24,865
Wood container and pallet	32192	53	1,764	33,309	43	4,069	95,356	9,154
All other wood products	32199	63	2,379	37,623	48	6,128	126,469	13,253
Manufactured (mobile) home	321991	21	778	37,590	17	1,833	106,949	4,134
Prefabricated wood building	321992	16	604	38,955	11	1,407	133,895	3,162
All other misc. wood product	321999	27	997	36,884	21	2,888	138,793	5,957
Paper manufacturing	322	336	20,737	61,805	261	85,852	329,187	185,510
Pulp, paper, and paperboard mills	3221	102	7,830	76,595	81	43,394	535,000	80,432
Pulp mills	32211	8	707	85,068	7	3,166	464,539	6,182
Paper mills	32212	59	4,319	73,145	48	22,638	476,468	44,415
Paperboard mills	32213	35	2,804	80,419	27	17,590	656,768	29,834
Converted paper product	3222	233	12,906	55,323	180	42,458	236,285	105,079
Paperboard container	32221	138	7,746	56,057	107	22,654	211,382	60,803
Paper bag and coated and treated paper	32222	46	2,609	57,065	34	9,542	278,068	21,242
Stationery product	32223	18	826	46,950	13	2,423	181,959	6,586
Other converted paper products	32229	32	1,725	54,269	25	7,839	314,958	16,448

X Not applicable. [1] North American Industry Classification System, 2012; see text, Section 15. [2] Includes other industries, not shown separately.

Source: U.S. Census Bureau, Annual Survey of Manufactures, "Statistics for Industry Groups and Industries: 2015 and 2014," <http://factfinder.census.gov>, accessed January 2017.

Table 914. Forest Land and Timberland by Type of Owner and Region: 2017

[Preliminary data. In thousands of acres (765,493 represents 765,493,000). As of January 1. Data are from the U.S. Forest Service's Forest Inventory and Analysis National Program. Forest land is land at least 10 percent stocked by forest trees of any size, including land that formerly had such tree cover and that will be naturally or artificially regenerated. The minimum area for classification of forest land is 1 acre or strips of timber with a crown width of at least 120 feet wide. Timberland is forest land that is producing or is capable of producing crops of industrial wood and that is not withdrawn from timber utilization by statute or administrative regulation]

Region	Forest land, total	Timberland Total	Timberland Federal Total	Timberland Federal National forest	Timberland Federal Bureau of Land Management lands	Timberland Federal Other	Timberland State, county, and municipal	Timberland Private [1]
Total	765,493	514,425	108,178	96,138	6,109	5,931	47,095	359,152
North	175,789	164,894	11,348	10,146	12	1,190	25,650	127,896
Northeast	84,727	78,539	2,852	2,355	0	498	10,102	65,586
North Central	91,062	86,355	8,495	7,792	12	692	15,549	62,310
South	245,513	208,092	16,397	12,258	0	4,138	9,561	182,135
Southeast	89,692	85,754	7,016	5,061	0	1,955	5,618	73,119
South Central	155,821	122,338	9,380	7,197	0	2,183	3,942	109,016
Rocky Mountains	130,641	69,654	47,111	44,206	2,688	217	3,193	19,350
Great Plains	6,797	6,084	1,217	1,051	18	148	265	4,602
Intermountain	123,844	63,569	45,894	43,154	2,670	70	2,927	14,748
Pacific Coast	213,549	71,784	33,323	29,527	3,409	386	8,691	29,771
Alaska	128,735	12,996	4,874	3,848	812	213	4,810	3,313
Pacific Northwest	51,827	41,462	19,200	16,802	2,299	98	3,637	18,625
Pacific Southwest [2]	32,986	17,326	9,249	8,877	297	75	245	7,833

[1] Includes Indian lands. [2] Includes Hawaii.

Source: U.S. Forest Service, National Assessment - Resources Planning Act (RPA), *Forest Resources of the United States, 2017: A Technical Document Supporting the Forest Service Update of the 2010 RPA Assessment*, March 2017. See also <https://www.fia.fs.fed.us/program-features/rpa/>.

Table 915. National Forest System Lands by State: 2016

[In thousands of acres (232,496 represents 232,496,000). As of September 30, 2016. Data do not include Delaware, District of Columbia, Hawaii, Iowa, Maryland, Massachusetts, New Jersey, or Rhode Island]

State	Total lands	National Forest System lands[1]	Other lands[2]	State	Total lands	National Forest System lands[1]	Other lands[2]
United States	**232,496**	**192,921**	**39,575**	Nevada	6,292	5,760	532
Alabama	1,290	671	620	New Hampshire	847	748	98
Alaska	24,007	22,143	1,864	New Mexico	10,249	9,224	1,025
Arizona	11,813	11,204	609	New York	17	16	–
Arkansas	3,549	2,593	956	North Carolina	3,027	1,256	1,771
California	24,286	20,772	3,514	North Dakota	1,103	1,103	–
Colorado	15,960	14,485	1,475	Ohio	856	244	612
Connecticut	–	–	–	Oklahoma	759	400	359
Florida	1,423	1,200	223	Oregon	17,655	15,697	1,958
Georgia	1,796	868	929	Pennsylvania	741	514	227
Idaho	21,713	20,445	1,268	South Carolina	1,381	633	749
Illinois	958	305	653	South Dakota	2,435	2,005	430
Indiana	647	204	443	Tennessee	1,291	720	571
Kansas	109	109	–	Texas	2,002	757	1,245
Kentucky	2,205	820	1,385	Utah	9,211	8,190	1,021
Louisiana	1,032	609	423	Vermont	837	410	427
Maine	94	54	41	Virginia	3,254	1,666	1,588
Michigan	4,887	2,874	2,013	Washington	11,990	9,331	2,658
Minnesota	5,488	2,844	2,643	West Virginia	1,893	1,046	847
Mississippi	2,374	1,191	1,183	Wisconsin	2,003	1,524	479
Missouri	3,093	1,507	1,585	Wyoming	9,726	9,215	511
Montana	19,189	17,183	2,006	Puerto Rico	56	29	27
Nebraska	562	351	211	Virgin Islands	–	–	–

– Represents or rounds to zero. [1] National Forest System is a nationally significant system of federally owned units of forest, range, and related land consisting of national forests, purchase units, national grasslands, land utilization project areas, experimental forest areas, experimental range areas, designated experimental areas, and other land areas; water areas; and interests in lands that are administered by USDA Forest Service or designated for administration through the Forest Service. [2] Other lands are lands within the unit boundaries in private, state, county, and municipal ownership and the federal lands over which the Forest Service has no jurisdiction. Also includes lands offered to the United States and approved for acquisition and subsequent Forest Service administration, but to which title has not yet been accepted by the United States.

Source: U.S. Forest Service, *Land Areas of the National Forest System as of September 30, 2016,* November 2016. See also <http://www.fs.fed.us/land/staff/lar/LAR2016/lar2016index.html>.

Table 916. Timber Volume, Growth, and Removal on Timberland by Species Group and Region: 2016 and 2017

[Preliminary data. In millions of cubic feet (1,116,012 represents 1,116,012,000,000). Data are from the U.S. Forest Service's Forest Inventory and Analysis National Program]

Region	2017 Net volume[1]						2016 Net growth and removals of growing stock					
	All timber[2]			Growing stock[3]			Timber growth[4]			Timber removals[5]		
	All species	Soft-woods	Hard-woods	All species	Soft-woods	Hard-woods	All species	Soft-woods	Hard-woods	All species	Soft-woods	Hard-woods
Total	**1,116,012**	**598,873**	**517,139**	**985,238**	**560,526**	**424,712**	**25,009**	**15,468**	**9,542**	**12,901**	**8,805**	**4,096**
North	314,204	68,278	245,926	270,041	60,601	209,440	5,932	1,546	4,386	2,399	624	1,774
Northeast	172,556	41,465	131,091	152,780	37,108	115,672	3,264	917	2,347	1,144	357	787
North Central	141,647	26,813	114,834	117,261	23,494	93,768	2,668	629	2,039	1,254	268	987
South	377,781	149,800	227,981	319,088	141,307	177,781	13,764	9,268	4,496	7,813	5,581	2,232
Southeast	167,894	71,539	96,355	142,603	67,540	75,063	6,393	4,285	2,108	3,458	2,667	791
South Central	209,887	78,261	131,626	176,485	73,767	102,717	7,371	4,983	2,388	4,355	2,914	1,441
Rocky Mountains	144,222	128,750	15,472	130,005	119,102	10,903	299	189	109	404	396	8
Great Plains	8,476	2,537	5,938	4,487	1,885	2,601	57	-2	59	34	29	5
Intermountain	135,747	126,213	9,534	125,518	117,217	8,301	242	192	50	370	367	3
Pacific Coast	279,805	252,044	27,760	266,104	239,515	26,589	5,015	4,465	550	2,286	2,204	82
Alaska	39,229	35,639	3,590	37,140	33,761	3,379	254	133	121	39	39	–
Pacific Northwest	166,844	153,680	13,163	159,238	146,480	12,758	3,707	3,423	284	1,892	1,811	81
Pacific Southwest[6]	73,732	62,725	11,007	69,726	59,273	10,452	1,054	909	145	355	355	–

– Represents or rounds to zero. [1] As of January 1. [2] Includes growing stock, live cull and sound dead. [3] Live trees of commercial species meeting specified standards of quality or vigor. Cull trees are excluded. Includes only trees 5.0-inches in diameter or larger at 4 1/2 feet above ground. [4] The net increase in the volume of trees during a specified year. Components include the increment in net volume of trees at the beginning of the specific year surviving to its end, plus the net volume of trees reaching the minimum size class during the year, minus the volume of trees that died during the year, and minus the net volume of trees that became cull trees during the year. [5] The net volume of trees removed from the inventory during a specified year by harvesting, cultural operations such as timber stand improvement, or land clearing. [6] Includes Hawaii.

Source: U.S. Forest Service, National Assessment - Resources Planning Act (RPA), *Forest Resources of the United States, 2017: A Technical Document Supporting the Forest Service Update of the 2010 RPA Assessment,* March 2017. See also <https://www.fia.fs.fed.us/program-features/rpa/>.

Table 917. Timber Removals—Roundwood Product Output by Source and Species Group: 2011

[In million cubic feet (12,808 represents 12,808,000,000). Data are from U.S. Forest Service's Forest Inventory and Analysis National Program]

Source and species group	Total	Sawlogs	Pulpwood	Veneer logs	Other products [1]	Fuelwood [2]
Total..................	**12,808**	**4,988**	**5,033**	**700**	**283**	**1,804**
Softwoods..................	8,362	3,647	3,353	624	223	515
Hardwoods..................	4,446	1,341	1,680	76	60	1,289
Growing stock [3]..................	10,758	4,752	4,483	680	209	633
Softwoods..................	7,460	3,494	3,064	608	159	135
Hardwoods..................	3,298	1,257	1,419	73	50	498
Other sources [4]..................	2,050	236	550	19	74	1,170
Softwoods..................	902	152	289	16	64	379
Hardwoods..................	1,149	84	261	3	10	791

[1] Includes poles, pilings, posts, cooperage and miscellaneous products. [2] Downed and dead wood volume left on the ground after trees have been cut on timberland. [3] Includes live trees of commercial species meeting specified standards of quality or vigor. Cull trees are excluded. Includes only trees 5.0-inches in diameter or larger at 4.5 feet above the ground. [4] Includes salvable dead trees, rough and rotten trees, trees of noncommercial species, trees less than 5.0-inches in diameter at 4.5 feet above the ground, tops, and roundwood harvested from nonforest land (for example, fence rows).

Source: U.S. Forest Service, National Assessment - Resources Planning Act (RPA), "2012 RPA Resource Tables," <http://www.fia.fs.fed.us/program-features/rpa/>, accessed August 2014.

Table 918. Timber Products—Production, Foreign Trade, and Consumption by Type of Product: 1990 to 2013

[In millions of cubic feet, roundwood equivalent (15,577 represents 15,577,000,000)]

Type of product	1990	1995	2000	2005	2008	2009	2010	2011	2012	2013
Industrial roundwood:										
Domestic production..............	15,577	15,454	15,528	14,075	11,721	10,384	10,727	11,299	11,611	11,971
Softwoods......................	10,968	10,166	10,327	10,406	8,880	7,716	8,218	8,640	8,978	9,225
Hardwoods......................	4,609	5,288	5,201	3,669	2,841	2,668	2,509	2,660	2,633	2,746
Imports.........................	3,044	3,929	4,619	5,511	3,148	2,388	2,496	2,466	2,577	2,597
Exports.........................	2,306	2,284	2,039	1,470	1,751	1,571	1,840	2,040	1,960	2,161
Consumption....................	16,315	17,099	18,108	18,116	13,117	11,201	11,384	11,725	12,228	12,407
Softwoods......................	11,736	11,955	12,830	14,021	10,278	8,520	8,895	9,097	9,598	9,925
Hardwoods......................	4,579	5,144	5,278	4,095	2,840	2,681	2,489	2,629	2,630	2,482
Lumber:										
Domestic production...........	7,317	6,857	7,384	7,680	5,395	4,576	4,569	5,005	5,219	5,607
Imports.........................	1,905	2,545	2,943	3,744	1,894	1,347	1,422	1,403	1,480	1,699
Exports.........................	589	462	435	362	345	288	341	387	374	406
Consumption....................	8,633	8,939	9,892	11,063	6,945	5,636	5,650	6,022	6,324	6,901
Plywood and veneer:										
Domestic production...........	1,423	1,303	1,187	1,068	745	616	655	653	679	702
Imports.........................	97	107	154	373	184	146	161	163	160	171
Exports.........................	109	89	51	37	45	34	55	52	57	57
Consumption....................	1,410	1,321	1,290	1,403	884	728	760	764	782	815
Pulp products:										
Domestic production...........	5,313	6,079	5,881	4,498	4,720	4,423	4,617	4,682	4,824	4,766
Imports.........................	1,038	1,245	1,448	1,272	1,029	857	873	861	879	672
Exports.........................	645	904	776	560	791	731	802	881	875	1,033
Consumption....................	5,705	6,420	6,553	5,211	4,959	4,550	4,688	4,661	4,842	4,406
Logs: [1]										
Imports.........................	4	13	72	113	35	28	32	30	49	47
Exports.........................	674	451	422	345	313	322	407	485	432	432
Pulpwood chips, exports..........	288	377	355	166	257	196	235	235	235	234
Other industrial timber products: [2]										
Production and consumption....	562	387	300	318	290	250	245	239	222	230
Fuelwood:										
Production and consumption....	2,900	2,150	1,622	1,550	1,510	1,400	1,380	1,366	1,440	1,520

[1] Prior to 2010, pulpwood logs are not included in logs. [2] Includes cooperage logs, poles and piling, fence posts, hewn ties, round mine timbers, box bolts, etc.

Source: U.S. Forest Service, *U.S. Timber Production, Trade, Consumption, and Price Statistics, 1965-2013*, February 2016. See also <https://www.treesearch.fs.fed.us/pubs/50895>.

Table 919. Selected Timber Products—Imports and Exports: 1990 to 2013

[In million board feet (13,107 represents 13,107,000,000), except as indicated]

Product	Unit	1990	1995	2000	2005	2009	2010	2011	2012	2013
IMPORTS										
Lumber, total..................	Mil. bd. ft.	13,107	17,556	20,243	25,753	9,236	9,769	9,633	10,172	11,666
Softwood....................	Mil. bd. ft.	12,875	17,202	19,449	24,678	8,855	9,468	9,289	9,864	11,358
Hardwood...................	Mil. bd. ft.	232	354	795	1,075	381	301	344	308	308
From Canada..............	Mil. bd. ft.	11,918	16,990	18,616	21,841	8,393	9,151	8,946	9,633	11,020
Logs, total [1]..................	Mil. bd. ft. [2]	23	80	450	704	178	199	188	307	291
Softwood....................	Mil. bd. ft.	13	55	390	609	90	99	91	136	120
Hardwood...................	Mil. bd. ft.	10	26	59	95	88	100	97	171	171
From Canada..............	Mil. bd. ft.	19	56	426	605	89	90	84	133	120
Paper and board [3]...........	1,000 tons	12,195	14,238	17,356	17,958	11,218	11,144	10,670	10,490	11,007
Woodpulp....................	1,000 tons	4,893	5,969	7,227	6,762	5,044	6,163	6,117	5,599	6,112
Plywood.....................	Mil. sq. ft. [4]	1,687	1,951	2,902	6,964	2,751	3,042	3,081	3,029	3,219
EXPORTS										
Lumber, total..................	Mil. bd. ft.	4,614	2,958	2,700	2,191	1,784	2,148	2,468	2,383	2,601
To: Canada.................	Mil. bd. ft.	658	650	701	649	455	621	573	634	640
Japan......................	Mil. bd. ft.	1,270	978	325	80	128	179	196	189	208
European Union...........	Mil. bd. ft.	686	513	507	346	175	209	196	166	166
Softwood....................	Mil. bd. ft.	3,753	1,872	1,400	897	983	1,347	1,667	1,582	1,788
Hardwood...................	Mil. bd. ft.	813	1,057	1,300	1,294	801	801	801	801	801
Logs, total [1]..................	Mil. bd. ft. [2]	4,213	2,820	2,638	2,157	2,014	2,542	3,031	2,698	2,698
To: Canada.................	Mil. bd. ft. [2]	396	716	1,350	1,168	876	835	719	754	811
Japan......................	Mil. bd. ft. [2]	2,626	1,728	934	574	435	425	458	469	523
China.......................	Mil. bd. ft. [2]	362	20	22	94	270	780	1,384	1,052	1,291
Softwood....................	Mil. bd. ft.	3,994	2,552	2,066	1,607	1,644	2,074	2,501	2,110	2,546
Hardwood...................	Mil. bd. ft.	220	268	573	550	369	468	409	418	418
Paper and board [3]...........	1,000 tons	5,163	7,621	8,701	7,125	7,750	8,781	9,331	9,036	12,890
Woodpulp....................	1,000 tons	5,905	8,261	6,409	6,413	7,519	8,265	9,068	8,125	8,146
Plywood.....................	Mil. sq. ft. [4]	1,766	1,517	916	686	619	1,004	949	1,039	1,035

[1] Prior to 2000, pulpwood logs are not included. [2] Log scale. [3] Includes paper and board products. Excludes hardboard. [4] 3/8 inch basis.

Source: U.S. Forest Service. *U.S. Timber Production, Trade, Consumption, and Price Statistics, 1965-2013*, February 2016. See also <http://www.treesearch.fs.fed.us/pubs/50895>.

Table 920. Lumber Production and Consumption by Species Group: 1990 to 2013

[In billion board feet (48.1 represents 48,100,000,000), except per capita in board feet. Per capita consumption based on estimated resident population as of July 1]

Item	1990	1995	2000	2005	2006	2007	2008	2009	2010	2011	2012	2013
Production, total.................	**48.1**	**44.9**	**48.6**	**50.9**	**49.7**	**45.8**	**36.0**	**30.2**	**30.5**	**33.3**	**34.8**	**37.3**
By species:												
Softwoods.......................	35.8	32.2	36.0	39.8	38.7	35.2	29.2	23.2	24.8	26.8	28.3	30.0
Hardwoods......................	12.3	12.6	12.6	11.2	11.0	10.6	6.8	7.0	5.7	6.6	6.5	7.3
Consumption, total..............	**57.4**	**59.5**	**66.1**	**74.5**	**70.9**	**62.5**	**46.9**	**37.7**	**38.1**	**40.5**	**42.4**	**45.6**
Per capita......................	230	226	234	251	245	207	154	123	123	130	135	144
By species:												
Softwoods.......................	45.7	47.6	54.0	63.6	60.6	52.6	40.7	31.1	32.9	34.4	36.4	39.6
Hardwoods......................	11.7	11.9	12.1	10.9	10.3	9.9	6.2	6.6	5.2	6.1	6.0	6.0

Source: U.S. Forest Service, *U.S. Timber Production, Trade, Consumption, and Price Statistics, 1965-2013*, February 2016. See also <https://www.treesearch.fs.fed.us/pubs/50895>.

Table 921. Pulpwood Consumption, Woodpulp Production, and Paper and Board Production and Consumption: 1990 to 2013

[In thousands (99,361 represents 99,361,000) except where otherwise indicated]

Item	Unit	1990	1995	2000	2005	2009	2010	2011	2012	2013
Pulpwood consumption.........	1,000 cords [1]	99,361	97,052	95,904	108,513	87,424	89,774	89,158	90,649	86,164
Woodpulp production [2].........	1,000 tons	60,311	63,507	62,599	59,121	50,598	52,832	53,175	53,001	53,099
Paper and board: [3]										
Production......................	1,000 tons	78,679	89,509	94,491	91,031	78,299	82,968	82,003	81,051	80,477
Consumption [4].................	1,000 tons	85,711	96,126	103,147	101,864	81,767	85,331	83,342	82,565	78,594
Per capita.....................	Pounds	686	731	731	687	532	551	534	525	498

[1] One cord equals 128 cubic feet. [2] Includes dissolving and special alpha pulps; excludes defibrated/exploded pulps and screenings. [3] Excludes wet machine board and construction grades. [4] Production plus imports, minus exports.

Source: U.S. Forest Service. *U.S. Timber Production, Trade, Consumption, and Price Statistics, 1965-2013*, February 2016. See also <https://www.treesearch.fs.fed.us/pubs/50895>.

Table 922. Selected Timber Products—Producer Price Indexes: 1990 to 2016

[1982=100. For information about producer prices, see text, Section 14]

Product	1990	1995	2000	2005	2010	2012	2014	2015	2016
Lumber and wood products [1].................	**129.7**	**178.1**	**178.2**	**196.5**	**192.7**	**214.9**	**224.2**	**221.9**	**222.7**
Lumber................................	124.6	173.4	178.8	198.6	167.3	198.7	214.9	199.3	201.8
Softwood lumber.........................	123.8	178.5	178.6	203.6	160.8	199.8	205.6	192.7	198.8
Hardwood lumber........................	131.0	167.0	185.9	196.6	187.3	208.4	241.9	221.1	218.1
Millwork [1].............................	130.4	163.8	176.4	197.2	207.0	225.8	232.3	237.2	240.6
General millwork........................	132.0	165.4	178.0	196.1	211.2	225.8	232.3	238.0	241.0
Prefabricated structural members....................	122.3	163.5	175.1	206.9	185.6	224.5	231.7	232.6	237.6
Plywood..............................	114.2	165.3	157.6	186.8	176.7	199.6	204.1	198.9	192.3
Softwood veneer and plywood..........	119.6	188.1	173.3	223.5	197.1	236.8	245.3	234.5	214.5
Hardwood veneer and plywood [2].................	(NA)	(NA)	(NA)	(NA)	103.6	108.0	108.4	108.6	112.9
Other wood products [1]................	114.7	143.7	130.5	139.2	142.5	151.3	159.8	161.4	159.3
Wood boxes...........................	119.1	145.0	155.2	164.9	183.0	196.5	199.2	199.4	199.7
Pulp, paper, and allied products [1].............	**141.2**	**172.2**	**183.7**	**202.6**	**236.9**	**248.8**	**250.5**	**248.8**	**247.7**
Pulp, paper, and prod., excl. bldg. paper [1].............	132.9	163.4	161.4	169.8	206.8	218.2	220.9	218.4	216.3
Woodpulp..............................	151.3	183.2	145.3	138.0	186.0	180.7	183.7	181.6	171.6
Wastepaper...........................	138.9	371.1	282.5	230.9	421.5	363.6	342.0	291.8	312.5
Paper [1]..............................	128.8	159.0	149.8	159.6	182.1	190.8	192.7	189.8	186.7
Writing and printing papers..........................	129.1	158.4	146.6	156.1	179.5	182.7	183.9	183.6	180.4
Newsprint.............................	119.6	161.8	127.5	138.5	125.6	(NA)	(NA)	113.6	114.7
Paperboard............................	135.7	183.1	176.7	175.5	224.9	243.7	248.6	243.1	233.4
Converted paper and paperboard products [1]........	135.2	157.0	162.7	176.1	209.0	224.7	228.4	228.2	228.5
Office supplies and accessories....................	121.4	134.9	133.8	143.1	159.9	171.1	174.1	174.0	176.1
Building paper & building board mill products........	112.2	144.9	138.8	184.9	168.4	207.9	188.9	186.3	201.0

NA Not available. [1] Includes other products not shown separately. [2] December 2005=100.

Source: U.S. Bureau of Labor Statistics, "Producer Price Indexes," <http://www.bls.gov/ppi/>, accessed June 2017.

Table 923. Paper and Paperboard—Production and New Supply: 1990 to 2016

[In millions of short tons (80.55 represents 80,550,000). 1 short ton = 2,000 lbs]

Item	1990	1995	2000	2005	2010	2013	2014	2015	2016
Production, total..................	**80.55**	**91.21**	**96.05**	**92.61**	**83.70**	**81.33**	**80.58**	**79.80**	**79.15**
Paper, total........................	39.36	42.90	45.52	41.40	35.51	32.33	30.74	29.60	28.61
Paperboard, total...................	39.42	46.55	48.97	49.71	47.46	48.15	49.04	49.40	49.73
Unbleached kraft..................	20.36	22.73	21.80	22.58	21.36	22.00	22.22	22.41	22.63
Semichemical.....................	5.64	5.67	5.95	6.41	5.44	5.31	4.87	4.75	4.42
Bleached kraft....................	4.26	5.16	5.30	5.58	5.62	5.40	5.47	5.35	5.21
Recycled..........................	9.03	12.84	15.79	15.06	15.05	15.44	16.48	16.89	17.48
Wet machine board and construction grades...........	1.82	1.82	1.56	1.50	0.73	0.85	0.79	0.80	0.81
New supply, all grades, excluding products..............	**87.68**	**98.08**	**105.02**	**101.81**	**84.16**	**80.92**	**80.92**	**79.99**	**79.46**
Paper, total........................	49.49	52.77	57.13	53.69	40.34	36.54	35.85	34.43	33.54
Newsprint........................	13.41	12.76	12.92	10.12	5.00	3.92	4.00	3.51	3.35
Printing/writing papers............	25.46	29.55	32.99	31.99	23.73	20.82	20.04	19.08	18.13
Packaging and industrial converting papers................	4.72	4.24	4.27	4.05	4.18	4.13	4.21	4.17	4.23
Tissue...........................	5.90	6.22	6.95	7.54	7.43	7.66	7.61	7.68	7.83
Paperboard, total..................	36.30	43.39	46.02	46.51	43.06	43.54	44.31	44.77	45.13

Source: American Forest and Paper Association, Washington, DC, *Paper Industry Annual Statistical Summary* ©.

Table 924. Fishery Products—Domestic Catch, Imports, and Disposition: 1990 to 2015

[Live weight, in millions of pounds (16,349 represents 16,349,000,000)]

Item	1990	1995	2000	2005	2010	2012	2013	2014	2015 (P)
Total supply	**16,349**	**16,484**	**17,340**	**20,612**	**19,748**	**20,757**	**20,988**	**21,431**	**21,426**
For human food	12,662	13,584	14,740	18,155	17,560	18,065	18,572	19,115	18,848
For industrial use [2]	3,687	2,900	2,600	2,457	2,188	2,692	2,416	2,317	2,579
Domestic catch	**9,404**	**9,788**	**9,069**	**9,707**	**8,231**	**9,634**	**9,870**	**9,486**	**9,718**
For human food	7,041	7,667	6,912	7,997	6,526	7,477	8,043	7,828	7,750
For industrial use [2]	2,363	2,121	2,157	1,710	1,705	2,157	1,827	1,658	1,968
Imports [1]	**6,945**	**6,696**	**8,271**	**10,905**	**11,517**	**11,123**	**11,118**	**11,945**	**11,709**
For human food	5,621	5,917	7,828	10,158	11,034	10,588	10,529	11,286	11,098
For industrial use [2]	1,324	779	443	747	483	535	589	659	611
Exports	**4,627**	**5,166**	**5,758**	**8,420**	**6,129**	**8,259**	**8,915**	**9,344**	**8,771**
For human food	3,832	4,175	4,587	6,385	5,170	6,474	7,066	7,365	6,936
For industrial use [2]	795	991	1,171	2,035	959	1,785	1,850	1,979	1,835
Disposition of domestic catch	**9,404**	**9,788**	**9,069**	**9,707**	**8,231**	**9,634**	**9,870**	**9,486**	**9,718**
Fresh and frozen [3]	6,501	7,099	6,657	7,776	6,515	7,541	8,019	7,916	7,622
Canned [3]	751	769	530	563	373	299	365	196	364
Cured	126	90	119	160	102	82	45	63	65
Reduced to meal, oil, etc.	2,026	1,830	1,763	1,208	1,241	1,712	1,451	1,311	1,667

P Preliminary. [1] Includes landings of tuna caught by foreign vessels in American Samoa. [2] Processed into meal, oil, solubles, and shell products, or used as bait and animal food. [3] Includes for human food, and bait and animal food.

Source: U.S. National Oceanic and Atmospheric Administration, National Marine Fisheries Service, *Fisheries of the United States 2015*, August 2016, and earlier editions. See also <http://www.st.nmfs.noaa.gov/commercial-fisheries/index>.

Table 925. Fisheries—Quantity and Value of Domestic Catch: 1980 to 2015

[In millions of pounds (6,482 represents 6,482,000,000), except as noted]

Year	Quantity (mil. lbs. [1]) Total	For human food	For industrial products [2]	Value (mil. dol.)	Average price per lb. (cents)	Year	Quantity (mil. lbs. [1]) Total	For human food	For industrial products [2]	Value (mil. dol.)	Average price per lb. (cents)
1980	6,482	3,654	2,828	2,237	34.5	2007	9,309	7,490	1,819	4,192	45.0
1985	6,258	3,294	2,964	2,326	37.2	2008	8,325	6,633	1,692	4,383	52.6
1990	9,404	7,041	2,363	3,522	37.5	2009	8,031	6,198	1,833	3,891	48.4
1995	9,788	7,667	2,121	3,770	38.5	2010	8,231	6,526	1,705	4,520	54.9
2000	9,069	6,912	2,157	3,550	39.1	2011	9,858	7,909	1,949	5,289	53.7
2003	9,507	7,521	1,986	3,347	35.2	2012	9,634	7,477	2,157	5,103	53.0
2004	9,683	7,794	1,889	3,756	38.8	2013	9,870	8,043	1,827	5,466	55.4
2005	9,707	7,997	1,710	3,942	40.6	2014	9,486	7,828	1,658	5,448	57.4
2006	9,483	7,842	1,641	4,024	42.4	2015 (P)	9,718	7,750	1,968	5,203	53.5

P Preliminary. [1] Live weight. [2] Processed into meal, oil, solubles, and shell products, or used as bait and animal food.

Source: U.S. National Oceanic and Atmospheric Administration, National Marine Fisheries Service, *Fisheries of the United States 2015*, August 2016, and earlier editions. See also <http://www.st.nmfs.noaa.gov/commercial-fisheries/index>.

Table 926. Domestic Fish and Shellfish Catch and Value by Major Species Caught: 2000 to 2015

[In thousands (9,068,985 represents 9,068,985,000)]

Species	Quantity (1,000 lbs.) 2000	2010	2014	2015 (P)	Value ($1,000) 2000	2010	2014	2015 (P)
Total [1]	**9,068,985**	**8,230,587**	**9,485,952**	**9,717,627**	**3,549,481**	**4,519,510**	**5,447,617**	**5,203,004**
Fish, total [1]	**7,689,661**	**6,918,013**	**8,229,221**	**8,582,612**	**1,594,815**	**2,155,593**	**2,385,213**	**2,369,384**
Cod, Atlantic	25,060	17,714	5,170	3,370	26,384	28,119	9,358	6,447
Cod, Pacific	530,505	539,635	717,548	699,106	142,330	146,941	153,724	257,744
Flounder	412,723	624,358	713,580	554,605	109,910	146,243	175,361	144,344
Halibut	75,190	56,497	23,235	24,539	143,826	206,553	114,858	119,271
Herring, Atlantic	160,269	144,513	205,246	177,397	9,972	21,275	29,247	25,558
Herring, Pacific	74,835	108,868	103,657	69,176	12,043	23,308	12,630	7,307
Menhaden	1,760,498	1,471,803	1,256,192	1,617,930	112,403	107,193	117,402	166,483
Pollock, Alaska	2,606,802	1,947,580	3,145,610	3,262,608	160,525	282,399	399,884	441,668
Salmon	628,638	787,740	720,201	1,066,047	270,213	554,816	616,658	460,166
Tuna	50,779	48,047	58,739	57,123	95,176	108,453	135,168	137,966
Whiting (Atlantic, silver)	26,855	17,564	16,213	14,229	11,370	10,862	11,467	10,492
Whiting (Pacific, hake)	452,718	355,272	574,923	333,298	18,809	27,316	58,588	25,208
Shellfish, total [1]	**1,379,324**	**1,276,366**	**1,220,730**	**1,107,367**	**1,954,666**	**2,341,902**	**3,035,400**	**2,810,252**
Clams	118,482	88,891	90,744	86,096	153,973	200,657	214,779	206,299
Crabs	299,006	349,604	295,224	326,393	405,006	572,797	685,703	678,727
Lobsters: American	83,180	115,433	147,786	145,921	301,300	396,757	566,563	617,187
Oysters	41,146	28,080	34,135	27,535	90,667	117,590	240,301	213,773
Scallops, sea	32,747	57,454	33,813	35,722	164,609	455,088	424,448	437,934
Shrimp	332,486	258,972	295,329	327,070	690,453	413,980	681,421	488,384
Squid, Pacific	259,508	286,403	226,934	81,069	27,077	70,706	72,509	24,447

P Preliminary. [1] Includes other species not shown separately.

Source: U.S. National Oceanic and Atmospheric Administration, National Marine Fisheries Service, *Fisheries of the United States 2015*, August 2016, and earlier editions. See also <http://www.st.nmfs.noaa.gov/commercial-fisheries/index>.

Table 927. U.S. Private Aquaculture—Trout and Catfish Production and Value: 1990 to 2016

[67.8 represents 67,800,000. Data are for calendar year and foodsize fish (trout at least 12 inches long; catfish weighing at least three quarters of a pound)]

Item	Unit	1990	1995	2000	2005	2010	2014	2015	2016
TROUT FOODSIZE									
Number sold	Mil.	67.8	60.2	58.4	55.6	38.7	48.3	45.4	46.3
Total weight	Mil. lb.	56.8	55.6	59.0	59.9	45.3	60.7	57.9	59.1
Total value of sales	Mil. dol.	64.6	60.8	63.3	63.5	63.2	95.7	96.4	97.0
Avg. price received by processors	Dol./lb.	1.14	1.09	1.07	1.06	1.40	1.58	1.66	1.64
Percent sold to processors	Percent	58	68	70	66	63	57	58	61
CATFISH FOODSIZE									
Number sold	Mil.	272.9	321.8	420.1	395.6	263.4	184.6	195.5	190.6
Total weight	Mil. lb.	392.4	481.5	633.8	605.5	478.9	307.5	317.4	320.2
Total value of sales	Mil. dol.	305.1	378.1	468.8	427.8	375.1	332.4	346.4	363.4
Avg. price received by processors	Dol./lb.	0.78	0.79	0.74	0.71	0.78	1.08	1.09	1.14

Source: U.S. Department of Agriculture, National Agricultural Statistics Service, *Trout Production*, February 2017, and *Catfish Production*, February 2017. See also <https://www.nass.usda.gov/Publications/Reports_by_Release_Day/index.php>.

Table 928. Supply of Selected Shellfish and Fish Products: 1990 to 2015

[In millions of pounds (734 represents 734,000,000). Totals available for U.S. consumption are supply minus exports plus imports. Round weight is the complete or full weight as caught]

Species	Unit	1990	1995	2000	2005	2010	2012	2013	2014	2015 (P)
Shrimp	Heads-off weight	734	832	1,173	1,559	1,739	1,635	1,565	1,733	1,797
Tuna, canned	Canned weight	856	875	980	895	834	735	726	728	704
Snow crab	Round weight	37	42	122	171	197	202	229	194	239
Clams	Meat weight	152	144	133	120	105	109	111	109	105
Salmon, canned	Canned weight	148	147	95	123	73	45	128	16	101
American lobster	Round weight	95	94	125	144	186	211	212	210	222
Spiny lobster	Round weight	89	89	99	83	60	51	31	12	13
Scallops	Meat weight	74	62	78	86	85	60	74	68	62
Oysters	Meat weight	56	63	71	65	57	54	60	58	57
King crab	Round weight	19	21	41	78	44	63	54	54	53
Crab meat, canned	Canned weight	9	12	29	59	66	67	61	62	63

P Preliminary.

Source: U.S. National Oceanic and Atmospheric Administration, National Marine Fisheries Service, *Fisheries of the United States 2015*, August 2016, and earlier editions. See also <http://www.st.nmfs.noaa.gov/commercial-fisheries/index>.

Table 929. Canned, Fresh, and Frozen Fishery Products—Production and Value: 1990 to 2015

[Production in millions of pounds (1,178 represents 1,178,000,000); value in millions of dollars (1,562 represents $1,562,000,000). Canned fishery products data are for natural pack only]

Product	Production (mil. lbs.)					Value (mil. dol.)				
	1990	2000	2010	2014	2015 (P)	1990	2000	2010	2014	2015 (P)
Canned, total	**1,178**	**1,747**	**956**	**733**	**878**	**1,562**	**1,626**	**1,414**	**1,376**	**1,424**
Tuna	581	671	395	391	400	902	856	724	783	773
Salmon	196	171	146	89	168	366	288	356	354	356
Clam products	110	127	110	77	120	76	120	98	74	147
Sardines, Maine	13	(Z)	[1] (D)	[1] (D)	[1] (D)	17	(Z)	[1] (D)	[1] (D)	[1] (D)
Shrimp	1	2	[1] (D)	1	[1] (D)	3	11	[1] (D)	4	[1] (D)
Crab [2]	1	(Z)	1	(Z)	(Z)	4	(Z)	8	(Z)	(Z)
Oysters [3]	1	(Z)	[1] (D)	[1] (D)	[1] (D)	1	1	[1] (D)	[1] (D)	[1] (D)
Other	275	776	303	175	191	193	350	228	160	147
Fish fillets and steaks [4]	**441**	**368**	**585**	**822**	**725**	**843**	**823**	**1,486**	**2,392**	**1,820**
Cod	65	56	49	79	70	132	167	131	266	253
Flounder	54	27	32	17	12	154	71	53	63	47
Haddock	7	6	23	14	14	24	24	89	69	65
Ocean perch, Atlantic	1	(Z)	1	2	1	1	1	3	5	4
Rockfish	33	11	2	2	3	53	25	6	7	8
Pollock, Atlantic	12	2	2	2	1	21	4	7	7	4
Pollock, Alaska	164	160	290	479	461	174	178	368	712	622
Other	105	106	186	226	163	284	353	829	1,262	816

P Preliminary. D Figure withheld to avoid disclosure pertaining to a specific organization or individual. Z Less than 500,000 pounds or $500,000. [1] Included with "other." [2] Includes crab meat specialties. [3] Includes oyster specialties. [4] Fresh and frozen.

Source: U.S. National Oceanic and Atmospheric Administration, National Marine Fisheries Service, *Fisheries of the United States 2015*, August 2016, and earlier editions. See also <http://www.st.nmfs.noaa.gov/commercial-fisheries/index>.

Table 930. Mineral and Mining Industries—Employment, Hours, and Earnings: 1990 to 2016

[In thousands (680 represents 680,000), except as noted. Industries based on North American Classification System (NAICS) 2012. Based on the Current Employment Statistics Program, see Appendix III]

Industry and item	Unit	1990	1995	2000	2005	2010	2014	2015	2016
All mining: [1]									
All employees............	1,000	680	558	520	562	655	839	760	626
Production workers...........	1,000	469	391	383	419	483	610	550	435
Avg. weekly hours...........	Number	46.1	46.8	45.5	46.4	44.8	47.8	46.1	45.5
Avg. weekly earnings........	Dollars	630	711	770	884	1,086	1,300	1,238	1,255
Oil and gas extraction:									
All employees............	1,000	190	152	125	126	159	198	193	180
Production workers...........	1,000	84	73	67	72	89	104	108	95
Avg. weekly hours...........	Number	44.4	43.6	41.3	44.3	39.0	45.9	43.9	42.6
Avg. weekly earnings........	Dollars	591	677	802	856	1,066	1,435	1,323	1,438
Coal mining:									
All employees............	1,000	136	97	72	74	81	73	64	51
Production workers...........	1,000	110	78	59	61	70	62	54	42
Avg. weekly hours...........	Number	44.7	45.7	45.6	48.5	48.4	47.6	45.3	44.4
Avg. weekly earnings........	Dollars	822	929	945	1,071	1,366	1,442	1,386	1,337
Metal ore mining:									
All employees............	1,000	53	48	38	29	37	44	42	39
Production workers...........	1,000	43	39	29	22	28	(NA)	(NA)	(NA)
Avg. weekly hours...........	Number	42.5	43.4	43.4	44.2	42.5	(NA)	(NA)	(NA)
Avg. weekly earnings........	Dollars	646	788	871	1,001	1,158	(NA)	(NA)	(NA)
Nonmetallic minerals mining, and quarrying:									
All employees............	1,000	113	108	115	110	87	90	92	92
Production workers...........	1,000	85	81	87	84	65	(NA)	(NA)	(NA)
Avg. weekly hours...........	Number	45.0	46.3	46.1	45.9	43.8	(NA)	(NA)	(NA)
Avg. weekly earnings........	Dollars	532	632	722	830	848	(NA)	(NA)	(NA)

NA Not available. [1] Includes other industries not shown separately.

Source: U.S. Bureau of Labor Statistics, Current Employment Statistics, "Employment, Hours, and Earnings—National," <http://www.bls.gov/ces/home.htm>, accessed June 2017.

Table 931. Mine Safety: 2010 to 2016

[Calendar year data]

Item	All Mines			Coal			Metal and non-metal		
	2010	2015	2016	2010	2015	2016	2010	2015	2016
Number of mines..............	14,283	13,299	13,089	1,944	1,460	1,289	12,339	11,839	11,800
Number of miners.............	361,176	349,898	318,723	135,500	102,804	81,883	225,676	247,094	236,840
Fatalities....................	72	29	25	48	12	8	24	17	17
Fatal injury rate [1]..........	0.024	0.010	0.010	0.038	0.013	0.012	0.013	0.008	0.009
All injury rate [1]............	2.81	2.30	2.19	3.43	2.91	2.89	2.37	2.02	1.94
Total mining area inspection hours per mine [2]........	63	56	55	259	245	246	23	23	23
Citations and orders [3]........	170,064	107,790	97,255	96,351	49,370	40,596	73,713	58,420	56,659
S&S [4] citations and orders (percent).....	32	24	22	32	23	21	31	24	23
Amount assessed [5] (mil. dol.)...........	162.3	65.4	52.0	110.2	37.3	25.9	52.1	28.1	26.1
Coal production (mil. tons).......	(X)	(X)	(X)	1,086	897	727	(X)	(X)	(X)

X Not applicable. [1] Reported injury rates per 200,000 employees. [2] Total Mining Area Time includes: On-site Inspection Time (metal/non-metal), MMU Pit Time (Coal), Outby Area Time (Coal), Surface Area Time (Coal), Citation/Order writing On-Site. On-site inspection hours represent hours entered by Authorized Representatives of the Secretary (AR) for certain inspection activities and task codes. [3] Citations and orders are those not vacated. [4] A violation that "significantly and substantially" contributes to the cause and effect of a coal or other mine safety or health hazard. [5] Government penalties or fines.

Source: U.S. Mine Safety and Health Administration, Office of Program Education and Outreach Services, Mine Safety and Health At a Glance: Calendar Year, July 2017, and earlier reports. See also <https://www.msha.gov/data-reports/statistics/mine-safety-and-health-glance>.

Table 932. Mining and Primary Metal Production Indexes: 1990 to 2016

[Index 2012=100]

Industry group	2012 NAICS [1] code	1990	1995	2000	2005	2010	2013	2014	2015	2016
Mining [2]....................	**21**	**91.9**	**90.0**	**89.1**	**84.3**	**87.6**	**106.0**	**117.3**	**112.2**	**102.1**
Oil and gas extraction [2]........	211	87.8	85.4	83.0	76.1	85.7	110.5	126.0	134.2	129.1
Crude oil and natural gas..........	211111	89.6	86.2	83.1	76.4	85.6	110.7	126.2	134.3	128.6
Coal mining.....................	2121	108.4	106.7	109.4	113.1	106.9	97.0	97.8	86.9	70.0
Metal ore mining.................	2122	111.7	122.2	118.8	101.8	97.1	101.7	104.9	100.3	101.3
Iron ore.......................	21221	106.6	118.1	118.5	102.1	93.4	96.8	104.1	82.8	76.4
Gold and silver ore..............	21222	127.7	136.6	152.2	110.0	99.7	97.9	90.7	91.8	101.5
Copper, nickel, lead, and zinc.......	21223	122.5	140.5	122.6	99.0	96.0	106.5	115.6	117.9	120.3
Oil and gas drilling.............	213111	57.9	50.6	64.7	80.6	79.3	93.6	98.6	52.6	28.0
Primary metal manufacturing [2]......	**331**	**91.2**	**100.4**	**104.9**	**99.0**	**95.0**	**103.3**	**104.1**	**96.8**	**93.7**
Iron and steel...................	3311, 3312	86.0	95.5	99.8	96.6	91.8	102.1	101.4	91.6	90.2
Aluminum.......................	3313	99.1	95.6	101.2	103.8	88.9	107.3	106.3	107.2	96.5
Nonferrous metals [2].............	3314	88.3	100.4	90.2	80.1	107.9	107.0	107.6	98.3	100.8

[1] Based on the 2012 North American Industry Classification System (NAICS). [2] Includes other industries not shown separately.

Source: Board of Governors of the Federal Reserve System, "Industrial Production and Capacity Utilization, Statistical Release G.17," <http://www.federalreserve.gov/datadownload/default.htm>, accessed July 2017.

Table 933. Mineral Production: 1990 to 2015

[In units as indicated (1,029.1 represents 1,029,100,000). Data represent production as measured by mine shipments, mine sales, or marketable production; see Appendix IV]

Minerals and metals	Unit	1990	2000	2010	2014	2015
FUEL MINERALS						
Coal, total..	Mil. sh. tons	1,029.1	1,073.6	1,084.4	1,000.0	896.9
Bituminous..	Mil. sh. tons	693.2	574.3	489.5	480.0	403.7
Subbituminous....................................	Mil. sh. tons	244.3	409.2	514.8	438.6	419.5
Lignite...	Mil. sh. tons	88.1	85.6	78.2	79.5	71.6
Anthracite...	Mil. sh. tons	3.5	4.6	1.8	1.9	2.1
Natural gas (marketed production)...................	Tril. cu. ft.	18.59	20.20	22.38	27.50	28.75
Petroleum (crude)...................................	Mil. bbl. [1]	2,685	2,131	1,998	3,199	3,437
Uranium concentrate (recoverable content).........	Mil. lb.	8.9	4.0	4.2	4.9	3.3
NONFUEL MINERALS						
Asbestos (sales)...................................	1,000 metric tons	(D)	5	–	–	–
Barite, primary, sold/used by producers............	1,000 metric tons	430	392	662	663	425
Boron minerals, sold or used by producers.........	1,000 metric tons	1,090	1,070	(D)	(D)	(D)
Bromine, sold or used by producers................	1,000 metric tons	177	228	(D)	(D)	(D)
Cement (excludes Puerto Rico): [2]..................	Mil. metric tons	(NA)	(NA)	66	83	84
Clays..	1,000 metric tons	42,900	40,800	25,600	25,600	25,400
Diatomite..	1,000 metric tons	631	677	595	901	832
Feldspar...	1,000 metric tons	630	790	500	530	520
Fluorspar, finished shipments......................	1,000 metric tons	64	–	(NA)	(NA)	(NA)
Garnet (industrial).................................	1,000 metric tons	47	60	53	44.2	55.6
Gypsum, crude.....................................	Mil. metric tons	15	20	10	14.9	15.2
Helium [3]...	Mil. cu. meters	65	98	75	75	66
Lime, sold or used by producers....................	Mil. metric tons	16	20	18	20	18
Mica, scrap/flake, sold or used by producers.......	1,000 metric tons	109	101	56	48	33
Peat, sales by producers...........................	1,000 metric tons	721	847	628	468	455
Perlite, processed, sold or used....................	1,000 metric tons	576	672	414	462	459
Phosphate rock, marketable........................	Mil. metric tons	46	39	26	25	27
Potash (K2O equivalent), marketable...............	1,000 metric tons	1,710	1,300	930	850	740
Pumice & pumicite, sold and used..................	1,000 metric tons	443	1,050	241	269	310
Salt...	Mil. metric tons	37	46	43	45	45
Sand & gravel:.....................................	Mil. metric tons	855	1,148	839	1,007	1,040
Construction [2]..................................	Mil. metric tons	829	1,120	807	897	937
Industrial...	Mil. metric tons	26	28	32	110	103
Soda ash (sodium carbonate).......................	1,000 metric tons	9,100	10,200	10,600	11,700	11,600
Stone:...	Mil. metric tons	2,230	2,810	2,830	3,720	3,960
Crushed and broken...............................	Mil. metric tons	1,110	1,560	1,160	1,250	1,330
Dimension [4].....................................	1,000 metric tons	1,120	1,250	1,670	2,470	2,630
Sulfur: total shipments.............................	1,000 metric tons	11,500	10,700	9,170	9,630	9,540
Talc and pyrophyllite, crude [5]....................	1,000 metric tons	1,270	851	604	608	687
Vermiculite concentrate............................	1,000 metric tons	209	150	100	100	100
METALS						
Aluminum..	1,000 metric tons	4,048	3,668	1,726	1,710	1,587
Copper (recoverable content).......................	1,000 metric tons	1,590	1,450	1,110	1,360	1,380
Gold (recoverable content).........................	Metric tons	294	353	231	210	214
Iron ore, usable (gross weight).....................	Mil. metric tons	57	61	50	56	46
Lead (recoverable content).........................	1,000 metric tons	484	449	369	379	367
Magnesium metal..................................	1,000 metric tons	139	(D)	(D)	(D)	(D)
Molybdenum, mine.................................	1,000 metric tons	62	41	59	68	47
Nickel ore, refinery byproduct......................	1,000 metric tons	330	(D)	(D)	(D)	(D)
Palladium metal....................................	Kilograms	5,930	10,300	11,600	12,400	12,500
Platinum metal.....................................	Kilograms	1,810	3,110	3,450	3,660	3,670
Silicon (Si content) [6].............................	1,000 metric tons	418	367	176	401	411
Silver (recoverable content)........................	Metric tons	2,120	1,860	1,280	1,180	1,090
Titanium concentrate, (TiO2 content)...............	1,000 metric tons	(D)	300	200	100	200
Vanadium (recoverable content)....................	Metric tons	2,310	–	1,060	–	–
Zinc, ore and concentrate..........................	1,000 metric tons	508	796	748	832	825

NA Not available. D Withheld to avoid disclosing individual company data. – Represents or rounds to zero. [1] 42-gal. bbl. [2] Data for 2015 are estimates. [3] Extracted from natural gas. Both grade A and crude helium. [4] Includes Puerto Rico. [5] After 1990, includes only talc. [6] For 2006-2010, ferrosilicon only; silicon metal withheld to avoid disclosing proprietary data. Beginning in 2011, silicon alloys and metal. Beginning 2012, includes statistics for ferrosilicon and silicon metal containing less than 99.9% silicon.

Source: Nonfuels, through 1994, U.S. Bureau of Mines, thereafter; U.S. Geological Survey, *Mineral Commodity Summaries 2017,* January 2017, and earlier reports. Fuels, U.S. Energy Information Administration, *Annual Energy Review 2011,* September 2012, and earlier reports; *Annual Coal Report, 2015,* November 2016; and "Natural Gas Gross Withdrawals and Production," <https://www.eia.gov/naturalgas/data.php>, "Uranium & Nuclear Fuel Summary Production Statistics," <https://www.eia.gov/nuclear/data.php>, and "Crude Oil Production," <https://www.eia.gov/petroleum/data.php>, accessed July 2017.

Table 934. Nonfuel Mineral Commodities—Summary: 2015

[4,540 represents 4,540,000. Data are for mine or crude production and average price or value are in dollars per metric ton, except as noted]

Mineral	Unit	Production	Exports	Net import reliance [1,2] (percent)	Consumption, apparent	Average price per unit (dollars)	Employment (number)
Alumina (metal equivalent)	1,000 metric tons	4,540	2,180	([3])	3,930	[7] 400	(NA)
Aluminum	1,000 metric tons	1,587	3,010	41	5,220	[4] .882	31,000
Antimony (contained)	Metric tons	–	[5] 3,190	83	23,300	[4] 3.27	27
Asbestos	Metric tons	(NA)	–	100	343	1,780	(NA)
Barite	1,000 metric tons	425	139	78	1,960	197	458
Bauxite (metal equiv.)	1,000 metric tons	(D)	20	>75	(D)	[8] 26	(NA)
Beryllium (contained)	Metric tons	205	29	12	233	[4] 220	(NA)
Bismuth (contained)	Metric tons	–	519	95	1,370	[4] 6.43	(NA)
Boron (B2O3 content)	1,000 metric tons	(D)	[9]198	([3])	(D)	[10] 400	1,180
Bromine (contained)	Metric tons	(D)	25,000	<50	(D)	(NA)	1,050
Cadmium (contained)	Metric tons	[6] (D)	[13] 350	([3])	(D)	[11, 14] 1.47	(NA)
Cement	1,000 metric tons	[15] 83,700	1,294	11	93,300	106	10,000
Chromium	1,000 metric tons	[12] 154	236	65	438	[17] 217	(NA)
Clays	1,000 metric tons	[18] 25,400	3,970	([3])	21,900	(NA)	5,860
Cobalt (contained)	Metric tons	[16] 2,750	3,830	73	10,300	[4] 13.44	(NA)
Copper (mine, recoverable)	1,000 metric tons	1,380	392	[6] 32	1,820	[4] 2.56	11,200
Diamond, stones (industrial)	Million carats	79	–	2	81	[19] 17.50	(NA)
Diatomite	1,000 metric tons	832	75	([3])	764	291	660
Feldspar	1,000 metric tons	520	15	20	625	73	370
Fluorspar	1,000 metric tons	(NA)	14	100	411	260-280	5
Garnet (industrial)	Metric tons	55,600	14,700	80	279,000	(NA)	110
Gemstones	Million dollars	[37] 63.6	18,500	99	6,660	(NA)	1,100
Germanium (contained)	Kilograms	(D)	5,000	85	(NA)	[11] 1,250	(NA)
Gold (contained)	Metric tons	214	494	([3])	(NA)	[20] 1,163	11,900
Graphite (natural)	1,000 metric tons	–	12	100	35	[21] 1,480	(NA)
Gypsum (crude)	1,000 metric tons	15,200	63	11	35,200	9	4,500
Iodine	Metric tons	(D)	1,190	>50	(D)	[11, 22] 27.74	60
Iron ore (usable)	Million metric tons	46	8	([3])	39.7	81	4,802
Iron and steel scrap (metal)	Million metric tons	[23] 73.3	[23] 13	([3])	64	[24] 213	30,000
Iron and steel slag (metal)	1,000 metric tons	[25] 17.7	(Z)	8	17.7	20	1,700
Lead (contained)	1,000 metric tons	367	349	31	1,540	[4] .912	3,640
Lime	1,000 metric tons	[26] 18,300	346	<1	18,300	[26] 120.00	(NA)
Lithium	Metric tons	(D)	1,790	>25	(D)	6,500	70
Magnesium compounds	1,000 metric tons	380	70	57	891	(NA)	260
Magnesium metal	1,000 metric tons	(D)	15	<40	(D)	[4] 2.15	420
Manganese (gross weight)	1,000 metric tons	–	1	100	707	[27] 3.53	(NA)
Mercury [38]	Metric tons	[16] (NA)	(Z)	(NA)	(NA)	[28] 1,850	(NA)
Mica, scrap and flake	Metric tons	86,300	7,380	44	58,400	142	(NA)
Molybdenum (contained)	Metric tons	47,400	41,400	([3])	24,400	[11] 15.01	950
Nickel (contained) [29]	Metric tons	27,200	61,480	38	120,000	[30] 11,831	(NA)
Niobium (columbium)	Metric tons	–	1,430	100	7,080	[11] 24	(NA)
Nitrogen (fixed)-ammonia	1,000 metric tons	9,590	93	30	13,700	[31] 481	1,200
Peat	1,000 metric tons	455	28	72	1,620	28	550
Perlite	1,000 metric tons	459	40	20	574	60	142
Phosphate rock	1,000 metric tons	27,400	(NA)	4	28,100	72	2,000
Platinum-group metals	Kilograms	[32] 16,170	[32] 37,400	[33] 69	[33] (NA)	[20, 34] 1,056	1,440
Potash (K2O equivalent)	1,000 metric tons	740	106	87	5,500	[35] 570	1,300
Pumice and pumicite	1,000 metric tons	310	11	15	362	33	140
Salt	1,000 metric tons	45,000	839	33	62,800	[36] 185.00	4,200
Silicon, metal	1,000 metric tons	[39] 411	37	<50	(D)	[4] 1.27	(NA)
Silver (contained)	Metric tons	1,090	818	71	8,000	[20] 15.72	750
Soda ash (sodium carbonate)	1,000 metric tons	11,600	6,390	([3])	5,220	[40] 140.88	2,500
Stone (crushed)	Million metric tons	1,330	(Z)	2	1,400	11	67,100
Sulfur (all forms)	1,000 metric tons	9,540	1,906	14	11,100	[41] 87.62	2,600
Talc	1,000 metric tons	687	206	14	803	169	269
Thallium (contained)	Kilograms	–	157	100	(NA)	[11] 7,400	(NA)
Tin (contained)	Metric tons	[16] 12,500	5,880	74	40,700	[4] 7.56	(NA)
Titanium dioxide	1,000 metric tons	1,220	648	([3])	792	(NA)	3,100
Tungsten (contained)	Metric tons	[16] (D)	3,758	>25	(D)	[42] 302	(NA)
Vermiculite	1,000 metric tons	100	2	20	120	140-575	68
Zinc (contained)	1,000 metric tons	825	570	81	931	[4, 43] .955	2,930
Zirconium (ZrO2)	Metric tons	50,000	5,619	>25	70,000	[44] 1,050	(NA)

– Represents or rounds to zero. < Less than. > Greater than. D Withheld to avoid disclosing company proprietary data. NA Not available. Z Less than .05 million metric tons or less than half a unit shown. [1] Data rounded to no more than three significant digits; except prices. [2] Calculated as percent of apparent consumption. [3] Net exporter. [4] Dollars per pound. [5] Ore and concentrates not included. [6] Refinery production. [7] Alumina, average value U.S. imports (f.a.s.). [8] Bauxite, average value U.S. imports (f.a.s.). [9] Boric acid, gross weight. [10] Average value of mineral imports at port of exportation. [11] Dollars per kilogram. [12] Recycling production, based on reported stainless steel scrap receipts. [13] Unwrought cadmium and powders. [14] Average New York dealer price for 99.95% purity in 5-short-ton lots. Source: Platts Metals Week. [15] Excludes Puerto Rico. [16] Secondary production. [17] Imported chromite ore. [18] Excludes attapulgite. [19] Value of imports, dollars per carat. [20] Dollars per troy ounce. [21] Price of flake imports. Graphite lump/chip (Sri Lankan) price $1,800 per ton. [22] Cost, insurance, and freight (c.i.f.) value, crude, per kilogram. [23] Production includes receipts for purchases. Exports exclude rails for rerolling and other uses, and ships, boats, and other vessels for scrapping. [24] Delivered, No. 1 Heavy Melting composite price. [25] Quantities sold, and exclude any entrained metal recovered during slag processing and sold separately or returned to iron, and especially, steel furnaces. Also includes sales of imported granulated blast furnace slag. [26] Lime production data are sold or used by producers. Price data are for quicklime only. [27] 46% to 48% Mn metallurgical ore, per metric ton unit, contained Mn; c.i.f. value, U.S. ports. [28] Dollars per 76-pound flask. [29] Primary and secondary materials. [30] London Metal Exchange cash price. [31] Dollars per short ton, f.o.b. Gulf Coast. [32] Platinum and palladium. [33] Platinum. [34] Dealer price of platinum. [35] Price of K2O, muriate. [36] Vacuum and open pan, bulk, pellets and packaged, f.o.b. mine and plant. [37] Natural production, $8.5 million; laboratory-created (synthetic) production, $55.1 million. [38] Mercury not produced as principal commodity in U.S. since 1992; secondary production (recycled) not reported. [39] Production for ferrosilicon and silicon metal containing less than 99.9% silicon. [40] Dollars per short ton, F.o.b. mine or plant. [41] Elemental sulfur, f.o.b. mine or plant. [42] A metric ton unit of tungsten trioxide (WO3) contains 7.93 kilograms of tungsten. Platts Metals Week. [43] Platts Metals Week North American price for Special High Grade zinc. [44] Domestic zircon.

Source: U.S. Geological Survey, *Mineral Commodity Summaries, 2017*, January 2017. See also <https://minerals.usgs.gov/minerals/>.

Table 935. Selected Fuel and Nonfuel Mineral Products—Average Prices: 1990 to 2016

	Nonfuel minerals									Fuels		
Year	Copper, cath-ode (cents/ lb.)	Plati-num [1] (dol./troy oz.)	Gold (dol./troy oz.) [2]	Silver (dol./troy oz.) [2]	Lead [3] (cents/ lb.)	Nickel [4] (cents/ lb.)	Tin (New York) [4] (cents/ lb.)	Zinc [5] (cents/ lb.)	Sulfur, crude [6] (dol./ metric ton)	Bitumi-nous coal [7] (dol./ short ton)	Crude petrol-eum [7] (dol./ bbl.)	Natural gas [8] (dol./ 1,000 cu. ft.)
1990.........	123	467	385	4.82	46	402	386	75	80	27.43	20.03	3.03
1995.........	138	425	386	5.15	42	373	416	56	44	25.56	14.62	2.78
2000.........	88	549	280	5.00	44	392	370	56	25	24.15	26.72	4.62
2001.........	77	533	272	4.39	44	270	315	44	10	25.36	21.84	5.72
2002.........	76	543	311	4.62	44	307	292	39	12	26.57	22.51	4.12
2003.........	85	694	365	4.91	44	437	340	41	29	26.57	27.56	5.85
2004.........	134	849	411	6.69	55	627	547	52	33	30.56	36.77	6.65
2005.........	174	900	446	7.34	61	669	483	67	31	36.80	50.28	8.67
2006.........	315	1,144	606	11.61	77	1,100	565	159	33	39.32	59.69	8.61
2007.........	328	1,308	699	13.43	124	1,688	899	154	36	40.80	66.52	8.16
2008.........	319	1,578	874	15.00	120	957	1,129	89	264	51.39	94.04	9.18
2009.........	241	1,208	975	14.69	87	665	837	78	2	55.44	56.35	6.48
2010.........	348	1,616	1,228	20.20	109	989	1,240	102	70	60.88	74.71	6.18
2011.........	406	1,725	1,572	35.28	122	1,038	1,575	106	160	68.50	95.73	5.63
2012.........	367	1,555	1,673	31.22	114	795	1,283	96	124	66.04	94.52	4.73
2013.........	340	1,490	1,415	23.87	110	681	1,352	96	69	60.61	95.99	4.88
2014.........	318	1,388	1,269	19.37	106	765	(NA)	107	80	55.99	87.39	5.71
2015.........	256	1,056	1,163	15.72	91	537	(NA)	96	88	51.57	44.39	4.26
2016 [9].......	220	1,000	1,270	19.62	90	422	(NA)	99	78	(NA)	38.29	3.72

NA Not available. [1] Average annual dealer prices. [2] 99.95 percent purity. [3] North American delivered basis. 1990-2012, North American producer price. Beginning 2013, North American market price. [4] Nickel: London metal Exchange. Tin: Metals Week composite. [5] Platt's Metals Week price for North American Special High Grade zinc. Average prices for 1990 are for U.S. High Grade Zinc. [6] F.o.b. (Free on Board) works. [7] Average value at the point of production or domestic first purchase price. [8] Citygate price. Citygate is a point or measuring station at which a distributing gas utility receives gas from a natural gas pipeline company or transmission system. [9] Estimated.

Source: Nonfuels, through 1994, U.S. Bureau of Mines; thereafter, U.S. Geological Survey, *Mineral Commodity Summaries 2017*, January 2017 and earlier reports. Fuels, U.S. Energy Information Administration, *Monthly Energy Review*, March 2017 and earlier reports; and *Annual Coal Report, 2015*, November 2016 and earlier reports. See also <http://minerals.usgs.gov/minerals/pubs/mcs/> and <http://www.eia.gov/totalenergy/data/monthly/>.

Table 936. Value of Domestic Nonfuel Mineral Production by State: 2000 to 2016
[In millions of dollars (39,400 represents $39,400,000,000)]

State	2000	2010	2015 [1]	2016 [1]	State	2000	2010	2015 [1]	2016 [1]
United States [2]........	**39,400**	**66,400**	**78,300**	**74,600**					
Alabama..................	930	969	1,250	1,370	Montana............	596	1,140	1,340	925
Alaska..................	1,140	3,400	3,090	3,090	Nebraska............	[3] 84	234	382	[3] 196
Arizona..................	2,510	6,790	6,800	5,550	Nevada.............	2,980	7,700	6,940	7,650
Arkansas..................	484	709	991	959	New Hampshire.....	[3] 57	[3] 94	111	131
California..............	3,270	2,890	3,300	3,520	New Jersey..........	[3] 291	[3] 258	[3] 309	333
Colorado...............	592	1,850	2,410	1,510	New Mexico........	786	1,020	1,760	1,460
Connecticut.............	[3] 112	[3] 148	[3] 232	[3] 352	New York..........	1,020	1,310	1,530	1,770
Delaware..............	[3] 14	[3] 12	[3] 15	[3] 20	North Carolina......	744	880	[3] 943	[3] 1,170
Florida..................	1,820	2,680	2,840	3,260	North Dakota........	35	[3] 70	[3] 243	[3] 132
Georgia..................	1,620	1,430	1,700	1,790	Ohio..................	999	1,170	[3] 1,310	[3] 1,270
Hawaii..................	[3] 92	106	129	133	Oklahoma...........	473	702	744	777
Idaho..................	358	1,180	713	654	Oregon.............	299	312	398	507
Illinois..................	913	924	2,150	[3] 1,720	Pennsylvania.......	[3] 1,250	[3] 1,670	[3] 1,700	[3] 1,830
Indiana..................	695	782	916	1,010	Rhode Island........	[3] 20	[3] 33	[3] 70	[3] 72
Iowa....................	503	583	817	[3] 644	South Carolina......	[3] 551	[3] 468	[3] 679	[3] 823
Kansas..................	629	1,090	1,050	[3] 623	South Dakota.......	233	258	293	363
Kentucky................	501	762	[3] 571	[3] 525	Tennessee..........	737	831	1,130	1,210
Louisiana................	325	549	[3] 689	[3] 530	Texas..............	1,950	2,780	5,270	4,830
Maine..................	96	110	[3] 96	[3] 102	Utah................	1,430	4,380	2,930	2,490
Maryland................	[3] 358	[3] 305	[3] 306	[3] 310	Vermont............	[3] 67	[3] 121	[3] 118	[3] 137
Massachusetts..........	[3] 200	[3] 233	[3] 305	[3] 405	Virginia.............	710	1,040	1,160	1,230
Michigan................	1,640	2,190	2,790	2,830	Washington.........	607	712	936	965
Minnesota..............	1,460	[3] 4,180	[3] 959	[3] 3,270	West Virginia.......	172	272	395	425
Mississippi..............	149	198	192	220	Wisconsin..........	[3] 372	509	3,600	1,730
Missouri................	1,370	2,010	2,560	2,490	Wyoming............	978	1,860	2,370	2,530

[1] Preliminary. [2] Includes data not distributed to States, not shown separately. [3] Partial data only; excludes values withheld to avoid disclosing individual company data.

Source: U.S. Geological Survey, *Minerals Yearbook, 2013,* October 2016, and earlier reports; and *Mineral Commodities Summaries 2017,* January 2017, and earlier reports. See also <http://minerals.er.usgs.gov/minerals/pubs/mcs/>.

Table 937. Principal Fuels, Nonmetals, and Metals—World Production, 2000 and 2015, and the U.S. Share, 2015

[In units as indicated (5,129 represents 5,129,000,000), except as indicated; see Appendix IV]

Mineral	Unit	2000	2005	2009	2010	2011	2012	2013	2014	2015	U.S. share 2015
FUELS [1]											
Coal	Mil. sh. tons	5,129	6,604	7,729	8,205	8,754	9,018	9,041	9,019	(NA)	(NA)
Petroleum (crude) [2]	Bil. bbl.	25.0	27.0	26.6	27.2	27.2	27.8	27.8	28.5	29.4	11.7
Natural gas (dry, marketable)	Tril. cu. ft.	87.1	98.3	105.4	112.3	116.5	119.4	120.9	122.3	(NA)	(NA)
Natural gas plant liquids	Bil. bbl.	2.3	2.9	3.1	3.3	3.3	3.5	3.5	3.7	3.9	31.7
NONMETALS											
Asbestos	1,000 metric tons	2,110	2,210	2,110	2,010	2,000	2,020	2,050	2,030	2,030	–
Barite	1,000 metric tons	6,560	7,870	7,050	6,820	8,370	9,220	8,240	8,390	7,410	5.7
Cement, hydraulic	Mil. metric tons	1,660	2,350	3,050	3,290	3,630	3,820	4,070	4,180	4,060	2.1
Feldspar	1,000 metric tons	9,540	16,800	19,000	21,600	21,200	20,700	21,800	22,900	22,900	2.3
Fluorspar	1,000 metric tons	4,450	5,360	6,290	7,000	9,080	6,870	6,330	6,720	6,670	(NA)
Gypsum	Mil. metric tons	108	147	232	241	243	244	252	260	260	12.0
Mica (incl. scrap)	1,000 metric tons	328	359	1,060	1,110	1,100	1,080	1,130	1,140	1,130	2.9
Nitrogen (N content)	Mil. metric tons	108	122	128	132	139	139	144	140	130	6.8
Phosphate rock (gross wt.)	Mil. metric tons	132	152	162	183	200	216	232	237	241	11.4
Potash (K2O equivalent)	Mil. metric tons	27	34	21	34	36	33	36	41	41	1.8
Sulfur, elemental basis	Mil. metric tons	59	69	68	70	70	70	68	69	69	13.8
METALS, mine basis											
Bauxite	Mil. metric tons	136	178	209	239	254	254	291	264	293	(NA)
Copper	1,000 metric tons	13,200	15,000	16,100	16,100	16,100	16,900	18,300	18,400	19,100	5.7
Gold	Metric tons	2,590	2,470	2,490	2,590	2,680	2,750	2,920	3,020	3,100	6.9
Iron ore (gross wt.)	Mil. metric tons	969	1,320	1,710	1,870	2,030	2,070	2,230	2,330	2,280	2.0
Lead [4]	1,000 metric tons	3,200	3,470	3,780	4,160	4,750	5,080	5,430	5,440	4,950	–
Mercury	Metric tons	1,360	1,520	1,880	2,180	1,970	1,830	2,320	2,750	3,270	–
Molybdenum [4]	1,000 metric tons	135	186	221	246	264	256	258	268	235	20.2
Nickel [4]	1,000 metric tons	1,290	1,460	1,410	1,710	2,340	2,570	2,790	2,350	2,280	1.2
Silver	1,000 metric tons	18	21	22	23	23	24	26	27	25	4.4
Tantalum concentrates (Ta content)	Metric tons	1,070	1,380	956	922	947	1,100	1,180	1,150	1,170	–
Titanium mineral concentrates (titanium content) [5]	1,000 metric tons	4,940	6,000	5,440	7,760	7,290	7,300	7,640	7,350	7,130	(NA)
Tungsten [4]	1,000 metric tons	44	60	61	68	74	77	84	87	89	(NA)
Vanadium [4]	1,000 metric tons	41	56	59	72	72	75	80	83	78	–
Zinc [4]	1,000 metric tons	8,770	10,000	11,600	12,300	12,500	12,900	13,100	13,300	12,800	6.4
METALS, smelter basis											
Aluminum	1,000 metric tons	24,300	31,900	37,200	41,800	46,800	49,200	51,900	54,000	57,500	2.8
Cadmium	1,000 metric tons	20	20	21	24	21	22	23	23	23	(NA)
Copper	1,000 metric tons	11,000	13,500	14,900	15,600	15,900	16,100	17,100	17,900	18,500	2.8
Iron, pig [5]	Mil. metric tons	573	802	919	1,040	1,100	1,120	1,170	1,180	1,160	2.2
Lead [6,7]	1,000 metric tons	6,580	7,660	8,850	9,610	10,300	10,500	10,600	10,600	(NA)	(NA)
Magnesium [6,7]	Mil. metric tons	422	622	588	765	806	840	909	1,000	972	(NA)
Raw Steel [8]	Mil. metric tons	850	1,140	1,230	1,430	1,520	1,520	1,620	1,670	1,610	4.9
Tin [8]	1,000 metric tons	272	324	310	318	321	314	313	369	326	(NA)
Zinc	1,000 metric tons	9,137	10,300	11,400	12,800	13,100	12,600	13,000	13,500	[3] 13,900	1.2

– Represents zero. NA Not available. [1] Source: Energy Information Administration, "International Energy Statistics." [2] Crude oil including lease condensate. [3] Starting 2005, no smelter processing necessary. [4] Content of ore and concentrate. [5] Estimated. [6] Primary production; no smelter processing necessary. [7] Starting 2005, excludes U.S. production. [8] Production from primary sources only.

Source: U.S. Energy Information Administration, Open Data, "International Energy Data," <http://www.eia.gov/opendata/>, accessed August 2017; and U.S. Geological Survey, *Minerals Commodity Survey 2017*, January 2017, and "Historical Statistics for Mineral and Material Commodities in the United States," <http://minerals.usgs.gov/minerals/pubs/historical-statistics/>, accessed August 2017.

Table 938. Petroleum Industry—Wells Drilled, Production, Foreign Trade, Reserves, and Refineries: 1990 to 2016

[602 represents 602,000. Includes all costs incurred for drilling and equipping wells to point of completion as productive wells or abandonment after drilling becomes unproductive. Based on sample of operators of different size drilling establishments]

Item	Unit	1990	1995	2000	2005	2010	2014	2015	2016
Crude oil producing wells, (Dec. 31)	1,000	602	574	534	498	520	(NA)	(NA)	(NA)
Daily output per well [1]	Bbl.	12.2	11.4	10.9	10.4	10.5	(NA)	(NA)	(NA)
Completed wells drilled, total	1,000	32.33	21.14	29.29	44.02	37.50	(NA)	(NA)	(NA)
Crude oil	1,000	12.84	8.25	8.09	10.78	16.25	(NA)	(NA)	(NA)
Natural gas	1,000	11.25	8.08	17.05	28.59	16.97	(NA)	(NA)	(NA)
Dry holes	1,000	8.25	4.81	4.15	4.65	4.28	(NA)	(NA)	(NA)
Average depth per well	Feet	4,827	5,542	4,932	5,459	7,183	(NA)	(NA)	(NA)
Average cost per well	$1,000	384	513	755	1,721	(NA)	(NA)	(NA)	(NA)
Average cost per foot	Dollars	76.07	87.22	142.16	306.50	(NA)	(NA)	(NA)	(NA)
Crude oil production, total [2]	Mil. bbl.	2,685	2,394	2,131	1,892	1,999	3,199	3,437	3,248
Value at wells [2, 3]	Bil. dol.	53.77	35.00	56.93	95.03	149.32	(NA)	(NA)	(NA)
Average price per barrel	Dollars	20.03	14.62	26.72	50.28	74.71	87.39	44.39	38.29
Lower 48 states [4]	Mil. bbl.	2,037	1,853	1,771	1,577	1,780	3,018	3,260	3,061
Alaska	Mil. bbl.	647	542	354	315	219	181	176	179
Onshore	Mil. bbl.	2,290	1,838	1,482	1,265	1,367	(NA)	(NA)	(NA)
Offshore	Mil. bbl.	395	556	649	625	632	(NA)	(NA)	(NA)
Imports: Crude oil [2, 5]	Mil. bbl.	2,151	2,639	3,320	3,696	3,363	2,681	2,687	2,883
Refined petroleum products	Mil. bbl.	775	586	874	1,310	942	692	761	798
Exports: Crude oil [2]	Mil. bbl.	40	35	18	12	15	128	170	190
Proved reserves	Bil. bbl.	26.3	22.4	22.0	21.8	23.3	36.4	32.3	(NA)
Operable refineries	Number	205	175	158	148	148	142	140	141
Daily capacity (Jan. 1)	1,000 bbl.	15,572	15,434	16,512	17,125	17,584	17,925	17,967	18,317
Refinery input, total	Mil. bbl.	5,325	5,555	5,964	6,136	6,345	6,779	6,871	6,938
Crude oil [2]	Mil. bbl.	4,894	5,100	5,514	5,555	5,374	5,785	5,909	5,930
Natural gas plant liquids	Mil. bbl.	171	172	139	161	161	187	189	196
Other liquids [6]	Mil. bbl.	260	283	311	420	810	808	773	813
Refinery output, total [7]	Mil. bbl.	5,574	5,838	6,311	6,497	6,735	7,174	7,258	7,344
Motor gasoline [8]	Mil. bbl.	2,540	2,722	2,910	3,036	3,306	3,493	3,560	3,656
Jet fuel (kerosene type)	Mil. bbl.	478	514	588	564	517	563	580	601
Distillate fuel oil	Mil. bbl.	1,067	1,152	1,310	1,443	1,542	1,794	1,819	1,773
Residual fuel oil	Mil. bbl.	347	288	255	229	213	159	152	153
Liquefied petroleum gases	Mil. bbl.	182	239	258	209	240	238	224	229
Utilization rate	Percent	87.1	92.0	92.6	90.6	86.4	90.4	91.0	89.8

NA Not available. [1] Based on number of wells producing at end of year. [2] Includes lease condensate. [3] Values based on domestic first purchase price. [4] Excluding Alaska and Hawaii. [5] Includes imports for the Strategic Petroleum Reserve. [6] Unfinished oils (net), other hydrocarbons, hydrogen, aviation and motor gasoline blending components (net). Beginning 1995, also includes oxygenates (net). [7] Includes other products not shown separately. [8] Finished motor gasoline. Beginning 1995, also includes ethanol blended into motor gasoline.

Source: U.S. Energy Information Administration, *Annual Energy Review 2011*, September 2012; and "Petroleum & Other Liquids Data," <http://www.eia.gov/naturalgas/data.cfm> and "Monthly Energy Review, Petroleum," <http://www.eia.gov/totalenergy/data/monthly/#petroleum>, accessed July 2017.

Table 939. Crude Oil and Petroleum Products Supply, Disposition, and Ending Stocks: 2016

[In millions of barrels (3,248.1 represents 3,248,100,000). Minus sign (-) indicates decrease]

Commodity	Supply				Disposition				Ending stocks
	Field production [1]	Refinery and blender net production	Imports	Adjustments [2]	Stock change	Refinery and blender net inputs	Exports	Products supplied [3]	
Crude oil	3,248.1	(X)	2,883.1	24.0	35.0	5,929.9	190.3	–	1,179.4
Natural gas liquids and LRG [4]	1,272.9	228.6	59.5	(X)	6.2	195.5	439.3	912.1	203.5
Pentanes plus	158.4	(X)	3.2	(X)	4.5	53.5	71.9	23.9	25.0
Liquefied petroleum gases	1,114.4	228.6	56.3	(X)	1.7	142.1	367.4	888.3	178.4
Ethane/ethylene	458.5	1.5	–	(X)	20.1	(NA)	34.7	405.2	54.0
Propane/propylene	424.3	213.3	47.8	(X)	-12.6	(NA)	291.4	406.6	84.1
Normal butane/butylene	117.4	16.8	4.9	(X)	-5.3	64.4	39.1	40.9	32.2
Isobutane/isobutylene	114.3	-3.0	3.6	(X)	-0.5	77.7	2.2	35.6	8.1
Finished motor gasoline	(X)	3,655.9	21.6	-33.9	0.2	(X)	231.0	3,413.5	28.6
Kerosene-type jet fuel	(X)	601.2	53.8	(X)	2.5	(X)	64.5	587.9	42.8
Distillate fuel oil [5]	(X)	1,773.1	53.8	32.4	4.7	(X)	435.5	1,419.1	165.5

– Represents or rounds to zero. NA Not available. X Not applicable. [1] Represents crude oil production on leases, natural gas liquids production at natural gas processing plants, new supply of other hydrocarbons/oxygenates and motor gasoline blending components, fuel ethanol, and distillate fuel oil. [2] Includes an adjustment for crude oil, previously referred to as "Unaccounted For Crude Oil." Also included is an adjustment for motor gasoline blending components, fuel ethanol, and distillate fuel oil. [3] Products supplied is equal to field production, plus refinery and blender net production, plus import, plus adjustments, minus stock change, minus refinery and blender net inputs, minus export. [4] Liquefied Refinery Gases (LRGs) are liquefied petroleum gases fractionated from refinery or still gases through compression and/or refrigeration. They are retained in the liquid state. Excludes still gas. [5] Distillate stocks located in the "Northeast Heating Oil Reserve" are not included.

Source: U.S. Energy Information Administration, "Petroleum Supply and Disposition," <http://www.eia.gov/petroleum/>, accessed May 2017.

Table 940. Crude Petroleum and Natural Gas—Production and Value for Major Producing States: 2010 to 2016

[In units as indicated (1,998 represents 1,998,000,000 barrels)]

State	Crude petroleum								Natural gas marketed production [1]			
	Quantity (mil. bbl.)				Value (mil. dol.) [2]				Quantity (bil. cu. ft.)			
	2010	2014	2015	2016	2010	2014	2015	2016	2010	2014	2015	2016
Total [3]	1,998	3,199	3,437	3,248	149,304	279,534	152,547	124,370	22,382	27,498	28,753	28,295
Alabama	7	10	10	8	540	882	432	318	223	181	168	(NA)
Alaska [4]	215	175	170	174	15,561	15,085	6,970	5,749	374	345	344	344
Arkansas	6	7	6	5	407	583	265	201	927	1,123	1,010	827
California	200	205	201	188	14,930	18,861	9,185	7,120	287	239	231	211
Colorado	33	96	126	115	2,399	7,901	5,114	4,362	1,578	1,643	1,705	1,703
Florida	2	2	2	2	(NA)	(NA)	(NA)	(NA)	12	(Z)	(Z)	(NA)
Illinois	9	10	10	9	664	837	419	335	2	2	2	(NA)
Indiana	2	3	2	2	134	220	99	71	7	7	7	(NA)
Kansas	40	50	45	37	2,931	4,297	1,963	1,404	325	286	285	250
Kentucky	3	3	3	3	178	292	130	104	135	93	86	(NA)
Louisiana	67	69	63	57	5,264	6,474	3,045	2,337	2,210	1,961	1,777	1,861
Michigan	7	7	6	6	517	655	292	244	131	115	108	(NA)
Mississippi	24	24	25	21	1,840	2,211	1,166	825	74	54	58	(NA)
Montana	25	30	29	23	1,779	2,408	1,153	822	88	59	57	51
Nebraska	2	3	3	2	162	253	116	82	2	(Z)	(Z)	(NA)
New Mexico	65	124	147	147	4,953	10,332	6,516	5,771	1,292	1,230	1,245	1,230
New York	(Z)	(Z)	(Z)	(Z)	(NA)	(NA)	(NA)	(NA)	36	20	18	(NA)
North Dakota	113	394	429	378	7,906	32,697	17,788	13,817	82	326	472	505
Ohio	5	15	26	22	351	1,253	995	815	78	512	1,015	1,467
Oklahoma	67	145	158	154	5,068	12,982	7,093	6,071	1,827	2,331	2,500	2,468
Pennsylvania	3	7	7	6	226	548	273	238	573	4,258	4,813	5,264
Texas	427	1,158	1,264	1,176	32,525	100,784	56,798	46,277	6,715	7,985	7,881	6,986
Utah	25	41	37	30	1,680	3,232	1,505	1,123	432	455	423	367
West Virginia	2	8	8	8	130	625	269	249	265	1,067	1,319	1,375
Wyoming	54	76	86	72	3,670	6,132	3,515	2,602	2,306	1,794	1,794	1,603
Federal offshore	588	528	564	595	(NA)	(NA)	(NA)	(NA)	(NA)	(NA)	(NA)	(NA)
Lower 48 states	1,783	3,024	3,267	3,075	133,820	264,459	145,641	118,802	22,008	27,152	28,409	27,951

Z Less than 500,000. NA Not available. [1] Excludes nonhydrocarbon gases. [2] Crude petroleum production value calculated using production quantity and domestic crude oil first purchase price. [3] Includes other states, not shown separately. State production includes state offshore production, as well as extractions from the Gulf not distributed to states. U.S. level totals shown in Table 938 and Table 945 may contain revisions not carried to state level. [4] Alaska crude oil production and value for North Slope only.

Source: U.S. Energy Information Administration, "Petroleum & Other Liquids Data," <http://www.eia.gov/petroleum/data.cfm>, and "Natural Gas Data," <http://www.eia.gov/naturalgas/data.cfm>; accessed June 2017.

Table 941. Crude Oil and Natural Gas—Reserves by State: 2010 to 2015

[23,267 mil. bbl. represents 23,267,000,000 barrels. As of December 31. Proved reserves are estimated quantities of the mineral, which geological and engineering data demonstrate with reasonable certainty, to be recoverable in future years from known reservoirs under existing economic and operating conditions. Based on a sample of operators of oil and gas wells]

Area	2010		2013		2014		2015	
	Crude oil proved reserves (mil. bbl.)	Natural gas (bil. cu. ft.)	Crude oil proved reserves (mil. bbl.)	Natural gas (bil. cu. ft.)	Crude oil proved reserves (mil. bbl.)	Natural gas (bil. cu. ft.)	Crude oil proved reserves (mil. bbl.)	Natural gas (bil. cu. ft.)
United States [1]	23,267	304,625	33,371	338,264	36,385	368,704	32,318	307,730
Alabama	42	2,629	44	1,597	66	2,036	64	2,182
Alaska	3,722	8,838	2,898	7,316	2,855	6,745	2,034	4,566
Arkansas	40	14,178	40	13,518	65	12,789	51	8,339
California	2,938	2,647	2,876	1,887	2,854	2,107	2,333	1,832
Colorado	386	24,119	896	22,381	1,200	20,851	1,212	17,139
Florida	18	56	38	15	70	–	16	–
Illinois	64	(NA)	42	(NA)	34	(NA)	31	(NA)
Indiana	8	(NA)	8	(NA)	8	(NA)	8	(NA)
Kansas	295	3,673	372	3,592	414	4,359	337	3,183
Kentucky	15	2,613	17	1,663	16	1,611	10	1,362
Louisiana	424	29,277	503	20,164	534	22,975	424	16,097
Michigan	40	2,919	64	1,807	53	1,845	43	1,386
Mississippi	247	853	223	595	230	558	158	480
Montana	369	944	413	575	444	667	326	692
Nebraska	10	(NA)	10	(NA)	15	(NA)	17	(NA)
New Mexico	823	15,412	1,171	13,576	1,476	15,283	1,486	14,364
New York	(NA)	281	(NA)	144	(NA)	143	(NA)	104
North Dakota	1,814	1,667	5,677	5,420	6,043	6,034	5,193	6,203
Ohio	42	832	42	3,161	78	6,723	62	12,104
Oklahoma	710	26,345	1,019	26,873	1,241	31,778	1,262	28,486
Pennsylvania	22	13,960	15	49,674	22	59,873	13	55,894
Texas	5,674	88,997	10,468	90,349	12,272	97,154	11,759	78,866
Utah	449	6,981	613	6,829	555	6,685	389	3,547
Virginia	(NA)	3,215	(NA)	2,373	(NA)	2,800	(NA)	2,496
West Virginia	17	7,000	17	22,765	11	29,432	12	20,553
Wyoming	567	35,074	723	33,618	953	27,553	725	20,436
Federal offshore	4,496	11,765	5,137	8,193	4,849	8,527	4,335	7,296
Lower 48 states	19,545	295,787	30,473	330,948	33,530	361,959	30,284	303,164

– Represents zero. NA Not available. [1] Includes other states, not shown separately.

Source: U.S. Energy Information Administration, "Petroleum & Other Liquids Data," <http://www.eia.gov/petroleum/data.cfm>; and "Natural Gas Data," <http://www.eia.gov/naturalgas/data.cfm>; accessed March 2017.

Table 942. Federal Offshore Leasing, Exploration, Production, and Revenue: 1990 to 2016

[In units, as indicated (56.79 represents 56,790,000). Data presented by fiscal year. See source for explanation of terms and for reliability statement]

Item	Unit	1990	1995	2000	2005	2010	2014	2015	2016
Tracts offered..........................	Number	10,459	10,995	7,992	11,447	6,958	11,671	11,871	12,910
Tracts leased..........................	Number	825	835	553	989	446	400	194	140
Acres offered..........................	Millions	56.79	59.70	42.89	61.08	36.96	61.07	63.21	68.69
Acres leased..........................	Millions	4.30	4.34	2.92	5.24	2.37	2.09	1.07	0.77
New wells being drilled:									
Active..........................	Number	120	237	236	135	48	(NA)	(NA)	(NA)
Suspended..........................	Number	266	155	139	59	76	(NA)	(NA)	(NA)
Cumulative wells (since 1953):									
Wells completed..........................	Number	13,167	13,423	13,733	13,398	10,404	(NA)	(NA)	(NA)
Wells plugged and abandoned.......	Number	14,677	21,478	26,893	31,884	36,695	(NA)	(NA)	(NA)
Revenue, total [1]..........................	Bil. dol.	3.4	2.7	5.2	6.3	5.3	7.4	5.1	2.8
Bonuses, oil and gas..................	Bil. dol.	0.8	0.4	0.4	0.6	1.0	1.0	0.6	0.2
Royalties, oil and gas..................	Bil. dol.	2.6	2.1	4.1	5.5	3.6	5.9	4.1	2.4
Rentals, oil and gas..................	Bil. dol.	0.1	0.1	0.2	0.2	0.2	0.2	0.2	0.2
Sales value [2]..........................	Bil. dol.	17.0	13.8	27.4	37.2	25.1	43.7	30.9	19.0
Oil..........................	Bil. dol.	7.0	6.3	11.5	15.4	21.3	40.0	27.8	17.4
Natural gas..........................	Bil. dol.	9.5	7.5	15.9	21.8	3.7	3.7	3.1	1.7
Sales volume: [3]									
Oil..........................	Mil. bbl.	324	409	566	332	261	396	444	451
Natural gas..........................	Bil. cu. ft.	5,093	4,692	4,723	3,504	1,043	852	914	738

NA Not available [1] Includes revenues from sources and commodities not shown separately, including oil condensate, salt, sulfur, and wind. [2] Sales value is value at time of sale, not current value. Excludes gas plant products. [3] Excludes sales volumes for gas plant products.

Source: U.S. Department of the Interior, Bureau of Ocean Energy Management, Regulation and Enforcement, *Outer Continental Shelf Lease Sale Statistics*, December 2016; and Office of Natural Resources Revenue, "Annual Reported Royalty Revenue," <http://statistics.onrr.gov/ReportTool.aspx>, accessed March 2017. See also <http://www.boem.gov/Outer-Continental-Shelf-Lease-Sale-Statistics/>.

Table 943. Natural Gas Plant Liquids—Production and Value: 1990 to 2016

[In units, as indicated. Barrels of 42 gallons (569 represents 569,000,000)]

Item	Unit	1990	1995	2000	2005	2010	2013	2014	2015	2016
Field production [1]........................	Mil. bbl.	569	643	699	627	757	951	1,100	1,220	1,273
Pentanes plus..........................	Mil. bbl.	113	122	112	97	101	127	144	158	158
Liquefied petroleum gases............	Mil. bbl.	456	521	587	529	656	824	956	1,062	1,114
Natural gas processed..................	Tril. cu. ft.	15	17	17	15	16	18	20	21	(NA)

NA Not available. [1] Includes other finished petroleum products, not shown separately.

Source: U.S. Energy Information Administration, "Natural Gas Plant Processing," <https://www.eia.gov/naturalgas/data.cfm>; and "Natural Gas Plant Field Production," <https://www.eia.gov/petroleum/data.cfm>; accessed March 2017.

Table 944. Net U.S. Imports of Selected Minerals and Metals as Percent of Apparent Consumption: 1980 to 2016

[In percent. Based on net imports which equal the difference between imports and exports plus or minus government stockpile and industry stock changes]

Minerals and metals	1980	1990	1995	2000	2005	2010	2014	2015	2016 [1]
Fluorspar...........................	87	91	92	100	100	100	100	100	100
Manganese........................	98	100	100	100	100	100	100	100	100
Niobium...........................	100	100	100	100	100	100	100	100	100
Strontium..........................	100	100	100	100	100	100	100	100	100
Tantalum..........................	90	86	80	80	100	100	100	100	100
Mica (sheet).......................	100	100	100	100	100	100	100	100	100
Vanadium..........................	35	(D)	84	100	100	82	100	100	100
Titanium..........................	(NA)	(NA)	70	79	71	65	92	83	91
Potash............................	65	68	75	80	80	83	85	87	90
Zinc..............................	60	64	71	72	67	73	81	81	82
Barite............................	44	71	65	84	84	75	79	78	78
Bauxite [2]........................	(NA)	98	99	100	100	100	>75	>75	>75
Tin...............................	79	71	84	88	78	73	74	74	75
Cobalt............................	93	84	79	78	83	81	75	73	74
Platinum..........................	(NA)	(NA)	(NA)	78	93	91	67	69	73
Silver............................	7	(NA)	(NA)	43	72	65	63	71	67
Chromium.........................	67	80	75	77	68	63	74	65	58
Aluminum.........................	([3])	([3])	23	33	41	14	33	41	52
Palladium.........................	(NA)	(NA)	(NA)	84	84	49	65	52	48
Copper...........................	16	15	27	37	42	32	32	32	34
Tungsten..........................	53	81	90	66	68	63	>25	>25	>25
Nickel............................	76	64	60	54	48	41	56	38	25
Iron and steel......................	13	13	21	18	15	6	30	22	16
Gypsum...........................	21	27	30	27	27	12	11	11	12
Sulfur............................	14	15	21	18	24	19	12	14	9

D Withheld to avoid disclosure. NA Not available. > Greater than. [1] Preliminary. [2] Includes alumina. [3] Net exporter.

Source: Through 1990, U.S. Bureau of Mines; thereafter, U.S. Geological Survey, *Mineral Commodity Summaries 2017*, January 2017, and earlier reports. See also <http://minerals.usgs.gov/minerals/pubs/mcs/>.

Table 945. Natural Gas—Supply, Consumption, Reserves, and Marketed Production: 1990 to 2016

[270 represents 270,000. Data are for dry natural gas, plus a small amount of supplemental gaseous fuels. Minus sign (-) indicates debit]

Item	Unit	1990	1995	2000	2005	2010	2014	2015	2016 (P)
Producing wells (year-end)............	1,000	270	299	342	426	488	566	555	(NA)
Production value at wells..............	Bil. dol.	31.8	30.3	74.3	138.8	100.3	(NA)	(NA)	(NA)
Avg. per 1,000 cu. ft..................	Dollars	1.71	1.55	3.68	7.33	4.48	(NA)	(NA)	(NA)
Proved reserves [1]......................	Tril. cu. ft.	169	165	177	204	305	369	308	(NA)
Marketed production [2].............	**Bil. cu. ft.**	**18,594**	**19,506**	**20,198**	**18,927**	**22,382**	**27,498**	**28,753**	**28,295**
Minus: Extraction losses [3]...........	Bil. cu. ft.	784	908	1,016	876	1,066	1,608	1,693	1,836
Equals: Dry production................	Bil. cu. ft.	17,810	18,599	19,182	18,051	21,316	25,890	27,060	26,459
Plus: Supplemental gas supplies.....	Bil. cu. ft.	123	110	90	64	65	60	59	59
Equals: Dry production with supplemental gas................	Bil. cu. ft.	17,932	18,709	19,272	18,114	21,380	25,949	27,118	26,518
Plus: Withdrawals from storage [4].....	Bil. cu. ft.	1,934	2,974	3,498	3,057	3,274	3,586	3,101	3,335
Plus: Imports.........................	Bil. cu. ft.	1,532	2,841	3,782	4,341	3,741	2,695	2,718	3,001
Plus: Balancing item [5]................	Bil. cu. ft.	307	396	-306	236	115	-283	-258	-66
Equals: Total supply..................	Bil. cu. ft.	21,706	24,920	26,246	25,748	28,511	31,947	32,678	32,788
Minus: Exports.......................	Bil. cu. ft.	86	154	244	729	1,137	1,514	1,784	2,315
Minus: Additions to storage [4].........	Bil. cu. ft.	2,433	2,566	2,684	3,002	3,291	3,839	3,639	2,977
Equals: Consumption, total........	**Bil. cu. ft.**	**19,174**	**22,207**	**23,333**	**22,014**	**24,087**	**26,593**	**27,306**	**27,490**
Lease and plant fuel..................	Bil. cu. ft.	1,236	1,220	1,151	1,112	1,286	1,512	1,587	1,561
Pipeline fuel [6].........................	Bil. cu. ft.	(NA)	(NA)	642	584	674	700	666	671
Residential...........................	Bil. cu. ft.	4,391	4,850	4,996	4,827	4,782	5,087	4,610	4,391
Commercial [7].........................	Bil. cu. ft.	2,623	3,031	3,182	2,999	3,103	3,466	3,199	3,123
Industrial............................	Bil. cu. ft.	(NA)	(NA)	8,142	6,601	6,826	7,646	7,535	7,719
Vehicle fuel..........................	Bil. cu. ft.	(NA)	(NA)	13	23	29	35	39	41
Electric power sector..................	Bil. cu. ft.	(NA)	(NA)	5,206	5,869	7,387	8,146	9,671	9,984
World production (dry).................	Tril. cu. ft.	74	78	87	98	112	122	(NA)	(NA)
U.S. production (dry).................	Tril. cu. ft.	18	19	19	18	21	26	27	26
U.S. percent of world...............	Percent	24.2	23.8	22.0	18.4	19.0	21.2	(NA)	(NA)

P Preliminary. NA Not available. [1] Estimated, end of year. [2] Marketed production includes gross withdrawals from reservoirs less quantities used for reservoir repressuring and quantities vented or flared. Excludes nonhydrocarbon gases subsequently removed. [3] Volumetric reduction in natural gas resulting from the removal of natural gas plant liquids, which are transferred to petroleum supply. [4] Underground storage. [5] Quantities lost and imbalances in data due to differences among data sources. Since 1980, excludes in-transit shipments that cross U.S.-Canada border (i.e., natural gas delivered to its destination via the other country). [6] Natural gas consumed in the operation of pipelines and delivery to consumers. [7] Includes deliveries to municipalities and public authorities for institutional heating and other purposes.

Source: U.S. Energy Information Administration, "Natural Gas Data," <http://www.eia.gov/naturalgas/data.cfm>; "Monthly Energy Review, Natural Gas," <http://www.eia.gov/totalenergy/data/monthly/#naturalgas>; and "International Energy Statistics," <http://www.eia.gov/countries/data.cfm>; accessed August 2017.

Table 946. Unconventional Dry Natural Gas Production and Proved Reserves: 2014 and 2015

[In billions of cubic feet (1,404 represents 1,404,000,000,000). For states not listed, no production or reserves were reported]

State	Production				Proved reserves [1]			
	Coalbed methane [2]		Shale gas [3]		Coalbed methane [2]		Shale gas [3]	
	2014	2015	2014	2015	2014	2015	2014	2015
United States........	**1,404**	**1,269**	**13,447**	**15,213**	**15,696**	**12,517**	**199,684**	**175,601**
Alabama...............	78	72	(NA)	(NA)	978	975	(NA)	(NA)
Alaska.................	–	–	–	–	–	–	–	–
Arkansas..............	2	1	1,038	923	15	5	11,695	7,164
California.............	–	–	3	2	–	–	44	31
Colorado..............	412	392	236	325	5,103	4,394	3,775	3,115
Florida................	–	–	(NA)	(NA)	–	–	–	(NA)
Kansas................	27	25	1	1	211	170	4	5
Kentucky..............	–	–	2	1	7	6	50	13
Louisiana..............	–	–	1,191	1,153	–	–	12,792	9,154
Michigan..............	–	–	96	65	–	–	1,432	1,006
Mississippi............	–	–	2	3	–	–	19	11
Montana...............	–	–	42	39	11	3	482	360
New Mexico...........	373	344	28	46	4,120	3,189	646	1,044
New York.............	–	–	(NA)	(NA)	–	–	(NA)	(NA)
North Dakota..........	–	–	426	545	–	–	6,442	6,904
Ohio..................	(NA)	(NA)	441	959	(NA)	(NA)	6,384	12,430
Oklahoma.............	61	48	869	993	602	328	16,653	18,672
Pennsylvania..........	11	10	4,009	4,597	158	135	56,210	53,484
Texas.................	9	10	4,156	4,353	61	63	54,158	42,626
Utah..................	47	42	(NA)	(NA)	538	352	(NA)	(NA)
Virginia...............	108	106	3	3	2,233	2,060	84	76
West Virginia..........	11	11	869	1,163	76	68	28,311	19,226
Wyoming..............	264	207	29	36	1,572	760	380	204

– Represents or rounds to zero. NA Not available. [1] Proved reserves of natural gas as of December 31 of the report year are the estimated quantities which analysis of geological and engineering data demonstrate with reasonable certainty to be recoverable in future years from known reservoirs under existing economic and operating conditions. [2] Methane is generated during coal formation and is contained in the coal microstructure. Typical recovery entails pumping water out of the coal to allow the gas to escape. Methane is the principal component of natural gas. Coal bed methane can be added to natural gas pipelines without any special treatment. [3] Natural gas produced from low permeability shale formations.

Source: U.S. Energy Information Administration, "Natural Gas Data," <http://www.eia.gov/naturalgas/data.cfm>, accessed June 2017.

Table 947. Coal Supply, Disposition, and Prices: 2000 to 2016

[In millions of short tons (1,073.6 represents 1,073,600,000). 1 short ton = 2,000 lbs]

Item	2000	2005	2010	2013	2014	2015	2016
United States, total supply	**1,073.6**	**1,131.5**	**1,084.4**	**984.8**	**1,000.0**	**896.9**	**728.2**
Consumption by sector:							
Total	1,084.1	1,126.0	1,048.5	924.4	917.7	798.1	729.5
Electric power	985.8	1,037.5	975.1	858.0	851.6	738.4	677.3
Coke plants	28.9	23.4	21.1	21.5	21.3	19.7	16.5
Other industrial plants	65.2	60.3	49.3	43.1	42.9	38.5	34.6
Combined heat and power (CHP)	28.0	25.9	24.6	19.8	19.1	17.0	14.3
Noncombined heat and power	37.2	34.5	24.7	23.3	23.9	21.5	20.3
Commercial	3.7	4.3	3.1	2.0	1.9	1.5	1.2
Residential [1]	0.5	0.4	(NA)	(NA)	(NA)	(NA)	(NA)
Year-end coal stocks:							
Total [2]	140.0	144.3	231.7	200.3	197.7	238.4	203.3
Electric power	102.0	101.1	174.9	147.9	151.5	195.5	163.9
Coke plants	1.5	2.6	1.9	2.2	2.6	2.2	1.7
Other industrial plants	4.6	5.6	4.5	4.1	4.2	4.4	3.6
Producers/distributors	31.9	35.0	49.8	45.7	38.9	35.9	33.7
U.S. coal trade:							
Net exports [3]	46.0	19.5	62.4	108.8	85.9	62.6	50.4
Exports	58.5	49.9	81.7	117.7	97.3	74.0	60.3
Steam coal	25.7	21.3	25.6	52.0	37.2	28.0	19.3
Metallurgical coal	32.8	28.7	56.1	65.7	60.1	46.0	40.9
Imports	12.5	30.5	19.4	8.9	11.4	11.3	9.9
Average delivered price (dollars per short ton):							
Electric utilities	24.28	31.22	44.27	45.02	45.67	42.6	40.64
Independent power producers	(NA)	30.39	41.49	(NA)	(NA)	(NA)	(NA)
Coke plants	44.38	83.79	153.59	156.99	131.41	118.69	(NA)
Other industrial plants	31.46	47.63	64.38	69.16	68.20	65.44	(NA)

NA Not available. [1] Beginning in 2008, residential coal consumption data are not collected by Energy Information Administration. [2] Includes other stocks, not shown separately. [3] Exports minus imports.

Source: U.S. Energy Information Administration, *Annual Coal Report 2015*, November 2016, and earlier reports; and "Coal Data," <http://www.eia.gov/coal/data.cfm>, and "Monthly Energy Review, Coal," <http://www.eia.gov/totalenergy/data/monthly/#coal>, accessed July 2017.

Table 948. Coal and Coke—Summary: 1990 to 2015

[In millions of short tons (1,029 represents 1,029,000,000), except as indicated. Includes coal consumed at mines. Recoverability varies between 40 and 90 percent for individual deposits; 50 percent or more of overall U.S. coal reserve base is believed to be recoverable]

Item	Unit	1990	1995	2000	2005	2010	2013	2014	2015
COAL									
Production, total [1, 2]	**Mil. sh. tons**	**1,029**	**1,033**	**1,074**	**1,131**	**1,084**	**985**	**1,000**	**897**
Average price per short ton	Dollars	21.76	18.83	16.78	23.59	35.61	37.24	34.83	31.83
Anthracite production [2]	Mil. sh. tons	3.5	4.7	4.6	1.7	1.7	2.1	1.9	2.1
Bituminous coal and lignite [3]	Mil. sh. tons	1,026	1,028	1,069	1,130	1,083	983	998	895
Underground	Mil. sh. tons	425	396	374	369	337	342	355	307
Surface [2]	Mil. sh. tons	605	637	700	763	745	641	644	589
Exports	Mil. sh. tons	106	89	58	50	82	118	97	74
Imports	Mil. sh. tons	3	9	13	30	19	9	11	11
Consumption [4]	Mil. sh. tons	904	962	1,084	1,126	1,049	924	918	798
Electric power sector [5]	Mil. sh. tons	783	850	986	1,037	975	858	852	738
Industrial	Mil. sh. tons	115	106	94	84	70	65	64	58
Number of mines	Number	3,243	2,104	1,453	1,415	1,285	1,061	985	853
Daily employment	1,000	131	90	72	79	86	80	75	66
Production, by state:									
Alabama	Mil. sh. tons	29	25	19	21	20	19	16	13
Illinois	Mil. sh. tons	60	48	33	32	33	52	58	56
Indiana	Mil. sh. tons	36	26	28	34	35	39	39	34
Kentucky	Mil. sh. tons	173	154	131	120	105	80	77	61
Montana	Mil. sh. tons	38	39	38	40	45	42	45	42
Ohio	Mil. sh. tons	35	26	22	25	27	25	22	17
Pennsylvania	Mil. sh. tons	71	62	75	67	59	54	61	50
Virginia	Mil. sh. tons	47	34	33	28	22	17	15	14
West Virginia	Mil. sh. tons	169	163	158	154	135	113	112	96
Wyoming	Mil. sh. tons	184	264	339	404	443	388	396	376
Other states	Mil. sh. tons	187	192	197	206	161	156	158	138
World production	Mil. sh. tons	5,281	4,957	5,129	6,604	8,205	9,041	9,019	(NA)
Percent U.S. of world	Percent	19.5	20.8	20.9	17.1	13.2	10.9	11.1	(NA)
COKE									
Production	Mil. sh. tons	27.6	23.7	20.8	16.7	15.0	15.3	15.2	13.8
Imports	Mil. sh. tons	0.8	3.8	3.8	3.5	1.2	0.1	0.1	0.1
Exports	Mil. sh. tons	0.6	1.4	1.1	1.7	1.5	0.8	0.9	0.9
Consumption [6]	Mil. sh. tons	27.8	25.8	23.2	18.2	14.8	14.4	14.4	13.1

NA Not available. [1] Includes bituminous coal, subbituminous coal, lignite, and anthracite. [2] Beginning 2005, includes a small amount of refuse recovery. [3] Includes subbituminous. [4] Includes some categories not shown separately. [5] Electricity-only and combined-heat-and-power (CHP) plants whose primary business is to sell electricity and/or heat to the public. [6] Consumption is calculated as the sum of production and imports minus exports and stock change.

Source: U.S. Energy Information Administration, *Annual Energy Review 2011*, September 2012; *Annual Coal Report 2015*, November 2016; *Quarterly Coal Report*, June 2017; and Open Data, "International Energy Data," <http://www.eia.gov/opendata/>, accessed September 2017. See also <http://www.eia.gov/totalenergy> and <http://www.eia.gov/coal/annual/>.

Table 949. Demonstrated Coal Reserves by Major Producing State: 2014 and 2015

[Reserves in millions of short tons (478,415 represents 478,415,000,000). As of January 1 the following year. The demonstrated reserve base represents the sum of coal in both measured and indicated resource categories of reliability. Measured resources of coal are estimates that have a high degree of geologic assurance from sample analyses and measurements from closely spaced and geological well-known sample sites. Indicated resources are estimates based partly from sample and analyses and measurements and partly from reasonable geologic projections]

	2014				2015			
		Reserves				Reserves		
			Method of mining				Method of mining	
State	Number of mines	Total reserves	Under-ground	Surface	Number of mines	Total reserves	Under-ground	Surface
United States [1]	**985**	**478,415**	**328,410**	**150,005**	**853**	**477,078**	**327,791**	**149,287**
Alabama	36	3,911	791	3,119	37	3,887	772	3,115
Alaska	1	6,091	5,423	668	1	6,089	5,423	666
Arkansas	2	416	271	144	2	415	271	144
Colorado	10	15,743	10,987	4,756	9	15,710	10,955	4,754
Illinois	22	103,783	87,294	16,489	23	103,674	87,190	16,484
Indiana	29	8,976	8,486	490	24	8,921	8,455	466
Iowa	(NA)	2,189	1,732	457	(NA)	2,189	1,732	457
Kansas	2	970	(NA)	970	1	970	(NA)	970
Kentucky	252	28,435	15,915	12,520	210	28,326	15,828	12,497
Kentucky, Eastern	231	9,528	568	8,960	193	9,482	539	8,943
Kentucky, Western	21	18,907	15,347	3,560	17	18,844	15,290	3,555
Maryland	20	606	561	45	18	603	560	43
Missouri	1	5,985	1,479	4,506	1	5,985	1,479	4,506
Montana	6	118,730	70,891	47,839	6	118,673	70,879	47,795
New Mexico	3	11,826	6,043	5,782	3	11,796	6,030	5,766
North Dakota	4	8,726	(NA)	8,726	4	8,690	(NA)	8,690
Ohio	28	22,901	17,240	5,661	25	22,870	17,215	5,655
Oklahoma	6	1,537	1,223	314	5	1,536	1,223	313
Pennsylvania	222	26,460	22,326	4,134	195	26,365	22,238	4,126
Anthracite [2]	61	7,178	3,841	3,337	58	7,175	3,841	3,334
Bituminous	161	19,283	18,485	797	137	19,190	18,398	792
Tennessee	7	749	497	252	10	748	496	251
Texas	16	11,911	(NA)	11,911	14	11,866	(NA)	11,866
Utah	8	5,023	4,757	265	9	4,994	4,729	265
Virginia	69	1,351	874	477	65	1,326	854	472
Washington	(NA)	1,340	1,332	8	(NA)	1,340	1,332	8
West Virginia	191	30,879	27,689	3,190	151	30,703	27,539	3,165
Wyoming	18	58,966	42,441	16,525	16	58,494	42,435	16,059

NA Not available. [1] Includes other states not shown separately. [2] All of the anthracite mines in the United States are located in northeastern Pennsylvania.

Source: U.S. Energy Information Administration, *Annual Coal Report 2015*, November 2016, and earlier reports. See also <http://www.eia.gov/coal/annual/>.

Table 950. Uranium Concentrate Industry—Summary: 1990 to 2016

[In units as indicated (1.7 represents 1,700,000). See also Section 19, Table 971]

Item	Unit	1990	1995	2000	2010	2012	2013	2014	2015	2016
Exploration and development, surface drilling	Mil. ft.	1.7	1.3	1.0	4.9	7.2	3.8	1.3	0.9	0.8
Expenditures	Mil. dol.	(NA)	2.6	5.6	44.6	66.6	49.9	28.2	28.7	22.3
Number of mines operated	Number	39	12	10	9	12	12	11	9	9
Underground	Number	27	–	1	4	6	3	2	1	–
Open pit	Number	2	–	–	–	–	–	–	–	–
In situ leaching	Number	7	5	4	4	5	7	8	7	8
Other sources [1]	Number	3	7	5	1	1	2	1	1	1
Mine production	1,000 pounds	5,876	3,528	3,123	4,237	4,335	4,577	4,912	3,711	2,545
Underground	1,000 pounds	(D)	–	(D)	(D)	(D)	(D)	(D)	(D)	(D)
Open pit	1,000 pounds	1,881	–	–	–	–	–	–	–	–
In situ leaching	1,000 pounds	(D)	3,372	2,995	(D)	(D)	(D)	(D)	(D)	(D)
Other sources [1]	1,000 pounds	3,995	156	128	(D)	(D)	(D)	(D)	(D)	(D)
Uranium concentrate production	1,000 pounds	8,886	6,043	3,958	4,228	4,146	4,659	4,891	3,343	2,886
Concentrate shipments from mills and plants	1,000 pounds	12,957	5,500	3,187	5,137	3,911	4,655	4,593	4,023	3,018
Employment	Person-years [2]	1,335	1,107	627	1,073	1,196	1,156	787	625	560

– Represents zero. D Data withheld to avoid disclosing figures for individual companies. NA Not available. [1] Includes mine water, mill site cleanup and mill tailings, and well field restoration as sources of uranium. [2] A person-year is defined as one whole year, or fraction thereof, worked by an employee, including contracted man power. 12 months worked is 1 person year.

Source: U.S. Energy Information Administration, through 2002, *Uranium Industry,* annual. Thereafter, *Domestic Uranium Production Report,* May 2017, and earlier reports. See also <http://www.eia.gov/uranium/production/annual/>.

Table 951. Crude Petroleum and Natural Gas Extraction Industry Establishments, Employees, and Payroll by State: 2015

[16,101,742 represents $16,101,742,000. Excludes self-employed individuals, employees of private households, railroad employees, agricultural production employees, and most government employees. See source for definitions and statement on reliability of data. An establishment is a single physical location where business is conducted or where services or industrial operations are performed. See Appendix III]

State	Crude petroleum and natural gas extraction (NAICS 211111) [1]			State	Crude petroleum and natural gas extraction (NAICS 211111) [1]		
	Establishments	Number of employees [2]	Annual payroll ($1,000)		Establishments	Number of employees [2]	Annual payroll ($1,000)
United States........	**7,477**	**124,847**	**16,101,742**	Mississippi...........	77	855	87,426
				Missouri.............	13	49	2,522
Alabama...............	29	344	30,328	Montana.............	85	1,032	122,755
Alaska.................	22	2,206	515,523	Nebraska............	20	95	4,812
Arizona................	19	53	4,350	Nevada..............	18	62	4,626
Arkansas..............	109	1,916	159,220	New Hampshire.....	2	([3])	(D)
California.............	243	5,693	782,354	New Mexico.........	150	3,674	359,110
Colorado..............	415	7,776	1,275,470	New York...........	39	323	25,079
Connecticut...........	5	22	2,052	North Carolina......	6	41	3,297
Delaware..............	4	18	3,059	North Dakota........	67	3,553	390,922
District of Columbia....	4	6	554	Ohio.................	179	1,731	106,399
Florida.................	27	184	14,997	Oklahoma...........	1,152	15,772	1,958,573
Georgia...............	5	([4])	(D)	Oregon.............	5	7	783
Hawaii................	2	([3])	(D)	Pennsylvania........	198	4,885	565,893
Idaho.................	2	([3])	(D)	Rhode Island........	1	([3])	(D)
Illinois...............	162	981	50,827	South Carolina......	(NA)	(NA)	(NA)
Indiana................	37	194	13,834	South Dakota.......	6	45	3,605
Iowa..................	2	([3])	(D)	Tennessee..........	11	107	8,084
Kansas................	384	2,660	174,105	Texas.................	3,047	56,342	7,927,100
Kentucky.............	81	579	53,066	Utah................	56	1,521	164,092
Louisiana.............	364	6,023	699,151	Virginia.............	21	307	35,284
Maryland..............	2	([3])	(D)	Washington..........	9	13	1,878
Massachusetts........	3	([3])	(D)	West Virginia........	167	2,275	181,480
Michigan.............	69	796	60,013	Wisconsin...........	3	([3])	(D)
Minnesota.............	6	19	1,586	Wyoming............	149	2,619	301,687

D Withheld to avoid disclosing data for individual companies; data are included in higher level totals. NA Not available. [1] North American Industry Classification System, 2012. [2] Covers full-time and part-time employees who are on the payroll in the pay period including March 12. [3] 0 to 19 employees. [4] 20 to 99 employees.

Source: U.S. Census Bureau, County Business Patterns, "Geography Area Series: County Business Patterns," <http://factfinder.census.gov>, accessed April 2017. See also <https://www.census.gov/programs-surveys/cbp.html>.

Table 952. Natural Gas Liquid Extraction Industry—Establishments, Employees, and Payroll by State: 2015

[1,182,390 represents $1,182,390,000. Excludes self-employed individuals, employees of private households, railroad employees, agricultural production employees, and most government employees. See source for definitions and statement on reliability of data. An establishment is a single physical location where business is conducted or where services or industrial operations are performed. See Appendix III]

State	Natural gas liquid extraction (NAICS 211112) [1]			State	Natural gas liquid extraction (NAICS 211112) [1]		
	Establishments	Number of employees [2]	Annual payroll ($1,000)		Establishments	Number of employees [2]	Annual payroll ($1,000)
United States......	**429**	**10,635**	**1,182,390**	Missouri.............	3	([5])	(D)
Alabama.............	1	([4])	(D)	Montana.............	4	79	9,550
Alaska...............	2	([6])	(D)	Nebraska............	1	([3])	(D)
Arizona..............	1	([3])	(D)	New Mexico.........	23	454	42,153
Arkansas.............	2	([4])	(D)	New York...........	1	([4])	(D)
California............	10	328	40,536	North Dakota........	4	134	17,713
Colorado.............	20	439	47,310	Ohio.................	12	([6])	(D)
Florida...............	1	([4])	(D)	Oklahoma...........	61	709	65,936
Illinois...............	3	([5])	(D)	Pennsylvania........	11	1,249	173,077
Indiana..............	2	([4])	(D)	Tennessee..........	1	([3])	(D)
Kansas..............	25	207	17,717	Texas.................	145	2,955	297,111
Kentucky............	3	([4])	(D)	Utah................	4	([6])	(D)
Louisiana............	47	659	69,301	Virginia.............	1	([4])	(D)
Michigan............	11	226	18,007	West Virginia........	9	174	18,353
Mississippi...........	3	318	50,598	Wyoming............	18	947	99,110

D Withheld to avoid disclosing data for individual companies; data are included in higher level totals. [1] North American Industry Classification System, 2012. [2] Covers full- and part-time employees who are on the payroll in the pay period including March 12. [3] 0 to 19 employees. [4] 20 to 99 employees. [5] 100 to 249 employees. [6] 250 to 499 employees.

Source: U.S. Census Bureau, County Business Patterns, "Geography Area Series: County Business Patterns," <http://factfinder.census.gov>, accessed April 2017. See also <https://www.census.gov/programs-surveys/cbp.html>.

Section 19
Energy and Utilities

This section presents statistics on fuel resources, energy production and consumption, electric energy, renewable energy, and the electric and gas utility industries. The principal sources are the U.S. Department of Energy's Energy Information Administration (EIA), the Edison Electric Institute, Washington, DC, and the American Gas Association, Arlington, VA. The Department of Energy was created in October 1977 and assumed and centralized the responsibilities of all or part of several agencies including the Federal Power Commission (FPC), the U.S. Bureau of Mines, the Federal Energy Administration, and the U.S. Energy Research and Development Administration. For additional data on transportation, see Section 23; on fuels, see Section 18; and on energy-related housing characteristics, see Section 20.

The EIA, in its *Annual Energy Review*, provides statistics and trend data on energy supply, demand, and prices. Information is included on petroleum and natural gas, coal, electricity, hydroelectric power, nuclear power, solar, wind, wood, and geothermal energy. Due to budget constraints, in 2013 the EIA suspended publication of the *Annual Energy Review*. In order to continue publishing similar data, the EIA expanded their coverage of data in their *Monthly Energy Review*, which presents current supply, disposition, and price data and monthly publications on petroleum, coal, natural gas, and electric power. Additional EIA reports include the *Electric Power Annual*; *Natural Gas Annual*; *Petroleum Supply Annual*; *U.S. Crude Oil, Natural Gas, and Natural Gas Liquids Reserves Annual Report*; *Electric Sales, Revenue, and Price*; *State Energy Consumption, Price, and Expenditure Data*; *Annual Energy Outlook*; *Uranium Marketing Annual Report*; *Domestic Uranium Production Report—Quarterly*; and *International Energy Statistics*. These various reports contain state, national, and international data on the production of electricity, net summer capability of generating plants, fuels used in energy production, energy sales and consumption, and hydroelectric power. The EIA also provides access to regular data updates through its Open Data program. For more information, please refer to the EIA's Open Data program's website <http://www.eia.gov/opendata/>.

Data on residential energy consumption, expenditures, and conservation activities are available from EIA's Residential Energy Consumption Survey (RECS) and are published every 4 years. The Commercial Buildings Energy Consumption Survey (CBECS), conducted on a quadrennial basis, collects information on the stock of U.S. commercial buildings, their energy-related characteristics, and their energy consumption and expenditures. Data on manufacturing energy consumption, use, and expenditures are also collected every 4 years from EIA's Manufacturing Energy Consumption Survey (MECS). Due to the long gaps between the RECS, CBECS, and MECS, tables are rotated in and out of Section 19 in an effort to keep the data as current as possible. The results from these surveys are published at <http://www.eia.gov/consumption/>.

The Edison Electric Institute's annual *Statistical Year Book of the Electric Power Industry* contains data on the distribution of electric energy by public utilities. The American Gas Association, in its annual yearbook, *Gas Facts*, presents data on gas utilities and financial and operating statistics.

Btu conversion factors—Various energy sources are converted from original units to the thermal equivalent using British thermal units (Btu). A Btu is the amount of energy required to raise the temperature of 1 pound of water 1 degree Fahrenheit (F) at or near 39.2 degrees F. Factors are calculated annually from the latest final annual data available; some are revised as a result.

Electric power industry—In recent years, EIA has restructured the industry categories it once used to gather and report electricity statistics. The electric power industry, previously divided into electric utilities and non-utilities, now consists of the Electric Power Sector, the Commercial Sector, and the Industrial Sector.

The Electric Power Sector is composed of electricity-only and combined-heat-and-power plants (CHPs) whose primary business is to sell electricity, or electricity and heat, to the public.

Electricity-only plants are composed of traditional electric utilities, and nontraditional participants, including energy service providers, power marketers, independent power producers (IPPs), and the portion of CHPs that produce only electricity.

A utility is defined as a corporation, person, agency, authority, or other legal entity or instrumentality aligned with distribution facilities for delivery of electric energy for use primarily by the public. Electric utilities include investor-owned electric utilities, municipal and state utilities, federal electric utilities, and rural electric cooperatives.

An independent power producer is an entity defined as a corporation, person, agency, authority, or other legal entity or instrumentality that owns or operates facilities whose primary business is to produce electricity for use by the public. They are not generally aligned with distribution facilities and are not considered electric utilities.

Combined-heat-and-power producers are plants designed to produce both heat and electricity from a single heat source. These types of electricity producers can be independent power producers or industrial or commercial establishments. As some independent power producers are CHPs, their information is included in the data for the combined-heat-and-power sector.

The Commercial Sector consists of commercial CHPs and commercial electricity-only plants. Industrial CHPs and industrial electricity-only plants make up the Industrial Sector. For more information, please refer to the *Electric Power Annual 2015* website at <http://www.eia.gov/electricity/annual/>.

Table 953. Utilities—Establishments, Revenue, Payroll, and Employees by Kind of Business: 2012

[531,891 represents $531,891,000,000. Includes only establishments or firms with payroll. Data based on the 2012 Economic Census. See Appendix III]

Kind of business	2012 NAICS code [1]	Establish-ments (number)	Revenue		Annual payroll		Paid employees for pay period including March 12 (number)
			Total (mil. dol.)	Per paid employee (dol.)	Total (mil. dol.)	Per paid employee (dol.)	
Utilities.............................	22	17,595	531,891	816,743	58,923	90,479	651,234
Electric power generation, transmission, & distribution.............................	2211	10,330	430,079	823,891	49,937	95,663	522,010
Electric power generation...........................	22111	2,678	120,025	818,164	14,847	101,207	146,701
Hydroelectric power generation..................	221111	405	2,452	707,938	274	79,151	3,464
Fossil fuel electric power generation............	221112	1,416	81,474	992,721	7,998	97,451	82,071
Nuclear electric power generation...............	221113	141	28,868	562,132	5,698	110,961	51,354
Solar electric power generation..................	221114	136	428	270,276	118	74,492	1,582
Wind electric power generation..................	221115	410	5,058	946,000	510	95,437	5,347
Geothermal electric power generation..........	221116	45	981	794,491	124	100,785	1,235
Biomass electric power generation..............	221117	107	721	506,643	106	74,218	1,424
Other electric power generation..................	221118	18	43	193,594	19	82,888	224
Electric power transmission, control & distribution.............................	22112	7,652	310,054	826,129	35,090	93,495	375,309
Electric bulk power transmission & control.............................	221121	250	9,959	798,970	1,408	112,949	12,465
Electric power distribution..........................	221122	7,402	300,095	827,062	33,682	92,827	362,844
Natural gas distribution.............................	2212	2,419	89,568	1,067,088	6,682	79,603	83,937
Water, sewage, & other systems....................	2213	4,846	12,243	270,348	2,304	50,883	45,287
Water supply & irrigation systems.................	22131	4,039	9,438	259,623	1,842	50,664	36,352
Sewage treatment facilities.........................	22132	712	1,377	201,056	301	43,951	6,849
Steam & air-conditioning supply...................	22133	95	1,428	684,768	162	77,473	2,086

[1] North American Industry Classification System, 2012; see text, Section 15.

Source: U.S. Census Bureau, 2012 Economic Census, EC1200A1, "All sectors: Geographic Area Series: Economy-Wide Key Statistics: 2012," <http://factfinder.census.gov/>, accessed May 2017.

Table 954. Utilities—Employees, Annual Payroll, and Establishments by Utility Type: 2015

[64,195 represents $64,195,000,000. Excludes most government employees, railroad employees, and self-employed persons. An establishment is a single physical location where business is conducted or where services or industrial operations are performed. See Appendix III]

Industry	2012 NAICS code [1]	Number of employ-ees [2]	Annual payroll (mil. dol.)	Average payroll per employ-ee (dol.)	Establishments by employment size-class				
					Total	Under 20 employ-ees	20 to 99 employ-ees	100 to 499 employ-ees	500 employ-ees and over
Utilities, total..........................	22	639,234	64,195	100,425	17,990	12,595	4,125	1,081	189
Electric power generation, transmission and distribution............	2211	510,028	53,854	105,590	10,617	6,506	3,088	845	178
Electric power generation................	22111	134,915	15,285	113,295	2,862	1,947	647	207	61
Hydroelectric power....................	221111	3,261	283	86,749	423	380	42	1	–
Fossil fuel electric power..............	221112	76,005	8,408	110,627	1,485	831	456	188	10
Nuclear electric power..................	221113	45,922	5,646	122,947	158	78	19	10	51
Solar electric power....................	221114	1,396	143	102,769	123	102	21	–	–
Wind electric power.....................	221115	3,148	351	111,441	233	206	21	6	–
Geothermal electric power.............	221116	1,134	112	98,545	37	21	14	2	–
Biomass electric power.................	221117	1,247	96	76,948	109	81	28	–	–
Other electric power generation.......	221118	2,802	246	87,861	294	248	46	–	–
Electric power transmission, control & distribution..............	22112	375,113	38,568	102,818	7,755	4,559	2,441	638	117
Electric bulk power transmission & control.............................	221121	13,048	1,661	127,309	268	166	68	27	7
Electric power distribution..............	221122	362,065	36,907	101,935	7,487	4,393	2,373	611	110
Natural gas distribution....................	2212	86,439	7,756	89,734	2,567	1,703	663	190	11
Water, sewage, & other systems.........	2213	42,767	2,585	60,449	4,806	4,386	374	46	–
Water supply & irrigation systems................................	22131	34,771	2,065	59,383	4,017	3,700	275	42	–
Sewage treatment facilities..............	22132	6,171	316	51,224	695	628	63	4	–
Steam & air-conditioning supply........	22133	1,825	204	111,953	94	58	36	–	–

– Represents zero. [1] North American Industry Classification System, 2012; see text, Section 15. [2] Covers full- and part-time employees who are on the payroll in the pay period including March 12.

Source: U.S. Census Bureau, County Business Patterns, "Geography Area Series: County Business Patterns by Employment Size Class," <http://factfinder.census.gov>, accessed April 2017. See also <https://www.census.gov/programs-surveys/cbp.html>.

Table 955. Energy Supply and Disposition by Type of Fuel: 1973 to 2016

[In quadrillion British thermal units (Btu) (63.56 represents 63,560,000,000,000,000). For definition of Btu, see source and text, this section]

Year	Production										Net imports, total [7]	Consumption					
	Total [1]	Crude oil [2]	Dry natural gas	Coal [3]	Nuclear electric power	Renewable energy [4]						Total [1,8]	Petroleum [9]	Dry natural gas [10]	Coal	Nuclear electric power	Renewable energy [4] total
						Total [1]	Hydroelectric power [5]	Biomass [6]	Solar/photovoltaic [4]	Wind							
1973	63.56	19.49	22.19	13.99	0.91	4.41	2.86	1.53	(NA)	(NA)	12.58	75.68	34.84	22.51	12.97	0.91	4.41
1975	61.32	17.73	19.64	14.99	1.90	4.69	3.15	1.50	(NA)	(NA)	11.71	71.96	32.73	19.95	12.66	1.90	4.69
1980	67.18	18.25	19.91	18.60	2.74	5.43	2.90	2.48	(NA)	(NA)	12.10	78.07	34.20	20.24	15.42	2.74	5.43
1985	67.70	18.99	16.98	19.33	4.08	6.08	2.97	3.02	(Z)	(Z)	7.58	76.39	30.92	17.70	17.48	4.08	6.08
1990	70.70	15.57	18.33	22.49	6.10	6.04	3.05	2.74	0.06	0.03	14.06	84.48	33.55	19.60	19.17	6.10	6.04
1995	71.17	13.89	19.08	22.13	7.08	6.56	3.21	3.10	0.07	0.03	17.68	91.03	34.44	22.67	20.09	7.08	6.56
1996	72.48	13.72	19.34	22.79	7.09	7.01	3.59	3.16	0.07	0.03	19.02	94.02	35.67	23.08	21.00	7.09	7.01
1997	72.47	13.66	19.39	23.31	6.60	7.02	3.64	3.11	0.07	0.03	20.63	94.60	36.16	23.22	21.45	6.60	7.01
1998	72.87	13.24	19.61	24.05	7.07	6.49	3.30	2.93	0.07	0.03	22.24	95.02	36.82	22.83	21.66	7.07	6.49
1999	71.74	12.45	19.34	23.30	7.61	6.52	3.27	2.97	0.07	0.05	23.48	96.65	37.84	22.91	21.62	7.61	6.51
2000	71.33	12.36	19.66	22.74	7.86	6.10	2.81	3.01	0.06	0.06	24.90	98.82	38.27	23.82	22.58	7.86	6.10
2001	71.73	12.28	20.17	23.55	8.03	5.16	2.24	2.62	0.06	0.07	26.32	96.17	38.19	23.77	21.91	8.03	5.16
2002	70.71	12.16	19.38	22.73	8.15	5.73	2.69	2.71	0.06	0.11	25.72	97.64	38.23	23.51	21.90	8.15	5.73
2003	69.93	11.96	19.63	22.09	7.96	5.94	2.79	2.80	0.06	0.11	26.99	97.92	38.79	22.83	22.32	7.96	5.94
2004	70.23	11.55	19.07	22.85	8.22	6.06	2.69	3.00	0.06	0.14	29.14	100.09	40.23	22.92	22.47	8.22	6.07
2005	69.43	10.97	18.56	23.19	8.16	6.22	2.70	3.10	0.06	0.18	30.20	100.19	40.30	22.57	22.80	8.16	6.23
2006	70.73	10.77	19.02	23.79	8.21	6.59	2.87	3.21	0.06	0.26	29.92	99.48	39.82	22.24	22.45	8.21	6.64
2007	71.40	10.75	19.79	23.49	8.46	6.51	2.45	3.47	0.07	0.34	29.34	101.01	39.49	23.66	22.75	8.46	6.52
2008	73.21	10.61	20.70	23.85	8.43	7.19	2.51	3.87	0.07	0.55	26.02	98.89	36.91	23.84	22.39	8.43	7.17
2009	72.65	11.33	21.14	21.62	8.36	7.62	2.67	3.95	0.08	0.72	22.77	94.12	34.96	23.42	19.69	8.36	7.60
2010	74.73	11.59	21.81	22.04	8.43	8.08	2.54	4.32	0.09	0.92	21.69	97.44	35.49	24.57	20.83	8.43	8.03
2011	77.91	11.95	23.41	22.22	8.27	9.10	3.10	4.50	0.11	1.17	18.38	96.84	34.82	24.95	19.66	8.27	9.00
2012	79.11	13.77	24.61	20.68	8.06	8.74	2.63	4.41	0.16	1.34	15.80	94.42	34.02	26.09	17.38	8.06	8.71
2013	81.70	15.81	24.86	20.00	8.24	9.25	2.56	4.65	0.23	1.60	12.84	97.16	34.61	26.81	18.04	8.24	9.28
2014	87.60	18.55	26.72	20.29	8.34	9.61	2.47	4.86	0.34	1.73	10.97	98.33	34.88	27.38	18.00	8.34	9.57
2015	88.05	19.65	28.06	17.95	8.34	9.49	2.32	4.75	0.43	1.78	10.89	97.37	35.60	28.20	15.55	8.34	9.47
2016	83.88	18.59	27.41	14.58	8.42	10.15	2.48	4.74	0.59	2.11	11.56	97.40	35.94	28.43	14.22	8.42	10.16

NA Not available. Z Less than 5 trillion. [1] Includes other types of fuel, not shown separately. [2] Includes lease condensate. [3] Beginning 1989, includes waste coal supplied. Beginning 2001, also includes a small amount of refuse recovery. [4] Electricity net generation from conventional hydroelectric power, geothermal, solar, and wind. Consumption of electricity from wood, biomass waste, and alcohol fuels; geothermal heat pump and direct use energy; and solar thermal direct use energy. [5] Conventional hydroelectricity net generation. [6] Organic nonfossil material of biological origin constituting a renewable energy source. [7] Imports minus exports. [8] Includes coal coke net imports and electricity net imports, not shown separately. [9] Petroleum products supplied, including natural gas plant liquids and crude oil burned as fuel. Does not include biofuels that have been blended with petroleum. [10] Excludes supplemental gaseous fuels.

Source: U.S. Energy Information Administration, *Monthly Energy Review*, May 2017. See also <http://www.eia.gov/totalenergy/data/monthly/>.

Table 956. Energy Supply and Disposition by Type of Fuel—Estimates, 2015 and 2016, and Projections, 2017 to 2035

[Quadrillion Btu (87.16 represents 87,160,000,000,000,000) per year. Btu = British thermal unit. For definition of Btu, see source and text, this section. Projections are "reference" or mid-level forecasts. See report for methodology and assumptions used in generating projections]

Type of fuel	2015	2016	Projections				
			2017	2020	2025	2030	2035
Production, total	**87.16**	**84.64**	**87.12**	**95.79**	**100.06**	**100.73**	**101.36**
Crude oil and lease condensate	19.69	18.28	18.22	20.67	21.69	22.02	21.37
Natural gas plant liquids	4.47	4.78	5.17	6.22	6.45	6.44	6.36
Natural gas, dry	27.92	27.40	28.77	31.81	34.15	36.06	37.73
Coal [1]	16.99	15.18	15.30	16.72	15.06	13.24	12.88
Nuclear power	8.34	8.34	8.28	7.97	8.09	8.03	7.54
Renewable energy [2]	9.29	9.73	10.07	11.52	13.60	14.09	14.60
Other [3]	0.46	0.92	1.30	0.88	1.03	0.85	0.87
Imports, total	**23.83**	**25.20**	**25.12**	**22.93**	**22.93**	**22.15**	**22.34**
Crude oil [4]	16.33	17.49	17.71	16.18	16.63	16.41	16.83
Petroleum products [5]	4.25	4.18	4.25	4.20	4.26	4.03	3.96
Natural gas	2.79	3.08	2.80	2.21	1.74	1.48	1.36
Other imports [6]	0.47	0.45	0.37	0.35	0.29	0.23	0.19
Exports, total	**12.93**	**13.74**	**14.34**	**19.13**	**22.70**	**24.00**	**24.30**
Petroleum [7]	9.17	10.19	10.50	11.97	14.60	15.41	15.27
Natural gas	1.80	2.09	2.46	5.57	6.47	6.86	7.14
Coal	1.96	1.46	1.38	1.59	1.64	1.73	1.89
Consumption, total	**96.93**	**96.47**	**97.31**	**99.66**	**100.24**	**98.73**	**99.21**
Petroleum products [8]	36.57	36.89	37.21	37.85	37.03	35.81	35.54
Natural gas	28.19	28.59	28.77	28.22	29.14	30.36	31.61
Coal	15.47	13.93	14.12	15.24	13.47	11.51	10.97
Nuclear power	8.34	8.34	8.28	7.97	8.09	8.03	7.54
Renewable energy [9]	7.91	8.29	8.59	9.96	12.07	12.58	13.11
Other [10]	0.45	0.42	0.34	0.42	0.45	0.44	0.43
Net imports of petroleum	**11.41**	**11.48**	**11.45**	**8.40**	**6.30**	**5.04**	**5.52**
Prices (2016 dollars per unit):							
Crude oil spot prices (dol. per barrel)							
Brent spot price	53.06	43.43	49.91	74.82	86.23	94.52	102.15
West Texas Intermediate spot price	49.35	42.78	48.94	68.85	80.08	87.59	95.58
Natural gas at Henry Hub (dol. per mil. BTU)	2.66	2.50	3.00	4.51	4.51	5.00	5.09
Coal minemouth price (dol. per ton) [11]	34.16	33.92	33.65	34.51	34.67	34.29	36.52
Electricity price (cents per kWh)	10.6	10.3	10.3	10.5	11.2	11.4	11.4

[1] Includes waste coal. [2] Includes grid-connected electricity from conventional hydroelectric; wood and wood waste; landfill gas; municipal solid waste; other biomass; wind; photovoltaic and solar thermal sources; and nonelectric energy from renewable sources, such as active and passive solar systems, and wood. Excludes electricity imports using renewable sources and nonmarketed renewable energy. [3] Includes nonbiogenic municipal solid waste, liquid hydrogen, methanol, and some domestic inputs to refineries. [4] Includes imports of crude oil for the Strategic Petroleum Reserve. [5] Includes imports of finished petroleum products, unfinished oils, alcohols, ethers, blending components, and renewable fuels such as ethanol. [6] Includes coal, coal coke (net), and electricity (net). [7] Includes crude oil, petroleum products, ethanol, and biodiesel. [8] Includes petroleum-derived fuels and non-petroleum-derived fuels, such as ethanol, biodiesel, and coal-based synthetic liquids. Petroleum coke, which is a solid, is included. Also included are hydrocarbon gas liquids and crude oil consumed as a fuel. [9] Includes grid-connected electricity from wood and wood waste, non-electric energy from wood, and biofuels heat and coproducts used in the production of liquid fuels, but excludes the energy content of the liquid fuels. Also includes non-biogenic municipal solid waste and net electricity imports. [10] Includes non-biogenic municipal solid waste and net electricity imports. [11] Includes reported prices for both open market and captive mines.

Source: U.S. Energy Information Administration, *Annual Energy Outlook 2017*, January 2017. See also <http://www.eia.gov/forecasts/aeo/index.cfm>.

Table 957. Energy Consumption by End-Use Sector: 1975 to 2016

[Trillion Btu (14,813.4 represents 14,813,400,000,000,000). Btu=British thermal unit. For residential and commercial, industrial, and transportation sectors. Represents consumption of fossil fuels and renewable energy, plus electricity retail sales and electrical system energy losses. For definition of Btu, see source and text, this section. See Appendix III]

Year	Residential	Commercial [1]	Industrial [2]	Trans-portation	Year	Residential	Commercial [1]	Industrial [2]	Trans-portation
1975	14,813.4	9,492.5	29,413.0	18,245.0	1996	19,501.8	15,171.9	34,903.2	24,439.2
1976	15,410.3	10,063.3	31,392.8	19,100.8	1997	18,962.3	15,681.2	35,199.4	24,751.3
1977	15,661.7	10,207.6	32,263.0	19,821.6	1998	18,951.9	15,967.5	34,841.6	25,260.1
1978	16,132.3	10,511.9	32,687.6	20,617.1	1999	19,553.5	16,376.3	34,762.8	25,949.5
1979	15,812.7	10,648.0	33,924.7	20,471.5	2000	20,421.0	17,175.4	34,662.5	26,555.3
1980	15,753.4	10,578.3	32,039.4	19,696.7	2001	20,037.6	17,136.8	32,719.2	26,282.2
1981	15,261.5	10,615.9	30,711.6	19,514.0	2002	20,785.8	17,345.8	32,661.1	26,845.7
1982	15,530.9	10,860.3	27,614.5	19,089.2	2003	21,119.3	17,346.1	32,553.1	26,900.2
1983	15,425.0	10,938.4	27,427.8	19,176.6	2004	21,081.4	17,655.4	33,515.6	27,842.8
1984	15,959.6	11,443.9	29,569.9	19,655.6	2005	21,612.7	17,853.4	32,441.5	28,280.3
1985	16,041.3	11,451.2	28,815.8	20,087.9	2006	20,670.3	17,707.2	32,390.8	28,716.7
1986	15,975.1	11,606.1	28,273.6	20,788.8	2007	21,519.0	18,252.9	32,385.2	28,858.3
1987	16,263.2	11,946.0	29,378.9	21,468.9	2008	21,667.7	18,402.1	31,334.2	27,486.3
1988	17,132.6	12,578.1	30,677.4	22,317.7	2009	21,077.4	17,887.3	28,465.9	26,687.1
1989	17,785.0	13,193.6	31,319.9	22,477.9	2010	21,794.6	18,058.3	30,525.6	27,059.1
1990	16,944.4	13,319.9	31,809.8	22,419.6	2011	21,300.5	17,978.6	30,843.1	26,712.1
1991	17,419.3	13,500.0	31,399.3	22,118.0	2012	19,858.1	17,421.9	30,914.8	26,219.3
1992	17,354.8	13,441.1	32,570.9	22,415.1	2013	21,067.6	17,932.0	31,409.4	26,749.8
1993	18,216.5	13,819.8	32,627.9	22,711.7	2014	21,429.3	18,254.6	31,643.2	26,996.5
1994	18,110.3	14,097.3	33,520.3	23,365.1	2015	20,511.8	18,151.9	31,327.2	27,355.2
1995	18,516.7	14,689.9	33,969.8	23,851.1	2016	20,413.1	18,214.0	30,843.8	27,925.5

[1] Commercial sector fuel use, including that at commercial combined-heat-and-power (CHP) and commercial electricity-only plants. [2] Industrial sector fuel use, including that at industrial combined-heat-and-power (CHP) and industrial electricity-only plants.

Source: U.S. Energy Information Administration, *Monthly Energy Review*, May 2017. See also <http://www.eia.gov/totalenergy/data/monthly/>.

Table 958. Energy Consumption by Mode of Transportation: 2010 to 2015

[27 represents 27,000,000,000,000. Btu = British thermal unit. For conversion rates for each fuel type, see source]

Mode	Trillion Btu				Physical units		
	2010	2014	2015	Unit	2010	2013	2014
AIR [1]							
Aviation gasoline.................	27	25	24	Mil. gal.	221	197	197
Jet fuel................................	1,686	1,587	1,637	Mil. gal.	12,492	11,416	11,691
HIGHWAY							
Light duty vehicle, short wheel base & motorcycle [2]...	10,902	11,163	11,252	Mil. gal.	87,215	88,611	89,301
Light duty vehicle, long wheel base [2]..................	4,531	4,668	4,555	Mil. gal.	36,251	35,159	37,343
Single-unit 2-axle 6-tire or more truck.	1,887	1,862	1,856	Mil. gal.	15,097	14,502	14,894
Combination truck [3]................	3,741	3,640	3,611	Mil. gal.	29,927	28,795	29,118
Bus....................................	240	279	279	Mil. gal.	1,921	2,117	2,233
TRANSIT [4]							
Electricity..............................	22	23	23	Mil. kWh	6,414	6,651	6,673
Diesel...................................	88	75	80	Mil. gal.	633	609	542
Gasoline and other nondiesel fuels [5]...................	12	14	14	Mil. gal.	98	107	108
Compressed natural gas............	18	19	22	Mil. gal.	126	132	138
RAIL [6]							
Distillate/diesel fuel.................	493	545	521	Mil. gal.	3,557	3,748	3,687
Electricity..............................	2	2	2	Mil. kWh	559	525	(NA)
WATER							
Residual fuel oil......................	770	576	503	Mil. gal.	5,143	4,212	3,847
Distillate/diesel fuel oil.............	278	221	335	Mil. gal.	2,003	1,676	1,593
Gasoline...............................	146	141	258	Mil. gal.	1,167	1,123	1,419
PIPELINE							
Natural gas...........................	695	722	687	Mil. cu. ft.	674,124	833,061	835,757

NA Not available. [1] Includes general aviation and certified carriers, domestic operations only; and fuel used in air taxi operations, but not commuter operations. [2] Beginning in 2007, data are calculated using a new methodology developed by the Federal Highway Administration (FHWA). Those data are based on new categories and are not comparable to previous years. The new category "Light duty vehicle, short wheel base" includes passenger cars, light trucks, vans and sport utility vehicles with a wheelbase (WB) equal to or less than 121 inches. The new category "Light duty vehicle, long wheel base" includes large passenger cars, vans, pickup trucks, and sport/utility vehicles with wheelbases (WB) larger than 121 inches. [3] A power unit (truck tractor) and one or more trailing units (a semitrailer or trailer). [4] Includes light, heavy, and commuter rail; motor bus; trolley bus; van pools; automated guideway; and demand-responsive vehicles. [5] Includes gasoline, liquefied petroleum gas, liquefied natural gas, methane, ethanol, bunker fuel, kerosene, grain additive, and other fuel. [6] Includes Amtrak and freight service carriers that have an annual operating revenue of $250 million or more.

Source: U.S. Department of Transportation, Bureau of Transportation Statistics, "National Transportation Statistics," <www.bts.gov/publications/national_trans_stats>, accessed July 2017.

Table 959. Renewable Energy Consumption Estimates by Source and Sector: 1990 to 2016

[In trillion Btu (6,040.0 represents 6,040,000,000,000,000). For definition of Btu, see source and text, this section. Renewable energy is obtained from sources that are essentially inexhaustible, unlike fossil fuels of which there is a finite supply]

Source and sector	1990	2000	2010	2013	2014	2015	2016
Consumption, total..........	**6,040.0**	**6,104.2**	**8,030.1**	**9,275.9**	**9,570.0**	**9,470.9**	**10,160.8**
Conventional hydroelectric power [1].........	3,046.4	2,811.1	2,538.5	2,562.4	2,466.6	2,321.2	2,477.3
Geothermal energy [2]...............	170.7	164.4	208.0	214.0	214.5	211.8	225.8
Biomass energy [3]..................	2,735.1	3,008.2	4,269.7	4,673.2	4,824.6	4,734.2	4,756.4
Solar energy [4]....................	58.8	63.4	90.5	225.0	336.8	426.5	587.1
Wind energy [5].....................	29.0	57.1	923.4	1,601.4	1,727.5	1,777.3	2,114.2
Residential [6].................	**640.2**	**486.3**	**541.5**	**711.5**	**738.8**	**607.4**	**572.9**
Wood [7]............................	580.0	420.0	440.0	580.0	590.4	439.9	372.6
Geothermal [2]......................	5.5	8.6	36.8	39.6	39.6	39.6	39.6
Solar [4]............................	54.7	57.7	64.7	91.9	108.8	127.9	160.7
Commercial [8].................	**98.4**	**128.3**	**141.8**	**181.8**	**199.4**	**232.4**	**251.2**
Biomass [3].........................	94.0	119.1	110.9	119.9	125.9	154.3	157.4
Geothermal [2]......................	2.8	7.6	18.5	19.7	19.7	19.7	19.7
Hydroelectric [1]....................	1.4	1.0	0.8	0.4	0.4	0.3	0.5
Industrial [9]..................	**1,717.1**	**1,928.2**	**2,207.8**	**2,272.2**	**2,314.1**	**2,321.3**	**2,317.5**
Biomass [3].........................	1,684.2	1,881.5	2,184.8	2,226.0	2,286.3	2,289.8	2,283.2
Geothermal [2]......................	1.9	4.4	4.2	4.2	4.2	4.2	4.2
Hydroelectric [1]....................	30.9	42.2	16.3	33.0	12.2	13.1	12.1
Transportation................	**60.4**	**134.9**	**1,074.7**	**1,277.7**	**1,291.9**	**1,325.3**	**1,433.9**
Fuel ethanol........................	60.4	134.9	1,041.4	1,071.6	1,093.5	1,109.4	1,145.3
Biodiesel [10].......................	(NA)	(NA)	33.2	182.3	180.8	190.6	262.8
Electric power [11]............	**3,523.9**	**3,426.5**	**4,064.4**	**4,832.7**	**5,025.7**	**4,984.5**	**5,585.3**
Biomass [3].........................	316.5	452.8	459.4	469.6	530.1	524.9	509.3
Geothermal [2]......................	160.5	143.8	148.5	150.5	151.0	148.3	162.3
Hydroelectric [1]....................	3,014.0	2,767.9	2,521.5	2,528.9	2,454.0	2,307.7	2,464.6
Solar [4]............................	3.8	5.0	11.8	83.2	164.6	227.9	336.9
Wind [5]............................	29.0	57.1	923.3	1,600.4	1,726.0	1,775.7	2,112.2

NA Not available. [1] Power produced from the kinetic energy of falling water. [2] As used at electric power plants, hot water or steam extracted from geothermal reservoirs in the Earth's crust that is supplied to steam turbines at electric power plants that drive generators to produce electricity. [3] Wood and wood-derived fuels, municipal solid waste (from biogenic sources, landfill gas, sludge waste, agricultural byproducts, and other biomass), fuel ethanol, and biodiesel. [4] The radiant energy of the sun, which can be converted into other forms of energy, such as heat or electricity. Solar thermal and photovoltaic electricity net generation and solar thermal direct use energy. [5] Energy present in wind motion that can be converted to mechanical energy for driving pumps, mills, and electric power generators. Wind pushes against sails, vanes, or blades radiating from a central rotating shaft. [6] Living quarters for private households; excludes institutional living quarters. [7] Wood and wood-derived fuels. [8] Service-providing facilities and equipment of businesses, governments, and other private and public organizations. Includes institutional living quarters and sewage treatment facilities. Includes commercial combined-heat-and-power and commercial electricity-only plants. [9] All facilities and equipment used for producing, processing, or assembling goods. Includes industrial combined-heat-and-power and industrial electricity-only plants. [10] Any liquid biofuel suitable as a diesel fuel substitute, additive, or extender. [11] Electricity-only and combined-heat-and-power plants whose primary business is to sell electricity and/or heat to the public. Includes sources not shown separately.

Source: U.S. Energy Information Administration, *Monthly Energy Review*, May 2017. See also <http://www.eia.gov/totalenergy/data/monthly/>.

Table 960. Energy Consumption—End-Use Sector and Selected Source by State: 2015

[In trillions of British thermal units (97,251 represents 97,251,000,000,000,000 Btu), except as indicated. For definition of Btu, see source and text, this section. U.S. totals may not equal sum of states due to independent rounding and/or interstate flows of electricity that are not allocated to the states. For technical notes and documentation, see source <http://www.eia.gov/state/seds/seds-technical-notes-updates.cfm>]

State	Total [1,2]	Per capita [3] (mil. Btu)	End-use sector [4] Residential	Commercial	Industrial [2]	Transportation	Source Petroleum [5]	Natural gas (dry) [6]	Coal	Hydroelectric power [7]	Nuclear electric power
U.S.	97,251	303	20,486	18,109	31,398	27,259	36,871	28,246	15,549	2,321	8,337
AL	1,910	393	353	264	808	485	546	696	494	92	439
AK	620	840	49	66	333	172	244	337	20	15	–
AZ	1,440	211	384	347	235	474	531	366	386	61	340
AR	1,056	354	230	180	371	275	328	297	227	33	145
CA	7,676	197	1,357	1,465	1,837	3,017	3,492	2,382	31	129	194
CO	1,480	272	343	290	439	408	484	497	340	15	–
CT	752	210	249	199	76	228	327	261	7	3	182
DE	278	294	66	57	89	66	106	108	7	–	–
DC	179	267	42	109	7	21	22	34	(Z)	–	–
FL	4,242	210	1,219	1,018	487	1,517	1,688	1,366	467	2	294
GA	2,851	280	704	553	767	828	917	713	395	28	354
HI	282	198	32	41	64	145	242	3	16	1	–
ID	524	317	114	88	173	149	178	108	4	82	–
IL	3,943	307	930	795	1,171	1,047	1,315	1,022	850	1	1,017
IN	2,846	430	532	376	1,306	632	804	738	1,007	4	–
IA	1,495	479	226	202	766	301	433	335	348	9	55
KS	1,083	372	220	213	372	279	355	260	273	(Z)	90
KY	1,725	390	363	266	633	463	608	275	796	32	–
LA	4,259	912	334	270	2,964	691	2,101	1,589	174	9	160
ME	406	305	95	66	116	129	203	54	3	31	–
MD	1,399	233	427	429	114	429	498	227	166	15	153
MA	1,445	213	434	404	160	447	585	457	24	8	52
MI	2,767	279	719	598	711	739	880	872	617	14	307
MN	1,770	323	373	350	606	441	594	449	272	8	126
MS	1,133	379	200	158	389	386	445	534	72	–	123
MO	1,827	301	502	416	359	551	645	271	696	15	109
MT	391	379	81	75	125	111	171	75	178	92	–
NE	853	450	148	137	367	201	243	170	266	16	108
NV	650	225	151	124	163	211	230	313	37	21	–
NH	305	229	94	71	41	100	156	71	11	12	99
NJ	2,288	256	588	597	251	852	1,015	779	23	(Z)	348
NM	676	325	115	125	225	212	247	260	216	1	–
NY	3,724	189	1,115	1,139	394	1,077	1,346	1,397	41	242	466
NC	2,524	251	694	587	545	698	827	516	406	44	440
ND	608	803	70	86	316	136	198	104	408	20	–
OH	3,741	322	890	709	1,204	937	1,169	1,034	866	4	182
OK	1,631	417	294	258	599	480	549	712	281	25	–
OR	957	238	224	184	249	300	339	245	27	291	–
PA	3,881	303	933	657	1,401	890	1,213	1,345	879	24	842
RI	203	192	67	49	24	61	90	97	–	(Z)	–
SC	1,648	337	364	275	544	464	532	282	241	24	556
SD	383	447	66	63	154	100	119	83	20	45	–
TN	2,167	329	534	448	571	614	711	322	371	89	261
TX	12,898	470	1,696	1,592	6,459	3,150	6,292	4,267	1,340	9	412
UT	791	264	156	162	224	248	286	241	330	7	–
VT	132	211	39	27	18	49	84	12	–	11	–
VA	2,368	283	611	615	445	696	804	525	232	11	293
WA	1,988	278	443	368	555	623	769	328	58	684	85
WV	775	421	167	114	313	181	195	193	731	13	–
WI	1,776	308	404	362	573	436	552	477	408	22	105
WY	524	893	45	62	304	113	163	147	487	8	–

– Represents zero. Z Less than 50 billion Btu. [1] Includes other sources, not shown separately. [2] U.S. total energy and U.S. industrial sector include net imports of coal coke that are not allocated to the states. [3] Based on estimated resident population as of July 1. [4] End-use sector data include electricity sales and associated electrical system energy losses. [5] Includes fuel ethanol blended into motor gasoline. [6] Includes supplemental gaseous fuels. [7] Conventional hydroelectric power. Does not include pumped-storage hydroelectricity.

Source: U.S. Energy Information Administration, "State Energy Data System," <http://www.eia.gov/state/seds/>, accessed July 2017.

Table 961. Energy Expenditures and Average Fuel Prices by Source and Sector: 1980 to 2015

[In millions of dollars (374,347 represents $374,347,000,000), except as indicated. Btu = British thermal units. For definition of Btu, see text, this section. End-use sector and electric utilities exclude expenditures and prices on energy sources such as hydropower, solar, wind, and geothermal. Also excludes expenditures for reported amounts of energy consumed by the energy industry for production, transportation, and processing operations]

Source and Sector	1980	1990	2000	2005	2010	2012	2013	2014	2015
EXPENDITURES (mil. dol.)									
Total [1,2,3]	**374,347**	**474,647**	**687,708**	**1,045,729**	**1,213,336**	**1,356,215**	**1,378,885**	**1,399,486**	**1,127,132**
Natural gas [4]	51,062	65,278	119,094	200,356	161,303	132,830	151,672	174,398	140,359
Petroleum products	237,676	237,672	359,400	596,286	716,627	884,703	882,034	868,154	622,524
Motor gasoline [5]	124,408	126,558	192,153	312,047	376,492	473,216	467,328	452,821	342,583
Coal	22,607	28,419	27,959	36,742	50,245	44,964	45,260	44,873	36,578
Retail electricity	98,095	176,691	231,578	295,787	365,913	360,863	372,068	389,872	388,344
Residential sector [6]	69,277	110,905	155,299	215,186	249,390	235,149	250,241	264,671	247,515
Commercial sector [2,3]	47,074	79,602	113,421	155,157	177,666	171,948	178,466	190,778	187,052
Industrial sector [2,3]	94,316	103,351	140,960	208,223	221,348	230,213	237,251	246,710	185,516
Transportation sector [2]	163,680	180,790	278,028	467,163	564,931	718,905	712,927	697,327	507,049
Motor gasoline [5]	121,809	123,845	189,836	304,875	369,433	464,635	458,655	445,572	329,466
Electric utilities [3]	38,027	40,627	60,053	95,916	94,799	82,169	89,117	95,820	76,351
AVERAGE FUEL PRICES (dol. per mil. Btu)									
All sectors	**6.89**	**8.28**	**10.31**	**15.55**	**18.94**	**21.86**	**21.47**	**21.39**	**17.31**
Residential sector [6]	7.46	11.87	14.21	19.16	22.42	23.49	22.73	23.39	23.03
Commercial sector [3]	7.83	11.87	13.90	18.59	20.92	21.03	20.67	21.46	20.85
Industrial sector [3]	4.71	5.29	6.47	10.39	12.19	12.43	12.59	12.92	9.83
Transportation sector	8.61	8.33	10.75	16.91	21.49	28.36	27.69	26.68	19.12
Electric utilities [3]	1.77	1.48	1.71	2.61	2.63	2.41	2.62	2.80	2.28

[1] Includes other sources not shown separately. [2] There is a discontinuity in this time series between 1988 and 1989 due to the expanded coverage of the use of wood and biomass waste beginning in 1989. [3] There are no direct fuel costs for hydroelectric, geothermal, wind, photovoltaic, or solar thermal energy. [4] Natural gas as it is consumed; includes supplemental gaseous fuels that are commingled with natural gas. [5] Beginning 1995, includes fuel ethanol blended into motor gasoline. [6] There are no direct fuel costs for geothermal, photovoltaic, or solar thermal energy.

Source: U.S. Energy Information Administration, "State Energy Data System (SEDS)," <http://www.eia.gov/state/seds/>, accessed July 2017.

Table 962. Fuel Ethanol and Biodiesel—Summary: 2000 to 2016

[233.1 represents 233,100,000,000,000. Btu=British thermal units. For definition of Btu, see source and text, this section. Minus sign (-) indicates an excess of exports over imports, except where noted]

Fuel	2000	2005	2010	2011	2012	2013	2014	2015	2016
FUEL ETHANOL									
Feedstock [1] (tril. Btu)	233.1	549.5	1,823.5	1,904.2	1,800.7	1,805.1	1,938.0	1,998.0	2,060.8
Production:									
1,000 barrels	38,627	92,961	316,617	331,646	314,714	316,493	340,781	352,553	364,979
Tril. Btu	137.6	331.2	1,127.5	1,180.7	1,120.4	1,126.4	1,212.5	1,254.4	1,298.6
Net imports [2] (1,000 barrels)	116	3,234	-9,115	-24,365	-5,891	-5,761	-18,371	-17,632	-24,049
Stocks [3] (1,000 barrels)	3,400	5,563	17,941	18,238	20,350	16,424	18,739	21,596	19,531
Stock change [4] (1,000 barrels)	-624	-439	1,347	297	2,112	-3,926	2,315	2,857	-1,907
Consumption:									
1,000 barrels	39,367	96,634	306,155	306,984	306,711	314,658	320,095	332,064	342,837
Tril. Btu	140.3	344.3	1,090.2	1,092.9	1,091.9	1,119.9	1,138.9	1,181.5	1,219.8
BIODIESEL									
Feedstock [5] (tril. Btu)	(NA)	11.7	44.4	125.2	128.2	175.9	165.4	163.4	201.2
Production:									
1,000 barrels	(NA)	2,162	8,177	23,035	23,588	32,368	30,452	30,080	37,037
Tril. Btu	(NA)	11.58	43.82	123.45	126.41	173.46	163.19	161.20	198.48
Net imports (1,000 barrels)	(NA)	1	-2,024	-908	-2,203	3,477	2,604	6,308	14,404
Stocks [6] (1,000 barrels)	(NA)	(NA)	672	2,005	1,984	3,810	3,131	6,308	6,217
Stock change [4] (1,000 barrels)	(NA)	(NA)	-39	1,028	-20	1,825	-679	813	2,403
Consumption:									
1,000 barrels	(NA)	2,163	6,192	21,099	21,406	34,020	33,735	35,575	49,038
Tril. Btu	(NA)	11.6	33.2	113.1	114.7	182.3	180.8	190.6	262.8

NA Not available. [1] Total corn and other biomass inputs to the production of undenatured ethanol used for fuel ethanol. [2] Through 2009, data are for fuel ethanol imports only; data for fuel ethanol exports are not available. Beginning in 2010, data are for fuel ethanol imports minus fuel ethanol exports. [3] Stocks are at end of year. [4] A negative number indicates a decrease in stocks. [5] Total vegetable oil and other biomass inputs to the production of biodiesel. [6] Stocks at end of year. Through 2010, includes stocks at bulk terminals only. Beginning in 2011, includes stocks at bulk terminals and biodiesel production plants.

Source: U.S. Energy Information Administration, *Monthly Energy Review*, May 2017. See also <http://www.eia.gov/totalenergy/data/monthly/>.

Table 963. Energy Expenditures—End-Use Sector and Selected Source by State: 2015

[In millions of dollars (1,127,132 represents $1,127,132,000,000). End-use sector and electric utilities exclude expenditures on energy sources such as hydroelectric, photovoltaic, solar thermal, wind, and geothermal. Also excludes expenditures for reported amounts of energy consumed by the energy industry for production, transportation, and processing operations. For technical notes and documentation, see source, <http://www.eia.gov/state/seds/seds-technical-notes-complete.cfm>]

| State | Total [1,2] | End-use sector | | | | Source | | | |
		Residential	Commercial	Industrial [2]	Transportation	Petroleum products [3]	Natural gas [4]	Coal	Electricity sales
U.S..............	1,127,132	247,515	187,052	185,516	507,049	622,524	140,359	36,578	388,344
AL.................	20,095	4,330	3,005	4,279	8,481	9,654	2,685	1,310	8,271
AK.................	5,523	750	897	909	2,968	4,122	501	98	1,074
AZ.................	20,022	4,707	3,693	2,001	9,621	10,929	1,923	802	8,000
AR.................	11,172	2,296	1,545	2,354	4,977	5,839	1,698	517	3,789
CA.................	121,894	20,417	22,336	14,323	64,819	70,898	13,393	110	39,979
CO.................	15,939	3,457	2,674	2,387	7,421	8,669	2,198	630	5,356
CT.................	13,109	4,701	2,896	891	4,622	6,637	1,818	23	5,239
DE.................	3,422	933	630	545	1,315	1,660	630	21	1,261
DC.................	2,164	507	1,194	82	380	440	361	–	1,362
FL.................	56,606	14,729	10,647	4,078	27,152	29,971	6,701	1,450	24,719
GA.................	33,379	8,469	5,524	4,380	15,006	16,784	4,064	1,168	13,070
HI.................	5,702	829	1,026	1,006	2,841	3,847	91	52	2,475
ID.................	5,981	1,079	710	1,239	2,953	3,516	595	14	1,865
IL.................	42,227	9,195	6,525	7,122	19,384	23,060	6,369	1,723	12,823
IN.................	27,832	5,239	3,221	7,526	11,846	13,737	4,442	2,671	9,298
IA.................	13,939	2,460	1,778	4,055	5,647	8,048	1,851	615	3,936
KS.................	11,299	2,390	1,952	1,971	4,986	6,077	1,308	468	3,957
KY.................	17,726	3,465	2,319	3,508	8,434	10,111	1,508	1,805	6,138
LA.................	30,536	3,382	2,535	13,954	10,665	20,442	4,382	562	6,488
ME.................	6,069	1,635	984	821	2,630	4,020	455	11	1,519
MD.................	19,431	5,419	4,332	1,161	8,519	10,076	1,993	475	7,459
MA.................	23,840	7,488	5,720	2,052	8,581	11,431	3,898	86	9,232
MI.................	33,225	8,305	5,698	5,230	13,993	16,735	5,651	1,592	10,992
MN.................	19,479	4,181	3,210	3,620	8,468	10,642	2,619	535	6,258
MS.................	12,646	2,453	1,805	2,102	6,286	7,061	1,805	222	4,579
MO.................	21,844	5,248	3,642	2,710	10,245	11,854	2,299	1,342	7,696
MT.................	4,337	810	705	610	2,212	2,717	404	309	1,218
NE.................	8,192	1,447	1,072	1,837	3,836	4,636	904	366	2,627
NV.................	9,004	2,071	1,310	1,352	4,270	4,715	1,549	95	3,413
NH.................	5,233	1,688	1,062	481	2,001	3,105	561	43	1,762
NJ.................	31,137	7,307	6,754	2,288	14,789	17,198	4,448	88	10,291
NM.................	7,139	1,233	1,159	865	3,882	4,426	737	506	2,201
NY.................	55,849	17,591	15,235	3,406	19,618	25,264	9,469	140	22,747
NC.................	30,841	7,922	5,308	3,990	13,621	16,140	3,163	1,422	12,547
ND.................	5,485	674	718	1,660	2,433	3,478	276	676	1,561
OH.................	41,822	9,904	6,349	7,770	17,799	21,329	5,662	2,079	14,759
OK.................	16,033	3,052	2,116	2,998	7,867	9,047	2,919	567	4,761
OR.................	12,652	2,549	1,846	1,787	6,471	7,267	1,396	65	4,134
PA.................	45,467	12,288	6,372	9,321	17,487	23,614	7,092	2,326	14,980
RI.................	3,596	1,260	811	334	1,191	1,789	738	–	1,304
SC.................	18,421	4,250	2,638	3,120	8,413	9,462	1,411	860	7,792
SD.................	3,860	692	537	764	1,867	2,305	418	44	1,146
TN.................	23,878	5,133	4,230	3,394	11,121	12,664	1,836	955	9,224
TX.................	116,142	19,538	13,220	31,440	51,944	75,125	12,061	2,686	33,371
UT.................	8,734	1,593	1,393	1,177	4,571	5,109	1,204	647	2,555
VT.................	2,675	821	532	299	1,023	1,730	114	–	795
VA.................	27,515	6,766	5,008	2,933	12,807	14,810	2,859	722	10,426
WA.................	21,798	4,209	3,243	2,487	11,859	13,145	2,119	146	6,602
WV.................	7,287	1,584	972	1,646	3,085	3,922	584	1,752	2,619
WI.................	20,732	4,628	3,423	3,950	8,731	10,672	2,787	972	7,363
WY.................	4,380	444	546	1,479	1,912	2,594	415	812	1,312

– Represents or rounds to zero. [1] Total expenditures are the sum of purchases for each source (including electricity sales) less electric power sector purchases of fuel. There are no direct fuel costs for hydroelectric, geothermal, wind, photovoltaic, or solar thermal energy. The U.S. total includes -$177 million for coal coke net imports, which are not allocated to the states. [2] Includes sources not shown separately, such as electricity imports and exports and coal coke net imports, which are not allocated to the states. [3] Includes fuel ethanol blended into motor gasoline. [4] Includes supplemental gaseous fuels.

Source: U.S. Energy Information Administration, "State Energy Data System," <http://www.eia.gov/state/seds/>, accessed July 2017.

Table 964. Energy Imports and Exports by Type of Fuel: 1980 to 2016

[In quadrillion Btu (12.10 represents 12,100,000,000,000,000 Btu). Btu=British thermal units; for definition, see text, this section]

Type of fuel	1980	1990	1995	2000	2005	2010	2012	2013	2014	2015	2016
Net imports, total [1]	**12.10**	**14.06**	**17.68**	**24.90**	**30.20**	**21.69**	**15.80**	**12.84**	**10.97**	**10.89**	**11.56**
Coal	-2.39	-2.70	-2.08	-1.21	-0.51	-1.62	-2.88	-2.70	-2.18	-1.60	-1.29
Natural gas (dry)	0.96	1.46	2.74	3.62	3.71	2.69	1.58	1.37	1.23	0.99	0.74
Petroleum [2]	13.50	15.29	16.82	22.31	26.85	20.58	16.96	13.96	11.79	11.29	11.86
Other [3]	0.04	0.01	0.20	0.18	0.14	0.04	0.14	0.21	0.13	0.21	0.25
Imports, total	15.80	18.82	22.18	28.87	34.66	29.87	27.07	24.62	23.24	23.79	25.42
Coal	0.03	0.07	0.24	0.31	0.76	0.48	0.21	0.20	0.25	0.26	0.22
Natural gas (dry)	1.01	1.55	2.90	3.87	4.45	3.83	3.22	2.96	2.76	2.79	3.08
Petroleum [2]	14.66	17.12	18.80	24.42	29.20	25.36	23.36	21.13	19.95	20.41	21.72
Other [3]	0.10	0.08	0.24	0.26	0.25	0.19	0.28	0.34	0.28	0.34	0.40
Exports, total	3.69	4.75	4.50	3.96	4.46	8.18	11.27	11.79	12.27	12.90	13.86
Coal	2.42	2.77	2.32	1.53	1.27	2.10	3.09	2.90	2.43	1.85	1.51
Natural gas (dry)	0.05	0.09	0.16	0.25	0.74	1.15	1.63	1.59	1.53	1.80	2.34
Petroleum	1.16	1.82	1.98	2.11	2.34	4.78	6.40	7.17	8.16	9.12	9.86
Other [3]	0.07	0.07	0.05	0.08	0.11	0.15	0.14	0.14	0.15	0.13	0.16

[1] Net imports equals imports minus exports. Minus sign (-) indicates exports are greater than imports. [2] Includes imports into the Strategic Petroleum Reserve. [3] Coal coke, small amounts of electricity transmitted across U.S. borders with Canada and Mexico, and small amounts of biodiesel.

Source: U.S. Energy Information Administration, *Monthly Energy Review*, March 2017. See also <http://www.eia.gov/totalenergy/>.

Table 965. U.S. Foreign Trade in Natural Gas, Crude Oil, Petroleum Products, and Coal: 1980 to 2016

[985 represents 985,000,000,000 cu. ft. Minus sign (-) indicates trade deficit]

Mineral fuel	Unit	1980	1990	1995	2000	2005	2010	2014	2015	2016 (P)
Natural gas:										
Imports	Bil. cu. ft.	985	1,532	2,841	3,782	4,341	3,741	2,695	2,718	3,001
Exports	Bil. cu. ft.	49	86	154	244	729	1,137	1,514	1,784	2,315
Net trade [1]	Bil. cu. ft.	-936	-1,447	-2,687	-3,538	-3,612	-2,604	-1,181	-935	-685
Crude oil: [2]										
Imports [3]	Mil. barrels	1,926	2,151	2,639	3,320	3,696	3,363	2,681	2,687	2,883
Exports	Mil. barrels	105	40	35	18	12	15	128	170	190
Net trade [1]	Mil. barrels	-1,821	-2,112	-2,604	-3,301	-3,684	-3,348	-2,552	-2,518	-2,693
Petroleum products:										
Imports	Mil. barrels	(NA)	775	586	874	1,310	942	692	761	798
Exports	Mil. barrels	(NA)	273	312	362	414	843	1,396	1,560	1,708
Net trade [1]	Mil. barrels	(NA)	-502	-274	-512	-896	-98	704	798	910
Coal:										
Imports	Mil. sh. tons	1	3	9	13	30	19	11	11	10
Exports	Mil. sh. tons	92	106	89	58	50	82	97	74	60
Net trade [1]	Mil. sh. tons	91	103	79	46	19	62	86	63	50

P Preliminary. NA Not available. [1] Exports minus imports. [2] Includes lease condensate. [3] Includes Strategic Petroleum Reserve imports.

Source: U.S. Energy Information Administration, *Monthly Energy Review*, May 2017; and "Petroleum and Other Liquids, Imports/Exports & Movements," <http://www.eia.gov/petroleum/data.cfm#imports>, accessed May 2017.

Table 966. Crude Oil Imports Into the U.S. by Country of Origin: 1993 to 2016

[In millions of barrels (2,477 represents 2,477,000,000). A barrel contains 42 gallons. Crude oil imports are reported by the Petroleum Administration for Defense (PAD) District in which they are to be processed. A PAD District is a geographic aggregation of the 50 states and D.C. into 5 districts. Includes crude oil imported for storage in the Strategic Petroleum Reserve (SPR). Total Organization of Petroleum Exporting Countries (OPEC) excludes, and non-OPEC includes, petroleum imported into the United States indirectly from members of OPEC, primarily from Caribbean and West European areas, as petroleum products that were refined from crude oil produced by OPEC]

Country of origin	1993	1995	2000	2005	2010	2011	2012	2013	2014	2015	2016
Total imports	**2,477**	**2,639**	**3,320**	**3,696**	**3,363**	**3,261**	**3,121**	**2,821**	**2,681**	**2,687**	**2,883**
OPEC, total [1,2]	**1,346**	**1,303**	**1,663**	**1,758**	**1,662**	**1,536**	**1,476**	**1,275**	**1,097**	**976**	**1,164**
Algeria	9	10	(Z)	83	120	65	44	10	2	1	19
Angola	123	131	108	166	140	122	81	73	51	45	58
Ecuador	28	35	46	101	76	74	65	85	78	82	87
Iraq	(NA)	(NA)	227	193	152	168	174	124	135	84	153
Kuwait	126	78	96	83	71	70	111	119	113	74	76
Nigeria	264	227	320	393	359	280	148	87	21	20	77
Saudi Arabia	468	460	558	527	395	433	498	484	423	384	402
Venezuela	369	420	448	453	333	317	334	275	268	283	271
Non-OPEC, total [2]	**1,131**	**1,336**	**1,657**	**1,938**	**1,701**	**1,725**	**1,645**	**1,546**	**1,584**	**1,712**	**1,719**
Brazil	(NA)	(NA)	2	34	93	85	69	40	53	69	53
Canada	329	380	493	596	719	812	888	941	1,052	1,157	1,192
Chad	(NA)	(NA)	(NA)	27	7	18	10	24	22	26	23
Colombia	52	75	116	57	124	145	147	134	107	136	162
Mexico	315	375	480	568	421	402	357	310	285	251	213
Norway	50	94	111	43	9	19	9	6	3	3	13
Oman	(NA)	7	1	8	4	15	3	1	(NA)	(NA)	11
Russia	(NA)	5	3	73	98	82	37	15	7	14	14

NA Not available. Z Represents less than 500,000 barrels. [1] Countries listed under OPEC and non-OPEC are based on current affiliations. OPEC and non-OPEC averages are based on affiliations for the stated period of time which may differ from current affiliations. Angola joined OPEC in January 2007, Ecuador withdrew from OPEC in January 1993 and rejoined in November 2007, Gabon withdrew from OPEC in 1995 and rejoined in July 2016, and Indonesia withdrew in January 2009 and rejoined in January 2016. [2] Includes countries not shown separately.

Source: U.S. Energy Information Administration, Petroleum & Other Liquids, "U.S. Imports by Country of Origin," <https://www.eia.gov/petroleum/data.cfm#imports>, accessed March 2017.

Table 967. Crude Oil and Refined Products—Summary: 1980 to 2016

[13,481 represents 13,481,000 bbl. Barrels (bbl.) contain 42 gallons. Data are averages]

Year	Crude oil [1] (1,000 bbl. per day)					Refined oil products (1,000 bbl. per day)			Total oil imports [5] (1,000 bbl. per day)	Crude oil stocks [1,2] (mil. bbl.)	
	Input to refiner- ies	Domestic produc- tion	Imports		Exports	Domestic demand	Imports	Exports		Total [6]	Strategic reserve [7]
			Total [3]	Strategic reserve [4]							
1980....	13,481	8,597	5,263	44	287	17,056	1,646	258	6,909	358	108
1981....	12,470	8,572	4,396	256	228	16,058	1,599	367	5,996	363	230
1982....	11,774	8,649	3,488	165	236	15,296	1,625	579	5,113	350	294
1983....	11,685	8,688	3,329	234	164	15,231	1,722	575	5,051	344	379
1984....	12,044	8,879	3,426	197	181	15,726	2,011	541	5,437	345	451
1985....	12,002	8,971	3,201	118	204	15,726	1,866	577	5,067	321	493
1986....	12,716	8,680	4,178	48	154	16,281	2,045	631	6,224	331	512
1987....	12,854	8,349	4,674	73	151	16,665	2,004	613	6,678	349	541
1988....	13,246	8,140	5,107	51	155	17,283	2,295	661	7,402	330	560
1989....	13,401	7,613	5,843	56	142	17,325	2,217	717	8,061	341	580
1990....	13,409	7,355	5,894	27	109	16,988	2,123	748	8,018	323	586
1991....	13,301	7,417	5,782	(NA)	116	16,714	1,844	885	7,627	325	569
1992....	13,411	7,171	6,083	10	89	17,033	1,805	861	7,888	318	575
1993....	13,613	6,847	6,787	15	98	17,237	1,833	904	8,620	335	587
1994....	13,866	6,662	7,063	12	99	17,718	1,933	843	8,996	337	592
1995....	13,973	6,560	7,230	(NA)	95	17,725	1,605	855	8,835	303	592
1996....	14,195	6,465	7,508	(NA)	110	18,309	1,971	871	9,478	284	566
1997....	14,662	6,452	8,225	(NA)	108	18,620	1,936	896	10,162	305	563
1998....	14,889	6,252	8,706	(NA)	110	18,917	2,002	835	10,708	324	571
1999....	14,804	5,881	8,731	8	118	19,519	2,122	822	10,852	284	567
2000....	15,067	5,822	9,071	8	50	19,701	2,389	990	11,459	286	541
2001....	15,128	5,801	9,328	11	20	19,649	2,543	951	11,871	312	550
2002....	14,947	5,744	9,140	16	9	19,761	2,390	975	11,530	278	599
2003....	15,304	5,649	9,665	(NA)	12	20,034	2,599	1,014	12,264	269	638
2004....	15,475	5,441	10,088	77	27	20,731	3,057	1,021	13,145	286	676
2005....	15,220	5,184	10,126	52	32	20,802	3,588	1,133	13,714	308	685
2006....	15,242	5,086	10,118	8	25	20,687	3,589	1,292	13,707	296	689
2007....	15,156	5,077	10,031	7	27	20,680	3,437	1,405	13,468	268	697
2008....	14,648	5,000	9,783	19	29	19,498	3,132	1,773	12,915	308	702
2009....	14,336	5,353	9,013	56	44	18,771	2,678	1,980	11,691	307	727
2010....	14,724	5,475	9,213	(NA)	42	19,180	2,580	2,311	11,793	312	727
2011....	14,806	5,646	8,935	(NA)	47	18,882	2,501	2,939	11,436	308	696
2012....	14,999	6,487	8,527	(NA)	67	18,490	2,071	3,137	10,598	338	695
2013....	15,312	7,468	7,730	(NA)	134	18,961	2,129	3,487	9,859	327	696
2014....	15,848	8,764	7,344	(NA)	351	19,106	1,897	3,824	9,241	361	691
2015....	16,188	9,415	7,363	(NA)	465	19,531	2,086	4,273	9,449	449	695
2016....	16,202	8,875	7,877	(NA)	520	19,631	2,181	4,668	10,058	484	695

NA Not available. [1] Includes lease condensate. [2] Crude oil at end of period. Includes commercial and Strategic Petroleum Reserve (SPR) stocks. [3] Includes Strategic Petroleum Reserve. [4] Through 2000, includes imports by SPR only; beginning in 2004, includes imports by SPR, and imports into SPR by others. [5] Crude oil (including Strategic Petroleum Reserve imports) plus refined products. [6] Beginning in 1981, includes stocks of Alaskan crude oil in transit. [7] Crude oil stocks in the Strategic Petroleum Reserve include non-U.S. stocks held under foreign or commercial storage agreements.

Source: U.S. Energy Information Administration, *Monthly Energy Review*, May 2017, and earlier reports. See also <http://www.eia.gov/totalenergy/data/monthly/>.

Table 968. Petroleum and Coal Products Corporations—Sales, Net Profit, and Profit Per Dollar of Sales: 1990 to 2016

[318.5 represents $318,500,000,000. Through 2000, covers Standard Industrial Classification (SIC) group 29. Beginning 2001, covers North American Industry Classification System (NAICS) 324. Profit rates are averages of quarterly figures at annual rates]

Item	Unit	1990	1995	2000	2005	2010	2012	2013	2014	2015	2016
Sales...................................	Bil. dol.	318.5	283.1	455.2	956.0	1,077.1	1,377.4	1,342.5	1,283.8	834.3	685.1
Net profit:											
Before income taxes...............	Bil. dol.	23.1	16.5	55.5	120.2	56.0	117.6	79.8	82.3	21.0	1.4
After income taxes..................	Bil. dol.	17.8	13.9	42.6	96.3	54.2	99.0	73.0	74.2	24.0	11.5
Depreciation [1].......................	Bil. dol.	18.7	16.7	15.5	18.6	30.8	29.1	29.2	32.0	33.6	34.6
Profits per dollar of sales:											
Before income taxes...............	Cents	7.3	5.8	12.2	12.6	5.3	8.5	5.9	6.3	2.4	0.2
After income taxes..................	Cents	5.6	4.9	9.4	10.1	5.1	7.2	5.4	5.7	2.8	0.3
Profits on stockholders' equity:											
Before income taxes...............	Percent	16.4	12.6	29.4	38.0	12.2	22.9	14.6	14.3	3.8	0.3
After income taxes..................	Percent	12.7	10.6	22.6	30.4	11.8	19.3	13.3	12.9	4.4	2.2

[1] Includes depletion and accelerated amortization of emergency facilities.

Source: U.S. Census Bureau, *Quarterly Financial Report for Manufacturing, Mining, Trade, and Selected Service Industries*. See also <http://www.census.gov/econ/qfr/>.

Table 969. Nuclear Power Plants—Number, Capacity, and Generation: 1980 to 2016

[51.8 represents 51,800,000 kilowatts (kW)]

Item	1980	1990	1995	2000	2005	2010	2013	2014	2015	2016 (P)
Operable generating units [1,2]	71	112	109	104	104	104	100	99	99	99
Net summer capacity [2,3] (mil. kW)	51.8	99.6	99.5	97.9	100.0	101.2	99.2	98.6	98.7	99.3
Net generation (bil. kWh)	251.1	576.9	673.4	753.9	782.0	807.0	789.0	797.2	797.2	805.3
Percent of total electricity net generation	11.0	19.0	20.1	19.8	19.3	19.6	19.4	19.5	19.6	19.7
Capacity factor [4] (percent)	56.3	66.0	77.4	88.1	89.3	91.1	89.9	91.7	92.3	92.5

P Preliminary. [1] Total of nuclear generating units holding full-power licenses, or equivalent permission to operate, at the end of the year. Includes units retaining full-power licenses during long, non-routine shutdowns that for a time rendered them unable to generate electricity. [2] As of year-end. [3] Net summer capacity is the peak steady hourly output that generating equipment is expected to supply to system load, exclusive of auxiliary and other power plant, as demonstrated by a test at the time of summer peak demand. [4] Weighted average of monthly capacity factors. Monthly factors are derived by dividing actual monthly generation by the maximum possible generation for the month (number of hours in the month multiplied by the net summer capacity at the end of the month).

Source: U.S. Energy Information Administration, *Monthly Energy Review*, May 2017. See also <http://www.eia.gov/totalenergy/data/monthly/>.

Table 970. Nuclear Power Plants—Number of Reactors, Net Generation, and Net Summer Capacity by State: 2015

[797,178 represents 797,178,000,000 kilowatt hours (kWh)]

State	Number of reactors	Nuclear net generation Total (mil. kWh)	Percent of total [1]	Nuclear net summer capacity Total (mil. kWh)	Percent of total [1]	State	Number of reactors	Nuclear net generation Total (mil. kWh)	Percent of total [1]	Nuclear net summer capacity Total (mil. kWh)	Percent of total [1]
U.S.	**99**	**797,178**	**19.6**	**98.7**	**9.3**	MN	3	12,039	21.1	1.6	10.5
						MS	1	11,715	18.1	1.4	8.7
AL	5	41,951	27.5	5.1	16.7	MO	1	10,440	12.5	1.2	5.5
AZ	3	32,526	28.7	3.9	14.0	NE	2	10,325	25.9	1.2	14.3
AR	2	13,838	24.9	1.8	12.3	NH	1	9,484	47.4	1.2	28.1
CA	2	18,505	9.4	2.2	3.0	NJ	4	33,262	44.6	4.1	21.9
CT	2	17,411	46.5	2.1	23.8	NY	6	44,603	32.2	5.4	13.4
FL	4	28,122	11.8	3.6	6.1	NC	5	42,097	32.8	5.1	16.3
GA	4	33,838	26.3	4.1	11.2	OH	2	17,377	14.3	2.1	7.4
IL	11	97,282	50.2	11.6	25.5	PA	9	80,517	37.5	9.7	23.0
IA	1	5,243	9.3	0.6	3.6	SC	7	53,156	55.1	6.6	28.9
KS	1	8,630	19.0	1.2	8.2	TN	3	24,960	33.2	3.4	16.8
LA	2	15,301	14.2	2.1	8.1	TX	4	39,355	8.7	5.0	4.2
MD	2	14,643	40.3	1.7	13.8	VA	4	28,060	33.2	3.6	14.2
MA	1	4,995	15.6	0.7	5.2	WA	1	8,161	7.5	1.2	3.7
MI	4	29,334	26.0	4.0	13.2	WI	2	10,008	15.1	1.2	7.2

[1] For total electric power generation and capacity by source, see Table 976.

Source: U.S. Energy Information Administration, *Electric Power Annual*, "Detailed State Data," <http://www.eia.gov/electricity/data/state/>, accessed January 2017.

Table 971. Uranium Concentrate—Supply, Inventories, and Average Prices: 1990 to 2016

[8.89 represents 8,890,000 pounds (lbs.). Years ending December 31. For additional data on uranium, see Table 933 and Table 950]

Item	Unit	1990	1995	2000	2005	2010	2013	2014	2015	2016
Production [1]	Mil. lbs.	8.89	6.04	3.98	2.69	4.23	4.66	4.89	3.34	2.92
Exports [2]	Mil. lbs.	2.0	9.8	13.6	20.5	23.1	18.9	20.0	25.7	17.2
Imports [2]	Mil. lbs.	23.7	41.3	44.9	65.5	55.3	57.3	58.6	64.1	50.7
Electric plant purchases from domestic suppliers	Mil. lbs.	20.5	22.3	24.3	27.3	16.2	23.3	20.5	19.6	18.8
Loaded into U.S. nuclear reactors [3]	Mil. lbs.	(NA)	51.1	51.5	58.3	44.3	42.6	50.5	47.4	42.5
Inventories, total	Mil. lbs.	129.1	72.5	111.3	93.8	111.3	134.4	135.5	135.5	143.9
At domestic suppliers	Mil. lbs.	26.4	13.7	56.5	29.1	24.7	21.3	18.7	14.3	15.3
At electric plants	Mil. lbs.	102.7	58.7	54.8	64.7	86.5	113.1	114.0	121.1	128.6
Average price per pound:										
Purchased imports [4]	Dollars	12.55	10.20	9.84	14.83	47.01	48.24	44.11	42.96	40.45
Domestic purchases	Dollars	15.70	11.11	11.45	13.98	44.88	52.51	43.99	43.03	41.64

NA Not available. [1] Data are for uranium concentrate, a yellow or brown powder obtained by the milling of uranium ore, processing of in situ leach mining solutions, or as a by-product of phosphoric acid production. [2] Includes transactions by uranium buyers (consumers). Buyer imports and exports prior to 1990 are believed to be small. [3] Does not include any fuel rods removed from reactors and later reloaded into the reactor. [4] For purchases made by U.S. suppliers and by U.S. owners and operators of civilian nuclear power plants.

Source: U.S. Energy Information Administration, through 2010, *Annual Energy Review*; thereafter, *Uranium Marketing Annual Report*, June 2017, and *Domestic Uranium Production Report–Quarterly*, May 2017. See also <http://www.eia.gov/nuclear/>.

Table 972. Renewable Energy Generating Capacity and Generation Projections: 2015 to 2050

[In gigawatts, unless otherwise noted. Reference case projections are business-as-usual trend estimates, given known technology, as well as market, demographic, and technological trends. Based on results from EIA's National Energy Modeling System]

Net summer capacity and generation	Reference case								Annual growth 2015-2050 (percent)
	2015	2020	2025	2030	2035	2040	2045	2050	
ELECTRIC POWER SECTOR [1]									
Total net summer capacity..................	**174.06**	**227.00**	**284.06**	**304.79**	**327.43**	**363.61**	**402.36**	**433.49**	**2.4**
Conventional hydroelectric power...............	78.97	79.56	79.85	80.12	80.36	80.53	80.72	80.90	0.1
Geothermal [2]......................................	2.50	2.67	3.96	5.28	6.41	7.00	7.47	7.92	3.5
Municipal waste [3].................................	3.73	3.78	3.78	3.78	3.78	3.78	3.78	3.78	–
Wood and other biomass [4]......................	3.56	3.73	3.71	3.71	3.76	4.03	4.19	4.57	0.7
Solar thermal......................................	1.80	1.96	1.96	1.96	1.96	1.96	1.96	1.96	0.3
Solar photovoltaic [5].............................	11.61	28.88	38.50	57.11	76.05	104.71	134.31	148.03	6.2
Wind..	71.89	106.39	152.27	152.82	155.09	161.57	169.91	186.30	2.5
Total generation (bil. kWh)..................	**511.07**	**728.07**	**937.90**	**991.89**	**1,050.00**	**1,138.76**	**1,233.09**	**1,321.77**	**2.6**
Conventional hydroelectric power...............	247.63	308.92	310.62	312.43	313.64	314.74	315.86	317.03	0.6
Geothermal [2]......................................	15.86	18.35	28.67	39.25	48.39	53.26	57.43	61.09	3.9
Biogenic municipal waste [6]....................	18.07	20.25	21.18	21.03	20.76	21.69	22.60	22.55	0.4
Wood and other biomass.......................	14.48	8.15	10.05	14.16	14.30	16.10	17.75	20.97	4.2
Dedicated plants............................	13.77	7.75	9.64	13.66	13.83	15.58	17.20	20.43	4.5
Co-firing....................................	0.71	0.39	0.40	0.50	0.47	0.52	0.55	0.53	-0.4
Solar thermal................................	3.25	3.65	3.65	3.57	3.53	3.42	3.35	3.39	0.1
Solar photovoltaic [5].........................	21.17	54.50	75.58	111.14	151.78	208.87	267.79	292.02	6.9
Wind..	190.60	314.15	488.05	490.22	497.51	520.58	548.22	604.64	3.0
END-USE SECTORS [7]									
Total net summer capacity..................	**19.03**	**35.51**	**51.38**	**72.74**	**101.00**	**136.33**	**180.50**	**236.43**	**7.1**
Conventional hydropower........................	0.28	0.28	0.28	0.28	0.28	0.28	0.28	0.28	–
Geothermal.......................................	–	–	–	–	–	–	–	–	(X)
Municipal waste [3]...............................	0.57	0.57	0.57	0.57	0.57	0.57	0.57	0.57	–
Biomass..	4.45	4.40	4.25	3.94	3.75	3.68	3.71	3.68	-0.5
Solar photovoltaic [5].............................	11.61	27.14	43.12	64.50	92.52	127.32	170.67	225.74	8.4
Wind..	2.12	3.12	3.16	3.44	3.88	4.47	5.28	6.17	2.0
Total generation (bil. kWh)..................	**48.69**	**70.38**	**92.60**	**122.49**	**163.32**	**215.42**	**281.57**	**365.70**	**5.8**
Conventional hydropower	1.32	1.32	1.32	1.32	1.32	1.32	1.32	1.32	–
Geothermal.......................................	–	–	–	–	–	–	–	–	(X)
Municipal waste [3]...............................	4.04	4.04	4.04	4.04	4.04	4.04	4.04	4.04	–
Biomass..	24.51	23.10	22.31	20.56	19.50	19.10	19.26	19.06	-0.7
Solar photovoltaic [5].............................	16.08	37.92	60.87	92.13	133.44	185.16	250.09	333.25	8.6
Wind..	2.74	4.01	4.07	4.45	5.02	5.81	6.86	8.03	2.1
ALL SECTORS									
Total net summer capacity..................	**193.09**	**262.51**	**335.44**	**377.53**	**428.43**	**499.93**	**582.87**	**669.92**	**3.4**
Conventional hydropower........................	79.24	79.84	80.12	80.39	80.63	80.81	80.99	81.18	0.1
Geothermal.......................................	2.50	2.67	3.96	5.28	6.41	7.00	7.47	7.92	3.5
Municipal waste..................................	4.31	4.36	4.35	4.35	4.35	4.35	4.35	4.35	–
Wood and other biomass [4].....................	8.01	8.12	7.97	7.65	7.51	7.72	7.90	8.25	0.1
Solar [5]..	25.02	57.98	83.58	123.57	170.53	233.98	306.93	375.72	7.2
Wind..	74.01	109.54	155.46	156.29	159.00	166.08	175.22	192.49	2.5
Total generation (bil. kWh)..................	**559.75**	**798.45**	**1,030.51**	**1,114.38**	**1,213.32**	**1,354.18**	**1,514.67**	**1,687.47**	**3.0**
Conventional hydropower........................	248.95	310.24	311.94	313.74	314.96	316.05	317.18	318.34	0.6
Geothermal.......................................	15.86	18.35	28.67	39.25	48.39	53.26	57.43	61.09	3.9
Municipal waste..................................	22.11	24.29	25.23	25.07	24.81	25.74	26.64	26.59	0.3
Wood and other biomass........................	38.99	31.25	32.35	34.72	33.80	35.20	37.01	40.03	0.9
Solar [5]..	40.49	96.06	140.10	206.84	288.75	397.44	521.22	628.66	7.5
Wind..	193.34	318.26	492.22	494.76	502.63	526.48	555.18	612.76	3.0

– Represents or rounds to zero. X Not applicable. [1] Includes electricity-only and combined heat and power plants that have a regulatory status. [2] Includes both hydrothermal resources and near-field enhanced geothermal systems (EGS). [3] Includes municipal waste, landfill gas, and municipal sewage sludge. [4] Facilities co-firing biomass and coal are classified as coal. [5] Does not include off-grid photovoltaics (PV). [6] Includes biogenic municipal waste, landfill gas, and municipal sludge. [7] Includes combined heat and power plants and electricity-only plants in the commercial and industrial sectors and small on-site generating systems in the residential, commercial, and industrial sectors used primarily for own-use generation, but which many also sell some power to the grid.

Source: U.S. Energy Information Administration, *Annual Energy Outlook 2017*, January 2017. See also <http://www.eia.gov/forecasts/aeo/>.

Table 973. Electricity Net Generation by Sector and Fuel Type: 1990 to 2016

[3,037.8 represents 3,037,800,000,000 kilowatt hours (kWh). Data are for fuels consumed to produce electricity. Also includes fuels consumed to produce useful thermal output at a small number of electric utility combined-heat-and-power (CHP) plants]

Source and sector	Unit	1990	1995	2000	2005	2010	2013	2014	2015	2016 (P)
Net generation, total	**Bil. kWh.**	**3,037.8**	**3,353.5**	**3,802.1**	**4,055.4**	**4,125.1**	**4,066.0**	**4,093.6**	**4,077.6**	**4,079.1**
Electric power sector, total	Bil. kWh.	2,901.3	3,194.2	3,637.5	3,902.2	3,972.4	3,903.7	3,937.0	3,919.3	3,919.8
Commercial sector[1]	Bil. kWh.	5.8	8.2	7.9	8.5	8.6	12.2	12.5	12.6	12.6
Industrial sector[2]	Bil. kWh.	130.8	151.0	156.7	144.7	144.1	150.0	144.1	145.7	146.6
Net generation by source, all sectors:										
Fossil fuels, total	Bil. kWh.	2,103.6	2,293.9	2,692.5	2,909.5	2,883.4	2,746.0	2,750.6	2,727.2	2,657.3
Coal[3]	Bil. kWh.	1,594.0	1,709.4	1,966.3	2,012.9	1,847.3	1,581.1	1,581.7	1,352.4	1,240.1
Petroleum[4]	Bil. kWh.	126.5	74.6	111.2	122.2	37.1	27.2	30.2	28.2	23.9
Natural gas[5]	Bil. kWh.	372.8	496.1	601.0	761.0	987.7	1,124.8	1,126.6	1,333.5	1,380.3
Other gases[6]	Bil. kWh.	10.4	13.9	14.0	13.5	11.3	12.9	12.0	13.1	13.0
Nuclear electric power	Bil. kWh.	576.9	673.4	753.9	782.0	807.0	789.0	797.2	797.2	805.3
Hydroelectric pumped storage[7]	Bil. kWh.	-3.5	-2.7	-5.5	-6.6	-5.5	-4.7	-6.2	-5.1	-6.7
Renewable energy, total	Bil. kWh.	357.1	384.8	356.5	357.7	427.4	522.1	538.6	544.2	609.4
Conventional hydroelectric power	Bil. kWh.	292.9	310.8	275.6	270.3	260.2	268.6	259.4	249.1	265.8
Biomass, total[8]	Bil. kWh.	45.8	56.9	60.7	54.3	56.1	60.9	64.0	63.6	62.6
Wood[8]	Bil. kWh.	32.5	36.5	37.6	38.9	37.2	40.0	42.3	41.9	40.5
Waste[9]	Bil. kWh.	13.3	20.4	23.1	15.4	18.9	20.8	21.6	21.7	22.1
Geothermal	Bil. kWh.	15.4	13.4	14.1	14.7	15.2	15.8	15.9	15.9	17.4
Solar[10]	Bil. kWh.	0.4	0.5	0.5	0.6	1.2	9.0	17.7	24.9	36.8
Wind	Bil. kWh.	2.8	3.2	5.6	17.8	94.7	167.8	181.7	190.7	226.9
Other[11]	Bil. kWh.	3.6	4.1	4.8	12.8	12.9	13.6	13.5	14.0	13.7
Consumption of fuels for electricity generation:										
Coal[3]	Mil. short tons	792.5	860.6	994.9	1,041.4	979.7	860.7	853.6	739.6	678.0
Petroleum, total	Mil. bbl.	218.8	132.6	195.2	206.8	65.1	47.5	53.6	49.1	42.6
Distillate fuel oil[12]	Mil. bbl.	18.1	19.6	31.7	20.7	14.1	9.8	14.5	12.4	9.4
Residual fuel oil[13]	Mil. bbl.	190.7	95.5	143.4	141.5	24.0	11.8	14.7	14.1	10.2
Other liquids[14]	Mil. bbl.	0.4	0.7	1.4	3.0	2.1	1.7	2.4	2.4	1.6
Petroleum coke	Mil. short tons	1.9	3.4	3.7	8.3	5.0	4.9	4.4	4.0	4.3
Natural gas[5]	Bil. cu. ft.	3,691.6	4,737.9	5,691.5	6,036.4	7,680.2	8,596.3	8,544.4	10,016.6	10,400.2
Other gases[6]	Tril. Btu.	111.8	132.5	126.0	109.9	90.1	115.3	110.0	106.0	102.2
Biomass	Tril. Btu.	653.5	795.6	825.9	585.3	630.3	695.8	744.8	719.6	697.8
Wood[8]	Tril. Btu.	442.3	479.9	495.8	355.3	349.5	397.9	431.3	406.7	381.6
Waste[9]	Tril. Btu.	211.2	315.7	330.1	230.1	280.8	297.9	313.5	313.0	316.2
Other[11]	Tril. Btu.	36.0	42.0	46.2	173.0	184.4	200.1	199.9	203.6	193.5

P Preliminary. [1] Commercial combined-heat-and-power (CHP) and commercial electricity-only plants. [2] Industrial CHP and industrial electricity-only plants. [3] Anthracite, bituminous coal, subbituminous coal, lignite, waste coal, and coal synfuel. [4] Distillate fuel oil, residual fuel oil, petroleum coke, jet fuel, kerosene, other petroleum, waste oil, and beginning in 2011, propane. [5] Includes a small amount of supplemental gaseous fuels that cannot be identified separately. [6] Blast furnace gas and other manufactured and waste gases derived from fossil fuels. Through 2010, also includes propane. [7] Pumped storage facility production minus energy used for pumping. [8] Wood and wood-derived fuels. [9] Municipal solid waste from biogenic sources, landfill gas, sludge waste, agricultural byproducts, and other biomass. Through 2000, also includes nonrenewable waste (municipal solid waste from non-biogenic sources and tire-derived fuels). [10] Solar thermal and photovoltaic energy. Does not include estimated distributed solar photovoltaic generation, which was 14,139 million kilowatthours in 2015 and 19,467 million kilowatthours in 2016. [11] Batteries, chemicals, hydrogen, pitch, purchased steam, sulfur, miscellaneous technologies, and beginning 2001, nonrenewable waste (municipal solid waste from nonbiogenic sources, and tire-derived fuels). [12] Fuel oil numbers 1, 2, and 4. For 1990 through 2000, electric utility data also include small amounts of kerosene and jet fuel. [13] Fuel oil numbers 5 and 6. For 1990 through 2000, electric utility data also include a small amount of fuel oil number 4. [14] Jet fuel, kerosene, other petroleum liquids, waste oil, and beginning in 2011, propane.

Source: U.S. Energy Information Administration, *Monthly Energy Review*, May 2017. See also <http://www.eia.gov/totalenergy/data/monthly>.

Table 974. Total Electric Net Summer Capacity for All Sectors by Energy Source: 1990 to 2015

[In million kilowatts (734.1 represents 734,100,000). Data are at end of year. For plants that use multiple sources of energy, capacity is assigned to the predominant energy source]

Source	1990	1995	2000	2005	2010	2012	2013	2014	2015
Net summer capacity, total.............	**734.1**	**769.5**	**811.7**	**978.0**	**1,039.1**	**1,063.0**	**1,060.1**	**1,068.4**	**1,064.1**
Fossil fuels, total................................	527.8	554.2	598.9	757.1	782.2	781.2	774.3	774.3	758.5
Coal [1]...	307.4	311.4	315.1	313.4	316.8	309.7	303.3	299.1	279.7
Petroleum [2].....................................	77.9	66.6	61.8	58.5	55.6	47.2	43.5	41.1	36.8
Natural gas [3]...................................	140.8	174.5	219.6	383.1	407.0	422.4	425.4	432.2	439.4
Other gases [4]..................................	1.6	1.7	2.3	2.1	2.7	1.9	2.1	1.9	2.5
Nuclear electric power.........................	99.6	99.5	97.9	100.0	101.2	101.9	99.2	98.6	98.7
Hydroelectric pumped storage..............	19.5	21.4	19.5	21.3	22.2	22.4	22.4	22.5	22.6
Renewable energy, total......................	86.8	93.9	94.9	98.7	132.6	155.9	161.8	93.2	192.3
Conventional hydroelectric power..........	73.9	78.6	79.4	77.5	78.8	78.7	79.2	79.7	79.7
Biomass, total...................................	8.1	10.3	10.0	9.8	11.4	12.3	13.4	13.5	14.1
Wood [5]..	5.5	6.7	6.1	6.2	7.0	7.5	8.4	8.4	9.0
Waste [6].......................................	2.5	3.5	3.9	3.6	4.4	4.8	5.0	5.2	5.1
Geothermal.......................................	2.7	3.0	2.8	2.3	2.4	2.6	2.6	2.5	2.5
Solar [7]...	0.3	0.3	0.4	0.4	0.9	3.2	6.6	17.6	23.4
Wind..	1.8	1.7	2.4	8.7	39.1	59.1	60.0	64.2	72.6
Other [8]..	0.5	0.5	0.5	0.9	0.9	1.7	2.3	2.8	1.8

[1] Coal includes anthracite, bituminous, subbituminous, lignite, and waste coal; coal synfuel and refined coal; and beginning in 2011, coal-derived synthesis gas. Prior to 2011, coal-derived synthesis gas was included in other gases. [2] Distillate fuel oil, residual fuel oil, petroleum coke, jet fuel, kerosene, other petroleum, waste oil, and beginning in 2011, synthetic gas and propane. Prior to 2011, synthetic gas and propane were included in other gases. [3] Includes a small amount of supplemental gaseous fuels that cannot be identified separately. [4] Blast furnace gas, propane gas, and other manufactured and waste gases derived from fossil fuels. [5] Wood and wood-derived fuels. [6] Municipal solid waste from biogenic sources, landfill gas, sludge gas, agricultural byproducts, and other biomass. Also includes nonrenewable waste (municipal solid waste from nonbiogenic sources, and tire-derived fuels). [7] Solar thermal and photovoltaic energy. [8] Batteries, hydrogen, purchased steam, sulfur, tire-derived fuels and other miscellaneous energy sources.

Source: U.S. Energy Information Administration, *Electric Power Annual 2015*, November 2016, and earlier reports. See also <http://www.eia.gov/electricity/annual/>.

Table 975. Electricity—End Use and Average Retail Prices: 1990 to 2015

[2,837.1 represents 2,837,100,000,000. Beginning 2003, the category "other" has been replaced by "transportation," and the categories "commercial" and "industrial" have been redefined. Data represent revenue from electricity retail sales divided by the amount of retail electricity sold (in kilowatt-hours). Prices include state and local taxes, energy or demand charges, customer service charges, environmental surcharges, franchise fees, fuel adjustments, and other miscellaneous charges applied to end-use customers during normal billing operations. Prices do not include deferred charges, credits, or other adjustments, such as fuel or revenue from purchased power, from previous reporting periods. Data are for a census of electric utilities. Beginning in 2000 data also include energy service providers selling to retail customers]

Item	1990	1995	2000	2005	2010	2012	2013	2014	2015
END USE (Billion kilowatt-hours)									
Total end use [1]........................	**2,837.1**	**3,164.0**	**3,592.4**	**3,811.0**	**3,886.8**	**3,832.3**	**3,868.3**	**3,903.3**	**3,900.2**
Direct use [2]................................	124.5	150.7	170.9	150.0	131.9	137.7	143.5	138.6	141.2
Retail sales, total [3]...................	**2,712.6**	**3,013.3**	**3,421.4**	**3,661.0**	**3,754.8**	**3,694.6**	**3,724.9**	**3,764.7**	**3,759.0**
Residential...................................	924.0	1,042.5	1,192.4	1,359.2	1,445.7	1,374.5	1,394.8	1,407.2	1,404.1
Commercial [4].............................	838.3	953.1	1,159.3	1,275.1	1,330.2	1,327.1	1,337.1	1,352.2	1,360.8
Industrial [5].................................	945.5	1,012.7	1,064.2	1,019.2	971.2	985.7	985.4	997.6	986.5
Transportation [6]...........................	4.8	5.0	5.4	7.5	7.7	7.3	7.6	7.8	7.6
AVERAGE RETAIL PRICES (Cents per kilowatt-hour)									
Total.......................................	**6.57**	**6.89**	**6.81**	**8.14**	**9.83**	**9.84**	**10.07**	**10.44**	**10.41**
Residential...................................	7.83	8.40	8.24	9.45	11.54	11.88	12.13	12.52	12.65
Commercial [7].............................	7.34	7.69	7.43	8.67	10.19	10.09	10.26	10.74	10.64
Industrial [5].................................	4.74	4.66	4.64	5.73	6.77	6.67	6.89	7.10	6.91
Transportation [6]...........................	(NA)	(NA)	(NA)	8.57	10.56	10.21	10.55	10.45	10.09
Other [8]......................................	6.40	6.88	6.56	(NA)	(NA)	(NA)	(NA)	(NA)	(NA)

NA Not available. [1] The sum of "total retail sales" and "direct use." [2] Use of electricity that is 1) self-generated, 2) produced by either the same entity that consumes the power or an affiliate, and 3) used in direct support of a service or industrial process located within the same facility or group of facilities that house the generating equipment. Direct use is exclusive of station use. [3] Electricity retail sales to ultimate customers reported by electric utilities and, beginning in 2000, other energy service providers. [4] Includes public street and highway lighting, interdepartmental sales, and other sales to public authorities. [5] Beginning 2003, includes agriculture and irrigation. [6] Includes sales to railroads and railways. [7] Beginning 2003, includes public street and highway lighting, interdepartmental sales, and other sales to public authorities. [8] Public street and highway lighting, interdepartmental sales, other sales to public authorities, agriculture and irrigation, and transportation including railroads and railways.

Source: U.S. Energy Information Administration, *Electric Power Annual 2015*, November 2016, and earlier reports. See also <http://www.eia.gov/electricity/>.

Table 976. Electric Power Industry—Net Generation and Net Summer Capacity by State: 2000 to 2015

[3,802.1 represents 3,802,100,000,000. Capacity as of December 31. Covers utilities for public use]

State	Net generation (billion kilowatt-hours)									Net summer capacity (million kilowatts)	
				2015							
				Total (bil. kWh)[1]	Percent from—						
	2000	2010	2014		Petro-leum	Natural gas	Hydro-electric	Nuclear	Coal	2014	2015
U.S.	**3,802.1**	**4,125.1**	**4,093.6**	**4,077.6**	**0.7**	**32.7**	**6.1**	**19.6**	**33.2**	**1,068.4**	**1,064.1**
AL	124.4	152.2	149.3	152.5	0.1	36.6	6.5	27.5	27.2	32.0	30.4
AK	6.2	6.8	6.0	6.3	11.9	49.2	25.0	–	10.6	2.5	2.6
AZ	88.9	111.8	112.3	113.1	(Z)	29.7	5.8	28.7	32.0	28.2	28.1
AR	43.9	61.0	61.6	55.6	0.1	26.8	6.4	24.9	39.1	14.8	14.7
CA	208.1	204.1	198.8	196.7	(Z)	59.0	7.0	9.4	0.2	74.6	74.9
CO	44.2	50.7	53.8	52.4	(Z)	22.2	3.1	–	60.2	14.9	15.8
CT	33.0	33.3	33.7	37.5	1.2	46.3	0.8	46.5	1.6	8.8	8.8
DE	6.0	5.6	7.7	7.8	2.0	85.6	–	–	7.7	3.1	3.4
DC	0.1	0.2	0.1	0.1	0.2	42.1	–	–	–	(Z)	(Z)
FL	191.8	229.1	230.0	237.4	0.9	65.6	0.1	11.8	18.1	59.4	58.6
GA	123.9	137.6	125.8	128.8	0.2	39.2	2.3	26.3	28.8	38.2	36.3
HI	10.6	10.8	10.2	10.1	69.4	0.0	1.2	–	13.2	2.7	2.7
ID	11.9	12.0	15.2	15.7	(Z)	24.3	55.9	–	0.5	4.9	4.9
IL	178.5	201.4	202.1	194.0	(Z)	5.6	0.1	50.2	38.0	44.7	45.5
IN	127.8	125.2	115.4	104.0	1.3	15.6	0.4	–	75.2	27.5	26.3
IA	41.5	57.5	56.9	56.7	0.2	4.2	1.7	9.3	52.6	16.5	16.9
KS	44.8	47.9	49.7	45.5	0.1	2.6	(Z)	19.0	54.0	14.2	14.3
KY	93.0	98.2	90.9	83.5	1.3	7.1	4.1	–	86.9	20.9	20.1
LA	92.9	102.9	104.2	107.8	3.9	61.4	0.9	14.2	14.1	26.7	26.2
ME	14.0	17.0	13.2	11.7	4.7	25.1	28.6	–	0.8	4.5	4.6
MD	51.1	43.6	37.8	36.4	0.6	12.5	4.5	40.3	38.3	12.3	12.4
MA	38.7	42.8	31.1	32.1	2.4	65.5	2.6	15.6	7.0	13.1	13.2
MI	104.2	111.6	106.8	113.0	0.7	17.7	1.3	26.0	46.8	30.4	30.1
MN	51.4	53.7	57.0	57.0	(Z)	13.0	1.5	21.1	43.3	15.6	15.7
MS	37.6	54.5	55.1	64.8	(Z)	69.7	–	18.1	9.9	16.1	16.1
MO	76.6	92.3	87.8	83.6	0.1	5.5	1.9	12.5	78.1	21.8	21.8
MT	26.5	29.8	30.3	29.3	1.7	2.0	33.7	–	54.6	6.3	6.2
NE	29.1	36.6	39.4	39.9	(Z)	1.1	4.2	25.9	60.6	8.7	8.7
NV	35.5	35.1	36.0	39.0	(Z)	74.3	5.8	–	6.8	10.5	10.9
NH	15.0	22.2	19.5	20.0	0.9	30.2	6.3	47.4	4.7	4.4	4.4
NJ	58.1	65.7	68.1	74.6	0.5	49.6	(Z)	44.6	2.4	19.4	18.8
NM	34.0	36.3	32.3	32.7	0.2	28.6	0.3	–	62.5	8.1	8.4
NY	138.1	137.0	137.1	138.6	1.4	41.1	18.8	32.2	1.7	40.4	40.2
NC	122.3	128.7	128.1	128.4	0.3	28.5	3.7	32.8	31.1	30.5	31.3
ND	31.3	34.7	36.5	37.2	0.1	1.9	5.6	0.0	74.6	6.8	7.4
OH	149.1	143.6	134.5	121.9	1.1	23.0	0.4	14.3	58.8	31.5	28.7
OK	55.6	72.3	70.2	76.1	(Z)	45.0	3.5	–	32.7	24.0	24.8
OR	51.8	55.1	60.1	57.9	(Z)	28.1	54.0	–	4.1	15.9	15.9
PA	201.7	229.8	221.1	214.6	0.3	27.7	1.2	37.5	30.1	42.7	42.3
RI	6.0	7.7	6.3	6.9	1.6	94.9	(Z)	–	–	1.8	1.8
SC	93.3	104.2	97.2	96.5	0.2	17.1	2.7	55.1	23.4	22.8	22.7
SD	9.7	10.0	11.0	9.6	0.2	8.0	50.4	–	15.5	3.9	4.1
TN	95.8	82.3	79.5	75.2	0.2	12.4	12.7	33.2	40.7	21.0	20.2
TX	377.7	411.7	437.6	449.8	0.1	52.8	0.2	8.7	27.0	112.9	117.1
UT	36.6	42.2	43.8	41.9	(Z)	19.6	1.8	–	75.5	8.3	8.3
VT	6.3	6.6	7.0	2.0	0.2	0.1	57.5	–	–	0.6	0.7
VA	77.2	73.0	77.1	84.4	1.3	39.4	1.4	33.2	20.4	26.3	25.2
WA	108.2	103.5	116.3	109.3	(Z)	11.9	67.2	7.5	4.6	30.9	31.0
WV	92.9	80.8	81.1	72.3	0.2	1.8	1.9	–	94.1	16.3	15.1
WI	59.6	64.3	61.1	66.4	0.3	20.2	3.5	15.1	56.0	17.2	16.7
WY	45.5	48.1	49.7	49.0	0.1	1.5	1.8	–	88.0	8.5	8.5

– Represents zero. Z Represents less than .05 percent of net electricity generation. [1] Includes other sources not shown separately.

Source: U.S. Energy Information Administration, *Electric Power Annual*, "Data Tables" and "Detailed State Data," <http://www.eia.gov/electricity/annual/>, accessed January 2017.

Table 977. Electric Power Industry—Capability, Peak Load, and Capacity Margin: 1980 to 2015

[558,237 represents 558,237,000 kilowatts (kW). Excludes Alaska and Hawaii. Capability represents the maximum kilowatt output with all power sources available and with hydraulic equipment under actual water conditions, allowing for maintenance, emergency outages, and system operating requirements. Capacity margin is the difference between capability and peak load. Minus sign (-) indicates decrease]

Year	Capability at the time of— Summer peak load (1,000 kW) Amount	Change from prior year	Winter peak load (1,000 kW) Amount	Change from prior year	Noncoincident peak load Summer (1,000 kW)	Winter (1,000 kW)	Capacity margin Summer Amount (1,000 kW)	Percent of capability	Winter Amount (1,000 kW)	Percent of capability
1980	558,237	13,731	572,195	17,670	427,058	384,567	131,179	23.5	187,628	32.8
1985	621,597	17,357	636,475	14,350	460,503	423,660	161,094	25.9	212,815	33.4
1990	685,091	11,775	696,757	11,508	546,331	484,231	138,760	20.3	212,526	30.5
1991	690,915	5,824	703,212	6,455	551,418	485,761	139,497	20.2	217,451	30.9
1992	695,436	4,521	707,752	4,540	548,707	492,983	146,729	21.1	214,769	30.3
1993	694,250	-1,186	711,957	4,205	575,356	521,733	118,894	17.1	190,224	26.7
1994	702,985	8,735	715,090	3,133	585,320	518,253	117,665	16.7	196,837	27.5
1995	714,222	11,237	727,679	12,589	620,249	544,684	93,973	13.2	182,995	25.1
1996	730,376	16,154	737,637	9,958	616,790	554,081	113,586	15.6	183,556	24.9
1997	737,855	7,479	736,666	-971	637,677	529,874	100,178	13.6	206,792	28.1
1998	744,670	6,815	735,090	-1,576	660,293	567,558	84,377	11.3	167,532	22.8
1999	765,744	21,074	748,271	13,181	682,122	570,915	83,622	10.9	177,356	23.7
2000	808,054	42,310	767,505	19,234	678,413	588,426	129,641	16.0	179,079	23.3
2001	788,990	-19,064	806,598	39,093	687,812	576,312	101,178	12.8	230,286	28.6
2002	833,380	44,390	850,984	44,386	714,565	604,986	118,815	14.3	245,998	28.9
2003	856,131	22,751	882,120	31,136	709,375	593,874	146,756	17.1	288,246	32.7
2004	875,870	19,739	864,849	-17,271	704,459	618,701	171,411	19.6	246,148	28.5
2005	882,125	6,255	878,110	13,261	758,876	626,365	123,249	14.0	251,745	28.7
2006	891,226	9,101	899,551	21,441	789,475	640,981	101,751	11.4	258,570	28.7
2007	914,397	23,171	913,650	14,099	782,227	637,905	132,170	14.5	275,745	30.2
2008	909,504	-4,893	927,781	14,131	752,470	643,557	157,034	17.3	284,224	30.6
2009	916,449	6,945	920,002	-7,779	725,958	668,818	190,491	20.8	251,184	27.3
2010	923,559	7,110	935,262	15,260	767,948	651,418	155,611	16.8	283,844	30.3
2011	892,426	-31,133	893,206	-42,056	782,469	648,190	109,957	12.3	245,016	27.4
2012	931,893	39,467	947,156	53,950	767,762	618,570	164,131	17.6	328,586	34.7
2013	944,515	12,622	956,984	9,828	758,953	686,202	185,562	19.6	270,782	28.3
2014	917,167	-27,348	928,477	-28,507	723,411	677,005	193,756	21.1	251,472	27.1
2015	916,439	-728	920,599	-7,878	741,056	636,387	175,383	19.1	284,212	30.9

Source: Edison Electric Institute, Washington, DC, *Statistical Yearbook of the Electric Power Industry*, annual ©. See also <http://www.eei.org>.

Table 978. Electric Energy Retail Sales by Class of Service and State: 2015

[In billions of kilowatt-hours (3,759.0 represents 3,759,000,000,000). Data include both bundled and unbundled consumers]

State	Total [1]	Residential	Commercial	Industrial	State	Total [1]	Residential	Commercial	Industrial
United States	**3,759.0**	**1,404.1**	**1,360.8**	**986.5**	Missouri	81.5	33.9	30.5	17.0
Alabama	88.8	31.9	23.4	33.5	Montana	14.2	4.8	4.9	4.5
Alaska	6.2	2.0	2.8	1.4	Nebraska	29.5	9.5	9.3	10.7
Arizona	77.3	33.2	29.3	14.9	Nevada	36.0	12.3	9.6	14.1
Arkansas	46.5	18.3	12.2	16.0	New Hampshire	11.0	4.5	4.5	2.0
California	261.2	89.4	118.4	52.6	New Jersey	75.5	29.1	38.7	7.3
Colorado	54.1	18.4	20.4	15.3	New Mexico	23.1	6.6	8.9	7.6
Connecticut	29.5	12.9	13.0	3.4	New York	148.9	51.0	77.0	18.1
Delaware	11.5	4.8	4.2	2.4	North Carolina	133.8	57.9	48.2	27.7
District of Columbia	11.3	2.5	8.2	0.2	North Dakota	18.1	4.9	6.3	7.0
Florida	235.6	122.8	95.8	16.9	Ohio	149.2	51.5	47.1	50.6
Georgia	135.9	56.4	47.2	32.1	Oklahoma	61.3	22.6	20.7	18.0
Hawaii	9.5	2.6	3.2	3.7	Oregon	47.3	18.3	16.0	12.9
Idaho	23.1	8.1	6.3	8.7	Pennsylvania	146.3	54.4	43.7	47.4
Illinois	138.6	44.6	50.3	43.1	Rhode Island	7.7	3.1	3.7	0.8
Indiana	104.5	32.4	24.0	48.0	South Carolina	81.3	30.1	21.9	29.3
Iowa	47.1	13.8	12.1	21.3	South Dakota	12.1	4.6	4.7	2.8
Kansas	39.8	13.2	15.4	11.2	Tennessee	99.6	41.7	35.0	23.0
Kentucky	76.0	26.2	19.6	30.3	Texas	392.3	145.7	136.3	110.2
Louisiana	91.7	31.5	25.0	35.1	Utah	30.2	9.1	11.6	9.4
Maine	11.9	4.7	4.0	3.2	Vermont	5.5	2.1	2.0	1.4
Maryland	61.8	27.4	30.0	3.9	Virginia	112.0	45.9	48.3	17.5
Massachusetts	54.6	20.2	26.2	7.9	Washington	90.1	34.1	29.3	26.8
Michigan	102.5	33.4	38.4	30.7	West Virginia	32.3	11.4	7.8	13.1
Minnesota	66.6	21.7	23.4	21.5	Wisconsin	68.7	21.2	23.5	24.0
Mississippi	48.7	18.6	14.4	15.7	Wyoming	16.9	2.7	3.9	10.3

[1] Includes transportation, not shown separately.

Source: U.S. Energy Information Administration, "Electric Sales, Revenue, and Average Price," <http://www.eia.gov/electricity/sales_revenue_price/index.cfm>, accessed December 2016.

Table 979. Electric Energy Average Retail Price by Class of Service and State: 2015

[In cents per kilowatt-hour (kWh). Data include both bundled and unbundled consumers]

State	Total [1]	Resi-dential	Com-mercial	Indus-trial	State	Total [1]	Resi-dential	Com-mercial	Indus-trial
United States.........	**10.41**	**12.65**	**10.64**	**6.91**	Missouri............	9.44	11.21	9.16	6.44
Alabama.................	9.33	11.70	10.83	6.03	Montana...........	8.90	10.88	10.23	5.32
Alaska...................	17.59	19.83	17.44	14.53	Nebraska..........	8.91	10.60	8.67	7.59
Arizona.................	10.34	12.13	10.39	6.26	Nevada.............	9.48	12.76	9.25	6.75
Arkansas...............	8.19	9.82	8.32	6.23	New Hampshire...	16.02	18.50	14.96	12.74
California...............	15.42	16.99	15.73	12.17	New Jersey........	13.74	15.81	12.79	10.64
Colorado...............	9.94	12.12	9.88	7.40	New Mexico.......	9.62	12.47	10.30	6.33
Connecticut...........	17.77	20.94	15.97	12.95	New York..........	15.28	18.54	15.31	6.31
Delaware...............	11.17	13.42	10.25	8.28	North Carolina....	9.37	11.28	8.73	6.51
District of Columbia. ...	12.07	12.99	12.01	8.78	North Dakota......	8.75	9.62	8.83	8.07
Florida..................	10.49	11.58	9.50	8.22	Ohio...............	9.98	12.80	10.07	7.02
Georgia.................	9.62	11.54	9.89	5.87	Oklahoma.........	7.90	10.14	7.68	5.35
Hawaii..................	26.17	29.60	26.93	23.06	Oregon............	8.75	10.66	8.80	5.97
Idaho...................	8.09	9.93	7.80	6.60	Pennsylvania......	10.31	13.64	9.60	7.20
Illinois..................	9.40	12.50	9.02	6.67	Rhode Island......	17.01	19.29	15.78	13.76
Indiana.................	8.99	11.57	9.78	6.86	South Carolina....	9.58	12.57	10.21	6.05
Iowa....................	8.35	11.63	8.92	5.90	South Dakota.....	9.47	11.08	9.16	7.37
Kansas.................	10.14	12.34	10.10	7.61	Tennessee.........	9.30	10.30	10.16	6.17
Kentucky...............	8.14	10.24	9.44	5.48	Texas..............	8.70	11.56	8.15	5.59
Louisiana...............	7.65	9.33	8.66	5.41	Utah................	8.54	10.88	8.62	6.17
Maine...................	12.78	15.61	12.47	9.05	Vermont............	14.41	17.09	14.54	10.27
Maryland...............	12.07	13.82	11.00	8.53	Virginia............	9.31	11.37	8.21	6.95
Massachusetts.........	16.90	19.83	15.79	13.54	Washington........	7.40	9.09	8.22	4.35
Michigan...............	10.76	14.42	10.55	7.02	West Virginia......	8.11	10.08	8.61	6.09
Minnesota..............	9.53	12.12	9.44	7.02	Wisconsin.........	10.73	14.11	10.89	7.58
Mississippi.............	9.53	11.27	10.55	6.56	Wyoming...........	7.97	10.97	9.12	6.76

[1] Includes transportation, not shown separately.

Source: U.S. Energy Information Administration, "Electric Sales, Revenue, and Average Price," <http://www.eia.gov/electricity/sales_revenue_price/index.cfm>, accessed December 2016.

Table 980. Total Electric Power Industry—Generation, Sales, Revenue, and Customers: 1990 to 2016

[2,808 represents 2,808,000,000,000 Kilowatt hours (kWh). Sales and revenue are to and from ultimate customers. Commercial and Industrial are not wholly comparable on a year-to-year basis due to changes from one classification to another. Beginning 2005, the Energy Information Administration replaced the "Other" sector with the Transportation sector. The Transportation sector consists entirely of electrified rail and urban transit systems. Data previously reported in "Other" have been relocated to the Commercial sector, except for Agriculture (i.e., irrigation load), which have been relocated to the Industrial sector]

Class	Unit	1990	2000	2005	2010	2012	2013	2014	2015	2016 [1]
Generation [2].........................	Bil. kWh	2,808	3,802	4,055	4,125	4,048	4,066	4,094	4,078	4,079
Sales [3]............................	Bil. kWh	2,713	3,421	3,661	3,755	3,695	3,752	3,792	3,786	3,711
Residential or domestic............	Bil. kWh	924	1,192	1,359	1,446	1,375	1,408	1,420	1,417	1,407
Percent of total...................	Percent	34.1	34.9	37.1	38.5	37.2	37.5	37.4	37.4	37.9
Commercial [4]......................	Bil. kWh	751	1,055	1,275	1,330	1,327	1,353	1,361	1,369	1,360
Industrial [5].......................	Bil. kWh	946	1,064	1,019	971	986	984	1,003	992	936
Revenue [3]...........................	Bil. dol.	178.2	233.2	298.0	368.9	366.8	377.9	396.3	394.3	381.4
Residential or domestic............	Bil. dol.	72.4	98.2	128.4	166.8	164.8	170.6	177.7	179.1	176.6
Percent of total...................	Percent	40.6	42.1	43.1	45.2	44.9	45.1	44.8	45.4	46.3
Commercial [4]......................	Bil. dol.	55.1	78.4	110.5	135.6	135.1	139.2	146.3	145.8	140.9
Industrial [5].......................	Bil. dol.	44.9	49.4	58.5	65.8	66.2	67.4	71.5	68.7	63.2
Ultimate customers [3]................	Million	110.6	127.6	138.4	144.1	145.3	147.9	149.0	150.1	150.4
Residential or domestic............	Million	97.1	111.7	120.8	125.7	126.8	129.1	130.1	131.0	131.3
Commercial [4]......................	Million	12.1	14.3	16.9	17.7	17.7	18.0	18.1	18.2	18.2
Industrial [5].......................	Million	0.5	0.5	0.7	0.7	0.7	0.8	0.9	0.8	0.8
Avg. kWh used per customer.......	1,000	24.5	26.8	26.5	26.1	25.4	25.4	25.4	25.2	24.7
Residential........................	1,000	9.5	10.7	11.3	11.5	10.8	10.9	10.9	10.8	10.7
Commercial [4].....................	1,000	62.2	73.5	75.4	75.1	75.0	75.2	75.2	75.2	74.7
Avg. annual bill per customer.......	Dollar	1,612	1,828	2,153	2,560	2,524	2,555	2,660	2,627	2,536
Residential........................	Dollar	745	879	1,063	1,327	1,300	1,321	1,366	1,367	1,345
Commercial [4].....................	Dollar	4,562	5,464	6,538	7,661	7,633	7,733	8,083	8,011	7,742
Avg. revenue per kWh sold.........	Cents	6.6	6.8	8.1	9.8	9.9	10.1	10.5	10.4	10.3
Residential........................	Cents	7.8	8.2	9.4	11.5	12.0	12.1	12.5	12.6	12.6
Commercial [4].....................	Cents	7.3	7.4	8.7	10.2	10.2	10.3	10.7	10.7	10.4
Industrial [5]......................	Cents	4.7	4.6	5.7	6.8	6.7	6.8	7.1	6.9	6.8

[1] Preliminary. [2] Includes batteries, chemicals, hydrogen, pitch, sulfur, purchased steam, and miscellaneous technologies, which are not separately displayed. [3] Includes other types, not shown separately. Data for 1990 are as of December 31; data for following years are average yearly customers. [4] Small light and power. [5] Large light and power.

Source: Edison Electric Institute, Washington, DC, *Statistical Yearbook of the Electric Power Industry*, annual ©. See also <http://www.eei.org>.

Table 981. Revenue and Expense Statistics for Major U.S. Investor-Owned Electric Utilities: 1995 to 2015

[In millions of dollars (199,967 represents $199,967,000,000). Covers investor-owned electric utilities that met any one or more of the following conditions, during each of the last 3 years: 1 million megawatt-hours of total sales, 100 megawatt-hours of annual sales for resale, 500 megawatt-hours of annual power exchange delivered, or 500 megawatt-hours of annual wheeling for others. Missing or erroneous respondent data may result in slight imbalances in some of the expense account subtotals]

Item	1995	2000	2005	2010	2012	2013	2014	2015
Utility operating revenues..........	**199,967**	**233,915**	**265,652**	**285,512**	**270,912**	**281,901**	**298,430**	**282,695**
Electric utility..........................	183,655	213,634	234,909	260,119	249,166	257,718	271,832	260,121
Other utility.............................	16,312	20,281	30,743	25,393	21,745	24,183	26,598	22,574
Utility operating expenses..........	**165,321**	**210,250**	**236,786**	**253,022**	**235,694**	**244,316**	**258,936**	**242,728**
Electric utility..........................	150,599	191,564	207,830	234,173	220,722	227,483	240,643	228,366
Operation...............................	91,881	132,607	150,645	166,922	152,379	156,077	165,989	149,939
Production............................	68,983	107,554	120,586	128,831	111,714	115,046	123,366	107,201
Cost of fuel........................	29,122	32,407	36,106	44,138	38,998	41,127	42,545	34,711
Purchased power..................	29,981	62,608	77,902	67,284	54,570	55,529	62,066	52,970
Other................................	9,880	12,561	6,599	17,409	18,146	18,390	18,755	19,521
Transmission.......................	1,425	2,713	5,664	6,948	7,183	7,881	8,902	9,624
Distribution.........................	2,561	3,092	3,502	4,007	4,181	4,197	4,331	4,406
Customer accounts.................	3,613	4,239	4,229	5,091	5,086	5,107	5,255	5,184
Customer service..................	1,922	1,826	2,291	4,741	5,640	5,906	6,396	6,445
Sales.................................	348	405	219	185	221	203	208	201
Administrative and general........	13,028	12,768	14,130	17,120	18,353	17,738	17,532	16,878
Maintenance...........................	11,767	12,064	12,033	14,957	15,489	15,505	16,801	16,392
Depreciation..........................	19,885	20,636	17,123	20,951	23,677	24,723	25,919	26,847
Taxes and other......................	27,065	24,479	26,805	31,343	29,177	31,179	31,934	35,188
Other utility..........................	14,722	18,686	28,956	18,849	14,972	16,833	18,293	14,362
Net utility operating income.......	**34,646**	**23,665**	**28,866**	**32,490**	**35,218**	**37,585**	**39,494**	**39,968**

Source: U.S. Energy Information Administration, *Electric Power Annual 2015*, November 2016, and earlier reports. See also <http://www.eia.gov/electricity/annual/>.

Table 982. Renewable Energy Net Generation of Electricity by Source and State: 2016

[In millions of kilowatt-hours (265,829 represents 265,829,000,000). Data based on results from the Energy Information Agency's annual survey form EIA-923. For more on net generation, see Table 976]

State	Hydro-electric	Other renewable				State	Hydro-electric	Other renewable			
		Total	Wind	Bio-mass [1]	Solar			Total	Wind	Bio-mass [1]	Solar
U.S......	265,829	363,082	226,872	62,572	56,221	MO.......	1,237	1,480	1,123	147	210
AL.......	7,721	3,293	(NA)	3,258	35	MT.......	10,183	2,163	2,130	22	11
AK.......	1,549	215	164	51	(NA)	NE........	1,725	3,895	3,793	94	8
AZ........	7,158	6,170	543	219	5,408	NV........	1,767	7,136	344	26	2,918
AR........	3,418	1,439	(NA)	1,402	37	NH.......	1,121	2,176	447	1,675	54
CA........	28,945	59,665	13,698	6,066	27,432	NJ........	(S)	3,735	22	967	2,746
CO........	1,918	10,445	9,425	(S)	1,020	NM.......	146	4,624	3,614	18	976
CT........	286	1,230	14	869	347	NY........	26,604	7,303	3,946	2,290	1,067
DE........	(NA)	247	(S)	75	172	NC........	4,529	6,445	6	2,423	4,016
DC.......	(NA)	54	(NA)	–	54	ND........	1,912	8,091	8,080	11	–
FL........	219	5,161	(NA)	4,560	601	OH........	517	2,212	1,255	764	193
GA........	3,082	5,733	(NA)	4,657	1,076	OK........	2,382	20,237	19,913	313	11
HI........	118	2,047	644	322	821	OR........	33,700	8,535	7,163	992	183
ID........	9,446	3,147	2,427	584	39	PA........	2,376	6,237	3,472	2,382	383
IL........	129	11,295	10,627	573	95	RI........	(S)	279	33	205	41
IN........	415	5,636	4,903	448	285	SC........	2,399	2,407	(NA)	2,372	35
IA........	956	20,105	20,049	(S)	56	SD........	4,134	3,147	3,145	–	2
KS........	(S)	14,196	14,113	71	12	TN........	7,418	1,190	38	1,001	151
KY........	3,450	481	(NA)	452	29	TX........	1,103	60,394	57,551	1,735	1,108
LA........	1,103	2,881	(NA)	2,687	194	UT........	816	2,464	827	84	1,023
ME.......	2,968	4,469	1,614	2,826	29	VT........	1,056	921	293	473	155
MD......	1,397	1,987	527	547	913	VA........	1,526	4,189	(NA)	4,124	65
MA.......	770	3,380	237	1,194	1,949	WA.......	76,843	10,148	8,042	2,017	89
MI........	1,548	7,256	4,693	2,503	60	WV.......	1,410	1,443	1,432	5	6
MN.......	884	12,500	10,637	1,806	57	WI........	2,405	2,981	1,521	1,422	38
MS.......	(NA)	1,498	(NA)	1,493	5	WY.......	998	4,366	4,363	(NA)	3

– Represents or rounds to zero. NA Not available. S Reporting standards not met. [1] Includes landfill gas and municipal solid waste biogenic (paper and paper board, wood, food, leather, textiles, and yard trimmings). Also includes agriculture by-products/crops, sludge waste, and other biomass solids, liquids, gases, black liquor and wood/wood waste solids and liquids.

Source: Energy Information Administration, "Electricity Data Browser," <http://www.eia.gov/electricity/data/browser/>, accessed June 2017.

Table 983. Major Power Outages by Type of Disturbance and Duration: 2016

[Data shown for power outages lasting longer than 16 hours]

Type of Disturbance	Month	Area affected	Duration	Number of customers affected [1]
Fuel Supply Deficiency....................	March	San Bernardino County, California	1,064 Hours, 47 Minutes	0
Fuel Supply Deficiency....................	September	Tompkins County, New York	399 Hours, 30 Minutes	(NA)
Fuel Supply Deficiency....................	May	Tompkins County, New York	311 Hours, 57 Minutes	(NA)
Severe Weather.........................	October	North Carolina, South Carolina	129 Hours, 9 Minutes	(NA)
Severe Weather.........................	October	Georgia	114 Hours, 38 Minutes	36,384
Fuel Supply Deficiency....................	December	California	73 Hours, 57 Minutes	0
Severe Weather.........................	September	Leon and Wakulla Counties, Florida	67 Hours, 20 Minutes	75,000
Weather................................	March	Denver City and County, Colorado	66 Hours, 59 Minutes	0
Public appeal to reduce electricity usage, transmission Interruption......	October	Utah	56 Hours, 30 Minutes	4,000
Distribution Interruption..................	May	Dallas, Tarrant, and Parker Counties, Texas	54 Hours, 15 Minutes	85,000
Distribution Interruption..................	May	Louisiana	53 Hours	85,000
Severe Weather.........................	October	Florida	53 Hours	165,000
Weather................................	April	Harris County, Texas	50 Hours, 50 Minutes	415,103
Severe Weather.........................	July	Oklahoma, Arkansas	50 Hours, 30 Minutes	7,300
Severe Weather.........................	October	Florida	46 Hours, 30 Minutes	1,200,000
Weather................................	January	North Carolina, South Carolina	44 Hours, 38 Minutes	150,000
Severe Weather.........................	July	Dallas County, Texas	44 Hours, 15 Minutes	62,000
Severe Weather.........................	July	Arkansas, Louisiana, Mississippi, Texas	31 Hours, 30 Minutes	170,244
Weather................................	February	Connecticut, Massachusetts, Rhode Island	28 Hours, 27 Minutes	115,057
Public appeal to reduce electricity usage................................	October	Texas	27 Hours, 51 Minutes	(NA)
Weather................................	February	Michigan	25 Hours, 13 Minutes	145,314
Severe Weather.........................	July	Dallas and Tarrant Counties, Texas	24 Hours, 15 Minutes	52,000
Severe Weather.........................	July	North Carolina	22 Hours, 35 Minutes	203,345
Severe Weather.........................	July	Minnesota, Wisconsin	22 Hours, 30 Minutes	250,000
Weather................................	April	Harris County, Texas	19 Hours, 45 Minutes	214,864
Severe Weather.........................	September	Georgia	18 Hours, 45 Minutes	57,000
Weather................................	June	Georgia, Alabama, Mississippi, Florida	16 Hours, 54 Minutes	91,260
Weather or natural disaster..............	December	Maine	16 Hours, 30 Minutes	85,263

NA Not available. [1] Number of customers affected are preliminary estimates.

Source: U.S. Energy Information Administration, *Electric Power Monthly*, March 2017. See also <http://www.eia.gov/electricity/monthly/>.

Table 984. Gas Utility Industry—Summary: 1990 to 2015

[54,261 represents 54,261,000. Covers natural, manufactured, mixed, and liquid petroleum gas. Based on a questionnaire mailed to all privately and municipally owned gas utilities in the United States, except those with annual revenues less than $25,000]

Item	Unit	1990	1995	2000	2005	2010	2013	2014	2015
End users [1].........................	1,000	**54,261**	**58,728**	**61,262**	**64,395**	**64,960**	**64,406**	**64,893**	**65,612**
Residential..........................	1,000	49,802	53,955	56,494	59,569	60,246	59,788	60,223	60,922
Commercial..........................	1,000	4,246	4,530	4,610	4,678	4,582	4,482	4,534	4,559
Industrial............................	1,000	166	181	157	145	129	123	122	120
Other...............................	1,000	48	61	2	2	3	12	14	10
Sales [2]............................	Tril. Btu [3]	**9,842**	**9,221**	**9,232**	**8,848**	**7,980**	**8,023**	**8,247**	**7,602**
Residential..........................	Tril. Btu	4,468	4,803	4,741	4,516	4,371	4,337	4,471	4,080
Percent of total...................	Percent	45	52	51	51	55	54	54	54
Commercial..........................	Tril. Btu	2,192	2,281	2,077	2,056	1,842	1,820	1,917	1,766
Industrial............................	Tril. Btu	3,010	1,919	1,698	1,654	1,209	1,263	1,245	1,172
Other...............................	Tril. Btu	171	218	715	622	558	603	614	584
Revenues [2].......................	Mil. dol.	**45,153**	**46,436**	**59,243**	**96,909**	**72,886**	**65,887**	**74,031**	**60,923**
Residential..........................	Mil. dol.	25,000	28,742	35,828	55,680	47,231	42,937	47,200	40,451
Percent of total...................	Percent	55	62	60	57	65	65	64	66
Commercial..........................	Mil. dol.	10,604	11,573	13,339	22,653	16,578	14,684	16,985	14,057
Industrial............................	Mil. dol.	8,996	5,571	7,432	13,751	6,437	5,711	6,730	4,434
Other...............................	Mil. dol.	553	549	2,645	4,825	2,640	2,556	3,115	1,982
Prices per mil. Btu [3]..............	Dollars	**4.59**	**5.05**	**6.42**	**10.95**	**9.13**	**8.21**	**8.98**	**7.99**
Residential..........................	Dollars	5.60	6.00	7.56	12.33	10.81	9.90	10.56	9.91
Commercial..........................	Dollars	4.84	5.07	6.42	11.02	9.00	8.07	8.86	7.96
Industrial............................	Dollars	2.99	2.98	4.38	8.31	5.32	4.52	5.41	3.78
Gas mains mileage.................	1,000	**1,189**	**1,278**	**1,369**	**1,438**	**1,531**	**1,574**	**1,584**	**1,594**
Field and gathering.................	1,000	32	31	27	23	19	17	18	18
Transmission........................	1,000	292	297	297	297	308	303	302	301
Distribution.........................	1,000	865	950	1,046	1,118	1,204	1,254	1,265	1,276
Construction expenditures.......	Mil. dol.	**7,899**	**10,760**	**8,624**	**10,089**	**11,042**	**17,382**	**16,655**	**21,074**
Transmission........................	Mil. dol.	2,886	3,380	1,590	3,368	3,524	6,580	4,619	6,578
Distribution.........................	Mil. dol.	3,714	5,394	5,437	5,129	5,674	8,002	9,669	11,614
Production and storage...........	Mil. dol.	309	367	138	179	151	326	190	135
General.............................	Mil. dol.	770	1,441	1,273	1,070	1,185	1,904	1,602	1,928
Underground storage..............	Mil. dol.	219	177	185	343	509	570	575	819

[1] Annual average. [2] Excludes sales for resale. [3] For definition of Btu, see text, this section.

Source: American Gas Association, Washington, DC, *Annual Statistics* ©. See also <http://www.aga.org>.

Table 985. Gas Utility Industry—Customers, Sales, and Revenues by State: 2015

[65,612 represents 65,612,000. See headnote, Table 984. For definition of Btu, see text, this section]

State	Customers [1] (1,000) Total	Resi-dential	Sales [2] (tril. Btu) Total	Resi-dential	Revenues [2] (mil. dol.) Total	Resi-dential	State	Customers [1] (1,000) Total	Resi-dential	Sales [2] (tril. Btu) Total	Resi-dential	Revenues [2] (mil. dol.) Total	Resi-dential
U.S....	65,612	60,922	7,621	4,080	60,923	40,451	MO......	1,512	1,369	154	99	1,579	1,108
AL.......	840	769	99	34	860	462	MT......	304	269	30	19	240	155
AK.......	142	129	59	19	460	179	NE.......	500	458	56	31	407	270
AZ.......	1,258	1,201	68	36	899	588	NV......	867	824	59	38	613	438
AR.......	619	550	57	34	563	382	NH......	118	103	16	8	216	127
CA.......	10,966	10,540	570	393	5,633	4,336	NJ......	2,755	2,559	318	229	2,509	1,843
CO......	1,864	1,712	198	126	1,475	1,012	NM......	626	579	50	34	383	286
CT.......	588	530	105	51	1,037	613	NY......	3,863	3,595	454	332	4,353	3,458
DE.......	175	162	19	12	208	142	NC......	1,330	1,207	126	67	1,200	746
DC.......	137	131	14	10	159	118	ND......	163	141	35	11	200	86
FL.......	724	686	49	15	555	287	OH.....	709	671	80	59	683	529
GA.......	353	320	63	17	456	194	OK......	1,034	941	82	61	768	608
HI........	32	29	3	1	91	23	OR......	800	718	73	38	768	463
ID........	415	375	38	24	301	202	PA......	2,572	2,388	277	210	2,843	2,247
IL........	3,792	3,545	455	357	3,417	2,758	RI......	258	236	28	21	368	285
IN........	1,782	1,635	193	132	1,582	1,137	SC......	679	621	152	28	905	347
IA........	1,007	908	122	65	798	534	SD......	207	183	23	12	160	98
KS........	945	861	88	59	782	584	TN......	1,259	1,125	153	70	1,218	648
KY........	825	742	98	49	852	518	TX......	4,845	4,524	1,369	218	5,985	2,240
LA........	946	888	112	37	740	393	UT......	958	892	92	60	813	569
ME........	41	31	9	3	131	45	VT......	49	43	12	4	114	56
MD......	930	875	84	62	928	724	VA......	1,213	1,125	127	79	1,240	890
MA......	1,600	1,472	213	130	2,367	1,639	WA.....	1,239	1,134	123	74	1,310	849
MI.......	3,245	3,017	409	299	3,338	2,554	WV.....	371	338	42	26	383	260
MN......	1,637	1,497	229	121	1,732	1,033	WI......	1,895	1,722	249	131	1,678	1,083
MS.......	490	439	69	24	490	225	WY......	131	116	16	9	132	79

[1] Averages for the year. [2] Excludes sales for resale.

Source: American Gas Association, Washington, DC, *Annual Statistics* ©, annual. See also <http://www.aga.org>.

Table 986. Privately Owned Gas Utility Industry—Balance Sheet and Income Account: 1990 to 2015

[In millions of dollars (121,686 represents $121,686,000,000). The gas utility industry consists of pipeline and distribution companies. Excludes operations of companies distributing gas in bottles or tanks]

Item	1990	1995	2000	2005	2010	2012	2013	2014	2015
COMPOSITE BALANCE SHEET									
Assets, total......................	121,686	141,965	165,709	196,215	220,860	259,806	251,284	255,928	255,356
Total utility plant.......................	112,863	143,636	162,206	207,976	239,718	269,676	268,750	276,999	284,728
Depreciation and amortization........	49,483	62,723	69,366	91,794	92,012	93,668	94,583	99,388	101,995
Utility plant (net).......................	63,380	80,912	92,839	116,183	147,707	176,009	174,167	177,611	182,732
Investment and fund accounts........	23,872	26,489	10,846	16,331	7,132	13,408	13,137	14,518	11,939
Current and accrued assets..........	23,268	18,564	35,691	32,325	27,288	26,646	26,784	23,319	20,386
Deferred debits [1].......................	9,576	13,923	24,279	29,574	37,307	41,856	35,485	38,930	38,915
Liabilities, total....................	121,686	141,965	165,709	196,215	220,860	259,806	251,284	255,928	255,356
Capitalization, total.....................	74,958	90,581	96,079	120,949	133,414	153,903	152,236	153,555	153,776
Capital stock.....................	43,810	54,402	47,051	62,470	74,157	87,463	87,781	86,458	85,224
Long-term debts.....................	31,148	35,548	48,267	58,264	59,223	66,268	64,402	67,894	68,543
Current and accrued liabilities........	29,550	28,272	42,312	34,936	28,564	32,133	32,506	26,615	25,264
Deferred income taxes [2].............	11,360	14,393	17,157	24,937	34,401	45,821	44,651	39,598	43,028
Other liabilities and credits............	5,818	8,715	10,161	15,393	24,515	28,121	21,944	36,161	33,288
COMPOSITE INCOME ACCOUNT									
Operating revenues, total........	66,027	58,390	72,042	102,018	82,315	68,359	75,541	77,774	69,137
Minus: Operating expenses [3]........	60,137	50,760	64,988	89,385	71,761	59,258	64,767	66,990	58,343
Operation and maintenance.........	51,627	37,966	54,602	77,673	57,758	44,413	49,332	51,444	43,420
Federal, state, and local taxes......	4,957	6,182	6,163	7,513	7,569	8,303	8,543	8,396	7,604
Equals: Operating income...........	5,890	7,630	7,053	12,632	10,554	9,100	10,774	10,784	10,794
Utility operating income..............	6,077	7,848	7,166	12,812	11,045	9,972	11,342	11,040	11,347
Income before interest charges......	8,081	9,484	7,589	13,972	12,368	10,241	11,318	11,413	11,780
Net income...........................	4,410	5,139	4,245	9,777	8,619	7,096	7,739	8,024	8,532
Dividends............................	3,191	4,037	3,239	2,419	2,080	1,799	1,454	1,107	1,411

[1] Includes capital stock discount and expense and reacquired securities. [2] Includes reserves for deferred income taxes. [3] Includes expenses not shown separately.

Source: American Gas Association, Washington, DC, *Annual Statistics* ©. See also <http://www.aga.org>.

Table 987. Sewage Treatment Facilities and Employees: 2014 and 2015

[Data based on the North American Industry Classification System (NAICS), 2012; see text, Section 15]

State	Sewage treatment facilities (NAICS 22132)				State	Sewage treatment facilities (NAICS 22132)			
	2014		2015			2014		2015	
	Number of establishments	Paid employees	Number of establishments	Paid employees		Number of establishments	Paid employees	Number of establishments	Paid employees
U.S.	**707**	**6,415**	**695**	**6,171**	MO	18	(2)	20	89
AL	17	217	18	254	MT	5	(2)	6	41
AK	2	(1)	3	(1)	NE	2	(2)	2	(2)
AZ	19	(3)	21	133	NV	1	(1)	1	(1)
AR	4	(1)	4	18	NH	5	(1)	5	21
CA	43	(4)	45	330	NJ	14	105	12	83
CO	10	(2)	8	44	NM	5	35	4	37
CT	13	276	13	99	NY	27	301	27	328
DE	4	57	4	59	NC	25	123	21	108
DC	(NA)	(NA)	(NA)	(NA)	ND	1	(1)	1	(1)
FL	58	588	53	574	OH	13	(3)	13	227
GA	13	121	13	61	OK	21	213	19	206
HI	18	(2)	18	91	OR	8	(2)	7	37
ID	7	(2)	5	33	PA	45	446	46	485
IL	33	260	32	262	RI	5	(2)	5	(2)
IN	35	441	36	397	SC	7	40	7	49
IA	7	(2)	6	(2)	SD	(NA)	(NA)	(NA)	(NA)
KS	2	(2)	2	(2)	TN	10	96	10	97
KY	8	(2)	7	(2)	TX	70	388	69	379
LA	28	345	26	356	UT	(NA)	(NA)	(NA)	(NA)
ME	1	(1)	1	(1)	VT	2	(1)	2	(1)
MD	6	45	7	71	VA	6	28	7	42
MA	17	(4)	17	311	WA	4	(2)	4	67
MI	23	177	24	145	WV	10	69	10	61
MN	10	(2)	10	90	WI	6	(1)	6	14
MS	18	(3)	17	218	WY	1	(1)	1	(1)

NA Not available. [1] 0 to 19 employees. [2] 20 to 99 employees. [3] 100 to 249 employees. [4] 250 to 499 employees.

Source: U.S. Census Bureau, County Business Patterns, "Geography Area Series: County Business Patterns," <http://factfinder.census.gov/>, accessed April 2017. See also <https://www.census.gov/programs-surveys/cbp.html>.

Section 20
Construction and Housing

This section presents data on the construction industry and on various indicators of its activity and costs; on housing units and their characteristics and occupants; and on the characteristics and vacancy rates for commercial buildings.

The principal source of these data is the U.S. Census Bureau, which issues a variety of current publications, as well as data from the decennial census. Current construction statistics compiled by the Census Bureau appear in its *New Residential Construction* and *New Residential Sales* press releases and websites at <www.census.gov/construction/nrc/> and <www.census.gov/construction/nrs/>. *Construction Spending* presents data on all types of construction. Reports of the censuses of construction industries (see below) are also issued on various topics.

Other Census Bureau publications include the quarterly *Housing Vacancies and Homeownership*, the quarterly *Survey of Market Absorption*, the biennial *American Housing Survey* (formerly *Annual Housing Survey*), and other reports of the censuses of housing and of construction industries.

Other sources include Dodge Data & Analytics, New York, NY, which presents national and state data on construction contracts; the National Association of Home Builders with data on housing starts; the NATIONAL ASSOCIATION OF REALTORS®, which presents data on existing home sales; the Bureau of Economic Analysis, which presents data on residential fixed assets; the U.S. Energy Information Administration, which provides data on commercial buildings through its periodic sample surveys; and the Federal Financial Institutions Examination Council, which provide data on home loans and home improvement loans.

Censuses and surveys—Censuses of the construction industry were first conducted by the Census Bureau for 1929, 1935, and 1939; beginning in 1967, a census has been taken every 5 years (through 2012, for years ending in "2" and "7"). Release of data from the 2012 Economic Census was completed in 2016. The construction sector of the Economic Census covers all employer establishments primarily engaged in (1) building construction by general contractors or operative builders; (2) heavy (nonbuilding) construction by general contractors; and (3) construction by special trade contractors. This sector includes construction management and land subdividers and developers. The 2007 census was conducted in accordance with the 2007 North American Industrial Classification System (NAICS). See text, Section 15, Business Enterprise.

The *American Housing Survey* (*Current Housing Reports* Series H-150 and H-170), which began in 1973, provided an annual and ongoing series of data on selected housing and demographic characteristics until 1983. In 1984, the name of the survey was changed from the *Annual Housing Survey*. Currently, national data are collected every other year, and data for selected metropolitan areas are collected on a rotating basis. The supplemental sample of housing units is selected for 25 metropolitan units and combined with the national sample in order to

produce metropolitan estimates using the national survey. All samples represent a cross section of the housing stock in their respective areas. Estimates are subject to both sampling and nonsampling errors; caution should therefore be used in making comparisons between years.

Data on residential mortgages were collected continuously from 1890 to 1970, except 1930, as part of the decennial census by the Census Bureau. Since 1973, mortgage status data have been presented in the *American Housing Survey*. Data on mortgage activity are covered in Section 25, Banking and Finance.

Housing units—In general, a housing unit is a house, an apartment, a group of rooms or a single room occupied or intended for occupancy as separate living quarters; that is, the occupants live separately from any other individual in the building, and there is direct access from the outside or through a common hall. Transient accommodations, barracks for workers, and institutional-type quarters are not counted as housing units.

Statistical reliability—For a discussion of statistical collection and estimation, sampling procedures, and measures of statistical reliability applicable to Census Bureau data, see Appendix III.

Table 988. Construction—Establishments, Employees, and Payroll by Kind of Business (NAICS Basis): 2014 and 2015

[5,705 represents 5,705,000. Covers establishments with payroll. Excludes most government employees, railroad employees, and self-employed persons. For statement on methodology, see Appendix III]

Kind of business	2012 NAICS code [1]	Establishments 2014	Establishments 2015	Paid employees [2] (1,000) 2014	Paid employees [2] (1,000) 2015	Annual payroll (mil. dol.) 2014	Annual payroll (mil. dol.) 2015
Construction................................	**23**	**667,099**	**682,390**	**5,705**	**6,008**	**319,443**	**348,599**
Construction of buildings............................	236	200,846	206,286	1,181	1,252	68,418	75,878
Residential building construction...................	2361	159,792	164,519	598	635	28,936	32,280
New single-family housing construction (except for-sale builders).........................	236115	51,462	50,262	176	179	7,886	8,459
New multifamily housing construction (except for-sale builders).........................	236116	2,788	2,818	31	33	2,199	2,430
New housing for-sale builders....................	236117	12,701	12,878	96	104	7,152	7,994
Residential remodelers...........................	236118	92,841	98,561	296	319	11,698	13,398
Nonresidential building construction..............	2362	41,054	41,767	583	616	39,481	43,598
Industrial building construction....................	23621	3,133	3,202	82	88	5,183	5,715
Commercial and institutional building construction...................................	23622	37,921	38,565	500	528	34,298	37,883
Heavy and civil engineering construction...........	237	38,724	38,959	899	922	61,917	65,266
Utility system construction.........................	2371	19,142	19,585	533	549	35,893	37,218
Water and sewer line and related structures....	23711	11,093	11,017	151	159	9,111	9,845
Oil and gas pipeline and related structures......	23712	2,090	2,166	168	178	12,718	13,260
Power and communication line and related structures.................................	23713	5,959	6,402	214	211	14,064	14,113
Land subdivision.................................	2372	5,354	5,239	25	25	1,587	1,742
Highway, street, and bridge construction..........	2373	9,920	9,804	260	261	18,863	20,429
Other heavy and civil engineering construction...	2379	4,308	4,331	82	87	5,575	5,877
Specialty trade contractors..........................	238	427,529	437,145	3,625	3,835	189,108	207,455
Foundation, structure, and building exterior contractors....................................	2381	85,680	87,703	709	759	33,588	37,888
Poured concrete foundation and structures contractors....................................	23811	18,853	19,120	185	198	9,206	10,430
Structural steel and precast concrete contractors....................................	23812	3,276	3,332	63	69	3,503	4,069
Framing contractors..............................	23813	10,319	10,650	66	71	2,451	2,755
Masonry contractors.............................	23814	18,086	18,263	124	130	5,456	6,090
Glass and glazing contractors....................	23815	5,069	5,305	48	53	2,499	2,866
Roofing contractors..............................	23816	17,457	18,193	149	158	6,869	7,739
Siding contractors................................	23817	7,275	7,491	30	31	1,191	1,307
Other foundation, structure, and building exterior contractors...........................	23819	5,345	5,349	45	49	2,413	2,633
Building equipment contractors....................	2382	172,604	176,142	1,739	1,824	98,818	106,922
Electrical contractors.............................	23821	70,350	71,848	733	762	41,832	44,521
Plumbing, heating, and air-conditioning contractors....................................	23822	95,201	97,181	883	934	48,694	53,521
Other building equipment contractors............	23829	7,053	7,113	122	128	8,293	8,880
Building finishing contractors.......................	2383	104,385	106,961	663	705	28,797	32,168
Drywall and insulation contractors................	23831	17,270	17,857	202	216	9,353	10,526
Painting and wall covering contractors...........	23832	31,607	31,943	174	184	7,185	7,859
Flooring contractors..............................	23833	14,091	14,601	64	68	2,746	3,078
Tile and terrazzo contractors.....................	23834	8,893	9,160	48	50	1,953	2,177
Finish carpentry contractors......................	23835	26,024	26,795	116	125	4,901	5,614
Other building finishing contractors..............	23839	6,500	6,605	60	62	2,658	2,914
Other specialty trade contractors..................	2389	64,860	66,339	514	547	27,905	30,478
Site preparation contractors......................	23891	33,816	34,413	301	318	16,835	18,234
All other specialty trade contractors..............	23899	31,044	31,926	213	229	11,070	12,243

[1] Data based on North American Industry Classification System (NAICS) 2012. See text, Section 15. [2] Employees on the payroll for the pay period including March 12.

Source: U.S. Census Bureau, County Business Patterns, "Geography Area Series: County Business Patterns," <http://factfinder.census.gov/>, accessed April 2017. See also <https://www.census.gov/programs-surveys/cbp.html>.

Table 989. Value of New Construction Put in Place: 1980 to 2016

[In millions of dollars (273,936 represents $273,936,000,000). Represents value of construction put in place during year; differs from building permit and construction contract data in timing and coverage. Includes installed cost of normal building service equipment and selected types of industrial production equipment (largely site fabricated). Excludes cost of shipbuilding, land, and most types of machinery and equipment. For methodology, see Appendix III]

Year	Total	Private Total	Private Residential buildings	Private Non-residential	Public Total	Public Federal	Public State and local
1980.................	273,936	210,290	100,381	109,909	63,646	9,642	54,004
1990.................	476,778	369,300	191,103	178,197	107,478	12,099	95,379
2000.................	802,756	621,431	346,138	275,293	181,325	14,168	167,157
2005.................	1,116,811	882,651	624,574	258,077	234,160	17,300	216,860
2010.................	809,256	505,290	242,035	263,255	303,966	31,133	272,833
2012.................	850,455	571,145	269,784	301,360	279,311	26,933	252,378
2013.................	906,351	635,669	323,381	312,288	270,682	23,727	246,955
2014.................	1,005,628	729,500	369,793	359,707	276,128	22,416	253,712
2015.................	1,113,648	823,303	422,143	401,160	290,345	22,455	267,890
2016.................	1,185,683	898,686	466,592	432,093	286,997	22,672	264,325

Source: U.S. Census Bureau, "Construction Spending," <http://www.census.gov/construction/c30/c30index.html>, accessed September 2017.

Table 990. New Privately Owned Housing Units Authorized by State: 2015 and 2016

[1,182.6 represents 1,182,600. 2016 data is forecast. Based on the 2014 Universe, which includes approximately 20,100 places in the United States that have building permit systems in 2014]

State	Housing units (1,000) 2015	2016 Total	2016 1-unit [1]	Valuation (mil. dol.) 2015	2016 Total	2016 1-unit [1]	State	Housing units (1,000) 2015	2016 Total	2016 1-unit [1]	Valuation (mil. dol.) 2015	2016 Total	2016 1-unit [1]
U.S.	1,182.6	1,206.6	750.8	223,611	237,102	182,207	MO	18.3	19.0	11.3	3,146	3,283	2,510
AL	14.1	15.0	11.7	2,417	2,723	2,342	MT	4.8	4.8	3.1	827	760	597
AK	1.3	1.5	1.0	325	369	302	NE	8.1	8.1	5.1	1,317	1,306	1,049
AZ	28.9	35.6	24.9	6,986	8,045	6,645	NV	14.1	18.0	11.4	2,142	2,872	2,334
AR	8.5	9.5	6.8	1,380	1,563	1,362	NH	3.8	3.8	2.7	737	760	617
CA	98.2	102.4	50.3	22,637	24,045	15,202	NJ	30.6	26.8	9.6	4,052	4,029	2,206
CO	31.9	39.0	21.6	7,533	8,929	6,676	NM	4.6	4.9	3.8	872	907	813
CT	6.1	5.5	2.5	1,282	1,197	797	NY	74.6	33.7	10.2	10,826	6,045	3,040
DE	5.2	5.8	4.7	642	722	619	NC	54.8	60.6	43.7	9,708	11,091	9,611
DC	5.0	4.7	0.3	495	511	76	ND	6.3	4.0	2.4	953	714	550
FL	109.9	116.2	75.1	23,439	25,864	20,335	OH	20.0	22.8	15.2	3,983	4,589	3,815
GA	45.5	51.7	36.5	7,955	9,381	7,684	OK	11.5	12.1	9.2	2,216	2,155	1,939
HI	5.4	3.4	2.0	1,582	1,266	820	OR	17.5	19.6	11.0	3,592	3,944	2,915
ID	10.0	12.2	9.7	1,934	2,368	2,140	PA	22.9	23.3	16.5	4,406	4,516	3,734
IL	19.6	22.6	10.2	4,137	4,388	2,720	RI	1.0	1.2	0.9	212	237	212
IN	18.5	18.7	14.1	3,737	3,876	3,418	SC	31.0	32.2	26.3	6,243	6,724	6,233
IA	12.1	14.3	8.2	2,243	2,661	1,934	SD	4.5	5.7	3.2	741	884	634
KS	8.6	9.8	5.2	1,646	1,770	1,336	TN	32.2	36.2	24.6	5,596	6,581	5,372
KY	10.6	12.7	7.3	1,468	1,727	1,368	TX	175.4	165.9	106.5	29,087	29,242	23,459
LA	13.8	14.5	12.5	2,777	2,767	2,561	UT	18.3	22.7	15.2	3,851	4,808	3,884
ME	3.7	4.0	3.3	683	777	699	VT	2.0	1.8	1.0	334	315	239
MD	17.1	17.0	11.1	3,081	3,167	2,354	VA	28.5	31.1	21.6	4,724	5,473	4,512
MA	17.4	16.3	7.6	3,981	3,946	2,377	WA	40.4	44.1	22.5	8,519	9,116	6,478
MI	18.2	20.4	14.5	3,850	4,272	3,575	WV	2.8	2.5	2.0	417	397	358
MN	19.5	21.4	12.1	4,135	4,593	3,328	WI	16.8	19.3	11.0	3,078	3,733	2,814
MS	6.8	6.9	6.1	1,078	1,126	1,064	WY	1.9	1.7	1.5	608	570	547

[1] The 1-unit structure category is a single-family home. It includes fully detached, semi-detached (semi-attached, side-by-side), row houses, and townhouses.

Source: U.S. Census Bureau, Construction Reports, "Building Permits Survey," <http://www.census.gov/construction/bps/>, accessed September 2017.

Table 991. Construction Contracts Started—Value of Construction and Floor Space of Buildings by Class of Construction: 2012 to 2016

[492.9 represents $492,900,000,000. Dollar value data includes new construction, additions, and alterations. Square footage data includes new construction and additions; alterations which create no net new square footage are not included]

Year	Total	Residential buildings	Nonresidential buildings Total	Commercial [1]	Manufacturing	Education [2]	Health	Public	Religious	Social and recreational	Miscellaneous	Nonbuilding construction
VALUE (bil. dol.)												
2012	492.9	166.6	160.2	55.3	13.1	43.3	22.9	8.7	1.9	8.6	6.4	166.1
2013	547.5	211.0	179.2	67.7	19.4	43.6	22.0	6.6	1.8	11.4	6.6	157.3
2014	605.7	233.8	224.7	83.9	35.8	50.8	23.0	7.7	1.7	13.9	7.8	147.2
2015	680.3	273.3	223.5	91.3	25.0	53.5	22.8	7.8	2.1	13.6	7.3	183.6
2016	709.3	294.8	243.8	108.4	19.2	54.2	25.7	7.9	1.6	17.6	9.1	170.8
FLOOR SPACE (mil. sq. ft.)												
2012	2,262	1,481	781	422	62	136	72	24	13	33	19	(X)
2013	2,715	1,839	876	535	55	131	73	16	11	36	19	(X)
2014	2,960	1,950	1,010	622	80	149	68	16	10	45	20	(X)
2015	3,247	2,229	1,017	642	70	148	71	14	10	41	21	(X)
2016	3,475	2,418	1,057	690	64	142	75	15	8	45	19	(X)

X Not applicable. [1] Includes nonindustrial warehouses. [2] Includes science facilities.

Source: Dodge Data & Analytics (copyright) 1-800-591-4462.

Table 992. Construction Contracts Started—Value by Region: 2012 to 2016

[In millions of dollars (492,872 represents $492,872,000,000). Includes new construction, additions and alterations]

Region	2012	2013	2014	2015	2016 Total [1]	2016 Residential	2016 Nonresidential
U.S.	492,872	547,477	605,671	680,332	709,337	294,775	243,776
New England	19,761	24,331	22,544	27,276	29,200	11,053	12,277
Middle Atlantic	54,093	63,824	70,693	84,215	82,196	27,566	35,141
East North Central	52,067	57,810	64,564	68,669	75,058	26,993	26,847
West North Central	38,686	45,045	43,902	47,952	52,013	18,024	15,914
South Atlantic	108,160	109,530	124,996	136,138	156,104	79,119	43,910
East South Central	24,996	26,775	28,314	29,518	33,972	14,653	11,418
West South Central	86,025	97,176	110,648	138,924	112,085	43,389	38,106
Mountain	40,760	45,010	53,776	56,225	61,438	30,576	18,373
Pacific	68,323	77,974	86,235	91,416	107,272	43,402	41,790

[1] Includes nonbuilding construction, not shown separately.

Source: Dodge Data & Analytics (copyright) 1-800-591-4462.

Table 993. Value of Private Construction Put in Place: 2000 to 2016

[In millions of dollars (621,431 represents $621,431,000,000). Represents value of construction put in place during year; differs from building permit and construction contract data in timing and coverage. See Appendix III]

Type of construction	2000	2005	2010	2011	2012	2013	2014	2015	2016
Total construction [1]	**621,431**	**882,651**	**505,290**	**501,925**	**571,145**	**635,669**	**729,500**	**823,303**	**898,686**
Residential	346,138	624,574	242,035	244,122	269,784	323,381	369,793	422,143	466,592
New single family	236,788	433,510	112,569	108,178	132,015	170,768	193,600	221,128	242,476
New multifamily	28,259	47,297	14,686	15,037	22,510	31,500	41,553	52,531	60,517
Improvements [2]	81,091	143,767	114,780	120,907	115,260	121,113	134,639	148,484	163,600
Nonresidential	275,293	258,077	263,255	257,803	301,360	312,288	359,707	401,160	432,093
Lodging	16,304	12,666	11,201	8,395	10,197	13,028	16,306	21,324	26,483
Office [1]	52,407	37,276	24,368	23,738	27,448	30,133	38,864	47,449	59,263
General	49,637	32,962	22,203	21,231	25,111	28,419	36,958	45,675	57,012
Financial	2,689	4,285	2,122	2,284	1,945	1,597	1,867	1,629	1,848
Commercial	64,055	66,584	37,154	39,153	44,312	50,947	60,890	63,404	73,457
Automotive [1]	5,967	5,614	3,546	4,270	4,834	4,639	4,830	5,527	7,119
Sales	1,629	2,834	1,355	1,816	2,079	1,956	2,117	2,123	3,063
Service/parts	3,009	1,805	1,679	1,977	2,221	2,313	2,047	2,646	3,065
Parking	1,330	975	511	478	534	370	666	758	990
Food/beverage	8,786	7,795	4,605	5,268	5,845	6,594	7,230	7,212	8,115
Food	4,792	3,128	2,027	2,840	2,430	2,937	3,447	3,103	3,476
Dining/drinking	2,935	4,078	1,911	1,650	2,436	2,141	2,170	2,574	2,899
Fast food	1,058	590	667	779	979	1,516	1,613	1,535	1,740
Multi-retail [1]	14,911	22,750	12,486	13,361	14,904	16,686	19,543	19,629	21,295
General merchandise	5,100	6,740	3,794	3,368	3,773	2,942	2,792	2,331	2,459
Shopping center	6,803	12,462	6,725	6,748	7,934	9,806	12,946	13,433	14,739
Shopping mall	2,523	2,631	1,332	2,356	2,288	2,938	2,868	2,988	3,369
Other commercial [1]	13,537	11,744	4,220	3,720	3,934	4,786	4,586	5,205	6,437
Drug store	1,682	1,315	1,077	721	765	893	943	531	515
Building supply store	2,592	2,416	772	611	493	506	495	596	563
Other stores	8,136	7,075	1,741	1,743	2,069	2,468	2,409	2,866	4,205
Warehouse [1]	14,822	12,827	5,661	6,543	7,047	8,766	13,698	16,552	21,178
General commercial	13,511	11,468	5,229	6,219	6,575	8,107	12,894	15,478	19,210
Ministorage	1,263	1,311	401	241	365	472	589	954	1,912
Farm	5,988	5,854	6,637	5,991	7,748	9,476	11,005	9,280	9,314
Health care	19,455	28,495	29,552	28,906	31,429	29,696	28,885	30,518	30,183
Hospital	10,183	18,250	21,528	20,483	21,223	19,199	17,680	19,348	19,103
Medical building	5,066	8,031	5,276	5,429	6,415	7,015	7,167	6,983	7,424
Special care	4,206	2,213	2,748	2,995	3,791	3,482	4,039	4,188	3,655
Educational [1]	11,683	12,788	13,418	14,081	16,625	16,919	16,583	17,559	19,895
Preschool	770	516	492	349	396	420	462	353	498
Primary/secondary	2,948	2,718	2,585	2,973	2,795	2,997	3,599	3,615	3,764
Higher education [1]	6,333	6,946	8,322	8,477	10,809	10,868	10,501	11,834	13,212
Instructional	3,058	3,556	4,993	4,658	5,786	4,928	4,944	5,394	6,107
Dormitory	1,356	1,537	1,654	2,165	2,902	3,924	3,559	3,931	4,618
Sports/recreation	645	821	790	660	709	981	974	1,056	1,064
Other educational [1]	1,318	2,294	1,687	1,869	2,206	2,226	1,656	1,488	1,986
Gallery/museum	920	1,745	1,522	1,468	1,407	1,486	1,224	1,054	1,532
Religious	8,030	7,715	5,237	4,205	3,819	3,565	3,380	3,568	3,501
House of worship	5,656	5,992	4,214	3,256	3,143	3,055	2,853	3,012	3,043
Other religious	2,347	1,723	1,023	950	675	510	527	556	458
Auxiliary building	1,280	1,251	795	651	521	419	391	466	345
Public safety	423	408	241	205	103	125	227	224	104
Amusement and recreation [1]	8,768	7,507	6,483	6,744	6,217	6,916	7,719	9,855	12,078
Theme/amusement park	747	200	353	472	512	670	943	1,225	1,930
Sports	1,068	807	1,596	1,096	1,043	1,336	1,889	3,456	4,493
Fitness	1,152	1,425	1,150	1,067	1,251	1,310	1,182	1,157	1,212
Performance/meeting center	732	1,072	565	510	517	673	657	566	753
Social center	2,368	1,626	914	662	614	789	757	868	846
Movie theater/studio	1,461	1,248	426	510	362	618	717	832	1,031
Transportation [1]	6,879	7,124	9,894	9,537	10,883	11,029	12,151	13,575	12,951
Air	1,804	748	259	535	1,044	921	729	828	1,873
Land	4,907	6,214	9,503	8,944	9,810	9,988	11,035	12,480	10,976
Railroad	4,263	5,816	8,973	8,546	9,279	9,272	10,225	11,653	9,872
Communication	18,799	18,846	17,689	17,536	15,952	17,619	17,105	21,505	21,880
Power	29,344	29,210	66,117	64,262	86,402	81,278	98,206	91,503	96,748
Electricity	23,374	22,678	48,972	50,291	68,967	54,411	69,970	67,123	73,037
Gas	4,891	5,239	8,297	10,357	10,317	10,897	11,033	12,546	11,956
Oil	1,003	1,293	8,848	3,614	7,118	15,970	17,203	11,834	11,755
Sewage and waste disposal	508	240	439	520	597	356	241	369	354
Water supply	714	326	717	635	373	591	573	539	192
Manufacturing	37,583	28,413	40,607	39,768	46,774	49,863	58,142	79,287	74,669
Food/beverage/tobacco	3,985	4,446	4,000	4,792	4,380	4,934	6,387	6,833	6,650
Textile/apparel/leather/furniture	561	487	591	301	171	377	799	605	960
Wood	483	933	438	369	335	732	619	335	341
Paper/printing/publishing	1,327	1,181	634	684	1,190	1,016	633	827	838
Petroleum/coal	1,255	734	11,612	5,453	4,777	4,036	5,048	4,274	4,145
Chemical	3,798	6,263	7,580	7,345	10,848	15,483	22,744	36,616	34,764
Plastic/rubber	1,645	834	728	947	1,686	1,537	2,173	3,200	3,385
Nonmetallic mineral	1,898	1,105	1,150	896	857	916	944	1,158	1,236
Primary metal	1,976	793	4,738	3,130	4,691	4,487	3,836	5,943	4,147
Fabricated metal	2,148	664	1,104	1,593	1,726	1,484	819	1,170	2,101
Machinery	864	872	1,030	1,373	1,631	1,442	1,163	1,855	1,432
Computer/electronic/electrical	6,392	4,039	4,614	8,815	9,592	7,312	4,962	3,376	1,923
Transportation equipment	6,318	3,518	1,962	3,260	3,869	5,132	6,988	12,136	11,831

[1] Includes other types of construction, not shown separately. [2] Private residential improvement does not include expenditures on rental, vacant, or seasonal properties.

Source: U.S. Census Bureau, "Construction Spending," <http://www.census.gov/construction/c30/c30index.html>, accessed September 2017.

Table 994. Value of State and Local Government Construction Put in Place: 2000 to 2016

[In millions of dollars (167,157 represents $167,157,000,000)]

Type of construction	2000	2005	2010	2011	2012	2013	2014	2015	2016
Total construction [1]	**167,157**	**216,860**	**272,833**	**254,753**	**252,378**	**246,955**	**253,712**	**267,890**	**264,325**
Residential	2,962	4,047	7,576	5,962	4,672	4,537	4,128	5,701	5,802
Multifamily	2,945	3,740	6,536	5,182	3,935	3,574	3,444	4,907	5,168
Nonresidential	164,196	212,813	265,256	248,791	247,705	242,418	249,585	262,189	258,523
Office	4,494	5,211	8,317	7,440	6,055	5,220	5,424	5,873	5,544
Commercial [1]	1,820	1,882	1,456	1,682	1,412	1,119	898	1,404	1,630
Automotive	1,233	1,490	769	840	942	696	499	844	670
Parking	1,143	1,357	675	680	799	621	443	800	543
Warehouse	330	218	286	319	171	133	184	244	370
Health care	2,829	5,059	6,193	7,009	7,040	6,928	6,174	5,440	5,300
Hospital	1,949	3,429	4,789	5,317	5,522	5,439	4,762	4,190	3,829
Medical building	490	1,168	747	906	982	970	990	808	874
Special care	390	463	657	785	536	520	422	442	596
Educational [1]	46,818	65,750	71,948	67,965	65,622	60,027	61,176	65,346	67,788
Primary/secondary [1]	33,764	44,184	44,559	40,760	39,389	36,050	35,936	38,022	41,320
Elementary	12,272	14,251	13,171	10,795	11,195	10,580	11,887	10,433	12,447
Middle/junior high	5,820	9,069	7,029	8,116	7,557	7,730	6,781	7,458	8,685
High	13,326	19,892	24,055	21,389	20,276	17,339	16,475	19,733	19,469
Higher education [1]	10,749	18,033	24,384	24,315	23,328	21,790	22,722	24,895	23,975
Instructional	6,317	9,275	14,138	13,373	11,931	11,755	11,948	13,365	13,365
Parking	514	1,013	593	717	532	398	391	548	447
Administration	294	387	357	433	430	409	528	588	659
Dormitory	1,078	2,918	3,371	3,965	4,435	3,845	3,468	4,109	4,125
Library	308	588	662	568	322	157	279	643	400
Student union/cafeteria	322	880	1,147	1,227	1,464	1,378	1,412	1,241	1,215
Sports/recreation	966	1,769	2,398	2,358	2,356	2,594	2,901	2,844	2,529
Infrastructure	835	1,138	1,381	1,461	1,735	1,065	1,683	1,549	1,200
Other educational [1]	1,645	2,735	2,223	1,831	2,054	1,500	2,062	1,895	1,761
Library/archive	976	2,098	1,386	1,159	1,385	1,016	1,079	1,143	1,278
Public safety [1]	5,854	6,013	7,586	7,245	7,641	6,592	6,414	5,829	5,594
Correctional	4,754	3,958	4,624	4,929	5,126	4,395	4,249	3,612	3,411
Detention	3,907	2,936	2,789	3,166	3,306	2,554	2,171	1,981	1,958
Police/sheriff	848	1,022	1,836	1,762	1,820	1,841	2,079	1,631	1,453
Other public safety	1,100	2,055	2,962	2,316	2,515	2,197	2,165	2,217	2,182
Fire/rescue	994	1,675	1,747	1,477	1,627	1,403	1,496	1,553	1,642
Amusement and recreation [1]	7,583	7,340	9,668	8,542	8,876	8,081	8,713	9,954	9,998
Sports	2,289	1,587	1,819	1,223	1,127	1,289	1,856	1,749	1,609
Performance/meeting center	2,075	1,921	1,841	1,805	1,804	1,474	1,780	1,588	1,687
Convention center	1,397	1,350	1,119	1,112	1,316	917	1,154	864	856
Social center	1,152	1,006	1,561	1,054	1,008	1,127	887	1,102	1,240
Neighborhood center	886	866	1,395	887	890	1,050	774	1,040	1,037
Park/camp	1,930	2,728	4,259	4,277	4,825	4,098	4,070	5,230	5,221
Transportation	13,000	16,256	26,493	23,340	24,797	25,871	27,757	29,087	26,902
Air [1]	6,700	8,993	11,897	9,867	9,799	9,768	10,821	10,828	10,274
Passenger terminal	2,930	3,310	6,503	5,681	4,992	5,310	4,922	5,005	5,819
Runway	3,196	4,861	4,710	3,760	4,313	3,780	4,980	5,244	3,850
Land [1]	5,165	5,936	12,954	11,811	13,047	13,984	15,106	16,597	15,118
Passenger terminal	1,253	907	3,380	3,223	2,978	2,946	3,666	4,558	4,355
Mass transit	1,484	3,208	6,447	5,846	7,033	7,189	7,161	7,559	6,712
Railroad	1,471	552	751	662	850	1,459	1,695	1,641	1,131
Water	1,136	1,327	1,642	1,661	1,952	2,118	1,829	1,662	1,510
Dock/marina	863	930	1,115	1,247	1,502	1,583	1,360	1,232	1,186
Dry dock/marine terminal	236	397	527	414	450	536	469	430	323
Power [1]	5,501	8,320	10,770	9,492	9,794	10,951	10,732	9,822	7,666
Electrical	5,257	7,091	9,972	7,886	7,136	8,334	8,946	8,551	6,698
Distribution	2,087	1,786	3,253	2,486	2,046	2,151	3,120	2,607	2,701
Highway and street	51,574	63,157	81,309	78,369	79,722	80,610	84,014	89,719	90,303
Pavement	37,929	45,177	51,433	47,954	47,566	46,282	50,509	53,266	53,986
Lighting	856	1,232	1,975	1,754	1,738	1,525	1,221	1,512	1,829
Retaining wall	1,099	675	1,250	1,033	845	895	878	1,048	819
Tunnel	894	373	810	873	1,359	1,477	1,038	825	1,186
Bridge	9,302	14,244	24,222	25,545	27,050	28,811	29,234	31,576	30,740
Toll/weigh	325	320	214	238	338	129	137	209	309
Maintenance building	293	96	275	237	187	373	282	392	431
Rest facility/streetscape	878	1,042	1,130	735	640	1,119	715	892	1,003
Sewage and waste disposal	14,000	18,336	24,555	21,196	20,946	21,037	21,870	23,182	21,795
Sewage/dry waste [1]	9,338	11,717	13,234	11,975	12,077	11,591	12,517	13,846	12,974
Plant	2,765	3,369	3,755	3,260	3,022	2,376	2,565	2,813	2,469
Line/pump station	6,326	8,243	9,375	8,619	8,956	9,072	9,815	10,855	10,286
Waste water	4,663	6,620	11,321	9,222	8,869	9,446	9,353	9,336	8,820
Plant	3,229	5,231	9,428	7,836	7,414	7,861	7,354	6,980	6,667
Line/drain	1,434	1,389	1,893	1,386	1,455	1,585	1,999	2,356	2,154
Water supply	9,528	13,483	14,420	13,393	12,746	12,919	12,731	12,560	12,231
Plant	3,067	4,943	5,683	5,391	4,833	4,358	4,221	4,379	4,023
Well	378	360	383	389	336	480	513	290	292
Line	4,644	6,234	6,246	5,867	5,631	5,777	5,816	6,026	5,625
Pump station	625	776	970	744	633	734	817	624	819
Reservoir	266	502	393	427	639	804	618	386	712
Tank/tower	548	668	744	574	674	765	747	855	760
Conservation and development [1]	933	1,752	2,035	2,289	2,225	2,500	3,071	3,095	3,052
Dam/levee	303	405	783	874	727	822	1,096	946	936
Breakwater/jetty	270	726	675	649	853	1,022	1,098	1,383	1,359
Dredging	140	211	173	198	184	214	259	298	289

[1] Includes other types of construction, not shown separately.

Source: U.S. Census Bureau, "Construction Spending," <http://www.census.gov/construction/c30/c30index.html>, accessed September 2017.

Table 995. Construction of New Privately Owned Housing Units Started: 1960 to 2016

[In thousands of units (1,252 represents 1,252,000). For composition of regions, see map inside front cover]

Year	Total	1 unit structures	Northeast	Midwest	South	West
1960	1,252	995	221	292	429	309
1970	1,434	813	218	294	612	311
1980	1,292	852	125	218	643	306
1990	1,193	895	131	253	479	329
1995	1,354	1,076	118	290	615	331
1996	1,477	1,161	132	322	662	361
1997	1,474	1,134	137	304	670	363
1998	1,617	1,271	149	331	743	395
1999	1,641	1,302	156	347	746	392
2000	1,569	1,231	155	318	714	383
2001	1,603	1,273	149	330	732	391
2002	1,705	1,359	158	350	782	416
2003	1,848	1,499	163	374	839	472
2004	1,956	1,611	175	356	909	516
2005	2,068	1,716	190	357	996	525
2006	1,801	1,465	167	280	910	444
2007	1,355	1,046	143	210	681	321
2008	906	622	121	135	453	196
2009	554	445	62	97	278	117
2010	587	471	72	98	298	120
2011	609	431	68	101	308	133
2012	781	535	80	128	398	175
2013	925	618	97	150	464	215
2014	1,003	648	110	163	496	235
2015	1,112	715	138	153	556	266
2016	1,174	782	116	182	585	291

Source: U.S. Census Bureau, "New Residential Construction," <http://www.census.gov/construction/nrc/historical_data/>, accessed June 2017.

Table 996. Characteristics of New Privately Owned Single-Family Houses Completed: 2000 to 2016

[Percent distribution, except as noted (1,242 represents 1,242,000). Data are percent distribution of characteristics for all houses completed (includes new houses completed, houses built for sale completed, contractor-built and owner-built houses completed, and houses completed for rent). Percents exclude houses for which characteristics specified were not reported]

Characteristic	2000	2010	2015	2016	Characteristic	2000	2010	2015	2016
Total houses (1,000)	1,242	496	648	738	Bedrooms	100	100	100	100
					2 or less	11	13	10	10
Construction type	100	100	100	100	3	54	52	42	45
Site built	94	95	97	97	4 or more	35	35	47	46
Modular	3	2	2	2	Bathrooms	100	100	100	100
Other	3	2	1	1	1-1/2 or less	7	8	4	3
Exterior wall material	100	100	100	100	2	39	36	29	31
Brick	20	23	23	22	2-1/2 or more	34	32	29	29
Wood	14	8	5	5	3 baths or more	20	25	38	37
Stucco	17	17	24	24	Heating fuel	100	100	100	100
Vinyl siding	39	36	27	27	Gas	70	54	60	60
Aluminum siding	1	(NA)	(NA)	(NA)	Electricity	27	43	39	39
Fiber cement	(NA)	13	19	20	Oil	3	1	(NA)	(NA)
Other	8	2	2	2	Other	1	2	1	1
Floor area	100	100	100	100	Heating system	100	100	100	100
Under 1,400 sq. ft	14	13	8	7	Warm air furnace	71	56	56	56
1,400 to 1,799 sq. ft	22	19	13	15	Electric heat pump	23	38	41	41
1,800 to 2,399 sq. ft	29	27	26	27	Other	6	5	3	3
2,400 to 2,999 sq. ft	17	18	21	21	Central air-conditioning	100	100	100	100
3,000 to 3,999 sq. ft	13	15	20	19	With	85	88	93	93
4,000 or more	5	7	11	11	Without	15	12	7	7
Average (sq. ft.)	2,266	2,392	2,687	2,640					
Median (sq. ft.)	2,057	2,169	2,467	2,422	Fireplaces	100	100	100	100
Number of stories	100	100	100	100	No fireplace	40	51	51	52
1	47	47	42	44	1 or more	59	49	49	48
2 or more [1]	52	53	57	56					
Foundation	100	100	100	100	Parking facilities	100	100	100	100
Full or partial basement	37	30	27	27	Garage	89	85	91	91
Slab	46	52	58	59	Carport	1	1	1	1
Crawl space	17	18	15	14	No garage or carport	11	13	9	8

NA Not available. [1] Includes houses with 1-1/2 and 2-1/2 stories and split-level houses.

Source: U.S. Census Bureau and U.S. Department of Housing and Urban Development, "Characteristics of New Housing," <http://www.census.gov/construction/chars/>, accessed June 2017.

Table 997. Construction Materials—Producer Price Indexes: 2005 to 2016

[1982 = 100, except as noted. This index, more formally known as the special commodity grouping index for construction materials, covers materials incorporated as integral part of a building or normally installed during construction and not readily removable. Excludes consumer durables such as kitchen ranges, refrigerators, etc. For discussion of producer price indexes, see text, Section 14]

Commodity	2005	2010	2011	2012	2013	2014	2015	2016
Construction materials	**169.6**	**194.5**	**201.1**	**205.8**	**209.3**	**214.4**	**213.6**	**213.9**
Architectural coatings	203.3	264.1	276.3	309.5	308.4	309.4	302.3	303.0
Plastic construction products	158.8	190.9	199.0	207.1	208.1	211.1	213.1	211.9
Softwood cut stock and dimension	205.1	206.0	202.5	194.1	203.9	207.4	199.7	200.0
Softwood lumber, not edge worked [1]	115.0	85.8	85.6	92.8	110.4	113.4	104.9	108.6
Softwood lumber, made from purchased lumber [1]	111.2	111.5	112.2	115.3	121.2	126.4	128.3	130.5
Hardwood cut stock and dimension	198.4	186.2	189.2	189.1	221.7	275.8	246.6	239.8
Hardwood flooring [2]	168.0	161.2	163.4	163.2	184.8	199.6	195.8	188.5
Millwork	197.2	207.0	210.1	216.5	225.8	232.3	237.2	240.6
Softwood veneer and plywood	223.5	197.1	185.8	218.6	236.8	245.3	234.5	214.5
Hardwood veneer and plywood [3]	(NA)	103.6	103.9	106.0	108.0	108.4	108.6	112.9
Prefabricated wood buildings and components [4]	206.1	215.6	216.2	224.0	231.6	236.4	240.4	243.3
Building paper and building board mill products	184.9	168.4	163.6	187.1	207.9	188.9	186.3	201.0
Pressure and soil pipe and fittings, cast iron	240.8	348.4	373.5	394.0	389.9	390.6	392.9	396.4
Hot rolled steel sheet and strip, incl. tin mill products [5]	125.4	150.7	161.6	149.9	136.1	140.3	115.9	107.2
Hot rolled steel bars, plates, and structural shapes [5]	159.8	192.9	223.0	213.3	199.8	206.8	185.2	164.5
Aluminum extruded and drawn pipe and tube [6]	102.2	98.1	110.9	103.2	96.0	101.1	95.6	90.2
Builders' hardware [7]	179.2	219.4	230.6	234.2	235.0	242.2	244.5	246.8
Plumbing fixtures and fittings	197.6	231.4	237.0	241.5	245.7	252.6	257.1	257.8
Heating equipment	179.9	221.5	227.6	235.3	239.8	243.6	248.2	253.1
Metal doors, sash, and trim	184.9	208.1	219.0	225.9	226.3	228.1	233.6	235.5
Sheet metal products	169.4	191.0	201.6	200.4	196.3	198.6	199.3	197.6
Fabricated structural metal bar joists and concrete reinforcing bars	163.0	176.1	179.9	183.0	183.3	187.9	190.5	194.0
Fabricated metal pipe, tube, and fittings [8]	(NA)	(NA)	(NA)	100.6	101.0	101.9	101.5	100.3
Residential electric lighting fixtures, except portable [9]	106.9	121.1	124.0	125.6	127.2	128.1	130.4	131.5
Elevators, escalators, and other lifts	123.5	133.8	135.6	138.0	140.1	143.1	145.4	147.1
Air purification equipment/industrial and commercial fans and blowers	170.9	192.2	199.8	204.0	206.0	211.7	217.3	218.4
Plumbing and heating valves (low pressure) [10]	182.2	249.5	262.1	272.4	277.6	285.8	292.6	296.9
Electric switches [11]	101.9	124.4	131.6	145.0	147.8	152.4	153.4	151.0
Wire connectors for electrical circuitry [11]	106.9	132.1	133.7	135.7	139.1	141.8	138.8	132.8
Current-carrying wiring devices not elsewhere classified [12]	(NA)	105.2	108.4	110.0	111.1	112.1	111.3	108.8
Noncurrent-carrying electrical conduit and fittings [6, 13]	106.6	119.2	128.6	133.3	134.6	135.4	134.1	134.1
Other noncurrent-carrying wiring devices [6, 14]	102.3	126.4	130.3	131.9	133.3	135.1	135.6	136.1
Carpets and rugs	145.3	167.5	173.8	177.4	178.4	182.8	184.1	183.9
Hard surface floor coverings	169.0	203.2	216.5	227.9	(NA)	(NA)	(NA)	(NA)
Float, sheet, and plate glass	96.0	88.2	86.7	83.9	85.8	88.8	91.0	97.3
Construction sand, gravel, and crushed stone	195.8	262.2	266.5	272.8	278.8	289.3	299.9	312.6
Cement, hydraulic	176.4	193.5	187.8	190.6	199.3	208.1	223.4	235.2
Concrete products	177.2	210.6	210.8	215.0	221.0	230.3	239.4	247.0
Clay construction products excluding refractories	165.4	179.4	176.1	173.6	175.8	178.1	182.4	184.7
Prepared asphalt and tar roofing and siding products	125.0	218.9	226.0	221.2	229.7	224.5	223.2	221.6
Roofing asphalts, pitches, coatings, and cement	155.0	227.5	258.7	277.8	265.7	265.8	234.3	201.3
Gypsum products	229.6	206.6	201.9	230.3	268.7	290.6	293.1	297.1
Insulation materials	142.2	146.6	155.9	164.7	173.4	182.9	182.6	187.8
Paving mixtures and blocks	156.9	279.4	296.2	316.5	317.9	323.6	313.0	294.6
Cut stone and stone products [4]	145.1	147.8	147.8	147.9	148.8	152.3	156.8	161.6

NA Not available. [1] December 2003 = 100. [2] June 1984 = 100. [3] December 2005 = 100. [4] June 1984 = 100. [5] June 1982 = 100. [6] December 2004 = 100. [7] Includes lock units, key blanks, door and window hardware, cabinet hardware, etc. [8] December 2011 = 100. [9] June 1998 = 100. [10] December 1982 = 100. [11] December 1999 = 100. [12] June 2006 = 100. [13] Includes plastic conduit and fittings. [14] Includes boxes, covers, bar hangers, etc.

Source: U.S. Bureau of Labor Statistics, "Producer Price Indexes," <http://www.bls.gov/ppi/data.htm>, accessed May 2017.

Table 998. Subsidized Apartments Completed, 1970 to 2015, and by Type of Subsidy, 2015

[Data shown for rental apartments in buildings with five units or more. Details may not sum to totals because of rounding. Based on sample and subject to sampling variability; see source for details]

Year	Total apartments completed	Subsidized apartments completed	Percent subsidized	Year and type of subsidy	Number
1970	526,000	55,900	11	**2015**	
1980	418,900	79,900	19	Total apartments completed	310,300
1990	294,400	13,800	5	**Subsidized apartments completed [1]**	**29,200**
2000	300,000	24,400	8	Section 8	10,700
2005	258,000	44,000	17	Housing for Elderly Direct Loan Program	1,200
2010	146,500	31,400	21	Low Income Housing Tax Credit (LHITC)	19,200
2013	186,200	38,600	21	Federal tax exempt multifamily bond financing	2,700
2014	255,700	26,400	10	Other subsidized programs	6,900

[1] Respondents were instructed to select all subsidies that applied to the building.

Source: U.S. Census Bureau, "Survey of Market Absorption of New Multifamily Units, Annual 2016 Absorptions: (Apartments Completed in 2015)," <http://www.census.gov/housing/soma/data/annual.html>, accessed June 2017.

Table 999. Housing Starts and Average Length of Time From Start to Completion of New Privately Owned Single-Family Homes: 1990 to 2016

[895 represents 895,000. For buildings started in permit-issuing places]

Year	Total [1]	Purpose of construction			Region [2]			
		Built for sale	Contractor built	Owner built	North-east	Mid-west	South	West
STARTS (1,000)								
1990	895	529	196	147	104	193	371	226
1994	1,198	763	245	169	123	268	522	286
1995	1,076	712	199	133	102	234	485	256
1996	1,161	774	218	144	112	254	524	271
1997	1,134	784	189	131	111	238	507	278
1998	1,271	882	209	144	122	273	574	303
1999	1,302	912	208	142	126	289	580	308
2000	1,231	871	195	128	118	260	556	297
2001	1,273	919	186	129	111	269	590	303
2002	1,359	999	198	125	118	277	628	336
2003	1,499	1,120	205	127	116	309	686	388
2004	1,611	1,240	198	130	128	306	743	433
2005	1,716	1,358	197	129	138	306	831	441
2006	1,465	1,121	189	119	118	235	757	356
2007	1,046	760	151	104	93	171	540	242
2008	622	408	107	74	63	102	324	133
2009	445	297	83	51	44	76	232	93
2010	471	306	83	55	52	79	247	93
2011	431	287	74	47	41	74	229	86
2012	535	373	82	47	46	92	283	114
2013	618	457	91	45	55	102	326	134
2014	648	460	110	50	51	106	346	145
2015	715	526	109	50	55	107	387	165
2016	782	579	116	49	60	121	421	179
COMPLETION (months)								
1990	6.4	5.9	5.3	10.3	9.3	5.6	5.7	6.9
1994	5.6	4.9	5.3	9.1	7.1	5.7	5.3	5.6
1995	5.9	5.2	5.8	9.5	7.4	6.0	5.4	6.0
1996	6.0	5.2	5.8	9.9	8.2	6.1	5.6	5.6
1997	6.0	5.2	5.9	9.8	7.3	6.2	5.6	5.8
1998	6.0	5.4	6.0	9.5	7.1	6.2	5.5	6.1
1999	6.1	5.5	6.4	9.2	7.0	6.4	5.7	6.3
2000	6.2	5.6	6.5	9.2	7.5	6.4	5.9	6.0
2001	6.2	5.6	7.0	9.2	7.6	6.5	5.8	6.3
2002	6.1	5.5	6.6	9.6	7.3	6.4	5.6	6.2
2003	6.2	5.5	6.8	9.9	7.5	6.7	5.7	6.2
2004	6.2	5.7	7.0	9.1	7.3	6.7	5.8	6.3
2005	6.4	5.9	7.6	9.8	7.7	6.6	6.0	6.8
2006	6.9	6.3	7.8	10.7	8.3	7.1	6.3	7.4
2007	7.1	6.5	7.9	10.2	8.5	7.4	6.5	8.0
2008	7.7	6.8	8.5	11.1	8.9	8.2	6.7	9.0
2009	7.9	6.6	8.7	11.9	10.7	8.2	6.7	9.0
2010	6.9	5.8	7.6	11.0	10.1	7.3	5.9	7.3
2011	6.6	5.4	7.7	10.8	8.9	6.9	5.9	6.8
2012	6.0	4.9	7.3	10.5	8.5	6.5	5.2	6.1
2013	6.0	5.0	7.5	11.0	8.4	6.7	5.5	5.6
2014	6.2	5.4	7.5	10.8	8.6	6.9	5.7	6.2
2015	6.3	5.5	7.6	11.1	8.9	7.0	5.8	6.1
2016	6.6	5.8	7.8	11.5	9.6	6.9	6.0	6.7

[1] Includes units built for rent not shown separately. [2] For composition of regions, see map, inside front cover.

Source: U.S. Census Bureau, "New Residential Construction," <http://www.census.gov/construction/nrc/>, accessed June 2017.

Table 1000. Price Indexes of New Single-Family Houses Sold by Region: 1970 to 2016

[2005=100. Based on kinds of homes sold in 2005. Includes value of the lot. For composition of regions, see map, inside front cover]

Year	Total	North-east	Midwest	South	West	Year	Total	North-east	Midwest	South	West
1970	14.9	13.4	17.9	18.2	10.2	2002	81.4	80.2	86.1	86.3	71.5
1975	22.1	19.6	25.4	26.4	15.9	2003	86.0	84.3	90.6	89.4	78.2
1980	38.9	30.2	41.2	44.4	31.9	2004	92.8	91.6	96.7	94.4	88.2
1985	46.2	43.1	48.2	53.9	36.4	2005	100.0	100.0	100.0	100.0	100.0
1990	55.7	58.0	58.6	60.6	46.2	2006	104.7	102.6	102.9	105.4	105.2
1992	57.2	60.5	61.2	62.4	46.7	2007	104.9	101.5	102.8	107.4	102.6
1993	59.4	57.4	65.2	65.5	47.8	2008	99.5	100.8	98.9	103.7	92.7
1994	62.9	62.0	69.4	68.1	51.9	2009	95.1	97.1	96.0	101.1	84.8
1995	64.3	62.3	70.9	70.1	52.7	2010	95.0	101.1	96.9	99.5	85.4
1996	66.0	63.2	72.5	71.2	55.3	2011	94.3	100.0	97.8	99.6	83.1
1997	67.5	65.9	74.3	72.7	56.5	2012	97.6	102.1	101.5	102.7	86.3
1998	69.2	66.1	76.0	74.4	58.4	2013	104.7	108.2	105.3	110.1	94.7
1999	72.8	69.1	79.5	78.1	62.0	2014	112.3	120.0	113.1	117.2	102.6
2000	75.6	73.0	83.5	80.6	64.4	2015	113.6	112.1	118.3	118.6	103.2
2001	77.9	76.7	84.4	82.8	67.1	2016	122.6	127.2	122.8	125.8	116.3

Source: U.S. Census Bureau, "Construction Price Indexes," <http://www.census.gov/construction/cpi/>, accessed June 2017.

Table 1001. New Privately Owned Single-Family Houses Sold by Region and Type of Financing, 2005 to 2016, and by Sales-Price Group, 2016

[In thousands (1,283 represents 1,283,000). Based on a national probability sample of monthly interviews with builders or owners of single-family houses for which building permits have been issued or, for nonpermit areas, on which construction has started. For details, see source and Appendix III. For composition of regions, see map inside front cover]

Year and sales-price group	Total sold	Region				Financing type			
		Northeast	Midwest	South	West	Conventional[1]	FHA insured[2]	VA guaranteed[3]	Cash
2005	1,283	81	205	638	358	1,150	51	28	52
2009	375	31	54	202	87	234	92	32	17
2010	323	31	45	173	74	189	81	35	19
2011	306	21	45	168	72	190	61	35	20
2012	368	29	47	195	97	234	75	35	20
2013	429	31	61	233	105	296	67	35	24
2014	437	28	59	243	108	311	51	36	31
2015	501	24	61	286	130	348	81	38	37
2016	**561**	**32**	**69**	**318**	**142**	**396**	**88**	**48**	**30**
Under $125,000	5	(Z)	(Z)	5	(Z)	4	1	0	29
$125,000 to $149,999	18	(Z)	2	15	1	12	6	(Z)	1
$150,000 to $199,999	73	2	11	56	5	36	27	6	1
$200,000 to $249,999	79	3	14	50	13	39	24	12	4
$250,000 to $299,999	78	2	10	48	19	51	14	11	4
$300,000 to $399,999	132	6	17	70	39	103	11	10	3
$400,000 to $499,999	79	6	7	35	30	65	4	5	7
$500,000 to $749,999	66	7	6	30	23	59	1	1	5
$750,000 and over	30	6	2	10	11	28	(Z)	(Z)	5
									2

Z Less than 500 units. [1] Includes houses reporting other types of financing, not shown separately. [2] Federal Housing Administration. [3] U.S. Department of Veterans Affairs.

Source: U.S. Census Bureau and U.S. Department of Housing and Urban Development, "Characteristics of New Housing," <http://www.census.gov/construction/chars/>, accessed June 2017.

Table 1002. Median Sales Price of New Privately Owned Single-Family Houses Sold by Region: 1980 to 2016

[In dollars. For definition of median, see Guide to Tabular Presentation. For composition of regions, see map inside front cover. Based on a national probability sample of monthly interviews with builders or owners of single-family houses selected from building permits and a canvassing of areas not requiring permits. For more details, see source]

Year	U.S.	Northeast	Midwest	South	West	Year	U.S.	Northeast	Midwest	South	West
1980	64,600	69,500	63,400	59,600	72,300	2010	221,800	329,900	197,700	196,800	259,300
1985	84,300	103,300	80,300	75,000	92,600	2011	227,200	322,800	203,300	211,400	256,000
1990	122,900	159,000	107,900	99,000	147,500	2012	245,200	368,800	230,600	227,000	270,000
1995	133,900	180,000	134,000	124,500	141,000	2013	268,900	371,200	255,300	246,600	310,500
2000	169,000	227,400	169,700	148,000	196,400	2014	282,800	402,800	269,700	257,700	333,900
2005	240,900	343,800	216,900	197,300	332,600	2015	296,400	459,600	278,200	274,600	348,800
2009	216,700	302,500	189,200	194,800	263,700	2016	316,200	448,200	284,400	284,000	381,300

Source: U.S. Census Bureau, "New Residential Sales," <http://www.census.gov/construction/nrs/>, accessed June 2017.

Table 1003. New Manufactured (Mobile) Homes Placed for Residential Use and Average Sales Price by Region: 1990 to 2016

[195.4 represents 195,400. A mobile home is a moveable dwelling, 8 feet or more wide and 40 feet or more long, designed to be towed on its own chassis, with transportation gear integral to the unit when it leaves the factory, and without need of permanent foundation. Excluded are travel trailers, motor homes, and modular housing. Data are based on a probability sample and subject to sampling variability; see source. For composition of regions, see map inside front cover]

Year	Units placed (1,000)					Average sales price (dollars)				
	Total	Northeast	Midwest	South	West	U.S.	Northeast	Midwest	South	West
1990	195.4	18.8	37.7	108.4	30.6	27,800	30,000	27,000	24,500	39,300
1995	319.4	15.0	57.5	203.2	43.7	35,300	35,800	35,700	33,300	44,100
2000	280.9	14.9	48.7	178.7	38.6	46,400	47,000	47,900	44,300	54,100
2001	196.2	12.2	37.6	116.4	30.0	48,900	50,000	49,100	46,500	58,000
2002	174.3	11.8	34.2	101.0	27.2	51,300	53,200	51,700	48,000	62,600
2003	139.8	11.2	25.2	77.2	26.1	54,900	57,300	55,100	50,500	67,700
2004	124.4	11.0	20.6	67.4	25.5	58,200	60,200	58,800	52,300	73,200
2005	122.9	9.2	17.1	68.1	28.5	62,600	67,000	60,600	55,700	79,900
2006	112.4	7.9	14.5	66.1	23.9	64,300	65,300	59,100	58,900	83,400
2007	94.8	7.0	10.8	59.4	17.7	65,400	66,100	64,900	59,900	85,500
2008	80.5	5.0	8.2	54.0	13.3	64,700	68,400	65,700	59,600	84,900
2009	54.5	3.5	5.3	37.8	7.9	63,100	61,600	65,400	59,300	81,500
2010	50.7	3.8	5.8	34.6	6.6	62,800	65,200	60,700	60,000	79,000
2011	47.6	3.3	6.3	31.5	6.5	60,500	62,700	60,800	58,400	70,600
2012	52.8	3.9	7.9	34.4	6.6	62,200	63,400	60,900	60,100	75,300
2013	56.3	4.0	7.5	37.4	7.5	64,000	66,500	62,900	61,200	79,100
2014 [1]	44.1	3.0	6.8	27.5	6.8	65,300	67,900	60,600	63,000	80,700
2015	45.6	3.1	6.6	28.5	7.5	68,000	72,100	60,800	65,100	88,200
2016	51.5	3.1	8.2	32.3	7.8	70,600	77,600	61,500	68,500	88,500

[1] Data not comparable to prior years due to a change in methodology. See source for details.

Source: U.S. Census Bureau, "Manufactured Housing Survey (MHS) Tables," <https://www.census.gov/programs-surveys/mhs/data/tables.All.html>, accessed August 2017.

Table 1004. Existing Single-Family Homes Sold and Price by Region: 1990 to 2016

[2,914 represents 2,914,000. Includes existing detached single-family homes and townhomes; excludes condos and co-ops. Based on data (adjusted and aggregated to regional and national totals) reported by participating real estate multiple listing services. For definition of median, see Guide to Tabular Presentation. See Table 1006 for data on condos and co-ops. For composition of regions, see map inside front cover]

Year	Homes sold (1,000)					Median sales price (dollars)				
	U.S.	Northeast	Midwest	South	West	U.S.	Northeast	Midwest	South	West
1990............	2,914	513	804	1,008	589	97,300	146,200	76,700	86,300	141,200
1995............	3,519	615	940	1,212	752	117,000	146,500	96,500	99,200	153,600
1996............	3,797	656	986	1,283	872	122,600	147,800	102,800	105,000	160,200
1997............	3,964	683	1,004	1,356	921	129,000	152,400	108,900	111,300	169,000
1998............	4,495	745	1,129	1,592	1,029	136,000	157,100	116,300	118,000	179,500
1999............	4,649	728	1,145	1,704	1,072	141,200	160,700	121,600	122,100	189,400
2000............	4,603	715	1,116	1,707	1,065	147,300	161,200	125,600	130,300	199,200
2001............	4,735	710	1,154	1,795	1,076	156,600	169,400	132,300	139,600	211,700
2002............	4,974	730	1,217	1,872	1,155	167,600	190,100	138,300	149,700	234,300
2003............	5,446	770	1,323	2,073	1,280	180,200	220,300	143,700	159,700	254,700
2004............	5,958	821	1,389	2,310	1,438	195,200	254,400	151,500	171,800	289,100
2005............	6,180	838	1,411	2,457	1,474	219,000	281,600	168,300	181,100	340,300
2006............	5,677	787	1,314	2,352	1,224	221,900	280,300	164,800	183,700	350,500
2007............	4,398	587	1,091	1,819	901	217,900	288,100	161,400	178,800	342,500
2008............	3,665	471	882	1,439	873	196,600	271,500	150,500	169,400	276,100
2009............	3,870	480	918	1,460	1,012	172,100	243,200	142,900	155,000	215,400
2010............	3,708	465	859	1,426	958	173,100	243,900	140,800	153,700	220,700
2011............	3,787	449	863	1,471	1,004	166,200	237,500	135,800	149,300	204,500
2012............	4,128	492	1,002	1,605	1,029	177,200	237,200	143,700	158,400	234,300
2013............	4,484	540	1,122	1,775	1,047	197,400	248,900	155,700	174,200	276,400
2014............	4,344	533	1,060	1,789	962	208,900	252,200	164,200	182,900	294,400
2015............	4,646	576	1,162	1,885	1,023	223,900	262,500	175,500	196,400	319,100
2016............	4,838	617	1,222	1,955	1,044	235,500	265,400	184,400	209,200	342,900

Source: NATIONAL ASSOCIATION OF REALTORS ®. See also <http://www.realtor.org/research-and-statistics>.

Table 1005. Median Sales Price of Existing Single-Family Homes by Selected Metropolitan Area: 2010 and 2016

[In thousands of dollars (173.1 represents $173,100). Includes existing detached single-family homes and townhouses. Areas are metropolitan statistical areas defined by Office of Management and Budget, though in some areas an exact match is not possible from available data]

Metropolitan area	2010	2016	Metropolitan area	2010	2016
United States, total............................	**173.1**	**235.5**	New Haven-Milford, CT............................	231.0	219.7
Allentown-Bethlehem-Easton, PA-NJ............	224.0	186.8	New Orleans-Metairie, LA........................	159.7	188.1
Anaheim-Santa Ana-Irvine, CA..................	546.4	740.0	New York-Newark-Jersey City, NY-NJ-PA......	393.7	388.5
Atlanta-Sandy Springs-Marietta, GA............	114.8	184.5	New York-Jersey City-White Plains, NY-NJ....	450.0	370.2
Atlantic City-Hammonton, NJ....................	226.4	187.5	Oklahoma City, OK................................	145.7	150.8
Baltimore-Columbia-Towson, MD.................	246.1	253.0	Omaha-Council Bluffs, NE-IA....................	137.3	168.8
Boston-Cambridge-Newton, MA-NH..............	357.3	421.1	Orlando-Kissimmee-Sanford, FL.................	137.0	224.0
Boulder, CO...	358.1	511.7	Philadelphia-Camden-		
Bridgeport-Stamford-Norwalk, CT................	408.6	373.5	Wilmington, PA-NJ-DE-MD.....................	214.9	225.4
Charleston-North Charleston, SC.................	200.5	252.2	Phoenix-Mesa-Scottsdale, AZ....................	139.2	232.7
Chicago-Naperville-Elgin, IL......................	191.4	234.9	Portland-South Portland, ME.....................	218.0	248.7
Cincinnati, OH-KY-IN..............................	128.0	152.3	Portland-Vancouver-Hillsboro, OR-WA.........	237.3	351.2
Cleveland-Elyria, OH..............................	114.5	132.2	Providence-Warwick, RI-MA......................	228.5	264.2
Colorado Springs, CO.............................	195.5	256.6	Raleigh, NC..	190.4	247.9
Dallas-Fort Worth-Arlington, TX..................	143.8	227.1	Reno, NV...	179.5	306.0
Deltona-Daytona Beach-Ormond Beach, FL....	115.0	172.5	Richmond, VA......................................	(NA)	235.4
Denver-Aurora-Lakewood, CO....................	232.4	384.3	Riverside-San Bernardino-Ontario, CA..........	179.3	313.5
Des Moines-West Des Moines, IA................	150.9	185.2	Sacramento-Roseville-Arden-Arcade, CA.....	184.2	320.0
Eugene-Springfield, OR...........................	196.3	239.7	Saint Louis, MO-IL................................	131.1	163.9
Hartford-West Hartford-East Hartford, CT.......	235.8	231.1	Salem, OR..	173.5	237.2
Honolulu, HI..	607.6	733.5	Salt Lake City, UT.................................	206.5	272.5
Houston-The Woodlands-Sugar Land, TX.......	155.0	217.4	San Diego-Carlsbad, CA..........................	385.7	565.0
Indianapolis-Carmel-Anderson, IN................	123.3	159.8	San Francisco-Oakland-Hayward, CA..........	525.6	838.6
Las Vegas-Henderson-Paradise, NV.............	138.0	237.8	San Jose-Sunnyvale-Santa Clara, CA..........	595.0	1,000.0
Little Rock-North Little Rock-Conway, AR.......	132.5	137.8	Seattle-Tacoma-Bellevue, WA...................	295.7	414.5
Los Angeles-Long Beach-Glendale, CA.........	323.3	507.1	Tampa-St. Petersburg-Clearwater, FL..........	130.0	198.0
Louisville/Jefferson County, KY-IN................	134.6	163.2	Trenton, NJ...	250.7	253.1
Madison, WI..	217.7	247.3	Tucson, AZ...	156.6	190.4
Memphis, TN-MS-AR..............................	120.2	155.3	Virginia Beach-Norfolk-		
Miami-Fort Lauderdale-West Palm Beach, FL...	199.9	305.0	Newport News, VA-NC.........................	205.0	215.0
Milwaukee-Waukesha-West Allis, WI.............	205.9	228.2	Washington-Arlington-		
Minneapolis-St. Paul-Bloomington, MN-WI......	170.6	237.0	Alexandria, DC-VA-MD-WV...................	325.3	390.6

NA Not available.

Source: NATIONAL ASSOCIATION OF REALTORS ®. See also <http://www.realtor.org/research-and-statistics>.

Table 1006. Existing Apartment Condos and Co-Ops—Units Sold and Median Sales Price by Region: 1990 to 2016

[272 represents 272,000. Data shown here reflect revisions from prior estimates. For definition of median, see Guide to Tabular Presentation. For composition of regions, see map inside front cover]

Year	Units sold (1,000)					Median sales price (dollars)				
	U.S.	Northeast	Midwest	South	West	U.S.	Northeast	Midwest	South	West
1990	272	73	55	80	64	86,900	107,500	70,200	64,200	114,600
1991	261	76	55	75	55	87,500	104,600	73,900	65,600	114,500
1992	282	88	61	77	56	87,700	100,600	79,000	65,600	114,500
1993	312	98	66	89	59	86,000	96,800	78,900	66,500	112,000
1994	343	108	68	101	66	88,800	97,100	86,200	66,700	118,600
1995	333	108	66	96	63	89,000	92,500	90,700	67,800	114,800
1996	370	120	72	105	73	92,600	95,100	95,200	70,600	119,800
1997	407	134	79	111	83	97,300	98,600	99,100	73,300	128,900
1998	470	157	92	126	95	102,500	100,900	106,400	76,800	137,700
1999	534	182	102	145	105	110,100	109,800	114,600	80,700	143,900
2000	571	197	106	160	108	114,000	108,500	121,700	84,200	149,100
2001	601	203	116	174	108	125,600	121,200	134,800	93,200	160,400
2002	657	221	129	193	114	144,900	143,500	148,600	109,900	187,000
2003	732	250	146	211	125	168,500	178,100	162,600	126,900	222,400
2004	820	292	161	230	137	197,100	214,100	181,000	156,600	258,000
2005	896	331	177	245	143	223,900	245,100	189,100	187,300	283,800
2006	801	299	169	211	122	221,900	249,700	190,900	184,000	264,700
2007	624	126	100	236	162	226,300	256,100	195,200	185,100	263,300
2008	459	103	71	164	121	209,800	252,500	188,200	166,800	218,500
2009	464	105	58	180	121	175,600	232,800	157,100	132,700	162,100
2010	474	95	53	202	124	171,700	242,200	150,500	118,500	154,700
2011	477	89	52	210	126	165,100	237,700	129,000	107,800	176,000
2012	528	104	66	229	129	173,700	240,100	127,800	123,900	196,700
2013	603	118	79	265	141	194,900	250,200	138,300	147,900	249,200
2014	591	112	76	262	141	204,300	254,900	149,300	154,700	273,300
2015	608	115	78	266	149	210,700	249,300	157,900	162,900	294,500
2016	614	116	82	263	153	220,700	256,600	166,200	172,600	321,300

Source: NATIONAL ASSOCIATION OF REALTORS ®. See also <http://www.realtor.org/research-and-statistics>.

Table 1007. New Unfurnished Apartments Completed and Rented in 3 Months by Region: 1990 to 2015

[214.3 represents 214,300. Structures with five or more units, privately financed, nonsubsidized, unfurnished rental apartments. Based on sample and subject to sampling variability; see source for details. For composition of regions, see map, inside front cover]

Year and rent	Number (1,000)					Percent rented in 3 months				
	U.S.	North-east	Midwest	South	West	U.S.	North-east	Midwest	South	West
1990	214.3	12.7	44.3	77.2	80.0	67	66	75	64	65
1995	155.0	7.1	31.7	78.5	37.7	73	74	75	72	73
2000	226.2	14.8	39.5	125.9	45.9	72	85	76	67	77
2005	113.0	4.7	20.5	57.8	30.0	64	75	64	62	64
2006	116.4	5.8	13.6	68.4	28.6	58	41	58	60	56
2007	104.8	5.6	9.5	61.8	28.0	55	66	58	52	58
2008	146.4	8.9	17.2	88.2	32.1	50	52	58	48	51
2009	163.0	10.0	17.2	93.3	42.4	51	56	74	49	44
2010	89.1	5.9	16.2	42.8	24.1	61	79	68	60	55
2011	74.7	10.9	18.6	38.8	6.4	59	67	53	60	54
2012	104.5	8.9	17.8	54.3	23.5	63	88	60	61	61
2013	134.2	14.2	14.3	75.8	29.9	63	63	78	60	64
2014	210.8	28.1	35.6	93.6	53.4	61	54	60	61	66
2015	**261.8**	**29.9**	**47.1**	**114.9**	**69.9**	**60**	**62**	**67**	**53**	**66**
Less than $850	22.4	3.8	7.1	9.4	2.1	68	72	73	58	88
$850 to $1,049	35.5	0.7	15.8	12.5	6.4	70	62	74	64	71
$1,050 to $1,249	43.2	0.9	10.5	22.8	9.0	65	70	68	60	76
$1,250 to $1,449	40.7	1.6	6.8	20.6	11.8	59	81	60	52	68
$1,450 to $1,649	30.4	3.4	2.5	16.6	7.8	59	81	56	51	68
$1,650 to $1,849	24.4	3.8	1.5	11.4	7.7	54	67	42	49	58
$1,850 to $2,409	16.4	3.3	0.6	6.4	6.1	57	59	51	47	68
$2,050 to $2,249	11.6	2.6	0.4	4.5	4.1	50	50	32	45	59
$2,250 to $2,449	8.5	1.3	0.7	3.4	3.1	57	55	65	49	63
$2,450 or more	28.8	8.6	1.2	7.1	11.9	49	49	34	36	58
Median asking rent (dol.)	1,396	1,896	1,062	1,373	1,596	(X)	(X)	(X)	(X)	(X)

X Not applicable.

Source: U.S. Census Bureau, "Survey of Market Absorption of New Multifamily Units, Annual 2016 Absorptions (Apartments Completed in 2015)," and earlier releases, <http://www.census.gov/housing/soma/data/annual.html>, accessed April 2017.

Table 1008. Total Housing Inventory for the United States: 1990 to 2016

[In thousands (106,283 represents 106,283,000), except percent. Data for 2000-2009 have been revised based on Vintage 2010 estimates. Data for 2010-2016 are based on Vintage 2015 estimates. Based on the Current Population Survey and the Housing Vacancy Survey and subject to sampling error; see source and Appendix III for details]

Item	1990	2000	2005	2010	2011	2012	2013	2014	2015	2016
All housing units..................	106,283	116,264	125,363	131,778	132,172	132,605	133,203	133,952	134,758	135,577
Vacant................................	12,059	13,680	15,880	18,903	18,740	18,240	18,180	17,900	17,362	17,302
Year-round vacant..................	9,128	10,315	12,060	14,419	14,225	13,781	13,736	13,447	12,983	12,961
For rent..........................	2,662	2,980	3,763	4,321	4,082	3,819	3,686	3,424	3,281	3,228
For sale only.....................	1,064	1,088	1,468	2,000	1,901	1,554	1,534	1,448	1,417	1,343
Rented or sold....................	660	935	1,073	915	983	986	1,072	1,070	1,079	1,055
Held off market...................	4,742	5,313	5,755	7,183	7,258	7,422	7,443	7,506	7,204	7,335
Occasional use..................	1,485	1,901	1,909	2,263	2,265	2,281	2,386	2,241	2,013	2,094
Usual residence elsewhere.....	1,068	1,050	1,142	1,266	1,195	1,260	1,253	1,361	1,351	1,445
Other.............................	2,189	2,363	2,703	3,654	3,797	3,881	3,803	3,906	3,841	3,795
Seasonal [1]........................	2,931	3,364	3,820	4,484	4,515	4,459	4,444	4,453	4,381	4,342
Total occupied........................	94,224	102,584	109,484	112,874	113,433	114,365	115,023	116,052	117,397	118,275
Owner..............................	60,248	69,223	75,411	75,443	75,023	74,834	74,892	74,805	74,737	75,016
Renter.............................	33,976	33,362	34,073	37,431	38,410	39,532	40,131	41,245	42,658	43,259
PERCENT DISTRIBUTION										
All housing units..................	100.0	100.0	100.0	100.0	100.0	100.0	100.0	100.0	100.0	100.0
Vacant................................	11.3	11.8	12.7	14.3	14.2	13.8	13.6	13.4	12.9	12.8
Total occupied........................	88.7	88.2	87.3	85.7	85.8	86.2	86.4	86.6	87.1	87.2
Owner..............................	56.7	59.5	60.2	57.3	56.8	56.4	56.2	55.8	55.5	55.3
Renter.............................	32.0	28.7	27.2	28.4	29.1	29.8	30.1	30.8	31.7	31.9

[1] Includes vacant seasonal mobile homes.

Source: U.S. Census Bureau, "Housing Vacancies and Home Ownership," <http://www.census.gov/housing/hvs/>, accessed February 2017.

Table 1009. Occupied Housing Inventory by Age of Householder: 1990 to 2016

[In thousands (94,224 represents 94,224,000). Data for 2000-2009 have been revised based on Vintage 2010 estimates. Data for 2010-2016 are based on Vintage 2015 estimates. Based on the Current Population Survey and Housing Vacancy Survey; see source for details]

Age of householder	1990	2000	2005	2010	2011	2012	2013	2014	2015	2016
Total...................	94,224	102,584	109,484	112,874	113,433	114,365	115,023	116,052	117,397	118,275
Under 25 years old.......	5,143	5,966	6,614	6,115	6,073	6,064	6,145	6,142	6,125	6,157
25 to 29 years old........	9,508	8,199	8,893	9,122	9,054	8,766	8,756	8,857	9,012	9,076
30 to 34 years old........	11,213	9,941	9,696	9,566	9,948	9,956	9,994	10,096	10,094	10,136
35 to 39 years old........	10,914	11,576	10,648	9,885	9,659	9,553	9,532	9,708	9,827	10,081
40 to 44 years old........	9,893	12,016	11,858	10,621	10,506	10,655	10,383	10,173	10,090	9,861
45 to 49 years old........	8,038	10,837	11,916	11,795	11,439	10,954	10,738	10,562	10,568	10,507
50 to 54 years old........	6,532	9,416	10,716	11,826	11,774	11,830	11,872	11,734	11,453	11,214
55 to 59 years old........	6,182	7,457	9,614	10,531	10,838	11,274	11,345	11,392	11,570	11,674
60 to 64 years old........	6,446	6,013	7,422	9,429	9,833	9,936	9,997	10,192	10,498	10,633
65 to 69 years old........	6,407	5,680	5,968	7,102	7,300	7,974	8,336	8,738	9,303	9,621
70 to 74 years old........	5,397	5,421	5,073	5,497	5,552	5,805	6,190	6,462	6,693	6,939
75 years old and over....	8,546	10,061	11,066	11,385	11,458	11,598	11,737	11,994	12,164	12,378

Source: U.S. Census Bureau, "Housing Vacancies and Home Ownership," <http://www.census.gov/housing/hvs/>, accessed February 2017.

Table 1010. Vacancy Rates for Housing Units—Characteristics: 2000 to 2016

[In percent. Rate is relationship between vacant housing for rent or for sale and the total rental and homeowner supply, which comprises occupied units, units rented or sold and awaiting occupancy, and vacant units available for rent or sale. Based on the Current Population/Housing Vacancy Survey; see source for details. For composition of regions, see map inside front cover]

Characteristic	Rental units					Homeowner units				
	2000	2010	2014	2015	2016	2000	2010	2014	2015	2016
Total units..............	8.0	10.2	7.6	7.1	6.9	1.6	2.6	1.9	1.8	1.7
Northeast..................	5.6	7.6	6.0	5.5	5.4	1.2	1.7	1.7	1.9	1.8
Midwest...................	8.8	10.8	8.0	7.6	7.5	1.3	2.6	1.8	1.7	1.6
South.....................	10.5	12.7	9.5	8.9	8.8	1.9	2.8	2.2	2.1	2.1
West......................	5.8	8.2	5.6	5.1	4.6	1.5	2.7	1.6	1.4	1.3
Units in structure:										
1 unit..................	7.1	9.2	7.3	7.1	6.8	1.5	2.2	1.7	1.7	1.6
2 units or more.........	8.7	11.1	7.9	7.2	7.0	4.7	9.2	5.2	5.1	4.5
5 units or more.........	9.2	11.7	8.3	7.4	7.4	5.8	9.2	4.7	4.5	4.0
Units with:										
3 rooms or less.........	10.3	13.8	10.6	9.9	9.7	10.4	14.8	12.3	13.6	13.1
4 rooms.................	8.2	10.5	7.7	7.0	6.6	2.9	5.7	4.3	4.4	4.0
5 rooms.................	6.9	8.9	6.7	6.1	6.1	2.0	3.0	2.4	2.2	2.1
6 rooms or more........	5.2	7.1	5.5	5.6	5.5	1.1	1.7	1.3	1.2	1.2

Source: U.S. Census Bureau, "Housing Vacancies and Home Ownership," <http://www.census.gov/housing/hvs/>, accessed February 2017.

Table 1011. Housing Units and Tenure—States: 2015

[134,794 represents 134,794,000. The American Community Survey universe includes the household population and the population living in institutions, college dormitories, and other group quarters. Based on a sample and subject to sampling variability; see Appendix III]

State	Housing units (1,000) Total	Occu-pied	Vacant Total	For sea-sonal use[1]	For rent only	For sale only	Owner-occupied units Total (1,000)	Average house-hold size (persons)	Renter-occupied units Total (1,000)	Average house-hold size (persons)
United States.............	134,794	118,208	16,585	5,465	2,757	1,410	74,507	2.71	43,702	2.54
Alabama..................	2,218	1,846	372	77	65	31	1,254	2.61	593	2.48
Alaska...................	309	250	59	31	6	4	160	2.94	90	2.66
Arizona..................	2,929	2,463	466	216	80	38	1,525	2.70	938	2.72
Arkansas.................	1,348	1,145	203	48	38	19	746	2.56	399	2.47
California...............	13,988	12,896	1,092	383	208	86	6,911	3.01	5,986	2.93
Colorado.................	2,309	2,075	234	114	36	16	1,323	2.65	752	2.44
Connecticut..............	1,496	1,344	152	28	34	19	889	2.70	455	2.36
Delaware.................	422	353	69	39	8	5	250	2.63	103	2.57
District of Columbia......	310	282	28	4	9	2	113	2.42	169	2.13
Florida..................	9,210	7,463	1,747	932	232	130	4,760	2.63	2,703	2.71
Georgia..................	4,182	3,656	526	96	98	55	2,261	2.76	1,395	2.67
Hawaii...................	532	446	86	35	23	4	252	2.94	194	2.94
Idaho....................	692	597	95	48	10	9	412	2.76	185	2.63
Illinois.................	5,318	4,795	523	50	112	68	3,130	2.70	1,665	2.46
Indiana..................	2,841	2,515	326	50	70	30	1,715	2.64	800	2.39
Iowa.....................	1,369	1,247	122	22	25	15	881	2.52	366	2.19
Kansas...................	1,254	1,112	142	16	32	13	738	2.65	373	2.34
Kentucky.................	1,957	1,716	241	43	38	22	1,138	2.54	578	2.42
Louisiana................	2,025	1,738	287	59	56	20	1,122	2.67	616	2.52
Maine....................	729	545	184	129	9	9	387	2.50	158	2.07
Maryland.................	2,434	2,178	257	60	45	27	1,436	2.76	742	2.56
Massachusetts............	2,846	2,560	286	129	36	15	1,580	2.72	980	2.29
Michigan.................	4,550	3,859	692	285	63	57	2,717	2.60	1,141	2.31
Minnesota................	2,397	2,147	250	131	29	23	1,523	2.60	624	2.23
Mississippi..............	1,301	1,104	197	44	36	18	744	2.61	360	2.65
Missouri.................	2,747	2,374	372	102	56	30	1,570	2.57	804	2.32
Montana..................	494	415	79	43	8	5	276	2.50	138	2.26
Nebraska.................	821	744	77	16	15	5	490	2.60	254	2.24
Nevada...................	1,210	1,042	168	49	45	15	563	2.75	479	2.73
New Hampshire............	623	518	105	70	5	7	367	2.61	151	2.19
New Jersey...............	3,594	3,188	406	132	71	37	2,009	2.86	1,179	2.56
New Mexico...............	915	762	153	49	24	13	514	2.72	248	2.60
New York.................	8,207	7,234	973	345	159	71	3,839	2.80	3,395	2.50
North Carolina...........	4,491	3,844	647	216	106	55	2,455	2.59	1,389	2.48
North Dakota.............	363	313	49	16	10	3	193	2.51	120	2.03
Ohio.....................	5,157	4,607	550	59	95	56	3,013	2.55	1,594	2.26
Oklahoma.................	1,712	1,466	246	38	43	19	958	2.64	508	2.50
Oregon...................	1,719	1,553	165	64	23	17	949	2.60	604	2.44
Pennsylvania.............	5,603	4,956	647	175	96	68	3,406	2.60	1,550	2.26
Rhode Island.............	463	407	55	16	12	6	241	2.66	167	2.25
South Carolina...........	2,210	1,858	352	125	63	26	1,266	2.57	592	2.53
South Dakota.............	380	339	41	14	6	3	231	2.54	108	2.19
Tennessee................	2,892	2,530	362	72	68	33	1,665	2.58	865	2.49
Texas....................	10,588	9,421	1,167	256	278	98	5,753	2.98	3,669	2.65
Utah.....................	1,038	931	107	47	15	8	641	3.30	290	2.88
Vermont..................	327	255	72	52	3	4	180	2.44	75	2.16
Virginia.................	3,469	3,107	362	93	60	37	2,020	2.67	1,087	2.52
Washington...............	2,992	2,729	263	99	35	28	1,703	2.66	1,025	2.44
West Virginia............	886	735	151	43	15	11	531	2.49	203	2.34
Wisconsin................	2,657	2,320	337	189	38	23	1,549	2.54	770	2.20
Wyoming..................	269	229	41	16	8	2	156	2.53	73	2.42

[1] For seasonal, recreational, or occasional use.

Source: U.S. Census Bureau, 2015 American Community Survey, B25002, "Occupancy Status"; B25003, "Tenure"; B25004, "Vacancy Status"; and B25010, "Average Household Size of Units by Tenure"; <http://factfinder.census.gov/>, accessed December 2016.

Table 1012. Homeowner and Rental Vacancy Rates by State: 2016

[In percent, see headnote Table 1010. From the Current Population Survey/Housing Vacancy Survey, and includes the civilian noninstitutionalized population, people in noninstitutional group quarters, and military households off post or with families on post (must include 1 household member who is a civilian adult). Based on a sample and subject to sampling variability, see Appendix III]

State	Homeowner vacancy rate	Rental vacancy rate	State	Homeowner vacancy rate	Rental vacancy rate	State	Homeowner vacancy rate	Rental vacancy rate
U.S.	1.7	6.9	Iowa	1.1	5.4	North Carolina	2.1	8.3
			Kansas	1.6	11.1	North Dakota	1.8	15.4
			Kentucky	1.9	7.3	Ohio	1.5	6.9
Alabama	2.5	14.6	Louisiana	2.1	11.4	Oklahoma	2.0	11.2
Alaska	1.3	8.1	Maine	2.1	4.0	Oregon	1.4	4.4
Arizona	1.8	6.8	Maryland	2.3	7.5	Pennsylvania	1.7	6.3
Arkansas	3.4	11.1	Massachusetts	1.2	4.1	Rhode Island	1.1	3.7
California	1.0	3.6	Michigan	1.3	7.5	South Carolina	1.9	8.8
Colorado	1.0	4.7	Minnesota	0.9	4.2	South Dakota	0.8	7.3
Connecticut	2.1	7.0	Mississippi	2.2	9.6	Tennessee	1.7	7.4
Delaware	2.1	8.1	Missouri	2.3	9.1	Texas	1.8	9.4
Dist. of Columbia	1.6	5.8	Montana	2.1	6.0	Utah	0.9	5.7
Florida	2.2	8.1	Nebraska	1.1	6.5	Vermont	1.6	4.5
Georgia	1.7	7.2	Nevada	1.8	6.7	Virginia	2.3	7.0
Hawaii	1.4	10.6	New Hampshire	1.6	4.6	Washington	1.3	3.8
Idaho	1.7	6.0	New Jersey	2.2	5.5	West Virginia	1.6	8.7
Illinois	2.2	7.6	New Mexico	2.0	9.5	Wisconsin	1.5	5.3
Indiana	1.7	9.8	New York	2.0	5.2	Wyoming	2.2	12.2

Source: U.S. Census Bureau, "Housing Vacancies and Home Ownership," <http://www.census.gov/housing/hvs/>, accessed February 2017.

Table 1013. Homeowner and Rental Vacancy Rates by Metropolitan Area: 2016

[In percent, see headnote Table 1010. Based on the Current Population Survey/Housing Vacancy Survey; see headnotes Table 1010 and Table 1012. Data are based on 2010 metropolitan/nonmetropolitan definitions and some MSA titles have changed from previous years; see source for details. Subject to sampling error; see source and Appendix III for details]

Metropolitan area	Homeowner vacancy rate	Rental vacancy rate	Metropolitan area	Homeowner vacancy rate	Rental vacancy rate
Inside metropolitan areas	1.6	6.5	Memphis, TN-AR-MS	1.4	9.4
Akron, OH	0.6	9.3	Miami-Fort Lauderdale-West Palm Beach, FL	1.4	7.2
Albany-Schenectady-Troy, NY	2.1	3.8	Milwaukee-Waukesha-West Allis, WI	1.3	5.2
Albuquerque, NM	1.9	8.1	Minneapolis-St. Paul-Bloomington, MN-WI	0.8	3.8
Allentown-Bethlehem-Easton, PA-NJ	1.1	4.2	Nashville-Davidson-Murfreesboro-Franklin, TN	1.5	4.8
Atlanta-Sandy Springs-Roswell, GA	1.6	6.2	New Haven-Milford, CT	2.5	7.3
Austin-Round Rock, TX	1.0	5.5	New Orleans-Metairie, LA	2.6	11.1
Baltimore-Columbia-Towson, MD	2.8	7.6	New York-Newark-Jersey City, NY-NJ-PA	2.2	4.7
Baton Rouge, LA	1.5	7.4	North Port-Bradenton-Sarasota, FL	1.2	9.8
Birmingham-Hoover, AL	2.1	15.1	Oklahoma City, OK	1.6	10.9
Boston-Cambridge-Newton, MA-NH	0.9	3.7	Omaha-Council Bluffs, NE-IA	0.7	6.7
Bridgeport-Stamford-Norwalk, CT	2.3	7.9	Orlando-Kissimmee-Sanford, FL	2.1	6.6
Buffalo-Cheektowaga-Niagara Falls, NY	1.2	9.3	Philadelphia-Camden-Wilmington, PA-NJ-DE-MD	1.4	6.8
Cape Coral-Fort Myers, FL	3.0	5.8	Phoenix-Mesa-Scottsdale, AZ	1.6	5.8
Charleston-N. Charleston-Summerville, SC	2.4	12.2	Pittsburgh, PA	1.8	7.4
Charlotte-Concord-Gastonia, NC-SC	1.1	7.4	Portland-Vancouver-Hillsboro, OR-WA	1.0	5.0
Chicago-Naperville-Elgin, IL	2.3	6.4	Providence-Warwick, RI-MA	1.3	3.8
Cincinnati, OH-KY-IN	1.4	5.8	Raleigh, NC	1.9	4.3
Cleveland-Elyria, OH	1.7	7.1	Richmond, VA	1.7	5.8
Columbia, SC	0.9	5.2	Riverside-San Bernardino-Ontario, CA	1.8	5.6
Columbus, OH	1.0	6.1	Rochester, NY	1.4	6.4
Dallas-Ft. Worth-Arlington, TX	1.4	6.8	Sacramento-Roseville-Arden-Arcade, CA	0.6	5.9
Dayton, OH	3.3	10.5	St. Louis, MO-IL	2.9	8.5
Denver-Aurora-Lakewood, CO	1.1	4.5	Salt Lake City, UT	0.5	6.4
Detroit-Warren-Dearborn, MI	0.6	7.1	San Antonio-New Braunfels, TX	1.9	10.3
Fresno, CA	0.8	3.8	San Diego-Carlsbad, CA	1.2	2.9
Grand Rapids-Wyoming, MI	0.5	5.1	San Francisco-Oakland-Hayward, CA	0.7	3.6
Greensboro-High Point, NC	1.7	12.5	San Jose-Sunnyvale-Santa Clara, CA	0.8	4.5
Hartford-West Hartford-East Hartford, CT	1.7	6.8	Seattle-Tacoma-Bellevue, WA	0.9	3.3
Houston-The Woodlands-Sugar Land, TX	1.8	9.3	Syracuse, NY	2.3	6.5
Indianapolis-Carmel-Anderson, IN	1.4	9.2	Tampa-St. Petersburg-Clearwater, FL	2.5	8.7
Jacksonville, FL	1.6	8.3	Toledo, OH	1.0	6.4
Kansas City, MO-KS	0.8	9.2	Tucson, AZ	1.6	9.8
Knoxville, TN	1.7	6.2	Tulsa, OK	1.3	8.2
Las Vegas-Henderson-Paradise, NV	2.0	6.6	Urban Honolulu, HI	1.1	9.4
Little Rock-North Little Rock-Conway, AR	2.4	12.2	Virginia Beach-Norfolk-Newport News, VA	2.1	8.2
Los Angeles-Long Beach-Anaheim, CA	0.8	2.9	Washington-Arlington-Alexandria, DC-VA-MD-WV	1.7	6.0
Louisville/Jefferson County, KY-IN	1.5	5.0	Worcester, MA	1.2	3.7

Source: U.S. Census Bureau, "Housing Vacancies and Home Ownership," <http://www.census.gov/housing/hvs/>, accessed February 2017.

Table 1014. Housing Units—Characteristics by Tenure and Region: 2015

[In thousands of units (134,790 represents 134,790,000), except as indicated. As of Fall. Based on the American Housing Survey; see Appendix III. For composition of regions, see map, inside front cover]

Characteristic	Total housing units	Sea-sonal units	Year-round units							Vacant units
			Occupied							
			Total	Owner	Renter	North-east	Mid-west	South	West	
Total units	**134,790**	**2,922**	**118,290**	**74,360**	**43,930**	**21,459**	**26,395**	**43,962**	**26,474**	**13,578**
Percent distribution	100.0	2.2	87.8	62.9	37.1	15.9	19.6	32.6	19.6	10.1
Units in structure:										
Single family detached	83,173	1,685	74,648	61,919	12,729	11,575	18,376	28,401	16,295	6,841
Single family attached	9,838	212	8,648	3,896	4,752	2,159	1,430	3,057	2,002	978
2 to 4 units	10,351	110	8,838	1,229	7,608	2,833	1,872	2,271	1,862	1,402
5 to 9 units	6,068	67	5,227	425	4,802	938	1,144	1,766	1,379	775
10 to 19 units	5,547	45	4,746	387	4,359	670	920	1,964	1,192	756
20 or more units	11,058	241	9,213	1,210	8,005	2,766	1,659	2,546	2,243	1,603
Manufactured/mobile home [1]	8,686	562	6,901	5,228	1,673	515	991	3,926	1,470	1,222
Year structure built:										
Median year (est.)	1976	1979	1976	1978	1973	(NA)	(NA)	(NA)	(NA)	(NA)
1980 or later	59,399	1,402	52,386	34,783	17,604	5,558	9,822	24,611	12,395	5,613
1970 to 1979	20,162	496	17,522	10,861	6,661	2,392	3,778	6,840	4,511	2,145
1960 to 1969	14,725	310	13,060	7,956	5,104	2,495	3,062	4,461	3,043	1,355
1950 and earlier	40,504	713	35,322	20,760	14,562	11,014	9,731	8,051	6,526	4,469
Stories in structure: [2]										
1 story	42,212	1,085	36,870	24,931	11,939	1,414	4,615	19,954	10,886	4,256
2 stories	46,256	793	41,022	25,628	15,394	6,984	10,645	13,172	10,221	4,440
3 stories	27,960	281	25,113	15,507	9,606	8,307	8,586	5,326	2,894	2,567
4 or more stories	9,607	200	8,314	2,999	5,316	4,237	1,554	1,549	975	1,092
Foundation: [3]										
Full basement	28,523	302	26,166	22,337	3,830	8,893	11,338	3,929	2,006	2,054
Partial building	9,582	118	8,839	7,658	1180	2,557	3,474	1,712	1,095	624
Crawlspace	19,891	537	17,416	13,472	3,944	773	2,631	8,395	5,616	1,940
Concrete slab	33,013	749	29,338	21,299	8,039	1,340	2,157	16,566	9,276	2,927
Equipment:										
With complete facilities [4]	129,269	2,503	116,290	73,843	42,448	21,057	25,974	43,316	25,943	10,477
Lacking complete facilities [4]	5,521	418	2,000	517	1,483	402	421	646	531	3,103
Kitchen sink	133,193	2,742	117,654	74,132	43,522	21,318	26,252	43,811	26,274	12,798
Refrigerator	131,082	2,582	117,662	74,091	43,571	21,334	26,259	43,789	26,279	10,840
Cooking stove or range	130,898	2,592	116,898	73,945	42,954	21,198	26,096	43,465	26,139	11,407
Microwave oven only	761	13	669	219	450	86	170	245	167	78
Dishwasher	89,395	1,463	80,723	57,436	23,286	12,864	17,238	31,492	19,130	7,209
Washing machine	105,309	1,679	97,655	71,445	26,210	15,506	22,154	38,434	21,562	5,974
Clothes dryer	103,278	1,664	95,755	70,569	25,186	14,904	22,032	37,692	21,126	5,859
Main heating equipment:										
Warm-air furnace	85,651	1,433	76,214	50,345	25,869	9,999	21,280	27,162	17,774	8,004
Steam or hot water system	12,173	142	10,917	6,038	4,879	7,965	1,730	658	565	1,114
Electric heat pump	16,475	489	13,980	9,443	4,537	499	959	10,849	1,672	2,007
Built-in electric units	5,429	159	4,614	1,765	2,849	1,366	989	747	1,511	657
Floor, wall, or pipeless furnace	6,820	153	5,962	2,881	3,081	848	866	1,633	2,615	705
Room heaters with flue	928	50	776	480	297	178	120	293	185	102
Room heaters without flue	803	48	648	386	262	43	32	507	66	108
Portable electric heaters	2,206	107	1,878	910	968	70	110	1150	549	221
Stoves	1,412	110	1,197	974	222	289	174	298	435	105
Fireplaces, with and without inserts	382	29	299	235	64	38	55	102	106	54
None	1,266	128	819	376	443	8	5	154	650	321
Main cooling equipment:										
Central air conditioning	89,464	1,500	79,918	55,056	24,862	7,918	19,381	38,104	14,515	8,046
One or more room units	27,125	323	25,318	12,640	12,678	10,913	5,362	5,118	3,926	1,485
Source of water:										
Public system or private company	(NA)	(NA)	104,619	62,760	41,860	18,060	22,327	39,646	24,587	(NA)
Individual well	(NA)	(NA)	13,135	11,181	1,954	3,313	4,019	4,171	1,631	(NA)
Means of sewage disposal:										
Public sewer	(NA)	(NA)	93,645	53,842	39,803	16,487	21,338	32,864	22,956	(NA)
Septic tank or cesspool	(NA)	(NA)	23,229	19,795	3,434	4,565	4,791	10,597	3,277	(NA)

NA Not available. [1] Includes trailers. Includes width not reported, not shown separately. [2] Excludes mobile homes; includes basements and finished attics. [3] Includes only single family homes (1 unit, attached or detached). [4] A complete kitchen includes sink, refrigerator, oven or burners.

Source: U.S. Census Bureau, "American Housing Survey: National Summary Tables – AHS 2015," <http://www.census.gov/programs-surveys/ahs/data.html>, accessed November 2016.

Table 1015. Housing Units by Units in Structure and State: 2015

[In percent, except as indicated (134,794 represents 134,794,000). The American Community Survey universe includes the household population and the population living in institutions, college dormitories, and other group quarters. Based on a sample and subject to sampling variability; see Appendix III]

State	Total housing units (1,000)	Percent of units by units in structures—								
		1-unit detached	1-unit attached	2 units	3 or 4 units	5 or 9 units	10 or 19 units	20 or more units	Mobile homes	Boat, RV, van, etc.
U.S................	134,794	61.4	5.8	3.7	4.5	4.8	4.6	8.8	6.3	0.1
AL..................	2,218	68.8	1.6	2.0	2.8	4.7	3.1	3.9	12.9	0.1
AK..................	309	61.8	7.3	5.2	7.3	5.3	3.1	4.6	5.1	0.1
AZ..................	2,929	63.2	4.9	1.4	3.5	4.2	5.3	6.6	10.6	0.3
AR..................	1,348	69.3	1.7	3.0	3.4	3.9	3.7	2.7	12.3	0.1
CA..................	13,988	57.7	7.0	2.5	5.6	6.2	5.4	11.7	3.8	0.1
CO..................	2,309	62.7	7.0	1.6	3.4	4.6	6.0	10.5	4.1	0.1
CT..................	1,496	58.7	5.2	8.7	8.8	5.4	3.8	8.5	0.8	(Z)
DE..................	422	59.5	13.9	1.7	2.5	3.3	5.7	4.7	8.6	(Z)
DC..................	310	12.1	25.0	3.7	6.9	6.1	11.6	34.6	(Z)	0.1
FL..................	9,210	53.8	6.1	2.3	4.1	5.1	6.1	13.3	9.1	0.1
GA..................	4,182	65.9	3.8	2.2	3.1	4.9	4.9	6.1	9.1	0.1
HI..................	532	52.2	9.4	2.5	4.1	6.5	5.5	19.4	0.3	0.1
ID..................	692	72.9	3.1	2.3	4.7	2.8	2.0	3.2	9.0	0.1
IL..................	5,318	58.5	5.8	5.7	6.7	6.5	3.8	10.5	2.5	(Z)
IN..................	2,841	72.3	3.6	2.6	3.7	4.7	3.7	4.4	5.0	(Z)
IA..................	1,369	72.9	3.8	2.5	3.5	3.7	4.2	5.6	3.8	(Z)
KS..................	1,254	72.6	4.3	2.5	3.9	3.7	3.8	4.6	4.6	0.1
KY..................	1,957	66.8	2.4	3.0	4.2	5.0	3.3	3.0	12.4	0.1
LA..................	2,025	65.0	2.6	4.5	4.1	3.2	3.2	4.3	13.0	0.1
ME..................	729	70.2	2.2	4.9	5.8	3.4	1.7	3.4	8.3	(Z)
MD..................	2,434	51.1	21.3	1.5	2.5	4.8	8.5	8.6	1.4	(Z)
MA..................	2,846	51.7	5.5	10.5	10.6	5.9	4.3	10.6	0.9	(Z)
MI..................	4,550	72.3	4.5	2.4	2.6	4.2	3.7	5.1	5.1	(Z)
MN..................	2,397	67.0	7.5	2.3	2.0	2.3	3.3	12.2	3.4	(Z)
MS..................	1,301	69.4	1.2	2.3	2.9	4.9	2.6	2.1	14.5	0.1
MO..................	2,747	70.5	3.3	3.3	4.9	4.0	3.4	4.7	6.0	0.1
MT..................	494	68.7	3.3	3.4	3.8	2.8	2.4	3.7	11.7	0.2
NE..................	821	72.5	3.7	1.9	2.7	4.2	4.9	6.5	3.5	0.1
NV..................	1,210	59.0	4.7	1.3	6.1	8.7	5.7	8.9	5.4	0.1
NH..................	623	63.1	5.6	5.7	5.6	5.1	3.2	6.1	5.6	(Z)
NJ..................	3,594	53.0	9.5	9.6	6.5	4.7	5.2	10.4	1.0	(Z)
NM..................	915	63.7	3.6	1.9	4.1	3.1	2.3	4.2	17.0	0.2
NY..................	8,207	41.6	4.9	10.5	7.4	5.3	4.0	23.9	2.3	(Z)
NC..................	4,491	64.6	3.9	2.2	2.9	4.3	4.5	4.3	13.3	0.1
ND..................	363	57.8	5.0	2.6	3.9	3.9	5.1	14.1	7.6	(Z)
OH..................	5,157	68.4	4.5	4.4	4.5	5.0	4.0	5.5	3.7	(Z)
OK..................	1,712	72.9	1.9	1.9	2.7	4.0	3.3	3.9	9.3	0.1
OR..................	1,719	63.4	4.3	3.1	4.2	4.7	3.6	8.3	8.1	0.2
PA..................	5,603	57.0	18.7	4.4	4.1	3.3	2.6	5.9	4.0	(Z)
RI..................	463	54.0	3.6	10.8	12.5	5.5	3.7	8.7	1.1	0.1
SC..................	2,210	62.8	3.1	2.1	2.8	4.7	3.7	4.4	16.4	0.1
SD..................	380	68.3	3.9	1.7	2.8	3.9	4.2	6.1	9.1	(Z)
TN..................	2,892	68.8	2.8	2.9	3.3	4.7	3.9	4.0	9.4	0.1
TX..................	10,588	65.0	2.6	2.0	3.3	4.9	6.6	8.3	7.2	0.2
UT..................	1,038	68.2	6.0	3.1	4.1	3.6	4.5	6.4	3.9	0.1
VT..................	327	66.6	3.8	6.5	6.0	4.7	1.6	4.0	6.8	(Z)
VA..................	3,469	61.5	10.7	1.8	2.9	4.9	6.0	7.2	5.1	(Z)
WA..................	2,992	63.5	3.8	2.5	3.5	4.6	5.1	10.2	6.6	0.2
WV..................	886	70.4	2.4	1.9	3.1	3.0	1.9	2.6	14.6	0.1
WI..................	2,657	66.5	4.3	6.7	3.7	5.0	3.3	6.9	3.5	(Z)
WY..................	269	64.7	4.7	1.5	4.5	4.2	3.0	3.3	13.8	0.2

Z Less than .05 percent.

Source: U.S. Census Bureau, 2015 American Community Survey, B25024, "Units in Structure," <http://factfinder.census.gov/>, accessed December 2016.

Table 1016. Housing Units—Size of Units and Lot: 2015

[In thousands (134,790 represents 134,790,000), except as indicated. As of Fall. Based on the American Housing Survey; see Appendix III. For composition of regions, see map inside front cover]

Item	Total housing units	Sea-sonal units	Year-round units Occupied Total	Owner	Renter	North-east	Mid-west	South	West	Vacant units
Total units	**134,790**	**2,922**	**118,290**	**74,360**	**43,930**	**21,459**	**26,395**	**43,962**	**26,474**	**13,578**
Rooms:										
1 room	667	49	513	24	488	120	81	114	198	105
2 rooms	1,508	79	1,177	90	1,087	303	172	258	444	251
3 rooms	11,247	367	9,202	1,019	8,183	2,200	1,760	2,933	2,310	1,679
4 rooms	24,119	886	19,723	6,064	13,659	3,745	4,244	7,005	4,728	3,511
5 rooms	30,497	714	26,261	15,507	10,754	4,129	5,866	10,616	5,651	3,522
6 rooms	28,315	451	25,354	19,501	5,853	4,293	5,679	10,126	5,256	2,509
7 rooms	18,250	187	16,957	14,593	2,364	3,086	4,014	6,063	3,795	1,105
8 or more rooms	20,186	188	19,103	17,560	1,543	3,584	4,580	6,847	4,092	895
Complete bathrooms:										
No bathrooms	100	20	50	19	32	21	8	9	13	29
1 bathroom	47,424	1,317	39,538	13,250	26,288	9,714	9,599	12,024	8,201	6,570
1 and one-half bathrooms	15,957	326	14,213	9,833	4,380	3,687	4,298	3,909	2,319	1,419
2 or more bathrooms	71,308	1,257	64,489	51,258	13,230	8,037	12,488	28,021	15,941	5,560
Square footage of unit: [1]										
Less than 500	2,748	133	2,228	330	1,898	619	398	574	639	388
500 to 749	7,930	339	6,358	1,106	5,253	1,317	1,187	2,098	1,756	1,234
750 to 999	13,759	383	11,363	3,538	7,826	2,014	2,405	4,145	2,799	2,012
1,000 to 1,499	27,068	664	23,532	14,934	8,598	3,580	5,191	8,967	5,793	2,871
1,500 to 1,999	21,662	356	19,685	16,410	3,276	2,840	4,116	7,837	4,892	1,621
2,000 to 2,499	14,006	167	13,026	11,652	1,374	2,153	3,016	5,008	2,850	813
2,500 to 2,999	7,293	83	6,820	6,325	496	1,120	1,469	2,651	1,579	390
3,000 to 3,999	7,077	93	6,595	6,205	390	931	1,744	2,522	1,397	389
4,000 or more	3,312	66	3,022	2,824	199	511	822	1,111	578	223
Not reported	29,934	638	25,660	11,038	14,622	6,373	6,048	9,048	4,191	3,637
Median square footage	1,500	1,150	1,500	1,800	975	(NA)	(NA)	(NA)	(NA)	(NA)
Lot size:										
Single detached and attached units and mobile homes [2]	98,753	2,295	87,783	69,456	18,327	13,791	20,249	34,654	19,089	8,675
Less than one-eighth acre	15,776	392	13,830	9,126	4,704	3,293	2,876	3,935	3,727	1,554
One-eighth to one-quarter acre	32,158	509	29,124	22,292	6,832	2,865	6,351	10,580	9,328	2,524
One-quarter to one-half acre	19,639	374	17,688	14,960	2,728	2,842	4,833	7,436	2,578	1,578
One-half up to one acre	9,090	220	7,995	6,833	1,162	1,619	1,630	3,874	873	874
1 up to 5 acres	14,642	415	12,860	10,825	2,035	2,226	2,701	6,319	1,614	1,367
5 up to 10 acres	2,834	97	2,510	2,274	236	345	646	1,143	375	229
10 or more acres	4,614	288	3,776	3,145	632	603	1,212	1,369	594	551

NA Not available. [1] Figures differ from previously published data in that square footage data has been expanded to include all units. [2] Does not include cooperatives or condominiums.

Source: U.S. Census Bureau, "American Housing Survey: AHS Table Creator," <http://www.census.gov/programs-surveys/ahs/data.html>, accessed December 2016.

Table 1017. Occupied Housing Units—Tenure by Race of Householder: 2001 to 2015

[In thousands (106,261 represents 106,261,000), except percent. As of Fall. Based on the American Housing Survey; see Appendix III]

Race of householder and tenure	2001	2003	2005	2007	2009	2011	2013	2015
ALL RACES [1]								
Occupied units, total	**106,261**	**105,842**	**108,871**	**110,692**	**111,806**	**114,907**	**115,852**	**118,290**
Owner-occupied	72,265	72,238	74,931	75,647	76,428	76,091	75,650	74,360
Percent of occupied	68.0	68.3	68.8	68.3	68.4	66.2	65.3	62.9
Renter-occupied	33,996	33,604	33,940	35,045	35,378	38,816	40,201	43,930
WHITE [2]								
Occupied units, total	**85,292**	**87,483**	**89,449**	**90,413**	**91,137**	**92,820**	**93,284**	**93,760**
Owner-occupied	62,465	63,126	65,023	65,554	65,935	65,357	65,088	63,103
Percent of occupied	73.2	72.2	72.7	72.5	72.3	70.4	69.8	67.3
Renter-occupied	22,826	24,357	24,426	24,859	25,202	27,463	28,196	30,657
BLACK [2]								
Occupied units, total	**13,292**	**13,004**	**13,447**	**13,856**	**13,993**	**14,694**	**15,015**	**15,998**
Owner-occupied	6,318	6,193	6,471	6,464	6,547	6,662	6,480	6,673
Percent of occupied	47.5	47.6	48.1	46.7	46.8	45.3	43.2	41.7
Renter-occupied	6,974	6,811	6,975	7,392	7,446	8,033	8,535	9,325
HISPANIC ORIGIN [3]								
Occupied units, total	**9,814**	**11,038**	**11,651**	**12,609**	**12,739**	**13,841**	**14,675**	**15,617**
Owner-occupied	4,731	5,106	5,752	6,364	6,439	6,530	6,897	7,114
Percent of occupied	48.2	46.3	49.4	50.5	50.5	47.2	47.0	45.6
Renter-occupied	5,083	5,931	5,899	6,244	6,300	7,311	7,778	8,503

[1] Includes other races not shown separately. [2] The 2003 American Housing Survey (AHS) allowed respondents to choose more than one race. Beginning in 2003, data represent householders who selected this race group only and exclude householders reporting more than one race. The AHS in prior years only allowed respondents to report one race group. See also comments on race in the text for Section 1 and the below cited source. [3] Persons of Hispanic origin may be of any race.

Source: U.S. Census Bureau, "American Housing Survey: AHS Table Creator," <http://www.census.gov/programs-surveys/ahs/data.html>, accessed December 2016.

Table 1018. Homeownership Rates by Age of Householder and Household Type: 1990 to 2016

[In percent. Represents the proportion of owner households to the total number of occupied households. Based on the Current Population Survey/Housing Vacancy Survey; see headnote, Table 1012, source, and Appendix III for details]

Age of householder and household type	1990	2000	2005	2010	2011	2012	2013	2014	2015	2016
United States	**63.9**	**67.4**	**68.9**	**66.9**	**66.1**	**65.4**	**65.1**	**64.5**	**63.7**	**63.4**
AGE OF HOUSEHOLDER										
Less than 25 years old	15.7	21.7	25.7	22.8	22.6	21.7	22.2	21.7	21.8	21.9
25 to 29 years old	35.2	38.1	40.9	36.8	34.6	34.3	34.1	32.7	31.7	30.9
30 to 34 years old	51.8	54.6	56.8	51.6	49.8	47.9	48.1	47.1	45.9	45.4
35 to 39 years old	63.0	65.0	66.6	61.9	59.8	56.9	55.8	56.0	55.3	55.3
40 to 44 years old	69.8	70.6	71.7	67.9	66.9	65.5	65.0	63.2	61.6	62.0
45 to 49 years old	73.9	74.7	75.0	72.0	71.0	69.9	69.6	68.5	68.0	66.7
50 to 54 years old	76.8	78.5	78.3	75.0	74.4	73.4	72.6	72.6	71.8	71.6
55 to 59 years old	78.8	80.4	80.6	77.7	77.3	76.2	75.8	75.4	74.7	74.0
60 to 64 years old	79.8	80.3	81.9	80.4	79.8	78.6	77.6	77.2	76.2	76.1
65 to 69 years old	80.0	83.0	82.8	81.6	81.7	81.1	80.5	80.3	79.3	79.0
70 to 74 years old	78.4	82.6	82.9	82.4	83.3	83.5	82.8	81.6	81.3	81.7
75 years old and over	72.3	77.7	78.4	78.9	79.3	80.0	80.0	78.6	77.2	77.0
Less than 35 years old	38.5	40.8	43.0	39.1	37.7	36.7	36.8	35.8	35.0	34.5
35 to 44 years old	66.3	67.9	69.3	65.0	63.5	61.4	60.6	59.7	58.5	58.6
45 to 54 years old	75.2	76.5	76.6	73.5	72.7	71.7	71.2	70.7	70.0	69.3
55 to 64 years old	79.3	80.3	81.2	79.0	78.5	77.3	76.6	76.3	75.4	75.0
65 years and over	76.3	80.4	80.6	80.5	80.9	81.1	80.8	79.9	78.9	78.8
TYPE OF HOUSEHOLD										
Family households:										
Married-couple families	78.1	82.4	84.2	82.1	81.5	80.8	80.7	80.3	79.6	80.0
Male householder, no spouse present	55.2	57.5	59.1	56.9	55.6	55.9	55.3	54.5	53.8	53.7
Female householder, no spouse present	44.0	49.1	51.0	48.6	48.1	46.7	46.7	46.2	45.9	45.7
Nonfamily households:										
One-person	49.0	53.6	55.6	55.3	55.0	54.5	53.9	53.3	52.2	51.3
Male householder	42.4	47.4	50.3	51.3	50.6	49.8	49.8	49.1	48.5	47.2
Female householder	53.6	58.1	59.6	58.6	58.5	58.3	57.2	56.6	55.3	54.6
Other:										
Male householder	31.7	38.0	41.7	40.7	39.5	39.8	39.8	37.7	36.6	36.1
Female householder	32.5	40.6	44.7	41.9	43.1	41.0	41.9	41.4	40.7	38.4

Source: U.S. Census Bureau, "Housing Vacancies and Home Ownership," <http://www.census.gov/housing/hvs/>, accessed February 2017.

Table 1019. Homeownership Rates by State: 1990 to 2016

[In percent. Represents the proportion of owner households to the total number of occupied households. See headnote, Table 1012]

State	1990	2000	2005	2010	2015	2016	State	1990	2000	2005	2010	2015	2016
United States	**63.9**	**67.4**	**68.9**	**66.9**	**63.7**	**63.4**	Missouri	64.0	74.2	72.3	71.2	68.5	66.7
Alabama	68.4	73.2	76.6	73.2	70.0	69.7	Montana	69.1	70.2	70.4	68.1	66.4	67.1
Alaska	58.4	66.4	66.0	65.7	62.3	65.2	Nebraska	67.3	70.2	70.2	70.4	68.1	68.0
Arizona	64.5	68.0	71.1	66.6	61.7	61.9	Nevada	55.8	64.0	63.4	59.7	54.8	54.5
Arkansas	67.8	68.9	69.2	67.9	67.1	67.6	New Hampshire	65.0	69.2	74.0	74.9	71.6	71.8
California	53.8	57.1	59.7	56.1	54.3	53.8	New Jersey	65.0	66.2	70.1	66.5	64.0	62.2
Colorado	59.0	68.3	71.0	68.5	63.6	62.4	New Mexico	68.6	73.7	71.4	68.6	66.5	67.4
Connecticut	67.9	70.0	70.5	70.8	66.5	64.2	New York	53.3	53.4	55.9	54.5	51.5	51.5
Delaware	67.7	72.0	75.8	74.7	73.3	73.0	North Carolina	69.0	71.1	70.9	69.5	65.2	65.7
Dist. of Columbia	36.4	41.9	45.8	45.6	40.4	40.8	North Dakota	67.2	70.7	68.5	67.1	61.8	61.4
Florida	65.1	68.4	72.4	69.3	64.8	64.3	Ohio	68.7	71.3	73.3	69.7	66.4	66.1
Georgia	64.3	69.8	67.9	67.1	62.9	62.3	Oklahoma	70.3	72.7	72.9	69.2	67.4	66.8
Hawaii	55.5	55.2	59.8	56.1	59.3	57.7	Oregon	64.4	65.3	68.2	66.3	61.1	62.6
Idaho	69.4	70.5	74.2	72.4	70.0	70.5	Pennsylvania	73.8	74.7	73.3	72.2	69.6	68.5
Illinois	63.0	67.9	70.9	68.8	65.4	65.3	Rhode Island	58.5	61.5	63.1	62.8	58.9	56.3
Indiana	67.0	74.9	75.0	71.2	69.4	70.9	South Carolina	71.4	76.5	73.9	74.8	67.1	68.9
Iowa	70.7	75.2	73.9	71.1	68.8	70.0	South Dakota	66.2	71.2	68.4	70.6	70.1	69.4
Kansas	69.0	69.3	69.5	67.4	64.9	67.1	Tennessee	68.3	70.9	72.4	71.0	66.5	66.4
Kentucky	65.8	73.4	71.6	70.3	67.9	67.9	Texas	59.7	63.8	65.9	65.3	61.9	61.5
Louisiana	67.8	68.1	72.5	70.4	63.3	64.2	Utah	70.1	72.7	73.9	72.5	69.9	71.3
Maine	74.2	76.5	73.9	73.8	69.9	72.6	Vermont	72.6	68.7	74.2	73.6	71.8	71.3
Maryland	64.9	69.9	71.2	68.9	67.1	66.5	Virginia	69.8	73.9	71.2	68.7	67.1	66.3
Massachusetts	58.6	59.9	63.4	65.3	60.5	59.7	Washington	61.8	63.6	67.6	64.4	62.6	61.6
Michigan	72.3	77.2	76.4	74.5	74.6	72.8	West Virginia	72.0	75.9	81.3	79.0	74.9	74.8
Minnesota	68.0	76.1	76.5	72.6	70.1	72.4	Wisconsin	68.3	71.8	71.1	71.0	66.6	67.7
Mississippi	69.4	75.2	78.8	74.8	70.7	69.7	Wyoming	68.9	71.0	72.8	73.4	69.9	70.2

Source: U.S. Census Bureau, "Housing Vacancies and Home Ownership," <http://www.census.gov/housing/hvs/>, accessed March 2017.

Table 1020. Occupied Housing Units—Costs by Region: 2015

[74,360 represents 74,360,000. As of Fall. See headnote, Table 1021, for an explanation of housing costs. Based on the American Housing Survey; see Appendix III. For composition of regions, see map inside front cover]

Category	Number (1,000)					Percent distribution				
	Total units	North-east	Mid-west	South	West	Total units	North-east	Mid-west	South	West
OWNER-OCCUPIED UNITS										
Total............................	**74,360**	**13,079**	**17,792**	**28,107**	**15,382**	**100.0**	**100.0**	**100.0**	**100.0**	**100.0**
Monthly housing costs:										
Less than $200......................	1,538	97	233	975	234	2.1	0.7	1.3	3.5	1.5
$200 to $299........................	3,705	251	758	2,158	538	5.0	1.9	4.3	7.7	3.5
$300 to $399........................	5,899	512	1,542	3,031	814	7.9	3.9	8.7	10.8	5.3
$400 to $499........................	6,053	617	1,809	2,584	1,043	8.1	4.7	10.2	9.2	6.8
$500 to $699........................	10,566	1,621	3,060	4,101	1,784	14.2	12.4	17.2	14.6	11.6
$700 to $999........................	12,892	2,445	3,573	4,680	2,192	17.3	18.7	20.1	16.7	14.3
$1,000 to $1,499....................	15,426	3,189	3,830	5,253	3,154	20.7	24.4	21.5	18.7	20.5
$1,500 to $2,499....................	12,483	2,914	2,209	3,849	3,512	16.8	22.3	12.4	13.7	22.8
$2,500 or more......................	5,798	1,434	778	1,475	2,109	7.8	11.0	4.4	5.2	13.7
RENTER-OCCUPIED UNITS										
Total............................	**43,930**	**8,380**	**8,602**	**15,855**	**11,093**	**100.0**	**100.0**	**100.0**	**100.0**	**100.0**
Monthly housing costs:										
Less than $200......................	1,206	222	282	496	205	2.7	2.6	3.3	3.1	1.8
$200 to $299........................	1,725	432	386	608	299	3.9	5.2	4.5	3.8	2.7
$300 to $399........................	1,347	303	322	460	261	3.1	3.6	3.7	2.9	2.4
$400 to $499........................	1,947	335	525	831	258	4.4	4.0	6.1	5.2	2.3
$500 to $699........................	6,414	779	1,822	2,804	1,010	14.6	9.3	21.2	17.7	9.1
$700 to $999........................	10,936	1,707	2,647	4,253	2,329	24.9	20.4	30.8	26.8	21.0
$1,000 to $1,499....................	10,442	2,238	1,483	3,532	3,187	23.8	26.7	17.2	22.3	28.7
$1,500 to $2,499....................	6,002	1,385	578	1,617	2,421	13.7	16.5	6.7	10.2	21.8
$2,500 or more......................	1,769	594	174	291	709	4.0	7.1	2.0	1.8	6.4
No cash rent.........................	2,140	382	383	964	410	4.9	4.6	4.5	6.1	3.7

Source: U.S. Census Bureau, "American Housing Survey: AHS Table Creator," <http://www.census.gov/programs-surveys/ahs/data.html>, accessed December 2016.

Table 1021. Occupied Housing Units—Financial Summary by Selected Characteristics of the Householder: 2015

[In thousands of units (118,290 represents 118,290,000), except as indicated. As of Fall. Housing costs include real estate taxes, property insurance, utilities, fuel, water, garbage collection, homeowner association fees, cooperative or condominium fees, mobile home fees, routine maintenance, mortgages, other charges in mortgages, and mortgage insurance. Based on the American Housing Survey; see Appendix III]

Characteristic	Total occupied units	Tenure		Black [1]		Hispanic origin [2]		Elderly [3]		Households below poverty level	
		Owner	Renter	Owner	Renter	Owner	Renter	Owner	Renter	Owner	Renter
Total units [4]...................	**118,290**	**74,360**	**43,930**	**6,673**	**9,325**	**7,114**	**8,503**	**21,989**	**6,245**	**6,751**	**11,372**
Monthly housing costs:											
$199 or less........................	2,745	1,538	1,206	221	437	141	214	667	238	559	829
$200 to $299........................	5,431	3,705	1,725	534	509	334	254	1,766	514	858	1,194
$300 to $399........................	7,246	5,899	1,347	681	391	497	207	2,840	403	1,019	674
$400 to $499........................	8,000	6,053	1,947	604	484	553	280	2,892	459	770	775
$500 to $699........................	16,980	10,566	6,414	908	1,679	946	1,064	4,144	884	1,119	2,150
$700 to $999........................	23,830	12,892	10,936	1,087	2,589	1,270	2,428	3,768	1,216	1,032	2,546
$1,000 to $1,499....................	25,868	15,426	10,442	1,311	1,954	1,537	2,389	3,102	1,016	787	1,613
$1,500 to $2,499....................	18,485	12,483	6,002	968	866	1,365	1,202	1,979	561	416	734
$2,500 or more......................	7,567	5,798	1,769	361	146	472	196	833	437	194	222
Median amount (dol.) [5]...........	917	912	922	794	810	953	958	(NA)	(NA)	(NA)	(NA)
Monthly housing costs as percent of income: [6]											
Less than 5 percent...............	3,502	3,089	413	265	72	230	58	733	57	3	23
5 to 9 percent......................	13,303	11,839	1,464	928	244	759	212	3,200	130	12	42
10 to 14 percent...................	17,580	14,450	3,130	1,105	531	1,204	486	3,803	218	90	94
15 to 19 percent...................	16,968	12,228	4,739	980	854	1,051	679	3,140	298	222	143
20 to 24 percent...................	13,702	8,898	4,804	780	924	926	878	2,513	415	284	198
25 to 29 percent...................	10,296	5,619	4,677	570	977	654	890	1,664	591	277	497
30 to 34 percent...................	7,680	3,803	3,877	421	899	494	883	1,224	669	291	522
35 to 39 percent...................	5,178	2,474	2,705	216	614	298	562	885	377	265	376
40 percent or more................	25,938	11,098	14,842	1,285	3,577	1,394	3,423	4,647	2,898	4,444	7,701
Median amount (percent) [5,7]...	21	17	31	19	34	21	34	(NA)	(NA)	(NA)	(NA)
Median monthly costs (dol.): [5]											
Electricity..........................	104	117	82	119	84	121	83	(NA)	(NA)	(NA)	(NA)
Piped gas..........................	53	58	42	58	44	46	37	(NA)	(NA)	(NA)	(NA)
Fuel oil.............................	133	150	100	167	125	142	83	(NA)	(NA)	(NA)	(NA)

NA Not available. [1] For persons who selected this race group only. See footnote 3, Table 1017. [2] Persons of Hispanic origin may be of any race. [3] Householders 65 years old and over. [4] Include units with no cash rents, not shown separately. [5] For explanation of median, see Guide to Tabular Presentation. [6] Money income before taxes. [7] Excludes households with zero or negative income and those with no cash rent.

Source: U.S. Census Bureau, "American Housing Survey: AHS Table Creator," <http://www.census.gov/programs-surveys/ahs/data.html>, accessed December 2016.

Table 1022. Owner-Occupied Housing Units—Value and Costs by State: 2015

[In percent, except as indicated (74,507 represents 74,507,000). The American Community Survey universe includes the household population and excludes the population living in institutions, college dormitories, and other group quarters. Based on a sample and subject to sampling variability; see Appendix III. For definition of median, see Guide to Tabular Presentation]

State	Total (1,000)	Percent of units with value of—			Median value (dol.)	Median selected monthly owner costs [1] (dol.)	Selected monthly owner costs as a percent income in the past 12 months			
		$99,999 or less	$100,000 to $199,999	$200,000 or more			Less than 15 percent	15.0 to 24.9 percent	25.0 to 29.9 percent	30.0 percent or more
U.S.	74,507	21.5	29.8	48.7	194,500	1,477	23.4	35.8	10.8	29.4
AL.	1,254	36.7	34.7	28.6	134,100	1,124	28.8	35.7	9.6	25.0
AK.	160	12.2	18.9	68.9	259,600	1,817	20.7	38.5	12.7	27.9
AZ.	1,525	19.4	32.4	48.3	194,300	1,319	24.1	35.4	9.7	29.7
AR.	746	40.3	36.9	22.8	120,700	1,029	30.1	35.0	9.6	24.6
CA.	6,911	5.9	9.0	85.1	449,100	2,123	16.1	31.4	12.6	39.3
CO.	1,323	8.1	19.3	72.5	283,800	1,558	24.3	37.1	10.8	27.6
CT.	889	5.3	24.8	69.9	270,900	2,020	18.8	35.6	12.0	33.2
DE.	250	10.4	26.7	62.9	240,200	1,506	24.3	35.8	8.8	30.7
DC.	113	2.3	4.5	93.2	551,300	2,312	25.7	35.9	11.7	26.6
FL.	4,760	23.7	31.4	44.9	179,800	1,394	19.9	33.3	10.7	35.3
GA.	2,261	26.8	36.4	36.8	159,300	1,299	25.8	35.5	10.0	27.9
HI.	252	2.1	5.4	92.5	566,900	2,248	17.5	30.5	11.5	39.8
ID.	412	16.2	42.9	41.0	176,300	1,170	24.1	35.3	10.5	28.5
IL.	3,130	22.3	32.9	44.8	180,300	1,588	23.0	36.5	11.0	29.1
IN.	1,715	34.3	41.3	24.4	131,000	1,089	32.5	37.2	8.8	21.0
IA.	881	33.2	40.0	26.7	136,100	1,170	30.6	40.1	9.1	19.9
KS.	738	34.0	36.6	29.4	141,200	1,279	27.5	40.7	10.3	21.2
KY.	1,138	36.3	38.6	25.1	130,000	1,089	29.3	37.3	9.1	23.8
LA.	1,122	30.1	36.3	33.6	155,600	1,219	30.8	33.6	9.1	25.9
ME.	387	20.9	35.8	43.4	180,300	1,340	21.9	36.5	11.6	29.7
MD.	1,436	6.6	18.3	75.1	299,800	1,909	21.7	36.6	11.7	29.4
MA.	1,580	3.3	12.5	84.2	352,100	2,048	19.3	35.8	12.1	32.5
MI.	2,717	34.9	36.1	29.0	137,500	1,220	27.4	37.3	9.8	25.0
MN.	1,523	14.4	35.6	50.0	200,000	1,459	25.8	40.1	10.7	23.1
MS.	744	44.4	34.1	21.5	112,700	1,083	26.4	33.0	9.8	30.1
MO.	1,570	29.9	39.0	31.1	147,800	1,200	27.1	39.5	9.4	23.6
MT.	276	18.0	29.0	53.0	209,500	1,316	22.0	36.2	11.8	29.4
NE.	490	28.9	43.2	27.8	141,600	1,269	27.5	40.8	10.8	20.4
NV.	563	12.8	30.4	56.8	221,400	1,396	21.9	35.6	12.2	29.8
NH.	367	9.0	25.9	65.1	244,500	1,828	18.3	39.5	12.5	29.6
NJ.	2,009	5.3	16.4	78.3	322,600	2,349	15.4	32.6	12.3	39.2
NM.	514	26.5	36.3	37.2	164,100	1,214	23.8	34.5	9.6	30.9
NY.	3,839	15.5	21.5	63.0	293,500	2,009	21.0	31.5	11.2	35.9
NC.	2,455	25.8	37.2	37.0	160,100	1,234	26.4	35.5	10.2	27.3
ND.	193	23.9	32.1	43.9	180,900	1,297	35.7	37.8	9.9	16.3
OH.	3,013	33.2	39.8	26.9	136,400	1,228	27.6	38.6	9.8	23.7
OK.	958	38.1	37.2	24.7	126,800	1,159	29.2	36.2	9.5	24.6
OR.	949	10.1	21.6	68.3	264,100	1,534	19.2	36.3	12.1	31.9
PA.	3,406	24.2	34.8	40.9	170,600	1,414	24.9	36.8	10.7	27.2
RI.	241	4.6	31.1	64.3	241,000	1,730	19.0	35.7	13.1	31.8
SC.	1,266	30.9	36.1	33.0	148,600	1,168	25.8	35.6	10.0	28.0
SD.	231	29.0	38.7	32.3	152,800	1,225	27.0	40.0	11.2	21.8
TN.	1,665	28.8	38.6	32.5	150,600	1,167	25.5	36.9	10.7	26.3
TX.	5,753	30.0	35.3	34.7	152,000	1,453	25.2	37.2	10.4	26.7
UT.	641	6.6	31.5	61.9	234,600	1,408	23.7	40.3	11.5	24.1
VT.	180	11.6	30.9	57.5	223,700	1,530	17.0	36.6	11.6	34.6
VA.	2,020	11.9	24.8	63.3	257,800	1,692	22.4	37.4	11.6	28.1
WA.	1,703	8.1	20.4	71.5	284,000	1,704	19.6	38.2	12.3	29.5
WV.	531	44.8	34.1	21.1	112,100	972	34.9	35.6	8.0	21.1
WI.	1,549	19.5	42.1	38.3	168,300	1,359	23.4	40.4	11.3	24.6
WY.	156	15.7	29.8	54.6	212,500	1,364	26.5	39.3	10.5	23.0

[1] For homes with a mortgage. Selected monthly owner costs are the sum of payments for mortgages, deeds of trust, contracts to purchase, or similar debts on the property (including payments for the first mortgage, second mortgages, home equity loans, and other junior mortgages); real estate taxes; fire, hazard, and flood insurance on the property; utilities; and fuels. It also includes, where appropriate, the monthly condominium fee for condominiums and mobile home costs.

Source: U.S. Census Bureau, 2015 American Community Survey, B25075, "Value"; B25077, "Median Value"; B25088, "Median Selected Monthly Owner Costs by Mortgage Status"; and B25091, "Mortgage Status by Selected Monthly Owner Cost as a Percentage of Household Income in the Past 12 Months"; <http://factfinder.census.gov>, accessed December 2016. See also <http://www.census.gov/acs/www/>.

Table 1023. Renter-Occupied Housing Units—Gross Rent by State: 2015

[In percent, except as indicated (43,702 represents 43,702,000). The American Community Survey universe includes the household population, and excludes the population living in institutions, college dormitories, and other group quarters. For definition of median, see Guide to Tabular Presentation. Based on a sample and subject to sampling variability; see Appendix III]

State	Total [1] (1,000)	Percent of units with gross rent of—					Median gross rent (dol.)	Gross rent as a percent of household income in the past 12 months [2]			
		$299 or less	$300 to $499	$500 to $749	$750 to $999	$1,000 or more		Less than 15.0 percent	15.0 to 24.9 percent	25.0 to 29.9 percent	30.0 percent or more
U.S............	43,702	4.1	6.3	18.1	22.3	43.8	959	11.7	23.4	10.6	46.8
AL.............	593	6.0	12.4	28.4	24.1	17.7	729	12.3	21.3	9.6	42.7
AK.............	90	1.6	4.3	8.5	17.9	59.7	1,163	12.9	24.9	10.3	43.9
AZ.............	938	2.1	5.0	21.1	25.8	40.8	933	11.2	25.1	10.7	44.9
AR.............	399	5.7	13.3	34.0	23.1	14.6	695	13.8	22.5	9.6	41.8
CA.............	5,986	2.3	3.0	7.6	15.5	68.4	1,311	9.2	21.8	11.0	52.9
CO.............	752	3.5	3.4	12.6	20.5	56.8	1,111	10.1	25.7	11.2	48.0
CT.............	455	4.6	5.8	8.9	19.7	57.1	1,108	9.8	22.8	11.9	49.1
DE.............	103	3.2	4.8	9.7	24.5	51.2	1,049	12.7	24.6	9.4	44.0
DC.............	169	5.8	4.5	5.6	11.1	69.8	1,417	12.2	24.8	11.7	45.6
FL.............	2,703	2.5	3.5	13.0	24.8	51.7	1,046	8.1	21.4	10.5	52.9
GA.............	1,395	3.5	5.9	20.2	27.5	37.3	909	11.2	24.3	10.4	45.8
HI.............	194	2.8	2.5	5.4	9.7	73.6	1,500	9.7	20.3	10.2	52.4
ID.............	185	3.6	10.2	29.9	27.6	21.6	770	13.2	25.8	8.8	42.5
IL.............	1,665	4.6	6.4	18.2	25.2	41.4	936	12.5	24.1	10.4	45.6
IN.............	800	4.5	9.4	32.2	28.2	20.2	758	13.2	23.8	11.0	43.9
IA.............	366	5.1	13.5	32.7	24.4	17.6	718	17.4	23.5	10.4	40.1
KS.............	373	4.5	11.1	27.9	26.1	24.7	782	14.3	26.7	11.6	38.9
KY.............	578	6.9	12.1	32.6	22.3	16.8	702	13.9	24.3	9.8	40.6
LA.............	616	5.1	9.5	24.0	24.9	25.0	800	11.1	20.0	7.9	46.0
ME.............	158	8.7	10.1	22.4	26.3	25.2	792	10.3	22.3	13.6	44.8
MD.............	742	4.0	3.6	6.9	13.1	68.5	1,278	10.3	25.0	11.4	47.7
MA.............	980	7.0	7.1	9.0	14.8	58.3	1,164	11.4	23.5	10.8	48.1
MI.............	1,141	5.5	7.5	28.0	27.0	26.6	803	12.4	22.9	10.7	46.1
MN.............	624	6.0	8.0	19.2	25.2	37.4	888	13.1	25.9	11.7	44.0
MS.............	360	6.3	10.9	29.9	22.5	17.4	724	10.9	20.2	8.1	43.6
MO.............	804	4.8	10.4	29.8	26.7	22.1	763	13.2	25.3	11.1	41.9
MT.............	138	6.0	12.4	25.4	25.0	22.0	763	14.1	24.4	10.2	40.5
NE.............	254	4.9	11.4	30.7	25.0	21.9	750	16.1	26.2	10.4	39.7
NV.............	479	1.3	3.1	18.4	28.0	46.2	980	10.6	25.9	11.2	46.8
NH.............	151	3.4	6.0	11.0	26.0	49.4	1,017	10.9	26.8	13.1	44.0
NJ.............	1,179	4.3	3.5	5.7	15.9	66.8	1,214	11.0	21.9	10.4	50.5
NM.............	248	5.1	9.3	28.6	22.3	27.4	783	12.4	22.6	9.5	45.3
NY.............	3,395	5.2	6.1	11.5	14.8	58.7	1,173	12.4	21.1	9.9	50.2
NC.............	1,389	4.0	7.8	25.8	27.1	28.3	827	11.7	23.7	10.6	44.9
ND.............	120	4.3	11.1	28.0	24.3	26.0	775	20.0	26.9	9.2	36.2
OH.............	1,594	6.1	9.8	32.1	26.1	20.9	746	14.0	24.4	10.9	43.3
OK.............	508	4.6	9.8	30.0	26.2	20.3	759	14.6	24.9	9.3	39.7
OR.............	604	3.5	5.2	17.0	28.3	41.6	943	11.0	24.1	10.5	48.2
PA.............	1,550	5.6	7.6	21.3	25.0	34.7	868	13.2	23.2	10.4	45.2
RI.............	167	9.1	8.0	12.5	26.7	40.1	938	10.4	24.0	13.5	44.6
SC.............	592	4.4	7.9	24.5	27.0	27.0	819	11.3	23.8	9.3	43.8
SD.............	108	7.6	15.6	32.5	21.2	15.6	675	14.6	29.7	9.7	37.2
TN.............	865	5.6	9.7	26.4	26.2	24.6	785	12.4	22.9	11.0	43.5
TX.............	3,669	2.8	4.8	19.8	26.9	40.4	932	12.8	24.9	10.7	43.9
UT.............	290	3.2	5.4	18.2	28.5	39.6	925	12.9	27.6	11.4	41.5
VT.............	75	5.9	7.2	15.7	24.9	39.2	923	10.4	23.9	11.2	46.3
VA.............	1,087	3.7	4.3	12.0	18.3	56.4	1,144	11.1	24.5	11.3	46.0
WA.............	1,025	3.8	4.5	13.0	21.1	53.6	1,080	11.4	26.0	11.6	45.4
WV.............	203	6.9	13.1	32.2	19.3	13.1	675	13.5	20.1	9.2	38.7
WI.............	770	4.2	8.2	29.0	30.0	24.2	792	14.3	25.8	10.7	43.0
WY.............	73	3.0	6.8	28.3	21.5	29.8	815	17.0	26.9	8.6	35.9

[1] Includes units with no cash rent. [2] Percent distribution of rental units by gross rent as a percent of household income. Percentage calculated from totals which include units "not computed"; therefore, rows will not total 100 percent.

Source: U.S. Census Bureau, 2015 American Community Survey, B25063, "Gross Rent"; B25064, "Median Gross Rent"; and B25070, "Gross Rent as a Percentage of Household Income in Past 12 Months"; <http://factfinder.census.gov>, accessed December 2016.

Table 1024. Mortgage Characteristics—Owner-Occupied Units: 2015

[In thousands (74,360 represents 74,360,000). As of Fall. Based on the American Housing Survey; see Appendix III]

Mortgage characteristic	Total owner occupied units	Housing unit characteristics		Household characteristics			
		New construc- tion [1]	Mobile homes	Black [2]	His- panic [3]	Elderly [4]	Below poverty level
ALL OWNERS							
Total.................................	**74,360**	**2,354**	**5,228**	**6,673**	**7,114**	**21,989**	**6,751**
Mortgages currently on property:							
None, owned free and clear.........................	30,415	625	3,730	2,568	2,528	14,430	4,392
Reverse mortgage...........................	357	–	7	44	19	323	57
Regular or home equity lump sum mortgage(s) [5, 6]............................	39,881	1,707	1,447	3,884	4,377	6,186	2,181
1 regular/lump sum mortgage......................	37,779	1,669	1,428	3,686	4,163	5,933	2,095
2 or more regular/lump sum mortgages............	2,101	37	19	198	213	254	86
Regular/home equity lump sum mortgage(s) and home equity line(s) of credit...................	2,245	18	11	110	125	366	56
Home equity line(s) of credit..........................	1,461	4	33	66	66	683	67
Number of regular and home equity mortgages:							
1 mortgage...	39,999	1,687	1,439	3,791	4,288	6,290	2,149
2 mortgages...	2,089	37	19	200	203	255	87
3 mortgages or more.................................	38	–	–	3	10	8	–
OWNERS WITH ONE OR MORE REGULAR OR LUMP SUM HOME EQUITY MORTGAGES							
Total.................................	**42,097**	**1,724**	**1,458**	**3,990**	**4,498**	**6,544**	**2,236**
Mortgage origination:							
Placed new mortgage(s)...........................	41,791	1,718	1,445	3,947	4,436	6,488	2,190
Primary obtained when property acquired.........	22,313	1,402	1,060	2,533	2,748	2,656	1,330
Obtained later......................................	19,478	315	385	1,415	1,689	3,832	860
Assumed...	16	–	–	4	3	5	1
Wrap-around..	64	–	7	1	14	14	16
Not reported..	227	7	6	38	45	38	28
Payment plan of primary mortgage:							
Fixed payment, self amortizing.....................	39,560	1,657	1,367	3,709	4,180	6,056	1,967
Payment option....................................	91	–	3	16	13	14	22
Interest only.......................................	137	2	–	8	32	32	24
Balloon...	89	5	3	12	3	14	10
Graduated payment mortgage.......................	267	6	21	25	34	60	32
Adjustable rate mortgage...........................	1,191	29	38	103	123	198	79
Other..	585	26	24	90	84	129	83
Interest only adjustable rate........................	13	–	–	1	3	3	1
Not reported..	163	1	2	27	25	36	18
Type of mortgage insurance:							
FHA...	9,647	428	216	1,565	1,416	1,168	531
VA..	2,179	199	27	302	214	362	87
RHS/RD [7]...	622	41	34	68	53	67	41
Other types...	27,822	990	1,077	1,859	2,489	4,671	1,407
Not reported..	1,827	66	104	196	325	276	169
Reason primary refinanced:							
Units with a refinanced primary mortgage [5].......	16,159	175	228	1,065	1,347	2,755	557
To get a lower interest rate.........................	11,502	130	119	626	831	1,823	308
To reduce monthly payment.........................	4,403	40	63	365	430	728	154
To reduce payment period...........................	2,814	18	37	134	230	374	85
To increase payment period.........................	386	2	4	19	33	68	21
To receive cash....................................	1,883	3	33	156	163	401	79
To suspend or temporarily reduce payments......	348	3	3	57	44	73	16
Other reason.......................................	1,589	27	53	90	109	301	78
Cash received in primary mortgage refinance:							
Units receiving refinance cash.......................	1,883	3	33	156	163	401	79
Median amount received (dol.).......................	28,000	50,000	10,000	30,000	40,000	54,000	45,000

– Represents or rounds to zero. [1] Constructed in the 2010-2015 period. [2] For persons who selected this race group only. See footnote 3, Table 1017. [3] Persons of Hispanic origin may be of any race. [4] 65 years old and over. [5] Figures may not add to total because more than one category may apply to a unit. [6] Regular mortgages include all mortgages not classified as home-equity line of credit or reverse. [7] Rural Housing Service/Rural Development mortgage.

Source: U.S. Census Bureau, "American Housing Survey: AHS Table Creator," <http://www.census.gov/programs-surveys/ahs/data.html>, accessed January 2017.

Table 1025. Home Purchase Loans by Race/Ethnicity and Sex: 2015

[Amount in millions of dollars (864,650 represents $864,650,000,000). Applicants are only shown in one race and one gender category. Data is the final 2015 National Aggregate data]

Race/ethnicity and gender	Applications received		Loans originated		Applications approved, not accepted		Applications denied		Applications withdrawn		Files closed for incompleteness	
	Number	Amount (million dollars)	Number	Amount (million dollars)	Number	Amount (million dollars)	Number	Amount (million dollars)	Number	Amount (million dollars)	Number	Amount (million dollars)
Total [1], [2]	**3,423,616**	**864,650**	**2,410,111**	**629,306**	**115,780**	**29,040**	**409,695**	**81,903**	**361,487**	**100,024**	**126,543**	**24,378**
White	2,565,554	612,888	1,856,719	456,252	85,284	19,668	278,613	53,746	261,534	67,937	83,404	15,285
Male	831,377	193,381	581,714	138,500	28,193	6,438	103,061	20,275	87,525	22,589	30,884	5,579
Female	538,909	99,598	379,320	73,110	17,703	3,075	67,574	9,669	55,843	11,164	18,469	2,579
Joint (male/female)	1,189,423	318,510	892,379	243,798	39,053	10,054	106,970	23,631	117,355	33,970	33,666	7,058
Black	131,989	21,926	67,061	13,165	4,548	801	36,169	4,310	13,404	2,588	10,807	1,062
Male	46,076	7,887	24,127	4,706	1,756	315	11,811	1,535	4,958	957	3,424	374
Female	55,243	7,875	27,391	4,659	1,783	268	16,061	1,664	5,514	907	4,494	377
Joint (male/female)	29,721	6,017	15,225	3,724	966	208	7,953	1,079	2,863	707	2,714	298
Hispanic or Latino	227,331	42,517	137,239	27,938	8,120	1,496	43,702	6,342	24,804	5,050	13,466	1,690
Male	102,222	19,169	61,635	12,507	3,730	705	19,398	2,891	11,252	2,305	6,207	762
Female	57,583	9,410	34,256	6,109	1,968	310	11,757	1,475	6,430	1,141	3,172	375
Joint (male/female)	66,596	13,793	41,003	9,254	2,392	478	12,228	1,941	7,003	1,576	3,970	543
Asian	247,322	87,854	173,741	61,581	9,424	3,380	26,813	9,178	29,614	10,953	7,730	2,763
Male	107,533	36,218	74,944	25,080	4,196	1,429	11,649	3,841	13,182	4,641	3,562	1,227
Female	51,593	15,320	36,006	10,724	1,981	600	6,027	1,690	6,010	1,827	1,569	480
Joint (male/female)	87,488	36,049	62,400	25,626	3,208	1,338	9,040	3,615	10,281	4,428	2,559	1,042
Native Hawaiian/Other Pacific Islander	7,976	2,066	5,219	1,425	296	76	1,210	266	942	235	309	64
Male	3,284	819	2,158	559	121	31	507	110	366	90	132	28
Female	2,315	521	1,490	365	94	19	353	60	282	62	96	15
Joint (male/female)	2,324	713	1,546	493	78	25	340	93	282	81	78	20
American Indian/Alaska Native	14,774	2,433	7,278	1,462	458	80	4,110	467	1,346	275	1,582	148
Male	6,059	1,041	3,057	617	192	33	1,584	200	591	127	635	64
Female	4,631	636	2,114	371	161	24	1,443	136	408	68	505	38
Joint (male/female)	3,338	606	1,583	359	105	23	955	116	272	63	423	44
Two or more minority races	1,978	492	1,141	317	75	20	422	77	225	54	115	23
Male	771	180	453	115	40	10	158	29	79	18	41	8
Female	665	134	355	82	21	5	160	23	85	18	44	7
Joint (male/female)	532	175	329	119	14	5	99	24	61	19	29	8
Joint [3]	57,306	18,443	40,487	13,674	1,959	611	6,419	1,522	6,272	2,165	2,169	471
Race not available [4]	396,717	118,548	258,465	81,430	13,736	4,403	55,939	12,336	48,150	15,817	20,427	4,562
Male	51,267	13,544	29,135		1,802	537	9,756	1,885	6,244	1,929	4,330	772
Female	31,134	6,547	17,675	4,157	1,066	238	6,366	952	3,841	872	2,186	328
Joint (male/female)	63,498	19,842	40,687	13,617	2,212	756	8,902	1,996	7,728	2,605	3,969	869

[1] Total includes those cases in which gender was reported and in those in which gender information was not available. [2] Includes all loans from other race/ethnicities not shown separately. [3] "Joint" means with two applicants, one reported a single designation of "White" and the other applicant reported one or more minority racial designations. [4] "Not available" includes situations in which information was not provided or not applicable.

Source: Federal Financial Institutions Examination Council, "Home Mortgage Disclosure Act National Aggregate Report," <http://www.ffiec.gov/Hmda/default.htm>, accessed September 2017.

Table 1026. Heating Equipment and Fuels for Occupied Units: 2005 to 2015

[108,871 represents 108,871,000. As of Fall. Data for 2005 to 2009 based on population controls from Census 2000. Beginning 2011, data based on Census 2010 controls. Based on American Housing Survey. See Appendix III]

Type of equipment or fuel	Number (1,000)					Percent distribution	
	2005	2009	2011	2013	2015	2013	2015
Occupied units, total.................	108,871	111,806	114,907	115,852	118,290	100.0	100.0
Heating equipment:							
Warm air furnace.......................	68,275	71,141	73,687	74,712	76,214	64.5	64.4
Steam or hot water.....................	12,880	12,506	12,624	12,448	10,917	10.7	9.2
Heat pumps.............................	12,484	13,264	13,523	13,526	13,980	11.7	11.8
Built-in electric units..................	4,699	4,761	4,865	5,064	4,614	4.4	3.9
Floor, wall, or pipeless furnace........	5,102	4,802	4,505	4,571	5,962	3.9	5.0
Room heaters with flue................	1,294	950	932	851	776	0.7	0.7
Room heaters without flue.............	1,327	1,109	1,094	1,034	648	0.9	0.5
Fireplaces, stoves, portable heaters or other....	2,411	2,887	3,208	3,260	4,360	2.8	3.7
None....................................	399	386	468	386	819	0.3	0.7
House main heating fuel:							
Electricity..............................	34,263	37,851	40,385	42,041	48,311	36.3	40.8
Utility gas..............................	56,317	56,806	57,721	58,225	54,797	50.3	46.3
Bottled, tank, or liquid propane gas...	6,228	5,817	5,415	5,198	4,706	4.5	4.0
Fuel oil, kerosene, etc.................	9,929	8,813	8,599	7,623	6,658	6.6	5.6
Coal or coke...........................	95	98	79	98	80	0.1	0.1
Wood and other fuel...................	1,640	2,035	2,240	2,280	2,919	2.0	2.5
None....................................	398	386	468	387	819	0.3	0.7
Cooking fuel:							
Electricity..............................	65,297	67,078	68,879	69,330	71,267	59.8	60.2
Gas [1].................................	43,316	44,477	45,759	46,294	46,381	40.0	39.2
Other fuel..............................	51	68	92	71	200	0.1	0.2
None....................................	206	183	177	158	442	0.1	0.4

[1] Includes utility, bottled, tank, and liquid propane gas.

Source: U.S. Census Bureau, "American Housing Survey: AHS Table Creator," <http://www.census.gov/programs-surveys/ahs/data.html>, accessed January 2017.

Table 1027. Occupied Housing Units—Housing Indicators by Selected Characteristics of the Householder: 2015

[In thousands of units (118,290 represents 118,290,000). As of Fall. Based on the American Housing Survey; see Appendix III]

Characteristic	Total occupied units	Tenure		Black [1]		Hispanic origin [2]		Elderly [3]		Households below poverty level	
		Owner	Renter	Owner	Renter	Owner	Renter	Owner	Renter	Owner	Renter
Total units.................	118,290	74,360	43,930	6,673	9,325	7,114	8,503	21,989	6,245	6,751	11,372
Selected amenities:											
Porch, deck, balcony or patio.........	96,039	66,332	29,707	5,601	5,924	5,805	5,277	19,649	3,652	5,669	6,932
Usable fireplace.......................	41,136	34,895	6,241	2,599	1,044	2,387	891	9,851	588	2,102	914
Separate dining room..................	57,105	42,614	14,491	4,206	3,359	3,968	2,900	12,328	1,589	3,365	3,366
With 2 or more living rooms or recreation rooms.....................	39,372	34,666	4,706	2,601	739	2,184	538	10,096	537	1,913	686
Garage or carport with home.........	74,475	58,289	16,186	4,335	2,393	5,123	3,063	17,501	2,063	4,397	2,908
Selected deficiencies:											
Signs of mice or rats in last 12 months...........................	13,257	8,823	4,433	710	1,159	720	968	2,465	482	906	1,433
Signs of cockroaches in last 12 months...........................	14,021	6,540	7,481	965	1,991	1,224	2,305	1,847	788	878	2,460
Holes in floors.........................	1,714	822	893	112	228	122	228	213	95	203	375
Open cracks or holes (interior).......	7,384	3,923	3,460	538	900	536	690	858	266	528	1,201
Broken/peeling paint or plaster (interior)............................	2,889	1,433	1,457	238	413	195	316	370	150	246	493
No electrical wiring....................	185	109	76	8	11	26	27	38	17	27	31
Exposed wiring........................	3,375	1,857	1,518	183	378	237	417	568	216	285	513
Rooms without electric outlet........	2,739	1,335	1,403	183	345	168	258	435	192	194	460
Units with mold in the last 12 months...........................	4,299	2,031	2,268	299	550	244	523	474	201	351	830
Water leakage from inside structure [4].....................	10,005	5,328	4,678	675	1,190	510	852	1,220	440	574	1,289
Water leakage from outside structure [4]....................	11,759	7,808	3,952	793	921	733	696	1,980	365	824	1,127
Sagging roof [5].......................	2,163	1,558	605	161	142	196	112	328	41	328	217
Missing roof material [5]...............	3,281	2,496	785	343	167	289	143	629	75	436	245
Hole in roof [5]........................	1,522	1,060	462	192	133	161	102	265	41	291	191
Missing bricks, siding, or other outside wall material [5]...............	2,641	1,864	777	261	182	217	144	390	75	356	273
Boarded up windows [5]...............	1,187	811	376	95	67	137	90	204	27	196	172
Broken windows [5]....................	4,310	3,025	1,285	358	272	413	244	679	78	542	451
Foundation crumbling or has open crack or hole [5].....................	6,095	4,556	1,539	602	349	446	264	1,229	191	529	479

[1] For persons who selected this race group only. See footnote 3, Table 1017. [2] Persons of Hispanic origin may be of any race. [3] Householders 65 years old and over. [4] During the 12 months prior to the survey. [5] Excludes multiunit structures.

Source: U.S. Census Bureau, "American Housing Survey: AHS Table Creator," <http://www.census.gov/programs-surveys/ahs/data.html>, accessed January 2017.

Table 1028. Home Remodeling—Number of Households With Work Done by Amount Spent: 2016

[In thousands (2,347 represents 2,347,000), except percent. As of Fall 2016. For work done in the prior 12 months. Based on household survey and subject to sampling error; see source]

Remodeling project	Total households with work done [1]		Households with work done by outside contractor	Number of households by amount spent		
	Number	Percent of households		Under $1,000	$1,000 to $2,999	Over $3,000
Conversion of garage/attic/basement into living space	2,347	0.96	739	411	305	774
Remodel bathroom	13,697	5.60	4,258	4,336	3,279	3,320
Remodel kitchen	8,388	3.43	3,356	1,407	1,568	3,508
Remodel bedroom	6,084	2.49	1,325	2,895	867	693
Add/extend garage	869	0.36	313	59	167	348
Aluminum windows	1,116	0.46	628	231	258	223
Vinyl windows	3,908	1.60	2,244	812	1,034	1,428
Clad-wood/wood windows	809	0.33	299	100	49	199
Ceramic tile floors	4,207	1.72	1,700	1,795	638	623
Skylights	1,264	0.52	468	416	175	204
Ceramic wall tile	2,134	0.87	679	1,227	157	105
Convert room to home office	2,580	1.06	299	1,379	314	75
Convert room to home theater	621	0.25	91	153	131	36
Remodel other rooms	5,096	2.08	1,364	2,014	821	1,088
Add bathroom	1,346	0.55	399	282	261	413
Add other rooms - exterior addition	1,179	0.48	487	51	229	598
Add deck/porch/patio	4,417	1.81	1,895	1,113	1,050	1,306
Roofing	8,705	3.56	6,279	936	1,127	4,829
Siding - vinyl/metal	1,817	0.74	1,031	208	244	669
Hardwood floors	5,032	2.06	2,191	1,004	1,145	1,458
Laminate flooring	5,584	2.28	1,714	2,279	1,076	928
Vinyl flooring	2,476	1.01	828	1,101	435	335
Carpeting	6,908	2.83	4,075	2,198	1,675	1,078
Kitchen cabinets	4,294	1.76	1,604	831	731	1,278
Kitchen counter tops	4,989	2.04	2,531	1,093	894	1,524
Exterior doors	4,317	1.77	2,051	1,828	698	538
Interior doors	3,284	1.34	1,044	1,669	360	189
Garage doors	2,538	1.04	1,502	930	582	141
Concrete or masonry work	3,246	1.33	1,413	1,271	527	611
Swimming pool - in ground	812	0.33	319	25	76	249

[1] Includes no response and amount unknown.

Source: © Fall 2016, GfK MRI a division of GfK US, LLC. See also <http://www.mri.gfk.com/>.

Table 1029. Home Improvement Loans by Race/Ethnicity: 2015

[Applications in thousands (921.2 represents 921,200); values in millions of dollars (80,252.2 represents $80,252,200,000). Applicants are categorized by the race of the first person listed on the application unless the 'joint' designation applies. Data is the final 2015 National Aggregate data]

Item	Unit	Total [1,2]	White, total [1]	Black, total [1]	Asian, total [1]	Joint, total [3]	Hispanic or Latino [4]
Applications received:							
Number	1,000	921.2	660.4	91.6	25.4	11.8	93.7
Amount	Mil. dol.	80,252.2	57,936.7	3,327.6	4,508.1	1,516.8	5,453.5
Loans originated:							
Number	1,000	473.6	369.8	29.8	12.2	6.6	35.9
Amount	Mil. dol.	49,371.7	36,856.1	1,410.2	2,698.7	965.7	2,753.2
Applications approved but not accepted:							
Number	1,000	31.1	22.4	2.2	1.0	0.4	3.5
Amount	Mil. dol.	2,290.7	1,600.6	89.1	141.9	44.0	174.6
Applications denied:							
Number	1,000	336.4	211.7	54.8	9.1	3.6	47.8
Amount	Mil. dol.	16,951.3	11,456.1	1,339.6	920.1	282.7	1,694.1
Applications withdrawn:							
Number	1,000	56.2	40.1	3.3	2.1	0.8	4.6
Amount	Mil. dol.	8,431.1	5,866.1	349.2	548.8	162.4	616.7
Files closed for incompleteness:							
Number	1,000	23.9	16.4	1.6	1.0	0.3	2.0
Amount	Mil. dol.	3,207.4	2,157.9	139.5	198.6	62.0	215.0

[1] Applicants are shown in only one race category. [2] Total includes other races, not shown separately. [3] Joint means one applicant on an application reports a single designation of "White" and the other applicant reports one or more minority racial designations. [4] Persons of Hispanic origin may be of any race.

Source: Federal Financial Institutions Examination Council, "Home Mortgage Disclosure Act National Aggregate Report," <http://www.ffiec.gov/Hmda/default.htm>, accessed September 2017.

Table 1030. Net Stock of Residential Fixed Assets: 1990 to 2015

[In billions of dollars (5,851 represents $5,851,000,000,000). End of year estimates]

Item	1990	1995	2000	2005	2010	2012	2013	2014	2015
Total residential fixed assets............	**5,851**	**7,416**	**10,041**	**15,483**	**16,115**	**16,712**	**17,907**	**18,891**	**19,199**
By type of owner and legal form of organization:									
Private...............................	5,702	7,228	9,810	15,148	15,783	16,364	17,533	18,496	18,800
Corporate...........................	63	73	100	151	170	174	183	190	193
Noncorporate.......................	5,639	7,154	9,710	14,997	15,613	16,189	17,350	18,306	18,607
Government...........................	149	188	232	335	332	348	374	395	399
Federal.............................	52	62	75	103	98	101	108	114	113
State and local....................	97	127	156	232	234	247	265	281	286
By tenure group:[1]									
Owner-occupied........................	4,184	5,485	7,596	12,052	12,527	13,036	14,033	14,863	15,135
Tenant-occupied.......................	1,641	1,902	2,410	3,379	3,533	3,616	3,806	3,955	3,988

[1] Excludes stocks of other nonfarm residential assets, which consists primarily of dormitories and of fraternity and sorority houses.

Source: U.S. Bureau of Economic Analysis, Fixed Assets Accounts Tables, "Table 5.1 Current-Cost Net Stock of Residential Fixed Assets by Type of Owner, Legal Form of Organization, and Tenure Group," <http://www.bea.gov/iTable/index_FA.cfm>, accessed January 2017.

Table 1031. Commercial Buildings—Summary: 2012

[5,557 represents 5,557,000. Includes mall buildings. Building type based on predominant activity in which the occupants were engaged. Based on the Commercial Buildings Energy Consumption Survey (CBECS), a sample survey of building representatives conducted in 2012; subject to sampling variability]

Characteristic	All buildings (1,000)	Total floor-space (mil. sq. ft.)	Total workers in all buildings (1,000)	Mean square foot per building [1] (1,000)	Mean square foot per worker [1]	Mean operating hours per week [1]
All buildings....................	**5,557**	**87,043**	**88,182**	**15.7**	**987**	**62**
Building floorspace (sq. ft.):						
1,001 to 5,000...............................	2,777	8,036	10,232	2.9	785	56
5,001 to 10,000.............................	1,231	8,910	9,231	7.2	965	62
10,001 to 25,000...........................	882	14,083	14,183	16.0	993	65
25,001 to 50,000...........................	332	11,917	11,327	35.9	1,052	72
50,001 to 100,000..........................	199	13,938	12,354	69.9	1,128	80
100,001 to 200,000.........................	90	12,415	11,310	137.9	1,098	89
200,001 to 500,000.........................	38	10,670	10,347	284.3	1,031	100
Over 500,000..............................	8	7,074	9,196	885.0	769	117
Principal activity within building:						
Education.................................	389	12,237	10,885	31.5	1,124	53
Food sales...............................	177	1,252	1,172	7.1	1,067	121
Food service.............................	380	1,819	3,431	4.8	530	82
Health care..............................	157	4,155	7,613	26.5	546	60
Inpatient.............................	10	2,374	4,281	247.8	555	168
Outpatient............................	147	1,781	3,333	12.1	535	53
Lodging..................................	158	5,826	3,066	36.9	1,900	165
Mercantile...............................	602	11,330	9,117	18.8	1,243	64
Retail (other than mall)...............	438	5,439	4,023	12.4	1,352	62
Enclosed and strip malls..............	164	5,890	5,094	35.9	1,156	69
Office...................................	1,012	15,952	33,756	15.8	473	55
Public assembly..........................	352	5,559	3,108	15.8	1,789	56
Public order and safety..................	84	1,440	1,854	17.2	776	113
Religious worship........................	412	4,557	1,940	11.1	2,350	31
Service..................................	619	4,627	4,031	7.5	1,148	56
Warehouse and storage....................	796	13,032	6,362	16.4	2,048	67
Other....................................	125	2,002	1,611	16.0	1,242	61
Vacant...................................	296	3,256	236	11.0	13,811	8
Number of establishments:						
One......................................	4,205	54,944	52,072	13.1	1,055	64
2 to 5...................................	862	17,756	18,916	20.6	939	65
6 to 10..................................	147	4,425	5,890	30.1	751	77
11 to 20.................................	68	3,704	5,276	54.8	702	70
More than 20.............................	27	3,821	6,028	140.9	634	84
Currently unoccupied.....................	248	2,393	–	9.6	(X)	–
Year constructed:						
Before 1920..............................	362	3,980	3,309	11.0	1,203	48
1920 to 1945.............................	488	6,020	6,003	12.3	1,003	52
1946 to 1959.............................	599	7,381	6,566	12.3	1,124	51
1960 to 1969.............................	639	10,362	9,851	16.2	1,052	61
1970 to 1979.............................	684	10,846	12,536	15.9	865	61
1980 to 1989.............................	915	15,185	17,468	16.6	869	65
1990 to 1999.............................	845	13,803	13,432	16.3	1,028	68
2000 to 2003.............................	375	7,215	7,471	19.2	966	66
2004 to 2007.............................	347	6,524	5,993	18.8	1,089	69
2008 to 2012.............................	303	5,726	5,552	18.9	1,031	76

– Represents zero. X Not applicable. [1] For explanation of mean, see Guide to Tabular Presentation.

Source: U.S. Energy Information Administration, "2012 CBECS Survey Data," <http://www.eia.gov/consumption/commercial/data/2012/>, accessed March 2015.

Manufactures

This section presents summary data for manufacturing as a whole and more detailed information for major industry groups and selected products. The types of measures shown at the different levels include data for establishments, employment and payroll, value and quantity of production and shipments, value added by manufacture, inventories, and various indicators of financial status.

The principal source of these data is the U.S. Census Bureau's *Annual Survey of Manufactures*. Reports on current activities of industries or current movements of individual commodities are also compiled by such government agencies as the Bureau of Economic Analysis; Bureau of Labor Statistics; the Department of Commerce, International Trade Administration; and by private research or trade associations.

The Census Bureau's *Quarterly Financial Report* publishes up-to-date aggregate statistics on the financial results and position of U.S. corporations. Based upon a sample survey, the QFR presents estimated statements of income and retained earnings, balance sheets, and related financial and operating ratios for manufacturing corporations with assets of $250,000 or over, and mining, wholesale trade and retail trade corporations with assets of $50 million and over or above industry-specific receipt cut-off values. These statistical data are classified by industry and by asset size.

Several private trade associations provide industry coverage for certain sections of the economy.

Censuses and annual surveys—The first census of manufactures covered the year 1809. Between 1809 and 1963, a census was conducted at periodic intervals. Since 1967, it has been conducted every 5 years for years ending in "2" and "7". Results from the 2012 census are presented in this section utilizing the North American Industry Classification System (NAICS). Release of data from the 2012 Economic Census was completed in 2016. For additional information see text, Section 15, Business Enterprise, and the Census Bureau website at <https://www.census.gov/econ/>. Census data, either directly reported or estimated from administrative records, are obtained for every manufacturing plant with one or more paid employees.

The *Annual Survey of Manufactures* (ASM), conducted for the first time in 1949, collects data for the years between censuses for the more general measure of manufacturing activity covered in detail by the censuses. The annual survey data are estimates derived from a scientifically selected sample of establishments. The *ASM* is a sample survey of approximately 50,000 establishments conducted annually, except for years ending in 2 and 7, at which time ASM statistics are included in the manufacturing sector of the Economic Census. In 2012, there were approximately 294,600 active manufacturing establishments. For sample efficiency and cost considerations, the manufacturing population is partitioned into two groups: (1) establishments eligible to be mailed a questionnaire, defined as the mail stratum, which is comprised of larger single-location manufacturing companies and all manufacturing establishments of multi-location companies, supplemented annually with new large single-location companies from IRS data and new multi-location companies from the Company Organization Survey; and (2) establishments not eligible to be mailed a questionnaire, defined as the nonmail stratum, which includes small- and medium-sized single establishment companies.

Establishments and classification—Each of the establishments covered in the 2012 Economic Census—Manufacturing was classified in accordance with the industry definitions in the 2012 NAICS manual. In NAICS, an industry is generally defined as a group of establishments that have similar production processes. To the extent practical, the system uses supply-based or production-oriented concepts in defining industries. The resulting group of establishments must be significant in terms of number, value added by manufacture, value of shipments, and number of employees. Establishments frequently make products classified both in their industry (primary products) and other industries (secondary products). Industry statistics (employment, payroll, value added by manufacture, value of shipments, etc.) reflect the activities of the establishments, which may make both primary and secondary products. Product statistics, however, represent the output of all establishments without regard for the classification of the producing establishment. For this reason, when relating the industry statistics, especially the value of shipments, to the product statistics, the composition of the industry's output should be considered.

Establishment—An establishment is a single physical location where business is conducted or where services or industrial operations are performed. Data in this sector includes those establishments where manufacturing is performed. A separate report is required for each manufacturing establishment (plant) with one employee or more that is in operation at any time during the year. An establishment not in operation for any portion of the year is requested to return the report form with the proper notation in the "Operational Status" section of the form. In addition, the establishment is requested to report data on any employees, capital expenditures, inventories, or shipment from inventories during the year.

Durable goods—Items with a normal life expectancy of 3 years or more. Automobiles, furniture, household appliances, and mobile homes are common examples.

Nondurable goods—Items which generally last for only a short time (3 years or less). Food, beverages, clothing, shoes, and gasoline are common examples.

Statistical reliability—For a discussion of statistical collection and estimation, sampling procedures, and measures of statistical reliability applicable to Census Bureau data, see Appendix III.

Table 1032. Manufacturing—Contribution to Gross Domestic Product in Current and Real (2009) Dollars by Industry: 2000 to 2016

[In billions of dollars (10,284.8 represents $10,284,800,000,000). Value added GDP is the contribution of each industry's labor and capital to its gross output and to the overall gross domestic product (GDP) of the United States. Value added is equal to an industry's gross output (sales or receipts and other operating income, commodity taxes, and inventory change) minus its intermediate inputs (consumption of goods and services purchased from other industries or imported). Current-dollar value added is calculated as the sum of distributions by an industry to its labor and capital which are derived from the components of gross domestic income]

Industry	2007 NAICS code [1]	2000	2005	2010	2014	2015	2016
CURRENT DOLLARS							
Gross domestic product, total [2]	(X)	**10,284.8**	**13,093.7**	**14,964.4**	**17,393.1**	**18,036.6**	**18,569.1**
Private industries	(X)	8,956.0	11,366.3	12,826.5	15,115.8	15,698.7	16,177.5
Manufacturing	**31–33**	**1,555.3**	**1,704.2**	**1,830.6**	**2,099.4**	**2,170.3**	**2,175.2**
Durable goods	33, 321, 327	927.0	959.5	956.6	1,129.2	1,176.4	1,184.7
Wood products	321	28.3	34.9	22.1	29.1	30.2	31.6
Nonmetallic mineral products	327	42.7	49.1	36.2	45.9	48.0	50.0
Primary metals	331	47.0	56.6	48.4	58.6	55.9	54.4
Fabricated metal products	332	121.7	122.9	120.3	146.2	149.2	149.0
Machinery	333	113.3	114.9	122.1	152.2	153.1	148.0
Computer and electronic products	334	225.9	211.0	249.0	266.3	278.2	282.3
Electrical equipment, appliances, and components	335	45.8	43.2	50.0	55.4	56.3	55.5
Motor vehicles, bodies and trailers, and parts	3361–63	138.1	136.9	92.9	144.2	163.2	175.9
Other transportation equipment	3364–66, 69	71.2	89.9	112.2	126.0	131.1	125.8
Furniture and related products	337	33.6	33.8	22.2	26.1	28.1	29.4
Miscellaneous manufacturing	339	59.4	66.2	81.2	79.2	83.1	82.8
Nondurable goods	31, 32 (except 321 and 327)	628.4	744.7	874.0	970.2	993.9	990.5
Food and beverage and tobacco products	311, 312	164.1	179.9	229.7	246.3	257.5	263.1
Textile mills and textile product mills	313, 314	28.0	20.8	15.6	18.0	18.1	18.3
Apparel and leather and allied products	315, 316	22.2	13.9	10.5	10.1	10.0	10.1
Paper products	322	62.4	51.9	55.3	56.6	59.6	59.3
Printing and related support activities	323	43.7	44.6	38.8	37.5	38.7	39.4
Petroleum and coal products	324	53.1	142.7	130.0	170.6	161.8	139.6
Chemical products	325	189.0	227.3	330.8	364.6	377.3	387.6
Plastics and rubber products	326	65.9	63.5	63.3	66.6	70.8	73.1
CHAINED (2009) DOLLARS							
Gross domestic product, total [2]	(X)	**12,559.7**	**14,234.2**	**14,783.8**	**15,982.3**	**16,397.2**	**16,662.1**
Private industries	(X)	10,826.2	12,311.1	12,650.2	13,754.4	14,144.3	14,381.8
Manufacturing	**31–33**	**1,603.3**	**1,776.7**	**1,818.2**	**1,883.1**	**1,912.0**	**1,909.2**
Durable goods	33, 321, 327	806.1	930.1	976.1	1,100.0	1,109.5	1,110.0
Wood products	321	25.1	26.1	21.4	21.9	23.4	24.4
Nonmetallic mineral products	327	51.3	55.1	37.3	43.4	42.7	42.1
Primary metals	331	46.9	44.3	38.4	47.8	54.7	60.5
Fabricated metal products	332	162.1	152.0	129.3	145.8	140.3	137.0
Machinery	333	130.2	129.9	127.8	142.3	134.3	125.7
Computer and electronic products	334	91.8	153.8	255.8	284.0	295.5	302.1
Electrical equipment, appliances, and components	335	53.6	51.9	51.3	52.7	51.8	51.2
Motor vehicles, bodies and trailers, and parts	3361–63	106.9	129.6	99.8	150.3	154.3	163.5
Other transportation equipment	3364–66, 69	92.3	98.6	112.3	114.8	115.5	108.9
Furniture and related products	337	40.6	39.6	23.3	26.0	26.3	26.9
Miscellaneous manufacturing	339	62.3	68.0	81.9	76.0	76.6	76.0
Nondurable goods	31, 32 (except 321 and 327)	807.1	850.6	843.8	795.7	814.2	811.2
Food and beverage and tobacco products	311, 312	209.8	212.1	233.3	220.3	219.5	210.9
Textile mills and textile product mills	313, 314	29.7	22.3	15.6	16.4	16.1	15.6
Apparel and leather and allied products	315, 316	19.7	13.3	10.8	10.2	9.3	9.3
Paper products	322	72.6	64.9	53.4	51.4	51.4	50.8
Printing and related support activities	323	40.7	44.6	39.7	39.8	38.7	38.8
Petroleum and coal products	324	75.9	127.5	98.5	96.8	109.9	113.8
Chemical products	325	263.4	284.7	330.4	296.9	301.9	302.6
Plastics and rubber products	326	78.5	75.9	65.3	63.6	62.5	64.3

X Not applicable. [1] North American Industry Classification System, 2007; see text, Section 15. [2] Includes industries, not shown separately. For additional industries, see Table 693.

Source: U.S. Bureau of Economic Analysis, Industry Economic Accounts, Gross Domestic Product by Industry, "Value Added," <http://www.bea.gov/industry/gdpbyind_data.htm>, accessed July 2017.

Table 1033. Manufacturing—Selected Industry Statistics by State: 2012

[11,214 represents 11,214,000. Based on the 2012 Economic Census and the 2012 Nonemployer Statistics. See Appendix III]

State	Employers				Nonemployers	
	Number of establishments	Number of employees (1,000)	Annual payroll (mil. dol.)	Sales, shipments, receipts or revenue (mil. dol.)	Number of establishments	Sales, shipments, receipts or revenue (mil. dol.)
United States	**297,191**	**11,214**	**593,397**	**5,696,730**	**344,658**	**16,164**
Alabama	4,283	233	11,099	124,810	4,472	185
Alaska	527	12	515	(D)	1,130	38
Arizona	4,269	132	8,193	51,243	6,897	302
Arkansas	2,688	154	6,291	62,713	2,733	118
California	38,741	1,163	69,317	512,303	45,927	2,640
Colorado	4,898	115	6,230	50,447	7,324	293
Connecticut	4,350	164	10,546	55,160	3,646	230
Delaware	573	26	1,393	22,597	643	39
District of Columbia	113	1	61	310	267	10
Florida	12,890	277	14,270	96,924	21,526	1,057
Georgia	7,456	334	15,317	155,837	10,179	453
Hawaii	796	11	465	(D)	2,163	89
Idaho	1,759	52	2,445	20,201	2,674	89
Illinois	13,868	542	28,414	281,038	10,978	493
Indiana	8,141	453	23,041	242,764	6,995	322
Iowa	3,598	204	10,021	116,669	3,053	115
Kansas	2,875	152	7,578	86,076	2,891	124
Kentucky	3,782	214	10,140	129,284	3,860	182
Louisiana	3,308	136	8,489	271,191	4,413	195
Maine	1,650	49	2,424	16,045	2,608	91
Maryland	3,096	100	5,909	39,533	4,517	180
Massachusetts	6,806	234	14,395	81,928	6,073	322
Michigan	12,444	514	27,611	238,892	12,399	582
Minnesota	7,313	298	15,823	123,076	7,623	300
Mississippi	2,252	133	5,919	66,442	2,497	95
Missouri	6,097	243	11,921	111,535	6,237	283
Montana	1,237	16	715	11,535	2,108	71
Nebraska	1,844	92	4,003	57,499	1,620	54
Nevada	1,706	38	1,979	14,719	2,301	134
New Hampshire	1,851	67	3,924	18,896	2,274	110
New Jersey	7,758	231	14,095	108,855	6,676	430
New Mexico	1,389	27	1,349	29,102	3,173	91
New York	16,475	427	22,073	148,880	18,373	876
North Carolina	8,953	404	18,191	202,345	10,352	384
North Dakota	745	24	1,043	14,427	640	25
Ohio	14,482	627	33,135	313,630	13,302	677
Oklahoma	3,610	133	6,416	74,295	4,012	193
Oregon	5,289	152	8,122	51,350	7,193	269
Pennsylvania	13,988	544	28,058	231,396	14,067	744
Rhode Island	1,509	40	2,076	11,262	1,184	51
South Carolina	3,854	207	10,082	99,161	4,152	180
South Dakota	1,025	42	1,765	16,883	968	31
Tennessee	5,823	294	14,181	139,960	6,300	292
Texas	19,782	767	42,530	702,603	32,514	1,557
Utah	3,163	108	5,763	50,046	4,024	160
Vermont	1,013	31	1,594	9,315	1,890	55
Virginia	5,101	228	11,586	96,390	5,610	212
Washington	6,992	248	14,462	131,531	8,816	338
West Virginia	1,245	49	2,604	24,553	1,295	44
Wisconsin	8,995	437	21,879	177,729	7,127	330
Wyoming	553	10	631	10,784	962	33
Puerto Rico	1,653	84	2,875	76,575	(NA)	(NA)

NA Not available. D Withheld to avoid disclosing data on individual companies.

Source: U.S. Census Bureau, "2012 Economic Census, EC1200A1: All sectors: Geographic Area Series: Economy-Wide Key Statistics: 2012," <http://factfinder.census.gov/>, accessed September 2015. See also <http://www.census.gov/econ/census/>.

Table 1034. Manufacturing—Establishments, Employees, and Annual Payroll by Industry: 2014 and 2015

[121,070 represents 121,070,000. Excludes most government employees, railroad employees, and self-employed persons. See Appendix III]

Industry	NAICS code [1]	Establishments		Employees (1,000) [2]		Payroll (mil. dol.)	
		2014	2015	2014	2015	2014	2015
All industries, total..........................	(X)	7,563,084	7,663,938	121,070	124,086	5,940,187	6,253,488
Manufacturing, total.....................	31–33	292,543	292,825	11,424	11,606	639,911	656,771
Percent of all industries..................	(X)	3.9	3.8	9.4	9.4	10.8	10.5
Food..	311	26,947	26,819	1,439	1,486	59,006	62,392
Beverage and tobacco products............	312	6,768	8,002	171	185	8,840	9,632
Textile mills................................	313	2,302	2,210	104	103	4,220	4,333
Textile product mills........................	314	6,211	6,195	113	114	3,967	4,128
Apparel manufacturing.....................	315	6,891	7,087	106	104	2,873	2,863
Leather and allied products................	316	1,174	1,180	25	26	881	944
Wood products.............................	321	13,719	14,071	365	378	14,370	15,243
Paper......................................	322	4,261	4,217	352	351	20,998	21,481
Printing and related support activities......	323	26,187	25,688	459	448	20,141	20,240
Petroleum and coal products...............	324	2,158	2,133	102	102	10,112	10,446
Chemical...................................	325	13,079	13,182	750	759	58,891	60,805
Plastics and rubber products...............	326	12,398	12,276	724	740	33,623	35,063
Nonmetallic mineral products..............	327	14,799	14,731	359	370	18,324	19,231
Primary metal..............................	331	4,558	4,533	394	399	24,411	24,204
Fabricated metal products..................	332	54,879	54,767	1,426	1,447	72,995	73,683
Machinery..................................	333	23,872	23,794	1,063	1,078	63,364	64,579
Computer and electronic products..........	334	12,825	12,677	820	796	66,862	65,423
Electrical equipment, appliance and components........	335	5,697	5,671	337	345	19,128	19,984
Transportation equipment..................	336	11,780	11,880	1,419	1,478	93,421	97,124
Furniture and related products.............	337	15,521	15,098	354	359	13,960	14,729
Miscellaneous.............................	339	26,517	26,614	541	539	29,526	30,247

X Not applicable. [1] Data based on North American Industry Classification System (NAICS) 2012; see text, Section 15. [2] Covers full- and part-time employees who are on the payroll in the pay period including March 12.

Source: U.S. Census Bureau, County Business Patterns, "Geography Area Series: County Business Patterns," <https://factfinder.census.gov/>, accessed April 2017. See also <https://www.census.gov/programs-surveys/cbp.html>.

Table 1035. Manufacturing—Establishments, Employees, and Annual Payroll by State: 2015

[11,606 represents 11,606,000. Excludes most government employees, railroad employees, and self-employed persons. Data are for North American Industry Classification System (NAICS) 2012, codes 31–33. See Appendix III]

State	Establish-ments	Employees (1,000) [1]	Payroll (mil. dol.)	State	Establish-ments	Employees (1,000) [1]	Payroll (mil. dol.)
United States.......	292,825	11,606	656,771	Missouri..............	5,907	260	13,861
Alabama.............	4,158	248	12,530	Montana.............	1,276	18	851
Alaska...............	535	12	588	Nebraska............	1,785	93	4,298
Arizona..............	4,268	141	8,615	Nevada..............	1,794	42	2,340
Arkansas............	2,605	155	6,744	New Hampshire.....	1,788	67	4,282
California............	38,532	1,163	74,690	New Jersey..........	7,413	219	14,138
Colorado............	5,040	121	7,355	New Mexico.........	1,358	26	1,361
Connecticut.........	4,135	149	11,079	New York...........	15,963	423	23,694
Delaware............	583	26	1,500	North Carolina......	8,739	424	20,848
District of Columbia...	101	1	53	North Dakota........	758	25	1,206
Florida..............	13,112	298	16,069	Ohio.................	14,139	664	36,324
Georgia.............	7,432	365	18,108	Oklahoma...........	3,510	141	7,122
Hawaii..............	764	12	531	Oregon..............	5,432	160	8,638
Idaho...............	1,754	58	3,068	Pennsylvania........	13,666	552	30,798
Illinois..............	13,470	541	31,563	Rhode Island........	1,397	39	2,211
Indiana.............	7,991	489	26,179	South Carolina......	3,750	225	12,320
Iowa................	3,525	212	10,846	South Dakota.......	1,038	45	2,012
Kansas..............	2,817	167	9,052	Tennessee..........	5,645	316	16,362
Kentucky............	3,692	232	12,275	Texas................	19,759	811	48,829
Louisiana...........	3,273	125	8,479	Utah.................	3,286	118	6,513
Maine...............	1,661	50	2,570	Vermont.............	1,000	30	1,567
Maryland............	2,968	98	6,324	Virginia..............	4,984	237	12,936
Massachusetts.......	6,544	222	15,551	Washington..........	7,021	262	16,933
Michigan............	12,437	567	32,278	West Virginia........	1,196	48	2,742
Minnesota...........	7,311	304	17,373	Wisconsin...........	8,821	451	24,061
Mississippi..........	2,117	141	6,476	Wyoming............	575	10	627

[1] Covers full- and part-time employees who are on the payroll in the pay period including March 12.

Source: U.S. Census Bureau, County Business Patterns, "Geography Area Series: County Business Patterns," <https://factfinder.census.gov>, accessed April 2017. See also <https://www.census.gov/programs-surveys/cbp.html>.

Table 1036. Manufactures—Summary by Selected Industry: 2015

[Employee data in thousands (11,167.0 represents 11,167,000); financial data in millions of dollars (636,504 represents $636,504,000,000), except as noted. Based on data from the 2015 Annual Survey of Manufactures]

Industry based on shipments	2012 NAICS code [1]	All employees Number [2] (1,000)	Payroll Total (mil. dol.)	Payroll Per employee (dol.)	Production workers [2] (1,000)	Value added by manufactures [3] (mil. dol.)	Value of shipments [4] (mil. dol.)
Manufacturing, total [5]	**31–33**	**11,167.0**	**636,504**	**56,999**	**7,808.0**	**2,430,098**	**5,546,998**
Food [5]	311	1,389.1	59,567	42,881	1,100.6	282,651	775,591
Grain and oil seed milling	3112	53.7	3,285	61,228	38.8	24,587	89,458
Sugar and confectionery products	3113	72.3	3,349	46,305	53.4	16,432	34,864
Fruit and vegetable preserving and specialty food	3114	162.4	7,040	43,359	136.3	34,272	74,154
Dairy products	3115	131.5	6,959	52,923	99.9	32,167	112,566
Animal slaughtering and processing	3116	477.1	16,925	35,479	415.0	60,084	215,984
Bakeries and tortilla	3118	241.5	9,734	40,309	171.9	39,563	69,820
Beverage and tobacco products	312	156.3	9,180	58,719	88.6	94,191	155,583
Beverage	3121	143.5	8,349	58,195	78.8	60,691	114,055
Textile mills	313	100.3	4,200	41,862	81.4	11,995	30,617
Textile product mills	314	111.3	4,118	36,989	85.8	11,262	25,631
Apparel [5]	315	87.2	2,667	30,576	68.8	6,253	11,489
Cut and sew apparel	3152	68.5	2,115	30,889	53.4	4,834	8,888
Leather and allied products	316	24.2	897	37,059	18.5	1,945	5,040
Wood products [5]	321	366.6	15,035	41,015	293.7	40,780	97,193
Sawmills and wood preservation	3211	76.4	3,595	47,032	64.3	10,650	28,974
Paper	322	335.5	20,737	61,805	260.8	85,852	185,510
Pulp, paper, and paperboard mills	3221	102.2	7,830	76,595	81.1	43,394	80,432
Converted paper products	3222	233.3	12,906	55,323	179.7	42,458	105,079
Printing and related support activities	323	416.5	19,963	47,935	293.1	48,503	82,674
Petroleum and coal products	324	102.9	10,367	100,723	67.4	102,293	507,907
Chemical [5]	325	746.3	56,622	75,870	439.2	396,494	751,623
Basic chemical	3251	150.3	12,827	85,356	91.2	95,562	217,765
Pharmaceutical and medicine	3254	259.7	21,312	82,051	131.7	153,720	222,677
Soap, cleaning compound, and toilet preparation	3256	87.1	5,469	62,818	54.3	53,183	88,894
Plastics and rubber products	326	728.7	34,559	47,426	560.6	111,505	236,362
Plastics products	3261	599.0	27,937	46,637	460.7	91,201	191,915
Rubber product	3262	129.7	6,622	51,067	99.9	20,305	44,447
Nonmetallic mineral products	327	367.0	18,596	50,676	280.1	67,438	118,029
Glass and glass product	3272	85.9	4,417	51,421	68.3	15,186	25,518
Cement and concrete products	3273	162.3	8,062	49,682	125.5	28,376	53,331
Primary metal [5]	331	378.0	23,353	61,782	296.7	81,072	228,334
Iron and steel mills and ferroalloy	3311	95.6	7,444	77,850	76.4	29,305	88,647
Foundries	3315	121.9	6,273	51,449	98.7	18,066	32,242
Fabricated metal products [5]	332	1,372.0	72,216	52,636	1,002.5	187,296	349,958
Forging and stamping	3321	112.6	5,902	52,418	83.6	14,925	33,123
Architectural and structural metals	3323	328.4	16,765	51,044	234.0	41,399	84,557
Machine shops, turned product and screw, nut, and bolt	3327	372.6	19,445	52,195	277.5	41,664	66,714
Coating, engraving, heat treating, and allied activities	3328	120.4	5,825	48,376	93.5	16,839	27,850
Machinery [5]	333	1,041.2	62,451	59,981	657.1	189,796	384,579
Agriculture, construction, and mining machinery	3331	199.3	11,240	56,386	132.3	43,409	98,334
Industrial machinery	3332	101.5	7,314	72,024	54.2	17,939	31,231
HVAC and commercial refrigeration equipment	3334	130.8	6,416	49,067	92.5	21,762	43,987
Metalworking machinery	3335	145.4	8,561	58,896	99.5	18,856	31,265
Computer and electronic products [5]	334	773.5	62,394	80,662	362.2	175,064	300,494
Computer and peripheral equipment	3341	36.6	2,844	77,636	14.6	12,529	26,341
Communications equipment	3342	85.9	7,903	91,953	33.5	20,535	36,098
Semiconductor and other electronic component	3344	255.0	18,274	71,656	154.6	49,154	90,127
Navigational, measuring, medical, and control instruments	3345	372.4	32,064	86,107	146.2	89,535	142,065
Electrical equipment, appliance, and component [5]	335	338.9	19,318	57,001	225.9	61,288	125,954
Electrical equipment	3353	114.1	6,659	58,365	72.0	18,386	37,754
Other electrical equipment and component	3359	136.5	8,262	60,550	87.8	26,113	54,364
Transportation equipment [5]	336	1,465.5	96,525	65,866	1,052.0	338,305	948,208
Motor vehicle	3361	188.7	14,175	75,112	163.5	76,772	337,158
Motor vehicle parts	3363	529.9	28,008	52,858	410.0	83,092	257,388
Aerospace product and parts	3364	419.9	36,830	87,716	237.5	130,119	236,863
Ship and boat building	3366	133.3	7,788	58,402	90.9	20,743	34,315
Furniture and related products [5]	337	345.9	14,519	41,973	257.0	39,299	73,484
Miscellaneous [5]	339	519.9	29,219	56,195	316.0	96,817	152,735
Medical equipment and supplies	3391	256.6	16,323	63,610	156.2	59,856	88,970

[1] North American Industrial Classification System, 2012; see text, Section 15. [2] Includes all full-time and part-time employees on payrolls of operating manufacturing establishments. All employees represents the average of production workers plus all other employees for the payroll period ended nearest the 12th of March. [3] Adjusted value added; takes into account (a) value added by merchandising operations (that is, difference between the sales value and cost of merchandise sold without further manufacture, processing, or assembly), plus (b) net change in finished goods and work-in-process inventories between beginning and end of year. [4] This item covers the received or receivable net selling values, "free on board" (FOB) plant (exclusive of freight and taxes), of all products shipped as well as all miscellaneous receipts. In the case of multiunit companies, the manufacturer was requested to report the value of products transferred to other establishments of the same company at full economic or commercial value. [5] Includes industries not shown separately.

Source: U.S. Census Bureau, Annual Survey of Manufactures, "Geographic Area Statistics: Statistics for All Manufacturing by State: 2015 and 2014," December 2016, <http://factfinder.census.gov/>, accessed March 2017. See also <https://www.census.gov/programs-surveys/asm.html>.

Table 1037. Manufactures—Summary by State: 2015

[Employment data in thousands (11,167.0 represents 11,167,000); financial data in millions of dollars (636,504 represents $636,504,000,000). Based on data from the 2015 Annual Survey of Manufactures. Data are for North American Industry Classification System (NAICS) 2012 codes 31–33. Sum of state totals may not add to U.S. total due to independent rounding. See Appendix III]

| State | All employees [1] | | | Production workers [1] | | Value added by manufactures [2] | | Value of shipments [3] (mil. dol.) |
	Number (1,000)	Payroll Total (mil. dol.)	Per employee (dol.)	Number (1,000)	Wages (mil. dol.)	Total (mil. dol.)	Per production worker (dol.)	
United States.............	11,167.0	636,504	56,999	7,808.0	360,741	2,430,098	311,233	5,546,998
Alabama....................	233.6	11,989	51,325	175.8	7,733	45,183	257,010	129,827
Alaska......................	12.8	584	45,629	10.4	412	(D)	(D)	5,807
Arizona.....................	133.8	8,813	65,876	81.6	3,837	27,667	338,956	52,940
Arkansas...................	150.2	6,671	44,415	120.4	4,731	25,468	211,596	59,267
California..................	1,123.9	72,133	64,182	715.7	33,570	253,830	354,668	511,912
Colorado...................	119.4	7,188	60,182	78.1	3,658	25,974	332,754	52,722
Connecticut................	156.4	10,827	69,227	91.0	4,738	35,105	385,790	57,995
Delaware...................	25.9	1,496	57,661	17.7	804	6,029	340,429	18,674
District of Columbia........	1.1	53	46,419	0.7	30	(D)	(D)	316
Florida......................	269.4	15,010	55,712	179.7	7,735	56,974	317,052	107,033
Georgia....................	346.4	17,386	50,186	261.9	10,845	68,622	262,007	167,762
Hawaii.....................	11.4	556	48,828	7.4	335	(D)	(D)	5,904
Idaho......................	53.5	3,041	56,862	39.4	1,810	8,588	217,789	20,421
Illinois.....................	541.7	30,906	57,049	378.8	17,290	108,600	286,686	258,510
Indiana.....................	473.3	25,599	54,086	357.1	16,619	105,755	296,131	250,419
Iowa.......................	207.4	10,789	52,021	150.4	6,516	48,847	324,853	117,584
Kansas.....................	160.1	8,934	55,800	114.6	5,453	34,517	301,190	88,193
Kentucky...................	227.4	12,212	53,714	176.1	8,428	46,416	263,601	133,362
Louisiana..................	121.1	8,254	68,167	86.5	5,150	49,642	573,570	174,288
Maine......................	47.6	2,567	53,889	35.2	1,677	7,689	218,420	15,909
Maryland...................	94.2	6,032	64,053	58.0	2,742	22,019	379,670	40,223
Massachusetts.............	226.3	15,446	68,257	133.2	6,698	45,709	343,237	83,616
Michigan...................	545.0	31,339	57,502	392.5	19,340	103,492	263,659	264,609
Minnesota.................	291.7	16,327	55,973	194.9	8,751	55,699	285,808	119,852
Mississippi................	130.1	6,160	47,347	102.0	4,191	21,572	211,402	58,500
Missouri...................	247.7	13,739	55,470	184.3	8,884	54,050	293,278	121,666
Montana...................	16.1	848	52,787	11.1	512	3,402	305,382	9,722
Nebraska..................	93.6	4,394	46,926	71.5	2,954	19,289	269,687	56,703
Nevada....................	39.9	2,244	56,214	27.0	1,273	8,249	305,038	16,216
New Hampshire.............	65.9	4,071	61,768	39.6	1,808	11,015	278,024	20,288
New Jersey.................	224.6	14,430	64,242	142.9	6,822	47,702	333,892	96,575
New Mexico................	23.5	1,275	54,308	15.6	731	5,639	360,440	13,627
New York..................	398.5	22,836	57,310	266.6	12,223	78,528	294,598	150,850
North Carolina.............	407.7	19,968	48,975	304.0	12,181	107,969	355,179	214,445
North Dakota...............	24.4	1,160	47,592	18.5	752	5,019	271,344	13,827
Ohio.......................	649.5	35,884	55,249	465.6	21,825	130,628	280,540	325,674
Oklahoma..................	128.4	6,861	53,452	94.7	4,269	24,953	263,489	63,408
Oregon....................	156.6	9,289	59,325	107.6	5,107	27,579	256,252	58,405
Pennsylvania..............	531.1	29,616	55,765	368.5	17,203	108,333	294,021	224,894
Rhode Island..............	37.5	2,175	58,027	25.2	1,172	5,925	235,586	11,907
South Carolina.............	219.4	11,768	53,647	162.7	7,471	45,054	276,856	112,930
South Dakota..............	43.9	2,006	45,743	32.2	1,267	7,479	231,979	17,106
Tennessee.................	302.7	15,580	51,466	224.0	9,745	63,708	284,452	144,722
Texas......................	744.6	45,047	60,498	513.4	25,072	219,272	427,096	566,356
Utah.......................	110.1	6,212	56,433	74.0	3,424	22,739	307,466	48,646
Vermont...................	27.4	1,502	54,801	18.6	827	4,134	221,702	8,579
Virginia....................	230.4	12,587	54,623	164.9	7,532	57,468	348,555	101,654
Washington................	249.7	16,351	65,480	165.7	8,975	69,611	420,159	144,903
West Virginia..............	44.2	2,605	58,904	31.3	1,599	11,536	368,093	24,595
Wisconsin.................	436.7	23,110	52,921	312.5	13,595	80,759	258,456	175,958
Wyoming..................	9.2	633	68,808	6.7	425	2,809	417,204	7,702

D Withheld to avoid disclosing data of individual companies, included in higher level totals. [1] Includes all full-time and part-time employees on the payrolls of operating manufacturing establishments during the pay period that included March 12. Included are employees on paid sick leave, paid holidays, and paid vacations; not included are proprietors and partners of unincorporated businesses. [2] Value added is derived by subtracting the cost of materials, supplies, containers, fuel, purchased electricity, and contract work from the value of shipments (products manufactured plus receipts for services rendered). The result of this calculation is adjusted by the addition of value added by merchandising operations (i.e., the difference between the sales value and the cost of merchandise sold without further manufacture, processing, or assembly) plus the net change in finished goods and work-in-process between the beginning and end of year inventories. [3] Includes extensive and unmeasurable duplication from shipments between establishments in the same industry classification.

Source: U.S. Census Bureau, Annual Survey of Manufactures, "Geographic Area Statistics for All Manufacturing by State: 2015 and 2014," December 2016, <http://factfinder.census.gov/>, accessed March 2017. See also <https://www.census.gov/programs-surveys/asm.html>.

Table 1038. Manufacturing Industries—Employees by Industry: 2000 to 2016

[Annual averages of monthly figures (132,024 represents 132,024,000). Covers all full- and part-time employees who worked during, or received pay for, any part of the pay period including the 12th of the month. Minus sign (-) indicates decrease. See also head note, Table 653]

Industry	2012 NAICS code [1]	All employees (1,000)					Percent change		
		2000	2010	2014	2015	2016	1990-2000	2000-2010	2010-2016
All industries..................................	(X)	132,024	130,361	138,958	141,843	144,306	20.5	-1.3	10.7
Manufacturing..................................	31–33	17,263	11,528	12,185	12,336	12,348	-2.4	-33.2	7.1
Percent of all industries.........................	(X)	13.1	8.8	8.8	8.7	8.6	-19.1	-32.4	-3.2
Durable goods................................	(X)	10,877	7,064	7,674	7,765	7,719	1.3	-35.1	9.3
Wood products [2].............................	321	615	342	372	383	392	13.3	-44.4	14.6
Sawmills & wood preservation.................	3211	134	82	91	92	92	-9.6	-38.5	11.3
Nonmetallic mineral products [2]...............	327	554	371	384	398	408	4.9	-33.1	9.9
Cement & concrete products....................	3273	234	170	175	185	191	20.1	-27.4	12.5
Primary metals [2].............................	331	622	362	399	394	378	-9.7	-41.7	4.3
Iron & steel mills & ferroalloy production.......	3311	135	87	91	88	84	-27.7	-35.9	-3.4
Steel products from purchased steel...........	3312	73	52	60	59	56	4.0	-28.7	7.3
Alumina & aluminum production.................	3313	101	54	59	59	59	-7.3	-46.3	9.8
Foundries....................................	3315	217	112	126	125	118	1.4	-48.4	5.1
Fabricated metal products [2]..................	332	1,753	1,282	1,454	1,458	1,425	8.9	-26.9	11.2
Architectural & structural metals...............	3323	428	321	362	368	367	20.0	-25.0	14.4
Machine shops & threaded products...........	3327	365	313	371	368	353	18.4	-14.4	12.8
Coating, engraving, & heat treating metals....	3328	175	122	139	141	136	22.7	-30.0	11.4
Machinery [2].................................	333	1,457	996	1,127	1,121	1,080	3.3	-31.6	8.5
Agricultural, construction, & mining machinery..............................	3331	222	208	254	239	209	-2.8	-6.4	0.3
HVAC & commercial refrigeration equipment...................................	3334	194	125	128	129	129	17.7	-35.9	3.1
Metalworking machinery.......................	3335	274	155	182	184	180	2.5	-43.3	16.3
Turbine & power transmission equipment......	3336	111	92	101	101	99	-2.4	-17.6	8.0
Other general purpose machinery..............	3339	344	226	264	266	260	2.4	-34.4	15.3
Computer & electronic products [2].............	334	1,820	1,095	1,049	1,053	1,048	-4.3	-39.9	-4.3
Computer & peripheral equipment..............	3341	302	158	160	160	164	-17.8	-47.8	4.1
Communications equipment....................	3342	239	117	93	88	86	7.0	-50.8	-27.1
Semiconductors & electronic components.....	3344	676	369	367	370	367	17.8	-45.4	-0.6
Electronic instruments........................	3345	488	406	391	399	396	-23.2	-16.7	-2.5
Electrical equipment & appliances [2]...........	335	591	360	378	384	383	-6.7	-39.2	6.6
Electrical equipment.........................	3353	210	136	144	144	139	-13.9	-35.1	2.4
Other electrical equipment & components.....	3359	191	119	127	130	132	-2.3	-37.8	11.2
Transportation equipment [2]...................	336	2,057	1,333	1,559	1,605	1,625	-3.6	-35.2	21.9
Motor vehicles...............................	3361	291	153	194	201	209	7.4	-47.6	36.9
Motor vehicle bodies & trailers.................	3362	183	107	141	148	151	40.8	-41.4	41.2
Motor vehicle parts...........................	3363	840	419	537	565	580	28.6	-50.1	38.5
Aerospace products & parts...................	3364	517	478	491	490	489	-38.5	-7.5	2.4
Ship & boat building..........................	3366	154	125	137	138	135	-11.3	-19.1	8.5
Furniture & related products [2]................	337	680	357	370	381	389	13.0	-47.5	8.9
Household & institutional furniture.............	3371	441	223	233	239	245	10.7	-49.3	9.8
Miscellaneous manufacturing..................	339	728	567	582	590	591	6.2	-22.1	4.3
Medical equipment & supplies.................	3391	305	303	307	309	308	7.7	-0.7	1.7
Other miscellaneous manufacturing...........	3399	423	264	275	281	283	5.1	-37.6	7.1
Nondurable goods..............................	(X)	6,386	4,464	4,512	4,571	4,629	-8.2	-30.1	3.7
Food manufacturing [2]........................	311	1,553	1,451	1,484	1,512	1,554	3.0	-6.6	7.1
Fruit & vegetable preserving & specialty.......	3114	197	173	169	170	173	-9.5	-12.6	0.5
Dairy products...............................	3115	136	130	134	136	141	-5.9	-4.2	8.0
Animal slaughtering & processing..............	3116	507	489	481	486	495	18.6	-3.5	1.1
Bakeries & tortilla manufacturing..............	3118	306	277	293	297	304	4.9	-9.7	9.9
Textile mills [2]...............................	313	378	119	117	117	114	-23.1	-68.5	-4.3
Fabric mills..................................	3132	192	53	55	55	53	-29.0	-72.2	-0.2
Textile product mills [2].......................	314	230	119	115	116	115	-2.5	-48.2	-3.4
Textile furnishings mills.......................	3141	129	57	52	52	52	1.3	-55.7	-8.6
Apparel [2]...................................	315	484	157	140	137	131	-46.4	-67.6	-16.2
Cut & sew apparel...........................	3152	380	124	115	111	106	-49.3	-67.4	-14.3
Paper & paper products........................	322	605	395	373	373	371	-6.6	-34.7	-6.1
Pulp, paper, & paperboard mills...............	3221	191	112	105	102	100	-19.7	-41.3	-11.0
Converted paper products.....................	3222	413	282	269	271	271	1.1	-31.7	-4.1
Printing & related support activities..............	323	807	488	454	450	447	-0.2	-39.6	-8.4
Petroleum & coal products.....................	324	123	114	112	113	112	-19.4	-7.5	-2.0
Chemicals [2].................................	325	980	787	803	807	811	-5.3	-19.8	3.1
Basic chemicals..............................	3251	188	142	147	149	148	-24.4	-24.5	3.9
Pharmaceuticals & medicines..................	3254	274	277	279	282	287	32.4	0.9	3.7
Soaps, cleaning compounds, and toiletries....	3256	129	102	104	105	106	-2.4	-20.6	3.5
Plastics & rubber products [2]..................	326	951	625	674	689	699	15.3	-34.3	11.8
Plastics products.............................	3261	737	502	541	556	566	19.2	-31.9	12.8
Rubber products.............................	3262	214	123	133	133	133	3.5	-42.5	8.0
Miscellaneous nondurable goods manufacturing...............................	312,6	276	211	239	258	276	-21.4	-23.5	30.6
Beverages...................................	3121	175	167	197	215	233	1.2	-4.5	39.7

X Not applicable. [1] Based on the North American Industry Classification System, 2012 (NAICS); see text, this section and Section 15. [2] Includes other industries, not shown separately.

Source: U.S. Bureau of Labor Statistics, Current Employment Statistics, "Employment, Hours, and Earnings—National," <http://www.bls.gov/ces/data.htm>, accessed March 2017.

Table 1039. Manufacturing—Value of Imports and Exports by Commodity: 2015

[In thousands of dollars (22,409,854 represents $22,409,854,000). Values are based on manufacturing data from the Annual Survey of Manufacturers and administrative records from official U.S. import and export merchandise trade statistics]

Commodity description	Product code [1]	Value of product shipments [2]	Total export value of goods [3]	General import value of goods [4]
Food manufacturing:				
Dog and cat food	311111	22,409,854	1,287,219	737,563
Other animal food	311119	32,846,154	1,517,848	632,924
Soybean and other oilseed products	311224	28,795,485	7,108,470	6,522,705
Fruit and vegetable canning products	311421	26,621,505	3,196,434	5,448,624
Fluid milk products	311511	33,998,142	239,791	42,057
Cheese products	311513	40,207,913	1,398,943	1,299,483
Animal (except poultry) slaughtering products	311611	97,084,333	14,546,602	10,026,131
Meat processed from carcasses	311612	47,888,835	(NA)	72,074
Poultry processing products	311615	63,018,574	4,052,994	512,071
Commercial bakery products	311812	29,952,883	(NA)	(NA)
Beverage and tobacco product manufacturing:				
Soft drinks	312111	38,647,525	1,113,342	2,642,339
Brewery products	312120	30,325,474	3,607,549	4,642,091
Tobacco products	312230	40,227,092	923,172	1,331,044
Wood product manufacturing:				
Sawmill products	321113	21,396,612	3,397,432	5,655,773
Paper manufacturing:				
Paper (except newsprint) mill products	322121	40,582,956	2,588,402	3,684,189
Paperboard mill products	322130	29,506,988	5,062,046	1,917,381
Corrugated and solid fiber boxes	322211	36,963,623	1,548,695	429,176
Paper bags and coated and treated paper	322220	21,229,008	5,158,175	3,500,584
Printing and related support activities manufacturing:				
Commercial printing products (except screen and books)	323111	63,372,672	3,175,303	3,587,987
Petroleum and coal products manufacturing:				
Petroleum refinery products	324110	437,725,182	77,446,490	52,413,504
Chemical manufacturing:				
Petrochemicals	325110	50,473,687	1,520,724	1,391,752
Other basic inorganic chemicals	325180	27,914,611	13,417,818	9,032,100
Ethyl alcohol	325193	25,338,392	1,751,887	561,352
All other basic organic chemical manufacturing	325199	75,968,016	33,629,068	30,227,538
Plastics materials and resins	325211	78,903,074	28,826,278	12,814,676
Pharmaceutical preparations	325412	153,661,122	30,884,362	74,578,051
Biological products (except diagnostic)	325414	26,375,045	17,594,737	16,923,031
Paints and coatings	325510	27,380,466	2,731,439	1,005,297
Soaps and other detergents	325611	23,547,476	1,557,802	1,008,145
Toilet preparations	325620	36,384,754	8,947,014	7,854,786
Plastics and rubber products manufacturing:				
All other plastics products	326199	89,726,417	11,032,664	18,563,824
Nonmetallic mineral product manufacturing:				
Ready-mix concrete	327320	26,489,187	2,877	164
Primary metal manufacturing:				
Iron and steel mill products and ferroalloys	331110	84,649,951	13,758,995	33,252,860
Fabricated metal product manufacturing:				
Fabricated structural metal products	332312	29,061,976	1,277,020	3,520,255
Machine shops	332710	37,565,043	(NA)	(NA)
Machinery manufacturing:				
Farm machinery and equipment	333111	31,045,342	7,332,184	7,975,020
Construction machinery	333120	29,395,846	14,007,012	17,874,922
Air-conditioning and warm air heating equipment and commercial and industrial refrigeration equipment	333415	31,575,743	5,781,764	9,734,997
Other engine equipment	333618	27,455,200	12,104,017	13,693,314
Computer and electronic product manufacturing:				
Semiconductors and related devices	334413	46,074,331	41,806,342	41,679,508
Electromedical and electrotherapeutic apparatus	334510	27,337,381	10,108,755	10,338,084
Search, detection, navigation, guidance, aeronautical, and nautical systems and instruments	334511	39,088,992	5,976,264	7,829,869
Transportation equipment manufacturing:				
Automobiles	336111	118,437,969	48,443,716	165,006,696
Light truck and utility vehicles	336112	181,976,776	8,789,310	15,823,197
Heavy duty trucks	336120	33,145,393	5,841,994	14,233,918
Motor vehicle gasoline engines and engine parts	336310	31,547,247	8,683,072	18,719,050
Motor vehicle electrical and electronic equipment	336320	22,503,960	6,584,124	20,122,515
Motor vehicle transmission and power train parts	336350	40,067,604	2,953,470	9,013,376
Motor vehicle seating and interior trim	336360	30,863,764	3,005,086	7,657,618
Motor vehicle metal stampings	336370	34,986,457	1,365,403	715,551
Other motor vehicle parts	336390	64,106,339	17,874,145	36,229,749
Aircraft	336411	123,786,705	67,020,073	18,266,927
Aircraft engines and engine parts	336412	39,223,293	36,799,610	19,579,510
Other aircraft parts and auxiliary equipment	336413	40,627,789	24,082,313	16,462,580
Guided missiles and space vehicles	336414	22,201,356	1,316,593	5,378
Ships and ship repair	336611	24,666,600	2,010,137	1,090,406
Miscellaneous manufacturing:				
Surgical and medical instruments	339112	37,774,961	16,480,828	12,354,835
Surgical appliances and supplies	339113	31,056,632	11,287,768	13,638,150

NA Not available. [1] Based on North American Industry Classification (NAICS) product codes. [2] Includes total value of all products produced and shipped by all producers. For selected products, this can represent value of receipts, value of production, or value of work done. [3] Exports measure total physical movement of merchandise out of the U.S. to foreign countries whether such merchandise is exported from within the U.S. Customs territory, from a U.S. Customs bonded warehouse, or a U.S. Foreign Trade Zone. [4] Imports include commodities of foreign origin as well as goods of domestic origin returned to the U.S. with no change in condition or after having been processed and/or assembled in other countries.

Source: U.S. Census Bureau, *Manufacturing and International Trade Report: 2015*, February 2017. See also <https://www.census.gov/foreign-trade/index.html>.

Table 1040. Manufacturing Industries—Average Weekly Hours and Average Weekly Overtime Hours of Production Workers: 2000 to 2016

[Covers all full- and part-time employees who worked during, or received pay for, any part of the pay period including the 12th of the month]

Industry	2012 NAICS code [1]	Average weekly hours of production workers					Average weekly overtime hours of production workers				
		2000	2010	2014	2015	2016	2000	2010	2014	2015	2016
Total	31–33	41.3	41.1	42.0	41.8	41.9	4.7	3.8	4.5	4.3	4.3
Durable goods	(X)	41.8	41.4	42.5	42.1	42.3	4.8	3.8	4.6	4.3	4.4
Wood products	321	41.0	39.1	42.0	41.3	41.8	4.1	3.0	4.3	4.1	4.3
Nonmetallic mineral products	327	41.6	41.7	43.3	42.4	42.0	6.1	4.7	5.8	4.9	4.7
Primary metals	331	44.2	43.7	44.2	43.8	43.4	6.5	5.7	7.1	6.5	6.2
Fabricated metal products	332	41.9	41.4	42.6	42.3	42.1	4.9	3.8	4.8	4.3	4.1
Machinery	333	42.3	42.1	43.0	41.9	42.1	5.1	3.9	4.8	4.0	3.9
Computer and electronic products	334	41.4	40.9	40.8	40.9	41.2	4.6	2.9	3.0	3.0	3.3
Electrical equipment and appliances	335	41.6	41.1	41.7	42.2	42.9	3.7	3.6	4.5	4.2	4.3
Transportation equipment	336	43.3	42.9	43.6	43.7	44.1	5.6	4.7	5.3	5.3	5.9
Furniture and related products	337	39.2	38.5	40.9	39.8	40.0	3.5	2.3	3.6	3.1	3.0
Miscellaneous manufacturing	339	39.0	38.7	40.2	40.1	40.8	3.1	2.7	3.2	3.1	3.4
Nondurable goods	(X)	40.3	40.8	41.3	41.4	41.2	4.5	3.8	4.3	4.3	4.1
Food manufacturing	311	40.1	40.7	40.8	41.0	41.4	4.9	4.5	4.5	4.5	4.7
Textile mills	313	41.4	41.2	41.5	42.5	41.2	4.8	3.3	4.3	5.2	4.3
Textile product mills	314	38.7	39.0	38.0	37.0	37.7	3.4	2.4	2.8	2.5	2.6
Apparel	315	35.7	36.6	38.5	38.2	36.4	2.1	1.1	2.0	2.0	2.1
Paper and paper products	322	42.8	42.9	43.7	43.0	42.7	5.7	4.9	4.9	4.8	4.5
Printing and related support activities	323	39.2	38.2	39.0	39.8	39.2	3.7	2.2	2.9	3.1	2.6
Petroleum and coal products	324	42.7	43.0	46.1	45.2	44.2	6.5	6.4	7.3	7.8	6.8
Chemicals	325	42.2	42.2	42.7	42.6	41.8	5.0	3.6	4.6	4.5	4.1
Plastics and rubber products	326	40.8	41.9	42.2	42.4	42.4	3.9	4.0	4.5	4.5	4.1
Misc. nondurable manufacturing	329	40.5	37.8	39.7	38.0	37.8	5.4	2.3	3.5	3.2	2.8

X Not applicable. [1] Based on the North American Industry Classification System (NAICS), 2012; see text, this section and Section 15.

Source: U.S. Bureau of Labor Statistics, Current Employment Statistics, "Employment, Hours, and Earnings - National," <http://www.bls.gov/ces/data.htm/>, accessed July 2017.

Table 1041. Indexes of Employment and Hours of All Persons in Manufacturing: 2010 to 2016

[2007=100. Based on Current Employment Statistics and supplemented with Current Population Survey. Employment and hours of all persons include those of paid employees, the self employed (partners and proprietors), and unpaid family workers. See text, Section 12]

Industry	2007 NAICS code [1]	Employment					Hours				
		2010	2013	2014	2015	2016	2010	2013	2014	2015	2016
Food manufacturing	311	97.4	100.4	99.6	102.6	104.8	97.6	100.0	99.2	102.9	106.3
Beverage and tobacco products	312	93.3	102.1	108.3	115.5	124.4	86.6	103.3	105.0	109.2	116.6
Textile mills	313	71.3	68.3	68.7	68.8	65.9	73.0	70.6	70.3	72.0	66.3
Textile product mills	314	72.5	72.5	68.5	74.0	75.4	76.5	71.1	69.9	71.5	73.5
Apparel manufacturing	315	72.4	65.9	64.2	63.9	60.2	72.0	65.1	64.8	64.9	58.0
Leather and allied products	316	83.2	88.3	79.0	84.2	85.8	82.7	94.0	83.2	86.3	84.3
Wood product manufacturing	321	66.7	67.9	70.9	72.9	74.9	67.7	73.3	75.5	76.1	78.4
Paper and paper products	322	86.4	82.9	81.8	81.4	81.0	86.9	82.7	82.4	81.4	80.3
Printing and related support activities	323	79.7	71.7	73.2	71.8	70.6	78.9	72.2	72.8	72.5	70.7
Petroleum and coal products	324	99.0	95.8	97.5	98.1	97.7	95.5	102.8	103.3	100.0	100.0
Chemical manufacturing	325	91.5	91.6	93.6	94.2	94.6	92.4	93.3	94.2	94.4	92.8
Plastics and rubber products	326	82.3	86.7	89.0	90.7	92.1	82.6	87.3	91.0	93.0	93.4
Nonmetallic mineral products	327	75.2	75.8	77.2	80.1	82.6	74.4	74.0	76.9	78.3	80.0
Primary metal products	331	79.8	87.2	87.8	86.5	82.7	81.7	89.0	91.3	88.2	84.6
Fabricated metal products	332	82.4	91.5	93.5	92.9	91.1	81.1	92.4	94.8	94.0	91.8
Machinery manufacturing	333	83.6	92.4	94.0	94.1	90.5	84.1	93.3	96.2	93.3	90.6
Computer and electronic products	334	86.2	83.6	82.3	82.4	82.6	87.5	84.0	83.6	84.0	84.1
Electrical equipment and appliances	335	83.8	87.4	88.0	88.9	89.6	83.8	89.2	88.5	91.1	92.0
Transportation equipment	336	78.1	87.8	91.1	93.4	94.6	79.2	90.9	93.7	96.6	98.6
Furniture and related products	337	67.7	68.1	70.5	72.2	72.0	66.4	70.4	73.8	73.4	74.0
Miscellaneous manufacturing	339	87.3	89.2	89.7	91.9	90.8	87.4	91.0	92.4	95.0	97.2

[1] North American Industry Classification System, 2007; see text, Section 15.

Source: U.S. Bureau of Labor Statistics, Labor Productivity and Costs, "Labor Productivity and Costs by Industry Tables," May 2017, <http://www.bls.gov/lpc/tables.htm>.

Table 1042. Average Hourly Earnings of Production Workers in Manufacturing Industries by State: 2013 to 2016

[In dollars. Data are based on the North American Industry Classification System (NAICS), 2012. Based on the Current Employment Statistics Program. Covers full- and part-time employees who received pay for any part of the pay period including the 12th of the month. Excludes proprietors, self-employed, unpaid family or volunteer workers, farm workers, and domestic workers. See source, and Appendix III]

State	2013	2014	2015	2016	State	2013	2014	2015	2016
United States	**19.30**	**19.56**	**19.91**	**20.43**	Montana	17.19	17.28	18.01	18.69
Alabama	18.15	18.32	18.79	19.38	Nebraska	16.76	17.19	17.73	17.79
Alaska	17.44	20.44	22.58	22.16	Nevada	15.83	16.39	17.48	19.13
Arizona	18.69	18.49	17.95	17.61	New Hampshire	18.53	18.76	19.74	20.67
Arkansas	15.43	15.96	16.19	15.84	New Jersey	19.00	19.60	20.03	21.26
California	20.91	20.92	21.36	21.89	New Mexico	16.32	16.71	16.56	16.87
Colorado	24.65	25.04	26.54	28.67	New York	19.25	19.42	19.40	19.51
Connecticut	21.79	22.42	25.68	26.72	North Carolina	16.72	16.71	16.98	17.39
Delaware	15.96	16.63	17.25	17.61	North Dakota	18.70	19.18	19.96	20.61
Florida	20.34	20.09	20.03	21.01	Ohio	19.46	19.80	19.85	20.59
Georgia	18.08	18.10	18.02	18.14	Oklahoma	17.82	18.08	18.47	18.62
Hawaii	19.38	18.37	20.14	21.40	Oregon	18.73	19.32	19.67	19.96
Idaho	21.33	21.49	22.18	19.74	Pennsylvania	19.16	19.02	18.95	19.29
Illinois	19.45	19.49	19.78	20.25	Rhode Island	18.93	18.38	17.69	18.22
Indiana	18.43	18.78	18.91	18.89	South Carolina	17.92	18.66	18.86	19.26
Iowa	17.95	18.91	19.03	18.66	South Dakota	17.16	17.32	18.01	18.59
Kansas	18.11	18.52	18.87	19.00	Tennessee	17.21	17.49	17.48	18.58
Kentucky	18.87	19.74	20.33	20.41	Texas	19.91	21.09	21.67	22.66
Louisiana	21.99	22.04	22.07	22.11	Utah	18.07	18.39	19.06	20.11
Maine	20.86	20.55	20.89	21.28	Vermont	18.40	18.45	18.93	20.14
Maryland	18.02	19.33	18.85	19.08	Virginia	19.08	19.45	19.97	19.56
Massachusetts	21.55	21.41	21.80	22.79	Washington	24.34	25.16	25.52	26.42
Michigan	20.10	20.46	20.80	20.50	West Virginia	18.75	19.28	19.19	19.83
Minnesota	19.85	19.88	20.22	20.03	Wisconsin	18.56	18.95	19.32	19.62
Mississippi	17.45	17.83	18.30	20.33	Wyoming	21.58	20.99	21.58	21.99
Missouri	18.55	19.02	19.62	20.26	Puerto Rico	13.03	13.78	13.03	12.27

Source: U.S. Bureau of Labor Statistics, Current Employment Statistics, "Employment, Hours, and Earnings – National," <http://www.bls.gov/ces/data.htm>; and "Employment, Hours, and Earnings – State and Metro Area," <http://www.bls.gov/sae/data.htm>; accessed April 2017.

Table 1043. Manufacturing Full-Time Equivalent (FTE) Employees and Wages by Industry: 2000 to 2016

[123,384 represents 123,384,000. Based on National Income and Product Account tables. Full-time equivalent employees equals the number of employees on full-time schedules plus the number of employees for part-time schedules converted to full-time basis]

Industry	2002 NAICS code [1]	Full-time equivalent (FTE) employees (1,000)				Wage and salary accruals per FTE worker (dol.)			
		2000	2010	2015	2016	2000	2010	2015	2016
Domestic industries, total	(X)	**123,384**	**120,594**	**132,416**	**134,291**	**39,166**	**52,951**	**59,439**	**60,308**
Manufacturing	31–33	**16,948**	**11,231**	**12,075**	**12,046**	**43,957**	**60,018**	**66,821**	**67,607**
Percent of all industries	(X)	13.7	9.3	9.1	9.0	112.2	113.3	112.4	112.1
Durable goods	(X)	10,713	6,908	7,625	7,556	46,573	63,346	70,016	71,199
Wood products	321	602	334	370	381	30,351	38,152	44,748	45,064
Nonmetallic mineral products	327	549	357	389	397	39,021	50,623	57,188	58,422
Primary metals	331	611	353	386	366	45,836	61,058	66,620	67,409
Fabricated metal products	332	1,735	1,249	1,430	1,387	37,766	51,441	56,030	56,997
Machinery	333	1,427	976	1,100	1,056	46,612	62,655	69,867	69,745
Computer and electronic products	334	1,779	1,079	1,042	1,033	70,449	95,998	111,345	117,014
Electrical equipment, appliances, and components	335	583	351	376	376	40,241	59,422	66,520	67,213
Motor vehicles, bodies and trailers, and parts	3361–3363	1,301	673	906	934	48,754	58,384	61,688	62,171
Other transportation equipment	3364–3365	740	645	684	673	53,294	79,409	90,191	90,859
Furniture and related products	337	671	346	370	380	29,571	39,985	44,956	45,921
Miscellaneous manufacturing	339	715	547	573	573	38,744	56,906	64,868	65,269
Nondurable goods	(X)	6,235	4,322	4,450	4,490	39,464	54,700	61,345	61,563
Food and beverage and tobacco products	311–312	1,727	1,561	1,674	1,720	33,956	44,711	49,380	50,131
Textile mills and textile product mills	313–314	588	230	226	223	29,013	39,110	44,206	45,358
Apparel and leather and allied products	315	539	179	160	153	24,198	38,238	41,827	43,217
Paper products	322	598	382	364	361	45,834	61,583	68,439	68,587
Printing and related support activities	323	757	472	441	438	39,142	45,793	49,634	50,489
Petroleum and coal products	324	120	109	109	109	62,998	97,164	115,938	115,761
Chemical products	325	967	775	797	798	61,314	84,795	98,500	96,411
Plastics and rubber products	326	938	615	680	689	35,624	47,775	52,561	53,828

X Not applicable. [1] North American Industry Classification System, 2002; see text, Section 15.

Source: U.S. Bureau of Economic Analysis, National Income and Product Accounts, "Table 6.5D. Full-Time Equivalent Employees by Industry," and "Table 6.6D. Wages and Salaries Per Full-Time Equivalent Employee by Industry," <http://www.bea.gov/itable/>, accessed August 2017.

Table 1044. Manufacturers' Shipments, Inventories, and New Orders: 1995 to 2016

[In billions of dollars (3,480 represents $3,480,000,000,000), except ratio. Based on the Manufacturers' Shipments, Inventories, and Orders (M3) survey. See source for details]

Year	Shipments	Inventories (December 31) [1]	Ratio of inventories to shipments [2]	New orders	Unfilled orders (December 31)
1995	3,480	415	1.41	3,427	443
1996	3,597	421	1.40	3,567	485
1997	3,835	433	1.36	3,780	508
1998	3,900	439	1.37	3,808	492
1999	4,032	453	1.34	3,957	501
2000	4,209	470	1.37	4,161	545
2001	3,970	417	1.33	3,869	506
2002	3,915	412	1.30	3,823	476
2003	4,015	398	1.20	3,976	503
2004	4,309	429	1.17	4,289	555
2005	4,742	461	1.14	4,764	652
2006	5,016	509	1.21	5,090	796
2007	5,319	547	1.22	5,397	946
2008	5,469	529	1.43	5,452	995
2009	4,424	491	1.29	4,206	825
2010	4,911	538	1.27	4,896	870
2011	5,492	589	1.29	5,512	953
2012	5,697	607	1.30	5,710	1,015
2013	5,810	612	1.29	5,827	1,077
2014	5,888	622	1.34	5,931	1,168
2015	5,547	623	1.43	5,476	1,144
2016	5,447	627	1.37	5,374	1,123

[1] Inventories are stated at current cost. [2] Ratio based on December seasonally adjusted inventory data.

Source: U.S. Census Bureau, Manufacturers' Shipments, Inventories, and Orders, "Historical Data," <http://www.census.gov/manufacturing/m3/historical_data/index.html>, accessed July 2017.

Table 1045. Ratios of Manufacturers' Inventories to Shipments and Unfilled Orders to Shipments by Industry Group: 2000 to 2016

[Based on the Manufacturers' Shipments, Inventories, and Orders (M3) survey. See source for details]

Industry	2012 NAICS code [1]	2000	2010	2012	2013	2014	2015	2016
INVENTORIES-TO-SHIPMENTS RATIO [2]								
All manufacturing industries	(X)	**1.37**	**1.27**	**1.30**	**1.29**	**1.34**	**1.43**	**1.37**
Durable goods	(X)	1.56	1.62	1.65	1.64	1.64	1.74	1.68
Wood products	321	1.41	1.39	1.31	1.35	1.35	1.35	1.26
Nonmetallic mineral products	327	1.26	1.50	1.40	1.42	1.32	1.27	1.24
Primary metals	331	1.77	1.54	1.63	1.64	1.76	1.90	1.70
Fabricated metals	332	1.56	1.57	1.61	1.60	1.61	1.69	1.55
Machinery	333	2.05	1.86	1.91	1.88	2.06	2.15	2.19
Computers and electronic products	334	1.47	1.59	1.70	1.63	1.69	1.73	1.64
Electrical equipment, appliances, and components	335	1.41	1.46	1.61	1.67	1.56	1.70	1.70
Transportation equipment	336	1.42	1.66	1.64	1.65	1.53	1.74	1.66
Furniture and related products	337	1.36	1.18	1.13	1.13	1.07	1.15	1.14
Miscellaneous products	339	1.83	1.73	1.70	1.56	1.70	1.70	1.85
Nondurable goods	(X)	1.13	0.98	1.00	0.99	1.05	1.11	1.07
Food products	311	0.86	0.78	0.81	0.81	0.80	0.85	0.83
Beverages and tobacco products	312	1.50	1.66	1.59	1.70	1.68	1.76	1.74
Textile mills	313	1.54	1.25	1.31	1.19	1.25	1.24	1.22
Textile product mills	314	1.87	1.65	1.61	1.52	1.49	1.62	1.50
Apparel	315	1.91	1.61	1.95	2.07	2.13	2.28	2.03
Leather and allied products	316	1.88	1.78	1.80	1.88	1.97	2.20	1.98
Paper products	322	1.11	0.98	1.01	1.00	1.01	1.03	1.01
Printing	323	0.78	0.77	0.74	0.81	0.82	0.80	0.84
Petroleum and coal products	324	0.68	0.72	0.72	0.69	0.81	0.90	0.85
Basic chemicals	325	1.35	1.23	1.26	1.25	1.27	1.31	1.27
Plastics and rubber products	326	1.24	1.20	1.29	1.29	1.27	1.26	1.26
UNFILLED ORDERS-TO-SHIPMENTS RATIO								
All manufacturing industries	(X)	**4.02**	**6.10**	**6.31**	**6.73**	**6.93**	**7.30**	**6.89**
Durable goods	(X)	4.02	6.10	6.31	6.73	6.93	7.30	6.89
Primary metals	331	1.52	1.87	1.56	1.49	1.52	1.61	1.59
Fabricated metals	332	2.13	2.80	2.83	2.72	2.67	2.73	2.52
Machinery	333	2.66	3.81	3.77	3.66	3.48	3.62	3.58
Computers and electronic products	334	4.24	5.94	6.58	5.92	5.97	5.74	5.84
Electrical equipment, appliances, and components	335	1.83	1.96	2.11	2.01	1.99	2.09	2.44
Transportation equipment	336	8.06	14.12	13.74	15.44	15.66	16.55	14.93
Furniture and related products	337	1.29	1.40	1.27	1.65	1.44	1.61	1.70

X Not applicable. [1] Based on the North American Industry Classification System, 2012; see text, this section and Section 15. [2] Ratio based on December seasonally adjusted inventory data.

Source: U.S. Census Bureau, Manufacturers' Shipments, Inventories, and Orders, "Historical Data," <http://www.census.gov/manufacturing/m3/historical_data/index.html>, accessed July 2017.

Table 1046. Value of Manufacturers' Shipments, Inventories, and New Orders by Industry: 2000 to 2016

[In billions of dollars (4,209 represents $4,209,000,000,000). Based on the Manufacturers' Shipments, Inventories, and Orders (M3) survey. See source for details]

Industry	2007 NAICS code [1]	2000	2010	2013	2014	2015	2016
SHIPMENTS							
All manufacturing industries	(X)	**4,209**	**4,911**	**5,810**	**5,888**	**5,547**	**5,447**
Durable goods	(X)	2,374	2,281	2,696	2,797	2,779	2,742
Wood products	321	94	69	89	95	97	102
Nonmetallic mineral products	327	97	90	106	113	118	124
Primary metals	331	157	231	263	265	228	211
Fabricated metals	332	268	295	347	357	350	357
Machinery	333	292	316	394	404	385	358
Computers and electronic products	334	511	328	309	302	300	310
Electrical equipment, appliances, and components	335	125	110	124	126	126	119
Transportation equipment	336	640	636	841	912	948	936
Furniture and related products	337	75	60	68	70	73	77
Miscellaneous products	339	115	145	156	152	153	149
Nondurable goods	(X)	1,835	2,631	3,114	3,091	2,768	2,705
Food products	311	435	654	763	794	776	780
Beverages and tobacco products	312	112	130	147	147	156	160
Textile mills	313	52	30	32	31	31	30
Textile product mills	314	34	21	23	25	26	26
Apparel	315	60	13	12	11	11	12
Leather and allied products	316	10	5	5	5	5	5
Paper products	322	165	172	186	187	186	186
Printing	323	104	83	82	82	83	81
Petroleum and coal products	324	235	628	853	786	508	420
Basic chemicals	325	449	705	786	787	752	764
Plastics and rubber products	326	178	189	226	234	236	240
INVENTORIES (as of December 31)							
All manufacturing industries	(X)	**470**	**538**	**612**	**622**	**623**	**627**
Durable goods	(X)	298	313	360	377	384	381
Wood products	321	10	8	10	11	11	11
Nonmetallic mineral products	327	10	11	12	12	13	13
Primary metals	331	22	31	36	38	33	31
Fabricated metals	332	34	40	45	48	48	47
Machinery	333	49	52	62	66	65	64
Computers and electronic products	334	63	42	41	40	42	42
Electrical equipment, appliances, and components	335	15	14	16	16	17	16
Transportation equipment	336	69	90	113	119	128	127
Furniture and related products	337	8	6	6	6	7	7
Miscellaneous products	339	18	20	20	21	22	22
Nondurable goods	(X)	172	225	251	245	239	246
Food products	311	32	44	52	53	53	55
Beverages and tobacco products	312	14	18	20	21	23	23
Textile mills	313	6	3	3	3	3	3
Textile product mills	314	5	3	3	3	3	3
Apparel	315	9	2	2	2	2	2
Leather and allied products	316	2	1	1	1	1	1
Paper products	322	15	14	15	16	16	16
Printing	323	6	5	5	5	5	5
Petroleum and coal products	324	13	43	47	37	29	34
Basic chemicals	325	52	73	80	79	79	80
Plastics and rubber products	326	18	19	24	25	24	24
NEW ORDERS							
All manufacturing industries	(X)	**4,161**	**4,896**	**5,827**	**5,931**	**5,476**	**5,374**
Durable goods	(X)	2,327	2,265	2,713	2,841	2,708	2,669
Wood products	321	94	(NA)	(NA)	(NA)	(NA)	(NA)
Nonmetallic mineral products	327	97	(NA)	(NA)	(NA)	(NA)	(NA)
Primary metals	331	154	244	261	266	223	212
Fabricated metals	332	270	304	345	360	347	356
Machinery	333	295	334	385	404	380	354
Computers and electronic products	334	436	270	251	251	252	263
Electrical equipment, appliances, and components	335	126	110	122	128	126	122
Transportation equipment	336	663	638	929	1,002	937	909
Furniture and related products	337	75	60	70	69	74	77
Miscellaneous products	339	117	(NA)	(NA)	(NA)	(NA)	(NA)
Nondurable goods	(X)	1,835	(NA)	(NA)	(NA)	(NA)	(NA)

NA Not available. X Not applicable. [1] Based on the North American Industry Classification System, 2007; see text, this section and Section 15.

Source: U.S. Census Bureau, Manufacturers' Shipments, Inventories, and Orders, "Annual Benchmark Data and Benchmark Procedures," <http://www.census.gov/manufacturing/m3/index.html>, and "Historical Data," <http://www.census.gov /manufacturing/m3/historical_data/index.html>; accessed July 2017.

Table 1047. Value of Manufacturers' Shipments, Inventories, and New Orders by Market Grouping: 2000 to 2016

[In billions of dollars (4,209 represents $4,209,000,000,000). Based on the Manufacturers' Shipments, Inventories, and Orders (M3) survey. See source for details]

Market grouping	2000	2010	2012	2013	2014	2015	2016
SHIPMENTS							
All manufacturing industries	**4,209**	**4,911**	**5,697**	**5,810**	**5,888**	**5,547**	**5,447**
Consumer goods	1,501	2,059	2,437	2,496	2,508	2,268	2,206
Consumer durable goods	391	323	373	403	436	462	456
Consumer nondurable goods	1,109	1,735	2,064	2,093	2,072	1,806	1,751
Aircraft and parts	112	147	184	197	211	210	193
Defense aircraft and parts	25	63	58	59	58	55	47
Nondefense aircraft and parts	87	84	126	138	153	155	146
Construction materials and supplies	445	444	501	524	547	554	570
Motor vehicles and parts	471	401	508	546	600	637	642
Computers and related products	110	42	30	29	27	26	24
Information technology industries	400	270	273	271	263	259	259
Nondefense capital goods	808	728	885	892	906	884	829
Excluding aircraft	758	675	800	799	804	780	735
Defense capital goods	67	130	116	116	111	111	115
INVENTORIES (December 31)							
All manufacturing industries	**470**	**538**	**607**	**612**	**622**	**623**	**627**
Consumer goods	128	169	186	187	181	181	188
Consumer durable goods	26	21	24	25	27	28	28
Consumer nondurable goods	102	148	162	162	155	153	160
Aircraft and parts	36	55	67	69	72	79	77
Defense aircraft and parts	9	12	13	12	12	12	12
Nondefense aircraft and parts	27	43	54	57	60	67	66
Construction materials and supplies	49	52	59	60	63	63	63
Motor vehicles and parts	22	22	28	30	32	34	34
Computers and related products	8	4	4	4	4	4	4
Information technology industries	51	36	38	37	35	36	36
Nondefense capital goods	127	135	158	159	166	172	171
Excluding aircraft	107	100	114	113	117	116	116
Defense capital goods	17	21	20	20	20	21	21
NEW ORDERS							
All manufacturing industries	**4,161**	**4,896**	**5,710**	**5,827**	**5,931**	**5,476**	**5,374**
Consumer goods	1,502	2,059	2,437	2,496	2,508	2,268	2,206
Consumer durable goods	393	323	374	403	436	462	456
Consumer nondurable goods	1,109	1,735	2,064	2,093	2,072	1,806	1,751
Aircraft and parts	131	155	249	277	292	202	170
Defense aircraft and parts	31	63	69	54	56	52	51
Nondefense aircraft and parts	99	91	180	223	235	150	120
Construction materials and supplies	447	451	501	524	548	554	570
Motor vehicles and parts	468	403	511	546	605	639	641
Computers and related products	108	40	30	29	28	26	24
Information technology industries	410	273	274	256	259	258	267
Nondefense capital goods	831	748	932	970	980	868	808
Excluding aircraft	768	685	803	804	808	772	738
Defense capital goods	80	137	119	92	108	106	119

Source: U.S. Census Bureau, Manufacturers' Shipments, Inventories, and Orders, "Historical Data," <http://www.census.gov/manufacturing/m3/historical_data/index.html>, accessed June 2017.

Table 1048. Finances and Profits of Manufacturing Corporations: 2005 to 2016

[In billions of dollars (5,411 represents $5,411,000,000,000). Data exclude estimates for corporations with less than $250,000 in assets at time of sample selection]

Item	2005 [1]	2008 [2]	2009 [2]	2010 [2]	2011 [2]	2012 [3]	2013 [3]	2014 [3]	2015 [3]	2016 [3]
Net sales	5,411	6,374	5,110	5,756	6,486	6,668	6,743	6,903	6,433	6,273
Net operating profit	359	358	289	420	479	508	497	538	516	505
Net profit:										
Before taxes	524	388	361	584	722	676	722	745	612	657
After taxes	401	266	286	478	594	564	601	609	506	550
Cash dividends	179	182	172	180	184	212	242	259	275	280
Net income retained in business	222	84	115	298	410	353	359	350	231	270

[1] Based on the North American Industry Classification System, 2002. [2] Based on the North American Industry Classification System, 2007. [3] Based on the North American Industry Classification System, 2012; see text, Section 15.

Source: U.S. Census Bureau, *Quarterly Financial Report for Manufacturing, Mining, Trade, and Selected Service Industries*. See also <http://www.census.gov/econ/qfr>.

Table 1049. Manufacturing Corporations—Assets and Profits by Asset Size: 1990 to 2016

[In millions of dollars (2,629,458 represents $2,629,458,000,000). Corporations and assets as of end of 4th quarter; profits for entire year. Through 2000, based on Standard Industrial Classification code (SIC); beginning 2001, based on the North American Industry Classification System; see text, Section 15. For corporations above a certain asset value based on complete canvass. The asset value for complete canvass was raised in 1988 to $50 million and in 1995 to $250 million. Asset sizes less than these values are sampled, except as noted. For details regarding survey description, data analysis, and methodology, see source, 4th quarter report. Minus sign (-) indicates loss]

Year	Total	Asset–size class						
		Under $10 million [1]	$10 to $25 million	$25 to $50 million	$50 to $100 million	$100 to $250 million	$250 million to $1 billion	$1 billion and over
Assets:								
1990	2,629,458	142,498	74,477	55,914	72,554	123,967	287,512	1,872,536
2000	4,852,106	171,666	85,482	72,122	90,866	149,714	389,537	3,892,720
2001	4,747,789	169,701	84,664	67,493	88,088	131,617	393,752	3,812,474
2002	4,823,219	166,191	82,369	62,654	81,667	134,821	407,423	3,888,095
2003	5,162,852	161,462	80,681	62,592	77,205	126,826	392,192	4,261,894
2004	5,538,113	163,072	80,085	71,674	81,741	126,950	414,144	4,600,447
2005	5,828,716	165,195	85,785	68,731	87,818	142,900	423,917	4,854,370
2006	6,179,142	168,537	93,786	72,494	91,877	146,651	418,501	5,187,295
2007	6,891,131	180,319	98,348	80,400	93,017	144,254	433,634	5,861,160
2008	6,819,681	180,025	99,430	80,757	98,478	137,907	420,104	5,802,981
2009	6,942,972	166,590	106,773	71,642	76,308	126,202	413,856	5,981,600
2010	7,432,384	165,598	105,661	74,081	82,713	130,428	405,113	6,468,791
2011	7,907,376	169,045	114,818	76,809	86,452	130,488	435,889	6,893,876
2012	8,331,651	173,043	112,237	81,304	90,724	130,768	440,070	7,303,505
2013	8,838,478	173,571	116,199	88,598	86,532	138,222	439,357	7,795,999
2014	9,088,807	174,633	118,458	94,843	85,856	134,269	456,857	8,023,891
2015	9,632,509	174,895	121,807	88,342	90,246	153,601	446,889	8,556,729
2016	10,174,579	182,581	121,030	95,112	90,948	137,719	455,536	9,091,653
Net profit: [2]								
1990	110,128	8,527	5,160	2,769	2,661	3,525	7,110	80,377
2000	275,313	16,578	6,820	3,403	2,742	3,510	15,121	227,136
2001	36,168	8,387	3,366	-408	403	-543	-6,782	31,746
2002	134,686	10,003	2,784	807	1,699	3,356	-1,227	117,262
2003	237,041	9,821	3,374	2,005	2,256	2,973	4,115	212,497
2004	348,151	14,970	5,745	3,858	3,080	5,140	12,787	302,571
2005	401,344	17,357	6,057	4,066	3,781	7,678	15,967	346,438
2006	470,282	22,301	8,685	5,260	4,601	8,901	21,405	399,131
2007	442,734	22,930	9,006	4,402	6,518	8,400	17,565	373,915
2008	266,346	18,182	7,472	5,820	3,739	3,403	2,239	225,492
2009	286,491	9,692	5,979	4,617	2,500	2,723	2,653	258,310
2010	477,884	16,637	7,670	4,181	5,880	5,390	19,494	417,121
2011	594,335	20,357	9,257	5,209	5,730	6,808	17,568	529,406
2012	564,191	23,042	11,500	6,452	6,727	5,820	19,727	490,924
2013	601,368	24,740	10,202	6,468	6,141	6,982	21,000	525,835
2014	608,722	26,754	12,012	5,782	5,841	6,676	18,976	532,680
2015	506,008	25,663	11,056	5,858	6,079	6,577	15,602	435,174
2016	549,883	25,227	11,262	6,781	7,117	6,794	20,403	472,300

[1] Excludes estimates for corporations with less than $250,000 in assets at time of sample selection. [2] After taxes.

Source: U.S. Census Bureau, *Quarterly Financial Report for Manufacturing, Mining, Trade, and Selected Service Industries*. See also <http://www.census.gov/econ/qfr>.

Table 1050. Manufacturing Corporations—Selected Finances: 1990 to 2016

[In billions of dollars (2,811 represents $2,811,000,000,000). Data are not necessarily comparable from year to year due to changes in accounting procedures, industry classifications, sampling procedures, etc.; for details, see source. See headnote, Table 1048. Minus sign (-) indicates loss]

Year	All manufacturing corporations			Durable goods			Nondurable goods		
	Sales	Profits [1]		Sales	Profits [1]		Sales	Profits [1]	
		Before taxes	After taxes		Before taxes	After taxes		Before taxes	After taxes
1990	2,811	158	110	1,357	57	41	1,454	101	69
2000	4,548	381	275	2,457	191	132	2,091	190	144
2001 [2]	4,295	83	36	2,321	-69	-76	1,974	152	112
2002	4,217	196	135	2,261	45	21	1,955	149	113
2003	4,397	306	237	2,283	118	88	2,114	188	149
2004	4,934	447	348	2,537	200	157	2,397	248	192
2005	5,411	524	401	2,731	211	161	2,681	313	240
2006	5,783	605	470	2,910	249	193	2,873	356	278
2007	6,060	603	443	3,016	247	159	3,044	356	283
2008	6,374	388	266	2,970	98	43	3,405	290	223
2009	5,110	361	286	2,427	84	55	2,683	276	232
2010	5,756	584	478	2,708	287	232	3,048	297	245
2011	6,486	722	594	2,927	335	284	3,558	387	310
2012	6,668	676	564	3,102	303	260	3,567	373	304
2013	6,743	722	601	3,178	358	294	3,566	365	308
2014	6,903	745	609	3,342	378	308	3,561	367	301
2015	6,433	612	506	3,367	324	265	3,065	289	241
2016	6,273	657	550	3,334	337	277	2,940	319	273

[1] Beginning 1998, profits before and after income taxes reflect inclusion of minority stockholders' interest in net income before and after income taxes. [2] Beginning 2001, data reported based on the North American Industry Classification System.

Source: U.S. Census Bureau, *Quarterly Financial Report for Manufacturing, Mining, Trade, and Selected Service Industries*. See also <http://www.census.gov/econ/qfr>.

Table 1051. Motor Vehicle Manufactures—Summary by Selected Industry: 2015

[48,458 represents $48,458,000,000. Based on the Annual Survey of Manufactures; see Appendix III]

Industry	2012 NAICS code [1]	All employees [2] Number	All employees [2] Payroll Total (mil. dol.)	All employees [2] Payroll Payroll per employee (dol.)	Production workers [2]	Value of product shipments [3] (mil. dol.)
Motor vehicle manufacturing, total	**3361-3363**	**849,384**	**48,458**	**57,051**	**679,616**	**636,621**
Motor vehicle, total	3361	188,721	14,175	75,112	163,462	337,158
Automobile and light duty motor vehicle	33611	156,933	12,378	78,874	137,117	304,009
Automobile	336111	78,262	6,086	77,770	67,333	124,774
Light truck and utility vehicle	336112	78,671	6,291	79,972	69,784	179,235
Heavy duty truck	33612	31,788	1,797	56,538	26,345	33,149
Motor vehicle body and trailer	3362	130,790	6,275	47,977	106,165	42,075
Motor vehicle body and trailer manufacturing	33621	130,790	6,275	47,977	106,165	42,075
Motor vehicle body	336211	45,341	2,208	48,701	35,162	13,966
Truck trailer	336212	31,150	1,421	45,614	26,487	10,022
Motor home	336213	9,511	495	52,033	7,507	4,141
Travel trailer and camper	336214	44,788	2,151	48,025	37,008	13,946
Motor vehicle parts	3363	529,873	28,008	52,858	409,989	257,388
Motor vehicle gasoline engine and engine parts	33631	54,245	3,510	64,707	43,121	34,239
Motor vehicle electrical and electronic equipment	33632	56,394	2,879	51,046	43,112	24,503
Motor vehicle steering and suspension	33633	37,451	1,932	51,581	27,876	15,351
Motor vehicle brake system	33634	21,470	1,014	47,239	15,892	10,460
Motor vehicle transmission and power train parts	33635	65,956	4,099	62,145	50,806	37,807
Motor vehicle seating and interior trim	33636	64,185	2,779	43,291	49,358	30,934
Motor vehicle metal stamping	33637	94,953	5,226	55,040	76,086	36,253
Other motor vehicle parts	33639	135,218	6,569	48,584	103,739	67,842

[1] North American Industry Classification System, 2012; see text, Section 15. [2] Includes all full-time and part-time employees on the payrolls of operating manufacturing establishments during any part of the pay period that included the 12th of the month specified on the report form. Included are employees on paid sick leave, paid holidays, and paid vacations; not included are proprietors and partners of unincorporated businesses. [3] Includes extensive and unmeasurable duplication from shipments between establishments in the same industry classification.

Source: U.S. Census Bureau, Annual Survey of Manufactures, "General Statistics: Statistics for Industry Groups and Industries: 2015, and 2014," <http://www.factfinder.census.gov/>, accessed February 2017.

Table 1052. Motor Vehicle Manufactures—Employees, Payroll, and Shipments by Major Producing State: 2015

[14,175,149 represents $14,175,149,000. Industry based on the 2012 North American Industry Classification System (NAICS); see text, Section 15. See footnote 3, Table 1051 for information regarding shipments. Based on the Annual Survey of Manufactures; see Appendix III]

State	Motor vehicle manufacturing (NAICS 3361) Employees	Payroll ($1,000)	Value of shipments ($1,000)	Motor vehicle parts manufacturing (NAICS 3363) Employees	Payroll ($1,000)	Value of shipments ($1,000)
United States [1]	**188,721**	**14,175,149**	**337,157,630**	**529,873**	**28,007,830**	**257,388,296**
Alabama	11,196	942,348	28,270,145	24,860	1,144,671	15,794,426
Arizona	162	5,754	16,258	2,124	123,129	886,646
Arkansas	(4)	(D)	(D)	5,085	213,539	1,685,907
California	6,599	621,658	5,607,048	14,283	751,991	5,801,643
Colorado	(3)	(D)	(D)	1,425	96,170	318,707
Florida	1,139	59,526	379,687	3,321	172,922	1,190,935
Georgia	(8)	(D)	(D)	13,277	658,719	8,626,005
Illinois	10,458	706,098	14,610,510	31,569	1,493,704	10,930,631
Indiana	15,108	1,125,951	33,113,600	53,329	2,918,193	24,897,451
Iowa	63	3,102	47,873	4,967	228,464	1,673,694
Kentucky	19,647	1,591,314	31,288,645	33,087	1,616,129	16,633,586
Maryland	(2)	(D)	(D)	629	43,298	364,766
Massachusetts	(3)	(D)	(D)	1,582	98,298	712,907
Michigan	35,952	2,857,156	66,574,102	108,249	6,274,088	53,794,198
Minnesota	(7)	(D)	(D)	2,870	140,209	968,590
Mississippi	(9)	(D)	(D)	5,301	250,319	2,406,875
Missouri	11,935	(D)	(D)	11,579	525,767	4,741,606
Nebraska	(3)	(D)	(D)	4,025	184,905	1,369,386
New Jersey	61	3,728	65,932	760	40,130	250,543
New York	29	1,783	22,041	9,183	677,990	4,928,388
North Carolina	(8)	(D)	(D)	17,216	880,001	9,929,378
Ohio	21,384	1,564,352	45,878,385	69,589	4,020,436	33,120,651
Oregon	(6)	(D)	(D)	1,355	67,201	513,488
Pennsylvania	(7)	(D)	(D)	8,554	370,914	3,575,399
South Carolina	(9)	(D)	(D)	14,861	840,528	9,488,243
South Dakota	(5)	(D)	(D)	882	38,468	248,064
Tennessee	6,968	556,011	11,209,360	37,129	1,816,427	20,656,138
Texas	8,485	675,085	28,782,395	14,929	728,431	7,663,348
Utah	(2)	(D)	(D)	3,896	158,163	2,034,912
Virginia	(8)	(D)	(D)	5,261	250,386	1,491,965
Washington	(5)	(D)	(D)	2,690	111,059	989,001
West Virginia	(4)	(D)	(D)	2,905	154,961	3,061,162
Wisconsin	(9)	(D)	(D)	9,479	441,837	3,871,057

D Withheld to avoid disclosing data on individual companies. [1] Includes states not shown separately. [2] Employee class size of 0 to 19. [3] Employee class size of 20 to 99. [4] Employee class size of 100 to 249. [5] Employee class size of 250 to 499. [6] Employee class size of 500 to 999. [7] Employee class size of 1,000 to 2,499. [8] Employee class size of 2,500 to 4,999. [9] Employee class size of 5,000 to 9,999.

Source: U.S. Census Bureau, Annual Survey of Manufactures, "Geographic Area Statistics: Statistics for All Manufacturing by State: 2015 and 2014," January 2017, <http://factfinder.census.gov/>, accessed July 2017.

Table 1053. Net Orders for U.S. Civil Jet Transport Aircraft: 1990 to 2013

[1990 data are net new firm orders; beginning 2000, net announced orders. Minus sign (-) indicates net cancellations. In 1997, Boeing acquired McDonnell Douglas]

Type of aircraft and customer	1990	2000	2005	2009	2010	2011	2012	2013
Total number [1]	**670**	**585**	**1,004**	**142**	**530**	**805**	**1,203**	**1,355**
U.S. customers	259	412	220	24	232	596	443	304
Foreign customers	411	193	811	118	298	209	760	1,051
Boeing 737, total	189	378	571	178	486	551	1,124	1,046
U.S. customers	38	302	152	34	206	525	407	196
Foreign customers	151	86	439	144	280	26	717	850
Boeing 747, total	153	24	43	2	-1	-1	1	12
U.S. customers	24	1	13	-2	-2	-1	–	–
Foreign customers	129	18	30	4	1	–	1	12
Boeing 757, total [2]	66	43	(X)	(X)	(X)	(X)	(X)	(X)
U.S. customers	33	38	(X)	(X)	(X)	(X)	(X)	(X)
Foreign customers	33	14	(X)	(X)	(X)	(X)	(X)	(X)
Boeing 767, total	60	6	15	2	3	42	22	2
U.S. customers	23	-2	–	-1	–	31	19	2
Foreign customers	37	14	20	3	3	11	3	–
Boeing 777, total	34	113	154	19	46	200	68	113
U.S. customers	34	60	10	-7	3	37	4	11
Foreign customers	–	53	146	26	43	163	64	102
Boeing 787, total	–	–	235	-59	-4	13	-12	182
U.S. customers	–	–	45	–	25	4	13	95
Foreign customers	–	–	190	-59	-29	9	-25	87
McDonnell Douglas MD-11, total [3]	52	–	–	(X)	(X)	(X)	(X)	(X)
U.S. customers	16	–	–	(X)	(X)	(X)	(X)	(X)
Foreign customers	36	–	–	(X)	(X)	(X)	(X)	(X)
McDonnell Douglas MD-80/90, total [3]	116	–	–	(X)	(X)	(X)	(X)	(X)
U.S. customers	91	–	–	(X)	(X)	(X)	(X)	(X)
Foreign customers	25	–	–	(X)	(X)	(X)	(X)	(X)
McDonnell Douglas MD-95, total [3]	–	21	–	(X)	(X)	(X)	(X)	(X)
U.S. customers	–	13	–	(X)	(X)	(X)	(X)	(X)
Foreign customers	–	8	–	(X)	(X)	(X)	(X)	(X)

X Not applicable. – Represents zero. [1] Beginning 2000, includes unidentified customers. [2] Boeing 757 is no longer in production; the last delivery occurred in 2005. [3] McDonnell Douglas aircraft are no longer in production; last aircraft were delivered in 2006.

Source: © 2014 Aerospace Industries Association of America, Inc. See also <http://www.aia-aerospace.org/research-center/>.

Table 1054. Aerospace Industry Sales by Product Group and Customer: 2005 to 2014

[In billions of dollars (168.6 represents $168,600,000,000). Data for 2014 are preliminary]

Group	2005	2008	2009	2010	2011	2012	2013	2014
CURRENT DOLLARS								
Total sales	**168.6**	**211.1**	**210.7**	**209.4**	**214.9**	**222.5**	**219.4**	**228.4**
Product group:								
Aircraft, total	86.6	112.2	110.8	110.2	113.1	120.7	121.8	127.8
Civil [1]	37.2	48.2	51.3	48.2	53.2	62.2	69.7	75.3
Military	49.4	64.0	59.5	62.1	59.9	58.6	52.2	52.6
Missiles	20.8	24.6	24.7	23.5	22.7	21.8	20.7	19.9
Space	35.8	44.1	45.8	46.0	49.1	48.8	46.3	48.8
Related products and services [2]	25.4	30.2	29.4	29.7	30.0	31.1	30.6	31.9
Customer group:								
Aerospace products and services, total	143.2	180.9	181.2	179.7	184.9	191.4	188.8	196.5
DOD [3]	80.7	103.4	101.7	103.5	101.1	95.7	87.3	87.3
NASA [4]	16.1	18.1	19.3	19.4	19.9	19.5	19.1	19.8
Other customers [5]	46.4	59.4	60.3	56.8	63.9	76.2	82.5	89.5
Related products and services [2]	25.4	30.2	29.4	29.7	30.0	31.1	30.6	31.9
CONSTANT (2009) DOLLARS [6]								
Total sales	**175.7**	**212.4**	**210.7**	**209.6**	**214.0**	**219.5**	**215.2**	**222.9**
Product group:								
Aircraft, total	90.2	112.9	110.8	110.3	112.6	119.2	119.5	124.7
Civil [1]	38.7	48.5	51.3	48.2	52.9	61.4	68.4	73.4
Military	51.5	64.4	59.5	62.1	59.7	57.8	51.1	51.3
Missiles	21.7	24.7	24.7	23.5	22.7	21.5	20.3	19.4
Space	37.3	44.4	45.8	46.1	48.9	48.2	45.4	47.7
Related products and services [2]	26.4	30.4	29.4	29.7	29.9	30.7	30.1	31.1
Customer group:								
Aerospace products and services, total	149.2	182.0	181.2	179.9	184.1	188.9	185.2	191.8
DOD [3]	84.1	104.1	101.7	103.6	100.7	94.4	85.6	85.2
NASA [4]	16.8	18.2	19.3	19.4	19.9	19.3	18.7	19.3
Other customers [5]	48.4	59.8	60.7	56.9	63.6	75.2	80.9	87.3
Related products and services [2]	26.4	30.4	29.4	29.7	29.9	30.7	30.1	31.1

[1] All civil sales of aircraft (domestic and export sales of jet transports, commuters, business, and personal aircraft and helicopters). [2] Electronics, software, and ground support equipment, plus sales of non-aerospace products which are produced by aerospace-manufacturing use technology, processes, and materials derived from aerospace products. [3] Department of Defense. [4] National Aeronautics and Space Administration. [5] Includes civil aircraft sales (see footnote 1), commercial space sales, all exports of military aircraft and missiles and related propulsion and parts. [6] Based on Aerospace Industry Association's aerospace composite price deflator (2009=100).

Source: © 2014 Aerospace Industries Association of America, Inc., *2014 Year-end Review and Forecast*, December 2014. See also <http://www.aia-aerospace.org>.

Table 1055. General Aviation Airplane Shipments and Billings: 1990 to 2016

[2,008 represents $2,008,000,000. Data are for U.S. manufactured airplanes. Totals may not add up due to rounding]

Type of airplane	1990	2000	2010	2012	2013	2014	2015	2016
Airplane units shipped (number)	**1,144**	**2,816**	**1,334**	**1,518**	**1,615**	**1,631**	**1,592**	**1,525**
Total piston	695	1,913	746	708	754	788	783	718
Single-engine	608	1,810	679	645	674	716	740	685
Multi-engine	87	103	67	63	80	72	43	33
Total turbine	449	903	588	810	861	843	809	807
Turboprop	281	315	224	463	527	468	420	411
Business jet	168	588	364	347	334	375	389	396
Factory net billings (mil. dol.)	**2,008**	**8,558**	**7,875**	**8,017**	**11,069**	**11,688**	**11,982**	**10,577**
Total piston	92	446	368	374	456	484	477	511
Single-engine	68	(NA)	(NA)	(NA)	(NA)	(NA)	(NA)	(NA)
Multi-engine	24	(NA)	(NA)	(NA)	(NA)	(NA)	(NA)	(NA)
Total turbine	1,916	8,112	7,506	7,643	10,613	11,204	11,506	10,067
Turboprop	644	934	724	867	1,358	1,316	1,282	1,180
Business jet	1,272	7,178	6,782	6,776	9,255	9,888	10,224	8,886

NA Not available.

Source: General Aviation Manufacturers Association, *2016 General Aviation Statistical Databook & 2017 Industry Outlook* ©, 2017, and earlier reports. See also <www.gama.aero>.

Table 1056. Semiconductors, Electronic Components, and Other Electronic Component Manufacturing Equipment—Value of Shipments: 2010 to 2015

[In millions of dollars (9,765 represents $9,765,000,000). Data are from the Annual Survey of Manufacturers (ASM) and are based on the North American Industry Classification System (NAICS). The ASM is conducted annually, except for years ending in 2 and 7, at which time ASM data are included in the manufacturing sector of the Economic Census]

Product description	Product code	2010	2011	2012	2013	2014	2015
Semiconductor machinery manufacturing	333242	(NA)	(NA)	9,765	8,795	6,970	5,777
Semiconductor machinery manufacturing	333295	9,210	11,870	(NA)	(NA)	(NA)	(NA)
Electron tube manufacturing	334411	1,157	1,174	(NA)	(NA)	(NA)	(NA)
Bare printed circuit board manufacturing	334412	4,589	4,445	4,773	4,449	4,121	4,188
Semiconductors and related device manufacturing	334413	71,847	79,456	47,211	43,411	45,443	46,074
Integrated circuit packages	3344131	53,636	62,297	33,611	29,360	31,073	31,014
Transistors	3344134	658	676	542	539	285	300
Diodes and rectifiers	3344137	417	379	286	215	243	274
Other semiconductor devices (incl. chips, wafers, and heat sinks)	334413A	14,341	13,467	10,524	11,316	12,517	13,049
Other semiconductor and related device [1]	334413W	2,794	2,639	2,249	1,981	1,325	1,438
Electronic capacitor manufacturing	334414	972	1,070	(NA)	(NA)	(NA)	(NA)
Electronic resistor manufacturing	334415	582	548	(NA)	(NA)	(NA)	(NA)
Capacitor, resistor, coil, transformer, and other inductor manufacturing	334416	1,744	2,120	3,522	3,323	3,343	3,346
Capacitors for electronic circuitry	3344161	(NA)	(NA)	1,025	916	946	1,010
Resistors for electronic circuitry	3344162	(NA)	(NA)	433	382	402	345
Electronic coils, transformers, and other inductors	3344163	(NA)	(NA)	1,977	1,936	1,889	1,880
Other capacitor, resistor, coil, transformer, and other inductor [1]	334416W	(NA)	(NA)	86	90	106	112
Electronic connector manufacturing	334417	4,587	4,985	5,393	5,488	5,157	5,447
Printed circuit assembly, electronic assembly manufacturing	334418	18,197	18,151	16,383	16,947	15,820	16,838
External modems, consumer	3344184	716	705	232	260	180	94
Printed circuit assemblies, loaded boards and modules	334418B	16,181	16,146	15,134	15,757	14,776	15,795
Other printed circuit assembly, electronic assembly	334418W	1,301	1,300	1,017	930	864	948
Other electronic component manufacturing	334419	8,664	9,331	10,717	10,684	11,340	11,795
Crystals, filters, piezoelectric, & other related electronic devices	3344191	878	998	992	937	880	902
Electron tubes and parts, excluding glass blanks	3344192	(NA)	(NA)	1,154	927	952	954
Transducers, incl. electrical-electronic input/output transducers	3344194	1,200	1,266	626	789	943	927
Switches, mechanical, for electronic circuitry	3344197	1,070	1,094	981	973	997	993
Microwave components and devices (excl. antennae, tubes, etc.)	334419A	1,276	1,601	1,807	1,684	1,707	1,666
All other miscellaneous electronic components	334419E	3,437	3,413	4,212	4,508	4,840	5,273
Other electronic component manufacturing [1]	334419W	802	959	946	866	1,022	1,081

NA Not available. [1] Not specified by kind.

Source: U.S. Census Bureau, Annual Survey of Manufactures, "Value of Products Shipments: Value of Shipments for Product Classes: 2015 and 2014," <http://factfinder.census.gov>, accessed July 2017, and earlier releases.

Table 1057. Computers and Peripheral Equipment Manufacturing—Value of Shipments: 2010 to 2015

[In millions of dollars (16,987 represents $16,987,000,000). Data are from the Annual Survey of Manufacturers (ASM) and are based on the North American Industry Classification System (NAICS). The ASM is conducted annually, except for years ending in 2 and 7, at which time ASM data are included in the manufacturing sector of the Economic Census]

Product description	Product code	2010	2011	2012	2013	2014	2015
Electronic computers manufacturing	334111	16,987	6,814	8,116	7,878	8,918	9,237
Host computers, multiusers (mainframes, servers, etc.)	3341111	12,008	3,911	4,769	4,559	5,464	5,899
Single user computers, microprocessor-based	3341117	4,295	2,255	2,550	2,534	2,531	2,361
Other computers (array, analog, hybrid, and special-use computers)	334111D	375	345	456	446	517	406
Other electronic computer [2]	334111W	[1] 309	[1] 303	341	340	407	571
Computer storage devices manufacturing	334112	7,942	8,545	8,619	9,072	8,138	7,441
Computer storage devices [3]	3341121	7,108	7,747	6,948	7,092	6,359	5,962
Parts, attachments, and accessories for computer storage devices	3341124	652	603	1,616	1,920	1,699	1,417
Other computer storage device manufacturing [2]	334112W	182	196	56	60	80	63
Computer terminal and other computer peripheral equipment manufacturing	334118	(NA)	(NA)	10,634	10,691	8,974	8,227
Computer terminals (excluding point-of-sale and funds-transfer devices, parts, attachments, and accessories)	3341181	(NA)	(NA)	353	514	579	704
Parts, attachments, and accessories for computer terminals (excluding point-of-sale and funds-transfer devices)	3341182	(NA)	(NA)	20	22	70	77
All other miscellaneous computer peripheral (input/output) equipment [3]	3341183	(NA)	(NA)	7,041	6,232	4,721	4,389
Parts, subassemblies, and accessories for computer peripheral equipment (excluding digital cameras) [3]	3341184	(NA)	(NA)	1445	2287	2,412	1957
Point-of-sale terminals and fund-transfer devices	3341185	(NA)	(NA)	906	855	592	463
Parts and attachments for point-of-sale terminals and fund-transfer devices	3341186	(NA)	(NA)	284	135	97	80
Other computer terminal and other computer peripheral equipment [2]	334118W	(NA)	(NA)	585	645	503	558
Magnetic and optical recording media	334613	753	603	321	[1] 233	452	435
Software and other prerecorded compact disc, tape, and record reproducing	334614	(NA)	(NA)	2,670	2,525	2,291	2,298
Software reproducing	3346141	(NA)	(NA)	684	649	648	613
Reproduction of recording media	3346142	(NA)	(NA)	1,904	1,749	1,554	1,595

NA Not available. [1] Sampling error exceeds 40 percent. [2] Not specified by kind. [3] Excluding parts, attachments, accessories, etc.

Source: U.S. Census Bureau, Annual Survey of Manufactures, "Value of Products Shipments: Value of Shipments for Product Classes: 2015 and 2014," <http://factfinder.census.gov>, accessed July 2017, and earlier releases.

Table 1058. Communications Equipment Manufacturing—Value of Shipments: 2009 to 2015

[In millions of dollars (7,623 represents $7,623,000,000). Data are from the Annual Survey of Manufacturers (ASM) and are based on the North American Industry Classification System (NAICS). The ASM is conducted annually, except for years ending in 2 and 7, at which time ASM data are included in the manufacturing sector of the Economic Census]

Product description	Product code	2009	2010	2011	2012	2013	2014	2015
Telephone apparatus manufacturing	334210	7,623	8,340	8,188	7,171	7,539	6,535	6,634
Telephone switching and switchboard equipment	3342101	1,693	1,719	1,562	654	1,368	1,333	1,392
Carrier line equipment and non-consumer modems	3342104	2,208	2,406	2,647	2,310	1,728	1,860	1,949
Wireline voice and data network equipment	3342107	3,036	3,453	3,197	3,348	3,621	2,530	2,228
Other telephone apparatus manufacturing	334210W	687	762	782	859	822	812	1,065
Radio and television broadcast and wireless communications equipment	334220	27,838	26,663	26,114	26,345	26,379	23,066	21,007
Broadcast, studio, and related electronic equipment	3342202	3,684	4,549	4,599	2,335	2,025	1,923	1,918
Wireless networking equipment	3342203	1,950	1,528	1,088	2,093	2,262	1,528	1,442
Radio station equipment	3342205	13,796	12,225	11,328	9,761	9,936	9,140	8,734
Other communications systems and equipment	3342209	7,397	7,804	8,465	10,571	10,582	9,142	7,627
Other radio and television broadcast and wireless communications equipment	334220W	[1] 1,011	(S)	(S)	1,586	1,574	1,334	1,285
Other communications equipment manufacturing	334290	3,482	4,801	4,906	4,663	4,909	4,923	4,445
Alarm systems (incl. electric sirens and horns)	3342901	1,423	1,258	1,377	2,015	2,177	1,951	1,613
Vehicular and pedestrian traffic control equipment	3342902	1,185	2,656	2,641	1,595	1,739	1,995	1,823
Intercommunications systems (incl. inductive paging systems)	3342903	336	453	455	562	465	450	525
Other communications equipment [2]	334290W	538	434	432	491	528	527	484
External modems, consumer	3344184	443	716	705	232	260	180	94

S Estimates do not meet publication standards. [1] Sampling error exceeds 40 percent. [2] Not specified by kind.

Source: U.S. Census Bureau, Annual Survey of Manufactures, "Value of Products Shipments: Value of Shipments for Product Classes: 2015 and 2014," <http://factfinder.census.gov>, accessed July 2017, and earlier releases.

Table 1059. Pharmaceutical Preparations—Value of Shipments: 2009 to 2015

[In millions of dollars (125,249 represents $125,249,000,000). Data are from the Annual Survey of Manufactures (ASM) and based on the North American Industry Classification System (NAICS). The ASM is conducted annually, except for years ending in 2 and 7, at which time ASM data are included in the manufacturing sector of the Economic Census]

Product description	Product code	2009	2010	2011	2012	2013	2014	2015
Pharmaceutical preparations, except biologicals......	**325412**	**125,249**	**114,131**	**123,950**	**115,776**	**120,032**	**137,663**	**153,661**
Affecting neoplasms, endocrine system, and metabolic disease........	3254121	33,225	27,167	27,957	24,432	27,019	26,101	30,265
Acting on the central nervous system and sense organs....	3254124	27,415	25,235	26,010	24,154	25,334	27,966	32,080
Acting on the cardiovascular system..........................	3254127	12,038	10,441	11,076	7,796	12,317	13,807	13,731
Acting on the respiratory system..........................	325412A	13,831	14,249	20,545	19,241	13,108	13,705	14,078
Acting on the digestive system or genito-urinary system.....	325412D	8,792	7,780	7,138	7,500	4,581	5,286	5,232
Acting on the skin...........................	325412G	3,884	4,148	3,586	2,986	2,624	2,771	4,157
Vitamin, nutrient, and hematinic preparations.................	325412L	8,898	8,980	10,244	9,298	8,103	10,665	11,299
Affecting parasitic and infective diseases (excl. diagnostics)........	325412P	9,287	8,400	8,892	8,355	15,634	28,032	33,180
Preparations for veterinary use (excl. diagnostics) [1].........	325412T	2,592	2,674	2,851	2,920	2,411	2,328	2,140
In vivo diagnostic substances..........................	325412V	1,917	1,660	1,904	2,692	2,504	1,259	1,318
Other pharmaceutical preparation manufacturing [2]...........	325412W	3,370	3,397	3,747	6,402	6,397	5,744	6,181

[1] Including medicinal premixes and medicated pet care products; excluding pet flea and tick products. [2] Not specified by kind.

Source: U.S. Census Bureau, Annual Survey of Manufactures, "Value of Products Shipments: Value of Shipments for Product Classes: 2015 and 2014," <http://factfinder.census.gov>, accessed July 2017, and earlier releases.

Table 1060. Household Appliances Manufacturing—Value of Shipments: 2009 to 2015

[In millions of dollars (3,674 represents $3,674,000,000). Data are from the Annual Survey of Manufacturers (ASM) and are based on the North American Industry Classification System (NAICS). The ASM is conducted annually, except for years ending in 2 and 7, at which time ASM data are included in the manufacturing sector of the Economic Census]

Product description	Product code	2009	2010	2011	2012	2013	2014	2015
Household cooking appliance manufacturing....................	335221	3,674	3,719	3,781	4,369	4,419	4,472	4,767
Electric household ranges, ovens, and surface cooking units & equipment........	3352211	1,980	1,895	1,908	2,494	2,376	2,452	2,614
Gas household ranges, ovens, and surface cooking units & equipment........	3352213	1,043	1,121	1,154	1,156	1,223	975	1,063
Other household ranges and cooking equipment..............	3352215	648	690	707	700	801	1,012	1,056
Other household cooking appliance manufacturing.............	335221W	3	13	12	18	19	33	34
Household refrigerator and home freezer manufacturing........	335222	3,538	3,481	3,512	3,497	3,364	3,824	4,095
Household refrigerators (incl. combination refrigerator-freezers)........	3352221	(D)	(D)	2,880	2,966	2,931	(D)	(D)
Household laundry equipment manufacturing...................	335224	3,551	3,528	3,578	3,553	3,529	3,497	3,526
Other major household appliance manufacturing................	335228	3,654	3,761	3,946	4,385	4,318	4,610	4,869
Household water heaters, electric, for permanent installation........	3352281	638	613	673	957	815	898	828
Household water heaters, except electric......................	3352283	923	983	1,092	1,251	1,144	1,253	1,429
All other misc. household appliances (including parts).........	3352285	2,065	2,151	2,168	2,161	2,317	2,437	2,590
Other major household appliance manufacturing [1].............	335228W	28	14	13	16	42	22	22

D Data withheld to avoid disclosing data of individual companies. [1] Not specified by kind.

Source: U.S. Census Bureau, Annual Survey of Manufactures, "Value of Products Shipments: Value of Shipments for Product Classes: 2015 and 2014," <http://factfinder.census.gov>, accessed July 2017, and earlier releases.

Wholesale and Retail Trade

This section presents statistics relating to the distributive trades, specifically wholesale trade and retail trade. Data shown for the trades are classified by kind of business and cover sales, establishments, employees, payrolls, and other items. The principal sources of these data are from the U.S. Census Bureau and include the *2007* and *2012 Economic Censuses*, annual and monthly surveys, and the *County Business Patterns* program. These data are supplemented by several tables from trade associations, such as the National Automobile Dealers Association.

Data on wholesale and retail trade also appear in several other sections. For instance, labor force employment and earnings data appear in Section 12, Labor Force, Employment, and Earnings; gross domestic product of the industry (Table 693) appears in Section 13, Income, Expenditures, Poverty, and Wealth; and financial data (several tables) from the quarterly *Statistics of Income Bulletin*, published by the Internal Revenue Service, appear in Section 15, Business Enterprise.

Censuses—Censuses of wholesale trade and retail trade have been taken at various intervals since 1929. Beginning with the 1967 census, legislation provides for a census of each area to be conducted every 5 years (for years ending in "2" and "7"). The industries covered in the censuses and surveys of business are defined in the North American Industry Classification System (NAICS). Retail trade refers to places of business primarily engaged in retailing merchandise to the general public; and wholesale trade, to establishments primarily engaged in selling goods to other businesses and normally operating from a warehouse or office that have little or no display of merchandise. Census Bureau tables in this section generally utilize either the 2007 or 2012 NAICS codes. NAICS codes are reviewed every 5 years to identify areas for revision, so that the classification system can keep pace with the changing economy. For information on this system and how it affects the comparability of wholesale and retail statistics historically, see text, Section 15, Business Enterprise, and especially the Census Bureau website at <http://www.census.gov/eos/www/naics>.

The *2007* and *2012 Economic Censuses* have three series of publications for these two sectors: 1) subject series with reports such as product lines and establishment and firm sizes, 2) geographic reports with individual reports for each state, and 3) industry series with individual reports for industry groups. Release of data from the *2012 Economic Census* was completed in 2016. For information on these series, see the Census Bureau website at <https://www.census.gov/programs-surveys/economic-census.html>.

Current surveys—Current sample surveys conducted by the Census Bureau cover various aspects of wholesale and retail trade. Its *Monthly Retail Trade and Food Services* release at <http://www.census.gov/retail/index.html> contains monthly estimates of sales, inventories, and inventory/sales ratios for the United States, by kind of business. Annual figures on retail sales, year-end inventories, purchases, accounts receivable, and gross margins by kind of business are located on the Census Bureau website at <https://www.census.gov/retail/index.html#arts>.

Statistics from the Census Bureau's monthly wholesale trade survey include national estimates of sales, inventories, and inventory/sales ratios for merchant wholesalers excluding manufacturers' sales branches and offices. Data are presented by major summary groups "durable and nondurable," and 4-digit NAICS industry groups. Merchant wholesalers excluding manufacturers' sales branches and offices are those wholesalers who take title to the goods they sell (e.g., jobbers, exporters, importers, industrial distributors). These data, based on reports submitted by a sample of firms, appear in the *Monthly Wholesale Trade Report*. This report, along with monthly sales, inventories, and inventories/sales ratios, also provides data on annual sales, inventories, and year-end inventories/sales ratios. The *Annual Wholesale Trade Survey* provides data on merchant wholesalers excluding manufacturer sales branches and offices as well as summary data for all merchant wholesalers. This report also provides separate data for manufacturer sales branches and offices, and electronic markets, agents, brokers, and commission merchants. Included in the *Annual Wholesale Trade Report* are data on annual sales, year-end inventories, inventories/sales ratios, operating expenses, purchases, and gross margins. Data are presented by major summary groups "durable and nondurable" and 4-digit NAICS industry groups. These reports are available on the Census Bureau website at <http://www.census.gov/wholesale/index.html>.

E-commerce—Electronic commerce (or e-commerce) is the sale of goods and services over the internet and extranet, electronic data interchange (EDI) network, electronic mail, or other online systems. Payment may or may not be made online. E-commerce data are collected in four separate Census Bureau surveys. These surveys use different measures of economic activity such as shipments for manufacturing, sales for wholesale and retail trade, and revenues for service industries. Data can be found at <http://www.census. gov/programs-surveys/e-stats.html>. Consequently, measures of total economic and e-commerce activity vary by economic sector, are conceptually and definitionally different, and therefore, are not additive. This edition has several tables on e-commerce sales, such as Tables 1064, 1074, and 1075 in this section; and Table 1297 in Section 27, Accommodation, Food Services, and Other Services.

Statistical reliability—For a discussion of statistical collection and estimation, sampling procedures, and measures of statistical reliability applicable to Census Bureau data, see Appendix III.

Table 1061. Wholesale and Retail Trade—Establishments, Sales, Payroll, and Employees: 2007 and 2012

[435.0 represents 435,000. Covers establishments with payroll. Based on data from the Economic Census; see Appendix III]

Kind of business	2007 NAICS code [1]	Establishments (1,000)		Sales (bil. dol.)		Annual payroll (bil. dol.)		Paid employees (1,000)	
		2007	2012	2007	2012	2007	2012	2007	2012
Wholesale trade................................	**42**	**435.0**	**419.5**	**6,516**	**7,900**	**336**	**362**	**6,227**	**5,882**
Wholesale trade, durable goods.....................	423	255.0	245.4	2,898	3,152	207	217	3,619	3,355
Wholesale trade, nondurable goods.................	424	134.6	130.7	2,991	4,108	116	132	2,320	2,244
Wholesale electronic markets and agents and brokers.........................	425	45.4	43.4	627	639	13	14	289	283
Retail trade....................................	**44–45**	**1,128.1**	**1,062.1**	**3,918**	**4,220**	**363**	**369**	**15,515**	**14,704**
Motor vehicle and parts dealers.....................	441	126.8	116.5	891	869	73	70	1,914	1,710
Furniture and home furnishings stores..............	442	65.1	51.6	108	89	15	11	557	425
Electronics and appliance stores....................	443	50.8	46.8	109	101	11	10	486	416
Building material and garden equipment and supplies dealers...............................	444	91.1	78.3	318	279	38	34	1,331	1,145
Food and beverage stores.........................	445	146.1	147.6	539	620	55	61	2,827	2,865
Health and personal care stores....................	446	88.5	91.0	234	270	28	31	1,068	1,002
Gasoline stations................................	447	118.8	114.5	450	554	15	16	891	857
Clothing and clothing accessories stores............	448	156.5	147.7	216	234	27	28	1,644	1,664
Sporting goods, hobby, book, and music stores.....	451	57.4	48.4	81	79	9	9	619	535
General merchandise stores.........................	452	45.9	49.1	577	641	54	58	2,763	2,773
Miscellaneous store retailers........................	453	121.9	107.0	104	98	14	14	792	713
Nonstore retailers................................	454	59.4	63.6	290	386	23	27	621	600

[1] North American Industrial Classification System; see text, Section 15.

Source: U.S. Census Bureau, 2012 Economic Census, "EC1200CCOMP1: All sectors: Core Business Statistics Series: Comparative Statistics for the U.S. (2007 NAICS Basis): 2012 and 2007," <http://factfinder.census.gov>, accessed July 2016.

Table 1062. Wholesale Trade—Nonemployer Firms and Receipts by Industry Type: 2015

[37,946,145 represents $37,946,145,000. Includes only firms subject to federal income tax. Nonemployers are businesses with no paid employees. Each distinct business income tax return filed by a nonemployer business is counted as a firm]

Industry type	2012 NAICS code [1]	Firms				Receipts ($1,000)
		Total	Corpora- tions [2]	Individual proprietor- ships [3]	Partner- ships [4]	
Wholesale trade, total...............................	**42**	**417,272**	**69,431**	**319,998**	**27,843**	**37,946,145**
Durable goods merchant wholesalers...............................	**423**	**202,260**	**37,584**	**150,276**	**14,400**	**19,416,097**
Motor vehicle and motor vehicle parts and supplies merchant wholesalers...............................	4231	18,076	3,601	13,378	1,097	2,459,864
Furniture and home furnishing merchant wholesalers..............	4232	12,999	1,977	10,288	734	1,078,137
Lumber and other construction materials merchant wholesalers...............................	4233	7,650	1,448	5,587	615	876,195
Professional and commercial equipment and supplies merchant wholesalers...............................	4234	11,419	2,225	8,241	953	1,207,472
Metal and mineral (except petroleum) merchant wholesalers...............................	4235	2,940	666	2,059	215	376,188
Household appliance and electrical and electronic goods merchant wholesalers...............................	4236	10,151	2,908	6,356	887	1,220,845
Hardware and plumbing and heating equipment and supplies merchant wholesalers...............................	4237	4,503	1,020	3,128	355	456,736
Machinery, equipment, and supplies merchant wholesalers...............................	4238	18,378	4,964	11,820	1,594	2,434,215
Miscellaneous durable goods merchant wholesalers..............	4239	116,144	18,775	89,419	7,950	9,306,445
Nondurable goods merchant wholesalers........................	**424**	**153,395**	**24,743**	**117,784**	**10,868**	**14,214,779**
Paper and paper product merchant wholesalers....................	4241	5,460	918	4,237	305	484,223
Drugs and druggists' sundries merchant wholesalers..............	4242	3,125	648	2,184	293	283,404
Apparel, piece goods, and notions merchant wholesalers...............................	4243	26,165	4,003	20,418	1,744	1,798,293
Grocery and related products merchant wholesalers..............	4244	29,616	5,327	22,183	2,106	4,267,909
Farm product raw material merchant wholesalers...................	4245	6,103	610	5,159	334	639,178
Chemical and allied products merchant wholesalers..............	4246	3,570	1,010	2,167	393	452,283
Petroleum and petroleum products merchant wholesalers...............................	4247	2,111	425	1,472	214	289,751
Beer, wine, and distilled alcoholic beverage merchant wholesalers...............................	4248	5,965	921	4,172	872	534,298
Miscellaneous nondurable goods merchant wholesalers...............................	4249	71,280	10,881	55,792	4,607	5,465,440
Wholesale electronic markets and agents and brokers..........	**425**	**61,614**	**7,104**	**51,935**	**2,575**	**4,315,255**
Business to business electronics markets...........................	42511	9,758	1,189	8,052	517	794,635
Wholesale trade agents and brokers................................	42512	51,856	5,915	43,883	2,058	3,520,620

[1] North American Industry Classification System, 2012; see text, Section 15. [2] A legally incorporated business under state laws. [3] Also referred to as "sole proprietorship," an unincorporated business with a sole owner. Includes self-employed persons. [4] An unincorporated business where two or more persons join to carry on a trade or business with each having a shared financial interest in the business.

Source: U.S. Census Bureau, Nonemployer Statistics, "Geographic Area Series: Nonemployer Statistics by Legal Form of Organization for the U.S. and States," <http://factfinder.census.gov>, accessed June 2017. See also <http://www.census.gov/econ/nonemployer/>.

Table 1063. Wholesale Trade—Establishments, Employees, and Payroll: 2014 and 2015

[416.6 represents 416,600. Covers establishments with payroll. Excludes self-employed individuals, employees of private households, railroad employees, agricultural production employees, and most government employees. For statement on methodology, see Appendix III]

Kind of business	NAICS code [1]	Establishments (1,000)		Employees [2] (1,000)		Payroll (bil. dol.)	
		2014	2015	2014	2015	2014	2015
Wholesale trade, total................................	42	416.6	413.4	5,967	6,076	404.8	423.1
Merchant wholesalers, durable goods......................	423	241.3	237.5	3,383	3,441	242.0	251.8
Motor vehicle and motor vehicle parts and supply merchant wholesalers................................	4231	24.5	24.1	376	389	20.1	21.3
Furniture and home furnishing merchant wholesalers..........	4232	12.3	12.1	148	151	8.4	9.0
Lumber and other construction materials merchant wholesalers................................	4233	16.9	16.8	207	217	11.7	12.5
Professional and commercial equipment and supplies merchant wholesalers................................	4234	35.9	34.1	655	643	59.5	60.2
Metal and mineral (except petroleum) merchant wholesalers................................	4235	10.2	10.0	153	157	9.5	9.7
Household appliances and electrical and electronic goods merchant wholesalers........................	4236	29.6	29.2	521	547	50.6	55.4
Hardware, plumbing and heating equipment and supplies merchant wholesalers................................	4237	19.2	19.1	229	235	14.5	15.1
Machinery, equipment, and supplies merchant wholesalers................................	4238	58.1	57.6	756	769	50.1	50.8
Miscellaneous durable goods merchant wholesalers...........	4239	34.6	34.3	337	334	17.6	17.8
Merchant wholesalers, nondurable goods....................	424	130.1	130.4	2,289	2,334	147.3	155.4
Paper and paper product merchant wholesalers.............	4241	10.1	10.1	147	147	8.4	8.8
Drugs and druggists' sundries merchant wholesalers.........	4242	10.0	10.1	298	307	35.6	38.6
Apparel, piece goods and notions merchant wholesalers......	4243	16.3	16.1	202	200	11.8	12.1
Grocery and related product merchant wholesalers...........	4244	34.7	35.3	787	815	40.3	43.2
Farm product raw material merchant wholesalers...........	4245	6.3	6.3	63	65	3.5	3.7
Chemical and allied products merchant wholesalers...........	4246	12.8	12.5	157	158	11.5	11.9
Petroleum and petroleum products merchant wholesalers.....	4247	6.7	6.7	103	103	7.6	7.8
Beer, wine, and distilled alcoholic beverages...............	4248	4.5	4.5	194	198	12.2	12.5
Miscellaneous nondurable goods merchant wholesalers......	4249	28.9	28.8	338	340	16.3	16.9
Wholesale electronic markets and agents and brokers.....	425	45.2	45.5	295	302	15.6	16.0

[1] Data based on 2012 North American Industry Classification System (NAICS). [2] Covers full- and part-time employees who are on the payroll in the pay period including March 12.

Source: U.S. Census Bureau, County Business Patterns, "Geography Area Series: County Business Patterns," <http://factfinder.census.gov/>, accessed April 2017. See also <https://www.census.gov/programs-surveys/cbp.html>.

Table 1064. Merchant Wholesale Trade Sales—Total and E-Commerce: 2015

[5,292,436 represents $5,292,436,000,000. Covers only businesses with paid employees. Excludes manufacturers' sales branches and offices. Based on the Annual Wholesale Trade Survey, see Appendix III]

Kind of business	2007 NAICS code [1]	Value of sales (mil. dol.)		E-commerce as percent of total sales	Percent distribution of E-commerce sales
		Total	E-commerce		
Total merchant wholesale trade..........................	42	5,292,436	1,314,122	24.8	100.0
Durable goods..	423	2,520,142	558,746	22.2	42.5
Motor vehicles, parts and supplies.......................	4231	430,183	185,843	43.2	14.1
Furniture and home furnishings..........................	4232	79,576	11,105	14.0	0.8
Lumber and other construction materials..................	4233	117,623	(S)	(S)	(S)
Professional and commercial equipment and supplies.................	4234	449,274	116,961	26.0	8.9
Computer equipment and supplies....................	42343	231,948	62,482	26.9	4.8
Metals and minerals (except petroleum)...................	4235	156,730	10,334	6.6	0.8
Electrical goods..	4236	548,890	133,037	24.2	10.1
Hardware, plumbing and heating equipment...............	4237	129,385	19,330	14.9	1.5
Machinery, equipment and supplies......................	4238	398,247	42,320	10.6	3.2
Miscellaneous durable goods............................	4239	210,234	31,692	15.1	2.4
Nondurable goods..	424	2,772,294	755,376	27.2	57.5
Paper and paper products..............................	4241	95,837	(S)	(S)	(S)
Drugs, drug proprietaries and druggists' sundries............	4242	604,440	(S)	(S)	(S)
Apparel, piece goods and notions........................	4243	165,477	43,908	26.5	3.3
Groceries and related products..........................	4244	629,113	121,487	19.3	9.2
Farm product raw materials.............................	4245	219,072	20,545	9.4	1.6
Chemical and allied products............................	4246	117,822	14,213	12.1	1.1
Petroleum and petroleum products.......................	4247	552,450	34,897	6.3	2.7
Beer, wine, and distilled alcoholic beverages..............	4248	136,490	10,570	7.7	0.8
Miscellaneous nondurable goods........................	4249	251,593	33,320	13.2	2.5

S Figure does not meet publication standards. [1] North American Industry Classification System, 2007. See text, Section 15.

Source: U.S. Census Bureau, "Annual Wholesale Trade Survey - 2015," <http://www.census.gov/wholesale/index.html>, and "2015 E-Commerce Multi-sector Data Tables," <http://www.census.gov/programs-surveys/e-stats/data/tables.html>; accessed June 2017.

Table 1065. Merchant Wholesalers' Sales and Inventories by Kind of Business: 2000 to 2015

[In billions of dollars (2,814.6 represents $2,814,600,000,000), except ratios. Inventories and inventories/sales ratios, as of December, not seasonally adjusted. Excludes manufacturers' sales branches and offices. Data adjusted using final results of the 2012 Economic Census. Based on data from the Annual Wholesale Trade Survey and the Monthly Wholesale Trade Survey; see Appendix III]

Kind of business	2007 NAICS code [1]	2000	2010	2011	2012	2013	2014	2015
SALES								
Merchant wholesalers	**42**	**2,814.6**	**4,337.4**	**4,885.1**	**5,208.0**	**5,370.6**	**5,564.2**	**5,292.4**
Durable goods	**423**	**1,486.7**	**1,999.2**	**2,229.7**	**2,389.6**	**2,461.0**	**2,556.6**	**2,520.1**
Motor vehicles, parts, and supplies	4231	222.2	303.0	337.8	393.6	401.6	415.0	430.2
Furniture and home furnishings	4232	52.7	57.4	61.1	67.5	71.6	76.7	79.6
Lumber and other construction materials	4233	87.2	86.5	88.3	94.1	105.0	111.5	117.6
Professional, commercial equipment and supplies	4234	282.2	397.8	412.1	412.6	425.5	437.9	449.3
Computer, peripheral equipment and software	42343	174.8	220.1	222.2	217.9	224.6	228.8	231.9
Metal and mineral (except petroleum)	4235	93.8	138.4	172.5	180.6	173.8	184.7	156.7
Electrical and electronic goods	4236	260.0	391.0	427.9	475.8	510.7	535.5	548.9
Hardware, plumbing, heating equipment and supplies	4237	72.1	96.2	103.9	112.5	117.5	124.7	129.4
Machinery, equipment, and supplies	4238	256.1	305.3	356.6	394.4	404.2	421.3	398.2
Miscellaneous durable goods	4239	160.3	223.7	269.4	258.4	251.1	249.4	210.2
Nondurable goods	**424**	**1,327.9**	**2,338.1**	**2,655.4**	**2,818.4**	**2,909.5**	**3,007.5**	**2,772.3**
Paper and paper products	4241	77.8	86.0	88.4	90.2	92.0	95.9	95.8
Drugs and druggists' sundries	4242	176.0	415.9	443.4	462.6	486.8	540.1	604.4
Apparel, piece goods, and notions	4243	96.5	137.0	143.3	148.9	156.2	162.4	165.5
Grocery and related products	4244	374.5	491.3	519.2	556.3	576.8	611.5	629.1
Farm product raw materials	4245	102.7	188.3	234.1	254.5	270.7	254.9	219.1
Chemical and allied products	4246	62.3	102.7	118.0	122.4	124.4	128.8	117.8
Petroleum and petroleum products	4247	195.8	591.0	759.8	811.6	818.5	834.5	552.5
Beer, wine, and distilled alcoholic beverages	4248	71.3	111.3	116.4	122.0	130.0	130.7	136.5
Miscellaneous nondurable goods	4249	170.9	214.5	232.8	249.9	254.1	248.7	251.6
INVENTORIES								
Merchant wholesalers	**42**	**309.7**	**442.6**	**487.0**	**522.4**	**541.8**	**573.3**	**579.5**
Durable goods	**423**	**198.5**	**256.7**	**285.9**	**311.1**	**326.3**	**348.8**	**349.6**
Motor vehicles, parts, and supplies	4231	28.8	41.4	48.4	50.0	52.0	56.5	64.4
Furniture and home furnishings	4232	6.4	8.2	8.5	9.2	9.8	10.3	10.7
Lumber and other construction materials	4233	8.3	10.2	10.3	11.0	12.2	12.9	13.7
Professional, commercial equipment and supplies	4234	27.3	32.1	33.3	35.5	37.0	40.1	39.1
Computer, peripheral equipment and software	42343	12.1	13.1	13.1	13.8	14.6	16.2	15.3
Metal and mineral (except petroleum)	4235	13.6	23.0	27.3	29.8	29.7	33.2	27.2
Electrical and electronic goods	4236	31.3	34.5	38.2	42.2	43.7	45.2	47.1
Hardware, plumbing, heating equipment and supplies	4237	11.5	16.7	18.2	18.9	19.3	21.1	21.9
Machinery, equipment, and supplies	4238	51.1	66.3	75.3	87.3	94.8	101.7	99.3
Miscellaneous durable goods	4239	20.2	24.4	26.4	27.2	27.8	27.9	26.1
Nondurable goods	**424**	**111.2**	**185.9**	**201.1**	**211.4**	**215.5**	**224.6**	**229.9**
Paper and paper products	4241	6.7	7.3	7.6	7.7	7.9	8.2	8.1
Drugs and druggists' sundries	4242	23.9	37.7	40.0	41.1	46.1	53.6	59.5
Apparel, piece goods, and notions	4243	14.2	20.4	22.7	23.3	24.5	26.1	28.5
Grocery and related products	4244	20.5	26.8	30.0	31.4	31.6	34.2	35.4
Farm product raw materials	4245	11.5	29.2	28.6	32.8	29.3	29.9	26.7
Chemical and allied products	4246	6.0	9.3	10.6	11.5	11.6	12.0	11.8
Petroleum and petroleum products	4247	5.2	22.5	25.2	25.3	24.3	18.4	17.0
Beer, wine, and distilled alcoholic beverages	4248	6.5	10.8	11.5	12.5	13.6	14.4	14.5
Miscellaneous nondurable goods	4249	16.6	21.9	24.7	25.9	26.5	27.9	28.4
INVENTORIES/SALES RATIO								
Merchant wholesalers	**42**	**1.10**	**1.02**	**1.00**	**1.00**	**1.01**	**1.03**	**1.09**
Durable goods	**423**	**1.34**	**1.28**	**1.28**	**1.30**	**1.33**	**1.36**	**1.39**
Motor vehicles, parts, and supplies	4231	1.30	1.37	1.43	1.27	1.29	1.36	1.50
Furniture and home furnishings	4232	1.22	1.43	1.39	1.36	1.38	1.34	1.35
Lumber and other construction materials	4233	0.96	1.17	1.17	1.17	1.16	1.16	1.16
Professional, commercial equipment and supplies	4234	0.97	0.81	0.81	0.86	0.87	0.92	0.87
Computer, peripheral equipment and software	42343	0.69	0.60	0.59	0.63	0.65	0.71	0.66
Metal and mineral (except petroleum)	4235	1.45	1.66	1.59	1.65	1.71	1.80	1.74
Electrical and electronic goods	4236	1.20	0.88	0.89	0.89	0.86	0.84	0.86
Hardware, plumbing, heating equipment and supplies	4237	1.60	1.74	1.75	1.68	1.64	1.69	1.69
Machinery, equipment, and supplies	4238	1.99	2.17	2.11	2.21	2.35	2.41	2.49
Miscellaneous durable goods	4239	1.26	1.09	0.98	1.05	1.11	1.12	1.24
Nondurable goods	**424**	**0.84**	**0.80**	**0.76**	**0.75**	**0.74**	**0.75**	**0.83**
Paper and paper products	4241	0.87	0.85	0.86	0.85	0.86	0.86	0.85
Drugs and druggists' sundries	4242	1.36	0.91	0.90	0.89	0.95	0.99	0.98
Apparel, piece goods, and notions	4243	1.47	1.49	1.59	1.56	1.57	1.61	1.72
Grocery and related products	4244	0.55	0.55	0.58	0.56	0.55	0.56	0.56
Farm product raw materials	4245	1.12	1.55	1.22	1.29	1.08	1.17	1.22
Chemical and allied products	4246	0.97	0.91	0.90	0.94	0.93	0.93	1.00
Petroleum and petroleum products	4247	0.27	0.38	0.33	0.31	0.30	0.22	0.31
Beer, wine, and distilled alcoholic beverages	4248	0.91	0.97	0.99	1.03	1.05	1.10	1.06
Miscellaneous nondurable goods	4249	0.97	1.02	1.06	1.03	1.04	1.12	1.13

[1] North American Industry Classification System, 2007. See text, Section 15.

Source: U.S. Census Bureau, "2015 Annual Wholesale Trade Report," <http://www.census.gov/wholesale/>, accessed March 2017.

Table 1066. Wholesale and Retail Trade—Establishments, Employees, and Payroll by State: 2014 and 2015

[5,967 represents 5,967,000. Covers establishments with payroll. Excludes self-employed individuals, employees of private households, railroad employees, agricultural production employees, and most government employees. Data based on 2012 North American Industry Classification System (NAICS). See text, Section 15. For statement on methodology, see Appendix III]

State	Wholesale trade (NAICS 42)						Retail trade (NAICS 44, 45)					
	Establishments		Employees [1] (1,000)		Annual payroll (mil. dol.)		Establishments		Employees [1] (1,000)		Annual payroll (mil. dol.)	
	2014	2015	2014	2015	2014	2015	2014	2015	2014	2015	2014	2015
U.S.........	416,593	413,437	5,967	6,076	404,842	423,133	1,065,368	1,070,209	15,373	15,704	406,625	428,218
AL...........	5,348	5,315	72	71	3,915	3,942	18,029	18,043	228	232	5,544	5,820
AK...........	745	729	9	9	602	588	2,496	2,514	34	35	1,049	1,105
AZ...........	6,607	6,488	92	92	5,428	5,856	17,944	18,103	307	314	8,331	8,788
AR...........	3,439	3,418	44	44	2,320	2,421	10,866	10,908	141	143	3,396	3,555
CA...........	59,379	59,353	840	854	70,149	72,916	107,469	108,542	1,638	1,690	47,759	51,641
CO...........	7,206	7,219	95	100	6,905	7,367	18,643	18,734	262	273	7,364	7,953
CT...........	4,324	4,261	72	73	5,554	5,724	12,542	12,524	186	184	5,395	5,476
DE...........	1,083	1,117	16	16	1,486	1,250	3,627	3,656	54	55	1,407	1,472
DC...........	452	419	4	4	344	384	1,740	1,751	21	22	666	635
FL...........	31,443	31,221	311	314	17,147	17,877	73,200	74,533	1,026	1,071	27,322	29,166
GA...........	13,058	12,928	199	205	12,387	13,010	33,666	34,041	453	469	11,408	12,091
HI...........	1,674	1,661	19	19	923	958	4,639	4,602	71	72	1,986	2,074
ID...........	2,050	2,064	29	30	1,785	1,855	5,818	6,004	80	82	2,123	2,206
IL...........	18,893	18,539	314	316	22,850	23,812	39,252	39,165	606	627	15,334	16,258
IN...........	7,684	7,668	116	129	6,545	8,440	21,431	21,426	315	318	7,611	7,974
IA...........	4,914	4,974	67	68	3,454	3,602	11,828	11,736	180	185	4,215	4,457
KS...........	4,497	4,459	65	63	3,712	3,760	10,391	10,327	150	150	3,618	3,712
KY...........	4,315	4,293	70	72	3,938	4,113	15,223	15,187	204	207	4,936	5,176
LA...........	5,482	5,463	77	78	4,429	4,400	16,596	16,525	229	238	5,799	6,099
ME...........	1,575	1,581	18	18	929	939	6,304	6,281	82	82	2,095	2,163
MD...........	5,678	5,581	87	88	5,910	6,235	18,171	18,273	292	290	7,705	7,992
MA...........	7,875	7,763	137	140	11,448	12,416	24,136	24,101	360	366	10,152	10,599
MI...........	11,234	11,053	172	177	11,125	11,813	34,686	34,711	457	466	11,460	12,037
MN...........	8,152	8,032	133	135	9,940	10,144	18,993	18,974	296	300	7,546	8,087
MS...........	2,788	2,756	35	37	1,731	1,838	11,555	11,587	141	143	3,234	3,392
MO...........	7,789	7,705	126	126	6,579	6,990	21,228	21,177	310	316	7,749	8,145
MT...........	1,580	1,594	16	16	762	805	4,757	4,791	59	60	1,500	1,587
NE...........	3,162	3,209	43	42	2,359	2,495	7,240	7,352	110	113	2,753	2,835
NV...........	2,984	2,969	34	35	2,005	2,086	8,512	8,682	141	147	3,881	4,077
NH...........	1,847	1,839	24	25	1,757	1,807	6,044	6,050	97	99	2,645	2,753
NJ...........	14,236	14,060	256	255	22,647	23,102	31,685	31,557	457	461	13,456	13,465
NM...........	1,855	1,847	21	21	1,140	1,105	6,557	6,536	96	97	2,446	2,537
NY...........	32,438	31,785	367	371	25,634	26,208	78,763	78,832	936	937	26,435	27,245
NC...........	11,674	11,602	175	180	11,878	12,344	34,246	34,527	469	482	11,548	12,293
ND...........	1,705	1,723	24	24	1,448	1,408	3,242	3,259	51	52	1,432	1,502
OH...........	14,217	14,035	231	236	13,914	14,334	36,260	36,339	560	565	13,998	14,592
OK...........	4,699	4,626	61	61	3,444	3,287	13,237	13,305	181	184	4,599	4,743
OR...........	5,345	5,352	74	82	4,685	6,077	13,994	14,159	197	203	5,269	5,743
PA...........	14,832	14,628	248	249	17,015	17,891	43,598	43,399	660	665	16,597	17,338
RI...........	1,337	1,328	20	21	1,445	1,504	3,744	3,748	49	50	1,347	1,398
SC...........	4,975	4,915	69	74	3,880	4,165	17,567	17,599	229	237	5,518	5,899
SD...........	1,522	1,507	18	19	939	997	3,866	3,941	52	53	1,281	1,373
TN...........	6,858	6,779	114	114	6,686	6,957	22,533	22,643	316	317	8,091	8,357
TX...........	33,235	33,380	511	524	34,910	35,987	79,814	80,298	1,242	1,280	33,055	34,965
UT...........	3,743	3,702	55	55	3,254	3,337	9,224	9,546	142	151	3,816	4,177
VT...........	813	824	11	12	618	629	3,400	3,351	39	40	1,058	1,099
VA...........	7,204	7,073	102	103	6,435	6,744	27,059	27,188	421	424	10,751	11,182
WA...........	9,288	9,283	127	131	8,196	8,636	21,586	21,778	322	331	9,594	10,082
WV...........	1,530	1,486	21	22	1,010	1,109	6,214	6,150	86	86	1,994	2,071
WI...........	6,985	6,987	115	117	6,703	6,950	19,143	19,114	306	309	7,477	7,934
WY...........	845	844	9	9	541	524	2,610	2,640	32	32	878	900

[1] Covers full- and part-time employees who are on the payroll in the pay period including March 12.

Source: U.S. Census Bureau, County Business Patterns, "Geography Area Series: County Business Patterns," <https://factfinder.census.gov/>, accessed April 2017. See also <https://www.census.gov/programs-surveys/cbp.html>.

Table 1067. Retail Trade—Establishments, Employees, and Payroll: 2014 and 2015

[1,065.4 represents 1,065,400. Covers establishments with payroll. Excludes self-employed individuals, employees of private households, railroad employees, agricultural production employees, and most government employees. For statement on methodology, see Appendix III]

Kind of business	NAICS code [1]	Establishments (1,000) 2014	Establishments (1,000) 2015	Employees (1,000) [2] 2014	Employees (1,000) [2] 2015	Payroll (bil. dol.) 2014	Payroll (bil. dol.) 2015
Retail trade, total.	**44–45**	**1,065.4**	**1,070.2**	**15,373**	**15,704**	**406.6**	**428.2**
Motor vehicle and parts dealers.	441	117.6	118.2	1,837	1,908	80.7	86.7
Automobile dealers.	4411	46.2	46.5	1,195	1,247	60.9	65.8
New car dealers.	44111	21.3	21.4	1,057	1,105	55.5	59.9
Used car dealers.	44112	24.8	25.1	138	142	5.3	5.9
Other motor vehicle dealers.	4412	13.9	13.8	133	138	5.5	6.0
Recreational vehicle dealers.	44121	2.6	2.6	37	39	1.7	2.0
Motorcycle and boat and other motor vehicle dealers.	44122	11.3	11.2	97	100	3.7	4.0
Motorcycle, ATV, and all other motor vehicle dealers.	441228	6.9	6.8	67	68	2.5	2.6
Automotive parts, accessories, and tire stores.	4413	57.6	57.8	509	523	14.3	14.9
Automotive parts and accessories stores.	44131	37.1	37.2	336	347	8.3	8.7
Tire dealers.	44132	20.5	20.7	173	177	6.0	6.2
Furniture and home furnishing stores.	442	50.6	50.3	429	445	12.8	13.6
Furniture stores.	4421	23.6	23.4	198	202	7.0	7.5
Home furnishings stores.	4422	27.0	27.0	231	243	5.8	6.1
Floor covering stores.	44221	10.8	10.6	63	65	2.5	2.7
Other home furnishings stores.	44229	16.3	16.4	168	178	3.3	3.4
Window treatment stores.	442291	1.8	2.2	6	7	0.2	0.2
Electronics and appliance stores.	443	46.8	46.7	410	407	11.3	11.8
Household appliance stores.	443141	7.8	7.6	62	60	2.0	2.0
Electronics stores.	443142	39.0	39.1	348	347	9.3	9.8
Building material & garden equipment & supplies dealers.	444	77.0	76.6	1,266	1,280	38.2	38.6
Building material & supplies dealers [3].	4441	59.2	58.9	1,121	1,131	33.7	33.9
Home centers.	44411	6.6	6.5	([5])	686	(D)	16.5
Hardware stores.	44413	15.3	15.4	139	143	3.4	3.6
Lawn & garden equipment & supplies stores [3].	4442	17.7	17.7	144	149	4.5	4.7
Nursery, garden center, and farm supply stores.	44422	13.9	13.9	120	124	3.6	3.8
Food & beverage stores.	445	150.2	152.5	3,017	3,130	64.7	68.3
Grocery stores.	4451	94.4	95.5	2,705	2,800	58.4	61.2
Supermarkets & grocery (except convenience) stores.	44511	66.0	66.3	2,578	2,667	56.2	58.8
Convenience stores.	44512	28.4	29.2	128	133	2.2	2.3
Specialty food stores.	4452	22.6	23.3	154	167	2.8	3.4
Beer, wine, & liquor stores [4].	4453	33.2	33.7	158	162	3.4	3.7
Health & personal care stores [3].	446	92.4	92.8	1,021	1,041	34.1	34.9
Pharmacies & drug stores.	44611	43.7	44.1	704	713	25.8	26.2
Cosmetics, beauty supplies, & perfume stores.	44612	16.0	16.3	131	140	2.5	2.7
Optical goods stores.	44613	12.4	11.9	78	78	2.2	2.3
Gasoline stations.	447	111.6	111.6	904	922	17.3	18.2
Gasoline stations with convenience stores.	44711	96.5	97.0	756	775	13.8	14.6
Other gasoline stations.	44719	15.1	14.6	148	147	3.5	3.6
Clothing & clothing accessories stores.	448	147.2	146.7	1,736	1,711	30.3	31.4
Clothing stores [3].	4481	98.4	98.5	1,381	1,348	22.2	22.9
Men's clothing stores.	44811	7.1	7.0	57	53	1.5	1.5
Women's clothing stores.	44812	35.9	35.3	354	330	5.6	5.5
Children's & infants' clothing stores.	44813	7.4	7.2	85	74	1.1	1.1
Family clothing stores.	44814	28.1	28.9	709	720	10.8	11.4
Shoe stores.	4482	25.2	25.0	224	234	3.9	4.1
Jewelry, luggage, & leather goods stores.	4483	23.6	23.2	131	129	4.3	4.4
Jewelry stores.	44831	22.7	22.2	125	123	4.0	4.1
Sporting goods, hobby, book, & music stores.	451	46.3	46.2	560	579	9.9	10.4
Sporting goods/hobby/musical instrument stores [3].	4511	38.3	38.2	458	479	8.4	8.9
Sporting goods stores.	45111	21.8	21.9	259	271	5.1	5.5
Hobby, toy, and game stores.	45112	8.1	8.1	128	141	2.0	2.1
Book stores and news dealers [3].	4512	8.0	8.0	101	100	1.5	1.5
Book stores.	451211	6.9	6.9	93	91	1.3	1.3
General merchandise stores.	452	52.4	53.0	2,836	2,902	63.0	67.6
Department stores.	4521	7.9	7.9	1,033	1,017	20.1	21.0
Other general merchandise stores.	4529	44.5	45.1	1,803	1,886	42.9	46.6
Warehouse clubs & superstores.	45291	5.3	5.6	1,434	1,502	36.9	40.3
All other general merchandise stores.	45299	39.2	39.6	369	384	6.0	6.3
Miscellaneous store retailers [3].	453	108.1	108.5	751	758	15.5	16.5
Florists.	4531	13.8	13.4	61	60	1.1	1.1
Office supplies, stationery, and gift stores.	4532	30.2	28.8	240	231	4.3	4.4
Office supplies and stationery stores.	45321	6.8	6.5	81	80	1.7	1.7
Gift, novelty, and souvenir stores.	45322	23.3	22.4	159	151	2.6	2.7
Used merchandise stores.	4533	20.0	20.1	194	198	3.5	3.7
Other miscellaneous store retailers [3].	4539	44.1	46.2	256	269	6.6	7.3
Pet and pet supplies stores.	45391	9.2	9.4	109	111	2.1	2.3
Nonstore retailers [3].	454	65.3	67.1	607	620	28.8	30.5
Electronic shopping & mail-order houses.	4541	32.5	34.6	397	414	20.4	22.0
Direct selling establishments.	4543	28.9	28.8	175	172	7.3	7.3
Fuel dealers.	45431	8.7	8.3	74	73	3.4	3.5

D Figure withheld to avoid disclosure. [1] Data based on North American Industry Classification System (NAICS), 2012. See text, Section 15. [2] Covers full- and part-time employees who are on the payroll in the pay period including March 12. [3] Includes other kinds of business, not shown separately. [4] Includes government employees. [5] 100,000 or more employees.

Source: U.S. Census Bureau, County Business Patterns, "Geography Area Series: County Business Patterns," <https://factfinder.census.gov>, accessed April 2017. See also <https://www.census.gov/programs-surveys/cbp.html>.

Table 1068. Retail Trade—Nonemployer Firms and Receipts by Industry Type: 2015

[87,351,860 represents $87,351,860,000. See headnote, Table 1062]

Industry type	2012 NAICS code [1]	Firms				Receipts ($1,000)
		Total	Corporations [2]	Individual proprietorships [3]	Partnerships [4]	
Retail trade, total.....	**44–45**	**1,985,553**	**117,179**	**1,795,090**	**73,284**	**87,351,860**
Motor vehicle & parts dealers.....	441	172,535	15,710	149,967	6,858	18,211,831
Furniture & home furnishings stores.....	442	41,477	5,010	33,785	2,682	2,505,579
Electronics and appliance stores.....	443	26,357	3,224	21,961	1,172	1,336,406
Building material & garden equipment & supplies dealers.......	444	38,595	3,692	33,173	1,730	2,440,506
Building material & supplies dealers.....	4441	26,315	2,942	22,100	1,273	1,865,982
Food & beverage stores.....	445	108,495	12,040	89,489	6,966	8,017,449
Grocery stores.....	4451	42,691	5,133	35,345	2,213	3,610,518
Specialty food stores.....	4452	54,136	5,016	45,574	3,546	2,746,736
Health & personal care stores.....	446	174,555	7,017	163,954	3,584	4,154,612
Gasoline stations.....	447	8,722	1,720	6,277	725	1,161,166
Clothing & clothing accessories stores.....	448	172,282	9,740	155,134	7,408	6,119,868
Clothing stores.....	4481	119,393	6,904	106,469	6,020	4,191,450
Jewelry, luggage, and leather goods stores.....	4483	47,586	2,362	44,072	1,152	1,642,598
Sporting goods, hobby, musical instrument, & book stores.....	451	76,756	5,255	66,948	4,553	3,445,971
Book stores and news dealer.....	4512	15,458	759	14,138	561	503,869
General merchandise stores.....	452	36,968	3,316	31,443	2,209	1,794,003
Miscellaneous store retailers.....	453	271,035	20,895	235,037	15,103	12,716,871
Office supplies, stationery, and gift stores.....	4532	48,889	3,644	42,556	2,689	1,842,791
Nonstore retailers.....	454	857,687	29,558	807,835	20,294	25,446,240
Electronic shopping & mail-order houses.....	4541	139,146	9,288	123,133	6,725	7,528,231
Direct selling establishments.....	4543	699,662	18,535	668,977	12,150	17,220,748

[1] North American Industry Classification System, 2012; see text, Section 15. [2] A legally incorporated business under state laws. [3] Also referred to as "sole proprietorship," an unincorporated business with a sole owner. Includes self-employed persons. [4] An unincorporated business where two or more persons join to carry on a trade or business with each having a shared financial interest in the business.

Source: U.S. Census Bureau, Nonemployer Statistics, "Geographic Area Series: Nonemployer Statistics by Legal Form of Organization for the U.S. and States," <http://factfinder.census.gov>, accessed June 2017. See also <https://www.census.gov/econ/nonemployer/index.html>.

Table 1069. Retail Industries—Employees, Average Weekly Hours, and Average Hourly Earnings: 2010 to 2016

[Annual averages of monthly figures (14,440 represents 14,440,000). Covers all full- and part-time employees who worked during, or received pay for, any part of the pay period including the 12th of the month]

Industry	2012 NAICS code [1]	Employees (1,000)			Average weekly hours [2]			Average hourly earnings [2] (dol.)		
		2010	2015	2016	2010	2015	2016	2010	2015	2016
Retail trade, total [3].....	**44,45**	**14,440**	**15,605**	**15,820**	**30.2**	**30.1**	**29.7**	**13.25**	**14.82**	**15.05**
Motor vehicle and parts dealers [3].....	441	1,629	1,929	1,982	36.5	37.5	37.0	17.06	18.93	19.01
Automobile dealers.....	4411	1,012	1,239	1,282	36.7	37.6	37.0	18.22	20.34	20.31
Auto parts, accessories, and tire stores.....	4413	489	545	550	36.9	37.7	37.1	14.54	15.88	16.05
Furniture and home furnishings stores.....	442	438	467	474	29.1	30.7	31.4	15.25	16.79	17.55
Electronics and appliance stores [3].....	443	522	522	522	31.6	37.4	36.1	16.83	21.90	22.70
Electronics stores.....	443142	465	466	466	31.3	37.8	36.4	17.02	22.56	23.34
Building material and garden supply stores [3].....	444	1,132	1,234	1,272	33.9	32.0	31.6	14.11	15.14	15.53
Building material and supplies dealers.....	4441	1,005	1,085	1,115	34.2	31.7	31.2	14.13	15.19	15.58
Lawn and garden equip. and supplies stores.....	4442	127	150	157	31.6	34.0	34.3	13.98	14.73	15.16
Food and beverage stores [3].....	445	2,808	3,062	3,089	29.0	28.4	27.9	12.03	12.71	12.71
Grocery stores.....	4451	2,461	2,682	2,703	29.0	28.5	28.0	12.12	12.76	12.76
Supermarkets and other grocery stores.....	44511	2,323	2,523	2,538	28.9	28.4	27.9	12.27	12.91	12.88
Convenience stores.....	44512	138	159	165	31.3	30.8	29.0	9.43	10.41	10.76
Specialty food stores.....	4452	211	227	230	29.7	27.8	27.4	11.13	12.42	12.32
Beer, wine, and liquor stores.....	4453	136	153	156	27.2	26.1	26.0	11.89	12.02	12.27
Health and personal care stores [3].....	446	981	1,034	1,050	29.4	28.8	28.9	16.99	17.31	17.45
Pharmacies and drug stores.....	44611	715	721	731	29.3	28.9	28.8	17.59	17.87	18.45
Gasoline stations [3].....	447	819	905	926	30.7	30.7	30.5	10.25	10.99	11.31
Gasoline stations with convenience stores.....	44711	719	799	820	30.4	30.5	30.3	9.99	10.76	11.10
Clothing and clothing accessories stores [3].....	448	1,353	1,354	1,346	21.2	21.7	21.7	11.59	12.87	13.49
Clothing stores.....	4481	1,040	1,006	996	20.1	20.2	20.0	10.91	12.12	12.72
Shoe stores.....	4482	182	212	214	23.3	24.0	24.3	11.80	14.01	14.77
Jewelry, luggage, and leather goods stores.....	4483	131	136	137	28.1	30.0	30.1	15.56	15.46	15.86
Sporting goods, hobby, book, and music stores [3].....	451	579	623	621	23.4	24.5	25.2	11.69	13.74	14.15
Sporting goods, hobby, and musical instrument stores.....	4511	459	538	536	23.8	24.6	25.6	11.82	13.92	14.23
Book stores and news dealers.....	4512	120	86	85	22.0	24.0	23.1	11.10	12.58	13.57
General merchandise stores.....	452	2,998	3,131	3,171	31.7	29.3	28.9	10.98	12.03	12.28
Miscellaneous store retailers [3].....	453	762	828	833	28.0	28.9	28.3	12.50	13.75	13.64
Florists.....	4531	69	63	62	22.4	27.4	26.5	11.05	11.66	11.61
Office supplies, stationary, and gift stores.....	4532	303	281	272	27.1	27.8	26.4	13.06	15.31	14.56
Used merchandise stores.....	4533	125	171	175	29.5	30.1	29.2	10.72	11.20	11.82
Other miscellaneous store retailers.....	4539	264	314	324	29.8	29.4	29.6	13.07	14.34	14.34
Pet and pet supplies stores.....	45391	99	114	117	27.4	28.8	29.5	12.83	14.09	13.74
Nonstore retailers [3].....	454	421	515	536	36.3	36.5	36.0	17.73	22.33	21.90
Electronic shopping and mail-order houses.....	4541	247	343	362	35.9	36.5	35.5	18.22	23.84	22.92

[1] Based on the North American Industry Classification System (NAICS), 2012; see text, this section and Section 15. [2] Data shown for production and nonsupervisory employees. [3] Includes other kind of businesses, not shown separately.

Source: U.S. Bureau of Labor Statistics, Current Employment Statistics, "Employment, Hours, and Earnings—National," <http://www.bls.gov/ces/data.htm>, accessed March 2017.

Table 1070. Retail Trade and Food Services—Sales by Kind of Business: 2000 to 2015

[In billions of dollars (3,287.5 represents $3,287,500,000,000). Data have been adjusted using final results of the 2012 Economic Census]

Kind of business	2007 NAICS code [1]	2000	2010	2011	2012	2013	2014	2015
Retail sales and food services, total	44, 45, 722	**3,287.5**	**4,285.0**	**4,598.3**	**4,826.4**	**5,001.8**	**5,215.7**	**5,350.5**
Retail sales, total	44, 45	2,983.3	3,818.0	4,103.0	4,302.2	4,458.5	4,639.4	4,727.4
GAFO, total [2]	(X)	862.7	1,114.4	1,155.7	1,191.8	1,212.5	1,238.7	1,258.5
Motor vehicle and parts dealers	441	796.2	742.9	812.9	886.5	959.3	1,020.9	1,095.4
Automobile dealers	4411	687.8	621.2	684.5	752.8	819.3	875.6	941.3
New car dealers	44111	630.1	549.5	608.8	672.6	735.4	785.1	842.1
Other motor vehicle dealers	4412	45.0	43.8	45.5	49.6	55.0	59.5	64.7
Auto parts, accessories, and tire stores	4413	63.4	77.9	83.0	84.1	85.0	85.8	89.3
Furniture and home furnishings stores	442	91.2	85.2	87.6	91.5	95.3	99.7	106.8
Furniture stores	4421	50.6	46.7	47.7	49.8	50.9	53.3	57.4
Home furnishings stores	4422	40.6	38.5	39.9	41.8	44.5	46.4	49.4
Electronics and appliance stores [3]	443	82.2	97.4	99.9	102.1	103.0	103.5	102.1
Appliances, televisions, and other electronics stores	44311	58.2	71.5	72.2	72.8	73.2	73.3	72.6
Building materials, garden equipment, and supply stores [3]	444	229.0	260.6	269.5	281.5	301.8	318.4	331.6
Hardware stores	44413	16.2	18.7	20.0	20.7	21.0	22.6	23.1
Food and beverage stores [3]	445	444.8	580.5	609.1	628.2	640.8	669.2	685.6
Grocery stores	4451	402.5	520.8	547.5	563.6	574.5	599.6	613.2
Supermarkets and other grocery (except convenience) stores	44511	381.4	498.0	523.4	539.2	549.1	573.8	587.9
Beer, wine and liquor stores	4453	28.5	41.4	42.4	44.4	46.1	48.3	50.7
Health and personal care stores [3]	446	155.2	260.4	271.6	274.0	281.8	299.3	315.3
Pharmacies and drug stores	44611	130.9	222.2	231.2	230.0	235.5	250.5	263.5
Gasoline stations	447	249.8	448.3	533.5	555.4	549.6	538.8	443.8
Clothing and clothing accessory stores [3]	448	167.7	213.3	228.6	239.5	244.7	250.4	255.8
Clothing stores [3]	4481	118.1	158.3	168.1	176.1	179.0	183.1	187.1
Women's clothing stores	44812	31.4	37.7	40.0	41.8	41.8	41.6	41.0
Shoe stores	4482	22.9	27.2	29.3	31.0	32.5	33.5	34.5
Jewelry stores	44831	24.8	25.9	29.1	29.9	30.5	31.2	31.5
Sporting goods, hobby, book & music stores [3]	451	75.8	80.4	80.7	83.0	84.6	85.5	87.4
Sporting goods stores	45111	25.3	37.4	39.0	42.1	44.4	44.7	46.4
Hobby, toy, and game stores	45112	16.9	15.8	16.1	16.6	16.9	17.4	18.0
General merchandise stores [3]	452	404.2	603.8	624.8	642.3	651.9	667.2	674.9
Department stores (excluding leased depts.)	4521	232.5	184.8	183.4	177.3	170.2	168.1	164.0
Discount department stores	452112	136.2	119.9	117.6	114.4	109.6	107.5	105.1
Department stores (including leased depts.) [4]	4521	239.9	187.1	185.6	179.4	172.4	170.4	166.4
Discount department stores	452112	139.6	120.6	118.0	114.5	109.7	107.7	105.3
Warehouse clubs and superstores	45291	139.6	368.0	386.3	406.3	419.4	433.3	441.7
Miscellaneous store retailers [3]	453	106.7	104.2	108.4	110.0	112.4	115.9	119.5
Office supplies, stationery, and gift stores	4532	41.7	34.3	34.1	33.5	33.0	32.4	31.5
Office supplies and stationery stores	45321	22.7	18.8	18.1	17.4	16.6	15.8	14.7
Used merchandise stores	4533	9.8	11.8	13.2	14.7	15.4	16.2	17.0
Nonstore retailers [3]	454	180.5	341.0	376.3	408.2	433.1	470.9	509.3
Electronic shopping and mail-order houses	4541	113.8	263.5	294.7	328.7	350.5	386.1	433.7
Fuel dealers	45431	26.7	35.5	39.5	35.9	37.7	39.6	29.7
Food services and drinking places [5]	722	**304.3**	**466.9**	**495.4**	**524.3**	**543.3**	**576.2**	**623.1**

X Not applicable. [1] North American Industry Classification System, 2007; see text, Section 15. [2] GAFO (General Merchandise, Apparel, Furniture, and Office Supplies) represents stores classified in the following NAICS codes: 442, 443, 448, 451, 452, and 4532. [3] Includes other kinds of businesses, not shown separately. [4] Includes data for leased departments operated within department stores. Data are not included in aggregate kind-of-business totals. [5] See also Table 1300.

Source: U.S. Census Bureau, "2015 Annual Retail Trade Report," <http://www.census.gov/retail/index.html>, accessed March 2017.

Table 1071. Retail Trade Corporations—Sales, Net Profit, and Profit Per Dollar of Sales: 2015 and 2016

[2,694 represents $2,694,000,000,000. Represents 2012 North American Industry Classification System (NAICS) groups 44 and 45. Profit rates are averages of quarterly figures at annual rates. Covers corporations with assets of $50,000,000 or more]

Item	Unit	Total retail trade		Food and beverage stores (NAICS 445)		Clothing and general merchandise stores (NAICS 448, 452)		All other retail stores	
		2015	2016	2015	2016	2015	2016	2015	2016
Sales	Bil. dol.	2,694	2,802	464	469	904	917	1,326	1,415
Net profit:									
Before income taxes	Bil. dol.	126.4	130.0	12.2	11.6	48.4	46.0	65.8	72.4
After income taxes	Bil. dol.	88.1	94.6	8.1	7.5	32.6	31.2	47.4	55.9
Profits per dollar of sales:									
Before income taxes	Cents	4.7	4.6	2.6	2.5	5.3	5.0	5.0	5.1
After income taxes	Cents	3.3	3.4	1.7	1.6	3.6	3.4	3.6	3.9
Profits on stockholders' equity:									
Before income taxes	Percent	25.8	26.7	21.8	19.4	26.0	25.7	26.6	29.3
After income taxes	Percent	18.0	19.5	14.4	12.5	17.5	17.5	19.2	22.6

Source: U.S. Census Bureau, *Quarterly Financial Report for Manufacturing, Mining, Trade, and Selected Service Industries*. See also <http://www.census.gov/econ/qfr/>.

Table 1072. Retail Trade and Food Services—Estimated Per Capita Sales by Selected Kind of Business: 2000 to 2015

[Estimates are shown in dollars and are based on data from the Annual Retail Trade Survey and the Census Bureau's Population Estimates Program. Based on estimated resident population estimates as of July 1. Data have been adjusted using final results of the 2012 Economic Census. For additional information, see source and Appendix III]

Kind of business	2007 NAICS code [1]	2000	2005	2010	2012	2013	2014	2015
Retail and food service, total	44–45, 722	**11,651**	**13,826**	**13,851**	**15,370**	**15,821**	**16,373**	**16,670**
Retail, total	44–45	**10,573**	**12,484**	**12,342**	**13,701**	**14,103**	**14,564**	**14,728**
Total excluding motor vehicle and parts dealers	44–45, ex 441	7,751	9,478	9,941	10,878	11,069	11,360	11,316
Motor vehicle and parts dealers	441	2,822	3,006	2,402	2,823	3,034	3,204	3,412
Furniture and home furnishings stores	442	323	369	275	292	302	313	333
Electronics and appliance stores	443	291	340	315	325	326	325	318
Building material and garden equipment and supplies dealers	444	812	1,086	842	897	954	999	1,034
Food and beverage stores	445	1,576	1,721	1,877	2,001	2,027	2,101	2,135
Health and personal care stores	446	550	711	842	873	891	939	982
Gasoline stations	447	885	1,282	1,449	1,769	1,738	1,692	1,383
Clothing and clothing accessories stores	448	594	680	689	763	777	786	797
Sporting goods, hobby, book, and music stores	451	269	274	260	264	267	268	272
General merchandise stores	452	1,433	1,788	1,952	2,046	2,062	2,094	2,103
Miscellaneous store retailers	453	378	363	337	350	356	364	372
Nonstore retailers	454	640	865	1,102	1,300	1,370	1,478	1,586
Food services and drinking places, total	722	**1,078**	**1,342**	**1,509**	**1,669**	**1,718**	**1,809**	**1,942**

[1] North American Industry Classification System, 2007; see text, Section 15.

Source: U.S. Census Bureau, "2015 Annual Retail Trade Report," <http://www.census.gov/retail/index.html>, accessed March 2017.

Table 1073. Retail Trade—Merchandise Inventories and Inventory/Sales Ratios by Kind of Business: 2013 to 2016

[Inventories in billions of dollars (542.2 represents $542,200,000,000). As of Dec. 31. Estimates exclude food services. Includes warehouses. Adjusted for seasonal variations. Sales data also adjusted for holiday and trading-day differences. Based on data from the Monthly Retail Trade Survey, Annual Retail Trade Survey, and administrative records; see Appendix III]

Kind of business	2007 NAICS code [1]	Inventories				Inventory/sales ratio			
		2013	2014	2015	2016	2013	2014	2015	2016
Retail inventories, total [2]	44–45	**542.2**	**558.6**	**588.4**	**608.4**	**1.44**	**1.44**	**1.48**	**1.46**
Total excluding motor vehicle and parts dealers	44–45 ex 441	365.6	375.2	390.3	395.3	1.24	1.25	1.28	1.25
Motor vehicle and parts dealers	441	176.6	183.5	198.2	213.1	2.17	2.10	2.14	2.15
Furniture, home furnishings, electronics, and appliance stores	442, 443	26.9	27.3	27.4	26.9	1.64	1.57	1.57	1.56
Building material and garden equipment and supplies dealers	444	48.0	49.8	52.4	54.9	1.91	1.85	1.79	1.80
Food and beverage stores	445	42.7	44.2	44.9	46.2	0.78	0.77	0.78	0.78
Clothing and clothing accessories stores	448	50.2	51.2	53.8	54.2	2.42	2.42	2.53	2.52
General merchandise stores	452	80.6	80.9	82.4	80.5	1.48	1.45	1.45	1.45
Department stores	4521	29.8	28.2	28.6	27.1	2.13	2.03	2.08	2.15

[1] North American Industry Classification System, 2007; see text, Section 15. [2] Includes other kind of businesses, not shown separately.

Source: U.S. Census Bureau, Monthly Retail Trade Report, "Retail Inventories and Inventories/Sales Ratios," <http://www.census.gov/retail/index.html>, accessed March 2017.

Table 1074. Retail Trade Sales—Total and E-Commerce by Kind of Business: 2015

[4,727,427 represents $4,727,427,000,000. Covers retailers with and without payroll. Based on the Annual Retail Trade Survey; see Appendix III]

Kind of business	2007 NAICS code [1]	Value of sales (mil. dol.)		E-commerce as percent of total sales	Percent distribution of E-commerce sales
		Total	E-commerce		
Retail trade, total [2]	**44–45**	**4,727,427**	**340,415**	**7.2**	**100.0**
Motor vehicle and parts dealers	441	1,095,412	29,716	2.7	8.7
Furniture and home furnishings stores	442	106,779	691	0.6	0.2
Electronics and appliance stores	443	102,108	1,331	1.3	0.4
Building material and garden equipment and supplies stores	444	331,644	1,708	0.5	0.5
Food and beverage stores	445	685,568	1,166	0.2	0.3
Health and personal care stores	446	315,257	(D)	(D)	(D)
Clothing and clothing accessories stores	448	255,831	4,107	1.6	1.2
Sporting goods, hobby, book, and music stores	451	87,355	2,265	2.6	0.7
General merchandise stores	452	674,928	107	–	–
Miscellaneous store retailers	453	119,461	2,938	2.5	0.9
Nonstore retailers	454	509,267	295,746	58.1	86.9
Electronic shopping and mail-order houses	45411	433,692	294,809	68.0	86.6

– Represents or rounds to zero. D Withheld to avoid disclosing individual company data. [1] North American Industry Classification System, 2007; see text, Section 15. [2] Includes other kinds of businesses, not shown separately.

Source: U.S. Census Bureau, "2015 E-Commerce Multi-sector Data Tables," <http://www.census.gov/programs-surveys/e-stats/data/tables.html>, accessed June 2017.

Table 1075. Electronic Shopping and Mail-Order Houses—Total and E-Commerce Sales by Merchandise Line: 2014 and 2015

[386,065 represents $386,065,000,000. Represents 2007 North American Industry Classification System code 45411, which comprises establishments primarily engaged in retailing all types of merchandise using nonstore means, including catalogs, toll-free telephone numbers, or electronic media, such as interactive television or computer. Covers businesses with and without paid employees. Based on the Annual Retail Survey; see Appendix III]

Merchandise lines	2014 Value of sales (million dollars) Total	2014 Value of sales (million dollars) E-commerce	2014 E-commerce as percent of total sales	2015 Value of sales (million dollars) Total	2015 Value of sales (million dollars) E-commerce	2015 E-commerce as percent of total sales
Total..	386,065	256,269	66.4	433,692	294,809	68.0
Books and magazines...............................	11,879	10,828	91.2	12,583	11,648	92.6
Clothing and clothing accessories (includes footwear)................................	53,751	46,830	87.1	58,188	52,128	89.6
Computer hardware................................	29,527	16,884	57.2	(S)	17,459	(S)
Computer software................................	9,594	6,491	67.7	(S)	(S)	(S)
Drugs, health aids, beauty aids....................	93,586	19,112	20.4	(S)	21,469	(S)
Electronics and appliances.........................	28,158	24,234	86.1	30,016	26,050	86.8
Food, beer, and wine...............................	8,636	6,349	73.5	9,841	7,579	77.0
Furniture and home furnishings....................	26,599	23,311	87.6	32,369	28,883	89.2
Music and videos.................................	(S)	(S)	(S)	(S)	(S)	(S)
Office equipment and supplies.....................	(S)	(S)	(S)	10,613	9,236	87.0
Sporting goods....................................	10,910	9,347	85.7	13,104	11,681	89.1
Toys, hobby goods, and games....................	10,623	8,997	84.7	12,110	10,682	88.2
Other merchandise [1].............................	55,104	41,543	75.4	68,378	52,893	77.4
Nonmerchandise receipts [2].......................	25,500	22,317	87.5	29,153	26,374	90.5

S Figure does not meet publication standards. [1] Includes jewelry, collectibles, souvenirs, auto parts and accessories, hardware, and lawn and garden equipment and supplies. [2] Includes auction commissions, shipping and handling, customer training, customer support, and advertising.

Source: U.S. Census Bureau, "2015 E-Commerce Multi-sector Data Tables," <https://www.census.gov/programs-surveys/e-stats/data/tables.html>, accessed June 2017.

Table 1076. Franchised New Car Dealerships—Summary: 2000 to 2016

[In units as indicated (46.1 represents $46,100,000,000)]

Item	Unit	2000	2005	2009	2010	2011	2012	2013	2014	2015	2016
Dealerships [1]........................	Number	20,490	19,898	16,918	16,181	16,049	16,125	16,170	16,396	16,545	16,708
Sales [2]..............................	Bil. dol.	(NA)	(NA)	(NA)	(NA)	(NA)	(NA)	(NA)	(NA)	(NA)	996
New light duty vehicle sales.......	Millions	(NA)	16.9	10.4	11.6	12.7	14.4	15.5	16.4	17.4	17.5
New cars sold....................	Millions	8.8	7.7	5.5	5.6	6.1	7.2	7.6	7.7	7.5	6.9
New light trucks sold..............	Millions	(NA)	9.3	4.9	5.9	6.6	7.2	7.9	8.7	9.9	10.6
Average retail new vehicle selling price....................	Dollars	(NA)	(NA)	(NA)	30,079	30,982	31,194	32,035	32,824	33,456	34,449
Used vehicles sold.................	Millions	20.5	19.7	14.9	15.3	15.6	17.1	17.4	(NA)	(NA)	15.0
Employment........................	1,000	1,114	1,138	913	892	934	963	1,009	1,056	1,111	1,132
Annual payroll......................	Bil. dol.	46.1	51.5	43.5	42.4	45.8	51.6	53.7	58.1	62.6	64.9
Advertising expenses..............	Bil. dol.	6.4	7.7	5.4	5.9	6.4	7.2	7.6	(NA)	(NA)	(NA)
Average dealer pretax profits as percent of sales [2].................	Percent	(NA)	(NA)	(NA)	(NA)	(NA)	(NA)	(NA)	2.6	2.7	2.5
Inventory: [3] Domestic: [4]											
Total.............................	1,000	3,183	2,991	1,697	1,687	(NA)	(NA)	(NA)	(NA)	2,868	2,056
Days' supply.....................	Days	68	70	72	60	57	62	66	(NA)	65	74
Imported: [4]											
Total.............................	1,000	468	566	519	494	(NA)	(NA)	(NA)	(NA)	656	1,853
Days' supply.....................	Days	50	52	61	55	46	52	58	(NA)	55	54

NA Not available. [1] Light-duty new vehicle dealerships, as of December 31. [2] Beginning 2016, new methodology for calculating sales was implemented. [3] Annual average. [4] Classification based on location of automobile production (i.e., automobiles manufactured by foreign companies but produced in the U.S., Canada, and Mexico are classified as domestic).

Source: National Automobile Dealers Association, <www.nada.org>. *NADA Data 2016: Annual Financial Profile of America's Franchised New-Car Dealerships*, annual ©.

Table 1077. New Motor Vehicle Sales and Car Production: 1990 to 2016

[In thousands (14,137 represents 14,137,000). Data are primarily from "Ward's Automotive Reports" published by Ward's Communications, Southfield, MI]

Type of vehicle	1990	2000	2010	2011	2012	2013	2014	2015	2016
New motor vehicle sales.........	**14,137**	**17,812**	**11,772**	**13,048**	**14,779**	**15,883**	**16,860**	**17,846**	**17,866**
New-car sales............................	9,300	8,778	5,636	6,093	7,245	7,586	7,708	7,517	6,873
Domestic..............................	6,897	6,762	3,791	4,146	5,120	5,433	5,610	5,595	5,169
Import.................................	2,403	2,016	1,844	1,947	2,125	2,153	2,098	1,922	1,703
New-truck sales.........................	4,837	9,034	6,137	6,956	7,534	8,296	9,152	10,329	10,993
Light...................................	4,560	8,572	5,919	6,649	7,188	7,944	8,744	9,879	10,592
Domestic............................	3,957	7,720	5,020	5,667	6,127	6,704	7,384	8,097	8,461
Import...............................	603	852	899	982	1,061	1,239	1,360	1,782	2,131
Heavy.................................	278	462	218	307	346	353	408	449	401
Domestic-car production.............	**6,231**	**5,471**	**2,731**	**2,977**	**4,109**	**4,369**	**4,253**	**4,163**	**3,917**

Source: U.S. Bureau of Economic Analysis, National Economic Accounts, "Supplemental Estimates: Motor Vehicles," <http://www.bea.gov/national/index.htm#supp>, accessed March 2017.

Table 1078. Food and Alcoholic Beverage Expenditures by Sales Outlet: 1990 to 2014

[In billions of dollars (569.6 represents $569,600,000,000)]

Sales outlet	1990	2000	2005	2009	2010	2011	2012	2013	2014
Food sales, total [1]	**569.6**	**834.2**	**1,055.6**	**1,205.2**	**1,238.6**	**1,304.8**	**1,363.2**	**1,407.1**	**1,459.0**
Food at home	324.6	443.1	548.0	622.1	637.2	669.6	693.5	709.5	727.8
Food stores [2]	256.4	302.8	338.9	377.1	385.0	404.5	416.8	425.2	436.7
Other stores [3]	25.6	74.8	133.8	161.6	166.2	175.0	183.4	187.6	193.1
Home-delivered, mail order	5.3	18.7	18.5	18.2	18.8	19.6	20.8	22.2	21.6
Farmers, manufacturers, wholesalers	25.6	32.4	38.9	44.5	45.9	48.2	49.7	51.0	52.3
Home production and donations	11.7	14.4	17.9	20.7	21.4	22.3	22.8	23.6	24.1
Food away from home [4]	245.0	391.1	507.6	583.1	601.4	635.2	669.7	697.6	731.3
Alcoholic beverage sales, total	**68.0**	**101.6**	**127.1**	**147.0**	**151.4**	**158.2**	**166.8**	**169.5**	**176.1**
Packaged alcoholic beverages	34.9	48.2	63.5	78.3	81.3	85.0	89.4	90.4	92.8
Liquor stores	18.6	24.4	32.1	39.0	40.2	40.8	43.3	45.0	47.5
Food stores	10.8	15.8	18.6	20.3	20.7	21.8	22.5	22.9	23.5
All other	5.4	8.0	12.8	19.0	20.3	22.4	23.6	22.4	21.8
Alcoholic drinks away from home	33.1	53.4	63.6	68.7	70.1	73.2	77.3	79.2	83.3
Eating and drinking places [5]	26.5	41.5	51.2	54.0	55.2	57.9	61.5	62.9	66.9
Hotels and motels [5]	3.2	6.4	4.7	4.7	4.7	4.8	4.9	4.9	4.9
All other	3.4	5.5	7.6	10.0	10.2	10.4	10.9	11.4	11.5

[1] Includes taxes and tips. [2] Excludes sales to restaurants and institutions. [3] Includes eating and drinking establishments, trailer parks, commissary stores, and military exchanges. [4] Includes food supplied and donated. [5] Includes tips.

Source: U.S. Department of Agriculture, Economic Research Service, "Food Expenditures," <http://www.ers.usda.gov/data-products/food-expenditures.aspx>, accessed February 2016.

Transportation

This section presents data on civil air transportation, both passenger and cargo, and on water transportation, including inland waterways, oceanborne commerce, the merchant marine, cargo, and vessel tonnages.

This section also presents statistics on revenues, passenger and freight traffic volume, and employment in various revenue-producing modes of the transportation industry, including motor vehicles, trains, and pipelines. Data are also presented on highway mileage and finances, motor vehicle travel, accidents, and registrations; and characteristics of public transit, railroads, and pipelines.

The principal source of transportation data is the annual *National Transportation Statistics* publication of the U.S. Bureau of Transportation Statistics. Principal sources of air and water transportation data are the *Annual Report* issued by Airlines for America, Washington, DC and the annual *Waterborne Commerce of the United States* issued by the Corps of Engineers of the Department of Army. In addition, the U.S. Census Bureau in its Commodity Flow Survey (part of the Economic Census, taken every 5 years through 2012, for years ending in "2" and "7") provides data on the type, weight, and value of commodities shipped by manufacturing establishments in the United States, by means of transportation, origin, and destination. Release of data from the 2012 Economic Census was completed in 2016. This census was conducted in accordance with the 2012 North American Industry Classification System (NAICS). See text, Section 15, Business Enterprise, for a discussion of the Economic Census and NAICS.

The Bureau of Transportation Statistics (BTS) was established within the U.S. Department of Transportation (DOT) in 1992 to collect, report, and analyze transportation data. Today, BTS is a component of the DOT Research and Innovative Technology Administration (RITA). BTS products include reports to Congress, the Secretary of Transportation, and stakeholders in the nation's transportation community. These stakeholders include: federal agencies, state and local governments, metropolitan planning organizations, universities, the private sector, and the general public. Congress requires, by congressional mandate laid out in 49 U.S.C. 111 (1), the BTS to report on transportation statistics to the President and Congress. *The Transportation Statistics Annual Report* (TSAR), provides a data overview of U.S. transportation issues. As required by Congress, each TSAR has two essential components: a review of the state of transportation statistics with recommendations for improvements, and a presentation of the data. The BTS publication *National Transportation Statistics* (NTS), a companion report to the TSAR, has more comprehensive and longer time-series data. NTS presents information on the U.S. transportation system, including its physical components, safety record, economic performance, energy use, and environmental impacts. The BTS publication *State Transportation Statistics* presents a statistical profile of transportation in the 50 states and the District of Columbia. This profile includes infrastructure, freight movement and passenger travel, system safety,

vehicles, transportation-related economy and finance, energy usage, and the environment.

The principal compiler of data on public roads and on operation of motor vehicles is the U.S. Department of Transportation's (DOT) Federal Highway Administration (FHWA). These data appear in FHWA's annual *Highway Statistics* and other publications.

The U.S. National Highway Traffic Safety Administration (NHTSA), through its *Traffic Safety Facts FARS/GES Annual Report*, presents descriptive statistics about traffic crashes of all severities, from those that result in property damage to those that result in the loss of life. This report compiles motor vehicle crash data from the Fatality Analysis Reporting System (FARS) and the General Estimates System (GES). Other publications and reports can be found at the National Center for Statistics and Analysis (NCSA), Publications and Data Request, located on the internet at <https://crashstats.nhtsa.dot.gov/#/>. DOT's Federal Railroad Administration (FRA), Office of Safety Analysis presents railroad safety information, including accidents and incidents, inspections, and highway-rail crossing data at its "Safety Database" located at <http://safetydata.fra.dot.gov/officeofsafety>.

Civil aviation—Federal promotion and regulation of civil aviation have been carried out by the Federal Aviation Administration (FAA) and the Civil Aeronautics Board (CAB). The CAB promoted and regulated the civil air transportation industry within the United States and between the United States and foreign countries. The Board granted licenses to provide air transportation service, approved or disapproved proposed rates and fares, and approved or disapproved proposed agreements and corporate relationships involving air carriers. In December 1984, the CAB ceased to exist as an agency. Some of its functions were transferred to the DOT, as outlined below. The responsibility for investigation of aviation accidents resides with the National Transportation Safety Board.

The Office of the Secretary, DOT aviation activities include: negotiation of international air transportation rights, selection of U.S. air carriers to serve capacity controlled international markets, oversight of international rates and fares, maintenance of essential air service to small communities, and consumer affairs. DOT's Bureau of Transportation Statistics (BTS) handles aviation information functions formerly assigned to CAB. Prior to BTS, the Research and Special Programs Administration handled these functions.

The principal activities of the FAA include: the promotion of air safety; controlling the use of navigable airspace; prescribing regulations dealing with the competency of airmen, airworthiness of aircraft, and air traffic control; operation of air route traffic control centers, airport traffic control towers, and flight service stations; the design, construction, maintenance, and inspection of navigation, traffic control, and communications equipment; and the development of general aviation.

The CAB published monthly and quarterly financial and traffic statistical data for the certificated route air carriers. BTS continues these publications, including both certificated and noncertificated (commuter) air carriers. The FAA annually publishes data on the use of airway facilities; data related to the location of airmen, aircraft, and airports; the volume of activity in the field of nonair carrier (general aviation) flying; and aircraft production and registration.

General aviation comprises all civil flying (including such commercial operations as small demand air taxis, agriculture application, powerline patrol, etc.) but excludes certificated route air carriers, supplemental operators, large-aircraft commercial operators, and commuter airlines.

Air carriers and service—The CAB previously issued "certificates of public convenience and necessity" under Section 401 of the Federal Aviation Act of 1958 for scheduled and nonscheduled (charter) passenger services and cargo services. It also issued certificates under Section 418 of the Act to cargo air carriers for domestic all-cargo service only. The DOT Office of the Secretary now issues the certificates under a "fit, willing, and able" test of air carrier operations. Carriers operating only a 60-seat-or-less aircraft are given exemption authority to carry passengers, cargo, and mail in scheduled and nonscheduled service under Part 298 of the DOT (formerly CAB) regulations. Exemption authority carriers who offer scheduled passenger service to an essential air service point must meet the "fit, willing, and able" test.

Vessel shipments, entrances, and clearances—Shipments by dry cargo vessels comprise shipments on all types of watercraft, except tanker vessels; shipments by tanker vessels comprise all types of cargo, liquid and dry, carried by tanker vessels. A vessel is reported as entered only at the first port which it enters in the United States, whether or not cargo is unloaded at that port.

A vessel is reported as cleared only at the last port at which clearance is made to a foreign port, whether or not it takes on cargo. Army and Navy vessels entering or clearing without commercial cargo are not included in the figures.

Units of measurement—Cargo (or freight) tonnage and shipping weight both represent the gross weight of the cargo, including the weight of containers, wrappings, crates, etc. However, shipping weight excludes lift and cargo vans and similar substantial outer containers. Other tonnage figures generally refer to stowing capacity of vessels, 100 cubic feet being called 1 ton. Gross tonnage comprises the space within the frames and the ceiling of the hull, together with those closed-in spaces above deck available for cargo, stores, passengers, or crew, with certain minor exceptions. Net or registered tonnage is the gross tonnage less the spaces occupied by the propelling machinery, fuel, crew quarters, master's cabin, and navigation spaces. Substantially, it represents space available for cargo and passengers. The net tonnage capacity of a ship may bear little relation to weight of cargo. Deadweight tonnage is the weight in long tons required to depress a vessel from light water line (that is, with only the machinery and equipment on board) to load line. It is, therefore, the weight of the cargo, fuel, etc., which a vessel is designed to carry with safety.

Federal-aid highway systems—The Intermodal Surface Transportation Efficiency Act (ISTEA) of 1991 eliminated the historical Federal-Aid Highway Systems and created the National Highway System (NHS) and other federal-aid highway categories. The final NHS was approved by Congress in December of 1995 under the National Highway System Designation Act.

Functional systems—Roads and streets are assigned to groups according to the character of service intended. The functional systems are (1) arterial highways that generally handle the long trips, (2) collector facilities that collect and disperse traffic between the arterials and the lower systems, and (3) local roads and streets that primarily serve direct access to residential areas, farms, and other local areas.

Regulatory bodies—The Federal Energy Regulatory Commission (FERC) is an independent agency that regulates the interstate transmission of electricity, natural gas, and oil. FERC also reviews proposals to build liquefied natural gas (LNG) terminals and interstate natural gas pipelines as well as licenses to hydropower projects. The Energy Policy Act of 2005 gave FERC additional responsibilities such as regulating the transmission and wholesale sales of electricity in interstate commerce.

The Surface Transportation Board (STB) was created in the Interstate Commerce Commission Termination Act of 1995, Pub. L. No.104-88, 109 Stat. 803 (1995) (ICCTA), and is the successor agency to the Interstate Commerce Commission. The STB is an economic regulatory agency that Congress charged with the fundamental missions of resolving railroad rate and service disputes and reviewing proposed railroad mergers. The STB makes decisions independently, although it is administratively affiliated with the Department of Transportation.

The STB serves as both an adjudicatory and a regulatory body. The agency has jurisdiction over railroad rate and service issues and rail restructuring transactions (mergers, line sales, line construction, and line abandonment); certain trucking company, moving van, and noncontiguous ocean shipping company rate matters; certain intercity passenger bus company structure, financial, and operational matters; and rates and services of certain pipelines not regulated by the Federal Energy Regulatory Commission. Other ICC regulatory functions were either eliminated or transferred to the Federal Highway Administration or the Bureau of Transportation Statistics within DOT.

Class I Railroads are regulated by the STB and subject to the Uniform System of Accounts and required to file annual and periodic reports. Railroads are classified based on their annual operating revenues. The class to which a carrier belongs is determined by comparing its adjusted operating revenues for 3 consecutive years to the following scale: Class I, $250 million or more; Class II, $20 million to $250 million; and Class III, $0 to $20 million. Operating revenue dollar ranges are indexed for inflation.

Postal Service—The U.S. Postal Service provides mail processing and delivery services within the United States. The Postal Accountability and Enhancement Act of 2006 was the first major legislative change to the Postal Service since 1971 when the Postal Reorganization Act of 1970 created the Postal Service as an independent establishment of the Federal Executive Branch. The Act of 2006 changed the way the U.S. Postal Service operates and conducts business. Now annual rate increases for market dominant products are linked to the Consumer Price Index and the Postal Service has more flexibility for pricing competitive products, enabling it to respond to dynamic market conditions and changing customer needs.

Revenue and cost analysis describes the Postal Service's system of attributing revenues and costs to classes of mail and service. This system draws primarily upon probability sampling techniques to develop estimates of revenues, volumes, and weights, as well as costs by class of mail and special service. The costs attributed to classes of mail and special services are primarily incremental costs which vary in response to changes in volume; they account for roughly 60 percent of the total costs of the Postal Service. The balance represents "institutional costs." Statistics on revenues, volume of mail, and distribution of expenditures are presented in the Postal Service's annual reports *Cost and Revenue Analysis, Annual Report to Congress,* and *Comprehensive Statement on Postal Operations.*

Statistical reliability—For a discussion of statistical collection and estimation, sampling procedures, and measures of statistical reliability applicable to Census Bureau data, see Appendix III.

Table 1079. Transportation-Related Components of U.S. Gross Domestic Product: 2000 to 2015

[In billions of dollars (1,059.9 represents $1,059,900,000,000), except percent. For explanation of chained dollars, see Section 13 text. Minus sign (-) indicates a decrease]

Item	2000	2010	2012	2013	2014	2015
CURRENT DOLLARS						
Total transportation-related final demand [1]	**1,059.9**	**1,320.2**	**1,560.5**	**1,608.0**	**1,661.1**	**1,630.6**
Total gross domestic product (GDP)	10,284.8	14,964.4	16,155.3	16,691.5	17,393.1	18,036.6
Transportation as a percent of GDP	10.3	8.8	9.7	9.6	9.6	9.0
Personal consumption of transportation	795.3	942.2	1,105.8	1,136.2	1,168.1	1,116.2
Motor vehicles and parts	363.2	342.0	395.8	416.1	442.8	464.8
Motor vehicle fuels, lubricants, and fluids	168.6	307.3	390.5	385.6	371.2	283.0
Transportation services	263.5	292.9	319.5	334.5	354.1	368.4
Gross private domestic investment	177.6	137.4	224.0	251.6	284.0	321.6
Transportation structures	6.8	9.9	10.9	11.0	12.2	13.5
Transportation equipment	170.8	127.5	213.1	240.6	271.8	308.1
Net exports of transportation-related goods and service [2]	-104.7	-75.9	-99.2	-102.7	-113.4	-143.8
Exports (+)	174.3	255.6	324.4	344.5	363.6	358.6
Civilian aircraft, engines, and parts	48.1	71.9	94.3	105.0	113.1	119.5
Automotive vehicles, engines, and parts	80.4	112.0	146.2	152.7	159.8	151.9
Other transportation	45.8	71.7	83.9	86.8	90.7	87.2
Imports (-)	279.0	331.5	423.6	447.2	477.0	502.4
Civilian aircraft, engines, and parts	26.4	31.3	40.1	47.0	53.3	55.2
Automotive vehicles, engines, and parts	195.0	225.6	298.5	309.6	329.5	350.1
Other transportation	57.6	74.6	85.0	90.6	94.2	97.1
Government transportation-related purchases	179.8	304.2	307.5	305.3	314.1	329.1
Federal purchases [3]	19.0	38.9	41.7	39.0	39.4	41.2
State and local purchases [3]	151.8	240.6	247.0	251.3	260.3	274.7
Defense-related purchases [4]	9.0	24.7	18.8	15.0	14.4	13.2
CHAINED (2009) DOLLARS						
Total transportation-related final demand [1]	**1,347.9**	**1,251.2**	**1,343.6**	**1,382.7**	**1,431.8**	**1,484.8**
Total gross domestic product (GDP)	12,559.7	14,783.8	15,354.6	15,612.2	15,982.3	16,397.2
Transportation as a percent of GDP	10.7	8.5	8.8	8.9	9.0	9.1
Personal consumption of transportation	945.0	870.4	910.8	942.1	980.1	1,020.7
Motor vehicles and parts	346.4	323.4	359.1	375.7	399.5	419.4
Motor vehicle fuels, lubricants, and fluids	265.8	259.9	252.5	257.6	257.7	266.6
Transportation services	332.8	287.1	299.2	308.8	322.9	334.7
Gross private domestic investment	212.9	146.7	229.3	253.4	282.1	314.4
Transportation structures	8.8	9.8	10.4	10.4	11.2	12.2
Transportation equipment	204.1	136.9	218.9	243.0	270.9	302.2
Net exports of transportation-related goods and service [2]	-104.7	-75.5	-94.1	-98.9	-112.1	-146.3
Exports (+)	217.0	247.5	295.8	311.6	324.1	321.1
Civilian aircraft, engines, and parts	69.9	70.1	86.2	94.2	98.4	101.2
Automotive vehicles, engines, and parts	86.8	111.5	140.5	145.9	151.9	144.5
Other transportation	60.3	65.9	69.1	71.5	73.8	75.4
Imports (-)	321.7	323.0	389.9	410.5	436.2	467.4
Civilian aircraft, engines, and parts	37.7	30.5	35.2	40.4	45.2	46.3
Automotive vehicles, engines, and parts	211.9	224.2	282.2	293.8	314.6	341.1
Other transportation	72.1	68.3	72.5	76.3	76.4	80.0
Government transportation-related purchases	283.0	297.9	277.1	269.9	274.0	289.1
Federal purchases [3]	25.3	37.8	38.9	35.8	35.6	36.9
State and local purchases [3]	245.5	236.0	221.4	220.7	225.8	240.4
Defense-related purchases [4]	12.2	24.1	16.8	13.4	12.6	11.8

[1] Sum of total personal consumption of transportation, total gross private domestic investment, net exports of transportation-related goods and services, and total government transportation-related purchases. [2] Exports minus imports. [3] Federal purchases and state and local purchases are the sum of consumption expenditures and gross investment. [4] Defense-related purchases are the sum of transportation of material and travel.

Source: U.S. Bureau of Transportation Statistics, "National Transportation Statistics," <https://www.rita.dot.gov/bts/sites/rita.dot.gov.bts/files/publications/national_transportation_statistics/index.html>, accessed February 2017.

Table 1080. Employment in Transportation and Warehousing: 2000 to 2016

[In thousands (4,410 represents 4,410,000). Annual average of monthly figures. Based on Current Employment Statistics program; see Appendix III]

Industry	NAICS code [1]	2000	2005	2010	2011	2012	2013	2014	2015	2016
Transportation and warehousing	**48–49**	**4,410**	**4,361**	**4,191**	**4,302**	**4,416**	**4,498**	**4,661**	**4,871**	**4,989**
Air transportation	481	614	501	458	457	459	444	444	459	476
Rail transportation	482	232	228	216	228	231	231	236	241	215
Water transportation	483	56	61	62	61	64	65	67	66	66
Truck transportation	484	1,406	1,398	1,250	1,301	1,349	1,382	1,417	1,452	1,454
Transit and ground passenger	485	372	389	430	440	440	449	467	478	478
Pipeline transportation	486	46	38	42	43	44	45	47	50	50
Scenic and sightseeing	487	28	29	27	28	28	29	31	33	35
Support activities	488	537	552	543	562	580	598	626	652	660
Couriers and messengers	492	605	571	528	529	534	544	577	613	642
Warehousing and storage	493	514	595	633	653	687	711	750	829	915

[1] North American Industry Classification System 2012, see text, Sections 12 and 15.

Source: U.S. Bureau of Labor Statistics, Current Employment Statistics, "Employment, Hours, and Earnings—National," <http://www.bls.gov/ces/data.htm/>, accessed March 2017.

Table 1081. Transportation and Warehousing—Establishments, Employees, and Payroll by Kind of Business: 2014 and 2015

[Employment in thousands (4,406.8 represents 4,406,800); payroll in millions of dollars ($207,352.3 represents $207,352,300,000). Covers establishments with payroll. Excludes self-employed individuals, railroad employees, and most government employees. For statement on methodology, see Appendix III. County Business Patterns excludes rail transportation (NAICS 482) and the National Postal Service (NAICS 491)]

Industry	NAICS code [1]	Establishments		Paid employees (1,000) [2]		Annual payroll (mil. dol.)	
		2014	2015	2014	2015	2014	2015
Transportation & warehousing.....................	**48–49**	**220,565**	**228,382**	**4,406.8**	**4,616.6**	**207,352.3**	**222,018.3**
Air transportation...................	481	4,873	4,877	428.8	453.4	28,786.5	32,614.3
Scheduled air transportation..............	4811	2,518	2,516	392.5	416.2	25,821.7	29,444.3
Scheduled passenger air transportation.............	481111	2,072	2,089	382.1	405.6	25,096.3	28,656.2
Scheduled freight air transportation...............	481112	446	427	10.4	10.7	725.3	788.1
Nonscheduled air transportation......................	4812	2,355	2,361	36.3	37.1	2,964.9	3,170.0
Water transportation.........................	483	1,689	1,710	68.5	67.9	5,287.5	5,495.9
Deep sea, coastal, & Great Lakes water transportation........................	4831	1,119	1,141	46.9	45.3	3,702.5	3,789.7
Inland water transportation....................	4832	570	569	21.5	22.6	1,585.0	1,706.3
Inland water freight transportation..............	483211	353	359	19.3	20.3	1,470.6	1,584.4
Inland water passenger transportation.......	483212	217	210	2.2	2.3	114.4	121.9
Truck transportation...................	484	116,429	121,653	1,392.6	1,448.6	65,329.2	68,039.8
General freight trucking................	4841	69,128	74,098	915.4	955.3	42,662.3	45,046.4
General freight trucking, local............	48411	28,035	29,884	185.5	195.9	7,599.1	8,202.1
General freight trucking, long distance...............	48412	41,093	44,214	729.9	759.3	35,063.3	36,844.4
Specialized freight trucking...................	4842	47,301	47,555	477.2	493.4	22,666.9	22,993.4
Used household & office goods moving...........	48421	7,858	7,933	94.7	96.9	3,296.6	3,474.2
Specialized freight (except used goods) trucking, local........................	48422	29,249	29,163	212.5	217.1	10,371.7	10,341.6
Specialized freight (except used goods) trucking, long-distance........................	48423	10,194	10,459	170.0	179.4	8,998.6	9,177.5
Transit & ground passenger transportation..............	485	19,682	20,249	479.8	492.6	12,470.4	13,614.8
Urban transit systems..........................	4851	838	794	51.9	53.5	2,357.1	2,462.6
Mixed mode systems........................	485111	24	27	([3])	0.7	(D)	27.6
Commuter rail........................	485112	12	14	3.1	3.4	264.5	303.2
Bus and other motor vehicle mode systems.........	485113	757	708	46.1	47.5	1,929.8	2,002.7
Other........................	485119	45	45	2.0	2.0	133.2	129.1
Interurban & rural bus transportation..................	4852	490	467	13.9	12.5	464.8	477.2
Taxi & limousine service......................	4853	8,335	8,553	76.4	77.5	2,061.7	2,452.8
Taxi service........................	48531	3,340	3,348	34.0	35.1	901.1	1,276.6
Limousine service........................	48532	4,995	5,205	42.4	42.4	1,160.6	1,176.2
School & employee bus transportation..............	4854	4,176	4,302	219.2	227.1	4,527.9	4,921.2
Charter bus industry........................	4855	1,347	1,315	33.0	34.0	939.5	1,010.1
Other transit & ground passenger transportation......	4859	4,496	4,818	85.4	87.9	2,119.4	2,290.9
Special needs transportation................	485991	2,970	3,085	65.7	66.6	1,630.9	1,758.4
Pipeline transportation.....................	486	4,189	3,671	([6])	52.2	6,290.2	5,909.3
Pipeline transportation of crude oil....................	4861	771	796	12.3	13.9	1,387.1	1,614.0
Pipeline transportation of natural gas.................	4862	2,729	2,179	([5])	30.3	(D)	3,376.1
Other pipeline transportation.....................	4869	689	696	6.9	8.0	793.5	919.2
Scenic & sightseeing transportation................	487	2,686	2,744	25.3	26.5	879.4	969.1
Scenic & sightseeing transportation, land.............	4871	688	715	10.3	11.2	317.9	352.7
Scenic & sightseeing transportation, water............	4872	1,769	1,803	12.7	13.0	463.4	508.8
Scenic & sightseeing transportation, other............	4879	229	226	2.3	2.3	98.1	107.6
Support activities for transportation....................	488	42,534	43,495	656.6	674.5	32,384.2	34,248.2
Support activities for air transportation................	4881	5,835	5,762	175.4	175.0	7,358.7	7,595.6
Airport operations............................	48811	2,116	2,076	89.4	94.9	2,604.4	2,923.5
Air traffic control............................	488111	192	191	([4])	1.4	(D)	96.0
Other support activities for air transportation.........	48819	3,719	3,686	86.0	80.1	4,754.3	4,672.1
Support activities for rail transportation..............	4882	1,428	1,403	36.6	39.4	1,854.2	2,026.2
Support activities for water transportation.............	4883	2,582	2,556	100.2	97.4	6,427.7	6,423.2
Port and harbor operations.................	48831	351	337	6.8	7.9	399.5	434.2
Marine cargo handling....................	48832	482	492	69.8	66.4	4,406.5	4,335.0
Navigational services to shipping....................	48833	881	889	12.1	11.9	907.8	923.3
Other support activities for water transportation.....	48839	868	838	11.4	11.2	713.9	730.7
Support activities for road transportation..............	4884	11,093	11,497	89.9	91.8	2,902.8	3,087.1
Motor vehicle towing........................	48841	8,581	8,878	56.0	57.6	1,865.7	2,022.7
Freight transportation arrangement....................	4885	20,008	20,606	238.3	253.9	13,309.2	14,530.2
Other support activities for transportation..............	4889	1,588	1,671	16.2	17.1	531.7	585.9
Couriers & messengers....................	492	13,864	14,853	540.5	591.4	23,626.9	25,661.5
Couriers........................	4921	9,409	10,402	504.5	553.2	22,573.0	24,435.2
Local messengers & local delivery....................	4922	4,455	4,451	36.1	38.2	1,053.9	1,226.3
Warehousing & storage.....................	493	14,619	15,130	761.0	809.4	32,298.0	35,465.4

D Data withheld to avoid disclosure. [1] Data based on 2012 North American Industry Classification System (NAICS). See text, Section 15. [2] Covers full- and part-time employees who are on the payroll in the pay period including March 12. [3] 500 to 999 employees. [4] 1,000 to 2,499 employees. [5] 25,000 to 49,999 employees [6] 50,000 to 99,999 employees.

Source: U.S. Census Bureau, County Business Patterns, "Geography Area Series: County Business Patterns," <https://factfinder.census.gov/>, accessed April 2017. See also <https://www.census.gov/programs-surveys/cbp.html>.

Table 1082. Transportation Sector—Estimated Revenue by Kind of Business: 2010 to 2015

[In millions of dollars (660,440 represents $660,440,000,000). For taxable employer firms. Estimates have been adjusted to results of the 2012 Economic Census. Based on the Service Annual Survey; see Appendix III]

Kind of business	NAICS code [1]	2010	2012	2013	2014	2015
Transportation and warehousing.............................	4849y	660,440	773,120	805,714	859,178	876,498
Air transportation [2].......................................	481	148,419	181,271	189,150	199,009	200,161
Scheduled passenger air transportation..........................	481111	126,902	157,177	165,509	173,250	174,099
Nonscheduled chartered passenger air transportation..........	481211	10,499	11,451	11,706	13,285	13,709
Water transportation [2]...................................	483	37,392	41,709	42,807	45,132	44,003
Deep sea freight transportation...............................	483111	9,281	9,640	9,530	9,215	8,443
Deep sea passenger transportation...........................	483112	14,393	16,325	16,875	17,985	18,593
Coastal and great lakes freight transportation....................	483113	6,254	7,006	7,657	7,909	7,509
Inland water freight transportation............................	483211	6,879	8,074	8,064	9,281	8,652
Truck transportation.......................................	484	197,963	238,003	245,520	263,875	263,249
General freight trucking, local...............................	48411	19,902	23,360	24,305	26,222	26,426
General freight trucking, long-distance, truckload................	484121	77,474	92,215	94,298	101,178	101,884
General freight trucking, long-distance, less than truckload.....	484122	31,698	37,453	38,805	41,378	41,221
Used household and office goods moving......................	48421	12,361	13,651	14,348	15,366	15,897
Specialized freight (except used goods) trucking, local.........	48422	28,465	36,171	37,631	40,873	38,828
Specialized freight (except used goods) trucking, long-distance.......................................	48423	28,063	35,153	36,133	38,858	38,993
Transit and ground passenger transportation [2].................	485	26,900	29,955	31,307	32,969	34,031
Urban transit systems.......................................	4851	4,460	4,940	5,178	5,443	5,596
Interurban and rural bus transportation........................	4852	1,037	1,151	1,175	1,188	1,146
Taxi service...	48531	2,225	2,477	2,558	2,640	2,678
Limousine service..	48532	3,554	4,138	4,361	4,572	4,564
School and employee bus transportation......................	4854	8,628	9,444	9,851	10,355	10,939
Charter bus industry..	4855	2,888	3,078	3,166	3,273	3,439
Pipeline transportation [2].................................	486	33,069	36,434	38,813	41,852	43,764
Pipeline transportation of crude oil............................	4861	5,004	6,801	7,863	9,029	10,004
Pipeline transportation of natural gas.........................	4862	21,831	22,987	23,782	25,097	25,230
Pipeline transportation of refined petroleum products............	48691	5,993	6,417	6,869	7,451	8,227
Scenic and sightseeing transportation [2].......................	487	2,545	3,093	3,271	3,368	3,666
Scenic and sightseeing transportation, land....................	4871	903	1,010	1,029	1,027	1,084
Scenic and sightseeing transportation, water...................	4872	1,236	1,580	1,669	1,727	1,906
Support activities for transportation [2].........................	488	125,423	144,749	153,744	167,478	177,816
Airport operations...	48811	5,699	6,929	7,022	7,709	7,936
Other support activities for air transportation...................	48819	15,072	15,546	16,217	16,723	16,826
Support activities for rail transportation.......................	4882	3,945	4,836	5,213	5,238	5,781
Port and harbor operations..................................	48831	1,856	2,359	2,565	2,625	2,809
Marine cargo handling......................................	48832	7,572	8,904	9,046	10,034	10,782
Navigational services to shipping.............................	48833	2,886	3,168	3,349	3,426	3,503
Motor vehicle towing..	48841	5,040	5,109	5,376	5,795	6,016
Freight transportation arrangement...........................	4885	77,359	91,455	98,108	108,392	116,044
Couriers and messengers..................................	492	63,855	69,362	71,570	75,118	78,424
Couriers and express delivery services........................	4921	60,917	65,801	67,849	71,280	74,117
Local messengers and local delivery..........................	4922	2,938	3,561	3,721	3,838	4,307
Warehousing and storage..................................	493	24,874	28,494	29,532	30,377	31,384
General warehousing and storage............................	49311	15,966	17,617	18,272	18,864	19,486
Refrigerated warehousing and storage........................	49312	4,083	4,098	4,071	4,310	(S)
Farm product warehousing and storage........................	49313	698	738	754	726	786
Other warehousing and storage..............................	49319	4,127	6,041	6,435	6,477	6,698

S Estimate does not meet publication standards. [1] Data are based on 2007 North American Industry Classification System (NAICS); see text, this section and Section 15. [2] Includes other kinds of business not shown separately.

Source: U.S. Census Bureau, Annual & Quarterly Services, "2015 Service Annual Survey," <http://www.census.gov/services/index.html>, accessed December 2016.

Table 1083. Transportation and Warehousing—Establishments, Revenue, Payroll, and Employees by Industry: 2012

[730,541 represents $730,541,000,000. For establishments with payroll. Based on the 2012 Economic Censuses. Paid employees for pay period including March 12. See Appendix III]

Industry type	NAICS code [1]	Number of establish- ments	Revenue (mil. dol.)	Annual payroll (mil. dol.)	Paid employees (1,000)
Transportation and warehousing total....................	48–49	213,809	730,541	183,841	4,305.5
Air transportation..	481	4,979	181,273	26,236	444.6
Water transportation.......................................	483	1,496	41,709	4,802	67.4
Truck transportation.......................................	484	111,899	238,003	57,861	1,363.1
Transit and ground passenger transportation..................	485	18,735	28,687	11,275	495.1
Pipeline transportation.....................................	486	3,391	36,483	5,086	47.4
Scenic and sightseeing transportation........................	487	2,573	3,092	832	27.9
Support activities for transportation...........................	488	42,489	103,439	28,435	617.7
Couriers and messengers...................................	492	13,799	69,362	21,157	529.5
Warehousing and storage...................................	493	14,448	28,494	28,157	712.8

[1] Data based on the 2007 North American Industry Classification System (NAICS); see text, Section 15.

Source: U.S. Census Bureau, 2012 Economic Census, Table EC1200CCOMP1, "All Sectors: Core Business Statistics Series: Comparative Statistics for the U.S. (2007 NAICS Basis): 2012 and 2007," <http://factfinder.census.gov/>, accessed September 2016.

Table 1084. Transportation and Warehousing—Nonemployer Establishments and Receipts by Kind of Business: 2010 to 2015

[1,021.2 represents 1,021,200. Includes only firms subject to federal income tax. Nonemployers are businesses with no paid employees. Data originate chiefly from administrative records of the Internal Revenue Service; see Appendix III]

Kind of business	NAICS code [1]	Establishments (1,000)			Receipts (mil. dol.)		
		2010	2014	2015	2010	2014	2015
Transportation and warehousing............	**48–49**	**1,021.2**	**1,250.9**	**1,528.3**	**60,746**	**81,851**	**83,890**
Air transportation....................................	481	19.1	18.9	19.5	1,219	1,355	1,385
Water transportation................................	483	6.6	6.7	6.7	490	539	548
Truck transportation................................	484	490.3	546.0	573.6	42,485	57,317	56,158
General freight trucking........................	4841	445.1	499.6	526.2	39,277	53,642	52,493
General freight trucking, local.................	48411	168.7	178.9	185.4	12,144	15,803	15,906
General freight trucking, long-distance........	48412	276.4	320.7	340.7	27,133	37,838	36,588
Specialized freight trucking......................	4842	45.2	46.4	47.4	3,207	3,676	3,662
Transit and ground passenger transportation....	485	218.4	362.4	577.8	7,463	11,727	14,301
Urban transit system............................	4851	1.1	3.1	1.4	39	76	21
Interurban and rural bus transportation..........	4852	1.5	1.7	2.1	67	74	76
Taxi and limousine service........................	4853	176.4	296.1	480.3	6,107	9,836	11,997
School and employee bus transportation........	4854	6.9	6.8	6.8	191	199	200
Charter bus industry..............................	4855	3.8	4.1	4.2	172	192	193
Other transit and ground passenger transportation...................................	4859	28.7	50.5	83.1	887	1,350	1,814
Pipeline transportation.............................	486	0.9	1.2	1.2	76	101	85
Scenic and sightseeing transportation...........	487	4.9	5.5	5.9	163	201	220
Support activities for transportation..............	488	105.2	131.8	153.3	4,624	6,031	6,422
Couriers and messengers..........................	492	166.6	167.2	178.6	3,772	4,041	4,208
Warehousing and storage..........................	493	9.2	11.0	11.0	455	537	550

[1] 2010 data based on the 2007 North American Industry Classification System (NAICS); beginning 2012, data based on 2012 NAICS.

Source: U.S. Census Bureau, Nonemployer Statistics, "Geographic Area Series: Nonemployer Statistics by Legal Form of Organization for U.S. and States," <https://factfinder.census.gov/>, accessed May 2017. See also <https://census.gov/programs-surveys/nonemployer-statistics.html>.

Table 1085. Transportation System Mileage Within the United States: 1980 to 2015

[3,860 represents 3,860,000. Numbers, except where indicated]

System	Unit	1980	1985	1990	1995	2000	2005	2010	2014	2015
Highway [1]........................	1,000	3,860	3,864	3,867	3,912	3,936	3,996	4,067	4,177	4,155
Class 1 rail [2]...................	Number	164,822	145,764	119,758	108,264	99,250	95,664	95,573	94,372	93,628
Amtrak [2]........................	Number	24,000	24,000	24,000	24,000	23,000	22,007	21,178	21,356	21,358
Transit: [3]										
Commuter rail [4]..............	Number	(NA)	3,574	4,132	4,160	5,209	7,118	7,630	7,795	(NA)
Heavy rail [5]...................	Number	(NA)	1,293	1,351	1,458	1,558	1,622	1,617	1,622	(NA)
Light rail [6].....................	Number	(NA)	384	483	568	834	1,188	1,497	1,877	(NA)
Navigable channels [7]..........	Number	25,000	25,000	25,000	25,000	25,000	25,000	25,000	25,000	25,000
Oil pipeline [8]..................	Number	(NA)	(NA)	(NA)	(NA)	(NA)	166,760	181,986	199,659	208,616
Gas pipeline [9].................	1,000	(NA)	1,315	1,547	1,700	1,788	1,962	2,102	2,169	2,190

NA Not available. [1] All public road and street mileage in the 50 states and the District of Columbia. Beginning in 1998, approximately 43,000 miles of Bureau of Land Management Roads are excluded. [2] Data represent miles of road owned (aggregate length of road, excluding yard tracks, sidings, and parallel lines). Portions of Class I freight railroads, Amtrak, and Commuter rail networks share common trackage. Amtrak data represent miles of road operated. [3] Transit system length is measured in directional route-miles; see source. [4] Urban passenger train service for short-distance travel between a central city and adjacent suburb. Does not include rapid rail transit or light rail service. [5] Also known as subway, elevated (railway), or metropolitan railway (metro). [6] A streetcar-type vehicle operated on city streets. Beginning in 2011, "Light rail" includes light rail, street car rail, and hybrid rail. [7] Estimated sums of domestic waterways which include rivers, bays, channels, and the inner route of the Southeast Alaskan Islands, but does not include the Great Lakes or deep ocean traffic. Beginning in 2007, includes waterways connecting the Great Lakes and the St. Lawrence Seaway inside the U.S. [8] Includes trunk and gathering lines for crude-oil pipeline. Oil pipeline data has been discontinued for years prior to 2001. [9] Excludes service pipelines.

Source: U.S. Bureau of Transportation Statistics, "National Transportation Statistics," <https://www.rita.dot.gov/bts/sites/rita.dot.gov.bts/files/publications/national_transportation_statistics/index.html>, accessed April 2017.

Table 1086. U.S. Aircraft, Vehicles, and Other Conveyances: 2000 to 2015

[Number, or in thousands (225,821 represents 225,821,000), as indicated]

Mode	2000	2008	2009	2010	2011	2012	2013	2014	2015
AIR									
Air carrier [1]	7,826	7,337	7,169	7,185	7,168	6,914	6,740	6,761	6,876
General aviation [2] (active fleet)	217,533	228,663	223,877	223,370	222,250	209,034	199,927	204,408	210,030
HIGHWAY									
Total registered vehicles (1,000)	225,821	255,918	254,213	250,070	253,216	253,639	255,877	260,351	263,610
Light duty vehicle, short wheel base [3]	(NA)	196,763	193,980	190,203	183,523	183,172	184,497	187,555	189,618
Passenger cars [3]	133,621	(NA)	(NA)	(NA)	(NA)	(NA)	(NA)	(NA)	(NA)
Motorcycle	4,346	7,753	7,930	8,010	8,438	8,455	8,405	8,418	8,601
Light duty vehicle, long wheel base [4]	(NA)	39,685	40,488	40,242	50,319	50,589	51,513	52,600	53,299
Other 2-axle 4-tire vehicles [4]	79,085	(NA)	(NA)	(NA)	(NA)	(NA)	(NA)	(NA)	(NA)
Trucks [5]	5,926	8,288	8,356	8,217	7,819	8,190	8,126	8,329	8,456
Truck, combination	2,097	2,585	2,617	2,553	2,452	2,469	2,471	2,577	2,747
Bus	746	843	842	846	666	765	865	872	889
TRANSIT									
Motor bus	58,578	63,151	63,343	63,108	61,127	61,245	66,823	62,449	(NA)
Light rail cars [6]	1,306	1,948	2,059	2,096	2,284	2,348	2,842	2,444	(NA)
Heavy rail cars [7]	10,311	11,377	11,461	11,510	14,942	10,469	10,380	10,551	(NA)
Trolley bus	652	590	531	571	479	570	560	537	(NA)
Commuter rail cars and locomotives	5,497	6,494	6,722	6,768	6,971	6,938	7,150	7,177	(NA)
Demand responsive	22,087	30,773	34,235	33,555	31,846	31,929	31,433	31,359	(NA)
Other [8]	7,705	14,953	17,766	18,066	18,965	16,996	17,793	17,994	(NA)
RAIL									
Class I, freight cars	560,154	450,297	416,180	397,730	380,699	380,641	373,838	371,642	330,996
Class I, locomotive	20,028	24,003	24,045	23,893	24,250	24,707	25,033	25,916	26,574
Nonclass I freight cars	132,448	109,487	108,233	101,755	95,972	92,742	88,122	(NA)	(NA)
Car companies' and shippers' freight cars	688,194	833,188	839,020	809,544	806,554	842,802	873,679	(NA)	(NA)
Amtrak, passenger train car	1,894	1,177	1,214	1,274	1,301	2,090	1,447	1,419	1,428
Amtrak, locomotive	378	278	274	282	287	485	418	428	423
WATER									
Non-self-propelled vessels [9]	31,360	31,238	31,008	31,412	31,498	31,550	31,081	31,043	(NA)
Self-propelled vessels [10]	8,202	9,063	9,101	9,100	9,023	8,980	8,918	9,039	(NA)
Ocean-going self-propelled vessels (1,000 gross tons and over) [11]	282	225	217	221	214	198	187	179	170
Recreational boats (1,000)	12,782	12,693	12,722	12,439	12,174	12,102	12,013	11,804	11,867

NA Not available. [1] Air carrier aircraft are those carrying passengers or cargo for hire under 14 CFR 121 and 14 CFR 135. [2] Includes air taxi aircraft. [3] Data for 2000-06 are for passenger cars. Beginning 2007, data are for Light Duty Vehicles Short Wheel Base—passenger cars, light trucks, vans and sport utility vehicles with a wheelbase of 121 inches or less. [4] Data for 2000-06 are for 2-axle, 4-tire vehicles other than passenger cars, motorcycles, and buses. Beginning 2007, data are for Light Duty Vehicles Long Wheel Base—large passenger cars, vans, pickup trucks, and sport/utility vehicles with wheelbases larger than 121 inches. [5] Includes trucks on a single frame with at least 2 axles and 6 tires. [6] Fixed rail streetcar or trolley, for example. [7] Metro, subway, or rapid transit, for example. [8] Includes Alaska railroad, automated guideway transit, cable car, ferry boat, inclined plane, monorail, and vanpool. [9] Includes dry-cargo barges, tank barges, and railroad-car floats. [10] Includes dry-cargo and/or passenger, offshore supply vessels, railroad-car ferries, tankers, and towboats. [11] 2000-06 data include private and government owned vessels of 1,000 gross tons or more. Beginning 2007, data are reported only for privately owned vessels of 1,000 gross tons or more. 2009 data include privately owned vessels of 10,000 deadweight tons or more, not including the Great Lakes vessels.

Source: U.S. Bureau of Transportation Statistics, "National Transportation Statistics," <https://www.rita.dot.gov/bts/publications/>, accessed August 2017.

Table 1087. Transportation Shipments by Mode: 2012 to 2045

[16,953 represents 16,953,000,000. All truck, rail, water, and pipeline movements that involve more than one mode, including exports and imports that change mode at international gateways, are included in multiple modes & mail to avoid double counting. Data do not include imports and exports that pass through the United States from a foreign origin to a foreign destination by any mode]

Mode	2012				2015 [1]				2045 [2]			
	Total	Domestic	Exports	Imports	Total	Domestic	Exports	Imports	Total	Domestic	Exports	Imports
WEIGHT (millions of tons)												
Total	**16,953**	**14,953**	**864**	**1,136**	**18,056**	**16,045**	**912**	**1,099**	**25,345**	**20,914**	**2,190**	**2,241**
Truck	10,166	9,970	107	89	10,859	10,649	110	100	14,866	14,270	291	305
Rail	1,613	1,487	52	74	1,607	1,458	54	85	1,921	1,597	108	216
Water	933	506	68	359	936	553	94	289	1,158	614	189	355
Air, air and truck	10	2	4	4	11	2	4	5	38	4	16	18
Multiple modes and mail [3]	1,320	311	596	413	1,353	327	613	412	2,971	434	1,519	1,018
Pipeline	2,870	2,641	36	194	3,258	3,017	37	204	4,361	3,978	63	319
Other and unknown	41	37	1	3	33	29	1	3	31	16	4	11
VALUE (billions of 2012 dollars)												
Total	**17,805**	**14,058**	**1,532**	**2,215**	**19,258**	**15,072**	**1,699**	**2,487**	**37,080**	**22,499**	**6,474**	**8,106**
Truck	11,011	10,333	367	311	11,718	10,994	382	342	18,735	16,270	1,247	1,218
Rail	569	417	59	93	617	451	62	104	1,058	652	153	253
Water	617	274	71	272	636	304	99	233	1,021	345	272	405
Air, air and truck	1,044	138	434	472	1,194	152	466	576	5,133	330	2,449	2,354
Multiple modes and mail [3]	3,275	1,752	573	949	3,599	1,875	658	1,065	9,152	3,404	2,262	3,485
Pipeline	1,250	1,143	9	97	1,410	1,295	10	105	1,656	1,498	15	144
Other and unknown	40	1	17	22	83	1	21	61	325	–	76	248

– Represents zero. [1] The 2015 data are provisional estimates that are based on selected modal and economic trend data. [2] Freight Analysis Framework forecasts. [3] Multiple modes and mail also includes some air movements.

Source: U.S. Department of Transportation, Bureau of Transportation Statistics, *Transportation Statistics Annual Report 2016*, February 2017. See also <https://www.bts.gov/product/transportation-statistics-annual-report>.

Table 1088. Shipment Characteristics by Mode of Transportation: 2007 and 2012

[11,684,872 represents $11,684,872,000,000, unless otherwise noted. For business establishments in mining, manufacturing, wholesale trade, and selected retail and services industries. 2012 industries classified by the 2007 North American Industry Classification System (NAICS). 2007 industries classified by 2002 NAICS. Selected auxiliary establishments are also included. Based on the Commodity Flow Survey, conducted as part of the Economic Census; see Appendix III]

Mode of transportation	Value (mil. dol.)		Tons (1,000)		Ton-miles (mil.)		Average miles per shipment	
	2007	2012	2007	2012	2007	2012	2007	2012
All modes	**11,684,872**	**13,852,143**	**12,543,425**	**11,299,409**	**3,344,658**	**2,969,506**	**619**	**630**
Single modes	**9,539,037**	**11,900,364**	**11,698,128**	**10,905,518**	**2,894,251**	**2,697,418**	**234**	**262**
Truck [1]	8,335,789	10,132,229	8,778,713	8,060,166	1,342,104	1,247,717	206	227
For-hire truck	4,955,700	6,504,636	4,075,136	4,298,693	1,055,646	1,050,942	599	508
Private truck	3,380,090	3,627,592	4,703,576	3,761,472	286,457	196,775	57	58
Rail	436,420	473,070	1,861,307	1,628,537	1,344,040	1,211,481	728	805
Water	114,905	301,554	403,639	575,996	157,314	192,866	520	908
Great Lakes	(S)	424	17,792	31,403	6,887	10,959	657	347
Inland water	91,004	218,927	343,307	424,542	117,473	118,742	144	275
Deep sea	23,058	59,878	42,540	72,987	32,954	22,130	923	1,157
Air (includes truck and air)	252,276	450,575	3,611	4,845	4,510	5,810	1,304	1,295
Pipeline [2]	399,646	542,936	650,859	635,975	(S)	(S)	(S)	(S)
Multiple modes	**1,866,723**	**1,950,753**	**573,729**	**357,047**	**416,642**	**271,832**		
Parcel, U.S. Postal Service or courier	1,561,874	1,688,242	33,900	28,490	27,961	22,716	975	922
Truck and rail	187,248	224,833	225,589	213,814	196,772	169,524	1,007	988
Truck and water	58,389	29,035	145,521	56,720	98,396	48,568	1,429	1,562
Rail and water	13,892	7,976	54,878	55,570	47,111	29,170	1,928	1,073
Other multiple modes	45,320	668	113,841	2,452	46,402	1,853	1,182	(S)
Other and unknown modes	**279,113**	**1,026**	**271,567**	**36,844**	**33,764**	**256**	**116**	**(S)**

S Data do not meet publication standards due to high sampling variability or other reasons. [1] Truck as a single mode includes shipments that went by private truck only, for-hire truck only, or a combination of private truck and for-hire truck. [2] Commodity Flow Survey data exclude shipments of crude oil.

Source: U.S. Department of Transportation, Bureau of Transportation Statistics, and U.S. Census Bureau, Commodity Flow Survey, "Shipment Characteristics by Origin Geography by Mode: 2012 and 2007," <http://factfinder.census.gov>, accessed July 2015. See also <http://www.census.gov/econ/cfs/>.

Table 1089. Hazardous Shipments—Value, Tons, and Ton-Miles: 2007 and 2012

[1,448,218 represents $1,448,218,000,000. For business establishments in mining, manufacturing, wholesale trade, and selected retail industries. 2012 data cover industries classified by the 2007 North American Industry Classification System (NAICS). 2007 data cover industries classified by 2002 NAICS. Also includes auxiliary establishments of multi-establishment companies. Based on the Commodity Flow Survey, conducted as part of the Economic Census; see Appendix III]

Mode of transportation and class of material	Value (mil. dol.)		Tons (1,000)		Ton-miles (mil.)		Average miles per shipment	
	2007	2012	2007	2012	2007	2012	2007	2012
All modes	**1,448,218**	**2,334,425**	**2,231,133**	**2,580,153**	**323,457**	**307,524**	**96**	**114**
Single modes	1,370,615	2,304,743	2,111,622	2,552,868	279,105	275,628		
Truck [1]	837,074	1,466,021	1,202,825	1,531,405	103,997	96,559	65	68
For-hire truck	358,792	870,893	495,077	882,288	63,288	62,018	59	56
Private truck	478,282	595,128	707,748	649,117	40,709	34,541	214	150
Rail	69,213	79,222	129,743	110,988	92,169	84,850	32	33
Water	69,186	217,816	149,794	283,561	37,064	54,902	578	808
Air (includes truck and air)	1,735	4,380	(S)	261	(S)	271	1,095	1,120
Pipeline [2]	393,408	537,304	628,905	626,652	(S)	(S)	(S)	(S)
Multiple modes [3]	71,069	29,682	111,022	27,285	42,886	31,896	834	654
Parcel, U.S. Postal Service or courier	7,675	10,294	236	305	151	178	836	650
Other and unknown modes	6,534	(NA)	8,489	(NA)	1,466	(NA)	58	(NA)
Class of Material	**1,448,218**	**2,334,425**	**2,231,133**	**2,580,153**	**323,457**	**307,524**	**96**	**114**
Class 1, Explosives	11,754	18,397	3,047	4,045	911	1,012	738	840
Class 2, Gases	131,810	125,054	250,506	164,794	55,260	33,157	51	57
Class 3, Flammable and combustible liquid	1,170,455	2,016,681	1,752,814	2,203,490	181,615	204,573	91	93
Class 4, Flammable solid; spontaneously combustible material; dangerous when wet material	4,067	5,415	20,408	11,321	5,547	5,804	309	565
Class 5, Oxidizers and organic peroxides	6,695	7,562	14,959	12,025	7,024	5,479	361	437
Class 6, Toxic materials and infectious substances	21,198	15,196	11,270	7,612	5,667	3,607	467	513
Class 7, Radioactive materials	20,633	12,288	515	(S)	37	39	(S)	34
Class 8, Corrosive materials	51,475	75,850	114,441	125,287	44,395	37,784	208	264
Class 9, Miscellaneous hazardous material	30,131	57,981	63,173	51,006	23,002	16,068	484	530

NA Not available. S Data do not meet publication standards. [1] Truck as a single mode includes shipments that went by private truck only, for-hire truck only, or a combination of private truck and for-hire truck. [2] Commodity Flow Survey Data exclude shipments of crude oil. [3] Includes other modes not shown. Multimode data for 2012 and 2007 are not comparable due to methodological changes; see source.

Source: U.S. Department of Transportation, Bureau of Transportation Statistics, and U.S. Census Bureau, *United States: 2012, Hazardous Materials*, February 2015; and 2012 Commodity Flow Survey, CF1200H01, "Hazardous Materials Series: HazMat Shipment Characteristics by Mode," and CF1200H02, "Hazardous Materials Series: HazMat Shipment Characteristics by Hazardous Class," <http://factfinder.census.gov>, accessed February 2015. See also <http://www.census.gov/econ/cfs/>.

Table 1090. Transportation Accidents, Deaths, and Injuries: 2000 to 2014

[Number, except in thousands (6,394 represents 6,394,000) as indicated. See source for more information]

Mode	Accidents					Deaths					Injuries				
	2000	2005	2010	2013	2014	2000	2005	2010	2013	2014	2000	2005	2010	2013	2014 (P)
Air [1]	1,985	1,782	1,506	1,298	1,288	764	603	477	430	439	359	305	278	248	266
Air carrier [2]	56	40	30	23	28	92	22	2	9	–	31	14	17	7	14
Commuter [2]	12	6	6	7	4	5	–	–	5	–	7	–	2	9	9
On-demand [3]	80	65	30	44	35	71	18	17	25	20	12	20	2	16	15
General aviation	1,837	1,671	1,440	1,224	1,221	596	563	458	391	419	309	271	256	216	237
Land:															
Highway crashes (1,000) [4]	6,394	6,159	5,419	5,687	6,064	41.9	43.5	33.0	32.8	32.7	3,189	2,699	2,239	2,313	2,338
Passenger car occupants	4,926	4,499	5,350	5,669	5,982	20.7	18.5	12.5	12.0	11.9	2,052	1,573	1,253	1,296	1,292
Motorcyclists	69	101	(NA)	106	110	2.9	4.6	4.5	4.7	4.6	58	87	82	88	92
Light truck occupants	3,208	3,382	2,285	3,869	4,184	11.5	13.0	9.8	9.2	9.1	887	872	733	750	782
Large truck occupants	438	423	276	342	438	0.8	0.8	0.5	0.7	0.7	31	27	20	24	27
Bus occupants	56	50	54	67	69	–	0.1	–	0.1	–	18	11	17	23	14
Pedestrians	(NA)	(NA)	(NA)	(NA)	(NA)	4.8	4.9	4.3	4.8	4.9	78	64	70	66	65
Pedalcyclists	(NA)	(NA)	(NA)	(NA)	(NA)	0.7	0.8	0.6	0.7	0.7	51	45	52	48	50
Other	(NA)	(NA)	(NA)	(NA)	(NA)	0.6	0.8	0.7	0.7	0.8	15	18	13	16	16
Railroad [5]	14,024	11,816	10,031	10,019	10,274	937	884	734	700	769	11,643	9,550	8,379	8,708	8,624
Highway-rail grade crossing [6]	607	571	453	515	531	425	359	261	232	264	1,219	1,053	888	975	861
Transit [7]	24,261	8,151	3,492	4,416	4,693	295	149	221	266	236	56,697	19,028	25,222	24,622	24,045
Waterborne [8]	13,143	9,946	9,889	9,789	10,112	701	829	821	650	674	(NA)	4,125	3,770	3,432	3,384
Recreational boating [9]	7,740	4,969	4,604	4,062	4,064	701	697	672	560	610	4,355	3,451	3,153	2,620	2,678
Pipeline:	380	719	588	619	699	38	16	19	9	19	81	48	108	44	96
Hazard liquid	146	369	350	401	445	1	2	1	1	–	4	2	3	6	–
Gas	234	350	238	218	254	37	14	18	8	19	77	46	105	38	96

– Represents or rounds to zero. NA Not available. P Preliminary. [1] See footnote 1, Table 1097. Injuries classified as serious. [2] See footnote 2, Table 1097. Injuries classified as serious. [3] See footnote 3, Table 1097. Injuries classified as serious. [4] Highway crashes often involve more than one motor vehicle, and hence "total highway crashes" is smaller than the sum of the components. Data on deaths are from U.S. National Highway Traffic Safety Administration and are based on deaths within 30 days of the accident. Includes only police reported crashes. For more details, see Table 1131. [5] Accidents and incidents resulting from freight and passenger rail operations including commuter rail. Grade crossing accidents are also included when classified as a train accident. Deaths and injuries exclude those in incidents resulting from freight and passenger rail operations including commuter rail. Injury figures also include occupational illness. [6] Accidents and incidents occurring at highway-rail crossings resulting from freight and highway-rail grade crossing accidents involving motor vehicles. Public highway-rail grade crossing incidents, fatalities, and injuries involving motor vehicles are excluded and counted under Highway. Highway-rail grade passenger rail operations including commuter rail. [7] Includes motor bus, commuter rail, heavy rail, light rail, demand response, van pool, and automated guideway. Starting with 2002, only injuries requiring immediate medical treatment away from the scene now qualify as reportable. [8] To include vessel-related deaths and injuries include those involving damage to vessels, such as collisions or groundings. Totals include deaths and injuries not related to vessel casualties, not shown separately. [9] Covers occurrences involving a vessel or its equipment that results in 1) a death; 2) an injury that requires medical treatment beyond first aid; 3) damage to a vessel and other property, totaling to more than $2,000 or complete loss of a vessel; or 4) the disappearance of the vessel under circumstances that indicate death or injury. Federal regulations (33 CFR 173-4) require the operator of any vessel that is numbered or used for recreational purposes to submit an accident report.

Source: U.S. Bureau of Transportation Statistics, "National Transportation Statistics," <http://www.bts.gov/publications/national_transportation_statistics>, accessed September 2016.

Table 1091. U.S. Scheduled Airline Industry—Summary: 2007 to 2014

[In units as indicated (769.6 represents $769,600,000). For calendar years or as of December 31. For domestic and international operations. Covers carriers certificated under Section 401 of the Federal Aviation Act. Minus sign (-) indicates loss]

Item	Unit	2007	2008	2009	2010	2011	2012	2013	2014
SCHEDULED SERVICE									
Revenue passengers enplaned	Mil.	769.6	743.3	703.9	720.5	730.8	736.7	743.2	762.1
Revenue passenger miles	Bil.	829.4	812.4	769.5	798.0	814.4	823.2	840.4	862.1
Available seat miles	Bil.	1,037.7	1,021.3	957.2	972.6	992.7	994.5	1,011.2	1,033.8
Revenue passenger load factor	Percent	79.9	79.5	80.4	82.1	82.0	82.8	83.1	83.4
Mean passenger trip length [1]	Miles	1,078	1,093	1,093	1,108	1,114	1,117	1,131	1,131
Cargo ton miles	Mil.	29,571	28,119	24,970	27,885	28,123	27,790	26,441	27,236
Aircraft departures	1,000	11,399	10,897	10,145	10,095	10,058	9,864	9,745	9,536
FINANCES									
Total operating revenue [2]	Mil. dol.	174,696	186,087	155,051	174,677	193,041	196,105	200,245	207,708
Passenger revenue	Mil. dol.	107,678	111,511	91,443	103,978	114,299	115,975	120,642	126,706
Cargo revenue	Mil. dol.	24,002	29,192	23,014	17,622	1,589	889	1,023	1,140
Charter revenue	Mil. dol.	5,544	4,338	3,841	3,254	604	976	877	930
Other revenue	Mil. dol.	37,472	41,047	36,753	49,824	76,548	78,265	77,703	78,932
Total operating expense	Mil. dol.	165,353	189,437	152,716	164,160	186,005	188,592	187,726	191,029
Operating profit (or loss)	Mil. dol.	9,344	-3,350	2,335	10,517	7,036	7,513	12,519	16,678
Interest income (or expense)	Mil. dol.	-3,915	-3,743	-4,214	-4,215	-3,970	-3,740	-3,334	-3,005
Net profit (or loss)	Mil. dol.	7,691.4	-23,749.8	-2,610.3	3,666.0	1,392.2	363.7	12,710.6	8,514.3
Passenger revenue per passenger mile	Cents	13.0	13.7	11.9	13.0	14.0	14.1	14.4	14.7
Operating profit margin	Percent	5.3	-1.8	1.5	6.0	3.6	3.8	6.3	8.0
Net profit margin	Percent	4.4	-12.8	-1.7	2.1	0.7	0.2	6.3	4.1
EMPLOYEES									
Average full-time equivalents	1,000	613.9	608.9	573.9	564.4	577.3	584.5	584.0	589.1

[1] For definition of mean, see Guide to Tabular Presentation. [2] Includes other types of revenues, not shown separately.

Source: Airlines for America, ©; and Bureau of Transportation Statistics, <http://www.transtats.bts.gov/>, accessed June 2015.

Table 1092. Passenger Airline Cost Indexes: 1980 to 2014

[2000=100. To be included in the cost index, carriers must have met the following criteria on an annual basis: 1) must report both passenger revenue and revenue passenger miles (RPMs), and 2) passenger revenue must be greater than or equal to 25 percent of total operating revenue]

Index	1980	1990	2000	2005	2006	2007	2008	2009	2010	2011	2012	2013	2014
Composite index [1]	77.4	101.1	100.0	136.1	149.7	153.0	203.6	145.7	158.0	190.6	195.3	187.6	190.7
Labor costs	52.0	73.1	100.0	117.3	119.0	119.1	119.7	127.4	135.3	136.9	145.6	148.9	157.5
Fuel	113.7	98.1	100.0	206.6	242.8	258.0	379.4	233.9	268.8	349.7	356.4	331.1	336.4
Aircraft ownership [2]	33.5	71.1	100.0	98.9	98.7	94.0	91.1	92.8	92.9	91.8	90.9	93.9	94.2
Nonaircraft ownership	40.4	88.1	100.0	106.1	104.2	106.6	118.8	115.2	111.4	111.5	106.7	108.5	106.2
Professional services	27.0	67.5	100.0	105.5	111.2	115.8	125.3	118.5	118.5	121.4	115.7	118.6	122.0
Food and beverage	88.5	125.5	100.0	61.3	57.9	57.8	60.0	59.7	59.5	61.7	60.6	61.9	62.0
Landing fees	49.2	81.0	100.0	130.7	135.6	136.7	148.5	158.9	169.8	166.5	165.4	165.4	169.6
Maintenance material	73.3	119.2	100.0	59.1	62.2	69.9	76.8	83.5	82.9	92.2	101.1	102.9	109.1
Aircraft insurance	246.1	161.0	100.0	157.1	181.0	152.3	124.0	150.7	164.9	163.8	158.0	132.0	96.9
Nonaircraft insurance	73.3	68.2	100.0	319.9	259.3	222.1	195.3	184.4	188.2	168.2	167.1	142.9	114.9
Passenger commissions	121.5	227.0	100.0	31.6	29.2	28.3	27.0	26.7	26.4	25.6	22.4	23.3	21.9
Communication	50.3	85.7	100.0	73.3	68.5	71.2	79.2	77.2	75.3	80.0	75.0	74.4	71.2
Advertising and promotion	112.9	165.0	100.0	75.5	80.9	67.3	59.0	61.7	61.0	65.3	63.2	65.0	56.8
Utilities and office supplies	67.9	97.7	100.0	87.6	94.3	102.2	108.9	99.8	118.4	119.2	110.8	122.5	125.2
Transportation-related expenses	46.0	55.0	100.0	159.8	171.3	168.6	196.2	158.9	157.7	185.0	184.0	191.0	191.8
Employee business expenses	40.9	70.5	100.0	101.0	107.4	118.6	123.3	116.8	120.7	128.0	135.5	146.1	163.0
Other operating expenses	56.0	87.4	100.0	122.2	121.5	129.7	173.8	140.0	138.4	159.2	162.6	161.0	158.9
Interest [3]	160.7	182.0	100.0	120.6	133.5	120.3	105.6	116.2	121.8	118.6	117.7	105.8	92.5

[1] Weighted average of all components, including interest. [2] Includes lease, aircraft and engine rentals, depreciation, and amortization. [3] Interest on long-term debt and capital and other interest expense.

Source: Airlines for America, Washington, DC, U.S. Passenger Airline Cost Index ©. See also <http://www.airlines.org/>.

Table 1093. Airline Fuel Consumption and Fuel Costs: 2004 to 2016

[19,683 represents 19,683,000,000. Data are shown aggregated for scheduled and unscheduled service on U.S. carriers with over $20 million in revenue per year]

Year	Total fuel consumption (million gallons)	Total fuel cost (million dollars)	Cost per gallon (dollars)	Domestic service			International service		
				Con-sumption (million gallons)	Cost (million dollars)	Cost per gallon (dollars)	Con-sumption (million gallons)	Cost (million dollars)	Cost per gallon (dollars)
2004........	19,683	22,758	1.16	14,091	16,027	1.14	5,592	6,732	1.20
2005........	19,950	33,175	1.66	13,976	22,951	1.64	5,975	10,224	1.71
2006........	19,712	38,772	1.97	13,694	26,480	1.93	6,018	12,292	2.04
2007........	19,886	41,862	2.11	13,682	28,411	2.08	6,205	13,451	2.17
2008........	18,872	57,888	3.07	12,686	37,876	2.99	6,187	20,013	3.23
2009........	17,061	32,331	1.90	11,339	21,544	1.90	5,721	10,787	1.89
2010........	17,298	39,350	2.27	11,257	25,571	2.27	6,042	13,779	2.28
2011........	17,558	53,515	3.05	11,035	33,730	3.06	6,523	19,785	3.03
2012........	16,946	53,415	3.15	10,440	33,189	3.18	6,506	20,227	3.11
2013........	16,824	50,629	3.01	10,337	31,513	3.05	6,487	19,117	2.95
2014........	16,780	48,037	2.86	10,459	30,114	2.88	6,321	17,923	2.84
2015........	17,349	32,196	1.86	10,929	20,006	1.83	6,421	12,190	1.90
2016........	17,668	25,742	1.46	11,374	16,636	1.46	6,295	9,106	1.45

Source: U.S. Bureau of Transportation Statistics, "Airline Fuel Cost and Consumption," <https://www.transtats.bts.gov/fuel.asp>, accessed April 2017.

Table 1094. Top 40 Airports in 2016—Passengers Enplaned: 2006 and 2016

[In thousands (754,131 represents 754,131,000), except rank. For calendar year. Intl = international. Airports ranked by total passengers enplaned on U.S. carrier scheduled domestic and international service and foreign carrier scheduled international service from the United States]

Airport	2006 Rank	2006 Total	2016 Rank	2016 Total	Airport	2006 Rank	2006 Total	2016 Rank	2016 Total
All airports....................	(X)	754,131	(X)	768,441	Philadelphia Intl, PA................	16	15,712	20	13,534
Total, top 40.............	(X)	570,748	(X)	613,107	Fort Lauderdale, FL (Hollywood Intl)....	23	10,561	21	13,002
Atlanta, GA (Hartsfield Intl).....	1	41,588	1	46,739	Baltimore, MD (BWI Intl)................	22	10,844	22	11,543
Los Angeles Intl, CA...........	3	30,190	2	36,740	Washington, DC (Ronald				
Chicago O'Hare Intl, IL.........	2	37,249	3	34,807	Reagan Washington Natl)..............	28	9,075	23	10,571
Dallas/Fort Worth Intl, TX......	4	29,006	4	28,892	Chicago, IL (Midway)...................	26	9,421	24	10,432
New York, NY (JFK Intl)........	8	21,330	5	26,763	Salt Lake City Intl, UT.................	24	10,538	25	10,286
Denver Intl, CO.................	5	23,123	6	26,282	Washington, DC (Dulles Intl)...........	21	11,207	26	9,750
San Francisco Intl, CA.........	14	16,561	7	23,690	San Diego, CA (San Diego Intl).........	29	8,862	27	9,640
Las Vegas, NV					Honolulu Intl, HI.....................	25	9,995	28	8,907
(McCarran Intl).................	6	22,611	8	21,245	Tampa, FL (Tampa Intl)..................	27	9,389	29	8,523
Seattle-Tacoma Intl, WA.....	18	15,017	9	20,180	Portland Intl, OR.......................	33	7,068	30	8,344
Charlotte-Douglas Intl, NC.....	17	15,021	10	20,004	Dallas, TX (Dallas Love Field)..........	48	3,813	31	7,223
Phoenix Sky Harbor Intl, AZ. ..	7	21,584	11	19,558	St. Louis, MO (Lambert-St Louis Intl). ..	31	7,475	32	6,420
Miami Intl, FL...................	15	15,840	12	19,056	Nashville Intl, TN......................	40	5,142	33	6,000
Orlando Intl, FL.................	13	17,013	13	18,642	Houston, TX (William P. Hobby).........	44	4,625	34	5,929
Houston, Intercontinental, TX..	9	20,589	14	18,403	Austin-Bergstrom Intl, TX..............	45	4,152	35	5,713
Newark, NJ (Liberty Intl).......	10	17,901	15	18,190	Oakland Intl, CA........................	32	7,335	36	5,560
Minneapolis-St. Paul Intl, MN..	12	17,378	16	16,827	New Orleans Intl, LA....................	56	3,162	37	5,219
Boston, MA (Logan Intl)........	19	13,585	17	16,385	Kansas City Intl, MO...................	34	5,915	38	5,086
Detroit, MI (Wayne Co)........	11	17,696	18	15,566	Raleigh, NC (Raleigh-Durham Intl)......	43	4,790	39	4,976
New York, NY (La Guardia)....	20	12,947	19	13,560	San Jose, CA (Norman Y. Mineta Intl)...	37	5,435	40	4,919

X Not applicable.

Source: U.S. Bureau of Transportation Statistics, "National Transportation Statistics," <https://www.rita.dot.gov/bts/sites/rita.dot.gov.bts/files/publications/national_transportation_statistics/index.html>, accessed August 2017.

Table 1095. Top 25 Domestic Airline Markets—Average Daily Passengers: 2014

[For calendar year. Data are for the top 25 markets and include all commercial airports in each metro area. Data represent traffic each way between origin and final destinations]

Market	Passengers	Market	Passengers
New York - Los Angeles.............................	3,531	New York - Miami...............................	1,593
Los Angeles - San Francisco........................	2,757	Boston - Washington............................	1,547
New York - Chicago.................................	2,654	Honolulu - Los Angeles..........................	1,546
New York - San Francisco...........................	2,569	Seattle - San Francisco..........................	1,514
Atlanta - New York.................................	2,072	Boston - Chicago................................	1,496
Honolulu - Kahului.................................	1,913	Las Vegas - Los Angeles.........................	1,493
Ft. Lauderdale - New York..........................	1,832	Las Vegas - San Francisco........................	1,485
Los Angeles - Seattle..............................	1,811	Denver - Las Vegas..............................	1,479
Los Angeles - Chicago..............................	1,793	New York - Orlando..............................	1,476
Denver - Phoenix...................................	1,774	Denver - Los Angeles............................	1,447
Boston - San Francisco.............................	1,684	Boston - Los Angeles............................	1,445
Chicago - San Francisco............................	1,617	Dallas - Chicago................................	1,398
		Orlando - Philadelphia...........................	1,395

Source: Airlines for America, Washington, DC, ©. See also <http://www.airlines.org>.

Table 1096. Commuter/Regional Airline Operations Summary: 2010 to 2015

[In units as indicated (164.1 represents 164,100,000). Calendar year data. Commuter/regional airlines primarily operate aircraft of 75 passengers or less and 18,000 pounds of payload capacity serving short haul and small community markets. Represents operations within all of North America by U.S. regional carriers. As of 2014, "operating carriers" is defined as those certificate holders operating scheduled passenger service under 14 CFR Parts 135 or 121 with capacities of fewer than 100 seats. As of 2015, Part 380 public charter operations are excluded. Averages are means. For definition of mean, see Guide to Tabular Presentation]

Item	Unit	2010	2011	2012	2013	2014	2015
Passenger certificated carriers operating.............	Number	66	68	66	63	65	64
Passengers enplaned....................................	Millions	164.1	162.2	161.3	159.1	157.6	156.6
Average passengers enplaned per carrier...........	1,000	2,486.4	2,385.0	2,444.5	2,525.9	2,424.0	2,446.3
Revenue passenger miles (RPM).....................	Billions	76.6	76.2	75.6	74.9	75.1	74.8
Average RPMs per carrier..............................	Millions	1,160.9	1,121.2	1,145.5	1,189.5	1,155.5	1,168.0
Available seat miles....................................	Billions	100.1	99.8	96.9	95.7	94.0	92.8
Average load factor.....................................	Percent	76.6	76.4	78.0	78.3	79.9	80.6
Departures completed...................................	Millions	4.69	4.59	4.46	4.34	4.11	3.87
Airports served..	Number	673	681	623	614	607	615
Average trip length......................................	Miles	467	471	469	471	477	478
Average seating capacity (seats).....................	Number	56	56	56	56	58	61
Fleet flying hours.......................................	1,000	5,048	5,021	4,853	4,782	4,522	4,302

Source: Regional Airline Association, *2016 Annual Report* ©, and previous editions. See also <http://www.raa.org/>.

Table 1097. U.S. Air Carrier Aircraft Accidents: 2000 to 2015

[For years ending December 31. See source for more details]

Item	Unit	2000	2010	2011	2012	2013	2014	2015 (P)
Air carrier accidents, all services [1].......	**Number**	**56**	**30**	**32**	**26**	**23**	**29**	**28**
Fatal accidents..............................	Number	3	1	–	–	2	–	–
Fatalities...................................	Number	92	2	–	–	9	–	–
Aboard......................................	Number	92	2	–	–	9	–	–
Rates per 100,000 flight hours:								
Accidents................................	Rate	0.31	0.17	0.18	0.15	0.13	0.16	0.16
Fatal accidents............................	Rate	0.02	0.01	–	–	0.01	–	–
Commuter air carrier accidents [2]............	Number	12	6	4	5	7	4	5
Fatal accidents..............................	Number	1	–	–	–	2	–	1
Fatalities...................................	Number	5	–	–	–	5	–	1
Aboard......................................	Number	5	–	–	–	5	–	1
Rates per 100,000 flight hours:								
Accidents................................	Rate	3.25	1.91	1.23	1.55	2.36	1.21	1.46
Fatal accidents............................	Rate	0.27	–	–	–	0.68	–	0.29
On-demand air taxi accidents [3].............	Number	80	30	50	36	44	35	38
Fatal accidents..............................	Number	22	6	16	8	10	8	7
Fatalities...................................	Number	71	17	41	12	25	20	27
Aboard......................................	Number	68	17	41	12	25	20	27
Rates per 100,000 flight hours:								
Accidents................................	Rate	2.04	0.96	(NA)	1.02	1.30	0.96	1.07
Fatal accidents............................	Rate	0.56	0.19	(NA)	0.23	0.30	0.22	0.20
General aviation accidents [4].................	Number	1,837	1,440	1,471	1,473	1,224	1,223	1,209
Fatal accidents..............................	Number	345	271	270	273	222	257	229
Fatalities...................................	Number	596	458	458	438	391	424	376
Aboard......................................	Number	585	455	447	438	386	414	373
Rates per 100,000 flight hours:								
Accidents................................	Rate	6.57	6.63	(NA)	7.05	6.26	6.23	5.85
Fatal accidents............................	Rate	1.21	1.24	(NA)	1.30	1.12	1.31	1.09

– Represents zero. NA Not available. P Preliminary. [1] U.S. air carriers operating aircraft with 10 or more seats under 14 CFR 121. [2] All scheduled service of U.S. air carriers operating aircraft with fewer than 10 seats under 14 CFR 135. [3] All nonscheduled service of U.S. air carriers operating aircraft fewer than 10 seats under 14 CFR 135. [4] U.S. civil registered aircraft not operated under 14 CFR 121 or 135.

Source: U.S. National Transportation Safety Board, Investigations Data and Stats, "Review of Accident Data—2015 Preliminary Aviation Statistics," <http://www.ntsb.gov/investigations/>, accessed November 2016.

Table 1098. U.S. Airline Carrier Delays, Cancellations, and Diversions: 2000 to 2015

[5,683.0 represents 5,683,000. For calendar year. See headnote, Table 1099]

Item	2000	2007	2008	2009	2010	2011	2012	2013	2014	2015
Total operations.......	**5,683.0**	**7,455.5**	**7,009.7**	**6,450.3**	**6,450.1**	**6,085.3**	**6,096.8**	**6,369.5**	**5,819.8**	**5,819.1**
NUMBER (1,000)										
Delayed departures [1].....	1,131.7	1,573.0	1,327.2	1,084.3	1,111.9	1,042.4	991.8	1,229.3	1,193.2	1,055.5
Delayed arrivals [2].........	1,356.0	1,804.0	1,524.7	1,218.3	1,174.9	1,109.9	1,015.2	1,269.3	1,240.5	1,063.4
Cancellations [3]...........	187.5	160.8	137.4	89.4	113.3	116.0	78.9	96.0	127.0	89.9
Diversions [4]...............	14.3	17.2	17.3	15.5	15.5	14.4	12.5	14.2	14.4	15.2
PERCENT										
Delayed departures [1].....	19.9	21.1	18.9	16.8	17.2	17.1	16.3	19.3	20.5	18.1
Delayed arrivals [2].........	23.9	24.2	21.8	18.9	18.2	18.2	16.7	19.9	21.3	18.3
Cancellations [3]...........	3.3	2.2	2.0	1.4	1.8	1.9	1.3	1.5	2.2	1.5
Diversions [4]...............	0.3	0.2	0.2	0.2	0.2	0.2	0.2	0.2	0.2	0.3

[1] Late departures comprise flights departing 15 minutes or more after the scheduled departure time. [2] Late arrivals comprise flights arriving 15 minutes or more after the scheduled arrival time. [3] A cancelled flight is one that was not operated, but was listed in a carrier's computer reservation system within seven days of the scheduled departure. [4] A diverted flight is one that left from the scheduled departure airport but flew to a destination point other than the scheduled destination point.

Source: U.S. Bureau of Transportation Statistics, "National Transportation Statistics," <https://www.rita.dot.gov/bts/sites/rita.dot.gov.bts/files/publications/national_transportation_statistics/index.html>, accessed February 2017.

Table 1099. On-Time Flight Arrivals and Departures at Major U.S. Airports: 2016

[In percent. Quarterly, based on gate arrival and departure times for domestic scheduled operations of U.S. major airlines. All U.S. airlines with 1 percent or more of total U.S. domestic scheduled airline passenger revenues are required to report on-time data. A flight is considered on time if it operated within 15 minutes of the scheduled time shown in the carrier's computerized reservation system. See source for data on individual airlines]

Airport	Code	On-time arrivals				On-time departures			
		1st quarter	2nd quarter	3rd quarter	4th quarter	1st quarter	2nd quarter	3rd quarter	4th quarter
Total, all airports............................	**(X)**	**82.1**	**81.9**	**79.2**	**82.5**	**82.5**	**82.4**	**79.9**	**82.9**
Total, major airports...........................	(X)	81.4	81.6	78.5	82.3	81.4	81.8	78.8	82.4
Atlanta, Hartsfield............................	ATL	86.4	86.6	83.3	89.0	84.0	83.3	79.6	86.7
Boston, Logan International..................	BOS	78.6	79.5	73.7	80.5	81.3	83.0	78.0	82.7
Baltimore/Washington International.........	BWI	83.1	82.9	79.7	87.3	80.1	79.8	77.9	84.5
Charlotte, Douglas............................	CLT	83.5	84.6	81.1	88.3	83.3	82.7	78.2	87.7
Washington, Reagan National................	DCA	78.0	78.8	75.0	84.5	81.1	83.1	80.4	86.2
Denver International..........................	DEN	84.7	81.6	81.5	83.9	82.2	79.8	79.1	81.3
Dallas-Fort Worth International..............	DFW	83.8	78.7	75.6	84.8	81.9	77.1	74.5	84.4
Detroit, Metro Wayne County................	DTW	83.5	87.4	84.7	86.0	82.5	87.1	83.7	84.3
Newark International..........................	EWR	76.4	77.4	71.5	73.2	76.6	79.1	72.3	74.8
Fort Lauderdale-Hollywood International....	FLL	74.5	79.8	76.5	81.1	75.3	79.0	76.3	80.0
Washington/Dulles...........................	IAD	84.3	83.7	81.0	86.9	83.2	83.6	81.5	86.2
Houston, George Bush.......................	IAH	85.5	80.6	82.3	86.5	84.6	79.9	81.5	84.0
New York, JFK International..................	JFK	75.8	78.6	71.8	81.2	76.2	80.5	73.4	80.8
Las Vegas, McCarran International..........	LAS	83.5	81.2	80.2	81.3	82.1	78.7	77.8	79.9
Los Angeles International.....................	LAX	80.5	76.6	74.7	72.2	79.7	76.8	75.1	74.2
New York, La Guardia.........................	LGA	68.9	73.2	70.0	75.9	74.3	79.4	74.6	80.7
Orlando International..........................	MCO	79.4	81.1	76.1	82.8	80.0	81.6	76.7	83.1
Chicago, Midway..............................	MDW	85.0	83.1	81.5	84.6	81.1	79.1	76.4	80.4
Miami International............................	MIA	76.7	78.8	74.6	83.2	75.8	77.9	72.8	82.6
Minneapolis-St. Paul International...........	MSP	84.3	85.7	82.2	84.3	85.4	87.4	83.7	84.7
Chicago, O'Hare...............................	ORD	80.4	81.9	74.8	81.7	76.3	79.7	72.9	78.7
Portland International.........................	PDX	86.1	85.3	83.7	80.6	88.3	87.6	86.3	82.7
Philadelphia International.....................	PHL	81.5	80.5	76.2	85.4	81.9	83.2	78.9	85.3
Phoenix, Sky Harbor International...........	PHX	86.7	84.3	81.4	77.5	86.0	83.5	81.8	81.0
San Diego International, Lindbergh Field. ..	SAN	84.1	81.9	81.7	81.1	83.9	83.2	83.2	82.2
Seattle-Tacoma International.................	SEA	85.9	84.8	82.6	80.9	87.2	86.5	85.0	83.7
San Francisco International...................	SFO	71.2	76.6	75.1	70.9	76.2	79.3	78.2	75.8
Salt Lake City International...................	SLC	86.7	89.3	87.2	85.2	87.8	88.8	87.5	85.9
Tampa, Tampa International..................	TPA	80.4	81.0	76.7	85.6	82.2	82.5	79.2	86.7

X Not applicable.

Source: U.S. Department of Transportation, Bureau of Transportation Statistics, "TranStats," <http://www.transtats.bts.gov>, accessed July 2017.

Table 1100. Consumer Complaints Filed Against U.S. Airlines: 2000 to 2016

[Calendar year data. Represents complaints filed by consumers to the U.S. Department of Transportation (DOT), Aviation Consumer Protection Division, regarding service problems with air carriers. See source for data on individual airlines]

Complaint category	2000	2005	2010	2011	2012	2013	2014	2015	2016
Total...........................	**20,564**	**6,900**	**10,988**	**11,546**	**15,338**	**13,176**	**15,539**	**20,175**	**17,904**
Flight problems [1].................	8,698	1,942	3,337	3,656	4,249	3,980	4,974	6,434	6,179
Baggage.........................	2,753	1,586	1,938	1,852	2,182	2,134	2,667	3,133	2,770
Ticketing/boarding [2]............	1,405	679	1,510	1,448	2,456	1,900	2,256	2,695	2,115
Customer service [3].............	4,074	800	1,345	1,287	1,988	1,836	1,708	2,276	1,933
Refunds.........................	803	530	730	985	1,185	920	1,156	1,573	1,362
Fares [4]........................	708	219	465	634	1,010	503	916	1,813	1,363
Disability [5].....................	612	430	572	628	741	683	784	944	862
Oversales [6]....................	759	284	544	508	503	426	514	648	597
Discrimination [7].................	(NA)	100	143	128	99	80	68	65	94
Advertising.......................	42	45	77	82	202	96	130	163	124
Animals..........................	1	3	8	9	5	6	2	3	1
Other [8].........................	684	282	319	329	717	612	364	428	504

NA Not available. [1] Cancellations, delays, and other deviations from schedule. [2] Errors in reservations and ticketing; and problems in making reservations, obtaining tickets, and boarding (except oversales). Prior to 1998, includes disability complaints. [3] Unhelpful employees, inadequate meals or cabin service, treatment of delayed passengers. [4] Incorrect or incomplete information about fares, discount fare conditions, and availability, etc. [5] Civil rights complaints by air travelers with disabilities. Prior to 2000, included in ticketing/boarding. [6] All bumping problems, whether or not airline complied with DOT regulations. [7] Civil rights complaints by air travelers (other than disability) based on factors such as race, religion, national origin or sex. [8] Frequent flyer, smoking, tours credit, cargo problems, security, airport facilities, claims for bodily injury, and others not classified above.

Source: U.S. Department of Transportation, Aviation Consumer Protection Division, *Air Travel Consumer Report*, February 2017, and earlier reports. See also <https://www.transportation.gov/airconsumer>.

Table 1101. Airports, Aircraft, and Airmen: 1980 to 2016

[As of December 31 or for years ending December 31]

Item	1990	2000	2010	2012	2013	2014	2015	2016
Airports, total [1]	**17,490**	**19,281**	**19,802**	**19,711**	**19,457**	**19,299**	**(NA)**	**19,536**
Public [1]	5,589	5,317	5,175	5,171	5,155	5,145	(NA)	5,136
Percent—with lighted runways	71.4	75.9	(NA)	(NA)	(NA)	(NA)	(NA)	(NA)
With paved runways	70.7	74.3	(NA)	(NA)	(NA)	(NA)	(NA)	(NA)
Private	11,901	13,964	14,353	14,269	14,009	13,863	(NA)	14,112
Percent—with lighted runways	7.0	7.2	(NA)	(NA)	(NA)	(NA)	(NA)	(NA)
With paved runways	31.5	32.0	(NA)	(NA)	(NA)	(NA)	(NA)	(NA)
Military	(NA)	(NA)	274	271	289	286	(NA)	288
Certificated [2]	680	651	551	542	542	537	(NA)	531
General aviation	16,810	18,630	19,251	19,169	18,915	18,762	(NA)	19,005
Active air carrier fleet [3]	**6,083**	**7,826**	**7,185**	**6,914**	**6,736**	**6,754**	**6,871**	**(NA)**
Fixed wing	6,072	8,010	(NA)	(NA)	(NA)	(NA)	(NA)	(NA)
Helicopter [4]	11	39	(NA)	(NA)	(NA)	(NA)	(NA)	(NA)
General aviation fleet [5]	**198,000**	**217,533**	**223,370**	**209,034**	**199,927**	**204,408**	**210,030**	**(NA)**
Fixed-wing	184,500	183,276	176,272	165,257	158,911	161,321	164,293	(NA)
Turbojet	4,100	7,001	11,484	11,793	11,637	12,362	13,440	(NA)
Turboprop	5,300	5,762	9,369	10,304	9,619	9,777	9,712	(NA)
Piston	175,200	170,513	155,419	143,160	137,655	139,182	141,141	(NA)
Rotorcraft	6,900	7,150	10,102	10,055	9,765	9,966	10,506	(NA)
Other	6,600	6,700	5,684	5,006	4,277	4,699	4,941	(NA)
Gliders	(X)	2,041	1,899	1,820	1,594	1,791	1,870	(NA)
Lighter than air	(X)	4,660	3,785	3,186	2,684	2,908	3,071	(NA)
Experimental	(X)	20,407	29,662	26,715	24,918	26,191	27,922	(NA)
Airman certificates held:								
Pilot, total	**702,659**	**625,581**	**627,588**	**610,576**	**599,086**	**593,499**	**590,039**	**584,362**
Female	40,515	35,607	42,218	40,621	39,621	39,322	39,287	39,187
Student [6]	128,663	93,064	119,119	119,946	120,285	120,546	122,729	128,501
Recreational	87	340	212	218	238	220	190	175
Sport	(X)	(X)	3,682	4,493	4,824	5,157	5,482	5,889
Airplane:								
Private	299,111	251,561	202,020	188,001	180,214	174,883	170,718	162,313
Commercial	149,666	121,858	123,705	116,400	108,206	104,322	101,164	96,081
Air transport	107,732	141,596	142,198	145,590	149,824	152,933	154,730	157,894
Rotorcraft only [7]	9,567	7,775	15,377	15,126	15,114	15,511	15,566	15,518
Glider only	7,833	9,387	21,275	20,802	20,381	19,927	19,460	17,991
Flight instructor certificates	63,775	80,931	96,473	98,328	98,842	100,993	102,628	104,382
Instrument ratings	297,073	311,944	318,001	311,952	307,120	306,066	304,329	302,572
Remote pilots [8]	(NA)	(NA)	(NA)	(NA)	(NA)	(NA)	(NA)	20,362
Nonpilot [9]	**492,237**	**547,453**	**686,717**	**701,291**	**707,155**	**717,399**	**728,329**	**652,943**
Mechanic	344,282	344,434	331,989	337,775	338,844	341,409	342,528	279,435
Repairmen	(X)	38,208	41,267	40,444	39,952	39,566	39,363	34,411
Parachute rigger	10,094	10,477	8,407	8,474	8,491	8,702	8,846	5,851
Ground instructor	66,882	72,326	75,205	73,599	72,493	71,755	70,957	65,053
Dispatcher	11,002	16,340	20,691	21,862	22,401	23,113	23,754	19,758
Flight navigator	1,290	570	174	141	126	115	102	67
Flight attendant	(X)	(X)	159,946	172,357	179,531	188,936	200,319	212,607
Flight engineer	58,687	65,098	49,038	46,639	45,317	43,803	42,460	35,761

NA Not available. X Not applicable. [1] Includes civil and joint-use civil-military airports, heliports, STOL (short takeoff and landing) ports, and seaplane bases in the U.S. and its territories. Sole-use military airports are included beginning in 2007. Public airports are under public agency control; private airports are owned by a private individual or corporation. [2] Certificated airports serve air-carriers with aircraft seating more than 9 passengers. As of 2005, the Federal Aviation Administration (FAA) no longer certificates military airports. [3] Air-carrier aircraft carry passengers or cargo for hire under 14 CFR 121 (large aircraft—more than 30 seats) and 14 CFR 135 (small aircraft—30 seats or fewer). Beginning in 1990, the number of aircraft is the monthly average reported in use for the last three months of the year. Prior to 1990, it was the number of aircraft reported in use during December of a given year. [4] 2000 change in helicopters due to estimating methods. [5] Beginning 1995, excludes commuters. [6] Beginning 2010, duration of validity for student pilot certificates for pilots under age 40 increased from 36 to 60 months. [7] Data for 1980 are for helicopters only. [8] Remote pilot certification started in August 2016. These numbers are not included in the pilot totals. [9] All certificates on record. No medical examination required.

Source: Prior to 2000: *FAA Statistical Handbook of Aviation*, annual. Thereafter: U.S. Bureau of Transportation Statistics, "National Transportation Statistics," <https://www.rita.dot.gov/bts/publications>, accessed September 2017. U.S. Federal Aviation Administration, "U.S. Civil Airmen Statistics," and "General Aviation and Air Tax (Part 135) Activity Surveys," <http://www.faa.gov/data_research/aviation_data_statistics/>, accessed September 2017.

Table 1102. Worldwide Airline Accidents and Fatalities by World Region: 2016

[Number, except departures in thousands (34,900 represents 34,900,000). Regions are Regional Aviation Safety Group (RASG) regions]

Region	Departures (1,000)	Accidents	Accident rates [1]	Fatalities	Fatal accidents
World	**34,900**	**75**	**2.1**	**182**	**7**
Africa (AFI)	900	1	1.2	1	1
Asia and Pacific (APAC)	10,700	19	1.8	50	2
Europe (EUR) [2]	8,700	24	2.8	64	2
Middle East (MID)	1,300	3	2.3	67	2
Americas (PA)	13,300	28	2.1	–	–

– Represents zero. [1] Number of accidents per million departures of scheduled commercial operations that involve the transportation of passengers, cargo and mail for remuneration or hire. [2] RASG EUR includes Algeria, Morocco, and Tunisia.

Source: International Civil Aviation Organization, Montreal, Canada, *Safety Report, 2017* ©, <http://www.icao.int/safety/Pages/Safety-Report.aspx>.

Table 1103. Water Transportation System Summary: 2000 to 2014

[12.8 represents 12,800,000. Data compiled from U.S. Army Corps of Engineers, Department of Homeland Security/Coast Guard, and Bureau of Transportation Statistics publications; see source for details]

Item or characteristic	Unit	2000	2010	2013	2014
U.S. flag privately owned merchant fleet [1]	Number	282	221	187	179
Recreational boats	Millions	12.8	12.4	12.0	11.8
Lock chambers	Number	276	239	239	239
Lock sites	Number	230	193	193	193
Average age of locks	Years	50.2	59.5	62.5	63.5
Waterway facilities (including cargo handling docks)	Number	9,309	8,060	8,231	8,229
Ports (handling over 250,000 tons)	Number	197	178	182	183
Miles of navigable waterways	Number	25,000	25,000	25,000	25,000
U.S. flag vessels:					
Total vessels [2]	Number	41,354	40,512	39,999	40,082
Barge/non-self-propelled vessels	Number	33,152	31,412	31,081	31,043
Self-propelled vessels	Number	8,202	9,078	8,918	9,039
U.S. flag vessels by age:					
Under 6 years old	Percent	19.6	18.5	19.3	17.7
6 to 10 years old	Percent	9.2	11.5	12.1	14.1
11 to 15 years old	Percent	5.1	17.0	14.3	12.4
16 to 20 years old	Percent	19.6	8.7	13.6	15.1
21 to 25 years old	Percent	18.3	4.2	7.7	8.3
25 years old and over	Percent	27.7	39.3	32.6	31.9

[1] Includes only oceangoing self-propelled, cargo-carrying vessels of 1,000 gross tons and above. [2] Includes unclassified vessels.

Source: U.S. Department of Transportation, Bureau of Transportation Statistics, *Transportation Statistics Annual Report 2016*, February 2017. See also <https://www.bts.dot.gov/product/transportation-statistics-annual-report>.

Table 1104. Freight Carried on Major U.S. Waterways: 2000 to 2015

[In millions of short tons (3.1 represents 3,100,000). One short ton equals 2,000 pounds]

Waterway	2000	2005	2010	2011	2012	2013	2014	2015
Atlantic Intracoastal Waterway	3.1	2.7	2.9	2.9	2.7	2.9	2.4	2.6
Great Lakes	187.5	169.4	129.5	134.7	126.8	127.6	132.3	123.7
Gulf Intracoastal Waterway	113.8	116.1	116.2	112.6	113.8	115.4	126.1	118.9
Mississippi River system [1]	715.5	678.0	663.2	672.5	683.5	670.0	718.6	684.4
Mississippi River main stem	515.6	464.6	483.2	499.0	508.6	493.7	536.2	521.1
Ohio River system [2]	274.4	280.1	245.2	239.6	239.1	239.4	246.0	223.1
Columbia River	55.2	51.5	54.7	54.2	56.8	55.3	61.7	54.7
Snake River	6.7	5.3	3.4	2.7	3.3	3.7	4.4	3.6

[1] Main channels and all tributaries of the Mississippi, Illinois, Missouri, and Ohio Rivers. [2] Main channels and all navigable tributaries and embayments of the Ohio, Tennessee, and Cumberland Rivers.

Source: U.S. Army Corps of Engineers, *Waterborne Commerce of the United States, 2015*, 2017, and earlier reports. See also <http://www.navigationdatacenter.us/wcsc/wcsc.htm>.

Table 1105. Waterborne Commerce by Type of Commodity: 2000 to 2015

[In millions of short tons (2,424.6 represents 2,424,600,000). One short ton is equal to 2,000 pounds. Domestic trade includes all commercial movements between United States ports and on inland rivers, the Great Lakes, canals, and connecting channels of the United States. Foreign commerce is waterborne import, export, and in-transit traffic between the United States, Puerto Rico and the Virgin Islands, and any foreign country; these statistics do not include traffic between any foreign country and selected United States territories and possessions (American Samoa, Guam, Northern Mariana Islands and U.S. outlying islands)]

Commodity	2000	2005	2010	2012	2013	2014	2015 Total	2015 Domestic	2015 Foreign imports	2015 Foreign exports
Total	2,424.6	2,527.6	2,334.4	2,306.8	2,274.8	2,345.8	2,278.8	904.6	751.6	622.5
Coal	297.0	316.6	309.6	328.9	312.3	292.2	233.9	155.9	10.6	67.4
Petroleum and petroleum products	1,044.0	1,111.4	1,018.8	943.4	927.5	906.0	917.3	346.5	369.0	201.8
Crude petroleum	571.4	602.7	508.5	440.3	418.9	396.8	382.7	110.4	259.0	13.3
Petroleum products [1]	472.4	508.8	510.4	503.1	508.6	509.1	534.6	236.1	110.0	188.5
Gasoline	125.2	156.1	137.8	135.3	124.6	118.7	131.4	69.4	32.1	29.9
Distillate fuel oil	91.7	141.1	185.4	195.7	198.7	192.7	191.6	64.9	55.4	71.3
Residual fuel oil	131.6	96.1	81.1	68.6	65.3	62.2	64.5	50.1	6.2	8.2
Chemicals and related products	172.4	174.9	180.1	184.9	180.5	180.4	181.8	72.6	50.6	58.7
Fertilizers	35.1	34.5	35.8	38.9	39.9	43.5	42.3	18.4	15.7	8.2
Other chemicals and related products	137.3	140.4	144.3	145.9	140.6	136.9	139.5	54.2	34.9	50.4
Crude material, inedible	380.3	386.0	307.0	323.2	331.4	354.3	347.6	177.5	100.0	70.1
Forest products, wood and chips	33.1	29.4	20.8	25.3	28.9	30.3	29.0	5.4	5.2	18.4
Pulp and waste paper	13.6	18.7	21.4	24.6	24.0	23.5	23.4	–	2.4	20.9
Soil, sand, gravel, rock, and stone [1]	165.0	177.9	120.3	120.1	126.2	134.1	140.9	103.2	35.9	1.8
Limestone	67.4	73.5	61.3	55.4	59.9	64.7	69.9	49.1	19.7	1.1
Phosphate rock	3.4	6.0	4.6	5.2	5.8	5.6	4.3	2.2	2.1	–
Sand & gravel	79.0	80.2	46.3	51.6	51.8	54.8	57.4	49.0	7.9	0.5
Iron ore and scrap	97.9	85.7	82.0	89.4	85.4	85.8	74.2	48.2	8.3	17.7
Marine shells	0.3	–	0.1	0.1	0.1	0.1	0.1	0.1	–	
Nonferrous ores and scrap	29.2	29.2	23.9	28.0	29.5	29.5	29.0	5.5	17.4	6.1
Sulphur, clay, and salt	11.3	8.7	6.3	7.5	7.6	7.9	7.9	1.2	2.2	4.5
Slag	4.0	6.0	4.3	4.5	5.0	5.2	5.2	2.0	3.2	–
Other nonmetal minerals	25.9	30.4	27.8	23.7	24.6	38.0	37.9	12.0	25.3	0.6
Primary manufactured goods	153.0	166.4	103.7	122.0	117.1	135.2	129.8	34.1	81.4	14.3
Papers products	12.1	13.7	13.7	13.5	13.1	12.8	12.8	0.3	5.5	6.9
Lime, cement, and glass	55.9	62.4	27.6	29.4	29.8	31.6	33.9	14.5	18.1	1.2
Primary iron and steel products	57.1	52.1	33.5	50.8	49.7	64.5	57.2	17.5	38.1	1.6
Primary nonferrous metal products	25.5	33.5	26.7	26.3	22.3	24.0	23.3	1.7	17.3	4.3
Primary wood products	2.5	4.8	2.2	2.1	2.1	2.3	2.7	0.1	2.4	0.2
Food and farm products	283.3	251.3	300.1	275.4	270.1	319.4	312.9	95.2	44.5	173.2
Fish	2.4	3.0	3.1	3.3	3.2	3.2	3.2	0.1	1.9	1.1
Grain [1]	145.2	124.0	131.8	97.7	100.6	131.0	120.3	44.9	2.2	73.2
Wheat	43.4	36.4	38.4	39.9	49.7	35.9	30.6	9.3	0.4	20.9
Corn	88.2	75.2	81.8	49.0	41.7	80.5	70.1	30.6	0.5	39.0
Oilseeds [1]	57.6	47.2	76.9	83.3	73.2	89.2	91.3	34.7	0.7	55.9
Soybeans	47.3	40.8	67.4	73.0	62.5	80.3	79.5	30.6	0.4	48.5
Vegetables products	8.9	8.3	12.9	13.8	13.1	12.7	12.5	1.3	6.2	5.0
Processed grain and animal feed	23.1	18.4	20.6	21.2	22.1	27.0	30.0	8.5	1.3	20.2
Other agricultural products	46.1	50.5	54.9	56.1	57.8	56.2	55.7	5.7	32.3	17.8
All manufactured equipment, machinery, and products	83.6	110.3	104.1	118.9	121.0	132.5	133.6	21.3	85.8	26.5
Waste and scrap, not elsewhere classified	4.3	2.0	1.3	1.3	1.3	1.3	1.2	1.2	–	
Unknown or not elsewhere classified	6.8	8.7	9.6	8.8	13.7	24.4	20.6	0.2	9.8	10.6

– Represents or rounds to zero. [1] Includes commodities not shown separately.

Source: U.S. Army Corps of Engineers, *Waterborne Commerce of the United States, 2015*, 2017, and earlier editions. See also <http://www.navigationdatacenter.us/wcsc/wcsc.htm>.

Table 1106. Top 30 U.S. Ports by Tons of Traffic: 2015

[In thousands of short tons (39,404 represents 39,404,000), except rank. One short ton equals 2,000 lbs. For calendar year. Represents tons of cargo shipped from or received by the specified port. Excludes cargo carried on general ferries; coal and petroleum products loaded from shore facilities directly onto bunkers of vessels for fuel; and amounts of less than 100 tons of government-owned equipment in support of Corps of Engineers projects]

Port name	Rank	Total	Domestic	Foreign Total	Inbound	Outbound
Baltimore, MD	17	39,404	6,973	32,431	14,641	17,791
Baton Rouge, LA	8	68,782	42,896	25,886	9,971	15,915
Beaumont, TX	5	87,170	35,337	51,833	32,352	19,481
Cincinnati-Northern KY, Ports of	14	44,968	44,968			
Corpus Christi, TX	6	85,675	40,404	45,271	25,455	19,816
Duluth-Superior, MN and WI	22	33,327	27,099	6,228	863	5,365
Houston, TX	2	240,933	77,522	163,411	71,388	92,024
Huntington - Tristate [1]	16	42,741	42,741	–		
Lake Charles, LA	12	56,692	27,438	29,255	19,576	9,678
Long Beach, CA	7	78,165	11,214	66,950	44,714	22,236
Los Angeles, CA	9	60,188	5,967	54,220	35,645	18,576
Mobile, AL	10	58,595	22,689	35,905	19,764	16,141
New Orleans, LA	4	87,810	48,117	39,692	18,891	20,802
New York, NY and NJ	3	126,690	47,357	79,334	62,495	16,839
Pascagoula, MS	25	26,590	9,131	17,459	9,177	8,282
Paulsboro, NJ	30	22,500	9,084	13,416	11,842	1,574
Pittsburgh, PA	26	26,369	26,369	–	–	–
Plaquemines, LA, Port of	13	53,506	33,800	19,706	2,866	16,840
Port Arthur, TX	19	35,787	9,691	26,096	8,597	17,499
Port Everglades, FL	27	23,058	9,914	13,144	9,858	3,286
Richmond, CA	23	28,529	10,292	18,237	13,093	5,144
Savannah, GA	20	35,205	1,049	34,155	17,441	16,715
Seattle, WA	29	22,607	5,540	17,066	7,961	9,105
South Louisiana, LA, Port of	1	259,102	139,078	120,024	38,312	81,712
St. Louis, MO and IL	21	34,965	34,965	–		
Tacoma, WA	28	22,626	4,551	18,075	8,053	10,022
Tampa, FL	18	35,934	22,383	13,551	7,989	5,562
Texas City, TX	15	42,924	15,327	27,597	12,353	15,244
Valdez, AK	24	26,747	26,591	156	10	147
Virginia, VA, Port of	11	57,762	6,509	51,253	10,378	40,876

– Represents or rounds to zero. [1] The Port of Huntington is the largest inland shipping port in the United States. Port operations occur in Ashland, KY; Ironton, OH; and Huntington, WV.

Source: U.S. Army Corps of Engineers, *Waterborne Commerce of the United States, 2015,* 2017. See also <http://www.navigationdatacenter.us/wcsc/wcsc.htm>.

Table 1107. Top 30 U.S. Ports/Waterways Ranked by Container Traffic: 2015

[In thousands of twenty-foot equivalent units (TEUs) (35,665.4 represents 35,665,400). For calendar year. For the 30 leading ports/waterways in total TEUs. A TEU is a measure of containerized cargo capacity equal to one standard 20-foot length by 8-foot width by 8-foot, 6 inch height container. Does not include empty foreign containers]

Port/waterway name	Rank	Total loaded	Domestic loaded Total [1]	Inbound	Outbound	Foreign loaded Total	Inbound
Total U.S. [2]	(X)	35,665.4	5,522.0	2,083.2	2,083.2	31,499.0	20,066.8
Anchorage, AK	18	320.5	360.9	244.6	75.6	0.3	0.3
Baltimore, MD	16	609.2	26.0	12.2	6.7	590.2	388.2
Boston, MA	22	191.2	–	–	–	191.2	115.6
Camden-Gloucester, NJ	25	117.4	107.7	20.6	60.6	36.1	31.8
Charleston, SC	9	1,551.6	–	–	–	1,551.6	835.7
Chester, PA	30	85.9	–	–	–	85.9	57.6
Gulfport, MS	26	115.2	–	–	–	115.2	66.0
Honolulu, HI	11	797.9	1,059.9	452.1	319.0	26.8	21.3
Houston, TX	6	1,753.0	0.4	0.3	–	1,752.7	844.5
Jacksonville, FL	13	755.5	559.7	86.3	371.9	297.3	181.6
Juneau, AK	27	104.9	149.6	76.9	28.0	–	–
Kahului, HI	29	87.4	135.2	71.5	15.9	(Z)	(Z)
Ketchikan, AK	28	92.3	140.8	20.8	71.5	(Z)	(Z)
Long Beach, CA	2	5,172.5	370.6	54.8	252.3	4,865.4	3,581.1
Los Angeles, CA	1	5,526.3	–	–	–	5,526.3	4,064.1
Miami, FL	12	766.0	–	–	–	766.0	407.9
Mobile, AL	23	182.7	–	–	–	182.7	81.9
New Orleans, LA	17	365.7	–	–	–	365.7	115.0
New York (NJ-NY), NY	3	4,613.1	96.7	42.2	42.2	4,528.6	3,205.2
Oakland, CA	7	1,656.4	206.4	28.5	109.9	1,518.1	818.0
Palm Beach, FL	24	140.9	–	–	–	140.9	26.8
Philadelphia, PA	19	305.7	26.7	7.9	9.3	288.4	214.2
Port Everglades, FL	14	716.2	–	–	–	716.2	319.5
Port of Virginia, VA	5	2,003.7	56.1	17.6	20.7	1,965.3	1,047.3
San Juan, PR	15	715.4	667.5	432.6	106.9	176.0	158.1
Savannah, GA	4	2,824.5	–	–	–	2,824.5	1,619.4
Seattle, WA	10	1,072.9	412.1	94.8	153.7	824.5	459.8
Tacoma, WA	8	1,646.5	370.9	81.0	249.4	1,316.2	845.3
Wilmington, NC	20	232.7	–	–	–	232.7	125.3
Wilmington, DE	21	193.5	–	–	–	193.5	164.9

– Represents zero. X Not applicable. Z Less than 50 TEUs. [1] Includes empty TEUs, not shown separately. [2] Includes other ports/waterways not shown separately.

Source: U.S. Army Corps of Engineers, Navigation Data Center, Waterborne Commerce Statistics Center, "2015 Waterborne Container Traffic for U.S. Ports," <http://www.navigationdatacenter.us/wcsc/wcsc.htm>, accessed February 2017.

Table 1108. Highway Mileage—Urban and Rural by Ownership: 1990 to 2015

[In thousands (3,880 represents 3,880,000). As of December 31. Includes Puerto Rico beginning 2000]

Type and control of roadways	1990	1995	2000	2010	2011	2012	2013	2014	2015
Total mileage [1]	**3,880**	**3,912**	**3,951**	**4,084**	**4,094**	**4,109**	**4,132**	**4,194**	**4,171**
Urban mileage	757	819	859	1,103	1,108	1,127	1,192	1,215	1,223
Under state control	96	112	112	(NA)	153	154	160	172	174
Under local control [1]	661	706	746	(NA)	945	960	1,021	1,036	1,042
Under federal control [2]	(NA)	(NA)	(NA)	(NA)	9	13	11	8	7
Rural mileage	3,123	3,093	3,092	2,980	2,985	2,983	2,941	2,978	2,949
Under state control	703	691	664	(NA)	631	631	625	616	612
Under local control [1]	2,242	2,231	2,311	(NA)	2,227	2,224	2,174	2,209	2,198
Under federal control [2]	178	170	117	(NA)	127	128	141	154	139

NA Not available. [1] Includes state park, state toll, other state agency, other local agency and other roadways not identified by ownership. [2] Includes roadways in federal parks, forest, and reservations that are not part of the state and local highway system.

Source: U.S. Federal Highway Administration, "Highway Statistics 2015," and earlier reports, <http://www.fhwa.dot.gov/policyinformation/statistics.cfm>, accessed February 2017.

Table 1109. Highway Mileage by State—Functional Systems and Urban/Rural Status: 2015

[As of December 31. Excludes Puerto Rico. For definition of functional systems, see text, this section]

State	Total	Functional systems					Urban	Rural
		Interstate	Other freeways and expressways	Arterial	Collector	Local		
United States	**4,154,727**	**48,053**	**17,986**	**403,081**	**811,231**	**2,874,376**	**1,209,214**	**2,945,513**
Alabama	102,019	1,001	27	9,693	22,645	68,654	26,231	75,788
Alaska	16,129	1,081	–	1,572	3,296	10,181	2,833	13,296
Arizona	66,122	1,169	232	5,972	8,245	50,505	26,322	39,800
Arkansas	102,609	703	201	7,426	21,142	73,137	17,128	85,481
California	195,834	2,451	1,984	27,067	33,127	131,205	109,485	86,349
Colorado	88,740	952	352	8,905	16,243	62,288	20,469	68,271
Connecticut	21,512	346	279	2,723	3,399	14,764	15,829	5,683
Delaware	6,416	41	56	624	1,131	4,563	3,406	3,010
District of Columbia	1,507	12	16	270	156	1,053	1,507	–
Florida	122,659	1,495	745	12,986	15,542	91,891	86,170	36,489
Georgia	128,134	1,247	163	14,331	22,835	89,557	50,346	77,788
Hawaii	4,455	55	34	791	759	2,817	2,788	1,668
Idaho	51,163	612	–	4,358	10,576	35,617	5,932	45,231
Illinois	145,840	2,185	139	14,518	22,424	106,573	49,655	96,185
Indiana	96,571	1,265	311	8,540	22,275	64,179	30,214	66,356
Iowa	114,442	788	–	9,874	31,554	72,225	12,473	101,969
Kansas	140,654	874	592	8,572	33,971	96,646	13,874	126,780
Kentucky	79,857	842	565	5,575	16,612	56,263	15,035	64,822
Louisiana	61,419	937	96	5,957	10,361	44,067	17,610	43,808
Maine	22,911	365	18	2,111	5,969	14,448	3,001	19,910
Maryland	32,037	480	305	3,796	5,058	22,398	18,576	13,461
Massachusetts	36,423	575	333	6,432	4,562	24,522	30,054	6,369
Michigan	122,286	1,252	701	14,329	24,598	81,406	37,964	84,322
Minnesota	138,767	914	166	13,520	30,408	93,759	22,144	116,624
Mississippi	76,777	807	64	7,566	15,833	52,507	12,865	63,912
Missouri	131,549	1,380	1,404	9,083	25,187	94,494	24,384	107,165
Montana	75,007	1,192	–	6,159	16,173	51,483	4,186	70,822
Nebraska	94,481	482	460	7,680	20,778	65,082	7,146	87,335
Nevada	43,900	597	55	3,471	5,826	33,950	9,638	34,263
New Hampshire	16,138	225	83	1,661	2,642	11,527	5,056	11,083
New Jersey	39,065	432	488	5,902	4,436	27,807	33,381	5,684
New Mexico	69,069	1,000	11	5,610	8,848	53,599	8,356	60,712
New York	114,365	1,744	928	13,671	20,710	77,313	49,967	64,398
North Carolina	106,334	1,271	873	10,056	17,303	76,830	40,832	65,502
North Dakota	87,128	571	–	5,970	12,317	68,271	2,125	85,003
Ohio	122,926	1,574	912	10,572	23,270	86,597	47,434	75,492
Oklahoma	112,711	933	198	8,291	25,725	77,565	17,922	94,790
Oregon	73,544	730	57	7,025	18,823	46,909	14,902	58,641
Pennsylvania	120,091	1,867	884	12,935	19,830	84,574	47,599	72,492
Rhode Island	6,046	70	91	854	894	4,137	4,686	1,361
South Carolina	76,250	851	129	7,365	14,960	52,945	18,569	57,681
South Dakota	82,576	679	309	6,120	19,018	56,451	3,383	79,193
Tennessee	95,637	1,104	165	9,212	18,197	66,958	31,301	64,336
Texas	313,596	3,417	1,514	32,943	66,913	208,808	108,373	205,222
Utah	46,299	937	53	3,795	8,301	33,214	11,052	35,246
Vermont	14,252	320	18	1,304	3,112	9,498	1,462	12,791
Virginia	75,061	1,122	447	8,916	15,631	48,945	27,789	47,273
Washington	80,338	764	1,031	7,487	17,266	53,791	24,033	56,305
West Virginia	38,770	554	23	3,484	8,630	26,080	7,143	31,627
Wisconsin	115,372	876	471	12,330	23,432	78,262	23,656	91,716
Wyoming	28,942	914	3	3,675	10,289	14,061	2,931	26,010

– Represents zero.

Source: U.S. Federal Highway Administration, "Highway Statistics 2015," <http://www.fhwa.dot.gov/policyinformation/statistics.cfm>, accessed February 2017.

Table 1110. Bridge Inventory—Total, Deficient, and by Condition: 2012 to 2016, and by State, 2016

[Based on the National Bridge Inventory program; for details, see source]

State and year	Number of bridges	Structurally deficient [1]		Bridge condition [2]					
				Number			Percent		
		Number	Percent	Good	Fair	Poor	Good	Fair	Poor
2012................	607,380	66,749	11.0	287,194	262,878	57,049	47.3	43.3	9.4
2013................	607,751	63,522	10.5	287,581	265,456	54,492	47.3	43.7	9.0
2014................	610,749	61,365	10.0	287,701	269,734	52,905	47.1	44.2	8.7
2015................	611,845	58,791	9.6	289,158	271,690	50,917	47.3	44.4	8.3
U.S. total, 2016......	**614,387**	**56,007**	**9.1**	**291,412**	**274,306**	**48,559**	**47.4**	**44.6**	**7.9**
Alabama................	16,098	1,229	7.6	7,040	8,338	720	43.7	51.8	4.5
Alaska.................	1,488	144	9.7	644	702	141	43.3	47.2	9.5
Arizona................	8,154	214	2.6	4,931	3,042	181	60.5	37.3	2.2
Arkansas..............	12,871	811	6.3	6,984	5,291	596	54.3	41.1	4.6
California.............	25,431	1,388	5.5	16,788	7,439	1,204	66.0	29.3	4.7
Colorado..............	8,682	497	5.7	3,861	4,364	455	44.5	50.3	5.2
Connecticut...........	4,214	338	8.0	1,250	2,628	336	29.7	62.4	8.0
Delaware..............	877	43	4.9	267	567	43	30.4	64.7	4.9
District of Columbia.....	245	9	3.7	67	169	9	27.3	69.0	3.7
Florida................	12,313	256	2.1	8,534	3,545	233	69.3	28.8	1.9
Georgia...............	14,835	700	4.7	7,021	7,275	539	47.3	49.0	3.6
Hawaii................	1,132	64	5.7	436	634	62	38.5	56.0	5.5
Idaho.................	4,445	411	9.2	1,218	2,867	360	27.4	64.5	8.1
Illinois................	26,704	2,243	8.4	13,815	10,732	2,157	51.7	40.2	8.1
Indiana...............	19,245	1,533	8.0	7,876	9,902	1,464	40.9	51.5	7.6
Iowa..................	24,184	4,968	20.5	9,182	10,300	4,671	38.0	42.6	19.3
Kansas...............	25,013	2,151	8.6	13,890	9,664	1,458	55.5	38.6	5.8
Kentucky..............	14,265	1,157	8.1	5,471	7,733	1,059	38.4	54.2	7.4
Louisiana.............	12,915	1,739	13.5	6,647	4,730	1,534	51.5	36.6	11.9
Maine.................	2,450	352	14.4	774	1,337	339	31.6	54.6	13.8
Maryland..............	5,321	308	5.8	1,782	3,242	297	33.5	60.9	5.6
Massachusetts.........	5,171	483	9.3	1,409	3,294	468	27.2	63.7	9.1
Michigan..............	11,156	1,234	11.1	4,674	5,274	1,202	41.9	47.3	10.8
Minnesota.............	13,355	800	6.0	8,431	4,144	776	63.1	31.0	5.8
Mississippi............	17,068	2,098	12.3	11,104	4,480	1,479	65.1	26.2	8.7
Missouri..............	24,468	3,195	13.1	11,009	11,335	2,124	45.0	46.3	8.7
Montana..............	5,276	465	8.8	1,841	3,066	369	34.9	58.1	7.0
Nebraska.............	15,334	2,361	15.4	7,899	5,945	1,478	51.5	38.8	9.6
Nevada...............	1,933	31	1.6	981	925	27	50.8	47.9	1.4
New Hampshire........	2,486	304	12.2	1,321	916	249	53.1	36.8	10.0
New Jersey............	6,730	609	9.0	1,882	4,280	568	28.0	63.6	8.4
New Mexico...........	3,973	258	6.5	1,511	2,212	250	38.0	55.7	6.3
New York.............	17,462	1,928	11.0	6,215	9,342	1,884	35.6	53.5	10.8
North Carolina.........	18,099	1,790	9.9	7,764	8,564	1,764	42.9	47.3	9.7
North Dakota..........	4,400	661	15.0	2,323	1,567	509	52.8	35.6	11.6
Ohio..................	28,284	1,942	6.9	15,957	10,445	1,882	56.4	36.9	6.7
Oklahoma.............	23,053	3,460	15.0	10,900	9,273	2,877	47.3	40.2	12.5
Oregon...............	8,118	429	5.3	3,063	4,655	398	37.7	57.3	4.9
Pennsylvania..........	22,791	4,506	19.8	6,539	11,821	4,430	28.7	51.9	19.4
Rhode Island..........	772	192	24.9	128	452	192	16.6	58.5	24.9
South Carolina........	9,358	964	10.3	4,256	4,276	826	45.5	45.7	8.8
South Dakota.........	5,849	1,147	19.6	1,879	2,915	1,055	32.1	49.8	18.0
Tennessee............	20,123	998	5.0	9,990	9,207	924	49.6	45.8	4.6
Texas................	53,488	900	1.7	28,168	24,667	653	52.7	46.1	1.2
Utah.................	3,039	95	3.1	1,760	1,191	88	57.9	39.2	2.9
Vermont..............	2,766	155	5.6	1,458	1,225	83	52.7	44.3	3.0
Virginia...............	13,892	935	6.7	4,857	8,154	881	35.0	58.7	6.3
Washington...........	8,178	392	4.8	4,337	3,477	364	53.0	42.5	4.5
West Virginia..........	7,217	1,247	17.3	2,641	3,353	1,222	36.6	46.5	16.9
Wisconsin.............	14,230	1,232	8.7	7,413	5,725	1,092	52.1	40.2	7.7
Wyoming..............	3,128	344	11.0	780	2,029	319	24.9	64.9	10.2
Puerto Rico...........	2,308	297	12.9	444	1,596	268	19.2	69.2	11.6

[1] Bridges are structurally deficient if they have been restricted to light vehicles, require immediate rehabilitation to remain open, or are closed. [2] Good: pavement and bridge infrastructure that is free of significant defects, and has a condition that does not adversely affect its performance; Fair: pavement and bridge infrastructure that has isolated surface defects or functional deficiencies on pavements; or minor deterioration of bridge elements; Poor: pavement and bridge infrastructure that is exhibiting advanced deterioration and conditions that impact structural capacity.

Source: U.S. Federal Highway Administration, Office of Bridges and Structures, "Deficient Bridges by Highway System" and "Highway Bridge Condition by Highway System," <https://www.fhwa.dot.gov/bridge/britab.cfm>, accessed February 2017.

Table 1111. Funding for Highways and Disposition of Highway–User Revenue: 1990 to 2015

[In millions of dollars (75,444 represents $75,444,000,000). Data compiled from reports of state and local authorities]

Type	1990	1995	2000	2010	2011	2012	2013	2014	2015
Total receipts	**75,444**	**96,269**	**131,115**	**220,977**	**204,939**	**216,561**	**(NA)**	**252,642**	**241,063**
Current income	69,880	87,620	119,815	187,960	177,861	195,307	(NA)	222,515	218,812
Highway-user revenues	44,346	59,331	81,335	93,830	95,138	105,153	(NA)	106,423	113,454
Other taxes and fees	19,827	21,732	31,137	80,220	66,968	69,273	(NA)	97,838	85,434
Investment income, other receipts	5,707	6,557	7,342	13,910	15,754	20,881	(NA)	18,253	19,924
Bond issue proceeds [1]	5,564	8,649	11,301	33,017	27,078	21,254	(NA)	30,127	22,251
Funds drawn from or placed in reserves [2]	-36	-2,791	-8,418	-15,664	1,501	4,758	(NA)	-14,213	-5,868
Total funds available	75,408	93,478	122,697	205,313	206,440	221,319	(NA)	238,429	235,195
Total disbursements	**75,408**	**93,478**	**122,697**	**205,313**	**206,440**	**221,319**	**(NA)**	**238,429**	**235,195**
Current disbursements	72,457	88,994	117,592	193,034	192,727	198,670	(NA)	204,976	207,537
Capital outlay	35,151	44,228	61,323	100,175	101,612	105,199	(NA)	105,452	106,539
Maintenance and traffic services	20,365	24,319	30,636	48,773	46,311	47,990	(NA)	51,593	51,817
Administration and research	6,501	8,419	10,020	16,165	16,590	16,023	(NA)	16,137	16,930
Highway law enforcement and safety	7,235	8,218	11,031	18,080	17,374	17,847	(NA)	19,629	20,165
Interest on debt	3,205	3,810	4,583	9,842	10,840	11,611	(NA)	12,164	12,087
Bond retirement [1]	2,951	4,484	5,105	12,279	13,713	22,649	(NA)	33,453	27,658

NA Not available. [1] Proceeds and redemptions of short-term notes and refunding issues are excluded. [2] Negative numbers indicate that funds were placed in reserves.

Source: U.S. Federal Highway Administration, "Highway Statistics 2015," and earlier reports, <http://www.fhwa.dot.gov/policyinformation/statistics.cfm>, accessed July 2017.

Table 1112. State Motor Fuel Tax and Related Receipts, 2012 to 2015; and Gasoline Tax Rates, 2015

[643 represents $643,000,000. Federal tax rate is 18.4 cents a gallon. This table includes revenues from State taxes on all motor-vehicle fuels and related receipts due to motor-fuel taxation and administration. In many States, however, the tax on special fuels (fuels other than gasoline and gasohol) is applicable only to the amount used on the highways. For the States that apply the tax to all fuel sold, the revenue and refunds covering the nonhighway portion of these special fuels have been excluded]

State	Adjusted total receipts (million dollars)				Tax rate, [1] 2015	State	Adjusted total receipts (million dollars)				Tax rate, [1] 2015
	2012	2013	2014	2015			2012	2013	2014	2015	
AL	643	635	645	667	18.00	MO	705	666	668	680	17.00
AK	32	32	32	32	8.00	MT	197	203	201	210	27.75
AZ	611	634	635	657	18.00	NE	320	314	331	332	26.10
AR	508	478	431	437	21.50	NV	481	486	511	579	24.00
CA	5,383	5,238	5,724	5,485	30.00	NH	144	143	146	180	23.83
CO	556	566	586	606	22.00	NJ	529	527	539	542	10.50
CT	700	681	786	869	25.00	NM	270	280	275	284	17.00
DE	113	113	113	117	23.00	NY	1,642	1,658	1,632	1,654	25.85
DC	23	22	23	25	23.50	NC	1,851	1,882	1,904	1,913	36.25
FL	2,189	2,276	2,345	2,452	17.30	ND	201	209	223	207	23.00
GA [2]	448	459	970	1,026	26.00	OH	1,817	1,764	1,777	1,819	28.00
HI	84	84	84	84	17.00	OK	462	433	451	455	17.00
ID	224	228	231	238	32.00	OR	479	571	586	601	30.00
IL	1,214	1,183	1,219	1,215	19.00	PA	2,115	2,089	2,252	2,991	50.50
IN	810	807	810	828	18.00	RI	137	136	139	144	33.00
IA	441	437	436	491	30.80	SC	538	537	551	566	16.00
KS	423	425	451	447	24.00	SD	141	135	140	171	30.00
KY	789	837	881	849	24.60	TN	842	836	843	863	20.00
LA	583	585	589	595	20.00	TX	3,174	3,209	3,339	3,445	20.00
ME	244	258	287	243	30.00	UT	357	353	359	362	24.50
MD	725	745	803	911	32.10	VT	103	104	122	122	19.20
MA	660	651	732	755	24.00	VA	889	899	702	773	16.20
MI	930	935	942	987	19.00	WA	1,160	1,177	1,198	1,198	44.50
MN	851	866	881	879	28.50	WV	346	373	386	383	34.60
MS	402	396	401	398	18.40	WI	964	964	980	993	30.90
						WY	93	108	169	168	24.00

[1] State gasoline tax rates in cents per gallon. In effect July 1. Includes other miscellanous tax (environmental, etc.). [2] Beginning 2014, Georgia receipts includes special fuel and use tax.

Source: U.S. Federal Highway Administration, "Highway Statistics 2015," and earlier reports, <http://www.fhwa.dot.gov/policyinformation/statistics.cfm>, accessed February 2017.

Table 1113. Public Obligations for Highways—Changes in Indebtedness During the Year: 2000 to 2015

[In millions of dollars (56,264 represents $56,264,000,000). Table summarizes state indebtedness from all state bond issues, including the toll facility issues and the state issues for local roads. This table is compiled from reports of state authorities. Table also summarizes the change in status of the highway obligations of local governments including toll authorities]

Item	2000	2005	2010	2011	2012	2013	2014	2015
STATE GOVERNMENT								
Obligations outstanding, beginning of year.........	56,264	82,476	138,798	157,728	166,402	181,075	201,462	211,692
Obligations issued.....................................	9,067	19,784	26,895	23,240	18,789	27,163	30,402	29,155
Obligations retired....................................	3,897	14,072	11,143	12,617	15,283	15,783	19,311	22,909
Obligations outstanding, end of year...............	61,434	88,187	154,550	168,351	169,908	192,455	212,553	217,938
LOCAL GOVERNMENT [1,2]								
Obligations outstanding, beginning of year.........	34,904	44,406	65,679	(NA)	75,668	83,776	(NA)	(NA)
Bonds outstanding, beginning of year.............	34,229	43,403	63,891	(NA)	73,547	81,461	(NA)	(NA)
Bonds outstanding, end of year....................	34,949	46,168	67,707	(NA)	79,244	70,415	(NA)	(NA)
Obligations outstanding, end of year...............	35,557	47,170	69,794	(NA)	81,552	72,108	(NA)	(NA)

NA Not available. [1] Short-term notes data not shown. The data are included in beginning and ending year obligations. [2] The number of local government data estimated varied year to year.

Source: U.S. Federal Highway Administration, "Highway Statistics 2015," and earlier reports, <http://www.fhwa.dot.gov/policyinformation/statistics.cfm>, accessed September 2017.

Table 1114. State Disbursements for Highways by State: 2000 to 2015

[In millions of dollars (89,832 represents $89,832,000,000). Comprises disbursements from current revenues or loans for construction, maintenance, interest and principal payments on highway bonds, transfers to local units, and miscellaneous. Includes transactions by state toll authorities. Data exclude amounts allocated for collection expenses and nonhighway purposes, and mass transit]

State	2000	2005	2010	2011	2012	2013	2014	2015
United States.............	**89,832**	**116,517**	**145,944**	**149,959**	**156,715**	**152,179**	**164,620**	**168,242**
Alabama.....................	1,246	1,519	1,781	1,840	1,987	1,988	2,285	2,281
Alaska.......................	501	643	756	806	819	991	1,173	1,185
Arizona......................	2,040	2,458	2,663	2,723	3,112	3,125	2,388	3,388
Arkansas....................	817	1,078	1,376	1,341	1,374	1,783	2,022	1,473
California....................	6,750	8,308	19,961	16,585	17,155	12,337	14,350	12,162
Colorado....................	1,392	1,652	2,249	2,577	2,485	2,580	2,571	2,632
Connecticut.................	1,304	1,434	1,761	1,733	1,939	1,982	1,943	2,097
Delaware....................	595	1,104	1,353	1,191	1,888	1,368	1,291	984
District of Columbia........	244	327	582	413	478	432	386	413
Florida......................	4,208	7,369	7,867	6,966	7,486	9,547	8,538	9,635
Georgia.....................	1,567	2,070	2,926	3,123	3,033	2,679	2,743	3,017
Hawaii.......................	272	506	460	414	465	463	397	568
Idaho........................	492	608	959	877	775	791	808	853
Illinois.......................	3,447	4,201	5,385	4,928	6,211	5,711	6,331	6,783
Indiana......................	1,932	2,235	2,839	3,023	2,709	2,825	2,613	2,636
Iowa.........................	1,494	1,392	1,888	1,698	1,980	1,837	2,025	2,183
Kansas......................	1,206	1,394	1,571	1,478	2,049	1,419	1,727	1,806
Kentucky....................	1,651	1,723	2,528	2,073	2,314	2,537	2,946	3,013
Louisiana....................	1,301	1,387	2,457	2,283	2,798	2,079	1,774	2,698
Maine........................	488	616	684	705	(NA)	(NA)	(NA)	988
Maryland....................	1,599	2,049	2,255	2,519	2,813	2,483	2,785	3,395
Massachusetts..............	3,524	3,196	2,923	(NA)	(NA)	(NA)	(NA)	(NA)
Michigan....................	2,748	3,561	3,484	3,015	3,014	3,022	3,419	3,111
Minnesota..................	1,692	2,131	2,625	3,336	2,585	2,840	2,997	3,486
Mississippi.................	1,039	1,081	1,345	1,262	1,305	1,414	1,413	1,200
Missouri.....................	1,818	2,069	2,814	3,007	2,707	2,408	3,421	2,364
Montana....................	474	664	778	754	891	723	764	783
Nebraska...................	745	876	1,409	1,443	1,423	1,508	1,555	1,595
Nevada......................	651	865	1,007	968	1,253	1,064	779	867
New Hampshire.............	387	389	793	(NA)	(NA)	(NA)	722	858
New Jersey.................	4,503	7,119	5,201	6,453	6,954	7,492	(NA)	7,146
New Mexico................	1,162	911	1,163	1,632	934	1,296	1,018	1,142
New York...................	5,307	9,638	7,711	8,516	(NA)	(NA)	11,391	9,821
North Carolina.............	2,621	3,698	3,646	4,312	4,346	4,505	4,414	4,324
North Dakota...............	385	456	559	618	854	1,022	880	950
Ohio.........................	3,351	4,040	4,520	4,754	4,950	4,835	5,151	5,838
Oklahoma...................	1,417	1,163	2,040	3,383	2,469	1,818	2,005	2,669
Oregon......................	1,010	1,628	1,522	1,382	1,937	1,263	2,223	2,265
Pennsylvania...............	4,517	4,567	8,835	9,220	7,320	7,134	8,200	8,592
Rhode Island...............	256	407	540	480	616	511	(NA)	(NA)
South Carolina.............	970	1,360	1,899	1,609	1,686	1,523	1,864	1,555
South Dakota...............	466	466	532	547	592	677	651	625
Tennessee..................	1,440	1,718	2,076	2,094	2,160	2,187	1,987	1,879
Texas.......................	5,665	8,918	9,365	11,693	13,411	15,024	19,682	21,222
Utah.........................	1,072	986	2,303	2,248	2,225	1,608	1,482	1,622
Vermont.....................	287	310	436	556	719	518	532	568
Virginia......................	2,678	3,384	3,334	3,882	4,465	4,487	5,316	5,235
Washington.................	1,871	2,625	4,149	4,937	5,768	6,491	4,802	5,489
West Virginia...............	1,170	1,425	1,327	1,388	1,395	1,275	1,315	1,227
Wisconsin...................	1,663	2,363	2,702	2,892	3,312	3,071	3,316	3,547
Wyoming....................	396	429	605	564	614	568	594	635

NA Not available.

Source: U.S. Federal Highway Administration, "Highway Statistics 2015," and earlier reports, <https://www.fhwa.dot.gov/policyinformation/statistics.cfm>, accessed April 2017.

Table 1115. Federal Highway Trust Fund-Receipts, Expenditures, and Balance: 1960 to 2015

[In billions of dollars (2.54 represents $2,540,000,000). For fiscal year ending September 30. Established as part of the Federal Aid Highway Act of 1956]

Year	Receipts	Expenditures	Balance	Year	Receipts	Expenditures	Balance
1960	2.54	2.94	0.12	2006	33.70	33.91	9.01
1970	5.47	4.38	2.61	2007	34.31	34.98	8.11
1980	7.65	9.21	11.00	2008	39.36	37.01	10.03
1990	13.45	14.38	9.63	2009	37.32	37.57	8.88
2000	30.35	27.00	22.55	2010	44.89	32.01	20.74
2001	26.92	29.10	20.37	2011	32.01	37.32	14.32
2002	27.98	32.22	16.14	2012	37.64	41.15	9.73
2003	28.96	32.11	12.99	2013	37.70	42.92	3.77
2004	29.79	31.97	10.81	2014	52.50	43.79	11.38
2005	32.91	33.12	10.59	2015	41.83	42.95	9.04

Source: U.S. Federal Highway Administration, "Highway Statistics 2015," <https://www.fhwa.dot.gov/policyinformation/statistics.cfm>, accessed August 2017.

Table 1116. Federal Highway Trust Fund Receipts from Highway Users by State: 2015

[In thousands of dollars (40,813,294 represents $40,813,294,000). For fiscal years ending September 30. Federal Highway Trust Fund receipts are reported by the U.S. Department of the Treasury. Payments into the Fund attributable to highway users in each State are estimated by the Federal Highway Administration]

State	Total	Highway account						Mass transit account	
		Motor fuel			Other				
		Motor fuel, total	Gasoline	Special fuels	Federal use tax	Trucks and trailers	Tires	Gasoline	Special fuels
Total	40,813,294	29,559,385	21,033,199	8,526,186	1,149,768	4,554,325	500,968	3,915,061	1,133,787
Alabama	782,738	564,745	397,428	167,317	22,563	89,374	9,831	73,976	22,249
Alaska	127,735	83,770	41,712	42,058	5,672	22,465	2,471	7,764	5,593
Arizona	795,082	576,276	410,935	165,341	22,296	88,318	9,715	76,490	21,987
Arkansas	503,746	349,865	218,295	131,570	17,742	70,279	7,731	40,633	17,496
California	3,847,268	2,887,113	2,260,439	626,674	84,508	334,742	36,821	420,751	83,333
Colorado	650,245	473,014	340,812	132,202	17,828	70,617	7,768	63,438	17,580
Connecticut	367,887	277,064	218,881	58,183	7,846	31,079	3,419	40,742	7,737
Delaware	102,083	78,261	64,543	13,718	1,850	7,328	806	12,014	1,824
Dist. of Columbia	25,842	19,627	15,831	3,796	512	2,028	223	2,947	505
Florida	2,088,960	1,585,048	1,275,420	309,628	41,754	165,390	18,192	237,403	41,173
Georgia	1,356,075	990,223	721,124	269,099	36,288	143,741	15,811	134,228	35,784
Hawaii	101,766	79,935	69,630	10,305	1,390	5,505	605	12,961	1,370
Idaho	234,327	165,092	108,014	57,078	7,697	30,489	3,354	20,105	7,590
Illinois	1,449,177	1,037,203	712,699	324,504	43,760	173,336	19,067	132,660	43,151
Indiana	1,067,446	742,453	465,557	276,896	37,340	147,906	16,269	86,657	36,821
Iowa	559,524	388,067	240,984	147,083	19,834	78,566	8,642	44,856	19,559
Kansas	439,714	309,729	202,506	107,223	14,459	57,274	6,300	37,694	14,258
Kentucky	705,637	496,986	324,820	172,166	23,217	91,963	10,116	60,461	22,894
Louisiana	679,609	490,556	345,668	144,888	19,538	77,393	8,513	64,342	19,267
Maine	213,693	158,063	119,213	38,850	5,239	20,752	2,283	22,190	5,166
Maryland	706,427	532,057	420,384	111,673	15,059	59,651	6,561	78,249	14,850
Massachusetts	662,505	507,618	418,085	89,533	12,074	47,825	5,261	77,821	11,906
Michigan	1,183,436	884,608	685,722	198,886	26,820	106,237	11,686	127,638	26,447
Minnesota	721,473	526,004	381,386	144,618	19,502	77,249	8,497	70,990	19,231
Mississippi	537,244	382,916	259,802	123,114	16,602	65,762	7,234	48,359	16,371
Missouri	972,231	697,159	481,766	215,393	29,046	115,053	12,656	89,675	28,642
Montana	201,218	136,559	78,391	58,168	7,844	31,071	3,418	14,591	7,735
Nebraska	336,456	229,629	134,632	94,997	12,810	50,743	5,582	25,060	12,632
Nevada	322,447	235,056	170,368	64,688	8,723	34,553	3,801	31,712	8,602
New Hampshire	167,310	129,147	108,210	20,937	2,823	11,184	1,230	20,142	2,784
New Jersey	1,076,297	807,136	630,849	176,287	23,772	94,165	10,358	117,424	23,442
New Mexico	386,789	261,326	147,452	113,874	15,356	60,827	6,691	27,446	15,143
New York	1,556,098	1,142,972	845,943	297,029	40,055	158,660	17,452	157,461	39,498
North Carolina	1,203,816	889,152	668,044	221,108	29,817	118,106	12,991	124,348	29,402
North Dakota	252,378	161,552	71,492	90,060	12,145	48,106	5,292	13,307	11,976
Ohio	1,535,410	1,104,115	769,433	334,682	45,132	178,773	19,665	143,220	44,505
Oklahoma	710,199	491,568	303,113	188,455	25,413	100,664	11,073	56,421	25,060
Oregon	482,052	341,949	228,620	113,329	15,283	60,536	6,659	42,555	15,070
Pennsylvania	1,539,102	1,103,185	761,394	341,791	46,091	182,570	20,082	141,724	45,450
Rhode Island	95,797	71,791	56,016	15,775	2,127	8,427	927	10,427	2,098
South Carolina	758,383	555,930	409,216	146,714	19,785	78,368	8,620	76,170	19,510
South Dakota	174,632	119,072	69,568	49,504	6,676	26,443	2,909	12,949	6,583
Tennessee	961,494	697,137	497,622	199,515	26,905	106,572	11,723	92,626	26,531
Texas	4,545,761	3,185,753	2,048,759	1,136,994	153,325	607,334	66,805	381,350	151,194
Utah	384,653	268,728	171,035	97,693	13,174	52,184	5,740	31,836	12,991
Vermont	80,440	60,691	48,162	12,529	1,690	6,692	736	8,965	1,666
Virginia	1,138,047	835,462	617,447	218,015	29,400	116,454	12,810	114,930	28,991
Washington	762,112	561,325	418,570	142,755	19,251	76,254	8,388	77,911	18,983
West Virginia	259,122	185,060	126,335	58,725	7,919	31,368	3,450	23,516	7,809
Wisconsin	793,705	571,215	399,017	172,198	23,221	91,981	10,118	74,272	22,898
Wyoming	207,706	130,423	51,855	78,568	10,595	41,968	4,616	9,654	10,450

Source: U.S. Federal Highway Administration, "Highway Statistics 2015," <http://www.fhwa.dot.gov/policyinformation/statistics.cfm>, accessed August 2017.

Table 1117. Motor Vehicle Distance Traveled by Type of Vehicle: 1970 to 2015

[1,110 represents 1,110,000,000,000. The travel data by vehicle type and stratification of trucks are estimated by the Federal Highway Administration (FHWA)]

Year	Vehicle miles of travel (bil.) [1]					Average miles traveled per vehicle (1,000) [1]				
	Total [2]	Light duty vehicle short WB [3]	Buses [4]	Light duty vehicle long WB [3]	Trucks [5, 6]	Total [2]	Light duty vehicle short WB [3]	Buses [4]	Light duty vehicle long WB [3]	Trucks [5, 6]
1970........	1,110	920	4.5	123	62	10.0	10.0	12.0	8.7	13.6
1975........	1,328	1,040	6.1	201	81	9.6	9.3	13.1	9.8	15.2
1980........	1,527	1,122	6.1	291	108	9.5	8.8	11.5	10.4	18.7
1985........	1,775	1,256	4.5	391	124	10.0	9.4	7.5	10.5	20.6
1990........	2,144	1,418	5.7	575	146	11.1	10.3	9.1	11.9	23.6
1991........	2,172	1,367	5.8	649	150	11.3	10.3	9.1	12.2	24.2
1992........	2,247	1,381	5.8	707	153	11.6	10.6	9.0	12.4	25.4
1993........	2,296	1,385	6.1	746	160	11.6	10.5	9.4	12.4	26.3
1994........	2,358	1,416	6.4	765	170	11.7	10.8	9.6	12.2	25.8
1995........	2,423	1,438	6.4	790	178	11.8	11.2	9.4	12.0	26.5
1996........	2,486	1,470	6.6	817	183	11.8	11.3	9.4	11.8	26.1
1997........	2,562	1,503	6.8	851	191	12.1	11.6	9.8	12.1	27.0
1998........	2,632	1,550	7.0	868	196	12.2	11.8	9.8	12.2	25.4
1999........	2,691	1,569	7.7	901	203	12.2	11.9	10.5	12.0	26.0
2000........	2,747	1,967	14.8	491	262	12.2	11.0	19.8	14.6	29.1
2001........	2,796	1,987	13.0	512	272	11.9	10.7	17.3	14.7	28.9
2002........	2,856	2,036	13.3	520	276	12.2	11.1	17.5	14.3	29.4
2003........	2,890	2,051	13.4	528	286	12.2	11.1	17.2	14.8	30.3
2004........	2,965	2,083	13.5	569	284	12.2	11.0	17.0	15.2	29.7
2005........	2,989	2,096	13.2	581	285	12.1	11.0	16.3	14.8	28.8
2006........	3,014	2,048	14.0	633	301	12.0	10.5	17.1	16.3	29.1
2007........	3,031	2,104	14.5	587	304	11.9	10.7	17.4	15.0	28.3
2008........	2,977	2,025	14.8	605	311	11.6	10.3	17.6	15.3	28.6
2009........	2,957	2,016	14.4	617	288	11.6	10.4	17.1	15.3	26.3
2010........	2,967	2,026	13.8	623	287	11.9	10.7	16.3	15.5	26.6
2011........	2,950	2,046	13.8	604	268	11.7	11.2	20.7	12.0	26.1
2012........	2,969	2,063	14.8	601	269	11.7	11.3	19.3	11.9	25.3
2013........	2,988	2,074	15.2	603	275	11.7	11.2	17.5	11.7	26.0
2014........	3,026	2,072	16.0	638	279	11.6	11.0	18.3	12.1	25.6
2015........	3,095	2,148	16.2	632	280	11.7	11.3	18.3	11.9	25.0

[1] Beginning with 2000 data, FHWA updated data using an enhanced methodology implemented in March 2011. Prior to 2000, "Light Duty Vehicles Short WB" were categorized as "Cars"; and "Light Duty Vehicles Long WB" were categorized as "Vans, pickups, sport utility vehicles." [2] Motorcycles included with "Cars" through 1994; thereafter in total, not shown separately. [3] Light Duty Vehicles Short WB—passenger cars, light trucks, vans and sport utility vehicles with a wheelbase (WB) equal to or less than 121 inches. Light Duty Vehicles Long WB—large passenger cars, vans, pickup trucks, and sport/utility vehicles with WB larger than 121 inches. [4] Includes school buses. [5] Includes combination trucks. [6] Beginning in 2000: Single-Unit—single frame trucks that have 2-axles and at least 6 tires or a gross vehicle weight rating exceeding 10,000 lbs.

Source: U.S. Federal Highway Administration, "Highway Statistics 2015," and earlier reports, <http://www.fhwa.dot.gov/policyinformation/statistics.cfm>, accessed February 2017.

Table 1118. State Motor Vehicle Registrations: 2000 to 2015

[In thousands (221,475 represents 221,475,000). Information obtained from state authorities, see source. For motorcycles; see Table 1119]

Type	2000	2010	2011	2012	2013	2014	2015
All motor vehicles...............	**221,475**	**242,061**	**244,778**	**245,184**	**247,417**	**251,933**	**255,009**
Private and commercial.............	217,567	237,784	241,068	241,457	243,487	247,849	250,967
Publicly owned......................	3,908	4,277	3,710	3,728	3,985	4,084	4,042
Automobiles [1]........................	133,621	130,892	125,657	111,290	113,676	113,899	112,864
Private and commercial.............	132,247	129,434	124,136	109,834	112,128	112,261	111,412
Publicly owned......................	1,374	1,458	1,520	1,456	1,548	1,638	1,453
Buses.................................	746	846	666	765	865	872	889
Private and commercial.............	314	347	312	301	361	467	466
Publicly owned......................	432	499	354	464	503	405	423
Trucks [1].............................	87,108	110,322	118,456	133,130	132,931	137,162	141,256
Private and commercial.............	85,005	108,003	116,620	131,322	130,998	135,121	139,090
Publicly owned......................	2,103	2,319	1,836	1,808	1,934	2,041	2,166

[1] Includes panel, delivery, personal, passenger vans, minivans, pickups, and utility vehicles.

Source: U.S. Federal Highway Administration, "Highway Statistics 2015," and earlier reports, <http://www.fhwa.dot.gov/policyinformation/statistics.cfm>, accessed February 2017.

Table 1119. State Motor Vehicle Registrations, 1990 to 2015; and Motorcycle Registrations and Licensed Drivers, 2015

[In thousands (188,798 represents 188,798,000). Motor vehicle registrations cover publicly, privately, and commercially owned vehicles. Some states did not provide complete current registration data. Table displays estimates by FHWA, transaction data, or previous year data; see source and earlier editions for more information. For uniformity, data have been adjusted to a calendar-year basis as registration years in states differ; figures represent net numbers where possible, excluding reregistrations and nonresident registrations. See also Table 1118. Data for farm trucks, which are registered at a nominal fee and restricted to use in the vicinity of the owner's farm, are not included for some States]

State	Motor vehicle registrations [1]						2015		Motor-cycle registra-tions [2], in 2015	Licensed drivers in 2015
	1990	2000	2010	2012	2013	2014	Total	Auto-mobile		
U.S.	188,798	221,475	242,061	253,639	247,472	251,933	255,009	112,864	8,601	218,084
AL.	3,744	3,960	4,654	4,845	4,669	5,251	5,285	2,278	115	3,907
AK.	477	594	710	775	754	768	783	193	32	533
AZ.	2,825	3,795	4,320	5,163	5,193	5,407	5,470	2,333	161	4,979
AR.	1,448	1,840	2,073	2,480	2,344	2,686	2,680	948	92	2,120
CA.	21,926	27,698	31,014	27,702	27,275	27,873	28,595	14,464	829	25,533
CO.	3,155	3,626	4,180	4,562	4,499	4,632	4,814	1,822	191	3,975
CT.	2,623	2,853	3,082	2,706	2,764	2,777	2,755	1,386	87	2,567
DE.	526	630	799	944	917	927	936	438	28	743
DC.	262	242	212	322	329	330	319	201	4	456
FL.	10,950	11,781	14,373	15,666	14,586	14,947	15,532	7,735	573	14,263
GA.	5,489	7,155	7,702	7,647	7,580	7,956	7,937	3,524	200	6,906
HI.	771	738	904	1,232	1,294	1,350	1,209	523	34	910
ID.	1,054	1,178	1,325	1,644	1,628	1,696	1,788	626	66	1,135
IL.	7,873	8,973	10,079	10,132	9,841	10,042	10,249	4,775	346	8,462
IN.	4,366	5,571	5,698	6,004	5,355	5,790	5,822	2,336	223	4,468
IA.	2,632	3,106	3,313	3,511	3,357	3,409	3,447	1,326	190	2,224
KS.	2,012	2,296	2,436	2,449	2,529	2,446	2,539	992	96	2,029
KY.	2,909	2,826	3,589	3,671	3,922	4,038	4,041	1,714	111	3,021
LA.	2,995	3,557	4,086	3,889	3,843	3,773	3,787	1,439	114	3,357
ME.	977	1,024	1,054	1,180	1,136	1,143	1,049	420	55	1,020
MD.	3,607	3,848	4,557	3,983	3,734	3,927	4,009	1,994	126	4,186
MA.	3,726	5,265	5,334	4,950	4,860	4,869	4,902	2,374	168	5,041
MI.	7,209	8,436	9,286	7,798	7,925	7,868	8,037	3,377	257	7,104
MN.	3,508	4,630	4,848	5,099	4,982	4,986	5,033	2,080	249	3,351
MS.	1,875	2,289	2,016	2,052	2,045	2,039	2,041	847	28	1,988
MO.	3,905	4,580	5,153	5,685	5,636	5,179	5,406	2,273	218	4,213
MT.	783	1,026	926	1,489	1,369	1,402	1,448	436	197	781
NE.	1,384	1,619	1,802	1,888	1,835	1,895	1,925	733	56	1,394
NV.	853	1,220	1,362	2,130	2,132	2,169	2,242	1,018	75	1,836
NH.	946	1,052	1,203	1,302	1,335	1,234	1,222	535	74	1,075
NJ.	5,652	6,390	6,628	7,911	6,909	6,724	5,786	2,919	152	6,179
NM.	1,301	1,529	1,612	1,806	1,817	1,866	1,760	668	63	1,468
NY.	10,196	10,235	10,255	10,449	10,329	10,557	10,284	4,869	355	11,690
NC.	5,162	6,223	5,743	7,793	7,618	7,682	7,740	3,439	189	7,161
ND.	630	694	736	810	809	833	852	247	39	545
OH.	8,410	10,467	9,801	10,116	9,958	10,049	10,152	4,739	405	7,923
OK.	2,649	3,014	3,357	3,440	3,333	3,388	2,859	1,157	129	2,622
OR.	2,445	3,022	3,050	3,527	3,514	3,330	3,479	1,433	128	2,809
PA.	7,971	9,260	9,991	10,471	10,060	10,108	10,205	4,680	393	8,943
RI.	672	760	782	854	821	833	843	447	32	745
SC.	2,521	3,095	3,661	3,897	3,873	3,903	4,046	1,784	116	3,684
SD.	704	793	926	1,004	928	943	986	329	96	656
TN.	4,444	4,820	5,114	5,393	5,288	5,331	5,446	2,318	166	4,621
TX.	12,800	14,070	17,194	20,238	19,727	20,432	21,478	8,451	387	15,880
UT.	1,206	1,628	2,655	1,981	1,996	2,076	2,150	919	79	1,914
VT.	462	515	567	607	583	582	624	253	31	549
VA.	4,938	6,046	6,149	7,117	6,861	6,965	7,046	3,270	193	5,820
WA.	4,257	5,116	4,683	5,850	6,166	6,176	6,489	2,841	236	5,516
WV.	1,225	1,442	1,436	1,459	1,395	1,496	1,555	566	59	1,167
WI.	3,815	4,366	4,968	5,215	5,015	5,059	5,142	2,189	325	4,195
WY.	528	586	663	799	799	789	784	207	31	422

[1] Automobiles, trucks, and buses (excludes motorcycles). Excludes vehicles owned by military services. [2] Private and commercial.

Source: U.S. Federal Highway Administration, "Highway Statistics 2015," and earlier reports, <http://www.fhwa.dot.gov/policyinformation/statistics.cfm>, accessed February 2017.

Table 1120. Domestic Motor Fuel Consumption by Type of Vehicle: 1970 to 2015

[Consumption in billions (92.3 represents 92,300,000,000 gallons). See Table 1117. Comprises all fuel types used for propulsion of vehicles under state motor fuels laws. Excludes federal purchases for military use. Minus sign (-) indicates decrease]

Year	Annual fuel consumption (bil. gal.) [1]						Average miles per gallon [1]				
	All vehi- cles [2]	Annual percent change [3]	Light duty vehicle short WB [2,4]	Buses [5]	Light duty vehicle long WB [4]	Trucks [6,7]	All vehi- cles [2]	Light duty vehicle short WB [2,4]	Buses [5]	Light duty vehicle long WB [4]	Trucks [6,7]
1970......	92.3	4.8	67.8	0.8	12.3	11.3	12.0	13.5	5.5	10.0	5.5
1980......	115.0	-5.9	70.2	1.0	23.8	20.0	13.3	16.0	6.0	12.2	5.4
1990......	130.8	-0.8	69.8	0.9	35.6	24.5	16.4	20.3	6.4	16.1	6.0
2000......	162.5	0.7	88.9	2.2	28.9	42.0	16.9	22.1	6.7	17.0	6.2
2001......	163.5	0.6	87.8	1.9	30.1	43.0	17.1	22.6	6.8	17.0	6.3
2002......	168.7	3.2	91.5	1.9	30.8	43.3	17.0	22.3	6.9	16.9	6.4
2003......	170.0	0.8	91.6	1.9	31.3	44.8	17.0	22.4	7.1	16.9	6.4
2004......	173.5	2.1	93.4	1.9	33.8	44.4	17.1	22.3	7.1	16.9	6.4
2005......	174.8	0.7	93.2	1.9	34.4	44.5	17.2	22.5	7.1	16.9	6.4
2006......	175.0	0.1	88.6	2.0	37.0	46.4	17.2	23.1	7.1	17.1	6.5
2007......	176.2	0.7	89.6	2.0	36.9	47.2	17.2	22.9	7.2	17.1	6.4
2008......	170.8	-3.1	85.6	2.1	34.9	47.7	17.4	23.7	7.2	17.3	6.5
2009......	168.1	-1.6	85.7	2.0	35.7	44.3	17.6	23.5	7.2	17.3	6.5
2010......	170.4	1.4	86.8	1.9	36.3	45.0	17.4	23.3	7.2	17.2	6.4
2011......	168.5	-1.1	88.4	1.9	35.3	42.4	17.5	23.2	7.1	17.1	6.3
2012......	168.6	0.1	88.6	2.1	35.1	42.4	17.6	23.3	7.2	17.1	6.4
2013......	169.7	0.6	88.6	2.1	35.2	46.8	17.6	23.4	7.2	17.2	6.4
2014......	173.3	2.2	89.3	2.2	37.3	44.0	17.5	23.2	7.2	17.1	6.3
2015......	172.9	-0.3	90.0	2.2	36.4	43.7	17.9	23.9	7.3	17.3	6.4

[1] See footnote 1, Table 1117. [2] Motorcycles included with "Cars" through 1994; thereafter in total, not shown separately. [3] Change from immediate prior year. [4] Light Duty Vehicles Short WB—passenger cars, light trucks, vans and sport utility vehicles with a wheelbase (WB) equal to or less than 121 inches. Light Duty Vehicles Long WB—large passenger cars, vans, pickup trucks, and sport/utility vehicles with (WB) larger than 121 inches. [5] Includes school buses. [6] Includes combination trucks. [7] Beginning 2000: Single-Unit—single frame trucks that have 2-axles and at least 6 tires or a gross vehicle weight rating over 10,000 lbs.

Source: U.S. Federal Highway Administration, "Highway Statistics 2015," and earlier reports, <http://www.fhwa.dot.gov/policyinformation/statistics.cfm>, accessed February 2017.

Table 1121. Alternative Fuel Vehicles—Models Available and Refueling Stations by Vehicle Fuel Type: 1995 to 2016

[The Energy Policy Act of 1992 defines alternative fuels and allows the U.S. Department of Energy (DOE) to add to the list of alternative fuels if the fuel is substantially nonpetroleum, yields substantial energy security benefits, and offers substantial environmental benefits]

Fuel type	1995	2000	2005	2010	2013	2014	2015	2016
MODELS AVAILABLE								
Total.........................	13	37	29	36	117	219	141	115
Propane [1]......................	–	2	–	–	6	14	10	5
Compressed natural gas (CNG) [1]..........	10	15	5	1	11	19	17	12
Ethanol (E85).............................	–	8	24	34	84	90	84	66
Methanol (M85)............................	2	–	–	–	–	–	–	–
Electric vehicle [2]........................	1	12	–	1	15	16	27	29
Hydrogen.................................	–	–	–	–	1	2	3	3
REFUELING STATIONS								
Total.........................	4,677	5,205	5,164	6,912	27,159	33,805	39,963	(NA)
Propane.................................	3,299	3,268	2,995	2,647	2,956	2,931	3,594	(NA)
Compressed Natural Gas (CNG)...........	1,065	1,217	787	841	1,263	1,495	1,563	(NA)
LNG (Liquid Natural Gas)...................	(NA)	44	40	39	81	103	111	(NA)
Biodiesel [3].............................	–	2	304	644	757	783	721	(NA)
Ethanol (E85).............................	37	113	436	2,142	2,639	2,840	2,990	(NA)
Methanol (M85)............................	88	3	–	–	–	–	–	(NA)
Electric vehicle [4]........................	188	558	588	541	19,410	25,602	30,945	(NA)
Hydrogen.................................	(NA)	(NA)	14	58	53	51	39	(NA)

– Represents zero. NA Not available. [1] Dedicated and bi-fuel vehicles. [2] Electric vehicles include plug-in hybrid-electric vehicles but do not include neighborhood electric vehicles, low-speed electric vehicles, or two-wheeled electric vehicles. [3] Stations selling biodiesel blends less than B20 are only included in the 2005-2007 station counts. [4] Beginning 2011, electric stations are counted by the plug rather than by the geographical location. This is different from the other fuels, which count only the geographical location regardless of how many dispensers or nozzles are on site.

Source: U.S. Department of Energy, Office of Energy Efficiency and Renewable Energy, *Transportation Energy Data Book*, Edition 35, October 2016. See also <http://cta.ornl.gov/data>

Table 1122. Traffic Fatalities—Number and Rate by State: 2000 to 2015

[For deaths within 30 days of the accident]

State	2000	2010	2014	2015	Fatality rate [1] 2010	2015	State	2000	2010	2014	2015	Fatality rate [1] 2010	2015
U.S.....	41,945	32,999	32,675	35,092	1.11	1.13	MO......	1,157	821	766	869	1.16	1.21
AL.......	996	862	820	849	1.34	1.26	MT......	237	189	192	224	1.69	1.81
AK.......	106	56	73	65	1.17	1.29	NE.....	276	190	225	246	0.98	1.22
AZ.......	1,036	759	770	893	1.27	1.37	NV.....	323	257	290	325	1.16	1.25
AR.......	652	571	466	531	1.70	1.52	NH.....	126	128	95	114	0.98	0.87
CA.......	3,753	2,720	3,074	3,176	0.84	0.95	NJ......	731	556	556	562	0.76	0.75
CO.......	681	450	488	546	0.96	1.08	NM.....	432	349	383	298	1.38	1.09
CT.......	341	320	248	266	1.02	0.84	NY......	1,460	1,201	1,039	1,121	0.92	0.88
DE.......	123	101	121	126	1.13	1.27	NC.....	1,557	1,320	1,284	1,379	1.29	1.23
DC.......	48	24	23	23	0.67	0.65	ND.....	86	105	135	131	1.27	1.31
FL.......	2,999	2,444	2,494	2,939	1.25	1.42	OH.....	1,366	1,080	1,006	1,110	0.97	0.98
GA.......	1,541	1,247	1,164	1,430	1.12	1.21	OK.....	650	668	669	643	1.40	1.35
HI.......	132	113	95	94	1.13	0.91	OR.....	451	317	357	447	0.94	1.24
ID.......	276	209	186	216	1.32	1.30	PA.....	1,520	1,324	1,195	1,200	1.32	1.19
IL.......	1,418	927	924	998	0.88	0.95	RI.....	80	67	52	45	0.81	0.57
IN........	886	754	746	821	1.00	1.04	SC.....	1,065	809	824	977	1.65	1.89
IA........	445	390	321	320	1.24	0.96	SD.....	173	140	136	133	1.58	1.43
KS.......	461	431	385	355	1.44	1.13	TN.....	1,307	1,032	962	958	1.47	1.25
KY.......	820	760	672	761	1.58	1.56	TX.....	3,779	3,023	3,538	3,516	1.29	1.36
LA.......	938	721	737	726	1.59	1.51	UT......	373	253	256	276	0.95	0.93
ME......	169	161	131	156	1.11	1.07	VT......	76	71	44	57	0.98	0.78
MD......	588	496	442	513	0.88	0.89	VA.....	929	740	703	753	0.90	0.91
MA......	433	347	328	306	0.64	0.52	WA.....	631	460	462	568	0.80	0.95
MI.......	1,382	942	901	963	0.97	0.98	WV.....	411	315	272	268	1.64	1.35
MN......	625	411	361	411	0.73	0.72	WI.....	799	572	507	566	0.96	0.91
MS......	949	641	607	677	1.61	1.70	WY......	152	155	150	145	1.66	1.51

[1] Deaths per 100 million vehicle miles traveled.

Source: U.S. National Highway Traffic Safety Administration, *Traffic Safety Facts 2015*, DOT-HS-812-384, 2017. See also <https://www.nhtsa.gov/research-data>.

Table 1123. Motor Vehicle Occupants and Nonoccupants Killed and Injured: 1990 to 2015

[Injuries in thousands (3,231 represents 3,231,000). For deaths within 30 days of the accident]

Year	Total	Occupants Total	Passenger cars	Light trucks [1]	Large trucks [1]	Buses	Other/ unknown [2]	Motorcycle occupants [3]	Nonoccupants Total	Pedestrian	Pedalcyclist	Other/ unknown [2]
KILLED												
1990................	44,599	33,890	24,092	8,601	705	32	460	3,244	7,465	6,482	859	124
2000................	41,945	33,451	20,699	11,526	754	22	450	2,897	5,597	4,763	693	141
2001................	42,196	33,243	20,320	11,723	708	34	458	3,197	5,756	4,901	732	123
2002................	43,005	34,105	20,569	12,274	689	45	528	3,270	5,630	4,851	665	114
2003................	42,884	33,627	19,725	12,546	726	41	589	3,714	5,543	4,774	629	140
2004................	42,836	33,276	19,192	12,674	766	42	602	4,028	5,532	4,675	727	130
2005................	43,510	33,070	18,512	13,037	804	58	659	4,576	5,864	4,892	786	186
2006................	42,708	32,119	17,925	12,761	805	27	601	4,837	5,752	4,795	772	185
2007................	41,259	30,527	16,614	12,458	805	36	614	5,174	5,558	4,699	701	158
2008................	37,423	26,791	14,646	10,816	682	67	580	5,312	5,320	4,414	718	188
2009................	33,883	24,526	13,135	10,312	499	26	554	4,469	4,888	4,109	628	151
2010................	32,999	23,371	12,491	9,782	530	44	524	4,518	5,110	4,302	623	185
2011................	32,479	22,510	12,014	9,302	640	55	499	4,630	5,339	4,457	682	200
2012................	33,782	23,017	12,361	9,418	697	39	502	4,986	5,779	4,818	734	227
2013................	32,893	22,483	12,037	9,186	695	54	511	4,692	5,718	4,779	749	190
2014................	32,744	22,307	11,947	9,103	656	44	557	4,594	5,843	4,910	729	204
2015................	35,092	23,695	12,628	9,813	667	49	538	4,976	6,421	5,376	818	227
INJURED (1,000)												
1990................	3,231	2,960	2,376	505	42	33	4	84	187	105	75	7
2000................	3,189	2,997	2,052	887	31	18	10	58	134	78	51	5
2001................	3,033	2,841	1,927	861	29	15	9	60	131	78	45	8
2002................	2,926	2,735	1,805	879	26	19	6	65	126	71	48	7
2003................	2,889	2,697	1,756	889	27	18	7	67	124	70	46	8
2004................	2,788	2,594	1,643	900	27	16	7	76	118	68	41	9
2005................	2,699	2,494	1,573	872	27	11	10	87	118	64	45	8
2006................	2,575	2,375	1,475	857	23	10	11	88	112	61	44	7
2007................	2,491	2,264	1,379	841	23	12	8	103	124	70	43	10
2008................	2,346	2,120	1,304	768	23	15	9	96	130	69	52	9
2009................	2,217	2,011	1,216	759	17	12	7	90	116	59	51	7
2010................	2,239	2,027	1,253	733	20	17	5	82	130	70	52	8
2011................	2,217	2,010	1,240	728	23	13	6	81	126	69	48	9
2012................	2,362	2,134	1,328	762	25	12	6	93	136	76	49	10
2013................	2,313	2,099	1,296	750	24	23	5	88	125	66	48	11
2014................	2,338	2,121	1,292	782	27	14	6	92	125	65	50	10
2015................	2,443	2,230	1,378	803	30	12	8	88	125	70	45	10

[1] See footnotes 2 and 3, Table 1125. [2] Includes combination trucks. [3] Includes mopeds, three wheel motorcycles, off-road motorcycles, etc.

Source: U.S. National Highway Traffic Safety Administration, *Traffic Safety Facts 2015*, DOT-HS-812-384, 2017. See also <https://www.nhtsa.gov/research-data>.

Table 1124. Fatal Motor Vehicle Accidents—National Summary: 2000 to 2015

[Based on data from the Fatality Analysis Reporting System (FARS). FARS gathers data on accidents that result in loss of human life. FARS is operated and maintained by National Highway Traffic Safety Administration's (NHTSA), National Center for Statistics and Analysis (NCSA). FARS data are gathered on motor vehicle accidents that occurred on a roadway customarily open to the public, resulting in the death of a person within 30 days of the accident. Collection of these data depend on the use of police, hospital, medical examiner/coroner, and Emergency Medical Services reports; state vehicle registration, driver licensing, and highway department files; and vital statistics documents and death certificates. See source for further detail]

Item	2000	2005	2010	2011	2012	2013	2014	2015
Fatal crashes, total...............................	**37,526**	**39,252**	**30,296**	**29,867**	**31,006**	**30,203**	**30,056**	**32,166**
One vehicle involved............................	21,117	22,678	18,156	17,991	18,705	18,074	17,885	18,683
Two or more vehicles involved..................	16,409	16,574	12,040	11,766	12,095	11,983	12,104	13,483
Occupants involved..............................	94,325	94,614	68,927	67,143	69,531	67,514	66,971	73,390
Drivers involved.................................	57,280	59,220	44,599	43,840	45,664	44,803	44,671	48,613
Persons killed in fatal crashes [1]...............	**41,945**	**43,510**	**32,999**	**32,479**	**33,782**	**32,893**	**32,744**	**35,092**
Occupants...	33,451	33,070	23,371	22,510	23,017	22,483	22,307	23,695
Drivers..	22,914	23,237	16,864	16,474	16,838	16,520	16,470	17,466
Passengers......................................	10,451	9,750	6,451	5,972	6,106	5,896	5,766	6,158
Other...	86	83	56	64	73	67	71	71
Motorcyclists....................................	2,897	4,576	4,518	4,630	4,986	4,692	4,594	4,976
Nonoccupants....................................	5,597	5,864	5,110	5,339	5,779	5,718	5,843	6,421
Pedestrians.....................................	4,763	4,892	4,302	4,457	4,818	4,779	4,910	5,376
Pedalcyclists....................................	693	786	623	682	734	749	729	818
Other..	141	186	185	200	227	190	204	227
Occupants killed by vehicle type:								
Passenger cars.................................	20,699	18,512	12,491	12,014	12,361	12,037	11,947	12,628
Mini-compact (95 inches)....................	1,113	452	171	185	188	159	145	125
Subcompact (95 to 99 inches)...............	3,660	2,536	1,252	1,166	1,156	1,047	924	988
Compact (100 to 104 inches)................	7,022	6,288	3,954	3,789	3,834	3,610	3,430	3,457
Intermediate (105 to 109) inches............	5,204	5,571	4,227	4,050	4,050	4,083	4,323	4,490
Full-size (110 to 114) inches................	2,287	2,491	1,982	1,958	2,098	2,108	2,094	2,295
Largest (115 inches and over)...............	897	796	681	669	751	722	736	770
Unknown.......................................	516	378	168	164	194	248	274	503
Motorcycles and other motorized cycles......	2,897	4,576	4,518	4,630	4,986	4,692	4,586	4,976
Motorcycles....................................	2,783	4,418	4,266	4,343	4,623	4,336	4,263	4,652
Other motorized cycles.......................	114	158	236	269	334	332	323	324
Light trucks [2]...................................	11,526	13,037	9,782	9,302	9,418	9,186	9,103	9,813
Pickup..	6,003	6,067	4,486	4,270	4,343	4,171	4,248	4,449
Utility...	3,358	4,831	3,942	3,884	3,885	3,811	3,796	4,182
Van..	2,129	2,112	1,346	1,128	1,167	1,136	1,020	1,116
Other..	36	27	8	20	23	37	32	66
Large trucks [3]................................	754	804	530	640	697	695	656	667
Buses...	22	58	44	55	39	54	44	49
Other/unknown vehicles.......................	450	659	524	499	502	511	557	538
Percent distribution of fatal accidents by the highest driver BAC in accident: [6]								
0.00 percent....................................	62.7	63.3	64.0	64.0	64.0	63.0	64.0	65.0
0.01 to 0.07 percent............................	5.6	5.4	5.0	5.0	5.0	6.0	5.0	5.0
0.08 percent and over...........................	31.4	31.1	31.0	30.0	31.0	31.0	30.0	29.0
Fatalities per 100,000 resident population								
Under 5 years old..............................	3.70	2.94	1.99	1.79	2.03	1.99	1.71	1.87
5 to 9 years old.................................	3.55	3.00	1.73	1.69	1.68	1.66	1.71	1.72
10 to 15 years old..............................	5.65	4.67	2.70	2.56	2.47	2.35	2.26	2.42
16 to 20 years old..............................	29.38	27.48	15.45	15.44	14.82	13.79	14.06	14.67
21 to 24 years old..............................	27.02	27.73	19.43	18.69	19.05	18.06	17.80	18.58
25 to 34 years old..............................	17.29	17.82	13.43	13.15	13.95	13.39	13.37	14.23
35 to 44 years old..............................	15.08	15.08	11.07	10.64	11.19	10.82	10.42	11.46
45 to 54 years old..............................	13.79	14.59	11.28	11.35	11.71	11.31	11.29	12.17
55 to 64 years old..............................	13.61	13.88	10.90	10.45	11.14	11.03	10.95	11.71
65 to 74 years old..............................	15.29	15.16	10.89	11.26	11.22	10.87	10.40	11.31
75 years old and over..........................	23.29	20.47	16.70	15.18	14.97	15.04	14.94	15.09
Fatalities per 100 million VMT [4]..................	1.53	1.46	1.11	1.10	1.14	1.10	1.08	1.13
Fatalities per 100,000 licensed drivers...........	22.00	21.70	15.71	15.33	15.95	15.50	15.29	16.09
VMT per registered vehicle [4].....................	12,657	12,169	11,531	11,130	11,176	11,096	11,010	11,003
Fatalities per 100,000 registered vehicles.......	19.33	17.71	12.82	12.25	12.72	12.21	11.92	12.47
Fatal crashes per 100 million VMT [4].............	1.37	1.31	1.02	1.01	1.04	1.01	1.01	0.96
Fatalities per 100,000 resident population.......	14.87	14.72	10.67	10.42	10.76	10.40	10.27	10.92
Vehicle miles traveled (VMT) (bil.)..............	2,747	2,989	2,967	2,950	2,970	2,988	3,026	3,095
Licensed drivers (1,000)........................	190,625	200,549	210,115	211,875	211,815	212,160	214,092	218,084
Registered vehicles (1,000) [5]..................	217,028	245,628	257,312	265,043	265,647	269,294	274,805	281,312

[1] Deaths within 30 days of the accident. Starting with 1995, total does not include motorcyclist data. [2] Trucks with a gross vehicle weight rating of 10,000 pounds or less, including pickups, vans, truck-based station wagons, and utility vehicles. [3] Trucks with a gross vehicle weight rating of over 10,000 pounds. [4] VMT = vehicle miles of travel. [5] Data on motor vehicle registrations for 2011 and beyond are not strictly comparable to data for prior years due to methodology changes. See source for details. [6] BAC = blood alcohol concentration.

Source: National Highway Traffic Safety Administration, *Traffic Safety Facts, 2015*, and earlier reports; and "Fatality Analysis Reporting System," <http://www.nhtsa.gov/FARS>, accessed September 2017.

Table 1125. Vehicles Involved in Crashes by Vehicle Type, Rollover Occurrence, and Crash Severity: 2015

[Excludes motorcycles]

Crash severity by vehicle type	Total Number	Rollover occurrence Yes Number	Yes Percent	No Number	No Percent
Vehicles involved in all crashes [1]	**11,172,000**	**210,000**	**1.9**	**10,962,000**	**98.1**
Passenger cars	6,243,000	86,000	1.4	6,157,000	98.6
Light trucks: [2]					
Pickup	1,508,000	43,000	2.8	1,465,000	97.2
Utility	2,255,000	57,000	2.5	2,198,000	97.5
Van	616,000	9,000	1.4	608,000	98.6
Other	35,000	1,000	3.1	34,000	96.9
Large truck [3]	433,000	12,000	2.7	421,000	97.3
Bus	68,000	(Z)	(Z)	68,000	100.0
Other/unknown	15,000	3,000	20.5	12,000	79.5
Fatal crashes	**43,847**	**7,947**	**18.1**	**35,900**	**81.9**
Passenger cars	19,534	2,676	13.7	16,858	86.3
Light trucks: [2]					
Pickup	8,698	2,066	23.8	6,632	76.2
Utility	7,636	2,058	27.0	5,578	73.0
Van	2,172	309	14.2	1,863	85.8
Other	169	29	17.2	140	82.8
Large truck [3]	4,050	533	13.2	3,517	86.8
Bus	261	8	3.1	253	96.9
Other/unknown	1,327	268	20.2	1,059	79.8
Injury crashes	**3,092,000**	**121,000**	**3.9**	**2,971,000**	**96.1**
Passenger cars	1,785,000	49,000	2.8	1,736,000	97.2
Light trucks: [2]					
Pickup	398,000	23,000	5.7	376,000	94.3
Utility	617,000	34,000	5.5	583,000	94.5
Van	175,000	5,000	2.9	170,000	97.1
Other	7,000	(Z)	4.0	7,000	96.0
Large truck [3]	87,000	6,000	7.3	81,000	92.7
Bus	15,000	(Z)	(Z)	15,000	100.0
Other/unknown	7,000	3,000	42.2	4,000	57.8

Z less than 500 or 0.05 percent. [1] Includes property-only crashes, not shown separately. [2] Light trucks of 10,000 pounds gross vehicle weight rating or less, including pickups, vans, truck-based station wagons and utility vehicles. [3] Large trucks over 10,000 pounds gross vehicle weight rating.

Source: U.S. National Highway Traffic Safety Administration, *Traffic Safety Facts 2015*, DOT-HS-812-384, 2017. See also <https://www.nhtsa.gov/research-data>.

Table 1126. Distracted Drivers—Crashes, Road Fatalities, and Injuries: 2009 to 2015

["Distraction" is defined as a specific type of inattention that occurs when drivers divert their attention from the driving task to focus on some other activity instead. "Distraction" is a subset of "inattention" (which also includes fatigue and physical and emotional conditions of the driver). For more information, including revision in coding of "distracted driving," see appendix in source report]

Description	2009	2010	2011	2012	2013	2014	2015
FATAL CRASHES [1]							
Total	30,797	30,196	29,867	31,006	30,202	30,056	32,166
Drivers involved	45,230	44,440	43,668	45,337	44,574	44,583	48,613
Fatalities	33,808	32,885	32,367	33,561	32,719	32,675	35,092
Crashes involving driver distraction [2]	**4,898**	**2,993**	**3,047**	**3,098**	**2,923**	**2,972**	**3,196**
Percent	16	10	10	10	10	10	10
Involving cell phone use	(NA)	366	354	380	411	387	442
Percent	(NA)	12	12	12	14	13	14
Drivers involved	5,084	2,912	3,085	3,119	2,959	3,000	3,263
Percent	11	7	7	7	7	7	7
Fatalities	5,474	3,092	3,331	3,328	3,154	3,179	3,477
Percent	16	9	10	10	10	10	10
INJURY CRASHES (ESTIMATED) [3]							
Total	1,517,000	1,542,000	1,530,000	1,634,000	1,591,000	1,648,000	1,715,000
People injured	2,217,000	2,239,000	2,217,000	2,362,000	2,313,000	2,338,000	2,443,000
In crashes involving driver distraction	448,000	416,000	387,000	421,000	424,000	431,000	391,000
Percent of total	20	19	17	18	18	18	16
In crashes involving cell phone use	(NA)	24,000	21,000	28,000	34,000	33,000	30,000
Percent of total distracted	(NA)	6	5	7	8	8	8

NA Not available. [1] Data from NHTSA's Fatality Analysis Reporting System (FARS). [2] For multi-vehicle crashes, the crash was reported as a distracted-driving crash if at least one driver was reported as distracted. In some of these multi-vehicle crashes, multiple drivers were reported as distracted. [3] Data from National Automotive Sampling System (NASS) General Estimates System (GES).

Source: U.S. National Highway Traffic Safety Administration, *Distracted Driving 2015*, March 2017, and earlier reports. See also <https://crashstats.nhtsa.dot.gov> and <https://www.nhtsa.gov/risky-driving/distracted-driving>.

Table 1127. Traffic Fatalities by State and Highest Driver Blood Alcohol Concentration (BAC) in the Crash: 2015

[A crash is a police-reported event that produces injury and/or property damage, involves a vehicle in transport and occurs on a trafficway or while the vehicle is in motion after running off the trafficway. A positive blood alcohol concentration (BAC level of .01 grams per deciliter and higher) indicates that alcohol was consumed by the person tested, and the incident is alcohol related or alcohol involved; a BAC level of .08 g/dL or more indicates that the person was alcohol impaired]

State	Traffic fatalities, total [1]	(BAC=.00)		Alcohol involved driving fatalities (BAC=.01–.07)		Alcohol impaired driving fatalities (BAC=.08 or more)		Total fatalities involving alcohol (BAC=.01 or more)	
		Number	Percent	Number	Percent	Number	Percent	Number	Percent
United States [2]	**35,092**	**22,912**	**65**	**1,808**	**5**	**10,265**	**29**	**12,074**	**34**
Alabama	849	564	66	39	5	247	29	286	34
Alaska	65	41	62	1	2	23	36	24	38
Arizona	893	552	62	50	6	272	31	322	36
Arkansas	531	356	67	26	5	149	28	175	33
California	3,176	2,101	66	156	5	914	29	1,070	34
Colorado	546	368	67	27	5	151	28	178	33
Connecticut	266	147	55	14	5	103	39	117	44
Delaware	126	80	63	4	3	41	33	45	36
District of Columbia	23	14	61	3	13	6	26	9	39
Florida	2,939	1,984	67	144	5	797	27	941	32
Georgia	1,430	1,010	71	54	4	366	26	419	29
Hawaii	94	54	58	6	6	33	35	39	41
Idaho	216	136	63	10	5	70	32	80	37
Illinois	998	633	63	56	6	307	31	363	36
Indiana	821	609	74	34	4	178	22	211	26
Iowa	320	226	71	16	5	78	24	94	29
Kansas	355	257	73	13	4	84	24	97	27
Kentucky	761	535	70	30	4	192	25	223	29
Louisiana	726	439	61	42	6	245	34	287	39
Maine	156	88	56	17	11	52	33	68	44
Maryland	513	316	62	37	7	159	31	196	38
Massachusetts	306	187	61	22	7	96	31	118	39
Michigan	963	649	67	47	5	267	28	314	33
Minnesota	411	262	64	29	7	115	28	144	35
Mississippi	677	465	69	37	5	175	26	212	31
Missouri	869	604	69	40	5	224	26	264	30
Montana	224	130	58	18	8	75	34	93	41
Nebraska	246	160	65	18	7	65	26	83	34
Nevada	325	210	65	17	5	97	30	114	35
New Hampshire	114	72	63	8	7	33	29	41	36
New Jersey	562	423	75	28	5	111	20	139	25
New Mexico	298	190	64	11	4	98	33	109	36
New York	1,121	748	67	60	5	311	28	370	33
North Carolina	1,379	902	65	65	5	411	30	476	35
North Dakota	131	67	51	11	8	50	38	61	46
Ohio	1,110	744	67	51	5	313	28	363	33
Oklahoma	643	441	69	31	5	170	27	201	31
Oregon	447	262	59	29	7	155	35	184	41
Pennsylvania	1,200	784	65	46	4	364	30	409	34
Rhode Island	45	22	49	4	8	19	43	23	51
South Carolina	977	633	65	42	4	301	31	343	35
South Dakota	133	86	65	3	2	43	33	46	35
Tennessee	958	655	68	48	5	252	26	300	31
Texas	3,516	1,954	56	229	7	1,323	38	1,552	44
Utah	276	222	80	10	4	43	16	53	19
Vermont	57	40	71	1	1	15	27	16	28
Virginia	753	498	66	46	6	208	28	254	34
Washington	568	380	67	39	7	148	26	187	33
West Virginia	268	185	69	12	4	71	27	83	31
Wisconsin	566	345	61	29	5	189	33	217	38
Wyoming	145	85	58	4	3	56	38	60	42
Puerto Rico	309	183	59	22	7	104	34	126	41

[1] Total fatalities include those in which there was no driver or motorcycle rider present. [2] U.S. total excludes Puerto Rico.

Source: U.S. National Highway Traffic Safety Administration, *Traffic Safety Facts 2015*, DOT-HS-812-384, 2017. See also <https://www.nhtsa.gov/research-data>.

Table 1128. Alcohol Involvement for Drivers in Fatal Crashes: 2000 to 2015

[BAC = blood alcohol concentration. NHTSA estimates alcohol involvement when alcohol test results are unknown, see source for more information]

Age, sex, and vehicle type	2000 Total drivers in fatal crashes	2000 Percent with .08% BAC or greater	2010 Total drivers in fatal crashes	2010 Percent with .08% BAC or greater	2013 Total drivers in fatal crashes	2013 Percent with .08% BAC or greater	2014 Total drivers in fatal crashes	2014 Percent with .08% BAC or greater	2015 Total drivers in fatal crashes	2015 Percent with .08% BAC or greater
Total drivers involved in fatal crashes [1]	**57,280**	**21**	**44,599**	**22**	**44,803**	**21**	**44,671**	**21**	**48,613**	**20**
Drivers by age group:										
Under 16 years old	320	10	159	6	139	7	137	6	154	10
16 to 20 years old	8,024	18	4,505	18	3,908	17	3,815	17	4,214	16
21 to 24 years old	5,950	32	4,608	34	4,630	32	4,664	30	4,942	28
25 to 34 years old	11,739	28	8,567	30	8,808	30	8,992	29	9,860	27
35 to 44 years old	11,132	26	7,333	25	7,220	24	6,910	24	7,675	23
45 to 54 years old	8,234	18	7,517	21	7,376	20	7,370	20	7,852	19
55 to 64 years old	4,766	12	5,577	14	5,947	14	6,004	16	6,453	14
65 to 74 years old	3,134	8	2,902	8	3,373	8	3,316	10	3,767	9
75 years old and over	3,147	4	2,688	4	2,586	5	2,650	5	2,723	6
Drivers by sex:										
Male	41,795	24	32,079	24	32,608	23	32,630	23	35,472	21
Female	14,790	13	11,859	15	11,429	14	11,293	15	12,220	14
Drivers by vehicle type:										
Passenger cars	27,661	24	17,710	24	17,850	23	17,802	22	19,413	21
Light trucks [2]	20,393	22	17,385	22	16,810	21	17,040	22	18,570	20
Large trucks [3]	4,948	1	3,456	1	3,872	2	3,702	2	3,996	2
Motorcycles	2,971	32	4,647	28	4,795	27	4,703	29	5,071	27

[1] Includes age and sex unknown, and other and unknown types of vehicles. [2] See footnote 2, Table 1125. [3] See footnote 3, Table 1125.

Source: U.S. National Highway Traffic Safety Administration, *Traffic Safety Facts 2015*, DOT-HS-812-384, 2017, and earlier reports. See also <https://www.nhtsa.gov/research-data>.

Table 1129. Fatalities by Highest Driver Blood Alcohol Concentration (BAC) in the Crash: 2000 to 2015

[A motor vehicle crash is alcohol impaired if at least one driver involved in the crash is determined to have a BAC of .08 gram per deciliter (g/dl) or higher. Thus, any fatality that occurs in an alcohol impaired crash is considered an alcohol impaired driving fatality. A person is considered to be legally impaired with a BAC of .08 g/dl or more. See source for more information]

Item	2000	2005	2010	2011	2012	2013	2014	2015
Total fatalities [1]	**41,945**	**43,510**	**32,999**	**32,479**	**33,782**	**32,893**	**32,744**	**35,092**
BAC=.00								
Number	26,082	27,423	21,005	20,848	21,563	20,865	20,913	22,912
Percent	62.2	63.0	63.7	64.2	63.8	63.4	63.9	65.3
BAC=.01–.07								
Number	2,422	2,404	1,771	1,662	1,782	1,834	1,800	1,808
Percent	5.8	5.5	5.4	5.1	5.3	5.6	5.5	5.2
Alcohol impaired driving fatalities: BAC=.08 or more								
Number	13,324	13,582	10,136	9,865	10,336	10,084	9,943	10,265
Percent	31.8	31.2	30.7	30.4	30.6	30.7	30.4	29.3

[1] Total fatalities include those in which there was no driver or motorcycle rider present.

Source: U.S. National Highway Traffic Safety Administration, *Traffic Safety Facts 2015*, DOT-HS-812-384, 2017. See also <https://www.nhtsa.gov/research-data>.

Table 1130. Motor Vehicle Crashes by Crash Severity: 2000 to 2015

[6,394 represents 6,394,000. A crash is a police-reported event that produces injury and/or property damage, involves a vehicle in transport, and occurs on a trafficway or while the vehicle is in motion after running off the trafficway. A fatal crash involves at least 1 person dying within 30 days of the crash]

Item	2000	2005	2009	2010	2011	2012	2013	2014	2015
Crashes (1,000)	**6,394**	**6,159**	**5,505**	**5,419**	**5,338**	**5,615**	**5,687**	**6,064**	**6,296**
Fatal	37.5	39.3	30.8	30.3	29.9	31.0	30.2	30.1	32.2
Nonfatal injury	2,070	1,816	1,517	1,542	1,530	1,634	1,591	1,648	1,715
Property damage only	4,286	4,304	3,957	3,847	3,778	3,950	4,066	4,387	4,548
Percent of total crashes:									
Fatal	0.6	0.6	0.6	0.6	0.6	0.6	0.5	0.5	0.5
Nonfatal injury	32.4	29.5	27.6	28.5	28.7	29.1	28.0	27.2	27.2
Property damage only	67.0	69.9	71.9	71.0	70.8	70.3	71.5	72.3	72.2

Source: U.S. National Highway Traffic Safety Administration, *Traffic Safety Facts 2015*, DOT-HS-812-384, 2017. See also <https://www.nhtsa.gov/research-data>.

Table 1131. Motor Vehicle Crashes—Number and Deaths: 2000 to 2015

[6,394 represents 6,394,000]

Item	Unit	2000	2005	2010	2011	2012	2013	2014	2015
CRASHES									
Total [1]	1,000	6,394	6,159	5,419	5,338	5,615	5,687	6,064	6,296
Fatal	1,000	37.5	39.3	30.3	29.9	31.0	30.2	30.1	32.2
Injury	1,000	2,070	1,816	1,542	1,530	1,634	1,591	1,648	1,715
Property damage only	1,000	4,286	4,304	3,847	3,778	3,950	4,066	4,387	4,548
DEATHS									
Deaths within 30 days of crash	1,000	41.9	43.5	33.0	32.5	33.8	32.9	32.7	35.1
Occupants	1,000	33.5	33.1	23.4	22.5	23.0	22.5	22.3	23.7
Passenger cars	1,000	20.7	18.5	12.5	12.0	12.4	12.0	11.9	12.6
Light trucks [2]	1,000	11.5	13.0	9.8	9.3	9.4	9.2	9.1	9.8
Large trucks [2]	1,000	0.8	0.8	0.5	0.6	0.7	0.7	0.7	0.7
Buses	1,000	(Z)	0.1	(Z)	0.1	(Z)	0.1	(Z)	(Z)
Other/unknown	1,000	0.5	0.7	0.5	0.5	0.5	0.5	0.6	0.5
Motorcycle riders [3]	1,000	2.9	4.6	4.5	4.6	5.0	4.7	4.6	5.0
Nonoccupants	1,000	5.6	5.9	5.1	5.3	5.8	5.7	5.8	6.4
Pedestrians	1,000	4.8	4.9	4.3	4.5	4.8	4.8	4.9	5.4
Pedalcyclist	1,000	0.7	0.8	0.6	0.7	0.7	0.7	0.7	0.8
Other/unknown	1,000	0.1	0.2	0.2	0.2	0.2	0.2	0.2	0.2
TRAFFIC DEATH RATES [4]									
Per 100 million vehicle miles	Rate	1.5	1.5	1.1	1.1	1.1	1.1	1.1	1.1
Per 100,000 licensed drivers	Rate	22.0	21.7	15.7	15.3	16.0	15.5	15.3	16.1
Per 100,000 registered vehicles	Rate	19.3	17.7	12.8	12.3	12.7	12.2	11.9	12.5
Per 100,000 resident population	Rate	14.9	14.7	10.7	10.4	10.8	10.4	10.3	10.9

(Z) Represents less than 50 deaths. [1] Covers police-reported accidents in which at least one person dies within 30 days of the crash; or no one dies but at least one person is injured; or no one is injured but property damage has occurred. [2] See footnotes 2 and 3 in Table 1125. [3] Includes motor scooters, minibikes, and mopeds. [4] Based on 30-day definition of traffic deaths.

Source: U.S. National Highway Traffic Safety Administration, *Traffic Safety Facts, 2015*, DOT-HS-812-384, 2017. See also <http://www.nhtsa.gov/NCSA>.

Table 1132. Licensed Drivers and Number in Fatal Accidents by Age and Sex: 2015

[107,650 represents 107,650,000]

Age group	Licensed drivers (1,000)			Drivers in fatal accidents			Accident rates per number of drivers [2]	
	Male	Female	Both sexes	Male	Female	Both sexes [1]	Male	Female
Total	107,650	110,435	218,084	35,472	12,220	48,613	33.0	11.1
19 years old and under	4,361	4,229	8,591	2,234	1,006	3,243	51.2	23.8
Under 16 years old	32	33	65	111	41	154	341.6	125.7
16 years old	527	538	1,065	248	139	387	47.0	25.9
17 years old	967	954	1,920	426	225	651	44.1	23.6
18 years old	1,305	1,246	2,550	658	297	955	50.4	23.8
19 years old	1,530	1,460	2,990	791	304	1,096	51.7	20.8
20 to 24 years old	8,914	8,717	17,630	4,458	1,606	6,067	50.0	18.4
20 years old	1,645	1,579	3,224	791	334	1,125	48.1	21.2
21 years old	1,708	1,661	3,368	889	311	1,203	52.1	18.7
22 years old	1,791	1,740	3,532	944	333	1,277	52.7	19.1
23 years old	1,857	1,831	3,688	914	328	1,242	49.2	17.9
24 years old	1,912	1,906	3,818	920	300	1,220	48.1	15.7
25 to 29 years old	9,600	9,666	19,266	4,032	1,327	5,361	42.0	13.7
30 to 34 years old	9,484	9,636	19,120	3,323	1,174	4,499	35.0	12.2
35 to 39 years old	8,948	9,139	18,088	2,944	1,035	3,980	32.9	11.3
40 to 44 years old	8,976	9,131	18,107	2,794	901	3,695	31.1	9.9
45 to 49 years old	9,440	9,548	18,988	2,887	856	3,743	30.6	9.0
50 to 54 years old	10,130	10,358	20,488	3,134	975	4,109	30.9	9.4
55 to 59 years old	9,859	10,209	20,068	2,850	823	3,676	28.9	8.1
60 to 64 years old	8,621	9,026	17,647	2,116	657	2,777	24.5	7.3
65 to 69 years old	7,218	7,571	14,788	1,657	577	2,235	23.0	7.6
70 to 74 years old	4,975	5,257	10,232	1,120	412	1,532	22.5	7.8
75 to 79 years old	3,267	3,567	6,834	737	351	1,088	22.6	9.8
80 to 84 years old	2,157	2,364	4,521	585	268	853	27.1	11.3
85 and over	1,700	2,017	3,716	537	245	782	31.6	12.1

[1] Total includes unknown/unreported instances. [2] Per 100,000 male or female licensed drivers. Rates for drivers 19 years old and under are likely overstated because of a higher proportion of unlicensed drivers.

Source: U.S. Federal Highway Administration, "Highway Statistics 2015," <http://www.fhwa.dot.gov/policy/ohpi/hss/index.cfm>; and National Highway Traffic Safety Administration, "Fatality Analysis Reporting System," <http://www.nhtsa.gov/FARS>; accessed September 2017.

Table 1133. Speeding-Related Traffic Fatalities by Road Type and State: 2015

[Speeding consists of exceeding the posted speed limit or driving too fast for the road conditions or any speed-related violation charged (racing, driving above speed limit, speed greater than reasonable, exceeding special speed limit)]

State	Traffic fatalities, total	Total[2]	Interstate		Non-interstate				
			Rural	Urban	Freeway and expressway	Other principal arterial	Minor arterial	Collector	Local
United States [1]	**35,092**	**9,557**	**537**	**754**	**527**	**2,168**	**1,631**	**1,658**	**1,594**
Alabama	849	236	10	6	1	35	54	66	36
Alaska	65	22	7	4	–	2	1	6	1
Arizona	893	307	37	23	18	83	57	38	51
Arkansas	531	90	4	5	7	17	15	12	30
California	3,176	955	51	127	203	206	172	123	72
Colorado	546	216	20	17	5	77	32	38	26
Connecticut	266	73	1	11	10	12	21	8	9
Delaware	126	34	–	–	–	6	2	12	5
District of Columbia	23	7	–	1	–	–	–	–	6
Florida	2,939	320	7	8	5	80	16	2	45
Georgia	1,430	268	6	26	5	48	54	61	68
Hawaii	94	40	–	4	–	25	11	–	–
Idaho	216	49	7	1	–	9	6	12	3
Illinois	998	369	17	42	2	94	78	74	62
Indiana	821	232	18	15	1	43	39	55	61
Iowa	320	49	2	2	1	13	9	9	13
Kansas	355	128	5	6	3	39	16	24	35
Kentucky	761	140	7	2	7	19	25	60	20
Louisiana	726	165	12	9	1	35	27	44	35
Maine	156	60	2	–	1	8	3	27	19
Maryland	513	121	–	11	1	4	11	9	7
Massachusetts	306	80	–	12	1	24	17	12	14
Michigan	963	264	19	15	16	52	61	45	55
Minnesota	411	82	5	1	1	11	25	23	16
Mississippi	677	96	1	3	1	10	35	22	24
Missouri	869	310	17	26	24	57	47	70	69
Montana	224	91	11	–	1	22	7	26	23
Nebraska	246	37	2	2	2	12	10	–	9
Nevada	325	111	6	12	7	26	37	8	13
New Hampshire	114	56	1	7	1	18	5	7	17
New Jersey	562	128	–	7	17	27	38	20	2
New Mexico	298	130	12	12	4	31	20	14	24
New York	1,121	343	12	21	17	80	39	25	149
North Carolina	1,379	547	24	30	17	275	33	49	119
North Dakota	131	43	2	–	1	15	12	6	7
Ohio	1,110	207	4	11	10	20	47	67	46
Oklahoma	643	171	9	11	6	28	22	40	55
Oregon	447	118	11	4	–	32	21	35	15
Pennsylvania	1,200	540	23	37	10	109	100	89	146
Rhode Island	45	20	1	3	4	5	3	–	4
South Carolina	977	361	47	17	16	63	119	59	40
South Dakota	133	31	6	3	–	9	2	8	3
Tennessee	958	187	4	26	1	31	43	45	37
Texas	3,516	1,105	78	130	80	214	125	151	–
Utah	276	58	4	11	4	15	2	12	6
Vermont	57	21	–	2	–	6	1	9	3
Virginia	753	104	4	6	4	28	25	25	8
Washington	568	156	6	15	7	26	27	47	27
West Virginia	268	66	2	6	2	8	17	16	15
Wisconsin	566	167	10	3	2	44	38	39	31
Wyoming	145	46	3	1	–	15	4	9	13
Puerto Rico	309	118	7	11	1	35	36	23	5

– Represents zero. [1] U.S. totals do not include Puerto Rico. [2] Includes fatalities that occurred on roads for which the type was unknown.

Source: U.S. National Highway Traffic Safety Administration, *Traffic Safety Facts 2015*, DOT-HS-812-384, 2017. See also <https://www.nhtsa.gov/research-data>.

Table 1134. Roadway Traffic Congestion by Urbanized Area: 2014

[15,142 represents 15,142,000. Various federal, state, and local information sources were used to develop the database with the primary source being the Federal Highway Administration's Highway Performance Monitoring System]

Urbanized area	Daily vehicle miles of travel (1,000)		Annual person hours of delay		Annual congestion cost [1]		
	Freeway	Arterial streets	Total hours (1,000)	Per auto commuter [2]	Delay and fuel cost (million dollars)	Per person (dollars) [2]	Fuel wasted (gal. per person) [2]
U.S., average	**15,142**	**14,786**	**59,767**	**52**	**1,371**	**1,189**	**23**
Akron, OH	5,847	4,493	12,283	27	284	634	15
Albany-Schenectady, NY	7,273	5,623	20,409	42	479	991	21
Albuquerque, NM	4,736	7,834	20,452	36	501	886	19
Allentown, PA-NJ	5,427	5,231	17,114	30	393	694	15
Atlanta, GA	51,003	46,002	148,666	52	3,214	1,130	20
Austin, TX	13,273	11,237	51,116	52	1,140	1,159	22
Baltimore, MD	28,412	19,258	87,620	47	2,075	1,115	21
Birmingham, AL	10,059	7,473	19,385	34	501	891	16
Boston, MA-NH-RI	41,097	36,127	153,994	64	3,363	1,388	30
Bridgeport-Stamford, CT-NY	10,030	5,649	37,119	49	898	1,174	22
Buffalo, NY	6,709	9,164	26,851	40	620	918	21
Charleston-North, Charleston, SC	3,971	6,141	18,422	41	470	1,047	20
Charlotte, NC-SC	12,776	10,348	34,153	43	770	963	17
Chicago, IL-IN	57,279	79,284	302,609	61	7,222	1,445	29
Cincinnati, OH-KY-IN	18,088	15,593	48,485	41	1,159	989	21
Cleveland, OH	18,297	13,364	45,051	38	1,046	887	22
Colorado Springs, CO	4,652	5,366	16,058	35	356	772	17
Columbus OH	16,360	11,421	40,025	41	921	933	20
Dallas-Fort, Worth-Arlington, TX	64,411	41,713	186,535	53	4,202	1,185	22
Dayton, OH	7,006	5,280	14,604	25	346	590	13
Denver-Aurora, CO	21,709	21,048	91,479	49	2,061	1,101	24
Detroit, MI	33,441	44,627	155,358	52	3,514	1,183	25
El Paso, TX-NM	5,777	5,633	19,127	33	439	760	16
Fresno, CA	3,160	7,289	11,823	23	251	495	11
Grand Rapids, MI	5,617	7,539	21,536	39	470	854	19
Hartford, CT	11,022	7,073	28,296	45	656	1,038	21
Honolulu, HI	6,066	3,252	27,672	50	616	1,125	26
Houston, TX	51,673	39,211	203,173	61	4,924	1,490	29
Indianapolis, IN	12,735	16,382	46,435	43	1,142	1,060	23
Jackson, MS	4,602	6,208	12,287	38	282	878	15
Jacksonville, FL	11,801	9,189	29,680	38	659	842	15
Kansas City, MO-KS	22,986	12,479	45,570	39	1,085	933	18
Las Vegas -Henderson, NV	11,297	14,267	63,693	46	1,375	984	21
Los Angeles-Long Beach-Anaheim, CA	121,603	119,049	622,509	80	13,318	1,711	25
Louisville-Jefferson Co., KY-IN	12,020	9,178	35,622	43	860	1,048	22
Memphis, TN-MS-AR	9,339	13,122	37,824	43	939	1,080	21
Miami, FL	40,928	49,525	195,946	52	4,444	1,169	24
Milwaukee, WI	11,170	14,241	37,659	38	984	987	22
Minneapolis-St Paul, MN-WI	30,259	26,451	99,710	47	2,196	1,035	18
Nashville-Davidson, TN	16,339	11,781	38,977	45	1,013	1,168	22
New Haven, CT	7,820	3,929	16,430	40	384	932	19
New Orleans, LA	5,422	8,239	39,159	45	1,014	1,161	22
New York-Newark, NY-NJ-CT	122,655	110,098	628,241	74	14,712	1,739	35
Oklahoma City, OK	11,088	13,287	45,652	49	1,030	1,110	23
Omaha, NE-IA	5,369	5,978	18,224	32	407	707	17
Orlando, FL	12,928	17,251	52,723	46	1,207	1,044	21
Oxnard, CA	2,093	3,255	6,282	23	134	494	8
Philadelphia, PA-NJ-DE-MD	36,224	45,884	157,183	48	3,669	1,112	23
Phoenix-Mesa, AZ	29,548	39,686	155,730	51	3,641	1,201	25
Pittsburgh, PA	9,093	14,740	44,758	39	1,030	889	21
Portland, OR-WA	13,874	13,882	72,341	52	1,763	1,273	29
Providence, RI-MA	11,302	10,286	37,809	43	846	951	21
Raleigh, NC	8,588	10,138	23,128	34	504	734	13
Richmond, VA	11,719	9,492	26,104	34	558	729	14
Riverside-San Bernardino, CA	32,679	17,079	99,058	59	2,201	1,316	18
Sacramento, CA	16,200	17,371	60,220	43	1,334	958	19
Salt Lake City-West Valley City, UT	8,600	8,400	26,925	37	779	1,059	22
San Antonio, TX	21,270	12,956	64,328	44	1,462	1,002	20
San Diego, CA	39,817	22,543	79,412	42	1,658	887	11
San Francisco-Oakland, CA	28,137	24,086	146,013	78	3,143	1,675	33
San Jose, CA	27,553	17,794	104,559	67	2,230	1,422	28
Seattle, WA	28,010	27,708	139,842	63	3,294	1,491	28
St Louis, MO-IL	31,260	19,537	69,350	43	1,637	1,020	21
Tampa-St Petersburg, FL	14,418	27,894	71,628	41	1,589	907	18
Toledo, OH-MI	4,332	4,729	15,905	38	381	920	20
Tucson, AZ	3,826	11,760	35,993	47	856	1,128	23
Tulsa, OK	8,036	9,129	30,341	44	682	984	20
Virginia Beach, VA	13,003	15,875	48,274	45	1,020	953	19
Washington, DC-VA-MD	39,071	45,433	204,375	82	4,560	1,834	35
Worcester, MA	6,107	5,243	13,143	38	302	865	18

[1] Value of extra time (delay) and the extra fuel consumed by vehicles traveling at slower speeds. Fuel cost per gallon is the average price for each state. [2] Per auto commuter data are based on estimated commuters in the urban area.

Source: Texas A&M Transportation Institute, College Station, Texas, *2015 Urban Mobility Report*, August 2015 ©. See also <http://mobility.tamu.edu/ums/>.

Table 1135. Commuting to Work by Transportation Method and State: 2015

[In percent, except as indicated. Workers in thousands (148,324 represents 148,324,000). For workers 16 years old and over. The American Community Survey universe includes the household population and the population living in institutions, college dormitories, and other group quarters. Based on a sample and subject to sampling variability; see Appendix III]

| State | Total workers (1,000) | Percent of workers who commuted to work by— | | | | | | Mean travel time to work (min.) |
| | | Car, truck, or van | | Public transportation [1] | Walking | Taxi, motorcycle, bicycle or other means | Working at home | |
		Drove alone	Car-pooled					
U.S............	148,324	76.6	9.0	5.2	2.8	1.2	4.6	26.4
AL............	2,012	85.5	9.0	0.3	1.1	0.9	3.2	24.6
AK............	363	67.9	12.6	1.5	7.9	4.5	4.4	19.2
AZ............	2,900	77.1	10.6	2.1	2.1	1.6	5.5	25.1
AR............	1,253	82.6	10.8	0.5	1.8	1.2	3.1	22.1
CA............	17,634	73.9	10.0	5.2	2.7	1.5	5.5	28.9
CO............	2,740	76.5	8.4	3.0	2.8	1.0	7.1	25.4
CT............	1,773	78.4	7.8	4.9	3.0	0.8	4.8	26.4
DE............	441	81.4	7.9	2.7	2.2	0.7	4.7	26.0
DC............	358	33.6	5.2	35.8	14.0	1.3	6.0	29.8
FL............	8,880	79.7	8.9	2.2	1.4	1.5	5.6	27.0
GA............	4,555	79.6	9.9	2.3	1.5	1.3	5.1	28.0
HI............	705	67.4	13.5	7.0	4.1	2.4	4.6	27.4
ID............	735	77.1	10.8	0.8	3.2	1.2	6.2	20.5
IL............	6,095	73.6	7.9	9.3	3.0	1.1	4.4	28.8
IN............	3,064	83.1	8.6	1.1	2.3	0.9	3.6	23.3
IA............	1,575	81.0	8.6	1.4	3.4	1.0	4.1	19.0
KS............	1,414	82.6	8.9	0.6	2.3	1.0	4.2	19.0
KY............	1,899	82.1	9.7	1.1	2.5	1.2	3.1	23.3
LA............	2,014	82.8	9.0	1.5	2.0	1.3	2.8	25.3
ME............	636	79.7	8.7	0.6	3.8	1.1	5.7	24.0
MD............	3,001	73.8	8.9	9.0	2.6	1.1	4.4	32.6
MA............	3,451	70.2	7.4	10.6	5.0	1.3	4.8	29.7
MI............	4,420	82.8	8.7	1.3	2.3	0.9	3.6	24.4
MN............	2,861	78.1	8.3	3.6	2.7	0.9	5.5	23.4
MS............	1,194	85.4	9.2	0.3	1.5	1.3	2.1	24.3
MO............	2,853	81.8	8.7	1.6	1.9	1.1	4.8	23.6
MT............	484	74.5	10.4	0.8	5.6	1.1	6.0	18.0
NE............	974	82.0	9.0	0.8	2.8	1.0	3.9	18.4
NV............	1,315	77.8	10.5	3.7	2.2	1.7	3.7	24.2
NH............	696	81.1	7.5	0.9	2.7	1.0	6.5	27.6
NJ............	4,285	71.8	7.5	11.6	3.3	1.4	4.1	31.3
NM............	877	81.4	9.0	0.9	2.3	1.0	4.8	21.7
NY............	9,276	52.7	6.6	28.6	6.3	1.2	4.0	33.1
NC............	4,525	81.4	9.4	1.1	1.8	1.1	5.0	24.3
ND............	404	82.0	8.6	0.4	3.8	0.5	4.5	16.6
OH............	5,381	83.2	7.8	1.8	2.4	0.9	3.7	23.4
OK............	1,740	82.5	10.2	0.4	1.7	1.2	3.7	21.4
OR............	1,840	71.2	10.2	4.8	3.8	1.0	6.3	23.6
PA............	5,978	76.3	8.5	5.7	3.9	0.8	4.2	26.8
RI............	510	79.0	9.7	2.9	3.7	1.0	3.3	24.7
SC............	2,145	83.0	9.3	0.5	2.0	1.2	3.8	24.2
SD............	431	80.6	8.4	0.8	3.1	0.8	5.8	16.9
TN............	2,954	83.9	9.0	0.8	1.2	1.2	3.8	24.8
TX............	12,557	80.8	10.2	1.5	1.6	1.4	4.4	26.3
UT............	1,395	75.8	11.2	2.7	2.8	1.0	5.5	21.3
VT............	320	76.9	8.2	1.3	5.8	0.9	6.1	23.0
VA............	4,116	77.5	9.1	4.7	2.3	1.3	4.6	28.2
WA............	3,371	72.4	9.8	6.2	3.7	1.2	5.6	27.1
WV............	722	82.7	8.7	1.1	2.7	1.3	3.2	25.5
WI............	2,912	81.2	7.9	1.9	3.2	0.9	4.1	22.0
WY............	289	77.3	10.0	2.2	4.6	1.1	4.2	19.0
PR............	999	82.3	8.6	1.9	3.0	1.8	2.2	29.2

[1] Excluding taxicabs.

Source: U.S. Census Bureau, 2015 American Community Survey, B08006, "Sex of Workers by Means of Transportation to Work" and GCT0801, "Mean Travel Time to Work of Workers 16 Years Old and Over Who Did Not Work At Home (Minutes)," <http://factfinder.census.gov>, accessed December 2016.

Table 1136. Passenger Transit Industry—Summary: 1990 to 2013

Table 1136. Passenger Transit Industry—Summary: 1990 to 2013

[16,053 represents $16,053,000,000. Includes Puerto Rico. Includes aggregate information for all transit systems in the United States. Excludes nontransit services such as taxicab, school bus, unregulated jitney (a small bus or automobile that transports passengers on a route for a small fare), sightseeing bus, intercity bus, and special application mass transportation systems (e.g., amusement parks, airports, island, and urban park ferries). Includes active vehicles only]

Item	Unit	1990	2000	2005	2010	2011	2012	2013
Operating systems	Number	5,078	6,000	6,429	7,300	7,100	7,200	6,804
Motor bus systems	Number	2,688	2,262	1,500	1,206	1,175	1,365	1,268
Revenue vehicles, active	Number	93,553	131,918	150,827	174,425	175,258	176,729	178,613
Motor bus	Number	58,714	75,013	82,027	66,239	69,175	70,187	71,139
Commuter rail	Number	5,007	5,498	6,392	6,927	7,237	7,103	7,369
Demand response [1]	Number	16,471	33,080	41,958	68,621	65,336	68,632	38,559
Heavy rail	Number	10,419	10,591	11,110	11,510	11,342	10,469	10,380
Light rail	Number	913	1,577	1,645	2,104	2,257	2,310	2,387
Trolley bus	Number	832	951	615	571	479	570	560
Other	Number	1,197	5,208	7,080	18,453	19,432	17,458	18,218
Operating funding, total	Mil. dol.	16,053	24,243	31,708	39,117	41,310	43,577	46,048
Agency funds	Mil. dol.	6,786	11,004	12,559	14,675	15,602	16,205	16,734
Passenger funding	Mil. dol.	5,891	8,746	10,269	12,556	13,558	14,180	14,984
Other	Mil. dol.	895	2,258	2,290	2,119	2,044	2,025	1,749
Government funds [2]	Mil. dol.	9,267	13,239	19,149	24,442	25,708	27,372	29,314
Directly generated [3]	Mil. dol.	(4)	1,959	2,694	2,549	2,563	2,825	2,936
Local	Mil. dol.	5,327	5,319	6,658	8,458	9,069	9,546	10,228
State	Mil. dol.	2,970	4,967	7,495	9,761	10,048	11,139	12,038
Federal	Mil. dol.	970	994	2,303	3,675	4,028	3,862	4,112
Operating expense	Mil. dol.	15,742	22,646	30,295	37,755	38,362	39,701	42,188
Vehicle operations	Mil. dol.	6,654	10,111	13,793	17,009	17,590	17,988	18,625
Maintenance	Mil. dol.	4,631	6,445	8,259	9,797	10,015	10,433	11,137
General administration	Mil. dol.	3,450	3,329	4,075	5,731	5,674	5,786	6,637
Purchased transportation	Mil. dol.	1,008	2,761	4,168	5,218	5,083	5,494	5,789
Capital expenditures	Mil. dol.	(NA)	9,587	12,383	17,824	17,057	18,168	18,229
Vehicle-miles operated	Million	3,242	4,081	4,601	5,455	5,378	5,392	5,392
Motor bus	Million	2,130	2,315	2,485	2,413	2,414	2,405	2,414
Trolley bus	Million	14	14	13	12	12	12	12
Heavy rail	Million	537	595	646	666	655	656	674
Light rail	Million	24	53	69	94	94	99	107
Commuter rail	Million	213	271	303	345	347	349	362
Demand response [1]	Million	306	759	978	1,694	1,612	1,618	1,565
Other	Million	18	74	107	232	244	253	259
Trips taken	Million	8,799	9,363	9,815	10,218	10,319	10,584	10,650
Motor bus	Million	5,677	5,678	5,855	5,256	5,234	5,367	5,330
Trolley bus	Million	126	122	107	99	98	99	96
Heavy rail	Million	2,346	2,632	2,808	3,550	3,647	3,743	3,817
Light rail	Million	175	320	381	457	479	498	510
Commuter rail	Million	328	413	423	464	472	477	487
Demand response [1]	Million	68	105	125	190	191	211	223
Other	Million	79	93	117	203	197	189	186
Avg. fare per trip	Cents	67	93	102	123	131	134	142
Employees, number (avg.) [5]	1,000	273	360	367	394	398	401	399
Payroll, employee	Mil. dol.	7,226	10,400	12,177	14,286	14,331	14,369	14,546
Fringe benefits, employee	Mil. dol.	3,986	5,413	8,093	10,342	10,597	11,048	11,066

NA Not available. [1] This operation (also called paratransit or dial-a-ride) is comprised of passenger cars, vans or small buses operating in response to calls from passengers or their agents to the transit operator, who then dispatches a vehicle to pick up the passengers and transport them to their destinations. [2] Represents the sum of federal, state, and local assistance, and that portion of directly generated funds that accrue from tax collections, toll transfers from other sectors of operations, and bond proceeds. [3] These are any funds generated from taxes controlled by the transit agency. [4] Funds data are included in local government data through 1993. [5] Through 1990, represents employee equivalents of 2,080 hours = one employee; beginning 1995, equals actual employees.

Source: American Public Transportation Association, Washington, DC, *Public Transportation Fact Book*, annual ©. See also <http://www.apta.com/resources/statistics/Pages/default.aspx>.

Table 1137. Top Twenty Cities—Public Transit Savings: 2017

[Individuals who ride public transportation can save on average $9,797 annually based on the June 2, 2017 national average gas price and the national unreserved monthly parking rate. On a per month basis, transit riders can save on average $816 per month versus driving. See source report and other monthly "Transit Savings" releases for information and methodology on how savings are calculated. The cities with the highest transit ridership are ranked in order of their transit savings based on the purchase of a monthly public transit pass and factoring in local gas prices and the local monthly unreserved parking rate]

City	Savings (dollars)		City	Savings (dollars)	
	Monthly	Annual		Monthly	Annual
New York	1,218	14,612	Minneapolis	858	10,300
San Francisco	1,097	13,167	Denver	843	10,120
Boston	1,060	12,726	Baltimore	840	10,079
Philadelphia	988	11,853	Washington, DC	819	9,834
Seattle	978	11,739	Pittsburgh	810	9,722
Chicago	970	11,643	Cleveland	795	9,542
Honolulu	944	11,325	Miami	771	9,247
Los Angeles	932	11,179	Atlanta	766	9,187
San Diego	844	10,605	Dallas	761	9,133
Portland	873	10,477	Las Vegas	760	9,122

Source: American Public Transportation Association, Media Center, Press Releases ©. See also <http://www.apta.com/mediacenter/pressreleases/2017/Pages/June-Transit-Savings.aspx>.

Table 1138. Characteristics of Rail Transit by Transit Authority: 2015

[8,946.3 represents $8,946,300,000]

Mode and transit agency	Metro area served	Directional route–miles [1,2]	Number of high-way-rail cross-ings [1]	Number of stations	Fare revenues earned (mil. dol.)	Total operating expenses (mil. dol.)	Unlinked passenger trips (million)
Total [3]	(X)	12,308.2	7,399	3,301	8,946.3	16,793.4	4,887.2
Heavy rail	(X)	1,646.2	27	1,051	5,399.7	8,950.2	3,860.1
Chicago Transit Authority	Chicago	207.8	25	145	299.3	569.1	241.7
Greater Cleveland Regional Transit Authority	Cleveland	38.1	–	18	6.5	32.7	6.4
Los Angeles County Metropolitan Transportation Authority, Metro	Los Angeles	31.9	–	16	36.3	127.2	47.5
Maryland Transit Administration	Baltimore	29.4	–	14	12.9	56.4	13.9
Massachusetts Bay Transportation Authority	Boston	76.3	–	54	215.5	349.4	174.9
Metropolitan Atlanta Rapid Transit Authority	Atlanta	96.1	–	38	78.2	213.0	72.5
Miami-Dade Transit	Miami	49.8	–	23	26.7	97.0	21.9
MTA New York City Transit	New York	489.4	–	469	3,313.6	5,200.2	2,662.4
Port Authority Trans-Hudson Corporation	New York	28.6	2	13	174.0	389.3	85.5
Port Authority Transit Corporation	Philadelphia	31.5	–	13	25.1	50.8	10.2
San Francisco Bay Area Rapid Transit District	San Francisco	209.0	–	44	459.0	575.5	134.7
Southeastern Pennsylvania Transportation Authority	Philadelphia	74.9	–	75	107.1	188.6	100.7
Staten Island Rapid Transit Operating Authority, MTA Staten Island Railway	New York	28.6	–	22	8.2	50.0	8.6
Washington Metropolitan Area Transit Authority	Washington	234.2	–	91	627.0	983.9	270.2
Alternativa de Transporte Integrado ATI	San Juan, PR	20.6	–	16	10.4	67.1	9.0
Commuter rail [4]	(X)	8,754.3	3,477	1,257	2,997.5	5,776.0	490.9
Alaska Railroad Corporation	Anchorage	959.9	133	11	19.9	43.3	0.2
Altamont Corridor Express	San Jose	172.0	127	10	8.0	16.7	1.2
Central Florida Commuter Rail	Orlando	63.5	91	12	2.1	33.7	1.0
Central Puget Sound Regional Transit Authority	Seattle	163.8	66	12	11.9	40.5	3.9
Connecticut Department of Transportation	Hartford	101.2	–	9	2.6	33.9	0.9
Dallas Area Rapid Transit	Dallas	72.3	44	10	9.4	24.0	2.2
Maryland Transit Administration	Baltimore	400.4	40	42	43.1	142.3	9.3
Massachusetts Bay Transportation Authority	Boston	776.1	258	138	189.0	404.7	32.9
Metro Transit	Minneapolis	77.9	36	7	2.5	15.7	0.7
Metro-North Commuter Railroad Company, MTA Metro-North Railroad	New York	545.7	157	112	677.6	1,134.7	85.8
MTA Long Island Rail Road	New York	638.2	334	124	700.7	1,290.6	98.7
New Jersey Transit Corporation	New York	1,001.8	328	165	541.2	943.5	89.3
North County Transit District	San Diego	82.2	31	8	7.4	19.7	1.6
Northeast Illinois Regional Commuter Railroad Corporation,	Chicago	975.0	568	241	337.4	706.7	72.6
Northern Indiana Commuter Transportation District	Chicago	179.8	117	19	20.7	44.5	3.6
Northern New England Passenger Rail Authority	Boston	287.6	103	12	7.9	19.8	0.4
Peninsula Corridor Joint Powers Board dba: Caltrain	San Francisco	153.7	54	32	83.4	115.4	19.0
Pennsylvania Department of Transportation	Philadelphia	144.4	1	12	38.3	52.4	1.4
Regional Transportation Authority	Nashville	62.8	35	6	0.8	4.7	0.3
Rio Metro Regional Transit District	Albuquerque	193.1	86	14	2.6	30.3	1.0
South Florida Regional Transportation Authority	Miami	142.2	73	18	12.8	76.4	4.3
Southeastern Pennsylvania Transportation Authority	Philadelphia	446.9	287	154	151.5	269.9	37.7
Southern California Regional Rail Authority	Los Angeles	777.8	423	55	83.1	207.6	14.0
Utah Transit Authority	Salt Lake City	174.5	65	16	7.1	39.3	4.6
Virginia Railway Express	Washington	161.5	20	18	36.7	65.8	4.5

– Represents zero. X Not applicable. [1] Vehicles operated in maximum services (VOMS) include directly operated (DO) and Purchase Transportation (PT) by mode. [2] The mileage in each direction over which public transportation vehicles travel while in revenue service. The mileage is computed without regard to the number of traffic lanes or rail tracks existing in the right-of-way. [3] Includes light rail, not shown separately. [4] Excludes commuter-type services operated independently by Amtrak.

Source: U.S. Department of Transportation, Federal Transit Administration, National Transit Database, Annual Data Tables, "Track and Roadway," "Service," "Metrics," and "Transit Station," <https://www.transit.dot.gov/ntd/ntd-data>, accessed September 2017.

Table 1139. Transit Ridership in Selected Urbanized Areas: 2013

[Passenger trips in thousands (10,574,238 represents 10,574,238,000)]

Urbanized areas	2010 Population Total	Annual unlinked passenger trips [1] (1,000)	Unlinked passenger trips per capita	Percent distribution Motor bus	Heavy rail [2]	Light rail [3]	Commuter rail [4]	Other [5]
U.S. urbanized areas.	209,569,050	10,574,238	50.5	49.2	36.1	4.6	4.5	3.2
Atlanta, GA.	4,515,419	140,132	31.0	46.8	49.7	–	–	1.4
Baltimore, MD.	2,203,663	108,096	49.1	63.8	14.1	8.0	8.4	1.9
Boston, MA-NH-RI.	4,181,019	403,160	96.4	30.2	41.8	17.4	8.7	1.8
Chicago, IL-IN.	8,608,208	648,055	75.3	51.6	35.4	–	11.9	1.1
Cincinnati, OH-KY-IN.	1,624,827	21,067	13.0	97.9	–	–	–	1.9
Cleveland, OH.	1,780,673	50,067	28.1	69.3	12.8	5.8	–	2.0
Dallas-Fort Worth-Arlington, TX.	5,121,892	80,648	15.7	56.4	–	36.5	2.6	3.9
Denver-Aurora, CO.	2,374,203	101,684	42.8	75.1	–	23.4	–	1.5
Detroit, MI.	3,734,090	45,838	12.3	88.1	–	–	–	11.9
Houston, TX.	4,944,332	84,791	17.1	71.8	–	13.4	–	5.2
Indianapolis, IN.	1,487,483	10,527	7.1	97.4	–	–	–	2.6
Kansas City, MO-KS.	1,519,417	17,010	11.2	86.1	–	–	–	3.5
Las Vegas-Henderson, NV.	1,886,011	65,874	34.9	84.9	–	–	–	8.4
Los Angeles-Long Beach-Anaheim, CA.	12,150,996	681,565	56.1	77.9	7.3	9.3	2.0	1.8
Miami, FL.	5,502,379	171,635	31.2	77.3	12.4	–	2.4	7.9
Milwaukee, WI.	1,376,476	128,516	93.4	66.4	–	–	–	0.5
Minneapolis-St. Paul, MN-WI.	2,650,890	95,088	35.9	85.9	–	10.7	0.8	2.5
New York-Newark, NY-NJ-CT.	18,351,295	4,299,316	234.3	27.7	63.6	0.4	6.1	0.9
Orlando, FL.	1,510,516	29,853	19.8	93.8	–	–	–	3.4
Philadelphia, PA-NJ-DE-MD.	5,441,567	380,981	70.0	51.2	29.3	–	9.9	2.4
Phoenix-Mesa, AZ.	3,629,114	76,807	21.2	78.6	–	18.6	–	2.8
Pittsburgh, PA.	1,733,853	65,462	37.8	83.4	–	12.3	–	3.2
Portland, OR-WA.	1,849,898	111,675	60.4	57.7	–	35.1	–	1.3
Riverside-San Bernardino, CA.	1,932,666	25,790	13.3	94.2	–	–	–	4.4
Sacramento, CA.	1,723,634	31,867	18.5	53.2	–	42.4	–	2.1
San Antonio, TX.	1,758,210	46,963	26.7	96.9	–	–	–	3.1
San Diego, CA.	2,956,746	154,010	52.1	54.0	–	41.3	1.1	2.2
San Francisco-Oakland, CA.	3,281,212	449,674	137.0	38.8	28.1	10.1	3.6	17.5
San Jose, CA.	1,664,496	44,221	26.6	74.1	–	24.3	–	1.7
Seattle, WA.	3,059,393	201,644	65.9	57.7	–	4.8	1.5	25.6
St. Louis, MO-IL.	2,150,706	49,900	23.2	64.0	–	34.2	–	1.8
Tampa-St. Petersburg, FL.	2,441,770	30,945	12.7	96.2	–	–	–	2.5
Virginia Beach, VA.	1,439,666	18,811	13.1	86.2	–	9.4	–	4.4
Washington, DC-VA-MD.	4,586,770	473,403	103.2	40.0	57.8	–	1.0	0.5

– Represents zero. [1] The number of times passengers board public transportation vehicles. A passenger is counted each time he or she boards a vehicle even if the boarding is part of the same journey from origin to destination. [2] Also called metro, subway, rapid transit, or rapid rail. [3] Also called hybrid rail, streetcar, tramway, or trolley. [4] Also called metropolitan rail or regional rail. [5] Other includes automated guideway, cable car, demand response (see footnote 1, Table 1136), ferry boat, inclined plane, monorail, trolley bus, and van pool.

Source: U.S. Bureau of Transportation Statistics, "State Transportation Statistics," <http://www.rita.dot.gov/bts/sites/rita.dot.gov.bts/files/publications/state_transportation_statistics/index.html>, accessed August 2016.

Table 1140. Federal Transit Administration (FTA) Funding Allocations by State: 2015 and 2016

[In millions of dollars (10,715.9 represents $10,715,900,000). For fiscal years ending September 30. Data shown are apportionments and allocations for formula and discretionary programs]

State	2015	2016	State	2015	2016	State	2015	2016	State	2015	2016
Total [1]	10,715.9	11,286.3	ID.	23.2	24.1	MO.	94.7	97.3	PA.	386.7	412.4
AL.	52.8	52.8	IL.	575.0	728.5	MT.	19.7	20.7	RI.	35.7	36.7
AK.	44.5	51.2	IN.	87.6	89.7	NE.	26.2	24.5	SC.	47.0	48.3
AZ.	129.2	111.2	IA.	41.1	39.7	NV.	57.6	65.2	SD.	16.0	16.2
AR.	30.7	31.8	KS.	35.1	35.4	NH.	15.7	16.8	TN.	85.3	86.9
CA.	1,738.0	2,155.8	KY.	60.2	52.6	NJ.	573.1	599.6	TX.	634.5	556.1
CO.	271.3	357.3	LA.	59.6	61.6	NM.	44.2	45.2	UT.	70.1	148.3
CT.	217.8	167.9	ME.	30.2	31.2	NY.	1,585.9	1,459.5	VT.	8.5	9.1
DE.	24.6	25.5	MD.	230.1	340.2	NC.	217.6	291.8	VA.	270.4	162.7
DC.	175.8	193.9	MA.	339.7	513.4	ND.	13.6	14.2	WA.	423.8	321.0
FL.	413.7	383.2	MI.	162.1	132.0	OH.	174.3	218.0	WV.	24.8	25.6
GA.	173.9	182.0	MN.	206.7	112.9	OK.	51.5	48.4	WI.	80.9	82.1
HI.	298.0	292.0	MS.	29.1	29.3	OR.	223.5	200.2	WY.	10.9	11.6

[1] Includes data for Island Areas of the U.S. and unallocated funds, not shown separately. Does not include oversight funds.

Source: U.S. Department of Transportation, Federal Transit Administration, Office of Budget and Policy, "FTA Allocations for Formula and Discretionary Programs by State FY1998-2016," <https://www.transit.dot.gov/funding/apportionments/funding-state>, accessed May 2017.

Table 1141. Commuters by Commuting Time to Work for Top Metropolitan Statistical Areas: 2015

[141,481 represents 141,481,000, except percent. For workers 16 years and over who did not work at home. Covers any mode of travel. Based on a sample, subject to sampling variability]

Metropolitan Statistical Area	Total commuters (1,000)	Percent over 35 minutes	Commuting time (in minutes)								
			Less than 10 minutes	10 to 14 minutes	15 to 19 minutes	20 to 24 minutes	25 to 29 minutes	30 to 34 minutes	35 to 44 minutes	45 to 59 minutes	60 or more minutes
United States	**141,481**	**24**	**17,843**	**19,270**	**21,666**	**20,664**	**8,883**	**19,422**	**9,532**	**11,473**	**12,727**
Atlanta-Sandy Springs-Roswell, GA	2,534	33	190	252	321	350	162	414	215	293	336
Baltimore-Columbia-Towson, MD	1,314	32	105	139	166	187	84	212	112	151	158
Boston-Cambridge-Newton, MA-NH	2,380	35	224	252	284	291	127	363	206	280	352
Charlotte-Concord-Gastonia, NC-SC	1,098	24	107	137	165	162	80	178	87	105	78
Chicago-Naperville-Elgin, IL-IN-WI	4,376	36	368	428	525	542	271	665	412	533	631
Dallas-Ft. Worth-Arlington, TX	3,279	28	305	381	461	477	206	543	274	345	286
Denver-Aurora-Lakewood, CO	1,366	27	116	144	204	211	102	223	124	135	286
Detroit-Warren-Dearborn, MI	1,856	25	177	225	281	286	134	281	166	180	126
Houston-The Woodlands-Sugar Land, TX	3,014	31	239	324	391	398	159	559	233	352	358
Los Angeles-Long Beach-Anaheim, CA	5,900	30	433	653	828	853	325	1,036	436	600	736
Miami-Ft. Lauderdale-West Palm Beach, FL	2,656	28	179	262	357	415	174	525	206	272	266
Minneapolis-St. Paul-Bloomington, MN-WI	1,779	22	185	220	271	292	148	271	151	143	99
New York-Newark-Jersey City, NY-NJ-PA	9,187	43	659	826	924	1,043	465	1,362	815	1,125	1,967
Orlando-Kissimmee-Sanford, FL	1,071	26	82	111	145	174	76	204	98	108	74
Philadelphia-Camden-Wilmington, PA-NJ-DE-MD	2,761	31	264	328	342	384	177	417	237	298	314
Phoenix-Mesa-Scottsdale, AZ	1,920	23	192	231	288	308	149	302	153	168	130
Pittsburgh, PA	1,078	25	128	134	157	155	79	152	86	101	87
Portland-Vancouver-Hillsboro, OR-WA	1,096	25	113	140	163	164	82	160	95	99	81
Riverside-San Bernardino-Ontario, CA	1,734	31	170	219	252	238	93	224	102	143	293
St. Louis, MO-IL	1,311	23	139	168	195	219	98	196	110	111	76
San Diego-Carlsbad, CA	1,476	21	134	180	247	259	110	235	102	104	106
San Francisco-Oakland-Hayward, CA	2,161	37	137	219	279	276	114	327	185	257	367
Seattle-Tacoma-Bellevue, WA	1,774	32	146	177	235	254	120	282	168	183	209
Tampa-St. Petersburg-Clearwater, FL	1,246	25	126	157	189	199	80	180	90	120	105
Washington-Arlington-Alexandria, DC-VA-MD-WV	3,059	41	188	255	340	366	178	470	311	423	529

Source: U.S. Census Bureau, 2015 American Community Survey, B08134, "Means of Transportation to Work by Travel Time to Work," <https://www.census.gov/programs-surveys/acs.html>, accessed February 2017.

Table 1142. Commuters Who Ride Bicycles or Walk to Work—Selected Cities: 2013

[Covers cities with the highest percent of commuters who walk or bike to work, based on the American Community Survey. Data are weighted 3-year averages for 2011-2013]

Leading cities (Walking)	Percent of commuters who walk to work	Leading cities (Bicycling)	Percent of commuters who bike to work	Percent male	Percent female
Boston	14.8	Portland, OR	6.1	66	34
Washington, DC	12.6	Washington, DC	4.0	63	37
San Francisco	10.2	Minneapolis	3.9	67	33
New York	10.2	San Francisco	3.7	68	32
Seattle	9.3	Seattle	3.7	69	31
Philadelphia	8.5	Oakland	3.0	62	38
Baltimore	6.8	Tucson	2.9	71	29
Chicago	6.7	Denver	2.4	72	28
Minneapolis	6.5	Sacramento	2.3	68	32
Portland, OR	5.9	Philadelphia	2.1	63	37
Milwaukee	5.6	Boston	1.9	74	26
Atlanta	4.9	Austin	1.6	72	28
Denver	4.8	Chicago	1.4	71	29
Miami	4.7	Albuquerque	1.3	69	31
Cleveland	4.6	Los Angeles	1.1	79	21
Oakland	4.6	Fresno	1.1	73	27
Los Angeles	3.7	New York	1.0	74	26
Tucson	3.6	Long Beach	1.0	70	30
Detroit	3.4	Mesa	1.0	76	24
Sacramento	3.3	Miami	0.9	69	31
San Diego	3.1	Milwaukee	0.9	68	32
Columbus	2.9	Atlanta	0.9	78	22
Omaha	2.7	San Diego	0.9	76	24
Austin	2.6	San Jose	0.9	74	26
Long Beach	2.5	Baltimore	0.9	70	30

Source: Alliance for Biking and Walking, *Bicycling and Walking in the United States: 2016 Benchmarking Report* ©. See also <http://bikingandwalkingbenchmarks.org/>.

Table 1143. Truck Transportation—Revenue and Equipment Inventory: 2010 to 2015

[In millions of dollars (197,963 represents $197,963,000,000), except where noted. For all employer firms regardless of tax status. Covers NAICS 484. Estimates have been adjusted to the results of the 2012 Economic Census. Data are based on the 2007 North American Industry Classification System (NAICS); see text, this section and Section 15]

Item	2010	2012	2013	2014	2015
Total operating revenue	**197,963**	**238,003**	**245,520**	**263,875**	**263,249**
Total motor carrier revenue	182,649	219,999	227,251	245,000	244,652
Revenue by commodities handled:					
Agricultural and fish products	19,195	23,763	23,835	23,428	25,493
Grains, alcohol, and tobacco products	9,294	10,585	10,916	11,577	12,455
Stone, nonmetallic minerals, and metallic ores	12,150	14,750	14,664	16,805	16,750
Coal and petroleum products	10,316	13,356	14,047	14,808	14,815
Pharmaceutical and chemical products	9,295	11,311	12,039	12,378	12,332
Wood products, textiles, and leathers	15,702	18,308	18,798	19,335	19,802
Base metal and machinery	19,672	23,411	23,319	25,815	24,829
Electronic, motorized vehicles, and precision instruments	10,817	12,475	12,888	13,797	13,598
Used household and office goods	10,190	11,210	12,032	12,947	14,220
New furniture and miscellaneous manufactured products	15,612	18,365	18,875	20,466	20,566
Other goods	50,406	62,465	65,838	73,644	69,792
Hazardous materials	11,203	15,871	16,256	16,646	17,177
Inventory of revenue-generating equipment (1,000):					
Trucks	164	204	223	228	(S)
Owned and/or leased with drivers	149	185	201	203	212
Leased without drivers	15	19	(S)	(S)	(S)
Truck-tractors	675	729	761	817	841
Owned and/or leased with drivers	588	634	666	717	728
Leased without drivers	87	95	95	100	113
Trailers	1,586	1,684	1,772	1,858	1,915
Owned and/or leased with drivers	1,389	1,476	1,577	1,677	1,727
Leased without drivers	197	208	195	181	188

S Estimate does not meet publication standards.

Source: U.S. Census Bureau, Annual & Quarterly Services, "2015 Service Annual Survey," <http://www.census.gov/services/index.html>, accessed December 2016.

Table 1144. Petroleum Pipeline Companies—Characteristics: 1980 to 2015

[173 represents 173,000. Covers pipeline companies operating in interstate commerce and subject to the jurisdiction of the Federal Energy Regulatory Commission]

Item	Unit	1980	1990	2000	2010	2011	2012	2013	2014	2015
Miles of pipeline, total	1,000	173	168	152	148	150	152	152	161	165
Gathering lines	1,000	36	32	18	10	13	14	15	15	16
Trunk lines	1,000	136	136	134	138	137	138	137	146	149
Total deliveries	Mil. bbl.	10,600	11,378	14,450	13,518	13,568	14,136	14,594	16,170	18,148
Crude oil	Mil. bbl.	6,405	6,563	6,923	7,204	7,032	7,471	8,122	9,289	10,865
Products	Mil. bbl.	4,195	4,816	7,527	6,314	6,537	6,665	6,471	6,881	7,283
Total trunk line traffic	Bil. bbl. miles	3,405	3,500	3,508	3,565	3,608	3,770	3,800	4,193	4,589
Crude oil	Bil. bbl. miles	1,948	1,891	1,602	1,634	1,653	1,760	1,760	2,059	2,339
Products	Bil. bbl. miles	1,458	1,609	1,906	1,931	1,955	2,009	2,053	2,134	2,250
Carrier property value	Mil. dol.	19,752	25,828	29,648	45,380	49,157	54,071	67,890	84,910	93,485
Operating revenues	Mil. dol.	6,356	7,149	7,483	11,219	12,562	14,007	15,734	19,281	22,019
Net income	Mil. dol.	1,912	2,340	2,705	4,582	6,109	6,423	6,981	9,573	6,689

Source: PennWell Publishing Co., Houston, TX, *Oil & Gas Journal*, annual ©. See also <http://www.ogj.com/>.

Table 1145. Pipelines—Mileage and Incident Summary: 2004 to 2015

[In miles except where indicated (267,837 represents $267,837,000)]

Year	Pipeline mileage								Pipeline incidents [2]	
	Natural gas systems			Hazardous liquid or carbon dioxide systems						
	Distri-bution [1]	Trans-mission	Gathering	Total [3]	Petro-leum/ refined products	HVLs (highly volatile liquids)	Crude oil	CO2 or other	Number of incidents	Total cost as reported ($1,000)
2004.......	1,925,748	303,001	24,992	166,669	62,391	51,794	49,264	3,221	671	267,837
2005.......	1,962,351	300,468	23,754	166,760	62,899	51,284	48,732	3,846	719	1,245,463
2006.......	2,022,474	300,324	20,898	166,719	61,905	52,533	48,453	3,827	639	151,984
2007.......	2,025,731	301,066	20,042	169,846	62,091	54,382	49,488	3,884	611	153,904
2008.......	2,075,191	303,181	20,663	173,789	61,599	57,024	50,963	4,203	659	565,519
2009.......	2,086,689	304,560	20,376	175,965	61,803	57,233	52,737	4,192	627	179,070
2010.......	2,102,366	304,805	19,621	181,986	64,800	57,980	54,631	4,560	586	1,692,501
2011.......	2,121,217	305,057	19,277	183,580	64,130	58,599	56,100	4,735	592	426,552
2012.......	2,137,866	303,341	16,532	186,221	64,042	59,861	57,463	4,840	573	229,613
2013.......	2,149,697	302,827	17,369	192,412	63,351	62,768	61,087	5,190	619	349,962
2014.......	2,169,254	301,804	17,509	199,659	61,767	65,787	66,813	5,276	707	310,257
2015.......	2,190,494	301,177	17,747	208,616	62,588	67,577	73,204	5,233	715	344,103

[1] Includes main and estimated service mileage. [2] Includes serious and significant incidents. Serious incidents include a fatality or injury requiring in-patient hospitalization. Significant incidents include serious incidents; those with $50,000 or more in total costs; highly volatile liquid releases of 5 barrels or more or other liquid releases of 50 barrels or more; and liquid releases resulting in an unintentional fire or explosion. [3] Beginning 2010, includes fuel grade ethanol, not shown separately.

Source: U.S. Department of Transportation, Pipeline and Hazardous Materials Safety Administration, "Pipeline Mileage and Facilities" and "Pipeline Incidents: 20 Year Trends," <http://www.phmsa.dot.gov/pipeline/library/data-stats>, accessed March 2017.

Table 1146. Crude Oil, Fuel Ethanol and Biodiesel Movements by Rail: 2010 to 2016

[In thousands of barrels (23,788 represents 23,788,000). Crude oil movements on railroads to and from Canada, within the 50 States and the District of Columbia (including interstate and intrastate). Estimates based on data from the Surface Transportation Board and other information]

Item	2010	2011	2012	2013	2014	2015	2016
Crude oil..................................	23,788	42,370	152,047	296,064	382,034	318,782	175,185
Intra-U.S. movements...................	23,712	41,371	138,024	259,194	316,276	275,218	142,094
U.S. exports to Canada...............	55	256	6,217	7,391	12,605	4,414	–
U.S. imports from Canada.............	21	743	7,807	29,479	53,153	39,149	33,091
Fuel ethanol.............................	208,061	219,324	207,870	202,412	211,692	220,823	236,278
Biodiesel.................................	2,606	6,387	7,855	7,950	9,473	8,332	12,188

– Represents zero.

Source: U.S. Energy Information Administration, Petroleum & Other Liquids, "Movements of Crude Oil and Selected Products by Rail," <http://www.eia.gov/petroleum/data.cfm>, accessed April 2017.

Table 1147. U.S. Postal Service Rates for Letters and Postcards: 1991 to 2017

[In dollars. For 1st class retail mail. Prior to 2013, international rates exclude Canada and Mexico]

Domestic mail date of rate change	Letters		Post-cards	Express mail— first 1/2 pound [1]	International air mail date of rate change	Letters	Post-cards
	First ounce	Each added ounce					
1991 (Feb. 3).................	0.29	0.23	0.19	9.95	**First 1/2 ounce**		
1995 (Jan. 1).................	0.32	0.23	0.20	10.75	1991 (Feb. 3)............	0.50	0.40
1999 (Jan. 10)...............	0.33	0.22	0.20	11.75	1995 (July 9).............	0.60	0.40
2001 (Jan. 7).................	0.34	0.21	0.20	12.25	1999 (Jan. 10)............	0.60	0.50
2001 (July 1).................	0.34	0.23	0.21	12.45	**First ounce [2]**		
2002 (June 30)...............	0.37	0.23	0.23	13.65	2001 (Jan. 7).............	0.80	0.70
2006 (Jan. 8).................	0.39	0.24	0.24	14.40	2006 (Jan. 8).............	0.84	0.75
2007 (May 14)...............	0.41	0.17	0.26	16.25	2007 (May 14)............	0.90	0.90
2008 (May 12)...............	0.42	0.17	0.27	[3] 12.60	2008 (May 12)............	0.94	0.94
2009 (May 11)...............	0.44	0.17	0.28	[4] 13.05	2009 (May 11)............	0.98	0.98
2010 (Jan. 4).................	0.44	0.17	0.28	[5] 13.65	2010 (no change)........	0.98	0.98
2011 (Apr. 17)...............	0.44	0.20	0.29	[6] 13.25	2011 (no change)........	0.98	0.98
2012 (Jan. 22)...............	0.45	0.20	0.32	[7] 12.95	2012 (Jan. 22)...........	1.05	1.05
2013 (Jan. 27)...............	0.46	0.20	0.33	[8] 14.10	2013 (Jan. 27)...........	1.10	1.10
2014 (Jan. 26)...............	0.49	0.21	0.34	[9] 16.95	2014 (Jan. 26)...........	1.15	1.15
2015 (May 31)...............	0.49	0.22	0.35	[9] 16.95	2015 (May 31)...........	1.20	1.20
2016 (Apr. 10)...............	0.47	0.21	0.34	[10] 22.95	2016 (Apr. 10)...........	1.15	1.15
2017 (Jan. 22)...............	0.49	0.21	0.34	[11] 23.75	2017 (no change)........	1.15	1.15

[1] On May 12, 2008, the Postal Service initiated a zoned pricing structure for Express Mail. [2] International letter prices after the first ounce vary according to the price group that is applicable to each destination country. [3] Prices increased on May 12, 2008. Prices range from $12.60 to zones 1 and 2 to $19.50 to zone 8. [4] Prices increased on January 18, 2009. Prices range from $13.05 to zones 1 and 2 to $21.20 to zone 8. [5] Prices range from $13.65 to zones 1 and 2 to $22.20 to zone 8. [6] Prices changed on January 2, 2011. Prices range from $13.25 to zones 1 and 2 to $26.65 to zone 8. [7] Prices range from $12.95 to zones 1 and 2 to $28.00 to zone 8. [8] Prices range from $14.10 to zones 1 and 2 to $30.60 to zone 8. [9] Beginning January 2014, the Postal Service implemented a Zone 9. Prices range from $16.95 to zones 1 and 2 to $38.05 to zone 9. [10] Prices range from $22.95 to zones 1 and 2 to $38.05 to zone 9. [11] Prices range from $23.75 to zones 1 and 2 to $39.40 to zone 9.

Source: U.S. Postal Service, *Domestic Rate History*, July 2009; and "Price List Notice 123," <http://pe.usps.com/text/dmm300/Notice123.htm>, accessed April 2017.

Table 1148. U.S. Postal Service—Summary: 1990 to 2016

[166,301 represents 166,301,000,000 except as indicated. For years ending September 30. Includes Puerto Rico and all Island Areas]

Item	1990	2000	2005	2010	2014	2015	2016
Offices, stations, and branches..........	**40,067**	**38,060**	**37,142**	**36,222**	**35,649**	**35,520**	**35,423**
Number of post offices.........................	28,959	27,876	27,385	27,077	26,669	26,615	26,611
Number of stations and branches..............	11,108	10,184	9,757	9,145	8,980	8,905	8,812
Delivery points (mil.)......................	**(NA)**	**135.9**	**144.3**	**150.9**	**153.9**	**155.0**	**156.1**
Residential...........................	(NA)	123.9	131.3	137.5	141.0	142.1	143.3
City...................................	(NA)	76.1	78.5	80.5	81.7	82.0	82.4
P.O. Box.............................	(NA)	15.9	15.6	15.7	15.9	15.9	15.9
Rural/highway contract......................	(NA)	31.9	37.2	41.2	43.5	44.2	44.9
Business.............................	(NA)	12.1	13.0	13.3	12.9	12.8	12.8
Pieces of mail handled (mil.).............	**166,301**	**207,882**	**211,743**	**170,859**	**155,532**	**154,322**	**154,323**
First-class mail [1, 2]........................	89,270	103,526	98,071	77,592	63,849	62,599	61,219
Periodicals (formerly 2nd class).............	10,680	10,365	9,070	7,269	6,045	5,838	5,586
Standard Mail (formerly Standard A) [2].........	63,725	90,057	100,942	81,841	80,308	80,030	80,885
U.S. Postal Service.........................	538	363	621	438	439	357	421
Free for the blind.........................	35	47	76	68	46	46	45
Shipping and Package Services [2, 3, 6]..........	(X)	(X)	(X)	3,057	3,970	4,539	5,161
Express mail [2, 3, 5].......................	59	71	56	43	36	36	33
Package Services (formerly Standard B).....	663	1,128	1,166	657	548	566	591
Priority mail [2, 3, 4]........................	518	1,223	888	779	934	1,007	1,028
International economy mail (surface) [3]........	166	79	23	([3])	([3])	([3])	([3])
International, airmail or total [3, 7].............	632	1,021	829	594	875	913	1,006
Employees, total (1,000)..................	**843**	**901**	**803**	**672**	**618**	**622**	**640**
Career.................................	**761**	**788**	**705**	**584**	**488**	**492**	**509**
Headquarters..............................	2	2	3	3	3	3	3
Headquarters support......................	6	6	4	5	4	4	4
Inspection Service.........................	4	4	3	2	2	2	2
Inspector General.........................	(X)	1	1	1	1	1	1
Field Career...............................	749	775	693	573	478	482	499
Postmasters...........................	27	26	25	23	17	15	14
Supervisors/managers..................	43	39	33	28	23	24	25
Professional, administrative, and technical...........................	10	10	9	6	4	4	5
Clerks.................................	290	282	222	157	119	126	130
Mail handlers.........................	51	61	56	49	39	38	39
City carriers..........................	236	241	228	192	165	164	171
Motor vehicle operators.................	7	9	9	7	7	7	8
Rural carriers.........................	42	57	64	67	66	67	68
Special delivery messengers..............	2	(X)	(X)	(X)	(X)	(X)	(X)
Building and equipment maintenance........	33	42	40	37	33	31	32
Vehicle maintenance....................	5	6	5	5	5	5	5
Other [8]...............................	1	2	2	(X)	(X)	(X)	(X)
Non-career.............................	**83**	**114**	**98**	**88**	**130**	**130**	**131**
Casuals.................................	27	30	19	7	2	2	2
Transitional.............................	(X)	13	8	16	–	–	–
Rural part-time..........................	43	58	57	52	48	51	53
Relief/leave replacements.................	12	12	12	11	13	5	4
Non-bargaining temporary.................	(Z)	1	1	2	(Z)	(Z)	(Z)
Compensation and employee benefits (mil. dol.).............................	34,214	49,532	53,932	48,909	46,000	47,519	48,689
Avg. salary per employee (dol.) [9]...........	37,570	50,103	62,635	72,099	(NA)	(NA)	(NA)
Pieces of mail per employee (1,000).........	197	231	264	254	252	248	241
Operating postal revenue...................	**39,201**	**64,476**	**69,798**	**67,052**	**67,764**	**68,790**	**71,429**
Mail revenue.............................	**37,891**	**62,285**	**66,648**	**63,262**	**63,925**	**65,410**	**67,806**
First-class mail [1, 2]........................	24,023	35,516	36,062	32,111	28,416	28,411	27,496
Periodicals (formerly 2nd class)..............	1,509	2,171	2,161	1,879	1,625	1,589	1,507
Standard Mail (formerly Standard A) [2].........	8,082	15,193	18,954	16,728	17,426	17,646	17,622
Shipping and Package Services [2, 3, 6].........	(X)	(X)	(X)	10,156	13,549	15,062	17,425
Express mail [2, 3, 5].......................	630	996	872	829	760	779	809
Package Services (formerly Standard B).....	919	1,912	2,201	1,531	812	785	797
Priority mail [2, 3, 4]........................	1,555	4,837	4,634	5,455	7,237	7,689	8,202
International economy mail (surface) [3]........	222	180	134	([3])	([3])	([3])	([3])
International, airmail or total [3, 7].............	941	1,477	1,631	2,388	2,909	2,702	2,695
Service revenue...........................	**1,310**	**2,191**	**3,150**	**3,790**	**3,839**	**3,380**	**3,623**
Certified [10]...............................	310	385	601	791	673	669	670
Insurance [10].............................	47	109	132	128	92	90	77
Money orders.............................	155	235	208	182	164	159	153
Other [10]................................	592	1,342	2,122	2,635	2,910	2,462	2,723
Operating expenses (million dollars) [11]..	**40,490**	**62,992**	**68,283**	**75,426**	**73,178**	**73,826**	**76,899**

– Represents zero. NA Not available. X Not applicable. Z Fewer than 500. [1] Items mailed at 1st class rates and weighing 11 ounces or less. [2] Beginning 2010, Express Mail, Priority Mail, First-Class Parcels, and Standard Parcels are not included in Mail categories but reclassified under Shipping and Package Services. [3] "Volume" and "Mailing & Shipping Revenue" restructured for the "Postal Accountability and Enhancement Act (PAEA) of 2006." Some categories eliminated. [4] Provides 2 to 3 day delivery service. [5] Overnight delivery of packages weighing up to 70 pounds. [6] Beginning 2010, also includes Package Services. [7] Airmail only, for 2005 and earlier. Beginning 2010, total international, including all international revenues and pieces formerly included in First-Class Mail, Standard Mail, and Package Services. [8] Includes discontinued operations, area offices, and nurses. Beginning 2010, nurses are included with clerks, and not "other" employment is reported. [9] For career bargaining unit employees. Includes fringe benefits. [10] Beginning 2000, return receipt revenue broken out from registry, certified, and insurance and included in "other." [11] Shown in year in which obligation was incurred.

Source: U.S. Postal Service, *FY2016 Annual Report to Congress,* 2016, and earlier reports, and unpublished data. See also <http://about.usps.com/who-we-are/financials/welcome.htm>.

Section 24
Information and Communications

This section presents statistics on the various information and communications media: publishing, including newspapers, periodicals, books, and software; motion pictures, sound recordings, broadcasting, and telecommunications; and information services, such as libraries. Statistics on computer use and internet access are also included.

Information industry—The U.S. Census Bureau's *Service Annual Survey*, provides estimates of revenues and expenses of firms in the information sector of the economy. Data are based on the North American Industry Classification System (NAICS). The information sector comprises establishments engaged in the following processes: (1) producing and distributing information and cultural products, (2) providing the means to transmit or distribute these products as well as data or communications, and 3) processing data. It includes establishments previously classified in the Standard Industrial Classification (SIC) in manufacturing (publishing); transportation, communications, and utilities (telecommunications and broadcasting); and services (software publishing, motion picture production, data processing, online information services, and libraries).

The main components of the information sector include the publishing industries, including software publishing, and both traditional publishing and publishing exclusively on the internet; the motion picture and sound recording industries; the broadcasting industries, including traditional broadcasting and broadcasting exclusively over the internet; the telecommunications industries; and web search portals, data processing industries, and information services.

Telecommunications encompasses wired (including broadband internet service providers), wireless (including mobile), and satellite telecommunications. Broadcasting covers radio, television, and cable and other subscription programming. Internet publishing and broadcasting, and web search portals are grouped together.

Service Annual Survey data from 1998 to 2003 are based on the 1997 NAICS; 2004 to 2010 data are based variously on 2002 and 2007 NAICS; beginning in 2011, data are all based on 2007 NAICS, with data for various previous years revised to accommodate the new NAICS codes. Major revisions in many communications industries affect the comparability of these data. The following URL contains detailed information about NAICS, see <http://www.census.gov/eos/www/naics/>. See also the text in Section 15, Business Enterprise.

The 1997 Economic Census was the first economic census to cover the new information sector of the economy. The census, conducted every 5 years, for the years ending "2" and "7," provides information on the number of establishments, receipts, payroll, and paid employees for the United States and various geographic levels. The most recent reports are from the 2012 Economic Census.

The Federal Communications Commission (FCC), established in 1934, regulates interstate and international communications by radio, television, wire, satellite, and cable across the entire U.S. Only the largest carriers and holding companies file annual financial reports which are publicly available. The FCC has jurisdiction over interstate and foreign communication services but not over intrastate or local services. Also, the gross operating revenues of the telephone carriers reporting publicly available data annually to the FCC are estimated to cover about 90 percent of the revenues of all U.S. telephone companies. Data are not comparable with Census Bureau's *Service Annual Survey* because of coverage and different accounting practices for those telephone companies which report to the FCC.

Reports filed by the broadcasting industry cover all radio and television stations operating in the United States. The private radio services represent the largest and most diverse group of licensees regulated by the FCC. These services provide voice, data communications, point-to-point, and point-to-multipoint radio communications for fixed and mobile communicators. Major users of these services are small businesses, the aviation industry, the maritime trades, the land transportation industry, the manufacturing industry, state and local public safety and governmental authorities, emergency medical service providers, amateur radio operators, and personal radio operations (CB and the General Mobile Radio Service). The FCC also licenses entities as private and common carriers. Private and common carriers provide fixed and land mobile communications service on a for-profit basis.

Statistics on publishing are available from the Census Bureau, as well as from various private agencies. Editor & Publisher Co., Irvine, CA, presents annual data on the number and circulation of daily and Sunday newspapers in its *Data Book*. Data on public libraries are from the Institute of Museums and Library Services. Data on media use among the general public, including recent trends in use of the internet and social media, and mobile electronic devices are collected by the Pew Research Center, Washington, DC. Gfk Mediamark Research and Intelligence also collects data on internet use, as well as use of other traditional media.

Statistical reliability—For a discussion of statistical collection and estimation, sampling procedures, and measures of statistical reliability applicable to Census Bureau data, see Appendix III.

Table 1149. Information Industries—Type of Establishment, Employees, and Payroll: 2015

[Employees in thousands (3,394.3 represents 3,394,300); payroll in millions of dollars (309,327 represents $309,327,000,000). Excludes self-employed individuals, employees of private households, railroad employees, agricultural production employees, and most government employees. For more information see source and Appendix III]

Industry	2012 NAICS code [1]	Establishments				Employees [6] (1,000)	Annual payroll (mil. dol.)
		Total [2]	Corpora-tions [3]	Sole proprietor-ships [4]	Non-profits [5]		
Information industries.................	**51**	**139,508**	**76,409**	**4,824**	**5,176**	**3,394.3**	**309,327**
Publishing industries (except internet)...............	511	26,859	12,587	1,331	731	877.3	96,601
Newspaper, periodical, book, and directory........	5111	17,260	6,618	1,105	716	407.5	25,508
Newspaper publishers...............................	51111	7,165	3,342	533	165	194.9	8,815
Periodical publishers................................	51112	5,840	1,939	329	302	105.3	9,167
Book publishers....................................	51113	2,555	807	149	219	64.5	4,999
Directory and mailing list publishers...............	51114	886	334	34	7	22.3	1,670
Other publishers....................................	51119	814	196	60	23	20.5	858
Greeting card publishers.........................	511191	100	31	8	(NA)	14.2	477
All other publishers..............................	511199	714	165	52	23	6.4	382
Software publishers.................................	5112	9,599	5,969	226	15	469.8	71,093
Motion picture and sound recording industries.......	512	25,522	6,318	1,281	586	431.6	17,216
Motion picture and video industries.................	5121	21,958	5,541	1,032	509	403.0	15,235
Motion picture and video production...............	51211	14,371	2,901	620	265	230.8	11,298
Motion picture and video distribution..............	51212	348	110	15	13	2.8	269
Motion picture and video exhibition...............	51213	4,620	1,993	286	219	141.7	1,692
Motion picture theaters (except drive-ins)........	512131	4,407	1,956	234	218	140.8	1,670
Drive-in motion picture theaters..................	512132	213	37	52	1	0.9	21
Postproduction and other motion picture and video industries.............................	51219	2,619	537	111	12	27.7	1,977
Teleproduction and other postproduction services...........................	512191	2,408	489	97	7	26.4	1,883
Other motion picture and video industries........	512199	211	48	14	5	1.2	95
Sound recording industries...........................	5122	3,564	777	249	77	28.5	1,981
Record production.................................	51221	356	62	17	3	1.1	71
Integrated record production/distribution..........	51222	400	140	19	7	13.4	1,034
Music publishers....................................	51223	707	189	62	6	6.2	448
Sound recording studios............................	51224	1,700	297	134	11	5.0	275
Other sound recording industries..................	51229	401	89	17	50	2.8	152
Broadcasting (except internet)........................	515	8,439	3,577	301	1,197	259.5	22,036
Radio and television broadcasting....................	5151	7,725	3,242	269	1,034	206.9	15,382
Radio broadcasting.................................	51511	5,556	2,061	213	754	88.9	4,898
Radio networks..................................	515111	857	302	31	202	11.2	920
Radio stations..................................	515112	4,699	1,759	182	552	77.6	3,977
Television broadcasting............................	51512	2,169	1,181	56	280	118.1	10,484
Cable and other subscription programming........	5152	714	335	32	163	52.6	6,654
Telecommunications...................................	517	53,010	42,757	651	256	1,026.3	81,685
Wired telecommunications carriers..................	5171	34,845	32,370	191	229	734.9	59,787
Wireless telecommunications carriers (except satellite)................................	5172	11,869	8,533	57	7	221.8	16,494
Satellite telecommunications.......................	5174	538	227	43	2	8.3	865
Other telecommunications..........................	5179	5,758	1,627	360	18	61.4	4,538
Telecommunications resellers.....................	517911	2,505	632	98	4	27.7	1,641
All other telecommunications.....................	517919	3,253	995	262	14	33.7	2,897
Data processing, hosting, and related services...	518	13,599	7,007	461	148	539.2	50,921
Other information services............................	519	12,079	4,163	799	2,258	260.4	40,869
News syndicates....................................	51911	474	323	10	16	6.9	612
Libraries and archives..............................	51912	2,264	94	58	2,032	26.8	841
Internet publishing and broadcasting and web search portals..................................	51913	7,796	3,425	377	166	212.9	38,521
All other information services.......................	51919	1,545	321	354	44	13.7	895

NA Not available. [1] 2012 North American Industry Classification System; see text, this section and Section 15. [2] Includes other types of establishments, not shown separately. [3] An incorporated business that is granted a charter recognizing it as a separate legal entity having its own privileges, and liabilities distinct from those of its members. [4] An unincorporated business with a sole owner. [5] An organization that does not distribute surplus funds to its owners or shareholders, but instead uses surplus funds to help pursue its goals. Most non-profit organizations are exempt from income taxes. [6] For employees on the payroll for the pay period including March 12.

Source: U.S. Census Bureau, County Business Patterns, "Geography Area Series: County Business Patterns by Legal Form of Organization," <http://factfinder.census.gov>, accessed April 2017.

Table 1150. Information Sector Services—Estimated Revenue and Expenses: 2013 to 2015

[In millions of dollars (1,284,064 represents $1,284,064,000,000). For all employer firms regardless of tax status. Estimates have been adjusted to the results of the 2012 Economic Census and are based on the 2007 North American Industry Classification System (NAICS). Based on the Service Annual Survey and administrative data; see Appendix III]

Industry	2007 NAICS[1] code	Operating revenue			Operating expenses		
		2013	2014	2015	2013	2014	2015
Information industries...	**51**	**1,284,064**	**1,351,616**	**1,405,882**	**979,003**	**1,040,721**	**1,075,164**
Publishing industries (except internet)...	511	279,253	291,575	293,771	192,162	201,242	197,948
Newspaper publishers...	51111	28,512	28,112	26,550	26,884	25,927	23,937
Periodical publishers...	51112	29,185	29,378	28,314	23,787	24,296	23,517
Book publishers...	51113	26,720	26,891	27,676	16,430	17,242	16,732
Directory and mailing list publishers...	51114	8,265	8,602	8,214	6,475	6,848	6,057
Greeting card publishers...	511191	3,585	3,501	3,457	2,424	2,363	2,529
All other publishers...	511199	1,252	1,269	1,219	866	841	847
Software publishers...	5112	181,734	193,822	198,341	115,296	123,725	124,329
Motion picture and sound recording industries...	512	95,084	94,745	98,982	75,096	74,546	77,694
Motion picture and video production and distribution[2]...	5121x	64,504	62,831	64,434	52,190	51,276	52,565
Motion picture and video exhibition...	51213	14,144	14,563	15,787	11,237	11,631	12,874
Teleproduction and other postproduction services...	512191	4,922	5,212	5,500	4,511	4,481	4,705
Other motion picture and video industries...	512199	379	448	398	290	344	227
Record production...	51221	297	338	392	210	192	243
Integrated record production/distribution...	51222	5,032	5,077	5,765	3,750	3,703	3,921
Music publishers...	51223	4,314	4,732	5,054	1,685	1,648	1,807
Sound recording studios...	51224	951	1,002	1,086	817	866	912
Other sound recording industries...	51229	541	542	566	406	405	440
Broadcasting (except internet)...	515	131,413	140,792	148,462	91,263	98,007	103,437
Radio networks...	515111	5,703	6,011	6,509	4,379	4,599	5,046
Radio stations...	515112	12,523	12,397	12,445	9,858	9,505	10,082
Television broadcasting...	51512	44,782	49,911	50,577	35,815	38,804	40,315
Cable and other subscription programming...	5152	68,405	72,473	78,931	41,211	45,099	47,994
Telecommunications...	517	558,935	588,172	601,970	438,363	467,168	477,282
Wired telecommunications carriers[3]...	5171	288,647	296,792	306,384	238,214	252,910	260,074
Wireless telecommunications carriers (except satellite)[4]...	5172	233,123	251,766	254,406	172,724	185,931	187,772
Satellite telecommunications...	5174	6,920	6,729	6,926	4,805	4,666	4,937
Telecommunications resellers[5]...	517911	16,263	17,595	18,708	11,649	12,184	12,582
All other telecommunications[6]...	517919	13,982	15,290	15,546	10,971	11,477	11,917
Data processing, hosting, and related services...	518	116,040	120,450	129,957	102,403	105,358	112,907
Other information services...	519	103,339	115,882	132,740	79,716	94,400	105,896
News syndicates...	51911	1,935	1,898	2,042	1,646	1,663	1,667
Libraries and archives...	51912	2,435	2,496	2,514	2,159	2,274	2,318
Internet publishing and broadcasting, and Web search portals[7]...	51913	96,951	109,414	125,868	74,344	88,716	99,829
Other information services...	51919	2,018	2,074	2,316	1,567	1,747	2,082

[1] North American Industry Classification System (NAICS), 2007; see text, Section 15. [2] Includes NAICS 51211 (Motion Picture and Video Production) and NAICS 51212 (Motion Picture and Video Distribution). [3] Includes 2002 NAICS 5171 (Wired Telecommunications Carriers), 2002 NAICS 5175 (Cable and Other Program Distribution), and a portion of 2002 NAICS 518111 (Internet Service Providers). [4] Includes 2002 NAICS 517211 (Paging), 2002 NAICS 517212 (Cellular and Other Wireless Telecommunications) and a portion of 2002 NAICS 518111 (Internet Service Providers). [5] Includes 2002 NAICS 5173 (Telecommunications Resellers). [6] Includes 2002 NAICS 51791 (Other Telecommunications) and a portion of 2002 NAICS 518111 (Internet Service Providers). [7] Includes 2002 NAICS 516 (Internet Publishing and Broadcasting) and 2002 NAICS 518112 (Web Search Portals).

Source: U.S. Census Bureau, Annual & Quarterly Services, "2015 Service Annual Survey," <http://www.census.gov/services/index.html>, accessed December 2016.

Table 1151. Information Industries—Establishments, Revenue, Payroll, and Employees by Kind of Business: 2012

[1,238,463 represents $1,238,463,000,000. For establishments with payroll. Based on the 2012 Economic Census; see Appendix III]

Kind of business	2012 NAICS code [1]	Establish-ments	Receipts [2] (mil. dol.)	Annual payroll (mil. dol.)	Paid employees (1,000)
Information industries............................	**51**	**138,341**	**1,238,463**	**269,070**	**3,321**
Publishing industries (except internet)................................	511	27,788	272,152	80,426	876
Newspaper, periodical, book, & directory publishers................	5111	18,940	101,076	25,050	466
Software publishers.................................	5112	8,848	171,075	55,376	411
Motion picture & sound recording industries............................	512	25,018	91,974	16,252	304
Motion picture & video industries..............................	5121	21,264	80,762	14,299	281
Sound recording industries..............................	5122	3,754	11,212	1,953	24
Broadcasting (except internet)............................	515	9,597	126,723	20,332	278
Radio broadcasting..............................	51511	6,735	18,000	5,182	104
Television broadcasting..............................	51512	2,090	45,126	8,934	119
Cable & other subscription programming............................	5152	772	63,596	6,217	56
Telecommunications............................	517	50,698	545,594	75,895	1,134
Wired telecommunications carriers..............................	5171	32,688	285,663	54,232	781
Wireless telecommunications carriers (except satellite)............	5172	13,458	225,397	17,041	293
Satellite telecommunications..............................	5174	535	6,802	859	10
Other telecommunications..............................	5179	4,017	27,732	3,763	51
Data processing, hosting, and related services......................	518	14,689	107,994	41,126	497
Other information services............................	519	10,551	94,026	35,038	231

[1] North American Industry Classification System, 2012; see text, this section and Section 15. [2] Includes value of sales, shipments, receipts, revenue, or business done.

Source: U.S. Census Bureau, 2012 Economic Census, "Table EC1200A1: All Sectors: Geographic Area Series: Economy-Wide Key Statistics: 2012," <http://factfinder.census.gov/>, accessed April 2016.

Table 1152. Information Industries—Establishments, Employees, and Payroll by State: 2015

[Annual payroll in millions of dollars (309,327 represents $309,327,000,000). Based on Census Bureau's County Business Patterns and Nonemployer Statistics programs. Data are for North American Industry Classification System (NAICS) 2012 code 51]

State	Establish-ments	Annual payroll (mil. dol.)	Paid employees [1]	Non-employer establish-ments	State	Establish-ments	Annual payroll (mil. dol.)	Paid employees [1]	Non-employer establish-ments
U.S..........	**139,508**	**309,327**	**3,394,317**	**328,995**	MO.........	2,392	3,707	56,075	4,331
AL...........	1,502	1,892	32,939	2,854	MT.........	638	419	8,724	945
AK...........	403	473	6,711	491	NE.........	885	1,259	20,980	1,326
AZ...........	2,121	3,552	49,040	5,814	NV.........	1,272	1,091	16,658	3,282
AR...........	1,014	1,324	24,670	1,709	NH.........	718	1,208	13,880	1,449
CA...........	22,943	84,080	684,853	61,246	NJ.........	3,715	8,904	87,708	10,365
CO...........	3,217	7,234	81,017	7,408	NM.........	727	553	11,413	1,532
CT...........	1,754	3,608	40,729	3,870	NY.........	11,473	30,561	283,737	30,163
DE...........	523	422	6,684	936	NC.........	3,591	5,619	79,884	8,308
DC...........	749	2,643	24,055	1,426	ND.........	329	424	6,798	432
FL...........	8,287	12,236	165,788	23,412	OH.........	3,752	5,771	84,415	8,694
GA...........	4,089	10,418	118,864	10,883	OK.........	1,456	1,609	29,302	2,636
HI...........	498	525	8,116	1,161	OR.........	2,041	2,482	36,436	4,995
ID...........	634	595	11,917	1,461	PA.........	5,047	10,258	113,699	10,277
IL...........	5,439	9,930	123,407	11,435	RI.........	456	456	6,733	934
IN...........	2,048	2,574	42,870	4,633	SC.........	1,376	2,057	33,880	3,451
IA...........	1,473	1,600	30,607	2,159	SD.........	445	324	6,877	590
KS...........	1,359	2,406	34,674	2,112	TN.........	2,440	2,771	48,149	6,709
KY...........	1,507	1,418	35,992	2,679	TX.........	9,238	18,756	238,809	23,287
LA...........	1,447	1,329	26,261	3,181	UT.........	1,471	2,868	44,211	3,923
ME...........	791	560	11,250	1,295	VT.........	485	417	6,839	813
MD...........	2,486	4,096	50,918	6,619	VA.........	3,870	8,565	94,665	7,846
MA...........	3,626	12,420	113,375	8,061	WA.........	3,387	19,641	127,377	7,226
MI...........	3,760	4,700	69,379	8,301	WV.........	660	505	10,517	875
MN...........	2,516	4,301	57,814	5,286	WI.........	2,186	3,925	56,824	4,067
MS...........	921	646	13,773	1,524	WY.........	351	198	4,024	583

[1] Number of paid employees for pay period including March 12.

Source: U.S. Census Bureau, County Business Patterns, "Geography Area Series: County Business Patterns, 2015"; and Nonemployer Statistics, "Geographic Area Series: Nonemployer Statistics for the U.S."; <http://factfinder.census.gov/>, accessed May 2017. See also <https://www.census.gov/programs-surveys/cbp.html> and <http://www.census.gov/econ/nonemployer/>.

Table 1153. Utilization and Number of Selected Media: 2000 to 2015

[100.2 represents 100,200,000]

Media	Unit	2000	2005	2008	2009	2010	2011	2012	2013	2014	2015
Households with—											
Telephones [1]	Millions	100.2	107.0	112.7	114.0	114.0	114.4	116.9	118.4	119.9	122.2
Telephone service [1]	Percent	94.1	92.9	95.0	95.7	95.5	95.6	95.8	95.7	96.1	96.3
Landline households with											
wireless telephone [2]	Percent	(X)	42.4	58.5	59.4	58.1	55.0	52.5	49.5	44.7	41.6
Wireless-only [2]	Percent	(X)	7.3	17.5	22.7	26.6	31.6	35.8	39.4	44.0	47.4
Total broadcast stations [3, 4]	Number	(NA)	27,354	29,832	30,503	30,630	30,411	30,470	30,432	30,592	31,032
Radio stations	Number	(NA)	13,660	14,253	14,420	14,619	14,952	15,196	15,358	15,432	15,480
AM stations	Number	4,685	4,757	4,786	4,790	4,782	4,766	4,738	4,727	4,705	4,684
FM commercial	Number	5,892	6,231	6,427	6,479	6,526	6,542	6,598	6,612	6,652	6,701
FM educational	Number	(NA)	2,672	3,040	3,151	3,311	3,644	3,860	4,019	4,075	4,095
Television stations [3]	Number	1,663	1,750	1,759	1,782	1,781	1,783	1,781	1,784	1,785	1,782
Commercial	Number	1,288	1,370	1,378	1,392	1,390	1,387	1,386	1,388	1,390	1,387
VHF TV band	Number	567	588	582	373	368	360	358	358	358	356
UHF TV band	Number	721	782	796	1,019	1,022	1,027	1,028	1,030	1,032	1,031
Educational	Number	(NA)	380	381	390	391	396	395	396	395	395
VHF TV band	Number	(NA)	126	129	107	107	107	107	107	106	106
UHF TV band	Number	(NA)	254	252	283	284	289	288	289	289	289
Broadband subscribers: [5]											
Total fixed broadband [6]	Millions	6.8	47.8	75.7	80.0	84.5	88.3	92.5	96.0	97.8	102.2
25 Mbps/3 Mbps [7]	Millions	(NA)	(NA)	(NA)	(NA)	(NA)	(NA)	(NA)	(NA)	42.4	54.0
Mobile wireless [8]	Millions	(NA)	(NA)	26.5	56.3	97.5	141.9	170.1	197.4	223.5	253.0
Residential fixed broadband [6]	Millions	5.2	44.0	69.0	73.4	76.9	80.7	84.4	87.6	89.2	93.4
25 Mbps/3 Mbps [7]	Millions	(NA)	(NA)	(NA)	(NA)	(NA)	(NA)	(NA)	(NA)	40.6	51.5
Residential mobile wireless	Millions	(NA)	(NA)	19.1	43.7	72.5	105.8	131.4	159.2	184.8	210.2

NA Not available. X Not applicable. [1] As of November. Based on Current Population Survey. Source: Federal Communications Commission, prior to 2012, *Telephone Subscribership in the United States*, December 2011, and earlier reports. Beginning 2012, *Universal Service Monitoring Report, 2016*, and earlier reports. See also <https://www.fcc.gov/general/federal-state-joint-board-monitoring-reports>. [2] For January to June. Based on National Health Interview Survey. For families living in the same housing unit. Source: U.S. National Center for Health Statistics, *Wireless Substitution: Early Release of Estimates From the National Health Interview Survey, January–June 2016*, December 2016, and earlier reports. See also <http://www.cdc.gov/nchs/nhis/releases.htm#wireless>. [3] As of December 31. Source: Federal Communications Commission Encyclopedia, "Broadcast Station Totals," <https://www.fcc.gov/encyclopedia/broadcast-radio-am-and-fm-application-status-lists>, accessed April 2017. [4] Includes Class A, Low Power TV, UHF and VHF Translators; FM Translators and Boosters; and Low Power FM stations. [5] As of December. Internet access over 200 kilobits per second in at least one direction. Based on FCC Form 477. Source: Federal Communications Commission, Wireline Competition Bureau, *Internet Access Services: Status as of December 31, 2015*, November 2016. [6] Includes aDSL, sDSL, cable modem, fiber-to-the-premises, satellite, fixed wireless, power line, and other. [7] Internet download and upload speeds, measured in megabits per second (Mbps). [8] Data prior to 2008 not shown due to reporting instruction changes on FCC Form 477 between June 2008 and December 2008; see source for details.

Source: Compiled from sources mentioned in footnotes.

Table 1154. Audience Use of Media by Type—Summary: 2016

[In percent, except total population (244,525 represents 244,525,000). As of Fall 2016. For persons age 18 and over. Represents the percent of persons using each media type during an average week, except as noted. Based on a sample and subject to sampling error]

Item	Total pop. (1,000)	TV viewing	TV prime time viewing	Cable/ pay TV viewing [1]	Radio listening	Newspaper reading [2]	Internet use
Total	**244,525**	**89.16**	**78.43**	**74.35**	**83.53**	**45.01**	**82.21**
18 to 24 years old	30,397	76.47	57.50	65.09	86.40	33.93	96.41
25 to 34 years old	43,409	83.05	70.01	63.60	89.59	35.13	95.22
35 to 44 years old	40,294	88.56	78.13	72.08	89.11	39.81	93.71
45 to 54 years old	43,197	92.60	83.22	77.66	88.39	45.64	85.66
55 to 64 years old	40,797	94.01	85.18	80.54	83.32	51.09	77.39
65 years old and over	46,432	96.25	89.90	83.92	66.79	60.10	51.81
Male	117,951	89.27	77.96	74.05	85.10	45.42	82.21
Female	126,574	89.06	78.88	74.62	82.06	44.64	82.22
White only	180,165	88.93	78.90	75.52	83.86	45.88	83.19
Black only	29,592	93.14	82.35	77.80	83.00	52.05	75.61
Other races/multiple classifications	34,768	86.95	72.71	65.35	82.25	34.53	82.80
Employed:							
Full time	120,160	88.90	77.75	74.49	90.56	42.48	92.38
Part time	29,152	84.24	70.60	70.99	85.77	44.12	90.99
Not employed	95,213	90.99	81.69	75.20	73.97	48.48	66.70
Household income:							
Less than $50,000	94,629	88.92	77.43	66.59	77.13	44.91	67.68
$50,000 to $74,999	43,398	89.31	77.93	75.57	86.31	45.43	86.43
$75,000 to $149,999	72,354	88.98	79.13	79.26	88.24	44.80	91.93
$150,000 or more	34,143	90.04	80.40	83.88	87.73	45.22	96.54

[1] In the past 7 days. [2] One or more issues over a 28-day period.

Source: © Fall 2016, GfK MRI a division of GfK US, LLC. See also <http://www.mri.gfk.com/>.

Table 1155. Books Published by Subject: 2005 to 2013

[Data shown are print ISBN (International Standard Book Number) counts, by year of publication. Data are compiled in June of the following year. Includes ISBNs that have not been assigned a subject, books that do not have prices, and books with alternative book bindings]

Subject	2005	2007	2008	2009	2010	2011	2012	2013 [1]
Total.	282,500	407,646	561,580	1,335,475	4,152,906	1,608,751	2,352,797	1,413,095
Agriculture.	1,483	1,259	1,556	1,363	1,833	1,773	2,194	1,470
Arts.	8,762	9,291	10,304	9,860	10,910	10,701	11,320	11,083
Biography.	8,904	11,414	11,375	13,795	12,291	12,163	11,333	10,842
Business.	7,885	7,722	8,873	9,351	10,194	10,109	13,989	11,116
Computers.	6,092	6,069	5,638	5,276	7,553	6,986	7,028	6,959
Cooking.	3,062	2,836	3,164	2,643	3,057	2,963	3,168	3,181
Education.	6,951	7,162	9,640	9,578	10,839	11,820	11,122	10,669
Fiction.	34,927	53,590	53,058	48,738	46,641	43,016	49,853	50,498
General works.	2,017	2,211	2,400	2,562	3,004	2,708	2,507	2,446
History.	12,686	14,406	13,477	15,480	14,659	12,270	11,959	12,471
Home economics.	1,634	1,775	1,644	1,656	1,699	1,579	1,664	1,508
Juveniles.	32,112	31,009	29,825	33,028	31,371	30,836	33,239	32,902
Language.	5,669	4,879	6,181	5,426	4,929	4,358	4,537	4,475
Law.	5,468	5,195	5,533	5,915	5,908	5,795	5,531	6,072
Literature.	6,297	9,974	10,843	11,456	9,315	7,054	7,004	8,591
Medicine.	11,688	10,777	11,022	11,093	12,869	13,690	15,077	13,400
Music.	4,076	3,540	4,131	4,570	3,927	3,948	4,273	5,294
Personal finance.	542	582	598	699	595	636	591	538
Philosophy and psychology.	10,556	13,098	12,605	13,949	14,277	14,011	15,018	15,479
Poetry and drama.	9,414	11,610	11,700	13,474	11,723	9,653	10,038	10,156
Religion.	16,785	19,540	18,296	20,527	18,937	18,518	19,854	18,653
Science.	12,626	12,714	14,100	15,608	20,706	19,010	18,852	18,684
Sociology and economics.	23,750	24,546	24,737	26,904	28,581	28,356	28,442	29,399
Sports and recreation.	6,438	6,362	6,262	5,971	6,639	6,198	6,197	5,807
Technology.	7,138	7,131	7,666	8,688	11,599	10,131	11,564	9,769
Travel.	4,941	5,678	5,101	4,800	4,572	3,755	3,603	3,450
Nontraditional/not classified [2]	30,597	123,276	271,851	1,033,065	3,844,278	1,316,714	2,042,840	1,108,183

[1] Projected. [2] Consists of reprints (often public domain), other titles printed on-demand, and wiki-based material. Also includes records not yet classified or not classifiable.

Source: © ProQuest LLC, Bowker®, a ProQuest affiliate, "ISBN Annual Output Reports," <http://www.bowker.com/tools-resources/Bowker-Data.html>, accessed June 2015.

Table 1156. Publishing Industries—Estimated Revenue by Source and Media Type: 2010 to 2015

[In millions of dollars (260,795 represents $260,795,000,000). For all employer firms regardless of tax status. Estimates adjusted to the 2012 Economic Census. Based on 2007 North American Industry Classification System (NAICS), covering NAICS 51111, 51112, 51113, 51114, and 511191. See text, this section and Section 15, and Appendix III]

Source of revenue and media type	2010	2012	2013	2014	2015
Publishing industries (except internet) [1]	260,795	272,152	279,253	291,575	293,771
Newspaper publishers.	33,360	29,790	28,512	28,112	26,550
Subscription and sales.	8,491	7,855	7,953	8,040	7,987
Advertising space.	20,378	17,245	16,081	15,667	14,868
Classified advertising.	5,082	4,909	3,627	3,288	3,464
All other advertising.	15,296	12,336	12,454	12,379	11,404
Other operating revenue.	4,491	4,690	4,478	4,405	3,695
Printing services.	1,214	1,331	1,452	1,454	1,391
Distribution services.	1,268	1,146	1,078	1,052	782
All other.	2,009	2,213	1,948	1,899	1,522
Print newspapers.	26,973	22,417	21,389	20,421	18,942
Online newspapers.	1,614	2,449	2,277	2,901	3,501
Other media newspapers.	282	234	368	385	412
Periodical publishers.	31,876	29,338	29,185	29,378	28,314
Subscription and sales.	10,764	10,869	10,691	10,435	10,253
Advertising space.	13,938	12,318	12,617	12,475	11,854
Other operating revenue.	7,174	6,151	5,877	6,468	6,207
Printing services for others.	1,241	922	924	966	854
Licensing of rights to content.	434	411	432	497	489
All other.	5,499	4,818	4,521	5,005	4,864
Print periodicals.	20,587	18,429	18,499	17,790	16,425
Online periodicals.	3,402	3,947	4,046	4,433	4,969
Other media periodicals.	713	811	763	687	713
Book publishers.	27,735	26,732	26,720	26,891	27,676
Textbooks.	8,596	8,158	8,581	8,616	8,456
Children's books.	3,189	3,429	3,223	3,234	3,460
General reference books.	637	561	548	625	674
Professional, technical, and scholarly books.	5,131	5,075	4,414	4,369	4,050
Adult trade books.	6,626	6,119	6,311	5,551	5,961
All other operating revenue.	3,556	3,390	3,643	4,496	5,075
Print books.	19,890	18,399	17,690	17,127	16,844
Online books.	3,297	4,213	4,630	4,274	4,744
Other media books.	992	730	757	994	1,013
Directory and mailing list publishers [2]	11,987	10,118	8,265	8,602	8,214
Subscription and sales.	2,067	(S)	3,378	3,436	3,339
Advertising space.	9,226	6,129	4,486	4,707	4,377
Print directories, databases, and other information collections.	7,360	6,034	4,851	4,387	3,939
Online directories, databases, and other information collections.	3,507	3,332	2,756	3,425	(S)

S Figure does not meet publication standards. [1] Includes other industries not shown separately. [2] Includes other revenue sources not shown separately.

Source: U.S. Census Bureau, Annual & Quarterly Services, "2015 Service Annual Survey," <http://www.census.gov/services/index.html>, accessed January 2017.

Table 1157. Daily and Sunday Newspapers—Number and Circulation: 1970 to 2016

[Circulation in millions (62.1 represents 62,100,000). Number of newspapers as of February 1 the following year, except as noted. Circulation figures as of 6-month period ended primarily September 30 of year shown. For English language newspapers only]

Type	1970	1980	1990	2000	2005	2010	2011	2012	2013 [3]	2014 [3]	2015 [3]	2016 [3]
NUMBER												
Total daily newspapers [1]	**1,748**	**1,745**	**1,611**	**1,480**	**1,452**	**(NA)**	**1,381**	**1,425**	**1,395**	**1,331**	**1,338**	**1,286**
Morning	334	387	559	766	817	(NA)	930	983	980	953	972	939
Evening	1,429	1,388	1,084	727	645	(NA)	451	442	444	402	389	369
Sunday newspapers	586	736	863	917	914	(NA)	899	980	934	923	904	866
NET PAID CIRCULATION (mil.)												
Total daily newspapers [1]	62.1	62.2	62.3	55.8	53.3	(NA)	44.2	43.2	40.7	40.4	34.9	33.4
Morning	25.9	29.4	41.3	46.8	46.1	(NA)	40.1	38.4	37.0	36.8	31.6	30.4
Evening	36.2	32.8	21.0	9.0	7.2	(NA)	4.1	4.7	3.7	3.7	3.3	3.1
Sunday newspapers	49.2	54.7	62.6	59.4	55.3	(NA)	48.3	44.6	43.3	42.8	40.0	37.8
PER CAPITA CIRCULATION [2]												
Total daily newspapers [1]	0.30	0.27	0.25	0.20	0.18	(NA)	0.14	0.14	0.13	0.13	0.11	0.10
Morning	0.13	0.13	0.17	0.17	0.16	(NA)	0.13	0.12	0.12	0.12	0.10	0.09
Evening	0.18	0.14	0.08	0.03	0.02	(NA)	0.01	0.02	0.01	0.01	0.01	0.01
Sunday newspapers	0.24	0.24	0.25	0.21	0.19	(NA)	0.16	0.14	0.14	0.13	0.12	0.12

NA Not available. [1] All-day newspapers are counted in both morning and evening rows but only once in total. Circulation is divided equally between morning and evening. [2] Based on U.S. Census Bureau estimated resident population as of July 1 as of year shown. [3] Number of newspapers as of January 1 of following year.

Source: Editor & Publisher, 17782 Cowan Ste C, Irvine, CA 92614, *Editor & Publisher Newspaper DataBook* ©, annual. See also <http://www.editorandpublisher.com/>.

Table 1158. Daily and Sunday Newspapers—Number and Circulation: Total, 1995 to 2016, and by State, 2016

[Circulation in thousands (58,193 represents 58,193,000). Number of newspapers as of February 1 the following year, except as noted. Circulation as of 6-month period ended primarily September 30 of year shown. For English language newspapers only]

State	Daily Number	Daily Net paid (1,000)	Daily Per capita [2]	Sunday Number	Sunday Net paid circulation [1] (1,000)	State	Daily Number	Daily Net paid (1,000)	Daily Per capita [2]	Sunday Number	Sunday Net paid circulation [1] (1,000)
1995	1,533	58,193	0.22	888	61,529	IN	67	842	0.13	32	1,026
1996	1,520	56,983	0.21	890	60,798	IA	33	380	0.12	14	396
1997	1,509	56,728	0.21	903	60,484	KS	29	258	0.09	12	210
1998	1,489	56,182	0.20	898	60,066	KY	22	351	0.08	15	389
1999	1,483	55,979	0.20	905	59,894	LA	19	300	0.06	13	318
2000	1,480	55,773	0.20	917	59,421	ME	8	121	0.09	5	97
2001	1,468	55,578	0.19	913	59,090	MD	9	241	0.04	8	371
2002	1,457	55,186	0.19	913	58,780	MA	31	799	0.12	18	782
2003	1,456	55,185	0.19	917	58,495	MI	45	524	0.05	23	629
2004	1,457	54,626	0.19	915	57,753	MN	22	615	0.11	14	846
2005	1,452	53,345	0.18	914	55,270	MS	18	190	0.06	17	202
2006	1,437	52,329	0.18	907	53,175	MO	35	520	0.09	17	637
2007	1,422	50,742	0.17	907	51,246	MT	11	122	0.12	8	124
2008	1,408	48,598	0.16	902	49,115	NE	15	233	0.12	6	221
2009	1,397	46,278	0.15	919	46,895	NV	6	446	0.15	5	400
2010	(NA)	(NA)	(NA)	(NA)	(NA)	NH	11	133	0.10	6	115
2011	1,381	44,243	0.14	899	48,301	NJ	16	758	0.08	14	950
2012	1,425	43,154	0.14	980	44,612	NM	15	165	0.08	12	164
2013 [3]	1,395	40,712	0.13	934	43,292	NY	55	6,595	0.33	38	7,285
2014 [3]	1,331	40,420	0.13	923	42,751	ND	44	679	0.07	39	819
2015 [3]	1,338	34,901	0.11	904	40,014	ND	10	96	0.13	7	103
						OH	80	1,177	0.10	43	1,320
Total, 2016 [3]	**1,286**	**33,419**	**0.10**	**866**	**37,771**	OK	33	357	0.09	25	411
AL	21	224	0.05	14	215	OR	16	193	0.05	12	196
AK	7	66	0.09	4	57	PA	71	1,565	0.12	47	1,592
AZ	12	351	0.05	10	508	RI	5	90	0.09	2	98
AR	26	304	0.10	15	311	SC	16	310	0.06	14	379
CA	69	2,532	0.06	53	3,381	SD	11	101	0.12	5	78
CO	27	590	0.11	17	685	TN	25	440	0.07	18	586
CT	18	383	0.11	14	463	TX	68	1,544	0.06	63	1,969
DE	2	77	0.08	2	94	UT	6	167	0.05	6	281
DC	3	604	0.89	1	770	VT	8	62	0.10	4	48
FL	38	1,548	0.08	35	2,161	VA	20	2,863	0.34	17	1,836
GA	30	500	0.05	23	640	WA	20	525	0.07	17	676
HI	6	209	0.15	5	222	WV	17	207	0.11	12	234
ID	12	150	0.09	10	247	WI	32	508	0.09	20	601
IL	57	1,339	0.10	29	1,569	WY	9	63	0.11	6	60

NA Not available. [1] Circulation figures based on the principal community served by a newspaper which is not necessarily the same location as the publisher's office. [2] Per capita based on estimated resident population as of July 1 of year shown. [3] Number of newspapers as of January 1 of following year.

Source: Editor & Publisher, 17782 Cowan Ste C, Irvine, CA 92614, *Editor & Publisher Newspaper DataBook* ©, annual. See also <http://www.editorandpublisher.com/>.

Table 1159. Software Publishers—Estimated Revenue by Type: 2010 to 2015

[In millions of dollars (150,459 represents $150,459,000,000). For all employer firms regardless of tax status. Data are based on the 2007 North American Industry Classification System (NAICS), and cover NAICS 5112. Estimates are adjusted to the 2012 Economic Census where applicable. See text, this section, and Section 15, Business Enterprise. See also Appendix III]

Item	2010	2012	2013	2014	2015
Operating revenue............................	**150,459**	**171,075**	**181,734**	**193,822**	**198,341**
By source:					
System software publishing [1]............................	50,626	53,629	59,447	61,352	62,171
Operating system software............................	18,439	17,144	19,813	19,127	19,041
Network software............................	14,870	17,089	17,614	18,163	18,362
Database management software............................	9,832	11,293	12,737	13,364	14,974
Development tools and programming languages software............	3,765	3,657	4,185	4,264	2,484
Application software publishing [1]................	56,882	65,171	68,088	75,125	75,834
General business productivity and home use applications............	25,766	30,466	32,173	35,803	35,030
Cross-industry application software............	13,635	15,725	17,973	18,713	20,568
Vertical market application software............	9,340	10,099	9,726	11,350	11,927
Utilities application software............	2,649	3,390	3,142	3,164	2,605
Other services [1]............	(NA)	52,275	(NA)	57,345	60,336
Custom application design and development............	4,551	6,021	(S)	5,667	5,602
Information technology technical consulting services............	4,621	5,685	6,560	6,516	6,681
Resale of computer hardware and software............	4,462	6,001	6,602	8,609	9,501
Information technology-related training services............	1,694	2,097	2,004	1,947	2,331
By software sales type:					
System software............	50,626	53,629	59,447	61,352	62,171
Personal computer software............	17,623	15,657	16,119	15,469	15,461
Enterprise or network software............	19,444	22,444	26,096	26,651	28,399
Mainframe computer software............	9,783	10,890	12,205	13,485	12,907
Other system software............	3,776	4,638	5,027	5,747	5,404
Application software............	56,882	65,171	68,088	75,125	75,834
Personal computer software............	16,946	19,786	22,360	23,107	20,511
Enterprise or network software............	28,622	32,792	34,937	38,555	40,236
Mainframe computer software............	1,976	1,643	1,541	1,619	2,492
Other application software............	9,338	10,950	(S)	(S)	(S)
Operating expenses, total [1]............	**98,348**	**109,889**	**115,296**	**123,725**	**124,329**
Personnel costs [1]............	59,538	69,627	73,364	77,344	77,488
Gross annual payroll............	45,013	53,143	55,852	58,875	60,185
Employer's cost for fringe benefits............	11,044	12,644	13,924	14,703	14,141
Health insurance............	(NA)	4,335	4,763	4,830	4,472
Defined benefit pension plans............	(NA)	151	(S)	100	92
Defined contribution plans............	(NA)	1,187	1,339	1,583	1,505
Payroll taxes, employer paid insurance premiums (except health), and other employer benefits............	(NA)	6,971	7,680	8,190	8,072
Temporary staff and leased employee expense............	3,481	3,840	3,588	3,766	3,162
Expensed equipment............	606	716	912	772	752
Expensed purchases of software............	816	931	936	1,174	1,392
Purchased electricity and fuels (except motor fuels)............	404	305	313	326	322
Lease and rental payments............	2,133	2,218	2,300	2,499	2,403
Purchased advertising and promotional services............	7,280	6,048	7,328	8,130	7,903
Depreciation and amortization charges............	5,452	5,973	6,867	7,544	7,650
Governmental taxes and license fees............	(S)	916	897	1,315	1,159
Inventories at end of year, total............	**1,876**	**2,238**	**(S)**	**3,961**	**3,791**

NA Not available. S Data do not meet publication standards. [1] Includes other sources of revenue and types of expenses, not shown separately.

Source: U.S. Census Bureau, Annual & Quarterly Services, "2015 Service Annual Survey," <http://www.census.gov/services/index.html>, accessed January 2017.

Table 1160. Internet Publishing and Broadcasting, and Web Search Portals—Estimated Revenue and Expenses: 2010 to 2015

[In millions of dollars (54,976 represents $54,976,000,000). For all employer firms regardless of tax status. Data are based on the 2007 North American Industry Classification System (NAICS), and cover NAICS 51913, which includes 2002 NAICS 516 (Internet Publishing and Broadcasting) and 2002 NAICS 518112 (Web Search Portals). Estimates are adjusted to the 2012 Economic Census. See text, Section 15, and Appendix III]

Item	2010	2012	2013	2014	2015
Operating revenue............	**54,976**	**87,946**	**96,951**	**109,414**	**125,868**
Source of revenue:					
Publishing and broadcasting of content on the internet............	19,238	29,006	30,765	34,079	42,287
Online advertising space............	27,406	44,085	49,805	54,670	64,330
Licensing of rights to use intellectual property............	1,320	3,409	3,782	4,133	3,109
All other operating revenue............	(S)	11,446	12,599	16,532	16,142
Revenue by type of customer:					
Household consumers and individual users............	(S)	23,097	25,125	31,741	36,451
Business firms, not-for-profit organizations, and government............	(S)	64,849	71,826	77,673	89,417
Operating expenses............	**40,417**	**65,524**	**74,344**	**88,716**	**99,829**

S Data do not meet publication standards.

Source: U.S. Census Bureau, Annual & Quarterly Services, "2015 Service Annual Survey," <http://www.census.gov/services/index.html>, accessed January 2017.

Table 1161. Motion Picture and Sound Recording Industries—Estimated Revenue and Sources of Revenue: 2010 to 2015

[In millions of dollars (89,323 represents $89,323,000,000). For all employer firms regardless of tax status. Data are based on the 2007 North American Industry Classification System (NAICS). Estimates have been adjusted to the results of the 2012 Economic Census. See text, this section, and Section 15, Business Enterprise. See also Appendix III]

Kind of business and revenue source	2010	2012	2013	2014	2015
Operating revenue	**89,323**	**91,259**	**94,246**	**93,865**	**98,024**
Motion picture and video industries	**77,520**	**80,762**	**83,949**	**83,054**	**86,119**
Motion picture and video production and distribution [1,2]	59,411	61,886	64,504	62,831	64,434
Domestic licensing of rights to motion picture films	13,113	12,863	13,282	12,156	14,419
Domestic licensing of rights to television programs	10,767	12,250	12,974	13,225	13,988
International licensing of rights to motion picture films	8,623	7,434	8,125	6,897	7,568
International licensing of rights to television programs	3,010	3,680	4,196	4,828	4,144
Sale of audiovisual works for wholesale, retail, and rental markets	10,619	8,825	8,164	6,395	6,159
Motion picture and video exhibition [1]	12,869	13,544	14,144	14,563	15,787
Admissions to feature film exhibitions	8,731	8,913	9,191	9,316	9,932
Food and beverage sales	3,615	3,916	4,140	4,388	4,960
Postproduction services and other motion picture and video industries [1]	5,240	5,332	5,301	5,660	5,898
Audiovisual postproduction services	3,125	3,414	3,572	3,674	3,728
Motion picture film laboratory services	428	(S)	140	166	134
Duplication and copying services	1,158	1,067	1,020	1,050	999
Sound recording industries	**11,803**	**10,497**	**10,297**	**10,811**	**11,905**
Integrated record production and distribution [1]	6,991	5,408	5,032	5,077	5,765
Licensing revenue	(NA)	(NA)	388	559	629
Sales of recordings	5,475	4,156	3,982	3,890	4,460
Music publishers [1]	3,964	4,176	4,314	4,732	5,054
Licensing of rights to use musical compositions	3,205	3,429	3,496	3,753	3,938
Print music	280	283	272	242	237
Sound recording studios [1]	848	913	951	1,002	1,086
Studio recording	627	651	647	644	683

NA Not available. S Data do not meet publication standards. [1] Includes other sources of revenue not shown separately. [2] Includes NAICS 51211 (Motion Picture and Video Production) and NAICS 51212 (Motion Picture and Video Distribution).

Source: U.S. Census Bureau, Annual & Quarterly Services, "2015 Service Annual Survey," <http://www.census.gov/services/index.html>, accessed January 2017.

Table 1162. Recording Media—Manufacturers' Shipments and Value: 2000 to 2016

[1,079.2 represents 1,079,200,000. Data are net after returns. Formats with no retail value equivalent included at wholesale value. Based on reports of Recording Industry Association of America member companies who distribute about 85 percent of the music sold in the U.S. Data are supplemented by other sources]

Medium	2000	2005	2010	2011	2012	2013	2014	2015	2016
UNIT SHIPMENTS (mil.)									
Total [1]	**1,079.2**	**1,301.9**	**1,739.5**	**1,825.0**	**1,803.4**	**1,691.1**	**1,481.0**	**1,272.3**	**977.2**
Physical [2]	**1,079.2**	**748.8**	**267.7**	**255.8**	**212.7**	**188.9**	**161.3**	**141.1**	**119.8**
Compact disk, album [3]	942.5	705.4	253.0	240.8	198.2	173.8	142.5	119.9	99.4
Compact disk, single	34.2	2.8	1.0	1.3	1.1	0.6	1.0	0.4	0.1
Vinyl LP/EP (long play/extended play)	2.2	1.0	4.2	5.5	6.9	9.4	13.1	16.9	17.2
Vinyl single	4.8	2.3	0.3	0.4	0.4	0.3	0.5	0.5	0.4
Music video [4]	18.2	33.8	9.1	7.7	6.0	4.8	4.1	3.2	2.5
Digital	(X)	554.4	1,473.3	1,571.0	1,594.1	1,508.5	1,327.4	1,142.0	880.0
Download single	(X)	366.9	1,177.4	1,332.3	1,392.2	1,332.8	1,167.1	994.5	751.2
Download album	(X)	13.6	85.8	103.9	116.7	118.0	117.5	109.3	86.0
Kiosk [5]	(X)	0.7	1.7	1.3	2.0	3.7	1.6	2.2	1.7
Music video	(X)	1.9	18.4	16.3	10.5	8.4	6.8	3.2	2.3
Mobile [6]	(X)	170.0	188.5	115.4	69.3	39.3	26.6	21.9	16.1
Paid subscription [7]	(X)	1.3	1.5	1.8	3.4	6.2	7.7	10.8	22.6
VALUE (mil. dol.)									
Total [8]	**14,323.7**	**12,289.9**	**7,013.8**	**7,135.6**	**7,015.5**	**7,034.5**	**6,877.1**	**6,868.8**	**7,650.5**
Physical [2]	**14,323.7**	**11,195.0**	**3,663.7**	**3,381.0**	**2,772.3**	**2,463.8**	**2,245.6**	**1,982.0**	**1,670.3**
Compact disk, album [3]	13,214.5	10,520.2	3,389.4	3,100.7	2,485.6	2,140.9	1,829.1	1,482.5	1,172.5
Compact disk, single	142.7	10.9	2.9	3.5	3.2	2.4	3.8	1.2	0.3
Vinyl LP/EP (long play/extended play)	27.7	14.2	88.9	119.4	160.7	210.7	313.0	414.5	429.7
Vinyl single	26.3	13.2	2.3	4.6	4.7	3.0	5.9	6.1	5.4
Music video [4]	281.9	602.2	177.6	151.0	116.6	106.3	90.9	71.2	58.4
Digital [9]	(X)	1,094.9	3,161.4	3,558.1	4,052.6	4,381.0	4,441.8	4,683.9	5,775.9
Download single	(X)	363.3	1,336.4	1,522.4	1,623.6	1,573.4	1,370.3	1,195.1	906.8
Download album	(X)	135.7	872.0	1,070.8	1,204.8	1,232.1	1,150.0	1,090.0	875.8
Kiosk [5]	(X)	1.0	6.4	2.7	3.7	6.2	2.6	3.7	2.9
Music video	(X)	3.7	36.6	32.4	20.8	16.7	13.6	6.4	4.5
Mobile [6]	(X)	421.6	448.0	276.2	166.9	97.9	66.3	54.5	40.1
Paid subscription [7]	(X)	149.2	212.4	247.8	399.9	643.3	778.8	1,158.8	2,258.3
SoundExchange distributions	(X)	20.4	249.2	292.0	462.0	590.4	773.4	802.6	883.9
On-demand streaming [10]	(X)	(X)	(X)	113.8	170.9	220.9	286.9	372.7	469.0

X Not applicable. [1] Total unit shipments exclude paid subscriptions. [2] Includes other media (DVD audio, super audio CD, and cassettes), not shown separately. [3] Prior to 2006, includes DualDisc. [4] Includes DVD video. [5] Singles and albums. [6] Master ringtones and ringbacks; prior to 2013, also included music videos, full length downloads, and other mobile. [7] Streaming, tethered, and other paid subscription services not operating under statutory licenses. Volume is annual average number of subscribers. [8] Total value includes synchronization royalties, not shown separately. [9] Beginning 2016, includes "other digital," "limited tier paid subscription," and "other advertising supported streaming," not shown separately. [10] Advertising supported audio and music video services not operating under statutory licenses.

Source: Recording Industry Association of America, Washington, D.C., *News and Notes on 2016 RIAA Shipment and Revenue Statistics* ©; and "RIAA U.S. Sales Database," <https://www.riaa.com/u-s-sales-database/> ©, accessed April 2017.

Table 1163. Radio and Television Broadcasting—Estimated Revenue and Expenses: 2010 to 2015

[In millions of dollars (4,626 represents $4,626,000,000). For all employer firms regardless of tax status. Based on the 2007 North American Industry Classification System (NAICS). Estimates have been adjusted to the results of the 2012 Economic Census. See text, this section, and Section 15, Business Enterprise]

Item	2010	2012	2013	2014	2015
RADIO NETWORKS (NAICS 51511)					
Total operating revenue	**4,626**	**5,158**	**5,703**	**6,011**	**6,509**
National/regional/local air time	748	849	961	1,005	997
Public and non-commercial programming services	420	432	421	427	452
All other operating revenue	3,458	3,877	4,321	4,579	5,060
RADIO STATIONS (NAICS 515112)					
Total operating revenue	**12,313**	**12,842**	**12,523**	**12,397**	**12,445**
National/regional/local air time	10,521	10,644	10,558	10,437	10,415
Public and non-commercial programming services	599	624	689	685	741
All other operating revenue	1,193	1,574	1,276	1,275	1,289
TELEVISION BROADCASTING (NAICS 51512)					
Total operating revenue	**38,926**	**45,126**	**44,782**	**49,911**	**50,577**
National/regional/local air time	30,803	35,640	34,240	37,274	36,121
Public and non-commercial programming services	1,853	1,883	2,121	2,246	2,367
All other operating revenue	6,270	7,603	8,421	10,391	12,089
RADIO AND TELEVISION BROADCASTING (NAICS 5151)					
Operating expenses, total	**47,087**	**49,926**	**50,052**	**52,908**	**55,443**
Personnel costs	14,370	16,105	16,379	17,361	17,901
Gross annual payroll	11,898	13,348	13,478	14,312	14,713
Employer's cost for fringe benefits	1,850	2,199	2,435	2,523	2,638
Temporary staff and leased employee expense	622	558	466	526	550
Expensed equipment	187	135	114	133	131
Expensed purchases of other materials, parts, and supplies	230	205	240	257	248
Expensed purchases of software	201	194	195	197	240
Purchased electricity and fuels (except motor fuel)	373	392	398	435	424
Lease and rental payments	901	913	959	1,018	1,065
Purchased repair and maintenance	275	317	334	368	354
Purchased advertising and promotional services	1,324	1,584	1,700	1,858	1,986
Broadcast rights and music license fees	13,177	14,859	14,781	15,131	16,039
Network compensation fees (networks only)	518	468	580	794	1,295
Depreciation and amortization charges	2,671	2,848	2,785	3,284	3,198
Governmental taxes and license fees	271	306	373	280	329
Other operating expenses	12,589	11,600	11,214	11,792	12,233
Data processing and other purchased computer services	(NA)	173	225	279	290
Purchased communication services	(NA)	365	407	402	410
Water, sewer, refuse removal, and other utility payments	(NA)	31	32	36	43
Purchased professional and technical services	(NA)	1,016	1,040	984	1,151
All other operating expenses	(NA)	10,015	9,510	10,091	10,339

NA Not available.

Source: U.S. Census Bureau, Annual & Quarterly Services, "2015 Service Annual Survey," <http://www.census.gov/services/index.html>, accessed January 2017.

Table 1164. Cable and Premium TV—Summary: 1990 to 2014

[In units as indicated (50,520 represents 50,520,000). Cable TV for calendar year. Premium TV as of December 31 of year shown]

Year	Cable TV Average basic subscribers (1,000)	Cable TV Average monthly basic rate (dol.)	Revenue [1] Total (mil. dol.)	Revenue [1] Basic (mil. dol.)	Units [2] Total premium [3] (1,000)	Units [2] Premium cable (1,000)	Units [2] Non-cable delivered premium (1,000)	Monthly rate [4] All premium weighted average [5] (dollars)	Monthly rate [4] Premium cable (dollars)	Monthly rate [4] Non-cable delivered premium (dollars)
1990	50,520	16.78	17,405	10,174	39,902	(NA)	(NA)	10.35	(NA)	(NA)
1995	60,550	23.07	23,669	16,763	60,098	51,173	8,925	8.32	8.54	6.99
1998	64,650	27.81	30,568	21,574	83,886	58,562	25,325	8.60	8.74	8.22
1999	65,500	28.92	33,392	22,732	89,655	60,205	29,450	8.75	8.85	8.50
2000	66,302	30.37	35,963	24,161	103,440	66,768	36,672	8.72	8.81	8.48
2001	66,884	32.87	41,374	26,384	115,525	75,633	39,892	8.97	9.10	8.66
2002	66,729	34.71	47,573	27,797	125,662	81,128	44,534	9.19	9.29	9.00
2003	66,374	36.59	52,123	29,142	127,377	83,421	43,956	9.38	9.45	9.23
2004	66,102	38.14	57,105	30,252	140,060	90,843	49,217	9.91	9.92	9.88
2005	65,764	39.63	62,515	31,278	149,067	96,910	52,157	9.95	9.97	9.93
2006	65,787	41.17	68,743	32,505	158,069	101,464	56,605	10.01	10.02	9.98
2007	65,655	42.72	75,218	33,657	171,043	109,960	61,083	10.05	10.06	10.02
2008	64,821	44.28	81,023	34,442	149,749	92,540	57,209	10.08	10.10	10.06
2009	63,432	46.13	84,425	35,113	150,651	85,975	64,676	10.12	10.13	10.09
2010	61,516	47.89	88,025	35,352	166,241	88,359	77,882	10.15	10.17	10.13
2011	59,489	49.90	91,458	35,623	175,322	90,425	84,896	10.19	10.21	10.17
2012	57,796	51.68	94,647	35,845	183,459	91,363	92,095	10.23	10.25	10.21
2013	56,041	53.28	96,312	35,833	186,785	91,124	95,660	10.24	10.26	10.23
2014	54,384	54.92	99,328	35,840	189,812	92,907	96,904	10.24	10.25	10.22

NA Not available. [1] Includes total video, residential telephony and high-speed internet access revenue. [2] Individual program services sold to subscribers with more than one unit often sold to an individual household. [3] Includes multipoint distribution service (MDS), satellite TV (STV), multipoint multichannel distribution service (MMDS), satellite master antenna TV (SMATV), C-band satellite, DBS satellite, and telecommunications video for full- and mini- premium services. [4] Weighted average representing 8 months of unregulated basic rate and 4 months of FCC rolled-back rate. [5] Includes average premium unit price based on data for major premium services.

Source: SNL Kagan, a division of SNL Financial, LC. From the *Broadband Cable Financial Databook* ©, annual; the *Cable Program Investor* and *Cable TV Investor: Deals & Finance* ©, monthly newsletters; and various other SNL Kagan publications ©. See also <http://www.snl.com/Sectors/Media/Default.aspx>.

Table 1165. Cable and Other Subscription Programming—Estimated Revenue and Expenses: 2010 to 2015

[In millions of dollars (54,869 represents $54,869,000,000). For all employer firms regardless of tax status. Based on the 2007 North American Industry Classification System. Covers NAICS 5152. Estimates have been adjusted to the results of the 2012 Economic Census. See text, this section and Section 15, and Appendix III]

Item	2010	2012	2013	2014	2015
Operating revenue, total	**54,869**	**63,596**	**68,405**	**72,473**	**78,931**
Source of revenue:					
Advertising and program revenue [1]	31,218	36,425	39,273	42,266	47,817
Air time	21,170	23,112	24,734	26,039	27,388
All other operating services revenue	2,481	4,059	4,398	4,168	3,726
Operating expenses, total	**34,124**	**38,640**	**41,211**	**45,099**	**47,994**
Personnel costs	6,729	7,162	7,478	7,914	8,531
Gross annual payroll	5,418	5,727	6,036	6,293	6,874
Employer's cost for fringe benefits	987	1,154	1,214	1,338	1,358
Health insurance	(NA)	339	392	515	482
Defined benefit pension plans	(NA)	128	138	93	130
Defined contribution plans	(NA)	237	232	255	252
Payroll taxes, employer paid insurance premiums (except health), and other employer benefits	(NA)	450	452	475	494
Temporary staff and leased employee expense	324	281	228	283	299
Expensed equipment	83	77	81	82	76
Expensed purchases of other materials, parts, and supplies	74	67	64	74	81
Expensed purchases of software	80	100	110	129	140
Purchased electricity and fuels (except motor fuels)	69	64	66	68	68
Lease and rental payments	613	647	680	725	751
Purchased repairs and maintenance	90	132	132	132	156
Purchased advertising and promotional services	2,606	2,722	2,663	2,893	3,216
Program and production costs	16,464	19,339	21,044	22,282	24,687
Depreciation and amortization charges	4,091	4,284	4,497	5,025	4,845
Governmental taxes and license fees	66	100	93	108	103
Other operating expenses	3,159	3,946	4,303	5,667	5,340
Data processing and other purchased computer services	(NA)	50	55	54	48
Purchased communication services	(NA)	98	97	104	101
Water, sewer, refuse removal, and other utility payments	(NA)	11	11	11	12
Purchased professional and technical services	(NA)	525	604	657	685
All other operating expenses	(NA)	3,262	3,536	4,841	4,494

NA Not available. [1] Licensing of rights to broadcast specialty programming protected by copyright.

Source: U.S. Census Bureau, Annual & Quarterly Services, "2015 Service Annual Survey," <http://www.census.gov/services/index.html>, accessed January 2017.

Table 1166. Telecommunications Industry Revenue by Service Type: 2010 to 2015

[Revenue in millions of dollars (446,386 represents $446,386,000,000). Data are based on carrier Form 499-A filings to the Federal Communications Commission, and are the basis for establishing Universal Service Fund (USF) program collections]

Category	Revenue (mil. dol.)					
	2010	2011	2012	2013	2014	2015
Total reported revenue	446,386	475,576	479,729	494,981	496,892	515,598
Total telecommunications revenue	**273,158**	**261,038**	**255,242**	**243,088**	**228,631**	**214,477**
Non-telecommunications revenue	173,228	214,538	224,487	251,892	268,260	301,121
Local service and payphone revenue	**102,847**	**98,313**	**95,422**	**93,105**	**90,994**	**90,495**
Local exchange and Federal/State USF support	56,993	52,718	50,598	49,016	47,495	46,515
Pay telephone	197	136	362	359	327	286
Local private line	26,809	28,243	29,101	29,632	31,194	32,191
Other local	3,032	3,145	2,408	1,746	1,456	1,493
Subscriber line charges	7,481	6,703	6,195	5,968	5,507	5,175
Access	8,336	7,368	6,759	6,384	5,016	4,836
Mobile service revenue	**111,643**	**107,393**	**105,183**	**98,160**	**86,998**	**75,263**
Toll service revenue	**50,006**	**46,347**	**44,624**	**42,837**	**41,555**	**39,678**
Operator	3,585	3,162	3,092	3,064	2,785	2,351
Non-operator switched toll	27,132	27,557	25,340	23,345	22,518	21,499
Long distance private line	14,344	11,443	12,262	12,542	12,362	12,778
Other long distance	4,945	4,186	3,929	3,886	3,891	3,050

Source: U.S. Federal Communications Commission, *Universal Service Monitoring Report, 2016,* January 2017. See also <https://www.fcc.gov/general/federal-state-joint-board-monitoring-reports>.

Table 1167. Wired and Wireless Telecommunications Carriers—Estimated Revenue: 2010 to 2015

[In millions of dollars (281,149 represents $281,149,000,000). For all employer firms regardless of tax status. Data are based on 2007 North American Industry Classification System (NAICS) and cover NAICS 5171 Wired Telecommunications Carriers and NAICS 5172 Wireless Telecommunications Carriers (except satellite). Estimates have been adjusted to the results of the 2012 Economic Census. See text, this section and Section 15, and Appendix III]

Item	2010	2012	2013	2014	2015
Wired telecommunications carriers operating revenue [1]	**281,149**	**285,663**	**288,647**	**296,792**	**306,384**
Fixed local telephony	43,765	35,990	31,201	30,395	31,365
Fixed long-distance telephony	19,964	18,068	16,447	15,478	16,188
Fixed all distance	2,640	1,894	1,249	1,131	1,190
Carrier services	18,183	17,663	16,386	18,588	18,451
Private network services	21,069	20,496	19,929	19,429	20,552
Subscriber line charges	3,289	3,988	3,555	3,430	3,579
Internet access services	51,588	63,069	70,146	73,048	79,670
Internet telephony	9,874	12,530	12,976	13,013	13,362
Telecommunications network installation services	503	399	504	654	1,002
Reselling services for telecommunications equipment, retail	1,696	1,273	1,305	1,143	1,351
Rental of telecommunications equipment	687	472	484	592	572
Repair and maintenance services for telecommunications equipment	373	638	566	904	966
Basic programming package	52,634	55,594	58,569	60,034	60,218
Premium programming package	20,367	21,752	21,181	21,124	19,792
Pay-per-view	3,303	3,200	(S)	3,086	2,743
Air time (advertising and program content)	4,843	(S)	(S)	5,021	4,765
Rental and reselling services for program distribution equipment	7,840	10,707	11,558	12,132	13,084
Installation services for connections to program distribution networks	1,081	1,245	1,360	1,658	1,403
Website hosting services	291	140	134	178	207
All other operating revenue	17,159	12,058	13,345	15,754	15,924
Wireless telecommunications carrier operating revenue [2]	**199,235**	**225,397**	**233,123**	**251,766**	**254,406**
Messaging (paging) services	921	554	(S)	(S)	530
Mobile telephony	58,238	54,716	62,015	59,890	60,967
Mobile long distance	3,387	(D)	(D)	4,184	4,020
Mobile all distance	(S)	65,493	59,666	54,093	46,260
Internet access services	(S)	62,878	66,274	77,373	80,290
Telecommunication network installation services	(S)	172	196	207	187
Reselling services for telecommunications equipment, retail	18,754	23,682	24,690	35,483	42,064
Rental of telecommunications equipment	333	342	433	489	473
Repair and maintenance services for telecommunications equipment	1,219	(D)	(D)	2,232	2,217
All other operating revenue	11,492	12,694	13,723	17,277	17,398

S Data do not meet publication standards. D Estimate in table is withheld to avoid disclosing data of individual companies; data are included in higher level totals. [1] Includes 2002 NAICS 5171 (Wired Telecommunications Carriers), 2002 NAICS 5175 (Cable and Other Program Distribution), and a portion of 2002 NAICS 518111 (Internet Service Providers). [2] Includes 2002 NAICS 517211 (Paging), 2002 NAICS 517212 (Cellular and Other Wireless Telecommunications), and a portion of 2002 NAICS 518111 (Internet Service Providers). Excludes satellite telecommunications.

Source: U.S. Census Bureau, Annual & Quarterly Services, "2015 Service Annual Survey," <http://www.census.gov/services/index.html>, accessed January 2017.

Table 1168. Average Annual Telephone Service Expenditures by All Consumer Units: 2001 to 2015

[In dollars except percent distribution. Based on the Consumer Expenditure Survey. Expenditures reported are direct out-of-pocket expenditures. A consumer unit is defined as members of a household related by blood, marriage, adoption, or some other legal arrangement; a single person living alone or sharing a household with others, but who is financially independent; or two or more persons living together who share responsibility for at least two out of the three major types of expenses: food, housing, and other expenses]

Year	Average annual telephone service (dollars)				Percent distribution			
	Total telephone services	Residential and other telephone services [1]	Cellular phone service	Other services [2]	Total telephone services	Residential and other telephone services [1]	Cellular phone service	Other services [2]
2001	914	686	210	19	100.0	75.1	23.0	2.1
2002	957	641	294	22	100.0	67.0	30.7	2.3
2003	956	620	316	20	100.0	64.9	33.1	2.1
2004	990	592	378	20	100.0	59.8	38.2	2.0
2005	1,048	570	455	23	100.0	54.4	43.4	2.2
2006	1,087	542	524	21	100.0	49.9	48.2	1.9
2007	1,110	482	608	20	100.0	43.4	54.8	1.8
2008	1,127	467	643	17	100.0	41.4	57.0	1.5
2009	1,162	434	712	17	100.0	37.3	61.2	1.4
2010	1,178	401	760	17	100.0	34.1	64.5	1.4
2011	1,226	381	826	20	100.0	31.1	67.3	1.6
2012	1,239	359	862	19	100.0	28.9	69.6	1.5
2013	1,271	358	913	(NA)	100.0	28.2	71.8	(NA)
2014	1,315	353	963	(NA)	100.0	26.8	73.2	(NA)
2015	1,347	324	1,023	(NA)	100.0	24.1	75.9	(NA)

NA Not available. [1] Beginning 2013, data are shown for residential telephone, phone cards, VoIP (Voice over Internet Protocol), and pay phone services combined. Prior to 2013, data are shown for residential and pay telephone services. [2] Phone cards, pager services, and for 2007-2012, VoIP.

Source: U.S. Bureau of Labor Statistics, Consumer Expenditure Survey, unpublished data; and "Annual Calendar Year Tables, 2015," <http://www.bls.gov/cex/home.htm>, accessed January 2017.

Table 1169. Cellular Telecommunications Industry: 2000 to 2016

[In units as indicated (109.5 represents 109,500,000). Calendar year data, except as noted. Based on a survey sent to facilities-based commercial mobile radio service providers, including cellular, personal communications services, advanced wireless service, mobile WiMAX, and enhanced special mobile radio (ESMR) systems. The number of operational systems beginning 2000 differs from that reported for previous periods as a result of the consolidated operation of ESMR systems in a broader service area instead of by a city-to-city basis]

Item	Unit	2000	2005	2010	2012	2013	2014	2015	2016
Wireless subscriber connections [1]	Millions	109.5	207.9	296.3	326.5	335.7	355.4	377.9	395.9
Wireless penetration [2]	Percent	38.0	69.0	94.2	102.2	104.3	109.7	115.7	120.6
Cell sites [3]	Number	104,288	183,689	253,086	301,779	304,360	298,055	307,626	308,334
Employees	Number	184,449	233,067	250,393	230,101	230,409	232,169	235,818	216,537
Service revenue	Mil. dol.	52,466	113,538	159,930	185,014	189,193	187,848	191,949	188,524
Capital investment [4]	Mil. dol.	89,624	199,025	310,015	365,426	398,568	430,624	462,605	488,997
Average monthly revenue per unit [5]	Dollars	48.55	50.65	47.53	48.99	48.79	46.64	44.65	41.50
Average length of call [5]	Minutes	2.6	3.0	1.8	1.8	(NA)	(NA)	(NA)	(NA)
Voice minutes, annual reported	Billions	258.9	1,495.5	2,241.3	2,299.9	2,618.2	2,454.9	2,881.0	2,751.0
Voice minutes, monthly [6]	Minutes	248.0	716.0	683.0	633.0	690.0	610.0	670.0	606.0
Wireless data usage (megabytes), annual	Billions	(NA)	(NA)	388.0	1,468.0	3,229.8	4,060.7	9,649.9	13,719.0
Number of text messages [7]	Billions	(Z)	9.8	187.7	171.3	153.1	169.3	156.7	132.7
Number of MMS [7, 8]	Billions	(NA)	0.2	4.3	7.0	10.1	15.4	19.8	25.7

NA Not available. Z Entry less than half the unit of measurement shown. [1] Number of active wireless devices. Does not represent individual subscribers. [2] Number of active wireless devices divided by total U.S. population (including U.S. territories). [3] The basic geographic unit for wireless telecommunications coverage. [4] Beginning 2005, cumulative capital investment figure reached by summing the incremental capital investment in year shown with cumulative capital investment of prior year. [5] As of December 31. [6] Derived, based on minutes divided by reported devices. [7] Number of messages in final month of survey (December). [8] Multimedia Messaging Service.

Source: CTIA-The Wireless Association, Washington, DC, *Annual Wireless Industry Survey* ©.

Table 1170. Landline and Wireless Telephone Status of Households and Adults: 2010 to 2016

[In percent. Data cover 6-month period from January to June. Estimates are preliminary. Based on in-person interviews of a sample of the civilian noninstitutionalized population, conducted for the National Health Interview Survey]

Telephone status and characteristics	2010	2011	2012	2013	2014	2015	2016
HOUSEHOLDS							
Landline with wireless	58.1	55.0	52.5	49.5	44.7	41.6	40.2
Landline without wireless	12.9	11.2	9.4	8.5	8.5	7.6	7.2
Wireless only	26.6	31.6	35.8	39.4	44.0	47.4	49.3
Without any telephone	2.0	2.0	2.1	2.3	2.6	3.4	3.1
Other [1]	0.3	0.3	0.2	0.1	0.1	0.1	0.1
ADULTS							
Landline with wireless	62.2	58.8	56.1	52.8	47.3	43.9	42.1
Wireless mostly [2]	17.7	18.2	17.6	17.7	16.6	16.3	16.6
Landline without wireless	10.9	9.0	7.8	6.9	7.0	6.2	5.8
Wireless only	24.9	30.2	34.0	38.0	43.1	46.7	49.0
Without any telephone	1.7	1.8	1.9	2.2	2.4	3.1	2.9
Other [1]	0.3	0.2	0.2	0.1	0.2	0.1	0.1
ADULTS IN WIRELESS ONLY HOUSEHOLDS							
Sex:							
Male	26.2	31.4	35.2	39.7	44.3	48.2	50.3
Female	23.7	29.1	32.9	36.5	41.9	45.3	47.8
Age:							
18 to 24 years	39.9	46.8	49.5	54.3	57.8	59.4	62.7
25 to 29 years	51.3	58.1	60.1	65.6	69.3	71.3	72.1
30 to 34 years	40.4	46.2	55.1	59.9	64.9	67.8	69.8
35 to 44 years	27.0	34.3	39.1	44.5	52.5	56.6	60.0
45 to 64 years	16.9	21.6	25.8	29.8	35.7	40.8	43.3
65 and over years	5.4	7.9	10.5	12.6	15.7	19.3	21.1
Race/ethnicity:							
White only, non-Hispanic	22.7	27.6	30.4	35.1	39.6	43.2	45.0
Black only, non-Hispanic	28.5	32.5	37.7	39.4	44.9	48.1	49.2
Asian only, non-Hispanic	18.8	27.7	33.4	35.2	41.3	47.9	51.4
Multiple race, non-Hispanic	36.0	39.3	40.2	46.2	52.5	53.6	53.9
Hispanic or Latino, any race	34.7	40.8	46.5	49.9	56.1	59.2	63.7
Education:							
Some high school or less	28.6	32.1	36.4	41.7	46.6	49.0	52.1
High school graduate or GED [3]	23.6	30.8	33.9	37.2	43.3	46.7	48.4
Some post-high school, no degree	26.5	31.8	36.7	40.6	45.6	49.0	50.8
4-year college degree or higher	22.7	26.9	30.1	34.5	39.0	43.5	46.5
Household poverty status: [4]							
Poor	39.3	46.8	51.8	54.7	59.1	59.3	63.1
Near poor	32.9	38.1	42.3	47.5	50.8	54.4	54.0
Not poor	21.7	27.7	30.7	35.3	40.8	45.7	48.2
Home ownership status:							
Owned or home being bought	15.5	20.6	23.2	27.2	32.9	37.2	39.0
Renting	47.1	52.5	58.2	61.5	64.6	67.0	69.7
Other arrangement	34.9	38.4	37.7	42.6	52.2	52.8	52.0

[1] Other includes landline and non-landline, each with unknown wireless telephone. [2] Wireless mostly is for adults living in households with both landline and cellular telephones but in which all families receive all or almost all calls on cell phones. [3] GED is General Educational Development (high school equivalency diploma). [4] Based on household income and household size using the U.S. Census Bureau's poverty thresholds. "Poor" persons are defined as those below the poverty threshold. "Near poor" persons have incomes of 100% to less than 200% of the poverty threshold. "Not poor" persons have incomes of 200% of the poverty threshold or greater.

Source: U.S. National Center for Health Statistics, *Wireless Substitution: Early Release of Estimates From the National Health Interview Survey, January–June 2016*, December 2016, and earlier reports. See also <http://www.cdc.gov/nchs/nhis/releases.htm#wireless>.

Table 1171. Data Processing, Hosting, and Related Services—Estimated Revenue and Expenses: 2010 to 2015

[In millions of dollars (85,201 represents $85,201,000,000). For all employer firms regardless of tax status. Data are based on the 2007 North American Industry Classification System (NAICS), and cover NAICS 518. Estimates have been adjusted to the results of the 2012 Economic Census. See text, Section 15, and Appendix III]

Item	2010	2012	2013	2014	2015
Total operating revenue	**85,201**	**107,994**	**116,040**	**120,450**	**129,957**
Data processing, information technology infrastructure provisioning, and hosting services	61,142	78,726	85,252	86,546	94,942
Information technology design and development services	2,452	3,515	3,223	4,141	4,113
Information technology technical support services	(S)	3,088	3,311	4,023	(S)
Information technology technical consulting services	4,133	4,729	5,214	5,421	4,585
Information and document transformation services	2,406	3,055	3,020	2,827	2,761
Software publishing	(S)	(S)	(S)	(S)	2,848
Reselling services for computer hardware and software, retail	794	(S)	(S)	(S)	688
All other operating revenue	9,286	(S)	13,178	14,138	16,183
Total operating expenses	**73,996**	**94,662**	**102,403**	**105,358**	**112,907**
Personnel costs	36,638	47,100	50,559	54,497	59,415
Gross annual payroll	29,710	37,787	40,602	43,706	47,879
Employer's cost for fringe benefits [1]	4,613	6,427	6,798	7,639	8,327
Temporary staff and leased employee expense	2,315	2,886	3,159	3,152	3,209
Expensed equipment	1,095	918	898	980	(S)
Expensed purchases of other materials, parts, and supplies	4,126	3,182	2,866	2,879	2,094
Expensed purchases of software	2,013	2,351	2,764	3,142	3,412
Purchased electricity and fuels (except motor fuels)	760	669	654	684	714
Lease and rental payments	2,823	3,074	3,390	3,447	3,477
Purchased repair and maintenance	1,019	1,071	1,168	1,203	(S)
Purchased advertising and promotional services	(S)	2,259	2,301	2,439	2,695
Depreciation and amortization charges	6,506	8,191	8,883	8,860	9,340
Governmental taxes and license fees	(S)	(S)	665	729	833
All other operating expenses	16,611	25,212	28,255	26,498	28,642

S Data do not meet publication standards. [1] Includes health insurance; defined benefit pension plans; defined contribution plans; and payroll taxes, employer paid insurance premiums (except health), and other employer benefits.

Source: U.S. Census Bureau, Annual & Quarterly Services, "2015 Service Annual Survey," <http://www.census.gov/services/index.html>, accessed January 2017.

Table 1172. Electronic Device Ownership by Device Type and Owner Characteristics: 2016

[In percent. Based on a September 29 to November 6, 2016 survey of 3,015 adults age 18 and older. Surveys are conducted in English and Spanish, on landline and cellular telephones]

Owner characteristic	Any cellular telephone	Smart-phone	Cellphone, not smart-phone	Tablet computer	E-book reader [1]	Computer [2]
Total	**95**	**77**	**18**	**51**	**22**	**78**
SEX						
Men	96	78	18	48	17	78
Women	94	75	19	54	26	78
RACE/ETHNICITY						
White, non-Hispanic	94	77	17	52	24	83
Black, non-Hispanic	94	72	23	48	18	66
Hispanic	98	75	23	47	15	60
AGE						
18 to 29 years	100	92	8	49	17	83
30 to 49 years	99	88	11	62	24	81
50 to 64 years	97	74	23	52	25	81
65 years and older	80	42	38	32	19	62
EDUCATION						
Less than high school	92	54	39	25	9	40
High school graduate	92	69	23	42	15	67
Some college	96	80	16	54	22	85
College or higher	97	89	8	67	32	95
HOUSEHOLD INCOME						
Less than $30,000	92	64	29	32	14	56
$30,000 to $49,999	95	74	21	50	17	78
$50,000 to $74,999	96	83	13	56	23	91
$75,000 and over	99	93	6	69	32	96
METRO STATUS						
Urban	95	77	17	52	21	77
Suburban	96	79	16	53	24	81
Rural	94	67	27	43	17	70

[1] Handheld electronic device for reading books in electronic format. [2] Desktop or laptop computer.

Source: Pew Research Center ©, "Mobile Fact Sheet," <http://www.pewinternet.org/fact-sheet/mobile/>, accessed June 2017; and unpublished data.

Table 1173. Cellular Telephone Activities and Applications Among Adults by Cell Phone User Characteristics: 2015

[In percent. Based on a survey conducted from June 10 to July 12, 2015 among 2,001 adults age 18 or older, including 1,300 cellular phone interviews]

Characteristic	Activities conducted on cell phone					
	Location-based services [1]	Listen to online radio or music service	Video call or chat	Buy a product online	Get sports scores or analysis	Watch movies or TV shows via paid subscription service
Total................................	**71**	**54**	**35**	**48**	**36**	**27**
SEX						
Male..................................	72	53	36	48	47	23
Female...............................	71	56	34	47	25	30
RACE/ETHNICITY						
White, non-Hispanic...................	68	47	33	46	33	23
Black, non-Hispanic...................	75	70	34	50	45	30
Hispanic..............................	78	68	40	46	40	33
AGE						
18 to 29 years old....................	90	80	61	67	47	47
30 to 49 years old....................	87	71	42	58	45	33
50 to 64 years old....................	57	36	19	33	29	14
65 years old and over.................	37	14	9	22	13	3
EDUCATION						
High school graduate or less..........	60	51	26	33	32	27
Some college.........................	75	56	39	54	33	28
College or higher.....................	82	57	43	59	45	24
HOUSEHOLD INCOME						
Less than $30,000....................	60	50	28	30	28	27
$30,000 to $49,999..................	78	57	38	55	37	31
$50,000 to $74,999..................	71	54	35	50	38	22
$75,000 and over.....................	88	64	48	66	48	30
METRO STATUS						
Urban................................	75	61	40	51	40	29
Suburban.............................	73	53	36	48	37	27
Rural................................	59	42	22	40	25	20

[1] Get directions, recommendations, or other information from cell phone based on location.

Source: Pew Research Center, Princeton Survey Research Associates International, July 2015 data ©. See also <http://www.pewinternet.org/>.

Table 1174. Social Media—Use of Social Networking Sites Among Adult Internet Users: 2016

[As percent of all internet users. Based on responses from 696 internet users participating in a survey of 1,520 adults age 18 and older, conducted March 7 to April 4, 2016, in English and Spanish on landline and cellular telephones. Margins of error for results range from plus or minus 4.2 to 8.7 percentage points]

Characteristic	Social networking site				
	Facebook	Pinterest	Instagram	LinkedIn	Twitter
Total...........................	**79**	**31**	**32**	**29**	**24**
SEX					
Male.............................	75	17	26	31	24
Female...........................	83	45	38	27	25
AGE					
18 to 29 years...................	88	36	59	34	36
30 to 49 years...................	84	34	33	33	23
50 to 64 years...................	72	28	18	24	21
65 years and over................	62	16	8	20	10
EDUCATION					
High school graduate or less.....	77	24	27	12	20
Some college.....................	82	34	37	27	25
College graduate or higher.......	79	34	33	50	29
INCOME					
Under $30,000....................	84	30	38	21	23
$30,000 to $49,999..............	80	32	32	13	18
$50,000 to $74,999..............	75	31	32	32	28
$75,000 and over.................	77	35	31	45	30
METRO STATUS					
Urban............................	81	30	39	34	26
Suburban.........................	77	34	28	30	24
Rural............................	81	25	31	18	24
EMPLOYMENT STATUS					
Employed.........................	(NA)	(NA)	(NA)	35	(NA)
Not employed [1].................	(NA)	(NA)	(NA)	17	(NA)

NA Not available. [1] Not employed includes those who are retired, not employed for pay, disabled persons, or students.

Source: Pew Research Center, *Social Media Update 2016*, November 2016 ©. See also <http://www.pewinternet.org/category/publications/report/>.

Table 1175. Computer and Internet Use by Selected Characteristics: 2015

[In thousands (253,149 represents 253,149,000), except as noted. Based on the American Community Survey. Data are based on a sample and are subject to sampling variability]

Characteristic	Population with computer in household [1]				No computer in household	Percent with no computer in household
	With broadband internet subscription [2]		No internet subscription [3]			
	Number	Percent	Number	Percent		
Total household population	**253,149**	**80.8**	**30,038**	**9.6**	**28,656**	**9.1**
AGE						
Under 18 years	61,150	83.3	7,824	10.7	4,214	5.7
18 to 64 years	161,039	83.1	18,404	9.5	13,478	7.0
65 years and over	30,960	67.0	3,810	8.2	10,964	23.7
RACE AND ETHNICITY						
White alone	189,137	82.4	19,599	8.5	19,739	8.6
Black or African American alone	27,120	69.7	6,016	15.5	5,602	14.4
American Indian and Alaska Native alone	1,637	65.3	397	15.8	459	18.3
Asian alone	15,465	91.3	786	4.6	632	3.7
Native Hawaiian/Other Pacific Islander alone	429	80.1	54	10.0	51	9.5
Some other race alone	11,111	73.5	2,255	14.9	1,681	11.1
Two or more races	8,251	85.0	932	9.6	493	5.1
Hispanic or Latino origin [4]	41,293	74.5	7,459	13.5	6,468	11.7
EDUCATIONAL ATTAINMENT						
Household population 25 years and over	168,505	79.5	19,176	9.0	23,058	10.9
Less than high school graduate	15,050	56.8	3,915	14.8	7,391	27.9
High school graduate/some college [5]	92,814	77.6	12,215	10.2	13,798	11.5
Bachelor's degree or higher	60,642	92.2	3,046	4.6	1,869	2.8
EMPLOYMENT STATUS						
Civilian population 16 years and over	198,519	80.2	22,880	9.2	24,795	10.0
In labor force	135,367	85.0	14,280	9.0	8,966	5.6
Employed	127,793	85.6	12,950	8.7	8,022	5.4
Unemployed	7,575	76.6	1,330	13.4	945	9.6
Not in labor force	63,152	71.6	8,600	9.7	15,828	17.9

[1] Includes desktop, laptop, netbook, or notebook computer; handheld computer including mobile smartphones or other handheld wireless computer, or some other type of computer which may include tablets or other devices. [2] Paid internet access services via DSL, cable, fiber optic, mobile broadband, satellite, or fixed wireless subscription. Includes data plans for mobile phones. [3] Includes those who accessed the internet without a subscription and also those with no internet access at all. [4] Persons of Hispanic or Latino origin may be of any race. [5] Includes persons with high school equivalency, and with associate's degree.

Source: U.S. Census Bureau, 2015 American Community Survey, S2802 "Types of Internet Subscriptions by Selected Characteristics," <https://factfinder.census.gov/>, accessed September 2017.

Table 1176. Percent of Households with a Computer and Paid Internet Subscription by State: 2015

[In percent. Survey respondents could select more than one type of computer and more than one type of internet subscription. Household computer can include desktop, laptop, netbook or notebook computer, and handheld computer including smartphone, tablet, and other devices. Based on the American Community Survey. Please note that although the ACS includes people living in group quarters, computer and internet use data were not collected from group quarters]

State	Total	Type of internet subscription			State	Total	Type of internet subscription		
		Dial-up internet service	Broadband internet service [1]	No paid internet service [2]			Dial-up internet service	Broadband internet service [1]	No paid internet service [2]
U.S.	**86.8**	**0.6**	**87.7**	**11.7**	MO	85.3	0.9	85.4	13.8
AL	80.8	0.7	83.8	15.5	MT	86.1	1.2	86.6	12.2
AK	92.4	0.5	88.1	11.4	NE	86.7	0.7	89.5	9.8
AZ	87.6	0.5	88.6	10.9	NV	89.7	0.6	87.6	11.9
AR	81.4	1.0	78.1	20.9	NH	91.1	0.5	92.1	7.4
CA	89.7	0.6	90.0	9.4	NJ	88.1	0.4	91.8	7.8
CO	91.5	0.7	90.3	9.1	NM	80.8	1.1	82.5	16.4
CT	88.5	0.5	91.6	7.9	NY	86.6	0.4	89.0	10.6
DE	87.3	0.7	88.0	11.4	NC	85.1	0.6	86.5	13.0
DC	89.3	0.4	85.4	14.2	ND	86.2	0.6	88.1	11.3
FL	87.5	0.6	87.8	11.6	OH	85.5	0.6	88.2	11.2
GA	86.7	0.4	85.5	14.0	OK	83.9	0.5	83.8	15.8
HI	89.1	0.5	91.7	7.8	OR	90.7	0.8	88.8	10.5
ID	89.2	1.0	85.5	13.4	PA	84.6	0.9	88.7	10.4
IL	86.3	0.6	88.6	10.8	RI	86.5	0.7	89.6	9.7
IN	85.0	0.9	85.6	13.6	SC	83.4	0.6	83.2	16.2
IA	85.7	1.1	87.0	11.8	SD	85.0	0.7	87.9	11.4
KS	86.0	0.7	88.0	11.3	TN	82.4	0.6	84.4	14.9
KY	82.1	0.9	85.3	13.8	TX	86.7	0.5	85.1	14.4
LA	80.8	0.7	84.2	15.1	UT	93.2	0.7	88.8	10.5
ME	86.9	1.0	88.2	10.8	VT	87.0	1.0	89.9	9.1
MD	89.9	0.6	90.0	9.5	VA	88.2	0.6	88.6	10.8
MA	89.0	0.5	92.2	7.3	WA	91.4	0.5	91.3	8.1
MI	86.2	0.7	85.6	13.7	WV	79.6	0.7	86.7	12.6
MN	89.2	0.9	88.7	10.3	WI	86.4	0.8	88.4	10.7
MS	78.3	0.7	77.2	22.1	WY	89.8	1.0	86.4	12.6

[1] Broadband (high-speed) internet service includes DSL, cable, fiber optic, mobile broadband, satellite, or fixed wireless subscription. [2] Includes households accessing the internet without a subscription and also households with no internet access.

Source: U.S. Census Bureau, 2015 American Community Survey, "B28003, Presence of a Computer and Type of Internet Subscription in Household," <http://factfinder.census.gov>, accessed January 2017.

Table 1177. Internet Access by Selected User Characteristics: 2016

[In percent, except as noted (244,525 represents 244,525,000). For persons aged 18 and over. As of Fall 2016. Based on sample and subject to sampling error]

Characteristic	Total adults	Accessed the internet					
		At home	At work	At school or library	At another place	Using a cellphone or smart-phone	Using WiFi or wireless connection outside of home
Total adults (1,000) [1]	**244,525**	**198,084**	**108,764**	**30,914**	**92,869**	**179,789**	**72,176**
PERCENT DISTRIBUTION							
Total	100.00	100.00	100.00	100.00	100.00	100.00	100.00
Age:							
18 to 34 years old	30.18	33.78	35.21	53.28	39.68	38.31	40.48
35 to 54 years old	34.14	37.11	45.76	32.48	38.38	39.31	38.92
55 years old and over	35.67	29.11	19.03	14.24	21.94	22.38	20.61
Sex:							
Male	48.24	48.35	51.76	44.72	49.05	48.15	49.28
Female	51.76	51.65	48.24	55.28	50.95	51.85	50.72
Census region: [2]							
Northeast	18.05	18.45	18.69	18.17	20.09	17.90	20.04
South	37.68	36.67	36.21	37.41	34.34	37.63	34.91
Midwest	21.35	21.06	21.01	19.55	19.21	20.01	20.22
West	22.92	23.82	24.09	24.88	26.36	24.46	24.83
Household size:							
1 to 2 persons	45.05	41.16	37.28	31.81	36.71	37.15	38.37
3 to 4 persons	37.22	40.27	44.49	47.31	42.38	42.39	43.27
5 or more persons	17.73	18.57	18.23	20.88	20.91	20.46	18.36
Any child in household	39.42	42.95	47.03	45.92	46.37	47.01	42.74
Marital status:							
Never married	28.26	29.30	29.00	49.75	33.52	32.18	35.50
Married	52.86	55.54	58.67	38.76	52.97	53.93	52.47
Other [3]	22.55	19.04	16.78	15.79	17.69	18.35	16.43
Education:							
Graduated college plus	29.80	34.68	44.39	38.99	38.42	34.89	44.58
Attended college	28.38	30.72	30.16	39.15	31.43	31.03	31.84
Did not attend college	41.82	34.60	25.45	21.87	30.15	34.08	23.57
Employment status:							
Employed full-time	49.14	54.54	84.13	41.97	57.97	58.50	59.35
Employed part-time	11.92	13.07	15.29	23.38	14.52	13.46	14.93
Occupation of employed:							
Professional	14.06	16.81	27.79	24.85	19.75	17.70	22.72
Management/business/financial	10.12	11.81	20.23	8.05	13.28	12.70	15.76
Sales/office	13.36	15.05	23.88	12.93	15.77	16.09	16.67
Natural resources/construction/maintenance	5.61	5.68	6.34	2.69	5.21	5.94	4.00
Other	17.92	18.26	21.17	16.83	18.47	19.52	15.14
Sector of employment:							
Business	31.59	34.83	51.44	23.72	37.87	37.32	37.49
Government	9.42	10.84	17.12	18.93	11.78	11.34	12.16
Other	15.04	16.20	21.75	14.64	16.42	17.26	17.66
Household income:							
Less than $50,000	38.70	31.42	18.57	37.82	27.48	30.03	25.63
$50,000 to $74,999	17.75	18.84	18.23	15.14	17.81	18.54	16.69
$75,000 to $149,999	29.59	33.21	40.62	31.60	35.26	33.97	35.58
$150,000 or more	13.96	16.53	22.58	15.43	19.46	17.46	22.11

[1] Includes other labor force status not shown separately. [2] For composition of regions, see map inside front cover. [3] Includes separated, divorced, and widowed, and also persons engaged to be married.

Source: © Fall 2016, GfK MRI a division of GfK US, LLC. See also <http://www.mri.gfk.com/>.

Table 1178. Home Internet Access—Broadband and Smartphone Only Service by Selected Characteristics: 2013 to 2016

[In percent. Based on a survey of 6,010 adults participating in a September 2013 survey (sampling error plus or minus 1.4 percentage points); a total of 6,687 adults participating in three surveys conducted April, July, and November 2015 (sampling error plus or minus 1.3 percentage points); and a survey of 4,535 adults conducted in April and November 2016 (sampling error plus or minus 1.7 percentage points). Surveys were conducted in English and Spanish on landline and cellular telephones]

Characteristic	Internet broadband service in the home			Internet via smartphone only [1]		
	2013	2015	2016	2013	2015	2016
Total............................	**70**	**67**	**72**	**8**	**13**	**12**
SEX						
Male................................	70	66	74	9	14	12
Female..............................	70	67	70	8	13	12
RACE/ETHNICITY						
White, non-Hispanic.................	74	72	77	6	10	9
Black, non-Hispanic.................	62	54	65	10	19	15
Hispanic...........................	56	50	55	16	23	23
AGE						
18 to 29 years.....................	81	75	78	12	19	17
30 to 49 years.....................	77	74	80	9	16	13
50 to 64 years.....................	68	65	72	7	11	11
65 years and older.................	47	45	51	3	7	7
EDUCATION						
High school graduate or less........	50	47	53	11	18	18
Some college or associate degree......	80	75	80	8	14	12
College graduate or higher.........	90	87	90	4	6	5
HOUSEHOLD INCOME						
Less than $20,000..................	46	41	48	13	21	23
$20,000 to $50,000.................	67	63	67	10	16	14
$50,000 to $75,000.................	85	80	82	5	10	10
$75,000 to $100,000................	88	88	90	6	8	6
$100,000 and over..................	93	90	93	4	6	5
METRO STATUS						
Urban..............................	70	67	73	9	15	12
Suburban...........................	74	70	74	7	12	12
Rural..............................	60	55	62	9	15	14
PARENTAL STATUS						
Parent of minor child..............	77	73	79	10	17	12
Not parent of minor child..........	67	64	69	8	12	12

[1] Persons without home broadband internet service who own a smartphone that can access the internet.

Source: Pew Research Center ©, *Home Broadband 2015*, December 2015; and unpublished data. See also <http://www.pewinternet.org/category/publications/report/>.

Table 1179. Adult Internet Users and Home Internet Connection by Selected Characteristics: 2000 to 2016

[In percent. Covers persons age 18 and over who use the internet at a workplace, school, home, or anywhere else, on at least an occasional basis. Based on telephone surveys of persons with landline telephones unless otherwise noted. Beginning 2011, surveys include interviews conducted in English and Spanish. Data for 2016 are from November 2016 interviews with 3,015 persons, including 2,258 cellphone users. Data for 2015 are from July 2015 interviews with 2,001 persons, including 1,300 cellphone users. Data for 2014 (except broadband vs. dial-up statistics) are from interviews with 1,006 persons, including 504 cellphone users. Data for 2010 are from interviews with 2,252 persons, including 744 cellphone users. For 2000, internet users include persons who ever go online to access the internet or to send and receive e-mail. For 2005, internet users include those who at least occasionally use the internet or send and receive e-mail]

Characteristic	Adult internet users						All adults, by type of home connection, 2016	
	2000	2005	2010	2014	2015	2016	Broadband	Dial-up
Total adults..........................	**53**	**69**	**79**	**87**	**87**	**90**	**73**	**4**
Age:								
18 to 29 years old..................	72	82	95	97	97	99	77	5
30 to 49 years old..................	62	80	87	93	97	96	81	3
50 to 64 years old..................	48	68	78	88	80	89	75	2
65 years old and over...............	15	28	42	57	65	67	51	4
Sex:								
Male................................	56	70	79	87	87	90	74	3
Female..............................	51	67	79	86	87	90	72	4
Race/ethnicity:								
White, non-Hispanic.................	55	70	80	85	87	90	78	2
Black, non-Hispanic.................	42	54	71	81	84	86	65	3
Hispanic............................	48	73	82	83	84	90	58	9
Education:								
Less than high school..............	19	35	52	[2]( )	68	71	34	8
High school graduate [1]............	41	59	67	[2]76	77	84	62	4
Some college.......................	69	80	90	91	93	94	80	3
College graduate or higher.........	79	88	96	97	97	98	91	2
Annual household income:								
Less than $30,000..................	35	50	63	77	78	81	53	7
$30,000 to $49,999.................	61	74	84	85	87	91	71	5
$50,000 to $74,999.................	74	86	89	93	94	96	83	2
$75,000 or more....................	81	91	95	99	97	98	93	1

[1] Includes those with a GED certificate. [2] Data are combined for respondents who completed and did not complete high school.

Source: Pew Research Center, Pew Internet & American Life Project Surveys conducted September–December 2000, September and December of 2005, May 2010, May 2013, January 2014, July 2015, and November 2016 ©. See also <http://www.pewinternet.org>.

Table 1180. Households Using Electronics, Internet Devices, and Cell Phones by Type and Household Income: 2015

[In millions (118.2 represents 118,200,000). Based on the Residential Energy Consumption Survey, a periodic household survey covering electronics in use in the respondent's primary residence in the 50 states and DC. Includes single-family homes, units in multifamily buildings, and mobile homes. Excludes secondary homes, vacant, seasonal and vacation homes, group quarters, and common areas of apartment buildings. Data may not sum to totals due to rounding]

Item	Total	Households by income (millions)							
		Less than $20,000	$20,000 to $39,999	$40,000 to $59,999	$60,000 to $79,999	$80,000 to $99,000	$100,000 to $119,999	$120,000 to $139,999	$140,000 or more
Total households.................	118.2	22.5	27.2	18.6	15.4	9.7	8.1	5.4	11.2
TELEVISION AND VIDEO									
Number of televisions:									
0..........................	3.1	0.9	1.0	0.4	0.3	(B)	(B)	(B)	(B)
1..........................	30.0	8.7	7.0	4.2	3.8	1.5	1.7	0.9	2.2
2..........................	39.1	7.5	9.6	6.4	4.9	3.4	2.5	1.8	2.9
3 or more..................	46.0	5.4	9.6	7.6	6.4	4.5	3.8	2.7	6.0
Hours TV used per weekday: [1]									
Less than 1 hour....................	3.7	0.9	0.8	0.5	0.5	0.2	0.3	(B)	0.5
1 to 3 hours........................	29.7	4.2	5.7	4.3	4.4	2.6	2.7	1.9	4.0
4 to 6 hours........................	43.0	6.6	9.2	6.9	6.0	4.1	3.1	2.4	4.6
7 to 10 hours.......................	21.5	4.6	5.8	3.9	2.4	1.7	1.3	0.6	1.3
More than 10 hours..................	17.2	5.4	4.7	2.6	1.9	0.9	0.6	0.4	0.6
Hours TV used per weekend day: [1]									
Less than 1 hour....................	3.1	1.0	0.8	0.4	0.4	(B)	0.2	(B)	(B)
1 to 3 hours........................	20.2	3.7	4.0	2.6	3.0	1.9	1.5	1.1	2.6
4 to 6 hours........................	38.4	5.7	8.6	5.9	5.0	3.4	3.0	2.1	4.7
7 to 10 hours.......................	30.4	5.3	7.0	5.4	4.1	2.6	2.3	1.3	2.4
More than 10 hours..................	23.0	6.1	5.7	4.0	2.7	1.6	1.0	0.7	1.2
Number of cable or satellite TV boxes: [2]									
1..........................	34.0	4.2	6.8	6.3	4.7	3.3	2.8	1.8	4.2
2 or more..................	20.0	1.6	3.3	3.0	2.9	2.5	1.9	1.7	3.1
Number of internet streaming devices:									
1..........................	24.9	3.0	4.6	4.1	3.7	2.2	2.5	1.3	3.5
2 or more..................	9.0	0.5	1.4	1.5	1.1	1.2	0.7	0.8	1.8
Number of home theater or audio systems:									
1..........................	26.0	2.5	3.8	3.6	3.9	3.0	2.9	1.9	4.5
2..........................	2.9	(B)	(B)	0.6	0.3	0.2	0.3	0.4	0.8
Number of video game consoles:									
1..........................	29.6	4.0	5.8	4.8	4.5	2.8	2.5	1.7	3.4
2..........................	9.5	1.3	1.8	1.6	1.0	1.1	0.8	0.5	1.5
3 or more..................	4.7	0.4	1.0	0.8	0.7	0.5	0.4	0.3	0.6
INTERNET AND DEVICES									
Have internet access in the home:									
Yes.......................	101.1	14.4	21.8	16.8	14.5	9.4	7.8	5.4	11.1
Have wireless access..............	87.8	10.4	17.8	14.5	13.1	8.8	7.3	5.0	10.8
No........................	17.1	8.1	5.4	1.8	0.9	0.3	0.3	(B)	(B)
Number of desktop computers:									
1..........................	41.3	5.2	9.2	6.7	5.4	3.8	3.3	2.6	5.0
2 or more..................	8.0	(NA)	1.1	(NA)	(NA)	(NA)	(NA)	(NA)	1.5
Number of laptop computers:									
1..........................	44.6	6.2	10.1	8.2	6.7	4.6	3.3	1.7	3.8
2..........................	21.2	1.8	3.3	3.2	3.6	2.1	2.1	1.9	3.3
3 or more..................	9.6	0.7	0.9	0.9	1.1	0.8	1.2	0.9	3.0
Number of tablets and e-readers:									
1..........................	38.2	5.2	9.1	6.9	5.5	3.9	2.8	1.8	3.0
2..........................	19.1	1.6	2.6	2.9	2.7	1.9	2.0	1.5	3.8
3 or more..................	10.5	0.4	1.1	1.1	1.7	1.1	1.3	1.1	2.5
Number of smartphones:									
1..........................	28.4	5.8	8.0	5.6	3.7	2.1	1.4	0.8	1.1
2..........................	37.6	4.0	6.5	6.3	5.9	4.1	3.3	2.6	4.9
3 or more..................	23.9	2.5	3.6	3.1	3.2	2.4	2.7	1.7	4.6
Number of other cell phones:									
1..........................	28.4	7.7	7.5	4.1	3.3	1.9	1.5	1.0	1.4
2 or more..................	14.2	3.3	4.0	2.3	1.8	1.0	0.7	(NA)	0.6

B Data withheld due to relative standard error being greater than 50 percent or fewer than 10 cases responded. NA Not available. [1] Data shown for primary television. [2] Cable and satellite boxes with digital video recorder (DVR).

Source: U.S. Energy Information Administration, Residential Energy Consumption Survey—2015 Data, "Table HC4.5 Electronics in U.S. Homes by Household Income, 2015," <https://www.eia.gov/consumption/residential/data/2015/>, accessed June 2017.

Table 1181. Number of Public Libraries and Library Services by State: 2014

[1,423,217 represents 1,423,217,000. Data are generally for the fiscal year ending in June; see source for reporting periods. Based on a census of all public libraries that meet the definition of a Federal State Cooperative System (FSCS) Public Library, which can have one or more outlets (central, branch, bookmobile) that provide direct service to the public]

State	Number of public libraries [1]	Library visits (1,000s)	Per capita visits [2]	Per capita circulation of materials [2]	Average number of public use internet computers [3]	State	Number of public libraries [1]	Library visits (1,000s)	Per capita visits [2]	Per capita circulation of materials [2]	Average number of public use internet computers [3]
U.S....	9,070	1,423,217	4.6	7.5	17.2	MO......	149	29,518	5.4	10.2	13.7
AL......	218	17,002	3.7	4.5	18.0	MT........	82	4,703	4.8	6.0	11.1
AK......	79	3,477	5.3	7.3	10.3	NE........	263	8,329	5.4	8.5	10.4
AZ......	90	27,610	4.1	6.6	25.4	NV.......	21	10,525	3.8	7.5	15.4
AR......	58	10,974	4.2	5.4	11.1	NH........	219	7,493	6.5	9.0	6.5
CA......	184	164,300	4.3	5.8	19.5	NJ........	281	45,302	5.3	6.7	18.6
CO.....	113	32,979	6.4	12.5	24.8	NM......	87	7,323	4.5	5.6	14.1
CT......	182	20,979	6.1	8.7	18.2	NY.......	756	106,454	5.5	7.4	18.2
DE......	21	3,835	4.1	6.7	24.1	NC.......	80	35,106	3.6	5.4	19.9
DC......	1	4,231	6.4	6.0	38.5	ND........	73	2,175	3.4	6.1	10.9
FL......	82	75,554	3.9	6.0	31.6	OH.......	251	82,495	7.2	15.9	18.2
GA......	63	29,490	2.9	3.8	21.8	OK.......	117	13,687	4.3	6.9	14.5
HI........	1	4,875	3.5	4.6	10.5	OR.......	129	21,638	5.8	15.2	14.2
ID........	102	8,730	6.4	10.6	12.5	PA........	455	44,792	3.6	5.3	13.0
IL........	623	72,590	6.2	9.8	20.3	RI........	48	6,026	5.7	6.8	20.0
IN........	237	35,441	5.8	12.7	20.5	SC.......	42	18,179	3.9	5.6	21.9
IA........	534	18,030	5.9	9.1	8.4	SD........	112	3,915	5.1	7.6	7.7
KS......	318	13,925	5.6	10.0	10.2	TN........	186	19,528	3.1	4.1	17.6
KY......	119	19,284	4.4	6.9	23.6	TX........	548	73,033	3.0	4.7	22.0
LA......	68	17,242	3.7	4.5	15.8	UT........	72	17,650	6.1	13.0	16.5
ME.....	228	6,834	5.9	8.1	7.9	VT........	155	3,702	6.4	7.6	6.7
MD.....	24	27,794	4.8	10.0	26.0	VA.......	91	37,406	4.6	9.2	19.3
MA.....	368	42,010	6.4	9.6	13.9	WA......	62	41,281	6.0	12.2	19.1
MI......	388	50,126	5.1	8.5	18.5	WV.......	97	5,368	2.9	3.4	8.4
MN.....	137	24,566	4.5	10.0	15.8	WI.......	381	32,854	5.7	10.5	13.7
MS.....	52	9,191	3.1	2.7	11.8	WY.......	23	3,667	6.3	8.4	11.4

[1] Of the 9,070 public libraries, 81.0 percent are single direct service outlets. There are 8,890 central library outlets, 7,669 branch library outlets, and 659 bookmobiles. [2] Per capita rate based on total unduplicated population of legal service area given by the state library agency of each state. [3] See footnote 5 in Table 1182.

Source: Institute of Museum and Library Services, Public Libraries Survey Data and Reports, "FY 2014 PLS: Supplementary Tables," <https://www.imls.gov/research-evaluation/data-collection/public-libraries-survey/explore-pls-data/pls-data>, accessed April 2017.

Table 1182. Public Libraries—Selected Characteristics: 2014

[Total operating income in thousands of dollars (12,054,030 represents $12,054,030,000). Data are generally for the fiscal year ending in June; see source for reporting periods. Based on a census of all public libraries in the 50 states and the District of Columbia. See source for details]

Population of service area	Number of—		Operating income			Paid staff [3]		Avg. number of public use internet computers per stationary outlet [5]
	Public libraries	Stationary outlets [1]	Total [2] (1,000)	Source (percentage)		Total	Librarians with ALA-MLS [4]	
				State government	Local government			
Total...................	9,070	16,559	12,054,030	7.0	85.2	138,332	32,064	17.2
Fewer than 1,000......	972	976	36,565	8.1	72.4	704	38	4.7
1,000 to 2,499........	1,477	1,491	112,551	5.1	78.2	2,068	155	6.3
2,500 to 4,999..........	1,246	1,282	186,470	5.8	80.3	3,090	384	8.0
5,000 to 9,999..........	1,498	1,641	457,628	6.6	82.2	6,757	1,219	10.9
10,000 to 24,999.......	1,760	2,246	1,244,149	5.9	86.3	16,067	3,804	15.3
25,000 to 49,999.......	977	1,717	1,474,941	6.6	86.7	17,687	4,422	18.5
50,000 to 99,999......	569	1,580	1,509,380	7.7	85.9	17,583	4,291	20.5
100,000 to 249,999....	374	2,073	1,910,472	7.5	85.6	22,503	5,081	21.6
250,000 to 499,999....	111	1,201	1,429,983	7.1	87.2	16,029	3,802	24.3
500,000 to 999,000....	56	1,128	1,805,978	7.4	86.1	18,708	4,308	29.0
1,000,000 or more.....	30	1,224	1,885,913	7.2	81.6	17,138	4,560	31.3

[1] The sum of central and branch libraries. The total number of central libraries is 8,890; the total of branch libraries is 7,669. [2] Total includes income from the federal government (0.4%) and other sources (7.4%), not shown separately. [3] Full-time equivalents. [4] Librarians with master's degrees from a graduate library education program accredited by the American Library Association (ALA). Total librarians, including those without ALA-MLS, is 47,195. [5] The average per stationary outlet was calculated by dividing the total number of public use internet computers in central and branch outlets by the total number of such outlets.

Source: Institute of Museum and Library Services, Public Libraries Survey Data and Reports, "FY 2014 PLS: Supplementary Tables," <https://www.imls.gov/research-evaluation/data-collection/public-libraries-survey/explore-pls-data/pls-data>, accessed April 2017.

Table 1183. Public Library Holdings by Type by State: 2014

[In thousands (765,490 represents 765,490,000), except as noted. Data are generally for the fiscal year ending in June; see source for reporting periods. Based on a census of all public libraries conducted by Institute of Museum and Library Services. Covers only libraries that meet the definition of a Federal State Cooperative System (FSCS) public library. State data comparisons should be made with caution because of differences in reporting periods and adherence to survey definitions. Data are not subject to sampling error; census results may contain nonsampling error]

State	Type of holding							
	Print materials [1] (1,000)	Current print serial subscriptions (1,000)	Electronic books, average [2]	Databases (1,000)	Audio		Video	
					Physical units (1,000)	Download-able titles, average [2]	Physical units (1,000)	Download-able titles, average [2]
U.S. total.	765,490	1,370	23,543.9	410.0	45,487	7,286.4	61,560	589.7
Alabama.	9,340	9	12,093.3	13.4	450	2,856.5	620	125.4
Alaska.	2,392	6	4,450.6	4.5	115	4,723.1	266	11.8
Arizona.	8,230	14	15,193.1	3.4	690	7,713.6	1,117	69.8
Arkansas.	6,304	10	9,179.9	3.6	230	3,199.7	401	172.9
California.	65,409	93	16,186.7	4.1	3,531	3,068.3	5,139	734.4
Colorado.	10,308	26	12,306.5	2.2	923	4,624.6	1,344	269.8
Connecticut.	13,813	20	6,826.0	8.7	795	5,357.4	1,079	66.9
Delaware.	1,643	4	19,770.0	0.7	115	2,565.0	176	−
District of Columbia.	1,816	2	177,086.0	0.1	86	16,154.0	141	804.0
Florida.	31,603	43	21,924.4	6.7	1,947	10,057.7	3,521	1,715.9
Georgia.	16,603	17	5,321.7	10.6	637	4,119.9	888	26.1
Hawaii.	3,313	3	22,966.0	0.1	232	9,338.0	156	−
Idaho.	4,314	6	2,373.5	5.4	234	642.6	316	5.2
Illinois.	43,486	85	11,480.8	21.4	2,688	3,634.6	3,493	297.6
Indiana.	24,369	46	17,836.2	18.0	1,584	2,974.4	2,113	175.0
Iowa.	11,928	29	8,725.8	8.3	672	4,674.4	937	7.1
Kansas.	9,242	15	950.8	16.9	480	142.7	818	58.1
Kentucky.	9,033	17	58,117.1	4.8	517	16,957.8	806	7,752.4
Louisiana.	11,896	23	12,934.4	5.0	466	4,350.2	1,056	659.7
Maine.	5,995	9	5,082.2	15.1	225	3,304.8	350	62.8
Maryland.	12,736	23	79,444.1	0.8	1,068	61,543.2	1,107	377.9
Massachusetts.	31,270	45	20,323.5	27.1	1,500	4,967.9	1,898	311.9
Michigan.	32,540	51	7,225.5	17.2	1,967	2,504.6	2,449	120.2
Minnesota.	14,613	26	25,340.9	7.6	883	3,349.5	985	200.7
Mississippi.	5,642	6	1,166.9	2.9	203	315.4	332	5.7
Missouri.	16,767	34	1,838.8	2.7	983	557.1	1,127	64.0
Montana.	2,566	4	11,622.6	2.9	107	8,392.1	184	263.2
Nebraska.	5,885	13	10,255.2	5.9	254	4,711.0	341	1.0
Nevada.	4,298	7	10,250.1	1.0	398	3,811.7	586	1,289.3
New Hampshire.	5,785	11	19,209.3	5.9	280	7,269.0	436	0.9
New Jersey.	27,816	49	11,040.3	12.2	1,702	8,544.4	2,074	971.3
New Mexico.	4,248	6	2,265.7	4.4	208	1,032.1	301	13.5
New York.	70,815	167	19,307.1	21.5	3,509	4,568.0	5,155	986.7
North Carolina.	16,752	22	41,695.6	5.8	710	5,883.4	814	1,074.0
North Dakota.	2,252	4	5,267.0	3.6	90	1,634.1	118	172.8
Ohio.	42,782	134	160,841.3	25.2	3,517	42,189.5	5,086	2,811.6
Oklahoma.	7,152	9	14,085.1	4.7	474	3,572.0	422	193.8
Oregon.	9,865	17	30,193.9	4.3	752	19,941.8	917	1,150.6
Pennsylvania.	25,780	46	11,652.7	10.8	2,141	5,016.7	1,857	916.8
Rhode Island.	4,233	5	25,553.0	2.0	148	9,658.9	226	285.5
South Carolina.	9,107	14	11,755.0	2.5	434	7,035.5	718	549.0
South Dakota.	2,807	5	8,714.1	6.1	111	2,727.1	150	58.0
Tennessee.	11,761	12	81,964.9	13.5	593	31,758.4	735	2,618.4
Texas.	40,314	52	6,235.3	28.7	2,059	1,743.9	2,792	104.8
Utah.	6,638	12	7,662.8	3.2	613	10,710.1	645	139.1
Vermont.	2,732	6	529.8	7.8	136	496.7	182	3.2
Virginia.	17,540	22	21,953.4	1.3	1,018	3,653.3	1,193	413.8
Washington.	13,430	41	28,834.9	1.8	1,192	12,635.3	1,531	467.5
West Virginia.	5,034	6	49,495.5	1.8	195	4,330.2	295	181.1
Wisconsin.	18,797	40	123,640.0	19.9	1,463	29,041.8	1,968	1,048.7
Wyoming.	2,497	4	7,470.2	1.9	165	5,887.8	197	12.3

− Represents zero. [1] Includes books, and non-serial government documents. [2] The average was calculated by dividing the total number of materials of each type by the total number of public libraries. Includes digital documents digitized by the library, licensed or not; and non-serial government documents.

Source: Institute of Museum and Library Services, Public Libraries Survey Data and Reports, "FY 2014 PLS: Supplementary Tables," <https://www.imls.gov/research-evaluation/data-collection/public-libraries-survey/explore-pls-data/pls-data>, accessed April 2017.

Table 1184. Public Library Technology Services and Resources Available for Patrons: 2014

[In percent, except as indicated. Based on sample survey of public libraries at the branch/outlet level; survey excludes bookmobiles. The 2014 survey collected responses from 2,304 libraries (44.4% response rate); see source for details. Items will not total 100% as categories are not mutually exclusive]

Item	Total	Metropolitan status			
		City	Suburb	Town	Rural
Average number of public access internet workstations (number)...................	18.8	37.0	23.6	17.9	8.8
Public library outlets offering public wireless internet access (percent)...............	97.8	100.0	98.5	99.4	95.5
Technology services and resources available (percent):					
E-books..	90.3	98.3	97.6	92.3	81.2
Digital media content...	53.1	82.7	67.7	43.9	36.0
Online homework assistance...	95.3	98.2	96.0	95.0	93.8
Online job/employment resources...	62.3	77.7	68.6	61.3	52.3
Online language learning...	56.0	84.0	75.3	48.6	35.5
Online health resources..	76.8	92.3	84.9	75.5	65.9
Video conferencing services..	11.6	6.3	6.5	17.3	14.3
Print on Demand (POD)...	2.1	2.3	1.9	3.4	1.4
Mobile device-enabled website...	46.5	59.8	59.6	44.3	33.6
Mobile apps to access library services and resources...........................	42.7	63.0	54.0	37.3	29.8
Scanned codes..	24.6	36.1	35.6	23.3	13.1

Source: Information Policy and Access Center, University of Maryland, College Park, MD, *2014 Digital Inclusion Survey: Survey Findings and Results*, by John Carlo Bertot, et al., October 2015 ©. See also <http://digitalinclusion.umd.edu/>.

Table 1185. Use of Public Libraries, Library Websites, and Library Mobile Applications by Demographic Characteristics: 2016

[In percent. Covers visits or use in past 12 months. Based on interviews with 3,015 adults conducted September 29 to November 6, 2016, in English and Spanish on landline and cellular telephones. Margin of sampling error plus or minus 2.0 percentage points]

Characteristics	Visited library or book-mobile	Used library website	Used library mobile app	Characteristics	Visited library or book-mobile	Used library website	Used library mobile app
Total............................	**46**	**31**	**8**	EDUCATION			
SEX				Less than high school............	30	12	4
Male.............................	39	24	5	High school graduate............	40	23	6
Female...........................	54	37	11	Some college.....................	49	35	6
RACE/ETHNICITY				College graduate or higher......	56	40	14
White, non-Hispanic.............	45	29	8				
Black, non-Hispanic.............	50	35	11	HOUSEHOLD INCOME			
Hispanic.........................	43	27	5	Less than $30,000................	42	28	7
AGE				$30,000 to $74,999...............	50	32	7
18 to 29 years...................	56	43	7	$75,000 to $99,999...............	48	34	11
30 to 49 years...................	46	35	10	$100,000 to $149,000............	49	35	11
50 to 64 years...................	43	25	9	$150,000 and over...............	46	32	11
65 years and older...............	39	15	6	METRO STATUS			
PARENTAL STATUS				Urban............................	46	32	10
Parent of minor child............	54	38	11	Suburban.........................	48	30	7
Not a parent of minor child.....	43	27	7	Rural............................	42	27	7

Source: Pew Research Center ©, unpublished data. See also <http://www.pewinternet.org>.

Section 25
Banking, Finance, and Insurance

This section presents data on the nation's finances, various types of financial institutions, money and credit, securities, insurance, and real estate. The primary sources of these data are publications of several departments of the federal government, especially the U.S. Treasury Department, and independent agencies such as the Federal Deposit Insurance Corporation, the Board of Governors of the Federal Reserve System, and the Securities and Exchange Commission. National data on insurance are available primarily from private organizations, such as the American Council of Life Insurers and the National Association of Insurance Commissioners.

Financial Accounts of the United States—The Federal Reserve Board brings together statistics on all of the major forms of financial instruments to present an economy-wide view of asset and liability relationships in the Financial Accounts of the United States. The accounts relate borrowing and lending to one another and to the nonfinancial activities that generate income and production. Each claim outstanding is included simultaneously as an asset of the lender and as a liability of the debtor. The accounts also indicate the balance between asset totals and liability totals over the economy as a whole. Several publications of the Federal Reserve Board contain information on these financial accounts: Summary data on flows and outstandings in the statistical release *Financial Accounts of the United States* (quarterly); and concepts and organization of the accounts in *Financial Accounts Guide* <http://www.federalreserve.gov/apps/fof/>. Data are also available on the Federal Reserve Board's website at <http://www.federalreserve.gov/releases/z1/>.

Survey of Consumer Finances (SCF)—The Federal Reserve Board, in cooperation with the Treasury Department, sponsors this survey, which is conducted every 3 years to provide detailed information on the finances of U.S. families. Among the topics covered are the balance sheet, pension, income, and other demographic characteristics of U.S. families. The survey also gathers information on the use of financial institutions. Since 1992, data for the SCF have been collected by the National Organization for Research at the University of Chicago. Data and information on the survey are available on the Federal Reserve Board's website at <http://www.federalreserve.gov/econresdata/scf/scfindex.htm>.

Banking system—Banks in this country are organized under the laws of both the states and the federal government and are regulated by several bank supervisory agencies. National banks are supervised by the Comptroller of the Currency. *Reports of Condition and Income*, commonly known as call reports, have been collected from national banks since 1863. Summaries of these reports are published in the Comptroller's *Annual Report*, which also presents data on the structure of the national banking system.

The Federal Reserve System was established in 1913 to exercise central banking functions, some of which are shared with the U.S. Treasury. It includes national banks and state banks that voluntarily join the system. Statements of state bank members are consolidated by the Federal Reserve Board with data for national

banks collected by the Comptroller of the Currency into totals for all member banks of the system. Balance sheet data for member banks and other commercial banks are available on the Federal Reserve Board's website at <www.federalreserve.gov/data.htm>.

The Federal Deposit Insurance Corporation (FDIC), established in 1933, insures each depositor up to $250,000. Major item balance sheet and income data for all insured financial institutions are published in the *FDIC Quarterly Banking Profile*. This publication is also available on the internet at <https://www.fdic.gov/bank/analytical/qbp/>. Quarterly financial information for individual institutions is available through the FDIC and Federal Financial Institutions Examination Council websites at <http://www.fdic.gov> and <http://www.ffiec.gov>.

Credit unions—Federally chartered credit unions are under the supervision of the National Credit Union Administration. State-chartered credit unions are supervised by the respective state supervisory authorities. The administration publishes comprehensive program and statistical information on all federal and federally insured state credit unions in the *Annual Report of the National Credit Union Administration*.

Other credit agencies—Insurance companies, finance companies dealing primarily in installment sales financing, and personal loan companies represent important sources of funds for the credit market. Statistics on loans, investments, cash, etc., of life insurance companies are published principally by the American Council of Life Insurers in its *Life Insurers Fact Book*. Consumer credit data are available on the Federal Reserve Board's website at <www.federalreserve.gov/data.htm>. Government corporations and credit agencies make available credit of specified types or to specified groups of private borrowers, either by lending directly or by insuring or guaranteeing loans made by private lending institutions. Data on operations of government credit agencies, along with other government corporations, are available in reports of individual agencies.

Securities—The Securities and Exchange Commission (SEC) was established in 1934 to protect the interests of the public and investors against malpractices in the securities and financial markets and to provide the fullest possible disclosure of information regarding securities to the investing public.

Data on the securities industry and securities transactions are also available from a number of private sources. The Securities Industry and Financial Markets Association (SIFMA), New York, NY, <http://www.sifma.org/>, publishes the *SIFMA Fact Book*. The Investment Company Institute, Washington, DC, <http://www.ici.org/>, publishes a reference book, research newsletters, and a variety of research reports that examine the industry, its shareholders, or industry issues. The annual *Investment Company Fact Book* is a guide to trends and statistics observed in the investment company industry. Institute research reports provide a detailed examination of shareholder demographics and other aspects of fund ownership.

Among the many sources of data on stock and bond prices and sales are the New York Stock Exchange, New York, NY, <http://www.nyse.com/>; NASDAQ, Washington, DC, <http://www.nasdaq.com/>; and Global Financial Data, Los Angeles, CA, <http://www.globalfinancialdata.com/>.

Insurance—Insuring companies, which are regulated by the various states or the District of Columbia, are classified as either life or property. Both life and property insurance companies may underwrite health insurance. Insuring companies, other than those classified as life, are permitted to underwrite one or more property lines provided they are so licensed and have the necessary capital or surplus. There are a number of published sources for statistics on the various classes of insurance—life, health, fire, marine, and casualty. Organizations representing certain classes of insurers publish reports for these classes. The American Council of Life Insurers publishes statistics on life insurance purchases, ownership, benefit payments, and assets in its *Life Insurers Fact Book*.

Statistical reliability—For a discussion of statistical collection, estimation, and sampling procedures and measures of reliability applicable to data from the Census Bureau and the Federal Reserve Board's Survey of Consumer Finances, see Appendix III.

Table 1186. Gross Domestic Product in Finance, Insurance, Real Estate, Rental and Leasing Industries in Current and Chained (2009) Dollars: 2000 to 2016

[In billions of dollars, except percent (750 represents $750,000,000,000.) Represents value added by industry. For definition of gross domestic product and explanation of chained dollars, see text, Section 13, Income]

Industry	2007 NAICS code [1]	Current dollars				Chained (2009) dollars			
		2000	2010	2015	2016	2000	2010	2015	2016
Finance & insurance, total...............	**52**	**750**	**1,006**	**1,293**	**1,356**	**783**	**969**	**1,028**	**1,042**
Percent of gross domestic product......	(X)	7.3	6.7	7.2	7.3	6.2	6.6	6.3	6.3
Federal Reserve banks, credit inter-									
mediation, and related activities..........	521, 522	328	410	504	(S)	311	388	374	(S)
Securities, commodity contracts, &									
investments.....................	523	131	200	236	(S)	146	192	164	(S)
Insurance carriers & related activities......	524	276	365	489	(S)	321	360	450	(S)
Funds, trusts, & other financial vehicles...	525	16	31	64	(S)	13	29	54	(S)
Real estate & rental & leasing, total. ..	**53**	**1,242**	**1,946**	**2,363**	**2,462**	**1,540**	**1,957**	**2,165**	**2,188**
Percent of gross domestic product......	(X)	12.1	13.0	13.1	13.3	12.3	13.2	13.2	13.1
Real estate.....................	531	1,105	1,784	2,158	(S)	1,372	1,795	1,960	(S)
Rental & leasing services and lessors of									
intangible assets.....................	532, 533	137	162	206	(S)	169	162	206	(S)

S Figure does not meet publication standards. X Not applicable. [1] Data based on the 2007 North American Industry Classification System (NAICS). See text, Section 15.

Source: U.S. Bureau of Economic Analysis, "Value Added by Industry" and "Real Value Added by Industry," <http://www.bea.gov/iTable/index_industry_gdpIndy.cfm>, accessed April 2017.

Table 1187. Finance, Insurance, Real Estate, and Rental and Leasing—Establishments, Revenue, Payroll, and Employees by Kind of Business: 2007 and 2012

[3,669 represents $3,669,000,000,000. For establishments with payroll. Based on the 2007 and 2012 Economic Censuses; see Appendix III]

Kind of business	2007 NAICS code [1]	Establishments (number)		Revenue (bil. dol.)		Annual payroll (bil. dol.)		Paid employees (1,000)	
		2007	2012	2007	2012	2007	2012	2007	2012
Finance & insurance [2].........................	**52**	**501,713**	**468,183**	**3,669**	**3,636**	**502.4**	**523.6**	**6,608**	**6,041**
Monetary authorities—central bank.............	521	47	56	45	100	1.3	1.7	19	17
Credit intermediation & related activities........	522	231,439	196,147	1,343	1,095	180.9	184.2	3,280	2,815
Security, commodity contracts, & like activity...	523	85,475	95,906	612	515	166.3	168.4	885	904
Insurance carriers & related activities...........	524	184,752	176,074	1,669	1,925	153.9	169.2	2,423	2,304
Real estate & rental & leasing...............	**53**	**384,297**	**354,106**	**485**	**488**	**84.8**	**85.3**	**2,188**	**1,924**
Real estate.....................	531	316,730	295,780	330	325	61.3	60.9	1,529	1,403
Rental & leasing services.........................	532	65,120	55,795	122	129	21.1	21.3	630	485
Lessors of other nonfinancial intangible									
assets.....................	533	2,447	2,531	33	33	2.3	3.1	29	36

[1] Based on the North American Industry Classification System (NAICS); see text, Section 15. [2] Total does not include NAICS 525, Funds, trusts, and other financial vehicles.

Source: U.S. Census Bureau, 2012 Economic Census, EC1253A2, "Geographic Area Series: Comparative Statistics for the U.S. (2007 NAICS Basis): 2012 and 2007," <http://factfinder.census.gov/>, accessed June 2016.

Table 1188. Finance and Insurance—Nonemployer Establishments and Receipts by Kind of Business: 2010 to 2015

[716.8 represents 716,800. Includes only firms subject to federal income tax. Nonemployers are businesses with no paid employees. Data originate chiefly from administrative records of the Internal Revenue Service; see Appendix III]

Kind of business	NAICS code [1]	Establishments (1,000)			Receipts (mil. dol.)		
		2010	2014	2015	2010	2014	2015
Finance and insurance.........................	**52**	**716.8**	**715.8**	**718.5**	**50,626**	**54,742**	**55,329**
Credit intermediation & related activities.........................	522	53.3	45.1	45.8	2,790	2,885	3,134
Depository credit intermediation.........................	5221	6.2	5.8	5.9	181	203	214
Nondepository credit intermediation.........................	5222	21.8	21.1	22.1	1,554	1,712	1,864
Activities related to credit intermediation.........................	5223	25.3	18.2	17.8	1,056	969	1,056
Security, commodity contracts, & like activity.................	523	273.4	272.5	272.2	29,202	30,574	30,204
Securities & commodity contracts interm. & brokerage.......	5231	29.8	28.1	27.6	4,969	4,914	4,812
Investment banking and securities dealing..................	52311	7.2	7.2	7.4	1,748	1,309	1,389
Securities brokerage.........................	52312	18.6	17.5	17.0	2,589	3,041	2,914
Commodity contracts dealing.........................	52313	1.1	1.1	1.0	236	198	175
Commodity contracts brokerage.........................	52314	2.9	2.4	2.2	397	365	334
Securities & commodity exchanges.........................	5232	1.9	1.9	1.8	660	335	354
Other financial investment activities.........................	5239	241.7	242.5	242.7	23,573	25,326	25,038
Insurance carriers & related activities.........................	524	390.1	398.2	400.5	18,634	21,283	21,991
Insurance carriers.........................	5241	2.7	1.8	1.8	185	171	172
Agencies & other insurance-related activities.................	5242	387.4	396.4	398.7	18,449	21,112	21,819
Insurance agencies & brokerages.........................	52421	270.5	276.9	279.0	13,854	15,779	16,340
Other insurance related activities.........................	52429	116.9	119.6	119.8	4,595	5,333	5,479

[1] Data for 2010 are based on 2007 North American Industry Classification System (NAICS); data for 2014 and 2015 based on 2012 NAICS. For more information, see text, Section 15.

Source: U.S. Census Bureau, Nonemployer Statistics, "Geographic Area Series: Nonemployer Statistics for the U.S., States, Metropolitan Areas, and Counties," <http://factfinder.census.gov/>, accessed May 2017. See also <http://www.census.gov/econ/nonemployer>.

Table 1189. Finance and Insurance—Establishments, Employees, and Payroll: 2010 and 2015

[473.5 represents 473,500. Covers establishments with payroll. Employees are for the week including March 12. Excludes most government employees, railroad employees, and self-employed persons. For statement on methodology, see Appendix III]

Kind of business	NAICS code [1]	Establishments (1,000)		Employees (1,000)		Payroll (bil. dol.)	
		2010	2015	2010	2015	2010	2015
Finance & insurance, total [2]	**52**	**473.5**	**470.1**	**5,929**	**6,136**	**472.4**	**595.8**
Monetary authorities—central bank	521	(Z)	0.1	18	19	1.6	2.1
Credit intermediation & related activities	522	199.1	191.7	2,757	2,761	160.2	212.5
Depository credit intermediation [2]	5221	124.4	119.4	1,982	1,910	111.6	140.5
Commercial banking	52211	92.7	91.8	1,528	1,512	91.2	118.3
Savings institutions	52212	13.8	9.0	199	125	9.8	8.5
Credit unions	52213	17.8	18.6	251	271	10.3	13.4
Nondepository credit intermediation [2]	5222	41.6	43.3	521	580	34.9	51.9
Real estate credit	522292	14.3	13.2	216	243	14.2	23.3
Activities related to credit intermediation	5223	33.1	29.0	254	271	13.7	20.2
Security, commodity contracts & like activity [2]	523	96.4	98.5	874	896	156.4	187.0
Security & commodity contracts intermediation & brokerage [2]	5231	45.4	42.7	435	405	82.0	86.1
Securities brokerage	52312	38.3	37.1	309	294	45.7	50.3
Other financial investment activities [2]	5239	50.9	55.7	434	486	73.6	99.8
Portfolio management	52392	19.1	23.6	232	279	51.0	73.9
Insurance carriers & related activities	524	176.9	178.7	2,273	2,453	153.1	193.0
Insurance carriers [2]	5241	33.3	32.8	1,421	1,491	104.7	131.6
Direct life insurance carriers	524113	8.9	8.5	360	360	28.6	37.7
Direct health & medical insurance carriers	524114	4.8	5.4	459	491	31.0	38.9
Direct property & casualty insurance carriers	524126	14.4	14.0	529	551	39.3	46.8
Agencies & other insurance-related activities [2]	5242	143.6	145.9	852	963	48.4	61.4
Insurance agencies & brokerages	52421	131.4	134.1	646	685	36.3	44.9

Z Less than 50. [1] 2010 data based on 2007 North American Industry Classification System (NAICS); 2015 data based on 2012 NAICS. For more information, see text, Section 15. [2] Includes other kinds of businesses, not shown separately.

Source: U.S. Census Bureau, County Business Patterns, "Geography Area Series: County Business Patterns," <http://factfinder.census.gov/>, accessed April 2017. See also <https://www.census.gov/programs-surveys/cbp.html>.

Table 1190. Revenues of Finance and Insurance Industries: 2010 to 2015

[In billions of dollars (3,495.7 represents $3,495,700,000,000). Covers taxable employer firms only. Based on Service Annual Survey. Estimates have been adjusted to the results of the 2012 Economic Census. See Appendix III]

Kind of business	NAICS code [1]	2010	2011	2012	2013	2014	2015
Finance & insurance, total	**52**	**3,495.7**	**3,517.3**	**3,636.1**	**3,727.9**	**3,948.2**	**4,101.3**
Monetary authorities—central bank	521	88.2	87.7	100.2	90.2	113.9	113.1
Credit intermediation & related activities [2]	522	1,161.3	1,111.3	1,095.2	1,085.1	1,075.0	1,104.8
Commercial banking	52211	407.9	393.3	390.2	383.3	384.7	391.5
Savings institutions	52212	48.2	44.0	(D)	35.8	(D)	(D)
Credit unions	52213	47.7	47.5	50.0	49.8	49.9	53.4
Credit card issuing	52221	81.5	82.2	81.8	87.4	83.6	85.1
Sales financing	52222	89.5	82.0	83.4	89.9	97.3	104.9
Mortgage & nonmortgage loan brokers	52231	6.3	5.4	7.9	8.1	7.2	9.5
Financial transactions processing, reserve, and clearinghouse activities	52232	52.7	53.1	56.7	61.7	62.4	65.0
Securities, commodity contracts, and other financial investment activities [2]	523	497.6	508.6	515.5	547.1	582.5	586.5
Investment banking and securities dealing	52311	119.6	108.5	104.1	104.1	105.9	107.3
Securities brokerage	52312	114.8	118.3	120.4	126.9	136.5	135.6
Commodity contracts dealing	52313	6.9	7.0	6.7	7.2	7.8	7.9
Commodity contracts brokerage	52314	6.2	6.7	5.4	5.0	5.3	5.1
Securities and commodity exchanges	5232	10.1	11.1	9.7	9.8	10.0	10.5
Miscellaneous intermediation	52391	17.2	18.5	18.9	20.1	22.2	22.5
Portfolio management	52392	172.3	183.8	193.2	213.1	227.2	227.2
Investment advice	52393	25.7	28.6	32.2	36.2	40.8	44.3
Insurance carriers & related activities [2]	524	1,748.6	1,809.6	1,925.3	2,005.6	2,176.9	2,296.9
Direct life, health, medical insurance carriers	52411	1,060.7	1,093.5	1,142.0	1,174.7	1,298.9	1,378.8
Other direct insurance carriers	52412	441.6	452.2	470.0	493.1	521.2	544.3
Reinsurance carriers	52413	45.7	45.5	49.4	52.2	55.0	55.8
Insurance agencies & brokerages	52421	98.4	102.6	106.8	115.0	120.1	130.0

D Estimate in table is withheld to avoid disclosing data of individual companies; data are included in higher level totals. [1] Data is based on 2007 NAICS; see text, this section and Section 15. [2] Includes other kinds of business, not shown separately.

Source: U.S. Census Bureau, Annual and Quarterly Services, "2015 Service Annual Survey," <http://www.census.gov/services/index.html>, accessed February 2017.

Table 1191. Financial Accounts of the United States—Financial Assets of Financial and Nonfinancial Institutions by Holder Sector: 2000 to 2016

[In billions of dollars (93,019 represents $93,019,000,000,000). As of Dec. 31]

Sector	2000	2005	2009	2010	2011	2012	2013	2014	2015	2016
All sectors	93,019	130,991	153,697	162,282	166,693	177,673	194,406	205,843	209,774	220,631
Households[1]	33,959	45,410	48,683	52,820	53,662	57,983	65,484	69,556	71,160	75,334
Nonfinancial business	11,233	14,497	16,894	17,745	18,434	19,315	20,791	22,248	24,009	25,645
Nonfinancial corporations	9,761	11,901	13,317	14,017	14,509	15,088	16,261	17,274	18,713	20,011
Nonfinancial noncorporate	1,473	2,597	3,576	3,728	3,925	4,226	4,531	4,973	5,296	5,634
Federal government	570	644	1,397	1,620	1,422	1,520	1,717	1,892	2,138	2,331
State and local government	1,661	2,321	2,682	2,777	2,751	2,855	2,866	2,967	3,070	3,218
Monetary authority	636	879	2,266	2,452	2,945	2,955	4,074	4,555	4,542	4,510
Private depository institutions	7,512	11,084	13,554	13,697	14,580	14,985	15,920	16,898	17,373	18,072
U.S.-chartered depository institutions	6,334	9,446	11,441	11,473	11,840	12,218	12,795	13,647	14,182	14,897
Foreign banking offices in U.S.	710	904	1,218	1,268	1,736	1,720	2,037	2,093	1,951	1,842
Banks in U.S.-affiliated areas	62	106	95	80	76		85	92	88	94
Credit unions	406	628	801	876	929	971	1,003	1,066	1,151	1,238
Property-casualty insurance companies	864	1,393	1,546	1,598	1,667	1,689	1,775	1,845	1,849	1,908
Life insurance companies	3,176	4,462	4,902	5,343	5,617	5,978	6,160	6,520	6,445	6,764
Private pension funds	4,283	5,391	5,958	6,600	6,714	7,241	8,099	8,426	8,631	9,099
Defined benefit plans	1,785	2,251	2,626	2,836	2,947	3,019	3,095	3,186	3,270	3,344
Defined contribution plans	2,497	3,140	3,331	3,764	3,767	4,222	5,004	5,239	5,361	5,755
Federal government retirement funds	2,003	2,495	2,923	3,156	3,264	3,382	3,537	3,656	3,764	3,894
State and local government employee retirement funds	2,270	3,478	4,282	4,776	4,929	5,122	5,337	5,559	5,819	6,103
Money market mutual funds[2]	1,845	2,027	3,316	2,804	2,691	2,693	2,718	2,725	2,755	2,728
Mutual funds[2]	5,119	6,865	7,797	9,030	8,941	10,364	12,333	13,151	12,897	13,616
Closed-end funds	143	276	223	238	242	264	279	289	261	262
Exchange-traded funds	66	301	777	992	1,048	1,337	1,675	1,974	2,101	2,524
Government-sponsored enterprises (GSE)[3]	1,965	2,822	3,048	6,722	6,480	6,275	6,361	6,400	6,488	6,685
Agency- and GSE-backed mortgage pools[4]	2,493	3,548	5,377	1,147	1,312	1,443	1,574	1,649	1,775	1,933
Asset-backed securities issuers[5]	1,509	3,500	3,392	2,345	2,071	1,843	1,511	1,424	1,347	1,233
Finance companies[5]	1,213	1,857	1,662	1,589	1,569	1,494	1,473	1,501	1,481	1,385
Real estate investment trusts	65	306	263	302	433	594	663	725	659	673
Security brokers and dealers	2,020	3,569	3,269	3,504	3,533	3,706	3,408	3,255	3,044	3,022
Holding companies[6]	908	1,674	3,366	3,355	3,424	4,330	4,300	4,391	3,956	4,330
Funding corporations[7]	1,303	1,569	1,830	1,655	1,458	1,367	1,288	1,305	1,454	1,559
Rest of the world	6,202	10,624	14,290	16,015	17,505	18,937	21,066	22,933	22,756	23,804

[1] Includes nonprofit organizations. [2] Open-end investment companies. Includes funding vehicles for variable annuities. [3] Federal Home Loan Banks, Federal National Mortgage Association (Fannie Mae), Federal Home Loan Mortgage Corporation (Freddie Mac), Federal Agriculture Mortgage Corporation, Farm Credit System, the Financing Corporation, and the Resolution Funding Corporation. The Student Loan Marketing Association (Sallie Mae), was included until it was fully privatized in 2004. [4] Government National Mortgage Association, Federal National Mortgage Association, Federal Home Loan Mortgage Corporation, Federal Agriculture Mortgage Corporation, and Farmers Home Administration pools. Also includes agency- and GSE-backed mortgage pool securities which are used as collateral for agency- and GSE-backed collateralized mortgage obligations (CMOs) and privately issued CMOs. Excludes Federal Financing Bank holdings of pool securities, which are included with federal government mortgages and other loans and advances. [5] Includes retail captive finance companies and mortgage companies. [6] Parent-only bank holding companies and savings and loan holding companies that file the Federal Reserve Board form FR Y-9LP, FR Y-9SP, or FR 2320. [7] Funding subsidiaries, custodial accounts for reinvested collateral of securities lending operations, Federal Reserve lending facilities, and funds associated with the Public-Private Investment Program (PPIP).

Source: Board of Governors of the Federal Reserve System, "Financial Accounts of the United States, Z.1," <https://www.federalreserve.gov/data.htm>, accessed July 2017.

Table 1192. Financial Accounts of the United States—Debt Securities and Debt Loans Outstanding By Sector: 2000 to 2016

[In billions of dollars (28,598 represents $28,598,000,000,000). As of December 31. Represents credit market debt owed by sectors shown. Some sectors only borrow/lend through debt securities or loans, but not both]

Item	2000	2005	2009	2010	2011	2012	2013	2014	2015	2016
Total debt outstanding.............	28,598	43,448	54,512	54,880	55,850	57,739	59,479	61,775	63,602	66,100
Total debt securities [1].............	16,359	24,727	32,422	33,553	34,595	36,221	37,381	38,744	39,767	41,314
Domestic nonfinancial.............	8,127	11,445	15,973	17,928	19,216	20,729	21,810	22,813	23,946	25,102
Household sector (nonprofits).............	138	217	273	272	264	250	236	229	221	217
Nonfinancial corporate business.............	2,710	3,006	3,724	3,961	4,164	4,516	4,809	5,120	5,527	5,816
Federal government.............	4,090	5,585	8,883	10,529	11,667	12,848	13,705	14,441	15,166	16,008
State and local governments [2].............	1,189	2,637	3,092	3,167	3,121	3,115	3,059	3,023	3,032	3,060
Financial sectors.............	7,529	12,074	14,600	13,549	13,120	12,926	12,921	13,063	13,104	13,421
U.S.-chartered depository institutions.............	99	134	177	490	500	383	281	263	254	233
Foreign banking offices in U.S.............	2	1	–	–	–	–	–	–	–	–
Government-sponsored enterprises (GSE).............	1,826	2,592	2,707	6,435	6,247	6,093	6,200	6,276	6,369	6,563
Agency- and GSE-backed mortgage pools.............	2,493	3,548	5,377	1,147	1,312	1,443	1,574	1,649	1,775	1,933
Asset-backed securities issuers.............	1,515	3,504	3,394	2,345	2,071	1,843	1,511	1,424	1,347	1,233
Finance companies.............	743	966	900	1,188	1,159	1,084	1,078	1,080	1,064	1,007
Real estate investment trusts.............	65	217	144	145	153	179	355	403	396	415
Brokers and dealers.............	41	62	93	130	92	90	112	124	131	129
Holding companies.............	243	430	1,090	1,047	966	1,220	1,192	1,200	1,057	1,168
Funding corporations.............	503	620	719	622	620	591	618	644	710	739
Rest of the world.............	703	1,209	1,849	2,076	2,259	2,566	2,649	2,867	2,717	2,792
Total loans [3].............	12,239	18,720	22,090	21,327	21,255	21,518	22,099	23,032	23,834	24,785
Domestic nonfinancial.............	10,930	16,924	19,982	19,359	19,230	19,469	19,819	20,564	21,341	22,216
Financial sectors.............	1,145	1,654	1,951	1,786	1,799	1,781	1,971	2,128	2,131	2,224
Rest of the world.............	164	142	157	182	226	268	308	339	363	345

– Represents zero. [1] Includes open market paper, Treasury securities, agency- and GSE-backed securities, municipal securities, and corporate and foreign bonds. [2] Excludes employee retirement funds. [3] Includes depository loans not elsewhere classified, other loans and advances, mortgages, and consumer credit.

Source: Board of Governors of the Federal Reserve System, "Financial Accounts of the United States, Z.1," <https://www.federalreserve.gov/data.htm>, accessed July 2017.

Table 1193. Financial Accounts of the United States—Financial Assets and Liabilities of Foreign Sector: 2000 to 2016

[In billions of dollars (6,202 represents $6,202,000,000,000). As of December 31. Minus sign (-) indicates loss]

Type of instrument	2000	2005	2009	2010	2011	2012	2013	2014	2015	2016
Total financial assets.............	6,202	10,624	14,290	16,015	17,505	18,937	21,066	22,933	22,756	23,804
Special Drawing Rights allocations.............	6	7	55	54	54	54	54	51	49	47
Net interbank assets.............	80	-17	14	-15	230	96	382	404	289	133
U.S. checkable deposits and currency.............	236	300	361	390	472	541	591	674	715	766
U.S. time deposits.............	226	223	299	308	356	394	445	499	499	547
Money market fund shares.............	11	23	77	70	74	97	108	113	114	113
Security repurchase agreements.............	91	705	489	582	678	671	705	811	668	729
Debt securities, excluding negotiable certificates of deposit.............	2,335	4,980	7,480	8,252	8,749	9,365	9,587	10,172	10,359	10,684
Commercial paper.............	114	157	117	102	103	103	101	108	104	140
Treasury securities.............	1,021	1,984	3,671	4,459	5,004	5,571	5,793	6,156	6,148	6,004
Treasury bills.............	178	265	750	710	648	662	686	672	725	670
Other Treasury securities.............	844	1,720	2,920	3,749	4,357	4,910	5,107	5,484	5,423	5,334
Agency- and GSE-backed securities [1].............	348	1,006	1,150	1,096	1,078	1,001	884	900	914	988
Municipal securities.............	8	29	59	72	72	72	76	81	87	95
U.S. corporate bonds.............	843	1,804	2,484	2,523	2,491	2,618	2,733	2,928	3,106	3,458
Nonfinancial business loans.............	117	163	182	162	196	144	140	171	208	206
U.S. corporate equities.............	1,483	2,118	2,657	3,213	3,397	3,953	5,204	5,922	5,507	5,747
Mutual fund shares.............	149	163	183	263	370	495	552	608	597	681
Trade receivables.............	46	53	93	112	129	141	148	162	176	185
Foreign direct investment in U.S. [2].............	1,421	1,906	2,398	2,624	2,799	2,987	3,148	3,346	3,576	3,966
Total liabilities.............	3,328	5,710	8,149	8,862	9,431	9,951	10,163	10,515	10,393	10,750
U.S. official reserve assets [3].............	57	54	119	121	137	139	133	119	106	106
U.S. private deposits.............	803	1,165	1,258	1,304	1,066	919	951	827	586	485
Security repurchase agreements.............	0	381	455	664	765	801	692	708	783	873
Debt securities.............	703	1,209	1,849	2,076	2,259	2,566	2,649	2,867	2,717	2,792
Commercial paper.............	121	384	401	399	345	373	407	386	445	366
Bonds.............	582	825	1,448	1,678	1,914	2,193	2,243	2,481	2,272	2,426
Loans.............	164	142	157	182	226	268	308	339	363	345
Depository institution loans n.e.c. [4].............	115	110	138	162	205	238	277	305	328	312
Other loans and advances.............	50	31	19	20	21	30	32	34	35	33
Trade credit and advances.............	37	34	45	51	55	56	53	47	45	45
U.S. direct investment abroad [2].............	1,532	2,652	4,077	4,274	4,599	5,018	5,215	5,458	5,649	5,952
Miscellaneous liabilities.............	31	74	188	191	324	184	161	150	145	152
U.S. equity in IBRD, etc. [5].............	36	44	50	53	55	58	60	62	65	67
Nonofficial U.S. currencies.............	3	3	13	3	102	12	3	4	4	8
Investment by holding companies.............	-7	27	125	136	166	115	98	83	76	77

[1] GSE = Government-sponsored enterprises. [2] Direct investment is valued on a current-cost basis. [3] Excludes monetary gold. [4] N.e.c. = not elsewhere classified. [5] IBRD is International Bank for Reconstruction and Development.

Source: Board of Governors of the Federal Reserve System, "Financial Accounts of the United States, Z.1," <https://www.federalreserve.gov/data.htm>, accessed July 2017.

Table 1194. Financial Accounts of the United States—Assets of Households and Nonprofit Organizations: 2000 to 2016

[In billions of dollars (33,959 represents $33,959,000,000,000). As of December 31. See also Table 746]

Type of instrument	Total (billion dollars)							Percent distribution		
	2000	2005	2010	2013	2014	2015	2016	2000	2010	2016
Total financial assets	33,959	45,410	52,820	65,484	69,556	71,160	75,334	100.0	100.0	100.0
Foreign deposits	48	64	67	52	46	32	25	0.1	0.1	—
Checkable deposits and currency	405	286	423	993	1,094	1,139	1,062	1.2	0.8	1.4
Time and savings deposits	3,068	4,962	6,442	7,390	7,891	8,357	9,079	9.0	12.2	12.1
Money market fund shares	933	941	1,127	1,161	1,113	1,069	1,126	2.7	2.1	1.5
Debt securities [1]	2,255	3,396	4,851	4,320	3,962	4,410	4,318	6.6	9.2	5.7
Treasury securities	589	419	1,098	1,140	838	1,138	1,409	1.7	2.1	1.9
Agency and GSE-backed securities [2]	618	559	274	266	283	504	423	1.8	0.5	0.6
Municipal securities	488	1,635	2,074	1,833	1,694	1,641	1,676	1.4	3.9	2.2
Corporate and foreign bonds	559	783	1,405	1,081	1,147	1,127	810	1.6	2.7	1.1
Loans [1]	558	759	955	1,017	1,063	1,002	993	1.6	1.8	1.3
Mortgages	96	127	132	124	122	115	113	0.3	0.3	0.1
Consumer credit (student loans) [3]	—	—	71	52	48	44	39	–	0.1	0.1
Corporate equities [3]	7,974	8,237	8,704	12,744	14,369	14,045	15,622	23.5	16.5	20.7
Mutual fund shares	2,466	3,279	4,473	6,250	6,747	6,523	6,999	7.3	8.5	9.3
Trade receivables	124	153	184	213	220	227	234	0.4	0.3	0.3
Life insurance reserves	819	1,083	1,137	1,233	1,283	1,309	1,340	2.4	2.2	1.8
Pension entitlements [4]	9,971	13,305	16,882	19,869	20,667	21,261	22,268	29.4	32.0	29.6
Equity in noncorporate business	4,959	8,336	6,765	9,332	10,185	10,836	11,268	14.6	12.8	15.0
Miscellaneous assets	379	609	808	910	917	952	1,000	1.1	1.5	1.3

– Represents or rounds to zero. [1] Includes other instruments not shown separately. [2] GSE = government-sponsored enterprises. [3] Directly held shares, including those in closed-end and exchange-traded funds shares. Other equities are included in mutual funds, life insurance reserves, and pension entitlements. [4] Includes public and private defined benefit and defined contribution plans and annuities, including those in IRAs and at life insurance companies. Excludes social security.

Source: Board of Governors of the Federal Reserve System, "Financial Accounts of the United States, Z.1," <https://www.federalreserve.gov/data.htm>, accessed July 2017.

Table 1195. Financial Assets Held by Families by Type of Asset: 2010 and 2013

[Median value in thousands of constant 2013 dollars (23.0 represents $23,000). All dollar figures are adjusted to 2013 dollars using the "current methods" version of the consumer price index for all urban consumers published by U.S. Bureau of Labor Statistics. Families include one-person units; for definition of family, see text, Section 1. Based on Survey of Consumer Finances; see Appendix III]

Age of family head and family income	Any financial asset [1]	Trans-action accounts [2]	Certifi-cates of deposit	Savings bonds	Stocks [3]	Pooled invest-ment funds [4]	Retire-ment accounts [5]	Life insur-ance [6]	Other man-aged [7]
PERCENT OF FAMILIES OWNING ASSET									
2010, total	94.1	92.5	12.2	12.0	15.1	8.7	50.4	19.7	5.7
2013, total	94.5	93.2	7.8	10.0	13.8	8.2	49.2	19.2	5.2
Under 35 years old	92.6	90.2	5.2	9.0	7.2	4.2	39.3	9.2	1.3
35 to 44 years old	93.1	91.8	4.4	12.5	14.3	6.3	55.4	13.3	2.0
45 to 54 years old	93.3	91.8	6.7	10.4	14.7	8.2	56.5	17.1	3.9
55 to 64 years old	95.7	94.6	5.8	10.8	15.5	10.6	59.3	24.4	7.1
65 to 74 years old	97.4	97.1	11.7	9.4	18.4	11.8	48.0	29.4	11.9
75 years old and over	97.2	96.7	18.8	6.8	15.3	10.3	29.0	30.4	9.2
Percentiles of income: [8]									
Less than 20	81.8	78.9	4.8	4.0	4.2	2.2	8.8	10.9	1.5
20 to 39.9	92.9	90.8	6.3	5.1	5.5	2.7	27.9	16.0	3.2
40 to 59.9	98.2	97.2	7.6	8.0	9.3	6.0	50.8	19.3	4.4
60 to 79.9	99.8	99.1	9.2	14.7	14.4	8.5	70.4	23.8	6.3
80 to 89.9	99.8	99.8	9.6	18.5	25.4	12.3	83.7	23.1	8.6
90 to 100	100.0	100.0	11.9	18.2	45.3	30.8	92.7	28.7	12.9
MEDIAN VALUE [9]									
2010, total	23.0	3.8	21.4	1.1	21.4	85.7	47.2	7.8	75.0
2013, total	21.3	4.1	16.0	1.0	27.0	80.0	59.0	8.0	100.0
Under 35 years old	5.8	2.2	4.0	0.7	6.6	11.0	12.0	2.5	13.0
35 to 44 years old	20.4	3.8	6.3	0.7	20.0	48.0	42.7	7.0	40.0
45 to 54 years old	31.8	4.0	10.0	1.0	16.0	53.0	87.0	8.0	70.0
55 to 64 years old	52.7	5.0	25.0	1.2	30.0	143.0	104.0	9.8	100.0
65 to 74 years old	72.0	7.0	31.0	3.0	50.0	155.0	149.0	9.0	125.0
75 years old and over	28.7	7.0	22.0	3.0	76.0	145.0	69.0	8.0	110.0

[1] Includes other types of financial assets, not shown separately. [2] Checking, savings, and money market deposit accounts, money market mutual funds, and call accounts at brokerages. [3] Covers only those stocks that are directly held by families outside mutual funds, retirement accounts, and other managed assets. [4] Excludes money market mutual funds and indirectly held mutual funds and includes all other types of directly held pooled investment funds, such as traditional open-ended and closed-end mutual funds, real estate investment trusts, and hedge funds. [5] The tax-deferred retirement accounts consist of IRAs, Keogh accounts, and certain employer-sponsored accounts. Employer-sponsored accounts include 401(k), 403(b), and thrift saving accounts from current or past jobs; other current job plans from which loans or withdrawals can be made; and accounts from past jobs from which the family expects to receive the account balance in the future. [6] The value of such policies according to their current cash value, not their death benefit. [7] Includes personal annuities and trusts with an equity interest and managed investment accounts. [8] Percentiles of income distribution in 2013 dollars: 20th: $23,300; 40th: $40,500; 60th: $63,100; 80th: $104,500; 90th: $154,600. Percentile: A value on a scale of zero to 100 that indicates the percent of a distribution that is equal to or below it. [9] Median value of financial asset for families holding such assets.

Source: Board of Governors of the Federal Reserve System, 2013 Survey of Consumer Finances, *Changes in U.S. Family Finances From 2010 to 2013: Evidence from the Survey of Consumer Finances*, Federal Reserve Bulletin, Vol. 100, No. 4, September 2014. See also <http://www.federalreserve.gov/econresdata/scf/scfindex.htm>.

Table 1196. Financial Accounts of the United States—Liabilities of Households and Nonprofit Organizations: 2000 to 2016

[In billions of dollars (7,359 represents $7,359,000,000,000). As of December 31. Minus sign (-) indicates decrease. See also Table 746]

Type of instrument	Total (billion dollars)							Percent distribution		
	2000	2005	2010	2013	2014	2015	2016	2000	2010	2016
Total liabilities	**7,359**	**12,201**	**13,875**	**13,921**	**14,288**	**14,652**	**15,116**	**100.0**	**100.0**	**100.0**
Debt securities (municipal securities)	138	217	272	236	229	221	217	1.9	2.0	1.4
Loans	7,054	11,758	13,304	13,361	13,727	14,090	14,552	95.9	95.9	96.3
Home mortgages [1]	4,814	8,935	9,983	9,472	9,456	9,556	9,769	65.4	72.0	64.6
Consumer credit	1,741	2,321	2,647	3,096	3,317	3,537	3,765	23.7	19.1	24.9
Depository institution loans, not elsewhere classified [2]	15	-17	61	91	212	326	351	0.2	0.4	2.3
Other loans and advances	354	352	414	481	514	437	427	4.8	3.0	2.8
Commercial mortgages	129	168	198	222	228	234	240	1.8	1.4	1.6
Trade payables	148	203	274	295	302	309	316	2.0	2.0	2.1
Deferred and unpaid life insurance premiums	20	23	25	29	30	32	31	0.3	0.2	0.2

[1] Includes loans made under home equity lines of credit and home equity loans secured by junior liens. [2] Includes loans extended by the Federal Reserve to financial institutions such as domestic hedge funds through the Term Asset-Backed Securities Loan Facility (TALF).

Source: Board of Governors of the Federal Reserve System, "Financial Accounts of the United States, Z.1," <https://www.federalreserve.gov/data.htm>, accessed July 2017.

Table 1197. Financial Debt Held by Families by Type of Debt: 2010 and 2013

[Median debt in thousands of constant 2013 dollars (75.7 represents $75,700). See headnote, Table 1195]

Age and race of family head and family income	Any debt	Secured by residential property		Installment loans	Credit card balances [2]	Lines of credit not secured by residential property	Other [3]
		Primary residence [1]	Other				
PERCENT OF FAMILIES HOLDING DEBT							
2010, total	74.9	47.0	5.4	46.4	39.4	2.1	6.4
2013, total	**74.5**	**42.9**	**5.3**	**47.2**	**38.1**	**1.9**	**6.6**
Under 35 years old	77.1	28.6	2.4	63.5	36.8	2.1	5.7
35 to 44 years old	84.8	53.5	5.0	58.2	41.7	2.6	7.7
45 to 54 years old	82.3	56.1	7.9	52.8	44.3	1.7	9.7
55 to 64 years old	78.7	48.9	7.8	43.3	43.4	1.7	7.7
65 to 74 years old	66.4	42.2	4.8	29.3	32.8	2.2	4.2
75 years old and over	41.4	19.9	2.7	15.7	21.1	0.7	2.0
White non-Hispanic	75.3	48.4	6.1	46.3	38.5	2.0	6.5
Nonwhite or Hispanic	72.9	31.6	3.5	49.0	37.4	1.6	6.8
Percentiles of income: [4]							
Less than 20	52.2	13.6	0.7	32.4	19.5	0.7	4.2
20 to 39.9	66.7	25.8	2.1	41.3	34.2	1.5	5.3
40 to 59.9	80.7	40.1	3.9	52.7	46.8	1.6	5.3
60 to 79.9	87.0	62.9	5.6	56.4	49.8	2.3	9.1
80 to 89.9	87.5	71.9	9.5	61.2	48.7	3.6	10.5
90 to 100	84.5	72.6	18.7	45.0	32.2	3.2	7.9
MEDIAN DEBT [5]							
2010, total	75.7	116.8	104.0	13.6	2.8	6.4	4.8
2013, total	**60.4**	**115.0**	**90.0**	**14.9**	**2.3**	**4.4**	**4.0**
Under 35 years old	31.0	120.0	83.0	18.0	1.5	1.2	2.0
35 to 44 years old	96.5	140.0	100.0	16.3	2.5	4.0	4.0
45 to 54 years old	100.0	121.0	90.0	14.4	2.6	10.0	4.9
55 to 64 years old	63.4	102.0	85.0	13.0	3.0	12.0	5.0
65 to 74 years old	44.0	81.0	55.0	10.2	2.3	17.0	5.6
75 years old and over	20.0	54.0	60.0	10.1	1.9	50.0	2.3
White non-Hispanic	82.2	118.0	99.0	15.1	2.7	8.5	5.0
Nonwhite or Hispanic	29.0	114.0	65.0	13.0	1.7	1.2	2.4

[1] Debt secured by residential property consists of first-lien and junior-lien mortgages and home equity lines of credit secured by the primary residence. [2] Families that had an outstanding balance on any of their credit cards after paying their most recent bills. [3] Includes loans on insurance policies, loans against pension accounts, borrowing on margin accounts, and unclassified loans. [4] See footnote 8, Table 1195. [5] Median amount of financial debt for families holding such debts.

Source: Board of Governors of the Federal Reserve System, 2013 Survey of Consumer Finances, *Changes in U.S. Family Finances From 2010 to 2013: Evidence from the Survey of Consumer Finances*, Federal Reserve Bulletin, Vol. 100, No. 4, September 2014. See also <http://www.federalreserve.gov/econresdata/scf/scfindex.htm>.

Table 1198. Amount of Debt Held by Families—Percent Distribution by Type and Purpose of Debt: 2007 to 2013

[See headnote, Table 1195]

Type and purpose of debt	2007	2010	2013	Type and purpose of debt	2007	2010	2013
TYPE OF DEBT				**PURPOSE OF DEBT**			
Total	100.0	100.0	100.0	Total	100.0	100.0	100.0
Secured by residential property:				Primary residence:			
Primary residence	74.6	74.2	73.8	Purchase	79.8	79.5	79.6
Other	10.1	9.8	9.0	Improvement	2.3	1.9	1.7
Lines of credit not secured				Other residential property	0.5	0.4	0.5
by residential property	0.4	1.0	0.7	Investments, excluding			
Installment loans	10.2	11.1	13.1	real estate	2.2	2.5	2.1
Credit card balances	3.5	2.9	2.4	Vehicles	5.5	4.7	5.1
Other	1.1	1.0	1.1	Goods and services	5.8	5.2	4.0
				Education	4.0	5.8	7.1

Source: Board of Governors of the Federal Reserve System, 2013 Survey of Consumer Finances, *Changes in U.S. Family Finances From 2010 to 2013: Evidence from the Survey of Consumer Finances*, Federal Reserve Bulletin, Vol. 100, No. 4, September 2014, and previous reports. See also <http://www.federalreserve.gov/econresdata/scf/scfindex.htm>.

Table 1199. Ratios of Debt Payments to Family Income: 2007 to 2013

[In percent. All dollar figures are adjusted to 2013 dollars using the "current methods" version of the consumer price index for all urban consumers published by the U.S. Bureau of Labor Statistics. Families include one-person units; for definition of family, see text, Section 1. Based on Survey of Consumer Finances, see Appendix III. For definition of median, see Guide to Tabular Presentation]

Age of family head and family income (constant 2013 dollars)	Ratio of debt payments to family income						Percent of debtors with—					
	Aggregate			Median for debtors			Ratios above 40 percent			Any payment 60 days or more past due		
	2007	2010	2013	2007	2010	2013	2007	2010	2013	2007	2010	2013
All families	**14.6**	**14.7**	**12.1**	**18.6**	**18.2**	**15.9**	**14.7**	**13.9**	**11.0**	**7.1**	**10.8**	**9.3**
Under 35 years old	19.7	17.0	14.9	17.6	16.3	13.7	15.0	11.7	8.0	9.4	10.4	11.6
35 to 44 years old	18.6	18.4	13.6	20.3	20.8	16.1	12.7	16.5	9.8	8.6	15.8	11.4
45 to 54 years old	15.1	16.2	13.9	19.6	19.2	18.7	16.3	15.4	11.8	7.3	12.6	12.0
55 to 64 years old	12.7	12.6	11.2	17.6	17.7	16.4	14.8	13.1	14.0	4.9	8.4	6.4
65 to 74 years old	9.7	11.3	8.9	18.4	17.0	14.3	15.3	12.0	12.3	4.4	6.1	4.7
75 years old and over	4.4	6.8	6.0	13.2	14.1	10.7	13.9	11.9	10.0	1.0	3.2	2.7
Percentiles of income: [1]												
Less than 20	17.6	23.5	15.7	18.8	16.0	13.1	26.7	26.2	23.4	15.1	21.1	16.4
20 to 39.9	17.2	16.8	14.7	16.7	17.5	15.2	19.7	18.6	18.1	11.3	15.2	14.1
40 to 59.9	19.9	19.5	16.2	20.4	20.1	16.4	14.5	15.3	11.2	8.3	10.4	10.0
60 to 79.9	21.8	19.4	16.6	21.9	20.4	17.7	12.8	11.1	5.9	4.3	8.8	7.3
80 to 89.9	19.7	18.1	16.6	19.1	19.3	18.5	8.1	5.3	4.1	1.9	5.3	4.3
90 to 100	8.5	9.4	7.4	12.6	13.1	11.8	3.8	2.9	1.6	0.2	2.1	1.0
Percentiles of net worth: [1]												
Less than 25	14.9	19.3	16.7	12.0	13.9	12.2	10.6	15.0	12.4	16.8	22.2	21.0
25 to 49.9	22.5	19.3	16.9	23.4	21.1	18.1	19.5	15.2	13.6	7.6	13.4	10.4
50 to 74.9	20.4	19.2	16.8	21.7	20.6	17.8	15.6	14.2	10.1	4.2	6.7	5.0
75 to 89.9	17.0	15.9	14.0	18.2	16.6	15.4	13.0	11.0	7.7	1.2	2.1	1.8
90 to 100	8.1	8.8	6.5	12.7	13.5	11.3	11.1	10.9	7.8	0.7	1.2	1.0
Owner occupied	15.7	16.2	13.2	22.9	22.2	19.7	18.1	17.1	13.8	4.8	8.7	6.5
Renter occupied or other	7.9	7.0	6.6	8.4	6.8	6.8	5.4	5.0	4.3	13.5	16.6	15.9

[1] See footnote 8, table 1195. Percentiles of distribution of net worth in 2013 dollars: 25th: $8,800; 50th: $81,200; 75th: $317,300; and 90th: $941,700.

Source: Board of Governors of the Federal Reserve System, 2013 Survey of Consumer Finances, *Changes in U.S. Family Finances from 2010 to 2013: Evidence from the Survey of Consumer Finances*, Federal Reserve Bulletin, Vol. 100, No. 4, September 2014. See also <http://www.federalreserve.gov/econresdata/scf/scfindex.htm>.

Table 1200. Household Debt-Service Payments and Financial Obligations as a Percentage of Disposable Personal Income: 1990 to 2016

[As of end of year, seasonally adjusted. Mortgage debt service ratio (DSR) is defined as the total quarterly required mortgage payments divided by total quarterly disposable personal income. The consumer DSR is defined as the total quarterly required consumer debt payments divided by total quarterly disposable personal income. The financial obligations ratio adds automobile lease payments, rental payments on tenant-occupied property, homeowners' insurance, and property tax payments to the debt service ratio]

Year	Financial obligations ratio	Household debt service ratio			Year	Financial obligations ratio	Household debt service ratio		
		Total	Mortgage	Consumer			Total	Mortgage	Consumer
1990	17.0	11.6	6.2	5.4	2010	16.2	11.1	6.0	5.1
2000	17.1	12.1	5.7	6.4	2011	15.7	10.5	5.5	5.1
2005	17.3	12.6	6.5	6.1	2012	15.0	9.9	5.0	4.9
2006	17.6	12.8	6.9	5.9	2013	15.5	10.2	4.9	5.3
2007	18.1	13.2	7.2	6.0	2014	15.2	9.9	4.6	5.3
2008	17.8	12.8	6.9	5.8	2015	15.4	10.0	4.5	5.5
2009	17.1	12.0	6.5	5.4	2016	15.4	10.0	4.4	5.6

Source: Board of Governors of the Federal Reserve System, "Household Debt Service and Financial Obligations Ratios," <https://www.federalreserve.gov/data.htm>, accessed April 2017.

Table 1201. FDIC-Insured Financial Institutions—Number and Assets by State and Island Area: 2016

[In billions of dollars, except as indicated (16,780.2 represents $16,780,200,000,000). As of December 31. Information is obtained primarily from the Federal Financial Institutions Examination Council (FFIEC) Call Reports and the Office of Thrift Supervision's Thrift Financial Reports. Data are based on the location of each reporting institution's main office. Reported data may include assets located outside of the reporting institution's home state]

State or Island Area	Number of institutions	Assets by asset size of bank				State or Island Area	Number of institutions	Assets by asset size of bank			
		Total	Less than $100 mil. [1]	$100 mil. to $1 bil. [1]	Greater than $1 bil. [1]			Total	Less than $100 mil. [1]	$100 mil. to $1 bil. [1]	Greater than $1 bil. [1]
Total......	5,913	16,780.2	91.5	1,173.9	15,514.8	NE..........	182	76.3	4.1	27.0	45.2
AL..........	127	258.2	2.5	24.7	231.0	NV..........	17	196.2	0.2	4.1	191.9
AK..........	5	6.3	–	1.2	5.1	NH..........	19	11.8	0.1	7.2	4.5
AZ..........	17	21.4	0.3	4.0	17.1	NJ..........	86	138.6	0.4	22.7	115.5
AR..........	101	88.1	1.5	19.6	67.1	NM..........	40	14.8	0.3	8.8	5.6
CA..........	178	716.9	0.8	46.1	670.0	NY..........	146	949.7	0.5	34.6	914.7
CO..........	88	57.6	1.4	14.5	41.6	NC..........	62	1,982.4	0.7	13.0	1,968.8
CT..........	42	104.9	0.2	12.6	92.1	ND..........	78	27.3	2.1	10.0	15.2
DE..........	22	1,020.7	0.1	2.3	1,018.3	OH..........	197	2,994.6	3.8	35.7	2,955.1
DC..........	3	1.1	–	1.1	–	OK..........	209	109.0	4.6	35.4	69.0
FL..........	149	184.2	1.4	37.5	145.3	OR..........	24	35.9	0.3	5.2	30.4
GA..........	183	306.4	2.5	32.4	271.5	PA..........	165	230.9	1.1	44.5	185.3
HI..........	8	51.1	–	1.4	49.8	RI..........	9	127.1	(Z)	1.0	126.0
ID..........	12	5.5	0.1	3.0	2.4	SC..........	56	28.1	0.9	14.2	13.0
IL..........	473	465.9	9.3	78.4	378.2	SD..........	69	3,129.9	1.8	10.6	3,117.5
IN..........	111	85.4	1.2	23.3	60.9	TN..........	157	102.9	1.7	39.7	61.4
IA..........	302	84.2	5.6	50.1	28.5	TX..........	464	476.4	6.3	101.4	368.7
KS..........	263	68.8	7.3	35.2	26.4	UT..........	47	602.1	0.5	7.8	593.8
KY..........	164	58.2	1.8	35.7	20.6	VT..........	12	6.8	0.1	4.7	2.1
LA..........	130	73.7	1.7	30.1	41.9	VA..........	85	712.8	0.4	20.2	692.3
ME..........	26	23.7	0.2	7.1	16.4	WA..........	49	70.5	0.6	12.2	57.7
MD..........	54	38.5	0.4	15.5	22.6	WV..........	58	35.1	0.6	10.5	23.9
MA..........	133	384.6	0.7	38.2	345.7	WI..........	222	108.9	3.1	46.5	59.3
MI..........	104	71.3	1.7	22.4	47.3	WY..........	32	8.2	0.4	7.8	–
MN..........	311	72.3	8.5	38.7	25.1	GU..........	3	2.4	–	0.5	1.9
MS..........	79	88.9	0.9	17.8	70.2	FM..........	1	0.1	–	0.1	–
MO..........	280	175.0	5.4	48.5	121.1	PR..........	5	57.6	–	–	57.6
MT..........	52	30.4	1.7	7.0	21.7	VI..........	2	0.3	–	0.3	–

– Represents zero. Z Less than $50 million. GU—Guam, FM—Federated States of Micronesia, PR—Puerto Rico, VI—Virgin Islands. [1] Asset size data for states not shown individually are included in the national totals.

Source: U.S. Federal Deposit Insurance Corporation, "Statistics on Banking," <http://www2.fdic.gov/sdi/sob/>, accessed April 2017.

Table 1202. FDIC-Insured Financial Institutions—Income and Selected Measures of Financial Condition: 2000 to 2016

[In billions of dollars, except as indicated (511.9 represents $511,900,000,000). Includes Island Areas. Includes foreign branches of U.S. banks. Minus sign (-) indicates decrease]

Item	2000	2005	2010	2011	2012	2013	2014	2015	2016
INCOME									
Interest income..........	511.9	522.2	536.9	507.5	486.7	470.4	469.8	478.5	515.8
Interest expense..........	276.6	205.1	106.9	84.8	65.9	53.3	47.1	46.9	54.4
Net interest income..........	235.3	317.0	430.0	422.7	420.8	417.1	422.7	431.6	461.4
Provisions for loan losses..........	32.1	29.8	158.0	77.6	57.8	32.4	29.8	37.1	47.8
Noninterest income..........	165.6	223.4	235.7	230.1	248.7	252.5	247.9	253.3	252.5
Noninterest expense..........	242.3	317.4	391.8	411.8	421.2	416.8	422.8	417.0	422.2
Income taxes..........	43.6	64.6	38.4	50.7	58.3	70.0	68.2	70.5	75.7
Net income attributable to bank..........	81.5	133.8	85.5	118.4	141.0	154.3	152.2	163.4	171.3
PERFORMANCE RATIOS									
Return on assets (percent) [1]..........	1.14	1.28	0.65	0.88	1.00	1.07	1.01	1.04	1.04
Return on equity (percent) [2]..........	13.53	12.43	5.85	7.79	8.90	9.54	9.01	9.29	9.32
Net interest margin (percent) [3]..........	3.77	3.47	3.76	3.60	3.42	3.26	3.14	3.07	3.13
Net charge-offs (bil. dol.) [4]..........	26.3	31.6	187.6	113.3	82.2	53.5	39.6	37.3	42.5
Net charge-offs to loans and leases, total (percent)..........	0.59	0.49	2.55	1.55	1.10	0.69	0.49	0.44	0.47
Net charge-off rate, credit card loans (percent)..........	4.36	4.74	10.08	5.45	3.95	3.35	3.12	2.92	3.16
CONDITION RATIOS									
Equity capital to assets (percent)..........	8.49	10.28	11.15	11.16	11.17	11.15	11.15	11.24	11.11
Noncurrent assets plus other real estate owned to assets (percent) [5]..........	0.71	0.50	3.11	2.61	2.20	1.63	1.20	0.97	0.86

[1] Net income (including securities transactions and nonrecurring items) as a percentage of average total assets. [2] Net income as a percentage of average total equity capital. [3] Interest income less interest expense as a percentage of average earning assets (i.e. the profit margin a bank earns on its loans and investments). [4] Total loans and leases charged off (removed from balance sheet because of uncollectibility), less amounts recovered on loans and leases previously charged off. [5] Noncurrent assets: the sum of loans, leases, debt securities and other assets that are 90 days or more past due, or in nonaccrual status. Other real estate owned, primarily foreclosed property.

Source: U.S. Federal Deposit Insurance Corporation, *Quarterly Banking Profile*, Fourth Quarter 2016, and earlier reports; and "QBP Time Series Spreadsheets, Annual Income," <https://www.fdic.gov/bank/analytical/qbp/>, accessed April 2017. See also <http://www5.fdic.gov/qbp/>.

Table 1203. FDIC-Insured Financial Institutions—Number, Assets, and Liabilities: 2000 to 2016

[In billions of dollars, except as indicated (7,463 represents $7,463,000,000,000). As of December 31. Includes Island Areas. Excludes insured branches of foreign banks. Includes foreign branches of U.S. banks]

Item	2000	2005	2010	2011	2012	2013	2014	2015	2016
Commercial bank offices, total..............	73,231	81,136	89,165	89,478	89,672	88,609	87,622	86,921	85,750
Number of main offices.....................	8,315	7,523	6,519	6,275	6,072	5,847	5,607	5,340	5,112
Number of branches.......................	64,916	73,613	82,646	83,203	83,600	82,762	82,015	81,581	80,638
Savings institutions, total....................	1,589	1,310	1,139	1,082	1,011	965	902	844	801
COMMERCIAL BANKS AND SAVINGS INSTITUTIONS									
Number of financial institutions reporting................................	**9,904**	**8,833**	**7,658**	**7,357**	**7,083**	**6,812**	**6,509**	**6,182**	**5,913**
Assets, total [1]..........................	**7,463**	**10,879**	**13,319**	**13,891**	**14,450**	**14,731**	**15,554**	**15,968**	**16,780**
Net loans and leases [1].....................	4,572	6,641	7,144	7,283	7,533	7,757	8,187	8,721	9,183
Real estate loans [1]......................	2,396	4,140	4,267	4,134	4,092	4,066	4,171	4,375	4,603
1-4 family residential mortgages...........	1,340	2,042	1,900	1,883	1,894	1,830	1,842	1,904	1,995
Nonfarm nonresidential..................	525	826	1,071	1,061	1,073	1,109	1,150	1,231	1,324
Construction and development............	197	450	321	240	203	210	238	275	313
Home equity loans......................	151	534	637	604	554	510	492	465	434
Multifamily residential real estate.......	117	188	213	219	233	263	297	344	383
Commercial and industrial loans............	1,086	1,086	1,184	1,345	1,494	1,567	1,715	1,841	1,935
Loans to individuals [1].....................	672	949	1,316	1,308	1,324	1,353	1,418	1,498	1,589
Credit cards and related plans.............	266	396	702	688	696	691	718	756	800
Other loans to individuals.................	406	553	614	620	628	662	700	741	790
Auto loans...........................	(NA)	(NA)	(NA)	300	320	353	385	415	442
Loans to depository institutions.............	118	162	109	119	103	114	101	98	88
Lease financing receivables................	167	139	102	100	105	111	114	116	127
Less: Reserve for losses...................	71	77	231	191	162	136	123	119	122
Securities................................	1,361	1,893	2,668	2,850	3,010	3,002	3,219	3,354	3,560
Domestic office assets.....................	6,702	9,825	11,693	12,097	12,572	12,948	13,866	14,408	15,177
Foreign office assets......................	760	1,054	1,626	1,794	1,878	1,782	1,688	1,560	1,603
Liabilities and capital, total [1]..............	**7,463**	**10,879**	**13,319**	**13,891**	**14,450**	**14,731**	**15,554**	**15,968**	**16,780**
Deposits...................................	4,915	7,141	9,423	10,186	10,817	11,192	11,764	12,190	12,895
Foreign office deposits.....................	707	921	1,550	1,428	1,370	1,401	1,396	1,285	1,247
Domestic office deposits...................	4,208	6,221	7,873	8,758	9,447	9,791	10,368	10,905	11,647
Interest-bearing deposits.................	3,437	5,004	6,184	6,493	6,906	7,180	7,516	7,905	8,495
Noninterest-bearing deposits..............	771	1,217	1,689	2,265	2,541	2,612	2,852	3,000	3,152
Equity capital.............................	633	1,119	1,511	1,569	1,629	1,654	1,741	1,801	1,869

NA Not available. [1] Includes other items not shown separately.

Source: U.S. Federal Deposit Insurance Corporation, "FDIC Quarterly Banking Profile," <www2.fdic.gov/qbp/>; and "Historical Statistics on Banking," <http://www2.fdic.gov/hsob/index.asp>; accessed September 2017.

Table 1204. FDIC-Insured Financial Institutions by Asset Size: 2016

[15,627.7 represents $15,627,700,000,000. Includes Island Areas. Includes foreign branches of U.S. banks]

Item	Unit	Total	Less than $100 mil.	$100 mil. to $1 bil.	$1 bil. to $10 bil.	Greater than $10 bil.
COMMERCIAL BANKS						
Institutions reporting...........................	Number	5,112	1,354	3,154	506	98
Assets, total....................................	Billion dollars	15,627.7	80.9	996.9	1,444.3	13,105.6
Deposits..	Billion dollars	11,982.3	68.6	839.4	1,159.2	9,915.1
Net income attributable to bank....................	Billion dollars	157.0	0.7	10.5	14.5	131.4
Return on assets................................	Percent	1.03	0.87	1.08	1.05	1.02
Return on equity................................	Percent	9.14	7.03	9.75	9.03	9.12
Equity capital to assets..........................	Percent	11.12	12.14	10.88	11.50	11.09
Noncurrent assets plus other real estate owned to assets............................	Percent	0.84	1.07	0.98	0.87	0.83
Net charge-offs to loans and leases...............	Percent	0.46	0.22	0.15	0.28	0.51
Percentage of banks losing money................	Percent	3.81	7.75	2.57	1.58	1.02
SAVINGS INSTITUTIONS						
Institutions reporting...........................	Number	801	187	483	115	16
Assets, total....................................	Billion dollars	1,151.9	10.6	177.0	317.5	646.9
Deposits..	Billion dollars	912.3	8.2	140.5	242.0	521.5
Net income attributable to bank....................	Billion dollars	13.8	0.1	1.8	2.6	9.3
Return on assets................................	Percent	1.26	1.07	1.07	0.85	1.52
Return on equity................................	Percent	11.45	6.26	8.40	7.13	15.25
Equity capital to assets..........................	Percent	10.85	17.04	12.65	11.79	9.80
Noncurrent assets plus other real estate owned to assets............................	Percent	1.10	1.30	0.83	0.69	1.37
Net charge-offs to loans and leases...............	Percent	0.62	0.11	0.08	0.10	1.17
Percentage of banks losing money................	Percent	8.36	21.39	5.38	0.87	(NA)

NA Not applicable.

Source: U.S. Federal Deposit Insurance Corporation, "Statistics on Depository Institutions," <https://www5.fdic.gov/sdi/main.asp>, accessed September 2017.

Table 1205. FDIC-Insured Financial Institutions—Deposit Insurance Fund (DIF) Indicators: 2007 to 2016

[In billions of dollars, except as indicated (6,922 represents $6,922,000,000,000). As of December 31. Includes Island Areas. Includes insured branches of foreign banks. Minus sign (-) indicates decrease]

Item	2007	2008	2009	2010	2011	2012	2013	2014	2015	2016
Number of institutions reporting..........	8,545	8,315	8,021	7,667	7,366	7,092	6,821	6,518	6,191	5,922
Domestic deposits, total [1]..................	6,922	7,505	7,705	7,888	8,782	9,475	9,825	10,408	10,950	11,692
Estimated insured deposits [2]...........	4,292	4,751	5,408	6,302	6,973	7,405	5,998	6,197	6,523	6,917
DIF balance (BIF/SAIF prior to 2006)....	52	17	-21	-7	12	33	47	63	73	83
Reserve ratio [3]............................	1.22	0.36	-0.39	-0.12	0.17	0.45	0.79	1.01	1.11	1.20
Number of problem institutions..........	76	252	702	884	813	651	467	291	183	123
Assets of problem institutions...........	22.2	159.4	402.8	390.0	319.4	232.7	152.7	86.7	46.8	27.6
Number of assisted institutions..........	–	5	8	–	–	–	–	–	–	–
Assets of assisted institutions...........	–	1,306.0	1,917.5	–	–	–	–	–	–	–
Number of failed institutions.............	3	25	140	157	92	51	24	18	8	5
Assets of assisted institutions...........	2.6	371.9	169.7	92.1	34.9	11.6	6.0	2.9	6.7	0.3

– Represents zero. [1] Excludes foreign office deposits, which are uninsured. [2] In general, insured deposits are total domestic deposits minus estimated uninsured deposits. Prior to September 30, 2009 insured deposits included deposits in accounts of $100,000 or less; beginning September 30, 2009, insured deposits include deposits in accounts of $250,000 or less. The Dodd-Frank Wall Street Reform and Consumer Protection Act (Dodd-Frank) temporarily provided unlimited coverage for noninterest bearing transaction accounts for two years beginning December 31, 2010, and ending December 31, 2012. [3] DIF balance as percent of DIF-insured deposits.

Source: U.S. Federal Deposit Insurance Corporation, *Quarterly Banking Profile*, Fourth Quarter 2016, and earlier reports. See also <http://www5.fdic.gov/qbp/index.asp>.

Table 1206. FDIC-Insured Financial Institutions—Number of Offices and Deposits by State: 2016

[11,274 represents $11,274,000,000,000. As of June 30. Includes insured U.S. branches of foreign banks. The term "offices" includes both main offices and branches. "Banking office" is defined to include all offices and facilities that actually hold deposits, and does not include loan production offices, computer centers, and other nondeposit installations, such as automated teller machines (ATMs). Several institutions have designated home offices that do not accept deposits; these have been included to provide a more complete listing of all offices. The figures for each geographical area only include deposits of offices located within that area. Based on the Summary of Deposits survey]

State	Number of offices	Total deposits (bil. dol.)	State	Number of offices	Total deposits (bil. dol.)	State	Number of offices	Total deposits (bil. dol.)
Total [1].....	91,838	11,274	IA..............	1,549	80	NC.............	2,482	347
			KS..............	1,465	70	ND.............	429	26
U.S...........	91,435	11,201	KY..............	1,689	77	OH.............	3,784	324
AL.............	1,520	97	LA..............	1,555	102	OK.............	1,350	84
AK.............	127	12	ME..............	486	27	OR.............	1,026	71
AZ.............	1,248	115	MD..............	1,592	136	PA.............	4,299	366
AR.............	1,354	61	MA..............	2,192	356	RI.............	262	29
CA.............	6,993	1,269	MI..............	2,714	200	SC.............	1,288	79
CO.............	1,517	125	MN..............	1,738	222	SD.............	470	454
CT.............	1,212	129	MS..............	1,160	51	TN.............	2,154	138
DE.............	270	357	MO..............	2,345	166	TX.............	6,682	769
DC.............	229	46	MT..............	385	22	UT.............	544	563
FL.............	5,285	542	NE..............	1,074	63	VT.............	243	13
GA.............	2,440	225	NV..............	503	204	VA.............	2,478	287
HI.............	276	41	NH..............	429	32	WA.............	1,758	143
ID.............	502	23	NJ..............	3,046	314	WV.............	647	32
IL.............	4,504	473	NM..............	487	31	WI.............	2,129	144
IN.............	2,125	119	NY..............	5,175	1,528	WY.............	224	15

[1] Includes outlying areas not shown separately.

Source: U.S. Federal Deposit Insurance Corporation, "Summary of Deposits, Reference Tables," <https://www5.fdic.gov/sod/sodSummary.asp?barItem=3>, accessed September 2017.

Table 1207. U.S. Banking Offices of Foreign Banks—Summary: 2000 to 2016

[In billions of dollars (1,358 represents $1,358,000,000,000), except as indicated. As of December. The U.S. offices of foreign banking organizations consist of U.S. branches and agencies of foreign banks and bank subsidiaries of foreign banking organizations. Foreign-owned institutions are those owned by a bank located outside of the United States and its affiliated insular areas. Bank subsidiaries of foreign banking organizations are U.S. commercial banks of which more than 25 percent are owned by a foreign banking organization or where the relationship is reported as being a controlling relationship by the filer of the FR Y-10 (Report of Changes in Organizational Structure) report form. Covers the U.S. offices of foreign banking organizations that are located in the 50 states and the District of Columbia; excludes offices located in Puerto Rico, American Samoa, Guam, the Virgin Islands and other U.S.-affiliated insular areas]

Item	2000	2005	2010	2012	2013	2014	2015	2016	Share [1]		
									2000	2010	2016
Assets......................	1,358	2,123	2,838	3,274	3,539	3,730	3,539	3,521	18.9	20.4	19.8
Loans, total.................	557	802	960	1,117	1,198	1,335	1,416	1,447	13.5	13.7	15.6
Business loans.............	308	276	326	415	445	519	581	592	25.0	25.1	26.5
Deposits....................	770	1,162	1,752	1,866	2,017	2,149	2,029	1,962	16.5	18.3	15.2

[1] Foreign owned banks plus U.S. branches and offices of foreign banks as percent of all banks in the United States.

Source: Board of Governors of the Federal Reserve System, "Share Data for U.S. Offices of Foreign Banks," March 2017, <http://www.federalreserve.gov/Releases/iba/fboshr.htm>, accessed September 2017.

Table 1208. Federal and State-Chartered Credit Unions—Summary: 2000 to 2016

[43,883 represents 43,883,000. As of December 31, except as noted. Federal data include District of Columbia, Puerto Rico, Guam, and Virgin Islands. Excludes state-insured, privately insured, and noninsured state-chartered credit unions and corporate central credit unions, which have mainly other credit unions as members]

Year	Operating credit unions Federal	State	Number of failed institutions [1]	Members (1,000) Federal	State	Assets (mil. dol.) Federal	State	Loans outstanding (mil. dol.) Federal	State	Savings (mil. dol.) Federal	State
2000......	6,336	3,980	29	43,883	33,705	242,881	195,363	163,851	137,485	210,188	169,053
2007......	5,036	3,065	12	48,474	38,363	417,578	335,885	289,169	237,755	349,101	283,298
2008......	4,847	2,959	19	49,130	39,453	447,124	364,132	309,277	256,720	373,366	307,762
2009......	4,714	2,840	31	49,604	40,333	482,684	402,069	311,154	261,285	408,832	343,835
2010......	4,589	2,750	29	50,081	40,447	500,075	414,395	306,276	258,555	427,603	358,877
2011......	4,447	2,647	16	50,743	41,093	525,633	436,121	308,845	262,640	449,316	378,093
2012......	4,272	2,547	22	51,797	42,043	557,119	464,612	322,675	275,066	474,903	402,948
2013......	4,105	2,449	17	52,499	43,762	571,326	490,588	343,780	301,440	485,500	424,587
2014......	3,927	2,346	15	53,374	45,873	596,143	525,948	373,387	338,939	499,681	451,106
2015......	3,764	2,257	16	54,306	48,369	628,012	576,272	404,729	382,293	522,109	493,892
2016......	3,608	2,177	14	56,637	50,254	670,185	622,357	444,524	424,591	559,825	532,762

[1] For calendar year. A failed institution is defined as a credit union which has ceased operation because it was involuntarily liquidated or merged with assistance from the National Credit Union Share Insurance Fund.

Source: National Credit Union Administration, *National Credit Union Administration 2016 Annual Report,* March 2017, and earlier reports; and "5300 Call Report Aggregate Financial Performance Report," December 2016, <https://www.ncua.gov/analysis/Pages/call-report-data. aspx>. See also <https://www.ncua.gov/NewsRoom/Pages/publications/annual-reports.aspx> and <http://www.ncua.gov/Legal/Documents/ Reports/2014-Historic-Stats.pdf>.

Table 1209. Noncash Payments by Method of Payment, and ATM Cash Withdrawals: 2012 and 2015

[123.5 represents 123,500,000,000. Estimates are based on survey data gathered from depository and financial institutions, payment networks, processors, and issuers by the Federal Reserve. The 2016 Study combines information gathered in three related survey efforts. Some estimates are based on data collected in the 2016 Depository and Financial Institutions Payments Survey (DFIPS), which was sent to a nationally representative, stratified random sample of depository and financial institutions. Other estimates are based on 2015 data collected in the 2016 Networks, Processors, and Issuers Payments Surveys (NPIPS) through a set of surveys of payment networks, processors, and card issuers. Finally, some estimates are from data collected in the 2016 Check Sample Survey (CSS), which are based on the information from a random sample of checks processed by a selected number of large commercial banks during 2015]

Method of payment	Transactions (billions) 2012	2015	Value (trillion dollars) 2012	2015	Average value per transaction (dollars) 2012	2015
Noncash payments, total..........................	**123.5**	**144.1**	**160.9**	**177.9**	**1,302**	**1,234**
Card payments......................................	**83.4**	**103.3**	**4.6**	**5.7**	**56**	**55**
Debit cards..	56.5	69.5	2.1	2.6	37	37
Non-prepaid..	47.3	59.6	1.9	2.3	40	38
Prepaid...	9.3	9.9	0.2	0.3	25	27
General purpose [1]...............................	3.1	3.7	0.1	0.1	35	34
Private label [2]...................................	3.7	3.6	(Z)	0.1	13	20
Electronic benefits transfers (EBT)...............	2.5	2.6	0.1	0.1	30	29
Credit cards..	26.8	33.8	2.5	3.2	95	93
General purpose [1]...............................	24.4	31.0	2.3	2.8	93	90
Private label [2]...................................	2.5	2.8	0.3	0.4	112	128
Automated Clearing House (ACH) payments......	**20.4**	**23.5**	**129.0**	**145.3**	**6,322**	**6,176**
Credit transfers.....................................	8.6	9.9	76.6	90.5	8,944	9,145
Network..	6.9	8.0	22.6	26.8	3,259	3,333
On-us [3]...	1.6	1.9	53.9	63.8	33,421	34,173
Debit transfers.....................................	11.8	13.6	52.5	54.8	4,427	4,018
Network..	9.8	11.3	14.2	14.9	1,456	1,321
On-us [3]...	2.1	2.4	38.2	39.9	18,493	16,784
Checks (paid)......................................	**19.7**	**17.3**	**27.2**	**26.8**	**1,378**	**1,554**
U.S. Treasury checks...............................	0.1	0.1	0.2	0.1	1,645	2,400
Postal money orders................................	0.1	0.1	(Z)	(Z)	204	225
Commercial checks.................................	19.5	17.1	27.0	26.7	1,383	1,558
Interbank..	13.9	12.6	17.2	17.9	1,239	1,420
On-us [3]..	5.6	4.5	9.8	8.8	1,740	1,941
Memo:						
ATM cash withdrawals.............................	**5.8**	**5.8**	**0.7**	**0.7**	**118**	**122**
Checks (written) [4].................................	22.5	19.4	27.8	27.3	1,239	1,410
Checks converted to ACH...........................	2.7	2.1	0.6	0.5	227	238

Z less than $50 billion. [1] Cards issued by depository institutions and processed over card networks. [2] Cards issued by merchants and processed over proprietary networks. [3] On-us payments are those payments processed by a depository institution between their own customers internally. [4] Total checks written are the sum of checks paid and checks converted to ACH, which uses the check as a source document to initiate the ACH payment.

Source: Board of Governors of the Federal Reserve System *The 2016 Federal Reserve Payments Study: Recent Developments in Consumer and Business Payment Choices,* June 2017. See also <http://www.frbservices.org/communications/payment_system_research. html>.

Table 1210. Debit Cards: Holders, Number, Transactions, and Volume: 2000 and 2010, and Projections, 2016

[160 represents 160,000,000]

Type of debit card	Cardholders (mil.)			Number of cards (mil.)			Number of point-of-sale transactions (mil.)			Purchase volume (bil. dol.)		
	2000	2010	2016 (P)	2000	2010	2016 (P)	2000	2010	2016 (P)	2000	2010	2016 (P)
Total [1]............	160	185	203	235	4,008	5,449	9,571	49,281	75,438	342	1,825	2,860
Bank [2]............	137	164	186	137	516	699	5,290	36,879	55,467	210	1,387	2,084
EFT networks [3]............	159	184	200	223	281	311	2,979	7,239	12,982	100	262	506
Private label prepaid [4]............	(NA)	(NA)	(NA)	(NA)	3,447	4,680	1,280	5,125	6,748	31	172	256
ACH network [5]............	11	13	31	11	13	32	22	39	241	1	3	14

NA Not available. P Projected. [1] Cardholders may hold more than one type of card. Bank cards and electronic funds transfer (EFT) cards are the same pieces of plastic that carry multiple brands. The total card figure shown does not include any duplication. [2] Visa and MasterCard debit cards, including prepaid cards. Beginning 2010, includes Interlink & MasterCard PIN debit. [3] Cards issued by financial institution members of regional and national switches such as Star, Interlink (for 2000), Pulse, Nyce, etc. EFT = Electronic funds transfer. [4] Prepaid cards without the Visa, MasterCard, American Express, or Discover logos. [5] ACH = Automated clearing house. Retail cards such as those issued by Target, Nordstrom, etc.

Source: The Nilson Report, Carpinteria, CA, twice-monthly newsletter. © Used by permission.

Table 1211. Credit Cards: Holders, Number, Purchase Volume, and Debt: 2000 and 2010, and Projections, 2016

[159 represents 159,000,000]

Type of credit card	Cardholders (mil.)			Number of cards (mil.)			Credit card purchase volume (bil. dol.)			Credit card debt outstanding (bil. dol.)		
	2000	2010	2016 (P)	2000	2010	2016 (P)	2000	2010	2016 (P)	2000	2010	2016 (P)
Total [1]............	159	152	178	1,425	877	1,041	1,242	2,061	3,340	680	811	1,001
Visa............	93	100	124	255	240	311	487	809	1,549	268	332	420
MasterCard............	86	75	91	200	171	200	281	479	693	212	240	278
Store............	114	95	108	597	318	381	120	138	196	92	92	118
Oil company............	76	38	28	98	35	33	45	47	61	5	6	7
Discover............	36	41	43	50	55	51	69	106	121	48	50	62
American Express............	23	34	35	33	49	48	221	476	695	50	90	101
The rest [2]............	7	6	16	192	9	19	18	5	24	5	1	16

P Projected. [1] Cardholders may hold more than one type of card. [2] Includes Universal Air Travel Plan (UATP), phone cards, automobile rental, and miscellaneous cards; credit card purchase volume and cardholders excludes phone cards.

Source: The Nilson Report, Carpinteria, CA, twice-monthly newsletter. © Used by permission.

Table 1212. Consumer Credit by Type of Holder: 2000 to 2016

[In billions of dollars (1,741 represents $1,741,000,000,000). As of December 31. Not seasonally adjusted]

Type of holder	2000	2005	2009	2010	2011	2012	2013	2014	2015	2016
Total............	1,741	2,321	2,555	2,647	2,758	2,920	3,096	3,317	3,537	3,765
Households (nonprofit organizations) [1]............	–	–	83	71	67	58	52	48	44	39
Nonfinancial corporate business............	81	60	43	44	47	47	43	44	45	44
Federal government [2]............	60	90	233	364	495	622	736	846	950	1,049
U.S.-chartered depository institutions............	616	816	906	1,186	1,193	1,219	1,272	1,343	1,428	1,532
Credit unions............	184	229	237	226	223	244	266	303	342	382
Government-sponsored enterprises............	37	–	–	–	–	–	–	–	–	–
Asset-backed securities issuers............	528	610	572	50	46	50	49	50	46	52
Finance companies............	234	517	481	705	688	680	679	684	682	668
Memo:										
Credit card loans [3]............	702	857	916	839	841	845	857	891	939	1,000
Auto loans............	581	823	719	713	751	809	879	958	1,039	1,112
Student loans [4]............	–	–	772	856	961	1,055	1,146	1,236	1,320	1,406
Other consumer credit [5]............	458	641	148	239	204	210	213	232	239	248

– Represents or rounds to zero. [1] Student loans originated under the Federal Family Education Loan Program. [2] Includes loans originated by the Department of Education under the Federal Direct Loan Program and Perkins Loans; as well as Federal Family Education Loan Program loans that the government purchased from depository institutions, finance companies, and nonprofit and educational institutions; and loans in default. [3] Revolving credit that also includes overdraft plans on checking accounts and other loans without a fixed repayment schedule. [4] Includes student loans held by nonprofit organizations, the federal government, depository institutions, and finance companies. Data begin in 2006. [5] Prior to 2006, includes student loans.

Source: Board of Governors of the Federal Reserve System, "Financial Accounts of the United States, Z.1," <https://www.federalreserve.gov/data.htm>, accessed July 2017.

Table 1213. Consumer Credit Outstanding and Finance Rates: 2000 to 2016

[In billions of dollars (1,717 represents $1,717,000,000,000), except percent. Covers most short- and intermediate-term credit extended to individuals, excluding loans secured by real estate. Estimated amounts of seasonally adjusted credit outstanding as of end of year; finance rates, annual averages]

Type of credit	2000	2005	2009	2010	2011	2012	2013	2014	2015	2016
Total	**1,717**	**2,291**	**2,555**	**2,647**	**2,758**	**2,920**	**3,096**	**3,317**	**3,537**	**3,766**
Revolving	683	830	916	839	841	845	857	891	939	1,000
Nonrevolving [1]	1,034	1,461	1,639	1,808	1,917	2,074	2,238	2,426	2,598	2,766
FINANCE RATES (percent)										
Commercial banks:										
New automobiles (48 months)	9.34	7.07	6.72	6.21	5.73	4.91	4.43	4.24	4.19	4.30
Personal loans (24 months)	13.90	12.06	11.10	10.87	10.88	10.71	10.20	10.22	9.75	9.69
Credit card plans, all accounts	15.78	12.51	13.40	13.78	12.74	12.06	11.91	11.87	12.09	12.35
Credit card plans, accounts assessed interest	14.92	14.55	14.31	14.26	13.09	12.96	12.95	13.19	13.66	13.56
Finance companies:										
New automobiles [2]	(NA)	(NA)	3.82	4.70	4.40	4.60	4.70	4.90	5.10	5.00

NA Not available. [1] Comprises automobile loans and all other loans not included in revolving credit, such as loans for mobile homes, education, boats, trailers, or vacations. These loans may be secured or unsecured. [2] Covers most of the captive and non-captive finance companies. Amount of finance weighted.

Source: Board of Governors of the Federal Reserve System, Data Releases, Household Finances, "Consumer Credit-G.19" and "Finance Companies-G.20," <http://www.federalreserve.gov/econresdata/statisticsdata.htm>, accessed May 2017.

Table 1214. Bank Account Status of Households by Selected Characteristics: 2013 and 2015

[In percent, except total households (123,750 represents 123,750,000). A household is 'unbanked' if no one in the household has a checking or savings account at an insured bank. An 'underbanked' household is one that had a bank account but also used the following products or services from an alternative financial services (AFS) provider in the past 12 months: money orders, check cashing, international remittances, payday loans, refund anticipation loans, rent-to-own services, pawn shop loans, or auto title loans. A 'fully banked' household is one that has a bank account and has not used an AFS in the past 12 months. Data collected through a Federal Deposit Insurance Corporation (FDIC)-sponsored supplement to the Current Population Survey]

Characteristic	Total households (1,000)		Unbanked households		Banked households					
					Underbanked		Fully banked		Underbanked status unknown [1]	
	2013	2015	2013	2015	2013	2015	2013	2015	2013	2015
Total households	**123,750**	**127,538**	**7.7**	**7.0**	**20.0**	**19.9**	**67.0**	**68.0**	**5.3**	**5.0**
RACE/ETHNICITY [2]										
White	84,310	85,428	3.6	3.1	15.9	15.6	75.4	76.6	5.0	4.7
Black	16,773	17,961	20.6	18.2	33.2	31.1	40.0	45.5	6.3	5.2
Hispanic	14,953	16,106	17.9	16.2	28.6	29.3	48.4	48.9	5.1	5.6
Asian	5,931	6,275	2.2	4.0	17.7	21.0	73.4	67.2	6.7	7.8
American Indian/Alaska Native	1,469	1,457	16.9	11.4	25.4	27.6	53.2	56.4	4.6	4.6
Native Hawaiian/Pacific Islander	314	310	6.1	9.5	25.1	27.1	64.5	58.5	4.2	4.9
AGE										
15 to 24 years	6,244	6,648	15.7	13.1	30.8	29.4	48.8	52.1	4.6	5.5
25 to 34 years	20,464	21,005	12.5	10.6	24.7	24.5	58.3	60.8	4.6	4.0
35 to 44 years	21,408	21,640	9.0	8.9	23.8	22.7	62.5	63.1	4.6	5.3
45 to 54 years	24,551	23,773	7.5	6.7	21.9	21.1	65.4	67.5	5.2	4.8
55 to 64 years	22,710	23,981	5.6	5.8	17.7	18.5	71.7	70.9	5.0	4.8
65 years or more	28,372	30,491	3.5	3.1	11.6	13.0	78.2	78.1	6.7	5.8
EDUCATION										
No high school diploma	13,871	13,802	25.1	23.2	24.1	25.9	46.3	46.4	4.6	4.5
High school diploma	33,684	33,239	10.8	9.7	21.9	22.2	61.7	62.9	5.6	5.3
Some college	36,007	37,512	5.6	5.5	23.0	22.0	66.2	67.7	5.2	4.8
College degree	40,188	42,985	1.1	1.1	14.3	14.5	79.3	79.1	5.3	5.2
EMPLOYMENT STATUS										
Employed	75,587	78,152	5.4	5.0	21.7	21.4	67.8	68.7	5.0	5.0
Unemployed	5,436	3,869	23.0	23.0	25.3	24.8	47.8	48.6	3.8	3.7
Not in labor force	42,727	45,517	9.9	9.2	16.3	17.1	67.9	68.5	5.9	5.3
FAMILY INCOME										
Less than $15,000	19,044	18,046	27.7	25.6	22.4	24.3	45.2	45.1	4.7	4.9
$15,000 to $30,000	21,763	21,392	11.4	11.8	25.0	23.6	57.9	59.5	5.7	5.1
$30,000 to $50,000	24,496	25,336	5.1	5.0	23.3	23.7	65.7	66.2	5.9	5.1
$50,000 to $75,000	22,552	23,003	1.7	1.6	19.8	20.2	73.2	73.0	5.2	5.1
At least $75,000	35,895	39,761	0.5	0.5	13.6	13.4	81.0	81.3	4.9	4.9
DISABILITY STATUS										
Disabled, age 25 to 64	10,841	11,497	18.4	17.6	28.1	28.4	49.0	49.7	4.5	4.3
Not disabled, age 25 to 64	78,293	78,902	7.2	6.5	21.1	20.6	66.8	68.1	4.9	4.8
HOUSING TENURE										
Homeowner	80,136	80,685	2.6	2.3	15.5	15.4	76.7	77.4	5.2	4.9
Non-homeowner	43,614	46,853	17.3	15.2	28.2	27.7	49.2	51.8	5.3	5.3
REGION										
Northeast	22,199	22,699	6.8	6.3	19.3	19.3	68.4	67.9	5.5	6.4
Midwest	27,315	27,625	6.4	5.7	16.9	17.5	71.4	72.5	5.2	4.3
South	46,738	48,382	9.2	8.7	23.5	21.6	62.1	65.0	5.2	4.7
West	27,498	28,832	7.4	5.9	17.6	19.9	69.6	68.9	5.3	5.3

[1] Banked households with underbanked status unknown. [2] Households are categorized into racial/ethnic classification as follows: if the householder is black, the household is classified as "black" regardless of whether the householder is also Hispanic or any other race. If the householder is not identified as black and is identified as Hispanic, the household is classified as "Hispanic." If the householder is identified as white and not any other race and not Hispanic, then the household is classified as "white." If the householder is identified as Asian and not black or Hispanic, then the household is classified as "Asian." Householders who are "American Indian/Alaska Native" excludes Asians. Householders who are "Native Hawaiian/Pacific Islander" excludes Asians and American Indians/Alaska Natives.

Source: Federal Deposit Insurance Corporation, Division of Depositor and Consumer Protection, *2015 FDIC Survey of Unbanked and Underbanked Households*, October 2016. See also <https://www.economicinclusion.gov/surveys/>.

Table 1215. Mortgage Debt Outstanding by Type of Property and Holder: 2000 to 2016

[In billions of dollars (6,761 represents $6,761,000,000,000). As of December 31]

Type of property and holder	2000	2005	2009	2010	2011	2012	2013	2014	2015	2016
MORTGAGES BY TYPE										
Total	**6,761**	**12,104**	**14,467**	**13,875**	**13,548**	**13,324**	**13,324**	**13,480**	**13,839**	**14,322**
Home [1]	5,122	9,443	10,987	10,514	10,272	10,046	9,951	9,939	10,052	10,282
Multifamily residential	402	670	860	858	858	889	924	986	1,082	1,189
Commercial	1,152	1,886	2,474	2,349	2,251	2,216	2,264	2,358	2,496	2,625
Farm	85	105	146	154	167	173	185	197	209	224
Total liabilities	6,761	12,104	14,467	13,875	13,548	13,324	13,324	13,480	13,839	14,322
Household sector	4,943	9,103	10,665	10,181	9,971	9,773	9,694	9,683	9,790	10,009
Nonfinancial business	1,734	2,856	3,627	3,518	3,388	3,357	3,416	3,566	3,813	4,077
Nonfinancial corporate business	353	763	758	665	573	448	431	395	443	478
Nonfinancial noncorporate business	1,381	2,093	2,869	2,853	2,814	2,909	2,985	3,170	3,370	3,599
Real estate investment trusts	84	145	175	176	190	194	214	231	235	236
Total assets	**6,761**	**12,104**	**14,467**	**13,875**	**13,548**	**13,324**	**13,324**	**13,480**	**13,839**	**14,322**
Household sector	96	127	127	132	138	125	124	122	115	113
Nonfinancial corporate business	44	68	30	28	27	26	27	29	51	57
Nonfinancial noncorporate business	23	36	38	42	36	34	35	34	37	39
Federal government	76	77	108	107	110	111	115	117	116	120
State and local governments	131	159	194	205	203	207	204	209	221	230
U.S.-chartered depository institutions	2,350	4,055	4,372	4,195	4,050	4,029	3,983	4,091	4,296	4,538
Foreign banking offices in U.S	17	21	38	35	33	31	30	38	51	67
Banks in U.S.-affiliated areas	16	35	42	36	33	35	32	30	27	26
Credit unions	120	226	317	317	321	328	346	372	405	442
Property-casualty insurance companies	2	3	4	4	5	6	8	10	12	15
Life insurance companies	236	285	326	318	333	344	363	385	427	461
Private pension funds	12	10	24	26	22	23	22	24	21	21
State and local government retirement funds	22	13	12	12	11	10	9	10	10	6
Government-sponsored enterprises	264	589	708	5,021	4,924	4,824	4,878	4,870	4,920	5,027
Agency- and GSE-backed mortgage pools	2,493	3,548	5,377	1,147	1,312	1,443	1,574	1,649	1,775	1,933
Asset-backed securities issuers	604	2,163	2,275	1,963	1,724	1,506	1,201	1,094	1,016	897
Finance companies	238	541	430	244	211	179	157	148	120	103
Real estate investment trusts	18	147	46	45	56	64	215	247	218	225
HOME MORTGAGES [1]										
Total liabilities	5,122	9,443	10,987	10,514	10,272	10,046	9,951	9,939	10,052	10,282
Household sector	4,814	8,935	10,468	9,983	9,767	9,560	9,472	9,456	9,556	9,769
Nonfinancial corporate business	14	31	20	14	10	10	10	11	13	15
Nonfinancial noncorporate business	294	477	499	518	495	476	469	472	482	499
Total assets	**5,122**	**9,443**	**10,987**	**10,514**	**10,272**	**10,046**	**9,951**	**9,939**	**10,052**	**10,282**
Household sector	87	118	117	124	121	118	114	111	107	104
Nonfinancial corporate business	21	41	18	17	16	15	16	17	31	34
Nonfinancial noncorporate business	9	13	14	15	13	12	13	13	14	14
Federal government	16	13	22	24	24	25	26	27	28	30
State and local governments	67	82	100	106	105	107	105	108	114	119
U.S.-chartered depository institutions	1,556	2,730	2,693	2,616	2,538	2,504	2,386	2,390	2,434	2,510
Foreign banking offices in U.S	–	–	1	1	1	2	1	3	2	1
Banks in U.S.-affiliated areas	9	16	23	20	18	20	19	17	16	15
Credit unions	120	226	317	317	321	328	346	372	405	442
Life insurance companies	7	7	9	9	9	11	11	15	19	22
Private pension funds	8	1	2	2	2	2	1	1	1	1
State and local government retirement funds	7	5	4	4	4	4	3	4	3	2
Government-sponsored enterprises	210	454	433	4,691	4,588	4,476	4,546	4,538	4,571	4,645
Agency- and GSE-backed mortgage pools	2,426	3,446	5,267	1,075	1,223	1,327	1,424	1,475	1,569	1,685
Asset-backed securities issuers	385	1,671	1,593	1,315	1,120	938	793	700	603	523
Finance companies	187	490	366	170	150	133	115	105	90	79
Real estate investment trusts	8	128	9	9	20	26	31	44	46	57
Memo:										
Home equity loans included above [2]	408	918	1,034	929	854	770	703	673	635	595
U.S.-chartered depository institutions	308	701	841	783	723	653	596	568	533	495
Foreign banking offices in U.S	–	–	(Z)	(Z)	(Z)	(Z)	(Z)	(Z)	(Z)	(Z)
Credit unions	41	76	95	88	82	76	72	74	76	79
Asset-backed securities issuers	10	43	32	23	18	15	12	10	8	6
Finance companies	49	98	66	34	30	27	23	21	18	16

– Represents zero. Z Less than $500,000,000. [1] Mortgages on one- to four-family properties including mortgages on farm houses. [2] Loans made under home equity lines of credit and home equity loans secured by junior liens. Excludes home equity loans held by individuals.

Source: Board of Governors of the Federal Reserve System, "Financial Accounts of the United States, Z.1," <https://www.federalreserve.gov/data.htm>, accessed July 2017.

Table 1216. Mortgage Originations and Delinquency and Foreclosure Rates: 2000 to 2015

[In percent, except as indicated (1,139 represents $1,139,000,000,000). Covers one- to four-family residential nonfarm mortgage loans. Mortgage origination is the making of a new mortgage, including all steps taken by a lender to attract and qualify a borrower, process the mortgage loan, and place it on the lender's books. Based on the National Delinquency Survey which covers 45 million loans on one- to four-unit properties, representing between 80 to 85 percent of all 'first-lien' residential mortgage loans outstanding. Loans surveyed were reported by approximately 120 lenders, including mortgage bankers, commercial banks, and thrifts]

Item	2000	2005	2008	2009	2010	2011	2012	2013	2014	2015
MORTGAGE ORIGINATIONS										
Total (bil. dol.)	**1,139**	**2,908**	**1,509**	**1,995**	**1,572**	**1,262**	**1,750**	**2,003**	**1,122**	**1,630**
Purchase (bil. dol.)	905	1,512	731	664	473	404	503	571	638	881
Refinance (bil. dol.)	234	1,397	777	1,331	1,099	858	1,247	1,432	484	749
DELINQUENCY RATES [1]										
Total	**4.4**	**4.5**	**6.9**	**9.4**	**9.3**	**8.0**	**7.4**	**6.7**	**5.9**	**5.1**
Prime conventional loans	2.3	2.3	4.3	6.5	6.5	5.3	4.6	3.9	3.4	3.0
Subprime conventional loans	11.9	10.8	19.9	25.5	25.9	23.0	20.6	21.0	19.1	16.5
Federal Housing Administration loans	9.1	12.5	13.0	14.0	12.8	12.3	11.6	10.6	9.7	9.0
Veterans Administration loans	6.8	7.0	7.2	7.9	7.5	6.8	6.4	5.8	5.2	4.5
FORECLOSURE RATES										
Total loans in foreclosure process [2]	**1.2**	**1.0**	**3.3**	**4.3**	**4.6**	**4.4**	**4.1**	**3.2**	**2.5**	**2.0**
Prime conventional loans	0.4	0.4	1.9	3.0	3.5	3.4	3.0	2.2	1.5	1.2
Subprime conventional loans	9.4	3.3	13.7	15.1	14.5	14.7	13.0	11.1	9.8	8.3
Federal Housing Administration loans	1.7	2.3	2.4	3.2	3.5	3.4	4.0	3.6	2.8	2.6
Veterans Administration loans	1.2	1.1	1.7	2.2	2.4	2.3	2.3	5.8	1.5	1.4
Loans entering foreclosure process [3]	**1.5**	**1.6**	**4.2**	**5.4**	**5.0**	**4.1**	**3.5**	**2.5**	**1.8**	**1.6**
Prime conventional loans	0.6	0.7	2.4	4.0	4.0	3.3	2.6	1.6	1.1	1.0
Subprime conventional loans	9.2	5.6	16.5	16.2	12.9	12.1	9.5	8.2	6.1	5.2
Federal Housing Administration loans	2.3	3.4	3.8	4.8	4.7	3.3	4.5	3.3	2.5	2.5
Veterans Administration loans	1.5	1.5	2.3	3.1	3.3	2.4	2.2	1.9	1.4	1.4

[1] Number of loans delinquent 30 days or more as percentage of mortgage loans serviced in survey. Annual average of quarterly figures. Delinquency rate does not include loans in the process of foreclosure. [2] Percentage of loans in the foreclosure process at year-end, not seasonally adjusted. [3] Percentage of loans entering foreclosure process at year-end, not seasonally adjusted.

Source: Mortgage Bankers Association of America, Washington, DC, "MBA Mortgage Originations Estimates," and National Delinquency Survey, <http://www.mortgagebankers.org/>; and unpublished data ©.

Table 1217. Delinquency Rates and Charge-Off Rates on Loans at Insured Commercial Banks: 2000 to 2016

[In percent. Annual averages of quarterly figures, not seasonally adjusted. Delinquent loans are those past due 30 days or more and still accruing interest as well as those in nonaccrual status. They are measured as a percentage of end-of-period loans. Charge-offs, which are the value of loans removed from the books and charged against loss reserves, are measured net of recoveries as a percentage of average loans and annualized. Includes only U.S.-chartered commercial banks]

Type of loan	2000	2005	2010	2011	2012	2013	2014	2015	2016
DELINQUENCY RATES									
Total loans	**2.20**	**1.57**	**6.96**	**5.83**	**5.02**	**3.96**	**3.00**	**2.34**	**2.10**
Real estate	1.87	1.37	9.69	8.81	8.01	6.44	4.83	3.62	2.79
Residential [1, 2]	2.08	1.55	10.81	10.40	10.37	8.97	7.20	5.64	4.46
Commercial [2, 3]	1.48	1.07	8.53	6.87	4.81	3.06	1.88	1.23	0.90
Consumer	3.55	2.81	4.15	3.23	2.80	2.45	2.22	2.00	2.07
Credit cards	4.51	3.70	4.90	3.55	2.88	2.50	2.23	2.14	2.25
Other	2.98	2.23	3.32	2.89	2.71	2.41	2.21	1.88	1.90
Leases	1.62	1.28	1.89	1.04	0.79	0.87	0.75	0.77	1.01
Business	2.30	1.51	3.46	2.01	1.34	1.00	0.80	0.87	1.56
Agricultural production	2.54	1.30	3.04	2.11	1.56	1.15	0.91	0.84	1.22
Farmland [2]	2.30	1.59	3.57	3.50	2.88	2.24	1.71	1.55	1.75
CHARGE-OFF RATES									
Total loans	**0.66**	**0.54**	**2.66**	**1.63**	**1.12**	**0.69**	**0.49**	**0.42**	**0.46**
Real estate	0.04	0.04	0.43	0.35	0.27	0.07	0.04	0.01	0.03
Residential [1, 2]	0.05	0.05	2.34	1.40	0.71	0.26	0.07	0.04	0.01
Commercial [2, 3]	0.76	0.26	1.71	0.85	0.48	0.30	0.22	0.24	0.43
Consumer	4.30	4.83	9.43	5.68	3.99	3.48	3.16	2.93	3.17
Credit cards	1.13	1.38	2.05	1.40	1.03	0.86	0.77	0.68	0.78
Other	0.27	0.07	0.77	0.24	0.25	0.05	0.04	0.05	0.21
Leases	0.09	0.06	2.15	1.46	1.07	0.48	0.20	0.13	0.06
Business	2.32	2.74	5.90	3.62	2.54	2.17	1.92	1.75	1.92
Agricultural production	0.31	0.58	0.72	0.21	0.21	0.15	0.08	0.18	0.24
Farmland [2]	0.12	0.08	2.11	1.57	1.36	0.65	0.29	0.21	0.10

[1] Residential real estate loans include loans secured by one- to four-family properties, including home equity lines of credit. [2] Booked in domestic offices only. [3] Commercial real estate loans include construction and land development loans, loans secured by multifamily residences, and loans secured by nonfarm, nonresidential real estate, only.

Source: Board of Governors of the Federal Reserve, Data Releases, Bank Assets and Liabilities, "Charge-Off and Delinquency Rates on Loans and Leases at Commercial Banks," <http://www.federalreserve.gov/releases/chargeoff/>, accessed February 2017.

Table 1218. Money Stock: 2000 to 2016

[In billions of dollars (1,089 represents $1,089,000,000,000). As of December. Seasonally adjusted averages of daily figures]

Item	2000	2005	2009	2010	2011	2012	2013	2014	2015	2016
M1, total	**1,089**	**1,375**	**1,699**	**1,843**	**2,170**	**2,461**	**2,660**	**2,930**	**3,080**	**3,323**
Currency [1]	531	725	864	919	1,002	1,091	1,160	1,252	1,338	1,418
Travelers' checks [2]	8.3	7.2	5.1	4.7	4.3	3.8	3.5	2.9	2.5	2.2
Demand deposits [3]	310	325	449	520	755	925	1,029	1,189	1,223	1,347
Other checkable deposits [4]	239	319	381	399	410	442	468	486	517	555
M2, total	**4,905**	**6,651**	**8,471**	**8,775**	**9,636**	**10,429**	**10,995**	**11,647**	**12,314**	**13,249**
M1	1,089	1,375	1,699	1,843	2,170	2,461	2,660	2,930	3,080	3,323
Non-M1 components of M2	3,817	5,276	6,773	6,933	7,466	7,967	8,335	8,717	9,234	9,927
Retail money funds	891	679	771	668	659	639	636	617	640	713
Savings deposits (including money market deposit accounts)	1,880	3,604	4,813	5,331	6,032	6,685	7,132	7,581	8,185	8,842
Commercial banks	1,425	2,778	3,980	4,412	5,036	5,729	6,111	6,502	7,039	7,575
Thrift institutions	454	826	834	920	996	956	1,021	1,079	1,146	1,268
Small time deposits [5]	1,046	994	1,188	933	776	644	567	519	408	372
Commercial banks	701	647	869	663	547	467	423	388	299	264
Thrift institutions	345	347	319	271	229	177	144	132	110	108

[1] Currency outside U.S. Treasury, Federal Reserve Banks and the vaults of depository institutions. [2] Outstanding amount of U.S. dollar-denominated travelers' checks of nonbank issuers. Travelers' checks issued by depository institutions are included in demand deposits. [3] Demand deposits at domestically chartered commercial banks, U.S. branches and agencies of foreign banks, and Edge Act corporations (excluding those amounts held by depository institutions, the U.S. government, and foreign banks and official institutions) less cash items in the process of collection and Federal Reserve float. [4] Negotiable order of withdrawal (NOW) and automatic transfer service (ATS) balances at domestically chartered commercial banks, U.S. branches and agencies of foreign banks, Edge Act corporations, and thrift institutions, credit union share draft balances, and demand deposits at thrift institutions. [5] Small-denomination time deposits are those issued in amounts of less than $100,000. All Individual Retirement Account (IRA) and Keogh account balances at commercial banks and thrift institutions are subtracted from small time deposits.

Source: Board of Governors of the Federal Reserve System, Data Releases, Money Stock and Reserve Balances, "Money Stock Measures – H.6," weekly releases, <http://www.federalreserve.gov/releases/h6/>, accessed January 2017.

Table 1219. Volume of Debt Markets by Type of Security: 2000 to 2016

[In billions of dollars (2,551 represents $2,551,000,000,000). Covers debt markets as represented by the source]

Type of security	2000	2005	2010	2012	2013	2014	2015	2016
NEW ISSUE VOLUME [1]								
Total	**2,551**	**5,792**	**7,283**	**7,276**	**6,812**	**6,239**	**6,649**	**7,252**
U.S. Treasury securities [2]	312	746	2,320	2,305	2,140	2,215	2,122	2,169
Federal agency debt [3]	447	635	1,346	823	584	530	634	915
Municipal	198	407	433	382	335	339	405	446
Mortgage-backed securities [4]	779	2,782	2,011	2,158	2,092	1,365	1,710	1,918
Asset-backed securities [5]	240	474	119	243	282	353	287	284
Corporate debt [6]	575	748	1,055	1,365	1,378	1,437	1,490	1,520
AVERAGE DAILY TRADING VOLUME								
Total	**357.6**	**918.6**	**893.7**	**849.0**	**816.1**	**729.2**	**728.8**	**771.2**
U.S. Treasury securities [2]	206.5	554.5	528.2	518.9	545.4	504.2	490.1	514.2
Federal agency debt [3, 7]	72.8	78.8	11.2	9.7	6.6	5.3	4.5	5.5
Municipal	8.8	16.9	13.3	11.3	11.2	9.9	8.6	10.6
Mortgage-backed securities [4, 7]	69.5	251.8	320.6	280.4	222.8	178.0	193.0	206.6
Corporate [6]	(NA)	16.6	20.5	22.6	24.7	26.7	27.9	30.0
Non-agency mortgaged-back securities [8]	(NA)	(NA)	(NA)	4.5	4.1	3.7	3.1	2.9
Asset-backed securities [5]	(NA)	(NA)	(NA)	1.5	1.3	1.5	1.4	1.3
VOLUME OF SECURITIES OUTSTANDING								
Total	**16,128**	**24,636**	**33,687**	**35,139**	**36,149**	**37,169**	**38,200**	**39,373**
U.S. Treasury securities [2]	2,952	4,170	8,853	11,046	11,854	12,505	13,192	13,908
Federal agency debt [3]	1,854	2,616	2,539	2,096	2,057	2,029	1,995	1,972
Municipal [9]	1,481	3,098	3,940	3,887	3,818	3,776	3,791	3,834
Mortgage-backed securities [4]	4,119	7,218	9,258	8,838	8,742	8,764	8,759	8,921
Asset-backed securities [5]	705	1,282	1,500	1,273	1,272	1,337	1,362	1,337
Money market instruments [10]	1,614	1,644	1,058	952	952	930	941	885
Corporate debt [6]	3,403	4,608	6,540	7,047	7,455	7,827	8,159	8,517

NA Not available. [1] Covers only long-term issuance. [2] Marketable public debt. [3] Beginning with 2004, Sallie Mae (Student Loan Marketing Assn) has been excluded due to privatization. [4] Includes Government National Mortgage Association (GNMA), Federal National Mortgage Association (FNMA), and Federal Home Loan Mortgage Corporation (FHLMC) mortgage-backed securities (MBS), and collateralized mortgage obligations (CMOs), and CMBS, and private-label MBS/CMOs. [5] Excludes mortgage-backed assets. Includes auto, credit card, home equity loans, manufacturing, student loan and other. Collateralized debt obligations are included. [6] Includes nonconvertible corporate debt, Yankee bonds, and MTNs (Medium-Term Notes), but excludes federal agency debt and certificates of deposit. [7] Primary dealer trading volume through March 2010 for federal agency debt and through May 2011 for mortgage-backed securities. After those dates, data from FINRA Trace. [8] Includes mortgage securities issued by private institutions, such as subsidiaries of investment banks, banks, financial institutions, non-bank mortgage lenders, and home builders. [9] Due to the change in underlying sourcing from the Federal Reserve, municipal securities outstanding has been restated from 2004 onward and revised upward by about $840 billion. [10] Commercial paper, bankers acceptances, and large time deposits.

Source: The Securities Industry and Financial Markets Association, New York, NY ©. Based on data supplied by Bloomberg, Dealogic, Thomson Reuters Eikon, Thomson Reuters SDC, U.S. Treasury, Fannie Mae (FNMA), Freddie Mac (FHLMC), Ginnie Mae (GNMA), Farmer Mac, Farm Credit, FHLB, Federal Reserve Bank of New York, Municipal Securities Rulemaking Board, and FINRA Trace (Financial Industry Regulatory Authority Trade Reporting and Compliance Engine). See also <http://www.sifma.org/>.

Table 1220. Bond Yields: 2000 to 2016

[Percent per year. Annual averages of daily figures]

Type	2000	2005	2009	2010	2011	2012	2013	2014	2015	2016
U.S. Treasury, constant maturities: [1]										
1-year	6.11	3.62	0.47	0.32	0.18	0.17	0.13	0.12	0.32	0.61
2-year	6.26	3.85	0.96	0.70	0.45	0.28	0.31	0.46	0.69	0.83
3-year	6.22	3.93	1.43	1.11	0.75	0.38	0.54	0.90	1.02	1.00
5-year	6.16	4.05	2.20	1.93	1.52	0.76	1.17	1.64	1.53	1.33
7-year	6.20	4.15	2.82	2.62	2.16	1.22	1.74	2.14	1.89	1.63
10-year	6.03	4.29	3.26	3.22	2.78	1.80	2.35	2.54	2.14	1.84
20-year	6.23	4.64	4.11	4.03	3.62	2.54	3.12	3.07	2.55	2.22
Municipal (Bond Buyer, 20 bonds)	5.71	4.40	4.62	4.29	4.51	3.73	4.27	4.23	3.66	(NA)
High-grade municipal bonds (Standard & Poor's) [2]	5.77	4.29	4.64	4.16	4.29	3.14	3.96	3.78	3.48	3.07

NA Not available. [1] Yields on actively traded non-inflation-indexed issues adjusted to constant maturities. Yields are based on closing indicative prices quoted by secondary market participants. [2] Source: U.S. Council of Economic Advisors, *Economic Indicators*, monthly, <https://www.gpo.gov/fdsys/browse/collection.action?collectionCode=ECONI>, accessed June 2017.

Source: Except as noted, Board of Governors of the Federal Reserve System, "H15, Selected Interest Rates," <http://www.federalreserve.gov/releases/h15/data.htm>, accessed June 2017.

Table 1221. Securities Industry—Financial Summary: 2000 to 2015

[In billions of dollars, except as indicated (349.5 represents $349,500,000,000). Minus sign (-) indicates loss]

Type	2000	2005	2009	2010	2011	2012	2013	2014	2015
Number of firms	7,258	6,016	5,132	4,907	4,708	4,761	4,555	4,380	4,247
Revenues, total	**349.5**	**332.5**	**287.0**	**262.0**	**245.8**	**264.4**	**272.5**	**279.4**	**275.7**
Commissions	54.1	46.8	49.0	47.0	47.7	40.6	40.1	39.5	37.3
Trading/investment gains	70.8	30.7	45.3	31.2	10.2	26.9	21.2	21.6	16.4
Underwriting profits	18.7	19.9	22.6	24.4	22.9	27.9	32.0	33.5	30.7
Margin interest	24.5	13.3	4.5	5.0	6.2	7.2	7.1	8.2	8.4
Mutual fund sales	19.4	20.7	17.2	18.8	19.4	20.1	21.6	22.8	22.1
Other	161.9	201.2	148.4	135.5	139.3	141.7	150.4	153.9	160.7
Expenses, total	**310.4**	**311.3**	**211.6**	**224.0**	**228.9**	**229.9**	**243.8**	**253.9**	**250.9**
Interest expense	131.9	140.2	21.9	22.4	20.3	20.6	16.6	15.9	16.1
Compensation	95.2	88.8	95.4	102.1	102.4	104.7	110.0	114.5	115.8
Commissions/clearance paid	15.5	18.6	23.3	24.0	25.4	24.2	25.1	25.7	25.1
Other	67.8	63.6	71.0	75.5	80.8	80.4	92.2	97.7	93.8
Net income, pretax	**39.1**	**21.2**	**75.4**	**38.0**	**16.8**	**34.6**	**28.6**	**25.6**	**24.8**
Pre-tax profit margin (percent)	11.2	6.4	26.3	14.5	6.9	13.1	10.5	9.2	9.0
Pre-tax return on equity (percent)	31.1	13.1	38.2	17.1	7.5	14.7	12.0	10.5	10.2
Assets	2,866	5,215	4,340	4,757	4,662	4,892	4,591	4,440	4,051
Liabilities	2,728	5,051	4,125	4,526	4,444	4,658	4,348	4,197	3,806
Ownership equity	138	164	214	231	218	234	243	243	245

Source: U.S. Securities and Exchange Commission, "Select SEC and Market Data Fiscal 2016," and earlier reports, <http://www.sec.gov/about.shtml>, accessed February 2017.

Table 1222. Total Returns of Stocks, Bonds, and Treasury Bills: 1980 to 2016

[Average annual percent change. Stock return data are based on the Standard & Poor's 500 index. Minus sign (-) indicates loss]

Period	Stocks				Treasury bills, total return	Bonds (10-year), total return
	Total return before inflation	Capital gains	Dividends and reinvestment	Total return after inflation		
1980 to 1989	17.55	12.59	4.40	11.85	9.13	13.01
1990 to 1999	18.21	15.31	2.51	14.85	4.95	8.02
2000 to 2009	-0.45	-2.73	2.27	-3.39	2.74	6.63
2001	-11.89	-13.04	1.32	-13.68	3.32	5.53
2002	-22.10	-23.37	1.65	-23.91	1.61	15.37
2003	28.68	26.38	1.82	26.31	1.03	0.46
2004	10.88	8.99	1.73	7.38	1.43	4.61
2005	4.91	3.00	1.85	1.45	3.30	3.09
2006	15.80	13.62	1.91	11.97	4.97	2.21
2007	5.49	3.53	1.89	1.35	4.52	10.54
2008	-37.00	-38.49	1.88	-37.10	1.24	20.23
2009	26.25	23.45	2.44	23.11	0.15	-9.50
2010	15.06	12.78	2.02	13.36	0.03	7.26
2011	2.96	0.00	2.96	0.83	0.06	16.89
2012	16.00	13.41	2.29	14.02	0.08	2.77
2013	32.39	29.60	2.15	30.43	0.05	-8.56
2014	13.69	11.39	2.06	12.83	0.03	10.74
2015	1.32	-0.73	2.05	0.58	0.06	11.27
2016	11.96	9.53	2.22	9.68	0.33	-5.40

Source: Global Financial Data, Los Angeles, CA, "GFD Guide to Total Returns," <http://www.globalfinancialdata.com> ©, and unpublished data.

Table 1223. New Security Issues of Corporations by Type of Offering: 2005 to 2016

[In billions of dollars (2,362 represents $2,362,000,000,000). Represents gross proceeds of issues maturing in more than one year. Figures are the principal amount or the number of units multiplied by the offering price. Excludes secondary offerings, employee stock plans, investment companies other than closed-end, intracorporate transactions, Yankee bonds, and private placements listed. Stock data include ownership securities issued by limited partnerships]

Type of offering	2005	2010	2015	2016	Type of offering	2005	2010	2015	2016
Total [1]	**2,362**	**1,025**	**1,664**	**1,522**	Nonfinancial	211	498	888	794
					Financial	2,036	396	723	694
Bonds, total	2,247	894	1,611	1,488	Stocks, total [2]	115	131	174	138
Sold in the U.S.	2,115	880	1,511	1,404	Nonfinancial	55	61	111	87
Sold abroad	131	14	100	83	Financial	61	70	63	51

[1] Total reflects the sum of the gross issuance of bonds and the gross proceeds of stocks in the domestic market. [2] Gross proceeds of stocks in all markets.

Source: Board of Governors of the Federal Reserve System, "New Security Issues, U.S. Corporations," <http://www.federalreserve.gov/econresdata/releases/corpsecure/current.htm>, accessed July 2017.

Table 1224. Equities, Corporate Bonds, and Municipal and Treasury Securities—Holdings and Net Purchases by Type of Investor: 2000 to 2016

[In billions of dollars (17,300 represents $17,300,000,000,000). Holdings as of December 31. Minus sign (-) indicates net sales]

Type of investor	Holdings					Net purchases				
	2000	2010	2014	2015	2016	2000	2010	2014	2015	2016
EQUITIES [1]										
Total [2]	**17,300**	**23,149**	**36,742**	**35,665**	**38,685**	**5.6**	**22.9**	**272.7**	**-125.5**	**-366.3**
Household sector [3]	7,974	8,704	14,369	14,045	15,622	-554.8	-225.1	167.9	-16.3	-195.5
State and local governments	93	127	174	178	191	6.1	–	2.0	5.1	3.9
Property-casualty insurance companies	191	217	331	323	342	0.3	-4.8	3.4	-1.9	-2.1
Life insurance companies	247	223	318	337	460	-11.1	9.3	-5.0	31.9	100.2
Private pension funds	1,823	1,778	2,284	2,164	2,327	64.4	21.6	-183.9	-112.6	-56.7
Federal government retirement funds	57	141	219	219	239	5.2	5.4	3.5	0.2	-5.7
State and local government retirement funds	1,299	1,729	2,258	2,157	2,237	11.6	-74.1	-132.2	-66.7	-91.8
Mutual funds	3,911	5,873	8,799	8,625	9,070	233.3	69.0	94.5	55.9	-116.6
Exchange-traded funds	66	753	1,620	1,710	2,033	42.4	80.1	190.7	173.5	188.4
Brokers and dealers	77	117	188	167	176	9.6	-18.5	8.7	-10.3	-3.6
Rest of the world [4]	1,483	3,213	5,922	5,507	5,747	197.8	130.9	116.5	-186.6	-179.7
CORPORATE & FOREIGN BONDS										
Total [2]	**4,855**	**10,441**	**11,667**	**11,719**	**12,088**	**353.6**	**-234.2**	**513.6**	**278.2**	**384.1**
Household sector [3]	559	1,405	1,147	1,127	810	106.3	-487.6	129.2	-206.5	-204.4
U.S.-chartered depository institutions	312	551	522	510	503	46.9	-98.2	-37.4	-12.2	-6.6
Foreign banking offices in U.S.	55	238	197	172	161	7.6	-9.4	0.9	-24.9	-11.5
Property-casualty insurance companies	188	338	448	437	454	6.4	24.0	22.7	18.0	15.3
Life insurance companies	1,209	2,112	2,468	2,442	2,601	54.7	90.5	78.8	80.9	99.5
Private pension funds	263	435	679	709	731	-76.9	81.2	26.3	29.5	22.2
State and local government retirement funds	314	377	509	542	572	4.2	6.5	28.2	7.5	30.0
Mutual funds	361	1,224	1,781	1,737	1,862	-39.2	211.5	75.1	55.8	96.8
Exchange-traded funds [4]	–	78	215	242	310	–	18.7	35.2	37.2	63.4
Rest of the world [4]	843	2,523	2,928	3,106	3,458	168.3	-36.8	209.6	359.7	350.1
MUNICIPAL SECURITIES [5]										
Total [2]	**1,481**	**3,945**	**3,781**	**3,796**	**3,837**	**23.6**	**106.7**	**-42.7**	**15.4**	**40.9**
Household sector [3]	488	2,074	1,694	1,641	1,676	17.9	70.0	-59.7	-56.2	8.8
U.S.-chartered depository institutions	117	255	452	499	549	3.4	30.3	32.7	47.4	50.3
Property-casualty insurance companies	184	358	340	346	338	-14.9	-22.7	-15.4	9.4	1.0
Money market mutual funds	242	388	282	268	162	32.5	-53.1	-26.9	-13.6	-106.2
Mutual funds	273	490	587	604	632	-20.5	33.0	15.1	16.2	41.4
TREASURY SECURITIES										
Total [2]	**4,063**	**10,504**	**14,417**	**15,141**	**15,984**	**-274.0**	**1,645.3**	**736.0**	**724.4**	**842.8**
Household sector [3]	589	1,098	838	1,138	1,409	-206.4	318.5	-226.6	224.8	204.5
State and local governments	310	596	622	665	721	5.5	8.4	33.8	43.6	55.8
Monetary authority	512	1,021	2,461	2,462	2,464	33.7	244.9	252.6	0.2	2.1
U.S.-chartered depository institutions	97	218	420	435	531	-36.4	93.0	203.3	14.8	96.0
Life insurance companies	60	160	200	204	217	-6.4	20.3	14.0	6.9	20.4
Private pension funds	111	200	296	317	326	-9.3	29.8	-4.3	21.5	8.7
Federal government retirement funds	739	1,273	1,618	1,709	1,808	22.9	75.8	87.0	91.3	99.3
State and local governments retirement funds	179	154	181	175	187	-19.8	8.3	-7.0	-6.5	12.4
Money market mutual funds	94	342	419	483	796	-13.2	-72.4	-77.1	63.9	313.2
Mutual funds	113	417	683	827	865	7.5	129.8	193.3	155.3	52.5
Rest of the world [4]	1,021	4,459	6,156	6,148	6,004	-75.2	740.4	318.5	48.3	-98.8

– Represents or rounds to zero. [1] Excludes mutual fund shares; see Table 1230. [2] Includes other types, not shown separately. [3] Includes nonprofit organizations. [4] Holdings and net purchases of U.S. issues by foreign residents. [5] Includes loans.

Source: Board of Governors of the Federal Reserve System, "Financial Accounts of the United States, Z.1," <https://www.federalreserve.gov/data.htm>, accessed July 2017.

Table 1225. Foreign Securities Held by U.S. Residents: 2010 to 2015

[In billions of dollars (6,763 represents $6,763,000,000,000). Estimates for end of calendar year. See also Table 1305]

Country	Total			Corporate stocks			Long-term and short-term debt		
	2010	2014	2015	2010	2014	2015	2010	2014	2015
Total holdings [1]	6,763	9,604	9,455	4,647	6,727	6,756	2,116	2,878	2,699
Australia	323	311	296	150	140	139	174	171	157
Belgium	35	63	68	29	50	56	7	13	12
Bermuda	160	227	217	134	198	187	25	30	30
Brazil	235	166	116	194	109	66	41	56	50
Canada	695	844	705	409	417	325	287	427	380
Cayman Islands	366	1,112	1,217	166	820	915	200	292	302
China [2]	102	133	108	101	129	103	2	4	5
Curacao [3]	(NA)	82	70	(NA)	78	67	(NA)	4	3
France	366	485	474	244	318	327	122	167	146
Germany	299	375	378	207	274	283	92	101	95
Hong Kong	135	151	136	133	142	129	2	9	7
India	91	129	130	86	122	120	5	7	10
Ireland	132	387	498	101	332	422	31	55	77
Israel	64	75	80	45	57	63	19	18	17
Italy	66	109	107	51	64	73	14	45	34
Japan	519	689	822	450	592	690	69	97	131
Jersey	42	91	92	21	82	80	21	9	12
Korea, South	148	178	171	122	141	139	26	37	32
Luxembourg	100	133	128	33	43	41	68	90	87
Mexico	109	166	148	77	67	56	32	99	91
Netherlands	233	388	404	120	233	250	112	155	154
Norway	56	73	58	23	25	22	33	48	36
Russia	62	41	40	56	31	32	7	10	8
Singapore	64	98	99	56	73	81	8	25	18
South Africa	78	83	63	70	71	54	8	12	9
Spain	87	133	115	66	93	90	22	40	25
Sweden	122	165	138	63	85	86	59	80	51
Switzerland	327	424	420	319	409	407	8	15	13
Taiwan	95	114	108	94	114	108	(Z)	(Z)	(Z)
United Kingdom	1,001	1,300	1,240	626	922	897	375	378	343

NA Not available. Z Less than $500 million. [1] Includes other countries, not shown separately. [2] Excludes Hong Kong, Macau, and Taiwan. [3] Separate reporting for Curacao began with the 2013 survey. In previous years, data were reported as part of Netherlands Antilles.

Source: U.S. Department of Treasury, "Securities (c): Annual Cross-U.S. Border Portfolio Holdings, PART B: U.S. Residents' Portfolio Holdings of Foreign Securities," <http://www.treasury.gov/resource-center/data-chart-center/tic/Pages/fpis.aspx#usclaims>, accessed February 2017.

Table 1226. U.S. Securities Held by Foreign Residents: 2010 and 2016

[In billions of dollars (10,691 represents $10,691,000,000,000). Estimates as of June. Long-term securities include all forms of equity and all debt securities with an original term-to-maturity of over one year]

Region and country	U.S. securities, total [1]		U.S Treasury long-term securities		Long-term corporate debt		U.S. corporate stocks	
	2010	2016	2010	2016	2010	2016	2010	2016
Total [2]	10,691	17,139	3,343	5,585	2,493	3,505	2,814	6,186
Australia	118	237	14	24	22	31	74	171
Belgium	408	589	31	95	342	398	19	31
Bermuda	249	307	42	50	91	114	44	86
Brazil	169	259	132	239	2	1	2	5
British Virgin Islands	85	161	4	20	22	20	42	105
Canada	424	951	29	69	80	160	298	695
Cayman Islands	743	1,525	36	175	303	420	290	796
China [3]	1,611	1,630	1,108	1,238	11	16	127	178
Denmark	49	117	5	22	14	25	26	68
France	194	229	15	41	52	53	115	120
Germany	195	373	46	78	65	114	57	155
Hong Kong	293	305	60	137	16	33	33	75
India	41	119	21	110	3	(Z)	1	2
Ireland	356	931	27	235	130	296	77	238
Israel	37	76	8	29	3	5	13	37
Italy	41	78	21	38	3	13	13	24
Japan	1,393	1,960	737	1,086	130	187	224	428
Korea, South	122	236	34	75	9	26	13	75
Luxembourg	622	1,349	49	180	302	526	172	516
Mexico	84	117	31	39	12	3	17	36
Netherlands	247	350	22	46	57	71	152	210
Norway	136	306	14	58	25	46	90	201
Russia	170	91	121	91	(Z)	(Z)	(Z)	(Z)
Singapore	176	321	47	103	28	60	91	137
Sweden	81	165	14	39	11	7	49	117
Switzerland	397	742	87	207	110	136	162	351
Taiwan	228	519	149	185	18	81	12	43
United Kingdom	798	1,427	72	199	369	437	324	741
International & regional organizations	78	96	43	57	15	13	5	4

Z Less than $500 million. [1] Includes short-term debt and other long-term debt. [2] Includes other countries not shown separately. [3] Excludes Hong Kong, Macau, and Taiwan.

Source: U.S. Department of Treasury, "Securities (c): Annual Cross-U.S. Border Portfolio Holdings, PART A: Foreign Residents' Portfolio Holdings of U.S. Securities," <http://www.treasury.gov/resource-center/data-chart-center/tic/Pages/fpis.aspx>, accessed June 2017.

Table 1227. Stock Prices and Yields: 2000 to 2016

[Closing values as of end of December, except as noted]

Index	2000	2005	2010	2013	2014	2015	2016
STOCK PRICES							
Standard & Poor's indices: [1]							
S&P 500 composite (1941–43 = 10)	1,320	1,248	1,257	1,848	2,059	2,044	2,239
S&P 400 MidCap Index (1982 = 100)	517	738	907	1,343	1,452	1,399	1,661
S&P 600 SmallCap Index (Dec. 31, 1993 = 100)	220	351	416	666	695	672	838
S&P 500 Citigroup Value Index (Dec. 31, 1974 = 35)	636	648	590	847	928	876	1,001
S&P 500 Citigroup Growth Index (Dec. 31, 1974 = 35)	688	597	659	992	1,122	1,164	1,223
Russell indices: [2]							
Russell 1000 (Dec. 31, 1986 = 130)	700	679	697	1,030	1,144	1,132	1,242
Russell 2000 (Dec. 31, 1986 = 135)	484	673	784	1,164	1,205	1,136	1,357
Russell 3000 (Dec. 31, 1986 = 140)	726	723	749	1,108	1,224	1,206	1,332
N.Y. Stock Exchange common stock index:							
Composite (Dec. 31, 2002 = 5000)	6,946	7,754	7,964	10,400	10,839	10,143	11,057
Yearly high	7,165	7,868	7,983	10,407	11,335	11,255	11,688
Yearly low	6,095	6,903	6,356	8,571	9,732	9,510	8,938
American Stock Exchange Composite Index (Dec. 29, 1995 = 550)	898	1,759	2,208	2,426	2,444	2,149	2,308
NASDAQ Composite Index (Feb. 5, 1971 = 100)	2,471	2,205	2,653	4,177	4,736	5,007	5,383
Nasdaq-100 (Jan. 31, 1985 = 125)	2,342	1,645	2,218	3,592	4,236	4,593	4,864
Industrial (Feb. 5, 1971 = 100)	1,483	1,860	2,184	3,715	3,789	4,101	4,445
Banks (Feb. 5, 1971 = 100)	1,939	3,078	1,847	2,602	2,676	2,853	3,852
Computers (Oct. 29, 1993 = 200)	1,295	992	1,372	2,046	2,453	2,606	2,926
Transportation (Feb. 5, 1971 = 100)	1,160	2,438	2,562	2,965	3,955	3,334	4,063
Telecommunications (Oct. 29, 1993 = 200)	463	184	226	249	271	251	288
Biotech (Oct. 29, 1993 = 200)	1,085	790	970	2,370	3,178	3,540	2,773
Dow Jones Averages:							
Composite (65 stocks)	3,317	3,638	4,033	5,642	6,474	5,978	6,902
Industrial (30 stocks)	10,787	10,718	11,578	16,577	17,823	17,425	19,763
Transportation (20 stocks)	2,947	4,196	5,107	7,401	9,140	7,509	9,044
Utility (15 stocks)	412	405	405	491	618	578	660
COMMON STOCK YIELDS (percent)							
Standard & Poor's Composite Index (500 stocks): [3]							
Dividend-price ratio [4]	1.15	1.83	1.98	2.14	2.04	2.20	2.11
Earnings-price ratio [5]	3.63	5.36	6.04	5.57	5.25	4.64	3.89

[1] Standard & Poor's Indices are market-value weighted and are chosen for market size, liquidity, and industry group representation. The S&P 500 index represents 500 large publicly-traded companies. The S&P MidCap Index tracks mid-cap companies. The S&P SmallCap Index consists of 600 domestic small-cap stocks. [2] The Russell 1000 and 3000 indices show respectively the 1000 and 3000 largest capitalization stocks in the United States. The Russell 2000 index shows the 2000 largest capitalization stocks in the United States after the first 1000. [3] Source: U.S. Council of Economic Advisors, *Economic Indicators*, monthly. [4] Aggregate cash dividends (based on latest known annual rate) divided by aggregate market value based on Wednesday closing prices. Averages of monthly figures. [5] Averages of quarterly ratios which are ratio of earnings (after taxes) for 4 quarters ending with particular quarter- to-price index for last day of that quarter.

Source: Except as noted, Global Financial Data, Los Angeles, CA ©, <http://www.globalfinancialdata.com/>.

Table 1228. Stock Ownership by Age of Head of Family and Family Income: 2007 to 2013

[Median value in thousands of constant (2013) dollars (38.2 represents $38,200). All dollar figures are adjusted to 2013 dollars using the "current methods" version of the consumer price index for all urban consumers published by U.S. Bureau of Labor Statistics. Families include one-person units; for definition of family, see text, Section 1. Based on Survey of Consumer Finance; see Appendix III. For definition of median, see Guide to Tabular Presentation]

Age of family head and family income (constant (2013) dollars)	Families having direct or indirect stock holdings [1] (percent)			Median value among families with holdings			Stock holdings share of group's financial assets (percent)		
	2007	2010	2013	2007	2010	2013	2007	2010	2013
All families	**53.2**	**49.8**	**48.8**	**38.2**	**31.1**	**35.8**	**53.6**	**46.8**	**51.3**
Under 35 years old	41.6	39.8	38.6	7.3	7.5	7.1	45.6	39.2	46.5
35 to 44 years old	55.9	50.0	53.9	28.1	21.2	23.5	54.7	50.5	53.6
45 to 54 years old	63.1	57.9	54.9	50.5	40.3	44.0	53.4	48.4	55.9
55 to 64 years old	60.8	59.7	57.2	87.6	60.8	60.0	55.4	48.2	51.5
65 to 74 years old	53.1	45.5	49.2	62.9	81.4	117.4	55.5	44.1	49.0
75 years old and over	40.2	41.9	34.5	50.5	58.5	81.4	47.8	43.9	48.3
Percentiles of income: [2]									
Less than 20	14.2	12.3	11.4	6.7	5.4	6.6	39.0	40.9	31.8
20 to 39.9	36.4	31.0	26.7	9.1	7.8	10.0	34.6	30.9	33.6
40 to 59.9	53.0	51.4	49.3	20.2	12.9	14.0	39.9	37.3	41.4
60 to 79.9	73.3	68.2	69.4	37.1	22.8	28.0	53.1	41.6	43.5
80 to 89.9	86.2	82.3	81.8	72.1	62.6	68.8	49.6	44.7	49.6
90 to 100	91.6	90.4	93.0	248.1	285.6	281.9	57.7	50.6	55.7

[1] Indirect holdings are those in pooled investment trusts, retirement accounts and other managed assets. [2] See footnote 8, Table 1195.

Source: Board of Governors of the Federal Reserve System, 2013 Survey of Consumer Finances, *Changes in U.S. Family Finances From 2010 to 2013: Evidence from the Survey of Consumer Finances,* Federal Reserve Bulletin, Vol. 100, No. 4, September 2014. See also <http://www.federalreserve.gov/econresdata/scf/scfindex.htm>.

Table 1229. Transaction Activity in Equities, Options, and Security Futures, 2000 to 2015, and by Exchange, 2015

[In billions of dollars (36,275 represents $36,275,000,000,000). Market value of all sales of equities and options listed on an exchange or subject to last-sale reporting. Also reported are the value of such options that were exercised and the value of single-stock futures that were delivered. Excludes options and futures on indexes]

Year and exchange	Market value of sales			
	Total	Equity trading	Option trading	Option exercises and futures deliveries
2000	36,275	35,557	485	233
2004	27,876	27,158	223	495
2005	34,568	33,223	350	995
2006	43,941	41,798	531	1,611
2007	66,136	63,064	861	2,211
2008	82,012	78,653	1,096	2,264
2009	59,850	57,566	710	1,574
2010	64,008	61,146	725	2,137
2011	70,100	66,683	923	2,494
2012	59,371	55,620	938	2,813
2013	62,899	59,515	752	2,633
2014	69,979	66,354	762	2,863
2015, total	**74,148**	**70,790**	**720**	**2,638**
BATS (Better Alternative Trading System) Exchange, Inc.	5,717	5,390	73	254
BATS Y-Exchange, Inc.	2,490	2,490	–	–
BOX Options Exchange LLC	73	–	16	57
C2 Options Exchange, Inc.	42	–	9	33
Chicago Board Options Exchange, Inc.	534	–	112	421
The Chicago Stock Exchange, Inc.	637	637	–	–
EDGA Exchange, Inc.	1,716	1,716	–	–
EDGX Exchange, Inc.	4,696	4,696	–	–
FINRA, Inc. [1]	23,635	23,635	–	–
International Securities Exchange, LLC	418	–	93	325
ISE Gemini, LLC	88	–	20	69
Miami International Securities Exchange, LLC	169	–	37	132
NASDAQ OMX BX	1,453	1,430	5	18
NASDAQ OMX PHLX	1,414	677	156	581
The Nasdaq Stock Market LLC	12,851	12,592	54	205
National Stock Exchange	–	–	–	–
New York Stock Exchange, Inc.	8,376	8,376	–	–
NYSE Amex LLC	391	59	71	261
NYSE Arca, Inc.	9,433	9,091	74	267
OneChicago, LLC	15	–	–	15

– Represents or rounds to zero. [1] Financial Industry Regulatory Authority.

Source: U.S. Securities and Exchange Commission, "Select SEC and Market Data, Fiscal 2016," <http://www.sec.gov/about.shtml>, accessed May 2017.

Table 1230. Mutual Fund Shares—Holdings and Net Purchases by Type of Investor: 2000 to 2016

[In billions of dollars (5,119.4 represents $5,119,400,000,000). Holdings as of Dec. 31. A mutual fund is an open-end investment company that continuously issues and redeems shares that represent an interest in a pool of financial assets. Excludes money market mutual funds and exchange-traded funds. Minus sign (-) indicates net sales]

Type of investor	Holdings					Net purchases				
	2000	2010	2014	2015	2016	2000	2010	2014	2015	2016
Total	**5,119.4**	**9,029.8**	**13,150.6**	**12,897.2**	**13,615.6**	**295.2**	**395.9**	**309.7**	**95.7**	**22.7**
Households, nonprofit organizations	2,466.2	4,473.0	6,747.1	6,522.6	6,998.9	77.4	214.3	262.7	56.5	142.2
Nonfinancial corporate business	118.0	186.8	234.6	235.7	238.1	0.3	11.1	15.2	7.4	-10.3
State and local governments	30.8	58.8	84.3	86.5	93.4	1.2	3.0	1.0	2.6	2.0
U.S.-chartered depository institutions	15.0	45.0	59.7	54.9	58.0	2.5	-5.8	-0.7	-0.9	-1.8
Credit unions	2.2	1.5	2.1	1.9	1.9	-0.7	–	-0.2	-0.1	-0.1
Property-casualty insurance companies	2.9	11.1	18.2	18.4	19.3	0.4	-0.6	1.2	0.7	0.6
Life insurance companies	726.1	1,301.5	1,680.9	1,608.4	1,538.0	62.9	62.2	-54.0	-34.6	-167.1
Private pension funds	1,246.1	2,220.2	3,175.5	3,217.3	3,435.0	106.9	55.4	40.6	34.8	40.6
State and local government retirement funds	362.5	469.5	540.5	554.4	551.4	51.5	1.2	11.3	22.3	-34.1
Rest of the world	149.5	262.5	607.8	597.1	681.5	-7.3	55.2	32.7	7.1	50.7

– Represents or rounds to zero.

Source: Board of Governors of the Federal Reserve System, "Financial Accounts of the United States, Z.1," <https://www.federalreserve.gov/data.htm>, accessed July 2017.

Table 1231. Household Ownership of Mutual Funds by Age and Income: 2006 and 2016

[In percent. Ownership includes money market, stock, bond, and hybrid mutual funds, variable annuities, and mutual funds owned through Individual Retirement Accounts (IRAs), Keoghs, and employer-sponsored retirement plans. In 2016, an estimated 54,900,000 households own mutual funds. A mutual fund is an open-end investment company that continuously issues and redeems shares that represent an interest in a pool of financial assets]

Age of household head [1]	Percent distribution, 2016 [3]	As percent of all households		Household income [2]	Percent distribution, 2016 [3]	As a percent of all households	
		2006	2016 [3]			2006	2016 [3]
Total.........................	100	45	44	Less than $25,000.........	5	14	9
				$25,000 to $34,999.......	4	28	18
Less than 35 years old....	16	34	35	$35,000 to $49,999.......	8	41	29
35 to 44 years old..........	18	49	46	$50,000 to $74,999.......	18	55	46
45 to 54 years old..........	23	60	54	$75,000 to $99,999.......	16	72	60
55 to 64 years old..........	22	49	50	$100,000 to $199,999.....	38	83	81
65 years old and over......	21	33	37	$200,000 and over.........	11	78	79

[1] Age is based on the sole or co-decision maker for household saving and investing. [2] Total reported is household income before taxes in prior year. [3] Starting in 2014, the survey was revised to include a dual frame random digit dial (RDD) sample design. See source for details.

Source: Holden, Sarah, Daniel Schrass, and Michael Bogdan, Investment Company Institute, Washington, DC, *ICI Research Perspective*, "Ownership of Mutual Funds, Shareholder Sentiment, and Use of the Internet, 2016"; Vol. 22, No. 6, October 2016, <www.ici.org/pdf/per22-06. pdf> ©.

Table 1232. Characteristics of Mutual Fund Owners: 2016

[In percent, except as indicated. Mutual fund ownership includes holdings of money market, stock, bond, and hybrid mutual funds; and funds owned through variable annuities, Individual Retirement Accounts (IRAs), Keoghs, and employer-sponsored retirement plans. The 2016 data are based on a national probability sample of 2,399 primary financial decision-makers in households with mutual fund investments. A mutual fund is an open-end investment company that continuously issues and redeems shares that represent an interest in a pool of financial assets. For definition of median, see Guide to Tabular Presentation]

Characteristic	Total	Age [1]				Household income [2]			
		Under 35 years	35 to 54 years	55 to 64 years	65 years and over	Less than $50,000	$50,000 to $99,000	$100,000 to $149,000	$150,000 or more
Median age [1] (years).............................	51	29	46	59	72	58	51	49	50
Median household income [2] (dol.).............	94,300	80,000	105,000	100,000	75,000	34,000	72,000	120,000	185,000
Median household financial assets [3] (dollars)..	200,000	50,000	200,000	425,000	400,000	50,000	125,000	275,000	500,000
Own an IRA...................................	63	53	59	66	74	55	57	65	75
Household with defined contribution retirement plan(s) [4]............................	85	88	91	87	68	69	86	88	92
401(k) plan.......................................	74	76	82	79	51	58	72	76	86
403(b), state, local, or federal government plan............................	35	33	39	28	37	26	36	38	39
Median mutual fund assets (dol.)..............	125,000	32,000	100,000	250,000	300,000	40,000	75,000	160,000	350,000
Own:									
Equity funds......................................	86	85	87	87	82	74	88	85	90
Bond funds.......................................	46	40	46	49	44	31	44	49	52

[1] See Table 1231, footnote 1. [2] See Table 1231, footnote 2. [3] Includes assets in employer-sponsored retirement plans but excludes value of primary residence. [4] For definition of defined contribution plan, see headnote, Table 574.

Source: Holden, Sarah, Daniel Schrass, and Michael Bogdan, Investment Company Institute, Washington, DC, *ICI Research Perspective*, "Ownership of Mutual Funds, Shareholder Sentiment, and Use of the Internet, 2016"; Vol. 22, No. 6, October 2016, <www.ici.org/pdf/per22-06. pdf> ©.

Table 1233. Mutual Funds—Summary: 2000 to 2016

[6,965 represents $6,965,000,000,000. Number of funds and assets as of December 31. A mutual fund is an open-end investment company that continuously issues and redeems shares that represent an interest in a pool of financial assets. Excludes data for funds that invest in other mutual funds. Minus sign (-) indicates net redemptions]

Type of fund	Unit	2000	2005	2010	2011	2012	2013	2014	2015	2016
Number of funds, total......................	**Number**	**8,155**	**7,977**	**7,556**	**7,590**	**7,590**	**7,715**	**7,927**	**8,115**	**8,066**
Equity funds.....................................	Number	4,370	4,571	4,515	4,526	4,497	4,539	4,647	4,762	4,752
Hybrid funds....................................	Number	508	481	495	520	562	605	665	717	717
Bond funds.......................................	Number	2,238	2,055	1,894	1,912	1,951	2,017	2,088	2,155	2,176
Money market funds, taxable [1]...........	Number	704	593	442	431	400	382	364	336	319
Money market funds, tax-exempt [2].........	Number	335	277	210	201	180	173	163	145	102
Assets, total.................................	**Bil. dol.**	**6,965**	**8,891**	**11,834**	**11,633**	**13,054**	**15,049**	**15,873**	**15,650**	**16,344**
Equity funds.....................................	Bil. dol.	3,934	4,885	5,597	5,213	5,939	7,763	8,314	8,148	8,577
Hybrid funds....................................	Bil. dol.	361	621	842	884	1,032	1,283	1,374	1,334	1,389
Bond funds.......................................	Bil. dol.	824	1,358	2,591	2,845	3,391	3,286	3,461	3,413	3,650
Money market funds, taxable [1]...........	Bil. dol.	1,611	1,690	2,474	2,400	2,406	2,448	2,464	2,500	2,598
Money market funds, tax-exempt [2].........	Bil. dol.	234	336	330	292	287	271	261	255	130
Net new cash flow:..........................	**Bil. dol.**	**388**	**254**	**-282**	**-96**	**200**	**177**	**104**	**-101**	**-229**
Equity funds.....................................	Bil. dol.	316	124	-24	-129	-153	160	25	-77	-260
Hybrid funds....................................	Bil. dol.	-37	43	36	40	46	74	29	-21	-46
Bond funds.......................................	Bil. dol.	-50	25	232	118	306	-71	44	-25	107
Money market funds............................	Bil. dol.	159	62	-525	-124	–	15	6	21	-30

– Represents zero. [1] Funds invest in short-term, high-grade securities sold in the money market. [2] Funds invest in municipal securities with relatively short maturities.

Source: Investment Company Institute. 2017. *2017 Investment Company Fact Book: A Review of Trends and Activities in the U.S. Investment Company Industry.* Washington, DC: Investment Company Institute. Available at <www.icifactbook.org> ©.

Table 1234. Retirement Assets by Type of Asset: 2000 to 2016

[In billions of dollars, except as indicated (11,558 represents $11,558,000,000,000). As of December 31]

Item	2000	2005	2010	2012	2013	2014	2015	2016
Retirement assets, total	**11,558**	**14,406**	**17,941**	**19,709**	**22,648**	**23,896**	**23,867**	**25,289**
IRA assets [1]	2,629	3,425	5,029	5,785	6,819	7,292	7,329	7,850
Bank and thrift deposits [2]	250	278	461	508	507	505	523	561
Life insurance companies [3]	202	301	309	329	356	377	391	411
Mutual funds	1,266	1,782	2,426	2,763	3,336	3,536	3,502	3,719
Other assets [1,4]	912	1,064	1,833	2,185	2,620	2,874	2,913	3,159
Traditional [1]	2,407	3,034	4,340	4,969	5,828	6,225	6,254	6,695
Roth [1]	78	156	355	439	548	600	605	660
SEP and SAR-SEP [1,5]	134	193	265	298	349	367	370	390
SIMPLE [1,6]	10	42	69	78	95	100	100	105
Defined contribution plans	2,959	3,736	4,758	5,242	6,132	6,480	6,539	7,034
401(k) plans	1,738	2,393	3,119	3,495	4,148	4,406	4,445	4,825
Other private-sector defined contribution plans [7]	500	413	464	452	500	514	520	550
403(b) plans	520	623	723	766	858	887	880	911
Thrift Savings Plan [8]	92	164	265	316	381	412	430	467
457 plans	110	143	189	212	245	261	263	282
Private-sector defined benefit plans	2,020	2,262	2,481	2,709	2,892	3,003	2,870	2,946
State and local government defined benefit plans	2,340	2,787	2,954	2,998	3,549	3,730	3,664	3,831
Federal defined benefit plans [9]	705	908	1,161	1,270	1,370	1,438	1,512	1,595
Annuities [10]	905	1,288	1,557	1,705	1,886	1,954	1,954	2,032
Memo:								
Mutual fund retirement assets	2,550	3,662	4,936	5,612	6,815	7,243	7,140	7,564
Percent of total retirement assets	22	25	28	28	30	30	30	30
Percent of all mutual funds	37	41	42	43	45	46	46	46

[1] Data for 2015 and 2016 are estimated. [2] Includes Keogh deposits. [3] Annuities held by IRAs, excluding variable annuity mutual fund IRA assets. [4] Excludes mutual fund assets held through brokerage accounts, which are included in mutual funds. [5] Simplified Employee Pension (SEP) IRAs and salary reduction (SAR) IRAs. [6] Savings Incentive Match Plan for Employees (SIMPLE) IRAs. [7] Includes Keoghs and other defined contribution plans (profit-sharing, thrift-savings, stock bonus, and money purchase) without 401(k) features. [8] Federal Employees Retirement System (FERS) Thrift Savings Plan (TSP) as reported by the Federal Reserve Board. [9] Federal pension plans include U.S. Treasury security holdings of the civil service retirement and disability fund, the military retirement fund, the judicial retirement funds, the Railroad Retirement Board, and the foreign service retirement and disability fund. These plans also include securities held in the National Railroad Retirement Investment Trust. [10] Annuities include all fixed and variable annuities held outside of retirement plans and IRAs.

Source: Investment Company Institute. 2017. "The U.S. Retirement Market, First Quarter 2017" (June), <https://www.ici.org/research/stats/retirement>.

Table 1235. Pension Funds—Summary: 2000 to 2016

[In billions of dollars (8,556 represents $8,556,000,000,000). As of end of year. Covers private pension funds, state and local government employee retirement funds, and federal government retirement funds in defined benefit plans and defined contribution plans (including 401(k) type plans). Excludes social security trust funds; see Table 568]

Item	2000	2005	2010	2011	2012	2013	2014	2015	2016
Total financial assets [1]	**8,556**	**11,364**	**14,533**	**14,906**	**15,745**	**16,972**	**17,641**	**18,214**	**19,096**
Money market fund shares	104	131	192	208	187	203	207	203	215
Debt securities [1]	2,058	2,319	2,861	3,037	3,233	3,520	3,649	3,806	3,994
Treasury securities [2]	1,029	1,215	1,627	1,766	1,894	2,019	2,095	2,201	2,321
Agency- and GSE (government-sponsored enterprises)-backed securities	374	433	339	304	283	278	271	256	261
Corporate and foreign bonds	578	621	818	886	983	1,142	1,196	1,259	1,311
Corporate equities	3,178	4,004	3,648	3,470	3,850	4,622	4,761	4,540	4,803
Mutual fund shares	1,609	2,235	2,690	2,589	2,894	3,513	3,716	3,772	3,986
Miscellaneous assets [1]	1,388	2,530	5,018	5,473	5,462	4,987	5,171	5,757	5,951
Unallocated insurance contracts [3]	462	533	626	634	654	676	672	661	690
Contributions receivable	73	45	91	94	81	79	76	72	70
Claims of pension fund on sponsor [4]	678	1,746	3,634	4,032	3,980	3,443	3,593	4,151	4,261
Pension entitlements (liabilities) [5]	**8,644**	**11,458**	**14,676**	**15,054**	**15,906**	**17,155**	**17,834**	**18,399**	**19,287**
Memo:									
Defined benefit plan funded status:									
Pension entitlements, total	**5,743**	**7,762**	**10,173**	**10,566**	**10,911**	**11,274**	**11,701**	**12,137**	**12,572**
Funded by assets [6]	5,065	6,016	6,539	6,534	6,933	7,831	8,108	7,986	8,310
Unfunded	678	1,746	3,634	4,032	3,978	3,443	3,593	4,151	4,261
Household retirement assets, total [7]	**12,266**	**16,256**	**21,323**	**21,859**	**23,479**	**25,958**	**27,196**	**27,831**	**29,325**
Defined benefit plans	5,655	7,669	10,030	10,419	10,750	11,091	11,509	11,952	12,381
Defined contribution plans	2,901	3,695	4,503	4,488	4,995	5,882	6,133	6,262	6,715
Individual retirement plans (IRAs) [8]	2,629	3,425	5,029	5,153	5,785	6,819	7,292	7,329	7,850
Annuities at life insurance companies [9]	1,081	1,467	1,761	1,800	1,949	2,167	2,263	2,288	2,380

[1] Includes other types of assets not shown separately. [2] Includes both marketable and nonmarketable government securities. [3] Assets of pension plans held at life insurance companies. [4] Unfunded defined benefit pension entitlements. [5] Actuarial value of accrued pension entitlements in defined benefit plans and assets of defined contribution plans. These liabilities are assets of the household sector. [6] Total defined benefit financial assets plus nonfinancial assets less claims of pension fund on sponsor. [7] Households' retirement assets in tax-deferred accounts, including employer sponsored pension plans, individual retirement accounts (IRAs), Roth IRAs, and annuities. [8] IRA assets are not included in above assets or entitlements. [9] Excludes annuities held in IRAs at life insurance companies.

Source: Board of Governors of the Federal Reserve System, "Financial Accounts of the United States, Z.1," <https://www.federalreserve.gov/data.htm>, accessed July 2017.

Table 1236. Private Pension Fund Assets by Type, and Liabilities: 2000 to 2016

[In billions of dollars (4,283 represents $4,283,000,000,000). As of December 31. Covers private defined benefit plans and defined contribution plans (including 401(k) type plans). Minus sign (-) indicates overfunding]

Type of instrument	2000	2005	2010	2011	2012	2013	2014	2015	2016
Total financial assets [1]	**4,283**	**5,391**	**6,600**	**6,714**	**7,241**	**8,099**	**8,426**	**8,631**	**9,099**
Money market fund shares	84	90	142	159	142	155	156	151	156
Debt securities [1]	596	665	852	927	1,070	1,160	1,181	1,227	1,258
Treasury securities	111	111	200	238	302	300	296	317	326
Agency and GSE-backed securities [2]	194	245	179	169	171	166	163	154	152
Corporate and foreign bonds	263	286	435	479	561	653	679	709	731
Corporate equities	1,823	2,288	1,778	1,680	1,891	2,244	2,284	2,164	2,327
Mutual fund shares	1,246	1,727	2,220	2,204	2,484	3,008	3,175	3,217	3,435
Miscellaneous assets [1]	387	518	1,535	1,668	1,583	1,459	1,548	1,792	1,839
Unallocated insurance contracts [3]	362	405	466	484	504	525	527	517	537
Pension entitlements (liabilities) [4]	**4,323**	**5,430**	**6,636**	**6,750**	**7,277**	**8,135**	**8,462**	**8,668**	**9,135**
Funded status of defined benefit plans:									
Pension entitlements	1,826	2,290	2,872	2,984	3,055	3,131	3,223	3,307	3,380
Funded by assets [5]	2,020	2,321	2,424	2,466	2,665	2,912	2,939	2,810	2,884
Unfunded	-193	-30	449	518	391	219	283	497	496
Defined benefit plan assets	1,785	2,251	2,836	2,947	3,019	3,095	3,186	3,270	3,344
Defined contribution plan assets	2,497	3,140	3,764	3,767	4,222	5,004	5,239	5,361	5,755

[1] Includes other types of assets not shown separately. [2] GSE=Government-sponsored enterprises. [3] Assets of private pension plans held at life insurance companies (e.g., GICs, variable annuities). [4] Actuarial value of accrued pension entitlements in defined benefit plans and assets of defined contribution plans. [5] Total defined benefit financial assets plus nonfinancial assets less claims of pension fund on sponsor.

Source: Board of Governors of the Federal Reserve System, "Financial Accounts of the United States, Z.1," <https://www.federalreserve.gov/data.htm>, accessed July 2017.

Table 1237. Public Employee Retirement Systems—Assets and Liabilities: 2000 to 2016

[In billions of dollars (2,270 represents $2,270,000,000,000). As of December 31. Includes claims of sponsor (unfunded pension entitlements. Minus sign (-) indicates overfunding]

Type of instrument	2000	2005	2010	2011	2012	2013	2014	2015	2016
STATE AND LOCAL GOVERNMENT EMPLOYEE RETIREMENT PLANS									
Total financial assets [1]	**2,270**	**3,478**	**4,776**	**4,929**	**5,122**	**5,337**	**5,559**	**5,819**	**6,103**
Debt securities [1]	721	693	724	729	726	816	836	856	913
Treasury securities	179	152	154	161	173	188	181	175	187
Agency and GSE-backed securities [2]	179	182	155	128	104	106	102	96	102
Corporate and foreign bonds	314	331	377	400	413	481	509	542	572
Corporate equities	1,299	1,606	1,729	1,655	1,811	2,172	2,258	2,157	2,237
Mutual fund shares	363	508	470	385	409	506	540	554	551
Miscellaneous assets [1]	-205	589	1,752	2,057	2,082	1,743	1,817	2,144	2,280
Claims of pension fund on sponsor [3]	-334	354	1,455	1,766	1,792	1,437	1,504	1,832	1,933
Pension entitlements (liabilities) [4]	**2,318**	**3,532**	**4,883**	**5,040**	**5,247**	**5,484**	**5,715**	**5,967**	**6,257**
Funded status of defined benefit plans:									
Pension entitlements	2,006	3,141	4,409	4,604	4,790	4,987	5,234	5,496	5,764
Funded by assets [5]	2,340	2,787	2,954	2,838	2,998	3,549	3,730	3,664	3,831
Unfunded [3]	-334	354	1,455	1,766	1,792	1,437	1,504	1,832	1,933
Defined benefit plan assets	1,959	3,087	4,302	4,493	4,665	4,840	5,078	5,348	5,609
Defined contribution plan assets	311	391	474	436	457	497	482	471	493
FEDERAL GOVERNMENT EMPLOYEE RETIREMENT FUNDS									
Total financial assets [1]	**2,003**	**2,495**	**3,156**	**3,264**	**3,382**	**3,537**	**3,656**	**3,764**	**3,894**
Debt securities [1]	740	961	1,285	1,381	1,437	1,545	1,631	1,723	1,823
Treasury securities [6]	739	951	1,273	1,367	1,420	1,531	1,618	1,709	1,808
Corporate equities	57	111	141	134	148	206	219	219	239
Claims of pension fund on sponsor [7]	1,206	1,423	1,731	1,748	1,797	1,786	1,806	1,822	1,832
Pension entitlements (liabilities) [8]	**2,003**	**2,495**	**3,156**	**3,264**	**3,382**	**3,537**	**3,656**	**3,764**	**3,894**
Funded status of defined benefit plans:									
Pension entitlements	1,911	2,331	2,892	2,978	3,066	3,155	3,244	3,334	3,428
Funded by assets [9]	705	908	1,161	1,230	1,270	1,370	1,438	1,512	1,595
Unfunded [7]	1,206	1,423	1,731	1,748	1,796	1,786	1,806	1,822	1,832
Defined benefit plan assets [10]	1,911	2,331	2,892	2,978	3,066	3,155	3,244	3,334	3,428
Defined contribution plan assets [11]	92	164	265	285	316	381	412	430	467

[1] Includes other types of instruments not shown separately. [2] GSE=Government sponsored enterprises. [3] Unfunded defined benefit pension entitlements. [4] Actuarial value of accrued defined benefit pension entitlements. [5] Total defined benefit financial assets plus nonfinancial assets less claims of pension fund on sponsor. [6] Includes marketable and nonmarketable Treasury securities. [7] Unfunded defined benefit pension entitlements and suspended investments in the Thrift Savings Plan G Fund by the Treasury. [8] Actuarial value of accrued pension entitlements in defined benefit plans and assets of defined contribution plans, including suspended investments in the Thrift Savings Plan G Fund. [9] Total defined benefit financial assets less defined benefit claims of pension fund on sponsor. [10] Includes the Civil Service Retirement and Disability Fund, Railroad Retirement Board, judicial retirement fund, Military Retirement Fund, Foreign Service Retirement and Disability Fund, and National Railroad Retirement Investment Trust. [11] Thrift Savings Plan.

Source: Board of Governors of the Federal Reserve System, "Financial Accounts of the United States, Z.1," <https://www.federalreserve.gov/data.htm>, accessed July 2017.

Table 1238. Life Insurance in Force and Purchases in the United States—Summary: 1990 to 2016

[389 represents 389,000,000. As of December 31 or calendar year, as applicable. Covers life insurance with life insurance companies only. Data represents all life insurance in force on lives of U.S. residents whether issued by U.S. or foreign companies]

Year	Number of policies, total (millions)	Life insurance in force			Life insurance purchases [1]					
		Value (bil. dol.)			Number (1,000)			Amount (bil. dol.)		
		Total [2]	Individual	Group	Total	Individual	Group	Total	Individual	Group
1990.......	389	9,393	5,391	3,754	28,791	14,199	14,592	1,529	1,070	459
2000.......	369	15,953	9,376	6,376	34,882	13,345	21,537	2,515	1,594	921
2005.......	373	18,399	9,970	8,263	34,519	11,407	23,112	2,836	1,796	1,040
2010.......	284	18,426	10,484	7,831	28,621	10,123	18,498	2,809	1,673	1,135
2011.......	286	19,219	10,994	8,120	27,177	10,309	16,867	2,832	1,673	1,160
2012.......	272	19,321	11,215	8,012	27,063	10,306	16,757	2,800	1,679	1,121
2013.......	275	19,662	11,365	8,215	25,264	9,929	15,336	2,779	1,640	1,139
2014.......	278	20,115	11,826	8,209	27,147	9,440	17,707	2,759	1,590	1,168
2015.......	281	20,779	12,342	8,361	28,315	10,305	18,010	2,877	1,647	1,229
2016.......	291	20,330	11,992	8,246	27,523	11,005	16,518	2,874	1,685	1,190

[1] Excludes revivals, increases, dividend additions, and reinsurance acquired. Includes long-term credit insurance (life insurance on loans of more than 10 years' duration). [2] Includes other types of policies not shown separately such as credit.

Source: American Council of Life Insurers, Washington, DC, *Life Insurers Fact Book*, annual ©.

Table 1239. U.S. Life Insurance Companies—Summary: 2000 to 2016

[811.5 represents $811,500,000,000. As of December 31 or calendar year, as applicable. Covers domestic and foreign business of U.S. companies. Includes annual statement data for companies that primarily are health insurance companies. Beginning in 2005, includes fraternal benefit societies]

Item	Unit	2000	2005	2010	2011	2012	2013	2014	2015	2016
U.S. companies [1]	Number	1,269	1,119	917	895	868	850	830	814	797
Income [2]	Bil. dol.	811.5	779.0	862.6	915.3	952.4	906.7	999.4	1,064.7	985.8
Life insurance premiums	Bil. dol.	130.6	142.3	104.6	127.5	135.4	130.6	138.3	155.9	119.3
Annuity considerations [3]	Bil. dol.	306.7	277.1	293.6	334.9	348.1	287.7	361.6	333.0	326.8
Health insurance premiums	Bil. dol.	105.6	118.3	172.7	171.6	172.3	175.1	158.4	159.9	164.0
Investment and other [4]	Bil. dol.	268.5	241.4	291.6	281.3	296.6	313.4	341.1	416.0	375.7
Payments under life insurance and annuity contracts	Bil. dol.	375.2	365.7	365.6	393.2	402.2	411.6	443.8	447.7	443.0
Payments to life insurance beneficiaries	Bil. dol.	44.1	53.0	58.4	62.1	63.3	64.3	67.9	74.3	76.0
Surrender values under life insurance [5]	Bil. dol.	27.2	39.2	35.8	33.5	31.5	28.7	27.8	28.8	30.2
Surrender values under annuity contracts [5, 6]	Bil. dol.	214.0	190.3	184.1	206.2	216.8	222.8	256.7	247.2	238.0
Policyholder dividends	Bil. dol.	20.0	17.9	15.9	15.5	15.5	16.0	16.7	18.5	18.4
Annuity payments [6]	Bil. dol.	68.7	63.9	70.1	74.5	74.0	78.8	73.8	77.8	79.1
Matured endowments	Bil. dol.	0.6	0.6	0.6	0.6	0.4	0.4	0.4	0.4	0.4
Other payments	Bil. dol.	0.6	0.7	0.7	0.7	0.6	0.7	0.7	0.7	0.7
Health insurance benefit payments	Bil. dol.	78.8	79.6	122.5	120.6	123.8	127.5	113.6	115.3	119.8
BALANCE SHEET										
Assets	Bil. dol.	3,182	4,482	5,311	5,493	5,777	6,150	6,406	6,478	6,772
Mortgage-backed securities	Bil. dol.	(NA)	(NA)	631	607	583	562	567	556	568
Government bonds	Bil. dol.	364	590	413	463	459	464	479	496	522
Corporate securities	Bil. dol.	2,238	3,136	3,271	3,353	3,619	3,978	4,133	4,150	4,313
Bonds	Bil. dol.	1,241	1,850	1,700	1,807	1,894	1,974	2,061	2,150	2,257
Stocks	Bil. dol.	997	1,285	1,570	1,546	1,725	2,004	2,072	2,001	2,056
Mortgages	Bil. dol.	237	295	327	343	354	374	395	437	472
Real estate	Bil. dol.	36	33	28	29	31	31	32	44	47
Policy loans	Bil. dol.	102	110	127	129	131	132	133	135	135
Other	Bil. dol.	204	319	515	568	601	610	666	659	715
Interest earned on assets [7]	Percent	7.05	4.90	4.33	4.35	4.25	4.20	4.61	4.81	4.50
Obligations and surplus funds [8]	Bil. dol.	3,182	4,482	5,311	5,493	5,777	6,150	6,406	6,478	6,772
Policy reserves	Bil. dol.	2,712	3,360	4,098	4,244	4,449	4,780	4,956	5,025	5,232
Annuities [9]	Bil. dol.	1,875	2,189	2,660	2,729	2,920	3,186	3,299	3,320	3,467
Group	Bil. dol.	960	758	863	871	958	1,029	1,050	1,022	1,053
Individual	Bil. dol.	881	1,415	1,780	1,840	1,943	2,137	2,228	2,276	2,391
Supplementary contracts [10]	Bil. dol.	34	16	17	18	19	20	22	23	23
Life insurance	Bil. dol.	742	1,029	1,224	1,286	1,302	1,365	1,423	1,463	1,500
Health insurance	Bil. dol.	96	141	214	229	228	228	234	242	264
Liabilities for deposit-type contracts [11]	Bil. dol.	21	456	420	413	431	450	468	470	495
Capital and surplus	Bil. dol.	188	256	319	321	340	348	368	383	398

NA Not available. [1] Includes life insurance companies that sell accident and health insurance. [2] Premiums are net of reinsurance business and fluctuate with reinsurance activities as well as sale changes. [3] Beginning 2005, excludes certain deposit-type funds from income due to codification. [4] Investment represents gross investment income. [5] "Surrender values" include annuity withdrawals of funds. [6] Beginning 2005, excludes payments under deposit-type contracts. [7] Net rate. [8] Includes other obligations not shown separately. [9] Beginning 2005, excludes reserves for guaranteed interest contracts (GICs). [10] Data for 2000 include reserves for contracts with and without life contingencies; beginning 2005, includes only reserves for contracts with life contingencies. [11] Policyholder dividend accumulations for all years. Beginning 2005, also includes liabilities for guaranteed interest contracts, supplementary contracts without life contingencies, and premium and other deposits.

Source: American Council of Life Insurers, Washington, DC, *Life Insurers Fact Book*, annual ©.

Table 1240. Property and Casualty Insurance—Summary: 2000 to 2014

[In billions of dollars (305.1 represents $305,100,000,000). Minus sign (-) indicates loss]

Item	2000	2005	2010	2011	2012	2013	2014
Premiums, net written [1]	305.1	427.6	423.8	438.0	456.7	477.0	502.6
Automobile, private [2]	120.0	159.6	160.3	163.3	168.0	174.9	183.4
Automobile, commercial [2]	19.8	26.8	21.1	21.0	22.1	23.9	25.7
Fire	(NA)	7.9	10.2	10.3	10.8	11.2	11.5
Homeowners' multiple peril	32.7	53.0	61.3	64.1	67.8	72.8	77.9
Commercial multiple peril	(NA)	29.7	28.9	30.0	31.5	33.2	34.4
Marine, inland and ocean	8.3	11.2	11.2	11.5	12.3	13.0	13.9
Workers' compensation	26.2	39.7	31.5	35.7	38.7	40.9	43.6
Other liability [3]	(NA)	39.4	35.7	36.5	38.3	42.1	44.2
Reinsurance	(NA)	6.6	12.3	13.2	14.7	12.5	11.5
Losses and expenses	321.3	421.4	430.4	468.8	462.1	449.6	472.8
Underwriting gain/loss	-27.3	-5.6	-10.5	-36.2	-15.4	15.2	12.3
Investment income earned	42.0	49.7	47.6	49.2	48.0	47.3	46.2
Net income after taxes	4.4	44.2	35.2	19.5	35.1	63.4	55.5

NA Not available. [1] Excludes state funds, after reinsurance transactions. Includes other lines of insurance not shown separately. [2] Includes premiums for automobile liability and physical damage. [3] Coverages protecting against legal liability resulting from negligence, carelessness, or failure to act.

Source: Insurance Information Institute, New York, NY, "Facts and Statistics," <http://www.iii.org/insurance-topics/features/facts-and-statistics> ©, accessed August 2015. See also <http://www.iii.org>.

Table 1241. Automobile Insurance—Average Expenditures Per Insured Vehicle by State: 2013 and 2014

[In dollars. Average expenditure equals total premiums written divided by liability car-years. A car-year is equal to 365 days of insured coverage for a single vehicle. The average expenditures for automobile insurance in a state are affected by a number of factors, including the underlying rate structure, the coverages purchased, the deductibles and limits selected, the types of vehicles insured, and the distribution of driver characteristics. The National Association of Insurance Commissioners does not rank state average expenditures and does not endorse any conclusions drawn from this data]

State	2013	2014	State	2013	2014	State	2013	2014	State	2013	2014
U.S.	841	866	ID.	553	572	MO.	704	724	PA.	841	858
AL.	674	695	IL.	745	775	MT.	679	695	RI.	1,066	1,106
AK.	889	884	IN.	622	642	NE.	639	663	SC.	794	825
AZ.	811	837	IA.	572	586	NV.	936	970	SD.	581	601
AR.	703	729	KS.	669	689	NH.	733	751	TN.	704	725
CA.	783	815	KY.	773	783	NJ.	1,254	1,264	TX.	895	906
CO.	778	821	LA.	1,146	1,193	NM.	723	749	UT.	734	766
CT.	1,011	1,032	ME.	593	607	NY.	1,182	1,205	VT.	656	665
DE.	1,101	1,126	MD.	979	1,001	NC.	625	644	VA.	719	743
DC.	1,187	1,192	MA.	1,008	1,036	ND.	605	630	WA.	838	872
FL.	1,144	1,141	MI.	1,131	1,227	OH.	659	683	WV.	859	871
GA.	801	840	MN.	745	773	OK.	768	808	WI.	621	646
HI.	739	752	MS.	768	797	OR.	783	819	WY.	640	669

Source: National Association of Insurance Commissioners (NAIC), Kansas City, MO, *Auto Insurance Database Report*, annual ©. Reprinted with permission of the NAIC. Further reprint or distribution strictly prohibited without prior written permission of the NAIC.

Table 1242. Renters and Homeowners Insurance—Average Premiums by State: 2014

[In dollars. Average premium equals premiums divided by exposure per house-years. A house-year is equal to 365 days of insured coverage for a single dwelling and is the standard measurement for homeowners insurance. The National Association of Insurance Commissioners does not rank state average expenditures and does not endorse any conclusions drawn from these data]

State	Renters [1]	Homeowners [2]	State	Renters [1]	Homeowners [2]	State	Renters [1]	Homeowners [2]	State	Renters [1]	Homeowners [2]
U.S.	190	1,132	ID.	156	590	MO.	181	1,199	PA.	158	893
AL.	245	1,340	IL.	177	987	MT.	142	1,003	RI.	179	1,398
AK.	168	976	IN.	187	944	NE.	150	1,226	SC.	194	1,240
AZ.	195	765	IA.	146	853	NV.	190	704	SD.	120	995
AR.	213	1,252	KS.	179	1,431	NH.	145	905	TN.	215	1,139
CA.	203	974	KY.	169	1,023	NJ.	168	1,092	TX [3].	259	1,947
CO.	174	1,273	LA.	255	1,847	NM.	191	937	UT.	145	634
CT.	205	1,337	ME.	147	811	NY.	205	1,256	VT.	152	844
DE.	154	736	MD.	161	942	NC.	155	1,056	VA.	157	946
DC.	160	1,151	MA.	198	1,314	ND.	114	1,136	WA.	169	695
FL.	202	2,055	MI.	203	865	OH.	188	797	WV.	180	877
GA.	226	1,089	MN.	144	1,219	OK.	248	1,772	WI.	132	686
HI.	210	1,018	MS.	262	1,447	OR.	164	574	WY.	154	1,021

[1] Based on the HO-4 renters insurance policy for tenants. Includes broad named-peril coverage for the personal property of tenants. [2] Based on the HO-3 homeowner package policy for owner-occupied dwellings, 1–4 family units. Provides "all risks" coverage (except those specifically excluded in the policy) on buildings, broad named-peril coverage on personal property, and is the most common package written. [3] The Texas Insurance Commissioner promulgates residential policy forms which are similar but not identical to the standard forms.

Source: National Association of Insurance Commissioners (NAIC), Kansas City, MO, *Dwelling Fire, Homeowners Owner-Occupied, and Homeowners Tenant and Condominium/Cooperative Unit Owners Insurance* ©. Reprinted with permission of the NAIC. Further reprint or distribution strictly prohibited without prior written permission of the NAIC.

Table 1243. Real Estate and Rental and Leasing—Nonemployer Establishments and Receipts by Kind of Business: 2010 to 2015

[2,343.1 represents 2,343,100. Includes only firms subject to federal income tax. Nonemployers are businesses with no paid employees. Data originate chiefly from administrative records of the Internal Revenue Service; see Appendix III]

Kind of business	NAICS code [1]	Establishments (1,000)			Receipts (mil. dol.)		
		2010	2014	2015	2010	2014	2015
Real estate & rental & leasing, total.............	53	2,343.1	2,543.8	2,635.8	209,549	247,884	259,768
Real estate..........................	531	2,262.2	2,461.3	2,552.5	203,065	240,743	252,450
Lessors of real estate..................	5311	989.3	1,124.0	1,156.2	135,015	153,686	158,624
Offices of real estate agents & brokers...........	5312	641.6	662.5	694.7	25,502	35,586	38,904
Activities related to real estate..............	5313	631.3	674.8	701.6	42,549	51,470	54,922
Rental & leasing services................	532	78.9	79.5	80.2	6,288	6,870	7,024
Automotive equipment rental & leasing...........	5321	18.3	18.1	18.6	990	1,085	1,171
Consumer goods rental..................	5322	18.3	19.1	19.1	779	865	887
General rental centers.................	5323	4.8	6.0	6.5	409	469	519
Commercial/industrial equipment rental & leasing........	5324	37.5	36.3	36.0	4,109	4,451	4,448
Lessors of other nonfinancial intangible assets........	533	2.0	3.0	3.1	197	271	293

[1] Data for 2010 based on 2007 North American Industry Classification System (NAICS); beginning in 2012, data based on 2012 NAICS. For more information, see text, Section 15.

Source: U.S. Census Bureau, Nonemployer Statistics, "Geographic Area Series: Nonemployer Statistics for the U.S., States, Metropolitan Areas, and Counties," <http://factfinder.census.gov>, accessed June 2017. See also <http://www.census.gov/econ/nonemployer/>.

Table 1244. Real Estate and Rental and Leasing—Establishments, Employees, and Payroll: 2010 and 2015

[347.3 represents 347,300. Covers establishments with payroll. Data for 2010 based on the North American Industry Classification System (NAICS) 2007; 2015 data based on NAICS 2012; see text, section 15, Business Enterprise. Employees are for the week including March 12. Most government employees are excluded. For statement on methodology, see Appendix III]

Kind of business	NAICS code	Establishments (1,000)		Employees (1,000)		Payroll (bil. dol.)	
		2010	2015	2010	2015	2010	2015
Real estate & rental & leasing, total.............	53	347.3	377.6	1,946.4	2,065.4	80.5	106.3
Real estate.......................	531	287.8	321.9	1,407.9	1,522.2	58.7	78.2
Lessors of real estate..................	5311	114.4	125.6	513.3	573.3	18.7	26.1
Offices of real estate agents & brokers...........	5312	89.2	102.8	278.0	281.8	12.7	18.4
Activities related to real estate [1].............	5313	84.2	93.5	616.6	667.1	27.4	33.7
Residential property managers..............	531311	39.2	47.1	380.5	427.3	13.6	17.7
Rental & leasing services................	532	57.2	53.2	509.4	508.8	19.3	24.4
Automotive equipment rental & leasing...........	5321	11.1	15.8	149.2	164.9	5.5	6.8
Passenger car rental & leasing.............	53211	5.6	10.3	([2])	102.2	3.5	3.8
Truck, utility trailer & RV rental & leasing........	53212	5.6	5.5	46.0	62.7	2.0	3.0
Consumer goods rental [1]...............	5322	27.9	20.0	193.0	143.7	5.1	5.1
Video tape & disc rental................	53223	10.9	2.1	79.9	15.3	1.2	0.4
Home health equipment rental.............	532291	3.8	3.2	36.6	32.0	1.6	1.3
General rental centers.................	5323	4.2	2.8	25.3	18.8	0.9	0.8
Commercial/industrial equipment rental & leasing [1]..........	5324	13.9	14.7	141.8	181.4	7.9	11.8
Construction, transportation, and mining equipment........	53241	5.5	5.2	55.4	69.4	3.4	5.2
Lessors of other nonfinancial intangible assets........	533	2.4	2.5	29.2	34.5	2.4	3.7

[1] Includes industries not shown separately. [2] Over 100,000 employees.

Source: U.S. Census Bureau, County Business Patterns, "Geography Area Series: County Business Patterns," <http://factfinder.census.gov>, accessed April 2017. See also <https://www.census.gov/programs-surveys/cbp.html>.

Table 1245. Real Estate and Rental and Leasing Services—Revenue by Kind of Business: 2010 to 2015

[In millions of dollars (431,216 represents $431,216,000,000). Covers taxable and tax-exempt employer firms. Data are based on the 2007 North American Industry Classification System (NAICS); see text, this section and Section 15. Estimates have been adjusted using the results of the 2012 Economic Census. Based on Service Annual Survey; see Appendix III]

Kind of business	NAICS code	2010	2011	2012	2013	2014	2015
Real estate and rental and leasing, total................	53	431,216	454,896	487,656	523,255	564,613	602,846
Real estate [1].......................	531	289,294	303,318	325,339	351,972	380,860	410,457
Lessors of residential buildings and dwellings..........	53111	73,899	79,917	85,980	91,448	98,130	105,318
Lessors of nonresidential buildings (excl. miniwarehouses)...	53112	86,933	91,764	96,132	100,759	107,747	114,499
Offices of real estate agents and brokers............	5312	55,966	57,020	65,094	75,928	84,199	92,869
Real estate property managers..............	53131	43,659	45,598	47,179	50,670	55,574	59,429
Offices of real estate appraisers.............	53132	5,225	5,248	5,824	5,734	5,464	5,881
Rental and leasing services [1]..................	532	112,020	119,310	129,336	135,753	145,799	152,544
Passenger car rental.................	532111	22,534	24,320	25,033	25,957	27,295	28,194
Passenger car leasing.................	532112	6,063	6,545	7,714	8,136	8,610	9,050
Truck, trailer, and recreational vehicle rental and leasing.....	53212	13,941	14,923	15,667	15,941	16,933	18,082
Consumer electronics and appliances rental..................	53221	5,253	5,880	6,667	6,809	7,462	7,991
Construction/transportation/mining equipment rental and leasing..............	53241	23,012	25,991	30,480	32,837	36,285	36,201
Lessors of other nonfinancial intangible assets..................	533	29,902	32,268	32,981	35,530	37,954	39,845

[1] Includes other kinds of business, not shown separately.

Source: U.S. Census Bureau, Annual and Quarterly Services, "2015 Annual Services," <http://www.census.gov/services/index.html>, accessed February 2017.

Section 26
Arts, Recreation, and Travel

This section presents data on the arts, entertainment, and recreation economic sector of the economy, and personal recreational activities, the arts and humanities, and domestic and foreign travel.

Arts, entertainment, and recreation industry—The U.S. Census Bureau surveys—County Business Patterns, Economic Census, Nonemployer Statistics, and Service Annual Survey—provide data on the arts, entertainment, and recreation sector. The *County Business Patterns'* annual data includes number of establishments, number of employees, first quarter and annual payrolls, and number of establishments by employment size class. The *Economic Census*, conducted every five years for the years ending in '2' and '7', provides information on the number of establishments, receipts, payroll, and paid employees for the United States and various geographic levels. Data from the 2012 Economic Census have been fully released as of September 2016 through the Census Bureau's American FactFinder® service on the Census Bureau website at <factfinder.census.gov>. Nonemployer statistics are an annual tabulation of economic data by industry for active businesses without paid employees that are subject to federal income tax. The *Service Annual Survey* provides estimates of operating revenue of taxable firms and revenues and expenses of firms exempt from federal taxes for industries in this sector of the economy. See Appendix III for more details.

Recreation and leisure activities—Data on the participation in various recreation and leisure time activities are based on several sample surveys. Data on the public's involvement with arts events and activities are published by the National Endowment for Arts (NEA). The NEA's *Survey of Public Participation in the Arts* remains the largest periodic study of arts participation in the United States. The most recent data are from the 2012 survey. Data on participation in fishing, hunting, and other forms of wildlife associated recreation are published periodically by the U.S. Department of Interior, Fish and Wildlife Service. The most recent data are from the 2011 survey. Data on participation in various sports recreation activities are published by the National Sporting Goods Association. GfK Mediamark Research and Intelligence, LLC also conducts periodic surveys on sports and leisure activities, as well as other topics.

Parks and recreation—The Department of the Interior has responsibility for administering the national parks. The National Park Service publishes information on visits to national park areas in its annual report, *National Park Statistical Abstract*. Additional data regarding acreage and visits for each area administered by the service, plus certain "related" areas can be found at <https://irma.nps.gov/Stats/>. Statistics for state parks are compiled by the National Association of State Park Directors in its annual *Statistical Report of State Park Operations*.

Travel—Statistics on arrivals and departures to the United States, cities and states visited by overseas travelers, and tourism sales and employment are reported by the International Trade Administration (ITA), Office of Travel & Tourism Industries (OTTI). Data on domestic travel and travel expenditures are published by the research department of the U.S. Travel Association. Other data on household transportation characteristics are in Section 23, Transportation.

Statistical reliability—For a discussion of statistical collection and estimation, sampling procedures, and measures of statistical reliability applicable to Census Bureau data, see Appendix III.

Table 1246. Arts, Entertainment, and Recreation Services—Estimated Revenue: 2010 to 2015

[In millions of dollars (188,117 represents $188,117,000,000). For taxable and tax-exempt employer firms. Data are based on the 2007 North American Industry Classification System (NAICS). Selected estimates have been adjusted using the results of the 2012 Economic Census. Based on the Service Annual Survey, see Appendix III]

Industry	2007 NAICS Code	2010	2011	2012	2013	2014	2015
Arts, entertainment, and recreation............	71	188,117	193,592	201,192	211,292	223,154	237,482
Performing arts, spectator sports, and related industries......................................	711	80,461	83,260	86,421	90,200	96,483	104,698
Performing arts companies..........................	7111	13,814	14,426	13,857	13,769	14,332	15,263
Spectator sports..	7112	31,737	32,940	33,298	34,977	37,264	40,095
Sports teams and clubs............................	711211	21,442	22,333	22,672	24,145	26,668	28,979
Racetracks..	711212	6,951	7,163	7,434	7,421	7,238	7,596
Other spectator sports............................	711219	3,344	3,444	3,192	3,411	3,358	3,520
Promoters of performing arts, sports, and similar events...	7113	16,312	16,643	18,474	19,916	22,020	24,538
Agents and managers for artists, athletes, entertainers and other public figures..............	7114	5,358	5,690	5,832	6,208	6,674	7,322
Independent artists, writers, and performers.......	7115	13,240	13,561	14,960	15,330	16,193	17,480
Museums, historical sites, and similar institutions. ..	712	14,241	12,279	13,725	15,080	15,900	15,168
Amusement, gambling, and recreation industries. ..	713	93,415	98,053	101,046	106,012	110,771	117,616
Amusement parks and arcades......................	7131	11,832	14,058	14,302	15,168	16,374	18,075
Amusement and theme parks......................	71311	10,205	12,400	12,597	13,524	14,694	16,252
Amusement arcades................................	71312	1,627	1,658	1,705	1,644	1,680	1,823
Gambling industries....................................	7132	23,432	24,202	24,385	25,698	26,607	27,923
Casinos (except casino hotels).....................	71321	15,367	15,722	15,688	16,617	17,094	18,323
Other gambling industries..........................	71329	8,065	8,480	8,697	9,081	9,513	9,600
Other amusement and recreation industries........	7139	58,151	59,793	62,359	65,146	67,790	71,618
Golf courses and country clubs....................	71391	19,788	19,832	20,812	20,918	21,224	21,821
Skiing facilities.......................................	71392	2,265	2,259	2,215	2,433	2,530	2,571
Marinas..	71393	3,604	3,742	3,891	3,999	4,203	4,291
Fitness and recreational sports centers............	71394	22,311	23,191	24,051	25,649	26,673	28,319
Bowling centers......................................	71395	3,007	3,072	3,083	3,224	3,403	3,629
All other amusement and recreation industries. ..	71399	7,176	7,697	8,307	8,923	9,757	10,987

Source: U.S. Census Bureau, Annual & Quarterly Services, "2015 Service Annual Survey," <http://www.census.gov/services.index.html>, accessed January 2017.

Table 1247. Arts, Entertainment, and Recreation—Establishments, Revenue, Payroll, and Employees by Kind of Business: 2007 and 2012

[189,417 represents $189,417,000,000. For establishments with payroll only. Definition of paid employees varies among NAICS sectors. Data are based on the 2007 and 2012 Economic Censuses which are subject to nonsampling error. For details on survey methodology, sampling and nonsampling errors, see Appendix III]

Kind of business	2007 NAICS code [1]	Number of establishments		Revenue (mil. dol.)		Annual payroll (mil. dol.)		Paid employees (1,000)	
		2007	2012	2007	2012	2007	2012	2007	2012
Arts, entertainment, and recreation, total..	71	124,620	124,591	189,417	201,193	58,359	64,052	2,061	2,082
Performing arts, spectator sports, and related industries [2]............................	711	43,868	45,612	77,773	86,421	27,839	31,545	438	434
Performing arts companies..........................	7111	8,838	8,508	13,574	13,857	3,980	3,950	128	119
Spectator sports..	7112	4,237	4,164	30,403	33,298	14,136	16,653	121	118
Promoters of performing arts, sports and similar events...	7113	6,647	6,846	16,122	18,474	2,957	3,211	121	137
Agents and managers for artists, athletes, entertainers and other public figures.............	7114	3,534	3,716	4,919	5,832	1,694	1,886	19	18
Museums, historical sites, and similar institutions [2]...	712	7,125	7,319	13,285	13,726	3,662	4,197	130	135
Amusement, gambling, and recreation industries [2].......................................	713	73,627	71,660	98,359	101,046	26,859	28,310	1,494	1,513
Amusement parks and arcades..................	7131	3,145	3,299	13,544	14,302	2,802	3,386	134	155
Gambling industries...............................	7132	2,327	2,886	25,135	24,385	4,566	4,272	170	149
Other amusement and recreation services......................................	7139	68,155	65,475	59,680	62,359	19,490	20,652	1,190	1,208

[1] Based on 2007 North American Industry Classification System (NAICS); see text, this section and section 15. [2] Includes other industries not shown separately.

Source: U.S. Census Bureau, 2012 Economic Census, EC1271A2, "Arts, Entertainment, and Recreation: Geographic Area Series: Comparative Statistics for the U.S. (2007 NAICS Basis): 2012 and 2007," <http://factfinder.census.gov/>, accessed September 2016.

Table 1248. Arts, Entertainment, and Recreation—Nonemployer Establishments and Receipts by Kind of Business (NAICS Basis): 2010 to 2015

[Firms in thousands (1,154.0 represents 1,154,000); receipts in millions of dollars (26,756 represents $26,756,000,000). Includes only firms subject to federal income tax. Nonemployers are businesses with no paid employees but with annual receipts of $1,000 or more]

Kind of business	NAICS code [1]	Firms (1,000)			Receipts (mil. dol.)		
		2010	2014	2015	2010	2014	2015
Arts, entertainment, and recreation..........	**71**	**1,154.0**	**1,311.4**	**1,341.7**	**26,756**	**33,308**	**34,549**
Performing arts, spectator sports, and related industries............	711	1,004.9	1,148.6	1,177.3	21,053	26,605	27,590
Performing arts companies........................	7111	61.2	87.6	93.8	1,249	1,713	1,832
Spectator sports................................	7112	151.9	167.5	169.8	2,515	3,110	3,242
Promoters of performing arts, sports, and similar events..........	7113	45.0	55.2	55.9	1,699	2,349	2,467
Agents/managers for artists, athletes, and other public figures....	7114	36.3	39.6	38.5	1,300	1,652	1,678
Independent artists, writers, and performers.....................	7115	710.3	798.7	819.2	14,290	17,781	18,371
Museums, historical sites, and similar institutions..................	712	5.8	6.3	6.5	95	116	122
Amusement, gambling, and recreation industries..................	713	143.4	156.5	158.0	5,607	6,587	6,837
Amusement parks and arcades.......................	7131	4.7	4.4	4.3	251	238	248
Gambling industries.................................	7132	10.2	10.4	10.5	1,185	1,297	1,325
Other amusement and recreation services.........................	7139	128.5	141.7	143.2	4,171	5,052	5,265

[1] Data for 2010 are based on 2007 North American Industry Classification System; beginning in 2012, data based on 2012 NAICS. see text, Section 15.

Source: U.S. Census Bureau, Nonemployer Statistics, "Geographic Area Series: Nonemployer Statistics for the U.S., States, Metropolitan Areas, and Counties," <http://factfinder.census.gov>, accessed June 2017. See also <http://www.census.gov/econ/nonemployer/>.

Table 1249. Arts, Entertainment, and Recreation—Establishments, Employees, and Payroll by Kind of Business (NAICS Basis): 2014 and 2015

[Employees in thousands (2,170.1 represents 2,170,100); payroll in millions of dollars (72,218 represents $72,218,000,000). Covers establishments with paid employees. Excludes self-employed individuals, employees of private households, railroad employees, agricultural production employees, and most government employees. For statement on methodology, see Appendix III]

Kind of business	2012 NAICS code [1]	Establishments		Employees [2] (1,000)		Payroll (mil. dol.)	
		2014	2015	2014	2015	2014	2015
Arts, entertainment, & recreation..................	**71**	**129,839**	**133,610**	**2,170.1**	**2,230.8**	**72,218**	**76,799**
Performing arts, spectator sports......................	711	48,273	50,239	474.3	483.3	35,605	38,070
Performing arts companies...........................	7111	8,690	8,908	121.8	124.1	4,376	4,607
Theater companies & dinner theaters..............	71111	3,347	3,355	68.6	69.1	2,177	2,258
Dance companies..................................	71112	590	668	9.4	9.9	261	278
Musical groups & artists..........................	71113	4,405	4,522	37.9	38.5	1,708	1,819
Other performing arts companies..................	71119	348	363	5.9	6.6	230	252
Spectator sports.....................................	7112	4,237	4,315	127.8	128.3	18,233	19,491
Sports teams & clubs.............................	711211	961	1,004	66.1	68.9	15,949	17,182
Racetracks..	711212	631	639	45.1	42.7	1,383	1,390
Other spectator sports............................	711219	2,645	2,672	16.6	16.7	901	919
Promoters of performing arts, sports, & similar events..	7113	7,329	7,600	158.4	163.9	4,024	4,410
Promoters of performing arts, sports, & similar events with facilities......................	71131	3,050	3,228	129.7	133.7	2,580	2,849
Promoters of performing arts, sports, & similar events without facilities...................	71132	4,279	4,372	28.7	30.2	1,444	1,561
Agents/managers for artists, athletes, and other public figures.....................................	7114	3,883	4,211	20.1	20.2	2,189	2,451
Independent artists, writers, & performers............	7115	24,134	25,205	46.1	46.8	6,784	7,111
Museums, historical sites, & similar institutions.......	712	7,498	7,594	143.3	146.0	4,569	4,835
Museums...	71211	5,051	5,125	92.0	93.3	2,978	3,141
Historical sites....................................	71212	1,142	1,139	10.2	10.5	266	280
Zoos & botanical gardens.........................	71213	625	632	34.4	35.2	1,088	1,164
Nature parks & other similar institutions.............	71219	680	698	6.7	7.1	236	250
Amusement, gambling, & recreation industries.......	713	74,068	75,777	1,552.6	1,601.5	32,045	33,895
Amusement parks & arcades........................	7131	3,194	3,280	182.3	196.9	4,177	4,513
Amusement & theme parks........................	71311	486	523	143.9	155.9	3,687	3,965
Amusement arcades..............................	71312	2,708	2,757	38.4	41.0	489	548
Gambling industries.................................	7132	2,866	2,828	153.4	152.9	4,995	5,208
Casinos (except casino hotels)....................	71321	319	338	100.0	99.0	3,257	3,407
Other gambling industries.........................	71329	2,547	2,490	53.5	53.9	1,738	1,801
Other amusement & recreation services.............	7139	68,008	69,669	1,216.9	1,251.7	22,873	24,174
Golf courses & country clubs......................	71391	11,407	11,280	293.9	295.2	8,626	8,958
Skiing facilities...................................	71392	385	373	75.0	73.2	797	821
Marinas...	71393	3,811	3,881	26.7	27.0	995	1,036
Fitness & recreational sports centers...............	71394	31,715	32,712	637.2	658.8	8,963	9,493
Bowling centers...................................	71395	3,870	3,820	69.1	69.2	976	1,026
All other amusement & recreation industries.......	71399	16,820	17,603	115.0	128.2	2,516	2,840

[1] Data based on 2012 North American Industry Classification System (NAICS) see text, this section and Section 15. [2] For employees on the payroll for the period including March 12.

Source: U.S. Census Bureau, County Business Patterns, "Geography Area Series: County Business Patterns," <http://factfinder.census.gov/>, accessed April 2017. See also <https://www.census.gov/programs-surveys/cbp.html>.

Table 1250. Expenditures Per Consumer Unit for Entertainment and Reading: 1985 to 2015

[Data are annual averages. In dollars, except as indicated. Based on the Consumer Expenditure Survey (CES). For description of survey, see text, Section 13; also see headnote, Table 709. For composition of regions, see map, inside front cover]

Year and characteristic	Entertainment and reading		Entertainment				Reading
	Total	Percent of total expenditures	Total	Fees and admissions	Audio and visual equipment and services	Other supplies, equipment & services [1]	
1985	1,311	5.6	1,170	320	371	479	141
1990	1,575	5.6	1,422	371	454	597	153
1995	1,775	5.5	1,612	433	542	637	163
1998	1,907	5.4	1,746	449	535	762	161
1999	2,050	5.5	1,891	459	608	824	159
2000	2,009	5.3	1,863	515	622	727	146
2001	2,094	5.3	1,953	526	660	767	141
2002	2,218	5.5	2,079	542	692	845	139
2003	2,187	5.4	2,060	494	730	835	127
2004	2,348	5.4	2,218	528	788	903	130
2005	2,514	5.4	2,388	588	888	912	126
2006	2,493	5.2	2,376	606	906	863	117
2007	2,816	5.7	2,698	658	987	1,053	118
2008	2,951	5.8	2,835	616	1,036	1,183	116
2009	2,803	5.7	2,693	628	975	1,090	110
2010	2,604	5.4	2,504	581	954	970	100
2011	2,687	5.4	2,572	594	977	1,001	115
2012	2,714	5.3	2,605	614	979	1,011	109
2013	2,584	5.1	2,482	569	964	949	102
2014	2,831	5.3	2,728	636	1,051	1,041	103
2015, total	**2,956**	**5.3**	**2,842**	**652**	**1,084**	**1,106**	**114**
Age of reference person:							
Under 25 years old	1,392	4.2	1,354	241	667	446	38
25 to 34 years old	2,561	4.9	2,475	545	983	947	86
35 to 44 years old	3,287	5.0	3,192	957	1,195	1,039	95
45 to 54 years old	3,423	4.9	3,317	879	1,239	1,201	106
55 to 64 years old	3,438	5.8	3,323	557	1,135	1,631	115
65 years old and older	2,639	5.9	2,464	510	1,011	943	175
65 to 74 years old	3,162	6.4	3,005	603	1,083	1,319	157
75 years old and over	1,927	5.1	1,728	382	912	435	199
Hispanic or Latino origin of reference person:							
Hispanic	1,819	3.8	1,771	386	895	490	48
Non-Hispanic	3,126	5.5	3,002	692	1,112	1,198	124
Race of reference person:							
White, and all other races [2]	3,200	5.5	3,075	708	1,108	1,259	125
Asian	2,468	3.9	2,371	910	853	608	97
Black	1,548	3.8	1,500	207	1,003	290	48
Region of residence:							
Northeast	2,884	4.9	2,754	742	1,124	888	130
Midwest	2,976	5.4	2,859	619	1,075	1,165	117
South	2,771	5.3	2,682	513	1,083	1,086	89
West	3,319	5.4	3,177	852	1,059	1,265	142
Size of consumer unit:							
One person	1,791	5.3	1,711	309	779	624	80
Two or more persons	3,435	5.3	3,307	794	1,209	1,305	128
Two persons	3,463	5.9	3,312	692	1,146	1,475	151
Three persons	3,320	4.9	3,219	714	1,242	1,262	101
Four persons	3,592	4.8	3,468	1,095	1,283	1,089	124
Five persons or more	3,323	4.7	3,229	877	1,283	1,068	94
Income before taxes:							
Quintiles of income:							
Lowest 20 percent	1,307	5.3	1,270	143	667	461	37
Second 20 percent	1,820	5.2	1,738	282	897	559	82
Third 20 percent	2,326	5.1	2,219	363	1,033	823	107
Fourth 20 percent	3,185	5.0	3,051	685	1,199	1,167	134
Highest 20 percent	6,129	5.5	5,919	1,782	1,619	2,517	210
Education:							
Less than a high school graduate	1,142	4.3	1,103	75	681	348	39
High school graduate	1,790	4.9	1,725	172	877	676	65
High school graduate with some college	2,442	5.3	2,359	347	1,068	944	83
Associate's degree	3,101	5.8	3,017	555	1,143	1,319	84
Bachelor's degree	3,541	5.1	3,398	982	1,209	1,208	143
Master's, professional, or doctoral degree	4,847	5.5	4,628	1,479	1,310	1,839	219

[1] Other entertainment supplies, equipment, and services include pets, toys, hobbies, and playground equipment; and other entertainment supplies, equipment, and services. [2] All other races includes Native Hawaiian or other Pacific Islander, American Indian or Alaska Native, and approximately 1 percent reporting more than one race.

Source: U.S. Bureau of Labor Statistics, Consumer Expenditure Survey, "Consumer Expenditures in 2015," <http://www.bls.gov/cex/home.htm#tables>, accessed February 2017.

Table 1251. Arts and Culture Production—Real Value Added In Chained (2009) Dollars and Employment by Industry: 2009 to 2014

[In millions of dollars (617,487 represents $617,487,000,000); employment in thousands (4,813 represents 4,813,000)]

Industry	2009	2010	2011	2012	2013	2014
REAL VALUE ADDED CHAINED (2009) DOLLARS						
Total	**617,487**	**650,432**	**649,040**	**657,402**	**673,431**	**686,243**
Core arts and cultural production	**115,844**	**119,946**	**123,165**	**125,603**	**127,345**	**131,478**
Performing arts	39,618	41,694	42,053	42,823	44,027	45,529
Performing arts companies	12,540	16,654	16,678	15,599	15,602	15,895
Promoters of performing arts and similar events	7,823	5,973	6,139	6,961	7,860	8,228
Agents/managers for artists	1,932	1,747	2,028	1,976	2,047	2,215
Independent artists, writers, and performers	17,323	17,367	17,259	18,314	18,548	19,210
Museums	4,929	4,068	4,046	4,522	4,765	4,799
Design services [1]	64,184	67,004	69,845	71,403	71,793	74,192
Advertising	23,221	24,822	25,749	28,914	28,817	28,965
Architectural services	15,047	14,472	14,961	13,974	13,949	15,013
Landscape architectural services	2,668	2,619	2,579	2,411	2,570	2,715
Interior design services	6,048	6,807	7,215	6,475	6,568	7,191
Industrial design services	1,109	1,325	1,611	1,429	1,438	1,614
Graphic design services	6,006	7,148	7,484	6,602	6,610	6,903
Computer systems design	1,965	2,180	2,436	2,831	2,889	3,205
Photography and photofinishing services	7,655	7,112	7,198	8,141	8,341	7,981
Fine arts education	2,735	2,942	2,900	2,516	2,534	2,654
Education services	4,378	4,232	4,325	4,408	4,301	4,378
Supporting arts and cultural production	**478,249**	**508,918**	**504,611**	**507,862**	**523,298**	**531,656**
Art support services [1]	98,870	96,119	94,172	93,668	93,414	93,941
Rental and leasing	6,759	5,396	4,588	5,480	5,265	5,501
Grant-making and giving services	513	494	481	484	519	513
Unions	1,067	1,017	1,063	1,154	1,130	1,153
Government	90,160	88,786	87,566	86,099	86,034	86,300
Information services [1]	288,157	314,128	313,951	320,985	336,995	344,481
Publishing	72,374	75,605	76,700	78,373	78,762	79,922
Motion pictures	77,011	92,036	90,741	92,583	95,414	95,252
Sound recording	13,047	14,475	14,038	16,095	15,878	16,078
Broadcasting	103,444	107,264	105,785	107,938	114,281	116,388
Manufacturing [1]	16,892	17,291	16,721	14,809	13,578	13,982
Jewelry and silverware manufacturing	3,277	3,297	2,618	2,095	1,369	1,569
Printed goods manufacturing	8,725	8,661	8,818	8,386	8,296	8,259
Musical instruments manufacturing	772	980	944	786	754	739
Custom architectural woodwork and metalwork manufacturing	2,010	2,057	1,999	1,893	1,864	1,888
Camera and motion picture equipment manufacturing	276	326	443	14	12	13
Construction	11,519	16,747	13,328	9,540	8,530	8,323
Wholesale and transportation industries	22,529	24,455	25,571	27,019	27,827	27,307
Retail industries	40,281	40,398	40,963	41,857	43,312	44,153
All other industries	**23,394**	**21,572**	**21,294**	**23,910**	**22,789**	**23,126**
EMPLOYMENT						
Total	**4,813**	**4,676**	**4,655**	**4,682**	**4,743**	**4,803**
Core arts and cultural production	**974**	**930**	**944**	**961**	**986**	**1,024**
Performing arts	235	229	234	236	247	260
Performing arts companies	103	101	101	101	102	104
Promoters of performing arts and similar events	76	73	76	77	84	92
Agents/managers for artists	21	21	21	22	23	24
Independent artists, writers, and performers	35	35	36	37	38	39
Museums	117	116	118	121	126	130
Design services [1]	492	457	460	466	472	489
Advertising	129	124	129	135	138	146
Architectural services	118	104	102	103	105	110
Landscape architectural services	25	22	21	22	22	23
Interior design services	21	18	19	19	20	22
Industrial design services	24	24	25	25	28	28
Graphic design services	65	61	62	61	62	63
Computer systems design	16	16	17	18	19	20
Photography and photofinishing services	93	85	83	81	76	74
Fine arts education	37	39	41	43	47	50
Education services	93	90	91	94	95	96
Supporting arts and cultural production	**3,633**	**3,561**	**3,528**	**3,515**	**3,559**	**3,579**
Art support services [1]	1,273	1,229	1,204	1,178	1,189	1,194
Rental and leasing	68	54	45	42	40	38
Grant-making and giving services	5	4	5	6	6	6
Unions	19	17	19	20	23	22
Government	1,178	1,150	1,132	1,108	1,117	1,124
Information services [1]	1,172	1,156	1,150	1,166	1,177	1,178
Publishing	367	348	343	341	334	327
Motion pictures	348	357	358	365	372	374
Sound recording	14	13	13	13	13	13
Broadcasting	405	397	393	400	409	410
Manufacturing [1]	205	191	187	176	175	175
Jewelry and silverware manufacturing	28	27	27	26	26	26
Printed goods manufacturing	116	106	103	95	93	92
Musical instruments manufacturing	8	8	8	8	8	8
Custom architectural woodwork and metalwork manufacturing	31	29	30	30	30	30
Camera and motion picture equipment manufacturing	2	2	2	–	–	–
Construction	103	124	104	89	95	100
Wholesale and transportation industries	172	176	183	193	196	191
Retail industries	708	686	700	711	727	741
All other industries	**206**	**185**	**183**	**205**	**197**	**200**

– Represents zero. [1] Includes other services or goods manufacturing, not shown separately.

Source: U.S. Bureau of Economic Analysis, Satellite Accounts, Arts and Cultural Production, <https://www.bea.gov/industry/index.htm#satellite>, accessed April 2017.

Table 1252. Personal Consumption Expenditures for Recreation: 1990 to 2016

[In billions of dollars (314.7 represents $314,700,000,000), except percent. Represents market value of purchases of goods and services by individuals and nonprofit institutions]

Type of product or service	1990	2000	2005	2010	2014	2015	2016
Total recreation expenditures	**314.7**	**633.7**	**804.6**	**888.3**	**1,041.9**	**1,085.9**	**1,137.6**
Percent of total personal consumption [1]	8.2	9.3	9.1	8.7	8.8	8.8	8.9
Video and audio equipment, computers, and related services	81.1	181.2	239.0	276.4	308.2	313.5	319.9
Video and audio equipment	43.7	79.9	101.4	99.5	102.8	103.0	103.3
Information processing equipment	9.6	44.1	67.0	90.3	105.8	110.8	116.3
Services related to video and audio goods and computers	27.8	57.2	70.6	86.6	99.6	99.7	100.3
Sports and recreational goods and related services	74.2	146.0	184.1	174.2	213.3	226.5	236.6
Sports and recreational vehicles	16.6	34.9	49.1	35.6	47.3	51.1	52.8
Other sporting and recreational goods	55.4	106.8	130.0	134.2	161.0	170.2	178.1
Maintenance and repair of recreational vehicles and sports equipment	2.1	4.2	4.9	4.4	5.1	5.2	5.7
Membership clubs, sports centers, parks, theaters, and museums	49.7	91.9	117.9	141.8	168.9	180.2	192.2
Membership clubs and participant sports centers	14.3	26.4	34.3	39.5	45.7	47.9	50.5
Amusements parks, campgrounds, and related recreational services	19.2	31.1	33.6	38.8	50.1	54.7	59.3
Admissions to specified spectator amusements	14.4	30.6	43.7	57.3	65.8	70.3	75.0
Motion picture theaters	5.1	8.6	9.7	11.8	13.0	13.7	14.4
Live entertainment, excluding sports	4.5	10.4	18.3	26.3	30.0	32.4	34.6
Spectator sports	4.8	11.6	15.7	19.2	22.8	24.2	26.0
Museums and libraries	1.9	3.8	6.4	6.1	7.2	7.3	7.3
Magazines, newspapers, books, and stationery	47.3	81.0	85.0	89.9	108.8	113.2	123.8
Gambling	23.7	67.6	96.5	105.6	121.1	124.4	128.6
Pets, pet products, and related services	18.8	39.7	57.2	75.9	93.4	98.9	106.7
Photographic goods and services	16.7	19.7	17.7	15.4	17.6	18.2	18.2
Package tours [2]	3.2	6.7	7.2	9.1	10.6	11.1	11.6

[1] See Table 700. [2] Consists of tour operators' and travel agents' margins. Purchases of travel and accommodations included in tours are accounted for separately in other personal consumption expenditures categories.

Source: U.S. Bureau of Economic Analysis, National Income and Product Accounts Tables, "Table 2.5.5. Personal Consumption Expenditures by Function," <http://www.bea.gov/iTable/index_nipa.cfm>, accessed August 2017.

Table 1253. Performing Arts—Selected Data: 1990 to 2017

[In units, as indicated (282 represents $282,000,000). For season ending in year shown, except as indicated]

Item	Unit	1990	1995	2000	2005	2010	2013	2014	2015	2016	2017
Legitimate theater: [1]											
Broadway shows:											
New productions	Number	39	34	36	39	39	46	44	37	39	45
Attendance	Millions	8.0	9.0	11.4	11.5	11.9	11.6	12.2	13.1	13.3	13.3
Playing weeks [2,3]	Number	1,070	1,120	1,464	1,494	1,464	1,430	1,496	1,626	1,648	1,580
Gross ticket sales	Mil. dol.	282	406	603	769	1,020	1,139	1,269	1,365	1,373	1,449
Broadway road tours: [4]	Number										
Attendance	Millions	11.1	9.9	11.4	12.9	15.9	13.8	13.9	13.7	14.0	13.9
Playing weeks	Number	944	882	854	1,027	1,250	983	994	953	1,014	983
Gross ticket sales	Mil. dol.	367	547	553	706	947	877	933	957	981	1,007
Nonprofit professional theatres: [5]											
Companies reporting [6]	Number	185	215	262	1,490	1,807	1,773	1,770	(NA)	(NA)	(NA)
Gross income	Mil. dol.	308	444	791	1,647	1,913	2,127	2,240	(NA)	(NA)	(NA)
Earned income	Mil. dol.	188	281	466	845	964	1,136	1,190	(NA)	(NA)	(NA)
Contributed income	Mil. dol.	119	163	325	802	948	991	1,050	(NA)	(NA)	(NA)
Gross expenses	Mil. dol.	306	445	708	1,530	1,870	2,051	2,150	(NA)	(NA)	(NA)
Productions	Number	2,265	2,646	3,241	12,000	16,000	21,600	22,000	(NA)	(NA)	(NA)
Performances	Number	46,131	56,608	66,123	169,000	163,000	215,800	216,000	(NA)	(NA)	(NA)
Total attendance	Millions	15.2	18.6	22.0	32.5	31.0	34.9	32.8	(NA)	(NA)	(NA)

NA Not available [1] Source: The Broadway League, New York, NY ©. For season ending in year shown. [2] All shows (new productions and holdovers from previous seasons). [3] Eight performances constitute one playing week. [4] North American Tours include U.S. and Canadian companies. [5] Source: Theatre Communications Group, New York, NY ©. For years ending on or prior to August 31. Beginning in 2007, for fiscal years ending on or prior to Sept. 30. [6] Beginning in 2002, nonprofit theatre data is based on survey responses and extrapolated data from IRS Form 990.

Source: Compiled from sources listed in footnotes. See also <http://www.livebroadway.com/> and <http://www.tcg.org/>.

Table 1254. Arts and Humanities—Selected Federal Aid Programs: 1990 to 2016

[In millions of dollars (170.8 represents $170,800,000), except as indicated. For fiscal year ending September 30. FY2010 include funds from the American Recovery and Reinvestment Act]

Type of fund and program	1990	1995	2000	2005	2010	2013	2014	2015	2016
National Endowment for the Arts:									
Funds available [1]	170.8	152.1	85.2	108.8	153.1	119.6	124.7	127.1	132.7
Program appropriation [2]	152.3	138.1	79.6	99.5	138.7	109.1	116.3	116.6	118.4
Grants awarded (number) [3]	4,252	3,534	1,906	2,161	2,731	2,152	2,261	2,346	2,446
Funds obligated [4, 5]	157.6	147.9	83.5	104.4	141.1	113.9	117.1	118.4	124.4
National Endowment for the Humanities:									
Funds available [1]	140.6	152.3	102.6	119.8	146.6	146.1	124.8	129.8	130.1
Program appropriation	114.2	125.7	82.7	99.9	125.7	102.2	107.9	108.1	109.8
Matching funds [6]	26.3	25.7	15.1	15.9	14.3	10.2	10.7	10.9	10.9
Grants awarded (number) [3]	2,195	1,871	1,230	1,174	1,204	854	762	822	920
Funds obligated [4, 5]	141.0	151.8	100.0	117.8	142.7	113.9	117.5	121.5	121.9
Education programs	16.3	19.2	13.0	14.6	16.0	13.8	13.3	13.8	13.5
State partnership	29.6	32.0	30.6	36.9	49.1	39.1	43.6	42.6	43.9
Research grants	22.5	22.2	6.9	7.1	12.5	10.1	10.8	10.1	10.1
Fellowships	15.3	16.5	6.1	8.9	6.8	5.0	4.4	7.0	5.8
Challenge [7]	14.6	13.8	10.8	12.7	10.5	8.5	9.1	7.8	8.8
Public programs	25.4	25.8	11.8	14.4	19.4	14.3	13.7	17.6	13.9
Digital Humanities	(NA)	(NA)	(NA)	(NA)	4.9	4.2	4.7	4.7	4.7
Preservation and access	17.5	22.2	20.7	22.4	22.6	17.4	17.1	17.1	15.7

NA Not available. [1] Includes other program funds not shown separately. Excludes administrative funds. [2] FY1990–FY1996 include Regular Program Funds, Treasury Funds, Challenge Grant Funds, and Policy, Planning, and Research Funds. FY1997 includes Regular Program Funds, Matching Grant Funds, and Policy, Research and Technology Funds. FY1998–FY 2000 includes Regular Program Funds and Matching Grant Funds. [3] Excludes cooperative agreements and interagency agreements. [4] Includes obligations for new grants, supplemental awards on previous years' grants, cooperative agreements, and interagency agreements. Excludes obligations funded with administrative funds. [5] Beginning with 1997 data, the grantmaking structure changed from discipline-based categories to thematic ones. [6] Represents federal funds obligated only upon receipt or certification by endowment of matching nonfederal gifts. Funds for matching grants are not allocated by program area because they are awarded on a grant-by-grant basis. [7] Program designed to stimulate new sources and higher levels of giving to institutions for the purpose of guaranteeing long-term stability and financial independence. Program usually requires a match of at least 3 private dollars to each federal dollar.

Source: U.S. National Endowment for the Arts, unpublished data; and U.S. National Endowment for the Humanities, unpublished data.

Table 1255. State Arts Agency Legislative Appropriations: 2016 to 2017

[In thousands of dollars (340,911 represents 340,911,000). For fiscal year ending June 30 in most states. The National Assembly of State Arts Agencies (NASAA) is the membership organization of the nations' state and jurisdictional arts agencies. Legislative appropriations include funds designated to the state arts agency by state legislatures. These include line items, which are not controlled by the agency but passed through to designated entities. State arts agencies also receive monies from other sources including other state funds, the federal government (primarily the National Endowment for the Arts), private funds, and legislative earmarks. Minus sign (-) indicates decrease in spending]

State	Legislative appropriations including line items 2016, revised	Legislative appropriations including line items 2017, enacted	Percent change, 2016 to 2017	State	Legislative appropriations including line items 2016, revised	Legislative appropriations including line items 2017, enacted	Percent change, 2016 to 2017	State	Legislative appropriations including line items 2016, revised	Legislative appropriations including line items 2017, enacted	Percent change, 2016 to 2017
U.S.	**340,911**	**368,223**	**8.0**	KY	2,670	2,626	-1.7	OK	3,511	2,938	-16.3
				LA	1,967	2,097	6.6	OR	2,052	2,101	2.4
AL	4,184	4,734	13.1	ME	975	894	-8.2	PA	9,590	9,590	–
AK	730	696	-4.6	MD	17,552	20,367	16.0	RI	2,750	2,255	-18.0
AZ [1]	–	1,500	(NA)	MA	14,160	14,299	1.0	SC	3,094	3,508	13.4
AR [2]	1,680	1,665	-0.9	MI	9,000	9,000	–	SD	836	846	1.1
CA [2]	10,759	17,637	63.9	MN	34,341	38,842	13.1	TN	6,999	7,060	0.9
CO	2,000	2,000	–	MS	1,986	1,743	-12.3	TX	7,771	8,360	7.6
CT [3]	5,723	4,238	-26.0	MO	7,297	7,373	1.0	UT [7]	3,040	3,218	5.8
DE	3,318	3,407	2.7	MT	571	512	-10.4	VT	645	675	4.6
DC	16,955	22,044	30.0	NE	1,507	1,561	3.6	VA	3,637	3,449	-5.2
FL	38,873	43,655	12.3	NV [6]	1,599	1,954	22.2	WA	1,143	1,166	2.0
GA	903	1,016	12.5	NH	291	310	6.4	WV	872	865	-0.9
HI	5,575	5,732	2.8	NJ	16,396	16,405	0.1	WI [8]	796	812	2.0
ID	759	783	3.1	NM	1,608	1,315	-18.2	WY	1,223	1,039	-15.0
IL [4]	(NA)	(NA)	(NA)	NY	45,174	45,174	–	GU [9]	451	451	–
IN	3,323	3,323	–	NC	7,649	8,399	9.8	MP [9]	216	550	155.1
IA [5]	1,234	1,234	–	ND	837	798	-4.6	PR [9, 10]	15,872	16,707	5.3
KS	190	189	-0.8	OH	14,222	14,722	3.5	VI [9]	329	315	-4.0

– Represents zero. NA Not available. [1] Since FY2012, the legislature has not appropriated funding to the state arts agency from the general fund. The state arts agency's FY2017 base appropriations were drawn from interest on the state's rainy-day fund and were nonrecurring. Other state funds are generated from state business license revenues. [2] One-time discretionary funds designated by the state legislature account for $6.8 million of the FY2017 appropriation. Other state funding includes support for the Arts in Corrections program. [3] The total appropriation for FY2017 does not include funding going through the agency's budget for line items to non-arts organizations. [4] The state of Illinois has operated without a full and permanent budget since July 1, 2015. [5] The Iowa Department of Cultural Affairs has sustained a mid-year de-appropriation for FY2017 of $210,958 as well as the complete elimination of the $6.1 million Iowa Cultural Trust as a result of efforts by the Iowa Legislature and Governor to address a projected state budget shortfall. The immediate impact on the Iowa Arts Council operating budget of approximately $41,000 is not captured in this report. [6] Fiscal year 2017 appropriations include nonrecurring funds from the Department of Tourism and Cultural Affairs of $267,254. [7] The agency's appropriation does not include state support for the Fine Arts Outreach POPS program and the Beverley Taylor Sorenson Arts Learning Program, which are administered by agencies other than the state arts agency. [8] State funds listed in FY2017 assume match to the NEA. The state arts agency must obtain legislative action and the governor's signature for an additional $29,700, which is the difference between NEA funds and the amount allocated in the state's biennial budget. [9] GU—Guam, MP—Northern Marianas, PR—Puerto Rico, VI—Virgin Islands. [10] Fiscal year 2017 figures were taken from the appropriated budget documented by Puerto Rico's Office of Management and Budget. The commonwealth's budget remains in distress due to uncertainty about long-term debt.

Source: National Assembly of State Arts Agencies, *State Arts Agency Revenues, Fiscal Year 2017* ©, February 2017. See also <http://www.nasaa-arts.org>.

Table 1256. Personal Participation in Various Arts or Creative Activities by Selected Characteristics: 2012

[In percent, except as indicated (235.0 represents 235,000,000). For persons 18 years old and over. Represents creating or performing at least once in the prior 12 months]

Item	Adult population (millions)	Music	Dance	Films/ videos	Photos	Visual Arts	Pottery/ jewelry	Weaving/ sewing [1]	Creative writing
Total................	235.0	5.0	1.3	2.8	12.4	5.7	4.5	13.2	5.9
Sex:									
Male..................	113.1	5.6	0.9	3.6	11.5	4.7	2.1	2.4	5.6
Female................	121.9	4.5	1.6	2.1	13.2	6.7	6.8	23.2	6.2
Race and ethnicity:									
White alone............	155.7	5.3	1.1	2.9	14.3	6.4	5.1	14.8	6.7
African American alone......	26.8	4.3	1.7	3.0	8.0	3.4	4.2	9.5	4.3
Hispanic................	35.0	4.1	1.5	2.2	7.9	3.7	2.5	9.4	4.1
Other alone.............	17.5	5.5	1.2	3.2	10.9	6.9	4.5	11.9	5.2
Age:									
18 to 24 years old...........	30.4	8.6	2.7	4.5	13.4	9.3	7.1	9.8	10.2
25 to 34 years old...........	41.0	5.0	1.0	3.6	15.4	6.0	4.2	10.6	6.4
35 to 44 years old...........	39.6	4.2	1.4	4.2	14.0	5.6	4.4	10.8	6.4
45 to 54 years old...........	43.7	5.3	1.0	2.5	12.4	5.0	4.6	13.5	4.3
55 to 64 years old...........	38.3	4.4	0.9	2.0	11.9	5.7	4.6	15.5	5.3
65 to 74 years old...........	23.8	3.0	1.2	1.2	10.0	4.0	3.6	19.0	4.1
75 years old and older.......	18.1	3.8	0.5	0.5	5.3	3.3	2.3	16.5	4.6

[1] Includes weaving, crocheting, knitting, quilting, needlepoint, and sewing.

Source: U.S. National Endowment for the Arts, *A Decade of Arts Engagement: Findings From the Survey of Public Participation in the Arts, 2002–2012*, January 2015. See also <http://arts.gov/publications/decade-arts-engagement-findings-survey-public-participation-arts-2002-2012>.

Table 1257. Attendance/Participation Rates for Various Arts Activities by Selected Characteristics: 2012

[In percent, except as indicated (235.0 represents 235,000,000). For persons 18 years old and over. Represents attendance at least once in the prior twelve months. Excludes elementary and high school performances]

Item	Adult population (million)	Jazz concert	Classical music concert	Musicals	Non-musical plays	Art museums/ galleries	Craft/ visual art festivals	Parks/ historic buildings [1]	Live book reading or story-telling [2]
Total................	235.0	8.1	8.8	15.2	8.3	21.0	22.4	23.9	4.1
Sex:									
Male..................	113.1	7.9	8.0	12.9	7.3	18.7	18.2	23.1	3.0
Female................	121.9	8.3	9.5	17.3	9.2	23.1	26.4	24.6	5.1
Race and ethnicity:									
White alone............	155.7	8.4	11.0	18.4	10.1	24.1	26.2	28.3	4.2
African American alone......	26.8	11.2	4.0	9.3	6.2	11.9	12.0	13.1	5.2
Hispanic................	35.0	5.0	3.3	7.3	3.6	14.3	16.8	13.8	2.5
Other alone.............	17.5	7.4	7.3	11.2	4.9	21.2	16.3	21.2	4.7
Age:									
18 to 24 years old...........	30.4	9.2	6.7	13.0	6.4	18.3	18.3	20.5	4.6
25 to 34 years old...........	41.0	8.0	7.3	13.6	7.5	22.0	21.6	25.1	5.2
35 to 44 years old...........	39.6	7.8	6.4	12.9	7.3	21.2	22.0	23.3	4.8
45 to 54 years old...........	43.7	7.9	8.2	16.9	9.5	22.0	24.6	26.2	3.3
55 to 64 years old...........	38.3	10.0	11.0	19.0	9.0	22.5	25.8	26.5	4.0
65 to 74 years old...........	23.8	7.9	13.9	17.7	10.6	22.4	26.1	25.5	3.6
75 years old and older.......	18.1	3.9	10.9	11.9	7.8	15.5	15.0	15.0	2.2
Education:									
Grade school................	9.9	0.9	0.9	1.6	0.3	3.6	5.9	3.9	1.2
Some high school............	19.0	1.3	1.6	2.9	1.8	4.3	8.0	5.9	1.5
High school graduate........	70.9	4.5	3.1	8.3	3.9	9.9	16.3	13.3	1.8
Some college................	68.7	8.2	7.3	14.6	7.8	19.7	23.6	25.0	4.2
College graduate............	43.0	13.1	15.9	26.7	14.6	37.2	32.9	38.4	6.6
Graduate school.............	23.5	17.9	26.0	32.1	20.0	49.3	36.9	48.8	9.2
Income:									
Less than $20,000...........	40.9	4.8	3.9	6.2	3.8	10.2	12.3	12.1	3.0
$20,000 to $50,000..........	76.0	5.3	5.6	9.6	5.8	14.0	17.9	16.2	3.5
$50,000 to $75,000..........	43.9	8.2	9.2	16.8	7.9	22.1	24.5	25.1	4.4
$75,000 to $100,000.........	27.6	10.2	10.3	20.1	11.6	26.5	28.9	30.1	5.4
$100,000 to $150,000........	27.1	12.6	15.1	24.6	13.5	33.8	30.5	38.8	4.7
$150,000 and over...........	19.6	16.3	19.4	32.4	16.6	43.2	36.4	46.6	5.5

[1] Visiting historic parks or monuments or touring buildings or neighborhoods for the historic or design value. [2] Examples include author readings, poetry, or storytelling events.

Source: U.S. National Endowment for the Arts, *A Decade of Arts Engagement: Findings From the Survey of Public Participation in the Arts, 2002–2012*, January 2015. See also <http://arts.gov/publications/decade-arts-engagement-findings-survey-public-participation-arts-2002-2012>.

Table 1258. Attendance at/Participation in Various Leisure Activities Including Reading by Selected Characteristics: 2012

[In percent, except as indicated (235.0 represents 235,000,000). See headnote, Table 1256]

Item	Adult popu-lation (mil.)	Attendance at—			Participation in—		Reading—		
		Movies	Sports events [1]	Film festival	Exercise/ playing sports	Book club/ reading group	Fiction books	Non-fiction books	Litera-ture [2]
Total............................	**235.0**	**59.4**	**30.3**	**2.4**	**45.7**	**3.5**	**44.4**	**42.7**	**47.0**
Sex:									
Male............................	113.1	58.2	34.7	2.4	47.5	1.9	33.3	36.8	37.0
Female..........................	121.9	60.4	26.4	2.5	44.0	5.1	54.5	48.2	56.1
Race and ethnicity:									
White alone..................	155.7	61.6	34.0	2.6	49.3	3.8	59.2	47.0	52.3
African American alone.....	26.8	53.3	21.9	1.6	37.7	5.0	36.8	38.0	40.2
Hispanic.......................	35.0	54.8	24.3	2.2	38.5	1.4	26.9	29.0	31.0
Other alone...................	17.5	57.5	21.4	3.1	40.8	2.9	37.9	38.6	41.7
Age:									
18 to 24 years old............	30.4	75.7	40.7	3.0	58.5	2.8	45.3	39.2	47.9
25 to 34 years old............	41.0	68.5	36.2	3.0	52.8	3.0	45.0	41.3	47.9
35 to 44 years old............	39.6	68.3	35.2	2.2	49.3	3.7	42.6	41.3	45.1
45 to 54 years old............	43.7	59.9	32.2	2.6	44.9	4.0	43.0	41.9	44.7
55 to 64 years old............	38.3	50.6	24.5	2.4	40.8	3.8	45.4	45.4	48.2
65 to 74 years old............	23.8	44.1	20.8	2.0	37.2	4.6	48.8	48.6	51.9
75 years old and older.......	18.1	30.6	11.2	1.2	24.1	3.0	40.4	42.6	43.8
Education:									
Grade school..................	9.9	21.6	7.8	1.0	12.2	1.7	12.1	19.2	16.9
Some high school.............	19.0	36.7	13.6	0.4	24.1	0.4	21.5	21.2	22.9
High school graduate........	70.9	48.6	22.0	0.9	35.0	2.2	33.1	31.0	36.9
Some college..................	68.7	64.9	33.1	2.6	49.2	2.8	49.1	45.7	50.3
College graduate.............	43.0	75.3	44.4	3.9	62.6	5.6	60.5	57.3	63.0
Graduate school..............	23.5	76.8	42.2	6.0	68.8	9.2	65.8	68.8	69.5
Income:									
Less than $20,000............	40.9	39.4	14.5	1.7	31.3	2.3	34.3	35.3	36.5
$20,000 to $50,000...........	76.0	50.3	32.9	1.8	35.4	2.4	37.6	36.7	42.2
$50,000 to $75,000...........	43.9	65.3	33.0	3.1	48.9	4.2	46.6	44.8	47.7
$75,000 to $100,000..........	27.6	74.8	42.4	3.1	56.1	3.9	41.9	39.7	52.8
$100,000 to $150,000.........	27.1	73.0	43.9	2.4	63.3	5.3	56.8	51.2	57.0
$150,000 and over............	19.6	77.9	49.9	3.7	69.4	6.1	61.3	58.6	63.3

[1] Includes amateur or professional sports events. [2] Includes plays, poetry, novels, or short stories.

Source: U.S. National Endowment for the Arts, *A Decade of Arts Engagement: Findings From the Survey of Public Participation in the Arts, 2002–2012*, January 2015. See also <http://arts.gov/publications/decade-arts-engagement-findings-survey-public-participation-arts-2002-2012>.

Table 1259. Household Pet Ownership: 2011

[In percent, except as indicated (69.9 represents 69,900,000). Based on a sample survey of 50,347 households]

Item	Unit	Dogs	Cats	Birds	Horses
Total companion pet population [1]..................................	**Million**	**69.9**	**74.1**	**8.3**	**4.9**
Number of households owning pets..................................	Million	43.3	36.1	3.7	1.8
Percent of households owning companion pets [1]....................	Percent	36.5	30.4	3.1	1.5
Average number owned per household................................	Number	1.6	2.1	2.3	2.7
PERCENT OF HOUSEHOLDS OWNING PETS					
Annual household income:					
Under $20,000..	Percent	34.5	34.1	4.3	1.4
$20,000 to $34,999...	Percent	40.0	36.8	4.0	2.1
$35,000 to $54,999...	Percent	42.4	35.6	3.9	1.9
$55,000 to $84,999...	Percent	43.8	34.0	3.3	1.9
$85,000 and over...	Percent	43.9	31.7	3.1	1.9
Household size: [1]					
One person...	Percent	26.8	29.8	2.6	1.3
Two persons..	Percent	40.1	34.6	3.2	1.8
Three persons..	Percent	50.0	38.3	4.2	2.2
Four persons...	Percent	53.7	34.9	4.3	2.0
Five or more persons...	Percent	54.2	38.1	6.8	2.6
VETERINARY CARE AND EXPENDITURES					
Households obtaining veterinary care [2]............................	Percent	81.3	55.1	12.4	53.8
Average visits per household per year.............................	Number	2.6	1.6	0.3	1.9
Expenditures per household per year (mean)........................	Dollars	378	191	33	373
Expenditures per animal (mean)...................................	Dollars	227	90	14	133

[1] As of December 31, 2011. [2] During the year.

Source: American Veterinary Medical Association, Schaumburg, IL, *U.S. Pet Ownership and Demographics Sourcebook, 2012*, ©. See also <http://www.avma.org/reference/marketstats/sourcebook.asp>.

Table 1260. Adult Participation in Selected Leisure Activities by Frequency: 2016

[In thousands (18,453 represents 18,453,000), except percent. For Fall 2016. Percent is based on total projected population of 244,525,000. Based on sample and subject to sampling error; see source]

| Activity | Participated in the last 12 months [1] | | Frequency of participation | | | | | | | |
| | | | Two or more times a week | | Once a week | | Two to three times a month | | Once a month | |
	Number (1,000)	Percent	Number (1,000)	Percent	Number (1,000)	Percent	Number (1,000)	Percent	Number (1,000)	Percent
Adult education courses	18,453	7.6	3,672	1.5	1,870	0.8	1,116	0.5	1,344	0.6
Aquarium attendance	12,090	4.9	223	0.1	71	(Z)	40	(Z)	226	0.1
Attend a circus	7,933	3.2	36	(Z)	156	0.1	36	(Z)	92	(Z)
Attend art galleries or shows	19,074	7.8	212	0.1	173	0.1	508	0.2	611	0.3
Attend auto shows	14,599	6.0	247	0.1	184	0.1	262	0.1	898	0.4
Attend classical music/opera performances	8,407	3.4	107	(Z)	50	(Z)	268	0.1	504	0.2
Attend country music performances	15,598	6.4	53	(Z)	160	0.1	266	0.1	493	0.2
Attend dance performances	9,651	4.0	53	(Z)	243	0.1	234	0.1	174	0.1
Attend horse races	5,858	2.4	148	0.1	149	0.1	859	0.4	2,450	1.0
Attend other music performances [2]	26,664	10.9	181	0.1	614	0.3	602	0.3	1,443	0.6
Attend rock music performances	22,051	9.0	92	(Z)	297	0.1	11,934	4.9	8,181	3.4
Baking	55,449	22.7	7,658	3.1	7,963	3.3	15,373	6.3	8,933	3.7
Barbecuing	70,598	28.9	9,552	3.9	10,456	4.3	1,581	0.7	1,332	0.5
Billiards/pool	15,591	6.4	970	0.4	1,030	0.4	802	0.3	704	0.3
Bird watching	10,474	4.3	4,357	1.8	756	0.3	5,574	2.3	7,398	3.0
Board games	35,675	14.6	1,804	0.7	3,315	1.4	351	0.1	2,356	1.0
Book clubs	6,245	2.6	174	0.1	215	0.1	822	0.3	987	0.4
Chess	8,453	3.5	1,048	0.4	481	0.2	365	0.2	609	0.3
Concerts on radio	6,059	2.5	1,111	0.5	302	0.1	5,874	2.4	3,609	1.5
Cooking for fun	49,348	20.2	17,533	7.2	7,914	3.2	2,404	1.0	1,438	0.6
Crossword puzzles	23,658	9.7	8,938	3.7	2,606	1.1	1,719	0.7	1,710	0.7
Dance/go dancing	18,364	7.5	1,582	0.7	1,656	0.7	30,997	12.7	16,242	6.6
Dining out	129,060	52.8	23,153	9.5	28,032	11.5	15,698	6.4	15,888	6.5
Entertain friends or relatives at home	79,400	32.5	6,705	2.7	8,957	3.7	1,017	0.4	703	0.3
Fantasy sports league	10,861	4.4	2,646	1.1	1,693	0.7	340	0.1	873	0.4
Furniture refinishing	8,411	3.4	353	0.1	131	0.1	6,639	2.7	6,731	2.8
Go to bars/night clubs	43,205	17.7	2,905	1.2	4,076	1.7	5,275	2.2	6,919	2.8
Go to beach	70,777	28.9	2,718	1.1	2,358	1.0	854	0.4	2,383	1.0
Go to live theater	26,087	10.7	231	0.1	182	0.1	995	0.4	3,110	1.3
Go to museums	30,261	12.4	279	0.1	263	0.1	2,600	1.1	3,613	1.5
Home decoration and furnishing	24,979	10.2	1,347	0.6	1,042	0.4	457	0.2	1,117	0.5
Karaoke	9,634	3.9	186	0.1	276	0.1	2,246	0.9	1,672	0.7
Painting, drawing	17,672	7.2	3,583	1.5	1,744	0.7	1,583	0.7	908	0.4
PC/computer games (play offline with software)	16,642	6.8	8,182	3.4	1,210	0.5	802	0.3	1,391	0.6
Photo album/scrap book	10,233	4.2	482	0.2	447	0.2	3,728	1.5	2,978	1.2
Photography	25,337	10.4	5,764	2.4	2,652	1.1	1,165	0.5	2,363	1.0
Picnic	19,151	7.8	427	0.2	717	0.3	557	0.2	997	0.4
Play bingo	10,458	4.3	915	0.4	809	0.3	4,975	2.0	5,854	2.4
Play cards	38,654	15.8	3,572	1.5	3,666	1.5	1,849	0.8	1,272	0.5
Play musical instrument	16,777	6.9	5,495	2.3	1,851	0.8	7,297	3.0	5,704	2.3
Reading books	82,881	33.9	43,297	17.7	7,709	3.2	576	0.3	657	0.3
Reading comic books	6,637	2.7	1,582	0.7	674	0.3	1,931	0.8	1,319	0.5
Sudoku puzzles	18,679	7.6	6,541	2.7	2,290	0.9	688	0.3	1,027	0.5
Tailgating	10,516	4.3	221	0.1	540	0.2	1,738	0.7	1,402	0.6
Trivia games	16,555	6.8	3,871	1.6	2,325	0.9	2,379	1.0	1,912	0.8
Video/electronic games (console)	21,656	8.9	8,925	3.7	2,326	1.0	774	0.6	873	0.4
Video/electronic games (portable)	12,781	5.2	5,637	2.3	1,395	0.6	964	0.4	1,238	0.5
Woodworking	10,512	4.3	1,492	0.6	1,002	0.4	2,554	1.0	1,412	0.6
Word games	24,953	10.2	9,821	4.0	2,502	1.0	843	0.3	1,909	0.8
Zoo attendance	30,310	12.4	59	(Z)	174	0.1				

Z Represents less than 0.05. [1] Includes those participating less than once a month, not shown separately. [2] Excluding country and rock.

Source: © Fall 2016, GfK MRI a division of GfK US, LLC. See also <http://www.mri.gfk.com/>.

Table 1261. Selected Recreational Activities: 1990 to 2016

[18,719 represents 18,719,000]

Activity	Unit	1990	2000	2005	2010	2012	2013	2014	2015	2016
Golf facilities [1]	Number	12,846	15,489	16,052	15,890	15,619	15,516	15,372	15,204	15,014
Tennis players: [2]	1,000	(NA)	(NA)	(NA)	18,719	17,020	17,678	17,904	17,963	18,079
Skiing: [3]										
Skier visits & snowboarder [4]	Million	50.0	52.2	56.9	59.8	51.0	56.9	56.5	53.6	52.8
Operating resorts	Number	591	503	492	471	474	478	470	470	463

NA Not available. [1] Source: National Golf Foundation, Jupiter, FL. [2] Source: Tennis Industry Association, Hilton Head, SC. Based on a nationwide telephone survey of households, in which all household members ages 6 and up are enumerated, with data on tennis participation collected for each person. Data prior to 2007 is not available due to new methodology being implemented after 2007. [3] Source: National Ski Areas Association, Lakewood, CO. ©. [4] Represents one person visiting a ski area for all or any part of a day or night, and includes full-and half-day, night, complimentary, adult, child, season, and other types of tickets. Data are estimated and are for the season ending in the year shown.

Source: Compiled from sources listed in footnotes.

Table 1262. Amusement Park Attendance at Top 15 U.S. Facilities: 2010 to 2016

[In thousands (109,321 represents 109,321,000). Covers gated (entry ticket required) commercial theme and amusement parks with annual attendance of one million or more]

Park name	Location	Attendance				
		2010	2013	2014	2015	2016
Total top 15	(X)	**109,321**	**119,951**	**123,039**	**130,441**	**131,512**
Magic Kingdom, Walt Disney World	Lake Buena Vista, FL	16,972	18,588	19,332	20,492	20,395
Disneyland	Anaheim, CA	15,980	16,202	16,769	18,278	17,943
EPCOT, Walt Disney World	Lake Buena Vista, FL	10,825	11,229	11,454	11,798	11,712
Disney's Animal Kingdom	Lake Buena Vista, FL	9,886	10,198	10,402	10,922	10,844
Disney's Hollywood Studios	Lake Buena Vista, FL	9,603	10,110	10,312	10,828	10,776
Universal Studios Florida	Orlando, FL	5,925	7,062	8,263	9,585	9,998
Universal's Islands of Adventure	Orlando, FL	5,949	8,141	8,141	8,792	9,362
Disney's California Adventure	Anaheim, CA	6,278	8,514	8,769	9,383	9,295
Universal Studios Hollywood	Universal City, CA	5,040	6,148	6,824	7,097	8,086
SeaWorld Florida	Orlando, FL	5,100	5,090	4,683	4,777	4,402
Busch Gardens	Tampa, FL	4,200	4,087	4,128	4,252	4,169
Knotts Berry Farm	Buena Park, CA	3,600	3,683	3,683	3,867	4,014
Cedar Point	Sandusky, OH	3,051	3,382	3,247	3,507	3,604
SeaWorld California	San Diego, CA	3,800	4,311	3,794	3,528	3,528
Kings Island	Kings Island, OH	3,112	3,206	3,238	3,335	3,384

X Not applicable.

Source: Themed Entertainment Association and AECOM, *2016 Theme Index and Museum Index: The Global Attractions Attendance Report* ©, and previous reports. See also <http://www.teaconnect.org/> and <http://www.aecom.com/services/economics/>.

Table 1263. Reading in Print, Electronic, and Audio Formats Among Adults: 2016

[In percent. Data shown for adults aged 18 years and older who read at least one book in the formats shown during the previous 12 months. Based on a telephone survey conducted March 7 through April 4, 2016 among a nationally representative sample of 1,520 adults]

Characteristic	Total	Print	E-book	Audio-book	Characteristic	Total	Print	E-book	Audio-book
Total	**73**	**65**	**28**	**14**	EDUCATION				
					Less than high school	45	38	11	12
SEX					High school graduate	62	55	19	9
Men	68	61	27	14	Some college	81	74	32	14
Women	77	70	29	14	College graduate	86	79	41	20
RACE/ETHNICITY					HOUSEHOLD INCOME				
White, non-Hispanic	76	70	31	15	Less than $30,000	65	59	19	9
Black, non-Hispanic	69	63	23	11	$30,000 to $49,999	74	68	26	16
Hispanic	58	48	18	12	$50,000 to $74,999	75	69	33	19
					$75,000 and higher	81	73	40	16
AGE									
18 to 29 years	80	72	35	16	METRO STATUS				
30 to 49 years	73	65	32	15	Urban	75	69	29	17
50 to 64 years	70	64	24	15	Suburban	73	64	30	14
65 years and older	67	61	19	9	Rural	66	61	22	10

Source: Pew Research Center, *Book Reading 2016*, September 2016 ©. See also <http://www.pewinternet.org/2016/09/01/book-reading-2016/>.

Table 1264. Leisure Time Use on Weekends and Holidays by Type of Activity and Selected Demographic Characteristics: 2016

[Data are based on interviews of approximately 10,500 individuals 15 years old and over who reported their activities for one 24-hour period. Respondents engaging in more than one activity at a time reported only their primary activity; except for child care, secondary activities were not reported]

Selected characteristics	Average hours per day spent on all leisure and sports activities			Percent distribution of leisure time on weekends and holidays						
	All days (hours)	Weekdays (hours)	Weekends and holidays (hours)	Sports, exercise, recreation	Socializing, communicating	Watching TV	Reading	Relaxing, thinking	Playing games, using computers for leisure	Other[1]
Total, 15 years old and over	**5.13**	**4.58**	**6.43**	**5.9**	**15.2**	**51.5**	**5.1**	**5.4**	**7.3**	**9.5**
Sex:										
Men	5.51	4.87	7.04	7.1	13.6	53.3	3.7	5.1	7.4	9.7
Women	4.77	4.31	5.86	4.4	17.1	49.3	6.8	5.6	7.2	9.4
Age:										
15 to 19 years	5.20	4.59	6.62	11.0	13.9	37.3	2.0	(S)	20.4	11.3
20 to 24 years	4.80	4.20	6.27	6.4	19.9	43.7	2.6	(S)	11.0	12.0
25 to 34 years	4.13	3.49	5.68	7.4	20.1	45.8	2.6	4.0	8.8	11.4
35 to 44 years	3.97	3.29	5.60	6.8	19.8	49.6	3.4	5.4	5.2	9.6
45 to 54 years	4.59	4.05	5.88	6.1	16.2	55.1	3.7	4.9	4.9	9.2
55 to 64 years	5.57	5.03	6.85	4.8	12.0	56.8	6.9	6.4	3.9	9.1
65 to 74 years	6.92	6.59	7.71	3.8	11.8	57.5	8.7	4.9	5.6	7.7
75 years and over	7.60	7.33	8.23	2.2	8.4	57.8	10.4	8.6	5.5	6.9
Race/ethnicity:										
White	5.11	4.56	6.43	6.2	15.1	51.2	5.6	4.8	7.2	9.8
Black	5.63	5.10	6.87	3.5	15.0	57.9	2.5	7.1	6.4	7.6
Asian	4.05	3.51	5.24	8.0	21.0	37.4	6.5	6.5	10.1	10.5
Hispanic origin	4.52	4.08	5.58	5.2	17.9	53.2	1.8	7.0	5.0	10.0
Employment status:										
Employed	4.16	3.48	5.83	7.0	17.7	48.7	4.3	4.8	6.7	10.8
Full-time workers	4.00	3.25	5.84	7.5	17.8	49.7	4.1	4.5	6.0	10.4
Part-time workers	4.69	4.24	5.81	5.2	17.4	45.1	4.8	6.5	8.8	12.2
Not employed	6.75	6.48	7.39	4.5	12.2	54.9	6.2	6.0	8.1	8.0
Weekly earnings:[2]										
$0 - $580	4.28	3.60	5.82	5.7	21.6	50.7	2.7	4.5	6.7	8.2
$581 - $920	3.99	3.16	6.01	5.7	17.6	50.4	4.0	4.7	7.5	10.3
$921 - $1,440	4.10	3.33	6.08	5.9	16.6	52.1	4.1	4.4	6.1	10.7
$1,441 and higher	3.90	3.04	5.95	10.4	17.1	46.6	5.9	3.2	4.9	11.9
Presence and age of children:										
No household children under 18	5.72	5.20	6.97	5.2	14.3	52.9	6.0	5.5	6.9	9.0
Household children under 18	4.06	3.48	5.47	7.5	17.6	47.7	3.1	5.1	8.2	10.6
Children 13 to 17 years, none younger	4.66	4.06	6.04	7.0	14.4	50.5	3.8	4.1	9.6	10.8
Children 6 to 12 years, none younger	4.10	3.53	5.59	9.3	17.2	45.6	3.6	6.4	7.5	10.4
Youngest child under 6 years	3.70	3.09	5.07	6.3	20.1	47.7	2.2	4.7	8.1	10.8
Educational attainment, 25 years and over:										
Less than a high school diploma	5.85	5.43	6.82	2.5	12.8	64.2	1.5	10.6	2.6	5.9
High school graduates, no college	5.72	5.28	6.79	4.4	11.6	60.1	4.9	6.3	5.6	7.1
Some college or associate degree	5.03	4.51	6.32	4.7	15.7	54.6	5.1	5.2	5.9	9.0
Bachelor's degree and higher	4.58	3.93	6.11	7.5	18.2	44.0	8.2	3.6	6.4	12.1

S Figure does not meet publication standards. [1] Includes other leisure and sports activities, not elsewhere classified, and travel related to leisure and sports activities. [2] These values are based on usual weekly earnings. The earnings data are limited to wage and salary workers (both incorporated and unincorporated self-employed workers are excluded). Each earnings range represents approximately 25 percent of full-time wage and salary workers who held only one job.

Source: U.S. Bureau of Labor Statistics, *American Time Use Survey, 2016*, Bulletin USDL-17-0880, June 2017. See also <http://www.bls.gov/tus/>.

Table 1265. Characteristics of Selected Spectator Sports: 1990 to 2016

[54,824 represents 54,824,000]

Sport	Unit	1990	1995	2000	2005	2010	2013	2014	2015	2016
Baseball, major leagues: [1]										
Regular season attendance........	1,000	54,824	50,469	72,749	74,926	73,054	74,028	73,730	73,760	73,159
National League..................	1,000	24,492	25,110	39,851	41,644	40,890	39,437	39,246	38,903	38,114
American League.................	1,000	30,332	25,359	32,898	33,282	32,164	34,591	34,484	34,857	35,045
Playoffs attendance [2]...........	1,000	479	533	1,314	1,191	1,210	1,424	1,127	1,420	1,275
World Series attendance...........	1,000	209	286	277	168	244	258	291	215	278
Basketball: [3, 4]										
NCAA—Men's college:										
Teams..........................	Number	768	866	937	984	1,027	1,050	1,060	1,067	1,075
Attendance......................	1,000	28,741	28,225	28,949	30,940	32,632	32,510	32,511	32,382	31,859
NCAA—Women's college:										
Teams..........................	Number	782	864	958	1,018	1,048	1,069	1,079	1,084	1,089
Attendance [5]..................	1,000	2,777	4,962	8,825	9,903	11,160	11,182	11,124	11,367	11,346
Football: [4]										
NCAA—Men's college:										
Teams..........................	Number	534	600	624	618	644	657	655	666	668
Attendance......................	1,000	35,330	35,638	39,059	43,487	49,671	50,291	49,073	49,058	49,316
National Hockey League: [6]										
Regular season attendance........	1,000	12,580	9,234	18,800	(NA)	20,996	12,793	21,759	21,533	21,615
Playoffs attendance................	1,000	1,356	1,329	1,525	(NA)	1,702	1,632	1,776	1,701	1,685
Professional rodeo: [7]										
Rodeos.........................	Number	754	739	688	662	570	611	607	624	618
Performances....................	Number	2,159	2,217	2,081	1,940	1,671	1,686	1,652	1,663	1,639
Members........................	Number	5,693	6,894	6,255	6,127	5,323	5,071	4,898	4,782	4,692
Permit-holders..................	Number	3,290	3,835	3,249	2,701	1,881	1,912	1,793	1,784	1,748
Total prize money................	Mil. dol.	18.2	24.5	32.3	36.6	39.9	39.6	41.1	46.3	45.1

NA Not available. [1] Source: Major League Baseball (previously, The National League of Professional Baseball Clubs), New York, NY, National League Green Book ©; and The American League of Professional Baseball Clubs, New York, NY, American League Red Book ©. [2] Beginning 1995, two rounds of playoffs were played. Prior years had one round. [3] Season beginning in year shown. [4] Source: National Collegiate Athletic Association, Indianapolis, IN ©. [5] Attendance for women's basketball includes doubleheaders with men's teams beginning with the 1997 season, if attendance was taken by halftime of the women's game. [6] For season ending in year shown. Source: National Hockey League, Montreal, Quebec ©. In September 2004, franchise owners locked out their players upon the expiration of the collective bargaining agreement. The entire season was cancelled in February 2005. [7] Source: Professional Rodeo Cowboys Association, Colorado Springs, CO, Official Professional Rodeo Media Guide, annual ©.

Source: Compiled from sources listed in footnotes.

Table 1266. Adult Attendance at Sports Events by Frequency: 2016

[In thousands (168 represents 168,000), except percent. For Fall 2016. Percent is based on total projected population of 244,525,000. Data not comparable to previous years. Pro is professional. Based on a survey and subject to sampling error; see source]

Event	Attend regularly Number (1,000)	Attend regularly Percent	Attend on occasion Number (1,000)	Attend on occasion Percent	Event	Attend regularly Number (1,000)	Attend regularly Percent	Attend on occasion Number (1,000)	Attend on occasion Percent
Alpine skiing and ski jumping...	168	0.07	808	0.33	Other golf......................	108	0.04	538	0.22
Auto racing – NASCAR.........	359	0.15	1,741	0.71	Greyhound racing..............	76	0.03	246	0.10
Auto racing – other.............	401	0.16	1,459	0.60	Gymnastics....................	269	0.11	625	0.26
Baseball:					High school sports............	4,046	1.65	7,902	3.23
College........................	494	0.20	1,459	0.60	Horse racing (track or OTB)...	352	0.14	1,487	0.61
Pro (MLB) regular season....	1,975	0.81	13,292	5.44	Ice hockey:				
Pro (MLB) playoffs/					NHL regular season.........	891	0.36	4,231	1.73
World Series.................	400	0.16	1,685	0.69	NHL playoffs and Stanley				
Basketball:					Cup finals.................	253	0.10	984	0.40
College........................	947	0.39	3,598	1.47	Lacrosse (MLL)..............	195	0.08	320	0.13
NCAA tournament.............	270	0.11	684	0.28	Marathon, triathlon & other				
Pro (NBA) regular season....	477	0.20	3,602	1.47	endurance events............	219	0.09	827	0.34
Pro (NBA) playoffs.............	266	0.11	961	0.39	Mixed martial arts (MMA).....	138	0.06	434	0.18
Pro (WNBA)..................	162	0.07	384	0.16	Motorcycle racing.............	209	0.09	690	0.28
Bicycle racing.................	194	0.08	560	0.23	Olympics – Summer...........	52	0.02	218	0.09
Bowling.......................	346	0.14	1,071	0.44	Olympics – Winter.............	27	0.01	217	0.09
Boxing.........................	247	0.10	693	0.28	Poker.........................	114	0.05	424	0.17
Bull riding (Pro)................	91	0.04	551	0.23	Rodeo........................	274	0.11	1,533	0.63
Equestrian events..............	200	0.08	710	0.29	Soccer:				
Extreme sports – Summer....	190	0.08	439	0.18	MLS.........................	340	0.14	1,741	0.71
Extreme sports – Winter........	111	0.05	460	0.19	World Cup...................	146	0.06	673	0.28
Figure skating.................	120	0.05	418	0.17	Tennis:				
Fishing........................	471	0.19	1,120	0.46	Men's.......................	206	0.08	527	0.22
Football:					Women's....................	126	0.05	615	0.25
College........................	2,997	1.23	8,192	3.35	Track & field.................	401	0.16	793	0.32
Pro (NFL) Monday					Truck and tractor				
or Thursday night games....	583	0.2	2557	1.1	pull/mud racing.............	58	0.02	473	0.19
NFL weekend games.........	1,015	0.42	5,059	2.07	Volleyball (Pro beach)........	69	0.03	255	0.10
NFL playoffs/Super Bowl......	247	0.10	1,020	0.42	Weightlifting..................	130	0.05	272	0.11
Golf:					Wrestling:				
PGA..........................	147	0.06	943	0.39	WWE........................	180	0.07	851	0.35
LPGA.........................	98	0.04	445	0.18	Other Pro....................	109	0.04	362	0.15

Source: © Fall 2016, GfK MRI a division of GfK US, LLC. See also <http://www.mri.gfk.com/>.

Table 1267. Participation in NCAA Sports by Sex: 2015 to 2016

[For the academic year]

Sport	Males			Females		
	Teams	Athletes	Average squad	Teams	Athletes	Average squad
Total	**9,180**	**278,445**	**(X)**	**10,541**	**214,086**	**(X)**
Baseball	948	34,554	36.4	(X)	(X)	(X)
Basketball	1,090	18,684	17.1	1,107	16,593	15.0
Bowling	1	4	4	68	599	8.8
Cross country [1]	994	14,412	14.5	1,071	15,958	14.9
Equestrian [1,2,3]	7	14	2.1	44	1,357	30.8
Fencing [1]	35	647	18.5	44	721	16.4
Field hockey	(X)	(X)	(X)	273	6,032	22.1
Football	672	73,660	109.6	(X)	(X)	(X)
Golf [1]	835	8,676	10.4	656	5,293	8.1
Gymnastics	16	320	20.0	83	1,502	18.1
Ice hockey	142	4,102	28.9	98	2,289	23.4
Lacrosse	362	13,446	37.1	483	11,375	23.6
Rifle [1]	23	163	7.1	30	194	6.5
Rowing [2,3]	57	2,343	41.1	146	7,469	51.2
Rugby [2,3]	3	164	54.7	12	372	31.0
Sailing [1,2]	23	458	19.9	(X)	(X)	(X)
Sand volleyball [2]	(X)	(X)	(X)	56	909	16.2
Skiing [1]	32	417	13.0	33	436	13.2
Soccer	832	24,803	29.8	1,034	27,358	26.5
Softball	(X)	(X)	(X)	1,004	19,680	19.6
Squash [2,3]	32	488	15.3	30	406	13.5
Swimming/diving [1]	426	9,455	22.2	541	12,356	22.8
Synchronized swimming [3]	(X)	(X)	(X)	2	44	22.0
Tennis	766	8,092	10.6	929	8,933	9.6
Track, indoor [1]	690	25,220	36.6	784	26,886	34.3
Track, outdoor [1]	795	28,334	35.6	880	29,048	33.0
Volleyball	122	1,899	15.6	1,070	17,119	16.0
Water polo	45	1,014	22.5	59	1,136	19.3
Wrestling	232	7,075	30.5	(X)	(X)	(X)

X Not applicable. [1] Co-ed sport. [2] Sport recognized by the NCAA but does not have an NCAA men's championship. [3] Sport recognized by the NCAA as an emerging sport for women.

Source: The National Collegiate Athletic Association (NCAA), Indianapolis, IN, *NCAA Sports Sponsorship and Participation Rates Report* ©. See also <http://www.ncaapublications.com/>.

Table 1268. Participation in High School Athletic Programs by Sex: 1980 to 2017

[For academic years. Data based on number of state associations reporting and may underrepresent the number of schools with and participants in athletic programs]

Year	Participants [1]		Sex and sport	Most popular sports, 2016–2017 [2]	
	Males	Females		Schools	Participants
1980 to 1981	3,503,124	1,853,789	**MALE**		
1985 to 1986	3,344,275	1,807,121	Football (11-player)	14,099	1,057,407
1990 to 1991	3,406,355	1,892,316	Track & field (outdoor)	16,699	600,136
1995 to 1996	3,634,052	2,367,936	Basketball	18,214	550,305
1996 to 1997	3,706,225	2,474,043	Baseball	15,979	491,790
1997 to 1998	3,763,120	2,570,333	Soccer	12,188	450,234
1998 to 1999	3,832,352	2,652,726	Cross country	15,087	266,271
1999 to 2000	3,861,749	2,675,874	Wrestling	10,629	244,804
2000 to 2001	3,921,069	2,784,154	Tennis	9,725	158,171
2001 to 2002	3,960,517	2,806,998	Golf	13,223	141,466
2002 to 2003	3,988,738	2,856,358	Swimming & diving	7,342	138,364
2003 to 2004	4,038,253	2,865,299			
2004 to 2005	4,110,319	2,908,390			
2005 to 2006	4,206,549	2,953,355	**FEMALE**		
2006 to 2007	4,321,103	3,021,807	Track & field (outdoor)	16,658	494,477
2007 to 2008	4,372,115	3,057,266	Volleyball	15,992	444,779
2008 to 2009	4,422,662	3,114,091	Basketball	17,934	430,368
2009 to 2010	4,455,740	3,172,637	Soccer	11,823	388,339
2010 to 2011	4,494,406	3,173,549	Softball (fast pitch)	15,440	367,405
2011 to 2012	4,484,987	3,207,533	Cross country	14,880	226,039
2012 to 2013	4,490,854	3,222,723	Tennis	10,121	187,519
2013 to 2014	4,527,994	3,267,664	Swimming & diving	7,721	170,797
2014 to 2015	4,519,312	3,287,735	Competitive spirit squads	6,541	144,243
2015 to 2016	4,544,574	3,324,326	Lacrosse	2,717	93,473
2016 to 2017	4,563,238	3,400,297			

[1] A participant is counted in each sport participated in. [2] Ten most popular sports for each gender, ranked by number of participants.

Source: National Federation of State High School Associations, Indianapolis, IN, *The 2016–2017 High School Athletics Participation Survey* ©. Reprinted with permission of the National Federation of State High School Associations. See also <http://www.nfhs.org/>.

Table 1269. Participants in Selected Sports Activities: 2015

[In thousands (290,841 represents 290,841,000). Data are based on an online survey of 35,000 individuals. The questionnaire asked the heads of households and up to three other household members who were at least seven years of age to indicate their age, the sports in which they participated in 2015, and the number of days of participation in 2015. A participant is defined as an individual years of age or older who participates in a sport more than once a year; selected fitness activities required participation of 6 or more days during 2015. See source for methodology]

Activity	Total (number)	Sex — Male	Sex — Female	Age 7–17	Age 18–24	Age 25–34	Age 35–44	Age 45–54	Age 55–64	Age 65–74	Age 75 and over	Income Under 25,000	Income 25,000–34,999	Income 35,000–49,999	Income 50,000–74,999	Income 75,000–99,999	Income 100,000–149,999	Income 150,000 and over
Total persons age 7 and older	290,841	142,627	148,214	45,567	31,464	43,517	40,513	43,459	40,078	34,599	11,644	68,639	29,375	38,100	49,443	33,447	38,973	32,865
Aerobic exercising [1]	45,138	15,835	29,303	4,185	5,229	9,504	7,881	6,623	5,376	5,354	985	6,514	3,258	5,105	8,193	5,930	7,568	8,568
Archery, target [2]	8,353	5,469	2,884	2,316	1,352	1,463	1,111	1,244	546	240	80	1,381	838	1,175	1,403	1,170	1,326	1,059
Backpacking [2]	12,309	7,560	4,749	2,528	1,753	2,659	2,125	1,931	993	262	59	1,699	958	1,467	2,449	1,811	2,148	1,776
Baseball	11,786	9,491	2,295	5,730	1,141	2,051	1,489	889	877	242	—	1,495	920	1,454	2,201	1,822	2,139	1,755
Basketball	24,812	18,536	6,276	9,742	3,774	4,546	3,643	1,988	—	93	—	4,170	2,103	3,069	4,982	3,462	3,951	3,075
Bicycle riding [1]	36,008	20,430	15,578	10,528	3,083	5,137	4,553	5,691	4,112	2,568	337	5,143	2,969	3,847	7,046	5,507	6,031	5,464
Billiards/pool [1]	21,465	13,586	7,879	2,310	3,257	4,548	4,340	3,614	2,145	1,036	216	4,006	2,278	2,261	4,104	2,854	3,078	2,884
Boating, motor/power	14,129	8,755	5,374	2,094	1,372	1,695	2,173	2,494	2,427	1,619	255	1,756	823	1,522	2,056	2,486	2,767	2,720
Bowling [1]	35,219	18,810	16,409	7,931	4,121	6,885	6,139	5,319	3,030	1,523	271	5,508	3,122	3,904	7,434	4,844	5,816	4,591
Camping [3]	40,129	21,810	18,319	8,676	4,525	6,681	6,999	6,353	4,324	2,164	407	6,234	3,888	5,162	8,425	5,708	6,383	4,331
Cheerleading	3,739	334	3,405	2,675	473	314	152	126	—	—	—	277	216	514	865	535	811	520
Dart throwing	10,197	6,576	3,621	1,316	1,471	2,187	2,189	1,860	868	201	104	2,065	1,078	1,323	1,869	1,389	1,292	1,181
Exercise walking [1]	106,321	46,216	60,104	8,014	8,804	15,279	16,060	19,280	19,057	15,488	4,339	20,786	10,477	13,820	19,168	12,914	15,371	13,785
Exercise with equipment [1]	56,275	28,785	27,490	4,066	7,816	10,056	9,150	9,309	7,583	6,777	1,518	7,658	4,691	6,549	10,619	7,960	9,726	9,071
Fishing, fresh water	29,451	20,520	8,931	4,715	2,506	3,881	5,067	5,336	4,143	3,159	644	4,884	3,228	4,337	6,389	3,937	4,152	2,525
Fishing, salt water	9,716	7,063	2,653	1,209	709	1,661	1,572	2,026	1,440	924	176	1,369	752	1,089	1,850	1,390	1,466	1,801
Football, tackle	7,830	7,105	725	4,379	1,018	1,235	817	324	57	—	—	1,240	540	848	1,637	1,250	1,307	1,009
Golf	18,565	13,859	4,706	1,648	1,206	2,641	3,127	3,254	3,238	3,012	439	1,091	917	1,404	3,536	2,982	4,352	4,283
Gymnastics	5,769	1,298	4,471	3,508	557	862	464	222	55	75	25	712	436	525	1,164	1,073	1,126	734
Hiking	41,976	21,468	20,507	5,682	5,065	7,826	7,217	6,994	5,396	3,426	370	6,116	3,514	4,221	7,608	6,158	7,340	6,959
Hockey, ice	3,336	2,643	693	1,057	523	735	547	294	179	—	—	187	228	240	627	657	613	784
Hunting with bow & arrow	5,734	4,470	1,264	519	715	1,091	1,243	1,084	743	317	22	945	540	907	998	719	900	724
Hunting with firearms	17,656	14,701	2,955	1,639	1,843	2,700	3,130	3,601	2,991	1,441	311	3,208	1,418	2,705	3,575	2,317	2,378	2,057
In-line roller skating	4,895	2,136	2,759	2,271	755	637	682	357	141	53	—	683	443	625	983	810	834	517
Kayaking	9,225	5,039	4,186	1,251	1,080	2,066	1,454	1,461	1,239	582	93	891	390	529	1,491	1,443	1,939	2,543
Lacrosse	2,940	1,625	1,315	1,522	627	340	236	181	36	—	—	231	192	129	365	486	564	973
Mountain biking, off road	5,623	3,644	1,979	894	525	1,443	1,126	937	575	123	—	751	388	510	895	867	1,333	879
Muzzleloading	2,703	2,355	348	138	364	449	322	297	368	318	43	587	254	505	486	264	564	364
Paintball games	5,094	3,415	1,679	1,797	938	1,393	601	583	39	29	—	763	527	476	646	83	1,023	460
Running/jogging [1]	44,545	23,546	20,999	8,664	7,579	9,590	8,724	5,682	2,937	1,202	168	6,558	3,466	4,670	8,257	6,260	7,696	7,638
Skateboarding	5,656	3,808	1,848	2,830	1,297	750	501	230	49	—	—	1,451	359	719	944	689	925	569
Skiing, alpine	6,058	3,501	2,557	1,433	720	838	666	1,028	956	385	32	376	81	341	566	730	1,508	2,458
Skiing, cross country	2,428	1,282	1,146	414	159	489	542	340	349	119	16	185	78	152	299	396	504	814
Snowboarding	4,276	2,927	1,349	1,070	725	1,281	703	341	155	—	—	325	207	410	711	725	930	968
Soccer	14,112	9,027	5,085	7,364	1,926	2,311	1,689	583	185	36	17	2,054	1,016	1,390	2,717	2,210	2,596	2,130
Softball [1]	9,751	4,943	4,808	3,971	1,009	1,450	1,420	1,161	646	95	—	974	746	873	2,316	1,379	1,797	1,667
Swimming [1]	46,283	23,322	22,956	12,806	4,052	6,505	6,062	6,036	5,693	4,402	722	5,454	4,031	5,239	8,699	6,607	8,528	7,721
Table tennis/ping pong	10,498	5,802	4,696	2,550	1,697	2,009	1,301	1,484	804	581	72	1,174	557	1,231	1,806	1,806	2,200	1,724
Target shooting, live ammunition	20,428	14,947	5,481	1,868	2,644	3,952	3,511	3,469	2,804	1,881	298	3,435	1,540	2,954	4,131	2,648	3,140	2,579
Target shooting, airgun	5,205	3,860	1,345	1,202	807	1,017	929	680	239	306	26	1,000	363	765	1,223	669	908	277
Tennis	12,771	6,597	6,174	2,946	1,197	2,987	1,923	2,136	977	492	114	847	834	1,096	2,302	2,307	2,749	2,637
Volleyball	10,699	4,423	6,276	4,453	1,673	1,908	1,310	947	335	53	21	1,336	785	1,067	2,310	2,116	2,116	1,491
Water skiing	3,487	1,991	1,496	943	571	728	577	341	273	54	—	243	119	371	586	830	598	740
Weightlifting [1]	34,803	23,235	11,568	3,155	5,875	7,354	5,995	5,681	3,685	2,776	776	5,174	2,589	3,795	6,312	4,593	6,042	6,298
Workout at club [1]	36,587	17,231	19,356	2,916	5,875	7,677	5,818	5,024	4,402	3,967	908	4,164	2,570	4,032	6,430	5,079	7,011	7,302
Wrestling [1]	3,045	2,377	668	1,345	535	636	345	157	27	—	—	759	288	364	564	457	397	216
Yoga	30,696	7,253	23,443	2,522	4,790	8,393	5,536	4,150	2,992	1,937	376	5,660	2,475	3,358	5,370	4,111	5,073	4,648

— Represents zero. [1] Participant engaged in activity at least six times in the year. [2] Includes wilderness camping. [3] Vacation/overnight.

Source: National Sporting Goods Association, Mt. Prospect, IL, *Sports Participation in the United States, 2016 Edition* ©. See also <http://www.nsga.org/research>.

Table 1270. Consumer Purchases of Sporting Goods by Consumer Characteristics: 2015

[Shown as percent of dollar purchases. Data are based on an online survey of over 16,000 households. Because surveys prior to 2010 were conducted by mail, current data may not be fully comparable to past years]

| Characteristic | Total | Footwear | | | | | Equipment | | | | |
		Cross-train/ fitness shoes	Gym shoes/ sneakers	Hiking shoes/ boots	Jogging/ running shoes	Walking shoes	Bi-cycles	Fitness trackers/ pedo-meters	Golf club sets	Hand-guns	Rod/ reel combi-nation
Total..........................	**100.0**	**100.0**	**100.0**	**100.0**	**100.0**	**100.0**	**100.0**	**100.0**	**100.0**	**100.0**	**100.0**
Age of user:											
Under 14 years old..............	17.8	3.9	11.8	2.9	5.1	4.4	11.7	0.9	3.9	0.2	3.9
14 to 17 years old...............	5.3	5.8	11.4	3.9	6.4	2.6	4.8	1.3	3.7	–	0.8
18 to 24 years old...............	9.9	11.2	11.4	6.6	11.0	5.2	8.1	8.1	0.5	5.8	4.8
25 to 34 years old...............	13.5	19.0	16.4	13.4	18.3	10.8	18.0	22.7	11.1	20.3	18.8
35 to 44 years old...............	12.7	15.2	12.1	15.5	18.0	12.0	13.8	16.3	9.7	14.7	20.4
45 to 64 years old...............	26.2	36.1	28.0	50.0	33.9	43.6	35.2	41.6	52.2	40.7	42.5
65 years old and over...........	14.5	8.8	8.9	7.7	7.3	21.4	8.4	9.1	18.9	18.3	8.8
Sex of user:											
Male..........................	49.2	46.6	44.8	64.2	50.4	45.1	62.7	40.3	68.6	71.3	80.3
Female........................	50.8	53.4	55.2	35.8	49.6	54.9	37.3	59.7	31.4	28.7	19.7
Annual household income:											
Under $15,000..................	12.6	3.7	7.1	6.7	4.1	7.0	9.5	2.6	4.0	4.8	5.7
$15,000 to $24,999.............	11.0	5.4	9.0	5.8	4.4	8.5	4.3	3.5	0.4	4.3	8.6
$25,000 to $34,999.............	10.1	5.3	8.9	7.8	7.0	9.2	5.0	7.2	1.8	7.2	8.3
$35,000 to $49,999.............	13.1	10.7	12.0	11.5	10.6	12.4	10.1	10.9	3.5	13.9	15.6
$50,000 to $74,999.............	17.0	20.3	19.3	16.7	17.3	18.0	14.7	15.8	18.9	20.9	20.6
$75,000 to $99,999.............	11.5	15.8	12.1	14.8	15.7	14.0	13.9	16.0	14.8	12.3	12.9
$100,000 to $149,999..........	13.4	21.1	17.1	19.5	20.3	16.9	20.7	19.3	18.9	18.2	16.3
$150,000 and over.............	11.3	17.7	14.5	17.2	20.6	14.0	21.8	24.7	37.7	18.4	12.0
Education of household head:											
Less than high school...........	12.2	0.6	1.0	0.8	0.7	1.7	0.7	0.8	–	1.5	0.9
High school.....................	29.6	10.2	14.9	10.9	9.6	15.0	8.7	8.1	5.1	13.3	19.4
Some college...................	28.4	26.2	32.8	31.5	26.5	29.0	26.1	24.3	10.3	28.5	32.5
College graduate...............	29.8	63.0	51.3	56.8	63.2	54.3	64.5	66.8	84.6	56.7	47.2

– Represents or rounds to zero.

Source: National Sporting Goods Association, Mt. Prospect, IL, *Sporting Goods Market: 2016 Edition* ©. See also <https://www.nsga.org/research/nsga-research-offerings/>.

Table 1271. National Park System—Summary: 1990 to 2016

[In units as indicated (986 represents $986,000,000). For year ending September 30, except as noted. Includes data for six areas in Puerto Rico and Virgin Islands, one area in American Samoa, and one area in Guam]

Item	1990	1995	2000	2005	2010	2014	2015	2016
FINANCES (mil. dol.): [1]								
Expenditures reported........................	986	1,445	1,833	2,451	3,239	2,737	2,949	2,964
Salaries and wages....................	459	633	799	984	1,237	1,174	1,167	1,196
Improvements, maintenance..............	160	234	299	361	531	507	532	559
Construction...........................	109	192	215	381	443	152	184	182
Other.................................	259	386	520	725	1,028	904	1,066	1,022
Funds available.............................	1,506	2,225	3,316	4,218	5,402	4,532	5,161	5,228
Appropriations.........................	1,053	1,325	1,881	2,425	2,848	2,804	2,967	3,233
Other [2]..............................	453	900	1,435	1,793	2,554	1,728	2,194	1,995
Revenue from operations................	79	106	234	286	387	473	589	548
RECREATION VISITS (millions): [3]								
All areas....................................	258.7	269.6	285.9	273.5	281.3	292.8	307.2	331.0
National parks [4]......................	57.7	64.8	66.1	63.5	64.6	68.9	75.3	82.9
National monuments....................	23.9	23.5	23.8	20.9	23.0	24.5	24.9	25.7
National historical, commemorative, archaeological [5]......................	57.5	56.9	72.2	74.9	80.0	88.9	93.9	99.5
National parkways......................	29.1	31.3	34.0	31.7	28.6	28.5	29.6	32.8
National recreation areas [4]............	47.2	53.7	50.0	46.8	49.0	45.2	46.2	50.3
National seashores and lakeshores.......	23.3	22.5	22.5	21.7	22.2	22.3	22.8	24.1
National Capital Parks..................	7.5	5.5	5.4	4.3	3.0	3.3	3.1	3.0
Recreation overnight stays (millions).......	17.6	16.8	15.4	13.5	14.4	14.0	14.9	15.3
In commercial lodgings [6]...............	3.9	3.8	3.7	3.4	3.5	4.7	4.8	4.6
In Park Service campgrounds...........	7.9	7.1	5.9	5.2	5.5	5.3	5.9	6.4
In backcountry.........................	1.7	2.2	1.9	1.7	1.8	1.9	2.0	2.2
Other [7]..............................	4.2	3.7	3.8	3.2	3.7	2.2	2.2	2.2
LAND (1,000 acres): [8]								
Total.......................................	76,362	77,355	78,153	79,048	80,527	80,469	80,603	80,726
Parks.................................	46,089	49,307	49,785	49,910	50,662	50,727	50,737	50,748
Recreation areas.......................	3,344	3,353	3,388	3,391	3,418	3,420	3,421	3,399
Other.................................	26,929	24,695	24,980	25,747	26,447	26,322	26,445	26,579
Acquisition, net.............................	21	27	186	17	23	8	127	125

[1] Financial data are those associated with the National Park System. Certain other functions of the National Park Service (principally the activities absorbed from the former Heritage Conservation and Recreation Service in 1981) are excluded. [2] Includes funds carried over from prior years. [3] For calendar year. Includes other areas, not shown separately. [4] For 1990, combined data for North Cascades National Park and two adjacent National Recreation Areas are included in National Parks total. [5] Includes National Battlefields, National Battlefield Parks, National Historic Sites, National Historical Parks, National Memorials, National Military Parks, National Preserves, and National Reserves. [6] Beginning in 2011, includes concessioner lodging and campgrounds. [7] Prior to 2011, includes concessioner campgrounds. [8] Federal land only, as of December 31. Federal land acreages, in addition to National Park Service administered lands, also include lands within national park system area boundaries but under the administration of other agencies. Year-to-year changes in the federal lands figures includes changes in the acreages of these other lands and hence often differ from "net acquisition."

Source: U.S. National Park Service, *National Park Statistical Abstract 2016*, March 2017, and earlier reports; and unpublished data. See also <https://irma.nps.gov/Stats/>.

Table 1272. National Park Service (NPS) Visits and Acreage by State: 2016

Table 1272. National Park Service (NPS) Visits and Acreage by State: 2016

State	Recreation visits[1]	Gross area acres	Federal land NPS fee acres[2]	Federal land NPS less than fee acres[3]	Federal land Other federal fee acres[4]	Nonfederal land Other public acres[5]	Nonfederal land Private acres
Total[6]	330,971,680	84,735,952	79,954,251	333,872	437,980	1,404,921	2,604,927
Alabama	1,022,696	22,737	17,507	202	13	3,288	1,726
Alaska	2,783,011	54,653,962	52,452,522	105,821	8	372,315	1,723,296
Arizona	12,007,543	2,947,585	2,657,413	115	76,800	56,833	156,424
Arkansas	3,787,198	104,976	98,347	3,428	20	2,746	435
California	41,977,184	8,168,077	7,609,746	165	11,035	373,439	173,692
Colorado	7,457,420	737,850	662,712	6,755	41,971	262	26,150
Connecticut	39,079	7,782	5,846	1,055	–	874	6
Delaware	–	904	890	6	–	2	6
District of Columbia	42,700,158	8,625	8,476	8	6	134	2
Florida	10,855,363	2,638,635	2,468,544	1,330	44,495	99,958	24,308
Georgia	7,040,865	64,129	39,875	167	1,461	17,379	5,247
Hawaii	5,786,318	369,320	357,937	1	22	11,228	132
Idaho	629,191	518,224	511,600	1,226	173	901	4,324
Illinois	239,719	116	12	–	–	17	86
Indiana	1,949,880	15,573	10,752	500	–	3,424	897
Iowa	229,577	2,713	2,708	–	–	5	1
Kansas	121,249	11,637	462	271	–	69	10,835
Kentucky	1,882,702	95,942	94,103	137	–	838	864
Louisiana	500,797	23,545	17,633	–	–	2,801	3,111
Maine	3,317,250	179,451	156,183	11,192	22	10,646	1,409
Maryland	6,668,215	74,278	41,524	5,832	480	23,791	2,651
Massachusetts	10,127,182	59,497	32,962	1,029	44	21,919	3,543
Michigan	2,702,934	718,143	632,177	685	46	58,515	26,719
Minnesota	1,016,336	301,330	139,760	3,193	142	98,663	59,573
Mississippi	6,618,913	118,544	104,006	5,228	–	72	9,238
Missouri	2,824,117	83,476	54,499	9,168	–	14,070	5,740
Montana	5,655,262	1,274,136	1,214,196	1,850	6,137	1,464	50,489
Nebraska	307,208	66,570	5,899	485	845	435	58,906
Nevada	5,526,764	801,162	797,603	–	2,508	44	1,008
New Hampshire	42,377	21,190	13,521	1,556	5,772	162	180
New Jersey	4,829,258	99,328	35,542	140	3,208	59,050	1,388
New Mexico	1,872,044	480,894	467,519	5	2,549	4,661	6,159
New York	18,904,528	97,380	33,716	3,903	148	19,988	39,625
North Carolina	18,493,719	409,878	366,578	12,272	20,782	3,289	6,957
North Dakota	784,710	72,568	71,192	256	151	122	847
Ohio	2,818,683	34,546	20,285	1,462	84	8,461	4,254
Oklahoma	1,688,733	10,241	10,008	9	189	8	27
Oregon	1,328,643	203,385	196,197	1,404	4,976	295	513
Pennsylvania	11,070,571	115,400	52,361	3,041	387	19,627	39,983
Rhode Island	65,588	331	5	–	–	–	326
South Carolina	1,680,015	32,348	31,972	61	5	51	259
South Dakota	4,464,251	296,584	148,010	122,324	–	78	26,173
Tennessee	9,401,901	387,327	358,227	1,714	9,665	4,162	13,558
Texas	5,432,749	1,251,559	1,205,775	87	1,013	8,669	36,015
Utah	14,409,739	2,117,683	2,097,866	833	1,142	12,808	5,035
Vermont	55,716	23,237	9,836	3,927	8,809	544	120
Virginia	27,092,479	364,672	306,278	7,137	24,867	7,101	19,290
Washington	8,522,006	1,967,559	1,834,594	2,144	100,222	12,815	17,785
West Virginia	1,683,649	92,684	65,210	370	386	6,893	19,825
Wisconsin	537,925	133,757	61,835	11,353	802	47,671	12,097
Wyoming	7,461,665	2,396,430	2,344,979	21	48,462	1,293	1,675

– Represents or rounds to zero. [1] See footnote 1, Table 1273. [2] See footnote 2, Table 1273. [3] See footnote 3, Table 1273. [4] See footnote 4, Table 1273. [5] See footnote 5, Table 1273. [6] Includes Island Areas of the U.S., not shown separately.

Source: U.S. National Park Service, Land Resources Division, unpublished data. See also <https://irma.nps.gov/Stats/>.

Table 1273. National Park Service (NPS) Visits and Acreage by Type of Area: 2016

Type of area	Recreation visits[1]	Gross area acres	Federal land NPS fee acres[2]	Federal land NPS less than fee acres[3]	Federal land Other federal fee acres[4]	Non-federal land Other public acres[5]	Non-federal land Private acres
Total[6]	330,971,689	84,735,952	79,954,251	333,872	437,982	1,404,920	2,604,926
National historic sites	11,019,908	34,615	22,362	856	42	399	10,956
National historical parks	33,020,999	188,648	135,756	4,137	550	29,235	18,970
National memorials	41,636,249	10,735	9,748	9	25	76	877
National monuments	25,728,513	2,136,763	1,967,724	14,808	27,068	8,496	118,667
National parks	82,895,409	52,202,789	50,475,208	226,621	45,766	568,212	886,982
National recreation areas	50,331,201	3,705,615	3,154,637	1,523	242,889	135,311	171,255
National seashores	19,797,234	596,933	404,611	14,947	61,226	106,820	9,328
National parkways	32,802,051	181,888	161,794	9,123	213	403	10,355

[1] Recreation visit represents the entry of a person onto lands or waters administered by the NPS for recreational purposes excluding government personnel, through traffic, tradespeople, and persons residing within park boundaries. [2] Complete Federal ownership of all rights in the land. [3] Federal ownership of some rights in the land. [4] Tracts under the administration of another federal agency (e.g., U.S. Forest Service, Department of the Army, etc.). Bureau of Land Management tracts are also identified as Other Fee (Federal) until they are withdrawn for NPS use; then status changes to Fee (Federal). [5] Non-federal tracts owned by the state, county, and/or other municipalities, including quasi-public entities. [6] Includes other areas, not shown separately.

Source: U.S. National Park Service, Land Resources Division, unpublished data. See also <https://irma.nps.gov/Stats/>.

Table 1274. State Parks and Recreation Areas by State: 2016

[In units as indicated (18,598 represents 18,598,000). For year ending June 30. Data are shown as reported by state park directors. In some states, the park agency has forests, fish and wildlife areas, and/or other areas under its control. In other states, the park agency is responsible for state parks only]

State	Acreage (1,000)	Visitors (1,000) [1]	Total revenue generated ($1,000)	Operating expenditures ($1,000)	Revenue share of operating expenditures
United States..................	18,598	791,410	1,238,587	2,463,811	50.3
Alabama............................	48	5,005	34,929	41,966	83.2
Alaska...............................	3,387	3,538	3,690	14,199	26.0
Arizona.............................	64	2,682	16,177	21,338	75.8
Arkansas...........................	55	8,088	28,281	61,258	46.2
California..........................	1,625	78,906	133,700	446,582	29.9
Colorado...........................	1,565	13,515	35,735	49,934	71.6
Connecticut.......................	209	8,435	7,811	18,162	43.0
Delaware...........................	26	5,548	17,458	26,450	66.0
Florida..............................	791	31,841	68,457	77,011	88.9
Georgia.............................	86	8,359	29,177	47,348	61.6
Hawaii...............................	32	1,050	4,986	9,196	54.2
Idaho................................	59	4,714	10,457	16,904	61.9
Illinois..............................	483	39,918	7,221	49,840	14.5
Indiana.............................	171	16,177	56,445	58,613	96.3
Iowa.................................	71	15,393	5,070	17,848	28.4
Kansas..............................	164	7,185	9,061	12,160	74.5
Kentucky...........................	46	6,233	49,560	89,893	55.1
Louisiana..........................	44	1,979	11,293	27,921	40.4
Maine...............................	98	2,828	4,322	8,933	48.4
Maryland...........................	138	12,937	19,321	40,465	47.7
Massachusetts...................	354	30,038	17,615	70,856	24.9
Michigan...........................	304	30,865	55,130	63,926	86.2
Minnesota.........................	287	9,656	22,831	73,546	31.0
Mississippi........................	28	1,186	9,193	15,319	60.0
Missouri............................	154	20,158	15,198	50,474	30.1
Montana............................	46	2,678	3,089	9,850	31.4
Nebraska...........................	170	12,291	25,150	24,922	100.9
Nevada.............................	151	3,255	4,754	11,848	40.1
New Hampshire..................	231	1,273	21,532	21,077	102.2
New Jersey........................	448	16,207	13,319	11,635	114.5
New Mexico........................	192	5,266	5,781	18,482	31.3
New York...........................	4,281	67,169	102,397	224,658	45.6
North Carolina...................	229	18,086	9,484	38,900	24.4
North Dakota.....................	35	1,351	4,693	12,183	38.5
Ohio.................................	174	44,243	26,215	62,813	41.7
Oklahoma..........................	69	9,675	20,351	29,211	69.7
Oregon.............................	108	54,192	26,511	59,850	44.3
Pennsylvania.....................	294	40,522	25,087	100,677	24.9
Rhode Island......................	10	7,885	6,557	10,658	61.5
South Carolina...................	90	8,597	28,054	29,298	95.8
South Dakota.....................	102	7,592	34,596	19,394	178.4
Tennessee.........................	196	35,865	35,053	82,380	42.6
Texas...............................	636	8,844	44,346	80,596	55.0
Utah.................................	151	4,528	20,054	15,624	128.4
Vermont............................	74	1,033	6,716	9,737	69.0
Virginia.............................	73	9,436	21,256	41,077	51.7
Washington........................	120	35,055	44,287	69,972	63.3
West Virginia.....................	151	7,364	21,856	42,409	51.5
Wisconsin..........................	157	17,901	12,011	16,983	70.7
Wyoming...........................	119	4,867	2,325	9,435	24.6

[1] Includes overnight visitors.

Source: National Association of State Park Directors, Raleigh NC, *Statistical Report of State Park Operations: 2015-2016, Annual Information Exchange for the Period July 1, 2015 through June 30, 2016* ©, May 2017. See also <http://www.stateparks.org/>.

Table 1275. Participants in Wildlife-Related Recreation Activities: 2011

[In thousands (37,397 represents 37,397,000). For persons 16 years old and over engaging in activity at least once in 2011. Based on survey and subject to sampling error; see source for details]

Participant	Number	Days of participation	Trips	Participant	Number	Days of participation
Total sportspersons [1]	**37,397**	**835,725**	**711,645**	**Wildlife watchers [1]**	**71,776**	**(X)**
Total anglers	33,112	553,841	455,005	Away from home [2]	22,496	335,625
Freshwater	27,547	455,862	368,805	Observe wildlife	19,808	268,798
Excluding Great Lakes	27,060	443,223	353,620	Photograph wildlife	12,354	110,459
Great Lakes	1,665	19,661	15,185	Feed wildlife	5,399	59,255
Saltwater	8,889	99,474	86,200			
				Around the home [3]	68,598	(X)
Total hunters	13,674	281,884	256,640	Observe wildlife	45,046	(X)
Big game	11,570	212,116	167,320	Photograph wildlife	25,370	(X)
Small game	4,506	50,884	43,135	Feed wildlife	52,817	(X)
Migratory birds	2,583	23,263	21,315	Visit public parks	12,311	(X)
Other animals	2,168	34,434	24,869	Maintain plantings or natural areas	13,399	(X)

X Not applicable. [1] Detail does not add to total due to multiple responses and nonresponse. [2] Persons taking a trip of at least 1 mile from home for activity. [3] Activity within 1 mile of home.

Source: U.S. Fish and Wildlife Service, *2011 National Survey of Fishing, Hunting, and Wildlife Associated Recreation*, December 2012. See also <http://www.census.gov/prod/www/fishing.html>.

Table 1276. Expenditures for Wildlife-Related Recreation Activities: 2011

[41,789 represents $41,789,000,000. For persons 16 years old and over. Based on survey and subject to sampling error; see source for details]

Expenditure item	Fishing			Hunting			Wildlife watching		
	Expenditures (mil. dol.)	Spenders		Expenditures (mil. dol.)	Spenders		Expenditures [1] (mil. dol.)	Spenders	
		Number (1,000)	Percent of anglers		Number (1,000)	Percent of hunters		Number (1,000)	Percent [2]
Total, all items [3]	**41,789**	**30,289**	**91**	**33,702**	**13,364**	**98**	**54,890**	**55,980**	**78**
Total trip-related	21,789	29,309	89	10,421	11,914	87	17,275	19,905	88
Food and lodging	7,711	25,158	76	3,881	10,289	75	9,349	17,017	76
Food	5,435	24,891	75	3,218	10,253	75	5,465	16,740	74
Lodging	2,276	5,983	18	663	1,881	14	3,884	6,851	30
Transportation	6,262	25,293	76	4,768	10,990	80	6,007	18,647	83
Public	804	2,222	7	304	648	5	2,521	3,029	13
Private	5,458	24,504	74	4,464	10,885	80	6,486	17,768	79
Other trip costs	7,817	25,143	76	1,772	4,581	34	1,918	9,359	42
Equipment expenditures:									
Equipment [4]	6,142	21,527	65	7,738	10,400	76	11,323	47,951	67
Auxiliary equipment	1,107	4,420	13	1,845	5,101	37	1,555	6,445	9
Special equipment [5]	8,258	2,296	7	4,389	613	4	14,272	2,219	3
Other expenditures:									
Magazines and books	108	2,483	8	107	1,934	14	420	8,480	12
Land leasing and ownership	3,434	924	3	7,129	2,279	17	5,677	1,233	2
Membership dues/contributions	322	1,728	5	383	1,885	14	2,164	10,756	15
Plantings	(X)	(X)	(X)	703	1,273	9	2,204	8,818	12
Licenses, stamps, tags, and permits	629	17,166	52	986	10,214	75	(X)	(X)	(X)

X Not applicable. [1] Information on trip-related expenditures for wildlife watching was collected for away-from-home participants only. Equipment and other expenditures for wildlife watching are base on information collected from both away-fro-home and around-the-home participants. [2] Percent of wildlife-watching participants column is base on away-from-home participants for trip-related expenditures. For equipment and other expenditures the percent of wildlife-watching participants is based on total participants. [3] Total not adjusted for multiple responses or nonresponse. [4] Includes fishing, hunting, and wild-life watching. [5] Special equipment includes boats, campers, cabins, trail bikes, etc.

Source: U.S. Fish and Wildlife Service, *2011 National Survey of Fishing, Hunting, and Wildlife Associated Recreation*, December 2012. See also <http://www.census.gov/prod/2012pubs/fwh11-nat.pdf>.

Table 1277. Tribal Gaming Revenues: 2010 to 2016

[Revenue in millions of dollars (26,503 represents $26,503,000,000). For year ending September 30]

Region	2010		2012		2013		2014		2015		2016	
	Number of operations	Revenue	Number of operations	Revenue	Number of operations	Revenue	Number of operations	Revenue	Number of operations	Revenue	Number of operations	Revenue
Total [1]	**422**	**26,503**	**425**	**27,900**	**449**	**28,032**	**459**	**28,459**	**474**	**29,882**	**484**	**31,196**
Region I	50	2,655	49	2,874	51	2,903	51	2,927	52	3,022	53	3,177
Region II	62	6,794	64	6,957	66	6,993	68	7,298	71	7,881	70	8,381
Region III	48	2,539	48	2,717	48	2,739	48	2,708	53	2,808	57	2,932
Region IV	119	4,452	120	4,798	128	4,745	130	4,675	134	4,829	132	4,884
Region V	116	3,352	117	3,816	128	3,900	132	4,078	133	4,348	135	4,560
Region VI	27	6,711	27	6,739	28	6,752	30	6,773	31	6,994	37	7,261

[1] Portland (Region I): Alaska, Idaho, Oregon, and Washington. Sacramento (Region II): California, and Northern Nevada. Phoenix (Region III): Arizona, Colorado, New Mexico, and Southern Nevada. St. Paul (Region IV): Iowa, Michigan, Minnesota, Montana, North Dakota, Nebraska, South Dakota, Wisconsin, and Wyoming. Oklahoma City/Tulsa (Region V): Oklahoma, Texas, Kansas. Washington (Region VI): Alabama, Connecticut, Florida, Louisiana, Mississippi, North Carolina, and New York.

Source: National Indian Gaming Commission, *Gross Gaming Revenues 2012-2016,* July 2017, and earlier reports; and *Gross Gaming Revenues by Region 2015 and 2016,* July 2017, and earlier reports. See also <http://www.nigc.gov/commission/gaming-revenue-reports>.

Table 1278. Real Tourism Output: 2005 to 2016

[In millions of dollars (681,024 represents $681,024,000,000)]

Commodity	Direct output (current dollars)			Real output (chained 2009 dollars)		
	2005	2010	2016	2005	2010	2016
Total.................................	**681,024**	**701,356**	**893,709**	**752,607**	**678,716**	**815,447**
Traveler accommodations............................	121,924	129,651	185,408	133,129	130,757	160,897
Food services and drinking places............................	101,965	105,700	124,343	118,378	104,448	105,701
Domestic passenger air transportation services...............	79,398	80,094	99,480	87,937	74,679	83,518
International passenger air transportation services............	30,371	43,096	52,701	30,477	38,785	50,190
Passenger rail transportation services.........................	1,460	1,862	2,234	1,726	1,847	1,905
Passenger water transportation services.......................	9,883	10,976	13,502	8,746	10,852	13,000
Interurban bus transportation.................................	1,636	1,370	1,531	1,953	1,310	1,348
Interurban charter bus transportation.........................	1,764	1,625	1,881	2,107	1,550	1,654
Urban transit systems and other transportation services......	4,298	4,227	5,047	4,965	4,060	4,183
Taxi service...	3,983	4,090	4,120	4,573	3,934	3,350
Scenic and sightseeing transportation services...............	2,496	2,467	3,632	2,767	2,459	3,282
Automotive rental...	26,940	28,007	36,698	34,863	28,234	41,815
Other vehicle rental...	762	763	1,000	853	747	996
Automotive repair services...................................	13,913	12,390	13,291	16,362	12,156	11,753
Parking lots and garages....................................	2,168	2,322	2,800	2,649	2,248	2,180
Highway tolls...	679	702	875	837	664	814
Travel arrangement and reservation services..................	31,665	36,771	50,092	33,766	36,765	47,589
Motion pictures and performing arts...........................	14,736	14,040	16,800	16,700	13,855	14,539
Spectator sports..	6,732	5,179	6,046	7,910	5,071	4,906
Participant sports...	12,183	10,073	12,186	13,045	10,171	11,505
Gambling...	37,721	41,286	51,165	41,452	40,614	45,723
All other recreation and entertainment........................	13,955	12,110	11,773	15,749	12,004	10,417
Gasoline...	54,926	61,592	75,626	56,865	51,958	81,530
Nondurable PCE [1] commodities other than gasoline..........	105,467	90,962	121,478	116,065	89,976	110,189

[1] Personal consumption expenditures.

Source: U.S. Bureau of Economic Analysis, Satellite Accounts Data, "Travel and tourism data files," <http://www.bea.gov/industry/tourism_data.htm>, accessed July 2017.

Table 1279. Travel Forecast Summary: 2013 to 2020

[In billions of dollars (16,663.2 represents $16,663,200,000,000)]

Indicator	Unit	2013	2014	2015	2016	2017 [1]	2018 [1]	2019 [1]	2020 [1]
Real GDP.............................	Billions	16,663.2	17,348.1	18,036.6	18,569.1	19,404.6	20,334.8	21,110.0	21,906.3
Unemployment rate..................	Percent	7.4	6.2	5.3	4.9	4.7	4.6	4.6	4.7
Consumer price index (CPI) [2].......	Percent	233.0	236.7	237.1	237.8	245.5	250.7	255.6	260.5
Travel price index (TPI) [2]............	Percent	275.6	279.6	272.4	272.3	282.0	292.0	300.5	308.2
Total travel expenditures in U.S.....	Billions	886.2	928.1	970.4	990.3	1,020.9	1,062.9	1,106.4	1,154.4
U.S. residents........................	Billions	751.2	792.4	813.4	836.6	865.9	901.3	937.0	975.4
International visitors [3]...............	Billions	135.0	135.7	157.0	153.7	155.1	161.6	169.4	179.0
Total international visitors to the United States.................	Millions	70.0	75.0	77.5	77.6	77.5	79.0	82.2	85.7
Overseas arrivals to the United States..............................	Millions	32.0	34.9	38.4	39.2	39.3	40.4	42.1	44.0
Total domestic person trips [4]........	Millions	2,059.6	2,109.3	2,178.7	2,206.5	2,245.9	2,286.3	2,322.4	2,356.2
Business.............................	Millions	444.9	451.0	459.8	458.9	466.2	471.2	475.0	478.2
Leisure..............................	Millions	1,614.7	1,658.3	1,718.9	1,747.5	1,779.7	1,815.1	1,847.4	1,878.1

[1] Projected. [2] 1982-1984=100. [3] Excludes international visitors' spending on traveling to the U.S. on U.S. flag carriers, and other miscellaneous transportation. [4] One person on one trip 50 miles or more, one way, away from home or including one or more nights away from home.

Source: U.S. Travel Association, *Travel Industry Forecasts,* June 2017. See also <https://www.ustravel.org/research>.

Table 1280. Chain–Type Price Indexes for Direct Tourism Output: 2000 to 2016

[Index numbers, 2009=100. For explanation of chain-type price indexes, see text, Section 13]

Tourism goods and services group	2000	2005	2009	2010	2011	2012	2013	2014	2015	2016
All tourism goods and services.......	**79.0**	**90.5**	**100.0**	**103.3**	**108.6**	**111.6**	**112.2**	**114.0**	**110.5**	**112.2**
Traveler accommodations..................	80.1	91.6	100.0	99.2	100.9	103.9	104.7	109.3	112.7	109.9
Transportation............................	77.7	91.6	100.0	107.5	117.4	120.7	120.4	120.9	109.3	117.6
Passenger air transportation.............	79.3	93.2	100.0	108.6	116.6	122.1	122.3	125.3	120.0	105.5
All other transportation-related commodities............................	76.5	90.4	100.0	106.7	117.9	119.9	119.2	118.2	102.8	117.6
Food services and drinking places........	74.8	86.1	100.0	101.2	103.6	106.8	109.1	111.7	114.8	111.1
Recreation, entertainment, and shopping...............................	82.5	90.5	100.0	101.1	103.6	106.0	106.3	107.7	108.6	112.0
Recreation and entertainment.............	78.5	90.1	100.0	101.2	103.0	105.2	106.9	108.4	109.0	110.3
Shopping.................................	85.7	90.9	100.0	101.1	104.2	106.6	107.4	108.9	109.4	112.2

Source: U.S. Department of Commerce, Bureau of Economic Analysis, Satellite Accounts, Travel and Tourism, News Release, *Travel and Tourism Satellite Account: Fourth Quarter and Annual 2016,* March 2017, <https://bea.gov/newsreleases/industry/tourism/tournewsrelease.htm>.

Table 1281. Tourism Sales and Employment by Industry Segment: 2000 to 2016

[Sales in billions of dollars (580.3 represents $580,300,000,000); employment in thousands (5,926 represents 5,926,000). Direct tourism-related sales comprise all output purchased directly by visitors (e.g., traveler accommodations, passenger air transportation, souvenirs). Direct tourism-related employment comprises all jobs where the workers are engaged in the production of direct tourism-related sales (output), such as hotel staff, airline pilots, and souvenir sellers]

Tourism commodity group	2000	2005	2009	2010	2011	2012	2013	2014	2015	2016
DIRECT TOURISM SALES (OUTPUT) (bil. dol.)										
All tourism goods and services	**580.3**	**681.0**	**669.7**	**701.4**	**780.7**	**812.8**	**854.2**	**892.4**	**905.7**	**937.9**
Traveler accommodations	106.3	121.9	127.9	129.7	137.8	146.3	153.3	162.3	176.0	185.2
Transportation	231.1	266.3	266.9	292.4	338.8	353.5	370.8	387.5	370.4	381.5
Passenger air transportation	100.6	109.8	110.8	123.2	136.4	138.1	141.7	148.9	152.1	152.9
All other transportation-related commodities	130.5	156.6	156.1	169.2	202.4	215.4	229.1	238.6	218.3	228.6
Food services and drinking places	87.4	102.0	99.3	105.7	114.0	118.7	123.0	129.9	139.1	146.9
Recreation, entertainment, and shopping	155.5	190.8	175.7	173.7	190.0	194.3	207.1	212.6	220.1	224.2
Recreation and entertainment	62.9	85.3	83.2	82.7	86.8	91.1	89.9	92.2	97.2	96.6
Shopping	92.6	105.5	92.5	91.0	103.2	103.2	117.2	120.4	123.0	127.7
DIRECT TOURISM EMPLOYMENT (1,000)										
All tourism industries	**5,926**	**5,589**	**4,994**	**4,925**	**5,107**	**5,176**	**5,376**	**5,374**	**5,352**	**5,385**
Traveler accommodations	1,386	1,324	1,257	1,268	1,300	1,328	1,357	1,383	1,384	1,389
Transportation	1,377	1,154	1,030	996	1,020	1,030	1,178	1,187	1,188	1,172
Air transportation services	569	474	434	424	436	440	449	455	455	461
All other transportation-related industries	809	680	596	572	584	591	729	732	733	711
Food services and drinking places	1,658	1,690	1,513	1,551	1,625	1,660	1,655	1,641	1,626	1,659
Recreation, entertainment, and shopping	1,257	1,197	998	932	969	957	972	951	943	958
Recreation and entertainment	590	621	520	505	520	527	501	479	474	484
Shopping	668	576	478	428	449	429	470	472	469	475
All other industries	247	224	195	178	193	201	214	212	211	213

Source: U.S. Department of Commerce, Bureau of Economic Analysis, Satellite Accounts, Travel and Tourism, News Release, *Travel and Tourism Satellite Account: Fourth Quarter and Annual 2016*, March 2017, <https://bea.gov/newsreleases/industry/tourism/tournewsrelease.htm>.

Table 1282. Top States and Cities Visited by Overseas Travelers: 2000 to 2016

[25,975 represents 25,975,000. Includes travelers for business and pleasure, international travelers in transit through the United States, and students. Excludes travel by international personnel and international businessmen employed in the United States. Starting with the 2006 data, the statistical policy for visitation estimates of international visitation requires a minimum sample of 400 respondents. States and cities are ranked by the latest overseas visitors data]

State and other area	Overseas visitors [1] (1,000)				City	Overseas visitors [1] (1,000)			
	2000	2010	2015	2016		2000	2010	2015	2016
Total overseas travelers [2,3]	**25,975**	**26,363**	**38,392**	**37,589**	New York, NY [4]	5,714	8,462	10,132	9,800
New York	5,922	8,647	10,385	10,014	Miami, FL	2,935	3,111	5,509	5,379
Florida	6,026	5,826	9,667	9,540	Los Angeles-Long Beach, CA	3,533	3,348	4,857	4,977
California	6,364	5,615	8,139	8,221	Orlando, FL	3,013	2,715	4,718	4,473
Nevada	2,364	2,504	3,505	3,417	San Francisco, CA	2,831	2,636	3,632	3,571
Hawaiian Islands	2,727	2,135	3,021	3,146	Las Vegas, NV	2,260	2,425	3,409	3,327
Texas	1,169	1,028	1,789	1,692	Oahu/Honolulu, HI	2,234	1,634	2,380	2,394
Massachusetts	1,429	1,292	1,789	1,643	Washington, DC	1,481	1,740	2,135	2,090
Guam	1,325	1,318	1,505	1,583	Boston, MA	1,325	1,186	1,609	1,526
Illinois	1,377	1,186	1,708	1,567	Chicago, IL	1,351	1,134	1,620	1,466
Arizona	883	765	1,044	1,158	San Diego, CA	701	765	1,159	1,169
New Jersey	909	975	994	1,105	Fort Lauderdale, FL	(X)	(X)	902	1,015
Pennsylvania	649	923	1,029	974	Houston, TX	442	448	864	819
Georgia	805	817	998	876	Flagstaff, AZ [5]	(B)	501	672	771
Washington	468	501	852	729	Atlanta, GA	701	712	837	725
Utah	(B)	475	595	643	Anaheim-Santa Ana, CA	494	369	610	695
Louisiana	(X)	(X)	518	519	Florida Keys, FL	(X)	(X)	637	662
Colorado	519	343	461	485	Seattle, WA	416	475	783	658
North Carolina	416	343	491	436	Philadelphia, PA	390	633	680	628

B Figure too small to meet statistical standards for reliability of a derived figure. X Not applicable (not ranked). [1] Excludes visitors from Canada and Mexico. [2] A person is counted in each area visited, but only once in the total. [3] Includes other states and cities, not shown separately. [4] Data include New York City-White Plains-Wayne, NY-NJ grouped together. [5] Data include Flagstaff, Grand Canyon, and Sedona grouped together.

Source: U.S. Department of Commerce, International Trade Administration, National Travel and Tourism Office, "2016 U.S. Travel and Tourism Statistics (Inbound), Overseas Visitation Estimates," <http://travel.trade.gov/outreachpages/inbound.general_information.inbound_overview.html>, accessed August 2017.

Table 1283. Domestic and International Travel Expenditures by State: 2015

[In millions of dollars (947,114 represents $947,114,000,000). Shows aggregate spending by foreign visitors and by U.S. residents on domestic overnight trips and day trips of 50 miles or more, one way, away from home]

State	Total (mil. dol.)	Percent distribution	Rank	State	Total (mil. dol.)	Percent distribution	Rank	State	Total (mil. dol.)	Percent distribution	Rank
U.S. total...	947,114	100.0	(X)	KS...........	7,426	0.8	35	ND..........	3,132	0.3	45
				KY...........	9,008	1.0	31	OH...........	19,000	2.0	14
AL...........	9,128	1.0	30	LA...........	11,396	1.2	24	OK...........	7,740	0.8	34
AK...........	2,633	0.3	48	ME.........	3,722	0.4	43	OR...........	11,030	1.2	25
AZ...........	18,455	1.9	16	MD.........	16,376	1.7	20	PA...........	25,008	2.6	8
AR...........	6,806	0.7	37	MA.........	20,233	2.1	13	RI...........	1,994	0.2	51
CA...........	128,930	13.6	1	MI.........	18,758	2.0	15	SC...........	13,368	1.4	23
CO...........	18,298	1.9	18	MN.........	13,672	1.4	22	SD...........	2,836	0.3	47
CT...........	10,900	1.2	27	MS.........	6,201	0.7	38	TN...........	18,417	1.9	17
DE...........	2,036	0.2	50	MO.........	13,860	1.5	21	TX...........	67,841	7.2	4
DC...........	10,703	1.1	29	MT.........	4,366	0.5	41	UT...........	8,169	0.9	33
FL...........	90,860	9.6	2	NE.........	4,870	0.5	39	VT...........	2,391	0.3	49
GA...........	27,547	2.9	7	NV.........	35,103	3.7	6	VA...........	23,688	2.5	9
HI...........	21,705	2.3	11	NH.........	3,969	0.4	42	WA.........	16,947	1.8	19
ID...........	4,414	0.5	40	NJ.........	20,834	2.2	12	WV.........	2,952	0.3	46
IL...........	37,280	3.9	5	NM.........	6,927	0.7	36	WI.........	10,880	1.1	28
IN...........	10,940	1.2	26	NY.........	69,808	7.4	3	WY.........	3,241	0.3	44
IA...........	8,275	0.9	32	NC..........	22,790	2.4	10	Other [1]......	10,253	1.1	(X)

X Not applicable. [1] This category includes foreign visitor spending in U.S. territories, and Canadian and Mexican visitor spending in the U.S. Those dollars are not represented in state totals.

Source: U.S. Travel Association, Washington, DC, *Impact of Travel on State Economies 2016* ©, January 2017. See also <http://www.ustravel.org/research>.

Table 1284. Average Cost of Airfare for Domestic Routes: 1995 to 2016

[In dollars, except percent. Fares based on domestic itinerary fares. Itinerary fares consist of round-trip fares unless the customer does not purchase a return trip. In that case, the one-way fare is included. Fares are based on the total ticket value which consists of the price charged by the airlines plus any additional taxes and fees levied by an outside entity at the time of purchase. Fares include only the price paid at the time of the ticket purchase and do not include other fees paid at the airport or onboard the aircraft. Averages do not include frequent-flyer or "zero fares" or a few abnormally high reported fares]

	Current dollars			Constant (2016) dollars [1]		
		Percent change			Percent change	
Year	Average fare	From previous year	Cumulative from 1995	Average fare	From previous year	Cumulative from 1995
1995..................	292	(NA)	(NA)	460	(NA)	(NA)
1996..................	277	-5.3	-5.3	423	-8.0	-8.0
1997..................	287	3.8	-1.7	430	1.5	-6.7
1998..................	309	7.6	5.8	455	6.0	-1.1
1999..................	324	4.7	10.8	467	2.5	1.4
2000..................	339	4.7	16.0	472	1.3	2.7
2001..................	321	-5.4	9.7	435	-8.0	-5.6
2002..................	312	-2.6	6.9	417	-4.1	-9.4
2003..................	315	1.0	7.9	411	-1.3	-10.6
2004..................	305	-3.2	4.5	388	-5.7	-15.7
2005..................	307	0.6	5.2	378	-2.7	-17.9
2006..................	329	6.9	12.4	391	3.6	-15.0
2007..................	325	-1.0	11.3	377	-3.7	-18.2
2008..................	346	6.5	18.5	386	2.6	-16.1
2009..................	310	-10.4	6.2	347	-10.1	-24.5
2010..................	336	8.3	15.0	370	6.5	-19.6
2011..................	364	8.3	24.5	388	4.9	-15.6
2012..................	375	3.0	28.3	392	0.9	-14.9
2013..................	382	1.9	30.7	394	0.5	-14.5
2014..................	392	2.5	34.1	397	0.9	-13.7
2015..................	377	-3.8	29.0	382	-3.9	-17.0
2016..................	349	-7.4	19.5	349	-8.5	-24.1

NA Not available. [1] Rate calculated using Bureau of Labor Statistics Consumer Price Index.

Source: U.S. Department of Transportation, Bureau of Transportation Statistics, Air Fares, "National Level Fares since 1995—Annual," <https://www.rita.dot.gov/bts/airfares>, accessed April 2017.

Table 1285. International Travel: 1990 to 2015

[In thousands (44,619 represents 44,619,000). U.S. travelers cover residents of the United States, its territories and possessions. International travelers to the U.S. include travelers for business and pleasure, and excludes travel by international personnel and international businessmen employed in the United States. Some traveler data revised since originally issued. 2015 visitor data are preliminary]

Item and area	1990	1995	2000	2005	2010	2012	2013	2014	2015
U.S. TRAVELERS TO FOREIGN COUNTRIES BY WORLD REGION OF DESTINATION [1]									
Total	44,619	51,285	61,327	63,502	61,060	60,697	61,344	68,185	73,997
Canada	12,252	13,005	15,189	14,390	11,871	11,887	11,478	11,523	12,475
Mexico	16,377	18,771	19,285	20,325	20,682	20,308	20,851	25,882	28,733
Total overseas	15,990	19,059	26,853	28,787	28,507	28,502	29,015	30,780	32,789
Europe	8,043	8,596	13,373	11,976	9,806	10,204	10,039	10,804	11,378
INTERNATIONAL TRAVELERS TO U.S. BY VISITOR REGION OF RESIDENCE									
Total	39,363	43,318	51,238	49,206	60,010	66,657	69,995	75,022	77,510
Canada	17,263	14,663	14,667	14,862	20,176	22,697	23,407	23,014	20,705
Mexico	7,041	8,016	10,596	12,665	13,472	14,199	14,547	17,070	18,414
Total overseas [2]	15,059	20,639	25,975	21,679	26,363	29,761	32,041	34,938	38,392
Europe	6,659	8,793	11,597	10,313	11,985	12,478	12,894	14,161	15,699
Asia	4,360	6,616	7,554	6,198	7,020	8,311	9,085	9,697	10,816
South America	1,328	2,449	2,941	1,820	3,250	4,416	5,142	5,481	5,654
Caribbean	1,137	1,044	1,331	1,135	1,201	1,131	1,156	1,339	1,490
Oceania	662	588	731	737	1,095	1,322	1,433	1,586	1,764
Central America	412	509	822	696	760	803	834	934	1,068
Middle East	365	454	702	527	736	925	1,058	1,226	1,343
Africa	137	186	295	252	316	373	439	514	557

[1] A person is counted in each area visited but only once in the total. [2] "Overseas" excludes Canada and Mexico.

Source: U.S. Department of Commerce, International Trade Administration, Office of Travel and Tourism, *2015 United States Resident Travel Abroad,* October 2016; and *International Visitation to the United States: A Statistical Summary of U.S. Visitation (2015),* June 2016. See also <http://tinet.ita.doc.gov/outreachpages/outbound.general_information.outbound_overview.asp> and <http://tinet.ita.doc.gov/outreachpages/inbound.general_information.inbound_overview.asp>.

Table 1286. International Travelers and Payments: 2000 to 2015

[In units as indicated (86,184 represents $86,184,000,000). See headnote, Table 1285]

Year	Travel and passenger fare (mil. dol.)				U.S. net travel and passenger receipts (mil. dol.)	U.S. travelers to international countries (1,000)	International travelers to the U.S. (1,000) [3]
	Payments by U.S. travelers		Receipts from international visitors				
	Total [1]	Travel payments [2]	Total [1]	Travel receipts [2]			
2000	86,184	65,787	120,384	100,187	34,200	61,327	44,681
2005	101,419	79,988	122,079	101,470	20,660	63,502	49,206
2007	112,788	89,235	144,224	119,037	31,436	64,049	56,135
2008	119,837	92,545	164,718	133,761	44,881	63,653	58,007
2009	102,953	81,421	146,005	119,902	43,052	62,050	55,103
2010	110,049	86,623	167,997	137,010	57,948	61,061	60,010
2011	116,447	89,700	187,630	150,867	71,183	59,209	62,821
2012	129,903	100,338	200,996	161,632	71,093	60,697	66,657
2013	136,136	104,107	214,543	172,901	78,407	61,370	69,995
2014	145,677	110,787	220,757	177,241	75,080	67,713	75,022
2015 [4]	155,965	120,471	216,867	178,297	60,902	73,459	77,510

[1] Includes passenger fares, not shown separately. [2] Travel payments and receipts cover purchases of goods and services by U.S. persons traveling abroad, and by foreign travelers in the U.S. Goods and services include food, lodging, recreation, gifts, entertainment, local transportation, and other items. [3] Beginning in 2014, prior years are not comparable due to a change in methodology for counting U.S. overseas arrivals. [4] Preliminary.

Source: U.S. Department of Commerce, International Trade Administration, National Travel and Tourism Office, *International Visitation to the United States: A Statistical Summary of U.S. Visitation (2015),* June 2016; and "U.S. Travel and Tourism Statistics," <http://tinet.ita.doc.gov/outreachpages/inbound.general_information.inbound_overview.asp>, accessed June 2016.

Table 1287. Top 20 U.S. Gateway Airports for Nonstop International Air Travel Passengers: 2016

[215,266 represents 215,266,000. International passengers are residents of any country traveling nonstop to and from the United States on U.S. and foreign carriers. The data cover all passengers arriving and departing from U.S. airports on nonstop commercial international flights with 60 seats or more]

Gateway airport	Airport code	Passengers, (1,000)	Gateway airport	Airport code	Passengers, (1,000)
Total, all airports	(X)	**215,266**	Dallas-Ft. Worth, TX	DFW	7,854
Total, top 20 airports	(X)	191,596	Washington (Dulles), DC	IAD	7,203
Top 20, percentage of total	(X)	89.0	Boston, MA	BOS	6,233
			Fort Lauderdale, FL	FLL	5,879
New York (JFK), NY	JFK	31,595	Orlando, FL	MCO	5,476
Los Angeles, CA	LAX	22,544	Honolulu, HI	HNL	5,131
Miami, FL	MIA	20,533	Seattle-Tacoma, WA	SEA	4,663
San Francisco, CA	SFO	12,197	Philadelphia, PA	PHL	3,692
Chicago (O'Hare), IL	ORD	12,118	Las Vegas, NV	LAS	3,509
Newark, NJ	EWR	11,867	Detroit, MI	DTW	3,331
Atlanta, GA	ATL	11,209	Guam Island, GU	GUM	2,986
Houston (G. Bush), TX	IAH	10,598	Charlotte, NC	CLT	2,980

X Not applicable.

Source: U.S. Department of Transportation, Research and Innovative Technology Administration, Bureau of Transportation Statistics, Office of Airline Information, "T-100 International Segment data," <http://www.transtats.bts.gov/Fields.asp?Table_ID=261>, accessed July 2017.

Table 1288. Crossings for Top 5 U.S.-Canadian and U.S.-Mexican Border Land Passenger Gateways: 2016

[27,320 represents 27,320,000]

Item and gateway	Entering the U.S. (1,000)	Item and gateway	Entering the U.S. (1,000)
All U.S.-Canadian land gateways: [1]		**All U.S.-Mexican land gateways:** [1]	
Personal vehicles	27,320	Personal vehicles	75,625
Personal vehicle passengers	49,812	Personal vehicle passengers	140,702
Buses	88	Buses	181
Bus passengers	1,939	Bus passengers	2,269
Train passengers	287	Train passengers	14
Pedestrians	447	Pedestrians	42,169
Top five gateways:		**Top five gateways:**	
Personal vehicles:		Personal vehicles:	
Buffalo-Niagara Falls, NY	4,792	San Ysidro, CA	13,702
Detroit, MI	4,041	El Paso, TX	12,526
Blaine, WA	3,901	Otay Mesa, CA	7,722
Port Huron, MI	1,562	Laredo, TX	5,092
Champlain-Rouses Pt., NY	1,012	Hidalgo, TX	4,721
Personal vehicle passengers:		Personal vehicle passengers:	
Buffalo-Niagara Falls, NY	10,247	San Ysidro, CA	24,014
Blaine, WA	7,672	El Paso, TX	20,768
Detroit, MI	6,789	Otay Mesa, CA	13,583
Port Huron, MI	3,034	Laredo, TX	10,746
Champlain-Rouses Pt., NY	2,254	Hidalgo, TX	9,635
Pedestrians:		Pedestrians:	
Buffalo-Niagara Falls, NY	341	San Ysidro, CA	7,382
Sumas, WA	34	El Paso, TX	7,033
Point Roberts, WA	27	Calexico, CA	4,271
International Falls, MN	12	Laredo, TX	3,574
Calais, ME	9	Otay Mesa, CA	3,505

[1] Data reflect all personal vehicles and buses, passengers, and pedestrians entering the U.S.-Canadian border and U.S.-Mexican border, regardless of nationality.

Source: U.S. Department of Transportation, Bureau of Transportation Statistics, "Border Crossing / Entry Data," <www.transtats.bts.gov/bordercrossing.aspx>, accessed September 2017.

Table 1289. Foreign Tourists Admitted by Country of Citizenship: 2000 to 2015

[In thousands (30,511 represents 30,511,000). For years ending September 30. Represents non-U.S. citizens admitted to the country for a temporary period of time, for pleasure (tourists). Includes nonimmigrant admission classes B2 (temporary visitors for pleasure), GMT (Commonwealth of the Northern Marianas Islands visa waiver program–temporary visitors for pleasure, Guam or Northern Mariana Islands), and WT (visa waiver program–temporary visitors for pleasure)]

Country and region	2000 [1]	2005	2010	2015	Country and region	2000 [1]	2005	2010	2015
All countries [2]	**30,511**	**23,815**	**35,131**	**61,017**	Thailand	76	37	48	72
Europe [3]	**11,806**	**10,016**	**11,741**	**13,552**	Turkey	93	57	74	143
Austria	182	116	166	181	United Arab Emirates	36	3	8	28
Belgium	254	154	227	244	**Africa** [3]	**327**	**212**	**274**	**540**
Czech Republic	44	26	58	87	Egypt	44	19	34	73
Denmark	150	153	244	281	Nigeria	27	40	62	170
Finland	95	76	106	128	South Africa	114	64	63	99
France [4]	1,113	1,007	1,371	1,658	**Oceania** [3]	**748**	**723**	**1,046**	**1,543**
Germany	1,925	1,248	1,599	1,786	Australia	535	527	843	1,245
Greece	60	40	54	57	New Zealand	170	184	191	281
Hungary	58	30	49	68	**North America** [3, 6]	**6,501**	**5,546**	**12,754**	**30,038**
Iceland	27	34	35	48	Canada [7]	277	23	87	9,977
Ireland	325	398	406	402	Mexico	3,972	4,070	11,010	17,904
Italy	626	636	924	1,052	**Caribbean**	**1,404**	**876**	**999**	**1,226**
Netherlands [4]	559	483	598	596	Bahamas, The	24	257	250	229
Norway	144	117	197	273	Dominican Republic	195	189	219	295
Poland	116	119	103	146	Haiti	72	65	90	126
Portugal	86	81	120	151	Jamaica	240	152	180	249
Russia	74	53	134	242	Trinidad and Tobago	133	106	129	163
Spain	370	402	692	846	**Central America**	**792**	**578**	**657**	**930**
Sweden	321	249	330	505	Costa Rica	172	109	143	202
Switzerland	400	207	315	409	El Salvador	175	147	105	150
United Kingdom [4]	4,671	4,232	3,768	3,991	Guatemala	177	135	159	209
Asia [3]	**7,853**	**5,688**	**6,255**	**9,827**	Honduras	87	75	101	156
China [5]	656	221	482	1,950	Nicaragua	47	33	38	56
India	253	247	490	921	Panama	106	64	94	136
Indonesia	62	42	44	84	**South America** [3]	**2,867**	**1,498**	**2,785**	**5,484**
Israel	319	220	253	340	Argentina	515	145	375	713
Japan	4,946	3,758	3,252	3,350	Bolivia	48	18	31	55
Korea, South	606	528	896	1,564	Brazil	706	385	976	2,222
Malaysia	64	32	37	59	Chile	194	82	119	298
Pakistan	47	34	39	87	Colombia	411	282	455	854
Philippines	163	144	179	255	Ecuador	122	119	169	351
Saudi Arabia	67	10	36	138	Peru	190	142	162	269
Singapore	131	57	72	97	Uruguay	66	24	35	70
Taiwan	(NA)	201	183	344	Venezuela	570	270	423	560

[1] Due to the expiration of the Visa Waiver Program during May-October 2000, data for business and pleasure not available separately. [2] Total includes visitors of unknown country of citizenship. [3] Total includes other countries, not shown separately. [4] As of 2005, includes overseas territories; see source for details. [5] Prior to 2005, data for China includes Taiwan. As of 2005, data for China includes Hong Kong and Macau. [6] The majority of short-term admissions from Canada and Mexico are excluded. [7] The number of admissions in 2015 greatly exceeds totals reported in previous years due to a more complete count of Canadian air and sea admissions.

Source: U.S. Department of Homeland Security, Office of Immigration Statistics, *2015 Yearbook of Immigration Statistics*, December 2016, and earlier reports. See also <https://www.dhs.gov/immigration-statistics/yearbook>.

Section 27
Accommodation, Food Services, and Other Services

This section presents statistics relating to services other than those covered in the previous sections on wholesale and retail trade, transportation, communications, financial services, and recreation services. Data shown for services are classified by kind of business and cover sales or receipts, establishments, employees, payrolls, and other items.

The principal sources of these data are from the U.S. Census Bureau and include the 2007 and 2012 Economic Census, annual surveys, and the County Business Patterns program. These data are supplemented by data from several sources including the National Restaurant Association on food and drink sales (Table 1298) and the American Hotel & Lodging Association on lodging (Table 1296).

Data on these services also appear in several other sections. For instance, labor force employment and earnings data appear in Section 12, Labor Force, Employment, and Earnings; gross domestic product of the industry (Table 693) appears in Section 13, Income, Expenditures, Poverty, and Wealth; and financial data (several tables) from the quarterly *Statistics of Income Bulletin*, published by the Internal Revenue Service, appear in Section 15, Business Enterprise.

Censuses—Limited coverage of the service industries started in 1933. Beginning with the 1967 census, legislation provides for a census of each area to be conducted every 5 years (for years ending in "2" and "7"). For more information on the most current census, see the Census Bureau's Economic Census website at <https://www.census.gov/programs-surveys/economic-census.html>. The industries covered in the censuses and surveys of business are defined in the North American Industry Classification System

(NAICS). For information on NAICS, see the Census website at <www.census.gov/eos/www/naics/>.

In general, the 2007 and 2012 Economic Censuses have three series of publications for these sectors: 1) subject series with reports such as product lines, and establishment and firm sizes, 2) geographic reports with individual reports for each state, and 3) industry series with individual reports for industry groups.

Release of data from the *2012 Economic Census* was completed in 2016.

Current surveys—The Service Annual Survey provides annual estimates of nationwide receipts for selected personal, business, leasing and repair, amusement and entertainment, social and health, and other professional service industries in the United States. For selected social, health, and other professional service industries, separate estimates are developed for receipts of taxable firms and revenue and expenses for firms and organizations exempt from federal income taxes. Several service sectors from this survey are covered in other sections of this publication. The estimates for tax exempt firms in these industries are derived from a sample of employer firms only. Estimates obtained from annual and monthly surveys are based on sample data and are not expected to agree exactly with results that would be obtained from a complete census of all establishments. Data include estimates for sampling units not reporting. Data are released in the *Quarterly Services Report* and the *Annual Services Report* at <http://www.census.gov/services/index.html>.

Statistical reliability—For a discussion of statistical collection and estimation, sampling procedures, and measures of statistical reliability applicable to Census Bureau data, see Appendix III.

Table 1290. Selected Service-Related Industries—Establishments, Sales, Payroll, and Employees by Kind of Business: 2012

[1,480,277,061 represents $1,480,277,061,000. Covers only establishments with payroll. Based on the 2012 Economic Census; for statement on methodology, see Appendix III]

Kind of business	2012 NAICS code [1]	Establish-ments, (number)	Sales or receipts ($1,000)	Annual payroll (1,000)	Paid employ-ees [2] (number)
Professional, scientific, and technical services............	54	856,463	1,480,277,061	581,406,127	8,203,735
Professional, scientific, and technical services..............	541	856,463	1,480,277,061	581,406,127	8,203,735
Management of companies and enterprises..............	55	53,765	115,513,632	308,764,261	3,082,292
Administrative and support and waste management and remediation services........	56	386,387	673,036,536	329,013,077	9,774,262
Administrative and support services...................	561	363,188	593,837,306	311,056,595	9,405,895
Waste management and remediation services..........	562	23,199	79,199,230	17,956,482	368,367
Accommodation and food services.................	72	662,489	708,138,598	196,103,341	12,007,689
Accommodation........	721	63,833	195,858,388	50,120,659	1,950,081
Food services and drinking places.................	722	598,656	512,280,210	145,982,682	10,057,608
Other services (except public administration)........	81	529,691	426,693,675	108,185,736	3,430,711
Repair and maintenance.......................	811	210,151	143,943,567	41,273,746	1,194,122
Personal and laundry services.................	812	212,568	87,031,329	28,674,529	1,349,371
Religious, grantmaking, civic, professional, and similar organizations................	813	106,972	195,718,779	38,237,461	887,218

[1] North American Industrial Classification System, 2012; see text, Section 15. [2] For employees on the payroll during the pay period including March 12.

Source: U.S. Census Bureau, 2012 Economic Census, "EC1200A1: All sectors: Geographic Area Series: Economy-Wide Key Statistics: 2012," <http://factfinder.census.gov>, accessed July 2016.

Table 1291. Selected Service-Related Industries—Nonemployer Establishments and Receipts by Kind of Business: 2013 to 2015

[3,236 represents 3,236,000. Includes only firms subject to federal income tax. Nonemployers are businesses with no paid employees. Data originate chiefly from administrative records of the Internal Revenue Service; see Appendix III]

Kind of business	NAICS code [1]	Firms (1,000)			Receipts (mil. dol.)		
		2013	2014	2015	2013	2014	2015
Professional, scientific, and technical services..............	54	3,236	3,363	3,411	143,067	153,887	157,584
Professional, scientific, and technical services [2]...............	541	3,236	3,363	3,411	143,067	153,887	157,584
Legal services.......................	5411	278	287	290	18,009	19,188	19,565
Accounting, tax preparation, bookkeeping, and payroll services........	5412	359	371	374	9,143	9,828	10,083
Architectural, engineering, and related services...........	5413	229	232	230	10,999	11,546	11,635
Specialized design services.................	5414	219	225	228	7,817	8,422	8,721
Computer systems design and related services..............	5415	306	308	305	14,145	14,872	14,955
Management, scientific and technical consulting..............	5416	668	711	729	31,973	34,963	35,925
Scientific research and development services..............	5417	35	38	39	1,269	1,324	1,420
Advertising, public relations, and related services.............	5418	142	145	147	7,490	7,958	8,071
Administrative and support and waste management and remediation services...........	56	2,033	2,075	2,069	42,969	45,390	46,393
Administrative and support services [2]..........	561	2,012	2,055	2,050	41,489	43,855	44,870
Office administrative services................	5611	223	230	233	3,723	3,963	4,132
Business support services................	5614	222	221	218	5,938	6,084	6,193
Services to buildings and dwellings............	5617	1,254	1,284	1,277	23,389	24,906	25,442
Waste management and remediation services..............	562	20	20	19	1,480	1,535	1,523
Accommodation and food services............	72	346	364	371	15,306	16,197	17,658
Accommodation........	721	58	63	66	3,191	3,364	3,826
Food services and drinking places..............	722	288	301	306	12,115	12,833	13,832
Special food services........	7223	169	178	183	4,504	4,801	5,113
Drinking places (alcoholic beverages)............	7224	28	27	25	1,641	1,649	1,671
Restaurants and other eating places............	7225	92	97	97	5,969	6,383	7,048
Full-service restaurants........	722511	42	43	43	2,918	3,040	3,373
Limited-service eating places............	722513	36	37	36	2,695	2,891	3,129
Other services (except public administration)............	81	3,584	3,680	3,695	90,754	95,823	98,971
Repair and maintenance [2]............	811	752	765	756	27,248	28,560	29,004
Automotive repair and maintenance..........	8111	325	330	328	13,918	14,591	14,856
Personal and household goods repair and maintenance.....	8114	325	335	330	9,044	9,546	9,759
Personal and laundry services [2]............	812	2,622	2,702	2,727	60,246	63,901	66,573
Personal care services..........	8121	1,301	1,344	1,352	27,931	29,621	31,051
Hair, nail, and skin care services.............	81211	1,081	1,105	1,104	23,820	25,063	26,118
Beauty salons.............	812112	733	748	746	15,043	15,714	16,280
Death care services...........	8122	17	17	17	849	880	913
Drycleaning and laundry services.............	8123	32	32	31	1,749	1,766	1,789
Other personal services.............	8129	1,272	1,309	1,327	29,717	31,633	32,820
Religious, grantmaking, civic, professional, and similar organizations.............	813	209	213	212	3,260	3,362	3,394

[1] North American Industry Classification System, see text, Section 15. Data based on NAICS 2012. [2] Includes other kinds of business not shown separately.

Source: U.S. Census Bureau, Nonemployer Statistics, "Geographic Area Series: Nonemployer Statistics by Legal Form of Organization for the U.S. and States," <http://factfinder.census.gov>, accessed June 2017. See also <http://www.census.gov/econ/nonemployer/>.

Table 1292. Selected Service-Related Industries—Establishments, Employees, and Payroll by Industry: 2014 and 2015

[In thousands (882.8 represents 882,800); payroll in billions of dollars (665.2 represents $665,200,000,000). Covers establishments with paid employees. Excludes self-employed individuals, employees of private households, railroad employees, agricultural production employees, and most government employees; see source for NAICS and other exclusions. For statement on methodology, see Appendix III]

Industry	2012 NAICS code [1]	Establishments (1,000)		Employees [2] (1,000)		Annual payroll (bil. dol.)	
		2014	2015	2014	2015	2014	2015
Professional, scientific, & technical services.............	**54**	**882.8**	**896.0**	**8,619.6**	**8,798.3**	**665.2**	**704.4**
Professional, scientific, & technical services.................	541	882.8	896.0	8,619.6	8,798.3	665.2	704.4
Legal services..	5411	186.7	186.2	1,150.5	1,139.3	97.1	100.3
Offices of lawyers.......................................	54111	173.2	172.8	1,071.0	1,060.5	92.9	95.9
Accounting, tax preparation, bookkeeping, and payroll services..................................	5412	132.1	132.9	1,422.4	1,453.8	68.2	74.3
Offices of certified public accountants.................	541211	56.6	56.5	454.5	481.2	33.0	36.3
Tax preparation services...............................	541213	31.1	31.4	198.5	193.7	2.2	2.4
Architectural, engineering, & related services [3].......	5413	109.0	111.6	1,415.4	1,438.0	117.0	119.5
Architectural services..................................	54131	21.3	21.5	157.4	163.2	11.9	12.9
Engineering services....................................	54133	59.0	60.9	1,021.3	1,029.4	91.0	91.9
Specialized design services [3]........................	5414	30.8	31.5	108.1	113.0	6.1	6.6
Graphic design services................................	54143	15.3	15.3	51.5	52.8	2.9	3.0
Computer systems design & related services [3]...........	5415	135.4	138.8	1,643.0	1,687.6	153.4	163.5
Custom computer programming services...................	541511	66.2	67.0	719.8	784.7	65.0	75.1
Computer systems design services......................	541512	50.5	53.0	623.4	653.1	59.7	64.0
Management, scientific, technical consulting services [3]....	5416	165.2	168.8	1,150.8	1,183.7	90.1	95.6
Management consulting services.......................	54161	130.6	134.1	949.6	976.5	75.1	79.9
Environmental consulting services......................	54162	10.0	10.0	78.1	78.9	5.1	5.2
Scientific research & development services...............	5417	18.2	19.0	670.6	710.1	75.3	84.5
Research & development in the physical engineering & life sciences...............................	54171	16.3	17.0	633.6	671.7	72.8	81.8
Advertising & related services [3].......................	5418	37.5	37.5	468.0	462.2	31.9	32.5
Advertising agencies....................................	54181	13.3	13.4	190.6	188.8	15.7	16.4
Public relations agencies................................	54182	8.3	8.5	53.8	55.1	5.3	5.4
Other professional, scientific, & technical services.........	5419	68.0	69.8	590.8	610.7	26.0	27.6
Veterinary services......................................	54194	30.6	31.0	323.2	338.7	11.3	12.4
Management of companies and enterprises...............	**55**	**53.8**	**53.9**	**3,236.0**	**3,308.8**	**350.2**	**367.0**
Administrative and support and waste management and remediation services.............	**56**	**398.2**	**404.3**	**10,579.3**	**11,112.5**	**395.5**	**428.2**
Administrative & support services [3].....................	561	374.4	380.4	10,200.5	10,728.6	375.1	407.0
Employment services....................................	5613	48.6	51.5	5,604.3	6,023.6	217.6	240.6
Temporary help services...............................	56132	32.1	34.7	3,094.8	3,320.0	91.1	98.4
Business support services [3]...........................	5614	33.1	32.8	763.8	787.2	25.3	26.6
Telephone call centers..................................	56142	5.2	5.2	434.5	449.0	11.5	11.8
Collection agencies.....................................	56144	4.4	4.2	128.1	124.3	4.9	4.9
Travel arrangement & reservation services...............	5615	25.2	23.4	231.9	229.9	12.7	12.7
Travel agencies...	56151	18.6	16.8	99.9	119.0	5.2	6.8
Investigation & security services.........................	5616	25.7	25.7	895.0	910.3	25.1	26.0
Investigation, guard, & armored car services.............	56161	14.8	14.8	766.7	779.4	19.1	19.7
Security systems services..............................	56162	10.9	10.9	128.3	130.9	5.9	6.3
Services to buildings & dwellings [3].....................	5617	184.7	189.1	1,763.4	1,805.8	46.6	49.8
Landscaping services...................................	56173	96.4	98.7	568.4	587.0	20.1	21.9
Waste management & remediation services..............	562	23.7	23.9	378.8	383.9	20.4	21.2
Waste collection..	5621	10.9	10.9	196.6	199.8	10.2	10.9
Waste treatment & disposal.............................	5622	2.6	2.6	51.8	51.3	3.3	3.3
Remediation & other waste management services.........	5629	10.2	10.4	130.4	132.7	6.8	7.0
Accommodation & food services..................	**72**	**679.3**	**687.6**	**12,791.9**	**13,196.9**	**228.5**	**245.2**
Accommodation...	721	65.1	66.0	1,998.7	2,032.0	54.9	57.8
Traveler accommodation.................................	7211	55.6	56.6	1,944.2	1,977.1	53.3	56.1
Hotels (except casino hotels) & motels..................	72111	50.7	51.7	1,503.0	1,540.0	39.0	41.5
RV (recreational vehicle) parks & recreational camps......	7212	7.3	7.4	42.6	43.4	1.4	1.4
Rooming & boarding houses.............................	7213	2.1	2.1	12.0	11.6	0.3	0.3
Food services & drinking places.........................	722	614.2	621.6	10,793.2	11,164.9	173.5	187.5
Drinking places (alcoholic beverages)...................	7224	41.0	40.7	362.2	367.6	5.7	6.1
Restaurants and other eating places.....................	7225	531.7	542.0	9,701.0	10,081.0	152.5	166.3
Full-service restaurants.................................	722511	239.0	243.1	5,063.9	5,253.9	89.8	97.9
Limited-service restaurants.............................	722513	228.7	233.4	3,893.9	4,043.2	51.9	56.6
Cafeterias, grill buffets, and buffets....................	722514	6.0	6.0	120.3	123.1	1.7	1.7
Snack and nonalcoholic beverage bars..................	722515	58.0	59.5	622.9	660.8	9.2	10.0
Other services (except public administration).............	**81**	**739.9**	**746.0**	**5,347.1**	**5,401.2**	**161.3**	**168.7**
Repair & maintenance [3]................................	811	212.1	213.5	1,226.6	1,244.7	46.8	49.4
Automotive repair & maintenance........................	8111	158.0	158.8	850.7	865.1	28.6	30.3
Personal & household goods repair & maintenance........	8114	20.5	20.8	68.1	69.9	2.1	2.3
Personal & laundry services [3].........................	812	220.3	225.6	1,365.0	1,398.1	31.7	33.7
Personal care services..................................	8121	122.7	125.9	658.8	669.9	13.0	13.9
Death care services....................................	8122	20.8	20.8	139.3	139.3	4.8	5.0
Drycleaning & laundry services.........................	8123	35.2	34.7	288.7	294.7	7.5	7.8
Religious/grantmaking/civic/professional [4].............	813	307.5	307.0	2,755.5	2,758.4	82.7	85.6
Religious organizations..................................	8131	184.3	184.2	1,685.0	1,679.6	34.6	35.6
Grantmaking & giving services..........................	8132	19.5	19.7	183.3	186.9	10.4	10.9
Social advocacy organizations..........................	8133	17.1	17.3	161.0	165.1	7.2	7.7
Civic & social organizations.............................	8134	26.2	26.3	235.1	238.8	4.8	5.1
Business/professional/labor/political [4]..................	8139	60.5	59.5	491.2	487.9	25.7	26.3
Labor unions [4]..	81393	14.3	14.2	150.2	149.0	5.4	5.5

[1] North American Industry Classification System (NAICS), 2012. See text, section 15. [2] Includes employees on the payroll for the pay period including March 12. [3] Includes other kinds of business, not shown separately. [4] Also includes other similar organizations.

Source: U.S. Census Bureau, County Business Patterns, "Geography Area Series: County Business Patterns," <https://factfinder.census.gov/>, accessed April 2017. See also <https://www.census.gov/programs-surveys/cbp.html>.

Table 1293. Employed Persons in Service Industries by Sex, Race, and Hispanic Origin and by Industry: 2016

[18,325 represents 18,325,000. Civilian noninstitutionalized population 16 years and older. Based on the Current Population Survey (CPS); see text, Section 1, and Appendix III. For information on employees in other sectors, see Table 638 and Table 655]

Industry	2012 NAICS code [1]	Total employed (1,000)	Percent of total			
			Female	Black [2]	Asian [2]	Hispanic or Latino [3]
Professional and business services..........................	**54-56**	**18,325**	**41.4**	**9.7**	**8.3**	**16.6**
Professional and technical services.......................	**54**	**11,228**	**42.2**	**6.5**	**11.2**	**8.8**
Legal services..........................	5411	1,610	55.3	6.3	3.7	10.6
Accounting, tax preparation, bookkeeping, and payroll services..........................	5412	1,110	60.2	6.9	7.8	10.6
Architectural, engineering, and related services...............	5413	1,652	23.6	5.7	7.3	9.0
Specialized design services..........................	5414	402	57.1	4.8	5.5	12.5
Computer systems design and related services................	5415	2,845	26.1	7.3	22.8	5.9
Management, scientific, and technical consulting services..........................	5416	1,652	43.7	7.3	9.8	7.5
Scientific research and development services................	5417	597	48.7	6.5	16.4	8.5
Advertising, public relations, and related services............	5418	548	51.4	4.1	5.0	12.3
Other professional, scientific, and technical services [4]........	5419	464	53.2	7.8	6.6	13.4
Veterinary services..........................	54194	347	81.2	2.9	2.3	8.4
Management, administrative, and waste services............	**55-56**	**7,097**	**40.0**	**14.9**	**3.6**	**28.9**
Management of companies and enterprises....................	55	188	44.2	7.6	5.5	13.5
Employment services..........................	5613	1,046	54.0	23.2	5.2	20.3
Business support services..........................	5614	808	64.2	18.8	4.5	18.5
Travel arrangement and reservation services.................	5615	304	62.1	9.0	9.0	13.2
Investigations and security services..........................	5616	828	24.1	24.8	4.2	16.6
Services to buildings and dwellings [5]..........................	5617	1,599	56.3	12.9	2.6	42.0
Landscaping services..........................	56173	1,412	8.3	6.8	1.2	43.7
Other administrative and support services....................	5611,2,9	334	49.5	11.2	6.1	16.9
Waste management and remediation services..............	562	577	17.2	13.2	2.0	24.1
Accommodation and food services..........................	**72**	**10,952**	**52.3**	**13.3**	**7.1**	**25.8**
Accommodation..........................	721	1,592	55.5	13.8	8.9	28.4
Traveler accommodation..........................	7211	1,488	56.1	14.4	9.6	29.6
Recreational vehicle parks and camps, and rooming and board houses..........................	7212,3	104	47.2	4.0	0.1	10.8
Food services and drinking places..........................	722	9,360	51.7	13.2	6.8	25.4
Restaurants and other food services [6]..........................	722, excl. 7224	9,134	51.7	13.4	6.9	25.6
Drinking places, alcoholic beverages..........................	7224	226	51.1	5.9	2.3	13.9
Other services..........................	**81**	**7,320**	**52.2**	**10.6**	**7.7**	**18.1**
Other services (except private households)....................	81	6,596	47.9	11.0	8.1	15.9
Repair and maintenance..........................	811	2,051	10.9	7.9	3.9	23.7
Automotive repair and maintenance [7]..........................	8111	1,205	8.3	7.7	3.3	24.3
Car washes..........................	811192	168	12.0	12.8	2.5	34.3
Electronic and precision equipment repair and maintenance..........................	8112	134	17.2	12.2	8.9	17.3
Commercial and industrial machinery and equipment repair and maintenance..........................	8113	322	7.0	5.6	2.5	23.3
Personal and household goods repair and maintenance [8]..........................	8114	218	26.5	6.1	7.0	16.1
Footwear and leather goods repair..........................	81143	5	(Z)	(Z)	(Z)	(Z)
Personal and laundry services..........................	812	2,481	71.7	12.6	14.2	15.5
Barber shops..........................	812111	134	20.5	34.6	2.8	19.5
Beauty salons..........................	812112	982	91.2	12.7	6.8	16.3
Nail salons and other personal care services.................	812113, 81219	541	75.4	7.3	43.2	7.2
Drycleaning and laundry services..........................	8123	286	56.6	14.6	10.5	31.2
Funeral homes, cemeteries, and crematories..................	8122	149	40.9	11.7	1.4	11.2
Other personal services..........................	8129	389	57.8	11.3	4.2	13.8
Membership associations and organizations....................	813	2,064	55.9	12.0	4.8	8.5
Religious organizations..........................	8131	1,088	47.2	10.3	4.8	8.4
Civic, social, advocacy organizations, grantmaking and giving services..........................	8132,3,4	754	68.9	15.3	5.2	8.6
Business, professional, political, and similar organizations [9]..........................	8139	164	56.9	8.5	3.4	6.0
Labor unions..........................	81393	58	46.3	12.0	3.1	17.4
Private households..........................	814	724	91.7	7.6	4.1	38.5

Z Base less than 50,000. [1] Based on the North American Industry Classification System, 2012; see Section 15. [2] The Current Population Survey (CPS) allows respondents to choose more than one race. Data represent persons who selected this race group only and exclude persons reporting more than one race. See also comments on race in text for Section 1. [3] Persons of Hispanic origin may be of any race. [4] Excludes NAICS 54194 (veterinary services). [5] Excludes NAICS 56173 (landscaping services). [6] Excludes NAICS 7224 (drinking places, alcoholic beverages). [7] Excludes NAICS 811192 (car washes). [8] Excludes NAICS 81143 (footwear and leather goods repair). [9] Excludes NAICS 81393 (labor unions).

Source: U.S. Bureau of Labor Statistics, CPS Tables, "Employed persons by detailed industry, sex, race, and Hispanic or Latino ethnicity," <http://www.bls.gov/cps/tables.htm>, accessed February 2017.

Table 1294. Selected Service-Related Industries—Establishments, Employees, and Annual Payroll by State: 2015

[Employees in thousands (8,798 represents 8,798,000); payroll in millions of dollars (704,390 represents $704,390,000,000). Covers establishments with paid employees. Excludes most government employees, railroad employees, and self-employed persons. Data are from Census Bureau's County Business Patterns program. For statement on methodology, see Appendix III]

State	Professional, scientific, and technical services (NAICS 54) [1]			Administrative and support and waste management and remediation services (NAICS 56) [1]			Accommodation and food services (NAICS 72) [1]		
	Establish-ments	Employ-ees [2] (1,000)	Annual payroll (mil. dol.)	Establish-ments	Employ-ees [2] (1,000)	Annual payroll (mil. dol.)	Establish-ments	Employ-ees [2] (1,000)	Annual payroll (mil. dol.)
United States........	896,026	8,798	704,390	404,282	11,112	428,199	687,619	13,197	245,248
Alabama................	9,404	97	6,590	4,304	135	3,670	8,551	171	2,512
Alaska..................	1,920	19	1,427	1,131	18	841	2,125	28	738
Arizona................	17,221	145	10,084	8,367	256	8,665	12,207	282	5,045
Arkansas..............	5,944	37	2,042	2,639	61	1,430	5,600	101	1,441
California..............	122,589	1,258	114,129	43,631	1,389	65,843	83,829	1,609	33,797
Colorado..............	25,558	191	16,847	8,877	251	11,337	13,262	271	5,221
Connecticut..........	9,286	108	9,350	5,381	86	3,553	8,459	141	2,966
Delaware..............	2,852	31	3,294	1,462	28	957	2,086	39	708
District of Columbia.....	5,532	100	12,461	1,114	32	1,366	2,504	69	1,910
Florida.................	76,416	488	32,376	35,004	1,509	62,153	39,324	908	17,691
Georgia...............	29,216	252	18,587	12,324	377	13,184	19,704	404	6,504
Hawaii.................	3,350	23	1,451	1,845	60	1,962	3,627	105	2,983
Idaho..................	4,551	33	1,801	2,296	40	1,091	3,605	59	898
Illinois.................	39,132	403	34,824	17,075	519	17,234	27,731	507	9,567
Indiana................	12,928	112	6,970	7,314	207	6,127	13,123	270	4,062
Iowa...................	6,324	55	3,219	3,649	77	2,349	6,933	119	1,742
Kansas................	7,184	64	4,039	3,630	77	2,578	6,034	114	1,640
Kentucky..............	8,290	73	3,492	4,058	119	2,951	7,910	170	2,506
Louisiana.............	12,263	106	6,598	4,738	105	3,913	9,390	212	3,756
Maine..................	3,504	23	1,427	2,132	23	715	4,122	51	1,077
Maryland..............	20,503	274	23,391	8,328	192	8,029	11,656	221	4,159
Massachusetts.......	21,512	277	29,669	10,549	200	9,905	17,230	288	6,178
Michigan..............	21,480	263	19,439	11,762	334	10,456	19,769	371	6,061
Minnesota............	16,767	179	14,185	7,519	164	6,457	11,482	236	4,108
Mississippi............	4,741	31	1,591	2,223	57	1,423	5,450	124	2,015
Missouri...............	13,858	157	11,099	7,629	168	5,206	12,472	254	4,081
Montana...............	3,711	20	960	1,770	25	882	3,480	50	826
Nebraska..............	4,629	99	5,004	2,672	61	2,172	4,426	74	1,074
Nevada................	8,758	58	3,598	4,297	112	3,658	6,306	318	9,313
New Hampshire.........	3,783	31	2,053	2,341	51	2,441	3,684	56	1,076
New Jersey............	29,351	322	28,654	13,991	317	12,685	20,610	296	5,938
New Mexico...........	4,724	(S)	(S)	1,855	32	1,056	4,247	86	1,475
New York..............	61,371	644	58,568	26,982	581	30,564	52,169	761	17,969
North Carolina.........	23,859	211	15,500	12,422	374	12,603	20,199	393	6,249
North Dakota...........	1,899	16	995	1142	15	545	2,077	40	665
Ohio...................	24,087	250	16,715	13,526	397	12,629	23,697	462	6,928
Oklahoma.............	9,794	71	4,314	4,497	104	3,778	7,781	149	2,230
Oregon................	12,068	91	6,693	5,740	99	3,334	11,057	170	3,177
Pennsylvania.........	29,792	324	25,079	15,629	332	11,245	27,997	458	7,412
Rhode Island..........	3,054	23	1,460	1,753	24	890	3,053	47	889
South Carolina.........	10,271	83	5,332	5,784	172	5,269	10,219	208	3,380
South Dakota..........	1,928	12	585	1,094	11	343	2,421	41	648
Tennessee.............	11,243	113	7,518	6,956	245	7,323	12,509	268	4,414
Texas..................	68,165	685	55,782	27,587	950	36,418	52,086	1,111	19,312
Utah...................	10,146	94	4,886	4,288	126	4,346	5,505	112	1,749
Vermont...............	2,125	19	922	1,111	8	255	1,951	33	594
Virginia................	30,859	438	40,494	10,642	245	9,805	17,398	340	5,952
Washington............	21,267	193	16,117	9,642	152	6,699	16,704	268	5,609
West Virginia..........	2,921	27	1,313	1,479	32	938	3,555	67	1,049
Wisconsin.............	11,581	108	6,916	7,069	158	4,706	14,462	234	3,379
Wyoming..............	2,315	10	559	1,032	7	217	1,841	29	574

S Data do not meet publication standards. [1] North American Industry Classification System, 2012. See text, section 15. [2] For employees on the payroll for the pay period including March 12.

Source: U.S. Census Bureau, County Business Patterns, "Geography Area Series: County Business Patterns," <https://factfinder.census.gov/>, accessed April 2017. See also <https://www.census.gov/programs-surveys/cbp.html>.

Table 1295. Professional, Scientific, and Technical Services—Estimated Revenue by Kind of Business: 2010 to 2015

[In millions of dollars (1,293,795 represents $1,293,795,000,000). For taxable employer firms. Estimates have been adjusted to the results of the 2012 Economic Census. Based on the Service Annual Survey and administrative data; see Appendix III]

Kind of business	2007 NAICS code [1]	2010	2011	2012	2013	2014	2015
Professional, scientific, and technical services (except notaries) [2, 3]	54	1,293,795	1,377,251	1,440,060	1,471,255	1,549,333	1,605,848
Offices of lawyers	54111	231,608	241,696	246,141	245,031	251,745	260,956
Other legal services	54119	11,228	10,907	12,810	14,121	13,193	14,092
Offices of certified public accountants	541211	68,702	70,834	76,911	79,715	84,586	91,321
Tax preparation services	541213	5,740	5,848	5,848	6,276	6,657	7,099
Payroll services	541214	25,748	27,095	29,306	31,020	32,803	35,097
Other accounting services	541219	15,742	16,912	18,196	19,126	20,733	22,498
Architectural services	54131	26,849	28,058	28,129	28,865	31,967	34,864
Landscape architectural services	54132	3,021	2,954	2,796	3,018	3,211	3,357
Engineering services	54133	191,660	209,570	208,124	205,874	217,178	225,517
Drafting services	54134	602	739	833	931	1,046	1,134
Building inspection services	54135	1,856	1,931	2,005	2,114	2,416	2,590
Surveying and mapping services [4]	5413z	7,534	7,979	8,735	9,083	9,871	9,130
Testing laboratories	54138	14,057	15,431	15,324	16,146	16,257	17,190
Interior design services	54141	6,594	7,144	7,671	8,172	9,479	10,351
Industrial design services	54142	1,308	1,579	1,629	1,690	1,827	1,941
Graphic design services	54143	7,378	7,544	7,552	7,497	8,157	8,761
Other specialized design services	54149	945	1,148	1,355	1,301	1,506	1,562
Computer systems design and related services	5415	283,362	306,119	326,032	331,025	347,637	348,245
Management consulting services [5]	54161	138,955	154,155	170,213	180,646	193,290	199,868
Environmental consulting services	54162	12,554	13,266	13,477	13,409	13,018	12,789
Other scientific and technical consulting services	54169	18,779	20,936	23,599	25,714	27,821	29,409
Research and development in physical, engineering and life sciences	54171	73,067	76,589	77,059	80,564	86,013	92,803
Research and development in social sciences and humanities	54172	1,848	1,902	1,907	2,142	2,293	2,168
Advertising agencies	54181	30,870	31,301	34,832	35,473	37,563	39,815
Public relations agencies	54182	9,515	9,569	10,135	10,633	11,405	11,863
Media buying agencies	54183	5,107	5,865	6,725	6,939	7,165	7,503
Media representatives	54184	2,992	3,016	2,936	3,153	3,311	3,296
Display advertising	54185	7,089	7,001	7,157	7,104	7,159	7,248
Direct mail advertising	54186	10,140	10,236	10,200	10,033	10,226	10,126
Advertising material distribution services	54187	3,616	3,052	2,703	3,102	3,475	3,976
Other services related to advertising	54189	11,964	12,443	12,656	12,820	13,369	13,630
Marketing research and public opinion polling	54191	16,531	17,107	16,378	16,450	17,695	17,769
Photography studios, portrait	541921	4,180	3,875	3,682	3,676	3,952	4,109
Commercial photography	541922	1,590	1,597	1,786	1,934	1,908	1,757
Translation and interpretation services	54193	3,740	3,883	4,187	3,797	3,654	3,627
Veterinary services	54194	27,033	27,713	29,533	30,825	33,390	35,421
All other professional, scientific, and technical services	54199	10,291	10,257	11,498	11,836	12,357	12,966

[1] Based on the North American Industry Classification System, 2007; see Section 15. [2] Data prior to 2011 have been restated to reflect comparable data on the 2007 NAICS basis for more detailed levels within this aggregate. [3] Excludes NAICS 54112 (Offices of Notaries). [4] Includes NAICS 54136 (Geophysical Surveying and Mapping Services) and NAICS 54137 (Surveying and Mapping Services, except Geophysical Services). [5] A portion of NAICS 54161 (Management Consulting Services) moved to NAICS 56131 (Employment Placement Agencies and Executive Search Services) with the 2007 NAICS update. Data prior to 2011 have been restated to reflect comparable data on the 2007 NAICS basis.

Source: U.S. Census Bureau, Annual & Quarterly Services, "2015 Service Annual Survey," <http://www.census.gov/services/index.html>, accessed February 2017.

Table 1296. Lodging Industry Summary: 1990 to 2014

Year	Average occupancy rate (percent)	Average room rate (dollars)	2014			2014		
			Item	Establish-ments [1]	Rooms	Item	Business traveler	Leisure traveler
1990	63.3	57.96	Total	53,432	4,978,705	Typical night:		
2000	63.7	85.89				Made reservations (%)	95	93
2005	63.1	91.04	By Size:			Amount paid (dol.)	$147.00	$131.00
2010	57.6	98.06	Under 75 rooms	29,403	1,259,399			
2011	60.0	101.70	75–149 rooms	17,888	1,873,391	Length of stay (%):		
2012	61.4	106.15	150–299 rooms	4,456	891,651	One night	41	49
2013	62.2	110.35	300–500 rooms	1,152	428,714	Two nights	25	27
2014	64.4	115.02	Over 500 rooms	533	525,550	Three or more	33	24

[1] Based on properties with 15 or more rooms.

Source: American Hotel & Lodging Association, Washington, DC, Lodging Industry Trends 2015 ©. See also <http://www.ahla.com/information/>.

Table 1297. Selected Service Industries—E-Commerce Revenue: 2014 and 2015

[511,814 represents $511,814,000,000. Includes data only for businesses with paid employees, except for accommodation and food services, which also includes businesses with and without paid employees. Except as noted, based on the Service Annual Survey. E-commerce is defined as the value of goods and services sold online. The term "online" includes the use of the internet, intranet, extranet, as well as proprietary networks that run systems such as Electronic Data Interchange (EDI)]

Kind of business	2007 NAICS code [1]	E-commerce revenue (mil. dol.) 2014	E-commerce revenue (mil. dol.) 2015	E-commerce as percent of total revenue, 2015	E-commerce revenue, percent distribution, 2015
Selected service industries, total [2]	(X)	**511,814**	**549,742**	**3.9**	**100.0**
Utilities [3]	22	302	286	–	0.1
Selected transportation and warehousing [4]	4849y	100,617	107,826	12.3	19.6
Air transportation	481	57,209	62,686	31.3	11.4
Water transportation	483	6,113	6,522	14.8	1.2
Truck transportation	484	19,778	19,957	7.6	3.6
Transit and ground passenger transportation	485	930	975	2.9	0.2
Pipeline transportation	486	3,267	3,234	7.4	0.6
Scenic and sightseeing transportation	487	400	488	13.3	0.1
Support activities for transportation	488	(S)	(S)	(S)	(S)
Information	51	139,180	150,435	10.7	27.4
Publishing industries (except internet)	511	76,564	78,316	26.7	14.2
Motion picture and sound recording industries	512	4,646	5,836	5.9	1.1
Broadcasting (except internet)	515	1,477	1,392	0.9	0.3
Telecommunications	517	9,318	8,476	1.4	1.5
Data processing, hosting, and related services	518	13,964	15,920	12.3	2.9
Finance and insurance [5]	52	109,237	113,507	2.8	20.6
Activities related to credit intermediation	5223	14,325	14,910	16.4	2.7
Securities and commodity contracts intermediation and brokerage	5231	17,278	17,042	6.7	3.1
Real estate and rental and leasing [6]	53	29,118	30,423	5.0	5.5
Rental and leasing services	532	23,484	24,230	15.9	4.4
Selected professional, scientific, and technical services [7]	54	28,510	29,835	1.8	5.4
Computer systems design and related services	5415	8,219	8,353	2.4	1.5
Administrative and support and waste management and remediation services	56	26,255	29,057	3.6	5.3
Travel arrangement and reservation services	5615	14,087	14,895	36.5	2.7
Educational services [8]	61	5,237	5,242	8.5	1.0
Health care and social assistance	62	1,092	1,162	0.1	0.2
Arts, entertainment, and recreation	71	8,385	9,516	4.0	1.7
Accommodation and food services [9]	72	(S)	(S)	(S)	(S)
Other services (except public administration) [10]	81	11,738	13,655	2.7	2.5
Repair and maintenance	811	(S)	1,182	0.7	0.2
Personal and laundry services	812	2,647	2,894	2.9	0.5
Religious, grantmaking, civic, professional, and similar organizations	813	8,039	9,579	4.1	1.7

– Represents or rounds to zero. X Not applicable. S Data do not meet publication standards. [1] North American Industry Classification System (NAICS), 2007; see text Section 15. [2] Includes other kinds of business, not shown separately. [3] Excludes government owned utilities. [4] Excludes NAICS 482 (Rail Transportation) and NAICS 491 (Postal Service). [5] Excludes NAICS 525 (Funds, Trusts, and Other Financial Vehicles). [6] 2007 NAICS definition includes equity Real Estate Investment Trusts (REITs). [7] Excludes NAICS 54112 (Offices of Notaries). [8] Excludes NAICS 6111 (Elementary and Secondary Schools), NAICS 6112 (Junior Colleges), and NAICS 6113 (Colleges, Universities, and Professional Schools). [9] Estimates are based on data from the 2015 Annual Retail Trade Survey. [10] Excludes NAICS 81311 (Religious Organizations), NAICS 81393 (Labor Unions and Similar Labor Organizations), NAICS 81394 (Political Organizations), and NAICS814 (Private Households).

Source: U.S. Census Bureau, "2015 E-Commerce Multi-sector Data Tables," <http://www.census.gov/programs-surveys/e-stats/data/tables.html>, accessed June 2017.

Table 1298. Commercial and Noncommercial Restaurant Groups—Food and Drink Sales: 2013 to 2017

[In millions of dollars (676,363 represents $676,363,000,000). Data refer to sales to consumers of food and alcoholic beverages. Sales are estimated. Minus (-) sign indicates decrease. For details, see source]

Type of place or service	Sales (mil. dol.) 2013	2014	2015	2016	2017 [2]	Percent change [1] 2015	2016	2017
Total [3]	**676,363**	**705,496**	**737,960**	**766,044**	**798,706**	**4.6**	**3.8**	**4.3**
Commercial restaurant services [3]	620,865	647,883	679,199	705,743	736,322	4.8	3.9	4.3
Eating and drinking places	481,649	502,828	527,570	547,901	571,479	4.9	3.9	4.3
Eating places	463,478	484,384	508,610	528,600	551,695	5.0	3.9	4.4
Full-service restaurants	226,787	236,993	246,946	254,108	263,002	4.2	2.9	3.5
Limited service restaurants	190,780	199,556	211,330	221,896	233,657	5.9	5.0	5.3
Cafeterias, grill-buffets and buffets	6,739	6,456	6,172	5,888	5,682	-4.4	-4.6	-3.5
Snack and nonalcoholic beverage bars	31,767	33,663	36,137	38,434	40,750	7.3	6.4	6.0
Social caterers	7,405	7,716	8,025	8,274	8,605	4.0	3.1	4.0
Bars and taverns [4]	18,171	18,443	18,960	19,301	19,784	2.8	1.8	2.5
Noncommercial restaurant services	53,013	55,089	56,177	57,648	59,651	2.0	2.6	3.5
Military restaurant services [5]	2,485	2,524	2,583	2,653	2,733	2.4	2.7	3.0

[1] Percent change from immediate prior year. [2] Projection. [3] Includes other groupings, not shown separately. [4] For establishments serving food. [5] Continental U.S. only.

Source: National Restaurant Association, Washington, DC, *2017 State of the Industry*, annual ©. See also <http://www.restaurant.org/>.

Table 1299. Administrative and Support and Waste Management and Remediation Services—Estimated Revenue by Kind of Business: 2010 to 2015

[In millions of dollars (614,178 represents $614,178,000,000). For taxable and tax-exempt employer firms. Estimates have been adjusted to results of the 2012 Economic Census. Based on the Service Annual Survey and administrative data; see Appendix III]

Kind of business	2007 NAICS code [1]	2010	2011	2012	2013	2014	2015
Administrative and support and waste management and remediation services [2]	**56**	**614,178**	**644,136**	**673,033**	**701,050**	**769,796**	**816,393**
Administrative and support services [2]	**561**	**535,359**	**564,521**	**593,835**	**619,716**	**683,527**	**728,883**
Office administrative services	5611	39,193	41,487	43,421	45,580	49,552	50,806
Facilities support services	5612	25,592	27,517	25,442	24,895	25,773	27,218
Employment placement agencies and executive search services [3]	56131	14,336	16,220	16,232	16,825	18,236	19,186
Temporary help services	56132	99,329	111,746	120,089	125,193	136,727	153,477
Professional employer organizations	56133	90,081	93,351	102,617	110,241	135,918	146,510
Document preparation services	56141	3,130	3,085	3,399	3,361	3,320	3,400
Telephone answering services	561421	2,167	2,169	1,946	1,911	1,982	2,086
Telemarketing bureaus and other contact centers	561422	14,729	15,459	16,919	17,252	18,269	18,626
Private mail centers	561431	2,107	2,179	2,329	2,327	2,491	2,626
Other business service centers (including copy shops)	561439	6,619	5,922	5,774	5,907	5,920	5,896
Collection agencies	56144	11,660	11,862	12,379	12,362	11,945	11,537
Credit bureaus	56145	6,604	6,433	7,062	7,443	8,084	9,330
Repossession services	561491	844	775	633	674	760	769
Court reporting and stenotype services	561492	2,252	2,246	2,116	2,097	2,175	2,240
All other business support services	561499	8,199	7,886	7,137	6,804	6,997	7,018
Travel agencies	56151	12,203	13,267	13,732	13,405	14,313	15,052
Tour operators	56152	5,125	5,108	5,373	5,649	5,826	6,084
Convention and visitors bureaus	561591	1,387	1,453	1,589	1,710	1,876	2,010
All other travel arrangement and reservation services	561599	12,846	13,205	13,652	15,397	16,393	17,640
Investigation services	561611	4,404	4,641	4,904	5,170	5,133	5,323
Security guards and patrol services	561612	20,820	21,582	23,040	23,589	23,604	24,012
Armored car services	561613	2,291	2,372	2,334	2,326	2,191	2,247
Security systems services (except locksmiths)	561621	13,833	14,725	15,030	15,888	17,861	19,045
Locksmiths	561622	1,542	1,579	1,637	1,659	1,767	1,803
Exterminating and pest control services	56171	9,444	9,608	10,307	10,972	11,525	11,929
Janitorial services	56172	34,559	35,917	36,681	37,885	40,015	41,676
Landscaping services	56173	47,674	49,640	51,908	55,609	63,570	67,549
Carpet and upholstery cleaning services	56174	2,746	2,958	3,083	3,193	3,446	3,537
Other services to buildings and dwellings	56179	4,758	4,901	5,477	6,040	6,609	7,141
Packaging and labeling services	56191	5,397	5,648	5,939	6,490	6,875	7,474
Convention and trade show organizers	56192	10,016	11,086	12,023	12,127	12,920	13,050
All other support services	56199	19,472	18,494	19,631	19,735	21,454	22,586
Waste management and remediation services	**562**	**78,819**	**79,615**	**79,198**	**81,334**	**86,269**	**87,510**
Solid waste collection	562111	36,431	37,097	36,560	37,435	39,409	39,503
Hazardous waste collection	562112	2,096	2,040	2,249	2,618	2,899	3,225
Other waste collection	562119	1,271	1,344	1,488	1,377	1,508	1,703
Hazardous waste treatment and disposal	562211	6,221	6,569	6,698	6,491	8,019	7,915
Solid waste landfill	562212	4,798	4,919	5,136	5,667	5,782	5,778
Solid waste combustors and incinerators	562213	(S)	(S)	2,489	2,520	2,517	(S)
Other nonhazardous waste treatment and disposal	562219	481	469	506	528	480	509
Remediation services	56291	16,422	14,680	14,193	14,500	14,940	15,532
Materials recovery facilities	56292	5,092	6,104	5,639	5,570	5,722	5,285
Septic tank and related services	562991	2,351	2,412	2,627	2,847	3,101	3,563
All other miscellaneous waste management services	562998	1,442	1,615	1,613	1,781	1,892	1,947

S Figure does not meet publication standards. [1] North American Industry Classification System, 2007; see text, Section 15. [2] Data prior to 2011 have been restated to reflect comparable data on the 2007 NAICS basis for more detailed levels within this aggregate. [3] Includes 2002 NAICS 561310 (Employment Placement Agencies) and a portion of 2002 NAICS 541612 (Human Resources and Executive Search Consulting Services).

Source: U.S. Census Bureau, Annual & Quarterly Services, "2015 Service Annual Survey," <http://www.census.gov/services/index.html>, accessed February 2017.

Table 1300. Estimated Accommodation and Food Service Sales by Kind of Business: 2000 to 2015

[In millions of dollars (441,944 represents $441,944,000,000). Estimates are based on data from the Annual Retail Trade Survey and administrative records and have been adjusted to final results of the 2012 Economic Census]

Kind of business	2007 NAICS code [1]	2000	2010	2011	2012	2013	2014	2015
Accommodation and food services, total	**72**	**441,944**	**642,653**	**682,847**	**723,159**	**752,481**	**798,024**	**857,726**
Accommodation	721	137,683	175,733	187,497	198,998	209,168	221,808	234,645
Traveler accommodations [2]	7211	133,118	169,594	181,129	192,032	202,088	214,406	226,944
Hotels and motels (excluding casinos)	72111	97,063	119,463	128,131	136,338	144,726	155,655	167,032
Casino hotels	72112	34,596	48,011	50,834	53,414	54,998	56,153	57,030
RV parks and recreational camps	7212	3,588	4,843	4,933	5,217	5,337	5,532	5,835
Rooming and boarding houses	7213	977	1,296	1,435	1,749	1,743	1,870	1,866
Food services and drinking places [2]	722	304,261	466,920	495,350	524,161	543,313	576,216	623,081
Full service restaurants	7221	133,579	198,699	213,880	227,210	235,818	253,256	272,892
Limited service eating places	7222	127,519	203,257	214,248	225,958	235,588	248,646	271,111
Special food places	7223	27,833	44,764	46,654	49,572	50,470	52,709	56,394
Drinking places	7224	15,330	20,200	20,568	21,421	21,437	21,605	22,684

[1] North American Industry Classification System, 2007; see text, Section 15. [2] Includes other kinds of business not shown separately.

Source: U.S. Census Bureau, "Annual Accommodation and Food Services—2015," <http://www.census.gov/retail/index.html>, accessed March 2017.

Table 1301. Other Services—Estimated Revenue for Employer Firms by Kind of Business: 2011 to 2015

[In millions of dollars (404,997 represents $404,997,000,000). For taxable and tax exempt employer firms. Estimates have been adjusted to results of the 2012 Economic Census. Based on the Service Annual Survey; see Appendix III]

Kind of business	2007 NAICS code [1]	2011	2012	2013	2014	2015
Other services (except public administration) [2, 3]	**81**	**404,997**	**426,694**	**450,492**	**482,548**	**498,951**
Repair and maintenance	811	137,612	143,945	148,202	157,449	162,955
General automotive repair	811111	38,720	40,515	42,602	46,655	47,718
Automotive exhaust system repair	811112	669	682	710	727	774
Automotive transmission repair	811113	2,310	2,290	2,262	2,369	2,313
Other automotive mechanical and electrical repair and maintenance	811118	1,983	1,890	1,932	2,053	2,054
Automotive body, paint, interior repair and maintenance	811121	27,288	28,570	29,345	30,244	32,009
Automotive glass replacement shops	811122	3,320	3,275	3,415	3,729	4,196
Automotive oil change and lubrication shops	811191	4,995	5,022	4,979	5,122	5,336
Car washes	811192	6,374	7,024	7,264	7,609	8,031
All other automotive repair and maintenance	811198	1,419	1,538	1,727	1,916	1,964
Consumer electronics repair and maintenance	811211	1,656	1,724	1,704	1,640	1,653
Computer and office machine repair and maintenance	811212	5,006	4,802	4,960	5,014	4,962
Communication equipment repair and maintenance	811213	2,648	2,627	2,670	3,015	3,145
Other electronic and precision equipment repair and maintenance	811219	6,736	6,566	6,365	6,727	7,187
Commercial and industrial machinery and equipment (except automotive and electronic) repair and maintenance	8113	28,682	31,065	31,539	33,679	34,270
Home and garden equipment and appliance repair and maintenance	81141	2,180	2,452	2,623	2,780	2,808
Reupholstery and furniture repair	81142	935	976	1,053	1,085	1,173
Footwear and leather goods repair	81143	179	197	211	217	230
Other personal and household goods repair and maintenance	81149	2,512	2,730	2,841	2,868	3,132
Personal and laundry services	812	83,691	87,030	91,165	96,608	101,406
Barber shops	812111	510	536	590	692	748
Beauty shops	812112	18,790	19,259	19,947	20,866	21,348
Nail salons	812113	2,399	2,989	3,393	3,834	4,415
Diet and weight reducing centers	812191	1,758	1,919	1,710	1,569	1,456
Other personal care services	812199	4,240	4,829	5,441	6,033	6,661
Funeral homes and funeral services	81221	12,829	13,004	13,542	13,733	14,476
Cemeteries and crematories	81222	3,183	3,297	3,425	3,646	3,782
Coin-operated laundries and drycleaners	81231	3,481	3,549	3,844	4,003	4,021
Dry-cleaning and laundry services (except coin-operated)	81232	7,644	7,583	7,708	7,956	7,908
Linen supply	812331	4,777	5,139	5,259	5,610	6,075
Industrial launders	812332	6,762	7,089	7,304	7,718	7,982
Pet care (except veterinary) services	81291	3,010	3,376	3,707	4,206	4,768
Photofinishing	81292	1,553	1,613	1,680	1,839	1,844
Parking lots and garages	81293	7,650	7,471	7,741	8,315	9,033
All other personal services	81299	5,105	5,377	5,874	6,588	6,889
Religious, grantmaking, civic, professional, and similar organizations [4]	813	183,694	195,719	211,125	228,491	234,590
Grantmaking and giving services	8132	82,717	90,708	102,359	114,180	117,547
Social advocacy organizations	8133	24,168	24,551	25,470	28,253	28,693
Civic and social organizations	8134	15,448	16,054	16,759	17,143	17,864
Business, professional, labor, political, and similar organizations [5]	8139	61,361	64,406	66,537	68,915	70,486

[1] Based on the North American Industry Classification System, 2007; see Section 15. [2] Data prior to 2011 have been restated to reflect comparable data on the 2007 NAICS basis. [3] Excludes NAICS 8131 (Religious Organizations), NAICS 81393 (Labor Unions and Similar Labor Organizations), NAICS 81394 (Political Organizations), and NAICS 814 (Private Households). [4] Excludes NAICS 8131 (Religious Organizations), NAICS 81393 (Labor Unions and Similar Labor Organizations), and NAICS 81394 (Political Organizations). [5] Excludes NAICS 81393 (Labor Unions and Similar Labor Organizations) and NAICS 81394 (Political Organizations).

Source: U.S. Census Bureau, Annual & Quarterly Services, "2015 Service Annual Survey," <http://www.census.gov/services/index.html>, accessed February 2017.

Table 1302. National Nonprofit Associations—Number by Type: 1980 to 2017

[Data compiled during last few months of year previous to year shown and the beginning months of year shown]

Type	1980	1990	2000	2005	2010 [1]	2014	2015	2016	2017
Total	**14,726**	**22,289**	**21,840**	**22,720**	**23,983**	**24,851**	**23,891**	**24,278**	**24,102**
Trade, business, commercial	3,118	3,918	3,880	3,789	3,761	3,673	3,487	3,548	3,521
Agriculture and environment	677	940	1,103	1,170	1,442	1,461	1,421	1,434	1,415
Legal, governmental, public admin., military	529	792	790	868	913	917	894	896	912
Scientific, engineering, technical	1,039	1,417	1,302	1,354	1,563	1,570	1,507	1,544	1,553
Educational	[2] 2,376	1,291	1,297	1,318	1,444	1,408	1,344	1,351	1,368
Cultural	([2])	1,886	1,786	1,733	1,717	1,674	1,610	1,631	1,681
Social welfare	994	1,705	1,829	2,072	2,673	3,254	3,166	3,174	3,067
Health, medical	1,413	2,227	2,495	2,982	3,481	4,099	4,069	4,232	4,274
Public affairs	1,068	2,249	1,776	1,854	1,734	1,740	1,601	1,568	1,513
Fraternal, nationality, ethnic	435	573	525	550	461	431	398	427	411
Religious	797	1,172	1,123	1,147	1,056	994	964	980	970
Veteran, hereditary, patriotic	208	462	835	774	585	583	545	556	543
Hobby, avocational	910	1,475	1,330	1,433	1,374	1,356	1,287	1,304	1,274
Athletic sports	504	840	717	762	946	940	899	902	892
Labor unions	235	253	232	208	188	173	162	168	163
Chambers of Commerce [3]	105	168	143	135	142	136	125	128	126
Greek and non-Greek letter societies	318	340	296	349	305	299	294	317	316
Fan clubs	(NA)	581	381	314	198	143	118	118	103

NA Not available. [1] Beginning in 2007, there was an increase in the number of associations due to an increase in newly discovered and established associations. [2] Data for cultural associations included with educational associations. [3] National and binational. Includes trade and tourism organizations.

Source: Gale, Cengage Learning. ENCYCLOPEDIA OF ASSOCIATIONS 56 NATIONAL ORG V1 3V NATL ORG, 56E. © 2017 Gale, a part of Cengage Learning, Inc. Reproduced by permission. www.cengage.com/permissions.

Foreign Commerce and Aid

This section presents data on the flow of goods, services, and capital between the United States and other countries; changes in official reserve assets of the United States; international investments; and foreign assistance programs.

The Bureau of Economic Analysis publishes current figures on U.S. international transactions and the U.S. international investment position in its monthly *Survey of Current Business* and in an interactive database on the internet at <http://www.bea.gov/iTable/index.cfm>. Statistics for the foreign aid programs are presented by the Agency for International Development (USAID) in its annual *U.S. Overseas Loans and Grants*.

The principal source of merchandise import and export data is the U.S. Census Bureau. Current data are presented monthly in *U.S. International Trade in Goods and Services Report* Series FT 900, as well as in the "USA Trade Online" database, at <https://usatrade.census.gov/>. The *Guide to Foreign Trade Statistics*, found on the Census Bureau website at <http://www.census.gov/foreign-trade/guide/index.html>, lists the Census Bureau's monthly and annual products and services in this field. In addition, the International Trade Administration and the Bureau of Economic Analysis present summary as well as selected commodity and country data for U.S. foreign trade on their websites: <http://www.trade.gov/mas/ian/tradestatistics/> and <http://www.bea.gov/international/index.htm>, respectively. The merchandise trade data published by the Bureau of Economic Analysis in the *Survey of Current Business* and on the web include balance of payments adjustments to the Census Bureau data. The U.S. Treasury Department's *Monthly Treasury Statement of Receipts and Outlays of the United States Government* contains information on import duties. The International Trade Commission, U.S. Department of Agriculture (agricultural products), U.S. Department of Energy (mineral fuels, like petroleum and coal), and the U.S. Geological Survey (minerals) release various reports and specialized products on U.S. trade.

International accounts—The international transactions tables (Tables 1303, 1306, and 1307) show, for given time periods, the transfer of goods, services, grants, and financial assets and liabilities between the United States and the rest of the world. The international investment position table (Table 1305) presents, for specific dates, the value of U.S. investments abroad and of foreign investments in the United States. The movement of foreign and U.S. capital as presented in the balance of payments is not the only factor affecting the total value of foreign investments. Among the other factors are changes in the valuation of assets or liabilities, including changes in prices of securities, defaults, expropriations, and write-offs.

Direct investment abroad means the ownership or control, directly or indirectly, by one person of 10 percent or more of the voting securities of an incorporated business enterprise or an equivalent interest in an unincorporated business enterprise. Direct investment position is the value of U.S. parents' claims on the equity of and receivables due from

foreign affiliates, less foreign affiliates' receivables due from their U.S. parents. Income consists of parents' shares in the earnings of their affiliates plus net interest received by parents on intercompany accounts, less withholding taxes on dividends and interest.

Foreign aid—Foreign assistance is divided into three major categories—grants (military supplies and services and other grants), credits, and other assistance (through net accumulation of foreign currency claims from the sale of agricultural commodities). *Grants* are transfers for which no payment is expected (other than a limited percentage of the foreign currency "counterpart" funds generated by the grant), or which at most involve an obligation on the part of the receiver to extend aid to the United States or other countries to achieve a common objective. *Credits* are loan disbursements or transfers under other agreements which give rise to specific obligations to repay, over a period of years, usually with interest. All known returns to the U.S. government stemming from grants and credits (reverse grants, returns of grants, and payments of principal) are taken into account in net grants and net credits, but no allowance is made for interest or commissions. *Other assistance* represents the transfer of U.S. farm products in exchange for foreign currencies (plus, since enactment of Public Law 87-128, currency claims from principal and interest collected on credits extended under the farm products program), less the government's disbursements of the currencies as grants, credits, or for purchases. The net acquisition of currencies represents net transfers of resources to foreign countries under the agricultural programs, in addition to those classified as grants or credits.

Exports—Export statistics consist of goods valued at more than $2,500 per commodity shipped by individuals and organizations (including exporters, freight forwarders, and carriers) from the U.S. to other countries. The Census Bureau compiles export data primarily from three sources: Shipper's Export Declaration documents filed with Customs and Border Protection and sent to the Census Bureau (3 percent of all transactions), data in electronic form submitted directly by exporters and their agents (63 percent); and special computer tapes from Canada for U.S. exports to Canada (34 percent). Estimates are made for low-value exports by country of destination, and based on bilateral trade patterns. They include U.S. exports under mutual security programs and exclude shipments to U.S. Armed Forces for their own use.

The value reported in the export statistics is generally equivalent to a free alongside ship (f.a.s.) value at the U.S. port of export, based on the transaction price, including inland freight, insurance, and other charges incurred in placing the merchandise alongside the carrier at the U.S. port of exportation. This value, as defined, excludes the cost of loading merchandise aboard the exporting carrier and also excludes freight, insurance, and any other charges or transportation and other costs beyond the U.S. port of exportation. The country of destination is defined as the country of ultimate destination or country where the merchandise is to be consumed, further processed, or manufactured, as known to the shipper at the time of exportation. When ultimate destination is not known, the shipment is statistically credited to the last country to which the shipper knows the merchandise will be shipped in the same form as exported.

Statistics for U.S. exports to Canada are based on import documents filed with Canadian agencies and forwarded to the U.S. Census Bureau under a 1987 data exchange agreement. Under this agreement, each country eliminated most cross-border export documents; maintains detailed statistics on cross-border imports; exchanges monthly files of cross-border import statistics; and publishes exchanged statistics in place of previously compiled export statistics.

Prior to 1989, exports were based on Schedule B, Statistical Classification of Domestic and Foreign Commodities Exported from the United States. Beginning in 1989, Schedule B classifications are based on the Harmonized System and coincide with the Standard International Trade Classification, Revision 3. This revision will affect the comparability of most export series beginning with the 1989 data for commodities.

Imports—Import statistics consist of goods valued at more than $2,000 per commodity shipped by individuals and organizations (including importers and customs brokers) into the U.S. from other countries. The Census Bureau compiles import data from records filed with Customs and Border Protection, usually within 10 days after the merchandise enters the United States. Estimates are made for low-value shipments by country of origin, based on previous bilateral trade patterns and periodically updated. Country of origin is defined as country where the merchandise was grown, mined, or manufactured. If country of origin is unknown, country of shipment is reported. Statistics for over 95 percent of all commodity transactions are compiled from records filed electronically with Customs and forwarded as computer tape files to the U.S. Census Bureau. Statistics for other transactions are compiled from

hard-copy documents filed with Customs and forwarded on a flow basis for U.S. Census Bureau processing.

Data on import values are presented on two valuations bases in this section: the c.i.f. (cost, insurance, and freight) and the customs import value (as appraised by the U.S. Customs Service in accordance with legal requirements of the Tariff Act of 1930, as amended). This latter valuation, primarily used for collection of import duties, frequently does not reflect the actual transaction value.

Imports are classified either as "General imports" or "Imports for consumption." *General imports* are a combination of entries for immediate consumption, entries into customs bonded warehouses, and entries into U.S. Foreign Trade Zones, thus generally reflecting total arrivals of merchandise. *Imports for consumption* are a combination of entries for immediate consumption, withdrawals from warehouses for consumption, and entries of merchandise into U.S. customs territory from U.S. Foreign Trade Zones, thus generally reflecting the total of the commodities entered into U.S. consumption channels.

Beginning in 1989, import statistics are based on the Harmonized Tariff Schedule of the United States, which coincides with import Standard International Trade Classification, Revision 3. This revision will affect the comparability of most import series beginning with the 1989 data.

Area coverage—Except as noted, the geographic area covered by the export and import trade statistics is the United States Customs area (includes the 50 states, the District of Columbia, and Puerto Rico), the U.S. Virgin Islands (effective January 1981), and U.S. Foreign Trade Zones (effective July 1982).

Statistical reliability—For a discussion of statistical collection and estimation, sampling procedures, and measures of statistical reliability applicable to Census Bureau data, see Appendix III.

Table 1303. U.S. International Transactions by Type of Transaction: 2000 to 2016

[In millions of dollars (1,469,648 represents $1,469,648,000,000). Minus sign (-) indicates debits. N.i.e. is not indicated elsewhere]

Type of transaction	2000	2005	2009	2010	2011	2012	2013	2014	2015	2016
Exports of goods and services and income receipts	**1,469,648**	**1,885,833**	**2,283,060**	**2,624,558**	**2,982,620**	**3,095,673**	**3,212,249**	**3,333,332**	**3,172,990**	**3,157,241**
Exports of goods and services	1,075,321	1,286,022	1,583,053	1,853,606	2,127,021	2,218,989	2,293,457	2,375,905	2,263,907	2,208,072
Goods	784,940	913,016	1,070,331	1,290,273	1,499,240	1,562,578	1,592,002	1,633,986	1,510,757	1,455,704
General merchandise	778,718	906,104	1,055,433	1,271,966	1,463,990	1,524,738	1,557,657	1,611,034	1,489,171	1,434,861
Foods, feeds, and beverages	47,871	58,955	93,908	107,719	126,247	133,049	136,163	143,721	127,735	130,555
Industrial supplies and materials	171,108	236,812	293,540	388,561	485,258	483,232	492,422	500,677	417,445	386,767
Capital goods except automotive	357,000	358,426	391,498	447,839	494,202	527,459	534,757	551,758	539,758	519,839
Automotive vehicles, parts, and engines	80,356	98,406	81,715	112,008	133,036	146,158	152,661	159,812	151,921	150,313
Consumer goods except food and automotive	89,305	115,228	149,287	164,909	174,719	180,994	188,093	198,398	197,407	193,440
Other general merchandise	33,078	38,276	45,486	50,931	50,529	53,846	53,562	56,669	54,904	53,948
Net exports of goods under merchanting	159	1,330	797	411	511	552	461	299	261	301
Nonmonetary gold	6,063	5,582	14,101	17,896	34,739	37,289	33,883	22,654	21,325	20,542
Services	290,381	373,006	512,722	563,333	627,781	656,411	701,455	741,919	753,150	752,368
Maintenance and repair services n.i.e.	5,011	7,624	12,863	14,549	16,436	17,186	18,568	21,149	23,406	25,628
Transport[1]	45,758	52,622	62,189	71,656	79,830	83,944	86,776	90,729	87,609	84,318
Travel (for all purposes including education)[2]	100,187	101,470	119,902	137,010	150,867	161,632	177,484	191,918	205,418	205,940
Insurance services	3,631	7,566	14,586	14,397	15,114	16,790	16,696	17,333	16,229	16,348
Financial services	22,117	39,878	64,437	72,348	78,271	76,692	95,131	106,949	102,595	98,180
Charges for the use of intellectual property n.i.e.	51,808	74,448	98,406	107,521	123,333	124,440	128,034	129,716	124,442	124,453
Telecommunications, computer, and information services	12,215	15,515	23,816	25,038	29,171	32,510	34,419	34,691	35,664	36,455
Other business services	40,497	58,302	95,984	101,029	112,568	120,382	121,530	128,915	136,622	142,231
Government goods and services n.i.e.[3,4]	9,156	15,582	20,538	19,784	22,191	22,835	22,816	20,518	21,165	18,814
Primary income receipts	356,706	534,215	613,249	680,169	755,937	767,972	792,819	817,348	782,985	813,977
Investment income	352,311	529,419	607,509	674,238	749,832	761,670	786,206	810,845	776,424	807,430
Compensation of employees	4,395	4,796	5,740	5,931	6,105	6,302	6,613	6,503	6,562	6,547
Secondary income (current transfer) receipts[5]	37,621	65,595	86,758	90,783	99,662	108,711	125,973	140,079	126,098	135,192
Imports of goods and services and income payments	**1,873,098**	**2,631,067**	**2,655,581**	**3,055,256**	**3,427,209**	**3,521,871**	**3,561,792**	**3,707,131**	**3,607,589**	**3,608,926**
Imports of goods and services	1,447,837	2,000,267	1,966,827	2,348,263	2,675,646	2,755,762	2,755,334	2,866,241	2,764,352	2,712,866
Goods	1,231,722	1,695,820	1,580,025	1,938,950	2,239,886	2,303,749	2,294,247	2,385,480	2,272,612	2,208,211
General merchandise	1,225,780	1,691,201	1,569,630	1,924,446	2,221,911	2,284,535	2,276,499	2,370,016	2,260,022	2,190,053
Foods, feeds, and beverages	46,489	69,072	82,861	92,492	108,257	111,127	116,003	126,805	128,768	131,046
Industrial supplies and materials	303,768	533,686	469,641	610,268	765,553	734,803	686,673	675,567	492,241	441,834
Capital goods except automotive	347,706	382,833	374,054	450,406	513,430	551,777	558,971	598,759	606,772	593,902
Automotive vehicles, parts, and engines	194,954	238,715	159,188	225,641	255,226	298,498	309,573	329,498	350,034	351,050
Consumer goods except food and automotive	284,634	412,734	429,853	485,121	515,868	518,821	532,876	558,700	596,553	585,363
Other general merchandise	48,229	54,161	54,034	60,519	63,578	69,508	72,402	80,688	85,654	86,858
Nonmonetary gold	5,942	4,618	10,395	14,504	17,975	19,214	17,748	15,464	12,590	18,159
Services	216,115	304,448	386,801	409,313	435,761	452,013	461,087	480,761	491,740	504,654
Maintenance and repair services n.i.e.	2,569	3,015	5,938	6,909	8,236	8,015	7,420	7,520	9,010	8,810
Transport[1]	57,606	75,643	64,133	74,628	81,377	84,985	90,634	94,188	97,061	96,827
Travel (for all purposes including education)[2]	65,787	79,988	81,421	86,623	89,700	100,338	98,120	105,668	114,723	123,618
Insurance services	11,284	28,710	63,801	61,478	55,654	55,513	53,420	51,011	47,822	48,077
Financial services	10,936	12,126	14,415	15,502	17,368	16,703	21,545	24,883	25,740	25,629
Charges for the use of intellectual property n.i.e.	16,606	25,577	31,297	32,551	36,087	38,661	38,860	41,983	39,858	44,392
Telecommunications, computer, and information services	12,397	15,975	25,784	29,015	32,756	32,779	35,034	36,502	36,270	36,851
Other business services	24,414	35,960	68,553	70,646	83,289	87,157	90,714	94,771	99,665	98,922
Government goods and services n.i.e.[3,6]	14,516	27,454	31,460	31,960	31,293	27,861	25,341	24,236	21,592	21,528
Primary income payments	338,637	480,317	498,089	511,986	544,853	560,497	586,842	606,573	602,023	640,751
Investment income	327,682	464,409	483,671	497,986	530,670	545,551	570,816	589,514	583,726	620,608
Compensation of employees	10,955	15,909	14,418	13,962	14,184	14,946	16,026	17,059	18,297	20,143
Secondary income (current transfer) payments[5]	86,624	150,482	190,665	195,045	206,709	205,611	219,616	234,317	241,214	255,309
Capital transfer receipts and other credits	**35**	**15,462**	**—**	**—**	**—**	**7,668**	**—**	**—**	**—**	**—**
Capital transfer payments and other debits	**36**	**2,346**	**140**	**157**	**1,186**	**764**	**412**	**45**	**42**	**59**
Net U.S. acquisition of financial assets[7]	**587,682**	**562,983**	**131,074**	**958,703**	**492,530**	**176,764**	**649,587**	**818,784**	**194,205**	**347,891**
Direct investment assets	186,371	52,591	312,597	349,829	436,615	377,239	392,796	338,853	311,139	311,581
Equity	170,011	42,287	260,928	338,294	397,743	321,228	334,706	330,364	296,487	329,732

See footnotes at end of table.

Table 1303. U.S. International Transactions by Type of Transaction: 2000 to 2016-Continued.

See headnote on page 817.

Type of transaction	2000	2005	2009	2010	2011	2012	2013	2014	2015	2016
Debt instruments	16,360	10,304	51,669	11,535	38,872	56,011	58,090	8,488	14,651	-18,151
Portfolio investment assets	159,713	267,290	375,883	199,620	85,365	248,760	481,298	582,677	160,911	40,638
Equity and investment fund shares	106,714	186,684	63,696	79,150	6,950	103,974	287,432	431,625	196,922	14,423
Debt securities [8]	52,999	80,606	312,186	120,469	78,415	144,786	193,866	151,052	-36,511	26,215
Other investment assets	241,308	257,196	-609,662	407,420	-45,327	-453,695	-221,408	-99,162	-271,052	-6,418
Currency and deposits	(NA)	82,879	-394,461	150,249	-89,161	-521,922	-126,959	-161,750	-201,635	-89,663
Loans	(NA)	173,031	-215,735	251,128	39,821	67,538	-104,254	68,411	-67,715	82,338
Insurance technical reserves	(NA)	(NA)	(NA)	(NA)	(NA)	(NA)	(NA)	(NA)	(NA)	(NA)
Trade credit and advances	680	1,286	535	6,043	4,013	689	9,805	-5,824	-1,702	907
Reserve assets	290	-14,094	52,256	1,835	15,877	4,460	-3,099	-3,583	-6,292	2,090
Special drawing rights	722	-4,511	48,230	31	-1,752	37	22	23	9	684
Reserve position in the International Monetary Fund	-2,308	-10,200	3,357	1,293	18,079	4,032	-3,438	-3,849	-6,485	1,348
Other reserve assets	1,876	617	669	511	-450	391	317	243	185	58
Currency and deposits	(NA)	224	138	55	110	24	3	5	-20	-56
Securities	(NA)	309	480	439	-598	365	313	234	205	114
Other claims	(NA)	84	51	17	39	3	1	4		
Net U.S. incurrence of liabilities [7]	1,066,074	1,277,056	325,644	1,391,039	983,160	632,685	1,055,789	1,091,350	502,112	741,393
Direct investment liabilities	349,124	142,345	161,082	264,039	263,499	250,343	288,131	237,655	506,161	479,415
Equity	258,438	116,476	155,760	207,842	191,138	211,419	211,769	146,413	390,160	351,769
Debt instruments	90,686	25,869	5,322	56,197	72,361	38,925	76,362	91,242	116,001	127,645
Portfolio investment liabilities	441,966	832,037	357,352	820,434	311,626	747,017	511,987	703,480	213,977	237,367
Equity and investment fund shares	193,600	89,258	219,302	178,952	123,357	239,065	-62,642	154,311	-187,306	-141,078
Debt securities [8]	248,366	742,779	138,050	641,481	188,269	507,952	574,629	549,170	401,284	378,445
Other investment liabilities	274,984	302,673	-192,789	306,566	408,036	-364,675	255,670	150,214	-218,027	24,612
Currency and deposits	(NA)	-124,782	-74,225	115,678	475,678	-246,001	202,838	59,723	-36,228	19,654
Loans	(NA)	415,824	-172,464	172,256	-84,789	-130,307	41,333	77,891	-262,615	-2,310
Insurance technical reserves	(NA)	(NA)	(NA)	(NA)	(NA)	(NA)	(NA)	(NA)	(NA)	(NA)
Trade credit and advances	(NA)	(NA)	6,301	18,632	17,147	11,633	11,499	12,600	8,360	7,268
Special drawing rights allocations	10,375	11,632	47,598							
Financial derivatives, net [9]	(NA)	(NA)	-44,816	-14,076	-35,006	7,064	2,222	-54,270	-25,248	15,817
Statistical discrepancy [10]	-74,941	18,045	133,275	-15,557	-79,862	-29,563	-54,025	47,009	101,486	74,059
Balance on current account (exports less imports)	-403,450	-745,234	-372,521	-430,698	-444,589	-426,198	-349,543	-373,800	-434,598	-451,685
Balance on goods and services	-372,517	-714,245	-383,774	-494,658	-548,625	-536,773	-461,876	-490,336	-500,445	-504,793
Balance on goods	-446,783	-782,804	-509,694	-648,678	-740,646	-741,171	-702,244	-751,494	-761,855	-752,507
Balance on services	74,266	68,558	125,920	154,020	192,020	204,398	240,368	261,157	261,410	247,714
Balance on primary income	18,069	53,898	115,160	168,221	211,084	207,475	205,977	210,774	180,962	173,225
Balance on secondary income	-49,003	-84,887	-103,907	-104,261	-107,047	-96,900	-93,643	-94,238	-115,116	-120,117
Balance on capital account	-1	13,116	-140	-157	-1,186	6,904	-412	-45	-42	-59
Net lending/borrowing from current- and capital-account transactions [11]	-403,451	-732,118	-372,661	-430,855	-445,774	-419,293	-349,955	-373,845	-434,641	-451,744
Net lending/borrowing from financial-account transactions [11, 12]	-478,392	-714,073	-239,386	-446,411	-525,636	-448,857	-403,979	-326,836	-333,155	-377,685

-- Represents zero. NA Not available. [1] Includes passenger fares. [2] All travel purposes include 1) business travel, including expenditures by border, seasonal, and other short-term workers and 2) personal travel, including health-related and education-related travel. [3] Includes goods and services supplied by and to embassies, consulates, and military bases; goods and services acquired from the host economy by diplomatic and military personnel; and services supplied by and to governments that are not included in other service categories. [4] Includes transfers under U.S. military sales contracts. [5] Secondary income (current transfer) receipts and payments include U.S. government grants and pensions, fines and penalties, withholding taxes, personal transfers (remittances), insurance-related transfers, and other current transfers. [6] Includes direct defense expenditures. [7] Excluding financial derivatives. [8] Includes transactions in U.S. Treasury and other U.S. securities. [9] Transactions for financial derivatives are only available as a net value equal to transactions for assets less transactions for liabilities. A positive value represents net U.S. cash payments arising from derivatives contracts, and a negative value represents net U.S. cash receipts. [10] The statistical discrepancy is the difference between total debits and total credits recorded in the current, capital, and financial accounts. In the current and capital accounts, credits and debits are labeled in the table. In the financial account, an acquisition of an asset or a repayment of a liability is a debit, and an incurrence of a liability or a disposal of an asset is a credit. [11] Net lending means that U.S. residents are net suppliers of funds to foreign residents, and net borrowing means the opposite. Net lending or net borrowing can be computed from current- and capital-account transactions or from financial-account transactions. The two amounts differ by the statistical discrepancy. [12] Net lending or net borrowing from financial-account transactions is the net U.S. acquisition of financial assets excluding financial derivatives less net U.S. incurrence of liabilities excluding financial derivatives plus financial derivatives other than reserves.

Source: U.S. Bureau of Economic Analysis, International Economic Accounts, "Table 1.2. U.S. International Transactions, Expanded Detail," <http://www.bea.gov/international/index.htm>, accessed June 2017.

Table 1304. U.S. Government Reserve Assets: 1990 to 2015

[In billions of dollars (83.3 represents $83,300,000,000). As of end of year]

Type	1990	2000	2007	2008	2009	2010	2011	2012	2013	2014	2015
Total	83.3	67.6	70.6	77.6	130.8	132.4	148.0	150.2	144.6	130.1	117.6
Gold stock	11.1	11.0	11.0	11.0	11.0	11.0	11.0	11.0	11.0	11.0	11.0
Special drawing rights	11.0	10.5	9.5	9.3	57.8	56.8	55.0	55.1	55.2	51.9	49.7
Reserve position in IMF [1]	52.2	14.8	4.2	7.7	11.4	12.5	30.1	34.2	30.8	25.2	17.6
Foreign currencies	9.1	31.2	45.8	49.6	50.5	52.1	51.9	49.9	47.6	41.9	39.2

[1] International Monetary Fund.

Source: Data prior to 2005, U.S. Department of the Treasury, *Treasury Bulletin*. Beginning in 2005, Board of Governors of the Federal Reserve System, "International Summary Statistics," January 2017 and earlier releases, <http://www.federalreserve.gov/econresdata/statisticsdata.htm>.

Table 1305. U.S. International Investment Position by Type of Investment: 2010 to 2016

[In billions of dollars (-2,512 represents -$2,512,000,000,000). Estimates as of end of 4th quarter. Minus sign (-) indicates loss or deficit]

Type of investment	2010	2011	2012	2013	2014	2015	2016
U.S. net international investment position	**-2,512**	**-4,455**	**-4,518**	**-5,373**	**-6,980**	**-7,493**	**-8,318**
Net international investment position excluding financial derivatives	-2,622	-4,541	-4,576	-5,450	-7,066	-7,550	-8,380
Financial derivatives other than reserves, net	110	86	58	78	86	56	61
U.S. assets	**21,768**	**22,209**	**22,562**	**24,145**	**24,833**	**23,352**	**23,849**
Assets excluding financial derivatives	18,116	17,492	18,942	21,128	21,580	20,924	21,640
Financial derivatives other than reserves, gross positive fair value	3,652	4,717	3,620	3,017	3,252	2,428	2,209
By functional category:							
Direct investment at market value	5,486	5,215	5,970	7,121	7,189	6,999	7,375
Equity	4,621	4,320	4,984	6,054	6,040	5,788	6,172
Debt instruments	866	895	986	1,066	1,149	1,211	1,203
Portfolio investment	7,160	6,872	7,984	9,206	9,704	9,570	9,879
Equity and investment fund shares	4,900	4,501	5,322	6,473	6,771	6,756	6,997
Debt securities	2,260	2,370	2,662	2,733	2,934	2,814	2,882
Financial derivatives other than reserves, gross positive fair value	3,652	4,717	3,620	3,017	3,252	2,428	2,209
Over-the-counter contracts	3,622	4,669	3,586	2,980	3,182	2,385	2,167
Exchange-traded contracts	31	48	34	37	70	43	42
Other investment	4,980	4,869	4,417	4,353	4,252	3,971	3,979
Currency and deposits	2,767	2,582	2,062	1,976	1,807	1,628	1,560
Loans	2,162	2,232	2,299	2,323	2,398	2,299	2,374
Trade credit and advances	51	55	56	53	47	45	45
Reserve assets	489	537	572	448	434	384	407
Monetary gold	368	400	433	315	315	277	301
Special drawing rights	57	55	55	55	52	50	49
Reserve position in the International Monetary Fund	12	30	34	31	25	18	18
Other reserve assets	52	52	50	47	42	39	39
U.S. liabilities	**24,280**	**26,664**	**27,080**	**29,517**	**31,813**	**30,846**	**32,168**
Liabilities excluding financial derivatives	20,738	22,033	23,518	26,578	28,646	28,474	30,020
Financial derivatives other than reserves, gross negative fair value	3,542	4,631	3,562	2,940	3,167	2,372	2,148
By functional category:							
Direct investment at market value	4,099	4,199	4,662	5,815	6,370	6,701	7,569
Equity	2,928	2,968	3,416	4,443	4,896	5,076	5,784
Debt instruments	1,171	1,231	1,247	1,372	1,474	1,624	1,786
Portfolio investment	11,869	12,647	13,979	15,541	16,921	16,646	17,352
Equity and investment fund shares	3,546	3,842	4,545	5,865	6,643	6,209	6,564
Debt securities	8,323	8,805	9,434	9,677	10,279	10,437	10,788
Financial derivatives other than reserves, gross negative fair value	3,542	4,631	3,562	2,940	3,167	2,372	2,148
Over-the-counter contracts	3,512	4,581	3,528	2,903	3,101	2,329	2,105
Exchange-traded contracts	30	49	34	37	66	43	43
Other investment	4,769	5,187	4,877	5,222	5,355	5,127	5,099
Currency and deposits	2,365	2,839	2,602	2,674	2,890	2,947	2,950
Loans	2,238	2,165	2,081	2,345	2,254	1,963	1,926
Trade credit and advances	112	129	141	148	160	168	175
Special drawing rights allocations	54	54	54	54	51	49	47

Source: U.S. Bureau of Economic Analysis, International Economic Accounts, International Investment Position, "Table 1.2 U.S. Net International Investment Position at the End of the Period, Expanded Detail," <http://www.bea.gov/iTable/index_ita.cfm>, accessed September 2017. See also <http://www.bea.gov/international/index.htm>.

Table 1306. International Service Transactions by Selected Type of Service and Selected Country: 2000 to 2016

[In millions of dollars (290,381 represents $290,381,000,000). Country data are based on information available from U.S. reporting sources. In some instances, the statistics may not necessarily reflect the ultimate foreign transactor. N.i.e. is not included elsewhere]

Type of service and country	Exports				Imports			
	2000	2010	2015	2016	2000	2010	2015	2016
Services, total	**290,381**	**563,333**	**753,150**	**752,368**	**216,115**	**409,313**	**491,740**	**504,654**
TYPE OF SERVICE								
Maintenance and repair services n.i.e. [1]	5,011	14,549	23,406	25,628	2,569	6,909	9,010	8,810
Transport	45,758	71,656	87,609	84,318	57,606	74,628	97,061	96,827
Sea transport	11,554	15,905	18,044	18,078	21,787	29,496	37,295	35,097
Air transport [2]	31,267	51,579	64,944	61,548	32,678	41,377	55,851	57,874
Passenger	20,197	30,987	41,976	38,770	20,397	23,426	35,494	37,198
Other modes of transport [3]	2,938	4,172	4,621	4,692	3,141	3,755	3,915	3,856
Travel	100,187	137,010	205,418	205,940	65,787	86,623	114,723	123,618
Business	42,664	39,523	43,201	40,960	22,640	21,274	16,152	15,879
Expenditures by border, seasonal, and other short-term workers	5,975	6,344	8,267	8,971	366	1,065	1,321	1,383
Other business travel	36,689	33,179	34,934	31,989	22,274	20,209	14,831	14,496
Personal	57,523	97,487	162,218	164,980	43,147	65,349	98,571	107,739
Health related	1,501	2,876	3,597	3,751	155	1,019	1,828	2,057
Education related	10,348	20,937	35,388	39,425	2,032	5,468	7,248	7,584
Other personal travel	45,674	73,674	123,232	121,804	40,960	58,862	89,495	98,097
Insurance services	3,631	14,397	16,229	16,348	11,284	61,478	47,822	48,077
Direct insurance	628	4,029	2,885	2,038	1,683	4,374	4,138	4,076
Reinsurance	3,002	8,981	11,834	13,050	9,601	55,660	41,840	41,835
Auxiliary insurance services [4]	(NA)	1,387	1,510	1,260	(NA)	1,444	1,844	2,165
Financial services [2]	22,117	72,348	102,595	98,180	10,936	15,502	25,740	25,629
Financial management, financial advisory, and custody services	(NA)	27,319	55,031	48,396	(NA)	4,105	12,171	10,876
Credit card and other credit-related services	(NA)	10,460	19,627	20,689	(NA)	3,702	6,352	7,152
Charges for the use of intellectual property n.i.e. [2]	51,808	107,521	124,442	124,453	16,606	32,551	39,858	44,392
Industrial processes	(NA)	36,333	45,640	47,512	(NA)	18,847	21,178	23,200
Computer software [5]	(NA)	36,008	36,761	36,621	(NA)	5,228	6,768	7,423
Trademarks and franchise fees	(NA)	19,131	20,577	19,869	(NA)	4,635	3,784	3,629
Telecommunications, computer, and information services	12,215	25,038	35,664	36,455	12,397	29,015	36,270	36,851
Telecommunications services	5,266	10,911	12,587	12,225	6,167	7,986	6,280	5,476
Computer services	4,358	8,991	15,828	17,283	5,934	19,407	27,507	28,989
Information services	2,591	5,137	7,249	6,947	295	1,622	2,484	2,386
Other business services	40,497	101,029	136,622	142,231	24,414	70,646	99,665	98,922
Research and development services	7,116	22,446	34,539	37,176	3,346	22,170	32,202	34,243
Professional and management consulting services	17,621	46,749	66,784	74,021	10,648	27,690	40,423	40,169
Technical, trade-related, and other business services [6]	15,760	31,834	35,299	31,034	10,420	20,786	27,040	24,510
Government goods and services n.i.e. [7]	9,156	19,784	21,165	18,814	14,516	31,960	21,592	21,528
AREA AND COUNTRY								
Europe	107,416	214,164	275,959	279,470	97,718	172,108	207,135	212,002
European Union	93,485	179,237	228,433	231,249	84,215	143,615	174,059	176,454
Euro Area [8]	56,433	110,572	144,062	148,142	52,511	90,824	108,335	112,712
France	10,351	16,761	19,755	19,674	10,842	15,820	16,311	16,451
Germany	15,848	24,896	29,983	31,638	15,822	28,397	31,777	33,395
Italy	5,706	8,452	9,157	8,860	6,824	9,552	10,786	11,339
Netherlands	7,052	12,990	16,245	15,569	5,978	8,061	10,237	9,794
United Kingdom	31,706	53,568	67,560	65,729	27,238	42,307	53,589	51,698
Canada	24,808	53,126	54,510	53,957	18,239	27,351	29,171	29,950
Latin America, other Western Hemisphere	54,194	106,293	159,639	148,780	38,752	87,596	100,412	100,219
Brazil	6,494	18,405	27,646	24,338	1,530	5,143	7,834	6,797
Mexico	15,780	24,614	31,604	32,045	11,200	13,966	22,878	24,569
Asia and Pacific	83,301	154,029	216,962	224,632	48,509	95,203	129,895	135,273
Australia	5,719	15,690	22,344	21,977	2,637	5,269	7,203	7,274
China	5,099	22,500	48,537	54,157	3,202	10,609	15,064	16,139
Hong Kong	3,652	5,775	9,842	10,053	4,017	6,419	8,838	8,748
India	2,789	10,322	18,374	20,632	1,909	14,711	24,610	25,808
Japan	36,862	43,259	44,746	44,154	16,326	24,589	29,519	31,004
Korea, South	6,661	15,451	20,645	21,055	5,699	9,334	11,237	10,974
Singapore	6,358	10,380	14,323	16,940	1,995	4,279	6,713	7,258
Taiwan	5,380	9,742	12,269	11,697	3,693	5,865	7,645	7,732
Middle East	9,101	21,148	29,145	29,397	5,234	18,049	16,632	17,246
Africa	6,184	11,997	14,566	13,799	3,710	7,934	8,279	8,552
International organizations and unallocated	5,377	2,576	2,369	2,331	3,954	1,071	216	1,413

NA Not available. [1] Covers maintenance and repair services by residents of country on goods owned by residents of another country. Excludes maintenance and repair of transportation equipment, construction maintenance and repair, and computer maintenance and repair. [2] Includes other types not shown separately. [3] Includes freight services performed by truck, rail, pipeline, in space, and port services for rail and water transport. [4] Includes agents' commissions, brokerage services, insurance consulting services, actuarial services, and other insurance services. [5] Includes receipts and payments for rights to reproduce and distribute. Excludes licenses for use; these licenses are included under computer services. [6] Includes construction, architectural and engineering services, waste treatment, operational leasing, trade-related, and other business services. [7] See footnote 3, Table 1303. Exports include transfers under U.S. military sales contracts; imports include direct defense expenditures. [8] Euro area refers to European Union member countries that have adopted the Euro as the common currency. Only those countries that are members of the Euro area in a given year are included in the data for that year. For list of countries included over time, see <http://www.bea.gov/international/bp_web/geographic_area_definitions.cfm>.

Source: U.S. Bureau of Economic Analysis, International Economic Accounts, International Transactions, "Table 3.1. U.S. International Trade in Services," and "Table 3.3. U.S. International Trade in Services by Area and Country, Not Seasonally Adjusted Detail," <http://www.bea.gov/international/index.htm>, accessed September 2017.

Table 1307. U.S. Balances on International Transactions by Area and Selected Country: 2015 and 2016

[In millions of dollars (-434,598 represents -$434,598,000,000). Country data are based on information available from U.S. reporting sources. In some instances, the statistics may not necessarily reflect the ultimate foreign transactor. With the June 2017 data release, the Bureau of Economic Analysis has incorporated a new data source, an improved estimation methodology, newly available and revised source data, and updated seasonal adjustments beginning with statistics for 1999. Data here are not comparable to data presented in previous editions; for details see <https://www.bea.gov/newsreleases/international/transactions/transnewsrelease.htm>. Minus sign (-) indicates debits]

Area or country	2015, balance on—				2016, balance on—			
	Current account	Goods	Services	Primary income [1]	Current account	Goods	Services	Primary income [1]
All areas	-434,598	-761,855	261,410	180,962	-451,685	-752,507	247,714	173,225
Europe	-5,035	-173,634	68,824	107,244	-8,051	-166,691	67,468	98,965
European Union	5,314	-156,974	54,374	106,225	5,736	-148,003	54,794	95,773
Euro Area [2]	-28,363	-133,564	35,727	70,278	-26,401	-127,564	35,430	66,428
Germany	-77,312	-75,359	-1,794	-5,541	-71,779	-65,250	-1,757	-7,978
Italy	-27,041	-28,113	-1,629	3,121	-28,409	-28,715	-2,479	2,907
Netherlands	80,817	23,092	6,009	51,952	81,395	23,297	5,776	52,060
United Kingdom	47,765	-2,081	13,971	35,122	46,457	671	14,031	29,194
Canada	10,229	-21,169	25,340	7,481	12,696	-16,276	24,007	6,912
Latin America, other Western Hemisphere	66,574	-29,927	59,227	64,924	38,689	-41,405	48,562	64,035
Brazil	27,102	5,060	19,812	3,175	25,004	5,402	17,541	2,380
Mexico	-75,010	-67,049	8,725	-2,128	-81,480	-70,527	7,476	-2,766
Asia and Pacific	-513,352	-546,898	87,068	-14,243	-488,200	-534,906	89,359	-7,102
Australia	38,228	13,613	15,141	9,630	37,766	12,511	14,702	11,017
China	-362,103	-367,495	33,473	-23,453	-332,661	-347,290	38,018	-18,821
Hong Kong	35,584	30,645	1,004	4,009	31,869	27,760	1,305	2,863
India	-35,664	-23,332	-6,236	3,520	-35,528	-24,501	-5,175	4,433
Japan	-79,813	-70,360	15,227	-25,615	-76,611	-70,233	13,150	-20,928
Korea, South	-20,196	-28,000	9,409	461	-18,995	-27,686	10,082	18
Singapore	37,034	9,893	7,611	19,442	37,355	8,586	9,682	18,878
Taiwan	-22,233	-15,010	4,624	-9,960	-21,259	-12,814	3,965	-10,817
Middle East	7,352	7,649	12,512	-1,639	6,072	11,198	12,151	-5,747
Africa	-5,722	1,865	6,287	4,162	-13,227	-4,728	5,248	2,488
International organizations and unallocated	5,356	261	2,153	13,032	336	301	918	13,676

[1] Primary income consists of investment income and compensation of employees. [2] Euro area refers to European Union member countries that have adopted the Euro as the common currency. For the 2015 and 2016 data, this includes the countries that had adopted the Euro as of January 1, 2015: Austria, Belgium, Cyprus, Estonia, Finland, France, Germany, Greece, Ireland, Italy, Latvia Luxembourg, Malta, Netherlands, Portugal, Slovakia, Slovenia, and Spain.

Source: U.S. Bureau of Economic Analysis, International Transactions (ITA), "Table 1.1. U.S. International Transactions" and "Table 1.3. U.S. International Transactions, Expanded Detail by Area and Country," <http://www.bea.gov/international/index.htm>, accessed June 2017.

Table 1308. Employment of Majority-Owned U.S. Affiliates of Foreign Companies by State: 2010 to 2015

[In thousands (5,435.4 represents 5,435,400). Covers full-time and part-time employees on the payroll, generally at the end of the fiscal year. A U.S. majority-owned affiliate is a U.S. business enterprise in which a foreign entity has a direct or indirect voting interest greater than 50 percent]

State and other area	2010	2013	2014	2015	State and other area	2010	2013	2014	2015
Total	5,435.4	6,181.4	6,613.3	6,820.7	Montana	6.3	7.5	7.2	7.0
					Nebraska	23.9	30.8	32.6	32.8
Alabama	81.9	91.7	93.0	97.2	Nevada	39.0	44.5	51.2	49.2
Alaska	14.1	16.5	17.9	17.4	New Hampshire	39.3	41.4	43.6	43.7
Arizona	77.0	86.8	95.7	103.4	New Jersey	222.9	235.2	265.6	276.4
Arkansas	35.9	44.8	47.0	48.1	New Mexico	15.3	22.4	20.8	20.2
California	584.0	647.2	689.2	715.8	New York	398.9	416.8	448.1	474.0
Colorado	80.9	87.9	100.6	103.2	North Carolina	194.7	232.0	242.0	251.8
Connecticut	100.9	101.0	102.5	103.6	North Dakota	11.5	14.6	13.5	12.7
Delaware	26.7	26.2	26.5	27.0	Ohio	210.2	243.6	254.2	259.0
District of Columbia	22.4	23.2	23.5	24.4	Oklahoma	38.6	48.7	48.8	50.0
Florida	232.9	262.7	312.7	327.2	Oregon	43.0	50.7	59.1	61.7
Georgia	189.5	210.6	218.4	226.9	Pennsylvania	261.3	287.6	296.0	300.8
Hawaii	26.8	34.6	37.2	37.5	Rhode Island	26.1	28.9	30.9	27.8
Idaho	13.4	16.1	17.3	17.5	South Carolina	108.4	128.7	129.0	133.0
Illinois	252.7	293.0	313.8	324.9	South Dakota	7.2	12.9	13.3	12.6
Indiana	136.0	161.2	186.2	190.9	Tennessee	117.2	135.5	152.5	163.5
Iowa	44.9	55.4	55.4	56.4	Texas	451.4	522.2	559.9	585.9
Kansas	54.5	71.3	57.3	57.6	Utah	31.4	37.1	40.8	42.2
Kentucky	89.2	101.9	112.4	117.3	Vermont	11.1	10.9	12.3	12.4
Louisiana	56.1	72.4	67.7	67.7	Virginia	147.8	171.3	173.3	182.4
Maine	30.3	31.9	33.4	34.7	Washington	94.4	103.6	109.1	112.7
Maryland	101.6	101.6	113.0	117.2	West Virginia	28.7	28.1	28.7	29.3
Massachusetts	187.3	203.6	216.2	215.1	Wisconsin	77.5	87.3	96.4	93.0
Michigan	145.4	209.0	238.4	238.1	Wyoming	7.8	9.0	8.5	7.9
Minnesota	90.7	103.0	107.8	111.7	Puerto Rico	21.9	20.5	24.4	24.9
Mississippi	26.8	34.2	37.3	38.4	Other U.S. areas	13.9	19.8	23.8	21.9
Missouri	81.7	100.6	105.0	110.0	Foreign	2.3	1.4	2.3	2.7

Source: U.S. Bureau of Economic Analysis, International Economic Accounts, "Direct Investment and Multinational Enterprises (MNEs)," <http://www.bea.gov/iTable/index_MNC.cfm>, accessed September 2017.

Table 1309. New Foreign Direct Investment in the U.S. by Industry of U.S. Business Enterprise and Country of Ultimate Beneficial Owner: 2015 and 2016

[In millions of dollars (439,563 represents $439,563,000,000). Data shown are first year expenditures by foreign direct investors to acquire, establish, or expand U.S. businesses. First year expenditures include those expenditures in the calendar year in which the transaction occurred. A U.S. business enterprise is categorized as "acquired" if a foreign entity acquired a 10 percent or more voting interest in an incorporated U.S. business, or an equivalent interest of an unincorporated U.S. business, either directly or indirectly through an existing U.S. affiliate. A U.S. business enterprise is categorized as "established" if a foreign entity or existing U.S. affiliate of a foreign entity establishes a new legal entity in the U.S. in which the foreign entity owns 10 percent or more of the new business enterprise's voting interest, or an equivalent interest if unincorporated. An existing U.S. affiliate is categorized as "expanded" if it expands its operations to include a new facility where business is conducted and the expansion has a projected total cost of more than $3 million]

Industry and country	2015 Total	2015 U.S. businesses acquired	2015 U.S. businesses established	2015 U.S. businesses expanded	2016 Total	2016 U.S. businesses acquired	2016 U.S. businesses established	2016 U.S. businesses expanded
Total [1]	439,563	425,788	10,739	3,037	373,440	365,700	5,565	2,175
INDUSTRY [2]								
Manufacturing	290,420	288,420	961	1,038	129,354	128,071	209	1,075
Wholesale trade	2,290	1,937	128	225	13,974	13,749	(D)	(D)
Retail trade	10,805	10,633	172	(Z)	10,332	10,306	23	3
Information	12,175	11,890	158	127	42,825	42,662	150	13
Finance and insurance	44,587	42,809	1,745	33	47,930	46,650	1,159	121
Real estate and rental and leasing	37,175	30,903	6,215	57	7,678	6,077	1,513	88
Professional, scientific, and technical services	22,019	21,860	124	36	59,061	58,890	126	46
Other industries	20,092	17,336	1,235	1,520	62,284	59,295	(D)	(D)
COUNTRY [3]								
Canada	88,735	86,994	839	902	58,502	56,910	1,263	329
Europe [1]	294,651	288,920	4,336	1,395	187,900	184,563	1,909	1,427
France	13,916	13,276	50	589	19,246	18,848	148	249
Germany	46,418	45,759	450	209	13,382	12,756	116	511
Ireland	175,978	175,885	92	(Z)	35,397	35,299	7	92
Netherlands	13,784	(D)	(D)	8	23,260	23,242	14	3
Switzerland	5,679	5,511	64	105	34,880	34,798	21	61
United Kingdom	20,758	20,354	341	63	54,496	54,352	117	28
Latin America/other Western Hemisphere	5,956	5,481	393	82	29,367	29,065	257	45
South and Central America [1]	433	281	(D)	(D)	680	(D)	(D)	(D)
Other Western Hemisphere [1]	5,523	5,200	(D)	(D)	28,686	(D)	(D)	(D)
Bermuda	3,077	2,967	109	–	(D)	(D)	6	–
Caribbean Islands (British)	2,351	2,147	(D)	(D)	3,800	(D)	(D)	(D)
Africa	494	(D)	(D)	(D)	(D)	(D)	21	–
Middle East	5,871	5,658	(D)	(D)	2,853	(D)	(D)	(D)
Asia and Pacific [1]	42,879	37,330	4,987	562	86,794	84,620	1,811	364
Australia	1,825	(D)	(D)	7	(D)	(D)	19	7
China	7,781	6,583	1,060	138	27,619	26,819	775	25
Hong Kong	1,329	1,129	197	2	(D)	(D)	76	(D)
Japan	26,855	24,180	2,272	403	18,206	17,123	824	259
South Korea	936	(D)	(D)	6	(D)	(D)	(D)	(D)
Singapore	2,806	2,095	711	–	(D)	(D)	6	1

– Represents zero. Z Less than $500,000. D Suppressed to avoid disclosure of data of individual companies. [1] Includes other countries not shown separately. [2] Based on 2012 North American Industry Classification System (NAICS); see text, Section 15. [3] Country of ultimate beneficial owner (UBO). The UBO is the entity proceeding up a U.S. affiliate's ownership chain, beginning with the foreign parents, which is not owned more than 50 percent by another entity.

Source: U.S. Bureau of Economic Analysis, International Economic Accounts, "Direct Investment and Multinational Enterprises," <http://www.bea.gov/iTable/index_MNC.cfm>, accessed September 2017.

Table 1310. Foreign Direct Investment Position in the United States on a Historical-Cost Basis: by Selected Country, 2000 to 2016, and by Industry, 2016

[In millions of dollars (1,256,867 represents $1,256,867,000,000). Foreign direct investment is defined as the ownership or control, directly or indirectly, by one foreign entity of 10 percent or more of the voting interest of a U.S. business enterprise. As used here, "entity" is synonymous with "person," used in a broad legal sense that includes any individual, branch, partnership, association, trust, corporation, or government. Data are based on surveys of U.S. affiliates of foreign companies]

Country	All industries total				2016			
	2000	2010	2014	2015	Total [1]	Manufac-turing	Wholesale trade	Finance and insurance [2]
All countries................	**1,256,867**	**2,280,044**	**2,945,795**	**3,303,586**	**3,725,418**	**1,532,365**	**367,596**	**504,780**
Canada................	114,309	192,463	273,896	322,118	371,468	114,760	21,677	62,441
Europe [3]................	887,014	1,659,774	2,004,199	2,276,695	2,605,559	1,195,643	187,257	333,427
Austria................	3,007	4,532	6,962	7,088	10,611	3,264	(D)	4
Belgium................	14,787	69,565	97,038	89,231	79,854	55,799	8,394	(D)
Denmark................	4,025	7,772	13,322	14,432	18,233	5,146	6,380	2
Finland................	8,875	4,943	4,284	6,482	5,874	1,906	2,486	(D)
France................	125,740	189,763	202,682	232,431	252,864	118,351	17,242	48,099
Germany................	122,412	203,077	251,009	279,735	291,697	104,161	28,177	41,643
Ireland................	25,523	24,097	26,431	35,814	85,460	21,727	-2,119	5,410
Italy................	6,576	20,142	23,508	27,690	30,010	8,285	2,193	(D)
Luxembourg................	58,930	170,309	232,288	347,864	417,386	251,828	25,659	11,544
Netherlands................	138,894	234,408	258,177	299,780	355,242	160,767	27,972	40,142
Norway................	2,665	10,478	19,539	20,706	25,548	1,432	(D)	(D)
Spain................	5,068	43,095	63,956	66,985	68,169	9,638	215	(D)
Sweden................	21,991	38,780	40,142	43,416	46,933	40,177	-4,223	117
Switzerland................	64,719	180,642	245,188	249,225	310,759	149,994	22,770	81,790
United Kingdom................	277,613	400,435	479,373	512,139	555,687	235,364	28,382	78,491
Latin America and other Western Hemisphere................	53,691	62,130	117,051	117,301	124,798	21,982	5,160	(D)
South and Central America [3].....	13,384	17,943	25,083	25,755	25,805	9,984	-1,056	(D)
Brazil................	882	1,357	1,444	551	-1,831	-67	-2,929	710
Mexico................	7,462	10,970	15,198	15,209	16,757	4,713	1,556	212
Venezuela................	792	3,122	3,926	4,187	4,457	(D)	19	(Z)
Other Western Hemisphere [3]....	40,307	44,187	91,967	91,546	98,993	11,997	6,216	19,959
Curacao................	(X)	(X)	1,982	1,630	1,660	(D)	(D)	17
Netherlands Antilles................	3,807	2,819	(X)	(X)	(X)	(X)	(X)	(X)
U.K. Islands, Caribbean................	15,191	38,477	87,344	94,773	86,054	14,625	9,277	22,188
Africa................	2,700	2,265	1,691	4,330	4,394	2,320	(D)	7
Middle East [3]................	6,506	16,808	16,467	18,169	19,826	3,731	(D)	(D)
Israel................	3,012	8,714	6,175	7,442	8,136	3,900	472	(D)
Asia and Pacific [3]................	192,647	346,605	532,491	564,974	599,373	193,928	146,923	87,047
Australia................	18,775	35,632	56,404	47,270	46,926	16,010	3,509	3,921
China................	(X)	3,300	10,071	16,769	27,475	14,038	1,142	425
Hong Kong................	1,493	4,440	9,776	10,991	11,649	1,680	2,772	-7
India................	(X)	4,102	8,927	9,629	9,852	978	345	(D)
Japan................	159,690	255,012	371,874	402,164	421,103	139,638	107,167	73,277
Korea, South................	3,110	15,746	39,966	40,585	40,937	7,194	27,180	489
Singapore................	5,087	21,517	20,665	21,654	23,933	9,743	2,812	(D)
Taiwan................	3,174	4,642	6,107	6,890	7,196	3,133	413	4

D Suppressed to avoid disclosure of data of individual companies. X Not applicable. Z Between -$500,000 and +$500,000. [1] Includes other industries, not shown separately. [2] Excludes depository institutions. [3] Includes other countries, not shown separately.

Source: U.S. Bureau of Economic Analysis, International Economic Accounts, "Direct Investment and Multinational Enterprises," <http://www.bea.gov/iTable/index_MNC.cfm>, accessed September 2017.

Table 1311. U.S. Majority-Owned Affiliates of Foreign Companies—Selected Financial and Operating Data by Industry of Affiliate: 2014

[In billions of dollars (13,659 represents $13,659,000,000,000), except as indicated. A majority-owned U.S. affiliate is a U.S. business enterprise in which a foreign entity ("entity" is used here in a broad legal sense including any individual, branch, partnership, association, trust, corporation, or government) has a direct or indirect voting interest greater than 50 percent]

Industry	NAICS code [2]	Total assets	Sales	Employ-ment (1,000)	Employee compen-sation	Gross property, plant, and equipment	Mer-chandise exports	Mer-chandise imports
All industries................	(X)	**13,659**	**4,165**	**6,613**	**521**	**2,132**	**423**	**716**
Manufacturing [1]................	31-33	2,449	1,781	2,410	213	914	230	297
Petroleum and coal products................	324	294	350	48	11	253	31	67
Chemicals................	325	808	355	337	45	163	41	55
Machinery................	333	153	108	223	22	27	20	18
Transportation equipment................	336	348	365	502	37	167	63	86
Wholesale trade................	42	803	1,154	609	54	294	177	399
Retail trade................	44-45	110	180	583	20	64	1	15
Information................	51	348	140	290	26	89	1	(Z)
Finance and insurance................	52	8,531	359	418	72	103	(D)	(Z)
Real estate and rental and leasing................	53	177	30	54	4	130	(D)	(D)
Professional, scientific, and technical services................	54	204	119	346	37	19	1	–
Other industries................	(X)	1,037	401	1,904	97	520	13	(D)

– Represents zero. D Suppressed to avoid disclosure of data of individual companies. X Not applicable. Z Less than $500,000. [1] Includes other industries not shown separately. [2] Based on the North American Industry Classification System (NAICS); see text, Section 15.

Source: U.S. Bureau of Economic Analysis, International Economic Accounts, "Foreign Direct Investment in the United States," <http://www.bea.gov/international/di1fdiop.htm>, accessed September 2017.

Table 1312. U.S. Direct Investment Position Abroad, Capital Outflows, and Income by Industry of Foreign Affiliates: 2000 to 2016

[In millions of dollars (1,316,247 represents $1,316,247,000,000). U.S. investment abroad is the ownership or control by one U.S. person of 10 percent or more of the voting securities of an incorporated foreign business enterprise or an equivalent interest in an unincorporated foreign business enterprise]

Industry	2000	2005	2010	2013	2014	2015	2016
DIRECT INVESTMENT POSITION ON A HISTORICAL-COST BASIS							
All industries, total [1]	1,316,247	2,241,656	3,741,910	4,579,713	4,910,065	5,048,773	5,332,225
Mining	72,111	109,280	172,819	213,081	218,054	198,800	198,742
Manufacturing [1]	343,899	430,737	518,321	623,700	613,079	620,746	666,580
Food	23,497	27,638	47,704	64,766	68,010	61,197	60,602
Chemicals	75,807	106,975	111,327	135,824	134,211	142,820	147,836
Primary and fabricated metals	21,644	23,013	18,674	27,138	26,590	26,949	25,512
Machinery	22,229	26,433	41,285	47,871	41,331	40,848	46,404
Computer and electronic products	59,909	50,773	72,935	88,448	86,758	90,293	97,015
Electrical equipment, appliances, and components	10,005	15,449	19,941	13,361	12,922	13,353	12,893
Transportation equipment	49,887	50,739	49,636	51,589	55,671	60,771	71,362
Other manufacturing	(NA)	129,716	156,819	194,704	187,585	184,516	204,956
Wholesale trade	93,936	132,915	168,722	228,582	228,727	227,815	244,296
Information	52,345	102,848	126,063	147,853	165,472	181,688	195,187
Depository institutions (banking)	40,152	66,707	118,585	126,595	135,129	123,194	129,319
Finance and insurance	217,086	463,981	734,859	629,357	695,696	657,685	674,664
Professional, scientific, and technical services	32,868	57,164	81,874	95,973	110,902	111,160	120,159
Holding companies (nonbank)	(NA)	710,386	1,584,903	2,228,127	2,450,117	2,622,873	2,761,524
Other industries	441,886	167,640	235,764	286,446	292,889	304,812	341,754
FINANCIAL OUTFLOWS [INFLOWS(-)] WITHOUT CURRENT-COST ADJUSTMENT							
All industries, total [1]	142,627	15,369	277,779	303,432	294,754	262,569	280,681
Mining	2,174	12,015	11,884	8,483	13,762	-61	1,365
Manufacturing [1]	43,002	28,121	33,320	58,865	51,135	41,383	50,472
Food	2,014	1,171	5,341	4,754	6,766	2,478	3,029
Chemicals	3,812	3,911	7,614	11,199	14,831	5,928	5,858
Primary and fabricated metals	1,233	-703	546	1,216	1,661	561	15
Machinery	2,659	2,077	4,229	3,861	5,266	1,246	3,231
Computer and electronic products	17,303	3,607	6,772	5,534	8,607	10,266	17,562
Electrical equipment, appliances, and components	2,100	1,662	1,743	2,075	1,278	1,265	340
Transportation equipment	7,814	-250	-380	7,780	3,481	11,518	10,528
Other manufacturing	(NA)	16,645	7,456	22,447	9,245	8,120	9,910
Wholesale trade	11,938	12,517	15,487	18,378	9,008	9,586	18,985
Information	16,531	2,831	8,777	16,605	19,751	14,884	19,382
Depository institutions	-1,274	-4,751	-4,811	-9,304	-3,736	-3,906	2,671
Finance and insurance	21,659	13,079	21,887	14,196	3,751	11,802	-35
Professional, scientific, and technical services	5,441	-2,055	2,774	11,981	12,197	5,614	10,544
Holding companies (nonbank)	(NA)	-66,351	169,743	164,551	167,178	160,168	141,802
Other industries	40,690	19,964	18,718	19,677	21,707	23,098	35,494
INCOME WITHOUT CURRENT-COST ADJUSTMENT [2]							
All industries, total [1]	133,692	271,877	417,605	448,890	445,815	406,691	409,966
Mining	13,164	24,559	29,138	26,047	19,383	3,665	2,107
Manufacturing [1]	42,230	46,896	61,240	63,772	59,565	60,508	64,966
Food	2,681	3,558	4,322	5,019	4,737	3,657	3,999
Chemicals	11,552	13,056	14,088	16,254	15,983	14,497	16,934
Primary and fabricated metals	1,536	1,815	1,349	1,668	1,216	1,635	1,655
Machinery	2,257	2,253	4,465	5,297	3,433	2,141	3,151
Computer and electronic products	8,860	7,714	11,440	9,503	11,976	12,738	12,677
Electrical equipment, appliances, and components	1,079	1,703	1,653	1,564	1,278	1,126	1,094
Transportation equipment	4,107	1,936	6,471	7,545	5,713	10,027	10,474
Other manufacturing	(NA)	14,862	17,452	16,921	15,229	14,685	14,982
Wholesale trade	14,198	24,494	24,538	24,716	27,442	19,697	21,832
Information	-964	10,832	12,229	15,367	15,571	13,634	14,468
Depository institutions	2,191	164	1,328	7,616	4,700	4,747	7,362
Finance and insurance	15,210	27,911	35,143	36,999	36,339	38,620	42,054
Professional, scientific, and technical services	3,548	9,272	8,856	10,906	11,177	11,327	14,478
Holding companies (nonbank)	(NA)	109,566	220,101	230,409	239,331	221,141	206,032
Other industries	42,504	18,184	25,033	33,058	32,307	33,353	36,668

NA Not available. [1] Includes other industries, not shown separately. [2] Prior to 2006, income is shown net of withholding taxes. Beginning 2006, income is shown gross of withholding taxes.

Source: U.S. Bureau of Economic Analysis, International Economic Accounts, "Direct Investment and Multinational Enterprises," <http://www.bea.gov/iTable/index_MNC.cfm>, accessed September 2017.

Table 1313. U.S. Direct Investment Position Abroad on a Historical-Cost Basis by Selected Country: 2000 to 2016

[In millions of dollars (1,316,247 represents $1,316,247,000,000). U.S. investment abroad is the ownership or control by one U.S. person of 10 percent or more of the voting securities of an incorporated foreign business enterprise or an equivalent interest in an unincorporated foreign business enterprise. Negative position can occur when a U.S. parent company's liabilities to the foreign affiliate are greater than its equity in and loans to the foreign affiliate]

Country	2000	2005	2010	2012	2013	2014	2015	2016
All countries	**1,316,247**	**2,241,656**	**3,741,910**	**4,410,015**	**4,579,713**	**4,910,065**	**5,048,773**	**5,332,225**
Canada	132,472	231,836	295,206	366,709	370,259	357,439	346,746	363,914
Europe [1]	687,320	1,210,679	2,034,559	2,445,652	2,604,776	2,796,982	2,919,510	3,174,885
Austria	2,872	11,236	11,485	14,327	15,630	10,118	11,814	15,891
Belgium	17,973	49,306	43,975	49,144	51,966	48,314	46,120	55,822
Czech Republic	1,228	2,729	5,268	6,016	6,383	6,377	5,847	5,524
Denmark	5,270	6,914	11,802	14,306	13,397	13,024	12,969	13,643
Finland	1,342	1,950	1,597	2,007	1,919	2,753	1,239	3,395
France	42,628	60,526	78,320	75,185	78,667	79,129	77,860	78,062
Germany	55,508	100,473	103,319	121,072	111,724	107,720	102,068	107,711
Greece	795	1,884	1,775	1,065	-584	-442	605	628
Hungary	1,920	2,795	4,237	7,500	6,317	5,851	6,302	6,552
Ireland	35,903	55,173	158,851	212,411	220,670	276,012	334,325	387,092
Italy	23,484	24,528	27,137	27,317	25,829	27,491	26,300	24,686
Luxembourg	27,849	79,937	272,206	408,205	460,029	537,881	553,066	607,849
Netherlands	115,429	240,205	514,689	647,365	740,740	737,653	783,309	847,391
Norway	4,379	8,533	28,541	43,326	40,617	37,614	34,736	32,318
Poland	3,884	5,575	13,152	13,137	12,480	11,529	11,239	11,621
Portugal	2,664	2,138	2,612	2,061	1,978	2,372	2,240	2,273
Russia	1,147	9,363	10,040	13,389	13,280	8,570	8,543	10,574
Spain	21,236	50,197	52,390	27,978	33,879	34,962	36,280	37,388
Sweden	25,959	30,153	23,275	33,635	31,675	29,467	30,497	27,145
Switzerland	55,377	100,692	119,891	122,417	128,490	140,427	155,710	172,608
Turkey	1,826	2,563	4,155	4,945	3,845	2,984	3,058	3,109
United Kingdom	230,762	351,513	501,247	537,041	537,714	621,663	625,124	682,361
Latin America and other Western Hemisphere	266,576	379,582	752,788	828,721	788,772	875,390	873,398	843,357
South America [1]	84,220	73,311	136,598	147,490	140,871	136,379	124,523	131,629
Argentina	17,488	10,103	11,747	13,393	13,427	13,911	13,600	13,721
Brazil	36,717	30,882	66,963	76,821	69,760	66,782	57,579	64,438
Chile	10,052	11,127	30,747	27,537	28,329	28,301	28,543	29,428
Colombia	3,693	4,292	6,181	7,251	7,523	7,139	6,522	6,217
Ecuador	832	941	1,283	571	581	566	491	509
Peru	3,130	5,542	7,196	6,651	5,559	6,122	5,743	6,187
Venezuela	10,531	8,934	10,255	12,781	13,267	11,005	9,568	7,984
Central America [1]	73,841	82,496	97,752	114,848	97,095	97,411	97,020	98,557
Costa Rica	1,716	1,598	1,827	1,034	999	1,404	1,423	1,565
Honduras	399	821	936	722	772	730	1,147	1,140
Mexico	39,352	73,687	85,751	104,388	86,433	86,976	86,795	87,635
Panama	30,758	4,826	5,156	4,709	4,682	4,002	3,751	4,377
Other Western Hemisphere [1]	108,515	223,775	518,438	566,384	550,806	641,600	651,855	613,171
Barbados	2,141	3,881	7,524	11,242	12,413	15,230	15,548	18,990
Bermuda	60,114	113,222	265,524	279,555	256,359	294,147	304,812	288,822
Dominican Republic	1,143	815	1,432	1,088	1,183	1,217	1,299	1,401
U.K. Islands, Caribbean	33,451	83,164	191,680	218,648	218,049	284,231	286,679	265,548
Africa [1]	11,891	22,756	54,816	55,849	60,884	66,403	59,266	57,465
Egypt	1,998	5,475	12,599	17,341	18,796	(D)	23,236	22,202
Nigeria	470	1,105	5,058	5,369	5,066	4,405	4,558	3,819
South Africa	3,562	3,969	6,017	5,471	6,457	5,921	5,336	5,061
Middle East [1]	10,863	21,115	34,431	40,306	45,399	49,775	46,583	45,925
Israel	3,735	7,978	9,464	8,977	8,934	8,500	9,119	9,669
Saudi Arabia	3,661	3,830	7,436	9,500	10,084	8,470	9,669	9,825
United Arab Emirates	683	2,285	4,935	8,481	11,401	15,921	15,625	13,355
Asia and Pacific [1]	207,125	375,689	570,111	672,777	709,623	764,077	803,269	846,680
Australia	34,838	75,669	125,421	165,106	168,300	170,897	158,726	165,347
China	11,140	19,016	58,996	54,514	60,454	73,660	84,525	92,481
Hong Kong	27,447	36,415	41,264	56,086	56,785	60,795	64,105	65,625
India	2,379	7,162	24,666	25,413	24,850	27,812	29,939	32,939
Indonesia	8,904	8,603	10,558	11,441	12,117	13,580	13,352	14,563
Japan	57,091	81,175	113,523	125,283	117,239	100,823	104,128	114,637
Korea, South	8,968	19,760	26,233	32,202	32,108	35,540	36,931	39,068
Malaysia	7,910	11,097	11,791	10,898	13,360	11,088	14,968	13,897
New Zealand	4,271	5,191	6,724	8,476	7,414	8,215	7,929	8,430
Philippines	3,638	6,522	5,399	3,988	4,091	4,057	5,390	5,896
Singapore	24,133	76,390	102,778	145,236	182,079	225,223	250,748	258,864
Taiwan	7,836	14,356	22,188	17,546	15,307	15,093	15,307	16,187
Thailand	5,824	10,252	12,999	10,773	9,957	11,054	10,594	11,774

[1] Includes other countries, not shown separately.

Source: U.S. Bureau of Economic Analysis, International Economic Accounts, "Direct Investment and Multinational Enterprises," <http://www.bea.gov/iTable/index_MNC.cfm>, accessed September 2017.

Table 1314. U.S. Foreign Economic and Military Aid by Major Recipient Country: 2000 to 2015

[In millions of dollars (17,111.9 represents $17,111,900,000). For years ending September 30. Annual figures are for obligations. Total aid may not add due to rounding]

Region/country	2000	2005	2010	2014	2015 Total	2015 Economic aid	2015 Military aid
Total [1]	17,111.9	35,270.1	48,236.4	43,077.9	42,957.2	34,299.4	8,657.8
Middle East & North Africa [1]	6,799.2	14,522.3	8,843.3	7,226.2	9,435.9	4,071.4	5,364.5
Egypt	2,076.1	1,790.5	1,617.2	179.5	1,525.5	222.6	1,302.8
Iraq	1.2	8,705.7	2,092.4	414.1	574.7	394.4	180.3
Israel	3,863.4	2,713.5	2,837.6	3,126.6	3,113.0	13.0	3,100.0
Jordan	448.3	647.3	765.8	1,143.4	1,517.1	1,048.8	468.3
Lebanon	35.0	25.2	158.7	437.0	506.4	351.9	154.5
Morocco	51.1	45.8	56.4	23.4	69.5	54.4	15.1
West Bank/Gaza [2]	122.0	347.0	686.9	497.3	556.7	556.6	0.2
Yemen	57.2	29.2	122.4	243.8	176.7	176.5	0.2
Sub-Saharan Africa [1]	2,025.1	4,904.6	8,305.0	10,175.9	11,644.1	11,156.3	487.8
Angola	105.4	64.8	99.9	55.1	58.3	57.6	0.7
Botswana	0.9	41.9	52.0	50.9	43.9	43.2	0.6
Burkina Faso	18.1	13.8	29.2	62.3	32.5	32.2	0.3
Chad	4.1	61.0	181.7	147.2	108.7	99.5	9.3
Congo, Democratic Republic of	32.6	117.6	360.8	438.6	467.5	459.9	7.6
Ethiopia	277.6	629.0	759.2	742.1	808.8	784.7	24.2
Ghana	66.8	69.1	110.1	184.7	297.5	293.1	4.4
Kenya	93.5	223.9	573.3	891.7	941.3	847.4	93.8
Lesotho	2.1	3.9	33.3	35.4	29.2	29.2	(Z)
Liberia	22.4	148.6	177.0	249.1	782.5	776.4	6.2
Madagascar	27.4	155.0	55.9	58.3	155.6	155.3	0.3
Malawi	44.4	58.4	170.5	207.9	245.0	244.7	0.3
Mali	43.7	57.6	123.2	169.3	207.0	206.3	0.7
Mozambique	82.1	104.6	292.8	337.1	338.9	338.2	0.7
Namibia	15.5	46.5	89.4	61.7	43.6	43.4	0.2
Nigeria	112.6	152.7	408.5	595.6	592.3	588.2	4.2
Rwanda	39.0	82.1	173.6	177.6	246.8	245.8	0.9
Senegal	37.4	49.2	657.0	119.0	116.7	110.4	6.3
Somalia	13.9	36.8	156.2	402.2	255.1	244.1	11.0
South Africa	56.8	172.8	467.2	515.6	362.4	359.2	3.2
South Sudan [3]	(X)	(X)	(X)	867.8	844.0	817.1	26.9
Sudan	51.0	1,030.0	891.7	263.8	230.9	230.9	−
Tanzania	44.5	120.5	422.6	589.4	591.6	586.8	4.8
Uganda	76.2	286.8	415.7	557.3	591.5	564.5	26.9
Zambia	35.4	171.5	264.3	672.9	245.8	245.4	0.4
Zimbabwe	20.9	57.3	215.5	172.7	190.1	190.1	−
Latin America & Caribbean [1]	2,301.2	2,564.8	4,328.8	2,534.0	3,956.9	3,711.7	245.2
Bolivia	241.1	171.3	91.7	7.5	56.6	56.6	−
Colombia	1,168.6	736.2	795.4	560.4	841.1	763.0	78.2
El Salvador	34.9	42.9	62.2	84.3	332.9	324.3	8.6
Guatemala	71.8	55.2	149.7	161.9	137.9	114.3	23.6
Haiti	84.5	223.0	1,351.3	355.0	504.5	503.4	1.1
Honduras	41.8	287.4	39.7	95.6	133.7	111.7	22.1
Mexico	43.9	104.2	718.2	332.3	585.9	530.5	55.3
Peru	204.2	133.5	203.7	165.5	304.0	294.8	9.2
Asia [1]	1,163.2	3,832.7	15,157.9	10,392.5	6,257.5	4,694.8	1,562.8
Afghanistan	54.1	1,729.9	10,866.5	7,259.3	3,104.5	2,020.6	1,084.0
Bangladesh	78.3	77.4	171.9	314.0	227.3	222.8	4.5
Cambodia	27.5	52.9	72.4	123.4	86.0	81.5	4.5
India	188.0	202.8	116.3	141.9	104.9	99.6	5.3
Indonesia	242.3	230.7	309.3	196.6	220.8	199.7	21.1
Mongolia	25.8	19.0	38.1	−	12.5	8.5	3.9
Nepal	22.6	73.3	66.8	83.8	263.3	258.3	5.0
Pakistan	23.8	712.4	2,681.4	999.0	1,135.2	840.2	295.0
Philippines	82.2	159.2	200.9	364.2	256.6	155.9	100.7
Sri Lanka	10.5	143.4	81.5	35.2	33.9	33.1	0.8
Oceania [1]	164.7	162.3	209.7	265.2	232.5	230.7	1.8
Micronesia, Federated States of	81.0	94.3	90.1	161.2	115.1	115.1	−
Central Asia [1]	1,461.9	2,335.8	2,140.1	1,416.1	1,030.3	726.1	304.1
Armenia	104.2	77.8	54.6	70.6	59.0	47.3	11.6
Georgia	112.4	108.9	229.4	289.5	112.6	53.6	59.0
Kazakhstan	53.4	68.5	331.4	191.8	191.0	112.8	78.3
Kyrgyzstan	47.3	51.3	128.3	75.4	61.8	60.4	1.4
Moldova	48.6	32.4	294.0	54.9	55.7	39.2	16.5
Russia	708.6	1,577.3	505.7	159.4	22.8	22.8	−
Ukraine	199.5	156.9	314.7	308.5	300.9	224.2	76.8
Eastern Europe [1]	1,045.3	717.5	707.5	434.5	343.2	235.0	108.2
Kosovo	−	−	35.0	72.3	56.2	50.9	5.3
Poland	84.8	96.0	221.2	53.7	32.4	21.3	11.1
Western Europe	24.0	132.6	78.7	125.2	146.2	141.3	5.0

− Represents zero. Z less than $50,000. X Not applicable. [1] Includes other countries, not shown separately, and aid not assigned to specific countries within their parent regions. [2] See footnote 6, Table 1353. [3] South Sudan seceded from Sudan in July 2011.

Source: U.S. Agency for International Development, *U.S. Overseas Loans and Grants: Obligations and Loan Authorizations, July 1, 1945–September 30, 2015*, and earlier reports. See also <https://explorer.usaid.gov/reports.html>.

Table 1315. U.S. Foreign Economic and Military Aid Programs: 1980 to 2015

[In millions of dollars (9,682 represents $9,682,000,000). For years ending September 30. Total foreign aid programs are the sum of economic and military assistance. Major components in recent years include U.S. Agency for International Development (USAID), U.S. Department of Agriculture (USDA), U.S. Department of State, and U.S. Department of Treasury. Annual figures are in obligations]

Year and world region	Total foreign assistance	Military assistance	Economic assistance, by funding agency					
			Total	USAID	USDA	State Department	Treasury Department	Other U.S. agencies
1980................................	9,682	2,110	7,572	4,062	1,437	459	1,478	137
1985................................	18,107	5,780	12,327	8,132	2,052	431	1,548	164
1990................................	16,003	4,959	11,044	6,964	1,643	590	1,469	377
1995................................	15,556	4,290	11,266	7,281	1,284	132	1,781	788
2000................................	17,112	5,149	11,963	5,907	1,936	2,278	1,110	731
2005................................	35,270	9,071	26,200	14,160	2,017	4,674	1,240	4,108
2006................................	37,061	12,889	24,172	11,389	1,789	5,270	1,127	4,596
2007................................	39,546	13,973	25,573	10,371	1,626	5,594	1,476	6,507
2008................................	46,545	16,458	30,087	9,814	2,539	8,969	1,217	7,549
2009................................	46,426	14,788	31,638	11,810	2,410	11,263	1,638	4,517
2010................................	48,236	14,855	33,381	12,071	2,386	11,558	2,245	5,121
2011................................	48,832	18,590	30,242	10,396	1,885	10,613	2,034	5,314
2012................................	49,983	17,841	32,143	11,357	1,898	12,629	2,829	3,429
2013................................	45,802	13,803	31,999	11,780	1,821	11,182	2,672	4,545
2014................................	43,078	10,453	32,625	10,856	1,728	13,919	2,735	3,387
2015, total..................	**42,957**	**8,658**	**34,299**	**13,234**	**1,681**	**13,403**	**2,642**	**3,340**
Asia................................	6,258	1,563	4,695	3,023	82	1,183	217	191
Eurasia............................	1,030	304	726	303	–	212	–	211
Eastern Europe.................	343	108	235	121	–	60	–	54
Latin America and Caribbean...	3,957	245	3,712	1,064	90	2,030	107	421
Middle East and North Africa. . .	9,436	5,365	4,071	2,507	76	1,449	10	30
Oceania...........................	233	2	231	25	–	8	–	198
Sub-Saharan Africa.............	11,644	488	11,156	3,540	1,374	5,044	215	984
Western Europe.................	146	5	141	2	–	107	–	32
Canada............................	11	–	11	–	–	–	–	11
World, not specified............	9,899	579	9,321	2,650	59	3,310	2,093	1,209

– Represents or rounds to zero.

Source: U.S. Agency for International Development, *U.S. Overseas Loans and Grants: Obligations and Loan Authorizations, July 1, 1945–September 30, 2015*, and earlier reports. See also <https://explorer.usaid.gov/reports.html>.

Table 1316. U.S. International Trade in Goods by Related Parties: 2005 to 2016

[In millions of dollars (1,662,380 represents $1,662,380,000,000). "Related party trade" is trade by U.S. companies with their subsidiaries abroad as well as trade by U.S. subsidiaries of foreign companies with their parent companies]

Country and commodity	NAICS code [2]	2005	2010	2014	2015	2016
IMPORTS FOR CONSUMPTION						
Total imports.......................	(X)	1,662,380	1,900,587	2,324,940	2,226,615	2,173,617
Related party trade, total [1]..............	**(X)**	**775,730**	**922,340**	**1,180,431**	**1,113,042**	**1,071,342**
Mexico............................	(X)	99,709	135,989	197,712	207,917	206,662
Canada...........................	(X)	127,719	138,210	182,437	148,425	139,075
China..............................	(X)	62,716	107,007	136,242	131,405	114,590
Japan..............................	(X)	108,322	94,001	102,419	101,722	103,182
Germany..........................	(X)	51,870	54,005	85,087	83,594	76,978
Korea, South.....................	(X)	24,920	29,291	43,382	43,456	45,508
Transportation equipment......	336	188,445	179,675	261,521	276,328	281,380
Computer & electronic products...	334	176,719	203,829	224,389	221,730	214,526
Chemicals.........................	325	84,459	134,018	153,482	152,463	142,598
Machinery, except electrical.....	333	56,804	53,722	84,744	81,786	77,466
Electrical equipment, appliances & components........	335	26,018	33,496	48,841	50,029	49,648
Miscellaneous manufactured commodities...............	339	22,922	36,298	41,144	42,972	43,695
EXPORTS						
Total exports.......................	(X)	803,992	1,122,567	1,398,850	1,285,939	1,226,482
Related party trade, domestic exports, total [1].......	**(X)**	**245,712**	**311,693**	**401,647**	**382,651**	**378,297**
Canada...........................	(X)	76,331	85,861	104,837	91,863	88,939
Mexico............................	(X)	44,570	49,612	78,395	77,858	74,595
China..............................	(X)	4,909	13,396	21,684	22,243	25,316
Netherlands......................	(X)	9,308	15,032	17,098	17,309	17,911
Japan..............................	(X)	17,427	16,690	18,417	17,702	16,818
Belgium...........................	(X)	7,382	9,691	15,535	17,229	15,842
Transportation equipment......	336	52,513	55,466	83,908	86,985	90,384
Chemicals.........................	325	48,121	64,361	79,736	79,696	77,226
Computer & electronic products...	334	41,863	42,795	37,357	38,517	37,003
Machinery, except electrical.....	333	25,492	32,318	37,838	34,337	31,094
Petroleum & coal products......	324	4,974	23,367	38,193	24,113	22,048
Miscellaneous manufactured commodities...............	339	9,914	13,693	16,943	17,748	17,565

X Not applicable. [1] Includes other countries and other commodities, not shown separately. [2] Based on the North American Industry Classification System (NAICS); see text, Section 15.

Source: U.S. Census Bureau, "NAICS Related Party Database," <https://relatedparty.ftd.census.gov/>, accessed August 2017. See also <https://www.census.gov/foreign-trade/index.html>.

Table 1317. U.S. International Trade in Goods and Services: 2000 to 2016

[In millions of dollars (-372,517 represents -$372,517,000,000). Data are presented on a balance of payments basis and will not agree with the following merchandise trade tables in this section. Minus sign (-) indicates deficit]

Category	2000	2005	2010	2013	2014	2015	2016
TRADE BALANCE							
Total..	**-372,517**	**-714,245**	**-494,658**	**-461,876**	**-490,336**	**-500,445**	**-504,793**
Goods......................................	-446,783	-782,804	-648,678	-702,244	-751,494	-761,855	-752,507
Services...................................	74,266	68,558	154,020	240,368	261,157	261,410	247,714
Maintenance and repair services, n.i.e. [1] ...	2,442	4,609	7,640	11,148	13,629	14,396	16,818
Transport [2]...............................	-11,848	-23,021	-2,972	-3,858	-3,459	-9,452	-12,509
Travel for all purposes [3].................	34,400	21,482	50,387	79,364	86,250	90,695	82,322
Insurance services.........................	-7,653	-21,144	-47,081	-36,724	-33,678	-31,593	-31,729
Financial services.........................	11,181	27,752	56,846	73,586	82,066	76,855	72,551
Charges for the use of intellectual property, n.i.e. [1,4]........................	35,202	48,871	74,970	89,174	87,733	84,584	80,061
Telecommunications, computer, and information services......................	-182	-460	-3,977	-615	-1,811	-606	-396
Other business services [5]...............	16,083	22,342	30,383	30,816	34,144	36,957	43,309
Government goods and services, n.i.e. [1,6]...............................	-5,360	-11,872	-12,176	-2,525	-3,718	-427	-2,714
EXPORTS							
Total..	**1,075,321**	**1,286,022**	**1,853,606**	**2,293,457**	**2,375,905**	**2,263,907**	**2,208,072**
Goods......................................	784,940	913,016	1,290,273	1,592,002	1,633,986	1,510,757	1,455,704
Services...................................	290,381	373,006	563,333	701,455	741,919	753,150	752,368
Maintenance and repair services, n.i.e. [1] ...	5,011	7,624	14,549	18,568	21,149	23,406	25,628
Transport [2]...............................	45,758	52,622	71,656	86,776	90,729	87,609	84,318
Travel for all purposes [3].................	100,187	101,470	137,010	177,484	191,918	205,418	205,940
Insurance services.........................	3,631	7,566	14,397	16,696	17,333	16,229	16,348
Financial services.........................	22,117	39,878	72,348	95,131	106,949	102,595	98,180
Charges for the use of intellectual property, n.i.e. [1,4]........................	51,808	74,448	107,521	128,034	129,716	124,442	124,453
Telecommunications, computer, and information services......................	12,215	15,515	25,038	34,419	34,691	35,664	36,455
Other business services [5]...............	40,497	58,302	101,029	121,530	128,915	136,622	142,231
Government goods and services, n.i.e. [1,6]...............................	9,156	15,582	19,784	22,816	20,518	21,165	18,814
IMPORTS							
Total..	**1,447,837**	**2,000,267**	**2,348,263**	**2,755,334**	**2,866,241**	**2,764,352**	**2,712,866**
Goods......................................	1,231,722	1,695,820	1,938,950	2,294,247	2,385,480	2,272,612	2,208,211
Services...................................	216,115	304,448	409,313	461,087	480,761	491,740	504,654
Maintenance and repair services, n.i.e. [1] ...	2,569	3,015	6,909	7,420	7,520	9,010	8,810
Transport [2]...............................	57,606	75,643	74,628	90,634	94,188	97,061	96,827
Travel for all purposes [3].................	65,787	79,988	86,623	98,120	105,668	114,723	123,618
Insurance services.........................	11,284	28,710	61,478	53,420	51,011	47,822	48,077
Financial services.........................	10,936	12,126	15,502	21,545	24,883	25,740	25,629
Charges for the use of intellectual property, n.i.e. [1,4]........................	16,606	25,577	32,551	38,860	41,983	39,858	44,392
Telecommunications, computer, and information services......................	12,397	15,975	29,015	35,034	36,502	36,270	36,851
Other business services [5]...............	24,414	35,960	70,646	90,714	94,771	99,665	98,922
Government goods and services, n.i.e. [1,6]...............................	14,516	27,454	31,960	25,341	24,236	21,592	21,528

[1] N.i.e. means not included elsewhere. [2] Includes passenger fares. [3] All travel purposes include 1) business travel, including expenditures by border, seasonal, and other short-term workers and 2) personal travel, including health-related and education-related travel. [4] Includes charges for the use of proprietary rights, such as patents, trademarks, and copyrights, and charges for licenses to use, reproduce, distribute, and sell or purchase intellectual property. [5] Includes three categories: "other business services" (including research and development, management, advertising, and so on); "construction"; and "personal, cultural and recreational services" (including fees related to the production of motion pictures, radio, and television programs, downloaded recording and manuscripts, telemedicine, online education, and receipts or payments for cultural, sporting, and performing arts activities, and so on). [6] Includes goods and services supplied by and to embassies, consulates, and military bases; goods and services acquired by diplomatic and military personnel in the host economy; and services supplied by and to governments not included in other categories of services.

Source: U.S. Bureau of Economic Analysis, "International Economic Accounts: Trade in Goods and Services," <http://www.bea.gov/international/index.htm#trade>, accessed September 2017.

Table 1318. U.S. Freight Gateways—Value of Shipments: 2016

[In billions of dollars (3,638.8 represents $3,638,800,000,000), except as indicated. For the top 40 gateways ranked by value of shipments]

Port	Rank	Total trade	Exports	Imports	Exports as a percent of total
Total U.S. merchandise trade	(X)	3,638.8	1,451.0	2,187.8	39.9
Top 40 gateways	(X)	3,087.7	1,214.9	1,872.8	39.3
As a percent of total	(X)	84.9	83.7	85.6	(X)
Los Angeles, CA	1	273.4	32.7	240.7	12.0
Laredo, TX	2	199.8	88.7	111.2	44.4
JFK International Airport, NY	3	186.7	88.8	97.9	47.6
Chicago, IL	4	169.5	45.5	124.0	26.8
Newark, NJ	5	162.7	14.9	147.8	9.2
Detroit, MI	6	145.7	73.3	72.4	50.3
New Orleans, LA	7	114.2	57.8	56.3	50.7
Houston, TX	8	112.8	63.1	49.7	55.9
Los Angeles International Airport, CA	9	102.9	51.9	51.0	50.4
Port Huron, MI	10	89.9	42.5	47.4	47.3
Long Beach, CA	11	88.0	32.4	55.6	36.9
Buffalo-Niagara Falls, NY	12	86.1	47.1	39.0	54.7
Savannah, GA	13	83.8	24.5	59.2	29.3
Charleston, SC	14	79.1	33.0	46.1	41.8
El Paso, TX	15	75.2	30.9	44.3	41.1
Norfolk-Newport News, VA	16	70.0	26.0	44.1	37.1
Miami International Airport, FL	17	58.8	32.7	26.1	55.6
Anchorage, AK	18	57.3	18.1	39.1	31.7
San Francisco International Airport, CA	19	54.6	26.9	27.8	49.2
Tacoma, WA	20	54.5	10.8	43.7	19.8
Dallas-Fort Worth, TX	21	52.5	21.8	30.7	41.5
Cleveland, OH	22	50.3	28.8	21.5	57.3
Baltimore, MD	23	50.0	14.1	35.9	28.1
Oakland, CA	24	48.9	18.7	30.2	38.3
Otay Mesa, CA	25	43.1	15.1	28.0	35.1
New York, NY	26	40.9	32.1	8.8	78.5
Atlanta, GA	27	40.2	15.3	24.9	38.0
Hidalgo, TX	28	30.6	10.4	20.3	33.9
Everett, WA	29	29.4	27.4	2.0	93.1
Eagle Pass, TX	30	29.3	8.1	21.2	27.7
Nogales, AZ	31	26.8	10.3	16.6	38.2
Seattle-Tacoma International Airport, WA	32	26.8	17.1	9.7	63.7
Blaine, WA	33	26.2	15.3	10.9	58.5
Champlain-Rouses Point, NY	34	25.5	8.9	16.6	34.9
Miami, FL	35	23.9	9.5	14.4	39.7
Jacksonville, FL	36	23.4	6.0	17.4	25.8
Santa Teresa, NM	37	23.2	10.7	12.4	46.3
Port Everglades, FL	38	22.1	11.7	10.4	52.9
Philadelphia, PA	39	22.0	4.3	17.7	19.6
Seattle, WA	40	21.7	6.5	15.2	30.0

X Not applicable.

Source: U.S. Census Bureau, Foreign Trade Division, "USA Trade Online," <https://usatrade.census.gov/>, accessed August 2017.

Table 1319. U.S. Agricultural Exports by State: 2000 to 2015

[In millions of dollars (51,265 represents $51,265,000,000). Calendar year. Export estimates based on U.S. farm cash receipts. Export values are calibrated such that the sum of state export estimates for a commodity equals the total U.S. export value for the commodity]

State	2000	2005	2010	2014	2015	State	2000	2005	2010	2014	2015
U.S.	51,265	63,182	115,820	149,986	133,052	MO.	1,329	1,680	3,472	4,322	3,605
						MT.	496	628	1,072	1,548	1,199
AL.	602	803	1,154	1,541	1,237	NE.	2,258	2,456	5,283	7,174	6,385
AK.	6	10	12	16	17	NV.	64	62	111	167	138
AZ.	484	661	1,071	1,334	1,378	NH.	33	38	66	86	82
AR.	1,296	1,925	3,180	3,609	3,110	NJ.	248	294	401	525	505
CA.	6,854	9,735	15,456	23,568	22,547	NM.	325	372	687	764	756
CO.	886	825	1,511	1,794	1,613	NY.	499	577	1,226	1,688	1,467
CT.	133	153	215	285	244	NC.	1,870	2,104	3,396	4,119	3,542
DE.	130	140	241	321	252	ND.	1,323	1,735	3,784	5,012	4,068
FL.	1,910	2,119	2,981	3,724	3,540	OH.	1,440	1,644	3,390	4,234	3,641
GA.	1,439	1,579	2,650	3,107	2,888	OK.	819	998	1,542	1,639	1,523
HI.	151	187	312	405	384	OR.	793	1,006	1,353	2,041	1,881
ID.	706	810	1,483	2,236	1,877	PA.	691	849	1,610	2,305	2,040
IL.	3,054	3,637	7,392	9,728	7,999	RI.	13	20	32	36	35
IN.	1,680	1,874	4,270	5,767	4,564	SC.	398	486	814	897	793
IA.	3,416	4,342	9,287	11,119	9,971	SD.	1,219	1,428	2,969	4,381	3,720
KS.	1,913	2,179	4,633	4,581	4,143	TN.	549	779	1,241	1,748	1,464
KY.	1,286	1,313	1,525	2,497	2,117	TX.	2,735	3,690	6,341	6,383	6,064
LA.	610	776	1,524	1,882	1,528	UT.	160	201	324	529	420
ME.	145	132	241	305	261	VT.	49	60	140	225	196
MD.	336	314	562	753	647	VA.	559	576	883	1,230	1,053
MA.	106	122	200	206	176	WA.	1,300	1,604	2,801	3,825	3,794
MI.	903	1,140	2,345	3,100	2,802	WV.	59	62	116	172	143
MN.	2,185	2,693	6,080	7,262	6,281	WI.	909	1,162	2,412	3,108	2,778
MS.	752	1,091	1,796	2,332	1,867	WY.	145	111	238	353	313

Source: U.S. Department of Agriculture, Economic Research Service, "State Export Data," <http://www.ers.usda.gov/data-products/state-export-data.aspx>, accessed November 2016.

Table 1320. U.S. Exports and General Imports of Merchandise by Customs District: 2005 to 2016

[In billions of dollars (901.1 represents $901,100,000,000). Exports are f.a.s. (free alongside ship) value basis; imports are on customs-value basis. These data may differ from those in Table 1316, Table 1322, and Table 1323. For methodology, see Foreign Trade Statistics in Appendix III]

Customs district	Exports					General imports				
	2005	2010	2014	2015	2016	2005	2010	2014	2015	2016
Total [1]	901.1	1,278.5	1,621.9	1,503.1	1,451.0	1,673.5	1,913.9	2,356.4	2,248.2	2,187.8
Anchorage, AK	12.1	14.5	17.9	18.7	18.8	10.4	16.2	14.7	16.9	16.8
Baltimore, MD	9.0	14.7	18.8	15.6	14.2	29.6	28.8	35.4	36.8	36.7
Boston, MA	10.4	8.2	7.6	7.4	7.7	21.7	19.2	23.2	25.2	21.8
Buffalo, NY	35.0	40.6	49.5	47.4	47.1	42.6	39.2	44.8	41.6	40.1
Charleston, SC	16.2	19.5	30.5	31.7	33.3	31.9	29.4	44.3	47.2	43.3
Chicago, IL	29.9	35.8	44.1	46.6	45.7	78.7	125.6	166.8	155.2	152.6
Cleveland, OH	20.8	25.4	33.7	34.1	36.7	49.0	69.2	98.2	95.8	95.2
Columbia-Snake, OR	6.3	12.3	15.1	12.1	13.2	14.2	12.2	13.4	12.3	14.7
Dallas-Fort Worth, TX	17.8	18.1	20.6	21.9	22.5	31.8	38.4	56.9	52.0	46.8
Detroit, MI	106.9	113.2	133.1	120.5	118.8	123.1	106.0	129.3	124.7	129.1
Duluth, MN	1.9	2.6	5.5	5.0	4.6	9.3	6.8	10.1	8.9	8.6
El Paso, TX	19.9	29.3	41.9	41.7	42.0	28.0	44.1	50.3	56.9	59.5
Great Falls, MT	9.8	17.4	18.4	14.3	9.6	27.1	26.9	29.9	24.2	22.3
Honolulu, HI	2.4	7.4	12.6	13.9	10.3	3.7	4.6	5.0	4.1	3.1
Houston-Galveston, TX	47.0	94.5	130.5	109.3	91.6	89.4	116.9	121.9	86.2	69.8
Laredo, TX	60.5	81.4	123.5	121.6	118.2	78.7	104.2	157.1	163.4	164.8
Los Angeles, CA	78.4	105.1	128.2	114.1	118.7	215.5	242.7	289.8	279.5	279.3
Miami, FL	34.1	58.9	65.6	58.6	56.1	31.8	36.6	50.1	48.2	48.2
Milwaukee, WI	0.1	0.1	0.3	0.3	0.5	1.3	0.9	1.2	1.0	0.9
Minneapolis, MN	2.3	2.6	2.8	2.6	2.1	6.9	13.6	17.0	12.6	12.3
Mobile, AL	5.0	8.7	12.0	10.6	10.1	14.3	20.8	24.9	22.8	23.3
New Orleans, LA	32.6	69.1	99.9	84.1	83.8	97.8	125.3	134.4	115.2	109.8
New York, NY	90.9	136.3	153.1	143.8	136.4	176.7	190.6	234.0	226.4	220.1
Nogales, AZ	6.9	8.9	13.8	14.9	13.1	13.0	17.4	20.9	21.7	21.9
Norfolk, VA	16.8	21.1	30.8	28.8	26.0	23.5	23.9	33.0	34.4	33.8
Ogdensburg, NY	13.3	16.2	18.3	17.2	16.1	28.2	27.8	29.6	29.3	29.3
Pembina, ND	13.6	21.3	32.5	25.6	22.4	12.8	14.7	20.2	17.3	15.5
Philadelphia, PA	10.2	14.3	18.0	15.8	15.8	47.8	56.9	54.9	56.0	53.8
Port Arthur, TX	2.1	6.5	16.0	12.2	10.4	20.9	26.4	29.7	14.3	10.2
Portland, ME	2.8	4.4	5.2	4.3	4.7	11.2	9.8	15.7	14.0	10.9
Providence, RI	0.1	0.3	0.5	0.2	0.2	4.4	5.8	8.3	8.6	7.7
San Diego, CA	15.0	16.2	22.2	22.7	24.1	28.4	32.4	42.2	47.4	46.3
San Francisco, CA	36.6	47.1	54.6	47.8	50.9	62.4	60.6	74.8	70.0	68.9
San Juan, PR	9.7	19.7	17.6	17.3	15.8	19.5	19.4	23.7	20.0	21.8
Savannah, GA	24.7	41.0	49.2	47.6	45.8	47.9	68.0	92.7	101.1	98.0
Seattle, WA	44.1	58.5	85.4	87.9	82.7	51.7	52.6	67.3	66.9	64.6
St. Albans, VT	4.3	3.3	2.8	2.1	2.2	12.6	6.9	10.1	9.3	7.6
St. Louis, MO	1.3	1.0	1.0	1.6	1.8	9.7	11.5	21.6	17.3	15.2
Tampa, FL	10.1	14.4	16.2	14.7	11.8	19.3	16.4	21.1	25.6	26.5
Virgin Islands, U.S.	0.5	1.9	1.4	0.1	0.3	9.1	10.5	0.7	0.1	0.6
Washington, DC	3.7	6.0	5.5	5.1	5.0	3.7	8.2	6.6	7.1	7.7
Wilmington, NC	2.2	5.3	5.3	5.1	5.6	15.4	12.8	13.3	13.6	11.5

[1] Totals include the following special districts, not shown separately: vessels under their own power or afloat, low valued imports and exports, and mail shipments. Totals may also include data for two or more Customs Districts that have been combined and published under an arbitrary designation, as a solution to disclosure situations.

Source: U.S. Census Bureau, U.S. Foreign Trade Division, "USA Trade Online," <https://usatrade.census.gov/>, accessed August 2017.

Table 1321. U.S. Exports of Goods by State of Origin: 2005 to 2016

[In millions of dollars (901,082 represents $901,082,000,000), except as indicated. Data are on a f.a.s. (free alongside ship) value basis and are based on origin of movement]

State	2005	2007	2008	2009	2010	2011	2012	2013	2014	2015	2016 Total	Rank
Total¹	901,082	1,148,199	1,287,442	1,056,043	1,278,495	1,482,508	1,545,821	1,578,517	1,621,874	1,503,101	1,451,011	(X)
United States	853,292	1,090,418	1,222,545	1,000,269	1,208,081	1,416,625	1,478,314	1,509,865	1,551,164	1,435,997	1,385,055	(X)
Alabama	10,879	14,407	15,879	12,355	15,495	17,928	19,577	19,301	19,450	19,328	20,422	22
Alaska	3,613	4,010	3,542	3,270	4,155	5,259	4,543	4,528	5,111	4,620	4,347	41
Arizona	14,947	19,228	19,784	14,023	15,721	17,885	18,405	19,478	21,247	22,655	22,016	19
Arkansas	3,871	4,887	5,776	5,267	5,219	5,611	7,615	7,161	6,866	5,869	5,707	35
California	116,690	134,319	144,806	120,080	143,208	159,421	161,757	168,192	173,869	165,380	163,513	2
Colorado	6,773	7,352	7,713	5,867	6,726	7,338	8,170	8,545	8,364	7,950	7,580	33
Connecticut	9,750	13,799	15,384	13,799	16,029	16,233	15,871	16,427	15,963	15,242	14,394	25
Delaware	2,535	4,024	4,898	4,312	4,945	5,516	5,114	5,327	5,267	5,267	4,532	40
District of Columbia	823	1,082	1,196	1,091	1,483	1,041	2,014	2,708	940	1,088	1,331	48
Florida	33,444	44,858	54,238	46,888	55,399	65,010	66,223	60,482	58,439	53,900	52,049	7
Georgia	20,657	23,366	27,514	23,743	28,893	34,863	36,039	37,578	39,413	38,595	35,644	11
Hawaii	1,032	560	960	563	684	884	732	599	1,447	1,896	795	51
Idaho	3,273	4,703	5,005	3,877	5,157	5,913	6,120	5,789	5,138	4,295	4,877	39
Illinois	36,169	48,896	53,677	41,626	50,061	64,903	68,158	66,213	68,394	63,402	59,758	5
Indiana	21,594	25,956	26,502	22,907	28,764	32,332	34,399	34,216	35,589	33,819	34,655	12
Iowa	7,373	9,656	12,125	9,042	10,880	13,317	14,622	13,903	15,112	13,234	12,115	27
Kansas	6,736	10,277	12,514	8,917	9,900	11,623	11,684	12,459	12,022	10,690	10,181	30
Kentucky	14,961	19,652	19,121	17,650	19,346	20,119	22,132	25,412	27,757	27,644	29,199	17
Louisiana	19,404	30,319	41,908	32,616	41,371	54,971	62,869	63,247	64,770	48,686	48,419	9
Maine	2,332	2,750	3,016	2,231	3,162	3,422	3,048	2,687	2,811	2,763	2,875	45
Maryland	7,138	8,949	11,383	9,225	10,167	10,863	11,745	11,747	12,228	10,052	9,658	32
Massachusetts	22,052	25,351	28,369	23,593	26,305	27,871	25,614	26,812	27,384	25,290	25,892	18
Michigan	37,849	44,555	45,136	32,655	44,851	51,064	57,051	59,400	57,573	53,954	54,713	6
Minnesota	14,736	18,062	19,186	15,532	18,904	20,732	20,827	20,760	21,398	20,016	19,202	23
Mississippi	4,021	5,184	7,323	6,316	8,224	10,939	11,794	12,415	11,485	10,848	10,495	29
Missouri	10,514	13,484	12,852	9,522	12,925	14,161	13,903	12,958	14,190	13,648	13,935	26
Montana	715	1,134	1,395	1,053	1,393	1,592	1,576	1,506	1,545	1,404	1,360	47
Nebraska	3,003	4,266	5,412	4,873	5,821	7,588	7,455	7,393	7,890	6,663	6,380	34
Nevada	3,941	5,714	6,121	5,672	5,913	7,990	10,261	8,701	7,692	8,666	9,763	31
New Hampshire	2,557	2,914	3,752	3,061	4,368	4,307	3,488	3,511	4,233	4,001	4,143	42
New Jersey	21,107	30,836	35,643	27,244	32,131	38,172	37,286	36,612	36,587	32,064	31,223	15
New Mexico	2,543	2,585	2,783	1,270	1,543	2,096	2,958	2,726	3,802	3,781	3,632	43
New York	51,841	71,116	81,386	58,743	69,685	84,999	81,338	86,407	88,834	83,134	76,720	4
North Carolina	19,507	23,356	25,091	21,793	24,918	27,067	28,839	29,347	31,420	30,202	30,161	16
North Dakota	1,192	2,047	2,772	2,193	2,532	3,393	4,310	4,402	5,513	4,027	5,313	36
Ohio	35,110	42,562	45,628	34,104	41,505	46,458	48,819	51,048	52,641	51,157	49,299	8
Oklahoma	4,322	4,579	5,077	4,415	5,354	6,228	6,579	6,920	6,308	5,251	5,048	37
Oregon	12,407	16,531	19,352	14,907	17,684	18,317	18,388	18,684	20,086	20,086	21,753	20
Pennsylvania	22,334	29,195	34,649	28,381	34,943	41,103	38,852	41,181	40,411	39,437	36,484	10
Rhode Island	1,268	1,649	1,974	1,496	1,949	2,289	2,366	2,164	2,388	2,133	2,278	46
South Carolina	13,960	16,575	19,853	16,488	20,336	24,733	25,115	26,341	29,773	30,989	31,322	14
South Dakota	948	1,510	1,654	1,011	1,259	1,462	1,557	1,582	1,578	1,420	1,223	49
Tennessee	19,174	21,865	23,238	20,484	25,948	30,016	31,143	32,474	33,251	32,588	31,433	13
Texas	129,346	168,229	192,222	162,995	206,992	251,104	264,665	277,716	285,559	248,606	231,107	1
Utah	6,067	7,815	10,306	10,337	13,808	18,968	19,260	16,111	12,224	13,308	12,078	28
Vermont	4,672	3,685	3,697	3,219	4,278	4,275	4,139	4,027	3,670	3,181	2,990	44
Virginia	12,238	16,864	18,942	15,052	17,169	18,125	18,277	17,896	19,391	17,801	16,313	24
Washington	33,078	52,089	54,498	51,851	53,345	64,800	75,654	81,630	90,558	86,379	79,559	3
West Virginia	3,161	3,987	5,643	4,826	6,443	9,039	11,407	8,732	7,597	5,833	5,045	38
Wisconsin	14,961	18,825	20,570	16,725	19,800	22,069	23,119	23,110	23,426	22,438	21,021	21
Wyoming	671	802	1,081	926	983	1,219	1,439	1,351	1,757	1,175	1,098	50

X Not applicable. ¹ Includes other areas, not shown separately, and exports with an unknown state or area of origin.

Source: U.S. Census Bureau, Foreign Trade Division, "USA Trade Online," <https://usatrade.census.gov/>, accessed June 2017. See also <http://www.census.gov/foreign-trade/data/index.html>.

Table 1322. U.S. Exports, Imports, and Trade Balance by Country: 2005 to 2016

[In millions of dollars (901,082 represents $901,082,000,000). Data reflect trade between foreign countries and the U.S., Puerto Rico, the U.S. Virgin Islands, and U.S. Foreign Trade Zones. Data are shown on a Census Basis. Country totals include exports of special category commodities, if any. For methodology, see Foreign Trade Statistics in Appendix III. Minus sign (-) denotes an excess of imports over exports]

Country	Exports, domestic and foreign					General imports					Merchandise trade balance				
	2005	2010	2014	2015	2016	2005	2010	2014	2015	2016	2005	2010	2014	2015	2016
Total [1]	901,082	1,278,495	1,621,874	1,503,101	1,451,011	1,673,455	1,913,857	2,356,356	2,248,183	2,187,805	-772,373	-635,362	-734,482	-745,082	-736,794
Afghanistan	262	2,151	813	479	913	67	85	74	24	34	195	2,066	738	455	879
Algeria	1,106	1,194	2,617	1,876	2,191	10,446	14,518	4,629	3,372	3,228	-9,340	-13,324	-2,012	-1,496	-1,037
Angola	929	1,293	2,039	1,166	1,251	8,484	11,940	5,720	2,806	2,856	-7,555	-10,646	-3,681	-1,640	-1,604
Antigua and Barbuda	190	158	217	678	260	4	5	8	7	17	186	153	209	671	244
Argentina	4,122	7,392	10,823	9,361	8,513	4,584	3,803	4,246	3,951	4,648	-462	3,589	6,577	5,410	3,865
Armenia	65	113	60	50	44	46	75	96	62	43	19	38	-36	-12	1
Aruba	559	540	1,300	1,168	801	2,920	19	60	55	16	-2,361	521	1,240	1,113	785
Australia	15,589	21,805	26,682	25,034	22,160	7,342	8,583	10,697	10,884	9,510	8,246	13,222	15,984	14,151	12,650
Austria	2,544	2,429	3,825	4,024	3,796	6,103	6,835	10,828	11,312	10,870	-3,558	-4,407	-7,003	-7,287	-7,075
Azerbaijan	132	253	950	478	434	45	1,989	1,012	507	142	87	-1,736	-62	-29	292
Bahamas, The	1,787	3,178	3,321	2,387	2,112	700	815	532	453	299	1,087	2,363	2,789	1,934	1,814
Bahrain	351	1,235	1,060	1,271	899	432	420	965	902	768	-81	815	95	368	131
Bangladesh	320	576	1,113	943	906	2,693	4,294	5,277	5,991	5,911	-2,373	-3,718	-4,164	-5,048	-5,005
Barbados	395	397	540	595	482	32	43	51	68	50	363	355	489	527	432
Belarus	35	133	93	59	195	345	175	132	158	134	-310	-41	-38	-99	61
Belgium	18,691	25,458	34,736	34,147	32,097	13,023	15,552	20,962	19,485	17,014	5,668	9,906	13,774	14,663	15,084
Belize	218	289	237	285	267	98	120	97	75	55	119	169	140	210	212
Benin	72	463	781	631	235	1	(Z)	5	5	7	72	462	775	626	228
Bermuda	490	637	647	601	628	87	22	37	109	24	403	614	610	492	604
Bolivia	219	508	1,009	932	657	293	680	1,935	1,006	975	-74	-172	-926	-75	-318
Botswana	67	48	53	39	42	178	170	318	212	434	-111	-121	-265	-173	-392
Brazil	15,372	35,418	42,432	31,641	30,107	24,436	23,958	30,021	27,441	26,054	-9,064	11,460	12,411	4,199	4,053
British Virgin Islands	125	146	388	260	333	34	19	11	16	31	91	127	377	243	302
Brunei	50	124	549	133	615	563	12	32	19	14	-513	112	517	114	601
Bulgaria	268	171	359	289	269	454	260	608	598	604	-186	-89	-249	-308	-335
Cambodia	70	154	328	391	361	1,767	2,301	2,848	3,025	2,814	-1,697	-2,147	-2,520	-2,634	-2,454
Cameroon	117	132	301	225	190	158	297	186	132	151	-41	-165	115	93	39
Canada	211,899	249,256	312,817	280,855	266,797	290,384	277,637	349,286	296,230	277,756	-78,486	-28,380	-36,469	-15,375	-10,958
Chad	54	90	66	57	33	1,498	2,044	2,329	1,303	899	-1,444	-1,954	-2,262	-1,247	-866
Chile	5,134	10,907	16,541	15,449	12,922	6,664	7,017	9,479	8,772	8,797	-1,531	3,889	7,062	6,677	4,125
China	41,192	91,911	123,657	115,932	115,602	243,470	364,953	468,475	483,189	462,618	-202,278	-273,042	-344,818	-367,257	-347,016
Colombia	5,462	12,068	20,067	16,303	13,067	8,849	15,659	18,316	14,075	13,794	-3,387	-3,592	1,751	2,228	-726
Congo, Rep. of	104	254	322	249	131	1,623	3,316	424	304	132	-1,519	-3,062	-103	-55	-1
Congo, Dem. Rep. of	65	93	182	136	83	264	528	154	154	174	-199	-434	27	-18	-91
Costa Rica	3,599	5,178	6,947	6,045	5,870	3,415	8,697	9,516	4,489	4,331	183	-3,519	-2,570	1,556	1,538
Cote d'Ivoire	124	163	239	266	291	1,198	1,177	1,193	1,028	1,164	-1,074	-1,014	-953	-761	-873
Croatia	159	312	340	332	286	364	336	464	577	510	-206	-24	-124	-245	-224
Cuba [2]	369	363	299	180	245	(X)	(X)	(Z)	(Z)	(Z)	369	363	299	180	245
Curacao [2]	(X)	(X)	612	521	877	(X)	(X)	369	335	261	(X)	(X)	242	186	616
Cyprus	84	134	152	102	182	31	11	64	32	53	54	123	87	70	129
Czech Republic	1,054	1,411	2,303	1,977	1,963	2,193	2,450	4,405	4,489	4,403	-1,139	-1,039	-2,103	-2,512	-2,440
Denmark	1,918	2,132	2,361	2,203	2,238	5,144	6,012	7,534	7,760	7,941	-3,226	-3,879	-5,174	-5,557	-5,703
Djibouti	48	123	111	145	133	1	3	3	35	28	46	120	99	109	105
Dominican Republic	4,719	6,579	7,928	7,115	7,756	4,604	3,672	4,528	4,665	4,680	115	2,908	3,400	2,449	3,076
Ecuador	1,964	5,409	8,254	5,819	4,153	5,759	7,451	10,870	7,467	6,059	-3,795	-2,042	-2,616	-1,648	-1,906
Egypt	3,159	6,833	6,483	4,759	3,483	2,091	2,238	1,411	1,406	1,493	1,068	4,594	5,072	3,353	1,990
El Salvador	1,854	2,434	3,306	3,249	2,933	1,989	2,206	2,398	2,532	2,496	-134	228	908	717	437
Equatorial Guinea	281	272	575	162	278	1,561	2,214	255	163	85	-1,280	-1,942	320	-1	193
Ethiopia	456	773	1,669	1,555	826	62	128	207	310	203	394	645	1,462	1,245	590
Fiji	28	44	80	57	55	169	179	184	203	203	-141	-135	-104	-146	-148
Finland	2,254	2,180	2,150	1,559	1,573	4,342	3,884	5,035	4,507	4,571	-2,088	-1,704	-2,885	-2,948	-2,998
France	22,259	26,970	31,289	30,055	31,132	33,842	38,355	47,105	47,752	46,710	-11,583	-11,386	-15,816	-17,697	-15,578
French Polynesia	112	122	130	120	100	60	53	40	43	34	52	69	89	77	67

See footnote at end of table.

Table 1322. U.S. Exports, Imports, and Trade Balance by Country: 2005 to 2016—Continued.

See headnote on page 832.

Country	Exports, domestic and foreign					General imports					Merchandise trade balance				
	2005	2010	2014	2015	2016	2005	2010	2014	2015	2016	2005	2010	2014	2015	2016
Gabon	99	243	417	204	85	2,816	2,212	798	337	107	-2,716	-1,969	-381	-133	-22
Georgia	214	301	628	341	324	194	198	409	181	95	20	103	218	159	230
Germany	34,184	48,155	49,419	49,945	49,363	84,751	82,450	124,182	124,819	114,099	-50,567	-34,295	-74,763	-74,873	-64,736
Ghana	337	989	1,186	950	832	158	273	272	309	321	179	716	914	641	511
Gibraltar	163	1,494	2,531	1,979	1,684	5	1	(Z)	2	(Z)	159	1,493	2,531	1,978	1,683
Greece	1,192	1,106	773	726	747	884	798	1,050	1,357	1,228	309	309	-277	-631	-481
Grenada	82	71	84	90	87	6	8	10	9	12	77	64	74	81	74
Guatemala	2,835	4,477	6,046	5,821	5,841	3,137	3,523	4,218	4,121	3,938	-302	954	1,828	1,700	1,903
Guyana	177	291	370	368	445	120	299	501	431	432	57	-8	-131	-63	12
Haiti	710	1,209	1,274	1,141	1,091	447	551	908	950	899	262	658	365	190	192
Honduras	3,254	4,606	5,961	5,216	4,830	3,749	3,933	4,646	4,760	4,618	-495	673	1,316	456	212
Hong Kong	16,351	26,570	40,913	37,183	34,895	8,892	4,296	5,897	6,793	7,407	7,459	22,274	35,016	30,390	27,487
Hungary	1,023	1,290	1,844	1,715	1,844	2,561	2,491	5,331	5,720	5,340	-1,538	-1,201	-3,488	-4,005	-3,495
Iceland	512	325	375	415	448	269	201	300	317	371	243	124	75	99	77
India	7,919	19,249	21,499	21,453	21,652	18,804	29,533	45,358	44,790	46,032	-10,886	-10,284	-23,859	-23,337	-24,380
Indonesia	3,054	6,948	8,281	7,118	6,024	12,014	16,478	19,390	19,600	19,194	-8,960	-9,530	-11,109	-12,482	-13,171
Iran	96	211	187	282	172	174	95	(Z)	11	88	-79	117	187	271	84
Iraq	1,374	1,643	2,106	1,971	1,266	9,054	12,143	13,827	4,353	5,983	-7,680	-10,500	-11,721	-2,383	-4,717
Ireland	8,447	7,276	7,808	8,931	9,565	28,733	33,848	33,988	39,336	45,528	-20,286	-26,572	-26,180	-30,405	-35,962
Israel	9,737	11,295	15,073	13,539	13,197	16,830	20,985	23,007	24,478	22,203	-7,093	-9,690	-7,934	-10,939	-9,007
Italy	11,524	14,220	16,969	16,212	16,707	31,009	28,514	42,378	44,164	45,273	-19,485	-14,294	-25,409	-27,951	-28,565
Jamaica	1,701	1,661	2,180	1,716	1,650	376	328	286	306	303	1,325	1,334	1,895	1,410	1,347
Japan	54,681	60,472	66,892	62,393	63,236	138,004	120,552	134,505	131,383	132,046	-83,323	-60,080	-67,613	-68,990	-68,810
Jordan	644	1,172	2,050	1,360	1,459	1,267	974	1,401	1,492	1,555	-623	198	649	-132	-96
Kazakhstan	538	730	1,008	510	1,111	1,101	1,872	1,411	816	750	-563	-1,142	-403	-306	361
Kenya	573	375	1,641	943	397	348	311	591	573	552	225	64	1,049	370	-156
Korea, South	27,572	38,821	44,650	43,484	42,309	43,781	48,875	69,677	71,758	69,881	-16,210	-10,055	-25,027	-28,273	-27,572
Kuwait	1,975	2,775	3,649	2,741	3,295	4,335	5,382	11,437	4,685	3,301	-2,360	-2,607	-7,788	-1,944	-6
Kyrgyzstan	31	79	72	32	20	5	10	2	16	3	27	69	70	16	17
Laos	10	13	29	25	31	4	59	33	45	55	6	-46	-4	-21	-24
Latvia	178	345	428	267	273	362	193	276	303	338	-185	152	152	-36	-65
Lebanon	466	2,009	1,268	1,286	1,171	86	84	72	93	108	379	1,925	1,196	1,193	1,063
Liberia	69	191	185	136	158	91	180	83	45	64	-22	11	101	91	94
Libya	84	666	532	231	190	1,590	2,117	225	155	224	-1,506	-1,451	307	76	-33
Liechtenstein	20	29	31	35	25	296	213	302	310	288	-276	-183	-270	-275	-264
Lithuania	390	628	681	528	464	634	637	1,096	1,059	1,182	-244	-9	-414	-531	-718
Luxembourg	711	1,440	1,516	1,394	1,453	389	451	757	639	499	323	989	759	755	954
Macau	102	33	433	542	632	1,249	141	75	122	119	-1,147	-108	359	420	513
Macedonia	32	34	34	31	46	48	37	167	203	230	-17	-4	-133	-173	-184
Madagascar	28	116	47	55	42	324	108	216	320	445	-295	8	-169	-265	-403
Malawi	28	37	51	37	47	116	72	67	61	74	-87	-35	-16	-24	-28
Malaysia	10,461	14,079	13,069	12,279	11,832	33,685	25,901	30,564	33,972	36,630	-23,224	-11,821	-17,495	-21,693	-24,798
Malta	194	457	918	491	292	283	262	174	241	1,294	-89	196	743	249	-1,001
Marshall Islands	75	91	95	54	283	17	12	14	29	39	58	79	80	25	244
Martinique	35	297	331	133	145	22	23	82	37	17	13	274	249	95	128
Mauritania	86	84	149	126	116	1	53	101	1	50	85	31	47	125	66
Mexico	120,248	163,665	241,007	236,204	229,702	170,109	229,986	295,730	296,401	294,056	-49,861	-66,321	-54,723	-60,197	-64,354
Mongolia	22	116	167	69	55	144	12	15	17	11	-122	104	153	52	44
Morocco	481	1,948	2,102	1,625	1,933	446	686	995	1,012	1,021	35	1,262	1,107	613	911
Mozambique	63	224	375	264	149	12	65	100	96	106	51	159	275	168	43
Namibia	112	110	343	128	213	129	195	256	85	92	-17	-85	87	42	121
Nepal	25	28	36	36	41	112	60	87	87	89	-87	-32	-51	-51	-48
Netherlands	26,468	34,740	43,141	40,211	39,690	14,862	19,055	20,899	16,841	16,114	11,606	15,685	22,242	23,370	23,576
New Zealand	2,592	2,820	4,284	3,631	3,574	3,155	2,764	3,985	4,293	4,047	-563	57	273	-662	-473
Nicaragua	625	981	1,009	1,267	1,479	1,181	2,008	3,105	3,189	3,293	-555	-1,026	-2,097	-1,921	-1,814
Niger	79	49	59	72	66	66	27	5	4	6	13	22	54	67	60
Nigeria	1,620	4,061	5,966	3,435	1,895	24,239	30,516	3,840	1,916	4,176	-22,620	-26,455	2,126	1,519	-2,281

See footnotes at end of table.

Table 1322. U.S. Exports, Imports, and Trade Balance by Country: 2005 to 2016-Continued.

See headnote on page 832.

Country	Exports, domestic and foreign					General imports					Merchandise trade balance				
	2005	2010	2014	2015	2016	2005	2010	2014	2015	2016	2005	2010	2014	2015	2016
Norway	1,942	3,100	4,421	3,570	3,924	6,776	6,950	5,366	4,760	4,408	-4,834	-3,850	-945	-1,190	-484
Oman	571	1,105	2,014	2,355	1,804	555	773	978	907	1,125	16	332	1,036	1,448	679
Pakistan	1,252	1,901	1,513	1,838	2,108	3,253	3,509	3,676	3,701	3,444	-2,002	-1,608	-2,163	-1,863	-1,336
Panama	2,162	6,066	10,140	7,674	6,128	327	381	432	408	410	1,835	5,685	9,708	7,266	5,718
Papua New Guinea	55	186	143	208	126	58	97	100	91	91	-3	89	43	117	35
Paraguay	896	1,810	2,116	1,492	1,970	52	62	196	163	149	844	1,748	1,919	1,329	1,821
Peru	2,309	6,750	10,055	8,724	7,955	5,119	5,243	6,079	5,053	6,252	-2,810	1,506	3,976	3,671	1,703
Philippines	6,895	7,377	8,453	7,902	8,200	9,250	7,982	10,190	10,232	10,044	-2,355	-605	-1,736	-2,331	-1,844
Poland	1,268	2,983	3,661	3,716	3,658	1,949	2,964	5,214	5,620	5,961	-681	19	-1,554	-1,905	-2,303
Portugal	1,132	1,058	1,121	943	948	2,329	2,142	3,226	3,270	3,206	-1,197	-1,084	-2,106	-2,328	-2,258
Qatar	987	3,160	5,173	4,222	4,926	448	466	1,742	1,354	1,160	539	2,693	3,430	2,868	3,765
Romania	609	730	977	754	695	1,208	1,008	2,134	2,149	1,963	-599	-278	-1,156	-1,395	-1,269
Russia	3,962	5,994	10,752	7,087	5,792	15,307	25,691	23,660	16,366	14,536	-11,344	-19,697	-12,907	-9,279	-8,744
Rwanda	11	31	21	14	75	6	21	41	46	26	4	9	-19	-31	49
Saudi Arabia	6,805	11,506	18,717	19,790	17,972	27,193	31,413	47,041	22,081	16,918	-20,387	-19,907	-28,324	-2,290	1,055
Senegal	141	219	171	199	184	4	5	26	72	55	138	214	145	127	130
Serbia	(Z)	104	135	126	145	(Z)	164	280	273	310	(Z)	-60	-145	-146	-164
Sierra Leone	38	61	88	77	63	9	29	29	40	30	29	32	59	38	33
Singapore	20,466	29,009	30,068	28,474	26,725	15,110	17,428	16,502	18,267	17,833	5,356	11,581	13,566	10,207	8,891
Sint Maarten [2]	(X)	(X)	778	741	711	(X)	(X)	50	52	92	(X)	(X)	728	689	619
Slovakia	150	256	445	380	293	961	1,073	2,118	2,300	2,526	-811	-817	-1,672	-1,920	-2,233
Slovenia	234	328	301	346	331	413	465	707	678	752	-179	-137	-405	-332	-421
South Africa	3,907	5,632	6,375	5,457	4,605	5,886	8,221	8,326	7,315	6,765	-1,979	-2,589	-1,950	-1,858	-2,160
Spain	6,839	10,355	10,200	10,310	10,398	8,724	8,554	14,459	14,129	13,424	-1,885	1,802	-4,259	-3,819	-3,027
Sri Lanka	198	179	351	362	368	2,083	1,748	2,678	2,890	2,784	-1,885	-1,569	-2,328	-2,528	-2,416
Suriname	246	362	519	444	302	165	191	453	146	67	80	171	66	297	236
Sweden	3,715	4,740	4,337	3,939	3,814	13,821	10,497	10,360	9,905	9,701	-10,106	-5,757	-6,024	-5,966	-5,887
Switzerland	10,718	20,704	22,204	22,154	22,777	13,000	19,137	31,322	31,401	36,349	-2,282	1,567	-9,118	-9,247	-13,572
Syria	155	503	7	3	3	324	429	12	7	7	-169	74	-6	-3	-3
Taiwan	21,614	26,050	26,675	25,823	26,037	34,826	35,847	40,840	40,905	39,248	-13,211	-9,797	-14,164	-15,082	-13,211
Tajikistan	29	57	25	19	21	241	1	4	31	1	-212	56	21	-12	21
Tanzania	96	163	302	173	158	34	43	86	105	148	63	121	216	68	9
Thailand	7,257	8,976	11,815	11,229	10,445	19,890	22,694	27,229	28,619	29,477	-12,633	-13,717	-15,414	-17,390	-19,032
Togo	28	158	1,025	312	229	6	4	9	14	11	21	149	1,015	298	219
Trinidad and Tobago	1,417	1,925	2,411	2,512	2,341	7,891	6,613	5,996	4,314	2,956	-6,474	-4,688	-3,584	-1,803	-615
Tunisia	261	573	831	602	527	264	405	524	546	392	-3	167	307	56	135
Turkey	4,239	10,538	11,650	9,520	9,388	5,182	4,207	7,413	7,878	8,046	-943	6,331	4,237	1,642	1,342
Turkmenistan	215	40	456	81	106	135	48	20	56	18	80	-8	435	25	88
Uganda	63	94	78	88	69	26	58	46	64	51	37	36	32	24	18
Ukraine	533	1,349	1,239	862	1,077	1,098	1,078	935	851	578	-565	271	304	11	499
United Arab Emirates	8,120	11,662	22,115	23,006	22,401	1,468	1,145	2,820	2,469	3,371	6,651	10,517	19,296	20,537	19,031
United Kingdom	38,568	48,410	53,913	56,095	55,289	51,033	49,805	54,689	57,993	54,272	-12,465	-1,395	-776	-1,898	1,017
Uruguay	357	975	1,660	1,295	1,115	732	235	457	605	536	-376	740	1,150	690	579
Uzbekistan	74	101	213	138	318	96	68	14	10	31	-22	33	199	128	287
Venezuela	6,421	10,645	11,178	8,344	5,233	33,978	32,707	30,220	15,564	10,893	-27,557	-22,063	-19,042	-7,220	-5,660
Vietnam	1,193	3,706	5,732	7,101	10,100	6,631	14,868	30,618	38,016	42,099	-5,438	-11,162	-24,885	-30,916	-31,998
Yemen	219	398	369	158	171	279	181	41	48	2	-60	216	328	110	169
Zambia	29	56	114	84	82	32	29	56	47	47	-3	27	58	37	35
Zimbabwe	46	68	49	38	30	94	59	65	67	23	-49	9	-16	-29	7

X Not applicable. Z Entry would amount to less than half the unit of measurement shown. [1] Includes additional countries, not shown separately. [2] The Netherlands Antilles dissolved on October 10, 2010. Curacao and Sint Maarten became autonomous territories of the Kingdom of the Netherlands.

Source: U.S. Census Bureau, "USA Trade Online," <https://usatrade.census.gov/>, accessed September 2017. See also U.S. International Trade in Goods and Services, Series FT-900, <http://www.census.gov/foreign-trade/Press-Release/ft900_index.html>.

Table 1323. U.S. Exports and General Imports by Selected Commodity Groups: 2014 to 2016

[In millions of dollars (1,621,874 represents $1,621,874,000,000). All data are presented on a Census basis. For methodology, see Foreign Trade Statistics in Appendix III]

Selected commodity	Exports 2014	Exports 2015	Exports 2016	General imports 2014	General imports 2015	General imports 2016
Total [1]	1,621,874	1,503,101	1,451,011	2,356,356	2,248,183	2,187,805
Manufactured goods [2]	1,192,266	1,110,725	1,049,243	1,930,685	1,946,303	1,912,316
Agricultural commodities [2]	149,982	133,057	134,723	111,959	113,808	114,443
Food and live animals [3]	108,567	97,924	96,059	97,148	98,649	99,936
Live animals other than fish	926	717	722	3,542	3,286	2,788
Meat and preparations	19,430	16,007	16,259	8,920	9,989	8,558
Cereals and preparations	26,868	22,880	22,896	9,243	8,988	9,016
Vegetables and fruits	22,242	22,066	21,684	28,233	30,164	32,632
Coffee, tea, cocoa, and spices	3,149	3,040	3,067	13,034	13,403	13,366
Feeding stuff for animals	13,180	12,599	11,295	3,111	2,944	2,779
Crude materials except fuels [3]	85,464	71,761	71,292	36,523	31,453	29,607
Hides, skins, and furskins, raw	2,926	2,436	1,921	307	242	165
Oil seeds and oleaginous fruits	26,136	20,733	24,687	2,198	1,250	1,028
Crude rubber	3,176	2,605	2,451	3,772	2,988	2,693
Cork and wood	7,272	6,580	6,704	7,189	6,947	8,019
Pulp and waste paper	8,687	8,469	8,290	3,588	3,293	3,010
Textile fibers including waste	6,916	5,999	5,878	1,419	1,446	1,280
Crude fertilizers	2,813	2,589	2,290	2,934	2,845	2,232
Metalliferous ores and metal scrap	24,487	19,317	16,145	8,850	6,830	5,864
Mineral fuels and lubricants [3]	154,498	103,458	92,623	347,474	190,501	153,822
Coal, coke, and briquettes	8,718	5,889	4,547	1,199	1,139	996
Petroleum products and preparations	127,818	85,733	74,636	326,709	177,455	142,933
Gas, natural and manufactured	17,399	11,595	13,246	16,897	9,446	7,701
Animal and vegetable oils [3]	2,798	2,596	2,618	5,778	5,664	6,049
Animal oil and fat	725	536	636	244	239	243
Fixed vegetable fats and oil, crude	1,687	1,729	1,715	5,382	5,249	5,621
Chemicals and related products [3]	201,513	194,332	185,909	207,797	216,183	217,283
Organic chemicals	39,544	34,387	31,240	52,205	49,146	47,157
Inorganic chemicals	11,436	10,412	10,116	13,125	12,025	10,933
Dyeing, tanning, and coloring materials	7,706	7,292	7,138	3,972	3,828	3,761
Medicinal and pharmaceutical products	44,607	48,401	46,667	76,173	89,280	95,485
Fertilizers	3,724	3,566	2,958	8,119	7,873	5,333
Plastics in primary forms	35,208	32,408	30,849	15,751	14,549	14,244
Plastics in nonprimary forms	12,805	12,914	12,599	9,630	9,638	9,472
Manufactured goods by material	117,765	109,578	101,910	254,658	244,112	232,281
Leather and leather manufactures	1,438	1,218	1,116	1,399	1,428	1,413
Rubber manufactures	10,181	9,280	8,378	21,829	21,239	20,090
Cork and wood manufactures	2,215	2,107	2,068	9,571	10,306	10,837
Paper and paperboard	16,046	15,414	14,604	16,761	16,487	16,061
Textile yarn, fabric	13,261	12,703	11,812	26,996	28,157	27,497
Nonmetallic mineral manufactures	13,043	13,703	13,427	45,184	45,040	45,808
Iron and steel	18,425	14,856	12,619	46,875	36,929	27,341
Nonferrous metals	15,547	14,314	13,466	38,559	34,511	33,455
Manufactures of metals	27,609	25,984	24,419	47,484	50,015	49,780
Machinery and transport equipment	534,388	517,920	493,575	941,886	971,371	954,022
Power generating machinery	40,159	37,197	33,828	66,484	67,331	64,521
Specialized industrial machinery	48,872	43,684	38,073	47,377	44,933	42,488
Metalworking machinery	5,813	5,439	4,736	9,949	9,783	9,309
General industrial machinery	70,262	66,202	58,635	92,811	93,250	89,930
Office machinery	21,867	20,629	19,356	118,224	116,858	110,533
Telecommunications equipment	23,715	22,924	20,733	152,783	159,474	157,878
Electrical machinery	80,902	80,114	78,182	159,571	164,522	168,324
Road vehicles	121,561	114,704	111,836	257,479	275,754	277,086
Transport equipment	121,238	127,026	128,195	37,209	39,466	33,952
Miscellaneous manufactured articles [3]	122,945	120,270	117,812	349,052	370,162	366,535
Prefabricated buildings	3,245	2,900	2,505	11,464	12,602	13,163
Furniture	6,477	6,464	6,269	41,480	45,565	47,140
Travel goods	568	592	612	10,995	11,509	10,733
Apparel and clothing accessories	3,424	3,348	3,080	90,154	93,617	88,212
Footwear	827	848	788	26,018	27,650	25,634
Scientific and controlling equipment	50,008	48,124	46,772	50,680	52,448	53,629
Photographic equipment	6,465	6,396	6,114	14,355	14,466	14,185
Miscellaneous commodities [4]	64,452	61,358	58,199	94,409	97,487	104,403
Re-exports	223,024	217,163	224,528	(X)	(X)	(X)

X Not applicable. [1] Total exports including re-exports (exports of foreign merchandise). [2] Manufactured goods is based on the North American Industry Classification System (NAICS) and Agricultural commodities is based on the Harmonized System commodities specified by the U.S. Department of Agriculture definition. All other commodity detail is based on Standard International Trade Classification (SITC). [3] Includes other commodities, not shown separately. [4] Includes special transactions, coin, nonmonetary gold, and the low value estimate.

Source: U.S. Census Bureau, *U.S. International Trade in Goods and Services, Annual Revision for 2016*, Series FT-900, June 2017. See also <http://www.census.gov/foreign-trade/Press-Release/ft900_index.html>.

Table 1324. U.S. Total and Aerospace Foreign Trade: 1990 to 2014

[In millions of dollars (-101,718 represents -$101,718,000,000), except percent. Data are reported as exports of domestic merchandise, including Department of Defense shipments and undocumented exports to Canada, f.a.s. (free alongside ship) basis, and imports for consumption, customs value basis. Minus sign (-) indicates deficit]

Year	U.S. merchandise trade			Aerospace trade					
						Exports			
	Trade balance [1]	Imports	Exports	Trade balance [1]	Imports	Total	Percent of U.S. exports	Civil	Military
1990.......	-101,718	495,311	393,592	27,282	11,801	39,083	9.9	31,517	7,566
1995.......	-158,801	743,543	584,742	21,562	11,509	33,071	5.7	25,079	7,991
2000.......	-436,104	1,218,022	781,918	26,735	27,944	54,679	7.0	45,566	9,113
2001.......	-411,899	1,140,999	729,100	26,035	32,473	58,508	8.0	49,371	9,137
2002.......	-468,263	1,161,366	693,103	29,533	27,242	56,775	8.2	47,348	9,427
2003.......	-532,350	1,257,121	724,771	27,111	25,393	52,504	7.2	44,366	8,138
2004.......	-654,830	1,469,704	814,875	31,002	25,815	56,817	7.0	47,772	9,045
2005.......	-772,373	1,673,455	901,082	39,783	27,649	67,433	7.5	57,587	9,845
2006.......	-827,971	1,853,938	1,025,967	54,809	30,453	85,262	8.3	71,857	13,404
2007.......	-808,763	1,956,962	1,148,199	60,614	36,610	97,224	8.5	83,977	13,247
2008.......	-816,199	2,103,641	1,287,442	57,389	37,694	95,082	7.4	82,264	12,819
2009.......	-503,582	1,559,625	1,056,043	56,034	25,132	81,166	7.7	70,500	10,666
2010.......	-635,362	1,913,857	1,278,495	43,188	34,569	77,757	6.1	66,936	10,821
2011.......	-725,447	2,207,954	1,482,508	46,750	38,879	85,630	5.8	75,065	10,565
2012.......	-730,446	2,276,267	1,545,821	55,754	43,940	99,694	6.4	86,610	13,083
2013.......	-689,931	2,268,371	1,578,439	61,027	49,806	110,833	7.0	97,331	13,502
2014.......	-727,153	2,347,685	1,620,532	61,185	57,708	118,893	7.3	104,145	14,748

[1] Exports minus imports.

Source: © 2014 Aerospace Industries Association of America, Inc., *2014 Year-End Review and Forecast*, <http://www.aia-aerospace.org/research-center/statistics/>; and U.S. Census Bureau, *U.S. International Trade in Goods and Services, Annual Revision for 2014*, Series FT-900, June 2015, and earlier reports, <http://www.census.gov/foreign-trade/Press-Release/ft900_index.html>.

Table 1325. U.S. Exporting and Importing Companies by Employment-Size Class: 2010 and 2015

[Value in millions of dollars (1,140,406 represents $1,140,406,000,000). Data include all companies that can be linked to import and/or export transactions. Trade values are taken from the transactions used to compile the official U.S. Trade statistics; company information is taken from the Business Register. For information on data limitations, see Technical Documentation in source]

Employment-size class and company type	Number		Known value [1] (mil. dol.)		Percent of—			
					Number		Known value	
	2010	2015	2010	2015	2010	2015	2010	2015
EXPORTERS								
All companies, total..........	**293,988**	**294,834**	**1,140,406**	**1,335,114**	**100.0**	**100.0**	**100.0**	**100.0**
By employment-size:								
1 to 19 employees..............	112,572	107,356	82,739	80,468	38.3	36.4	7.3	6.0
20 to 49 employees.............	30,984	30,872	45,037	41,503	10.5	10.5	3.9	3.1
50 to 99 employees.............	15,179	15,316	43,710	43,843	5.2	5.2	3.8	3.3
100 to 249 employees..........	11,581	12,104	59,349	84,384	3.9	4.1	5.2	6.3
250 to 499 employees..........	4,336	4,763	46,254	67,899	1.5	1.6	4.1	5.1
500 or more employees.........	6,490	6,999	755,466	895,248	2.2	2.4	66.2	67.1
Unknown [2]......................	112,846	117,424	107,851	121,770	38.4	39.8	9.5	9.1
IMPORTERS								
All companies, total..........	**181,648**	**196,925**	**1,679,522**	**1,969,469**	**100.0**	**100.0**	**100.0**	**100.0**
By employment-size:								
1 to 19 employees..............	77,796	82,516	112,664	143,998	42.8	41.9	6.7	7.3
20 to 49 employees.............	18,487	20,284	71,093	79,839	10.2	10.3	4.2	4.1
50 to 99 employees.............	9,472	10,467	58,075	70,492	5.2	5.3	3.5	3.6
100 to 249 employees..........	7,820	8,818	96,080	108,003	4.3	4.5	5.7	5.5
250 to 499 employees..........	3,174	3,664	69,812	97,428	1.7	1.9	4.2	4.9
500 or more employees.........	5,013	5,584	1,148,183	1,338,468	2.8	2.8	68.4	68.0
Unknown [2]......................	59,886	65,592	123,616	131,242	33.0	33.3	7.4	6.7

[1] Known value is defined as the portion of U.S. total exports and general imports that could be matched to specific companies. Export values are on f.a.s. or "free alongside ship basis." [2] Includes missing employment data, nonemployers, and companies that reported annual payroll but did not report any employees on their payroll.

Source: U.S. Census Bureau, *Profile of U.S. Importing and Exporting Companies 2014-2015*, April 2017, and earlier reports. See also <http://www.census.gov/foreign-trade/statistics/press-release/>.

Table 1326. Domestic Exports and Imports for Consumption of Merchandise by Selected NAICS Product Category: 2005 to 2016

[In millions of dollars (799,957 represents $799,957,000,000). Includes nonmonetary gold. For methodology, see Foreign Trade Statistics in Appendix III. NAICS = North American Industry Classification System; see text, Section 15. N.e.c. = Not elsewhere classified]

Product category	2005	2010	2013	2014	2015	2016
Domestic exports, total....................	**799,957**	**1,122,567**	**1,371,134**	**1,398,850**	**1,285,939**	**1,226,482**
Agricultural, forestry, and fishery products.................	37,109	65,753	76,378	80,265	69,780	74,040
Agricultural products, total....................	30,683	58,023	66,121	69,885	60,215	64,852
Livestock and livestock products..........................	1,118	1,539	2,367	2,209	2,031	1,804
Forestry products, n.e.c................................	1,686	2,181	2,767	2,846	2,354	2,336
Fish, fresh or chilled, and other marine products.........	3,622	4,011	5,122	5,324	5,180	5,048
Mining, total....................	12,629	26,394	37,820	47,860	34,192	34,278
Oil and gas....................	4,547	9,248	17,497	28,981	19,806	22,586
Minerals and ores....................	8,082	17,146	20,322	18,879	14,386	11,692
Manufacturing, total....................	708,205	952,360	1,176,942	1,192,266	1,110,725	1,049,243
Food and kindred products....................	28,937	50,902	67,561	69,385	61,982	60,165
Beverages and tobacco products....................	3,423	5,339	8,143	8,184	8,476	7,438
Textiles and fabrics....................	8,483	7,833	9,055	9,386	8,968	8,243
Textile mill products....................	2,344	2,583	2,829	2,863	2,793	2,676
Apparel and accessories....................	4,075	3,070	3,179	3,190	3,104	2,880
Leather and allied products....................	2,300	2,421	3,229	3,363	3,041	2,887
Wood products....................	4,463	5,075	6,497	7,229	6,812	6,813
Paper products....................	16,640	22,962	23,864	23,963	23,321	22,208
Printed, publishing, & similar products....................	5,526	6,021	5,847	5,472	5,088	4,846
Petroleum and coal products....................	17,979	61,010	118,429	116,804	78,010	65,799
Chemicals....................	114,821	171,365	189,476	190,037	182,417	173,532
Plastics and rubber products [1]....................	18,784	24,262	29,806	30,962	29,971	28,852
Nonmetallic mineral products [1]....................	6,663	9,226	10,451	11,060	10,700	10,527
Primary metal products....................	27,455	49,725	69,515	58,722	51,697	46,038
Fabricated metal products....................	23,370	32,690	41,311	43,691	41,603	39,075
Machinery, except electrical....................	97,001	126,023	135,434	136,775	123,737	108,609
Computers and electronic products [1]....................	122,744	121,121	122,431	123,126	119,889	115,441
Electrical equipment, appliances, and components [1]....	26,457	31,035	45,277	47,774	46,564	42,476
Transportation equipment [1]....................	144,985	176,337	235,681	250,048	252,316	252,240
Furniture and fixtures....................	2,844	3,979	4,990	5,168	4,959	4,615
Miscellaneous manufactured commodities....................	28,909	39,381	43,937	45,064	45,277	43,882
Newspapers, books, & other published matter, n.e.c.....	960	851	–	–	–	–
Special classification provisions....................	41,055	77,210	79,995	78,460	71,243	68,921
Waste and scrap....................	10,389	29,420	23,641	20,961	17,548	16,729
Used or second-hand merchandise....................	2,570	4,711	14,076	14,028	12,435	12,149
Goods returned or reimported....................	65	30	26	35	32	25
Special classification provision, n.e.c....................	28,030	43,049	42,251	43,436	41,228	40,020
Imports for consumption, total....................	**1,664,625**	**1,900,587**	**2,241,103**	**2,324,940**	**2,226,615**	**2,173,617**
Agricultural, forestry, and fishery products.................	30,761	42,686	53,923	58,474	56,315	58,001
Agricultural products, total....................	15,818	24,017	31,731	33,663	33,435	35,142
Livestock and livestock products....................	3,277	4,116	5,219	6,392	6,124	5,818
Forestry products, n.e.c....................	2,250	3,356	3,390	2,759	2,380	2,241
Fish, fresh or chilled, and other marine products.........	9,416	11,198	13,582	15,661	14,376	14,800
Mining, total....................	192,115	235,401	230,543	206,873	115,949	92,836
Oil and gas....................	185,621	228,066	222,413	198,022	109,006	87,618
Minerals and ores....................	6,494	7,335	8,130	8,851	6,943	5,218
Manufacturing, total....................	1,372,004	1,550,204	1,867,084	1,960,054	1,948,349	1,918,244
Food and kindred products....................	29,779	41,039	52,860	57,158	58,434	57,924
Beverages and tobacco products....................	12,849	15,515	19,088	20,088	21,201	22,364
Textiles and fabrics....................	7,450	6,525	8,000	8,412	8,569	8,186
Textile mill products....................	13,508	15,825	18,733	19,605	20,753	20,596
Apparel and accessories....................	74,478	75,411	83,818	86,282	89,283	84,299
Leather and allied products....................	26,559	30,859	36,735	38,503	40,297	37,942
Wood products....................	23,654	11,364	15,320	16,631	17,100	18,782
Paper products....................	22,094	21,029	19,985	20,924	20,305	19,548
Printed, publishing, & similar products....................	5,599	5,324	5,234	5,311	5,531	5,472
Petroleum and coal products....................	81,359	102,169	124,370	113,112	67,950	55,213
Chemicals....................	131,936	187,576	206,944	214,403	217,057	215,144
Plastics and rubber products....................	28,072	34,364	46,741	49,147	49,709	49,220
Nonmetallic mineral products....................	18,445	16,075	18,929	20,971	21,796	21,674
Primary metal products....................	64,666	79,617	92,607	101,566	85,078	79,775
Fabricated metal products....................	41,026	46,712	61,321	65,472	67,395	65,468
Machinery, except electrical....................	109,619	104,832	145,595	159,640	156,738	150,357
Computers and electronic products....................	269,921	324,379	347,749	365,311	372,194	372,780
Electrical equipment, appliances, and components......	55,179	68,465	92,282	98,163	101,929	102,278
Transportation equipment....................	251,386	239,870	332,576	354,722	375,280	375,420
Furniture and fixtures....................	25,096	25,702	30,752	33,301	36,867	38,392
Miscellaneous manufactured commodities....................	79,329	97,554	107,448	111,331	114,882	117,410
Newspapers, books, & other published matter, n.e.c.....	128	35	–	–	–	–
Special classification provisions....................	69,617	72,261	89,553	99,538	106,002	104,536
Waste and scrap....................	3,207	5,261	6,469	6,765	5,089	4,672
Used or second-hand merchandise....................	6,026	6,403	9,837	10,246	13,149	11,459
Goods returned or reimported....................	37,024	40,992	56,532	61,711	66,829	68,167
Special classification provision, n.e.c....................	23,359	19,605	16,716	20,816	20,935	20,239

– Represents zero or rounds to less than half the unit of measurement shown. [1] Beginning 2009, export statistics for certain commodity classifications related to the aircraft industry are subject to suppression and have been aggregated in a manner that prevents the disclosure of confidential information.

Source: U.S. Census Bureau, Foreign Trade Division, USA Trade Online, <https://usatrade.census.gov/>, accessed August 2017. See also U.S. International Trade in Goods and Services, Series FT-900, <http://www.census.gov/foreign-trade/data/index.html>.

Table 1327. Export and Import Unit Value Indexes—Selected Countries: 2011 to 2015

[Indexes in U.S. dollars, 2000=100. A unit value is an implicit price derived from value and quantity data]

Country	Export unit value					Import unit value				
	2011	2012	2013	2014	2015	2011	2012	2013	2014	2015
United States........	**189.6**	**197.7**	**202.0**	**207.3**	**192.5**	**179.9**	**185.5**	**184.9**	**191.6**	**183.3**
Australia..............	425.4	401.9	396.1	377.7	295.0	340.7	364.8	338.5	331.2	291.4
Belgium..............	253.1	237.3	249.5	251.4	211.9	263.7	248.0	255.1	256.7	211.9
Canada..............	163.2	164.7	165.7	171.6	147.7	189.4	194.6	194.4	196.1	178.3
France..............	182.5	174.0	177.8	177.6	154.8	213.0	199.5	201.6	200.1	169.4
Germany..............	267.8	254.5	262.5	271.5	241.5	253.0	232.8	238.2	243.4	211.7
Greece..............	288.5	302.4	312.3	308.5	244.1	202.0	189.6	186.1	191.0	145.0
Ireland..............	162.8	151.2	148.1	154.0	156.0	130.8	123.3	129.3	143.5	140.1
Italy..............	217.6	208.4	215.5	220.3	190.9	234.0	204.6	200.8	198.6	171.3
Japan..............	171.7	166.6	149.2	144.0	130.4	225.4	233.4	219.5	214.0	170.9
Korea, South........	322.3	318.0	324.9	332.4	305.8	326.8	323.8	321.3	327.5	272.0
Netherlands..........	286.9	281.8	288.8	289.3	243.9	273.0	269.6	270.8	270.7	232.3
Norway..............	267.1	268.0	259.8	240.8	175.5	264.0	253.9	261.1	259.3	221.7
Spain..............	266.6	256.8	276.5	282.3	245.1	241.8	216.6	218.7	230.4	198.6
Sweden..............	215.1	198.3	192.8	189.1	160.9	243.5	226.2	220.9	223.1	189.3
Switzerland..........	291.7	388.2	444.5	386.6	360.1	252.3	358.6	389.6	334.1	305.2
United Kingdom......	177.9	166.1	189.9	177.4	161.7	195.0	200.2	190.1	198.9	180.2

Source: World Bank, "World Development Indicators" database ©, <http://data.worldbank.org/>, accessed September 2017.

Table 1328. U.S. Trade with China—Leading Commodity Imports and Exports: 2010 to 2016

[In billions of dollars (365.0 represents $365,000,000,000), except as noted]

Commodity	NAICS code [1]	2010	2013	2014	2015	2016	2015-2016 percent change
IMPORTS FROM CHINA							
Total imports [2].............................	(X)	**365.0**	**440.4**	**468.5**	**483.2**	**462.6**	**-4.3**
Communications equipment.............................	3342	33.5	58.9	64.2	67.3	65.8	-2.3
Computer equipment.............................	3341	59.8	68.1	67.2	63.4	57.4	-9.6
Misc. manufactured commodities........................	3399	34.2	32.4	33.6	35.8	34.9	-2.5
Apparel.............................	3152	26.6	27.4	27.1	27.5	25.1	-8.6
Semiconductors and other electronic components.....	3344	18.3	19.4	22.5	23.4	22.4	-3.9
Furniture and kitchen cabinets..........................	3371	11.1	13.2	14.0	15.8	16.4	3.9
Footwear.............................	3162	15.7	16.8	16.8	17.1	14.6	-14.3
Audio and video equipment.............................	3343	19.5	13.8	14.6	14.9	13.8	-7.5
Motor vehicle parts.............................	3363	7.0	10.5	12.2	13.6	13.4	-1.2
Household appliances and misc. machines............	3352	9.1	11.7	12.2	13.3	12.3	-7.1
EXPORTS TO CHINA							
Total exports [2].............................	(X)	**85.8**	**114.0**	**115.3**	**107.3**	**107.0**	**-0.3**
Oilseeds and grains.............................	1111	11.3	15.7	16.3	13.0	15.5	19.5
Aerospace products and parts.........................	3364	5.7	12.1	13.3	15.1	14.2	-5.9
Motor vehicles.............................	3361	3.2	8.3	11.0	9.1	8.9	-2.0
Semiconductors and other electronic components.....	3344	6.1	4.4	4.9	5.5	5.5	-0.1
Waste and scrap.............................	9100	8.5	8.7	7.1	5.9	5.2	-12.8
Navigational, measuring, electromedical, and control instruments..............	3345	3.5	5.3	4.9	4.8	4.8	0.1
Basic chemicals.............................	3251	4.1	5.1	4.4	4.4	4.5	3.9
Resin, synthetic rubber, artificial and synthetic fibers and filaments...................	3252	4.3	4.2	4.3	3.7	3.5	-4.3
Other general purpose machinery.......................	3339	2.4	3.1	3.3	3.0	2.8	-4.3
Motor vehicle parts.............................	3363	1.0	1.8	2.1	1.9	2.3	22.6

X Not applicable. [1] Based on the North American Industry Classification System (NAICS); see text, Section 15. [2] Includes items not shown separately.

Source: U.S. International Trade Commission, "Interactive Tariff and Trade DataWeb," <http://dataweb.usitc.gov/>, accessed September 2017.

Table 1329. U.S. Trade in Processed Foods By Commodity: 2000 to 2016

[Includes Puerto Rico, U.S. territories, and shipments under foreign aid programs. Metric ton = 1.102 short tons or .984 long tons]

Product category	Units	2000	2010	2014	2015	2016
Processed foods imports, total [1,2]	**Metric tons**	**11,054,749**	**16,834,276**	**19,899,087**	**20,889,677**	**22,070,557**
Beer and wine	Kiloliters	2,771,174	4,078,532	4,511,272	4,752,894	5,000,120
Beer	Kiloliters	2,331,185	3,146,395	3,443,068	3,658,196	3,897,276
Wine	Kiloliters	439,989	932,137	1,068,203	1,094,698	1,102,844
Distilled spirits and other alcoholic beverages	Kiloliters	47,708	36,640	64,271	96,827	107,704
Chocolate and confectionery [2]	Metric tons	858,136	1,362,569	1,461,835	1,445,896	1,575,339
Chocolate	Metric tons	525,437	820,017	858,177	857,595	944,498
Sugar confectionery	Metric tons	293,105	499,236	565,617	552,216	596,046
Condiments and sauces	Metric tons	351,000	569,652	630,725	688,683	743,386
Fats and oils [2]	Metric tons	1,698,793	3,518,341	4,320,967	4,518,986	4,935,937
Olive oil	Metric tons	203,960	275,435	310,712	312,317	331,418
Soybean oil	1,000 kilograms	35,949	53,697	69,424	141,979	137,528
Vegetable oils (excl. soybean)	Metric tons	1,427,711	3,075,082	3,786,185	3,911,047	4,292,355
Food preparations [2]	Metric tons	1,111,342	2,052,605	2,587,368	2,610,715	2,643,388
Baking inputs, mixes, and types of dough [3]	Metric tons	682,340	1,097,081	1,290,504	1,449,030	1,548,271
Non-alcoholic beverages [2]	Kiloliters	3,689,991	5,552,744	6,027,458	6,316,795	6,609,317
Bottled drinks [4]	Kiloliters	555,954	1,222,531	1,635,841	1,853,012	2,051,772
Juices	Kiloliters	3,134,037	4,330,213	4,391,618	4,463,783	4,557,545
Pasta and processed cereals [2]	Metric tons	517,471	881,572	1,095,337	1,117,142	1,076,957
Breakfast cereals and other breakfast products	Metric tons	113,024	277,763	338,819	345,427	321,168
Pasta	Metric tons	316,886	367,974	438,216	452,592	462,503
Prepared/preserved meats	Metric tons	197,083	143,248	148,838	183,457	191,727
Prepared/preserved seafood	Metric tons	876,402	1,283,775	1,289,069	1,302,694	1,323,660
Processed fruit	Metric tons	865,350	1,422,793	1,808,179	2,032,694	1,974,900
Processed vegetables and pulses [2]	Metric tons	1,695,961	2,455,785	2,645,850	2,814,386	2,954,199
Frozen potato products [5]	Metric tons	527,642	725,033	820,697	836,805	897,730
Processed/prepared dairy products [2]	Metric tons	245,530	230,269	281,158	332,609	371,180
Cheese	Metric tons	188,707	138,539	164,778	197,768	205,333
Cream & powdered/condensed milk	Metric tons	18,897	33,250	39,446	43,062	51,693
Ice cream	Metric tons	9,151	30,263	23,920	24,253	27,023
Yogurt and dairy drinks	Liters	23,060	11,197	401,208	766,532	734,353
Snack foods	Metric tons	627,030	1,126,307	1,222,310	1,392,481	1,619,384
Baked snack foods [6]	Metric tons	480,515	899,781	1,059,310	1,203,117	1,420,059
Mixes of nuts and fruit [7]	Metric tons	92,782	156,182	82,359	97,200	100,920
Potato chips	Metric tons	23,758	40,569	42,416	49,443	47,222
Prepared peanuts and peanut butter	Metric tons	29,976	29,774	38,226	42,721	51,184
Spices	Metric tons	192,577	300,902	338,073	373,529	387,561
Syrups and sweeteners [2]	Metric tons	1,106,543	866,613	1,136,688	1,109,100	1,170,543
Fructose and fructose syrup	Metric tons	66,513	92,496	118,776	128,660	90,786
Glucose and glucose syrup	Metric tons	113,647	217,058	245,517	250,667	250,331
Processed foods exports, total [2]	**Metric tons**	**10,908,071**	**17,719,580**	**20,421,619**	**19,642,372**	**19,666,421**
Beer and wine	Kiloliters	526,828	703,995	927,056	1,037,534	992,843
Beer	Kiloliters	262,305	320,694	529,103	623,417	619,456
Wine	Kiloliters	264,523	383,301	397,954	414,117	373,387
Distilled spirits and other alcoholic beverages	Kiloliters	23,884	23,969	44,768	47,166	39,202
Chocolate and confectionery [2]	Metric tons	302,600	420,212	541,470	507,671	511,133
Chocolate	Metric tons	192,742	303,757	393,617	359,821	359,724
Sugar confectionery	Metric tons	98,043	108,527	140,143	139,194	144,149
Condiments and sauces	Metric tons	363,963	638,943	918,949	1,035,365	1,046,442
Fats and oils [2]	Metric tons	1,998,801	3,356,665	2,369,151	2,388,025	2,426,527
Soybean oil	1,000 kilograms	586,786	1,656,926	892,743	957,404	1,003,634
Vegetable oils (excl. soybean)	Metric tons	1,044,199	1,066,611	831,275	916,581	879,541
Food preparations [2]	Metric tons	2,492,061	3,397,278	4,914,371	4,475,542	4,348,206
Baking inputs, mixes, and types of dough [3]	Metric tons	1,904,460	2,280,017	3,616,726	3,247,708	3,094,034
Non-alcoholic beverages [2]	Kiloliters	1,661,547	1,617,263	1,659,815	1,540,447	1,290,729
Bottled drinks [4]	Kiloliters	487,448	636,964	688,680	752,027	663,133
Juices	Kiloliters	1,174,098	980,299	971,135	788,420	627,596
Pasta and processed cereals [2]	Metric tons	683,017	983,674	828,188	812,351	797,834
Breakfast cereals and other breakfast products	Metric tons	265,399	568,666	447,712	447,769	421,324
Pasta	Metric tons	102,295	181,765	206,617	208,630	175,030
Prepared/preserved meats	Metric tons	313,041	643,614	727,861	733,106	733,897
Prepared/preserved seafood	Metric tons	434,173	457,886	550,418	499,509	468,097
Processed fruit	Metric tons	388,844	571,165	655,077	619,768	575,368
Processed vegetables and pulses [2]	Metric tons	1,272,076	1,679,157	2,405,058	2,376,737	2,496,817
Frozen potato products [5]	Metric tons	568,709	790,607	1,046,781	1,047,741	1,096,930
Processed/prepared dairy products [2]	Metric tons	398,655	1,179,545	1,615,242	1,441,144	1,503,834
Cheese	Metric tons	47,760	173,327	368,200	316,889	286,659
Cream & powdered/condensed milk	Metric tons	114,847	466,853	625,381	612,477	642,540
Ice cream	Metric tons	41,652	35,680	68,198	69,668	65,929
Snack foods	Metric tons	490,079	784,168	1,011,343	1,035,126	1,009,461
Baked snack foods [6]	Metric tons	274,577	476,137	663,111	658,148	646,958
Mixes of nuts and fruit [7]	Metric tons	72,748	160,303	169,505	195,594	156,365
Potato chips	Metric tons	106,040	86,510	83,841	90,800	91,640
Prepared peanuts and peanut butter	Metric tons	36,713	61,218	94,886	90,583	114,499
Soups	1,000 kilograms	97,212	140,420	171,914	172,054	169,351
Syrups and sweeteners [2]	Metric tons	726,427	2,525,583	2,524,207	2,386,374	2,409,379
Fructose and fructose syrup	Metric tons	322,904	1,395,278	1,405,903	1,339,450	1,384,193
Glucose and glucose syrup	Metric tons	209,686	738,966	618,301	521,434	490,728
Molasses	Kiloliters	199,070	203,841	78,785	61,713	102,508

[1] Imports for consumption. Excludes merchandise entered into bonded warehouses of Foreign Trade Zones under Customs custody; see source for details. [2] Includes commodities not shown separately. [3] Includes pudding. [4] Includes soda, juice mixes, beer, milk-based drinks, etc. [5] Includes French fries. [6] Pastries, pretzels, corn chips, etc. [7] Includes packaged and microwaveable popcorn.

Source: U.S. Department of Agriculture, Foreign Agricultural Service, "Global Agricultural Trade System," <http://www.fas.usda.gov/gats>, accessed September 2017.

Puerto Rico and the Island Areas

This section presents summary economic and social statistics for Puerto Rico, the U.S. Virgin Islands, Guam, American Samoa, and the Northern Mariana Islands. Primary sources include the decennial censuses of population and housing and the annual Puerto Rico Community Survey conducted by the U.S. Census Bureau; County Business Patterns and other Census Bureau publications and databases; other U.S. government publications, such as the *National Vital Statistics Reports* (NSVR) series, issued by the National Center for Health Statistics; and the annual *Economic Report for the Governor and Legislative Assembly* of the Puerto Rico Planning Board.

Jurisdiction—The United States gained jurisdiction over these areas as follows: the islands of Puerto Rico and Guam, surrendered by Spain in December 1898, were ceded to the United States by the Treaty of Paris, ratified in 1899. Puerto Rico became a commonwealth on July 25, 1952, thereby achieving a high degree of local autonomy under its own constitution. The U.S. Virgin Islands, comprising approximately 50 islands and cays, was purchased by the United States from Denmark in 1917. American Samoa, a group of seven islands, was acquired in accordance with a convention among the United States, Great Britain, and Germany, ratified in 1900 (Swains Island was annexed in 1925). By an agreement approved by the United Nations Security Council and the United States, the Northern Mariana Islands, previously under Japanese mandate, was administered by the United States between 1947 and 1986 under the United Nations trusteeship system. The Northern Mariana Islands became a U.S. commonwealth in 1986.

Censuses—Because characteristics of Puerto Rico and the island areas differ, the presentation of census data for them is not uniform. The 1960 Census of Population covered all the territories listed above except the Northern Mariana Islands (their census was conducted in April 1958 by the Office of the High Commissioner of the Trust Territory of the Pacific Islands), while the 1960 Census of Housing excluded American Samoa. The 1970, 1980, 1990, 2000, and 2010 censuses of population and housing covered all five areas. Beginning in 1967, Congress authorized the Economic Censuses, to be taken at 5-year intervals, for years ending in "2" and "7." Prior economic censuses were conducted in Puerto Rico for 1949, 1954, 1958, and 1963 and in Guam and the U.S. Virgin Islands for 1958 and 1963. In 1967, the census of construction industries was added for the first time in Puerto Rico; in 1972, the U.S. Virgin Islands and Guam were covered; and in 1982, the Economic Census was taken for the first time for the Northern Mariana Islands. Agricultural censuses have been conducted with increasing regularity in Puerto Rico since 1910, in the U.S. Virgin Islands since 1917, and in Guam and American Samoa since 1920; the first agricultural census in the Northern Mariana Islands was conducted in 1970.

Puerto Rico Community Survey—The Puerto Rico Community Survey (PRCS) began in 2005 and was an important element in the Census Bureau's re-engineered 2010 census plan. The American Community Survey (ACS) is the equivalent of the PRCS for the United States (50 states and District of Columbia). The PRCS collects and produces population and housing information every year instead of every 10 years. About 36,000 households are surveyed each year from across every municipio in Puerto Rico.

Information in other sections—In addition to the statistics presented in this section, other data on Puerto Rico and the island areas are included in many tables showing distribution by states in various sections of the *Abstract*. See "Puerto Rico" and "Island Areas of the U.S." in the Index.

Selected Island Areas of the United States

Caribbean Region

United States

ATLANTIC OCEAN

The Bahamas

Turks and Caicos Islands (U.K.)

Cuba

Cayman Islands (U.K.)

Haiti | Dominican Republic

PUERTO RICO (U.S.)

B.V.I. (U.K.)

Jamaica

VIRGIN ISLANDS (U.S.)

Caribbean Sea

Pacific Region

NORTHERN MARIANA ISLANDS (U.S.)

Wake Island (U.S.)

Johnston Atoll (U.S.)

GUAM (U.S.)

PACIFIC OCEAN

Kingman Reef (U.S.)

Marshall Islands

Palmyra Atoll (U.S.)

Federated States of Micronesia

Kiribati

Nauru

Howland Island (U.S.)

Baker Island (U.S.)

Papua New Guinea

Solomon Islands

Tuvalu

Vanuatu

Samoa

Coral Sea

Australia

Fiji

AMERICAN SAMOA (U.S.)

Table 1330. Estimated and Projected Resident Population of Puerto Rico and Island Areas: 2000 to 2030

[In thousands (58 represents 58,000). Population as of July 1. Population data generally are de facto figures for the present territory. Data are adjusted to the 2010 Census of Population. See text, Section 30, for general comments regarding the data. For details of methodology, coverage, and reliability, see source]

Area	2000	2005	2010	2013	2014	2015	2016	Projected 2020	Projected 2025	Projected 2030
American Samoa...............	58	57	56	54	53	53	52	49	46	43
Guam........................	155	160	163	165	166	166	167	168	170	169
Northern Mariana Islands......	70	68	55	53	53	53	53	51	50	48
Puerto Rico...................	3,811	3,822	3,722	3,589	3,534	3,473	3,411	3,189	2,980	2,809
Virgin Islands................	109	108	108	108	108	108	108	106	104	100

Source: U.S. Census Bureau, "International Data Base (IDB)," <http://www.census.gov/population/international/data/>, accessed September 2017.

Table 1331. Births, Deaths, and Infant Deaths for Puerto Rico and the Island Areas: 2000 to 2015

[Births, deaths, and infant deaths by place of residence. Rates for 2000 and 2010 based on population enumerated as of April 1; for other years, on population estimated as of July 1]

Area and year	Births Number	Births Rate [1]	Deaths Number	Deaths Rate [2]	Infant deaths Number	Infant deaths Rate [3]
Puerto Rico:						
2000.............................	59,333	15.6	28,365	7.4	574	9.7
2010.............................	42,153	11.3	29,153	7.8	341	8.1
2013.............................	36,486	10.1	29,009	8.0	261	7.2
2014.............................	34,434	9.7	30,152	8.5	241	7.0
2015.............................	31,157	9.0	(NA)	(NA)	(NA)	(NA)
Guam:						
2000.............................	3,766	24.2	648	4.2	22	5.8
2010.............................	3,416	21.4	857	5.4	48	14.1
2013.............................	3,285	20.5	873	5.4	31	9.4
2014.............................	3,395	21.1	939	5.8	28	8.3
2015.............................	3,366	20.8	(NA)	(NA)	(NA)	(NA)
Virgin Islands:						
2000.............................	1,564	14.4	641	5.9	21	13.4
2010.............................	1,600	15.1	715	6.7	13	(B)
2013.............................	(NA)	(NA)	(NA)	(NA)	(NA)	(NA)
2014.............................	(NA)	(NA)	(NA)	(NA)	(NA)	(NA)
2015.............................	1,325	12.8	(NA)	(NA)	(NA)	(NA)
American Samoa:						
2000.............................	1,731	30.0	219	3.8	11	(B)
2010.............................	1,234	22.2	224	4.0	14	(B)
2013.............................	1,077	19.7	262	4.8	10	(B)
2014.............................	1,077	19.8	246	4.5	9	(B)
2015.............................	1,078	19.8	(NA)	(NA)	(NA)	(NA)
Northern Marianas:						
2000.............................	1,431	20.5	136	2.0	11	(B)
2010.............................	1,072	20.0	174	3.3	4	(B)
2013.............................	686	13.4	185	3.6	8	(B)
2014.............................	517	10.0	202	3.9	7	(B)
2015.............................	427	8.2	(NA)	(NA)	(NA)	(NA)

B Base figure too small to meet statistical standards of reliability. NA Not available. [1] Birth rates are births per 1,000 women of child-bearing age. [2] Death rates are deaths per 1,000 population. [3] Infant death rates are infant deaths (under 1 year) per 1,000 live births.

Source: U.S. National Center for Health Statistics, National Vital Statistics Reports (NVSR), *Births: Final Data for 2015*, Vol. 66, No. 1, January 2017, and earlier reports; and *Deaths: Final Data for 2014*, Vol. 65, No. 4, June 2016, and earlier reports. See also <http://www.cdc.gov/nchs/nvss.htm>.

Table 1332. Public Elementary and Secondary Schools by Island Area: 2014

[Enrollment and staff are for Fall of year shown. Revenues and expenditures are for school year ending in year shown]

Item	Puerto Rico	Guam	U.S. Virgin Islands	American Samoa	Northern Marianas
Enrollment...........................	410,950	31,144	14,241	[1] 16,400	[2] 10,638
Elementary (pre-kindergarten to grade 8 and elementary ungraded)............	284,246	21,112	9,724	[1] 11,763	[2] 7,340
Secondary (grades 9 to 12)....................	126,704	10,032	4,517	[1] 4,637	[2] 3,298
Total staff (Fall)........................	50,099	3,938	2,212	[1] 1,869	[2] 876
School district staff...................	1,347	401	116	[1] 186	[2] 98
School staff..........................	36,773	3,287	1,648	[1] 1,364	[2] 679
Teachers.........................	31,186	2,286	1,131	[1] 971	[2] 417
Student support staff................	4,661	126	58	[1] 218	[2] 22
Other support services staff.........	7,318	124	390	[1] 101	[2] 77
Revenues, total [3] ($1,000)...........	3,521,851	295,639	195,405	87,593	58,326
Current expenditures [4] ($1,000).........	3,510,706	286,844	175,022	71,709	62,502
Per pupil [4] (dollars)................	8,281	8,585	11,705	[1] 3,481	5,875

[1] 2006 data. [2] 2013 data. [3] Includes federal, territorial, local, and private revenues. [4] Includes current expenditures only, and excludes capital expenditures, interest on school debt, community services, private school programs, adult education, and other expenditures not directly allocable to public school operations.

Source: U.S. National Center for Education Statistics, *Digest of Education Statistics*, "Advance Release of Selected 2016 Digest Tables," <http://www.nces.ed.gov/programs/digest/>, accessed April 2017.

Table 1333. Occupational Employment and Average Annual Wages in Guam, Puerto Rico, and Virgin Islands: 2016

[The Occupational Employment Survey (OES) program conducts a semiannual mail survey designed to produce estimates of employment and wages for specific occupations. Excludes self-employed persons. For more details on the survey, see <https://www.bls.gov/oes/oes_emp.htm>]

Selected occupation	SOC code [1]	Guam		Puerto Rico		Virgin Islands	
		Employ-ment	Average annual wages [2]	Employ-ment	Average annual wages [2]	Employ-ment	Average annual wages [2]
Total, all occupations [3].........................	(X)	**61,520**	**34,790**	**883,360**	**28,740**	**37,320**	**37,640**
Management occupations............................	11	5,170	65,900	38,470	72,210	3,160	71,300
Business and financial operations..................	13	2,450	50,530	41,270	38,460	1,390	54,120
Computer and mathematical occupations..........	15	510	50,050	10,390	44,210	350	57,070
Architecture and engineering........................	17	1,050	56,010	13,340	55,320	210	59,710
Life, physical, and social sciences..................	19	420	52,700	6,140	47,430	290	47,700
Community and social services......................	21	870	44,180	15,520	28,880	450	41,850
Legal occupations.....................................	23	370	67,660	4,250	64,950	480	97,730
Education, training, and library occupations.........	25	4,420	43,150	67,220	35,340	2,510	41,400
Arts, design, entertainment, sports, and media.....	27	680	32,410	7,380	31,400	260	44,600
Healthcare practitioner and technical occupations..	29	1,690	61,810	51,290	36,910	1,100	64,870
Healthcare support.....................................	31	820	24,890	10,240	20,620	390	28,540
Protective service occupations......................	33	2,720	37,000	54,210	25,400	2,500	33,560
Food preparation and serving related occupations..	35	6,540	20,250	71,310	18,610	4,460	25,340
Buildings and grounds cleaning and maintenance...	37	3,160	20,610	40,660	19,940	2,130	23,330
Personal care and service occupations..............	39	1,370	22,500	16,060	19,170	1,110	23,370
Sales and related occupations.......................	41	4,810	23,160	110,120	22,610	4,080	27,750
Office and administrative support...................	43	10,790	28,720	166,660	24,420	6,660	32,190
Farming, fishing, and forestry.......................	45	70	27,800	1,750	22,290	30	31,760
Construction and extraction..........................	47	5,230	30,450	28,550	21,270	1,190	42,330
Installation, maintenance, and repair...............	49	3,010	33,940	28,810	26,730	1,640	36,150
Production occupations...............................	51	1,670	29,750	57,990	24,020	670	31,710
Transportation and material moving................	53	3,700	28,370	41,730	21,830	2,250	27,450

X Not applicable. [1] Office of Management and Budget's Standard Occupational Classification (SOC) is used to define occupations. SOC categorizes workers into one of over 800 detailed occupations, which are classified into 23 major occupational groups. [2] Annual wages have been calculated by multiplying the hourly mean wage by a "year-round, full-time" hours figure of 2,080 hours; for those occupations where there is not an hourly mean wage published, the annual wage has been directly calculated from the reported survey data. [3] Estimates do not sum to the total because the total may include data for occupations for which separate employment estimates could not be published. See source for more information.

Source: U.S. Bureau of Labor Statistics, "Occupational Employment Statistics," <http://www.bls.gov/oes/current/oessrcst.htm>, accessed April 2017.

Table 1334. Prisoners in Custody of Correctional Authorities in U.S. Territories and Commonwealths: 2005 to 2015

[As of December 31]

Jurisdiction	Total inmates				Sentenced to more than 1 year			
	2005	2012	2014	2015	2005	2012	2014	2015
American Samoa.............	222	192	[1] 212	(NA)	174	(NA)	(NA)	(NA)
Guam............................	505	(NA)	754	[2] 754	238	(NA)	316	[2] 316
Northern Mariana Islands....	149	168	175	218	83	109	143	153
Puerto Rico....................	14,263	12,244	12,327	11,364	11,469	9,781	9,797	8,893
U.S. Virgin Islands............	596	577	(NA)	(NA)	435	378	(NA)	(NA)

NA Not available. [1] Data for 2013. [2] Guam did not submit 2015 data. Counts were imputed.

Source: U.S. Department of Justice, Bureau of Justice Statistics, *Prisoners in 2015*, NCJ 250229, December 2016, and earlier reports; and *Correctional Populations in the United States, 2012*, NCJ 243936, December 2013. See also <http://www.bjs.gov/index.cfm?ty=tp&tid=1>.

Table 1335. Puerto Rico—Selected Social, Demographic, and Housing Characteristics: 2010 and 2015

[The Puerto Rico Community Survey universe includes the household population and the population living in institutions, college dormitories, and other group quarters. Based on a sample and subject to sampling variability; see text, this section and Appendix III]

Characteristic	2010 Number	2010 Percent	2015 Number	2015 Percent
Total population...........	3,722,133	100.0	3,474,182	100.0
SEX				
Male........	1,785,266	48.0	1,657,467	47.7
Female........	1,936,867	52.0	1,816,715	52.3
AGE				
Under 5 years....	223,247	6.0	172,896	5.0
5 to 9 years....	236,531	6.4	203,080	5.8
10 to 14 years....	268,378	7.2	217,606	6.3
15 to 19 years....	284,254	7.6	244,432	7.0
20 to 24 years....	264,790	7.1	253,642	7.3
25 to 34 years....	482,756	13.0	421,169	12.1
35 to 44 years....	487,539	13.1	448,443	12.9
45 to 54 years....	486,273	13.1	455,086	13.1
55 to 59 years....	219,460	5.9	216,773	6.2
60 to 64 years....	223,184	6.0	214,090	6.2
65 to 74 years....	313,604	8.4	357,541	10.3
75 to 84 years....	170,712	4.6	194,256	5.6
85 years and over....	61,405	1.6	75,168	2.2
MARITAL STATUS				
Males 15 years and over....	1,410,023	100.0	1,349,963	100.0
Never married....	566,489	40.2	589,872	43.7
Married, not separated....	610,584	43.3	523,411	38.8
Separated....	39,169	2.8	33,197	2.5
Widowed....	39,752	2.8	41,173	3.0
Divorced....	154,029	10.9	162,310	12.0
Females 15 years and over....	1,583,954	100.0	1,530,637	100.0
Never married....	523,558	33.1	555,020	36.3
Married, not separated....	601,632	38.0	522,307	34.1
Separated....	50,458	3.2	48,180	3.1
Widowed....	171,416	10.8	163,281	10.7
Divorced....	236,890	15.0	241,849	15.8
HOUSEHOLDS				
Total households....	1,319,448	100.0	1,221,851	100.0
Family households (families)....	966,123	73.2	844,538	69.1
With own children under 18 years....	405,933	30.8	314,058	25.7
Married-couple families....	557,851	42.3	471,172	38.6
With own children under 18 years....	200,406	15.2	143,565	11.7
Male householder, no wife present....	82,129	6.2	80,957	6.6
With own children under 18 years....	39,285	3.0	32,035	2.6
Female householder, no husband present....	326,143	24.7	292,409	23.9
With own children under 18 years....	166,242	12.6	138,458	11.3
Nonfamily households....	353,325	26.8	377,313	30.9
Householder living alone....	306,036	23.2	330,379	27.0
65 years and over....	125,754	9.5	151,873	12.4
Average household size....	2.79	(X)	2.81	(X)
Average family size....	3.28	(X)	3.46	(X)
DISABILITY STATUS				
Total civilian noninstitutionalized population....	3,695,636	100.0	3,447,794	100.0
With a disability....	726,334	19.7	737,665	21.4

X Not applicable.

Source: U.S. Census Bureau, 2015 Puerto Rico Community Survey, DP02PR, "Selected Social Characteristics in Puerto Rico," and DP05, "Demographic and Housing Estimates," <http://factfinder.census.gov>, accessed May 2017. See also <http://census.gov/programs-surveys/acs/about/puerto-rico-community-survey.html>.

Table 1336. Puerto Rico—Owner and Renter Occupied Housing by Household Type: 2015

[The Puerto Rico Community Survey universe includes the household population and the population living in institutions, college dormitories, and other group quarters. Based on a sample and subject to sampling variability; see text, this section and Appendix III]

Household type	Owner occupied	Renter occupied	Household type	Owner occupied	Renter occupied
Total households....	836,820	385,031			
Family households....	605,158	239,380	Householder 15 to 34 years....	13,785	49,570
Married-couple family....	395,004	76,168	Householder 35 to 64 years....	95,675	69,552
Householder 15 to 34 years....	23,983	19,279	Householder 65 years and over....	52,194	11,633
Householder 35 to 64 years....	234,608	44,949	Nonfamily households....	231,662	145,651
Householder 65 years and over....	136,413	11,940	Householder living alone....	204,286	126,093
Other family....	210,154	163,212	Householder 15 to 34 years....	5,214	16,323
Male householder, no wife present..	48,500	32,457	Householder 35 to 64 years....	88,952	68,017
Householder 15 to 34 years....	5,216	10,473	Householder 65 years and over....	110,120	41,753
Householder 35 to 64 years....	29,161	17,968	Householder not living alone....	27,376	19,558
Householder 65 years and over....	14,123	4,016	Householder 15 to 34 years....	2,606	7,716
Female householder,			Householder 35 to 64 years....	18,071	8,484
no husband present....	161,654	130,755	Householder 65 years and over....	6,699	3,358

Source: U.S. Census Bureau, 2015 Puerto Rico Community Survey, B25011, "Tenure by Household Type and Age of Householder," <http://factfinder.census.gov>, accessed May 2017. See also <http://census.gov/programs-surveys/acs/about/puerto-rico-community-survey.html>.

Table 1337. Puerto Rico—Socioeconomic Summary: 1990 to 2016

[3,512 represents 3,512,000]

Item	Unit	1990	2000	2005	2010	2013	2014	2015	2016 (P)
POPULATION									
Total [1]	1,000	3,512	3,808	3,824	3,731	3,614	3,564	3,504	3,442
Persons per family	Number	3.7	3.4	3.3	3.2	3.1	3.1	3.1	3.0
LABOR FORCE									
Total [2]	1,000	1,124	1,303	1,357	1,285	1,180	1,159	1,130	1,134
Employed [3]	1,000	963	1,159	1,213	1,075	1,015	993	984	1,002
Agriculture [4]	1,000	36	24	25	17	17	17	17	17
Manufacturing	1,000	168	159	135	101	94	85	82	85
Trade	1,000	185	239	256	237	225	231	239	238
Government	1,000	222	249	268	250	213	204	197	190
Unemployed	1,000	161	143	144	210	165	166	147	133
Unemployment rate [5]	Rate	14.0	11.0	10.6	16.3	14.0	14.3	13.0	11.7
Compensation of employees	Mil. dol.	13,639	23,504	29,372	29,870	29,841	29,349	28,862	28,840
Average compensation	Dollar	14,854	20,280	24,214	27,786	29,400	29,556	29,331	28,782
Salary and wages	Mil. dol.	13,639	23,504	25,393	25,793	25,710	25,189	24,800	24,646
INCOME [6]									
Personal income:									
Current dollars	Mil. dol.	21,105	38,856	49,929	59,983	64,160	63,116	63,854	63,878
Constant (1954) dollars	Mil. dol.	5,551	8,491	10,030	9,958	10,235	9,846	9,763	9,671
Disposable personal income:									
Current dollars	Mil. dol.	19,914	36,239	46,597	57,111	61,866	60,781	61,334	61,634
Constant (1954) dollars	Mil. dol.	5,238	7,919	9,173	9,481	9,869	9,482	9,378	9,331
Average family income:									
Current dollars	Dollar	22,232	34,693	43,086	51,446	55,035	54,899	56,492	55,671
Constant (1954) dollars	Dollar	5,847	7,581	8,655	8,541	8,780	8,564	8,637	8,428
TOURISM [6]									
Number of visitors	1,000	3,426	4,566	5,073	4,379	4,210	4,456	5,051	5,077
Visitor expenditures	Mil. dol.	1,366	2,388	3,239	3,211	3,311	3,439	3,825	3,985
Average per visitor	Dollar	399	523	638	733	786	772	757	785
Net income from tourism	Mil. dol.	383	615	771	(NA)	(NA)	(NA)	(NA)	(NA)

P Preliminary. NA Not available. [1] 1990 and 2000 enumerated as of April 1; for all other years the population is the average of population estimates at the beginning and the end of the fiscal year. [2] For population 16 years old and over. [3] Includes employment in other industries, not shown separately. [4] Includes forestry and fisheries. [5] Unemployed as percent of the labor force. [6] For fiscal years.

Source: Puerto Rico Planning Board, San Juan, PR, *Economic Report for the Governor and Legislative Assembly, 2016*, March 2017, and earlier reports. See also <http://www.gdb-pur.com/economy/statistical-appendix.html>.

Table 1338. Puerto Rico—Business Summary by Industry: 2014 and 2015

[Payroll in millions of dollars (17,244.3 represents $17,244,300,000). Covers establishments with payroll. Excludes self-employed individuals, employees of private households, railroad employees, agricultural production employees, and most government employees. For statement on methodology, see Appendix III]

Kind of business	NAICS code [1]	Establishments		Paid employees [2]		Annual payroll (mil. dol.)	
		2014	2015	2014	2015	2014	2015
Total, all industries	(X)	**44,169**	**43,620**	**681,058**	**677,974**	**17,244.3**	**17,315.9**
Agriculture, forestry, fishing and hunting	11	16	14	231	172	1.7	1.4
Mining, quarrying, and oil and gas extraction	21	47	43	627	516	12.0	10.7
Utilities	22	26	26	341	344	24.4	21.7
Construction	23	1,889	1,773	25,571	24,510	553.6	527.9
Manufacturing	31–33	1,750	1,730	74,076	73,706	2,906.6	2,885.2
Wholesale trade	42	2,047	1,986	30,021	29,568	1,122.0	1,129.0
Retail trade	44–45	9,837	9,569	131,674	130,558	2,367.4	2,388.4
Transportation and warehousing	48–49	1,012	988	15,391	14,312	439.2	414.8
Information	51	668	681	19,071	18,019	786.7	749.7
Finance and insurance	52	1,808	1,814	34,898	31,708	1,532.6	1,432.4
Real estate and rental and leasing	53	1,614	1,581	10,610	10,414	252.3	257.5
Professional, scientific, and technical services	54	4,328	4,327	30,364	32,389	1,123.2	1,218.9
Management of companies and enterprises	55	104	102	4,637	7,129	252.2	341.3
Administrative, support, waste mgmt, and remediation services	56	1,910	1,928	77,456	77,062	1,490.7	1,469.2
Educational services	61	939	920	40,621	40,866	863.0	853.9
Health care and social assistance	62	7,601	7,646	82,432	84,261	2,013.8	2,065.3
Arts, entertainment, and recreation	71	454	452	4,402	3,543	74.3	71.4
Accommodation and food services	72	4,443	4,434	78,608	79,246	1,059.0	1,100.3
Other services (except public administration)	81	3,383	3,313	19,621	18,841	362.2	363.8
Industries not classified	99	293	293	([3])	810	7.4	12.9

X Not applicable. [1] Based on the 2012 North American Industry Classification System. See text, Section 15. [2] Covers full- and part-time employees who are on the payroll in the pay period including March 12. [3] 250 to 499 employees.

Source: U.S. Census Bureau, County Business Patterns, "Geography Area Series: County Business Patterns for Puerto Rico and the Island Areas," <http://factfinder.census.gov/>, accessed April 2017. See also <https://www.census.gov/programs-surveys/cbp.html>.

Table 1339. Puerto Rico—Gross Product and Net Income: 1990 to 2016

[In millions of dollars (21,619 represents $21,619,000,000). For fiscal years ending June 30. Minus sign (-) indicates decrease]

Item	1990	2000	2010	2013	2014	2015	2016 (P)
Gross product	**21,619**	**41,419**	**64,295**	**68,945**	**68,798**	**69,570**	**70,135**
Agriculture	434	407	822	847	867	855	840
Manufacturing	12,126	24,489	46,577	47,581	47,876	48,648	49,664
Contract construction and mining [1]	720	2,157	1,518	1,252	1,150	1,129	1,044
Transportation, warehousing, and utilities	2,468	2,579	2,923	2,575	3,042	3,044	2,957
Trade (wholesale and retail)	4,728	6,093	7,466	7,626	7,849	7,804	7,966
Finance, insurance, and real estate	3,896	10,511	19,026	21,185	20,210	20,464	20,747
Services [2]	3,015	9,987	11,993	12,743	13,391	13,581	13,882
Government	3,337	5,478	8,350	8,238	7,825	7,268	7,354
Commonwealth	2,884	4,601	6,862	6,665	6,286	5,741	5,804
Municipalities	453	877	1,488	1,573	1,540	1,527	1,550
Rest of the world	-8,985	-20,283	-34,087	-33,505	-33,648	-33,573	-34,900
Statistical discrepancy	-121	585	-294	405	235	350	580
Net income	**17,941**	**32,610**	**50,246**	**55,390**	**55,379**	**55,670**	**55,457**
Agriculture	486	385	824	848	870	860	845
Manufacturing	11,277	22,627	43,292	44,178	44,417	45,127	46,040
Mining [1]	26	34	21	23	13	22	20
Contract construction	679	1,764	1,206	1,047	924	897	806
Transportation, warehousing, and utilities	1,778	1,961	2,128	1,747	2,146	2,139	2,045
Trade (wholesale and retail)	3,420	4,995	6,155	6,515	6,615	6,570	6,617
Finance, insurance, and real estate	3,280	8,175	13,099	16,162	15,559	15,549	15,763
Services [2]	2,643	7,475	9,257	10,138	10,658	10,813	10,868
Government	3,337	5,478	8,350	8,238	7,825	7,268	7,354
Rest of the world	-8,985	-20,283	-34,087	-33,505	-33,648	-33,573	-34,900

P Preliminary. [1] Mining includes only quarries. [2] Includes all other services not elsewhere classified.

Source: Puerto Rico Planning Board, San Juan, PR, *Economic Report for the Governor and Legislative Assembly, 2016*, March 2017, and earlier reports. See also <http://www.gdb-pur.com/economy/statistical-appendix.html>.

Table 1340. Puerto Rico—Transfer Payments: 2000 to 2016

[In millions of dollars (8,659 represents $8,659,000,000). Data represent transfer payments between federal and state governments and other nonresidents]

Item	2000	2005	2010	2013	2014	2015	2016 (P)
Total receipts	**8,659**	**10,551**	**16,504**	**18,106**	**17,981**	**18,017**	**18,152**
Federal government	7,966	9,673	15,585	16,967	16,953	17,091	17,222
Transfers to individuals [1]	7,868	9,547	15,352	16,751	16,739	16,863	16,983
Veterans benefits	491	491	733	807	869	1,416	1,230
Medicare	1,196	1,825	2,529	4,148	4,481	4,467	4,511
Social security	3,863	5,118	7,074	7,929	7,354	7,718	7,820
Nutritional assistance	1,193	1,306	1,605	1,868	1,869	1,846	1,908
Industry subsidies	98	127	233	216	214	228	239
U.S. state governments	15	15	29	30	30	34	34
Other nonresidents	679	863	890	1,109	998	892	896
Total payments	**2,763**	**3,583**	**3,804**	**3,745**	**3,870**	**3,988**	**3,967**
Federal government	2,693	3,516	3,586	3,653	3,763	3,848	3,837
Transfers from individuals [1]	1,326	1,792	1,862	1,924	1,936	1,982	1,946
Contribution to Medicare	191	303	392	451	415	464	443
Employee contribution for social security	1,133	1,483	1,467	1,469	1,516	1,514	1,500
Transfers from industries	51	74	92	104	127	133	137
Unemployment insurance	234	221	207	214	217	248	283
Employer contribution for social security	1,081	1,429	1,424	1,411	1,482	1,485	1,471
Other nonresidents [2]	70	67	215	91	108	141	130
Net balance	**5,897**	**6,968**	**12,700**	**14,362**	**14,110**	**14,029**	**14,184**
Federal government	5,273	6,157	11,999	13,314	13,190	13,244	13,385
U.S. state governments	10	10	26	27	27	31	31
Other nonresidents	614	801	675	1,021	893	754	768

P Preliminary. [1] Includes other receipts and payments not shown separately. [2] Includes U.S. state governments.

Source: Puerto Rico Planning Board, San Juan, PR, *Economic Report to the Governor and Legislative Assembly, 2016*, March 2017, and earlier reports. See also <http://www.gdb-pur.com/economy/statistical-appendix.html>.

Table 1341. Puerto Rico—Merchandise Imports and Exports: 1980 to 2016

[In millions of dollars (9,018 represents $9,018,000,000). Data shown is trade for the San Juan, Puerto Rico Customs District. Imports are imports for consumption; see text, Section 28]

Item	1980	1990	2000	2005	2009	2010	2011	2012	2013	2014	2015	2016
Imports	9,018	16,200	27,006	40,499	38,780	39,766	44,736	45,407	43,811	42,768	42,260	45,871
From U.S.	5,345	10,792	15,172	20,994	20,038	20,641	20,346	19,808	20,314	20,848	22,882	25,151
From other	3,673	5,408	11,834	19,505	18,742	19,125	24,391	25,599	23,497	21,920	19,378	20,720
Exports	6,576	20,402	43,191	56,836	59,594	67,347	56,767	58,646	61,632	66,699	70,769	71,985
To U.S.	5,643	17,915	38,335	47,121	40,779	47,630	40,942	42,308	44,229	49,194	53,281	56,136
To other	933	2,487	4,856	9,715	18,815	19,717	15,825	16,337	17,404	17,504	17,488	15,849

Source: U.S. Census Bureau, Foreign Trade Division, *U.S. Trade with Puerto Rico and U.S. Possessions* (FT 895), 2016 and earlier reports; *U.S. Merchandise Trade: Selected Highlights* (FT 920), December 2011 and earlier reports; and "USA Trade Online," <https://usatrade.census.gov/>, accessed May 2017.

Table 1342. Puerto Rico—Agricultural Summary: 2007 and 2012

[1 cuerda = 0.97 acre]

All farms	Unit	2007	2012	All farms	Unit	2007	2012
Farms.......................	Number	15,745	13,159	Tenants...................	Number	2,425	2,728
Farm land..................	Cuerdas	557,530	584,988	Farms by type of			
Average size of farm.....	Cuerdas	35.4	44.5	organization:			
Approximate land area....	Cuerdas	2,254,365	2,254,365	Individual or family......	Number	13,958	11,938
Proportion in farms.......	Percent	24.7	25.9	Partnership.............	Number	49	117
Farms by size:				Corporation..............	Number	575	738
Less than 10 cuerdas....	Number	7,502	5,129	Other.....................	Number	1,163	366
10 to 19 cuerdas.........	Number	3,545	2,859	Farms by value of sales:			
20 to 49 cuerdas.........	Number	2,680	2,872	Less than $1,000........	Number	4,442	1,837
50 to 99 cuerdas.........	Number	865	940	$1,000 to $2,499.........	Number	2,771	2,015
100 to 174 cuerdas......	Number	524	563	$2,500 to $4,499.........	Number	2,428	1,986
175 to 259 cuerdas......	Number	207	401	$5,000 to $7,499.........	Number	1,206	1,209
260 cuerdas or more.....	Number	422	395	$7,500 to $9,999.........	Number	882	771
Tenure of operator:				$10,000 to $19,999......	Number	1,497	1,521
Operators..................	Number	15,745	13,159	$20,000 to $39,999.......	Number	1,030	968
Full owners.............	Number	11,402	9,362	$40,000 to $59,999......	Number	281	394
Part owners.............	Number	1,918	1,069	$60,000 or more..........	Number	1,208	1,322

Source: U.S. Department of Agriculture, National Agricultural Statistics Service (NASS), *2012 Census of Agriculture: Puerto Rico, Island and Municipio Data*, Geographic Area Series, Volume 1: Part 52, June 2014. See also <http://www.agcensus.usda.gov/Publications>.

Table 1343. Puerto Rico—Farms and Market Value of Agricultural Products Sold: 2012

[For market value, 547,629 represents $547,629,000]

Type of product	Number of farms	Market value ($1,000)	Average value per farm (dol.)	Type of product	Number of farms	Market value ($1,000)	Average value per farm (dol.)
Total......................	**13,159**	**547,629**	**41,616**	Horticultural specialties.........	657	37,534	57,129
Crops........................	9,367	271,320	(NA)	Grasses and other crops.......	532	14,589	27,422
Coffee.....................	4,478	29,273	6,537	Livestock, poultry, and their			
Pineapples.................	42	1,906	45,375	products....................	4,119	276,309	67,081
Plantains...................	3,628	80,505	22,190	Cattle and calves...............	2,911	33,606	11,544
Bananas....................	1,474	12,106	8,213	Poultry and poultry products. ..	706	40,376	57,189
Grains.....................	781	8,539	10,934	Dairy products...................	318	189,425	595,677
Root crops or tubers............	1,242	8,192	6,596	Hogs and pigs..................	532	8,019	15,074
Fruits and coconuts..............	1,926	31,541	16,377	Aquaculture......................	51	688	13,490
Vegetables and melons [1]........	1,528	47,135	30,848	Other............................	630	4,195	6,659

NA Not available. [1] Includes hydroponic crops.

Source: U.S. Department of Agriculture, National Agricultural Statistics Service (NASS), *2012 Census of Agriculture: Puerto Rico, Island and Municipio Data*, Geographic Area Series, Volume 1: Part 52, June 2014. See also <http://www.agcensus.usda.gov/Publications>.

Table 1344. Guam, Virgin Islands, Northern Mariana Islands, and American Samoa—Economic Summary by Sector: 2012

[Sales and payroll in millions of dollars (7,737 represents $7,737,000,000). Data for establishments with annual payroll. Based on the 2012 Economic Census of Island Areas; see Appendix III]

Kind of business	Guam	Virgin Islands	Northern Mariana Islands	American Samoa	Kind of business	Guam	Virgin Islands	Northern Mariana Islands	American Samoa
Total: [1]					Paid employees [2].....	2,505	686	716	253
Establishments........	3,099	2,414	1,339	377	Retail trade:				
Sales..................	7,737	6,831	1,324	1,154	Establishments........	630	560	284	136
Annual payroll..........	1,287	1,129	208	114	Sales..................	1,980	1,318	314	210
Paid employees [2].....	53,579	32,465	14,215	7,070	Annual payroll..........	184	142	31	17
Construction:					Paid employees [2].....	8,879	6,596	2,463	1,435
Establishments........	320	161	62	20	Professional, scientific,				
Sales..................	750	238	37	31	& technical services:				
Annual payroll..........	167	58	8	5	Establishments........	241	232	105	22
Paid employees [2].....	6,722	1,729	821	432	Sales..................	294	307	29	20
Manufacturing:					Annual payroll..........	105	95	10	5
Establishments........	54	57	39	25	Paid employees [2]....	2,737	2,108	602	254
Sales..................	123	1,963	21	(D)	Accommodation &				
Annual payroll..........	28	168	7	(D)	food services:				
Paid employees [2].....	1,282	1,984	592	([3])	Establishments........	450	279	142	36
Wholesale trade:					Sales..................	790	539	180	29
Establishments........	177	64	74	16	Annual payroll..........	189	161	38	6
Sales..................	982	221	247	275	Paid employees [2]....	12,575	6,864	3,195	574
Annual payroll..........	66	25	11	5					

D Withheld to avoid disclosing data for individual companies; data are included in higher level totals. [1] Includes other industries, not shown separately. [2] For pay period including March 12. [3] 1,000 to 2,499 employees.

Source: U.S. Census Bureau, 2012 Economic Census of the Island Areas, Geographic Area Series, "General Statistics by Kind of Business," <http://factfinder.census.gov/>, accessed July 2014. See also <http://www.census.gov/econ/islandareas/>.

ProQuest Statistical Abstract of the United States: 2018

Table 1345. Puerto Rico—School Enrollment and Educational Attainment by Level: 2005 to 2015

[The Puerto Rico Community Survey universe includes the household population and the population living in institutions, college dormitories, and other group quarters. Based on a sample and subject to sampling variability; see text, this section and Appendix III]

Characteristic	2005	2010	2011	2012	2013	2014	2015
EDUCATIONAL ENROLLMENT							
Population 3 years and over enrolled in school.....	1,138,768	995,743	991,812	983,155	942,530	921,168	892,872
Nursery school, preschool.........................	69,731	55,298	56,486	58,639	55,475	55,250	52,792
Kindergarten....................................	52,261	45,366	45,657	44,606	42,217	37,899	37,989
Elementary school (grades 1-8).....................	486,546	414,233	400,439	394,200	376,924	362,625	340,580
High school (grades 9-12).........................	242,548	213,581	212,136	207,820	199,044	187,227	189,446
College or graduate school.......................	287,682	267,265	277,094	277,890	268,870	278,167	272,065
EDUCATIONAL ATTAINMENT							
Population 25 years and over.......................	2,431,653	2,444,933	2,443,515	2,432,137	2,417,418	2,400,677	2,382,526
Less than 9th grade..............................	547,055	484,138	461,611	440,807	419,215	398,760	391,558
9th to 12th grade, no diploma......................	269,039	262,682	243,839	225,826	234,868	229,019	210,220
High school graduate (includes equivalency)......	588,130	623,709	648,204	650,650	653,505	669,936	647,581
Some college, no degree.........................	290,283	317,797	304,832	306,603	291,031	292,524	314,431
Associate's degree..............................	231,848	212,186	215,478	219,146	233,730	223,726	228,508
Bachelor's degree...............................	377,437	389,954	416,008	428,778	416,877	417,133	424,255
Graduate or professional degree..................	127,861	154,467	153,543	160,327	168,192	169,579	165,973
Percent high school graduate or higher.............	66.4	69.5	71.1	72.6	72.9	73.8	74.7
Percent bachelor's degree or higher...............	20.8	22.3	23.3	24.2	24.2	24.4	24.8

Source: U.S. Census Bureau, 2015 Puerto Rico Community Survey, DP02PR, "Selected Social Characteristics in Puerto Rico," <http://factfinder.census.gov>, accessed May 2017. See also <http://census.gov/programs-surveys/acs/about/puerto-rico-community-survey.html>.

Table 1346. Virgin Islands—Business Summary by Industry: 2014 and 2015

[Payroll in thousands of dollars (969,022 represents $969,022,000). Covers establishments with payroll. Excludes self-employed individuals, employees of private households, railroad employees, agricultural production employees, and most government employees. For statement on methodology, see Appendix III]

Industry	NAICS code [1]	Establishments		Paid employees [2]		Annual payroll ($1,000)	
		2014	2015	2014	2015	2014	2015
Total, all industries......................................	(X)	**2,609**	**2,572**	**29,541**	**29,118**	**969,022**	**969,738**
Agriculture, forestry, fishing and hunting...............	11	1	2	([3])	([3])	(D)	(D)
Mining, quarrying, and oil and gas extraction..........	21	2	2	([3])	([3])	(D)	(D)
Utilities..	22	8	6	([5])	37	(D)	2,498
Construction...	23	166	160	1,190	1,293	47,000	47,089
Manufacturing...	31-33	51	49	642	602	30,407	27,131
Wholesale trade.......................................	42	65	58	796	771	43,861	44,001
Retail trade...	44-45	541	535	6,300	6,086	138,875	136,588
Transportation and warehousing.......................	48-49	108	108	1,733	1,677	52,611	53,187
Information..	51	43	41	([6])	775	(D)	38,667
Finance and insurance................................	52	115	116	1,179	1,082	75,757	69,927
Real estate and rental and leasing.....................	53	197	196	1,116	1,002	40,582	39,465
Professional, scientific, and technical services........	54	245	240	982	979	51,056	52,316
Management of companies and enterprises...........	55	8	8	([5])	126	(D)	5,503
Administrative, support, waste mgmt, and remediation services..................................	56	169	165	2,196	2,132	68,126	78,406
Educational services..................................	61	38	33	702	673	19,062	18,636
Health care and social assistance.....................	62	268	259	3,084	3,152	133,073	136,423
Arts, entertainment, and recreation....................	71	58	55	600	676	13,849	15,625
Accommodation and food services....................	72	297	297	6,822	6,966	168,995	175,918
Other services (except public administration)..........	81	212	214	1,150	1,015	30,661	27,112
Industries not classified...............................	99	17	28	([4])	56	(D)	888

X Not applicable. D Withheld to avoid disclosing data for individual companies; data are included in total. [1] Based on the 2012 North American Industry Classification System. See text, Section 15. [2] Covers full- and part-time employees who are on the payroll in the pay period including March 12. [3] 0 to 19 employees. [4] 20 to 99 employees. [5] 100 to 249 employees. [6] 500 to 999 employees.

Source: U.S. Census Bureau, County Business Patterns, "Geography Area Series: County Business Patterns for Puerto Rico and the Island Areas," <http://factfinder.census.gov/>, accessed April 2017. See also <https://www.census.gov/programs-surveys/cbp.html>.

Table 1347. Guam—Business Summary by Industry: 2014 and 2015

[Payroll in thousands of dollars (1,421,411 represents $1,421,411,000). Covers establishments with payroll. Excludes self-employed individuals, employees of private households, railroad employees, agricultural production employees, and most government employees. For statement on methodology, see Appendix III]

Industry	NAICS code [1]	Establishments		Paid employees [2]		Annual payroll ($1,000)	
		2014	2015	2014	2015	2014	2015
Total, all industries..........................	(X)	3,474	3,475	56,814	57,902	1,421,411	1,494,258
Agriculture, forestry, fishing and hunting........	11	2	2	([3])	([3])	(D)	(D)
Mining, quarrying, and oil and gas extraction...	21	1	1	([3])	([3])	(D)	(D)
Utilities..	22	6	5	([4])	61	(D)	3,216
Construction......................................	23	341	346	6,628	6,380	171,515	164,934
Manufacturing....................................	31-33	60	57	972	911	22,239	22,040
Wholesale trade.................................	42	205	200	2,749	2,849	75,729	80,587
Retail trade......................................	44-45	684	684	9,613	9,801	207,605	217,246
Transportation and warehousing................	48-49	100	99	([5])	2,782	(D)	106,025
Information.......................................	51	50	52	1,306	1,227	46,410	46,167
Finance and insurance..........................	52	130	128	2,195	2,230	86,941	89,093
Real estate and rental and leasing.............	53	259	263	1,904	2,083	48,333	52,006
Professional, scientific, and technical services..	54	259	262	2,525	2,646	104,691	111,557
Management of companies and enterprises....	55	10	9	135	68	7,239	3,340
Administrative, support, waste mgmt, and remediation services..........................	56	177	172	4,101	4,479	89,381	93,001
Educational services............................	61	65	60	1,209	1,255	25,825	26,390
Health care and social assistance..............	62	198	204	3,506	3,758	136,442	163,813
Arts, entertainment, and recreation.............	71	67	69	1,178	1,174	20,801	21,243
Accommodation and food services.............	72	519	518	13,314	13,496	211,827	231,928
Other services (except public administration)...	81	294	293	2,526	2,500	57,137	58,624
Industries not classified.........................	99	47	51	111	196	2,093	2,715

X Not applicable. D Withheld to avoid disclosing data for individual companies; data are included in total. [1] Based on the 2012 North American Industry Classification System. See text, Section 15. [2] Covers full- and part-time employees who are on the payroll in the pay period including March 12. [3] 0 to 19 employees. [4] 20 to 99 employees. [5] 2,500 to 4,999 employees.

Source: U.S. Census Bureau, County Business Patterns, "Geography Area Series: County Business Patterns for Puerto Rico and the Island Areas," <http://factfinder.census.gov/>, accessed April 2017. See also <http://www.census.gov/econ/cbp/>.

Table 1348. Northern Marianas—Business Summary by Industry: 2014 and 2015

[Payroll in thousands of dollars (194,709 represents $194,709,000). Covers establishments with payroll. Excludes self-employed individuals, employees of private households, railroad employees, agricultural production employees, and most government employees. For statement on methodology, see Appendix III]

Industry	NAICS code [1]	Establishments		Paid employees [2]		Annual payroll ($1,000)	
		2014	2015	2014	2015	2014	2015
Total, all industries..........................	(X)	1,425	1,724	12,078	16,276	194,709	301,267
Agriculture, forestry, fishing and hunting.........	11	3	2	([3])	([3])	45	(D)
Mining, quarrying, and oil and gas extraction. ..	21	1	1	([4])	([4])	(D)	(D)
Utilities..	22	4	4	([5])	([5])	(D)	(D)
Construction......................................	23	56	80	233	842	3,109	14,618
Manufacturing....................................	31-33	41	48	392	442	5,108	7,562
Wholesale trade.................................	42	71	83	573	681	8,694	12,208
Retail trade......................................	44-45	310	346	1,900	2,475	30,255	40,571
Transportation and warehousing................	48-49	42	48	991	1,038	15,948	18,614
Information.......................................	51	20	23	297	409	9,417	11,928
Finance and insurance..........................	52	50	47	328	277	7,172	7,468
Real estate and rental and leasing.............	53	115	163	435	563	5,716	8,355
Professional, scientific, and technical services..	54	86	102	321	556	8,777	11,868
Management of companies and enterprises....	55	5	5	([3])	24	(D)	689
Administrative, support, waste mgmt, and remediation services..........................	56	125	147	1,013	1,646	16,280	24,453
Educational services............................	61	61	68	291	340	4,576	5,905
Health care and social assistance..............	62	44	45	782	1,042	15,555	34,101
Arts, entertainment, and recreation.............	71	49	53	432	459	6,754	7,302
Accommodation and food services.............	72	168	195	3,086	4,203	38,400	69,733
Other services (except public administration). ..	81	137	166	445	651	6,412	9,570
Industries not classified.........................	99	37	98	73	217	639	2,267

X Not applicable. D Withheld to avoid disclosing data for individual companies; data are included in total. [1] Based on the 2012 North American Industry Classification System. See text, Section 15. [2] Covers full- and part-time employees who are on the payroll in the pay period including March 12. [3] 0 to 19 employees. [4] 20 to 99 employees. [5] 250 to 499 employees.

Source: U.S. Census Bureau, County Business Patterns, "Geography Area Series: County Business Patterns for Puerto Rico and the Island Areas," <http://factfinder.census.gov/>, accessed April 2017. See also <https://www.census.gov/programs-surveys/cbp.html>.

Table 1349. American Samoa—Business Summary by Industry: 2014 and 2015

[Payroll in thousands of dollars (133,551 represents $133,551,000). Covers establishments with payroll. Excludes self-employed individuals, employees of private households, railroad employees, agricultural production employees, and most government employees. For statement on methodology, see Appendix III]

Industry	NAICS code [1]	Establishments		Paid employees [2]		Annual payroll ($1,000)	
		2014	2015	2014	2015	2014	2015
Total, all industries.................................	(X)	480	486	7,761	8,156	133,551	140,751
Agriculture, forestry, fishing and hunting..........	11	2	1	([3])	([3])	(D)	(D)
Construction...	23	28	30	375	500	7,668	9,113
Manufacturing...	31-33	35	38	([7])	3,160	(D)	50,943
Wholesale trade..	42	23	25	240	264	4,329	4,784
Retail trade..	44-45	170	170	1,347	1,465	19,188	20,655
Transportation and warehousing....................	48-49	26	27	338	326	4,619	4,649
Information...	51	10	6	176	168	3,734	4,024
Finance and insurance...............................	52	11	10	([5])	110	(D)	2,735
Real estate and rental and leasing................	53	13	13	79	67	999	878
Professional, scientific, and technical services...	54	25	26	([5])	199	(D)	5,788
Management of companies and enterprises.....	55	2	2	([3])	([3])	(D)	(D)
Administrative, support, waste mgmt, remediation services................................	56	22	24	166	116	2,370	1,679
Educational services..................................	61	5	4	([5])	127	1,689	1,760
Health care and social assistance................	62	15	15	([6])	([6])	(D)	(D)
Arts, entertainment, and recreation...............	71	2	1	([3])	([3])	(D)	(D)
Accommodation and food services...............	72	41	40	556	448	6,228	6,335
Other services (except public administration)....	81	44	45	404	399	4,880	4,627
Industries not classified.............................	99	6	9	([4])	26	237	269

X Not applicable. D Withheld to avoid disclosing data for individual companies; data are included in total. [1] Based on the 2012 North American Industry Classification System. See text, Section 15. [2] Covers full- and part-time employees who are on the payroll in the pay period including March 12. [3] 0 to 19 employees. [4] 20 to 99 employees. [5] 100 to 249 employees. [6] 500 to 999 employees. [7] 2,500 to 4,999 employees.

Source: U.S. Census Bureau, County Business Patterns, "Geography Area Series: County Business Patterns for Puerto Rico and the Island Areas," <http://factfinder.census.gov/>, accessed April 2017. See also <https://www.census.gov/programs-surveys/cbp.html>.

Section 30
International Statistics

This section presents statistics for the world as a whole and for many countries on a comparative basis with the United States. Data are shown for population, births and deaths, social and economic indicators, finances, agriculture, energy, climate, science and technology, communications, and military affairs.

Statistics for individual countries may be found primarily in official national publications, generally in the form of yearbooks, issued by most countries in their own national languages and expressed in their own customary units of measure. For a listing of selected publications, see Appendix I table under international statistical abstracts from a foreign agency.

For international comparisons, the United Nations Statistics Division compiles data as submitted by member countries and issues a number of summary publications, generally in English and French. Among these are the annual *Statistical Yearbook; Demographic Yearbook; Population and Vital Statistics Report; International Trade Statistics Yearbook; Energy Statistics Yearbook; Industrial Commodity Statistics Yearbook; National Accounts Statistics;* and the *Monthly Bulletin of Statistics.* Specialized agencies of the United Nations also issue international summary publications on various topics, including agricultural, labor, health, and trade statistics. Among these are *Food Outlook* and the *Statistical Pocketbook* issued by the Food and Agriculture Organization (FAO); *World Employment and Social Outlook* issued by the International Labor Organization (ILO); *World Health Statistics* issued by the World Health Organization (WHO); and the *Handbook of Statistics* issued by the Conference on Trade and Development (UNCTAD).

The U.S. Census Bureau publishes estimates and projections of key demographic measures for countries and regions of the world in its International Data Base at <http://www.census.gov/population/international/>.

The International Monetary Fund (IMF), the World Bank, and the Organisation for Economic Co-operation and Development (OECD) also compile international statistics. The IMF publishes a series of reports related to financial data. These include *World Economic Outlook, Global Financial Stability Report,* and *Fiscal Monitor.* The World Bank publishes many reports on a wide range of topics related to international development. Three of their flagship statistical publications are *World Development Report, World Development Indicators,* and *Global Economic Prospects.* The OECD also produces numerous statistical publications in fields including economics, health, and education. Among these are the *OECD Factbook; Economic Outlook; National Accounts of OECD Countries; Science, Technology and Innovation Outlook; International Migration Outlook; Employment Outlook;* and *Education at a Glance.*

Statistical coverage and country classifications—
Problems of space and availability of data limit the number of countries and the extent of statistical coverage shown. The lists of countries and territories

included in individual tables are generally based on source publications and databases, as cited.

In the last quarter-century, several important changes took place in the status of the world's nations. In 1991, the Soviet Union broke up into 15 independent countries: Armenia, Azerbaijan, Belarus, Estonia, Georgia, Kazakhstan, Kyrgyzstan, Latvia, Lithuania, Moldova, Russia, Tajikistan, Turkmenistan, Ukraine, and Uzbekistan.

Germany was reunified in 1990, when the German Democratic Republic (former East Germany) joined the Federal Republic of Germany (former West Germany) to form a single country. On January 1, 1993, Czechoslovakia was succeeded by two independent countries: the Czech Republic and Slovakia.

Following the breakup of the Socialist Federal Republic of Yugoslavia in 1992, the United States recognized Bosnia and Herzegovina, Croatia, Slovenia, and Macedonia as independent countries. Serbia and Montenegro, both former republics of Yugoslavia, became independent of one another on May 31, 2006. This separation is reflected in the population estimates of Table 1353, but some tables may still show both countries as combined. On February 17, 2008, Kosovo declared its independence from Serbia.

The Treaty of Maastricht created the European Union (EU) in 1992 with 12 member countries. The EU is not a state intended to replace existing states, but it is more than just an international organization. Its member states have set up common institutions to which they delegate some of their sovereignty so that decisions on specific matters of joint interest can be made democratically at a European level. This pooling of sovereignty is also called "European integration." The EU has grown in size with successive waves of accessions in 1995, 2004, 2007, and 2013. The 28 current members of the EU are: Austria, Belgium, Bulgaria, Croatia, Cyprus, Czech Republic, Denmark, Estonia, Finland, France, Germany, Greece, Hungary, Ireland, Italy, Latvia, Lithuania, Luxembourg, Malta, the Netherlands, Poland, Portugal, Romania, Slovakia, Slovenia, Spain, Sweden, and the United Kingdom. In June 2016, the electorate of the United Kingdom voted to withdraw from the EU. Negotiations for the exit have begun, but withdrawal is not expected to be complete until 2019. Until that time, the UK remains a full member of the EU.

In 1992, the EU decided to establish an economic and monetary union (EMU), with the introduction of a single European currency managed by a European Central Bank. The single currency—the euro—became a reality on January 1, 2002, when euro notes and coins replaced national currencies in 12 of the then 15 countries of the European Union (Belgium, Germany, Greece, Spain, France, Ireland, Italy, Luxembourg, the Netherlands, Austria, Portugal, and Finland). Since then, 13 additional countries have acceded to EU membership, but Cyprus, Estonia, Latvia, Lithuania, Malta, Slovakia, and Slovenia have been the only new members of the EU to adopt the euro as the national currency.

Elsewhere in the world, Eritrea announced its independence from Ethiopia in April 1993 and was subsequently recognized as an independent nation by the United States. In the South Pacific, the Marshall Islands, Micronesia, and Palau gained independence from the United States in 1991. In May of 2002, Timor-Leste won independence from Indonesia. The Netherlands Antilles dissolved on October 10, 2010. As a result, Curaçao and Sint Maarten became autonomous territories of the Netherlands. Most recently, Sudan and South Sudan became separate countries as of July 2011.

The population estimates and projections used in Tables 1350 through 1353, 1355, and 1356 were prepared by the U.S. Census Bureau. For each country, available data on population by age and sex, fertility, mortality, and international migration were evaluated and, where necessary, adjusted for inconsistencies and errors in the data. Comprehensive population projections were made by the cohort-component method based on an assessment of probable future trends.

Economic associations—The Organisation for European Economic Co–operation (OEEC) was originally a regional grouping of Western European countries established in 1948 for the purpose of harmonizing national economic policies and conditions. It was succeeded on September 30, 1961 by the Organisation for Economic Co-operation and Development (OECD). The current member nations of the OECD are Australia, Austria, Belgium, Canada, Chile, Czech Republic, Denmark, Estonia, Finland, France, Germany, Greece, Hungary, Iceland, Ireland, Israel, Italy, Japan, Latvia, Luxembourg, Mexico, the Netherlands, New Zealand, Norway, Poland, Portugal, Slovak Republic, Slovenia, South Korea, Spain, Sweden, Switzerland, Turkey, the United Kingdom, and the United States.

Quality and comparability of the data—The quality and comparability of the data presented here are affected by a number of factors:

1. The year for which data are presented may not be the same for all subjects for a particular country or for a given subject for different countries, though the data shown are the most recent available. All such variations have been noted. The data shown are for calendar years except as otherwise specified.

2. The statistical bases, methods of estimating, methods of data collection, extent of coverage, precision of definition, scope of territory, and margins of error may vary for different items within a particular country, and for like items for different countries. Footnotes and headnotes to the tables describe some of the major coverage qualifications attached to the figures; considerably more detail is presented in the source publications. Many of the measures shown are merely rough indicators of magnitude.

3. Figures shown in this section for the United States may not always agree with figures shown in the preceding sections. Discrepancies may be attributable to the use of differing original sources,

differences in the definition of geographic limits (the 50 states, continental U.S. only, or the U.S. including certain outlying areas and possessions), or to possible adjustments made to the U.S. figures in order to make them more comparable with figures from other countries.

International comparisons of national accounts data—To compare national accounts data for different countries, it is necessary to convert each country's data into a common unit of currency, usually the U.S. dollar. The market exchange rates, which often are used in converting national currencies, do not necessarily reflect the relative purchasing power in the various countries. It is necessary that the goods and services produced in different countries be valued consistently if the differences observed are meant to reflect real differences in the volumes of goods and services produced. The use of purchasing power parities (see Tables 1364, 1365, and 1371) instead of exchange rates is intended to achieve this objective.

The method used to present the data shown in Table 1371 is to construct volume measures directly by revaluing the goods and services sold in different countries at a common set of international prices. By dividing the ratio of the gross domestic products of two countries expressed in their own national currencies by the corresponding ratio calculated at constant international prices, it is possible to derive the implied purchasing power parity (PPP) between the two currencies concerned. PPPs show how many units of currency are needed in one country to buy the same amount of goods and services that one unit of currency will buy in the other country. For further information, see *National Accounts of OECD Countries, Volume I, Main Aggregates*, issued annually by the Organisation for Economic Co-operation and Development (OECD), Paris, France.

International Standard Industrial Classification—The original version of the International Standard Industrial Classification of All Economic Activities (ISIC) was adopted in 1948. A number of countries have utilized ISIC as the basis for devising their industrial classification schemes. Substantial comparability has been attained among the industrial classification schemes of many countries, including the United States, by ensuring that national classification categories correspond to ISIC categories. The United Nations, the International Labour Organization, the Food and Agriculture Organization, and other international bodies use ISIC in publishing and analyzing statistical data. Revisions of ISIC were issued in 1958, 1968, 1989, 2002, and 2008.

International Maps—A series of regional world maps is provided within this section. References are included in Table 1353 for easy location of individual countries on the maps. Map projection will be distorted due to being portrayed on a flat surface. For additional information and maps see the Central Intelligence Agency's *The World Factbook*, at <https://www.cia.gov/library/publications/the-world-factbook/docs/refmaps.html>.

Political Map of the World, June 2012

Scale: 1:36,000,000

Lambert Conformal Conic Projection,
standard parallels 25°N and 77°N

803541AI(G00694)6-12

Scale 1:35,000,000
Azimuthal Equal-Area Projection

0   500 Kilometers

0   500 Miles

Boundary representation is
not necessarily authoritative.

Scale 1:19,300,000
Lambert Conformal Conic Projection,
standard parallels 40°N and 68°N

803539AI (G00772) 6-12

Golan Heights is Israeli-occupied Syria.

West Bank is Israeli-occupied with current status subject to the Israeli-Palestinian Interim Agreement; permanent status to be determined through further negotiation.

The status of the Gaza Strip is a final status issue to be resolved through negotiations.

Israel proclaimed Jerusalem as its capital in 1950, but the US, like nearly all other countries, maintains its Embassy in Tel Aviv-Yafo.

Scale 1:21,000,000
Lambert Conformal Conic Projection, standard parallels 12°N and 38°N

0   300 Kilometers
0   300 Miles

Boundary representation is not necessarily authoritative.

803540AI (G00412) 6-12

Scale 1:48,000,000

Azimuthal Equal-Area Projection

0 800 Kilometers
0 800 Miles

Boundary representation is
not necessarily authoritative.

803537AI (G00543) 6-12

North Pacific Ocean

South Pacific Ocean

AUSTRALIA

INDONESIA

PHILIPPINES

PAPUA NEW GUINEA

NEW ZEALAND

KIRIBATI

TUVALU

VANUATU

TONGA

French Polynesia (FRANCE)

Cook Islands (N.Z.)

SOLOMON ISLANDS

FEDERATED STATES OF MICRONESIA

MARSHALL ISLANDS

PALAU

NAURU

FIJI

SAMOA

Indian Ocean

Tasman Sea

Coral Sea

Philippine Sea

CHINA

Scale 1:41,000,000

Miranda Projection

Table 1350. Total World Population and Population Projections: 1980 to 2050

[4,445.4 represents 4,445,400,000. As of midyear]

Year	Population (mil.)	Average annual [1] Growth rate (percent)	Average annual [1] Population change (mil.)	Year	Population (mil.)	Average annual [1] Growth rate (percent)	Average annual [1] Population change (mil.)
1980............	4,445.4	1.83	81.39	2020............	7,636.1	0.98	74.54
1990............	5,284.3	1.58	83.24	2025............	7,997.5	0.86	68.90
2000............	6,084.7	1.25	76.19	2030............	8,330.5	0.76	63.18
2005............	6,467.4	1.20	77.79	2035............	8,636.2	0.67	58.11
2010............	6,858.6	1.13	77.41	2040............	8,917.3	0.60	53.31
2015............	7,247.9	1.08	78.10	2045............	9,174.1	0.53	48.28
2017............	**7,405.1**	**1.05**	**77.94**	2050............	9,404.8	(NA)	(NA)

NA Not available. [1] Represents change from year shown to immediate succeeding year.

Source: U.S. Census Bureau, International Programs Data, "World Population Summary," <http://www.census.gov/population/international/data/>, accessed September 2017.

Table 1351. Population by Continent: 1980 to 2050

[In millions, except percent (4,445.4 represents 4,445,400,000). As of midyear. For geographic classification of individual countries, see source]

Year	World	Africa	North America [1]	South America	Asia	Europe	Oceania
1980.................................	4,445.4	479.5	370.8	239.7	2,637.7	695.2	22.5
1990.................................	5,284.3	632.0	423.3	295.4	3,184.5	722.6	26.4
2000.................................	6,084.7	805.9	485.5	346.3	3,686.1	730.5	30.4
2010.................................	6,858.6	1,031.7	538.9	391.3	4,121.5	740.2	34.9
2017.................................	**7,405.1**	**1,222.2**	**574.6**	**418.5**	**4,404.4**	**747.4**	**38.0**
2020.................................	7,636.1	1,309.9	589.8	429.3	4,518.2	749.6	39.3
2030.................................	8,330.5	1,624.8	635.8	460.2	4,819.7	747.0	43.0
2040.................................	8,917.3	1,972.1	671.4	480.9	5,011.1	735.8	46.1
2050.................................	9,404.8	2,341.0	697.7	490.1	5,110.9	716.7	48.4
PERCENT DISTRIBUTION							
1980.................................	100.0	10.8	8.3	5.4	59.3	15.6	0.5
1990.................................	100.0	12.0	8.0	5.6	60.3	13.7	0.5
2000.................................	100.0	13.2	8.0	5.7	60.6	12.0	0.5
2010.................................	100.0	15.0	7.9	5.7	60.1	10.8	0.5
2017.................................	**100.0**	**16.5**	**7.8**	**5.7**	**59.5**	**10.1**	**0.5**
2020.................................	100.0	17.2	7.7	5.6	59.2	9.8	0.5
2030.................................	100.0	19.5	7.6	5.5	57.9	9.0	0.5
2040.................................	100.0	22.1	7.5	5.4	56.2	8.3	0.5
2050.................................	100.0	24.9	7.4	5.2	54.3	7.6	0.5

[1] Data for North America include Central America and Caribbean area.

Source: U.S. Census Bureau, "International Data Base (IDB)," <http://www.census.gov/population/international/data/>, accessed September 2017.

Table 1352. Population and Population Change by Development Status: 1950 to 2050

[2,557.6 represents 2,557,600,000. As of midyear. Minus sign (-) indicates decrease. "Less developed" countries include all of Africa, all of Asia except Japan, the Transcaucasian and Central Asian republics, all of Latin America and the Caribbean, and all of Oceania except Australia and New Zealand. For details on classification of individual countries, see source]

Year	Number (millions) World	Number (millions) Less developed countries	Number (millions) More developed countries	Percent of world Less developed countries	Percent of world More developed countries
POPULATION					
1950............................	2,557.6	1,750.6	807.1	68.4	31.6
1960............................	3,043.0	2,132.2	910.8	70.1	29.9
1970............................	3,713.3	2,709.7	1,003.6	73.0	27.0
1980............................	4,445.4	3,363.7	1,081.7	75.7	24.3
1990............................	5,284.3	4,140.2	1,144.1	78.3	21.7
2000............................	6,084.7	4,891.2	1,193.5	80.4	19.6
2010............................	6,858.6	5,621.8	1,236.8	82.0	18.0
2017............................	**7,405.1**	**6,141.2**	**1,263.9**	**82.9**	**17.1**
2020............................	7,636.1	6,361.4	1,274.7	83.3	16.7
2030............................	8,330.5	7,033.7	1,296.8	84.4	15.6
2040............................	8,917.3	7,613.8	1,303.5	85.4	14.6
2050............................	9,404.8	8,107.1	1,297.7	86.2	13.8
POPULATION CHANGE					
1950 to 1960..................	485.4	381.7	103.7	78.6	21.4
1960 to 1970..................	670.3	577.5	92.9	86.1	13.9
1970 to 1980..................	732.1	654.0	78.1	89.3	10.7
1980 to 1990..................	838.8	776.5	62.3	92.6	7.4
1990 to 2000..................	800.5	751.0	49.5	93.8	6.2
2000 to 2010..................	773.9	730.6	43.3	94.4	5.6
2010 to 2020..................	777.5	739.6	37.9	95.1	4.9
2020 to 2030..................	694.4	672.3	22.1	96.8	3.2
2030 to 2040..................	586.8	580.1	6.6	98.9	1.1
2040 to 2050..................	487.6	493.3	-5.8	101.2	-1.2

Source: U.S. Census Bureau, "International Data Base (IDB)," <http://www.census.gov/population/international/data>, accessed September 2017.

Table 1353. Population and Land Area by Country or Territory: 2000 to 2020

[6,084,704 represents 6,084,704,000. Covers countries or territories with populations of 5,000 or more in 2017. Population estimates were derived from information available as of August 2017. See text of this section for general comments concerning the data. For details of methodology, coverage, and reliability, see source. Minus sign (-) indicates decrease]

Country or territory	Map refer-ence [1]	Mid-year population (1,000)				Popula-tion rank, 2017	Annual growth rate [2], 2010 to 2020	Popula-tion per sq. mile, 2017	Land area [3], (sq. mile)
		2000	2010	2017	2020 (P)				
World	**S0**	**6,084,704**	**6,858,585**	**7,405,108**	**7,636,084**	**(X)**	**1.07**	**146**	**50,854,965**
Afghanistan	S7	22,461	29,121	34,125	36,644	39	2.30	136	251,827
Albania	S4	3,158	2,987	3,048	3,075	136	0.29	288	10,578
Algeria	S5	30,638	35,950	40,969	42,973	33	1.78	45	919,595
Andorra	S4	65	85	86	86	200	0.13	474	181
Angola	S5	15,657	22,641	29,310	32,522	46	3.62	61	481,354
Antigua and Barbuda	S2	75	87	95	98	197	1.24	554	171
Argentina	S3	37,336	41,358	44,293	45,479	31	0.95	42	1,056,642
Armenia	S6	3,100	3,072	3,045	3,021	137	-0.17	280	10,889
Australia	S8	19,053	21,516	23,232	23,939	56	1.07	8	2,966,153
Austria	S4	8,113	8,448	8,754	8,859	95	0.48	275	31,832
Azerbaijan	S6	8,463	9,302	9,961	10,206	90	0.93	312	31,903
Bahamas, The	S2	283	310	330	338	179	0.84	85	3,865
Bahrain	S6	655	1,180	1,411	1,505	155	2.43	4,808	293
Bangladesh	S7	128,735	146,616	157,827	162,651	8	1.04	3,140	50,259
Barbados	S2	274	286	292	295	180	0.31	1,761	166
Belarus	S4	10,033	9,680	9,550	9,478	93	-0.21	122	78,340
Belgium	S4	10,264	10,866	11,491	11,721	77	0.76	983	11,690
Belize	S2	248	315	360	380	177	1.88	41	8,805
Benin	S5	6,619	9,056	11,039	11,956	82	2.78	258	42,711
Bhutan	S7	606	700	758	782	165	1.11	51	14,824
Bolivia	S3	8,195	9,947	11,138	11,640	81	1.57	27	418,265
Bosnia and Herzegovina	S4	3,806	3,885	3,856	3,836	128	-0.13	195	19,763
Botswana	S5	1,655	1,978	2,215	2,317	144	1.58	10	218,816
Brazil	S3	174,315	195,834	207,353	211,716	5	0.78	64	3,227,096
Brunei	S8	325	395	444	464	174	1.62	218	2,033
Bulgaria	S4	7,909	7,391	7,102	6,967	103	-0.59	170	41,888
Burkina Faso	S5	11,588	16,242	20,108	21,978	59	3.02	190	105,715
Burma	S7	46,641	51,415	55,124	56,590	24	0.96	218	252,321
Burundi	S5	6,716	9,121	11,467	12,632	78	3.26	1,156	9,915
Cabo Verde	S5	430	509	561	583	173	1.37	360	1,557
Cambodia	S7	12,351	14,454	16,204	16,927	68	1.58	238	68,153
Cameroon	S5	15,818	20,822	24,995	26,969	53	2.59	137	182,514
Canada	S1	31,100	33,760	35,624	36,387	38	0.75	10	3,511,023
Central African Republic	S5	3,980	4,845	5,625	5,991	115	2.12	23	240,535
Chad	S5	7,943	10,543	12,076	12,756	75	1.90	25	486,180
Chile	S3	15,175	16,760	17,789	18,187	65	0.82	62	287,187
China	S7	1,268,302	1,336,681	1,379,303	1,394,016	1	0.42	383	3,600,947
Colombia	S3	38,910	44,205	47,699	49,085	29	1.05	119	401,044
Comoros	S5	545	706	808	846	163	1.81	936	863
Congo, Republic of	S5	2,939	4,238	4,955	5,293	122	2.22	38	131,854
Congo, Democratic Republic	S5	52,445	69,851	83,301	89,250	16	2.45	95	875,312
Costa Rica	S2	3,883	4,516	4,930	5,098	123	1.21	250	19,714
Cote d'Ivoire	S5	16,885	21,059	24,185	25,504	54	1.92	197	122,782
Croatia	S4	4,390	4,417	4,292	4,228	127	-0.44	199	21,612
Cuba	S2	11,147	11,262	11,147	11,059	80	-0.18	263	42,402
Cyprus	S6	920	1,103	1,222	1,267	159	1.39	342	3,568
Czech Republic	S4	10,269	10,551	10,675	10,702	87	0.14	358	29,825
Denmark	S4	5,337	5,516	5,606	5,642	116	0.23	342	16,384
Djibouti	S5	669	741	865	922	162	2.19	97	8,950
Dominica	S2	71	73	74	74	202	0.19	255	290
Dominican Republic	S2	8,469	9,824	10,734	11,109	86	1.23	575	18,656
Ecuador	S3	12,446	14,791	16,291	16,905	67	1.34	152	106,889
Egypt	S5	65,504	81,239	97,041	104,124	14	2.48	252	384,345
El Salvador	S2	5,850	6,052	6,172	6,217	108	0.27	771	8,000
Equatorial Guinea	S5	491	651	778	836	164	2.51	72	10,831
Eritrea	S5	3,884	5,365	5,919	6,081	112	1.25	152	38,996
Estonia	S4	1,380	1,303	1,252	1,229	158	-0.59	76	16,366
Ethiopia	S5	64,365	86,043	105,350	114,640	12	2.87	273	386,102
Fiji	S8	805	876	921	936	161	0.66	131	7,056
Finland	S4	5,169	5,355	5,518	5,572	117	0.40	47	117,304
France	S4	61,255	64,941	67,106	67,848	21	0.44	271	247,270
Gabon	S5	1,236	1,545	1,772	1,877	153	1.94	18	99,486
Gambia, The	S5	1,357	1,755	2,051	2,174	146	2.14	525	3,907
Georgia	S6	4,819	4,903	4,926	4,930	124	0.06	183	26,911
Germany	S4	82,184	81,644	80,594	80,160	19	-0.18	599	134,623
Ghana	S5	18,981	23,571	27,500	29,340	49	2.19	313	87,851
Greece	S4	10,559	10,750	10,768	10,742	85	-0.01	213	50,443
Grenada	S2	102	108	112	113	190	0.48	841	133
Guatemala	S2	11,085	13,550	15,461	16,264	70	1.83	374	41,374
Guinea	S5	8,350	10,324	12,414	13,420	74	2.62	131	94,872
Guinea-Bissau	S5	1,279	1,565	1,792	1,893	152	1.90	165	10,857
Guyana	S3	785	746	738	750	166	0.06	10	76,004
Haiti	S2	8,279	9,553	10,647	11,068	88	1.47	1,001	10,641
Honduras	S2	6,359	7,989	9,039	9,465	94	1.69	209	43,201
Hungary	S4	10,147	9,992	9,851	9,772	92	-0.22	285	34,598
Iceland	S1	281	318	340	351	178	0.98	9	38,707
India	S7	1,006,300	1,173,108	1,281,936	1,326,093	2	1.23	1,117	1,147,956
Indonesia	S8	214,091	243,423	260,581	267,026	4	0.93	373	699,451
Iran	S6	66,482	75,035	82,022	84,923	17	1.24	139	591,352
Iraq	S6	23,128	30,526	39,192	42,213	35	3.24	232	168,868

See footnotes at end of table.

Table 1353. Population and Land Area by Country or Territory: 2000 to 2020-Continued.

See headnote on page 865.

Country or territory	Map refer-ence [1]	Mid-year population (1,000)				Popula-tion rank, 2017	Annual growth rate [2], 2010 to 2020	Popula-tion per sq. mile, 2017	Land area [3], (sq. mile)
		2000	2010	2017	2020 (P)				
Ireland....................	S4	3,822	4,623	5,011	5,177	121	1.13	188	26,596
Israel.....................	S6	6,097	7,368	8,300	8,675	97	1.63	1,057	7,849
Italy.....................	S4	57,784	60,749	62,138	62,403	23	0.27	547	113,568
Jamaica...................	S2	2,616	2,847	2,991	3,051	138	0.69	715	4,182
Japan.....................	S7	126,776	127,579	126,451	125,507	10	-0.16	899	140,728
Jordan....................	S6	4,785	6,800	10,248	10,821	89	4.64	299	34,287
Kazakhstan................	S7	15,687	17,085	18,557	19,092	62	1.11	18	1,042,360
Kenya.....................	S5	30,606	40,843	47,616	49,858	30	1.99	217	219,746
Kiribati..................	S8	85	99	108	112	191	1.17	345	313
Korea, North..............	S7	22,785	24,326	25,248	25,643	51	0.53	543	46,490
Korea, South..............	S7	46,841	49,258	51,181	51,835	27	0.51	1,368	37,421
Kosovo....................	S4	1,700	1,815	1,895	1,933	150	0.63	451	4,203
Kuwait....................	S6	1,972	2,543	2,875	2,994	139	1.63	418	6,880
Kyrgyzstan................	S6	4,937	5,410	5,789	5,965	114	0.98	78	74,055
Laos......................	S7	5,397	6,368	7,127	7,447	101	1.57	80	89,112
Latvia....................	S4	2,368	2,115	1,945	1,881	149	-1.17	81	24,034
Lebanon...................	S6	3,834	4,492	6,230	5,470	107	1.97	1,577	3,950
Lesotho...................	S5	1,916	1,920	1,958	1,969	148	0.26	167	11,720
Liberia...................	S5	2,847	3,817	4,689	5,073	125	2.84	126	37,189
Libya.....................	S5	5,025	6,110	6,653	6,943	106	1.28	10	679,362
Liechtenstein.............	S4	33	36	38	39	213	0.80	619	62
Lithuania.................	S4	3,489	3,089	2,824	2,731	140	-1.23	117	24,201
Luxembourg................	S4	438	509	594	628	171	2.10	595	998
Macedonia.................	S4	2,015	2,072	2,104	2,113	145	0.19	214	9,820
Madagascar................	S5	15,712	20,847	25,054	26,956	52	2.57	112	224,534
Malawi....................	S5	11,129	15,183	19,196	21,197	61	3.34	528	36,324
Malaysia..................	S8	23,151	28,275	31,382	32,652	41	1.44	247	126,895
Maldives..................	S7	300	396	393	392	176	-0.10	3,413	115
Mali......................	S5	10,844	14,514	17,885	19,553	64	2.98	38	471,118
Malta.....................	S4	390	407	416	419	175	0.30	3,412	122
Marshall Islands..........	S8	53	66	75	78	201	1.68	1,067	70
Mauritania................	S5	2,501	3,205	3,759	4,005	129	2.23	9	397,955
Mauritius.................	S5	1,186	1,294	1,356	1,379	156	0.64	1,731	784
Mexico....................	S1	99,775	114,061	124,575	128,650	11	1.20	166	750,561
Micronesia, Federated States of....	S8	108	107	104	102	194	-0.45	384	271
Moldova...................	S4	4,180	3,732	3,474	3,364	131	-1.04	274	12,699
Monaco....................	S4	32	31	31	31	217	0.12	39,685	1
Mongolia..................	S7	2,461	2,783	3,068	3,168	135	1.29	5	599,831
Montenegro................	S4	732	667	643	639	168	-0.42	124	5,194
Morocco...................	S5	28,113	31,627	33,987	34,956	40	1.00	197	172,317
Mozambique................	S5	17,997	22,417	26,574	28,603	50	2.44	88	303,623
Namibia...................	S5	1,878	2,183	2,485	2,630	142	1.86	8	317,874
Nauru.....................	S8	10	9	10	10	223	0.54	1,189	8
Nepal.....................	S7	23,487	26,664	29,384	30,328	45	1.29	531	55,348
Netherlands...............	S4	15,930	16,574	17,085	17,280	66	0.42	1,306	13,086
New Zealand...............	S8	3,802	4,252	4,510	4,615	126	0.82	44	102,138
Nicaragua.................	S2	4,866	5,604	6,026	6,203	111	1.02	130	46,328
Niger.....................	S5	10,725	15,270	19,245	21,151	60	3.26	39	489,076
Nigeria...................	S5	123,945	160,341	190,632	204,909	7	2.45	542	351,649
Norway....................	S4	4,492	4,891	5,320	5,467	120	1.11	45	117,484
Oman......................	S6	2,432	2,968	3,424	3,635	132	2.03	29	119,499
Pakistan..................	S6	152,429	184,405	204,925	213,719	6	1.48	689	297,637
Palau.....................	S8	19	21	21	22	219	0.38	121	177
Panama....................	S2	2,900	3,411	3,753	3,894	130	1.33	131	28,703
Papua New Guinea..........	S8	4,813	6,065	6,910	7,259	105	1.80	40	174,850
Paraguay..................	S3	5,418	6,376	6,944	7,192	104	1.20	45	153,399
Peru......................	S3	25,797	28,948	31,037	31,915	43	0.98	63	494,209
Philippines..............	S7	76,452	93,137	104,256	109,181	13	1.59	906	115,124
Poland....................	S4	38,654	38,616	38,476	38,282	36	-0.09	328	117,474
Portugal..................	S4	10,336	10,736	10,840	10,842	84	0.10	307	35,317
Qatar.....................	S6	640	1,719	2,314	2,444	143	3.52	517	4,473
Romania...................	S4	22,447	21,959	21,530	21,303	58	-0.30	243	88,761
Russia....................	S7	147,054	142,527	142,258	141,722	9	-0.06	22	6,323,482
Rwanda....................	S5	8,047	9,923	11,901	12,712	76	2.48	1,250	9,524
Saint Kitts and Nevis.....	S2	46	50	53	54	207	0.76	523	101
Saint Lucia...............	S2	153	161	165	166	187	0.34	705	234
Saint Vincent and the Grenadines..	S2	108	104	102	101	195	-0.28	680	150
Samoa.....................	S8	176	192	200	204	185	0.60	184	1,089
San Marino................	S4	27	31	34	34	215	0.84	1,424	24
Sao Tome and Principe.....	S5	141	176	201	211	184	1.83	540	372
Saudi Arabia..............	S6	21,312	25,732	28,572	29,819	47	1.47	34	830,000
Senegal...................	S5	9,469	12,323	14,669	15,736	71	2.44	197	74,336
Serbia....................	S4	7,604	7,345	7,111	7,012	102	-0.46	238	29,913
Seychelles................	S5	79	88	94	96	198	0.83	535	176
Sierra Leone..............	S5	3,809	5,246	6,163	6,625	109	2.33	223	27,653
Singapore.................	S8	4,063	5,140	5,889	6,210	113	1.89	22,201	265
Slovakia..................	S4	5,400	5,426	5,446	5,441	118	0.03	293	18,573
Slovenia..................	S4	2,011	2,003	1,972	1,951	147	-0.26	253	7,780
Solomon Islands...........	S8	434	559	648	685	167	2.03	60	10,805
Somalia...................	S5	7,501	9,768	11,031	11,757	83	1.85	46	242,216
South Africa..............	S5	44,913	51,123	54,842	56,464	25	0.99	117	468,909
South Sudan [4]...........	S5	6,296	9,584	13,026	14,558	73	4.18	52	248,777

See footnotes at end of table.

Table 1353. Population and Land Area by Country or Territory: 2000 to 2020-Continued.

See headnote on page 865.

Country or territory	Map refer- ence [1]	Mid-year population (1,000)				Popula- tion rank, 2017	Annual growth rate [2], 2010 to 2020	Popula- tion per sq. mile, 2017	Land area [3], (sq. mile)
		2000	2010	2017	2020 (P)				
Spain	S4	40,589	46,506	48,958	50,016	28	0.73	254	192,657
Sri Lanka	S7	19,041	21,084	22,409	22,889	57	0.82	898	24,954
Sudan [4]	S5	27,067	32,997	37,346	39,161	37	1.71	52	718,723
Suriname	S3	464	546	592	610	172	1.10	10	60,232
Swaziland	S5	1,144	1,354	1,467	1,513	154	1.11	221	6,643
Sweden	S4	8,924	9,432	9,960	10,202	91	0.78	63	158,431
Switzerland	S4	7,277	7,770	8,236	8,404	98	0.78	533	15,443
Syria	S6	16,514	21,766	18,029	22,346	63	0.26	254	70,900
Taiwan	S7	22,185	23,127	23,508	23,603	55	0.20	1,887	12,456
Tajikistan	S7	6,230	7,487	8,469	8,874	96	1.70	155	54,637
Tanzania	S5	33,193	44,288	53,951	58,553	26	2.79	158	342,009
Thailand	S7	62,902	66,720	68,414	68,997	20	0.33	347	197,256
Timor-Leste	S8	767	1,088	1,291	1,384	157	2.41	225	5,743
Togo	S5	4,992	6,587	7,965	8,608	99	2.68	379	20,998
Tonga	S8	100	106	106	106	193	0.04	385	277
Trinidad and Tobago	S2	1,252	1,229	1,218	1,209	160	-0.16	615	1,980
Tunisia	S5	9,546	10,526	11,404	11,721	79	1.08	190	59,985
Turkey	S6	65,970	74,687	80,845	82,018	18	0.94	272	297,157
Turkmenistan	S6	4,385	4,941	5,351	5,529	119	1.12	29	181,441
Tuvalu	S8	10	10	11	11	222	0.80	1,101	10
Uganda	S5	22,916	31,507	39,570	43,518	34	3.23	520	76,101
Ukraine	S4	49,014	45,768	44,034	43,923	32	-0.41	197	223,681
United Arab Emirates	S6	3,219	4,976	6,072	6,495	110	2.67	188	32,278
United Kingdom	S4	59,140	62,348	64,769	65,761	22	0.53	693	93,410
United States	**S1**	**282,162**	**309,348**	**326,626**	**334,503**	**3**	**0.78**	**92**	**3,531,905**
Uruguay	S3	3,220	3,301	3,360	3,388	133	0.26	50	67,574
Uzbekistan	S6	25,042	27,866	29,749	30,565	44	0.92	181	164,248
Vanuatu	S8	191	245	283	298	182	1.96	60	4,706
Venezuela	S3	24,249	28,481	31,304	32,442	42	1.30	92	340,561
Vietnam	S7	79,178	89,571	96,160	98,721	15	0.97	803	119,719
Yemen	S6	17,236	23,210	28,037	29,884	48	2.53	138	203,850
Zambia	S5	9,984	13,042	15,972	17,427	69	2.90	56	287,028
Zimbabwe	S5	12,047	12,722	13,805	14,546	72	1.34	92	149,362
TERRITORIES AND DEPENDENCIES									
American Samoa	S8	58	56	52	49	210	-1.16	670	77
Anguilla	S1	11	15	17	18	220	2.03	486	35
Aruba	S1	90	105	115	119	189	1.33	1,656	69
Bermuda	S1	63	68	71	72	203	0.50	3,399	21
Cayman Islands	S1	38	50	58	62	205	2.10	573	102
Cook Islands	S8	16	11	9	9	224	-2.93	102	91
Curacao [5]	S2	134	143	150	151	188	0.54	873	171
Faroe Islands	S4	46	49	51	52	211	0.51	94	538
French Polynesia	S8	236	269	288	295	181	0.93	195	1,478
Gaza Strip [6]	S6	1,128	1,503	1,795	1,918	151	2.44	12,915	139
Gibraltar	S4	27	29	29	30	218	0.24	10,876	3
Greenland	S1	57	58	58	58	206	(-Z)	(Z)	836,330
Guam	S8	155	163	167	168	186	0.31	797	210
Guernsey	S4	62	65	67	67	204	0.35	2,208	30
Hong Kong	S7	6,656	7,029	7,192	7,250	100	0.31	17,359	414
Isle of Man	S4	76	84	89	90	199	0.76	402	221
Jersey	S4	87	93	99	101	196	0.79	2,207	45
Macau	S7	432	568	602	614	170	0.79	55,682	11
Montserrat	S2	4	5	5	5	228	0.49	134	39
New Caledonia	S8	211	252	279	290	183	1.39	40	7,056
Northern Mariana Islands	S8	70	55	52	51	209	-0.69	292	179
Puerto Rico	S2	3,811	3,722	3,352	3,189	134	-1.54	979	3,425
Saint Barthelemy	S2	7	7	7	7	226	-0.39	744	10
Saint Helena	S5	7	8	8	8	225	0.25	66	119
Saint Martin	S2	28	30	32	33	216	0.74	1,541	21
Saint Pierre and Miquelon	S1	6	6	6	5	227	-1.06	59	93
Sint Maarten [5]	S2	31	38	42	44	212	1.46	3,206	13
Turks and Caicos Islands	S2	19	43	53	56	208	2.58	144	366
Virgin Islands, British	S2	23	30	35	37	214	2.32	601	58
Virgin Islands, U.S	S2	109	108	107	106	192	-0.20	803	134
Wallis and Futuna	S8	15	15	16	16	221	0.33	287	55
West Bank [6]	S6	1,947	2,404	2,748	2,900	141	1.87	1,262	2,178
Western Sahara	S5	336	492	603	652	169	2.83	6	102,703

P Projected. X Not applicable. Z Less than 0.05 percent or less than 1 person per square mile. [1] See maps for geographic locations, as indicated. [2] Computed by the exponential method. For explanation of average annual percent change, see Guide to Tabular Presentation. [3] Data converted from square kilometers to square miles. [4] Sudan and South Sudan became separate countries in July 2011. [5] The Netherlands Antilles dissolved on October 10, 2010. Curacao and Sint Maarten became autonomous territories of the Kingdom of the Netherlands. [6] The Gaza Strip and West Bank are Israeli occupied with interim status subject to Israeli/Palestinian negotiations. The final status is yet to be determined.

Source: U.S. Census Bureau, "International Data Base (IDB)," <http://www.census.gov/population/international/data/>, accessed September 2017.

Table 1354. Foreign or Foreign-Born Population in Selected OECD Countries: 1990 to 2015

[19,767 represents 19,767,000. In Australia, Mexico, and the United States, the data refer to residents who are foreign born. In the European countries, South Korea, and Japan, they represent the legal nationality or citizenship status of residents. Data are based on censuses, population registers, and residence permits. For details about data methodology for individual countries, see source]

Country	1990	2000	2005	2010	2011	2012	2013	2014	2015
United States	**19,767**	**30,273**	**35,770**	**39,917**	**40,382**	**40,738**	**41,344**	**42,391**	**43,290**
Australia	3,886	4,412	4,877	5,881	6,018	6,210	6,399	6,558	6,711
Austria	(NA)	702	797	913	951	1,004	1,066	1,146	1,268
Belgium	905	862	900	1,119	1,169	1,257	1,268	1,305	1,363
Denmark	161	259	270	346	359	375	397	423	463
France	3,597	(NA)	3,542	3,893	3,981	4,084	4,178	4,351	4,400
Germany	5,343	7,297	6,756	6,754	6,931	7,214	7,634	8,153	9,108
Italy	781	1,380	2,671	3,879	4,052	4,388	4,921	5,014	5,027
Japan	1,075	1,686	2,012	2,133	2,079	2,034	2,066	2,122	2,232
Korea	50	210	511	1,003	982	933	986	1,092	1,143
Luxembourg	113	162	191	221	230	239	249	259	269
Mexico	341	493	612	961	967	974	991	940	1,007
Netherlands	692	668	691	760	786	796	816	847	901
Spain	(NA)	1,371	4,144	5,751	5,736	5,546	5,023	4,730	4,601
Sweden	484	472	480	633	655	667	695	739	783
Switzerland	1,100	1,384	1,512	1,720	1,772	1,825	1,887	1,947	1,994
United Kingdom	1,723	2,342	3,035	4,524	4,785	4,788	4,941	5,592	5,951

NA Not available.

Source: Organisation for Economic Co-operation and Development (OECD), 2017, "International Migration Database," OECD International Migration Statistics (database) ©, <http://dx.doi.org/10.1787/data-00342-en>, accessed September 2017.

Table 1355. Youth and Elderly Population Distribution by Country: 2017 and 2020

[Percent of total population, as of mid-year. Covers countries with 11 million or more population in 2017]

Country	2017 Under 15 years old	2017 65 years old and over	2020 (P) Under 15 years old	2020 (P) 65 years old and over	Country	2017 Under 15 years old	2017 65 years old and over	2020 (P) Under 15 years old	2020 (P) 65 years old and over
World	**25.4**	**8.9**	**24.9**	**9.6**	Madagascar	39.9	3.3	38.9	3.5
Afghanistan	40.9	2.6	40.6	2.7	Malawi	46.3	2.7	45.9	2.7
Algeria	29.3	5.7	29.6	6.2	Malaysia	27.8	6.1	26.8	6.9
Angola	48.1	2.3	47.8	2.3	Mali	48.2	3.0	47.7	3.0
Argentina	24.6	11.6	24.0	12.1	Mexico	26.9	7.1	26.0	7.7
Australia	17.8	16.1	17.6	17.0	Morocco	25.8	6.7	24.9	7.5
Bangladesh	27.8	6.2	26.5	6.8	Mozambique	44.7	2.9	44.1	2.9
Belgium	17.2	18.6	17.2	19.2	Nepal	30.2	5.2	28.4	5.7
Benin	42.6	2.9	41.5	2.9	Netherlands	16.4	18.7	16.1	19.8
Bolivia	31.8	5.3	30.3	5.7	Niger	49.0	2.6	47.9	2.7
Brazil	22.3	8.3	21.1	9.2	Nigeria	42.5	3.1	41.7	3.2
Burkina Faso	44.9	2.4	44.3	2.4	Pakistan	31.4	4.5	29.7	4.8
Burma	26.9	5.5	26.0	6.0	Peru	26.3	7.4	25.4	8.0
Burundi	45.6	2.6	45.3	2.8	Philippines	33.4	4.5	32.4	4.9
Cambodia	31.0	4.3	30.2	4.6	Poland	14.8	16.9	14.8	18.7
Cameroon	42.4	3.2	41.6	3.3	Romania	14.4	16.4	14.1	17.6
Canada	15.4	18.6	15.4	20.1	Russia	17.1	14.3	17.2	15.5
Chad	43.0	3.0	41.4	3.1	Rwanda	41.4	2.4	40.0	2.6
Chile	20.1	10.8	19.8	11.8	Saudi Arabia	26.1	3.4	25.0	3.8
China	17.2	10.8	17.3	12.3	Senegal	41.5	3.0	40.4	3.1
Colombia	24.2	7.4	23.3	8.4	Somalia	43.1	2.2	42.4	2.3
Congo, Dem. Rep.	41.7	2.7	40.3	2.7	South Africa	28.3	5.7	27.9	6.1
Cote d'Ivoire	37.0	3.5	35.6	3.7	South Sudan [1]	44.4	2.1	42.8	2.2
Cuba	16.6	14.9	16.3	15.8	Spain	15.4	18.0	15.0	18.5
Ecuador	27.1	7.5	25.8	8.1	Sri Lanka	24.1	9.7	23.1	10.6
Egypt	33.3	4.2	33.6	4.4	Sudan [1]	38.7	3.3	36.5	3.4
Ethiopia	43.5	2.9	42.7	3.0	Syria	31.6	4.2	30.8	4.5
France	18.5	19.5	18.4	20.5	Taiwan	12.9	13.7	12.4	15.7
Germany	12.8	22.1	12.9	23.0	Tanzania	43.7	3.0	42.7	3.1
Ghana	38.0	4.2	37.4	4.4	Thailand	16.9	10.6	16.4	11.8
Guatemala	34.5	4.5	33.0	4.9	Tunisia	25.1	7.9	25.3	8.9
Guinea	41.5	3.7	41.0	3.8	Turkey	24.7	7.5	23.4	8.4
India	27.3	6.2	26.3	6.7	Uganda	48.0	2.0	47.4	1.9
Indonesia	25.0	7.0	23.9	7.8	Ukraine	15.8	16.3	16.2	17.0
Iran	24.2	5.3	24.1	5.9	United Kingdom	17.5	18.0	17.6	18.5
Iraq	39.5	3.5	38.1	3.8	**United States**	**18.7**	**15.6**	**18.4**	**16.9**
Italy	13.6	21.5	13.4	22.1	Uzbekistan	23.9	5.2	23.2	5.9
Japan	12.8	27.9	12.5	29.2	Venezuela	27.4	7.1	26.4	8.0
Kazakhstan	25.9	7.6	26.1	8.4	Vietnam	23.5	6.1	22.6	6.9
Kenya	40.0	3.0	36.8	3.3	Yemen	39.8	2.7	37.7	2.9
Korea, North	20.8	9.6	20.5	9.7	Zambia	46.0	2.3	45.7	2.3
Korea, South	13.2	14.1	12.8	15.9	Zimbabwe	38.9	4.5	38.3	4.5

P Projected. [1] Data for Sudan exclude South Sudan, which became an independent country in July 2011.

Source: U.S. Census Bureau, "International Data Base (IDB)," <http://www.census.gov/population/international/data/>, accessed September 2017.

Table 1356. Births, Deaths, and Life Expectancy by Country or Territory: 2017 and 2020

[Covers countries with 12 million or more population in 2017]

Country or territory	Crude birth rate [1] 2017	Crude birth rate [1] 2020 (P)	Crude death rate [2] 2017	Crude death rate [2] 2020 (P)	Expectation of life at birth (years) 2017	Expectation of life at birth (years) 2020 (P)	Infant mortality rate [3] 2017	Infant mortality rate [3] 2020 (P)	Total fertility rate per woman [4] 2017	Total fertility rate per woman [4] 2020 (P)
World	**18.3**	**17.7**	**7.8**	**7.8**	**69.3**	**70.0**	**32.9**	**30.8**	**2.42**	**2.38**
Afghanistan	37.9	36.7	13.4	12.7	51.7	52.8	110.6	104.3	5.12	4.82
Algeria	22.2	20.0	4.3	4.4	77.0	77.5	19.6	17.6	2.70	2.59
Angola	44.2	42.7	9.2	8.5	60.2	61.3	67.6	62.3	6.16	5.96
Argentina	16.7	16.0	7.5	7.4	77.3	77.8	9.8	9.0	2.26	2.21
Australia	12.1	11.9	7.3	7.5	82.3	82.5	4.3	4.1	1.77	1.76
Bangladesh	18.8	18.1	5.4	5.5	73.4	74.2	31.7	28.3	2.17	2.11
Brazil	14.1	13.6	6.7	6.9	74.0	74.7	17.5	15.9	1.75	1.73
Burkina Faso	41.2	39.9	11.2	10.6	55.9	56.9	72.2	67.8	5.71	5.49
Burma	18.1	17.0	7.4	7.2	68.2	69.3	35.8	31.7	2.17	2.07
Cambodia	23.0	21.3	7.5	7.3	64.9	65.9	47.4	43.7	2.52	2.39
Cameroon	35.4	34.2	9.6	9.0	59.0	60.3	51.0	47.6	4.64	4.46
Canada	10.3	10.1	8.7	9.0	81.9	82.2	4.5	4.4	1.60	1.61
Chad	35.6	33.8	13.8	13.1	50.6	51.7	85.4	80.6	4.34	4.03
Chile	13.6	13.1	6.2	6.5	78.9	79.4	6.6	6.2	1.80	1.77
China	12.3	11.6	7.8	8.2	75.7	76.1	12.0	11.4	1.60	1.60
Colombia	16.1	15.4	5.5	5.6	75.9	76.6	13.6	12.3	2.00	1.94
Congo, Dem. Rep	33.5	31.3	9.6	9.1	57.7	58.8	68.2	63.6	4.39	3.99
Cote d'Ivoire	27.7	26.1	9.4	9.1	59.0	59.9	55.8	51.6	3.38	3.15
Ecuador	17.9	17.0	5.1	5.2	77.0	77.5	16.4	15.0	2.19	2.09
Egypt	29.6	27.2	4.6	4.4	73.0	73.7	19.0	17.1	3.47	3.29
Ethiopia	36.5	35.2	7.7	7.2	62.6	63.7	49.6	45.6	4.99	4.75
France	12.2	11.9	9.3	9.6	81.9	82.2	3.2	3.2	2.07	2.06
Germany	8.6	8.6	11.7	12.1	80.8	81.1	3.4	3.3	1.45	1.47
Ghana	30.5	29.6	7.0	6.6	67.0	68.2	35.2	32.1	4.00	3.90
Guatemala	24.1	22.7	4.7	4.6	72.6	73.4	21.3	19.2	2.77	2.57
Guinea	35.1	34.2	9.0	8.4	61.0	62.4	50.0	45.2	4.77	4.60
India	19.0	18.2	7.3	7.3	68.8	69.7	39.1	35.4	2.43	2.35
Indonesia	16.2	15.4	6.5	6.6	73.0	73.7	22.7	20.4	2.11	2.04
Iran	17.9	16.3	5.3	5.3	74.0	74.5	15.9	14.9	1.97	1.94
Iraq	30.4	29.1	3.8	3.8	74.9	74.9	37.5	37.5	4.00	3.82
Italy	8.6	8.4	10.4	10.7	82.3	82.5	3.3	3.2	1.44	1.47
Japan	7.7	7.3	9.8	10.2	85.3	86.0	2.0	1.9	1.41	1.43
Kazakhstan	18.1	16.4	8.1	8.2	71.1	72.0	19.6	17.9	2.25	2.16
Kenya	23.9	20.8	6.7	6.6	64.3	65.1	37.1	34.0	2.98	2.57
Korea, North	14.6	14.5	9.3	9.4	70.7	71.6	22.1	20.0	1.95	1.92
Korea, South	8.3	8.2	6.0	6.8	82.5	82.6	3.0	3.0	1.26	1.29
Madagascar	31.6	29.9	6.5	6.2	66.3	67.3	41.2	37.8	4.03	3.78
Malawi	41.0	40.1	7.9	7.2	61.7	63.2	43.4	39.5	5.49	5.31
Malaysia	19.1	18.3	5.1	5.3	75.2	75.9	12.5	11.4	2.50	2.43
Mali	43.9	42.2	9.8	9.0	60.3	61.6	69.5	64.0	6.01	5.72
Mexico	18.3	17.6	5.3	5.4	76.1	76.7	11.6	10.7	2.24	2.19
Morocco	17.7	16.9	4.9	5.0	77.1	77.7	21.9	19.5	2.11	2.07
Mozambique	38.1	37.2	11.6	10.9	53.7	54.8	65.9	60.5	5.08	4.90
Nepal	19.5	18.1	5.6	5.7	71.0	71.8	27.9	25.1	2.12	1.96
Netherlands	10.9	11.0	8.9	9.2	81.4	81.7	3.6	3.5	1.78	1.77
Niger	44.2	42.5	11.8	11.0	55.9	57.1	81.1	76.1	6.49	6.08
Nigeria	36.9	35.9	12.4	11.7	53.8	55.0	69.8	65.6	5.07	4.88
Pakistan	21.9	20.7	6.3	6.2	68.1	69.0	52.1	47.2	2.62	2.42
Peru	17.8	17.0	6.1	6.2	74.0	74.7	18.4	16.7	2.12	2.04
Philippines	23.7	22.9	6.1	6.0	69.4	70.0	21.4	20.0	3.02	2.92
Poland	9.5	8.9	10.4	10.6	77.8	78.3	4.4	4.3	1.35	1.38
Romania	8.9	8.5	12.0	12.0	75.4	76.0	9.4	8.7	1.35	1.38
Russia	11.0	10.0	13.5	13.4	71.0	71.9	6.8	6.5	1.61	1.60
Saudi Arabia	18.3	17.8	3.4	3.4	75.5	76.1	13.2	12.0	2.09	2.04
Senegal	33.4	31.8	8.1	7.6	62.1	63.2	49.1	45.7	4.28	4.04
South Africa	20.2	19.2	9.4	9.3	63.8	64.8	31.0	27.8	2.29	2.22
South Sudan	35.5	33.6	7.7	7.2	61.6	62.7	62.8	57.8	5.07	4.72
Spain	9.2	8.7	9.1	9.3	81.8	82.0	3.3	3.2	1.50	1.51
Sri Lanka	15.2	14.2	6.2	6.5	76.9	77.5	8.4	7.8	2.07	2.01
Sudan	27.9	26.0	7.3	6.9	64.4	65.5	48.8	45.0	3.57	3.24
Syria	21.2	19.7	4.0	4.0	75.1	75.6	14.8	13.7	2.50	2.34
Taiwan	8.3	8.0	7.4	7.9	80.2	80.6	4.3	4.2	1.13	1.14
Tanzania	35.6	34.6	7.6	7.1	62.6	63.9	39.9	36.4	4.77	4.59
Thailand	11.0	10.7	8.0	8.3	74.9	75.6	9.2	8.6	1.52	1.54
Turkey	15.7	14.8	6.0	6.1	75.0	75.7	17.6	15.8	2.01	1.96
Uganda	42.9	41.4	10.2	9.4	55.9	57.2	56.1	51.8	5.71	5.44
Ukraine	10.3	9.6	14.4	14.0	72.1	72.9	7.8	7.4	1.54	1.56
United Kingdom	12.1	11.9	9.4	9.5	80.8	81.1	4.3	4.1	1.88	1.86
United States	**12.5**	**12.4**	**8.2**	**8.3**	**80.0**	**80.4**	**5.8**	**5.6**	**1.87**	**1.87**
Uzbekistan	16.8	16.1	5.3	5.4	74.0	74.7	18.0	16.3	1.76	1.74
Venezuela	18.8	17.9	5.3	5.4	76.0	76.6	12.2	11.3	2.32	2.26
Vietnam	15.5	14.5	5.9	6.0	73.7	74.4	17.3	15.7	1.81	1.77
Yemen	28.4	25.8	6.0	5.6	65.9	66.9	46.0	41.9	3.63	3.20
Zambia	41.5	40.4	12.2	11.6	52.7	53.6	61.1	56.0	5.63	5.49
Zimbabwe	34.2	33.6	10.2	9.3	60.4	62.3	32.7	30.3	3.98	3.93

P Projection. [1] Number of births during 1 year per 1,000 persons (based on midyear population). [2] Number of deaths during 1 year per 1,000 persons (based on midyear population). [3] Number of deaths of children under 1 year of age per 1,000 live births in a calendar year. [4] Average number of children that would be born if all women lived to the end of childbearing age, based on birth rates for each specified year.

Source: U.S. Census Bureau, "International Data Base (IDB)," <http://www.census.gov/population/international/data/>, accessed September 2017.

Table 1357. Life Expectancy at Birth and at Age 65 by Sex—Selected Countries: 2010 and 2015

Country	Life expectancy at birth (years)				Life expectancy at age 65 (years)			
	Females		Males		Females		Males	
	2010	2015	2010	2015	2010	2015	2010	2015
United States............	81.0	[1] 81.2	76.2	[1] 76.3	20.3	[1] 20.6	17.7	[1] 18.0
Australia...................	84.0	84.5	79.5	80.4	21.8	22.3	18.9	19.5
Austria....................	83.5	83.7	77.8	78.8	21.4	21.3	17.9	18.1
Belgium...................	83.0	83.4	77.5	78.7	21.3	21.5	17.6	18.2
Brazil.....................	77.2	78.5	69.6	71.0	19.2	19.8	16.4	16.7
Canada...................	83.3	(NA)	78.8	(NA)	21.5	(NA)	18.3	(NA)
Czech Republic...........	80.9	81.6	74.5	75.7	19.0	19.4	15.5	15.9
Denmark..................	81.4	82.7	77.2	78.8	19.7	20.7	17.0	18.0
Finland...................	83.5	84.4	76.9	78.7	21.5	21.9	17.5	18.3
France....................	85.3	85.5	78.3	79.2	23.4	23.5	18.9	19.4
Germany..................	83.0	83.1	78.0	78.3	20.9	21.0	17.8	17.9
Greece....................	83.3	83.7	78.0	78.5	21.0	21.3	18.2	18.5
Hungary...................	78.6	79.0	70.7	72.3	18.2	18.2	14.1	14.5
Iceland....................	84.1	83.8	79.8	81.2	21.5	21.3	18.3	19.5
Ireland....................	83.1	83.4	78.5	79.6	20.8	21.0	17.7	18.4
Israel [2].................	83.6	84.1	79.7	80.1	21.2	21.5	18.9	18.9
Italy......................	84.7	84.9	79.5	80.3	22.1	22.2	18.3	18.9
Japan.....................	86.3	87.1	79.6	80.8	23.8	24.3	18.7	19.5
Korea, South.............	83.6	85.2	76.8	79.0	21.2	22.4	16.8	18.2
Mexico....................	77.0	77.7	71.1	72.3	18.5	18.6	16.6	16.8
Netherlands..............	83.0	83.2	78.9	79.9	21.0	21.1	17.7	18.4
New Zealand.............	82.7	[1] 83.4	78.9	[1] 79.9	21.0	[1] 21.5	18.5	[1] 19.3
Norway...................	83.3	84.2	79.0	80.5	21.2	21.6	18.0	18.9
Poland....................	80.7	81.6	72.2	73.5	19.5	20.1	15.1	15.7
Portugal..................	83.2	84.3	76.8	78.1	21.0	21.7	17.2	18.0
Russia....................	74.9	76.7	63.1	65.9	16.5	17.6	12.1	13.3
South Africa.............	56.1	59.5	52.7	55.5	(NA)	(NA)	(NA)	(NA)
Spain.....................	85.5	85.8	79.2	80.1	22.9	23.0	18.6	19.0
Sweden...................	83.6	84.1	79.6	80.4	21.2	21.5	18.3	18.9
Switzerland..............	84.9	85.1	80.3	80.8	22.5	22.4	19.0	19.4
Turkey....................	76.8	80.7	71.8	75.3	16.0	19.4	14.0	16.1
United Kingdom..........	82.6	82.8	78.6	79.2	20.8	20.8	18.2	18.6

NA Not available. [1] Estimated. [2] The statistical data for Israel are supplied by and under the responsibility of the relevant Israeli authorities. The use of such data by the OECD is without prejudice to the status of the Golan Heights, East Jerusalem and Israeli settlements in the West Bank under the terms of international law.

Source: Organisation for Economic Co-operation and Development (OECD), 2017, "OECD Health Data: Health Status," OECD Health Statistics (database) ©, <http://dx.doi.org/10.1787/data-00546-en>, accessed July 2017.

Table 1358. Percent of the Adult Population Considered to Be Obese: 2005 to 2015

[Obesity rates are defined as the percentage of the population with a Body Mass Index (BMI) over 30 kg/m^2. The BMI is a single number that evaluates an individual's weight status in relation to height (weight/height^2). Obesity estimates derived from health examinations are generally higher and more reliable than those coming from self-reports because they preclude any misreporting of people's height and weight. However, health examinations are only conducted regularly in a few countries. For more information on methods, see source]

Country	2005	2009	2010	2011	2012	2013	2014	2015
OBESITY, MEASURED								
United States...................	(NA)	(NA)	36.1	(NA)	35.3	(NA)	38.2	(NA)
Australia.........................	(NA)	(NA)	(NA)	28.3	(NA)	(NA)	27.9	(NA)
Canada..........................	23.7	(NA)	25.4	(NA)	(NA)	25.8	(NA)	(NA)
Hungary..........................	(NA)	28.5	(NA)	(NA)	(NA)	(NA)	30.0	(NA)
Ireland..........................	(NA)	(NA)	(NA)	(NA)	(NA)	(NA)	(NA)	23.0
Japan...........................	3.9	3.9	3.5	4.1	3.6	3.7	3.9	3.7
Korea, South....................	3.5	3.8	4.1	4.3	4.6	4.7	4.3	5.3
Luxembourg......................	18.6	[1] 22.1	22.5	23.5	23.0	22.7	22.6	(NA)
Mexico..........................	30.2	(NA)	(NA)	(NA)	32.4	(NA)	(NA)	(NA)
New Zealand.....................	(NA)	27.8	(NA)	(NA)	28.6	30.8	29.9	30.7
Slovak Republic..................	17.6	(NA)	(NA)	(NA)	(NA)	(NA)	(NA)	(NA)
United Kingdom..................	23.2	23.0	26.1	24.8	24.7	24.9	25.6	26.9
OBESITY, SELF REPORTED								
United States...................	25.1	27.7	28.1	28.5	28.6	28.7	29.5	30.1
Austria..........................	(NA)	(NA)	(NA)	(NA)	(NA)	(NA)	14.7	(NA)
Belgium..........................	(NA)	(NA)	(NA)	(NA)	(NA)	13.7	14.0	(NA)
Canada..........................	15.2	17.2	17.5	17.7	17.7	18.2	19.6	(NA)
Finland..........................	14.1	14.9	15.6	16.6	15.8	15.7	18.3	[1] 18.8
France...........................	(NA)	(NA)	12.9	(NA)	14.5	(NA)	15.3	(NA)
Germany.........................	13.6	14.7	(NA)	(NA)	(NA)	15.7	16.4	(NA)
Iceland..........................	(NA)	(NA)	21.0	(NA)	22.2	(NA)	(NA)	[1] 19.0
Ireland..........................	(NA)	(NA)	(NA)	(NA)	(NA)	(NA)	(NA)	18.0
Israel [2].......................	(NA)	(NA)	15.7	(NA)	(NA)	15.7	17.8	(NA)
Italy............................	9.9	10.3	10.3	10.0	10.4	10.3	10.3	9.8
Korea, South....................	(NA)	2.0	2.0	2.1	2.2	2.4	2.6	2.8
Netherlands.....................	10.7	11.8	11.4	11.4	12.0	11.1	[1] 13.3	12.8
Norway..........................	9.0	(NA)	(NA)	(NA)	10.0	(NA)	(NA)	12.0
Spain............................	(NA)	15.7	(NA)	16.6	(NA)	(NA)	16.7	(NA)
Sweden..........................	10.9	10.9	11.3	11.0	11.8	11.7	12.2	12.3
Turkey..........................	(NA)	(NA)	16.9	(NA)	17.2	(NA)	19.9	(NA)

NA Not available. [1] Break in series. [2] See footnote 2, Table 1357.

Source: Organisation for Economic Co-operation and Development (OECD), 2017, "OECD Health Data: Non-medical Determinants of Health," OECD Health Statistics (database) ©, <http://dx.doi.org/10.1787/data-00546-en>, accessed July 2017.

Table 1359. Daily Tobacco Consumption by Country and Sex: 2000 to 2015

[Daily smokers as percent of population aged over 15. Covers only tobacco forms consumed by smoking]

Country	Total				Females				Males			
	2000	2010	2014	2015	2000	2010	2014	2015	2000	2010	2014	2015
United States	**19.1**	**15.1**	**12.9**	**11.4**	**17.3**	**13.6**	**11.8**	**10.7**	**21.2**	**16.7**	**14.0**	**12.2**
Brazil	(NA)	14.1	[1] 8.7	7.2	(NA)	11.7	[1] 7.3	5.4	(NA)	16.8	[1] 10.3	9.5
China	29.7	26.2	(NA)	24.7	3.5	2.2	(NA)	1.8	55.8	50.1	(NA)	47.6
Czech Republic	(NA)	22.8	22.3	18.2	(NA)	16.5	18.5	14.8	(NA)	29.3	26.4	21.8
Denmark	30.5	[1] 20.9	17.0	17.0	29.0	[1] 19.3	17.0	17.0	32.0	[1] 22.7	17.0	16.0
Finland	23.4	19.0	15.4	[1] 17.4	20.3	15.7	14.0	[1] 14.5	27.3	23.2	17.2	[1] 18.7
France	27.0	23.3	22.4	(NA)	21.0	20.7	19.4	(NA)	33.0	26.4	25.8	(NA)
Iceland	22.4	14.2	[1] 12.6	10.9	22.0	13.9	[1] 13.0	11.0	22.8	14.5	[1] 12.1	10.7
India	21.6	13.7	(NA)	11.2	7.3	2.9	(NA)	1.9	35.9	24.4	(NA)	20.4
Indonesia	31.1	36.3	(NA)	39.9	6.0	4.2	(NA)	3.6	56.2	68.4	(NA)	76.2
Italy	24.4	23.1	19.7	19.8	17.4	17.1	14.9	15.8	31.9	29.6	24.8	24.9
Japan	27.0	19.5	19.6	18.2	11.5	8.4	8.5	7.9	47.4	32.2	32.2	30.1
Korea	(NA)	22.9	20.0	17.3	(NA)	5.2	4.0	3.4	(NA)	40.8	36.6	31.4
Luxembourg	(NA)	18.3	15.3	15.0	(NA)	15.7	13.7	13.9	(NA)	20.9	17.0	16.0
Netherlands	32.0	[1] 20.9	[1] 19.1	19.0	29.0	[1] 18.8	[1] 16.7	16.9	35.0	[1] 23.1	[1] 21.7	21.2
New Zealand	25.0	(NA)	15.7	15.0	25.0	(NA)	14.3	13.9	25.0	(NA)	17.2	16.1
Norway	32.0	19.0	13.0	13.0	32.0	19.0	13.0	13.0	31.0	19.0	14.0	13.0
South Africa	23.9	20.3	(NA)	19.0	12.5	8.0	(NA)	6.5	35.3	32.5	(NA)	31.4
Sweden	18.9	13.6	11.9	11.2	21.0	12.5	12.1	10.7	16.8	14.7	11.7	11.7
United Kingdom	27.0	20.0	19.0	(NA)	25.0	20.0	17.0	(NA)	29.0	21.0	20.0	(NA)

NA Not available. [1] Break in series or difference in methodology.

Source: Organisation for Economic Co-operation and Development (OECD), 2017, "OECD Health Data: Non-medical Determinants of Health," OECD Health Statistics (database) ©, <http://dx.doi.org/10.1787/data-00546-en>, accessed July 2017.

Table 1360. Road Traffic Fatalities by Country: 2000 to 2015

[Fatalities include any person killed immediately or dying within 30 days as a result of an injury accident. For countries that do not apply the threshold of 30 days, conversion coefficients are estimated so that comparisons on the basis of the 30 day-definition can be made]

Country	2000	2005	2010	2014	2015	Country	2000	2005	2010	2014	2015
United States	**41,945**	**43,510**	**32,999**	**32,675**	[2] **35,200**	Japan	10,410	7,997	5,828	4,838	4,859
Albania	280	308	353	264	270	Korea, South	10,236	6,376	5,505	4,762	4,621
Armenia	214	310	[2] 294	297	346	Latvia	588	442	218	212	187
Australia	1,817	1,627	1,353	1,150	1,205	Lithuania	641	773	299	267	241
Austria	976	768	552	430	479	Mexico	5,224	4,710	5,032	(NA)	(NA)
Belgium	1,470	1,089	841	727	732	Moldova	406	391	452	324	300
Bulgaria	1,012	957	776	660	708	Netherlands	1,166	817	640	570	621
Canada	2,904	2,898	2,238	[2] 1,834	(NA)	New Zealand	462	405	375	293	319
China	(NA)	98,738	65,225	(NA)	(NA)	Norway	341	224	208	147	117
Croatia	655	597	426	308	348	Poland	6,294	5,444	3,907	3,202	2,938
Czech Republic	1,486	1,286	802	688	738	Portugal	1,857	1,247	937	638	593
Finland	396	379	272	229	266	Romania	2,499	2,641	2,377	1,818	(NA)
France	8,079	5,318	3,992	3,384	(NA)	Russia	29,594	33,957	26,567	26,958	23,114
Georgia	500	581	685	511	602	Serbia	1,048	841	656	536	601
Germany	7,503	5,361	3,648	3,377	3,459	Slovak Republic	648	600	353	295	310
Greece	2,037	1,658	1,258	795	[2] 805	Slovenia	313	258	138	108	120
Hungary	1,200	1,278	740	626	644	Spain	5,776	4,442	2,478	1,688	1,689
Iceland	32	19	8	4	16	Sweden	591	440	[1] 266	270	259
India	78,911	94,968	134,513	139,671	146,133	Switzerland	592	409	327	243	253
Ireland	415	396	212	[2] 193	166	Turkey	5,510	4,505	4,045	3,524	[1] 7,530
Italy	7,061	5,818	4,114	3,381	(NA)	United Kingdom	3,580	3,336	1,905	1,854	1,804

NA Not available. [1] Break in series. [2] Estimated or provisional.

Source: International Transport Forum (ITF) / Organisation for Economic Co-operation and Development (OECD), 2017, "Road injury accidents," Transport Statistics ©. See also <http://www.internationaltransportforum.org/>.

Table 1361. Suicide Rates by Sex and Country: 2014

[Deaths due to intentional self-harm per 100,000 persons]

Country	Total	Men	Women	Country	Total	Men	Women
United States	**13.5**	**21.6**	**6.0**	Italy [2]	6.3	10.5	2.6
Australia	12.2	18.8	6.0	Japan	17.6	25.4	10.2
Austria	13.9	22.7	6.4	Korea, South [3]	28.7	43.3	16.8
Belgium	16.1	23.6	9.1	Lithuania	29.8	55.3	8.6
Brazil	5.7	9.5	2.3	Mexico	5.5	9.5	1.9
Canada [2]	10.9	16.7	5.3	Netherlands	10.4	14.5	6.6
Chile	10.4	18.1	3.5	New Zealand [2]	12.5	18.8	6.4
Czech Republic	13.3	22.6	4.9	Norway	10.5	15.5	5.7
Denmark	10.6	16.3	5.2	Poland	14.8	26.7	3.8
Estonia	17.5	31.9	6.0	Portugal	10.0	16.5	4.6
Finland	14.1	21.9	6.7	Russia [1]	21.0	39.0	6.9
France [3]	14.3	23.1	6.7	Slovak Republic	9.7	18.1	2.7
Germany	10.8	17.3	5.2	South Africa	1.2	2.1	0.5
Greece	4.7	7.8	1.9	Spain	7.6	12.0	3.7
Hungary	17.8	30.7	7.5	Sweden	11.4	15.8	7.2
Ireland [3]	10.9	17.7	4.2	Switzerland [3]	12.2	18.9	6.3
Israel [4]	5.5	8.8	2.4	United Kingdom [3]	7.5	12.2	3.0

[1] 2011 data. [2] 2012 data. [3] 2013 data. [4] See footnote 2, Table 1357.

Source: Organisation for Economic Co-operation and Development (OECD), 2017, "Health Status," OECD Health Statistics database ©, <http://dx.doi.org/10.1787/data-00540-en>, accessed July 2017.

Table 1362. Health Expenditures by Country: 1990 to 2016

[In percent. GDP = gross domestic product]

Country	Total expenditures on health (percent of GDP)					Public (government) expenditures on health (percent of total)				
	1990	2000	2010	2015	2016 [1]	1990	2000	2010	2015	2016 [1]
United States.............	**(NA)**	**12.5**	**16.4**	**16.9**	**17.2**	**(NA)**	**44.2**	**48.4**	**49.4**	**49.1**
Australia....................	6.5	7.6	8.5	9.4	9.6	66.2	68.4	68.6	67.3	67.8
Austria.....................	7.7	9.2	10.1	10.3	10.4	74.4	75.5	76.1	75.6	75.7
Belgium....................	7.1	7.9	9.9	10.5	10.4	(NA)	74.6	77.4	77.5	77.3
Canada....................	8.4	8.3	10.6	10.3	10.3	74.3	70.0	69.8	70.2	70.0
Czech Republic...........	3.8	5.7	6.9	7.2	7.2	97.1	89.8	83.3	83.5	83.4
Denmark...................	8.0	8.1	10.4	10.3	10.4	82.4	83.1	84.6	84.1	84.1
Finland....................	7.2	6.8	8.9	9.4	9.4	80.0	71.2	74.3	74.4	74.2
France.....................	8.0	9.5	10.7	11.1	11.0	76.0	78.9	78.4	78.9	78.8
Germany [2]...............	8.0	9.8	11.0	11.2	11.3	75.4	79.4	83.5	84.5	84.6
Greece....................	6.1	7.2	9.6	8.4	8.2	54.1	61.6	69.1	59.1	59.3
Hungary...................	(NA)	6.8	7.6	7.2	7.6	(NA)	69.6	67.1	66.7	68.3
Iceland....................	7.4	9.0	8.8	8.6	8.6	86.2	80.6	80.4	81.5	82.1
Ireland....................	5.6	5.9	10.5	7.8	7.8	73.2	77.5	76.2	70.0	70.2
Italy.......................	7.0	7.6	9.0	9.0	8.9	81.3	72.6	78.5	74.9	75.0
Japan.....................	5.7	7.2	9.2	10.9	10.9	77.6	80.4	81.9	84.0	84.1
Korea, South..............	3.7	4.0	6.5	7.4	7.7	40.1	53.9	57.9	56.4	56.4
Luxembourg...............	5.1	5.9	7.0	6.0	6.3	93.1	82.0	84.9	82.0	83.0
Mexico....................	(NA)	4.9	6.0	5.9	5.8	(NA)	45.2	48.6	52.2	51.7
Netherlands...............	7.1	7.1	10.4	10.7	10.5	71.2	66.4	82.6	80.7	80.8
New Zealand..............	6.7	7.5	9.7	9.3	9.2	82.4	78.0	80.6	80.3	80.2
Norway....................	7.1	7.7	8.9	10.0	10.5	82.8	81.7	84.7	85.4	85.2
Poland....................	4.3	5.3	6.4	6.3	6.4	90.9	68.9	71.7	70.0	69.0
Portugal...................	5.5	8.4	9.8	9.0	8.9	64.9	70.5	69.8	66.2	66.2
Slovak Republic...........	(NA)	5.3	7.8	6.9	6.9	(NA)	89.2	71.9	79.7	79.8
Spain......................	6.1	6.8	9.0	9.2	9.0	78.4	71.4	74.8	71.0	70.6
Sweden....................	7.3	7.4	8.5	11.0	11.0	79.6	85.5	81.9	83.7	83.9
Switzerland................	7.4	9.3	10.7	12.1	12.4	51.0	55.4	62.5	64.0	63.6
Turkey.....................	2.5	4.6	5.1	4.1	4.3	59.9	61.7	78.0	78.1	79.4
United Kingdom...........	5.1	6.0	8.5	9.9	9.7	84.3	79.3	83.1	79.7	79.2

NA Not available. [1] Data are estimated or provisional. [2] Data prior to 1991 are for former West Germany.

Source: Organisation for Economic Co-operation and Development (OECD), 2017, "Health expenditure and financing: Health expenditure indicators," OECD Health Statistics (database) ©, <http://dx.doi.org/10.1787/data-00349-en>, accessed July 2017.

Table 1363. Physicians and Inpatient Hospital Care—Selected Countries: 2000 to 2015

Country	Practicing physicians per 1,000 population				Acute (curative) inpatient hospital care							
					Beds per 1,000 population				Average length of stay (days)			
	2000	2010	2014	2015	2000	2010	2014	2015	2000	2010	2014	2015
United States........	**2.3**	**2.4**	**2.6**	**(NA)**	**3.0**	**2.7**	**2.5**	**(NA)**	**5.8**	**5.4**	**5.5**	**(NA)**
Australia................	2.5	(NA)	[1] 3.5	[1] 3.5	(NA)	(NA)	(NA)	(NA)	6.1	5.0	4.7	(NA)
Austria..................	3.9	4.8	5.1	5.1	6.9	6.2	5.8	5.7	7.6	6.6	6.5	6.5
Belgium.................	2.8	2.9	3.0	3.0	7.3	5.9	5.7	5.7	7.7	7.2	6.9	(NA)
Canada..................	(NA)	(NA)	[1] 2.5	[1] 2.6	3.5	2.1	2.1	2.0	7.2	7.7	7.6	7.4
Czech Republic........	[2] 3.4	3.6	(NA)	(NA)	[2] 5.8	4.9	4.3	4.3	7.9	7.1	6.6	6.6
Denmark................	2.9	3.6	3.7	(NA)	4.3	3.4	[2] 2.6	2.5	3.8	(NA)	(NA)	(NA)
Estonia.................	3.1	3.2	3.3	3.4	[2] 6.0	3.8	3.7	3.7	7.3	5.5	5.4	5.5
Finland.................	2.5	[1] 3.0	[1] 3.2	(NA)	[2] 3.9	3.4	3.1	3.1	[2] 6.9	7.0	6.7	6.6
France..................	(NA)	(NA)	3.1	3.1	5.1	4.3	4.2	4.1	5.6	5.8	5.7	(NA)
Germany................	3.3	3.7	4.1	4.1	6.8	6.2	6.2	6.1	10.1	8.1	7.6	7.6
Hungary.................	[1,2] 2.7	[2] 2.9	3.3	[2] 3.1	[1] 6.2	4.5	4.3	4.3	7.1	5.8	5.7	5.6
Ireland.................	(NA)	(NA)	[1] 2.8	[1] 2.9	2.8	2.5	2.4	2.4	6.4	6.0	5.6	6.1
Israel [3]...............	3.5	3.3	3.5	3.4	2.9	2.4	2.3	2.3	9.0	5.2	5.1	5.2
Italy....................	(NA)	(NA)	3.9	3.8	[2] 4.2	3.0	2.7	2.6	7.0	6.7	6.8	6.9
Japan...................	1.9	2.2	2.4	(NA)	9.8	8.1	7.9	7.9	24.8	18.2	[2] 16.9	16.5
Korea, South..........	1.3	2.0	2.2	2.2	[2] 4.6	[2] 6.4	[2] 7.3	(NA)	11.0	10.0	8.3	8.0
Mexico..................	1.6	2.0	2.2	2.4	[2] 1.8	[2] 1.5	[2] 1.6	[2] 1.5	(NA)	(NA)	(NA)	(NA)
Netherlands............	(NA)	(NA)	3.4	3.5	3.1	[2] 2.9	(NA)	(NA)	9.0	5.6	6.7	6.2
New Zealand...........	2.2	2.6	2.8	[2] 3.0	(NA)	2.8	2.7	2.7	4.3	6.0	4.6	(NA)
Norway..................	3.4	4.1	4.4	[2] 4.4	3.8	3.8	3.4	3.4	6.0	6.3	5.5	[2] 6.2
Poland..................	2.2	2.2	2.3	2.3	5.2	[2] 5.0	5.0	4.9	(NA)	7.3	6.6	6.9
Portugal................	(NA)	(NA)	(NA)	(NA)	3.7	3.3	3.3	[1] 3.3	7.8	7.0	7.2	[1] 7.1
Russia..................	4.6	5.0	[2] 4.2	4.0	(NA)	(NA)	(NA)	(NA)	13.5	10.8	[2] 9.9	9.7
Slovak Republic........	3.2	(NA)	(NA)	(NA)	6.4	5.4	4.9	4.9	8.4	6.6	[2] 7.0	6.9
Slovenia................	2.2	2.4	2.8	2.8	5.2	4.3	4.2	4.2	7.1	5.5	6.6	6.5
Spain...................	3.1	3.8	3.8	3.9	2.9	2.5	2.4	2.4	7.1	6.3	5.9	5.9
Sweden.................	3.1	3.9	4.2	(NA)	3.1	2.5	2.4	2.3	6.6	5.8	5.6	5.7
Switzerland.............	(NA)	3.8	4.1	4.2	5.3	[2] 4.1	3.8	3.7	9.3	[2] 6.6	5.8	5.7
Turkey..................	(NA)	(NA)	(NA)	(NA)	2.0	2.5	2.7	2.7	5.6	4.0	4.0	3.9
United Kingdom........	2.0	2.7	2.8	[2] 2.8	(NA)	(NA)	(NA)	(NA)	(NA)	6.1	6.0	6.0

NA Not available. [1] Estimated. [2] Break in series or difference in methodology. [3] The statistical data for Israel are supplied by and under the responsibility of the relevant Israeli authorities. The use of such data by the OECD is without prejudice as to the status of the Golan Heights, East Jerusalem and Israeli settlements in the West Bank under the terms of international law.

Source: Organisation for Economic Co-Operation and Development (OECD), 2017, "Health care resources," OECD Health Statistics (database) ©, <http://dx.doi.org/10.1787/data-00541-en>; and "Health care utilisation," OECD Health Statistics (database) ©, <http://dx.doi.org/10.1787/data-00542-en>; accessed July 2017.

Table 1364. Gross National Income (GNI) by Country: 2010 and 2016

[For total GNI, 65,031,660 represents $65,031,660,000,000. GNI is the sum of value added by all resident producers, plus any product taxes (less subsidies) not included in the valuation of output, plus net receipts of primary income from abroad]

Country	Gross national income [1]				GNI on purchasing power parity basis [2]			
	Total (mil. dol.)		Per capita (dol.)		Total (mil. dol.)		Per capita (dol.)	
	2010	2016	2010	2016	2010	2016	2010	2016
World [3]	**65,031,660**	**76,643,886**	**9,383**	**10,299**	**88,657,553**	**119,822,859**	**12,792**	**16,101**
United States	**15,143,137**	**18,153,487**	**48,950**	**56,180**	**15,121,133**	**18,749,688**	**48,880**	**58,030**
Afghanistan	14,430	19,937	500	580	45,732	65,772	1,590	1,900
Algeria	161,081	173,452	4,460	4,270	454,344	597,853	12,580	14,720
Angola	75,707	98,982	3,240	3,440	121,741	179,338	5,210	6,220
Argentina	378,200	524,532	9,170	11,960	729,948	853,994	17,710	19,480
Australia	1,025,762	1,313,016	46,560	54,420	829,927	1,109,159	37,670	45,970
Azerbaijan	48,952	46,455	5,410	4,760	133,025	157,428	14,690	16,130
Bangladesh	118,314	216,291	780	1,330	393,638	617,088	2,590	3,790
Belarus	57,702	53,200	6,080	5,600	148,072	163,612	15,600	17,210
Belgium	521,870	475,046	47,900	41,860	451,014	522,113	41,390	46,010
Brazil	1,890,905	1,835,993	9,610	8,840	2,721,058	3,075,470	13,830	14,810
Cambodia	10,701	17,934	750	1,140	33,750	55,266	2,360	3,510
Canada	1,508,743	1,584,301	44,370	43,660	1,334,171	1,575,432	39,230	43,420
Chile	183,264	242,312	10,780	13,530	289,787	416,770	17,050	23,270
China	5,810,913	11,393,571	4,340	8,260	12,431,613	21,366,057	9,290	15,500
Colombia	254,324	307,430	5,540	6,320	471,246	676,847	10,260	13,910
Congo, Dem. Rep	19,715	32,705	310	420	36,816	57,825	570	730
Costa Rica	32,868	52,644	7,230	10,840	56,016	76,515	12,320	15,750
Cote d'Ivoire	24,421	35,968	1,200	1,520	51,803	85,581	2,540	3,610
Czech Republic	201,170	185,560	19,210	17,570	267,922	345,478	25,580	32,710
Denmark	339,645	325,104	61,220	56,730	242,919	292,504	43,790	51,040
Dominican Republic	51,741	68,030	5,230	6,390	103,961	154,183	10,500	14,480
Ecuador	65,924	95,343	4,410	5,820	134,792	181,375	9,030	11,070
Egypt	196,206	331,297	2,330	3,460	796,126	1,063,421	9,470	11,110
Ethiopia	33,248	67,515	380	660	91,939	177,039	1,050	1,730
France	2,847,644	2,605,813	43,790	38,950	2,390,566	2,835,242	36,760	42,380
Germany	3,662,448	3,609,439	44,790	43,660	3,274,082	4,094,787	40,040	49,530
Ghana	30,540	38,864	1,250	1,380	72,257	117,162	2,950	4,150
Greece	307,604	203,733	27,660	18,960	307,228	289,058	27,630	26,900
Guatemala	39,442	62,846	2,700	3,790	93,344	128,544	6,380	7,750
Hong Kong	236,168	317,690	33,620	43,240	338,090	444,695	48,130	60,530
India	1,507,911	2,220,043	1,220	1,680	5,254,842	8,594,226	4,270	6,490
Indonesia	612,254	888,958	2,520	3,400	1,950,593	2,929,425	8,040	11,220
Iraq	136,158	202,002	4,430	5,430	387,717	641,453	12,600	17,240
Ireland	204,639	250,866	44,880	52,560	165,015	271,422	36,190	56,870
Israel	225,795	309,342	29,620	36,190	215,147	319,670	28,220	37,400
Italy	2,234,110	1,914,131	37,690	31,590	2,075,055	2,316,529	35,010	38,230
Japan	5,562,863	4,825,207	43,440	38,000	4,597,756	5,443,843	35,900	42,870
Kazakhstan	121,371	154,947	7,440	8,710	279,328	407,647	17,110	22,910
Kenya	40,444	66,886	980	1,380	99,935	151,459	2,420	3,130
Korea, South	1,053,302	1,414,400	21,260	27,600	1,506,812	1,833,915	30,410	35,790
Lebanon	36,645	46,129	8,450	7,680	68,260	83,230	15,740	13,860
Malaysia	231,517	307,242	8,240	9,850	562,878	838,888	20,020	26,900
Mexico	1,048,985	1,152,770	8,940	9,040	1,748,866	2,262,920	14,910	17,740
Morocco	96,295	102,159	2,930	2,850	204,771	275,738	6,230	7,700
Netherlands	889,469	788,108	53,530	46,310	746,805	856,401	44,950	50,320
New Zealand	129,107	183,341	29,680	39,070	129,264	177,667	29,710	37,860
Nigeria	233,074	456,389	1,470	2,450	757,884	1,067,765	4,780	5,740
Norway	432,368	430,823	88,430	82,330	286,585	327,136	58,620	62,510
Pakistan	184,123	291,845	1,080	1,510	743,098	1,078,212	4,360	5,580
Peru	127,619	189,001	4,340	5,950	264,767	396,685	9,010	12,480
Philippines	256,027	369,969	2,730	3,580	684,793	970,830	7,310	9,400
Poland	484,234	481,280	12,730	12,680	773,568	1,015,858	20,330	26,770
Portugal	242,730	204,909	22,960	19,850	279,561	309,638	26,440	29,990
Romania	173,890	186,559	8,590	9,470	342,602	452,317	16,920	22,950
Russia	1,425,123	1,425,703	9,980	9,720	2,837,672	3,305,726	19,860	22,540
Saudi Arabia	514,152	702,099	18,750	21,750	1,236,786	1,799,741	45,100	55,760
Serbia	42,656	37,258	5,850	5,280	86,223	96,558	11,830	13,680
Singapore	227,377	290,909	44,790	51,880	356,614	476,878	70,240	85,050
South Africa	317,112	306,555	6,220	5,480	588,011	718,880	11,530	12,860
Spain	1,496,332	1,277,961	32,130	27,520	1,468,836	1,687,663	31,540	36,340
Sri Lanka	48,796	80,110	2,430	3,780	166,962	253,800	8,300	11,970
Sudan [4]	55,350	84,876	1,250	2,140	135,153	169,621	3,040	4,290
Sweden	505,495	540,960	53,900	54,630	402,211	495,166	42,890	50,000
Thailand	308,010	388,308	4,580	5,640	850,877	1,106,823	12,660	16,070
Turkey	754,125	888,818	10,430	11,180	1,252,138	1,907,487	17,310	23,990
Uganda	19,112	27,296	560	660	50,322	75,413	1,480	1,820
Ukraine	137,090	98,629	2,990	2,310	346,461	349,434	7,550	8,190
United Kingdom	2,597,893	2,782,338	41,390	42,390	2,272,129	2,763,382	36,200	42,100
Uruguay	35,060	52,449	10,390	15,230	54,371	72,647	16,110	21,090
Uzbekistan	38,346	70,841	1,340	2,220	122,251	211,563	4,280	6,640
Venezuela	335,817	(NA)	11,570	(NA)	464,747	(NA)	16,010	(NA)
Vietnam	110,302	190,497	1,270	2,050	367,548	560,984	4,230	6,050
Zambia	18,278	21,643	1,320	1,300	41,506	62,841	3,000	3,790

NA Not available. [1] Gross national income calculated using the World Bank Atlas conversion factor; for details, see source. [2] For explanation of purchasing power parity (PPP), see headnote, Table 1365. [3] Includes other countries not shown separately. [4] Sudan and South Sudan became separate countries in July 2011. Data for 2016 exclude South Sudan.

Source: The World Bank, Washington, DC, "World Development Indicators" database ©, <https://data.worldbank.org/data-catalog/world-development-indicators>, accessed September 2017.

Table 1365. Real Gross Domestic Product (GDP) Per Capita and Per Employed Persons by Country: 1960 to 2016

[U.S. figures based on the System of National Income and Product Accounts (NIPA) from the Bureau of Economic Analysis. Data for all other countries are based on the 1993 or 2008 United Nations System of National Accounts (SNA). Per capita data based on total resident population. Real GDP is a macroeconomic measure of the size of an economy adjusted for price changes and inflation. Employment data include people serving in the armed forces. Real dollars are calculated based on 2016 Purchasing Power Parities (PPPs). PPPs are currency conversion rates used to convert GDP expressed in different currencies to a common value (U.S. dollars in this case). A PPP for a given country is the number of national currency units needed to buy the specific basket of goods and services that one dollar will buy in the United States. See text, this section]

Country	1960	1970	1980	1990	2000	2005	2010	2012	2013	2014	2015	2016
REAL GDP PER CAPITA (2016 U.S. dollars)												
United States........	19,482	25,847	31,948	39,899	49,506	53,571	53,152	54,368	54,874	55,738	56,738	57,196
Canada.............	15,625	21,513	28,877	33,692	40,222	43,461	43,618	44,800	45,379	46,027	46,039	46,172
Australia............	16,205	22,164	26,566	31,656	39,772	44,136	46,351	47,685	47,940	48,566	49,063	49,558
Japan..............	6,943	16,919	23,388	32,726	36,513	38,441	38,728	39,381	40,238	40,441	40,987	41,468
Korea, South........	1,768	3,125	5,931	12,549	22,391	27,526	32,742	34,279	35,112	36,057	36,869	37,740
Singapore..........	6,017	11,564	23,596	37,044	55,283	61,909	76,824	81,386	83,785	85,110	85,116	85,205
Austria.............	12,958	19,377	27,352	33,585	41,692	44,208	46,378	47,657	47,438	47,396	47,345	47,519
Belgium............	13,274	20,259	27,622	32,834	39,841	42,642	43,984	44,119	43,921	44,494	44,890	45,120
Czech Republic......	(NA)	13,189	18,598	21,377	22,646	27,571	30,309	30,563	30,406	31,198	32,549	33,275
Denmark...........	16,900	24,330	29,205	35,390	44,348	46,685	46,088	46,442	46,681	47,223	47,644	47,858
Finland.............	11,404	17,530	23,702	30,872	37,261	41,777	42,560	42,629	42,111	41,673	41,647	42,102
France.............	13,380	20,638	26,708	31,918	37,557	39,320	39,713	40,228	40,255	40,239	40,502	40,817
Germany [1].........	16,555	23,289	30,325	34,224	40,179	41,206	44,220	46,075	46,175	46,716	47,110	47,531
Ireland.............	8,732	12,642	17,416	24,098	44,325	53,126	49,588	48,736	49,149	53,090	54,730	57,069
Italy...............	12,024	19,752	26,724	33,154	38,897	40,034	38,540	37,504	36,431	36,139	36,458	36,789
Netherlands........	16,705	24,124	29,643	34,799	45,243	47,180	49,367	49,244	49,006	49,523	50,267	51,086
Norway............	18,243	25,393	38,179	46,763	63,400	68,664	67,987	68,715	68,567	69,099	69,517	69,602
Spain..............	6,392	13,151	19,152	25,088	32,323	35,489	35,062	33,553	33,089	33,646	34,749	35,874
Sweden............	16,545	24,484	28,257	33,460	39,865	44,595	46,450	46,845	47,027	47,775	49,204	50,231
United Kingdom......	15,301	19,057	22,887	29,079	35,806	40,114	39,319	39,844	40,334	41,261	41,832	42,277
REAL GDP PER EMPLOYED PERSON (2016 U.S. dollars)												
United States........	50,688	63,929	71,127	81,752	100,597	110,904	116,705	118,052	118,908	119,821	121,161	121,244
Canada.............	41,931	55,872	63,211	69,616	82,299	85,289	84,890	86,660	87,473	89,157	89,273	89,884
Australia............	42,705	54,209	64,327	71,620	88,047	92,385	94,180	96,726	97,854	99,401	99,879	100,694
Japan..............	13,713	32,269	46,335	62,586	70,640	75,001	75,411	76,822	77,914	77,719	78,380	78,392
Korea, South........	6,426	10,475	16,525	29,746	49,797	58,029	68,090	69,723	70,637	71,478	72,518	73,719
Singapore..........	20,300	36,822	51,901	77,919	106,341	126,131	129,492	132,967	133,509	133,253	132,972	134,268
Austria.............	26,646	44,485	59,236	72,832	89,440	94,448	95,110	95,993	95,793	95,520	95,821	95,962
Belgium............	34,672	52,484	72,156	85,244	99,419	105,029	107,030	107,162	107,447	108,761	109,356	109,250
Czech Republic......	(NA)	25,204	36,398	42,887	47,681	57,060	62,631	63,283	62,775	64,125	66,119	66,522
Denmark...........	36,735	49,737	59,490	69,073	85,954	90,911	91,708	93,852	94,762	95,384	95,717	95,332
Finland.............	22,992	35,454	48,112	62,061	83,919	90,919	91,900	90,949	90,904	90,766	91,323	92,066
France.............	30,895	50,181	64,885	78,441	88,978	94,000	95,796	96,886	97,190	97,356	98,134	98,645
Germany [1].........	32,428	48,137	61,462	68,555	82,696	86,354	88,025	89,426	89,297	90,011	90,720	91,270
Ireland.............	23,117	34,930	50,533	71,903	99,297	112,438	119,911	119,891	118,239	126,120	128,452	131,575
Italy...............	28,753	53,007	70,360	82,941	96,249	94,760	92,286	90,205	90,257	90,298	90,395	90,049
Netherlands........	40,604	56,166	69,231	76,413	87,762	92,333	93,445	93,378	94,310	95,880	96,851	97,924
Norway............	42,708	59,999	80,032	96,343	122,742	134,874	128,309	128,501	128,397	129,288	131,036	132,235
Spain..............	15,874	33,160	56,798	70,123	79,540	79,280	84,188	86,624	87,438	87,856	88,454	88,934
Sweden............	33,859	49,793	54,866	62,270	82,243	92,597	96,854	96,371	96,640	97,784	100,248	101,860
United Kingdom......	33,571	43,231	51,378	62,218	77,053	84,344	84,799	85,835	86,462	87,051	87,429	87,760

NA Not available. [1] Prior to 1991, data are for the former West Germany.

Source: The Conference Board, Inc., "Total Economy Database™," May 2017 update. Reproduced with permission from The Conference Board, Inc. © 2017 The Conference Board, Inc.

Table 1366. Sectoral Contributions to Gross Value Added: 2010 and 2016

[In percent. According to the 2008 System of National Accounts (SNA) and the International Standard Industrial Classification (ISIC), Revision 4 (2008), with some exceptions, value added is estimated at basic prices and includes financial intermediation services indirectly measured (FISIM). Value added represents an industry's contribution to national GDP and is calculated as the difference between production and intermediate inputs. Value added comprises labor costs, consumption of fixed capital, indirect taxes less subsidies, and net operating surplus and mixed income. Selected data are estimated or provisional; see source for details]

Country	Agriculture [1]		Industry [2]				Services	
			Total		Manufacturing			
	2010	2016	2010	2016	2010	2016	2010	2016
United States [3]	1.2	[4] 1.1	16.7	[4] 15.8	12.4	[4] 12.3	78.4	[4] 78.9
Australia	2.5	[4] 2.6	20.5	[4] 15.6	7.9	[4] 6.6	69.0	[4] 73.1
Austria	1.4	1.3	22.2	21.6	18.7	18.7	69.9	70.7
Belgium	0.9	0.7	17.6	16.7	14.7	14.2	76.0	77.0
Chile	3.9	4.3	32.3	24.1	11.7	12.0	57.3	64.4
China	9.8	[4] 9.2	40.0	[4] 34.3	(NA)	(NA)	43.6	[4] 49.7
Czech Republic	1.7	2.5	29.9	32.3	23.4	27.1	61.5	59.8
Denmark	1.4	1.1	18.4	18.8	12.7	15.5	75.8	75.3
Estonia	3.2	2.9	22.0	20.7	15.7	15.8	68.8	70.4
Finland	2.7	2.7	23.5	20.3	19.5	16.9	67.3	70.2
France	1.8	1.6	13.5	14.1	11.3	11.4	78.6	78.8
Germany	0.7	0.6	25.9	25.6	22.2	22.6	69.1	69.0
Greece	3.3	4.0	11.2	13.4	8.2	9.8	81.1	80.2
Hungary	3.5	4.5	25.8	27.0	21.6	23.9	66.4	65.1
Ireland	1.1	1.0	24.4	38.9	21.6	36.7	72.9	57.5
Italy	2.0	2.1	18.7	19.3	15.8	16.3	73.7	73.8
Japan [5]	1.1	[4] 1.1	23.7	[4] 23.3	20.9	[4] 20.5	70.4	[4] 70.0
Korea	2.5	[4] 2.3	33.1	[4] 32.9	30.7	[4] 29.5	59.3	[4] 59.7
Latvia	4.4	3.2	18.9	16.7	13.4	12.5	71.7	74.9
Mexico	3.3	[4] 3.3	27.1	[4] 25.3	17.4	[4] 18.9	61.5	[4] 63.9
Netherlands	1.9	1.8	16.8	15.2	11.8	12.1	76.0	78.2
Norway	1.8	2.5	33.7	24.9	8.1	7.9	59.2	65.8
Poland	2.9	2.4	24.7	26.5	17.7	20.4	63.9	64.2
Portugal	2.2	2.2	16.8	18.5	13.2	13.6	75.2	75.3
Slovak Republic	2.8	3.8	26.3	27.3	20.8	22.8	62.0	61.4
Slovenia	2.0	2.3	24.2	27.6	20.2	23.9	67.4	65.4
Spain	2.6	2.6	17.2	17.8	13.3	14.1	71.4	74.1
Sweden	1.6	1.3	23.0	19.9	18.6	16.5	69.4	72.7
Switzerland	0.7	0.7	21.2	20.1	19.2	18.1	73.0	73.8
United Kingdom	0.7	0.6	14.4	13.0	10.0	9.7	79.2	80.2

NA Not available. [1] Includes forestry, fishing, and hunting sectors. [2] Includes energy. [3] Value added is estimated at factor cost for U.S. [4] Data is for 2015. [5] Value added is estimated approximately at market prices for Japan.

Source: Organisation for Economic Co-operation and Development (OECD), 2017, "National Accounts at a Glance," OECD National Accounts Statistics (database) ©, <http://dx.doi.org/10.1787/data-00369-en>, accessed July 2017.

Table 1367. Index of Industrial Production by Country: 2000 to 2016

[Annual averages of monthly data. Industrial production indexes generally measure output in the manufacturing, mining, electric, gas, and water utilities sectors. Minus sign (-) indicates decrease]

Country	Index (2010=100)								Annual percent change				
	2000	2005	2010	2012	2013	2014	2015	2016	2010 to 2011	2012 to 2013	2013 to 2014	2014 to 2015	2015 to 2016
United States	101.5	105.9	100.0	106.1	108.2	111.6	110.8	109.4	3.1	2.0	3.1	-0.7	-1.2
Australia	84.6	90.5	100.0	103.9	105.0	109.3	110.5	111.7	1.0	1.1	4.0	1.2	1.0
Austria	77.4	90.7	100.0	107.7	108.1	108.1	110.4	112.6	5.9	0.4	–	2.1	2.0
Belgium	70.9	85.3	100.0	102.6	103.5	104.5	104.6	109.0	4.7	0.9	1.0	0.1	4.2
Brazil	74.7	87.1	100.0	98.1	100.1	97.1	89.1	83.3	0.4	2.1	-3.0	-8.2	-6.5
Canada	111.7	113.0	100.0	104.9	106.4	110.8	110.0	110.4	4.9	1.5	4.1	-0.7	0.4
Chile	79.2	99.0	100.0	113.3	113.5	112.2	112.4	111.6	5.4	0.2	-1.2	0.2	-0.8
Czech Republic	69.6	90.6	100.0	105.2	105.2	110.5	115.8	119.1	0.4	0.5	0.5	–	0.4
Denmark	110.7	116.3	100.0	101.9	102.4	103.2	104.5	108.1	1.8	0.4	0.8	1.2	3.5
Finland	91.2	100.0	100.0	99.6	96.5	94.7	93.8	96.1	1.7	-3.1	-1.8	-1.0	2.5
France	114.4	111.5	100.0	100.1	99.4	98.5	100.4	100.8	2.4	-0.8	-0.9	2.0	0.4
Germany	89.4	95.3	100.0	108.0	108.4	110.5	110.9	112.3	8.7	0.3	2.0	0.4	1.3
Greece	123.9	119.4	100.0	92.2	89.2	87.5	88.3	90.6	-5.8	-3.2	-2.0	1.0	2.6
Hungary	70.8	92.7	100.0	104.3	105.8	113.5	121.5	122.4	5.7	1.4	7.2	7.0	0.8
India	48.8	[2] 65.8	100.0	105.5	106.2	108.1	111.6	111.9	4.8	0.6	1.8	3.2	0.3
Ireland	68.1	90.9	100.0	98.1	95.9	116.0	158.8	159.9	-0.4	-2.2	20.9	36.9	0.7
Italy	118.0	113.0	100.0	95.0	92.1	91.6	92.4	94.2	1.3	-3.0	-0.6	0.9	1.9
Japan	104.3	106.1	100.0	97.7	96.9	98.7	97.4	97.1	-2.9	-0.9	1.9	-1.3	-0.3
Korea, South	53.4	71.9	100.0	107.4	108.2	108.4	108.1	109.2	6.0	0.7	0.2	-0.3	1.0
Mexico [1]	92.5	96.8	100.0	106.3	105.9	108.7	109.8	109.6	3.5	-0.4	2.7	1.0	-0.1
Netherlands	89.6	93.7	100.0	99.0	99.5	96.7	93.5	95.4	-0.5	0.5	-2.8	-3.3	2.0
New Zealand	90.4	102.1	100.0	98.2	98.7	101.7	102.6	103.2	-2.4	0.5	3.1	0.8	0.7
Norway	118.6	113.5	100.0	96.7	94.1	96.1	97.5	96.4	-5.0	-2.7	2.1	1.5	-1.2
Poland	56.9	74.3	100.0	108.1	110.6	114.4	119.9	123.3	6.8	2.3	3.4	4.9	2.8
Russia	69.1	91.4	100.0	108.5	110.2	112.9	112.1	113.6	5.0	1.6	2.4	-0.7	1.4
Spain	116.5	119.3	100.0	92.1	90.6	91.7	94.7	96.5	-1.5	-1.6	1.2	3.2	2.0
Sweden	98.6	107.3	100.0	100.5	95.8	94.0	97.5	99.0	2.7	-4.7	-1.8	3.7	1.6
Switzerland	82.4	83.7	100.0	106.3	107.1	108.6	105.9	105.8	3.6	0.8	1.4	-2.5	-0.1
Turkey	63.2	86.2	100.0	112.4	116.2	120.3	123.8	126.1	9.6	3.4	3.5	2.9	1.9
United Kingdom	111.9	107.9	100.0	96.7	96.0	97.5	98.7	99.8	-0.6	-0.7	1.5	1.3	1.1

– Represents or rounds to zero. [1] Including construction. [2] Break in series.

Source: Organisation for Economic Co-operation and Development (OECD), 2017, "Key short-term indicators," Main Economic Indicators (database) ©, <http://dx.doi.org/10.1787/data-00039-en>, accessed July 2017.

Table 1368. Selected Indexes of Manufacturing Productivity, Unit Labor Costs, Employment, and Hours Worked by Country: 2000 to 2016

[2002=100. Data for all countries are prepared according to the System of National Accounts (SNA) 2008 or its European counterpart, the European System of Accounts 2010 (ESA 2010). Data refer to all employed persons (including employees, self-employed, and unpaid family workers). Minus sign (-) indicates decrease]

Index	United States	Aus-tralia	Canada	France	Ger-many	Italy	Japan	Nether-lands	South Korea	Swe-den	United King-dom
Output per hour worked: [1]											
2000	89.5	94.2	99.2	94.3	97.8	100.1	98.9	96.5	89.7	93.5	95.3
2010	152.0	113.8	106.8	128.1	124.6	110.5	131.1	123.9	181.3	150.8	129.7
2014	147.3	118.1	118.4	138.5	131.8	117.7	138.4	130.7	192.0	155.2	131.3
2015	148.2	118.2	117.3	143.4	132.5	119.9	141.0	132.5	191.8	162.3	129.8
2016	148.0	116.1	119.1	145.7	135.4	118.7	138.6	135.5	195.9	163.8	132.0
Average annual percent change:											
1999-2006	6.1	2.1	2.4	4.4	3.9	1.5	3.6	4.2	7.5	6.7	4.7
2007-2014	1.8	1.0	1.4	1.8	0.9	1.2	1.6	1.1	4.3	1.5	0.9
2015-2016	-0.1	-1.8	1.5	1.6	2.2	-1.0	-1.7	2.2	2.1	1.0	1.6
Hourly labor cost, national currency basis: [2]											
2000	94.0	92.0	93.9	91.7	96.4	93.8	102.9	93.0	85.9	90.5	93.1
2010	130.3	141.3	126.4	129.0	117.7	130.6	101.1	124.4	193.7	127.8	142.9
2014	138.8	159.4	143.8	141.7	128.7	142.8	104.3	137.8	219.3	144.5	154.2
2015	142.2	161.6	147.4	143.3	130.8	144.2	105.1	138.5	222.1	150.1	159.5
2016	146.5	166.6	151.3	145.4	133.4	143.1	105.5	141.0	229.6	152.0	166.2
Average annual percent change:											
1999-2006	4.1	4.3	3.6	3.8	2.4	2.9	-0.5	3.5	7.1	3.8	5.4
2007-2014	2.2	3.1	2.7	2.7	2.2	3.0	0.3	2.6	5.3	2.9	2.4
2015-2016	3.0	3.0	2.6	1.4	2.0	-0.7	0.3	1.8	3.3	1.3	4.2
Real hourly compensation, CPI deflated, national currency basis:											
2000	98.2	98.8	98.4	95.0	99.7	98.8	101.2	100.0	92.4	94.7	96.3
2010	107.5	112.8	107.9	112.1	104.3	111.0	102.1	109.7	154.8	117.7	112.6
2014	105.4	114.8	114.1	116.1	106.9	113.0	102.5	111.9	159.4	128.8	106.1
2015	107.9	114.6	115.7	117.4	108.4	114.0	102.5	111.8	159.7	134.0	108.7
2016	109.8	116.6	117.1	119.0	110.0	113.2	103.1	113.5	163.2	132.8	111.3
Average annual percent change:											
1999-2006	1.4	1.2	1.3	2.1	1.0	0.7	-0.2	1.3	4.6	2.9	3.0
2007-2014	0.2	0.4	0.9	1.2	0.6	1.1	0.1	0.8	2.6	1.9	-0.8
2015-2016	1.7	1.7	1.1	1.3	1.5	-0.6	0.5	1.5	2.2	-0.8	2.4
Unit labor costs, national currency basis: [2]											
2000	105.0	97.7	94.6	97.3	98.6	93.7	104.0	96.4	95.8	96.8	97.6
2010	85.7	124.1	118.4	100.7	94.5	118.3	77.1	100.4	106.9	84.8	110.2
2014	94.2	134.9	121.4	102.3	97.6	121.4	75.4	105.4	114.2	93.1	117.5
2015	95.9	136.8	125.6	100.0	98.7	120.2	74.6	104.5	115.8	92.5	122.8
2016	98.9	143.5	127.0	99.8	98.5	120.5	76.1	104.1	117.2	92.8	126.0
Average annual percent change:											
1999-2006	-2.0	2.2	1.2	-0.6	-1.5	1.5	-4.1	-0.7	-0.3	-2.9	0.7
2007-2014	0.4	2.1	1.3	0.9	1.3	1.7	-1.3	1.6	1.0	1.4	1.5
2015-2016	3.1	4.8	1.0	-0.2	-0.2	0.3	2.0	-0.4	1.2	0.3	2.5
Output per employed person: [1]											
2000	90.4	94.2	99.5	98.0	98.9	101.2	99.5	97.3	92.0	95.8	94.0
2010	143.4	111.2	104.2	128.3	121.5	103.3	130.3	123.1	169.6	154.4	131.8
2014	138.8	112.3	115.8	137.2	129.9	108.5	138.4	132.0	172.8	154.5	135.0
2015	138.7	114.1	115.1	142.4	131.1	112.0	141.3	133.2	173.2	162.3	133.6
2016	138.6	109.8	116.8	144.3	133.6	112.3	139.3	137.2	174.9	164.6	135.4
Average annual percent change:											
1999-2006	5.9	1.9	2.2	3.6	3.7	1.1	4.0	3.9	7.6	6.9	4.5
2007-2014	1.2	0.5	1.2	1.7	0.6	0.4	1.3	1.2	3.4	1.1	1.2
2015-2016	-0.1	-3.8	1.5	1.3	1.9	0.3	-1.5	2.9	1.0	1.4	1.3
All employed persons:											
2000	114.0	100.6	103.8	101.2	101.8	99.6	106.9	102.5	96.3	100.8	110.4
2010	81.7	92.7	80.6	81.1	92.9	90.7	93.2	86.3	98.5	82.8	72.7
2014	87.6	87.3	78.1	78.4	97.4	84.2	89.0	82.6	113.1	79.6	72.9
2015	89.0	84.2	78.7	77.5	97.7	83.6	88.3	82.8	114.8	79.1	73.5
2016	89.0	85.1	78.0	76.7	97.7	84.2	88.7	83.0	116.3	78.5	73.1
Average annual percent change:											
1999-2006	-2.5	-0.4	-0.3	-1.3	-1.0	-0.2	-1.8	-1.4	1.7	-1.3	-4.2
2007-2014	-1.0	-1.1	-2.5	-1.9	0.5	-2.1	-1.1	-1.2	1.6	-1.7	-1.9
2015-2016	(-Z)	1.1	-0.9	-1.0	(-Z)	0.8	0.5	0.3	1.3	-0.8	-0.6
Hours worked of all employed persons:											
2000	115.1	100.5	104.1	105.2	103.1	100.7	107.5	103.3	98.8	103.3	108.9
2010	77.1	90.6	78.7	81.3	90.6	84.9	92.6	85.7	92.1	84.8	73.9
2014	82.6	83.0	76.4	77.6	96.0	77.7	89.0	83.4	101.8	79.2	75.0
2015	83.3	81.3	77.2	77.0	96.7	78.0	88.5	83.3	103.6	79.1	75.7
2016	83.3	80.5	76.5	76.0	96.4	79.7	89.1	84.1	103.8	78.8	75.0
Average annual percent change:											
1999-2006	-2.8	-0.6	-0.5	-2.2	-1.2	-0.5	-1.4	-1.7	1.7	-1.1	-4.4
2007-2014	-1.7	-1.6	-2.8	-2.0	0.2	-3.0	-1.4	-1.1	0.7	-2.0	-1.5
2015-2016	(-Z)	-0.9	-0.9	-1.2	-0.3	2.1	0.7	1.0	0.2	-0.4	-0.9

Z less than 0.05 percent. [1] Output is defined as value added. [2] "Compensation" data are used as a proxy for "Labor Cost" when payroll tax and subsidies data are not available to adjust worker compensation to an employer labor cost basis.

Source: The Conference Board, Inc., International Labor Comparisons program, "International Comparisons of Manufacturing Productivity and Unit Labor Cost Trends 2016, Summary and Time Series Tables," May 2017, <https://www.conference-board.org/ilcprogram>. Reproduced with permission from The Conference Board, Inc. © 2017 The Conference Board, Inc.

Table 1369. Indexes of Hourly Compensation Costs for Employees in Manufacturing by Country: 2000 to 2015

[United States=100. Compensation costs include pay for time worked (base wages and salaries, overtime pay, bonuses and premiums paid each pay period, and cost of living adjustments), directly-paid benefits (pay for leave time, irregular bonuses, and pay in kind), employer social insurance expenditures (legally required, private, and contractual social benefit costs), and labor-related taxes (minus subsidies). Data are adjusted for exchange rates. Regional averages are trade-weighted to account for differences in countries' relative importance to total world trade in manufactured goods. See source for detail]

Area or country	2000	2010	2013	2014	2015	Area or country	2000	2010	2013	2014	2015
United States..........	100	100	100	100	100	Hungary.............	12	24	26	26	22
						Ireland................	66	117	115	117	96
ILC economies ¹.....	78	91	93	93	(NA)	Israel.................	49	55	61	62	58
OECD ²................	83	96	98	98	(NA)	Italy...................	67	97	101	101	83
Europe................	82	103	108	108	(NA)	Japan ⁶...............	100	91	79	73	63
Euro Area ³..........	83	112	117	117	98	Mexico...............	19	18	19	18	16
Eastern Europe ⁴.....	13	28	29	29	25	Netherlands.........	85	111	113	114	97
East Asia ex-Japan ⁵..	35	44	52	54	51	New Zealand........	36	59	71	73	62
Argentina ⁶............	33	37	55	48	55	Norway..............	98	165	180	170	132
Australia..............	67	114	130	124	103	Philippines...........	4	5	6	6	6
Austria................	88	115	122	123	104	Poland...............	14	24	25	27	23
Belgium...............	105	146	151	150	123	Portugal..............	24	35	35	34	29
Brazil..................	17	29	29	28	21	Singapore............	47	56	71	72	67
Canada................	73	99	100	93	82	Slovakia..............	10	31	34	35	30
Czech Republic........	14	33	33	32	27	South Korea.........	39	51	61	64	60
Denmark...............	89	140	141	142	118	Spain................	50	77	77	76	63
Estonia................	10	27	32	34	29	Sweden..............	94	123	141	135	111
Finland................	79	116	122	122	102	Switzerland..........	108	147	173	175	(NA)
France.................	85	112	119	119	100	Taiwan ⁶.............	29	24	26	26	25
Germany...............	101	126	132	134	112	Turkey...............	(NA)	18	17	17	15
Greece................	40	64	52	52	41	United Kingdom......	83	83	85	89	83

NA Not available. ¹ ILC (International Labor Comparisons) economies refers to the 35 national economies included in ILC compensation comparisons, excluding China and India that are not strictly comparable with each other or with data for other countries. Data for 2000 excludes Turkey. ² Organisation for Economic Co-operation and Development; see text, this section. Includes only those countries that are also ILC economies. ³ Euro Area includes Austria, Belgium, Estonia, Finland, France, Germany, Greece, Ireland, Italy, the Netherlands, Portugal, Slovakia and Spain. ⁴ Czech Republic, Estonia, Hungary, Poland, and Slovakia. ⁵ South Korea, Philippines, Singapore, and Taiwan. Excludes Japan. ⁶ Except for Argentina, Japan, and Taiwan, data relate to manufacturing as defined by the International Standard Industrial Classification of All Economic Activities (ISIC) Revision 4.

Source: The Conference Board, Inc., International Labor Comparisons program, "International Comparisons of Hourly Compensation Costs in Manufacturing, 2015," April 2016, <https://www.conference-board.org/ilcprogram/compensation>. Reproduced with permission from The Conference Board, Inc. © 2017 The Conference Board, Inc.

Table 1370. Annual Percent Change in Labor Productivity and Hours Worked by Country: 1995 to 2016

[Annual percent change for period shown. Labor productivity growth refers to the growth in gross domestic product (GDP) per hour worked. Data are derived from The Conference Board Total Economy Database. Regional labor productivity growth rates are aggregated using shares in nominal PPP converted GDP; regional hours growth is weighted using total hours shares. Growth rates are the averages of yearly growth rates. Minus sign (-) indicates decrease]

Country	Labor productivity		Total hours worked		Country	Labor productivity		Total hours worked	
	1995-2005	2006-2016	1995-2005	2006-2016		1995-2005	2006-2016	1995-2005	2006-2016
Advanced economies ¹........	2.1	1.0	0.6	0.3	Czech Republic.......	3.5	1.6	-0.4	0.4
United States.......	2.4	0.9	1.0	0.5	Estonia................	6.2	2.1	-0.2	-0.5
Japan...............	1.9	0.8	-0.6	-0.2	Hungary..............	3.2	0.7	0.3	0.3
					Latvia................	6.0	2.4	(Z)	-0.8
European Union (EU-15, old) ²......	1.6	0.6	0.8	0.2	Lithuania.............	5.2	2.8	0.4	-0.4
Austria..............	2.0	1.0	0.4	0.2	Malta.................	3.4	1.7	0.4	1.9
Belgium.............	1.3	0.5	1.1	0.7	Poland...............	4.4	2.7	0.1	1.1
Denmark............	1.3	0.7	0.9	(Z)	Romania..............	4.4	4.0	-1.9	-1.0
Finland..............	2.6	0.4	1.2	0.1	Slovakia..............	5.0	2.7	-0.4	0.8
France..............	1.9	0.7	0.4	0.1	Slovenia..............	3.8	1.0	-0.2	0.2
Germany............	1.7	0.8	-0.4	0.6	European Union (EU-28, enlarged) ⁵...	1.8	0.9	0.5	0.2
Greece..............	2.4	-0.4	1.2	-1.6	Addenda:				
Ireland..............	4.3	2.2	3.4	-0.3	Other advanced economies ¹..........	2.9	2.0	1.1	0.8
Italy.................	0.8	(Z)	0.8	-0.3	Australia..............	2.0	1.4	1.7	1.3
Luxembourg........	0.8	0.3	3.3	2.6	Canada...............	1.5	0.8	1.7	0.8
Netherlands........	1.6	0.5	1.2	0.6	Hong Kong............	1.7	2.8	1.6	0.5
Portugal............	1.2	1.0	1.2	-1.0	Iceland...............	3.0	1.2	1.4	1.1
Spain...............	0.4	1.2	3.4	-0.5	Israel.................	1.6	1.2	2.6	2.7
Sweden.............	2.7	0.8	0.4	1.2	New Zealand.........	1.3	1.0	2.2	1.3
United Kingdom....	2.1	0.4	0.9	0.9	Norway..............	2.3	-0.2	0.7	1.4
European Union (EU-13, new) ³....	3.8	2.4	-0.4	0.2	Singapore............	2.5	1.1	2.8	3.9
Bulgaria.............	2.1	2.8	-0.3	-0.2	South Korea..........	5.3	3.3	0.2	0.2
Croatia ⁴...........	4.7	-0.5	-0.5	0.7	Switzerland...........	1.5	0.6	0.2	1.2
Cyprus..............	1.7	0.5	1.7	(Z)	Taiwan...............	4.4	2.8	0.7	0.4

Z Less than 0.05 percent. ¹ "Advanced" includes the U.S., EU-15, Japan, and "other advanced" economies. ² Referring to membership of the European Union until April 30, 2004. ³ Referring to membership of the European Union as of January 1, 2007. ⁴ Referring to labor productivity based on persons engaged, not hours worked. ⁵ Referring to all 28 current members of the European Union. See text, this section.

Source: The Conference Board, New York, NY, "The Conference Board Total Economy Database™," May 2017 (Original version). Reproduced with permission from The Conference Board, Inc. © 2017 The Conference Board, Inc.

Table 1371. Comparative Price Levels—Selected OECD Countries: June 2017

[Purchasing power parities (PPPs) are rates of currency conversion that eliminate the differences in price levels between countries. Comparative price levels are defined as the ratios of PPPs to exchange rates. The PPPs are given in national currency units per U.S. dollar. This table should be read vertically. Each column shows the number of specified monetary units needed in each of the countries listed to buy the same representative basket of consumer goods and services. In each case the representative basket costs a hundred units in the country whose currency is specified. For example, in June 2017, an item that costs $1.00 in the United States would cost $0.96 (U.S. dollars) in Japan]

Country	United States (USD)	Australia (AUD)	Canada (CAD)	Chile (Chilean peso)	France (EUR)	Germany (EUR)	Italy (EUR)	Japan (JPY)	Korea (KRW)	Mexico (MXN)	Spain (EUR)	Turkey (TRY)	United Kingdom (GBP)
United States	100	86	99	155	105	109	110	104	110	177	121	201	98
Australia [1]	117	100	116	181	123	128	129	122	128	207	141	235	115
Austria	96	82	95	149	101	105	106	100	105	170	116	193	94
Belgium	98	84	97	152	103	107	108	102	107	174	119	197	96
Canada	101	86	100	156	106	110	111	105	110	179	122	203	99
Chile	65	55	64	100	68	71	71	67	71	114	78	130	63
Czech Republic	60	51	59	93	63	65	66	62	66	106	72	121	59
Denmark	123	105	122	191	130	135	136	129	135	218	149	248	121
Estonia	67	58	67	104	71	74	74	70	74	119	82	136	66
Finland	108	92	107	167	114	118	119	112	118	191	130	217	106
France	95	81	94	147	100	104	105	99	104	168	115	191	93
Germany	91	78	91	142	96	100	101	95	100	162	111	184	90
Greece	77	66	76	119	81	84	85	80	84	136	93	155	75
Hungary	52	45	52	81	55	57	58	55	58	93	64	106	52
Iceland	154	131	152	238	162	168	170	160	168	272	186	309	151
Ireland	110	94	109	170	116	120	122	115	121	195	133	222	108
Israel [2]	119	102	118	185	126	130	132	125	131	212	144	240	117
Italy	91	77	90	140	95	99	100	95	99	160	110	182	89
Japan	96	82	95	148	101	105	106	100	105	170	116	193	94
Korea, South	91	78	91	141	96	100	101	95	100	162	110	184	89
Latvia	64	55	63	99	67	70	70	67	70	113	77	128	63
Luxembourg	110	94	109	171	116	120	122	115	121	195	133	222	108
Mexico	56	48	56	87	59	62	62	59	62	100	68	114	55
Netherlands	98	84	97	152	104	107	108	102	108	174	119	198	96
New Zealand [1]	116	99	115	179	122	126	128	121	127	205	140	233	113
Norway	123	105	122	191	130	135	136	129	135	218	149	248	121
Poland	49	42	48	76	51	53	54	51	53	86	59	98	48
Portugal	75	64	74	116	79	82	83	78	82	133	91	151	74
Slovak Republic	60	51	59	92	63	65	66	62	65	106	72	120	58
Slovenia	72	62	72	112	76	79	80	76	80	129	88	146	71
Spain	83	71	82	128	87	90	91	86	91	146	100	166	81
Sweden	107	92	106	166	113	117	118	112	117	190	130	216	105
Switzerland	144	123	143	223	152	157	159	150	158	255	174	290	141
Turkey	50	42	49	77	52	54	55	52	54	88	60	100	49
United Kingdom	102	87	101	158	107	111	113	106	112	181	123	205	100

[1] Estimates based on quarterly consumer prices. [2] The statistical data for Israel are supplied by and under the responsibility of the relevant Israeli authorities. The use of such data by the OECD is without prejudice to the status of the Golan Heights, East Jerusalem and Israeli settlements in the West Bank under the terms of international law.

Source: Organisation for Economic Co-operation and Development (OECD), 2017 "Prices: Comparative Price Levels," Main Economic Indicators (database) ©, <http://dx.doi.org/10.1787/data-00536-en>, accessed August 2017.

Table 1372. Indexes of Living Costs Abroad by Selected City: 2017

[As of January 2017. Washington, DC=100. Indexes compare the costs in dollars of representative goods and services (excluding housing and education) purchased at the foreign location and the cost of comparable goods and services in the Washington, DC area. The indexes are place-to-place comparisons at specific times and currency exchange rates. They cannot be used for measuring cost changes over time at a foreign location. Since the indexes reflect only the expenditure pattern and living costs of American families, they are not comparable to the living costs of foreign nationals living in their own country. Survey dates show month/day/year]

Country/territory	City	Survey date	Local index [1]	Country/territory	City	Survey date	Local index [1]
Algeria	Algiers	12/13/2015	88	Kyrgyzstan	Bishkek	7/30/2013	133
Angola	Luanda	9/27/2015	184	Laos	Vientiane	1/15/2016	127
Argentina	Buenos Aires	6/21/2015	152	Latvia	Riga	5/11/2014	143
Armenia	Yerevan	11/22/2015	140	Lebanon	Beirut	12/17/2014	130
Australia	Canberra	4/16/2015	147	Liberia	Monrovia	8/8/2012	143
Austria	Vienna	12/3/2013	176	Libya	Tripoli	1/5/2007	116
Azerbaijan	Baku	1/5/2015	156	Lithuania	Vilnius	2/5/2015	98
Bahamas	Nassau	4/11/2016	160	Luxembourg	(X)	6/8/2015	140
Bangladesh	Dhaka	7/1/2015	130	Macedonia	Skopje	7/8/2015	82
Belarus	Minsk	9/27/2013	136	Madagascar	Antananarivo	1/13/2016	156
Belgium	Brussels	3/23/2015	132	Malawi	Lilongwe	3/12/2014	132
Belize	Belmopan	3/20/2014	131	Malaysia	Kuala Lumpur	9/25/2014	116
Bolivia	La Paz	7/21/2011	120	Mali	Bamako	2/12/2014	154
Bosnia-Herzegovina	Sarajevo	2/23/2015	102	Mauritania	Nouakchott	4/12/2015	132
Botswana	Gaborone	11/5/2014	129	Mexico	Mexico City	9/27/2012	122
Brazil	Sao Paulo	6/5/2014	155	Moldova	Chisinau	5/1/2012	122
Bulgaria	Sofia	11/11/2014	141	Mongolia	Ulaanbaatar	4/6/2014	141
Burma	Rangoon	12/1/2015	90	Montenegro	Podgorica	9/14/2015	116
Burundi	Bujumbura	12/2/2014	128	Morocco	Casablanca	2/11/2014	151
Cambodia	Phnom Penh	3/4/2013	128	Mozambique	Maputo	9/8/2014	148
Cameroon	Yaounde	5/11/2015	143	Nepal	Kathmandu	3/17/2014	109
Canada	Ottawa	10/19/2012	158	Netherlands	The Hague	4/21/2014	159
Chad	Ndjamena	5/22/2014	158	New Zealand	Wellington	2/8/2016	126
Chile	Santiago	9/7/2015	134	Nicaragua	Managua	8/11/2014	115
China	Beijing	5/26/2016	139	Niger	Niamey	5/16/2016	135
Colombia	Bogota	12/15/2014	138	Nigeria	Abuja	10/6/2013	163
Costa Rica	San Jose	1/26/2016	146	Norway	Oslo	1/25/2016	153
Cote d'Ivoire	Abidjan	2/23/2015	142	Oman	Muscat	9/28/2014	131
Croatia	Zagreb	6/15/2016	108	Pakistan	Islamabad	12/10/2004	102
Cuba	Havana	12/26/2014	137	Panama	Panama City	12/31/2015	127
Cyprus	Nicosia	9/17/2014	148	Papua New Guinea	Port Moresby	1/22/2015	170
Czech Republic	Prague	7/12/2012	140	Paraguay	Asuncion	11/26/2015	116
Dem. Rep. of Congo	Kinshasa	2/16/2012	194	Peru	Lima	6/5/2015	138
Denmark	Copenhagen	5/4/2015	160	Philippines	Manila	4/19/2015	115
Djibouti	Djibouti City	2/11/2014	155	Poland	Warsaw	7/31/2012	131
Dominican Republic	Santo Domingo	11/5/2012	125	Portugal	Lisbon	10/5/2014	137
Ecuador	Quito	4/13/2016	157	Qatar	Doha	9/9/2015	133
Egypt	Cairo	3/13/2006	96	Romania	Bucharest	6/14/2012	116
El Salvador	San Salvador	4/21/2014	137	Russia	Moscow	3/11/2016	147
Equatorial Guinea	Malabo	2/18/2010	177	Rwanda	Kigali	5/27/2015	150
Eritrea	Asmara	4/12/2015	184	Samoa	(X)	6/20/2011	137
Estonia	Tallinn	7/21/2015	138	Saudi Arabia	Riyadh	6/2/2014	141
Ethiopia	Addis Ababa	4/19/2014	112	Senegal	Dakar	9/17/2014	179
Fiji	Suva	9/10/2014	136	Serbia	Belgrade	3/28/2016	97
Finland	Helsinki	2/3/2015	133	Sierra Leone	Freetown	5/14/2014	155
France	Paris	2/19/2015	162	Singapore	(X)	12/11/2013	152
Gabon	Libreville	10/21/2015	153	Slovakia	Bratislava	6/17/2012	135
Georgia	Tbilisi	7/27/2014	130	Slovenia	Ljubljana	3/18/2016	139
Germany	Berlin	12/17/2015	156	South Africa	Pretoria	10/23/2014	128
Ghana	Accra	5/16/2012	163	Spain	Madrid	8/28/2014	151
Greece	Athens	10/22/2013	150	Sri Lanka	Colombo	3/4/2015	98
Guatemala	Guatemala City	2/10/2014	125	Sudan	Khartoum	12/14/2013	168
Guyana	Georgetown	4/13/2012	155	Sweden	Stockholm	5/13/2010	185
Haiti	Port-au-Prince	3/23/2016	147	Switzerland	Geneva	11/17/2015	169
Honduras	Tegucigalpa	7/20/2015	119	Syria	Damascus	10/13/2010	116
Hong Kong	(X)	6/8/2014	147	Taiwan	Taipei	12/29/2015	126
Hungary	Budapest	5/3/2015	114	Tajikistan	Dushanbe	4/7/2016	117
Iceland	Reykjavik	1/29/2015	132	Tanzania	Dar es Salaam	10/14/2014	147
India	New Delhi	4/21/2016	105	Thailand	Bangkok	3/10/2015	122
Indonesia	Jakarta	11/17/2015	107	Tunisia	Tunis	1/9/2014	121
Iraq	Baghdad	7/21/2004	74	Turkey	Istanbul	3/9/2014	129
Ireland	Dublin	12/4/2014	147	Uganda	Kampala	9/23/2012	137
Israel	Tel Aviv	3/4/2014	153	Ukraine	Kyiv	10/28/2015	130
Italy	Rome	2/5/2012	171	United Arab Emirates	Dubai	7/21/2016	131
Jamaica	Kingston	3/31/2016	118	United Kingdom	London	9/11/2014	220
Japan	Tokyo City	2/18/2014	180	Uruguay	Montevideo	1/29/2014	157
Jordan	Amman	3/12/2013	140	Uzbekistan	Tashkent	8/4/2014	143
Kazakhstan	Astana	5/9/2014	146	Venezuela	Caracas	9/4/2014	173
Kenya	Nairobi	10/20/2014	144	Vietnam	Hanoi	5/27/2014	117
Korea, South	Seoul	11/1/2014	150	Yemen	Sanaa	4/25/2009	92
Kosovo	Pristina	8/16/2009	129	Zambia	Lusaka	6/15/2014	143
Kuwait	Kuwait City	11/30/2013	129	Zimbabwe	Harare	4/19/2015	155

X Not applicable. [1] The local index measures living costs for private American citizens and excludes special price advantages available only to U.S. government employees. The local index is a comparison of prices at the foreign post and in Washington, DC, with the price ratios weighted by the expenditure pattern of American employees living at the foreign post. This is the index most appropriate for use by business firms and other private organizations to establish cost-of-living allowances for their American employees stationed abroad.

Source: U.S. Department of State, Bureau of Administration, "Indexes of Living Costs Abroad, Quarters Allowances, and Hardship Differentials," January 2017, <http://aoprals.state.gov/content.asp?content_id=186&menu_id=81>.

Table 1373. Percent of Consumer Expenditures Spent on Food, Alcohol, and Tobacco Consumed at Home by Selected Country: 2015

Country/territory	Food [1]	Alcoholic beverages and tobacco	Country/territory	Food [1]	Alcoholic beverages and tobacco	Country/territory	Food [1]	Alcoholic beverages and tobacco
United States	**6.4**	**2.0**	Georgia	31.6	5.3	Peru	36.4	6.0
			Germany	10.3	3.2	Philippines	41.9	1.2
Algeria	42.5	2.1	Greece	16.9	4.9	Poland	16.5	7.4
Argentina	20.3	4.5	Guatemala	40.6	1.7	Portugal	17.3	3.2
Australia	9.8	3.4	Hong Kong	14.1	1.2	Qatar	11.7	0.3
Austria	9.9	3.4	Hungary	18.6	8.5	Romania	27.7	3.6
Azerbaijan	40.1	1.6	India	30.5	2.3	Russia	28.0	9.2
Bahrain	12.9	0.4	Indonesia	32.9	5.2	Saudi Arabia	25.0	0.6
Belarus	36.4	7.7	Iran	24.2	0.4	Serbia	24.5	7.1
Belgium	12.9	4.2	Ireland	9.6	5.7	Singapore	6.7	1.9
Bolivia	28.5	1.8	Israel	14.8	2.5	Slovakia	17.7	5.0
Bosnia-Herzegovina	31.1	6.3	Italy	14.4	4.4	Slovenia	14.6	5.6
Brazil	15.5	2.2	Japan	14.2	2.5	South Africa	18.9	5.9
Bulgaria	18.4	6.9	Jordan	37.9	6.6	South Korea	13.0	2.2
Cameroon	45.6	2.1	Kazakhstan	43.0	1.1	Spain	13.0	4.0
Canada	9.1	3.3	Kenya	46.7	3.3	Sweden	12.6	3.6
Chile	15.3	2.8	Kuwait	18.2	0.5	Switzerland	8.7	3.6
China	25.0	3.5	Latvia	20.0	8.0	Taiwan	14.0	2.0
Colombia	17.4	2.9	Lithuania	23.2	6.9	Thailand	25.7	3.3
Costa Rica	19.9	0.9	Macedonia	31.7	5.7	Tunisia	22.3	3.2
Croatia	30.5	3.7	Malaysia	20.6	1.8	Turkey	21.5	5.1
Czech Republic	15.9	8.2	Mexico	23.1	2.6	Turkmenistan	38.2	2.2
Denmark	11.1	3.8	Montenegro	19.0	3.5	Ukraine	38.1	8.1
Dominican Republic	23.2	4.2	Morocco	35.2	3.9	United Arab Emirates	13.8	0.2
Ecuador	22.7	0.8	Netherlands	11.7	3.4	United Kingdom	8.2	3.9
Egypt	35.2	4.4	New Zealand	14.9	5.0	Uruguay	18.2	1.2
Estonia	20.4	8.6	Nigeria	56.4	1.3	Uzbekistan	30.5	2.5
Finland	12.8	4.7	Norway	12.3	4.1	Venezuela	19.6	3.7
France	13.2	3.5	Pakistan	40.9	1.0	Vietnam	35.0	2.8

[1] Includes nonalcoholic beverages.

Source: U.S. Department of Agriculture, Economic Research Service, Food Expenditure Series, "Expenditures on food and alcoholic beverages that were consumed at home by selected countries," <http://www.ers.usda.gov/data-products/food-expenditures.aspx>, accessed August 2016.

Table 1374. Gross Public Debt, Expenditures, and Receipts as Percent of GDP by Country: 2000 to 2018

[Percent of nominal gross domestic product. Gross debt, expenditures, and receipts refer to the general government sector, which is a consolidation of accounts for the central, state, and local governments plus social security. Expenditures, or total outlays, are defined as current outlays plus capital outlays. Receipts cover current receipts, but exclude capital receipts. Nontax receipts consist of property income (including dividends and other transfers from public enterprises), fees, charges, sales, fines, and capital transfers received by the general government, etc.]

Country	Gross debt			Expenditures			Receipts		
	2000	2010	2018 (P)	2000	2010	2018 (P)	2000	2010	2018 (P)
United States [1]	**52.8**	**95.4**	**109.2**	**33.9**	**43.2**	**37.9**	**34.7**	**31.0**	**32.7**
Australia	27.1	30.3	46.0	34.6	36.6	35.7	36.1	32.0	34.5
Austria	70.5	96.1	100.9	50.7	53.1	49.6	48.6	48.6	48.9
Belgium	120.3	107.8	124.6	49.0	53.3	52.0	49.0	49.3	50.2
Canada	84.7	86.3	99.5	40.7	43.2	39.9	43.3	38.4	38.6
Czech Republic	24.0	46.3	47.2	40.3	43.0	40.0	36.9	38.6	40.5
Denmark	60.5	53.4	53.1	52.7	56.7	52.8	54.6	54.0	52.5
Estonia	6.8	12.0	13.4	36.4	40.5	41.0	36.3	40.7	40.2
Finland	50.9	55.9	81.8	48.0	54.8	54.2	54.9	52.1	52.8
France	71.9	96.9	125.7	51.1	56.5	55.9	49.8	49.7	53.1
Germany	59.5	84.6	71.0	44.7	47.4	44.5	45.6	43.1	45.1
Greece	113.2	127.3	174.1	46.3	52.4	48.0	42.3	41.2	47.7
Hungary	60.9	85.9	94.3	46.8	49.2	47.1	43.8	44.7	44.3
Iceland	40.4	90.8	59.3	41.2	49.3	39.9	42.5	39.6	41.4
Ireland	38.4	85.2	87.6	30.9	65.3	26.9	35.8	33.2	26.8
Israel [2]	79.6	70.7	62.1	48.0	41.1	40.2	44.8	37.7	37.6
Italy	118.8	126.2	156.2	45.4	49.9	48.7	44.1	45.7	47.3
Japan	132.3	181.4	227.9	37.5	39.3	38.0	30.2	30.1	33.6
Korea	(NA)	33.5	45.5	24.7	31.0	32.5	29.1	32.0	34.3
Latvia	14.5	53.3	45.2	37.3	45.0	37.2	34.5	36.3	36.8
Luxembourg	12.6	26.8	32.1	37.8	44.2	39.5	43.7	43.5	40.1
Netherlands	60.5	68.1	70.2	41.8	48.2	42.6	43.6	43.2	44.2
New Zealand	36.2	37.0	38.2	37.5	47.9	39.2	39.2	40.7	40.0
Norway	32.2	48.4	59.4	42.0	45.0	50.6	57.1	56.0	55.0
Poland	45.4	61.0	73.6	42.1	45.8	41.9	39.1	38.5	38.9
Portugal	62.0	104.1	144.2	42.6	51.8	43.2	39.4	40.6	42.2
Slovak Republic	57.9	47.4	57.3	52.0	42.1	39.9	40.0	34.7	39.3
Slovenia	(NA)	46.8	95.7	46.1	49.3	44.1	42.5	43.6	43.8
Spain	65.2	66.8	116.1	39.1	45.6	40.6	38.1	36.2	38.2
Sweden	57.3	46.0	48.3	53.6	51.3	49.6	56.9	51.2	50.5
Switzerland	52.7	44.9	43.5	34.2	32.9	34.2	33.7	33.3	34.7
United Kingdom	48.8	89.3	122.6	35.9	48.3	41.3	37.0	38.7	38.9

NA Not available. P Projection. [1] Receipts exclude the operating surpluses of public enterprises, while expenditures include them. [2] See footnote 2, Table 1371.

Source: Organisation for Economic Co-operation and Development (OECD), 2017, "OECD Economic Outlook No. 101 (Edition 2017/1)," OECD Economic Outlook: Statistics and Projections (database) ©, <http://dx.doi.org/10.1787/639d73ee-en>, accessed August 2017.

Table 1375. Percent Distribution of Tax Receipts by Country and Tax Type: 2010 to 2015

Country	Total[1]	Income and profits taxes[2]			Social security contributions			Taxes on goods and services[5]		
		Total[3]	Individual	Corporate	Total[4]	Employees	Employers	Total[3]	General consumption taxes[6]	Taxes on specific goods, services[7]
United States:										
2010.............	100.0	42.4	34.8	7.6	26.1	11.6	13.1	18.3	8.4	7.0
2015[8].............	100.0	49.1	40.8	8.3	23.7	10.5	11.8	16.8	7.7	6.7
Australia:										
2010.............	100.0	56.7	38.4	18.3	0.0	0.0	0.0	28.9	13.7	11.8
2014.............	100.0	57.9	41.0	16.8	0.0	0.0	0.0	26.9	12.9	10.4
Canada:										
2010.............	100.0	46.6	35.0	10.5	14.9	5.9	8.4	24.0	14.0	8.5
2015[8].............	100.0	47.6	36.8	9.8	15.3	6.1	8.6	23.2	13.9	7.9
Chile:										
2010.............	100.0	38.1	6.8	20.4	6.8	6.6	0.3	51.2	38.5	9.8
2015[8].............	100.0	36.4	7.1	23.7	6.9	6.7	0.2	54.0	40.8	9.9
Czech Republic:										
2010.............	100.0	20.2	10.2	10.0	44.8	9.1	28.2	33.2	20.5	10.8
2015[8].............	100.0	21.4	10.8	10.6	43.3	8.8	27.4	33.6	21.9	10.1
France:										
2010.............	100.0	22.7	17.1	5.6	38.4	9.3	26.0	24.9	16.7	7.4
2015[8].............	100.0	23.5	18.9	4.6	37.1	9.4	24.8	24.4	15.7	8.0
Germany:										
2010.............	100.0	28.5	24.3	4.3	39.2	17.2	18.5	29.5	20.0	8.4
2015[8].............	100.0	31.5	26.7	4.7	37.9	16.9	17.8	27.2	18.9	7.3
Greece:										
2010.............	100.0	21.9	12.3	7.8	34.6	13.5	15.7	38.0	23.0	11.5
2014.............	100.0	23.7	16.4	5.3	28.7	11.8	12.5	43.4	21.0	12.5
Italy:										
2010.............	100.0	32.6	26.8	5.5	31.1	5.6	21.5	26.3	14.5	9.1
2015[8].............	100.0	32.0	26.2	4.8	30.2	5.6	20.1	27.1	14.3	9.7
Japan:										
2010.............	100.0	30.2	18.6	11.6	41.1	17.8	18.6	18.7	9.6	7.2
2014.............	100.0	31.8	18.9	12.9	39.7	17.3	18.1	19.8	12.2	6.0
Korea, South:										
2010.............	100.0	28.0	14.2	13.8	23.3	9.5	10.4	33.7	17.5	15.1
2015[8].............	100.0	30.3	17.4	12.8	26.6	11.3	12.2	28.0	15.3	10.9
Turkey:										
2010.............	100.0	21.3	14.0	7.3	24.9	9.4	13.7	47.7	21.7	24.1
2015[8].............	100.0	20.3	14.6	5.7	29.0	11.0	16.2	44.3	20.6	22.0
United Kingdom:										
2010.............	100.0	37.5	28.7	8.7	19.0	7.6	10.9	30.9	18.8	10.8
2015[8].............	100.0	35.4	27.9	7.5	18.6	7.3	10.9	32.9	21.2	10.6

[1] Includes property taxes, employer payroll taxes other than social security contributions, and miscellaneous taxes not shown separately. [2] Includes taxes on capital gains. [3] Includes other taxes, not shown separately. [4] Includes contributions of self-employed persons, not shown separately. [5] Taxes on the production, sales, transfer, leasing, and delivery of goods and services and rendering of services. [6] Primarily value-added and sales taxes. [7] For example, excise taxes on alcohol, tobacco, and gasoline. [8] Data are provisional/estimates.

Source: Organisation for Economic Co-operation and Development (OECD), 2017, "Revenue Statistics: Comparative tables," OECD Tax Statistics (database) ©, <http://dx.doi.org/10.1787/data-00262-en>, accessed August 2017.

Table 1376. Household Tax Burden by Country: 2016

[As percent of gross wage earnings of the average worker. The tax burden reflects income tax plus employee social security contributions less cash benefits]

Country	Single person without children	One-earner family with two children	Country	Single person without children	One-earner family with two children
OECD average[1].............	25.52	19.93	Italy....................	31.12	24.23
United States.................	**25.98**	**14.10**	Japan....................	22.20	20.79
Australia.........................	24.32	24.32	Korea, South.............	14.14	11.70
Austria..........................	31.87	29.67	Latvia...................	29.05	19.55
Belgium..........................	40.75	29.10	Luxembourg.............	30.96	19.28
Canada..........................	23.08	18.26	Mexico...................	10.84	10.84
Chile............................	7.00	7.00	Netherlands.............	30.45	28.39
Czech Republic..................	23.57	6.84	New Zealand............	17.89	17.89
Denmark.........................	36.19	32.25	Norway..................	27.93	26.84
Estonia..........................	18.29	12.59	Poland....................	25.00	19.19
Finland..........................	30.79	30.73	Portugal.................	27.57	15.25
France[2].........................	29.10	22.16	Slovak Republic.........	23.24	11.91
Germany.........................	39.66	21.29	Slovenia.................	33.43	25.09
Greece..........................	25.39	25.92	Spain....................	21.38	14.07
Hungary..........................	33.50	24.44	Sweden..................	24.85	24.85
Iceland..........................	29.19	21.83	Switzerland.............	16.88	10.42
Ireland..........................	19.25	10.80	Turkey...................	27.26	25.25
Israel[3].........................	17.80	17.80	United Kingdom.........	23.34	22.74

[1] As of 2016, the Organisation for Economic Co-operation and Development (OECD) is comprised of the 35 member countries shown above. See text, this section. [2] Figures correspond to tax calculations that are based on the tax legislation relating to the income earned in the selected year. [3] See footnote 2, Table 1371.

Source: Organisation for Economic Co-operation and Development (OECD), 2017, "Taxing Wages: Comparative tables," OECD Tax Statistics (database) ©, <http://dx.doi.org/10.1787/data-00265-en>, accessed July 2017.

Table 1377. Household Net Saving Rates by Country: 2000 to 2015

[As a percentage of household disposable income. Household savings are estimated by subtracting household consumption expenditure from household disposable income, plus the change in net equity of households in pension funds. Households include households plus nonprofit institutions serving households. Net saving rates are measured after deducting consumption of fixed capital (depreciation), with respect to assets used in enterprises operated by households, as well as owner-occupied dwellings. The household saving rate is calculated as the ratio of household savings to household disposable income (plus the change in net equity of households in pension funds). Minus sign (-) indicates an excess of expenditures over income]

Country	2000	2005	2009	2010	2011	2012	2013	2014	2015
United States..............	4.3	2.7	6.3	5.8	6.2	7.9	5.2	5.8	6.0
EU-28 [1]...............	6.4	5.3	6.9	5.9	5.1	4.6	4.5	4.1	(NA)
Australia [2]................	1.9	-0.1	7.9	8.9	9.7	8.7	9.0	8.0	6.8
Austria......................	10.5	10.7	11.3	9.3	7.9	8.7	7.0	7.0	7.3
Belgium.....................	10.4	8.5	11.3	8.1	6.6	5.7	4.9	4.6	4.2
Canada......................	5.3	1.5	4.7	4.4	4.3	4.8	5.3	4.0	4.3
Chile........................	(NA)	11.6	11.6	7.7	8.7	10.3	10.2	10.1	8.9
Czech Republic............	6.0	6.1	8.5	7.6	6.0	6.0	5.6	6.6	6.6
Denmark....................	-5.6	-4.3	0.7	1.8	0.8	0.1	2.3	-1.8	4.4
France......................	10.0	9.4	10.8	10.4	10.0	9.5	8.7	8.7	8.9
Germany....................	9.0	10.1	10.0	10.0	9.6	9.3	9.0	9.4	9.7
Greece [3]...................	-1.4	-2.9	-1.1	-6.9	-8.9	-10.9	-16.1	-15.3	-19.3
Hungary.....................	5.2	5.6	3.4	3.4	4.1	2.6	4.3	5.7	4.3
Ireland......................	-4.0	1.1	9.6	7.6	4.7	7.3	5.6	6.1	5.8
Italy........................	7.4	9.1	7.1	4.2	3.7	2.0	3.6	3.9	3.1
Japan.......................	8.9	3.4	4.0	3.7	4.0	2.7	0.3	-0.4	0.7
Korea, South...............	(NA)	6.7	4.8	4.7	3.9	3.9	5.6	7.2	(NA)
Latvia.......................	-9.8	-6.5	5.9	-4.4	-15.0	-15.6	-16.1	-14.7	-12.7
Mexico......................	(NA)	8.2	8.4	8.8	6.9	6.1	5.6	6.4	6.6
Netherlands................	5.6	3.7	7.1	4.9	5.8	7.2	7.3	7.9	6.5
New Zealand [2]............	-2.5	-5.4	1.4	2.4	2.6	0.9	0.7	[3] -1.0	(NA)
Norway......................	4.3	9.7	5.1	4.0	5.8	7.1	7.6	8.2	10.4
Poland......................	11.0	2.2	2.8	2.4	-1.1	-1.1	-0.1	-0.5	-1.0
Spain.......................	5.8	3.2	7.3	3.7	4.6	2.3	3.8	3.2	2.3
Sweden.....................	4.3	5.2	12.3	11.1	12.6	15.3	15.3	15.9	16.2
Switzerland................	15.3	14.0	17.1	17.0	17.8	18.5	19.1	20.1	19.0
United Kingdom............	4.3	-0.2	3.8	5.7	3.4	2.7	0.6	0.5	0.2

NA Not available. [1] See footnote 3, Table 1390 for list of EU-28 countries. [2] Data refer to fiscal year. [3] Data are estimates.

Source: Organisation for Economic Co-operation and Development (OECD), 2017, "National Accounts at a Glance," OECD National Accounts Statistics (database) ©, <http://dx.doi.org/10.1787/data-00369-en>, accessed July 2017.

Table 1378. Insurance and Pensions by Country: 2015

[5,270,840 represents $5,270,840,000,000]

Country	Insurance						Pensions [2]	
	Investment assets (mil. U.S. dollars) [1]	Direct gross premiums (percent of GDP)	Total gross premiums (mil. U.S. dollars)		Gross claims payments (mil. U.S. dollars)		Investment assets (mil. U.S. dollars)	Benefits paid (percent of GDP)
			Life	Non-life	Life	Non-life		
United States.........	5,270,840	11.3	973,634	1,647,449	343,018	922,356	23,860,553	6.7
Australia...............	72,063	5.7	46,633	32,163	40,141	23,049	1,511,771	5.8
Austria.................	89,394	5.1	7,437	13,645	9,368	8,013	(NA)	0.3
Belgium................	249,115	6.1	17,038	11,642	21,863	10,029	25,956	0.2
Canada.................	488,043	4.4	23,996	59,596	3,249	27,788	2,248,545	3.5
Czech Republic.......	(NA)	3.4	2,537	3,695	2,081	1,972	15,028	0.4
Denmark...............	289,157	10.8	22,055	9,943	17,055	7,114	598,574	0.8
Finland.................	25,730	5.1	6,941	4,972	4,389	3,185	132,905	1.3
France.................	1,842,461	9.4	160,881	89,891	131,580	62,368	212,254	(Z)
Germany...............	1,570,742	6.3	99,588	193,381	81,302	86,138	218,473	0.2
Greece.................	12,114	2.0	1,999	1,963	1,461	746	(NA)	(NA)
Hungary................	3,894	2.5	1,529	1,462	1,182	742	4,819	0.1
Iceland.................	981	2.5	35	384	10	274	26,651	5.1
Ireland.................	57,957	20.1	38,837	9,945	31,703	6,601	122,324	(NA)
Israel [3]...............	39,063	(NA)	(NA)	(NA)	(NA)	(NA)	165,228	1.7
Italy....................	614,455	9.0	129,025	36,762	79,299	25,049	154,991	0.3
Japan..................	3,214,102	7.3	311,854	(NA)	268,119	39,424	(NA)	(NA)
Korea, South..........	676,310	12.7	104,801	78,841	59,306	23,361	343,315	2.1
Luxembourg...........	59,268	36.5	19,633	1,637	13,639	2,111	1,572	0.2
Mexico.................	52,016	2.1	11,530	13,399	6,421	5,893	175,939	0.5
Netherlands...........	528,996	4.9	16,300	21,084	25,038	15,312	1,266,434	4.1
New Zealand..........	7,131	2.6	(NA)	4,657	1,077	4,395	(NA)	(NA)
Norway.................	138,805	5.3	11,383	9,264	6,201	6,965	(NA)	0.2
Poland..................	26,498	3.0	7,302	7,237	5,135	4,109	40,470	(Z)
Portugal................	40,680	6.7	9,407	4,532	11,061	3,114	21,288	0.3
Slovak Republic.......	4,839	2.7	1,229	1,170	749	587	8,750	0.1
Spain...................	289,030	5.0	28,520	36,967	30,387	21,234	168,046	0.3
Sweden................	326,869	7.9	29,507	10,746	7,684	7,651	374,146	(NA)
Switzerland............	417,499	9.2	34,407	35,959	28,884	22,364	794,358	5.0
Turkey..................	4,294	1.6	1,390	10,386	757	5,093	37,196	(NA)
United Kingdom.......	1,303,510	10.5	246,702	90,041	296,353	47,829	2,741,924	2.9

NA Not available or not applicable. Z Less than 0.05 percent. [1] Includes total investment assets of direct insurance companies (excludes re-insurance). [2] Includes public and private autonomous pension funds of all types (occupational and personal, mandatory and voluntary). [3] See footnote 2, Table 1371.

Source: Organisation for Economic Co-operation and Development (OECD), 2017, Insurance Statistics (database) ©, <http://www.oecd.org/daf/fin/insurance/oecdinsurancestatistics.htm>; and Global Pension Statistics (database) ©, <http://www.oecd.org/daf/fin/private-pensions/globalpensionstatistics.htm>; accessed September 2017.

Table 1379. Annual Percent Changes in Consumer Prices by Country: 2010 to 2016

[Percent change from previous year. Inflation as measured by the consumer price index reflects the annual percentage change in the cost to the average consumer of acquiring a basket of goods and services that may be fixed or adjusted at specified intervals, such as yearly. For general comments concerning the data, see text, this section. For additional qualifications of the data for individual countries, see source. Minus sign (-) indicates decrease]

Country	2010	2013	2014	2015	2016	Country	2010	2013	2014	2015	2016
World [1]	**3.5**	**2.8**	**2.8**	**1.6**	**1.6**	Kenya	4.0	5.7	6.9	6.6	6.3
United States	**1.6**	**1.5**	**1.6**	**0.1**	**1.3**	Korea, South	2.9	1.3	1.3	0.7	1.0
Afghanistan	0.9	7.7	4.6	-1.5	2.2	Malaysia	1.7	2.1	3.2	2.1	2.1
Australia	2.8	2.4	2.5	1.5	1.3	Mexico	4.2	3.8	4.0	2.7	2.8
Austria	1.8	2.0	1.6	0.9	0.9	Mongolia	10.1	8.6	13.0	5.8	0.6
Bangladesh	8.1	7.5	7.0	6.2	5.5	Morocco	1.0	1.9	0.4	1.6	1.6
Belarus	7.7	18.3	18.1	13.5	11.8	Netherlands	1.3	2.5	1.0	0.6	0.3
Brazil	5.0	6.2	6.3	9.0	8.7	New Zealand	2.3	1.3	0.9	0.3	0.5
Cambodia	4.0	2.9	3.9	1.2	3.0	Nigeria	13.7	8.5	8.1	9.0	15.7
China	3.3	2.6	2.0	1.4	2.0	Norway	2.4	2.1	2.0	2.2	3.6
Colombia	2.3	2.0	2.9	5.0	7.5	Pakistan	13.9	7.7	7.2	2.5	3.8
Croatia	1.0	2.2	-0.2	-0.5	-1.1	Peru	1.5	2.8	3.2	3.6	3.6
Czech Republic	1.4	1.4	0.3	0.3	0.6	Philippines	3.8	3.0	4.1	1.4	1.8
Denmark	2.3	0.8	0.6	0.5	0.2	Poland	2.7	1.0	0.1	-1.0	-0.6
Egypt	11.3	9.4	10.1	10.4	13.8	Romania	6.1	4.0	1.1	-0.6	-1.5
Ethiopia	8.1	8.1	7.4	10.1	7.3	Russia	6.9	6.8	7.8	15.5	7.1
France	1.5	0.9	0.5	(Z)	0.2	Saudi Arabia	5.3	3.5	2.7	2.2	3.5
Germany	1.1	1.5	0.9	0.2	0.5	Singapore	2.8	2.4	1.0	-0.5	-0.5
Ghana	10.7	11.6	15.5	17.1	17.5	South Africa	4.3	5.8	6.1	4.6	6.3
Greece	4.7	-0.9	-1.3	-1.7	-0.8	Spain	1.8	1.4	-0.2	-0.5	-0.2
Haiti	5.7	5.9	4.6	9.0	13.8	Sri Lanka	6.2	6.9	3.3	0.9	3.7
Honduras	4.7	5.2	6.1	3.2	2.7	Sweden	1.2	(Z)	-0.2	(Z)	1.0
India	12.0	10.9	6.6	4.9	4.9	Switzerland	0.7	-0.2	(-Z)	-1.1	-0.4
Indonesia	5.1	6.4	6.4	6.4	3.5	Thailand	3.2	2.2	1.9	-0.9	0.2
Iran	10.1	39.3	17.2	13.7	8.6	Tunisia	4.4	5.8	4.9	4.9	3.7
Ireland	-0.9	0.5	0.2	-0.3	(Z)	Turkey	8.6	7.5	8.9	7.7	7.8
Israel	2.7	1.5	0.5	-0.6	-0.5	Ukraine	9.4	-0.3	12.2	48.7	13.9
Italy	1.5	1.2	0.2	(Z)	-0.1	United Kingdom	3.3	2.6	1.5	0.1	0.6
Japan	-0.7	0.3	2.8	0.8	-0.1	Venezuela	28.2	40.6	62.2	109.7	(NA)
Jordan	5.0	4.8	2.9	-0.9	-0.8	Vietnam	8.9	6.6	4.1	0.9	(NA)

NA Not available. Z Less than 0.05 percent. [1] Includes other countries not shown separately.

Source: The World Bank, Washington, DC, World Development Indicators database, "Inflation, consumer prices (annual %)" ©, <http://data.worldbank.org/data-catalog/world-development-indicators>, accessed August 2017.

Table 1380. Unemployment Rates by Country: 1990 to 2015

[Annual averages. The standardized unemployment rates shown here are calculated as the number of unemployed persons as a percentage of the civilian labor force. The unemployed are persons of working age who, in the reference period, are without work, are available for work, and have taken specific steps to find work]

Country	1990	2000	2005	2008	2009	2010	2011	2012	2013	2014	2015
OECD, total [1]	(NA)	6.1	6.6	5.9	8.1	8.3	7.9	8.0	7.9	7.3	(NA)
EU-28 [2]	(NA)	9.2	8.9	7.0	8.9	9.5	9.6	10.4	10.8	10.2	9.4
United States	**5.6**	**4.0**	**5.1**	**5.8**	**9.3**	**9.6**	**8.9**	**8.1**	**7.4**	**6.2**	**5.3**
Australia	6.9	6.3	5.0	4.2	5.6	5.2	5.1	5.2	5.7	6.1	6.1
Austria	3.3	3.5	5.6	4.1	5.3	4.8	4.6	4.9	5.3	5.6	5.7
Belgium	8.9	7.0	8.4	7.0	7.9	8.3	7.1	7.5	8.4	8.5	8.5
Canada	8.1	6.8	6.8	6.1	8.3	8.1	7.5	7.3	7.1	6.9	6.9
Chile	(NA)	9.2	8.0	7.8	9.7	8.1	7.1	6.4	5.9	6.4	6.2
Czech Republic	0.8	8.9	8.0	4.4	6.7	7.3	6.7	7.0	7.0	6.1	5.1
Denmark	8.3	4.5	4.8	3.4	6.0	7.5	7.6	7.5	7.0	6.6	6.2
Estonia	0.7	14.6	8.1	5.5	13.6	16.8	12.4	10.1	8.7	7.4	6.2
Finland	3.2	9.8	8.4	6.4	8.3	8.4	7.8	7.7	8.2	8.7	9.4
France	7.6	8.0	8.3	7.0	8.6	8.8	8.7	9.2	9.7	9.7	(NA)
Germany	4.8	7.8	11.2	7.6	7.8	7.1	5.9	5.4	5.2	5.0	4.6
Greece	7.0	11.2	9.8	7.3	9.0	12.0	16.5	23.8	27.3	26.6	24.6
Hungary	(NA)	6.5	7.3	7.9	10.1	11.2	11.1	11.0	10.2	7.8	6.8
Iceland	1.8	2.3	2.6	3.0	7.2	7.6	7.1	6.0	5.4	5.0	4.0
Ireland	13.0	4.6	4.8	5.8	12.3	13.9	14.6	15.0	13.9	11.8	9.8
Israel [3]	(NA)	8.8	9.0	6.1	7.5	6.6	5.6	6.9	6.2	5.9	5.3
Italy	11.5	10.7	7.8	6.8	7.8	8.5	8.4	10.8	12.3	12.8	12.0
Japan	2.1	4.7	4.4	4.0	5.1	5.0	4.6	4.3	4.0	3.6	3.4
Korea, South	2.4	4.4	3.7	3.2	3.6	3.7	3.4	3.2	3.1	3.5	3.6
Luxembourg	1.1	2.4	4.1	4.2	5.4	5.8	5.7	6.1	6.9	7.1	6.8
Mexico	2.7	2.6	3.5	3.5	5.2	5.2	5.2	4.8	5.0	4.9	4.3
Netherlands	7.7	3.0	4.7	2.8	3.4	4.5	5.0	5.8	7.2	7.4	6.9
New Zealand	8.0	6.2	3.8	4.2	6.1	6.5	6.5	6.9	6.2	5.8	5.8
Norway	5.3	3.5	4.6	2.6	3.2	3.6	3.3	3.2	3.5	3.5	4.4
Poland	6.5	16.1	17.7	7.1	8.2	9.6	9.6	10.1	10.3	9.0	7.5
Portugal	4.6	4.0	7.6	7.6	9.5	10.8	12.8	15.6	16.3	14.0	12.5
Slovak Republic	(NA)	18.8	16.2	9.6	12.1	14.4	13.6	13.9	14.2	13.2	11.5
Spain	16.3	13.9	9.2	11.3	17.9	19.9	21.5	24.9	26.2	24.5	22.1
Sweden	1.8	5.9	7.8	6.2	8.3	8.6	7.8	8.0	8.0	7.9	7.4
Switzerland	0.5	2.6	4.2	3.2	4.1	4.3	3.8	3.9	4.1	4.2	4.2
Turkey	8.0	6.5	10.6	11.0	14.0	11.9	9.8	9.2	9.7	9.9	10.3
United Kingdom	6.9	5.5	4.7	5.3	7.7	7.8	7.9	7.9	7.7	6.2	5.6

NA Not available. [1] For complete OECD membership listing, see Section 30 introduction. [2] See footnote 2, Table 1383. [3] See footnote 2, Table 1371.

Source: Organisation for Economic Co-operation and Development (OECD), 2017, "Labour Force Statistics: Summary tables," OECD Employment and Labour Market Statistics (database) ©, <http://dx.doi.org/10.1787/data-00286-en>, accessed September 2017.

Table 1381. Civilian Labor Force, Employment, and Unemployment by Country: 1970 to 2013

[Labor force and employment in thousands (82,771 represents 82,771,000). Data are based on U.S. labor force definitions (see source) except that age limits of the working-age population vary as follows: Data for the United States, Canada, Spain, and the United Kingdom refer to persons aged 16 years and over. Data for Australia, France, Germany, Japan, Netherlands, and South Korea refer to persons aged 15 years and over. Data may not be comparable to prior years due to breaks in series resulting from changes in methodology. For specific methodological information for individual countries, see source]

Year	United States	Canada	Aus-tralia	Japan	South Korea	France	Ger-many [1]	Nether-lands	Spain	United King-dom
Civilian labor force (1,000):										
1970.........................	82,771	8,395	5,478	50,957	10,094	21,428	26,247	(NA)	(NA)	(NA)
1980.........................	106,940	11,725	6,693	55,895	14,485	23,499	27,256	5,769	13,279	26,762
1990.........................	125,840	14,047	8,444	62,986	18,572	24,581	29,412	6,650	15,154	28,777
2000.........................	142,583	15,632	9,498	66,710	22,135	25,969	39,343	7,906	17,482	28,962
2005.........................	149,321	17,056	10,404	65,386	23,743	27,028	40,786	8,308	20,735	30,148
2010.........................	153,889	18,263	11,628	65,521	24,749	28,018	41,639	8,723	22,941	31,405
2011.........................	153,616	18,434	11,815	65,067	25,099	28,056	42,100	8,720	22,971	31,642
2012.........................	154,975	18,616	11,972	64,642	25,501	28,313	42,189	8,859	22,924	31,992
2013.........................	155,389	18,823	12,152	64,765	25,873	28,468	42,534	8,936	22,634	32,291
Labor force participation rate: [2]										
1970.........................	60.4	57.8	62.1	64.8	57.8	57.9	56.9	(NA)	(NA)	(NA)
1980.........................	63.8	65.0	62.1	62.7	59.2	57.9	54.7	54.5	50.4	62.8
1990.........................	66.5	67.4	64.7	62.6	60.1	55.7	55.0	56.0	50.2	64.4
2000.........................	67.1	66.0	64.2	61.7	61.2	55.4	56.8	62.2	52.3	62.8
2005.........................	66.0	67.3	65.4	59.5	62.0	55.3	57.6	63.5	57.1	63.1
2010.........................	64.7	67.0	66.3	59.1	61.0	55.7	58.8	65.0	59.8	63.2
2011.........................	64.1	66.8	66.4	58.7	61.1	55.5	59.3	64.6	59.8	63.2
2012.........................	63.7	66.7	66.1	58.4	61.3	55.8	59.2	65.1	59.8	63.4
2013.........................	63.2	66.5	65.9	58.5	61.5	55.8	59.5	65.1	59.4	63.5
Civilian employment (1,000):										
1970.........................	78,678	7,919	5,388	50,146	9,617	20,898	26,107	(NA)	(NA)	(NA)
1980.........................	99,303	10,872	6,284	54,598	13,683	22,223	26,486	5,418	11,778	24,929
1990.........................	118,793	12,964	7,859	61,706	18,085	22,605	27,952	6,134	12,857	26,724
2000.........................	136,891	14,677	8,902	63,790	21,156	23,730	36,211	7,660	15,387	27,375
2005.........................	141,730	16,032	9,881	62,910	22,856	24,596	36,202	7,867	18,822	28,681
2010.........................	139,064	16,969	11,022	62,421	23,829	25,383	38,688	8,333	18,309	28,929
2011.........................	139,869	17,238	11,215	62,332	24,244	25,452	39,596	8,331	17,972	29,078
2012.........................	142,469	17,445	11,347	62,152	24,681	25,502	39,873	8,390	17,155	29,444
2013.........................	143,929	17,669	11,465	62,565	25,066	25,501	40,264	8,336	16,638	29,831
Employment-population ratio: [3]										
1970.........................	57.4	54.5	61.1	63.8	55.1	56.5	56.6	(NA)	(NA)	(NA)
1980.........................	59.2	60.3	58.3	61.3	55.9	54.7	53.1	51.1	44.7	58.5
1990.........................	62.8	62.2	60.2	61.3	58.6	51.2	52.3	51.7	42.6	59.8
2000.........................	64.4	62.0	60.2	59.0	58.5	50.6	52.3	60.3	46.0	59.4
2005.........................	62.7	63.3	62.1	57.3	59.7	50.3	51.2	60.1	51.8	60.0
2010.........................	58.5	62.3	62.9	56.3	58.7	50.5	54.6	62.1	47.7	58.2
2011.........................	58.4	62.5	63.0	56.2	59.1	50.4	55.8	61.8	46.8	58.0
2012.........................	58.6	62.5	62.7	56.1	59.4	50.2	56.0	61.7	44.8	58.3
2013.........................	58.6	62.5	62.2	56.5	59.5	50.0	56.3	60.7	43.7	58.7
Unemployment rate:										
1970.........................	4.9	5.7	1.7	1.6	4.7	2.5	0.5	(NA)	(NA)	(NA)
1980.........................	7.1	7.3	6.1	2.3	5.5	5.4	2.8	6.1	11.3	6.8
1990.........................	5.6	7.7	6.9	2.0	2.6	8.0	5.0	7.8	15.2	7.1
2000.........................	4.0	6.1	6.3	4.4	4.4	8.6	8.0	3.1	12.0	5.5
2005.........................	5.1	6.0	5.0	3.8	3.7	9.0	11.2	5.3	9.2	4.9
2010.........................	9.6	7.1	5.2	4.7	3.7	9.4	7.1	4.5	20.2	7.9
2011.........................	8.9	6.5	5.1	4.2	3.4	9.3	5.9	4.5	21.8	8.1
2012.........................	8.1	6.3	5.2	3.9	3.2	9.9	5.5	5.3	25.2	8.0
2013.........................	7.4	6.1	5.6	3.4	3.1	10.4	5.3	6.7	26.5	7.6
Men.........................	7.6	6.6	5.7	3.2	3.3	10.4	5.7	7.1	26.0	8.1
Women......................	7.1	5.6	5.6	3.6	2.9	10.4	4.9	6.3	27.1	7.1
Under 25 years old.......	15.5	12.4	12.2	6.3	9.4	24.4	8.0	11.1	56.2	20.8
Teenagers [4].............	22.9	18.0	16.3	5.9	10.4	32.1	8.5	14.0	75.0	29.8
20 to 24 years old.......	12.8	9.5	9.6	6.4	9.2	22.5	7.8	8.9	52.3	17.0
25 years old and over....	6.1	5.1	4.3	3.1	2.7	8.9	5.0	5.9	24.1	5.5

NA Not available. [1] Unified Germany for 1991 onward. Prior to 1991, data relate to the former West Germany. [2] Civilian labor force as a percent of the civilian working-age population. Germany includes the institutionalized population as part of the working-age population. [3] Civilian employment as a percent of the civilian working-age population. Germany includes the institutionalized population as part of the working-age population. [4] 16 to 19-year-olds in the United States, Canada, Spain, and the United Kingdom; 15 to 19-year-olds in Australia, Japan, South Korea, France, Germany, and Netherlands.

Source: The Conference Board, Inc., International Labor Comparisons program, "International Comparisons of Annual Labor Force Statistics, 2013," August 2014, <https://www.conference-board.org/ilcprogram/laborforceannual>. Reproduced with permission from The Conference Board, Inc. © 2017 The Conference Board, Inc.

Table 1382. Youth Educational Enrollment and Employment Status by Country: 2010 and 2016

[Percent of total youth population for selected age groups]

Country	2010 15 to 29 year olds In education, total	2010 15 to 29 year olds Not in education Employed	2010 15 to 29 year olds Not in education Not employed	2010 20 to 24 year olds In education, total	2010 20 to 24 year olds Not in education Employed	2010 20 to 24 year olds Not in education Not employed	2016 15 to 29 year olds In education, total	2016 15 to 29 year olds Not in education Employed	2016 15 to 29 year olds Not in education Not employed	2016 20 to 24 year olds In education, total	2016 20 to 24 year olds Not in education Employed	2016 20 to 24 year olds Not in education Not employed
United States	46.1	37.8	16.1	38.6	42.0	19.4	44.8	41.1	14.1	39.0	45.6	15.3
Australia	45.6	42.6	11.8	41.5	47.3	11.2	48.2	40.4	11.4	46.1	41.9	12.0
Canada	44.1	42.3	13.6	39.4	45.1	15.6	43.3	43.5	13.2	41.3	43.8	14.9
Denmark	57.2	32.3	10.5	53.4	34.5	12.1	62.1	29.7	8.2	61.5	29.0	9.5
France	44.0	39.4	16.6	40.4	38.9	20.6	47.5	35.3	17.2	42.7	35.4	21.9
Germany	51.3	36.7	12.0	47.5	38.8	13.7	52.5	37.9	9.6	53.5	35.7	10.8
Greece	44.8	37.2	18.1	47.6	31.3	21.1	51.8	24.6	23.5	56.9	18.1	25.0
Ireland [1]	41.1	38.1	20.8	36.9	37.0	26.1	48.7	35.1	16.2	43.9	36.3	19.8
Italy	45.3	31.7	23.0	40.8	32.1	27.1	47.6	26.4	26.0	42.9	24.8	32.2
Mexico	34.1	42.2	23.7	25.6	48.3	26.1	37.1	41.1	21.8	28.9	46.2	24.9
Netherlands	55.4	37.9	6.8	55.3	37.3	7.4	55.8	36.4	7.8	57.6	34.0	8.5
Norway	46.2	45.4	8.4	42.2	48.8	9.0	45.4	45.2	9.4	44.0	45.1	10.9
Poland	50.2	34.8	15.0	52.9	29.5	17.6	43.3	41.7	15.1	44.0	38.0	18.0
Spain	39.7	36.6	23.6	39.7	33.3	27.0	50.5	27.8	21.7	51.0	23.5	25.5
Sweden	54.5	35.2	10.3	46.0	39.8	14.2	50.2	41.6	8.2	46.1	43.0	10.8
Switzerland	48.5	41.7	9.8	44.3	44.6	11.0	48.9	42.4	8.7	45.3	44.6	10.1
Turkey	31.4	32.0	36.6	25.2	31.1	43.7	41.2	30.6	28.2	35.6	31.5	32.9
United Kingdom	42.1	42.0	15.9	33.7	46.9	19.3	40.2	46.6	13.2	33.3	51.7	15.0

[1] Year of reference is 2015 instead of 2016.

Source: Organisation for Economic Co-operation and Development (OECD), 2017, "Indicator C5: Transition from school to work," Education at a Glance 2017: OECD Indicators, OECD Publishing ©, <http://dx.doi.org/10.1787/eag-2017-en>, accessed September 2017.

Table 1383. Female Labor Force Participation Rates by Country: 1990 to 2014

[In percent. Female labor force of all ages divided by female population 15-64 years old]

Country	1990	2000	2010	2013	2014	Country	1990	2000	2010	2013	2014
OECD, total [1]	(NA)	60.4	63.0	(NA)	(NA)	Ireland	43.3	57.0	63.2	64.2	63.5
EU–28 [2]	(NA)	60.3	64.3	66.0	(NA)	Italy	46.1	47.1	51.5	54.1	55.0
United States	68.6	70.8	68.9	68.8	68.8	Japan	60.3	64.0	68.6	71.5	(NA)
Australia	62.2	65.9	71.4	72.3	72.4	Korea	51.2	54.9	58.3	60.2	61.9
Austria	55.1	61.9	69.4	71.2	(NA)	Luxembourg	50.5	69.4	96.3	(NA)	(NA)
Belgium	52.4	56.6	62.0	62.5	63.1	Mexico	23.4	43.3	48.6	50.0	48.5
Canada	67.5	69.8	74.3	75.3	75.0	Netherlands	52.4	65.5	72.8	75.2	(NA)
Chile	(NA)	38.5	51.9	55.1	56.2	New Zealand	65.4	67.9	73.8	76.1	77.4
Czech Republic	69.1	64.2	62.3	66.2	66.6	Norway	71.2	76.2	77.1	77.9	77.9
Denmark	78.3	75.7	76.7	76.5	(NA)	Poland	(NA)	60.5	55.7	57.2	58.0
Estonia	74.9	68.3	73.9	75.5	74.4	Portugal	62.4	67.4	73.6	72.5	(NA)
Finland	73.8	72.2	73.3	74.6	75.3	Slovak Republic	(NA)	63.1	62.3	63.0	(NA)
France	59.1	64.5	67.0	68.5	(NA)	Spain	41.5	51.5	66.4	68.9	68.9
Germany [3]	56.7	63.6	71.5	73.5	73.9	Sweden	80.9	75.0	77.5	80.8	(NA)
Greece	43.3	49.5	58.0	(NA)	(NA)	Switzerland	65.7	76.1	81.4	83.4	(NA)
Hungary	(NA)	52.1	55.8	58.3	60.4	Turkey	36.3	30.3	30.4	34.1	33.8
Iceland	(NA)	82.8	82.1	83.1	83.4	United Kingdom	66.4	67.8	70.4	72.1	73.0

NA Not available. [1] For complete OECD membership listing, see Section 30 introduction. [2] European Union-28: Austria, Belgium, Bulgaria, Croatia, Cyprus, Czech Republic, Denmark, Estonia, Finland, France, Germany, Greece, Hungary, Ireland, Italy, Latvia, Lithuania, Luxembourg, Malta, Netherlands, Poland, Portugal, Romania, Slovak Republic, Slovenia, Spain, Sweden, and United Kingdom. [3] Prior to 1991, data are for former West Germany.

Source: Organisation for Economic Co-operation and Development (OECD), 2016, "Labour Force Statistics: Summary tables," OECD Employment and Labour Market Statistics (database) ©, <http://dx.doi.org/10.1787/data-00286-en>, accessed September 2016.

Table 1384. Civilian Employment-Population Ratio: 1990 to 2013

[Civilian employment as a percent of the civilian working-age population. Data may not be comparable to prior years due to breaks in series resulting from changes in methodology; for information for individual countries, see source. See headnote, Table 1381]

Country	Women 1990	Women 2000	Women 2005	Women 2010	Women 2013	Men 1990	Men 2000	Men 2005	Men 2010	Men 2013
United States	54.3	57.5	56.2	53.6	53.2	72.0	71.9	69.6	63.7	64.4
Canada	54.1	56.0	58.1	58.5	58.6	70.6	68.2	68.6	66.2	66.5
Australia	49.4	52.3	55.0	56.5	56.4	71.3	68.2	69.4	69.4	68.2
Japan	48.0	46.4	45.7	45.7	46.5	75.4	72.5	69.7	67.7	67.3
South Korea	46.2	47.0	48.4	47.8	48.8	71.8	70.7	71.6	70.1	70.8
France	42.0	44.0	45.0	46.0	46.0	61.5	57.9	56.3	55.4	54.4
Germany [1,2]	40.5	44.0	44.7	48.9	51.0	65.6	61.2	58.1	60.6	61.9
Italy	29.2	32.7	34.1	34.5	34.4	60.0	57.0	56.8	54.4	51.7
Netherlands	38.5	50.6	52.5	56.2	55.6	65.4	70.2	68.0	68.2	66.0
Sweden	61.8	56.1	56.0	55.3	56.9	70.7	64.2	63.8	63.3	63.7
United Kingdom	50.3	52.5	53.7	52.9	53.4	70.0	66.9	66.8	63.8	64.1

[1] Unified Germany for 1991 onward. Prior to 1991, data relate to the former West Germany. [2] Germany includes institutionalized population as part of the working-age population.

Source: The Conference Board, Inc., International Labor Comparisons program, "International Comparisons of Annual Labor Force Statistics, 2013," August 2014, <https://www.conference-board.org/ilcprogram/laborforceannual>. Reproduced with permission from The Conference Board, Inc. © 2017 The Conference Board, Inc.

Table 1385. Civilian Employment by Sector and Country: 2010 and 2013

[139,064 represents 139,064,000. Civilian employment approximating U.S. concepts. Data based on U.S. labor force definitions except that age limits of the working-age population vary as follows: Data for the United States, Canada, and the United Kingdom refer to persons aged 16 years and over. Data for Australia, France, Germany, Italy, Japan, and South Korea refer to persons aged 15 years and over. Data may not be comparable to prior years due to breaks in series resulting from changes in methodology. For specific methodological information for individual countries, see source. Sectors are based on International Standard Industrial Classification (ISIC), unless otherwise indicated]

Sector and Year	United States [1]	Canada [1]	Australia	Japan [2]	South Korea	France	Germany	Italy	United Kingdom
TOTAL EMPLOYMENT (1,000)									
2010, total	**139,064**	**16,969**	**11,022**	**62,421**	**23,829**	**25,383**	**38,688**	**22,597**	**28,929**
Agriculture, forestry, fishing [3]	2,206	369	367	2,420	1,566	750	632	856	351
Industry [4]	23,889	3,216	2,172	15,620	5,802	5,313	10,415	6,175	5,173
Manufacturing	14,081	1,743	981	10,580	4,028	3,383	7,737	4,214	2,849
Services [5]	112,969	13,384	8,484	44,381	16,461	19,321	27,641	15,566	23,404
2013, total	**143,929**	**17,669**	**11,465**	**62,565**	**25,066**	**25,501**	**40,264**	**22,167**	**29,831**
Agriculture, forestry, fishing [3]	2,130	378	314	2,200	1,520	790	578	804	314
Industry [4]	25,205	3,356	2,207	15,360	5,954	4,964	10,630	5,693	5,208
Manufacturing	14,869	1,733	925	10,370	4,184	3,168	7,804	4,082	2,918
Services [5]	116,594	13,936	8,945	45,005	17,592	19,747	29,056	15,669	24,310
PERCENT DISTRIBUTION [6]									
2010, total	**100.0**	**100.0**	**100.0**	**100.0**	**100.0**	**100.0**	**100.0**	**100.0**	**100.0**
Agriculture, forestry, fishing [3]	1.6	2.2	3.3	3.9	6.6	3.0	1.6	3.8	1.2
Industry [4]	17.2	19.0	19.7	25.0	24.3	20.9	26.9	27.3	17.9
Manufacturing	10.1	10.3	8.9	16.9	16.9	13.3	20.0	18.6	9.8
Services [5]	81.2	78.9	77.0	71.1	69.1	76.1	71.4	68.9	80.9
2013, total	**100.0**	**100.0**	**100.0**	**100.0**	**100.0**	**100.0**	**100.0**	**100.0**	**100.0**
Agriculture, forestry, fishing [3]	1.5	2.1	2.7	3.5	6.1	3.1	1.4	3.6	1.1
Industry [4]	17.5	19.0	19.2	24.6	23.8	19.5	26.4	25.7	17.5
Manufacturing	10.3	9.8	8.1	16.6	16.7	12.4	19.4	18.4	9.8
Services [5]	81.0	78.9	78.0	71.9	70.2	77.4	72.2	70.7	81.5

[1] Data for the United States and Canada are based on the North American Industry Classification System (NAICS). [2] Data for Japan are based on the Japanese Standard Industrial Classification System (JSIC). [3] Includes hunting. [4] Includes manufacturing, mining, and construction. [5] Transportation, communication, public utilities, trade, finance, public administration, private household services, and miscellaneous services. [6] Percent of total civilian employment.

Source: The Conference Board, Inc., International Labor Comparisons program, "International Comparisons of Annual Labor Force Statistics, 2013," August 2014, <https://www.conference-board.org/ilcprogram/laborforceannual>. Reproduced with permission from The Conference Board, Inc. © 2017 The Conference Board, Inc.

Table 1386. Educational Performance and Attainment by Country: 2015

Country	Student mean scores in reading, science, and mathematics proficiency [1]			Educational attainment of adult population 25 to 64 years old (percent)		
	Reading scale	Mathematics scale	Science scale	Below upper secondary	Upper secondary and vocational	Tertiary and higher [2]
United States	**496.9**	**469.6**	**496.2**	**10.5**	**44.9**	**44.6**
Australia	502.9	493.9	510.0	21.0	36.1	42.9
Austria	484.9	496.7	495.0	15.4	54.1	30.6
Belgium	498.5	507.0	502.0	25.3	37.8	36.9
Canada	526.7	515.6	527.7	9.6	35.2	55.2
Chile	458.6	422.7	447.0	(NA)	(NA)	(NA)
Czech Republic	487.3	492.3	492.8	6.8	71.0	22.2
Denmark	499.8	511.1	501.9	19.6	43.3	37.1
France	499.3	492.9	495.0	(NA)	(NA)	(NA)
Germany	509.1	506.0	509.1	13.2	59.2	27.6
Greece	467.0	453.6	454.8	29.8	41.2	29.1
Ireland	520.8	503.7	502.6	20.2	37.0	42.8
Israel [3]	479.0	469.7	466.6	14.5	36.7	48.8
Italy	484.8	489.7	480.5	40.1	42.3	17.5
Japan	516.0	532.4	538.4	(NA)	(NA)	(NA)
Korea	517.4	524.1	515.8	14.2	40.3	45.5
Mexico	423.3	408.0	415.7	64.5	19.2	16.3
Netherlands	503.0	512.3	508.6	23.6	41.1	35.3
New Zealand	509.3	495.2	513.3	25.3	40.7	34.0
Norway	513.2	501.7	498.5	17.6	39.7	42.7
Poland	505.7	504.5	501.4	9.2	63.0	27.7
Portugal	498.1	491.6	501.1	54.9	22.3	22.9
Spain	495.6	485.8	492.8	42.6	22.4	35.1
Sweden	500.2	493.9	493.4	18.0	42.2	39.8
Switzerland	492.2	521.3	505.5	11.8	46.5	41.7
Turkey	428.3	420.5	425.5	63.0	19.0	18.0
United Kingdom	498.0	492.5	509.2	20.9	35.6	43.5

NA Not available. [1] Proficiency scores are based on the Program for International Student Assessment (PISA), an international standardized test which takes place in three-year cycles. PISA tests are administered to a nationally representative sample of fifteen-year-old students in each country. [2] Tertiary education entails completion of an advanced course of study or research program leading to an associate's, bachelor's, master's, or doctorate degree, usually 2 years or longer in duration. [3] See footnote 2, Table 1371.

Source: Organisation for Economic Co-operation and Development (OECD), 2017, "Education at a glance: Educational Attainment and Labour-force Status," OECD Education Statistics (database) ©, <http://dx.doi.org/10.1787/889e8641-en>; and "Annex B1. Results (tables)" in PISA 2015 Results (Volume 1), OECD Publishing, <http://dx.doi.org/10.1787/9789264266490-en>; accessed August 2017.

Table 1387. World Supply and Utilization of Major Crops and Livestock: 2005 to 2017

[In millions of units (215.8 represents 215,800,000). For major crops, data are for marketing or trade year ending in year shown, unless otherwise indicated. For livestock and dairy, data are for calendar year]

Commodity	2005	2010	2012	2013	2014	2015	2016	2017 [1]
Wheat:								
Area harvested (hectares)	215.8	225.6	221.0	215.9	219.7	221.5	225.1	222.4
Production (metric tons)	626.8	687.2	697.3	658.6	715.1	728.0	737.0	754.3
Exports (metric tons)	113.2	135.3	153.6	147.2	162.5	161.9	172.0	181.4
Consumption (metric tons)	606.2	652.8	697.4	679.9	697.9	705.1	711.8	739.1
Ending stocks (metric tons)	156.5	203.7	198.9	177.7	194.8	217.7	242.8	258.0
Corn:								
Area harvested (hectares)	145.3	158.6	172.3	178.0	181.1	180.3	178.4	183.6
Production (metric tons)	716.8	826.4	891.6	873.0	994.7	1,019.4	968.8	1,068.8
Exports (metric tons)	76.0	92.7	103.7	100.7	130.8	128.4	144.7	144.5
Consumption (metric tons)	688.7	822.9	870.5	871.9	946.5	967.5	985.4	1,031.3
Ending stocks (metric tons)	131.0	141.0	128.0	133.2	174.9	209.6	212.8	227.5
Rice, milled:								
Area harvested (hectares)	151.4	155.8	160.1	158.7	161.4	160.6	158.9	160.1
Production (metric tons)	400.8	440.1	467.4	472.5	478.3	478.4	471.9	483.8
Exports (metric tons)	28.9	31.8	40.0	39.5	44.1	42.6	40.4	42.5
Consumption (metric tons)	406.2	435.0	456.4	462.6	473.9	475.4	468.9	477.4
Ending stocks (metric tons)	74.0	95.2	106.6	113.9	114.0	115.0	115.8	118.5
Coarse grains: [2]								
Area harvested (hectares)	299.0	308.1	317.5	317.0	322.2	326.3	322.5	324.1
Production (metric tons)	1,015.8	1,118.0	1,158.2	1,139.8	1,284.3	1,311.6	1,259.0	1,362.1
Exports (metric tons)	101.2	118.8	133.3	132.4	165.2	173.9	184.6	182.9
Consumption (metric tons)	979.7	1,115.8	1,157.2	1,137.7	1,237.1	1,276.1	1,256.5	1,348.6
Ending stocks (metric tons)	179.2	192.7	161.7	163.9	211.1	246.6	249.2	262.7
Oilseeds:								
Area harvested (hectares)	219.0	235.8	248.1	255.9	259.8	264.6	262.5	264.7
Production (metric tons)	383.0	447.2	447.5	475.5	504.0	537.3	521.1	571.5
Exports (metric tons)	74.4	107.0	111.7	118.5	133.8	147.1	153.2	168.4
Consumption (metric tons)	368.3	425.4	467.6	470.1	494.1	518.9	524.8	552.0
Ending stocks (metric tons)	59.5	74.6	66.7	68.4	78.0	92.9	90.0	105.9
Coffee, green:								
Production (60 kg bags)	121.9	129.8	144.8	158.0	160.1	153.7	153.2	159.1
Exports (60 kg bags)	94.8	106.3	117.7	122.8	128.9	123.6	133.4	130.0
Consumption (60 kg bags)	116.5	138.3	141.5	142.1	142.4	145.7	152.3	155.6
Ending stocks (60 kg bags)	41.1	28.8	25.7	35.4	41.2	43.0	34.7	35.1
Sugar, centrifugal:								
Production (metric tons)	140.7	153.2	172.3	177.8	175.9	177.4	164.7	170.8
Exports (metric tons)	47.0	48.3	55.0	55.7	57.8	54.9	53.8	57.8
Consumption (metric tons)	141.6	154.1	159.6	165.3	165.8	167.9	169.4	171.9
Ending stocks (metric tons)	34.7	28.0	35.2	42.3	44.9	48.8	43.9	38.8
Cotton:								
Area harvested (hectares)	35.8	30.2	36.1	34.3	32.6	34.1	30.3	29.4
Production (480 lb. bales)	121.5	103.4	127.7	123.9	120.4	119.2	96.8	106.5
Exports (480 lb. bales)	34.9	35.8	46.0	46.5	41.1	35.3	35.3	36.6
Consumption (480 lb. bales)	108.0	119.5	103.9	107.6	109.4	111.5	111.3	113.6
Ending stocks (480 lb. bales)	61.1	47.8	74.7	92.1	103.2	111.8	97.2	90.3
Beef:								
Beef cow beginning stocks (head)	217.3	204.6	206.7	208.3	206.5	200.0	202.2	206.3
Production (metric tons) [3]	56.1	59.3	59.5	60.6	60.8	59.7	60.5	61.6
Exports (metric tons) [3]	7.4	7.8	8.1	9.1	10.0	9.5	9.4	9.6
Consumption (metric tons) [3]	55.6	58.2	58.1	58.9	58.8	57.9	58.7	59.7
Ending stocks (metric tons) [3]	0.5	0.7	0.7	0.7	0.6	0.6	0.6	0.6
Pork:								
Sow beginning stocks (head)	82.2	79.3	78.8	79.5	78.8	76.1	73.0	69.8
Production (metric tons) [3]	93.8	103.0	106.9	108.9	110.7	110.6	109.9	110.7
Exports (metric tons) [3]	5.0	6.0	7.3	7.0	7.0	7.2	8.3	8.8
Consumption (metric tons) [3]	93.3	102.8	106.4	108.5	110.0	110.1	109.6	110.2
Ending stocks (metric tons) [3]	0.8	0.6	0.7	0.7	0.7	0.7	0.6	0.7
Chicken (broilers):								
Beginning stocks (metric tons)	0.6	0.5	0.6	0.7	0.6	0.6	0.7	0.7
Production (metric tons)	64.3	78.1	83.3	84.4	86.7	88.9	88.7	89.5
Exports (metric tons)	6.9	8.9	10.1	10.3	10.5	10.3	10.7	11.2
Consumption (metric tons)	63.5	76.9	81.6	82.9	85.0	87.2	86.9	87.6
Ending stocks (metric tons)	0.6	0.5	0.7	0.6	0.6	0.7	0.7	0.7
Dairy:								
Dairy cows beginning stocks (head)	228.0	233.5	240.0	242.3	247.0	248.3	250.4	251.2
Milk production (metric tons) [4]	483.5	512.7	543.0	550.3	570.7	592.1	596.3	606.9
Milk exports (metric tons) [4]	0.4	0.7	1.1	1.1	1.4	1.6	1.9	1.9
Milk consumption (metric tons) [4]	483.4	512.3	542.5	550.0	570.3	591.6	595.7	606.2

[1] Preliminary. [2] Coarse grains include corn, barley, sorghum, oats, rye, millet, and mixed grains. [3] Carcass weight equivalent (CWE). [4] Includes milk from cows as well as other bovines.

Source: U.S. Department of Agriculture, Foreign Agricultural Service, "Production, Supply and Distribution Online," <http://www.fas.usda.gov/psdonline/>, accessed July 2017.

Table 1388. World Crop Production Summary: 2015 to 2017

[In millions of metric tons (737.0 represents 737,000,000). Data are for marketing or trade year]

Country	Wheat 2015–2016	Wheat 2016–2017 prel.	Coarse grains [1] 2015–2016	Coarse grains [1] 2016–2017 prel.	Rice (milled) 2015–2016	Rice (milled) 2016–2017 prel.	Oilseeds [2] 2015–2016	Oilseeds [2] 2016–2017 prel.	Cotton 2015–2016	Cotton 2016–2017 prel.
World	**737.0**	**754.1**	**1,258.5**	**1,360.1**	**471.9**	**483.1**	**521.2**	**570.2**	**96.8**	**106.0**
Total foreign	680.9	691.2	891.5	957.5	465.7	476.0	405.3	442.9	83.9	88.8
United States	**56.1**	**62.9**	**367.0**	**402.6**	**6.1**	**7.1**	**115.9**	**127.3**	**12.9**	**17.2**
Canada	27.6	31.7	25.6	25.6	([3])	([3])	24.8	25.1	([3])	([3])
Mexico	3.8	3.9	32.4	33.2	0.2	0.2	1.0	1.1	0.9	0.8
Russia	61.0	72.5	37.4	40.8	0.7	0.7	12.9	15.0	([3])	([3])
Ukraine	27.3	26.8	33.4	39.3	([3])	([3])	17.6	19.3	([3])	([3])
European Union	([3])	([3])	([3])	([3])	([3])	([3])	([3])	([3])	1.3	1.3
China	130.2	128.9	231.4	227.4	145.8	144.9	54.5	55.0	22.0	22.8
India	86.5	87.0	38.7	44.2	104.4	108.0	29.6	37.8	26.4	26.5
Indonesia	([3])	([3])	10.5	10.9	36.2	37.2	11.8	12.3	([3])	([3])
Pakistan	25.1	25.6	5.7	6.1	6.8	6.8	3.5	3.7	7.0	7.7
Thailand	([3])	([3])	4.8	5.3	15.8	18.6	0.9	0.9	([3])	([3])
Argentina	11.3	17.0	37.9	47.7	0.9	0.9	60.8	62.7	0.8	0.7
Brazil	5.5	6.7	69.1	99.9	7.2	8.2	99.0	116.8	5.9	6.8
Australia	24.2	35.0	12.4	16.6	0.2	0.6	3.9	5.6	2.9	4.4
South Africa	1.4	1.9	8.7	17.0	([3])	([3])	1.5	2.2	([3])	0.1
Turkey	19.5	17.3	14.2	10.9	0.5	0.5	2.3	2.7	2.7	3.2
All others	257.4	237.0	329.2	332.7	147.0	149.4	81.4	82.8	14.0	14.6

[1] Includes corn, barley, sorghum, oats, rye, millet, and mixed grains. [2] Includes soybean, cottonseed, peanut (in shell), sunflower seed, and rapeseed for individual countries. Copra and palm kernel are added to world totals. [3] Indicates no reported or insignificant production.

Source: U.S. Department of Agriculture, Foreign Agricultural Service, *World Agricultural Production*, June 2017. See also <http://www.fas.usda.gov/data/world-agricultural-production>.

Table 1389. Meat Production by Type and Country: 2015 and 2016

[In thousands of metric tons (59,720 represents 59,720,000). Carcass weight equivalent basis for beef, veal, and pork. Chicken (16-week-old broiler) weight based on ready-to-cook equivalent]

Country	Beef and veal [1] 2015	Beef and veal [1] 2016	Country	Pork 2015	Pork 2016	Country	Chicken [2] 2015	Chicken [2] 2016
World	**59,720**	**60,466**	**World**	**110,614**	**109,853**	**World**	**88,936**	**88,728**
United States	**10,817**	**11,502**	China	54,870	52,990	**United States**	**17,971**	**18,261**
Brazil	9,425	9,284	EU-28 [3]	23,249	23,400	Brazil	13,146	12,910
EU-28 [3]	7,684	7,830	**United States**	**11,121**	**11,319**	China	13,400	12,300
China	6,700	7,000	Brazil	3,519	3,700	EU-28 [3]	10,890	11,330
India	4,100	4,200	Russia	2,615	2,870	India	3,900	4,200
Argentina	2,720	2,650	Vietnam	2,572	2,675	Russia	3,600	3,720
Australia	2,547	2,125	Canada	1,899	1,955	Mexico	3,175	3,285
Mexico	1,850	1,879	Philippines	1,463	1,540	Argentina	2,080	2,055
Pakistan	1,710	1,750	Mexico	1,323	1,376	Turkey	1,909	1,871
Turkey	1,423	1,642	Japan	1,254	1,279	Thailand	1,700	1,780
Other countries	10,744	10,604	Other countries	6,729	6,749	Other countries	17,165	17,016

[1] May include meat of other bovines. [2] Excludes chicken paws. [3] See footnote 3, Table 1390.

Source: U.S. Department of Agriculture, Foreign Agricultural Service, "Production, Supply and Distribution Online," <http://apps.fas.usda.gov/psdonline>, accessed July 2017.

Table 1390. Meat Consumption by Type and Country: 2015 and 2016

[In thousands of metric tons (57,877 represents 57,877,000). Carcass weight equivalent basis for beef, veal, and pork. Chicken (16-week-old broiler) weight based on ready-to-cook equivalent]

Country	Beef and veal [1] 2015	Beef and veal [1] 2016	Country	Pork 2015	Pork 2016	Country	Chicken [2] 2015	Chicken [2] 2016
World	**57,877**	**58,739**	**World**	**110,143**	**109,554**	**World**	**87,160**	**86,908**
United States	**11,276**	**11,676**	China	55,668	54,980	**United States**	**15,094**	**15,331**
EU-28 [3]	7,744	7,854	EU-28 [3]	20,872	20,286	China	13,267	12,344
China	7,339	7,759	**United States**	**9,341**	**9,477**	EU-28 [3]	10,442	10,815
Brazil	7,781	7,652	Russia	3,016	3,192	Brazil	9,309	9,024
India	2,294	2,436	Brazil	2,893	2,870	India	3,892	4,196
Argentina	2,534	2,434	Vietnam	2,550	2,650	Mexico	3,960	4,071
Russia	1,966	1,843	Japan	2,568	2,626	Russia	3,804	3,836
Mexico	1,797	1,809	Mexico	2,176	2,256	Japan	2,321	2,394
Pakistan	1,636	1,676	Korea, South	1,813	1,894	Argentina	1,894	1,905
Turkey	1,457	1,654	Philippines	1,637	1,734	South Africa	1,690	1,775
Other countries	12,053	11,946	Other countries	7,609	7,589	Other countries	21,487	21,217

[1] May include meat of other bovines. [2] Excludes chicken paws. [3] European Union-28: Austria, Belgium, Bulgaria, Croatia, Cyprus, Czech Republic, Denmark, Estonia, Finland, France, Germany, Greece, Hungary, Ireland, Italy, Latvia, Lithuania, Luxembourg, Malta, Netherlands, Poland, Portugal, Romania, Slovakia, Slovenia, Spain, Sweden, and United Kingdom.

Source: U.S. Department of Agriculture, Foreign Agricultural Service, "Production, Supply and Distribution Online," <http://apps.fas.usda.gov/psdonline>, accessed July 2017.

Table 1391. Wheat, Rice, and Corn—Exports and Imports of Leading Countries: 2010 to 2017

[In thousands of metric tons (24,143 represents 24,143,000). Wheat data represent trade years ending in June of year shown; corn data represent trade years ending in September of year shown; rice data represent trade years ending in December of year shown. Countries listed are the ten leading exporters or importers in 2017]

Leading country	Exports			Leading country	Imports		
	2010	2016	2017 [1]		2010	2016	2017 [1]
WHEAT				**WHEAT**			
United States	**24,143**	**21,811**	**29,300**	Egypt	10,500	11,925	11,500
Russia	18,556	25,543	27,800	Indonesia	5,364	10,116	9,900
European Union [2]	22,293	34,686	27,000	Algeria	5,167	8,153	8,000
Australia	13,764	15,782	22,000	Brazil	6,691	5,922	7,788
Canada	18,992	22,136	20,000	Bangladesh	3,353	4,693	6,000
Ukraine	9,337	17,431	18,000	India	291	300	6,000
Argentina	5,255	8,750	12,000	Japan	5,502	5,715	5,900
Kazakhstan	7,871	7,600	6,750	Morocco	2,304	4,503	5,500
Turkey	4,363	5,605	6,200	Philippines	3,197	4,850	5,500
Mexico	839	1,568	1,500	European Union [2]	5,358	6,916	5,300
RICE				**RICE**			
India	2,228	10,040	10,500	China	366	4,600	5,100
Thailand	9,047	9,867	10,000	Nigeria	2,000	2,100	2,100
Vietnam	6,734	5,088	5,800	European Union [2]	1,235	1,816	1,850
Pakistan	4,000	4,300	4,000	Philippines	2,400	800	1,400
United States	**3,868**	**3,373**	**3,600**	Saudi Arabia	1,069	1,300	1,400
Burma	700	1,300	1,900	Cote d'Ivoire	840	1,300	1,350
Uruguay	808	996	925	Iran	1,520	1,100	1,100
China	619	368	800	Iraq	1,188	930	1,000
Brazil	430	641	650	Senegal	685	980	1,000
Argentina	468	527	550	South Africa	733	954	925
CORN				**CORN**			
United States	**49,696**	**51,198**	**55,000**	Japan	15,971	15,194	15,000
Argentina	16,973	21,678	26,500	Mexico	8,298	14,011	14,800
Brazil	8,623	35,382	22,000	European Union [2]	2,758	13,768	13,100
Ukraine	5,072	16,595	20,500	Korea, South	8,461	10,121	9,800
Paraguay	1,359	2,662	2,100	Egypt	5,832	8,776	9,000
European Union [2]	1,569	1,949	2,000	Vietnam	1,600	8,600	9,000
South Africa	1,586	759	2,000	Iran	4,300	6,600	8,500
Burma	300	1,000	1,100	Colombia	3,651	4,458	4,700
Canada	186	1,764	1,100	Taiwan	4,521	4,656	4,600
Mexico	642	1,559	750	Algeria	2,569	4,329	4,500

[1] Preliminary. [2] See footnote 3, Table 1390.

Source: U.S. Department of Agriculture, Foreign Agricultural Service, "Production, Supply and Distribution Online," <http://www.fas.usda.gov/psdonline>, accessed July 2017.

Table 1392. World Production of Major Mineral Commodities: 2012 to 2015

[Units are as noted. Th. represents thousand, mil. represents million, and bil. represents billion]

Commodity	Unit	2012	2013	2014	2015	Leading producers, 2015
MINERAL FUELS						
Coal	mil. short tons	9,018	9,041	9,019	(NA)	China, United States, India [4]
Dry natural gas	bil. cubic feet	119,351	120,936	122,336	(NA)	United States, Russia, Iran [4]
Natural gas plant liquids	mil. barrels [1]	3,479	3,521	3,689	3,853	United States, Saudi Arabia, Russia
Petroleum, crude	mil. barrels [1]	27,762	27,809	28,496	29,366	Russia, Saudi Arabia, United States
NONMETALLIC MINERALS						
Cement, hydraulic	mil. metric tons	3,820	4,070	4,180	4,060	China, India, United States
Diamond, gem and industrial	mil. carats	128	130	(NA)	(NA)	Russia, Botswana, Congo (Dem. Rep. of) [5]
Nitrogen in ammonia	mil. metric tons	139.0	144	140	141	China, Russia, India
Phosphate rock, marketable	mil. metric tons	216	232	237	241	China, Morocco/Western Sahara, U.S.
Potash, marketable	mil. metric tons	32.8	35.6	40.8	40.6	Canada, Russia, Belarus
Salt	mil. metric tons	259	273	272	271	China, United States, India
Sulfur, elemental basis	mil. metric tons	69.8	68.0	69.0	68.9	United States, China, Russia
METALS						
Aluminum	mil. metric tons	49.2	51.9	54.0	57.5	China, Russia, Canada
Bauxite, gross weight	mil. metric tons	254	291	264	293	Australia, China, Malaysia
Chromium (chromite), gross weight	th. metric tons	26,000	28,700	27,300	30,400	South Africa, Kazakhstan, Turkey
Copper, metal content [2]	th. metric tons	16,900	18,300	18,400	19,100	Chile, China, Peru
Gold, metal content	metric tons	2,750	2,920	3,020	3,100	China, Australia, Russia
Iron ore, gross weight [3]	mil. metric tons	2,070	2,230	2,330	2,280	Australia, Brazil, China
Lead, metal content [2]	th. metric tons	5,080	5,430	5,440	4,950	China, Australia, United States
Manganese ore, metal content	th. metric tons	15,500	17,500	17,400	17,500	South Africa, China, Australia
Nickel, metal content [2]	th. metric tons	2,570	2,790	2,350	2,280	Philippines, Russia, Canada
Steel, crude	mil. metric tons	1,520	1,620	1,670	1,610	China, Japan, India
Tin, metal content [2]	th. metric tons	254	246	285	291	China, Indonesia, Burma
Zinc, metal content	th. metric tons	12,900	13,100	13,300	12,800	China, Australia, Peru

NA Not available. [1] 42-gallon barrels. [2] Mine output. [3] Includes iron ore concentrates and iron ore agglomerates. [4] Leading producers in 2014. [5] Leading producers in 2013.

Source: Mineral fuels, U.S. Energy Information Administration, Open Data, "International Energy Data", <www.eia.gov/opendata/>, accessed September 2017. Nonmetallic minerals and metals, U.S. Geological Survey, *Minerals Yearbook*, annual; *Mineral Commodity Summaries*, annual; and "Historical Statistics for Mineral and Material Commodities in the United States," <https://minerals.usgs.gov/minerals/pubs/historical-statistics/>, accessed September 2017.

Table 1393. Net Electricity Generation by Energy Source and Country: 2014

[22,657.1 represents 22,657,100,000,000. kWh = kilowatt hours. Ranked for top 40 countries]

Country	Total [1] (bil. kWh)	Amount				Percent distribution			
		Fossil fuels [2]	Hydro	Nuclear	Non-hydro renew-ables [3]	Fossil fuels [2]	Hydro	Nuclear	Non-hydro renew-ables [3]
World, total [4].........	22,657.1	14,941.2	3,858.7	2,408.9	1,477.5	65.9	17.0	10.6	6.5
China....................	5,388.2	3,985.0	1,041.5	123.8	242.8	74.0	19.3	2.3	4.5
United States...........	4,103.1	2,750.6	259.4	797.2	302.2	67.0	6.3	19.4	7.4
India....................	1,217.7	989.0	128.0	33.2	67.5	81.2	10.5	2.7	5.5
Russia..................	1,005.6	660.3	173.5	169.1	3.7	65.7	17.3	16.8	0.4
Japan...................	979.8	832.9	81.0	–	67.7	85.0	8.3	–	6.9
Canada.................	632.8	126.0	378.6	98.6	29.7	19.9	59.8	15.6	4.7
Germany................	591.1	331.7	19.4	91.8	150.4	56.1	3.3	15.5	25.4
Brazil...................	577.1	134.7	369.7	14.5	58.3	23.3	64.1	2.5	10.1
France..................	533.6	25.0	62.2	418.0	30.6	4.7	11.7	78.3	5.7
Korea, South...........	513.3	356.6	2.7	149.2	6.4	69.5	0.5	29.1	1.2
United Kingdom........	316.9	192.1	5.8	57.9	62.1	60.6	1.8	18.3	19.6
Saudi Arabia...........	293.1	293.1	–	–	–	100.0	–	–	–
Mexico..................	286.4	224.5	38.5	9.3	14.1	78.4	13.4	3.3	4.9
Italy....................	267.0	145.1	58.0	–	64.6	54.3	21.7	–	24.2
Spain...................	264.3	100.3	38.8	54.9	71.8	37.9	14.7	20.8	27.2
Iran.....................	258.4	240.5	13.7	3.7	0.4	93.1	5.3	1.4	0.2
Taiwan..................	242.4	192.2	4.3	40.8	5.7	79.3	1.8	16.8	2.4
Turkey..................	239.4	187.0	40.2	–	12.1	78.1	16.8	–	5.0
South Africa...........	235.4	218.3	1.0	14.8	2.5	92.7	0.4	6.3	1.1
Australia...............	235.4	198.6	18.2	–	18.6	84.4	7.7	–	7.9
Indonesia...............	216.3	190.3	15.0	–	11.0	88.0	6.9	–	5.1
Ukraine.................	171.3	78.4	8.4	83.1	1.7	45.8	4.9	48.5	1.0
Thailand................	164.1	148.4	5.5	–	10.2	90.4	3.3	–	6.2
Egypt...................	162.2	146.8	13.8	–	1.6	90.5	8.5	–	1.0
Sweden.................	150.2	1.6	63.1	62.3	23.2	1.1	42.0	41.5	15.5
Poland..................	149.8	130.2	2.2	–	17.7	86.9	1.4	–	11.8
Norway.................	140.5	2.6	135.5	–	2.6	1.9	96.5	–	1.9
Malaysia................	139.3	125.2	13.3	–	0.9	89.9	9.5	–	0.6
Vietnam.................	135.4	77.3	58.0	–	0.1	57.1	42.8	–	0.1
Argentina...............	126.2	85.5	32.1	5.3	3.5	67.8	25.4	4.2	2.8
Venezuela..............	124.4	38.1	86.3	–	–	30.6	69.4	–	–
United Arab Emirates...	103.4	103.1	–	–	0.3	99.7	–	–	0.3
Pakistan................	100.4	64.3	31.1	4.6	0.4	64.0	31.0	4.6	0.4
Kazakhstan.............	99.2	91.0	8.2	–	–	91.7	8.2	–	–
Netherlands............	97.9	80.7	0.1	3.9	13.2	82.4	0.1	4.0	13.5
Czech Republic........	80.2	42.7	1.9	28.6	7.3	53.2	2.4	35.7	9.1
Philippines.............	73.7	54.0	9.0	–	10.7	73.2	12.3	–	14.5
Chile...................	70.6	40.5	22.9	–	7.3	57.3	32.4	–	10.3
Colombia...............	68.3	16.9	49.2	–	2.2	24.8	72.0	–	3.2
Switzerland.............	67.9	0.5	37.7	26.5	3.9	0.8	55.5	39.0	5.8

– Represents or rounds to zero. [1] Electricity generated from fossil fuels, hydro, nuclear, geothermal, solar, wind, tidal, biomass, and waste resources. [2] Electricity generated from coal, oil, and gas resources. [3] Electricity generated from geothermal, solar, wind, tidal and wave, biomass, and waste resources. [4] Includes countries not shown separately.

Source: U.S. Energy Information Administration, Open Data, "International Energy Data," <https://www.eia.gov/opendata/>, accessed August 2017.

Table 1394. World Primary Energy Production by Region and Type: 1980 to 2014

[In quadrillion Btu (286.5 represents 286,500,000,000,000,000). Btu = British thermal unit. For Btu conversion factors, see source]

Region and type	1980	1990	1995	2000	2005	2010	2012	2013	2014
World total........................	286.5	349.6	361.7	393.9	423.3	468.3	492.2	495.1	501.9
REGION									
North America.....................	83.0	91.4	95.8	98.5	91.6	93.4	97.5	100.4	106.6
United States [1].................	67.2	70.7	71.2	71.3	66.7	70.4	74.1	76.4	82.0
Central and South America..........	12.0	16.6	21.1	25.8	21.6	23.2	24.4	24.7	25.3
Europe..........................	36.9	44.3	47.7	49.4	41.9	35.5	33.2	31.9	31.1
Eurasia [2].......................	59.5	75.3	53.1	54.3	63.8	67.4	71.1	71.7	71.6
Middle East.......................	42.3	41.0	48.3	57.5	66.0	71.9	78.2	77.8	79.3
Africa............................	17.0	21.2	23.5	26.9	32.6	35.1	34.2	32.4	31.5
Asia and Oceania..................	35.9	59.8	72.1	81.6	105.8	141.8	153.6	156.2	156.4
TYPE OF FUEL									
Petroleum [3].....................	133.1	136.2	141.8	156.4	169.8	172.8	177.6	177.5	182.1
Dry natural gas....................	50.3	76.0	80.4	89.6	101.6	116.0	123.5	125.2	126.8
Coal.............................	70.4	91.0	86.5	90.5	118.3	148.0	163.0	164.0	163.8
Hydroelectric power................	17.9	22.3	25.3	26.8	29.1	33.2	34.6	35.9	(NA)
Nuclear electric power..............	7.6	20.4	23.3	25.7	27.3	27.4	24.5	24.7	(NA)
Non-hydroelectric renewables [4]......	0.3	1.6	2.1	2.7	4.0	7.7	10.5	12.3	(NA)

NA Not available. [1] Includes biomass, geothermal, and solar energy produced in the United States and not used for generating electricity. [2] Prior to 1992, data were for the former U.S.S.R. [3] Includes crude oil, lease condensate, and natural gas plant liquids. [4] Including geothermal, solar, wind, tidal and wave, biomass, and waste resources.

Source: U.S. Energy Information Administration, Open Data, "International Energy Data," <http://www.eia.gov/opendata/>, accessed September 2017.

Table 1395. World Primary Energy Consumption by Region and Type: 1980 to 2014

[In quadrillion Btu (282.8 represents 282,800,000,000,000,000). Btu = British thermal unit. For Btu conversion factors, see source]

Region and type	1980	1990	2000	2005	2009	2010	2011	2012	2013	2014
World, total [1]	**282.8**	**348.0**	**395.1**	**453.2**	**481.5**	**509.0**	**522.4**	**533.4**	**542.7**	**545.8**
REGION										
North America	91.3	99.7	117.7	120.2	114.4	118.0	118.2	115.6	119.0	120.1
United States [2]	**78.1**	**84.5**	**98.8**	**100.2**	**94.2**	**97.4**	**96.8**	**94.4**	**97.1**	**98.0**
Central and South America	11.5	14.5	20.9	22.7	25.5	27.1	28.2	28.8	29.4	29.8
Europe	71.9	76.8	80.8	84.2	80.6	83.5	81.3	80.6	80.0	77.6
Eurasia [3]	48.5	62.6	39.0	42.6	39.7	43.1	44.8	45.5	44.6	44.4
Middle East	5.9	11.2	17.8	23.4	28.9	30.4	31.5	33.4	33.9	35.1
Africa	6.6	9.6	12.0	14.3	15.6	16.4	16.5	17.7	18.1	18.8
Asia and Oceania	47.1	73.5	106.9	145.9	176.7	190.6	201.9	211.6	217.8	220.0
TYPE OF FUEL										
Petroleum [4]	131.9	136.2	156.4	159.5	161.4	178.4	179.7	182.4	183.9	185.6
Dry natural gas	50.8	75.3	89.8	102.6	109.1	118.1	121.3	125.1	127.2	127.5
Coal	70.4	91.0	90.5	118.3	138.4	148.0	158.0	163.0	164.0	163.8

NA Not available. [1] Includes nuclear electric power, not shown separately. [2] Includes biomass, geothermal, and solar energy consumed in the United States and not used for generating electricity. [3] Prior to 1992, data were for the former U.S.S.R. [4] Includes all refined petroleum products.

Source: U.S. Energy Information Administration, Open Data, "International Energy Data," <http://www.eia.gov/opendata/>, accessed September 2017.

Table 1396. Energy Consumption by Country: 2010 to 2014

[For total consumption, 509.04 represents 509,040,000,000,000,000. Btu = British thermal units. Total primary energy consumption includes the consumption of petroleum, dry natural gas, coal, and net nuclear, hydroelectric, and non-hydroelectric renewable electricity. See text of this section for general comments about the data. For data qualifications for countries and Btu conversion factors, see source]

Country	Total (quad. Btu) 2010	2012	2013	2014	Country	Total (quad. Btu) 2010	2012	2013	2014
World, total [1]	**509.04**	**533.36**	**542.68**	**545.78**	Kuwait	1.41	1.64	1.62	1.75
United States	**97.43**	**94.37**	**97.06**	**98.04**	Libya	0.91	0.74	0.78	0.77
Algeria	1.79	2.12	2.03	2.36	Malaysia	3.03	3.15	3.26	3.48
Argentina	3.53	3.65	3.71	3.76	Mexico	7.26	7.41	7.51	7.52
Australia	5.42	5.55	5.67	5.66	Morocco	0.71	0.76	0.76	0.82
Austria	1.49	1.46	1.46	1.42	Netherlands	4.24	4.03	4.04	3.85
Azerbaijan	0.57	0.60	0.61	0.60	New Zealand	0.85	0.84	0.85	0.90
Bahrain	0.55	0.59	0.69	0.74	Nigeria	0.81	1.14	1.23	1.33
Bangladesh	0.95	1.08	1.11	1.14	Norway	1.83	1.90	1.86	1.91
Belarus	1.13	1.15	1.19	1.12	Oman	0.95	1.15	1.07	1.14
Belgium	2.85	2.57	2.62	2.45	Pakistan	2.59	2.64	2.64	2.65
Brazil	11.47	12.26	12.67	12.84	Paraguay	0.44	0.48	0.48	0.45
Bulgaria	0.76	0.80	0.74	0.78	Peru	0.88	0.99	1.02	1.06
Canada	13.33	13.80	14.44	14.57	Philippines	1.19	1.29	1.35	1.39
Chile	1.26	1.34	1.37	1.39	Poland	3.99	4.01	4.00	3.92
China	99.61	117.19	122.45	122.91	Portugal	1.10	0.96	1.03	1.03
Colombia	1.41	1.60	1.61	1.67	Qatar	1.25	1.91	2.07	2.11
Cuba	0.40	0.41	0.40	0.42	Romania	1.40	1.39	1.32	1.33
Czech Republic	1.73	1.68	1.65	1.63	Russia	29.67	30.96	30.53	30.88
Denmark	0.81	0.74	0.74	0.72	Saudi Arabia	8.89	9.87	9.86	10.21
Ecuador	0.59	0.65	0.68	0.71	Serbia \1	0.77	0.76	0.76	0.67
Egypt	3.31	3.67	3.60	3.58	Singapore	2.87	3.09	3.13	3.29
Finland	1.27	1.20	1.20	1.16	Slovakia	0.76	0.70	0.72	0.68
France	10.94	10.54	10.59	10.17	South Africa	5.47	5.66	5.65	5.68
Germany	13.67	13.19	13.34	12.87	Spain	6.15	5.83	5.57	5.48
Greece	1.31	1.17	1.09	1.05	Sweden	2.20	2.22	2.11	2.11
Hong Kong	1.33	1.17	1.16	1.19	Switzerland	1.32	1.28	1.29	1.24
Hungary	1.05	0.96	0.94	0.95	Syria	1.03	0.74	0.59	0.55
India	21.85	24.07	24.08	24.90	Taiwan	4.61	4.47	4.46	4.60
Indonesia	6.13	6.67	7.04	7.38	Thailand	4.41	4.91	5.12	5.16
Iran	9.32	9.90	10.15	10.59	Trinidad and Tobago	0.94	0.93	1.04	1.03
Iraq	1.47	1.72	1.78	1.86	Turkey	4.74	5.26	5.22	5.25
Ireland	0.62	0.57	0.57	0.56	Turkmenistan	1.02	1.38	1.41	1.39
Israel	0.90	0.91	0.90	0.93	Ukraine	5.02	5.02	4.69	4.22
Italy	7.61	6.99	6.64	6.41	United Arab Emirates	3.66	4.04	4.12	4.26
Japan	21.07	19.90	19.62	19.07	United Kingdom	8.84	8.54	8.53	8.03
Kazakhstan	2.38	2.72	2.71	2.73	Uzbekistan	1.96	2.19	1.95	1.99
Korea, North	0.75	0.57	0.58	0.64	Venezuela	3.22	3.37	3.25	3.31
Korea, South	10.59	11.19	11.13	11.22	Vietnam	1.94	2.30	2.13	2.29

[1] Includes countries not shown separately.

Source: U.S. Energy Information Administration, Open Data, "International Energy Data," <http://www.eia.gov/open/data>, accessed August 2017.

Table 1397. World Energy Consumption by Region and Energy Source: 2015, and Projections, 2020 to 2050

[In quadrillion Btu (575.4 represents 575,400,000,000,000,000). Btu = British thermal units. For Btu conversion factors, see source. Energy totals include net imports of coal coke and electricity generated from biomass in the United States. The electricity portion of the national consumption values consists of generation for domestic use plus an adjustment for electricity trade based on a fuel's share of total generation in the exporting country. OECD = Organisation for Economic Co-operation and Development; see text, this section]

Region and energy source	2015	Projections 2020	2025	2030	2035	2040	2045	2050	Average annual percent change 2015-2050
World, total........................	**575.4**	**604.9**	**634.9**	**663.2**	**697.3**	**736.5**	**775.2**	**813.7**	**1.00**
OECD, total....................	239.9	244.0	247.8	250.3	254.8	261.8	268.3	276.6	0.40
OECD Americas..................	121.9	124.4	125.5	124.8	126.3	129.5	133.0	136.9	0.30
United States.................	**97.5**	**100.2**	**100.7**	**99.1**	**99.5**	**101.6**	**104.1**	**106.9**	**0.30**
OECD Europe....................	79.8	80.5	81.0	83.0	84.8	87.2	88.8	91.4	0.40
OECD Asia.....................	38.3	39.1	41.3	42.5	43.7	45.1	46.5	48.3	0.70
Non-OECD, total................	335.5	360.9	387.1	413.0	442.4	474.7	506.9	537.1	1.40
Non-OECD Europe and Eurasia..	47.7	47.5	47.4	47.6	48.4	48.7	48.6	48.7	0.10
Non-OECD Asia.................	200.1	221.8	241.8	260.3	280.0	302.3	324.5	344.6	1.60
China.......................	133.1	146.4	155.9	161.2	166.8	172.5	177.9	181.6	0.90
India.......................	28.4	33.3	38.0	44.3	51.9	60.7	69.2	76.5	2.90
Middle East....................	33.9	36.4	39.0	41.8	45.4	49.3	53.5	57.2	1.50
Africa........................	22.7	24.2	25.5	27.9	31.0	34.2	37.5	41.1	1.70
Non-OECD Americas.............	31.1	31.0	33.4	35.4	37.6	40.2	42.8	45.6	1.10
Liquids........................	190.6	200.0	203.9	208.1	216.0	226.0	235.8	244.9	0.70
Natural gas....................	128.9	131.7	143.4	154.3	168.6	184.0	200.9	218.2	1.50
Coal..........................	158.2	161.9	161.9	158.8	159.3	160.5	162.5	164.6	0.10
Nuclear.......................	26.0	28.5	30.9	33.5	35.4	37.9	38.7	39.4	1.20
Other.........................	71.7	82.7	94.8	108.4	117.9	128.0	137.3	146.6	2.10

Source: U.S. Energy Information Administration, *International Energy Outlook 2017*, September 2017. See also <http://www.eia.gov/forecasts/ieo/index.cfm>.

Table 1398. World Daily Crude Oil Production by Major Producing Country: 1980 to 2016

[In thousands of barrels per day (59,558 barrels represents 59,558,000 barrels). Includes lease condensate. Ranked for top 35 countries, as of current year]

Country	1980	1990	2000	2005	2010	2012	2013	2014	2015	2016
World, total [1].............	**59,558**	**60,498**	**68,527**	**73,866**	**74,573**	**76,060**	**76,190**	**78,070**	**80,455**	**80,578**
Russia..........................	(X)	(X)	6,479	9,043	9,694	9,922	10,054	10,107	10,253	10,551
Saudi Arabia...................	9,900	6,410	8,404	9,550	8,900	9,832	9,693	9,735	10,168	10,461
United States...............	**8,597**	**7,355**	**5,822**	**5,184**	**5,475**	**6,487**	**7,468**	**8,764**	**9,415**	**8,875**
Iraq...........................	2,514	2,040	2,571	1,878	2,399	2,983	3,054	3,368	4,054	4,452
Iran...........................	1,662	3,088	3,696	4,139	4,080	3,387	3,113	3,239	3,300	4,068
China..........................	2,114	2,774	3,249	3,609	4,078	4,074	4,164	4,208	4,278	3,981
Canada.........................	1,435	1,553	1,977	2,369	2,741	3,138	3,325	3,613	3,677	3,679
United Arab Emirates.........	1,709	2,117	2,368	2,535	2,415	2,804	2,820	2,894	3,019	3,106
Kuwait.........................	1,656	1,175	2,079	2,529	2,300	2,635	2,650	2,642	2,804	2,924
Brazil.........................	182	631	1,269	1,634	2,055	2,061	2,024	2,255	2,437	2,515
Venezuela......................	2,168	2,137	3,155	2,565	2,410	2,500	2,500	2,500	2,500	2,277
Mexico.........................	1,936	2,553	3,104	3,423	2,621	2,593	2,562	2,469	2,302	2,187
Nigeria........................	2,055	1,810	2,165	2,627	2,408	2,457	2,307	2,347	2,171	1,871
Angola.........................	150	475	746	1,239	1,909	1,787	1,803	1,742	1,802	1,770
Norway.........................	486	1,630	3,222	2,698	1,871	1,612	1,533	1,562	1,610	1,648
Kazakhstan.....................	(X)	(X)	718	1,288	1,525	1,514	1,573	1,632	1,653	1,595
Qatar..........................	472	406	742	978	1,459	1,551	1,553	1,540	1,532	1,523
Algeria........................	1,106	1,180	1,214	1,692	1,540	1,532	1,462	1,420	1,429	1,348
Oman..........................	282	685	970	774	865	919	940	943	982	1,007
United Kingdom................	1,622	1,820	2,275	1,649	1,233	888	801	787	893	933
Colombia.......................	126	440	691	526	786	944	1,003	988	1,003	886
Indonesia......................	1,577	1,462	1,428	1,059	945	860	828	789	785	834
Azerbaijan.....................	(X)	(X)	280	433	1,035	922	871	847	848	834
India..........................	182	660	646	665	751	779	772	767	761	735
Malaysia.......................	283	619	690	726	638	586	576	603	654	667
Ecuador........................	204	285	395	532	486	504	526	556	543	548
Argentina......................	491	483	761	704	626	551	540	532	532	511
Egypt..........................	595	873	768	623	568	539	524	517	511	494
Libya..........................	1,787	1,375	1,410	1,633	1,650	1,367	918	471	404	385
Congo, Republic of...........	65	165	280	229	305	280	261	262	269	308
Vietnam........................	–	50	316	372	299	331	332	307	333	302
Australia......................	380	575	722	456	479	405	335	353	322	290
Thailand.......................	–	44	110	183	242	239	241	233	248	258
Turkmenistan..................	(X)	(X)	142	183	178	215	228	239	243	231
Equatorial Guinea.............	–	–	168	363	298	289	270	260	250	227

X Not applicable. – Represents zero or rounds to zero. [1] Includes countries not shown separately.

Source: U.S. Energy Information Administration, Open Data, "International Energy Data," <http://www.eia.gov/opendata/>, accessed August 2017.

Table 1399. World Dry Natural Gas Production by Major Producing Country: 1980 to 2014

[In billions of cubic feet (53,378 represents 53,378,000,000,000). Ranked for top 30 countries, as of current year]

Country	Natural gas production								
	1980	1990	2000	2005	2010	2011	2012	2013	2014
World, total [1]	**53,378**	**73,695**	**87,097**	**98,291**	**112,338**	**116,516**	**119,351**	**120,936**	**122,336**
United States	**19,403**	**17,810**	**19,182**	**18,051**	**21,332**	**22,902**	**24,033**	**24,334**	**25,890**
Russia	(X)	(X)	19,335	21,224	20,915	22,213	21,764	22,139	21,225
Iran	250	837	2,127	3,655	5,161	5,361	5,640	5,696	6,162
Qatar	184	276	1,028	1,617	4,121	5,198	5,546	5,800	5,650
Canada	2,759	3,849	6,470	6,561	5,390	5,218	5,070	5,129	5,349
China	505	508	962	1,763	3,334	3,629	3,666	3,986	4,360
Norway	917	976	1,867	3,072	3,756	3,576	4,052	3,841	3,843
Saudi Arabia	334	1,077	1,759	2,516	3,096	3,258	3,508	3,533	3,616
Algeria	411	1,787	2,940	3,151	2,988	2,923	3,053	2,813	2,942
Turkmenistan	(X)	(X)	1,642	2,225	1,600	2,338	2,316	2,543	2,684
Indonesia	654	1,602	2,237	2,001	2,917	2,693	2,619	2,606	2,594
Netherlands	3,398	2,693	2,559	2,773	3,131	2,851	2,843	3,053	2,482
Malaysia	56	654	1,600	1,967	2,171	2,180	2,190	2,292	2,310
Australia	313	723	1,159	1,266	1,859	1,992	1,908	2,179	2,212
Uzbekistan	(X)	(X)	1,992	2,108	2,123	2,226	2,222	2,106	2,180
United Arab Emirates	200	780	1,355	1,659	1,811	1,847	1,918	1,928	1,916
Egypt	30	286	646	1,501	2,166	2,163	2,144	2,009	1,723
Mexico	900	903	1,314	1,349	1,769	1,744	1,626	1,594	1,567
Nigeria	38	131	440	791	1,024	1,107	1,503	1,356	1,548
Thailand	–	208	658	837	1,281	1,306	1,457	1,474	1,488
Trinidad and Tobago	81	177	493	1,069	1,499	1,434	1,431	1,511	1,486
Pakistan	286	482	856	1,088	1,400	1,383	1,457	1,391	1,380
United Kingdom	1,323	1,754	3,826	3,118	1,988	1,546	1,452	1,361	1,362
Argentina	280	630	1,321	1,611	1,416	1,369	1,329	1,256	1,254
Oman	28	99	322	699	957	937	1,060	1,073	1,091
India	51	399	795	1,056	1,848	1,682	1,448	1,240	1,074
Bangladesh	50	162	343	494	711	710	778	807	844
Venezuela	517	761	961	828	697	887	784	746	773
Bolivia	79	107	117	436	507	558	632	723	756
Brazil	42	97	257	345	445	515	598	744	719

X Not applicable. – Represents zero. [1] Includes countries not shown separately.

Source: U.S. Energy Information Administration, Open Data, "International Energy Data," <https://www.eia.gov/opendata/>, accessed July 2017.

Table 1400. World Coal Production by Major Producing Country: 1980 to 2014

[In thousands of short tons (4,161,123 represents 4,161,123,000). Coal includes anthracite, bituminous, subbituminous, metallurgical and lignite. Ranked for top 30 countries, as of current year]

Country	Coal production								
	1980	1990	2000	2005	2010	2011	2012	2013	2014
World, total [1]	**4,161,123**	**5,280,797**	**5,129,468**	**6,603,555**	**8,205,496**	**8,754,416**	**9,017,865**	**9,040,786**	**9,019,365**
China	683,587	1,189,725	1,525,800	2,607,124	3,779,212	4,149,575	4,348,754	4,380,935	4,270,260
United States	**829,700**	**1,029,076**	**1,073,612**	**1,131,498**	**1,084,368**	**1,095,628**	**1,016,458**	**984,842**	**1,000,049**
India	127,989	239,035	372,518	481,825	627,599	638,588	658,864	670,471	735,836
Australia	115,196	225,491	338,103	408,505	467,823	461,799	492,786	521,121	553,283
Indonesia	627	11,628	87,498	187,989	358,251	445,984	489,966	537,364	518,690
Russia	(X)	(X)	264,912	311,823	329,258	325,887	363,058	359,339	393,765
South Africa	126,898	192,684	247,138	270,053	283,521	278,616	285,031	282,812	288,142
Germany	(X)	(X)	226,047	226,993	202,286	208,846	217,144	210,493	205,597
Poland	253,517	237,082	178,247	174,987	146,257	152,680	158,197	156,875	150,374
Kazakhstan	(X)	(X)	85,367	96,118	122,278	128,364	132,858	131,808	127,271
Colombia	4,590	23,562	42,155	65,107	81,957	94,582	98,132	94,247	97,640
Canada	40,442	75,323	76,239	72,582	74,835	73,980	73,299	75,958	74,595
Turkey	20,531	52,280	69,741	64,309	80,908	83,903	78,772	66,572	70,702
Greece	25,571	57,205	70,423	76,498	62,303	64,668	69,397	59,441	56,047
Czech Republic	(X)	(X)	71,829	68,372	60,857	64,002	61,566	53,990	51,651
Ukraine	(X)	(X)	68,787	66,537	63,558	69,097	72,227	71,019	49,997
Korea, North	33,367	36,542	24,802	26,522	39,683	45,195	45,746	46,297	45,230
Vietnam	5,732	5,100	12,797	37,581	49,422	51,380	46,389	45,233	39,437
Bulgaria	33,304	34,916	29,136	27,222	32,413	40,927	36,847	31,537	34,506
Mongolia	5,818	7,889	5,715	8,285	27,793	32,625	29,113	28,552	33,960
Serbia	(X)	(X)	(X)	(X)	41,861	45,310	42,146	44,420	33,081
Romania	38,762	42,090	32,281	34,288	34,312	39,145	37,418	27,250	25,976
Thailand	1,681	13,692	19,520	23,014	20,221	23,509	19,918	19,391	19,820
Mexico	3,405	7,642	12,505	11,855	12,397	15,122	15,053	14,402	14,810
United Kingdom	143,407	102,252	34,390	22,595	20,223	20,450	18,703	13,969	12,839
Hungary	28,688	19,654	15,469	10,549	10,045	10,533	10,240	10,536	10,528
Philippines	363	1,370	1,491	3,487	8,088	8,390	8,987	7,817	10,487
Mozambique	–	–	26	13	39	680	4,993	6,992	10,031
Kosovo	(X)	(X)	(X)	(X)	9,534	9,141	9,572	9,060	7,941
Macedonia	(X)	(X)	8,285	7,585	7,412	9,049	8,058	7,370	7,857

– Represents zero. X Not applicable. [1] Includes countries not shown separately.

Source: U.S. Energy Information Administration, Open Data, "International Energy Data," <http://www.eia.gov/opendata/>, accessed August 2017.

Table 1401. Carbon Dioxide Emissions From Consumption of Fossil Fuels by Country: 1980 to 2014

[In millions of metric tons of carbon dioxide (18,401 represents 18,401,000,000). Ranked for top 25 countries, as of current year. Includes carbon dioxide emissions from the consumption of petroleum, natural gas, coal, and the flaring of natural gas]

Region/country	1980	1990	2000	2005	2010	2011	2012	2013	2014
World, total [1]	18,401	21,731	23,643	27,841	31,157	32,364	33,084	33,707	33,733
China	1,486	2,363	3,163	5,431	7,746	8,627	9,119	9,521	9,377
United States	4,680	4,981	5,829	6,026	5,642	5,569	5,355	5,455	5,508
India	263	529	874	1,093	1,614	1,662	1,805	1,822	1,895
Russia	(X)	(X)	1,484	1,576	1,651	1,690	1,742	1,722	1,756
Japan	939	1,044	1,157	1,199	1,108	1,149	1,205	1,203	1,177
Germany	(X)	(X)	813	806	773	763	775	788	756
Iran	118	201	320	449	564	591	597	619	646
Korea, South	138	245	435	483	563	622	629	643	643
Canada	430	438	525	573	558	573	569	602	607
Saudi Arabia	177	208	291	401	511	551	584	550	576
Indonesia	85	158	264	314	411	437	471	514	548
Brazil	185	238	347	372	461	476	503	529	547
South Africa	225	324	386	425	461	451	471	473	472
United Kingdom	597	575	555	569	521	481	494	487	446
Mexico	239	300	379	395	437	434	433	437	436
Australia	191	261	335	373	387	390	379	382	378
Italy	371	410	442	463	416	407	384	359	343
France	482	364	399	411	378	366	353	356	329
Thailand	34	91	165	245	280	281	290	325	325
Turkey	75	152	231	250	292	319	315	305	317
Taiwan	69	117	233	265	265	281	274	295	305
Poland	359	330	283	289	300	304	298	299	289
Spain	204	236	321	384	311	314	304	269	264
Netherlands	201	208	244	250	232	237	236	241	234
Ukraine	(X)	(X)	329	352	279	315	295	268	232

X Not applicable. [1] Includes other countries not shown separately.

Source: U.S. Energy Information Administration, Open Data, "International Energy Data," <http://www.eia.gov/countries/data.cfm>, accessed August 2017.

Table 1402. Average Temperatures and Precipitation—Selected International Cities

[In degrees Fahrenheit, except as noted. Data are generally based on a standard 30-year period; for details, see source. Minus sign (-) indicates degrees below zero]

City	January					July				
	Average high	Average low	Warmest	Coldest	Average precipitation (inches)	Average high	Average low	Warmest	Coldest	Average precipitation (inches)
Amsterdam, Netherlands	41	34	57	3	3.1	69	55	90	39	2.9
Athens, Greece	55	44	70	28	1.9	89	73	108	61	0.2
Baghdad, Iraq	58	38	75	25	1.1	110	78	122	61	–
Bangkok, Thailand	89	71	95	54	0.4	90	78	99	72	6.2
Beijing, China	34	17	54	1	0.2	86	72	104	63	8.8
Berlin, Germany	35	26	58	-11	(NA)	73	56	95	41	(NA)
Bogota, Colombia	66	43	84	27	1.9	64	47	82	32	1.8
Brasilia, Brazil	81	64	95	54	(NA)	79	52	97	37	(NA)
Buenos Aires, Argentina	85	64	104	44	4.2	58	41	88	23	2.3
Cairo, Egypt	65	49	86	32	0.2	93	72	108	63	–
Frankfurt, Germany	38	30	56	-4	1.8	75	57	97	38	2.4
Geneva, Switzerland	39	29	57	-2	2.2	77	56	96	41	2.8
Hong Kong, China	67	58	79	43	1.1	89	81	97	70	14.3
Istanbul, Turkey	46	37	64	16	3.7	82	66	100	50	0.7
Jakarta, Indonesia	83	75	92	72	(NA)	88	74	92	67	(NA)
Karachi, Pakistan	76	55	93	39	0.3	89	83	109	68	3.5
Lagos, Nigeria	82	79	93	64	(NA)	79	76	88	70	(NA)
London, England	45	36	61	15	2.4	72	56	93	45	1.8
Madrid, Spain	51	32	68	14	1.8	90	61	104	46	0.4
Manila, Philippines	86	71	95	61	0.8	88	76	99	70	15.9
Mexico City, Mexico	70	45	86	26	0.3	74	56	86	37	5.1
Montreal, Canada	21	7	52	-31	2.8	79	61	93	43	3.4
Moscow, Russia	21	11	46	-33	1.4	71	55	95	41	3.2
Nairobi, Kenya	77	58	88	45	1.8	71	54	85	43	0.5
New Delhi, India	68	48	85	32	0.9	93	81	111	70	7.9
Paris, France	43	34	59	1	(NA)	75	58	95	41	(NA)
Rio De Janeiro, Brazil	91	74	109	64	5.3	81	64	102	52	1.8
Rome, Italy	55	39	64	19	3.2	83	66	100	55	0.6
Seoul, Korea	33	21	55	-1	(NA)	82	71	97	55	(NA)
Singapore, Singapore	85	73	100	66	9.4	86	76	99	70	5.9
Sydney, Australia	79	65	109	49	4.0	62	44	80	32	2.5
Tel Aviv, Israel	62	46	84	32	(NA)	87	69	100	50	(NA)
Tokyo, Japan	48	35	66	25	2.0	82	71	95	55	5.3
Toronto, Canada	28	15	59	-24	1.9	79	60	99	45	2.8

– Represents zero. NA Not available.

Source: U.S. National Oceanic and Atmospheric Administration, *Climates of the World*. See also <http://www.ncdc.noaa.gov/oa/oldpubs/>.

Table 1403. Telephones, Cellular Phones, and Internet Use by Country: 2015

[For data qualifications for individual countries, see source]

Country	Telephone subscriptions per 100 people [1]	Cell phone subscriptions per 100 people [2]	Internet users (as percent of population) [3]	Country	Telephone subscriptions per 100 people [1]	Cell phone subscriptions per 100 people [2]	Internet users (as percent of population) [3]
United States	**38.40**	**117.59**	**74.45**	Jordan	4.80	179.43	53.40
Afghanistan	0.34	61.58	8.26	Kenya	0.18	80.68	45.62
Argentina	23.90	146.70	69.40	Korea, South	58.06	118.46	89.65
Australia	37.95	132.80	84.56	Malaysia	14.65	143.89	71.06
Azerbaijan	18.68	111.28	77.00	Mexico	15.88	85.99	57.43
Bangladesh	0.54	81.90	14.40	Morocco	6.55	126.87	57.08
Brazil	21.45	126.59	59.08	Myanmar	0.95	75.68	21.80
Canada	43.52	82.98	88.47	Netherlands	41.27	123.54	93.10
China	16.48	92.18	50.30	Nigeria	0.10	82.19	47.44
Croatia	34.70	103.77	69.80	Pakistan	1.88	66.92	18.00
Cuba	11.52	29.65	37.31	Panama	15.56	174.19	51.21
Egypt	7.36	110.99	37.82	Poland	23.69	142.69	68.00
France	59.91	102.61	84.69	Russia	25.02	159.95	70.10
Germany	54.93	116.71	87.59	Saudi Arabia	12.53	176.59	69.62
Greece	47.28	112.95	66.84	South Africa	7.72	164.51	51.92
Haiti	0.05	68.84	12.20	Spain	41.52	108.20	78.69
Hong Kong	59.23	228.68	84.95	Switzerland	50.25	136.47	87.48
India	1.99	78.06	26.00	Syria	15.90	64.28	29.98
Indonesia	8.75	132.35	21.98	Thailand	7.88	152.73	39.32
Iran	38.27	93.38	45.33	Turkey	14.99	96.02	53.74
Iraq	5.58	93.83	17.22	Ukraine	21.62	144.02	48.88
Israel	43.08	133.47	77.35	United Kingdom	52.02	124.13	92.00
Italy	33.05	142.12	65.57	Venezuela	24.86	92.97	61.87
Japan	50.23	126.54	91.06	Vietnam	6.32	130.64	52.72

[1] Refers to the sum of active number of analogue fixed telephone lines, voice-over-IP (VoIP) subscriptions, fixed wireless local loop (WLL) subscriptions, ISDN voice-channel equivalents and fixed public payphones. [2] Subscriptions to a public mobile telephone service that provide access to the public switched telephone network (PSTN) using cellular technology. Includes number of postpaid subscriptions and active prepaid accounts. Applies to all mobile cellular subscriptions that offer voice communications. Excludes subscriptions via data cards or USB modems, subscriptions to public mobile data services, private trunked mobile radio, telepoint, radio paging, and telemetry services. [3] Internet users are individuals who have used the internet (from any location) in the last 3 months. The internet can be used via a computer, mobile phone, personal digital assistant, games machine, digital TV etc.

Source: The World Bank, Washington, DC, "World Development Indicators" database ©, <http://data.worldbank.org/data-catalog/world-development-indicators>, accessed September 2017.

Table 1404. Global Telecommunications Indicators: 2000 to 2015

[975 represents 975,000,000]

Indicators	2000	2005	2010	2011	2012	2013	2014	2015
NUMBER (million)								
Fixed telephone subscriptions [1]	975	1,244	1,229	1,202	1,179	1,144	1,094	1,057
Mobile cellular subscriptions [1]	738	2,206	5,296	5,890	6,261	6,662	7,008	7,194
Fixed broadband internet subscriptions [2]	(NA)	220	532	598	649	692	730	839
Secure internet servers [3]	(NA)	0.40	1.06	1.27	1.27	1.14	1.37	1.53
PERCENT OF POPULATION								
Internet users [1]	6.8	15.8	29.1	31.7	34.9	37.4	40.6	43.9
PER 100 INHABITANTS								
Fixed telephone subscriptions [1]	16.0	19.4	17.8	17.2	16.7	16.0	15.1	14.4
Mobile cellular subscriptions [1]	12.1	33.9	76.5	84.2	88.5	93.1	96.9	98.3
Fixed broadband internet subscriptions [2]	(NA)	3.7	7.9	9.0	9.4	9.9	10.3	11.6

NA Not available. [1] See footnotes, Table 1403. [2] Refers to fixed subscriptions to high-speed access to the public internet (a TCP/IP connection), at downstream speeds equal to, or greater than, 256 kbit/s. Including cable modem, DSL, fiber-to-the-home/building, other fixed (wired)-broadband subscriptions, satellite broadband and terrestrial fixed wireless broadband. Excludes subscriptions that have access to data communications (including the internet) via mobile-cellular networks. [3] Includes servers using encryption technology in internet transactions.

Source: The World Bank, Washington, DC, "World Development Indicators" database ©, <http://data.worldbank.org/data-catalog/world-development-indicators>, accessed September 2017.

Table 1405. Patents by Country: 2016

[Includes only U.S. patents granted to residents of areas outside of the United States and its territories. For information on types of patents, see <http://www.uspto.gov/web/offices/ac/ido/oeip/taf/patdesc.htm>. Countries are in rank order. See also Table 804 and Table 805]

Country	Total [1]	Utility (inventions)	Designs	Country	Total [1]	Utility (inventions)	Designs
Total	**173,045**	**159,327**	**12,734**	Netherlands	2,955	2,567	171
				Switzerland	2,857	2,592	262
Japan	51,938	49,800	1,984	Australia	1,843	1,549	241
Korea, South	22,047	19,494	2,509	Finland	1,624	1,503	117
Germany	17,307	15,928	1,196	Austria	1,492	1,365	124
Taiwan	12,463	11,541	906	Belgium	1,319	1,232	75
China	11,737	10,462	1,273	Denmark	1,222	1,070	113
United Kingdom	7,345	6,458	822	Singapore	1,040	979	61
Canada	7,155	6,544	596	Hong Kong	886	657	229
France	6,879	6,426	418	Spain	879	768	99
Israel	3,904	3,713	163	Norway	663	599	61
India	3,715	3,657	55	Ireland	607	562	44
Italy	3,145	2,668	456	Russia	537	511	24
Sweden	3,094	2,820	266	Other countries	4,392	3,862	469

[1] Includes patents for botanical plants and reissues, not shown separately.

Source: U.S. Patent and Trademark Office, "General Patent Statistics Reports Available for Viewing," <http://www.uspto.gov/web/offices/ac/ido/oeip/taf/reports_stco.htm>, accessed September 2017; and unpublished data.

Table 1406. Foreign Exchange Rates by Country and Currency: 2016

[Foreign currency units per U.S. dollar. Rates shown are annual averages, including market and official exchange rates]

Country	Currency	2016 [1]	Country	Currency	2016 [1]
Afghanistan	Afghani	61.14	Kuwait	Kuwaiti dinar	0.30
Albania	Lek	127.40	Kyrgyzstan	Som	69.08
Algeria	Algerian dinar	110.10	Laos	Kip	8,190.20
Angola	Kwanza	172.00	Latvia	Lat	0.91
Argentina	Argentine peso	14.92	Lebanon	Lebanese pound	1,507.50
Armenia	Dram	492.70	Lesotho	Loti	16.15
Australia	Australian dollar	1.35	Liberia	Liberian dollar	92.33
Austria	Euro	0.92	Libya	Libyan dinar	1.69
Azerbaijan	Manat	1.53	Lithuania	Lita	0.91
Bahrain	Bahrain dinar	0.38	Macedonia	Denar	56.82
Bangladesh	Taka	78.50	Madagascar	Malagasy ariary	3,243.40
Belarus	Belarusian ruble	18,500.00	Malawi	Kwacha	671.60
Belgium	Euro	0.92	Malaysia	Ringgit	4.08
Benin	CFA franc	605.70	Mali	CFA franc	605.70
Bhutan	Ngultrum	68.39	Mauritania	Ouguiya	341.60
Bolivia	Boliviano	6.91	Mauritius	Mauritian rupee	35.56
Bosnia and Herzegovina	Konvertibilna marka	1.81	Mexico	Peso	18.34
Botswana	Pula	10.21	Moldova	Leu	20.40
Brazil	Real	3.39	Mongolia	Togrog	2,011.00
Brunei	Brunei dollar	1.39	Morocco	Dirham	9.93
Bulgaria	Leva	1.80	Mozambique	Metical	62.07
Burkina Faso	CFA franc	605.70	Namibia	Namibia dollar	16.15
Burma	Kyat	1,205.90	Nepal	Nepalese rupee	108.80
Burundi	Burundi franc	1,665.00	Netherlands	Euro	0.92
Cambodia	Riel	4,066.00	New Zealand	New Zealand dollar	1.44
Cameroon	CFA franc	605.70	Nicaragua	Cordoba	28.68
Canada	Canadian dollar	1.33	Niger	CFA franc	605.70
Central African Republic	CFA franc	605.70	Nigeria	Naira	305.00
Chad	CFA franc	605.70	Norway	Krone	8.62
Chile	Chilean peso	673.20	Oman	Omani rial	0.38
China	Renminbi yuan	6.63	Pakistan	Pakistan rupee	103.77
Colombia	Colombian peso	3,051.10	Panama	Balboa	1.00
Congo, Dem. Republic	Congolese franc	971.60	Papua New Guinea	Kina	3.16
Congo, Republic of	CFA franc	605.70	Paraguay	Guarani	5,689.10
Costa Rica	Colon	543.40	Peru	Nuevo sol	3.36
Cote d'Ivoire	CFA franc	605.70	Philippines	Philippine peso	47.08
Croatia	Kuna	6.97	Poland	Zloty	4.06
Cuba	Peso	(NA)	Portugal	Euro	0.92
Czech Republic	Koruna	25.02	Qatar	Riyal	3.64
Denmark	Krone	6.87	Romania	Leu	4.15
Djibouti	Djibouti franc	177.70	Russia	Ruble	68.06
Dominican Republic	Dominican peso	46.20	Rwanda	Rwandan franc	787.90
Ecuador	U.S. dollar	1.00	Saint Lucia	East Caribbean dollar	2.70
Egypt	Egyptian pound	9.71	Saudi Arabia	Riyal	3.75
El Salvador	U.S. dollar	1.00	Senegal	CFA franc	605.70
Eritrea	Nakfa	15.38	Serbia	Serbian dinar	112.40
Estonia	Euro	0.92	Sierra Leone	Leone	2,601.40
Ethiopia	Birr	23.25	Singapore	Singapore dollar	1.38
Fiji	Fijian dollar	2.11	Slovakia	Euro	0.92
Finland	Euro	0.92	Slovenia	Euro	0.92
France	Euro	0.92	Somalia	Somali shilling	(NA)
Gabon	CFA franc	605.70	South Africa	Rand	15.70
Gambia, The	Dalasi	44.50	Spain	Euro	0.92
Georgia	Lari	2.18	Sri Lanka	Sri Lankan rupee	146.60
Germany	Euro	0.92	Sudan	Sudanese dinar	6.32
Ghana	Cedi	3.99	Suriname	Suriname dollar	6.17
Greece	Euro	0.92	Swaziland	Emalangeni	16.15
Guatemala	Quetzal	7.65	Sweden	Krona	8.57
Guinea	Guinean franc	8,230.00	Switzerland	Swiss franc	1.00
Guyana	Guyana dollar	206.60	Syria	Syrian pound	497.80
Haiti	Gourde	63.16	Taiwan	New Taiwan dollar	32.85
Honduras	Lempira	23.07	Tajikistan	Tajik somoni	8.36
Hong Kong	Hong Kong dollar	7.78	Tanzania	Tanzania shilling	2,182.30
Hungary	Forint	287.70	Thailand	Baht	35.40
Iceland	Krona	129.30	Trinidad and Tobago	Tr. and Tob. dollar	6.71
India	Rupee	68.30	Tunisia	Tunisian dinar	2.14
Indonesia	Rupiah	13,483.00	Turkey	Lira	3.50
Iran	Rial	30,462.10	Turkmenistan	Manat	4.25
Iraq	Dinar	1,179.30	Uganda	Uganda shilling	3,427.00
Ireland	Euro	0.92	Ukraine	Hryvnia	25.26
Israel	Shekel	3.87	United Arab Emirates	Dirham	3.67
Italy	Euro	0.92	United Kingdom	Pound sterling	0.74
Jamaica	Jamaican dollar	125.20	Uruguay	Uruguayan peso	32.03
Japan	Yen	107.10	Uzbekistan	Soum	2,963.70
Jordan	Jordanian dinar	0.71	Venezuela	Bolivar	56.57
Kazakhstan	Tenge	348.50	Vietnam	Dong	22,347.00
Kenya	Kenyan shilling	102.00	West Bank and Gaza	Israeli shekel	3.87
Korea, North	North Korean won	(NA)	Yemen	Yemeni rial	284.90
Korea, South	Won	1,167.60	Zambia	Zambian kwacha	10.80

NA Not available. [1] End-of-year values were used if annual averages were unavailable. Some values were estimated using partial year data.

Source: Central Intelligence Agency, "The World Factbook," <https://www.cia.gov/library/publications/the-world-factbook/>, accessed September 2017.

Table 1407. Foreign Stock Market Indices: 1980 to 2016

[As of year end. The DAX-30 index is a total return index which includes dividends, whereas the other foreign indices are price indices which exclude dividends]

Year	London FTSE 100	Tokyo Nikkei 225	Hong Kong Hang Seng	Germany DAX-30	Paris CAC-40	Dow Jones Europe STOXX 50
1980.............	647	7,116	1,477	481	(X)	(X)
1985.............	1,413	13,113	1,752	1,366	(X)	(X)
1990.............	2,144	23,849	3,025	1,398	1,518	835
1995.............	3,689	19,868	10,073	2,254	1,872	1,538
2000.............	6,223	13,786	15,096	6,434	5,926	4,557
2005.............	5,619	16,111	14,876	5,408	4,715	3,349
2010.............	5,900	10,229	23,035	6,914	3,805	2,586
2011.............	5,572	8,455	18,434	5,898	3,160	2,370
2012.............	5,898	10,395	22,657	7,612	3,641	2,578
2013.............	6,749	16,291	23,306	9,552	4,296	2,919
2014.............	6,566	17,451	23,605	9,806	4,273	3,004
2015.............	6,242	19,034	21,914	10,743	4,637	3,100
2016.............	7,143	19,114	22,001	11,481	4,862	3,011

X Not applicable.

Source: Global Financial Data, Los Angeles, CA ©, <http://www.globalfinancialdata.com>.

Table 1408. Research and Development (R&D) Expenditures by Sector and Country: 2015

[Total and per capita expenditures in millions of dollars (1,247,981 represents $1,247,981,000,000). Gross domestic expenditure on R&D (GERD) may include financing from abroad. Selected data are preliminary or estimated. For methodological information for individual countries, see source. GDP = gross domestic product]

Country	Gross domestic expenditure on R&D (GERD)			Percent of GERD performed by:			
	Total (million current PPP U.S. dollars) [1]	Per capita (million current PPP U.S. dollars) [1]	Percent of GDP	Government sector	Business enterprise sector	Higher education sector	Private non-profit sector
OECD total [2]...........	1,247,981	977	2.4	11.0	69.1	17.6	2.4
EU-28 [2]................	386,467	758	2.0	12.3	63.6	23.2	1.0
EU-15 [3]................	356,166	880	2.1	11.4	64.6	23.0	1.0
United States [4].......	**502,893**	**1,563**	**2.8**	**11.2**	**71.5**	**13.2**	**4.1**
Argentina.............	5,577	132	0.6	51.2	21.2	26.0	1.6
Australia [5].............	20,573	921	2.2	12.4	58.2	26.4	3.0
Austria................	13,321	1,544	3.1	4.4	70.8	24.3	0.4
Belgium...............	12,625	1,126	2.5	7.8	71.9	19.9	0.3
Canada................	27,071	755	1.7	8.5	52.7	38.4	0.4
Chile..................	1,604	89	0.4	7.8	34.3	38.5	19.4
China.................	408,829	297	2.1	16.2	76.8	7.0	(NA)
Czech Republic........	6,927	657	1.9	20.4	54.3	24.9	0.4
Denmark..............	8,236	1,450	3.0	2.3	64.0	33.4	0.4
Estonia...............	569	433	1.5	10.8	46.1	41.4	1.8
Finland...............	6,712	1,225	2.9	8.2	66.7	24.4	0.8
France................	60,819	913	2.2	13.1	65.1	20.3	1.5
Germany..............	114,778	1,405	2.9	14.1	68.7	17.3	(NA)
Greece................	2,766	256	1.0	28.1	33.0	37.8	1.1
Hungary..............	3,585	364	1.4	13.3	73.4	12.1	(NA)
Iceland...............	346	1,045	2.2	4.8	64.7	30.5	(NA)
Ireland [6].............	3,639	788	1.5	4.4	71.0	24.7	(NA)
Israel [7]...............	13,024	1,555	4.3	1.7	85.4	11.7	1.2
Italy..................	30,102	496	1.3	13.3	55.3	28.6	2.9
Japan.................	170,003	1,339	3.3	7.9	78.5	12.3	1.3
Korea, South..........	74,051	1,463	4.2	11.7	77.5	9.1	1.6
Latvia................	308	156	0.6	25.6	24.8	49.6	(NA)
Luxembourg...........	761	1,337	1.3	31.1	51.0	17.8	(NA)
Mexico................	11,563	96	0.5	37.9	30.0	26.8	5.4
Netherlands...........	16,910	999	2.0	12.3	55.6	32.1	(NA)
New Zealand..........	2,228	482	1.3	20.3	49.8	29.9	(NA)
Norway...............	6,218	1,198	1.9	15.0	53.9	31.1	(NA)
Poland................	10,240	266	1.0	24.4	46.6	28.9	0.2
Portugal..............	3,922	379	1.3	5.9	47.1	45.5	1.5
Romania..............	2,137	108	0.5	38.3	44.0	17.4	0.3
Russia................	38,136	261	1.1	31.1	59.2	9.6	0.1
Singapore [6]...........	10,102	1,847	2.2	11.4	61.2	27.4	(NA)
Slovak Republic.......	1,912	353	1.2	27.9	28.0	43.8	0.4
Slovenia..............	1,459	707	2.2	13.5	76.3	10.2	0.0
South Africa [5].........	4,433	87	0.7	22.7	49.7	26.8	0.8
Spain.................	19,735	425	1.2	19.1	52.5	28.1	0.2
Sweden...............	15,372	1,569	3.3	3.4	69.7	26.7	0.2
Switzerland...........	17,688	2,136	3.4	0.9	71.0	26.7	1.5
Taiwan................	33,564	1,429	3.0	12.5	77.8	9.4	0.3
Turkey................	16,604	214	0.9	10.3	50.0	39.7	(NA)
United Kingdom.......	46,260	710	1.7	6.8	65.7	25.6	1.9

NA Not available or not applicable. [1] Purchasing power parities (PPPs) are currency conversion rates used to convert different currencies to a common value (U.S. dollars in this case). See introductory text, this section. [2] For full membership listing of the Organisation for Economic Co-operation and Development (OECD) and the European Union-28, see introductory text, this section. [3] European Union-15: Austria, Belgium, Denmark, Finland, France, Germany, Greece, Ireland, Italy, Luxembourg, Netherlands, Portugal, Spain, Sweden, and United Kingdom. [4] Excludes all or most capital expenditures. [5] 2010 data. [6] 2014 data. [7] Excludes defense expenditures. The statistical data for Israel are supplied by and under the responsibility of the relevant Israeli authorities. The use of such data by the OECD is without prejudice to the status of the Golan Heights, East Jerusalem and Israeli settlements in the West Bank under the terms of international law.

Source: Organisation for Economic Co-cooperation and Development (OECD), 2017, "Main Science and Technology Indicators," OECD Science, Technology and R&D Statistics (database) ©, <http://dx.doi.org/10.1787/data-00182-en>, accessed August 2017.

Table 1409. Development Assistance Outlays by Donor Country: 2015

[131,555 represents $131,555,000,000 except percent. Official development assistance (ODA) includes concessional loans and grants made by donor governments to developing countries and to multilateral institutions such as the United Nations or the World Bank]

| Country | Official development assistance (ODA) | | | Multilateral ODA (mil. current U.S. dol.) | Net private grants (mil. current U.S. dol.) |
	Net disbursements (mil. current U.S. dollars)	Percent of GNI [1]	Percent of total DAC [2] ODA		
DAC countries, total [2]..........	131,555	0.30	100.0	37,343	35,388
United States.....................	30,986	0.17	23.6	4,331	28,816
Australia...........................	3,494	0.29	2.7	741	(NA)
Austria.............................	1,324	0.35	1.0	541	(NA)
Belgium............................	1,904	0.42	1.4	793	388
Canada............................	4,277	0.28	3.3	1,305	2,488
Czech Republic...................	199	0.12	0.2	129	(NA)
Denmark...........................	2,566	0.85	2.0	685	16
Finland.............................	1,288	0.55	1.0	590	48
France.............................	9,039	0.37	6.9	3,882	(NA)
Germany...........................	17,940	0.52	13.6	3,827	1,381
Greece.............................	239	0.12	0.2	167	(NA)
Hungary............................	156	0.13	0.1	108	(NA)
Iceland.............................	40	0.24	–	9	(NA)
Ireland.............................	718	0.32	0.5	291	509
Italy.................................	4,003	0.22	3.0	2,174	128
Japan..............................	9,203	0.20	7.0	3,055	498
Korea, South......................	1,915	0.14	1.5	447	402
Luxembourg.......................	363	0.95	0.3	100	(NA)
Netherlands.......................	5,726	0.75	4.4	1,563	38
New Zealand......................	442	0.27	0.3	84	122
Norway.............................	4,278	1.05	3.3	971	(NA)
Poland.............................	441	0.10	0.3	341	(NA)
Portugal...........................	308	0.16	0.2	162	13
Slovak Republic...................	85	0.10	0.1	68	(NA)
Slovenia...........................	63	0.15	–	38	(NA)
Spain..............................	1,397	0.12	1.1	1,042	(NA)
Sweden............................	7,089	1.40	5.4	2,262	(NA)
Switzerland........................	3,529	0.51	2.7	803	540
United Kingdom...................	18,545	0.70	14.1	6,835	(NA)

– Represents or rounds to zero. NA Not available. [1] Gross national income. See headnote, Table 1364. [2] Development Assistance Committee (DAC) of the Organisation for Economic Co-operation and Development (OECD) is comprised of 29 developed countries, as shown above, and European Union institutions, not shown separately.

Source: Organisation for Economic Co-operation and Development (OECD), 2017, "Detailed aid statistics: Official and private flows," OECD International Development Statistics (database) ©, <http://dx.doi.org/10.1787/data-00072-en>, accessed August 2017.

Table 1410. Net Flow of Financial Resources to Developing Countries and Multilateral Organizations by Donor Country: 2000 to 2015

[134,228 represents $134,228,000,000. Net flow covers official and private loans, grants, development assistance, and technical assistance, minus amortization on loans. Military flows are excluded. GNI = gross national income. For explanation of GNI, see headnote, Table 1364]

| Country | Amount (million dollars) | | | | Percent of GNI | | | |
	2000	2010	2014	2015	2000	2010	2014	2015
DAC countries total [1]...............	134,228	512,678	587,816	315,325	0.54	1.25	1.26	0.71
United States......................	25,252	216,950	238,648	38,520	0.25	1.48	1.34	0.21
Australia.............................	1,891	14,531	31,975	13,840	0.51	1.23	2.29	1.15
Austria..............................	1,135	6,372	3,475	4,529	0.61	1.70	0.80	1.21
Belgium.............................	2,281	7,896	8,725	3,635	1.00	1.68	1.65	0.79
Canada.............................	6,483	22,642	17,876	3,718	0.95	1.46	1.02	0.24
Czech Republic.....................	16	228	106	263	0.03	0.13	0.06	0.16
Denmark............................	2,176	4,794	4,194	2,931	1.39	1.52	1.20	0.97
Finland..............................	1,087	4,312	3,027	-48	0.91	1.78	1.10	-0.02
France..............................	5,557	35,198	19,222	1,234	0.41	1.35	0.67	0.05
Germany............................	12,331	41,637	53,003	47,627	0.66	1.24	1.34	1.39
Greece..............................	229	761	-438	-85	0.20	0.26	-0.19	-0.04
Iceland..............................	9	29	37	40	0.10	0.26	0.22	0.24
Ireland..............................	740	2,695	1,203	1,228	0.93	1.57	0.55	0.54
Italy.................................	10,846	9,608	8,706	15,621	1.01	0.47	0.41	0.86
Japan..............................	11,423	48,249	40,718	37,909	0.24	0.86	0.85	0.83
Korea...............................	44	11,834	11,649	12,318	0.01	1.17	0.82	0.89
Luxembourg........................	129	411	423	363	0.73	1.07	1.06	0.95
Netherlands........................	6,947	13,013	68,874	68,160	1.85	1.67	7.85	8.91
New Zealand.......................	142	426	667	621	0.32	0.32	0.36	0.37
Norway.............................	1,437	5,876	5,040	4,565	0.87	1.41	0.99	1.12
Poland..............................	29	378	452	499	0.02	0.08	0.09	0.11
Portugal............................	4,622	162	2,369	128	4.45	0.07	1.04	0.07
Slovak Republic....................	6	74	83	85	0.03	0.09	0.09	0.10
Slovenia............................	(NA)	59	62	156	(NA)	0.13	0.12	0.37
Spain...............................	23,471	10,340	13,669	22,041	4.25	0.74	0.98	1.84
Sweden.............................	3,952	5,127	9,325	10,365	1.76	1.10	1.64	2.05
Switzerland.........................	1,765	23,444	12,916	6,518	0.64	4.01	1.85	0.95
United Kingdom....................	10,230	25,632	31,809	18,545	0.72	1.12	1.16	0.70

NA Not available. [1] The OECD Development Assistance Committee (DAC) is comprised of the above-listed member countries plus Hungary and the European Union.

Source: Organisation for Economic Co-operation and Development (OECD), 2017, "Detailed aid statistics: Official and private flows," OECD International Development Statistics (database) ©, <http://dx.doi.org/10.1787/data-00072-en>, accessed August 2017.

Table 1411. External Debt by Developing Country: 2000 to 2015

[In millions of U.S. dollars (9,763 represents $9,763,000,000). Total external debt is debt owed to nonresidents repayable in foreign currency, goods, or services. Total external debt is the sum of public, publicly guaranteed, and private nonguaranteed long-term debt, use of International Monetary Fund (IMF) credit, and short-term debt. Short-term debt includes all debt having an original maturity of one year or less and interest in arrears on long-term debt]

Country	2000	2010	2014	2015	Country	2000	2010	2014	2015
Angola....................	9,763	16,949	28,903	27,991	Malaysia................	41,946	133,800	196,587	190,951
Argentina................	150,063	126,641	144,972	159,694	Mauritius................	967	2,734	15,202	14,643
Azerbaijan...............	1,585	7,159	11,788	13,215	Mexico..................	152,558	245,906	441,564	426,334
Bangladesh..............	15,603	26,881	35,665	38,640	Mongolia................	960	5,928	20,826	21,542
Belarus..................	2,620	28,412	40,014	37,876	Morocco................	20,790	27,259	42,809	42,989
Bosnia and Herzegovina..	2,791	14,032	14,115	12,887	Nigeria.................	32,374	15,484	24,756	29,029
Brazil....................	242,512	352,364	556,921	543,399	Pakistan................	33,022	64,003	62,262	65,482
Bulgaria.................	12,009	50,635	47,834	37,492	Panama................	6,608	48,882	78,023	87,724
China...................	145,666	734,465	1,770,543	1,418,291	Papua New Guinea. ...	2,325	5,987	20,429	20,031
Colombia................	34,272	64,097	101,376	111,050	Paraguay...............	3,106	15,895	16,493	16,162
Costa Rica...............	4,692	8,154	19,640	23,667	Peru...................	28,834	42,154	61,270	65,938
Dominican Republic.......	4,618	13,499	26,262	26,632	Philippines..............	58,456	65,303	77,104	77,725
Ecuador.................	19,637	16,248	24,399	27,273	Romania................	11,259	115,393	111,824	95,955
Egypt...................	29,194	36,742	41,677	46,585	Russia [1]..............	146,665	417,892	549,631	467,720
El Salvador..............	4,535	11,060	14,533	14,982	Serbia [1]...............	11,573	32,935	33,079	30,807
Ethiopia.................	5,516	7,335	16,589	20,414	South Africa...........	25,435	108,392	141,103	137,887
Georgia.................	1,826	9,656	14,035	14,854	Sri Lanka..............	9,250	21,684	42,264	43,920
Ghana..................	6,743	9,114	18,363	20,677	Sudan [2]...............	16,076	22,286	21,762	21,406
Guatemala..............	3,948	15,039	19,286	20,182	Tanzania...............	7,186	8,893	14,352	15,049
India...................	101,131	290,428	457,553	479,559	Thailand...............	79,830	106,358	135,292	129,654
Indonesia...............	144,032	198,268	292,969	308,540	Tunisia................	11,355	22,472	26,372	27,363
Jamaica................	4,828	14,193	14,078	14,122	Turkey.................	116,799	300,526	400,874	397,923
Jordan..................	11,063	17,073	24,281	25,746	Ukraine................	13,910	124,297	131,206	122,825
Kazakhstan..............	12,890	119,145	157,651	154,288	Uzbekistan.............	4,948	7,802	13,308	14,838
Kenya..................	6,148	8,848	16,683	19,148	Venezuela.............	42,753	101,766	135,748	123,666
Lebanon................	10,073	24,676	29,943	30,896	Vietnam................	12,785	44,902	72,423	77,798

[1] Data from 2000 to 2005 are for Serbia and Montenegro. In June 2006, Serbia and Montenegro became separate countries; beginning 2006, data exclude Montenegro. Data from 2008 onward exclude Kosovo, which declared independence that year. [2] Data for Sudan include South Sudan, which became an independent state in July 2011.

Source: The World Bank, Washington, DC, "External debt stocks, total," World Development Indicators (database) ©, <http://data. worldbank.org/data-catalog/world-development-indicators>, accessed August 2017.

Table 1412. Foreign Direct Investment Flows in Selected Countries: 2010 to 2016

[In millions of dollars (210,554 represents $210,554,000,000). Data are converted to U.S. dollars using the yearly average exchange rate]

Country	Inflows					Outflows				
	2010	2013	2014	2015	2016	2010	2013	2014	2015	2016
United States..........	**210,544**	**217,274**	**212,324**	**476,684**	**468,330**	**296,334**	**321,937**	**313,524**	**281,661**	**300,496**
Australia................	36,442	56,946	39,613	22,268	(NA)	19,803	1,580	3	-16,741	(NA)
Austria.................	-21,694	-3,765	32	5,597	-32,033	-14,065	6,704	-2,586	12,504	-33,159
Belgium................	43,233	25,188	-8,917	21,281	33,094	-8,313	29,480	-2,700	30,361	18,263
Brazil..................	83,749	53,060	73,086	64,267	57,933	22,060	-1,180	2,230	3,092	-12,434
Canada................	28,399	69,372	59,137	41,538	35,257	34,721	57,365	60,542	67,079	70,549
Chile..................	17,227	19,331	23,784	15,866	11,266	10,534	8,127	12,573	12,139	6,165
China..................	243,703	290,928	268,097	242,489	170,557	57,954	72,971	123,130	174,391	217,203
Czech Republic........	6,147	3,641	5,492	465	6,752	1,168	4,021	1,620	2,488	984
Denmark...............	-12,559	635	2,157	2,561	1,015	-1,407	6,948	5,759	7,865	15,051
Estonia................	1,509	750	604	130	864	167	505	-159	323	352
Finland................	7,359	[1] -169	18,270	1,568	(NA)	10,189	[1] -2,401	1,182	-16,031	(NA)
France.................	13,891	34,264	2,669	47,334	28,343	48,158	20,365	49,785	44,695	57,311
Germany...............	65,646	[1] 12,796	-3,374	27,221	12,243	125,453	[1] 39,492	92,195	87,202	37,265
Greece................	330	2,817	2,683	1,140	3,125	1,558	-785	3,015	2,127	-638
Hungary...............	-37,264	-2,687	9,041	-27,915	46,443	-41,146	-2,747	5,189	-30,578	43,300
Iceland................	(NA)	412	439	670	-479	(NA)	460	-295	-29	-1,191
Indonesia..............	13,771	18,817	21,811	16,641	3,649	2,664	6,652	7,077	5,937	-12,372
Ireland................	42,807	46,616	37,417	188,361	22,298	22,350	29,360	41,440	166,321	44,535
Italy...................	9,179	[1] 24,267	23,224	19,332	28,951	32,657	[1] 25,130	26,318	22,315	22,792
Japan.................	-1,252	2,303	10,622	-2,251	11,388	56,276	135,745	129,157	128,698	145,230
Korea, South..........	(NA)	6,083	-917	3,076	(NA)	(NA)	31,488	19,994	18,490	(NA)
Latvia.................	379	904	783	666	125	20	413	288	32	179
Luxembourg...........	222,023	[1] 498,870	129,469	410,185	37,892	205,556	[1] 360,341	189,962	618,931	49,625
Netherlands............	135,774	381,217	131,746	98,159	85,045	210,620	468,440	87,576	162,602	166,225
New Zealand..........	-61	1,860	2,529	-337	2,420	716	530	472	89	-52
Norway................	(NA)	-5,916	19,504	(NA)	(NA)	(NA)	6,213	32,939	(NA)	(NA)
Poland................	12,799	2,734	17,509	11,819	11,880	6,148	-1,346	4,598	1,928	7,508
Portugal...............	2,424	2,701	2,977	6,935	6,062	-9,783	-1,205	-517	5,686	1,582
Russia.................	31,668	53,397	29,152	12,798	36,951	41,116	70,685	64,203	28,030	26,727
Slovak Republic........	1,770	[1] -604	-512	-196	49	946	[1] -313	43	-183	375
Slovenia...............	106	-151	1,050	1,675	1,260	-19	-214	275	267	287
Spain..................	(NA)	37,429	25,656	11,911	(NA)	(NA)	12,821	36,326	44,497	(NA)
Sweden...............	141	4,125	4,032	6,206	18,746	20,364	30,279	9,162	14,946	19,955
Switzerland............	28,750	646	[1] 8,070	70,406	(NA)	85,718	38,568	[1] -1,058	104,016	(NA)
Turkey.................	9,086	12,771	12,458	17,259	12,009	1,469	3,528	6,664	4,807	2,858
United Kingdom........	58,180	51,673	44,845	33,005	253,700	48,075	40,481	-148,383	-82,144	-12,607

NA Not available. [1] Break in series.

Source: Organisation for Economic Co-operation and Development (OECD), 2017, "Benchmark definition, 4th edition (BMD4): Foreign direct investment: financial flows, main aggregates," OECD International Direct Investment Statistics (database) ©, <http://dx.doi.org/10.1787/data-00741-en>, accessed August 2017.

Table 1413. International Transaction Balances, Reserve Assets, and Trade in Relation to Gross Domestic Product (GDP) by Country: 2015 and 2016

[In millions of U.S. dollars (-462,961 represents -$462,961,000,000), except as noted. Minus sign (-) indicates deficit]

Country	Current account balance		Reserve assets [1]		Goods and services trade balance		Exports as percent of GDP		Imports as percent of GDP	
	2015	2016	2015	2016	2015	2016	2015	2016	2015	2016
United States.........	-462,961	-481,210	106,540	106,291	-521,971	(NA)	12.6	(NA)	15.4	(NA)
Algeria.................	-27,229	(NA)	144,677	114,391	-21,792	-16,700	23.6	23.7	36.8	34.4
Angola.................	-10,273	(NA)	23,791	23,741	-2,281	307	33.9	33.0	36.1	32.7
Argentina.............	-16,806	(NA)	23,417	36,323	-4,910	-3,778	11.0	12.7	11.8	13.4
Australia..............	-57,990	-32,893	46,540	52,093	-19,457	-26,694	19.7	18.9	21.1	21.1
Austria................	7,241	6,618	12,698	12,940	15,110	14,718	53.1	52.2	49.1	48.4
Azerbaijan............	-222	-1,363	6,291	5,836	1,586	1,052	37.8	46.5	34.8	43.7
Bangladesh...........	2,687	(NA)	27,023	31,776	-14,460	-10,307	17.3	16.6	24.7	21.3
Belgium...............	1,935	-1,913	16,352	15,103	7,599	11,180	82.9	84.5	81.3	82.1
Brazil.................	-59,434	-23,530	354,175	362,505	-21,237	6,516	12.9	12.5	14.1	12.1
Bulgaria...............	-69	2,238	20,783	23,691	74	1,602	64.1	63.6	64.0	60.5
Canada................	-53,083	-51,195	79,695	82,718	-37,104	-36,191	31.6	31.0	34.0	33.4
Chile..................	-4,670	-3,574	38,633	40,484	-267	2,076	29.7	28.5	29.8	27.6
China.................	304,164	196,380	3,345,194	3,029,775	385,502	249,601	22.0	19.6	18.5	17.4
Colombia..............	-18,780	-12,541	46,104	45,962	-23,684	-18,653	15.2	14.0	23.4	20.6
Czech Republic.......	461	2,139	64,148	85,366	11,350	14,216	83.0	80.3	76.8	73.0
Denmark..............	27,582	24,837	62,917	61,764	22,301	21,050	55.2	53.1	47.8	46.2
Dominican Republic...	-1,280	-978	5,247	6,113	-3,108	-2,675	24.7	25.2	29.3	28.9
Ecuador...............	-2,120	1,414	2,085	3,781	-2,992	-334	20.7	19.3	23.7	19.7
Egypt.................	-16,787	(NA)	13,282	20,858	-28,207	-31,105	13.2	10.4	21.7	19.6
Finland...............	-1,394	-2,551	8,341	8,678	-692	-2,859	36.8	35.4	37.1	36.6
France................	-4,863	-22,749	55,192	56,125	-33,314	-42,411	29.8	29.4	31.2	31.2
Georgia...............	-1,673	(NA)	2,521	2,756	-2,453	-2,242	44.7	43.5	62.3	59.1
Germany..............	288,151	289,159	58,507	59,582	254,574	264,096	46.8	46.0	39.2	38.4
Ghana.................	-2,809	(NA)	(NA)	(NA)	-4,335	-3,041	43.9	40.7	55.4	47.9
Greece................	218	-1,131	2,189	2,695	280	-1,305	31.9	30.2	31.8	30.8
Honduras..............	-1,291	(NA)	3,731	3,788	-3,564	-3,294	46.0	42.7	63.1	58.0
Hong Kong, China....	10,264	(NA)	358,702	386,164	7,392	6,834	195.9	187.4	193.5	185.2
India.................	-22,457	(NA)	334,311	341,145	-48,815	-33,003	19.9	19.2	22.3	20.6
Indonesia.............	-17,519	-16,347	103,268	113,493	3,695	7,225	21.2	19.1	20.7	18.3
Iraq..................	4,121	(NA)	50,991	42,014	-10,800	-11,487	35.0	32.6	41.0	39.3
Ireland...............	28,967	14,349	1,999	3,368	90,070	68,203	124.0	119.9	92.2	96.7
Israel................	13,642	12,260	90,575	95,446	9,036	7,289	30.7	29.8	27.7	27.5
Italy.................	26,120	47,705	47,034	44,803	53,116	64,027	30.0	30.0	27.1	26.5
Jamaica...............	-430	-103	2,914	3,291	-2,191	-2,261	29.8	31.1	45.2	47.3
Japan.................	134,134	187,265	1,207,019	1,188,327	-14,158	(NA)	17.6	(NA)	18.0	(NA)
Jordan................	-3,332	(NA)	15,162	14,019	-8,592	-8,048	37.6	35.1	60.5	55.9
Kazakhstan............	-5,464	(NA)	20,295	19,915	7,345	4,648	28.5	32.6	24.5	29.2
Kenya.................	(NA)	(NA)	7,548	(NA)	-7,058	-6,199	16.7	14.6	27.7	23.4
Korea, South..........	105,940	98,677	363,149	366,308	96,258	95,912	45.3	42.2	38.4	35.4
Kuwait................	8,584	930	28,270	31,027	10,395	(NA)	54.4	(NA)	45.3	(NA)
Lebanon...............	-8,146	(NA)	38,756	43,338	-3,768	-5,695	57.0	54.5	65.0	66.5
Malaysia..............	8,960	(NA)	93,979	93,072	22,677	18,957	70.9	67.2	63.3	60.8
Mexico................	-33,347	-27,858	173,458	173,536	-22,564	-19,150	35.1	38.2	37.1	40.0
Mongolia..............	-948	(NA)	1,247	1,240	118	443	45.7	50.8	44.7	46.8
Morocco...............	-2,161	-4,531	22,254	24,541	-7,837	-10,522	34.3	34.7	42.1	45.1
Netherlands...........	66,155	64,754	17,341	13,342	80,881	83,949	82.5	80.8	71.7	69.9
New Zealand..........	-5,500	-5,152	14,700	17,808	1,245	(NA)	27.9	(NA)	27.2	(NA)
Nigeria...............	-15,763	(NA)	30,606	29,243	671	(NA)	10.6	(NA)	10.5	(NA)
Norway................	33,746	18,069	57,456	60,445	20,974	4,593	37.4	33.8	32.0	32.5
Pakistan..............	-1,603	(NA)	17,830	19,650	-17,440	-20,216	10.6	8.7	17.0	15.8
Panama................	-3,809	-3,098	3,378	3,847	-3,515	-2,650	49.5	44.8	56.2	49.6
Peru..................	-9,210	(NA)	60,413	60,524	-4,565	170	21.3	22.4	23.7	22.4
Philippines...........	7,266	601	73,964	73,433	-17,269	-27,346	28.4	28.0	34.3	36.9
Poland................	-2,932	-1,395	91,395	110,535	14,771	18,248	49.5	52.3	46.4	48.4
Portugal..............	140	1,708	6,367	10,899	1,448	2,446	40.6	40.3	39.8	39.1
Romania...............	-2,171	-4,385	35,167	36,133	-1,092	-1,752	41.1	41.4	41.7	42.3
Russia................	68,943	25,006	319,835	317,544	110,136	66,191	28.7	25.7	20.6	20.6
Saudi Arabia..........	-56,724	-24,914	615,985	535,364	-35,544	3,182	33.3	30.7	38.8	30.2
Serbia................	-1,751	(NA)	10,727	10,060	-3,624	-2,767	46.7	50.9	56.4	58.2
Singapore.............	53,757	56,501	247,534	246,365	76,943	76,848	177.9	172.1	152.0	146.3
South Africa..........	-13,911	-9,479	41,620	42,566	-3,448	430	30.4	30.3	31.5	30.2
Spain.................	16,207	24,076	44,378	52,666	29,219	35,855	33.2	33.1	30.7	30.2
Sri Lanka.............	-2,009	(NA)	6,543	5,189	-6,072	-6,208	21.0	21.4	28.5	29.1
Sudan.................	-5,933	(NA)	174	(NA)	-2,659	-2,579	8.2	9.8	10.9	12.5
Sweden................	23,277	23,653	53,814	54,730	23,529	23,638	45.6	44.4	40.8	39.8
Switzerland...........	77,378	70,632	566,960	640,594	78,574	(NA)	62.9	(NA)	51.2	(NA)
Tanzania..............	-3,312	(NA)	4,073	(NA)	-2,155	-782	21.6	17.6	26.3	19.2
Thailand..............	32,149	(NA)	151,266	166,157	46,265	59,946	69.1	68.9	57.5	54.2
Tunisia...............	-3,850	(NA)	7,328	5,887	-4,727	-4,564	40.7	40.2	51.6	51.0
Turkey................	-32,118	-32,626	92,921	92,055	-22,573	-25,426	23.3	22.1	26.0	25.0
Ukraine...............	-189	(NA)	12,368	14,598	-1,717	-5,812	52.6	49.3	54.5	55.5
United Kingdom.......	-122,571	-115,527	119,026	123,500	-45,509	-49,718	27.6	28.1	29.2	30.0
Venezuela.............	-20,360	(NA)	6,324	(NA)	(NA)	(NA)	(NA)	(NA)	(NA)	(NA)
Vietnam...............	906	(NA)	28,250	36,527	1,529	5,190	89.8	93.6	89.0	91.1

NA Not available. [1] Reserve assets are comprised of special drawing rights and reserve position in International Monetary Fund (IMF), and foreign exchange holdings. Gold holdings are excluded.

Source: The World Bank, Washington, DC, "World Development Indicators" database ©, <http://data.worldbank.org/data-catalog/world-development-indicators>, accessed August 2017.

Table 1414. International Tourism Arrivals, Expenditures, and Receipts—Leading Countries: 2000 to 2015

[Arrivals at national borders in thousands of non-resident tourists (677,311 represents 677,311,000). Expenditures and receipts in millions of current U.S. dollars (451,775 represents $451,775,000,000). Receipts are money spent by foreign tourists while traveling inside the country shown and include prepayment for goods or services in destination country. Expenditures are money spent by tourists from a given country of origin while traveling outside their home country. Data exclude receipts and expenditures for international transport. Ranked for top 50 countries in tourist arrivals as of 2015. Sources and collection methods differ, thus caution should be used in comparing data across countries]

Country	Arrivals (1,000)					Expenditures (mil. dol.)					Receipts (mil. dol.)				
	2000	2005	2010	2014	2015	2000	2005	2010	2014	2015	2000	2005	2010	2014	2015
World ¹	677,311	807,796	954,967	1,150,505	1,200,058	451,775	662,905	866,789	1,241,856	1,219,228	498,868	713,949	965,471	1,315,922	1,264,973
France	77,190	74,988	76,647	83,701	84,452	22,533	31,354	38,304	48,733	38,406	32,855	43,947	46,466	57,668	45,888
United States	51,238	49,206	60,010	75,022	77,510	67,860	79,990	86,623	105,529	112,872	100,716	101,469	137,010	191,325	204,525
Spain	46,403	55,914	52,677	64,939	68,215	5,922	15,175	16,930	17,969	17,347	29,802	49,565	54,305	65,100	56,426
China	31,229	46,809	55,664	55,622	56,886	13,114	21,759	54,880	234,662	292,200	16,231	29,296	45,814	105,380	114,109
Italy	41,181	36,513	43,626	48,576	50,732	15,685	22,370	26,908	28,857	24,417	27,493	35,319	38,438	45,547	39,420
Turkey	9,586	20,273	31,364	39,811	39,478	1,713	3,104	5,194	5,072	5,368	7,636	19,191	22,585	29,552	26,616
Germany	18,983	21,500	26,875	32,999	34,970	52,824	74,189	77,580	93,253	76,278	18,611	29,121	34,564	43,263	36,842
United Kingdom	23,212	28,039	28,295	32,613	34,436	38,262	62,566	54,879	62,794	63,426	21,769	31,012	32,891	46,628	45,532
Russian Federation	21,169	22,201	22,281	32,421	33,729	8,848	16,972	26,693	50,428	34,934	3,429	5,870	8,830	11,759	8,465
Mexico	20,641	21,915	23,290	29,346	32,093	5,499	7,600	7,255	9,606	10,098	8,294	11,803	11,992	16,208	17,734
Thailand	9,579	11,567	15,936	24,810	29,923	2,772	3,803	5,627	7,071	7,718	7,483	9,576	20,104	38,418	44,922
Austria	17,982	19,952	22,004	25,291	26,719	6,232	9,316	10,122	10,849	9,100	9,899	16,243	18,758	20,907	18,273
Hong Kong, China	8,814	14,773	20,085	27,770	26,686	12,502	13,305	17,357	22,011	23,059	5,868	10,179	21,689	39,243	35,574
Malaysia	10,222	16,431	24,577	27,437	25,721	2,075	3,711	8,324	12,442	10,589	5,011	8,846	18,152	22,600	17,614
Greece	13,096	14,765	15,007	22,033	23,599	4,558	3,039	2,854	2,754	2,259	9,219	13,334	12,479	17,813	15,662
Japan	4,757	6,728	8,611	13,413	19,737	31,884	37,565	27,950	19,314	15,971	3,373	12,430	13,224	18,812	24,968
Saudi Arabia	6,585	8,037	10,850	18,260	17,994	(NA)	9,087	21,135	24,118	20,725	(NA)	4,626	6,712	8,238	10,130
Canada	19,627	18,771	16,219	16,537	17,971	12,438	18,021	29,727	33,817	29,514	10,778	13,651	15,829	17,476	16,203
Poland	17,400	15,200	12,470	16,000	16,722	3,315	5,547	8,570	8,868	7,939	5,677	6,304	9,576	11,847	10,473
Netherlands	10,003	10,012	10,883	13,925	15,007	12,191	13,724	19,044	20,435	19,385	7,197	8,770	11,653	12,951	13,560
Macao, China	5,197	9,014	11,926	14,566	14,308	(NA)	412	800	1,210	1,265	(NA)	6,924	22,276	42,724	31,476
India	2,649	3,919	5,776	13,107	13,284	2,690	6,187	10,490	14,595	14,838	3,460	7,493	14,490	19,700	21,013
Korea, South	5,322	6,023	8,798	14,202	13,232	7,132	15,406	18,766	23,192	24,958	6,834	5,806	10,328	17,836	15,285
Croatia	5,831	7,743	9,111	11,623	12,683	568	754	832	846	755	2,758	7,370	8,069	9,863	8,833
Ukraine	6,431	17,631	21,203	12,712	12,428	470	2,805	3,742	5,061	4,443	394	3,125	3,788	1,612	1,082
Singapore	6,062	7,079	9,161	11,864	12,051	4,535	10,070	18,700	24,360	22,056	5,142	6,209	14,178	19,134	16,743
Bahrain	3,869	6,313	11,952	10,452	11,621	224	414	506	718	(NA)	573	920	1,362	1,197	(NA)
Denmark	3,535	9,587	9,425	10,267	10,424	4,669	6,850	9,082	10,443	8,918	3,671	5,293	5,704	7,617	6,685
Indonesia	5,064	5,002	7,003	9,435	10,407	3,197	3,584	6,395	7,682	7,292	4,975	4,522	6,958	10,261	10,761
Morocco	4,278	5,843	9,288	10,283	10,177	425	612	1,203	1,401	1,402	2,039	4,610	6,702	7,060	6,260
Portugal	5,599	5,769	6,756	9,092	9,957	2,228	3,050	3,906	4,407	4,005	5,243	7,676	10,006	13,777	12,692
Ireland	6,646	7,333	7,134	8,813	9,528	2,525	6,074	6,059	6,059	5,679	2,615	4,782	4,086	4,862	4,785
Romania	5,264	5,839	7,498	8,442	9,331	425	923	1,637	2,412	2,059	359	1,051	1,136	1,826	1,711
Switzerland	7,821	7,229	8,628	9,158	9,305	5,419	8,803	11,173	16,869	16,031	6,652	10,044	14,724	17,827	16,377
Egypt	5,116	8,244	14,051	9,628	9,139	1,072	1,629	2,240	3,140	3,442	4,345	6,851	12,528	7,208	6,065
South Africa	5,872	7,369	8,074	9,549	8,904	2,085	3,374	5,595	3,169	2,998	2,677	7,516	9,085	9,338	8,259
Czech Republic	4,773	6,336	6,334	8,096	8,707	1,276	2,405	4,252	5,133	4,867	2,973	4,813	7,172	6,822	6,048
Belgium	6,457	6,747	7,186	7,887	8,355	9,429	14,948	18,866	23,815	18,924	6,592	9,845	11,395	13,914	11,963
Vietnam	2,140	3,477	5,050	7,874	7,944	(NA)	(NA)	(NA)	(NA)	(NA)	(NA)	(NA)	(NA)	(NA)	(NA)
Australia	4,931	5,499	5,790	6,868	7,444	6,387	11,749	22,558	26,416	23,418	9,289	16,750	28,472	31,948	29,303
Bulgaria	2,785	4,837	6,047	7,311	7,099	538	1,309	826	1,202	1,116	1,074	2,412	3,343	3,927	3,154
Sweden	3,828	4,883	5,183	5,660	6,482	8,048	10,014	12,126	15,823	14,410	4,064	6,554	8,336	11,846	11,307
Brazil	5,313	5,358	5,161	6,430	6,306	3,894	4,720	15,965	25,567	17,357	1,810	3,861	5,261	6,843	5,844
Georgia	387	560	2,032	5,516	5,901	110	169	199	299	330	97	241	659	1,787	1,936
Argentina	2,909	3,823	5,325	5,931	5,736	4,425	2,790	4,878	5,362	5,920	2,904	2,729	4,942	4,635	4,400
Dominican Republic	2,978	3,691	4,125	5,141	5,600	309	352	395	417	463	2,860	3,518	4,163	5,630	6,118
Norway	3,104	3,824	4,767	4,855	5,361	4,601	9,678	13,472	18,539	15,821	2,050	3,494	4,692	5,579	4,883
Philippines	1,992	2,623	3,520	4,833	5,361	1,642	3,018	5,487	10,598	11,660	2,156	2,287	2,645	5,030	5,276
Tunisia	5,058	6,378	7,828	7,163	5,359	263	374	547	681	696	1,682	2,143	2,438	2,359	1,381
Iran	1,342	1,889	2,938	4,967	5,237	668	3,724	9,655	8,533	(NA)	467	791	(NA)	3,483	(NA)

NA Not available. ¹ Includes other countries not shown separately.

Source: The World Bank, Washington, DC, "World Development Indicators" database ©, <http://data.worldbank.org/data-catalog/world-development-indicators>, accessed September 2017.

Table 1415. Military Expenditures as a Percent of GDP, Selected Years 2014 to 2017, and Manpower, 2010, by Country

[120,022 represents 120,022,000. Manpower covers males and females deemed fit for military service, ages 16–49, who are not otherwise disqualified for health reasons]

Country	Expenditures Data as of year	Expenditures Percent of GDP [1]	Manpower in 2010 (1,000)	Country	Expenditures Data as of year	Expenditures Percent of GDP [1]	Manpower in 2010 (1,000)
United States............	**2016**	**3.29**	**120,022**	Kenya......................	2016	1.32	12,468
Afghanistan...............	2016	0.89	7,847	Korea, South.............	2016	2.30	21,033
Albania....................	2016	1.23	1,283	Kuwait....................	2015	4.83	1,364
Algeria....................	2016	6.55	17,249	Lebanon...................	2015	4.76	1,863
Angola....................	2016	2.95	3,039	Macedonia.................	2016	0.97	870
Argentina.................	2016	0.95	16,873	Malaysia..................	2016	1.41	12,423
Armenia...................	2016	4.09	1,362	Mexico....................	2016	0.58	48,882
Australia.................	2016	2.00	8,652	Montenegro................	2016	1.61	281
Austria...................	2016	0.68	3,134	Morocco...................	2016	3.28	14,403
Azerbaijan................	2016	3.64	3,738	Nepal.....................	2016	1.52	11,208
Bahrain...................	2015	4.59	669	Netherlands...............	2017	1.17	6,324
Bangladesh................	2016	1.44	66,102	New Zealand...............	2016	1.13	1,672
Brazil....................	2016	1.32	83,836	Nigeria...................	2016	0.43	40,708
Bulgaria..................	2016	1.44	2,659	Oman......................	2016	13.73	1,480
Canada....................	2016	0.99	13,023	Pakistan..................	2016	3.56	75,327
Chile.....................	2016	1.87	7,183	Peru......................	2016	1.29	12,354
China.....................	2016	1.90	618,589	Philippines...............	2016	1.28	41,571
Colombia..................	2016	3.39	19,012	Poland....................	2016	1.99	15,584
Congo, Dem. Rep.........	2016	1.34	20,500	Romania...................	2016	1.42	9,058
Czech Republic...........	2016	0.98	4,061	Russia....................	2016	5.40	46,813
Denmark...................	2016	1.15	2,018	Saudi Arabia..............	2016	9.85	13,043
Ecuador...................	2016	2.21	6,104	South Africa..............	2016	1.07	14,093
Egypt.....................	2016	1.67	35,305	Spain.....................	2016	0.91	18,721
France....................	2016	2.26	23,747	Sri Lanka.................	2016	2.44	8,752
Georgia...................	2016	2.23	1,825	Tanzania..................	2016	1.14	11,743
Germany...................	2016	1.19	29,538	Thailand..................	2016	1.45	27,491
Ghana.....................	2016	0.38	8,357	Tunisia...................	2016	2.32	4,882
Greece....................	2016	2.56	4,049	Turkey....................	2016	1.73	35,005
India.....................	2016	2.47	489,571	Uganda....................	2016	1.57	8,514
Indonesia.................	2016	0.88	107,539	Ukraine...................	2016	3.67	15,686
Iraq......................	2016	3.63	13,013	United Arab Emirates....	2014	5.66	3,072
Ireland...................	2016	0.34	1,944	United Kingdom..........	2016	1.84	24,035
Israel....................	2016	5.64	2,964	Venezuela.................	2015	1.00	11,690
Italy.....................	2016	1.51	22,596	Vietnam...................	2016	2.44	41,504
Japan.....................	2016	0.93	43,931	Yemen.....................	2014	3.97	8,174
Jordan....................	2016	4.58	2,824	Zambia....................	2016	1.53	3,434
Kazakhstan................	2016	0.82	6,438	Zimbabwe..................	2016	2.20	3,174

[1] Spending on defense programs as percent of Gross Domestic Product (GDP), calculated on an exchange rate basis. For countries with no military forces, this figure can include expenditures on public security and police. Some data include estimates.

Source: Central Intelligence Agency, *The World Factbook*, <https://www.cia.gov/library/publications/the-world-factbook/index.html>, accessed September 2017.

Table 1416. Terrorism Attacks, Fatalities, Injuries, and Hostages Taken for Top 10 Countries and Perpetrator Groups: 2015 and 2016

[Data shown for top 10 countries and perpetrator groups of attacks in 2016. Based on data collected by the National Consortium for the Study of Terrorism and Responses to Terrorism (START) and maintained in the Global Terrorism Database (GTD). Any assessments and descriptions, including those regarding the nature of the incidents or the factual circumstances thereof, are offered only as part of the analytic work product of the National Consortium START and may not reflect the views of the U.S. Government]

Country and perpetrator group	2015 Attacks	2015 Fatalities [1]	2015 Injuries [1]	2015 Kidnapped/ hostages taken	2016 Attacks	2016 Fatalities [1]	2016 Injuries [1]	2016 Kidnapped/ hostages taken
Worldwide total...........................	**12,121**	**29,424**	**37,419**	**12,264**	**11,072**	**25,621**	**33,814**	**15,543**
By country:								
Iraq......................................	2,417	6,973	11,900	4,008	2,965	9,764	13,314	8,586
Afghanistan...............................	1,716	5,312	6,250	1,134	1,340	4,561	5,054	1,673
India.....................................	798	289	500	866	927	337	636	317
Pakistan..................................	1,010	1,087	1,338	279	734	955	1,729	450
Philippines...............................	490	260	430	127	482	272	418	216
Nigeria...................................	588	4,940	2,786	858	466	1,832	919	265
Syria [2].................................	387	2,767	2,830	1,476	363	2,088	2,656	1,406
Turkey....................................	309	337	828	141	363	657	2,282	18
Yemen.....................................	460	1,517	2,599	456	363	628	793	173
Somalia...................................	241	659	463	161	359	740	943	373
By perpetrator:								
Islamic State of Iraq and Syria (ISIS) [3]....	969	6,178	6,608	4,805	1,133	9,114	7,671	8,379
Taliban...................................	1,104	4,535	4,758	975	848	3,615	3,572	1,498
Maoists/Communist Party of India-Maoist....	347	177	156	707	336	174	141	171
Al-Shabaab................................	226	836	561	559	332	740	921	375
Houthi Extremists.........................	292	978	1,704	387	267	374	568	137

[1] Includes perpetrators. [2] Given the limitations of media coverage in Syria, the data presented here are conservative estimates of terrorism in Syria. Consistent with START's practice of including in the GTD only those attacks that have been verified by at least one well-regarded source, these statistics represent those incidents that were reported by independent news outlets. [3] Excludes attacks attributed to branches of ISIS or ISIS-inspired individuals.

Source: U.S. State Department, Bureau of Counterterrorism, *Annex of Statistical Information: Country Reports on Terrorism 2016*, July 2017. See also <http://www.state.gov/j/ct/rls/crt/index.htm>.

Guide to Sources of Statistics, State Statistical Abstracts, and Foreign Statistical Abstracts

Alphabetically arranged, this guide contains references to important primary sources of statistical information for the United States and other countries. Secondary sources have been included if the information contained in them is presented in a particularly convenient form or if primary sources are not readily available. Nonrecurrent publications presenting compilations or estimates for years later than 2010, or types of data not available in regular series, are also included. Data are also available in press releases.

Valuable information may also be found in state reports and foreign statistical abstracts, which are included at the end of this appendix, and in reports for particular commodities, industries, or similar segments of our economic and social structures, many of which are not included here.

Publications listed under each subject are divided into two main groups: "U.S. Government" and "Nongovernment." The location of the publisher of each report is given except for federal agencies located in Washington, DC. Most federal publications may be purchased from the Superintendent of Documents, U.S. Government Printing Office, Washington, DC, tel. 1-866-512-1800, or at <http://bookstore.gpo.gov>. In some cases, federal publications may be obtained from the issuing agency.

Appendix I Table: Sources of Statistics, State Statistical Abstracts, and Foreign Statistical Abstracts

Title	Frequency	Paper	Internet	
			PDF	Other Formats
U.S. GOVERNMENT				
Administrative Office of the United States Courts				
http://www.uscourts.gov				
Calendar Year Reports on Authorized Wiretaps (state and federal)	Annual		X	X
Federal Court Management Statistics	Quarterly		X	X
Federal Judicial Caseload Statistics	Annual		X	X
Judicial Business of the United States Courts	Annual		X	X
Statistical Tables for the Federal Judiciary	Semiannual		X	
Agency for International Development				
http://www.usaid.gov				
U.S. Overseas Loans and Grants: Obligations and Loan Authorizations	Annual		X	X
Army Corps of Engineers				
http://www.usace.army.mil				
Waterborne Commerce of the United States Waterways and Harbors (in five parts)	Annual		X	X
Board of Governors of the Federal Reserve System				
http://www.federalreserve.gov				
Assets and Liabilities of Commercial Banks in the United States H.8	Weekly		X	X
Consumer Credit G.19	Monthly		X	X
Federal Reserve Bulletin	Periodic	X	X	X
Financial Accounts of the United States Z.1	Quarterly	X	X	X
Foreign Exchange Rates H.10	Weekly			X
Industrial Production and Capacity Utilization G.17	Monthly		X	X
Money Stock Measures H.6	Weekly		X	X
Survey of Consumer Finances	Triennial		X	X
Bureau of Economic Analysis				
http://www.bea.gov				
Arts and Cultural Production Satellite Accounts	Ongoing		X	X
Health Care Satellite Account	Ongoing		X	X
International Economic Accounts	Ongoing		X	X
National Economic Accounts	Ongoing		X	X
Regional Economic Accounts	Ongoing		X	X
Survey of Current Business	Monthly	X	X	X
Bureau of Justice Statistics				
http://www.bjs.gov/				
Background Checks for Firearm Transfers	Annual		X	X
Capital Punishment	Annual		X	X
Census of Problem-Solving Courts	Periodic		X	X
Census of Publicly Funded Forensic Crime Laboratories, 2009, August 2012	Periodic		X	X
Census of State and Federal Correctional Facilities, 2005, October 2008	Periodic		X	X
Civil Rights Complaints in U.S. District Courts, 1990-2006, August 2008	Periodic	X	X	X
Civil Trial Cases and Verdicts in Large Counties, 2005, September 2009	Periodic	X	X	X
Compendium of Federal Justice Statistics, 2009, December 2011	Periodic	X	X	X
Crimes Against the Elderly, 2003-2013, November 2014	Periodic		X	X
Criminal Victimization	Annual		X	X
Family Violence Statistics	Periodic	X	X	X
Federal Law Enforcement Officers, 2008, June 2012	Periodic		X	X
Felony Defendants in Large Urban Counties, 2009, December 2013	Biennial		X	X
Felony Sentences in State Courts, 2006, December 2009	Biennial		X	X
HIV in Prisons, 2015, August 2017	Periodic		X	X
Homicide in the U.S. Known to Law Enforcement, 1992 to 2011, December 2013	Periodic		X	X
Immigration Offenders in the Federal Criminal Justice System, 2010, July 2012	Periodic		X	X
Indicators of School Crime and Safety, 2016, May 2017	Annual		X	X

See footnotes at end of table.

Title	Frequency	Paper	Internet PDF	Internet Other Formats
Intimate Partner Violence, 1993-2011, November 2013	Periodic	X	X	X
Jail Inmates at Midyear, 2014, June 2015	Annual		X	X
Jails in Indian Country, 2015, November 2016	Annual		X	X
Justice Expenditure and Employment Extract Series, 2012, February 2015	Annual			X
Local Police Departments, 2013: Personnel, Policies, and Practices, May 2015	Periodic		X	X
Prisoners in 2015, December 2016	Annual		X	X
Probation and Parole in the United States, 2015, December 2016	Annual		X	X
Publicly Funded Forensic Crime Laboratories: Resources and Services, 2014, November 2016	Periodic		X	X
Prosecutors in State Courts, 2007, December 2011	Biennial		X	X
Rape and Sexual Assault Victimization Among College-Age Females, 1995-2013	Periodic		X	X
Recidivism Of Offenders Placed On Federal Community Supervision In 2005: Patterns From 2005 To 2010	Periodic		X	X
Sheriffs' Offices Personnel, 1993-2013, June 2016	Periodic	X	X	X
Sourcebook of Criminal Justice Statistics	Periodic		X	X
Survey of State Criminal History Information Systems, 2014, December 2015	Biennial	X	X	X
Survey of State Procedures Related to Firearm Sales, 2005, November 2006	Periodic	X	X	X
Tribal Crime Data Collection Activities, 2017, July 2017	Annual		X	X
Victims of Identity Theft, 2014, September 2015	Periodic		X	X
Bureau of Labor Statistics				
http://www.bls.gov				
100 Years of U.S. Consumer Spending: Data for the Nation, New York City, and Boston, Report 991	Periodic	X	X	
College Enrollment and Work Activity of High School Graduates	Annual		X	X
Compensation and Working Conditions	Periodic		X	X
Consumer Expenditure Survey, Integrated Diary and Interview Survey data	Annual		X	X
Consumer Price Index (CPI) Detailed Report	Monthly		X	X
Consumer Prices	Monthly		X	X
Employer Costs for Employee Compensation	Quarterly		X	X
Employment and Earnings	Monthly		X	X
Employment and Wages	Annual		X	X
Employment Characteristics of Families	Annual		X	X
Employment Cost Index	Quarterly		X	X
The Employment Situation	Monthly		X	X
Geographic Profile of Employment and Unemployment	Annual		X	X
Metropolitan Area Employment and Unemployment	Monthly		X	X
Monthly Labor Review	Monthly		X	X
National Compensation Survey	Annual		X	X
Occupational Employment and Wages	Annual		X	X
Occupational Injuries and Illnesses	Annual		X	X
Occupational Projections Data	Biennial		X	X
Producer Price Index (PPI) Detailed Report	Monthly		X	X
Productivity and Costs by Industry	Annual		X	X
Real Earnings	Monthly		X	X
Regional and State Employment and Unemployment	Monthly		X	X
Relative Importance of Components in the Consumer Price Indexes	Annual		X	X
U.S. Import and Export Price Indexes	Monthly		X	X
Union Membership	Annual		X	X
Usual Weekly Earnings of Wage and Salary Workers	Quarterly		X	X
Work Experience of the Population	Annual		X	X
Bureau of Land Management				
http://www.blm.gov				
Public Land Statistics	Annual		X	
Census Bureau				
http://www.census.gov				
2012 Economic Census, Bridge Between 2012 NAICS and 2007 NAICS Report	Quinquennial			X
2012 Economic Census, Company Statistics Series, Survey of Business Owners	Quinquennial			X
2012 Economic Census, Company Statistics Series, Survey of Business Owners: American Indian- and Alaska Native-Owned Firms	Quinquennial			X
2012 Economic Census, Company Statistics Series, Survey of Business Owners: Asian-Owned Firms	Quinquennial			X
2012 Economic Census, Company Statistics Series, Survey of Business Owners: Black-Owned Firms	Quinquennial			X
2012 Economic Census, Company Statistics Series, Survey of Business Owners: Hispanic-Owned Firms	Quinquennial			X
2012 Economic Census, Company Statistics Series, Survey of Business Owners: Native Hawaiian- and other Pacific Islander-Owned Firms	Quinquennial			X
2012 Economic Census, Comparative Statistics	Quinquennial			X
2012 Economic Census, Industry/Geography	Quinquennial			X
America's Families and Living Arrangements: 2016	Annual			X
Annual Revision of Monthly Retail and Food Services: Sales and Inventories	Annual		X	X
Annual Survey of Entrepreneurs	Annual		X	X
Annual Revision of Monthly Wholesale Distributors: Sales and Inventories	Annual		X	X
Annual Survey of Manufactures	Annual		X	
Census of Governments	Quinquennial		X	
Census of Population and Housing Decennial (2010, most recent)	Decennial	X	X	X
Computer and Internet Access in the United States: 2015	Biennial		X	X
Consumer Income and Poverty, P60, and Household Economic Studies, P70	Periodic	X	X	
County Business Patterns	Annual		X	X
Current Construction Reports: New Residential Construction and New Residential Sales	Monthly		X	X
Current Construction Reports: Value of Construction Put in Place, C30	Monthly		X	X

See footnotes at end of table.

Appendix I Table: Sources of Statistics, State Statistical Abstracts, and Foreign Statistical Abstracts-Continued.

See headnote on page 903.

Title	Frequency	Paper	Internet PDF	Internet Other Formats
Current Housing Reports, American Housing Survey for Selected Metropolitan Areas, H170	Biennial			X
Current Housing Reports, American Housing Survey for the United States, H150	Biennial			X
Current Housing Reports, Housing Vacancies and Homeownership, H111	Quarterly			X
Current Housing Reports, Survey of Market Absorption of New Multifamily Units (SOMA)	Quarterly		X	X
Current Housing Reports, Who Can Afford to Buy a Home in 2009, H121	Periodic	X	X	X
Current Population Reports (Series P20 and P23)	Periodic		X	X
Economic Census of Island Areas	Quinquennial			X
Fertility of American Women in the United States: 2016	Annual			X
Health Insurance Coverage in the United States: 2016	Annual		X	X
Income and Poverty in the United States: 2016	Annual		X	X
International Data Base	Annual			X
International Population Reports (Series P95)	Periodic		X	
Manufacturing and International Trade Report: 2015	Annual		X	X
Manufacturer's Shipments, Inventories, and Orders	Monthly		X	X
Manufacturer's Shipments, Inventories, and Orders: 1992-2016	Annual			X
New York City Housing and Vacancy Survey, 2014	Triennial			X
Nonemployer Statistics	Annual			X
Population Estimates and Projections	Annual			X
Quarterly Financial Report for Manufacturing, Mining, and Trade Corporations	Quarterly		X	X
Service Annual Survey Report	Annual			X
Survey of Plant Capacity Utilization	Quarterly			X
U.S. International Trade in Goods and Services (FT900)	Annual		X	X
U.S. Trade with Puerto Rico and U.S. Possessions (FT 895)	Annual		X	

Centers for Disease Control and Prevention, Atlanta, Georgia
http://www.cdc.gov

Title	Frequency	Paper	Internet PDF	Internet Other Formats
Morbidity and Mortality Weekly Report	Weekly	X	X	X
National Health Interview Survey	Ongoing		X	X
National Immunization Survey (NIS) – Children (19-35 months)	Annual		X	X
Surveillance for Foodborne Disease Outbreaks	Annual		X	

Centers for Medicare and Medicaid Services (CMS)
http://www.cms.gov

Title	Frequency	Paper	Internet PDF	Internet Other Formats
CMS Program Statistics	Annual		X	X
Medicare and Medicaid Statistical Supplement	Annual	X	X	X
Trustees Report	Annual	X	X	X

Central Intelligence Agency
http://www.cia.gov

Title	Frequency	Paper	Internet PDF	Internet Other Formats
World Factbook	Annual		X	X

Coast Guard (See Department of Homeland Security)

Council of Economic Advisers
http://www.whitehouse.gov/cea

Title	Frequency	Paper	Internet PDF	Internet Other Formats
Economic Indicators	Monthly	X	X	X
Economic Report of the President	Annual	X	X	X

Department of Agriculture, Economic Research Service
http://www.ers.usda.gov

Title	Frequency	Paper	Internet PDF	Internet Other Formats
Agricultural Income and Finance	Annual	X	X	
Amber Waves	Monthly		X	X
America's Diverse Family Farms	Annual	X	X	X
Cotton and Wool Yearbook	Annual			X
Feed Grains Yearbook	Annual		X	X
Food Availability (Per Capita) Data System	Ongoing			X
Food Expenditures	Annual			X
Fruit and Tree Nut Yearbook	Annual		X	X
Household Food Security in the United States in 2016: Statistical Supplement, No. 237	Annual		X	X
Oil Crops Yearbook	Annual		X	X
Rice Yearbook	Annual			X
Situation and Outlook Reports. Issued for: agricultural exports, feed, fruit and tree nuts, livestock and poultry, oil crops, rice, sugar and sweeteners, vegetables, wheat, and world agriculture	Periodic	X	X	X
Structure and Finances of U.S. Farms: Family Farm Report	Periodic	X	X	X
Sugar and Sweeteners Yearbook	Annual			X
Vegetable and Pulses Yearbook	Annual		X	X
World Agricultural Supply and Demand Estimates	Monthly	X	X	X

Department of Agriculture, Food and Nutrition Service
http://www.fns.usda.gov/fns/

Title	Frequency	Paper	Internet PDF	Internet Other Formats
Characteristics of Supplemental Nutrition Assistance Program Households	Annual	X	X	
WIC Participant and Program Characteristics	Biennial	X	X	

Department of Agriculture, Foreign Agricultural Service
http://www.fas.usda.gov

Title	Frequency	Paper	Internet PDF	Internet Other Formats
Livestock and Poultry World Markets and Trade	Semiannual	X	X	

Department of Agriculture, National Agricultural Statistics Service
http://www.nass.usda.gov

Title	Frequency	Paper	Internet PDF	Internet Other Formats
Agricultural Chemical Usage	Periodic			X
Agricultural Statistics	Annual	X	X	
Catfish Production	Semiannual	X	X	X
Cattle	Semiannual	X	X	X
Census of Agriculture	Quinquennial	X	X	X
Census of Agriculture: Organic Survey 2014	Periodic		X	X
Certified Organic Survey	Annual	X	X	X
Cherry Production	Annual	X	X	X

See footnotes at end of table.

Appendix I Table: Sources of Statistics, State Statistical Abstracts, and Foreign Statistical Abstracts-Continued.

See headnote on page 903.

Title	Frequency	Paper	Internet PDF	Internet Other Formats
Chickens and Eggs	Monthly	X	X	X
Citrus Fruits	Annual	X	X	X
Cranberries	Annual	X	X	X
Crop Production	Monthly	X	X	X
Crop Progress	Weekly	X	X	X
Crop Values	Annual	X	X	X
Dairy Products	Monthly	X	X	X
Farm Labor	Semiannual	X	X	X
Farms and Land in Farms	Annual	X	X	X
Floriculture Crops	Annual	X	X	X
Agricultural Land Values	Annual	X	X	X
Livestock Slaughter	Monthly	X	X	X
Meat Animals Production, Disposition, and Income	Annual	X	X	X
Milk Production	Monthly	X	X	X
Milk Production, Disposition, and Income	Annual	X	X	X
Noncitrus Fruits and Nuts	Semiannual	X	X	X
Poultry: Production and Value	Annual	X	X	X
Stock Reports. Stocks of grain, peanuts, potatoes, and rice	Periodic	X	X	X
Trout Production	Annual	X	X	X
Turkey Hatchery	Monthly	X	X	X
Turkeys Raised	Annual	X	X	X
Usual Planting and Harvesting Dates	Periodic	X	X	X
Vegetables	Periodic	X	X	X
Weekly Weather and Crop Bulletin	Weekly	X	X	
Winter Wheat and Rye Seedlings	Annual	X	X	X
Department of Agriculture, Natural Resources and Conservation Service http://www.nrcs.usda.gov				
National Resources Inventory	Periodic		X	X
Department of Defense http://www.dod.gov/				
Base Structure Report Fiscal Year 2015 Baseline, A Summary of the Real Property Inventory	Annual		X	X
2015 Demographics Report, Profile of the Military Community	Annual		X	X
Department of Defense, Defense Manpower Data Center https://www.dmdc.osd.mil/appj/dwp/dwp_reports.jsp				
Personnel Statistics	Periodic		X	X
Department of Defense, Defense Security Cooperation Agency http://www.dsca.mil/resources/dsca-historical-facts-book-fiscal-year-series				
Historical Facts Book & Fiscal Year Series	Annual		X	
Department of Education http://www.ed.gov				
Annual Report for Federal Student Aid	Annual		X	
Annual Report on Teacher Quality	Annual		X	
Federal Campus-Based Programs Data Book	Annual			X
Federal Pell Grant Program, End of Year Report	Annual		X	X
Department of Energy https://energy.gov/				
Transportation Energy Data Book	Annual		X	X
Department of Health and Human Services http://www.hhs.gov				
Health Care Fraud and Abuse Control Program Annual Report	Annual	X	X	
Profile of Older Americans	Annual	X	X	X
Department of Homeland Security https://www.dhs.gov/				
Budget in Brief	Annual	X	X	
Entry/Exit Overstay Report	Annual		X	
Department of Homeland Security, Coast Guard https://www.uscg.mil/				
State of the Coast Guard, 2016	Annual	X	X	
Department of Homeland Security, Office of Immigration Statistics http://www.dhs.gov/immigration-statistics				
Yearbook of Immigration Statistics	Annual	X	X	X
Department of Housing and Urban Development http://www.hud.gov				
National Housing Market Summary	Quarterly		X	X
Department of Justice https://www.justice.gov				
Asset Forfeiture Fund Report to Congress	Annual		X	X
Department of Justice, Bureau of Alcohol, Tobacco, Firearms and Explosives http://www.atf.gov/				
Firearms Commerce in the U.S. [Annual Firearms Manufacturing and Export Report]	Annual		X	
Firearms Trace Data (by State)	Annual		X	
Department of Labor http://www.dol.gov				
Agency Financial Report	Annual	X	X	
Annual Performance Report	Annual	X	X	
Health Insurance Coverage Bulletin	Annual		X	X

See footnotes at end of table.

Title	Frequency	Paper	Internet PDF	Internet Other Formats
Retirement Bulletins	Annual		X	X
Department of State				
http://www.state.gov				
Country Reports on Terrorism 2016	Annual		X	X
United States Contributions to International Organizations	Annual		X	X
Annex of Statistical Information: Country Reports on Terrorism 2015	Annual		X	X
Department of Transportation				
http://www.dot.gov				
Air Travel Consumer Report	Monthly	X	X	
Annual U.S Domestic Average Itinerary Fare in Current and Constant Dollars	Annual			X
National Transportation Statistics	Quarterly		X	X
Transportation Statistics Annual Report: 2016	Annual	X	X	
U.S. International Air Travel Statistics	Quarterly	X	X	X
Department of the Treasury, Alcohol and Tobacco Tax and Trade Bureau				
http://www.ttb.gov				
Tobacco Products Monthly Statistical Releases	Monthly	X	X	
Department of the Treasury, Bureau of the Fiscal Service				
https://www.fiscal.treasury.gov/				
Combined Statement of Receipts, Outlays, and Balances	Annual	X	X	X
Financial Report of the United States Government	Annual	X	X	X
Monthly Statement of the Public Debt of the United States	Monthly	X	X	X
Monthly Treasury Statement of Receipts and Outlays of the United States Government	Monthly	X	X	X
Treasury Bulletin	Quarterly	X	X	X
Department of Veterans Affairs				
http://www.va.gov				
Annual Benefits Report	Annual		X	
Annual Performance Plan and Report	Annual		X	
Compensation and Pension Data by County	Annual			X
Employment and Training Administration				
http://www.doleta.gov				
Unemployment Insurance Weekly Claims	Weekly		X	X
Energy Information Administration				
http://www.eia.gov				
Annual Coal Report	Annual		X	X
Annual Energy Outlook	Annual	X	X	X
Annual Energy Review (suspended for 2013)	Annual	X	X	X
Electric Power Annual	Annual		X	X
Electric Power Monthly	Monthly		X	X
Electric Sales, Revenue and Average Price	Annual		X	X
International Energy Outlook	Annual	X	X	X
International Energy Statistics portal	Ongoing		X	X
Monthly Energy Review	Monthly		X	X
Petroleum Marketing Monthly	Monthly		X	X
Petroleum Supply Annual	Annual		X	X
Petroleum Supply Monthly	Monthly		X	X
Quarterly Coal Report	Quarterly		X	X
Residential Energy Consumption Survey	Quadrennial		X	X
State Electricity Profiles	Annual		X	X
State Energy Data System Reports	Annual		X	X
U.S. Crude Oil and Natural Gas Proved Reserves	Annual		X	X
Weekly Coal Production	Weekly			X
Environmental Protection Agency				
http://www.epa.gov				
Air Quality Statistics Report	Annual		X	X
Clean Watersheds Needs Survey	Quadrennial		X	
Drinking Water Infrastructure Needs Survey and Assessment	Periodic		X	
National Water Quality Inventory Report to Congress	Periodic			X
Toxics Release Inventory National Analysis	Annual		X	X
Export-Import Bank of the United States				
http://www.exim.gov				
Annual Report	Annual	X	X	
Report to the U.S. Congress on Global Export Credit Competition and the Export-Import Bank of the United States	Annual	X	X	
Farm Credit Administration				
http://www.fca.gov/index.html				
Annual Report on the Farm Credit System	Annual	X	X	
Federal Bureau of Investigation				
https://ucr.fbi.gov/				
Crime in the United States	Annual		X	X
Hate Crime Statistics	Annual		X	X
Law Enforcement Officers Killed and Assaulted	Annual		X	X
Federal Communications Commission				
http://www.fcc.gov				
Annual Assessment of the Status of Competition in the Market for the Delivery of Video Programming	Annual		X	X
International Telecommunications Traffic and Revenue Data Report	Annual		X	X
Internet Access Services	Semi-Annual		X	X
Quarterly Report on Informal Consumer Inquiries and Complaints	Quarterly		X	X

See footnotes at end of table.

Appendix I Table: Sources of Statistics, State Statistical Abstracts, and Foreign Statistical Abstracts-Continued.

See headnote on page 903.

Title	Frequency	Paper	Internet PDF	Internet Other Formats
Report on Cable Industry Prices	Annual		X	X
Voice Telephone Services Report	Semi-Annual		X	X
Federal Deposit Insurance Corporation				
http://www.fdic.gov				
Annual Report	Annual	X	X	X
FDIC Survey of Unbanked and Underbanked Households	Biennial		X	X
FDIC Quarterly	Quarterly	X	X	X
Historical Statistics on Banking	Annual			X
Quarterly Banking Profile	Quarterly		X	X
Statistics on Banking	Quarterly			X
Summary of Deposits	Annual			X
Federal Highway Administration				
http://www.fhwa.dot.gov				
Highway Statistics	Annual	X	X	X
Federal Railroad Administration				
http://safetydata.fra.dot.gov/OfficeofSafety/default.aspx				
Railroad Safety Statistics	Annual	X	X	
Fish and Wildlife Service				
http://www.fws.gov				
National Survey of Fishing, Hunting, and Wildlife Associated Recreation	Quinquennial	X	X	
Forest Service				
http://www.fs.fed.us				
An Analysis of the Timber Situation in the United States 1952-2050	Periodic	X	X	
Land Areas of the National Forest System	Annual	X	X	X
RPA Assessment Tables	Periodic	X	X	X
U.S. Timber Production, Trade, Consumption, and Price Statistics 1965-2013	Biennial	X	X	
General Services Administration				
http://www.gsa.gov				
Federal Real Property Profile	Annual		X	X
Geological Survey				
http://www.usgs.gov/				
Estimated Use of Water in the United States	Quinquennial	X	X	X
Mineral Commodity Summaries	Annual	X	X	
Mineral Industry Surveys	Monthly/ Quarterly		X	X
Minerals Yearbook	Annual	X	X	X
Internal Revenue Service				
http://www.irs.gov/uac/Tax-Stats				
Corporation Income Tax Returns	Annual	X	X	X
Individual Income Tax Returns	Annual	X	X	X
IRS Data Book	Annual	X	X	X
Statistics of Income Bulletin	Quarterly	X	X	X
International Trade Administration, Office of Travel and Tourism Industries				
http://tinet.ita.doc.gov				
U.S. Travel and Tourism Statistics	Annual		X	X
International Trade Commission				
http://www.usitc.gov				
Recent Trends in U.S. Services Trade	Annual	X	X	
Library of Congress				
http://www.loc.gov				
Annual Report	Annual	X	X	
Maritime Administration				
http://www.marad.dot.gov				
Annual Report to Congress	Annual	X	X	
Fleet Statistics	Annual			X
U.S. Waterborne Foreign Trade	Annual			X
Vessel Calls	Annual		X	X
Mine Safety and Health Administration				
http://www.msha.gov				
Informational Reports by Mining Industry: Coal, Metallic Minerals, Nonmetallic Minerals (except stone and coal), Sand and Gravel, and Stone	Annual		X	X
Mine Injuries and Worktime	Quarterly	X	X	X
National Aeronautics and Space Administration				
http://www.nasa.gov				
Annual Procurement Report	Annual	X	X	
National Center for Education Statistics				
http://nces.ed.gov				
Academic Libraries	Biennial		X	X
After the Post-9/11 GI Bill: A Profile of Military Service Members and Veterans Enrolled in Undergraduate and Graduate Education	Periodic		X	X
Characteristics of Private Schools in the United States	Annual	X	X	X
Characteristics of Schools, Districts, Teachers, Principals, and School Libraries in the United States	Annual	X	X	X
The Condition of Education	Annual	X	X	X
Digest of Education Statistics	Annual	X	X	X
Enrollment in Postsecondary Institutions, Graduation Rates, and Financial Statistics	Annual		X	
Indicators of School Crime and Safety	Annual	X	X	X

See footnotes at end of table.

Appendix I Table: Sources of Statistics, State Statistical Abstracts, and Foreign Statistical Abstracts-Continued.

See headnote on page 903.

Title	Frequency	Paper	Internet PDF	Internet Other Formats
National Teacher and Principal Survey	Periodic		X	X
Profile and Financial Aid Estimates of Graduate Students	Quadrennial		X	X
Programs and Services for High School English Learners in Public School Districts: 2015-16	Annual		X	X
Schools and Staffing Survey	Periodic		X	X
The Nation's Report Card: Civics 2014	Periodic	X	X	
The Nation's Report Card: Economics 2012	Periodic	X	X	
The Nation's Report Card: Geography 2014	Periodic	X	X	
The Nation's Report Card: U.S. History 2014	Periodic	X	X	
The Nation's Report Card: Mathematics 2015	Periodic	X	X	
The Nation's Report Card: Reading 2015	Periodic	X	X	
The Nation's Report Card: Science 2015	Periodic	X	X	
The Nation's Report Card: Writing 2011	Periodic	X	X	
Trends in Undergraduate Nonfederal Grant and Scholarship Aid by Demographic and Enrollment Characteristics	Quadrennial		X	X
Trends in Pell Grant Receipt and the Characteristics of Pell Grant Recipients	Quadrennial		X	X
Projections of Education Statistics	Annual	X	X	X
Status and Trends in the Education of Racial and Ethnic Groups	Irregular	X	X	X
Trends in High School Dropout and Completion Rates in the United States	Annual		X	X
National Center for Health Statistics http://www.cdc.gov/nchs/				
Health: United States	Annual	X	X	X
National Health Statistics Reports	Periodic	X	X	
National Vital Statistics Reports	Periodic	X	X	
Vital and Health Statistics:				
Series 3: Analytical and Epidemiological Studies	Irregular	X	X	
Series 11: Health and Nutrition Examination Survey Statistics	Irregular	X	X	
Series 13: Data on Health Resources Utilization	Irregular	X	X	
Series 20: Data on Mortality	Irregular	X	X	
Series 21: Data on Natality, Marriage, and Divorce	Irregular	X	X	
Series 23: Data from the National Survey of Family Growth	Irregular	X	X	
National Credit Union Administration http://www.ncua.gov				
Annual Report	Annual	X	X	
Call Report Quarterly Summary Reports	Quarterly		X	
National Endowment for the Arts https://www.arts.gov/				
Annual Report	Annual	X	X	
Appropriations Request	Annual	X	X	
National Endowment for the Humanities http://www.neh.gov				
Annual Report	Annual	X	X	
Appropriations Request	Annual	X	X	
National Guard Bureau http://www.nationalguard.mil/				
Posture Statement	Annual		X	
National Highway Traffic Safety Administration http://www.nhtsa.gov				
Traffic Safety Facts	Annual	X	X	
National Oceanic and Atmospheric Administration http://www.noaa.gov				
Climatic Data for the World	Monthly			X
Comparative Climatic Data	Annual		X	X
Daily Normals of Temperature, Precipitation, Heating Degree Days (HDD), and Cooling Degree Days (CDD)	Periodic			X
Fisheries of the United States	Annual	X	X	
Hourly Precipitation Data. Monthly with annual summary; for each state	Monthly		X	X
Local Climatological Data. Monthly with annual summary; for major cities	Monthly		X	X
Monthly Normals of Temperature, Precipitation, Heating Degree Days (HDD), and Cooling Degree Days (CDD)	Periodic			X
Our Living Oceans	Periodic	X	X	
Storm Data	Monthly		X	
Tornado Summaries	Monthly			
U.S. Climate Normals	Decennial	X	X	X
National Park Service http://www.nps.gov				
National Park Statistical Abstract	Annual	X	X	
National Science Foundation http://www.nsf.gov/statistics				
Academic Institutional Profiles	Annual			X
Academic Research and Development Expenditures	Annual		X	X
Characteristics of Doctoral Scientists and Engineers in the United States	Biennial		X	X
Characteristics of Recent Science/Engineering Graduates	Biennial		X	X
Doctorate Recipients from U.S. Universities	Annual		X	X
Federal Funds for Research and Development	Annual		X	X
Federal Research and Development Funding by Budget Function	Annual		X	X
Federal Science and Engineering Support to Universities, Colleges, and Nonprofit Institutions	Annual		X	X
Graduate Students and Postdoctorates in Science and Engineering	Annual		X	X
National Patterns of Research and Development Resources	Annual		X	X

See footnotes at end of table.

Appendix I Table: Sources of Statistics, State Statistical Abstracts, and Foreign Statistical Abstracts-Continued.

See headnote on page 903.

Title	Frequency	Paper	Internet PDF	Internet Other Formats
Research and Development in Industry	Annual		X	X
Science and Engineering Degrees	Biennial		X	X
Science and Engineering Degrees, by Race/Ethnicity of Recipients	Biennial		X	X
Science and Engineering Doctorate Awards	Annual		X	X
Science and Engineering Indicators	Biennial	X	X	X
Science and Engineering State Profiles	Annual			X
Science Resources Statistics Info Briefs (various topics)	Frequent	X	X	X
Scientific and Engineering Research Facilities at Universities and Colleges	Biennial		X	X
Women, Minorities, and Persons with Disabilities in Science and Engineering	Biennial		X	X
National Transportation Safety Board				
http://www.ntsb.gov				
Review of U.S. Civil Aviation Accidents	Annual		X	X
Office of Juvenile Justice and Delinquency Prevention				
http://ojjdp.gov				
Highlights of the National Youth Gang Survey	Annual	X	X	X
Juvenile Arrests	Annual	X	X	X
Juvenile Offenders and Victims	Periodic	X	X	X
Office of Management and Budget				
http://www.whitehouse.gov/omb				
The Budget of the United States Government	Annual	X	X	X
Office of Personnel Management				
http://www.opm.gov				
Demographic Profile of the Federal Workforce	Biennial		X	
Employment and Trends	Bimonthly		X	X
Executive Branch Retirement Statistics	Annual		X	
Office of the Clerk, U.S. House of Representatives				
http://clerk.house.gov				
Statistics of the Presidential and Congressional Election	Biennial	X	X	
Patent and Trademark Office				
http://www.uspto.gov				
All Technologies (Utility Patents)	Annual	X	X	X
Patent Counts by Country/State and Year	Annual	X		X
Patenting Trends in the United States	Annual	X		X
Railroad Retirement Board				
https://secure.rrb.gov/				
Annual Report	Annual	X	X	
Quarterly Benefit Statistics	Quarterly	X	X	
Securities and Exchange Commission				
http://www.sec.gov/about.shtml				
Select SEC and Market Data	Annual		X	
Small Business Administration				
http://www.sba.gov				
Loan Program Performance Reports	Annual		X	
Quarterly Bulletin	Quarterly		X	X
Small Business Lending in the United States	Annual	X	X	X
Small Business Economy	Annual		X	
Small Business Profiles for States and Territories	Annual		X	
Social Security Administration				
http://www.ssa.gov				
Annual Statistical Report on the Social Security Disability Insurance Program	Annual	X	X	X
Annual Statistical Supplement to the Social Security Bulletin	Annual	X	X	X
Congressional Statistics	Annual	X	X	X
Fast Facts & Figures about Social Security	Annual	X	X	X
Income of the Population 55 and over	Biennially	X	X	X
OASDI Beneficiaries by State and County	Annual	X	X	X
Social Security Bulletin	Quarterly	X	X	X
SSI Annual Statistical Report	Annual	X	X	X
SSI Recipients by State and County	Annual	X	X	X
Substance Abuse and Mental Health Services Administration				
http://www.samhsa.gov				
Behavioral Health Barometer, United States	Annual	X	X	
National Mental Health Services Survey (N-MHSS)	Annual	X	X	X
National Survey on Drug Use and Health (NSDUH)	Annual	X	X	
National Survey on Substance Abuse Treatment Services (N-SSATS)	Annual	X	X	X
U.S. Copyright Office				
http://www.copyright.gov/				
Annual Report	Annual	X	X	
U.S. Sentencing Commission				
https://www.ussc.gov/				
2016 Sourcebook of Federal Sentencing Statistics	Annual		X	X
NONGOVERNMENT				
Aerospace Industries Association, Arlington, VA				
http://www.aia-aerospace.org				
Aerospace Industry Year-End Review and Forecast	Annual		X	
Economic Impact Study of the U.S. Aerospace and Defense Industry	Annual		X	
Quarterly Trade Bulletin	Quarterly		X	
U.S. Aerospace Manufacturing Update	Quarterly		X	

See footnotes at end of table.

Appendix I Table: Sources of Statistics, State Statistical Abstracts, and Foreign Statistical Abstracts-Continued.

See headnote on page 903.

Title	Frequency	Paper	Internet PDF	Internet Other Formats
Airlines for America, Washington, DC http://www.airlines.org				
American Bureau of Metal Statistics, Inc., Chatham, NJ http://www.abms.com Non-Ferrous Metal Yearbook	Annual	X		X
American Council of Life Insurers, Washington, DC http://www.acli.com Life Insurers Fact Book	Annual		X	
American Dental Association, Chicago, IL http://www.ada.org Survey of Dental Practice	Annual			X
American Forest and Paper Association, Washington, DC http://www.afandpa.org Monthly Exports/Imports Report Monthly Statistics of Paper, Paperboard and Wood Pulp Paper Industry Annual Capacity and Fiber Consumption Paper Industry Annual Statistical Summary	Monthly Monthly Annual Annual		X X X X	 X
American Gas Association, Washington, DC http://www.aga.org Gas Facts	Annual	X	X	
American Iron and Steel Institute, Washington, DC http://www.steel.org Annual Statistical Report	Annual	X	X	
American Medical Association, Chicago, IL http://www.ama-assn.org State Medical Licensure Statistics and License Requirements	Annual	X		X
American Osteopathic Association, Chicago, IL http://www.osteopathic.org/ Osteopathic Medical Profession Report	Annual		X	
American Public Transportation Association, Washington, DC http://www.apta.com Public Transportation Fact Book	Annual		X	X
Association of American Railroads, Washington, DC http://www.aar.org Analysis of Class I Railroads Freight Commodity Statistics Railroad Facts	Annual Annual Annual	X X X	X X X	X X
Berman Jewish Data Bank, Storrs, CT http://www.jewishdatabank.org Jewish Population in the United States	Annual		X	X
Bloomberg BNA, Washington, DC http://www.bna.com BNA's Labor and Employment Outlook Report BNA's Job Absence and Turnover Report Directory of U.S. Labor Organizations Source Book on Collective Bargaining Union Membership and Earnings Data Book	Annual Quarterly Annual Annual Annual	X X X X X		
Boy Scouts of America, Irving, TX http://www.scouting.org Scouting Annual Report	Annual		X	
Bowker, Ann Arbor, MI http://www.bowker.com ISBN Annual Output Reports	Annual		X	
Brookings Institution, Washington, DC https://www.brookings.edu/ Vital Statistics on Congress	Biennial		X	X
Chronicle of Higher Education, Inc., Washington, DC http://chronicle.com Almanac of Higher Education	Annual	X		X
College Board, New York, NY https://www.collegeboard.org/ College-Bound Seniors Total Group Profile Report	Annual		X	
Commodity Research Bureau, Chicago, IL http://www.crbtrader.com CRB Commodity Index Report CRB Commodity Yearbook CRB Futures Perspective CRB Infotech CD Final Markets End-of-Day Data Fundamental Market Service Trends In Futures	Weekly Annual Weekly Monthly Daily Weekly Daily	 X X 	X X X X X	X X X X X X
Conference Board, New York, NY http://www.conference-board.org Business Cycle Indicators Corporate Contributions Report	Monthly Annual		X X	X

See footnotes at end of table.

Appendix I Table: Sources of Statistics, State Statistical Abstracts, and Foreign Statistical Abstracts-Continued.

See headnote on page 903.

Title	Frequency	Paper	Internet PDF	Internet Other Formats
International Comparisons of Annual Labor Force Statistics	Annual		X	X
International Comparisons of Hourly Compensation Costs for Production Workers in Manufacturing	Annual		X	X
International Comparisons of Manufacturing Productivity and Unit Labor Cost Trends	Annual		X	X
Performance: Productivity, Employment, and Growth in the World's Economies	Irregular		X	
Congressional Quarterly (CQ) Press, Washington, DC https://us.sagepub.com/en-us/nam/cqpress				
America Votes	Biennial	X		
Consumer Technology Association, Arlington, VA https://www.cta.tech/				
U.S. Consumer Electronics Sales and Forecasts	Semiannual		X	
Council of State Governments, Lexington, KY http://www.csg.org				
Book of the States	Annual	X	X	
Credit Union National Association, Madison, WI http://www.cuna.org				
Operating Ratios and Spreads	Quarterly	X	X	
Dodge Data & Analytics, New York, NY http://analyticsstore.construction.com/				
Construction Potentials Bulletin	Monthly		X	
Dow Jones and Company, New York, NY http://www.dowjones.com/				
Wall Street Journal	Daily	X		X
Duncan McIntosh Company, Inc., Irvine, CA http://www.editorandpublisher.com				
Editor and Publisher	Monthly	X		X
Newspaper Databook	Annual	X		X
Edison Electric Institute, Washington, DC http://www.eei.org				
Statistical Yearbook of the Electric Power Industry	Annual	X	X	X
Euromonitor International, London, England http://www.euromonitor.com				
Consumer Americas	Annual	X	X	
Federal National Mortgage Association, Washington, DC http://www.fanniemae.com				
Annual Report on Form 10-K	Annual		X	
Food and Agriculture Organization of the United Nations, Rome, Italy http://www.fao.org				
World Fertilizer Trends and Outlook	Annual		X	
FAO Statistical Yearbook: World Food and Agriculture	Annual	X	X	
FAO Yearbook: Fishery and Aquaculture Statistics	Periodic	X	X	X
Yearbook of Forest Products	Annual	X	X	
Foundation Center, New York, NY http://www.foundationcenter.org				
FC Stats	Annual			X
General Aviation Manufacturers Association, Washington, DC http://www.gama.aero				
General Aviation Aircraft Shipment Report	Quarterly		X	
General Aviation Statistical Databook & Industry Outlook	Annual		X	
Girl Scouts of the USA, New York, NY http://www.girlscouts.org				
Annual Report	Annual		X	
Giving USA Foundation, Chicago, IL http://www.givingusa.org/				
Giving USA	Annual	X	X	X
Guttmacher Institute, New York, NY http://www.guttmacher.org				
Perspectives on Sexual and Reproductive Health	Quarterly		X	
Health Forum, an American Hospital Association Company, Chicago, IL http://www.ahadataviewer.com/				
AHA Annual Survey Data Base	Annual			X
AHA Hospital Statistics	Annual	X		X
IHS Global, Inc., Englewood, CO http://www.janes.com				
IHS Jane's All the World's Aircraft: Development & Production	Annual	X		X
IHS Jane's Defence: C4ISR & Mission Systems	Annual	X		X
IHS Jane's Fighting Ships	Annual	X		X
IHS Jane's Flight Avionics	Annual	X		X
IHS Jane's Land Warfare Platforms: Armoured Fighting Vehicles	Annual	X		X
IHS Jane's Land Warfare Platforms: Logistics, Support & Unmanned	Annual	X		X
IHS Jane's Merchant Ships	Annual	X		X
IHS Jane's Simulation & Training Systems	Annual	X		X
IHS Jane's Space Systems & Industry	Annual	X		X
IHS Jane's Weapons: Air-Launched	Annual	X		X
IHS Jane's Weapons: Infantry	Annual	X		X

See footnotes at end of table.

Appendix I Table: Sources of Statistics, State Statistical Abstracts, and Foreign Statistical Abstracts-Continued.

See headnote on page 903.

Title	Frequency	Paper	Internet	
			PDF	Other Formats
Independent Petroleum Association of America, Washington, DC				
http://www.ipaa.org				
IPAA Oil & Gas Producing Industry in Your State	Annual	X	X	
U.S. Petroleum Statistics	Annual	X	X	
Infobase Publishing, New York, NY				
http://www.worldalmanac.com				
The World Almanac and Book of Facts	Annual	X		
Information Today, Inc., Medford, NJ				
http://www.infotoday.com				
American Library Directory	Annual	X		
Library and Book Trade Almanac (formerly The Bowker Annual)	Annual	X		
Institute for Criminal Justice Ethics, New York, NY				
http://johnjayresearch.org/cje/				
Criminal Justice Ethics	Thrice yearly	X	X	
Insurance Information Institute, New York, NY				
http://www.iii.org				
The I.I.I. Insurance Fact Book	Annual	X	X	X
Inter-American Development Bank, Washington, DC				
http://www.iadb.org				
Annual Report	Annual	X	X	
Development in the Americas	Periodic	X	X	X
International Air Transport Association, Montreal, Canada and Geneva, Switzerland				
http://www.iata.org				
World Air Transport Statistics	Annual	X	X	X
International City Management Association, Washington, DC				
http://www.icma.org				
ICMA Chief Administrative Officers Salary & Compensation Survey	Annual		X	
Municipal Year Book	Annual		X	
International Labour Organization, Geneva, Switzerland				
http://www.ilo.org				
Yearbook of Labour Statistics	Annual	X		X
International Monetary Fund, Washington, DC				
http://www.imf.org				
Annual Report	Annual	X	X	X
Balance of Payments Statistics	Monthly	X	X	X
Direction of Trade Statistics	Quarterly	X		X
Government Finance Statistics Yearbook	Annual	X	X	X
International Financial Statistics	Monthly	X	X	X
International Telecommunication Union, Geneva, Switzerland				
http://www.itu.int/home/index.html				
ITU Yearbook of Statistics	Annual	X	X	
World Telecommunication/ICT Indicators	Annual	X	X	X
Investment Company Institute, Washington, DC				
http://www.ici.org				
Investment Company Fact Book	Annual		X	X
Joint Center for Housing Studies of Harvard University, Cambridge, MA				
http://www.jchs.harvard.edu/				
The State of the Nation's Housing	Annual		X	X
Media Source, Inc., New York, NY				
http://www.mediasourceinc.net/				
Library Journal	Semimonthly	X		X
School Library Journal	Monthly	X		X
National Academy of Social Insurance, Washington, DC				
http://www.nasi.org/				
Workers Compensation: Benefits, Coverage, and Costs	Annual	X	X	
National Association of Home Builders, Washington, DC				
http://www.nahb.org				
HousingEconomics.com (online subscription)	Ongoing			X
National Association of Latino Elected and Appointed Officials, Los Angeles, CA				
http://www.naleo.org				
National Directory of Latino Elected Officials	Annual		X	X
National Association of Realtors, Chicago, IL				
http://www.realtor.org				
Economist's Outlook	Daily			X
Investment and Vacation Home Buyers Survey	Annual	X	X	
NAR Member Profile	Annual	X	X	X
NAR Profile of Home Buyer and Sellers	Annual	X	X	
National Association of State Budget Officers, Washington, DC				
http://www.nasbo.org				
Fiscal Survey of the States	Semiannual	X	X	
State Expenditure Report	Annual	X	X	
National Association of State Park Directors, Raleigh, NC				
http://www.naspd.org				
Statistical Report of State Park Operations: Annual Information Exchange	Annual	X	X	
National Catholic Educational Association, Arlington, VA				

See footnotes at end of table.

Title	Frequency	Paper	Internet PDF	Internet Other Formats
http://www.ncea.org				
Dollars & Sense: A Report for the National Catholic Educational Association Secondary Schools Department	Biennial	X	X	
U.S. Catholic Elementary and Secondary Schools: The Annual Statistical Report on Schools, Enrollment and Staffing	Annual	X	X	
National Education Association, Washington, DC				
http://www.nea.org				
Rankings & Estimates: Rankings of the States and Estimates of School Statistics	Annual	X	X	
National Fire Protection Association, Quincy, MA				
http://www.nfpa.org				
National Fire Protection Association (NFPA) Journal	Bimonthly	X		X
National Golf Foundation, Jupiter, FL				
http://www.ngf.org				
Golf Facilities in the U.S.	Annual	X	X	
National Restaurant Association, Washington, DC				
http://www.restaurant.org				
Restaurant Industry 2020	Recurring		X	
Restaurant Industry Operations Report	Recurring	X	X	
Restaurant Industry Pocket Factbook	Annual	X	X	X
Restaurant Performance Index	Monthly		X	
Restaurant Trendmapper (online subscription)	Ongoing			X
State of the Industry	Annual	X	X	
National Safety Council, Itasca, IL				
http://www.nsc.org				
Injury Facts	Annual	X	X	
National Sporting Goods Association, Mount Prospect, IL				
http://www.nsga.org				
Sporting Goods Market	Annual	X	X	
Sports Participation in the U.S.	Annual	X	X	
NYSE Euronext, New York, NY				
https://www.nyse.com				
NYSE Facts & Figures (formerly the online NYSE Fact Book)	Ongoing			X
Organisation for Economic Cooperation and Development, Paris, France				
http://www.oecd-ilibrary.org/				
www.data.oecd.org				
CO2 Emissions From Fuel Combustion	Annual	X	X	X
Coal Information	Annual	X	X	X
Digital Economy Outlook	Biennial	X	X	X
Education at a Glance: OECD Indicators	Annual	X	X	X
Electricity Information	Annual	X	X	X
Energy Balances of Non-OECD Countries	Annual	X	X	X
Energy Balances of OECD Countries	Annual	X	X	X
Energy Prices and Taxes	Quarterly	X	X	
Energy Statistics of Non-OECD Countries	Annual	X	X	
Energy Statistics of OECD Countries	Annual	X	X	
Environmental Outlook	Periodic	X	X	X
Financial Accounts	Annual	X	X	X
Financial Balance Sheets	Annual	X	X	X
General Government Accounts	Annual	X	X	X
Geographical Distribution of Financial Flows to Developing Countries	Annual	X	X	X
International Migration Outlook	Annual	X	X	X
International Trade by Commodity Statistics	Ongoing	X	X	X
Issue 1: Main Aggregates	Annual	X	X	X
Issue 2: Detailed Tables	Annual	X	X	X
ITF Transport Outlook	Annual	X	X	X
Main Economic Indicators	Monthly	X	X	X
Main Science and Technology Indicators	Semiannual	X	X	X
National Accounts at a Glance	Annual	X	X	X
National Accounts of OECD Countries	Annual	X	X	X
Natural Gas Information	Annual	X	X	
Nuclear Energy Data	Annual	X	X	X
OECD Central Government Debt Statistics	Annual	X	X	X
OECD Communications Outlook	Biennial	X	X	X
OECD Economic Outlook	Semiannual	X	X	X
OECD Economic Surveys	Periodic	X	X	X
OECD Employment Outlook	Annual	X	X	X
OECD Factbook	Annual	X	X	X
OECD-FAO Agricultural Outlook	Annual	X	X	X
OECD Health Statistics	Annual			X
OECD Insurance Statistics	Annual	X	X	X
OECD International Development Statistics	Annual			X
OECD Journal: Economic Studies	Periodic	X	X	
OECD Journal: Financial Market Trends	Periodic	X	X	X
OECD Quarterly International Trade Statistics	Quarterly	X	X	X
OECD Review of Fisheries: Policies and Summary Statistics	Annual	X	X	X
OECD Science, Technology, and Industry Outlook	Biennial	X	X	X
OECD Science, Technology and R&D Statistics	Ongoing			X
OECD Society at a Glance	Biennial	X	X	X
OECD Territorial Reviews	Periodic	X	X	X
Oil Information	Annual	X	X	

See footnotes at end of table.

See headnote on page 903.

Title	Frequency	Paper	Internet PDF	Internet Other Formats
Oil, Gas, Coal, and Electricity Quarterly Statistics	Quarterly	X	X	X
Pensions at a Glance	Biennial	X	X	X
PISA (OECD Programme for International Student Assessment)	Periodic	X	X	X
Quarterly National Accounts	Quarterly	X	X	X
Revenue Statistics	Ongoing			X
Taxing Wages	Annual	X	X	X
Uranium: Resources Production and Demand	Biennial	X	X	X
World Energy Outlook	Annual	X	X	
PennWell Corporation, Tulsa, OK				
http://www.pennwell.com				
Offshore	Monthly	X	X	X
Oil and Gas Journal	Weekly	X	X	X
Pew Research Center				
http://www.pewinternet.org				
Book Reading	Periodic		X	X
Home Broadband	Periodic		X	X
Libraries and Learning	Periodic		X	X
Social Media Update	Periodic		X	X
Technology Device Ownership	Periodic		X	X
Puerto Rico Planning Board, San Juan, PR				
http://www.jp.gobierno.pr				
Construction Industry	Periodic	X		
Economic Report to the Governor	Annual	X	X	X
External Trade Statistics	Annual	X	X	
Income and Production	Annual	X	X	
Statistical Appendix-Economic Report to the Governor	Annual	X	X	X
PWxyz, LLC, New York, NY				
http://www.publishersweekly.com				
Publishers Weekly	Weekly	X		X
Radio Advertising Bureau, Dallas, TX				
http://www.rab.com				
Why Radio: Fact Sheets	Ongoing			X
Regional Airline Association, Washington, DC				
http://www.raa.org				
Regional Airlines Association Annual Report	Annual		X	
Securities Industry and Financial Markets Association, New York, NY				
http://www.sifma.org				
SIFMA Fact Book	Annual	X		X
U.S. Foreign Activity Report	Quarterly		X	X
Standard and Poor's Financial Services LLC, New York, NY				
http://www.standardandpoors.com				
Analyst's Handbook	Monthly	X		X
Corporation Records: Corporate Description	Monthly	X	X	X
Corporation Records: Daily News	Daily	X	X	X
Daily Stock Price Records	Quarterly			X
United Nations Conference on Trade and Development, Geneva, Switzerland				
http://www.unctad.org				
Development and Globalization: Facts and Figures	Periodic	X	X	X
Handbook of Statistics	Annual	X	X	X
United Nations Statistics Division, New York, NY				
http://unstats.un.org/unsd/default.htm				
Demographic Yearbook (Series R)	Annual	X	X	
Energy Balances and Electricity Profiles (Series W)	Annual	X	X	
Energy Statistics Yearbook (Series J)	Annual	X	X	
Industrial Commodity Statistics Yearbook: Production Statistics	Annual	X	X	
International Trade Statistics Yearbook (Series G)	Annual	X	X	
Main Aggregates and Detailed Tables	Annual	X	X	X
Monthly Bulletin of Statistics (Series Q)	Monthly	X	X	
National Accounts Statistics: Analysis of Main Aggregates	Annual	X		
National Accounts Statistics (Series X)	Annual	X	X	
Population and Vital Statistics Report (Series A)	Quarterly	X	X	
Statistical Yearbook	Annual	X	X	
World Statistics Pocketbook (Series V)	Annual	X	X	
The World's Women: Progress in Statistics	Quinquennial	X	X	
University of Michigan, Institute for Social Research, Inter-University Consortium for Political and Social Research, Ann Arbor, MI				
http://www.icpsr.umich.edu/icpsrweb/ICPSR/studies/8475				
American National Election Studies Cumulative Data File	Biennial			X
Warren Communications News, Washington, DC				
http://www.warren-news.com				
Cable and TV Station Coverage Atlas	Annual			X
Television and Cable Factbook	Ongoing			X
World Bank Group, Washington, DC				
http://www.worldbank.org				
Atlas of Global Development	Periodic	X	X	
Global Development Finance	Annual	X	X	X
The Little Data Book	Annual	X	X	
World Development Indicators	Annual	X	X	X

See footnotes at end of table.

Appendix I Table: Sources of Statistics, State Statistical Abstracts, and Foreign Statistical Abstracts-Continued.

See headnote on page 903.

Title	Frequency	Paper	Internet PDF	Internet Other Formats
World Health Organization, Geneva, Switzerland http://www.who.int/en/ World Health Statistics Report	Annual	X	X	
World Trade Organization, Geneva, Switzerland http://www.wto.org International Trade Statistics	Annual	X	X	X
STATE STATISTICAL ABSTRACTS FROM UNIVERSITIES				
Pennsylvania State University, Pennsylvania State Data Center, Middletown, PA http://pasdc.hbg.psu.edu/ Pennsylvania Abstract: A Statistical Fact Book	Annual	X	X	X
State University of New York: Nelson A. Rockefeller Institute of Government, Albany, NY http://www.rockinst.org/ New York State Statistical Yearbook	Annual	X	X	X
University of Florida: Bureau of Economic and Business Research, Gainesville, FL http://www.bebr.ufl.edu/ Florida Statistical Dashboards	Ongoing			X
University of Georgia: Selig Center for Economic Growth, Athens, GA http://www.terry.uga.edu/selig/ Georgia Economic Outlook	Annual	X	X	X
University of Kansas: Institute for Policy and Social Research, Lawrence, KS http://www.ipsr.ku.edu/ksdata/ksah/ Kansas Statistical Abstract	Annual		X	X
University of Missouri-Columbia: Economic and Policy Analysis Research Center, Columbia, MO http://eparc.missouri.edu/ Missouri Statistical Data Archive (online)	Ongoing		X	
University of Oklahoma: Center for Economic and Management Research, Norman, OK http://www.ou.edu/content/price/centersresearch/cemr/cemr_publications.html Oklahoma Statistical Abstract	Annual	X		
STATE STATISTICAL ABSTRACT FROM AN ASSOCIATION				
Texas State Historical Association, Austin, TX http://texasalmanac.com/ Texas Almanac	Biennial	X	X	X
STATE STATISTICAL ABSTRACTS FROM STATE AGENCIES				
Hawaii State Department of Business, Economic Development & Tourism, Honolulu, HI http://dbedt.hawaii.gov/economic/databook/ State of Hawaii Data Book	Annual		X	X
Maryland State Data Center, Maryland Department of Planning, Baltimore, MD http://www.mdp.state.md.us/msdc/ Maryland Statistical Handbook	Periodic		X	
Mississippi Secretary of State http://www.sos.ms.gov/ 2016-2020 Mississippi Blue Book	Quadrennial	X	X	
South Carolina, Revenue and Fiscal Affairs Office, Columbia, SC http://abstract.sc.gov/ South Carolina Statistical Abstract	Ongoing			X
INTERNATIONAL STATISTICAL ABSTRACTS FROM A FOREIGN AGENCY				
Australia **Australian Bureau of Statistics, Canberra** http://www.abs.gov.au/ Year Book Australia, 2012	Annual	X	X	X
Austria **Statistik Austria, Vienna** http://www.statistik.at/web_en/ Statistisches Jahrbuch Österreichs, 2017	Annual	X	X	X
Belgium **Statistics Belgium, Brussels** http://statbel.fgov.be/en Key Figures: Statistical Overview of Belgium, 2016	Annual	X	X	X
Canada **Statistics Canada, Ottawa** http://www.statcan.gc.ca/pub/11-402-x/index-eng.htm Canada Year Book, 2012 (Discontinued)	Annual		X	X
Czech Republic **Czech Statistical Office, Praha** http://www.czso.cz Statistical Yearbook of the Czech Republic, 2016	Annual	X	X	X
Denmark **Statistics Denmark, Copenhagen** http://www.dst.dk/en				

See footnotes at end of table.

Appendix I Table: Sources of Statistics, State Statistical Abstracts, and Foreign Statistical Abstracts-Continued.

See headnote on page 903.

Title	Frequency	Paper	Internet PDF	Internet Other Formats
Statistical Yearbook, 2017	Annual		X	
Finland **Statistics Finland, Helsinki** http://www.stat.fi/index_en.html Statistical Yearbook of Finland, 2015	Annual	X		
France **National Institute of Statistics and Economic Studies, Paris** http://www.insee.fr/en/ Tableaux de l'Economie Francaise, 2017	Annual		X	X
Germany **Statistisches Bundesamt, Wiesbaden** https://www.destatis.de/EN/Homepage.html Statistisches Jahrbuch: Deutschland und Internationales, 2015	Annual		X	
Greece **Hellenic Statistical Authority, Pireus** http://www.statistics.gr/en/home/ Statistical Yearbook of Greece, 2009/2010	Annual	X	X	
Hungary **Hungarian Central Statistical Office, Budapest** http://www.ksh.hu/?lang=en Statistical Yearbook of Hungary, 2016	Annual	X	X	X
Iceland **Statistics Iceland, Reykjavik** http://www.statice.is/ Statistical Yearbook of Iceland, 2015 (Discontinued)	Annual	X	X	X
Ireland **Central Statistics Office, Cork** http://www.cso.ie/en/ Statistical Yearbook of Ireland, 2016	Annual			X
Italy **Italian National Institute of Statistics, Rome** http://www.istat.it/en/ Annuario Statistico Italiano, 2016	Annual	X	X	X
Japan **Statistics Bureau, Ministry of Internal Affairs and Communications, Tokyo** http://www.stat.go.jp/english/data/index.htm Japan Statistical Yearbook, 2017	Annual	X	X	X
Korea, South **Statistics Korea, Daejeon** http://kostat.go.kr/eng/ Korea Statistical Yearbook, 2011	Annual	X		
Luxembourg **Service Central de la Statistique et des Etudes Economiques, Luxembourg** http://www.statistiques.public.lu/fr/acteurs/statec/index.html Annuaire statistique du Luxembourg, 2012	Annual	X	X	
Mexico **Instituto Nacional de Estadistica y Geografia, Aguascalientes** http://www.inegi.org.mx/ Anuario Estadistico de los Estados Unidos Mexicanos, 2015	Annual		X	X
Netherlands **Statistics Netherlands, The Hague** https://www.cbs.nl/nl-nl Statistical Yearbook of the Netherlands, 2014	Annual		X	X
New Zealand **Statistics New Zealand, Wellington** http://www.stats.govt.nz/ New Zealand Official Yearbook, 2012	Biennial		X	X
Norway **Statistics Norway, Oslo** https://www.ssb.no/en/ Statistical Yearbook of Norway, 2013 (Discontinued)	Annual		X	
Poland **Central Statistical Office of Poland, Warsaw** http://stat.gov.pl/en/intrastat Concise Statistical Yearbook of Poland, 2017 Statistical Yearbook of the Republic of Poland, 2016	Annual Annual	X X	X X	
Portugal **Statistics Portugal, Lisbon** https://www.ine.pt/ Statistical Yearbook of Portugal, 2015	Annual	X	X	X
Russia **Russian Federation Federal State Statistics Service, Moscow** http://www.gks.ru/ Russia in Figures	Ongoing			X
Slovakia				

See footnotes at end of table.

Appendix I Table: Sources of Statistics, State Statistical Abstracts, and Foreign Statistical Abstracts-Continued.

See headnote on page 903.

Title	Frequency	Paper	Internet	
			PDF	Other *Formats*
Statistical Office of the Slovak Republic, Bratislava http://slovak.statistics.sk/ Statisticka Rocenka Slovenskej Republiky, 2016	Annual	X	X	X
Spain **Instituto Nacional de Estadistica, Madrid** http://www.ine.es/en/welcome_en.htm Anuario Estadistico de España, 2017	Annual	X	X	
Sweden **Statistics Sweden, Stockholm** http://www.scb.se/en_/ Statistical Yearbook of Sweden, 2014 (Discontinued)	Annual	X	X	X
Switzerland **Federal Statistical Office, Neuchâtel** http://www.bfs.admin.ch/bfs/portal/en/index.html Statistisches Jahrbuch der Schweiz, 2017	Annual	X		
Turkey **Turkish Statistical Institute, Ankara** http://www.turkstat.gov.tr Turkey's Statistical Yearbook, 2013 Turkey in Statistics, 2016	Annual Annual	X X	X X	X X
United Kingdom **Office for National Statistics, London** http://www.ons.gov.uk Annual Abstract of Statistics, 2011	Annual		X	

Source: ProQuest research.

Guide to State Statistical Abstracts

This bibliography includes the most recent statistical abstracts for states published since 2000, plus those that will be issued in 2018. For some states, a near equivalent has been listed in substitution for, or in addition to, a statistical abstract. All sources contain statistical tables on a variety of subjects for the state as a whole, its component parts, or both. Internet sites also contain statistical data.

Alabama

University of Alabama, Center for Business and Economic Research, Box 870221, Tuscaloosa, AL 35487-0221. 205-348-6191. Fax: 205-348-2951. Internet site <http://cber.cba.ua.edu/>.
Alabama Economic Outlook, 2017. Annual. Print.

Alaska

Department of Commerce, Community and Economic Development, P.O. Box 110804, Juneau, AK 99811. 907-465-2510. Fax: 907-465-3767. Internet site <http://www.commerce.alaska.gov/web/ded/>.
The Alaska Economic Performance Report, 2013. Online.

Arizona

University of Arizona, Economic and Business Research Center, Eller College of Management, 1130 East Helen Street, McClelland Hall, Room 103, P.O. Box 210108, Tucson, AZ 85721-0108. 520-621-2155. Internet site <http://ebr.eller.arizona.edu/>.
Arizona's Economy. Quarterly. Online.

Arkansas

University of Arkansas at Little Rock, Institute for Economic Advancement, Economic Research, 2801 South University Avenue, Little Rock, AR 72204-1099. 501-569-8519. Fax: 501-569-8538. Internet site <http://iea.ualr.edu/economic-research-publications.html>.
Arkansas State and Country Economic Data, 2013. Annual. Print and Online.
Arkansas Personal Income Handbook, 2013. Annual. Print and Online.

California

Department of Finance, 915 L Street, Sacramento, CA 95814. 916-445-3878. Internet site <http://www.dof.ca.gov/>.

Colorado

Colorado Department of Local Affairs, Division of Local Government, State Demography Office, 1313 Sherman Street, Room 521, Denver, CO 80203. 303-864-7720. Fax: 303-353-0751. Internet site <http://dola.colorado.gov/demog-cms/content/region-profiles>.
2015 Region Profiles and Reports. Online.

Connecticut

Connecticut Department of Economic and Community Development, 450 Columbus Boulevard, Hartford, CT 06103. 860-270-8000. Internet site <http://www.ct.gov/ecd/site/default.asp>.
Connecticut Town Profiles, 2017. Recurring. Online.

Delaware

Delaware Economic Development Office, 99 Kings Highway, Dover, DE 19901-7305. 302-739-4271. Fax: 302-739-5749. Internet site <http://business.delaware.gov>.
Delaware Data Book, 2017. Online.

District of Columbia

Office of the City Administrator, John A. Wilson Building, 1350 Pennsylvania Avenue, NW, Suite 521, Washington, DC 20004. 202-478-9200. Fax: 202-727-9878. Internet site <http://opendata.dc.gov/>.
Open Data Catalog. Online.

Florida

University of Florida, Bureau of Economic and Business Research, P.O. Box 117148, Gainesville, FL 32611. 352-392-0171. Fax: 888-534-2404. Internet site <http://www.bebr.ufl.edu/data>.
Florida Statistical Dashboards. Online.

Georgia

University of Georgia, Terry College of Business, Selig Center for Economic Growth, 602 Bank of America, 110 E. Clayton Street, Athens, GA 30602-6269. 706-542-4085. Internet site <http://www.terry.uga.edu/about/centers-institutes/selig>.
Georgia Economic Outlook, 2017. Annual. Online.

University of Georgia, Carl Vinson Institute of Government, 201 N. Milledge Avenue, Athens, GA 30602. 706-542-2736. Fax: 706-542-9301. Internet site <http://www.countyguide.uga.edu/>.
The Georgia County Guide, 2017. Annual. Print.

Hawaii

Hawaii State Department of Business, Economic Development & Tourism, Research and Economic Analysis Division, Statistics and Data Support Branch, P.O. Box 2359, Honolulu, HI 96804. 808-586-2355. Internet site <http://dbedt.hawaii.gov/economic/databook/>.
2016 State of Hawaii Data Book. Annual. Online.

Idaho

University of Idaho Extension, 875 Perimeter Drive. MS 2338, Moscow, ID 83844-2338. 208-885-5883. Internet site <http://indicatorsidaho.org/>.
Indicators Idaho. Online.

Illinois

University of Illinois, Institute of Government and Public Affairs, 1007 W. Nevada Street, Urbana, IL 61801, MC-037. 217-333-3340. Fax: 217-244-4817. Internet site <http://www.igpa.uillinois.edu/>.

Indiana

Indiana University, Kelley School of Business, Indiana Business Research Center, 1309 E. 10th Street, Suite 4048, Bloomington, IN 47405. 812-855-5507. Internet site <http://www.stats.indiana.edu/>.
STATS Indiana. Online.

Iowa

Iowa State University of Science and Technology: Community Indicators Program, 17 East Hall, Ames, IA 50010. 515-294-9903. Fax: 515-294-0592. Internet site <http://www.icip.iastate.edu/>.
Community Indicators. Online.

State Library of Iowa, State Data Center, Ola Babcock Miller Building, 1112 East Grand, Des Moines, IA 50319-0233. 800-248-4483. Fax: 515-242-6543. Internet site <http://www.iowadatacenter.org>.

Kansas

University of Kansas, Institute for Policy and Social Research, 1541 Lilac Lane, 607 Blake Hall, Lawrence, KS 66045-3129. 785-864-3701. Fax: 785-864-3683. Internet site <http://www.ipsr.ku.edu/ksdata/ksah/>.
Kansas Statistical Abstract, 2016. Online.

Kentucky

Kentucky Cabinet for Economic Development, Old Capitol Annex, 300 West Broadway, Frankfort, KY 40601. 800-626-2930. Fax:502-564-3256. Internet site <http://www.thinkkentucky.com/>.

Louisiana

Louisiana State Census Data Center, Office of Electronic Services, 1201 N. Third Street, Suite 7-210, Baton Rouge, LA, 70802. 225-342-7000. Internet site <http://www.louisiana.gov/Explore/Demographics_and_Geography/>.

Maine

Department of Administrative and Financial Services, 78 State House Station, Augusta, ME 04333. 207-624-7800. Fax: 207-624-7804. Internet site <http://www.maine.gov/portal/about_me/statistics.html >.

Maryland

Maryland Department of Planning, 301 W. Preston Street Suite 702, Baltimore, MD 21201. 410-767-4500. Internet site <http://www.mdp.state.md.us/msdc/>.
2014 Maryland Statistical Handbook. Annual. Online.

Massachusetts

MassCHIP, Massachusetts Department of Public Health, 250 Washington Street, Boston, MA 02108-4619. 617-624-5512. Internet site <http://mass.gov/dph/masschip>. Instant Topics. Online.

Michigan

Michigan Economic Development Corporation, 300 N. Washington Square, Lansing, MI 48913. 1-888-522-0103. Internet site <http://www.michiganbusiness.org>.

Minnesota

Minnesota Department of Employment and Economic Development, 1st National Bank Building, 332 Minnesota Street, Suite E200, Saint Paul, MN 55101-1351. 800-657-3858. Internet site <http://mn.gov/deed/data />.
Compare Minnesota: Profiles of Minnesota's Economy & Population. Online.

Minnesota State Demographic Center, 658 Cedar Street, Room 300, Saint Paul, MN 55155, 651-296-2557. Internet site <http://www.demography.state.mn.us/>.

Mississippi

Mississippi Secretary of State, 401 Mississippi Street, Jackson, MS 39201. 601-359-1350. Internet site <http://www.sos.ms.gov/Education-Publications/Pages/Blue-Book-2016-2020.aspx >
2016-2020 Mississippi Blue Book. Quadrennial. Online.

Missouri

University of Missouri—Columbia, Economic and Policy Analysis Research Center, 10 Professional Building, Columbia, MO 65211. 573-882-4805. Fax: 573-882-5563. Internet site <http://eparc.missouri.edu/>.
Missouri Statistical Data Archive. Online.

Montana

Montana Department of Commerce, Census and Economic Information Center, 301 S. Park Avenue, Helena, MT 59620-0505. 406-841-2030. Fax: 406-841-2731. Internet site <http://ceic.mt.gov/>.

Nebraska

Nebraska Department of Economic Development, P.O. Box 94666, 301 Centennial Mall South, Lincoln, NE 68509-4666. 800-426-6505. Fax: 402-471-3778. Internet site <http://info.neded.org/>.

Nevada

Nevada Department of Administration, Budget Division, 209 East Musser Street, Room 200, Carson City, NV 89701-4298. 775-684-0222. Fax: 775-684-0260. Internet site <http://budget.nv.gov/>.

New Hampshire

New Hampshire Office of Energy and Planning, 107 Pleasant Street, Concord, NH 03301-8501. 603-271-2155. Fax: 603-271-2615. Internet site <http://www.nh.gov/oep/index.htm>.

New Jersey

State of New Jersey Department of Labor and Workforce Development, Bureau of Labor Market Information, 1 John Fitch Plaza, P.O. Box 110, Trenton, NJ 08625-0110. 609-292-2582. Fax: 609-633-9240. Internet site <http://lwd.dol.state.nj.us/labor/lpa/LMI_index.html>.
Labor Market Information. Online.

New Mexico

University of New Mexico, Bureau of Business and Economic Research, 303 Girard Boulevard NE, Suite 116, Albuquerque, NM 87106. 505-277-6626. Fax: 505-277-2773. Internet site <http://bber.unm.edu/>.
New Mexico Business, Current Economic Report . Print and Online. FOR-UNM Bulletin. Quarterly. Online.

New York

Nelson A. Rockefeller Institute of Government, 411 State Street, Albany, NY 12203-1003. 518-443-5522. Fax: 518-443-5788. Internet site <http://www.rockinst.org/>.
New York State Statistical Yearbook, 2015. Annual. Print and Online.

North Carolina

Office of State Budget and Management, MSC 20320, Raleigh, NC 27699-0320. 919-807-4700. Internet site <http://www.osbm.nc.gov/>.
State Comparisons. Online.

North Dakota

University of North Dakota, College of Business and Public Administration, Gamble Hall Room 110, 293 Centennial Drive, Stop 8098, Grand Forks, ND 58202-8098. 701-777-2135. Fax: 701-777-2019. Internet site <http://business.und.edu/>.

Ohio

Office of Research, Ohio Development Services Agency, 77 South High Street, Columbus, OH 43215-6130. 614-466-2116. Internet site <https://development.ohio.gov>.
Research Products and Services. Updated continuously.
Ohio County Trends. Online.

Oklahoma

University of Oklahoma, Center for Economic and Management Research, Michael F. Price College of Business, 307 West Brooks, Room 3, Norman, OK 73019-4004. 405-325-2931. Fax: 405-325-7688. Internet site <http://www.ou.edu/price/centersresearch/cemr.html>.
Statistical Abstract of Oklahoma, Annual. Print.

Oregon

Secretary of State, Archives Division, Archives Bldg., 800 Summer Street, NE, Salem, OR 97310. 503-373-0701 ext.1. Fax: 503-378-4118. Internet site <http://arcweb.sos.state.or.us/>.
Oregon Blue Book. 2017-2018 . Biennial. Online.

Pennsylvania

Pennsylvania State Data Center, Institute of State and Regional Affairs, Penn State Harrisburg, 777 West Harrisburg Pike, Middletown, PA 17057-4898. 717-948-6336. Fax: 717-948-6754. Internet site <http://pasdc.hbg.psu.edu>.
Pennsylvania Statistical Abstract, 2017. Print and electronic.

Rhode Island

Rhode Island Department of Labor and Training, Labor Market Information, 1511 Pontiac Avenue, Cranston, RI 02920. 401-462-8740. Fax: 401-462-8766. Internet site <http://www.dlt.ri.gov/lmi/>.
State of the State: A Statistical Profiles of Rhode Island's Cities and Towns. Online.

South Carolina

South Carolina Revenue and Fiscal Affairs Offices, Health and Demographics Section, 1000 Assembly Street, Suite 402, Columbia, SC 29201. 803-898-9940. Internet site <http://abstract.sc.gov>.
South Carolina Statistical Abstract. Ongoing. Online.

South Dakota

South Dakota State University, Rural Life and Census Data Center, Box 504, Brookings, SD 57007. 605-688-4899. Internet site <http://www.sdstate.edu/soc/rlcdc/index.cfm>.
Preliminary Population Projections 2010-2035. Online.
South Dakota State and Demographic Profiles 2008. Online.

Tennessee

Tennessee State Data Center, 916 Volunteer Blvd., 716 Stokely Management Center, Knoxville, TN 37996-0570. 865-974-6070. Fax: 865-974-3100. Internet site <http://tndata.utk.edu/>.

Texas

Texas State Historical Association, 3001 Lake Austin Blvd. Suite 3.116, Austin, TX 78703. 512-471-2600. Fax: 512-473-8691. Internet site <http://www.tshaonline.org/publications/books/3196>.
Texas Almanac, 2018-2019. Biennial. Print and Online.

Texas State Data Center and Office of the State Demographer, Institute for Demographic and Socioeconomic Research (IDSER), 501 W. César E. Chavez Blvd., San Antonio, TX 78207-4415. 210-458-6543. Fax: 210-458-6541. Internet site <http://txsdc.utsa.edu/>.

Utah

The University of Utah, Thomas S. Monson Center, 411 East South Temple Street, Salt Lake City, UT 84111. 801-585-5618. Internet site <http://gardner.utah.edu/economic-report-to-the-governor/>.
2017 Economic Report to the Governor. Annual. Online.

Vermont

Department of Labor, Labor Market Information, P.O. Box 488, Montpelier, VT 05601-0488. 802-828-4202. Fax: 802-828-4050. Internet site <http://www.vtlmi.info/>.
Vermont Economic-Demographic Profile, 2017. Annual. Online.

Virginia

University of Virginia, Weldon Cooper Center for Public Service, 2400 Old Ivy Road, P.O. Box 400206, Charlottesville, VA 22904-4206. 434-982-5522. Fax: 434-982-5524. Internet site <http://www.coopercenter.org/publications>.
Virginia Population Estimates. Online.
Virginia Population Projections. Online.

Washington

Washington State Office of Financial Management, Forecasting Division, P.O. Box 43113, Olympia, WA 98504-3113. 360-902-0555. Internet site <http://www.ofm.wa.gov/>.
Washington State Data Book, 2015. Biennial. Online.

West Virginia

West Virginia University, College of Business and Economics, Bureau of Business and Economic Research, P.O. Box 6527, Morgantown, WV 26506-6025. 304-293-7831. Internet site <http://be.wvu.edu/bber/index.htm>.
West Virginia Data Profile 2016. Annual. Online.
West Virginia Economic Outlook, 2018-2022. Annual. Online.

Wisconsin

Wisconsin Legislative Reference Bureau, One East Main Street, Suite 200, Madison, WI 53703. 608-266-0341. Internet site <http://legis.wisconsin.gov/lrb/>.
2015-2016 Wisconsin Blue Book. Biennial. Online.

Wyoming

Department of Administration and Information, Economic Analysis Division, 2800 Central Avenue, Cheyenne, WY 82002-0060. 307-777-7504. Fax: 307-632-1819. Internet site <http://eadiv.state.wy.us/>.
The Equality State Almanac, 2010. Annual. Online.

Metropolitan and Micropolitan Statistical Areas: Concepts, Components, and Population

The United States Office of Management and Budget (OMB) defines metropolitan and micropolitan statistical areas according to published standards that are applied to U.S. Census Bureau data. The general concept of a metropolitan or micropolitan statistical area is that of a core area containing a substantial population nucleus, together with adjacent communities having a high degree of economic and social integration with that core. Currently defined metropolitan and micropolitan statistical areas are based on application of 2010 standards (which appeared in the Federal Register on June 28, 2010) to 2010 decennial census data. Current metropolitan and micropolitan statistical area definitions were announced by OMB effective July 2015.

Standard definitions of metropolitan areas were first issued in 1949 by the then Bureau of the Budget (predecessor of OMB), under the designation "standard metropolitan area" (SMA). The term was changed to "standard metropolitan statistical area" (SMSA) in 1959 and to "metropolitan statistical area" (MSA) in 1983. The term "metropolitan area" (MA) was adopted in 1990 and referred collectively to metropolitan statistical areas (MSAs), consolidated metropolitan statistical areas (cMSAs), and primary metropolitan statistical areas (PMSAs). The term "core-based statistical area" (CBSA) became effective in 2000 and refers collectively to metropolitan and micropolitan statistical areas.

OMB has been responsible for the official metropolitan areas since they were first defined, except for the period 1977 to 1981, when they were the responsibility of the Office of Federal Statistical Policy and Standards, U.S. Department of Commerce. The standards for defining metropolitan areas were modified in 1958, 1971, 1975, 1980, 1990, 2000, and 2010.

Defining Metropolitan and Micropolitan Statistical Areas—The 2010 standards provide that each CBSA must contain at least one urban area of 10,000 or more population. Each metropolitan statistical area must have at least one urbanized area of 50,000 or more inhabitants. Each micropolitan statistical area must have at least one urban cluster of at least 10,000 but less than 50,000 population.

Under the standards, the county (or counties) in which at least 50 percent of the population resides within urban areas of 10,000 or more population, or that contain at least 5,000 people residing within a single urban area of 10,000 or more population, is identified as a "central county" (counties). Additional "outlying counties" are included in the CBSA if they meet specific requirements of commuting to or from the central counties. Counties or equivalent entities form the geographic "building blocks" for metropolitan and micropolitan statistical areas throughout the United States and Puerto Rico.

If specific criteria are met, a metropolitan statistical area containing a single core with a population of 2.5 million or more may be subdivided to form smaller groupings of counties referred to as "metropolitan divisions."

As of July 2015, there are 382 metropolitan statistical areas and 551 micropolitan statistical areas in the United States. In addition, there are 7 metropolitan statistical areas and 5 micropolitan statistical areas in Puerto Rico.

Principal Cities and Metropolitan and Micropolitan Statistical Area Titles—The largest city in each metropolitan or micropolitan statistical area is designated a "principal city." Additional cities qualify if specific requirements are met concerning population size and employment. The title of each metropolitan or micropolitan statistical area consists of the names of up to three of its principal cities in order of descending population size and the name of each state into which the metropolitan or micropolitan statistical area extends. Titles of metropolitan divisions also typically are based on principal city names, but in certain cases consist of county names.

Defining New England City and Town Areas—Cities and towns are the primary units of local government in the six New England states, where counties, unlike elsewhere, have little or no official governmental functions. The 2010 standards provide for a set of geographic areas that are defined using cities and towns in the New England states. The New England city and town areas (NECTAs) are defined using the same criteria as metropolitan and micropolitan statistical areas and are identified as either metropolitan or micropolitan, based, respectively, on the presence of either an urbanized area of 50,000 or more population or an urban cluster of at least 10,000 but less than 50,000 population. If the specific criteria are met, a NECTA containing a single core with a population of at least 2.5 million may be subdivided to form smaller groupings of cities and towns referred to as New England city and town area divisions.

Changes in Definitions Over Time—Changes in the definitions of these statistical areas since the 1950 census have consisted chiefly of (1) the recognition of new areas as they reached the minimum required city or urbanized area population and (2) the addition of counties (or cities and towns in New England) to existing areas as new decennial census data showed them to qualify.

In some instances, formerly separate areas have been merged, components of an area have been transferred from one area to another, or components have been dropped from an area. The large majority of changes have taken place on the basis of decennial census data. However, Census Bureau data serve as the basis for intercensal updates in specific circumstances.

Because of these historical changes in geographic definitions, users must be cautious in comparing data for these statistical areas from different dates. For some purposes, comparisons of data for areas as defined at given dates may be appropriate; for other purposes, it may be preferable to maintain consistent area definitions. Historical metropolitan area definitions are available for 1999, 1993, 1990, 1983, 1981, 1973, 1970, 1963, 1960, and 1950.

Excluding Tables 21 through 23 in the Population section; Table 618 in the Labor Force section; Table 706 in the Income section, and the tables that follow in this appendix, the tables presenting data for metropolitan areas in this edition of the Statistical Abstract may be based on earlier metropolitan area definitions. See the Census Bureau website at <http://www.census.gov/population/metro/data/pastmetro.html> for information on historical delineations and component counties.

Table A. Metropolitan Statistical Areas and Components—Population: 2016

[In thousands (170 represents 170,000). Population as of July 2016. Metropolitan Statistical Areas defined by the U.S. Office of Management and Budget as of July 2015. All Metropolitan Statistical Areas are arranged alphabetically]

Metropolitan Statistical Area ~~Metropolitan Division ~~~~Component county	Population, 2016 (1,000)
Abilene, TX	**170**
Callahan County, TX	14
Jones County, TX	20
Taylor County, TX	137
Akron, OH	**702**
Portage County, OH	162
Summit County, OH	540
Albany, GA	**152**
Baker County, GA	3
Dougherty County, GA	90
Lee County, GA	29
Terrell County, GA	9
Worth County, GA	21
Albany, OR	**123**
Linn County, OR	123
Albany-Schenectady-Troy, NY	**882**
Albany County, NY	309
Rensselaer County, NY	160
Saratoga County, NY	227
Schenectady County, NY	155
Schoharie County, NY	31
Albuquerque, NM	**910**
Bernalillo County, NM	677
Sandoval County, NM	142
Torrance County, NM	15
Valencia County, NM	76
Alexandria, LA	**155**
Grant Parish, LA	22
Rapides Parish, LA	132
Allentown-Bethlehem-Easton, PA-NJ	**836**
Warren County, NJ	107
Carbon County, PA	64
Lehigh County, PA	363
Northampton County, PA	302
Altoona, PA	**125**
Blair County, PA	125
Amarillo, TX	**263**
Armstrong County, TX	2
Carson County, TX	6
Oldham County, TX	2
Potter County, TX	121
Randall County, TX	133
Ames, IA	**97**
Story County, IA	97
Anchorage, AK	**403**
Anchorage Municipality, AK	298
Matanuska-Susitna Borough, AK	104
Ann Arbor, MI	**365**
Washtenaw County, MI	365
Anniston-Oxford-Jacksonville, AL	**115**
Calhoun County, AL	115
Appleton, WI	**234**
Calumet County, WI	50
Outagamie County, WI	185
Asheville, NC	**452**
Buncombe County, NC	256
Haywood County, NC	61
Henderson County, NC	114
Madison County, NC	21
Athens-Clarke County, GA	**205**
Clarke County, GA	125
Madison County, GA	29
Oconee County, GA	37
Oglethorpe County, GA	15
Atlanta-Sandy Springs-Roswell, GA	**5,790**
Barrow County, GA	77
Bartow County, GA	104
Butts County, GA	24
Carroll County, GA	116
Cherokee County, GA	242
Clayton County, GA	279
Cobb County, GA	748
Coweta County, GA	141
Dawson County, GA	24
DeKalb County, GA	740
Douglas County, GA	142
Fayette County, GA	112
Forsyth County, GA	221
Fulton County, GA	1,023
Gwinnett County, GA	907
Haralson County, GA	29
Heard County, GA	11
Henry County, GA	222
Jasper County, GA	14
Lamar County, GA	18
Meriwether County, GA	21
Morgan County, GA	18
Newton County, GA	107
Paulding County, GA	156
Pickens County, GA	31
Pike County, GA	18
Rockdale County, GA	89
Spalding County, GA	65
Walton County, GA	90
Atlantic City-Hammonton, NJ	**271**
Atlantic County, NJ	271
Auburn-Opelika, AL	**159**
Lee County, AL	159
Augusta-Richmond County, GA-SC	**595**
Burke County, GA	23
Columbia County, GA	147
Lincoln County, GA	8
McDuffie County, GA	21
Richmond County, GA	202
Aiken County, SC	167
Edgefield County, SC	26
Austin-Round Rock, TX	**2,056**
Bastrop County, TX	83
Caldwell County, TX	41
Hays County, TX	204
Travis County, TX	1,199
Williamson County, TX	529
Bakersfield, CA	**885**
Kern County, CA	885
Baltimore-Columbia-Towson, MD	**2,799**
Anne Arundel County, MD	568
Baltimore County, MD	831
Carroll County, MD	168
Harford County, MD	251
Howard County, MD	317
Queen Anne's County, MD	49
Baltimore city, MD	615
Bangor, ME	**152**
Penobscot County, ME	152
Barnstable Town, MA	**214**
Barnstable County, MA	214
Baton Rouge, LA	**835**
Ascension Parish, LA	122
East Baton Rouge Parish, LA	447
East Feliciana Parish, LA	20
Iberville Parish, LA	33
Livingston Parish, LA	140
Pointe Coupee Parish, LA	22
St. Helena Parish, LA	11
West Baton Rouge Parish, LA	26
West Feliciana Parish, LA	15
Battle Creek, MI	**134**
Calhoun County, MI	134
Bay City, MI	**105**
Bay County, MI	105
Beaumont-Port Arthur, TX	**410**
Hardin County, TX	56
Jefferson County, TX	255
Newton County, TX	14
Orange County, TX	85
Beckley, WV	**121**
Fayette County, WV	44
Raleigh County, WV	77
Bellingham, WA	**217**
Whatcom County, WA	217
Bend-Redmond, OR	**181**
Deschutes County, OR	181
Billings, MT	**170**
Carbon County, MT	10
Golden Valley County, MT	1
Yellowstone County, MT	158
Binghamton, NY	**244**
Broome County, NY	195
Tioga County, NY	49
Birmingham-Hoover, AL	**1,147**
Bibb County, AL	23
Blount County, AL	58
Chilton County, AL	44
Jefferson County, AL	660
St. Clair County, AL	88
Shelby County, AL	211
Walker County, AL	65
Bismarck, ND	**132**
Burleigh County, ND	94
Morton County, ND	31
Oliver County, ND	2
Sioux County, ND	4
Blacksburg-Christiansburg-Radford, VA	**183**
Floyd County, VA	16
Giles County, VA	17
Montgomery County, VA	99
Pulaski County, VA	34
Radford city, VA	17
Bloomington, IL	**189**
De Witt County, IL	16
McLean County, IL	172
Bloomington, IN	**166**
Monroe County, IN	145
Owen County, IN	21
Bloomsburg-Berwick, PA	**85**
Columbia County, PA	66
Montour County, PA	18
Boise City, ID	**691**
Ada County, ID	444
Boise County, ID	7
Canyon County, ID	212
Gem County, ID	17
Owyhee County, ID	11
Boston-Cambridge-Newton, MA-NH	**4,794**
Boston, MA	**1,995**
Norfolk County, MA	697
Plymouth County, MA	514
Suffolk County, MA	784
Cambridge-Newton-Framingham, MA	**2,369**
Essex County, MA	779
Middlesex County, MA	1,590
Rockingham County-Strafford County, NH	**431**
Rockingham County, NH	303
Strafford County, NH	127
Boulder, CO	**322**
Boulder County, CO	322
Bowling Green, KY	**171**
Allen County, KY	21
Butler County, KY	13
Edmonson County, KY	12
Warren County, KY	126
Bremerton-Silverdale, WA	**265**
Kitsap County, WA	265
Bridgeport-Stamford-Norwalk, CT	**944**
Fairfield County, CT	944
Brownsville-Harlingen, TX	**422**
Cameron County, TX	422
Brunswick, GA	**117**
Brantley County, GA	18
Glynn County, GA	85
McIntosh County, GA	14
Buffalo-Cheektowaga-Niagara Falls, NY	**1,133**
Erie County, NY	921
Niagara County, NY	212
Burlington, NC	**160**
Alamance County, NC	160
Burlington-South Burlington, VT	**217**

See footnotes at end of table.

Table A. Metropolitan Statistical Areas and Components—Population: 2016-Continued.

See headnote on page 925.

Metropolitan Statistical Area ~~Metropolitan Division ~~~~Component county	Population, 2016 (1,000)
Chittenden County, VT	162
Franklin County, VT	49
Grand Isle County, VT	7
California-Lexington Park, MD	**113**
St. Mary's County, MD	113
Canton-Massillon, OH	**401**
Carroll County, OH	28
Stark County, OH	374
Cape Coral-Fort Myers, FL	**722**
Lee County, FL	722
Cape Girardeau, MO-IL	**97**
Alexander County, IL	6
Bollinger County, MO	12
Cape Girardeau County, MO	79
Carbondale-Marion, IL	**126**
Jackson County, IL	59
Williamson County, IL	68
Carson City, NV	**55**
Carson City, NV	55
Casper, WY	**81**
Natrona County, WY	81
Cedar Rapids, IA	**268**
Benton County, IA	26
Jones County, IA	20
Linn County, IA	222
Chambersburg-Waynesboro, PA	**154**
Franklin County, PA	154
Champaign-Urbana, IL	**239**
Champaign County, IL	208
Ford County, IL	14
Piatt County, IL	17
Charleston, WV	**218**
Boone County, WV	23
Clay County, WV	9
Kanawha County, WV	186
Charleston-North Charleston, SC	**761**
Berkeley County, SC	211
Charleston County, SC	396
Dorchester County, SC	154
Charlotte-Concord-Gastonia, NC-SC	**2,474**
Cabarrus County, NC	202
Gaston County, NC	217
Iredell County, NC	173
Lincoln County, NC	81
Mecklenburg County, NC	1,055
Rowan County, NC	140
Union County, NC	227
Chester County, SC	32
Lancaster County, SC	90
York County, SC	259
Charlottesville, VA	**231**
Albemarle County, VA	107
Buckingham County, VA	17
Fluvanna County, VA	26
Greene County, VA	19
Nelson County, VA	15
Charlottesville city, VA	47
Chattanooga, TN-GA	**552**
Catoosa County, GA	66
Dade County, GA	16
Walker County, GA	68
Hamilton County, TN	358
Marion County, TN	28
Sequatchie County, TN	15
Cheyenne, WY	**98**
Laramie County, WY	98
Chicago-Naperville-Elgin, IL-IN-WI	**9,513**
Chicago-Naperville-Arlington Heights, IL	**7,305**
Cook County, IL	5,203
DuPage County, IL	929
Grundy County, IL	50
Kendall County, IL	125
McHenry County, IL	307
Will County, IL	690
Elgin, IL	**636**
DeKalb County, IL	105
Kane County, IL	532
Gary, IN	**701**
Jasper County, IN	33
Lake County, IN	486
Newton County, IN	14
Porter County, IN	168
Lake County-Kenosha County, IL-WI	**871**
Lake County, IL	703
Kenosha County, WI	168
Chico, CA	**227**
Butte County, CA	227
Cincinnati, OH-KY-IN	**2,165**
Dearborn County, IN	49
Ohio County, IN	6
Union County, IN	7
Boone County, KY	129
Bracken County, KY	8
Campbell County, KY	92
Gallatin County, KY	9
Grant County, KY	25
Kenton County, KY	165
Pendleton County, KY	15
Brown County, OH	44
Butler County, OH	378
Clermont County, OH	203
Hamilton County, OH	809
Warren County, OH	227
Clarksville, TN-KY	**282**
Christian County, KY	72
Trigg County, KY	14
Montgomery County, TN	196
Cleveland, TN	**121**
Bradley County, TN	104
Polk County, TN	17
Cleveland-Elyria, OH	**2,056**
Cuyahoga County, OH	1,249
Geauga County, OH	94
Lake County, OH	229
Lorain County, OH	306
Medina County, OH	177
Coeur d'Alene, ID	**154**
Kootenai County, ID	154
College Station-Bryan, TX	**255**
Brazos County, TX	220
Burleson County, TX	18
Robertson County, TX	17
Colorado Springs, CO	**712**
El Paso County, CO	688
Teller County, CO	24
Columbia, MO	**177**
Boone County, MO	177
Columbia, SC	**817**
Calhoun County, SC	15
Fairfield County, SC	23
Kershaw County, SC	64
Lexington County, SC	286
Richland County, SC	410
Saluda County, SC	20
Columbus, GA-AL	**309**
Russell County, AL	58
Chattahoochee County, GA	11
Harris County, GA	34
Marion County, GA	9
Muscogee County, GA	197
Columbus, IN	**81**
Bartholomew County, IN	81
Columbus, OH	**2,042**
Delaware County, OH	196
Fairfield County, OH	153
Franklin County, OH	1,265
Hocking County, OH	28
Licking County, OH	172
Madison County, OH	43
Morrow County, OH	35
Perry County, OH	36
Pickaway County, OH	58
Union County, OH	55
Corpus Christi, TX	**455**
Aransas County, TX	26
Nueces County, TX	361
San Patricio County, TX	68
Corvallis, OR	**89**
Benton County, OR	89
Crestview-Fort Walton Beach-Destin, FL	**267**
Okaloosa County, FL	201
Walton County, FL	66
Cumberland, MD-WV	**100**
Allegany County, MD	72
Mineral County, WV	27
Dallas-Fort Worth-Arlington, TX	**7,233**
Dallas-Plano-Irving, TX	**4,794**
Collin County, TX	940
Dallas County, TX	2,575
Denton County, TX	806
Ellis County, TX	168
Hunt County, TX	92
Kaufman County, TX	118
Rockwall County, TX	94
Fort Worth-Arlington, TX	**2,440**
Hood County, TX	57
Johnson County, TX	163
Parker County, TX	129
Somervell County, TX	9
Tarrant County, TX	2,017
Wise County, TX	64
Dalton, GA	**144**
Murray County, GA	39
Whitfield County, GA	105
Danville, IL	**78**
Vermilion County, IL	78
Daphne-Fairhope-Foley, AL	**209**
Baldwin County, AL	209
Davenport-Moline-Rock Island, IA-IL	**382**
Henry County, IL	49
Mercer County, IL	16
Rock Island County, IL	145
Scott County, IA	172
Dayton, OH	**801**
Greene County, OH	165
Miami County, OH	105
Montgomery County, OH	531
Decatur, AL	**152**
Lawrence County, AL	33
Morgan County, AL	119
Decatur, IL	**107**
Macon County, IL	107
Deltona-Daytona Beach-Ormond Beach, FL	**638**
Flagler County, FL	108
Volusia County, FL	529
Denver-Aurora-Lakewood, CO	**2,853**
Adams County, CO	498
Arapahoe County, CO	637
Broomfield County, CO	67
Clear Creek County, CO	9
Denver County, CO	693
Douglas County, CO	329
Elbert County, CO	25
Gilpin County, CO	6
Jefferson County, CO	572
Park County, CO	17
Des Moines-West Des Moines, IA	**635**
Dallas County, IA	85
Guthrie County, IA	11
Madison County, IA	16
Polk County, IA	474
Warren County, IA	50
Detroit-Warren-Dearborn, MI	**4,298**
Detroit-Dearborn-Livonia, MI	**1,749**
Wayne County, MI	1,749
Warren-Troy-Farmington Hills, MI	**2,548**
Lapeer County, MI	88
Livingston County, MI	189
Macomb County, MI	868
Oakland County, MI	1,244
St. Clair County, MI	160
Dothan, AL	**148**
Geneva County, AL	27
Henry County, AL	17

See footnotes at end of table.

Table A. Metropolitan Statistical Areas and Components—Population: 2016-Continued.

See headnote on page 925.

Metropolitan Statistical Area ~~Metropolitan Division ~~~~Component county	Population, 2016 (1,000)
Houston County, AL.	104
Dover, DE.	**175**
Kent County, DE.	175
Dubuque, IA.	**97**
Dubuque County, IA.	97
Duluth, MN-WI.	**279**
Carlton County, MN.	36
St. Louis County, MN.	200
Douglas County, WI.	44
Durham-Chapel Hill, NC.	**560**
Chatham County, NC.	72
Durham County, NC.	306
Orange County, NC.	142
Person County, NC.	39
East Stroudsburg, PA.	**166**
Monroe County, PA.	166
Eau Claire, WI.	**167**
Chippewa County, WI.	64
Eau Claire County, WI.	103
El Centro, CA.	**181**
Imperial County, CA.	181
Elizabethtown-Fort Knox, KY.	**150**
Hardin County, KY.	107
Larue County, KY.	14
Meade County, KY.	28
Elkhart-Goshen, IN.	**204**
Elkhart County, IN.	204
Elmira, NY.	**86**
Chemung County, NY.	86
El Paso, TX.	**842**
El Paso County, TX.	838
Hudspeth County, TX.	4
Enid, OK.	**63**
Garfield County, OK.	63
Erie, PA.	**276**
Erie County, PA.	276
Eugene, OR.	**370**
Lane County, OR.	370
Evansville, IN-KY.	**316**
Posey County, IN.	25
Vanderburgh County, IN.	182
Warrick County, IN.	62
Henderson County, KY.	46
Fairbanks, AK.	**101**
Fairbanks North Star Borough, AK.	101
Fargo, ND-MN.	**238**
Clay County, MN.	63
Cass County, ND.	175
Farmington, NM.	**115**
San Juan County, NM.	115
Fayetteville, NC.	**380**
Cumberland County, NC.	327
Hoke County, NC.	53
Fayetteville-Springdale-Rogers, AR-MO.	**525**
Benton County, AR.	258
Madison County, AR.	16
Washington County, AR.	228
McDonald County, MO.	23
Flagstaff, AZ.	**141**
Coconino County, AZ.	141
Flint, MI.	**409**
Genesee County, MI.	409
Florence, SC.	**206**
Darlington County, SC.	67
Florence County, SC.	139
Florence-Muscle Shoals, AL.	**147**
Colbert County, AL.	54
Lauderdale County, AL.	92
Fond du Lac, WI.	**102**
Fond du Lac County, WI.	102
Fort Collins, CO.	**340**
Larimer County, CO.	340
Fort Smith, AR-OK.	**281**
Crawford County, AR.	62
Sebastian County, AR.	128
Le Flore County, OK.	50
Sequoyah County, OK.	41
Fort Wayne, IN.	**432**

Metropolitan Statistical Area ~~Metropolitan Division ~~~~Component county	Population, 2016 (1,000)
Allen County, IN.	370
Wells County, IN.	28
Whitley County, IN.	33
Fresno, CA.	**980**
Fresno County, CA.	980
Gadsden, AL.	**103**
Etowah County, AL.	103
Gainesville, FL.	**281**
Alachua County, FL.	263
Gilchrist County, FL.	17
Gainesville, GA.	**197**
Hall County, GA.	197
Gettysburg, PA.	**102**
Adams County, PA.	102
Glens Falls, NY.	**126**
Warren County, NY.	65
Washington County, NY.	62
Goldsboro, NC.	**124**
Wayne County, NC.	124
Grand Forks, ND-MN.	**103**
Polk County, MN.	32
Grand Forks County, ND.	71
Grand Island, NE.	**85**
Hall County, NE.	62
Hamilton County, NE.	9
Howard County, NE.	6
Merrick County, NE.	8
Grand Junction, CO.	**150**
Mesa County, CO.	150
Grand Rapids-Wyoming, MI.	**1,047**
Barry County, MI.	60
Kent County, MI.	642
Montcalm County, MI.	63
Ottawa County, MI.	282
Grants Pass, OR.	**86**
Josephine County, OR.	86
Great Falls, MT.	**82**
Cascade County, MT.	82
Greeley, CO.	**295**
Weld County, CO.	295
Green Bay, WI.	**318**
Brown County, WI.	260
Kewaunee County, WI.	20
Oconto County, WI.	37
Greensboro-High Point, NC.	**756**
Guilford County, NC.	521
Randolph County, NC.	143
Rockingham County, NC.	91
Greenville, NC.	**177**
Pitt County, NC.	177
Greenville-Anderson-Mauldin, SC.	**885**
Anderson County, SC.	197
Greenville County, SC.	499
Laurens County, SC.	67
Pickens County, SC.	123
Gulfport-Biloxi-Pascagoula, MS.	**391**
Hancock County, MS.	47
Harrison County, MS.	203
Jackson County, MS.	141
Hagerstown-Martinsburg, MD-WV.	**264**
Washington County, MD.	150
Berkeley County, WV.	114
Hammond, LA.	**131**
Tangipahoa Parish, LA.	131
Hanford-Corcoran, CA.	**150**
Kings County, CA.	150
Harrisburg-Carlisle, PA.	**568**
Cumberland County, PA.	249
Dauphin County, PA.	274
Perry County, PA.	46
Harrisonburg, VA.	**133**
Rockingham County, VA.	80
Harrisonburg city, VA.	53
Hartford-West Hartford-East Hartford, CT.	**1,207**
Hartford County, CT.	892
Middlesex County, CT.	163

Metropolitan Statistical Area ~~Metropolitan Division ~~~~Component county	Population, 2016 (1,000)
Tolland County, CT.	151
Hattiesburg, MS.	**149**
Forrest County, MS.	76
Lamar County, MS.	61
Perry County, MS.	12
Hickory-Lenoir-Morganton, NC.	**364**
Alexander County, NC.	37
Burke County, NC.	89
Caldwell County, NC.	81
Catawba County, NC.	156
Hilton Head Island-Bluffton-Beaufort, SC.	**212**
Beaufort County, SC.	183
Jasper County, SC.	28
Hinesville, GA.	**81**
Liberty County, GA.	63
Long County, GA.	18
Homosassa Springs, FL.	**144**
Citrus County, FL.	144
Honolulu, HI.	**993**
Honolulu County, HI.	993
Hot Springs, AR.	**97**
Garland County, AR.	97
Houma-Thibodaux, LA.	**212**
Lafourche Parish, LA.	98
Terrebonne Parish, LA.	113
Houston-The Woodlands-Sugar Land, TX.	**6,772**
Austin County, TX.	30
Brazoria County, TX.	354
Chambers County, TX.	40
Fort Bend County, TX.	741
Galveston County, TX.	329
Harris County, TX.	4,590
Liberty County, TX.	82
Montgomery County, TX.	556
Waller County, TX.	50
Huntington-Ashland, WV-KY-OH.	**360**
Boyd County, KY.	48
Greenup County, KY.	36
Lawrence County, OH.	61
Cabell County, WV.	96
Lincoln County, WV.	21
Putnam County, WV.	57
Wayne County, WV.	41
Huntsville, AL.	**450**
Limestone County, AL.	93
Madison County, AL.	357
Idaho Falls, ID.	**143**
Bonneville County, ID.	112
Butte County, ID.	3
Jefferson County, ID.	28
Indianapolis-Carmel-Anderson, IN.	**2,004**
Boone County, IN.	65
Brown County, IN.	15
Hamilton County, IN.	316
Hancock County, IN.	74
Hendricks County, IN.	161
Johnson County, IN.	152
Madison County, IN.	129
Marion County, IN.	941
Morgan County, IN.	70
Putnam County, IN.	37
Shelby County, IN.	44
Iowa City, IA.	**169**
Johnson County, IA.	147
Washington County, IA.	22
Ithaca, NY.	**105**
Tompkins County, NY.	105
Jackson, MI.	**158**
Jackson County, MI.	158
Jackson, MS.	**579**
Copiah County, MS.	28
Hinds County, MS.	241
Madison County, MS.	105

See footnotes at end of table.

Metropolitan Statistical Area ~~Metropolitan Division ~~~~Component county	Popu- lation, 2016 (1,000)
Rankin County, MS	150
Simpson County, MS	27
Yazoo County, MS	27
Jackson, TN	**130**
Chester County, TN	17
Crockett County, TN	14
Madison County, TN	98
Jacksonville, FL	**1,478**
Baker County, FL	28
Clay County, FL	208
Duval County, FL	926
Nassau County, FL	81
St. Johns County, FL	235
Jacksonville, NC	**187**
Onslow County, NC	187
Janesville-Beloit, WI	**162**
Rock County, WI	162
Jefferson City, MO	**151**
Callaway County, MO	45
Cole County, MO	77
Moniteau County, MO	16
Osage County, MO	14
Johnson City, TN	**202**
Carter County, TN	57
Unicoi County, TN	18
Washington County, TN	127
Johnstown, PA	**135**
Cambria County, PA	135
Jonesboro, AR	**130**
Craighead County, AR	106
Poinsett County, AR	24
Joplin, MO	**178**
Jasper County, MO	119
Newton County, MO	59
Kahului-Wailuku-Lahaina, HI	**165**
Kalawao County, HI	(Z)
Maui County, HI	165
Kalamazoo-Portage, MI	**337**
Kalamazoo County, MI	262
Van Buren County, MI	75
Kankakee, IL	**110**
Kankakee County, IL	110
Kansas City, MO-KS	**2,105**
Johnson County, KS	584
Leavenworth County, KS	80
Linn County, KS	10
Miami County, KS	33
Wyandotte County, KS	164
Bates County, MO	16
Caldwell County, MO	9
Cass County, MO	103
Clay County, MO	239
Clinton County, MO	21
Jackson County, MO	692
Lafayette County, MO	33
Platte County, MO	98
Ray County, MO	23
Kennewick-Richland, WA	**284**
Benton County, WA	194
Franklin County, WA	90
Killeen-Temple, TX	**436**
Bell County, TX	340
Coryell County, TX	75
Lampasas County, TX	21
Kingsport-Bristol-Bristol, **TN-VA**	**306**
Hawkins County, TN	57
Sullivan County, TN	157
Scott County, VA	22
Washington County, VA	54
Bristol city, VA	17
Kingston, NY	**179**
Ulster County, NY	179
Knoxville, TN	**869**
Anderson County, TN	76
Blount County, TN	129
Campbell County, TN	40
Grainger County, TN	23
Knox County, TN	456
Loudon County, TN	51
Morgan County, TN	22
Roane County, TN	53
Union County, TN	19

Metropolitan Statistical Area ~~Metropolitan Division ~~~~Component county	Popu- lation, 2016 (1,000)
Kokomo, IN	**83**
Howard County, IN	83
La Crosse-Onalaska, WI-MN	**137**
Houston County, MN	19
La Crosse County, WI	118
Lafayette, LA	**492**
Acadia Parish, LA	63
Iberia Parish, LA	73
Lafayette Parish, LA	241
St. Martin Parish, LA	54
Vermilion Parish, LA	60
Lafayette-West Lafayette, IN	**217**
Benton County, IN	9
Carroll County, IN	20
Tippecanoe County, IN	188
Lake Charles, LA	**207**
Calcasieu Parish, LA	201
Cameron Parish, LA	7
Lake Havasu City-Kingman, **AZ**	**205**
Mohave County, AZ	205
Lakeland-Winter Haven, FL	**666**
Polk County, FL	666
Lancaster, PA	**539**
Lancaster County, PA	539
Lansing-East Lansing, MI	**475**
Clinton County, MI	78
Eaton County, MI	109
Ingham County, MI	288
Laredo, TX	**271**
Webb County, TX	271
Las Cruces, NM	**214**
Doña Ana County, NM	214
Las Vegas-Henderson- **Paradise, NV**	**2,156**
Clark County, NV	2,156
Lawrence, KS	**119**
Douglas County, KS	119
Lawton, OK	**128**
Comanche County, OK	122
Cotton County, OK	6
Lebanon, PA	**139**
Lebanon County, PA	139
Lewiston, ID-WA	**63**
Nez Perce County, ID	40
Asotin County, WA	22
Lewiston-Auburn, ME	**107**
Androscoggin County, ME	107
Lexington-Fayette, KY	**507**
Bourbon County, KY	20
Clark County, KY	36
Fayette County, KY	318
Jessamine County, KY	52
Scott County, KY	54
Woodford County, KY	26
Lima, OH	**104**
Allen County, OH	104
Lincoln, NE	**327**
Lancaster County, NE	310
Seward County, NE	17
Little Rock-North Little **Rock-Conway, AR**	**735**
Faulkner County, AR	122
Grant County, AR	18
Lonoke County, AR	72
Perry County, AR	10
Pulaski County, AR	393
Saline County, AR	119
Logan, UT-ID	**136**
Franklin County, ID	13
Cache County, UT	123
Longview, TX	**217**
Gregg County, TX	124
Rusk County, TX	53
Upshur County, TX	41
Longview, WA	**105**
Cowlitz County, WA	105
Los Angeles-Long **Beach-Anaheim, CA**	**13,310**
Anaheim-Santa Ana-Irvine, CA	3,173

Metropolitan Statistical Area ~~Metropolitan Division ~~~~Component county	Popu- lation, 2016 (1,000)
Orange County, CA	3,173
Los Angeles-Long **Beach-Glendale, CA**	**10,138**
Los Angeles County, CA	10,138
Louisville/Jefferson County, **KY-IN**	**1,283**
Clark County, IN	116
Floyd County, IN	77
Harrison County, IN	40
Scott County, IN	24
Washington County, IN	28
Bullitt County, KY	79
Henry County, KY	16
Jefferson County, KY	765
Oldham County, KY	66
Shelby County, KY	46
Spencer County, KY	18
Trimble County, KY	9
Lubbock, TX	**315**
Crosby County, TX	6
Lubbock County, TX	303
Lynn County, TX	6
Lynchburg, VA	**260**
Amherst County, VA	32
Appomattox County, VA	15
Bedford County, VA	78
Campbell County, VA	55
Lynchburg city, VA	80
Macon-Bibb County, GA	**229**
Bibb County, GA	153
Crawford County, GA	12
Jones County, GA	29
Monroe County, GA	27
Twiggs County, GA	8
Madera, CA	**155**
Madera County, CA	155
Madison, WI	**649**
Columbia County, WI	57
Dane County, WI	531
Green County, WI	37
Iowa County, WI	24
Manchester-Nashua, NH	**408**
Hillsborough County, NH	408
Manhattan, KS	**97**
Pottawatomie County, KS	24
Riley County, KS	73
Mankato-North Mankato, MN	**100**
Blue Earth County, MN	66
Nicollet County, MN	34
Mansfield, OH	**121**
Richland County, OH	121
McAllen-Edinburg-Mission, **TX**	**850**
Hidalgo County, TX	850
Medford, OR	**217**
Jackson County, OR	217
Memphis, TN-MS-AR	**1,343**
Crittenden County, AR	49
Benton County, MS	8
DeSoto County, MS	176
Marshall County, MS	36
Tate County, MS	28
Tunica County, MS	10
Fayette County, TN	40
Shelby County, TN	935
Tipton County, TN	61
Merced, CA	**269**
Merced County, CA	269
Miami-Fort Lauderdale-West **Palm Beach, FL**	**6,066**
Fort Lauderdale-Pompano **Beach-Deerfield Beach, FL**	**1,910**
Broward County, FL	1,910
Miami-Miami Beach-Kendall, **FL**	**2,713**
Miami-Dade County, FL	2,713
West Palm Beach-Boca **Raton-Delray Beach, FL**	**1,444**
Palm Beach County, FL	1,444
Michigan City-La Porte, IN	**110**

Metropolitan Statistical Area ~~Metropolitan Division ~~~~Component county	Popu- lation, 2016 (1,000)
LaPorte County, IN	110
Midland, MI	**83**
Midland County, MI	83
Midland, TX	**168**
Martin County, TX	6
Midland County, TX	163
Milwaukee-Waukesha-West Allis, WI	**1,572**
Milwaukee County, WI	951
Ozaukee County, WI	88
Washington County, WI	134
Waukesha County, WI	398
Minneapolis-St. Paul-Bloomington, MN-WI	**3,551**
Anoka County, MN	346
Carver County, MN	100
Chisago County, MN	55
Dakota County, MN	417
Hennepin County, MN	1,232
Isanti County, MN	39
Le Sueur County, MN	28
Mille Lacs County, MN	26
Ramsey County, MN	541
Scott County, MN	144
Sherburne County, MN	94
Sibley County, MN	15
Washington County, MN	253
Wright County, MN	133
Pierce County, WI	41
St. Croix County, WI	88
Missoula, MT	**116**
Missoula County, MT	116
Mobile, AL	**415**
Mobile County, AL	415
Modesto, CA	**542**
Stanislaus County, CA	542
Monroe, LA	**179**
Ouachita Parish, LA	157
Union Parish, LA	22
Monroe, MI	**149**
Monroe County, MI	149
Montgomery, AL	**374**
Autauga County, AL	55
Elmore County, AL	82
Lowndes County, AL	10
Montgomery County, AL	226
Morgantown, WV	**138**
Monongalia County, WV	105
Preston County, WV	34
Morristown, TN	**117**
Hamblen County, TN	64
Jefferson County, TN	54
Mount Vernon-Anacortes, WA	**124**
Skagit County, WA	124
Muncie, IN	**116**
Delaware County, IN	116
Muskegon, MI	**173**
Muskegon County, MI	173
Myrtle Beach-Conway-North Myrtle Beach, SC-NC	**449**
Brunswick County, NC	127
Horry County, SC	322
Napa, CA	**142**
Napa County, CA	142
Naples-Immokalee-Marco Island, FL	**365**
Collier County, FL	365
Nashville-Davidson-Murfreesboro-Franklin, TN	**1,865**
Cannon County, TN	14
Cheatham County, TN	40
Davidson County, TN	684
Dickson County, TN	52
Hickman County, TN	24
Macon County, TN	23
Maury County, TN	90
Robertson County, TN	69
Rutherford County, TN	308
Smith County, TN	19
Sumner County, TN	180
Trousdale County, TN	8

Metropolitan Statistical Area ~~Metropolitan Division ~~~~Component county	Popu- lation, 2016 (1,000)
Williamson County, TN	219
Wilson County, TN	133
New Bern, NC	**126**
Craven County, NC	103
Jones County, NC	10
Pamlico County, NC	13
New Haven-Milford, CT	**857**
New Haven County, CT	857
New Orleans-Metairie, LA	**1,269**
Jefferson Parish, LA	437
Orleans Parish, LA	391
Plaquemines Parish, LA	23
St. Bernard Parish, LA	46
St. Charles Parish, LA	53
St. James Parish, LA	22
St. John the Baptist Parish, LA	44
St. Tammany Parish, LA	254
New York-Newark-Jersey City, NY-NJ-PA	**20,154**
~~**Dutchess County-Putnam County, NY**~~	**393**
Dutchess County, NY	294
Putnam County, NY	99
~~**Nassau County-Suffolk County, NY**~~	**2,854**
Nassau County, NY	1,362
Suffolk County, NY	1,493
~~**Newark, NJ-PA**~~	**2,507**
Essex County, NJ	797
Hunterdon County, NJ	125
Morris County, NJ	498
Somerset County, NJ	334
Sussex County, NJ	143
Union County, NJ	556
Pike County, PA	56
~~**New York-Jersey City-White Plains, NY-NJ**~~	**14,399**
Bergen County, NJ	939
Hudson County, NJ	678
Middlesex County, NJ	837
Monmouth County, NJ	626
Ocean County, NJ	592
Passaic County, NJ	508
Bronx County, NY	1,456
Kings County, NY	2,629
New York County, NY	1,644
Orange County, NY	379
Queens County, NY	2,333
Richmond County, NY	476
Rockland County, NY	327
Westchester County, NY	975
Niles-Benton Harbor, MI	**154**
Berrien County, MI	154
North Port-Sarasota-Bradenton, FL	**788**
Manatee County, FL	376
Sarasota County, FL	413
Norwich-New London, CT	**270**
New London County, CT	270
Ocala, FL	**349**
Marion County, FL	349
Ocean City, NJ	**94**
Cape May County, NJ	94
Odessa, TX	**157**
Ector County, TX	157
Ogden-Clearfield, UT	**654**
Box Elder County, UT	53
Davis County, UT	342
Morgan County, UT	11
Weber County, UT	248
Oklahoma City, OK	**1,373**
Canadian County, OK	137
Cleveland County, OK	279
Grady County, OK	55
Lincoln County, OK	35
Logan County, OK	47
McClain County, OK	39
Oklahoma County, OK	783
Olympia-Tumwater, WA	**275**
Thurston County, WA	275
Omaha-Council Bluffs, NE-IA	**924**

Metropolitan Statistical Area ~~Metropolitan Division ~~~~Component county	Popu- lation, 2016 (1,000)
Harrison County, IA	14
Mills County, IA	15
Pottawattamie County, IA	94
Cass County, NE	26
Douglas County, NE	555
Sarpy County, NE	179
Saunders County, NE	21
Washington County, NE	21
Orlando-Kissimmee-Sanford, FL	**2,441**
Lake County, FL	335
Orange County, FL	1,314
Osceola County, FL	336
Seminole County, FL	455
Oshkosh-Neenah, WI	**170**
Winnebago County, WI	170
Owensboro, KY	**118**
Daviess County, KY	100
Hancock County, KY	9
McLean County, KY	9
Oxnard-Thousand Oaks-Ventura, CA	**850**
Ventura County, CA	850
Palm Bay-Melbourne-Titusville, FL	**579**
Brevard County, FL	579
Panama City, FL	**200**
Bay County, FL	184
Gulf County, FL	16
Parkersburg-Vienna, WV	**91**
Wirt County, WV	6
Wood County, WV	86
Pensacola-Ferry Pass-Brent, FL	**486**
Escambia County, FL	315
Santa Rosa County, FL	170
Peoria, IL	**376**
Marshall County, IL	12
Peoria County, IL	185
Stark County, IL	6
Tazewell County, IL	134
Woodford County, IL	39
Philadelphia-Camden-Wilmington, PA-NJ-DE-MD	**6,071**
~~**Camden, NJ**~~	**1,252**
Burlington County, NJ	449
Camden County, NJ	510
Gloucester County, NJ	292
~~**Montgomery-Bucks-Chester, PA**~~	**1,964**
Bucks County, PA	626
Chester County, PA	516
Montgomery County, PA	822
~~**Philadelphia, PA**~~	**2,131**
Delaware County, PA	563
Philadelphia County, PA	1,568
~~**Wilmington, DE-MD-NJ**~~	**723**
New Castle County, DE	557
Cecil County, MD	103
Salem County, NJ	63
Phoenix-Mesa-Scottsdale, AZ	**4,662**
Maricopa County, AZ	4,243
Pinal County, AZ	419
Pine Bluff, AR	**92**
Cleveland County, AR	8
Jefferson County, AR	70
Lincoln County, AR	14
Pittsburgh, PA	**2,342**
Allegheny County, PA	1,225
Armstrong County, PA	66
Beaver County, PA	167
Butler County, PA	187
Fayette County, PA	133
Washington County, PA	208
Westmoreland County, PA	355
Pittsfield, MA	**127**
Berkshire County, MA	127
Pocatello, ID	**84**
Bannock County, ID	84
Portland-South Portland, ME	**530**

Metropolitan Statistical Area ~~Metropolitan Division ~~~~Component county	Population, 2016 (1,000)
Cumberland County, ME	292
Sagadahoc County, ME	35
York County, ME	202
Portland-Vancouver-Hillsboro, OR-WA	**2,425**
Clackamas County, OR	408
Columbia County, OR	51
Multnomah County, OR	800
Washington County, OR	583
Yamhill County, OR	105
Clark County, WA	467
Skamania County, WA	12
Port St. Lucie, FL	**465**
Martin County, FL	159
St. Lucie County, FL	307
Prescott, AZ	**226**
Yavapai County, AZ	226
Providence-Warwick, RI-MA	**1,615**
Bristol County, MA	558
Bristol County, RI	49
Kent County, RI	165
Newport County, RI	83
Providence County, RI	634
Washington County, RI	126
Provo-Orem, UT	**603**
Juab County, UT	11
Utah County, UT	592
Pueblo, CO	**165**
Pueblo County, CO	165
Punta Gorda, FL	**178**
Charlotte County, FL	178
Racine, WI	**195**
Racine County, WI	195
Raleigh, NC	**1,303**
Franklin County, NC	65
Johnston County, NC	191
Wake County, NC	1,047
Rapid City, SD	**146**
Custer County, SD	9
Meade County, SD	28
Pennington County, SD	109
Reading, PA	**415**
Berks County, PA	415
Redding, CA	**180**
Shasta County, CA	180
Reno, NV	**458**
Storey County, NV	4
Washoe County, NV	454
Richmond, VA	**1,282**
Amelia County, VA	13
Caroline County, VA	30
Charles City County, VA	7
Chesterfield County, VA	339
Dinwiddie County, VA	28
Goochland County, VA	23
Hanover County, VA	104
Henrico County, VA	327
King William County, VA	16
New Kent County, VA	21
Powhatan County, VA	28
Prince George County, VA	38
Sussex County, VA	12
Colonial Heights city, VA	18
Hopewell city, VA	23
Petersburg city, VA	32
Richmond city, VA	223
Riverside-San Bernardino-Ontario, CA	**4,528**
Riverside County, CA	2,388
San Bernardino County, CA	2,140
Roanoke, VA	**314**
Botetourt County, VA	33
Craig County, VA	5
Franklin County, VA	56
Roanoke County, VA	94
Roanoke city, VA	100
Salem city, VA	26
Rochester, MN	**216**
Dodge County, MN	21
Fillmore County, MN	21
Olmsted County, MN	153
Wabasha County, MN	21
Rochester, NY	**1,079**

Metropolitan Statistical Area ~~Metropolitan Division ~~~~Component county	Population, 2016 (1,000)
Livingston County, NY	64
Monroe County, NY	748
Ontario County, NY	110
Orleans County, NY	41
Wayne County, NY	91
Yates County, NY	25
Rockford, IL	**339**
Boone County, IL	54
Winnebago County, IL	286
Rocky Mount, NC	**147**
Edgecombe County, NC	53
Nash County, NC	94
Rome, GA	**97**
Floyd County, GA	97
Sacramento-Roseville-Arden-Arcade, CA	**2,296**
El Dorado County, CA	186
Placer County, CA	381
Sacramento County, CA	1,514
Yolo County, CA	216
Saginaw, MI	**192**
Saginaw County, MI	192
St. Cloud, MN	**196**
Benton County, MN	40
Stearns County, MN	156
St. George, UT	**160**
Washington County, UT	160
St. Joseph, MO-KS	**127**
Doniphan County, KS	8
Andrew County, MO	17
Buchanan County, MO	89
DeKalb County, MO	13
St. Louis, MO-IL [1]	**2,807**
Bond County, IL	17
Calhoun County, IL	5
Clinton County, IL	38
Jersey County, IL	22
Macoupin County, IL	46
Madison County, IL	266
Monroe County, IL	34
St. Clair County, IL	263
Franklin County, MO	103
Jefferson County, MO	224
Lincoln County, MO	55
St. Charles County, MO	391
St. Louis County, MO	999
Warren County, MO	34
St. Louis city, MO	311
Salem, OR	**418**
Marion County, OR	336
Polk County, OR	82
Salinas, CA	**435**
Monterey County, CA	435
Salisbury, MD-DE	**400**
Sussex County, DE	220
Somerset County, MD	26
Wicomico County, MD	103
Worcester County, MD	51
Salt Lake City, UT	**1,186**
Salt Lake County, UT	1,121
Tooele County, UT	65
San Angelo, TX	**120**
Irion County, TX	2
Tom Green County, TX	118
San Antonio-New Braunfels, TX	**2,430**
Atascosa County, TX	49
Bandera County, TX	22
Bexar County, TX	1,929
Comal County, TX	135
Guadalupe County, TX	155
Kendall County, TX	43
Medina County, TX	49
Wilson County, TX	48
San Diego-Carlsbad, CA	**3,318**
San Diego County, CA	3,318
San Francisco-Oakland-Hayward, CA	**4,679**
Oakland-Hayward-Berkeley, CA	**2,783**
Alameda County, CA	1,648

Metropolitan Statistical Area ~~Metropolitan Division ~~~~Component county	Population, 2016 (1,000)
Contra Costa County, CA	1,135
San Francisco-Redwood City-South San Francisco, CA	**1,636**
San Francisco County, CA	871
San Mateo County, CA	765
San Rafael, CA	**261**
Marin County, CA	261
San Jose-Sunnyvale-Santa Clara, CA	**1,979**
San Benito County, CA	59
Santa Clara County, CA	1,919
San Luis Obispo-Paso Robles-Arroyo Grande, CA	**283**
San Luis Obispo County, CA	283
Santa Cruz-Watsonville, CA	**275**
Santa Cruz County, CA	275
Santa Fe, NM	**149**
Santa Fe County, NM	149
Santa Maria-Santa Barbara, CA	**446**
Santa Barbara County, CA	446
Santa Rosa, CA	**503**
Sonoma County, CA	503
Savannah, GA	**384**
Bryan County, GA	36
Chatham County, GA	289
Effingham County, GA	59
Scranton-Wilkes-Barre-Hazleton, PA	**555**
Lackawanna County, PA	211
Luzerne County, PA	316
Wyoming County, PA	28
Seattle-Tacoma-Bellevue, WA	**3,799**
Seattle-Bellevue-Everett, WA	**2,938**
King County, WA	2,150
Snohomish County, WA	788
Tacoma-Lakewood, WA	**861**
Pierce County, WA	861
Sebastian-Vero Beach, FL	**152**
Indian River County, FL	152
Sebring, FL	**101**
Highlands County, FL	101
Sheboygan, WI	**115**
Sheboygan County, WI	115
Sherman-Denison, TX	**128**
Grayson County, TX	128
Shreveport-Bossier City, LA	**442**
Bossier Parish, LA	126
Caddo Parish, LA	249
De Soto Parish, LA	27
Webster Parish, LA	40
Sierra Vista-Douglas, AZ	**126**
Cochise County, AZ	126
Sioux City, IA-NE-SD	**169**
Plymouth County, IA	25
Woodbury County, IA	103
Dakota County, NE	20
Dixon County, NE	6
Union County, SD	15
Sioux Falls, SD	**256**
Lincoln County, SD	54
McCook County, SD	6
Minnehaha County, SD	187
Turner County, SD	8
South Bend-Mishawaka, IN-MI	**321**
St. Joseph County, IN	269
Cass County, MI	52
Spartanburg, SC	**329**
Spartanburg County, SC	301
Union County, SC	28
Spokane-Spokane Valley, WA	**557**
Pend Oreille County, WA	13
Spokane County, WA	499
Stevens County, WA	44
Springfield, IL	**210**
Menard County, IL	13
Sangamon County, IL	197
Springfield, MA	**630**
Hampden County, MA	468

See footnotes at end of table.

Table A. Metropolitan Statistical Areas and Components—Population: 2016-Continued.

See headnote on page 925.

Metropolitan Statistical Area ~~Metropolitan Division ~~~~Component county	Population, 2016 (1,000)
Hampshire County, MA	162
Springfield, MO	**459**
Christian County, MO	84
Dallas County, MO	16
Greene County, MO	289
Polk County, MO	31
Webster County, MO	38
Springfield, OH	**135**
Clark County, OH	135
State College, PA	**161**
Centre County, PA	161
Staunton-Waynesboro, VA	**121**
Augusta County, VA	75
Staunton city, VA	24
Waynesboro city, VA	22
Stockton-Lodi, CA	**734**
San Joaquin County, CA	734
Sumter, SC	**107**
Sumter County, SC	107
Syracuse, NY	**657**
Madison County, NY	71
Onondaga County, NY	466
Oswego County, NY	119
Tallahassee, FL	**380**
Gadsden County, FL	46
Jefferson County, FL	14
Leon County, FL	288
Wakulla County, FL	32
Tampa-St. Petersburg-Clearwater, FL	**3,032**
Hernando County, FL	183
Hillsborough County, FL	1,376
Pasco County, FL	512
Pinellas County, FL	961
Terre Haute, IN	**171**
Clay County, IN	26
Sullivan County, IN	21
Vermillion County, IN	16
Vigo County, IN	108
Texarkana, TX-AR	**150**
Little River County, AR	12
Miller County, AR	44
Bowie County, TX	94
The Villages, FL	**124**
Sumter County, FL	124
Toledo, OH	**605**
Fulton County, OH	43
Lucas County, OH	432
Wood County, OH	130
Topeka, KS	**233**
Jackson County, KS	13
Jefferson County, KS	19
Osage County, KS	16
Shawnee County, KS	178
Wabaunsee County, KS	7
Trenton, NJ	**371**
Mercer County, NJ	371
Tucson, AZ	**1,016**
Pima County, AZ	1,016
Tulsa, OK	**987**
Creek County, OK	71
Okmulgee County, OK	39
Osage County, OK	48
Pawnee County, OK	16
Rogers County, OK	92
Tulsa County, OK	643
Wagoner County, OK	78
Tuscaloosa, AL	**241**
Hale County, AL	15
Pickens County, AL	20

Metropolitan Statistical Area ~~Metropolitan Division ~~~~Component county	Population, 2016 (1,000)
Tuscaloosa County, AL	206
Tyler, TX	**225**
Smith County, TX	225
Utica-Rome, NY	**294**
Herkimer County, NY	63
Oneida County, NY	231
Valdosta, GA	**145**
Brooks County, GA	16
Echols County, GA	4
Lanier County, GA	10
Lowndes County, GA	115
Vallejo-Fairfield, CA	**440**
Solano County, CA	440
Victoria, TX	**100**
Goliad County, TX	8
Victoria County, TX	92
Vineland-Bridgeton, NJ	**154**
Cumberland County, NJ	154
Virginia Beach-Norfolk-Newport News, VA-NC	**1,727**
Currituck County, NC	26
Gates County, NC	11
Gloucester County, VA	37
Isle of Wight County, VA	37
James City County, VA	74
Mathews County, VA	9
York County, VA	68
Chesapeake city, VA	238
Hampton city, VA	135
Newport News city, VA	182
Norfolk city, VA	245
Poquoson city, VA	12
Portsmouth city, VA	95
Suffolk city, VA	89
Virginia Beach city, VA	453
Williamsburg city, VA	15
Visalia-Porterville, CA	**460**
Tulare County, CA	460
Waco, TX	**265**
Falls County, TX	17
McLennan County, TX	248
Walla Walla, WA	**64**
Columbia County, WA	4
Walla Walla County, WA	60
Warner Robins, GA	**190**
Houston County, GA	152
Peach County, GA	27
Pulaski County, GA	11
Washington-Arlington-Alexandria, DC-VA-MD-WV	**6,132**
Silver Spring-Frederick-Rockville, MD	**1,291**
Frederick County, MD	248
Montgomery County, MD	1,044
Washington-Arlington-Alexandria, DC-VA-MD-WV	**4,841**
District of Columbia, DC	681
Calvert County, MD	91
Charles County, MD	158
Prince George's County, MD	908
Arlington County, VA	230
Clarke County, VA	14
Culpeper County, VA	50
Fairfax County, VA	1,139
Fauquier County, VA	69
Loudoun County, VA	386
Prince William County, VA	455
Rappahannock County, VA	7
Spotsylvania County, VA	132
Stafford County, VA	144

Metropolitan Statistical Area ~~Metropolitan Division ~~~~Component county	Population, 2016 (1,000)
Warren County, VA	39
Alexandria city, VA	156
Fairfax city, VA	24
Falls Church city, VA	14
Fredericksburg city, VA	28
Manassas city, VA	41
Manassas Park city, VA	16
Jefferson County, WV	56
Waterloo-Cedar Falls, IA	**170**
Black Hawk County, IA	133
Bremer County, IA	25
Grundy County, IA	12
Watertown-Fort Drum, NY	**114**
Jefferson County, NY	114
Wausau, WI	**136**
Marathon County, WI	136
Weirton-Steubenville, WV-OH	**119**
Jefferson County, OH	67
Brooke County, WV	23
Hancock County, WV	30
Wenatchee, WA	**118**
Chelan County, WA	76
Douglas County, WA	41
Wheeling, WV-OH	**143**
Belmont County, OH	69
Marshall County, WV	32
Ohio County, WV	43
Wichita, KS	**645**
Butler County, KS	67
Harvey County, KS	35
Kingman County, KS	7
Sedgwick County, KS	512
Sumner County, KS	23
Wichita Falls, TX	**151**
Archer County, TX	9
Clay County, TX	10
Wichita County, TX	132
Williamsport, PA	**115**
Lycoming County, PA	115
Wilmington, NC	**283**
New Hanover County, NC	223
Pender County, NC	59
Winchester, VA-WV	**135**
Frederick County, VA	84
Winchester city, VA	28
Hampshire County, WV	23
Winston-Salem, NC	**662**
Davidson County, NC	165
Davie County, NC	42
Forsyth County, NC	372
Stokes County, NC	46
Yadkin County, NC	38
Worcester, MA-CT	**936**
Windham County, CT	116
Worcester County, MA	820
Yakima, WA	**250**
Yakima County, WA	250
York-Hanover, PA	**444**
York County, PA	444
Youngstown-Warren-Boardman, OH-PA	**545**
Mahoning County, OH	230
Trumbull County, OH	202
Mercer County, PA	113
Yuba City, CA	**172**
Sutter County, CA	97
Yuba County, CA	75
Yuma, AZ	**206**
Yuma County, AZ	206

Z Represents less than 500. [1] The portion of Sullivan city in Crawford County, Missouri, is legally part of the St. Louis, MO-IL Metropolitan Statistical Area. The estimate shown here for the St. Louis, MO-IL Metropolitan Statistical Area does not include this area.

Source: U.S. Census Bureau, 2016 Population Estimates, <https://www.census.gov/programs-surveys/metro-micro/data/tables.html>.

Table B. Micropolitan Statistical Areas and Components—Population: 2016

[In thousands (43 represents 43,000). Population as of July 2016. Micropolitan Statistical Areas defined by the U.S. Office of Management and Budget as of July 2015. All Micropolitan Statistical Areas are arranged alphabetically]

Micropolitan Statistical Area ~~Component county	Population, 2016 (1,000)	Micropolitan Statistical Area ~~Component county	Population, 2016 (1,000)	Micropolitan Statistical Area ~~Component county	Population, 2016 (1,000)
Aberdeen, SD	**43**	Morehouse Parish, LA	26	Minidoka County, ID	21
Brown County, SD	39	**Batavia, NY**	**58**	**Burlington, IA-IL**	**47**
Edmunds County, SD	4	Genesee County, NY	58	Henderson County, IL	7
Aberdeen, WA	**72**	**Batesville, AR**	**37**	Des Moines County, IA	40
Grays Harbor County, WA	72	Independence County, AR	37	**Butte-Silver Bow, MT**	**35**
Ada, OK	**38**	**Bay City, TX**	**37**	Silver Bow County, MT	35
Pontotoc County, OK	38	Matagorda County, TX	37	**Cadillac, MI**	**48**
Adrian, MI	**99**	**Beatrice, NE**	**22**	Missaukee County, MI	15
Lenawee County, MI	99	Gage County, NE	22	Wexford County, MI	33
Alamogordo, NM	**65**	**Beaver Dam, WI**	**88**	**Calhoun, GA**	**57**
Otero County, NM	65	Dodge County, WI	88	Gordon County, GA	57
Albemarle, NC	**61**	**Bedford, IN**	**46**	**Cambridge, MD**	**32**
Stanly County, NC	61	Lawrence County, IN	46	Dorchester County, MD	32
Albert Lea, MN	**30**	**Beeville, TX**	**33**	**Cambridge, OH**	**39**
Freeborn County, MN	30	Bee County, TX	33	Guernsey County, OH	39
Albertville, AL	**95**	**Bellefontaine, OH**	**45**	**Camden, AR**	**29**
Marshall County, AL	95	Logan County, OH	45	Calhoun County, AR	5
Alexander City, AL	**41**	**Bemidji, MN**	**46**	Ouachita County, AR	24
Tallapoosa County, AL	41	Beltrami County, MN	46	**Campbellsville, KY**	**25**
Alexandria, MN	**37**	**Bennettsville, SC**	**27**	Taylor County, KY	25
Douglas County, MN	37	Marlboro County, SC	27	**Cañon City, CO**	**47**
Alice, TX	**41**	**Bennington, VT**	**36**	Fremont County, CO	47
Jim Wells County, TX	41	Bennington County, VT	36	**Canton, IL**	**36**
Alma, MI	**41**	**Berlin, NH-VT**	**38**	Fulton County, IL	36
Gratiot County, MI	41	Coos County, NH	32	**Carlsbad-Artesia, NM**	**58**
Alpena, MI	**29**	Essex County, VT	6	Eddy County, NM	58
Alpena County, MI	29	**Big Rapids, MI**	**43**	**Carroll, IA**	**20**
Altus, OK	**25**	Mecosta County, MI	43	Carroll County, IA	20
Jackson County, OK	25	**Big Spring, TX**	**38**	**Cedar City, UT**	**50**
Americus, GA	**35**	Glasscock County, TX	1	Iron County, UT	50
Schley County, GA	5	Howard County, TX	37	**Cedartown, GA**	**42**
Sumter County, GA	30	**Big Stone Gap, VA**	**58**	Polk County, GA	42
Amsterdam, NY	**49**	Dickenson County, VA	15	**Celina, OH**	**41**
Montgomery County, NY	49	Wise County, VA	39	Mercer County, OH	41
Andrews, TX	**18**	Norton city, VA	4	**Central City, KY**	**31**
Andrews County, TX	18	**Blackfoot, ID**	**45**	Muhlenberg County, KY	31
Angola, IN	**34**	Bingham County, ID	45	**Centralia, IL**	**38**
Steuben County, IN	34	**Bluefield, WV-VA**	**103**	Marion County, IL	38
Arcadia, FL	**36**	Tazewell County, VA	42	**Centralia, WA**	**77**
DeSoto County, FL	36	Mercer County, WV	60	Lewis County, WA	77
Ardmore, OK	**49**	**Blytheville, AR**	**43**	**Charleston-Mattoon, IL**	**63**
Carter County, OK	49	Mississippi County, AR	43	Coles County, IL	52
Arkadelphia, AR	**23**	**Bogalusa, LA**	**46**	Cumberland County, IL	11
Clark County, AR	23	Washington Parish, LA	46	**Chillicothe, OH**	**77**
Arkansas City-Winfield, KS	**36**	**Bonham, TX**	**34**	Ross County, OH	77
Cowley County, KS	36	Fannin County, TX	34	**Claremont-Lebanon, NH-VT**	**216**
Ashland, OH	**54**	**Boone, IA**	**27**	Grafton County, NH	89
Ashland County, OH	54	Boone County, IA	27	Sullivan County, NH	43
Ashtabula, OH	**98**	**Boone, NC**	**54**	Orange County, VT	29
Ashtabula County, OH	98	Watauga County, NC	54	Windsor County, VT	55
Astoria, OR	**39**	**Borger, TX**	**22**	**Clarksburg, WV**	**94**
Clatsop County, OR	39	Hutchinson County, TX	22	Doddridge County, WV	8
Atchison, KS	**16**	**Bozeman, MT**	**105**	Harrison County, WV	68
Atchison County, KS	16	Gallatin County, MT	105	Taylor County, WV	17
Athens, OH	**66**	**Bradford, PA**	**42**	**Clarksdale, MS**	**24**
Athens County, OH	66	McKean County, PA	42	Coahoma County, MS	24
Athens, TN	**53**	**Brainerd, MN**	**93**	**Clearlake, CA**	**64**
McMinn County, TN	53	Cass County, MN	29	Lake County, CA	64
Athens, TX	**80**	Crow Wing County, MN	64	**Cleveland, MS**	**33**
Henderson County, TX	80	**Branson, MO**	**86**	Bolivar County, MS	33
Atmore, AL	**38**	Stone County, MO	31	**Clewiston, FL**	**39**
Escambia County, AL	38	Taney County, MO	55	Hendry County, FL	39
Auburn, IN	**43**	**Breckenridge, CO**	**30**	**Clinton, IA**	**47**
DeKalb County, IN	43	Summit County, CO	30	Clinton County, IA	47
Auburn, NY	**78**	**Brenham, TX**	**35**	**Clovis, NM**	**50**
Cayuga County, NY	78	Washington County, TX	35	Curry County, NM	50
Augusta-Waterville, ME	**121**	**Brevard, NC**	**33**	**Coffeyville, KS**	**33**
Kennebec County, ME	121	Transylvania County, NC	33	Montgomery County, KS	33
Austin, MN	**39**	**Brookhaven, MS**	**35**	**Coldwater, MI**	**43**
Mower County, MN	39	Lincoln County, MS	35	Branch County, MI	43
Bainbridge, GA	**27**	**Brookings, OR**	**23**	**Columbus, MS**	**60**
Decatur County, GA	27	Curry County, OR	23	Lowndes County, MS	60
Baraboo, WI	**64**	**Brookings, SD**	**34**	**Columbus, NE**	**33**
Sauk County, WI	64	Brookings County, SD	34	Platte County, NE	33
Bardstown, KY	**46**	**Brownsville, TN**	**18**	**Concord, NH**	**149**
Nelson County, KY	46	Haywood County, TN	18	Merrimack County, NH	149
Barre, VT	**59**	**Brownwood, TX**	**38**	**Connersville, IN**	**23**
Washington County, VT	59	Brown County, TX	38	Fayette County, IN	23
Bartlesville, OK	**52**	**Bucyrus, OH**	**42**	**Cookeville, TN**	**110**
Washington County, OK	52	Crawford County, OH	42	Jackson County, TN	12
Bastrop, LA	**26**	**Burley, ID**	**44**	Overton County, TN	22
		Cassia County, ID	24	Putnam County, TN	76

See footnotes at end of table.

Micropolitan Statistical Area ~~Component county	Population, 2016 (1,000)	Micropolitan Statistical Area ~~Component county	Population, 2016 (1,000)	Micropolitan Statistical Area ~~Component county	Population, 2016 (1,000)
Coos Bay, OR	**64**	Union County, AR	40	Cherokee County, SC	57
Coos County, OR	64	**Elizabeth City, NC**	**64**	**Gainesville, TX**	**39**
Cordele, GA	**23**	Camden County, NC	10	Cooke County, TX	39
Crisp County, GA	23	Pasquotank County, NC	40	**Galesburg, IL**	**51**
Corinth, MS	**37**	Perquimans County, NC	13	Knox County, IL	51
Alcorn County, MS	37	**Elk City, OK**	**23**	**Gallup, NM**	**75**
Cornelia, GA	**44**	Beckham County, OK	23	McKinley County, NM	75
Habersham County, GA	44	**Elkins, WV**	**29**	**Garden City, KS**	**41**
Corning, NY	**97**	Randolph County, WV	29	Finney County, KS	37
Steuben County, NY	97	**Elko, NV**	**54**	Kearny County, KS	4
Corsicana, TX	**49**	Elko County, NV	52	**Gardnerville Ranchos, NV**	**48**
Navarro County, TX	49	Eureka County, NV	2	Douglas County, NV	48
Cortland, NY	**48**	**Ellensburg, WA**	**45**	**Georgetown, SC**	**61**
Cortland County, NY	48	Kittitas County, WA	45	Georgetown County, SC	61
Coshocton, OH	**37**	**Emporia, KS**	**34**	**Gillette, WY**	**49**
Coshocton County, OH	37	Lyon County, KS	34	Campbell County, WY	49
Craig, CO	**13**	**Enterprise, AL**	**51**	**Glasgow, KY**	**54**
Moffat County, CO	13	Coffee County, AL	51	Barren County, KY	44
Crawfordsville, IN	**38**	**Escanaba, MI**	**36**	Metcalfe County, KY	10
Montgomery County, IN	38	Delta County, MI	36	**Glenwood Springs, CO**	**77**
Crescent City, CA	**28**	**Española, NM**	**40**	Garfield County, CO	59
Del Norte County, CA	28	Rio Arriba County, NM	40	Pitkin County, CO	18
Crossville, TN	**59**	**Eufaula, AL-GA**	**28**	**Gloversville, NY**	**54**
Cumberland County, TN	59	Barbour County, AL	26	Fulton County, NY	54
Cullman, AL	**82**	Quitman County, GA	2	**Grand Rapids, MN**	**45**
Cullman County, AL	82	**Eureka-Arcata-Fortuna, CA**	**137**	Itasca County, MN	45
Cullowhee, NC	**42**	Humboldt County, CA	137	**Grants, NM**	**27**
Jackson County, NC	42	**Evanston, WY**	**21**	Cibola County, NM	27
Danville, KY	**54**	Uinta County, WY	21	**Great Bend, KS**	**27**
Boyle County, KY	30	**Fairfield, IA**	**18**	Barton County, KS	27
Lincoln County, KY	24	Jefferson County, IA	18	**Greeneville, TN**	**69**
Danville, VA	**104**	**Fairmont, MN**	**20**	Greene County, TN	69
Pittsylvania County, VA	62	Martin County, MN	20	**Greenfield Town, MA**	**70**
Danville city, VA	42	**Fairmont, WV**	**57**	Franklin County, MA	70
Dayton, TN	**32**	Marion County, WV	57	**Greensburg, IN**	**27**
Rhea County, TN	32	**Fallon, NV**	**24**	Decatur County, IN	27
Decatur, IN	**35**	Churchill County, NV	24	**Greenville, MS**	**47**
Adams County, IN	35	**Faribault-Northfield, MN**	**66**	Washington County, MS	47
Defiance, OH	**38**	Rice County, MN	66	**Greenville, OH**	**52**
Defiance County, OH	38	**Farmington, MO**	**67**	Darke County, OH	52
Del Rio, TX	**49**	St. Francois County, MO	67	**Greenwood, MS**	**40**
Val Verde County, TX	49	**Fergus Falls, MN**	**58**	Carroll County, MS	10
Deming, NM	**24**	Otter Tail County, MN	58	Leflore County, MS	30
Luna County, NM	24	**Fernley, NV**	**53**	**Greenwood, SC**	**95**
DeRidder, LA	**37**	Lyon County, NV	53	Abbeville County, SC	25
Beauregard Parish, LA	37	**Findlay, OH**	**76**	Greenwood County, SC	70
Dickinson, ND	**31**	Hancock County, OH	76	**Grenada, MS**	**21**
Stark County, ND	31	**Fitzgerald, GA**	**17**	Grenada County, MS	21
Dixon, IL	**34**	Ben Hill County, GA	17	**Guymon, OK**	**21**
Lee County, IL	34	**Forest City, NC**	**66**	Texas County, OK	21
Dodge City, KS	**34**	Rutherford County, NC	66	**Hailey, ID**	**28**
Ford County, KS	34	**Forrest City, AR**	**26**	Blaine County, ID	22
Douglas, GA	**43**	St. Francis County, AR	26	Camas County, ID	1
Coffee County, GA	43	**Fort Dodge, IA**	**37**	Lincoln County, ID	5
Dublin, GA	**57**	Webster County, IA	37	**Hannibal, MO**	**39**
Johnson County, GA	10	**Fort Leonard Wood, MO**	**53**	Marion County, MO	29
Laurens County, GA	48	Pulaski County, MO	53	Ralls County, MO	10
DuBois, PA	**81**	**Fort Madison-Keokuk, IA-IL-MO**	**60**	**Harrison, AR**	**45**
Clearfield County, PA	81	Hancock County, IL	19	Boone County, AR	37
Dumas, TX	**22**	Lee County, IA	35	Newton County, AR	8
Moore County, TX	22	Clark County, MO	7	**Hastings, NE**	**32**
Duncan, OK	**44**	**Fort Morgan, CO**	**28**	Adams County, NE	32
Stephens County, OK	44	Morgan County, CO	28	**Hays, KS**	**29**
Dunn, NC	**131**	**Fort Payne, AL**	**71**	Ellis County, KS	29
Harnett County, NC	131	DeKalb County, AL	71	**Heber, UT**	**31**
Durango, CO	**56**	**Fort Polk South, LA**	**51**	Wasatch County, UT	31
La Plata County, CO	56	Vernon Parish, LA	51	**Helena, MT**	**79**
Durant, OK	**46**	**Frankfort, IN**	**32**	Jefferson County, MT	12
Bryan County, OK	46	Clinton County, IN	32	Lewis and Clark County, MT	67
Dyersburg, TN	**38**	**Frankfort, KY**	**73**	**Helena-West Helena, AR**	**19**
Dyer County, TN	38	Anderson County, KY	22	Phillips County, AR	19
Eagle Pass, TX	**58**	Franklin County, KY	51	**Henderson, NC**	**44**
Maverick County, TX	58	**Fredericksburg, TX**	**27**	Vance County, NC	44
Easton, MD	**37**	Gillespie County, TX	27	**Hereford, TX**	**19**
Talbot County, MD	37	**Freeport, IL**	**46**	Deaf Smith County, TX	19
Edwards, CO	**54**	Stephenson County, IL	46	**Hermiston-Pendleton, OR**	**88**
Eagle County, CO	54	**Fremont, NE**	**37**	Morrow County, OR	11
Effingham, IL	**34**	Dodge County, NE	37	Umatilla County, OR	76
Effingham County, IL	34	**Fremont, OH**	**59**	**Hillsdale, MI**	**46**
El Campo, TX	**42**	Sandusky County, OH	59	Hillsdale County, MI	46
Wharton County, TX	42	**Gaffney, SC**	**57**	**Hilo, HI**	**198**
El Dorado, AR	**40**			Hawaii County, HI	198

See footnotes at end of table.

Micropolitan Statistical Area ~~Component county	Population, 2016 (1,000)
Hobbs, NM	**70**
Lea County, NM	70
Holland, MI	**116**
Allegan County, MI	116
Hood River, OR	**23**
Hood River County, OR	23
Hope, AR	**30**
Hempstead County, AR	22
Nevada County, AR	8
Houghton, MI	**39**
Houghton County, MI	37
Keweenaw County, MI	2
Hudson, NY	**61**
Columbia County, NY	61
Huntingdon, PA	**46**
Huntingdon County, PA	46
Huntington, IN	**36**
Huntington County, IN	36
Huntsville, TX	**86**
Trinity County, TX	14
Walker County, TX	71
Huron, SD	**18**
Beadle County, SD	18
Hutchinson, KS	**63**
Reno County, KS	63
Hutchinson, MN	**36**
McLeod County, MN	36
Indiana, PA	**86**
Indiana County, PA	86
Indianola, MS	**26**
Sunflower County, MS	26
Ionia, MI	**64**
Ionia County, MI	64
Iron Mountain, MI-WI	**30**
Dickinson County, MI	26
Florence County, WI	4
Jackson, OH	**33**
Jackson County, OH	33
Jackson, WY-ID	**34**
Teton County, ID	11
Teton County, WY	23
Jacksonville, IL	**39**
Morgan County, IL	34
Scott County, IL	5
Jacksonville, TX	**52**
Cherokee County, TX	52
Jamestown, ND	**21**
Stutsman County, ND	21
Jamestown-Dunkirk-Fredonia, NY	**130**
Chautauqua County, NY	130
Jasper, IN	**55**
Dubois County, IN	43
Pike County, IN	12
Jefferson, GA	**65**
Jackson County, GA	65
Jennings, LA	**31**
Jefferson Davis Parish, LA	31
Jesup, GA	**30**
Wayne County, GA	30
Junction City, KS	**36**
Geary County, KS	36
Juneau, AK	**32**
Juneau City and Borough, AK	32
Kalispell, MT	**98**
Flathead County, MT	98
Kapaa, HI	**72**
Kauai County, HI	72
Kearney, NE	**56**
Buffalo County, NE	49
Kearney County, NE	7
Keene, NH	**76**
Cheshire County, NH	76
Kendallville, IN	**48**
Noble County, IN	48
Kennett, MO	**31**
Dunklin County, MO	31
Kerrville, TX	**52**
Kerr County, TX	52
Ketchikan, AK	**14**
Ketchikan Gateway Borough, AK	14
Key West, FL	**79**

Micropolitan Statistical Area ~~Component county	Population, 2016 (1,000)
Monroe County, FL	79
Kill Devil Hills, NC	**40**
Dare County, NC	36
Tyrrell County, NC	4
Kingsville, TX	**32**
Kenedy County, TX	(Z)
Kleberg County, TX	32
Kinston, NC	**57**
Lenoir County, NC	57
Kirksville, MO	**30**
Adair County, MO	25
Schuyler County, MO	4
Klamath Falls, OR	**66**
Klamath County, OR	66
Laconia, NH	**61**
Belknap County, NH	61
La Grande, OR	**26**
Union County, OR	26
LaGrange, GA	**70**
Troup County, GA	70
Lake City, FL	**69**
Columbia County, FL	69
Lamesa, TX	**13**
Dawson County, TX	13
Laramie, WY	**38**
Albany County, WY	38
Las Vegas, NM	**28**
San Miguel County, NM	28
Laurel, MS	**85**
Jasper County, MS	17
Jones County, MS	68
Laurinburg, NC	**35**
Scotland County, NC	35
Lawrenceburg, TN	**43**
Lawrence County, TN	43
Lebanon, MO	**35**
Laclede County, MO	35
Levelland, TX	**23**
Hockley County, TX	23
Lewisburg, PA	**46**
Union County, PA	46
Lewisburg, TN	**32**
Marshall County, TN	32
Lewistown, PA	**46**
Mifflin County, PA	46
Lexington, NE	**26**
Dawson County, NE	24
Gosper County, NE	2
Liberal, KS	**23**
Seward County, KS	23
Lincoln, IL	**30**
Logan County, IL	30
Lock Haven, PA	**39**
Clinton County, PA	39
Logan, WV	**34**
Logan County, WV	34
Logansport, IN	**38**
Cass County, IN	38
London, KY	**128**
Knox County, KY	32
Laurel County, KY	60
Whitley County, KY	36
Los Alamos, NM	**18**
Los Alamos County, NM	18
Ludington, MI	**29**
Mason County, MI	29
Lufkin, TX	**88**
Angelina County, TX	88
Lumberton, NC	**133**
Robeson County, NC	133
Macomb, IL	**31**
McDonough County, IL	31
Madison, IN	**32**
Jefferson County, IN	32
Madisonville, KY	**46**
Hopkins County, KY	46
Magnolia, AR	**24**
Columbia County, AR	24
Malone, NY	**50**
Franklin County, NY	50
Malvern, AR	**33**
Hot Spring County, AR	33

Micropolitan Statistical Area ~~Component county	Population, 2016 (1,000)
Manitowoc, WI	**80**
Manitowoc County, WI	80
Marietta, OH	**61**
Washington County, OH	61
Marinette, WI-MI	**64**
Menominee County, MI	23
Marinette County, WI	40
Marion, IN	**67**
Grant County, IN	67
Marion, NC	**45**
McDowell County, NC	45
Marion, OH	**65**
Marion County, OH	65
Marquette, MI	**66**
Marquette County, MI	66
Marshall, MN	**26**
Lyon County, MN	26
Marshall, MO	**23**
Saline County, MO	23
Marshall, TX	**67**
Harrison County, TX	67
Marshalltown, IA	**40**
Marshall County, IA	40
Martin, TN	**34**
Weakley County, TN	34
Martinsville, VA	**65**
Henry County, VA	51
Martinsville city, VA	13
Maryville, MO	**23**
Nodaway County, MO	23
Mason City, IA	**51**
Cerro Gordo County, IA	43
Worth County, IA	8
Mayfield, KY	**37**
Graves County, KY	37
Maysville, KY	**17**
Mason County, KY	17
McAlester, OK	**44**
Pittsburg County, OK	44
McComb, MS	**52**
Amite County, MS	12
Pike County, MS	40
McMinnville, TN	**41**
Warren County, TN	41
McPherson, KS	**29**
McPherson County, KS	29
Meadville, PA	**86**
Crawford County, PA	86
Menomonie, WI	**45**
Dunn County, WI	45
Meridian, MS	**104**
Clarke County, MS	16
Kemper County, MS	10
Lauderdale County, MS	78
Merrill, WI	**28**
Lincoln County, WI	28
Mexico, MO	**26**
Audrain County, MO	26
Miami, OK	**32**
Ottawa County, OK	32
Middlesborough, KY	**27**
Bell County, KY	27
Milledgeville, GA	**54**
Baldwin County, GA	45
Hancock County, GA	9
Mineral Wells, TX	**28**
Palo Pinto County, TX	28
Minot, ND	**79**
McHenry County, ND	6
Renville County, ND	3
Ward County, ND	70
Mitchell, SD	**23**
Davison County, SD	20
Hanson County, SD	3
Moberly, MO	**25**
Randolph County, MO	25
Montrose, CO	**41**
Montrose County, CO	41
Morehead City, NC	**69**
Carteret County, NC	69
Morgan City, LA	**52**
St. Mary Parish, LA	52

See footnotes at end of table.

Table B. Micropolitan Statistical Areas and Components—Population: 2016-Continued.

See headnote on page 932.

Micropolitan Statistical Area ~~Component county	Population, 2016 (1,000)
Moscow, ID	**39**
Latah County, ID	39
Moses Lake, WA	**94**
Grant County, WA	94
Moultrie, GA	**46**
Colquitt County, GA	46
Mountain Home, AR	**41**
Baxter County, AR	41
Mountain Home, ID	**26**
Elmore County, ID	26
Mount Airy, NC	**72**
Surry County, NC	72
Mount Pleasant, MI	**71**
Isabella County, MI	71
Mount Pleasant, TX	**33**
Titus County, TX	33
Mount Sterling, KY	**47**
Bath County, KY	12
Menifee County, KY	6
Montgomery County, KY	28
Mount Vernon, IL	**38**
Jefferson County, IL	38
Mount Vernon, OH	**61**
Knox County, OH	61
Murray, KY	**38**
Calloway County, KY	38
Muscatine, IA	**43**
Muscatine County, IA	43
Muskogee, OK	**69**
Muskogee County, OK	69
Nacogdoches, TX	**66**
Nacogdoches County, TX	66
Natchez, MS-LA	**51**
Concordia Parish, LA	20
Adams County, MS	31
Natchitoches, LA	**39**
Natchitoches Parish, LA	39
Newberry, SC	**38**
Newberry County, SC	38
New Castle, IN	**49**
Henry County, IN	49
New Castle, PA	**87**
Lawrence County, PA	87
New Philadelphia-Dover, OH	**92**
Tuscarawas County, OH	92
Newport, OR	**48**
Lincoln County, OR	48
Newport, TN	**35**
Cocke County, TN	35
Newton, IA	**37**
Jasper County, IA	37
New Ulm, MN	**25**
Brown County, MN	25
Nogales, AZ	**46**
Santa Cruz County, AZ	46
Norfolk, NE	**48**
Madison County, NE	35
Pierce County, NE	7
Stanton County, NE	6
North Platte, NE	**37**
Lincoln County, NE	36
Logan County, NE	1
McPherson County, NE	(Z)
North Vernon, IN	**28**
Jennings County, IN	28
North Wilkesboro, NC	**69**
Wilkes County, NC	69
Norwalk, OH	**58**
Huron County, OH	58
Oak Harbor, WA	**83**
Island County, WA	83
Ogdensburg-Massena, NY	**110**
St. Lawrence County, NY	110
Oil City, PA	**53**
Venango County, PA	53
Okeechobee, FL	**40**
Okeechobee County, FL	40
Olean, NY	**78**
Cattaraugus County, NY	78
Oneonta, NY	**60**
Otsego County, NY	60
Ontario, OR-ID	**53**

Micropolitan Statistical Area ~~Component county	Population, 2016 (1,000)
Payette County, ID	23
Malheur County, OR	30
Opelousas, LA	**84**
St. Landry Parish, LA	84
Orangeburg, SC	**88**
Orangeburg County, SC	88
Oskaloosa, IA	**22**
Mahaska County, IA	22
Othello, WA	**19**
Adams County, WA	19
Ottawa, KS	**26**
Franklin County, KS	26
Ottawa-Peru, IL	**150**
Bureau County, IL	33
LaSalle County, IL	111
Putnam County, IL	6
Ottumwa, IA	**44**
Davis County, IA	9
Wapello County, IA	35
Owatonna, MN	**37**
Steele County, MN	37
Owosso, MI	**69**
Shiawassee County, MI	69
Oxford, MS	**54**
Lafayette County, MS	54
Oxford, NC	**59**
Granville County, NC	59
Ozark, AL	**49**
Dale County, AL	49
Paducah, KY-IL	**97**
Massac County, IL	15
Ballard County, KY	8
Livingston County, KY	9
McCracken County, KY	65
Pahrump, NV	**43**
Nye County, NV	43
Palatka, FL	**72**
Putnam County, FL	72
Palestine, TX	**58**
Anderson County, TX	58
Pampa, TX	**23**
Gray County, TX	23
Paragould, AR	**45**
Greene County, AR	45
Paris, TN	**32**
Henry County, TN	32
Paris, TX	**50**
Lamar County, TX	50
Parsons, KS	**20**
Labette County, KS	20
Payson, AZ	**54**
Gila County, AZ	54
Pecos, TX	**15**
Reeves County, TX	15
Pella, IA	**33**
Marion County, IA	33
Peru, IN	**36**
Miami County, IN	36
Picayune, MS	**55**
Pearl River County, MS	55
Pierre, SD	**22**
Hughes County, SD	18
Stanley County, SD	3
Sully County, SD	1
Pinehurst-Southern Pines, NC	**96**
Moore County, NC	96
Pittsburg, KS	**39**
Crawford County, KS	39
Plainview, TX	**34**
Hale County, TX	34
Platteville, WI	**52**
Grant County, WI	52
Plattsburgh, NY	**81**
Clinton County, NY	81
Plymouth, IN	**47**
Marshall County, IN	47
Point Pleasant, WV-OH	**57**
Gallia County, OH	30
Mason County, WV	27
Ponca City, OK	**45**
Kay County, OK	45

Micropolitan Statistical Area ~~Component county	Population, 2016 (1,000)
Pontiac, IL	**37**
Livingston County, IL	37
Poplar Bluff, MO	**43**
Butler County, MO	43
Portales, NM	**19**
Roosevelt County, NM	19
Port Angeles, WA	**75**
Clallam County, WA	75
Port Clinton, OH	**41**
Ottawa County, OH	41
Port Lavaca, TX	**22**
Calhoun County, TX	22
Portsmouth, OH	**76**
Scioto County, OH	76
Pottsville, PA	**144**
Schuylkill County, PA	144
Price, UT	**20**
Carbon County, UT	20
Prineville, OR	**23**
Crook County, OR	23
Pullman, WA	**49**
Whitman County, WA	49
Quincy, IL-MO	**77**
Adams County, IL	67
Lewis County, MO	10
Raymondville, TX	**22**
Willacy County, TX	22
Red Bluff, CA	**63**
Tehama County, CA	63
Red Wing, MN	**47**
Goodhue County, MN	47
Rexburg, ID	**52**
Fremont County, ID	13
Madison County, ID	39
Richmond, IN	**67**
Wayne County, IN	67
Richmond-Berea, KY	**106**
Madison County, KY	90
Rockcastle County, KY	17
Rio Grande City, TX	**64**
Starr County, TX	64
Riverton, WY	**40**
Fremont County, WY	40
Roanoke Rapids, NC	**72**
Halifax County, NC	52
Northampton County, NC	20
Rochelle, IL	**51**
Ogle County, IL	51
Rockingham, NC	**45**
Richmond County, NC	45
Rock Springs, WY	**44**
Sweetwater County, WY	44
Rolla, MO	**45**
Phelps County, MO	45
Roseburg, OR	**108**
Douglas County, OR	108
Roswell, NM	**65**
Chaves County, NM	65
Ruidoso, NM	**19**
Lincoln County, NM	19
Russellville, AR	**85**
Pope County, AR	64
Yell County, AR	22
Ruston, LA	**48**
Lincoln Parish, LA	48
Rutland, VT	**59**
Rutland County, VT	59
Safford, AZ	**38**
Graham County, AZ	38
St. Marys, GA	**53**
Camden County, GA	53
St. Marys, PA	**30**
Elk County, PA	30
Salem, OH	**104**
Columbiana County, OH	104
Salina, KS	**61**
Ottawa County, KS	6
Saline County, KS	55
Sandpoint, ID	**43**
Bonner County, ID	43
Sandusky, OH	**75**
Erie County, OH	75

Table B. Micropolitan Statistical Areas and Components—Population: 2016-Continued.

See headnote on page 932.

Micropolitan Statistical Area ~~Component county	Population, 2016 (1,000)
Sanford, NC	**60**
Lee County, NC	60
Sault Ste. Marie, MI	**38**
Chippewa County, MI	38
Sayre, PA	**61**
Bradford County, PA	61
Scottsbluff, NE	**38**
Banner County, NE	1
Scotts Bluff County, NE	36
Sioux County, NE	1
Scottsboro, AL	**52**
Jackson County, AL	52
Searcy, AR	**79**
White County, AR	79
Sedalia, MO	**42**
Pettis County, MO	42
Selinsgrove, PA	**40**
Snyder County, PA	40
Selma, AL	**40**
Dallas County, AL	40
Seneca, SC	**76**
Oconee County, SC	76
Seneca Falls, NY	**35**
Seneca County, NY	35
Sevierville, TN	**97**
Sevier County, TN	97
Seymour, IN	**44**
Jackson County, IN	44
Shawano, WI	**46**
Menominee County, WI	5
Shawano County, WI	41
Shawnee, OK	**72**
Pottawatomie County, OK	72
Shelby, NC	**97**
Cleveland County, NC	97
Shelbyville, TN	**47**
Bedford County, TN	47
Shelton, WA	**62**
Mason County, WA	62
Sheridan, WY	**30**
Sheridan County, WY	30
Show Low, AZ	**110**
Navajo County, AZ	110
Sidney, OH	**49**
Shelby County, OH	49
Sikeston, MO	**39**
Scott County, MO	39
Silver City, NM	**28**
Grant County, NM	28
Snyder, TX	**17**
Scurry County, TX	17
Somerset, KY	**64**
Pulaski County, KY	64
Somerset, PA	**75**
Somerset County, PA	75
Sonora, CA	**54**
Tuolumne County, CA	54
Spearfish, SD	**25**
Lawrence County, SD	25
Spencer, IA	**16**
Clay County, IA	16
Spirit Lake, IA	**17**
Dickinson County, IA	17
Starkville, MS	**50**
Oktibbeha County, MS	50
Statesboro, GA	**75**
Bulloch County, GA	75
Steamboat Springs, CO	**25**
Routt County, CO	25
Stephenville, TX	**42**
Erath County, TX	42
Sterling, CO	**22**
Logan County, CO	22
Sterling, IL	**57**
Whiteside County, IL	57
Stevens Point, WI	**70**
Portage County, WI	70
Stillwater, OK	**81**
Payne County, OK	81
Storm Lake, IA	**20**
Buena Vista County, IA	20
Sturgis, MI	**61**
St. Joseph County, MI	61

Micropolitan Statistical Area ~~Component county	Population, 2016 (1,000)
Sulphur Springs, TX	**36**
Hopkins County, TX	36
Summerville, GA	**25**
Chattooga County, GA	25
Summit Park, UT	**40**
Summit County, UT	40
Sunbury, PA	**93**
Northumberland County, PA	93
Susanville, CA	**31**
Lassen County, CA	31
Sweetwater, TX	**15**
Nolan County, TX	15
Tahlequah, OK	**49**
Cherokee County, OK	49
Talladega-Sylacauga, AL	**91**
Coosa County, AL	11
Talladega County, AL	80
Taos, NM	**33**
Taos County, NM	33
Taylorville, IL	**33**
Christian County, IL	33
The Dalles, OR	**26**
Wasco County, OR	26
Thomaston, GA	**26**
Upson County, GA	26
Thomasville, GA	**45**
Thomas County, GA	45
Tiffin, OH	**55**
Seneca County, OH	55
Tifton, GA	**41**
Tift County, GA	41
Toccoa, GA	**26**
Stephens County, GA	26
Torrington, CT	**183**
Litchfield County, CT	183
Traverse City, MI	**149**
Benzie County, MI	18
Grand Traverse County, MI	92
Kalkaska County, MI	17
Leelanau County, MI	22
Troy, AL	**33**
Pike County, AL	33
Truckee-Grass Valley, CA	**99**
Nevada County, CA	99
Tullahoma-Manchester, TN	**103**
Coffee County, TN	55
Franklin County, TN	42
Moore County, TN	6
Tupelo, MS	**140**
Itawamba County, MS	24
Lee County, MS	85
Pontotoc County, MS	32
Twin Falls, ID	**107**
Jerome County, ID	23
Twin Falls County, ID	84
Ukiah, CA	**88**
Mendocino County, CA	88
Union City, TN-KY	**37**
Fulton County, KY	6
Obion County, TN	31
Urbana, OH	**39**
Champaign County, OH	39
Uvalde, TX	**27**
Uvalde County, TX	27
Valley, AL	**34**
Chambers County, AL	34
Van Wert, OH	**28**
Van Wert County, OH	28
Vermillion, SD	**14**
Clay County, SD	14
Vernal, UT	**36**
Uintah County, UT	36
Vernon, TX	**13**
Wilbarger County, TX	13

Micropolitan Statistical Area ~~Component county	Population, 2016 (1,000)
Vicksburg, MS	**56**
Claiborne County, MS	9
Warren County, MS	47
Vidalia, GA	**36**
Montgomery County, GA	9
Toombs County, GA	27
Vincennes, IN	**38**
Knox County, IN	38
Vineyard Haven, MA	**17**
Dukes County, MA	17
Wabash, IN	**32**
Wabash County, IN	32
Wahpeton, ND-MN	**23**
Wilkin County, MN	6
Richland County, ND	16
Wapakoneta, OH	**46**
Auglaize County, OH	46
Warren, PA	**40**
Warren County, PA	40
Warrensburg, MO	**54**
Johnson County, MO	54
Warsaw, IN	**79**
Kosciusko County, IN	79
Washington, IN	**33**
Daviess County, IN	33
Washington, NC	**48**
Beaufort County, NC	48
Washington Court House, OH	**29**
Fayette County, OH	29
Watertown, SD	**28**
Codington County, SD	28
Watertown-Fort Atkinson, WI	**85**
Jefferson County, WI	85
Wauchula, FL	**27**
Hardee County, FL	27
Waycross, GA	**55**
Pierce County, GA	19
Ware County, GA	36
Weatherford, OK	**29**
Custer County, OK	29
West Plains, MO	**40**
Howell County, MO	40
West Point, MS	**20**
Clay County, MS	20
Whitewater-Elkhorn, WI	**103**
Walworth County, WI	103
Williston, ND	**34**
Williams County, ND	34
Willmar, MN	**42**
Kandiyohi County, MN	42
Wilmington, OH	**42**
Clinton County, OH	42
Wilson, NC	**82**
Wilson County, NC	82
Winnemucca, NV	**17**
Humboldt County, NV	17
Winona, MN	**51**
Winona County, MN	51
Wisconsin Rapids-Marshfield, WI	**73**
Wood County, WI	73
Woodward, OK	**21**
Woodward County, OK	21
Wooster, OH	**116**
Wayne County, OH	116
Worthington, MN	**22**
Nobles County, MN	22
Yankton, SD	**23**
Yankton County, SD	23
Zanesville, OH	**86**
Muskingum County, OH	86
Zapata, TX	**14**
Zapata County, TX	14

Z Represents less than 500.

Source: U.S. Census Bureau, 2016 Population Estimates, <https://www.census.gov/programs-surveys/metro-micro/data/tables.html>.

Introduction—The data presented in this *Statistical Abstract* come from not only federal statistical bureaus and other organizations that collect and issue statistics as their principal activity, but also governmental administrative and regulatory agencies, private research bodies, trade associations, insurance companies, health associations, private organizations, and philanthropic foundations. Consequently, the data vary considerably as to reference periods, definitions of terms and, for ongoing series, the number and frequency of time periods for which data are available.

The statistics presented were obtained and tabulated by various methods. Some statistics are based on complete enumerations or censuses while others are based on samples. Some information is extracted from records kept for administrative or regulatory purposes (school enrollment, hospital records, securities registration, financial accounts, social security records, income tax returns, etc.), while other information is obtained explicitly for statistical purposes through surveys.

Each set of data relates to a group of individuals or units of interest referred to as the *target universe,* or *target population*, or simply as the *universe* or *population*.

Prior to data collection, the target universe is clearly defined. For example, if data are to be collected for the universe of households in the United States, it is necessary to define a "household." The target universe may not be completely tractable. Cost and other considerations may restrict data collection to a *survey universe* based on an available list. This list is called a *survey frame, sampling frame, or survey sample.*

Tables may present data obtained for all population units, *a census*, or data obtained for only a portion, or *sample*, of the population units. When data are based on a sample, the sample is usually a scientifically selected *probability sample.* This is a sample selected from a list or sampling frame in such a way that every possible sample has a known chance of selection and usually each unit selected can be assigned a number, greater than zero and less than or equal to one, representing its likelihood or probability of selection.

For large-scale sample surveys, the probability sample of units is often selected as a multistage sample. The first stage of a multistage sample is the selection of a probability sample of large groups of population members, referred to as primary sampling units (PSUs). For example, in a national multistage household sample, PSUs are often counties or groups of counties. The second stage of a multistage sample is the selection, within each PSU selected at the first stage, of smaller groups of population units, referred to as secondary sampling units. In subsequent stages of selection, smaller and smaller nested groups are chosen until the ultimate sample of population units is obtained. To qualify a multistage sample as a probability sample, all stages of sampling must be carried out using probability sampling methods.

Prior to selection at each stage of a multistage (or a single stage) sample, a list of the sampling units or sampling frame for that stage must be obtained. For example, for the first stage of selection of a national household sample, a list of the counties and county groups that form the PSUs must be compiled. For the final stage of selection, lists of households, and sometimes persons within the households, have to be compiled in the field. For surveys of economic entities and for the economic censuses, the U.S. Census Bureau generally uses a frame constructed from the Bureau's Business Register. The Business Register contains all establishments with payroll in the United States, including small single-establishment firms as well as larger firms with multiple establishments.

Wherever the quantities in a table refer to an entire universe, but are constructed from data collected in a sample survey, the table quantities are referred to as *sample estimates.* In constructing a sample estimate, an attempt is made to come as close as is feasible to the corresponding universe quantity that would be obtained from a complete census of the universe. Estimates based on a sample will, however, generally differ from the hypothetical census figures. Two classifications of errors are associated with estimates based on sample surveys:

1 *Sampling error*—the error arising from the use of a sample, rather than a census, to estimate population quantities and

2 *Nonsampling error*—those errors arising from nonsampling sources. Nonsampling errors can include mistakes made in data collection or data processing, misunderstandings of the interviewer or the respondent, and data entry errors. As discussed below, the magnitude of the sampling error for an estimate can usually be estimated from the sample data. However, the magnitude of the nonsampling error for an estimate can rarely be estimated. Consequently, actual error in an estimate exceeds the error that can be estimated.

The particular sample used in a survey is only one of a large number of possible samples of the same size which could have been selected using the same sampling procedure. Estimates derived from the different samples would, in general, differ from each other. The *standard error* (SE) is a measure of the variation among the estimates derived from all possible samples. The standard error is the most commonly used measure of the sampling error of an estimate. Valid estimates of the standard errors of survey estimates can usually be calculated from the data collected in a probability sample. For convenience, the standard error is sometimes expressed as a percent of the estimate and is called the relative standard error or *coefficient of variation* (CV). For example, an estimate of 200 units with an estimated standard error of 10 units has an estimated CV of 5 percent.

A sample estimate and an estimate of its standard error or CV can be used to construct interval estimates that have a prescribed confidence that the interval includes the average of the estimates derived from all possible samples with a known probability. To illustrate, if all possible samples were selected under essentially the same general conditions, and using the same sample design, and if an estimate and its estimated standard error were calculated from each sample, then: 1) approximately 68 percent of the intervals from one standard error below the estimate to one standard error above the estimate would include the average estimate derived from all possible samples; 2) approximately 90 percent of the intervals from 1.6 standard errors below the estimate to 1.6 standard errors above the estimate would include the average estimate derived from all possible samples; and 3) approximately 95 percent of the intervals from two standard errors below the estimate to two standard errors above the estimate would include the average estimate derived from all possible samples.

Thus, for a particular sample, one can say with the appropriate level of confidence (e.g., 90 percent or 95 percent) that the average of all possible samples is included in the constructed interval. Example of a confidence interval: an estimate is 200 units with a standard error of 10 units. An approximately 90 percent confidence interval (plus or minus 1.6 standard errors) is from 184 to 216.

All surveys and censuses are subject to nonsampling errors. Nonsampling errors are of two kinds—*random* and *nonrandom*. Random nonsampling errors arise because of the varying interpretation of questions (by respondents or interviewers) and varying actions of coders, keyers, and other processors. Some randomness is also introduced when respondents must estimate. Nonrandom nonsampling errors result from total nonresponse (no usable data obtained for a sampled unit), partial or item nonresponse (only a portion of a response may be usable), inability or unwillingness on the part of respondents to provide correct information, difficulty interpreting questions, mistakes in recording or keying data, errors of collection or processing, and coverage problems (overcoverage and undercoverage of the target universe). Random nonresponse errors usually, but not always, result in an understatement of sampling errors and thus an overstatement of the precision of survey estimates. Estimating the magnitude of nonsampling errors would require special experiments or access to independent data and, consequently, the magnitudes are seldom available.

Nearly all types of nonsampling errors that affect surveys also occur in complete censuses. Since surveys can be conducted on a smaller scale than censuses, nonsampling errors can presumably be controlled more tightly. Relatively more funds and effort can perhaps be expended toward eliciting responses, detecting and correcting response error, and reducing processing errors. As a result, survey results can sometimes be more accurate than census results.

To compensate for suspected nonrandom errors, adjustments of the sample estimates are often made. For example, adjustments are frequently made for nonresponse, both total and partial. Adjustments made for either type of nonresponse are often referred to as *imputations*. Imputation for total nonresponse is usually made by substituting for the questionnaire responses of the nonrespondents the "average" questionnaire responses of the respondents. These imputations usually are made separately within various groups of sample members, formed by

attempting to place respondents and nonrespondents together that have "similar" design or ancillary characteristics. Imputation for item nonresponse is usually made by substituting for a missing item the response to that item of a respondent having characteristics that are "similar" to those of the nonrespondent.

For an estimate calculated from a sample survey, the *total error* in the estimate is composed of the sampling error, which can usually be estimated from the sample, and the nonsampling error, which usually cannot be estimated from the sample. The total error present in a population quantity obtained from a complete census is composed of only nonsampling errors. Ideally, estimates of the total error associated with data given in the *Statistical Abstract* tables should be given. However, due to the unavailability of estimates of nonsampling errors, only estimates of the levels of sampling errors, in terms of estimated standard errors or coefficients of variation, are available. To obtain estimates of the estimated standard errors from the sample of interest, see the source cited at the end of each table.

Source of Additional Material: The Federal Committee on Statistical Methodology (FCSM) is an interagency committee dedicated to improving the quality of federal statistics, online at <http://fcsm.sites.usa. gov>.

Principal data sources—Beginning below are brief descriptions of over 30 of the sample surveys and censuses that provide a substantial portion of the data contained in this *Abstract*.

U.S. DEPARTMENT OF AGRICULTURE, National Agricultural Statistics Service

Census of Agriculture

Universes, Frequency, and Types of Data: Complete count of U.S. farms and ranches conducted once every 5 years, with data at the national, state, and county level. Data cover number of farms and related items and characteristics for any place from which $1,000 or more of agricultural products were produced and sold, or normally would have been sold, during the census year.

Type of Data Collection Operation: Complete census for number of farms; land in farms; farm income; agriculture products sold; farms by type of organization; total cropland; irrigated land; farm operator characteristics; livestock and poultry inventory and sales; and selected crops harvested. Market value of land, buildings, and products sold, total farm production expenses, machinery and equipment, and fertilizer and chemicals.

Data Collection and Imputation Procedures: Data collection is by mailing questionnaires to all farmers and ranchers. Producers can return their forms by mail or online. Nonrespondents are contacted by telephone and correspondence follow-ups. Collection is supplemented by electronic data reporting on the internet, and personal enumeration for special classes of records in census operations. Imputations were made for all nonresponse items/characteristics and coverage adjustments were made to account for missed farms and ranches. The response rate for the 2012 Census was 80.1 percent.

Estimates of Sampling Error: Weight adjustments were made to account for the undercoverage and whole-unit nonresponse of farms on the Census Mail List (CML), and misclassification as to whether a farm or not a farm. These were treated as sampling errors.

Nonsampling Errors: Nonsampling errors are due to incompleteness of the census mailing list, duplications on the list, respondent reporting errors, errors in editing reported data, and in imputation for missing data. Evaluation studies are conducted to measure certain nonsampling errors such as list coverage and classification error. It is a reasonable assumption that the net effect of non-measurable errors is zero (the positive errors cancel the negative errors).

Sources of Additional Material: U.S. Department of Agriculture (NASS), 2012 Census of Agriculture, Appendix A Census of Agriculture Methodology, and Appendix B General Explanation and Census of Agriculture Report Form, at <http://www.agcensus.usda.gov/Publications/2012/>.

June Area Survey

Universe, Frequency, and Types of Data: The annual June Area survey utilizes an area sampling frame, and is designed to account for every acre of land, all agricultural activities, and land uses within segment boundaries. Data are collected annually from the 48 contiguous states and Hawaii on crop acreage, grain stocks, cattle inventory, hog inventory, sheep inventory, poultry inventory, land values, cash rents, farm numbers, and sales. The survey also serves to measure list incompleteness and is subsampled for multiple frame surveys.

Type of Data Collection Operation: Stratified probability sample of about 11,000 land area units of about 1 sq. mile (range from 0.1 sq. mile in cities to several sq. miles in open grazing areas). All farm operators within the boundaries of selected segments are interviewed. Sample represents 42,000 operating arrangements; over 35,000 interviews are conducted. Approximately 20 percent of the sample is replaced annually.

Data Collection and Imputation Procedures: Data collection for the June Area survey is completed entirely by personal interview during the 1st two weeks in June. Imputation is based on enumerator observation or data reported by respondents having similar agricultural characteristics.

Estimates of Sampling Error: Estimated CVs range from 1 to 2 percent for regional estimates and 3 to 6 percent for state estimates of major crop acres and livestock inventories.

Nonsampling Errors: These are minimized through rigid quality controls on the collection process and careful review of all reported data.

Sources of Additional Material: U.S. Department of Agriculture, National Agricultural Statistics Service, *Area Frame Design for Agricultural Surveys,* June 2009, <https://www.nass.usda.gov/Publications/Methodology_and_Data_Quality/index.php>, and <https://www.nass.usda.gov/Surveys/Guide_to_NASS_Surveys/June_Area/index.php>.

Objective Yield Surveys

Universe, Frequency, and Types of Data: Monthly forecasts and end-of-season estimates of planted and harvested acres, yield, and production of winter wheat, corn for grain, soybeans, fall potatoes, and upland cotton. All acres for harvest as grain in the leading producing states are eligible for this survey. Survey samples are selected from participants in the March Crops/Stocks Survey or the June Agricultural Survey, and include only the top producing states that together produce the majority of a given crop in the U.S.

Type of Data Collection Operation: Random location of plots in probability sample. Field work begins April 25 for winter wheat and July 25 for all the other crops. Sample units are visited at the end of each month during the growing season.

Data Collection and Imputation Procedures: Enumerators count and measure plant characteristics in sample fields. Production is measured from plots at harvest. Harvest loss is measured from post harvest gleanings.

Estimates of Sampling Error: CVs for national estimates of production are about 2 to 3 percent.

Nonsampling Errors: In addition to above, replicated sampling procedures are used to monitor effects of changes in survey procedures.

Sources of Additional Material: U.S. Department of Agriculture, National Agricultural Statistics Service, Statistical Methods Branch, *The Yield Forecasting Program of NASS,* May 2012, <https://www.nass.usda.gov/Publications/Methodology_and_Data_Quality/index.php>.

U.S. BUREAU OF JUSTICE STATISTICS (BJS)

National Crime Victimization Survey (NCVS)

Universe, Frequency, and Types of Data: Annual survey of U.S. household members age 12 and older to obtain data on criminal victimization for compilation of annual estimates; approximately 160,000 persons in 90,000 households are interviewed. The NCVS covers violent and property victimization, and the characteristics of crimes and victims. Violent crimes include rape or sexual assault, robbery, aggravated assault, and simple assault. Property crimes include household burglary, motor vehicle theft, and theft. The survey covers crimes that are both reported and not reported to the police. The Survey does not include homicide, arson, and commercial crimes.

Type of Data Collection Operation: The Census Bureau collects data for the Bureau of Justice Statistics. Persons interviewed are asked about the number and characteristics of victimization experiences during the prior 6 months.

Data Collection and Imputation Procedures: Eligible household members age 12 and older are interviewed every 6 months for a total of 7 interviews. Households stay in the sample for about 3 years. New households rotate into the sample on an ongoing basis. Personal interviews are used in the first interview; subsequent interviews are conducted either in person or by telephone. NCVS data include both person and household weights to provide estimates of the population and households represented by each person and each household in the sample. In 2015, 95,760 households and 163,880 persons age 12 or older were interviewed for the NCVS. The response rate was 82% for households and 86% for eligible persons.

Estimates of Sampling Error: Selected standard of errors for 2015 victimization rates per 1,000 persons age 12/older or 1,000 households are: 1.16 for all violent crime; 0.24 for rape/sexual assault; 0.29 for robbery; 1.00 for assault; 0.50 for domestic violence; 0.71 for all serious violent crime; 0.20 for nonfatal firearm violence; 2.65 for all property crimes; 1.03 for burglary; 0.40 for motor vehicle theft; and 2.27 for theft.

Nonsampling Errors: Respondent recall errors may include reporting incidents for other than the reference period; interviewer coding and processing errors; and possible mistaken reporting or classifying of events.

Sources of Additional Material: U.S. Bureau of Justice Statistics, *Criminal Victimization in the United States, 2015*, October 2016. <https://www.bjs.gov/content/pub/pdf/cv15.pdf>.

U.S. BUREAU OF LABOR STATISTICS

Consumer Expenditure Survey (CE)

Universe, Frequency and Types of Data: The Consumer Expenditure Survey (CE) is a nationwide household survey on family expenditures for goods and services. The CE also collects information on amount and sources of family income, changes in assets and liabilities, and demographic and economic characteristics of family members. The CE has two components: a quarterly interview survey, and a weekly diary survey. Estimates covering 12-month periods are released twice a year. Samples are national probability samples of households that are representative of the civilian noninstitutional population.

Type of Data Collection Operation: Both the Interview Survey and the Diary survey are conducted primarily by personal visit, with some telephone interviewing. The Interview Survey is a panel rotation survey. Each panel is interviewed for four quarters and then dropped from the survey. The measurement unit is the set of eligible individuals constituting a consumer unit (CU). The CU is defined as 1) all members in a housing unit who make up a family (includes foster children); 2) a person living alone or sharing a household with others, or living as a roomer in a private home or other lodging (includes hotel or motel), but who is financially independent; or 3) two or more unrelated persons living together who pool their income to make joint expenditure decisions. Students living in university-sponsored housing are also included in the sample as separate consumer units. The Census Bureau selects a sample of approximately 12,000 addresses per year to participate in the Diary Survey; approximately 6,900 households provide usable diaries (two 1-week diaries per household). For the Interview Survey, approximately 12,000 addresses are contacted each quarter. One-fourth of the addresses that are contacted each quarter are new to the survey. Approximately 6,900 households provide usable interviews.

Data Collection and Imputation Procedures: For the Interview Survey, data are collected by personal interview with each consumer unit interviewed once

per quarter. The Interview Survey is designed to collect information that respondents can recall for the past 3 months or longer regarding large or recurring expenditures. For the Diary Survey, respondents record all their expenditures in a self-reporting diary for two consecutive 1-week periods. The Diary Survey is designed to pick up small, frequently purchased items which can be difficult to recall over a long period of time. These items include food, beverages, and household and personal care products and services. Missing or invalid attributes, expenditures, or incomes are imputed. Assets and liabilities are not imputed. Beginning with 2014 data, the CES imputes federal and state income taxes. The U.S. Census Bureau collects the data for the Bureau of Labor Statistics.

Estimates of Sampling Error: Standard errors measure the uncertainty in the survey estimates caused by the fact that a random sample of consumer units from across the United States is used instead of every consumer unit in the nation. Beginning with the release of 2012 data, separate standard error tables are no longer issued; standard errors are included in the combined expenditure, share, and standard error tables.

Nonsampling Errors: Includes differences in the interpretation of questions, inability or unwillingness of respondents to provide correct information, and data processing errors. They occur regardless of whether data are collected from a sample or from the entire population.

Sources of Additional Material: Bureau of Labor Statistics, <http://www.bls.gov/cex>; and "BLS Handbook of Methods," <http://www.bls.gov/opub/hom/cex/home.htm>.

Consumer Price Index (CPI)

Universe, Frequency, and Types of Data: The Consumer Price Index (CPI) is a measure of the average change over time in the prices paid by urban consumers for a market basket of consumer goods and services. The CPI is derived from a monthly survey. The CPI reflects spending patterns of two population groups: all urban consumers (CPI-U), and urban wage earners and clerical workers (CPI-W). The all urban consumer group represents about 89 percent of the total U.S. population. The CPI-W population represents about 28 percent of the total U.S. population and is a subset of the CPI-U population. Not included in the CPI are the spending patterns of people living in rural non-metropolitan areas, farm families, Armed Forces personnel, and those in institutions, such as prisons and mental hospitals. The BLS calculates CPI indexes for the U.S., the 4 census regions, urban areas by population size, and selected metropolitan and local areas. The CPI covers over 200 item categories of consumer purchases.

Type of Data Collection Operation: BLS data collectors called economic assistants visit or call thousands of retail stores, service establishments, rental units, and doctors' offices, all over the United States, to obtain information on the prices of the thousands of items used for the CPI. Each month prices are collected in 87 urban areas from about 6,000 housing units and approximately 24,000 retail establishments.

Data Collection and Imputation Procedures: Each month the BLS collects prices for approximately 80,000 items. The BLS also collects rents from about 50,000 landlords or tenants; rent information is collected every 6 months. Prices of food, fuel, and a few other items are obtained monthly; prices of most other commodities and services are collected every month in the three largest geographic areas and every other month in others. The CPI uses imputation for missing information, which can be due to refusals of responses, inability to collect data for some other reason (the item may be out of season), and the inability to make a satisfactory estimate of the quality change. For noncomparable substitutions, an estimate of constant-quality price change is made by imputation.

Estimates of Sampling Error: The CPI is a statistical estimate that is subject to sampling error because it is based upon a sample of retail prices and not the complete universe of all prices. BLS calculates and publishes estimates of the 1-month, 2-month, 6-month, and 12-month percent change standard errors annually for the CPI-U. These standard error estimates can be used to construct confidence intervals for hypothesis testing. For the latest data, including information on how to use the estimates of standard error, see <www.bls.gov/cpi/cpivar2016.pdf>.

Nonsampling Errors: These errors occur from a variety of sources. Unlike sampling errors, they can cause persistent bias in measurements of the index. Nonsampling errors are caused by problems of price data collection, logistical lags in conducting surveys, difficulties in defining basic concepts and their operational implementation, and difficulties in handling the problems of quality change. Nonsampling errors can be far more hazardous to the accuracy of a price index than sampling errors. The BLS expends much effort to minimize these errors. Highly trained personnel ensure the comparability of quality of items from period to period; collection procedures are extensively documented, and recurring audits are conducted. The CPI program has an ongoing research and evaluation program in order to identify and implement improvements in the index.

Sources of Additional Material: U.S. Bureau of Labor Statistics, <http://www.bls.gov/cpi/cpi_methods. htm>; and "BLS Handbook of Methods," Chapter 17, <http://www.bls.gov/opub/hom/pdf/homch17. pdf>.

Current Employment Statistics (CES) Program

Universe, Frequency, and Types of Data: Monthly survey of approximately 147,000 businesses and government agencies representing approximately 634,000 worksites drawn from a sampling frame of Unemployment Insurance (UI) tax accounts covering roughly 9.7 million establishments. The active CES sample includes approximately one-third of all nonfarm payroll employees in the 50 states and the District of Columbia. A semiannual update is performed each summer to select units from the population of business openings and other units not previously eligible for selection. The CES collects data on employment, hours, and earnings at detailed industry levels. The CES series are estimates of nonfarm wage and salary jobs, not of employed persons; an individual with 2 jobs is counted twice by the payroll survey. The CES

excludes employees in agriculture and private households, and the self-employed.

Type of Data Collection Operation: The BLS uses various collection techniques. Data collection centers (DCCs) perform initial enrollment of each firm via telephone, collect the data for several months via Computer Assisted Telephone Interviewing (CATI), and, where possible, transfer respondents to a self-reporting mode such as touch-tone data entry (TDE), facsimile, or internet collection. Very large, multi-establishment firms are often enrolled via personal visit, and ongoing reporting is established via electronic data interchange (EDI). These firms provide electronic files to BLS that include data from all their worksites. All firms with 1,000 or more employees are asked to participate in the survey, as is a sample of firms across all employment sizes. When firms are rotated into the sample, they are retained for 2 years or more. When a respondent is rotated out of the sample, BLS will not ask the firm to participate for at least 3 years. Approximately 67 percent of the CES sample for the private industries overlaps from the previous sample to the current year sample.

Data Collection and Imputation Procedures: Each month, respondents extract the employment, hours, and earnings data from their payroll records and submit it to the BLS. Data are collected for the pay period that includes the 12th of each month. BLS staff prepare national estimates of employment, hours, and earnings. State agencies cooperate with the BLS to develop state and metropolitan area estimates.

Estimates of Sampling Errors: The magnitude of sampling error, or variance, is directly related to the size of the sample and the percentage of universe coverage achieved by the sample. The establishment survey sample covers over one-third of total universe employment; this yields a relatively small variance on the total nonfarm estimates. Information on measurements of error associated with sample estimates are available online under "CES Technical Notes" at <http://www.bls.gov/ces/home.htm>.

Nonsampling Errors: The benchmark error is used as a proxy measure of total error for the CES survey, and it represents the difference between two employment estimates derived from separate statistical processes (the CES sample process, and the Unemployment Insurance administrative process), and thus reflects the net of the errors present in each program. For total nonfarm employment over the past 10 years, absolute percentage benchmark error has averaged 0.3 percent, with an absolute range from less than 0.05 percent to 0.7 percent.

Sources of Additional Material: U.S. Bureau of Labor Statistics, "BLS Handbook of Methods," Chapter 2, <http://www.bls.gov/opub/hom/homch2.htm>; and Current Employment Statistics, "Technical Notes," <http://www.bls.gov/web/empsit/cestn. htm>.

National Compensation Survey (NCS)

Universe, Frequency, and Types of Data: The NCS is an establishment-based survey that provides comprehensive measures of 1) employer costs for employee compensation, 2) compensation trends, and 3) the incidence of employer-provided benefits among workers, with an emphasis on health insurance and retirement benefits. The NCS includes establishments in private industry and in state and local government; major exclusions are workers in federal and quasi-federal agencies, military personnel, agricultural workers, workers in private households, the self-employed, and unpaid workers. The NCS produces information on workers' earnings and benefits in a variety of occupations at different work levels. NCS is responsible for two quarterly releases: the Employment Cost Index (ECI), which measures percent changes in the cost of employment, and the Employer Costs for Employee Compensation (ECEC), which measures costs per hour worked for individual benefits. The survey provides data by industry, occupational group, labor union status, metropolitan area status, census region, and census division. ECEC also provides data by establishment-size class. Incidence and detailed provisions of employee benefit plans in private establishments are issued for broad occupational groups and selected industries, by selected employer and employee characteristics.

Type of Data Collection Operation: The sample of establishments is drawn by dividing the sample by industry and ownership. Number of establishments and occupations covered are reported monthly in NCS news releases. Each sample establishment is selected using a method of sampling called probability proportional to employment size. A probability sample of occupations within a sampled establishment is performed using a method called probability selection of occupations. The methodology and procedures used to estimate vary by product line. NCS replaces its sample on a continual basis. Private industry establishments are in the survey for approximately 5 years, with one fifth of the sample rotating out and replaced by a new panel each year.

Data Collection and Imputation Procedures: BLS field economists employ a variety of methods, including personal visits, mail, telephone, and email, to obtain data from NCS survey respondents. Quarterly updates are obtained via mail, facsimile, and telephone. Imputation is done for individual benefits. To address the problems of nonresponse and missing data, the NCS adjusts the weights of the remaining establishments and imputes missing values; missing values for an initially responding establishment are replaced by values from the original interview; missing values for an item are replaced by values derived from establishments with similar characteristics.

Estimates of Sampling Error: NCS uses standard errors to evaluate published series. These standard errors are available at <http://www.bls.gov/ncs/ect/ectvar.htm>.

Nonsampling Errors: Nonsampling errors have a number of potential sources. The primary sources are (1) survey nonresponse and (2) data collection and processing errors. Nonsampling errors are not measured. Quality assurance programs reduces the potential for nonsampling errors. These programs include the use of reinterviews, interview observations, validating data, and the systematic professional review of data. The programs also serve as a training device that provides feedback on errors for field economists (or data collectors). Quality assurance programs also provide

information on sources of error. This information is used to improve procedures that result in fewer errors.

Sources of Additional Material: Bureau of Labor Statistics, "BLS Handbook of Methods," Chapter 8, see <http://www.bls.gov/opub/hom//pdf/homch8.pdf>.

Producer Price Index (PPI)

Universe, Frequency, and Types of Data: Monthly survey of producing companies to determine price changes of all commodities and services produced in the United States for sale in commercial transactions. Price changes are from the perspective of the seller. Covers agriculture, forestry, fishing, manufacturing, mining, natural gas, electricity, construction, wholesale trade, retail trade, transportation, healthcare, and other services. Domestic production of goods for the military is included, as are goods shipped between establishments owned by the same company. The PPI covers over 70 percent of the service sector's output. The BLS releases each month about 10,000 PPIs for individual products and groups of products.

Type of Data Collection Operation: PPIs are based on selling prices reported by establishments of all sizes selected by probability sampling, with the probability of selection proportionate to employment size. Individual items and services from these firms are chosen by disaggregation, a process to select items based on their proportionate value to the manufacturer's overall revenue; further steps involve the item's characteristics. BLS periodically updates the PPI sample of survey respondents to reflect current conditions when the structure, membership, technology, or product mix of an industry shifts significantly, and to spread reporting burden among smaller firms. Results of these resampling efforts are incorporated into the PPI with the release of data for January and July. More than 100,000 price quotations per month are organized into three sets of PPIs: (1) Final demand-Intermediate demand (FD-ID) indexes, (2) commodity indexes, and (3) indexes for the net output of industries and their products. The FD-ID structure organizes products by class of buyer and degree of fabrication, as well as by stage of production. The commodity structure organizes products by similarity of end use or product type. The entire output of various industries is sampled to derive price indexes for the net output of industries and their products.

Data Collection and Imputation Procedures: Participation in the PPI program is voluntary. The BLS strongly encourages cooperating companies to supply actual transaction prices at the time of shipment to minimize the use of list prices. Prices submitted by survey respondents are effective on the Tuesday of the week containing the 13th day of the month. This survey is conducted via mail, facsimile, and the internet. Each month approximately 100,000 prices are solicited from roughly 25,000 reporters. Missing prices are estimated by those received for similar products or services. The current standard base period for most commodity-oriented PPI series is 1982, but many indexes that began after 1982 are based on the month of their introduction. The FD-ID indexes typically have a reference base of November 2009 =

100. All unadjusted PPIs are routinely subject to revision only once, 4 months after their original publication, to reflect late reports and corrections by company respondents. Once revised, indexes are considered final.

Estimates of Sampling Error: The Producer Price Index (PPI) program began publishing variance estimates in 2016 based on data for 2015. PPI intends to publish variance estimates on an annual basis. The median absolute value of the percent change is provided as the reference statistic and the corresponding median standard error is provided as the measure of variance. A report on variance estimates for PPI price changes is available online at <https://www.bls.gov/ppi/ppi_variance_methodology.htm>.

Nonsampling Errors: Nonsampling error occurs in many forms, but whatever the form, nonsampling error does not affect the spread of the sample estimates. Nonsampling error can, however, cause the estimate to be consistently higher (or lower) than the true population estimate. When this occurs, it is called the bias of a sample estimate. The PPI program, along with other programs at BLS, analyzes estimates for the presence of bias and mitigates nonsampling error by conducting dedicated research into the population of interest, by clearly documenting data collection procedures, and by performing quality checks throughout the collection process.

Sources of Additional Material: U.S. Bureau of Labor Statistics, PPI methodology, <http://www.bls.gov/ppi/methodology.htm>; <https://www.bls.gov/ppi/ppi_variance_methodology.htm>; and "BLS Handbook of Methods," Chapter 14, <http://stats.bls.gov/opub/hom/homch14.htm>.

BOARD OF GOVERNORS OF THE FEDERAL RESERVE SYSTEM

Survey of Consumer Finances

Universe, Frequency, and Types of Data: Triennial sample survey of families. At the time of compiling this *Statistical Abstract*, the 2013 Survey of Consumer Finances was the most recent survey conducted. In this survey a given household is divided into a primary economic unit (the family), and everyone else in the household. The primary economic unit is the economically dominant single person or couple (married or cohabiting) and all other persons in the household who are financially interdependent with the economically dominant person or couple. The primary economic unit is used as the reference family. The survey collects detailed data on the composition of family balance sheets, pensions, income, the terms of loans, and relationships with financial institutions. It also gathers information on the employment history and pension rights of the survey respondent and the spouse or partner of the respondent. Data include respondent demographic characteristics.

Type of Data Collection Operation: The survey employs a two-part strategy for sampling families. Some families are selected by standard multistage area probability sampling methods applied to all 50 states. The remaining families in the survey are selected using statistical records derived from tax returns, under the strict rules governing confidentiality and the rights of potential

respondents to refuse participation. The sample is designed to oversample wealthy households. For the 2013 Survey of Consumer Finances, 6,026 interviews were completed: 4,568 from the area probability sample, and 1,458 from the list sample. Response rates for the area-probability sample was about 70 percent and for the list sample about 33 percent.

Data Collection and Imputation Procedures: National Opinion Research Center (NORC) at the University of Chicago has collected data for the survey since 1992. The majority of interviews for SCF 2013 were conducted in person. Since 1995, interviews have been conducted via telephone if more convenient for respondents. Interviews were computer-assisted. Adjustments for nonresponse are made through multiple imputation of unanswered questions and through weighting adjustments based on data used in the sample design for families that refused participation.

Estimates of Sampling Error: The SCF attempts to reduce sampling error by designing the sample to reduce important sources of variability. Sampling error is estimated using replication methods. Replication methods draw samples, called replicates, from the set of actual respondents, and compute weights for all cases in each of the replicates.

Nonsampling Errors: Proper training and monitoring of interviewers, careful design of questionnaires, and systematic editing of the resulting data were used to control for nonsampling errors.

Sources of Additional Material: Board of Governors of the Federal Reserve System, "Changes in U.S. Family Finances from 2010 to 2013: Evidence from the Survey of Consumer Finances," *Federal Reserve Bulletin*, September 2014, <https://www.federalreserve.gov/econres/scf_2013.htm>.

U.S. CENSUS BUREAU

2012 Economic Census

Universe, Frequency, and Types of Data: Conducted every 5 years to obtain data on number of establishments, number of employees, payroll, total sales/receipts/revenue, and other industry-specific statistics. The universe is all establishments with paid employees excluding agriculture, forestry, fishing and hunting, and government. (Non-employer Statistics, discussed separately, covers establishments without paid employees.) For the 2012 Economic Census, 3.9 million businesses received economic census forms. See also <http://www.census.gov/econ/census/about/history.html>

The 2007 Economic Census used a cutoff of 5,000 or more population or jobs to identify the economic places valid for publication. The 2012 Economic Census reduced the cutoff to 2,500 resulting in nearly 5,000 new places to be published in the Census.

Type of Data Collection Operation: For most economic census sectors and programs, all large- and medium-size firms and all multi-establishment firms were sent report forms to be completed for each of their establishments. For most sectors and programs, report forms were also mailed to a sample of small employers (those with paid employees). This sample consists of single-establishment firms with payroll below a specified cut-off. The cut-off and sampling rate varies by economic census sector, industry, and geography. Data for firms with no paid employees were obtained from administrative records of other federal agencies.

Data Collection and Imputation Procedures: Mail questionnaires were used, with both mail and telephone follow-ups for nonrespondents. Businesses also had the option to respond electronically. Data for nonrespondents and for small employer firms not mailed a questionnaire were obtained from administrative records of other federal agencies, or imputed.

Estimates of Sampling Error: No measures of sampling variability are provided for sample-based estimates derived from the economic census, except for the construction sector. For additional information about sampling errors, see the methodology text for the sector of interest. Estimates of sampling error for construction industries are included with the data as published on the Census Bureau website.

Nonsampling Errors: Nonsampling errors may be attributed to an inability to identify all cases in the actual universe; definition and classification difficulties; differences in interpretation of questions; errors in recording or coding data; and other errors of collection, response, coverage, processing, and estimation for missing or misreported data.

Sources of Additional Material: U.S. Census Bureau, see <https://www.census.gov/EconomicCensus>.

American Community Survey (ACS)

Universe, Frequency, and Types of Data: Nationwide survey of approximately 3.54 million households in the U.S. and 36,000 households in Puerto Rico, per year, to obtain data about demographic, social, economic, and housing characteristics of housing units and the people residing in them. It covers the household population and, beginning in 2006, also includes the group quarter population living in correctional facilities, skilled-nursing homes, military barracks, college residence halls, and other group quarters. Sampling frames are drawn from the Census Bureau's Master Address File.

Type of Data Collection Operation: Housing unit address sampling is performed twice a year in both August and January. First-phase of sampling defines the universe for the second stage of sampling through two steps. First, all addresses that were eligible for the second-phase sampling within the past four years are excluded from eligibility. This ensures that no address is in sample more than once in any 5-year period. The second step is to select a 20 percent systematic sample of "new" units, i.e. those units that have never appeared on a previous Master Address File (MAF) extract. All new addresses are systematically assigned to either the current year or to one of four back-samples. This procedure maintains five equal partitions of the universe. The second-phase sampling is done on the current year's partition and results in approximately 3,540,000 housing unit addresses in the U.S. and 36,000 in Puerto Rico (PR).

Group quarter sampling is performed separately from the housing unit sampling. The sampling begins with separating the small (15 persons or fewer) and

the large (more than 15 persons) group quarters. The target sampling rate for both groups is a 2.5% sample of the group quarters population. It results in approximately 195,000 group quarter residents being selected.

Data Collection and Imputation Procedures: The American Community Survey is conducted every month on independent samples. The data collection operation for housing units (HUs) consists of four modes: internet, mail, telephone, and personal visit. For most housing units, the first phase includes a mailed request to respond by internet, followed later by an option to complete a paper questionnaire and return it by mail. If no response is received by mail or internet, the Census Bureau follows up with computer-assisted telephone interviewing (CATI) when a telephone number is available. If the Census Bureau is unable to reach an occupant using CATI, or if the household refuses to participate, the address may be selected for computer-assisted personal interviewing (CAPI). Mailable addresses with neither a response to the mail-out nor a telephone interview are sampled at a rate of 1 in 2, 2 in 5, or 1 in 3 based on the expected rate of completed interviews at the tract level. Unmailable addresses are sampled at a rate of 2 in 3. Those addresses selected through this process are assigned to Field Representatives (FRs), who visit the addresses, verify their existence, determine their occupancy status, and conduct interviews.

Collection of group quarters data is conducted primarily through FR interviews. Their methods include completing the questionnaire while speaking to the resident in person or over the telephone, or leaving paper questionnaires for residents to complete for themselves and then pick up later. This last option is used for data collection in federal prisons. If needed, a personal interview can be conducted with a proxy, such as a relative or guardian. After data collection is completed, any remaining incomplete or inconsistent information on the questionnaire are imputed during the final automated edit of the collected data.

Estimates of Sampling Error: The data in the ACS products are estimates and can vary from the actual values that would have been obtained by conducting a census of the entire population. The estimates from the chosen sample addresses can also vary from those that would have been obtained from a different set of addresses. This variation causes uncertainty, which can be measured using statistics such as standard errors, margins of error, and confidence intervals. All ACS estimates are accompanied by margins of errors to assist users.

Nonsampling Errors: Other types of errors may occur during any of the various complex operations used to select, collect and process survey data. An important goal of the ACS is to minimize the amount of nonsampling error introduced through coverage issues in the sample list, nonresponse from sample housing units, and transcribing or editing data. One way of accomplishing this is by finding additional sources of addresses, following up on nonrespondents, and maintaining quality control systems.

Sources of Additional Material: U.S. Census Bureau, American Community Survey, <http://www.census.gov/programs-surveys/acs/>; U.S. Census Bureau, American Community Survey Accuracy of the Data documents available on the internet, <http://www.census.gov/programs-surveys/acs/methodology.html>.

American Housing Survey

Universe, Frequency, and Types of Data: Conducted biennially in odd numbered years to obtain data on occupied or vacant housing units in the United States (group quarters are excluded). The AHS provides information on a wide range of "core" housing subjects, including size and composition of the nation's housing inventory, vacancies, fuel usage, physical condition of housing units, characteristics of occupants, equipment breakdowns, home improvements, mortgages and other housing costs, persons eligible for and beneficiaries of assisted housing, home values, and characteristics of recent movers. Beginning 2011, the AHS includes topical supplements. For the 2015 AHS, the Department of Housing and Urban Development (HUD) and the Census Bureau selected a integrated national sample that includes a representative sample of the nation, and oversamples of the top 15 metro areas and HUD-assisted housing units. The integrated national sample contained 85,393 units to interview; 3,382 were ineligible and about 12,500 did not yield an interview. The overall unweighted response rate was 85 percent; the weighted reponse was also 85 percent. The AHS sample was spread over 309 PSUs (including 85 largest core based statistical areas and 353 county and county equivalents), with a minimum of 7,500 population each.

Type of Data Collection Operation: Census Bureau interviewers visit or telephone the household occupying each housing unit in the sample. For unoccupied units, they obtain information from landlords, rental agents, or neighbors. The 2015 American Housing Survey underwent a major redesign – a new sample was redrawn, the questionnaire was redesigned, variables were dropped, added or modified, recodes and imputation methods were streamlined, and weighting methodology changed. Tables were redesigned and some estimates may not be comparable with previous years.

Data Collection and Imputation Procedures: Housing units participating in the AHS are scientifically selected to represent a cross section of all housing in the nation. The same basic sample of housing units is interviewed every two years until a new sample is selected. The U.S. Census Bureau updates the sample by adding newly constructed housing units and units discovered through coverage improvement efforts. Each housing unit in the AHS sample represents itself and between 450 to 4,000 other units. The mean value of the weights is 1,940. The median value of the weights is 1,309. The lower bound 5th percentile of weights is 464. The upper bound 95th percentile of weights is 3,982.

Estimates of Sampling Error: Error from sampling reflects how estimates from a sample vary from the actual value if all housing units had been interviewed under the same conditions. The AHS provides documentation for users to use to calculate sampling errors. See source Website under Technical Documentation, "Accuracy of the Data."

Nonsampling Errors: These may arise from a variety of factors, including errors in coverage, nonresponse, missing response, and inaccurate responses, and processing errors. The AHS takes numerous steps to minimize these types of errors.

Sources of Additional Material: U.S. Census Bureau, "American Housing Survey, Methodology and other Technical Documentation," <https://www.census.gov/programs-surveys/ahs/tech-documentation.html>.

Annual Survey of Public Employment and Payroll, and Census of Governments

Universe, Frequency, and Types of Data: The survey is conducted annually except in years ending in '2' and '7', when a census of all state and local governments is done. Covers civilian employees of all Federal Government agencies (except the Central Intelligence Agency, the National Security Agency, and the Defense Intelligence Agency), all agencies of the 50 state governments, and about 90,056 local governments (i.e., counties, municipalities, townships, special districts, and school districts) including the District of Columbia. The survey measures the number of state, local and federal civilian government employees and their gross payrolls for the pay period including March 12. The survey provides state and local government data on full-time and part-time employment, part-time hours worked, full-time equivalent employment, and payroll statistics by governmental function. The survey provides Federal Government data on total employees, full-time employees, and total March payroll by governmental function. The 2015 survey sample included 10,543 state and local governments. Overall response rate for the 2015 Census of Governments was 79.2 percent. All 50 state governments responded to the survey.

Type of Data Collection Operations: Census Bureau staff compiled Federal Government data from records of the U.S. Office of Personnel Management. For the 2015 survey, 45 of the state governments provided data from central payroll records for all or most of their agencies/institutions. Data for agencies and institutions for the remaining state governments were obtained by mail canvass questionnaires. Local governments were also canvassed using a mail questionnaire. However, elementary and secondary school system data in Delaware, Florida, and North Dakota were supplied by special arrangements with the state education agency in each of these states. All respondents receiving the mail questionnaire had the option of completing the survey online. The 2015 online survey instrument was completed by 27.6% of the state-level responding units and 83.3% of the local government respondents.

Editing and Imputation Procedures: Editing ensures survey data are accurate, complete, and consistent. Efforts are made at all phases of collection, processing, and tabulation to minimize errors. Although some edits are built into the internet data collection instrument and the data entry programs, the majority of edits are performed after the case has been loaded into the Census Bureau's database. Edits consist primarily of two types: consistency, and a ratio of the current years reported value to the prior year's value. The consistency edits check the logical relationships of reported data items. For example, if part-time employees and payroll are reported, then part-time hours must be reported. The current year/prior year edits compare data for the number of employees, the function reported for the employees, and the average salary between reporting years. If data fall outside of acceptable tolerance levels, the item is flagged for review. Some additional checks are made by comparing data from the Annual Finance Survey to data reported on the Annual Survey of Public Employment and Payroll to verify that employees reported on the Annual Survey of Public Employment and Payroll at a particular function have a corresponding expenditure on the Finance Survey. For both types of edits, the edit results are reviewed by analysts and adjusted when needed. When the analyst is unable to resolve or accept the edit failure, contact is made with the respondent to verify or correct data.

Imputation: For general purpose governments, school districts, and special districts, imputations were based on recent historical data from either a prior year annual survey or the most recent Census of Governments, as available. These data were adjusted by a growth rate that was determined by the growth of units that were similar (in size, geography, and type of government) to the nonrespondent. If no recent historical data were available, imputations were based on the data from a randomly selected donor that was similar to the nonrespondent.

Estimates of Sampling Error: The estimated coefficients of variation (CVs), which are provided for each estimate in data tables available online, are an estimate of this sampling variability. The CVs are expressed as percentages. The CV is the ratio of the standard error to the expectation of the estimate. State government employment and payroll data are not subject to sampling error. Consequently, state and local government aggregates for individual states are more reliable statistically than the local government only estimates.

Nonsampling Errors: Sample data are subject to nonsampling errors such as inability to obtain data for every variable from all units in the sample, inaccuracies in classification, response errors, misinterpretation of questions, mistakes in keying and coding, and coverage errors. These same errors may be evident in census collections and may affect the Census of Governments data used to adjust the sample during the estimation phase and used in the imputation process.

Sources of Additional Material: Census Bureau, Annual Survey of Public Employment and Payroll (ASPEP), <https://www.census.gov/programs-surveys/apes/technical-documentation.html>.

Annual Survey of State and Local Government Finances

Universe, Frequency, and Types of Data: In the years ending in "2" and "7," the Census Bureau conducts a census of the entire universe of all 50 state governments and 90,056 local governments (counties, municipalities, townships, special districts, and school districts). In intervening years, the Bureau conducts an annual survey of a sample of state and local governments. The survey collects data on government revenue (including taxes, charges, interest, and other earnings), expenditures by function and accounting category, debt, and financial assets by type.

Type of Data Collection Operations: Data for the annual survey were collected via mail canvass, internet, and central collection from State sources. Collection methods vary by state and type of government. Reviews of government accounting records provide data for most state government agencies and the 48 largest and most complex county and municipal governments. Data for local governments in about 28 states are consolidated and submitted by state agencies (central collections), usually as electronic transmissions or mutually developed questionnaires. Data for the balance of local governments in this annual survey were obtained via mail questionnaires sent to county, municipal, township, school district, and special district governments. In some cases, data could be obtained from state Comprehensive Annual Financial Reports.

Imputation Procedures: Imputations for nonresponding general purpose governments are based on recently reported historical data from either a prior year annual survey or the most recent census, adjusted by a growth rate. If no historical data are available, or the unit has not responded in over five years, data from a randomly selected similar unit are adjusted by the ratio of the populations of the non-responding and randomly selected donor governments. The imputations for non-responding special districts are done similarly. If prior year reported data are available, the prior year data for the non-respondent are adjusted by a growth rate that is determined from reporting units that are similar to the non-respondent. The overall unit response rate of the 2015 Annual Survey of Local Government Finances was 88.8 percent. The overall unit response rate of the 2015 Annual Survey of State Government Finances was 100.0 percent.

Estimates of Sampling Error: The local government statistics in the intercensal survey years are developed from a sample survey. Therefore, the local totals, as well as aggregates of state and local government data, are considered estimated amounts subject to sampling error. State government finance data are not subject to sampling. Consequently, state-local aggregates shown here have a relative standard error less than or equal to the local government estimates they include. Estimates of major United States totals for local governments are subject to a computed sampling variability of less than one-half of 1 percent. State and local government totals are generally subject to sampling variability of less than 3 percent. The coefficient of variations are available from the source tables, and can be used to derive the standard error of the estimates.

Nonsampling Errors: The estimates are subject to inaccuracies in classification, response, and processing. Efforts were made at all phases of collection, processing, and tabulation to minimize errors. Data are also subject to errors from imputations for missing data, errors from misreported data, errors from miscoding, and difficulties in identifying every unit that should be included in the report. Every effort was made to keep such errors to a minimum through examining, editing, and tabulating the data reported by government officials.

Annual Survey of Manufactures (ASM)

Universe, Frequency, and Types of Data: The Annual
Survey of Manufactures is a sample survey
conducted annually, except for years ending in '2'
and '7' when the survey is included in the Economic
Census, for all manufacturing establishments
having one or more paid employees. Survey
includes approximately 50,000 establishments
selected from a universe of approximately 297,000
manufacturing establishments within North
American Industry Classification System (NAICS)
codes 31-33 with records in the 2012 Economic
Census. The unit response rate for the 2014 ASM
was about 74 percent. The purpose of the ASM is to
provide key intercensal measures of manufacturing
activity, products, and location for the public and
private sectors. The ASM provides statistics on
employment, payroll, worker hours, payroll
supplements, cost of materials, value added by
manufacturing, capital expenditures, inventories,
and energy consumption. It also provides estimates
of value of shipments for 1,390 seven-digit NAICS
product classes.

Type of Data Collection Operation: The ASM is
conducted by mail with telephone and mail
follow-ups of nonrespondents. The ASM surveys
approximately 50,000 establishments; about
15,600 establishments are selected with certainty,
and the remaining establishments are selected with
probability proportional to a composite measure of
establishment size. The sample universe is updated
from two sources: Internal Revenue Service
administrative records are used to include new
single-establishment manufacturers, and the
Company Organization Survey identifies new
establishments of companies with multiple
establishments. The unit response rate for the 2014
ASM was about 74%; weighted item response rates
were over 70%.

Imputation Procedures: Imputation (for all
nonresponse items) is based on previous year
reports, or for new establishments in the survey, on
industry averages.

Estimates of Sampling Error: Statistics for the industry
groups and industries, and product shipments
include estimated relative standard errors. Relative
standard errors vary by industry and product
category.

Nonsampling Errors: Includes errors due to collection,
reporting, and transcription errors, many of which
are corrected through computer and clerical checks.

Sources of Additional Material: Census Bureau, Annual
Survey of Manufactures Methodology,
<http://www.census.gov/programs-surveys/asm/
technical-documentation/methodology.html>.

Census of Population and Housing

Universe, Frequency, and Types of Data: Complete
count of the U.S. population conducted every 10
years since 1790. Data obtained on number and
characteristics of people in the United States, U.S.
outlying territories, and Federally affiliated
Americans overseas.

Type of Data Collection Operation: In the 1990, 2000,
and 2010 censuses the 100 percent items included:
age, date of birth, sex, race, Hispanic origin, and
relationship to householder. In 1980,
approximately 19 percent of the housing units were
included in the sample; in 1990 and 2000,
approximately 17 percent.

Data Collection and Imputation Procedures: In 1980,
1990, 2000, and 2010 mail questionnaires were
used extensively with personal interviews in the
remainder. Extensive telephone and personal
follow-up for nonrespondents was done in the
censuses. Imputations were made by using
reported data for a person or housing unit with
similar characteristics.

Estimates of Sampling Error: Sampling errors for data
are estimated for all items collected by sample and
vary by characteristic and geographic area. The
coefficients of variation (CVs) for national and state
estimates are generally very small.

Nonsampling Errors: Since 1950, evaluation programs
have been conducted to provide information on the
magnitude of some sources of nonsampling errors
such as response bias and undercoverage in each
census. Results from the evaluation program for the
1990 census indicated that the estimated net
undercoverage amounted to about 1.61 percent of
the total resident population. Census 2000 had a
national overcount of 0.49 percent (0.20 percent
standard error) for the household population. For
the 2010 Census, the Census Coverage
Measurement Program found a net overcount of
0.01 percent (0.14 percent standard error) of the
resident population.

Sources of Additional Material: U.S. Census Bureau,
The Coverage of Population in the 1980 Census,
PHC80-E4; *Content Reinterview Study: Accuracy of
Data for Selected Population and Housing
Characteristics as Measured by Reinterview*,
PHC80-E2; *1980 Census of Population*, Vol. 1,
(PC80-1), Appendixes B, C, and D. *Content
Reinterview Survey: Accuracy of Data for Selected
Population and Housing Characteristics as
Measured by Reinterview*, 1990, CPH-E-1;
Effectiveness of Quality Assurance, CPH-E-2;
Programs to Improve Coverage in the 1990 Census,
1990, CPH-E-3. Documentation regarding the 2010
Census is available at <http://www.census.gov/
2010census/news/press-kits/ccm/ccm.html>.

County Business Patterns

Universe, Frequency, and Types of Data: County
Business Patterns is an annual series that contains
data on number of establishments, number of
employees, and first quarter and annual payrolls.
Data cover over 6 million single-unit establishments
and 1.8 million multi-unit establishments, and are
available by geographic area (state, county, and
metropolitan areas), 6-digit NAICS industry, legal
form of organization (U.S. and state only), and
employment size class. Most industries are covered;
excluded are crop and animal production; rail
transportation; National Postal Service; pension,
health, welfare, and vacation funds; trusts, estates,
and agency accounts; private households; and
public administration. CBP also excludes most
establishments reporting government employees.

Type of Data Collection Operation: Most basic data
items are extracted from the Census Bureau's
Business Register, a database of all known

employer companies. The annual Company Organization Survey provides individual establishment data for multilocation companies. Data for single establishment companies are obtained from various Census Bureau programs, such as the Economic Census, Annual Survey of Manufactures, and Current Business Surveys, as well as from administrative records of the Internal Revenue Service, the Social Security Administration, and the Bureau of Labor Statistics.

Estimates of Sampling Error: Payroll and employment data are not subject to sampling error.

Nonsampling Errors: The data are subject to nonsampling errors, such as inability to identify all cases in the universe; definition and classification difficulties; differences in interpretation of questions; errors in recording or coding the data obtained; and estimation of employers who reported too late to be included in the tabulations and for records with missing or misreported data. Employment data are missing from approximately 12 percent of incoming administrative payroll records. For these records, employment is imputed as the average employment of the two adjacent quarters, using average wage data for the prior year, or, based on average wage for the industry and geographic area. Payroll data is imputed for less than 1 percent of all incoming administrative records. Other missing data are also imputed through various methods.

Sources of Additional Material: U. S. Census Bureau, County Business Patterns, <http://www.census.gov/programs-surveys/cbp/about.html> and <http://www.census.gov/programs-surveys/cbp/technical-documentation/methodology.html>.

Current Population Survey (CPS)

Universe, Frequency, and Types of Data: Nationwide monthly sample designed primarily to produce national and state estimates of labor force and other characteristics of the civilian noninstitutionalized population 16 years of age and older, including sex, age, race, marital status, educational attainment, and family structure. In addition to the monthly survey, each March the CPS produces the Annual Social and Economic (ASEC) Supplement, which contains the basic monthly demographic and labor force data covered by the CPS, plus additional data on work experience, income, health insurance coverage, poverty, receipt of noncash benefits, and migration.

Type of Data Collection Operation: Multistage probability sample that currently includes 60,000 households from 824 sample areas. Sample size increased in some states to improve data reliability for those areas on an annual average basis. A continual sample rotation system is used. Households are in sample 4 months, out for 8 months, and in for 4 more. The CPS questionnaire is a completely computerized document that is administered by Census Bureau field representatives across the country through both personal and telephone interviews. One person, usually the person who owns or rents the housing unit, generally responds for all eligible members in a household regarding activities during the prior week (the week including the 12th of the month).

Data Collection and Imputation Procedures: For the 1st and 5th months that a household is in sample, personal interviews; other months, approximately

85 percent of the data collected by phone. The CPS makes imputations for missing and inconsistent data items. The CPS uses 3 imputation methods for item nonresponse: relational imputation, which infers the missing value from other characteristics on the person's record or within the household; longitudinal edits for most of the labor force edits, as appropriate; and "hot deck" allocation, a method of assigning a missing value from a record with similar characteristics, which is the hot deck. Hot decks are defined by variables such as age, race, and sex.

Estimates of Sampling Error: Sufficient sample is allocated to maintain, at most, a 1.9 percent coefficient of variation on national monthly estimates of unemployment, assuming a 6 percent unemployment rate. This translates into a change of 0.2 percentage point in the unemployment rate being significant at a 90 percent confidence level. For each of the 50 States and for the District of Columbia, the design maintains a coefficient of variation of at most 8 percent on the annual average estimate of unemployment, assuming a 6 percent unemployment rate.

Nonsampling Errors: Estimates of response bias on unemployment are available. Estimates of unemployment rate from reinterviews range from -2.4 percent to 1.0 percent of the basic CPS unemployment rate (over a 30-month span from January 2004 through June 2006). Eligible CPS households are approximately 82 percent of the assigned households, with a corresponding response rate of 92 percent.

Sources of Additional Material: U.S. Census Bureau and Bureau of Labor Statistics, *Current Population Survey: Design and Methodology*, (Technical Paper 66), <http://www.census.gov/prod/2006pubs/tp-66.pdf> and the Bureau of Labor Statistics, <http://www.bls.gov/cps/>; "BLS Handbook of Methods," Chapter 1, <http://www.bls.gov/opub/hom/homch1_a.htm>; and <http://www.census.gov/programs-surveys/cps/technical-documentation.html>.

Foreign Trade—Export Statistics

Universe, Frequency, and Types of Data: Export statistics cover goods valued at more than $2,500 per commodity shipped by individuals and organizations (including exporters, freight forwarders, and carriers) from the U.S. to other countries. Data are compiled in terms of commodity classification, quantities, values, shipping weights, method of transportation (air or vessel), state of (movement) origin, customs district, customs port, country of destination, and whether contents are domestic goods or reexports. Data are continuously compiled and processed. Documents are collected as shipments depart, and processed on a flow basis. Reports summarize shipments made during calendar months, quarters, and years. Statistics are reported monthly approximately 35 days after the end of the reference month and on a year-to-date basis.

Type of Data Collection Operation: Statistics for exported goods transactions are compiled from three sources: Shipper's Export Declaration documents filed with Customs and Border Protection (CBP) and sent to the U.S. Census Bureau (3 percent of all transactions), comparable data in electronic form submitted directly by exporters and their agents (63 percent), and special computer tapes from Canada for U.S. exports to Canada (34 percent). Estimates are made for low-value exports by country of destination, and based on bilateral trade patterns. Statistics for U.S. exports to Canada are based on import documents filed with Canadian agencies and forwarded to the U.S. Census Bureau under a 1987 data exchange agreement. Under this agreement, each country eliminated most cross-border export documents; maintains detailed statistics on cross-border imports; exchanges monthly files of cross-border import statistics; and publishes exchanged statistics in place of previously compiled export statistics.

Estimates of Sampling Error: Not applicable.

Nonsampling Errors: The goods data are a complete enumeration of electronic export information (EEI) reported in the automated export system (AES) and are not subject to sampling errors, but they are subject to several types of nonsampling errors. Quality assurance procedures are performed at every stage of collection, processing and tabulation; however the data are still subject to several types of nonsampling errors. The most significant of these include reporting errors, undocumented shipments, timeliness, data capture errors, and errors in the estimation of low-valued transactions.

Sources of Additional Material: Foreign Trade Statistics Overview, <http://www.census.gov/foreign-trade/about/index.html>.

Foreign Trade—Import Statistics

Universe, Frequency, and Types of Data: The import statistics consist of goods valued at more than $2,000 per commodity shipped by individuals and organizations (including importers and customs brokers) into the U.S. from other countries. Data are compiled in terms of commodity classification, quantities, values, shipping weights, methods of transportation (air or vessel), duties collected, unit prices, and market share, country of origin, customs district, customs port, import charges and duties. Data are continuously compiled and processed. Documents are collected as shipments arrive and processed on a flow basis. Reports summarize shipments made during calendar months and years. Statistics are reported monthly approximately 35 days after the end of the reference month and on a year-to-date basis.

Type of Data Collection Operation: A full compilation (i.e., a census) is taken of import shipments, plus U.S. Census Bureau estimates of low-valued imports and BEA estimates of trade in services. Statistics for imported goods shipments are compiled from the records filed with Customs and Border Protection (CBP), usually within 10 days after the merchandise enters the United States. Estimates are made for low-value shipments by country of origin, based on previous bilateral trade patterns and periodically updated. Statistics for over 95 percent of all commodity transactions are compiled from records filed electronically with CBP and forwarded as computer tape files to the U.S. Census Bureau. Statistics for other transactions are compiled from hard-copy documents filed with CBP and forwarded on a flow basis for U.S. Census Bureau processing.

Estimates of Sampling Error: Not applicable.

Nonsampling Errors: The goods data are a complete enumeration of documents collected by the U.S. Customs and Border Protection and are not subject to sampling errors; but they are subject to several types of nonsampling errors. Quality assurance procedures are performed at every stage of collection, processing, and tabulation; however the data are still subject to several types of nonsampling errors. The most significant of these include reporting errors, undocumented shipments, timeliness, data capture errors, and errors in the estimation of low-valued transactions.

Sources of Additional Material: Foreign Trade Statistics Overview, <http://www.census.gov/foreign-trade/about/index.html>.

Monthly and Annual Retail Trade Survey

Universe, Frequency, and Types of Data: The size of the Monthly Retail Trade Survey (MRTS) sample is approximately 12,000 employer firms. Data cover sales at retail and food services stores, and inventories held by retail stores. Statistics are available at the national level only. The Annual Retail Trade Survey (ARTS) covers employer businesses in the retail trade sector and the accommodation and food services sector, and requests data on sales, inventories, purchases, operating expenses, and other financial items.

Type of Data Collection Operation: Probability sample of all firms from a list frame. The list frame is the Bureau's Business Register, which is updated quarterly for recent birth Employer Identification Numbers (EINs) issued by the Internal Revenue Service and assigned an industry classification by the Social Security Administration. The largest firms are included monthly; a sample of others is included every month also. New samples were introduced with the 2011 Annual Retail Trade Survey (ARTS) and the April 2013 Monthly Retail Trade Survey (MRTS). These samples are designed to produce estimates based on the 2007 North American Industry Classification System (NAICS). The information used to create these sampling units was extracted from data collected as part of the 2007 Economic Census and from establishment records contained in the Census Bureau's Business Register as updated to December 2010.

Data Collection and Imputation Procedures: Data are collected by mail questionnaire with telephone follow-ups and fascimile reminders for nonrespondents. Imputation is made for each nonresponse item and each item failing edit checks. For both unit and item nonresponse, a missing value is replaced by a predicted value obtained from an appropriate model for nonresponse. This imputation uses survey data and administrative data as input. In any given month, imputed data amount to about 30.3 percent of the total monthly retail and food services sales estimate and about 32.9 percent of the total retail end-of-month inventory estimate. For the annual survey, imputed data amount to about 7.1 percent of the total retail sales and food services estimate and about 8.5 percent of the total retail end-of-year inventory estimate.

Estimates of Sampling Error: Estimated CVs and standard errors are included in monthly reports available online at <http://www.census.gov/retail/index.html#mrts>.

Nonsampling Errors: Nonsampling errors are difficult to measure and can be attributed to many sources: the inclusion of erroneous units in the survey (overcoverage), the exclusion of eligible units from the survey (undercoverage), nonresponse, misreporting, mistakes in recording and coding responses, misinterpretation of questions, and other errors of collection, response, coverage, or processing. Although nonsampling errors are not measured directly, the Census Bureau employs quality control procedures throughout the process to minimize these types of errors.

Sources of Additional Material: Census Bureau, Monthly and Annual Retail Trade, <http://www.census.gov/retail/index.html> and <http://www.census.gov/retail/how_surveys_are_collected.html>.

Survey of Construction

Universe, Frequency, and Types of Data: The Survey of Construction provides current national and regional statistics on starts, completions, and characteristics of new, privately-owned single-family and multifamily housing units and on sales of new single-family houses. Data collected include start and completion dates, sales date, sales price (single-family houses only), and the physical characteristics of housing units. Survey data are available monthly and annually for housing starts since 1959, for new home sales since 1963, and for completions since 1968. Reported data are for building or sales activity taking place during the applicable reference period. Monthly data collection begins the first day after the reference month and continues through the 7th working day.

Type of Data Collection Operation: A multistage probability sample of approximately 900 permit-issuing jurisdictions in the U.S. was selected. Each month in each of these permit offices, field representatives list and select a sample of permits for which to collect data. To obtain data in areas where building permits are not required, a multistage probability sample of over 70 land areas (census tracts or subsections of census tracts) is selected. All roads in these areas are canvassed and data are collected on all new residential construction found. Sampled buildings are followed up until they are completed (and sold, if for sale), or abandoned. Permits for one-to-four-unit buildings are sampled at an overall rate of 1 in 50. All permits authorizing buildings with 5 or more housing units in the sampled permit offices are selected.

Data Collection and Imputation Procedures: Data are obtained by telephone and/or field visit. Nonresponse/undercoverage adjustment factors are used to account for late reported data. Each month, housing starts, completions, and sales estimates derived from this survey are adjusted by the total numbers of authorized housing units (obtained from the Building Permits Survey) to develop national and regional estimates. Estimates are adjusted to reflect variations by region and type of construction, and to account for late reports and houses started or sold before a permit has been issued. Reported data are seasonally adjusted.

Estimates of Sampling Error: Data are subject to sampling errors. Estimates of the standard errors have been computed from the sample data for selected statistics. They are presented in the source tables in the form of average relative standard errors (RSEs). The relative standard error equals the standard error divided by the estimated value to which it refers.

Nonsampling Errors: Nonsampling errors are attributed to definitional problems, differences in interpretation of questions, incorrect reporting, inability to obtain information about all cases in the sample, and processing errors. Although not measured directly, the Census Bureau employs quality control procedures to minimize nonsampling errors.

Sources of Additional Material: Census Bureau, Survey of Construction, <https://www.census.gov/econ/overview/co0400.html>.

Nonemployer Statistics

Universe, Frequency, and Types of Data: Nonemployer statistics are an annual tabulation of economic data by industry for active businesses without paid employees or payroll, that are subject to federal income taxes, and that have receipts of $1,000 or more ($1 or more for the construction sector). Excluded are corporations and partnerships with over $1 million in receipts (except for service-type industries, maximum is $2 million). Maximum receipts for sole proprietorships depends on industry classification. Data showing the number of firms and receipts by industry are available for the U.S., states, counties, and metropolitan areas. Most types of businesses covered by the Census Bureau's economic statistics programs are included in the nonemployer statistics. Tax-exempt and agricultural-production businesses are excluded from nonemployer statistics.

Type of Data Collection Operation: The universe of nonemployer firms is created annually as a byproduct of the Census Bureau's Business Register processing for employer establishments. If a business is active but without paid employees, then it becomes part of the potential nonemployer universe. Industry classification and receipts are available for each potential nonemployer business. These data are obtained primarily from the annual business income tax returns of the Internal Revenue Service (IRS). The potential nonemployer universe undergoes a series of complex processing, editing, and analytical review procedures at the Census Bureau to distinguish nonemployers from employers, and to correct and complete data items used in creating the data tables.

Estimates of Sampling Error: Data are tabulated from administrative records, and are not subject to sampling error.

Nonsampling Errors: The data are subject to nonsampling errors, such as inability to identify all cases that should be included, difficulties with definitions and classification, errors in recording or coding data, and other coverage and processing errors. The improper inclusion of possible employer establishments in the nonemployer universe is a primary source of nonsampling error. The Census Bureau takes several steps to identify and remove these establishments from the nonemployer universe.

Sources of Additional Material: U. S. Census Bureau, Nonemployer Statistics, <https://www.census.gov/programs-surveys/nonemployer-statistics/technical-documentation.html>.

Service Annual Survey

Universe, Frequency, and Types of Data: The U.S. Census Bureau conducts the Service Annual Survey (SAS) to provide nationwide estimates of revenues and expenses for selected service industries. Estimates are summarized by industry classification based on the 2007 North American Industry Classification System (NAICS). Selected service industries covered by the Service Annual Survey include all or part of the following NAICS sectors: Utilities (NAICS 22), Transportation and Warehousing (NAICS 48-49); Information (NAICS 51); Finance and Insurance (NAICS 52); Real Estate and Rental and Leasing (NAICS 53); Professional, Scientific, and Technical Services (NAICS 54); Administrative and Support and Waste Management and Remediation Services (NAICS 56); Educational Services (NAICS 61); Health Care and Social Assistance (NAICS 62); Arts, Entertainment, and Recreation (NAICS 71); and Other Services, except Public Administration (NAICS 81). Covers taxable firms and firms exempt from Federal income taxes. Questionnaires are mailed in January and request annual data for the prior year. Estimates are published approximately 12 months after the initial survey mailing.

Type of Data Collection Operation: The Service Annual Survey estimates are developed from a probability sample of approximately 72,000 employer firms, and administrative records for nonemployers. Service Annual Survey questionnaires are mailed to a probability sample that is periodically reselected from a universe of firms located in the United States and having paid employees. The sample includes firms of all sizes and covers both taxable firms and firms exempt from federal income taxes. Updates to the sample are made on a quarterly basis to account for new and closed businesses. Firms without paid employees, or nonemployers, are included in the estimates through imputation and/or administrative records data provided by other federal agencies.

Estimates of Sampling Error: Estimates are based on a sample and subject to sampling error. The most recent Service Annual Survey results, including coefficients of variations (CVs), can be found on the internet at <http://www.census.gov/services/index.html>. Additional information regarding sampling error may also be found online at <http://www.census.gov/services/sas/sastechdoc.html>.

Nonsampling Errors: For both unit and item nonresponse, a missing value is replaced by a predicted value obtained from an appropriate model for nonresponse. The imputation uses survey data and administrative data as input.

Sources of Additional Material: U.S. Census Bureau, "Service Annual Survey," <http://www.census.gov/services/sas/about_the_surveys.html>.

Survey of Business Owners (SBO)

Universe, Frequency, and Types of Data: The Survey of Business Owners (SBO), conducted every 5 years since 1972 in the years ending in "2" and "7," provides statistics that describe the composition of U.S. businesses by owner characteristics. Data are presented for nonfarm businesses by sex, detailed ethnic and Hispanic group, and veteran status of the owner with 51 percent or more of stock or equity in the business. All U.S. firms with receipts of $1,000 or more, with and without paid employees, which are classified by the North American Industry Classification System (NAICS) codes 11 through 99, are represented, except for the following: NAICS 111, 112, 482, 491, 521, 525, 813, 814, and 92. The published data include the number of firms, sales and receipts, number of paid employees, and annual payroll. Data are presented by industry classifications, geographic area (states, metropolitan and micropolitan statistical areas, counties, and corporate municipalities [places] including cities, towns, townships, villages, and boroughs), and size of firm (employment and receipts). Please note that businesses can be tabulated in more than one racial group if the owners report more than one race; Hispanic owned firms may be of any race.

Type of Data Collection Operation: The Survey of Business Owners (SBO) sends letters to a random sample of businesses asking recipients to respond to the survey electronically. The list of all firms (or universe) was compiled from a combination of business tax returns and data collected on other economic census reports. The Survey of Business Owners (SBO) is conducted on a company or firm basis rather than an establishment basis. Several methodology changes were made for the 2012 SBO, in comparison to the previous 2007 SBO. The Census Bureau expanded the use of direct data substitution from existing sources, such as the American Community Survey and the decennial Census, to reduce the 2012 SBO sample size to 1.75 million firms from 2.3 million in 2007. The small sample size yielded sufficient quality, reduced overall respondent burden, and reduced costs associated with conducting a mail survey. Approximately half of the 2012 SBO sample was asked to respond to the survey electronically.

Data Collection and Imputation Procedures: The Census Bureau conducted follow-up mailings to nonrespondents, including sending letters to prompt electronic responses and paper forms. For the most recent SBO, responses came from approximately 66.2 percent of the 1.75 million businesses included in the SBO. For 2012 nonrespondents, 2007 data were substituted if available. For other nonrespondents, the Bureau used administrative data, and also imputed gender, ethnicity, race, and veteran status from donor respondents in the same sampling frame with similar characteristics. Imputed data account for approximately 24 percent of the firm count estimates by gender, ethnicity, race, and veteran status, and approximately 21 percent for the estimates of sales.

Estimates of Sampling Error: Sampling error is present in these estimates because they are based on the results of a sample survey and not on an enumeration of the entire universe. Since these estimates are based on a probability sample, it is possible to estimate the sampling variability of the survey estimates. The standard error (SE) provides a measure of the variation. The relative standard error (RSE) or coefficient of variation (CV) provides a measure of the magnitude of the variation relative to the estimate and is calculated as 100 multiplied by the ratio of the estimate to the SE. Relative standard errors for select data items are included in the data tables.

Nonsampling Errors: These stem from many sources: inability to obtain information for all cases in the universe, adjustments to the weights of respondents to compensate for nonrespondents, imputation for missing data, data errors and biases, mistakes in recording or keying data, errors in collection or processing, and coverage problems. Explicit measures of the effects of these nonsampling errors are not available. The Census Bureau detects and corrects most operational and data errors through an automated data edit designed to review the data for reasonableness and consistency. Quality control techniques were used to verify that operating procedures were carried out as specified.

Sources of Additional Materials: U.S. Census Bureau, Survey of Business Owners, <https://www.census.gov/programs-surveys/sbo/about.html>.

Annual Survey of Entrepreneurs

Universe, Frequency, and Types of Data: The Annual Survey of Entrepreneurs (ASE) includes all nonfarm businesses filing Internal Revenue Service tax forms as individual proprietorships, partnerships, or any type of corporation, with receipts of $1,000 or more. The ASE samples approximately 290,000 employer businesses in operation any time during the survey year. The ASE is conducted on a company or firm basis rather than an establishment basis. The survey is designed to sample the same in-scope businesses each survey year. Approximately 90 percent of the businesses selected for the 2014 ASE continued for the 2015 ASE. Businesses that closed or were otherwise out of scope are removed from the sample, and new businesses are added. The ASE collects statistics on the characteristics of businesses and their owners. Additionally, estimates are produced for employer businesses on the number of firms, sales and receipts, annual payroll, and employment. Data are presented by gender, ethnicity, race, and veteran status by 2-digit 2012 North American Industry Classification System (NAICS) code and other business characteristics. The survey covers 20 NAICS industries except for crop and animal production; rail transportation; postal service; monetary authorities-central bank; funds, trusts, and other financial vehicles; religious, grantmaking, civic, professional, and similar organizations; private households; and public administration. The survey will revise prior year estimates annually. The annual survey is a supplement to the Survey of Business Owners (SBO), which is conducted every 5 years.

Type of Data Collection Operation: The ASE collection is electronic only. Title 13 of the United States Code authorizes this survey and provides for mandatory responses. Those selected for the survey receive an initial letter informing the respondents of their requirement to complete the survey as well as instructions on accessing the survey. The ASE does not directly collect receipts, payroll, or employment; payroll and employment figures are derived from administrative sources.

Data Collection and Imputation Procedures: Approximately 66.9 percent of the 290,000 businesses in the ASE 2015 sample responded to the survey. For the 2015 ASE, 69.1 percent of businesses submitted an online questionnaire, but 6.9 percent of submissions did not contain enough information to be considered a response for the estimates by gender, ethnicity, race and veteran status. Of the 2015 ASE nonrespondents, approximately 41.5 percent responded to the 2012 SBO or 2014 ASE and had prior survey response data substituted for missing 2015 ASE responses. The remaining nonrespondents' information was imputed from donor respondents in the same sampling frame with similar characteristics (industry, legal form of organization, geography). Imputed data accounted for approximately 23.9 percent of the firm count estimates by gender, ethnicity, race, and veteran status and approximately 25.2 percent of the estimates of sales. For the 2014 ASE, approximately 74.0 percent of the 290,000 businesses responded to the survey; of the nonrespondents, about 8.2 percent responded to the 2012 SBO and had 2012 SBO data substituted for missing 2014 ASE responses. See source for detailed 2014 methodology.

Estimates of Sampling Error: The sample used for this survey is one of many possible samples of the same size that could have been selected using the same sample design. Estimates derived from the different samples would differ from each other. The relative standard error and standard error are measures of the variability among the estimates from all possible samples. The estimated relative standard errors and estimated standard errors are included in the data tables; they estimate the sampling variability, and thus measure the precision with which an estimate from the particular sample selected for this survey approximates the average result of all possible samples. Relative standard errors and standard errors are applicable only to those published cells in which sample cases are tabulated. A relative standard error is an expression of the standard error as a percent of the quantity being estimated.

Nonsampling Errors: Nonsampling errors are attributable from various sources, including the inability to obtain information for all cases in the universe, imputation for missing data, data errors and biases, mistakes in recording or keying data, errors in collection or processing, and coverage problems. While explicit measures of the effects of these nonsampling errors are not available, adjustments are made to the published relative standard errors to account for errors associated with imputation of missing data. It is believed that most of the important operational and data errors were detected and corrected through an automated data edit designed to review the data for reasonableness and consistency. Quality control techniques were used to verify that operating procedures were carried out as specified.

Sources of Additional Materials: U.S. Census Bureau, Annual Survey of Entrepremeurs Methodology online at, <https://www.census.gov/programs-surveys/ase/technical-documentation/methodology.html>.

U.S. DEPARTMENT OF EDUCATION National Center for Education Statistics

Integrated Postsecondary Education Data Survey (IPEDS), Completions

Universe, Frequency, and Types of Data: The IPEDS collects institution-level data from postsecondary institutions across the U.S. on tuition and fees, number and types of degrees and certificates conferred, number of students applying and enrolled, number of employees, financial statistics, graduation rates, student financial aid, and academic libraries. The survey consists of 12 components which are administered across the fall, winter, and spring reporting seasons. Submission of data to IPEDS is mandatory for any institution that participates in or is an applicant for participation in any federal financial assistance program authorized by Title IV of the Higher Education Act of 1965. IPEDS response rates for each component are nearly 100 percent. Over 7,000 institutions participate in the annual survey.

Type of Data Collection Operation: The IPEDS collects data via the internet. As respondents enter data online, the data collection system automatically calculates totals, averages, and percentages, and compares the responses with the previous year's submission for the same institution to ensure the data are reasonable. The system also compares data with other related values to ensure consistency of reporting within each survey component and across the data collection program. If data are still missing, analysts conduct imputations to complete the database.

Imputation Procedures: Missing data are imputed by using data of similar institutions. With the exception of the Institutional Characteristics component, all items collected in each component were eligible for imputation. Within the Institutional Characteristics component, only cost of attendance and other institutional charges data were eligible for imputation. IPEDS applies a single imputation method for both unit and item nonresponse. The Nearest Neighbor procedure identifies data related to the key statistics of interest for each component (the distance measure), then uses those data to identify a responding institution similar to the nonresponding institution and uses the respondent's data as a substitute for the nonrespondent's missing items.

Estimates of Sampling Error: Not applicable.

Nonsampling Errors: Nonsampling errors may arise when respondents or interviewers interpret questions differently; when respondents must estimate values, or when coders, keyers, and other processors handle answers differently; when people who should be included in the universe are not; or when people fail to respond (completely or partially). Estimating the magnitude of nonsampling errors often would require special experiments or access to independent data, thus nonsampling errors are seldom measured. For universe surveys,

an adjustment made for either type of nonresponse, total or partial, is often referred to as an imputation, which is often a substitution of the "average" questionnaire response for the nonresponse. For universe surveys, imputations are usually made separately within various groups of sample members that have similar survey characteristics.

Sources of Additional Material: U.S. Department of Education, National Center for Education Statistics, IPEDS Technical/Methodological reports, <http://nces.ed.gov/pubsearch/getpubcats.asp?sid=010>.

National Household Education Surveys (NHES) Program

Universe, Frequency, and Types of Data: The National Household Education Surveys Program is a system of surveys of the noninstitutionalized civilian population of the United States. NHES surveys have been conducted various years 1991 to 2012 and have varying universes of interest depending on the particular survey. Some surveys are recurring, others are fielded as 1-time surveys. Specific topics covered by each survey are at the NHES website <http://nces.ed.gov/nhes>. A list of the surveys fielded as part of NHES, each universe, and the years they were fielded is provided below.

1 Adult Education—Interviews were conducted with a representative sample of civilian, noninstitutionalized persons aged 16 and older who were not enrolled in grade 12 or below (1991, 1995, 1999, 2001, 2003, 2005).

2 Before- and After-School Programs and Activities—Interviews were conducted with parents of a representative sample of students in grades K through 8 (1999, 2001, 2005).

3 Civic Involvement—Interviews were conducted with representative samples of parents, youth, and adults (1996, 1999).

4 Early Childhood Program Participation—Interviews were conducted with parents of a representative sample of children from birth through grade 3, with the specific age groups varying by survey year (1991, 1995, 1999, 2001, 2005, and 2012).

5 Household Library Use—Interviews were conducted with a representative sample of U.S. households (1996).

6 Parent and Family Involvement in Education—Interviews were conducted with parents of a representative sample of children age three through grade 12 or in grades K through 12 depending on the survey year (1996, 1999, 2003, 2007, and 2012). Separate questionnaires are administered for children enrolled in public and private schools, and for children who are home schooled.

7 School Readiness—Interviews were conducted with parents of a representative sample of 3-7 year-old children (1993 and 1999) and of 3-5 year old children, not yet in kindergarten (2007).

8 School Safety and Discipline—Interviews were conducted with a representative sample of students in grades 6-12, their parents, and the parents of a representative sample of students in grades 3-12 (1993).

Type of Data Collection Operation: Through 2007, the NHES used telephone interviews to collect data. In 2012, the NHES switched to a mail survey, and samples were developed using household address information for all 50 states and the District of Columbia. The NHES 2012 sample was selected using a 2-stage address-based sampling frame. Black and Hispanic American households were sampled at a higher rate than other households. Data were collected using printed questionnaires mailed to sampled respondents.

Data Collection and Imputation Procedures: For telephone surveys, telephone numbers are selected using random digit dialing (RDD) techniques. Approximately 45,000 to 64,000 households are contacted in order to identify persons eligible for the surveys. Data are collected using computer-assisted telephone interviewing (CATI) procedures. Missing data are imputed using hot-deck imputation procedures. For the 2012 NHES, 159,994 addresses were sampled, with 99,426 screenings completed, and 32,086 screened households with eligible children. NHES nonrespondents received shortened versions of the survey, as a follow-up strategy to increase participation. The 2012 NHES used 3 imputation methods for missing data items: unweighted sequential hot deck imputation, for the majority of the missing data; weighted random imputation, for a small number of variables; and manual imputation, in a very small number of cases for most variables. The 2012 Parent and Family Involvement in Education survey received 17,563 completed questionnaires; overall response rate was 57.6 percent.

Estimates of Sampling Error: Reports presenting NHES data include tables on standard errors.

Nonsampling Errors: For each NHES survey, efforts were made to prevent nonsampling errors and errors from bias from occurring and to compensate for them, where possible. For instance, during the survey design phase, cognitive interviews are conducted to assess respondents' knowledge of the survey topics, their comprehension of questions and terms, and the sensitivity of items. Data from the 2012 NHES went through a series of processing procedures; these procedures include data capture and imaging; the reformatting of keyed data; a preliminary interview status classification; and a series of computer edits; and other editing procedures.

Sources of Additional Material: Please see the NHES website at <http://nces.ed.gov/nhes>; technical notes in "Parent and Family Involvement in Education, from the National Household Education Surveys Program of 2012," NCES 2013-028.REV, May 2015, <http://nces.ed.gov/pubs2013/2013028rev.pdf>; and *National Household Education Surveys Program of 2012, Data File User's Manual,* May 2015, <https://nces.ed.gov/nhes/pdf/userman/NHES_2012_UsersManual.pdf>.

Schools and Staffing Survey (SASS)

Universe, Frequency and Types of Data: NCES designed the SASS survey system to emphasize teacher demand and shortage, teacher and administrator characteristics, school programs, and general conditions in schools. SASS also collects data on many other topics, including principals' and teachers' perceptions of school climate and problems in their schools; teacher compensation; district hiring practices; basic characteristics of the student population; and instructional time and teacher and school performance. The SASS has four core components: the School Questionnaire, the Teacher Questionnaire, the Principal Questionnaire, and the School District Questionnaire. The SASS was conducted seven times during 1987-2011. During various survey cycles, SASS included Bureau of Indian Education schools, libraries, and charter schools. Please note that after 2010-2011, the National Center for Education Statistics redesigned the SASS and renamed it the National Teacher and Principal Survey. The first National Teacher and Principal Survey was conducted in 2015-2016; coverage will be provided as available and applicable.

Type of Data Collection Operation and Imputation Procedures: The 2007-08 SASS consisted of 5 questionnaires: district, principal, school, teacher, and school library media center questionnaires. The 2007-08 SASS was a mail-based survey, with telephone and field follow-up. The U.S. Census Bureau performs the data collection and begins by sending advance letters to the sampled Local Education Agencies (LEAs) and schools in August and September of collection years. Beginning in October, questionnaires are delivered by U.S. Census Bureau field representatives. The sampling frame for the public school sample is the most recent Common Core of Data (CCD) school file. CCD is a universe file that includes all elementary and secondary schools in the United States. Schools operated by the Department of Defense or those that offered only kindergarten or pre-kindergarten or adult education were excluded from the SASS sample. The list frame used for the private school sample is the most recent Private School Universe Survey (PSS) list, updated with association lists. An area frame supplement is based on the canvassing of private schools within specific geographical areas. A separate universe of schools funded by the Bureau of Indian Education (BIE) is drawn from the Program Education Directory maintained by the BIE. To avoid duplicates in the BIE files, BIE schools in the CCD school file are treated as public schools. SASS used four methods to impute values for questionnaire items that respondents did not answer. These were: (1) using data from other items on the questionnaire; (2) extracting data from a related component of SASS; (3) extracting data from the sampling frame (CCD or PSS); and (4) extracting data from the record of a sampled case with similar characteristics (commonly known as the "hot deck" method for imputing item response).

Estimates of Sampling Error: Sample errors can be calculated using replicate weights and Balanced Repeated Replication complex survey design methodology. Errors depend on cell sizes and range from less than 1 percent to over 5 percent (for reasonable cell sizes).

Nonsampling Errors: Because of unit nonresponse, bias may exist in some sample cells. However, bias has been adjusted for in the weighting process. Analysis of bias has been studied and no significant bias has been detected.

Sources of Additional Material: Please see the SASS website at <http://nces.ed.gov/surveys/sass/>.

U.S. DEPARTMENT OF JUSTICE, FEDERAL BUREAU OF INVESTIGATION

Uniform Crime Reporting (UCR) Program

Universe, Frequency, and Types of Data: Monthly reports on the number of criminal offenses that become known to law enforcement agencies. In

2015, a total of 16,643 city, university and college, county, state, tribal, and federal law enforcement agencies contributed data to the FBI. In 2015, law enforcement agencies active in the UCR Program represented over 321 million U.S. inhabitants. The UCR Program collects information regarding the violent crimes of murder and nonnegligent manslaughter, rape, robbery, and aggravated assault as well as the property crimes of burglary, larceny-theft, motor vehicle theft, and arson. (Although the FBI classifies arson as a property crime, it does not estimate arson data because of variations in the level of participation by the reporting agencies. Consequently, arson is not included in the property crime estimate.) The program also collects arrest data for the offenses listed above plus 20 offenses that include all other crimes except traffic violations.

Type of Data Collection Operation: Crime statistics are based on reports of crime data submitted either directly to the FBI by contributing law enforcement agencies or through cooperating state UCR Programs. UCR program participation is voluntary. Beginning with the 2013 data collections, all data must be submitted electronically, and after July 2013, the UCR Program no longer accepted paper submissions or the electronic submission of documents (i.e., Portable Document Format files).

Data Collection and Imputation Procedures: States with UCR programs collect data directly from individual law enforcement agencies and forward reports, prepared in accordance with UCR standards, to the FBI. Accuracy and consistency edits are performed by the FBI.

Estimates of Sampling Error: Not applicable.

Nonsampling Errors: Due to computer problems, changes in records management systems, personnel shortages, or a number of other reasons, some agencies cannot provide data for publication.

Sources of Additional Material: U.S. Department of Justice, Federal Bureau of Investigation, <https://ucr.fbi.gov/crime-in-the-u.s/2015/crime-in-the-u.s.-2015>; and *Crime in the United States*, annual, *Hate Crime Statistics*, annual, and *Law Enforcement Officers Killed and Assaulted*, annual, <https://ucr.fbi.gov/ucr>.

U.S. INTERNAL REVENUE SERVICE, TAX STATISTICS

Corporation Income Tax Returns

Universe, Frequency, and Types of Data: Annual study of unaudited corporation income tax returns, Forms 1120, 1120-F, 1120-L, 1120-PC, 1120-REIT, 1120-RIC, and 1120S, filed by corporations or businesses legally defined as corporations. The IRS Statistics of Income (SOI) Division collects data on corporations by size, industry, total assets, business receipts, deductions, liabilities, net income, income tax liability, tax credits, and other financial data. SOI aggregates these data for C corporations and passthrough entities, such as S corporations. The target population consists of all returns of active corporations organized for profit that are required to file one of the 1120 forms that are part of the SOI study.

Type of Data Collection Operation: For the 2013 tax year, the target sample was approximately 118,000 corporate tax returns (including inactive and non-eligible corporations), allocated to sample classes which are based on type of return, and either size of total assets alone or both size of total assets and a measure of income. Sampling rates for sample classes varied from 0.25 percent to 100 percent. The total realized sample for 2013, including inactive and noneligible corporations, is 118,105 returns.

Data Collection and Imputation Procedures: Computer selection of sample of tax return records. Data are adjusted during editing for incorrect, missing, or inconsistent entries to ensure consistency with other entries on return and to comply with statistical definitions. If the missing data items are from the balance sheet, then imputation procedures are used. If data for a whole return are missing because the return is unavailable to SOI during the data capture process, imputation procedures are also used in certain cases. Beginning with the Tax Year 2012 sample, the criteria for imputing balance sheets for returns with incomplete balance sheets changed significantly. Now, only the largest returns with incomplete balance sheets are subject to a balance sheet imputation procedure. As a result, the number of returns with imputed balance sheets will be negligible, and the IRS's Statistics of Income (SOI) division will perform imputation on an ad hoc basis only

Estimates of Sampling Error: Statistics of Income reports do not directly present the standard error. Instead, the ratio of the standard error to the estimate itself is presented in percentage form. This ratio is called the coefficient of variation (CV). The user of SOI data may multiply an estimate by its CV to recreate the standard error and to construct confidence intervals. Estimated CVs for Tax Year 2013 are published in the Statistics of Income, *Corporation Complete Report*, for 2013 in "Section 3: Description of the Sample and Limitation of the Data."

Nonsampling Errors: These may include coverage errors, processing errors, and response errors.

Sources of Additional Material: U.S. Internal Revenue Service, Statistics of Income, *Corporation Income Tax Returns*, <http://www.irs.gov/uac/SOI-Tax-Stats-Corporation-Tax-Statistics>.

Individual Income Tax Returns

Universe, Frequency, and Types of Data: Annual study of unaudited individual income tax returns, Forms 1040, 1040A, and 1040EZ, filed by U.S. citizens and residents. Data provided on various financial characteristics by size of adjusted gross income, marital status, and by taxable and nontaxable returns.

Type of Data Collection Operation: Stratified probability sample of 343,748 returns for tax year 2014. The sample is classified into sample strata based on the larger of total income or total loss amounts, the size of business plus farm receipts, and other criteria such as the potential usefulness of the return for tax policy modeling. Sampling rates for sample strata varied from 0.10 percent to 100 percent.

Data Collection and Imputation Procedures: Computer selection of sample of tax return records. Data adjusted during editing for incorrect, missing, or inconsistent entries to ensure consistency with other entries on return.

Estimates of Sampling Error: Coefficients of variation are available from source tables. Briefly, estimated CVs for tax year 2014 are: adjusted gross income less deficit, 0.09 percent; salaries and wages, 0.16 percent; and total income before tax credits, 0.13 percent. (State data not subject to sampling error.)

Nonsampling Errors: Processing errors and errors arising from the use of tolerance checks for the data.

Sources of Additional Material: U.S. Internal Revenue Service, Statistics of Income, *Individual Income Tax Returns* (Publication 1304), annual, <http://www.irs.gov/uac/SOI-Tax-Stats-Individual-Income-Tax-Return-Form-1040-Statistics>.

Partnership Income Tax Returns

Universe, Frequency, and Types of Data: Annual study of unaudited income tax returns of active partnerships related to financial and tax-related activity during tax year 2014 and reported on Forms 1065 and 1065B to the IRS. Data are provided by industry, based on the NAICS industry coding used by IRS.

Type of Data Collection Operation: Tax Year 2014 statistics are estimates based on a stratified probability sample of 45,946 returns selected from a population of 3,857,208 partnerships. However, 574 returns were "out of scope," yielding a final sample of 45,372 returns and an estimated overall active population of 3,621,155 partnerships. Statistics of Income (SOI) stratified the population into classes based on industry, type of return, size of total assets, and size of certain receipt or income amounts from both ordinary business income (loss) and portfolio income (loss). From these classes, SOI selected returns at various probabilities (from 0.02 percent to 100 percent) and weighted them to represent the total population.

Data Collection and Imputation Procedures: The sample of tax return records are selected via computer after data are transcribed by IRS and placed on an administrative file. Data are manually adjusted during editing for incorrect, missing, or inconsistent entries to ensure consistency with other entries on return. Data not available due to regulations are handled with weighting adjustments.

Estimates of Sampling Error: Some of the estimated coefficients of variation (the estimated standard error of the total divided by the estimated total) for tax year 2014: number of partnerships, 0.62 percent; number of partners, 1.57 percent; total assets, 0.11 percent; total income, 0.18 percent; total deductions, 0.19 percent; and business receipts, 0.16 percent.

Nonsampling Errors: The potential exists for coverage error due to unavailable returns; processing errors; and taxpayer reporting errors.

Sources of Additional Material: U.S. Internal Revenue Service, Statistics of Income, *Partnership Returns, 2014,* Fall 2016, <https://www.irs.gov/statistics/soi-tax-stats-soi-bulletin-articles-index-by-topic>.

Sole Proprietorship Income Tax Returns

Universe, Frequency, and Types of Data: Annual study of unaudited income tax returns of nonfarm sole proprietorships, Form 1040 with business

schedules. Data provided on various financial characteristics by industry.

Type of Data Collection Operation: Stratified probability sample of 91,665 returns from sole proprietorships for tax year 2014. The sample is classified based on presence or absence of certain business schedules; the larger of total income or loss; size of business plus farm receipts, and other criteria such as the potential usefulness of the return for tax policy modeling. Sampling rates vary from 0.1 percent to 100 percent.

Data Collection and Imputation Procedures: Computer selection of sample of tax return records. Data adjusted during editing for incorrect, missing, or inconsistent entries to ensure consistency with other entries on return.

Estimates of Sampling Error: Coefficients of variation for tax year 2014 are available in source documentation. In brief, CVs for sole proprietorships, all nonfarm industries are: total business receipts, 0.55 percent; total business deductions, 0.62; depreciation, 1.50 percent; and net income, 0.72 percent.

Nonsampling Errors: Processing errors and errors arising from the use of tolerance checks for the data.

Sources of Additional Material: U.S. Internal Revenue Service, Statistics of Income, Nonfarm Sole Proprietorship Statistics, <https://www.irs.gov/statistics/soi-tax-stats-nonfarm-sole-proprietorship-statistics>.

U.S. NATIONAL CENTER FOR HEALTH STATISTICS (NCHS)

National Health Interview Survey (NHIS)

Universe, Frequency, and Types of Data: Since 1957, the NHIS has been a continuous data collection covering the civilian noninstitutional population to obtain information on demographic characteristics, conditions, injuries, impairments, use of health services, health behaviors, and other health topics. Excluded are persons in long-term care institutions, correctional facilities, and U.S. nationals living abroad; active-duty armed forces personnel are also excluded unless at least one other family member is a civilian eligible for the survey.

Type of Data Collection Operation: Trained interviewers from the U.S. Census Bureau visit each selected household and administer the NHIS in person. The current NHIS sample design oversamples black, Hispanic, and Asian Americans. The annual NHIS questionnaire (also called the Core) consists of four main components: Household Composition, Family Core, Sample Adult Core, and Sample Child Core. The Census Bureau collects data using a computer assisted personal interviewing mode. Follow-up interviews may be conducted via telephone. The normal annual sample size for the 2006 to 2015 sample design is about 35,000 households containing about 87,500 persons. The sample size has been augmented each year for 2011 to 2015 to increase the number of states for which reliable state-level estimates can be made. In 2015, the sample was augmented by 19%. The 2015 NHIS contains data for 41,493 households containing 103,789 persons in 42,288 families. The number of sample children is 12,291 and the number of sample adults is 33,672. The total household response rate was 70.1 percent.

Data Collection and Imputation Procedures: The computer assisted personal interviewing program incorporated range and consistency checks of the data. Some missing data items (e.g., race, ethnicity) are imputed using a hot deck imputation value. Sequential regression models are used to create multiple imputation files for family income. Unit nonresponse is compensated for by an adjustment to the survey weights. Since 2004, imputation has been performed for injury and poisoning episodes for which the respondent did not provide sufficient information to determine a month, day, and year of occurrence.

Estimates of Sampling Error: Because NHIS data are based on a sample of the population, they are subject to sampling error. Standard errors are reported to indicate the reliability of the estimates. Estimates and standard errors were calculated using SUDAAN software, which takes into account the complex sampling design of NHIS. The Taylor series linearization method was used for variance estimation in SUDAAN. Standard errors are shown in source tables.

Nonsampling Errors: Nonsampling errors such as response errors, defective sample frames, nonresponse, and undercoverage, are difficult quantities to measure, but every effort is made to minimize such errors at each step of the NHIS operation.

Sources of Additional Material: National Center for Health Statistics, National Health Interview Survey, <http://www.cdc.gov/nchs/nhis/about_nhis.htm>. See also <http://www.cdc.gov/nchs/nhis/methods.htm>, and <http://www.cdc.gov/nchs/nhis/data-questionnaires-documentation.htm>.

National Survey of Family Growth (NSFG)

Universe, Frequency, and Types of Data: The National Survey of Family Growth (NSFG) is designed to provide national-level data that supplement and complement National Vital Statistics System data on registered births in the United States, by collecting data on the factors affecting those rates, including sexual activity, marriage, divorce, cohabitation, contraceptive use, infertility, and use of reproductive medical care. The NSFG also collects data on sexual behavior and attraction, and sexual orientation. The NSFG began in 1973 as a periodic survey of women age 15-44 among the civilian noninstitutionalized population. In 2002, the NSFG included men age 15-44. Beginning with the 2006-2010 NSFG, the program switched from periodic surveys to continuous interviewing. The 2011-2013 NSFG conducted in-person interviews with 5,601 women and 4,815 men. The response rates were 72.8 percent for all respondents, 73.4 percent for women, and 72.1 percent for men. The 2013-2015 NSFG included 5,699 interviews with women and 4,506 interviews with men; response rates were 71.2 percent for women and 67.1 percent for men.

Type of Data Collection Operation: Survey participation is voluntary. Only one person is interviewed in a selected household. Signed consent is required for minors age 15-17. Data are collected using personal interviews conducted using computer-assisted personal interviewing (CAPI). Selected data items are also collected using

audio computer-assisted self-interviewing (ACASI). In ACASI, the respondent listens to the questions through headphones, reads them on the screen, or both, and enters the response directly into the computer. This method avoids asking the respondent to give his or her answers to the interviewer, and it has been found to yield more complete reporting of sensitive behaviors.

Imputation Procedures: Imputation is the process of assigning answers to cases with missing data. In the NSFG, item imputation is performed on approximately 600 "recoded variables," or "recodes," rather than all of the thousands of variables in the data set. The purposes of imputation are to make the data more complete, more consistent, easier to use, and to reduce bias caused by differential failure to respond. Imputation is done in two ways for the 2013-2015 NSFG, logical and regression imputation. Regression imputation uses a regression equation to estimate a value for a case with missing data. Regression imputation was used to assign most of the imputed values. Logical imputation uses a subject-matter expert to assign a value based on the value of other variables for the case with missing data. For nearly all the recoded variables for which imputation is done in the continuous NSFG, less than 2 percent of the cases received an imputed value.

Estimates of Sampling Error: Standard errors are generally released along with data in NCHS reports. The source website has numerous documents discussing the survey sample design, sample error estimation design, examples of variance estimation, and other methodological issues under "2013-2015 NSFG: Public Use Data Files, Codebooks, and Documentation." See also "Responsive Design, Weighting, and Variance Estimation in the 2006–2010 National Survey of Family Growth," *Vital and Health Statistics*, Series 2, No. 158, June 2013.

Nonsampling Errors: Detailed discussion of variance estimation is available in "Responsive Design, Weighting, and Variance Estimation in the 2006–2010 National Survey of Family Growth," *Vital and Health Statistics*, Series 2, No. 158, June 2013.

Sources of Additional Material: National Center for Health Statistics, National Survey of Family Growth, <http://www.cdc.gov/nchs/nsfg/about_nsfg.htm>. See also materials available online at <https://www.cdc.gov/nchs/nsfg/nsfg_questionnaires.htm>.

National Vital Statistics System

Universe, Frequency, and Types of Data: Annual data on births, deaths, marriages, divorces, and fetal deaths in the United States. Legal authority for the registration of these events resides individually with the 50 States, 2 cities (Washington, DC, and New York City), and 5 territories (Puerto Rico, the Virgin Islands, Guam, American Samoa, and the Commonwealth of the Northern Mariana Islands). These jurisdictions are responsible for maintaining registries of vital events and for issuing copies of birth, marriage, divorce, and death certificates.

Type of Data Collection Operation: Mortality data based on complete file of death records, except 1972, based on 50 percent sample. Natality statistics 1951-1971, based on 50 percent sample of birth certificates, except a 20 percent to 50 percent sample in 1967, received by NCHS.

Data Collection and Imputation Procedures: Reports based on records from registration offices of the jurisdictions listed above. Data pertaining to causes of death are classified and coded according to the International Classification of Diseases (ICD).

Estimates of Sampling Error: For recent years, there is no sampling for these files; the files are based on 100 percent of certificates registered.

Nonsampling Errors: Generally more than 99 percent of the births and deaths occurring in this country are registered.

Sources of Additional Material: U.S. National Center for Health Statistics, *Vital Statistics of the United States*, Vol. I and Vol. II, annual, and the *National Vital Statistics Reports*. See the NCHS website at <http://www.cdc.gov/nchs/nvss/index.htm>.

National Highway Traffic Safety Administration (NHTSA)

Fatality Analysis Reporting System (FARS)

Universe, Frequency, and Types of Data: FARS is a census of all fatal motor vehicle traffic crashes that occur throughout the United States, including the District of Columbia and Puerto Rico, on roadways customarily open to the public. The crash must be reported to the state/jurisdiction, and is classified as fatal if a directly related fatality occurs within thirty days of the crash.

Type of Data Collection Operation: One or more analysts, in each state, extract data from the official documents and enter the data into a standardized electronic database.

Data Collection and Imputation Procedures: Data are from various state documents, including police accident reports, death certificates, state vehicle registration files, coroner/medical examiner reports, vital statistics, and other records. Computerized edit checks monitor the accuracy and completeness of the data. The FARS incorporates a sophisticated mathematical multiple imputation procedure to develop a probability distribution of missing blood alcohol concentration (BAC) levels in the database for drivers, pedestrians, and cyclists.

Estimates of Sampling Error: Since this is census data, there are no sampling errors.

Nonsampling Errors: FARS represents a census of all police-reported crashes and captures all data reported at the state level. FARS data undergo a rigorous quality control process to prevent inaccurate reporting. However, these data are highly dependent on the accuracy of the police accident reports. Errors or omissions within police accident reports may not be detected.

Sources of Additional Material: Fatality Analysis Reporting System (FARS), <http://www.nhtsa.gov/FARS>.

Appendix IV
Weights and Measures

U.S. Customary/Metric Conversion Table
[Conversions provided in the table are approximate]

Symbol	When you know U.S. customary	Multiply by	To find metric	Symbol
in	inches	2.54	centimeters	cm
ft	feet	30.48	centimeters	cm
yd	yards	0.91	meters	m
mi	miles	1.61	kilometers	km
in^2	square inches	6.45	square centimeters	cm^2
ft^2	square feet	0.09	square centimeters	cm^2
yd^2	square yards	0.84	square meters	m^2
mi^2	square miles	2.59	square kilometers	km^2
	acre	0.41	hectare	ha
oz	ounces	28.35	grams	g
lb	pounds	0.45	kilograms	kg
oz (troy)	troy ounces	31.1	grams	g
	short tons (2,000 lb)	0.91	metric tons	t
	long tons (2,240 lb)	1.02	metric tons	t
fl oz	fluid ounces	29.57	mililiters	mL
c	cups	0.24	liters	L
pt	pints	0.47	liters	L
qt	quarts	0.95	liters	L
gal	gallons	3.79	liters	L
ft^3	cubic feet	0.03	cubic meters	m^3
yd^3	cubic yards	0.76	cubic meters	m^3
°F	degrees Fahrenheit (subtract 32)	0.55	degrees Celsius	°C

Symbol	When you know metric	Multiply by	To find U.S. customary	Symbol
cm	centimeters	0.39	inches	in
cm	centimeters	0.03	feet	ft
m	meters	1.09	yards	yd
km	kilometers	0.62	miles	mi
cm^2	square centimeters	0.16	square inches	in^2
cm^2	square centimeters	10.76	square feet	ft^2
m^2	square meters	1.2	square yards	yd^2
km^2	square kilometers	0.39	square miles	mi^2
ha	hectare	2.47	acre	
g	grams	0.04	ounces	oz
kg	kilograms	2.20	pounds	lb
g	grams	0.04	troy ounces	oz (troy)
t	metric tons	1.1	short tons (2,000 lb)	
t	metric tons	0.98	long tons (2,240 lb)	
mL	mililiters	0.03	fluid ounces	fl oz
L	liters	4.23	cups	c
L	liters	2.11	pints	pt
L	liters	1.06	quarts	qt
L	liters	0.26	gallons	gal
m^3	cubic meters	35.31	cubic feet	ft^3
m^3	cubic meters	1.31	cubic yards	yd^3
°C	degrees Celsius (after multiplying, add 32)	1.8	degrees Fahrenheit	°F

Source: National Institute of Standards and Technology (NIST), Weights and Measures Division. See <https://www.nist.gov/pml/weights-and-measures/metric-si/unit-conversion>

Index

A

Agricultural science, degrees, 319, 320, 321
Agriculture (See also Farms):
    Employees, 638
    Foreign trade, 763, 877, 878, 879, 880, 881, 882,
        883, 884, 885, 1319, 1323, 1326
    Government payments, 467, 500, 868, 869, 870
    Value added, 869
Agriculture, construction, and mining machinery
    manufacturing (see also Machine tools, and
    Machinery manufacturing), 655, 661, 1036
Agriculture, forestry, and fishing industry:
    Capital, 784, 807, 809
    Earnings, 664, 794, 795, 796, 797, 798, 799, 800,
        909
    Employees, 644, 782, 785, 794, 795, 796, 797,
        798, 799, 800, 909
    Establishments, 779, 781, 782, 784, 785, 801,
        909
    Finances, 768, 771, 1339
    Gross domestic product, 693, 911
    Occupational safety, 682, 684
    Profits, 818
    Sales, 768, 771, 776, 777, 779, 800
Aid to families with dependent children,
    (See Temporary Assistance for Needy Families.)
AIDS (Acquired Immuno-Deficiency Syndrome), 127,
    133, 197, 198, 199, 200
Air conditioning, homes with, 1014
Air Force, personnel, 530
Air pollution:
    Air pollution control equipment, 416
    Emissions, 408, 409, 410, 417, 418, 419, 1401
    Greenhouse gases, 411, 412
    Toxic chemicals, 417, 418, 419
Air transportation:
    Accidents and deaths, 1090, 1097, 1102
    Airfare costs, 1284
    Airports, 1094, 1095, 1099, 1101, 1287
    Carrier delays, cancellations, 1098
    Civil aviation, 1101
    Consumer complaints, 1100
    Cost indexes, 1092
    Employees, 1080, 1091, 1101
    Federal outlays, 500
    Finances, 1091
    Fleet size, 1086, 1101
    Freight, 1091, 1318
    Fuel consumption and costs, 958, 1093
    Jet transport aircraft, orders, 1053
    Price indexes, 751, 761
    Regional airlines, 1096
    Revenue, 1082
    Traffic carried, 1091, 1096, 1287
Air transportation industry:
    Capital, 807
    Earnings, 655, 1083
    Employees, 655, 1081, 1083, 1281
    Establishments, 1081, 1083
    Foreign trade, 1087
    Finances, 1091, 1092
    Gross domestic product, 693
    Productivity, 661
    Profits, 1091
    Revenues, 1091, 1281

Shipments, 1087, 1088
Aircraft manufacturing. (See Aerospace industry.)
Airline operations (see also Air transportation), 1091,
    1093, 1095, 1096, 1098
Airplanes, 1055
Airports or airfields, 1101
    Federal aid to state and local government, 467
    Serving regional airlines, 1096
    Traffic, 1094, 1099, 1287
Alaska Native. (See American Indian, Alaska Native
    population.)
Alcoholic beverages (see also individual types; and
    Beer, wine, and liquor stores):
    Alcoholism treatment, 213
    Consumer expenditures, 700, 709, 712, 713, 1078
    Consumption, 214, 215
    Foreign trade, 882
    Price indexes, 751, 760
    Sales, 1064, 1075, 1078
Alcohol-induced deaths, 125
Alcohol involvement in fatal crashes, 1124, 1127,
    1128, 1129
Alcoholism treatment, 213
Aleut population. (See American Indian, Alaska Native
    population.)
Algeria (See Foreign countries.)
Aliens, illegal, 362, 551, 552, 553, 554
Alimony, 514
Allergies, 203, 226
Almonds, 871, 892, 893, 896
Alternative medicine, 202
Alternative minimum tax, 510
Altitudes, geographical, 402
Aluminum:
    Consumption, 934
    Employment, 934
    Foreign trade, 764, 765, 934, 944
    Prices, 760, 764, 765
    Production, 932, 933, 934
    Recycling, 414, 415
    World production, 937, 1392
Alzheimer's disease, deaths, 122, 123, 124, 125,
    126, 127, 128
Ambulatory health care services industry:
    Capital, 807
    Earnings, 172, 655, 778
    Employees, 173, 655, 778
    Establishments, 778
    Gross domestic product, 693
    Sales, receipts, 778
American College Testing Program (ACT), 281
American Indian, Alaska Native population, 5, 7, 9,
    10, 11, 13, 20, 42, 43, 70
    Age and/or sex, 7, 9, 10, 11
    AIDS, 200
    Births, birth rates, 5, 83, 85, 86, 87, 88, 89, 95
    Business owners, 793, 800
    Children, 9, 10, 11, 596
    College enrollment, 292, 323
    Criminal victimizations, 338
    Deaths, death rates, 5, 114, 115, 116, 129, 132,
        133, 135, 338
    Degrees conferred, 318, 839
    Educational attainment, 35, 70
    Elderly, 9, 10, 11

Note: Index citations refer to **table** numbers, not **page** numbers

Food stamp participants, 591
Gaming revenue, 1277
Grandparents living with grandchildren, 67
Health and dental care visits, 184, 224
Heart disease, deaths, 129
HIV disease, 133
Housing tenure, 35, 70
Income, 35
Immunization of children, 232
Marital status, 70
Migration, 5
Occupation, 35
Physical activity, 221
Poverty, 35
Public assistance, 598
Reservations, 42
States, 20
Suicides, death, 123, 132, 535
Tribes, 43
Teachers, 271, 274
Veterans, 545
Weapons in school, 327
American Samoa. (See Island areas of the U.S.)
American Sign Language, 296
American Stock Exchange, 1227
Amusement and recreation services. (See Arts, recreation, and travel.)
Amusement, gambling, and recreation industry:
Capital, 807
Earnings, 655, 778, 1248
Employees, 655, 778, 1249
Establishments, 778, 1248, 1249
Gaming revenue, 1277
Gross domestic product, 693
Nonemployer establishments, 1248
Occupational safety, 682
Productivity, 661
Receipts, revenue, 778, 1248
Amusement parks, 993, 1246, 1248, 1249, 1262
Amphetamines, 355
Analgesics, 214
Ancestry, 52
Andorra. (See Foreign countries.)
Anemia, deaths, 125
Anesthesiologists, 175
Angola. (See Foreign countries.)
Animal oils and fats. (See Oils, animal.)
Animal slaughtering and processing industry, 655, 661
Animals, domestic (see also individual classes):
Livestock, 849, 897, 900
Pets, 655, 1259, 1301
Annuities. (See Pensions and retirement benefits.)
Antigua and Barbuda. (See Foreign countries.)
Antimony, 934
Apparel goods (see also Clothing and accessory stores):
Consumer expenditures, 700, 709, 712, 713
Foreign trade, 1323, 1326
Prices, 749, 750, 751, 760, 761
Sales, 1064, 1075
Apparel manufacturing:
Capital, 807
Earnings, 655, 1036, 1043
Employees, 655, 1034, 1036, 1038, 1043

Establishments, 1034, 1035
Finances, 819
Foreign trade, 1326
Gross domestic product, 693, 1032
Industrial production index, 814
Productivity, 661
Profits, 819
Shipments, 1036, 1045, 1046
Toxic chemical releases, 418
Appeals Courts, U.S., 369, 371
Apples, 237, 756, 871, 892, 896
Appliances, household:
Consumer expenditures, 712, 713
Homes with, 1014
Injuries associated, 208
Price indexes, 751, 760
Sales and shipments, 1075
Appliances (household) manufacturing:
Inventories, 1046
Shipments, 1046, 1060
Aquaculture, 871, 927
Archery, 1269
Architects, 319, 320, 321, 638
Architectural services. (See Engineering and architectural services.)
Area of:
Developed land, 403, 404
Foreign countries, 1353
Forest land, 403, 404, 405, 914
Horticultural crops, 898
Island areas of the U.S., 394
Lakes, 395, 396, 397
Parks, 1271, 1272, 1273, 1274
States, 394
Timberland, 914
United States, 1, 394, 1353
Water, 1, 394, 403, 404, 406
World, 1353
Argentina. (See Foreign countries.)
Arizona. (See State data.)
Arkansas. (See State data.)
Armed Forces, 528, 529, 530, 531, 532, 534, 1415
Armenia. (See Foreign countries.)
Army, personnel, 530
Arrests (See Law enforcement)
Arson, 357, 358, 392
Arthritis, 204
Artists, employed, 638
Arts and humanities:
Aid to, 1254
Appropriations by state, 1255
Attendance, 1253, 1257
Charitable contributions, 604
Federal aid, 1254
Participation, 1256
Philanthropy, 604
States, 1255
Arts, recreation, and travel:
Capital, 784, 807, 809
Earnings, 653, 655, 664, 778, 794, 795, 796, 797, 798, 799, 800, 1248
Electronic commerce, 1297
Employees, 644, 653, 655, 778, 782, 785, 794, 795, 796, 797, 798, 799, 800, 1247, 1249, 1251

Note: Index citations refer to **table** numbers, not **page** numbers

Note: Index citations refer to **table** numbers, not **page** numbers

Price indexes, 751, 760
Production, 1077
Racing, 1266
Sales, 1076, 1077
Automotive equipment rental and leasing, 655, 661, 1278
Automotive products. (See Motor vehicles, Tires and tubes, etc.)
Automotive repair and maintenance service:
Earnings, 655
Employees, 655, 1292, 1293
Establishments, 1292
Nonemployers, 1291
Receipts/revenue, 1291, 1301
Aviation. (See Air transportation.)
Avocados, 237, 892, 896
Azerbaijan. (See Foreign countries.)

B

Backpacking, 1269
Bacon, 756
Bahamas, The. (See Foreign countries.)
Bahrain. (See Foreign countries.)
Bakeries and tortilla manufacturing, 655, 661, 1036
Bakery products, 712, 713, 751, 760
Balance of payments, 1303, 1306, 1307, 1317, 1413
Balance sheet, 746, 772, 773, 775
Bananas, 237, 756
Bangladesh. (See Foreign countries.)
Bankruptcies, 369, 802, 803
Banks, commercial:
Consumer credit, 1212, 1213
Credit cards, 1203, 1211
Debit cards, 1210
Debit held by families, 1198
Delinquency rates, repossessions, loans, 1217
Deposits, 1203, 1204, 1205, 1206, 1207
Earnings, 655, 1189
Employees, 655, 1189
Establishments, 1189, 1201, 1203, 1206
Finances, 1191, 1192, 1201, 1202, 1203, 1204, 1205, 1206, 1207, 1215, 1218, 1230
Flow of funds, 1191, 1192, 1230
Foreign banking offices in United States, 1207
Gross domestic product, 1186
Household banking status, 1214
Individual Retirement Accounts (IRAs); 401(k) plans, 570, 575, 576, 577, 1234
Insured banks, 1201, 1202, 1203, 1204, 1205, 1206
Loans, 1203
Productivity, 661
Profits, 1202, 1204
Robbery, 347
State data, 1201, 1206
Stock and bond prices and yields, 1227
Barbados. (See Foreign countries.)
Barite, 933, 934, 937, 944
Bars. (See Food Services and drinking places.)
Baseball, 1265, 1266, 1267, 1268, 1269
Basketball, 1265, 1266, 1267, 1268, 1269
Bauxite, 934, 937, 944, 1392
Beans, 237, 871, 874, 891, 895, 896

Beauty shops, 783, 1293, 1301
Bee colonies, 894
Beef (see also Meat and meat products):
Consumer expenditures, 712, 713
Consumption, 238, 899, 1387, 1390
Foreign trade, 879, 899, 1387
Price indexes, 751
Prices, 751, 756, 760
Production, 899, 1387, 1389
Beer. (See Malt beverages.)
Beer, wine, and liquor stores:
Earnings, 655, 1069
Employees, 489, 655, 1067, 1069
Establishments, 1067
Productivity, 661
Sales, 1070, 1078
Belarus. (See Foreign countries.)
Belgium. (See Foreign countries.)
Belize. (See Foreign countries.)
Benin. (See Foreign countries.)
Beryllium, 934
Beverages (see also Alcoholic beverages):
Expenditure, 712, 713
Price indexes, 749, 750, 751, 760, 764, 765
Beverages and tobacco product manufacturing:
Earnings, 655, 1034, 1036
Employees, 655, 1034, 1036, 1038
Finances, 819
Gross domestic product, 693
Industrial production index, 814
Productivity, 661
Profits, 819
Shipments, 1036, 1045, 1046
Bhutan. (See Foreign countries.)
Bicycles, 208, 347, 1090, 1123, 1131, 1142, 1266, 1269, 1270
Billiards, 1269
Biodiesel, 861, 959, 962, 1121, 1146
Biofuels, 955, 962, 1121, 1146
Biological sciences:
Degrees conferred, 319, 320, 321, 839, 840
Employment, 638
Enrollment, 835
Biomass, 959, 973, 974, 982
Bird ownership, 1259
Births and birth rates, 3, 4, 5, 22, 81, 82, 83, 84, 85, 86, 87, 88, 90, 91, 92, 94, 95, 96, 97, 98, 99, 100
American Indian, Eskimo, and Aleut population, 5, 83, 85, 86, 87, 88, 89, 95
Asian and Pacific Islander population, 83, 85, 86, 87, 88, 89
Asian population, 5, 95, 96
Assisted reproductive technology, 109
Birth defects, 92
Birth weight, 91
Births to single or unmarried women, 88, 89, 91, 94, 96, 97, 100
Births to teenage mothers, 83, 87, 88, 89, 91, 95, 96, 97
Black, African American population, 5, 82, 83, 84, 85, 86, 87, 88, 89, 90, 94, 95, 96, 97
Cesarean section deliveries, 90
Characteristics of mother, 83, 87, 88, 89, 90, 94, 95, 96, 97, 98, 99, 100
Citizenship, 95, 99

Note: Index citations refer to **table** numbers, not **page** numbers

Note: Index citations refer to **table** numbers, not **page** numbers

Prices, yields, sales, and issues, 1220, 1222
U.S. savings, 1195
Book, periodical, and music stores, 655, 661, 1067, 1068
Book publishing industry, 760, 1149, 1150, 1156
Bookkeeping. (See Accounting, tax preparation, bookkeeping, and payroll services.)
Books (see also Book publishing industry, Libraries, and Reading), 1075, 1155, 1156, 1183
Boots. (See Footwear.)
Borders, Canada and Mexico, 399, 1288
Border Patrol activities, 551, 552
Boron, 933, 934
Bosnia and Herzegovina. (See Foreign countries.)
Botox, 193
Botswana. (See Foreign countries.)
Botulism, 197
Bowling, 1266, 1267, 1269
Bowling center industry, 1246, 1249
Boxing, 1266
Brazil. (See Foreign countries.)
Bread, 751, 756
Breastfeeding, 108
Bridges, 1110
Broadband, 1153, 1176, 1178, 1179, 1404
Broadcasting industry:
    Capital, 807
    Earnings, 655, 778, 1149, 1151
    Employees, 655, 778, 1149, 1151
    Establishments, 778, 1149, 1151
    Finances, 768, 1150
    Gross domestic product, 693
    Multinational companies, 821, 822
    Number of stations, 1153
    Productivity, 661
    Receipts, revenue, 768, 778, 1150, 1151
Broadway and off-Broadway shows, 1253
Broccoli, 237, 871, 891
Broilers (see also Poultry), 760, 871, 899, 907, 908
Bromine, 933, 934
Bronchitis, 203
Brunei. (See Foreign countries.)
Buddhist population. (See Religion.)
Budget, federal:
    Debt, 497
    Outlays, 496, 498, 499, 500
    Receipts, 496, 502
    Taxes, 502
Building construction:
    Earnings, 655
    Employees, 655, 988
    Occupational safety, 684
Building materials, and garden supplies stores:
    Earnings, 655, 778, 1067, 1069
    Electronic commerce, 1064, 1074
    Employees, 655, 778, 1061, 1067, 1069
    Establishments, 778, 1061, 1067, 1068
    Inventories, 1047, 1073
    Nonemployers, 1068
    Price indexes, 997
    Productivity, 661
    Sales, 778, 1047, 1061, 1068, 1070, 1072, 1073
Building permits. (See Construction industry, and Housing and housing units.)

Buildings (see also Construction industry, and Housing and housing units):
    Characteristics of, 1031
    Construction value, 989, 991, 993, 994
    Federal, 524
    Fires and property loss, 391, 392, 423
    Floor space, 524, 991, 1031
Bulgaria. (See Foreign countries.)
Bullying, 329
Burglaries, 332, 333, 334, 335, 346, 347
Burkina Faso. (See Foreign countries.)
Burma. (See Foreign countries.)
Burundi. (See Foreign countries.)
Buses and bus transportation. (See Passenger transit industry, and Motor vehicles.)
Business cycles, 811
Business enterprises (see also individual types of business and industry):
    Ages of firms, 789
    Age of owner, 781
    American Indian- and Alaska Native-owned businesses, 793, 800, 801
    Asian-owned businesses, 793, 798, 801
    Bankruptcies filed, 802, 803
    Births and deaths of, 790, 791, 845
    Black-owned businesses, 793, 797, 801
    Capital, 807, 808, 809
    Corporations, partnerships, and proprietorships, 604, 766, 768, 769, 770, 771, 776, 777, 1062
    Employees, 780, 785, 786, 787, 788, 789, 791, 795, 796, 797, 798, 799, 800, 820, 845, 1293
    Establishments, 778, 780, 781, 782, 784, 785, 786, 788, 789, 791, 801
    Expansions and contractions, 791
    Family owned, 781
    Finances, 766, 769, 770, 771, 772, 773, 816, 817, 818, 819, 821, 822, 1048, 1049, 1050, 1071
    Firms, 786, 787, 788, 789, 791, 795, 796, 797, 798, 799, 800
    Flow of funds, 1191
    Foreign investment in the U.S., 1308, 1309, 1310
    Franchises, 782, 783
    High technology, 845
    Hispanic-owned businesses, 793, 796, 801
    Leading indicators, 812
    Loans to minority-operated small businesses, 792
    Minority-owned, 793, 795
    Multinational companies, 820, 821, 822, 823
    Native Hawaiian and Other Pacific Islander-owned business, 793, 799, 801
    Patents, 804, 805, 1405
    Payroll, 780, 785, 786, 787, 788
    Profits, 816, 817, 818, 819, 1048, 1049, 1050, 1071
    Sales, shipments, receipts, 1044, 1046, 1047, 1050, 1071
    Small business, 786, 787, 788, 790, 792
    Startups, 789
    Veteran-owned, 793, 801
    White-owned, 793
    Women-owned businesses, 793, 794, 801
Business management, degrees, 316, 319, 320, 321
Butane, 939
Butter, 238, 756, 905

Note: Index citations refer to **table** numbers, not **page** numbers

C

Cabbage, 237, 891, 896
Cable and other pay television services, 751, 1164
Cable and other subscription programming:
    Earnings, 655, 1149
    Employees, 655, 1149, 1151
    Establishments, 1149, 1151
    Finances, 1150, 1165
    Revenue, 1150, 1151, 1164, 1165
Cadmium, 934, 937
Cafeterias. (See Food services and drinking places.)
California. (See State data.)
Calves, 871, 899, 900, 903
Cambodia. (See Foreign countries.)
Cameroon. (See Foreign countries.)
Campaigns, fundraising, 460, 461, 462
Camping, 1269
Canada, (See also Foreign countries.), 396, 399
Cancer (malignancies), 195, 196
    Deaths, 122, 123, 124, 125, 126, 127, 128, 131
Candy, 751
Cantaloupes, 871, 891
Capacity utilization, index, 815
Cape Verde. (See Foreign countries.)
Capital (see also individual industries):
    Banking, 1202, 1203
    Expenditures, 808, 809, 810, 820
    New security issues, 1223
    Residential, 1030
    Stocks, 807, 1044
    Utilities, 981, 986
Capital equipment, producer price indexes, 760
Capital gains, 508, 509
Capital punishment, 383, 384, 385
Carbohydrates, 239, 240
Carbon dioxide emissions, 411, 412, 1401
Cardiovascular disease. (See Heart disease.)
Carpal tunnel syndrome, 685
Carrots, 237, 871, 891, 896
Cars. (See Automobiles.)
Casualty insurance, 1240
Catalog and mail order sales, 1068, 1070, 1074, 1075
Catfish, 927
Catholic population. (See Religion.)
Cat ownership, 1259
Cattle:
    Dairy cows, 897, 901, 904, 905
    Farm marketings, sales, 871, 872, 897
    Imports, 879
    Number on farms, 897, 900, 901, 903
    Prices, 760, 900
    Production, 900, 903
    Slaughter, 903
    Value on farms, 900
Cauliflower, 237, 891
Celery, 237, 891
Cellular and other wireless telecommunications, 1149, 1150, 1166, 1167, 1169, 1170, 1173
Cellular telephones, 1168, 1169, 1170, 1172, 1173, 1177, 1178, 1180, 1403, 1404
Cement (see also Nonmetallic mineral product manufacturing), 933, 934, 937
    Earnings, 655

Employment, 655, 934
Prices, 760, 934
Productivity, 661
World production, 1392
Central African Republic. (See Foreign countries.)
Central America. (See Foreign countries.)
Central and South American population (see also, Hispanic or Latino origin population), 36, 82, 89
Cereal and bakery products:
    Expenditures, prices, 709, 712, 713, 751
    Per capita consumption, 238
Cerebrovascular diseases, 122, 123, 124, 125, 126, 127, 128, 130, 205
Certificates of deposit, 1195
Certification and license status of workers, 675
Cesarean section deliveries, 90
Chad. (See Foreign countries.)
Charitable contributions (see also Philanthropy), 513, 515, 604, 605, 606, 607, 608
Charter schools, 276, 277
Checks, payments made, 1209
Cheerleading, 1268, 1269
Cheese (see also Dairy products), 238, 756, 905
Chemical engineering, degrees conferred, 840
Chemical products:
    Foreign trade, 877, 1316, 1323, 1326
    Price indexes, 760, 764, 765
    Production, 814
Chemicals manufacturing (see also individual chemicals):
    Capital, 807
    Earnings, 655, 1036, 1043
    Employees, 655, 1034, 1036, 1038, 1043
    Establishments, 1034
    Finances, 819
    Foreign trade, 764, 765, 1039, 1326
    Gross domestic product, 693, 1032
    Industrial production index, 814
    Inventories, 1045, 1046
    Multinational companies, 821, 822, 823
    Productivity, 661
    Profits, 819
    Research and development, 830, 831
    Shipments, 1036, 1045, 1046
    Toxic chemical releases, 417, 418
    Waterborne commerce, 1105
Chemistry (see also Physical sciences):
    Degrees conferred, 839, 840
    Employment, 638
    Salary offers, 316
Cherries, 237, 871, 892
Chicken pox, 197, 231, 232
Chickens. (See Poultry.)
Child abuse, 378, 379
Child care, 592, 595, 597, 638, 751
    Expenditures for, 595, 597, 715
    Tax credit, 516
Child day care services, 600, 638, 655
Child support, 562, 593, 594, 595
Children (see also Births, Deaths, Marriages, Divorces, and Population):
    Adopted, 46, 74, 75, 596
    Age and/or sex, 6, 8, 9, 10, 11, 17, 74, 76
    Aid, social welfare programs, 560, 562, 564, 566, 584, 585, 587, 588, 590, 591, 593, 594, 598, 600

Note: Index citations refer to **table** numbers, not **page** numbers

Note: Index citations refer to **table** numbers, not **page** numbers

Note: Index citations refer to **table** numbers, not **page** numbers

Computers and electronic product manufacturing:
  Capital, 807
  Earnings, 655, 1036, 1043
  Employees, 655, 1034, 1036, 1038, 1043
  Establishments, 1034
  Finances, 819
  Foreign trade, 1326
  Gross domestic product, 693, 1032
  Industrial production index, 814
  Inventories, 1045, 1046, 1047
  Multinational companies, 821, 822
  Productivity, 661
  Prices, 764
  Profits, 819
  Research and development, 830, 831
  Shipments, 1036, 1045, 1046, 1047, 1056, 1057
Condensed and evaporated milk, 238
Congestion, on roads, 1134
Congo (Brazzaville). (See Foreign countries.)
Congo (Kinshasa). (See Foreign countries.)
Congress, U.S.:
  Apportionment of, 447
  Asians, 450
  Bills, acts, resolutions, 452, 453
  Blacks, 450
  Campaign finances, 461, 462
  Composition of, 448, 449, 451
  Congressional districts, 446
  Hispanics, 450
  Seniority, 449
  Time, in sessions, 452
  Women, 450
  Votes cast, 436, 444, 445, 446
Connecticut. (See State data.)
Construction industry (see also Building construction, and Highways):
  Building permits, 990
  Capital, 784, 807, 809
  Construction contracts, 991, 992
  Earnings, 653, 655, 664, 665, 778, 794, 795, 796, 797, 798, 799, 800, 1344
  Employees, 640, 644, 653, 654, 655, 778, 781, 785, 786, 794, 795, 796, 797, 798, 799, 800, 843, 988, 1344
  Establishments, 778, 779, 781, 782, 784, 785, 786, 801, 988, 1344
  Finances, 768, 771, 1339
  Gross domestic product, 693, 1339
  Hires and separations, 659, 660
  Hours, 653
  Nonemployers, 779
  Occupational safety, 682, 684
  Profits, 818
  Residential, 990, 993, 994, 995, 996, 999
  Shipments, receipts, 768, 771, 776, 777, 778, 779, 794, 795, 796, 797, 798, 799, 800
  Unions, 687
  Value, of, 989, 991, 993, 994
Construction machinery, manufacturing:
  Earnings, 655, 1036
  Employees, 655, 1036
  Productivity, 661
  Shipments, 1036
Construction materials. (See Building materials.)

Consumers:
  Consumer complaints, 345, 1100
  Consumer goods, 208, 760
  Credit, 772, 773, 1194, 1197, 1200, 1211, 1212, 1213, 1217
  Expenditures:
    Entertainment, 700, 709, 712, 713, 1250, 1252
    Education, 700, 709, 712, 713
    Food, 700, 709, 710, 712, 713, 714, 761, 875
    Health insurance, 150, 700
    Housing, 700, 709, 710, 712, 713, 714, 761
    Medical care, 144, 145, 146, 147, 150, 151, 700, 709, 710, 712, 713, 714, 761
    Metropolitan areas, 710
    Pets, 1252
    Reading material, 709, 712, 713, 1250, 1252, 1263
    Sporting goods, 1252, 1270
    Transportation, 700, 709, 710, 712, 713, 714, 761
Consumer price indexes, 748, 749, 750, 751
  Foreign countries, 1372, 1379
  Medical care, 149, 749, 750, 751
  Purchasing power of the dollar, 748
Consumption. (See individual commodities, and Personal consumption expenditures.)
Contraception, use of, 101, 104
Convenience stores. (See Food and beverage stores.)
Copper:
  Consumption, 934, 944
  Foreign trade, 934, 944
  Prices, 760, 764, 765, 934, 935
  Production and value, 933, 934, 937, 1392
Copyrights, registration, 806
Corn:
  Acreage, 887, 888, 896, 1387
  Consumption, 237, 238, 1387
  Ethanol, 887
  Farm marketings, sales, 871, 872, 896
  Foreign trade, 881, 883, 884, 887, 1323, 1387, 1391
  Genetically engineered, 864
  Prices, 760, 764, 887, 888
  Production, 881, 887, 888, 891, 896, 1387
  Supply and disappearance, 887
Corporations:
  Bonds, 1219
  Capital, 775
  Dividend payments, 816
  Finances, 766, 767, 768, 769, 770, 771, 773, 774, 775, 776, 777, 1048, 1049, 1050, 1071, 1191, 1186, 1230
  Manufacturing, 1048, 1049, 1050
  Nonfinancial, 773
  Philanthropy, 604
  Profits, 766, 816, 817, 818, 819, 1048, 1049, 1050, 1071
  Receipts, 766
  Sales, 771, 776, 777, 1048
  Taxes:
    Corporate income tax, 468, 469, 482, 483, 485, 816
    Returns, 766, 767, 768, 775, 776, 777

Note: Index citations refer to **table** numbers, not **page** numbers

Correctional institutions (see also Prisoners):
    Construction, 994
    Employment, 489, 492, 638
    Expenditures, 361, 476, 482, 484, 486
    Population, 68, 386, 388
Cosmetic surgery, 193
Cosmetics, price indexes, 751
Costa Rica. (See Foreign countries.)
Cost-of-living indexes, 1372
Cote d'Ivoire. (See Foreign countries.)
Cotton:
    Acreage, 887, 1387
    Consumption, 1387
    Farm marketings, sales, 869, 871
    Foreign trade, 876, 881, 884, 887, 1387
    Genetically engineered, 864
    Prices, 760, 874, 887
    Production, 881, 887, 1387, 1388
    Supply and disappearance, 887
Countries (See Foreign countries.)
County governments, 463, 464
    Elected officials, 459
    Employees, 495
Couriers and messengers:
    Earnings, 655, 1083
    Employees, 655, 1080, 1081, 1083
    Establishments, 1081, 1083
    Revenue, 1082
Courts:
    Appeals courts, 369, 371
    District courts, U.S., 369, 370, 373
    Judicial officers, 369
    Juror service, 373
    Juveniles, 376, 377
    Problem solving, 374
    Public corruption, 367
    Sentencing Commission, U.S., 375
    State courts, 372
    Supreme Court, U.S., 368
Cows (see Cattle, and Dairy products.)
Crabs, 926, 928, 929
Crack cocaine. (See cocaine.)
Cranberries, 871, 892
Credit cards, 1198, 1209, 1211, 1213, 1217
Credit intermediation industry:
    Capital, 807
    Earnings, 1187, 1189, 1190
    Employees, 1187, 1189
    Establishments, 1187, 1188, 1189
    Nonemployers, 1188
    Receipts, 1187, 1188
Credit markets, 1213
Credit unions:
    Consumer credit, 1212
    Earnings, 1189
    Employees, 1189
    Establishments, 1189, 1208
    Finances, 1191, 1208, 1215, 1230
Crime (see also Criminal victimizations, and Law
    enforcement):
    Aliens, crimes committed, 553
    Assault, 332, 333, 334, 335, 340, 344, 357, 358
    Asset forfeiture, 356
    Burglary, 332, 333, 334, 335, 340, 346, 347, 357,
      358

    Child abuse and neglect, 378, 379
    Drug abuse violations, 357, 358
    Financial crime, 357, 358
    Firearm application denials, 354, 362
    Forensic service requests, 347
    Hate crimes, 348, 349
    Homicides, 330, 337, 338, 339, 350
    Larceny-theft, 332, 333, 334, 335, 340, 347, 357, 358
    Motor vehicle theft, 332, 333, 334, 335, 340, 346,
      347, 357, 358
    Murders, 332, 333, 334, 335, 336, 337, 357, 358
    Place of occurrence, 349, 351
    Police officers assaulted, killed, 359
    Property crime, 332, 333, 334, 335, 340, 342, 346,
      347, 357, 358
    Rape, 331, 332, 333, 334, 335, 340, 343, 357, 358,
      536
    Robbery, 332, 333, 334, 335, 340, 347, 357, 358
    Schools, 325, 327, 328, 330, 331
    Value lost, 347
    Violent crime, 332, 333, 334, 335, 336, 337, 340,
      342, 344, 350, 351, 357, 358
    Workplace, 683
Criminal cases, U.S. Courts, 369, 371, 372
Criminal justice expenditures, 361
Criminal victimizations, 340, 341, 344, 346, 347,
    348, 349, 350, 351
Croatia. (See Foreign countries.)
Crops (see also Farms and individual crops):
    Acreage, 886, 887, 891, 1342, 1387
    Farm marketings, sales, 849, 869, 871, 872, 873
    Foreign trade, 876, 879, 882, 884, 887, 1387
    Horticultural specialty crops, 898
    Prices, 874, 887
    Production, 887, 891, 1387, 1388
    Productivity, 886
    Supply and disappearance, 887, 1387
Cross country (running), 1267, 1268
Crude materials, prices, 758, 760
Crude oil (see also Petroleum and products):
    Foreign trade, 938, 939, 956, 965, 966, 967, 1323
    Pipelines, 1145
    Prices, 753, 760, 935, 938
    Production, 933, 938, 939, 942, 955, 956, 967, 1398
    Rail movements, 1146
Crustaceans, 926, 928, 929
Cryptosporidiosis, 197
Cuba. (See Foreign countries.)
Cuban population, 36, 82, 89, 611
Cucumbers, 237, 891
Currency:
    Comparative price levels, 1371
    Foreign exchange rate, 1406
    Personal saving component, 698
    Supply, 1218
Customs and Border Protection (CBP), 551, 552, 553,
    557, 558
Cyber-bullying, 329
Cyprus. (See Foreign countries.)
Czech Republic. (See Foreign countries.)

D

Dairy products (see also individual products):
    Consumer expenditures, 709, 712, 713

Note: Index citations refer to **table** numbers, not **page** numbers

ProQuest Statistical Abstract of the United States: 2018

Consumption, 238, 906, 1387
Farm marketings, sales, 869, 871, 872, 905
Foreign trade, 879, 882, 1387
Manufacture, 661, 905, 1036
Prices, 760, 874
Production, 905, 906, 1387
Dance, 1256, 1257
Data processing services. (See Computer programming and data processing services.)
Dates, 892
Day care. (See Child day care services.)
DAX, German stock index, 1407
Death care services, 655, 751, 1291, 1292, 1293, 1301
Death penalty, 383, 384, 385
Deaths and death rates (see also Accidents and fatalities), 3, 4, 22, 81
Age and sex, 112, 114, 115, 116, 117, 126, 127, 129, 130, 131, 132, 133, 134, 135
American Indian, Alaska Native population, 5, 114, 115, 116, 123, 129, 132, 133, 135
Asian population, 5, 114, 115, 116, 123, 129, 132, 133
Black, African American population, 5, 112, 114, 115, 116, 120, 121, 123, 124, 129, 132, 133, 135
Causes of death, 122, 123, 124, 125, 126, 127, 128, 129, 130, 131, 132, 133, 135, 136, 1090
Fetal and neonatal, 119, 120
Foreign countries, 1356, 1360, 1361
Heart disease, 122, 123, 124, 125, 126, 127, 128, 129
Hispanic or Latino origin, 5, 114, 116, 117, 124, 129, 132, 133, 135
Industrial, 684
Infant, 81, 119, 120, 121
Injuries, 123, 125
Island areas of the U.S., 121, 1331
Maternal, 120
Military deaths, 533, 535
Native Hawaiian, Other Pacific Islander population, 5
Race, 5, 112, 114, 115, 116, 120, 121, 123, 124, 129, 132, 133, 135
States, 16, 118, 121, 128
Suicide, 122, 123, 125, 126, 127, 132, 134, 533, 535, 1361
Traffic fatalities, 1090, 1122, 1123, 1124, 1126, 1127, 1129, 1131, 1132, 1133, 1360
Weather related, 423, 426
Workers' deaths, 393, 683, 684, 931
Deaths, of businesses, 790, 791
Debit cards, 1209, 1210
Debt (see also Loans and mortgages):
Consumer, 1200, 1213
Credit card, 1197, 1198, 1211, 1213
Credit market, 1192
Farm, 867
Federal government, 497
Foreign countries, 1374, 1411
Households, 1197
Individual, 741
Local government, 472, 486
State and local government, 472, 476, 482, 484, 1113, 1192
Student loan debt, 305

Deductions, taxes, 513, 514, 515
Business, 769, 770, 771, 775
Defense, Department of (see also Army, Air Force, Marine Corps, and Navy):
Budget authority, outlays, 498, 499, 500, 525, 526
Expenditures, 142, 145, 148
Military personnel, 297, 528, 529, 530, 531, 534, 535, 536
Military retirees, 532, 562
Property, sites and acreage, 527
Defined benefit and contribution plans, 569, 572, 573, 574, 577, 1191, 1234, 1235, 1236, 1237
Degrees conferred (see also individual fields), 317, 318, 319, 320, 321, 322, 836, 837, 838, 839, 840
Salary offers, 316
Delaware. (See State data.)
Delinquency. (See Juvenile delinquency.)
Dengue fever, 197
Denmark. (See Foreign countries.)
Dentists, 638
Care visits, 224
Charges and expenditures for, 141, 143, 144, 145, 149, 151, 761
Dental schools, students, and graduates, 322
Employment, 173, 642, 655
Medicaid payments, recipients, 161
Offices, 172, 174
Department stores:
Earnings, 655
Employees, 655, 1067
Establishments, 1067
Inventories, 1073
Productivity, 661
Sales, 1070, 1073
Deportations, illegal immigrants, 551, 552, 553
Deposit Insurance Fund, 1205
Deposits. (See Banks, commercial)
Depression, 223, 230
Dermatologists, 175
Development aid, 1409, 1410
Diabetes, 92, 122, 123, 124, 125, 126, 127, 128, 204
Diamonds, 934, 1392
Diatomite, 933, 934
Diesel, fuel, 958, 962
Dietitians and nutritionists, 638
Direct mail advertising industry, 1295
Directory and mailing list publications industry, 1149, 1150, 1156
Disabilities:
Age, 34, 201
Beneficiaries, 562, 566, 567
Benefits paid, 566, 567, 568
Elderly, 34, 201
Food stamp participants, 590, 591
Government transfer payments, 559, 560, 561
Hate crimes, 348, 349
Labor force status, 614
Learning, 227
Medicaid payments and/or recipients, 161
Military retirement system, 532
Payments, 568
Persons with disability, 34, 201

Note: Index citations refer to **table** numbers, not **page** numbers

Note: Index citations refer to **table** numbers, not **page** numbers

Note: Index citations refer to **table** numbers, not **page** numbers

Note: Index citations refer to **table** numbers, not **page** numbers

---

Note: Index citations refer to **table** numbers, not **page** numbers

Research and development, 827, 833
Salary, 316, 846
English, ability to speak, 53, 54, 55, 256, 266, 279
Entertainment:
    Consumer expenditures, 700, 709, 712, 713, 1250
    Consumer price indexes, 751
    Gaming, 1277
    Personal expenditures, 700, 712, 713, 1252
Environment (see also Pollution):
    Charitable contributions, 604
    Environmental industries, 416
    Volunteers, 603
    Wetlands, 404, 406
Environmental science, 827, 833, 835
Equatorial Guinea. (See Foreign countries.)
Equestrian, 1267
Eritrea. (See Foreign countries.)
Eskimo population. (See American Indian, Alaska, Native population.)
Establishments. (See Business enterprise, and individual industries.)
Estate and gift taxes, 504
Estonia. (See Foreign countries.)
Ethane, 939
Ethanol, 887, 962, 1121, 1146
Ethiopia. (See Foreign countries.)
Ethnicities. (See Hispanic or Latino origin, population.)
Ethylene, 939
Europe. (See Foreign countries.)
European Union. (See Foreign countries.)
Exchange-traded funds, 1191, 1224
Excise taxes, 502, 504
Executions of prisoners, 384, 385
Executive Office of the President (federal), 521
Exercise, 221, 1258, 1264, 1269
Exercise equipment, 208, 1270
Expectation of life (average lifetime), 110, 111, 112, 113
    Foreign countries, 1356
    Projections, 110
Expenditures. (See individual subjects.)
Expenditures of state and local government. (See individual governmental units.)
Expenditures of U.S. government, 466, 467, 500, 699, 1314, 1315
    Aid to the arts and humanities, 1254
    Aid to state and local government, 466, 467
    Budget outlays, 496, 498, 499, 500, 501
    Education. (See Federal aid to education.)
    Food programs, federal, 588, 589
    Health, 141, 142, 143, 144, 145, 467
    Homeland security, 467, 546, 547, 548, 549, 550
    Hospitals, 190
    National defense, 525, 526, 762
    Outlays, 496, 498, 499, 500, 501
    Payrolls, 488, 518, 519, 520
    Price indexes, 762
    Public debt, 497
    Research and development, 824, 825, 826, 827, 828, 829
    Schools, 242, 467
    Science/space, 847
    Veterans benefits. (See Veterans Affairs.)

Exports. (See Foreign trade.)
Express mail, 1147, 1148

F

Fabricated metal product manufacturing:
    Capital, 807, 1312
    Earnings, 655, 1036, 1043
    Employees, 655, 1034, 1036, 1038, 1043
    Establishments, 1034
    Finance, 819
    Foreign trade, 1039, 1326
    Gross domestic product, 693, 1032
    Industrial production index, 814
    Productivity, 661
    Profits, 819
    Shipments, 1036, 1045, 1046
    Toxic chemical releases, 418
Fabrics. (See Textile mill products.)
Falls, accidental deaths, 125, 126
Families. (See Households.)
Family and consumer sciences, degrees conferred, 319, 320, 321
Family courts, 374
Family farms, 859, 860
Farm mortgage loans, 1215
Farms:
    Acreage, 850, 851, 852, 853, 854, 855, 856, 857, 860, 863
        Cropland, 403, 405, 849, 853, 886
        Crops harvested (see also individual crops), 886, 887, 888, 889, 890, 891, 1387
        Farm type, 860
    Agrichemicals, 869, 874, 877
    Agricultural products:
        Exports, 1391
        Foreign countries, production, 1388, 1389
        Market value, 849
        Prices. (See Prices received by farmers.)
        Waterborne commerce, 1105
        World production, 1387, 1388, 1389
    Assets and liabilities, 867
    Corporate, 852, 855, 860
    Crops (see also individual crops):
        Acreage, 886, 887, 896, 1342
        Fruits and nuts, 892, 893, 896, 1343
        Income, 871, 872, 873, 1342
        Production, 881, 886, 887, 896, 1387, 1388
        Vegetables, 891, 895, 896
    Debt, 867, 1215
    Expenses, 865, 869
    Family or individual, 852, 854, 859, 1342
    Farm land and buildings value, 854, 855, 856, 867
    Farm operators, 856
    Farm products sold, marketing receipts, 854, 855, 856, 857, 858, 862, 868, 869, 871, 872, 873
        Fertilizers:
            Farm expenditures for, 869
            Foreign trade, 877, 1323
            Prices, 760, 874
    Farm to school programs, 866
    Government payments to farmers, 856, 858, 868, 869, 870

Note: Index citations refer to **table** numbers, not **page** numbers

Note: Index citations refer to **table** numbers, not **page** numbers

Note: Index citations refer to **table** numbers, not **page** numbers

Note: Index citations refer to **table** numbers, not **page** numbers

Note: Index citations refer to **table** numbers, not **page** numbers

Gemstones, 934
General merchandise stores:
    Earnings, 655, 778, 1069
    Electronic commerce, 1074
    Employees, 655, 778, 1061, 1067, 1069
    Establishments, 778, 1061, 1067, 1068
    Finances, 819
    Inventories, 1073
    Productivity, 661
    Profits, 819
    Sales, 778, 1061, 1068, 1070, 1072, 1073, 1074
Geography and cartography. (See Land.)
Genetically engineered crops, 864
Georgia. (See Foreign countries, and State data.)
Geothermal energy, 959, 972, 973, 974
Germanium, 934
German stock market index (DAX), 1407
Germany. (See Foreign countries.)
Ghana. (See Foreign countries.)
Giardiasis, 197
Gift and estate taxes, 469, 504
Glass, 413, 414, 415, 760
Gold:
    Consumption, 934
    Employment, 934
    Foreign trade, 934, 1323
    Prices, 760, 765, 934, 935
    Production and value, 932, 933, 934, 937, 1392
    Reserve assets, 1304
Golf, 1261, 1266, 1267, 1268, 1269, 1270
Golf courses, industry, 1246, 1249
Gonorrhea, 197
Government (see also Expenditures of U.S.
    government, Receipts, and individual
    governmental units):
    Buildings, 524
    Capital stock, 747
    Consumer credit holdings, 1212
    Earnings, 493, 653, 664, 666
    Employees, 491, 653, 654, 655, 666, 843
        Benefits, 490
        Characteristics, 522
        City government, 494
        County government, 495
        Federal, civilian, 488, 518, 519, 520, 521,
          522, 523
        Hours, 653
        Local government, 488, 489, 492, 493
        Retirement, 523
        Retirement systems, 523, 562, 571
        State government, 488, 489, 492, 493
    Employment cost index, 671, 757
    Expenditures:
        Capital outlays, 470, 471
        City government, 494
        Consumption, 699, 762
        County government, 495
        Federal, 496, 498, 499, 500, 501
          Agriculture, 868, 869, 870
          Aid to state and local government, 466, 467,
            468,
        Local government, 470, 471, 486
        State and local government, 468, 469, 470,
          471, 474, 476
        State government, 469, 470, 471, 481, 482
        Transfer payments, 559, 560, 561

Federally owned land, 524
Flow of funds, 1191
Freedom of Information Act, 364
Highways, 476, 484, 486, 1085, 1108, 1111,
    1112, 1113, 1114, 1115, 1116
Hires and separations, 659, 660
Hospitals, 190, 476
Insurance. (See Social insurance.)
Land. (See Public lands.)
Local government:
    Cities, 494
    Counties, 495
    Employees, 488, 489, 492, 493, 494, 495, 666
    Number, by type, 463, 464
    Payroll, 488, 489, 493, 494, 495
Number of units, by type of government, 463, 464
Occupational safety, 682, 684
Payrolls, 488, 489, 494, 495
Purchases of goods and services, 690, 691
Reserve assets, 1304
Salaries and wages (see also Income, and
    individual industries):
    Federal, 518, 664
    State and local government employees, 262,
      491, 493, 664, 666
Securities, 473, 1220
State and local government:
    Benefits, 490
    Employees, 488, 489, 491
    Federal aid, 466, 467
    Finances, 468, 469, 470, 471, 472, 474,
      475, 476
    Payroll, 488, 489, 493
    Revenue from pari-mutuel and amusement
      taxes and lotteries, 479
State government, 481, 483, 484, 487, 666
Government National Mortgage Association loans,
    1215
Governors, 454, 455
Graduates:
    College, 317, 318, 319, 320, 321, 322, 839,
      840, 842
    High school, 245, 283, 286, 290
Grain (see also individual classes):
    Consumption, 238, 1387
    Farm marketings, sales, 862, 871, 896
    Foreign trade, 876, 879, 881, 882, 884, 1387
    Prices, 874
    Production, 869, 881, 887, 896, 1387, 1388
Grandparents, living with grandchildren, 64, 67, 75
Grants, by foundations, 604, 605, 606
Grapefruit, 237, 756, 871, 892
Grapes, 237, 756, 871, 892, 896
Graphite, 934
Great Britain. (See Foreign countries.)
Great Lakes, 27, 28, 395, 396, 397,
    1104
Greece. (See Foreign countries.)
Greenhouse gases, 411, 412
Grocery stores (see also Food and beverage stores),
    655, 661, 1067, 1068, 1069, 1070
Gross domestic product (GDP):
    Components, annual growth rates, 690, 691,
      692, 1079
    Foreign countries, 1365
    Foreign trade, 1413

Note: Index citations refer to **table** numbers, not **page** numbers

---

Note: Index citations refer to **table** numbers, not **page** numbers

Note: Index citations refer to **table** numbers, not **page** numbers

Living arrangements, 33, 58, 66, 73, 76
Male householder, 59, 61, 62, 63, 64, 71, 72
Marital status of householder, 59, 61, 63
Married couples with or without own children, 59, 60, 61, 63
Media users, 1154
Mobility status, 30
Mortgages, 1196, 1197, 1198
Mutual fund ownership, 1231
Net worth, 744, 745, 746
Nonfamily, 59, 61
Participation in education, 266
Persons living alone (one-person households), 58, 59, 61, 62
Pets, 1259
Poverty, 35, 739, 740
Public assistance to families, 564
Race, 59, 64, 70
Region of householder, 724
Same-sex couple, 70
Savings rate, 1377
Single parent, 59, 63, 64
Size, 39, 59, 62
Stay-at-home parents, 65
Stock ownership, 1195, 1228
Telephones, 1153, 1170
Tenure, 35, 70, 718
Unmarried partners, 71, 72
Wealth, 744, 745
Household work, 676
Housekeeping supplies expenditures, 712, 713
Housing and household operations, price indexes, 751, 761
Housing and housing units (see also Households or families):
Age of housing stocks, 1014
Amenities, 996, 1027
Apartments, 998, 1006, 1007
Appliances, 751
Building permit value, 990
Capital, 1030
Coastal counties, 28
Condominiums, 1006
Construction:
Apartments completed and rented, 998, 1007
New units, 990, 995, 996, 999
Time to completion, 999
Value, 989, 991, 993, 994
Consumer expenditures, 700, 709, 710, 712, 713, 714
Consumer price indexes, 749, 750, 751
Costs, 1020, 1021, 1022
Deficiencies, 1027
Elderly, 1018, 1021, 1027
Energy, 957, 959, 960, 961, 963, 996
Fires, and property loss, 391
Floor space, 996
Government expenditures, 468, 469, 476, 500
Heating equipment used, 996, 1014, 1026
Heating fuel used, 1026
Homeless, 601, 602
Hurricanes, 398
Improvements, 1028
Kitchen equipment, 1014

Loans and mortgages, 1001, 1024, 1025, 1029, 1215, 1216, 1217
Lot size, 1016
Maintenance and repair expenditures, 712, 713
Metropolitan area data, 1005
Mobile homes, 1003, 1014, 1015, 1024
New privately owned homes, characteristics, 996
Ownership, 29, 35, 39, 718, 1008, 1009, 1011, 1014, 1016, 1017, 1018, 1019, 1020, 1021, 1022
Plumbing, 1014
Price indexes, 749, 750, 751, 752, 1000
Prices, or costs, 1000, 1001, 1002, 1003, 1004, 1005, 1006, 1020, 1021
Puerto Rico, 1336
Remodeling, 1028
Rent, rental value, 1007, 1020, 1021, 1023
Rooms, 1016
Sales, 1001, 1004, 1006
Shelters, 601
Square footage, 1016
State data, 1011, 1012, 1015, 1019, 1022, 1023
Structural type, 1010, 1014, 1015
Subsidized, 998
Supportive, 601
Tenure, 29, 35, 39, 718, 744, 745, 1008, 1009, 1010, 1011, 1012, 1013, 1014, 1016, 1017, 1018, 1019, 1020, 1021, 1022, 1023, 1336
Transitional, 601
Vacancies, 1008, 1010, 1011, 1012, 1013, 1014, 1016
Value, 746, 1022
Year built, 1014
Housing assistance, 563, 564, 601
Human immunodeficiency virus (HIV) infection (see also AIDS), 125, 126, 127, 133, 198, 199, 200
Human services, 601
Hungary. (See Foreign countries.)
Hunger, 209
Hunting and fishing, 909, 911, 1269, 1275
Hurricanes, 398, 423, 426
Hydroelectric power, 959, 982
Capacity, 972
Consumption, 955, 959, 960
Net generation, 973, 976, 982
Net summer capacity, 972, 974, 976
Production, 955, 972, 1393, 1394
Hypertension, 92, 125, 126, 205

I

Ice cream, 238, 756, 905
Ice hockey, 1265, 1266, 1267, 1269
Iceland. (See Foreign countries.)
Idaho. (See State data.)
Identity theft, 345, 352
Illegal aliens, 362, 551, 552, 553, 554
Illinois. (See State data.)
Immigrants (see also Foreign-born population):
Class of admission, 44, 48, 49
Country of birth, 46, 49, 50, 51

Note: Index citations refer to **table** numbers, not **page** numbers

Note: Index citations refer to **table** numbers, not **page** numbers

Note: Index citations refer to **table** numbers, not **page** numbers

Note: Index citations refer to **table** numbers, not **page** numbers

Note: Index citations refer to **table** numbers, not **page** numbers

---

Note: Index citations refer to **table** numbers, not **page** numbers

Lung disease. (See Pulmonary or respiratory disease.)
Luxembourg. (See Foreign countries.)
Lyme disease, 197, 198

M

Macadamia nuts, 892
Macedonia. (See Foreign countries.)
Machine tools, 751, 760
Machinery manufacturing:
  Capital, 807
  Earnings, 655, 1034, 1036, 1043
  Employees, 655, 1034, 1036, 1038, 1043
  Establishments, 1034
  Finances, 819
  Foreign trade, 764, 765, 1039, 1316, 1323
  Gross domestic product, 693, 1032
  Industrial production index, 814
  Inventories, 1045, 1046
  Price indexes, 764, 765
  Productivity, 661
  Profits, 819
  Research and development, 830, 831
  Shipments, 1036, 1045, 1046
  Toxic chemical releases, 418
Madagascar. (See Foreign countries.)
Magnesium, 934, 937
Mail, 1147, 1148
Mail order houses (including electronic shopping):
  Earnings, 655, 1069
  Employees, 655, 1067, 1069
  Establishments, 1067, 1068
  Productivity, 661
  Sales, 1068, 1070, 1074, 1075
Maine. (See State data.)
Malaria, 197
Malawi. (See Foreign countries.)
Malaysia. (See Foreign countries.)
Maldives. (See Foreign countries.)
Male householders. (See Households or families.)
Mali. (See Foreign countries.)
Malignant neoplasms. (See Cancer.)
Malt beverages (see also Beverages), 751, 876, 879
Malta. (See Foreign countries.)
Mammography testing, 210
Managed care health plans, 162
Management of companies and enterprises:
  Capital, 807, 809
  Earnings, 655, 664
  Employees, 638, 655, 778, 785, 786, 794, 795, 796, 797, 798, 799, 800, 1290, 1292, 1293
  Establishments, 778, 785, 786, 794, 795, 796, 797, 798, 799, 800, 1290, 1291, 1292
  Finances, 768, 771, 776, 777
  Gross domestic product, 693
  Occupational safety, 682
  Profits, 778, 818
  Sales, receipts, 768, 771, 776, 777, 794, 795, 796, 797, 798, 799, 800, 1290, 1291
Managers. (See Proprietors.)
Manganese, 934, 944, 1392
Manganiferous ore, 933

Manufacturing industry (see also individual industries):
  Capital, 784, 807, 809
  Construction value, 993
  Earnings, 653, 655, 664, 665, 778, 794, 795, 796, 797, 798, 799, 800, 1036, 1042, 1043, 1344
  Economic indicators, 812
  Employees, 644, 653, 654, 655, 778, 782, 785, 786, 794, 795, 796, 797, 798, 799, 800, 843, 1034, 1035, 1037, 1038, 1041, 1043, 1344
  Establishments, 778, 779, 781, 782, 784, 785, 786, 801, 1033, 1035, 1036, 1344
  Finances, 768, 771, 819, 1048, 1049, 1050, 1312, 1339
  Foreign countries, 1368, 1369
  Foreign investments in U.S., 1309, 1310
  Foreign trade, 1039
  Gross domestic product, 693, 695, 1032, 1339
  Hires and separations, 659, 660
  Hours, 653, 1040, 1041
  Industrial production index, 814, 1041
  Inventories, 813, 1044, 1045, 1046, 1047
  Investment abroad, 1312
  Island areas of the United States, 1338, 1344
  Multinational companies, 821, 822, 823
  Nonemployers, 779, 1033
  Occupational safety, 682, 684
  Productivity, 661, 662, 814, 815, 1041, 1368
  Profits, 817, 818, 819, 1048, 1049, 1050
  Sales, shipments, receipts, 768, 771, 776, 777, 778, 779, 794, 795, 796, 797, 798, 799, 800, 813, 1036, 1037, 1039, 1044, 1045, 1046, 1047, 1050, 1056, 1057, 1058, 1059, 1060
  State data, 1035, 1037, 1042
  Toxic chemical releases, 418
  Union membership, 687
Margarine, 238, 756
Marijuana (see also Drugs, illegal), 214, 215, 355, 365
Marine Corps, 530
Marital status, 56, 57
  Asian population, 56, 70
  Black, African American population, 56, 60, 70
  Computer use, 1177
  Couples with or without own household, 59
  Elderly, 32, 57, 70
  Employed persons, 621, 622, 624
  Foreign-born population, 39
  Hispanic origin population, 56, 60
  Householder status, 59, 61
  Internet access, 1177
  Interracial, 60
  Labor force participation rates, 620, 621, 622, 623
  Male householder, 59, 61
  Same-sex couple households, 70
  Unmarried partners, 70, 71, 72
  Women in the labor force, 620, 621, 622, 623
Marriages (see also Marital status), 81, 137, 138, 139, 140

Note: Index citations refer to **table** numbers, not **page** numbers

---

Note: Index citations refer to **table** numbers, not **page** numbers

Note: Index citations refer to **table** numbers, not **page** numbers

---

Note: Index citations refer to **table** numbers, not **page** numbers

Gross domestic product, 911
Mineral industry, 930
Oil and gas extraction, 951, 952
Payroll and earnings, 655, 909, 910
Petroleum industry, 938
Sales and revenue, 910
Timber-related industry, 912, 913
Naturalized citizens, 39, 47, 439
Nauru. (See Foreign countries.)
Navy, personnel, 530
Nebraska. (See State data.)
Nectarines, 237, 892
Neonatal deaths (see also Deaths and death rates), 120
Nepal. (See Foreign countries.)
Nephritis, nephrotic syndrome, and nephrosis (See Kidney disease), 123, 124, 125, 126, 127
Netherlands. (See Foreign countries.)
Neurologists, 175
Nevada. (See State data.)
New Hampshire. (See State data.)
New Jersey. (See State data.)
New Mexico. (See State data.)
New York. (See State data.)
New York Stock Exchange, 1227, 1229
New Zealand. (See Foreign countries.)
Newspaper, book, and directory publishers:
    Earnings, 655, 1149
    Employees, 655, 1149, 1151
    Establishments, 1149, 1151
    Finances, 1150, 1156
    Productivity, 661
    Revenue, 1150, 1151, 1156
Newspapers (See also Publishing industry):
    Number and circulation, 1157, 1158
    Reading, 1154
    Recycling, 415
Newsprint, 922, 923
Nicaragua. (See Foreign countries.)
Nickel:
    Consumption, 934
    Employment, 934
    Foreign trade, 934, 944
    Prices, 934, 935
    Production and value, 933, 934, 937
    World production, 937, 1392
Niger. (See Foreign countries.)
Nigeria. (See Foreign countries.)
Niobium, 934, 944
Nitrogen in ammonia, 934, 937, 1392
Nonalcoholic beverages, 712, 713
Nonemployer establishments, 599, 779, 1033, 1062, 1068, 1084, 1152, 1188, 1243, 1248, 1291
Nonmetallic mineral mining and quarrying, except fuels, 807, 909, 930
Nonmetallic mineral product manufacturing (see also Metals and metal products):
    Earnings, 655, 1034, 1036, 1043
    Employees, 655, 1034, 1036, 1038, 1043
    Establishments, 1034
    Foreign trade, 1039, 1323, 1326
    Gross domestic product, 693, 1032
    Productivity, 661, 814
    Profits, 819
    Sales, shipments, receipts, 1036, 1045, 1046

Toxic chemical releases, 418
Nonprofit organizations, 604, 605, 606, 607, 655, 1301, 1302
North Carolina. (See State data.)
North Dakota. (See State data.)
North Korea. (See Foreign countries.)
Northern Mariana Islands. (See Island areas of the U.S.)
Norway. (See Foreign countries.)
Notifiable diseases, 197
Nuclear power, 969, 970, 971
    Capacity, 969, 970
    Consumption, 955, 956, 960, 1397
    Production, 955, 956, 969, 970, 973, 976, 1394
    Reactors, 969, 970
    State data, 970, 976
Nursing and residential care facilities:
    Capital, 807
    Earnings, 655, 778
    Employees, 173, 655, 778
    Establishments, 178, 181, 778
    Expenditures, 141, 143, 144, 145, 148, 151
    Gross domestic product, 693
    Medicare utilization, 155
    Population, 68, 178
    Receipts, 172, 174, 778
Nursing personnel, 176, 638, 641
Nutrients and nutritional intake, 239, 240
Nutritional deficiencies, deaths, 125
Nuts, 238, 871, 882, 884, 892, 893

O

Obesity, 220, 225, 234, 1358
Obstetricians (see also Physicians), 175
Occupational safety, 681, 682, 684, 931
Occupations (see also individual occupations):
    American Indian, Alaska Native population, 35
    Asian population, 35, 638, 643
    Black, African American population, 35, 638, 643
    Earnings, 639, 668, 670,
    Employment, 35, 638, 639, 640, 643, 644, 670
    Employment cost index, 671, 757
    Hispanic origin population, 35, 638, 643
    Island areas of the U.S., 1333
    Mobility status, 29
    Native Hawaiian, Other Pacific Islander population, 35
    Pension plan/health plan coverage, 679
    Self-employed, 629
    Science and engineering, 841, 842, 843, 846
    Women, 638
Office buildings. (See Commercial buildings.)
Office equipment, 1075
Office supplies, stationery, and gift stores, 655, 661, 1067, 1068, 1070
Offshore leases, 942
Ohio. (See State data.)
Oil. (See Petroleum and products.)
Oil and gas extraction industry:
    Capital, 807
    Earnings, 655, 778, 909, 910, 930
    Employees, 655, 778, 909, 910, 930, 951, 952
    Establishments, 778, 909, 910, 951, 952

Note: Index citations refer to **table** numbers, not **page** numbers

Note: Index citations refer to **table** numbers, not **page** numbers

Note: Index citations refer to **table** numbers, not **page** numbers

Note: Index citations refer to **table** numbers, not **page** numbers

Black, African American population:
    Families, 35, 739, 740
    Households, 564
    Persons, 35, 735, 736, 737
    Children, 736, 737
    Families, 35, 732, 733, 739, 740
        American Indian, Alaska Native population, 35
        Asian and Pacific Islander population, 739
        Asian population, 35, 739, 740
        Black, African American population, 35, 739, 740
        Hispanic origin population, 35, 739, 740
        Housing, 564
        Native Hawaiian, Other Pacific Islander population, 35
    Foreign born, 39
    Health insurance coverage, 166
    Hispanic origin population:
        Families, 35, 740
        Households, 564
        Persons, 35, 735, 736, 737
    Native Hawaiian, Other Pacific Islander population, 35
    Persons, 732, 733
        Age, 737, 738
        American Indian, Alaska Native population, 35
        Asian population, 35, 735, 736, 737
        Black, African American population, 35, 735, 736, 737
        Children, 736, 737
        City, 732
        Educational attainment, 737
        Elderly, 32, 737
        Hispanic origin population, 35, 735, 736, 737
        Labor force, 738
        Native Hawaiian and Other Pacific Islander population, 35
    State, 733
    Threshold, 734
Power (see also Electric light and power industry):
    Electric, 973, 976, 977, 978, 979, 980, 981
    Hydro-electric, 960, 982
    Nuclear, 960, 969
    Prices, 753, 760, 961
Power generation and supply industry, 655, 661
Power plants. (See Electric light and power industry.)
Precipitation, selected cities, 430, 1402
Pregnancies, (see also Births and birth rates), 92, 109, 127
    Teen pregnancies, 83, 87, 88, 89, 91, 93, 94
Prescription drugs, 141, 143, 144, 145, 148, 149, 216, 217, 751
Presidents, U.S., elections for, 436, 440, 441, 442, 443
    Pardons and commutations, 360
Prices (see also individual commodities):
    Electricity, 753, 961, 975, 979
    Energy, 749, 751, 759, 760
    Fish, 925
    Food, 749, 750, 751, 755, 756, 875
    Foreign countries, 1371, 1372, 1379
    Fuel, 750, 751, 753
    Gas, 751, 754
    Housing, 1000, 1002, 1003, 1004, 1005

Indexes:
    Airline cost, 1092
    Consumer prices, 748, 749, 750, 751, 1379
        Foreign countries, 1372, 1379
            Medical care, 149, 749, 750, 751
            Metropolitan areas, 750
    Exports, 762, 764
    Gross domestic product, 762
    Higher education, 312
    Housing price index, 752, 1000
    Imports, 762, 765
    Personal consumption, 761
    Producer prices, 748, 759, 760, 997
        Timber, 922
    Purchasing power of the dollar, 748
    Received by farmers, 874
    Spot market price, 758
    Tourism commodities, 1280
    Living abroad, 1372
    Mineral products (see also individual minerals), 934
    Received by farmers:
        Crops, 887
        Indexes, 874
        Livestock and poultry, 900, 907
    Stocks, 1227
Primary metal manufacturing:
    Capital, 807
    Earnings, 655, 1036, 1043
    Employees, 655, 1034, 1036, 1038, 1043
    Establishments, 1034
    Finance, 819
    Foreign trade, 1039, 1326
    Gross domestic product, 693, 1032
    Industrial production index, 814, 932
    Productivity, 661
    Profits, 819
    Shipments, 1036, 1045, 1046
    Toxic chemical releases, 418
Printing and related support activities. (See Publishing industry.)
Prisoners (see also Correctional institutions), 380, 382, 383, 384, 385, 387, 1334
    Death sentences, 383, 384, 385
    Executions, 384, 385
    Jail inmates, 380, 381, 382
    Pardons, presidential, 360
    Recidivism, 387
    Sentencing Commission, U.S., 375
Probation, 375, 386, 387, 388
Problem solving courts, 374
Producer price indexes, 759, 760, 997
    Timber, 922
Productivity (see also individual industries):
    Capacity utilization, 815
    Farm output, 886
    Labor, 661, 662, 1041, 1368, 1369, 1370
    Mining industries, 948
Professional and business services:
    Consumer expenditures, 700
    Earnings, 655, 665
    Employees, 640, 644, 654, 655, 1293
    Hires and separations, 659, 660
Professional, scientific and technical services:
    Capital, 784, 807, 809

Note: Index citations refer to **table** numbers, not **page** numbers

Note: Index citations refer to **table** numbers, not **page** numbers

Q

R

Note: Index citations refer to **table** numbers, not **page** numbers

---

Note: Index citations refer to **table** numbers, not **page** numbers

Note: Index citations refer to **table** numbers, not **page** numbers

---

Note: Index citations refer to **table** numbers, not **page** numbers

Note: Index citations refer to **table** numbers, not **page** numbers

---

Note: Index citations refer to **table** numbers, not **page** numbers

Note: Index citations refer to **table** numbers, not **page** numbers

Note: Index citations refer to **table** numbers, not **page** numbers

Note: Index citations refer to **table** numbers, not **page** numbers

Note: Index citations refer to **table** numbers, not **page** numbers

Note: Index citations refer to **table** numbers, not **page** numbers

Note: Index citations refer to **table** numbers, not **page** numbers